LITERATURE
IN
ENGLISH

W.H. NEW & W.E. MESSENGER

LITERATURE IN ENGLISH

Edited by

W.H. NEW AND
W.E. MESSENGER

University of British Columbia

Prentice Hall Canada Inc., Scarborough, Ontario

Canadian Cataloguing in Publication Data

Main entry under title:

Literature in English

Includes bibliographical references and index.
ISBN 0-13-534777-7

1. College readers.   I. New, W.H. (William Herbert),
1938-   .   II. Messenger, William E., 1931-

PE1122.L58 1993   808.8   C92-095322-0

© 1993 Prentice-Hall Canada Inc., Scarborough, Ontario

Prentice-Hall, Inc., Englewood Cliffs, New Jersey
Prentice-Hall International, Inc., London
Prentice-Hall of Australia, Pty., Ltd., Sydney
Prentice-Hall of India Pvt., Ltd., New Delhi
Prentice-Hall of Japan, Inc., Tokyo
Prentice-Hall of Southeast Asia (Pte.) Ltd., Singapore
Editora Prentice-Hall do Brasil Ltda., Rio de Janeiro
Prentice-Hall Hispanoamericana, S.A., Mexico

ISBN: 0-13-534777-7

Acquisitions Editor: Marjorie Munroe
Developmental Editor: Maryrose O'Neill
Production Editor: Kelly Dickson
Copy Editor: Ruth Bradley-St-Cyr
Permissions Research: Robyn Craig and Sharon Houston
Cover and Interior Design: Gail Ferreira-Ng-A-Kien
Cover Image Credit: David Rankine
Page Layout: Olena Serbyn

1 2 3 4 5   AGI   97 96 95 94 93

Printed and bound in the USA by Arcata Graphics Inc.

Pages 1635-1640 constitute an extention of the copyright page.

Preface

1. Purpose

Literature in English brings together a wide range of literary works. It is primarily a collection of poems, stories, and essays, but readers will also find here examples of a number of less conventional literary genres: travel-writing, writing for children, letters, songs, dictionary definitions, and popular performance pieces. A few translations of works from other languages—adaptations which have themselves become noteworthy writings in English—add to the variety, and the variety directly reflects the range and accomplishment of literature in English. Indeed, in some ways "translation" or "transformation" is a principle that underlies the selection of texts for this book. Defined broadly, "translation" means "change," and readers will recognize that the "literature in English" collected in this anthology represents many kinds of change: changes over time, as history has altered the English language, questioned taste and fashion, and constructed "traditions"; changes in critical and artistic practice, including the judgment of what constitutes "literature"; and changes—or "translations"—from place to place, as writers in several societies have begun to use English as a medium of artistic expression, have responded both to history and to the present, and have variously reinforced and resisted European conventions, while developing their own.

2. Organization and Selection

The main Table of Contents lists works chronologically by authors' birthdates. Anonymous works are collected in appropriate groups, at the approximate time of their composition. There are also two Alternative Tables of Contents. The first one focusses on *manner*, offering a guide to the range of *forms* and *modes* represented in the anthology; the second focusses on *matter*, indicating many of the recurrent motifs, subjects, and ideas in the selections. Taken together, these three organizations allow for the individual works to be read and studied chronologically, separately, and comparatively; but some

entirely different principle might also guide your reading. For instance, you might choose to emphasize the consistency of an individual author's work, to analyze the structural features of particular texts, to probe the historical and social contexts of literary expression and literary production, to study the relation between theories of aesthetics and systems of language, or to examine various features of a literary "problem" such as class, gender, race, power, nature, convention, or authority. Whatever approach you take, the selections will provide enjoyment, and the various notes and apparatuses will heighten your appreciation and understanding.

One could consider the works assembled in this anthology as "representative" texts from Anglo-Saxon times to the late 20th century. But if so, the word "representative" has to be understood in several ways, all of which suggest different approaches to using this book.

As the various tables of contents suggest, the selections "represent" not only the formal variety of literature in English but also its wide reach around the world and its wide range of ideas. The book provides enough examples of different kinds of poetry and prose to show the historical changes (in both literature and language) that have taken place over 1200 years—though we deliberately do not divide literature into conventional periods and along strictly national lines (see *Literary Periods* in the Glossary). It includes a generous selection of texts by writers whom standard literary histories call "major": Chaucer, Spenser, Shakespeare, Milton, Pope, Keats, Dickinson, Tennyson, and others—though space limitations allow only excerpts from such longer works as Spenser's *The Faerie Queene*, Milton's *Paradise Lost*, and Tennyson's *In Memoriam*. Economics of space also dictates the omission of plays and novels, which are readily available as supplementary texts. The particular works brought together here, omissions notwithstanding, "represent" the range of these writers' accomplishments—a range demonstrated sometimes through variations in form or genre, sometimes through variations in subject over an entire career. By drawing on the writings of other (and often lesser-known) writers, however, the anthology demonstrates further that artistry is not limited to the work of the writers conventionally regarded as "major"; appreciating a wider range of the skilled accomplishments at any given time can increase readers' appreciation of literature and literary history.

The selections, along with the notes and cross-references, also provide opportunities to consider the social and cultural contexts of literature and to examine ways in which literary works can "represent" their place or time—or, indeed, represent opinions and attitudes that run counter to prevailing values and conventions. Writers frequently disagree with each other—probably as often with their predecessors as with their contemporaries—and this book samples several literary quarrels and debates: between Whigs and Tories, pastoral idealists and anti-pastoral satirists, High Church clergymen and Nonconformist preachers, monarchist apologists for empire and their republican or anti-colonial opposition. Alongside literary works that express the enthusiasms born of European expansionism, for example—the romantic appeals to adventure, the conventional attitudes regarding racial superiority—one can read slave narratives and condemnations of plantation politics. Alongside a series of class-marked reflections on art, nature, literary style, and the characteristics of civil order, one can read attacks on the assumptions that underlie such order and praise for alternative codes of taste and systems of governance. Alongside the writings that literary histories have conventionally emphasized, one can read works (many by women) whose perspective has long been made to seem peripheral.

This anthology, in other words, collects numerous works of literature that are both interesting and entertaining, and that "represent" both the multiple forms of tradition and the equally plural forces of change.

3. ANNOTATIONS AND REFERENCE GUIDES

Throughout, we provide several kinds of editorial annotations. At the foot of the page, we gloss obsolete words and usages, archaisms, most proper names, and many allusions. While we also gloss many words that, while not obsolete, are now rarely used, we generally do not explain words found in standard "college" or "desk" dictionaries, nor do we annotate allusions already familiar to most readers. The glosses and annotations translate some early English words that will not be readily understood, and explain facts that will facilitate the reading of the texts, but they do not interpret. We leave to each reader the pleasure of recognizing the effectiveness of literary design and of learning to appreciate what each work—sometimes intricately, and sometimes directly and simply—has to say.

You will also find many cross-references suggesting comparisons with other works in the book (indicated by page number) or possible additional readings outside the book which you might find relevant or enjoy pursuing. At the end of the anthology you will also find three useful addenda: Appendix I, Notes on Authors; Appendix II, a Chronology of events and accomplishments; and Appendix III, a Glossary of technical literary terms, with many cross-references back to examples in the book.

Most works in the anthology are followed by one or more dates, in parentheses. A single date indicates the year of composition and publication, or of one or the other when the two are near each other. Where the dates of composition and publication differ significantly from each other (as with Hopkins), both are given, separated by a semicolon. If a work underwent significant revision at a time substantially later than the original composition, then the dates are separated by a comma (or, in the case of continuous revision over a period of time, as with Bacon's essays, by a hyphen). In a few instances, where the dates of composition and first publication are unknown, as with Donne's poetry, a footnote explains special publication histories.

For further information on particular *words*, we urge you to consult the multi-volume *Oxford English Dictionary*, which traces changes in meaning and usage. (There are, in addition, several readily available histories of the English *language*, which can provide you with further information about changes in sound pattern, structure, dialect, and lexicon, and numerous specialized dictionaries of, for example, Middle English, regional speech, and slang. Two such works are Celia Millward's *A Biography of the English Language* and the latest edition of Thomas Pyles and John Algeo's *The History and Development of the English Language*.)

For further information on individual writers and their careers, Appendix I provides brief biographical data about the authors in the anthology. We also recommend that you consult the following:

The Oxford Companions to *English, American, Australian, Canadian, Welsh, Classical*, and *Children's Literature*, and to the *English Language;*
The Cambridge Guide to Literature in English;
The Feminist Companion to Literature in English;
The Dictionary of Literary Biography;
The Reader's Encyclopedia.

Here are a few other references you might find useful:

Brewer's Dictionary of Phrase and Fable;
The Oxford Classical Dictionary;
The Encyclopaedia Britannica, especially the 11th edition (1911), for its articles on history and literature;
The Columbia Encyclopedia.

Such books of course do not resolve all questions about writers or writing, but they do provide some information and often suggest valuable *approaches* to answering questions. It is also worth remembering that one of the better ways to learn about literature is to keep reading literary works themselves—because literary works often refer not just outwards into history but back to other works of literature. For example, among the best resource books for reading Milton's *Paradise Lost* are Homer's *Iliad* and *Odyssey*, Virgil's *Aeneid*, Ovid's *Metamorphoses*, and the Authorized or "King James" Version of the Bible (which is one reason we include some passages from these works). Similarly, some of the most useful companions for reading 19th- and 20th-century literature in English—not only of England but also of Canada, Australia, India, Africa, New Zealand, the West Indies, Southeast Asia, and the U.S.A.—include the Bible, and the works of Milton, Shakespeare, Bunyan, Blake, and Pope that we have sampled in this collection.

4. TEXTS

For most of the texts that were written before about the middle of the 18th century, we have modernized spelling, capitalization, punctuation, and paragraphing for the convenience and ease of the modern reader. However readable some of the older forms might be (see for example the note to Malory's *Morte Darthur*), they sometimes pose unnecessary difficulties. (As Caxton printed Malory, for example, each chapter was rendered as a single paragraph.) But we have left some

earlier works in their original form, or something approximating their original form—namely the following:

"Caedmon's Hymn"; "Aelfric's Colloquy"; "The Wanderer"; "The Parable of the Prodigal Son" (from the West Saxon Gospels); "The Bookworm"; "The Wife's Lament"; medieval lyrics and ballads; the excerpt from *Mandeville's Travels*; "The Prodigal Son" (Wyclif's translation); the opening stanza of *Sir Gawain and the Green Knight*; the works by Chaucer, Hoccleve, Henryson, Dunbar, Skelton, Cabot, More, David Lindsay, Tyndale, and Spenser; Hakluyt's translation of Vaz's account of Sir Francis Drake; Donne's "The Sunne Rising."

While we almost always provide glosses or translations (word-by-word in the case of Caedmon, to illustrate the grammar; looser in the case of "The Wanderer," to emphasize the sense), we leave these works in their early forms for two main reasons:

1. Some works depend for their effects upon their use of an early form of the language. Modernizing Spenser's vocabulary, for example, would destroy his conscious archaisms; modernizing Chaucer would radically alter his poetic rhythms;

2. The examples of original format (most obviously the several versions of the parable of the prodigal son) provide an opportunity to trace some of the changes that have taken place in the English language over the centuries (e.g., changes in sound, syntax, structure, and diction).

But even when we modernize spelling, something of the original remains. Because we have not altered their word order, syntax, or diction, for example, the prose of Margery Kempe, John Bourchier, and Thomas Malory still sounds clearly (and literally) old-fashioned.

Old and Middle English used several letters which Modern English has abandoned (though it still retains most of the sounds). Although we have frequently kept the thorn (þ), the eth (ð), the yogh (ȝ), the aesc (æ), and the wynn (ƿ), we have silently standardized several other orthographic variations. We have not kept all early abbreviations, for example, nor reproduced the inconsistency of early spelling. You will find some brief comments on early orthography and Middle English pronunciation, respectively, in the footnote to Caedmon and the headnote to Chaucer.

Even keeping the original spelling of early works, however, does not preserve their actual appearance. To help students visualize the changes in text and script, we therefore also include some sample pages of early print (see the List of Plates). For further information on printing history and on literary handwriting, you might wish to consult Anthony G. Petti's book, *English Literary Hands from Chaucer to Dryden*.

5.   ACKNOWLEDGMENTS

We are grateful to the owners of copyrighted material for permission to reprint works (the specific indication of sources appears on the copyright page and its extensions). Our indebtedness to others is long, deep, and wide: to our own teachers and students over many years; to numerous colleagues and friends for helpful conversations, comments, and suggestions; and to earlier compilers and editors who have cumulatively over the years helped us arrive at our own understanding of the texts. In particular, for their suggestions and their help with specific problems, we wish to thank our colleagues in the English, Classics, German, and Hispanic and Italian Studies Departments at the University of British Columbia: Andrew Busza, Marguerite Chiarenza, Bill Dusing, Harry Edinger, Jack Foster, Marketa Goetz-Stankiewicz, Iain Higgins, Herbert J. Rosengarten, Peter Taylor, Gernot Wieland, Paul Yachnin, and the late Ann Munton; our colleagues at other institutions: Lorraine McMullen, Raymond J.S. Grant, and Mervyn Nicholson; Joseph Jones and the staff of the Humanities Division of the University of British Columbia Library; and David New. Most especially, we thank Ann Messenger and Peggy New for their constant support and encouragement, and for their own expertise in reading literature. Peggy New discussed the project with us and made valuable suggestions for inclusion and commentary; Ann Messenger read the entire text in draft, and (while the responsibility for any remaining errors and omissions is our own) her careful textual and editorial advice clarifed many difficulties, corrected a number of inconsistencies, and enabled us to address social and historical disparities with more understanding than would otherwise have been possible. We thank them both, for helping make the preparation of this anthology, over several years, a discovery and a pleasure.

W.H.N., W.E.M.

TABLE OF CONTENTS

*Items marked with an asterisk are in prose; all others are in verse. See the Alternative Tables of
Contents, which follow, for more specific classifications by form and subject.

LIST OF PLATES

ALTERNATIVE TABLES OF CONTENTS

Even though not intended to be all-inclusive, these lists are necessarily long. Each presents you with a different sort of map of the anthology, and each invites you to roam around, to get acquainted with at least some of the various ways of thinking about the works it contains. (Many titles have been shortened in order to conserve space.)

1. TABLE OF CONTENTS ACCORDING TO FORMS AND MODES

Literary works have both form and content (see the Glossary). Some descriptive terms refer directly to content ("war," "romantic love"; see the subject categories in list 2); other terms refer directly to form, as in the list of stanzaic and other poetic forms in the opening section of this first list; but many literary terms describe or define or refer to characteristics of both form and content together. That is, the different "kinds" of literary works lie on a broad continuum from the formal to the content-driven, with a large area in between occupied by what can be called modes (see the Glossary). Mode sometimes overlaps with form (as satire and ode did in classical times, and as epic and pastoral in part still do) and sometimes overlaps with content (as in travel writing and autobiography). (Note: For the more common formal categories—heroic couplet, blank verse, and free verse—we include only a few examples; you may want to add others as your reading progresses; the other categories are relatively full. For terms not defined here, see the Glossary, which also augments some of these definitions.)

A guide to the categories listed in this section.

2. TABLE OF CONTENTS ACCORDING TO SUBJECTS AND MOTIFS

The categories that follow are intended as a guide to your reading and study; for example, they will help you locate ideas and texts for possible comparisons. They are not intended to limit your interpretation of any particular work, nor are they exhaustive. You may wish to add other works to these lists, or to classify works in more categories, or different ones. And you may wish to narrow these categories, or to devise new ones; here are some possibilities: anger, artifice, belief, benevolence, ceremony, choice, confession, democracy, discovery, dress or costume, duty, equality, escape, evolution, guilt, hypocrisy, illusion and reality, indirection, inspiration, jealousy, men and masculinity, nothingness, orality, popular culture, ritual, selfishness, sense of loss, sin, sincerity, social reform, the soul, sympathy and pity, tyranny, utopia. This too is not a definitive list; you can devise still other categories to help you pursue a particular project.

A guide to the categories listed in this section.

CÆDMON

England, 7th century

CÆDMON'S HYMN

Nu we sculan herian   heofonrices Weard,
Now we shall [must] praise   heaven-kingdom's Ward [Guardian],

Metodes mihte   and his modgeþonc,
the Creator-God's might   and his mood [mind]-thought,

weorc Wuldorfæder,   swa he wundra gehwæs,
the work of the Glory-Father,   so [how] he of wonders, each,

ece Dryhten,   ord onstealde.
the eternal Lord,   the beginning installed [established, ordained].

He ærest gesceop   eorðan bearnum   5
He first shaped [created]   for earth's bairns

heofon to hrofe,   halig Scyppend,
heaven to [for, as a] roof,   holy Shaper [Creator],

ða middangeard,   moncynnes Weard;
then middle-earth [the earth, the world],   mankind's Guardian;

ece Dryhten,   æfter teode
the eternal Lord   after ordained

firum foldan,   Frea ælmihtig.
for men earth [ground, dry land],   Lord [King] almighty.

CÆDMON'S HYMN   The letters Þ, þ (thorn) and Ð, ð (eth) are both pronounced *th*; *sc* is pronounced *sh*; the ligature or digraph æ (æsc, ash) is pronounced either like *a* in *man* (short) or *e* in *berry* (long). The interlinear translation follows Cædmon word for word, adding only an occasional definite article [and a few more-easily understood equivalents in brackets]. The sense sometimes parallels that of Genesis 1:1-10 (see pp. 241-42). Note the extra space marking the caesura in each line, and the alliteration connecting each pair of half-lines. Bede in his *Historia Ecclesiastica Gentis Anglorum* (*Ecclesiastical History of the English People*, 731) included a Latin translation of Cædmon's poem, and various manuscripts of Bede's Latin work and Anglo-Saxon translations of it include versions of the poem in the vernacular. The above is a West-Saxon version from the 11th century; following is a Northumbrian version, probably closer to Cædmon's original, from the 8th century; note in line 5 the phrase *aelda barnum*, "the children of men," instead of the other's "earth's children"; note also the letter ȝ (yogh), pronounced here as *y* or hard *g*, and elsewhere (see e.g. the excerpt from *Gawain*, p. 26) as *s* or the once standard palatal or guttural spirant represented e.g. by *gh* in modern *night:*

Nu scylun herȝan   hefaenricaes uard,
metudæs maecti   end his modȝidanc,
uerc uuldurfadur   sue he uundra ȝihuaes,
eci dryctin,   or astelidæ;
he aerist scop   aelda barnum
heben til hrofe,   haleȝ scepen,
tha middunȝeard   moncynnæs uard;
eci dryctin   æfter tiadæ
firum foldu,   frea allmectiȝ.

Plate 1.   The Chi-Rho page from the Gospel according to St. Mark, c. 698, showing the
Latin text with the Old English interlinear gloss, in the Northumbrian dialect,
which was added in the 10th century.

A̶ELFRIC

England, c.955–c.1020

AELFRIC'S COLLOQUY (abridged)

Þe cildra biddaþ þe, eala lareoþ, þæt þu tæce us
sprecan forþam unᵹelærede þe syndon and
ᵹeþæmmodlice þe sprecaþ.

Hþæt þille ᵹe sprecan?

Hþæt rece þe hþæt þe sprecan, buton hit riht
spræc sy and behefe, næs idel oþþe fracod.

Þille bespunᵹen on leornunᵹe?

Leofre ys us beon bespunᵹen for lare þænne hit
ne cunnan. Ac þe þitun þe bileþitne þesan and
nellan onbelæden spincᵹla us, buton þu bi
toᵹenydd fram us.

Ic axie þe, hþæt sprycst þu? Hþæt hæfst þu
þeorkes?

Ic eom ᵹeanþyrde monuc, and ic sincᵹe ælce
dæᵹ seofon tida mid ᵹebroþrum, and ic eom
bysᵹod and on sanᵹe, ac þeahhþæþere ic þolde
betþenan leornian sprecan on leden
ᵹereorde.

Hþæt cunnon þas þine ᵹeferan?

Sume synt yrþlincᵹas, sume scephyrdas, sume
oxanhyrdas, sume eac spylce huntan, sume
fisceras, sume fuᵹeleras, sume cypmenn, sume
scepyrhtan, sealteras, bæceras.

Hþæt sæᵹest þu, yrþlinᵹc? Hu beᵹæst þu þeorc
þin?

Eala, leof hlaford, þearle ic deorfe. Ic ᵹa ut on
dæᵹræd þyþende oxon to felda, and iuᵹie hiᵹ to
syl; nys hit spa stearc þinter þæt ic durre lutian
æt ham for eᵹe hlafordes mines, ac ᵹeiukodan
oxan, and ᵹefæstnodon sceare and cultre mit
þære syl, ælce dæᵹ ic sceal erian fulne æcer oþþe
mare.

Hæfst þu æniᵹne ᵹeferan?

We children beg thee, O teacher, that thou teach
us to speak [Latin right], because we are untaught
and we speak corruptly.

What do ye wish to speak about?

5 What reck we what we speak about as long as it
be right speech and necessary, not idle or wicked?

Would ye be beaten into learning?

We would liefer be beaten for lore than not to
know it. But we perceive thee to be gentle and
10 unwilling to inflict whips on us, unless thou art
compelled through ourselves.

I ask thee, what speakest thou? What work hast
thou?

I am a confessed monk, and I sing each day
15 seven times with the brothers, and I am busy in
reading and in song, but nevertheless I would
between-times learn to speak in the Latin
language.

What do these thy companions know?

20 Some are farmers, some shepherds, some
oxherds, some also likewise hunters, some fishers,
some fowlers, some chapmen, some shoe-wrights,
salters, bakers.

What sayest thou, farmer? How performest thou
25 thy work?

Alas, dear lord! I work hard. I go out at dawn,
drive oxen to the field, and yoke them to the
plough; there is no winter so stark that I dare idle
at home for fear of my master, but having yoked
30 oxen and fastened ploughshare and coulter to the
plough, each day I must plough a full acre or
more.

Hast thou any companions?

AELFRIC'S COLLOQUY Originally written in Latin as a colloquy between the master and his pupils, each of whom would take one or more of the parts. One of the surviving manuscripts includes this interlinear translation, which is complete except for a few gaps where it leaves a word or phrase untranslated. Where such a word or phrase is needed for understanding, we have translated it in brackets in our modern version. Note: The letter Þ is called a *wynn*, and is an orthographic representation of *w*. It should not be confused with the thorn (þ), which is pronounced like *th*. The yogh (ᵹ) is variously equivalent to *g, gh*, and *y*. **1. children:** (Latin *pueri*) i.e., boys. **22. chapmen:** merchants.

Ic hæbbe sumne cnapan þypende oxan mid zadisene, þe eac spilce nu has ys for cylde and hreame.

Hpæt mare dest þu on dæz?

Zepyslice þænne mare ic do. Ic sceal fyllan binnan oxan mid hiz, and pæterian hiz, and scearn heora beran ut.

Hiz! Hiz! micel zedeorf ys hyt.

Zeleof, micel zedeorf hit ys, forþam ic neom freoh.

Sceaphyrde, hæfst þu æniz zedeorf?

Zea, leof, ic hæbbe: on foreperdne morzen ic drife sceap mine to heora læse, and stande ofer hiz on hæte and on cyle mid hundum, þe læs pulfas forspelzen hiz, and ic azenlæde hiz on heora loca, and melke hiz tpeopa on dæz, and heora loca ic hæbbe, on þærto and cyse and buteran ic do; and ic eom zetrype hlaforde minon.

Eala, oxanhyrde, hpæt pyrst þu?

Eala, hlaford min, micel ic zedeorfe. Þænne se yrþlinzc unscenþ þa oxan, ic læde hiz to læse, and ealle niht ic stande ofer hiz paciende for þeofan, and eft on ærnemergen ic betæce hiz þam yrþlincze þel zefylde and zepæterode.

Ys þæs of þinum zeferum?

Zea, he ys.

Canst þu æniz þinz?

Ænne cræft ic cann.

Hpylcne?

Hunta ic eom.

Hpæs?

Cinczes.

Hu bezæst þu cræft þinne?

Ic brede me max and sette hiz on stope zehæppre, and zetihte hundas mine þæt pildeor hiz ehton, oþþæt hiz becuman to þam nettan unforsceapodlice and þæt hiz spa beon bezrynodo, and ic ofslea hiz on þam maxum.

Ne canst þu huntian buton mid nettum?

Zea, butan nettum huntian ic mæz.

Hu?

Mid spiftum hundum ic betæce pildeor.

Hpilce pildeor spypost zefehst þu?

Ic zefeo heortas and baras and rann and ræzan and hpilon haran.

I have one boy who drives the oxen with a goad-iron, who likewise now is hoarse from cold and shouting. [35]

What more dost thou in a day?

Certainly then I do more. I must fill the oxen's bins with hay and water them and carry out their dung. [40]

Hey! Hey! That is much labour.

Yea, sire; much labour it is, because I'm not free.

Shepherd, hast thou any labour?

Yea, sire, I have. In the early morning I drive [45] my sheep to their pasture, and stand over them in heat and in cold with dogs, lest wolves swallow them, and I lead them back to their fold, and milk them twice a day, and in their fold I have thereto both the cheese and butter I make, and I am true, [50] my lord.

O oxherd! What workest thou?

O my lord, I labour much. When the farmer unhitches the oxen, I lead them to the pasture, and all night I stand over them watching for thieves, [55] and afterwards in the early morning I take them home to the farmer well filled and watered.

Is this one of thy companions?

Yea, he is.

Knowest thou anything? [60]

One craft I know.

Which is?

I am a hunter.

Whose?

The king's. [65]

How do you practise your craft?

I braid my nets and set them in suitable places, and urge my dogs that they chase wild animals until they come to those nets unaware, [70] and they thus are trapped, and I slay them in the nets.

Canst thou not hunt except with nets?

Yea, I can hunt without nets.

How?

I take wild animals with swift dogs. [75]

Which wild animals catchest thou most often?

I catch harts and boars and reindeer and roes and sometimes hare.

Þære þu todæʒ on huntnoþe?

Ic næs, forþam sunnandæʒ ys, ac ʒyrstandæʒ ic pæs on huntunʒe.

 Hpæt ʒelæhtest þu?

Tpeʒen heortas and ænne bar.

Hu ʒefencʒe þu hiʒ?

Heortas ic ʒefenʒc on nettum and bar ic ofsloh.

Hu pære þu dyrstiʒ ofstikian bar?

Hundas bedrifon hyne to me, and ic þær toʒeanes standende færlice ofstikode hyne.

Spyþe þryste þu pære þa.

Ne sceal hunta forhtfull pesan, forþam mislice pildeor puniað on pudum.

Hpæt dest þu be þinre huntunʒe?

Ic sylle cynce spa hpæt spa ic ʒefo, forþam ic eom hunta hys.

Hpæt sylþ he þe?

He scryt me pel and fett and hpilon sylþ me hors oþþe beah, þæt þe lustlicor cræft minne ic beʒancʒe.

Hpylcne cræft canst þu?

Ic eom fiscere.

Hpæt beʒyst þu of þinum cræfte?

Biʒleofan and scrud and feoh.

Hu ʒefehst þu fixas?

Ic astiʒie min scyp and pyrpe max mine on ea, and ancʒil *vel* æs ic pyrpe and spyrtan, and spa hpæt spa hiʒ ʒehæftað ic ʒenime.

Hpæt ʒif hit unclæne beoþ fixas?

Ic utpyrpe þa unclænan ut, and ʒenime me clæne to mete.

Hpær cypst þu fixas þine?

On ceastre.

Hpa biʒþ hi?

Ceasterpara. Ic ne mæʒ spa fela spa ic mæʒ ʒesyllan.

Hpilce fixas ʒefehst þu?

Ælas and hacodas, mynas and æleputan, sceotan and lampredan, and spa pylce spa on pætere spymmaþ. Sprote.

Forhpi ne fixast þu on sæ?

Wert thou hunting today?

80 I wasn't, because it is Sunday; but yesterday I was hunting.

What didst thou catch?

Two harts and one boar.

How didst thou catch them?

85 The harts I caught in nets and the boar I slew.

How wert thou bold enough to stab the boar?

The dogs drove him toward me, and standing there before him, I suddenly stabbed him.

Very brave thou wert, then.

90 A hunter mustn't be fearful because various wild animals live in the woods.

What dost thou with thy hunting?

I give the king whatsoever I catch, because I am his hunter.

95 What does he give thee?

He clothes and feeds me well and sometimes gives me a horse or a bracelet, so that the more willingly I perform my craft.

Which craft do you know?

100 I am a fisher.

What gettest thou from thy craft?

Food and dress and money.

How dost thou catch fish?

I step into my ship and cast my nets into the *105* water, or I cast fishhook and bait, and whatsoever they catch, I take in baskets.

What if the fish are unclean?

I throw out the unclean and take the clean for meat.

110 Where dost thou sell thy fish?

In the town.

Who buys them?

The city-dwellers. I can't catch as many as I might sell.

115 Which fish dost thou catch?

Eels and pikes, minnows and eelpouts, trout and lampreys, and whichsoever swims in the water. Sprats.

Why dost thou not fish in the sea?

---

92. hunting: i.e., game. **109. meat:** i.e., food.

Hpilon ic do, ac seldon, forþam micel repyt me
ys to sæ.

Hpæt fehst þu on sæ?

Hærinczas and leaxas, merespyn and stirian,
ostran and crabban, muslan, pinepinclan,
sæcoccas, fazc and floc and lopystran and fela
spylces.

Þylt þu fon sumne hpæl?

Nic.

Forhpi?

Forþam plyhtlic þinzc hit ys zefon hpæl.
Ʒebeorhlicre ys me faran to ea mid scype mynan,
þænne faran mid manezum scypum on huntunze
hranes.

Forhpi spa?

Forþam leofre ys me zefon fisc þæne ic mæz
ofslean, þonne fisc, þe na þæt an me ac eac spylce
mine zeferan mid anum sleze he mæz besencean
oþþe zecpylman.

And þeah mænize zefoþ hpælas, and ætberstaþ
frecnysse, and micelne sceat þanon bezytaþ.

Soþ þu sezst, ac ic ne zeþristze for modes mines
nytenyssæ.

. . . .

Hpæt sæzst þu, manczere?

Ic secze þæt behefe ic eom ze cinzce and
eoldormannum and pelizum and eallum follce.

And hu?

Ic astize min scyp mid hlæstum minum, and
rope ofer sælice dælas, and cype mine þinzc, and
bicze þincz dyrpyrðe þa on þisum lande ne beoþ
acennede, and ic hit tozelæde eop hider mid
micclan plihte ofer sæ, and hpylon forlidenesse ic
þolie mid lyre ealra þinza minra, uneaþe cpic
ætberstende.

Hpylce þinc zelædst þu us?

Pællas and sidan, deorpyrþe zymmas and zold,
selcuþe reaf and pyrtzemanzc, pin and ele,
ylpesban and mæstlinzc, ær and tin, spefel and
zlæs, and þylces fela.

Pilt þu syllan þinzc þine her eal spa þu hi
zebohtest þær?

Ic nelle. Hpæt þænne me fremode zedeorf min?
Ac ic pille heora cypen her luflicor þonne zebicze

120 Sometimes I do, but seldom, because there's much rowing for me to the sea.

What dost thou catch in the sea?

Herring and salmon, dolphins and sturgeons, oysters and crabs, mussels, periwinkles, sea-
125 cockles, plaice and flounders, and lobsters and many such.

Wilt thou catch a whale?

Not I.

Why?

130 Because it is a dangerous thing to catch a whale. It is safer for me to go on the river with my ship than to fare with many ships in hunting whales.

Why so?

135 Because I had liefer catch a fish that I can kill, but not one that is able with one blow to sink or kill not only me but also my companions.

And even though many catch whales and escape
140 harm and get much money thereby?

Thou sayest the truth, but I dare not, because of my heart's cowardice.

. . . .

What sayest thou, merchant?

I say that I am useful to the king and the
145 noblemen and the rich and all folk.

And how so?

I board my ship with my cargo, and row over the expanses of the sea, and sell my things, and buy valuable things that are not produced in this
150 land, and I transport them hither to you with much risk over the sea, and sometimes I suffer shipwreck with loss of all my things, not easily escaping alive.

Which things bringest thou us?

155 Purple cloth and silk, precious gems and gold, little-known garments and mixed spices, wine and oil, ivory and brass, bronze and tin, sulphur and glass, and many such.

Wilt thou sell thy things here for just what thou
160 boughtest them there?

I won't. What then would my labour gain me? But I will sell them here dearer than I buy there,

þær, þæt sum ʒestreon me ic beʒyte, þanon ic me afede and min pif and minne sunu.

so that I get some profit, with which I feed myself and my wife and my son.

Þu, sceopyrhta, hpæt pyrcst þu us nytpyrþnessæ?

Thou, shoemaker, what workest thou useful to us?

Ys, pitodlice, cræft min behefe þearle eop and neodþearf.

Truly, my craft is extremely useful to you, and necessary.

Hu?

How?

Ic bicʒe hyda and fell, and ʒearkie hiʒ mid cræfte minon, and pyrce of him ʒescy mistlices cynnes, spyftleras and sceos, leþerhosa and butericas, bridelþpancʒas and ʒeræda, flaxan *vel* pinnan and hiʒdifatu, spurleþera and hælftra, pusan and fætelsas; and nan eoper nele oferpintran buton minon cræfte.

I buy hides and skins, and prepare them with my craft, and make of them various kinds of footwear, slippers and shoes, leather leggings and leather containers, bridle-reins and trappings, flasks and vessels and leather bottles, spur-straps and halters, bags and purses; and none of ye will get through the winter without my craft.

Sealtera, hpæt us fremaþ cræft þin?

Salter, what benefit to us is thy craft?

Þearle fremaþ cræft min eop eallum. Nan eoper blisse brycð on ʒererduncʒe oþþe mete, buton cræft min ʒistliþe him beo.

My craft is of very much benefit to you all. None of you enjoy satisfaction in a meal or meat unless he be hospitable to my craft.

Hu?

How so?

Hpylc manna þurhperodum þurhbrycþ mettum buton spæcce sealtes? Hpa ʒefylþ cleafan his oþþe hedderna buton cræfte minon? Efne, buterʒeþpeor ælc and cysʒerunn losaþ eop buton ic hyrde ætpese eop, þe ne furþon þæt an pyrtum eoprum butan me brucaþ.

Which man fully enjoys very delicious meat unless it is flavoured with salt? Who fills his cellar or storehouse except by my craft? Lo, all butter and cheese-curd spoils for you unless I the keeper be present with you, who can't even use your vegetables without me.

. . . .

. . . .

Eala, munuc, þe me tospycst, efne, ic hæbbe afandod þe habban ʒode ʒeferan and þearle neodþearfe; and ic ahsie þa.

Oh, monk who speaketh to me, lo, I have found that you have good and very necessary companions, and I ask [you if you also have others?

Indeed, I have more.

Who are they?

Ic hæbbe smiþas, isene smiþas, ʒoldsmiþ, seoloforsmiþ, arsmiþ, treoppyrhtan and maneʒra oþre mistlicra cræfta biʒʒenceras.

I have smiths: iron-smiths, a goldsmith, a silversmith, a coppersmith, a tree-wright, and many other various craft-workers.

Hæfst æniʒne pisne ʒeþeahtan?

Hast any wise counsellor?

Ʒepislice ic hæbbe. Ure ʒeʒaderunʒc buton ʒeþeahtynde beon pissod?

Certainly I have. [How may] our gathering be guided without a counsellor?

Þisa, hpilc cræft þe ʒeþuht betpux þas furþra pesan?

[What sayest thou], wise man: which craft amongst these seems to thee to be superior?

Me ys ʒeþuht Ʒodes þeopdom betpeoh þas cræftas ealdorscype healdan, spa spa hit ʒeræd on

[I say that] to me it seems God's service amongst those crafts holds supremacy, just as it

---

195. tree-wright: i.e., carpenter. **198. gathering:** i.e., community.

ȝodspelle: "Fyrmest sceceað rice Ȝodes and
rihtƿisnesse hys, and þas þinȝc ealle beoþ
toȝehyhte eoƿ."

And hƿilc þe ȝeþuht betƿux ƿoruldcræftas
heoldan ealdordom?

Eorþtilþ, forþam se yrþlinȝ us ealle fett.

Se smiþ secȝð: Hƿanon sylan scear oþþe
culter, þe na ȝade hæfþ buton of cræfte
minon? Hƿanon fiscere ancȝel, oþþe
sceopyrhton æl, oþþe seamere nædl? Nis
hit of minon ȝepeorce?

Se ȝeþeahtend ansƿeraþ: Soþ ƿitodlice sæȝst, ac
eallum us leofre ys ƿikian mid þe, yrþlincȝe,
þonne mid þe, forþam se yrþlinȝ sylð us hlaf and
drenc; þu, hƿæt sylst us on smiþþan þinre buton
isenne fyrspearcan and speȝincȝa beatendra
slecȝea and blaƿendra byliȝa?

Se treoppyrhta seȝð: Hƿilc eoƿer ne notaþ
cræfte minon, þonne hus and mistlice fata and
scypa eoƿ eallum ic ƿyrce?

Se ȝolsmiþ ansƿyrt: Eala, tryppyrhta, forhƿi spa
sprycst þu, þonne ne furþon an þyrl þu ne miht
don?

Se ȝeþeahtend sæȝþ: Eala, ȝeferan and ȝode
ƿyrhtan, uton toƿurpon hƿætlicor þas ȝeflitu, and
sy sibb and ȝeþþærnyss betƿeoh us, and framiȝe
anra ȝehƿylc oþron on cræfte hys, and ȝeðƿærian
symble mid þam yrþlinȝe, þær þe biȝleofan us and
foddor horsum urum habbaþ. And þis ȝeþeaht ic
sylle eallum ƿyrhtum, þæt anra ȝehƿylc cræft his
ȝeornlice beȝanȝe, forþam se þe cræft his forlæt,
he byþ forlæten fram þam cræfte. Spa hƿæðer þu
sy, spa mæsseprest, spa munuc, spa ceorl, spa
kempa, beȝa oþþe behƿyrf þe sylfne on þisum,
and beo þæt þu eart; forþam micel hynð and
sceamu hyt is menn nellan ƿesan þæt þæt he ys
and þæt þe he ƿesan sceal.

Eala, cild, hu eoƿ licaþ þeos spæc?

Þel heo licaþ us, ac þearle deoplice sprycst and
ofer mæþe ure þu forþtyhst spræce: ac sprec us
æfter urum andȝyte, þæt ƿe maȝon understandan
þa þinȝ þe þu specst.

---

reads in the gospel: "Seek ye first the kingdom of
God, and his righteousness, and all these things
shall be added unto you."

And which amongst worldly crafts seems to
thee to hold supremacy?

Earth-tilling, because the farmer feeds us all.

The smith sayeth: Whence does the
ploughman get ploughshare or coulter, who not
a goad has except from my craft? Whence the
fisher his hook, or the shoe-wright his awl, or
the seamer his needle? Isn't it from my work?

The counsellor answereth: Truth indeed thou
sayest, but all of us would liefer dwell with thee,
farmer, than with thee, because the farmer gives
us loaf and drink; thou, what givest us in thy
smithy but iron fire-sparks and the sound of
beating sledges and blowing bellows?

The tree-wright sayeth: Which of you doth not
use my craft, when I make houses and various
vats and ships for all of you?

The goldsmith answers: O carpenter, why
speakest thou so, when not even one hole canst
thou make [without my craft]?

The counsellor sayeth: O companions and good
wrights, let us cease quickly this argument, and
may there be peace and concord between us, and
from each one to the other in his craft, and agree
always with the farmer, where we get food for us
and fodder for our horses. And this thought I give
to all wrights, that each one diligently practise his
craft, for he who forsakes his craft, he is forsaken
by that craft. So whichever thou art, mass-priest,
or monk, or churl, or warrior, practise or exercise
thyself in this, and be what thou art, because
much humiliation and shame it is for a man
unwilling to be that that he is and that which he
ought to be.

O children, how liketh you this speech?

Well it pleaseth us, but thou speakest very
deeply and over our measure; but speak to us
according to our understanding, that we may
understand the thing thou speakest.

Line numbers: 205, 210, 215, 220, 225, 230, 235, 240, 245

204-06: Matthew 6:33. **224. goldsmith:** evidently a scribal error, since the Latin has *ferrarius* (blacksmith) here (and in line 210).

Ic ahsiʒe eop, forhpi spa ʒeornlice leorni ʒe?

Forþam þe nellaþ pesan spa stunte nytenu, þa nan þinʒ pitaþ, buton ʒærs and pæter.

And hpæt pille ʒe?

Þyllaþ pesan pise.

On hpilcon pisdome? Þille ʒe beon prættiʒe oþþe þusenthipe on leasunʒum, lytiʒe on spræcum, onʒlæplice, hinderʒepe, pel sprecende and yfele þencende, spæsum pordum underþeodde, facn piðinnan tyddriende, spa spa berʒyls metton oferʒepeorke, piþinnan full stence?

Þe nellaþ spa pesan pise, forþam he nys pis, þe mid dydrunʒe hyne sylfne bespicð.

Ac hu pille ʒe?

Þe pyllaþ beon bylepite butan licetunʒe, and pise þæt pe buʒon fram yfele and don ʒoda. Ʒyt þeahhpæþere deoplicor mid us þu smeaʒst, þonne yld ure onfon mæʒe; ac sprec us æfter uran ʒepunon, næs spa deoplice.

And ic do æal spa ʒe biddaþ. Þu, cnapa, hpæt dydest todæʒ?

Maneʒa þinʒ ic dyde. On þisse niht, þa þa cnyll ic ʒehyrde, ic aras on minon bedde and eode to cyrcean, and sanʒ uhtsanʒ mid ʒebroþrum; æfter þa þe sunʒon be eallum halʒum and dæʒredlice lofsanʒas; æfter þysum prim and seofon seolmas mid letanian and capitolmæssan; syþþan undertide, and dydon mæssan be dæʒe; æfter þisum þe sunʒan middæʒ, and æton and druncon and slepon, and eft þe arison and sunʒon non; and nu þe synd her ætforan þe, ʒearupe ʒehyran hpæt þu us secʒe.

Hpænne pylle ʒe synʒan æfen oþþe nihtsanʒc?

Þonne hyt tima byþ.

Þære þu todæʒ bespunczen?

Ic næs, forþam pærlice ic me heold.

And hu þine ʒeferan?

Hpæt me ahsast be þam? Ic ne dear yppan þe diʒla ure. Anra ʒehpylc pat ʒif he bespunczen pæs oþþe na.

. . . .

I ask you, why learn you so diligently?

Because we are unwilling to be like brute beasts, who know nothing except grass and water.

And what will ye?

We want to be wise.

In which wisdom? Will ye be sly or shifty in lying, skillful in speech, shrewd, clever, well speaking and evilly thinking, addicted to suave words, full of fakery within, like a painted sepulchral outer-work, full of stench within?

We don't want thus to be wise, because he is not wise who deceives himself with delusions.

But how will ye?

We would be sincere, without hypocrisy, and wise that we may turn from evil and do good. Yet, though, more deeply thou dost discuss with us than our age may grasp; but speak to us after our custom, not so deeply.

And I do just as ye biddeth. Thou, boy, what didst today?

Many things I did. On this night, when I heard the knell, I arose from bed and went to church, and sang matins with the brethren; after that we sang about all the saints and the morning hymns; after this, prime and seven psalms with the litanies and chapter-mass; after that tierce, and we did mass for the day; after this we sang midday, and ate and drank and slept, and afterwards we arose and sang nones; and now we are here before thee, ready to hear what thou sayest to us.

When will you sing evensong or compline? When it is time.

Wert thou beaten today?

I wasn't, because I hold myself warily.

And how about thy companions?

What dost thou ask me about that? I don't dare reveal our secrets to thee. Each one knows if he was beaten or not.

. . . .

250
255
260
265
270
275
280
285

---

274. midday: i.e., sext, the fourth of the seven canonical hours, at noon. **278. evensong:** vespers. **281. hold myself warily:** i.e., behave myself carefully.

Eala, ʒe cildra and ƿynsume leorneras, eoƿ manaþ eoƿer lareoƿ þæt ʒe hyrsumian ʒodcundum larum and þæt ʒe healdan eoƿ sylfe ænlice on ælcere stoƿe. Ʒaþ þeaplice þonne ʒe ʒehyran cyricean bellan, and ʒaþ into cyrcean, and abuʒaþ eadmodlice to halʒum ƿefodum, and standaþ þeaplice, and sinʒað anmodlice, and ʒebiddaþ for eoƿrum synnum, and ʒaþ ut butan hyʒeleaste to claustre oþþe to leorninʒa.

O ye [good] children and winsome learners, your teacher exhorts you that ye be obedient to divine teaching and that ye hold yourselves properly in every place. Go obediently when ye 290 hear the church-bell, and go into the church, and bow reverently to the holy altar, and stand obediently, and sing in unison, and pray for your sins, and go out without clowning to the cloister or to study.

Anonymous

(10th-11th centuries)

THE WANDERER

Oft him anhaga are gebideð,		Oft the solitary man favour awaits,
Metudes miltse, þeah þe he modcearig		Lord's mercy, though he, sorrowful of heart,
geond lagulade longe sceolde		throughout the ocean-way long must
hreran mid hondum hrimcealde sæ,		stir with hands the rime-cold sea,
wadan wræclastas: wyrd bið ful aræd.	5	wade paths of exile: fate is fully decreed.
Swa cwæð eardstapa earfeþa gemyndig,		So quoth the earth-stepper, of hardships mindful,
wraþra wælsleahta, winemæga hryre:		wrathful slaughter, friendly kinsmen's fall:
"Oft ic sceolde ana uhtna gehwylce		"Oft I must alone each dawn
mine ceare cwiþan: nis nu cwicra nan,		my cares bewail; there is none now alive
þe ic him modsefan minne durre	10	to whom I my heart dare
sweotule asecgan. Ic to soþe wat		clearly tell. I for sooth know
þæt biþ in eorle indryhten þeaw,		that it is in a warrior a noble custom
þæt he his ferðlocan fæste binde,		that he his heart-chamber fast bind,
healde his hordcofan, hycge swa he wille.		hold his thoughts, think as he will.
Ne mæg werigmod wyrde wiðstondan	15	Nor may the spirit-weary withstand fate,
ne se hreo hyge helpe gefremman:		nor the sad heart provide help;
for ðon domgeorne dreorigne oft		therefore the eager for glory sad thoughts oft
in hyra breostcofan bindað fæste.		bind fast in their breast-coffers.
Swa ic modsefan minne sceolde		So I my heart must
oft earmcearig eðle bidæled,	20	oft, careworn, of native country deprived,
freomægum feor feterum sælan,		free kinsmen afar, in fetters bind,
siþþan geara iu goldwine minne		since years ago my gold-friend
hrusan heolster biwrah and ic hean þonan		earth's darkness covered, and I wretchedly thence
wod wintercearig ofer waþema gebind,		travelled with winter-care over frosty waves,

THE WANDERER   **4. stir with hands:** i.e., row.

sohte sele dreorig   sinces bryttan,   25
hwær ic feor oþþe neah   findan meahte
þone þe in meoduhealle   mine wisse,
oþþe mec freondleasne   frefran wolde,
weman mid wynnum.   Wat se þe cunnað
hu sliþen bið   sorg to geferan   30
þam þe him lyt hafað   leofra geholena:
warað hine wræclast,   nales wunden gold,
ferðloca freorig,   nalæs foldan blæd;
gemon he selesecgas   and sincþege,
hu hine on geoguðe   his goldwine   35
wenede to wiste: wyn eal gedreas.
For þon wat se þe sceal   his winedryhtnes
leofes larcwidum   longe forþolian,
ðonne sorg and slæp   somod ætgædre
earmne anhagan   oft gebindað: 40
þinceð him on mode   þæt he his mondryhten
clyppe and cysse,   and on cneo lecge
honda and heafod,   swa he hwilum ær
in geardagum   giefstoles breac;
ðonne onwæcneð eft   wineleas guma,   45
gesihð him biforan   fealwe wægas,
baþian brimfuglas,   brædan feþra,
hreosan hrim and snaw   hægle gemenged.
Þonne beoð þy hefigran   heortan benne,
sare æfter swæsne;   sorg bið geniwad,   50
þonne maga gemynd   mod geondhweorfeð,
greteð gliwstafum,   georne geondsceawað.
Secga geseldan   swimmað eft on weg,
fleotendra ferð   no þær fela bringeð
cuðra cwidegiedda: cearo bið geniwad   55
þam þe sendan sceal   swiþe geneahhe
ofer waþema gebind   werigne sefan.
For þon ic geþencan ne mæg   geond þas woruld
for hwan modsefa   min ne gesweorce,
þonne ic eorla lif   eal geondþence,   60
hu hi færlice   flet ofgeafon,
modge maguþegnas.   Swa þes middangeard
ealra dogra gehwam   dreoseð and fealleþ.
For þon ne mæg weorþan wis   wer, ær he age
wintra dæl in woruldrice.   Wita sceal geþyldig,   65

ne sceal no to hatheort   ne to hrædwyrde,
ne to wac wiga   ne to wanhydig,

sought drearily the hall of a treasure-giver,
wherever I far or nigh might find
one who in mead-hall might know me,
or me friendless would comfort,
entertain with delights. Knows he that tries
how cruel is sorrow as companion
for him who has few beloved protectors;
for him is the path of exile, not at all wound gold,
a heart-chamber chilled, not at all earth's riches.
He remembers hall-retainers and receiving treasure,
how him in youth his gold-friend
entertained with feast: all joy is fallen away.
Wherefore he knows, who must his friend-lord's
loved lore-sayings long go without,
that when sorrow and sleep together
the wretched solitary often bind,
he imagines in his mind that he his liege-lord
embraces and kisses, and on his knee lays
hand and head, as he whilom before
in days of yore the gift-stool enjoyed;
then he awakens again the friendless man,
seeing before him dark waves,
bathing sea-birds spreading feathers,
falling rime and snow with hail mingled.
Then are they heavier, the heart's wounds,
sore for his beloved; sorrow is renewed;
then memory of kinsmen passes across his mind,
he greets them joyfully, eagerly looks upon them;
the warrior hall-companions swim again away;
the floating spirits bring there not many
familiar words; care is renewed
for him who must send very often
over the frosty waves his weary spirit.
Wherefore I cannot think for all the world
why my mind shouldn't become dark,
when I all the life of earls consider,
how they suddenly the hall-floor have given up,
brave thanes. So this middle-earth
each of all days perishes and falls.
Wherefore a man cannot become wise before he has
his share of winters in the world-kingdom. A wise
    man must be patient,
must be neither too hot-hearted nor too quick-spoken,
nor too weak a warrior nor too heedless,

---

32. wound: i.e., twisted, curved, as in rings and bracelets. **62. middle-earth:** See "Cædmon's Hymn," line 7 (p. 1); cf. "Midgard" in Old Norse mythology. **63. each of all days:** i.e., every day.

ne to forht ne to fægen   ne to feohgifre,
ne næfre gielpes to georn,   ær he geare cunne.

Beorn sceal gebidan,   þonne he beot spriceð,   70
oþ þæt collenferð   cunne gearwe
hwider hreþra gehygd   hweorfan wille.
Ongietan sceal gleaw hæle   hu gæstlic bið,
þonne eall þisse worulde wela   weste stondeð,
swa nu missenlice   geond þisne middangeard   75
winde biwaune   weallas stondaþ,
hrime bihrorene,   hryðge þa ederas.
Woriað þa winsalo,   waldend licgað
dreame bidrorene;   duguð eal gecrong
wlonc bi wealle: sume wig fornom,   80
ferede in forðwege;   sumne fugel oþbær
ofer heanne holm;   sumne se hara wulf
deaðe gedælde;   sumne dreorighleor
in eorðscræfe   eorl gehydde:
yþde swa þisne eardgeard   ælda Scyppend,   85
oþ þæt burgwara   breahtma lease,
eald enta geweorc   idlu stodon.
Se þonne þisne wealsteal   wise geþohte,
and þis deorce lif   deope geondþenceð,
frod in ferðe   feor oft gemon   90
wælsleahta worn,   and þas word acwið:
'Hwær cwom mearg, hwær cwom mago?   Hwær
      cwom maþþumgyfa?
Hwær cwom symbla gesetu?   Hwær sindon seledreamas?
Eala beorht bune,   eala byrnwiga,
eala þeodnes þrym!   Hu seo þrag gewat,   95
genap under nihthelm,   swa heo no wære!
Stondeð nu on laste   leofre duguþe
weal wundrum heah,   wyrmlicum fah:
eorlas fornomon   æsca þryþe,
wæpen wælgifru,   wyrd seo mære,   100
and þas stanhleoþu   stormas cnyssað;
hrið hreosende   hrusan bindeð,
wintres woma,   þonne won cymeð,
nipeð nihtscua,   norþan onsendeð
hreo hæglfare   hæleþum on andan.   105
Eall is earfoðlic   eorþan rice,
onwendeð wyrda gesceaft   weoruld under heofonum.
Her bið feoh læne,   her bið freond læne,
her bið mon læne,   her bið mæg læne:

nor too afraid nor too glad nor too avaricious,
nor never of boasting too eager, before he well
      understands.
A man must wait, when he a boast speaks,
until, proud-minded, he knows well
whither heart's thoughts will turn.
The wise man must understand how ghastly it will be
when all this world's wealth stands waste,
as now in various places throughout this middle-earth
winds blow upon walls that stand,
frost covered, ruins of dwellings.
Crumbled the wine-halls, rulers lie dead,
of joy deprived; doughty retainers all fallen,
proud by the wall: some war destroyed,
carried away to death; one a bird bore away
over the high sea; to one the hoary wolf
dealt out death; one with sad face
in earth-cave an earl hid.
Thus he lay waste this earth, man's Shaper,
until, from burghers' revelry free,
the old works of giants stood idle.
He who then of this wall-place has wise thought,
and this dark life deeply thinks over,
wise in heart, from afar back oft calls to mind
many slaughters, and these words speaks:
'Where went the horse, where went the man?
      Where went the treasure-giver?
Where went the banquet's seat? Where are the hall-joys?
Alas the bright cup! Alas the mailed warrior!
Alas the prince's glory! How that time has passed away,
become dark under night-helm, as if it never were!
Now, long after the beloved retainers, stands
a wall wondrous high, with hostile serpent-shape:
the earls carried off by mighty ash-spears,
a weapon slaughter-greedy, a fate well-known;
and on the stone-shelters storms beat;
snow-storms falling bind the earth,
winter's terror, then darkness comes,
night-shadow grows dark, from the north sends
harsh hail-storms to men, in hostility.
All is full of hardship in earth's kingdom;
fate's decree overturns the world under the heavens:
here are riches transitory, here are friends transitory,
here is man transitory, here are kinfolk transitory;

81-82: Perhaps referring to a ship burial. **87. the old works of giants:** probably Roman ruins. **88. wall-place:** or *foundation* — i.e., the earth. **98. serpent-shape:** perhaps ornamental depictions of dragons, or perhaps serpentine ("worm-like") insect tunnels under the now-fallen bark of wooden Viking ruins.

eall þis eorþan gesteal   idel weorþeð.'"   *110*
  Swa cwæð snottor on mode,   gesæt him sundor æt
    rune.
Til biþ se þe his treowe gehealdeð: ne sceal næfre his
    torn to rycene
beorn of his breostum acyþan,   nemþe he ær þa bote
    cunne,
eorl mid elne gefremman.   Wel bið þam þe him are
    seceð,
frofre to Fæder on heofonum,   þær us eal seo fæstnung
    stondeð.   *115*

all this earthly foundation becomes idle.'"
  So quoth the wise in mind, and sat apart in
    meditation.
Good is he who holds his faith, nor shall ever his
    anger too quickly
a man from his breast reveal, unless he first its remedy
    knows how,
this earl, with courage to effect. Well is it for him who
    mercy seeks,
comfort from the Father in heaven, where for us all
    security stands.

from *The West Saxon Gospels*

St. Luke, XV, 11-32: The Prodigal Son

11. He cwæð, Soðlice sum man hæfde twegen suna.

12. Þa cwæð se gingra to his fæder, "Fæder, syle me minne dæl minre æhte þe me to gebyreþ." Þa dælde he him his æhte.

13. Ða æfter feawum dagum ealle his þing gegaderude se gingra sunu, and ferde wræclice on feorlen rice, and forspilde þar his æhta, lybbende on his gælsan.

14. Ða he hig hæfde ealle amyrrede, þa wearð mycel hunger on þam rice, and he wearð wædla.

15. Þa ferde he and folgude anum burhsittendan men þæs rices; ða sende he hine to his tune þæt he heolde his swyn.

16. Ða gewilnode he his wambe gefyllan of þam beancoddum þe ða swyn æton; and him man ne sealde.

17. Þa beþohte he hine, and cwæð, "Eala, hu fela hyrlinga on mines fæder huse hlaf genohne habbað; and ic her on hungre forwurðe!

18. Ic arise, and ic fare to minum fæder, and ic secge him, 'Eala, fæder, ic syngode on heofenas and beforan þe;

19. Nu ic neom wyrðe þæt ic beo þin sunu nemned; do me swa anne of þinum hyrlingum.' "

20. And he aras þa and com to his fæder. And þa gyt þa he wæs feorr his fæder, he hyne geseah, and wearð mid mildheortnesse astyrod, and agen hine arn and hine beclypte and cyste hine.

21. Ða cwæð his sunu, "Fæder, ic syngude on heofon and beforan ðe; nu ic ne eom wyrþe þæt ic þin sunu beo genemned."

22. Ða cwæþ se fæder to his þeowum, "Bringað raðe þone selestan gegyrelan and scrydað hyne, and syllað him hring on his hand and gescy to his fotum;

23. And bringað an fætt styric and ofsleað, and utun etan and gewistfullian;

24. For þam þes min sunu wæs dead, and he geedcucude; he forwearð, and he is gemet." Ða ongunnon hig gewistlæcan.

25. Soðlice hys yldra sunu wæs on æcere; and he com, and þa he þam huse genealæhte, he gehyrde þone sweg and þæt weryd.

26. Þa clypode he anne þeow and axode hine hwæt þæt wære.

27. Ða cwæð he, "Þin broðor com; and þin fæder ofsloh an fæt celf, for þam þe he hyne halne onfeng."

28. Ða bealh he hine and nolde in gan. Þa eode his fæder ut and ongan hine biddan.

29. Ða cwæþ he his fæder andswarigende, "Efne swa fela geara ic þe þeowude, and ic næfre þin bebod ne forgymde; and ne sealdest þu me

næfre an ticcen þæt ic mid minum freondum
gewistfullude;

30. Ac syððan þes þin sunu com þe hys spede
mid myltystrum amyrde, þu ofsloge him fætt
celf."

31. Ða cwæþ he, "Sunu, þu eart symle mid
me, and ealle mine þing synt þine;

32. Þe gebyrede gewistfullian and geblissian,
for þam þes þin broðor wæs dead, and he
geedcucede; he forwearð, and he is gemet."

RIDDLE: THE BOOKWORM

Moððe word fræt.   Me þæt þuhte
wrætlicu wyrd,   þa ic þæt wundor gefrægn,
þæt se wyrm forswealg   wera gied sumes,
þeof in þystro,   þrymfæstne cwide
ond þæs strangan staþol.   Stælgiest ne wæs
wihte þy gleawra,   þe he þam wordum swealg.

A moth ate a word.   I thought that [That seemed to me]
marvelously weird,   when I heard of that wonder,
that the worm swallowed up   some words of a man,
a thief in darkness,   glorious speech
5   and strongly established.   The thievish stranger was not
a whit the wiser   after he swallowed those words.

THE WIFE'S LAMENT

Ic þis giedd wrece   bi me ful geomorre,
minre sylfre sið.   Ic þæt secgan mæg
hwæt ic yrmþa gebad,   siþþan ic up weox,
niwes oþþe ealdes,   no ma þonne nu.
A ic wite wonn   minra wræcsiþa.
    Ærest min hlaford gewat   heonan of leodum
ofer yþa gelac;   hæfde ic uhtceare
hwær min leodfruma   londes wære.
Ða ic me feran gewat   folgað secan,
wineleas wræcca   for minre weaþearfe,
ongunnon þæt þæs monnes   magas hycgan
þurh dyrne geþoht   þæt hy todælden unc,
þæt wit gewidost   in woruldrice
lifdon laðlicost;   and mec longade.
    Het mec hlaford min   her eard niman;
ahte ic leofra lyt   on þissum londstede,
holdra freonda;   forþon is min hyge geomor.
Ða ic me ful gemæcne   monnan funde,
heardsæligne,   hygegeomorne,
mod miþendne,   morþor hycgendne,
bliþe gebæro.   Ful oft wit beotedan
þæt unc ne gedælde   nemne deað ana,
owiht elles;   eft is þæt onhworfen,
is nu fornumen   swa hit no wære
freondscipe uncer.   Sceal ic feor ge neah
mines felaleofan   fæhðu dreogan.
    Heht mec mon wunian   on wuda bearwe.
under actreo   in þam eorðscræfe.
Eald is þes eorðsele,   eal ic eom oflongad;
sindon dena dimme,   duna uphea,

I make known this song full sadly about myself,
my selfsame journey; I tell, that can,
what hardship I have endured since I grew up
— new or old, never more than now.
5   Ay I know my dark exile-journey.
    First my lord departed hence from his people
over the bounding waves; I had dawn-care about
where, in what land, my prince was.
Then I went away myself, to seek the place,
10   a friendless exile, in my grievous need.
Then began this man's kinsmen to think
through secret thoughts that they would separate us two,
so that we two widest apart in the world-kingdom
would live — most loathsome to me in my longing.
15   My lord commanded me to take a dwelling here;
I have few beloved in this country,
faithful friends; therefore is my heart sad.
Thus I found a man full congenial to me
unfortunate, sad-hearted,
20   concealing his mind, thinking evil.
With blithe cries full oft we vowed
that nothing would separate us two except death alone,
not anything else; afterwards that is overturned;
now it is as if it never were,
25   our friendship. I must far and near
my much beloved's enmity endure.
    A man ordered me to dwell in a forest grove,
under an oak-tree, in this earth-cave.
Old is this earth-hall; I am all heavy with longing.
30   The valleys are gloomy, the downs up high,

bitre burgtunas   brerum beweaxne,
wic wynna leas.   Ful oft mec her wraþe begeat
fromsiþ frean.   Frynd sind on eorþan,
leofe lifgende,   leger weardiað,
þonne ic on uhtan   ana gonge   35
under actreo   geond þas eorðscrafu.
Þær ic sittan mot   sumorlangne dæg,
þær ic wepan mæg   mine wræcsiþas,
earfoþa fela;   forþon ic æfre ne mæg
þære modceare   minre gerestan   40
ne ealles þæs longaþes   þe mec on þissum life begeat.
    A scyle geong mon   wesan geomormod,
heard heortan geþoht;   swylce habban sceal
bliþe gebæro,   eac þon breostceare,
sinsorgna gedreag;   sy æt him sylfum gelong   45
eal his worulde wyn.   Sy ful wide fah
feorres folclondes   þæt min freond siteð
under stanhliþe   storme behrimed,
wine werigmod,   wætre beflowen
on dreorsele,   dreogeð se min wine   50
micle modceare;   he gemon to oft
wynlicran wic.   Wa bið þam þe sceal
of langoþe   leofes abidan.

the town's walls with bitter briers overgrown,
wick without joy. Full oft it comes over me hard here,
my lord's departure. Friends are on earth,
loved ones, living, keeping their beds,
while I at dawn alone go
under the oak-tree, through this earth-cave.
There I must sit the summerlong day,
there I weep mightily over my exile-journey
and many troubles, for I may not ever
rest from these mind-cares of mine,
nor all these longings that beset me in this life.
    Ay shall a young man be of sorrowful mood,
hard thoughts in heart, though he may have
a blithe bearing, and besides that breast-care,
continual masses of sorrow, and depend on himself for
all his worldly joy. It is an outcast, full widely
far from homeland, that my friend sits
under a stone-cliff be-rimed by storm,
spirit-weary friend, surrounded with water,
in a dreary hall. My friend he endures
much mind-care; he remembers too often
a happy wick. Woe be to one who must
abide, longing for loved ones.

from THE BESTIARY: THE LION

The Lion's Nature

Ðe leun stant on hille;   and he man hunten here,
Oðer ðurg his nese smel   smake ðat he negge,
Bi wilc weie so he wile   to dele niðer wenden,
Alle hise fetsteppes   after him he filleð;
Drageð dust wið his stert   ðer he dun steppeð,   5
Oðer dust oðer deu,   ðat he ne cunne is finden;
Driveð dun to his den   ðar he him bergen wille.
    An oðer kinde he haveð.   Wanne he is ikindled
Stille lið ðe leun,   ne stireð he nout of slepe,
Til ðe sunne haveð sinen   ðries him abuten;   10
Ðanne reiseð his fader him   mit te rem ðat he makeð.
    Ðe ðridde lage haveð ðe leun;   ðanne he lieð to slepen
Sal he nevre luken   ðe lides of hise egen.

The lion stands on a hill;   if he a man hunting hears,
Or through his nose's smell   scents that he draws nigh,
By whichever way that he wants   to the dale downwards to go,
All his footsteps   behind him he fills;
He drags dust with his tail   where he steps,
Either dust or dew,   so that he [the hunter] can't find him;
He drives down to his den   where he will shelter himself.
    Another kind [nature, characteristic] he has.   When he is born
The lion lies still,   not stirring out of his sleep
Till the sun has shone   thrice about him;
Then his father raises [rouses] him   with the roar that he makes.
    This third law [habit] has the lion: when he lies down to sleep
He never will lock [shut]   the lids of his eyes.

Signification

    Welle heg is tat hil   ðat is hevenriche;
Ure Loverd is te leun   ðe liveð ðer abuven;   15
Hu ðo him likede   to ligten her on erðe,
Migte nevre divel witen,   ðo he be derne hunte,
Hu he dun come,   ne hu he dennede him
In ðat defte meiden,   Marie bi name,

    Well high is that hill   that is the kingdom of Heaven;
Our Lord is the lion   that lives there above.
How, when it pleased him,   to alight here on earth,
The devil might never know,   though he be a cunning hunter,
How he came down,   nor how he sheltered himself as in a den
In that gentle maiden,   Mary by name,

Þe him bar to manne frame.   *20*
Ðo ure Drigten ded was,   and dolven also his wille was,
In a ston stille he lai   til it kam ðe ðridde dai;
His fader him filstnede swo   ðat he ros fro dede ðo,
         us to lif holden.
Wakeð so his wille is,   so hirde for his folde;   *25*
He is hirde, we ben sep;   silden he us wille
If we heren to his word   ðat we ne gon nowor wille.

Who bore him for man's benefit.
When our Lord was dead,   and buried also was his will,
In a stone still he lay   till it came the third day;
His father helped him so   that he rose from the dead then,
         to hold us to life.
He watches as is his will,   like a shepherd for his sheep;
He is shepherd, we are sheep; he   will shield us
If we obey his word   that we go nowhere wild [astray].

CHARMS

Against A Wen

Wenne, wenne, wenchichenne,
  her ne scealt þu timbrien,   ne nenne tun habben,
  ac þu scealt north eonene   to þan nihgan berhge,
  þer þu hauest, ermig,   enne broþer.
  He þe sceal legge   leaf et heafde.   *5*
  Under fot wolues,   under ueþer earnes,
  under earnes clea,   a þu geweornie.
  Clinge þu   alswa col on heorþe,
  scring þu   alswa scerne awage,
  and weorne   alswa weter on anbre.   *10*
  Swa litel þu gewurþe   alswa linsetcorn,
and miccli lesse alswa anes handwurmes hupeban, and
alswa litel þu gewurþe þet þu nawiht gewurþe.

Wen, wen,   little wen,
  here thou shalt not build,   nor no town have,
  but thou shalt north hence   to that nearby hill,
  where thou havest, poor wretch,   a brother.
  He thee shall lay   leaf at head.
  Under foot of wolf,   under feather of eagle,
  under eagle's claw,   aye thou wane.
  Shrivel thou   as coal on hearth,
  shrink thou   as sheerly away,
  and wane   as water in jug.
  So little thou become   as a linseed-grain,
and mickle less than a handworm's hipbone, and
so little thou become that thou art naught.

For A Swarm Of Bees

Wið ymbe nim eorþan, oferweorp mid þinre swiþran
handa under þinum swiþran fet, and cweð:
  Fo ic under fot,   funde ic hit.
  Hwæt, eorðe mæg   wið ealra wihta gehwilce
  and wið andan   and wið æminde   *5*
  and wið þa micelan   mannes tungan.
And wiððon forweorp ofer greot, þonne hi swirman, and
cweð:
  Sitte ge, sigewif,   sigað to eorþan!   *10*
  Næfre ge wilde   to wuda fleogan.
  Beo ge swa gemindige   mines godes,
  swa bið manna gehwilc   metes and eþeles.

For a swarm of bees: Take earth, throw over with thy right
hand under thy right foot, and say:
  Take I under foot,   try I it,
  lo! earth is mighty   against all creatures, every one,
  and against envy   and against malice,
  and against that mickle   tongue of man.
And with that throw over them grit, when they swarm, and
say:
  Sit ye, victory-women,   settle to earth.
  Never ye wild   to wood fly.
  Be ye as mindful   of my goods
  as is every man   of meat and property.

Medieval Lyrics
12th-15th centuries

Adam Lay Ybounden

Adam lay ybounden,
Bounden in a bond;
Four thousand winter
Thought he not too long.

And all was for an appil,   5
An appil that he tok,
As clerkes finden writen
In here book.

Ne hadde the appil take ben,
The appil take ben,   10
Ne hadde never Our Lady
A ben hevene quene.

Blessed be the time
That appil take was.
Therefore we moun singen   15
"Deo gracias."

I Sing of a Maiden

I Sing of a maiden
   That is makeles;
King of alle kinges
   To her son she ches.
He cam also stille   5
   Ther His moder was,
As dewe in Aprille
   That falleth on the gras.
He cam also stille
   To His moderes bowr,   10
As dewe in Aprille
   That falleth on the flowr.

He cam also stille
   There His moder lay,
As dewe in Aprille   15
   That falleth on the spray.
Moder and maiden
   Was never none but she;
Wel may swich a lady
   Godes moder be.   20

"Sumer is icumen in"
(The Cuckoo Song)

Sumer is icumen in,
   Lhude sing cuccu!
Groweth sed and bloweth med
   And springth the wude nu.
      Sing cuccu!   5

Awe bleteth after lomb,
   Lhouth after calve cu,
Bulluc sterteth, bucke verteth,
   Murie sing cuccu!
      Cuccu, cuccu,   10
   Wel singes thu cuccu.
   Ne swik thu naver nu!

Alysoun

Bytuene Mersh and Averil,
   When spray biginneth to springe,
The lutel foul hath hire wyl
   On hire lud to synge.
Ich libbe in love-longinge   5
   For semlokest of alle thinge;

Adam Lay Ybounden **8. here:** their. **15. moun:** may. **16. Deo gracias:** Thanks be to God. **I Sing of a Maiden** **2. makeles:** mateless, matchless. **4. To:** as; **ches:** chose. **5. also:** as. **6. Ther:** Where. **Sumer Is Icumen In** **1. is icumen:** i.e., has come. **2. Lhude:** loud. **3. bloweth:** bloometh; **med:** meadow. **4. wude:** wood; **nu:** now. **6. Awe:** Ewe. **7. Lhouth:** Loweth; **cu:** cow. **8. sterteth:** springeth, leapeth; **verteth:** farteth (i.e., from eating fresh grass). **9. Murie:** Merrily. **12. swik:** cease. **Alysoun** **4. On hire lud:** In her own language. **5. Ich libbe:** I live. **6. semlokest:** seemliest, fairest.

He may me blisse bringe,
Icham in hire baundoun.
   An hendy hap ichabbe yhent,
   Ichot from hevene it is me sent;   *10*
   From alle wymmen my love is lent
   And lyht on Alysoun.

On heu hire her is fayr ynoh,
   Hire browe broune, hire eye blake;
With lossum chere he on me loh,   *15*
   With middel smal and wel ymake.
   Bote he me wolle to hire take
   For to ben hire owen make,
   Longe to lyven ichulle forsake,
      And feye fallen adoun.   *20*
      An hendy hap, etc.

Nihtes when I wende and wake,
   Forthi myn wonges waxeth won;
Levedi, al for thine sake
   Longinge is ylent me on.   *25*
   In world nis non so wyter mon
   That al hire bounte telle con;
   Hire swyre is whittore then the swon,
      And feyrest may in toune.
      An hendy hap, etc.   *30*

Icham for wowing al forwake,
   Wery so water in wore;
Lest eny reve me my make,
   Ichabbe y-yerned yore.
   Betere is tholien whyle sore   *35*
   Then mournen evermore.
   Geynest under gore,
      Herkne to my roun:
      An hendy hap, etc.

UBI SUNT QUI ANTE NOS FUERENT?

Were beeth they that biforen us weren,
Houndes ladden and haukes beren
   And hadden feld and wode?
The riche leuedies in here bour,
That wereden gold in here tressour   *5*
   With here brighte rode;

Eten and drounken and maden hem glad;
Here lif was al with gamen ylad,
   Men kneleden hem biforen,
They beren hem wel swithe heye —   *10*
And in a twincling of on eye
   Here soules weren forloren.

Were is that lawing and that song,
That trayling and that proude gong,
   Tho haukes and tho houndes?   *15*
Al that joye is went away,
That wele is comen to weylaway,
   To manie harde stoundes.

Here paradis they nomen here,
And nou they lien in helle yfere,   *20*
   The fyr hit brennes evere.
Long is *ay* and long is *ho*,
Long is *wy* and long is *wo*—
   Thennes ne cometh they nevere.

WESTERN WIND

Westron wind, when wilt thou blow,
The small rain down can rain?
Christ, that my love were in my arms,
And I in my bed again.

---

7. he: i.e., she. **8. Icham:** I am; **baundoun:** power. **9. hendy:** gracious; **hap:** fortune; **ichabbe:** I have; **yhent:** received. **10. Ichot:** I know. **11. lent:** taken away. **12. lyht:** alighted, settled. **13. heu:** hue; **her:** hair. **15. lossum:** lovesome; **chere:** face; **loh:** laughed, smiled. **17. Bote:** Unless. **18. make:** mate. **19. ichulle:** I shall. **20. feye:** doomed to die. **22. wende:** toss, turn. **23. Forthi:** therefore; **wonges:** cheeks. **24. Levedi:** Lady. **25. ylent me on:** come upon me. **26. wyter:** wise. **27. bounte:** excellence. **28. swyre:** neck. **29. may:** maiden. **31. wowing:** wooing; **forwake:** worn out with lying awake. **32. wery so:** weary as; **wore:** weir, millpond, or other turbid pool? **33. reve me:** reave, deprive me of. **34. yore:** long while. **35. tholien whyle sore:** suffer a while sorely. **37. Geynest:** Fairest; **under gore:** in gown (i.e., among women). **38. roun:** voice, song.   UBI SUNT Title: translated by the first line. **1. Were:** where. **2. ladden:** led; **haukes:** hawks. **4. leuedies:** ladies; **here:** their; **bour:** bower. **5. tressour:** headdress. **6. rode:** face, complexion. **7. hem:** them. **10. swithe:** very. **13. lawing:** laughing. **14. trayling:** (trailing of robes? travelling?); **gong:** going, walking. **15. tho:** those. **17. wele:** well-being, wealth, prosperity; **weylaway:** Alas! Woe is me! **18. stoundes:** times. **19. nomen:** took. **20. yfere:** together. **22. ay:** alas!; **ho:** oh! **23. wy, wo:** woe! **24. thennes:** thence.

Medieval Ballads
13th-15th centuries

Sir Patrick Spens

The king sits in Dumferling toune,
  Drinking the blude-reid wine:
"O whar will I get guid sailor,
  To sail this ship of mine?"

Up and spak an eldern knicht,   *5*
  Sat at the king's richt knee:
"Sir Patrick Spens is the best sailor
  That sails upon the sea."

The king has written a braid letter,
  And signed it wi' his hand,   *10*
And sent it to Sir Patrick Spens,
  Was walking on the sand.

The first line that Sir Patrick read,
  A loud lauch lauched he;
The next line that Sir Patrick read,   *15*
  The teir blinded his ee.

"O wha is this has don this deid,
  This ill deid done to me,
To send me out this time o' the year,
  To sail upon the sea!   *20*

"Mak haste, mak haste, my mirry men all,
  Our guid ship sails the morn."
"O say na sae, my master deir,
  For I feir a deadly storm.

"Late late yestreen I saw the new moon   *25*
  Wi' the auld moon in her arm,
And I feir, I feir, my deir master,
  That we will come to harm."

O our Scots nobles wer richt laith
  To weet their cork-heild schoon;   *30*
Bot lang owre a' the play wer played
  Their hats they swam aboon.

O lang, lang may their ladies sit,
  Wi' their fans into their hand,
Or eir they see Sir Patrick Spens   *35*
  Come sailing to the land.

O lang, lang may the ladies stand,
  Wi' their gold kems in their hair,
Waiting for their ain deir lords,
  For they'll see thame na mair.   *40*

Haf owre, haf owre to Aberdour,
  It's fifty fadom deip,
And their lies guid Sir Patrick Spens,
  Wi' the Scots lords at his feit.

The Three Ravens

There were three ravens sat on a tree.
  Down a down, hey down, hey down,
There were three ravens sat on a tree,
  With a down;
There were three ravens sat on a tree,   *5*
They were as black as they might be,
  With a down derry, derry, derry, down, down.

The one of them said to his make,
  "Where shall we our breakfast take?"

"Down in yonder greenë field   *10*
There lies a knight slain under his shield;

Medieval Ballads Since folk ballads were long passed down orally before being recorded in writing, many exist in different versions, and printed texts often combine elements from two or more of these. You may want to look at others. Francis James Child's *The English and Scottish Popular Ballads* (1857-58, rev. 1883-98) includes different versions of hundreds of ballads, along with interesting comparisons and other discussion. **Sir Patrick Spens** Child #58. **9. braid:** broad. **29. laith:** loath. **32. aboon:** above. **The Three Ravens** Child #26. Each stanza should be sung with the twice repeated first line and the refrain lines ("Down a down" etc.), as shown with the first stanza. **8. make:** mate.

"His hounds they lie down at his feet,
So well do they their master keep;

"His hawks they fly so eagerly,
There's no fowl dare him come nigh."   *15*

Down there comes a fallow doe,
As great with young as she might go.

She lift up his bloudy head
And kissed his wounds that were so red.

She got him up upon her back   *20*
And carried him to earthen lake.

She buried him before the prime —
She was dead herself ere evensong time.

God send every gentleman
Such hounds, such hawks, and such a leman.   *25*

THOMAS RHYMER

True Thomas lay on Huntlie Bank;
   A ferlie he spied wi' his e'e;
And there he saw a lady bright
   Come riding down by the Eildon Tree.

Her skirt was o' the grass-green silk,   *5*
   Her mantle o' the velvet fine;
At ilka tett o' her horse's mane
   Hung fifty siller bells and nine.

True Thomas he pu'd aff his cap,
   And bowed him low down to his knee: *10*
"All hail, thou mighty Queen of Heaven!
   For thy peer on earth I never did see."

"O no, O no, True Thomas," she said,
   "That name does not belang to me;
I'm but the Queen o' fair Elfland,   *15*
   That am hither come to visit thee.

"Harp and carp, Thomas," she said;
   "Harp and carp along wi' me;
And if ye dare to kiss my lips,
   Sure of your body I will be."   *20*

"Betide me weal, betide me woe,
   That weird shall never daunten me."
Syne he has kissed her rosy lips,
   All underneath the Eildon Tree.

"Now ye maun go wi' me," she said,   *25*
   "True Thomas, ye maun go wi' me;
And ye maun serve me seven years,
   Thro' weal or woe as may chance to be."

She's mounted on her milk-white steed,
   She's ta'en True Thomas up behind;   *30*
And aye, whene'er her bridle rang,
   The steed flew swifter than the wind.

It was mirk, mirk night, there was nae starlight,
   And they waded rivers aboon the knee;
And they saw neither sun nor moon,   *35*
   But they heard the roaring of the sea.

O they rade on, and farther on,
   Until they came to a garden green:
He's put up his hand for to pull some fruit:
   For lack o' food he was like to tyne.   *40*

"O no, O no, True Thomas," she says.
   "Hold your hand, that must not be;
It was a' that cursed fruit o' thine
   Beggared man and woman in your country.

"But I have a loaf here in my lap,   *45*
   Likewise a bottle of guid red wine;
And now ere we go farther on,
   We'll rest a while, and ye may dine."

When he had eaten and drunk his fill,
   "Lay down your head upon my knee,"   *50*
The lady said, "ere we climb yon hill,
   And I will show you ferlies three.

"O see ye not yon narrow road,
   So thick beset wi' thorns and briers?
That is the Path of Righteousness,   *55*
   Though after it but few inquires.

---

25. leman: sweetheart.   **THOMAS RHYMER**   Child #37. **2. ferlie:** marvel, wonder. **7. ilka tett:** each tuft. **17. Harp and carp:** play, sing, talk. **22. weird:** fate, doom. **23. syne:** then. **25. maun:** must. **40. tyne:** die.

"And see not ye that braid, braid road
    That lies across the lily leven?
That is the Path of Wickedness,
    Though some call it the Road to Heaven.   *60*

"And see not ye yon bonny road
    That winds about the fernie brae?
That is the road to fair Elfland,
    Where you and I this night maun gae.

"But, Thomas, ye maun haud your tongue,   *65*
    Whatever ye may hear or see;
For gin ae word you should chance to speak,
    You'll ne'er get back to your ain country."

He's gotten a coat of the even cloth,
    And a pair of shoes of velvet green;   *70*
And till seven years were gane and past,
    True Thomas on earth was never seen.

RIDDLES WISELY EXPOUNDED

There were three sisters fair and bright,
    Jennifer, Gentle, and Rosemary,
And they three loved one valiant knight,
    As the dove flies over the mulberry tree.

The eldest sister let him in,   *5*
And barred the door with a silver pin.

The second sister made his bed,
And placed soft pillows under his head.

The youngest sister, fair and bright,
Was resolved for to wed with this valiant knight.   *10*

"And if you can answer questions three,
O then, fair maid, I will marry with thee.

"What is louder than an horn,
And what is sharper than a thorn?"

"Thunder is louder than an horn,   *15*
And hunger is sharper than a thorn."

"What is longer than the way,
And what is deeper than the sea?"

"Love is longer than the way,
And hell is deeper than the sea."   *20*

"What is greener than the grass,
And what is worse than a woman was?"

"Poison is greener than the grass,
And the Devil is worse than woman was."

"You have answered my questions three;   *25*
And now, fair maid, I will marry with thee."

LORD RANDAL

"O where hae ye been, Lord Randal, my son?
O where hae ye been, my handsome young man?"
"I ha been to the wild wood; mother, make my bed soon,
For I'm weary wi' hunting, and fain wald lie down."

"Where gat ye your dinner, Lord Randal, my son?   *5*
Where gat ye your dinner, my handsome young man?"
"I dined wi' my true-love; mother, make my bed soon,
For I'm weary wi' hunting, and fain wald lie down."

"What gat ye to your dinner, Lord Randal, my son?
What gat ye to your dinner, my handsome young man?"   *10*
"I gat eels boiled in broo'; mother, make by bed soon,
For I'm weary wi' hunting, and fain wald lie down."

"And what gat your leavings, Lord Randal, my son?
And wha gat your leavings, my handsome young man?"
"My hawks and my hounds; mother, make my bed soon,   *15*
For I'm wearied wi' hunting, and fain wald lie down."

"And what became of them, Lord Randal, my son?
And what became of them, my handsome young man?"
"O they swelled and they died; mother, make my bed soon,
For I'm weary wi' hunting, and fain wald lie down."   *20*

"O I fear ye are poisoned, Lord Randal, my son!
O I fear ye are poisoned, my handsome young man!"
"O yes! I am poisoned; mother, make my bed soon,
For I'm sick at the heart, and I fain wald lie down."

"What d' ye leave to your mother, Lord Randal, my son?   *25*
What d' ye leave to your mother, my handsome young man?"
"Four and twenty milk-kine; mother, make my bed soon,
For I'm sick at the heart, and I fain wald lie down."

---

58. lily leven: lovely lea. **67. gin:** if.   **RIDDLES WISELY EXPOUNDED** Child #1.   **LORD RANDAL** Child #12. **11. broo':** broth. **13. wha:** who.

"What d' ye leave to your sister, Lord Randal, my son?
What d' ye leave to your sister, my handsome young man?" *30*
"My gold and my silver; mother, make my bed soon,
For I'm sick at the heart, and I fain wald lie down."

"What d' ye leave to your brother, Lord Randal, my son?
What d' ye leave to your brother, my handsome young man?"
"My houses and my lands; mother, make my bed soon,   *35*
For I'm sick at the heart, and I fain wald lie down."

"What d' ye leave to your true-love, Lord Randal, my son?
What d' ye leave to your true-love, my handsome young man?"
"I leave her hell and fire; mother, make my bed soon,
For I'm sick at the heart, and I fain wald lie down."   *40*

"SIR JOHN MANDEVILLE"
France, c.1300-1372

from *THE VOIAGE AND TRAVAILE*
OF SIR JOHN MAUNDEVILLE, KT.

Ethiope is departed in two princypall parties; and that is in the Est partie, and in the
Meridionall partie, the whiche partie meridionall is clept Moretane And the folk of that
contree ben blake ynow, and more blake than in the tother partie, and thei ben clept
Mowres. In that partie is a well that in the day it is so cold that no man may drynke
thereoffe, and in the nyght it is so hoot that no man may suffre hys hond therein. And   *5*
beyonde that partie, toward the South, to passe by the See Occean, is a gret lond and a
gret contrey. But men may not duell there, for the fervent brennynge of the sonne, so is
it passynge hoot in that contrey.

In Ethiope all the ryveres and all the watres ben trouble, and they ben somdell salte,
for the gret hete that is there. And the folk of that contree ben lyghtly dronken, and han   *10*
but litill appetyt to mete. . . . In Ethiope ben many dyverse folk, and Ethiope is clept
"Cusis." In that contree ben folk that han but o foot, and thei gon so blyve that it is
mervaylle; and the foot is so large that it schadeweth all the body agen the sonne,
whanne thei wole lye and reste hem. In Ethiope, whan the children ben yonge and lytill,
thei ben all yalowe; and whan that thei wexen of age that yalownesse turneth to ben all   *15*
blak. In Ethiope is the cytee of Saba and the lond of the whiche on of the thre Kynges,
that presented oure Lord in Bethleem, was kyng offe.

Fro Ethiope men gon into Ynde be manye dyverse contreyes. And men clepen the
high Ynde "Emlak." And Ynde is devyded in three princypall parties; that is, the more,

THE VOIAGE AND TRAVAILE   The name "Sir John Mandeville" was real, but it was adopted as a persona by a 14th-century Frenchman. His book is a compilation of many travel and other writings (some of which were originally in English); the popular work was soon translated into English and other languages. **2. Moretane:** Mauritania. **3. ynow:** enough. **4. Mowres:** Moors. **9. trouble:** troubled, muddied, unclear. **11. mete:** food, meals. **12. "Cusis":** alleged early name of Ethiopia; cf. "Cush"; **o:** one; **blyve:** quickly. **14. hem:** them. **16. Saba:** Saba, Sheba (see Psalms 72:10). **19. Emlak:** error for *Euilak* (from *Havilah*; see Genesis 2:11, p. 243).

that is a full hoot contree, and Ynde the lesse, that is a full atempree contree that 20
streccheth to the lond of Medé; and the thridde part, toward the Septentrion, is full cold,
so that for pure cold and contynuell frost the water becometh cristall. And upon tho
roches of cristall growen the gode dyamandes, that ben of trouble colour. Yalow cristall
draweth colour lyke oylle. And thei ben so harde that no man may pollysch hem; and
men clepen hem "dyamandes" in that contree, and "hamese" in another contree. Othere 25
dyamandes men fynden in Arabye that ben not so gode, and thei ben more broun and
more tendre. And other dyamandes also men fynden in the Ile of Cipre that ben yit more
tendre, and hem men may wel pollische. And in the lond of Macedoyne men fynden
dyamaundes also. But the beste and the moste precyiouse ben in Ynde.

And men fynden many tyme harde dyamandes in a masse, that cometh out of gold 30
whan men puren it and fynen it out of the myne, whan men breken that masse in smale
peces. And sum tyme it happeneth that men fynden summe as grete as a pese, and
summe lasse; and thei ben als harde as tho of Ynde.

And all be it that men fynden gode dyamandes in Ynde, yit natheles men fynden
hem more comounly upon the roches in the see, and upon hilles where the myne of gold 35
is. And thei growen many togedre, on lytill, another gret. And ther ben summe of the
gretnesse of a bene, and summe als grete as an hasell-note. And thei ben square and
poynted of here owne kynde, bothe aboven and benethen, withouten worchinge of
mannes hond. And thei growen togedre, male and femele. And thei ben norysscht with
the dew of hevene. And thei engendren comounly, and bryngen forth smale children, 40
that multiplyen and growen all the yeer. I have often tymes assayed that yif a man kepe
hem with a lityll of the roche, and wete hem with May dew oftesithes, thei schull growe
everyche yeer, and the smale wole wexen grete. For right as the fyn perl congeleth and
wexeth gret of the dew of hevene, right so doth the verray dyamand; and right as the
perl, of his owne kynde, taketh roundnesse, right so the dyamand, be vertu of God, 45
taketh squarenesse.

And men schall bere the dyamaund on his left syde, for it is of grettere vertue
thanne, than on the right syde. For the strengthe of here growynge is toward the North,
that is the left syde of the world, and the left partie of man is, whan he turneth his face
toward the Est. 50

And yif you lyke to knowe the vertues of the dyamand, as men may fynden in the
Lapidarye, that many men knowen noght, I schall telle you, as thei beyond the see seyn
and affermen, of whom all science and all philosophie cometh from.

He that bereth the dyamand upon him, it yeveth him hardynesse and manhode, and
it kepeth the lemes of his body hole. It yeveth him victorye of his enemyes, in plee and 55
in werre, yif his cause be rightfull; and it kepeth him that bereth it in gode wytt; and it
kepeth him fro strif and ryot, fro evyll swevenes, from sorwes, and from enchaun-
tementes, and from fantasyes and illusiouns of wykked spirites. And yif ony cursed
wycche or enchauntour wolde bewycche him that bereth the dyamand, all that sorwe

---

20. atempree: temperate. **21. Medé:** Media; **Septentrion:** northern regions. **22. tho:** those. **32. pese:** pease, pea. **33. als:** as. **38. here:** their. **42. oftesithes:** oftentimes, often. **51. yif you lyke:** Cf. French *s'il vous plaît.* **55. lemes:** limbs; **plee:** plea, lawsuit. **57. swevenes:** dreams.

and myschance schall turne to himself, thorgh vertue of that ston. And also no wylde   *60*
best dar assaylle the man that bereth it on him. Also the dyamand scholde ben yoven
frely, withouten coveytynge and withouten byggynge, and than it is of grettere vertue.
And it maketh a man more strong and more sad agenst his enemyes. And it heleth him
that is lunatyk, and hem that the fend pursueth or travayleth. And yif venym or poysoun
be brought in presence of the dyamand, anon it begynneth to wexe moyst and for to   *65*
swete.

There ben also dyamandes in Ynde that ben clept "violastres" — for here colour is
liche vyolet, or more browne than the violettes — that ben full harde and full precyous.
But yit sum men love not hem so wel as the othere. But in soth, to me, I wolde loven hem
als moche as the othere, for I have seen hem assayed. Also there is another maner of   *70*
dyamandes that ben als white as cristall, but thei ben a lityll more trouble; and thei ben
gode and of gret vertue, and all thei ben square and poynted of here owne kynde. And
summe ben six squared, summe four squared, and summe thre, as nature schapeth hem.
And therfore whan grete lordes and knyghtes gon to seche worschipe in armes, thei beren
gladly the dyamaund upon hem.   *75*

I schal speke a litill more of the dyamandes, allthough I tarye my matere for a tyme,
to that ende that thei that knowen hem not be not disceyved be gabberes that gon be the
contree, that sellen hem. For whoso wil bye the dyamand, it is nedefull to him that he
knowe hem, because that men counterfeten hem often of cristall that is yalow, and of
saphires of cytryne colour, that is yalow also, and of the saphire loupe, and of many   *80*
other stones. But, I tell you, theise contrefetes ben not so harde, and also the poyntes wil
breken lightly, and men may esily pollische hem. But summe werkmen, for malice, wil
not pollische hem, to that entent to maken men beleve that thei may not ben pollisscht.
But men may assaye hem in this manere: First schere with hem, or write with hem, in
saphires, in cristall, or in other precious stones. After that men taken the ademand, that   *85*
is the schipmannes ston, that draweth the nedle to him, and men leyn the dyamand upon
the ademand, and leyn the nedle before the ademand; and yif the dyamand be gode and
vertuous, the ademand draweth not the nedle to him whils the dyamand is there present.
And this is the preef that thei beyonde the see maken.

Natheles it befalleth often tyme that the gode dyamand leseth his vertue, be synne   *90*
and for incontynence of him that bereth it. And thanne is it nedfull to make it to
recoveren his vertue agen, or els it is of litill value.

(c. 1357)

---

62. **byggynge:** buying. 63. **sad:** strong, able to resist, valiant, steadfast. 75. **gladly:** gladly, preferably, usually. 77. **gabberes:** liars, swindlers. 80. **loupe:** imperfect gem. 84. **schere:** shear, cut, score. 85. **ademand:** adamant — i.e., magnet, loadstone.

JOHN WYCLIF
England, c.1330-1384

from his translation of *THE BIBLE*

The Prodigal Son

A man hadde two sones; and þe ʒonger of hem seide unto his fadir, Fadir, ʒyve me a porcioun of þe substance þat falliþ me. And þe fadir departide him his goodis. And soone aftir, þis ʒonge sone gederide al þat fel to him, and wente forþ in pilgrimage in to a fer contré; and þer he wastide his goodis, lyvynge in lecherie. And after þat he hadde endid alle his goodis, þer fel a gret hungre in þat lond, and he bigan to be nedy. And he wente oute, and clevede to oon of þe citizeins of þat contré, and þis citisein sente him into his toun, to kepe swyn. And þis sone coveitide to fille his beli wiþ pese holes þat þe hogges eten, and no man ʒaf him. And he, turninge aʒen, seide, How many hynen in my fadirs hous ben ful of loves, and Y perishe here for hungre. Y shal rise, and go to my fadir, and seie to him, Fadir, I have synned in heven, and bifore þee; now Y am not worþi to be clepid þi sone, make me as oon of þin hynen. And he roos, and cam to his fadir. And ʒit whanne he was fer, his fadir sawe him, and was moved bi mercy, and rennyng aʒens his sone, fel on his nekke, and kiste him. And þe sone seide to him, Fadir, Y have synned in hevene, and bifore þee; now Y am not worþi to be clepid þi sone. And þe fadir seide to his servauntis anoon, Bringe ʒe forþ þe firste stoole, and cloþe ʒe him, and ʒyve ʒe a ryng in his hond, and shoon upon his feet. And bringe ʒe a fat calf, and sle him, and ete we, and fede us; for þis sone of myn was deed, and is quykened aʒen, and he was perishid, and is foundun. And þei bigunne to feede hem. And his eldere sone was in þe feeld; and whanne he cam, and was nyʒ þe hous, he herde a symphonie and oþer noise of mynystralcye. And þis eldere sone clepide oon of þe servauntis, and axide what weren þes þingis. And he seide to him, Þi broþir is comen, and þi fadir haþ slayn a fat calf, for he haþ resceyved him saaf. But þis eldere sone hadde dedeyn, and wolde not come in; þerfore his fadir wente out, and bigan to preie him. And he answeride, and seide to his fadir, Lo, so many ʒeeris Y serve to þee, Y passide nevere þi mandement; and þou ʒavest me nevere a kide, for to fede me wiþ my frendis. But after þat he, þis þi sone, þat murþeride his goodis wiþ hooris, is come, þou hast killid to him a fat calf. And þe fadir seide to him, Sone, þou art ever more wiþ me, and alle my goodis ben þine. But it was nede to ete and to make mery, for he, þis þi broþir was deed, and lyvede aʒen; he was perishid, and is founden.

(c. 1388)

Anonymous
late 14th century

from *Sir Gawain and the Green Knight*

Stanza 1

Siþen þe sege and þe assaut watz sesed at Troye,
Þe borz brittened and brent to brondez and askez,
Þe tulk þat þe trammes of tresoun þer wrozt
Watz tried for his tricherie, þe trewest on erthe:
Hit watz Ennias þe athel and his highe kynde,   5
Þat siþen depreced prouinces, and patrounes bicome
Welneze of al þe wele in þe West Iles.
Fro riche Romulus to Rome ricchis hym swyþe,
With gret bobbaunce þat burze he biges vpon fyrst,
And neuenes hit his aune nome, as hit now hat;   10

Ticius to Tuskan and teldes bigynnes,
Langaberde in Lumbardie lyftes vp homes,
And fer ouer þe French flod Felix Brutus
On mony bonkkes ful brode Bretayn he settez
    wyth wynne,   15
Where werre and wrake and wonder
Bi syþez hatz wont þerinne,
And oft boþe blysse and blunder
Ful skete hatz skyfted synne.

Geoffrey Chaucer
England, c.1340-1400

NOTE: We base our text of Chaucer's works on that of *The Riverside Chaucer*, Third Edition; General Editor, Larry D. Benson (Houghton Mifflin, 1987) — itself based on the first two editions (1933, 1957), edited by F. N. Robinson. We have made only a few small changes in spelling and punctuation for ease of reading. And we urge readers to consult Benson's edition for information about Chaucer and his work and his age, for a full glossary and extended discussion of Chaucer's language, and for much greater annotation, including frequent references to points made in Chaucer criticism. DATING: Chaucer probably began composing *The Canterbury Tales* about 1386 and continued working on them until near the end of his life. The short poems included here were likely written during the same period.

SIR GAWAIN AND THE GREEN KNIGHT   The "Gawain" poet wrote in a West-Midland dialect contemporary with though different from Chaucer's London dialect, which evolved into modern English. A word-for-word translation reads somewhat stiffly, but preserves some of the alliteration of the first fourteen lines, and even one of the rhymes in the so-called "bob and wheel" (the concluding five lines): "Since the siege and the assault was ceased at Troy, / The borough broken and burnt to brands and ashes, / The knight that the devices of treason there wrought / Was tried for his treachery, the truest on earth. / It was Aeneas the noble and his high kindred / That since depressed provinces, and patrons became / Well-nigh of all the wealth of the West Isles. / Afterwards high-ranked Romulus to Rome betook himself hastily, / With great pride that borough he builds up first, / And names it his own name, as it now has; / Ticius to Tuscany and buildings begins, / Langobard in Lombardy lifts up homes, / And far over the French flood Felix Brutus / On many banks full broad Britain he sets / with joy, / Where war and wrack and wonder / At times has dwelt therein, / And oft both bliss and blunder / Full swiftly have alternated since." The entire poem contains 101 stanzas. **6. depressed:** i.e., subjugated; **patrons:** lords. **7. West Isles:** i.e., Britain. **11. Ticius:** unknown — perhaps a fictitious eponymous founder of Tuscany. **12. Langobard:** eponymous ancestor of the Langobards and founder of Lombardy; **lifts up:** i.e., raises, builds. **14. banks:** banks, shores — or slopes, hills. **18. blunder:** i.e., trouble, turmoil. For a summary of the story, see Yvor Winter's poem of the same title (p. 1348)

NOTE ON PRONUNCIATION: Because pronunciation varies from region to region, it isn't possible to provide a universally accurate guide to the pronunciation of Chaucer's English, which in any event, like its spelling, is not entirely consistent, and about which there isn't absolute certainty. Nevertheless, here are hints about some key vowel sounds and a few other tips that should help you to at least approximate it.

vowel	*IPA symbol*	*pronunciation*	*examples*
a, aa	[a]	like *a* in *father*	whan, bathed, caas
a	[æ]	shorter, as in *that*	that, can
e, ee	[e]	like *a* in *late*	sweete, seke
e	[ɛ]	shorter, as in *met*	every, tendre
e (unstressed)	[ə]	like *a* in *above*	shoures, sonne
i, y	[i]	like *ee* in *sheet*	every, shires, **I**
i, y	[ɪ]	shorter, as in *sit*	swich, is, thyng
o, oo	[o]	like *o* in *rode*	to, roote, good
o, oo	[ɔ]	shorter, like *o* in *hot*	folk, goon, londes
ou, ow	[u]	like *oo* in *shoot*	licour, fowles
u, eu, ew, uw	[y]	like *ü* in German *grün*	vertu, mortreux, muwe
au, aw	[au]	like *ow* in *cow*	straunge, cause, lawe
ai, ay, ei, ey	[aɪ]	sometimes as in *way*	veyne, leyd, sayde
		sometimes as in *aisle*	batailled, vitaille

Pronounce final unstressed *e* (and sometimes *es*) as a separate syllable when it occurs at the end of a line *(soot-e, lond-es)*, and elsewhere when the syllable is required for the metre — e.g. *smal-e, fowl-es, mel-o-dy-e* ("General Prologue," line 9); in contrast, *pal-meres* (line 13) should be pronounced as a two-syllable word; final *e* within a line is usually elided before words beginning with a vowel or an unpronounced *h* *(droghte of, veyne in)*. Otherwise, pronounce all syllables: *bath-ed, y-en, pil-grim-a-ges, con-di-ci-oun, ar-wes, thil-ke, squi-er, pynch-ed, lokk-es, shour-es*; scanning lines will help you decide — e.g. *Of trib-u-la-ci-on in mar-i-age* ("The Wife of Bath's Prologue," line 173). Pronounce the *gh* in *ynogh* and other such words *(droghte, nyght)* like the *ch* in Scottish *loch*. Sound both letters in combinations such as *kn*: *knight, knyves, knowen, gnawen, hal-fe*. Note too that though most lines are fairly regular iambic pentameter, some are acephalous (e.g. line 1), and some have an extra syllable or two (even in addition to a pronounced *e* at the end), since Chaucer often substitutes a trisyllabic foot for the iamb — though elision will often enable you to read such lines as having ten syllables — e.g. in line 15 *every* reads as *ev'ry*, and the final syllables of *many* (212) and *ordre* (214) are elided. Further, you'll find that many words are stressed in ways at variance with modern usage; e.g. for rhyme it is necessary to stress the last syllable of such words as *licour* (line 2), *langage* (211), and *resoun* and *condicioun* (37-38), and the penultimate (i.e. third) syllable of such words as *chivalrie* and *curteisie* (45-46) and *hethenesse* and *worthynesse* (49-50).

To supplement these suggestions, listen to recordings of people reading from Chaucer's work. In addition, read the poetry *aloud*: frequently words that look unfamiliar on the page will sound familiar.

The prologues.

Hanne that Aprpll
with his shoures sote
The drought of Marche
had perced the rote
And bathed euery vapne
in suche lycoure
Of whiche vertue/ engen=
dred is the floure
Whan zephirus eke with his sote breth
Enspired hath euery holte and heth
The tendre croppes/and the ponge sonne
Hath in the Ram halfe his course ronne
And smale foules maken melodpe
That slepen al npght with open eye
So prpcketh hem nature in her courage
Than longen folke to go on pplgrymage
And palmers to seken straunge strondes
To serue halowes couthe in sondry londes
And specyally fro euery shpres ende
Of Englonde to Launterbury they wende
The holp blysful martyr for to seke
That hem hath holpen/whan they were seke.

It befel that season on a day
In South warke at þ taberde as I lay
Redy to go in my pplgrymage
To Launterbury with deuoute courage
That npght was come in to that hostelrye
Wel npne and twenty in a companye
Of sondry folke by auenture yfal
In felyshyp/and pplgrymes were they al
That towarde Launterbury wolde ryde
The chambres and stables weren wyde
And wel weren they eased at the best
And shortly whan the sonne was at rest
So had I spoken with hem euerychone
That I was of her felyshyp anone
And made forwarde erly for to ryse
To take our way there as I you deuyse
But netheles/whyle I haue tyme and space
Or that I ferther in this tale pace
Me thynke it accordaunt to reason
To tel you al the condycyon
Of eche of hem so as it semed me
And whiche they were/and of what degre
And eke in what aray that they were in
And at a knpght than wyl I fyrst begyn.

The knyght.   i.

A knpght there was/ a þ a worthy man
That fro the tyme that he fyrst began
To ryden out/he loued cheualrye
Trouthe /honour /fredom /and curtefye
Ful worthy was he in his lordes warre
And therto had he rydden no man farre
As wel in chrpstendome as in hethenesse
And euer had honour for his worthynesse
At Alysaundre he was/ whan it was won
Ful ofte tyme he had the Bourde begon
Abouen al nacyons in Pruce
In Lettowe had he rydden and in Luce
No crystẽ man so ofte of his degre
In Garnade at the syege had he be
At Algezer/and rydden in Belmarye
At Leyes was he/and also at Satalye
Whan they were wonne/and in the great see
At many a noble armye had he be
At mortal batailles had he ben fyftene
And foughten for our fayth at Tramyssene
In lystes thues /and aye slayne his fo
This ilke worthy knpght had ben also
Somtyme with the lorde of Palathye
Ayenst another hethen in Turkye
And euermore he had a soueraync pryse
And though he was worthy he was wise
And of his porte as meke as is a mayde
He neuer yet no vilanye ne sayde
In al his lyfe/vnto no maner wight
He was a very perfyte gentyl knpght
For to tel you of his aray
His hors were good/but he was nothyng gay
Of fustyan he wered a gyppon
Al besmottred with his haubergion
For he was late come fro his vyage
And wente for to don his pplgrymage.

The Squyer.   ii.

With hym there was his sone a yong squyre
A louer and a lufty bachelere
Wt his lockes crul as they were layde in presse
Of twenty yere of age he was I gesse
Of his stature he was of euen length
And wonderly delyuer/and of great strength
                    D.ii.   And

from THE CANTERBURY TALES

GENERAL PROLOGUE

Whan that Aprill with his shoures soote
The droghte of March hath perced to the roote,
And bathed every veyne in swich licour
Of which vertu engendred is the flour;
Whan Zephirus eek with his sweete breeth   5
Inspired hath in every holt and heeth
The tendre croppes, and the yonge sonne
Hath in the Ram his halve cours yronne,
And smale fowles maken melodye,
That slepen al the nyght with open ye   10
(So priketh hem nature in hir corages),
Thanne longen folk to goon on pilgrimages,
And palmeres for to seken straunge strondes,
To ferne halwes, kowthe in sondry londes;
And specially from every shires ende   15
Of Engelond to Caunterbury they wende,
The hooly blisful martir for to seke,
That hem hath holpen whan that they were seeke.
    Bifil that in that seson on a day,
In Southwerk at the Tabard as I lay   20
Redy to wenden on my pilgrymage
To Caunterbury with ful devout corage,
At nyght was come into that hostelrye
Wel nyne and twenty in a compaignye
Of sondry folk, by aventure yfalle   25
In felaweshipe, and pilgrimes were they alle,
That toward Caunterbury wolden ryde.
The chambres and the stables weren wyde,
And wel we weren esed atte beste.
And shortly, whan the sonne was to reste,   30
So hadde I spoken with hem everichon
That I was of hir felaweshipe anon,

And made forward erly for to ryse,
To take oure wey ther as I yow devyse.
    But nathelees, whil I have tyme and space,   35
Er that I ferther in this tale pace,
Me thynketh it acordaunt to resoun
To telle yow al the condicioun
Of ech of hem, so as it semed me,
And whiche they weren, and of what degree,   40
And eek in what array that they were inne;
And at a knyght than wol I first bigynne.
    A KNYGHT ther was, and that a worthy man,
That fro the tyme that he first bigan
To riden out, he loved chivalrie,   45
Trouthe and honour, fredom and curteisie.
Ful worthy was he in his lordes werre,
And therto hadde he riden, no man ferre,
As wel in Cristendom as in hethenesse,
And evere honoured for his worthynesse;   50
At Alisaundre he was whan it was wonne.
Ful ofte tyme he hadde the bord bigonne
Aboven alle nacions in Pruce;
In Lettow hadde he reysed and in Ruce,
No Cristen man so ofte of his degree.   55
In Gernade at the seege eek hadde he be
Of Algezir, and riden in Belmarye.
At Lyeys was he and at Satalye,
Whan they were wonne, and in the Grete See
At many a noble armee hadde he be.   60
At mortal batailles hadde he been fiftene,
And foughten for oure feith at Tramyssene
In lystes thries, and ay slayn his foo.
This ilke worthy knyght hadde been also

GENERAL PROLOGUE   **1. his:** its; **soote:** sweet, gentle. **4. Of which vertu:** through which power. **5. Zephirus:** the west wind (see the poem "Western Wind," p. 18); **eek:** also. **8. Ram:** the zodiacal sign of Aries. **10. ye:** eye. **11. hem:** them; **hir:** their; **corages:** hearts. **13. straunge:** foreign. **14. ferne halwes:** far (distant) hallowed places (shrines); **kowthe:** known. **17. martir:** Thomas à Becket. **18. seeke:** sick. **20. Southwerk:** Southwark, on the south bank of the Thames; **Tabard:** Tabard Inn. **25. aventure:** chance. **29. esed atte beste:** accommodated in the best way. **31. everichon:** every one. **33. made forward:** agreed. **34. devyse:** relate. **36. er:** ere. **46. fredom:** liberality. **47. werre:** war. **48. ferre:** farther. **49. hethenesse:** heathen lands. **51. Alisaundre:** Alexandria. **52. bord bigonne:** sat in the place of honour. **53. Pruce:** Prussia. **54. Lettow:** Lithuania; **reysed:** raided; **Ruce:** Russia. **56. Gernade:** Granada. **57. Algezir:** Algeciras; **Belmarye:** Belmarin or Benmarin, a Moorish kingdom in what is now Morocco. **58. Lyeys:** Ayash (Turkey); **Satalye:** Attalia (Turkey). **59. Grete See:** Mediterranean. **62. Tramyssene:** Tremessen, Tlemcen (Algeria). **63. lystes:** lists (for jousting tournaments); **ay:** aye, ever, always. **64. ilke:** same.

Somtyme with the lord of Palatye 65
Agayn another hethen in Turkye;
And everemoore he hadde a sovereyn prys.
And though that he were worthy, he was wys,
And of his port as meeke as is a mayde.
He nevere yet no vileynye ne sayde 70
In al his lyf unto no maner wight.
He was a verray, parfit gentil knyght.
But for to tellen yow of his array,
His hors were goode, but he was nat gay.
Of fustian he wered a gypon 75
Al bismotered with his habergeon,
For he was late ycome from his viage,
And wente for to doon his pilgrymage.
    With hym ther was his sone, a yong SQUIER,
A lovyere and a lusty bacheler, 80
With lokkes crulle as they were leyd in presse.
Of twenty yeer of age he was, I gesse.
Of his stature he was of evene lengthe,
And wonderly delyvere, and of greet strengthe.
And he hadde been somtyme in chyvachie 85
In Flaundres, in Artoys, and Picardye,
And born hym wel, as of so litel space,
In hope to stonden in his lady grace.
Embrouded was he, as it were a meede
Al ful of fresshe floures, whyte and reede. 90
Syngynge he was, or floytynge, al the day;
He was as fressh as is the month of May.
Short was his gowne, with sleves longe and wyde.
Wel koude he sitte on hors and faire ryde.
He koude songes make and wel endite, 95
Juste and eek daunce, and wel purtreye and write.
So hoote he lovede that by nyghtertale
He sleep namoore than dooth a nyghtyngale.
Curteis he was, lowely, and servysable,
And carf biforn his fader at the table. 100
    A YEMAN hadde he and servantz namo
At that tyme, for hym liste ride so,

And he was clad in cote and hood of grene.
A sheef of pecok arwes, bright and kene,
Under his belt he bar ful thriftily 105
(Wel koude he dresse his takel yemanly;
His arwes drouped noght with fetheres lowe),
And in his hand he bar a myghty bowe.
A not-heed hadde he, with a broun visage.
Of wodecraft wel koude he al the usage. 110
Upon his arm he bar a gay bracer,
And by his syde a swerd and a bokeler,
And on that oother syde a gay daggere
Harneised wel and sharp as point of spere;
A Cristopher on his brest of silver sheene. 115
An horn he bar, the bawdryk was of grene;
A forster was he, soothly, as I gesse.
    Ther was also a Nonne, a PRIORESSE,
That of hir smylyng was ful symple and coy;
Hir gretteste ooth was but by Seinte Loy; 120
And she was cleped Madame Eglentyne.
Ful wel she soong the service dyvyne,
Entuned in hir nose ful semely;
And Frenssh she spak ful faire and fetisly,
After the scole of Stratford atte Bowe, 125
For Frenssh of Parys was to hire unknowe.
At mete wel ytaught was she withalle;
She leet no morsel from hir lippes falle,
Ne wette hir fyngres in hir sauce depe;
Wel koude she carie a morsel and wel kepe 130
That no drope ne fille upon hire brest.
In curteisie was set ful muchel hir lest.
Hir over-lippe wyped she so clene
That in hir coppe ther was no ferthyng sene
Of grece, whan she dronken hadde hir draughte.
Ful semely after hir mete she raughte. 136
And sikerly she was of greet desport,
And ful plesaunt, and amyable of port,
And peyned hire to countrefete cheere
Of court, and to been estatlich of manere, 140

---

65. **Palatye:** Balat (Turkey). 67. **prys:** reputation. 69. **port:** bearing. 70. **vileynye:** coarseness, rudeness. 71. **no maner wight:** any sort of person. 72. **verray:** true; **parfit:** perfect; **gentil:** gentle, noble. 74. **gay:** gaily caparisoned. 75. **gypon:** tunic. 76. **bismotered:** besmutted, dirty, rust-smeared. 77. **viage:** journey. 81. **crulle:** curly. 83. **evene:** moderate. 84. **delyvere:** agile. 85. **chyvachie:** cavalry expedition. 87. **as of so litel space:** for such a short time. 91. **floytynge:** playing the flute or whistling. 94. **koude:** knew how to, could. 95. **endite:** indite, compose verse. 96. **Juste:** joust; **purtreye:** draw. 97. **by nyghtertale:** at nighttime. 101. **Yeman:** yeoman; **namo:** no more. 102. **hym liste:** it pleased him to. 105. **bar:** bore. 109. **not-heed:** close-cropped head. 112. **bokeler:** buckler. 115. **Cristopher:** a St. Christopher medal. 116. **bawdryk:** baldric. 120. **Loy:** Eloi, Eligius. 121. **cleped:** called, named. 124. **fetisly:** elegantly. 127. **mete:** food, meals. 132. **ful muchel her lest:** her greatest pleasure. 134. **ferthyng:** speck. 136. **raught:** reached. 137. **sikerly:** securely, surely, truly; **greet desport:** good cheer, pleasant behaviour. 139. **countrefete cheere:** imitate the bearing or manners. 140. **estatlich:** stately, dignified.

And to ben holden digne of reverence.
But for to speken of hir conscience,
She was so charitable and so pitous
She wolde wepe, if that she saugh a mous
Kaught in a trappe, if it were deed or bledde.   *145*
Of smale houndes hadde she that she fedde
With rosted flessh, or milk and wastel-breed.
But soore wepte she if oon of hem were deed,
Or if men smoot it with a yerde smerte;
And al was conscience and tendre herte.   *150*
Ful semely hir wympul pynched was,
Hir nose tretys, hir eyen greye as glas,
Hir mouth ful smal, and therto softe and reed.
But sikerly she hadde a fair forheed;
It was almoost a spanne brood, I trowe;   *155*
For, hardily, she was nat undergrowe.
Ful fetis was hir cloke, as I was war.
Of smal coral aboute hir arm she bar
A peire of bedes, gauded al with grene,
And theron heng a brooch of gold ful sheene,   *160*
On which ther was first write a crowned A,
And after *Amor vincit omnia.*
    Another NONNE with hire hadde she,
That was hir chapeleyne, and preestes thre.
    A MONK ther was, a fair for the maistrie,   *165*
An outridere, that lovede venerie,
A manly man, to been an abbot able.
Ful many a deyntee hors hadde he in stable,
And whan he rood, men myghte his brydel heere
Gynglen in a whistlynge wynd als cleere   *170*
And eek as loude as dooth the chapel belle
Ther as this lord was kepere of the celle.
The reule of Seint Maure or of Seint Beneit —
By cause that it was old and somdel streit
This ilke Monk leet olde thynges pace,   *175*
And heeld after the newe world the space.

He yaf nat of that text a pulled hen,
That seith that hunters ben nat hooly men,
Ne that a monk, whan he is recchelees,
Is likned til a fissh that is waterless —   *180*
This is to seyn, a monk out of his cloystre.
But thilke text heeld he nat worth an oystre;
And I seyde his opinion was good.
What sholde he studie and make hymselven wood,
Upon a book in cloystre alwey to poure,   *185*
Or swynken with his handes, and laboure,
As Austyn bit? How shal the world be served?
Lat Austyn have his swynk to hym reserved!
Therfore he was a prikasour aright:
Grehoundes he hadde as swift as fowel in flight; *190*
Of prikyng and of huntyng for the hare
Was al his lust, for no cost wolde he spare.
I seigh his sleves purfiled at the hond
With grys, and that the fyneste of a lond;
And for to festne his hood under his chyn,   *195*
He hadde of gold ywroght a ful curious pyn;
A love-knotte in the gretter ende ther was.
His heed was balled, that shoon as any glas,
And eek his face, as he hadde been enoynt.
He was a lord ful fat and in good poynt;   *200*
His eyen stepe, and rollynge in his heed,
That stemed as a forneys of a leed;
His bootes souple, his hors in greet estaat.
Now certeinly he was a fair prelaat;
He was nat pale as a forpyned goost.   *205*
A fat swan loved he best of any roost.
His palfrey was as broun as is a berye.
    A FRERE ther was, a wantowne and a merye,
A lymytour, a ful solempne man.
In alle the ordres foure is noon that kan   *210*
So muchel of daliaunce and fair langage.
He hadde maad ful many a mariage

---

141. digne: worthy. **147. wastel-breed:** good quality white bread. **149. yerde:** rod, staff. **151. wympul:** wimple; **pynched:** pleated. **152. tretys:** slender, well-formed. **153. therto:** in addition, moreover. **159. peire of bedes, gauded:** set of beads, rosary, with gaudes, large ornamental beads, separating groups of others and marking paternosters. **162.** *Amor vincit omnia:* (Latin) "Love conquers all." **165. fair for the maistrie:** excellent, surpassing all others. **166. outridere:** monk with duties outside the monastery; **venerie:** venery, the hunt. **168. deyntee:** worthy, fine. **172. celle:** a separate, subordinate monastery. **173:** the Benedictine rule, founded by St. Benedict and furthered by his follower St. Maurus. **174. somdel streit:** somewhat strict. **175. pace:** pass. **176:** and followed the (easier) ways of modern times. **177. pulled:** plucked. **182. thilke:** that same. **184. What:** why; **wood:** mad. **186. swynken:** work. **187: Austyn bit:** St. Augustine bids; **world:** i.e., secular world. **189. prikasour:** hard-riding hunter. **192. lust:** pleasure. **193. seigh:** saw; **purfiled:** fur-lined. **194. grys:** gray squirrel fur. **199. enoynt:** anointed. **200. in good point:** Cf. French *enbonpoint.* **201. stepe:** large, prominent, bright (and see line 753 below). **202. stemed:** shone; **forneys:** furnace; **leed:** cauldron. **205. forpyned:** wasted. **209. lymytour:** friar licensed to beg within a specified area. **210. ordres foure:** Dominicans, Franciscans, Carmelites, Augustinians — the mendicant friars; **kan:** knows.

Of yonge wommen at his owene cost.
Unto his ordre he was a noble post.
Ful wel biloved and famulier was he 215
With frankeleyns over al in his contree,
And eek with worthy wommen of the toun;
For he hadde power of confessioun,
As seyde hymself, moore than a curat,
For of his ordre he was licenciat. 220
Ful swetely herde he confessioun,
And plesaunt was his absolucioun:
He was an esy man to yive penaunce,
Ther as he wiste to have a good pitaunce.
For unto a povre ordre for to yive 225
Is signe that a man is wel yshryve;
For if he yaf, he dorste make avaunt,
He wiste that a man was repentaunt;
For many a man so hard is of his herte,
He may nat wepe, althogh hym soore smerte. 230
Therfore in stede of wepynge and preyeres
Men moote yeve silver to the povre freres.
His tipet was ay farced ful of knyves
And pynnes, for to yeven faire wyves.
And certeinly he hadde a murye note: 235
Wel koude he synge and pleyen on a rote;
Of yeddynges he bar outrely the pris.
His nekke whit was as the flour-de-lys;
Therto he strong was as a champioun.
He knew the tavernes wel in every toun 240
And everich hostiler and tappestere
Bet than a lazar or a beggestere,
For unto swich a worthy man as he
Acorded nat, as by his facultee,
To have with sike lazars aqueyntaunce. 245
It is nat honest; it may nat avaunce,
For to deelen with no swich poraille,
But al with riche and selleres of vitaille.
And over al, ther as profit sholde arise,
Curteis he was and lowely of servyse; 250

Ther nas no man nowher so vertuous.
He was the beste beggere in his hous;
For thogh a wydwe hadde noght a sho,
So plesaunt was his "*In principio*,"
Yet wolde he have a ferthyng, er he wente. 255
His purchas was wel bettre than his rente.
And rage he koude, as it were right a whelp.
In love-dayes ther koude he muchel help,
For ther he was nat lyk a cloysterer
With a thredbare cope, as is a povre scoler, 260
But he was lyk a maister or a pope.
Of double worstede was his semycope,
That rounded as a belle out of the presse.
Somwhat he lipsed, for his wantownesse,
To make his Englissh sweete upon his tonge; 265
And in his harpyng, whan that he hadde songe,
His eyen twynkled in his heed aright
As doon the sterres in the frosty nyght.
This worthy lymytour was cleped Huberd.
A MARCHANT was ther with a forked berd, 270
In mottelee, and hye on horse he sat;
Upon his heed a Flaundryssh bever hat,
His bootes clasped faire and fetisly.
His resons he spak ful solempnely,
Sownynge alwey th'encrees of his wynnyng. 275
He wolde the see were kept for any thyng
Bitwixe Middelburgh and Orewelle.
Wel koude he in eschaunge sheeldes selle.
This worthy man ful wel his wit bisette:
Ther wiste no wight that he was in dette, 280
So estatly was he of his governaunce
With his bargaynes and with his chevyssaunce.
For sothe he was a worthy man with alle,
But, sooth to seyn, I noot how men hym calle.
A CLERK ther was of Oxenford also, 285
That unto logyk hadde longe ygo.
As leene was his hors as is a rake,
And he nas nat right fat, I undertake,

---

220. licenciat: licensed to hear confession. **224. wiste to have:** knew he would get; **pitaunce:** donation, especially food. **226. yshryve:** shriven. **227. make avaunt:** boast. **236. rote:** or *rotte, crwth, crowd* — an old Celtic bowed stringed instrument, early kind of fiddle. **237:** for ballads he utterly took the prize. **241. tappestere:** barmaid. **242. Bet:** better; **beggestere:** beggar-woman. **244. facultee:** official position. **246. honest:** honourable, respectable. **247. poraille:** poor people. **248. vitaille:** victuals. **251. nas:** (contraction of *ne was*) wasn't. **253. sho:** shoe. **254. *In principio*:** "In the beginning" — the first words of both Genesis and John, the latter being the more likely point of this reference. **256. purchas:** proceeds from begging etc.; **rente:** regular income. **257. rage:** flirt wantonly. **258. love-dayes:** days for settling legal disputes. **264. lipsed:** lisped. **271. mottelee:** motley. **272. Flaundryssh:** Flemish. **276. kept for any thyng:** protected at any cost. **277:** Middelburg and Orwell, Dutch and English ports across the Channel from each other. **278. sheeldes:** shields, or écus — coins used as a medium of exchange. **279. bisette:** bestowed, applied, used. **282. chevyssaunce:** borrowing. **284. noot:** *(ne woot)* don't know. **285. clerk:** cleric, student. **286:** Logic was the principal subject of the trivium.

But looked holwe, and therto sobrely.
Ful thredbare was his overeste courtepy, 290
For he hadde geten hym yet no benefice,
Ne was so worldly for to have office.
For hym was levere have at his beddes heed
Twenty bookes, clad in blak or reed,
Of Aristotle and his philosophie 295
Than robes riche, or fithele, or gay sautrie.
But al be that he was a philosophre,
Yet hadde he but litel gold in cofre;
But al that he myghte of his freendes hente,
On bookes and on lernynge he it spente, 300
And bisily gan for the soules preye
Of hem that yaf hym wherwith to scoleye.
Of studie took he moost cure and moost heede.
Noght o word spak he moore than was neede,
And that was seyd in forme and reverence, 305
And short and quyk and ful of hy sentence;
Sownynge in moral vertu was his speche,
And gladly wolde he lerne and gladly teche.
  A SERGEANT OF THE LAWE, war and wys,
That often hadde been at the Parvys, 310
Ther was also, ful riche of excellence.
Discreet he was and of greet reverence —
He semed swich, his wordes weren so wise.
Justice he was ful often in assise,
By patente and by pleyn commissioun. 315
For his science and for his heigh renoun,
Of fees and robes hadde he many oon.
So greet a purchasour was nowher noon:
Al was fee symple to hym in effect;
His purchasyng myghte nat been infect. 320
Nowher so bisy a man as he ther nas,
And yet he semed bisier than he was.
In termes hadde he caas and doomes alle
That from the tyme of kyng William were falle.
Therto he koude endite and make a thyng, 325

Ther koude no wight pynche at his writyng;
And every statut koude he pleyn by rote.
He rood but hoomly in a medlee cote,
Girt with a ceint of silk, with barres smale;
Of his array telle I no lenger tale. 330
  A FRANKELEYN was in his compaignye.
Whit was his berd as is the dayesye;
Of his complexioun he was sangwyn.
Wel loved he by the morwe a sop in wyn;
To lyven in delit was evere his wone, 335
For he was Epicurus owene sone,
That heeld opinioun that pleyn delit
Was verray felicitee parfit.
An housholdere, and that a greet, was he;
Seint Julian he was in his contree. 340
His breed, his ale, was alweys after oon;
A bettre envyned man was nowher noon.
Withoute bake mete was nevere his hous,
Of fissh and flessh, and that so plentevous
It snewed in his hous of mete and drynke; 345
Of alle deyntees that men koude thynke,
After the sondry sesons of the yeer,
So chaunged he his mete and his soper.
Ful many a fat partrich hadde he in muwe,
And many a breem and many a luce in stuwe. 350
Wo was his cook but if his sauce were
Poynaunt and sharp, and redy al his geere.
His table dormant in his halle alway
Stood redy covered al the longe day.
At sessiouns ther was he lord and sire; 355
Ful ofte tyme he was knyght of the shire.
An anlaas and a gipser al of silk
Heeng at his girdel, whit as morne milk.
A shirreve hadde he been, and a contour.
Was nowher swich a worthy vavasour. 360
  AN HABERDASSHERE and a CARPENTER,
A WEBBE, a DYERE, and a TAPYCER —

---

290. overeste courtepy: outermost short coat. **292. office:** secular employment. **293. levere:** rather. **296. fithele:** fiddle; **sautrie:** psaltery. **297. philosophre:** The word also referred to an alchemist. **299. hente:** get, take. **301. gan:** did. **302. scoleye:** go to school, be a scholar. **304. o:** one. **306. sentence:** meaning, significance, content. **310. Parvys:** porch of St. Paul's, a meeting place for such dignified, high-ranking lawyers. **315. patente:** royal appointment; **pleyn:** full. **320. infect:** defective, invalid. **323. termes:** records, year-books; **caas:** cases; **doomes:** decisions. **325. thyng:** legal document. **326. pynche at:** find fault with. **328. medlee:** parti-coloured. **329. ceint:** cincture, belt. **333:** See note to line 420 below. **334. sop:** soaked bread. **335. wone:** wont. **340:** Julian the Hospitaller was the legendary patron saint of hospitality. **341. after oon:** of uniformly good quality. **342. envyned:** wine-stocked. **349. muwe:** mew, cage. **350. luce:** pike; **stuwe:** stew, fish-tank or -pond. **353. dormant:** left up rather than put away between meals. **355. sessiouns:** i.e., of court. **356. knyght of the shire:** i.e., member of Parliament. **357. anlaas:** broad dagger; **gipser:** purse. **359. contour:** accountant, auditor. **360. vavasour:** feudal landowner. **362. Webbe:** weaver; **Tapycer:** tapestry- or rug-maker.

And they were clothed alle in o lyveree
Of a solempne and a greet fraternitee.
Ful fressh and newe hir geere apiked was;   *365*
Hir knyves were chaped noght with bras
But al with silver, wroght ful clene and wel,
Hir girdles and hir pouches everydeel.
Wel semed ech of hem a fair burgeys
To sitten in a yeldehalle on a deys.   *370*
Everich, for the wisdom that he kan,
Was shaply for to been an alderman.
For catel hadde they ynogh and rente,
And eek hir wyves wolde it wel assente;
And elles certeyn were they to blame.   *375*
It is ful fair to been ycleped "Madame,"
And goon to vigilies al bifore,
And have a mantel royalliche ybore.

   A Cook they hadde with hem for the nones
To boille the chiknes with the marybones,   *380*
And poudre-marchant tart and galyngale.
Wel koude he knowe a draughte of Londoun ale.
He koude rooste, and sethe, and broille, and frye,
Maken mortreux, and wel bake a pye.
But greet harm was it, as it thoughte me,   *385*
That on his shyne a mormal hadde he.
For blankmanger, that made he with the beste.

   A Shipman was ther, wonynge fer by weste;
For aught I woot, he was of Dertemouthe.
He rood upon a rouncy, as he kouthe,   *390*
In a gowne of faldyng to the knee.
A daggere hangynge on a laas hadde he
Aboute his nekke, under his arm adoun.
The hoote somer hadde maad his hewe al broun;
And certeinly he was a good felawe.   *395*
Ful many a draughte of wyn had he ydrawe
Fro Burdeux-ward, whil that the chapman sleep.

Of nyce conscience took he no keep.
If that he faught and hadde the hyer hond,
By water he sente hem hoom to every lond.   *400*
But of his craft to rekene wel his tydes,
His stremes, and his daungers hym bisides,
His herberwe, and his moone, his lodemenage,
Ther nas noon swich from Hulle to Cartage.
Hardy he was and wys to undertake;   *405*
With many a tempest hadde his berd been shake.
He knew alle the havenes, as they were,
Fro Gootlond to the cape of Fynystere,
And every cryke in Britaigne and in Spayne.
His barge ycleped was the Maudelayne.   *410*

   With us ther was a Doctour of Phisik;
In al this world ne was ther noon hym lik,
To speke of phisik and of surgerye,
For he was grounded in astronomye.
He kepte his pacient a ful greet deel   *415*
In houres by his magyk natureel.
Wel koude he fortunen the ascendent
Of his ymages for his pacient.
He knew the cause of everich maladye,
Were it of hoot, or coold, or moyste, or drye,   *420*
And where they engendred, and of what humour.
He was a verray, parfit praktisour:
The cause yknowe, and of his harm the roote,
Anon he yaf the sike man his boote.
Ful redy hadde he his apothecaries   *425*
To sende hym drogges and his letuaries,
For ech of hem made oother for to wynne—
Hir frendshipe nas nat newe to bigynne.
Wel knew he the olde Esculapius,
And Deyscorides, and eek Rufus,   *430*
Olde Ypocras, Haly, and Galyen,
Serapion, Razis, and Avycen,

---

365. apiked: cleaned, trimmed, adorned. **366. chaped:** mounted. **369. burgeys:** burgher. **370. yeldehalle:** guildhall; **deys:** dais. **372. shaply:** shapely, suitable. **373. catel:** chattels, property. **377. al bifore:** before everyone, at the head of the procession (see lines 449-52 below). **381. poudre-marchant:** a flavouring powder. **384. mortreux:** stews. **386. mormal:** scabbed sore, ulcer. **387. blankmanger:** "white food" — creamed fowl or fish with rice etc., perhaps a stew or mousse. **388. wonynge:** dwelling. **390. rouncy:** carthorse, nag; **as:** as best. **391. faldyng:** coarse woollen cloth. **392. laas:** lace, leash, cord. **402. stremes:** currents; **hym bisides:** nearby, around him. **403. lodemenage:** pilotage, navigation. **404. Cartage:** Cartagena or Carthage. **409. Britaigne:** Brittany. **414. astronomye:** i.e., astrology. **416. in houres:** i.e., according to astrology; **natureel:** i.e., as opposed to black magic. **417-18. fortunen . . . ymages:** choose propitious astrological times for making and using his talismanic images. **420-21:** In medical theory based on Hippocrates and Galen, these are the qualities that pair off variously in the four elements, corresponding to the four body-fluids or "humours" (sanguine: air/blood, hot & moist; phlegmatic: water/phlegm, cold & moist; choleric: fire/choler, or red or yellow bile, hot & dry; melancholy: earth/black bile, cold & dry). Imbalances in these humours were believed to account for particular complexions and temperaments and also to cause various diseases (see "The Nun's Priest's Tale," lines 104ff., p. 65; and Pope's *The Rape of the Lock,* I, 58-66, p. 524). **424. boote:** remedy. **426. letuaries:** electuaries, sweetened drugs. **429-34:** Aesculapius, Dioscorides, Rufus of Ephesus, Hippocrates, Galen,

Averrois, Damascien, and Constantyn,
Bernard, and Gatesden, and Gilbertyn.
Of his diete mesurable was he,   *435*
For it was of no superfluitee,
But of greet norissyng and digestible.
His studie was but litel on the Bible.
In sangwyn and in pers he clad was al,
Lyned with taffata and with sendal.   *440*
And yet he was but esy of dispence;
He kepte that he wan in pestilence.
For gold in phisik is a cordial,
Therefore he lovede gold in special.
    A good WIF was ther OF biside BATHE,   *445*
But she was somdel deef, and that was scathe.
Of clooth-makyng she hadde swich an haunt
She passed hem of Ypres and of Gaunt.
In al the parisshe wif ne was ther noon
That to the offrynge bifore hire sholde goon;   *450*
And if ther dide, certeyn so wrooth was she
That she was out of alle charitee.
Hir coverchiefs ful fyne weren of ground;
I dorste swere they weyeden ten pound
That on a Sonday weren upon hir heed.   *455*
Hir hosen weren of fyn scarlet reed,
Ful streite yteyd, and shoes ful moyste and newe.
Boold was hir face, and fair, and reed of hewe.
She was a worthy womman al hir lyve:
Housbondes at chirche dore she hadde fyve,   *460*
Withouten oother compaignye in youthe—
But thereof nedeth nat to speke as nowthe.
And thries hadde she been at Jerusalem;
She hadde passed many a straunge strem;
At Rome she hadde been, and at Boloigne,   *465*
In Galice at Seint-Jame, and at Coloigne.
She koude muchel of wandrynge by the weye.
Gat-tothed was she, soothly for to seye.
Upon an amblere esily she sat,

Ywympled wel, and on hir heed an hat   *470*
As brood as is a bokeler or a targe;
A foot-mantel aboute hir hipes large,
And on hir feet a paire of spores sharpe.
In felaweshipe wel koude she laughe and carpe.
Of remedies of love she knew per chaunce,   *475*
For she koude of that art the olde daunce.
    A good man was ther of religioun,
And was a povre PERSOUN OF A TOUN,
But riche he was of hooly thoght and werk.
He was also a lerned man, a clerk,   *480*
That Cristes gospel trewely wolde preche;
His parisshens devoutly wolde he teche.
Benygne he was, and wonder diligent,
And in adversitee ful pacient,
And swich he was ypreved ofte sithes.   *485*
Ful looth were hym to cursen for his tithes,
But rather wolde he yeven, out of doute,
Unto his povre parisshens aboute
Of his offryng and eek of his substaunce.
He koude in litel thyng have suffisaunce.   *490*
Wyd was his parisshe, and houses fer asonder,
But he ne lefte nat, for reyn ne thonder,
In siknesse nor in meschief to visite
The ferreste in his parisshe, muche and lite,
Upon his feet, and in his hand a staf.   *495*
This noble ensample to his sheep he yaf,
That first he wroghte, and afterward he taughte.
Out of the gospel he tho wordes caughte,
And this figure he added eek therto,
That if gold ruste, what shal iren do?   *500*
For if a preest be foul, on whom we truste,
No wonder is a lewed man to ruste;
And shame it is, if a prest take keep,
A shiten shepherde and a clene sheep.
Wel oghte a preest ensample for to yive,   *505*
By his clennesse, how that his sheep sholde lyve.

Serapion, Hali ibn el Abbas, Rhazes of Baghdad, Avicenna, Averroës, Johannes of Damascus, Constantinus Afer, Bernard of Gordon, John of Gaddesden, Gilbertus Anglicus — an imposing list of medical authorities from the legendary or mythical Asclepius/Aesculapius to a Scot and two British figures of the 13th and 14th centuries. **439. sangwyn:** blood-red (cloth); **pers:** Persian blue (cloth). **441. esy:** moderate. **446. scathe:** a misfortune, a pity. **447. haunt:** skill. **448:** Ypres and Ghent were cloth-making centres in Flanders. **453. ground:** texture. **463-66:** Jerusalem, Rome, Boulogne, Saint James of Compostella (Galicia), and Cologne — all with shrines much visited by pilgrims. **468. gat-tothed:** gap-toothed. **469. amblere:** slow-paced horse. **472. foot-mantel:** riding overskirt. **474. carpe:** talk, chatter. **475-76:** possibly alluding to Ovid's *Remedia Amoris* and *Ars Amatoria*. **478. povre Persoun:** poor parson. **485. ypreved:** proven; **sithes:** times. **486. cursen:** excommunicate, or threaten to, to induce people to pay their tithes. **493. meschief:** misfortune. **494. much and lite:** great and small. **498. tho:** those. **502. lewed:** ignorant, uneducated. **503. keep:** care, notice. **505-14:** See John 10:12-13.

He sette nat his benefice to hyre
And leet his sheep encombred in the myre
And ran to Londoun unto Seinte Poules
To seken hym a chaunterie for soules,   *510*
Or with a bretherhed to been withholde;
But dwelte at hoom, and kepte wel his folde,
So that the wolf ne made it nat myscarie;
He was a shepherde and noght a mercenarie.
And though he hooly were and vertuous,   *515*
He was to synful men nat despitous,
Ne of his speche daungerous ne digne,
But in his techyng discreet and benygne.
To drawen folk to hevene by fairnesse,
By good ensample, this was his bisynesse.   *520*
But it were any persone obstinat,
What so he were, of heigh or lough estat,
Hym wolde he snybben sharply for the nonys.
A bettre preest I trowe that nowher noon ys.
He waited after no pompe and reverence,   *525*
Ne maked him a spiced conscience,
But Cristes loore and his apostles twelve
He taughte; but first he folwed it hymselve.
    With hym ther was a PLOWMAN, was his brother,
That hadde ylad of dong ful many a fother;   *530*
A trewe swynkere and a good was he,
Lyvynge in pees and parfit charitee.
God loved he best with al his hoole herte
At alle tymes, thogh him gamed or smerte,
And thanne his neighebor right as hymselve.   *535*
He wolde thresshe, and therto dyke and delve,
For Cristes sake, for every povre wight,
Withouten hire, if it lay in his myght.
His tithes payde he ful faire and wel,
Bothe of his propre swynk and his catel.   *540*
In a tabard he rood upon a mere.
    Ther was also a REVE, and a MILLERE,
A SOMNOUR, and a PARDONER also,
A MAUNCIPLE, and myself—ther were namo.

    The MILLERE was a stout carl for the nones;   *545*
Ful byg he was of brawn, and eek of bones.
That proved wel, for overal ther he cam,
At wrastlynge he wolde have alwey the ram.
He was short-sholdred, brood, a thikke knarre;
Ther was no dore that he nolde heve of harre,   *550*
Or breke it at a rennyng with his heed.
His berd as any sowe or fox was reed,
And therto brood, as though it were a spade.
Upon the cop right of his nose he hade
A werte, and theron stood a toft of herys,   *555*
Reed as the brustles of a sowes erys;
His nosethirles blake were and wyde.
A swerd and a bokeler bar he by his syde.
His mouth as greet was as a greet forneys.
He was a janglere and a goliardeys,   *560*
And that was moost of synne and harlotries.
Wel koude he stelen corn and tollen thries;
And yet he hadde a thombe of gold, pardee.
A whit cote and a blew hood wered he.
A baggepipe wel koude he blowe and sowne,   *565*
And therwithal he broghte us out of towne.
    A gentil MAUNCIPLE was ther of a temple,
Of which achatours myghte take exemple
For to be wise in byynge of vitaille;
For wheither that he payde or took by taille,   *570*
Algate he wayted so in his achaat
That he was ay biforn and in good staat.
Now is nat that of God a ful fair grace
That swich a lewed mannes wit shal pace
The wisdom of an heep of lerned men?   *575*
Of maistres hadde he mo than thries ten,
That weren of lawe expert and curious,
Of which ther were a duszeyne in that hous
Worthy to been stywardes of rente and lond
Of any lord that is in Engelond,   *580*
To make hym lyve by his propre good
In honour dettelees (but if he were wood),

---

510. chaunterie: chantry. **511. bretherhed:** i.e., guild; **withholde:** i.e., hired as chaplain. **517. daungerous:** disdainful, severe; **digne:** haughty. **523. snybben:** snub, rebuke. **526. spiced:** overly fastidious or scrupulous. **530. ylad:** carried; **fother:** load. **531. swynkere:** worker. **534. thogh him gamed or smerte:** whether in pleasure or pain, i.e., whatever the circumstances. **536. dyke and delve:** make dykes and dig ditches. **547. overal ther:** wherever. **548. ram:** i.e., as the prize. **550. nolde:** (*ne wolde*) wouldn't; **harre:** hinges. **554. cop:** tip. **560. janglere:** chatterer, quarreler. **562. tollen:** take his toll, or cut. **563. thombe of gold:** alluding to the proverb "an honest miller has a thumb of gold"; **pardee:** (*par dieu,* "by God") i.e., certainly, indeed!. **567. Maunciple:** maniciple — one who buys provisions for a **temple:** an Inn of Court. **568. achatours:** buyers. **570. by taille:** (tally) on credit. **571: algate:** always; **wayted:** attended, watched; **achaat:** purchases. **577. curious:** careful, skilful. **581. propre good:** own goods, wealth. **582. but if:** unless.

Or lyve as scarsly as hym list desire;
And able for to helpen al a shire
In any caas that myghte falle or happe. *585*
And yet this Manciple sette hir aller cappe.
 The REVE was a sclendre colerik man.
His berd was shave as ny as ever he kan;
His heer was by his erys ful round yshorn;
His top was dokked lyk a preest biforn. *590*
Ful longe were his legges and ful lene,
Ylyk a staf; ther was no calf ysene.
Wel koude he kepe a gerner and a bynne;
Ther was noon auditour koude on him wynne.
Wel wiste he by the droghte and by the reyn *595*
The yeldynge of his seed and of his greyn.
His lordes sheep, his neet, his dayerye,
His swyn, his hors, his stoor, and his pultrye
Was hoolly in this Reves governynge,
And by his covenant yaf the rekenynge, *600*
Syn that his lord was twenty yeer of age.
Ther koude no man brynge hym in arrerage.
Ther nas baillif, ne hierde, nor oother hyne,
That he ne knew his sleighte and his covyne;
They were adrad of hym as of the deeth. *605*
His wonyng was ful faire upon an heeth;
With grene trees yshadwed was his place.
He koude bettre than his lord purchace.
Ful riche he was astored pryvely.
His lord wel koude he plesen subtilly, *610*
To yeve and lene hym of his owene good,
And have a thank, and yet a cote and hood.
In youthe he hadde lerned a good myster:
He was a wel good wrighte, a carpenter.
This Reve sat upon a ful good stot *615*
That was al pomely grey and highte Scot.
A long surcote of pers upon he hade,
And by his syde he baar a rusty blade.
Of Northfolk was this Reve of which I telle,
Biside a toun men clepen Baldeswelle. *620*

Tukked he was as is a frere aboute,
And evere he rood the hyndreste of oure route.
 A SOMONOUR was ther with us in that place,
That hadde a fyr-reed cherubynnes face,
For saucefleem he was, with eyen narwe. *625*
As hoot he was and lecherous as a sparwe,
With scalled browes blake and piled berd.
Of his visage children were aferd.
Ther nas quyk-silver, lytarge, ne brymstoon,
Boras, ceruce, ne oille of tartre noon, *630*
Ne oynement that wolde clense and byte,
That hym myghte helpen of his whelkes white,
Nor of the knobbes sittynge on his chekes.
Wel loved he garleek, oynons, and eek lekes,
And for to drynken strong wyn, reed as blood; *635*
Thanne wolde he speke and crie as he were wood.
And whan that he wel dronken hadde the wyn,
Thanne wolde he speke no word but Latyn.
A fewe termes hadde he, two or thre,
That he had lerned out of som decree — *640*
No wonder is, he herde it al the day;
And eek ye knowen wel how that a jay
Kan clepen "Watte" as wel as kan the pope.
But whoso koude in oother thyng hym grope,
Thanne hadde he spent al his philosophie; *645*
Ay "*Questio quid iuris*" wolde he crie.
He was a gentil harlot and a kynde;
A bettre felawe sholde men noght fynde.
He wolde suffre for a quart of wyn
A good felawe to have his concubyn *650*
A twelfmonth, and excuse hym atte fulle;
Ful prively a fynch eek koude he pulle.
And if he foond owher a good felawe,
He wolde techen him to have noon awe
In swich caas of the ercedekenes curs, *655*
But if a mannes soule were in his purs;
For in his purs he sholde ypunysshed be.
"Purs is the ercedekenes helle," seyde he.

---

583. scarsly: scarcely — i.e., economically. **585. falle:** befall. **586. sette hir aller cappe:** made fools of them all. **587. Reve:** Reeve — a steward or manager of a manor or estate; **colerik:** choleric. **593. gerner:** granary. **597. neet:** neat, cattle. **598. stoor:** store, stock, livestock. **603. hyne:** hind — farm labourer. **604. sleighte:** craftiness, cunning, trickery; **covyne:** deceitfulness. **605. deeth:** death in general, or possibly the plague. **613. myster:** occupation, craft. **615. stot:** stallion. **616. pomely:** dappled; **highte:** was called. **621. Tukked:** with long coat tucked up. **622. route:** rout, company. **623. Somonour:** Summoner — an ecclesiastical court's summons-server. **625. saucefleem:** pimply (presumed to be caused by salty phlegm). **627. piled:** patchy, partly bare. **629. lytarge:** litharge. **630. boras:** borax; **ceruce:** ceruse; **oille of tartre;** cream of tartar. **643. "Watte":** Walter (cf. parrots taught to say "Polly"). **644. grope:** i.e. search out, examine. **646. "*Questio quid iuris*":** "The question is, what point of law" — a common court phrase. **647. harlot:** rascal. **652:** probably referring to his own lechery or to his ability to pull off a clever swindle. **653. owher:** anywhere.

But wel I woot he lyed right in dede;
Of cursyng oghte ech gilty man him drede,   660
For curs wol slee right as assoillyng savith,
And also war hym of a *Significavit*.
In daunger hadde he at his owene gise
The yonge girles of the diocise,
And knew hir conseil, and was al hir reed.   665
A gerland hadde he set upon his heed,
As greet as it were for an ale-stake.
A bokeleer hadde he maad hym of a cake.
  With hym ther rood a gentil PARDONER
Of Rouncivale, his freend and his compeer,   670
That streight was comen fro the court of Rome.
Ful loude he soong "Com hider, love, to me!"
This Somonour bar to hym a stif burdoun;
Was nevere trompe of half so greet a soun.
This Pardoner hadde heer as yelow as wex,   675
But smothe it heeng as dooth a strike of flex;
By ounces henge his lokkes that he hadde,
And therwith he his shuldres overspradde;
But thynne it lay, by colpons oon and oon.
But hood, for jolitee, wered he noon,   680
For it was trussed up in his walet.
Hym thoughte he rood al of the newe jet;
Dischevelee, save his cappe, he rood al bare.
Swiche glarynge eyen hadde he as an hare.
A vernycle hadde he sowed upon his cappe.   685
His walet lay biforn hym in his lappe,
Bretful of pardoun comen from Rome al hoot.
A voys he hadde as smal as hath a goot.
No berd hadde he, ne nevere sholde have;
As smothe it was as it were late shave.   690
I trowe he were a geldyng or a mare.
But of his craft, fro Berwyk into Ware
Ne was ther swich another pardoner.
For in his male he hadde a pilwe-beer,
Which that he seyde was Oure Lady veyl;   695
He seyde he hadde a gobet of the seyl

That Seint Peter hadde, whan that he wente
Upon the see, til Jhesu Crist hym hente.   660
He hadde a croys of latoun ful of stones,
And in a glas he hadde pigges bones.   700
But with thise relikes, whan that he fond
A povre person dwellynge upon lond,
Upon a day he gat hym moore moneye
Than that the person gat in monthes tweye;
And thus, with feyned flaterye and japes,   705
He made the person and the peple his apes.
But trewely to tellen atte laste,
He was in chirche a noble ecclesiaste.
Wel koude he rede a lessoun or a storie,
But alderbest he song an offertorie;   710
For wel he wiste, whan that song was songe,
He moste preche and wel affile his tonge
To wynne silver, as he ful wel koude;
Therefore he song the murierly and loude.
  Now have I toold you soothly, in a clause,   715
Th'estaat, th'array, the nombre, and eek the cause
Why that assembled was this compaignye
In Southwerk at this gentil hostelrye
That highte the Tabard, faste by the Belle.
But now is tyme to yow for to telle   720
How that we baren us that ilke nyght,
Whan we were in that hostelrie alyght;
And after wol I telle of our viage
And al the remenaunt of oure pilgrimage.
But first I pray yow, of youre curteisye,   725
That ye n'arette it nat my vileynye,
Thogh that I pleynly speke in this mateere,
To telle yow hir wordes and hir cheere,
Ne thogh I speke hir wordes proprely.
For this ye knowen al so wel as I: 730
Whoso shal telle a tale after a man,
He moot reherce as ny as evere he kan
Everich a word, if it be in his charge,
Al speke he never so rudeliche and large,

662. *Significavit*: a writ for imprisonment of one excommunicated. **663. In daunger:** under his power, control; **gise:** way, pleasure. **665. al hir reed:** their sole adviser. **667. ale-stake:** an alehouse's signpost, with its bush. **668. cake:** loaf of bread. **669. Pardoner:** seller of papal indulgences. **670. Rouncivale:** hospital near Charing Cross, connected with one in Roncesvalles, in Spain, near where, according to the 12th-century *Chanson de Roland*, Roland and part of Charlemagne's army were betrayed and killed. **676. strike:** hank. **677. ounces:** i.e., small portions. **679. colpons:** strips, strands. **681. walet:** wallet, i.e., bag, knapsack. **682. jet:** fashion. **685. vernycle:** a *veronica* worn as a badge by pilgrims. **687. Bretful:** brimful. **692. from Berwyk** (Berwick-upon-Tweed) **into Ware** (in the south): i.e., from one end of the country to the other. **694. male:** bag; **pilwe-beer:** pillowcase. **698. hente:** took. **699. latoun:** latten. **705. japes:** tricks. **712. affile:** file, i.e., smooth or sharpen. **715. in a clause:** i.e., briefly. **719. the Belle:** a tavern. **726. n'arette:** don't attribute.

Or ellis he moot telle his tale untrewe, 735
Or feyne thyng, or fynde wordes newe.
He may nat spare, althogh he were his brother;
He moot as wel seye o word as another.
Crist spak hymself ful brode in hooly writ,
And wel ye woot no vileynye is it. 740
Eek Plato seith, whoso kan hym rede,
The wordes moote be cosyn to the dede.
Also I prey yow to foryeve it me,
Al have I nat set folk in hir degree
Heere in this tale, as that they sholde stonde. 745
My wit is short, ye may wel understonde.
    Greet chiere made oure Hoost us everichon,
And to the soper sette he us anon.
He served us with vitaille at the beste;
Strong was the wyn, and wel to drynke us leste. 750
A semely man OURE HOOSTE was withalle
For to been a marchal in an halle.
A large man he was with eyen stepe —
A fairer burgeys was ther noon in Chepe —
Boold of his speche, and wys, and wel ytaught, 755
And of manhod hym lakkede right naught.
Eek therto he was right a myrie man;
And after soper pleyen he bigan,
And spak of myrthe amonges othere thynges,
Whan that we hadde maad oure rekenynges, 760
And seyde thus: "Now, lordynges, trewely,
Ye been to me right welcome, hertely;
For by my trouthe, if that I shal nat lye,
I saugh nat this yeer so myrie a compaignye
Atones in this herberwe as is now. 765
Fayn wolde I doon yow myrthe, wiste I how.
And of a myrthe I am right now bythoght,
To doon yow ese, and it shal coste noght.
    "Ye goon to Caunterbury — God yow speede,
The blisful martir quite yow youre meede! 770
And wel I woot, as ye goon by the weye,
Ye shapen yow to talen and to pleye;
For trewely, confort ne myrthe is noon
To ride by the weye doumb as a stoon;
And therfore wol I maken yow disport, 775
As I seyde erst, and doon yow som confort.
And if yow liketh alle by oon assent

For to stonden at my juggement,
And for to werken as I shal yow seye,
Tomorwe, whan ye riden by the weye, 780
Now, by my fader soule that is deed,
But ye be myrie, I wol yeve yow myn heed!
Hoold up youre hondes, withouten moore speche."
    Oure conseil was nat longe for to seche.
Us thoughte it was noght worth to make it wys, 785
And graunted hym withouten moore avys,
And bad him seye his voirdit as hym leste.
"Lordynges," quod he, "now herkneth for the beste;
But taak it nought, I prey yow, in desdeyn.
This is the poynt, to speken short and pleyn, 790
That ech of yow, to shorte with oure weye,
In this viage shal telle tales tweye
To Caunterbury-ward, I mene it so,
And homward he shal tellen othere two,
Of aventures that whilom han bifalle. 795
And which of yow that bereth hym best of alle —
That is to seyn, that telleth in this caas
Tales of best sentence and moost solaas —
Shal have a soper at oure aller cost
Heere in this place, sittynge by this post, 800
Whan that we come agayn fro Caunterbury.
And for to make yow the moore mury,
I wol myselven goodly with yow ryde,
Right at myn owene cost, and be youre gyde;
And whoso wole my juggement withseye 805
Shal paye al that we spenden by the weye.
And if ye vouche sauf that it be so,
Tel me anon, withouten wordes mo,
And I wol erly shape me therfore."
    This thyng was graunted, and oure othes swore
With ful glad herte, and preyden hym also 811
That he wolde vouche sauf for to do so,
And that he wolde been oure governour,
And of oure tales juge and reportour,
And sette a soper at a certeyn pris, 815
And we wol reuled been at his devys
In heigh and lough; and thus by oon assent
We been acorded to his juggement.
And therupon the wyn was fet anon;
We dronken, and to reste wente echon, 820

---

754. Chepe: Cheapside. **763. trouthe:** troth. **770. quite:** requite. **772. talen:** tell tales. **785. make it wys:** bring wisdom into it, make a fuss. **786. avys:** deliberation. **798. solaas:** delight, pleasure. **805. withseye:** gainsay. **816. devys:** will, direction. **819. fet:** fetched.

Withouten any lenger taryynge.

Amorwe, whan that day bigan to sprynge,
Up roos oure Hoost, and was oure aller cok,
And gadrede us togidre alle in a flok,
And forth we riden a litel moore than paas   *825*
Unto the Wateryng of Seint Thomas;
And there oure Hoost bigan his hors areste
And seyde, "Lordynges, herkneth, if yow leste.
Ye woot youre foreward, and I it yow recorde.
If even-song and morwe-song accorde,   *830*
Lat se now who shal telle the firste tale.
As evere mote I drynke wyn or ale,
Whoso be rebel to my juggement
Shal paye for al that by the wey is spent.
Now draweth cut, er that we ferrer twynne;   *835*
He which that hath the shorteste shal bigynne.
Sire Knyght," quod he, "my mayster and my lord,
Now draweth cut, for that is myn accord.
Cometh neer," quod he, "my lady Prioresse.
And ye, sire Clerk, lat be youre shamefastnesse, *840*
Ne studieth noght; ley hond to, every man!"
Anon to drawen every wight bigan,
And shortly for to tellen as it was,
Were it by aventure, or sort, or cas,
The sothe is this: the cut fil to the Knyght,   *845*
Of which ful blithe and glad was every wyght,
And telle he moste his tale, as was resoun,
By foreward and by composicioun,
As ye han herd; what nedeth wordes mo?
And whan this goode man saugh that it was so,   *850*
As he that wys was and obedient
To kepe his foreward by his free assent,
He seyde, "Syn I shal bigynne the game,
What, welcome be the cut, a Goddes name!
Now lat us ryde, and herkneth what I seye."   *855*
And with that word we ryden forth oure weye,
And he bigan with right a myrie cheere
His tale anon, and seyde as ye may heere.

. . . .

THE WIFE OF BATH'S PROLOGUE

"Experience, though noon auctoritee
Were in this world, is right ynogh for me
To speke of wo that is in mariage;
For, lordynges, sith I twelve yeer was of age,
Thonked be God that is eterne on lyve,   *5*
Housbondes at chirche dore I have had fyve —
If I so ofte myghte have ywedded bee —
And alle were worthy men in hir degree.
But me was toold, certeyn, nat longe agoon is,
That sith that Crist ne wente nevere but onis   *10*
To weddyng, in the Cane of Galilee,
That by the same ensample taughte he me
That I ne sholde wedded be but ones.
Herkne eek, lo, which a sharp word for the nones,
Biside a welle, Jhesus, God and man,   *15*
Spak in repreeve of the Samaritan:
'Thou hast yhad fyve housbondes,' quod he,
'And that ilke man that now hath thee
Is noght thyn housbonde,' thus seyde he certeyn.
What that he mente therby, I kan nat seyn;   *20*
But that I axe, why that the fifthe man
Was noon housbonde to the Samaritan?
How manye myghte she have in mariage?
Yet herde I nevere tellen in myn age
Upon this nombre diffinicioun.   *25*
Men may devyne and glosen, up and doun,
But wel I woot, expres, withoute lye,
God bad us for to wexe and multiplye;
That gentil text kan I wel understonde.
Eek wel I woot, he seyde myn housbonde   *30*
Sholde lete fader and mooder and take to me.
But of no nombre mencion made he,
Of bigamye, or of octogamye;
Why sholde men thanne speke of it vileynye?
Lo, heere the wise kyng, daun Salomon;   *35*
I trowe he hadde wyves mo than oon.
As wolde God it leveful were unto me
To be refresshed half so ofte as he!

826: a brook two miles along the way. **829. foreward:** promise, agreement; **recorde:** remind. **835. draweth cut:** draw lots; **twynne:** depart, go. **840. shamefastnesse:** modesty, shyness. **844. aventure:** chance, luck; **sort:** chance, destiny; **caas:** accident, chance. **848. composicioun:** agreement, arrangement.   **THE WIFE OF BATH'S PROLOGUE AND TALE   1. auctoritee:** i.e., written authority. **11. Cane:** Cana (see John 2). **15ff:** See John 4:6ff. **26. glosen:** gloss, interpret. **27. expres:** expressly, clearly. **28:** See Genesis 1:28 (p. 243). **31. lete:** leave (see Matthew 19:5). **35. daun:** sir. **36:** See I Kings 11:3. **37. leveful:** lawful, permissible.

Which yifte of God hadde he for alle his wyvys!
No man hath swich that in this world alyve is. *40*
God woot, this noble kyng, as to my wit,
The firste nyght had many a myrie fit
With ech of hem, so wel was hym on lyve.
Yblessed be God that I have wedded fyve!
Welcome the sixte, whan that evere he shal. *45*
For sothe, I wol nat kepe me chaast in al.
Whan myn housbonde is fro the world ygon,
Som Cristen man shal wedde me anon,
For thanne th'apostle seith that I am free
To wedde, a Goddes half, where it liketh me. *50*
He seith that to be wedded is no synne;
Bet is to be wedded than to brynne.
What rekketh me, thogh folk seye vileynye
Of shrewed Lameth and his bigamye?
I woot wel Abraham was an hooly man, *55*
And Jacob eek, as ferforth as I kan;
And ech of hem hadde wyves mo than two,
And many another holy man also.
Wher can ye seye, in any manere age,
That hye God defended mariage *60*
By expres word? I pray yow, telleth me.
Or where comanded he virginitee?
I woot as wel as ye, it is no drede,
Th'apostel, whan he speketh of maydenhede,
He seyde that precept therof hadde he noon. *65*
Men may conseille a womman to been oon,
But conseillyng is no comandement.
He putte it in oure owene juggement;
For hadde God comanded maydenhede,
Thanne hadde he dampned weddyng with the dede.
And certes, if ther were no seed ysowe, *71*
Virginitee, thanne wherof sholde it growe?
Poul dorste nat comanden, atte leeste,
A thyng of which his maister yaf noon heeste.
The dart is set up for virginitee; *75*
Cacche whoso may, who renneth best lat see.
    But this word is nat taken of every wight,
But ther as God lust gyve it of his myght.

I woot wel that th'apostel was a mayde;
But nathelees, thogh that he wroot and sayde *80*
He wolde that every wight were swich as he,
Al nys but conseil to virginitee.
And for to been a wyf he yaf me leve
Of indulgence; so nys it no repreve
To wedde me, if that my make dye, *85*
Withouten excepcion of bigamye.
Al were it good no womman for to touche—
He mente as in his bed or in his couche,
For peril is bothe fyr and tow t'assemble;
Ye knowe what this ensample may resemble. *90*
This is al and som: he heeld virginitee
Moore parfit than weddyng in freletee.
Freletee clepe I, but if that he and she
Wolde leden al hir lyf in chastitee.
    I graunte it wel; I have noon envie, *95*
Thogh maydenhede preferre bigamye.
It liketh hem to be clene, body and goost;
Of myn estaat I nyl nat make no boost,
For wel ye knowe, a lord in his houshold,
He nath nat every vessel al of gold; *100*
Somme been of tree, and doon hir lord servyse.
God clepeth folk to hym in sondry wyse,
And everich hath of God a propre yifte—
Som this, som that, as hym liketh shifte.
    Virginitee is greet perfeccion, *105*
And continence eek with devocion,
But Crist, that of perfeccion is welle,
Bad nat every wight he sholde go selle
Al that he hadde, and gyve it to the poore,
And in swich wise folwe hym and his foore. *110*
He spak to hem that wolde lyve parfitly;
And lordynges, by youre leve, that am nat I.
I wol bistowe the flour of al myn age
In the actes and in fruyt of mariage.
    Telle me also, to what conclusion *115*
Were membres maad of generacion,
And of so parfit wys a wright ywroght?
Trusteth right wel, they were nat maad for noght.

---

39. Which: What a. **49. th'apostle:** St. Paul — the Wife frequently draws on I Corinthians (see especially chapter 7). **52. brynne:** burn. **54. shrewed:** wicked, cursed; **Lamath:** Lamech — see Genesis 4:19-24 (p. 245). **60. defended:** forbade. **74. heeste:** behest. **75. dart:** i.e., as prize for winner of a race. **77. taken of:** i.e., applicable to. **79. mayde:** virgin. **85. make:** mate. **86. excepcion of:** objection because of. **92. freletee:** frailty. **96. preferre:** have preference over; **bigamye:** i.e., remarriage of a widow. **98. nyl:** *(ne wyl)* won't. **99-101:** See II Timothy 2:20. **104. shifte:** provide, distribute. **107-12:** See Matthew 19:21. **107. welle:** well, wellspring. **110. foore:** footsteps.

Glose whoso wole, and seye bothe up and doun

That they were maked for purgacioun   *120*

Of uryne, and oure bothe thynges smale

Were eek to knowe a femele from a male,

And for noon oother cause — say ye no?

The experience woot wel it is noght so.

So that the clerkes be nat with me wrothe,   *125*

I sey this: that they maked ben for bothe;

That is to seye, for office and for ese

Of engendrure, ther we nat God displese.

Why sholde men elles in hir bookes sette

That man shal yelde to his wyf hire dette?   *130*

Now wherwith sholde he make his paiement,

If he ne used his sely instrument?

Thanne were they maad upon a creature

To purge uryne, and eek for engendrure.

But I seye noght that every wight is holde,   *135*

That hath swich harneys as I to yow tolde,

To goon and usen hem in engendrure.

Thanne sholde men take of chastitee no cure.

Crist was a mayde and shapen as a man,

And many a seint, sith that the world bigan;   *140*

Yet lyved they evere in parfit chastitee.

I nyl envye no virginitee.

Lat hem be breed of pured whete-seed,

And lat us wyves hoten barly-breed;

And yet with barly-breed, Mark telle kan,   *145*

Oure Lord Jhesu refresshed many a man.

In swich estaat as God hath cleped us

I wol persevere; I nam nat precius.

In wyfhod I wol use myn instrument

As frely as my Makere hath it sent.   *150*

If I be daungerous, God yeve me sorwe!

Myn housbonde shal it have bothe eve and morwe,

Whan that hym list come forth and paye his dette.

An housbonde I wol have — I wol nat lette —

Which shal be bothe my dettour and my thral, *155*

And have his tribulacion withal

Upon his flessh, whil that I am his wyf.

I have the power durynge al my lyf

Upon his propre body, and noght he.

Right thus the Apostel tolde it unto me,   *160*

And bad oure housbondes for to love us weel.

Al this sentence me liketh every deel" —

  Up stirte the Pardoner, and that anon;

"Now, dame," quod he, "by God and by Seint John!

Ye been a noble prechour in this cas.   *165*

I was aboute to wedde a wyf; allas!

What sholde I bye it on my flessh so deere?

Yet hadde I levere wedde no wyf to-yeere!"

  "Abyde!" quod she, "my tale is nat bigonne.

Nay, thou shalt drynken of another tonne,   *170*

Er that I go, shal savoure wors than ale.

And whan that I have toold thee forth my tale

Of tribulacion in mariage,

Of which I am expert in al myn age —

This is to seyn, myself have been the whippe — *175*

Than maystow chese wheither thou wolt sippe

Of thilke tonne that I shal abroche.

Be war of it, er thou to ny approche;

For I shal telle ensamples mo than ten.

'Whoso that nyl be war by othere men,   *180*

By hym shul othere men corrected be.'

The same wordes writeth Ptholomee;

Rede in his Almageste, and take it there."

  "Dame, I wolde praye yow, if youre wyl it were,"

Seyde this Pardoner, "as ye bigan,   *185*

Telle forth youre tale, spareth for no man,

And teche us yonge men of youre praktike."

  "Gladly," quod she, "sith it may yow like;

But yet I praye to al this compaignye,

If that I speke after my fantasye,   *190*

As taketh not agrief of that I seye,

For myn entente nys but for to pleye.

  Now, sire, now wol I telle forth my tale.

As evere moote I drynken wyn or ale,

I shal seye sooth; tho housbondes that I hadde, *195*

As thre of hem were goode, and two were badde.

The thre were goode men, and riche, and olde;

Unnethe myghte they the statut holde

In which that they were bounden unto me.

Ye woot wel what I meene of this, pardee!   *200*

---

127. office: i.e., business of excretion. **132. sely:** happy, blessed, innocent, poor. **138. cure:** care. **144. hoten:** be called. **145-46:** not Mark, but John 6:9-14. **151. daungerous:** niggardly, grudging. **154. lette:** hinder, be hindered. **168. to-yeere:** this year. **170. tonne:** tun. **177. abroche:** broach. **180-83:** See *Ptolemaic* in the Glossary. This and the "proverbe" quoted at 326-27 are not in the *Almagest*, but rather in a collection of sayings later attributed to Ptolemy. **190. fantasye:** fancy, desire. **198. unnethe:** not easily, hardly.

As help me God, I laughe whan I thynke
How pitously a-nyght I made hem swynke!
And, by my fey, I tolde of it no stoor.
They had me yeven hir lond and hir tresoor;
Me neded nat do lenger diligence   *205*
To wynne hir love, or doon hem reverence.
They loved me so wel, by God above,
That I ne tolde no deyntee of hir love!
A wys womman wol bisye hire evere in oon
To gete hire love, ye, ther as she hath noon.   *210*
But sith I hadde hem hoolly in myn hond,
And sith they hadde me yeven al hir lond,
What sholde I taken keep hem for to plese,
But it were for my profit and myn ese?
I sette hem so a-werke, by my fey,   *215*
That many a nyght they songen 'Weilawey!'
The bacon was nat fet for hem, I trowe,
That som men han in Essex at Dunmowe.
I governed hem so wel, after my lawe,
That ech of hem ful blisful was and fawe   *220*
To brynge me gaye thynges fro the fayre.
They were ful glad whan I spak to hem faire,
For, God it woot, I chidde hem spitously.
    Now herkneth hou I baar me proprely,
Ye wise wyves, that kan understonde.   *225*
Thus shulde ye speke and bere hem wrong on honde,
For half so boldely kan ther no man
Swere and lyen, as a womman kan.
I sey nat this by wyves that been wyse,
But if it be whan they hem mysavyse.   *230*
A wys wyf, if that she kan hir good,
Shal beren hym on honde the cow is wood,
And take witnesse of hir owene mayde
Of hir assent. But herkneth how I sayde:
    'Sire olde kaynard, is this thyn array?   *235*
Why is my neighebores wyf so gay?
She is honoured overal ther she gooth;
I sitte at hoom; I have no thrifty clooth.
What dostow at my neighebores hous?

Is she so fair? Artow so amorous?   *240*
What rowne ye with oure mayde? Benedicite!
Sire olde lecchour, lat thy japes be!
And if I have a gossib or a freend,
Withouten gilt, thou chidest as a feend,
If that I walke or pleye unto his hous!   *245*
Thou comest hoom as dronken as a mous,
And prechest on thy bench, with yvel preef!
Thou seist to me it is a greet meschief
To wedde a povre womman, for costage;
And if that she be riche, of heigh parage,   *250*
Thanne seistow that it is a tormentrie
To soffre hire pride and hire malencolie.
And if that she be fair, thou verray knave,
Thou seyst that every holour wol hire have;
She may no while in chastitee abyde,   *255*
That is assailled upon ech a syde.
    Thou seyst som folk desiren us for richesse,
Somme for oure shap, and somme for oure fairnesse,
And som for she kan outher synge or daunce,
And som for gentillesse and daliaunce;   *260*
Som for hir handes and hir armes smale;
Thus goth al to the devel, by thy tale.
Thou seyst men may nat kepe a castel wal,
It may so longe assailled been overal.
    And if that she be foul, thou seist that she   *265*
Coveiteth every man that she may se,
For as a spanyel she wol on hym lepe,
Til that she fynde som man hire to chepe.
Ne noon so grey goos gooth ther in the lake
As, seistow, wol been withoute make.   *270*
And seyst it is an hard thyng for to welde
A thyng that no man wole, his thankes, helde.
Thus seistow, lorel, whan thow goost to bedde,
And that no wys man nedeth for to wedde,
Ne no man that entendeth unto hevene.   *275*
With wilde thonder-dynt and firy levene
Moote thy welked nekke be tobroke!
    Thow seyst that droppyng houses, and eek smoke,

---

203. fey: faith; **tolde of:** set by. **208. tolde no deyntee:** set no value on. **209. bisye hire evere in oon:** always busy herself. **217-18:** The "Dunmow flitch" was awarded to any man and wife who had lived a year without quarrelling or wishing to part. **220. fawe:** fain. **226. bere hem wrong on honde:** accuse them falsely. **232:** deceive him into thinking the chough is mad (the bird that supposedly tattles of a wife's infidelity). **235. kaynard:** dotard. **241. rowne:** whisper. **243. gossib:** gossip. **247. with yvel preef:** bad luck to you. **250. parage:** birth, lineage. **254. holour:** lecher. **268. chepe:** buy. **271. welde:** wield, control. **272. his thankes:** of his will, willingly. **273. lorel:** lost cause, worthless fellow, rogue. **276. levene:** lightning. **277. welked:** withered. **278. droppyng:** leaking (and see Proverbs 27:15).

And chidyng wyves maken men to flee
Out of hir owene houses; a, benedicitee!   *280*
What eyleth swich an old man for to chide?

    Thow seyst we wyves wol oure vices hide
Til we be fast, and thanne we wol hem shewe —
Wel may that be a proverbe of a shrewe!

    Thou seist that oxen, asses, hors, and houndes,
They been assayed at diverse stoundes;   *286*
Bacyns, lavours, er that men hem bye,
Spoones and stooles, and al swich housbondrye,
And so been pottes, clothes, and array;
But folk of wyves maken noon assay,   *290*
Til they be wedded — olde dotard shrewe! —
And thanne, seistow, we wol oure vices shewe.

    Thou seist also that it displeseth me
But if that thou wolt preyse my beautee,
And but thou poure alwey upon my face,   *295*
And clepe me "faire dame" in every place.
And but thou make a feeste on thilke day
That I was born, and make me fressh and gay;
And but thou do to my norice honour,
And to my chamberere withinne my bour,   *300*
And to my fadres folk and his allyes —
Thus seistow, olde barel-ful of lyes!

    And yet of oure apprentice Janekyn,
For his crispe heer, shynynge as gold so fyn,
And for he squiereth me bothe up and doun,   *305*
Yet hastow caught a fals suspecioun.
I wol hym noght, thogh thou were deed tomorwe!

    But tel me this: why hydestow, with sorwe,
The keyes of thy cheste awey fro me?
It is my good as wel as thyn, pardee!   *310*
What, wenestow make an ydiot of oure dame?
Now by that lord that called is Seint Jame,
Thou shalt nat bothe, thogh that thou were wood,
Be maister of my body and of my good;
That oon thou shalt forgo, maugree thyne yen.
What helpith it of me to enquere or spyen?   *316*
I trowe thou woldest loke me in thy chiste!

Thou sholdest seye, "Wyf, go wher thee liste;
Taak youre disport; I wol nat leve no talys.
I knowe yow for a trewe wyf, dame Alys."   *320*
We love no man that taketh kep or charge
Wher that we goon; we wol ben at oure large.

    Of alle men yblessed moot he be,
The wise astrologien, Daun Ptholome,
That seith this proverbe in his Almageste: *325*
"Of alle men his wysdom is the hyeste
That recceth nevere who hath the world in honde."
By this proverbe thou shalt understonde,
Have thou ynogh, what thar thee recche or care
How myrily that othere folkes fare?   *330*
For, certeyn, olde dotard, by youre leve,
Ye shul have queynte right ynogh at eve.
He is to greet a nygard that wolde werne
A man to lighte a candle at his lanterne;
He shal have never the lasse light, pardee.   *335*
Have thou ynogh, thee thar nat pleyne thee.

    Thou seyst also, that if we make us gay
With clothyng, and with precious array,
That it is peril of oure chastitee;
And yet — with sorwe! — thou most enforce thee,
And seye thise wordes in the Apostles name: *341*
"In habit maad with chastitee and shame
Ye wommen shul apparaille yow," quod he,
"And noght in tressed heer and gay perree,
As perles, ne with gold, ne clothes riche."   *345*
After thy text, ne after thy rubriche,
I wol nat wirche as muchel as a gnat.

    Thou seydest this, that I was lyk a cat;
For whoso wolde senge a cattes skyn,
Thanne wolde the cat wel dwellen in his in;   *350*
And if the cattes skyn be slyk and gay,
She wol nat dwelle in house half a day,
But forth she wole, er any day be dawed,
To shewe hir skyn and goon a-caterwawed.
This is to seye, if I be gay, sire shrewe,   *355*
I wol renne out my borel for to shewe.

---

283. fast: secure (i.e., married). **284. shrewe:** wicked person, scoundrel, wretch. **286. stoundes:** times. **287. Bacyns:** basins; **lavours:** washbowls. **295. poure:** pore. **299. norice:** nurse. **301. allyes:** kinsmen by marriage. **308. with sorwe:** i.e., sorrow be to you for it! **311. wenestow:** weenest thou. **315. maugree:** in spite of. **319. leve:** believe. **329. thar:** need. **332. queynte:** pudendum (possibly also a euphemism from French *coint*, "neat, dainty, pleasant"). **333. werne:** refuse. **336. pleyne:** complain. **344. perree:** jewelry. **350. in his in:** in his inn, lodging. **356. borel:** coarse woollen clothing.

Sire olde fool, what helpeth thee to spyen?
Thogh thou preye Argus with his hundred yen
To be my warde-cors, as he kan best,
In feith, he shal nat kepe me but me lest;   360
Yet koude I make his berd, so moot I thee!
    Thou seydest eek that ther been thynges thre,
The whiche thynges troublen al this erthe,
And that no wight may endure the ferthe.
O leeve sire shrewe, Jhesu shorte thy lyf!   365
Yet prechestow and seyst an hateful wyf
Yrekened is for oon of thise meschances.
Been ther none othere maner resemblances
That ye may likne youre parables to,
But if a sely wyf be oon of tho?   370
    Thou liknest eek wommenes love to helle,
To bareyne lond, ther water may nat dwelle.
Thou liknest it also to wilde fyr;
The moore it brenneth, the moore it hath desir
To consume every thyng that brent wole be.   375
Thou seyest, right as wormes shende a tree,
Right so a wyf destroyeth hire housbonde;
This knowe they that been to wyves bonde.'
    Lordynges, right thus, as ye have understonde,
Baar I stifly myne olde housbondes on honde   380
That thus they seyden in hir dronkenesse;
And al was fals, but that I took witnesse
On Janekyn, and on my nece also.
O Lord! The peyne I dide hem and the wo,
Ful giltelees, by Goddes sweete pyne!   385
For as an hors I koude byte and whyne.
I koude pleyne, and yit was in the gilt,
Or elles often tyme hadde I been spilt.
Whoso that first to mille comth, first grynt;
I pleyned first, so was oure werre ystynt.   390
They were ful glade to excuse hem blyve
Of thyng of which they nevere agilte hir lyve.
Of wenches wolde I beren hem on honde,
Whan that for syk unnethes myghte they stonde.
    Yet tikled I his herte, for that he   395
Wende that I hadde of hym so greet chiertee!
I swoor that al my walkynge out by nyghte

Was for t'espye wenches that he dighte;
Under that colour hadde I many a myrthe.
For al swich wit is yeven us in oure byrthe;   400
Deceite, wepyng, spynnyng God hath yive
To wommen kyndely, whil that they may lyve.
And thus of o thyng I avaunte me:
Atte ende I hadde the bettre in ech degree,
By sleighte, or force, or by som maner thyng,   405
As by continueel murmur or grucchyng.
Namely abedde hadden they meschaunce:
Ther wolde I chide and do hem no plesaunce;
I wolde no lenger in the bed abyde,
If that I felte his arm over my syde,   410
Til he had maad his raunson unto me;
Thanne wolde I suffre hym do his nycetee.
And therfore every man this tale I telle,
Wynne whoso may, for al is for to selle;
With empty hand men may none haukes lure.   415
For wynnyng wolde I al his lust endure,
And make me a feyned appetit;
And yet in bacon hadde I nevere delit.
That made me that evere I wolde hem chide,
For thogh the pope hadde seten hem biside,   420
I wolde nat spare hem at hir owene bord,
For, by my trouthe, I quitte hem word for word.
As helpe me verray God omnipotent,
Though I right now sholde make my testament,
I ne owe hem nat a word that it nys quit.   425
I broghte it so aboute by my wit
That they moste yeve it up, as for the beste,
Or elles hadde we nevere been in reste;
For thogh he looked as a wood leon,
Yet sholde he faille of his conclusion.   430
    Thanne wolde I seye, 'Goode lief, taak keep
How mekely looketh Wilkyn, oure sheep!
Com neer, my spouse, lat me ba thy cheke!
Ye sholde been al pacient and meke,
And han a sweete spiced conscience,   435
Sith ye so preche of Jobes pacience.
Suffreth alwey, syn ye so wel kan preche;
And but ye do, certein we shal yow teche

---

359. **warde-cors:** bodyguard. 361. **make his berd:** i.e., fool him; **thee:** thrive. 362-67: See Proverbs 30:21-23. 365. **leeve:** dear. 373: **wilde fyr:** "Greek fire." 376. **shende:** destroy. 385. **pyne:** pain, suffering. 391. **blyve:** quickly. 396. **chiertee:** charity, affection. 398. **dighte:** slept with. 412. **nycetee:** folly, lust. 418. **bacon:** i.e., old meat. 431. **lief:** dear. 433. **ba:** kiss.

That it is fair to have a wyf in pees.
Oon of us two moste bowen, doutelees,   *440*
And sith a man is moore resonable
Than womman is, ye moste been suffrable.
What eyleth yow to grucche thus and grone?
Is it for ye wolde have my queynte allone?
Wy, taak it al! Lo, have it every deel!   *445*
Peter! I shrewe yow, but ye love it weel;
For if I wolde selle my *bele chose,*
I koude walke as fressh as is a rose;
But I wol kepe it for youre owene tooth.
Ye be to blame, by God! I sey yow sooth.'   *450*
    Swiche manere wordes hadde we on honde.
Now wol I speken of my fourthe housbonde.
    My fourthe housbonde was a revelour —
This is to seyn, he hadde a paramour —
And I was yong and ful of ragerye,   *455*
Stibourn and strong, and joly as a pie.
How koude I daunce to an harpe smale,
And synge, ywis, as any nyghtyngale,
Whan I had dronke a draughte of sweete wyn!
Metellius, the foule cherl, the swyn,   *460*
That with a staf birafte his wyf hir lyf,
For she drank wyn, thogh I hadde been his wyf,
He sholde nat han daunted me fro drynke!
And after wyn on Venus moste I thynke,
For al so siker as cold engendreth hayl,   *465*
A likerous mouth moste han a likerous tayl.
In wommen vinolent is no defence —
This knowen lecchours by experience.
    But — Lord Crist! — whan that it remembreth me
Upon my yowthe, and on my jolitee,   *470*
It tikleth me aboute myn herte roote.
Unto this day it dooth myn herte boote
That I have had my world as in my tyme.
But age, allas, that al wole envenyme,
Hath me biraft my beautee and my pith.   *475*
Lat go. Farewel! The devel go therwith!
The flour is goon; ther is namoore to telle;
The bren, as I best kan, now moste I selle;

But yet to be right myrie wol I fonde.
Now wol I tellen of my fourthe housbonde.   *480*
    I seye, I hadde in herte greet despit
That he of any oother had delit.
But he was quit, by God and by Seint Joce!
I made hym of the same wode a croce;
Nat of my body, in no foul manere,   *485*
But certeinly, I made folk swich cheere
That in his owene grece I made hym frye
For angre, and for verray jalousye.
By God, in erthe I was his purgatorie,
For which I hope his soule be in glorie.   *490*
For, God it woot, he sat ful ofte and song,
Whan that his shoo ful bitterly hym wrong.
Ther was no wight, save God and he, that wiste,
In many wise, how soore I hym twiste.
He deyde whan I cam fro Jerusalem,   *495*
And lith ygrave under the roode beem,
Al is his tombe noght so curyus
As was the sepulcre of hym Daryus,
Which that Appelles wroghte subtilly;
It nys but wast to burye hym preciously.   *500*
Lat hym fare wel; God yeve his soule reste!
He is now in his grave and in his cheste.
    Now of my fifthe housbonde wol I telle.
God lete his soule nevere come in helle!
And yet was he to me the mooste shrewe;   *505*
That feele I on my ribbes al by rewe,
And evere shal unto myn endyng day.
But in oure bed he was so fressh and gay,
And therwithal so wel koude he me glose,
Whan that he wolde han my *bele chose;*   *510*
That thogh he hadde me bete on every bon,
He koude wynne agayn my love anon.
I trowe I loved hym best, for that he
Was of his love daungerous to me.
We wommen han, if that I shal nat lye,   *515*
In this matere a queynte fantasye:
Wayte what thyng we may nat lightly have,
Therafter wol we crie al day and crave.

---

442. **suffrable:** patient. 446. **Peter:** i.e., By St. Peter. 447. *bele chose: belle chose,* beautiful thing. 449. **tooth:** taste, pleasure. 455. **ragerye:** wantonness. 457ff.: See Ovid, *Ars Amatoria* I, 229ff. 458. **ywis:** truly, certainly. 460. **Metellius:** story told by Valerius Maximus (see line 1165 and note, below); **cherl:** churl. 466. **likerous:** gluttonous; lecherous. 467. **vinolent:** winy. 472. **boote:** good. 478. **bren:** bran. 479. **fonde:** try. 483. **Joce:** or Judocus, a Breton saint. 490. **hope:** hope, expect. 492. **wrong:** wrung. 498-99: The incident alluded to in these lines, recounted in a medieval work called *Alexandreis*, is unauthenticated. 506. **al by rewe:** all in a row. 509. **glose:** flatter. 514. **daungerous:** coy, playing hard to get. 517. **Wayte what:** whatever.

Forbede us thyng, and that desiren we;
Preesse on us faste, and thanne wol we fle.   *520*
With daunger oute we al oure chaffare;
Greet prees at market maketh deere ware,
And to greet cheep is holde at litel prys:
This knoweth every womman that is wys.

My fifthe housbonde — God his soule blesse! —
Which that I took for love, and no richesse,   *526*
He som tyme was a clerk of Oxenford,
And hadde left scole, and wente at hom to bord
With my gossib, dwellynge in oure toun;
God have hir soule! Hir name was Alisoun.   *530*
She knew myn herte, and eek my privetee,
Bet than oure parisshe preest, so moot I thee!
To hire biwreyed I my conseil al.
For hadde myn housbonde pissed on a wal,
Or doon a thyng that sholde han cost his lyf,   *535*
To hire, and to another worthy wyf,
And to my nece, which that I loved weel,
I wolde han toold his conseil every deel.
And so I dide ful often, God it woot,
That made his face often reed and hoot   *540*
For verray shame, and blamed hymself for he
Had toold to me so greet a pryvetee.

And so bifel that ones in a Lente —
So often tymes I to my gossyb wente,
For evere yet I loved to be gay,   *545*
And for to walke in March, Averill, and May,
Fro hous to hous, to heere sondry talys —
That Jankyn clerk, and my gossyb dame Alys,
And I myself, into the feeldes wente.
Myn housbonde was at Londoun al that Lente;
I hadde the bettre leyser for to pleye,   *551*
And for to se, and eek for to be seye
Of lusty folk. What wiste I wher my grace
Was shapen for to be, or in what place?
Therfore I made my visitaciouns   *555*
To vigilies and to processiouns,
To prechyng eek, and to thise pilgrimages,
To pleyes of myracles, and to mariages,
And wered upon my gaye scarlet gytes.

Thise wormes, ne thise motthes, ne thise mytes,
Upon my peril, frete hem never a deel;   *561*
And wostow why? For they were used weel.

Now wol I tellen forth what happed me.
I seye that in the feeldes walked we,
Til trewely we hadde swich daliance,   *565*
This clerk and I, that of my purveiance
I spak to hym and seyde hym how that he,
If I were wydwe, sholde wedde me.
For certeinly — I sey for no bobance —
Yet was I nevere withouten purveiance   *570*
Of mariage, n'of othere thynges eek.
I holde a mouses herte nat worth a leek
That hath but oon hole for to sterte to,
And if that faille, thanne is al ydo.

I bar hym on honde he hadde enchanted me —
My dame taughte me that soutiltee —   *576*
And eek I seyde I mette of hym al nyght,
He wolde han slayn me as I lay upright,
And al my bed was ful of verray blood;
'But yet I hope that ye shal do me good,   *580*
For blood bitokeneth gold, as me was taught.'
And al was fals; I dremed of it right naught,
But as I folwed ay my dames loore,
As wel of this as of othere thynges moore.

But now, sire, lat me se what I shal seyn.   *585*
A ha! By God, I have my tale ageyn.

Whan that my fourthe housbonde was on beere,
I weep algate, and made sory cheere,
As wyves mooten, for it is usage,
And with my coverchief covered my visage,   *590*
But for that I was purveyed of a make,
I wepte but smal, and that I undertake.

To chirche was myn housbonde born a-morwe
With neighebores, that for hym maden sorwe;
And Jankyn, oure clerk, was oon of tho.   *595*
As help me God, whan that I saugh hym go
After the beere, me thoughte he hadde a paire
Of legges and of feet so clene and faire
That al myn herte I yaf unto his hoold.
He was, I trowe, twenty wynter oold,   *600*

---

521. oute: spread out, offer; **chaffare:** wares. **523. to greet cheep:** too good a bargain. **533. biwreyed:** revealed; **conseil:** secrets. **552:** See Ovid, *Ars Amatoria* I, 98. **553. grace:** favour, fortune. **558. pleyes of myracles:** miracle plays, based on legends of saints and stories of miracles; the term is sometimes loosely applied also to "mystery plays," which dramatized scenes from the Bible. **559. gytes:** robes, dresses. **560-62:** Cf. Matthew 6:19-20. **566. purveiance:** foresight, provision. **569. bobance:** boast. **574. ydo:** done, finished — i.e., that's that. **577. mette:** dreamed. **587. beere:** bier.

And I was fourty, if I shal seye sooth;
But yet I hadde alwey a coltes tooth.
Gat-tothed I was, and that bicam me weel;
I hadde the prente of seinte Venus seel.
As help me God, I was a lusty oon,   605
And faire, and riche, and yong, and wel bigon,
And trewely, as myne housbondes tolde me,
I hadde the beste *quoniam* myghte be.
For certes, I am al Venerien
In feelynge, and myn herte is Marcien.   610
Venus me yaf my lust, my likerousnesse,
And Mars yaf me my sturdy hardynesse;
Myn ascendent was Taur, and Mars therinne.
Allas, allas! That evere love was synne!
I folwed ay myn inclinacioun   615
By vertu of my constellacioun;
That made me I koude noght withdrawe
My chambre of Venus from a good felawe.
Yet have I Martes mark upon my face,
And also in another privee place.   620
For God so wys be my savacioun,
I ne loved nevere by no discrecioun,
But evere folwede myn appetit,
Al were he short, or long, or blak, or whit;
I took no kep, so that he liked me,   625
How poore he was, ne eek of what degree.
    What sholde I seye but, at the monthes ende,
This joly clerk, Jankyn, that was so hende,
Hath wedded me with greet solempnytee,
And to hym yaf I al the lond and fee   630
That evere was me yeven therbifoore.
But afterward repented me ful soore;
He nolde suffre nothyng of my list.
By God, he smoot me ones on the lyst,
For that I rente out of his book a leef,   635
That of the strook myn ere wax al deef.
Stibourn I was as is a leonesse,
And of my tonge a verray jangleresse,

And walke I wolde, as I had doon biforn,
From hous to hous, although he had it sworn;   640
For which he often tymes wolde preche,
And me of olde Romayn geestes teche;
How he Symplicius Gallus lefte his wyf,
And hire forsook for terme of al his lyf,
Noght but for open-heveded he hir say   645
Lookynge out at his dore upon a day.
    Another Romayn tolde he me by name,
That, for his wyf was at a someres game
Withouten his wityng, he forsook hire eke.
And thanne wolde he upon his Bible seke   650
That ilke proverbe of Ecclesiaste
Where he comandeth and forbedeth faste
Man shal nat suffre his wyf go roule aboute.
Thanne wolde he seye right thus, withouten doute:
    'Whoso that buyldeth his hous al of salwes,   655
And priketh his blynde hors over the falwes,
And suffreth his wyf to go seken halwes,
Is worthy to been hanged on the galwes!'
But al for noght, I sette noght an hawe
Of his proverbes n'of his olde sawe,   660
Ne I wolde nat of hym corrected be.
I hate hym that my vices telleth me,
And so doo mo, God woot, of us than I.
This made hym with me wood al outrely;
I nolde noght forbere hym in no cas.   665
    Now wol I seye yow sooth, by Seint Thomas,
Why that I rente out of his book a leef,
For which he smoot me so that I was deef.
    He hadde a book that gladly, nyght and day,
For his desport he wolde rede alway;   670
He cleped it Valerie and Theofraste,
At which book he lough alwey ful faste.
And eek ther was somtyme a clerk at Rome,
A cardinal, that highte Seint Jerome,
That made a book agayn Jovinian;   675
In which book eek ther was Tertulan,

---

606. wel bigon: well provided, contented (opposite of *woebegone*). **608. quoniam:** Latin for *since, because* — nonsense euphemism for *queynte*. **613:** Taurus, the bull, was the ascendant house of the zodiac at her birth, with Mars in it. **619. Martes:** Mars's. **628. hende:** handy, courteous. **634. lyst:** ear. **640. had it sworn:** had sworn to the contrary. **642ff., 647ff.:** anecdotes related by Valerius Maximus (see line 1165 and note, below). **645. open-heveded:** bare-headed; **say:** saw. **651. Ecclesiaste:** Ecclesiasticus 25:25 (in the Apocrypha). **652. faste:** firmly, strictly. **653. roule:** roll, gad, wander. **655. salwes:** osiers. **656. falwes:** fallow land. **665. forbere:** endure, tolerate. **669ff.:** Jankyn's "book of wikked wyves" is a manuscript anthology of antifeminist works, the following people and works being specified: the *Epistola Valerii* (Valerius, "Valerie"), by Walter Map, Theophrastus's *Liber de Nuptis* ("Theofraste"), and St. Jerome's *Epistola Adversus Jovinianum* ("agayn Jovinian") — all anti-marriage, and all made use of by Chaucer elsewhere in this Prologue; works by Tertullian ("Tertulan"), probably those condemning marriage and promoting female

Crisippus, Trotula, and Helowys,
That was abbesse nat fer fro Parys,
And eek the Parables of Salomon,
Ovides Art, and bookes many on,   *680*
And alle thise were bounden in o volume.
And every nyght and day was his custume,
Whan he hadde leyser and vacacioun
From oother worldly occupacioun,
To reden on this book of wikked wyves.   *685*
He knew of hem mo legendes and lyves
Than been of goode wyves in the Bible.
For trusteth wel, it is an impossible
That any clerk wol speke good of wyves,
But if it be of hooly seintes lyves,   *690*
Ne of noon oother womman never the mo.
Who peyntede the leon, tel me who?
By God, if wommen hadde writen stories,
As clerkes han withinne hire oratories,
They wolde han writen of men moore wikkednesse
Than al the mark of Adam may redresse.   *696*
The children of Mercurie and of Venus
Been in hir wirkyng ful contrarius;
Mercurie loveth wysdam and science,
And Venus loveth ryot and dispence.   *700*
And, for hire diverse disposicioun,
Ech falleth in otheres exaltacioun.
And thus, God woot, Mercurie is desolat
In Pisces, wher Venus is exaltat,
And Venus falleth ther Mercurie is reysed.   *705*
Therfore no womman of no clerk is preysed.
The clerk, whan he is oold, and may noght do
Of Venus werkes worth his olde sho,
Thanne sit he doun, and writ in his dotage
That wommen kan nat kepe hir mariage!   *710*
    But now to purpos, why I tolde thee
That I was beten for a book, pardee!
Upon a nyght Jankyn, that was oure sire,

Redde on his book, as he sat by the fire,
Of Eva first, that for hir wikkednesse   *715*
Was al mankynde broght to wrecchednesse,
For which that Jhesu Crist hymself was slayn,
That boghte us with his herte blood agayn.
Lo, heere expres of womman may ye fynde
That womman was the los of al mankynde.   *720*
    Tho redde he me how Sampson loste his heres:
Slepynge, his lemman kitte it with hir sheres;
Thurgh which treson loste he bothe his yen.
    Tho redde he me, if that I shal nat lyen,
Of Hercules and of his Dianyre,   *725*
That caused hym to sette hymself afyre.
    No thyng forgat he the care and the wo
That Socrates hadde with his wyves two,
How Xantippa caste pisse upon his heed.
This sely man sat stille as he were deed;   *730*
He wiped his heed, namoore dorste he seyn,
But 'Er that thonder stynte, comth a reyn!'
    Of Phasipha, that was the queene of Crete,
For shrewednesse, hym thoughte the tale swete;
Fy! Spek namoore — it is a grisly thyng —   *735*
Of hire horrible lust and hir likyng.
    Of Clitermystra, for hire lecherye,
That falsly made hire housbonde for to dye,
He redde it with ful good devocioun.
    He tolde me eek for what occasioun   *740*
Amphiorax at Thebes loste his lyf.
Myn housbonde hadde a legende of his wyf,
Eriphilem, that for an ouche of gold
Hath prively unto the Grekes told
Wher that hir housbonde hidde hym in a place,   *745*
For which he hadde at Thebes sory grace.
    Of Lyvia tolde he me, and of Lucye:
They bothe made hir housbondes for to dye,
That oon for love, that oother was for hate.
Lyvia hir housbonde, on an even late,   *750*

---

modesty and chastity; "Crisippus," mentioned by Jerome; Trotula, a female physician and author from Salerno whose book *De Passionibus Mulierum* (*On the Illnesses of Women*) came out in the 13th century; Héloïse ("Helowys"), famous for the letters between her and her lover, later husband, Pierre Abélard; the book of Proverbs in the Bible ("Parables of Salomon"), and Ovid's *Ars Amatoria* ("Ovides Art"). **692:** what the lion in the Aesopian fable asked when shown a picture of a man killing a lion. **696. the mark of Adam:** i.e., all men. **701-05:** In astrology, because of their "diverse disposicioun," Mercury is "desolat," weakest, and Venus "exaltat," strongest, when in Pisces. **713. sire:** husband and master. **721-23:** For the story of Samson and Delilah, see Judges 13-16. **725-26:** For the story of Hercules and Deianira, see e.g. Ovid's *Metamorphoses*, IX. **729. Xantippa:** Xantippe, the philosopher Socrates's notoriously shrewish wife. **733. Phasipha:** Pasiphaë, mother of the Minotaur; see e.g. Ovid's *Ars Amatoria*, I, 295ff. **737. Clitermystra:** Clytemnestra, who with her lover, Aegisthus, murdered her husband, Agamemnon, who had led the Greeks against Troy. **741. Amphiorax:** Amphiaraus, whose wife Eriphyle betrayed him. **743. an ouche:** *a nowche*, a piece of jewelry. **747. Lyvia:** Livia, lover of Sejanus; **Lucye:** Lucia, or Lucilia, wife of the poet Lucretius (*De Rerum Natura*), who according to Jerome gave her husband a love-potion

Empoysoned hath, for that she was his fo;
Lucia, likerous, loved hire housbonde so
That, for he sholde alwey upon hire thynke,
She yaf hym swich a manere love-drynke
That he was deed er it were by the morwe;   755
And thus algates housbondes han sorwe.
    Thanne tolde he me how oon Latumyus
Compleyned unto his felawe Arrius
That in his gardyn growed swich a tree
On which he seyde how that his wyves thre   760
Hanged hemself for herte despitus.
'O leeve brother,' quod this Arrius,
'Yif me a plante of thilke blissed tree,
And in my gardyn planted shal it bee.'
    Of latter date, of wyves hath he red   765
That somme han slayn hir housbondes in hir bed,
And lete hir lecchour dighte hire al the nyght,
Whan that the corps lay in the floor upright.
And somme han dryve nayles in hir brayn,   769
Whil that they slepte, and thus they had hem slayn.
Somme han hem yeve poysoun in hire drynke.
He spak moore harm than herte may bithynke,
And therwithal he knew of mo proverbes
Than in this world ther growen gras or herbes.
'Bet is,' quod he, 'thyn habitacioun   775
Be with a leon or a foul dragoun,
Than with a womman usynge for to chyde.
Bet is,' quod he, 'hye in the roof abyde,
Than with an angry wyf doun in the hous;
They been so wikked and contrarious,   780
They haten that hir housbondes loven ay.'
He seyde, 'A womman cast hir shame away,
Whan she cast of hir smok'; and forthermo,
'A fair womman, but she be chaast also,
Is lyk a gold ryng in a sowes nose.'   785
Who wolde wene, or who wolde suppose,
The wo that in myn herte was, and pyne?
    And whan I saugh he wolde nevere fyne
To reden on this cursed book al nyght,
Al sodeynly thre leves have I plyght   790

Out of his book, right as he radde, and eke
I with my fest so took hym on the cheke
That in oure fyr he fil bakward adoun.
And he up stirte as dooth a wood leoun,
And with his fest he smoot me on the heed   795
That in the floor I lay as I were deed.
And whan he saugh how stille that I lay,
He was agast and wolde han fled his way,
Til atte laste out of my swogh I breyde.
'O! hastow slayn me, false theef?' I seyde,   800
'And for my land thus hastow mordred me?
Er I be deed, yet wol I kisse thee.'
    And neer he cam, and kneled faire adoun,
And seyde, 'Deere suster Alisoun,
As help me God, I shal thee nevere smyte!   805
That I have doon, it is thyself to wyte.
Foryeve it me, and that I thee biseke!'
And yet eftsoones I hitte hym on the cheke,
And seyde, 'Theef, thus muchel am I wreke;
Now wol I dye, I may no lenger speke.'   810
But atte laste, with muchel care and wo,
We fille acorded by us selven two.
He yaf me al the bridel in myn hond,
To han the governance of hous and lond,
And of his tonge, and of his hond also;   815
And made hym brenne his book anon right tho.
And whan that I hadde geten unto me,
By maistrie, al the soveraynetee,
And that he seyde, 'Myn owene trewe wyf,
Do as thee lust the terme of al thy lyf;   820
Keep thyn honour, and keep eek myn estaat'—
After that day we hadden never debaat.
God helpe me so, I was to hym as kynde
As any wyf from Denmark unto Inde,
And also trewe, and so was he to me.   825
I prey to God, that sit in magestee,
So blesse his soule for his mercy deere.
Now wol I seye my tale, if ye wol heere."
    The Frere lough, whan he hadde herd al this;
"Now dame," quod he, "so have I joye or blis,   830

---

that made him insane and drove him to suicide (a story retold by Tennyson in a dramatic monologue, "Lucretius"). **757ff.:** The story of Latumyus and Arrius is told in the *Epistola Valerii*. **769-70:** probably referring to Jael and Sisera — see Judges 4. **775-77:** See Ecclesiasticus 25:16. **778-79:** See Proverbs 21:9. **784-85:** See Proverbs 11:22. **788. fyne:** finish, stop. **790. plyght:** plucked. **799. swogh:** swoon; **breyde:** started, awoke. **806. wyte:** blame. **809. wreke:** avenged.

This is a long preamble of a tale!"
And whan the Somonour herde the Frere gale,
"Lo," quod the Somonour, "Goddes armes two!
A frere wol entremette hym everemo.
Lo, goode men, a flye and eek a frere   835
Wol falle in every dyssh and eek mateere.
What spekestow of preambulacioun?
What! amble, or trotte, or pees, or go sit doun!
Thou lettest oure disport in this manere."

    "Ye, woltow so, sire Somonour?" quod the Frere;
"Now, by my feith I shal, er that I go,   841
Telle of a somonour swich a tale or two
That alle the folk shal laughen in this place."

    "Now elles, Frere, I bishrewe thy face,"
Quod this Somonour, "and I bishrewe me,   845
But if I telle tales two or thre
Of freres er I come to Sidyngborne
That I shal make thyn herte for to morne,
For wel I woot thy pacience is gon."

    Oure Hooste cride "Pees! And that anon!"   850
And seyde, "Lat the womman telle hire tale.
Ye fare as folk that dronken ben of ale.
Do, dame, telle forth youre tale, and that is best."

    "Al redy, sire," quod she, "right as yow lest,
If I have licence of this worthy Frere."   855

    "Yis, dame," quod he, "tel forth, and I wol heere."

THE WIFE OF BATH'S TALE

    In th'olde dayes of the Kyng Arthour,
Of which that Britons speken greet honour,
Al was this land fulfild of fayerye.
The elf-queene, with hir joly compaignye,   860
Daunced ful ofte in many a grene mede.
This was the olde opinion, as I rede;
I speke of manye hundred yeres ago.
But now kan no man se none elves mo,
For now the grete charitee and prayeres   865
Of lymytours and othere hooly freres,
That serchen every lond and every streem,
As thikke as motes in the sonne-beem,
Blessynge halles, chambres, kichenes, bowres,
Citees, burghes, castels, hye toures,   870
Thropes, bernes, shipnes, dayeryes —
This maketh that ther ben no fayeryes.
For ther as wont to walken was an elf
Ther walketh now the lymytour hymself
In undermeles and in morwenynges,   875
And seyth his matins and his hooly thynges
As he gooth in his lymytacioun.
Wommen may go saufly up and doun.
In every bussh or under every tree
Ther is noon oother incubus but he,   880
And he ne wol doon hem but dishonour.

    And so bifel that this kyng Arthour
Hadde in his hous a lusty bacheler,
That on a day cam ridynge fro ryver,
And happed that, allone as he was born,   885
He saugh a mayde walkynge hym biforn,
Of which mayde anon, maugree hir heed,
By verray force, he rafte hire maydenhed;
For which oppressioun was swich clamour
And swich pursute unto the kyng Arthour   890
That dampned was this knyght for to be deed,
By cours of lawe, and sholde han lost his heed —
Paraventure swich was the statut tho —
But that the queene and other ladyes mo
So longe preyeden the kyng of grace   895
Til he his lyf hym graunted in the place,
And yaf hym to the queene, al at hir wille,
To chese wheither she wolde hym save or spille.
The queene thanketh the kyng with al hir myght,
And after this thus spak she to the knyght,   900
Whan that she saugh hir tyme, upon a day:
"Thou standest yet," quod she, "in swich array
That of thy lyf yet hastow no suretee.
I grante thee lyf, if thou kanst tellen me
What thyng is it that wommen moost desiren.   905
Be war, and keep thy nekke-boon from iren!
And if thou kanst nat tellen it anon,
Yet wol I yive thee leve for to gon
A twelf-month and a day, to seche and leere

---

832. gale: exclaim. **834. entremette hym:** interfere, intrude himself. **847. Sidyngborne:** Sittingbourne (town about two-thirds of the way from London to Canterbury). **871. Thropes:** thorps, hamlets, villages; **bernes:** barns; **shipnes:** stables. **875. undermeles:** afternoons. **884. fro ryver:** from hawking or hawking-ground by the river. **888. rafte:** bereft, took. **893. paraventure:** peradventure. **898. spille:** spill, waste, destroy. **909. leere:** learn.

An answere suffisant in this mateere;   910
And suretee wol I han, er that thou pace,
Thy body for to yelden in this place."

Wo was this knyght, and sorwefully he siketh;
But what! He may nat do al as hym liketh.
And at the laste he chees hym for to wende   915
And come agayn, right at the yeres ende,
With swich answere as God wolde hym purveye;
And taketh his leve, and wendeth forth his weye.

He seketh every hous and every place
Where as he hopeth for to fynde grace   920
To lerne what thyng wommen loven moost,
But he ne koude arryven in no coost
Wher as he myghte fynde in this mateere
Two creatures accordynge in-feere.
Somme seyde wommen loven best richesse,   925
Somme seyde honour, somme seyde jolynesse,
Somme riche array, somme seyden lust abedde,
And oftetyme to be wydwe and wedde.
Somme seyde that oure hertes been moost esed
Whan that we been yflatered and yplesed.   930
He gooth ful ny the sothe, I wol nat lye.
A man shal wynne us best with flaterye,
And with attendance and with bisynesse
Been we ylymed, bothe moore and lesse.

And somme seyen that we loven best   935
For to be free and do right as us lest,
And that no man repreve us of oure vice,
But seye that we be wise and no thyng nyce.
For trewely ther is noon of us alle,
If any wight wol clawe us on the galle,   940
That we nyl kike, for he seith us sooth.
Assay, and he shal fynde it that so dooth;
For, be we never so vicious withinne,
We wol been holden wise and clene of synne.

And somme seyn that greet delit han we   945
For to been holden stable, and eek secree,
And in o purpos stedefastly to dwelle,
And nat biwreye thyng that men us telle.
But that tale is nat worth a rake-stele.
Pardee, we wommen konne no thyng hele;   950

Witnesse on Myda — wol ye heere the tale?

Ovyde, amonges othere thynges smale,
Seyde Myda hadde, under his longe heres,
Growynge upon his heed two asses eres,
The whiche vice he hydde as he best myghte   955
Ful subtilly from every mannes sighte,
That, save his wyf, ther wiste of it namo.
He loved hire moost, and trusted hire also;
He preyede hire that to no creature
She sholde tellen of his disfigure.   960

She swoor him, "Nay"; for al this world to wynne,
She nolde do that vileynye or synne,
To make hir housbonde han so foul a name.
She nolde nat telle it for hir owene shame.
But nathelees, hir thoughte that she dyde   965
That she so longe sholde a conseil hyde;
Hir thoughte it swal so soore aboute hir herte
That nedely som word hire moste asterte;
And sith she dorste telle it to no man,
Doun to a mareys faste by she ran —   970
Til she cam there hir herte was afyre —
And as a bitore bombleth in the myre,
She leyde hir mouth unto the water doun:
"Biwreye me nat, thou water, with thy soun,"
Quod she; "to thee I telle it and namo;   975
Myn housbonde hath longe asses erys two!
Now is myn herte al hool; now is it oute.
I myghte no lenger kepe it, out of doute."
Heere may ye se, thogh we a tyme abyde,
Yet out it moot; we kan no conseil hyde.   980
The remenant of the tale if ye wol heere,
Redeth Ovyde, and ther ye may it leere.

This knyght, of which my tale is specially,
Whan that he saugh he myghte nat come therby —
This is to seye, what wommen love moost —   985
Withinne his brest ful sorweful was the goost.
But hoom he gooth; he myghte nat sojourne;
The day was come that homward moste he tourne.
And in his wey it happed hym to ryde,
In al this care, under a forest syde,   990
Wher as he saugh upon a daunce go

---

913. siketh: sighs. **922. coost:** coast, region. **924. in-feere:** together. **934. ylymed:** caught (as with birdlime). **938. nyce:** foolish, wanton. **949. rake-stele:** rake-handle. **950. hele:** conceal. **951. Myda:** Midas. **968. asterte:** escape. **970. mareys:** marsh. **972. bitore:** bittern; **bombleth:** boom. **982:** See Ovid's *Metamorphoses*, Book XI, which tells a different version.

Of ladyes foure and twenty, and yet mo;
Toward the whiche daunce he drow ful yerne,
In hope that som wysdom sholde he lerne.
But certeinly, er he cam fully there,   *995*
Vanysshed was this daunce, he nyste where.
No creature saugh he that bar lyf,
Save on the grene he saugh sittynge a wyf —
A fouler wight ther may no man devyse.
Agayn the knyght this olde wyf gan ryse,   *1000*
And seyde, "Sire knyght, heer forth ne lith no wey.
Tel me what that ye seken, by youre fey!
Paraventure it may the bettre be;
Thise olde folk kan muchel thyng," quod she.
    "My leeve mooder," quod this knyght, "certeyn
I nam but deed but if that I kan seyn   *1006*
What thyng it is that wommen moost desire.
Koude ye me wisse, I wolde wel quite youre hire."
    "Plight me thy trouthe heere in myn hand," quod
        she,
"The nexte thyng that I requere thee,   *1010*
Thou shalt it do, if it lye in thy myght,
And I wol telle it yow er it be nyght."
    "Have heer my trouthe," quod the knyght, "I
        grante."
    "Thanne," quod she, "I dar me wel avante
Thy lyf is sauf, for I wol stonde therby;   *1015*
Upon my lyf, the queene wol seye as I.
Lat se which is the proudeste of hem alle
That wereth on a coverchief or a calle
That dar seye nay of that I shal thee teche.
Lat us go forth withouten lenger speche."   *1020*
Tho rowned she a pistel in his ere,
And bad hym to be glad and have no fere.
    Whan they be comen to the court, this knyght
Seyde he had holde his day, as he hadde hight,
And redy was his answere, as he sayde.   *1025*
Ful many a noble wyf, and many a mayde,
And many a wydwe, for that they been wise,
The queene hirself sittynge as a justise,
Assembled been, his answere for to heere;
And afterward this knyght was bode appeere.   *1030*

To every wight comanded was silence,
And that the knyght sholde telle in audience
What thyng that worldly wommen loven best.
This knyght ne stood nat stille as doth a best,
But to his questioun anon answerde   *1035*
With manly voys, that al the court it herde:
    "My lige lady, generally," quod he,
"Wommen desiren to have sovereynetee
As wel over hir housbond as hir love,
And for to been in maistrie hym above.   *1040*
This is youre mooste desir, thogh ye me kille.
Dooth as yow list; I am heer at youre wille."
In al the court ne was ther wyf, ne mayde,
Ne wydwe that contraried that he sayde,
But seyden he was worthy han his lyf.   *1045*
And with that word up stirte the olde wyf,
Which that the knyght saugh sittynge on the grene:
"Mercy," quod she, "my sovereyn lady queene!
Er that youre court departe, do me right.
I taughte this answere unto the knyght;   *1050*
For which he plighte me his trouthe there,
The firste thyng that I wolde hym requere
He wolde it do, if it lay in his myghte.
Bifore the court thanne preye I thee, sir knyght,"
Quod she, "that thou me take unto thy wyf,   *1055*
For wel thou woost that I have kept thy lyf.
If I seye fals, sey nay, upon thy fey!"
    This knyght answerde, "Allas and weylawey!
I woot right wel that swich was my biheste.
For Goddes love, as chees a newe requeste!   *1060*
Taak al my good and lat my body go."
    "Nay, thanne," quod she, "I shrewe us bothe
        two!
For thogh that I be foul, and oold, and poore
I nolde for al the metal, ne for oore
That under erthe is grave or lith above,   *1065*
But if thy wyf I were, and eek thy love."
    "My love?" quod he, "nay, my dampnacioun!
Allas, that any of my nacioun
Sholde evere so foule disparaged be!"
But al for noght; the ende is this, that he   *1070*

---

993. yerne: eagerly, quickly. **1000. Agayn:** towards. **1008. wisse:** instruct, inform. **1018. calle:** hairnet, headdress. **1021. pistel:** epistle, message. **1024. hight:** promised. **1026ff.:** This assembly and the knight's appearance before it is similar to the "courts of love" purportedly held as part of the system of Courtly Love and presided over by Eleanor of Aquitaine, among others. **1068. nacioun:** family.

Constreyned was; he nedes moste hire wedde,
And taketh his olde wyf, and gooth to bedde.
    Now wolden som men seye, paraventure,
That for my necligence I do no cure
To tellen yow the joye and al th'array   *1075*
That at the feeste was that ilke day.
To which thyng shortly answeren I shal:
I seye ther nas no joye ne feeste at al;
Ther nas but hevynesse and muche sorwe.
For prively he wedded hire on morwe,   *1080*
And al day after hidde hym as an owle,
So wo was hym, his wyf looked so foule.
    Greet was the wo the knyght hadde in his thoght,
Whan he was with his wyf abedde ybroght;
He walweth and he turneth to and fro.   *1085*
His olde wyf lay smylynge everemo,
And seyde, "O deere housbonde, benedicitee!
Fareth every knyght thus with his wyf as ye?
Is this the lawe of kyng Arthures hous?
Is every knyght of his so dangerous?   *1090*
I am youre owene love and youre wyf;
I am she which that saved hath youre lyf,
And, certes, yet ne dide I yow nevere unright;
Why fare ye thus with me this firste nyght?
Ye faren lyk a man had lost his wit.   *1095*
What is my gilt? For Goddes love, tel it,
And it shal been amended, if I may."
    "Amended?" quod this knyght, "Allas, nay, nay!
It wol nat been amended nevere mo.
Thou art so loothly, and so oold also,   *1100*
And therto comen of so lough a kynde,
That litel wonder is thogh I walwe and wynde.
So wolde God myn herte wolde breste!"
    "Is this," quod she, "the cause of youre unreste?"
    "Ye, certeinly," quod he, "no wonder is."   *1105*
    "Now, sire," quod she, "I koude amende al this,
If that me liste, er it were dayes thre,
So wel ye myghte bere yow unto me.
    "But, for ye speken of swich gentillesse
As is descended out of old richesse,   *1110*
That therfore sholden ye be gentil men,
Swich arrogance is nat worth an hen.

Looke who that is moost vertuous alway,
Pryvee and apert, and moost entendeth ay
To do the gentil dedes that he kan;   *1115*
Taak hym for the grettest gentil man.
Crist wole we clayme of hym oure gentillesse,
Nat of oure eldres for hire old richesse.
For thogh they yive us al hir heritage,
For which we clayme to been of heigh parage,
Yet may they nat biquethe for no thyng   *1121*
To noon of us hir vertuous lyvyng,
That made hem gentil men ycalled be,
And bad us folwen hem in swich degree.
    "Wel kan the wise poete of Florence,   *1125*
That highte Dant, speken in this sentence.
Lo, in swich maner rym is Dantes tale:
'Ful selde up riseth by his branches smale
Prowesse of man, for God, of his goodnesse,
Wole that of hym we clayme oure gentillesse';   *1130*
For of oure eldres may we no thyng clayme
But temporel thyng, that man may hurte and
    mayme.
    "Eek every wight woot this as wel as I,
If gentillesse were planted natureelly
Unto a certeyn lynage doun the lyne,   *1135*
Pryvee and apert thanne wolde they nevere fyne
To doon of gentillesse the faire office;
They myghte do no vileynye or vice.
    "Taak fyr and ber it in the derkeste hous
Bitwix this and the mount of Kaukasous,   *1140*
And lat men shette the dores and go thenne;
Yet wole the fyr as faire lye and brenne
As twenty thousand men myghte it biholde;
His office natureel ay wol it holde,
Up peril of my lyf, til that it dye.   *1145*
    "Heere may ye se wel how that genterye
Is nat annexed to possessioun,
Sith folk ne doon hir operacioun
Alwey, as dooth the fyr, lo, in his kynde.
For, God it woot, men may wel often fynde   *1150*
A lordes sone do shame and vileynye;
And he that wole han pris of his gentrye,
For he was boren of a gentil hous

1109. **gentillesse:** nobility — see Chaucer's poem of that title. 1114. **pryvee and apert:** in private and in public. 1120. **parage:** birth, lineage. 1126. **Dant:** Dante (see his *Convivio*). 1152. **pris:** praise.

And hadde his eldres noble and vertuous,
And nyl hymselven do no gentil dedis   1155
Ne folwen his gentil auncestre that deed is,
He nys nat gentil, be he duc or erl,
For vileyns synful dedes make a cherl.
Thy gentillesse nys but renomee
Of thyne auncestres, for hire heigh bountee,   1160
Which is a strange thyng to thy persone.
For gentillesse cometh fro God allone.
Thanne comth oure verray gentillesse of grace;
It was no thyng biquethe us with oure place.
    "Thenketh hou noble, as seith Valerius,   1165
Was thilke Tullius Hostillius,
That out of poverte roos to heigh noblesse.
Reedeth Senec, and redeth eek Boece;
Ther shul ye seen expres that it no drede is
That he is gentil that dooth gentil dedis.   1170
And therfore, leeve housbonde, I thus conclude:
Al were it that myne auncestres were rude,
Yet may the hye God, and so hope I,
Grante me grace to lyven vertuously.
Thanne am I gentil, whan that I bigynne   1175
To lyven vertuously and weyve synne.
    "And ther as ye of poverte me repreeve,
The hye God, on whom that we bileeve,
In wilful poverte chees to lyve his lyf.
And certes every man, mayden, or wyf   1180
May understonde that Jhesus, hevene kyng,
Ne wolde nat chese a vicious lyvyng.
Glad poverte is an honest thyng, certeyn;
This wole Senec and othere clerkes seyn.
Whoso that halt hym payd of his poverte,   1185
I holde hym riche, al hadde he nat a sherte.
He that coveiteth is a povre wight,
For he wolde han that is nat in his myght;
But he that noght hath, ne coveiteth have,
Is riche, although ye holde hym but a knave.   1190
Verray poverte, it syngeth proprely;
Juvenal seith of poverte myrily:
'The povre man, whan he goth by the weye,
Bifore the theves he may synge and pleye.'

Poverte is hateful good and, as I gesse,   1195
A ful greet bryngere out of bisynesse;
A greet amendere eek of sapience
To hym that taketh it in pacience.
Poverte is this, although it seme alenge:
Possessioun that no wight wol chalenge.   1200
Poverte ful ofte, whan a man is lowe,
Maketh his God and eek hymself to knowe.
Poverte a spectacle is, as thynketh me,
Thurgh which he may his verray freendes see.
And therfore, sire, syn that I noght yow greve,
Of my poverte namoore ye me repreve.   1206
    "Now, sire, of elde ye repreve me;
And certes, sire, thogh noon auctoritee
Were in no book, ye gentils of honour
Seyn that men sholde an oold wight doon favour
And clepe hym fader, for youre gentillesse;   1211
And auctours shal I fynden, as I gesse.
    "Now ther ye seye that I am foul and old,
Than drede you noght to been a cokewold;
For filthe and eelde, also moot I thee,   1215
Been grete wardeyns upon chastitee.
But nathelees, syn I knowe youre delit,
I shal fulfille youre worldly appetit.
    "Chese now," quod she, "oon of thise thynges
        tweye:
To han me foul and old til that I deye,   1220
And be to yow a trewe, humble wyf,
And nevere yow displese in al my lyf,
Or elles ye wol han me yong and fair,
And take youre aventure of the repair
That shal be to youre hous by cause of me,   1225
Or in som oother place, may wel be.
Now chese yourselven, wheither that yow liketh."
    This knyght avyseth hym and sore siketh,
But atte laste he seyde in this manere:
"My lady and my love, and wyf so deere,   1230
I put me in youre wise governance;
Cheseth youreself which may be moost plesance
And moost honour to yow and me also.
I do no fors the wheither of the two,

1159. renomee: renown. **1160. bountee:** goodness. **1161. strange:** foreign. **1165. Valerius:** Valerius Maximus, 1st-century Roman historian and compiler of sayings and anecdotes for rhetoricians (see lines 460, 642ff., 647ff., above). **1166:** Tullus Hostilius, the partly legendary third king of Rome. **1168. Senek:** Seneca; **Boece:** Boethius. **1185. halt hym payd:** holds himself satisfied. **1192-94:** in Juvenal's *Satire X*, but also in Dante's *Convivio.* **1199. alenge:** wretched, miserable. **1214. cokewold:** cuckold. **1234. fors:** force, importance.

For as yow liketh, it suffiseth me."   *1235*
　　"Thanne have I gete of yow maistrie," quod she,
"Syn I may chese and governe as me lest?"
　　"Ye, certes, wyf," quod he, "I holde it best."
　　"Kys me," quod she, "we be no lenger wrothe,
For, by my trouthe, I wol be to yow bothe —   *1240*
This is to seyn, ye, bothe fair and good.
I prey to God that I moote sterven wood,
But I to yow be also good and trewe
As evere was wyf, syn that the world was newe.
And but I be to-morn as fair to seene   *1245*
As any lady, emperice, or queene,
That is bitwixe the est and eke the west,
Dooth with my lyf and deth right as yow lest.
Cast up the curtyn, looke how that it is."
　　And whan the knyght saugh verraily al this,
That she so fair was, and so yong therto,   *1251*
For joye he hente hire in his armes two.
His herte bathed in a bath of blisse.
A thousand tyme a-rewe he gan hire kisse,
And she obeyed hym in every thyng   *1255*
That myghte doon hym plesance or likyng.
　　And thus they lyve unto hir lyves ende
In parfit joye; and Jhesu Crist us sende
Housbondes meeke, yonge, and fressh abedde,
And grace t'overbyde hem that we wedde,   *1260*
And eek I praye Jhesu shorte hir lyves
That noght wol be governed by hir wyves;
And olde and angry nygardes of dispence,
God sende hem soone verray pestilence!

THE PARDONER'S PROLOGUE

　　"Lordynges," quod he, "in chirches whan I
　　　preche,
I peyne me to han an hauteyn speche,
And rynge it out as round as gooth a belle,

For I kan al by rote that I telle.
My theme is alwey oon, and evere was —   *5*
Radix malorum est Cupiditas.
　　"First I pronounce whennes that I come,
And thanne my bulles shewe I, alle and some.
Oure lige lordes seel on my patente,
That shewe I first, my body to warente,   *10*
That no man be so boold, ne preest ne clerk,
Me to destourbe of Cristes hooly werk.
And after that thanne telle I forth my tales;
Bulles of popes and of cardynales,
Of patriarkes and bishopes I shewe,   *15*
And in Latyn I speke a wordes fewe,
To saffron with my predicacioun,
And for to stire hem to devocioun.
Thanne shewe I forth my longe cristal stones,
Ycrammed ful of cloutes and of bones —   *20*
Relikes been they, as wenen they echoon.
Thanne have I in latoun a sholder-boon
Which that was of an hooly Jewes sheep.
'Goode men,' I seye, 'taak of my wordes keep;
If that this boon be wasshe in any welle,   *25*
If cow, or calf, or sheep, or oxe swelle
That any worm hath ete, or worm ystonge,
Taak water of that welle and wassh his tonge,
And it is hool anon; and forthermoore,
Of pokkes and of scabbe, and every soore   *30*
Shal every sheep be hool that of this welle
Drynketh a draughte. Taak kep eek what I telle:
If that the good-man that the beestes oweth
Wol every wyke, er that the cok hym croweth,
Fastynge, drynken of this welle a draughte,   *35*
As thilke hooly Jew oure eldres taughte,
His beestes and his stoor shal multiplie.
　　'And, sires, also it heeleth jalousie;
For though a man be falle in jalous rage,
Lat maken with this water his potage,   *40*

1242. sterven: starve, die. **1260. overbyde:** outlive.　**THE PARDONER'S PROLOGUE AND TALE**　During the interlude between the Physician's tale and the Pardoner's tale, the Host, after commenting on the Physician's "pitous tale," turns to the Pardoner: "'Thou beel amy, thou Pardoner,' he sayde, / 'Telle us som myrthe or japes right anon.' / 'It shal be doon,' quod he, 'by Seint Ronyon! / But first,' quod he, 'heere at this alestake / I wol bothe drynke and eten of a cake.' / But right anon thise gentils gonne to crye, / 'Nay, lat hym telle us of no ribaudye! / Telle us som moral thyng, that we may leere / Som wit, and thanne wol we gladly heere.' / 'I graunte, ywis,' quod he, 'but I moot thynke / Upon some honest thyng while that I drynke.' " **2. hauteyn:** haughty, loud. **6:** The love of money is the root of [all] evil (I Timothy 6:10). **8:** The Pardoner's bulls are of course indulgences. **17. saffron:** colour, spice; **predicacioun:** preaching. **19. cristal stones:** glass containers. **30. pokkes:** pocks. **33. oweth:** owns. **40. potage:** soup.

And nevere shal he moore his wyf mystriste,
Though he the soothe of hir defaute wiste,
Al had she taken prestes two or thre.
   'Heere is a miteyn eek, that ye may se.
He that his hand wol putte in this miteyn,   45
He shal have multipliyng of his grayn,
Whan he hath sowen, be it whete or otes,
So that he offre pens, or elles grotes.
   'Goode men and wommen, o thyng warne I yow:
If any wight be in this chirche now   50
That hath doon synne horrible, that he
Dar nat, for shame, of it yshryven be,
Or any womman, be she yong or old,
That hath ymaked hir housbonde cokewold,
Swich folk shal have no power ne no grace   55
To offren to my relikes in this place.
And whoso fyndeth hym out of swich blame,
He wol come up and offre a Goddes name,
And I assoille him by the auctoritee
Which that by bulle ygraunted was to me.'   60
   "By this gaude have I wonne, yeer by yeer,
An hundred mark sith I was pardoner.
I stonde lyk a clerk in my pulpet,
And whan the lewed peple is doun yset,
I preche so as ye han herd bifoore   65
And telle an hundred false japes moore.
Thanne peyne I me to strecche forth the nekke,
And est and west upon the peple I bekke,
As dooth a dowve sittynge on a berne.
Myne handes and my tonge goon so yerne   70
That it is joye to se my bisynesse.
Of avarice and of swich cursednesse
Is al my prechyng, for to make hem free
To yeven hir pens, and namely unto me.
For myn entente is nat but for to wynne,   75
And nothyng for correccioun of synne.
I rekke nevere, whan that they been beryed,
Though that hir soules goon a-blakeberyed!
For certes, many a predicacioun
Comth ofte tyme of yvel entencioun;   80
Som for plesance of folk and flaterye,
To been avaunced by ypocrisye,
And som for veyne glorie, and som for hate.

For whan I dar noon oother weyes debate,
Thanne wol I stynge hym with my tonge smerte
In prechyng, so that he shal nat asterte   86
To been defamed falsly, if that he
Hath trespased to my bretheren or to me.
For though I telle noght his propre name,
Men shal wel knowe that it is the same,   90
By signes, and by othere circumstances.
Thus quite I folk that doon us displesances;
Thus spitte I out my venym under hewe
Of hoolynesse, to semen hooly and trewe.
   "But shortly myn entente I wol devyse: 95
I preche of no thyng but for coveityse.
Therfore my theme is yet, and evere was,
Radix malorum est Cupiditas.
Thus kan I preche agayn that same vice
Which that I use, and that is avarice.   100
But though myself be gilty in that synne,
Yet kan I maken oother folk to twynne
From avarice and soore to repente.
But that is nat my principal entente;
I preche nothyng but for coveitise.   105
Of this mateere it oghte ynogh suffise.
   "Thanne telle I hem ensamples many oon
Of olde stories longe tyme agoon.
For lewed peple loven tales olde;
Swiche thynges kan they wel reporte and holde.
What, trowe ye, that whiles I may preche,   111
And wynne gold and silver for I teche,
That I wol lyve in poverte wilfully?
Nay, nay, I thoghte it nevere, trewely!
For I wol preche and begge in sondry landes;   115
I wol nat do no labour with myne handes,
Ne make baskettes and lyve therby,
By cause I wol nat beggen ydelly.
I wol noon of the apostles countrefete;
I wol have moneie, wolle, chese, and whete,   120
Al were it yeven of the povereste page,
Or of the povereste wydwe in a village,
Al sholde hir children sterve for famyne.
Nay, I wol drynke licour of the vyne
And have a joly wenche in every toun.   125
But herkneth, lordynges, in conclusioun:

---

48. pens: pence; **grotes:** groats. **61. gaude:** gaud, trick. **68. bekke:** beckon, nod. **107. ensamples:** exempla. **119-20:** See Mark 6:8.

Youre likyng is that I shal telle a tale.
Now have I dronke a draughte of corny ale,
By God, I hope I shal yow telle a thyng
That shal by reson been at youre likyng.   *130*
For though myself be a ful vicious man,
A moral tale yet I yow telle kan,
Which I am wont to preche for to wynne.
Now hoold youre pees! My tale I wol bigynne."

THE PARDONER'S TALE

   In Flaundres whilom was a compaignye   *135*
Of yonge folk that haunteden folye,
As riot, hasard, stywes, and tavernes,
Where as with harpes, lutes, and gyternes,
They daunce and pleyen at dees bothe day and
    nyght,
And eten also and drynken over hir myght,   *140*
Thurgh which they doon the devel sacrifise
Withinne that develes temple in cursed wise
By superfluytee abhomynable.
Hir othes been so grete and so dampnable
That it is grisly for to heere hem swere.   *145*
Oure blissed Lordes body they totere —
Hem thoughte that Jewes rente hym noght
    ynough —
And ech of hem at otheres synne lough.
And right anon thanne comen tombesteres
Fetis and smale, and yonge frutesteres,   *150*
Syngeres with harpes, bawdes, wafereres,
Whiche been the verray develes officeres
To kyndle and blowe the fyr of lecherye,
That is annexed unto glotonye.
The hooly writ take I to my witnesse   *155*
That luxurie is in wyn and dronkenesse.
   Lo, how that dronken Looth, unkyndely,
Lay by his doghtres two, unwityngly;
So dronke he was, he nyste what he wroghte.
   Herodes, whoso wel the stories soghte,   *160*
Whan he of wyn was repleet at his feeste,
Right at his owene table he yaf his heeste

To sleen the Baptist John, ful giltelees.
   Senec seith a good word doutelees;
He seith he kan no difference fynde   *165*
Bitwix a man that is out of his mynde
And a man which that is dronkelewe,
But that woodnesse, yfallen in a shrewe,
Persevereth lenger than doth dronkenesse.
O glotonye, ful of cursednesse!   *170*
O cause first of oure confusioun!
O original of oure dampnacioun,
Til Crist hadde boght us with his blood agayn!
Lo, how deere, shortly for to sayn,
Aboght was thilke cursed vileynye!   *175*
Corrupt was al this world for glotonye.
   Adam oure fader, and his wyf also,
Fro Paradys to labour and to wo
Were dryven for that vice, it is no drede.
For whil that Adam fasted, as I rede,   *180*
He was in Paradys; and whan that he
Eet of the fruyt deffended on the tree,
Anon he was out cast to wo and peyne.
O glotonye, on thee wel oghte us pleyne!
O, wiste a man how manye maladyes   *185*
Folwen of excesse and of glotonyes,
He wolde been the moore mesurable
Of his diete, sittynge at his table.
Allas, the shorte throte, the tendre mouth,
Maketh that est and west and north and south,   *190*
In erthe, in eir, in water, men to swynke
To gete a glotoun deyntee mete and drynke!
Of this matiere, O Paul, wel kanstow trete:
"Mete unto wombe, and wombe eek unto mete,
Shal God destroyen bothe," as Paulus seith.   *195*
Allas, a foul thyng is it, by my feith,
To seye this word, and fouler is the dede,
Whan man so drynketh of the white and rede
That of his throte he maketh his privee
Thurgh thilke cursed superfluitee.   *200*
   The apostel wepyng seith ful pitously,
"Ther walken manye of whiche yow told have I —

---

136. haunteden: habitually practised or resorted to. **137. stywes:** stews, brothels. **146. totere:** tear in pieces (i.e., using oaths referring to various parts of God's body — see 323ff. below). **149. tombesteres:** dancing girls. **150. frutesteres:** girls selling fruit. **151. waferers:** makers and sellers of wafer-cakes. **155-56:** See Ephesians 5:18. **157. Looth:** Lot (see Genesis 19). **159. nyste:** (*ne wyste*) didn't know. **160. Herodes:** Herod (see e.g. Matthew 14 and Mark 6). **171. confusioun:** ruin. **182. deffended:** forbidden. **184-88:** See e.g. Ecclesiasticus 37:29-31. **194-95:** See I Corinthians 6:13.

I seye it now wepyng, with pitous voys —
They been enemys of Cristes croys, 204
Of whiche the ende is deeth; wombe is hir god!"
O wombe! O bely! O stynkyng cod,
Fulfilled of dong and of corrupcioun!
At either ende of thee foul is the soun.
How greet labour and cost is thee to fynde!
Thise cookes, how they stampe, and streyne, and
    grynde, 210
And turnen substaunce into accident
To fulfille al thy likerous talent!
Out of the harde bones knokke they
The mary, for they caste noght awey
That may go thurgh the golet softe and swoote.
Of spicerie of leef, and bark, and roote 216
Shal been his sauce ymaked by delit,
To make hym yet a newer appetit.
But, certes, he that haunteth swiche delices
Is deed, whil that he lyveth in tho vices. 220
    A lecherous thyng is wyn, and dronkenesse
Is ful of stryvyng and of wrecchednesse.
O dronke man, disfigured is thy face,
Sour is thy breeth, foul artow to embrace,
And thurgh thy dronke nose semeth the soun 225
As though thou seydest ay "Sampsoun, Sampsoun!"
And yet, God woot, Sampsoun drank nevere no wyn.
Thou fallest as it were a styked swyn;
Thy tonge is lost, and al thyn honeste cure,
For dronkenesse is verray sepulture 230
Of mannes wit and his discrecioun.
In whom that drynke hath dominacioun
He kan no conseil kepe; it is no drede.
Now kepe yow fro the white and fro the rede,
And namely fro the white wyn of Lepe 235
That is to selle in Fysshstrete or in Chepe.
This wyn of Spaigne crepeth subtilly
In othere wynes, growynge faste by,
Of which ther ryseth swich fumositee
That whan a man hath dronken draughtes thre,
And weneth that he be at hoom in Chepe, 241

He is in Spaigne, right at the toune of Lepe —
Nat at the Rochele, ne at Burdeux toun —
And thanne wol he seye "Sampsoun, Sampsoun!"
    But herkneth, lordynges, o word, I yow preye,
That alle the sovereyn actes, dar I seye, 246
Of victories in the Olde Testament,
Thurgh verray God, that is omnipotent,
Were doon in abstinence and in preyere.
Looketh the Bible, and ther ye may it leere. 250
    Looke, Attilla, the grete conquerour,
Deyde in his sleep, with shame and dishonour,
Bledynge ay at his nose in dronkenesse.
A capitayn sholde lyve in sobrenesse.
And over al this, avyseth yow right wel 255
What was comaunded unto Lamuel —
Nat Samuel, but Lamuel, seye I;
Redeth the Bible, and fynde it expresly
Of wyn-yevyng to hem that han justise.
Namoore of this, for it may wel suffise. 260
    And now that I have spoken of glotonye,
Now wol I yow deffenden hasardrye.
Hasard is verray mooder of lesynges,
And of deceite, and cursed forswerynges,
Blaspheme of Crist, manslaughtre, and wast also
Of catel and of tyme; and forthermo, 266
It is repreve and contrarie of honour
For to ben holde a commune hasardour.
And ever the hyer he is of estaat,
The moore is he yholden desolaat. 270
If that a prynce useth hasardrye,
In alle governaunce and policye
He is, as by commune opinioun,
Yholde the lasse in reputacioun.
    Stilboun, that was a wys embassadour, 275
Was sent to Corynthe in ful greet honour
Fro Lacidomye to make hire alliaunce.
And whan he cam, hym happede, par chaunce,
That alle the gretteste that were of that lond,
Pleyynge atte hasard he hem fond. 280
For which, as soone as it myghte be,

202-05: See Philippians 3:18-19. **206. cod:** bag. **209. finde:** provide for. **211:** In philosophy, *substance* is the inner essence, *accident* the outward appearance. **212. talent:** appetite. **214. mary:** marrow. **219-20:** See I Timothy 5:6. **222. stryvyng:** strife, quarrelling. **227:** because he was a Nazarite. **239. fumositee:** rising fumes, vapours. **243:** i.e., French wines from La Rochelle and Bordeaux have been adulterated. **256. Lamuel:** Lemuel (see Proverbs 31:4-7). **263. lesynges:** lies. **267. repreve:** reproach, shame. **275. Stilboun:** changed from *Chilon* in Chaucer's source; possibly he was thinking of Stilpon, a minor Greek philosopher of the 4th century B.C. **277. Lacidomye:** Lacedaemon (Sparta).

He stal hym hoom agayn to his contree,
And seyde, "Ther wol I nat lese my name,
Ne I wol nat take on me so greet defame,
Yow for to allie unto none hasardours.   285
Sendeth othere wise embassadours;
For, by my trouthe, me were levere dye
Than I yow sholde to hasardours allye.
For ye, that been so glorious in honours,
Shul nat allyen yow with hasardours   290
As by my wyl, ne as by my tretee."
This wise philosophre, thus seyde hee.
      Looke eek that to the kyng Demetrius
The kyng of Parthes, as the book seith us,
Sente him a paire of dees of gold in scorn,   295
For he hadde used hasard ther-biforn;
For which he heeld his glorie or his renoun
At no value or reputacioun.
Lordes may fynden oother maner pley
Honest ynough to dryve the day awey.   300
      Now wol I speke of othes false and grete
A word or two, as olde bookes trete.
Gret sweryng is a thyng abhominable,
And fals sweryng is yet moore reprevable.
The heighe God forbad sweryng at al,   305
Witnesse on Mathew; but in special
Of sweryng seith the hooly Jeremye,
"Thou shalt swere sooth thyne othes, and nat lye,
And swere in doom and eek in rightwisnesse";
But ydel sweryng is a cursednesse.   310
Bihoold and se that in the firste table
Of heighe Goddes heestes honurable,
Hou that the seconde heeste of hym is this:
"Take nat my name in ydel or amys."
Lo, rather he forbedeth swich sweryng   315
Than homycide or many a cursed thyng;
I seye that, as by ordre, thus it stondeth;
This knoweth, that his heestes understondeth,
How that the seconde heeste of God is that.
And forther over, I wol thee telle al plat   320
That vengeance shal nat parten from his hous
That of his othes is to outrageous.

"By Goddes precious herte," and "By his nayles,"
And "By the blood of Crist that is in Hayles,
Sevene is my chaunce, and thyn is cynk and treye!"
"By Goddes armes, if thou falsly pleye,   326
This daggere shal thurghout thyn herte go!" —
This fruyt cometh of the bicched bones two,
Forsweryng, ire, falsnesse, homycide.
Now, for the love of Crist, that for us dyde,   330
Lete youre othes, bothe grete and smale.
But, sires, now wol I telle forth my tale.
      Thise riotoures thre of whiche I telle,
Longe erst er prime rong of any belle,
Were set hem in a taverne to drynke,   335
And as they sat, they herde a belle clynke
Biforn a cors, was caried to his grave.
That oon of hem gan callen to his knave:
"Go bet," quod he, "and axe redily
What cors is this that passeth heer forby;   340
And looke that thou reporte his name weel."
      "Sire," quod this boy, "it nedeth never-a-deel;
It was me toold er ye cam heer two houres.
He was, pardee, an old felawe of youres,
And sodeynly he was yslayn to-nyght,   345
Fordronke, as he sat on his bench upright.
Ther cam a privee theef men clepeth Deeth,
That in this contree al the peple sleeth,
And with his spere he smoot his herte atwo,
And wente his wey withouten wordes mo.   350
He hath a thousand slayn this pestilence.
And, maister, er ye come in his presence,
Me thynketh that it were necessarie
For to be war of swich an adversarie.
Beth redy for to meete hym everemoore;   355
Thus taughte me my dame; I sey namoore."
"By Seinte Marie!" seyde this taverner,
"The child seith sooth, for he hath slayn this yeer,
Henne over a mile, withinne a greet village,
Bothe man and womman, child, and hyne, and page;
I trowe his habitacioun be there.   361
To been avysed greet wysdom it were,
Er that he dide a man a dishonour."

---

294. Parthes: Parthia, or the Parthians. **305-06:** See Matthew 5:34-36. **307-09:** See Jeremiah 4:2. **311. firste table** (tablet): first section of the Ten Commandments. **313. second:** for Protestants, the third. **314:** See Exodus 20:7. **315. rather:** earlier. **320. al plat:** flatly. **321-22:** See Ecclesiasticus 23:11. **324. Hayles:** abbey supposed to possess a vial of Christ's blood. **325. cynk:** five. **339. bet:** better, faster — i.e., hurry. **359. Henne:** hence.

"Ye, Goddes armes!" quod this riotour,
"Is it swich peril with hym for to meete?   *365*
I shal hym seke by wey and eek by strete,
I make avow to Goddes digne bones!
Herkneth, felawes, we thre been al ones;
Lat ech of us holde up his hand til oother,
And ech of us bicomen otheres brother,   *370*
And we wol sleen this false traytour Deeth.
He shal be slayn, he that so manye sleeth,
By Goddes dignitee, er it be nyght!"
    Togidres han thise thre hir trouthes plight
To lyve and dyen ech of hem for oother,   *375*
As though he were his owene ybore brother.
And up they stirte, al dronken in this rage,
And forth they goon towardes that village
Of which the taverner hadde spoke biforn.
And many a grisly ooth thanne han they sworn, *380*
And Cristes blessed body they torente —
Deeth shal be deed, if that they may hym hente!
    Whan they han goon nat fully half a mile,
Right as they wolde han troden over a stile,
An oold man and a povre with hem mette.   *385*
This olde man ful mekely hem grette,
And seyde thus, "Now, lordes, God yow see!"
    The proudeste of thise riotoures three
Answerde agayn, "What, carl, with sory grace!
Why artow al forwrapped save thy face?   *390*
Why lyvestow so longe in so greet age?"
    This olde man gan looke in his visage,
And seyde thus: "For I ne kan nat fynde
A man, though that I walked into Inde,
Neither in citee ne in no village,   *395*
That wolde chaunge his youthe for myn age;
And therfore moot I han myn age stille,
As longe tyme as it is Goddes wille.
Ne Deeth, allas, ne wol nat han my lyf.
Thus walke I, lyk a restelees caityf,   *400*
And on the ground, which is my moodres gate,
I knokke with my staf, bothe erly and late,
And seye 'Leve mooder, leet me in!
Lo how I vanysshe, flessh, and blood, and skyn!
Allas, whan shul my bones been at reste?   *405*

Mooder, with yow wolde I chaunge my cheste
That in my chambre longe tyme hath be,
Ye, for an haire-clout to wrappe me!'
But yet to me she wol nat do that grace,
For which ful pale and welked is my face.   *410*
    "But, sires, to yow it is no curteisye
To speken to an old man vileynye,
But he trespasse in word or elles in dede.
In Hooly Writ ye may yourself wel rede:
'Agayns an oold man, hoor upon his heed,   *415*
Ye sholde arise;' wherfore I yeve yow reed,
Ne dooth unto an oold man noon harm now,
Namoore than that ye wolde men did to yow
In age, if that ye so longe abyde.
And God be with yow, where ye go or ryde!   *420*
I moot go thider as I have to go."
    "Nay, olde cherl, by God, thou shalt nat so,"
Seyde this oother hasardour anon;
"Thou partest nat so lightly, by Seint John!
Thou spak right now of thilke traytour Deeth. *425*
That in this contree alle oure freendes sleeth.
Have heer my trouthe, as thou art his espye,
Telle where he is or thou shalt it abye,
By God and by the hooly sacrement!
For soothly thou art oon of his assent   *430*
To sleen us yonge folk, thou false theef!"
    "Now, sires," quod he, "if that yow be so leef
To fynde Deeth, turne up this croked wey,
For in that grove I lafte hym, by my fey,
Under a tree, and there he wole abyde;   *435*
Noght for youre boost he wole him no thyng hyde.
Se ye that ook? Right there ye shal hym fynde.
God save yow, that boghte agayn mankynde,
And yow amende!" Thus seyde this olde man;
And everich of thise riotoures ran   *440*
Til he cam to that tree, and ther they founde
Of floryns fyne of gold ycoyned rounde
Wel ny an eighte busshels, as hem thoughte.
No lenger thanne after Deeth they soughte,
But ech of hem so glad was of that sighte,   *445*
For that the floryns been so faire and brighte,
That doun they sette hem by this precious hoord.

---

387. see: i.e., look after. **389. with sory grace:** may you have sorry luck. **415-16:** See Leviticus 19:32. **428. abye:** buy, pay for. **432. leef:** lief, ready, desirous.

The worste of hem, he spak the firste word.

   "Bretheren," quod he, "taak kep what that I seye;
My wit is greet, though that I bourde and pleye.
This tresor hath Fortune unto us yiven   *451*
In myrthe and jolitee oure lyf to lyven,
And lightly as it comth, so wol we spende.
Ey, Goddes precious dignitee! Who wende
To-day that we sholde han so fair a grace?   *455*
But myghte this gold be caried fro this place
Hoom to myn hous, or elles unto youres —
For wel ye woot that al this gold is oures —
Thanne were we in heigh felicitee.
But trewely, by daye it may nat bee.   *460*
Men wolde seyn that we were theves stronge,
And for oure owene tresor doon us honge.
This tresor moste ycaried be by nyghte
As wisely and as slyly as it myghte.
Wherfore I rede that cut among us alle   *465*
Be drawe, and lat se wher the cut wol falle;
And he that hath the cut with herte blithe
Shal renne to the town, and that ful swithe,
And brynge us breed and wyn ful prively.
And two of us shul kepen subtilly   *470*
This tresor wel; and if he wol nat tarie,
Whan it is nyght, we wol this tresor carie,
By oon assent, where as us thynketh best."
That oon of hem the cut broghte in his fest,
And bad hem drawe and looke where it wol falle;
And it fil on the yongeste of hem alle,   *476*
And forth toward the toun he wente anon.
And also soone as that he was gon,
That oon of hem spak thus unto that oother:
"Thow knowest wel thou art my sworen brother;
Thy profit wol I telle thee anon.   *481*
Thou woost wel that oure felawe is agon.
And heere is gold, and that ful greet plentee,
That shal departed been among us thre.
But nathelees, if I kan shape it so   *485*
That it departed were among us two,
Hadde I nat doon a freendes torn to thee?"

   That oother answerde, "I noot hou that may be.
He woot that the gold is with us tweye;   *489*
What shal we doon? What shal we to hym seye?"

   "Shal it be conseil?" seyde the firste shrewe,
"And I shal tellen in a wordes fewe
What we shal doon, and brynge it wel aboute."

   "I graunte," quod that oother, "out of doute,
That, by my trouthe, I wol thee nat biwreye."   *495*

   "Now," quod the firste, "thou woost wel we be tweye,
And two of us shul strenger be than oon.
Looke whan that he is set, that right anoon
Arys as though thou woldest with hym pleye,
And I shal ryve hym thurgh the sydes tweye   *500*
Whil that thou strogelest with hym as in game,
And with thy daggere looke thou do the same;
And thanne shal al this gold departed be,
My deere freend, bitwixen me and thee.
Thanne may we bothe oure lustes all fulfille,   *505*
And pleye at dees right at oure owene wille."
And thus acorded been thise shrewes tweye
To sleen the thridde, as ye han herd me seye.

   This yongeste, which that wente to the toun,
Ful ofte in herte he rolleth up and doun   *510*
The beautee of thise floryns newe and brighte.
"O Lord!" quod he, "if so were that I myghte
Have al this tresor to myself allone,
Ther is no man that lyveth under the trone
Of God that sholde lyve so murye as I!"   *515*
And atte laste the feend, oure enemy,
Putte in his thought that he sholde poyson beye,
With which he myghte sleen his felawes tweye;
For-why the feend foond hym in swich lyvynge
That he hadde leve him to sorwe brynge.   *520*
For this was outrely his fulle entente,
To sleen hem bothe and nevere to repente.
And forth he gooth, no lenger wolde he tarie,
Into the toun, unto a pothecarie,
And preyde hym that he hym wolde selle   *525*
Som poyson, that he myghte his rattes quelle;
And eek ther was a polcat in his hawe,
That, as he seyde, his capouns hadde yslawe,
And fayn he wolde wreke hym, if he myghte,
On vermyn that destroyed hym by nyghte.   *530*

   The pothecarie answerde, "And thou shalt have
A thyng that, also God my soule save,

---

450. bourde: jest. **500. ryve:** stab. **526. quelle:** kill. **527. hawe:** hedge, yard. **529. wreke:** revenge.

In al this world ther is no creature
That eten or dronken hath of this confiture
Noght but the montance of a corn of whete,   *535*
That he ne shal his lif anon forlete;
Ye, sterve he shal, and that in lasse while
Than thou wolt goon a paas nat but a mile,
This poysoun is so strong and violent."
  This cursed man hath in his hond yhent   *540*
This poysoun in a box, and sith he ran
Into the nexte strete unto a man,
And borwed of hym large botelles thre,
And in the two his poyson poured he;
The thridde he kepte clene for his drynke.   *545*
For al the nyght he shoop hym for to swynke
In cariynge of the gold out of that place.
And whan this riotour, with sory grace,
Hadde filled with wyn his grete botels thre,
To his felawes agayn repaireth he.   *550*
  What nedeth it to sermone of it moore?
For right as they hadde cast his deeth bifoore,
Right so they han hym slayn, and that anon.
And whan that this was doon, thus spak that oon:
"Now lat us sitte and drynke, and make us merie,
And afterward we wol his body berie."   *556*
And with that word it happed hym, par cas,
To take the botel ther the poyson was,
And drank, and yaf his felawe drynke also,
For which anon they storven bothe two.   *560*
  But certes, I suppose that Avycen
Wroot nevere in no canon, ne in no fen,
Mo wonder signes of empoisonyng
Than hadde thise wrecches two, er hir endyng.
Thus ended been thise homycides two,   *565*
And eek the false empoysonere also.
  O cursed synne of alle cursednesse!
O traytours homycide, O wikkednesse!
O glotonye, luxurie, and hasardrye!
Thou blasphemour of Crist with vileynye   *570*
And othes grete, of usage and of pride!
Allas, mankynde, how may it bitide
That to thy creatour, which that thee wroghte
And with his precious herte-blood thee boghte,

Thou art so fals and so unkynde, allas?   *575*
  Now, goode men, God foryeve yow youre
    trespas,
And ware yow fro the synne of avarice!
Myn hooly pardoun may yow alle warice,
So that ye offre nobles or sterlynges,
Or elles silver broches, spoones, rynges.   *580*
Boweth youre heed under this hooly bulle!
Cometh up, ye wyves, offreth of youre wolle!
Youre names I entre heer in my rolle anon;
Into the blisse of hevene shul ye gon.
I yow assoille, by myn heigh power,   *585*
Yow that wol offre, as clene and eek as cleer
As ye were born. — And lo, sires, thus I preche.
And Jhesu Crist, that is oure soules leeche,
So graunte yow his pardoun to receyve,
For that is best; I wol yow nat deceyve.   *590*
  But, sires, o word forgat I in my tale:
I have relikes and pardoun in my male,
As faire as any man in Engelond,
Whiche were me yeven by the popes hond.
If any of yow wole, of devocion,   *595*
Offren and han myn absolucion,
Com forth anon, and kneleth heere adoun,
And mekely receyveth my pardoun;
Or elles taketh pardoun as ye wende,
Al newe and fressh at every miles ende,   *600*
So that ye offren, alwey newe and newe,
Nobles or pens, whiche that be goode and trewe.
It is an honour to everich that is heer
That ye mowe have a suffisant pardoneer
T'assoille yow in contree as ye ryde,   *605*
For aventures whiche that may bityde.
Paraventure ther may fallen oon or two
Doun of his hors and breke his nekke atwo.
Looke which a seuretee is it to yow alle
That I am in youre felaweshipe yfalle,   *610*
That may assoille yow, bothe moore and lasse,
Whan that the soule shal fro the body passe.
I rede that oure Hoost heere shal bigynne,
For he is moost envoluped in synne.
Com forth, sire Hoost, and offre first anon,   *615*

561-62. Avycen: Avicenna, author of *The Book of the Canon in Medicine,* whose subdivisions were called *fens.* **575. unkynde:** unnatural. **578. warice:** save, cure.

And thou shalt kisse the relikes everychon,
Ye, for a grote! Unbokele anon thy purs."
   "Nay, nay!" quod he, "thanne have I Cristes
      curs!
Lat be," quod he, "it shal nat be, so theech!
Thou woldest make me kisse thyn olde breech,   620
And swere it were a relyk of a seint,
Though it were with thy fundement depeint!
But, by the croys which that Seint Eleyne fond,
I wolde I hadde thy coillons in myn hond
In stide of relikes or of seintuarie.   625
Lat kutte hem of, I wol thee helpe hem carie;
They shul be shryned in an hogges toord!"
   This Pardoner answerde nat a word;
So wrooth he was, no word ne wolde he seye.
   "Now," quod oure Hoost, "I wol no lenger pleye
With thee, ne with noon oother angry man."   631
But right anon the worthy Knyght bigan,
Whan that he saugh that al the peple lough,
"Namoore of this, for it is right ynough!
Sire Pardoner, be glad and myrie of cheere;   635
And ye, sire Hoost, that been to me so deere,
I prey yow that ye kisse the Pardoner.
And Pardoner, I prey thee, drawe thee neer,
And, as we diden, lat us laughe and pleye."
Anon they kiste, and ryden forth hir weye.   640

The Nun's Priest's Tale

A povre wydwe, somdeel stape in age,
Was whilom dwellyng in a narwe cotage,
Biside a grove, stondynge in a dale.
This wydwe, of which I telle yow my tale,
Syn thilke day that she was last a wyf   5
In pacience ladde a ful symple lyf,

For litel was hir catel and hir rente.
By housbondrie of swich as God hire sente
She foond hirself and eek hir doghtren two.
Thre large sowes hadde she, and namo,   10
Three keen, and eek a sheep that highte Malle.
Ful sooty was hir bowr and eek hir halle,
In which she eet ful many a sklendre meel.
Of poynaunt sauce hir neded never a deel.
No deyntee morsel passed thurgh hir throte;   15
Hir diete was accordant to hir cote.
Repleccioun ne made hire nevere sik;
Attempree diete was al hir phisik,
And exercise, and hertes suffisaunce.
The goute lette hire nothyng for to daunce,   20
N'apoplexie shente nat hir heed.
No wyn ne drank she, neither whit ne reed;
Hir bord was served moost with whit and blak —
Milk and broun breed, in which she foond no lak,
Seynd bacoun, and somtyme an ey or tweye,   25
For she was, as it were, a maner deye.
   A yeerd she hadde, enclosed al aboute
With stikkes, and a drye dych withoute,
In which she hadde a cok, hight Chauntecleer.
In al the land, of crowyng nas his peer.   30
His voys was murier than the murie orgon
On messe-dayes that in the chirche gon.
Wel sikerer was his crowyng in his logge
Than is a clokke or an abbey orlogge.
By nature he knew ech ascencioun   35
Of the equynoxial in thilke toun;
For whan degrees fiftene weren ascended,
Thanne crew he that it myghte nat been amended.
His coomb was redder than the fyn coral,
And batailled as it were a castel wal;   40
His bile was blak, and as the jeet it shoon;
Lyk asure were his legges and his toon;

---

619. **so theech:** (*so thee ich*) as I may thrive. **623:** According to tradition, St. Helena, mother of Constantine the Great, found the true cross and the site of the Holy Sepulchre. **624. coillons:** testicles. **625. seintuarie:** box for relics.   **The Nun's Priest's Tale**   The interlude between the Monk's tale and the Nun's Priest's tale begins with the Knight and the Host stopping the Monk's grim and boring parade of tragedies and asking him for something lighter, maybe about hunting. " 'Nay,' quod this Monk, 'I have no lust to pleye. / Now lat another telle, as I have toold.' / Thanne spak oure Hoost with rude speche and boold, / And seyde unto the Nonnes Preest anon, / 'Com neer, thou preest, com hyder, thou sir John! / Telle us swich thyng as may oure hertes glade. / Be blithe, though thou ryde upon a jade. / What thogh thyn hors be bothe foul and lene? / If he wol serve thee, rekke nat a bene. / Looke that thyn herte be murie everemo.' / 'Yis, sir,' quod he, 'yis, Hoost, so moot I go, / But I be myrie, ywis I wol be blamed.' / And right anon his tale he hath attamed [tamed, begun], / And thus he seyde unto us everichon, / This sweete preest, this goodly man sir John." **1. stape:** stepped, advanced. **9. foond:** provided for. **11. keen:** kine. **16. cote:** cottage, small farm. **21. shente:** harmed. **24. lak:** lack, fault. **25. Seynd:** singed, cooked; **ey:** egg. **26. deye:** dairywoman. **33. logge:** lodge, dwelling. **34. orlogge:** horologe, timepiece. **35-37:** He sensed when the celestial equator (a circle thought to rotate every 24 hours) had moved its hourly 15 degrees. **40. batailled:** notched, crenelated (like battlements).

His nayles whitter than the lylye flour,
And lyk the burned gold was his colour.
This gentil cok hadde in his governaunce   *45*
Sevene hennes for to doon al his plesaunce,
Whiche were his sustres and his paramours,
And wonder lyk to hym, as of colours;
Of whiche the faireste hewed on hir throte
Was cleped faire damoysele Pertelote.   *50*
Curteys she was, discreet, and debonaire,
And compaignable, and bar hyrself so faire
Syn thilke day that she was seven nyght oold
That trewely she hath the herte in hoold
Of Chauntecleer, loken in every lith;   *55*
He loved hire so that wel was hym therwith.
But swich a joye was it to here hem synge,
Whan that the brighte sonne gan to sprynge,
In sweete accord, "My lief is faren in londe!"
For thilke tyme, as I have understonde,   *60*
Beestes and briddes koude speke and synge.
   And so bifel that in a dawenynge,
As Chauntecleer among his wyves alle
Sat on his perche, that was in the halle,
And next hym sat this faire Pertelote,   *65*
This Chauntecleer gan gronen in his throte,
As man that in his dreem is drecched soore.
And whan that Pertelote thus herde hym roore,
She was agast and seyde, "Herte deere,
What eyleth yow, to grone in this manere?   *70*
Ye been a verray sleper; fy, for shame!"
   And he answerde, and seyde thus: "Madame,
I pray yow that ye take it nat agrief.
By God, me mette I was in swich meschief
Right now that yet myn herte is soore afright.   *75*
Now God," quod he, "my swevene recche aright,
And kepe my body out of foul prisoun!
Me mette how that I romed up and doun
Withinne our yeerd, wheer as I saugh a beest
Was lyk an hound, and wolde han maad areest   *80*
Upon my body, and wolde han had me deed.
His colour was bitwixe yelow and reed,
And tipped was his tayl and bothe his eeris

With blak, unlyk the remenant of his heeris;
His snowte smal, with glowynge eyen tweye.   *85*
Yet of his look for feere almoost I deye;
This caused me my gronyng, doutelees."
   "Avoy!" quod she, "fy on yow, hertelees!
Allas," quod she, "for, by that God above,
Now han ye lost myn herte and al my love!   *90*
I kan nat love a coward, by my feith!
For certes, what so any womman seith,
We alle desiren, if it myghte bee,
To han housbondes hardy, wise, and free,
And secree — and no nygard, ne no fool,   *95*
Ne hym that is agast of every tool,
Ne noon avauntour, by that God above!
How dorste ye seyn, for shame, unto youre love
That any thyng myghte make yow aferd?
Have ye no mannes herte, and han a berd?   *100*
Allas! And konne ye been agast of swevenys?
Nothyng, God woot, but vanitee in sweven is.
Swevenes engendren of replecciouns,
And ofte of fume and of complecciouns,
Whan humours been to habundant in a wight.   *105*
Certes this dreem, which ye han met to-nyght,
Cometh of the greete superfluytee
Of youre rede colera, pardee,
Which causeth folk to dreden in hir dremes
Of arwes, and of fyr with rede lemes,   *110*
Of rede beestes, that they wol hem byte,
Of contek, and of whelpes, grete and lyte;
Right as the humour of malencolie
Causeth ful many a man in sleep to crie
For feere of blake beres, or boles blake,   *115*
Or elles blake develes wole hem take.
Of othere humours koude I telle also
That werken many a man sleep ful wo;
But I wol passe as lightly as I kan.
Lo Catoun, which that was so wys a man,   *120*
Seyde he nat thus, 'Ne do no fors of dremes'?
Now sire," quod she, "whan we flee fro the bemes,
For Goddes love, as taak som laxatyf.
Up peril of my soule and of my lyf,

---

55. lith: limb. **59:** "My love is travelling in the country" (a popular song). **67. drecched:** troubled. **74. mette:** dreamed. **76. swevene:** dream; **recche:** interpret. **88. Avoy:** fie, shame; **hertelees:** lacking in heart, i.e., courage. **96. tool:** weapon. **104. fume:** vapours rising from stomach (i.e., gas). **104ff.:** See note to line 420 of the "General Prologue" (p. 34). **110. lemes:** flames. **112. contek:** strife, conflict. **120. Catoun:** Marcus Porcius Cato, supposed author of a book of Latin distichs from which this quotation is translated. **122. flee:** fly.

I conseille yow the beste — I wol nat lye —   *125*
That bothe of colere and of malencolye
Ye purge yow; and for ye shal nat tarie,
Though in this toun is noon apothecarie,
I shal myself to herbes techen yow
That shul been for youre hele and for youre prow;
And in oure yeerd tho herbes shal I fynde   *131*
The whiche han of hire propretee by kynde
To purge yow bynethe and eek above.
Foryet nat this, for Goddes owene love!
Ye been ful coleryk of compleccioun;   *135*
Ware the sonne in his ascencioun
Ne fynde yow nat repleet of humours hoote.
And if it do, I dar wel leye a grote,
That ye shul have a fevere terciane,
Or an agu that may be youre bane.   *140*
A day or two ye shul have digestyves
Of wormes, er ye take youre laxatyves
Of lawriol, centaure, and fumetere,
Or elles of ellebor, that groweth there,
Of katapuce, or of gaitrys beryis,   *145*
Of herbe yve, growyng in oure yeerd, ther mery is;
Pekke hem up right as they growe and ete hem yn.
Be myrie, housbonde, for youre fader kyn!
Dredeth no dreem; I kan sey yow namoore."
    "Madame," quod he, "graunt mercy of youre
        loore.   *150*
But nathelees, as touchyng daun Catoun,
That hath of wysdom swich a greet renoun,
Though that he bad no dremes for to drede,
By God, men may in olde bookes rede
Of many a man moore of auctorite   *155*
Than evere Caton was, so moot I thee,
That al the revers seyn of this sentence,
And han wel founden by experience
That dremes been significaciouns
As wel of joye as of tribulaciouns   *160*
That folk enduren in this lif present.
Ther nedeth make of this noon argument;
The verray preeve sheweth it in dede.
    "Oon of the gretteste auctour that men rede

Seith thus: that whilom two felawes wente   *165*
On pilgrimage, in a ful good entente,
And happed so, they coomen in a toun
Wher as ther was swich congregacioun
Of peple, and eek so streit of herbergage,
That they ne founde as muche as o cotage   *170*
In which they bothe myghte ylogged bee.
Wherfore they mosten of necessitee,
As for that nyght, departen compaignye;
And ech of hem gooth to his hostelrye,
And took his loggyng as it wolde falle.   *175*
That oon of hem was logged in a stalle,
Fer in a yeerd, with oxen of the plough;
That oother man was logged wel ynough,
As was his aventure or his fortune,
That us governeth alle as in commune.   *180*
    "And so bifel that, longe er it were day,
This man mette in his bed, ther as he lay,
How that his felawe gan upon hym calle,
And seyde, 'Allas, for in an oxes stalle
This nyght I shal be mordred ther I lye!   *185*
Now help me, deere brother, or I dye.
In alle haste com to me!' he sayde.
This man out of his sleep for feere abrayde;
But whan that he was wakened of his sleep,
He turned hym and took of this no keep.   *190*
Hym thoughte his dreem nas but a vanitee.
Thus twies in his slepyng dremed hee;
And atte thridde tyme yet his felawe
Cam, as hym thoughte, and seide, 'I am now slawe.
Bihoold my bloody woundes depe and wyde!   *195*
Arys up erly in the morwe tyde,
And at the west gate of the toun,' quod he,
'A carte ful of dong ther shaltow se,
In which my body is hid ful prively;
Do thilke carte arresten boldely.   *200*
My gold caused my mordre, sooth to sayn,'
And tolde hym every point how he was slayn,
With a ful pitous face, pale of hewe.
And truste wel, his dreem he foond ful trewe,
For on the morwe, as soone as it was day,   *205*

---

130. hele: health; **prow:** profit. **139. terciane:** tertian. **143:** spurge laurel, centaury, and fumitory. **144. ellebor:** hellebore. **145:** caper-spurge (euphorbia); gaiter-berry (buckthorn). **164:** probably Cicero or Valerius Maximus. **169. streit of herbergage:** short of lodging. **188. abrayde:** awoke, started up.

To his felawes in he took the way;
And whan that he cam to this oxes stalle,
After his felawe he bigan to calle.
  "The hostiler answerede hym anon,
And seyde, 'Sire, your felawe is agon.   *210*
As soone as day he wente out of the toun.'
  "This man gan fallen in suspecioun,
Remembrynge on his dremes that he mette,
And forth he gooth — no lenger wolde he lette —
Unto the west gate of the toun, and fond   *215*
A dong-carte, wente as it were to donge lond,
That was arrayed in that same wise
As ye han herd the dede man devyse.
And with an hardy herte he gan to crye
Vengeance and justice of this felonye: *220*
'My felawe mordred is this same nyght,
And in this carte he lith gapyng upright.
I crye out on the ministres,' quod he,
'That sholden kepe and reulen this citee.
Harrow! Allas! Heere lith my felawe slayn!'   *225*
What sholde I moore unto this tale sayn?
The peple out sterte and caste the cart to grounde,
And in the myddel of the dong they founde
The dede man, that mordred was al newe.
  "O blisful God, that art so just and trewe,   *230*
Lo, how that thou biwreyest mordre alway!
Mordre wol out; that se we day by day.
Mordre is so wlatsom and abhomynable
To God, that is so just and resonable,
That he ne wol nat suffre it heled be,   *235*
Though it abyde a yeer, or two, or thre.
Mordre wol out, this my conclusioun.
And right anon, ministres of that toun
Han hent the carter and so soore hym pyned,
And eek the hostiler so soore engyned,   *240*
That they biknewe hire wikkednesse anon,
And were anhanged by the nekke-bon.
  "Heere may men seen that dremes been to drede.
And certes in the same book I rede,
Right in the nexte chapitre after this —   *245*
I gabbe nat, so have I joye or blis —

Two men that wolde han passed over see,
For certeyn cause, into a fer contree,
If that the wynd ne hadde been contrarie,
That made hem in a citee for to tarie   *250*
That stood ful myrie upon an haven-syde;
But on a day, agayn the even-tyde,
The wynd gan chaunge, and blew right as hem leste.
Jolif and glad they wente unto hir reste,
And casten hem ful erly for to saille.   *255*
But herkneth! To that o man fil a greet mervaille:
That oon of hem, in slepyng as he lay,
Hym mette a wonder dreem agayn the day.
Hym thoughte a man stood by his beddes syde,
And hym comanded that he sholde abyde,   *260*
And seyde hym thus: 'If thou tomorwe wende,
Thow shalt be dreynt; my tale is at an ende.'
He wook, and tolde his felawe what he mette,
And preyde hym his viage for to lette;
As for that day, he preyde hym to byde.   *265*
His felawe, that lay by his beddes syde,
Gan for to laughe, and scorned him ful faste.
'No dreem,' quod he, 'may so myn herte agaste
That I wol lette for to do my thynges.
I sette nat a straw by thy dremynges,   *270*
For swevenes been but vanytees and japes.
Men dreme alday of owles and of apes,
And of many a maze therwithal;
Men dreme of thyng that nevere was ne shal.
But sith I see that thou wolt heere abyde,   *275*
And thus forslewthen wilfully thy tyde,
God woot, it reweth me; and have good day!'
And thus he took his leve, and wente his way.
But er that he hadde half his cours ysailed,
Noot I nat why, ne what myschaunce it ailed,   *280*
But casuelly the shippes botme rente,
And ship and man under the water wente
In sighte of othere shippes it bisyde,
That with hem sailed at the same tyde.
And therfore, faire Pertelote so deere,   *285*
By swiche ensamples olde maistow leere
That no man sholde been to recchelees

---

216. donge: spread dung, fertilize. **233. wlatsom:** disgusting, loathsome. **239. pyned:** pained, tortured. **240. engyned:** tortured (e.g. on the rack). **241. biknewe:** acknowledged. **246. gabbe:** speak loosely, lie. **264. lette:** postpone, cease. **276. forslewthen:** waste slothfully; **tyde:** time. **281. casuelly:** accidentally.

Of dremes; for I seye thee, doutelees,
That many a dreem ful soore is for to drede.
  "Lo, in the lyf of Seint Kenelm I rede,   290
That was Kenulphus sone, the noble kyng
Of Mercenrike, how Kenelm mette a thyng.
A lite er he was mordred, on a day,
His mordre in his avisioun he say.
His norice hym expowned every deel   295
His sweven, and bad hym for to kepe hym weel
For traisoun; but he nas but seven yeer oold,
And therfore litel tale hath he toold
Of any dreem, so hooly was his herte.
By God! I hadde levere than my sherte   300
That ye hadde rad his legende, as have I.
  "Dame Pertelote, I sey yow trewely,
Macrobeus, that writ the avisioun
In Affrike of the worthy Cipioun,
Affermeth dremes, and seith that they been   305
Warnynge of thynges that men after seen.
And forthermoore, I pray yow, looketh wel
In the olde testament, of Daniel,
If he heeld dremes any vanitee.
Reed eek of Joseph, and ther shul ye see   310
Wher dremes be somtyme — I sey nat alle —
Warnynge of thynges that shul after falle.
Looke of Egipte the kyng, daun Pharao,
His bakere and his butiller also,
Wher they ne felte noon effect in dremes.   315
Whoso wol seken actes of sondry remes
May rede of dremes many a wonder thyng.
Lo Cresus, which that was of Lyde kyng,
Mette he nat that he sat upon a tree,
Which signified he sholde anhanged bee?   320
Lo heere Andromacha, Ectores wyf,
That day that Ector sholde lese his lyf,
She dremed on the same nyght biforn
How that the lyf of Ector sholde be lorn,
If thilke day he wente into bataille.   325
She warned hym, but it myghte nat availle;
He wente for to fighte natheles,
But he was slayn anon of Achilles.

But thilke tale is al to longe to telle,
And eek it is ny day; I may nat dwelle.   330
Shortly I seye, as for conclusioun,
That I shal han of this avisioun
Adversitee; and I seye forthermoor
That I ne telle of laxatyves no stoor,
For they been venymes, I woot it weel;   335
I hem diffye, I love hem never a deel!
  "Now let us speke of myrthe, and stynte al this.
Madame Pertelote, so have I blis,
Of o thyng God hath sent me large grace;
For whan I se the beautee of youre face,   340
Ye been so scarlet reed aboute youre yen,
It maketh al my drede for to dyen;
For al so siker as *In principio,*
Mulier est hominis confusio —
Madame, the sentence of this Latyn is,   345
'Womman is mannes joye and al his blis.'
For whan I feele a-nyght your softe syde —
Al be it that I may nat on yow ryde,
For that oure perche is maad so narwe, allas —
I am so ful of joye and of solas,   350
That I diffye bothe sweven and dreem."
  And with that word he fley doun fro the beem,
For it was day, and eke his hennes alle,
And with a chuk he gan hem for to calle,
For he hadde founde a corn, lay in the yerd.   355
Real he was, he was namoore aferd.
He fethered Pertelote twenty tyme,
And trad hire eke as ofte, er it was pryme.
He looketh as it were a grym leoun,
And on his toos he rometh up and doun;   360
Hym deigned nat to sette his foot to grounde.
He chukketh whan he hath a corn yfounde,
And to hym rennen thanne his wyves alle.
Thus roial, as a prince is in his halle,
Leve I this Chauntecleer in his pasture,   365
And after wol I telle his aventure.
  Whan that the month in which the world bigan,
That highte March, whan God first maked man,
Was compleet, and passed were also,

---

292. Mercenrike: Mercia. **294. avisioun:** prophetic dream, vision. **298-99. little . . . of:** he cared little about. **300. levere:** rather. **303-04:** Macrobius, author of a commentary on Cicero's account of the dream of Scipio Africanus. **308:** See Daniel 7-12. **310-15:** See Genesis 37, 40-42. **316. remes:** realms. **318:** Croesus, king of Lydia. **321:** Andromache, Hector's wife. **343:** See "General Prologue," 254. **344:** (Latin) "Woman is man's ruin." **356. Real:** regal, royal. **357. feathered:** i.e., embraced with his wings. **358. trad:** trod. **362. chukketh:** clucks.

Syn March bigan, thritty dayes and two,   370
Bifel that Chauntecleer in al his pryde,
His sevene wyves walkynge by his syde,
Caste up his eyen to the brighte sonne,
That in the signe of Taurus hadde yronne   374
Twenty degrees and oon, and somwhat moore,
And knew by kynde, and by noon oother loore,
That it was pryme, and crew with blisful stevene.
"The sonne," he seyde, "is clomben up on hevene
Fourty degrees and oon, and moore ywis.
Madame Pertelote, my worldes blis,   380
Herkneth thise blisful briddes how they synge,
And se the fresshe floures how they sprynge;
Ful is myn herte of revel and solas!"
But sodeynly hym fil a sorweful cas,
For evere the latter ende of joye is wo.   385
God woot that worldly joye is soone ago;
And if a rethor koude faire endite,
He in a cronycle saufly myghte it write
As for a sovereyn notabilitee.
Now every wys man, lat him herkne me;   390
This storie is also trewe, I undertake,
As is the book of Launcelot de Lake,
That wommen holde in ful greet reverence.
Now wol I torne agayn to my sentence.
    A col-fox, ful of sly iniquitee,   395
That in the grove hadde woned yeres three,
By heigh ymaginacioun forncast,
The same nyght thurghout the hegges brast
Into the yerd ther Chauntecleer the faire
Was wont, and eek his wyves, to repaire;   400
And in a bed of wortes stille he lay
Til it was passed undren of the day,
Waitynge his tyme on Chauntecleer to falle,
As gladly doon thise homycides alle
That in await liggen to mordre men.   405
O false mordrour, lurkynge in thy den!
O newe Scariot, newe Genylon,

False dissymulour, o Greek Synon,
That broghtest Troye al outrely to sorwe!
O Chauntecleer, acursed be that morwe   410
That thou into that yerd flaugh fro the bemes!
Thou were ful wel ywarned by thy dremes
That thilke day was perilous to thee;
But what that God forwoot moot nedes bee,
After the opinioun of certein clerkis.   415
Witnesse on hym that any parfit clerk is,
That in scole is greet altercacioun
In this mateere, and greet disputisoun,
And hath been of an hundred thousand men.
But I ne kan nat bulte it to the bren   420
As kan the hooly doctour Augustyn,
Or Boece, or the Bisshop Bradwardyn,
Wheither that Goddes worthy forwityng
Streyneth me nedely for to doon a thyng —
"Nedely" clepe I symple necessitee —   425
Or elles, if free choys be graunted me
To do that same thyng, or do it noght,
Though God forwoot it er that I was wroght;
Or if his wityng streyneth never a deel
But by necessitee condicioneel.   430
I wol nat han to do of swich mateere;
My tale is of a cok, as ye may heere,
That tok his conseil of his wyf, with sorwe,
To walken in the yerd upon that morwe
That he hadde met that dreem that I yow tolde.
Wommennes conseils been ful ofte colde;   436
Wommannes conseil broghte us first to wo
And made Adam fro Paradys to go,
Ther as he was ful myrie and wel at ese.
But for I noot to whom it myght displese,   440
If I conseil of wommen wolde blame,
Passe over, for I seyde it in my game.
Rede auctours, where they trete of swich mateere,
And what they seyn of wommen ye may heere.
Thise been the cokkes wordes, and nat myne; 445

---

376. kynde: nature. **377. stevene:** voice. **384. cas:** case, accident, mischance. **387. rethor:** rhetorician. **395. col-fox:** coal-fox, i.e., one with black markings like those of the beast in Chauntecleer's dream. **396. woned:** dwelt. **402. undren:** the third hour (i.e., 9 a.m.). **404. gladly:** i.e., willingly, customarily. **407. Scariot:** Judas Iscariot (see e.g. Matthew 26-27); **Genylon:** Ganelon, betrayer of part of Charlemagne's army, under Roland (see note to "General Prologue," line 670, p. 38). **408. Synon:** Sinon, who deceived the Trojans into taking in the wooden horse (see e.g. Virgil's *Aeneid*, II). **420. bulte it to the bren:** bolt it to the bran — i.e., sift out the truth. **421-22:** Augustine, Boethius, and Thomas Bradwardyne, archbishop of Canterbury (d. 1349), all took part in the discussion of the problem of foreknowledge and free will; see also Milton's *Paradise Lost*, II, 557-61 (p. 343), III, 96-128 (p. 350). **424. streyneth:** constrains. **433. conseil:** counsel, advice. **436. colde:** baneful, fatal.

I kan noon harm of no womman divyne.
   Faire in the sond, to bathe hire myrily,
Lith Pertelote, and alle hire sustres by,
Agayn the sonne, and Chauntecleer so free
Soong murier than the mermayde in the see   *450*
(For Phisiologus seith sikerly
How that they syngen wel and myrily).
And so bifel that, as he caste his ye
Among the wortes on a boterflye,
He was war of this fox, that lay ful lowe.   *455*
Nothyng ne liste hym thanne for to crowe,
But cride anon, "Cok! cok!" and up he sterte
As man that was affrayed in his herte.
For natureelly a beest desireth flee
Fro his contrarie, if he may it see,   *460*
Though he never erst hadde seyn it with his ye.
   This Chauntecleer, whan he gan hym espye,
He wolde han fled, but that the fox anon
Seyde, "Gentil sire, allas, wher wol ye gon?
Be ye affrayed of me that am youre freend?   *465*
Now, certes, I were worse than a feend,
If I to yow wolde harm or vileynye!
I am nat come youre conseil for t'espye,
But trewely, the cause of my comynge
Was oonly for to herkne how that ye synge.   *470*
For trewely, ye have as myrie a stevene
As any aungel hath that is in hevene.
Therwith ye han in musyk moore feelynge
Than hadde Boece, or any that kan synge.
My lord youre fader — God his soule blesse! —
And eek youre mooder, of hire gentillesse,   *476*
Han in myn hous ybeen to my greet ese;
And certes, sire, ful fayn wolde I yow plese.
But, for men speke of syngyng, I wol seye —
So moote I brouke wel myne eyen tweye —   *480*
Save yow, I herde nevere man so synge
As dide youre fader in the morwenynge.
Certes, it was of herte, al that he song.
And for to make his voys the moore strong,
He wolde so peyne hym that with bothe his yen   *485*

He moste wynke, so loude he wolde cryen,
And stonden on his tiptoon therwithal,
And strecche forth his nekke long and smal.
And eek he was of swich discrecioun
That ther nas no man in no regioun   *490*
That hym in song or wisedom myghte passe.
I have wel rad in 'Daun Burnel the Asse,'
Among his vers, how that ther was a cok,
For that a preestes sone yaf hym a knok
Upon his leg whil he was yong and nyce,   *495*
He made hym for to lese his benefice.
But certeyn, ther nys no comparisoun
Bitwixe the wisedom and discrecioun
Of youre fader and of his subtiltee.
Now syngeth, sire, for seinte charitee;   *500*
Lat se; konne ye youre fader countrefete?"
   This Chauntecleer his wynges gan to bete,
As man that koude his traysoun nat espie,
So was he ravysshed with his flaterie.
   Allas, ye lordes, many a fals flatour   *505*
Is in youre courtes, and many a losengeour,
That plesen yow wel moore, by my feith,
Than he that soothfastnesse unto yow seith.
Redeth Ecclesiaste of flaterye;
Beth war, ye lordes, of hir trecherye.   *510*
   This Chauntecleer stood hye upon his toos,
Strecchynge his nekke, and heeld his eyen cloos,
And gan to crowe loude for the nones.
And daun Russell the fox stirte up atones,
And by the gargat hente Chauntecleer,   *515*
And on his bak toward the wode hym beer,
For yet ne was ther no man that hym sewed.
   O destinee, that mayst nat been eschewed!
Allas, that Chauntecleer fleigh fro the bemes!
Allas, his wyf ne roghte nat of dremes!   *520*
And on a Friday fil al this meschaunce.
   O Venus, that art goddesse of plesaunce,
Syn that thy servant was this Chauntecleer,
And in thy servyce dide al his poweer,
Moore for delit than world to multiplye,   *525*

---

451. Phisiologus: a Latin bestiary. **459-61:** referring to the belief that everything has a contrary, a natural opposite or enemy. **474:** Boethius wrote a book on music. **480. brouke:** make use of. **486. wynke:** i.e., close. **492-96.** In *Burnellus,* a 12th-century satirical poem by Nigel Wireker, the cock omitted to crow early in the morning, causing the young man to oversleep, miss his ordination, and fail to get his benefice. **500. seinte:** holy. **506. losengeour:** flatterer, lying rascal, deceiver. **509:** See Ecclesiasticus 12:10-11, 16, and perhaps also Proverbs 29:5. **515. gargat:** throat. **517. sewed:** pursued. **520. roghte:** recked.

Why woldestow suffre hym on thy day to dye?
  O Gaufred, deere maister soverayn,
That whan thy worthy kyng Richard was slayn
With shot, compleynedest his deeth so soore,
Why ne hadde I now thy sentence and thy loore,
The Friday for to chide, as diden ye?   *531*
For on a Friday, soothly, slayn was he.
Thanne wolde I shewe yow how that I koude
    pleyne
For Chauntecleres drede and for his peyne.
  Certes, swich cry ne lamentacion   *535*
Was nevere of ladyes maad whan Ilion
Was wonne, and Pyrrus with his streite swerd,
Whan he hadde hent kyng Priam by the berd,
And slayn hym, as seith us *Eneydos,*
As maden alle the hennes in the clos,   *540*
Whan they had seyn of Chauntecleer the sighte.
But sovereynly dame Pertelote shrighte
Ful louder than dide Hasdrubales wyf,
Whan that hir housbonde hadde lost his lyf
And that the Romayns hadde brend Cartage.   *545*
She was so ful of torment and of rage
That wilfully into the fyr she sterte
And brende hirselven with a stedefast herte.
  O woful hennes, right so criden ye
As whan that Nero brende the citee   *550*
Of Rome cryden senatoures wyves
For that hir husbondes losten alle hir lyves —
Withouten gilt this Nero hath hem slayn.
Now wole I turne to my tale agayn.
  This sely wydwe and eek hir doghtres two   *555*
Herden thise hennes crie and maken wo,
And out at dores stirten they anon,
And syen the fox toward the grove gon,
And bar upon his bak the cok away,
And cryden, "Out! Harrow and weylaway!   *560*
Ha, ha! The fox!" and after hym they ran,
And eek with staves many another man.

Ran Colle oure dogge, and Talbot and Gerland,
And Malkyn, with a dystaf in hir hand;
Ran cow and calf, and eek the verray hogges,   *565*
So fered for the berkyng of the dogges
And shoutyng of the men and wommen eeke
They ronne so hem thoughte hir herte breeke.
They yolleden as feendes doon in helle;
The dokes cryden as men wolde hem quelle;   *570*
The gees for feere flowen over the trees;
Out of the hyve cam the swarm of bees.
So hydous was the noyse — a, benedicitee! —
Certes, he Jakke Straw and his meynee
Ne made nevere shoutes half so shrille   *575*
Whan that they wolden any Flemyng kille,
As thilke day was maad upon the fox.
Of bras they broghten bemes, and of box,
Of horn, of boon, in whiche they blewe and
    powped,   *579*
And therwithal they skriked and they howped.
It semed as that hevene sholde falle.
  Now, goode men, I prey yow herkneth alle:
Lo, how Fortune turneth sodeynly
The hope and pryde eek of hir enemy!
This cok, that lay upon the foxes bak,   *585*
In al his drede unto the fox he spak,
And seyde, "Sire, if that I were as ye,
Yet sholde I seyn, as wys God helpe me,
'Turneth agayn, ye proude cherles alle!
A verray pestilence upon yow falle!   *590*
Now I am come unto the wodes syde;
Maugree youre heed, the cok shal heere abyde.
I wol hym ete, in feith, and that anon!'"
  The fox answerde, "In feith, it shal be don."
And as he spak that word, al sodeynly   *595*
This cok brak from his mouth delyverly,
And heighe upon a tree he fleigh anon.
And whan the fox saugh that the cok was gon,
"Allas!" quod he, "O Chauntecleer, allas!

527-32: Geoffrey of Vinsauf's *Poetria Nova* contained a specimen lament on the death of Richard I, including lines chiding Friday. **536-39. Ilion:** Ilium (Troy), whose king, Priam, Pyrrhus killed (see *Aeneid*, II). **543. Hasdrubales wyf:** the wife of Hasdrubal, king of Carthage. **560. Out!:** Alas! **Harrow:** Help! **weylaway:** alas. **561. Ha, ha!:** standard cry to scare away foxes, wolves, and the like. **563. Talbot; Gerland:** other dogs' names. **566. fered:** frightened. **574. Jakke Straw:** Jack Straw, supposedly one of the leaders of the Peasants' Revolt of 1381 (sometimes called "Jack Straw's Rebellion") — possibly a nickname for the principal leader, Wat Tyler; **meynee:** army, crew, company. **576:** The Flemings in England were among the rebels' targets because they were foreign labour during hard post-plague times. **578. bemes:** trumpets; **box:** boxwood. **579. powped:** puffed, blew. **592. Maugree youre heed:** in spite of your head — i.e., in spite of all you can do.

I have to yow," quod he, "ydoon trespas,   *600*
In as muche as I maked yow aferd
Whan I yow hente and broghte out of the yerd.
But, sire, I dide it in no wikke entente.
Com doun, and I shal telle yow what I mente;
I shal seye sooth to yow, God help me so!"   *605*
    "Nay thanne," quod he, "I shrewe us bothe two.
And first I shrewe myself, bothe blood and bones,
If thou bigyle me ofter than ones.
Thou shalt namoore thurgh thy flaterye
Do me to synge and wynke with myn ye;   *610*
For he that wynketh, whan he sholde see,
Al wilfully, God lat him nevere thee!"
    "Nay," quod the fox, "but God yeve hym
        meschaunce,
That is so undiscreet of governaunce
That jangleth whan he sholde holde his pees." *615*
    Lo, swich it is for to be recchelees
And necligent, and truste on flaterye.
    But ye that holden this tale a folye,
As of a fox, or of a cok and hen,
Taketh the moralite, goode men.   *620*
For Seint Paul seith that al that writen is,
To oure doctrine it is ywrite, ywis;
Taketh the fruyt, and lat the chaf be stille.
Now, goode God, if that it be thy wille,
As seith my lord, so make us alle goode men, *625*
And brynge us to his heighe blisse! Amen.

CHAUCERS WORDES UNTO ADAM, HIS OWNE SCRIVEYN

Adam scriveyn, if ever it thee bifalle
Boece or Troylus for to wryten newe,
Under thy long lokkes thou most have the scalle,
But after my makyng thow wryte more trewe;
So ofte adaye I mot thy werk renewe,   *5*
It to correcte and eke to rubbe and scrape,
And al is thorugh thy negligence and rape.

THE FORMER AGE

A blisful lyf, a paisible and a swete,
Ledden the peples in the former age.
They helde hem payed of the fruites that they ete,
Which that the feldes yave hem by usage;
They ne were nat forpampred with outrage;   *5*
Unknowen was the quern and ek the melle;
They eten mast, hawes, and swich pounage,
And dronken water of the colde welle.

Yit nas the ground nat wounded with the plough,
But corn up-sprong, unsowe of mannes hond,   *10*
The which they gnodded and eete nat half ynough.
No man yit knew the forwes of his lond,
No man the fyr out of the flint yit fond,
Unkorven and ungrobbed lay the vyne;
No man yit in the morter spyces grond   *15*
To clarre ne to sause of galantyne.

No mader, welde, or wood no litestere
Ne knew; the flees was of his former hewe;
No flesh ne wiste offence of egge or spere.
No coyn ne knew man which was fals or trewe,
No ship yit karf the wawes grene and blewe,   *21*
No marchaunt yit ne fette outlandish ware.
No trompes for the werres folk ne knewe,
Ne toures heye and walles rounde or square.

What sholde it han avayled to werreye?   *25*
Ther lay no profit, ther was no richesse;
But cursed was the tyme, I dare wel seye,
That men first dide hir swety bysinesse
To grobbe up metal, lurkinge in derknesse,
And in the riveres first gemmes soghte.   *30*
Allas, than sprong up al the cursednesse
Of coveytyse, that first our sorwe broghte.

Thise tyraunts putte hem gladly nat in pres
No wildnesse ne no busshes for to winne;
Ther poverte is, as seith Diogenes,   *35*
Ther as vitaile is ek so skars and thinne

621-22: See Romans 15:4. **CHAUCER'S WORDS UNTO ADAM, HIS OWN SCRIVEYN** **1. scriveyn:** scribe. **2. Boece:** Chaucer's translation of Boethius's *De Consolatione Philosophiae* (*The Consolation of Philosophy*); **Troylus:** Chaucer's long narrative poem *Troilus and Criseyde*. **4. But:** unless. **7. rape:** haste.   **THE FORMER AGE** One of Chaucer's sources for this poem was Ovid's *Metamorphoses*: see lines 91-167 in the opening section, as translated by George Sandys (pp. 268-69). **5. outrage:** excess. **6. melle:** mill. **7. pounage:** food for pigs. **11. gnodded:** rubbed, husked. **12. forwes:** furrows. **14. unkorven:** uncut, unpruned; **ungrobbed:** not dug about, uncultivated. **16. clarre:** spiced wine with honey; **galantyne:** sauce for fish and poultry. **17. wood:** woad — like madder and weld, a plant used for making dyes; **litestere:** dyer. **19. egge:** edge, sword. **22. outlandish:** foreign. **25. werreye:** make war. **33. putte hem . . . nat in pres:** didn't press or exert themselves.

That noght but mast or apples is therinne;
But, ther as bagges ben and fat vitaile,
Ther wol they gon, and spare for no sinne
With al hir ost the cite for to asayle. *40*

Yit was no paleis-chaumbres ne non halles;
In caves and wodes softe and swete
Slepten this blissed folk withoute walles
On gras or leves in parfit quiete.
Ne doun of fetheres ne no bleched shete *45*
Was kid to hem, but in seurtee they slepte.
Hir hertes were al oon withoute galles;
Everich of hem his feith to other kepte.

Unforged was the hauberk and the plate;
The lambish peple, voyd of alle vyce, *50*
Hadden no fantasye to debate,
But ech of hem wolde other wel cheryce.
No pryde, non envye, non avaryce,
No lord, no taylage by no tyrannye;
Humblesse and pees, good feith the emperice. *55*

Yit was not Jupiter the likerous,
That first was fader of delicacye,
Come in this world; ne Nembrot, desirous
To regne, had nat maad his toures hye.
Allas, allas, now may men wepe and crye! *60*
For in oure dayes nis but covetyse,
Doublenesse, and tresoun, and envye,
Poyson, manslawhtre, and mordre in sondry wyse.

TRUTH
Balade de Bon Conseyl

Flee fro the prees and dwelle with sothfastnesse;
Suffyce unto thy thing, though it be smal,
For hord hath hate, and climbing tikelnesse,
Prees hath envye, and wele blent overal.
Savour no more than thee bihove shal, *5*
Reule wel thyself that other folk canst rede,
And trouthe thee shal delivere, it is no drede.

Tempest thee noght al croked to redresse
In trust of hir that turneth as a bal;
Gret reste stant in litel besinesse. *10*
Be war therfore to sporne ayeyns an al,
Stryve not, as doth the crokke with the wal.
Daunte thyself, that dauntest otheres dede,
And trouthe thee shal delivere, it is no drede.

That thee is sent, receyve in buxumnesse; *15*
The wrastling for this world axeth a fal.
Her is non hoom, her nis but wildernesse:
Forth, pilgrim, forth! Forth, beste, out of thy stal!
Know thy contree, look up, thank God of al;
Hold the heye wey and lat thy gost thee lede, *20*
And trouthe thee shal delivere, it is no drede.

Envoy

Therfore, thou Vache, leve thyn old wrecchednesse;
Unto the world leve now to be thral.
Crye him mercy, that of his hy goodnesse
Made thee of noght, and in especial *25*
Draw unto him, and pray in general
For thee, and eek for other, hevenlich mede;
And trouthe thee shal delivere, it is no drede.

LAK OF STEDFASTNESSE

Somtyme the world was so stedfast and stable
That mannes word was obligacioun,
And now it is so fals and deceivable
That word and deed, as in conclusioun,
Ben nothing lyk, for turned up-so-doun *5*
Is al this world for mede and wilfulnesse,
That al is lost for lak of stedfastnesse.

What maketh this world to be so variable
But lust that folk have in dissensioun?
For among us now a man is holde unable, *10*
But if he can by som collusioun
Don his neighbour wrong or oppressioun.

---

40. ost: host, army. **46. kid:** known. **54. taylage:** tax. **55:** To supply the missing line after line 55, language historian Walter W. Skeat suggested "Fulfilled erthe of olde curtesye." **57. delicacye:** voluptuousness. **58-59:** Nimrod, among others, was traditionally thought to have built the Tower of Babel. **TRUTH 1. prees:** crowd. **3. tikelnesse:** instability. **4. wele blent:** wealth blinds. **7:** See John 8:32. **9:** i.e., Fortune with her wheel. **11. sporne:** kick; **al:** awl (cf. Acts 9:5). **13. Daunte:** rule, tame, overcome. **15. in buxumnesse:** bending, i.e., with bowed head or on bended knee — i.e., humbly, obediently, submissively. **22. Vache:** French for cow (see line 18), but probably the poem is addressed to Sir Philip de la Vache, Chaucer's contemporary and acquaintance, at a time when he was out of favour at court. **27. mede:** meed, reward. **LAK OF STEDFASTNESSE 6. mede:** meed, bribery, payoff.

What causeth this but wilful wrecchednesse,
That al is lost for lak of stedfastnesse?

Trouthe is put doun, resoun is holden fable,   *15*
Vertu hath now no dominacioun;
Pitee exyled, no man is merciable.
Through covetyse is blent discrecioun.
The world hath mad a permutacioun
Fro right to wrong, fro trouthe to fikelnesse,   *20*
That al is lost for lak of stedfastnesse.

Lenvoy to King Richard

O prince, desyre to be honourable,
Cherish thy folk and hate extorcioun.
Suffre nothing that may be reprevable
To thyn estat don in thy regioun.   *25*
Shew forth thy swerd of castigacioun,
Dred God, do law, love trouthe and worthinesse,
And wed thy folk agein to stedfastnesse.

THE COMPLAINT OF CHAUCER TO HIS PURSE

To yow, my purse, and to noon other wight
Complayne I, for ye be my lady dere.
I am so sory, now that ye been lyght;

For certes but yf ye make me hevy chere,
Me were as leef be layd upon my bere;   *5*
For which unto your mercy thus I crye,
Beth hevy ageyn, or elles mot I dye.

Now voucheth sauf this day or hyt be nyght
That I of yow the blisful soun may here
Or see your colour lyk the sonne bryght   *10*
That of yelownesse hadde never pere.
Ye be my lyf, ye be myn hertes stere.
Quene of comfort and of good companye,
Beth hevy ageyn, or elles moot I dye.

Now purse that ben to me my lyves lyght   *15*
And saveour as doun in this world here,
Out of this toune helpe me thurgh your myght,
Syn that ye wole nat ben my tresorere;
For I am shave as nye as any frere.
But yet I pray unto your curtesye,   *20*
Beth hevy agen, or elles moot I dye.

Lenvoy de Chaucer

O conquerour of Brutes Albyon,
Which that by lyne and free eleccion
Been verray kyng, this song to yow I sende,
And ye, that mowen alle oure harmes amende,   *25*
Have mynde upon my supplicacion.

DAME JULIAN OF NORWICH
England, c.1342–after 1413

from *REVELATIONS OF DIVINE LOVE*

The Thirty-Second Chapter

One time our good Lord said: "All thing shall be well"; and another time he said: "Thou shalt see thyself that all manner of thing shall be well." And in these two the soul took sundry manner of understanding. One was that he willeth we wit that not only he taketh

---

THE COMPLAINT OF CHAUCER TO HIS PURSE   **8. or hyt:** before it. **22. conqueror:** Henry IV; **Brutes Albyon:** Brutus's Albion (Brutus, descendant of Aeneas, was according to legend the founder of Britain; see the opening stanza of *Sir Gawain and the Green Knight,* p. 26). REVELATIONS OF DIVINE LOVE   **3. wit:** know.

heed to noble things and to great, but also to little and to small, to low and to simple, and to one and to other. And so meaneth he in that he saith: "All manner thing shall be well." For he willeth that we wit that the least thing shall not be forgotten. Another understanding is this: that there be many deeds evil done in our sight and so great harms taken that it seemeth to us that it were unpossible that ever it should come to a good end. And upon this we look, sorrowing and mourning therefor, so that we cannot rest us in the blissful beholding of God as we should do. And the cause is this: that the use of our reason is now so blind, so low, and so simple that we cannot know the high marvellous wisdom, the might and the goodness of the blissful Trinity. And thus meaneth he when he saith: "Thou shalt see thyself that all manner thing shall be well," as if he said, "Take now faithfully and trustfully, and at the last end thou shalt see verily in fullness of joy."

And thus in the same words before said: "I may make all thing well," I understand a mighty comfort of all works of our Lord God that are yet to come. There is a deed the which the blessed Trinity shall do in the last day, as to my sight, and what the deed shall be, and how it shall be done, it is unknown of all creatures which are beneath Christ, and shall be till when it shall be done. The goodness and the love of our Lord God will that we wit that it shall be, and the might and the wisdom of him by the same love will hill it and hide it from us what it shall be and how it shall be done. And the cause why he willeth we wit it thus is for he willeth we be the more eased in our souls and peaceable in love, leaving the beholding of all tempests that might let us from true enjoying in him.

This is the great deed ordained of our Lord God from without beginning, treasured and hid in his blessed breast, only known to himself, by which deed he shall make all things well. For right as the blessed Trinity made all things of nought, right so the same blessed Trinity shall make well all that is not well. And in this sight I marvelled greatly and beheld our faith, meaning thus: Our faith is grounded in God's word, and it belongeth to our faith that we believe that God's word shall be saved in all things. And one point of our faith is that many creatures shall be damned, as the angels that fell out of heaven for pride, which be now fiends, and many on earth that dieth out of the faith of Holy Church — that is to say, those that be heathen, and also many that hath received christendom and liveth unchristian life and so dieth out of charity. All these shall be damned to hell without end, as Holy Church teacheth me to believe.

And standing all this, methought it was unpossible that all manner of things should be well, as our Lord showed in this time. And as to this I had no other answer in showing of our Lord God but this: "That that is unpossible to thee is not unpossible to me. I shall save my word in all things and I shall make all things well." Thus I was taught, by the grace of God, that I should steadfastly hold me in the faith as I had before understood, and therewith that I should stand and sadly believe that all manner thing shall be well, as our Lord showed in that same time. For this is the great deed that our Lord God shall do, in which deed he shall save his word in all things and he shall make well all that is not well. What the deed shall be and how it shall be done there is no creature beneath Christ that wot it, nor shall wit it till it is done, as to the understanding that I took of our Lord's meaning in this time.

(c. 1373)

---

17. as to my sight: as I see it. **20. hill:** cover, conceal. **23. let:** hinder, prevent. **30. as:** such as. **35. standing all this:** all this being so. **37. showing:** revelation. **37-38:** See Luke 18:27. **40. sadly:** solemnly. For a 20th-century allusion to this chapter, see T. S. Eliot's "Little Gidding (p. 1315).

THOMAS HOCCLEVE
England, c.1369–c.1430

THOMAS HOCCLEVE'S COMPLAINT (abridged)

After that hervest inned had his sheves,
And that the broun season of mihelmesse
Was come and gan the trees robbe of ther leves
That grene had ben and in lusty fresshnesse,
And them into colour of yelownesse   5
Had dyed and doun throwen undir foote,
That chaunge sanke into myn herte roote.

For fresshly broughte it to my remembraunce
That stablenes in this worlde is ther none;
Ther is no thing but chaunge and variaunce.   10
How welthy a man be or wel be-goon,
Endure it shall not: he shall it forgoon.
Deeth undir foote shall him thrist adoun;
That is every wightes conclusyon.

Whiche for to weyve is in no mannes myght,   15
How riche he be, stronge, lusty, fressh, and gay.
And in the ende of Novembre, upon a nyght,
Sighynge sore as I in my bed lay,
For this and othir thoughtis whiche many a day
Before I tooke, sleep cam noon in myn eye,   20
So vexid me the thoughtful maladie.

I sy wel, sithin I with sicknes last
Was scourged, cloudy hath bene the favour
That shoon on me ful bright in times past;
The sunne abated and the derke shour   25
Hilded down right on me, and in langour
Made swymme, so that my spirite
To lyve no lust had ne no delite.

The greef aboute myn herte so sore swal,
And bolned ever to and to so sore,   30
That nedis oute I muste ther withal.
I thought I nolde kepe it cloos no more,

Ne let it in me for to eelde and hore.
And for to preve I cam of a woman,
I braste oute on the morwe and thus began.   35

*Here endith my prolog, and folwith
my complaint.*

Almyghty god, as liketh his goodnesse,
Visiteth folke alday, as men may se,
With los of good and bodily sikenesse;
And amonge othir he forgat not me.
Witnesse uppon the wilde infirmitie   40
Whiche that I had, as many a man wel knewe,
And whiche me out of my silfe caste and threwe.

It was so knowen to the peple and kouthe
That counseil was it noon, ne not be might;
How it with me stood was in every mannes mouthe,
And that ful sore my frendis affright.   46
They for myn helthe pilgrimages hight,
And soughte hem, some on hors and some on foote
(God yelde it them!), to gete me my boote.

But although the substaunce of my memory   50
Went to pley as for a certaine space,
Yit the lorde of vertue, the kyng of glory,
Of his highe myght and his benigne grace,
Made it to returne into the place
Whens it cam, whiche at all halwemesse   55
Was five yeere, neither more ne lesse.

And evere sithin (thanked be god oure lord
Of his good reconsiliacioun),
My wit and I have ben of such accord
As we were or the alteracioun   60

THOMAS HOCCLEVE'S COMPLAINT   **2. mihelmesse:** Michaelmas. **3. gan:** did. **11. How:** However; **wel be-goon:** well off. **15. weyve:** waive, avoid. **20. tooke:** took note of. **21. vexid:** worried. **22. sy:** saw; **sithin:** since. **26. Hilded:** Poured. **29. swal:** swelled. **30. bolned:** swelled, bulged. **33. eelde and hore:** grow old and hoary. **36. as liketh:** as it pleases. **37. alday:** always, anytime. **43. kouth:** known. **44. conseil:** secret. **47. hight:** promised. **49. yelde:** pay, requite; **boote:** good, cure. **51. a certain space:** a while. **55. halwemesse:** Hallowmas (All Saints' Day). **58. Of:** For. **60. or:** ere, before.

Of it was; but, by my salvacioun,
Sith that time have I be sore sett on fire,
And lyved in great torment and martire.

For though that my wit were hoom come again,
Men wolde it not so understond or take;   *65*
With me to dele hadden they disdain.
A riotous person I was, and forsake.
Myn olde frendshipe was all overshake;
No wight with me list make daliaunce.
The worlde me made a straunge continance.   *70*

With that myn herte sore gan to torment,
For often whan I in Westmynster Halle
And eke in Londoun amonge the prese went,
I sy the chere abaten and apalle
Of hem that weren wonte me for to calle   *75*
To companye; her heed they caste awry
Whan I hem mette, as they not me sy.

As seide is in the sauter might I say,
They that me sy fledden awey fro me;
Forgeten I was, all oute of mynde away,   *80*
As he that deed was from hertes cherte;
To a lost vessel lickened might I be;
For many a wight aboute me dwelling
Herde I me blame and putte in dispreising.

Thus spake many oone and seide by me: *85*
"Although from him his siknesse savage
Withdrawen and passed as for a time be,
Resorte it wole, namely in such age
As he is of." And thanne my visage
Bigan to glowe for the woo and fere.   *90*
Tho wordis, hem unwar, cam to myn eere.

. . . .

As that I oones fro Westmynster cam,
Vexid ful grevously with thoughtful hete,
Thus thought I: "A great fool I am   *185*
This pavyment a dayes thus to bete,
And in and out laboure fast and swete,
Wondringe and hevinesse to purchace,
Sithin I stonde out of al favour and grace."

And then thought I on that othir side: *190*
"If that I not be sen amonge the prees,
Men deme wole that I myn heed hide,
And am werse than I am, it is no lees."
O lorde, so my spirite was resteleees,
I soughte reste and I not it fonde,   *195*
But aye was trouble redy at myn honde.

I may not lett a man to ymagine
Ferre above the mone, if that him liste;
Therby the sothe he may not determine,
But by the prefe ben thingis knowen and wiste.
Many a doom is wrappid in the miste.   *201*
Man by his dedes and not by his lookes
Shal knowen be, as it is writen in bookes.

By taste of fruit men may wel wite and knowe
What that it is; othir preef is there noon.   *205*
Every man woote well that, as that I trowe.
Right so, they that deemen my wit is goon
(As yit this day there deemeth many oon
I am not wel) may, as I by them goo,
Taste and assay if it be so or noo.   *210*

Upon a look is harde men them to grounde
What a man is; therby the sothe is hid.
Whethir his wittes seke bene or sounde,
By countynaunce it is not wist ne kid.
Though a man harde have oones ben bitid,   *215*
God shilde it shuld on him contynue alway.
By communynge is the best assay.

. . . .

If a man oones fall in drunkenesse,   *225*
Shal he contynue therein ever mo?
Nay, though a man do in drinking excesse
So ferforthe that not speke he ne can, ne goo,
And his wittes welny ben refte him fro
And buried in the cuppe, he aftirward   *230*
Cometh to him selfe again; ellis were it hard.

Right so, though that my witte were a pilgrim
And wente fer from home, he cam again.
God me devoided of the grevous venim

---

63. martire: suffering. **67. forsake:** forsaken, abandoned. **68. overshake:** shaken off. **69. daliaunce:** conversation. **72. in Westmynster Halle:** Hoccleve was employed as a clerk in the office of the Privy Seal. **73. eke:** also; **prese:** press, crowd, throng. **74. apalle:** grow pale, weaken. **76. her heed:** their heads. **77. as:** as if. **78. sauter:** Psalter. **81. deed:** dead; **cherte:** charity, affection. **88. namely:** especially. **91. Tho:** Those. **193. lees:** lie. **197. lett:** prevent. **201. doom:** fate. **211. grounde:** base an opinion. **214. wist ne kid:** known. **215. harde:** hardship; **bitid:** befallen. **228. So ferforthe:** to such a degree. **229. welny:** well-nigh.

That had enfectid and wildid my brain.   *235*
See how the curteise leche moste soverain
Unto the seke geveth medicine
In nede, and him releveth of his pine.

                    . . . .

But algates, howe so be my countenaunce,
Debate is nowe noon betwixt me and my wit,
Although that ther were a disseveraunce
As for a time betwixt me and it.
The greater harme is myne, that nevere yit   *250*
Was I wel lettered, prudent and discreet;
There never stood yit wyse man on my feet.

The sothe is this: suche conceit as I had,
And undirstonding, al were it but smal,
Bifore that my wittis weren unsad,   *255*
Thanked be oure lorde Ihesu crist of al,
Suche have I now. But blowe is ny overal
The reverse, wherethorugh moch is my mornynge,
Which causeth me thus syghe in complainynge.

Sithen my good fortune hath chaunged hir chere,
Hie time is me to crepe into my grave.   *261*
To lyve joyless what do I here?
I in myn herte can no gladness have.
I may but smal sey but if men deme I rave.
Sithin othir thing than woo may I none gripe,   *265*
Unto my sepulcre am I nowe ripe.

                    . . . .

This troubly lyf hath al to longe endurid;
Not have I wist how in my skyn to tourne.
But now my silfe to my silfe have ensured
For no suche wondringe aftir this to mourne.   *305*
As longe as my lyf shal in me sojourne,
Of suche ymaginynge I not me recche;
Let them deeme as them list, and speke and drecche.

This othir day, a lamentacioun
Of a woful man in a book I sy,   *310*
To whom wordis of consolacioun
Resoun gaf, spekynge effectually;
And wel esid myhn herte was therby,

For when I had a while in the book red,
With the speche of resoun was I wel fed.   *315*

                    . . . .

Lenger I thoughte red have in this book,
But so it shope that I ne mighte naught:
He that it oughte again it to him took,
Me of his haste unwar; yet have I caught   *375*
Sum of the doctrine by resoun taught
To the man, as above have I said,
Whereof I holde me ful wel apaid.

For ever sithin, set have I the lesse
By the peples ymaginacioun,   *380*
Talkinge this and that of my siknesse
Whiche cam of goddis visitacioun;
Mighte I have be founde in probacioun
Not grucching, but han take it in souffraunce,
Holsum and wyse had be my governaunce.   *385*

Farwel, my sorowe! I caste it to the cok.
With pacience I hensforthe thinke unpike
Of such thoughtful dissese and woo the lok
And let them out, that han me made to sike.
Hereafter our lorde god may, if him like,   *390*
Make al myn olde affection resorte,
And in hope of that wole I me comforte.

Thorugh goddis just doom and his jugement,
And for my best, nowe I take and deem,
Gaf that good lorde me my punischement.   *395*
In welthe I tooke of him noon hede or yeme
Him for to please and him honoure and queme,
And he me gaf a boon on for to gnawe,
Me to correcte and of him to have awe.

He gaf me wit, and he tooke it away   *400*
Whanne that he sy that I it mis dispent,
And gaf again whanne it was to his pay.
He grauntid my giltis to repente,
And hensforwarde to set myn entente
Unto his deitee to do plesaunce   *405*
And to amende my sinful governaunce.

---

236. leche: leech, physician. **246. algates:** anyway, nevertheless. **255. unsad:** unsettled. **257. blowe:** blown, blustered, said. **260. chere:** face, behaviour. **264. but if men deme:** without men thinking. **307. recche:** reck, care. **308. drecche:** be tedious, vexing. **373. shope:** shaped, happened. **374. oughte:** owned. **396. yeme:** care. **397. queme:** please, subserve.

Laude and honour and thanke unto thee be,
Lorde god that salve art to al hevinesse.
Thanke of my welthe and myn adversitee,
Thanke of myn elde and of my seeknesse.   *410*
And thanke be to thin infinit goodnesse
For thi giftis and benefices alle;
And unto thi mercy and grace I calle.

(c. 1421)

THREE ROUNDELS

Cy ensuent trois chaunceons: lune conpleynante a
la dame monoie, et lautre la response dele a cellui
qui se conpleyet, et la tierce la commendacion de
ma dame.

1. [Complaint to Money]

Wel may I pleyne on yow, Lady moneye,
    That in the prison of your sharp scantnesse
    Souffren me bathe in wo and hevynesse,
And deynen nat of socour me purveye.

Whan that I baar of your prison the keye,   *5*
    Kepte I yow streite? Nay, god to witnesse!
Wel may I. . . .

I leet yow out. O, now, of your noblesse,   *11*
    Seeth unto me. In your deffaute, I deye.
Wel may I. . . .

Yee saillen al to fer. Retourne, I preye!
    Conforteth me ageyn this Cristemesse,
    Elles I moot in right a feynt gladnesse
Synge of yow thus and yow accuse, and seye: *20*
Wel may I. . . .

2. La Response

Hoccleve, I wole it to thee knowen be,
    I, lady moneie, of the world goddesse,
    That have al thyng undir my buxumnesse,
Nat sette by thy pleynte risshes three.

Myn hy might haddest thow in no cheertee   *5*
    Whyle I was in thy slipir sikirnesse.
Hoccleve. . . .

At instance of thyn excessif largesse,   *11*
    Becam I of my body delavee.
Hoccleve. . . .

And syn that lordes grete obeien me,
    Sholde I me dreede of thy poore symplesse?
    My golden heed akith for thy lewdnesse.
Go, poore wrecche. Who settith aght by thee? *20*
Hoccleve. . . .

Cest tout.   *25*

3. [Hoccleve's Humorous Praise of His Lady]

Of my lady, wel me rejoise I may:
    Hir golden forheed is ful narw and smal;
    Hir browes been lyk to dym reed coral;
And as the jeet hir yen glistren ay.

Hir bowgy cheekes been as softe as clay,
    With large jowes and substancial.   *6*
Of my lady. . . .

Hir nose a pentice is, that it ne shal
Reyne in hir mowth thogh shee uprightes lay. *12*
Of my lady. . . .

Hir mowth is nothyng scant, with lippes gray; *17*
    Hir chin unnethe may be seen at al;
    Hir comly body shape as a footbal,
And shee syngith ful lyk a papejay.   *20*
Of my lady. . . .

Cest tout.

THREE ROUNDELS   The form of these poems is a variant of the standard rondeau or rondel. **Argument:** "Here follow three songs: the one complains to the Lady Money, and the other the response given to him who complained, and the third the praise of my lady." **ROUNDEL 1 12. deffaute:** default, lack.   **ROUNDEL 2 3. buxumnesse:** bowing, obedient to me. **4. risshes:** rushes, straws. **6. slipir sikirnesse:** slippery security. **12. delavee:** dissolved, poured away. **19. lewdnesse:** ignorance. **25. Cest tout:** *C'est tout,* "That's all" — i.e., The End.   **ROUNDEL 3 4. yen:** eyes. **5. bowgy:** bulgy, baggy. **11. pentice:** penthouse, sloping roof, overhang. **18. unnethe:** scarcely. **20. papejay:** parrot.

MARGERY KEMPE
England, c.1373-c.1439

from *THE BOOK OF MARGERY KEMPE*

Chapter 1

When this creature was twenty year of age or somewhat more, she was married to a worshipful burgess of Lynn and was with child within short time, as nature would. And, after that she had conceived, she was laboured with great accesses till the child was born, and then, what for labour she had in childing and for sickness going before, she despaired of her life, weening she might not live. And then she sent for her ghostly   5
father, for she had a thing in conscience which she had never showed before that time in all her life; or she was ever letted by her enemy, the Devil, evermore saying to her while she was in good health she needed no confession but to do penance by herself alone, and all should be forgiven, for God is merciful enough. And therefore this creature oftentimes did great penance in fasting bread and water, and other deeds of alms, with   10
devout prayers, save she would not show it in confession. And when she was any time sick or diseased, the Devil said in her mind that she should be damned, for she was not shriven of that default. Wherefore, after that her child was born, she, not trusting her life, sent for her ghostly father, as said before, in full will to be shriven of all her lifetime as near as she could. And, when she came to the point for to say that thing   15
which she had so long concealed, her confessor was a little too hasty and began sharply to undermine her ere that she had fully said her intent, and so she would no more say for nought he might do. And anon, for dread she had of damnation on the one side and his sharp reproving on the other side, this creature went out of her mind and was wonderly vexed and laboured with spirits half year eight weeks and odd days. And in this time she   20
saw, as she thought, devils open their mouths all inflamed with burning flames of fire as they should have swallowed her in, sometimes ramping at her, sometimes threatening her, sometimes pulling her hair and haling her both night and day during the foresaid time. And also the devils cried upon her with great threatenings and bidding her she should forsake her Christianity, her faith, and deny her God, his mother, and all the   25
saints in heaven, her good works and all good virtues, her father, her mother, and all her

---

THE BOOK OF MARGERY KEMPE is the first genuine autobiography in English, dictated by Margery, herself illiterate, transcribed in the fifteenth century and handed down in private hands until discovered, in 1934, by Hope Emily Allen, in the possession of Colonel William Butler-Bowden, who published a modern version in 1936 (reprinted 1944 with introduction by R. W. Chambers). Brief edited extracts from the manuscript were printed by Wynken de Worde (1501) and Henry Pepwell (1521), but the only complete and dependable text is that prepared by Sanford Brown Meech and Hope Emily Allen, with full introduction, notes, appendices, and glossary, published by Oxford University Press for the Early English Text Society in 1940 (reprinted 1961). Although Margery's priestly amanuensis or a copyist no doubt did some rephrasing, the text is basically her own, including her consistently referring to herself in the third person as "this creature," "the said creature," and the like. **2. would:** i.e., would have it. **3. accesses:** attacks, sickness. **4. what for:** with the. **5. weening:** thinking. **5-6. ghostly father:** i.e., spiritual father, priest. **7. letted:** hindered, prevented. **10. fasting:** fasting on. **13. default:** fault, sin. **15. for to say:** of saying. **17. ere that:** before. **22. ramping:** threatening, raging. **23. haling:** pulling.

friends. And so she did. She slandered her husband, her friends, and her own self; she spake many a reproving word and many a shrewd word; she knew no virtue nor goodness; she desired all wickedness; like as the spirits tempted her to say and do so she said and did. She would have fordone herself many a time at their stirring and have been *30* damned with them in hell, and into witness thereof she bit her own hand so violently that it was seen all her life after. And also she rived her skin on her body against her heart with her nails despitously, for she had no other instruments; and worse she would have done save she was bound and kept with strength both day and night that she might not have her will. And, when she had long been laboured in these and many other *35* temptations that men thought she should never have escaped nor lived, then on a time, as she lay alone and her keepers were from her, our merciful Lord Christ Jesus, ever to be trusted, worshipped be his name, never forsaking his servant in time of need, appeared to his creature, which had forsaken him, in likeness of a man, most seemly, most beauteous, and most amiable that ever might be seen with man's eye, clad in a *40* mantle of purple silk, sitting upon her bed's side, looking upon her with so blessed a cheer that she was strengthened in all her spirits, said to her these words: "Daughter, why hast thou forsaken me, and I forsook never thee?" And anon, as he had said these words, she saw verily how the air opened as bright as any lightning, and he rose up into the air, not right hastily and quickly, but fair and easily that she might well behold him *45* in the air till it was closed again. And anon the creature was stabilized in her wits and in her reason as well as ever she was before, and prayed her husband as so soon as he came to her that she might have the keys of the buttery to take her meat and drink as she had done before. Her maids and her keepers counselled him he should deliver her no keys, for they said she would but give away such good as there was, for she wist not what she *50* said, as they thought. Nevertheless, her husband, ever having tenderness and compassion of her, commanded they should deliver to her the keys. And she took her meat and drink as her bodily strength would serve her and knew her friends and her household and all other that came to her to see how our Lord Jesus Christ had wrought his grace in her, so blessed might he be that ever is near in tribulation. When men think *55* he is far from them, he is full near by his grace. Afterward this creature did all other occupations as fell for her to do wisely and sadly enough, save she knew not verily the draught of our Lord.

Chapter 2

And, when this creature was thus graciously come again to her mind, she thought she was bound to God and that she would be his servant. Nevertheless, she would not leave her *60* pride nor her pompous array that she had used before, neither for her husband nor for none other man's counsel. And yet she wist full well that men said her full much villainy, for she wore gold pipes on her head and the edges of the tippets of her hoods had fancy long

---

28. shrewd: sharp. **30. stirring:** instigation. **31. into witness:** as evidence, a sign. **32. rived:** tore; **against:** over. **34. that:** so that. **35. laboured:** troubled, tormented. **37. from:** i.e., away from. **42. cheer:** facial expression. **48. meat:** i.e., food. **50. good:** goods; **wist:** knew. **52. of:** for. **57. sadly:** soberly. **57-58. knew . . . Lord:** i.e., had not yet experienced being truly "drawn" to the Lord, had not had a real spiritual or mystical experience. **62. said her:** i.e., said about her. **63. pipes:** wires or netting.

points. Her cloaks were also cut that way and covered with divers colours between the
points that it should be more stunning to men's sight and herself the more be worshipped. *65*
And, when her husband would speak to her for to leave her pride, she answered sharply
and shortly and said that she was come of worthy kindred — it ill beseemed him for to
have wedded her, for her father was sometime mayor of the town N. and afterward he was
alderman of the high Guild of the Trinity in N. And therefore she would save the worship
of her kindred whatsoever any man said. She had full great envy at her neighbours that *70*
they should be arrayed so well as she. All her desire was for to be worshipped of the
people. She would not once take any notice of chastising or be content with the goods that
God had sent her, as her husband was, but ever desired more and more. And then, for pure
covetousness and for to maintain her pride, she began to brew and was one of the greatest
brewers in the town N. for three or four years till she lost much good, for she had never *75*
used thereto. For, though she had never so good servants and cunning in brewing, yet it
would never prove with them. For, when the ale was as fair standing under barm as any
man might see, suddenly the barm would fall down that all the ale was lost every brewing
after other, that her servants were ashamed and would not dwell with her. Then this
creature thought how God had punished her beforetime and she could not be ware, and *80*
now eftsoons by losing of her goods, and then she left and brewed no more. And then she
asked her husband mercy for she would not follow his counsel aforetime, and she said that
her pride and sin was cause of all her punishing and she would amend what she had
trespassed with good will. But yet she left not the world wholly, for now she bethought her
of a new housewifery. She had a horse-mill. She got herself two good horses and a man to *85*
grind men's corn, and thus she trusted to get her living. This provision endured not long,
for in short time after on Corpus Christi Eve fell this marvel. This man, being in good
health of body and his two horses husky and likely that well had drawn in the mill
beforetime, as now he took one of these horses and put him in the mill as he had done
before, and this horse would draw no draught in the mill for nothing the man might do. *90*
The man was sorry and assayed with all his wits how he should make this horse draw.
Sometimes he led him by the head, sometimes he beat him, and sometimes he cherished
him, and all availed not, for he would rather go backward than forward. Then this man set
a sharp pair spurs on his heels and rode on the horse's back for to make him draw, and it
was never the better. When this man saw it would be in no way, then he set up this horse *95*
again in the stable and gave him meat, and he ate well and freshly. And then he took the
other horse and put him in the mill. And like as his fellow did so did he, for he would not
draw for anything that the man might do. And then this man forsook his service and would
no longer abide with the aforesaid creature. Anon as it was noised about the town of N.
that there would neither man nor beast do service to the said creature, then some said she *100*
was accursed; some said God took open vengeance on her; some said one thing; some said
another. And some wise men, whose mind was more grounded in the love of our Lord,
said it was the high mercy of our Lord Jesus Christ summoned and called her from the

---

65. worshipped: esteemed. **68. town N:** Lynn (King's Lynn), in Norfolk. **69. save:** preserve. **75. good:** money. **75-76. had never used thereto:** i.e., lacked experience or know-how. **76:** i.e., servants who had cunning. **77. prove:** be successful. **80. could not be ware:** was unable to understand. **81. left:** i.e., left off. **82. for . . . follow:** for not following. **88. likely:** suitable, in good shape. **95. be:** i.e., work.

pride and vanity of the wretched world. And then this creature, seeing all these adversities coming on every side, thought it was the scourges of our Lord that would chastise her for *105* her sin. Then she asked God mercy and forsook her pride, her covetousness, and desire that she had of the worship of the world, and did great bodily penance, and began to enter the way of everlasting life, as shall be said after.

Chapter 3

On a night, as this creature lay in her bed with her husband, she heard a sound of melody so sweet and delectable, it seemed to her as she had been in paradise. And *110* therewith she started out of her bed and said, "Alas, that ever I did sin, it is full merry in heaven." This melody was so sweet that it passed all the melody that might be heard in this world without any comparison, and caused this creature when she heard any mirth or melody afterward for to have full plenteous and abundant tears of high devotion with great sobbings and sighings after the bliss of heaven, not dreading the shames and the *115* spites of the wretched world. And ever after this draught she had in her mind the mirth and the melody that was in heaven, so much that she could not well restrain herself from the speaking thereof. For, where she was in any company, she would say oftentime, "It is full merry in heaven." And they that knew her governance beforetime and now heard her speaking so much of the bliss of heaven said unto her, "Why speak ye so of the *120* mirth that is in heaven; ye know it not and ye have not been there no more than we," and were wroth with her for she would not hear anyone speak of worldly things as they did and as she did beforetime. And after this time she had never desire to commune fleshly with her husband, for the debt of matrimony was so abominable to her that she had liefer, it seemed to her, eat or drink the ooze, the muck in the channel, than to consent to *125* any fleshly communing save only for obedience. And so she said to her husband, "I may not deny you my body, but the love of my heart and my affection is drawn from all earthly creatures and set only in God." He would have his will, and she obeyed with great weeping and sorrowing for that she might not live chaste. And oftentimes this creature counselled her husband to live chaste, and said that they oftentimes, she wist *130* well, had displeased God by their inordinate love and the great delectation that they had either of them in using of other, and now it were good that they should by their both will and consenting of them both, punish and chastise themselves willfully by abstaining from their lust of their bodies. Her husband said it were good to do so, but he might not yet; he should when God willed. And so he used her as he had done before, he would *135* not spare. And ever she prayed to God that she might live chaste, and three or four years after, when it pleased our Lord, he made a vow of chastity, as shall be written after by the leave of Jesus. And also, after this creature heard this heavenly melody, she did great bodily penance. She was shriven sometimes twice or thrice on the day, and in special of that sin which she so long had concealed and covered, as it is written in the beginning of *140* the book. She gave her to great fasting and to great waking; she rose at two or three of the clock and went to church and was there in her prayers until time of noon, also all the

---

116. **draught:** i.e., drawing, being pulled toward heaven. 125. **liefer:** rather; **channel:** gutter. 132. **both:** mutual.

afternoon. And then was she slandered and reproved of much people for she kept so strait a living. Then she got her a haircloth of a kiln such as men dry malt on and laid it in her kirtle as subtly and privily as she might, that her husband should not espy it, nor *145* no more he did, and yet she lay by him every night in his bed, and wore the haircloth every day, and bore children in the time. Then she had three years of great labour with temptations which she bore as meekly as she could, thanking our Lord for all his gifts, and was as merry when she was reproved, scorned, or japed for our Lord's love, and much more merry than she was beforetime in the worships of the world. For she wist *150* right well she had sinned greatly against God and was worthy more shame and sorrow than any man could do to her, and despite of the world was the right way heavenward since Christ himself chose that way. All his apostles, martyrs, confessors, and virgins and all that ever came to heaven passed by the way of tribulation, and she desired nothing so much as heaven. Then was she glad in her conscience when she believed that *155* she was entering the way which would lead her to the place that she most desired. And this creature had contrition and great compunction with plenteous tears and many boisterous sobbings for her sins and for her unkindness against her Maker. She bethought her from her childhood for her unkindness as our Lord would put it in her mind full many a time. And then, she beholding her own wickedness, she might but *160* sorrow and weep and ever pray for mercy and forgiveness. Her weeping was so plenteous and so continuing that much people weened that she might weep and leave when she would, and therefore many men said she was a false hypocrite and wept for the world for succour and for worldly good. And then full many forsook her that loved her before, while she was in the world, and would not know her, and ever she thanked *165* God of all, nothing desiring but mercy and forgiveness of sin.

Chapter 4

The first two years when this creature was thus drawn to our Lord, she had great quiet of spirit as for any temptations. She might well endure to fast; it grieved her not. She hated the joys of the world. She felt no rebellion in her flesh. She was strong, as it seemed to her, that she dreaded no devil in hell, for she did so great bodily penance. She thought *170* that she loved God more than he her. She was smitten with the deadly wound of vainglory and felt it not, for she desired many times that the crucifix should loosen his hands from the cross and embrace her in token of love. Our merciful Lord Christ Jesus, seeing this creature's presumption, sent her, as is writ before, three years of great temptations, of the which one of the hardest I purpose to write for example of them that *175* come after, that they should not trust in their own selves nor have any joy in themselves as this creature had, for no dread, our ghostly enemy sleepeth not, but he full busily searcheth our complexions and our dispositions, and where that he findeth us most frail there by our Lord's sufferance he layeth his snare, which may no man escape by his own power. And so he laid before this creature the snare of lechery, when she weened *180* that all fleshly lust had been wholly quenched in her. And so long she was tempted with

---

143. for she kept: for keeping, because she kept. **147. in the time:** during this period. **151. worthy:** deserving of. **158. boisterous:** noisy, violent; **unkindness:** unnaturalness. **162-63. leave . . . would:** leave off whenever she wanted. **163. for:** before.

the sin of lechery for aught that she could do. And yet she was often shriven, she wore the haircloth, and did great bodily penance, and wept many a bitter tear and prayed full often to our Lord that he should preserve her and keep her that she should not fall into temptation, for she thought she had liefer be dead than consent thereto. And in all this *185* time she had no lust to commune with her husband, but it was very painful and horrible unto her. In the second year of her temptations it fell so that a man which she loved well said unto her on Saint Margaret's Eve before evensong that for anything he would lie by her and have his lust of his body, and she should not withstand him, for, if he might not have his will that time, he said, he should else have it another time, she should not *190* choose. And he did it for to prove her what she would do, but she weened that he had meant full earnest at that time and said but little thereto. So they parted asunder as then and went both for to hear evensong, for her church was of Saint Margaret. This woman was so laboured with the man's words that she might not hear her evensong, nor say her Pater Noster, or think any other good thought, but was more laboured than ever she was *195* before. The Devil put in her mind that God had forsaken her, and else should she not so been tempted. She believed the Devil's suasions and began to consent for because she could think no good thought. Therefore weened she that God had forsaken her. And, when evensong was done, she went to the man beforesaid that he should have his lust, as she weened that he had desired, but he made such simulation that she could not know *200* his intent, and so they parted asunder for that night. This creature was so laboured and vexed all that night that she wist never what she might do. She lay by her husband, and for to commune with him it was so abominable unto her that she might not endure it, and yet was it lawful unto her in lawful time if she had wanted. But ever she was laboured with the other man for to sin with him inasmuch as he had spoken to her. At *205* the last through importunity of temptation and lacking of discretion she was overcome, and consented in her mind, and went to the man to know if he would then consent to her. And he said he would not for all the good in this world; he had liefer be hewn as small as flesh to the pot. She went away all shamed and confused in herself, seeing his stableness and her own unstableness. Then thought she of the grace that God had given *210* her beforetime, how she had two years of great quiet in soul, repentance of her sin with many bitter tears of compunction, and perfect will never to turn again to her sin, but rather to be dead, it seemed to her. And now she saw how she had consented in her will for to do sin. Then fell she half in despair. She thought she would have been in hell for the sorrow that she had. She thought she was worthy no mercy, for her consenting was *215* so willfully done, nor never worthy to do him service, for she was so false unto him. Nevertheless she was shriven many times and often, and did her penance whatsoever her confessor would enjoin her to do, and was governed after the rules of the Church. That grace God gave this creature, blessed may he be, but he withdrew not her temptation but rather increased it, as it seemed to her. And therefore weened she that he had forsaken *220* her and durst not trust to his mercy, but was laboured with horrible temptations of lechery and of despair nigh all the next year following, save our Lord of his mercy, as

---

186. but: rather. **189. lust:** pleasure. **191. prove:** test.

she said herself, gave her each day for the most part two hours of compunction for her sins with many bitter tears. And afterwards she was laboured with temptations of despair as she was before and was as far from feelings of grace as they that never felt 225 none. And that could she not bear, and therefore always she despaired. Save for the time that she felt grace, her labours were so wonderful that she could evil fare with them, but ever mourning and sorrowing as though God had forsaken her.

Chapter 5

Then on a Friday before Christmas Day, as this creature, kneeling in a chapel of Saint John within a church of Saint Margaret in N., wept wondrous sorely, asking mercy and 230 forgiveness of her sins and her trespass, our merciful Lord Christ Jesus, blessed may he be, ravished her spirit and said unto her: "Daughter, why weepest thou so sorely? I am come to thee, Jesus Christ, that died on the Cross suffering bitter pains and passions for thee. I, the same God, forgive thee thy sins to the utterest point. And thou shalt never come in hell nor in purgatory, but, when thou shalt pass out of this world, within the 235 twinkling of an eye thou shalt have the bliss of heaven, for I am the same God that have brought thy sins to thy mind and made thee to be shriven thereof. And I grant thee contrition unto thy life's end. Therefore I bid thee and command thee, boldly call me Jesus, thy love, for I am thy love and shall be thy love without end. And, daughter, thou hast an haircloth upon thy back. I will thou do it away, and I shall give thee an haircloth 240 in thine heart that shall like thee much better than all the haircloths in the world. Also, my dearworthy daughter, thou must forsake that thou lovest best in this world, and that is eating of flesh. And instead of that flesh thou shalt eat my flesh and my blood, that is the very body of Christ in the sacrament of the altar. This is my will, daughter, that thou receive my body every Sunday, and I shall flow so much grace in thee that all the world 245 shall marvel thereof. Thou shalt be eaten and gnawed of the people of the world as any rat gnaweth the stockfish. Dread thee naught, daughter, for thou shalt have the victory of all thine enemies. I shall give thee grace enough to answer every clerk in the love of God. I swear to thee by my majesty that I shall never forsake thee in weal nor in woe. I shall help thee and keep thee that there shall never devil in hell part thee from me, nor 250 angel in heaven, nor man in earth, for devils in hell may not, nor angels in heaven will not, nor man in earth shall not. And, daughter, I will thou leave thy praying of many prayers and think such thoughts as I will put in thy mind. I shall give thee leave to pray till six of the clock to say what thou would. Then shalt thou lie still and speak to me by thought, and I shall give to thee high meditation and true contemplation. And I bid thee 255 go to the anchorite at the Friar Preachers, and show him my privities and my counsels which I show to thee, and work after his counsel, for my spirit shall speak in him to thee." Then this creature went forth to the anchorite, as she was commanded, and showed him the revelations such as were shown to her. Then the anchorite with great reverence and weeping, thanking God, said, "Daughter, ye suck even on Christ's breast, 260 and ye have an earnest-penny of heaven. I charge you receiveth such thoughts as when

---

240. do: put. **241. like:** please. **242. dearworthy:** dearly esteemed; **that:** that which. **256. Friar Preachers:** i.e., the Dominicans.

God will give them as meekly and as devoutly as ye can and cometh to me and telleth me what they be, and I shall, with the leave of our Lord Jesus Christ, tell you whether they be of the Holy Ghost or else of your enemy the Devil."

Chapter 11

It befell upon a Friday on Midsummer Eve in right hot weather, as this creature was coming from York bearing a bottle with beer in her hand and her husband a cake in his bosom, he asked his wife this question: "Margery, if here came a man with a sword and would smite off my head unless I should commune in the natural way with you as I have done before, tell me the truth of your conscience — for ye say ye will not lie — whether would ye suffer mine head to be cut off or else suffer me to meddle with you again as I did sometime?" "Alas, sir," she said, "why move ye this matter and have we been chaste these eight weeks?" "For I will know the truth of your heart." And then she said with great sorrow, "Forsooth I had liefer see you be slain than we should turn again to our uncleanness." And he said again, "Ye are no good wife." And then she asked her husband what was the cause that he had not meddled with her eight weeks before, since she lay with him every night in his bed. And he said he was so made afeard when he would have touched her that he durst no more do. "Now, good sir, amend you and ask God mercy, for I told you near three years since that ye should be slain suddenly, and now is this the third year, and yet I hope I shall have my desire. Good sir, I pray you grant me what I shall ask, and I shall pray for you that ye shall be saved through the mercy of our Lord Jesus Christ, and ye shall have more meed in heaven than if ye wore a haircloth or a habergeon. I pray you, suffer me to make a vow of chastity in what bishop's hand that God wills." "Nay," he said, "that will I not grant you, for now may I use you without deadly sin and then might I not so." Then she said again, "If it be the will of the Holy Ghost to fulfill what I have said, I pray God ye may consent thereto; and, if it be not the will of the Holy Ghost, I pray God ye never consent thereto." Then went they forth to-Bridlington-ward in right hot weather, the foresaid creature having great sorrow and great dread for her chastity. And, as they came by a cross, her husband sat himself down under the cross, calling his wife unto him and saying these words unto her: "Margery, grant me my desire, and I shall grant you your desire. My first desire is that we shall lie still together in one bed as we have done before; the second, that ye shall pay my debts ere ye go to Jerusalem; and the third, that ye shall eat and drink with me on the Friday as ye were wont to do." "Nay, sir," she said, "to break the Friday I will never grant you while I live." "Well," he said, "then shall I meddle you again." She prayed him that he would give her leave to make her prayers, and he granted it well. Then she kneeled down beside a cross in the field and prayed in this manner with great abundance of tears: "Lord God, thou knowest all things; thou knowest what sorrow I have had to be chaste in my body to thee all these three years, and now might I have my will and I dare not for love of thee. For, if I would break that manner of fasting which thou commandest me to keep on the Friday without meat or drink, I should now have my desire. But, blessed Lord, thou knowest I will not go contrary to thy will, and much now is

265

270

275

280

285

290

295

300

---

271. **sometime:** in times past; **and have we:** now that we have. 277. **do:** i.e., do so. 281. **habergeon:** i.e., one worn as a form of penance.

my sorrow unless I find comfort in thee. Now, blessed Jesus, make thy will known to me, unworthy, that I may follow thereafter and fulfill it with all my might." And then our Lord Jesus Christ with great sweetness spake to this creature, commanding her to go again to her husband and pray him to grant her what she desired. "And he shall have what he desireth. For, my dearworthy daughter, this was the cause that I bade thee fast, for thou *305* shouldst the sooner obtain and get thy desire, and now it is granted thee. I will no longer thou fast; therefore I bid ye in the name of Jesus eat and drink as thy husband doth." Then this creature thanked our Lord Jesus Christ for his grace and his goodness, then rose up and went to her husband, saying unto him, "Sir, if it like you, ye shall grant me my desire, and ye shall have your desire. Granteth me that ye shall not come in my bed, and I grant *310* you to quit your debts ere I go to Jerusalem. And maketh my body free to God so that ye never make no challenge to me to ask no debt of matrimony after this day while ye live, and I shall eat and drink on the Friday at your bidding." Then said her husband again to her, "As free may your body be to God as it hath been to me." This creature thanked God greatly, enjoying that she had her desire, praying her husband that they should say three *315* Pater Nosters in the worship of the Trinity for the great grace that he had granted them. And so they did, kneeling under a cross, and then they ate and drank together in great gladness of spirit. . . .

Chapter 28

. . . . And so they went forth into the Holy Land till they could see Jerusalem. And, when this creature saw Jerusalem, riding on an ass, she thanked God with all her heart, *320* praying him for his mercy that like as he had brought her to see this earthly city Jerusalem he would grant her grace to see the blissful city Jerusalem above, the city of heaven. Our Lord Jesus Christ, answering to her thought, granted her to have her desire. Then for joy that she had and the sweetness that she felt in the conversation of our Lord, she was in point to have fallen off her ass, for she might not bear the *325* sweetness and grace that God wrought in her soul. Then two pilgrims of Dutchmen went to her and kept her from falling, of which the one was a priest. And he put spices in her mouth to comfort her, thinking she had been sick. And so they helped her forth to Jerusalem. And when she came there she said, "Sirs, I pray you be not displeased though I weep sore in this holy place where our Lord Jesus Christ was quick and dead." *330* Then went they to the temple in Jerusalem, and they were let in on the one day at evensong-time and abided therein till the next day at evensong-time. Then the friars lifted up a cross and led the pilgrims about from one place to another where our Lord had suffered his pains and his passions, every man and woman bearing a wax candle in their hand. And the friars always as they went about told them what our Lord suffered *335* in every place. And the foresaid creature wept and sobbed so plenteously as though she had seen our Lord with her bodily eye suffering his passion at that time. Before her in her soul she saw him verily by contemplation, and that caused her to have compassion. And when they came up onto the Mount of Calvary, she fell down that she could not

---

325. **in point to have fallen:** on the point of falling. 326. **Dutchmen:** Germans. 339. **that:** because.

stand nor kneel, but wallowed and wrested with her body, spreading her arms abroad, *340* and cried with a loud voice as though her heart should have burst asunder, for in the city of her soul she saw verily and freshly how our Lord was crucified. Before her face she heard and saw in her spiritual sight the mourning of our Lady, of Saint John and Mary Magdalene, and of many others that loved our Lord. And she had so great compassion and so great pain to see our Lord's pain that she could not keep herself *345* from crying and roaring though she should have been dead therefor. And this was the first cry that ever she cried in any contemplation. And this manner of crying endured many years after this time for aught that any man might do, and therefore suffered she much despite and much reproof. The crying was so loud and so wonderful that it made the people astonished unless they had heard it before or unless they knew the cause of *350* the crying. And she had them so oftentimes that they made her right weak in her bodily strength, and namely if she heard of our Lord's passion. And sometimes, when she saw the crucifix, or if she saw a man had a wound, or a beast, whether it were, or if a man beat a child before her or smote a horse or another beast with a whip, if she might see it or hear it, it seemed to her she saw our Lord being beaten or wounded like as she saw *355* in the man or in the beast, as well in the field as in the town, and by herself alone as well as among the people. First when she had her cryings at Jerusalem, she had them oftentimes, and in Rome also. And, when she came home into England, first at her coming home it came but seldom, as it were once in a month, then once in the week, afterward quotidianly, and once she had fourteen on one day, and another day she had *360* seven, and so as God would visit her, sometimes in the church, sometimes in the street, sometimes in the chamber, sometimes in the field when God would send them, for she knew never time nor hour when they should come. And they came never without passing great sweetness of devotion and high contemplation. And as soon as she perceived that she should cry, she would keep it in as much as she might that the *365* people should not have heard it, for annoying of them. For some said it was a wicked spirit vexed her; some said it was a sickness; some said she had drunk too much wine; some banned her; some wished she had been in the haven; some would she had been on the sea in a bottomless boat; and so each man as he thought. Other spiritual men loved her and favoured her the more. Some great clerks said our Lady cried never so, *370* nor no saint in heaven, but they knew full little what she felt, nor they would not believe but that she might have abstained her from crying if she had wanted. And therefore, when she knew that she should cry, she kept it in as long as she might and did all that she could to withstand it or else to put it away till she waxed as blue as any lead, and ever it should labour in her mind more and more until the time that it broke *375* out. And when the body might no longer endure the spiritual labour, but was overcome with the unspeakable love that wrought so fervently in the soul, then fell she down and cried wondrous loud. And the more that she would labour to keep it in or to put it away, much the more should she cry and the more louder. And thus she did on the Mount of Calvary, as it is written before. . . . *380*

---

353. whether: whichever. **368. banned:** cursed, scolded; **haven:** i.e., harbour, bay — now The Wash.

Chapter 52

There was a monk should preach in York, the which had heard much slander and much evil language of the said creature. And, when he should preach, there was much multitude of people to hear him, and she present with them. And so, when he was in his sermon, he rehearsed many matters so openly that the people conceived well it was for cause of her, wherefore her friends that loved her well were full sorry and heavy thereof, *385* and she was much the more merry, for she had matter to prove her patience and her charity wherethrough she trusted to please our Lord Christ Jesus. When the sermon was done, a doctor of divinity who loved her well with many others also came to her and said, "Margery, how have ye done this day?" "Sir," she said, "right well, blessed be God. I have cause to be right merry and glad in my soul that I may anything suffer for *390* his love, for he suffered much more for me." Anon after came a man who loved her right well of good will with his wife and others more, and led her seven miles thence to the Archbishop of York, and brought her into a fair chamber, where came a good clerk, saying to the good man who had brought her thither, "Sir, why have ye and your wife brought this woman hither? She shall steal away from you, and then shall ye have a *395* villainy of her." The good man said, "I dare well say she will abide and be at her answer with good will." On the next day she was brought into the archbishop's chapel, and there came many of the archbishop's household, despising her, calling her "Lollard" and "heretic," and swearing many a horrible oath that she should be burnt. And she, through the strength of Jesus, said again to them, "Sirs, I dread me ye shall be burnt in hell *400* without end unless ye amend you of your oaths swearing, for ye keep not the commandments of God. I would not swear as ye do for all the good of this world." Then they went away, as if they had been ashamed. She then, making her prayer in her mind, asked grace so to be demeaned that day as was most pleasing to God and profit to her own soul and good example to her fellow Christians. Our Lord, answering her, said it *405* should be right well. At the last the said archbishop came into the chapel with his clerks and sharply he said to her, "Why goest thou in white? Art thou a maiden?" She, kneeling on her knees before him, said, "Nay, sir, I am no maiden; I am a wife." He commanded his men to fetch a pair of fetters and said she should be fettered because she was a false heretic. And then she said, "I am no heretic, nor ye shall none prove me." *410* The archbishop went away and let her stand alone. Then she made her prayers to our Lord God almighty for to help her and succour her against all her enemies, spiritual and bodily, a long while, and her flesh trembled and quaked wondrously that she was fain to put her hands under her clothes that it should not be espied. Then the archbishop came again into the chapel with many worthy clerks, amongst whom was the same doctor *415* who had examined her before and the monk that had preached against her a little time before in York. Some of the people asked whether she were a Christian woman or a Jew; some said she was a good woman, and some said nay. Then the archbishop took his seat, and his clerks also, each of them in his degree, many people being present. And in the time while the people were gathering together and the archbishop taking his seat, *420* the said creature stood all behind, making her prayers for help and succour against her enemies with high devotion so long that she melted all into tears. And at the last she cried loud therewith, so that the archbishop and his clerks and many people had great wonder of her, for they had not heard such crying before. When her crying was passed,

she came before the archbishop and fell down on her knees, the archbishop saying full 425
boisterously to her, "Why weepest thou so, woman?" She, answering, said, "Sir, ye shall
wish some day that ye had wept as sore as I." And then anon, after the archbishop put to
her the articles of our faith, to the which God gave her grace to answer well and truly
and readily without any great study so that he might not blame her, then he said to the
clerks, "She knoweth her faith well enough. What shall I do with her?" The clerks said, 430
"We know well that she knows the articles of the faith, but we will not suffer her to
dwell among us, for the people hath great faith in her conversation, and peradventure she
might pervert some of them." Then the archbishop said unto her, "I am evilly informed
of thee; I hear say thou art a right wicked woman." And she said again, "Sir, so I hear
said that ye are a wicked man. And, if ye be as wicked as men say, ye shall never come 435
in heaven unless ye amend yourself while ye are here." Then said he full boisterously,
"Why, thou, what say men of me?" She answered, "Other men, sir, can tell you well
enough." Then said a great clerk with a furred hood, "Peace! Thou speak of thyself and
let him be." Then said the archbishop to her, "Lay thine hand on the book here before
me and swear that thou shalt go out of my diocese as soon as thou may." "Nay, sir," she 440
said, "I pray you, give me leave to go again into York to take my leave of my friends."
Then he gave her leave for one day or two. She thought it was too short a time,
wherefore she said again, "Sir, I may not go out of this diocese so hastily, for I must
tarry and speak with good men ere I go, and I must, sir, with your leave, go to
Bridlington and speak with my confessor, a good man, the which was the good prior's 445
confessor that is now canonised." Then said the archbishop to her, "Thou shalt swear
that thou shalt neither teach nor challenge the people in my diocese." "Nay, sir, I shall
not swear," she said, "for I shall speak of God and undermine them that swear great
oaths wheresoever I go unto the time that the pope and holy church hath ordained that
no man shall be so hardy to speak of God, for God almighty forbiddeth not, sir, that we 450
shall speak of him. And also the gospel maketh mention that, when the woman had
heard our Lord preach, she came before him with a loud voice and said, 'Blessed be the
womb that bare thee and the teats that gave thee suck.' Then our Lord said again to her,
'Forsooth, so are they blessed that hear the word of God and keep it.' And therefore, sir,
me thinketh that the gospel giveth me leave to speak of God." "Ah, sir," said the clerks, 455
"here wot we well that she hath a devil within her, for she speaketh of the gospel."
Quickly a great clerk brought forth a book and laid Saint Paul for his part against her,
that no woman should preach. She, answering thereto, said, "I preach not, sir, I come in
no pulpit. I use but communication and good words, and that will I do while I live."
Then said a doctor who had examined her beforetime, "Sir, she told me the worst tales 460
of priests that ever I heard." The bishop commanded her to tell that tale. "Sir, with your

---

452-54: See Luke 11:27-28; in Wyclif's translation, the relevant part reads as follows: "Blessid be the wombe that bar thee, and blessid be the teetis whiche thou hast sokun. And he seide, Rathere blessid ben thei, that heeren Goddis word, and kepen it." **457-58:** See I Corinthians 14:34-35: "Wymmen in chirchis be stille; sothli it is not suffrid to hem for to speke, but for to be suget, as the lawe seith. Forsoth if thei wolen ony thing lerne, at hom axe thei her hosebondis; forsoth it is foul thing to womman for to speke in chirche" (Wyclif). **459. communication and good words:** She is probably thinking of Wyclif's translation of part of II Corinthians 9:13, which speaks of "glorifiynge God in the obedience of youre knowleching in the gospel of Crist, and in symplenesse of comynycacioun into hem and into alle."

reverence, I spake but of one priest by the manner of example, the which as I have learned went wild in a wood through the sufferance of God for the profit of his soul, till the night came upon him. He, destitute of his harbour, found a fair arbour in the which he rested that night, having a fair pear-tree in the midst all flourishing with flowers and *465* embellished, and blooms full delectable to his sight, where came a bear, great and boisterous, huge to behold, shaking the pear-tree and knocking down the flowers. Greedily this grievous beast ate and devoured those fair flowers. And when he had eaten them, turning his tail end in the priest's presence, voided them out again at the hinder part. The priest, having great abomination of that loathly sight, conceiving great *470* heaviness for doubt what it might mean, on the next day he wandered forth in his way all heavy and pensive, whom it fortuned to meet with a seemly aged man like to a palmer or a pilgrim, the which enquired of the priest the cause of his heaviness. The priest, rehearsing the matter before written, said he conceived great dread and heaviness when he beheld that loathly beast befouling and devouring such fair flowers and *475* afterward so horribly voiding them before him at his tail end, and he not understanding what this might mean. Then the palmer, showing himself the messenger of God, thus addressed him: "Priest, thou thyself art the pear-tree, somedeal flourishing and flowering through thy service saying and the sacraments ministering, though thou do undevoutly, for thou takest full little heed how thou saist thy matins and thy service, so *480* it be blabbered to an end. Then goest thou to thy mass without devotion, and for thy sins hast thou full little contrition. Thou receivest there the fruit of everlasting life, the sacrament of the altar, in full feeble disposition. Then all the day after thou misspendest thy time: thou givest thyself to buying and selling, chopping and changing, as it were a man of the world. Thou sittest at thy ale, giving thyself to gluttony and excess, to lust of *485* thy body, through lechery and uncleanness. Thou breakest the commandments of God through swearing, lying, detraction, and backbiting, and such other sins using. Thus by thy misgovernance, like unto the loathly bear, thou devourest and destroyest the flowers and blooms of virtuous living to thine endless damnation and many men's hindering unless thou have grace of repentance and amending." Then the archbishop liked well the *490* tale and commended it, saying it was a good tale. And the clerk who had examined her beforetime, in the absence of the archbishop, said, "Sir, this tale smiteth me to the heart." The foresaid creature said to the clerk, "Ah, worshipful doctor, sir, in place where my dwelling is most, is a worthy clerk, a good preacher, who boldly speaketh against the misgovernance of the people and will flatter no man. He sayeth many times *495* in the pulpit, 'If any man be evil pleased with my preaching, note him well, for he is guilty.' And right so, sir," said she to the clerk, "fare ye by me, God forgive it you." The clerk wist not well what he might say to her. Afterward the same clerk came to her and prayed her of forgiveness that he had so been against her. Also he prayed her specially to pray for him. And then anon after the archbishop said, "Where shall I have a man that *500* might lead this woman from me?" Quickly there started up many young men, and every man of them said, "My lord, I will go with her." The archbishop answered, "Ye be too

---

463. wild: astray. **471. doubt:** uncertainty of.

young; I will not have you." Then a good sad man of the archbishop's household asked his lord what he would give him and he should lead her. The archbishop proffered him five shillings and the man asked a noble. The archbishop, answering, said, "I will not *505* spend so much on her body." "Yes, good sir," said the said creature, "our Lord shall reward you right well in return." Then the archbishop said to the man, "See, here is five shillings, and lead her fast out of this country." She, kneeling down on her knees, asked his blessing. He, praying her to pray for him, blessed her and let her go. Then she, going again to York, was received of much people and of full worthy clerks, which rejoiced in *510* our Lord that had given her, not lettered, wit and wisdom to answer to many learned men without villainy or blame, thanks be to God.

Chapter 88

When this book was first in writing, the said creature was more at home in her chamber with her writer and said fewer beads for speed of writing than she had done years before. And, when she came to church and should hear mass, purposing to say her *515* matins and such other devotions as she had used aforetime, her heart was drawn away from the saying and set much on meditation. She being afeard of displeasance of our Lord, he said to her soul, "Dread thee not, daughter, for as many beads as thou wouldst say I accept them as though thou saidst them, and thy study that thou studiest for to write the grace that I have shown to thee pleaseth me right much and he that writeth *520* both. For, though ye were in the church and wept both together as sore as ever thou didst, yet should ye not please me more than ye do with your writing, for, daughter, by this book many a man shall be turned to me and believe therein. . . . "

Chapter 89

Also, while the foresaid creature was occupied about the writing of this treatise, she had many holy tears and weepings, and oftentimes there came a flame of fire about her *525* breast full hot and delectable, and also he that was her writer could not sometimes keep himself from weeping. And often in the meantime, when the creature was in church, our Lord Jesus Christ with his glorious mother and many saints also came into her soul and thanked her, saying that they were well pleased with the writing of this book. And also she heard many times a voice of a sweet bird singing in her ear, and oftentimes she *530* heard sweet sounds and melodies that passed her wit for to tell them. And she was many times sick while this treatise was in writing, and, as soon as she would go about the writing of this treatise, she was hale and whole suddenly in a manner. . . . Here endeth this treatise, for God took him to his mercy that wrote the copy of this book, and though that he wrote not clearly nor openly to our manner of speaking, he in his manner of *535* writing and spelling made true sentences the which, through the help of God and of herself that had all this treatise in feeling and working, is truly drawn out of the copy into this little book.

(*c. 1425*)

---

508. country: region.

CHARLES D'ORLÉANS
France, 1394-1465

ROUNDEL 57

My ghostly father, I me confess,
   First to God, and then to yow,
   That at a window — wot ye how?
I stole a kiss of great sweetness,
Which done was out avisedness;   5
   But it is done, not undone, now.
My ghostly father, I me confess,
   First to God, and then to you.

But I restore it shall doubtless
   Again, if so be that I mow,   10
   And that to God I make avow,
And else I ask forgiveness.
My ghostly father, I me confess,
   First to God, and then to yow,
   That at a window — wot ye how?   15
I stole a kiss of great sweetness.

(c. 1437)

SIR THOMAS MALORY
England, d. 1471

from *LE MORTE DARTHUR*

(The Death of King Arthur)

As Sir Mordred was ruler of all England, he let make letters as though that they had come from beyond the sea, and the letters specified that King Arthur was slain in battle with Sir Lancelot. Wherefore Sir Mordred made a parliament, and called the lords together, and there he made them to choose him king. And so was he crowned at Canterbury, and held a feast there fifteen days.   5

ROUNDEL 57 (Actually a *rondel,* but even then a variant form, since the first four lines, rather than just the first two, are repeated at the end.) **1. ghostly father:** spiritual father, priest. **2. yow:** you. **3. wot:** know. **5. out avisedness:** not advisedly, without deliberation. **10. mow:** may, am able. **MORTE DARTHUR** The title of Malory's work was given it by William Caxton, who printed it in 1485, giving it also his own book and chapter divisions and making some editorial changes. In 1934 a manuscript closer to the original was found at Winchester College. The section given here corresponds to Caxton's Book XXI, Chapters 1-7. Among the events leading up to those narrated here are Mordred's and others' exposure of Lancelot's affair with Queen Guinevere; Lancelot's escape and subsequent rescue of Guinevere, who has been sentenced to death, in the process unknowingly killing Gawain's brothers Gareth and Gaheris; Arthur's being commanded by the Pope to forgive Guinevere and Lancelot; Gawain's insistence on vengeance; Lancelot's flight to France and Arthur's following and attacking him (having left Sir Mordred in charge in his absence); Gawain's being wounded by Lancelot. Although the mechanics have been modernized, the flavour of the original remains; here for example is how the opening sentences read in the original: "As sir Mordred was rular of all Inglonde, he lete make lettirs as thoughe that they had com frome beyonde the see, and the lettirs specifyed that kynge Arthur was slayne in batayle with sir Launcelot. Wherefore sir Mordred made a parlemente, and called the lordys togydir, and there he made them to chose hym kynge; and so was he crowned at Caunturbury, and hylde a feste there fiftene dayes; and aftirwarde he drew hym unto Wynchester, and there he toke quene Gwenyver, and seyde playnely that he wolde wedde her (which was hys unclys wyff and hys fadirs wyff)." **1. let make:** had made.

And afterward he drew him unto Winchester, and there he took Queen Guinevere, and said plainly that he would wed her — which was his uncle's wife and his father's wife. And so he made ready for the feast, and a day prefixed that they should be wedded, wherefore Queen Guinevere was passing heavy. But she durst not discover her heart, but spake fair, and agreed to Sir Mordred's will. And anon she desired of Sir *10* Mordred to go to London to buy all manner things that longed unto the bridal. And because of her fair speech Sir Mordred trusted her and gave her leave. And so when she came to London she took the Tower of London, and suddenly in all haste possible she stuffed it with all manner of victual and well garnished it with men, and so kept it. And when Sir Mordred wist this he was passing wroth out of measure; and short tale to *15* make, he laid a mighty siege about the Tower and made many assaults, and threw engines unto them and shot great guns. But all might not prevail, for Queen Guinevere would never, for fair speech nor for foul, never to trust unto Sir Mordred to come in his hands again.

Then came the Bishop of Canterbury, which was a noble clerk and an holy man, *20* and thus he said to Sir Mordred: "Sir, what will ye do? Will ye first displease God and sithen shame yourself and all knighthood? For is not King Arthur your uncle, and no farther but your mother's brother, and upon her he himself begat you, upon his own sister? Therefore how may you wed your own father's wife? And therefore, sir," said the Bishop, "leave this opinion, or else I shall curse you with book, bell, and candle." *25*

"Do thou thy worst," said Sir Mordred, "and I defy thee."

"Sir," said the Bishop, "wit you well I shall not fear me to do that me ought to do. And also ye noise that my lord Arthur is slain, and that is not so, and therefore ye will make a foul work in this land."

"Peace, thou false priest," said Sir Mordred, "for and thou chafe me any more, I *30* shall strike off thy head!"

So the Bishop departed, and did the cursing in the most orgulous wise that might be done. And then Sir Mordred sought the Bishop of Canterbury for to have slain him. Then the Bishop fled, and took part of his goods with him, and went nigh unto Glastonbury. And there he was a priest-hermit in a chapel, and lived in poverty and in *35* holy prayers, for well he understood that mischievous war was at hand.

Then Sir Mordred sought upon Queen Guinevere by letters and sendings, and by fair means and foul means, to have her to come out of the Tower of London; but all this availed nought, for she answered him shortly, openly and privily, that she had liefer slay herself than to be married with him. *40*

Then came there word unto Sir Mordred that King Arthur had raised the siege from Sir Lancelot and was coming homeward with a great host to be avenged upon Sir Mordred; wherefore Sir Mordred made writs unto all the barony of this land, and much people drew unto him, for then was the common voice among them that with King Arthur was never other life but war and strife, and with Sir Mordred was great joy and *45* bliss. Thus was King Arthur depraved, and evil said of; and many there were that King

---

6-8: Mordred was Arthur's illegitimate son by Arthur's half-sister, hence also his nephew (Arthur was earlier unaware of her relation to him). **11. longed:** belonged. **15. wist:** knew. **22. sithen:** since, then. **30. and:** if. **32. orgulous:** proud, haughty. **37. sendings:** messengers. **39. liefer:** rather. **46. depraved:** disparaged.

Arthur had brought up of nought, and given them lands, that might not then say him a good word.

Lo, ye all Englishmen, see ye not what a mischief here was? For he that was the most king and noblest knight of the world, and most loved the fellowship of noble knights, and by him they all were upholden, and yet might not these Englishmen hold them content with him. Lo thus was the old custom and usages of this land, and men say that we of this land have not yet lost that custom. Alas, this is a great default of us Englishmen, for there may no thing us please no term.

And so fared the people at that time. They were better pleased with Sir Mordred than they were with the noble King Arthur, and much people drew unto Sir Mordred, and said they would abide with him for better and for worse. And so Sir Mordred drew with a great host to Dover, for there he heard say that King Arthur would arrive. And so he thought to beat his own father from his own lands. And the most part of all England held with Sir Mordred, for the people were so new-fangle.

And so as Sir Mordred was at Dover with his host, so came King Arthur with a great navy of ships and galleys and carracks; and there was Sir Mordred ready awaiting upon his landing, to let his own father to land upon the land that he was king over. Then there was launching of great boats and small, and full of noble men of arms, and there was much slaughter of gentle knights, and many a full bold baron was laid full low, on both parties. But King Arthur was so courageous that there might no manner of knight let him to land, and his knights fiercely followed him. And so they landed maugre Sir Mordred's head and all his power, and put Sir Mordred aback, that he fled and all his people.

So when this battle was done, King Arthur let search his people that were hurt and dead. And than was noble Sir Gawain found in a great boat, lying more than half dead. When King Arthur knew that he was laid so low, he went unto him and so found him. And there the king made great sorrow out of measure, and took Sir Gawain in his arms, and thrice he there swooned. And then when he was waked, King Arthur said, "Alas, Sir Gawain, my sister's son, here now thou liest, the man in the world that I loved most. And now is my joy gone, for now, my nephew Sir Gawain, I will discover me unto you, that in your person and in Sir Lancelot I most had my joy and mine affiance, and now have I lost my joy of you both, wherefore all mine earthly joy is gone from me."

"Ah, mine uncle," said Sir Gawain, "now I will that ye wit that my death-day be come. And all, I may wit, mine own hastiness and my wilfulness, for through my wilfulness I was causer of mine own death, for I was this day hurt and smitten upon mine old wound the which Sir Lancelot gave me, and I feel myself that I must needs be dead by the hour of noon. And through me and my pride ye have all this shame and disease, for had that noble knight Sir Lancelot been with you, as he was and would have been, this unhappy war had never been begun, for he, through his noble knighthood and his noble blood, held all your cankered enemies in subjection and daunger. And now," said Sir Gawain, "ye shall miss Sir Lancelot. But alas that I would not accord with him! And therefore, fair uncle, I pray you that I may have paper, pen, and ink, that I may

---

63. let: hinder, prevent. **67–68. maugre . . . head:** in spite of Mordred's wish. **77. affiance:** trust. **84. disease:** trouble. **86. daunger:** captivity, obligation.

write unto Sir Lancelot a letter written with mine own hand." So when paper, pen, and ink was brought, then Sir Gawain was set up weakly by King Arthur, for he was shriven a little afore. And then he took his pen and wrote thus, as the French book maketh mention:

"Unto thee, Sir Lancelot, flower of all noble knights that ever I heard of or saw by my days, I, Sir Gawain, King Lot's son of Orkney, and sister's son unto the noble King Arthur, send thee greeting, letting thee to have knowledge that the tenth day of May I was smitten upon the old wound that thou gave me afore the city of Benwick, and through that wound I am come to my death-day. And I will that all the world wit that I, Sir Gawain, knight of the Table Round, sought my death, and not through thy deserving, but it was mine own seeking; wherefore I beseech thee, Sir Lancelot, to return again unto this realm and see my tomb and pray some prayer more or less for my soul. And this same day that I wrote this schedule, I was hurt to the death, which wound was first given of thine hand, Sir Lancelot, for of a more nobler man might I not be slain. Also, Sir Lancelot, for all the love that ever was between us, make no tarrying, but come over the sea in all goodly haste, that ye may with your noble knights rescue that noble king that made thee knight, for he is straitly bestad with an false traitor, which is my half-brother, Sir Mordred. For he hath crowned himself king, and would have wedded my lady Queen Guinevere, and so had he done had she not kept the Tower of London with strong hand. And so the tenth day of May last past my lord King Arthur and we all landed upon them at Dover, and there he put that false traitor Sir Mordred to flight. And so it there misfortuned me to be smitten upon the stroke that ye gave me of old. And the date of this letter was written but two hours and an half afore my death, written with mine own hand and subscribed with part of my heart's blood. And therefore I require thee, most famous knight of the world, that thou would see my tomb."

And then he wept and King Arthur both, and swooned. And when they were awaked both, the King made Sir Gawain to receive his sacrament, and then Sir Gawain prayed the King for to send for Sir Lancelot and to cherish him above all other knights. And so at the hour of noon Sir Gawain yielded up the ghost, and then the King let inter him in a chapel within Dover Castle, and there yet all men may see the skull of him, and the same wound is seen that Sir Lancelot gave him in battle.

Then was it told the King that Sir Mordred had pitched a new field upon Barham Down, and so upon the morn King Arthur rode thither to him, and there was a great battle betwixt them, and much people were slain on both parties; but at the last King Arthur's party stood best, and Sir Mordred and his party fled unto Canterbury. And then the King let search all the downs for his knights that were slain and interred them, and salved them with soft salves that full sore were wounded. Then much people drew unto King Arthur, and then they said that Sir Mordred warred upon King Arthur with wrong. And anon King Arthur drew him with his host down by the seaside westward, toward Salisbury. And there was a day assigned betwixt King Arthur and Sir Mordred, that they should meet upon a down beside Salisbury and not far from the seaside; and this day was assigned on Monday after Trinity Sunday, whereof King Arthur was passing glad that he might be avenged upon Sir Mordred. Then Sir Mordred raised much people

---

91. French book: i.e., one of the French Arthurian romances Malory was using as sources. **101. schedule:** note. **105. bestad:** beset.

about London, for they of Kent, Sussex, and Surrey, Essex, Suffolk, and Norfolk held the most part with Sir Mordred; and many a full noble knight drew unto him and also to the King, but they that loved Sir Lancelot drew unto Sir Mordred.

So upon Trinity Sunday at night King Arthur dreamed a wonderful dream, and in his dream him seemed that he saw upon a chaflet a chair, and the chair was fast to a wheel, and thereupon sat King Arthur in the richest cloth of gold that might be made. And the king thought there was under him, far from him, an hideous deep black water, and therein was all manner of serpents and worms and wild beasts foul and horrible. And suddenly the King thought that the wheel turned up-so-down, and he fell among the serpents, and every beast took him by a limb. And then the King cried as he lay in his bed, "Help! Help!" And then knights, squires, and yeomen awaked the King, and then he was so amazed that he wist not where he was, and then so he awaked until it was nigh day, and then he fell on slumbering again, not sleeping nor thoroughly waking. So the King seemed verily that there came Sir Gawain unto him with a number of fair ladies with him, so when King Arthur saw him he said, "Welcome, my sister's son; I weened ye had been dead, and now I see thee on-live, much am I beholden unto almighty Jesu. Ah, fair nephew, what been these ladies that hither come with you?"

"Sir," said Sir Gawain, "all these be ladies for whom I have foughten for when I was man living, and all these are those that I did battle for in righteous quarrels, and God hath given them that grace at their great prayer, because I did battle for them for their right, that they should bring me hither unto you. Thus much hath given me leave God for to warn you of your death, for and you fight as to-morn with Sir Mordred, as ye both have assigned, doubt ye not that ye must be slain, and the most part of your people on both parties. And for the great grace and goodness that Almighty Jesu hath unto you, and for pity of you and many more other good men there shall be slain, God hath sent me to you of his special grace to give you warning that in no wise ye do battle as to-morn, but that ye take a treaty for a month-day, and proffer you largely so that to-morn ye put in a delay, for within a month shall come Sir Lancelot with all his noble knights and rescue you worshipfully and slay Sir Mordred and all that ever will hold with him."

Then Sir Gawain and all the ladies vanished, and anon the King called upon his knights, squires, and yeomen and charged them wightly to fetch his noble lords and wise bishops unto him. And when they were come the King told them of his avision, that Sir Gawain had told him and warned him that and he fought on the morn he should be slain. Then the King commanded Sir Lucan the Butler and his brother Sir Bedivere the Bold, with two bishops with them, and charged them in any wise to take a treaty for a month-day with Sir Mordred. "And spare not: proffer him lands and goods as much as ye think reasonable."

So then they departed and came to Sir Mordred where he had a grim host of an hundred thousand, and there they entreated Sir Mordred long time. And at the last Sir Mordred was agreed for to have Cornwall and Kent by King Arthur's days, and after that all England, after the days of King Arthur. Then were they condescended that King Arthur and Sir Mordred should meet betwixt both their hosts, and everich of them

---

136. him seemed: it seemed to him; **chaflet:** scaffold, platform. **139. worms:** snakes, dragons. **147. weened:** thought. **158. proffer:** request. **162. wightly:** quickly. **163. avision:** dream. **172. condescended:** agreed. **173. everich:** each.

should bring fourteen persons. And so they came with this word unto Arthur. Then said he, "I am glad that this is done," and so he went into the field. *175*

And when King Arthur should depart he warned all his host that and they see any sword drawn, "look ye come on fiercely and slay that traitor, Sir Mordred, for I in no wise trust him." In like wise Sir Mordred warned his host that "And ye see any manner of sword drawn, look that ye come on fiercely and so slay all that ever before you standeth, for in no wise I will not trust for this treaty." And in the same wise said Sir *180* Mordred unto his host: "For I know well my father will be avenged upon me."

And so they met as their appointment was, and were agreed and accorded thoroughly. And wine was fetched and they drank together. Right so came out an adder of a little heath-bush, and it stung a knight in the foot; and so when the knight felt him so stung, he looked down and saw the adder, and anon he drew his sword to slay the *185* adder, and thought none other harm. And when the host on both parties saw that sword drawn, then they blew beams, trumpets, and horns and shouted grimly; and so both hosts dressed them together. And King Arthur took his horse and said, "Alas, this unhappy day!" and so rode to his party, and Sir Mordred in like wise.

And never since was there never seen a more dolefuller battle in no Christian land, *190* for there was but rushing and tiding, foining and striking, and many a grim word was there spoken of either to other, and many a deadly stroke. But ever King Arthur rode throughout the battle of Sir Mordred many times and did full nobly, as a noble king should do, and at all times he fainted never. And Sir Mordred did his devoir that day and put himself in great peril. And thus they fought all the long day, and never stinted till the *195* noble knights were laid to the cold earth. And ever they fought still till it was near night, and by then was there an hundred thousand laid dead upon the earth. Then was King Arthur wood-wroth out of measure, when he saw his people so slain from him. And so he looked about him and could see no more of all his host and good knights left, no more on-live but two knights; the one was Sir Lucan the Butler, and his brother Sir *200* Bedivere; and yet they were full sore wounded.

"Jesu mercy," said the King, "where are all my noble knights become? Alas, that ever I should see this doleful day! For now," said King Arthur, "I am come to mine end. But would to God," said he, "that I wist now where was that traitor Sir Mordred that hath caused all this mischief." Then King Arthur looked about and was ware where *205* stood Sir Mordred leaning upon his sword among a great heap of dead men. "Now give me my spear," said King Arthur unto Sir Lucan, "for yonder I have espied the traitor that all this woe hath wrought."

"Sir, let him be," said Sir Lucan, "for he is unhappy. And if ye pass this unhappy day ye shall be right well revenged upon him. And, good lord, remember ye of your *210* night's dream and what the spirit of Sir Gawain told you tonight, and yet God of his great goodness hath preserved you hitherto. And for God's sake, my lord, leave off by this, for, blessed be God, ye have won the field, for yet we been here three on-live, and with Sir Mordred is not one on-live. And therefore if ye leave off now, this wicked day of destiny is past." *215*

---

187. beams: clarions. **191. foining:** thrusting. **193. battle:** battalion, host. **194. devoir:** duty. **198. wood-wroth:** mad with anger. **209. unhappy:** harmful, unlucky (i.e., for Arthur).

"Now tide me death, tide me life," said the King, "now I see him yonder alone, he shall never escape mine hands, for at a better avail shall I never have him."

"God speed you well!" said Sir Bedivere.

Then the King got his spear in both his hands and ran toward Sir Mordred, crying and saying, "Traitor, now is thy death-day come!" And when Sir Mordred saw King 220 Arthur he ran until him with his sword drawn in his hand, and there King Arthur smote Sir Mordred under the shield with a foin of his spear, throughout the body more than a fathom. And when Sir Mordred felt that he had his death's wound he thrust himself with the might that he had up to the burr of King Arthur's spear, and right so he smote his father King Arthur, with his sword holden in both his hands, upon the side of the head, 225 that the sword pierced the helmet and the tay of the brain. And therewith Sir Mordred dashed down stark dead to the earth, and noble King Arthur fell in a swoon to the earth, and there he swooned oftentimes, and Sir Lucan and Sir Bedivere oftentimes hove him up. And so weakly betwixt them they led him to a little chapel not far from the sea, and when the King was there, him thought him reasonably eased. 230

Then heard they people cry in the field. "Now go thou, Sir Lucan," said the King, "and do me to wit what betokens that noise in the field." So Sir Lucan departed, for he was grievously wounded in many places, and so as he yede he saw and hearkened by the moonlight how that pillagers and robbers were come into the field to pillage and to rob many a full noble knight of brooches and bees and of many a good ring and many a rich 235 jewel. And who that were not dead all out, there they slew them for their harness and their riches.

When Sir Lucan understood this work, he came to the King as soon as he might and told him all what he had heard and seen. "Therefore by my rede," said Sir Lucan, "it is best that we bring you to some town." 240

"I would it were so," said the King, "but I may not stand, my head works so. Ah, Sir Lancelot," said King Arthur, "this day have I sore missed thee. And alas that ever I was against thee, for now have I my death, whereof Sir Gawain warned in my dream."

Then Sir Lucan took up the king the one part and Sir Bedivere the other part, and in the lifting up the King swooned, and in the lifting Sir Lucan fell in a swoon, that part of his guts 245 fell out of his body, and therewith the noble knight's heart burst. And when the King awoke he beheld Sir Lucan, how he lay foaming at the mouth and part of his guts lay at his feet.

"Alas," said the King, "this is to me a full heavy sight, to see this noble duke so die for my sake, for he would have helped me that had more need of help than I. Alas that he would not complain him, for his heart was so set to help me. Now Jesu have mercy 250 upon his soul." Then Sir Bedivere wept for the death of his brother. "Now leave this mourning and weeping, gentle knight," said the King, "for all this will not avail me. For wit thou well, and I might live myself, the death of Sir Lucan would grieve me evermore. But my time passeth on fast," said the King. "Therefore," said King Arthur unto Sir Bedivere, "take thou here Excalibur my good sword, and go with it to yonder 255 water's side, and when thou commest there, I charge thee throw my sword in that water, and come again and tell me what thou seest there."

---

221. until: unto, to. **226. tay:** case, outer membrane (i.e., skull). **233. yede:** went. **235. bees:** arm or neck bracelets. **241. works:** aches.

"My lord," said Sir Bedivere, "your commandment shall be done, and lightly bring you word again." So Sir Bedivere departed, and by the way he beheld that noble sword, and the pommel and the haft was all precious stones. And then he said to himself, "If I throw this rich sword in the water, thereof shall never come good, but harm and loss." And then Sir Bedivere hid Excalibur under a tree, and so as soon as he might he came again unto the King and said he had been at the water and had thrown the sword in to the water.   *260*

"What saw thou there?" said the King.   *265*

"Sir," he said, "I saw nothing but waves and winds."

"That is untruly said of thee," said the King. "And therefore go thou lightly again, and do my commandment; as thou art to me lief and dear, spare not, but throw it in."

Then Sir Bedivere returned again and took the sword in his hand; and yet him thought sin and shame to throw away that noble sword, and so eft he hid the sword and returned again and told the King that he had been at the water and done his commandment.   *270*

"What sawest thou there?" said the King.

"Sir," he said, "I saw nothing but waters wap and waves wan."

"Ah, traitor unto me and untrue," said King Arthur, "now hast thou betrayed me twice. Who would have weened that thou that hast been to me so lief and dear, and thou art named a noble knight, that thou would betray me for the riches of this sword. But now go again lightly, for thy long tarrying putteth me in great jeopardy of my life, for I have taken cold. And but if thou do now as I bid thee, if ever I may see thee I shall slay thee mine own hands, for thou wouldst for my rich sword see me dead."   *275*

280

Then Sir Bedivere departed and went to the sword and lightly took it up, and so he went unto the water's side, and there he bound the girdle about the hilt, and threw the sword as far into the water as he might. And there came an arm and an hand above the water and took it and clenched it, and shook it thrice and brandished; and then vanished away the hand with the sword into the water. So Sir Bedivere came again to the King and told him what he saw. "Alas," said the King, "help me hence, for I dread me I have tarried overlong." Then Sir Bedivere took the King upon his back and so went with him to that water's side. And when they were at the water's side, even fast by the bank hove a little barge with many fair ladies in it, and among them all was a queen, and all they had black hoods, and all they wept and shrieked when they saw King Arthur. "Now put me into that barge," said the King. And so he did softly, and there received him three ladies with great mourning. And so they set him down, and in one of their laps King Arthur laid his head.   *285*

290

And then the Queen said, "Ah, my dear brother, why have ye tarried so long from me? Alas, thy wound on your head hath caught overmuch cold."   *295*

And anon they rowed fromward the land, and Sir Bedivere beheld all those ladies go fromward him. Then Sir Bedivere cried and said, "Ah, my lord Arthur, what shall become of me, now ye go from me and leave me here alone among mine enemies?"

"Comfort thyself," said the King, "and do as well as thou mayest, for in me is no trust for to trust in. For I must into the vale of Avalon to heal me of my grievous wound.   *300*

---

258. lightly: quickly. **274. wap . . . wan:** lap . . . dark.

And if thou hear nevermore of me, pray for my soul." But ever the Queen and ladies wept and shrieked, that it was pity to hear.

And as soon as Sir Bedivere had lost the sight of the barge he wept and wailed, and so took the forest and went all that night. And in the morning he was ware, betwixt two holts hoar, of a chapel and an hermitage. Then was Sir Bedivere fain, and thither he 305 went, and when he came into the chapel he saw where lay an hermit grovelling on all four; fast thereby a tomb was new graven. When the hermit saw Sir Bedivere he knew him well, for he was but little tofore Bishop of Canterbury that Sir Mordred fleamed. "Sir," said Sir Bedivere, "what man is there here interred that ye pray so fast for?"

"Fair son," said the hermit, "I wot not verily but by deeming. But this same night, at 310 midnight, here came a number of ladies and brought here a dead corse and prayed me to inter him. And here they offered an hundred tapers, and they gave me a thousand bezants."

"Alas," said Sir Bedivere, "that was my lord King Arthur, which lieth here graven in this chapel." Then Sir Bedivere swooned, and when he awoke he prayed the hermit 315 that he might abide with him still, there to live with fasting and prayers, "for from hence will I never go," said Sir Bedivere, "by my will, but all the days of my life here to pray for my lord Arthur."

"Sir, ye are welcome to me," said the hermit, "for I know you better than ye ween that I do, for ye are Sir Bedivere the Bold, and the full noble duke Sir Lucan de Butler 320 was your brother." Then Sir Bedivere told the hermit all as ye have heard tofore, and so he belaft with the hermit that was beforehand Bishop of Canterbury. And there Sir Bedivere put upon him poor clothes, and served the hermit full lowly in fasting and in prayers.

Thus of Arthur I find no more written in books that been authorized, nor more of 325 the very certainty of his death heard I never read, but thus was he led away in a ship wherein were three queens; that one was King Arthur's sister, Queen Morgan le Fay, the tother was the Queen of North Galis, and the third was the Queen of the Waste Lands. Also there was Nimue, the chief lady of the lake, which had wedded Sir Pelleas, the good knight; and this lady had done much for King Arthur. And this Dame Nimue 330 would never suffer Sir Pelleas to be in no place where he should be in danger of his life, and so he lived unto the uttermost of his days with her in great rest.

Now more of the death of King Arthur could I never find, but that these ladies brought him to his burials, and such one was buried there that the hermit bore witness that sometime was Bishop of Canterbury. But yet the hermit knew not in certain that he 335 was verily the body of King Arthur, for this tale Sir Bedivere, a knight of the Table Round, made it to be written. Yet some men say in many parts of England that King Arthur is not dead, but had by the will of our Lord Jesu into another place; and men say that he shall come again, and he shall win the Holy Cross. Yet I will not say that it shall be so, but rather I will say, here in this world he changed his life. And many men say 340 that there is written upon his tomb this verse: *Hic jacet Arthurus, Rex Quondam Rexque Futurus.*

---

307. graven: dug. **308. fleamed:** caused to flee. **314. graven:** buried. **322. belaft:** remained. **341-42:** *Hic . . . Futurus:* (Latin) Here lies Arthur, once King, future King.

And thus leave I here Sir Bedivere with the hermit that dwelled that time in a chapel beside Glastonbury, and there was his hermitage. And so they lived in prayers and fastings and great abstinence. *345*

And when Queen Guinevere understood that King Arthur was dead and all the noble knights, Sir Mordred and all the remnant, then she stole away and five ladies with her, and so she went to Amesbury, and there she let make herself a nun, and wore white clothes and black, and great penance she took upon her, as ever did sinful woman in this land. And never creature could make her merry, but ever she lived in fasting, prayers, *350* and alms-deeds, that all manner of people marvelled how virtuously she was changed.

(1469; 1485)

 WILLIAM CAXTON
England, c.1422-1491

from translation of *THE FABLES OF AESOP*

THE WOLF AND THE CRANE

Whosoever doth any good to the evil man, he sinneth, as Aesop saith; for of any good which is done to the evil cometh no profit, whereof Aesop rehearseth to us such a fable: A wolf ate and devoured a sheep of whose bones he had one in his throat which he could not have out, and sore it grieved him. Then went the wolf and prayed the crane that she would draw out of his throat the bone, and the crane put her neck into his throat *5* and drew out the bone, whereby the wolf was whole. And the crane demanded of him to be paid of her salary. And the wolf answered to her, "Thou art well uncunning, and no good cunning, remembering the good that I have done to thee, for when thou haddest thy neck within my throat, if I would I might have eat thee." And thus it appeareth by the fable how no profit cometh of any good which is done to the evil. *10*

THE RAVEN AND THE FOX

They that be glad and joyful of the praising of flatterers ofttimes repent them thereof, whereof Aesop rehearseth to us such a fable: A raven which was upon a tree and held with his bill a cheese, the which cheese the fox desired much to have; wherefore the fox went and praised him by such words as follow. "O gentle raven, thou art the fairest bird of all other birds, for thy feathers been so fair, so bright, and so resplendishing, and can also so *5* well sing; if thou hadst the voice clear and small thou shouldst be the most happy of all

WOLF AND CRANE   7. uncunning: foolish.   RAVEN AND FOX   Cf. Chaucer's "Nun's Priest's Tale" (pp. 64-72).

other birds." And the fool which heard the flattering words of the fox began to open his bill for to sing. And then the cheese fell to the ground and the fox took and ate it. And when the raven saw that for his vainglory he was deceived, waxed heavy and sorrowful and repented him of that he had believed the fox. And this fable teacheth us how men ought not to be *10* glad nor take rejoicing in the words of caitiff folk nor also to believe flattery nor vainglory.

THE FROGS AND JUPITER

Nothing is so good as to live justly and at liberty, for freedom and liberty is better than any gold or silver, whereof Aesop rehearseth to us such a fable: There were frogs which were in ditches and ponds at their liberty; they altogether of one assent and of one will made a request to Jupiter that he would give them a king. And Jupiter began thereof to marvel. And for their king he casted to them a great piece of wood, which made a great *5* sound and noise in the water, whereof all the frogs had great dread and feared much. And after they approached to their king for to make obeisance unto him, and when they perceived that it was but a piece of wood they turned again to Jupiter, praying him sweetly that he would give to them another king. And Jupiter gave to them the heron for to be their king. And then the heron began to enter into the water and eat them one after *10* other. And when the frogs saw that their king destroyed and ate them thus, they began tenderly to weep, saying in this manner to the god Jupiter: "Right high and right mighty god Jupiter, please thee to deliver us from the throat of this dragon and false tyrant which eateth us the one after another." And he said to them, "The king which ye have demanded shall be your master, for when men have that which men ought to have, they ought to be *15* joyful and glad; and he that hath liberty ought to keep it well, for nothing is better than liberty, for liberty should not be well sold for all the gold and silver of all the world."

THE FOX AND THE RAISINS

He is not wise that desireth to have a thing which he may not have, as reciteth this fable of a fox which looked and beheld the raisins that grew upon an high vine, the which raisins he much desired for to eat them. And when he saw that none he might get, he turned his sorrow into joy and said, "These raisins been sour, and if I had some I would not eat them." And therefore this fable sheweth that he is wise which faineth not to *5* desire that thing the which he may not have.

THE ANT AND THE CIGALE

It is good to purvey himself in the summer season of such things whereof he shall miss and have need of in winter season, as thou mayest see by this present fable of the cigale which in the winter-time went and demanded of the ant some of her corn for to eat. And then the ant said to the cigale, "What hast thou done all the summer last passed?" And the cigale answered, "I have sung." And after said the ant to her, "Of my corn shalt not *5* thou none have. And if thou has sung all the summer, dance now in winter." And

---

11. caitiff: vile, base, basely wicked. **FOX AND RAISINS** Raisins: i.e. grapes. **ANT AND CIGALE** Cigale: cicada (better known as "The Fable of the Ant and the Grasshopper"). **1. purvey:** provide.

therefore there is one time for to do some labour and work, and one time for to have rest; for he that worketh not nor doth no good shall have oft at his teeth great cold and lack at his need.

THE TREE AND THE REED

None ought to be proud against his lord, but ought to humble himself toward him, as this fable rehearseth to us of a great tree which would never bow him for none wind, and a reed which was at his foot bowed himself as much as the wind would. And the tree said to him, "Why dost thou not abide still as I do?" And the reed answered, "I have not the might which thou hast." And the tree said to the reed proudly, "Then have I more *5* strength than thou." And anon after came a great wind which threw down to the ground the said great tree, and the reed abode in his own being. For the proud shall be always humbled and the meek and humble shall be enhanced, for the root of all virtue is obedience and humility.

THE CHILD WHICH KEPT THE SHEEP

He which is accustomed to make lesings, howbeit that he say truth, yet men believe him not, as rehearseth this fable of a child which sometime kept sheep, the which cried oft without cause, saying, "Alas, for God's love succour you me, for the wolf will eat my sheep." And when the labourers that cultivated and ered the earth about him heard his cry, they come to help him, the which came so many times and found nothing; and as *5* they saw that there were no wolves, they returned to their labourage. And the child did so many times for to play him. It happed on a day that the wolf came, and the child cried as he was accustomed to do, and because that the labourers supposed that it had not been truth, abode still at their labour, wherefore the wolf did eat the sheep. For men believe not lightly him which is known for a liar. *10*

THE ANT AND THE COLUMBE

None ought to be slowful of the good which he receiveth of other, as rehearseth this fable of an ant which came to a fountain for to drink, and as she would have drunk she fell within the fountain, upon the which was a columbe or dove which, seeing that the ant should have been drowned without help, took a branch of a tree and cast it to her for to save herself. And the ant went anon upon the branch and saved her. And anon after *5* came a falconer which would have take the dove. And then the ant, which saw that the falconer dressed his nets, came to his foot and so fast pricked it that she caused him to smite the earth with his foot, and therewith made so great noise that the dove heard it, wherefore she flew away or the gin and nets were all set. And therefore none ought to forget the benefit which he hath received of some other, for slowfulness is a great sin. *10*

(1484)

THE CHILD WHICH KEPT THE SHEEP   (Better known as "The Boy Who Cried Wolf.") **1. lesings:** lies. **4. ered:** ploughed.   **ANT AND COLUMBE** **1. slowful:** ungrateful. **9. or:** ere, before.

Prologue to the English translation of Virgil's AENEID
(from the French *Livre des Eneydes*, 1483)

After diverse works made, translated, and achieved, having no work in hand, I, sitting in
my study where as lay many diverse pamphlets and books, happened that to my hand
came a little book in French, which late was translated out of Latin by some noble clerk
of France, which book is named *Aeneid*, made in Latin by that noble poet and great
clerk Virgil, which book I saw over and read therein, how after the general destruction   5
of the great Troy, Aeneas departed, bearing his old father Anchises upon his shoulders,
his little son Ascanius on his hand, his wife with much other people following, and how
he shipped and departed, with all the history of his adventures that he had ere he came to
the achievement of his conquest of Italy, as all along shall be showed in this present
book. In which book I had great pleasure, because of the fair and honest terms and   10
words in French which I never saw before like, nor none so pleasant nor so well
ordered; which book, as me seemed, should be much requisite to noble men to see, as
well for the eloquence as the histories. How well that many hundred years past was the
said book of *Aeneid*, with other works, made and learned daily in schools, especially in
Italy and other places, which history the said Virgil made in metre.   15

    And when I had advised me in this said book, I deliberated and concluded to
translate it into English, and forthwith took a pen and ink and wrote a leaf or twain
which I oversaw again to correct it. And when I saw the fair and strange terms therein, I
doubted that it should not please some gentlemen which late blamed me, saying that in
my translations I had overcurious terms which could not be understood of common   20
people, and desired me to use old and homely terms in my translations. And fain would
I satisfy every man, and so to do, took an old book and read therein, and certainly the
English was so rude and broad that I could not well understand it. And also my Lord
Abbot of Westminster did do show to me late, certain evidences written in Old English,
for to reduce it into our English now used. And certainly it was written in such wise that   25
it was more like to Dutch than English; I could not reduce nor bring it to be understood.

    And certainly our language now used varyeth far from that which was used and
spoken when I was born. For we Englishmen be born under the domination of the moon,
which is never steadfast but ever wavering, waxing one season and waneth and
decreaseth another season. And that common English that is spoken in one shire varyeth   30
from another. Insomuch that in my days happened that certain merchants were in a ship
in Thames, for to have sailed over the sea into Zeeland, and for lack of wind they tarried
at a foreland, and went to land for to refresh them. And one of them named Sheffield, a
mercer, came into an house and asked for meat, and especially he asked after eggs. And
the good wife answered that she could speak no French. And the merchant was angry,   35
for he also could speak no French, but would have had eggs and she understood him not.
And then at last another said that he would have eyren; then the good wife said that she
understood him well. Lo, what should a man in these days now write, *eggs* or *eyren*?

PROLOGUE TO VIRGIL'S AENEID   **3. clerk:** scholar. **19. doubted:** feared.

Certainly it is hard to please every man, because of diversity and change of
language. For in these days every man that is in any reputation in his country will utter   *40*
his communication and matters in such manners and terms that few men shall
understand them. And some honest and great clerks have been with me, and desired me
to write the most curious terms that I could find. And thus between plain rude and
curious, I stand abashed. But in my judgment the common terms that be daily used been
lighter to be understood than the old and ancient English. And for as much as this   *45*
present book is not for a rude uplandish man to labour therein nor read it, but only for a
clerk and a noble gentleman that feeleth and understandeth in feats of arms, in love, and
in noble chivalry, therefore in a mean between both I have reduced and translated this
said book into our English, not over rude nor curious, but in such terms as shall be
understood, by God's grace, according to my copy. And if any man will entermete in   *50*
reading of it, and findeth such terms that he can not understand, let him go read and
learn Virgil or the epistles of Ovid, and there he shall see and understand lightly all — if
he have a good reader and informer. For this book is not for every rude and uncunning
man to see but to clerks and very gentlemen that understand gentleness and science.

Then I pray all them that shall read in this little treatise, to hold me excused for the   *55*
translating of it, for I acknowledge myself ignorant of cunning to enprise on me so high
and noble a work. But I pray master John Skelton, late created poet laureate in the
University of Oxford, to oversee and correct this said book, and to address and expound
where as shall be found fault to them that shall require it. For he hath late translated the
epistles of Tully and the book of Diodorus Siculus, and diverse other works out of Latin   *60*
into English, not in rude and old language but in polished and ornate terms craftily, as
he that hath read Virgil, Ovid, Tully, and all the other noble poets and orators to me
unknown. And also he hath read the nine muses, and understands their musical sciences,
and to whom of them each science is appropriated. I suppose he hath drunken of
Helicon's well. Then I pray him, and such other, to correct, add, or minish where as he   *65*
or they shall find fault. For I have but followed my copy in French as nigh as me is
possible. And if any word be said therein well, I am glad; and if otherwise, I submit my
said book to their correction.

Which book I present unto the high born my tocoming natural and sovereign lord,
Arthur, by the grace of God, Prince of Wales, Duke of Cornwall, and Earl of Chester,   *70*
first begotten son and heir unto our most dread natural and sovereign lord, and most
Christian king, Henry the VII, by the grace of God, King of England and of France, and
Lord of Ireland, beseeching his noble grace to receive it in thank of me, his most humble
subject and servant. And I shall pray unto almighty God for his prosperous increasing in
virtue, wisdom, and humanity, that he may be equal with the most renowned of all his   *75*
noble progenitors. And so to live in this present life that after this transitory life he and
we all may come to everlasting life in heaven. Amen.

(1490)

---

45. lighter: easier. **50. entermete:** introduce himself, meddle, i.e., busy himself. **53. informer:** teacher and adviser. **56. enprise:** enterprise,
undertake. **65. minish:** diminish. **69. tocoming:** future.

ROBERT HENRYSON
Scotland, c.1424-c.1506

ROBENE AND MAKYNE

Robene sat on gud grene hill,
Kepand a flok of fe.
Mirry Makyne said him till,
"Robin, thow rew on me!
I haif the luvit lowd and still, 5
Thir yeiris two or thre;
My dule in dern bot gif thow dill,
Dowtles but dreid I de."

Robene ansert, "Be the rude,
Nathing of lufe I knaw, 10
Bot keipis my scheip undir yone wud;
Lo, quhair thay raik on raw.
Quhat hes marrit the in thy mude,
Makyne, to me thow schaw.
Or quhat is lufe, or to be lude? 15
Fane wald I leir that law."

"At luvis lair gife thow will leir,
Tak thair ane A B C:
Be heynd, courtass, and fair of feir,
Wyse, hardy, and fre, 20
So that no denger do the deir
Quhat dule in dern thow dre.
Preiss the with pane at all poweir,
Be patient and previe."

Robene anserit hir agane, 25
"I wait nocht quhat is luve.
Bot I haif mervell incertane
Quhat makis the this wanrufe:
The weddir is fair, and I am fane,
My scheip gois haill aboif; 30
And we wald play us in this plane,
They wald us bayth reproif."

"Robene, tak tent unto my taill,
And wirk all as I reid,
And thow sall haif my hairt all haill, 35
Eik and my madinheid.
Sen God sendis bute for baill,
And for murning remeid,
I dern with the bot gif I daill,
Dowtless I am bot deid." 40

"Makyne, tomorne this ilk a tyde
And ye will meit me heir,
Peraventure my scheip ma gang besyd,
Quhill we haif liggit full neir;
Bot mawgre haif I and I byd, 45
Fra thay begin to steir;
Quhat lyis on hairt I will nocht hyd;
Makyn, than mak gud cheir."

"Robene, thow reivis me roif and rest;
I luve bot the allone." 50
"Makyne, adew; the sone gois west;
The day is neir hand gone."
"Robene, in dule I am so drest
That lufe wilbe my bone."
"Ga lufe, Makyne, quhair evir thow list, 55
For lemman I lue none."

"Robene, I stand in sic a styll;
I sicht, and that full sair."
"Makyne, I haif bene heir this quhyle;
At hame God gif I wair." 60
"My huny, Robene, talk ane quhill,
Gif thow will do no mair."
"Makyne, sum othir man begyle,
For hamewart I will fair."

ROBENE AND MAKYNE   **2. fe:** animals, sheep. **3. till:** to. **4. rew:** rue. **5. the:** thee. **6. thir:** these. **7. dule:** grief, misery; **dern:** secret; **dill:** soothe, assuage. **9. be the rude:** by the rood. **12. raik on raw:** wander in a row. **13. marrit:** marred, upset; **mude:** mood, mind. **15. lude:** loved. **16. leir:** learn. **17. lair:** lore. **19. heynd:** gentle; **feir:** appearance, demeanour. **21. denger:** power, disdain; **deir:** harm. **22. dre:** endure. **23. preiss:** press, strive. **24. previe:** privy, secret. (Lines 19-24 constitute a succinct statement of the rules of Courtly Love.) **26. wait:** know. **28. wanrufe:** restless, distressed. **29. fane:** happy. **30. haill:** whole, healthy. **33. tent:** attention. **34. reid:** advise. **37. bute:** boot, remedy, comfort; **baill:** bale. **39. I dern:** in secret; **bot gif:** but if, unless; **daill:** deal. **43. besyd:** beside, astray. **45. mawgre:** ill will, displeasure; **byd:** bide. **46. steir:** stir. **49. reivis:** reave; **roif:** quiet, ease (i.e., **roif and rest:** peace of mind). **54. bone:** bane. **56. lemman:** lover, sweetheart. **57. styll:** plight. **58. sicht:** sigh.

Robene on his wayis went, 65
Als licht as leif of tre;
Makyne murnit in hir intent,
And trowd him nevir to se.
Robene brayd attour the bent;
Than Makyne cryit on hie, 70
"Now ma thow sing, for I am schent.
Quhat alis lufe at me?"

Makyne went hame withowttin faill,
Full wery eftir cowth weip.
Than Robene in a fulfair daill 75
Assemblit all his scheip.
Be that sum pairte of Makynis aill
Outthrow his hairt cowd creip,
He fallowit hir fast thair till assaill,
And till hir tuke gude keip. 80

"Abyd, abyd, thow fair Makyne,
A word for ony thing!
For all my luve it salbe thyne,
Withowttin depairting.
All haill thy harte for till haif myne 85
Is all my cuvating;
My scheip tomorne quhill houris nyne
Will neid of no keping."

"Robene, thow hes hard soung and say,
In gestis and storeis auld, 90
The man that will nocht quhen he may
Sall haif nocht quhen he wald.
I pray to Jesu every day,
Mot eik thair cairis cauld
That first preissis with the to play 95
Be firth, forrest or fawld."

"Makyne, the nicht is soft and dry,
The wedder is warme and fair,
And the grene woid rycht neir us by
To walk attour all quhair. 100
Thair ma na janglour us espy,
That is to lufe contrair;
Thairin, Makyne, bath ye and I
Unsene we ma repair."

"Robene, that warld is all away, 105
And quyt brocht till ane end,
And nevir agane thairto perfay
Sall it be as thow wend;
For of my pane thow maid it play,
And all in vane I spend. 110
As thow hes done, sa sall I say,
Murne on; I think to mend."

"Makyne, the howp of all my heill,
My hairt on the is sett,
And evirmair to the be leill, 115
Quhill I may leif but lett;
Nevir to faill, as utheris feill,
Quhat grace that evir I gett."
"Robene, with the I will nocht deill.
Adew, for thus we mett." 120

Makyne went hame blyth annewche,
Attour the holtis hair;
Robene murnit, and Makyne lewche;
Scho sang, he sichit sair;
And so left him, bayth wo and wrewche, 125
In dolour and in cair,
Kepand his hird under a huche,
Amang the holtis hair.

---

67. intent: mind, thought. **69. brayd:** hurried off; **attour:** over; **bent:** grass. **71. schent:** destroyed. **72. alis:** ails. **74. cowth:** could, did. **77. be that:** by that time, by then. **78. outthrow:** throughout. **80. tuke . . . keip:** paid . . . heed, notice, attention. **89. hard:** heard. **90. gestis:** gest(e)s, tales. **94. eik:** eke, increase. **96. firth:** coppice, small wood. **99. woid:** wood. **100. attour:** about. **101. janglour:** gossip, talebearer. **107. perfay:** parfay, by my faith. **108. wend:** weened, thought. **113. heill:** health. **115. leill:** loyal, true. **116. leif:** love, praise; **but lett:** without hindrance. **121. annewche:** enough. **122. holtis:** holts, copses; **hair:** hoar. **123. lewche:** laughed. **127. huche:** cliff.

WILLIAM DUNBAR
Scotland, c.1460-c.1513

LAMENT FOR THE MAKARIS

I that in heill wes and gladnes
Am trublit now with gret seiknes
And feblit with infermite;
  Timor mortis conturbat me.

Our plesance heir is all vane glory,   5
This fals warld is bot transitory,
The flesch is brukle, the Fend is sle;
  Timor mortis conturbat me.

The stait of man dois change and vary,
Now sound, now seik, now blith, now sary,
Now dansand mery, now like to dee;   11
  Timor mortis conturbat me.

No stait in erd heir standis sickir;
As with the wynd wavis the wickir
Wavis this warldis vanite;   15
  Timor mortis conturbat me.

On to the ded gois all estatis,
Princis, prelotis, and potestatis,
Baith riche and pur of al degre;
  Timor mortis conturbat me.   20

He takis the knychtis in the feild,
Anarmyt under helme and scheild;
Victour he is at all mellie;
  Timor mortis conturbat me.

That strang unmercifull tyrand   25
Takis, on the moderis breist sowkand,
The bab full of benignite;
  Timor mortis conturbat me.

He takis the campion in the stour,
The capitane closit in the tour,   30
The lady in bour full of bewte;
  Timor mortis conturbat me.

He sparis no lord for his piscence,
Na clerk for his intelligence;
His awfull strak may no man fle;   35
  Timor mortis conturbat me.

Art-magicianis, and astrologgis,
Rethoris, logicianis, and theologgis,
Thame helpis no conclusionis sle;
  Timor mortis conturbat me.   40

In medicyne the most practicianis,
Lechis, surrigianis, and phisicianis,
Thame self fra ded may not supple;
  Timor mortis conturbat me.

I se that makaris amang the laif   45
Playis heir ther pageant, syne gois to graif;
Sparit is nocht ther faculte;
  Timor mortis conturbat me.

He hes done petuously devour
The noble Chaucer, of makaris flour,   50
The Monk of Bery, and Gower, all thre;
  Timor mortis conturbat me.

The gude Syr Hew of Eglintoun,
And eik Heryot, and Wyntoun,
He hes tane out of this cuntre;   55
  Timor mortis conturbat me.

LAMENT FOR THE MAKARIS   1. heill: health. **4:** Latin, meaning "The fear of death distresses me" — part of the response in the seventh lesson of the Office of the Dead. **7. brukle:** brittle, i.e., weak, frail; **Fend:** Fiend (i.e., Devil); **sle:** sly, cunning. **11. dansand:** dancing. **13. erd:** earth; **sickir:** secure. **14. wickir:** willow. **18. potestatis:** potentates. **22. Anarmyt:** armed. **23. mellie:** melee. **26. sowkand:** sucking. **29. stour:** battle. **31. bour:** bower. **33. piscence:** puissance. **35. strak:** stroke. **38. Rethoris:** rhetors. **41. most:** chief, greatest. **42. Lechis:** leeches, doctors. **43. supple:** help, deliver. **45. makaris:** makers, i.e., poets; **laif:** those left, rest, remainder. **46. syne:** then. **50. flour:** flower. **51. Monk of Bery:** John Lydgate, of Bury St. Edmunds; **Gower:** John Gower. Chaucer, Lydgate (c.1370-1449), and Gower (c.1330-1408) were three of the major poets of their time; except for Henryson, the poets referred to in succeeding stanzas were comparatively minor — several even entirely unknown now. **54. eik:** eke, also.

That scorpion fell hes done infek
Maister Johne Clerk, and James Afflek,
Fra balat making and tragidie;
   Timor mortis conturbat me.   60

Holland and Barbour he hes berevit;
Allace, that he nocht with us levit
Schir Mungo Lokert of the Le;
   Timor mortis conturbat me.

Clerk of Tranent eik he hes tane,   65
That maid the Anteris of Gawane;
Schir Gilbert Hay endit hes he;
   Timor mortis conturbat me.

He hes Blind Hary and Sandy Traill
Slaine with his schour of mortall haill,   70
Quhilk Patrik Johnestoun myght nocht fle;
   Timor mortis conturbat me.

He hes reft Merseir his endite,
That did in luf so lifly write,
So Schort, so quyk, of sentence hie;   75
   Timor mortis conturbat me.

He hes tane Roull of Aberdene,
And gentill Roull of Corstorphin;

Two bettir fallowis did no man se;
   Timor mortis conturbat me.   80

In Dumfermelyne he hes done roune
With Maister Robert Henrisoun;
Schir Johne the Ros enbrast hes he;
   Timor mortis conturbat me.

And he hes now tane, last of aw,   85
Gud gentill Stobo and Quintyne Schaw,
Of quham all wichtis hes pete;
   Timor mortis conturbat me.

Gud Maister Walter Kennedy
In poynt of dede lyis veraly,   90
Gret reuth it wer that so suld be;
   Timor mortis conturbat me.

Sen he hes all my brether tane,
He will nocht lat me lif alane,
On forse I man his nyxt pray be;   95
   Timor mortis conturbat me.

Sen for the deid remeid is none,
Best is that we for dede dispone,
Eftir our deid that lif may we;
   Timor mortis conturbat me.   100

                  (1508)

JOHN SKELTON

England, c.1460-1529

MANERLY MARGERY MYLK AND ALE

Ay, beshrewe yow, be my fay,
This wanton clarkes be nyse allway.
Avent, avent, my popagay!
"What, will ye do nothyng but play?"

Tully vally, strawe, let be I say!   5
  Gup, Cristian Clowte, gup, Jak of the Vale,
  With manerly Margery mylk and ale.

---

57. infek: i.e., stopped [from ballad-making, etc.]. **66. Anteris:** Adventures; King Arthur's nephew Gawain appears in many Arthurian romances, such as the *Morte Darthur* (see p. 94) and notably in *Sir Gawain and the Green Knight* (see the first stanza, p. 26; and see Yvor Winters's poem of the same title, p. 1348). **71. Quhilk:** which. **73. endite:** inditing. **78. gentill:** noble. **81. roune:** whispered. **83. enbrast:** embraced. **85. aw:** all. **87. quham:** whom; **wichtis:** wights; **pete:** pity. **90:** verily lies at the point of death. **91. reuth:** ruth. **95. On forse I man:** perforce I must. **97. Sen:** since. **98. dispone:** dispose, get ready.   **MANERLY MARGERY** A song for three voices; the refrains are sung by a third party, those in quotation marks by the clerk, and the rest by Margery the serving maid. **1. beshrewe:** curse; **be my fay:** by my faith. **2. nyse:** nice, i.e., foolish. **3. avent:** avaunt; **popagay:** popinjay. **5. Tully vally, strawe:** contemptuous expressions — "Fiddle-faddle, rubbish!" **6. Gup:** gee-up, giddyap — a command for horses; the two names are nicknames of character-types.

"Be Gad, ye be a praty pode,
And I love you an hole cart lode."
Strawe, Jamys foder, ye play the fode;   *10*
I am no hakney for your rode.
Go watch a bole, your bak is brode.
    Gup, Cristian Clowte, gup, Jak of the Vale,
    With manerly Margery mylk and ale.

Iwiss, ye deal uncurtesly;   *15*
What, wolde ye frompill me? Now, fy!
"What, and ye shall be my piggesnye?"
Be Crist, ye shall not, no, hardely!
I will not be japed bodely.
    Gup, Cristian Clowte, gup, Jak of the Vale,   *20*
    With manerly Margery mylk and ale.

"Walke forth your way, ye cost me nought;
Now have I fownd that I have sought:
The best chepe flessh that evyr I bought."
Yet, for His love that all hath wrought,   *25*
Wed me or els I dye for thought.
    Gup, Cristian Clowte, your breth is stale,
    With manerly Margery mylk and ale.
    Gup, Cristian Clowte, gup, Jak of the Vale,
    With manerly Margery mylk and ale.   *30*

                    (c. 1490; 1523)

"KNOLEGE, AQUAYNTANCE, RESORT, FAVOUR, WITH GRACE"

Knolege, aquayntance, resort, favour, with grace;
Delyte, desyre, respyte, wyth lyberte;
Corage wyth lust, convenient tyme and space;
Disdayns, dystres, exylyd cruelte;
Wordys well set with good habylyte;   *5*
Demure demenaunce, womanly of porte;
Transcendyng plesure, surmountyng all dysporte;

Allectuary arrectyd to redres
These feverous axys, the dedely wo and payne
Of thoughtfull hertys plungyd in dystres;   *10*

Refresshyng myndys the Aprell shoure of rayne;
Condute of comforte, and well most soverayne;
Herber enverduryd, contynuall fressh and grene;
Of lusty somer the passyng goodly quene;

The topas rych and precyouse in vertew;   *15*
Your ruddys wyth ruddy rubys may compare;
Saphyre of sadnes, envayned wyth Indy blew;
The pullyshed perle youre whytenes doth declare;
Dyamand poyntyd to rase oute hartly care;
Geyne surfetous suspecte the emeraud comendable;   *20*
Relucent smaragd, objecte incomperable;

Encleryd myrroure and perspectyve most bryght,
Illumynyd wyth feturys far passyng my reporte;
Radyent Esperus, star of the clowdy nyght,
Lodestar to lyght these lovers to theyr porte,   *25*
Gayne dangerous stormys theyr anker of supporte,
Theyr sayll of solace most comfortably clad,
Whych to behold makyth hevy hartys glad;

Remorse have I of youre most goodlyhod,
Of youre behavoure curtes and benynge,   *30*
Of your bownte and of youre womanhod,
Which makyth my hart oft to lepe and sprynge
And to remember many a praty thynge;
But absens, alas, wyth tremelyng fere and drede,
Abashyth me, albeit I have no nede.   *35*

You I assure, absens is my fo,
My dedely wo, my paynfull hevynes;
And if ye lyst to know the cause why so,
Open myne hart, beholde my mynde expres.
I wold you coud! Then shuld ye se, mastres,   *40*
How there nys thynge that I covet so fayne
As to enbrace you in myne armys twayne.

Nothynge yerthly to me more desyrous
Than to beholde youre bewteouse countenaunce.
But hateful absens, to me so envyous,   *45*
Though thou withdraw me from her by long dystaunce,
Yet shall she never oute of remembraunce,
For I have gravyd her wythin the secret wall
Of my trew hart, to love her best of all.

                    (c. 1495)

---

8. Be: by; **praty:** pretty; **pode:** toad (used affectionately). **10. Jamys foder:** James-fodder (i.e., St. James's wort, Jameswort, Jamesweed, ragwort); **fode:** deceiver. **11. hakney:** hackney; **rode:** riding. **12. bole:** bull. **15. Iwiss:** certainly. **16. frompill:** frumple, wrinkle. **17. piggesnye:** pig's eye (a flower, and a term of endearment, like "sweetheart"). **18. hardely:** certainly, indeed. **19. japed:** tricked, deceived. **24. chepe:** purchase, bargain. **26. thought:** anxiety, sadness.   **KNOLEGE, AQUAYNTANCE, RESORT** **3. Corage:** desire; **lust:** pleasure. **6. demenaunce:** demeanour. **8. Allectuary:** electuary; **arrectyd:** made up, prepared. **9. axys:** access, attack of illness. **12. condute:** conduit. **13. Herber:** arbour; **enverduryd:** made green. **16. ruddys:** reddish parts of complexion, as cheeks or lips. **17. sadnes:** seriousness; **Indy blew:** indigo or azure. **20. Geyne:** against; **surfetous:** overmuch; **suspecte:** suspicion. **21. smaragd:** emerald-like stone. **22. perspective:** an optical instrument for looking through, or here perhaps one that reflects. **24. Esperus:** Hesperus. **29. Remorse:** regretful remembrance. **38. lyst:** wish, desire. **39. expres:** clear, unmistakable. **41. nys:** is not. **45. envyous:** malicious, spiteful. Note the acrostic that spells the name of a woman, presumably the one the poem is about, with the first letter of each stanza.

To Maystres Margaret Hussey

Mirry Margaret,
As mydsomer flowre,
Jentill as fawcoun
Or hawke of the towre.
With solace and gladnes,   5
Moche mirthe and no madnes,
All good and no badnes,
So joyously,
So maydenly,
So womanly   10
Her demenyng
In every thynge;
Far, far passynge
That I can endyght,
Or suffice to wryght   15
Of mirry Margaret,
As mydsomer flowre,
Jentyll as fawcoun
Or hawke of the towre.
As pacient and as styll   20
And as full of good wyll
As fayre Isaphill;
Colyaunder,
Swete pomaunder;
Good Cassaunder,   25
Stedfast of thought,
Wele made, wele wrought;
Far may be sought
Erst that ye can fynde
So corteise, so kynde   30
As mirry Margaret,
This midsomer flowre,
Jentyll as fawcoun
Or hawke of the towre.

(c. 1490; 1523)

from Colyn Clout

Here after foloweth a lytell boke called
Colyn Clout compyled by Mayster Skelton,
Poete Laureate

*Quis con surget mihi adversus malignantes,
aut quis mecum adversus operantes
iniquitatem? Nemo, Domine!*

What can it avayle
To dryve forth a snayle,
Or to make a sayle
Of a herynges tayle?
To ryme or to rayle,   5
To wryte or to indyte,
Eyther for delyte
Or elles for despyte,
Or bokes to compyle
Of dyvers maner style,   10
Vyce to revyle
And synne to exyle?
To teche or to preche
As reason wyll reche?
Sey this and sey that,   15
"His hed is so fat
He wotteth never what
Nor whereof he speketh";
"He cryeth and he creketh,
He pryeth and he peketh,   20
He chydeth and he chatters,
He prateth and he patters,
He clyttreth and he clatters,
He medleth and he smatters,
He gloseth and he flatters."   25
Or if he speke playne,
Than he lacketh brayne:
"He is but a foole;
Let him go to scole,

To Maystres Margaret Hussey **2. mydsomer flowre:** i.e., the daisy, also called margaret. **3. Jentill:** gentle, noble, well-bred — though the term "falcon gentle" was used of the female and young of the goshawk. **4:** Referring either to the towering flight of the hawk or to certain hawks associated with a tower containing the royal mews. **5. solace:** comfort, pleasure. **14. That:** that which, anything that; **endyght:** indite. **22. Isaphill:** Hypsipyle, Queen of Lemnos, who saved her father's life, and was also devoted to the two sons she later had by Jason of the Argonauts. **23. Colyaunder:** coriander. **25. Cassaunder:** Cassandra, daughter of King Priam of Troy, who stuck to her dismal (and accurate) prophecies even though no one believed her. **29. Erst:** ere, before. **Colyn Clout** This introductory section (from a poem of over 1200 lines) illustrates the rough style Skelton used in his satires (somewhat evident also in the preceding poem), a style later called Skeltonics (also called "tumbling verse"): short and often irregular lines, with rhymes that come in irregular bunches. **Epigraph:** (Latin, from the Vulgate) "Who will rise up for me against the evil-doers? or who will stand up for me against the workers of iniquity? No man, Lord!" (See Psalms 94:16 and John 8:11.) **19. creketh:** croaks. **23. clyttreth:** chatters; **clatters:** babbles. **25. gloseth:** glozes — i.e., deceives, flatters.

On a thre-foted stole 30
That he may downe syt,
For he lacketh wyt."
And yf that he hyt
The nayle on the hede
It standeth in no stede: 35
"The devyll, they say, is dede;
The devyll is dede."
   It may well so be,
Or elles they wolde se
Otherwyse, and fle 40
From worldly vanyte
And foule covytousnesse
And other wretchednesse,
Fyckell falsenesse,
Varyablenesse, 45
With unstablenesse.
   And yf ye stande in doute
Who brought this ryme aboute,
My name is Colyn Cloute.
I purpose to shake oute 50
All my connyng bagge
Lyke a clerkely hagge,
For though my ryme be ragged,
Tattered and jagged,
Rudely rayne-beaten, 55
Rusty and mothe-eaten,
If ye take well therwith
It hath in it some pyth.
For, as farre as I can se,
It is wronge with eche degre: 60

For the temporalte
Accuseth the spiritualte;
The spiritualte agayne
Dothe grudge and complayne
Upon the temporall men. 65
Thus eche of other blother,
The tone against the tother.
Alas, they make me shoder,
For in hoder-moder
The churche is put in faute. 70
The prelates ben so haute,
They say, and loke so hye,
As though they wolde flye
About the sterry skye.
   Laye men say, indede, 75
How they take no hede
Theyr sely shepe to fede,
But plucke away and pull
Theyr fleces of wull.
Unneth they leve a locke 80
Of wolle amongest theyr flocke.
And as for theyr connynge,
A glommynge and a mommynge,
And make therof a jape!
They gaspe and they gape 85
All to have promocyon;
There is theyr hole devocyon,
With money, yf it wyll happe
To catche the forked cappe.
Forsothe, they are to lewde 90
To say so, all beshrewde!

(c. 1522; 1530)

JOHN BOURCHIER, LORD BERNERS
England, c.1467-1533

Preface to translation of *FROISSART'S CHRONICLES*

The Preface of John Bourchier, Knight, Lord Berners,
Translator of This Present Chronicle

What condign graces and thanks ought men to give to the writers of histories, who with their great labours have done so much profit to the human life! They show, open, manifest, and declare to the reader, by example of old antiquity, what we should enquire, desire, and

---

35: It does no good. **51. connyng bagge:** bag, accumulation, of learning or knowledge. **52. clerkely hagge:** i.e., pedantic old man. **66. blother:** blather. **67. tone . . . tother:** one . . . other. **68. shoder:** shudder. **69. hoder-moder:** hugger-mugger. **70. faute:** fault. **71. haute:** haughty. **77. sely:** simple, foolish. **80. Unneth:** scarcely. **83. glommynge:** glumming — i.e., looking glum, scowling; **mommynge:** mumbling, murmuring. **89. forked cap:** i.e., bishop's mitre. **90. lewde:** base, wicked, ignorant. **91. all:** altogether.

follow, and also what we should eschew, avoid, and utterly fly; for when we (being
unexpert of chances) see, behold, and read the ancient acts, gestes, and deeds, how and   *5*
with what labours, dangers, and perils they were gested and done, they right greatly
admonish, ensign, and teach us how we may lead forth our lives. And farther, he that hath
the perfect knowledge of others' joy, wealth, and high prosperity, and also trouble, sorrow,
and great adversity, hath the expert doctrine of all perils. And albeit that mortal folk are
marvelously separated, both by land and water, and right wondrously situate, yet are they   *10*
and their acts (done peradventure by the space of a thousand year) compact together by the
historiographer, as it were the deeds of one self city and in one man's life. Wherefore I say
that history may well be called a divine providence, for as the celestial bodies above
complect all and at every time the universal world, the creatures therein contained, and all
their deeds, semblably so doth history. Is it not a right noble thing for us, by the faults and   *15*
errors of others, to amend and erect our life into better? We should not seek and acquire
that other did; but what thing was most best, most laudable, and worthily done, we should
put before our eyes to follow. Be not the sage counsels of two or three old fathers in a city,
town, or country, whom long age hath made wise, discreet, and prudent, far more praised,
lauded, and dearly loved than of the young men? How much more then ought histories to   *20*
be commended, praised, and loved, in whom is included so many sage counsels, great
reasons, and high wisdoms of so innumerable persons, of sundry nations, and of every age,
and that in so long space as four or five hundred year. The most profitable thing in this
world for the institution of the human life is history. Once, the continual reading thereof
maketh young men equal in prudence to old men, and to old fathers stricken in age it   *25*
ministereth experience of things. More, it yieldeth private persons worthy of dignity, rule,
and governance. It compelleth the emperors, high rulers, and governors to do noble deeds,
to the end they may obtain immortal glory. It exciteth, moveth, and stirreth the strong
hardy warriors, for the great laud that they have after they been dead, promptly to go in
hand with great and hard perils in defence of their country. And it prohibiteth reprovable   *30*
persons to do mischievous deeds, for fear of infamy and shame. So thus, through the
monuments of writing, which is the testimony unto virtue, many men have been moved,
some to build cities, some to devise and establish laws right profitable, necessary, and
behoveful for the human life, some other to find new arts, crafts, and sciences very
requisite to the use of mankind. But above all things whereby man's wealth riseth, special   *35*
laud and praise ought to be given to history: it is the keeper of such things as have been
virtuously done, and the witness of evil deeds; and by the benefit of history all noble, high,
and virtuous acts be immortal. What moved the strong and fierce Hercules to enterprise in
his life so many great incomparable labours and perils? Certainly naught else but that for
his merit immortality might be given to him of all folk. In semblable wise did his imitator,   *40*
noble Duke Theseus, and many other innumerable worthy princes and famous men, whose
virtues been redeemed from oblivion and shine by history. And whereas other monuments
in process of time by variable chances are confused and lost, the virtue of history diffused
and spread through the universal world hath to her custos and keeper it (that is to say,

---

PREFACE TO FROISSART'S CHRONICLES   **7. ensign:** show, inform, teach (French *enseigner*). **14. complect:** embrace. **17. that:** i.e., that which. **24. Once:** i.e., first. **44. to:** i.e., for; **custos:** custodian, keeper.

time) which consumeth the other writings. And albeit that those men are right worthy of   *45*
great laud and praise who by their writings show and lead us the way to virtue, yet
nevertheless the poems, laws, and other acts that they found devised and writ, been mixed
with some damage, and sometimes for the truth they ensign a man to lie. But only history,
truly with words representing the acts, gestes, and deeds done, complecteth all profit. It
moveth, stirreth, and compelleth to honesty; detesteth, irketh, and abhorreth vices. It   *50*
extolleth, enhanceth, and lifteth up such as been noble and virtuous; depresseth, poistereth,
and thrusteth down such as been wicked, evil, and reprovable. What knowledge should we
have of ancient things past and history were not? which is the testimony thereof, the light
of truth, the mistress of the life human, the president of remembrance, and the messenger
of antiquity. Why moved and stirred Phalerius the king Ptolemy, oft and diligently to read   *55*
books? Forsooth for none other cause but that those things are found written in books that
the friends dare not show to the prince. Much more I would fain write of the incomparable
profit of history, but I fear me that I should too sore torment the reader of this my preface;
and also I doubt not but that the great utility thereof is better known than I could declare;
wherefore I shall briefly come to a point. Thus, when I advertised and remembered the   *60*
manifold commodities of history, how beneficial it is to mortal folk, and eke how laudable
and meritorious a deed it is to write histories, fixed my mind to do something therein; and
ever when this imagination came to me, I volved, turned, and read many volumes and
books containing famous histories. And among all other, I read diligently the four volumes
or books of Sir John Froissart of the country of Hainault, written in the French tongue,   *65*
which I judged commodious, necessary, and profitable to be had in English, since they
treat of the famous acts done in our parts; that is to say, in England, France, Spain,
Portugal, Scotland, Brittany, Flanders, and other places adjoining; and specially they
redound to the honour of Englishmen. What pleasure shall it be to the noble gentlemen of
England to see, behold, and read the high enterprises, famous acts, and glorious deeds   *70*
done and achieved by their valiant ancestors! Forsooth and God, this hath moved me at the
high commandment of my most redoubted sovereign lord King Henry the VIII, King of
England and of France, and high defender of the Christian faith, etc., under his gracious
supportation, to do my devoir to translate out of French into our maternal English tongue
the said volumes of Sir John Froissart, which chronicle beginneth at the reign of the most   *75*
noble and valiant King Edward the Third, the year of our Lord a thousand three hundred
and sixteen, and continueth to the beginning of the reign of King Henry the Fourth, the
year of our Lord God a thousand and four hundred — the space between is threescore and
fourteen years — requiring all the readers and hearers thereof to take this my rude
translation in gree. And in that I have not followed mine author word by word, yet I trust I   *80*
have ensued the true report of the sentence of the matter. And as for the true naming of all
manner of personages, countries, cities, towns, rivers, or fields, whereas I could not name
them properly nor aptly in English, I have written them according as I found them in

---

51. poistereth: fetters, entangles, encumbers. **53. and:** i.e., if. **55. Phalerius:** Demetrius of Phalerum (Demetrius Phalereus) was said to have suggested the great Library of Alexandria to Ptolemy I, its founder, and was for a time its librarian. **60. advertised:** took note of, observed, considered. **61. eke:** also. **63. volved:** turned over, turned over the pages of, turned over in my mind (considered). **66. commodious:** convenient, suitable. **77. sixteen:** a slip — needs to be twenty-six for the spread of 74 years to be correct, though Edward actually became king in 1327. **80. in gree:** in good will, kindly. **81. ensued:** followed; **sentence:** sense, significance. **82. whereas:** where.

French; and though I have not given every lord, knight, or squire his true addition, yet I trust I have not swerved from the true sentence of the matter. And thereas I have named *85* the distance between places by miles and leagues, they must be understood according to the custom of the countries whereas they be named, for in some place they be longer than in some other: in England a league or mile is well known; in France a league is two miles, and in some place three, and in other country is more or less; every nation hath sundry customs. And if any fault be in this my rude translation, I remit the correction thereof to *90* them that discreetly shall find any reasonable default; and in their so doing, I shall pray God to send them the bliss of heaven. Amen.

(1523)

Sebastian Cabot
England, 1474-1557

Ordinances, instructions, and advertisements

Ordinances, instructions, and advertisements of and for the direction of the intended voyage for Cathay, compiled, made, and delivered by the right worshipfull M. Sebastian Cabota Esquier, governour of the mysterie and companie of the Marchants adventurers for the discoverie of Regions, Dominions, Islands and places unknowen, the 9. day of May, in the yere of our Lord God 1553. And in the 7. yeere of the reigne of our most dread soveraigne Lord Edward the 6. by the grace of God, king of England, Fraunce and Ireland, defender of the faith, and of the Church of England and Ireland, in earth supreame head.

First the Captaine general, with the pilot major, the masters, marchants & other officers, to be so knit and accorded in unitie, love, conformitie, and obedience in every degree on all sides, that no dissention, variance, or contention may rise or spring betwixt them and the mariners of this companie, to the damage or hinderance of the voyage: for that dissention (by many experiences) hath overthrown many notable intended and *5* likely enterprises and exploits.

    2 Item, for as much as every person hath given an othe to be true, faithfull, and loial subjects, and liege men to the kings most excellent Majestie, his heires and

---

84. addition: something added to a person's name to show rank, occupation, residence, or the like — e.g. Demetrius *Phalareus*; John Bourchier, *Knight*. **85. thereas:** where. **90. remit:** refer a matter to someone else competent to deal with it. **Ordinances, instructions, and advertisements** (As printed in Hakluyt's collection; see p. 168.) Sebastian Cabot was the son of John Cabot (Giovanni Caboto, 1450-1498), Italian-born explorer for England. **Extended title: advertisements:** instructions, notifications, announcements. **Cathay:** The object of the voyage was to seek out the Northeast Passage to the Orient. **mysterie:** trade, occupation. **Marchants adventurers:** Cabot had founded, in 1551, the company of Merchant Adventurers.

successors, and for the observation of all lawes & statutes, made for the preservation of
his most excellent Majestie, & his crown Imperiall of his realmes of England and   *10*
Ireland, and to serve his grace, the Realme, and this present voyage truely, and not to
give up, intermit, or leave off the said voyage and enterprise untill it shalbe
accomplished, so farre forth as possibilitie and life of man may serve or extend:
Therfore it behoveth every person in his degree, as well for conscience, as for dueties
sake to remember his said charge, and the accomplishment thereof.   *15*

    3 Item, where furthermore every mariner or passenger in his ship hath given like
othe to bee obedient to the Captaine generall, and to every Captaine and master in his
ship, for the observation of these present orders contained in this booke, and all other
which hereafter shalbe made by the 12. counsailers in this present book named, or the
most part of them, for the better conduction, and preservation of the fleete, and   *20*
atchieving of the voyage, and to be prompt, ready and obedient in all acts and feates of
honesty, reason, and duetie to be ministred, shewed & executed, in advancement and
preferment of the voyage and exploit: therfore it is convenient that this present booke
shall once every weeke (by the discretion of the Captaine) be read to the said companie,
to the intent that every man may the better remember his othe, conscience, duetie and   *25*
charge.

    4 Item, every person by vertue of his othe, to doe effectually & with good wil (as
farre forth as him shall complie) all, and every such act and acts, deede and deeds, as
shalbe to him or them from time to time commanded, committed and enjoyned (during
the voyage) by the Captain generall, with the assent of the Counsell and assistants, as   *30*
well in and during the whole Navigation and voyage, as also in discovering and landing,
as cases and occasions shall require.

    5 Item, all courses in Navigation to be set and kept, by the advice of the Captaine,
Pilot major, masters, & masters mates, with the assents of the counsailers and the most
number of them, and in voyces uniformely agreeing in one to prevaile, and take place,   *35*
so that the Captaine generall, shall in all counsailes and assemblies have a double voyce.

    6 Item, that the fleete shal keep together, and not separate themselves asunder, as
much as by winde & weather may be done or permitted, & that the Captaines, Pilots &
masters shall speedily come aboord the Admiral, when and as often as he shall seeme to
have just cause to assemble them for counsaile or consultation to be had concerning the   *40*
affaires of the fleete and voyage.

    7 Item, that the marchants, and other skilful persons in writing, shal daily write,
describe, and put in memorie the Navigation of every day and night, with the points, and
observation of the lands, tides, elements, altitude of the sunne, course of the moon and
starres, and the same so noted by the order of the Master and pilot of every ship to be   *45*
put in writing, the captaine generall assembling the masters together once every weeke
(if winde and weather shal serve) to conferre all the observations, and notes of the said
ships, to the intent it may appeare wherein the notes do agree, and wherein they dissent,
and upon good debatement, deliberation, and conclusion determined, to put the same
into a common leger, to remain of record for the company: the like order to be kept in   *50*

---

39. **Admiral:** flagship. 47. **conferre:** compare.

proportioning of the Cardes, Astrolabes, and other instruments prepared for the voyage, at the charge of the companie.

8 Item, that all enterprises and exploits of discovering or landing to search Iles, regions, and such like, to be searched, attempted, and enterprised by good deliberation, and common assent, determined advisedly. And that in all enterprises, notable ambassages, suites, requests, or presentment of giftes, or presents to Princes, to be done and executed by the captaine generall in person or by such other, as he by common assent shall appoint or assigne to doe or cause to be done in the same.

9 Item, the steward and cooke of every ship, and their associats, to give and render to the captaine and other head officers of their shippe weekely (or oftner) if it shall seeme requisite, a just or plaine and perfect accompt of expenses of the victuals, as wel flesh, fish, bisket, meate, or bread, as also of beere, wine, oyle, or vineger, and all other kinde of victualling under their charge, and they, and every of them so to order and dispende the same, that no waste or unprofitable excesse be made otherwise then reason and necessitie shall command.

10 Item, when any inferiour or meane officer of what degree or condition he shalbe, shalbe tried untrue, remisse, negligent, or unprofitable in or about his office in the voyage, or not to use him selfe in his charge accordingly, then every such officer to be punished or removed at the discretion of the captaine and assistants, or the most part of them, and the person so removed not to be reputed, accepted, or taken from the time of his remove, any more for an officer, but to remaine in such condition and place, as hee shall be assigned unto, and none of the companie, to resist such chastisement or worthie punishment, as shalbe ministred unto him moderately, according to the fault or desert of his offence, after the lawes and common customes of the seas, in such cases heretofore used and observed.

11 Item, if any Mariner or officer inferiour shalbe found by his labour not meete nor worthie the place that he is presently shipped for, such person may bee unshipped and put on lande at any place within the kings Majesties realme & dominion, and one other person more able and worthy to be put in his place, at the discretion of the captaine and masters, & order to be taken that the partie dismissed shalbe allowed proportionably the value of that he shall have deserved to the time of his dismission or discharge, & he to give order with sureties, pawn, or other assurance, to repay the overplus of that he shall have received, which he shall not have deserved, & such wages to be made with the partie newly placed as shalbe thought reasonable, and he to have the furniture of al such necessaries as were prepared for the partie dismissed, according to right and conscience.

12 Item, that no blaspheming of God, or detestable swearing be used in any ship, nor communication of ribaldrie, filthy tales, or ungodly talke to be suffred in the company of any ship, neither dicing, carding, tabling, nor other divelish games to be frequented, whereby ensueth not onely povertie to the players, but also strife, variance, brauling, fighting, and oftentimes murther to the utter destruction of the parties, and provoking of Gods most just wrath, and sworde of vengeance. These and all such like

67. tried: proved.

pestilences, and contagions of vices, and sinnes to bee eschewed, and the offenders once monished, and not reforming, to bee punished at the discretion of the captaine and master, as appertaineth.   *95*

13 Item, that morning and evening prayer, with other common services appointed by the kings Majestie, and lawes of this Realme to be read and saide in every ship daily by the minister in the Admirall, and the marchant or some other person learned in other ships, and the Bible or paraphrases to be read devoutly and Christianly to Gods honour, and for his grace to be obtained, and had by humble and heartie praier of the Navigants   *100* accordingly.

14 Item, that every officer is to be charged by Inventorie with the particulars of his charge, and to render a perfect accompt of the diffraying of the same together with modest & temperate dispending of powder, shot, and use of all kinde of artillery, which is not to be misused, but diligently to be preserved for the necessary defence of the   *105* fleete and voyage, together with due keeping of all instruments of your Navigation, and other requisites.

15 Item, no liquor to be spilt on the balast, nor filthines to be left within boord: the cook room, and all other places to be kept cleane for the better health of the companie, the gromals & pages to bee brought up according to the laudable order and use of the Sea, as   *110* well in learning of Navigation, as in exercising of that which to them appertaineth.

16 Item, the liveries in apparel given to the mariners be to be kept by the marchants, and not to be worne, but by the order of the captaine, when he shall see cause to muster or shewe them in good aray, for the advancement and honour of the voyage, and the liveries to bee redelivered to the keeping of the marchants, untill it shal be thought   *115* convenient for every person to have the ful use of his garment.

17 Item, when any mariner or any other passenger shal have neede of any necessarie furniture of apparell for his body, and conservation of his health, the same shall bee delivered him by the Marchant, at the assignement of the captaine and Master of that shippe, wherein such needie person shall be, at such reasonable price as the same   *120* cost, without any gaine to be exacted by the marchants, the value therof to be entred by the marchant in his booke, and the same to be discounted off the parties wages, that so shal receive, and weare the same.

18 Item the sicke, diseased, weake, and visited person within boord, to be tendred, relieved, comforted, and holpen in the time of his infirmitie, and every maner of person,   *125* without respect, to beare anothers burden, and no man to refuse such labour as shall be put to him, for the most benefite, and publike wealth of the voyage, and enterprise, to be atchieved exactly.

19 Item if any person shal fortune to die, or miscary in the voyage, such apparell, and other goods, as he shall have at the time of his death, is to be kept by the order of the   *130* captaine and Master of the shippe, and an inventorie to be made of it, and conserved to the use of his wife, and children, or otherwise according to his mind, and wil, and the day of his death to be entred in the Marchants and Stewards bookes: to the intent it may be knowen what wages he shall have deserved to his death, and what shall rest due to him.

---

100. Navigants: navigators, voyagers. **110. gromals:** grooms. **124. visited:** afflicted with illness, attacked by plague or other disease. **129. miscary:** perish, come to destruction.

20 Item, that the Marchants appointed for this present voyage, shall not make any shew or sale of any kind of marchandizes, or open their commodities to any forrein princes, or any of their subjects, without the consent, privitie, or agreement of the Captaines, the cape Marchants and the assistants, or foure of them, whereof the captaine generall, the Pilot Major, and cape marchant to be three, and every of the pettie marchants to shewe his reckoning to the cape marchant, when they, or any of them shall be required: and no commutation or trucke to be made by any of the petie marchants, without the assent abovesaid: and all wares, and commodities trucked, bought or given to the companie, by way of marchandise, trucke, or any other respect, to be booked by the marchants, and to be wel ordred, packed, and conserved in one masse entirely, and not to be broken or altered, until the shippes shall returne to the right discharges, and inventorie of al goods, wares, and marchandises so trucked, bought, or otherwise dispended, to be presented to the Governor, Consuls, and Assistants in London, in good order, to the intent the Kings Majestie may be truly answered of that which to his grace by his grant of corporation is limited, according to our most bound dueties, and the whole companie also to have that which by right unto them appertaineth, and no embezelment shall be used, but the truth of the whole voyage to bee opened, to the common wealth and benefite of the whole companie, and mysterie, as appertaineth, without guile, fraude, or male engine.

21 Item, no particular person, to hinder or prejudicate the common stocke of the company, in sale or preferment of his own proper wares, and things, and no particular emergent or purchase to be employed to any severall profite, untill the common stocke of the companie shall be furnished, and no person to hinder the common benefite in such purchases or contingents, as shal fortune to any one of them, by his owne proper policie, industrie, or chance, nor no contention to rise in that behalfe, by any occasion of jewel, stone, pearles, precious mettals, or other things of the region, where it shall chance the same to rise, or to be found, bought, trucked, permuted, or given: but every person to be bounden in such case, and upon such occasion, by order, and direction, as the generall captaine, and the Councell shall establish and determine, to whose order and discretion the same is left: for that of things uncertaine, no certaine rules may or can be given.

22 Item not to disclose to any nation the state of our religion, but to passe it over in silence, without any declaration of it, seeming to beare with such lawes, and rites, as the place hath, where you shall arrive.

23 Item for as much as our people, and shippes may appeare unto them strange and wonderous, and theirs also to ours: it is to be considered, how they may be used, learning much of their natures and dispositions, by some one such person, as you may first either allure, or take to be brought aboord your ships, and there to learne as you may, without violence or force, and no woman to be tempted, or intreated to incontinencie, or dishonestie.

24 Item the person so taken, to be well entertained, used, and apparelled, to be set on land, to the intent that he or she may allure other to draw nigh to shewe the

---

138. cape Marchants: head merchants, supercargoes. **141. trucke:** trading by exchange of commodities, barter. **153. male engine:** malengine — evil machination, ill-intent, deceit. **154. prejudicate:** prejudice, affect prejudicially or unfavourably. **156. emergent:** outcome, incidental result. **161. permuted:** changed one for another, exchanged. **164. for that:** because.

commodities: and if the person taken may be made drunke with your beere, or wine, you shal know the secrets of his heart.

25 Item our people may not passe further into a lande, then that they may be able to recover their pinnesses, or ships, & not to credit the faire words of the strange people, which be many times tried subtile, and false, nor to be drawen into perill of losse, for the *180* desire of golde, silver, or riches, and esteeme your owne commodities above al other, and in countenance shew not much to desire the forren commodities: neverthelesse take them as for friendship, or by way of permutation.

26 Item every nation and region is to be considered advisedly, & not to provoke them by any disdaine, laughing, contempt, or such like, but to use them with prudent *185* circumspection, with al gentlenes, and curtesie, and not to tary long in one place, untill you shall have attained the most worthy place y^t may be found, in such sort, as you may returne w^t victuals sufficient prosperously.

27 Item the names of the people of every Island, are to be taken in writing, with the commodities, and incommodities of the same, their natures, qualities, and dispositions, *190* the site of the same, and what things they are most desirous of, & what commodities they wil most willingly depart with, & what mettals they have in hils, mountaines, streames, or rivers, in, or under the earth.

28 Item if people shal appeare gathering of stones, gold, mettall, or other like, on the sand, your pinnesses may drawe nigh, marking what things they gather, using or *195* playing upon the drumme, or such other instruments, as may allure them to harkening, to fantasie, or desire to see, and heare your instruments and voyces, but keepe you out of danger, and shewe to them no poynt or signe of rigour and hostilitie.

29 Item if you shall be invited into any Lords or Rulers house, to dinner, or other parliance, goe in such order of strength, that you may be stronger then they, and be *200* warie of woods and ambushes, and that your weapons be not out of your possessions.

30 Item if you shall see them weare Lyons or Beares skinnes, having long bowes, and arrowes, be not afraid of that sight: for such be worne oftentimes more to feare strangers, then for any other cause.

31 Item there are people that can swimme in the sea, havens, & rivers, naked, *205* having bowes and shafts, coveting to draw nigh your ships, which if they shal finde not wel watched, or warded, they wil assault, desirous of the bodies of men, which they covet for meate: if you resist them, they dive, and so will flee, and therefore diligent watch is to be kept both day & night, in some Islands.

32 Item if occasion shal serve, that you may give advertisements of your pro- *210* ceedings in such things as may correspond to the expectation of the company, and likelihood of successe in the voyage, passing such dangers of the seas, perils of ice, intollerable coldes, and other impediments, which by sundry authors & writers, have ministred matter of suspition in some heads, that this voyage could not succede for the extremitie of the North pole, lacke of passage, & such like, which have caused wavering *215* minds, and doubtful heads, not onely to withdraw themselves from the adventure of this

---

179. pinnesses: pinnaces. **187. yt:** that. **188. wt:** with. **190. commodities:** things commodious, advantages; **incommodities:** things incommodious, inconveniences, disadvantages.

voyage, but also disswaded others from the same, the certaintie wherof, when you shall have tried by experience, (most certaine Master of all worldly knowledge) then for declaration of the trueth, which you shall have experted, you may by common assent of counsell, sende either by land, or otherwaies, such two or one person, to bring the same 220 by credite, as you shal think may passe in safetie: which sending is not to be done, but upon urgent causes, in likely successe of the voyage, in finding of passage, in towardlines of beneficiall traffike, or such other like, whereby the company being advertised of your estates and proceedings, may further provide, foresee, and determine that which may seeme most good and beneficiall for the publike wealth of the same: 225 either providing before hand such things, as shall bee requisite for the continuance of the voyage, or else otherwise to dispose as occasion shall serve: in which things your wisedomes and discretions are to be used, and shewed, and the contents of this capitule, by you much to be pondred, for that you be not ignorant, how many persons, as well the kings Majestie, the Lords of his honorable Counsel, this whole companie, as also your 230 wives, children, kinsfolkes, allies, friends and familiars, be replenished in their hearts with ardent desire to learne and know your estates, conditions, and welfares, and in what likelihood you be in, to obtain this notable enterprise, which is hoped no lesse to succeed to you, then the Orient or Occident Indias have to the high benefite of the Emperour, and kings of Portingal, whose subjects industries, and travailes by sea, have 235 inriched them, by those lands and Islands, which were to all Cosmographers, and other writers both unknowne, and also by apparances of reason voide of experience thought and reputed unhabitable for extremities of heates, and colds, and yet indeed tried most rich, peopled, temperate, and so commodious, as all Europe hath not the like.

    33 Item no conspiracies, parttakings, factions, false tales, untrue reports, which be 240 the very seedes, and fruits of contention, discord, & confusion, by evill tongues to be suffered, but the same, & all other ungodlines to be chastened charitably with brotherly love, and alwaies obedience to be used and practised by al persons in their degrees, not only for duetie and conscience sake towards God, under whose mercifull hand navigants above all other creatures naturally bee most nigh, and vicine, but also for prudent and 245 worldly pollicie, and publike weale, considering and alwaies having present in your mindes that you be all one most royall kings subjects, and naturals, with daily remembrance of the great importance of the voyage, the honour, glorie, praise, and benefite that depend of, and upon the same, toward the common wealth of this noble Realme, the advancement of you the travailers therein, your wives, and children, and so 250 to endevour your selves as that you may satisfie the expectation of them, who at their great costs, charges, and expenses, have so furnished you in good sort, and plentie of all necessaries, as the like was never in any realme seene, used, or knowen requisite and needful for such an exploit, which is most likely to be atchieved, and brought to good effect, if every person in his vocation shall endevour himselfe according to his charge, 255 and most bounden duetie: praying the living God, to give you his grace, to accomplish your charge to his glorie, whose merciful hand shal prosper your voyage, and preserve you from all dangers.

---

219. experted: experienced, known by experience. **228. capitule:** ordinances. **245. vicine:** neighbouring, adjacent, near.

In witnes whereof I Sebastian Cabota, Governour aforesaide, to these present
ordinances, have subscribed my name, and put my seale, the day and yeere above   260
written.

The names of the twelve Counsellors appointed in this voyage.
1 SIR Hugh Willoughby Knight, Captaine generall.
2 Richard Chancelour Captaine of the Edward Bonaventure,
   and Pilot generall of the fleete.   265
3 George Burton Cape marchant.
4 Master Richard Stafford Minister.
5 Thomas Langlie Marchant.
6 James Dalabere Gentleman.
7 William Gefferson Master of the Bona Speranza Admirall.   270
8 Stephen Borrough Master of the Edward Bonaventure.
9 Cornelius Durfurth Master of the Confidentia.
10 Roger Wilson.
11 John Buckland.   } Masters mates.
12 Richard Ingram.   }   275

SIR THOMAS MORE
England, 1478-1535

A letter written with a cole by Sir Thomas More to hys doughter
maistres Margaret Roper, within a whyle after he was prisoner in
the towre.

Myne own good doughter, our lorde be thanked I am in good helthe of bodye, and in
good quiet of minde: and of worldly thynges I no more desyer than I have. I beseche
hym make you all mery in the hope of heaven. And such thynges as I somewhat longed
to talke with you all, concerning the worlde to come, our Lorde put theim into your
myndes, as I truste he dothe and better to by hys holy spirite: who blesse you and   5
preserve you all. Written with a cole by your tender loving father, who in hys pore
prayers forgetteth none of you all, nor your babes, nor your nurses, nor your good
husbandes nor your good husbandes shrewde wyves, nor your fathers shrewde wyfe
neither, nor our other frendes. And thus fare ye hartely well for lacke of paper.

Thomas More, knight
(1534; 1557)

264-65: Chancellor's ship made it to the White Sea; the other two ships were caught in the ice and their crews froze to death. Chancellor went
overland to Moscow, and began opening up trade with Russia; the Merchant Adventurers soon became the Muscovy Company.   **LETTER BY**
SIR THOMAS MORE   **5. to:** too. **6. cole:** coal.

Lewys the Lost Lover

Eye-flattering Fortune, look thou never so fair,
Or never so pleasantly begin to smile,
As though thou wouldst my ruin all repair,
During my life thou shalt me not beguile.
Trust shall I God, to enter in a while   5
His haven of heaven sure and uniform.
Ever after thy calm, look I for a storm.

(c. 1535; 1557)

Davy the Dicer

Long was I, Lady Luck, your serving man,
and now have lost again all that I gat;
wherefore when I think on you now and than,
and in my mind remember this and that,
ye may not blame me though I beshrew your cat,   5
but in faith I bless you again a thousand times
for lending me now some leisure to make rhymes.

(c. 1535; 1557)

SIR DAVID LINDSAY
Scotland, c.1486-1555

THE JUSTING BETWIX JAMES WATSOUN AND JHONE BARBOUR, SERVITOURIS TO KING JAMES THE FYFT

In Sainctandrois, on Whitsoun Monnunday,
Twa campionis thair manheid did assay,
Past to the barres, enarmit heid and handis.
Was never sene sic justing in na landis,
In presence of the Kingis grace and Quene,   5
Quhare mony lustie lady micht be sene.
Mony ane knicht, barroun, and banrent
Came for to se that awfull tornament.
The ane of thame was gentill James Watsoun,
And Johne Barbour the uther campioun;   10
Unto the King they war familiaris,
And of his chalmer baith cubicularis.
James was ane man of greit intelligence,
Ane medicinar full of experience;
And Jhone Barbour, he was ane nobill leche;   15
Crukit carlingis, he wald gar thame get speche.

From tyme thay enterit war into the feild,
Full womanlie thay weildit speir and scheild,
And wichtlie waiffit in the wynd thair heillis,
Hobland lyke cadgeris, rydand on thair creillis;   20
Bot ather ran at uther with sic haist,
That thay could never thair speir get in the raist.
Quhen gentil James trowit best with Johne to meit,
His speir did fald amang his horsis feit.
I am richt sure gude James had bene undone,   25
War nocht that Johne his mark tuke be the mone.
Quod Johne, "Howbeit you think my leggis lyke rokkis,
My speir is gude; now keip ye fra my knokkis."
"Tary," quod James, "ane quhyle, for be my thrift,
The feind ane thing I can se bot the lift."   30
"No more can I," quod Johne, "be Goddis breid;
I see na thing except the steipill heid."

LEWYS THE LOST LOVER DAVY THE DICER These two poems are described in the 1557 *Workes* as "two short ballettes which Sir Thomas More made for hys pastime while he was prisoner in the tower of London." **THE JUSTING** This bizarre mock-tournament probably took place as part of the celebration of the marriage of King James with Marie de Lorraine, in 1538, or within a year or two thereafter. Part of the satire lies in the fact that participants in true joustings were men of noble birth, not men such as the barber/physicians Watson and Barbour. **1. Sainctandrois:** Saint Andrews. **3. barres:** barrace, barriers — i.e., lists, the enclosure in which such show-combats took place. **6. lustie:** pleasant, lovely. **7. banrent:** knight banneret. **12. chalmer . . . cubicularis:** gentlemen of the bedchamber. **15. leche:** leech, physician. **16: crukit carlingis:** crooked (bent) old women — I.e., he would worm medical lore out of old women, still then the traditional healers. **19. wichtlie:** stoutly, swiftly; **waiffit:** waved; **heillis:** heels. **20. cadgeris:** itinerant hucksters; **creillis:** panniers, carried on horses' backs. **21. sic:** such. **22. raist:** rest. **23. trowit best:** believed most strongly. **26:** I.e., John takes aim by the moon (see lines 30-31: obviously both men's helmets severely limit their vision). **27. rokkis:** distaffs. **30. feind ane thing:** devil-a-thing; **lift:** sky. **31. breid:** bread, portion, or possibly beard or altar (board).

Yit, thocht thy braunis be lyk twa barrow trammis,
Defend the, man." Than ran thay to, lyke rammis.
At that rude rink, James had ben strykin doun,   *35*
War not that Johne for feirisness fell in swoun;
And richt sa James to Johne had done greit deir,
War not amangis his hors feit he brak his speir.
Quod James to Johne, "Yit for our ladyis saikis,
Lat us togidder straik thre market straikis."   *40*
"I had," quod Johne, "that sall on the be wrokin,"
Bot or he spurrit his hors, his speir was brokin.
From tyme with speiris nane could his marrow meit,
James drew ane sweird, with ane richt awful spreit,
And ran till Johne, till haif raucht him ane rout.   *45*
Johnis sweird was roustit, and wald na way cum out.
Than James leit dryfe at Johne with baith his fistis;
He myst the man and dang upon the listis.
And with that straik he trowit that Johne was slane;
His sweird stak fast, and gat it never agane.   *50*

Be this, gude Johne had gottin furth his sword,
And ran to James with mony awfull word:
"My furiousnes, forsuith, now sall thow find."
Straikand at James, his swerd flew in the wind.
Than gentil James began to crak greit wordis: *55*
"Allace!" quod he, "this day for falt of swordis."
Than ather ran at uther with new racis.
With gluifis of plait thay dang at uther facis.
Quha wan this feild, na creature culd ken,
Till at the last Johne cryit "Fy! red the men."   *60*
"Ye red," quod James, "for that is my desyre;
It is ane hour sen I began to tyre."
Sone be thay had endit that royall rink,
Into the feild micht na man stand for stink.
Than every man that stude on far cryit "Fy!"   *65*
Sayand "Adew!" for dirt partis cumpany.
Thair hors, harnes, and all geir was so gude,
Lovyng to God, that day, was sched no blude.

(1538)

WILLIAM TYNDALE
England, c.1495-1536

from his NEW TESTAMENT

The Prodigal Son
And he sayde: A certayne man had two sonnes & the yonger of them sayde to his father: father geve me the parte of the goodes y^t to me belongeth. And he devyded unto them his substance. And not long after, the yõger sonne gaddered all y^t he had to geder, & toke his jorney into a farre countre and there he wasted his goodes w^t ryetous lyvynge. And when he had spent all that he had ther arose a greate derth thorow out all that same   *5*
lãde, & he began to lacke. And he went & clave to a cytesyn of y^t same countre which

---

33. braunis: calves; **trammis:** shafts. **34. Defend the[e], man:** Cf. the fencing term *en garde*. **35. rink:** ring, place for tournament, or the contest itself. **36. feirisness:** fearfulness. **37. deir:** hurt, injury. **40. straik:** strike; **straikis:** strokes; **market** may mean good, notable, clearly intended or visible, or possibly just exchanged. **41. wrokin:** wreaked, inflicted. **43ff.: From tyme . . . :** i.e., since both had lost their spears, they turn to swords; **marrow:** mate, fellow. **44. spreit:** spirit, perhaps in the sense of a rush of air or wind. **45. till:** toward; **till:** to; **haif:** have; **raucht:** reached; **rout:** blow. **47. baith his fistis:** i.e., gripping the handle of his sword with both hands, either because the sword is a (perhaps inappropriately) heavy broadsword, intended for two hands, or because he doesn't know how to handle a sword properly — probably the former, since John's sword flies out of his hand[s], which a heavy sword would more likely do. **48. dang:** beat, struck. **56. falt:** want. **57. racis:** blows. **58. gluifis of plait:** gloves of mail. **60. red:** separate, part. **66. dirt partis company** (proverbial): i.e., such rude fellows (and *dirt* here may also be more literal) inevitably break up the party.

sent him to his felde to kepe his swyne. And he wolde fayne have fylled his bely with the coddes y^t the swyne ate: and no man gave to hym.

Then he came to hymselfe and sayde: how many hyred servauntes at my fathers have breed enough, & I dye for hõger. I will aryse & go to my father, & wyll saye unto *10* him: father I have synned agaynst hevẽ & before y^e, & am no more worthy to be called thy sonne; make me as one of thy hyred servaũtes. And he arose and went to his father. And when he was yet a greate waye of hys father sawe him & had cõpassyon & ran & fell on his neck & kyssed hym. And the sonne sayd unto hym: father, I have synned agaynst hevẽ & in thy sight, & am no moare worthy to be called thy sonne. But his *15* father sayd to his servaũtes: brynge forth that best garment and put it on him, & put a ringe on his hande, & showes on his fete. And brynge hydder that fatted caulfe & kill hym, & let us eate and be mery: for this my sonne was deed, and is alyve agayne; he was loste, & is now founde. And they began to be merye. The elder brother was in the felde, & whẽ he came & drewe nye to ye housse, he herde minstrelsy & daunsyng, & *20* called one of his servaũtes, & asked what those thinges meãte. And he sayde unto him: thy brother is come, & thy father had killed ye fatted caulfe, because he hath receaved him safe & sounde. And he was angry, & wolde not go in. Then came his father out & entreated him. He answered & sayde to hys father: Lo these many yeares have I done the service, nether brake at any tyme thy cõmaundment, & yet gavest thou me never so *25* moche as a kyd to make mery with my lovers: but assone as this thy sonne was come, whych hath devoured thy goodes with harlotes, thou haste for his pleasure kylled ye fatted caulfe. And he sayd unto him: Sonne, thou wast ever wyth me, and all that I have is thyne: it was mete that we shuld make mery and be glad: for thys thy brother was deed and is alyve agayne; and was loste, and is founde. *30*

JOHN HEYWOOD
England, c.1497-c.1580

EPIGRAMS

A Fool's Tongue

Upon a fool's provocation
A wise man will not talk,
But every light instigation
May make a fool's tongue walk.

Of Birds and Birders

Better one bird in hand than ten in the wood —
Better for birders, but for birds not so good.

Of Loving a Dog

Love me, love my dog; by love to agree,
I love thy dog as well as I love thee.

Of Enough and a Feast

As good enough as a feast; yea, God save it!
Enough were even as good, if we might have it.

(pub. 1562)

Anonymous
16th century

Of a New-Married Student

A student at his book so placed
That wealth he might have won,
From book to wife did fleet in haste,
From wealth to woe to run.
Now, who hath played a feater cast   5
Since juggling first begun?
In knitting of himself so fast,
Himself he hath undone.

The Poor Estate to Be Holden for Best

Experience now doth show what God us taught before,
Desired pomp is vain, and seldom doth it last;
Who climbs to reign with kings may rue his fate full sore;
Alas, the woeful end that comes with care full fast.
Reject him doth renown, his pomp full low is cast;   5
Deceived is the bird by sweetness of the call;
Expel that pleasant taste wherein is bitter gall.

Such as with oaten cakes in poor estate abides,
Of care have they no cure, the crab with mirth they roast;
More ease feel they than those that from their height down
    slides.   10
Excess doth breed their woe, they sail in Scylla's coast,
Remaining in the storms till ship and all be lost.
Serve God therefore thou poor, for lo, thou lives in rest,
Eschew the golden hall: thy thatched house is best.

Upon Consideration of the State of This Life He Wisheth Death

The longer life, the more offence;
The more offence, the greater pain;
The greater pain, the less defence;
The less defence, the lesser gain.
The loss of gain long ill doth try;   5
Wherefore come death, and let me die.

The shorter life, less count I find;
The less account, the sooner made;
The count soon made, the merrier mind;
The merrier mind doth thought evade.   10
Short life in truth this thing doth try;
Wherefore come death, and let me die.

Come gentle death, the ebb of care,
The ebb of care, the flood of life,
The flood of life, the joyful fare,   15
The joyful fare, the end of strife;
The end of strife, that thing wish I;
Wherefore come death, and let me die.

"Back and side go bare, go bare"

Back and side go bare, go bare,
    Both foot and hand go cold;
But, belly, God send thee good ale enough,
    Whether it be new or old.

I cannot eat but little meat,   5
    My stomach is not good;
But sure I think that I can drink
    With him that wears a hood.
Though I go bare, take ye no care,
    I am nothing a-cold;   10
I stuff my skin so full within
    Of jolly good ale and old.

Back and side go bare, etc.

I love no roast but a nut-brown toast,
    And a crab laid in the fire;   15
A little bread shall do me stead,
    Much bread I not desire.
No frost nor snow, no wind, I trow,

OF A NEW-MARRIED STUDENT   From *Songs and Sonnets* (or *Tottel's Miscellany*), 1557.   THE POOR ESTATE   From *Songs and Sonnets*, 1557. The first letter of each line and the final letter of the poem spell out "Edwarde Somerset," probably referring to Edward Seymour, Duke of Somerset, who was Protector to the young Edward VI, but who was imprisoned in 1550 and executed in 1552. **9. cure:** care; **crab:** crab apple.   UPON CONSIDERATION   From *Songs and Sonnets*, 1557. **11. try:** try out, test, prove. For another example of this technique of repetition, called *anadiplosis*, see Googe's "Out of Sight, Out of Mind" (p. 146).   BACK AND SIDE GO BARE   From *Gammer Gurton's Needle*, 1575, but almost surely known, probably in different versions, before being used in that play. **5. meat:** i.e., food. **8:** i.e., a monk. **14. toast:** i.e., for dipping. **15. crab:** crab apple.

Can hurt me if it would,
I am so wrapped, and throughly lapped   20
    Of jolly good ale and old.

Back and side go bare, etc.

And Tib, my wife, that as her life
    Loveth well good ale to seek,
Full oft drinks she till ye may see   25
    The tears run down her cheek;
Then doth she troll to me the bowl,
    Even as a malt-worm should,
And saith, "Sweetheart, I took my part
    Of this jolly good ale and old."   30

Back and side go bare, etc.

Now let them drink till they nod and wink,
    Even as good fellows should do;
They shall not miss to have the bliss
    Good ale doth bring men to.   35
And all poor souls that have scoured bowls
    Or have them lustily trolled,
God save the lives of them and their wives,
    Whether they be young or old.

Back and side go bare, etc.   40

Crabbed Age and Youth

Crabbed Age and Youth
Cannot live together.
Youth is full of pleasure,
Age is full of care;
Youth like summer morn,   5
Age like winter weather;
Youth like summer brave,
Age like winter bare.
Youth is full of sport,
Age's breath is short;   10
Youth is nimble, Age is lame;
Youth is hot and bold,
Age is weak and cold;
Youth is wild, and Age is tame.
Age, I do abhor thee;   15
Youth, I do adore thee.
O, my Love, my Love is young!
Age, I do defy thee.
O, sweet shepherd, hie thee!
For methinks thou stay'st too long.   20

SIR THOMAS WYATT
England, 1503-1542

"My galley charged with forgetfulness"

My galley charged with forgetfulness
Thorough sharp seas in winter nights doth pass,
'Tween rock and rock, and eke mine enemy, alas,
That is my lord, steereth with cruelness;
And every oar a thought in readiness,   5
As though that death were light in such a case.
And endless wind doth tear the sail apace
Of forced sighs and trusty fearfulness.
A rain of tears, a cloud of dark disdain,
Hath done the wearied cords great hinderance;   10
Wreathed with error and eke with ignorance,
The stars be hid that led me to this pain.
Drowned is reason that should me consort,
And I remain despairing of the port.

---

27. troll: pass. **28. malt-worm:** drinker. **CRABBED AGE AND YOUTH** From *The Passionate Pilgrim*, 1599. **MY GALLEY** Translated from Petrarch. This and the following poems by Wyatt were first printed in *Tottel's Miscellany*, 1557. **2. Thorough:** Through. **3. eke:** also; **enemy:** i.e., Love. For comparison, here is Petrarch's original: "Passa la nave mia colma d'oblio / per aspro mare, a mezza notte, il verno, / enfra Scilla e Caribdi; et al governo / siede 'l signore, anzi 'l nimico mio; / a ciascun remo un penser pronto et rio / che la tempesta e 'l fin par ch' abbi a scherno; / la vela rompe un vento umido, eterno / di sospir, di speranze et di desio; / pioggia di lagrimar, nebbia di sdegni / bagna e rallenta le già stanche sarte, / che son d'error con ignoranzia attorto. / Celansi i duo mei dolci usati segni; / morta fra l'onde è la ragion et l'arte: / tal ch' i' 'ncomincio a desperar del porto."

"I find no peace, and all my war is done"

I find no peace, and all my war is done;
I fear and hope, I burn and freeze like ice;
I fly above the wind, yet can I not arise;
And nought have I and all the world I season.
That looseth nor locketh holdeth me in prison   5
And holdeth me not, yet can I 'scape nowise;
Nor letteth me live nor die at my devise,
And yet of death it giveth none occasion.
Without eyen I see, and without tongue I plain;
I desire to perish, and yet I aske health;   10
I love another, and thus I hate myself;
I feed me in sorrow, and laugh in all my pain.
Likewise displeaseth me both death and life;
And my delight is causer of this strife.

"The long love that in my thought doth harbour"

The long love that in my thought doth harbour,
And in mine heart doth keep his residence,
Into my face presseth with bold pretence
And therein campeth, spreading his banner.
She that me learneth to love and suffer   5
And wills that my trust and lust's negligence
Be reined by reason, shame, and reverence,
With his hardiness taketh displeasure.
Wherewithal unto the heart's forest he fleeth,
Leaving his enterprise with pain and cry,   10
And there him hideth, and not appeareth;
What may I do when my master feareth,
But in the field with him to live and die?
For good is the life ending faithfully.

"They flee from me that sometime did me seek"

They flee from me that sometime did me seek,
With naked foot stalking in my chamber.
I have seen them gentle, tame, and meek
That now are wild and do not remember
That sometime they put themself in danger   5
To take bread at my hand; and now they range,
Busily seeking with a continual change.

Thanked be fortune, it hath been otherwise
Twenty times better; but once in special,
In thin array after a pleasant guise,   10
When her loose gown from her shoulders did fall,
And she me caught in her arms long and small,
Therewithal sweetly did me kiss,
And softly said, "Dear heart, how like you this?"

It was no dream; I lay broad waking.   15
But all is turned thorough my gentleness
Into a strange fashion of forsaking;
And I have leave to go of her goodness,
And she also to use newfangleness.
But since that I so kindly am served,   20
I would fain know what she hath deserved.

"My lute awake!"

My lute, awake! perform the last
Labour that thou and I shall waste,
And end that I have now begun;
For when this song is sung and past,
My lute, be still, for I have done.   5

I FIND NO PEACE   Translated from Petrarch. **4. season:** seize upon (particularly of a hawk or other bird of prey, to "flesh" its claws). **9. eyen:** eyes; **plain:** complain. Petrarch's original: "Pace non trovo, e non ò da far guerra; / e temo e spero, ed ardo, e son un ghiaccio; / et volo sopra 'l cielo, e giaccio in terra; / e nulla stringo, e tutto 'l mondo abbraccio. / Tal m'à in prigion che non m'apre né serra, / né per suo me riten né scioglie il laccio; / e non m'ancide Amore et non me sferra, / né me vuol vivo né me trae d'impaccio. / Veggio senz' occhi, e non ò lingua et grido; / et bramo di perir, et cheggio aita; / et ò in odio me stesso et amo altrui. / Pascomi di dolor, piangendo rido; / egualmente me spiace morte e vita. / In questo stato son, Donna, per vui."   THE LONG LOVE   Translated from Petrarch. **13. field:** i.e., field of battle. Petrarch's original: "Amor, che nel penser mio vive e regna / e 'l suo seggio maggior nel mio cor tene, / talor armato ne la fronte vene, / ivi si loca, et ivi pon sua insegna. / Quella ch'amare e sofferir ne 'nsegna / e vol che 'l gran desio, l'accesa spene, / ragion, vergogna, e reverenza affrene, / di nostro ardir fra se stessa si sdegna. / Onde Amor paventoso fugge al core, / lasciando ogni sua impresa, e piange e trema; / ivi s'asconde, e non appar più fore. / Che poss'io far, temendo il mio signore, / se non star seco infin a l'ora estrema? / Che bel fin fa chi ben amando more." Compare Surrey's translation of the same sonnet ("Love that liveth and reigneth in my thought," p. 135).

As to be heard where ear is none,
As lead to grave in marble stone,
My song may pierce her heart as soon;
Should we then sigh, or sing, or moan?
No, no, my lute, for I have done.   *10*

The rocks do not so cruelly
Repulse the waves continually
As she my suit and affection,
So that I am past remedy,
Whereby my lute and I have done.   *15*

Proud of the spoil that thou hast got
Of simple hearts thorough love's shot,
By whom, unkind, thou hast them won,
Think not he hath his bow forgot,
Although my lute and I have done.   *20*

Vengeance shall fall on thy disdain,
That makest but game on earnest pain;
Think not alone under the sun

Unquit to cause thy lovers plain,
Although my lute and I have done.   *25*

Perchance thee lie weathered and old,
The winter nights that are so cold,
Plaining in vain unto the moon;
Thy wishes then dare not be told;
Care then who list, for I have done.   *30*

And then may chance thee to repent
The time that thou hast lost and spent
To cause thy lovers sigh and swoon;
Then shalt thou know beauty but lent,
And wish and want as I have done.   *35*

Now cease, my lute, this is the last
Labour that thou and I shall waste,
And ended is that we begun;
Now is this song both sung and past;
My lute, be still, for I have done.   *40*

THOMAS, LORD VAUX

England, 1509-1556

OF THE MEAN ESTATE

The higher that the cedar tree under the heavens do grow,
The more in danger is the top when sturdy winds gan blow;
Who judges then in princely throne to be devoid of hate
Doth not yet know what heaps of ill lies hid in such estate.
Such dangers great, such gripes of mind, such toil do they sustain,   *5*
That oftentimes of God they wish to be unkinged again.

For as the huge and mighty rocks withstand the raging seas,
So kingdoms in subjection be whereas Dame Fortune please;
Of brittle joy, of smiling cheer, of honey mixed with gall,
Allotted is to every prince, in freedom to be thrall.   *10*
What watches long, what steps unsure, what griefs and cares of mind,
What bitter broils, what endless toils, to kingdoms be assigned.

MY LUTE, AWAKE **7. grave:** engrave. **24. unquit:** unpunished, unrevenged; **plain:** complain.   **OF THE MEAN ESTATE** **2. gan:** did.
5. gripes: pinches of pain or grief.

The subject then may well compare with prince for pleasant days,
Whose silent night brings quiet rest, whose might no storm bewrays.
How much be we then bound to God, who such provision makes   *15*
To lay our cares upon the prince; thus doeth he for our sakes.
To him therefore let us lift up our hearts and pray amain
That every prince that he hath placed may long in quiet reign.

(1576)

SIR ROGER ASCHAM
England, 1515-1568

from *THE SCHOOLMASTER*

. . . .

If your scholar do miss sometimes. . . , chide not hastily, for that shall both dull his wit and discourage his diligence; but admonish him gently, which shall make him both willing to amend and glad to go forward in love and hope of learning.

I have now wished, twice or thrice, this gentle nature to be in a Schoolmaster. And, that I have done so neither by chance nor without some reason, I will now declare at   *5* large why, in my opinion, love is fitter than fear, gentleness better than beating, to bring up a child rightly in learning.

With the common use of teaching and beating in common schools of England, I will not greatly contend — which if I did, it were but a small grammatical controversy, neither belonging to heresy nor treason, nor greatly touching God nor the Prince;   *10* although in very deed, in the end, the good or ill bringing up of children doth as much serve to the good or ill service of God, our Prince, and our whole country, as any one thing doth beside.

I do gladly agree with all good Schoolmasters in these points: to have children brought to good perfectness in learning, to all honesty in manners, to have all faults   *15* rightly amended, to have every vice severely corrected; but for the order and way that leadest rightly to these points, we somewhat differ. For commonly, many schoolmasters — some, as I have seen; more, as I have heard tell — be of so crooked a nature as, when they meet with a hard-witted scholar, they rather break him than mend him. For when the schoolmaster is angry with some other matter, then will he soonest fall to beat his   *20* scholar; and though he himself should be punished for his folly, yet must he beat some scholar for his pleasure, though there be no cause for him to do so, nor yet fault in the scholar to deserve so. These, ye will say, be fond schoolmasters, and few they be that be found to be such. They be fond indeed, but surely overmany such be found everywhere. But this will I say, that even the wisest of your great beaters do as oft punish nature as   *25* they do correct faults. Yea, many times the better nature is sorer punished. For if one by quickness of wit take his lesson readily, another by hardness of wit taketh it not so speedily; the first is always commended, the other is commonly punished, when a wise schoolmaster should rather discreetly consider the right disposition of both their natures and not so much weigh what either of them is able to do now, as what either of them is likely to do hereafter. For this I know, not only by reading of books in my study, but also by experience of life abroad in the world: that those which be commonly the wisest, the best learned, and best men also, when they be old, were never commonly the quickest of wit when they were young. The causes why, amongst other, which be many, that move me thus to think, be these few, which I will reckon. Quick wits commonly be apt to take, unapt to keep; soon hot and desirous of this and that, as cold and soon weary of the same again; more quick to enter speedily than able to pierce far, even like our sharp tools, whose edges be very soon turned. Such wits delight themselves in easy and pleasant studies, and never pass far forward in high and hard sciences. And therefore the quickest wits commonly may prove the best poets, but not the wisest orators; ready of tongue to speak boldly, not deep of judgment, either for good counsel or wise writing. Also, for manners and life, quick wits commonly be in desire, newfangle, in purpose, unconstant; light to promise anything, ready to forget everything, both benefit and injury, and thereby neither fast to friend nor fearful to foe; inquisitive of every trifle, not secret in greatest affairs; bold with any person; busy in every matter; soothing such as be present, nipping any that is absent; of nature also always flattering their betters, envying their equals, despising their inferiors; and by quickness of wit very quick and ready to like none so well as themselves. 30 35 40 45

Moreover commonly men very quick of wit be also very light of conditions, and thereby very ready of disposition to be carried over quickly by any light company to any riot and unthriftiness when they be young, and therefore seldom either honest of life or rich in living when they be old. For quick in wit and light in manners be either seldom troubled or very soon weary in carrying a very heavy purse. Quick wits also be, in most part of all their doings, overquick, hasty, rash, heady, and brainsick. These two last words, *heady* and *brainsick*, be fit and proper words, rising naturally of the matter, and termed aptly by the condition of overmuch quickness of wit. In youth also they be ready scoffers, privy mockers, and ever overlight and merry. In age, soon testy, very waspish, and always over-miserable; and yet few of them come to any great age, by reason of their misordered life when they were young, but a great deal fewer of them come to show any great countenance or bear any great authority abroad in the world, but either live obscurely, men know not how, or die obscurely, men mark not when. They be like trees that show forth fair blossoms and broad leaves in springtime, but bring out small and not long-lasting fruit in harvest time. . . . 50 55 60

. . . .

Learning teacheth more in one year than experience in twenty. And learning teacheth safely, when experience maketh more miserable than wise. He hazardeth sore that waxeth wise by experience. An unhappy master he is that is made cunning by many shipwrecks; a miserable merchant, that is neither rich nor wise but after some bankruptcies. It is costly wisdom that is bought by experience. We know by experience itself that it is a marvelous pain to find out but a short way by long wandering. And surely he that would prove wise by experience, he may be witty indeed, but even like a 65 70 swift runner that runneth fast out of his way and upon the night, he knoweth not whither. And verily they be fewest of number that be happy or wise by unlearned experience. And look well upon the former life of those few, whether your example be old or young, who without learning have gathered, by long experience, a little wisdom, and some happiness; and when you do consider what mischief they have committed, what dangers   *75* they have escaped (and yet twenty for one do perish in the adventure), then think well with yourself whether ye would that your own son should come to wisdom and happiness by the way of such experience or no.

(1570)

HENRY HOWARD, EARL OF SURREY
England, 1517-1547

Epitaph for Sir Thomas Wyatt

W. resteth here, that quick could never rest;
Whose heavenly gifts increased by disdain,
And virtue sank the deeper in his breast;
Such profit he by envy could obtain.

A head where wisdom mysteries did frame,   *5*
Whose hammers beat still in that lively brain
As on a stithy, where that some work of fame
Was daily wrought to turn to Britain's gain.

A visage stern and mild, where both did grow
Vice to contemn, in virtue to rejoice;   *10*
Amid great storms whom grace assured so
To live upright and smile at fortune's choice.

A hand that taught what might be said in rhyme,
That reft Chaucer the glory of his wit;
A mark the which, unparfited, for time,   *15*
Some may approach, but never none shall hit.

A tongue that served in foreign realms his king,
Whose courteous talk to virtue did inflame
Each noble heart; a worthy guide to bring
Our English youth by travail unto fame.   *20*

An eye whose judgment none affect could blind,
Friends to allure and foes to reconcile;
Whose piercing look did represent a mind
With virtue fraught, reposed, void of guile.

A heart where dread was never so impressed   *25*
To hide the thought that might the truth advance;
In neither fortune loft nor yet repressed,
To swell in wealth or yield unto mischance.

A valiant corps where force and beauty met;
Happy, alas, too happy, but for foes;   *30*
Lived and ran the race that Nature set,
Of manhood's shape, where she the mould did lose.

But to the heavens that simple soul is fled,
Which left with such as covet Christ to know
Witness of faith that never shall be dead;   *35*
Sent for our health, but not received so.

Thus, for our guilt, this jewel have we lost;
The earth his bones, the heavens possess his ghost.

(1542; 1557)

EPITAPH FOR SIR THOMAS WYATT   (Our title: in Tottel, it was one of two poems called "Of the death of Sir T. W. the elder.") **1. quick:** alive. **4. envy:** malevolence. **6. hammers:** in a poem beginning "Since you will needs that I shall sing," Wyatt wrote, "Such hammers work within my head / That sound nought else unto my ears / But fast at board and wake abed." **9. both:** i.e., sternness and mildness. **15. unparfited, for time:** unperfected, unfinished, for lack of sufficient time. **21. affect:** feeling, emotion, passion. **27. loft:** raised aloft, lofty, proud. **29. corps:** body (living; not a corpse).

"Love that liveth and reigneth in my thought"

Love that liveth and reigneth in my thought,
That built his seat within my captive breast,
Clad in the arms wherein with me he fought,
Oft in my face he doth his banner rest.
She that me taught to love and suffer pain,   5
My doubtful hope and eke my hot desire
With shamefast cloak to shadow and refrain,

Her smiling grace converteth straight to ire;
And coward Love then to the heart apace
Taketh his flight, where he doth lurk and plain, *10*
His purpose lost, and dare not show his face.
For my lord's guilt thus faultless bide I pain,
Yet from my lord shall not my foot remove:
Sweet is the death that taketh end by love.

(1557)

THOMAS TUSSER
England, c.1524-1580

THE LADDER TO THRIFT

1. To take thy calling thankfully,
   and shun the path to beggary.

2. To grudge in youth no drudgery,
   to come by knowledge perfectly.

3. To count no travail slavery,   5
   that brings in penny saverly.

4. To follow profit earnestly,
   but meddle not with pilfery.

5. To get by honest practisy,
   and keep thy gettings covertly.   *10*

6. To lash not out too lashingly,
   for fear of pinching penury.

7. To get good plot to occupy,
   And store and use it husbandly.

8. To show to landlord courtesy,   *15*
   and keep thy covenants orderly.

9. To hold that thine is lawfully,
   for stoutness or for flattery.

10. To wed good wife for company,
    and live in wedlock honestly.   *20*

11. To furnish house with householdry,
    and make provision skilfully.

12. To join to wife good family,
    and none to keep for bravery.

13. To suffer none live idlely,   *25*
    for fear of idle knavery.

14. To courage wife in huswifery,
    and use well-doers gentlely.

15. To keep no more but needfully,
    and count excess unsavoury.   *30*

16. To raise betimes the lubberly,
    both snorting Hob and Margery.

17. To walk thy pastures usually,
    To spy ill neighbour's subtilty.

18. To hate revengement hastily,   *35*
    for losing love and amity.

19. To love thy neighbour neighbourly,
    and show him no discourtesy.

20. To answer stranger civilly,
    but show him not thy secrecy.   *40*

LOVE THAT LIVETH AND REIGNETH   Translated from Petrarch; compare this version (also printed in *Tottel's Miscellany*, 1557) with that of Wyatt ("The long love that in my thought doth harbour," p. 130). **6. eke:** also. **7. shamefast:** shamefaced. **10. plain:** complain.   **THE LADDER TO THRIFT   11:** To not spend too lavishly. **17. that thine is:** what is thine. **18. for stoutness:** against or in spite of strength, arrogance. **23. family:** servants. **24. for bravery:** for show, to impress people. **31. lubberly:** coarse, dull, clumsy, stupid. **32. snorting:** snoring; **Hob and Margery:** servants' names.

21. To use no man deceitfully,
    to offer no man villainy.

22. To learn how foe to pacify,
    but trust him not too hastily.

23. To keep thy touch substantially,   45
    and in thy word use constancy.

24. To make thy bands advisedly,
    and come not bound through surety.

25. To meddle not with usury,
    nor lend thy money foolishly.   50

26. To hate to live in infamy,
    through craft, and living naughtily.

27. To shun all kind of treachery,
    for treason endeth horribly.

28. To learn to shun ill company,   55
    and such as live dishonestly.

29. To banish house of blasphemy,
    lest crosses cross unluckily.

30. To stop mischance through policy,
    for chancing too unhappily.   60

31. To bear thy crosses patiently,
    for worldly things are slippery.

32. To lay to keep from misery,
    age coming on so creepingly.

33. To pray to God continually,   65
    for aid against thine enemy.

34. To spend thy Sabbath holily,
    and help the needy poverty.

35. To live in conscience quietly,
    and keep thyself from malady.   70

36. To ease thy sickness speedily,
    ere health be past recovery.

37. To seek to God for remedy,
    for witches prove unluckily.

These be the steps, unfeignedly,   75
    to climb to thrift by husbandry.

These steps both reach and teach thee shall,
    To come by thrift, to shift withal.

                                            (1573)

THE DESCRIPTION OF AN ENVIOUS AND NAUGHTY NEIGHBOUR

An envious neighbour is easy to find,
His cumbersome fetches are seldom behind.
His hatred procureth from naughty to worse,
His friendship like Judas that carried the purse.
His head is a storehouse, with quarrels full fraught,   5
His brain is unquiet till all comes to naught.
His memory pregnant, old evils to recite,
His mind ever fixed, each evil to requite.
His mouth full of venom, his lips out of frame,
His tongue a false witness his friend to defame.   10
His eyes be promoters, some trespass to spy,
His ears be as spials, alarum to cry.
His hands be as tyrants, revenging each thing,
His feet at thine elbow, as serpent to sting.
His breast full of rancour, like canker to freat,   15
His heart like a lion, his neighbour to eat.
His gait like a sheepbiter, fleering aside,
His look like a coxcomb, up-puffed with pride.
His face made of brass, like a vice in a game,
His gesture like Davus, whom Terence doth name.   20
His brag as Thersites, with elbows abrode,
His cheeks in his fury shall swell like a toad.
His colour like ashes, his cap in his eyes,
His nose in the air, his snout in the skies.
His promise to trust to, as slippery as ice,   25
His credit much like to the chance of the dice.
His knowledge, or skill, is in prating too much,
His company shunned, and so be all such.
His friendship is counterfeit, seldom to trust,
His doings unlucky and ever unjust,   30
His fetch is to flatter, to get what he can,
His purpose once gotten, a pin for thee than.

                                            (1573)

---

45. keep thy touch: keep covenant, keep faith, keep one's promise. **47. bands:** bonds, agreements. **48. surety:** i.e., being surety for another. **59. policy:** prudence, shrewdness, stratagem. **63. lay:** lay by, save up.   **THE DESCRIPTION OF AN ENVIOUS AND NAUGHTY NEIGHBOUR 1. envious:** malevolent. **2. fetches:** strategems, tricks. **9. frame:** order, shape, regular condition. **11. promoters:** professional accusers, informers. **12. spials:** spies. **15. freat:** fret. **17. sheepbiter:** dog that worries or bites sheep, hence any malicious, shifty, sneaking person; **fleering:** making a wry face, distorting the face, grinning, grimacing. **19. vice:** character in a morality play representing some vice, hence a stage jester or buffoon; **game:** amusement, diversion. **20. Davus:** the conniving slave in *Andria* (166 B.C.), the first play by the Roman dramatist Terence. **21. Thersites:** scurrilous Greek soldier in Homer's *Iliad;* **abrode:** abroad (left in original spelling for the rhyme).

QUEEN ELIZABETH I

England, 1533-1603

THE DOUBT OF FUTURE FOES

The doubt of future foes exiles my present joy,
And wit me warns to shun such snares as threaten mine annoy;
For falsehood now doth flow and subject faith doth ebb,
Which would not be if reason ruled or wisdom weaved the web.
But clouds of toys untried do cloak aspiring minds,   *5*
Which turn to rain of late repent by course of changed winds.
The top of hope supposed, the root of ruth will be,
And fruitless all their graffed guiles, as shortly ye shall see.
The dazzled eyes with pride, which great ambition blinds,
Shall be unseeled by worthy wights whose foresight falsehood finds.   *10*
The daughter of debate that eke discord doth sow
Shall reap no gain where former rule hath taught still peace to grow.
No foreign banished wight shall anchor in this port;
Our realm it brooks no stranger's force; let them elsewhere resort.
Our rusty sword with rest shall first his edge employ   *15*
To poll the tops that seek such change and gape for joy.

(c. 1570; 1589)

ON MONSIEUR'S DEPARTURE

I grieve and dare not show my discontent;
I love and yet am forced to seem to hate;
I do, yet dare not say I ever meant;
I seem stark mute but inwardly do prate;
   I am and not; I freeze and yet am burned,   *5*
   Since from myself another self I turned.

My care is like my shadow in the sun,
Follows me flying, flies when I pursue it,
Stands and lies by me, doth what I have done.
His too familiar care doth make me rue it.   *10*
   No means I find to rid him from my breast,
   Till by the end of things it be suppressed.

Some gentler passion slide into my mind,
For I am soft and made of melting snow;
Or be more cruel, love, and so be kind.   *15*
Let me or float or sink, be high or low,
   Or let me live with some more sweet content,
   Or die and so forget what love ere meant.

(c. 1582)

---

32. than: then (left in original for the rhyme).   **THE DOUBT OF FUTURE FOES**   The poem refers mainly to Mary Queen of Scots, Elizabeth's cousin, who had abdicated and fled to England; a Catholic, she posed a threat to Elizabeth, who finally had her beheaded in 1587 after discovering her involvement in the Babington Plot (see also "Tichborne's Elegy," p. 204). **1. doubt:** fear. **5. toys:** tricks. **8. graffed:** grafted. **11. eke:** also. **16. poll the tops:** i.e., behead.   **ON MONSIEUR'S DEPARTURE**   Possibly referring to the Earl of Essex, though more likely to the Duke of Anjou, with whom in 1582 Elizabeth broke off negotiations about marriage.

GEORGE GASCOIGNE
England, c.1539-1577

GASCOIGNE'S WOODSMANSHIP

My worthy Lord, I pray you wonder not
To see your woodsman shoot so oft awry,
Nor that he stands amazed like a sot
And lets the harmless deer (unhurt) go by.
Or if he strike a doe which is but carren,   5
Laugh not, good Lord, but favour such a fault;
Take well in worth, he would fain hit the barren,
But though his heart be good, his hap is naught.
And therefore now I crave your Lordship's leave
To tell you plain what is the cause of this.   10
First, if it please your honour to perceive,
What makes your woodsman shoot so oft amiss,
Believe me, Lord, the case is nothing strange:
He shoots awry almost at every mark;
His eyes have been so used for to range,   15
That now God knows they be both dim and dark.
For proof he bears the note of folly now,
Who shot sometimes to hit Philosophy,
And ask you why? Forsooth I make avow,
Because his wanton wits went all awry.   20
Next that, he shot to be a man of law,
And spent some time with learned Littleton;
Yet in the end he proved but a daw,
For law was dark and he had quickly done.
Then could he wish Fitzherbert such a brain   25
As Tully had, to write the law by art,
So that with pleasure, or with little pain,
He might perhaps have caught a truant's part.
But all too late, he most misliked the thing
Which most might help to guide his arrow straight;   30

He winked wrong, and so let slip the string,
Which cast him wide, for all his quaint conceit.
From thence he shot to catch a courtly grace,
And thought even there to wield the world at will;
But out alas, he much mistook the place,   35
And shot awry at every rover still.
The blazing baits which draw the gazing eye
Unfeathered there his first affection;
No wonder then although he shot awry,
Wanting the feathers of discretion.   40
Yet more than them, the marks of dignity
He much mistook and shot the wronger way,
Thinking the purse of prodigality
Had been best mean to purchase such a prey.
He thought the flattering face which fleareth still   45
Had been full fraught with all fidelity,
And that such words as courtiers use at will
Could not have varied from the verity.
But when his bonnet buttoned with gold,
His comely cape begarded all with gay,   50
His bombast hose with linings manifold,
His knit silk stocks and all his quaint array,
Had picked his purse of all the Peter pence
Which might have paid for his promotion,
Then (all too late) he found that light expense   55
Had quite quenched out the court's devotion.
So that since then the taste of misery
Hath been always full bitter in his bit.
And why? Forsooth because he shot awry,
Mistaking still the marks which others hit.   60

GASCOIGNE'S WOODSMANSHIP   Written to Lord Grey of Wilton, who had furnished Gascoigne with a crossbow, called him his woodsman, and expected him to help in hunting deer; but Gascoigne never hit a deer, and often simply stood and let them go by as if he hadn't even seen them. **3. amazed:** dazed, bewildered, stupefied. **5. carren:** carrion, i.e. unfit for eating because pregnant (see line 130). **18:** Gascoigne was at Trinity College, Cambridge. **21:** Gascoigne studied law at Gray's Inn around 1555-57, and again after 1565. **22. Littleton:** Sir Thomas Littleton (c.1422-1481), jurist, author of *Treatise on Tenures* (in French), first text on English property law. **23. daw:** jackdaw — simpleton, sluggard. **25. Fitzherbert:** Sir Anthony Fitzherbert (1470-1538), jurist, author of works on law (e.g. *La Grande Abridgement*, 1514, brief accounts of important legal cases) and other subjects. **26. Tully:** Marcus Tullius Cicero, 1st-century B.C. Roman orator, philosopher, politician, and prolific author. **31. winked wrong:** i.e., closed the wrong eye when taking aim. **33-36:** from 1558-63 Gascoigne tried being a courtier. **35. out:** alas. **36. rover:** a mark used as a target, but at no fixed distance. **45. fleareth:** makes a wry face, grins, grimaces; **still:** always, constantly. **49. buttoned:** adorned with buttons. **50. begarded:** variegated for adornment; **gay:** i.e., ornaments, colours. **51. bombast:** stuffed, padded. **53. Peter pence:** i.e., small change (strictly used, the term "Peter pence" or "Peter's pence" referred to an annual tax or tribute of one penny per household, paid to the pope). **58. bit:** bite, mouth.

But now behold what mark the man doth find:
He shoots to be a soldier in his age,
Mistrusting all the virtues of the mind,
He trusts the power of his personage,
As though long limbs led by a lusty heart 65
Might yet suffice to make him rich again;
But Flushing frays have taught him such a part
That now he thinks the wars yield no such gain.
And sure I fear, unless your Lordship deign
To train him yet into some better trade, 70
It will be long before he hit the vein
Whereby he may a richer man be made.
He cannot climb as other catchers can,
To lead a charge before himself be led;
He cannot spoil the simple sackless man 75
Which is content to feed him with his bread.
He cannot pinch the painful soldier's pay
And shear him out his share in ragged sheets;
He cannot stop to take a greedy prey
Upon his fellows grovelling in the streets. 80
He cannot pull the spoil from such as pill
And seem full angry at such foul offence,
Although the gain content his greedy will
Under the cloak of contrary pretence.
And nowadays the man that shoots not so 85
May shoot amiss, even as your woodsman doth;
But then you marvel why I let them go
And never shoot, but say farewell, forsooth.
Alas, my Lord, while I do muse hereon,
And call to mind my youthful years misspent, 90
They give me such a bone to gnaw upon
That all my senses are in silence pent.
My mind is rapt in contemplation,
Wherein my dazzled eyes only behold
The black hour of my constellation, 95
Which framed me so luckless on the mould.
Yet therewithal I cannot but confess
That vain presumption makes my heart to swell,

For thus I think, not all the world (I guess)
Shoots bet than I; nay some shoots not so well. 100
In Aristotle somewhat did I learn
To guide my manners all by comeliness,
And Tully taught me somewhat to discern
Between sweet speech and barbarous rudeness.
Old Parkins, Rastall, and Dan Bracton's books 105
Did lend me somewhat of the lawless law;
The crafty courtiers with their guileful looks
Must needs put some experience in my maw.
Yet cannot these with many maistries mo
Make me shoot straight at any gainful prick, 110
Where some that never handled such a bow
Can hit the white, or touch it near the quick,
Who can nor speak nor write in pleasant wise,
Nor lead their life by Aristotle's rule,
Nor argue well on questions that arise, 115
Nor plead a case more than my Lord Mayor's mule;
Yet can they hit the marks that I do miss,
And win the mean which may the man maintain.
Now when my mind doth mumble upon this,
No wonder then although I pine for pain; 120
And whiles mine eyes behold this mirror thus,
The herd goeth by, and farewell gentle does;
So that your Lordship quickly may discuss
What blinds mine eyes so oft (as I suppose).
But since my Muse can to my Lord rehearse 125
What makes me miss, and why I do not shoot,
Let me imagine in this worthless verse:
If right before me, at my standing's foot,
There stood a doe, and I should strike her dead,
And then she prove a carrion carcass too, 130
What figure might I find within my head
To scuse the rage which ruled me so to do?
Some might interpret by plain paraphrase
That lack of skill or fortune led the chance,
But I must otherwise expound the case; 135
I say Jehovah did this doe advance,

---

62. soldier: Gascoigne served in the Netherlands (hence **Flushing** in line 67) with English volunteers supporting William of Orange against the Spanish. **64. personage:** bodily frame, stature. **73. catchers:** those who chase or drive, huntsmen; also, those who deceive, take in, e.g. to obtain money. **75. sackless:** innocent, guileless. **77. pinch:** limit or restrict narrowly. **79. stop:** possibly meaning "stoop." **81. pill:** pillage, plunder. **95-96:** I.e., the astrological signs were unfavourable at his birth. **96. mould:** earth. **100. bet:** better. **105:** John Parkins, jurist and author of a law text (1530); John Rastell (or Rastall, d.1536), printer, author, and barrister (*Expositiones terminorum legum Angliae*), who married Thomas More's sister; or possibly his son William Rastell (c.1508-1565), printer and judge, who brought out some law books (e.g. *A Collection of All the Statutes*); Henry de Bracton (d.1268; real name Henry of Bratton), English judge and author of a major treatise on English law (*De Legibus et Consuetudinibus Angliae*, published by Tottel in 1569). **109. maistries:** masteries, skills; **mo:** more. **110. prick:** the mark aimed at by an archer, the spot in the centre of the target, the bull's-eye. **112. white:** the white target itself or the white circle at the centre or around the bull's-eye. **118. mean:** means, pecuniary resources. **119. mumble:** chew or bite softly, as with toothless gums. **123. discuss:** examine, judge. **128. standing:** a hunter's station or stand, from which to shoot game. **132. scuse:** excuse.

And made her bold to stand before me so
Till I had thrust mine arrow to her heart,
That by the sudden of her overthrow
I might endeavour to amend my part,   *140*
And turn mine eyes that they no more behold
Such guileful marks as seem more than they be,
And though they glister outwardly like gold,
Are inwardly but brass, as men may see.

And when I see the milk hang in her teat,   *145*
Methinks it saith: old babe, now learn to suck,
Who in thy youth couldst never learn the feat
To hit the whites which live with all good luck.
Thus have I told my Lord (God grant in season)
A tedious tale in rime, but little reason.   *150*

(*1573*)

RAPHAEL HOLINSHED
England, fl. 1577

from *THE HISTORY OF ENGLAND*

Chapter 10: *A catalogue of causes or grievances inciting the Britons to rebel against the Romans, wherein is showed what injuries they sustained; of divers strange wonders and apparitions; the chief cause of the Britons insurging against the Romans; they admitted as well women as men to public government. A description of queen Boadicea, her personage and manner of attire.*

The Britons indeed were occasioned to do as they purposed, through many evil parts practised by the Romans greatly to their griefs and displeasures. For whereas Prasutagus (who is supposed by Hector Boethius to be Arviragus, king of the people called Iceni) had made the emperor and two of his own daughters his heirs, supposing by that means to have his kingdom and family preserved from all injury: it happened quite contrary to   5
that his expectation. For his kingdom was spoiled by the Roman captains, his wife named Boadicea beaten by the soldiers, his daughters ravished, the peers of the realm bereft of their goods, and the king's friends made and reputed as bondslaves.

There was also another great cause that stirred the Britons to this rebellion, which was the confiscating of their goods: for whereas Claudius himself had pardoned the   10
chiefest persons of the forfeitures, Decianus Catus the procurator of the Isle maintained that the same ought to be renewed again. To this another grief was added, that where Seneca had lent to the nobility of the Isle four hundred sesterces, each hundred being

---

THE HISTORY OF ENGLAND   Part of *The Chronicles of England, Scotland and Ireland* (1577), written by Holinshed and others; *The History of England* is by Holinshed. **3. Hector Boethius** (c.1465-c.1536): Scottish historian; **Iceni:** a tribe in what is now Norfolk and Suffolk. **7. Boadicea:** Holinshed's spelling is *Voadicia* (she is also called *Boudicca*, or *Bonduca*, as in the play by Beaumont and Fletcher).

500,000 pounds sterling, or thereabout, upon great interest, he required the whole sum together by great rigour and violence, although he forced them at the first to take this *15* money to usury.

Also such old soldiers as were placed by way of a colony, to inhabit the town of Camulodunum, expelled many of the Britons out of their houses, drove them out of their possessions and lands, and accounted the Britons as slaves, and as though they had been captive prisoners or bondmen. Besides this, the temple there that was built in honour of *20* Claudius, as an altar of eternal rule and government, was served with priests, the which under colour of religion did spoil, consume and devour the goods of all men.

Moreover, such strange sights and wonders as chanced about the same time, pricked the Britons the rather forward. For the image of the goddess Victoria in the temple at Camulodunum, slipping down, turned her back (as who should say she gave *25* place as vanquished) to the enemies. Also in the hall where the courts of justice were kept, there was a marvellous great noise heard, with much laughing, and a stir in the theatre, with great weeping and lamentable howling, at such time as it was certainly known that there was no creature there to make any noise. The sea at a spring tide appeared of a bloody colour, and when the tide was gone back, there were seen on the *30* sands the shapes and figures of men's bodies. Women also as ravished of their wits, and being as it were in a fury, prophesied that destruction was at hand, so that the Britons were put greatly in hope, and the Romans in fear.

But those things, whether they chanced by the craft of man, or illusion of the devil; or whether they proceeded of some natural cause, which the common people oftentimes *35* taketh superstitiously, in place of strange wonders signifying things to follow, we would let pass, lest we might be thought to offend religion; the which teaching all things to be done by the providence of God, despiseth the vain predictions of haps to come, if the order of an history (saith Polydor Virgil) would so permit, the which requireth all things to be written in manner as they fall out and come to pass. *40*

But the Britons were chiefly moved to rebellion by the just complaint of Boadicea, declaring how unseemly she had been used and treated at the hands of the Romans: and because she was most earnestly bent to seek revenge of their injuries, and hated the name of the Romans most of all other, they chose her to be captain (for they in rule and government made no difference then of sex, whether they committed the same to man or *45* woman) and so by a general conspiracy, the more part of the people having also allured the Essex men into rebellion, rose and assembled themselves together to make war against the Romans. There were of them a hundred and twenty thousand got together in one army under the leading of the said Boadicea, or Bunduica (as some name her).

She therefore to encourage her people against the enemies, mounted up into an high *50* place raised up of turfs and sods made for the nonce, out of the which she made a long and very pithy oration. Her mighty tall personage, comely shape, severe countenance, and sharp voice, with her long and yellow tresses of hair reaching down to her thighs,

---

18. Camulodunum: modern Colchester, in Essex. **39. Polydor Virgil** (or Polydore Vergil) (c.1470-c.1555): Italian historian, author of a history of England published in 1534.

her brave and gorgeous apparel also caused the people to have her in great reverence. She wore a chain of gold, great and very massy, and was clad in a loose kirtle of sundry $\quad$ 55 colours, and aloft thereupon she had a thick Irish mantle: hereto in her hand (as her custom was) she bore a spear, to shew herself the more dreadful.

Chapter 11: *The oration of queen Boadicea full of prudence and spirit to the Britons, for their encouragement against the Romans, wherein she rippeth up the vile servitude and shameful wrongs which their enemies inflicted upon them, with other matters very motive, both concerning themselves and their enemies; her supplication and prayer for victory.*

Now Boadicea being prepared (as you hear) set forth with such majesty, that she greatly encouraged the Britons; unto whom for their better animating and emboldening, she uttered this gallant oration in manner and form following. $\quad$ 60
   "I do suppose (my lovers and friends) that there is no man here but doth well understand how much liberty and freedom is to be preferred before thraldom and bondage. But if there have been any of you so deceived with the Roman persuasions, that ye did not for a time see a difference between them, and judged whether of both is most to be desired: now I hope that having tried what it is to be under both, ye will with $\quad$ 65 me reform your judgment, and by the harms already taken, acknowledge your oversight, and forsake your former error. Again, in that a number of you have rashly preferred an external sovereignty before the customs and laws of your own country, you do at this time (I doubt not) perfectly understand how much free poverty is to be preferred before great riches whereunto servitude is annexed; and much wealth in respect of captivity $\quad$ 70 under foreign magistrates whereupon slavery attendeth. For what thing (I beseech you) can there be so vile and grievous unto the nature of man, that hath not happened unto us, since the time that the Romans have been acquainted with this Island?
   "Are we not all in manner bereaved of our riches and possessions? Do not we (besides other things that we give, and the land that we till for their only profit) pay $\quad$ 75 them all kinds of tributes, yea for our own carcases? How much better is it to be once aloft and fortunate in deed, than under the forged and false title of liberty continually to pay for our redemption a freedom? How much is it more commendable to lose our lives in defense of our country, than to carry about not so much as our heads toll free, but daily oppressed and laden with innumerable exactions? But to what end do I remember $\quad$ 80 and speak of these things, since they will not suffer by death to become free? For what and how much we pay for them that are dead, there is not one here but he doth well understand. Among other nations such as are brought into servitude, are always by death discharged of their bondage: only to the Romans the dead do still live, and all to increase their commodity and gain. $\quad$ 85
   "If any of us be without money (as I know not well how and which way we should come by any) then are we left naked, and spoiled of that which remaineth in our houses,

---

56. Irish mantle: a sort of heavy cape or blanket worn by Irish rustics.

and we ourselves as men left desolate and dead. How shall we look for better dealing at their hand hereafter, that in the beginning deal so uncourteously with us: since there is no man that taketh so much as a wild beast, but at the first he will cherish it, and with some gentleness win it to familiarity? But we ourselves (to say the truth) are authors of our own mischief, which suffered them at the first to set foot within our Island, and did not by and by drive them back as we did Caesar, or slew them with our swords when they were yet far off, and that the adventuring hither was dangerous: as we did sometime to Augustus and Caligula. *95*

"We therefore that inhabit this Island, which for the quantity thereof may well be called a main, although it be environed about with the Ocean sea, dividing us from other nations, so that we seem to live upon another earth, and under a several heaven: we, even we (I say) whose name hath been long kept hid from the wisest of them all, are now contemned and trodden under foot, of them who study nothing else but how to *100* become lords and have rule of other men. Wherefore my well-beloved citizens, friends, and kinsfolk (for I think we are all of kin, since we were born and dwell in this Isle, and have one name common to us all), let us now, even now (I say, because we have not done it heretofore, and whilst the remembrance of our ancient liberty remaineth), stick together, and perform that thing which doth pertain to valiant and hardy courage, to the *105* end we may enjoy, not only the name of liberty, but also freedom itself, and thereby leave our force and valiant acts for an example to our posterity: for if we which have been liberally and in honest manner brought up, should utterly forget our pristinate felicity, what may we hope for in those that shall succeed us, and are like to be brought up in misery and thraldom? *110*

"I do not make rehearsal of these things unto you, to the end I would provoke you to mislike of this present estate of things (for well I know you abhor it sufficiently already), neither to put you in fear of those things that are likely to fall hereafter (because you do fear and see them very well beforehand), but to the end I may give you hearty thanks and worthy commendations, for that of your own accord and means you *115* determine so well to provide for things necessary (thereby to help both me and yourselves with willing minds) as men that are nothing in doubt of all the Roman puissance.

"If you consider the number of your enemies, it is not greater than yours: if you regard their strength, they are no stronger than you: and all this doth easily appear by the *120* basinets, habergeons, and grieves wherewith you be armed; and also by the walls, ditches, and trenches that you have made for your own defense, to keep off their excursions, who had rather fight with us afar off, than cope and deal with us at handstrokes, as our custom of the wars and martial discipline doth require. Wherefore we do so far exceed them in force, that in mine opinion, our army is more strong than *125* stone walls, and one of our targets worth all the armour that they do bear upon them: by means whereof, if the victory be ours, we shall soon make them captives: or if we lose the field, we shall easily escape the danger.

93-95. Caesar . . . Augustus . . . Caligula: Julius Caesar's raids into Britain occurred in 55 and 54 B.C.; Augustus planned an invasion, and Caligula led an invasion force as far as Boulogne. Claudius's conquest commenced in A.D. 43 and was complete by 85. The uprising inspired by Boadicea took place in 61. **121. basinets, habergeons, grieves:** helmets, mail jackets, leg armour (greaves).

"Furthermore, if after the flight we shall endeavour to meet anywhere, we have the marshes here beneath to hide us in, and the hills round about to keep them off, so that by 130 no means they shall have their purpose of us, whereas they being overcharged with heavy armour, shall neither be able to follow, if we flee, nor escape out of our danger, if they be put to flight; if they happen to break out at any time as desirous to make a raid, they return by and by to their appointed places, where we may take them as birds already in cage. In all which things, as they are far inferior to us, so most of all in this, 135 that they can not endure hunger, thirst, cold, heat, and sunshine, as we can do.

"In their houses also and tents, they make much account of their baked meats, wine, oil, and abroad of the shadow, that if any of these do fail them, they either die forthwith, or else in time they languish and consume: whereas to us every herb and root is meat, every juice an oil, all water pleasant wine, and every tree an house. Besides this, there is 140 no place of the land unknown to us, neither yet unfriendly to succour us at need; whereas to the Romans they are for the most part unknown and altogether dangerous, if they should stand in need; we can with ease swim over every river both naked and clad, which they with their great ships are scarce able to perform. Wherefore with hope and good luck let us set upon them courageously, and teach them to understand, that since 145 they are no better than hares and foxes, they attempt a wrong match when they endeavour to subdue the greyhounds and wolves." With which words the queen let an hare go out of her lap, as it were thereby to give prognostication of her success, which coming well to pass, all the company shouted, and cried out upon such as not long before had done such violence to so noble a personage. Presently upon this action, 150 Boadicea calling them together again, proceeded forward with her prayer, which she made before them all, holding up her hands, after this manner:

"I give thee thanks, O Adraste, and call upon thee thou woman of women, which reignest not over the burthen-bearing Egyptians, as Nitocris; neither over their merchants, as doth Semiramis, for these trifles we have learned lately of the Romans; 155 neither over the people of Rome, as a little heretofore Messalina, then Agrippina, and now Nero, who is called by the name of a man, but is indeed a very woman, as doth appear by his voice, his harp, and his woman's attire: but I call upon thee as a goddess which governest the Britons, that have learned not to till the field, nor to be handicraftsmen, but to lead their lives in the wars after the best manner: who also as 160 they have all other things, so have they likewise their wives and children common, whereby the women have the like audacity with the men, and no less boldness in the wars than they.

"Therefore since I have obtained a kingdom among such a mighty people, I beseech thee to grant them victory, health, and liberty, against these contentious, wicked, and 165 unsatiable men (if they may be called men, which use warm bathings, delicate fare, hot wines, sweet oils, soft beds, fine music, and so unkindly lusts) who are altogether given to covetousness and cruelty, as their doings do declare. Let not, I beseech thee, the Neronian or Domitian tyranny any more prevail upon me, or (to say truth) upon thee,

---

153. **Adraste:** probably *Adrasteia* (meaning perhaps "one whom no one escapes" or "the inevitable"), another name for Nemesis. 154. **Nitocris:** obscure Egyptian queen of about the 8th dynasty. 167. **unkindly:** unnatural.

but let them rather serve thee, whose heavy oppression thou hast born withal a long *170*
season, and that thou wilt still be our helper only, our defender, our favourer, and our
furtherer, O noble lady, I heartily beseech thee.'"

Chapter 12: *Queen Boadicea marcheth against the Romans, to whom she*
giveth a shameful and bloody overthrow without any motion of mercy;
dreadful examples of the Britons' cruelty indifferently executed without
exception of age or sex.

When Boadicea had made an end of her prayer, she set forward against her enemies,
who at that time were destitute indeed of their lieutenant Paulinus Suetonius, being as
then in Anglesey (as before ye have heard). Wherefore the Romans that were in *175*
Camulodunum sent for aid unto Catus Decianus the procurator, that is, the emperor's
agent, treasurer, or receiver, for in that city (although it were inhabited by Romans)
there was no great garrison of able men. Whereupon the procurator sent them such aid
as he thought he might well spare, which was not past two hundred men, and those not
sufficiently furnished either with weapon or armour. *180*

The city was not compassed with any rampart or ditch for defense, such as happily
were privy to the conspiracy having put into the heads of the Romans that no
fortification needed; neither were the aged men nor women sent away, whereby the
young able personages might without trouble of them the better attend to the defense of
the city; but even as they had been in all surety of peace, and free from suspicion of any *185*
war, they were suddenly beset with the huge army of Britons, and so all went to spoil
and fire that could be found without the enclosure of the temple, into the which the
Roman soldiers (stricken with sudden fear by this sudden coming of the enemies) had
thronged themselves. Where being besieged by the Britons, within the space of two days
the place was won, and they that were found within it slain, every mother's son. *190*

After this, the Britons, encouraged with the victory, went to meet with Petus
Cerealis, lieutenant of the legion, surnamed the ninth, and boldly encountering with the
same legion, gave the Romans the overthrow and slew all the footmen, so that Cerealis
with much ado escaped with his horsemen, and got him back to the camp, and saved
himself within the trenches. Catus the procurator being put in fear with this overthrow, *195*
and perceiving what hatred the Britons bare towards him, having with his covetousness
thus brought the war upon the head of the Romans, got him over into Gallia.

But Suetonius, advertised of these doings, came back out of Anglesey, and with
marvellous constancy marched through the midst of his enemies to London, being as
then not greatly peopled with Romans, though there was a colony of them, but full of *200*
merchants, and well provided of vittles: he was in great doubt at his coming thither,
whether he might best stay there as in a place most convenient, or rather seek some
other more easy to be defended. At length considering the small number of his men of
war, and remembering how Cerealis had sped by his too much rashness, he thought
better with the losing of one town to save the whole, than to put all in danger of *205*
irrecoverable loss. And therewith nothing moved at the prayer and tears of them which

197. **Gallia:** Gaul.

besought him of aid and succour, he departed, and those that would go with him he received into his army, those that tarried behind were oppressed by the enemies: and the like destruction happened to them of Verulamium, a town in those days of great fame, situate near to the place where the town of Saint Albans now standeth.   *210*

The Britons, leaving the castles and fortresses unassaulted, followed their gain in spoiling of those places which were easy to get, and where great plenty of riches was to be found, using their victory with such cruelty, that they slew (as the report went) to the number of 70 thousand Romans, and such as took their part in the said places by the Britons thus won and conquered. For there was nothing with the Britons but slaughter, *215* fire, gallows, and such like, so earnestly were they set on revenge. They spared neither age nor sex: women of great nobility and worthy fame they took and hanged up naked, and cutting off their paps, sewed them to their mouths, that they might seem as if they sucked and fed on them, and some of their bodies they stretched out in length, and thrust them on sharp stakes. All these things they did in great despite whilst they sacrificed in *220* their temples, and made feasts, namely in the wood consecrated to the honour of Andates, for so they called the goddess of victory whom they worshipped most reverently.

(1577)

[Note: Paulinus soon gathered reinforcements and crushed the revolt; Boadicea swallowed poison.]

Barnabe Googe
England, 1540-1594

OUT OF SIGHT, OUT OF MIND

The oftener seen, the more I lust,	The lesser grief, the greater gain, *10*
The more I lust, the more I smart,	The greater gain, the merrier I;
The more I smart, the more I trust,	Therefore I wish thy sight to fly.
The more I trust, the heavier heart,	
The heavy heart breeds mine unrest; *5*	The further off, the more I joy,
Thy absence therefore like I best.	The more I joy, the happier life,
	The happier life, less hurts annoy, *15*
The rarer seen, the less in mind,	The lesser hurts, pleasure most rife;
The less in mind, the lesser pain,	Such pleasures rife shall I obtain
The lesser pain, less grief I find,	When distance doth depart us twain.
	(1563)

OUT OF SIGHT, OUT OF MIND   **18. depart:** separate. For another example of such repetition (anadiplosis), see the anonymous "Upon Consideration of the State of This Life He Wisheth Death" (p. 128).

SIR EDWARD DYER
England, 1543-1607

"The lowest trees have tops, the ant her gall"
The lowest trees have tops, the ant her gall,
The fly her spleen, the little spark his heat;
The slender hairs cast shadows, though but small,
And bees have stings, although they be not great;
    Seas have their source, and so have shallow springs,   *5*
    And love is love, in beggars and in kings.
Where waters smoothest run, there deepest are the fords;
The dial stirs, yet none perceives it move;
The firmest faith is found in fewest words,
The turtles do not sing, and yet they love;   *10*
    True hearts have ears and eyes, no tongues to speak;
    They hear and see, and sigh, and then they break.
                              (c. 1580)

GEORGE TURBERVILLE
England, c.1544-c.1597

He declares that albeit he were imprisoned in Russia, yet his mind was at liberty and did daily repair to his friend

Now find I true that hath been often told,
No man may reave the freedom of the mind.
Though keeper's charge in chains the captive hold,
Yet can he not the soul in bondage bind.
That this is true I find the proof in me,   *5*
Who captive am and yet at liberty.

Though at my heel a cruel clog they tie,
And ranging out by rigour be restrained,
Yet maugre might, my mind doth freely fly

Home to my friend; it will not be enchained.   *10*
No churle's check, no tyrant's threat can stay
A lover's heart that longs to be away.

I do desire no aid of Dædalus
By feat to forge such waxen wings anew
As erst he gave his son, young Icarus,   *15*
When they from Crete for fear of Minos flew;
Dame Fancy hath such feathers still in store
For me to fly, as I desire no more.
                           (1587)

THE LOWEST TREES HAVE TOPS 12. turtles: turtledoves. **HE DECLARES THAT...** 9. maugre: in spite of.

EDMUND SPENSER
England, 1552-1599

from *THE SHEPHEARDES CALENDER*

JANUARYE

Aegloga prima.

Argument.

In this fyrst Æglogue Colin Cloute a shepheardes boy complaineth him of his unfortunate love, being but newly (as semeth) enamoured of a countrie lasse called Rosalinde: with which strong affection being very sore traveled, he compareth his carefull case to the sadde season of the yeare, to the frostie ground, to the frosen trees, and to his owne winterbeaten flocke. And lastlye, fynding himselfe robbed of all former pleasaunce and delights, hee breaketh his Pipe in peeces and casteth him selfe to the ground.

SPENSER   Because Spenser deliberately made his poetic style look and sound archaic, in the selections from his poetry we have left his spelling intact except for using *j*'s (which were then printed as *i*'s) and regularizing *u*'s and *v*'s (which were then often interchanged). We have also altered punctuation in a few instances where the original might have made comprehension difficult. As with Chaucer, reading aloud will often enable you to understand a word that looks strange. Unlike with Chaucer, final *e*'s are seldom pronounced; but a final *ed* is almost always pronounced; and some combinations are given multisyllabic value not present in modern English (e.g. *pu-is-sance*). As usual, scansion will prove a useful guide in these matters, as also in alerting you to the occasional need to elide vowel sounds.   **JANUARY**   An elaborate introduction to the twelve eclogues of *The Shepheardes Calender* was provided by one "E. K." — probably Edward Kirke, a fellow-student of Spenser's at Cambridge, though some scholars think "E. K." is a fiction for Spenser himself. E. K. also wrote the "Argument" preceding each eclogue and, after each, provided a "Glosse" defining or explaining some of the more difficult terms (e.g. the deliberate archaisms), pointing out sources and allusions, and expatiating on various features of the poems. Rather than include the complete "Glosse" for the January eclogue, we have incorporated a few of E. K.'s more helpful points in our own Gloss. **Argument: traveled:** travailed, troubled; **carefull:** full of care, sorrowful, sad.

Colin Cloute

A Shepeheards boye (no better doe him call)
When Winters wastful spight was almost spent,
All in a sunneshine day, as did befall,
Led forth his flock, that had bene long ypent.
So faynt they woxe, and feeble in the folde,   5
That now unnethes their feete could them uphold.

All as the Sheepe, such was the shepheards looke,
For pale and wanne he was, (alas the while),
May seeme he lovd, or els some care he tooke;
Well couth he tune his pipe, and frame his stile.   10
Tho to a hill his faynting flocke he ledde,
And thus him playnd, the while his shepe there fedde.

Ye Gods of love, that pitie lovers payne,
(If any gods the paine of lovers pitie),
Looke from above, where you in joyes remaine,   15
And bowe your eares unto my dolefull dittie.
And Pan thou shepheards God, that once didst love,
Pitie the paines, that thou thy selfe didst prove.

Thou barrein ground, whome winters wrath hath wasted,
Art made a myrrhour, to behold my plight;   20
Whilome thy fresh spring flowrd, and after hasted
Thy sommer prowde with Daffadillies dight.
And now is come thy wynters stormy state,
Thy mantle mard, wherein thou maskedst late.

Such rage as winters reigneth in my heart,   25
My life bloud friesing with unkindly cold;
Such stormy stoures do breede my balefull smart,
As if my year were wast, and woxen old.
And yet alas, but now my spring begonne,
And yet alas, yt is already donne.   30

You naked trees, whose shady leaves are lost,
Wherein the byrds were wont to build their bowre,
And now are clothd with mosse and hoary frost,
Instede of bloosmes, wherwith your buds did flowre;
I see your teares, that from your boughes doe raine,   35
Whose drops in drery ysicles remaine.

All so my lustfull leafe is drye and sere,
My timely buds with wayling all are wasted;
The blossome, which my braunch of youth did beare,
With breathed sighes is blowne away, and blasted,   40

And from mine eyes the drizling teares descend,
As on your boughes the ysicles depend.

Thou feeble flocke, whose fleece is rough and rent,
Whose knees are weake through fast and evill fare,
Mayst witnesse well by thy ill governement,   45
Thy maysters mind is overcome with care.
Thou weake, I wanne; thou leane, I quite forlorne;
With mourning pyne I, you with pyning mourne.

A thousand sithes I curse that carefull hower,
Wherein I longd the neighbour towne to see,   50
And eke tenne thousand sithes I blesse the stoure,
Wherein I sawe so fayre a sight, as shee.
Yet all for naught: such sight hath bred my bane.
Ah God, that love should breede both joy and payne.

It is not Hobbinol, wherefore I plaine,   55
Albee my love he seeke with dayly suit:
His clowning gifts and curtsies I disdaine,
His kiddes, his cracknelles, and his early fruit.
Ah foolish Hobbinol, thy gyfts bene vayne;
Colin them gives to Rosalind againe.   60

I love thilke lasse, (alas why doe I love?)
And am forlorne, (alas why am I lorne?)
Shee deignes not my good will, but doth reprove,
And of my rurall musick holdeth scorne.
Shepheards devise she hateth as the snake,   65
And laughes the songes, that Colin Clout doth make.

Wherefore my pype, albee rude Pan thou please,
Yet for thou pleasest not, where most I would;
And thou unlucky Muse, that wontst to ease
My musing mynd, yet canst not, when thou should;   70
Both pype and Muse, shall sore the while abye.
So broke his oaten pype, and downe dyd lye.

By that, the welked Phoebus gan availe
His weary waine, and nowe the frosty Night
Her mantle black through heaven gan overhaile.   75
Which seene, the pensife boy halfe in despight
Arose, and homeward drove his sonned sheep,
Whose hanging heads did seeme his carefull case to weepe.

Colins Embleme.
Anchóra speme.

(1579)

---

4. ypent: pent up. **5. woxe:** waxed. **6. unnethes:** scarcely [E. K.]. **10. couth:** "commeth of the verbe Conne, that is, to know or to have skill" [E. K.]; **stile:** composition. **11. Tho:** then. **12. playnd:** complained. **24. mard:** marred, spoiled. **27. stoures:** tumult, disturbance. **37. lustfull:** lusty, vigorous. **42. depend:** hang. **49. sithes:** times [E. K.]. **51. eke:** also. **58. cracknelles:** crackers, biscuits. **61. thilke:** this (that), this (that) same. **61-62:** "a prety Epanorthosis in these two verses, and withall a Paronomasia or playing with the word, where he sayth (I love thilke lasse (alas &c." [E. K.]; the rhetorical term *epanorthosis* refers to the changing of a statement while making it, e.g. recalling a term in order to correct or otherwise alter it. **63. deignes:** condescends to accept. **65. devise:** arts. **73. welked:** waning, fading; **avail:** "bring downe" [E. K.]. **75. overhaile:** "drawe over" [E. K.]. **76. despight:** anger. **77. sonned:** sunned, exposed to the sun. E. K. explains the emblem as follows: "His embleme or Poesye is here under added in Italian, Anchóra speme: the meaning whereof is, that notwithstanding his extreme passion and lucklesse love, yet leaning on hope, he is some what recomforted."

from *The Faerie Queene*

A Letter of the Authors expounding his whole intention in the course of this work, which for that it giveth great light to the reader, for the better understanding is hereunto annexed.

To the right noble and valorous Sir Walter Raleigh, knight, Lord Warden of the Stannaries and Her Majesty's lieutenant of the County of Cornwall.

Sir, knowing how doubtfully all allegories may be construed, and this book of mine, which I have entitled *The Faerie Queene*, being a continued allegory, or dark conceit, I have thought good as well for avoiding of jealous opinions and misconstructions, as also for your better light in reading thereof (being so by you commanded), to discover unto you the general intention and meaning, which in the whole course thereof I have   *5* fashioned, without expressing of any particular purposes or by-accidents therein occasioned.

The general end therefore of all the book is to fashion a gentleman or noble person in virtuous and gentle discipline; which for that I conceived should be most plausible and pleasing, being coloured with an historical fiction, the which the most part of men   *10* delight to read, rather for variety of matter than for profit of the example, I chose the history of King Arthur as most fit for the excellency of his person, being made famous by many men's former works, and also furthest from the danger of envy and suspicion of present time. In which I have followed all the antique poets historical: first Homer, who in the persons of Agamemnon and Ulysses hath exampled a good governor and a   *15* virtuous man, the one in his *Iliad*, the other in his *Odyssey*; then Virgil, whose like intention was to do in the person of Aeneas; after him Ariosto comprised them both in his Orlando; and lately Tasso dissevered them again, and formed both parts in two persons, namely that part which they in Philosophy call Ethic, or virtues of a private man, coloured in his Rinaldo, the other named Politic in his Goffredo. By example of   *20* which excellent poets I labour to portray in Arthur, before he was king, the image of a brave knight, perfected in the twelve private moral virtues, as Aristotle hath devised, the which is the purpose of these first twelve books; which if I find to be well accepted, I may be perhaps encouraged to frame the other part of politic virtues in his person after that he came to be king.   *25*

To some I know this method will seem displeasant, which had rather have good discipline delivered plainly in way of precepts, or sermoned at large, as they use, than thus cloudily enwrapped in allegorical devices. But such, meseems, should be satisfied with the use of these days, seeing all things accounted by their shows, and nothing esteemed of that is not delightful and pleasing to common sense. For this cause is   *30* Xenophon preferred before Plato, for that the one in the exquisite depth of his judgment

---

A **Letter of the Authors** 6. **by-accidents:** incidentals. 9. **for that:** because. 18. **Orlando:** in *Orlando Furioso.* 20. **Rinaldo . . . Goffredo:** in *Gerusalemme Liberata.* 22. **Aristotle:** The allusions in this and the preceding sentence are to Aristotle's *Nichomachean Ethics* and *Politics.* 29. **shows:** appearance. 31. **Xenophon . . . Plato:** The references are to Xenophon's *Cyropaedia* and Plato's *Republic.*

formed a commonwealth such as it should be, but the other in the person of Cyrus and the Persians fashioned a government such as might best be. So much more profitable and gracious is doctrine by example than by rule.

So have I laboured to do in the person of Arthur, whom I conceive after his long 35 education by Timon, to whom he was by Merlin delivered to be brought up, so soon as he was born of the Lady Igrayne, to have seen in a dream or vision the Faery Queen, with whose excellent beauty ravished, he awaking resolved to seek her out, and so being by Merlin armed, and by Timon thoroughly instructed, he went to seek her forth in Faeryland. In that Faery Queen I mean glory in my general intention, but in my 40 particular I conceive the most excellent and glorious person of our sovereign the Queen, and her kingdom in Faeryland. And yet in some places else I do otherwise shadow her. For considering she beareth two persons, the one of a most royal queen or empress, the other of a most virtuous and beautiful lady, this latter part in some places I do express in Belphoebe, fashioning her name according to your own excellent concept of Cynthia 45 (Phoebe and Cynthia being both names of Diana).

So in the person of Prince Arthur I set forth magnificence in particular, which virtue for that (according to Aristotle and the rest) it is the perfection of all the rest, and containeth in it them all, therefore in the whole course I mention the deeds of Arthur applicable to that virtue which I write of in that book. But of the twelve other virtues I 50 make twelve other knights the patrons, for the more variety of the history; of which these three books contain three: the first of the Knight of the Redcross, in whom I express Holiness; the second of Sir Guyon, in whom I set forth Temperance; the third of Britomartis, a Lady Knight, in whom I picture Chastity.

But because the beginning of the whole work seemeth abrupt and as depending 55 upon other antecedents, it needs that ye know the occasion of these three knights' several adventures. For the method of a poet historical is not such as of an historiographer. For an historiographer discourseth of affairs orderly as they were done, accounting as well the times as the actions; but a poet thrusteth into the midst, even where it most concerneth him, and there recoursing to the things forepast and divining of things 60 to come, maketh a pleasing analysis of all. The beginning therefore of my history, if it were to be told by an historiographer, should be the twelfth book, which is the last, where I devise that the Faery Queen kept her annual feast twelve days, upon which twelve several days the occasions of the twelve several adventures happened, which being undertaken by twelve several knights, are in these twelve books severally handled 65 and discoursed.

The first was this. In the beginning of the feast, there presented himself a tall clownish young man, who falling before the Queen of Faeries desired a boon (as the manner then was) which during that feast she might not refuse, which was that he might have the achievement of any adventure which during that feast should happen; that 70 being granted, he rested him on the floor, unfit through his rusticity for a better place.

---

42. shadow: portray allegorically. **45. Cynthia:** in a surviving fragment of a long poem usually called *The Ocean to Cynthia,* or *Cynthia, the Lady of the Sea.* **52. these three books:** The first three books of *The Faerie Queene* were published in 1590, the second three in 1596; the rest were never finished, though a part of Book VII appeared in 1609. **59. into the midst:** See *in medias res* in the Glossary. **68. clownish:** rustic, awkward, coarse.

Soon after entered a fair lady in mourning weeds, riding on a white ass, with a dwarf behind her leading a warlike steed that bore the arms of a knight, and his spear in the dwarf's hand. She falling before the Queen of Faeries, complained that her father and mother, an ancient King and Queen, had been by an huge dragon many years shut up in   *75* a brazen castle, who thence suffered them not to issue; and therefore besought the Faery Queen to assign her some one of her knights to take on him that exploit. Presently that clownish person upstarting, desired that adventure, whereat the Queen much wondering, and the lady much gainsaying, yet he earnestly importuned his desire. In the end the lady told him that unless that armour which she brought would serve him (that is the   *80* armour of a Christian man specified by Saint Paul, v. *Ephes.*) that he could not succeed in that enterprise; which being forthwith put upon him with due furnitures thereunto, he seemed the goodliest man in all that company, and was well liked of the lady. And eftsoons taking on him knighthood, and mounting on that strange courser, he went forth with her on that adventure; where beginneth the first book, viz.   *85*

A gentle knight was pricking on the playne, &c.

The second day there came in a palmer bearing an infant with bloody hands, whose parents he complained to have been slain by an enchantress called Acrasia, and therefore craved of the Faery Queene to appoint him some knight to perform that adventure, which being assigned to Sir Guyon, he presently went forth with that same   *90* palmer; which is the beginning of the second book and the whole subject thereof. The third day there came in a groom who complained before the Faery Queen that a vile enchanter called Busirane had in hand a most fair lady called Amoretta, whom he kept in most grievous torment because she would not yield him the pleasure of her body. Whereupon Sir Scudamour, the lover of that lady, presently took on him that adventure.   *95* But being unable to perform it by reason of the hard enchantments, after long sorrow, in the end met with Britomartis, who succoured him and rescued his love.

But by occasion hereof, many other adventures are intermeddled, but rather as accidents than intendments. As the love of Britomart, the overthrow of Marinell, the misery of Florimell, the virtuousness of Belphoebe, the lasciviousness of Hellenora, and   *100* many the like.

Thus much, Sir, I have briefly overrun to direct your understanding to the well-head of the history, that from thence gathering the whole intention of the conceit, ye may as in a handful grip all the discourse, which otherwise may happily seem tedious and confused. So humbly craving the continuance of your honourable favour towards me,   *105* and th'eternal establishment of your happiness, I humbly take leave.

23 January 1589.
Yours most humbly affectionate,
Ed. Spenser.

---

81. v. *Ephes.*: *vide* (see) *Ephesians* 6:11-17. 82. due furnitures: necessary equipment. 99. intendments: principal intentions. 104. happily: haply, perchance.

from BOOK I

The First Booke of The Faerie Queene. Contayning The Legende
of the Knight of the Red Crosse, or of Holinesse.

1

Lo I the man, whose Muse whilome did maske,
   As time her taught, in lowly Shepheards weeds,
   Am now enforst a far unfitter taske,
   For trumpets sterne to chaunge mine Oaten reeds,
   And sing of Knights and Ladies gentle deeds;   5
   Whose prayses having slept in silence long,
   Me, all too meane, the sacred Muse areeds
   To blazon broad emongst her learned throng:
Fierce warres and faithfull loves shall moralize my song.

2

Helpe then, O holy Virgin chiefe of nine,   10
   Thy weaker Novice to performe thy will,
   Lay forth out of thine everlasting scryne
   The antique rolles, which there lye hidden still,
   Of Faerie knights and fairest *Tanaquill*,
   Whom that most noble Briton Prince so long   15
   Sought through the world, and suffered so much ill,
   That I must rue his undeserved wrong:
O helpe thou my weake wit, and sharpen my dull tong.

3

And thou most dreaded impe of highest *Jove*,
   Faire *Venus* sonne, that with thy cruell dart   20
   At that good knight so cunningly didst rove,
   That glorious fire it kindled in his hart,
   Lay now thy deadly Heben bow apart,
   And with thy mother milde come to mine ayde;
   Come both, and with you bring triumphant *Mart*,   25
   In loves and gentle jollities arrayd,
After his murdrous spoiles and bloudy rage allayd.

4

And with them eke, O Goddesse heavenly bright,
   Mirrour of grace and Majestie divine,
   Great Lady of the greatest Isle, whose light   30
   Like *Phoebus* lampe throughout the world doth shine,
   Shed thy faire beames into my feeble eyne,
   And raise my thoughts too humble and too vile,
   To thinke of that true glorious type of thine,
   The argument of mine afflicted stile;   35
The which to heare, vouchsafe, O dearest dred a-while.

Canto I

The Patron of true Holinesse,
   foule Errour doth defeate:
Hypocrisie him to entrappe,
   doth to his home entreate.

1

A Gentle Knight was pricking on the plaine,
   Ycladd in mightie armes and silver shielde,
   Wherein old dints of deepe wounds did remaine,
   The cruell markes of many' a bloudy fielde;
   Yet armes till that time did he never wield: 5
   His angry steede did chide his foming bitt,
   As much disdayning to the curbe to yield:
   Full jolly knight he seemd, and faire did sitt,
As one for knightly giusts and fierce encounters fitt.

2

But on his brest a bloudie Crosse he bore,   10
   The deare remembrance of his dying Lord,
   For whose sweete sake that glorious badge he wore,

BOOK 1 (INVOCATION)   **3. enforst:** probably by Sir Philip Sidney. **7. Muse:** Calliope, muse of epic poetry, or perhaps Clio, muse of history;
areeds: teaches, advises. **12. scryne:** chest for books and papers. **14. Tanaquill:** wife of Tarquinius Priscus, legendary fifth king of Rome, she was
commonly thought of as a model of a noble queen — here one of Spenser's names for Queen Elizabeth. **15. Briton Prince:** Arthur. **19-20: impe . . .
Faire Venus sonne:** Cupid. **21. rove:** shoot. **23. Heben:** ebon. **25. Mart:** Mars, god of war. **28. eke:** also; **Goddesse:** Elizabeth. **31. Phoebus:** the sun,
after Phoebus Apollo, god of the sun. **32. eyne:** eyes. **34. glorious type:** Gloriana, the Faerie Queene, as "type" or foreshadowing of Elizabeth. **35.
afflicted:** humble; **stile:** style, composition, or perhaps pen (stylus). **36. dred:** dread, object of reverence.   **CANTO I**   **1. Gentle:** noble, chivalrous,
of gentle birth; **pricking:** spurring, riding. **8. jolly:** gallant, brave. **9. giusts:** jousts.

And dead as living ever him ador'd:
Upon his shield the like was also scor'd,
For soveraine hope, which in his helpe he had;   *15*
Right faithfull true he was in deede and word,
But of his cheere did seeme too solemne sad;
Yet nothing did he dread, but ever was ydrad.

3
Upon a great adventure he was bond,
That greatest *Gloriana* to him gave,   *20*
That greatest Glorious Queene of *Faerie* lond,
To winne him worship, and her grace to have,
Which of all earthly things he most did crave;
And ever as he rode, his hart did earne
To prove his puissance in battell brave   *25*
Upon his foe, and his new force to learne;
Upon his foe, a Dragon horrible and stearne.

4
A lovely Ladie rode him faire beside,
Upon a lowly Asse more white then snow,
Yet she much whiter, but the same did hide   *30*
Under a vele, that wimpled was full low,
And over all a blacke stole she did throw,
As one that inly mournd: so was she sad,
And heavie sat upon her palfrey slow;
Seemed in heart some hidden care she had,   *35*
And by her in a line a milke white lambe she lad.

5
So pure an innocent, as that same lambe,
She was in life and every vertuous lore,
And by descent from Royall lynage came
Of ancient Kings and Queenes, that had of yore   *40*
Their scepters stretcht from East to Westerne shore,
And all the world in their subjection held;
Till that infernall feend with foule uprore
Forwasted all their land, and them expeld: *44*
Whom to avenge, she had this Knight from far compeld.

6
Behind her farre away a Dwarfe did lag,
That lasie seemd in being ever last,
Or wearied with bearing of her bag

Of needments at his backe. Thus as they past,
The day with cloudes was suddeine overcast,   *50*
And angry *Jove* an hideous storme of raine
Did poure into his Lemans lap so fast,
That every wight to shrowd it did constrain,
And this faire couple eke to shroud themselves were fain.

7
Enforst to seeke some covert nigh at hand,   *55*
A shadie grove not far away they spide,
That promist ayde the tempest to withstand:
Whose loftie trees yclad with sommers pride,
Did spred so broad that heavens light did hide,
Not perceable with power of any starre: *60*
And all within were pathes and alleies wide,
With footing worne, and leading inward farre:
Faire harbour that them seemes; so in they entred arre.

8
And foorth they passe, with pleasure forward led,
Joying to heare the birdes sweete harmony,   *65*
Which therein shrouded from the tempest dred,
Seemd in their song to scorne the cruell sky.
Much can they prayse the trees so straight and hy,
The sayling Pine, the Cedar proud and tall,
The vine-prop Elme, the Poplar never dry,   *70*
The builder Oake, sole king of forrests all,
The Aspine good for staves, the Cypresse funerall.

9
The Laurell, meed of mightie Conquerours
And Poets sage, the Firre that weepeth still,
The Willow worne of forlorne Paramours,   *75*
The Eugh obedient to the benders will,
The Birch for shaftes, the Sallow for the mill,
The Mirrhe sweete bleeding in the bitter wound,
The warlike Beech, the Ash for nothing ill,
The fruitfull Olive, and the Platane round,   *80*
The carver Holme, the Maple seeldom inward sound.

10
Led with delight, they thus beguile the way,
Untill the blustring storme is overblowne;
When weening to returne, whence they did stray,

---

17. **cheere:** countenance; **sad:** serious, grave, pensive. 18. **ydrad:** dreaded. 19. **bond:** bound. 22. **worship:** honour, glory. 24. **earne:** yearn. 28. **lovely Lady:** later identified as Una (Latin "one"); she represents truth, or the one true faith. 36. **in:** on; **lad:** led. 44. **forwasted:** laid waste, ravaged. 46. **Dwarfe:** He stands for prudence. 52. **Lemans:** lover's, i.e., the earth's. 53. **shrowd:** shelter, protect. 63. **them:** to them. 68. **can:** did. 73. **meed:** reward. 76. **Eugh:** yew. 80. **Platane:** Plane-tree. 81. **Holme:** holm oak, holly oak.

They cannot finde that path which first was showne,   *85*
But wander too and fro in wayes unknowne,
Furthest from end then, when they neerest weene,
That makes them doubt their wits be not their owne:
So many pathes, so many turnings seene,   *89*
That which of them to take, in diverse doubt they been.

11

At last resolving forward still to fare,
Till that some end they finde or in or out,
That path they take, that beaten seemd most bare,
And like to lead the labyrinth about;
Which when by tract they hunted had throughout,   *95*
At length it brought them to a hollow cave,
Amid the thickest woods. The Champion stout
Eftsoones dismounted from his courser brave,
And to the Dwarfe a while his needlesse spere he gave.

12

Be well aware, quoth then that Ladie milde,   *100*
Least suddaine mischiefe ye too rash provoke:
The danger hid, the place unknowne and wilde,
Breedes dreadfull doubts: Oft fire is without smoke,
And perill without show: therefore your stroke
Sir knight with-hold, till further triall made.   *105*
Ah Ladie (said he) shame were to revoke
The forward footing for an hidden shade:
Vertue gives her selfe light, through darkenesse for to wade.

13

Yea but (quoth she) the perill of this place
I better wot then you, though now too late   *110*
To wish you backe returne with foule disgrace,
Yet wisedome warnes, whilest foot is in the gate,
To stay the steppe, ere forced to retrate.
This is the wandring wood, this *Errours den*,
A monster vile, whom God and man does hate: *115*
Therefore I read beware. Fly fly (quoth then
The fearefull Dwarfe:) this is no place for living men.

14

But full of fire and greedy hardiment,
The youthfull knight could not for ought be staide,
But forth unto the darksome hole he went,   *120*
And looked in: his glistring armor made
A litle glooming light, much like a shade,
By which he saw the ugly monster plaine,
Halfe like a serpent horribly displaide,
But th'other halfe did womans shape retaine,   *125*
Most lothsom, filthie, foule, and full of vile disdaine.

15

And as she lay upon the durtie ground,
Her huge long taile her den all overspred,
Yet was in knots and many boughtes upwound,
Pointed with mortall sting. Of her there bred   *130*
A thousand yong ones, which she dayly fed,
Sucking upon her poisonous dugs, eachone
Of sundry shapes, yet all ill favored:
Soone as that uncouth light upon them shone,
Into her mouth they crept, and suddain all were gone.   *135*

16

Their dam upstart, out of her den effraide,
And rushed forth, hurling her hideous taile
About her cursed head, whose folds displaid
Were stretcht now forth at length without entraile.
She lookt about, and seeing one in mayle   *140*
Armed to point, sought backe to turne againe;
For light she hated as the deadly bale,
Ay wont in desert darknesse to remaine,
Where plaine none might her see, nor she see any plaine.

17

Which when the valiant Elfe perceiv'd, he lept   *145*
As Lyon fierce upon the flying pray,
And with his trenchand blade her boldly kept
From turning backe, and forced her to stay:
Therewith enrag'd she loudly gan to bray,
And turning fierce, her speckled taile advaunst,   *150*
Threatning her angry sting, him to dismay:
Who nought aghast, his mightie hand enhaunst:
The stroke down from her head unto her shoulder glaunst.

---

88. doubt: fear. **92. or . . . or:** either . . . or. **94. about:** i.e., to the outside of. **95. tract:** trace, track. **100. aware:** wary. **101. least:** lest. **106. revoke:** hold back. **112. gate:** path. **116. read:** rede, advise. **118. hardiment:** hardihood. **126. disdaine:** loathsomeness. **129. boughtes:** coils, folds. **134. uncouth:** unfamiliar, strange, unusual. **138. displaid:** stretched out. **139. entraile:** twisting, coiling. **141. to point:** completely. **143. ay:** always. **145. Elfe:** the knight (in elfin- or faery-land). **152. enhaunst:** raised.

18

Much daunted with that dint, her sence was dazd,
    Yet kindling rage, her selfe she gathered round,   *155*
    And all attonce her beastly body raizd
    With doubled forces high above the ground:
    Tho wrapping up her wrethed sterne arownd,
    Lept fierce upon his shield, and her huge traine
    All suddenly about his body wound,   *160*
    That hand or foot to stirre he strove in vaine:
God helpe the man so wrapt in *Errours* endlesse traine.

19

His Lady sad to see his sore constraint,
    Cride out, Now, now, Sir knight, shew what ye bee,
    Add faith unto your force, and be not faint: *165*
    Strangle her, else she sure will strangle thee.
    That when he heard, in great perplexitie,
    His gall did grate for griefe and high disdaine,
    And knitting all his force got one hand free,
    Wherewith he grypt her gorge with so great paine,   *170*
That soone to loose her wicked bands did her constraine.

20

Therewith she spewd out of her filthy maw
    A floud of poyson horrible and blacke,
    Full of great lumpes of flesh and gobbets raw,
    Which stunck so vildly, that it forst him slacke   *175*
    His grasping hold, and from her turne him backe:
    Her vomit full of bookes and papers was,
    With loathly frogs and toades, which eyes did lacke,
    And creeping sought way in the weedy gras:
Her filthy parbreake all the place defiled has.   *180*

21

As when old father *Nilus* gins to swell
    With timely pride above the *Aegyptian* vale,
    His fattie waves do fertile slime outwell,
    And overflow each plaine and lowly dale:
    But when his later spring gins to avale,   *185*
    Huge heapes of mudd he leaves, wherein there breed
    Ten thousand kindes of creatures, partly male
    And partly female of his fruitfull seed;
Such ugly monstrous shapes elswhere may no man reed.

22

The same so sore annoyed has the knight,   *190*
    That welnigh choked with the deadly stinke,
    His forces faile, ne can no longer fight.
    Whose corage when the feend perceiv'd to shrinke,
    She poured forth out of her hellish sinke
    Her fruitfull cursed spawne of serpents small,   *195*
    Deformed monsters, fowle, and blacke as inke,
    Which swarming all about his legs did crall,
And him encombred sore, but could not hurt at all.

23

As gentle Shepheard in sweete even-tide,
    When ruddy *Phoebus* gins to welke in west,   *200*
    High on an hill, his flocke to vewen wide,
    Markes which do byte their hasty supper best;
    A cloud of combrous gnattes do him molest,
    All striving to infixe their feeble stings,
    That from their noyance he no where can rest,   *205*
    But with his clownish hands their tender wings
He brusheth oft, and oft doth mar their murmurings.

24

Thus ill bestedd, and fearefull more of shame
    Then of the certaine perill he stood in,
    Halfe furious unto his foe he came,   *210*
    Resolv'd in minde all suddenly to win,
    Or soone to lose, before he once would lin,
    And strooke at her with more then manly force,
    That from her body full of filthie sin
    He raft her hatefull head without remorse;   *215*
A streame of cole black bloud forth gushed from her
    corse.

25

Her scattred brood, soone as their Parent deare
    They saw so rudely falling to the ground,
    Groning full deadly, all with troublous feare,
    Gathred themselves about her body round,   *220*
    Weening their wonted entrance to have found
    At her wide mouth: but being there withstood
    They flocked all about her bleeding wound,
    And sucked up their dying mothers blood,
Making her death their life, and eke her hurt their good. *225*

---

154. dint: dent, stroke, blow. **168. griefe:** anger. **180. parbreake:** vomit. **185. avale:** fall, sink. **189. reed:** see. **200. welke:** fade, sink. **208. bestedd:** beset, placed. **212. lin:** stop, desist. **215. raft:** reft, severed.

26

That detestable sight him much amazde,
　To see th'unkindly Impes of heaven accurst
　Devoure their dam; on whom while so he gazd,
　Having all satisfide their bloudy thurst,
　Their bellies swolne he saw with fulnesse burst,　*230*
　And bowels gushing forth: well worthy end
　Of such as drunke her life, the which them nurst;
　Now needeth him no lenger labour spend,
His foes have slaine themselves, with whom he should
　contend.

27

His Ladie seeing all that chaunst from farre　*235*
　Approcht in hast to greet his victorie,
　And said, Faire knight, borne under happy starre,
　Who see your vanquisht foes before you lye;
　Well worthy be you of that Armorie,
　Wherein ye have great glory wonne this day,　*240*
　And proov'd your strength on a strong enimie,
　Your first adventure: many such I pray,
And henceforth ever wish, that like succeed it may.

28

Then mounted he upon his Steede againe,
　And with the Lady backward sought to wend;　*245*
　That path he kept, which beaten was most plaine,
　Ne ever would to any by-way bend,
　But still did follow one unto the end,
　The which at last out of the wood them brought.
　So forward on his way (with God to frend)　*250*
　He passed forth, and new adventure sought;
Long way he travelled, before he heard of ought.

29

At length they chaunst to meet upon the way
　An aged Sire, in long blacke weedes yclad,
　His feete all bare, his beard all hoarie gray,　*255*
　And by his belt his booke he hanging had;
　Sober he seemde, and very sagely sad,
　And to the ground his eyes were lowly bent,
　Simple in shew, and voyde of malice bad,
　And all the way he prayed, as he went,　*260*
And often knockt his brest, as one that did repent.

30

He faire the knight saluted, louting low,
　Who faire him quited, as that courteous was:
　And after asked him, if he did know
　Of straunge adventures, which abroad did pas.　*265*
　Ah my deare Sonne (quoth he) how should, alas,
　Silly old man, that lives in hidden cell,
　Bidding his beades all day for his trespas,
　Tydings of warre and worldly trouble tell?
With holy father sits not with such things to mell.　*270*

31

But if of daunger which hereby doth dwell,
　And homebred evill ye desire to heare,
　Of a straunge man I can you tidings tell,
　That wasteth all this countrey farre and neare.
　Of such (said he) I chiefly do inquere,　*275*
　And shall you well reward to shew the place,
　In which that wicked wight his dayes doth weare;
　For to all knighthood it is foule disgrace,
That such a cursed creature lives so long a space.

32

Far hence (quoth he) in wastfull wildernesse　*280*
　His dwelling is, by which no living wight
　May ever passe, but thorough great distresse.
　Now (sayd the Lady) draweth toward night,
　And well I wote, that of your later fight
　Ye all forwearied be: for what so strong,　*285*
　But wanting rest will also want of might?
　The Sunne that measures heaven all day long,
At night doth baite his steedes the *Ocean* waves emong.

33

Then with the Sunne take, Sir, your timely rest,
　And with new day new worke at once begin:　*290*
　Untroubled night they say gives counsell best.
　Right well Sir knight ye have advised bin,
　(Quoth then that aged man); the way to win
　Is wisely to advise: now day is spent.
　Therefore with me ye may take up your In　*295*
　For this same night. The knight was well content:
So with that godly father to his home they went.

---

227. unkindly Impes: unnatural offspring. **231:** Cf. Acts 1:18. **236. greet:** congratulate. **250. to frend:** as friend. **262. louting:** bowing. **263. quited:** requited, i.e., returned the salutation. **267. silly:** simple. **268. bidding his beades:** saying his prayers — i.e., saying (telling, counting) rosary beads. **270. sits not:** isn't fitting; **mell:** meddle. **274. wasteth:** lays waste to. **277. weare:** pass, spend. **280. wastfull:** desolate, waste, barren. **282. thorough:** through. **284. later:** last, recent. **288. baite:** feed and refresh. **294. advise:** consider, bethink oneself. **295. In:** inn, lodging.

34

A little lowly Hermitage it was,
   Downe in a dale, hard by a forests side,
   Far from resort of people, that did pas   *300*
   In travell to and froe: a little wyde
   There was an holy Chappell edifyde,
   Wherein the Hermite dewly wont to say
   His holy things each morne and eventyde:
   Thereby a Christall streame did gently play,   *305*
Which from a sacred fountaine welled forth alway.

35

Arrived there, the little house they fill,
   Ne looke for entertainement, where none was:
   Rest is their feast, and all things at their will;
   The noblest mind the best contentment has.   *310*
   With faire discourse the evening so they pas:
   For that old man of pleasing wordes had store,
   And well could file his *tongue as* smooth as glas;
   He told of Saintes and Popes, and evermore
He strowd an *Ave-Mary* after and before.   *315*

36

The drouping Night thus creepeth on them fast,
   And the sad humour loading their eye liddes,
   As messenger of *Morpheus* on them cast
   Sweet slombring deaw, the which to sleepe them biddes.
   Unto their lodgings then his guestes he riddes: *320*
   Where when all drownd in deadly sleepe he findes,
   He to his study goes, and there amiddes
   His Magick bookes and artes of sundry kindes,
He seekes out mighty charmes, to trouble sleepy mindes.

37

Then choosing out few wordes most horrible,   *325*
   (Let none them read) thereof did verses frame,
   With which and other spelles like terrible,
   He bade awake blacke *Plutoes* griesly Dame,
   And cursed heaven, and spake reprochfull shame
   Of highest God, the Lord of life and light;   *330*
   A bold bad man, that dar'd to call by name
   Great *Gorgon*, Prince of darknesse and dead night,
At which *Cocytus* quakes, and *Styx* is put to flight.

38

And forth he cald out of deepe darknesse dred
   Legions of Sprights, the which like little flyes   *335*
   Fluttring about his ever damned hed,
   A-waite whereto their service he applyes,
   To aide his friends, or fray his enimies:
   Of those he chose out two, the falsest twoo,
   And fittest for to forge true-seeming lyes;   *340*
   The one of them he gave a message too,
The other by him selfe staide other worke to doo.

39

He making speedy way through spersed ayre,
   And through the world of waters wide and deepe,
   To *Morpheus* house doth hastily repaire.   *345*
   Amid the bowels of the earth full steepe
   And low, where dawning day doth never peepe,
   His dwelling is; there *Tethys* his wet bed
   Doth ever wash, and *Cynthia* still doth steepe
   In silver deaw his ever-drouping hed,   *350*
Whiles sad Night over him her mantle black doth spred.

40

Whose double gates he findeth locked fast,
   The one faire fram'd of burnisht Yvory,
   The other all with silver overcast;
   And wakefull dogges before them farre do lye,   *355*
   Watching to banish Care their enimy,
   Who oft is wont to trouble gentle Sleepe.
   By them the Sprite doth passe in quietly,
   And unto *Morpheus* comes, whom drowned deepe
In drowsie fit he findes: of nothing he takes keepe.   *360*

41

And more, to lulle him in his slumber soft,
   A trickling streame from high rocke tumbling downe
   And ever-drizling raine upon the loft,
   Mixt with a murmuring winde, much like the sowne
   Of swarming Bees, did cast him in a swowne;   *365*
   No other noyse, nor peoples troublous cryes,
   As still are wont t'annoy the walled towne,
   Might there be heard; but carelesse Quiet lyes,
Wrapt in eternall silence farre from enemyes.

---

301. wyde: apart, to one side. **302. edifyde:** built. **315. strowd:** strewed, scattered. **317. sad humour:** heavy fluid, moisture. **318. Morpheus:** god of sleep. **320. riddes:** dispatches, sends. **321. deadly:** death-like. **328. Plutoes griesly Dame:** Proserpine (Persephone). **332. Gorgon:** Demogorgon. **333. Cocytus, Styx:** two of the rivers of the underworld (see *Paradise Lost*, II, 575ff., p. 343). **338. fray:** frighten, terrify. **343. spersed:** dispersed. **348. Tethys:** wife of Oceanus — here personifying the ocean itself. **349. Cynthia:** the moon (Artemis was born on Mt. Cynthus); **still:** always, constantly. **352. double gates:** in Greek myth, the two gates of Sleep, through which dreams come, false ones through the gate of ivory, true ones through the gate of horn (here, note, "with silver overcast"). **360. keepe:** heed, notice.

42

The messenger approaching to him spake,   *370*
   But his waste wordes returnd to him in vaine:
   So sound he slept, that nought mought him awake.
   Then rudely he him thrust, and pusht with paine,
   Whereat he gan to stretch: but he againe
   Shooke him so hard, that forced him to speake.   *375*
   As one then in a dreame, whose dryer braine
   Is tost with troubled sights and fancies weake,
He mumbled soft, but would not all his silence breake.

43

The Sprite then gan more boldly him to wake,
   And threatned unto him the dreaded name   *380*
   Of *Hecate*: whereat he gan to quake,
   And lifting up his lumpish head, with blame
   Halfe angry asked him, for what he came.
   Hither (quoth he) me *Archimago* sent,
   He that the stubborne Sprites can wisely tame,   *385*
   He bids thee to him send for his intent
A fit false dreame, that can delude the sleepers sent.

44

The God obayde, and calling forth straight way
   A diverse dreame out of his prison darke,
   Delivered it to him, and downe did lay   *390*
   His heavie head, devoide of carefull carke,
   Whose sences all were straight benumbd and starke.
   He backe returning by the Yvorie dore,
   Remounted up as light as chearefull Larke,
   And on his litle winges the dreame he bore   *395*
In hast unto his Lord, where he him left afore.

45

Who all this while with charmes and hidden artes,
   Had made a Lady of that other Spright,
   And fram'd of liquid ayre her tender partes
   So lively, and so like in all mens sight,   *400*
   That weaker sence it could have ravisht quight;
   The maker selfe for all his wondrous witt,

Was nigh beguiled with so goodly sight:
   Her all in white he clad, and over it
Cast a blacke stole, most like to seeme for *Una* fit.   *405*

46

Now when that ydle dreame was to him brought,
   Unto that Elfin knight he bad him fly,
   Where he slept soundly void of evill thought,
   And with false shewes abuse his fantasy,
   In sort as he him schooled privily;   *410*
   And that new creature borne without her dew,
   Full of the makers guile, with usage sly
   He taught to imitate that Lady trew,
Whose semblance she did carrie under feigned hew.

47

Thus well instructed, to their worke they hast,   *415*
   And comming where the knight in slomber lay,
   The one upon his hardy head him plast,
   And made him dreame of loves and lustfull play,
   That nigh his manly hart did melt away,
   Bathed in wanton blis and wicked joy: *420*
   Then seemed him his Lady by him lay,
   And to him playnd, how that false winged boy
Her chast hart had subdewd, to learne Dame pleasures toy.

48

And she her selfe of beautie soveraigne Queene,
   Faire *Venus* seemde unto his bed to bring   *425*
   Her, whom he waking evermore did weene
   To be the chastest flowre, that ay did spring
   On earthly braunch, the daughter of a king,
   Now a loose Leman to vile service bound:
   And eke the *Graces* seemed all to sing,   *430*
   Hymen iô Hymen, dauncing all around,
Whilst freshest *Flora* her with Yvie girlond crownd.

49

In this great passion of unwonted lust,
   Or wonted feare of doing ought amis,
   He started up, as seeming to mistrust   *435*

---

376. dryer braine: i.e., lacking the "sad humour" (line 317) that supposedly promotes sound sleep. **381. Hecate:** a goddess of the underworld associated with witchcraft. **384. Archimago:** i.e., the "holy father," the hermit, in whose abode the knight is sleeping; Archimago is the great enchanter, symbolizing hypocrisy and false religion. **387. sent:** senses, perception. **389. diverse:** diverting, distracting. **391. carke:** burden, load, grief, sorrow. **392. starke:** stiff. **400. lively:** lifelike. **405. Una:** See note to line 28, above. **410. in sort as:** in the way that. **411. dew:** (without her) due — i.e., improperly, unnaturally. **422. winged boy:** Cupid. **423. toy:** dalliance, amorous sport. **430. Graces:** the (usually three) Graces (Latin *Gratiae*, Greek *Charites*), goddesses personifying grace, charm, and beauty, often associated with Aphrodite (Venus); the standard three are Aglaia (splendour, radiance), Euphrosyne (mirth, joy), and Thaleia (flowering). **431. Hymen iô Hymen:** ritual wedding song to Hymen, god of marriage. **432. Flora:** goddess of flowers. **435. mistrust:** suspect.

Some secret ill, or hidden foe of his:
Lo there before his face his Lady is,
Under blake stole hyding her bayted hooke,
And as halfe blushing offred him to kis,
With gentle blandishment and lovely looke,   440
Most like that virgin true, which for her knight him took.

50

All cleane dismayd to see so uncouth sight,
  And halfe enraged at her shamelesse guise,
  He thought have slaine her in his fierce despight:
  But hasty heat tempring with sufferance wise,   445
  He stayde his hand, and gan himselfe advise
  To prove his sense, and tempt her faigned truth.
  Wringing her hands in wemens pitteous wise,
  Tho can she weepe, to stirre up gentle ruth,
Both for her noble bloud, and for her tender youth.   450

51

And said, Ah Sir, my liege Lord and my love,
  Shall I accuse the hidden cruell fate,
  And mightie causes wrought in heaven above,
  Or the blind God, that doth me thus amate,
  For hoped love to winne me certaine hate?   455
  Yet thus perforce he bids me do, or die.
  Die is my dew: yet rew my wretched state
  You, whom my hard avenging destinie
Hath made judge of my life or death indifferently.

52

Your owne deare sake forst me at first to leave   460
  My Fathers kingdome. There she stopt with teares;
  Her swollen hart her speach seemd to bereave,
  And then againe begun, My weaker yeares
  Captiv'd to fortune and frayle wordly feares,
  Fly to your faith for succour and sure ayde: 465
  Let me not dye in languor and long teares.
  Why Dame (quoth he) what hath ye thus dismayd?
What frayes ye, that were wont to comfort me affrayd?

53

Love of your selfe, she said, and deare constraint
  Lets me not sleepe, but wast the wearie night   470
  In secret anguish and unpittied plaint,
  Whiles you in carelesse sleepe are drowned quight.
  Her doubtfull words made that redoubted knight
  Suspect her truth: yet since no'untruth he knew,
  Her fawning love with foule disdainefull spight   475
  He would not shend, but said, Deare dame I rew,
That for my sake unknowne such griefe unto you grew.

54

Assure your selfe, it fell not all to ground;
  For all so deare as life is to my hart,
  I deeme your love, and hold me to you bound;   480
  Ne let vaine feares procure your needlesse smart,
  Where cause is none, but to your rest depart.
  Not all content, yet seemd she to appease
  Her mournefull plaintes, beguiled of her art,
  And fed with words, that could not chuse but please,
So slyding softly forth, she turned as to her ease.   486

55

Long after lay he musing at her mood,
  Much griev'd to thinke that gentle Dame so light,
  For whose defence he was to shed his blood.
  At last dull wearinesse of former fight   490
  Having yrockt a sleepe his irkesome spright,
  That troublous dreame gan freshly tosse his braine,
  With bowres, and beds, and Ladies deare delight:
  But when he saw his labour all was vaine,   494
With that misformed spright he backe returnd againe.

(1590)

---

440. lovely: loving. **443. guise:** behaviour. **445. sufferance:** patience. **447. prove:** try, test. **449. Tho can:** Then did. **454. blind God:** i.e., Cupid; **amate:** dismay, overwhelm. **469. deare:** dire, grievous. **473. doubtfull:** fearful, questionable. **476. shend:** put to shame, blame, reproach. **483. appease:** cease, quiet. **491. spright:** spirit, mind.

from *AMORETTI*

1

Happy ye leaves when as those lilly hands,
   which hold my life in their dead doing might,
   shall handle you and hold in loves soft bands,
   lyke captives trembling at the victors sight.
And happy lines, on which with starry light   5
   those lamping eyes will deigne sometimes to look
   and reade the sorrowes of my dying spright,
   written with teares in harts close bleeding book.
And happy rymes bath'd in the sacred brooke
   of *Helicon* whence she derived is,   10
   when ye behold that Angels blessed looke,
   my soules long lacked foode, my heavens blis.
Leaves, lines, and rymes, seeke her to please alone,
   whom if ye please, I care for other none.

6

Be nought dismayd that her unmoved mind
   doth still persist in her rebellious pride:
   such love not like to lusts of baser kynd,
   the harder wonne, the firmer will abide.
The durefull Oake, whose sap is not yet dride,   5
   is long ere it conceive the kindling fyre;
   but when it once doth burne, it doth divide
   great heat, and makes his flames to heaven aspire.
So hard it is to kindle new desire
   in gentle brest that shall endure for ever;   10
   deepe is the wound that dints the parts entire
   with chast affects, that naught but death can sever.
Then thinke not long in taking little paine,
   to knit the knot, that ever shall remaine.

9

Long-while I sought to what I might compare
   those powrefull eies, which lighten my dark spright,
   yet find I nought on earth to which I dare
   resemble th'image of their goodly light.
Not to the Sun: for they doo shine by night;   5

nor to the Moone: for they are changed never;
   nor to the Starres: for they have purer sight;
   nor to the fire: for they consume not ever;
Nor to the lightning: for they still persever;
   nor to the Diamond: for they are more tender;   10
   nor unto Christall: for nought may them sever;
   nor unto glasse: such basenesse mought offend her;
Then to the Maker selfe they likest be,
   whose light doth lighten all that here we see.

15

Ye tradefull Merchants, that with weary toyle
   do seeke most pretious things to make your gain,
   and both the Indias of their treasures spoile,
   what needeth you to seeke so farre in vaine?
For loe my love doth in her selfe containe   5
   all this worlds riches that may farre be found:
   if Saphyres, loe her eies be Saphyres plaine;
   if Rubies, loe hir lips be Rubies sound;
If Pearles, hir teeth be pearles both pure and round;
   if Yvorie, her forhead yvory weene;   10
   if Gold, her locks are finest gold on ground;
   if silver, her faire hands are silver sheene.
But that which fairest is, but few behold:
   her mind adornd with vertues manifold.

34

Lyke as a ship that through the Ocean wyde,
   by conduct of some star doth make her way,
   whenas a storme hath dimd her trusty guyde,
   out of her course doth wander far astray;
So I whose star, that wont with her bright ray   5
   me to direct, with cloudes is overcast,
   doe wander now in darknesse and dismay,
   through hidden perils round about me plast.
Yet hope I well, that when this storme is past
   my *Helice* the lodestar of my lyfe   10
   will shine again, and looke on me at last
   with lovely light to cleare my cloudy grief.
Till then I wander carefull comfortlesse,
   in secret sorow and sad pensivenesse.

AMORETTI   The sequence (89 sonnets in all) was written to and about Elizabeth Boyle, who in 1594 became Spenser's second wife (*Epithalamion*, which was published along with the sonnets in 1595, celebrates the marriage).   **SONNET 1   2. dead doing:** death-dealing, killing.   **6. lamping:** flashing, resplendent.   **10. *Helicon:*** Mount Helicon, the home of the Muses — the "sacred brooke" flows from the fountain Hippocrene, sacred to the Muses and standing for poetic inspiration.   **SONNET 6   5. durefull:** enduring.   **7. divide:** give forth in various directions.   **12. affects:** affectionate feelings, passions.   **SONNET 9   12. mought:** might.   **SONNET 34   8. plast:** placed.   **10. *Helice:*** a Greek name for Ursa Major (because it revolves around the North Star), though "lodestar" suggests that Spenser intends Polaris itself.

37

What guyle is this, that those her golden tresses
  She doth attyre under a net of gold,
  and with sly skill so cunningly them dresses,
  that which is gold or heare may scarse be told?
Is it that mens frayle eyes, which gaze too bold,   *5*
  she may entangle in that golden snare,
  and being caught may craftily enfold
  theyr weaker harts, which are not wel aware?
Take heed therefore, myne eyes, how ye doe stare
  henceforth too rashly on that guilefull net,   *10*
  in which if ever ye entrapped are,
  out of her bands ye by no meanes shall get.
Fondness it were for any being free
  to covet fetters, though they golden bee.

56

Fayre ye be sure, but cruell and unkind,
  As is a Tygre that with greedinesse
  hunts after bloud, when he by chance doth find
  a feeble beast, doth felly him oppresse.
Fayre be ye sure, but proud and pittilesse,   *5*
  as is a storme, that all things doth prostrate;
  finding a tree alone all comfortlesse,
  beats on it strongly it to ruinate.
Fayre be ye sure, but hard and obstinate,
  as is a rocke amidst the raging floods;   *10*
  gainst which a ship of succour desolate,
  doth suffer wreck both of her selfe and goods.
That ship, that tree, and that same beast am I,
  whom ye doe wreck, doe ruine, and destroy.

75

One day I wrote her name upon the strand,
  but came the waves and washed it away;
  agayne I wrote it with a second hand,
  but came the tyde, and made my paynes his pray.
Vayne man, sayd she, that doest in vaine assay   *5*
  a mortall thing so to immortalize,
  for I my selve shall lyke to this decay,
  and eek my name bee wyped out lykewise.

No so (quod I), let baser things devize
  to dy in dust, but you shall live by fame: *10*
  my verse your vertues rare shall eternize,
  and in the hevens wryte your glorious name.
Where whenas death shall all the world subdew,
  our love shall live, and later life renew.

79

Men call you fayre, and you doe credit it,
  For that your selfe ye dayly such doe see;
  but the trew fayre, that is the gentle wit,
  and vertuous mind, is much more praysd of me.
For all the rest, how ever fayre it be,   *5*
  shall turne to nought and loose that glorious hew;
  but onely that is permanent and free
  from frayle corruption, that doth flesh ensew.
That is true beautie: that doth argue you
  to be divine and borne of heavenly seed;   *10*
  deriv'd from that fayre Spirit, from whom al true
  and perfect beauty did at first proceed.
He onely fayre, and what he fayre hath made,
  all other fayre lyke flowres untymely fade.

EPITHALAMION

Ye learned sisters which have oftentimes
Beene to me ayding, others to adorne,
Whom ye thought worthy of your gracefull rymes,
That even the greatest did not greatly scorne
To heare theyr names sung in your simple layes,   *5*
But joyed in theyr prayse.
And when ye list your owne mishaps to mourne,
Which death, or love, or fortunes wreck did rayse,
Your string could soone to sadder tenor turne,
And teach the woods and waters to lament   *10*
Your dolefull dreriment.
Now lay those sorrowfull complaints aside,
And having all your heads with girland crownd,
Helpe me mine owne loves prayses to resound,
Ne let the same of any be envide: *15*

SONNET 37   13. **Fondness:** foolishness.   **SONNET 56**   4. **felly:** in a fell manner, fiercely, cruelly. 11. **desolate:** devoid, forlorn.   **SONNET 75**   8. **eek:** also.   **EPITHALAMION**   Title: "bridal song" (Greek *epi,* at, *thalamos,* bridal chamber). 1. **learned sisters:** the Muses. 2. **others to adorne:** referring to his poems praising others, such as Queen Elizabeth (*The Faerie Queene*) and Sir Philip Sidney (*Astrophell*). 7. **list:** wish, choose; **your owne . . . to mourne:** referring to his "The Teares of the Muses." 9. **tenor:** character, tone. 15. **ne:** nor; **of,** by.

So Orpheus did for his owne bride,
So I unto my selfe alone will sing,
The woods shall to me answer and my Eccho ring.

Early before the worlds light giving lampe,
His golden beame upon the hils doth spred, *20*
Having disperst the nights unchearefull dampe,
Doe ye awake, and with fresh lustyhed,
Go to the bowre of my beloved love,
My truest turtle dove,
Bid her awake; for Hymen is awake, *25*
And long since ready forth his maske to move,
With his bright Tead that flames with many a flake,
And many a bachelor to waite on him,
In theyr fresh garments trim.
Bid her awake therefore and soone her dight, *30*
For lo the wished day is come at last,
That shall for al the paynes and sorrowes past,
Pay to her usury of long delight:
And whylest she doth her dight,
Doe ye to her of joy and solace sing, *35*
That all the woods may answer and your eccho ring.

Bring with you all the Nymphes that you can heare
Both of the rivers and the forrests greene:
And of the sea that neighbours to her neare,
Al with gay girlands goodly wel beseene. *40*
And let them also with them bring in hand,
Another gay girland
For my fayre love of lillyes and of roses,
Bound truelove wize with a blew silke riband.
And let them make great store of bridale poses, *45*
And let them eeke bring store of other flowers
To deck the bridale bowers.
And let the ground whereas her foot shall tread,
For feare the stones her tender foot should wrong
Be strewed with fragrant flowers all along, *50*
And diapred lyke the discolored mead.
Which done, doe at her chamber dore awayt,
For she will waken strayt,
The whiles doe ye this song unto her sing,
The woods shall to you answer and your Eccho ring.

Ye Nymphes of Mulla which with carefull heed, *56*
The silver scaly trouts doe tend full well,
And greedy pikes which use therein to feed,
(Those trouts and pikes all others doo excell)
And ye likewise which keepe the rushy lake, *60*
Where none doo fishes take,
Bynd up the locks the which hang scatterd light,
And in his waters which your mirror make,
Behold your faces as the christall bright,
That when you come whereas my love doth lie, *65*
No blemish she may spie.
And eke ye lightfoot mayds which keepe the deere,
That on the hoary mountayne use to towre,
And the wylde wolves which seeke them to devoure,
With your steele darts doo chace from comming neer,
Be also present heere, *71*
To helpe to decke her and to help to sing,
That all the woods may answer and your eccho ring.

Wake, now my love, awake: for it is time,
The Rosy Morne long since left Tithones bed, *75*
All ready to her silver coche to clyme,
And Phoebus gins to shew his glorious hed.
Hark how the cheerefull birds do chaunt theyr laies
And carroll of loves praise.
The merry Larke hir mattins sings aloft, *80*
The thrush replyes, the Mavis descant playes,
The Ouzell shrills, the Ruddock warbles soft,
So goodly all agree with sweet consent,
To this dayes merriment.
Ah my deere love why doe ye sleepe thus long, *85*
When meeter were that ye should now awake,
T'awayt the comming of your joyous make,
And hearken to the birds love-learned song,
The deawy leaves among.
For they of joy and pleasance to you sing, *90*
That all the woods them answer and theyr eccho ring.

My love is now awake out of her dreame,
And her fayre eyes like stars that dimmed were
With darksome cloud, now shew theyr goodly beams
More bright then Hesperus his head doth rere. *95*

16: Orpheus's bride was Eurydice. **22. lustyhed:** energy, vigour. **25. Hymen:** See note to line 431 of *The Faerie Queene*. **26. maske:** masque or celebratory procession. **27. Tead:** torch; **flake:** flash, spark. **30. dight:** dress, adorn. **35. solace:** pleasure, comfort. **37. you can heare:** i.e., can hear you. **39:** Elizabeth Boyle lived at Kilcoran, near Youghal Bay, County Cork, Ireland; Spenser's own estate was at Kilcolman Castle, near the Mulla (Spenser's name for the River Abweg; see line 56), about 35 km north of Cork. **44:** i.e., with a truelove knot. **45. poses:** posies. **46. eeke:** also. **51. diapred:** flowered (from cloth woven in flowers); **discolored:** varicoloured. **53. strayt:** straightway. **68. towre:** climb high, like a hawk or falcon (see Skelton's "To Maystres Margaret Hussey," p. 113). **75:** Tithonos was the husband of Eos (Aurora), goddess of the dawn. **80. mattins:** matins. **87. make:** mate. **95. Hesperus:** the evening star (usually, the planet Venus).

Come now ye damzels, daughters of delight,
Helpe quickly her to dight,
But first come ye fayre houres which were begot
In Jove's sweet paradice, of Day and Night,
Which doe the seasons of the yeare allot,   *100*
And al that ever in this world is fayre
Doe make and still repayre.
And ye three handmayds of the Cyprian Queene,
The which doe still adorne her beauties pride,
Helpe to addorne my beautifullest bride: *105*
And as ye her array, still throw betweene
Some graces to be seene,
And as ye use to Venus, to her sing,
The whiles the woods shal answer and your eccho ring.

Now is my love all ready forth to come,   *110*
Let all the virgins therefore well awayt,
And ye fresh boyes that tend upon her groome
Prepare your selves; for he is comming strayt.
Set all your things in seemely good aray
Fit for so joyfull day,   *115*
The joyfulst day that ever sunne did see.
Faire Sun, shew forth thy favourable ray,
And let thy lifull heat nor fervent be
For feare of burning her sunshyny face,
Her beauty to disgrace.   *120*
O fayrest Phoebus, father of the Muse,
If ever I did honour thee aright,
Or sing the thing that mote thy mind delight,
Doe not thy servants simple boone refuse,
But let this day, let this one day be myne,   *125*
Let all the rest be thine.
Then I thy soverayne prayses loud wil sing,
That all the woods shal answer and theyr eccho ring.

Harke how the Minstrels gin to shrill aloud
Their merry Musick that resounds from far,   *130*
The pipe, the tabor, and the trembling Croud,
That well agree withouten breach or jar.
But most of all the Damzels doe delite,
When they their tymbrels smyte,
And thereunto doe daunce and carrol sweet,   *135*

That all the sences they doe ravish quite,
The whyles the boyes run up and downe the street,
Crying aloud with strong confused noyce,
As if it were one voyce.
Hymen, iô Hymen, Hymen they do shout,   *140*
That even to the heavens theyr shouting shrill
Doth reach, and all the firmament doth fill,
To which the people standing all about,
As in approvance doe thereto applaud
And loud advaunce her laud,   *145*
And evermore they Hymen, Hymen sing,
That al the woods them answer and theyr eccho ring.

Loe where she comes along with portly pace
Lyke Phoebe from her chamber of the East,
Arysing forth to run her mighty race,   *150*
Clad all in white, that seemes a virgin best.
So well it her beseemes that ye would weene
Some angell she had beene.
Her long loose yellow locks lyke golden wyre,
Sprinckled with perle, and perling flowres a tweene,
Doe lyke a golden mantle her attyre,   *156*
And being crowned with a girland greene,
Seeme lyke some mayden Queene.
Her modest eyes abashed to behold
So many gazers, as on her do stare,   *160*
Upon the lowly ground affixed are.
Ne dare lift up her countenance too bold,
But blush to heare her prayses sung so loud,
So farre from being proud.
Nathlesse doe ye still loud her prayses sing.   *165*
That all the woods may answer and your eccho ring.

Tell me ye merchants daughters did ye see
So fayre a creature in your towne before,
So sweet, so lovely, and so mild as she,
Adornd with beautyes grace and vertues store,   *170*
Her goodly eyes lyke Saphyres shining bright,
Her forehead yvory white,
Her cheekes lyke apples which the sun hath rudded,
Her lips lyke cherryes charming men to byte,
Her brest like to a bowle of creame uncrudded,   *175*

---

98. hours: The Horai (Horae), goddesses of the seasons, often in attendance at weddings and births, are daughters of Zeus (sky) and Themis (earth), whom Spenser contrives to call Day and Night. **102. still:** always, constantly. **103:** See note to line 430 of *The Faerie Queene* (p. 159). **106. betweene:** at intervals. **118. lifull:** lifegiving. **120. disgrace:** mar the grace of, disfigure. **121:** According to Hesiod, the standard source, the Muses were daughters of Zeus and Mnemosyne; but Spenser may well have meant this loosely, since Apollo, as god of music, was a sort of spiritual father, director of the choir of Muses; "the Muse" here may simply mean "music." **123. mote:** might. **131. Croud:** crowd (see note to Chaucer's General Prologue, line 236, p. 32). **148. portly:** stately. **149. Phoebe:** the moon (other names: Artemis, Selene, Cynthia, Diana, Luna). **149-50:** Cf. Psalms 19:4-5. **151. seemes:** beseems. **155. perle . . . perling:** pearl . . . pearl-like; or possibly referring to pearling-lace formed into flower-like ornaments. **173. rudded:** made ruddy, reddened. **175. uncrudded:** uncurdled.

Her paps lyke lyllies budded,
Her snowie necke lyke to a marble towre,
And all her body like a pallace fayre,
Ascending uppe with many a stately stayre,
To honours seat and chastities sweet bowre.   *180*
Why stand ye still ye virgins in amaze,
Upon her so to gaze,
Whiles ye forget your former lay to sing,
To which the woods did answer and your eccho ring.

But if ye saw that which no eyes can see,   *185*
The inward beauty of her lively spright,
Garnisht with heavenly guifts of high degree,
Much more then would ye wonder at that sight,
And stand astonisht lyke to those which red
Medusaes mazeful hed.   *190*
There dwels sweet love and constant chastity,
Unspotted fayth and comely womanhood,
Regard of honour and mild modesty;
There vertue raynes as Queene in royal throne,
And giveth lawes alone.   *195*
The which the base affections doe obay,
And yeeld theyr services unto her will;
Ne thought of thing uncomely ever may
Thereto approch to tempt her mind to ill.
Had ye once seene these her celestial threasures,   *200*
And unrevealed pleasures,
Then would ye wonder and her prayses sing,
That al the woods should answer and your eccho ring.

Open the temple gates unto my love,
Open them wide that she may enter in,   *205*
And all the postes adorne as doth behove,
And all the pillours deck with girlands trim,
For to recyve this Saynt with honour dew,
That commeth in to you.
With trembling steps and humble reverence,   *210*
She commeth in, before th'almighties vew;
Of her ye virgins learne obedience,
When so ye come into those holy places,
To humble your proud faces:
Bring her up to th'high altar, that she may   *215*
The sacred ceremonies there partake,
The which do endlesse matrimony make,
And let the roring Organs loudly play

The praises of the Lord in lively notes,
The whiles with hollow throates   *220*
The Choristers the joyous Antheme sing,
That al the woods may answere and their eccho ring.

Behold while she before the altar stands
Hearing the holy priest that to her speakes
And blesseth her with his two happy hands,   *225*
How the red roses flush up in her cheekes,
And the pure snow with goodly vermill stayne,
Like crimsin dyde in grayne,
That even th'Angels which continually,
About the sacred Altare doe remaine,   *230*
Forget their service and about her fly,
Ofte peeping in her face that seemes more fayre,
The more they on it stare.
But her sad eyes still fastened on the ground,
Are governed with goodly modesty,   *235*
That suffers not one looke to glaunce awry,
Which may let in a little thought unsownd.
Why blush ye love to give to me your hand,
The pledge of all our band?
Sing, ye sweet Angels, Alleluya sing,   *240*
That all the woods may answere and your eccho ring.

Now al is done; bring home the bride againe,
Bring home the triumph of our victory,
Bring home with you the glory of her gaine,
With joyance bring her and with jollity.   *245*
Never had man more joyfull day then this,
Whom heaven would heape with blis.
Make feast therefore now all this live long day,
This day for ever to me holy is,
Poure out the wine without restraint or stay,   *250*
Poure not by cups, but by the belly full,
Poure out to all that wull,
And sprinkle all the postes and wals with wine,
That they may sweat, and drunken be withall.
Crowne ye God Bacchus with a coronall,   *255*
And Hymen also crowne with wreathes of vine,
And let the Graces daunce unto the rest;
For they can doo it best:
The whiles the maydens doe theyr carroll sing,
To which the woods shal answer and theyr eccho ring. *260*

177: Cf. The Song of Solomon 7:4. **186. lively:** living. **189. red:** saw. **189-90:** Those who looked upon Medusa, the Gorgon with snakes for hair, were turned to stone. **206. postes:** doorposts. **227. vermill:** vermeil, vermilion. **228. grayne:** fast dye. **234. sad:** serious, grave. **239. band:** bond. **244. her gaine:** i.e., gaining her. **246. then:** than. **253:** echoes the Roman custom of anointing the doorposts when a bride is brought home. **255. Bacchus:** god of wine and revelry.

Ring ye the bels, ye young men of the towne,
And leave your wonted labors for this day:
This day is holy; doe ye write it downe,
That ye for ever it remember may.
This day the sunne is in his chiefest hight,   *265*
With Barnaby the bright,
From whence declining daily by degrees,
He somewhat loseth of his heat and light,
When once the Crab behind his back he sees.
But for this time it ill ordained was,   *270*
To chose the longest day in all the yeare,
And shortest night, when longest fitter weare;
Yet never day so long, but late would passe.
Ring ye the bels, to make it weare away,
And bonefiers make all day,   *275*
And daunce about them, and about them sing:
That all the woods may answer, and your eccho ring.

Ah when will this long weary day have end,
And lende me leave to come unto my love?
How slowly do the houres theyr numbers spend!   *280*
How slowly does sad Time his feathers move!
Hast thee O fayrest Planet to thy home
Within the Westerne fome;
Thy tyred steedes long since have need of rest.
Long though it be, at last I see it gloome,   *285*
And the bright evening star with golden creast
Appeare out of the East.
Fayre childe of beauty, glorious lampe of love
That all the host of heaven in rankes doost lead,
And guydest lovers through the nightes dread,   *290*
How chearefully thou lookest from above,
And seemst to laugh atweene thy twinkling light
As joying in the sight
Of these glad many which for joy doe sing,
That all the woods them answer and their eccho ring.   *295*

Now ceasse ye damsels your delights forepast;
Enough is it, that all the day was youres:
Now day is doen, and night is nighing fast:
Now bring the Bryde into the brydall boures.
Now night is come, now soone her disaray,   *300*
And in her bed her lay;
Lay her in lillies and in violets,
And silken courteins over her display,
And odoured sheetes, and Arras coverlets.
Behold how goodly my faire love does ly   *305*
In proud humility;
Like unto Maia, when as Jove her tooke,
In Tempe, lying on the flowry gras,
Twixt sleepe and wake, after she weary was,
With bathing in the Acidalian brooke.   *310*
Now it is night, ye damsels may be gon,
And leave my love alone,
And leave likewise your former lay to sing:
The woods no more shal answere, nor your eccho ring.

Now welcome night, thou night so long expected,   *315*
That long daies labour doest at last defray,
And all my cares, which cruell love collected,
Hast sumd in one, and cancelled for aye:
Spread thy broad wing over my love and me,
That no man may us see,   *320*
And in thy sable mantle us enwrap,
From feare of perrill and foule horror free.
Let no false treason seeke us to entrap,
Nor any dread disquiet once annoy
The safety of our joy: *325*
But let the night be calme and quietsome,
Without tempestuous storms or sad afray;
Lyke as when Jove with fayre Alcmena lay,
When he begot the great Tirynthian groome:
Or lyke as when he with thy selfe did lie,   *330*

265-66: St. Barnabas's Day, 11 June, was the summer solstice in the Old Style calendar. **269. Crab:** the constellation Cancer, the fourth sign of the zodiac, the sign of the summer solstice. **273. late:** i.e., finally, at last. **279. lende:** give, grant. **282. Planet:** In the Ptolemaic system, before the heliocentric Copernican system was adopted, the sun was considered one of the planets revolving about the earth (see *Ptolemaic* in the Glossary). **300. disaray:** undress. **304. Arras:** i.e., tapestry work from Arras, France. **307. Maia:** eldest and most beautiful of the Pleiades, the seven daughters of Atlas and Pleione; she became the mother of Hermes (Mercury), by Zeus (Jove). **308-10:** The Vale of Tempe lies between Mounts Olympus and Ossa, in Thessaly. (The Greek story has Zeus visit Maia on Mount Cyllene, in Arcadia. The "Acidalian brooke" in Boeotia is associated with Venus.) **329: Tirynthian groome:** Herakles (Hercules), son of Zeus and Alcmene; though commonly accepted as a native of Tiryns, he was also claimed by Thebes; in any event, he entered the service of Eurystheus, king of Mycenae and Tiryns, for whom he performed his "Twelve Labours." **330-31:** Evidently Spenser invented this myth.

And begot Majesty.
And let the mayds and yongmen cease to sing:
Ne let the woods them answer, nor theyr eccho ring.

Let no lamenting cryes, nor dolefull teares,
Be heard all night within nor yet without;   *335*
Ne let false whispers, breeding hidden feares,
Breake gentle sleepe with misconceived dout.
Let no deluding dreames, nor dreadful sights
Make sudden sad affrights;
Ne let housefyres, nor lightnings helpelesse harmes,
Ne let the Pouke, nor other evill sprights,   *341*
Ne let mischivous witches with theyr charmes,
Ne let hob Goblins, names whose sence we see not,
Fray us with things that be not.
Let not the shriech Oule, nor the Storke be heard: *345*
Nor the night Raven that still deadly yels,
Nor damned ghosts cald up with mighty spels,
Nor griesly vultures make us once affeard:
Ne let th'unpleasant Quyre of Frogs still croking
Make us to wish theyr choking.   *350*
Let none of these theyr drery accents sing;
Ne let the woods them answer, nor theyr eccho ring.

But let stil Silence trew night watches keepe,
That sacred peace may in assurance rayne,
And tymely sleep, when it is tyme to sleepe,   *355*
May poure his limbs forth on your pleasant playne,
The whiles an hundred little winged loves,
Like divers fethered doves,
Shall fly and flutter round about your bed,
And in the secret darke, that none reproves,   *360*
Their prety stealthes shal worke, and snares shal spread
To filch away sweet snatches of delight,
Conceald through covert night.
Ye sonnes of Venus, play your sports at will,
For greedy pleasure, carelesse of your toyes,   *365*
Thinks more upon her paradise of joyes,

Then what ye do, albe it good or ill.
All night therefore attend your merry play,
For it will soone be day;
Now none doth hinder you, that say or sing,   *370*
Ne will the woods now answer, nor your Eccho ring.

Who is the same, which at my window peepes?
Or whose is that faire face, that shines so bright?
Is it not Cinthia, she that never sleepes,
But walkes about high heaven al the night?   *375*
O fayrest goddesse, do thou not envy
My love with me to spy,
For thou likewise didst love, though now unthought,
And for a fleece of woll, which privily,
The Latmian shephard once unto thee brought,   *380*
His pleasures with thee wrought.
Therefore to us be favorable now;
And sith of wemens labours thou hast charge,
And generation goodly dost enlarge,
Encline thy will t'effect our wishfull vow,   *385*
And the chast wombe informe with timely seed,
That may our comfort breed;
Till which we cease our hopefull hap to sing,
Ne let the woods us answere, nor our Eccho ring.

And thou great Juno, which with awful might   *390*
The lawes of wedlock still dost patronize,
And the religion of the faith first plight
With sacred rites hast taught to solemnize;
And eeke for comfort often called art
Of women in their smart,   *395*
Eternally bind thou this lovely band,
And all thy blessings unto us impart.
And thou glad Genius, in whose gentle hand
The bridale bowre and geniall bed remaine,
Without blemish or staine,   *400*
And the sweet pleasures of theyr loves delight
With secret ayde dost succour and supply,
Till they bring forth the fruitfull progeny,
Send us the timely fruit of this same night.

---

337. dout: fear. **341. Pouke:** Puck; perhaps Spenser was thinking of the pooka, or phooka — in Irish folklore, a malignant spirit; in any event, the prankish Puck, or Robin Goodfellow, as portrayed in Shakespeare's *A Midsummer Night's Dream*, is much changed from the evil demon referred to here. **342. mischivous:** intending harm or evil. **344. fray:** frighten. **345-46:** The owl and the raven are birds of ill omen; Spenser evidently thought of the stork as one also, perhaps because it is listed, along with raven and owl, as among the "unclean" birds in Deuteronomy 14:12-19. **365. toyes:** amorous sports. **380. Latmian shepherd:** Endymion (but in the myth it was she who fell in love with the shepherd; and Virgil in his third Georgic refers to the story of Pan wooing the moon-goddess with a gift of fleece). **383:** As a goddess of light, Diana Lucina, like Juno Lucina (see lines 390ff.), was a goddess of birth. **392. religion:** religious sanction, sanctity. **395. smart:** pain, labour. **398. Genius:** the creative principle, a male spirit, counterpart of Juno Lucina as goddess of childbirth; protector of generation, and of the "geniall bed" named after him, as well as tutelary spirit throughout each person's life. **399. geniall:** nuptial.

And thou fayre Hebe, and thou Hymen free,   *405*
Grant that it may so be.
Til which we cease your further prayse to sing,
Ne any woods shal answer, nor your Eccho ring.

And ye high heavens, the temple of the gods,
In which a thousand torches flaming bright   *410*
Doe burne, that to us wretched earthly clods,
In dreadful darknesse lend desired light;
And all ye powers which in the same remayne,
More then we men can fayne,
Poure out your blessings on us plentiously,   *415*
And happy influence upon us raine,
That we may raise a large posterity,
Which from the earth, which they may long possesse,

With lasting happinesse,
Up to your haughty pallaces may mount,   *420*
And for the guerdon of theyr glorious merit
May heavenly tabernacles there inherit,
Of blessed Saints for to increase the count.
So let us rest, sweet love, in hope of this,
And cease till then our tymely joyes to sing,   *425*
The woods no more us answer, nor our eccho ring.

Song made in lieu of many ornaments,
With which my love should duly have bene dect,
Which cutting off through hasty accidents,
Ye would not stay your dew time to expect,   *430*
But promist both to recompens,
Be unto her a goodly ornament,
And for short time an endlesse moniment.

(1595)

RICHARD HAKLUYT
England, 1552-1616

from *THE PRINCIPALL NAVIGATIONS*

Opening passage from "A discourse of the West Indies and South sea written by Lopez Vaz a Portugal, borne in the citie of Elvas, continued unto the yere 1587. Wherein among divers certaine voyages of our Englishmen are truely reported: which was intercepted with the author thereof at the river of Plate, by Captaine Withrington and Captaine Christopher Lister, in the fleete set foorth for the South sea in the yeere 1586."

Francis Drake an Englishman being on the sea, and having knowledge of the small strength of the towne of Nombre de Dios, came into the harborough on a night with foure pinnesses, and landed an hundreth and fifty men: and leaving one halfe of his men with a trumpet in a fort which was there, hee with the rest entred the towne without doing any harme till hee came at the market place: and there his company discharging   *5* their calivers, and sounding their trumpets (which made a great noyse in the towne) were answered by their fellowes in the forte, who discharged and sounded in like maner. This attempt put the townsmen in such extreme feare, that leaving their houses, they

---

405. Hebe: daughter of Zeus and Hera, and goddess of youth. **414. fayne:** imagine. **420. haughty:** high, noble. **THE PRINCIPALL NAVIGATIONS** Translated by Richard Hakluyt. The full title is *The Principall Navigations, Voiages, and Discoveries of the English Nation made by Sea or over Land to the most remote and farthest distant quarters of the earth, at any time within the compass of these 1500 years.* Hakluyt's massive compilation is assembled and translated from various sources and is commonly referred to simply as *The Principal Navigations* or *Voyages and Discoveries*. Drake's expedition took place about 1572. **3. pinnesses:** pinnaces. **6. calivers:** light muskets or harquebusses.

fled into the mountaines, and there bethought themselves what the matter should be in
the towne, remaining as men amazed at so sudden an alarme. But the Spaniards being   *10*
men for the most part of good discretion joyned foureteene or fifteene of them together
with their pieces, to see who was in the towne: and getting to a corner of the market-
place they discovered the Englishmen, and perceiving that they were but a few,
discharged their pieces at them; and their fortune was such, that they slew the
trumpetter, and shot the captaine (whose name was Francis Drake) into the legge: who   *15*
feeling himselfe hurt retired toward the Fort, where he had left the rest of his men: but
they in the Fort sounded their trumpet, and being not answered againe, and hearing the
calivers discharged in the towne, thought that their fellowes in the towne had been
slaine, and thereupon fled to their Pinnesses. Now Francis Drake (whom his men carried
because of his hurt) when he came to the fort where he left his men and saw them fled,   *20*
he and the rest of his company were in so great feare, that leaving their furniture
behinde them, and putting off their hose, they swamme & waded all to their Pinnesses,
and departed forth of the harbour, so that if the Spaniards had followed them, they might
have slaine them all. Thus Captaine Drake did no more harme at Nombre de Dios,
neither was there in this skirmish any more than one Spaniard slaine, and of the   *25*
Englishmen onely their Trumpetter, whom they left behind with his trumpet in his hand.

From hence the coast lieth all along till you come to Cartagena. Betweene Nombre
de Dios and Cartagena is a great sound or gulfe, where the first Spaniardes that ever
dwelt upon the firme land built and inhabited the towne of Dariene: howbeit they abode
not long there, because of the unholesomenesse of the place.   *30*

But Captaine Drake being discontent with the repulse that the men of Nombre de
Dios gave him, went with his Pinnesses into the said bay or sound of Dariene, where
having conference with certaine Negros which were ranne away from their masters of
Panama and Nombre de Dios, he was informed that at the very same time many mules
were comming from Panama to Nombre de Dios laden with gold and silver. Upon this   *35*
newes Francis Drake taking with him an hundred shot, and the said Negros, stayed in
the way till the treasure came by, accompanied and guarded onely by those that drove
the mules, who mistrusted nothing at all. When captaine Drake met with them, he tooke
away their golde: but the silver he left behinde, because he could not carrie it over the
mountaines. And two dayes after this he went to the house of crosses called by the   *40*
Spaniards Venta de Cruzes, where all the merchants leave their goods, where he slew
sixe or seven of the marchants, but found neither gold nor silver, but great store of
marchandize: and so he fired the said house, with all the goods, which were judged to be
worth above two hundred thousand ducats. Thus not finding golde in this house to
satisfie his minde, hee burned the marchants goods, and foorthwith recovered his   *45*
Pinnesses: where fortune so favoured his proceedings, that he had not bene aboord halfe
an houre, but there came to the sea side above three hundred souldiers, which were sent
of purpose to take him: but God suffered him to escape their hands, to be a farther
plague unto the Spaniards.

(1589)

---

21. furniture: equipment. **36. shot:** balls, pellets, charges of powder. **38. mistrusted:** suspected.

SIR WALTER RALEGH
England, c.1552-1618

from *THE DISCOVERY OF GUIANA*

On Thursday the 6th of February, in the year 1595, we departed England, and the Sunday following had sight of the north cape of Spain, the wind for the most part continuing prosperous. We passed in sight of the Burlings and the rock, and so onwards for the Canaries, and fell with Fuerte Ventura the 17th of the same month, where we spent two or three days, and relieved our companies with some fresh meat. From thence   5
we coasted by the Gran Canaria, and so to Tenerife, and stayed there for the *Lion's Whelp*, your Lordship's ship, and for Captain Amys Preston and the rest. But when after seven or eight days we found them not, we departed and directed our course for Trinidado with mine own ship, and a small bark of Captain Cross's only (for we had before lost sight of a small gallego on the coast of Spain, which came with us from   10
Plymouth). We arrived at Trinidado the 22nd of March, casting anchor at Point Curiapan, which the Spaniards call Punto de Gallo.

. . . .

This island of Trinidado hath the form of a sheep-hook, and is but narrow; the north part is very mountainous; the soil is very excellent and will bear sugar, ginger, or any other commodity that the Indies yield. It hath store of deer, wild porks, fruits, fish, and   15
fowl. It hath also for bread sufficient maize, cassavi, and of those roots and fruits which are common everywhere in the West Indies. It hath divers beasts which the Indies have not. The Spaniards confessed that they found grains of gold in some of the rivers, but they having a purpose to enter Guiana (the magazine of all rich metals), cared not to spend time in the search thereof any farther.   20

. . . .

On both sides of this river [the Orinoco] we passed the most beautiful country that ever mine eyes beheld; and whereas all that we had seen before was nothing but woods, prickles, bushes, and thorns, here we beheld plains of twenty miles in length, the grasses short and green, and in divers parts groves of trees by themselves, as if they had been by all the art and labour in the world so made of purpose. And still as we rowed, the deer   25
came down feeding by the water's side, as if they had been used to a keeper's call. Upon this river there were great store of fowl, and of many sorts. We saw in it divers sorts of

---

THE DISCOVERY OF GUIANA   The full title is as follows: *The Discovery of the Large, Rich and Beautiful Empire of Guiana, with a Relation of the Great and Golden City of Manoa, which the Spaniards called El Dorado, and the Provinces of Emeria, Aromaia, Amapaia, and Other Countries, with their Rivers Adjoining. Performed in the Year 1595 by Sir Walter Ralegh, Knight, Captain of her Majesty's Guard, Lord Warden of the Stannaries, and Her Highness' Lieutenant General of the County of Cornwall.* **3. Burlings . . . rock:** Islas Berlengas and Cabo da Roca, near Lisbon. **4:** Fuerteventura is one of the Canary Islands. **7. your Lordship:** The epistle dedicatory is, first, to Charles Howard (1536-1624), lord admiral of England since 1585, commander in chief against the Spanish Armada (1588) and commander with Essex for the attack on Cadiz (see Thomas Deloney's "The Winning of Cales," p. 206), and made Earl of Nottingham in 1596 (the prominent family included the poet Surrey and Catherine Howard, Henry VIII's fifth queen, both of whom were executed), and also to Sir Robert Cecil.

strange fishes, and of marvellous bigness, but for *lagartos* it exceeded, for there were thousands of those ugly serpents, and the people call it for the abundance of them the River of Lagartos, in their language. I had a Negro, a very proper young fellow, that *30* leaping out of the galley to swim in the mouth of this river, was in all our sights taken and devoured with one of those *lagartos*.

In the meanwhile our companies in the galley thought we had been all lost (for we promised to return before night), and sent the *Lion's Whelp*'s ship's boat with Captain Whiddon to follow us up the river, but the next day, after we had rowed up and down *35* some four score miles, we returned and went on our way up the great river, and when we were even at the last cast for want of victuals, Captain Gifford being before the galley and the rest of the boats, seeking out some place to land upon the banks to make fire, espied four *canoas* coming down the river, and with no small joy caused his men to try the uttermost of their strengths, and after a while two of the four gave over, and ran *40* themselves ashore, every man betaking himself to the fastness of the woods; the two other lesser got away while he landed to lay hold on these, and so turned into some by-creek, we knew not whither. Those *canoas* that were taken were loaden with bread, and were bound for Marguerita in the West Indies, which those Indians (called Arwacas) purposed to carry thither for exchange. But in the lesser there were three Spaniards, who *45* having heard of the defeat of their governor in Trinidado, and that we purposed to enter Guiana, came away in those *canoas*. One of them was a *cavallero*, as the captain of the Arwacas after told us, another a soldier, and the third a refiner.

In the meantime nothing on the earth could have been more welcome to us, next unto gold, than the great store of very excellent bread which we found in these *canoas*, *50* for now our men cried, "Let us go on, we care not how far." After that Captain Gifford had brought the two *canoas* to the galley, I took my barge and went to the bank's side with a dozen shot, where the *canoas* first ran themselves ashore, and landed there, sending out Captain Gifford and Captain Thyn on one hand, and Captain Calfield on the other, to follow those that were fled into the woods, and as I was creeping through the *55* bushes, I saw an Indian basket hidden, which was the refiner's basket, for I found in it his quicksilver, saltpetre, and divers things for the trial of metals, and also the dust of such ore as he had refined. But in those *canoas* which escaped there was a good quantity of ore and gold.

I then landed more men, and offered 500 pound to what soldier soever could take *60* one of those three Spaniards that we thought were landed. But our labours were in vain in that behalf, for they put themselves into one of the small *canoas*, and so while the greater *canoas* were in taking, they escaped. But seeking after the Spaniards, we found the Arwacas hidden in the woods, which were pilots for the Spaniards and rowed their *canoas*; of which I kept the chiefest for a pilot, and carried him with me to Guiana, by *65* whom I understood where and in what countries the Spaniards had laboured for gold, though I made not the same known to all; for when the springs began to break, and the rivers to raise themselves so suddenly, as by no means we could abide the digging of any mine, especially for that the richest are defended with rocks of hard stone, which we

---

28. lagartos: alligators (from Spanish *el lagarto*).

call the white spar, and that it required both time, men, and instruments fit for such a   *70*
work, I thought it best not to hover thereabouts, lest if the same had been perceived by
the company, there would have been by this time many barks and ships set out, and
perchance other nations would also have gotten of ours for pilots, so as both ourselves
might have been prevented, and all our care taken for good usage of the people been
utterly lost by those that only respect present profit, and such violence or insolence   *75*
offered, as the nations which are borderers would have changed their desire of our love
and defence into hatred and violence. And for any longer stay to have brought a more
quantity (which I hear hath been often objected), whosoever had seen or proved the fury
of that river after it began to arise, and had been a month and odd days as we were from
hearing aught from our ships, leaving them meanly manned above 400 miles off, would   *80*
perchance have turned somewhat sooner than we did, if all the mountains had been gold
or rich stones. And to say the truth, all the branches and small rivers which fell into
Oroonoko were raised with such speed, as, if we waded them over the shoes in the
morning outward, we were covered to the shoulders homeward the very same day; and
to stay to dig out gold with our nails had been *opus laboris,* but not *ingenii.* Such a   *85*
quantity as would have served our turns we could not have had, but a discovery of the
mines to our infinite disadvantage we had made, and that could have been the best profit
of farther search or stay; for those mines are not easily broken nor opened in haste, and I
could have returned a good quantity of gold ready cast, if I had not shot at another mark
than present profit.   *90*

. . . .

(1596)

THE LIE

Go, Soul, the body's guest,	Not strong but by a faction.
Upon a thankless arrant.	If potentates reply,
Fear not to touch the best;	Give potentates the lie.
The truth shall be thy warrant.	
Go, since I needs must die, *5*	Tell men of high condition
And give the world the lie.	That manage the estate, *20*
	Their purpose is ambition,
Say to the court it glows	Their practice only hate,
And shines like rotten wood;	And if they once reply,
Say to the church it shows	Then give them all the lie.
What's good, and doth no good. *10*	
If church and court reply,	Tell them that brave it most, *25*
Then give them both the lie.	They beg for more by spending,
	Who in their greatest cost
Tell potentates they live	Like nothing but commending.
Acting by others' action:	And if they make reply,
Not loved unless they give, *15*	Then give them all the lie. *30*

---

74. prevented: anticipated. **85.** *opus . . . ingenii:* a work of labour, but not ingenuity.   **THE LIE**   Some scholars claim that this poem is not by
Ralegh. **2. arrant:** errand. **20. estate:** state. **25. brave it:** spend on showy attire.

Tell zeal it wants devotion;
Tell love it is but lust;
Tell time it metes but motion;
Tell flesh it is but dust.
And wish them not reply,   *35*
For thou must give the lie.

Tell age it daily wasteth;
Tell honour how it alters;
Tell beauty how she blasteth;
Tell favour how it falters.   *40*
And as they shall reply,
Give every one the lie.

Tell wit how much it wrangles
In tickle points of niceness;
Tell wisdom she entangles   *45*
Herself in over-wiseness.
And when they do reply,
Straight give them both the lie.

Tell physic of her boldness;
Tell skill it is pretension;   *50*
Tell charity of coldness;
Tell law it is contention.
And as they do reply,
So give them still the lie.

Tell fortune of her blindness;   *55*
Tell nature of decay;
Tell friendship of unkindness;
Tell justice of delay.
And if they will reply,
Then give them all the lie.   *60*

Tell arts they have no soundness,
But vary by esteeming;
Tell schools they want profoundness,
And stand too much on seeming.
If arts and schools reply,   *65*
Give arts and schools the lie.

Tell faith it's fled the city;
Tell how the country erreth;
Tell manhood shakes off pity;

Tell virtue least preferreth.   *70*
And if they do reply,
Spare not to give the lie.

So when thou hast, as I
Commanded thee, done blabbing,
Although to give the lie   *75*
Deserves no less than stabbing,
Stab at thee, he that will;
No stab the soul can kill.
                          (c. 1593; 1608)

THE NYMPH'S REPLY
TO THE SHEPHERD

If all the world and love were young,
And truth in every shepherd's tongue,
These pretty pleasures might me move
To live with thee and be thy love.

Time drives the flocks from field to fold, *5*
When rivers rage, and rocks grow cold,
And Philomel becometh dumb;
The rest complains of cares to come.

The flowers do fade, and wanton fields
To wayward winter reckoning yields;   *10*
A honey tongue, a heart of gall,
Is fancy's spring, but sorrow's fall.

Thy gowns, thy shoes, thy beds of roses,
Thy cap, thy kirtle, and thy posies,
Soon break, soon wither, soon forgotten: *15*
In folly ripe, in reason rotten.

Thy belt of straw and ivy buds,
Thy coral clasps and amber studs,
All these in me no means can move
To come to thee and be thy love.   *20*

But could youth last, and love still breed,
Had joys no date, nor age no need,
Then these delights my mind might move
To live with thee and be thy love.
                                    (1600)

---

44. tickle: delicate. **70. preferreth:** gets preferment, promotion.   THE NYMPH'S REPLY   See Marlowe's "The Passionate Shepherd to His Love" (p. 226) and cf. Donne's "The Bait" (p. 255); see also Walton's *The Compleat Angler* (pp. 295-97). **7. Philomel:** Philomela, the nightingale.

"WHAT IS OUR LIFE?"

What is our life? A play of passion;
Our mirth, the music of division;
Our mothers' wombs the tiring houses be
Where we are dressed for this short comedy.
Heaven the judicious sharp spectator is,   5

That sits and marks still who doth act amiss;
Our graves that hide us from the searching sun
Are like drawn curtains when the play is done.
Thus march we playing to our latest rest —
Only we die in earnest; that's no jest.   10

(1612)

from *THE HISTORY OF THE WORLD, BOOK V*

Chapter 2, Section 2, part 1: Of tyranny, and how tyrants are driven
to use help of mercenaries.

Here let us rest a while, as in a convenient breathing-place, whence we may take
prospect of the subject over which we travel. Behold a tyrannical city, persecuted by her
own mercenaries with a deadly war. It is a common thing, as being almost necessary,
that a tyranny should be upheld by mercenary forces; it is common that mercenaries
should be false; and it is common that all war made against tyrants should be exceeding   5
full of hate and cruelty. Yet we seldom hear that the ruin of a tyranny is procured or
sought by those that were hired to maintain the power of it, and seldom or never do we
read of any war that hath been prosecuted with such inexpiable hatred as this that is now
at hand.

That which we properly call tyranny is a violent form of government, not respecting   10
the good of the subject but only the pleasure of the commander. I purposely forbear to
say that it is the unjust rule of one over many, for very truly doth Cleon in Thucydides
tell the Athenians that their dominion over their subjects was none other than a mere
tyranny, though it were so that they themselves were a great city and a popular estate.
Neither is it peradventure greatly needful that I should call this form of commanding   15
"violent," since it may well and easily be conceived that no man willingly performs
obedience to one regardless of his life and welfare, unless himself be either a madman
or (which is little better) wholly possessed with some extreme passion of love. The
practice of tyranny is not always of a like extremity, for some lords are more gentle than
others to their very slaves, and he that is most cruel to some is mild enough towards   20
others, though it be but for his own advantage. Nevertheless, in large dominions,
wherein the ruler's discretion cannot extend itself unto notice of the difference which
might be found between the worth of several men, it is commonly seen that the taste of
sweetness, drawn out of oppression, hath so good a relish as continually inflames the
tyrant's appetite, and will not suffer it to be restrained with any limits of respect. Why   25

"WHAT IS OUR LIFE?"   **2. division:** rapid musical passage, run, similar to descant; execution of such a passage (i.e., dividing a succession
of long notes into numerous short ones). **3. tiring houses:** dressing (attiring) rooms in theatres.   **THE HISTORY OF THE WORLD**   Written
during Ralegh's long imprisonment in the Tower of London.   **CHAPTER 2, SECTION 2, PART 1**   **8-9:** in the preceding section Ralegh tells
"Of the cruel war begun between the Carthaginians and their own mercenaries." **12-14:** in his *History of the War Fought Between Athens and Sparta*
(*The Peloponnesian War*), I, 6.

should he seek out bounds to prescribe unto his desires, who cannot endure the face of one so honest as may put him in remembrance of any moderation? It is much that he hath gotten by extorting from some few; by sparing none, he should have riches in goodly abundance. He hath taken a great deal from everyone; but everyone could have spared more. He hath wrung all their purses, and now he hath enough; but (as covetousness is never satisfied) he thinks that all this is too little for a stock, though it were indeed a good yearly income. Therefore he deviseth new tricks of robbery, and is not better pleased with the gains than with the art of getting. He is hated for this, and he knows it well; but he thinks by cruelty to change hatred into fear. So he makes it his exercise to torment and murder all whom he suspecteth, in which course, if he suspect none unjustly, he may be said to deal craftily; but if innocency be not safe, how can all this make any conspirator to stand in fear, since the traitor is no worse rewarded than the quiet man? Wherefore he can think upon none other security than to disarm all his subjects, to fortify himself within some strong place, and for defence of his person and state, to hire as many lusty soldiers as shall be thought sufficient. These must not be of his own country, for if not everyone, yet someone or other might chance to have a feeling of the public misery. This considered, he allures unto him a desperate rabble of strangers, the most unhonest that can be found, such as have neither wealth nor credit at home, and will therefore be careful to support him by whose only favour they are maintained. Now, lest any of these, either by detestation of his wickedness or (which in wicked men is most likely) by promise of greater reward than he doth give, should be drawn to turn his sword against the tyrant himself, they shall all be permitted to do as he doth: to rob, to ravish, to murder, and to satisfy their own appetites in most outrageous manner, being thought so much the more assured to their master by how much the more he sees them grow hateful to all men else.

Considering in what age and in what language I write, I must be fain to say that these are not dreams, though some Englishmen perhaps that were unacquainted with history, lighting upon this leaf, might suppose this discourse to be little better. This is to show both how tyranny grows to stand in need of mercenary soldiers, and how those mercenaries are, by mutual obligation, firmly assured unto the tyrant.

Chapter 2, Section 2, part 2: That the tyranny of a city over her subjects is worse than the tyranny of one man; and that a tyrannical city must likewise use mercenary soldiers.

. . . .

Chapter 2, Section 2, part 3: The dangers growing from the use of mercenary soldiers and foreign auxiliaries.

. . . .

Chapter 2, Section 2, part 4: That the moderate government of the Romans gave them assurance to use the service of their own subjects in their wars. That in man's nature there is an affection breeding tyranny, which hindereth the use and benefit of the like moderation.

Here may it be demanded whether also the Romans were not compelled to use service of other soldiers in their many great wars, but performed all by their own citizens? For if it were their manner to arm their own subjects, how happened it that they feared no rebellion? If strangers, how then could they avoid the inconveniences above rehearsed? The answer is that their armies were compounded usually of their own citizens and of   *5* the Latins, in equal number, to which they added, as occasion required, some companies of the Campanes, Hetrurians, Samnites, or other of their subjects as were either interested in the quarrel or might best be trusted. They had, about these times (though seldom they did employ so many), ten Roman legions — a good strength, if all other help had been wanting — which served to keep in good order their subjects, that were   *10* always fewer in the army than themselves. As for the Latins, if consanguinity were not a sufficient obligation, yet many privileges and immunities, which they enjoyed, made them assured unto the state of Rome, under which they lived almost at liberty, as being bound to little else than to serve it in war.

It is true that a yoke, how easy soever, seems troublesome to the neck that hath   *15* been accustomed to freedom. Therefore many people of Italy have taken occasion of several advantages to deliver themselves from the Roman subjection. But still they have been reclaimed by war, the authors of rebellion have been sharply punished, and the people by degrees have obtained such liberty as made them esteem none otherwise of Rome than as the common city of all Italy. Yea, in process of time it was granted unto   *20* many cities, and those far off removed, even to Tarsus in Cilicia, where St. Paul was born, that all the burgesses should be free of Rome itself. This favour was conferred absolutely upon some; upon some with restraint of giving voice in election of magistrates, or with other such limitation as was thought fit. Hereunto may be added, that it was their manner, after a great conquest, to release unto their new subjects half of   *25* their tribute which they had been wont to pay unto their former lords, which was a ready way to bring the multitude into good liking of their present condition, when the review of harder times past should rather teach them to fear a relapse than to hope for better in the future by seeking innovation. Neither would it be forgotten, as a special note of the Romans' good government, that when some, for their well-deserving, have had the offer   *30* to be made citizens of Rome, they have refused it, and held themselves better contented with their own present estate. Wherefore it is no marvel that Petellia, a city of the Brutians in Italy, chose rather to endure all extremity of war than upon any condition to forsake the Romans, even when the Romans themselves had confessed that they were unable to help these their subjects and therefore willed them to look to their own good,   *35* as having been faithful to the utmost. Such love purchased these mild governors without impairing their majesty thereby. The sum of all is, they had of their own a strong army, they doubled it by adjoining thereunto the Latins, and they further increased it, as need required, with other help of their own subjects, all, or the most of their followers, accounting the prosperity of Rome to be the common good.   *40*

The moderate use of sovereign power being so effectual in assuring the people unto their lords, and consequently in the establishment or enlargement of dominion, it may seem strange that the practice of tyranny, whose effects are contrary, hath been so

---

CHAPTER 2, SECTION 2, PART 4 **7. Campanes:** Campanians; **Hetrurians:** Etrurians (Etruscans). **29ff.:** For these examples, Ralegh draws on the Roman historian Livy.

common in all ages. The like, I know, may be said of all vice and irregularity whatsoever, for it is less difficult (whosoever think otherwise) and more safe to keep the way of justice and honesty than to turn aside from it; yet commonly our passions lead us into bypaths. But where lust, anger, fear, or any the like affection seduceth our reason, the same unruly appetite either bringeth with it an excuse or at leastwise taketh away all cause of wonder. In tyranny it is not so, forasmuch as we can hardly descry the passion that is of force to insinuate itself into the whole tenor of a government. It must be confessed that lawless desires have bred many tyrants, yet so that these desires have seldom been hereditary or long lasting, but have ended commonly with the tyrant's life, sometimes before his death, by which means the government hath been reduced to a better form. In such cases, the saying of Aristotle holds, that tyrannies are of short continuance. But this doth not satisfy the question in hand: Why did the Carthaginians exercise tyranny? Why did the Athenians? Why have many other cities done the like? If in respect of their general good, how could they be ignorant that this was an ill course for the safety of the weal public? If they were led hereunto by any affection, what was that affection wherein so many thousand citizens, divided and subdivided within themselves by factions, did all concur, notwithstanding the much diversity of temper and the vehemency of private hatred among them? Doubtless we must be fain to say that tyranny is, by itself, a vice distinct from others.

A man, we know, is *animal politicum*, apt, even by nature, to command or obey, every one in his proper degree. Other desires of mankind are common likewise unto brute beasts, and some of them to bodies wanting sense; but the desire of rule belongeth unto the nobler part of reason, whereunto is also answerable an aptness to yield obedience. Now as hunger and thirst are given by nature, not only to man and beast but unto all sorts of vegetables, for the sustentation of their life; as fear, anger, lust, and other affections are likewise natural, in convenient measure, both unto mankind and to all creatures that have sense, for the shunning or repelling of harm and seeking after that which is requisite; even so is this desire of ruling or obeying engrafted by nature in the race of man, and in man only as a reasonable creature, for the ordering of his life in a civil form of justice.

All these inbred qualities are good and useful; nevertheless, hunger and thirst are the parents of gluttony and drunkenness, which, in reproach, are called beastly — by an unproper term, since they grow from appetites found in less worthy creatures than beasts, and are yet not so common in beasts as in men. The effects of anger, and of such other passions as descend no lower than unto brute beasts, are held less vile, and perhaps not without good reason; yet are they more horrible, and punished more grievously by sharper laws, as being in general more pernicious. But as no corruption is worse than of that which is best, there is not any passion that nourisheth a vice more hurtful unto mankind than that which issueth from the most noble root, even the depraved affection of ruling.

Hence arise those two great mischiefs, of which hath been an old question in dispute, whether be the worse: that all things, or that nothing, should be lawful. Of these a dull spirit, and overladen by fortune with power whereof it is not capable, occasioneth

---

54-55: Aristotle's *Politics*, V, 12. **63:** "Man is by nature a political animal" (Aristotle, *Politics*, I, 2).

the one; the other proceedeth from a contrary distemper, whose vehemency the bounds of reason cannot limit. Under the extremity of either, no country is able to subsist; yet the defective dullness, that permitteth anything, will also permit the execution of law, to which mere necessity doth enforce the ordinary magistrate, whereas tyranny is more 90 active, and pleaseth itself in the excess with a false colour of justice. Examples of stupidity and unaptness to rule are not very frequent, though such natures are everywhere found; for this quality troubles not itself in seeking empire; or if, by some error of fortune, it encounter therewithal (as when Claudius, hiding himself in a corner, found the empire of Rome), some friend, or else a wife, is not wanting to supply the 95 defect, which also cruelty doth help to shadow. Therefore this vice, as a thing unknown, is without a name.

Tyranny is more bold, and feareth not to be known, but would be reputed honourable; for it is *prosperum et foelix scelus*, "a fortunate mischief," as long as it can subsist. "There is no reward or honour," saith Peter Charron, "assigned to those that 100 know how to increase, or to preserve human nature; all honours, greatness, riches, dignities, empires, triumphs, trophies, are appointed for those that know how to afflict, trouble, or destroy it." Caesar and Alexander have unmade and slain, each of them, more than a million of men; but they made none, nor left none behind them. Such is the error of man's judgment, in valuing things according to common opinion. But the true 105 name of tyranny, when it grows to ripeness, is none other than *ferity*; the same that Aristotle saith to be worse than any vice. It exceedeth indeed all other vices issuing from the passions incident both to man and beast, no less than perjury, murder, treason, and the like horrible crimes exceed in villainy the faults of gluttony and drunkenness, that grow from more ignoble appetites. Hereof Sciron, Procrustes, and Pityocamptes, that 110 used their bodily force to the destruction of mankind, are not better examples than Phalaris, Dionysius, and Agathocles, whose mischievous heads were assisted by the hands of detestable ruffians. The same barbarous desire of lordship transported those old examples of ferity and these latter tyrants beyond the bounds of reason; neither of them knew the use of rule, nor the difference between freemen and slaves. 115

The rule of the husband over the wife, and of parents over their children, is natural, and appointed by God himself, so that it is always, and simply, allowable and good. The former of these is as the dominion of reason over appetite; the latter is the whole authority which one free man can have over another. The rule of a king is no more nor none other than of a common father over his whole country, which he that knows what 120 the power of a father is, or ought to be, knows to be enough. But there is a greater and more masterly rule, which God gave unto Adam when he said, "Have dominion over the fish of the sea, and over the fowl of the air, and over every living thing that moveth upon the earth," which also he confirmed unto Noah and his children, saying, "The fear

---

94-95: When the emperor Gaius (Caligula), his nephew, was murdered, soldiers found Claudius hiding in fear behind a curtain, and the Praetorian Guard saluted him, as it were drafting the otherwise unpopular minor consul as successor. **100.** Pierre Charron (1541-1603), French philosopher and theologian. **110:** three mythical brigands: Sciron made travellers wash his feet and then kicked them over his cliff; Procrustes stretched or lopped his involuntary guests to fit one of his beds; Pityocamptes ("pine-bender"), or Sinis, tied people to bent-down pine trees which when released tore them apart; the hero Theseus killed all three. **112:** Phalaris, 6th-century B.C. tyrant of Acragas, had people put in a hollow bull made of brass and roasted alive; Dionysius (c.430-367 B.C.), was tyrant of Syracuse and a notable war-maker (with mercenaries); Agathocles (361-289 B.C.), cruel tyrant and warmonger of Syracuse. **122-24:** Genesis 1:28 (p. 243). **124-27:** Genesis 9:2 (p. 249).

of you and the dread of you shall be upon every beast of the earth, and upon every fowl *125*
of the air, upon all that moveth upon the earth, and upon all the fishes of the sea; into
your hands are they delivered." He who gave this dominion to man gave also an aptitude
to use it. The execution of this power hath since extended itself over a great part of
mankind. There are indeed no small numbers of men whose disability to govern
themselves proves them, according to Aristotle's doctrine, to be naturally slaves. *130*

Yet find I not in scripture any warrant to oppress men with bondage, unless the
lawfulness thereof be sufficiently intimated where it is said that a man shall not be
punished for the death of a servant, whom he hath slain by correction, if the servant live
a day or two, because "he is his money"; or else by the captivity of the Midianitish girls,
which were made bondslaves, and the sanctuary had a part of them for the Lord's *135*
tribute. Doubtless the custom hath been very ancient, for Noah laid this curse upon
Canaan, that he should be "a servant of servants"; and Abraham had of Pharaoh, among
other gifts, "menservants and maidservants," which were none other than slaves.

Christian religion is said to have abrogated this old kind of servility, but surely they
are deceived that think so. St. Paul desired the liberty of Onesimus, whom he had won *140*
unto Christ; yet wrote he for this unto Philemon by way of request, craving it as a
benefit, not urging it as a duty. Agreeable hereto is the direction which the same St. Paul
giveth unto his servants: "Let every man abide in the same calling wherein he was
called. Art thou called being a servant? care not for it: but if thou mayest be made free,
use it rather." It is true that Christian religion hath procured liberty unto many, not only *145*
in regard of piety, but for that the Christian masters stood in fear of being discovered by
their slaves unto the persecutors of religion. Mahomet likewise, by giving liberty to his
followers, drew many unto his impiety; but whether he forbade it as unlawful unto his
sectators to hold one another of them in bondage, I cannot tell, save that by the practice
of the Turks and Moors it seems he did not. In England we had many bondservants until *150*
the times of our last civil wars, and I think the laws concerning villeinage are still in
force, of which the latest are the sharpest. And now, since slaves were made free, which
were of great use and service, there are grown up a rabble of rogues, cutpurses, and
other the like trades; slaves in nature, though not in law.

But whether this kind of dominion be lawful or not, Aristotle hath well proved that *155*
it is natural. And certainly we find not such a latitude of difference in any creature as in
the nature of man, wherein (to omit the infinite distance in estate of the elect and
reprobate) the wisest excel the most foolish by far greater degree than the most foolish
of men doth surpass the wisest of beasts. Therefore when commiseration hath given way
to reason, we shall find that nature is the ground even of masterly power and of servile *160*
obedience, which is thereto correspondent. But it may be truly said that some countries
have subsisted long without the use of any servility, as also it is true that some countries
have not the use of any tame cattle. Indeed the affections which uphold civil rule are
(though more noble) not so simply needful unto the sustentation either of our kind, as
are lust and the like, or of everyone, as are hunger and thirst, which notwithstanding are *165*
the lowest in degree. But where most vile and servile dispositions have liberty to show

---

132-34: Exodus 21:20-21. 134-36: Numbers 31. 136-37: Genesis 9:25 (p. 250). 137-38: Genesis 12:16. 140-42: Epistle to Philemon. 143-45: I
Corinthians 7:20-21. 149. **sectators:** followers, disciples, sectaries.

themselves begging in the streets, there may we more justly wonder how the dangerous toil of seafaring men can find enough to undertake them, than how the swarm of idle vagabonds should increase by access of those that are weary of their own more painful condition. This may suffice to prove that in mankind there is found, engrafted even by *170* nature, a desire of absolute dominion, whereunto the general custom of nations doth subscribe, together with the pleasure which most men take in flatterers, that are the basest of slaves.

This being so, we find no cause to marvel how tyranny hath been so rife in all ages, and practised not only in the single rule of some vicious prince, but ever by consent of *175* whole cities and estates, since other vices have likewise gotten head, and borne a general sway, notwithstanding that the way of virtue be more honourable and commodious. Few there are that have used well the inferior passions; how then can we expect that the most noble affections should not be disordered? In the government of wife and children, some are utterly careless, and corrupt all by their dull connivancy; *180* others, by masterly rigour, hold their own blood under condition of slavery.

To be a good governor is a rare commendation, and to prefer the weal public above all respects whatsoever is the virtue justly termed heroical. Of this virtue many ages afford not many examples. Hector is named by Aristotle as one of them, and deservedly, if this praise be due to extraordinary height of fortitude used in defence of a man's own *185* country. But if we consider that a love of the general good cannot be perfect without reference unto *the fountain of all goodness*, we shall find that no moral virtue, how great soever, can by itself deserve the commendation of more than virtue, as the heroical doth. Wherefore we must search the scriptures for patterns hereof, such as David, Josaphat, and Josias were. Of Christian kings if there were many such, the world would soon be *190* happy. It is not my purpose to wrong the worth of any by denying the praise where it is due, or by preferring a less excellent. But he that can find a king religious and zealous in God's cause, without enforcement either of adversity or of some regard of state; a procurer of the general peace and quiet; who not only useth his authority but adds the travail of his eloquence in admonishing his judges to do justice; by the vigorous *195* influence of whose government civility is infused, even into those places that have been the dens of savage robbers and cutthroats; one that hath quite abolished a slavish Brehon law, by which an whole nation of his subjects were held in bondage; and one whose higher virtue and wisdom doth make the praise, not only of nobility and other ornaments, but of abstinence from the blood, the wives, and the goods of those that are *200* under his power, together with a world of chief commendations, belonging unto some good princes, to appear less regardable; he, I say, that can find such a king, findeth an example worthy to add unto virtue an honourable title, if it were formerly wanting. Under such a king it is likely, by God's blessing, that a land shall flourish, with increase of trade, in countries before unknown; that civility and religion shall be propagated into *205* barbarous and heathen countries; and that the happiness of his subjects shall cause the nations far off removed to wish him their sovereign. I need not add hereunto, that all the

---

189-90: David's story is told in the books of Samuel (beginning at I Samuel 16), Kings, and Chronicles; Jehoshaphat (Josaphat), king of Judah (873-849 B.C.) — see I Kings 15:24, I Kings 22, II Kings 3, II Chronicles 17-20; Josiah (Josias), king of Judah (640-609 B.C.) — see II Kings 21-23, II Chronicles 33-35. **197-98. Brehon law:** Anglo-Irish term for the *Feineachas*, the ancient laws of Ireland.

actions of such a king, even his bodily exercises, do partake of virtue, since all things tending to the preservation of his life and health or to the mollifying of his cares (who, fixing his contemplation upon God, seeketh how to imitate the unspeakable goodness, *210* rather than the inaccessible majesty, with both of which himself is endued, as far as human nature is capable) do also belong to the furtherance of that common good which he procureth. Lest any man should think me transported with admiration, or other affection, beyond the bounds of reason, I add hereunto that such a king is nevertheless a man, must die, and may err; yet wisdom and fame shall set him free from error and from *215* death, both with and without the help of time. One thing I may not omit, as a singular benefit (though there be many other besides) redounding unto this king, as the fruit of his goodness. The people that live under a pleasant yoke are not only loving to their sovereign lord, but free of courage, and no greater in muster of men than of stout fighters, if need require; whereas on the contrary, he that ruleth as over slaves shall be attended, in *220* time of necessity, by slavish minds, neither loving his person nor regarding his or their honour. Cowards may be furious, and slaves outrageous for a time; but among spirits that have once yielded unto slavery universally, it is found truth that Homer saith, "God bereaveth a man of half his virtue that day, when he casteth him into bondage."

Of these things I might perhaps more seasonably have spoken in the general *225* discourse of government; but where so lively an example of the calamity following a tyrannical rule, and the use of mercenaries thereupon depending, did offer itself, as is this present business of the Carthaginians, I thought that the note would be more effectual than being barely delivered as out of a common place.

(1614)

LETTERS TO HIS WIFE, LADY RALEGH

Letter 1

You shall now receive, my dear wife, my last words in these my last lines. My love I send you, that you may keep it when I am dead, and my counsel, that you may remember it when I am no more. I would not, with my last will, present you with sorrows, dear Bess. Let them go into the grave with me and be buried in the dust. And seeing it is not the will of God that ever I shall see you in this life, bear my destruction *5* gently, and with a heart like thyself.

First, I send you all the thanks my heart can conceive or my words express, for your many travails and cares taken for me, which though they have not taken effect as you wished, yet my debt is to you not the less; but pay it I never shall in this world.

Secondly, I beseech you, for the love you bore me living, that you do not hide *10* yourself many days, but by your travail seek to help your miserable fortune, and the right of your poor child. Your mourning cannot avail me; I am but dust.

---

219. free of courage: ready, willing, open, liberal, of heart, spirit, mind, disposition. **223-24:** *Odyssey*, xvii, 322-23. **LETTER 1** Ralegh had been imprisoned in the Tower in 1592 when he married Elizabeth (Bess) Throckmorton, one of Queen Elizabeth's maids of honour, without the Queen's permission. In 1603 he was again sent to the Tower, this time on a charge of treason for plotting against King James, though the case against him was weak. He wrote this letter in prison in Winchester (where the trial had been moved because of the plague in London) in early December 1603, a few days before his scheduled execution; but he was reprieved at the last minute, and lived in the Tower, with his family, until 1616 (his second son, Carew, named after Ralegh's brother, was born there in 1604).

Thirdly, you shall understand that my lands were conveyed, *bona fide*, to my child. The writings were drawn at midsummer was twelvemonths; my honest cousin Brett can testify so much, and Dalberry too can remember somewhat therein; and I trust my blood 15 will quench their malice that have thus cruelly murdered me, and that they will not seek also to kill thee and thine with extreme poverty. To what friend to direct thee I know not, for all mine have left me in the true time of trial, and I plainly perceive that my death was determined from the first day. Most sorry I am, as God knows, that being thus surprised with death, I can leave you no better estate. God is my witness, I meant you all 20 my office of wines, or that I could have purchased by selling it; half my stuff and all my jewels, but some one for the boy. But God hath prevented all my resolutions, even that great God that worketh all in all. But if you can live free from want, care for no more, for the rest is but vanity. Love God, and begin betimes to repose yourself on him; therein shall you find true and lasting riches, and endless comfort. For the rest, when 25 you have travailed and wearied your thoughts on all sorts of worldly cogitations, you shall but sit down by sorrow in the end. Teach your son also to serve and fear God whilst he is yet young, that the fear of God may grow up with him; and then will God be a husband unto you and a father unto him, a husband and a father which can never be taken from you. 30

Bailey oweth me £200, and Adrian Gilbert £600. In Jersey also I have much owing me. Besides, the arrearages of the wines will pay my debts; and howsoever you do, for my soul's sake pay all poor men. When I am gone, no doubt you shall be sought to by many, for the world thinks that I was very rich; but take heed of the pretences of men and their affections, for they last but in honest and worthy men; and no greater misery 35 can befall you in this life than to become a prey, and afterwards to be despised. I speak not this, God knows, to dissuade you from marriage, for it will be best for you, both in respect of the world and of God. As for me, I am no more yours, nor you mine. Death hath cut us asunder, and God hath divided me from the world, and you from me.

Remember your poor child for his father's sake, who chose you and loved you in 40 his happiest times.

Get those letters, if it be possible, which I writ to the lords, wherein I sued for my life. God is my witness, it was for you and yours that I desired life; but it is true that I disdain myself for begging it, for know it, dear wife, that your son is the son of a true man, and one who in his own respect despiseth death and all his misshapen and ugly 45 forms.

I cannot write much. God he knoweth how hardly I steal this time while others sleep; and it is also high time that I should separate my thoughts from the world. Beg my dead body, which living was denied thee, and either lay it at Sherborne, if the land continue, or in Exeter church, by my father and mother. I can say no more; time and 50 death call me away.

The everlasting God, infinite, powerful, and inscrutable; that Almighty God which is goodness itself, mercy itself, the true life and light, keep thee and thine, and have mercy on me, and teach me to forgive my persecutors and false accusers, and send us to

---

14. was twelvemonths: i.e., of last year. **21. office of wines:** Ralegh had been granted a monopoly in the wine trade in 1583. **31. Jersey:** Ralegh had been made Governor of the island of Jersey in 1600. **49. Sherborne:** the large Dorsetshire estate granted Ralegh in 1592; it did not "continue," but was taken away from him and given to someone else.

meet again in his glorious kingdom. My true wife, farewell. Bless my poor boy, pray for   55
me, and let my good God hold you both in his arms.

Written with the dying hand of sometime thy husband, but now (alas!) overthrown.

Yours that was; but now not my own.
Walter Ralegh

Letter 2

I was loath to write, because I know not how to comfort you; and God knows, I never
knew what sorrow meant till now. All that I can say to you is this: that you must obey
the will and providence of God, and remember that the Queen's majesty bore the loss of
Prince Henry with a magnanimous spirit, as the Lady Harington of her only son.
Comfort your heart, dearest Bess, I shall sorrow for us both; and I shall sorrow the less   5
because I have not long to sorrow, because not long to live. I refer you to Mr Secretary
Winwood's letter, who will give you a copy of it, if you send for it; therein you shall
know what hath passed. I have written but that letter, for my brains are broken, and it is
a torment to me to write, especially of misery. I have desired Mr Secretary to give my
Lord Carew a copy of his letter. I have cleansed my ship of sick men, and sent them   10
home, and hope that God will send us somewhat before we return. Commend me to all
at Lothbury. You shall hear from me, if I live, from Newfoundland, where I mean to
clean my ships and revictual, for I have tobacco enough will pay for it. The Lord bless
and comfort you, that you may bear patiently the death of your most valiant son.

This 22nd of March, 1618, from the Isle of Christophers, yours,   15

Walter Ralegh

Postscript:

I protest before the majesty of God, that as Sir Francis Drake and Sir John Hawkins
died heartbroken when they failed of their enterprise, I could willingly do the like, did I
not contend against sorrow for your sake, in hope to provide somewhat for you, to
comfort and relieve you. If I live to return, resolve yourself that it is the care for you that
hath strengthened my heart. It is true that Keymis might have gone directly to the mine,   20
and meant it; but after my son's death, he made them believe he knew not the way, and
excused himself upon the want of water in the river, and, counterfeiting many
impediments, left it unfound. When he came back, I told him that he had undone me,

---

LETTER 2   Ralegh had been released in 1616 in order to return to South America and bring back gold from the mine he had found during his
earlier voyage (see the excerpt from *The Discovery of Guiana*, p. 170). In spite of orders not to stir up trouble with the Spanish, hostilities proved
unavoidable, and Ralegh's eldest son, Walter, was killed. Ralegh himself, though he had stayed behind at Trinidad with a fever, is certain that he
too, as commander of the expedition, is doomed to die upon his return (see 6). **3-4. loss of Prince Henry:** Henry, Prince of Wales, died in 1612; it
was primarily for him that Ralegh had begun *The History of the World* (see p. 174). **6-7. Secretary Winwood:** Sir Ralph Winwood (c.1563-1617),
secretary of state from 1614; he was instrumental in getting Ralegh released in 1616, and urged him to attack the Spanish; Ralegh is unaware of his
death the preceding October. **10. Lord Carew:** George Carew, Baron Carew and later Earl of Totnes (1555-1629), soldier, statesman, antiquary, and
Ralegh's friend. **15. Christophers:** St. Kitts. **20. Keymis:** Laurence (or Lawrence) Keymis (or Kemys), Ralegh's second-in-command, as he had
been during the Guiana expedition of 1595.

and that my credit was lost forever. He answered, that seeing my son was slain, and that he left me so weak that he thought not to find me alive, he had no reason to enrich a company of rascals who, after my son's death, made no account of him. He further told me that the English sent up into Guiana could hardly defend the Spanish town of St. Thomas which they had taken, and therefore for them to pass through thick woods it was impossible, and more impossible to have victuals brought them to the mountains. And it is true that the governor, Diego Palomeque, and other four captains being slain, whereof my son Wat slew one, Plessington, Wat's sergeant, another, and John of Morocco, one of his men, slew two other. I say, five of them slain in the entrance into the town, the rest went off in a whole body, and took more care to defend the passages to their mines (of which they had three within a league of the town, besides a mine that was about five miles off) than they did of the town itself. Yet Keymis at the first was resolved to go to the mine; but when he came to the bank-side to land, he had two of his men slain outright from the bank, and six others hurt, and Captain Thornix shot in the head, of which wound, and the accident thereof, he hath pined away these twelve weeks.

Now when Keymis came back and gave me the former reasons which moved him not to open the mine: the one, the death of my son; a second, the weakness of the English and their impossibilities to work it and to be victualled; a third, that it were a folly to discover it for the Spaniards; and, lastly, my weakness, and being unpardoned; and that I rejected all these his arguments, and told him that I must leave him to himself, to answer it to the King and the state, he shut himself into his cabin, and shot himself with a pocket pistol, which broke one of his ribs; and finding that he had not prevailed, he thrust a long knife under his short ribs up to the handle, and died. Thus much I have written to Mr Secretary, to whose letters I refer you; but because I think my friends will rather hearken after you than any other to know the truth, I did after the sealing break open the letter again to let you know in brief the state of that business, which I pray you impart to my Lord of Northumberland, and Silvanus Skory, and to Sir John Leigh.

For the rest, there was never poor man so exposed to the slaughter as I was, for being commanded upon my allegiance to set down, not only the country, but the very river by which I was to enter it, to name my ships, number my men, and my artillery, this was sent by the Spanish ambassador to his master the King of Spain. The King wrote his letters to all parts of the Indies, especially to the governor Palomeque of Guiana, El Dorado, and Trinidado, of which the first letter bore date the 19th of March, 1617, at Madrid, when I had not yet left the Thames; which letter I have sent Mr Secretary. I have also two other letters of the King's which I reserve, and of the council's. The King also sent a commission to levy 300 soldiers out of his garrisons of Nuevo Regno de Granadoes and Puerto Rico, with ten pieces of brass ordnance to entertain us; he also prepared an armada by sea to set upon us. It were too long to tell you how we were preserved; if I live, I shall make it known. My brains are broken, and I cannot write much; I live yet, and I told you why. Whitney, for whom I sold my plate at Plymouth, and to whom I gave more credit and countenance than to all the captains of my fleet, ran from me at Granadoes, and Woolaston with him; so as I have now but five

25

30

35

40

45

50

55

60

65

---

42. **being unpardoned:** The sentence of death passed on Ralegh in 1603 was still in effect. 50. **Northumberland:** Henry Percy (1564-1632), the 9th earl; **Skory:** a friend who had tried to dissuade Ralegh from embarking on the expedition.

ships, and one of those I have sent home, and in my fly-boat, a rabble of idle rascals, which I know will not spare to wound me; but I care not. I am sure there is never a base slave in all the fleet hath taken the pains and care that I have done, that hath slept so little, and travailled so much. My friends will not believe them, and for the rest I care not. God in heaven bless you and strengthen your heart.   *70*

Yours,
Walter Ralegh

Letter from Lady Ralegh to Sir Nicholas Carew, October 30, 1618

I desire, good brother, that you will be pleased to let my bury the worthy body of my noble husband, Sir Walter Ralegh, in your church at Beddington, where I desire to be buried. The Lords have given me his dead body, though they denied me his life. This night he shall be brought you with two or three of my men. Let me hear presently. God hold me in my wits.   *5*

JOHN FLORIO
England, c.1553-1625

from *A SHORT AND BRIEF NARRATION OF THE TWO NAVIGATIONS AND DISCOVERIES TO THE NORTHWEST PARTS CALLED NEW FRANCE*

. . . .

Of the Port called S. Antony's Port, S. Servan's Port, James Cartier's Port; of the river called S. James; of the customs and apparel of the inhabitors in the Island of White Sands.

The next day we passed the said Islands, and beyond them all we found a good haven, which we named S. Antony's Haven, and how one or two leagues beyond, we found a little river toward the southwest coast, that is between two other islands, and is a good harbour. There we set up a cross, and named it S. Servan's Port; and on the southwest side of the said port and river, about one league, there is a small island as round as any   *5*

---

66. fly-boat: a fast vessel used for rapid shipment, or a kind of frigate used in battle or on voyages of discovery.   **LETTER FROM LADY RALEGH**   After their father's death in 1571, Lady Ralegh's brother Nicholas was adopted by a maternal uncle named Carew, and took that surname; Beddington is on the south side of London, near Croydon. Ralegh was executed on October 29, 1618.   **A SHORT AND BRIEF NARRATION...**   Jacques Cartier (1491-1557) made three trips to what is now Canada: in 1534, 1535-36, and 1541-42; the second is the one described in the *Narration*. Florio is translating Giovanni Ramusio's Italian version of a French text attributed to Cartier.

oven, environed about with many other little islands, that give notice to the said ports. Further about two leagues, there is another greater river, in which they took good store of salmon, that we named S. James his River. Being in the said river, we saw a ship of Rochell that the night before had passed the port of Brest, where they thought to have gone a-fishing; but the mariners not knowing where they were, we with our boats *10* approached near unto it, and did direct it to another port one league more toward the west than the said river of S. James, which I take to be one of the best in all the world, and therefore we named it James Cartier's sound. If the soil were as good as the harbours are, it were a great commodity; but it is not to be called the new land, but rather stones, and wild furs, and a place fit for wild beasts, for in all the north island I did not see a cartload *15* of good earth; yet went I on shore in many places, and in the island of White Sands there is nothing else but moss, and small thorns scattered here and there, withered and dry. To be short, I believe that this was the land that God allotted to Cain. There are men of an indifferent good stature and bigness, but wild and unruly; they wear their hair tied on the top like a wreath of hay, and put a wooden pin within it, or any other such thing, instead *20* of a nail, and with them they bind certain birds' feathers. They are clothed with beasts' skins, as well the men as women, but that the women go somewhat straightlier and closer in their garments than men do, with their waists girded; they paint themselves with certain roan colours; their boats are made of the bark of a tree called *boul*, with the which they fish, and take great store of seals, and as far as we could understand since our *25* coming thither, that is not their habitation, but they come from the mainland out of hotter countries, to take of the said seals and other necessaries for their living.

(1580)

from ESSAYS, OR MORAL, POLITICAL, AND MILITARY DISCOURSES
Translated from *Essais* (1580-1595),
by Michel Eyquem de Montaigne (1533-1592)

THE PROFIT OF ONE MAN IS THE DAMAGE OF ANOTHER

Demades the Athenian condemned a man of the city whose trade was to sell such necessaries as belonged to burials, under colour he asked too much profit for them, and that such profit could not come unto him without the death of many people. This judgment seemeth to be ill taken, because no man profiteth but by the loss of others, by which reason a man should condemn all manner of gain. The merchant thrives not but *5*

---

8. S. James his: i.e., St. James's. **9. Rochell:** La Rochelle, French port on the Bay of Biscay; **passed the port of Brest:** The French text that was translated in 1556 from Ramusio's edition suggests that the ship spent the night *searching* for the port of Brest. Cartier was at this time exploring the south shore of Labrador and the adjacent coastline of what is now Quebec. "Brest" (named after the French seaport) was the name given to a harbour now called Baie de Bonne Espérance. The harbours of Saint Anthony and Saint Servan were later renamed Rocky Bay and Lobster Bay. The river Cartier named for Saint James historians take to be the Shecatica; the harbour he named for himself was renamed Cumberland Harbour in the 18th century, and then renamed again, once more after Cartier, in the 20th century. **22. straightlier:** more tightly. **THE PROFIT OF ONE MAN 1. Demades:** 4th-century B.C. Athenian politician.

by the licentiousness of youth; the husbandman by dearth of corn; the architect but by the ruin of houses; the lawyer by suits and controversies between men; honour itself, and practice of religious ministers, is drawn from our death and vices. No physician delighteth in the health of his own friend, saith the ancient Greek comic, nor no soldier is pleased with the peace of his city; and so of the rest. And which is worse, let every *10* man sound his own conscience, he shall find that our inward desires are for the most part nourished and bred in us by the loss and hurt of others — which when I considered, I began to think how nature doth not gainsay herself in this, concerning her general policy; for physicians hold that the birth, increase, and augmentation of every thing is the alteration and corruption of another. *15*

> *Nam quodcunque suis mutatum finibus exit,*
> *Continuò hoc mors est illius, quod fuit ante.*
>> Lucretius i. 687, 813; ii. 762; iii. 536

> Whatever from its bounds doth changed pass,
> That strait is death of that which erst it was. *20*

from OF COACHES

. . . .

If whatsoever hath come unto us by report of what is past were true and known of anybody, it would be less than nothing in respect of that which is unknown. And even of this image of the world, which whilst we live therein glideth and passeth away, how wretched, weak, and how short is the knowledge of the most curious? Not only of the particular events, which fortune often maketh exemplar and of consequence, but of the *5* state of mighty commonwealths, large monarchies, and renowned nations, there escapeth our knowledge a hundred times more than cometh unto our notice. We keep a coil, and wonder at the miraculous invention of our artillery, and amazed at the rare device of printing — whenas unknown to us, other men, and another end of the world named China, knew and had perfect use of both, a thousand years before. If we saw as *10* much of this vast world as we see but a least part of it, it is very likely we should perceive a perpetual multiplicity and ever-rolling vicissitude of forms. Therein is nothing singular and nothing rare, if regard be had unto nature, or to say better, if relation be had unto our knowledge, which is a weak foundation of our rules, and which doth commonly present us a right false image of things. *15*

How vainly do we nowadays conclude the declination and decrepitude of the world by the fond arguments we draw from our own weakness, drooping, and declination:

> *Jamque adeo affecta est ætas, affectaque tellus.*
>> Lucretius ii. 1159.

> And now both age and land
> So sick affected stand. *20*

---

6. licentiousness: lack of restraint, extravagance. **8-9. No physician. . . comic:** In *On Benefits*, vi, 38, which Montaigne follows here, the Roman writer Seneca (c.4 B.C. – A.D. 65) states: *"medicis gravis annus in quaestu est"* (doctors profit from a bad season); the "Greek comic" Montaigne refers to is the prolific dramatist Philemon (c.361-262 B.C.), fragments of whose lost works are quoted by the 5th-century compiler Stobaeus. **19. Lucretius** (c.94-55 B.C.): Roman poet and philosopher, author of *De Rerum Natura* (*Of the Nature of Things*). OF COACHES **7-8. keep a coil:** make a fuss.

And as vainly did another conclude its birth and youth by the vigour he perceiveth in the wits of his time, abounding in novelties and invention of divers arts:

> *Verùm ut opinor, habet novitatem, summa, recensque*
> *Natura est mundi, neque pridem exordia cepit:*   25
> *Quare etiam quædam nunc artes expoliuntur,*
> *Nunc etiam augescunt, nunc addita navigiis sunt*
> *Multa.* — Ibid. v. 330.

> But all this world is new, as I suppose,
> World's nature fresh, nor lately it arose: 30
> Whereby some arts refined are in fashion,
> And many things now to our navigation
> Are added, daily grown to augmentation.

Our world hath of late discovered another (and who can warrant us whether it be the last of his brethren, since both the demons, the sibyls, and all we have hitherto been   35
ignorant of this?), no less large, fully peopled, all-things-yielding, and mighty in strength than ours, nevertheless so new and infantine that he is yet to learn his A.B.C. It is not yet full fifty years that he knew neither letters, nor weight, nor measures, nor apparel, nor corn, nor vines, but was all naked, simply pure, in Nature's lap, and lived but with such means and food as his mother-nurse afforded him. If we conclude aright   40
of our end, and the foresaid poet of the infancy of this age, this late-world shall but come to light when ours shall fall into darkness. The whole universe shall fall into a palsy or convulsion of sinews: one member shall be maimed or shrunken, another nimble and in good plight.

I fear that by our contagion we shall directly have furthered his declination and   45
hastened his ruin, and that we shall too dearly have sold him our opinions, our new-fangles, and our arts. It was an unpolluted, harmless infant world; yet have we not whipped and submitted the same unto our discipline, or schooled him by the advantage of our valour or natural forces, nor have we instructed him by our justice and integrity, nor subdued by our magnanimity. Most of their answers, and a number of the   50
negotiations we have had with them, witness that they were nothing short of us, nor beholding to us for any excellency of natural wit or perspicuity, concerning pertinency.

The wonderful, or as I may call it amazement-breeding magnificence of the never-like seen cities of Cuzco and Mexico, and amongst infinite such like things, the admirable garden of that king where all the trees, the fruits, the herbs and plants,   55
according to the order and greatness they have in a garden, were most artificially framed in gold, as also in his cabinet all the living creatures that his country or his seas produced were cast in gold; and the exquisite beauty of their works in precious stones, in feathers, in cotton, and in painting show that they yielded as little unto us in cunning and industry. But concerning unfeigned devotion, awful observance of laws, unspotted   60
integrity, bounteous liberality, due loyalty and free liberty, it hath greatly availed us that we had not so much as they — by which advantage they have lost, cast away, sold, undone, and betrayed themselves.

---

44. plight: condition. **60. awful:** reverential.

Touching hardiness and undaunted courage, and as for matchless constancy, unmoved assuredness, undismayed resolution against pain, smarting, famine, and death *65* itself, I will not fear to oppose the examples which I may easily find amongst them to the most famous ancient examples we may with all our industry discover in all the annals and memories of our known Old World. For as for those which have subdued them, let them lay aside the wiles, the policies and stratagems which they have employed to cozen, to cony-catch, and to circumvent them, and the just astonishment *70* which those nations might justly conceive by seeing so unexpected an arrival of bearded men, divers in language, in habit, in religion, in behaviour, in form, in countenance, and from a part of the world so distant, and where they never heard any habitation was, mounted upon great and unknown monsters, against those who had never so much as seen any horse, and less any beast whatsoever apt to bear or taught to carry either man *75* or burden, covered with a shining and hard skin, and armed with slicing-keen weapons and glittering armour, against them who for the wonder of the glistering of a looking-glass or of a plain knife would have changed or given inestimable riches in gold, precious stones, and pearls, and who had neither the skill nor the matter wherewith at any leisure they could have pierced our steel; to which you may add the flashing-fire *80* and thundering roar of shot and harquebuses, able to quell and daunt even Caesar himself, had he been so suddenly surprised and as little experienced as they were; and thus to come unto and assault silly-naked people, saving where the invention of weaving of cotton cloth was known and used, for the most altogether unarmed, except some bows, stones, staves, and wooden bucklers, unsuspecting poor people, surprised under *85* colour of amity and well-meaning faith, overtaken by the curiosity to see strange and unknown things — I say, take this disparity from the conquerors and you deprive them of all the occasions and cause of so many unexpected victories.

When I consider that stern, untamed obstinacy and undaunted vehemence wherewith so many thousands of men, of women and children, do so infinite times present *90* themselves unto inevitable dangers for the defence of their gods and liberty, this generous obstinacy to endure all extremities, all difficulties and death, more easily and willingly than basely to yield unto their domination of whom they have so abominably been abused — some of them choosing rather to starve with hunger and fasting, being taken, than to accept food at their enemies' hands, so basely victorious — I perceive that whosoever had *95* undertaken them man to man, without odds of arms, of experience, or of number, should have had as dangerous a war, or perhaps more, as any we see amongst us.

Why did not so glorious a conquest happen under Alexander, or during the time of the ancient Greeks and Romans? Or why befell not so great a change and alteration of empires and people under such hands as would gently have polished, reformed, and *100* civilized what in them they deemed to be barbarous and rude, or would have nourished and fostered those good seeds which nature had there brought forth, adding not only to the manuring of their grounds and ornaments of their cities such arts as we had, and that no further than had been necessary for them, but therewithal joining unto the original virtues of the country those of the ancient Grecians and Romans? What reformation *105*

---

70. cony-catch: cheat, trick (trap a rabbit). **83. silly-:** simple, innocent, happy. **103. manuring . . . grounds:** cultivation . . . soil.

would all that far spreading world have found if the examples, demeanours, and policies wherewith we first presented them had called and allured those uncorrupted nations to the admiration and imitation of virtue, and had established between them and us a brotherly society and mutual correspondency? How easy a matter had it been profitably to reform and christianly to instruct minds yet so pure and new, so willing to be taught, *110* being for the most part endowed with so docile, so apt and so yielding natural beginnings? Whereas contrariwise, we have made use of their ignorance and inexperience to draw them more easily unto treason, fraud, luxury, avarice, and all manner of inhumanity and cruelty by the example of our life and pattern of our customs. Who ever raised the service of merchandise and benefit of traffic to so high a rate? So *115* many goodly cities ransacked and razed; so many nations destroyed and made desolate; so infinite millions of harmless people of all sexes, states, and ages massacred, ravaged, and put to the sword; and the richest, the fairest, and the best part of the world topsiturvied, ruined, and defaced for the traffic of pearls and pepper. Oh mechanical victories, oh base conquest! Never did greedy revenge, public wrongs, or general *120* enmities so moodily enrage and so passionately incense men against men unto so horrible hostilities, bloody dissipations, and miserable calamities.

. . . .

(1603)

SIR PHILIP SIDNEY
England, 1554-1586

Poems from *THE COUNTESS OF PEMBROKE'S ARCADIA*

"YE GOAT-HERD GODS, THAT LOVE THE GRASSY MOUNTAINS"

STREPHON.   KLAIUS.

STREPHON: Ye goat-herd gods, that love the grassy mountains,
Ye nymphs that haunt the springs in pleasant valleys,
Ye satyrs joyed with free and quiet forests,
Vouchsafe your silent ears to plaining music,
Which to my woes gives still an early morning,   *5*
And draws the dolour on till weary evening.

THE COUNTESS OF PEMBROKE'S ARCADIA   Sidney wrote his *Arcadia* for his sister, the Countess of Pembroke (see p. 210). The version that is now known as the *Old Arcadia*, not published as such until the 20th century, was finished by about 1580. Sidney's revised and much expanded version of approximately the first half of the work was published in 1590 and is now known as the *New Arcadia*; in 1593 the Countess of Pembroke undertook to correct errors in the 1590 publication and added the last parts of the first version in order to make a more-or-less complete work.   YE GOAT-HERD GODS   As the *Arcadia*'s narrator remarks in introducing this pastoral lament, it is a double sestina — i.e., twelve stanzas and an envoy instead of six. **4. plaining:** complaining.

KLAIUS: O Mercury, foregoer to the evening,
              O heavenly huntress of the savage mountains,
              O lovely star, entitled of the morning,
              While that my voice doth fill these woeful valleys,   *10*
              Vouchsafe your silent ears to plaining music,
              Which oft hath Echo tired in secret forests.

STREPHON: I that was once free burgess of the forests,
              Where shade from sun, and sports I sought at evening,
              I that was once esteemed for pleasant music,   *15*
              Am banished now among the monstrous mountains
              Of huge despair, and foul affliction's valleys,
              Am grown a screech-owl to myself each morning.

KLAIUS: I that was once delighted every morning,
              Hunting the wild inhabiters of forests;   *20*
              I that was once the music of these valleys,
              So darkened am, that all my day is evening,
              Heart-broken so, that mole-hills seem high mountains,
              And fill the vales with cries instead of music.

STREPHON: Long since, alas, my deadly swannish music   *25*
              Hath made itself a crier of the morning,
              And hath with wailing strength climbed highest mountains;
              Long since my thoughts more desert be than forests;
              Long since I see my joys come to their evening,
              And state thrown down to over-trodden valleys.   *30*

KLAIUS: Long since the happy dwellers of these valleys
              Have prayed me leave my strange exclaiming music,
              Which troubles their day's work, and joys of evening;
              Long since I hate the night, more hate the morning;
              Long since my thoughts chase me like beasts in forests,   *35*
              And make me wish myself laid under mountains.

STREPHON: Me seems I see the high and stately mountains
              Transform themselves to low dejected valleys;
              Me seems I hear in these ill-changed forests
              The nightingales do learn of owls their music;   *40*
              Me seems I feel the comfort of the morning
              Turned to the mortal serene of an evening.

---

7. Mercury: the evening star. **8. huntress:** Diana, the moon. **9. star . . . morning:** Venus. **25. swannish:** A swan supposedly sang only just before dying. **30. state:** estate, status, high rank, or position. **37. Me seems:** It seems to me. **42. mortal serene:** fine evening rain or dew in warm climates, thought to be noxious.

KLAIUS: Me seems I see a filthy cloudy evening
          As soon as sun begins to climb the mountains;
          Me seems I feel a noisome scent, the morning,   45
          When I do smell the flowers of these valleys;
          Me seems I hear, when I do hear sweet music,
          The dreadful cries of murdered men in forests.

STREPHON: I wish to fire the trees of all these forests;
          I give the sun a last farewell each evening;   50
          I curse the fiddling finders out of music;
          With envy I do hate the lofty mountains,
          And with despite despise the humble valleys;
          I do detest night, evening, day, and morning.

KLAIUS: Curse to myself my prayer is, the morning;   55
          My fire is more than can be made with forests;
          My state more base than are the basest valleys;
          I wish no evenings more to see, each evening;
          Shamed I hate myself in sight of mountains,
          And stop mine ears lest I grow mad with music.   60

STREPHON: For she whose parts maintain a perfect music,
          Whose beauty shined more than the blushing morning,
          Who much did pass in state the stately mountains,
          In straightness passed the cedars of the forests,
          Hath cast me, wretch, into eternal evening,   65
          By taking her two suns from these dark valleys.

KLAIUS: For she to whom compared the alps are valleys,
          She whose least word brings from the spheres their music,
          At whose approach the sun rose in the evening,
          Who where she went bare in her forehead morning,   70
          Is gone, is gone from these our spoiled forests,
          Turning to deserts our best pastured mountains.

STREPHON: These mountains witness shall, so shall these valleys,
          These forests eke, made wretched by our music.

KLAIUS: Our morning hymn is this, and song at evening.   75

                                                    (c. 1580; 1590)

---

52. envy: malice, anger. **63. pass:** surpass. **66. two suns:** i.e., eyes. **68:** See note to line 164 of *The Defence of Poesy*, below. **70. bare:** bore. **74. eke:** also.

"IF MINE EYES CAN SPEAK, TO DO HEARTY ERRAND"

If mine eyes can speak, to do hearty errand,
Or mine eyes' language she do hap to judge of,
So that eyes' message be of her received,
        Hope, we do live yet.

But if eyes fail then, when I most do need them,   *5*
Of if eyes' language be not unto her known,
So that eyes' message do return rejected,
        Hope, we do both die.

Yet dying, and dead, do we sing her honour;
So become our tombs monuments of her praise;   *10*
So becomes our loss the triumph of her gain;
        Hers be the glory.

If the spheres senseless do yet hold a music,
If the swan's sweet voice be not heard but at death,
If the mute timber when it hath the life lost   *15*
        Yieldeth a lute's tune;

Are then human minds privileged so meanly,
As that hateful death can abridge them of power
With the vow of truth to record to all worlds
        That we be her spoils?   *20*

Thus not ending, ends the due praise of her praise;
Fleshly veil consumes, but a soul hath his life,
Which is held in love; love it is that hath joined
        Life to this our soul.

But if eyes can speak to do hearty errand,   *25*
Or mine eyes' language she do hap to judge of,
So that eyes' message be of her received,
        Hope, we do live yet.
            (c. 1580; 1590)

from ASTROPHEL AND STELLA

1

Loving in truth, and fain in verse my love to show,
That the dear she might take some pleasure of my pain,
Pleasure might cause her read, reading might make her
   know,
Knowledge might pity win, and pity grace obtain,
I sought fit words to paint the blackest face of woe;   *5*
Studying inventions fine, her wits to entertain,
Oft turning others' leaves to see if thence would flow
Some fresh and fruitful showers upon my sunburned
   brain.
But words came halting forth, wanting invention's stay;
Invention, Nature's child, fled step-dame Study's blows,   *10*
And others' feet still seemed but strangers in my way.
Thus great with child to speak, and helpless in my throes,
Biting my truant pen, beating myself for spite,
"Fool," said my Muse to me, "look in thy heart and
   write."

5

It is most true that eyes are formed to serve
The inward light, and that the heavenly part
Ought to be king, from whose rules who do swerve,
Rebels to nature, strive for their own smart.
It is most true, what we call Cupid's dart   *5*
An image is, which for ourselves we carve;
And, fools, adore in temple of our heart,
Till that good god make church and churchman starve.
True, that true beauty virtue is indeed,
Whereof this beauty can be but a shade,   *10*
Which elements with mortal mixture breed.
True, that on earth we are but pilgrims made,
And should in soul up to our country move;
True, and yet true that I must Stella love.

14

Alas, have I not pain enough, my friend,
Upon whose breast a fiercer gripe doth tire
Than did on him who first stole down the fire,
While love on me doth all his quiver spend;
But with your rhubarb words ye must contend,   *5*
To grieve me worse, in saying that desire
Doth plunge my well-formed soul even in the mire
Of sinful thoughts which do in ruin end?
If that be sin which doth the manners frame,
Well stayed with truth in word and faith of deed,   *10*

IF MINE EYES CAN SPEAK   1. hearty: heart's **13:** See note to line 115 of *The Defence of Poesy*, below.   **ASTROPHEL AND STELLA Title:** "Star-lover" (Greek *astron* + *philos*) and "Star" (Latin *stella*). Sidney evidently addressed the sequence to Penelope Rich (*née* Devereaux, sister of the Earl of Essex), but the nature of their relationship isn't clearly known.   **SONNET 1** Sidney opens his sonnet sequence unconventionally, with a sonnet written in alexandrines. **1. fain:** eager, wanting. **6. inventions:** rhetorical term for things invented or discovered, namely topics to be treated, arguments to be used.   **SONNET 5 2. inward light:** i.e., reason. **4. smart:** hurt, pain.   **SONNET 14 2. gripe:** vulture; **tire:** of hawks or other birds, to pull or tear with the beak, tear flesh in feeding. **3. him . . . fire:** Prometheus. **5. rhubarb:** bitter-tasting.

Ready of wit and fearing nought but shame;
If that be sin which in fixed hearts doth breed
A loathing of all loose unchastity,
Then love is sin, and let me sinful be.

39

Come Sleep, O Sleep, the certain knot of peace,
The baiting place of wit, the balm of woe,
The poor man's wealth, the prisoner's release,
Th' indifferent judge between the high and low;
With shield of proof shield me from out the prease   5
Of those fierce darts Despair at me doth throw;
O make in me those civil wars to cease;
I will good tribute pay, if thou do so.
Take thou of me smooth pillows, sweetest bed,
A chamber deaf to noise and blind to light,   10
A rosy garland, and a weary head;
And if these things, as being thine by right,
Move not thy heavy grace, thou shalt in me
Livelier than elsewhere, Stella's image see.

71

Who will in fairest book of Nature know
How virtue may best lodged in beauty be,
Let him but learn of love to read in thee,
Stella, those fair lines which true goodness show.
There shall he find all vices' overthrow,   5
Not by rude force, but sweetest sovereignty
Of reason, from whose light those night-birds fly;
That inward sun in thine eyes shineth so.
And not content to be perfection's heir
Thyself, dost strive all minds that way to move,   10
Who mark in thee what is in thee most fair.
So while thy beauty draws the heart to love,
As fast thy Virtue bends that love to good;
"But ah," Desire still cries, "give me some food."

(c. 1582; 1591)

from THE DEFENCE OF POESY

. . . .

There is no art delivered unto mankind that hath not the works of nature for his principal object, without which they could not consist, and on which they so depend as they become actors and players, as it were, of what nature will have set forth. So doth the astronomer look upon the stars, and by that he seeth set down what order nature hath taken therein. So do the geometrician and arithmetician, in their divers sorts of   5
quantities. So doth the musician in times tell you which by nature agree, which not. The natural philosopher thereon hath his name, and the moral philosopher standeth upon the natural virtues, vices, or passions of man; and follow nature, saith he, therein, and thou shalt not err. The lawyer saith what men have determined; the historian, what men have done. The grammarian speaketh only of the rules of speech; and the rhetorician and   10
logician, considering what in nature will soonest prove and persuade, thereon give artificial rules which still are compassed within the circle of a question according to the proposed matter. The physician weigheth the nature of man's body, and the nature of things helpful or hurtful unto it. And the metaphysic, though it be in the second and abstract notions, and therefore be counted supernatural, yet doth he indeed build upon   15
the depth of nature. Only the poet, disdaining to be tied to any such subjection, lifted up with the vigour of his own invention, doth grow in effect into another nature in making

---

Sonnet 39   2. **baiting place:** feeding and resting place on a journey. 5. **of proof:** proven; **prease:** press, crowd.   **The Defence of Poesy**   Written in response to Stephen Gosson's *The School of Abuse* (1579), an attack upon poetry and drama. 7. **natural philosopher:** what we now call a scientist.

things either better than nature bringeth forth, or quite anew, forms such as never were in nature, as the Heroes, Demigods, Cyclops, Chimeras, Furies, and such like — so as he goeth hand in hand with nature, not enclosed within the narrow warrant of her gifts, but freely ranging within the zodiac of his own wit. Nature never set forth the earth in so rich tapestry as divers poets have done, neither with so pleasant rivers, fruitful trees, sweet-smelling flowers, nor whatsoever else may make the too-much-loved earth more lovely. Her world is brazen; the poets only deliver a golden. 20

. . . .

Now therein of all sciences (I speak still of human, and according to the human conceit) is our poet the monarch, for he doth not only show the way, but giveth so sweet a prospect into the way as will entice any man to enter into it. Nay, he doth, as if your journey should lie through a fair vineyard, at the very first give you a cluster of grapes, that, full of the taste, you may long to pass further. He beginneth not with obscure definitions, which must blur the margin with interpretations and load the memory with doubtfulness, but he cometh to you with words set in delightful proportion, either accompanied with or prepared for the well-enchanting skill of music, and with a tale forsooth he cometh unto you, with a tale which holdeth children from play and old men from the chimney corner; and pretending no more, doth intend the winning of the mind from wickedness to virtue. Even as the child is often brought to take most wholesome things by hiding them in such other as have a pleasant taste — which, if one should begin to tell them the nature of the aloes or rhubarb they should receive, would sooner take their physic at their ears than at their mouth, so is it in men (most of which are childish in the best things, till they be cradled in their graves): glad they will be to hear the tales of Hercules, Achilles, Cyrus, Aeneas, and hearing them, must needs hear the right description of wisdom, value, and justice, which if they had been barely (that is to say philosophically) set out, they would swear they be brought to school again. 25 30 35 40

That imitation whereof poetry is, hath the most conveniency to nature of all other, insomuch that, as Aristotle saith, those things which in themselves are horrible, as cruel battles, unnatural monsters, are made, in poetical imitation, delightful. Truly I have known men that even with reading *Amadis de Gaule* (which, God knoweth, wanteth much of a perfect poesy) have found their hearts moved to the exercise of courtesy, liberality, and especially courage. Who readeth Aeneas carrying old Anchises on his back, that wisheth not it were his fortune to perform so excellent an act? Whom doth not those words of Turnus move (the tale of Turnus having planted his image in the imagination): *fugientum hæc terra videbit? Usque adeone mori miserum est?* Where the philosophers, as they think, scorn to delight, so must they be content little to move, saving wrangling whether virtue be the chief or the only good, whether the contemplative or the active life do excel: which Plato and Boethius well knew, and 45 50 55

24: referring to the Four Ages (see the description of them in the excerpt from Sandys's translation of Ovid's *Metamorphoses*, p. 267). **30:** i.e., glosses and notes in the margins, as was then customary. **42. barely:** i.e., nakedly, simply, unadorned. **45-46. Aristotle . . . delightful:** at the beginning of Chapter IV of his *Poetics*. **47. *Amadis de Gaule*:** 15th-16th-century Spanish or Portuguese chivalric romance. **49-50. Aeneas . . . back:** See Virgil's *Aeneid*, II, 701ff. **52. *fugientum . . . est?*:** Shall this land see me fleeing? Is it always so miserable to die? (*Aeneid*, XII, 645-46).

therefore made mistress Philosophy very often borrow the raiment of Poesy. For even those hard-hearted evil men who think virtue a school-name, and know no other good but *indulgere genio*, and therefore despise the austere admonitions of the philosopher, and feel not the inward reason they stand upon, yet will be content to be delighted, which is all the good fellow poet seems to promise, and so steal to see the form of goodness (which seen, they cannot but love) ere themselves be aware, as if they took a medicine of cherries.   *60*

. . . .

Since then poetry is of all human learnings the most ancient, and of most fatherly antiquity, as from whence other learnings have taken their beginnings; since it is so universal that no learned nation doth despise it, nor barbarous nation is without it; since   *65* both Roman and Greek gave such divine names unto it, the one of prophesying, the other of making; and that indeed that name of making is fit for him, considering that where all other arts retain themselves within their subject, and receive as it were the being from it, the poet only bringeth his own stuff, and doth not learn a conceit out of a matter, but maketh matter for a conceit; since neither his description nor his end   *70* containeth any evil, the thing described cannot be evil; since his effects be so good as to teach goodness and delight the learners of it; since therein (namely in moral doctrine, the chief of all knowledges) he doth not only far pass the historian, but for instructing is well nigh comparable to the philosopher, and for moving leaveth him behind him; since the holy scripture (wherein there is no uncleanness) hath whole parts in it poetical, and   *75* that even our Saviour Christ vouchsafed to use the flowers of it; since all his kinds are not only in their united forms but in their severed dissections fully commendable: I think (and think I think rightly) the laurel crown appointed for triumphant captains doth worthily of all other learnings honour the poet's triumph.

. . . .

Let it suffice to have showed [poesy] is a fit soil for praise to dwell upon; and what   *80* dispraise may set upon it is either easily overcome or transformed into just commendation. So that since the excellencies of it may be so easily and so justly confirmed, and the low-creeping objections so soon trodden down, it not being an art of lies, but of true doctrine; not of effeminateness, but of notable stirring of courage; not of abusing man's wit, but of strengthening man's wit; not banished, but honoured by Plato;   *85* let us rather plant more laurels for to engarland the poets' heads (which honour of being laureate, as besides them only triumphant captains were, is a sufficient authority to show the price they ought to be held in) than suffer the ill-savoured breath of such wrong-speakers once to blow upon the clear springs of poesy.

. . . .

So that since the ever-praiseworthy poesy is full of virtue-breeding delightfulness,   *90* and void of no gift that ought to be in the noble name of learning; since the blames laid against it are either false or feeble; since the cause why it is not esteemed in England is the fault of the poet-apes, not poets; since, lastly, our tongue is most fit to honour

---

55. Boethius: (c.470-525), author of *De Consolatione Philosophiae*, translated by King Alfred, Chaucer, and Queen Elizabeth. **58. indulgere genio:** indulge one's own nature (Persius, *Satires*, V, 151). **65-67:** The Romans called a poet *vates* (seer, prophet), the Greeks *poietes* (maker).

poesy and to be honoured by poesy, I conjure you all that have had the evil luck to read this ink-wasting toy of mine, even in the name of the nine Muses, no more to scorn the *95* sacred mysteries of poesy; no more to laugh at the name of poets, as though they were next inheritors to fools; no more to jest at the reverent title of a Rhymer; but to believe, with Aristotle, that they were the ancient treasurers of the Grecians' divinity; to believe, with Bembus, that they were first bringers in of all civility; to believe, with Scaliger, that no philosopher's precepts can sooner make you an honest man than the *100* reading of Virgil; to believe, with Clauserus, the translator of Cornutus, that it pleased the heavenly deity, by Hesiod and Homer, under the veil of fables to give us all knowledge, logic, rhetoric, philosophy natural and moral, and *quid non?* To believe, with me, that there are many mysteries contained in poetry which of purpose were written darkly, lest by profane wits it should be abused; to believe, with Landino, that *105* they are so beloved of the gods that whatsoever they write proceeds of a divine fury. Lastly, to believe themselves when they tell you they will make you immortal by their verses.

Thus doing, your name shall flourish in the printers' shops. Thus doing, you shall be of kin to many a poetical preface. Thus doing, you shall be most fair, most rich, most *110* wise, most all: you shall dwell upon superlatives. Thus doing, though you be *Libertino patre natus*, you shall suddenly grow *Herculea proles, Si quid mea Carmina possunt*. Thus doing, your soul shall be placed with Dante's Beatrix, or Virgil's Anchises. But if (fie of such a but) you be born so near the dull-making cataract of Nilus that you cannot hear the planet-like music of poetry; if you have so earth-creeping a mind that it cannot *115* lift itself up to look to the sky of poetry, or rather by a certain rustical disdain will become such a mome as to be a Momus of poetry; then though I will not wish unto you the ass's ears of Midas, nor to be driven by a poet's verses, as Bubonax was, to hang himself, nor to be rhymed to death, as is said to be done in Ireland, yet thus much curse I must send you, in the behalf of all poets, that while you live, you live in love, and never *120* get favour for lacking skill of a sonnet; and when you die, your memory die from the earth for want of an epitaph.

(c. 1580-83; 1595)

---

99. Bembus: Cardinal Pietro Bembo (1470-1547), philosopher, poet, and man of letters. **100. Scaliger:** Julius Caesar Scaliger (1484-1558), Italian moralist and literary critic, author of *Poetices* (1561). **101. Clauserus:** Conrad Clauser (c.1520-1611), German translator (in Latin) of a Greek treatise by Lucius Annaeus Cornutus, 1st-century Roman philosopher, rhetorician, and writer on literature and myth. **103. *quid non?*:** what not? **105. Landino:** Cristoforo Landino (c.1424-1504), Italian scholar, Lorenzo de Medici's tutor. **111-12. *Libertino . . . natus*:** born of a freedman father (from Horace, *Satires*, 1, 6, 6). **112. *Herculea proles*:** offspring (descendant) of Hercules; *Si . . . possunt*: if my songs are at all effective (*Aeneid* IX, 446). **114:** Cicero in his "Dream of Scipio" says the Nile's noisy cataracts deafened anyone near. **115. planet-like:** i.e., like the celestial harmony or "music of the spheres" posited by Pythagoras (and see *Ptolemaic* in the Glossary). **117. mome:** lout, fool; **Momus:** Greek god of blame and ridicule — i.e., a critic. **118:** When Midas judged the satyr Pan's music superior to Apollo's, Apollo gave him ass's ears (Ovid tells the story in Book 11 of *Metamorphoses*). **118-19:** referring (with a confusion of the names) to a story about Hipponax (6th century B.C.), who supposedly satirized the sculptors Bupalus and Athenis for a statue caricaturing him, so upsetting them that they committed suicide. **119. rhymed . . . Ireland:** ancient Irish bards were supposedly able to kill their enemies with rhymed satire and curses, but the popular notion in Elizabethan times was that the Irish used such rhymes to get rid of rats; see e.g. Rosalind's comment in Shakespeare's *As You Like It*, III, ii: "I was never so berhymed since Pythagoras' time that I was an Irish rat."

"Thou blind man's mark, thou fool's self-chosen snare"

Thou blind man's mark, thou fool's self-chosen snare,
Fond fancy's scum, and dregs of scattered thought,
Band of all evils, cradle of causeless care,
Thou web of will, whose end is never wrought;
Desire, Desire! I have too dearly bought,   5
With price of mangled mind, thy worthless ware;
Too long, too long, asleep thou hast me brought,
Who should my mind to higher things prepare.
But yet in vain thou hast my ruin sought;
In vain thou madest me to vain things aspire;   10
In vain thou kindlest all thy smoky fire;
For Virtue hath this better lesson taught:
Within myself to seek my only hire,
Desiring nought but how to kill desire.

(c. 1581; 1598)

"Ring out your bells, let mourning shows be spread"

Ring out your bells, let mourning shows be spread,
For Love is dead —
    All Love is dead, infected
With plague of deep disdain;
    Worth, as nought worth, rejected,   5
And Faith fair scorn doth gain.
    From so ungrateful fancy,
    From such a female franzy,
    From them that use men thus,
    Good Lord, deliver us!   10

Weep, neighbours, weep; do you not hear it said
That Love is dead?
    His death-bed, peacock's folly;
His winding-sheet is shame;
    His will, false-seeming holy;   15
His sole executor, blame.
    From so ungrateful fancy,
    From such a female franzy,
    From them that use men thus,
    Good Lord, deliver us!   20

Let dirge be sung and trentals rightly read,
For Love is dead;
    Sir Wrong his tomb ordaineth
My mistress' marble heart,
    Which epitaph containeth,   25
"Her eyes were once his dart."
    From so ungrateful fancy,
    From such a female franzy,
    From them that use men thus,
    Good Lord, deliver us!   30

Alas, I lie; rage hath this error bred;
Love is not dead;
    Love is not dead, but sleepeth
In her unmatched mind,
    Where she his counsel keepeth,   35
Till due desert she find.
    Therefore from so vile fancy,
    To call such wit a franzy,
    Who Love can temper thus,
    Good Lord, deliver us!   40

(c. 1584; 1598)

FULKE GREVILLE, LORD BROOKE
England, 1554-1628

from *CÆLICA*

VII

The world, that all contains, is ever moving,
The stars within their spheres forever turned,
Nature, the Queen of Change, to change is loving,
And form to matter new is still adjourned.

Fortune, our fancy-God, to vary liketh,   5
Place is not bound to things within it placed,
The present time upon time passed striketh,
With Phoebus' wand'ring course the earth is graced.

THOU BLIND MAN'S MARK **1. mark:** target. **3. Band:** i.e., swaddling band.   **RING OUT YOUR BELLS** **6. fair scorn:** fair one's scorn. **8. franzy:** frenzy. **21. trentals:** Roman Catholic office for the dead, consisting of thirty consecutive daily masses; loosely, any dirge or elegy.   **CÆLICA** "Cælica" is probably a name used for more than one woman; similarly, "Myra" (in poem VII) figures in the sequence as well.   **VII** **1. world:** i.e., the Ptolemaic universe of spheres (see line 2) moved by the *primum mobile* (see *Ptolemaic* in the Glossary). **4. still adjourned:** continually summoned (i.e., a Platonic "form" or "idea" is ever called upon to manifest itself in new material; or a literary "form," such as the sonnet, is continually used to express different matter). **8. Phoebus:** the sun.

The air still moves, and by its moving cleareth,
The fire up ascends, and planets feedeth,   *10*
The water passeth on, and all lets weareth,
The earth stands still, yet change of changes breedeth.

Her plants, which summer ripes, in winter fade,
Each creature in unconstant mother lieth,
Man made of earth, and for whom earth is made,   *15*
Still dying lives, and living ever dieth;
    Only like fate sweet Myra never varies,
    Yet in her eyes the doom of all change carries.

XLIV

The Golden Age was when the world was young,
Nature so rich, as earth did need no sowing,
Malice not known, the serpents had not stung,
Wit was but sweet affection's overflowing.

Desire was free, and beauty's first-begotten;   *5*
Beauty then neither net, nor made by art,
Words out of thoughts brought forth, and not forgotten,
The laws were inward that did rule the heart.

The Brazen Age is now when earth is worn,
Beauty grown sick, nature corrupt and nought,   *10*
Pleasure untimely dead as soon as born,
Both words and kindness strangers to our thought.

If now this changing world do change her head,
Cælica, what have her new lords for to boast?
The old lord knows desire is poorly fed,   *15*
And sorrows not a wavering province lost,
    Since in the gilt-age Saturn ruled alone,
    And in this painted, planets every one.

LIX

Who ever sails near to Bermuda coast,
Goes hard aboard the monarchy of fear,
Where all desires (but Life's desire) are lost,
For wealth and fame put off their glories there.

    Yet this isle poison-like, by mischief known,   *5*
Weans not desire from her sweet nurse, the sea,
But unseen shows us where our hopes be sown,
With woeful signs declaring joyful way.
    For who will see the wealth of western sun,
    Oft by Bermuda's miseries must run.   *10*

Who seeks the god of love in beauty's sky
Must pass the empire of confused passion,
Where our desires to all but horrors die
Before that joy and peace can take their fashion.

    Yet this fair heaven that yields this soul-despair   *15*
Weans not the heart from his sweet god, affection,
But rather shows us what sweet joys are there,
Where constancy is servant to perfection.
    Who Cælica's chaste heart then seeks to move,
    Must joy to suffer all the woes of love.   *20*

XCII

Virgula divina, sorcerers call a rod
Gathered with vows and magic sacrifice,
Which borne about, by influence doth nod
Unto the silver, where it hidden lies;
    Which makes poor men to these black arts devout,   *5*
    Rich only in the wealth which hope finds out.

Nobility, this precious treasure, is
Laid up in secret mysteries of state,
King's creature, subjection's gilded bliss,
Where grace, not merit, seems to govern fate.   *10*
    Mankind I think to be this rod divine,
    For to the greatest ever they incline.

Eloquence, that is but wisdom speaking well,
(The poets feign) did make the savage tame;
Of ears and hearts chained unto tongues they tell;   *15*
I think nobility to be the same;
    For be they fools, or speak they without wit,
    We hold them wise; we fools be-wonder it.

Invisible there is an art to go
(They say that study nature's secret works),   *20*
And art there is to make things greater show;
In nobleness I think this secret lurks,
    For place a coronet on whom you will,
    You straight see all great in him, but his ill.

CVIII

What is the cause, why states, that war and win,
Have honour, and breed men of better fame
Than states in peace, since war and conquest sin
In blood, wrong liberty, all trades of shame?
    Force-framing instruments, which it must use,   *5*
    Proud in excess, and glory to abuse.

---

11. lets: obstacles, impediments. **XLIV** Cf. Chaucer's "The Former Age" (p. 72) and the excerpt from Sandys's Ovid (p. 267). **6. net:** i.e., snare for the unwary. **12. kindness:** naturalness. **17:** Saturn (identified with the Greek Kronos), god of sowing and harvest, oversaw the Golden Age, celebrated with the annual festival called *Saturnalia* (in Greece, *Kronia*). **LIX** The Bermudas were known as stormy and dangerous. **XCII** **1.** *Virgula divina*: divining or dowsing rod.

The reason is, peace is a quiet nurse
Of idleness, and idleness the field
Where wit and power change all seeds to the worse,
By narrow self-will upon which they build,   *10*
    And thence bring forth captived inconstant ends,
    Neither to princes nor to people friends.

Besides, the sins of peace on subjects feed,
And thence wound power, which for it all things can,
With wrong to one despairs in many breed,   *15*
For while laws' oaths, powers' creditors to man,
    Make humble subjects dream of native right,
    Man's faith abused adds courage to despite.

Where conquest works by strength, and stirs up fame,
A glorious echo, pleasing doom of pain,   *20*
    Which in the sleep of death yet keeps a name,
    And makes detracting loss speak ill in vain.

For to great actions time so friendly is,
As o'er the means (albeit the means be ill)
It casts forgetfulness, veils things amiss,   *25*
With power and honour to encourage will.

Besides, things hard a reputation bear,
To die resolved though guilty wonder breeds;
Yet what strength those be which can blot out fear,
And to self-ruin joyfully proceeds;   *30*
    Ask them that from the ashes of this fire
    With new lives still to such new flames aspire.

                                        (publ. 1633)

NICHOLAS BRETON
England, c.1555-1626

PHILLIDA AND CORIDON

In the merry month of May,
In a morn by break of day,
Forth I walked by the wood-side,
Whenas May was in his pride.
There I spied, all alone,   *5*
Phillida and Coridon.
Much ado there was, God wot,
He would love and she would not.
She said, Never man was true;
He said, None was false to you.   *10*
He said he had loved her long.
She said, Love should have no wrong.
Coridon would kiss her then.

She said maids must kiss no men
Till they did for good and all.   *15*
Then she made the shepherd call
All the heavens to witness truth,
Never loved a truer youth.
Thus with many a pretty oath,
Yea and nay, and faith and troth,   *20*
Such as silly shepherds use
When they will not love abuse,
Love which had been long deluded
Was with kisses sweet concluded,
And Phillida with garlands gay   *25*
Was made the Lady of the May.

                                        (1591)

PHILLIDA AND CORIDON   A three-part song written to be sung to Queen Elizabeth at an entertainment.

from FANTASTICS: SERVING FOR A PERPETUAL PROGNOSTICATION

January

It is now January, and Time begins to turn the wheel of his revolution. The woods begin to lose the beauty of their spreading boughs, and the proud oak must stoop to the axe. The squirrel now surveyeth the nut and the maple, and the hedgehog rolls up himself like a football. An apple and a nutmeg make a gossip's cup, and the ale and the faggot are the victualler's merchandise. The northern black dust is the during fuel, and the fruit of the grape heats the stomach of the aged. Down beds and quilted caps are now in the pride of their service, and the cook and the pantler are men of no mean office. The ox and the fat wether now furnish the market, and the cony is so ferreted that she cannot keep in her burrow. The currier and the lime-rod are the death of the fowl, and the falcon's bells ring the death of the mallard. The trotting gelding makes a way through the mire, and the hare and the hound put the huntsman to his horn. The barren doe subscribes to the dish, and the smallest seed makes sauce to the greatest flesh. The dried grass is the horse's ordinary, and the meal of the beans makes him go through with his travel. Fishermen now have a cold trade and travellers a foul journey. The cook room now is not the worst place in the ship, and the shepherd hath a bleak seat on the mountain. The blackbird leaveth not a berry on the thorn, and the garden earth is turned up for her roots. The water floods run over the proud banks, and the gaping oyster leaves his shell in the streets, while the proud peacock leaps into the pie. Moscovia commodities are now much in request, and the water spaniel is a necessary servant. The load-horse to the mill hath his full back-burden, and the thresher in the barn tries the strength of his flail. The woodcock and the pheasant pay their lives for their feed, and the hare after a course makes his hearse in a pie. The shoulder of a hog is a shoeing-horn to good drink, and a cold alms makes a beggar shrug. To conclude, I hold it a time of little comfort, the rich man's charge and the poor man's misery. Farewell.

March

It is now March, and the northern wind drieth up the southern dirt. The tender lips are now masked for fear of chapping, and the fair hands must not be ungloved. Now riseth the sun a pretty step to his fair height, and Saint Valentine calls the birds together where nature is pleased in the variety of love. The fishes and the frogs fall to their manner of generation, and the adder dies to bring forth her young. The air is sharp, but the sun is comfortable, and the day begins to lengthen. The forward gardens give the fine sallets, and a nosegay of violets is a present for a lady. Now beginneth Nature, as it were, to wake out of her sleep and send the traveller to survey the walks of the world. The sucking rabbit is good for weak stomachs, and the diet for the rheum doth many a great cure. The farrier now is the horse's physician, and the fat dog feeds the falcon in the mew. The tree begins to bud and

FANTASTICS   **4. gossip's cup:** caudle; **faggot:** here, a bundle of herbs or spices for the caudle. **5. northern black dust:** coal, probably from Newcastle-upon-Tyne; **during:** enduring, lasting, continuing. **7. pantler:** servant in charge of the pantry. **9. currier:** small fire-arm, similar to harquebus or musket; **lime-rod:** lime-twig, twig smeared with bird-lime. **12. subscribes:** agrees, submits, is a party, contributes; **smallest seed:** mustard. **13. ordinary:** meal provided at fixed time and price. **20. load-horse:** pack-horse. **30. sallets:** salads.

the grass to peep abroad, while the thrush with the blackbird make a charm in the young   *35*
springs. The milkmaid with her best-beloved talk away weariness to the market, and in an
honest meaning kind words do no hurt. The football now trieth the legs of strength, and
merry matches continue good fellowship. It is a time of much work and tedious to
discourse of, but in all I find of it I thus conclude in it: I hold it the servant of nature and
the schoolmaster of art, the hope of labour and the subject of reason. Farewell.   *40*

May

It is now May, and the sweetness of the air refresheth every spirit. The sunny beams
bring forth fair blossoms, and the dripping clouds water Flora's great garden. The male
deer puts out the velvet head, and the bagged doe is near her fawning. The sparhawk
now is drawn out of the mew, and the fowler makes ready his whistle for the quail. The
lark sets the morning watch, and the evening the nightingale. The barges, like bowers,   *45*
keep the streams of the sweet rivers, and the mackerel with the shad are taken prisoners
in the sea. The tall young oak is cut down for the maypole. The scythe and the sickle are
the mower's furniture, and fair weather makes the labourer merry. The physician now
prescribes the cold whey, and the apothecary gathers the dew for a medicine. Butter and
sage make the wholesome breakfast, but fresh cheese and cream are meat for a dainty   *50*
mouth, and the strawberry and the peasecod want no price in the market. The chicken
and the duck are fattened for the market, and many a gosling never lives to be a goose. It
is the month wherein Nature hath her full of mirth, and the senses are filled with
delights. I conclude it is from the heavens a grace and to the earth a gladness. Farewell.

October

It is now October, and the lofty winds make bare the trees of their leaves, while the hogs   *55*
in the woods grow fat with the fallen acorns. The forward deer begin to go to rut, and the
barren doe groweth good meat. The basket-makers now gather their rods, and the fishers
lay their leaps in the deep. The load-horses go apace to the mill, and the meal-market is
seldom without people. The hare on the hill makes the greyhound a fair course, and the
fox in the woods calls the hounds to a full cry. The multitude of people raiseth the price of   *60*
wares, and the smooth tongue will sell much. The sailor now bestirreth his stumps, while
the merchant liveth in fear of the weather. The great feasts are now at hand for the city, but
the poor must not beg for fear of the stocks. A fire and a pair of cards keep the guests in
the ordinary, and tobacco is held very precious for the rheum. The coaches now begin to
rattle in the streets, but the cry of the poor is unpleasing to the rich. Muffs and cuffs are   *65*
now in request, and the shuttlecock with the battledore is a pretty house exercise. Tennis
and balloon are sports of some charge, and a quick bandy is the court-keeper's
commodity. Dancing and fencing are now in some use, and kind hearts and true lovers lie
close to keep off cold. The titmouse now keeps in the hollow tree, and the blackbird sits
close in the bottom of a hedge. In brief, for the little pleasure I find in it, I thus conclude of   *70*
it: I hold it a messenger of ill news and a second service to a cold dinner. Farewell.

---

36. springs: young trees. **43. bagged:** pregnant; **sparhawk:** sparrowhawk. **45. barges, like bowers:** i.e., barges with families living aboard are like
bowers. **46. keep:** stay or remain in or on. **57. rods:** slender shoots or wands. **58. leaps:** baskets for catching or keeping fish. **63. pair:** set, pack. **64.
ordinary:** tavern or inn serving meals. **67. balloon:** game in which a large leather ball is knocked or kicked to and fro; **charge:** importance,
moment; **bandy:** bandy-ball, game similar to field-hockey; **court-keeper:** the master at a ball or racquet game.

December

It is now December, and he that walks the streets shall find dirt on his shoes, except he go all in boots. Now doth the lawyer make an end of his harvest and the client of his purse. Now capons and hens, besides turkeys, geese, and ducks, besides beef and mutton, must all die for the great feast, for in twelve days a multitude of people will not   *75* be fed with a little. Now plums and spice, sugar and honey, square it among pies and broth, and Gossip, I drink to you, and you are welcome, and I thank you, and how do you, and I pray you be merry. Now are the tailors and tire-makers full of work against the holidays, and music now must be in tune or else never. The youth must dance and sing and the aged sit by the fire. It is the law of nature and no contradiction in reason.   *80* The ass that hath borne all the year must now take a little rest, and the lean ox must feed till he be fat. The footman now shall have many a foul step, and the ostler shall have work enough about the heels of the horses, while the tapster, if he take not heed, will lie drunk in the cellar. The prices of meat will rise apace, and the apparel of the proud will make the tailor rich. Dice and cards will benefit the butler, and if the cook do not lack   *85* wit he will sweetly lick his fingers. Starchers and launderers will have their hands full of work, and periwigs and paintings will not be a little set by.

> Strange stuffs will be well sold,
> Strange tales well told,
> Strange sights much sought,   *90*
> Strange things much bought,
> And what else as falls out.

To conclude, I hold it the costly purveyor of excess and the after-breeder of necessity, the practice of folly and the purgatory of reason. Farewell.

(c. 1604; 1626)

from *The Good and the Bad*

A Drunkard

A drunkard is a known adjective, for he cannot stand alone by himself; yet in his greatest weakness a great trier of strength, whether health or sickness will have the upper hand in a surfeit. He is a spectacle of deformity and a shame of humanity, a view of sin and a grief of nature. He is the annoyance of modesty and the trouble of civility, the spoil of wealth and the spite of reason. He is only the brewer's agent and the   *5* alehouse benefactor, the beggar's companion and the constable's trouble. He is his wife's woe, his children's sorrow, his neighbours' scoff, and his own shame. In sum, he is a tub of swill, a spirit of sleep, a picture of a beast, and a monster of a man.

(1616)

---

75. twelve days: i.e., of Christmas. **77. Gossip:** familiar acquaintance, close friend — usually a woman. **78. tire-makers:** makers of headdresses. **87. paintings:** i.e., of the face; **set by:** esteemed, valued, set store by.

GEORGE PEELE
England, 1556-1596

"His golden locks time hath to silver turned"

His golden locks time hath to silver turned;
  Oh time too swift, oh swiftness never ceasing!
His youth 'gainst time and age hath ever spurned,
  But spurned in vain; youth waneth by increasing.
Beauty, strength, youth, are flowers but fading seen;   *5*
Duty, faith, love, are roots, and ever green.

His helmet now shall make a hive for bees,
  And lover's sonnets turned to holy psalms;
A man-at-arms must now serve on his knees,
  And feed on prayers, which are age his alms;   *10*

But though from court to cottage he depart,
His saint is sure of his unspotted heart.

And when he saddest sits in homely cell,
  He'll teach his swains this carol for a song:
Blest be the hearts that wish my sovereign well,   *15*
  Curst be the souls that think her any wrong.
Goddess, allow this aged man his right
To be your beadsman now, that was your knight.
                              (1590)

THOMAS MORLEY
England, 1557-1602

"April is in my mistress' face"

April is in my mistress' face,
And July in her eyes hath place.
Within her bosom is September,
But in her heart a cold December.
          (1594)

CHIDIOCK TICHBORNE
England, c.1558-1586

TICHBORNE'S ELEGY
written with his own hand in the Tower before his execution

My prime of youth is but a frost of cares,
My feast of joy is but a dish of pain,
My crop of corn is but a field of tares,

And all my good is but vain hope of gain;
The day is past, and yet I saw no sun,   *5*
And now I live, and now my life is done.

HIS GOLDEN LOCKS   **10. age his:** i.e., age's. **15, 17. my sovereign, Goddess:** i.e., Queen Elizabeth. **18. beadsman:** one who prays for another, e.g. one hired to do so.   APRIL IS IN MY MISTRESS' FACE   Morley, principally known as a musician, set this madrigal to music in 1594.   TICHBORNE'S ELEGY   Tichborne, a Roman Catholic, was imprisoned and executed for his involvement in the Babington Plot to

My tale was heard, and yet it was not told;
My fruit is fall'n, and yet my leaves are green;
My youth is spent, and yet I am not old;
I saw the world, and yet I was not seen;   *10*
My thread is cut, and yet it is not spun,
And now I live, and now my life is done.

I sought my death and found it in my womb,
I looked for life and saw it was a shade,
I trod the earth and knew it was my tomb,   *15*
And now I die, and now I was but made;
My glass is full, and now my glass is run,
And now I live, and now my life is done.

(1586)

THOMAS LODGE
England, 1558-1625

OLD DAMON'S PASTORAL

From Fortune's frowns and change removed,
  Wend silly flocks in blessed feeding;
None of Damon more beloved,
  Feed, gentle lambs, while I sit reading.

Careless worldlings, outrage quelleth   *5*
  All the pride and pomp of city,
But true peace with shepherds dwelleth
  (Shepherds who delight in pity).
Whether grace of heaven betideth,
  On our humble minds such pleasure,   *10*
Perfect peace with swains abideth;
  Love and faith is shepherd's treasure.
On the lower plains the thunder
  Little thrives, and nought prevaileth;
Yet in cities breedeth wonder,   *15*
  And the highest hills assaileth.

Envy of a foreign tyrant
  Threateneth kings, not shepherds humble;
Age makes silly swains delirant;
  Thirst of rule gars great men stumble.   *20*
What to other seemeth sorry,
  Abject state and humble biding,
Is our joy and country glory;
  Highest states have worse betiding.

Golden cups do harbour poison,   *25*
  And the greatest pomp, dissembling;
Court of seasoned words hath foison,
  Treason haunts in most assembling.

Homely breasts do harbour quiet,
  Little fear, and mickle solace;   *30*
States suspect their bed and diet;
  Fear and craft do haunt the palace.
Little would I, little want I,
  Where the mind and store agreeth;
Smallest comfort is not scanty;   *35*
  Least he longs that little seeth.
Time hath been that I have longed,
  Foolish I, to like of folly:
To converse where honour thronged,
  To my pleasures linked wholly.   *40*

Now I see, and seeing sorrow,
  That the day consumed returns not;
Who dare trust upon tomorrow
  When nor time nor life sojourns not?

(1600)

assassinate the Queen (Mary Queen of Scots was also involved: see Elizabeth I's "The Doubt of Future Foes," p. 137). Although the poem was said to be his, it is conceivable that someone else composed it. **11:** alluding to the work of the three Fates — spinning, measuring, and cutting the thread of life. **17: glass:** i.e., hourglass.   OLD DAMON'S PASTORAL   **19. delirant:** delirious, mad. **20. gars:** makes. **27. foison:** abundance. **31. States:** people of estate, status, high rank.

Thomas Deloney
England, c.1560-1600

THE WINNING OF CALES

Long had the proud Spaniard advanced to conquer us,
  Threatening our country with fire and sword,
Often preparing their navy most sumptuous
  With all the provision Spain could afford.
    Dub a dub, dub a dub, thus strikes the drums: 5
    Tantara, tantara, Englishmen comes.

To the seas presently went our lord admiral,
  With knights courageous and captains full good;
The Earl of Essex, a prosperous general,
  With him prepared to pass the salt flood.   10
    Dub a dub, dub a dub, thus strikes the drums;
    Tantara, tantara, Englishmen comes.

At Plymouth speedily took they ship valiantly;
  Braver ships never were seen under sail,
With their colours spread, and streamers o'er their head.
  Now bragging Spaniards, take heed of your tale.   16
    Dub a dub, dub a dub, thus strikes the drums;
    Tantara, tantara, Englishmen comes.

Unto Cales cunningly came we most happily,
  Where the king's navy did secretly ride,   20
Being upon their back, piercing their butts of sack,
  Ere that the Spaniard our coming descried.
    Tantara-rara, Englishmen comes,
    Bounce-abounce, bounce-abounce, off went the guns.

Great was the crying, the running and riding,   25
  Which at that season was made in that place;
The beacons were fired, as need was required;
  To hide their great treasure they had little space.
    Dub a dub, dub a dub, thus strikes the drums;
    "Alas!" they cried, "Englishmen comes."   30

There you might see their ships, how they were fired fast,
  And how their men drowned themselves in the sea;
There might you hear them cry, wail and weep piteously,
  When they saw no shift to 'scape thence away.
    Dub a dub....   35

The great *St. Philip*, the pride of the Spaniards,
  Was burnt to the bottom, and sunk in the sea;
But the *St. Andrew* and eke the *St. Matthew*
  We took in fight manly and brought them away.
    Dub a dub....   40

The Earl of Essex, most valiant and hardy,
  With horsemen and footmen marched towards the town;
The enemies which saw them, full greatly affrighted,
  Did fly for their saveguard, and durst not come down.
    Dub a dub....   45

"Now," quoth the noble Earl, "courage, my soldiers all;
  Fight and be valiant, the spoil you shall have,
And be well rewarded all, from the great to the small;
  But look that the women and children you save."
    Dub a dub....   50

The Spaniards at that sight saw 'twas in vain to fight,
  Hung up their flags of truce, yielding the town;
We marched in presently, decking the walls on high
  With our English colours which purchase renown.
    Dub a dub....   55

Entering the houses then of the most richest men,
  For gold and treasure we searched each day;
In some places we did find pies baking in the oven,
  Meat at the fire roasting, and men run away.
    Dub a dub....   60

Full of rich merchandise every shop we did see:
  Damasks and satins and velvet full fair,
Which soldiers measured out by the length of their swords;
  Of all commodities each had a share.
    Dub a dub....   65

Thus Cales was taken, and our brave general
  Marched to the market-place; there he did stand;
There many prisoners of good account were took;
  Many craved mercy, and mercy they found.
    Dub a dub....   70

When as our brave general saw they delayed time,
  And would not ransom the town as they said,
With their fair wainscots, their presses and bedsteads,
  Their joint-stools and tables a fire we made;
    And when the town burnt in a flame,   75
    With tara, tantara, from thence we came.

THE WINNING OF CALES This broadside ballad celebrates the raid on Cadiz ("Cales") in June 1596, led by the lord admiral, Charles Howard, and Robert Devereux, Earl of Essex (Deloney also wrote three broadsides on the 1588 defeat of the Spanish Armada). **21. butts of sack:** casks of dry Spanish wine. **29-30:** This refrain is repeated in the next eight stanzas. **38. eke:** also. **73. presses:** free-standing closets or chests for clothes, books, etc. **74. joint-stools:** stools made by a joiner, well-made stools.

ANTHONY MUNDAY
England, 1560-1633

THE WOODMAN'S WALK, BY "SHEPHERD TONIE"

Through a fair forest as I went
    upon a summer's day,
I met a woodman quaint and gent,
    yet in a strange array.
I marvelled much at his disguise,   *5*
    whom I did know so well,
But thus in terms both grave and wise
    his mind he gan to tell:
"Friend, muse not at this fond array,
    but list a while to me,   *10*
For it hath helped me to survey
    what I shall show to thee.
Long lived I in this forest fair,
    till weary of my weal,
Abroad in walks I would repair,   *15*
    as now I will reveal.
My first day's walk was to the Court,
    where beauty fed mine eyes;
Yet found I that the courtly sport
    did mask in sly disguise.   *20*
For falsehood sat in fairest looks,
    and friend to friend was coy;
Court-favour filled but empty books,
    and there I found no joy.
Desert went naked in the cold   *25*
    when crouching craft was fed;
Sweet words were cheaply bought and sold,
    but none that stood in stead.
Wit was employed for each man's own;
    plain meaning came too short;   *30*
All these devices seen and known
    made me forsake the Court.
Unto the City next I went,
    in hope of better hap;
Where liberally I launched and spent,   *35*
    as set on Fortune's lap.

The little stock I had in store
    methought would ne'er be done;
Friends flocked about me more and more,
    as quickly lost as won.   *40*
For when I spent, they then were kind,
    but when my purse did fail
The foremost man came last behind;
    thus love with wealth doth quail.
Once more for footing yet I strove,   *45*
    although the world did frown;
But they before that held me up,
    together trod me down.
And lest once more I should arise,
    they sought my quite decay;   *50*
Then got I into this disguise,
    and thence I stole away.
And in my mind (methought) I said,
    'Lord bless me from the city,
Where simpleness is thus betrayed,   *55*
    and no remorse or pity.'
Yet would I not give over so,
    but once more try my fate:
And to the Country then I go,
    to live in quiet state.   *60*
There did appear no subtle shows,
    but yea and nay went smoothly;
But lord, how country-folks can gloze
    when they speak most soothly!
More craft was in a buttoned cap,   *65*
    and in an old wive's rail,
Than in my life it was my hap
    to see on down or dale.
There was no open forgery,
    but underhanded gleaning,   *70*
Which they call country policy,
    but hath a worser meaning.

THE WOODMAN'S WALK **3. quaint:** wise, knowing, skilled; **gent:** polite, well-bred. **35. launched:** entered boldly, rushed into expense. **63. gloze:** talk speciously, deceive with smooth talk. **66. rail:** neckerchief. **71. policy:** prudence, skill; cunning craftiness.

Some good bold-face bears out the wrong
 because he gains thereby;
The poor man's back is cracked ere long, *75*
 yet there he lets him lie.
And no degree among them all,
 but had such close intending
That I upon my knees did fall,
 and prayed for their amending. *80*
Back to the woods I got again,
 in mind perplexed sore,

Where I found ease of all this pain,
 and mean to stray no more.
There, City, Court, nor Country too, *85*
 can any way annoy me,
But as a woodman ought to do,
 I freely may employ me.
There live I quietly alone,
 and none to trip my talk; *90*
Wherefore when I am dead and gone,
 think on the woodman's walk."

(1600)

ROBERT SOUTHWELL
England, c.1561-1595

THE BURNING BABE

As I in hoary winter's night stood shivering in the snow,
Surprised I was with sudden heat which made my heart to glow;
And lifting up a fearful eye to view what fire was near,
A pretty babe all burning bright did in the air appear,
Who, scorched with excessive heat, such floods of tears did shed, *5*
As though his floods should quench his flames which with his tears were fed.
"Alas," quoth he, "but newly born in fiery heats I fry,
Yet none approach to warm their hearts or feel my fire but I!
My faultless breast the furnace is, the fuel wounding thorns,
Love is the fire and sighs the smoke, the ashes shame and scorns; *10*
The fuel justice layeth on, and mercy blows the coals;
The metal in this furnace wrought are men's defiled souls,
For which, as now on fire I am to work them to their good,
So will I melt into a bath to wash them in my blood."
With this he vanished out of sight and swiftly shrunk away, *15*
And straight I called unto mind that it was Christmas day.

(c. 1595)

---

73. bold-face: impudent person; **bears out:** supports, backs up.

HUMPHREY GIFFORD
England, fl. 1580

"A woman's face is full of wiles"

A woman's face is full of wiles;
   Her tears are like the crocadill;
With outward cheer on thee she smiles,
   When in her heart she thinks thee ill.

Her tongue still chats of this and that;   *5*
   Than aspen leaf it wags more fast;
And as she talks she knows not what,
   There issues many a truthless blast.

Thou far dost take thy mark amiss
   If thou think faith in them to find;   *10*
The weathercock more constant is,
   Which turns about with every wind.

O how in pity they abound!
   Their heart is mild, like marble stone;
If in thyself no hope be found,   *15*
   Be sure of them thou gettest none.

I know some peppernosed dame
   Will term me fool and saucy jack,
That dare their credit so defame,
   And lay such slanders on their back.   *20*

What though on me they pour their spite?
   I may not use the glozer's trade;
I cannot say the crow is white,
   But needs must call a spade a spade.
(1580)

SIR JOHN HARINGTON
England, c.1561-1612

from *ELEGANT AND WITTY EPIGRAMS*

COMPARISON OF THE SONNET AND THE EPIGRAM

Once by mishap two poets fell a-squaring,
The sonnet and our epigram comparing;
And Faustus, having long demurred upon it,
Yet at the last gave sentence for the sonnet.
Now for such censure this his chief defence is,   *5*
Their sugared taste best likes his lick'rish senses.
   Well, though I grant sugar may please the taste,
   Yet let my verse have salt to make it last.

AGAINST WRITERS THAT CARP AT OTHER MEN'S BOOKS

The readers and the hearers like my books,
But yet some writers cannot them digest.
But what care I? For when I make a feast,
I would my guests should praise it, not the cooks.

OF TREASON

Treason doth never prosper; what's the reason?
For if it prosper, none dare call it treason.

A WOMAN'S FACE IS FULL OF WILES This appears as a song in a longer poem called "A Delectable Dream"; a character sings it to some fairies, who curse him for so criticizing women. **2. crocadill:** crocodile. **17. peppernosed:** apt to take offence. **22. glozer:** flatterer, deceiver. **COMPARISON OF THE SONNET** **6. likes:** pleases.

OF CLERGYMEN AND THEIR LIVINGS

In ancient time old men observed that
The clergymen were lean, their livings fat;
But in these days the case is altered clean:
The clergymen are fat, their livings lean.
   I, searching, find this cause that change to breed: *5*
   Now they feed fast, then they did fast and feed.

(1618)

MARY SIDNEY HERBERT, COUNTESS OF PEMBROKE
England, 1561-1621

A DIALOGUE BETWEEN TWO SHEPHERDS, THENOT AND PIERS, IN PRAISE OF ASTREA

Made by the Excellent Lady Mary, Countess of Pembroke,
at the Queen's Majesty's Being at Her House

THENOT
I sing divine Astrea's praise,
O Muses! help my wits to raise
And heave my verses higher.

PIERS
Thou needst the truth, but plainly tell,
Which much I doubt thou canst not well,   *5*
Thou art so oft a liar.

THENOT
If in my song no more I show
Than heav'n and earth and sea do know,
Then truly I have spoken.

PIERS
Sufficeth not no more to name,   *10*
But being no less, the like, the fame,
Else laws of truth be broken.

THENOT
Then say, she is so good, so fair,
With all the earth she may compare,
Not Momus' self denying.   *15*

PIERS
Compare may think where likeness holds,
Nought like to her the earth enfolds;
I looked to find you lying.

THENOT
Astrea sees with Wisdom's sight,
Astrea works by Virtue's might,   *20*
And jointly both do stay in her.

PIERS
Nay, take from them her hand, her mind;
The one is lame, the other blind;
Shall still your lying stain her?

THENOT
Soon as Astrea shows her face,   *25*
Straight every ill avoids the place,
And every good aboundeth.

PIERS
Nay, long before her face doth show,
The last doth come, the first doth go;
How loud this lie resoundeth!   *30*

A DIALOGUE BETWEEN TWO SHEPHERDS   **15. Momus:** See note to Sidney's *The Defence of Poesy*, line 117.

THENOT
Astrea is our chiefest joy,
Our chiefest guard against annoy,
Our chiefest wealth, our treasure.

PIERS
Where chiefest are, there others be,
To us none else but only she; _35_
When wilt thou speak in measure?

THENOT
Astrea may be justly said,
A field in flowery robe arrayed,
In season freshly springing.

PIERS
That spring endures but shortest time, _40_
This never leaves Astrea's clime;
Thou liest, instead of singing.

THENOT
As heavenly light that guides the day,
Right so doth thine each lovely ray,
That from Astrea flyeth. _45_

PIERS
Nay, darkness oft that light enclouds;
Astrea's beams no darkness shrouds;
How loudly Thenot lieth!

THENOT
Astrea rightly term I may
A manly palm, a maiden bay, _50_
Her virtue never dying.

PIERS
Palm oft is crooked, bay is low;
She still upright, still high doth grow;
Good Thenot, leave thy lying.

THENOT
Then Piers, of friendship tell my why, _55_
My meaning true, my words should lie,
And strive in vain to raise her.

PIERS
Words from conceit do only rise;
Above conceit her honour flies;
But silence: nought can praise her. _60_
(before 1600; 1602)

from PSALMS

Psalm 23

The Lord, the Lord my shepheard is,
    And so can never I
        Taste misery.
He rests me in green pasture his,
    By waters still and sweet _5_
        He guides my feet.

He me revives, leads me the way
    Which righteousness doth take,
        For his name's sake.
Yea though I should through valleys stray _10_
    Of death's dark shade, I will
        No whit fear ill.

For thou, dear Lord, thou me besett'st;
    Thy rod and thy staff be
        To comfort me; _15_
Before me thou a table sett'st,
    Even when foe's envious eye
        Doth it espy.

Thou oil'st my head, thou fill'st my cup;
    Nay, more, thou endless good _20_
        Shalt give me food.
To thee I say, ascended up,
    Where thou, the Lord of all,
        Dost hold thy hall.

PSALMS   Compare these versions with those in the King James Bible (p. 251). Sir Philip Sidney began translating the Psalms and rendering them in English verse, finishing 43 before his death, after which his sister did 107 more, as well as revising the first 43; the bulk of them weren't published until the early 19th century.   **PSALM 23**   **13. besett'st:** surround (but obviously not with hostile intent), accompany.

Psalm 121

What? and do I behold the lovely mountains,
Whence comes all my relief, my aid, my comfort?
O there, O there abides the world's Creator,
Whence comes all my relief, my aid, my comfort.

March, march lustily on, redoubt no falling;   *5*
God shall guide thy goings; the Lord thy keeper
Sleeps not, sleeps not a whit, no sleep no slumber
Once shall enter in Israel's true keeper.

But whom named I Israel's true keeper?
Whom? but only Jehovah, whose true keeping   *10*
Thy saving shadow is, not ever absent
When present period his relief requireth.

March then boldly; by day no sun shall hurt thee
With beams too violently right reflected.
Fear no journey by night; the moony vapours   *15*
Shall not cast any mist to breed thy grievance.

Nay from ev'ry mishap, from ev'ry mischief
Safe thou shalt by Jehovah's hand be guarded;
Safe in all thy goings, in all thy comings,
Now thou shalt by his hand, yea, still be guarded.   *20*

SIR FRANCIS BACON
England, 1561-1626

from *ESSAYS OR COUNSELS, CIVIL AND MORAL*

OF STUDIES

Studies serve for delight, for ornament, and for ability. Their chief use for delight is in privateness and retiring; for ornament, is in discourse; and for ability, is in the judgment and disposition of business. For expert men can execute, and perhaps judge of particulars, one by one; but the general counsels, and the plots and marshalling of affairs, come best from those that are learned. To spend too much time in studies is   *5* sloth; to use them too much for ornament is affectation; to make judgment wholly by their rules is the humour of a scholar. They perfect nature, and are perfected by experience, for natural abilities are like natural plants, that need pruning by study; and studies themselves do give forth directions too much at large, except they be bounded in by experience. Crafty men contemn studies, simple men admire them, and wise men use   *10* them, for they teach not their own use; but that is a wisdom without them and above them, won by observation. Read not to contradict and confute, nor to believe and take for granted, nor to find talk and discourse, but to weigh and consider. Some books are to be tasted, others to be swallowed, and some few to be chewed and digested; that is, some books are to be read only in parts, others to be read, but not curiously, and some   *15* few to be read wholly, and with diligence and attention. Some books also may be read by deputy, and extracts made of them by others; but that would be only in the less

---

PSALM 121   **5. redoubt:** fear.   OF STUDIES   **3. expert:** experienced, trained by experience or practice. **15. curiously:** carefully.

important arguments and the meaner sort of books; else distilled books are, like common distilled waters, flashy things. Reading maketh a full man, conference a ready man, and writing an exact man. And therefore if a man write little, he had need have a *20* great memory; if he confer little, he had need have a present wit; and if he read little, he had need have much cunning, to seem to know that he doth not. Histories make men wise; poets, witty; the mathematics, subtle; natural philosophy, deep; moral, grave; logic and rhetoric, able to contend. *Abeunt studia in mores.* Nay, there is no stond or impediment in the wit but may be wrought out by fit studies, like as diseases of the body *25* may have appropriate exercises. Bowling is good for the stone and reins, shooting for the lungs and breast, gentle walking for the stomach, riding for the head, and the like. So if a man's wit be wandering, let him study the mathematics, for in demonstrations, if his wit be called away never so little, he must begin again. If his wit be not apt to distinguish or find differences, let him study the Schoolmen, for they are *cymini* *30* *sectores.* If he be not apt to beat over matters, and to call up one thing to prove and illustrate another, let him study the lawyers' cases. So every defect of the mind may have a special receipt.

(1597-1625)

OF TRAVEL

Travel in the younger sort is a part of education; in the elder, a part of experience. He that travelleth into a country before he hath some entrance into the language, goeth to school, and not to travel. That young men travel under some tutor or grave servant, I allow well, so that he be such a one that hath the language, and hath been in the country before; whereby he may be able to tell them what things are worthy to be seen in the *5* country where they go, what acquaintances they are to seek, what exercises or discipline the place yieldeth; for else young men shall go hooded, and look abroad little. It is a strange thing that in sea voyages, where there is nothing to be seen but sky and sea, men should make diaries, but in land travel, wherein so much is to be observed, for the most part they omit it, as if chance were fitter to be registered than observation. Let diaries, *10* therefore, be brought in use. The things to be seen and observed are the courts of princes, specially when they give audience to ambassadors; the courts of justice, while they sit and hear causes, and so of consistories ecclesiastic; the churches and monasteries, with the monuments which are therein extant; the walls and fortifications of cities and towns, and so the havens and harbours, antiquities and ruins, libraries, *15* colleges, disputations and lectures, where any are; shipping and navies; houses and gardens of state and pleasure, near great cities; armouries, arsenals, magazines, exchanges, burses, warehouses; exercises of horsemanship, fencing, training of soldiers, and the like; comedies, such whereunto the better sort of persons do resort; treasuries of jewels and robes; cabinets and rarities; and, to conclude, whatsoever is memorable in *20* the places where they go; after all which the tutors or servants ought to make diligent

---

23. **witty:** i.e., keen, imaginative. 24. *Abeunt studia in mores:* Studies change into habits; i.e., studies affect character (Ovid); **stond:** impediment, obstacle. 26. **reins:** kidneys. 30-31. *cymini sectores:* cumin-seed splitters, i.e., hairsplitters. 31. **beat over:** hammer away at, reason about. **OF TRAVEL** 4. **allow:** approve. 7. **hooded:** i.e., like a falcon. 18. **burses:** bourses. 19. **comedies:** The term could refer to any plays, or drama in general.

inquiry. As for triumphs, masks, feasts, weddings, funerals, capital executions, and such shows, men need not to be put in mind of them; yet are they not to be neglected. If you will have a young man to put his travel into a little room, and in short time to gather much, this you must do: First, as was said, he must have some entrance into the language before he goeth; then he must have such a servant, or tutor, as knoweth the country, as was likewise said; let him carry with him also some card or book describing the country where he travelleth, which will be a good key to his inquiry. Let him keep also a diary. Let him not stay long in one city or town, more or less as the place deserveth, but not long; nay, when he stayeth in one city or town, let him change his lodging from one end and part of the town to another, which is a great adamant of acquaintance; let him sequester himself from the company of his countrymen, and diet in such places where there is good company of the nation where he travelleth. Let him, upon his removes from one place to another, procure recommendation to some person of quality residing in the place whither he removeth, that he may use his favour in those things he desireth to see or know. Thus he may abridge his travel with much profit. As for the acquaintance which is to be sought in travel, that which is most profitable is acquaintance with the secretaries and employed men of ambassadors, for so in travelling in one country he shall suck the experience of many. Let him also see and visit eminent persons in all kinds, which are of great name abroad, that he may be able to tell how the life agreeth with the fame. For quarrels, they are with care and discretion to be avoided; they are commonly for mistresses, healths, place, and words. And let a man beware how he keepeth company with choleric and quarrelsome persons, for they will engage him into their own quarrels. When a traveller returneth home, let him not leave the countries where he hath travelled altogether behind him, but maintain a correspondence by letters with those of his acquaintance which are of most worth. And let his travel appear rather in his discourse than in his apparel or gesture; and in his discourse let him be rather advised in his answers than forward to tell stories. And let it appear that he doth not change his country manners for those of foreign parts, but only prick in some flowers of that he hath learned abroad into the customs of his own country.

25

30

35

40

45

50

(1625)

from *Novum Organum*
Aphorisms — Book I

[The Idols]

. . . .

38.   The idols and false notions which are now in possession of the human understanding, and have taken deep root therein, not only so beset men's minds that truth can hardly find entrance, but even after entrance obtained, they will again in the

---

27. card: chart, map. **31. adamant:** loadstone, magnet. **42. healths:** drinking of healths, toasts. **49. prick in:** i.e., as one would in needlework. **50. that:** that which, what.   **Novum Organum (*The New Organon*)**   Since Bacon wrote this work in Latin, its inclusion here constitutes an exception among all the other items of "literature in English"; nevertheless, this section of it has become a classic in its own right, an often cited piece of Bacon's thinking which occupies an important place in the history of philosophy and in the growth of modern scientific thought. We base our text on what has become the standard translation, that in Ellis, Spedding, and Heath's mid-nineteenth-century edition of Bacon's works, making only a few minor changes in phrasing and punctuation. **Title:** i.e., in opposition to Aristotle's *Organon*. **1. idols:** (Latin *idolum, idola*; cf. *eidolon*)

very instauration of the sciences meet and trouble us, unless men being forewarned of the danger fortify themselves as far as may be against their assaults.   *5*

39.   There are four classes of idols which beset men's minds. To these for distinction's sake I have assigned names, calling the first class *Idols of the Tribe*; the second, *Idols of the Cave*; the third, *Idols of the Marketplace*; the fourth, *Idols of the Theatre*.

40.   The formation of ideas and axioms by true induction is no doubt the proper remedy to be applied for the keeping off and clearing away of idols. To point them out,   *10* however, is of great use, for the doctrine of idols is to the interpretation of nature what the doctrine of the refutation of sophisms is to common logic.

41.   The Idols of the Tribe have their foundation in human nature itself and in the tribe or race of men. For it is a false assertion that the sense of man is the measure of things. On the contrary, all perceptions as well of the sense as of the mind are according to the   *15* measure of the individual and not according to the measure of the universe. And the human understanding is like a false mirror which, receiving rays irregularly, distorts and discolours the nature of things by mingling its own nature with it.

42.   The Idols of the Cave are the idols of the individual man. For everyone (besides the errors common to human nature in general) has a cave or den of his own, which   *20* refracts and discolours the light of nature, owing either to his own proper and peculiar nature, or to his education and conversation with others, or to the reading of books and the authority of those whom he esteems and admires, or to the differences of impressions accordingly as they take place in a mind preoccupied and predisposed or in a mind indifferent and settled, or the like. So that the spirit of man (according as it is   *25* meted out to different individuals) is in fact a thing variable and full of perturbation, and governed as it were by chance. Whence it was well observed by Heraclitus that men look for sciences in their own lesser worlds and not in the greater or common world.

43.   There are also idols formed by the intercourse and association of men with each other, which I call Idols of the Marketplace on account of the commerce and consort of   *30* men there. For it is by discourse that men associate, and words are imposed according to the apprehension of the vulgar. And therefore the ill and unfit choice of words wonderfully obstructs the understanding. Nor do the definitions or explanations, wherewith in some things learned men are wont to guard and defend themselves, by any means set the matter right. But words plainly force and overrule the understanding, and   *35* throw all into confusion, and lead men away into numberless empty controversies and idle fancies.

44.   Lastly, there are idols which have immigrated into men's minds from the various dogmas of philosophies and also from wrong laws of demonstration. These I call Idols of the Theatre, because in my judgment all the received systems are but so many stage-   *40* plays, representing worlds of their own creation after an unreal and scenic fashion. Nor is it only of the systems now in vogue or only of the ancient sects and philosophies that I speak, for many more plays of the same kind may yet be composed and in like artificial manner set forth, seeing that errors the most widely different have nevertheless causes for the most part alike. Neither again do I mean this only of entire systems, but also of   *45*

---

in logic, false mental images or conceptions; fallacies; phantoms, fancies. **4. instauration:** institution. **12. sophisms:** i.e., logical fallacies. **14:** "Man is the measure of all things," said Protagoras (5th century B.C.). **27. Heraclitus:** See note to line 300 below.

many principles and axioms in science which by tradition, credulity, and negligence have come to be received.

But of these several kinds of idols I must speak more largely and exactly, that the understanding may be duly cautioned.

45.   The human understanding is of its own nature prone to suppose the existence of 50 more order and regularity in the world than it finds. And though there be many things in nature which are singular and unmatched, yet it devises for them parallels and conjugates and relatives which do not exist. Hence the fiction that all celestial bodies move in perfect circles, spirals, and dragons being (except in name) utterly rejected. Hence too the element of fire with its orb is brought in to make up the square with the 55 other three which the sense perceives. Hence also the ratio of density of the so-called elements is arbitrarily fixed at ten to one. And so on of other dreams. And these fancies affect not dogmas only, but simple notions also.

46.   The human understanding when it has once adopted an opinion (either as being the received opinion or as being agreeable to itself) draws all things else to support and 60 agree with it. And though there be a greater number and weight of instances to be found on the other side, yet these it either neglects and despises or else by some distinction sets aside and rejects in order that by this great and pernicious predetermination the authority of its former conclusions may remain inviolate. And therefore it was a good answer that was made by one who, when they showed him 65 hanging in a temple a picture of those who had paid their vows as having escaped shipwreck, and would have him say whether he did not now acknowledge the power of the gods, "Aye," asked he again, "but where are they painted that were drowned after their vows?" And such is the way of all superstition, whether in astrology, dreams, omens, divine judgments, or the like, wherein men, having a delight in such vanities, 70 mark the events where they are fulfilled, but where they fail, though this happen much oftener, neglect and pass them by. But with far more subtlety does this mischief insinuate itself into philosophy and the sciences, in which the first conclusion colours and brings into conformity with itself all that come after, though far sounder and better. Besides, independently of that delight and vanity which I have described, it is the 75 peculiar and perpetual error of the human intellect to be more moved and excited by affirmatives than by negatives, whereas it ought properly to hold itself indifferently disposed towards both alike. Indeed, in the establishment of any true axiom, the negative instance is the more forcible of the two.

47.   The human understanding is moved by those things most which strike and enter 80 the mind simultaneously and suddenly, and so fill the imagination, and then it feigns and supposes all other things to be somehow, though it cannot see how, similar to those few things by which it is surrounded. But for that going to and fro to remote and heterogeneous instances, by which axioms are tried as in the fire, the intellect is altogether slow and unfit, unless it be forced thereto by severe laws and overruling 85 authority.

---

54. dragons: presumably this term refers to some sort of serpentine patterns. **55-56:** Of the supposed four elements — earth, water, air, and fire — fire's "orb" or sphere was outermost and invisible. **65ff:** anecdote related by Cicero about Diagoras, 5th-century B.C. poet and philosopher of Melos, noted for his atheism.

48.   The human understanding is unquiet; it cannot stop or rest, and still presses onward, but in vain. Therefore it is that we cannot conceive of any end or limit to the world, but always as of necessity it occurs to us that there is something beyond. Neither again can it be conceived how eternity has flowed down to the present day, for that *90* distinction which is commonly received of infinity in time past and in time to come can by no means hold, for it would thence follow that one infinity is greater than another, and that infinity is wasting away and tending to become finite. The like subtlety arises touching the infinite divisibility of lines, from the same inability of thought to stop. But this inability interferes more mischievously in the discovery of causes, for although the *95* most general principles in nature ought to be held merely positive, as they are discovered, and cannot with truth be referred to a cause, nevertheless the human understanding, being unable to rest, still seeks something prior in the order of nature. And then it is that in struggling towards that which is further off it falls back upon that which is more nigh at hand, namely on final causes, which have relation clearly to the *100* nature of man rather than to the nature of the universe, and from this source have strangely defiled philosophy. But he is no less an unskilled and shallow philosopher who seeks causes of that which is most general, than he who in things subordinate and subaltern omits to do so.

49.   The human understanding is no dry light, but receives an infusion from the will *105* and affections, whence proceed sciences which may be called "sciences as one would." For what a man had rather were true he more readily believes. Therefore he rejects difficult things from impatience of research; sober things because they narrow hope; the deeper things of nature from superstition; the light of experience from arrogance and pride, lest his mind should seem to be occupied with things mean and transitory; things *110* not commonly believed, out of deference to the opinion of the vulgar. Numberless, in short, are the ways, and sometimes imperceptible, in which the affections colour and infect the understanding.

50.   But by far the greatest hindrance and aberration of the human understanding proceeds from the dullness, incompetency, and deceptions of the senses, in that things *115* which strike the sense outweigh things which do not immediately strike it, though they be more important. Hence it is that speculation commonly ceases where sight ceases, insomuch that of things invisible there is little or no observation. Hence all the working of the spirits enclosed in tangible bodies lies hid and unobserved of men. So also all the more subtle changes in form in the parts of coarser substances (which they commonly *120* call alteration, though it is in truth local motion through exceedingly small spaces) is in like manner unobserved. And yet unless these two things just mentioned be searched out and brought to light, nothing great can be achieved in nature, as far as the production of works is concerned. So again the essential nature of our common air and of all bodies less dense than air (which are very many) is almost unknown. For the sense by itself is a *125* thing infirm and erring; neither can instruments for enlarging or sharpening the senses do much; but all the truer kind of interpretation of nature is effected by instances and

---

100: Aristotle's four causes are the material, the formal, the efficient, and the final. **118-19:** The presence of such spiritual essences was then commonly believed in.

experiments fit and apposite, wherein the sense decides touching the experiment only, and the experiment touching the point in nature and the thing itself.

51.   The human understanding is of its own nature prone to abstractions and gives a *130* substance and reality to things which are fleeting. But to resolve nature into abstractions is less to our purpose than to dissect her into parts, as did the school of Democritus, which went further into nature than the rest. Matter rather than forms should be the object of our attention — its configurations and changes of configurations, and simple action, and law of action or motion — for forms are figments of the human mind, unless *135* you will call those laws of action forms.

52.   Such then are the idols which I call *Idols of the Tribe*, and which take their rise either from the homogeneity of the substance of the human spirit, or from its preoccupation, or from its narrowness, or from its restless motion, or from an infusion of the affections, or from the incompetency of the senses, or from the mode of *140* impression.

53.   The *Idols of the Cave* take their rise in the peculiar constitution, mental or bodily, of each individual, and also in education, habit, and accident. Of this kind there is a great number and variety, but I will instance those the pointing out of which contains the most important caution, and which have most effect in disturbing the clearness of the *145* understanding.

54.   Men become attached to certain particular sciences and speculations, either because they fancy themselves the authors and inventors thereof or because they have bestowed the greatest pains upon them and become most habituated to them. But men of this kind, if they betake themselves to philosophy and contemplations of a general *150* character, distort and colour them in obedience to their former fancies, a thing especially to be noticed in Aristotle, who made his natural philosophy a mere bond-servant to his logic, thereby rendering it contentious and well-nigh useless. The race of chemists again out of a few experiments of the furnace have built up a fantastic philosophy, framed with reference to a few things, and Gilbert, also, after he had employed himself most *155* laboriously in the study and observation of the loadstone, proceeded at once to construct an entire system in accordance with his favourite subject.

55.   There is one principal and as it were radical distinction between different minds in respect of philosophy and the sciences, which is this: that some minds are stronger and apter to mark the differences of things, others to mark their resemblances. The steady *160* and acute mind can fix its contemplations and dwell and fasten on the subtlest distinction; the lofty and discursive mind recognizes and puts together the finest and most general resemblances. Both kinds however easily err in excess, by catching the one at gradations, the other at shadows.

56.   There are found some minds given to an extreme admiration of antiquity, others to *165* an extreme love and appetite for novelty, but few so duly tempered that they can hold the mean, neither carping at what has been well laid down by the ancients nor despising what is well introduced by the moderns. This however turns to the great injury of the

---

132: The physical philosopher Democritus (5th century B.C.) is best known for his primitive atomic theory which he adopted from his master Leucippus (see lines 177 and 299 below). **133. forms:** e.g., for the Pythagoreans, a part of the essential nature of things; for Plato, the "Ideas" or universal principles and truths; for Aristotle, the immanent potential and purpose of things. **153. chemists:** i.e., alchemists. **155-57:** William Gilbert (1540-1603), scientist and court physician, published *De Magnete* (1600).

sciences and philosophy, since these affectations of antiquity and novelty are the humours of partisans rather than judgments, and truth is to be sought for not in the felicity of any age, which is an unstable thing, but in the light of nature and experience, which is eternal. These factions therefore must be abjured, and care must be taken that the intellect be not hurried by them into assent. *170*

57.   Contemplations of nature and of bodies in their simple form break up and distract the understanding, while contemplations of nature and bodies in their composition and *175* configuration overpower and dissolve the understanding — a distinction well seen in the school of Leucippus and Democritus as compared with the other philosophies. For that school is so busied with the particles that it hardly attends to the structure, while the others are so lost in admiration of the structure that they do not penetrate to the simplicity of nature. These kinds of contemplation should therefore be alternated and *180* taken by turns, so that the understanding may be rendered at once penetrating and comprehensive, and the inconveniences above mentioned, with the idols which proceed from them, may be avoided.

58.   Let such then be our provision and contemplative prudence for keeping off and dislodging the *Idols of the Cave*, which grow for the most part either out of the *185* predominance of a favourite subject, or out of an excessive tendency to compare or to distinguish, or out of partiality for particular ages, or out of the largeness or minuteness of the objects contemplated. And generally let every student of nature take this as a rule, that whatever his mind seizes and dwells upon with peculiar satisfaction is to be held in suspicion, and that so much the more care is to be taken in dealing with such questions *190* to keep the understanding even and clear.

59.   But the *Idols of the Marketplace* are the most troublesome of all, idols which have crept into the understanding through the alliances of words and names. For men believe that their reason governs words, but it is also true that words react on the understanding, and this it is that has rendered philosophy and the sciences sophistical and inactive. Now *195* words, being commonly framed and applied according to the capacity of the vulgar, follow those lines of division which are most obvious to the vulgar understanding. And whenever an understanding of greater acuteness or a more diligent observation would alter those lines to suit the true divisions of nature, words stand in the way and resist the change. Whence it comes to pass that the high and formal discussions of learned men *200* end oftentimes in disputes about words and names, with which (according to the use and wisdom of the mathematicians) it would be more prudent to begin, and so by means of definitions reduce them to order. Yet even definitions cannot cure this evil in dealing with natural and material things, since the definitions themselves consist of words, and those words beget others, so that it is necessary to recur to individual instances, and *205* those in due series and order, as I shall say presently when I come to the method and scheme for the formation of notions and axioms.

60.   The idols imposed by words on the understanding are of two kinds. They are either names of things which do not exist (for as there are things left unnamed through lack of observation, so likewise are there names which result from fantastic suppositions and to *210*

193ff.: One result of the distrust of words Bacon elaborates upon in this and the following section was the Royal Society's later insisting upon a clear, plain style; see the excerpt from Thomas Sprat's *History* (p. 455).

which nothing in reality corresponds) or they are names of things which exist, but yet confused and ill-defined and hastily and irregularly derived from realities. Of the former kind are Fortune, the Prime Mover, Planetary Orbits, Element of Fire, and like fictions which owe their origin to false and idle theories. And this class of idols is more easily expelled, because to get rid of them it is only necessary that all theories should be steadily rejected and dismissed as obsolete. *215*

But the other class, which springs out of a faulty and unskilful abstraction, is intricate and deeply rooted. Let us take for example such a word as *humid*, and see how far the several things which the word is used to signify agree with each other, and we shall find the word *humid* to be nothing else than a mark loosely and confusedly applied to denote a variety of actions which will not bear to be reduced to any constant meaning. *220* For it both signifies that which easily spreads itself round any other body, and that which in itself is indeterminate and cannot solidize, and that which readily yields in every direction, and that which easily divides and scatters itself, and that which easily unites and collects itself, and that which readily flows and is put in motion, and that *225* which readily clings to another body and wets it, and that which is easily reduced to a liquid, or being solid easily melts. Accordingly, when you come to apply the word, if you take it in one sense, flame is humid; if in another, air is not humid; if in another, fine dust is humid; if in another, glass is humid. So that it is easy to see that the notion is taken by abstraction only from water and common and ordinary liquids without any due *230* verification.

There are however in words certain degrees of distortion and error. One of the least faulty kinds is that of names of substances, especially of lowest species and well-deduced (for the notion of *chalk* and of *mud* is good, of *earth* bad); a more faulty kind is that of actions, as *to generate*, *to corrupt*, *to alter*; the most faulty is of qualities (except *235* such as are the immediate objects of the sense), as *heavy*, *light*, *rare*, *dense*, and the like. Yet in all these cases some notions are of necessity a little better than others, in proportion to the greater variety of subjects that fall within the range of the human sense.

61.   But the *Idols of the Theatre* are not innate, nor do they steal into the understanding *240* secretly, but are plainly impressed and received into the mind from the play-books of philosophical systems and the perverted rules of demonstrations. To attempt refutations in this case would be merely inconsistent with what I have already said, for since we agree neither upon principles nor upon demonstrations, there is no place for argument. And this is so far well, inasmuch as it leaves the honour of the ancients untouched. For *245* they are no wise disparaged, the question between them and me being only as to the way. For as the saying is, the lame man who keeps the right road outstrips the runner who takes a wrong one. Nay, it is obvious that when a man runs the wrong way, the more active and swift he is the further he will go astray.

But the course I propose for the discovery of sciences is such as leaves but little to *250* the acuteness and strength of wits, but places all wits and understandings nearly on a level. For as in the drawing of a straight line or a perfect circle much depends on the

---

213. **Prime Mover:** primum mobile, in the Ptolemaic system the outermost sphere, which makes the others move (for this and the following item, see *Ptolemaic* in the Glossary); **Planetary Orbits:** the inner spheres in which the various planets are fixed; **Element of Fire:** see note to 55-56 above.

steadiness and practice of the hand, if it be done by aim of hand only, but if with the aid of rule or compass, little or nothing; so is it exactly with my plan. But though particular confutations would be of no avail, yet touching the sects and general divisions of such 255 systems I must say something, something also touching the external signs which show that they are unsound, and finally something touching the causes of such great infelicity and of such lasting and general agreement in error, so that the access to truth may be made less difficult and the human understanding may the more willingly submit to its purgation and dismiss its idols.　　　　　260

62.　Idols of the Theatre, or of Systems, are many, and there can be and perhaps will be yet many more. For were it not that now for many ages men's minds have been busied with religion and theology, and were it not that civil governments, especially monarchies, have been averse to such novelties, even in matters speculative, so that men labour therein to the peril and harming of their fortunes, not only unrewarded but 265 exposed also to contempt and envy, doubtless there would have arisen many other philosophical sects like to those which in great variety flourished once among the Greeks. For as on the phenomena of the heavens many hypotheses may be constructed, so likewise (and more also) many various dogmas may be set up and established on the phenomena of philosophy. And in the plays of this philosophical theatre you may 270 observe the same thing which is found in the theatre of the poets, that stories invented for the stage are more compact and elegant, and more as one would wish them to be, than true stories out of history.

In general however there is taken for the material of philosophy either a great deal out of a few things, or a very little out of many things, so that on both sides philosophy 275 is based on too narrow a foundation of experiment and natural history, and decides on the authority of too few cases. For the Rational School of philosophers snatches from experience a variety of common instances, neither duly ascertained nor diligently examined and weighed, and leaves all the rest to meditation and agitation of wit.

There is also another class of philosophers, who having bestowed much diligent and 280 careful labour on a few experiments, have thence made bold to educe and construct systems, wresting all other facts in a strange fashion to conformity therewith.

And there is yet a third class, consisting of those who out of faith and veneration mix their philosophy with theology and traditions, among whom the vanity of some has gone so far aside as to seek the origin of sciences among spirits and genii. So that this 285 parent stock of errors — this false philosophy — is of three kinds: the Sophistical, the Empirical, and the Superstitious.

63.　The most conspicuous example of the first class was Aristotle, who corrupted natural philosophy by his logic, fashioning the world out of categories, assigning to the human soul, the noblest of substances, a genus from words of the second intention, 290 doing the business of density and rarity (which is to make bodies of greater or less dimensions, that is, occupy greater or less space) by the frigid distinction of act and power, asserting that single bodies have each a single and proper motion, and that if they participate in any other, then this results from an external cause, and imposing

---

289: Aristotle's ten categories are substance, quality, quantity, relation, time, place, action, position, condition, passivity (the state of being acted upon). **290. words . . . intention:** i.e., discussions of discussions of things, at one remove from examining the thing itself.

countless other arbitrary restrictions on the nature of things, being always more *295*
solicitous to provide an answer to the question and affirm something positive in words
than about the inner truth of things, a failing best shown when his philosophy is
compared with other systems of note among the Greeks. For the Homœomera of
Anaxagoras, the Atoms of Leucippus and Democritus, the Heaven and Earth of
Parmenides, the Strife and Friendship of Empedocles, Heraclitus's doctrine how bodies *300*
are resolved into the indifferent nature of fire, and remoulded into solids, have all of
them some taste of the natural philosopher, some savour of the nature of things, and
experience, and bodies; whereas in the physics of Aristotle you hear hardly anything but
the words of logic, which in his metaphysics also, under a more imposing name, and
more forsooth as a realist than a nominalist, he has handled over again. Nor let any *305*
weight be given to the fact that in his books on animals and his problems and other of
his treatises there is frequent dealing with experiments. For he had come to his
conclusion before; he did not consult experience, as he should have done, in order to the
framing of his decisions and axioms, but having first determined the question according
to his will, he then resorts to experience, and bending her into conformity with his *310*
placets leads her about like a captive in a procession, so that even on this count he is
more guilty than his modern followers, the schoolmen, who have abandoned experience
altogether.

64.   But the Empirical school of philosophy gives birth to dogmas more deformed and
monstrous than the Sophistical or Rational school. For it has its foundations not in the *315*
light of common notions (which though it be a faint and superficial light, is yet in a
manner universal, and has reference to many things) but in the narrowness and darkness
of a few experiments. To those therefore who are daily busied with these experiments,
and have infected their imagination with them, such a philosophy seems probable and
all but certain; to all men else incredible and vain. Of this there is a notable instance in *320*
the alchemists and their dogmas, though it is hardly to be found elsewhere in these
times, except perhaps in the philosophy of Gilbert. Nevertheless, with regard to
philosophies of this kind there is one caution not to be omitted, for I foresee that if ever
men are roused by my admonitions to betake themselves seriously to experiment and
bid farewell to sophistical doctrines, then indeed through the premature hurry of the *325*
understanding to leap or fly to universals and principles of things, great danger may be
apprehended from philosophies of this kind, against which evil we ought even now to
prepare.

65.   But the corruption of philosophy by superstition and an admixture of theology is
far more widely spread, and does the greatest harm whether to entire systems or to their *330*
parts. For the human understanding is obnoxious to the influence of the imagination no
less than to the influence of common notions. For the contentious and sophistical kind

---

298. Homœomera: Aristotle's name for the *spermata* or "seeds" which Anaxagoras (5th century B.C.) proposed as the constituent elements of everything. **300:** Parmenides (6th-5th century B.C.) discounted sense impressions in favour of reason, and referred to the belief that everything came from the contrasting "forms" of (a) heavenly fire or light and (b) heavy, earthly night or darkness; Empedocles (c.490-c.430 B.C.) claimed that the opposing forces of Love and Strife, acting upon the four elements or "roots," caused the creation and destruction of all things; Heraclitus (c.540-c.475 B.C.) held that everything is in flux, and that the universal substance was — or was like — fire, itself a process of change. **310-11. his placets:** i.e., that which pleases him (from Latin *placet*, "it pleases"; hence the conventional meaning of *placet* to mean "expression or vote of assent"). **322. Gilbert:** See 155-57, and note, above.

of philosophy ensnares the understanding, but this kind, being fanciful and tumid and half poetical, misleads it more by flattery. For there is in man an ambition of the understanding no less than of the will, especially in high and lofty spirits.   *335*

Of this kind we have among the Greeks a striking example in Pythagoras, though he united with it a coarser and more cumbrous superstition; another in Plato and his school, more dangerous and subtle. It shows itself likewise in parts of other philosophies, in the introduction of abstract forms and final causes and first causes, with the omission in most cases of causes intermediate, and the like. Upon this point the greatest caution   *340* should be used. For nothing is so mischievous as the apotheosis of error, and it is a very plague of the understanding for vanity to become the object of veneration. Yet in this vanity some of the moderns have with extreme levity indulged so far as to attempt to found a system of natural philosophy on the first chapter of Genesis, on the book of Job, and other parts of the sacred writings, seeking for the dead among the living, which also   *345* makes the inhibitions and repression of it the more important, because from this unwholesome mixture of things human and divine there arises not only a fantastic philosophy but also an heretical religion. Very meet it is therefore that we be sober-minded, and give to faith that only which is faith's.

. . . .

68.   So much concerning the several classes of idols and their equipage, all of which   *350* must be renounced and put away with a fixed and solemn determination, and the understanding thoroughly freed and cleansed — the entrance into the kingdom of man, founded on the sciences, being not much other than the entrance into the kingdom of heaven, whereinto none may enter except as a little child.

. . . .

(1620)

SAMUEL DANIEL
England, 1563-1619

Sonnets from *DELIA*

VI

Fair is my love, and cruel as she's fair;
Her brow shades frowns, although her eyes are sunny;
Her smiles are lightning, though her pride despair,
And her disdains are gall, her favours honey.
    A modest maid decked with a blush of honour,   *5*
Whose feet do tread green paths of youth and love;
The wonder of all eyes that look upon her,
Sacred on earth, designed a saint above.
    Chastity and Beauty, which were deadly foes,
Live reconciled friends within her brow;   *10*
And had she Pity to conjoin with those,
Then who had heard the plaints I utter now?
    O had she not been fair and thus unkind,
    My muse had slept, and none had known my mind.

---

345. seeking . . . living: Cf. Luke 24:5. **353-54:** See Matthew 18:3.   **DELIA**   The identity of "Delia" is not known, if indeed she is intended for a real woman; it may be that Daniel simply means to honour his patroness, the Countess of Pembroke (see p. 210).

XIII

Behold what hap Pygmalion had to frame,
And carve his proper grief upon a stone;
My heavy fortune is much like the same:
I work on flint, and that's the cause I moan.
    For hapless, lo even with mine own desires,   *5*
I figured on the table of my heart
The fairest form the world's eye admires,
And so did perish by my proper art.
    And still I toil to change the marble breast
Of her whose sweetest grace I do adore,   *10*
Yet cannot find her breathe unto my rest;
Hard is her heart and woe is me therefore.
    O happy he that joyed his stone and art;
    Unhappy I to love a stony heart.

XXIX

O why doth Delia credit so her glass,
Gazing her beauty deigned her by the skies,
And doth not rather look on him (alas!)
Whose state best shows the force of murthering eyes?
    The broken tops of lofty trees declare   *5*
The fury of a mercy-wanting storm;

And of what force your wounding graces are,
Upon myself you best may find the form.
    Then leave your glass, and gaze yourself on me;
That mirror shows what power is in your face;   *10*
To view your form too much may danger be:
Narcissus changed t'a flower in such a case.
    And you are changed, but not t'a hyacint;
    I fear your eye hath turned your heart to flint.

XXXIII

When men shall find thy flower, thy glory pass,
And thou with careful brow sitting alone,
Received hast this message from thy glass,
That tells thee truth, and says that all is gone,
    Fresh shalt thou see in me the wounds thou madest,   *5*
Though spent thy flame, in me the heat remaining;
I that have loved thee thus before thou fadest,
My faith shall wax when thou art in thy waning.
    The world shall find this miracle in me,
That fire can burn when all the matter's spent;   *10*
Then what my faith hath been thyself shalt see,
And that thou wast unkind thou mayst repent.
    Thou mayst repent that thou has scorned my tears,
    When winter snows upon thy golden hairs.

(1592)

MICHAEL DRAYTON
England, 1563-1631

TO THE VIRGINIAN VOYAGE

You brave heroic minds,
Worthy your country's name,
    That honour still pursue,
    Go, and subdue,
Whilst loit'ring hinds   *5*
Lurk here at home, with shame.

Britons, you stay too long;
Quickly aboard bestow you,
    And with a merry gale

    Swell your stretched sail,   *10*
With vows as strong
As the winds that blow you.

Your course securely steer,
West and by south forth keep;
    Rocks, lee-shores, nor shoals,   *15*
    When Æolus scowls,
You need not fear,
So absolute the deep.

SONNET XIII **1. Pygmalion:** legendary king of Cyprus who made a statue of a woman and fell in love with it; Aphrodite brought the statue to life as Galatea. SONNET XXIX **12-13:** In Greek myth, Narcissus fell in love with his own reflection in water and was later changed into the flower that bears his name, and Hyacinthus was a beautiful youth accidentally killed by Apollo and from whose blood sprang the flower of his name. TO THE VIRGINIAN VOYAGE Announced in April, 1606, the expedition of three ships sailed in December. **5. hinds:** servants, rustics, boors. **16. Æolus:** in Greek myth, keeper of the winds.

And cheerfully at sea,
Success you still entice   20
   To get the pearl and gold,
   And ours to hold,
Virginia,
Earth's only paradise,

Where nature hath in store   25
Fowl, venison, and fish,
   And the fruitfull'st soil,
   Without your toil,
Three harvests more,
All greater than you wish.   30

And the ambitious vine
Crowns with his purple mass
   The cedar reaching high
   To kiss the sky,
The cypress, pine,   35
And useful sassafras.

To whose the golden age
Still nature's laws doth give,
   No other care that tend
   But them to defend   40
From winter's age,
That long there doth not live.

When as the luscious smell
Of that delicious land,
   Above the seas that flows   45
   The clear wind throws,
Your hearts to swell,
Approaching the dear strand.

In kenning of the shore
(Thanks to God first given),   50
   O you the happiest men,
   Be frolic then,
Let cannons roar,
Frighting the wide heaven.

And in regions far   55
Such heroes bring ye forth

As those from whom we came,
   And plant our name
Under that star
Not known unto our north.   60

And as there plenty grows
Of laurel everywhere,
   Apollo's sacred tree,
   You it may see
A poet's brows   65
To crown, that may sing there.

Thy voyages attend,
Industrious Hakluyt,
   Whose reading shall inflame
   Men to seek fame,   70
And much commend
To after-times thy wit.

               (1606)

Sonnets from *IDEA*

12

As other men, so I myself do muse
Why in this sort I wrest invention so,
And why these giddy metaphors I use;
Leaving the path the greater part do go.
I will resolve you: I am lunatic,   5
And ever this in madmen you shall find,
What they last thought of, when the brain grew sick,
In most distraction they keep that in mind.
Thus talking idly in this bedlam fit,
Reason and I, you must conceive, are twain;   10
'Tis nine years now since first I lost my wit;
Bear with me, then, though troubled be my brain.
   With diet and correction, men distraught
   (Not too far past) may to their wits be brought.

               (1600)

68: Richard Hakluyt was the compiler of *The Principal Navigations, Voyages, Traffics, and Discoveries of the English Nation* (see pp. 117, 168). **IDEA** In "Idea," Drayton honours his close friend, Anne Goodere.

61

Since there's no help, come, let us kiss and part.
Nay, I have done; you get no more of me;
And I am glad, yea glad with all my heart,
That thus so cleanly I myself can free.
Shake hands forever, cancel all our vows,   *5*
And when we meet at any time again,
Be it not seen in either of our brows
That we one jot of former love retain.

Now at the last gasp of Love's latest breath,
When, his pulse failing, Passion speechless lies,   *10*
When Faith is kneeling by his bed of death,
And Innocence is closing up his eyes,
  Now if thou wouldst, when all have given him
    over,
  From death to life thou mightst him yet recover.

(1619)

CHRISTOPHER MARLOWE
England, 1564-1593

THE PASSIONATE SHEPHERD TO HIS LOVE

Come live with me, and be my love,
And we will all the pleasures prove
That valleys, groves, hills, and fields,
Woods, or steepy mountain yields.

And we will sit upon the rocks,   *5*
Seeing the shepherds feed their flocks
By shallow rivers, to whose falls
Melodious birds sing madrigals.

And I will make thee beds of roses,
And a thousand fragrant posies;   *10*
A cap of flowers, and a kirtle
Embroidered all with leaves of myrtle;

A gown made of the finest wool,
Which from our pretty lambs we pull;
Fair lined slippers for the cold,   *15*
With buckles of the purest gold;

A belt of straw and ivy buds,
With coral clasps and amber studs.
And if these pleasures may thee move,
Come live with me, and be my love.   *20*

The shepherds' swains shall dance and sing
For thy delight each May morning;
If these delights thy mind may move,
Then live with me, and be my love.

(1600)

WILLIAM SHAKESPEARE
England, 1564-1616

from Sonnets

18

Shall I compare thee to a summer's day?
Thou art more lovely and more temperate.

Rough winds do shake the darling buds of May,
And summer's lease hath all too short a date.
Sometime too hot the eye of heaven shines,   *5*

THE PASSIONATE SHEPHERD Cf. Ralegh's "The Nymph's Reply to the Shepherd" (p. 173) and Donne's "The Bait" (p. 255); see also Walton's *The Compleat Angler* (pp. 295-97). **2. prove:** experience.   **SONNETS** Shakespeare's works, like the Bible and the works of

And often is his gold complexion dimmed;
And every fair from fair sometime declines,
By chance or nature's changing course untrimmed.
But thy eternal summer shall not fade,
Nor lose possession of that fair thou ow'st,   *10*
Nor shall Death brag thou wander'st in his shade
When in eternal lines to time thou grow'st.
   So long as men can breathe, or eyes can see,
   So long lives this, and this gives life to thee.

29

When in disgrace with fortune and men's eyes
I all alone beweep my outcast state,
And trouble deaf heaven with my bootless cries,
And look upon myself and curse my fate,
Wishing me like to one more rich in hope,   *5*
Featured like him, like him with friends possessed,
Desiring this man's art and that man's scope,
With what I most enjoy contented least,
Yet in these thoughts myself almost despising,
Haply I think on thee, and then my state,   *10*
Like to the lark at break of day arising
From sullen earth, sings hymns at heaven's gate,
   For thy sweet love remembered such wealth brings
   That then I scorn to change my state with kings.

30

When to the sessions of sweet silent thought
I summon up remembrance of things past,
I sigh the lack of many a thing I sought,
And with old woes new wail my dear time's waste.
Then can I drown an eye, unused to flow,   *5*
For precious friends hid in death's dateless night,
And weep afresh love's long since cancelled woe,
And moan the expense of many a vanished sight.
Then can I grieve at grievances foregone,
And heavily from woe to woe tell o'er   *10*
The sad account of forebemoaned moan,
Which I new pay as if not paid before.
   But if the while I think on thee, dear friend,
   All losses are restored and sorrows end.

33

Full many a glorious morning have I seen
Flatter the mountaintops with sovereign eye,
Kissing with golden face the meadows green,
Gilding pale streams with heavenly alchemy,
Anon permit the basest clouds to ride   *5*
With ugly rack on his celestial face,
And from the forlorn world his visage hide,
Stealing unseen to west with this disgrace.
Even so my sun one early morn did shine
With all-triumphant splendour on my brow.   *10*
But out, alack! he was but one hour mine;
The region cloud hath masked him from me now.
   Yet him for this my love no whit disdaineth.
   Suns of the world may stain when heaven's sun
     staineth.

55

Not marble, nor the gilded monuments
Of princes shall outlive this powerful rhyme;
But you shall shine more bright in these contents
Than unswept stone, besmeared with sluttish time.
When wasteful war shall statues overturn,   *5*
And broils root out the work of masonry,
Nor Mars his sword nor war's quick fire shall burn
The living record of your memory.
'Gainst death and all-oblivious enmity
Shall you pace forth. Your praise shall still find room *10*
Even in the eyes of all posterity
That wear this world out to the ending doom.
   So, till the judgment that yourself arise,
   You live in this, and dwell in lovers' eyes.

65

Since brass, nor stone, nor earth, nor boundless sea
But sad mortality o'ersways their power,
How with this rage shall beauty hold a plea,
Whose action is no stronger than a flower?
O how shall summer's honey breath hold out   *5*
Against the wrackful siege of battering days
When rocks impregnable are not so stout,
Nor gates of steel so strong, but Time decays?

Milton and numerous other writers, have furnished many subsequent writers with titles; phrases in these sonnets, e.g."the darling buds of May" (18), "summer's lease" (18), "fortune and men's eyes" (29), and "remembrance of things past" (30), have become titles of 20th-century works by H. E. Bates, John Mortimer, John Herbert, and Marcel Proust (in the standard English translation).   **SONNET 18** **7. fair** (1, n.): fair one, beautiful one, beauty; **fair** (2): beautiful (adj.) or beauty (n.) (cf. Spenser's sonnet 79, p. 162). **8. untrimmed:** stripped of ornament or beauty. **10. ow'st:** ownest.   **SONNET 30** **1. sessions:** i.e., of a law court. **6. dateless:** endless. **8. expense:** loss. **9. foregone:** gone before, past. **10. tell:** count.   **SONNET 55** **7. Mars his:** Mars's. **12. ending doom:** Judgment Day (see also sonnet 116, below).

O fearful meditation! Where, alack,
Shall Time's best jewel from Time's chest lie hid?　　*10*
Or what strong hand can hold his swift foot back?
Or who his spoil of beauty can forbid?
　　O none, unless this miracle have might,
　　That in black ink my love may still shine bright.

71

No longer mourn for me when I am dead
Than you shall hear the surly sullen bell
Give warning to the world that I am fled
From this vile world, with vilest worms to dwell.
Nay, if you read this line, remember not　　*5*
The hand that writ it, for I love you so
That I in your sweet thoughts would be forgot
If thinking on me then should make you woe.
O, if, I say, you look upon this verse
When I perhaps compounded am with clay,　　*10*
Do not so much as my poor name rehearse,
But let your love even with my life decay,
　　Lest the wise world should look into your moan,
　　And mock you with me after I am gone.

73

That time of year thou mayst in me behold
When yellow leaves, or none, or few, do hang
Upon those boughs which shake against the cold,
Bare ruined choirs where late the sweet birds sang.
In me thou see'st the twilight of such day　　*5*
As after sunset fadeth in the west,
Which by and by black night doth take away,
Death's second self, that seals up all in rest.
In me thou see'st the glowing of such fire
That on the ashes of his youth doth lie,　　*10*
As the death-bed whereon it must expire,
Consumed with that which it was nourished by.
　　This thou perceiv'st, which makes thy love more strong,
　　To love that well which thou must leave ere long.

94

They that have power to hurt and will do none,
That do not do the thing they most do show,
Who, moving others, are themselves as stone,

Unmoved, cold, and to temptation slow;
They rightly do inherit heaven's graces,　　*5*
And husband nature's riches from expense;
They are the lords and owners of their faces,
Others but stewards of their excellence.
The summer's flower is to the summer sweet,
Though to itself it only live and die;　　*10*
But if that flower with base infection meet,
The basest weed outbraves his dignity:
　　For sweetest things turn sourest by their deeds;
　　Lilies that fester smell far worse than weeds.

97

How like a winter hath my absence been
From thee, the pleasure of the fleeting year!
What freezings have I felt, what dark days seen!
What old December's bareness everywhere!
And yet this time removed was summer's time,　　*5*
The teeming autumn, big with rich increase,
Bearing the wanton burthen of the prime,
Like widowed wombs after their lords' decease.
Yet this abundant issue seemed to me
But hope of orphans and unfathered fruit,　　*10*
For summer and his pleasure wait on thee,
And, thou away, the very birds are mute;
　　Or if they sing, 'tis with so dull a cheer
　　That leaves look pale, dreading the winter's near.

98

From you have I been absent in the spring,
When proud-pied April, dressed in all his trim,
Hath put a spirit of youth in everything,
That heavy Saturn laughed and leaped with him.
Yet nor the lays of birds, nor the sweet smell　　*5*
Of different flowers in odour and in hue,
Could make me any summer's story tell,
Or from their proud lap pluck them where they grew;
Nor did I wonder at the lily's white,
Nor praise the deep vermilion in the rose;　　*10*
They were but sweet, but figures of delight,
Drawn after you, you pattern of all those.
　　Yet seemed it winter still and, you away,
　　As with your shadow I with these did play.

SONNET 71　2. bell: death bell, or passing bell — one ring for each year of a parishioner's life (see Donne's Meditations XVI and XVII, pp. 260-62).　**SONNET 94　2. show:** appear capable of. **6. expense:** waste, loss, unnecessary expenditure.　**SONNET 98　4. That:** so that; **heavy:** dull, sad, gloomy, morose — i.e. *saturnine* (alchemists and astrologers associated the planet Saturn with lead, and thought it a bad sign to be born under).

106

When in the chronicle of wasted time
I see descriptions of the fairest wights,
And beauty making beautiful old rhyme
In praise of ladies dead and lovely knights,
Then, in the blazon of sweet beauty's best,   5
Of hand, of foot, of lip, of eye, of brow,
I see their antique pen would have expressed
Even such a beauty as you master now.
So all their praises are but prophecies
Of this our time, all you prefiguring;   10
And, for they looked but with divining eyes,
They had not skill enough your worth to sing.
    For we, which now behold these present days,
    Have eyes to wonder, but lack tongues to praise.

116

Let me not to the marriage of true minds
Admit impediments. Love is not love
Which alters when it alteration finds,
Or bends with the remover to remove.
Oh no! It is an ever-fixed mark   5
That looks on tempests and is never shaken;
It is the star to every wandering bark,
Whose worth's unknown, although his height be taken.
Love's not Time's fool, though rosy lips and cheeks
Within his bending sickle's compass come;   10
Love alters not with his brief hours and weeks,
But bears it out even to the edge of doom.
    If this be error and upon me proved,
    I never writ, nor no man ever loved.

129

The expense of spirit in a waste of shame
Is lust in action, and till action, lust
Is perjured, murderous, bloody, full of blame,
Savage, extreme, rude, cruel, not to trust;
Enjoyed no sooner but despised straight;   5
Past reason hunted, and no sooner had,
Past reason hated, as a swallowed bait,
On purpose laid to make the taker mad;

Mad in pursuit, and in possession so;
Had, having, and in quest to have, extreme,   10
A bliss in proof, and proved, a very woe;
Before, a joy proposed; behind, a dream.
    All this the world well knows, yet none knows well
    To shun the heaven that leads men to this hell.

130

My mistress' eyes are nothing like the sun;
Coral is far more red than her lips' red.
If snow be white, why then her breasts are dun;
If hairs be wires, black wires grow on her head.
I have seen roses damasked, red and white,   5
But no such roses see I in her cheeks;
And in some perfumes is there more delight
Than in the breath that from my mistress reeks.
I love to hear her speak, yet well I know
That music hath a far more pleasing sound.   10
I grant I never saw a goddess go;
My mistress when she walks treads on the ground.
    And yet, by heaven, I think my love as rare
    As any she belied with false compare.

146

Poor soul, the centre of my sinful earth,
[   ] these rebel powers that thee array,
Why dost thou pine within and suffer dearth,
Painting thy outward walls so costly gay?
Why so large cost, having so short a lease,   5
Dost thou upon thy fading mansion spend?
Shall worms, inheritors of this excess,
Eat up thy charge? Is this thy body's end?
Then, soul, live thou upon thy servant's loss,
And let that pine to aggravate thy store;   10
Buy terms divine in selling hours of dross;
Within be fed, without be rich no more.
    So shalt thou feed on Death, that feeds on men,
    And Death once dead, there's no more dying then.
                              (1590's; 1609)

SONNET 106   **11. for:** for the reason that, because.   SONNET 116   **1-2:** Cf. the marriage ceremony in the Book of Common Prayer: "If any of you know cause, or just impediment, why these two persons should not be joined together in holy matrimony, ye are to declare it." **5. mark:** i.e., seamark, landmark.   SONNET 130   **8. reeks:** is emitted, emanates. **11. go:** walk.   SONNET 146   **2:** A compositor erred here in setting type for the Quarto, repeating "My sinful earth" from line 1; scholars and students have offered many suggestions for the necessary two syllables, among them *Bearing, Feeding, Starved by, Slave of, Thrall to, Lord of, Gulled by, Fooled by, Tricked by*; you may wish to weigh the relative aptness or other virtues of these and any others you may think of.

Songs from Plays

Spring

When daisies pied and violets blue
 And lady-smocks all silver-white
And cuckoo-buds of yellow hue
 Do paint the meadows with delight,
The cuckoo then, on every tree,   5
Mocks married men; for thus sings he:
    Cuckoo,
Cuckoo, cuckoo — Oh, word of fear,
Unpleasing to a married ear!

When shepherds pipe on oaten straws,   10
 And merry larks are ploughmen's clocks,
When turtles tread, and rooks, and daws,
 And maidens bleach their summer smocks,
The cuckoo then, on every tree,
Mocks married men; for thus sings he: 15
    Cuckoo,
Cuckoo, cuckoo — Oh, word of fear,
Unpleasing to a married ear.

Winter

When icicles hang by the wall,
 And Dick the shepherd blows his nail, 20
And Tom bears logs into the hall,
 And milk comes frozen home in pail,
When blood is nipped and ways be foul,
Then nightly sings the staring owl,
    Tu-whit,   25
Tu-who, a merry note,
While greasy Joan doth keel the pot.

When all aloud the wind doth blow,
 And coughing drowns the parson's saw,
And birds sit brooding in the snow,   30
 And Marian's nose looks red and raw,
When roasted crabs hiss in the bowl,
Then nightly sings the staring owl,
    Tu-whit,
Tu-who, a merry note,   35
While greasy Joan doth keel the pot.

"Fear no more the heat o' the sun"

Fear no more the heat o' the sun,
 Nor the furious winter's rages;
Thou thy worldly task hast done,
 Home art gone and ta'en thy wages.
Golden lads and girls all must,   5
As chimney-sweepers, come to dust.

Fear no more the frown o' the great;
 Thou art past the tyrant's stroke;
Care no more to clothe and eat;
 To thee the reed is as the oak.   10
The sceptre, learning, physic, must
All follow this, and come to dust.

Fear no more the lightning flash,
 Nor the all-dreaded thunder-stone;
Fear not slander, censure rash;   15
 Thou hast finished joy and moan:
All lovers young, all lovers must
Consign to thee, and come to dust.

No exorciser harm thee!
 Nor no witchcraft charm thee!   20
Ghost unlaid forbear thee!
 Nothing ill come near thee!
Quiet consummation have,
And renowned be thy grave!

"Full fathom five"

Full fathom five thy father lies;
Of his bones are coral made;
Those are pearls that were his eyes:
Nothing of him that doth fade,
But doth suffer a sea-change   5
Into something rich and strange.
Sea-nymphs hourly ring his knell:
Ding-dong.
Hark! now I hear them — Ding-dong, bell.

SPRING   WINTER   Sung at the end of *Love's Labour's Lost* (1595). **2. lady-smocks:** cuckoo-flowers. **3. cuckoo-buds:** buttercups or the like. **9:** because the bird's name bears associations with cuckoldry. **10. oaten straws:** oat-reed pipes; see Spenser's "Januarye," line 72 (p. 149). **11:** because larks sing at sunrise, and early-risers are said to be "up with the lark" or to "rise with the lark" (see sonnet 29 above). **12. turtles tread:** turtledoves mate. **20. blows his nail:** idly passes the time by warming cold fingers. **27. keel:** cool, as by stirring, to prevent its boiling over. **32. crabs:** crabapples.   **FEAR NO MORE**   Sung in IV.ii of *Cymbeline* (c.1610) for Imogen, thought to be dead. **6. as:** like. **11. sceptre, learning, physic:** rulers, scholars, physicians. **14. thunder-stone:** thunderbolt (various kinds of stones, such as meteorites, were thought to accompany or even cause thunder). **18. consign to thee:** perhaps "submit like thee."   **FULL FATHOM FIVE**   Sung in I.ii of *The Tempest* (1611) by invisible Ariel to Ferdinand, misleading him about his father's supposed drowning.

KING JAMES I
Scotland/England, 1566-1625

from *AMATORIA*

Sonnet 8

As man, a man am I composed all
Of brethren four which did this world compone,
Yet unto me doth such a chance befall
As I of mankind all am he alone
Who of the four possesseth only one.   *5*
My flames of love to fiery heaven be past;
My air in sighs evanished is and gone;
My moisture into tears distilling fast;
Now only earth remains with me at last,
That am denuded of the other three.   *10*
Then cruel Dame, since unto such a cast
Your only beauty thus compelleth me,
    Send all my earth, with earth for to remain,
    Or else restore me to my self again.

                                                    (publ. 1911)

THOMAS NASHE
England, 1567-1601

"Adieu, farewell, earth's bliss"

Adieu, farewell, earth's bliss;
This world uncertain is;
Fond are life's lustful joys;
Death proves them all but toys;
None from his darts can fly.   *5*
I am sick, I must die.
    Lord, have mercy on us!

Rich men, trust not in wealth;
Gold cannot buy you health;
Physic himself must fade;   *10*
All things to end are made.
The plague full swift goes by;
I am sick, I must die.
    Lord, have mercy on us!

Beauty is but a flower   *15*
Which wrinkles will devour;
Brightness falls from the air;
Queens have died young and fair;
Dust hath closed Helen's eye.
I am sick, I must die.   *20*
    Lord, have mercy on us!

Strength stoops unto the grave;
Worms feed on Hector brave;
Swords may not fight with fate;
Earth still holds ope her gate.   *25*
"Come, come!" the bells do cry.
    I am sick, I must die.
    Lord, have mercy on us!

SONNET 8   **2. compone:** compose.   **ADIEU, FAREWELL, EARTH'S BLISS**   This poem is also commonly known as "A Litany in Time of Plague"; probably written during the plague of 1592, and included in the comedy *Summer's Last Will and Testament*. For the paradigm this poem follows, see *The Litany* in the Church of England's *Book of Common Prayer* (first issued 1549). See also Dunbar's "Lament for the Makaris" (p. 110). **3. Fond:** foolish. **4. toys:** trifles. **10. Physic:** the profession of medicine. **19. Helen:** Helen of Troy, known for her great beauty. **23. Hector:** Trojan hero in Homer's *Iliad*. **26. bells:** passing bells, death bells (see Donne's Meditations XVI and XVII, pp. 260-62).

Wit with his wantonness
Tasteth death's bitterness;   30
Hell's executioner
Hath no ears for to hear
What vain art can reply.
I am sick, I must die.
    Lord, have mercy on us!   35

Haste, therefore, each degree,
To welcome destiny;
Heaven is our heritage,
Earth but a player's stage;
Mount we unto the sky.   40
I am sick, I must die.
    Lord, have mercy on us!
                  (c. 1592; 1600)

Thomas Campion
England, 1567-1620

"My sweetest Lesbia"

My sweetest Lesbia, let us live and love,
And though the sager sort our deeds reprove,
Let us not weigh them; heav'n's great lamps do dive
Into their west, and straight again revive,
But soon as once set is our little light,   5
Then must we sleep one ever-during night.
If all would lead their lives in love like me,
Then bloody swords and armour should not be;
No drum nor trumpet peaceful sleeps should move,
Unless alarm came from the camp of love.   10
But fools do live, and waste their little light,
And seek with pain their ever-during night.
When timely death my life and fortune ends,
Let not my hearse be vexed with mourning friends,
But let all lovers rich in triumph come,   15
And with sweet pastimes grace my happy tomb;
And Lesbia, close up thou my little light,
And crown with love my ever-during night.
                    (1601)

"Bravely decked, come forth, bright day"

Bravely decked, come forth, bright day,
Thine hours with roses strew thy way,
    As they well remember.

Thou received shalt be with feasts:
Come, chiefest of the British guests,   5
    Thou fift of November.
Thou with triumph shalt exceed
    In the strictest ember;
For by thy return the Lord records his blessed deed.

Britons, frolic at your board;   10
But first sing praises to the Lord
    In your congregations.
He preserved your state alone;
His loving grace hath made you one
    Of his chosen nations.   15
But this light must hallowed be
    With your best oblations;
Praise the Lord, for only great and merciful is he.

Death had entered in the gate,
And ruin was crept near the State;   20
    But heav'n all revealed.
Fiery powder hell did make,
Which, ready long the flame to take,
    Lay in shade concealed.
God us helped, of his free grace: 25
    None to him appealed;
For none was so bad to bear the treason or the place.

---

39. player: actor.   **CAMPION** Campion also composed the music for these songs.   **MY SWEETEST LESBIA** Cf. Jonson's "Come my Celia" (p. 263); both poems are partly translations of a poem by the Roman poet Catullus (c.84–c.54 B.C.). **14. hearse:** frame placed over a coffin or tomb, for holding candles and epitaphs.   **BRAVELY DECKED** This song celebrates the thwarting of the Gunpowder Plot of 1605, an event still commemorated on Guy Fawkes Day ("Remember, remember, the fifth of November"). **8. ember:** referring to one of the special days for fasting and prayer. **18. only:** i.e., alone. **20:** The gunpowder was secretly stowed under the Houses of Parliament.

God his peaceful monarch chose,
To him the mist he did disclose,
      To him, and none other.   *30*
This he did, O King, for thee,
That thou thine own renown might'st see,
      Which no time can smother.
May blest Charles thy comfort be,
      Firmer than his brother;   *35*
May his heart the love of peace and wisdom
  learn from thee.

                  (c. 1613)

"Jack and Joan they think no ill"

Jack and Joan they think no ill,
But loving live, and merry still;
Do their weekday's work, and pray
Devoutly on the holy day;
Skip and trip it on the green,   *5*
And help to choose the Summer Queen;
Lash out at a country feast
Their silver penny with the best.

Well can they judge of nappy ale,
And tell at large a winter tale;   *10*
Climb up to the apple loft,
And turn the crabs till they be soft.
Tib is all the father's joy,
And little Tom the mother's boy;
All their pleasure is content,   *15*
And care to pay their yearly rent.

Joan can call by name her cows,
And deck her windows with green boughs;
She can wreaths and tutties make,
And trim with plums a bridal cake.   *20*

Jack knows what brings gain or loss,
And his long flail can stoutly toss,
Make the hedge, which others break,
And ever thinks what he doth speak.

Now you Courtly Dames and Knights,   *25*
That study only strange delights,
Though you scorn the home-spun gray,
And revel in your rich array,
Though your tongues dissemble deep,
And can your heads from danger keep;   *30*
Yet for all your pomp and train,
Securer lives the silly swain.

                  (c. 1613)

"There is a garden in her face"

There is a garden in her face,
Where roses and white lilies grow;
A heav'nly paradise is that place,
Wherein all pleasant fruits do flow.
    There cherries grow which none may buy,   *5*
    Till "Cherry ripe!" themselves do cry.

Those cherries fairly do enclose
Of orient pearl a double row,
Which when her lovely laughter shows,
They look like rosebuds filled with snow.   *10*
    Yet them nor peer nor prince can buy,
    Till "Cherry ripe!" themselves do cry.

Her eyes like angels watch them still;
Her brows like bended bows do stand,
Threat'ning with piercing frowns to kill   *15*
All that attempt with eye or hand
    Those sacred cherries to come nigh,
    Till "Cherry ripe!" themselves do cry.

                  (c. 1617)

"Silly boy, 'tis full moon yet"

Silly boy, 'tis full moon yet, thy night as day shines clearly;
Had thy youth but wit to fear, thou couldst not love so dearly.
Shortly wilt thou mourn when all thy pleasures are bereaved;
Little knows he how to love that never was deceived.

34-35: Prince Henry died in 1612, making Charles heir to the throne.   **JACK AND JOAN** **7. lash out:** spend freely. **19. tutties:** posies. **32. silly:** simple, rustic, innocent. **THERE IS A GARDEN IN HER FACE** **6. "Cherry ripe!":** a cry of London street vendors. **SILLY BOY** **3. bereaved:** taken away.

This is thy first maiden flame that triumphs yet unstained;   *5*
All is artless now you speak, not one word yet is feigned.
All is heav'n that you behold, and all your thoughts are blessed,
But no Spring can want his Fall, each Troilus hath his Cressid.

Thy well-ordered locks ere long shall rudely hang neglected;
And thy lively pleasant cheer, read grief on earth dejected.   *10*
Much then wilt thou blame thy Saint that made thy heart so holy,
And with sighs confess, in love, that too much faith is folly.

Yet be just and constant still, Love may beget a wonder;
Not unlike a Summer's frost, or Winter's fatal thunder.
He that holds his Sweetheart true unto his day of dying,   *15*
Lives of all that ever breathed most worthy the envying.

(c. 1617)

SIR HENRY WOTTON
England, 1568-1639

from A LETTER TO THE EARL OF SALISBURY

13 March 1610

Now touching the occurrences of the present, I send herewith unto his Majesty the strangest piece of news (as I may justly call it) that he hath ever yet received from any part of the world; which is the annexed book (come abroad this very day) of the Mathematical Professor at Padua, who by the help of an optical instrument (which both enlargeth and approximateth the object), invented first in Flanders, and bettered by himself, hath   *5* discovered four new planets rolling about the sphere of Jupiter, besides many other unknown fixed stars; likewise, the true cause of the *Via Lactae*, so long searched; and lastly, that the moon is not spherical, but endued with many prominences, and, which is of all the strangest, illuminated with the solar light by reflection from the body of the earth, as he seemeth to say. So as upon the whole subject he hath first overthrown all former   *10* astronomy — for we must have a new sphere to save the appearances — and next all astrology. For the virtue of these new planets must needs vary the judicial part, and why may there not yet be more? These things I have been bold thus to discourse unto your Lordship, whereof here all corners are full. And the author runneth a fortune to be either exceeding famous or exceeding ridiculous. By the next ship your Lordship shall receive   *15* from me one of the above-named instruments, as it is bettered by this man.

8: The story of Troilus and Cressida was told by Chaucer and Shakespeare, among others. **10. cheer:** facial expression.   **LETTER TO THE EARL OF SALISBURY**   Robert, 1st Earl of Salisbury (c.1563-1612), was Elizabeth I's minister of state, who negotiated the succession of James VI of Scotland to the English throne (as James I); named Lord Treasurer in 1608, he remained chief minister until his death. Wotton had been named ambassador to Venice in 1604, a post he held for twenty years. **3-4. Mathematical Professor at Padua:** Galileo Galilei (1564-1642), who built the first practical astronomical telescope in 1609; he reported his discoveries in the *Sidereus Nuncius* ("starry messenger"), published at Venice in 1610. **6. sphere of Jupiter:** See *Ptolemaic* in the Glossary. **7. Via Lactae:** Milky Way.

SIR JOHN DAVIES
England, 1569-1626

Epigram 36: Of Tobacco

Homer of Moly and Nepenthe sings:
Moly, the gods' most sovereign herb divine;
Nepenthe, Helen's drink, which gladness brings,
Heart's grief expels, and doth the wits refine.
But this our age another world hath found,   5
From whence an herb of heavenly power is brought;
Moly is not so sovereign for a wound,
Nor hath Nepenthe so great wonders wrought:
It is Tobacco, whose sweet substantial fume
The hellish torment of the teeth doth ease   10
By drawing down and drying up the rheum,
The mother and the nurse of each disease:
It is Tobacco, which doth cold expel,
And clears the obstructions of the arteries,
And surfeits, threat'ning death, digesteth well,   15
Decocting all the stomach's crudities:
It is Tobacco, which hath power to clarify
The cloudy mists before dim eyes appearing:
It is Tobacco, which hath power to rarefy
The thick gross humour which doth stop the hearing;   20
The wasting hectic, and the quartaine fever,
Which doth of physic make a mockery;
The gout it cures, and helps ill breaths for ever,
Whether the cause in teeth or stomach be;
And though ill breaths were by it but confounded,   25
Yet that vile medicine it doth far excel,
Which by Sir Thomas Moore hath been propounded,
For this is thought a gentleman-like smell.
O, that I were one of those Mountebanks
Which praise their oils and powders which they sell!   30
My customers would give me coin with thanks;

I for this ware, for sooth a tale would tell,
Yet would I use none of these terms before;
I would but say, that it the pox will cure.
This were enough, without discoursing more,   35
All our brave gallants in the town t'allure.

(c. 1590)

Epigram 47: Meditations of a Gull

See yonder melancholy gentleman,
Which, hood-winked with his hat, alone doth sit!
Think what he thinks, and tell me if you can,
What great affairs trouble his little wit.
He thinks not of the war 'twixt France and Spain,   5
Whether it be for Europe's good or ill;
Nor whether the Empire can itself maintain
Against the Turkish power encroaching still;
Nor what great town in all the Netherlands
The States determine to besiege this spring;   10
Nor how the Scottish policy now stands,
Nor what becomes of the Irish mutining.
But he doth seriously bethink him whether
Of the gulled people he be more esteemed
For his long cloak or for his great black feather,   15
By which each gull is now a gallant deemed;
Or of a journey he deliberates,
To Paris-garden, Cock-pit, or the Play;
Or how to steal a dog he meditates,
Or what he shall unto his mistress say: 20
    Yet with these thoughts he thinks himself most fit
    To be of counsel with a king for wit.

(c. 1590)

OF TOBACCO   Tobacco was used in South America in pre-Columbian times, and was taken to Europe in the mid-16th century; it had been introduced to England probably as early as 1565, and by 1604 King James I was attacking it and its supposed virtues in *A Counterblast to Tobacco.* Cf. also Charles Cotton's "On Tobacco" (p. 432). **1. Moly:** See note to Pope's *Rape of the Lock,* IV, 56 (p. 529); **Nepenthe:** See *Odyssey,* IV, 220ff., where Helen slips a "grief-banishing" drug into Telemachus's wine. **9. substantial:** partaking of the substance. **16. decocting:** digesting by the heat of the stomach. **20. humour:** body fluid. **21. wasting hectic:** consumption; **quartaine:** quartan, i.e., with paroxysms recurring every four days (or 72 hours). **22. physic:** medicine. **27:** One of Sir Thomas More's Latin epigrams dealt with bad breath, noting that onions can get rid of the smell of leeks, and garlic the smell of onions, but that only defecation could remove the smell of garlic. **34. pox:** syphilis. **MEDITATIONS OF A GULL** **7. Empire:** i.e., the Holy Roman Empire. **10. States:** the States or States-General, the body of powerful men who constitute the legislature of a country — here, of the Netherlands, which in the 1590s succeeded in recapturing most of its territory from the Spanish. **18. Paris-garden:** the Bear-Garden, on Bankside in Southwark, near the Globe Theatre — a site referred to in 1632 (in Donald Lupton's *London and the Country Carbonadoed*) as a place of rendezvous for "the swaggering Roarer; the amusing Cheater; the swearing Drunkard; and the bloody Butcher."

from *HYMNS TO ASTRAEA*

HYMN VIII: TO ALL THE PRINCES OF EUROPE

E urope, the earth's sweet Paradise,
L et all thy kings that would be wise
I n *politique devotion*,
S ail hither to observe her eyes,
A nd mark her heav'nly motion.   *5*

B rave Princes of this civil age,
E nter into this pilgrimage;
T his saint's tongue is an oracle,
H er eye hath made a Prince a page,
A nd works each day a miracle.   *10*

R aise but your looks to her, and see
E ven the true beams of majesty;
G reat Princes, mark her duly:
I f all the world you do survey,
N o forehead spreads so bright a ray,   *15*
A nd notes a Prince so truly.

(1599)

AMELIA LANYER
England, 1569-1645

from *SALVE DEUS REX JUDÆORUM*

EVE'S APOLOGY IN DEFENCE OF WOMEN

. . . .

Now Pontius Pilate is to judge the cause
Of faultless Jesus, who before him stands;
Who neither hath offended prince nor laws,
Although he now be brought in woeful bands.
O noble Governor, make thou yet a pause,   *5*
Do not in innocent blood imbrue thy hands;
  But hear the words of thy most worthy wife,
  Who sends to thee to beg her Saviour's life.

Let barb'rous cruelty far depart from thee,
And in true justice take affliction's part;   *10*
Open thine eyes, that thou the truth may'st see;
Do not the thing that goes against thy heart.
Condemn not him that must thy Saviour be,
But view his holy life, his good desert.
  Let not us women glory in men's fall,   *15*
  Who had power given to over-rule us all.

HYMNS TO ASTRAEA **Astraea:** i.e., Queen Elizabeth.   SALVE DEUS REX JUDÆORUM   ("Hail Lord, King of the Jews," which Lanyer said came to her in sleep long before she wrote the poem) **1. cause:** case. **6. imbrue:** stain. **7:** See Matthew 27:19; from line 5 on, the words are those of Pilate's wife.

Till now your indiscretion sets us free,
And makes our former fault much less appear;
Our Mother Eve, who tasted of the Tree,
Giving to Adam what she held most dear,   20
Was simply good, and had no power to see;
The after-coming harm did not appear,
    The subtile Serpent that our sex betrayed,
    Before our fall so sure a plot had laid.

That undiscerning Ignorance perceived   25
No guile or craft that was by him intended,
For had she known of what we were bereaved,
To his request she had not condescended.
But she, poor soul, by cunning was deceived;
No hurt therein her harmless heart intended,   30
    For she alleged God's word, which he denies,
    That they should die, but even as gods, be wise.

But surely Adam can not be excused;
Her fault though great, yet he was most to blame;
What Weakness offered, Strength might have refused;
Being Lord of all, the greater was his shame.   36
Although the Serpent's craft had her abused,
God's holy word ought all his actions frame,
    For he was Lord and King of all the earth
    Before poor Eve had either life or breath.   40

Who being framed by God's eternal hand
The perfect'st man that ever breathed on earth,
And from God's mouth received that strait command,
The breach whereof he knew was present death;
Yea, having power to rule both sea and land,   45
Yet with one apple won to lose that breath
    Which God had breathed in his beauteous face,
    Bringing us all in danger and disgrace.

And then to lay the fault on Patience' back,
That we, poor women, must endure it all;   50
We know right well he did discretion lack,
Being not persuaded thereunto at all.
If Eve did err, it was for knowledge sake;
The fruit being fair persuaded him to fall:
    No subtile Serpent's falsehood did betray him;   55
    If he would eat it, who had power to stay him?

Not Eve, whose fault was only too much love,
Which made her give this present to her Dear,
That what she tasted he likewise might prove,
Whereby his knowledge might become more clear;   60
He never sought her weakness to reprove
With those sharp words which he of God did hear;
    Yet men will boast of knowledge, which he took
    From Eve's fair hand, as from a learned book.

If any evil did in her remain,   65
Being made of him, he was the ground of all;
If one of many worlds could lay a stain
Upon our sex, and work so great a fall
To wretched man, by Satan's subtile train,
What will so foul a fault amongst you all?   70
    Her weakness did the Serpent's words obey,
    But you in malice God's dear Son betray,

Whom, if unjustly you condemn to die,
Her sin was small to what you do commit;
All mortal sins that do for vengeance cry   75
Are not to be compared unto it.
If many worlds would altogether try
By all their sins the wrath of God to get,
    This sin of yours surmounts them all as far
    As doth the sun another little star.   80

Then let us have our liberty again,
And challenge to yourselves no sov'reignty;
You came not in the world without our pain;
Make that a bar against your cruelty.
Your fault being greater, why should you disdain   85
Our being your equals, free from tyranny?
    If one weak woman simply did offend,
    This sin of yours hath no excuse, nor end.

To which, poor souls, we never gave consent;
Witness thy wife, O Pilate, speaks for all,   90
Who did but dream, and yet a message sent
That thou shouldst have nothing to do at all
With that just man, which, if thy heart relent,
Why wilt thou be a reprobate with Saul,
    To seek the death of him that is so good,   95
    For thy soul's health to shed his dearest blood?

      . . . .

        (1611)

---

27. bereaved: deprived. **28. condescended:** yielded, assented. **31-32:** See Genesis 3:3-5 (p. 244); **alleged:** cited. **43. strait:** strict. **53. knowledge:** i.e., knowledge's. **59. prove:** experience. **67. worlds:** multitudes. **69. train:** i.e., of persuasive, though specious, reasoning. **82. challenge:** claim. **94:** For the story of Saul, see I Samuel 9-31, especially 18ff.; the reference is to Saul's jealousy and pursuit of David, and perhaps also his slaughter of the priests and others of Nob.

THOMAS DEKKER
England, c.1570-c.1632

from *THE GULL'S HORN-BOOK*

Chapter VI: How a Gallant Should Behave Himself in a Playhouse

The theatre is your poets' royal exchange, upon which their muses (that are now turned
to merchants) meeting, barter away that light commodity of words for a lighter ware
than words, plaudities, and the breath of the great beast, which (like the threatenings of
two cowards) vanish all into air. Players and their factors, who put away the stuff, and
make the best of it they possibly can (as indeed 'tis their parts so to do), your gallant,   *5*
your courtier, and your captain had wont to be the soundest paymasters, and I think are
still the surest chapmen; and these, by means that their heads are well stocked, deal
upon this comical freight by the gross, when your groundling and gallery-commoner
buys his sport by the penny and, like a haggler, is glad to utter it again by retailing.

    Since then the place is so free in entertainment, allowing a stool as well to the farmer's   *10*
son as to your templar, that your stinkard has the selfsame liberty to be there in his tobacco
fumes which your sweet courtier hath, and that your carman and tinker claim as strong a
voice in their suffrage, and sit to give judgment on the play's life and death as well as the
proudest momus among the tribes of critic, it is fit that he whom the most tailor's bills do
make room for, when he comes should not be basely (like a viol) cased up in a corner.   *15*

    Whether therefore the gatherers of the public or private playhouse stand to receive the
afternoon's rent, let our gallant (having paid it) presently advance himself up to the throne
of the stage. I mean not into the lord's room (which is now but the stage's suburbs); no,
those boxes, by the iniquity of custom, conspiracy of waiting women and gentlemen ushers
that there sweat together, and the covetousness of sharers, are contemptibly thrust into the   *20*
rear, and much new satin is there damned by being smothered to death in darkness. But on
the very rushes where the comedy is to dance, yea and under the state of Cambyses himself
must our feathered ostrich, like a piece of ordnance, be planted, valiantly (because
impudently) beating down the mews and hisses of the opposed rascality.

    For do but cast up a reckoning, what large comings-in are pursed up by sitting on   *25*
the stage. First a conspicuous eminence is got, by which means the best and most
essential parts of a gallant (good clothes, a proportionable leg, white hand, the Persian
lock, and a tolerable beard) are perfectly revealed.

HOW A GALLANT SHOULD BEHAVE   **3. plaudities:** plaudits, applause, or appeals for applause; **great beast:** the masses, the audience. **7. chapmen:** merchants. **8. groundling:** spectator who stood in the pit or "yard" (line 52), on the ground; **gallery-commoner:** similarly, occupier of a cheap seat in the gallery. **9. utter:** vend, sell; **retailing:** selling in small quantities. **11. templar:** a lawyer or law-student, a member of either the Inner Temple or the Middle Temple, two of the four Inns of Court (in quarters once occupied by the Knights Templar). **14. momus:** fault-finder. **16. gatherers:** collectors of admission. **18. lord's room:** specially good seats (cf. "royal box"), but for some reason no longer considered fashionable ("suburbs" are tantamount to slums). **20. sharers:** shareholders. **22. rushes:** Loose rushes were used as floor-coverings; **state:** canopy, as over a throne; Cambyses, King of Persia, was the subject of a play (1569, by Thomas Preston) notable for its bombastic style. **23. feathered ostrich:** A gallant's costume might well include a plumed hat. **24. rascality:** no doubt the groundlings and gallery-commoners. **27-28. Persian lock:** probably a sort of love-lock.

By sitting on the stage, you have a signed patent to engross the whole commodity of censure, may lawfully presume to be a girder, and stand at the helm to steer the *30* passage of scenes; yet no man shall once offer to hinder you from obtaining the title of an insolent, overweening coxcomb.

By sitting on the stage, you may (without travelling for it) at the very next door ask whose play it is, and by that quest of inquiry the law warrants you to avoid much mistaking; if you know not the author you may rail against him, and peradventure so *35* behave yourself that you may enforce the author to know you.

By sitting on the stage, if you be a knight you may happily get you a mistress; if a mere Fleet Street gentleman, a wife; but assure yourself, by continual residence you are the first and principal man in election to begin the number of We Three.

By spreading your body on the stage, and by being a justice in examining of plays, *40* you shall put yourself into such true scenical authority that some poet shall not dare to present his muse rudely upon your eyes without having first unmasked her, rifled her, and discovered all her bare and most mystical parts before you at a tavern, when you most knightly shall, for his pains, pay for both their suppers.

By sitting on the stage, you may (with small cost) purchase the dear acquaintance of *45* the boys, have a good stool for sixpence, at any time know what particular part any of the infants present, get your match lighted, examine the play-suits' lace, and perhaps win wagers upon laying 'tis copper, etc. And to conclude, whether you be a fool or a justice of peace, a cuckold or a captain, a lord-mayor's son or a dawcock, a knave or an under-sheriff — of what stamp soever you be, current or counterfeit, the stage, like time, *50* will bring you to most perfect light and lay you open; neither are you to be hunted from thence, though the scarecrows in the yard hoot at you, hiss at you, spit at you, yea throw dirt even in your teeth; 'tis most gentlemanlike patience to endure all this and to laugh at the silly animals; but if the rabble, with a full throat, cry "Away with the fool!" you were worse than a madman to tarry by it, for the gentleman and the fool should never sit *55* on the stage together.

Marry, let this observation go hand in hand with the rest; or rather, like a country serving-man, some five yards before them. Present not yourself on the stage (especially at a new play) until the quaking prologue hath (by rubbing) got colour into his cheeks, and is ready to give the trumpets their cue that he's upon point to enter; for then it is *60* time, as though you were one of the properties or that you dropped out of the hangings, to creep from behind the arras with your tripos or three-footed stool in one hand and a teston mounted between a forefinger and thumb in the other; for if you should bestow your person upon the vulgar when the belly of the house is but half full, your apparel is quite eaten up, the fashion lost, and the proportion of your body in more danger to be *65* devoured than if it were served up in the counter amongst the poultry; avoid that as you would the bastome.

---

30. girder: one who jeers or mocks. **37. happily:** by chance. **39. We Three:** referring to a picture of two loggerheads (blockheads, dolts) inscribed "We three loggerheads be," or a picture of two asses inscribed "When shall we three meet again?" **46. boys:** boy actors. **47. match:** piece of slow-burning material, like punk, for lighting a pipe. **49. dawcock:** male jackdaw, fool. **59. prologue:** the actor who is to speak the play's prologue. **60. trumpets:** See note to line 100. **63. teston:** coin stamped with the head of Henry VIII. **65. eaten up:** wasted, to little purpose. **66. in the counter:** i.e., on the counters in the marketplace. **67. bastome:** bastinado.

It shall crown you with rich commendation to laugh aloud in the midst of the most
serious and saddest scene of the terriblest tragedy, and to let that clapper (your tongue)
be tossed so high that all the house may ring of it. Your lords use it; your knights are *70*
apes to the lords, and do so too; your inn-a-court-man is zany to the knights, and (marry
very scurvily) comes likewise limping after it; be thou a beagle to them all and never lin
snuffing till you have scented them, for talking and laughing (like a ploughman in a
morris) you heap Pelion upon Ossa, glory upon glory. As first, all the eyes in the
galleries will leave walking after the players and only follow you; the simplest dolt in *75*
the house snatches up your name, and when he meets you in the streets, or that you fall
into his hands in the middle of a watch, his word shall be taken for you: he'll cry "He's
such a gallant," and you pass. Secondly, you publish your temperance to the world, in
that you seem not to resort thither to taste vain pleasures with a hungry appetite, but
only as a gentleman to spend a foolish hour or two, because you can do nothing else. *80*
Thirdly, you mightily disrelish the audience and disgrace the author; marry, you take up
(though it be at the worst hand) a strong opinion of your own judgment, and enforce the
poet to take pity of your weakness, and by some dedicated sonnet to bring you into a
better paradise, only to stop your mouth.

If you can (either for love or money), provide yourself a lodging by the waterside, *85*
for above the convenience it brings to shun shoulder-clapping and to ship away your
cockatrice betimes in the morning, it adds a kind of state unto you to be carried from
thence to the stairs of your playhouse; hate a sculler (remember that) worse than to be
acquainted with one o' th' scullery. No, your oars are your only sea-crabs; board them,
and take heed you never go twice together with one pair: often shifting is a great credit *90*
to gentlemen, and that dividing of your fare will make the poor watersnakes be ready to
pull you in pieces to enjoy your custom. No matter whether upon landing you have
money or no; you may swim in twenty of their boats over the river upon ticket; marry,
when silver comes in, remember to pay treble their fare, and it will make your flounder-
catchers to send more thanks after you when you do not draw than when you do, for *95*
they know it will be their own another day.

Before the play begins, fall to cards; you may win or lose (as fencers do in a prize)
and beat one another by confederacy, yet share the money when you meet at supper;
notwithstanding, to gull the ragamuffins that stand aloof gaping at you, throw the cards
(having first torn four or five of them) round about the stage, just upon the third sound, *100*
as though you had lost; it skills not if the four knaves lie on their backs and outface the
audience; there's none such fools as dare take exceptions at them, because ere the play
go off, better knaves than they will fall into the company.

Now, sir, if the writer be a fellow that hath either epigrammed you, or hath had a
flirt at your mistress, or hath brought either your feather, or your red beard, or your little *105*

---

71. inn-a-court-man: See note to line 11. **72. lin:** cease, leave off. **74. heap Pelion upon Ossa:** alluding to the Greek myth in which the Titans piled one mountain on top of another in order to try to reach heaven. **77. watch:** one of the periods when a watchman is on duty. **85. waterside:** i.e., beside the Thames. **86. shoulder-clapping:** i.e., by a sheriff's officer making an arrest for debt. **87. cockatrice:** whore. **89. oars:** boats, oarsmen, or literally oars (see *pair* in line 90); **sea-crabs:** boatmen. **90. often shifting:** i.e., shifting often. **93. upon ticket:** (in modern British, "on tick") on credit. **95. draw:** draw out one's purse, pay. **97. prize:** athletic or other contest, here a fencing match. **100. third sound:** the last of three spaced signals, such as flourishes or fanfares on a trumpet, signalling that the play is about to begin. **101. skills:** matters; **four knaves:** potentially valuable cards. **105. feather:** plumage, fancy attire (see line 23 and note).

legs, etc. on the stage, you shall disgrace him worse than by tossing him in a blanket or giving him the bastinado in a tavern if, in the middle of his play (be it pastoral or comedy, moral or tragedy), you rise with a screwed and discontented face from your stool to be gone; no matter whether the scenes be good or no; the better they are the worse do you distaste them; and being on your feet, sneak not away like a coward, but *110* salute all your gentle acquaintance that are spread either on the rushes or on stools about you, and draw what troop you can from the stage after you; the mimics are beholden to you for allowing them elbow room; their poet cries, perhaps, "a pox go with you," but care not for that; there is no music without frets.

Marry, if either the company or indisposition of the weather bind you to sit it out, my *115* counsel is then that you turn plain ape, take up a rush, and tickle the earnest ears of your fellow gallants to make other fools fall a-laughing; mew at passionate speeches, blare at merry, find fault with the music, whew at the children's action, whistle at the songs, and above all curse the sharers, that whereas the same day you had bestowed forty shillings on an embroidered felt and feather (Scotch fashion) for your mistress in the court or your *120* punk in the city, within two hours after, you encounter with the very same block on the stage, when the haberdasher swore to you the impression was extant but that morning.

To conclude, hoard up the finest play-scraps you can get, upon which your lean wit may most savourly feed for want of other stuff, when the Arcadian and Euphuized gentlewomen have their tongues sharpened to set upon you; that quality (next to your *125* shuttlecock) is the only furniture to a courtier that's but a new beginner, and is but in his A B C of compliment. The next places that are filled after the playhouses be emptied are (or ought to be) taverns; into a tavern then let us next march, where the brains of one hogshead must be beaten out to make up another.

(1609)

THE BIBLE

from *THE AUTHORIZED VERSION*

GENESIS 1-9 (creation; fall; flood)

Chapter 1

In the beginning God created the heaven and the earth.

2 And the earth was without form, and void; and darkness was upon the face of the deep. And the Spirit of God moved upon the face of the waters.

3 And God said, Let there be light: and there was light.

4 And God saw the light, that it was good: and God divided the light from the darkness.

---

121. block: style of hat (moulded — "impression" — on a block). **122. extant:** in existence, in vogue, current. **124. Arcadian and Euphuized:** referring to the witty, lush, and often foolishly imitated styles of Sir Philip Sidney's *Arcadia* and John Lyly's *Euphues*. **126. shuttlecock:** perhaps referring to the game itself, and perhaps to the banter or "shuttlecock of conversation." **127ff.:** The final sentence serves as a transition to the next chapter.   **BIBLE**   While the phrasing of the *Authorized Version* or "King James" Bible has extensively influenced English literature, this

5 And God called the light Day, and the darkness he called Night. And the evening and the morning were the first day.

6 And God said, Let there be a firmament in the midst of the waters, and let it divide the waters from the waters.

7 And God made the firmament, and divided the waters which were under the firmament from the waters which were above the firmament: and it was so.

8 And God called the firmament Heaven. And the evening and the morning were the second day.

9 And God said, Let the waters under the heaven be gathered together unto one place, and let the dry land appear: and it was so.

10 And God called the dry land Earth; and the gathering together of the waters called he Seas: and God saw that it was good.

11 And God said, Let the earth bring forth grass, the herb yielding seed, and the fruit tree yielding fruit after his kind, whose seed is in itself, upon the earth: and it was so.

12 And the earth brought forth grass, and herb yielding seed after his kind, and the tree yielding fruit, whose seed was in itself, after his kind: and God saw that it was good.

13 And the evening and the morning were the third day.

14 And God said, Let there be lights in the firmament of the heaven to divide the day from the night; and let them be for signs, and for seasons, and for days, and years:

15 And let them be for lights in the firmament of the heaven to give light upon the earth: and it was so.

16 And God made two great lights; the greater light to rule the day, and the lesser light to rule the night: he made the stars also.

17 And God set them in the firmament of heaven to give light upon the earth,

18 And to rule over the day and over the night, and to divide the light from the darkness: and God saw that it was good.

19 And the evening and the morning were the fourth day.

20 And God said, Let the waters bring forth abundantly the moving creature that hath life, and fowl that may fly above the earth in the open firmament of heaven.

21 And God created great whales, and every living creature that moveth, which the waters brought forth abundantly, after their kind, and every winged fowl after his kind: and God saw that it was good.

22 And God blessed them, saying, Be fruitful, and multiply, and fill the waters in the seas, and let fowl multiply in the earth.

23 And the evening and the morning were the fifth day.

24 And God said, Let the earth bring forth the living creature after his kind, cattle, and creeping thing, and beast of the earth after his kind: and it was so.

25 And God made the beast of the earth after his kind, and cattle after their kind, and every thing that creepeth upon the earth after his kind: and God saw that it was good.

26 And God said, Let us make man in our image, after our likeness: and let them have dominion over the fish of the sea, and over the fowl of the

---

translation was neither the first nor the last. Aelfric had translated some portions into Anglo-Saxon; John Wyclif (see p. 25) initiated in the 14th century a translation of the Latin (or "Vulgate") version of the entire Bible; and translations of the New Testament that William Tyndale (see p. 126) made from the Greek version of Erasmus appeared in 1526, and of the Pentateuch and the book of Jonah in 1530 and 1531. Miles Coverdale (c.1488-1569), whose English version of the Psalms is retained in the *Book of Common Prayer*, produced in 1535 the first entire Bible to be *printed* in English, and Coverdale was also involved in one of the most influential of subsequent Protestant versions, the Geneva Bible (presented to Elizabeth I in 1560), which was answered by the Roman Catholic French-language version of the Old and New Testaments (the Douai version of 1609 and the Rheims version of 1582 respectively). King James I, also objecting to the Geneva Bible, authorized in 1604 a new translation of the entire Bible into English. A panel of fifty-four scholars, one of the leaders being Lancelot Andrewes (1555-1626), prepared the text that appeared in 1611, drawing substantially on the scholarship that produced the Geneva Bible and the phrasing of Tyndale's version. And another 150 English-language versions of the Bible appeared before the Revised Version of 1881-85, and an equal number since that time, among which are the New English Bible (1970), the Good News Bible (1976), and the New International Version (1979).

air, and over the cattle, and over all the earth, and over every creeping thing that creepeth upon the earth.

27 So God created man in his own image, in the image of God created he him; male and female created he them.

28 And God blessed them, and God said unto them, Be fruitful, and multiply, and replenish the earth, and subdue it: and have dominion over the fish of the sea, and over the fowl of the air, and over every living thing that moveth upon the earth.

29 And God said, Behold, I have given you every herb bearing seed, which is upon the face of all the earth, and every tree, in the which is the fruit of a tree yielding seed; to you it shall be for meat.

30 And to every beast of the earth, and to every fowl of the air, and to every thing that creepeth upon the earth, wherein there is life, I have given every green herb for meat: and it was so.

31 And God saw every thing that he had made, and, behold, it was very good. And the evening and the morning were the sixth day.

Chapter 2

Thus the heavens and the earth were finished, and all the host of them.

2 And on the seventh day God ended his work which he had made; and he rested on the seventh day from all his work which he had made.

3 And God blessed the seventh day, and sanctified it: because that in it he had rested from all his work which God created and made.

4 These are the generations of the heavens and of the earth when they were created, in the day that the Lord God made the earth and the heavens,

5 And every plant of the field before it was in the earth, and every herb of the field before it grew: for the Lord God had not caused it to rain upon the earth, and there was not a man to till the ground.

6 But there went up a mist from the earth, and watered the whole face of the ground.

7 And the Lord God formed man of the dust of the ground, and breathed into his nostrils the breath of life; and man became a living soul.

8 And the Lord God planted a garden eastward in Eden; and there he put the man whom he had formed.

9 And out of the ground made the Lord God to grow every tree that is pleasant to the sight, and good for food; the tree of life also in the midst of the garden, and the tree of knowledge of good and evil.

10 And a river went out of Eden to water the garden; and from thence it was parted, and became into four heads.

11 The name of the first is Pison: that is it which compasseth the whole land of Havilah, where there is gold;

12 And the gold of that land is good: there is bdellium and the onyx stone.

13 And the name of the second river is Gihon: the same is it that compasseth the whole land of Ethiopia.

14 And the name of the third river is Hiddekel: that is it which goeth toward the east of Assyria. And the fourth river is Euphrates.

15 And the Lord God took the man, and put him into the garden of Eden to dress it and to keep it.

16 And the Lord God commanded the man, saying, Of every tree of the garden thou mayest freely eat:

17 But of the tree of the knowledge of good and evil, thou shalt not eat of it: for in the day that thou eatest thereof thou shalt surely die.

18 And the Lord God said, It is not good that the man should be alone; I will make him an help meet for him.

19 And out of the ground the Lord God formed every beast of the field, and every fowl of the air; and brought them unto Adam to see what he would call them: and whatsoever Adam called every living creature, that was the name thereof.

20 And Adam gave names to all cattle, and to the fowl of the air, and to every beast of the field; but for Adam there was not found an help meet for him.

21 And the Lord God caused a deep sleep to fall upon Adam, and he slept: and he took one of his ribs, and closed up the flesh instead thereof;

22 And the rib, which the Lord God had taken from man, made he a woman, and brought her unto the man.

23 And Adam said, This is now bone of my bones, and flesh of my flesh: she shall be called Woman, because she was taken out of Man.

24 Therefore shall a man leave his father and his mother, and shall cleave unto his wife: and they shall be one flesh.

25 And they were both naked, the man and his wife, and were not ashamed.

Chapter 3

Now the serpent was more subtil than any beast of the field which the Lord God had made. And he said unto the woman, Yea, hath God said, Ye shall not eat of every tree of the garden?

2 And the woman said unto the serpent, We may eat of the fruit of the trees of the garden:

3 But of the fruit of the tree which is in the midst of the garden, God hath said, Ye shall not eat of it, neither shall ye touch it, lest ye die.

4 And the serpent said unto the woman, Ye shall not surely die:

5 For God doth know that in the day ye eat thereof, then your eyes shall be opened, and ye shall be as gods, knowing good and evil.

6 And when the woman saw that the tree was good for food, and that it was pleasant to the eyes, and a tree to be desired to make one wise, she took of the fruit thereof, and did eat, and gave also unto her husband with her, and he did eat.

7 And the eyes of them both were opened, and they knew that they were naked; and they sewed fig leaves together, and made themselves aprons.

8 And they heard the voice of the Lord God walking in the garden in the cool of the day: and Adam and his wife hid themselves from the presence of the Lord God amongst the trees of the garden.

9 And the Lord God called unto Adam, and said unto him, Where art thou?

10 And he said, I heard thy voice in the garden, and I was afraid, because I was naked; and I hid myself.

11 And he said, Who told thee that thou wast naked? Hast thou eaten of the tree, whereof I commanded thee that thou shouldest not eat?

12 And the man said, The woman whom thou gavest to be with me, she gave me of the tree, and I did eat.

13 And the Lord God said unto the woman, What is this that thou hast done? And the woman said, The serpent beguiled me, and I did eat.

14 And the Lord God said unto the serpent, Because thou hast done this, thou art cursed above all cattle, and above every beast of the field; upon thy belly shalt thou go, and dust shalt thou eat all the days of thy life:

15 And I will put enmity between thee and the woman, and between thy seed and her seed; it shall bruise thy head, and thou shalt bruise his heel.

16 Unto the woman he said, I will greatly multiply thy sorrow and thy conception: in sorrow thou shalt bring forth children; and thy desire shall be to thy husband, and he shall rule over thee.

17 And unto Adam he said, Because thou hast hearkened unto the voice of thy wife, and hast eaten of the tree of which I commanded thee, saying, Thou shalt not eat of it: cursed is the ground for thy sake; in sorrow shalt thou eat of it all the days of thy life;

18 Thorns also and thistles shall it bring forth to thee; and thou shalt eat the herb of the field;

19 In the sweat of thy face shalt thou eat bread, till thou return unto the ground; for out of it wast thou taken: for dust thou art, and unto dust shalt thou return.

20 And Adam called his wife's name Eve; because she was the mother of all living.

21 Unto Adam also and to his wife, did the Lord God make coats of skins, and clothed them.

22 And the Lord God said, Behold, the man is become as one of us, to know good and evil: and now, lest he put forth his hand, and take also of the tree of life, and eat, and live for ever:

23 Therefore the Lord God sent him forth from the garden of Eden, to till the ground from whence he was taken.

24 So he drove out the man; and he placed at the east of the garden of Eden Cherubims, and a flaming sword which turned every way, to keep the way of the tree of life.

Chapter 4

And Adam knew Eve his wife; and she conceived, and bare Cain, and said, I have gotten a man from the Lord.

2 And she again bare his brother Abel. And Abel was a keeper of sheep, but Cain was a tiller of the ground.

3 And in process of time it came to pass, that Cain brought of the fruit of the ground an offering unto the Lord.

4 And Abel, he also brought of the firstlings of his flock and of the fat thereof. And the Lord had respect unto Abel and to his offering:

5 But unto Cain and to his offering he had not respect. And Cain was very wroth, and his countenance fell.

6 And the Lord said unto Cain, Why art thou wroth? and why is thy countenance fallen?

7 If thou doest well, shalt thou not be accepted? and if thou doest not well, sin lieth at the door. And unto thee shall be his desire, and thou shalt rule over him.

8 And Cain talked with Abel his brother: and it came to pass, when they were in the field, that Cain rose up against Abel his brother, and slew him.

9 And the Lord said unto Cain, Where is Abel thy brother? And he said, I know not: Am I my brother's keeper?

10 And he said, What hast thou done? the voice of thy brother's blood crieth unto me from the ground.

11 And now art thou cursed from the earth, which hath opened her mouth to receive thy brother's blood from thy hand:

12 When thou tillest the ground, it shall not henceforth yield unto thee her strength; a fugitive and a vagabond shalt thou be in the earth.

13 And Cain said unto the Lord, My punishment is greater than I can bear.

14 Behold, thou hast driven me out this day from the face of the earth; and from thy face shall I be hid; and I shall be a fugitive and a vagabond in the earth; and it shall come to pass, that every one that findeth me shall slay me.

15 And the Lord said unto him, Therefore whosoever slayeth Cain, vengeance shall be taken on him sevenfold. And the Lord set a mark upon Cain, lest any finding him should kill him.

16 And Cain went out from the presence of the Lord, and dwelt in the land of Nod, on the east of Eden.

17 And Cain knew his wife; and she conceived, and bare Enoch: and he builded a city, and called the name of the city, after the name of his son, Enoch.

18 And unto Enoch was born Irad: and Irad begat Mehujael: and Mehujael begat Methusael: and Methusael begat Lamech.

19 And Lamech took unto him two wives: the name of the one was Adah, and the name of the other Zillah.

20 And Adah bare Jabal: he was the father of such as dwell in tents, and of such as have cattle.

21 And his brother's name was Jubal: he was the father of all such as handle the harp and organ.

22 And Zillah, she also bare Tubal-cain, an instructor of every artificer in brass and iron: and the sister of Tubal-cain was Naamah.

23 And Lamech said unto his wives, Adah and Zillah, Hear my voice; ye wives of Lamech, hearken unto my speech: for I have slain a man to my wounding, and a young man to my hurt.

24 If Cain shall be avenged sevenfold, truly Lamech seventy and sevenfold.

25 And Adam knew his wife again; and she bare a son, and called his name Seth: For God, said she, hath appointed me another seed instead of Abel, whom Cain slew.

26 And to Seth, to him also there was born a son; and he called his name Enos: then began men to call upon the name of the Lord.

Chapter 5

This is the book of the generations of Adam. In the day that God created man, in the likeness of God made he him;

2 Male and female created he them; and blessed them, and called their name Adam, in the day when they were created.

3 And Adam lived an hundred and thirty years, and begat a son in his own likeness, after his image; and called his name Seth:

4 And the days of Adam after he had begotten Seth were eight hundred years: and he begat sons and daughters:

5 And all the days that Adam lived were nine hundred and thirty years: and he died.

6 And Seth lived an hundred and five years, and begat Enos:

7 And Seth lived after he begat Enos eight hundred and seven years, and begat sons and daughters:

8 And all the days of Seth were nine hundred and twelve years: and he died.

9 And Enos lived ninety years, and begat Cainan:

10 And Enos lived after he begat Cainan eight hundred and fifteen years, and begat sons and daughters:

11 And all the days of Enos were nine hundred and five years: and he died.

12 And Cainan lived seventy years, and begat Mahalaleel:

13 And Cainan lived after he begat Mahalaleel eight hundred and forty years, and begat sons and daughters:

14 And all the days of Cainan were nine hundred and ten years: and he died.

15 And Mahalaleel lived sixty and five years, and begat Jared:

16 And Mahalaleel lived after he begat Jared eight hundred and thirty years, and begat sons and daughters:

17 And all the days of Mahalaleel were eight hundred ninety and five years: and he died.

18 And Jared lived an hundred sixty and two years, and he begat Enoch:

19 And Jared lived after he begat Enoch eight hundred years, and begat sons and daughters:

20 And all the days of Jared were nine hundred sixty and two years: and he died.

21 And Enoch lived sixty and five years, and begat Methuselah:

22 And Enoch walked with God after he begat Methuselah three hundred years, and begat sons and daughters:

23 And all the days of Enoch were three hundred sixty and five years:

24 And Enoch walked with God; and he was not; for God took him.

25 And Methuselah lived an hundred eighty and seven years, and begat Lamech:

26 And Methuselah lived after he begat Lamech seven hundred eighty and two years, and begat sons and daughters:

27 And all the days of Methuselah were nine hundred sixty and nine years: and he died.

28 And Lamech lived an hundred eighty and two years, and begat a son;

29 And he called his name Noah, saying, This same shall comfort us concerning our work and toil of our hands, because of the ground which the Lord hath cursed.

30 And Lamech lived after he begat Noah five hundred ninety and five years, and begat sons and daughters:

31 And all the days of Lamech were seven hundred seventy and seven years: and he died.

32 And Noah was five hundred years old: and Noah begat Shem, Ham, and Japheth.

Chapter 6

And it came to pass, when men began to multiply on the face of the earth, and daughters were born unto them,

2 That the sons of God saw the daughters of men that they were fair; and they took them wives of all which they chose.

3 And the Lord said, My Spirit shall not always strive with man, for that he also is flesh: yet his days shall be an hundred and twenty years.

4 There were giants in the earth in those days; and also after that, when the sons of God came in unto the daughters of men, and they bare children to them, the same became mighty men which were of old, men of renown.

5 And God saw that the wickedness of man was great in the earth, and that every imagination of the thoughts of his heart was only evil continually.

6 And it repented the Lord that he had made man on the earth, and it grieved him at his heart.

7 And the Lord said, I will destroy man whom I have created from the face of the earth; both man, and beast, and the creeping thing, and the fowls of the air; for it repenteth me that I have made them.

8 But Noah found grace in the eyes of the Lord.

9 These are the generations of Noah: Noah was a just man, and perfect in his generations, and Noah walked with God.

10 And Noah begat three sons, Shem, Ham, and Japheth.

11 The earth also was corrupt before God, and the earth was filled with violence.

12 And God looked upon the earth, and, behold, it was corrupt; for all flesh had corrupted his way upon the earth.

13 And God said unto Noah, The end of all flesh is come before me; for the earth is filled with violence through them; and, behold, I will destroy them with the earth.

14 Make thee an ark of gopher wood: rooms shalt thou make in the ark, and shalt pitch it within and without with pitch.

15 And this is the fashion which thou shalt make it of: The length of the ark shall be three hundred cubits, the breadth of it fifty cubits, and the height of it thirty cubits.

16 A window shalt thou make to the ark, and in a cubit shalt thou finish it above; and the door of the ark shalt thou set in the side thereof: with lower, second, and third stories shalt thou make it.

17 And, behold, I, even I, do bring a flood of waters upon the earth, to destroy all flesh, wherein is the breath of life, from under heaven; and every thing that is in the earth shall die.

18 But with thee will I establish my covenant; and thou shalt come into the ark, thou, and thy sons, and thy wife, and thy sons' wives with thee.

19 And of every living thing of all flesh, two of every sort shalt thou bring into the ark, to keep them alive with thee; they shall be male and female.

20 Of fowls after their kind, and of cattle after their kind; of every creeping thing of the earth after his kind, two of every sort shall come unto thee, to keep them alive.

21 And take thou unto thee of all food that is eaten, and thou shalt gather it to thee; and it shall be for food for thee, and for them.

22 Thus did Noah; according to all that God commanded him, so did he.

Chapter 7

And the Lord said unto Noah, Come thou and all thy house into the ark; for thee have I seen righteous before me in this generation.

2 Of every clean beast thou shalt take to thee by sevens, the male and his female: and of beasts that are not clean by two, the male and his female.

3 Of fowls also of the air by sevens, the male and the female; to keep seed alive upon the face of all the earth.

4 For yet seven days, and I will cause it to rain upon the earth forty days and forty nights; and every living substance that I have made will I destroy from off the face of the earth.

5 And Noah did according unto all that the Lord commanded him.

6 And Noah was six hundred years old when the flood of waters was upon the earth.

7 And Noah went in, and his sons, and his wife, and his sons' wives with him, into the ark, because of the waters of the flood.

8 Of clean beasts, and of beasts that are not clean, and of fowls, and of every thing that creepeth upon the earth,

9 There went in two and two unto Noah into the ark, the male and the female, as God had commanded Noah.

10 And it came to pass after seven days, that the waters of the flood were upon the earth.

11 In the six hundredth year of Noah's life, in the second month, the seventeenth day of the month, the same day were all the fountains of the great deep broken up, and the windows of heaven were opened.

12 And the rain was upon the earth forty days and forty nights.

13 In the selfsame day entered Noah, and Shem, and Ham, and Japheth, the sons of Noah, and Noah's wife, and the three wives of his sons with them, into the ark;

14 They, and every beast after his kind, and all the cattle after their kind, and every creeping thing that creepeth upon the earth after his kind, and every fowl after his kind, every bird of every sort.

15 And they went in unto Noah into the ark, two and two of all flesh, wherein is the breath of life.

16 And they that went in, went in male and female of all flesh, as God had commanded him: and the Lord shut him in.

17 And the flood was forty days upon the earth; and the waters increased, and bare up the ark, and it was lift up above the earth.

18 And the waters prevailed, and were increased greatly upon the earth; and the ark went upon the face of the waters.

19 And the waters prevailed exceedingly upon the earth; and all the high hills, that were under the whole heaven, were covered.

20 Fifteen cubits upward did the waters prevail; and the mountains were covered.

21 And all flesh died that moved upon the earth, both of fowl, and of cattle, and of beast, and of every creeping thing that creepeth upon the earth, and every man:

22 All in whose nostrils was the breath of life, of all that was in the dry land, died.

23 And every living substance was destroyed which was upon the face of the ground, both man, and cattle, and the creeping things, and the fowl of the heaven; and they were destroyed from the earth: and Noah only remained alive, and they that were with him in the ark.

24 And the waters prevailed upon the earth an hundred and fifty days.

Chapter 8

And God remembered Noah, and every living thing, and all the cattle that was with him in the ark: and God made a wind to pass over the earth; and the waters asswaged;

2 The fountains also of the deep and the windows of heaven were stopped, and the rain from heaven was restrained;

3 And the waters returned from off the earth continually: and after the end of the hundred and fifty days the waters were abated.

4 And the ark rested in the seventh month, on the seventeenth day of the month, upon the mountains of Ararat.

5 And the waters decreased continually until the tenth month: in the tenth month, on the first day of the month, were the tops of the mountains seen.

6 And it came to pass at the end of forty days, that Noah opened the window of the ark which he had made:

7 And he sent forth a raven, which went forth to and fro, until the waters were dried up from off the earth.

8 Also he sent forth a dove from him, to see if the waters were abated from off the face of the ground;

9 But the dove found no rest for the sole of her foot, and she returned unto him into the ark, for the waters were on the face of the whole earth: then he put forth his hand, and took her, and pulled her in unto him into the ark.

10 And he stayed yet other seven days; and again he sent forth the dove out of the ark:

11 And the dove came in to him in the evening; and, lo, in her mouth was an olive leaf pluckt off: so Noah knew that the waters were abated from off the earth.

12 And he stayed yet other seven days; and sent forth the dove; which returned not again unto him any more.

13 And it came to pass in the six hundredth and first year, in the first month, the first day of the month, the waters were dried up from off the earth: and Noah removed the covering of the ark, and looked, and, behold, the face of the ground was dry.

14 And in the second month, on the seven and twentieth day of the month, was the earth dried.

15 And God spake unto Noah, saying,

16 Go forth of the ark, thou, and thy wife, and thy sons, and thy sons' wives with thee.

17 Bring forth with thee every living thing that is with thee, of all flesh, both of fowl, and of cattle, and of every creeping thing that creepeth upon the earth; that they may breed abundantly in the earth, and be fruitful, and multiply upon the earth.

18 And Noah went forth, and his sons, and his wife, and his sons' wives with him:

19 Every beast, every creeping thing, and every fowl, and whatsoever creepeth upon the earth, after their kinds, went forth out of the ark.

20 And Noah builded an altar unto the Lord; and took of every clean beast, and of every clean fowl, and offered burnt offerings on the altar.

21 And the Lord smelled a sweet savour; and the Lord said in his heart, I will not again curse the ground any more for man's sake; for the imagination of man's heart is evil from his youth; neither will I again smite any more every thing living, as I have done.

22 While the earth remaineth, seedtime and harvest, and cold and heat, and summer and winter, and day and night shall not cease.

Chapter 9

And God blessed Noah and his sons, and said unto them, Be fruitful, and multiply, and replenish the earth.

2 And the fear of you and the dread of you shall be upon every beast of the earth, and upon every fowl of the air, upon all that moveth upon the earth, and upon all the fishes of the sea; into your hand are they delivered.

3 Every moving thing that liveth shall be meat for you; even as the green herb have I given you all things.

4 But flesh with the life thereof, which is the blood thereof, shall ye not eat.

5 And surely your blood of your lives will I require; at the hand of every beast will I require it, and at the hand of man; at the hand of every man's brother will I require the life of man.

6 Whoso sheddeth man's blood, by man shall his blood be shed: for in the image of God made he man.

7 And you, be ye fruitful, and multiply; bring forth abundantly in the earth, and multiply therein.

8 And God spake unto Noah, and to his sons with him, saying,

9 And I, behold, I establish my covenant with you, and with your seed after you;

10 And with every living creature that is with you, of the fowl, of the cattle, and of every beast of the earth with you; from all that go out of the ark, to every beast of the earth.

11 And I will establish my covenant with you; neither shall all flesh be cut off any more by the waters of a flood; neither shall there any more be a flood to destroy the earth.

12 And God said, This is the token of the covenant which I make between me and you and every living creature that is with you, for perpetual generations:

13 I do set my bow in the cloud, and it shall be for a token of a covenant between me and the earth.

14 And it shall come to pass, when I bring a cloud over the earth, that the bow shall be seen in the cloud:

15 And I will remember my covenant, which is between me and you and every living creature of all flesh; and the waters shall no more become a flood to destroy all flesh.

16 And the bow shall be in the cloud; and I will look upon it, that I may remember the everlasting covenant between God and every living creature of all flesh that is upon the earth.

17 And God said unto Noah, This is the token of the covenant, which I have established between me and all flesh that is upon the earth.

18 And the sons of Noah, that went forth of the ark, were Shem, and Ham, and Japheth: and Ham is the father of Canaan.

19 These are the three sons of Noah: and of them was the whole earth overspread.

20 And Noah began to be an husbandman, and he planted a vineyard:

21 And he drank of the wine, and was drunken; and he was uncovered within his tent.

22 And Ham, the father of Canaan, saw the nakedness of his father, and told his two brethren without.

23 And Shem and Japheth took a garment, and laid it upon both their shoulders, and went backward, and covered the nakedness of their father; and their faces were backward, and they saw not their father's nakedness.

24 And Noah awoke from his wine, and knew what his younger son had done unto him.

25 And he said, Cursed be Canaan; a servant of servants shall he be unto his brethren.

26 And he said, Blessed be the Lord God of Shem; and Canaan shall be his servant.

27 God shall enlarge Japheth, and he shall dwell in the tents of Shem; and Canaan shall be his servant.

28 And Noah lived after the flood three hundred and fifty years.

29 And all the days of Noah were nine hundred and fifty years: and he died.

EXODUS 19:20-20:22
(the ten commandments)

Chapter 19

20 And the Lord came down upon mount Sinai, on the top of the mount: and the Lord called Moses up to the top of the mount; and Moses went up.

21 And the Lord said unto Moses, Go down, charge the people, lest they break through unto the Lord to gaze, and many of them perish.

22 And let the priests also, which come near to the Lord, sanctify themselves, lest the Lord break forth upon them.

23 And Moses said unto the Lord, The people cannot come up to mount Sinai: for thou chargedst us, saying, Set bounds about the mount, and sanctify it.

24 And the Lord said unto him, Away, get thee down, and thou shalt come up, thou, and Aaron with thee: but let not the priests and the people break through to come up unto the Lord, lest he break forth upon them.

25 So Moses went down unto the people, and spake unto them.

Chapter 20

And God spake all these words, saying,

2 I am the Lord thy God, which have brought thee out of the land of Egypt, out of the house of bondage.

3 Thou shalt have no other gods before me.

4 Thou shalt not make unto thee any graven image, or any likeness of any thing that is in heaven above, or that is in the earth beneath, or that is in the water under the earth:

5 Thou shalt not bow down thyself to them, nor serve them: for I the Lord thy God am a jealous God, visiting the iniquity of the fathers upon the children unto the third and fourth generation of them that hate me;

6 And shewing mercy unto thousands of them that love me, and keep my commandments.

7 Thou shalt not take the name of the Lord thy God in vain; for the Lord will not hold him guiltless that taketh his name in vain.

8 Remember the sabbath day, to keep it holy.

9 Six days shalt thou labour, and do all thy work:

10 But the seventh day is the sabbath of the Lord thy God: in it thou shalt not do any work, thou, nor thy son, nor thy daughter, thy manservant, nor thy maidservant, nor thy cattle, nor thy stranger that is within thy gates:

11 For in six days the Lord made heaven and earth, the sea, and all that in them is, and rested the seventh day: wherefore the Lord blessed the

sabbath day, and hallowed it.

12 Honour thy father and thy mother: that thy days may be long upon the land which the Lord thy God giveth thee.

13 Thou shalt not kill.

14 Thou shalt not commit adultery.

15 Thou shalt not steal.

16 Thou shalt not bear false witness against thy neighbour.

17 Thou shalt not covet thy neighbour's house, thou shalt not covet thy neighbour's wife, nor his manservant, nor his maidservant, nor his ox, nor his ass, nor any thing that is thy neighbour's.

18 And all the people saw the thunderings, and the lightnings, and the noise of the trumpet, and the mountain smoking: and when the people saw it, they removed, and stood afar off.

19 And they said unto Moses, Speak thou with us, and we will hear: but let not God speak with us, lest we die.

20 And Moses said unto the people, Fear not: for God is come to prove you, and that his fear may be before your faces, that ye sin not.

21 And the people stood afar off: and Moses drew near unto the thick darkness where God was.

22 And the Lord said unto Moses, Thus thou shalt say unto the children of Israel, Ye have seen that I have talked with you from heaven.

PSALMS

23

The Lord is my shepherd; I shall not want.

2 He maketh me to lie down in green pastures: he leadeth me beside the still waters.

3 He restoreth my soul: he leadeth me in the paths of righteousness for his name's sake.

4 Yea, though I walk through the valley of the shadow of death, I will fear no evil: for thou art with me; thy rod and thy staff they comfort me.

5 Thou preparest a table before me in the presence of mine enemies: thou anointest my head with oil; my cup runneth over.

6 Surely goodness and mercy shall follow me all the days of my life: and I will dwell in the house of the Lord for ever.

121

I will lift up mine eyes unto the hills, from whence cometh my help.

2 My help cometh from the Lord, which made heaven and earth.

3 He will not suffer thy foot to be moved: he that keepeth thee will not slumber.

4 Behold, he that keepeth Israel shall neither slumber nor sleep.

5 The Lord is thy keeper: the Lord is thy shade upon thy right hand.

6 The sun shall not smite thee by day, nor the moon by night.

7 The Lord shall preserve thee from all evil: he shall preserve thy soul.

8 The Lord shall preserve thy going out and thy coming in from this time forth, and even for evermore.

MATTHEW 4:23, 5:1-17 (from the sermon on the mount: the beatitudes)

Chapter 4

23 And Jesus went about all Galilee, teaching in their synagogues, and preaching the gospel of the kingdom, and healing all manner of sickness and all manner of disease among the people.

Chapter 5

And seeing the multitudes, he went up into a mountain: and when he was set, his disciples came unto him:

2 And he opened his mouth, and taught them, saying,

3 Blessed are the poor in spirit: for theirs is the kingdom of heaven.

4 Blessed are they that mourn: for they shall be comforted.

5 Blessed are the meek: for they shall inherit the earth.

6 Blessed are they which do hunger and thirst after righteousness: for they shall be filled.

7 Blessed are the merciful: for they shall obtain mercy.

8 Blessed are the pure in heart: for they shall see God.

9 Blessed are the peacemakers: for they shall be called the children of God.

10 Blessed are they which are persecuted for righteousness' sake: for theirs is the kingdom of heaven.

11 Blessed are ye, when men shall revile you, and persecute you, and shall say all manner of evil against you falsely, for my sake.

12 Rejoice, and be exceeding glad: for great is your reward in heaven: for so persecuted they the prophets which were before you.

13 Ye are the salt of the earth: but if the salt have lost his savour, wherewith shall it be salted? it is thenceforth good for nothing, but to be cast out, and to be trodden under foot of men.

14 Ye are the light of the world. A city that is set on an hill cannot be hid.

15 Neither do men light a candle, and put it under a bushel, but on a candlestick; and it giveth light unto all that are in the house.

16 Let your light so shine before men, that they may see your good works, and glorify your Father which is in heaven.

17 Think not that I am come to destroy the law, or the prophets: I am not come to destroy, but to fulfil.

LUKE 15:11-32 (the prodigal son)

Chapter 15

11 And he said, A certain man had two sons:

12 And the younger of them said to his father, Father, give me the portion of goods that falleth to me. And he divided unto them his living.

13 And not many days after the younger son gathered all together, and took his journey into a far country, and there wasted his substance with riotous living.

14 And when he had spent all, there arose a mighty famine in that land; and he began to be in want.

15 And he went and joined himself to a citizen of that country; and he sent him into his fields to feed swine.

16 And he would fain have filled his belly with the husks that the swine did eat: and no man gave unto him.

17 And when he came to himself, he said, How many hired servants of my father's have bread enough and to spare, and I perish with hunger!

18 I will arise and go to my father, and will say unto him, Father, I have sinned against heaven, and before thee,

19 And am no more worthy to be called thy son: make me as one of thy hired servants.

20 And he arose, and came to his father. But when he was yet a great way off, his father saw him, and had compassion, and ran, and fell on his neck, and kissed him.

21 And the son said unto him, Father, I have sinned against heaven, and in thy sight, and am no more worthy to be called thy son.

22 But the father said to his servants, Bring forth the best robe, and put it on him; and put a ring on his hand, and shoes on his feet:

23 And bring hither the fatted calf, and kill it; and let us eat, and be merry:

24 For this my son was dead, and is alive again; he was lost, and is found. And they began to be merry.

25 Now his elder son was in the field: and as he came and drew nigh to the house, he heard musick and dancing.

26 And he called one of the servants, and asked what these things meant.

27 And he said unto him, Thy brother is come; and thy father hath killed the fatted calf, because he hath received him safe and sound.

28 And he was angry, and would not go in: therefore came his father out, and intreated him.

29 And he answering said to his father, Lo, these many years do I serve thee, neither transgressed I at any time thy commandment: and yet thou

never gavest me a kid, that I might make merry with my friends:

30 But as soon as this thy son was come, which hath devoured thy living with harlots, thou hast killed for him the fatted calf.

31 And he said unto him, Son, thou art ever with me, and all that I have is thine.

32 It was meet that we should make merry, and be glad: for this thy brother was dead, and is alive again; and was lost, and is found.

(1611)

JOHN DONNE
England, 1572-1631

from *SONGS AND SONNETS*

THE GOOD-MORROW

I wonder, by my troth, what thou and I
Did till we loved? Were we not weaned till then,
But sucked on country pleasures, childishly?
Or snorted we in the seven sleepers' den?
'Twas so; but this, all pleasures fancies be.   5
If ever any beauty I did see
Which I desired and got, 'twas but a dream of thee.

And now good morrow to our waking souls,
Which watch not one another out of fear;
For love all love of other sights controls,   10
And makes one little room an everywhere.
Let sea-discoverers to new worlds have gone;
Let maps to other worlds on worlds have shown;
Let us possess one world: each hath one, and is one.

My face in thine eye, thine in mine appears,   15
And true plain hearts do in the faces rest;
Where can we find two better hemispheres
Without sharp north, without declining west?
Whatever dies was not mixed equally;
If our two loves be one, or thou and I   20
Love so alike that none do slacken, none can die.

SONG

Go and catch a falling star,
   Get with child a mandrake root,
Tell me where all past years are,
   Or who cleft the Devil's foot,
Teach me to hear mermaids singing,   5
Or to keep off envy's stinging,
         And find
         What wind
Serves to advance an honest mind.

If thou beest born to strange sights,   10
   Things invisible to see,
Ride ten thousand days and nights,
   Till age snow white hairs on thee,
Thou, when thou return'st, wilt tell me
All strange wonders that befell thee,   15
         And swear
         No where
Lives a woman true, and fair.

If thou findst one, let me know,
   Such a pilgrimage were sweet;   20

DONNE Most of Donne's poems were not collected and published until 1633, after his death. But since most of them were written much earlier — in the 1590s and the first decade of the 17th century — we print them here ahead of the Meditations. And though it is impossible to determine the actual order of composition of the poems, we follow the standard order, that of the 1635 edition, which conveniently places the poems from *Songs and Sonnets* before the *Divine Poems*, reflecting Donne's movement from secular to sacred subjects. All the poems included here appeared in 1633 except for "Hymn to God My God, in My Sickness," which was first published in 1635. For purposes of illustration, we leave "The Sun Rising" with its original spelling and punctuation. **THE GOOD-MORROW 4. snorted:** snored; **seven sleepers:** in old legend, seven Christian youths of Ephesus who fled persecution and hid in a cave and slept for about 200 years. **5. but:** except for. **SONG** See William Habington's reply (p. 309). **2:** The mandrake, or mandragora, has a forked root thought to resemble a human body, and was thought, as a narcotic, to have magical powers, including that of aiding conception. **5. mermaids:** related to or identified with the Sirens, whose song only Odysseus heard without perishing (Homer's *Odyssey*, XII).

Yet do not, I would not go,
   Though at next door we might meet;
Though she were true when you met her,
And last till you write your letter,
    Yet she   *25*
    Will be
False, ere I come, to two, or three.

THE SUNNE RISING

    Busie old foole, unruly Sunne,
     Why dost thou thus,
Through windowes, and through curtaines call on us?
Must to thy motions lovers seasons run?
    Sawcy pedantique wretch, goe chide   *5*
    Late schoole boyes, and sowre prentices,
  Goe tell Court-huntsmen, that the King will ride,
  Call countrey ants to harvest offices;
Love, all alike, no season knowes, nor clyme,
Nor houres, dayes, moneths, which are the rags of time. *10*

    Thy beames, so reverend, and strong
     Why shouldst thou thinke?
I could eclipse and cloud them with a winke,
But that I would not lose her sight so long:
    If her eyes have not blinded thine,   *15*
    Looke, and to morrow late, tell mee,
  Whether both the'India's of spice and Myne
  Be where thou leftst them, or lie here with mee.
Aske for those Kings whom thou saw'st yesterday,
And thou shalt heare, All here in one bed lay.   *20*

    She'is all States, and all Princes, I,
     Nothing else is.
Princes doe but play us; compar'd to this,
All honor's mimique, All wealth alchimie.
    Thou sunne art halfe as happy'as wee,   *25*
    In that the world's contracted thus;
  Thine age askes ease, and since thy duties bee
  To warme the world, that's done in warming us.
Shine here to us, and thou art every where;
This bed thy center is, these walls, thy sphaere. *30*

THE CANONIZATION

For God's sake hold your tongue, and let me love,
   Or chide my palsy, or my gout,
My five gray hairs, or ruined fortune flout;
   With wealth your state, your mind with arts improve,
    Take you a course, get you a place,   *5*
    Observe His Honour, or His Grace,
Or the King's real, or his stamped face
   Contemplate; what you will, approve,
   So you will let me love.

Alas, alas, who's injured by my love?   *10*
   What merchant's ships have my sighs drowned?
Who says my tears have overflowed his ground?
   When did my colds a forward spring remove?
    When did the heats which my veins fill
    Add one more to the plaguy bill?   *15*
Soldiers find wars, and lawyers find out still
   Litigious men, which quarrels move,
   Though she and I do love.

Call us what you will, we are made such by love;
   Call her one, me another fly;   *20*
We're tapers too, and at our own cost die,
   And we in us find the eagle and the dove.
    The phoenix riddle hath more wit
    By us: we two being one, are it.
So to one neutral thing both sexes fit;   *25*
   We die and rise the same, and prove
   Mysterious by this love.

We can die by it, if not live by love,
   And if unfit for tombs and hearse
Our legend be, it will be fit for verse;   *30*
   And if no piece of chronicle we prove,
    We'll build in sonnets pretty rooms;
    As well a well-wrought urn becomes
The greatest ashes, as half-acre tombs,
   And by these hymns all shall approve   *35*
   Us canonized for love.

And thus invoke us: You whom reverend love
   Made one another's hermitage;
You, to whom love was peace, that now is rage;
   Who did the whole world's soul contract, and drove *40*

THE SUNNE RISING **6. prentices:** apprentices. **17:** from India or the East Indies, spices; from the West Indies, gold ("Myne": mine). **THE CANONIZATION** **5:** Settle on some course or career, get yourself appointed to a position at court or elsewhere. **7. stamped face:** i.e., on coins. **8. approve:** prove, test, try. **15. plaguy bill:** weekly list of those who have died of the plague. **21:** referring to the superstition that each act of intercourse took a day off one's life, and punning on the then common meaning of *die* as having an orgasm. **22. eagle . . . dove:** common multivalent emblems or symbols of maleness and femaleness and of such qualities as strength and majesty, peace and purity. **27. mysterious:** including the theological sense of *mystery*. **32. sonnets:** here probably referring to love lyrics in general; **rooms:** the term *stanza* is Italian for "room."

Into the glasses of your eyes —
   So made such mirrors and such spies
That they did all to you epitomize —
   Countries, towns, courts; beg from above
   A pattern of your love!   45

THE FLEA

Mark but this flea, and mark in this,
How little that which thou deny'st me is;
It sucked me first, and now sucks thee,
And in this flea our two bloods mingled be;
Thou know'st that this cannot be said   5
A sin, nor shame, nor loss of maidenhead,
   Yet this enjoys before it woo,
   And pampered swells with one blood made of two,
   And this, alas, is more than we would do.

Oh stay, three lives in one flea spare,   10
Where we almost, yea more than married are.
This flea is you and I, and this
Our marriage bed and marriage temple is;
Though parents grudge, and you, w'are met,
And cloistered in these living walls of jet.   15
   Though use make you apt to kill me,
   Let not to that, self-murder added be,
   And sacrilege, three sins in killing three.

Cruel and sudden, hast thou since
Purpled thy nail in blood of innocence?   20
Wherein could this flea guilty be,
Except in that drop which it sucked from thee?
Yet thou triumph'st, and say'st that thou
Find'st not thyself nor me the weaker now;
   'Tis true; then learn how false fears be: 25
   Just so much honour, when thou yield'st to me,
   Will waste, as this flea's death took life from thee.

THE BAIT

Come live with me, and be my love,
And we will some new pleasures prove
Of golden sands, and crystal brooks,
With silken lines, and silver hooks.

There will the river whispering run,   5
Warmed by thy eyes more than the sun,
And there th'enamoured fish will stay,
Begging themselves they may betray.

When thou wilt swim in that live bath,
Each fish, which every channel hath,   10
Will amorously to thee swim,
Gladder to catch thee, than thou him.

If thou to be so seen beest loath,
By sun or moon, thou darknest both,
And if myself have leave to see,   15
I need not their light, having thee.

Let others freeze with angling reeds,
And cut their legs with shells and weeds,
Or treacherously poor fish beset
With strangling snare, or windowy net.   20

Let coarse bold hands from slimy nest
The bedded fish in banks out-wrest,
Or curious traitors, sleave-silk flies,
Bewitch poor fishes' wand'ring eyes.

For thee, thou needst no such deceit,   25
For thou thyself art thine own bait;
That fish that is not catched thereby.
Alas, is wiser far than I.

A VALEDICTION: FORBIDDING MOURNING

As virtuous men pass mildly away,
   And whisper to their souls to go,
Whilst some of their sad friends do say,
   The breath goes now, and some say, No;

So let us melt, and make no noise,   5
   No tear-floods nor sigh-tempests move;
'Twere profanation of our joys
   To tell the laity our love.

Moving of th'earth brings harms and fears;
   Men reckon what it did and meant;   10
But trepidation of the spheres,
   Though greater far, is innocent.

---

41. glasses: i.e., as both mirrors and telescopes.   **THE BAIT**   See Marlowe's "The Passionate Shepherd to His Love" (p. 226) and Ralegh's "The Nymph's Reply to the Shepherd" (p. 173).   **A VALEDICTION: FORBIDDING MOURNING**   Said by Izaak Walton in his 1640 biography of Donne to have been written to Donne's wife as he prepared for a trip to France in 1612; Donne's wife's name was Ann More (or Moore).   **11:** in the Ptolemaic system, an oscillatory movement of the universe's concentric spheres that accounted for supposed variations in the precession of the equinoxes; see *Ptolemaic* in the Glossary.

Dull sublunary lovers' love,
    Whose soul is sense, cannot admit
Absence, because it doth remove   15
    Those things which elemented it.

But we by a love so much refined
    That ourselves know not what it is,
Inter-assured of the mind,
    Care less eyes, lips, and hands to miss.   20

Our two souls therefore, which are one,
    Though I must go, endure not yet
A breach, but an expansion,
    Like gold to airy thinness beat.

If they be two, they are two so   25
    As stiff twin compasses are two;
Thy soul, the fixed foot, makes no show
To move, but doth if th'other do.

And though it in the centre sit,
    Yet when the other far doth roam,   30
It leans, and hearkens after it,
    And grows erect as that comes home.

Such wilt thou be to me, who must,
    Like th'other foot, obliquely run;
Thy firmness makes my circle just,   35
    And makes me end where I begun.

THE RELIC

    When my grave is broke up again,
    Some second guest to entertain
    (For graves have learned that woman-head,
    To be to more than one a bed),
        And he that digs it spies   5
A bracelet of bright hair about the bone,
        Will he not let'us alone,
And think that there a loving couple lies,
Who thought that this device might be some way
To make their souls, at the last busy day,   10
Meet at this grave, and make a little stay?

If this fall in a time, or land,
    Where mis-devotion doth command,
    Then he that digs us up will bring
    Us to the Bishop and the King   15
        To make us relics; then
Thou shalt be a Mary Magdalen, and I
        A something else thereby;
All women shall adore us, and some men;
And since at such time miracles are sought,   20
I would have that age by this paper taught
What miracles we harmless lovers wrought.

    First, we loved well and faithfully,
    Yet knew not what we loved, nor why;
    Difference of sex no more we knew   25
    Than our guardian angels do;
        Coming and going, we
Perchance might kiss, but not between those meals;
        Our hands ne'er touched the seals
Which nature, injured by late law, sets free;   30
These miracles we did, but now, alas,
All measure and all language I should pass,
Should I tell what a miracle she was.

SATIRE III [RELIGION]

Kind pity chokes my spleen; brave scorn forbids
Those tears to issue which swell my eyelids;
I must not laugh, nor weep sins, and be wise;
Can railing then cure these worn maladies?
Is not our mistress, fair Religion,   5
As worthy of all our souls' devotion
As virtue was to the first blinded age?
Are not heaven's joys as valiant to assuage
Lusts as earth's honour was to them? Alas,
As we do them in means, shall they surpass   10
Us in the end, and shall thy father's spirit
Meet blind philosophers in heaven, whose merit
Of strict life may be imputed faith, and hear
Thee, whom he taught so easy ways and near
To follow, damned? O if thou dar'st, fear this;   15
This fear great courage and high valour is.

---

16. elemented: composed. **35. just:** exact, perfect (a circle with a central dot is the symbol for the sun and for gold; a circle itself has from ancient times been a symbol of perfection). **THE RELIC 1-2:** graves were commonly used over and over again. **3. woman-head:** womanhood; disposition or character natural to a woman. **27-28:** i.e., the conventional kisses of greeting and farewell. **SATIRE III** See *satire* in the Glossary. **1. spleen:** considered the seat of mirth and melancholy. **7. blinded:** i.e., pagan, pre-Christian. **13. imputed:** considered, regarded as.

Dar'st thou aid mutinous Dutch, and dar'st thou lay
Thee in ships, wooden sepulchres, a prey
To leaders' rage, to storms, to shot, to dearth?
Dar'st thou dive seas, and dungeons of the earth? *20*
Hast thou courageous fire to thaw the ice
Of frozen North discoveries? and thrice
Colder than salamanders, like divine
Children in th'oven, fires of Spain, and the Line,
Whose countries limbecks to our bodies be, *25*
Canst thou for gain bear? And must every he
Which cries not "Goddess!" to thy mistress, draw,
Or eat thy poisonous words? Courage of straw!
O desperate coward, wilt thou seem bold, and
To thy foes and his (who made thee to stand *30*
Sentinel in his world's garrison) thus yield,
And for forbidden wars, leave the appointed field?
Know thy foes: The foul Devil (whom thou
Strivest to please) for hate, not love, would allow
Thee fain his whole realm to be quit; and as *35*
The world's all parts wither away and pass,
So the world's self, thy other loved foe, is
In her decrepit wane, and thou, loving this,
Dost love a withered and worn strumpet; last,
Flesh (itself's death) and joys which flesh can taste *40*
Thou lovest; and thy fair goodly soul, which doth
Give this flesh power to taste joy, thou dost loathe.
Seek true religion. O where? Mirreus,
Thinking her unhoused here and fled from us,
Seeks her at Rome; there, because he doth know *45*
That she was there a thousand years ago;
He loves her rags so, as we here obey
The statecloth where the Prince sat yesterday.
Crantz to such brave loves will not be enthralled,
But loves her only who at Geneva is called *50*
Religion, plain, simple, sullen, young,
Contemptuous, yet unhandsome; as among
Lecherous humours there is one that judges
No wenches wholesome but coarse country drudges.
Graius stays still at home here, and because *55*
Some preachers, vile ambitious bawds, and laws

Still new like fashions, bid him think that she
Which dwells with us is only perfect, he
Embraceth her whom his godfathers will
Tender to him, being tender, as wards still *60*
Take such wives as their guardians offer, or
Pay values. Careless Phrygius doth abhor
All, because all cannot be good, as one
Knowing some women whores dares marry none.
Graccus loves all as one, and thinks that so *65*
As women do in divers countries go
In divers habits, yet are still one kind,
So doth, so is Religion; and this blind-
ness too much light breeds; but unmoved, thou
Of force must one, and forced but one allow, *70*
And the right; ask thy father which is she;
Let him ask his; though truth and falsehood be
Near twins, yet truth a little elder is;
Be busy to seek her; believe me this,
He's not of none, nor worst, that seeks the best. *75*
To adore or scorn an image, or protest,
May all be bad; doubt wisely; in strange way
To stand inquiring right, is not to stray;
To sleep, or run wrong, is. On a huge hill,
Cragged and steep, Truth stands, and he that will *80*
Reach her, about must, and about must go,
And what the hill's suddenness resists, win so;
Yet strive so, that before age, death's twilight,
Thy soul rest, for none can work in that night.
To will implies delay; therefore now do. *85*
Hard deeds, the body's pains; hard knowledge too
The mind's endeavours reach, and mysteries
Are like the sun, dazzling, yet plain to all eyes.
Keep the truth which thou hast found; men do not stand
In so ill case here that God hath with his hand *90*
Signed kings' blank charters to kill whom they hate;
Nor are they vicars, but hangmen to fate.
Fool and wretch, wilt thou let thy soul be tied
To man's laws, by which she shall not be tried
At the last day? Oh, will it then boot thee *95*
To say a Philip, or a Gregory,

---

17. mutinous Dutch: i.e., rebelling against Spanish dominion. **23-24. divine Children in th'oven:** Shadrach, Meshach, and Abednego (see Daniel 3:12ff.). **24. fires of Spain:** the Inquisition; **Line:** equator. **25. limbecks:** alembics. **27. draw:** i.e., his sword. **35. be quit:** i.e., have the run of. **43ff. Mirreus, Crantz,** etc.: fictional, representative followers — for weak reasons — of various religions or philosophies (Mirreus, Roman Catholicism; Crantz, Calvinist Puritanism; Graius, Anglicanism; Phrygius, skepticism, against all religions; Graccus, Universalism, embracing all religions equally). **48. statecloth:** canopy over the throne. **58. only:** alone. **62. values:** compensatory fine, perhaps giving up an inheritance. **82. suddenness:** i.e., steepness. **91. blank charters:** Cf. French *carte blanche.* **95. boot:** profit. **96-97:** Philip II of Spain; most likely Gregory XIII (pope 1572-85) or XIV (pope 1590-91); Henry VIII of England; Martin Luther.

A Harry, or a Martin taught thee this?
Is not this excuse for mere contraries
Equally strong? Cannot both sides say so?   99
That thou mayest rightly obey power, her bounds know;
Those passed, her nature and name is changed; to be
Then humble to her is idolatry.
As streams are, power is; those blest flowers that dwell

At the rough stream's calm head thrive and do well,
But having left their roots, and themselves given   105
To the stream's tyrannous rage, alas, are driven
Through mills, and rocks, and woods, and at last, almost
Consumed in going, in the sea are lost.
So perish souls, which more choose men's unjust   109
Power from God claimed, than God himself to trust.

from *DIVINE POEMS*
HOLY SONNETS

7

At the round earth's imagined corners, blow
Your trumpets, angels, and arise, arise
From death, you numberless infinities
Of souls, and to your scattered bodies go,
All whom the flood did, and fire shall, o'erthrow,   5
All whom war, dearth, age, agues, tyrannies,
Despair, law, chance hath slain, and you whose eyes
Shall behold God, and never taste death's woe.
But let them sleep, Lord, and me mourn a space,
For if above all these my sins abound,   10
'Tis late to ask abundance of thy grace
When we are there; here on this lowly ground
Teach me how to repent; for that's as good
As if thou'hadst sealed my pardon with thy blood.

10

Death, be not proud, though some have called thee
Mighty and dreadful, for thou art not so;
For those whom thou think'st thou dost overthrow
Die not, poor death, nor yet canst thou kill me.
From rest and sleep, which but thy pictures be,   5
Much pleasure; then from thee much more must flow,
And soonest our best men with thee do go,
Rest of their bones, and soul's delivery.
Thou art slave to fate, chance, kings, and desperate men,
And dost with poison, war, and sickness dwell,   10
And poppy or charms can make us sleep as well,
And better, than thy stroke; why swell'st thou then?
One short sleep past, we wake eternally,
And death shall be no more; Death, thou shalt die.

14

Batter my heart, three-personed God; for you
As yet but knock, breathe, shine, and seek to mend;
That I may rise and stand, o'erthrow me,'and bend
Your force to break, blow, burn, and make me new.
I, like an usurpt town to'another due,   5
Labour to'admit you, but Oh, to no end;
Reason, your viceroy in me, me should defend,
But is captived, and proves weak or untrue.
Yet dearly'I love you, and would be loved fain,
But am betrothed unto your enemy;   10
Divorce me,'untie, or break that knot again;
Take me to you, imprison me, for I,
Except that you enthrall me, never shall be free,
Nor ever chaste, except you ravish me.

HYMN TO GOD MY GOD,
IN MY SICKNESS

Since I am coming to that holy room
   Where, with thy choir of saints for evermore,
I shall be made thy music, as I come
   I tune the instrument here at the door,
      And what I must do then, think now before.   5

Whilst my physicians by their love are grown
   Cosmographers, and I their map, who lie
Flat on this bed, that by them may be shown
   That this is my southwest discovery
      Per fretum febris, by these straits to die,   10

SONNET 7 **1-2:** See Revelation 7:1. **8:** See Luke 9:27.   **HYMN TO GOD MY GOD, IN MY SICKNESS** Although Walton in his "Life" of Donne says this hymn was written only days before Donne's death, it and the following hymn were probably composed in 1623, during his serious illness, when he also wrote the Meditations which follow. **9. southwest discovery:** probably alluding to the Strait of Magellan. **10. *Per fretum febris*:** (Latin) through/by the strait/raging heat of fever.

I joy that in these straits I see my West;
  For though their currents yield return to none,
What shall my West hurt me? As West and East
  In all flat maps (and I am one) are one,
  So death doth touch the resurrection.   *15*

Is the Pacific Sea my home? Or are
  The Eastern riches? Is Jerusalem?
Anyan, and Magellan, and Gibraltar,
  All straits, and none but straits, are ways to them,
  Whether where Japhet dwelt, or Cham, or Shem.

We think that Paradise and Calvary,   *21*
  Christ's cross, and Adam's tree, stood in one place;
Look Lord, and find both Adams met in me;
  As the first Adam's sweat surrounds my face,
  May the last Adam's blood my soul embrace.   *25*

So, in his purple wrapped receive me, Lord,
  By these his thorns give me his other crown;
And as to others' souls I preached the word,
  Be this my text, my sermon to mine own,   *29*
  Therefore that he may raise, the Lord throws down.

A HYMN TO GOD THE FATHER

Wilt thou forgive that sin where I begun,
  Which is my sin, though it were done before?
Wilt thou forgive those sins through which I run,
  And do them still, though still I do deplore?
    When thou hast done, thou hast not done,   *5*
    For I have more.

Wilt thou forgive that sin by which I won
  Others to sin? and made my sin their door?
Wilt thou forgive that sin which I did shun
  A year, or two, but wallowed in a score?   *10*
    When thou hast done, thou hast not done,
    For I have more.

I have a sin of fear, that when I have spun
  My last thread, I shall perish on the shore;
Swear by thy self, that at my death thy Son   *15*
  Shall shine as he shines now, and heretofore;
    And, having done that, thou hast done;
    I have no more.

from *DEVOTIONS UPON EMERGENT OCCASIONS*

MEDITATION XV

*Interea insomnes noctes Ego
duco, Diesque.*

I sleep not day
nor night.

Natural men have conceived a twofold use of sleep: that it is a refreshing of the body in this life; that it is a preparing of the soul for the next; that it is a feast, and it is the grace at that feast; that it is our recreation, and cheers us, and it is our catechism and instructs us; we lie down in a hope that we shall rise the stronger, and we lie down in a knowledge that we may rise no more. Sleep is an opiate which gives us rest, but such an   *5* opiate as perchance being under it, we shall wake no more. But though natural men, who have induced secondary and figurative considerations, have found out this second, this emblematical use of sleep, that it should be a representation of death, God, who wrought and perfected his work before Nature began (for Nature was but his apprentice, to learn in the first seven days, and now is his foreman, and works next under him),   *10* God, I say, intended sleep only for the refreshing of man by bodily rest, and not for a figure of death, for he intended not death itself then. But man having induced death

---

18. Anyan: the Strait of Anian, an imaginary waterway across or north of North America, leading from the west coast to Hudson Bay or the Polar Ocean, and thence to the Atlantic — i.e., the fabled Northwest Passage first referred to and shown on maps in the 1560s (much later it was confused with the Bering Strait). **20:** the three sons of Noah who inherited and began repopulating the earth (see Genesis 9-10), supposedly Japhet in Europe, Ham (Cham) in Africa, Shem in Asia. **25. last Adam:** Christ, also known as the "second" or "new" Adam. **26. purple:** blood, also the colour for royalty, and see Mark 15:17: "And they clothed him with purple, and platted a crown of thorns, and put it about his head."

upon himself, God hath taken man's creature, death, into his hand, and mended it; and whereas it hath in itself a fearful form and aspect, so that man is afraid of his own creature, God presents it to him in a familiar, in an assiduous, in an agreeable and 15 acceptable form, in sleep, that so when he awakes from sleep and says to himself, "Shall I be no otherwise when I am dead than I was even now, when I was asleep?" he may be ashamed of his waking dreams, and of his melancholy fancying out a horrid and an affrightful figure of that death which is so like sleep. As then we need sleep to live out our threescore and ten years, so we need death to live that life which we cannot outlive. 20 And as death being our enemy, God allows us to defend ourselves against it (for we victual ourselves against death twice every day, as often as we eat), so God having so sweetened death unto us as he hath in sleep, we put ourselves into our enemy's hands once every day, so far as sleep is death, and sleep is as much death as meat is life. This then is the misery of my sickness, that death as it is produced from me, and is mine own 25 creature, is now before mine eyes; but in that form in which God hath mollified it to us and made it acceptable, in sleep I cannot see it. How many prisoners, who have even hollowed themselves their graves upon that earth on which they have lain long under heavy fetters, yet at this hour are asleep, though they be yet working upon their own graves by their own weight! He that hath seen his friend die today, or knows he shall see 30 it tomorrow, yet will sink into a sleep between. I cannot; and oh, if I be entering now into eternity, where there shall be no more distinction of hours, why is it all my business now to tell clocks? Why is none of the heaviness of my heart dispensed into mine eyelids, that they might fall as my heart doth? And why, since I have lost my delight in all objects, cannot I discontinue the faculty of seeing them by closing mine eyes in 35 sleep? But why rather, being entering into that presence where I shall wake continually and never sleep more, do I not interpret my continual waking here to be a parasceve and a preparation to that?

Meditation XVI

Et properare meum clamant,
   e Turre propinqua,
Obstreperæ Campanæ aliorum
in funere, funus.

From the bells of the church adjoining, I am daily remembered of my burial in funerals of others.

We have a convenient author, who writ a discourse of bells when he was prisoner in Turkey. How would he have enlarged himself if he had been my fellow-prisoner in this sickbed, so near to that steeple which never ceases, no more than the harmony of the spheres, but is more heard. When the Turks took Constantinople, they melted the bells into ordnance; I have heard both bells and ordnance, but never been so much affected 5 with those as with these bells. I have lain near a steeple in which there are said to be more

---

Meditation XV   37. parasceve: the day of preparation for the Jewish sabbath, sabbath eve, Friday, especially Good Friday (see Mark 15:42ff.); day of preparation.   **Meditation XVI**   Epigraph. **remembered:** reminded

than thirty bells, and near another where there is one so big as that the clapper is said to weigh more than six hundred pound, yet never so affected as here. Here the bells can scarce solemnize the funeral of any person but that I knew him, or knew that he was my neighbour; we dwelt in houses near to one another before, but now he is gone into that house into which I must follow him. There is a way of correcting the children of great persons, that other children are corrected in their behalf, and in their names, and this works upon them who indeed had more deserved it. And when these bells tell me that now one, and now another is buried, must not I acknowledge that they have the correction due to me, and paid the debt that I owe? There is a story of a bell in a monastery which, when any of the house was sick to death, rung always voluntarily, and they knew the inevitableness of the danger by that. It rung once when no man was sick, but the next day one of the house fell from the steeple and died, and the bell held the reputation of a prophet still. If these bells that warn to a funeral now were appropriated to none, may not I, by the hour of the funeral, supply? How many men that stand at an execution, if they would ask, "For what dies that man?" should hear their own faults condemned and see themselves executed by attorney? We scarce hear of any man preferred but we think of ourselves, that we might very well have been that man. Why might not I have been that man that is carried to his grave now? Could I fit myself to stand or sit in any man's place, and not to lie in any man's grave? I may lack much of the good parts of the meanest, but I lack nothing of the mortality of the weakest. They may have acquired better abilities than I, but I was born to as many infirmities as they. To be an incumbent by lying down in a grave, to be a doctor by teaching mortification by example, by dying, though I may have seniors, others may be elder than I, yet I have proceeded apace in a good university, and gone a great way in a little time, by the furtherance of a vehement fever; and whomsoever these bells bring to the ground today, if he and I had been compared yesterday, perchance I should have been thought likelier to come to the preferment, then, than he. God hath kept the power of death in his own hands, lest any man should bribe death. If man knew the gain of death, the ease of death, he would solicit, he would provoke death to assist him by any hand which he might use. But as when men see many of their own professions preferred it ministers a hope that that may light upon them, so when these hourly bells tell me of so many funerals of men like me, it presents, if not a desire that it may, yet a comfort whensoever mine shall come.

MEDITATION XVII

Nunc lento sonitu dicunt,
  Morieris.

Now this Bell tolling softly
for another, says to me,
Thou must die.

Perchance he for whom this bell tolls may be so ill as that he knows not it tolls for him; and perchance I may think myself so much better than I am as that they who are about me, and see my state, may have caused it to toll for me, and I know not that. The church is catholic, universal; so are all her actions; all that she does belongs to all. When she

baptizes a child, that action concerns me, for that child is thereby connected to that 5
head which is my head too, and engrafted into that body whereof I am a member. And
when she buries a man, that action concerns me: All mankind is of one author, and is
one volume; when one man dies, one chapter is not torn out of the book, but translated
into a better language; and every chapter must be so translated. God employs several
translators; some pieces are translated by age, some by sickness, some by war, some by 10
justice; but God's hand is in every translation, and his hand shall bind up all our
scattered leaves again, for that library where every book shall lie open to one another.
As therefore the bell that rings to a sermon calls not upon the preacher only, but upon
the congregation to come, so this bell calls us all — but how much more me, who am
brought so near the door by this sickness. There was a contention as far as a suit (in 15
which both piety and dignity, religion and estimation, were mingled) which of the
religious orders should ring to prayers first in the morning; and it was determined that
they should ring first that rose earliest. If we understand aright the dignity of this bell
that tolls for our evening prayer, we would be glad to make it ours by rising early, in
that application, that it might be ours as well as his whose indeed it is. The bell doth 20
toll for him that thinks it doth; and though it intermit again, yet from that minute that
that occasion wrought upon him, he is united to God. Who casts not up his eye to the
sun when it rises? but who takes off his eye from a comet when that breaks out? Who
bends not his ear to any bell which upon any occasion rings? but who can remove it
from that bell which is passing a piece of himself out of this world? No man is an 25
island, entire of itself; every man is a piece of the continent, a part of the main. If a
clod be washed away by the sea, Europe is the less, as well as if a promontory were, as
well as if a manor of thy friends or of thine own were. Any man's death diminishes me,
because I am involved in mankind. And therefore never send to know for whom the
bell tolls; it tolls for thee. Neither can we call this a begging of misery or a borrowing 30
of misery, as though we were not miserable enough of ourselves but must fetch in more
from the next house, in taking upon us the misery of our neighbours. Truly it were an
excusable covetousness if we did, for affliction is a treasure, and scarce any man hath
enough of it. No man hath affliction enough that is not matured and ripened by it, and
made fit for God by that affliction. If a man carry treasure in bullion, or in a wedge of 35
gold, and have none coined into current monies, his treasure will not defray him as he
travels. Tribulation is treasure in the nature of it, but it is not current money in the use
of it except we get nearer and nearer our home, heaven, by it. Another man may be sick
too, and sick to death, and this affliction may lie in his bowels, as gold in a mine, and
be of no use to him; but this bell, that tells me of his affliction, digs out and applies that 40
gold to me, if by this consideration of another's danger I take mine own into
contemplation, and so secure myself by making my recourse to my God, who is our
only security.

(1624)

MEDITATION XVII   **8ff.:** etymologically, *translated* means "carried across." **25-26. No man is an island:** see Arnold's "To Marguerite —
Continued" (p. 1058), Rukeyser's "Islands" (p.1373), and Macpherson's "The Island" (p. 1453). **26. main:** mainland.

BEN JONSON
England, 1573-1637

ON MY FIRST DAUGHTER

Here lies, to each her parents' ruth,
Mary, the daughter of their youth;
Yet, all heaven's gifts being heaven's due,
It makes the father less to rue.
At six months' end she parted hence   5
With safety of her innocence;
Whose soul heaven's Queen (whose name she bears)
In comfort of her mother's tears,
Hath placed amongst her virgin-train:
Where, while that severed doth remain,   10
This grave partakes the fleshly birth.
Which cover lightly, gentle earth.

(c. 1598; 1616)

ON MY FIRST SON

Farewell, thou child of my right hand, and joy;
    My sin was too much hope of thee, loved boy.
Seven years thou wert lent to me, and I thee pay,
    Exacted by thy fate, on the just day.
Oh, could I lose all father now! For why   5
    Will man lament the state he should envy?
To have so soon 'scaped world's and flesh's rage,
    And if no other misery, yet age!
Rest in soft peace, and asked, say, Here doth lie
    Ben Jonson his best piece of poetry.   10
For whose sake henceforth all his vows be such
    As what he loves may never like too much.

(1603; 1616)

SONG, TO CELIA (1)

Come, my Celia, let us prove
While we may the sports of love;
Time will not be ours forever;

He at length our good will sever.
Spend not then his gifts in vain;   5
Suns that set may rise again,
But if once we lose this light,
'Tis with us perpetual night.
Why should we defer our joys?
Fame and rumour are but toys.   10
Cannot we delude the eyes
Of a few poor household spies?
Or his easier ears beguile,
So removed by our wile?
'Tis no sin love's fruit to steal,   15
But the sweet theft to reveal;
To be taken, to be seen,
These have crimes accounted been.

(1605)

SONG: "STILL TO BE NEAT"

Still to be neat, still to be dressed
As you were going to a feast;
Still to be powdered, still perfumed:
Lady, it is to be presumed,
Though art's hid causes are not found,   5
All is not sweet, all is not sound.

Give me a look, give me a face
That makes simplicity a grace;
Robes loosely flowing, hair as free:
Such sweet neglect more taketh me   10
Than all th'adulteries of art;
They strike mine eyes, but not my heart.

(1609)

ON MY FIRST DAUGHTER Jonson's daughter Mary died c.1598. **ON MY FIRST SON** **1. right hand:** See Genesis 35:18: *Benjamin* means "son of my right hand"; Jonson's son Benjamin died of the plague in 1603, on his birthday ("the just day"). **10. Jonson his:** i.e., Jonson's. **SONG, TO CELIA (1)** From the play *Volpone; or, The Fox*, III.vii. 165-83. Cf. Campion's "My sweetest Lesbia," and the note (p. 232). **1. prove:** experience. **STILL TO BE NEAT** From the play *Epicoene; or, The Silent Woman*, I.i. (and known as "Clerimont's song"). Cf. Herrick's "Delight in Disorder" (p. 285).

Song, to Celia (2)

Drink to me only with thine eyes,
  And I will pledge with mine;
Or leave a kiss but in the cup,
  And I'll not look for wine.
The thirst that from the soul doth rise   5
  Doth ask a drink divine;
But might I of Jove's nectar sup,
  I would not change for thine.

I sent thee late a rosy wreath,
  Not so much honouring thee   10
As giving it a hope that there
  It could not withered be.
But thou thereon didst only breathe,
  And sent'st it back to me,
Since when it grows and smells, I swear,   15
  Not of itself, but thee.

(1616)

To Penshurst

Thou art not, Penshurst, built to envious show
  Of touch or marble, nor canst boast a row
Of polished pillars, or a roof of gold;
  Thou hast no lantern whereof tales are told,
Or stairs or courts; but stand'st an ancient pile,   5
  And these grudged at, art reverenced the while.
Thou joy'st in better marks, of soil, of air,
  Of wood, of water; therein thou art fair.
Thou hast thy walks for health as well as sport;
  Thy mount, to which the Dryads do resort,   10
Where Pan and Bacchus their high feasts have made
  Beneath the broad beech, and the chestnut shade;
That taller tree, which of a nut was set
  At his great birth, where all the Muses met.
There in the writhed bark are cut the names   15
  Of many a sylvan, taken with his flames;
And thence the ruddy satyrs oft provoke
  The lighter fauns to reach thy Lady's oak.

Thy copse too, named of Gamage, thou hast there,
  That never fails to serve thee seasoned deer   20
When thou wouldst feast, or exercise thy friends.
  The lower land, that to the river bends,
Thy sheep, thy bullocks, kine, and calves do feed;
  The middle grounds thy mares and horses breed.
Each bank doth yield thee conies; and the tops,   25
  Fertile of wood, Ashore and Sidney's copse,
To crown thy open table, doth provide
  The purpled pheasant with the speckled side;
The painted partridge lies in every field,
  And for thy mess is willing to be killed.   30
And if the high-swollen Medway fail thy dish,
  Thou hast thy ponds that pay thee tribute fish:
Fat aged carps that run into thy net;
  And pikes, now weary their own kind to eat,
As loath the second draught or cast to stay,   35
  Officiously at first themselves betray;
Bright eels that emulate them, and leap on land
  Before the fisher, or into his hand.
Then hath thy orchard fruit, thy garden flowers
  Fresh as the air, and new as are the hours.   40
The early cherry, with the later plum,
  Fig, grape, and quince, each in his time doth come;
The blushing apricot and woolly peach
  Hang on thy walls, that every child may reach.
And though thy walls be of the country stone,   45
  They are reared with no man's ruin, no man's groan;
There's none that dwell about them wish them down,
  But all come in, the farmer and the clown,
And no one empty-handed, to salute
  Thy lord and lady, though they have no suit.   50
Some bring a capon, some a rural cake,
  Some nuts, some apples; some that think they make
The better cheeses bring 'em, or else send
  By their ripe daughters, whom they would commend
This way to husbands, and whose baskets bear   55
  An emblem of themselves in plum or pear.
But what can this, more than express their love,
  Add to thy free provisions, far above
The need of such, whose liberal board doth flow

Song, to Celia (2) Composed from various passages in the *Epistles* of Philostratus (e.g. the opening line is from Epistle 33). **To Penshurst** **1. Penshurst:** estate in Kent owned by Sir Robert Sidney (1563-1626), Viscount Lisle, later (1618) Earl of Leicester, younger brother of Sir Philip Sidney; it had been in the Sidney family since 1552. **2. touch:** touchstone. **13-14. taller tree, his great birth:** An oak tree was planted at the time of Sir Philip Sidney's birth at Penshurst in 1554. **18. Lady's oak:** Tradition relates that Lady Leicester (wife of Sir Robert Sidney) once went into labour under this tree. **19:** Barbara Gamage (d. 1621), Sir Robert's wife (their eldest child was Lady Mary Wroth). **26. wood:** i.e., woods, two of them being "Ashore and Sidney's copse." **31:** The village of Penshurst is at the confluence of the Medway and Eden Rivers. **48. clown:** peasant, rustic.

With all that hospitality doth know? 60
Where comes no guest but is allowed to eat
    Without his fear, and of thy lord's own meat;
Where the same beer and bread and self-same wine
    That is his lordship's shall be also mine.
And I not fain to sit, as some this day 65
    At great men's tables, and yet dine away.
Here no man tells my cups, nor, standing by,
    A waiter doth my gluttony envy,
But gives me what I call and lets me eat;
    He knows below he shall find plenty of meat. 70
Thy tables hoard not up for the next day,
    Nor when I take my lodging need I pray
For fire or lights or livery; all is there
    As if thou then wert mine, or I reigned here;
There's nothing I can wish, for which I stay. 75
    That found King James when, hunting late this way
With his brave son, the Prince, they saw thy fires
    Shine bright on every hearth as the desires
Of thy Penates had been set on flame
    To entertain them, or the country came 80
With all their zeal to warm their welcome here.

What, great I will not say, but sudden cheer
Didst thou then make 'em! and what praise was heaped
    On thy good lady then! who therein reaped
The just reward of her high huswifery; 85
    To have her linen, plate, and all things nigh
When she was far, and not a room but dressed
    As if it had expected such a guest!
These, Penshurst, are thy praise, and yet not all.
    Thy lady's noble, fruitful, chaste withal; 90
His children thy great lord may call his own,
    A fortune in this age but rarely known.
They are and have been taught religion; thence
    Their gentler spirits have sucked innocence.
Each morn and even they are taught to pray 95
    With the whole household, and may every day
Read, in their virtuous parents' noble parts,
    The mysteries of manners, arms, and arts.
Now, Penshurst, they that will proportion thee
    With other edifices, when they see 100
Those proud, ambitious heaps and nothing else,
    May say, their lords have built, but thy lord dwells.

(1616)

JOSEPH HALL
England, 1574-1656

from *CHARACTERS OF VIRTUES AND VICES*

HE IS A HAPPY MAN

That hath learned to read himself more than all books, and hath so taken out this lesson that he can never forget it; that knows the world, and cares not for it; that, after many traverses of thoughts, is grown to know what he may trust to, and stands now equally armed for all events; that hath got the mastery at home, so as he can cross his will without a mutiny, and so please it that he makes it not a wanton; that in earthly things 5 wishes no more than nature, in spiritual is ever graciously ambitious; that for his condition stands on his own feet, not needing to lean upon the great, and can so frame his thoughts to his estate that when he hath least he cannot want, because he is as free from desire as superfluity; that hath seasonably broken the headstrong restiness of prosperity,

---

66. dine away: i.e., on inferior fare at another table or at the other end of a long table. **67. tells:** counts. **79. Penates:** Roman household gods. **99. proportion:** compare. **101. heaps:** Cf. *pile*, line 5.   HE IS A HAPPY MAN   **4-5: that hath got . . . a wanton:** i.e., his will is subservient to his reason. **9. restiness:** restiveness.

and can now manage it at pleasure; upon whom all smaller crosses light as hailstones   *10*
upon a roof; and for the greater calamities, he can take them as tributes of life and tokens
of love; and if his ship be tossed, yet he is sure his anchor is fast. If all the world were
his, he could be no other than he is, no whit gladder of himself, no whit higher in his
carriage, because he knows contentment lies not in the things he hath, but in the mind
that values them. The powers of his resolution can either multiply or subtract at pleasure.   *15*
He can make his cottage a manor or a palace when he lists, and his home-close a large
dominion, his stained cloth arras, his earth plate, and can see state in the attendance of
one servant, as one that hath learned a man's greatness or baseness is in himself; and in
this he may even contest with the proud, that he thinks his own best. Or if he must be
outwardly great, he can but turn the other end of the glass, and make his stately manor a   *20*
low and straight cottage, and in all his costly furniture he can see not richness but use; he
can see dross in the best metal and earth through the best clothes, and in all his troupe he
can see himself his own servant. He lives quietly at home out of the noise of the world,
and loves to enjoy himself always, and sometimes his friend, and hath as full scope to his
thought as to his eyes. He walks ever even in the midway betwixt hopes and fears,   *25*
resolved to fear nothing but God, to hope for nothing but what which he must have. He
hath a wise and virtuous mind in a serviceable body, which that better part affects as a
present servant and a future companion, so cherishing his flesh as one that would scorn to
be all flesh. He hath no enemies; not for that all love him, but because he knows to make
a gain of malice. He is not so engaged to any earthly thing that they two cannot part on   *30*
even terms; there is neither laughter in their meeting, nor in their shaking of hands tears.
He keeps ever the best company, the God of Spirits and the spirits of that God, whom he
entertains continually in an awful familiarity, not being hindered either with too much
light or with none at all. His conscience and his hand are friends, and (what devil soever
tempt him) will not fall out. That divine part goes ever uprightly and freely, not stooping   *35*
under the burden of a willing sin, not fettered with the gyves of unjust scruples. He would
not, if he could, run away from himself or from God; not caring from whom he lies hid,
so he may look these two in the face. Censures and applauses are passengers to him, not
guests; his ear is their thoroughfare, not their harbour; he hath learned to fetch both his
counsel and his sentence from his own breast. He doth not lay weight upon his own   *40*
shoulders, as one that loves to torment himself with the honour of much employment; but
as he makes work his game, so doth he not list to make himself work. His strife is ever to
redeem and not to spend time. It is his trade to do good, and to think of it his recreation.
He hath hands enough for himself and others, which are ever stretched forth for
beneficence, not for need. He walks cheerfully in the way that God hath chalked, and   *45*
never wishes it more wide or more smooth. Those very temptations whereby he is foiled
strengthen him; he comes forth crowned and triumphing out of the spiritual battles, and
those scars that he hath make him beautiful. His soul is every day dilated to receive that
God, in whom he is; and hath attained to love himself for God, and God for His own
sake. His eyes stick so fast in heaven that no earthly object can remove them; yea, his   *50*
whole self is there before his time, and sees with Stephen, and hears with Paul, and

---

16. home-close: i.e., the enclosure around his house. **17. earth:** earthenware. **21. straight:** strait. **33. awful:** reverential, admiring. **51-52:** For
Stephen, see Acts 7:55-56; for Paul, Acts 9:3-7, 22:6-15, 26:12-14; for Lazarus, John 12:2, Luke 16:19-25.

enjoys with Lazarus, the glory that he shall have, and takes possession beforehand of his room amongst the saints; and these heavenly contentments have so taken him up that now he looks down displeasedly upon the earth as the region of his sorrow and banishment, yet joying more in hope than troubled with the sense of evils. He holds it no *55* great matter to live, and his greatest business to die; and is so well acquainted with his last guest that he fears no unkindness from him: neither makes he any other of dying than of walking home when he is abroad, or of going to bed when he is weary of the day. He is well provided for both worlds, and is sure of peace here, of glory hereafter; and therefore hath a light heart and a cheerful face. All his fellow-creatures rejoice to serve *60* him; his betters, the angels, love to observe him; God Himself takes pleasure to converse with him, and hath sainted him before his death, and in his death crowned him.

(1615)

ROBERT HAYMAN
England, 1575-1629

"The Air in Newfound-land is wholesome, good"

The Air in Newfound-land is wholesome, good;
The Fire, as sweet as any made of wood;
The Waters, very rich, both salt and fresh;
The Earth more rich, you know it is no less.
Where all are good, Fire, Water, Earth, and Air,   *5*
What man made of these four would not live there?

(1628)

GEORGE SANDYS
England, 1578-1644

from Book One of *OVID'S METAMORPHOSES ENGLISHED*

Of bodies changed to other shapes I sing.
Assist, you Gods (from you these changes spring),
And, from the world's first fabric to these times,
Deduce my never-discontinued rhymes.

The sea, the Earth, all-covering Heaven unframed,   *5*
One face had nature, which they Chaos named:
An undigested lump; a barren load,
Where jarring seeds of things ill-joined abode.

OVID'S METAMORPHOSES ENGLISHED   The following are adapted from Sandys's notes to his translation of Ovid's Latin text. Of the proper names which Sandys does not define, the only ones not included in standard dictionaries are the Greek place names Aonia (line 323), which refers to Euboea and Boeotia; Oetean (line 323), which refers to the modern province of Fthiotis; and Cephisus (line 384), a river in Phocis associated with the Graces. **3. these times:** the reign of Augustus.

No Titan yet the world with light adorns,
Nor waxing Phoebe filled her waned horns, 10
Nor hung the self-poised earth in thin air placed,
Nor Amphitrite the vast shore embraced.
With Earth was air and sea: the Earth unstable,
The air was dark, the sea unnavigable,
No certain form to any one assigned; 15
This, that resists. For, in one body joined,
The cold and hot, the dry and humid fight,
The soft and hard, the heavy with the light.
But God, the better nature, this decides,
Who Earth from Heaven, the sea from earth divides, 20
And purer Heaven extracts from grosser air.
All which unfolded by his prudent care
From that blind mass; the happily disjoined
With strifeless peace He to their seats confined.
Forthwith up sprung the quick and weightless fire, 25
Whose flames unto the highest arch aspire;
The next, in levity and place, is air;
Gross elements to thicker earth repair,
Self-clogged with weight; the waters flowing round
Possess the last, and solid Tellus bound. 30
　　What God soever this division wrought,
And every part to due proportion brought;
First lest the Earth unequal should appear,
He turned it round, in figure of a sphere;
Then seas diffused, commanding them to roar 35
With ruffling winds, and give the land a shore.
To these he addeth springs, ponds, lakes immense,
And rivers, whom their winding borders fence.
Of these, not few Earth's thirsty jaws devour;
The rest their streams into the ocean pour; 40
When, in that liquid plain, with freer wave,
The foamy cliffs, instead of banks, they lave;
Bids trees increase to woods, the plains extend,
The rocky mountains rise, and vales descend.
　　Two equal zones, on either side, dispose 45
The measured heavens; a fifth, more hot than those.
As many lines th' included globe divide:
I'th' midst unsufferable beams reside;
Snow clothes the other two; the temperate hold
'Twixt these their seats, the heat well mixed with cold. 50
As earth, as water, upper air outweighs,
So much doth air fire's lighter balance raise.
There, He commands the changing clouds to stray;

There, thundering terrors mortal minds dismay,
And with the lightning, winds engendering snow, 55
　　Yet not permitted every way to blow,
Who hardly now to tear the world refrain
(So brothers jar!) though they divided reign.
To Persis and Sabaea, Eurus flies,
Whose gums perfume the blushing morn's uprise; 60
Next to the evening, and the coast that glows
With setting Phoebus, flowery Zeph'rus blows;
In Scythia horrid Boreas holds his reign
Beneath Boötes and the frozen Wain;
The land to this opposed doth Auster steep 65
With fruitful show'rs, and clouds which ever weep.
Above all these he placed the liquid skies,
Which, void of earthly dregs, did highest rise.
　　Scarce had He all thus orderly disposed,
Whenas the stars their radiant heads disclosed 70
(Long hid in night) and shone through all the sky.
Then, that no place should unpossessed lie,
Bright constellations, and fair figured gods,
In heavenly mansions fixed their blessed abodes;
The glittering fishes to the floods repair; 75
The beasts to earth, the birds resort to air.
　　The nobler creature, with a mind possessed,
Was wanting yet, that should command the rest.
That Maker, the best world's original,
Either him framed of seed celestial, 80
Or Earth, which late he did from Heaven divide,
Some sacred seeds retained, to Heaven allied,
Which with the living stream Prometheus mixed;
And in the artificial structure fixed
The form of all th' all-ruling deities. 85
And whereas others see with downcast eyes,
He with a lofty look did man indue,
And bade him Heaven's transcending glories view.
So that rude clay, which had no form afore,
Thus changed, of man the unknown figure bore. 90
　　The Golden Age was first, which uncompelled
And without rule, in faith and truth excelled.
As then there was nor punishment, nor fear,
Nor threatening laws in brass prescribed were,
Nor suppliant crouching pris'ners shook to see 95
Their angry judge, but all was safe and free.
To visit other worlds, no wounded pine
Did yet from hills to faithless seas decline.

---

9. Titan: the sun. **10. Phoebe:** the moon, as Phoebus the sun. **12. Amphitrite:** the daughter of Oceanus and wife to Neptune, here taken for the sea. **30. Tellus:** the earth, or goddess thereof. **45. zones:** so called of compassing the heavens like girdles. **59. Eurus:** an eastern wind that blows from the Orient; **Persis** (ancient Fars, in Iran) and **Sabaea:** (Sheba) lying east from Italy. **62. Zephyrus:** the west wind, importing a nourisher of life, for all vegetables by the temperature thereof more luxuriously prosper. **63. Boreas:** the north wind. **64. Boötes:** a constellation near the Arctic Circle. **65. Auster:** the southern wind. **83. Prometheus:** see note to line 363. **97. pine:** whereof masts are made for ships, a part of the ship here taken for the whole.

Then, unambitious mortals knew no more
But their own country's nature-bounded shore.   *100*
Nor swords, nor arms were yet; no trenches round
Besieged towns, nor strifeful trumpets sound;
The soldier, of no use. In firm content
And harmless ease, their happy days were spent.
The yet free Earth did of her own accord   *105*
(Untorn with ploughs) all sorts of fruit afford.
Content with nature's unenforced food,
They gather wildings, strawb'ries of the wood,
Sour cornels, what upon the bramble grows,
And acorns, which Jove's spreading oak bestows.   *110*
'Twas always spring: warm Zeph'rus sweetly blew
On smiling flowers, which without setting grew.
Forthwith the earth corn, unmanured, bears,
And every year renews her golden ears;
With milk and nectar were the rivers filled,   *115*
And honey from green holly-oaks distilled.
   But after Saturn was thrown down to Hell,
Jove ruled, and then the Silver Age befell:
More base than Gold, and yet than Brass more pure.
Jove changed the spring (which always did endure)   *120*
To winter, summer, autumn hot and cold;
The shortened springs the year's fourth part uphold.
Then first the glowing air with fervor burned
The rain to icicles by bleak winds turned.
Men houses built, late housed in caves profound,   *125*
In plashed bowers, and sheds with osiers bound.
Then first was corn into long furrows thrown,
And oxen under heavy yokes did groan.
   Next unto this succeeds the Brazen Age,
Worse natured, prompt to horrid war, and rage,   *130*
But yet not wicked. Stubborn Ir'n the last.
Then blushless crimes, which all degrees surpassed,
The world surround. Shame, truth, and faith depart;
Fraud enters, ignorant in no bad art,
Force, treason, and the wicked love of gain.   *135*
Their sails, those winds, which yet they knew not, strain,
And ships, which long on lofty mountains stood,
Then ploughed th' unpractised bosom of the flood.
The ground, as common erst as light, or air,
By limit-giving geometry they snare.   *140*
Nor with rich Earth's just nourishments content,
For treasure they her secret entrails rent;
The powerful evil, which all power invades,
By her well hid, and wrapped in Stygian shades.

Cursed steel, more cursed gold she now forth brought,   *145*
And bloody-handed war, who with both fought;
All live by spoil. The host his guest betrays,
Sons, fathers-in-law; 'twixt brethren love decays.
Wives husbands, husbands wives attempt to kill,
And cruel step-mothers pale poisons fill.   *150*
The son his father's hasty death desires;
Foiled piety, trod underfoot, expires.
Astraea, last of all the heavenly birth,
Affrighted, leaves the blood-defiled Earth.
   And that the Heavens their safety might suspect,   *155*
The giants now celestial thrones affect,
Who to the skies congested mountains rear;
Then Jove with thunder did Olympus tear,
Steep Pelion from under Ossa thrown.
Pressed with their burthen their huge bodies groan,   *160*
And with her children's blood the Earth imbrued;
Which she, scarce throughly cold, with life indued,
And gave thereto, t'uphold her stock, the face
And form of man, a God-contemning race,
Greedy of slaughter, not to be withstood;   *165*
Such, as well shows, that they were born of blood.
   Which when from Heaven Saturnius did behold,
He sighed, revolving what was yet untold,
Of fell Lycaon's late inhuman feast.
Just anger, worthy Jove, inflamed his breast.   *170*
A synod called, the summoned appear.
There is a way, well seen when skies be clear,
The Milky named; by this, the Gods resort
Unto th' almighty Thunderer's high court.
With ever-open doors, on either hand,   *175*
Of nobler deities the houses stand.
The vulgar dwell dispersed; the chief and great
In front of all, their shining mansions seat.
(This glorious roof I would not doubt to call,
Had I but boldness lent me, Heaven's Whitehall.)   *180*
All sat on marble seats; He, leaning on
His ivory sceptre, in a higher throne,
Did twice or thrice his dreadful tresses shake;
The earth, the sea, the stars (though fixed) quake;
Then thus, inflamed with indignation, spake: *185*
   "I was not more perplexed in that sad time
For this world's monarchy, when, bold to climb,
The serpent-footed giants durst invade,
And would on Heaven their hundred hands have laid.
Though fierce the foe, yet did that war depend   *190*

---

109. cornels: a red fruit with a hard shell growing on a thick shrub, for the most part in mountainous places. **110. oak:** either that which was the symbol of empire, or because Jove first introduced the feeding upon acorns. **137:** i.e., the trees whereof they were made. **139-40:** See Genesis 10:25. **153. Astraea:** Justice, the daughter of Jupiter and Themis, or of Astraeus and Hemera; that is, the daughter of the day, or goddess of civility, because Justice maketh men civil. **167. Saturnius:** Jupiter (Jove) the son of Saturn.

But of one body, and had soon an end.
Now all the race of man I must confound,
Wherever Nereus walks his wavy round;
And this I vow by those infernal floods,
Which slowly glide through silent Stygian woods.   *195*
All cures first sought, such parts as health reject
Must be cut off, lest they the sound infect.
Our demigods, nymphs, sylvans, satyrs, fauns,
Who haunt clear springs, high mountains, woods and lawns
(On whom since yet we please not to bestow   *200*
Celestial dwellings) must subsist below.
Think you, you gods, they can in safety rest,
When me (of lightning, and of you possessed,
Who both at our imperial pleasure sway)
The stern Lycaon practised to betray?"   *205*
All bluster, and in rage the wretch demand.
So when bold treason sought, with impious hand,
By Caesar's blood t'out-race the Roman name,
Mankind, and all the world's affrighted frame,
Astonished at so great a ruin, shook.   *210*
Nor thine, for thee, less thought, Augustus, took,
Than they for Jove. He, when he had suppressed
Their murmur, thus proceeded to the rest.
    "He hath his punishment; remit that care;
The manner how, I will in brief declare.   *215*
The time's accused (but as I hoped belied);
To try, I down from steep Olympus slide.
A god, transformed like one of human birth,
I wandered through the many-peopled Earth.
'Twere long to tell, what crimes of every sort   *220*
Swarmed in all parts; the truth exceeds report.
Now past den-dreadful Maenalus' confines,
Cyllene, cold Lycaeus clad with pines,
There where the Arcadians dwell, when doubtful light
Drew on the dewy chariot of the night,   *225*
I entered his unhospitable court.
The better vulgar to their prayers resort
When I by signs had shown a god's repair.
Lycaon first derides their zealous prayer,
Then said, 'We straight the undoubted truth will try,   *230*
Whether he be immortal or may die.'
In dead of night, when all was whist and still,
Me in my sleep he purposeth to kill.
Nor with so foul an enterprise content,
An hostage murders, from Molossia sent: *235*
Part of his severed scarce-dead limbs he boils,
Another part on hissing embers broils;

This set before me, I the house o'erturned
With vengeful flames, which round about him burned.
He, frighted, to the silent desert flies;   *240*
There howls, and speech with lost endeavour tries.
His self-like jaws still grin; more than for food
He slaughters beasts, and yet delights in blood.
His arms to thighs, his clothes to bristles changed;
A wolf, not much from his first form estranged: *245*
So hoary haired, his looks so full of rape,
So fiery eyed, so terrible his shape.
    One house that fate which all deserve sustains;
For through the world the fierce Erinys reigns.
You'ld think they had conspired to sin. But all   *250*
Shall swiftly by deserved vengeance fall."
    Jove's words a part approve, and his intent
Exasperate; the rest give their consent.
Yet all for man's destruction grieved appear,
And ask what form the widowed Earth shall bear?   *255*
Who shall with odours their cold altars feast?
Must Earth be only by wild beasts possessed?
The king of gods recomforts their despair,
And biddeth them impose on him that care,
Who promised, by a strange original   *260*
Of better people to supply their fall.
And now about to let his lightning fly,
He feared lest so much flame should catch the sky,
And burn Heaven's axletree. Besides, by doom
Of certain fate he knew the time should come   *265*
When sea, Earth, ravished Heaven, the curious frame
Of this world's mass, should shrink in purging flame.
He therefore those Cyclopean darts rejects,
And different-natured punishments elects:
To open all the flood-gates of the sky,   *270*
And man by inundation to destroy.
    Rough Boreas in Aeolian prison laid,
And those dry blasts which gathered clouds invade,
Out flies the south, with dropping wings, who shrouds
His terrible aspect in pitchy clouds.   *275*
His white hair streams, his beard big-swoll'n with showers,
Mists bind his brows, rain from his bosom pours,
As with his hands the hanging clouds he crushed;
They roared, and down in showers together rushed.
All-coloured Iris, Juno's messenger,   *280*
To weeping clouds doth nourishment confer.
The corn is lodged, the husbandmen despair,
Their long year's labour lost, with all their care.
Jove, not content with his aetherial rages,

---

193. Nereus: a sea god, here taken for the ambient ocean. **222-23:** Mountains of Arcadia — Maenalus celebrated for wild beasts, Cyllene for the birth of Mercury, and Lycaeus for pine trees. **224. doubtful light:** twilight. **235. Molossia:** a region of Epirus. **245:** *Lycaon* signifies a wolf. **249. Erinys:** a Fury. **268. Cyclopean darts:** lightning bolts forged by the Cyclops.

His brother's auxil'ary floods engages.   285
The streams convented, "'Tis too late to use
Much speech," said Neptune; "All your powers effuse,
Your doors unbar, remove whate'er restrains
Your liberal waves, and give them the full reins."
Thus charged, they return, their springs unfold,   290
And to the sea with headlong fury rolled.
He with his trident strikes the earth; she shakes,
And way for water by her motion makes.
Through open fields now rush the spreading floods,
And hurry with them cattle, people, woods,   295
Houses, and temples with their gods enclosed.
What such a force, unoverthrown, opposed,
The higher-swelling water quite devours,
Which hides th' aspiring tops of swallowed towers.
Now land and sea no different visage bore,   300
For all was sea, nor had the sea a shore.
One takes a hill; one in a boat deplores,
And where he lately ploughed, now strikes his oars;
O'er corn, o'er drowned villages he sails;
This from high elms entangled fishes hales.   305
In fields they anchor cast, as chance did guide,
And ships the underlying vineyards hide.
Where mountain-loving goats did lately graze,
The sea-calf now his ugly body lays.
Groves, cities, temples, covered by the deep,   310
The nymphs admire; in woods the dolphins keep,
And chase about the boughs; the wolf doth swim
Amongst the sheep; the lion (now not grim)
And tigers tread the waves. Swift feet no more
Avail the hart, nor wounding tusks the boar.   315
The wand'ring birds hid earth long sought in vain,
With weary wings descend into the main.
Licentious seas o'er drowned hills now fret,
And unknown surges airy mountains beat.
The waves the greater part devour; the rest   320
Death with long-wanted sustenance oppressed.
    The land of Phocis, fruitful when a land,
Divides Aonia from th' Oetean strand;
But now a part of the insulting main,
Of sudden-swelling waters a vast plain,   325
There his two heads Parnassus doth extend
To touched stars, whose tops the clouds transcend.
On this Deucalion's little boat was thrown;
With him his wife, the rest all overflown.
Corycian nymphs and hill-gods he adores,   330
And Themis, then oraculous, implores.
None was there better, none more just than he,

And none more reverenced the gods than she.
Jove, when he saw that all a lake was grown,
And of so many thousand men but one,   335
One, of so many thousand women, left,
Both guiltless, pious both, and all bereft,
The clouds (now chased by Boreas) from him throws,
And Earth to Heaven, Heaven unto Earth he shows.
Nor seas persist to rage: their awful guide   340
The wild waves calms, his trident laid aside,
And calls blue Triton, riding on the deep
(Whose mantle nature did in purple steep)
And bids him his loud sounding shell inspire,
And give the floods a signal to retire.   345
He his wreathed trumpet takes (as given in charge)
That from the turning bottom grows more large,
To which when he gives breath, 'tis heard by all,
From far-uprising Phoebus to his fall.
When this the watery deity had set   350
To his large mouth, and sounded a retreat,
All floods it heard, that earth or ocean knew,
And all the floods that heard the same withdrew.
Seas now have shores; full streams their channels keep;
They sink, and hills above the waters peep.   355
Earth re-ascends; as waves decrease, so grow
The forms of things, and late-hid figures show.
And after a long day, the trees extend
Their bared tops; with mud their branches bend.
The world's restored. Which when in such a state,   360
So deadly silent, and so desolate,
Deucalion saw, with tears which might have made
Another flood, he thus to Pyrrha said:
    "O Sister! O my wife! the poor remains
Of all thy sex, which all in one contains!   365
Whom human nature, one paternal line,
Then one chaste bed, and now like dangers join!
Of what the sun beholds from east to west.
We two are all: the sea entombs the rest.
Nor yet can we of life be confident;   370
The threatening clouds strange terrors still present.
O what a heart wouldst thou have had, if fate
Had ta'en me from thee and prolonged thy date!
So wild a fear, such sorrows, so forlorn
And comfortless, how couldest thou have borne!   375
If seas had sucked thee in, I would have followed
My wife in death, and sea should me have swallowed.
O would I could my father's cunning use,
And souls into well-moduled clay infuse!
Now all our mortal race we two contain,   380

---

330. Corycian: Corycus is a cave in Parnassus, consecrated to the nymphs. **363. Pyrrha:** Prometheus and Epimetheus were the sons of Iaphet, Epimetheus the father of Pyrrha and Prometheus of Deucalion; yet he calls her sister, as of old they did cousin-germans.

And but a pattern of mankind remain."
    This said, both wept; both, prayers to Heaven address,
And seek the oracle in their distress.
Forthwith descending to Cephisus' flood,   384
Which in known banks now ran, though thick with mud,
They on their heads and garments water throw,
And to the temple of the goddess go,
At that time all defiled with moss and mire,
The unfrequented altar without fire.
Then, humbly on their faces prostrate laid,   390
And kissing the cold stones, with fear thus prayed:
"If powers divine to just desires consent,
And angry gods do in the end relent,
Say, Themis, how shall we our race repair?
O, help the drowned in water and despair!"   395
The goddess, with compassion moved, replied:
"Go from my temple; both your faces hide;
Let garments all unbraced loosely flow,
And your great-parent's bones behind you throw."
Amazed, first Pyrrha silence breaks, and said: 400
"By me the goddess must not be obeyed,"
And, trembling, pardon craves: her mother's ghost
She fears would suffer, if her bones were tossed.
Meanwhile they ponder and reiterate
The words proceeding from ambiguous fate;   405
Then Promethides, Epimethida
Thus recollecteth, lost in her dismay:

"Or I the oracle misunderstand,
Or the just gods no wicked thing command,
The Earth is our great-mother, and the stones   410
Therein contained I take to be her bones.
These, sure, are those we should behind us throw."
Although Titania thought it might be so,
Yet she misdoubts. Both with weak faith rely
On aiding Heaven. What hurt was it to try?   415
Departing with heads veiled, and clothes unbraced,
Commanded stones they o'er their shoulders cast.
Did not antiquity avouch the same,
Who would believe't! The stones less hard became.
And as their natural hardness them forsook,   420
So by degrees they man's dimensions took,
And gentler-natured grew as they increased;
And yet not manifestly man expressed,
But, like rough-hewn rude marble statues stand,
That want the workman's last life-giving hand.   425
The earthy parts, and what had any juice,
Were both converted to the body's use.
The unflexible and solid, turn to bones;
The veins remain that were when they were stones.
Those thrown by man, the form of men indue;   430
And those were women which the woman threw.
Hence we, a hardy race, inured to pain:
Our actions our original explain.
                                            . . . .
                                                        (1626)

JOHN TAYLOR
England, 1580-1653

EPIGRAM

Walking along the streets the other day,
A ragged soldier crossed me on the way;
And though my purse's lining was but scant,
Yet somewhat I bestowed to ease his want.
For which he kindly thanked me, with his heart,   5
And took his leave, and friendly we did part.
When straight mine eyes a horse and foot-cloth spied,
Upon whose back in pompous state did ride
One whom I thought was deputy to Jove;

Yet not this soldier's wants could pity move,   10
But with disdainful looks and terms of scorn
Commands him travel whither he was born.
'Twill almost make a Puritan to swear
To see an ass's horse a cloak to wear
When Christians must go naked bare, and thin,   15
Wanting apparel t' hide their mangled skin.
Vain world, unto thy chaos turn again,
Since brutish beasts are more esteemed than men.
                                                        (1612)

---

406. **Promethides:** son of Prometheus; **Epimethida:** daughter of Epimetheus. 413. **Titania:** Pyrrha, of her great-grandfather Titan. **EPIGRAM**   Taylor was known as "The Water Poet" from his occupation of Thames "waterman" — i.e., he transported people and goods by boat (this epigram is from *The Sculler*); he was also an inn-keeper, a traveller, and a prolific pamphleteer.

BARTHOLOMEW GRIFFIN
England, fl. 1596

from *FIDESSA, MORE CHASTE THAN KIND*

"Fly to her heart, hover about her heart"

Fly to her heart, hover about her heart,
With dainty kisses mollify her heart,
Pierce with thy arrows her obdurate heart,
With sweet allurements ever move her heart,
At mid-day and at midnight touch her heart,   5
Be lurking closely, nestle about her heart,
With power (thou art a god) command her heart,

Kindle thy coals of love about her heart,
Yea, even into thyself transform her heart.
Ah, she must love! Be sure thou have her heart,   *10*
And I must die if thou have not her heart,
Thy bed, if thou rest well, must be her heart,
He hath the best part sure that hath the heart.
What have I not, if I have but her heart!

(1596)

SIR THOMAS OVERBURY
England, 1581-1613

from *SIR THOMAS OVERBURY'S CHARACTERS*

A MELANCHOLY MAN

Is a strayer from the drove: one that Nature made a sociable, because she made him man, and a crazed disposition hath altered. Unpleasing to all, as all to him; straggling thoughts are his content, they make him dream waking, there's his pleasure. His imagination is never idle, it keeps his mind in a continual motion, as the poise the clock: he winds up his thoughts often, and as often unwinds them; Penelope's web thrives   *5* faster. He'll seldom be found without the shade of some grove, in whose bottom a river dwells. He carries a cloud in his face, never fair weather; his outside is framed to his inside, in that he keeps a decorum, both unseemly. Speak to him; he hears with his eyes, ears follow his mind, and that's not at leisure. He thinks business, but never does any; he is all contemplation, no action. He hews and fashions his thoughts, as if he meant   *10* them to some purpose, but they prove unprofitable, as a piece of wrought timber to no

---

SIR THOMAS OVERBURY'S CHARACTERS   was first published in 1614 as "written by himself and other learned gentlemen his friends"; there were sixteen more editions by 1664, often with additions of new characters by still other authors. "A Fair and Happy Milkmaid," e.g., was written by the playwright John Webster (c.1578-c.1632).   **A MELANCHOLY MAN   4. poise:** weight. **5. Penelope's web:** As a ruse to put off her unwelcome suitors, Odysseus's wife promised to decide among them when she'd finished a piece of weaving — but each night she undid what she'd done that day (see *Odyssey*, II, 93ff., XIX, 137ff., XXIV, 128ff.)

use. His spirits and the sun are enemies: the sun bright and warm, his humour black and cold; variety of foolish apparitions people his head, they suffer him not to breathe according to the necessities of nature, which makes him sup up a draught of as much air at once as would serve at thrice. He denies nature her due in sleep, and nothing pleaseth   *15* him long, but that which pleaseth his own fantasies; they are the consuming evils, and evil consumptions that consume him alive. Lastly, he is a man only in show; but comes short of the better part, a whole reasonable soul, which is man's chief pre-eminence and sole mark from creatures sensible.

(1614)

A Fair and Happy Milkmaid

Is a country wench, that is so far from making herself beautiful by art, that one look of hers is able to put all face physic out of countenance. She knows a fair look is but a dumb orator to commend virtue, therefore minds it not. All her excellences stand in her so silently, as if they had stolen upon her without her knowledge. The lining of her   *5* apparel (which is herself) is far better than outsides of tissue; for though she be not arrayed in the spoil of the silk-worm, she is decked in innocency, a far better wearing. She doth not, with lying long a-bed, spoil both her complexion and conditions; Nature hath taught her too immoderate sleep is rust to the soul; she rises therefore with chanticleer, her dame's cock, and at night makes lamb her curfew. In milking a cow and   *10* straining the teats through her fingers, it seems that so sweet a milk-press makes the milk the whiter or sweeter; for never came almond glove or aromatic ointment off her palm to taint it. The golden ears of corn fall and kiss her feet when she reaps them, as if they wished to be bound and led prisoners by the same hand that felled them. Her breath is her own, which scents all the year long of June, like a new made haycock. She makes   *15* her hand hard with labour, and her heart soft with pity; and when winter's evenings fall early (sitting at her merry wheel) she sings a defiance to the giddy wheel of fortune. She doth all things with so sweet a grace, it seems ignorance will not suffer her to do ill, because her mind is to do well. She bestows her year's wages at next fair; and, in choosing her garments, counts no bravery in the world like decency. The garden and   *20* beehive are all her physic and chirurgery, and she lives the longer for it. She dares go alone and unfold sheep in the night, and fears no manner of ill because she means none; yet, to say truth, she is never alone, for she is still accompanied with old songs, honest thoughts, and prayers, but short ones; yet they have their efficacy, in that they are not palled with ensuing idle cogitations. Lastly, her dreams are so chaste that she dare tell   *25* them: only a Friday's dream is all her superstition; that she conceals for fear of anger. Thus lives she, and all her care is that she may die in the spring-time, to have store of flowers stuck upon her winding-sheet.

(1615)

12-13. humour black and cold: See note to Chaucer's "General Prologue," line 420 (p. 34).   **A Fair and Happy Milkmaid   2. face physic:** i.e., cosmetics (*physic*, "medicine").   **12. corn:** grain.   **18. bestows . . . fair:** i.e., shops for clothes at the next district fair.   **19. bravery:** decorative dress.   **20. chirurgery:** surgery.

PHINEAS FLETCHER
England, 1582-1650

from *A FATHER'S TESTAMENT*

57

Me, Lord? Canst thou mispend
One word, misplace one look on me?
  Call'st me thy Love, thy Friend?
Can this poor soul the object be
Of these love-glances, those life-kindling eyes?   5
What? I the centre of thy arms' embraces?
  Of all thy labour I the prize?
  Love never mocks, Truth never lies.
Oh how I quake: Hope fear, fear hope displaces:
I would, but cannot hope: such wondrous love amazes. *10*

   See, I am black as night,
See, I am darkness: dark as hell.
  Lord, thou more fair than light;
Heaven's sun thy shadow: can suns dwell
With shades? 'twixt light and darkness what commerce? *15*

True: thou art darkness, I thy Light: my ray
  Thy mists and hellish fogs shall pierce.
  With me, black soul, with me converse;
I make the foul December flowery May.
Turn thou thy night to me: I'll turn thy night to day. *20*

   See, Lord, see, I am dead:
Tombed in my self: my self my grave.
  A drudge: so born, so bred:
My self even to my self a slave.
Thou Freedom, Life: can Life and Liberty   *25*
Love bondage, death? *Thy Freedom I: I tied*
  To loose thy bonds: be bound to me:
  My yoke shall ease, my bonds shall free.
Dead soul, thy Spring of life, my dying side:
There die with me to live: to live in thee I died. *30*

(1670)

SIR JOHN BEAUMONT
England, 1583-1627

TO HIS LATE MAJESTY, CONCERNING THE TRUE FORM OF ENGLISH POETRY

Great king, the sov'reign ruler of this land,
By whose grave care our hopes securely stand,
Since you descending from that spacious reach
Vouchsafe to be our master, and to teach
Your English poets to direct their lines,   5
To mix their colours, and express their signs;
Forgive my boldness that I here present
The life of muses yielding true content
In pondered numbers, which with ease I tried
When your judicious rules have been my guide. *10*

  He makes sweet music who, in serious lines,
Light dancing tunes and heavy prose declines;
When verses like a milky torrent flow,
They equal temper in the poet show.
He paints true forms, who with a modest heart *15*
Gives lustre to his work, yet covers art.
Uneven swelling is no way to fame,
But solid joining of the perfect frame,
So that no curious finger there can find
The former chinks, or nails that fastly bind; *20*

TO HIS LATE MAJESTY **9. numbers:** metrical feet, versification. **10:** James I had published, in 1584, *Ane Schort Treatise*, whose rules regarding poetry this work follows.

Yet most would have the knots of stitches seen,
And holes where men may thrust their hands between.
On halting feet the ragged poem goes
With accents neither fitting verse nor prose;
The style mine ear with more contentment fills   25
In lawyers' pleadings, or physicians' bills.
For though in terms of art their skill they close,
And joy in darksome words as well as those,
They yet have perfect sense more pure and clear
Than envious muses, which sad garlands wear   30
Of dusky clouds, their strange conceits to hide
From human eyes; and, lest they should be spied
By some sharp Œdipus, the English tongue
For this their poor ambition suffers wrong.
In ev'ry language now in Europe spoke   35
By nations which the Roman Empire broke,
The relish of the muse consists in rhyme;
One verse must meet another like a chime.
Our Saxon shortness hath peculiar grace
In choice of words fit for the ending place,   40
Which leave impression in the mind as well
As closing sounds of some delightful bell.
These must not be with disproportion lame,

Nor should an echo still repeat the same.
In many changes these may be expressed,   45
But those that join most simply run the best;
Their form, surpassing far the fettered staves,
Vain care and needless repetition saves.
These outward ashes keep those inward fires
Whose heat the Greek and Roman works inspires;   50
Pure phrase, fit epithets, a sober care
Of metaphors, descriptions clear yet rare,
Similitudes contracted smooth and round,
Not vexed by learning, but with nature crowned;
Strong figures drawn from deep invention's springs,   55
Consisting less in words and more in things;
A language not affecting ancient times,
Nor Latin shreds, by which the pedant climbs;
A noble subject which the mind may lift
To easy use of that peculiar gift   60
Which poets in their raptures hold most dear,
When actions by the lively sound appear:
Give me such helps, I never will despair
But that our heads which suck the freezing air,
As well as hotter brains, may verse adorn,   65
And be their wonder, as we were their scorn.

(1629)

EDWARD HERBERT, LORD HERBERT OF CHERBURY
England, 1583-1648

SONNET OF BLACK BEAUTY

Black beauty, which above that common light,
    Whose power can no colours here renew
    But those which darkness can again subdue,
Dost still remain unvary'd to the sight,
And like an object equal to the view,   5
    Art neither chang'd with day, nor hid with night;
    When all these colours which the world call bright,
And which old Poetry doth so pursue,
Are with the night so perished and gone,
    That of their being there remains no mark,   10
Thou still abidest so entirely one,
    That we may know thy blackness is a spark
Of light inaccessible, and alone
    Our darkness which can make us think it dark.

(1665)

ANOTHER SONNET TO BLACK ITSELF

Thou Black, wherein all colours are compos'd,
    And unto which they all at last return,
    Thou colour of the Sun where it doth burn,
And shadow, where it cools, in thee is clos'd
Whatever nature can, or hath dispos'd   5
    In any other hue: from thee do rise
Those tempers and complexions, which disclos'd
    As parts of thee, do work as mysteries,
Of that thy hidden power; when thou dost reign,
    The characters of fate shine in the skies,   10
And tell us what the Heavens do ordain;
    But when Earth's common light shines to our eyes,
Thou so retir'st thy self, that thy disdain
    All revelation unto Man denies.

(1665)

---

47. fettered staves: i.e., stanzas; Beaumont is arguing in favour of couplets. **64-65:** Cf. Milton's remark about the harmful effect a "cold climate" might have on his poetry (*Paradise Lost*, IX, 44-46, p. 356).

WILLIAM DRUMMOND OF HAWTHORNDEN
Scotland, 1585-1649

"Sound hoarse, sad lute, true witness of my woe"

Sound hoarse, sad lute, true witness of my woe,
And strive no more to ease self-chosen pain
With soul-enchanting sounds; your accents strain
Unto these tears uncessantly which flow;
Shrill treble, weep; and you dull basses show   5
Your master's sorrow in a deadly vein;
Let never joyful hand upon you go,

Nor consort keep but when you do complain;
Fly Phœbus' rays, nay, hate the irksome light —
Woods' solitary shades for thee are best,   10
Or the black horrors of the blackest night,
When all the world, save thou and I, doth rest.
    Then sound, sad lute, and bear a mourning part;
    Thou hell mayst move, though not a woman's heart.

(1616)

LADY MARY WROTH
England, c.1587-c.1652

from *PAMPHILIA TO AMPHILANTHUS*

2

Dear eyes, how well (indeed) you do adorn
    That blessed sphere, which gazing souls hold dear,
    The loved place of sought-for triumphs near,
    The court of glory, where Love's force was born.

How may they term you April's sweetest morn   5
    When pleasing looks from those bright lights appear:
    A sun-shine day, from clouds and mists still clear;
    Kind nursing fires for wishes yet unborn!

Two stars of Heaven, sent down to grace the Earth,
    Placed in that throne which gives all joys their birth;   10
    Shining, and burning; pleasing yet their charms;

Which wounding, even in hurts are deem'd delights,
    So pleasant is their force! So great their mights
    As, happy, they can triumph in their harms.

(1621)

5

Can pleasing sight misfortune ever bring?
    Can firm desire a painful torment try?
    Can winning eyes prove to the heart a sting?
    Or can sweet lips in treason hidden lie?

The Sun most pleasing blinds the strongest eye   5
    If too much look'd on, breaking the sight's string;
    Desires still crossed must unto mischief hie,
    And as despair, a luckless chance may fling.

Eyes, having won, rejecting proves a sting,
    Killing the bud before the tree doth spring;   10
    Sweet lips not loving do as poison prove.

Desire, sight, eyes, lips, seek, see, prove, and find
    You love may win, but curses if unkind;
    Then show you harms dislike, and joy in Love.

(1621)

6

My pain, still smother'd in my grieved breast,
  Seeks for some ease, yet cannot passage find
  To be discharg'd of this unwelcome guest;
  When most I strive, more fast his burdens bind,

Like to a ship on Goodwins cast by wind,   5
  The more she strives, more deep in sand is pressed
  Till she be lost; so am I in this kind
  Sunk, and devour'd, and swallow'd by unrest,

Lost, shipwrackt, spoil'd, debar'd of smallest hope,
  Nothing of pleasure left, save thoughts have scope,   10
  Which wander may: Go then, my thoughts, and cry

Hope's perish'd; Love tempest-beaten, Joy lost,
  Killing despair hath all these blessings crossed,
  Yet faith still cries, Love will not falsify.

(1621)

GEORGE WITHER
England, 1588-1667

TIME IS A FADING FLOWER THAT'S FOUND WITHIN ETERNITY'S WIDE ROUND

Five terms there be, which five I do apply
To all that was, and is, and shall be done.
The first and last is that ETERNITY
Which neither shall have end nor was begun.
BEGINNING is the next, which is a space   5
(Or moment rather) scarce imaginary,
Made when the first material formed was,
And then forbidden longer time to tarry.
TIME entered when *Beginning* had an *Ending,*
And is a Progress, all the works of Nature   10
Within the circuit of it comprehending,
Ev'n till the period of the outward-creature.
END is the fourth of those five terms I mean
(As brief as was *Beginning*) and ordained
To set the last of moments to that scene   15
Which on this world's wide stage is entertained.
The fifth we EVERLASTING fitly call,
For though it once *begun,* yet shall it never
Admit of any *future-end* at all,
But be extended onward, still, forever.   20
  The knowledge of these terms, and of what actions
To each of them belongs, would set an end
To many controversies and distractions
Which do so many trouble and offend.
TIME'S nature by the fading flower appears,   25
Which is a type of transitory things;
The circled snake ETERNITY declares,
Within whose round each fading creature springs.
  Some riddles more to utter I intended,
  But lo, a sudden stop, my words have ended.   30

"Shall I, wasting in despair"

Shall I, wasting in despair,
Die because a woman's fair?
Or make pale my cheeks with care
'Cause another's rosy are?
Be she fairer than the day,   5
Or the flow'ry meads in May,
  If she be not so to me,
  What care I how fair she be?

PAMPHILIA TO AMPHILANTHUS SONNET 6 **5. Goodwins:** the Goodwin Sands, frequently the scene of shipwrecks, a few miles off the coast of Kent, near Deal.   **TIME IS A FADING FLOWER** **25:** See the emblem illustrating this poem in the accompanying facsimile reproduction. **26. type:** example, model. **27:** The image of a "circled snake" (e.g. the Ouroboros, the serpent with its tail in its mouth) has been a symbol of eternity since ancient times. The Greek legend encircling the illustration, *ainion kai proskairon,* means "everlasting and for a time," i.e., "eternal and temporary."   **SHALL I, WASTING IN DESPAIR** Ben Jonson wrote an amusing "Answer" to this poem, beginning "Shall I mine affections slack, / 'Cause I see a woman's black?" And see Stevie Smith's "Egocentric" (p. 1350).

Plate 3.   George Wither's "Time Is a Fading Flower," as it appeared in the first edition of *A Collection of Emblemes, Ancient and Moderne*, 1635.

Shall my heart be grieved or pined
'Cause I see a woman kind?   10
Or a well-disposed nature
Joined with a lovely feature?
Be she meeker, kinder, than
Turtle-dove or pelican,
   If she be not so to me,   15
   What care I how kind she be?

Shall a woman's virtues move
Me to perish for her love?
Or her well-deserving known
Make me quite forget mine own?   20
Be she with that goodness blest
Which may gain her name of best,
   If she be not such to me,
   What care I how good she be?

'Cause her fortune seems too high,   25
Shall I play the fool and die?
Those that bear a noble mind,
Where they want of riches find,
Think what with them they would do
That without them dare to woo;   30
   And unless that mind I see,
   What care I how great she be?

Great, or good, or kind, or fair,
I will ne'er the more despair;
If she love me, this believe,   35
I will die ere she shall grieve;
If she slight me when I woo,
I can scorn and let her go;
   For if she be not for me,
   What care I for whom she be?   40

(1622)

THOMAS HOBBES
England, 1588-1679

from *LEVIATHAN*

The Introduction

Nature, the art whereby God hath made and governs the world, is by the art of man, as in many other things, so in this also imitated, that it can make an artificial animal. For seeing life is but a motion of limbs, the beginning whereof is in some principal part within, why may we not say that all *automata* (engines that move themselves by springs and wheels as doth a watch) have an artificial life? For what is the heart but a spring,   5
and the nerves so many strings, and the joints but so many wheels, giving motion to the whole body, such as was intended by the artificer? Art goes yet further, imitating that rational and most excellent work of nature, man. For by art is created that great Leviathan called a Commonwealth, or State, in Latin *Civitas,* which is but an artificial man, though of greater stature and strength than the natural, for whose protection and   10
defense it was intended; and in which the sovereignty is an artificial soul, as giving life and motion to the whole body; the magistrates and other officers of judicature and execution, artificial joints; reward and punishment, by which fastened to the seat of the sovereignty every joint and member is moved to perform his duty, are the nerves, that do the same in the body natural; the wealth and riches of all the particular members are   15

LEVIATHAN   The full title is *Leviathan, or The Matter, Form, and Power of a Commonwealth, Ecclesiastical and Civil.*

the strength; *salus populi*, the people's safety, its business; counsellors, by whom all things needful for it to know are suggested unto it, are the memory; equity and laws, an artificial reason and will; concord, health; sedition, sickness; and civil war, death. Lastly, the pacts and covenants by which the parts of this body politic were at first made, set together, and united, resemble that *fiat,* or the first "Let us make man," pronounced by God in the Creation.

To describe the nature of this artificial man, I will consider

First, the matter thereof, and the artifice, both which is man.

Secondly, how and by what covenants it is made, what are the rights and just power or authority of a sovereign, and what it is that preserveth and dissolveth it.

Thirdly, what is a Christian commonwealth.

Lastly, what is the kingdom of darkness.

Concerning the first, there is a saying much usurped of late that wisdom is acquired, not by reading of books, but of men. Consequently whereunto, those persons that for the most part can give no other proof of being wise, take great delight to show what they think they have read in men by uncharitable censures of one another behind their backs. But there is another saying not of late understood, by which they might learn truly to read one another if they would take the pains; that is, *Nosce teipsum*, Read thyself — which was not meant, as it is now used, to countenance either the barbarous state of men in power towards their inferiors, or to encourage men of low degree to a saucy behaviour toward their betters, but to teach us that for the similitude of the thoughts and passions of one man to the thoughts and passions of another, whosoever looketh into himself, and considereth what he doth when he does think, opine, reason, hope, fear, etc., and upon what grounds, he shall thereby read and know what are the thoughts and passions of all other men upon like occasions. I say the similitude of the objects of the passions, which are the things desired, feared, hoped, etc.; for these the constitution individual and particular education do so vary, and they are so easy to be kept from our knowledge, that the characters of man's heart, blotted and confounded as they are with dissembling, lying, counterfeiting, and erroneous doctrines, are legible only to him that searcheth hearts. And though by men's actions we do discover their design sometimes, yet to do it without comparing them with our own and distinguishing all circumstances by which the case may come to be altered, is to decipher without a key, and be for the most part deceived by too much trust or too much diffidence, as he that reads is himself a good or evil man.

But let one man read another by his actions never so perfectly, it serves him only with his acquaintance, which are but few. He that is to govern a whole nation must read in himself, not this or that particular man, but mankind; which, though it be hard to do, harder than to learn any language or science, yet when I shall have set down my own reading orderly and perspicuously, the pains left another will be only to consider if he also find not the same in himself. For this kind of doctrine admitteth no other demonstration.

INTRODUCTION **16.** *salus populi*: a Latin saying, *Salus populi suprema est lex*, "The welfare of the people is the highest law." **33.** *Nosce teipsum*: more often translated as "Know thyself" (the Latin version of the Delphic inscription *Gnothi seauton*). **48. diffidence**: distrust.

Part I: Of Man
Chapter 13: Of the Natural Condition of Mankind,
as Concerning Their Felicity and Misery

Nature hath made men so equal in the faculties of body and mind as that, though there
be found one man sometimes manifestly stronger in body or of quicker mind than
another, yet when all is reckoned together, the difference between man and man is not
so considerable as that one man can thereupon claim to himself any benefit to which
another may not pretend as well as he. For as to the strength of body, the weakest has   *5*
strength enough to kill the strongest, either by secret machination, or by confederacy
with others that are in the same danger with himself.

And as to the faculties of the mind — setting aside the arts grounded upon words,
and especially that skill of proceeding upon general and infallible rules, called science,
which very few have, and but in few things, as being not a native faculty, born with us,   *10*
nor attained, as prudence, while we look after somewhat else — I find yet a greater
equality amongst men than that of strength. For prudence is but experience, which equal
time equally bestows on all men, in those things they equally apply themselves unto.
That which may perhaps make such equality incredible is but a vain conceit of one's
own wisdom, which almost all men think they have in a greater degree than the vulgar   *15*
— that is, than all men but themselves and a few others, whom by fame, or for
concurring with themselves, they approve. For such is the nature of men, that howsoever
they may acknowledge many others to be more witty, or more eloquent, or more
learned, yet they will hardly believe there be many so wise as themselves; for they see
their own wit at hand, and other men's at a distance. But this proveth rather that men are   *20*
in that point equal, than unequal. For there is not ordinarily a greater sign of the equal
distribution of anything than that every man is contented with his share.

From this equality of ability ariseth equality of hope in the attaining of our ends.
And therefore if any two men desire the same thing, which nevertheless they cannot
both enjoy, they become enemies; and in the way to their end (which is principally their   *25*
own conservation, and sometimes their delectation only) endeavour to destroy or subdue
one another. And from hence it comes to pass that where an invader hath no more to
fear than another man's single power, if one plant, sow, build, or possess a convenient
seat, others may probably be expected to come prepared with forces united, to
dispossess and deprive him, not only of the fruit of his labour, but also of his life or   *30*
liberty. And the invader again is in the like danger of another.

And from this diffidence of one another, there is no way for any man to secure
himself so reasonable as anticipation; that is, by force or wiles to master the persons of
all men he can, so long till he see no other power great enough to endanger him, and this
is no more than his own conservation requireth, and is generally allowed. Also because   *35*
there be some, that taking pleasure in contemplating their own power in the acts of
conquest, which they pursue farther than their security requires; if others that otherwise
would be glad to be at ease within modest bounds, should not by invasion increase their
power, they would not be able long time, by standing only on their defence, to subsist.

And by consequence, such augmentation of dominion over men being necessary to a 40
man's conservation, it ought to be allowed him.

Again, men have no pleasure, but on the contrary a great deal of grief, in keeping company, where there is no power able to overawe them all. For every man looketh that his companion should value him at the same rate he sets upon himself; and upon all signs of contempt, or undervaluing, naturally endeavours, as far as he dares (which 45 amongst them that have no common power to keep them in quiet, is far enough to make them destroy each other), to extort a greater value from his contemners by damage, and from others by the example.

So that in the nature of man, we find three principal causes of quarrel. First, competition; secondly, diffidence; thirdly, glory. 50

The first maketh men invade for gain; the second, for safety; and the third, for reputation. The first use violence to make themselves masters of other men's persons, wives, children, and cattle; the second, to defend them; the third, for trifles, as a word, a smile, a different opinion, and any other sign of undervalue, either direct in their persons, or by reflection in their kindred, their friends, their nation, their profession, or 55 their name.

Hereby it is manifest that during the time men live without a common power to keep them all in awe, they are in that condition which is called war; and such a war as is of every man against every man. For war consisteth not in battle only, or the act of fighting, but in a tract of time wherein the will to contend by battle is sufficiently 60 known, and therefore the notion of time is to be considered in the nature of war, as it is in the nature of weather. For as the nature of foul weather lieth not in a shower or two of rain, but in an inclination thereto of many days together, so the nature of war consisteth not in actual fighting, but in the known disposition thereto, during all the time there is no assurance to the contrary. All other time is peace. 65

Whatsoever therefore is consequent to a time of war, where every man is enemy to every man, the same is consequent to the time wherein men live without other security than what their own strength and their own invention shall furnish them withal. In such condition there is no place for industry, because the fruit thereof is uncertain, and consequently no culture of the earth; no navigation, nor use of the commodities that may 70 be imported by sea; no commodious building; no instruments of moving, and removing, such things as require much force; no knowledge of the face of the earth; no account of time; no arts; no letters; no society; and which is worst of all, continual fear, and danger of violent death; and the life of man, solitary, poor, nasty, brutish, and short.

It may seem strange to some man that has not well weighed these things, that nature 75 should thus dissociate, and render men apt to invade and destroy one another; and he may therefore, not trusting to this inference, made from the passions, desire perhaps to have the same confirmed by experience. Let him therefore consider with himself; when taking a journey, he arms himself and seeks to go well accompanied; when going to sleep, he locks his doors; when even in his house he locks his chests; and this when he 80 knows there be laws, and public officers, armed, to revenge all injuries shall be done him; what opinion he has of his fellow subjects, when he rides armed; of his fellow citizens, when he locks his doors; and of his children and servants, when he locks his chests. Does he not there as much accuse mankind by his actions, as I do by my words? But neither of us accuse man's nature in it. The desires and other passions of man are in themselves no sin. No more are the actions that proceed from those passions, till they know a law that forbids them; which, till laws be made, they cannot know; nor can any law be made, till they have agreed upon the person that shall make it.   85

It may peradventure be thought there was never such a time nor condition of war as this; and I believe it was never generally so, over all the world; but there are many places where they live so now. For the savage people in many places of America, except the government of small families, the concord whereof dependeth on natural lust, have no government at all, and live at this day in that brutish manner, as I said before. Howsoever, it may be perceived what manner of life there would be, where there were no common power to fear; by the manner of life which men that have formerly lived under a peaceful government use to degenerate into in a civil war.   90   95

But though there had never been any time wherein particular men were in a condition of war one against another, yet in all times, kings and persons of sovereign authority, because of their independency, are in continual jealousies, and in the state and posture of gladiators; having their weapons pointing, and their eyes fixed on one another; that is, their forts, garrisons, and guns upon the frontiers of their kingdoms; and continual spies upon their neighbours; which is a posture of war. But because they uphold thereby the industry of their subjects, there does not follow from it that misery which accompanies the liberty of particular men.   100

To this war of every man against every man, this also is consequent: that nothing can be unjust. The notions of right and wrong, justice and injustice, have there no place. Where there is no common power, there is no law; where no law, no injustice. Force and fraud are in war the two cardinal virtues. Justice and injustice are none of the faculties neither of the body nor mind. If they were, they might be in a man that were alone in the world, as well as his senses and passions. They are qualities that relate to men in society, not in solitude. It is consequent also to the same conditions that there be no propriety, no dominion, no *mine* and *thine* distinct; but only that to be every man's, that he can get; and for so long as he can keep it. And thus much for the ill condition which man by mere nature is actually placed in; though with a possibility to come out of it, consisting partly in the passions, partly in his reason.   105   110   115

The passions that incline men to peace are fear of death, desire of such things as are necessary to commodious living, and a hope by their industry to obtain them. And reason suggesteth convenient articles of peace, upon which men may be drawn to agreement. These articles are they which otherwise are called the Laws of Nature, whereof I shall speak more particularly in the two following chapters.   120

(1651)

CHAPTER 13   112. **propriety:** property, ownership.

ROBERT HERRICK
England, 1591-1644

TO FIND GOD

Weigh me the Fire; or, canst thou find
A way to measure out the Wind;
Distinguish all those Floods that are
Mixt in that wat'ry Theater;
And taste thou them as saltless there,   5
As in their Channel first they were?
Tell me the People that do keep
Within the Kingdoms of the Deep;
Or fetch me back that Cloud again,
Beshiver'd into seeds of Rain;   10
Tell me the motes, dust, sands, and spears
Of Corn, when Summer shakes his ears;
Show me that world of Stars, and whence
They noiseless spill their Influence:
This if thou canst; then show me Him   15
That rides the glorious Cherubim.

(1647)

from *HESPERIDES*

THE ARGUMENT OF HIS BOOK

I sing of *Brooks*, of *Blossoms, Birds,* and *Bowers:*
Of *April, May,* of *June,* and *July*-Flowers.
I sing of *May-poles, Hock-carts, Wassails, Wakes,*
Of *Bride-grooms, Brides,* and of their *Bridal-cakes.*
I write of *Youth,* of *Love,* and have access   5
By these, to sing of cleanly *Wantonness.*
I sing of *Dews,* of *Rains,* and piece by piece
Of *Balm,* of *Oil,* of *Spice,* and *Ambergris.*
I sing of *Times trans-shifting;* and I write
How *Roses* first came *Red,* and *Lilies White.*   10

I write of *Groves,* of *Twilights,* and I sing
The Court of *Mab,* and of the *Fairie-King.*
I write of *Hell;* I sing (and ever shall)
Of *Heaven,* and hope to have it after all.

DELIGHT IN DISORDER

A sweet disorder in the dress
Kindles in clothes a wantonness:
A Lawn about the shoulder thrown
Into a find distraction;
An erring Lace, which here and there   5
Enthrals the Crimson Stomacher;
A Cuff neglectful, and thereby
Ribbands to flow confusedly;
A winning wave (deserving note)
In the tempestuous petticoat;   10
A careless shoe-string, in whose tie
I see a wild civility;
Do more bewitch me, than when Art
Is too precise in every part.

TO THE VIRGINS, TO MAKE MUCH OF TIME

Gather ye Rosebuds while ye may,
    Old Time is still a-flying;
And this same flower that smiles to-day
    To-morrow will be dying.

The glorious Lamp of Heaven, the Sun,   5
    The higher he's a-getting,
The sooner will his race be run,
    And nearer he's to setting.

TO FIND GOD   12. Corn: grain.   **THE ARGUMENT OF HIS BOOK   3. Hock-carts:** carts that carry home the last load of the harvest, decorated like a float in a parade (from *hockey,* the festival at harvest home); **Wakes:** parish festivals. **12. Mab:** in some contexts, wife of Oberon and Queen of the fairies.   **DELIGHT IN DISORDER   3. Lawn:** i.e., a scarf made of fine cotton or linen. **5. erring:** wandering, straying. **8. ribbands:** ribbons.

That Age is best which is the first,
   When Youth and Blood are warmer;   *10*
But being spent, the worse, and worst
   Times still succeed the former.

Then be not coy, but use your time,
   And while ye may, go marry;
For having lost but once your prime,   *15*
   You may for ever tarry.

THE COMING OF GOOD LUCK

So Good-luck came, and on my roof did light,
Like noiseless Snow, or as the dew of night:
Not all at once, but gently, as the trees
Are by the Sun-beams tickled by degrees.

UPON A CHILD THAT DIED

Here she lies, a pretty bud,
Lately made of flesh and blood,
Who, as soon, fell fast asleep,
As her little eyes did peep.
Give her strewings, but not stir   *5*
The earth, that lightly covers her.

TO DAFFODILS

Fair Daffodils, we weep to see
   You haste away so soon;
As yet the early-rising Sun

Has not attain'd his Noon.
   Stay, stay,   *5*
   Until the hasting day
     Has run
   But to the even-song;
And, having pray'd together, we
   Will go with you along.   *10*

We have short time to stay, as you,
   We have as short a Spring;
As quick a growth to meet Decay,
   As you, or any thing.
     We die,   *15*
   As your hours do, and dry
     Away,
   Like to the Summer's rain;
Or as the pearls of Morning's dew
   Ne'er to be found again.   *20*

UPON JULIA'S CLOTHES

Whenas in silks my Julia goes,
Then, then, methinks, how sweetly flows
That liquefaction of her clothes.

Next, when I cast mine eyes and see
That brave Vibration each way free,   *5*
O how that glittering taketh me!

             (1648)

FRANCIS QUARLES
England, 1592-1644

ON THE PLOUGHMAN

I hear the whistling Ploughman, all day long,
Sweet'ning his labour with a cheerful song.
His bed's a pad of straw, his diet coarse;
In both, he fares not better than his horse.

He seldom slakes his thirst but from the pump,   *5*
And yet his heart is blithe, his visage plump;
His thoughts are ne'er acquainted with such things
As griefs or fears; he only sweats, and sings.

UPON A CHILD THAT DIED   **5. strewings:** flowers and leaves scattered on a grave.

Whenas the Landed Lord, that cannot dine
Without a qualm, if not refreshed with wine;   *10*
That cannot judge that controverted case,
'Twixt meat and mouth, without the bribe of sauce;
That claims the service of the purest linen
To pamper and to shroud his dainty skin in,
Groans out his days in lab'ring to appease   *15*
The rage of either business, or disease:

Alas, his silken robes, his costly diet,
Can lend a little pleasure, but no quiet;
The untold sums of his descended wealth
Can give his body plenty, but not health.   *20*
The one, in pains and want, possesses all;
T' other, in plenty, finds no peace at all;
'Tis strange! And yet the cause is eas'ly shown:
T' one's at God's finding; t' other, at his own.

(1635)

HENRY KING
England, 1592-1669

THE EXEQUY

To his matchlesse never to be forgotten friend

Accept, thou Shrine of my dead Saint!
Instead of Dirges this complaint;
And for sweet flowers to crown thy hearse,
Receive a strew of weeping verse
From thy griev'd friend, whom thou might'st see   *5*
Quite melted into tears for thee.

   Dear loss! since thy untimely fate
My task hath been to meditate
On thee, on thee: thou art the book,
The library whereon I look   *10*
Though almost blind. For thee (lov'd clay!)
I languish out, not live the day,
Using no other exercise
But what I practise with mine eyes:
By which wet glasses I find out   *15*
How lazily time creeps about
To one that mourns: this, only this
My exercise and bus'ness is:
So I compute the weary hours
With sighs dissolved into showers.   *20*

   Nor wonder if my time go thus
Backward and most preposterous;
Thou hast benighted me. Thy set

This Eve of blackness did beget,
Who wast my day (though overcast   *25*
Before thou had'st thy Noon-tide past),
And I remember must in tears,
Thou scarce had'st seen so many years
As Day tells hours. By thy clear Sun
My love and fortune first did run;   *30*
But thou wilt never more appear
Folded within my Hemisphere,
Since both thy light and motion
Like a fled Star is fall'n and gone;
And twixt me and my soul's dear wish   *35*
An earth now interposed is,
Which such a strange eclipse doth make
As ne'er was read in Almanake.

   I could allow thee for a time
To darken me and my sad Clime,   *40*
Were it a month, a year, or ten,
I would thy exile live till then;
And all that space my mirth adjourn,
So thou wouldst promise to return;
And putting off thy ashy shroud   *45*
At length disperse this sorrow's cloud.

ON THE PLOUGHMAN   **24. finding:** keep, maintenance, provision. THE EXEQUY   **Subtitle. friend:** Anne, his first wife, was buried in
January 1623. **23. set:** setting, i.e., death.

But woe is me! the longest date
Too narrow is to calculate
These empty hopes. Never shall I
Be so much blest as to descry   50
A glimpse of thee, till that day come
Which shall the earth to cinders doom,
And a fierce fever must calcine
The body of this world like thine,
(My Little World!). That fit of fire   55
Once off, our bodies shall aspire
To our souls' bliss: then we shall rise,
And view our selves with clearer eyes
In that calm Region, where no night
Can hide us from each other's sight.   60

   Mean time, thou hast her, earth: much good
May my harm do thee. Since it stood
With Heaven's will I might not call
Her longer mine, I give thee all
My short-liv'd right and interest   65
In her, whom living I lov'd best:
With a most free and bounteous grief,
I give thee what I could not keep.
Be kind to her, and prithee look
Thou write into thy Doomsday book   70
Each parcel of this Rarity
Which in thy Casket shrin'd doth lie:
See that thou make thy reck'ning straight,
And yield her back again by weight;
For thou must audit on thy trust   75
Each grain and atom of this dust,
As thou wilt answer Him that lent,
Not gave thee, my dear Monument.

   So close the ground, and 'bout her shade
Black curtains draw, my Bride is laid.   80

   Sleep on (my Love!) in thy cold bed
Never to be disquieted.
My last good-night! Thou wilt not wake

Till I thy fate shall overtake:
Till age, or grief, or sickness must   85
Marry my body to that dust
It so much loves; and fill the room
My heart keeps empty in thy tomb.
Stay for me there; I will not fail
To meet thee in that hollow vale.   90
And think not much of my delay;
I am already on the way,
And follow thee with all the speed
Desire can make, or sorrows breed.
Each minute is a short degree,   95
And ev'ry hour a step towards thee.
At night when I betake to rest,
Next morn I rise nearer my West
Of life, almost by eight hours' sail,
Than when sleep breath'd his drowsy gale.   100

   Thus from the Sun my Bottom steers,
And my day's Compass downward bears.
Nor labour I to stem the tide
Through which to Thee I swiftly glide.

   'Tis true, with shame and grief I yield,   105
Thou, like the Van, first took'st the field,
And gotten hast the victory
In thus adventuring to die
Before me, whose more years might crave
A just precedence in the grave.   110
But hark! My pulse like a soft Drum
Beats my approach, tells Thee I come;
And, slow howe'er my marches be,
I shall at last sit down by Thee.

   The thought of this bids me go on,   115
And wait my dissolution
With hope and comfort. Dear! (forgive
The crime) I am content to live
Divided, with but half a heart,
Till we shall meet and never part.   120

                                        (1657)

---

106. Van: foremost division in the field, vanguard.

GEORGE HERBERT
England, 1593-1633

EASTER-WINGS

Lord, who createdst man in wealth and store,
  Though foolishly he lost the same,
    Decaying more and more,
      Till he became
        Most poor: 5
        With thee
      O let me rise
    As larks, harmoniously,
  And sing this day thy victories:
Then shall the fall further the flight in me.   10

My tender age in sorrow did begin:
  And still with sicknesses and shame
    Thou didst so punish sin,
      That I became
        Most thin.   15
        With thee
      Let me combine
    And feel this day thy victory:
  For, if I imp my wing on thine,
Affliction shall advance the flight in me.   20
         (1633)

JORDAN (I)

Who says that fictions only and false hair
Become a verse? Is there in truth no beauty?
Is all good structure in a winding stair?
May no lines pass, except they do their duty
 Not to a true, but painted chair?   5

Is it no verse, except enchanted groves
And sudden arbours shadow coarse-spun lines?
Must purling streams refresh a lover's loves?
Must all be veiled, while he that reads, divines,
 Catching the sense at two removes?   10

Shepherds are honest people; let them sing:
Riddle who list, for me, and pull for prime:
I envy no man's nightingale or spring;
Nor let them punish me with loss of rhyme,
 Who plainly say, *My God, My King*.   15
       (1633)

EASTER WINGS Originally printed sideways, i.e., with the lines running vertically. **19. imp:** add on, graft (term from falconry).   **JORDAN (I) 12. pull for prime:** draw for a winning hand in the card game primero.

THE COLLAR

I struck the board, and cried, "No more.
              I will abroad."
What? shall I ever sigh and pine?
My lines and life are free; free as the road,
    Loose as the wind, as large as store.   5
          Shall I be still in suit?
Have I no harvest but a thorn
To let me bloud, and not restore
What I have lost with cordial fruit?
          Sure there was wine   10
Before my sighs did dry it: there was corn
    Before my tears did drown it.
  Is the year only lost to me?
    Have I no bays to crown it?
No flowers, no garlands gay? all blasted?   15
          All wasted?
Not so, my heart: but there is fruit,
      And thou hast hands.
Recover all thy sigh-blown age
On double pleasures: leave thy cold dispute   20
Of what is fit, and not. Forsake thy cage,
      Thy rope of sands,
Which petty thoughts have made, and made to thee
    Good cable, to enforce and draw,
        And be thy law,   25
While thou didst wink and wouldst not see.
      Away! take heed:
      I will abroad.

Call in thy death's head there: tie up thy fears.
      He that forbears   30
    To suit and serve his need,
      Deserves his load.
But as I rav'd and grew more fierce and wild
      At every word,
Methought I heard one calling, *Child!*   35
    And I replied, *My Lord.*

                      (1633)

LOVE (3)

Love bade me welcome; yet my soul drew back,
    Guilty of dust and sin.
But quick-eyed Love, observing me grow slack
    From my first entrance in,
Drew nearer to me, sweetly questioning   5
    If I lack'd any thing.

"A guest," I answered, "worthy to be here":
    Love said, "You shall be he."
"I the unkind, ungrateful? Ah my dear,
    I cannot look on thee."   10
Love took my hand, and smiling did reply,
    "Who made the eyes but I?"

"Truth, Lord, but I have marred them; let my shame
    Go where it doth deserve."   14
"And know you not," says Love, "who bore the blame?"
    "My dear, then I will serve."
"You must sit down," says Love, "and taste my meat."
    So I did sit and eat.

                      (1633)

IZAAK WALTON
England, 1593-1683

from *THE COMPLEAT ANGLER*

Chapter IV: Observations of the Nature and Breeding of the Trout, and how to fish for him, and the Milk-Maid's Song

PISCATOR.   The Trout is a fish highly valued, both in this and foreign nations. He may be justly said, as the old poet said of wine, and we English say of venison, to be a generous fish: a fish that is so like the buck, that he also has his seasons; for it is observed, that he comes in and goes out of season with the stag and buck. Gesner says

---

THE COLLAR **8. bloud:** blood, bleed. **29. death's head:** i.e., a *memento mori*.   THE COMPLEAT ANGLER **Piscator:** i.e., fisherman (line 1); **Venator:** i.e., hunter (line 128). **4. Gesner:** Konrad von Gesner (1516-1565), Swiss writer, naturalist, scholar, and doctor, author of the pioneering *Historia animalium* (1551-58).

his name is of a German offspring; and says he is a fish that feeds clean and purely, in *5*
the swiftest streams, and on the hardest gravel; and that he may justly contend with all
fresh-water fish, as the Mullet may with all sea fish, for precedency and daintiness of
taste; and that being in right season, the most dainty palates have allowed precedency to
him.

And before I go farther in my discourse, let me tell you, that you are to observe, that *10*
as there be some barren does that are good in summer, so there be some barren Trouts
that are good in winter; but there are not many that are so, for usually they be in their
perfection in the month of May, and decline with the buck. Now you are to take notice,
that in several countries, as in Germany, and in other parts, compared to ours, fish do
differ much in their bigness, and shape, and other ways; and so do Trouts. It is well *15*
known that in the Lake Leman, the Lake of Geneva, there are Trouts taken of three cubits
long, as is affirmed by Gesner, a writer of good credit; and Mercator says the Trouts that
are taken in the Lake of Geneva are a great part of the merchandize of that famous city.
And you are further to know, that there be certain waters that breed Trouts remarkable,
both for their number and smallness. I know a little brook in Kent that breeds them to a *20*
number incredible, and you may take them twenty or forty in an hour, but none greater
than about the size of a Gudgeon. There are also, in divers rivers, especially that relate to
or be near to the sea, as Winchester, or the Thames about Windsor, a little Trout called a
Samlet, or Skegger Trout, in both which places I have caught twenty or forty at a
standing, that will bite as fast and as freely as Minnows: these be by some taken to be *25*
young Salmons, but in those waters they never grow to be bigger than a Herring.

There is also in Kent, near to Canterbury, a Trout called there a Fordidge Trout, a
Trout that bears the name of the town where it is usually caught, that is accounted the
rarest of fish; many of them near the bigness of a Salmon, but known by their different
colour; and in their best season they cut very white; and none of these have been known *30*
to be caught with an angle, unless it were one that was caught by Sir George Hastings,
an excellent angler, and now with God; and he hath told me, he thought that Trout bit
not for hunger but wantonness; and it is the rather to be believed, because both he, then,
and many others before him, have been curious to search into their bellies, what the
food was by which they lived, and have found out nothing by which they might satisfy *35*
their curiosity.

Concerning which you are to take notice, that it is reported by good authors, that
grasshoppers and some fish have no mouths, but are nourished and take breath by the
porousness of their gills, man knows not how; and this may be believed, if we consider
that when the raven hath hatched her eggs, she takes no further care, but leaves her *40*
young ones to the care of the God of nature, who is said, in the Psalms, "to feed the
young ravens that call upon him." And they be kept alive and fed by a dew, or worms
that breed in their nests, or some other ways that we mortals know not. And this may be
believed of the Fordidge Trout, which, as it is said of the stork, that he knows his

---

5. German offspring: actually, from Old English *truht,* from late Latin *tructus, truta,* etc., from Greek *troktes,* "gnawer" — though there was also a
Low-Dutch form *trort.* **17. Mercator:** probably Gerard Mercator (1512-1594), Flemish geographer, mathematician, and cartographer. **31. Hastings:**
probably Sir George Hastings (d. 1641), grandson of George Hastings the 4th Earl of Huntingdon (d. 1605) and nephew of the Henry Hastings
(1551-1650) who is the subject of Shaftesbury's "character" (p. 407). **41-42:** See Psalms 147:9.

season, so he knows his times (I think almost his day) of coming into that river out of   *45*
the sea, where he lives, and, it is like, feeds nine months in the year, and fasts three in
the river of Fordidge. And you are to note, that those townsmen are very punctual in
observing the time of beginning to fish for them, and boast much, that their river affords
a Trout that exceeds all others. And just so does Sussex boast of several fish; as,
namely, a Shelsey Cockle, a Chichester Lobster, an Arundel Mullet, and an Amerly   *50*
Trout.

And, now, for some confirmation of the Fordidge Trout: you are to know that this
Trout is thought to eat nothing in the fresh water; and it may be the better believed,
because it is well known that swallows, and bats, and wagtails, which are called half-year
birds, and not seen to fly in England for six months in a year, but about Michaelmas leave   *55*
us for a hotter climate, yet some of them that have been left behind their fellows, have
been found, many thousands at a time, in hollow trees, or clay caves, where they have
been observed to live, and sleep out the whole winter, without meat. And so Albertus
observes, that there is one kind of frog that hath her mouth naturally shut up about the end
of August, and that she lives so all the winter; and though it be strange to some, yet it is   *60*
known to too many among us to be doubted.

And so much for these Fordidge Trouts, which never afford an angler sport, but either
live their time of being in the fresh water, by their meat formerly gotten in the sea, not
unlike the swallow or frog; or, by the virtue of the fresh water only; or, as the birds of
Paradise and the chameleon are said to live, by the sun and the air.   *65*

There is also in Northumberland a Trout called a Bulltrout, of a much greater length
and bigness than any in these southern parts; and there are, in many rivers that relate to the
sea, Salmon-trouts, as much different from others, both in shape and in their spots, as we
see sheep in some countries differ one from another in their shape and bigness, and in the
fineness of the wool; and, certainly, as some pastures breed larger sheep, so do some   *70*
rivers, by reason of the ground over which they run, breed larger Trouts.

Now the next thing that I will commend to your consideration is, that the Trout is of a
more sudden growth than other fish. Concerning which, you are also to take notice, that he
lives not so long as the Perch and divers other fishes do, as Sir Francis Bacon hath
observed in his *History of Life and Death*.   *75*

And next you are to take notice, that he is not like the Crocodile, which if he lives
never so long, yet always thrives till his death; but 'tis not so with the Trout, for after he is
come to his full growth, he declines in his body, and keeps his bigness, or thrives only in
his head till his death. And you are to know, that he will, about (especially before) the time
of his spawning, get almost miraculously through weirs and flood-gates, against the   *80*
stream, even through such high and swift places as is almost incredible. Next, that the
Trout usually spawns about October or November, but in some rivers a little sooner or

---

58. meat: i.e., food (in a note Walton says the foregoing information comes from the book by Bacon that he cites in the text at lines 74-75); **Albertus:** Albert of Cologne, Count of Bollstädt, called Albertus Magnus (1193 or 1206-1280), German scholastic philosopher, Dominican preacher (and briefly bishop of Regensburg), and scientist, author of *de Animalibus* and *de Vegetabilibus*, largely paraphrases and translations of Aristotle; in a note here Walton refers the reader to Edward Topsell (1572-1625), author of *The History of Four-footed Beasts* (1607) and *The History of Serpents* (1608), which collected material from Gesner and many other writers. **74-75:** Bacon's *Historia Vitae et Mortis*, published in 1623, was translated into English by W. Rowley in 1638, as *History, Natural and Experimental, of Life and Death; or of the Prolongation of Life*.

later; which is the more observable, because most other fish spawn in the spring or summer, when the sun hath warmed both the earth and water, and made it fit for generation. And you are to note, that he continues many months out of season; for it may *85* be observed of the Trout, that he is like the buck or the ox, that will not be fat in many months, though he go in the very same pastures that horses do, which will be fat in one month: and so you may observe, that most other fishes recover strength, and grow sooner fat and in season than the Trout doth.

And next you are to note, that till the sun gets to such a height as to warm the earth *90* and the water, the Trout is sick, and lean, and lousy, and unwholesome; for you shall, in winter, find him to have a big head, and, then, to be lank and thin and lean; at which time many of them have sticking on them Sugs, or Trout-lice, which is a kind of a worm, in shape like a clove, or pin with a big head, and sticks close to him, and sucks his moisture; those, I think, the Trout breeds himself, and never thrives till he free himself from them, *95* which is when warm weather comes; and, then, as he grows stronger, he gets from the dead still water into the sharp streams and the gravel, and, there, rubs off these worms or lice; and then, as he grows stronger, so he gets him into swifter and swifter streams, and there lies at the watch for any fly or minnow that comes near to him; and he especially loves the May-fly, which is bred of the cod-worm, or cadis; and these make the Trout bold *100* and lusty, and he is usually fatter and better meat at the end of that month than at any time of the year. Now you are to know that it is observed, that usually the best Trouts are either red or yellow; though some, as the Fordidge Trout, be white and yet good; but that is not usual; and it is a note observable, that the female Trout hath usually a less head, and a deeper body than the male Trout, and is usually the better meat. And note, that a hog-back *105* and a little head, to either Trout, Salmon, or any other fish, is a sign that that fish is in season.

But yet you are to note, that as you see some willows or palm-trees bud and blossom sooner than others do, so some Trouts be, in rivers, sooner in season; and as some hollies, or oaks, are longer before they cast their leaves, so are some Trouts, in rivers, longer *110* before they go out of season.

And you are to note, that there are several kinds of Trouts; but these several kinds are not considered but by very few men; for they go under the general name of Trouts; just as pigeons do, in most places, though it is certain, there are tame and wild pigeons, and of the tame, there be helmits and runts, and carriers and cropers, and indeed too many to name. *115* Nay, the Royal Society have found and published lately, that there be thirty and three kinds of spiders; and yet all, for aught I know, go under that one general name of spider. And it is so with many kinds of fish, and of Trouts especially, which differ in their bigness, and shape, and spots, and colour. The great Kentish hens may be an instance, compared to other hens; and, doubtless, there is a kind of small Trout, which will never *120* thrive to be big, that breeds very many more than others do, that be of a larger size; which you may rather believe, if you consider that the little wren and titmouse will have twenty

---

100. cod-worm: i.e., bait for cod; in the preceding chapter also called a case-worm **115. helmits:** helmets, fancy pigeons with different coloured head plumage; **runts:** domestic pigeons of large stout build; **cropers:** croppers, pouters, breed of pigeons that puff up their crops. **116-17:** *A Table of Spiders Found in England by Dr. M. Lister* (1671).

young ones at a time, when, usually, the noble hawk, or the musical thrassel or blackbird, exceed not four or five.

And now you shall see me try my skill to catch a Trout; and at my next walking, *125* either this evening or to-morrow morning, I will give you direction how you yourself shall fish for him.

VENATOR.   Trust me, master, I see now it is a harder matter to catch a Trout than a Chub; for I have put on patience, and followed you these two hours, and not seen a fish stir, neither at your minnow nor your worm. *130*

PISCATOR.   Well, scholar, you must endure worse luck sometime, or you will never make a good angler. But what say you now? There is a Trout now, and a good one too, if I can but hold him; and two or three turns more will tire him. Now you see he lies still, and the sleight is to land him: reach me that landing-net. So, Sir, now he is mine own; what say you now, is not this worth all my labour and your patience? *135*

VENATOR.   On my word, master, this is a gallant Trout; what shall we do with him?

PISCATOR.   Marry, e'en eat him to supper. We'll go to my hostess from whence we came; she told me, as I was going out of door, that my brother Peter, a good angler and a cheerful companion, had sent word he would lodge there to-night, and bring a friend with him. My hostess has two beds, and I know you and I may have the best. We'll *140* rejoice with my brother Peter and his friend, tell tales, or sing ballads, or make a catch, or find some harmless sport to content us, and pass away a little time without offence to God or man.

VENATOR.   A match, good master, let's go to that house, for the linen looks white, and smells of lavender, and I long to lie in a pair of sheets that smell so. Let's be going, *145* good master, for I am hungry again with fishing.

PISCATOR.   Nay, stay a little, good scholar. I caught my last Trout with a worm; now I will put on a minnow, and try a quarter of an hour about yonder trees for another; and, so, walk towards our lodging. Look you, scholar, thereabout we shall have a bite presently, or not at all. Have with you, Sir: o' my word I have hold of him. Oh! it is a *150* great logger-headed Chub; come, hang him upon that willow twig, and let's be going. But turn out of the way a little, good scholar! toward yonder high honeysuckle hedge; there we'll sit and sing, whilst this shower falls so gently upon the teeming earth, and gives yet a sweeter smell to the lovely flowers that adorn these verdant meadows.

Look! under that broad beech-tree I sat down, when I was last this way a-fishing; *155* and the birds in the adjoining grove seemed to have a friendly contention with an echo, whose dead voice seemed to live in a hollow tree near to the brow of that primrose-hill. There I sat viewing the silver streams glide silently towards their centre, the tempestuous sea; yet sometimes opposed by rugged roots and pebble-stones, which broke their waves, and turned them into foam; and sometimes I beguiled time by *160* viewing the harmless lambs; some leaping securely in the cool shade, whilst others sported themselves in the cheerful sun; and saw others craving comfort from the swollen

---

123. thrassel: throstle. **141. catch:** complex song for several voices, in which one singer picks up lines from another. **144. match:** something that suits or tallies with another — i.e., an agreeable notion. **150. o':** for "on."

udders of their bleating dams. As I thus sat, these and other sights had so fully possessed my soul with content, that I thought, as the poet has happily expressed it,

> I was for that time lifted above earth;   *165*
> And possessed joys not promised in my birth.

As I left this place, and entered into the next field, a second pleasure entertained me; 'twas a handsome milk-maid, that had not yet attained so much age and wisdom as to load her mind with any fears of many things that will never be, as too many men too often do; but she cast away all care, and sung like a nightingale. Her voice was good, and the ditty *170* fitted for it; it was that smooth song which was made by Kit Marlow, now at least fifty years ago; and the milk-maid's mother sung an answer to it, which was made by Sir Walter Raleigh, in his younger days. They were old-fashioned poetry, but choicely good; I think much better than the strong lines that are now in fashion in this critical age. Look yonder! on my word, yonder, they both be a-milking again. I will give her the Chub, and persuade *175* them to sing those two songs to us.

God speed you, good woman! I have been a-fishing; and am going to Bleak-Hall to my bed; and having caught more fish than will sup myself and my friend, I will bestow this upon you and your daughter, for I use to sell none.

MILK-WOMAN.   Marry! God requite you, Sir, and we'll eat it cheerfully. And if *180* you come this way a-fishing two months hence, a grace of God! I'll give you a syllabub of new verjuice, in a new-made haycock, for it. And my Maudlin shall sing you one of her best ballads; for she and I both love all anglers, they be such honest, civil, quiet men. In the meantime will you drink a draught of red cow's milk? You shall have it freely.   *185*

PISCATOR.   No, I thank you; but, I pray, do us a courtesy that shall stand you and your daughter in nothing, and yet we will think ourselves still something in your debt: it is but to sing us a song that was sung by your daughter when I last passed over this meadow, about eight or nine days since.

MILK-WOMAN.   What song was it, I pray? Was it, 'Come, Shepherds, deck your *190* heads'? or, 'As at noon Dulcina rested'? or, 'Phillida flouts me'? or, 'Chevy Chase'? or, 'Johnny Armstrong'? or, 'Troy Town'?

PISCATOR.   No, it is none of those; it is a song that your daughter sung the first part, and you sung the answer to it.

MILK-WOMAN.   O, I know it now. I learned the first part in my golden age, when I *195* was about the age of my poor daughter; and the latter part, which indeed fits me best now, but two or three years ago, when the cares of the world began to take hold of me: but you shall, God willing, hear them both, and sung as well as we can, for we both love

---

171-73: See Marlowe's "The Passionate Shepherd to His Love" (p. 226) and Ralegh's "The Nymph's Reply to the Shepherd" (p. 173); the versions that follow here (with Walton's titles) differ slightly from the standard versions, each e.g. having an extra stanza. **181-82. a syllabub of new verjuice:** a drink made by combining cream with the acidic juice of unripe fruit. **182. in . . . haycock:** i.e., where they may sit comfortably; **Maudlin:** English contraction of *Magdalen.* **190-92:** popular songs and ballads of the time ("Chevy Chase" is probably the best-known). Most such works can be found in one or another of such collections as Thomas Percy's *Reliques of Ancient English Poetry,* Joseph Ritson's *Ancient Songs and Ballads,* Sir Arthur Quiller-Couch's *The Oxford Book of Ballads,* and Hyder E. Rollins's *The Pepys Ballads*; "Troy Town," e.g., is in Percy, under the title "Queen Dido," as is "As at noon," with the title "Dulcina."

anglers. Come, Maudlin, sing the first part to the gentlemen, with a merry heart; and I'll
sing the second when you have done.   200

The Milk-Maid's Song
Come, live with me, and be my love,
And we will all the pleasures prove,
That valleys, groves, or hills, or fields,
Or woods, and steepy mountains yields;   205

Where we will sit upon the rocks,
And see the shepherds feed our flocks,
By shallow rivers, to whose falls
Melodious birds sing madrigals.

And I will make thee beds of roses;   210
And, then, a thousand fragrant posies,
A cap of flowers, and a kirtle,
Embroidered all with leaves of myrtle;

A gown made of the finest wool,
Which from our pretty lambs we pull;   215
Slippers lin'd choicely for the cold,
With buckles of the purest gold;

A belt of straw and ivy-buds,
With coral clasps, and amber studs.
And if these pleasures may thee move,   220
Come, live with me, and be my love.

Thy silver dishes, for thy meat,
As precious as the Gods do eat,
Shall, on an ivory table, be
Prepared each day for thee and me.   225

The shepherd swains shall dance and sing
For thy delight each May morning.
If these delights thy mind may move,
Then live with me, and be my love.

VENATOR.   Trust me, master, it is a choice song, and sweetly sung by honest   230
Maudlin. I now see it was not without cause that our good Queen Elizabeth did so often
wish herself a milk-maid all the month of May, because they are not troubled with fears
and cares, but sing sweetly all the day, and sleep securely all the night; and without
doubt, honest, innocent, pretty Maudlin does so. I'll bestow Sir Thomas Overbury's
milk-maid's wish upon her, "that she may die in the Spring; and, being dead, may have   235
good store of flowers stuck round about her winding-sheet."

The Milk-Maid's Mother's Answer
If all the world and love were young,
And truth in every shepherd's tongue,

234-36: See the end of Overbury's character of the milkmaid, p. 274.

These pretty pleasures might me move
To live with thee, and be thy love.

But time drives flocks from field to fold;
When rivers rage, and rocks grow cold;
Then Philomel becometh dumb;
And age complains of cares to come.

The flowers do fade, and wanton fields
To wayward winter reckoning yields.
A honey tongue, a heart of gall,
Is fancy's spring, but sorrow's fall.

Thy gowns, thy shoes, thy beds of roses,
Thy cap, thy kirtle, and thy posies,
Soon break, soon wither, soon forgotten;
In folly ripe, in reason rotten.

Thy belt of straw, and ivy buds,
Thy coral clasps, and amber studs,
All these in me no means can move
To come to thee, and be thy love.

What should we talk of dainties, then,
Of better meat than's fit for men?
These are but vain: that's only good
Which God hath blessed, and sent for food.

But could youth last, and love still breed;
Had joys no date, nor age no need;
Then those delights my mind might move
To live with thee, and be thy love.

MOTHER.   Well! I have done my song. But stay, honest anglers, for I will make Maudlin sing you one short song more. Maudlin! sing that song that you sung last night, when young Coridon the shepherd played so purely on his oaten pipe to you and your cousin Betty.

MAUDLIN.   I will, mother.

> I married a wife of late,
> The more's my unhappy fate:
> I married her for love,
>   As my fancy did me move,
>   And not for a worldly estate:
> But oh! the green sickness
> Soon changed her likeness;
> And all her beauty did fail.
>   But 'tis not so
>   With those that go
>   Thro' frost and snow,
>   As all men know,
> And carry the milking-pail.

271-83: For this song, Walton adapts lines from two ballads by the early 17th-century writer of broadside ballads, Martin Parker (d. 1656).

PISCATOR.   Well sung, good woman; I thank you. I'll give you another dish of fish one of these days; and then beg another song of you. Come, scholar! let Maudlin alone: *285* do not you offer to spoil her voice. Look! yonder comes mine hostess, to call us to supper. How now! is my brother Peter come?

HOSTESS.   Yes, and a friend with him. They are both glad to hear that you are in these parts; and long to see you; and long to be at supper, for they be very hungry.

(1653-76)

THOMAS CAREW
England, c.1595-1640

A SONG

Ask me no more where Jove bestows,
When June is past, the fading rose;
For in your beauty's orient deep
These flowers, as in their causes, sleep.

Ask me no more whither doth stray   *5*
The golden atoms of the day;
For in pure love heaven did prepare
Those powders to enrich your hair.

Ask me no more whither doth haste
The nightingale when May is past;   *10*

For in your sweet dividing throat
She winters, and keeps warm her note.

Ask me no more where those stars light
That downwards fall in dead of night;
For in your eyes they sit, and there   *15*
Fixed become as in their sphere.

Ask me no more if east or west
The phoenix builds her spicy nest;
For unto you at last she flies,
And in your fragrant bosom dies.   *20*

(1640)

ANONYMOUS
17th century

Weep you no more, sad fountains

Weep you no more, sad fountains;
  What need you flow so fast?
Look how the snowy mountains
  Heaven's sun doth gently waste!
But my sun's heavenly eyes,   *5*

View not your weeping,
That now lies sleeping
Softly, now softly lies
  Sleeping.

A SONG   11. dividing: musical, from the term *division*, referring to a rapid succession of short notes.   **WEEP YOU NO MORE**   Set to music by John Dowland (1562-c.1615) in his *Third and Last Book of Songs or Airs* (1603).

Sleep is a reconciling, *10*
    A rest that peace begets;
Doth not the sun rise smiling
    When fair at ev'n he sets?
Rest you then, rest, sad eyes!
    Melt not in weeping, *15*
    While she lies sleeping,
Softly, now softly lies
            Sleeping.

                    (1603)

The Silver Swan

The silver swan, who living had no note,
When death approached, unlocked her
    silent throat,
Leaning her breast against the reedy shore, *4*
Thus sung her first and last, and sung no more:
"Farewell all joys! O death, come close mine
    eyes;
More geese than swans now live, more
    fools than wise."

                    (1612)

Epigram: On Sir Francis Drake

Sir Drake, whom well the world's end knew,
    Which thou didst compass round,
And whom both poles of heaven once saw,
    Which north and south do bound,
The stars above would make thee known, *5*
    If men here silent were;
The Sun himself cannot forget
    His fellow traveller.

                    (1640)

London Mourning in Ashes

Of Fire, Fire, Fire I sing,
    that have more cause to cry,
In the Great Chamber of the King
    (a City mounted high);
Old London that *5*
Hath stood in state
    above six hundred years,

In six days' space,
Woe and alas!
    is burned and drowned in tears. *10*

The second of September in
    the middle time of night,
In Pudding Lane it did begin
    to burn and blaze outright;
Where all that gazed *15*
Were so amazed
    at such a furious flame,
They knew not how
Or what to do
    that might expel the same. *20*

It swallowed Fish Street Hill, and straight
    it licked up Lombard Street;
Down Canon Street in blazing state
    it flew with flaming feet;
Down to the Thames *25*
Whose shrinking streams
    began to ebb away,
As thinking that
The power of Fate
    had brought the latter day. *30*

Eurus the God of eastern gales
    was Vulcan's bellows now,
And did so fill the flagrant sails
    that high-built churches bow;
The leads they bear *35*
Dropped many a tear
    to see their fabrics burn;
The sins of men
Made churches then
    in dust and ashes mourn. *40*

With hand and feet, in every street,
    they pack up goods and fly;
Pitch, tar, and oil increase the spoil
    old Fish Street 'gins to fry;
The Fire doth range *45*

THE SILVER SWAN   Set to music by Orlando Gibbons (1583-1625) in *The First Set of Madrigals and Motets* (1612).   **EPIGRAM**   First printed in *Wit's Recreations* (1640).   **LONDON MOURNING IN ASHES**   A broadside ballad printed and sold shortly after the fire it describes (in September 1666) and one of the ballads collected by Samuel Pepys; see *The Pepys Ballads*, ed. Hyder E. Rollins, vol. 3 (Cambridge, Mass.: Harvard Univ. Press, 1930), pp. 3-10. Pepys himself wrote a description of The Great Fire of London in his diary; and see John Evelyn's account, p. 397. **30. latter day:** i.e., the last day, Judgment Day, the end of the world. **33. flagrant:** ardent, burning. **35. leads:** i.e., roofs covered with lead sheets. **37. fabrics:** structures, i.e., walls, roofs, etc.

Up to the Change,
  and every King commands,
But in despite
Of all its might,
  the stout old Founder stands.   *50*

Out of the shops the goods are ta'en,
  and haled from every shelf,
As in a shipwrack every man
  doth seek to save himself;
The Fire so hot,   *55*
A strength hath got
  no water can prevail;
An hundred ton
Were it poured on,
  would prove but like a pail.   *60*

The crackling flames do fume and roar,
  as billows do retire;
The City, though upon the shore,
  doth seem a sea of fire,
Where steeple spires   *65*
Show in the Fires
  like vessels sinking down.
The open fields
More safety yields,
  and thither fly the Town.   *70*

Up to the head of aged Paul's
  the flame doth fluttering fly;
Above a hundred thousand souls
  upon the ground do lie;
Sick souls and lame   *75*
All fly the flame;
  women with child we know
Are forced to run,
The Fire to shun,
  have not a day to go.   *80*

Cradles were rocked in every field,
  and food was all their cry,
Till the King's bowels bread did yield,
  and sent them a supply;
A Father he   *85*
Of his country,
  himself did sweetly show,
Both day and night,
With all his might,
  he sought to ease our woe.   *90*

The King himself in person there
  was, and the Duke of York,
And likewise many a Noble Peer
  assisted in the work;
To quell the ire   *95*
Of this wild Fire,
  whose army was so high,
And did invade,
So that it made
  ten hundred thousand fly.   *100*

From Sunday morn till Thursday at night
  it roared about the Town;
There was no way to quell its might
  but to pull houses down;
And so they did,   *105*
As they were bid
  By Charles, his great command;
The Duke of York
Some say did work
  with bucket in his hand.   *110*

At Temple Church, and Holborn Bridge,
  and Pie corner 'tis stenched;
The water did the Fire besiege,
  at Aldersgate it quenched;
At Cripplegate   *115*

---

46. the Change: the Royal Exchange, where merchants, brokers, etc., meet to transact business. **47-50:** I.e., the fire topples the statues of all the English rulers lined up around the quadrangle at the Exchange, from Edward the Confessor to Charles II, leaving standing only that of Sir Thomas Gresham (c.1519-1579), its founder (in 1566) and supposed originator of "Gresham's law" (but cf. Evelyn's remarks, lines 125-27, p. 401). **52. haled:** pulled, dragged. **70. Town:** the inhabitants of the metropolis. **83. bowels:** the seat of pity and other such emotions; the King was then Charles II (1630-1685). **92:** The Duke of York (1633-1701), Charles' younger brother, reigned as James II (1685-88). **111ff.:** Temple Church, at the western edge of the fire's ravages, in the grounds of The Temple (see note to line 11 of Dekker's essay, p. 238); the other names are of places along the northern rim, where the fire was "stenched" (i.e., stanched, stopped); the places named in the next stanza are at the eastern edge. Evelyn lists many of the same places, as well as others.

(Though very late)
   and eke at Coleman Street,
At Basinghall
The Fire did fall;
   we all were joyed to see't.   *120*

Bishopsgate Street to Cornhill end,
   And Leadenhall's secure;
It to the postern did extend;
   Fenchurch doth still endure;
Clothworker's Hall   *125*
Did ruined fall,
   yet stopped the Fire's haste;
Mark Lane, Tower Dock,
Did stand the shock,
   And all is quenched at last.   *130*

Many of French and Dutch were stopped,
   and also are confined;
'Tis said that they their fire-balls dropped,
   and this plot was designed
By them and those   *135*
That are our foes;
   yet some think nothing so,
But that our God

With his flaming rod
   for sin sends all this woe.   *140*

Although the Fire be fully quenched,
   yet if our sins remain,
And that in them we still are drenched,
   the Fire will rage again;
Or what is worse,   *145*
A heavier curse,
   in Famine will appear;
Where shall we tread
When want of bread
   and hunger draweth near?   *150*

If this do not reform our lives,
   a worse thing will succeed;
Our kindred, children, and our wives
   will die for want of bread;
When Famine comes,   *155*
'Tis not our drums,
   our ships, our horse or foot
That can defend;
But if we mend,
   we never shall come to't.   *160*

Bathsua (Reynolds) Makin

England, 1600-c.1675

from *An Essay to Revive the Ancient Education of Gentlewomen, in Religion, Manners, Arts, and Tongues*

Dedication:
To All Ingenious and Virtuous Ladies,
More especially to Her Highness the Lady Mary,
Eldest Daughter of His Royal Highness the Duke of York.

Custom, when it is inveterate, hath a mighty influence: it hath the force of Nature itself. The barbarous custom to breed women low is grown general amongst us, and hath prevailed so far, that it is verily believed (especially amongst a sort of debauched sots) that women are not endued with such reason as men, nor capable of improvement by

---

131ff.: As Evelyn says, England was then at war with them; but not only Dutch and French were among the "them and those" rumoured to have started the fire; the Catholics were also accused — even, the following January, by Parliament. **157:** i.e., navy or army. **An Essay to Revive . . . 2. breed:** educate.

education as they are. It is looked upon as a monstrous thing to pretend the contrary. A   *5*
learned woman is thought to be a comet that bodes mischief whenever it appears. To
offer to the world the liberal education of women is to deface the image of God in man,
it will make women so high and men so low; like fire in the housetop, it will set the
whole world in a flame.

These things and worse than these are commonly talked of, and verily believed by   *10*
many who think themselves wise men; to contradict these is a bold attempt, where the
attempter must expect to meet with much opposition. Therefore, ladies, I beg the candid
opinion of your sex, whose interest I assert. More especially, I implore the favour of
Your Royal Highness, a person most eminent amongst them, whose patronage alone
will be a sufficient protection. What I have written is not out of humour to show how   *15*
much may be said of a trivial thing to little purpose. I verily think women were formerly
educated in the knowledge of arts and tongues, and by their education many did rise to a
great height in learning. Were women thus educated now, I am confident the advantage
would be very great. The women would have honour and pleasure, their relations profit,
and the whole nation advantage. I am very sensible it is an ill time to set on foot this   *20*
design, wherein not only learning but virtue itself is scorned and neglected as pedantic
things fit only for the vulgar. I know no better way to reform these exorbitancies than to
persuade women to scorn those toys and trifles they now spend their time about, and to
attempt higher things, here offered. This will either reclaim the men, or make them
ashamed to claim the sovereignty over such as are more wise and virtuous than   *25*
themselves.

Were a competent number of schools erected to educate ladies ingenuously,
methinks I see how ashamed men would be of their ignorance, and how industrious the
next generation would be to wipe off their reproach.

I expect to meet with many scoffs and taunts from inconsiderate and illiterate men   *30*
that prize their own lusts and pleasure more than your profit and content. I shall be the
less concerned at these, so long as I am in your favour; and this discourse may be a
weapon in your hands to defend yourselves whilst you endeavour to polish your souls,
that you may glorify God, and answer the end of your creation, to be meet helps to your
husbands. Let not your Ladyships be offended that I do not (as some have wittily done)   *35*
plead for female preeminence. To ask too much is the way to be denied all. God hath
made the man the head; if you be educated and instructed as I propose, I am sure you
will acknowledge it, and be satisfied that you are helps, that your husbands do consult
and advise with you (which if you be wise they will be glad of) and that your husbands
have the casting voice, in whose determinations you will acquiesce. That this may be the   *40*
effect of this education in all ladies that shall attempt it, is the desire of

Your servant.
(1673)

JOHN EARLE
England, c.1601-1665

from *MICROCOSMOGRAPHY*

A DISCONTENTED MAN

Is one that is fallen out with the world, and will be revenged on himself. Fortune has denied him in something, and he now takes pet, and will be miserable in spite. The root of his disease is a self-humouring pride, and an accustomed tenderness not to be crossed in his fancy; and the occasion commonly of one of these three, a hard father, a peevish wench, or his ambition thwarted. He considered not the nature of the world till he felt it,   *5* and all blows fall on him heavier, because they light not first on his expectation. He has now foregone all but his pride, and is yet vain-glorious in the ostentation of his melancholy. His composure of himself is a studied carelessness, with his arms across, and a neglected hanging of his head and cloak; and he is as great an enemy to a hat-band, as fortune. He quarrels at the time, and up-starts, and sighs at the neglect of men   *10* of parts, that is, such as himself. His life is a perpetual satire, and he is still girding the age's vanity, when this very anger shews he too much esteems it. He is much displeased to see men merry, and wonders what they can find to laugh at. He never draws his own lips higher than a smile, and frowns wrinkle him before forty. He at last falls into that deadly melancholy to be a bitter hater of men, and is the most apt companion for any   *15* mischief. He is the spark that kindles the commonwealth, and the bellows himself to blow it: and if he turn any thing, it is commonly one of these, either friar, traitor, or mad-man.

A YOUNG MAN

He is now out of Nature's protection, though not yet able to guide himself; but left loose to the world and fortune, from which the weakness of his childhood preserved him; and now his strength exposes him. He is indeed just of age to be miserable, yet in his own conceit first begins to be happy; and he is happier in this imagination, and his misery not felt is less. He sees yet but the outside of world and men, and conceives them according   *5* to their appearing glister, and out of this ignorance believes them. He pursues all vanities for happiness, and enjoys them best in this fancy. His reason serves not to curb, but understand his appetite, and prosecute the motions thereof with a more eager earnestness. Himself is his own temptation, and needs not Satan; and the world will

---

A DISCONTENTED MAN   **2. takes pet:** takes offense and becomes sulky and peevish. **3. accustomed tenderness:** habitual oversensitivity. **8. melancholy:** For this and for choleric in line 3 of "A Cook," below, see the note to Chaucer's "General Prologue," line 420 (p. 34). **9-10. hat-band:** ornamental string or ribbon around a hat; not to wear one was to present oneself as a melancholy malcontent, as was also crossing one's arms. **10. time:** i.e., times, age. **11. girding:** mocking.   A YOUNG MAN   **4. conceit:** conception, opinion.

come hereafter. He leaves repentance for gray hairs, and performs it in being covetous. *10*
He is mingled with the vices of the age as the fashion and custom, with which he longs to
be acquainted; and sins to better his understanding. He conceives his youth as the season
of his lust, and the hour wherein he ought to be bad; and because he would not lose his
time, spends it. He distastes religion as a sad thing, and is six years elder for a thought of
heaven. He scorns and fears, and yet hopes for old age, but dare not imagine it with *15*
wrinkles. He loves and hates with the same inflammation; and when the heat is over, is
cool alike to friends and enemies. His friendship is seldom so steadfast, but that lust,
drink, or anger may overturn it. He offers you his blood today in kindness, and is ready to
take yours tomorrow. He does seldom anything which he wishes not to do again, and is
only wise after a misfortune. He suffers much for his knowledge, and a great deal of folly *20*
it is makes him a wise man. He is free from many vices, by being not grown to the
performance, and is only more virtuous out of weakness. Every action is his danger, and
every man his ambush. He is a ship without pilot or tackling, and only good fortune may
steer him. If he escape this age, he has escaped a tempest, and may live to be a man.

A Cook

The kitchen is his hell, and he the devil in it, where his meat and he fry together. His
revenues are showered down from the fat of the land, and he interlards his own grease
among, to help the drippings. Choleric he is not by nature so much as his art, and it is a
shrewd temptation that the chopping-knife is so near. His weapons ofter offensive are a
mess of hot broth and scalding water, and woe be to him that comes in his way. In the *5*
kitchen he will domineer and rule the roast in spite of his master, and curses in the very
dialect of his calling. His labour is mere blustering and fury, and his speech like that of
sailors in a storm, a thousand businesses at once; yet, in all this tumult, he does not love
combustion, but will be the first man that shall go and quench it. He is never a good
Christian till a hissing pot of ale has slacked him, like water cast on a firebrand, and for *10*
that time he is tame and dispossessed. His cunning is not small in architecture, for he
builds strange fabrics in paste, towers and castles, which are offered to the assault of
valiant teeth, and like Darius' palace in one banquet demolished. He is a pitiless
murderer of innocents, and he mangles poor fowls with unheard-of tortures; and it is
thought the martyrs' persecutions were devised from hence: sure we are, St. Lawrence's *15*
gridiron came out of his kitchen. His best faculty is at the dresser, where he seems to
have great skill in the tactics, ranging his dishes in order military, and placing with great
discretion in the fore-front meats more strong and hardy, and the more cold and
cowardly in the rear; as quaking tarts and quivering custards, and such milk-sop dishes,
which scape many times the fury of the encounter. But now the second course is gone *20*
up and he down in the cellar, where he drinks and sleeps till four o'clock in the
afternoon, and then returns again to his regiment.

(1628)

---

14. sad: serious, grave. **A Cook** **4. ofter:** more often. **10. slacked:** slaked. **13:** referring to Alexander's sack of Persepolis in 331 B.C.; see
Plutarch's account in his life of Alexander (see also Dryden's treatment of the event in his 1697 ode for St. Cecilia's Day, "Alexander's Feast"). **15:**
St. Lawrence, Roman martyr (d. 258), was, according to legend, roasted to death on a gridiron. **16. dresser:** buffet table, on which meats and other
foods are dressed and laid out for use.

OWEN FELLTHAM
England, c.1602-1668

from *RESOLVES: DIVINE, MORAL, AND POLITICAL*

OF PURITANS

I find many that are called Puritans; yet few or none that will own the name. Whereof
the reason sure is this, that 'tis for the most part held a name of infamy, and is so new,
that it hath scarcely yet obtained a definition; nor is it an appellation derived from one
man's name, whose tenets we may find digested into a volume; whereby we do much
err in the application. It imports a kind of excellency above another, which man (being   5
conscious of his own frail bendings) is ashamed to assume to himself. So that I believe
there are men which would be Puritans, but indeed not any that are. One will have him
one that lives religiously, and will not revel it in a shoreless excess. Another, him that
separates from our divine assemblies. Another, him that in some tenets only is peculiar.
Another, him that will not swear. Absolutely to define him, is a work, I think, of   10
difficulty; some I know that rejoice at the name; but sure they be such as least
understand it. As he is more generally in these times taken, I suppose we may call him a
Church-rebel, or one that would exclude order, that his brain might rule. To decline
offenses, to be careful and conscionable in our several actions, is a purity that every man
ought to labour for, which we may well do without a sullen segregation from all society.   15
If there be any privileges, they are surely granted to the children of the king, which are
those that are the children of heaven. If mirth and recreations be lawful, sure such a one
may lawfully use it. If wine were given to cheer the heart, why should I fear to use it for
that end? Surely, the merry soul is freer from intended mischief than the thoughtful man.
A bounded mirth is a patent, adding time and happiness to the crazed life of man. Yet if   20
Laertius reports him rightly, Plato deserves a censure for allowing drunkenness at
festivals; because, says he, as then, the gods themselves reach wines to present men.
God delights in nothing more than in a cheerful heart, careful to perform him service.
What parent is it that rejoiceth not to see his child pleasant, in the limits of a filial duty?
I know, we read of Christ's weeping, not of his laughter: yet we see, he graceth a feast   25
with his first miracle, and that a feast of joy; and can we think that such a meeting could
pass without the noise of laughter? What a lump of quickened care is the melancholic
man! Change anger into mirth, and the precept will hold good still: Be merry but sin not.
As there be many that in their life assume too great a liberty, so I believe there are some
that abridge themselves of what they might lawfully use. Ignorance is an ill steward, to   30

OF PURITANS   **Title:** The term "Puritans," first used in the 1560s, was mainly a term of reproach applied to members of the Church of England who wanted more purification of the early, unreformed, church — i.e., wanted the Reformation pushed further, in the direction of Presbyterianism; in the 17th century many Puritans, whether Presbyterians or other sects, separated from the Church of England. **14. conscionable:** conscientious, reasonable. **20. patent:** license, privilege; **crazed:** broken or crushed, confused. **21:** Diogenes Laertius (c.200-250) wrote a *History of Philosophy: The Lives and Opinions of Famous Philosophers.* **25:** See John 11:35. **25-26:** See John 2:1-11. **27-28:** See Ephesians 4:26.

provide for either soul or body. A man that submits to reverent order, that sometimes unbends himself in a moderate relaxation, and in all, labours to approve himself in the sereneness of a healthful conscience, such a Puritan I will love immutably. But when a man, in things but ceremonial, shall spurn at the grave authority of the Church, and out of a needless nicety be a thief to himself of those benefits which God hath allowed him,   *35* or out of a blind and uncharitable pride, censure and scorn others as reprobates, or out of obstinacy fill the world with brawls about undeterminable tenets, I shall think him one of those whose opinion hath fevered his zeal to madness and distraction. I have more faith in one Solomon, than in a thousand Dutch parlours of such opinionists. "Behold then; what I have seen good! — That it is comely to eat, and to drink, and to take   *40* pleasure in all his labour wherein he travaileth under the sun, the whole number of the days of his life, which God giveth him. For this is his portion. Nay, there is no profit to man, but that he eat, and drink, and delight his soul with the profit of his labour." For, he that saw other things but *vanity,* saw this also, that it was the hand of God. Methinks the reading of Ecclesiastes should make a Puritan undress his brain, and lay off all those   *45* fanatic toys that jingle about his understanding. For my own part, I think the world hath not better men than some that suffer under that name; nor withal, more scelestique villains. For when they are once elated with that pride, they so contemn others, that they infringe the laws of all human society.

OF WOMEN

Some are so uncharitable as to think all women bad; and others are so credulous as they believe they all are good. Sure, though every man speaks as he finds, there is reason to direct our opinion, without experience of the whole sex; which, in a strict examination, makes more for their honour than most men have acknowledged. At first, she was created his equal; only the difference was in the sex; otherwise they both were man. If   *5* we argue from the text that male and female made man, so the man being put first was worthier, I answer, so the evening and morning was the first day; yet few will think the night the better. That man is made her governor, and so above her, I believe rather the punishment of her sin, than the prerogative of his worth. Had they both stood, it may be thought, she had never been in that subjection; for then had it been no curse, but a   *10* continuance of her former estate, which had nothing but blessedness in it. Peter Martyr, indeed, is of opinion that man before the Fall had priority; but Chrysostom, he says, does doubt it. All will grant her body more admirable, more beautiful than man's; fuller of curiosities and noble Nature's wonders; both for conception, and fostering the producted birth. And can we think God would put a worser soul into a better body?   *15* When man was created, 'tis said, God made man; but when woman, 'tis said, God builded her, as if he had then been about a frame of rarer rooms, and more exact composition. And, without doubt, in her body she is much more wonderful, and by this

---

39-44: See Ecclesiastes 2, and 1:2-3. **47. scelestique:** wicked.   **OF WOMEN   11. Peter Martyr:** probably Pietro Martire Vermigli (1500-1562), reformist preacher and teacher who left the Catholic church, taught at Oxford, Strasbourg, and Zurich, and wrote many Biblical commentaries (named after the earlier Peter Martyr, St. Peter of Verona, 1205-1252, Dominican Friar and Inquisitor). **12. Chrysostom:** St. John Chrysostom (347-407), Archbishop of Constantinople.

we may think so in her mind. Philosophy tells us though the soul be not caused by the body, yet in the general it follows the temperament of it; so the comeliest outsides are naturally (for the most part) more virtuous within. If place can be any privilege, we shall find her built in Paradise, when man was made without it. 'Tis certain they are by constitution colder than the boiling man; so by this more temperate; 'tis heat that transports man to immoderation and fury; 'tis that which hurries him to a savage and libidinous violence. Women are naturally the more modest; and modesty is the seat and dwelling place of virtue. Whence proceed the most abhorred villainies, but from a masculine unblushing impudence? What a deal of sweetness do we find in a mild disposition! When a woman grows bold and daring, we dislike her, and say, she is too like a man; yet in ourselves we magnify what we condemn in her. Is not this injustice? Every man is so much the better by how much he comes nearer to God. Man in nothing is more like him than in being merciful. Yet woman is far more merciful than man, it being a sex wherein pity and compassion have dispersed far brighter rays. God is said to be love; and I am sure everywhere woman is spoken of for transcending in that quality. It was never found but in two men only, that their love exceeded that of the feminine sex; and if you observe them you shall find they were both of melting dispositions. I know when they prove bad, they are a sort of the vilest creatures, yet still the same reason gives it; for, *optima corrupta pessima,* the best things corrupted become the worst. They are things whose souls are of a more ductible temper than the harder metal of man; so may be made both better and worse. The representations of Sophocles and Euripides may be both true; and for the tongue-vice, talkativeness, I see not but at meetings men may very well vie words with them. 'Tis true, they are not of so tumultuous a spirit, so not so fit for great actions. Natural heat does more actuate the stirring genius of man. Their easy natures make them somewhat more unresolute; whereby men have argued them of fear and inconstancy. But men have always held the parliament, and have enacted their own wills, without ever hearing them speak; and then, how easy is it to conclude them guilty! Besides, education makes more difference between men and them than Nature; and all their aspersions are less noble for that they are only from their enemies, men. Diogenes snarled bitterly when, walking with another, he spied two women talking, and said, "See, the viper and the asp are changing poison." The poet was conceited that said, after they were made ill, that God made them fearful, that man might rule them; otherwise they had been past dealing with. Catullus his conclusion was too general, to collect a deceit in all women, because he was not confident of his own.

> *Nulli se dicit mulier mea nubere malle*
> *Quam mihi; non si se Jupiter ipse petat.*
> *Dicit: sed mulier Cupido quod dicit amanti,*
> *In vento et rapida scribere oportet aqua.*

---

34. two men only: i.e., David and Jonathan (see II Samuel 1:26). **48. Diogenes:** Greek philosopher (4th century B.C.), founder of the Cynics. **51. Catullus his:** i.e., Catullus's; Gaius Valerius Catullus (c.84-c.54 B.C.), Roman poet; the poem cited is poem LXX.

My mistress swears, she'd leave all men for me:
Yea, though that Jove himself should suitor be.   *60*
She says it: but what women swear to kind
Loves, may be writ in rapid streams and wind.

I am resolved to honor virtue, in what sex soever I find it. And I think, in the general,
I shall find it more in women than men, though weaker and more infirmly guarded. I
believe they are better, and may be wrought to be worse. Neither shall the faults of many   *65*
make me uncharitable to all; nor the goodness of some make me credulous of the rest.
Though hitherto, I confess, I have not found more sweet and constant goodness in man
than I have found in woman; and yet of these, I have not found a number.

(1623, 1628)

THE SYMPATHY

Soul of my soul! it cannot be,
That you should weep, and I from tears be free.
   All the vast room between both Poles,
   Can never dull the sense of souls,
     Knit in so fast a knot.   *5*
   Oh! can you grieve, and think that I
   Can feel no smart, because not nigh,
     Or that I know it not?

Th'are heretic thoughts. Two Lutes are strung,
And on a Table tuned alike for song;   *10*
   Strike one, and that which none did touch,
   Shall sympathizing sound as much,
     As that which toucht you see.
   Think then this world (which Heaven enrols)
   Is but a Table round, and souls   *15*
     More apprehensive be.

Know they that in their grossest parts,
Mix by their hallowed loves intwined hearts,
   This privilege boast, that no remove
   Can e'er infringe their sense of love.   *20*
     Judge hence then our estate,
   Since when we loved there was not put
   Two earthen hearts in one breast, but
     Two souls Co-animate.

(1661)

ON A GENTLEWOMAN, WHOSE NOSE WAS PITTED WITH THE SMALL POX

Why (foul Disease) in cheek or eye
Durst not thy small Impressions lye?
Or why aspired'st thou to that place,
The graceful Promont of her face?
Alas! we see the Rose and Snow   *5*
In one thou couldst not overthrow:
And where the other did but please
To look and shine, they killed disease.
Then as some sulphurous spirit sent
By the torn Air's distemperment,   *10*
To a rich Palace; finds within
Some Sainted maid or *Sheba* Queen;
And, not of power for her offence,
Rifles the Chimney going hence.
So thou too feeble to control   *15*
The Guest within, her purer soul,
Hast out of spleen to things of grace,
Left thy sunk footsteps in the place.
Yet fear not Maid, since so much fair
Is left, that these can those impair.   *20*
Face-scars do not disgrace, but show
Valour well freed from a bold foe.
Like Jacob's lameness, this shall be
Honour and Palm to Time and Thee.

(1661)

THE SYMPATHY **14. enrols:** i.e., enwraps, encircles.   ON A GENTLEWOMAN Cf. Lady Mary Wortley Montagu's "Saturday: The
Small Pox" (p. 555). **23. Jacob's lameness:** See Genesis 32:24-32.

WILLIAM HABINGTON
England, 1605-1654

AGAINST THEM WHO LAY UNCHASTITY TO THE SEX OF WOMEN

They meet but with unwholesome Springs,
And Summers which infectious are:
They hear but when the Mermaid sings,
And only see the falling star:
    Who ever dare   *5*
Affirm no woman chaste and fair.

Go cure your fevers, and you'll say
The Dog-days scorch not all the year;
In Copper Mines no longer stay,
But travel to the West, and there   *10*
    The right ones see,
And grant all gold's not Alchemy.

What madman 'cause the glow-worm's flame
Is cold, swears there's no warmth in fire?
'Cause some make forfeit of their name,   *15*
And slave themselves to man's desire,
    Shall the sex free
From guilt, damned to the bondage be?

Nor grieve, Castara, though 'twere frail,
Thy virtue then would brighter shine,   *20*
When thy example should prevail,
And every woman's faith be thine.
    And were there none,
'Tis majesty to rule alone.

(1634)

SIR THOMAS BROWNE
England, 1605-1682

from *PSEUDODOXIA EPIDEMICA: OR, ENQUIRIES INTO VERY MANY RECEIVED TENETS, AND COMMONLY PRESUMED TRUTHS*

Book V, Chapter 4: Of the Picture of the Serpent Tempting Eve

In the picture of Paradise, and delusion of our first Parents, the Serpent is often described with human visage, not unlike unto Cadmus, or his wife, in the act of their metamorphosis, which is not a mere pictorial contrivance or invention of the picturer, but an ancient tradition and conceived reality, as it stands delivered by Beda and authors

---

AGAINST THEM WHO . . .   **3-6:** See Donne's "Song" ("Go and catch a falling star"), p. 253. **19. Castara:** poetic name for Lucy Herbert, whom Habington married; his 1634 (anonymous) collection of love poems was entitled *Castara*.   PSEUDODOXIA EPIDEMICA is more commonly known as *Vulgar Errors*.   OF THE PICTURE OF THE SERPENT TEMPTING EVE   **2-3:** For the metamorphosis of Cadmus and his wife, see Ovid's *Metamorphoses*, IV, 562ff.   **4. Beda:** Bede, or "The Venerable Bede" (673-735), English historian and scholar, author of *Historia Ecclesiastica Gentis Anglorum* (731).

of some antiquity; that is, that Satan appeared not unto Eve in the naked form of a   *5*
Serpent, but with a virgin's head, that thereby he might become more acceptable, and
his temptation find the easier entertainment; which nevertheless is a conceit not to be
admitted, and the plain and received figure is with better reason embraced.

For first, as Pererius observeth from Barcephas, the assumption of human shape had
proved a disadvantage unto Satan, affording not only a suspicious amazement in Eve,   *10*
before the fact, in beholding a third humanity beside herself and Adam, but leaving
some excuse unto the woman, which afterward the man took up with lesser reason; that
is, to have been deceived by another like herself.

Again, there was no inconvenience in the shape assumed, or any considerable
impediment that might disturb that performance in the common form of a Serpent; for   *15*
whereas it is conceived the woman must needs be afraid thereof, and rather fly than
approach it, it was not agreeable unto the condition of Paradise and state of innocency
therein, if in that place, as most determine, no creature was hurtful or terrible unto man,
and those destructive effects they now discover succeeded the curse, and came in with
thorns and briars; and therefore Eugubinus (who affirmeth this Serpent was a Basilisk)   *20*
incurreth no absurdity, nor need we infer that Eve should be destroyed immediately
upon that vision; for noxious animals could offend them no more in the Garden than
Noah in the Ark: as they peaceably received their names, so they friendly possessed
their natures; and were their conditions destructive unto each other, they were not so
unto man, whose constitutions then were antidotes, and needed not fear poisons. And if   *25*
(as most conceive) there were but two created of every kind, they could not at that time
destroy either man or themselves, for this had frustrated the command of multiplication,
destroyed a species, and imperfected the Creation; and therefore also if Cain were the
first man born, with him entered not only the act, but the first power of murther; for
before that time neither could the Serpent nor Adam destroy Eve, nor Adam and Eve   *30*
each other, for that had overthrown the intention of the world, and put its Creator to act
the sixth day over again.

Moreover, whereas in regard of speech, and vocal conference with Eve, it may be
thought he would rather assume an human shape and organs, than the improper form of
a Serpent, it implies no material impediment; nor need we to wonder how he contrived a   *35*
voice out of the mouth of a Serpent who hath done the like out of the belly of a
Pythonissa, and the trunk of an oak, as he did for many years at Dodona.

Lastly, whereas it might be conceived that an human shape was fitter for this
enterprise, it being more than probable she would be amazed to hear a Serpent speak,
some conceive she might not yet be certain that only man was privileged with speech,   *40*
and being in the novity of the Creation, and inexperience of all things, might not be
affrighted to hear a Serpent speak. Beside she might be ignorant of their natures who

---

9. Pererius: Benedictus Pererius (Benito Pereira, c.1535-1610), Spanish Jesuit, author of *Commentariorum and disputationum in Genesim* (4 vols.,
c.1590-98), in which he brought together many writings by earlier authorities; **Barcephas:** Moses Bar-Cepha (c.813-903), Syrian bishop and
Biblical scholar. **20. Eugubinus:** Latin name of Agostino Steuco, or Steuchus (1496-1549), Italian scholar and divine who wrote much on Biblical
exegesis. **37. Pythonissa:** Pythoness, a prophetess, especially the one at the oracle of Apollo at Delphi; **Dodona:** in northern Greece, site of an
ancient oracle of Zeus. **41. novity:** newness, novelty.

was not versed in their names, as being not present at the general survey of animals, when Adam assigned unto every one a name concordant unto its nature; nor is this my opinion, but the determination of Lombard and Tostatus, and also the reply of Cyril unto   *45* the objection of Julian, who compared this story unto the fables of the Greeks.

(1646)

EDMUND WALLER
England, 1606-1687

Song: "Go, Lovely Rose"

Go, lovely Rose —
Tell her that wastes her time and me,
   That now she knows,
When I resemble her to thee,
How sweet and fair she seems to be.   *5*

   Tell her that's young,
And shuns to have her graces spied,
   That hadst thou sprung
In deserts where no men abide,
Thou must have uncommended died.   *10*

   Small is the worth
Of beauty from the light retired:
   Bid her come forth,
Suffer herself to be desired,
And not blush so to be admired.   *15*

   Then die — that she
The common fate of all things rare
   May read in thee;
How small a part of time they share
That are so wondrous sweet and fair!   *20*

(1645)

Of English Verse

Poets may boast, as safely vain,
Their work shall with the world remain;
Both, bound together, live or die,
The verses and the prophecy.

But who can hope his lines should long   *5*
Last in a daily changing tongue?
While they are new, envy prevails;
And as that dies, our language fails.

When architects have done their part,
The matter may betray their art;   *10*
Time, if we use ill-chosen stone,
Soon brings a well-built palace down.

Poets that lasting marble seek
Must carve in Latin or in Greek;
We write in sand, our language grows   *15*
And like the tide our work o'erflows.

Chaucer his sense can only boast,
The glory of his numbers lost!
Years have defaced his matchless strain,
And yet he did not sing in vain.   *20*

45-46: Peter Lombard (Petrus Lombardus, c.1100-c.1160), Italian theologian — also called Magister Sententiarum because of his *Sententiae* (c.1155-58), a compilation of the work of earlier theologians, which was a standard textbook of medieval theology; Tostatus, or Alonso Tostado (Alphonsus Abulensis, i.e., Alphonse of Avila, c.1400-55), Spanish theologian, author of the 13-volume *Commentaries on the Scriptures* (1508); Saint Cyril (c.376-444), patriarch of Alexandria, known for his antagonism toward heretics and heathens, wrote among other works a reply to the attack on the church by Julian the Apostate (Flavius Claudius Julianus, 332-363), Roman emperor, Constantine I's nephew, who abandoned Christianity and tried to restore pre-Christian religion; all of these are cited by Pererius.   **OF ENGLISH VERSE   18. numbers:** metrical feet, versification.

The beauties which adorned that age,
The shining subjects of his rage,
Hoping they should immortal prove,
Rewarded with success his love.

This was the generous poet's scope,   *25*
And all an English pen can hope,
To make the fair approve his flame,
That can so far extend their fame.

Verse, thus designed, has no ill fate
If it arrive but at the date   *30*
Of fading beauty; if it prove
But as long-lived as present love.

                          (1668)

THOMAS FULLER
England, 1608-1661

from *THE HOLY STATE AND THE PROFANE STATE*

THE GOOD SCHOOLMASTER

There is scarce any profession in the commonwealth more necessary which is so slightly performed. The reasons whereof I conceive to be these: First, young scholars make this calling their refuge, yea, perchance, before they have taken any degree in the university, commence schoolmasters in the country, as if nothing else were required to set up this profession but only a rod and a ferula. Secondly, others who are able use it only as a   *5* passage to better preferment, to patch the rents in their present fortune till they can provide a new one, and betake themselves to some more gainful calling. Thirdly, they are disheartened from doing their best with the miserable reward which in some places they receive, being masters to the children and slaves to their parents. Fourthly, being grown rich, they grow negligent, and scorn to touch the school but by the proxy of an   *10* usher. But see how well our schoolmaster behaves himself.

1. His genius inclines him with delight to his profession. Some men had as lief be schoolboys as schoolmasters, to be tied to the school as Cooper's Dictionary and Scapula's Lexicon are chained to the desk therein; and though great scholars, and skilful in other arts, are bunglers in this: but God of his goodness hath fitted several men for   *15* several callings, that the necessity of church and state, in all conditions, may be provided for. So that he who beholds the fabric thereof may say, God hewed out this stone, and appointed it to lie in this very place, for it would fit none other so well, and here it doth most excellent. And thus God moldeth some for a schoolmaster's life, undertaking it with desire and delight, and discharging it with dexterity and happy   *20* success.

---

27. fair: beautiful women.   **THE GOOD SCHOOLMASTER 5. ferula:** ferule, a flat stick used, like a rod, for inflicting punishment. **11. usher:** a schoolteacher's assistant.

2. He studies his scholars' natures as carefully as they their books; and ranks their dispositions into several forms. And though it may seem difficult for him in a great school to descend to all particulars, yet experienced schoolmasters may quickly make a grammar of boys' natures, and reduce them all, saving some few exceptions, to these general rules: *25*

(a) Those that are ingenious and industrious. The conjunction of two such planets in a youth presage much good unto him. To such a lad a frown may be a whipping, and a whipping a death; yea, where their master whips them once, shame whips them all the week after. Such natures he useth with all gentleness. *30*

(b) Those that are ingenious and idle. These think, with the hare in the fable, that, running with snails (so they count the rest of their schoolfellows), they shall come soon enough to the post, though sleeping a good while before their starting. Oh, a good rod would finely take them napping!

(c) Those that are dull and diligent. Wines, the stronger they be, the more lees they *35* have when they are new. Many boys are muddy-headed till they be clarified with age, and such afterwards prove the best. Bristol diamonds are both bright and squared and pointed by nature, and yet are soft and worthless; whereas orient ones in India are rough and rugged naturally. Hard, rugged, and dull natures of youth acquit themselves afterwards the jewels of the country, and therefore their dullness at first is to be borne with, if they be *40* diligent. That schoolmaster deserves to be beaten himself who beats nature in a boy for a fault. And I question whether all the whipping in the world can make their parts, which are naturally sluggish, rise one minute before the hour nature hath appointed.

(d) Those that are invincibly dull and negligent also. Correction may reform the latter, not amend the former. All the whetting in the world can never set a razor's edge *45* on that which hath no steel in it. Such boys he consigneth over to other professions. Shipwrights and boatmakers will choose those crooked pieces of timber which other carpenters refuse. Those may make excellent merchants and mechanics who will not serve for scholars.

3. He is able, diligent, and methodical in his teaching; not leading them rather in a *50* circle than forwards. He minces his precepts for children to swallow, hanging clogs on the nimbleness of his own soul, that his scholars may go along with him.

4. He is and will be known to be an absolute monarch in his school. If cockering mothers proffer him money to purchase their sons an exemption from his rod (to live as it were in a peculiar, out of their master's jurisdiction), with disdain he refuseth it, and *55* scorns the late custom, in some places, of commuting whipping into money, and ransoming boys from the rod at a set price. If he hath a stubborn youth, correction-proof, he debaseth not his authority by contesting with him, but fairly, if he can, puts him away before his obstinacy hath affected others.

5. He is moderate in inflicting deserved correction. Many a schoolmaster better *60* answereth the name παιδοτρίβης than παιδαγωγός, rather tearing his scholars' flesh

---

27. conjunction . . . planets: a metaphor using the language of astrology. **42. parts:** endowments, abilities, talents. **48. mechanics:** manual labourers (other than agricultural). **51. clogs:** weights used to hinder an animal's movements. **53. cockering:** coddling, pampering. **55. peculiar:** a church or parish that has jurisdiction over itself, exempt from that of a bishop's or other court. **61:** i.e., a wrestling or gymnastics master rather than a regular teacher or tutor (pedagogue).

with whipping than giving them good education. No wonder if his scholars hate the muses, being presented unto them in the shapes of fiends and furies. Junius complains *de insolenti carnificina* of his schoolmaster, by whom *conscindebatur flagris septies aut octies in dies singulos.* Yea, hear the lamentable verses of poor Tusser, in his own Life: *65*

> From Paul's I went, to Eton sent,
> To learn straightways the Latin phrase,
> Where fifty-three stripes given to me
>> At once I had.

> For fault but small, or none at all, *70*
> It came to pass thus beat I was;
> See, Udal, see the mercy of thee
>> To me, poor lad.

Such an Orbilius mars more scholars than he makes: their tyranny hath caused many tongues to stammer, which spake plain by nature, and whose stuttering at first was *75* nothing else but fears quavering on their speech at their master's presence; and whose mauling them about their heads hath dulled those who in quickness exceeded their master.

6. He makes his school free to him who sues to him *in forma pauperis.* And surely learning is the greatest alms that can be given. But he is a beast who because the poor *80* scholar cannot pay him wages, pays the scholar in his whipping. Rather are diligent lads to be encouraged with all excitements to learning. This minds me of what I have heard concerning Mr. Bust, that worthy late schoolmaster of Eton, who would never suffer any wandering begging scholar, such as justly the statute hath ranked in the forefront of rogues, to come into his school, but would thrust him out with earnestness (however *85* privately charitable unto him) lest his schoolboys should be disheartened from their books, by seeing some scholars, after their studying in the university, preferred to beggary.

7. He spoils not a good school to make thereof a bad college, therein to teach his scholars logic. For besides that logic may have an action of trespass against grammar for *90* encroaching on her liberties, syllogisms are solecisms taught in the school, and oftentimes they are forced afterwards in the university to unlearn the fumbling skill they had before.

8. Out of his school he is no whit pedantical in carriage or discourse; contenting himself to be rich in Latin, though he doth not jingle with it in every company wherein *95* he comes.

To conclude, let this amongst other motives make schoolmasters careful in their place, that the eminencies of their scholars have commended the memories of their

---

63. Junius: 1st-century schoolmaster and rhetor. **64.** *de . . . carnificina:* immoderate punishment. **64-65.** *conscindebatur . . . singulos:* beaten severely seven or eight times a day. **65. Tusser:** Thomas Tusser, author of *A Hundred Points of Good Husbandry* (see p. 135). **72. Udal:** Nicholas Udal, or Udall (1505-1556), English playwright and headmaster at Eton 1534-41. **74. Orbilius:** Orbilius Pupillus, teacher whom Horace criticizes for the beatings that accompanied his lessons. **79.** *in forma pauperis:* in the condition of a pauper. **83. Bust:** Matthew Bust (c.1576-1638), master of Eton (1611-30). **87. preferred:** moved on, advanced.

schoolmasters to posterity, who otherwise in obscurity had altogether been forgotten. Who had ever heard of R. Bond in Lancashire, but for the breeding of learned Ascham 100 his scholar; or of Hartgrave in Brundley school, in the same county, but because he was the first to teach worthy Dr. Whitaker? Nor do I honor the memory of Mulcaster for anything so much as for his scholar, that gulf of learning, Bishop Andrews. This made the Athenians, the day before the great feast of Theseus their founder, to sacrifice a ram to the memory of Conidas his schoolmaster that first instructed him. 105

(1642)

JOHN MILTON
England, 1608-1674

SONNET VII

How soon hath Time, the subtle thief of youth,
    Stol'n on his wing my three and twentieth year!
    My hasting days fly on with full career,
    But my late spring no bud or blossom shew'th.
Perhaps my semblance might deceive the truth,   5
    That I to manhood am arrived so near,
    And inward ripeness doth much less appear,
    That some more timely-happy spirits endu'th.
Yet be it less or more, or soon or slow,
    It shall be still in strictest measure ev'n   10
    To that same lot, however mean or high,
Toward which Time leads me, and the will of Heav'n;
    All is, if I have grace to use it so,
    As ever in my great Taskmaster's eye.

(1631 or 1632; 1645)

LYCIDAS

In this monody the author bewails a learned friend,
unfortunately drowned in his passage from Chester on
the Irish Seas, 1637. And by occasion foretells the ruin
of our corrupted clergy, then in their height.

Yet once more, O ye laurels, and once more
Ye myrtles brown, with ivy never sere,
I come to pluck your berries harsh and crude,
And with forced fingers rude
Shatter your leaves before the mellowing year.   5
Bitter constraint, and sad occasion dear,
Compels me to disturb your season due:
For Lycidas is dead, dead ere his prime,
Young Lycidas, and hath not left his peer.
Who would not sing for Lycidas? He knew   10

100-01: As Ascham tells us in his *Toxophilus,* he was educated until about age 15 not in a school but, along with other children, in the home of Sir Humphry Wingfield, under a tutor named R. Bond; for Ascham, see p. 132. **102:** William Whitaker (1548-1595), master of St. John's College and regius professor of divinity at Cambridge. **102-03:** Richard Mulcaster (c.1530-1611) was an influential educator, first headmaster of the Merchant Taylors' School, and author of two books on education; Lancelot Andrewes (1555-1626) was successively bishop of Chichester, Ely, and Winchester, and a principal among the scholars who produced the Authorized Version of the Bible (see p. 241). **104-05:** The honouring of Connidas is referred to by Plutarch near the beginning of his life of Theseus, legendary founder and national hero of Athens.　**SONNET VII　8. endu'th:** endoweth.　**LYCIDAS　Title:** "Lycidas" was a traditional name in pastorals (e.g. Theocritus's Idyll VII). **Introductory note** (added for the second edition, 1645): The "learned friend" was Edward King (1612-1637), fellow student at Cambridge, who had written a few poems and planned to enter the church. Though he and King were not close friends, Milton joined others in preparing a memorial volume; his pastoral elegy came last of thirty-six poems. **1-2:** Laurels, myrtles, and ivy are evergreens symbolic both of poetry and of immortality. **6. dear:** costly, hard, heavy, grievous, dire.

Himself to sing, and build the lofty rhyme.
He must not float upon his wat'ry bier
Unwept, and welter to the parching wind,
Without the meed of some melodious tear.
    Begin then, Sisters of the sacred well   *15*
That from beneath the seat of Jove doth spring,
Begin, and somewhat loudly sweep the string.
Hence with denial vain, and coy excuse;
So may some gentle Muse
With lucky words favour my destined urn,   *20*
And as he passes turn,
And bid fair peace be to my sable shroud.
For we were nursed upon the selfsame hill,
Fed the same flock, by fountain, shade, and rill.
    Together both, ere the high lawns appeared   *25*
Under the opening eyelids of the morn,
We drove afield, and both together heard
What time the grey-fly winds her sultry horn,
Batt'ning our flocks with the fresh dews of night,
Oft till the star that rose, at ev'ning, bright   *30*
Toward Heav'n's descent had sloped his westering wheel.
Meanwhile the rural ditties were not mute,
Tempered to th'oaten flute;
Rough satyrs danced, and fauns with cloven heel
From the glad sound would not be absent long,   *35*
And old Damoetas loved to hear our song.
    But O the heavy change, now thou art gone,
Now thou art gone, and never must return!
Thee, Shepherd, thee the woods and desert caves,
With wild thyme and the gadding vine o'ergrown, *40*
And all their echoes mourn.
The willows, and the hazel copses green,
Shall now no more be seen
Fanning their joyous leaves to thy soft lays.
As killing as the canker to the rose,   *45*
Or taint-worm to the weanling herds that graze,
Or frost to flowers that their gay wardrop wear,
When first the white-thorn blows;
Such, Lycidas, thy loss to shepherd's ear.

    Where were ye, Nymphs, when the remorseless deep
Closed o'er the head of your loved Lycidas?   *51*
For neither were ye playing on the steep
Where your old bards, the famous Druids, lie,
Nor on the shaggy top of Mona high,
Nor yet where Deva spreads her wizard stream.   *55*
Ay me, I fondly dream!
Had ye been there — for what could that have done?
What could the Muse herself that Orpheus bore,
The Muse herself, for her enchanting son
Whom universal nature did lament,   *60*
When the rout that made the hideous roar,
His gory visage down the stream was sent,
Down the swift Hebrus to the Lesbian shore.
    Alas! What boots it with uncessant care
To tend the homely slighted shepherd's trade,   *65*
And strictly meditate the thankless Muse?
Were it not better done as others use,
To sport with Amaryllis in the shade,
Or with the tangles of Neaera's hair?
Fame is the spur that the clear spirit doth raise   *70*
(That last infirmity of noble mind)
To scorn delights, and live laborious days;
But the fair guerdon when we hope to find,
And think to burst out into sudden blaze,
Comes the blind Fury with th'abhorred shears,   *75*
And slits the thin-spun life. "But not the praise,"
Phoebus replied, and touched my trembling ears;
"Fame is no plant that grows on mortal soil,
Nor in the glistering foil
Set off to th'world, nor in broad rumour lies,   *80*
But lives and spreads aloft by those pure eyes
And perfect witness of all-judging Jove;
As he pronounces lastly on each deed,
Of so much fame in Heav'n expect thy meed."
    O fountain Arethuse, and thou honoured flood, *85*
Smooth-sliding Mincius, crowned with vocal reeds,
That strain I heard was of a higher mood;
But now my oat proceeds,

15: the nine Muses, associated with both the fountain Aganippe, on Mt. Helicon, with its altar to Zeus (Jove), and the Pierian Spring, on Mt. Olympus, the home of the gods (in line 19 the "Muse," a "he," means simply a poet); cf. the refrain in Theocritus's first Idyll and in Moschus's "Lament for Bion." **36. old Damoetas:** another traditional name in pastoral, here perhaps referring to a particular tutor at Cambridge. **45. canker:** cankerworm. **47. wardrop:** wardrobe. **48. white-thorn:** hawthorn; **blows:** blooms. **50:** Cf. Theocritus, Idyll I, 66. **52. steep:** a mountain in Wales, probably Kerig-y-Druidion. **54. Mona:** Anglesey. **55. Deva:** Dee ("wizard" because its changes of course were thought prophetic of the fortunes of the region). **58. Muse:** Calliope. **61-63:** Orpheus was dismembered by Thracian Bacchantes; his head, still singing, floated down the river Hebrus and out to the island of Lesbos (see Ovid's *Metamorphoses*, XI, 1ff.). **66:** Cf. Virgil's "*musam meditaris*" (Eclogue I, 2). **68-69: Amaryllis, Neaera:** pastoral names. **75. blind Fury:** Atropos, the one of the three Fates who cuts the thread of life. **77. Phoebus:** Apollo. **85. Arethuse:** Arethusa, a Sicilian fountain on the island of Ortygia, near Syracuse and the birthplace of Theocritus, father of pastoral poetry. **86. Mincius:** river in Lombardy, near the birthplace of Virgil, master of Latin pastoral. **88. oat:** i.e., the oaten pipe or song of the shepherd/pastoral poet (see "oaten flute" of line 33).

And listens to the Herald of the Sea
That came in Neptune's plea.   *90*
He asked the waves, and asked the felon winds,
What hard mishap hath doomed this gentle swain?
And questioned every gust of rugged wings
That blows from off each beaked promontory;
They knew not of his story,   *95*
And sage Hippotades their answer brings,
That not a blast was from his dungeon strayed;
The air was calm, and on the level brine
Sleek Panope with all her sisters played.
It was that fatal and perfidious bark   *100*
Built in th'eclipse, and rigged with curses dark,
That sunk so low that sacred head of thine.
     Next Camus, reverend Sire, went footing slow
His mantle hairy, and his bonnet sedge,
Inwrought with figures dim, and on the edge   *105*
Like to that sanguine flower inscribed with woe.
"Ah! Who hath reft," quoth he, "my dearest pledge?"
Last came, and last did go,
The Pilot of the Galilean lake;
Two massy keys he bore of metals twain   *110*
(The golden opes, the iron shuts amain);
He shook his mitred locks, and stern bespake,
"How well could I have spared for thee, young swain,
Enow of such as for their bellies' sake
Creep and intrude and climb into the fold!   *115*
Of other care they little reck'ning make
Than how to scramble at the shearers' feast,
And shove away the worthy bidden guest.
Blind mouths! that scarce themselves know how to hold
A sheep-hook, or have learned ought else the least   *120*
That to the faithful herdman's art belongs!
What recks it them? What need they? They are sped;

And when they list, their lean and flashy songs
Grate on their scrannel pipes of wretched straw;
The hungry sheep look up, and are not fed,   *125*
But swoln with wind, and the rank mist they draw,
Rot inwardly, and foul contagion spread;
Besides what the grim Wolf with privy paw
Daily devours apace, and nothing said;
But that two-handed engine at the door   *130*
Stands ready to smite once, and smite no more."
     Return, Alpheus, the dread voice is past
That shrunk thy streams; return, Sicilian Muse,
And call the vales, and bid them hither cast
Their bells, and flow'rets of a thousand hues.   *135*
Ye valleys low where the mild whispers use,
Of shades and wanton winds, and gushing brooks,
On whose fresh lap the swart star sparely looks,
Throw hither all your quaint enamelled eyes
That on the green turf suck the honeyed show'rs,   *140*
And purple all the ground with vernal flow'rs.
Bring the rathe primrose that forsaken dies,
The tufted crow-toe, and pale jessamine,
The white pink, and the pansy freaked with jet,
The glowing violet,   *145*
The musk-rose, and the well-attired woodbine,
With cowslips wan that hang the pensive head,
And every flower that sad embroidery wears.
Bid amaranthus all his beauty shed,
And daffadillies fill their cups with tears,   *150*
To strew the laureate hearse where Lycid lies.
For so to interpose a little ease,
Let our frail thoughts dally with false surmise.
Ay me! Whilst thee the shores and sounding seas
Wash far away, where'er thy bones are hurled,   *155*
Whether beyond the stormy Hebrides,

---

89. Herald of the Sea: Triton. **96. Hippotades** (son of Hippotes): Aeolus, keeper of the winds. **99. Panope . . . sisters:** sea-nymphs, the many Nereids (daughters of Nereus). **101. Built in th'eclipse:** i.e., ill-omened (cf. *Paradise Lost,* I, 597; p. 334). **103. Camus:** god of the Cam, the river of Cambridge. **106:** the hyacinth, "sanguine" because sprung from the blood of Hyacinthus, accidentally killed by Apollo, and supposedly marked or "inscribed" with *aiai,* the Greek exclamation of grief (see Ovid's *Metamorphoses,* X, 163ff., especially 214-17). **109:** St. Peter, former fisherman on the Sea of Galilee (Lake Tiberias; see Luke 5). **110:** Peter was promised the keys of heaven (Matthew 16:19). **111:** Cf. *Paradise Lost,* II, 327-28 (p. 340). **112. mitred:** Peter wears the mitre as first bishop of the church. **113ff.:** On good and bad shepherds, see John 10:1-15; I Peter 5:2; Ezekiel 34; see also the excerpt from Skelton's *Colyn Clout,* lines 75-81 (p. 113); and see Ruskin's close-reading analysis of the passage (pp. 1051ff.). **122. They are sped:** they prosper. **123. flashy:** insipid, tasteless, vapid. **124. scrannel:** thin, meagre, miserable. **128. Wolf:** Roman Catholicism, but also Catholic leanings within some elements of the Anglican Church (e.g. Archbishop Laud and his followers); see *Paradise Lost,* XII, line 508 (p. 370). **130. two-handed engine:** The general import is clear enough (some powerful instrument of divine justice or vengeance), though any specific intention on Milton's part remains uncertain; some possibilities: the two Houses of Parliament? an executioner's sword or axe (in *Paradise Lost,* VI, line 251, Michael brandishes his sword "with huge two-handed sway"; and cf. Matthew 3:10)? what Milton in *Of Reformation in England* (1641) called "the axe of God's Reformation" chopping away at the papacy and episcopacy? the blind Fury's shears (see line 75)? Father Time's scythe? Christ's "sharp sickle" (Revelation 14:14ff.)? Other suggestions have been offered. **132. Alpheus:** river in Arcadia whose god pursued Arethusa under the sea and rose with her in Sicily (see line 85; see Ovid's *Metamorphoses,* V, 570ff.). **133. Sicilian Muse:** i.e., that of Theocritus and other pastoral poets. **138. swart star:** the Dog Star, Sirius (from Greek *seirios,* hot, burning), associated with late summer heat and parching vegetation. **142. rathe:** early. **144. freaked:** freckled, flecked.

Where thou perhaps under the whelming tide
Visit'st the bottom of the monstrous world;
Or whether thou, to our moist vows denied,
Sleep'st by the fable of Bellerus old,   160
Where the great vision of the guarded Mount
Looks toward Namancos and Bayona's hold;
Look homeward Angel now and melt with ruth,
And, O ye dolphins, waft the hapless youth.   164
   Weep no more, woeful shepherds, weep no more,
For Lycidas your sorrow is not dead,
Sunk though he be beneath a wat'ry floor;
So sinks the day-star in the ocean bed,
And yet anon repairs his drooping head,
And tricks his beams, and with new-spangled ore   170
Flames in the forehead of the morning sky:
So Lycidas sunk low, but mounted high,
Through the dear might of him that walked the waves,
Where other groves and other streams along
With nectar pure his oozy locks he laves,   175

And hears the unexpressive nuptial song
In the blest kingdoms meek of joy and love.
There entertain him all the saints above,
In solemn troops, and sweet societies
That sing, and singing in their glory move,   180
And wipe the tears forever from his eyes.
Now, Lycidas, the shepherds weep no more;
Henceforth thou art the Genius of the shore,
In thy large recompense, and shalt be good
To all that wander in that perilous flood.   185
   Thus sang the uncouth swain to th'oaks and rills,
While the still morn went out with sandals gray;
He touched the tender stops of various quills,
With eager thought warbling his Doric lay.
And now the sun had stretched out all the hills,   190
And now was dropped into the western bay;
At last he rose, and twitched his mantle blue:
Tomorrow to fresh woods, and pastures new.

(1638, 1645)

from *OF EDUCATION*

. . . .

The end then of learning is to repair the ruins of our first parents by regaining to know
God aright, and out of that knowledge to love him, to imitate him, to be like him, as we
may the nearest by possessing our souls of true virtue, which being united to the
heavenly grace of faith makes up the highest perfection. But because our understanding
cannot in this body found itself but on sensible things, nor arrive so clearly to the   5
knowledge of God and things invisible, as by orderly conning over the visible and
inferior creature, the same method is necessarily to be followed in all discreet teaching.
And seeing every nation affords not experience and tradition enough for all kinds of
learning, therefore we are chiefly taught the languages of those people who have at any
time been most industrious after wisdom; so that language is but the instrument   10
conveying to us things useful to be known. And though a linguist should pride himself
to have all the tongues that Babel cleft the world into, yet if he have not studied the solid
things in them, as well as the words and lexicons, he were nothing so much to be

---

158. **monstrous world:** i.e., world of sea-monsters. **160. Bellerus:** a giant imagined to account for *Bellerium,* the Roman name of the Land's End part of Cornwall. **161-62:** St. Michael's Mount, off the southern coast of Cornwall — "guarded" by the Archangel Michael looking south toward northwest Spain (Nemancos, near Cape Finisterre; Bayona's stronghold, on the coast near the border with Portugal). **164:** One or more dolphins were said to have wafted the Greek poet and musician Arion (7th century B.C.) safely to shore after he leaped overboard to avoid being killed for his wealth (see e.g. Herodotus, I, 23-24). **170. tricks:** tricks out, ornaments. **173:** See Matthew 14:25-26. **174-76:** Cf. Revelation 22:2, 19:7-9; **unexpressive:** inexpressible. **181:** Cf. Revelation 7:17, 21:4. **188. quills:** i.e., hollow reeds of the "oaten flute" or Pan-pipe. **189. Doric:** the Greek dialect of the Sicilian pastoral poets Theocritus, Bion, and Moschus. **190:** i.e., lengthened their shadows (cf. end of Virgil's Eclogue I). See also Samuel Johnson's criticism of *Lycidas* (p. 607).   **OF EDUCATION   1. ruins of our first parents:** the Fall of Adam and Eve. **7. creature:** creation.

esteemed a learned man as any yeoman or tradesman competently wise in his mother dialect only. . . . And for the usual method of teaching arts, I deem it to be an old error 15 of universities, not yet well recovered from the scholastic grossness of barbarous ages, that instead of beginning with arts most easy, and those be such as are most obvious to the sense, they present their young unmatriculated novices, at first coming, with the most intellective abstractions of logic and metaphysics; so that they having but newly left those grammatic flats and shallows where they stuck unreasonably to learn a few 20 words with lamentable construction, and now on the sudden transported under another climate to be tossed and turmoiled with their unballasted wits in fathomless and unquiet deeps of controversy, do for the most part grow into hatred and contempt of learning, mocked and deluded all this while with ragged notions and babblements, while they expected worthy and delightful knowledge; till poverty or youthful years call them 25 importunately their several ways and hasten them, with the sway of friends, either to an ambitious and mercenary or ignorantly zealous divinity; some allured to the trade of law, grounding their purposes not on the prudent and heavenly contemplation of justice and equity, which was never taught them, but on the promising and pleasing thoughts of litigious terms, fat contentions, and flowing fees; others betake them to state affairs, 30 with souls so unprincipled in virtue and true generous breeding that flattery and court-shifts and tyrannous aphorisms appear to them the highest points of wisdom, instilling their barren hearts with a conscientious slavery, if, as I rather think, it be not feigned. Others lastly of a more delicious and airy spirit retire themselves, knowing no better, to the enjoyments of ease and luxury, living out their days in feast and jollity; which 35 indeed is the wisest and safest course of all these, unless they were with more integrity undertaken. And these are the errors and these are the fruits of mispending our prime youth at the schools and universities as we do, either in learning mere words, or such things chiefly as were better unlearnt.

I shall detain you now no longer in the demonstration of what we should not do, but 40 straight conduct ye to a hillside where I will point ye out the right path of a virtuous and noble education; laborious indeed at the first ascent, but else so smooth, so green, so full of goodly prospect and melodious sounds on every side, that the harp of Orpheus was not more charming. I doubt not but ye shall have more ado to drive our dullest and laziest youth, our stocks and stubs, from the infinite desire of such a happy nurture, than 45 we have now to hale and drag our choicest and hopefullest wits to that asinine feast of sowthistles and brambles which is commonly set before them as all the food and entertainment of their tenderest and most docible age. I call therefore a complete and generous education that which fits a man to perform justly, skilfully, and magna-nimously all the offices, both private and public, of peace and war. And how all this 50 may be done between twelve and one and twenty, less time than is now bestowed in pure trifling at grammar and sophistry, is to be thus ordered.

. . . .

---

15. arts: the *quadrivium* (arithmetic, music, geography, astronomy) and the *trivium* (grammar, rhetoric, logic) made up the traditional "Seven Liberal Arts" from mediaeval times, with languages such as Latin and Greek added during the Renaissance. **34. delicious:** given to sensual indulgence, pleasure-seeking. **40. you:** This tractate was written in the form of an open letter to Samuel Hartlib, author of *A Reformation of Schools* (1642). **45. stocks and stubs:** senseless, stupid persons; blockheads.

For their studies, first they should begin with the chief and necessary rules of some
good grammar, either that now used or any better; and while this is doing, their speech
is to be fashioned to a distinct and clear pronunciation, as near as may be to the Italian,   *55*
especially in the vowels. For we Englishmen being far northerly, do not open our
mouths in the cold air wide enough to grace a southern tongue, but are observed by all
other nations to speak exceeding close and inward, so that to smatter Latin with an
English mouth is as ill a hearing as law French. . . . But here the main skill and ground-
work will be to temper them such lectures and explanations upon every opportunity as   *60*
may lead and draw them in willing obedience, inflamed with the study of learning and
the admiration of virtue, stirred up with high hopes of living to be brave men and
worthy patriots, dear to God, and famous to all ages. That they may despise and scorn
all their childish and ill-taught qualities, to delight in manly and liberal exercises, which
he who hath the art and proper eloquence to catch them with, what with mild and   *65*
effectual persuasions, and what with the intimation of some fear, if need be, but chiefly
by his own example, might in a short space gain them to an incredible diligence and
courage, infusing into their young breasts such an ingenuous and noble ardour as would
not fail to make many of them renowned and matchless men. At the same time, some
other hour of the day, might be taught them the rules of arithmetic, and soon after the   *70*
elements of geometry, even playing, as the old manner was. After evening repast, till
bedtime, their thoughts would be best taken up in the easy grounds of religion and the
story of scripture. The next step would be to the authors of agriculture, Cato, Varro, and
Columella, for the matter is most easy; and if the language be difficult, so much the
better: it is not a difficulty above their years. And here will be an occasion of inciting   *75*
and enabling them hereafter to improve the tillage of their country, to recover the bad
soil and to remedy the waste that is made of good. . . . And at the same time might be
entering into the Greek tongue, after the same manner as was before prescribed in the
Latin, whereby the difficulties of grammar being soon overcome, all the historical
physiology of Aristotle and Theophrastus are open before them. . . . And having . . .   *80*
passed the principles of arithmetic, geometry, astronomy, and geography, with a general
compact of physics, they may descend in mathematics to the instrumental science of
trigonometry, and from thence to fortification, architecture, enginery, or navigation.
And in natural philosophy they may proceed leisurely from the history of meteors,
minerals, plants, and living creatures as far as anatomy.   *85*

. . . .

By this time, years and good general precepts will have furnished them more
distinctly with that act of reason which in ethics is called Proairesis, that they may with
some judgment contemplate upon moral good and evil. . . . The next remove must be to
the study of politics, to know the beginning, end, and reasons of political societies, that

---

60. temper: fit, adapt, regulate suitably. **71. playing:** In Book VII of Plato's *Republic,* Socrates advises Glaucon not to use compulsion but to make children's lessons take the form of play. **73-74:** Marcus Porcius Cato (Cato the Elder, or the Censor, 234-149 B.C.), *De Re Rustica* (or *De Agri Cultura*); Marcus Terentius Varro (116-27 B.C.), *Rerum Rusticarum* (or *De Agricultura*); Lucius Junius Moderatus Columella (fl. mid-first century A.D.), *De Re Rustica, De Arboribus.* **83. enginery:** engineering, the art of constructing engines, especially perhaps military ones. **87. Proairesis:** (transliterated from the Greek of Plato and Aristotle) a choosing of one thing before another, an act of deliberate choice; see *Areopagitica,* below, lines 37-38 ("reason is but choosing"), and *Paradise Lost,* III, 108 ("reason also is choice").

they may not in a dangerous fit of the commonwealth be such poor, shaken, uncertain *90* reeds, of such a tottering conscience, as many of our great counsellors have lately shown themselves, but steadfast pillars of the state. After this they are to dive into the grounds of law and legal justice, delivered first and with best warrant by Moses, and as far as human prudence can be trusted, in those extolled remains of Grecian lawgivers, Lycurgus, Solon, Zaleucus, Charondas, and thence to all the Roman edicts and tables *95* with their Justinian, and so down to the Saxon and common laws of England, and the statutes. Sundays also and every evening may be now understandingly spent in the highest matters of theology and church history ancient and modern; and ere this time the Hebrew tongue at a set hour might have been gained, that the scriptures may be now read in their own original, whereto it would be no impossibility to add the Chaldee and *100* the Syrian dialect. When all these employments are well conquered, then will the choice histories, heroic poems, and Attic tragedies of stateliest and most regal argument, with all the famous political orations, offer themselves; which, if they were not only read but some of them got by memory, and solemnly pronounced with right accent and grace, as might be taught, would endue them even with the spirit and vigour of Demosthenes or *105* Cicero, Euripides or Sophocles. And now, lastly, will be the time to read with them those organic arts which enable men to discourse and write perspicuously, elegantly, and according to the fitted style, of lofty, mean, or lowly. . . . These are the studies wherein our noble and our gentle youth ought to bestow their time in a disciplinary way from twelve to one and twenty, unless they rely more upon their ancestors dead than *110* upon themselves living.

. . . .

Thus . . . you have a general view . . . concerning the best and noblest way of education; not beginning, as some have done, from the cradle, which yet might be worth many considerations, if brevity had not been my scope; many other circumstances also I could have mentioned, but this to such as have the worth in them to make trial, for light *115* and direction may be enough. Only I believe that this is not a bow for every man to shoot in that counts himself a teacher, but will require sinews almost equal to those which Homer gave Ulysses; yet I am withal persuaded that it may prove much more easy in the assay than it now seems at distance, and much more illustrious; howbeit not more difficult than I imagine, and that imagination presents me with nothing but very *120* happy and very possible according to best wishes, if God have so decreed, and this age have spirit enough to apprehend.

(1644)

95-96: Lycurgus (before 600 B.C.), traditionally, a Spartan legislator, founder of the constitution, though possibly a deity rather than a real person; Solon (late seventh-early sixth centuries B.C.), Athenian statesmen, poet, lawmaker and reformer; Zaleucus (mid-seventh century B.C.), lawgiver of the Greeks in Locri, in the "toe" of Italy; Charondas (c. sixth century B.C.), lawgiver of Catana, in Sicily; Justinian, Roman emperor A.D. 527-65, whose major achievement was the codification of Roman law. **100-01. Chaldee:** Biblical Aramaic; **Syrian:** Syriac. **102. Attic tragedies:** i.e., those of the Athenian dramatists Aeschylus, Sophocles, and Euripides. **105. Demosthenes:** a 4th-century B.C. Athenian orator. **106. Cicero:** a 1st-century B.C. Roman orator. **107. organic:** instrumental, serving as instruments toward a desired end. **108. lofty, mean, or lowly:** high, middle, or low style, similar to *formal, informal,* and *colloquial*; a style was "fitted" when it was appropriate to subject matter and occasion according to the principles of *decorum* (see Glossary). **117-18:** for the story of Odysseus (Ulysses) bending the bow, see Homer's *Odyssey*, XXI.

from *AREOPAGITICA:*
A *SPEECH FOR THE LIBERTY OF UNLICENSED PRINTING.*
TO THE PARLIAMENT OF ENGLAND

. . . .

I deny not but that it is of greatest concernment in the church and commonwealth to have a vigilant eye how books demean themselves, as well as men, and thereafter to confine, imprison, and do sharpest justice on them as malefactors; for books are not absolutely dead things, but do contain a potency of life in them to be as active as that soul was whose progeny they are; nay, they do preserve as in a vial the purest efficacy *5* and extraction of that living intellect that bred them. I know they are as lively and as vigorously productive as those fabulous dragon's teeth, and being sown up and down may chance to spring up armed men. And yet, on the other hand, unless wariness be used, as good almost kill a man as kill a good book: who kills a man kills a reasonable creature, God's image; but he who destroys a good book kills reason itself, kills the *10* image of God, as it were, in the eye. Many a man lives a burden to the earth; but a good book is the precious life-blood of a master-spirit, embalmed and treasured up on purpose to a life beyond life.

. . . .

Good and evil we know in the field of this world grow up together almost inseparably; and the knowledge of good is so involved and interwoven with the knowledge *15* of evil, and in so many cunning resemblances hardly to be discerned, that those confused seeds which were imposed upon Psyche as an incessant labour to cull out and sort asunder were not more intermixed. It was from out the rind of one apple tasted that the knowledge of good and evil as two twins cleaving together leaped forth into the world. And perhaps this is that doom which Adam fell into of knowing good and evil, *20* that is to say of knowing good by evil. As therefore the state of man now is, what wisdom can there be to choose, what continence to forbear, without the knowledge of evil? He that can apprehend and consider vice with all her baits and seeming pleasures, and yet abstain, and yet distinguish, and yet prefer that which is truly better, he is the true warfaring Christian. I cannot praise a fugitive and cloistered virtue, unexercised and *25* unbreathed, that never sallies out and seeks her adversary, but slinks out of the race where that immortal garland is to be run for, not without dust and heat. Assuredly we bring not innocence into the world, we bring impurity much rather; that which purifies us is trial, and trial is by what is contrary. That virtue therefore which is but a youngling

---

AREOPAGITICA   The title refers to the Areopagus ("Hill of Mars") in ancient Athens, meeting-place of both a government council and a judicial court. Milton was opposing Parliament's 1643 "Ordinance for Printing," which required that everything published be licensed and entered in the Stationers' Register — in effect, the government exercising prior censorship over anything it disapproved of. Although the law was widely ignored (*Areopagitica,* e.g., was not licensed), Milton's opposition to the principle remained strong. **7-8:** When the teeth of the dragon slain by Cadmus were sown, they sprang up armed men who proceeded to slay one another until only five were left (see Ovid's *Metamorphoses,* III, 1ff.; in VII, 121ff., the motif occurs again in the story of Jason and Medea). **17-18:** Apuleius in *The Golden Ass* (or *Metamorphoses*), IV-VI, tells of Venus's imposing seemingly impossible tasks on Psyche, among them the sorting of a heap of different kinds of seeds by sundown; friendly ants did the job for her. **25. warfaring:** the first edition read *wayfaring,* which some think preferable. **27. that immortal garland:** Milton may have in mind a specific "garland," analogous to the garland of laurel awarded victorious athletes and poets (several such prizes are mentioned in the Bible; see e.g. Philippians 3:14, II Timothy 4:8, James 1:12), or he may be referring to something as simple as "truth" or "virtue" (see line 59).

in the contemplation of evil, and knows not the utmost that vice promises to her   *30*
followers, and rejects it, is but a blank virtue, not a pure; her whiteness is but an
excremental whiteness. Which was the reason why our sage and serious poet Spenser,
whom I dare be known to think a better teacher than Scotus or Aquinas, describing true
temperance under the person of Guyon, brings him in with his palmer through the cave
of Mammon and the bower of earthly bliss, that he might see and know, and yet abstain.   *35*

. . . .

Many there be that complain of divine Providence for suffering Adam to transgress.
Foolish tongues! When God gave him reason, he gave him freedom to choose, for
reason is but choosing; he had been else a mere artificial Adam, such an Adam as he is
in the motions. We ourselves esteem not of that obedience, or love, or gift, which is of
force. God therefore left him free, set before him a provoking object, ever almost in his   *40*
eyes; herein consisted his merit, herein the right of his reward, the praise of his
abstinence. Wherefore did he create passions within us, pleasures round about us, but
that these rightly tempered are the very ingredients of virtue? They are not skilful
considerers of human things, who imagine to remove sin by removing the matter of sin;
for besides that it is a huge heap increasing under the very act of diminishing, though   *45*
some part of it may for a time be withdrawn from some persons, it cannot from all, in
such a universal thing as books are; and when this is done, yet the sin remains entire.
Though ye take from a covetous man all his treasure, he has yet one jewel left: ye
cannot bereave him of his covetousness. Banish all objects of lust, shut up all youth into
the severest discipline that can be exercised in any hermitage, ye cannot make them   *50*
chaste that came not hither so; such great care and wisdom is required to the right
managing of this point. Suppose we could expel sin by this means; look how much we
thus expel of sin, so much we expel of virtue, for the matter of them both is the same;
remove that, and ye remove them both alike. This justifies the high providence of God,
who, though he command us temperance, justice, continence, yet pours out before us   *55*
even to a profuseness all desirable things, and gives us minds that can wander beyond
all limit and satiety. Why should we then affect a rigour contrary to the manner of God
and of nature, by abridging or scanting those means which books freely permitted are,
both to the trial of virtue and the exercise of truth?

. . . .

Truth indeed came once into the world with her divine Master, and was a perfect   *60*
shape most glorious to look on; but when he ascended, and his apostles after him were
laid asleep, then straight arose a wicked race of deceivers, who, as that story goes of the
Egyptian Typhon with his conspirators, how they dealt with the good Osiris, took the
virgin Truth, hewed her lovely form into a thousand pieces, and scattered them to the
four winds. From that time ever since, the sad friends of Truth, such as durst appear,   *65*
imitating the careful search that Isis made for the mangled body of Osiris, went up and
down gathering up limb by limb still as they could find them. We have not yet found

---

32. excremental: like an outgrowth or excrescence, outside (perhaps with a glance at the "whited sepulchres" of Matthew 23:27). **33:** John Duns Scotus (c.1265-1308) and Saint Thomas Aquinas (1225-1274). **33-35:** in *The Faerie Queene*, II, vii-viii and xii. **37-38:** See "Of Education" above (line 87), and *Paradise Lost*, III, 108 (p. 350). **39. motions:** puppet shows. **56-57:** Note Belial's use of a similar phrase, *Paradise Lost*, II, line 148 (p. 338). **62ff.:** a story told by Plutarch in *On Isis and Osiris*; the monster Typhon, or Typhoeus, was identified with Set, or Seth, the Egyptian god who was brother and killer of Osiris. **66. careful:** anxious.

them all, Lords and Commons, nor ever shall do, till her Master's second coming; he shall bring together every joint and member, and shall mould them into an immortal feature of loveliness and perfection. Suffer not these licensing prohibitions to stand at *70* every place of opportunity, forbidding and disturbing them that continue seeking, that continue to do our obsequies to the torn body of our martyred saint. We boast our light; but if we look not wisely on the sun itself, it smites us into darkness. Who can discern those planets that are oft combust, and those stars of brightest magnitude that rise and set with the sun, until the opposite motion of their orbs bring them to such a place in the *75* firmament where they may be seen evening or morning? The light which we have gained was given us not to be ever staring on, but by it to discover onward things more remote from our knowledge.

. . . .

What should ye do then, should ye suppress all this flowery crop of knowledge and new light sprung up and yet springing daily in this city?. . . . Ye cannot make us now *80* less capable, less knowing, less eagerly pursuing of the truth, unless ye first make yourselves, that made us so, less the lovers, less the founders of our true liberty. . . . Give me the liberty to know, to utter, and to argue freely according to conscience, above all liberties.

. . . .

And now the time in special is, by privilege to write and speak what may help to the *85* further discussing of matters in agitation. The temple of Janus with his two controversial faces might now not unsignificantly be set open. And though all the winds of doctrine were let loose to play upon the earth, so Truth be in the field, we do injuriously by licensing and prohibiting to misdoubt her strength. Let her and Falsehood grapple; who ever knew Truth put to the worse, in a free and open encounter? Her confuting is the *90* best and surest suppressing. . . . For who knows not that Truth is strong, next to the Almighty? She needs no policies, nor stratagems, nor licensings to make her victorious; those are the shifts and the defences that error uses against her power. Give her but room, and do not bind her when she sleeps, for then she speaks not true, as the old Proteus did, who spake oracles only when he was caught and bound, but then rather she *95* turns herself into all shapes except her own, and perhaps tunes her voice according to the time, as Micaiah did before Ahab, until she be adjured into her own likeness.

. . . .

This I know: that errors in a good government and in a bad are equally almost incident; for what magistrate may not be misinformed, and much the sooner, if liberty of printing be reduced into the power of a few? But to redress willingly and speedily what *100* hath been erred, and in highest authority to esteem a plain advertisement more than others have done a sumptuous bribe, is a virtue (honoured Lords and Commons) answerable to your highest actions, and whereof none can participate but greatest and wisest men.

(1644)

---

74. combust: burned or scorched — and not visible — because of proximity to the sun. **86-87:** The double doors or gates of Janus's sanctuary in the Forum in Rome were opened only during wartime. **87. winds of doctrine:** See Ephesians 4:14, **89ff.:** Cf. Donne's "Satire III," 72ff. (p. 256). **90. her confuting:** i.e., confuting her (Falsehood). **95. Proteus:** see *Odyssey*, IV, 384ff. **97. Micaiah, Ahab:** see I Kings 22 and II Chronicles 18. **101. advertisement:** warning, notification.

SONNET XIX [ON HIS BLINDNESS]

When I consider how my light is spent,
  Ere half my days, in this dark world and wide,
  And that one talent which is death to hide
  Lodged with me useless, though my soul more bent
To serve therewith my Maker, and present   5
  My true account, lest he returning chide,
  "Doth God exact day-labour, light denied?"
  I fondly ask. But Patience, to prevent
That murmur, soon replies, "God doth not need
  Either man's work or his own gifts; who best   10
  Bear his mild yoke, they serve him best; his state
Is kingly: thousands at his bidding speed
  And post o'er land and ocean without rest;
  They also serve who only stand and wait."
                       (1652?; 1673)

SONNET XVIII: ON THE LATE MASSACRE IN PIEDMONT

Avenge, O Lord, thy slaughtered saints, whose bones
  Lie scattered on the Alpine mountains cold;
  Ev'n them who kept thy truth so pure of old
  When all our fathers worshipped stocks and stones,
Forget not; in thy book record their groans   5
  Who were thy sheep, and in their ancient fold

Slain by the bloody Piemontese that rolled
  Mother with infant down the rocks. Their moans
The vales redoubled to the hills, and they
  To Heav'n. Their martyred blood and ashes sow   10
  O'er all th'Italian fields, where still doth sway
The triple tyrant, that from these may grow
  A hundredfold, who having learnt thy way,
  Early may fly the Babylonian woe.
                      (1655; 1673)

SONNET XXIII

Methought I saw my late espoused saint
  Brought to me like Alcestis from the grave,
  Whom Jove's great son to her glad husband gave,
  Rescued from death by force though pale and faint.
Mine, as whom washed from spot of child-bed taint, 5
  Purification in the old law did save,
  And such as yet once more I trust to have
  Full sight of her in Heaven without restraint,
Came vested all in white, pure as her mind.
  Her face was veiled, yet to my fancied sight   10
  Love, sweetness, goodness, in her person shined
So clear, as in no face with more delight.
  But O, as to embrace me she inclined,
  I waked, she fled, and day brought back my night.
                      (1658; 1673)

from *PARADISE LOST*

The Verse

The measure is English heroic verse without rhyme, as that of Homer in Greek and of Virgil in Latin, rhyme being no necessary adjunct or true ornament of poem or good verse, in longer works especially, but the invention of a barbarous age, to set off wretched matter and lame metre — graced indeed since by the use of some famous modern poets, carried away by custom, but much to their own vexation, hindrance, and constraint to express many things otherwise, and for the   5 most part worse, than else they would have expressed them. Not without cause, therefore, some both Italian and Spanish poets of prime note have rejected rhyme both in longer and shorter works, as have also long since our best English tragedies, as a thing of itself, to all judicious ears, trivial and of no true musical delight; which consists only in apt numbers, fit quantity of syllables,

---

SONNET XIX Milton's blindness, encroaching for about fifteen years, was total by 1652. **3:** See Matthew 25:14-30. **7:** See John 9:4. **11. mild yoke:** See Matthew 11:29-30.   **SONNET XVIII** In April 1655, at Easter, soldiers massacred the dissenting Waldenses who lived in the Piedmont. **10ff.:** See Matthew 13:3-8; see also the note to lines 7-8 of *Areopagitica* above. **12. triple tyrant:** the pope, wearer of the triple crown. **14:** Roman Catholicism was often identified with the Babylon of Revelation 14:8, 17, 18.   **SONNET XXIII** Milton's second wife, Katherine Woodcock, bore a child in October 1657 and died in February 1658, not yet thirty; a few weeks later the child also died. **2-4. Alcestis:** wife of Admetus, rescued from the underworld by Heracles (Hercules), who fought against Death (see Euripides, *Alcestis*). **5-6:** See Leviticus 12. **10:** Because she was veiled, Admetus didn't recognize Alcestis; Milton married Katherine in 1656, years after losing his sight.

and the sense variously drawn out from one verse into another, not in the jingling sound of like   *10*
endings, a fault avoided by the learned ancients both in poetry and all good oratory. This neglect
then of rhyme so little is to be taken for a defect, though it may seem so perhaps to vulgar readers,
that it rather is to be esteemed an example set, the first in English, of ancient liberty recovered to
heroic poem from the troublesome and modern bondage of rhyming.

BOOK I

The Argument

This first book proposes, first in brief, the whole subject, man's disobedience, and the loss
thereupon of Paradise wherein he was placed: then touches the prime cause of his fall, the
Serpent, or rather Satan in the Serpent; who, revolting from God, and drawing to his side many
legions of angels, was by the command of God driven out of heaven with all his crew into the
great deep. Which action passed over, the poem hastes into the midst of things, presenting Satan   *5*
with his angels now fallen into Hell — described here, not in the centre (for Heaven and Earth
may be supposed as yet not made, certainly not yet accursed), but in a place of utter darkness,
fitliest called Chaos. Here Satan with his angels lying on the burning lake, thunderstruck and
astonished, after a certain space recovers, as from confusion; calls up him who, next in order and
dignity, lay by him; they confer of their miserable fall. Satan awakens all his legions, who lay till   *10*
then in the same manner confounded. They rise: their numbers, array of battle, their chief leaders
named, according to the idols known afterwards in Canaan and the countries adjoining. To these
Satan directs his speech, comforts them with hope yet of regaining heaven, but tells them lastly of
a new world and new kind of creature to be created, according to an ancient prophecy or report in
heaven; for that angels were long before this visible creation was the opinion of many ancient   *15*
fathers. To find out the truth of this prophecy, and what to determine thereon, he refers to a full
council. What his associates thence attempt. Pandemonium, the palace of Satan, rises, suddenly
built out of the deep; the infernal peers there sit in council.

Of man's first disobedience, and the fruit
Of that forbidden tree, whose mortal taste
Brought death into the world, and all our woe,
With loss of Eden, till one greater Man
Restore us, and regain the blissful seat,   *5*
Sing, Heav'nly Muse, that on the secret top
Of Oreb, or of Sinai, didst inspire
That shepherd who first taught the chosen seed
In the beginning how the Heav'ns and Earth
Rose out of Chaos; or if Sion hill   *10*
Delight thee more, and Siloa's brook that flowed
Fast by the oracle of God, I thence
Invoke thy aid to my advent'rous song,

That with no middle flight intends to soar
Above th' Aonian mount, while it pursues   *15*
Things unattempted yet in prose or rhyme.
And chiefly thou, O Spirit, that dost prefer
Before all temples th' upright heart and pure,
Instruct me, for thou know'st; thou from the first
Wast present, and with mighty wings outspread   *20*
Dove-like sat'st brooding on the vast abyss
And mad'st it pregnant: what in me is dark
Illumine, what is low raise and support;
That to the highth of this great argument
I may assert Eternal Providence,   *25*
And justify the ways of God to men.

PARADISE LOST   BOOK I   **4. one greater Man:** Christ. **6. Heav'nly Muse:** Urania (Greek, "heavenly one"), the classical Muse of
Astronomy, sometimes also of Fate, traditionally also associated with Knowledge or Wisdom (see VII, 8-9 below); here partaking also of the "Spirit
of God" (see 17, 21, below). **7. Oreb:** Horeb. **8. shepherd:** Moses, who supposedly wrote the Pentateuch. **11. Siloa:** See Isaiah 8:6, John 9:7 and 11.
12. oracle: in the temple (see I Kings 7:19-20). **15. Aonian mount:** Helicon, home of the Muses. **16. rhyme:** i.e., verse. **17, 21. Spirit . . . dove-like
sat'st brooding:** See Genesis 1:2 (p. 241), Matthew 3:16, Mark 1:10, Luke 3:22, John 1:32. **19-20:** Cf. Homer's *Iliad*, II, 484-85. **25. assert:**
includes sense of "defend, vindicate."

Say first, for heav'n hides nothing from thy view,
Nor the deep tract of Hell, say first what cause
Moved our grand parents in that happy state,
Favoured of Heav'n so highly, to fall off 30
From their Creator, and transgress his will
For one restraint, lords of the world besides?
Who first seduced them to that foul revolt?
Th' infernal Serpent; he it was whose guile,
Stirred up with envy and revenge, deceived 35
The mother of mankind, what time his pride
Had cast him out from Heav'n, with all his host
Of rebel angels, by whose aid aspiring
To set himself in glory above his peers,
He trusted to have equaled the Most High, 40
If he opposed; and with ambitious aim
Against the throne and monarchy of God
Raised impious war in Heav'n and battle proud
With vain attempt. Him the Almighty Power
Hurled headlong flaming from th' ethereal sky 45
With hideous ruin and combustion down
To bottomless perdition, there to dwell
In adamantine chains and penal fire,
Who durst defy th' Omnipotent to arms.
Nine times the space that measures day and night 50
To mortal men, he with his horrid crew
Lay vanquished, rolling in the fiery gulf
Confounded though immortal. But his doom
Reserved him to more wrath; for now the thought
Both of lost happiness and lasting pain 55
Torments him; round he throws his baleful eyes,
That witnessed huge affliction and dismay
Mixed with obdurate pride and steadfast hate.
At once as far as angels ken he views
The dismal situation waste and wild: 60
A dungeon horrible, on all sides round
As one great furnace flamed, yet from those flames
No light, but rather darkness visible
Served only to discover sights of woe,
Regions of sorrow, doleful shades, where peace 65
And rest can never dwell, hope never comes

That comes to all; but torture without end
Still urges, and a fiery deluge, fed
With ever-burning sulphur unconsumed:
Such place Eternal Justice had prepared 70
For those rebellious, here their prison ordained
In utter darkness, and their portion set
As far removed from God and light of heav'n
As from the centre thrice to th' utmost pole.
O how unlike the place from whence they fell! 75
There the companions of his fall, o'erwhelmed
With floods and whirlwinds of tempestuous fire,
He soon discerns, and welt'ring by his side
One next himself in power, and next in crime,
Long after known in Palestine, and named 80
Beelzebub. To whom th' Arch-Enemy,
And thence in Heav'n called Satan, with bold words
Breaking the horrid silence thus began:
   "If thou beest he — but O how fall'n! how changed
From him, who in the happy realms of light 85
Clothed with transcendent brightness didst outshine
Myriads though bright — if he whom mutual league,
United thoughts and counsels, equal hope
And hazard in the glorious enterprise,
Joined with me once, now misery hath joined 90
In equal ruin: into what pit thou seest
From what highth fall'n, so much the stronger proved
He with his thunder, and till then who knew
The force of those dire arms? Yet not for those,
Nor what the potent Victor in his rage 95
Can else inflict, do I repent or change,
Though changed in outward lustre, that fixed mind
And high disdain, from sense of injured merit,
That with the mightiest raised me to contend,
And to the fierce contention brought along 100
Innumerable force of Spirits armed
That durst dislike his reign, and me preferring,
His utmost power with adverse power opposed
In dubious battle on the plains of Heav'n,
And shook his throne. What though the field be lost? 105
All is not lost; the unconquerable will,

27-33: the "epic question(s)," which in effect the rest of the poem answers; cf. the invocations at the beginning of the *Iliad* (p. 534) and of Virgil's *Aeneid* (p. 440). **34ff.:** See Revelation 12:9, 20:1-3; Isaiah 14:12ff.; II Peter 2:4. **50:** In Hesiod's *Theogony*, Zeus overcomes Kronos and other Titans, who then fall nine days and nights to earth, then nine more days and nights to Tartarus. **57. witnessed:** bore witness to, expressed. **70-71:** See Matthew 25:41. **72. utter:** the main sense is "outer" (see Matthew 8:12, 22:13; see also the Argument, above: Milton's cosmology posits a universe with Heaven, or the Empyrean, at the top and a vast Chaos below; at the bottom of Chaos, Hell has been created, and in its upper part a Ptolemaic world of concentric spheres will be created, hanging from heaven by a golden chain; see *Ptolemaic* in the Glossary). **74. centre, pole:** i.e., the created world's centre (Earth) and pole (one end of the axis on which the whole turns). **81-82:** The name *Satan* means "adversary"; see I Peter 5:8, and III, 81; IX, 947, below. **84-85:** See Isaiah 14:12; *Aeneid*, II, 274.

And study of revenge, immortal hate,
And courage never to submit or yield:
And what is else not to be overcome?
That glory never shall his wrath or might   110
Extort from me. To bow and sue for grace
With suppliant knee, and deify his power
Who from the terror of this arm so late
Doubted his empire, that were low indeed,
That were an ignominy and shame beneath   115
This downfall; since by fate the strength of gods
And this Empyreal substance cannot fail,
Since through experience of this great event,
In arms not worse, in foresight much advanced,
We may with more successful hope resolve   120
To wage by force or guile eternal war
Irreconcilable to our grand Foe,
Who now triumphs, and in th' excess of joy
Sole reigning holds the tyranny of Heav'n."
    So spake th' apostate Angel, though in pain,   125
Vaunting aloud, but racked with deep despair;
And him thus answered soon his bold compeer:
    "O Prince, O Chief of many thronèd Powers,
That led th' embattled Seraphim to war
Under thy conduct, and in dreadful deeds   130
Fearless, endangered Heav'n's perpetual King,
And put to proof his high supremacy,
Whether upheld by strength, or chance, or fate;
Too well I see and rue the dire event,
That with sad overthrow and foul defeat   135
Hath lost us Heav'n, and all this mighty host
In horrible destruction laid thus low,
As far as Gods and Heav'nly essences
Can perish: for the mind and spirit remains
Invincible, and vigour soon returns,   140
Though all our glory extinct, and happy state
Here swallowed up in endless misery.
But what if he our Conqueror (whom I now
Of force believe almighty, since no less   144
Than such could have o'erpow'red such force as ours)
Have left us this our spirit and strength entire
Strongly to suffer and support our pains,
That we may so suffice his vengeful ire,
Or do him mightier service as his thralls
By right of war, whate'er his business be,   150

Here in the heart of Hell to work in fire,
Or do his errands in the gloomy deep?
What can it then avail though yet we feel
Strength undiminished, or eternal being
To undergo eternal punishment?"   155
    Whereto with speedy words th' Arch-Fiend replied:
"Fall'n Cherub, to be weak is miserable,
Doing or suffering: but of this be sure,
To do aught good never will be our task,
But ever to do ill our sole delight,   160
As being the contrary to his high will
Whom we resist. If then his providence
Out of our evil seek to bring forth good,
Our labour must be to pervert that end,
And out of good still to find means of evil;   165
Which ofttimes may succeed, so as perhaps
Shall grieve him, if I fail not, and disturb
His inmost counsels from their destined aim.
But see, the angry Victor hath recalled
His ministers of vengeance and pursuit   170
Back to the gates of Heav'n; the sulphurous hail
Shot after us in storm, o'erblown hath laid
The fiery surge, that from the precipice
Of Heav'n received us falling, and the thunder,
Winged with red lightning and impetuous rage,   175
Perhaps hath spent his shafts, and ceases now
To bellow through the vast and boundless deep.
Let us not slip th' occasion, whether scorn
Or satiate fury yield it from our Foe.
Seest thou yon dreary plain, forlorn and wild,   180
The seat of desolation, void of light,
Save what the glimmering of these livid flames
Casts pale and dreadful? Thither let us tend
From off the tossing of these fiery waves,
There rest, if any rest can harbour there,   185
And reassembling our afflicted powers,
Consult how we may henceforth most offend
Our Enemy, our own loss how repair,
How overcome this dire calamity,
What reinforcement we may gain from hope;   190
If not, what resolution from despair."
    Thus Satan talking to his nearest mate
With head uplift above the wave, and eyes
That sparkling blazed; his other parts besides

---

107. **study of:** ardent striving for, pursuit of. 114. **Doubted:** feared for. 115. **ignominy:** probably pronounced "ignomy." 128-29: the traditional nine orders of angels in their three hierarchies: the first hierarchy with seraphim, cherubim, and thrones; the second with dominations (or dominions), virtues, and powers; the third with principalities, archangels, and angels (see 737 below). 134. **event:** outcome, result. 144. **Of force:** Perforce. 158. **Doing or suffering:** i.e., whether being active or passive. 167. **fail:** mistake. 186. **afflicted:** struck down, overthrown. 187. **offend:** strike at, attack, harm.

Prone on the flood, extended long and large   *195*
Lay floating many a rood, in bulk as huge
As whom the fables name of monstrous size,
Titanian or Earth-born, that warred on Jove,
Briareos or Typhon, whom the den
By ancient Tarsus held, or that sea-beast   *200*
Leviathan, which God of all his works
Created hugest that swim th' ocean stream:
Him haply slumb'ring on the Norway foam,
The pilot of some small night-foundered skiff,
Deeming some island, oft, as seamen tell,   *205*
With fixed anchor in his scaly rind
Moors by his side under the lee, while night
Invests the sea, and wished morn delays:
So stretched out huge in length the Arch-Fiend lay
Chained on the burning lake; nor ever thence   *210*
Had ris'n or heaved his head, but that the will
And high permission of all-ruling Heaven
Left him at large to his own dark designs,
That with reiterated crimes he might
Heap on himself damnation, while he sought   *215*
Evil to others, and enraged might see
How all his malice served but to bring forth
Infinite goodness, grace and mercy shown
On man by him seduced, but on himself
Treble confusion, wrath and vengeance poured.   *220*
     Forthwith upright he rears from off the pool
His mighty stature; on each hand the flames
Driv'n backward slope their pointing spires, and rolled
In billows, leave i' th' midst a horrid vale.
Then with expanded wings he steers his flight   *225*
Aloft, incumbent on the dusky air
That felt unusual weight, till on dry land
He lights, if it were land that ever burned
With solid, as the lake with liquid fire,
And such appeared in hue; as when the force   *230*
Of subterranean wind transports a hill
Torn from Pelorus, or the shattered side
Of thund'ring Etna, whose combustible
And fueled entrails thence conceiving fire,
Sublimed with mineral fury, aid the winds,   *235*
And leave a singed bottom all involved

With stench and smoke: such resting found the sole
Of unblest feet. Him followed his next mate,
Both glorying to have scaped the Stygian flood
As Gods, and by their own recovered strength,   *240*
Not by the sufferance of supernal power.
     "Is this the region, this the soil, the clime,"
Said then the lost Archangel, "this the seat
That we must change for Heav'n, this mournful gloom
For that celestial light? Be it so, since he   *245*
Who now is sovran can dispose and bid
What shall be right: fardest from him is best,
Whom reason hath equaled, force hath made supreme
Above his equals. Farewell, happy fields,
Where joy for ever dwells! Hail, horrors, hail,   *250*
Infernal world, and thou, profoundest Hell,
Receive thy new possessor: one who brings
A mind not to be changed by place or time.
The mind is its own place, and in itself
Can make a Heav'n of Hell, a Hell of Heav'n.   *255*
What matter where, if I be still the same,
And what I should be, all but less than he
Whom thunder hath made greater? Here at least
We shall be free; th' Almighty hath not built
Here for his envy, will not drive us hence: *260*
Here we may reign secure, and in my choice
To reign is worth ambition, though in Hell:
Better to reign in Hell than serve in Heav'n.
But wherefore let we then our faithful friends,
Th' associates and copartners of our loss,   *265*
Lie thus astonished on th' oblivious pool,
And call them not to share with us their part
In this unhappy mansion, or once more
With rallied arms to try what may be yet
Regained in Heav'n, or what more lost in Hell?"   *270*
     So Satan spake, and him Beelzebub
Thus answered: "Leader of those armies bright,
Which but th' Omnipotent none could have foiled,
If once they hear that voice, their liveliest pledge
Of hope in fears and dangers, heard so oft   *275*
In worst extremes, and on the perilous edge
Of battle when it raged, in all assaults
Their surest signal, they will soon resume

196-208: the first of many epic similes in *Paradise Lost*. **197-99:** Titans and Giants, alike earth-born (offspring of Uranus and Ge, heaven and earth) and often confused with each other, both warred on the gods. **201ff. Leviathan:** the sea-monster of Job 41, Psalms 74:14 and 104:26, Isaiah 27:1. **202. ocean stream:** the old idea of Ocean as a stream flowing around a flat earth (see e.g. *Iliad*, XIV, 245-46). **224. horrid:** also signifying "bristling, rough" (often in Milton, a word of Latin origin has its etymological sense either alone or, as here, in addition to its later English sense). **230-37:** another epic simile. **232. Pelorus:** a promontory at the NE tip of Sicily (Cape Faro). **235. sublimed:** vaporized (a term from alchemy); also "raised up." **246. sovran:** sovereign. **255:** Cf. Helena's remark in Shakespeare's *A Midsummer Night's Dream*, II.i.243. **257. all but less than:** nearly equal to. **266. astonished:** astonied, stunned, dazed; **oblivious:** i.e., oblivion-causing (suggesting Lethe: see II, 583).

New courage and revive, though now they lie
Groveling and prostrate on yon lake of fire,   *280*
As we erewhile, astounded and amazed;
No wonder, fall'n such a pernicious highth!"

He scarce had ceased when the superior Fiend
Was moving toward the shore; his ponderous shield,
Ethereal temper, massy, large, and round,   *285*
Behind him cast; the broad circumference
Hung on his shoulders like the moon, whose orb
Through optic glass the Tuscan artist views
At ev'ning from the top of Fesole,
Or in Valdarno, to descry new lands,   *290*
Rivers or mountains in her spotty globe.
His spear, to equal which the tallest pine
Hewn on Norwegian hills, to be the mast
Of some great ammiral, were but a wand,
He walked with to support uneasy steps   *295*
Over the burning marl, not like those steps
On Heaven's azure; and the torrid clime
Smote on him sore besides, vaulted with fire.
Nathless he so endured, till on the beach
Of that inflamed sea, he stood and called   *300*
His legions, angel forms, who lay entranced,
Thick as autumnal leaves that strow the brooks
In Vallombrosa, where th' Etrurian shades
High over-arched embow'r; or scattered sedge
Afloat, when with fierce winds Orion armed   *305*
Hath vexed the Red Sea coast, whose waves o'erthrew
Busiris and his Memphian chivalry,
While with perfidious hatred they pursued
The sojourners of Goshen, who beheld
From the safe shore their floating carcasses   *310*
And broken chariot wheels; so thick bestrown,
Abject and lost lay these, covering the flood,
Under amazement of their hideous change.
He called so loud that all the hollow deep
Of Hell resounded: "Princes, Potentates,   *315*
Warriors, the flow'r of heav'n, once yours, now lost,
If such astonishment as this can seize

Eternal Spirits; or have ye chos'n this place
After the toil of battle to repose
Your wearied virtue, for the ease you find   *320*
To slumber here, as in the vales of Heav'n?
Or in this abject posture have ye sworn
To adore the Conqueror, who now beholds
Cherub and Seraph rolling in the flood
With scattered arms and ensigns, till anon   *325*
His swift pursuers from Heav'n gates discern
Th' advantage, and descending tread us down
Thus drooping, or with linked thunderbolts
Transfix us to the bottom of this gulf?
Awake, arise, or be for ever fall'n!"   *330*

They heard, and were abashed, and up they sprung
Upon the wing, as when men wont to watch
On duty, sleeping found by whom they dread,
Rouse and bestir themselves ere well awake.
Nor did they not perceive the evil plight   *335*
In which they were, or the fierce pains not feel;
Yet to their general's voice they soon obeyed
Innumerable. As when the potent rod
Of Amram's son in Egypt's evil day
Waved round the coast, up called a pitchy cloud   *340*
Of locusts, warping on the eastern wind,
That o'er the realm of impious Pharaoh hung
Like night, and darkened all the land of Nile:
So numberless were those bad angels seen
Hovering on wing under the cope of Hell   *345*
'Twixt upper, nether, and surrounding fires;
Till, as a signal giv'n, th' uplifted spear
Of their great Sultan waving to direct
Their course, in even balance down they light
On the firm brimstone, and fill all the plain;   *350*
A multitude, like which the populous North
Poured never from her frozen loins, to pass
Rhene or the Danaw, when her barbarous sons
Came like a deluge on the South, and spread
Beneath Gibraltar to the Libyan sands.   *355*
Forthwith from every squadron and each band

287-91: a briefer epic simile, referring to Galileo and his telescopic observations from Fiesole, a hill town above the Val d'Arno (valley of the Arno), near Florence; Milton had visited him there during a trip abroad in 1638-39; see also Wotton's letter (p. 234). **294. ammiral:** admiral's ship, flagship. **299. Nathless:** nevertheless. **302-11:** another epic simile (the last to be pointed out in these notes). **303. Vallombrosa:** "shady valley" and site (at that time) of a monastery in the Appenines east of Florence in Tuscany (part of what was ancient Etruria), visited by Milton in autumn of 1638. **304. sedge:** The Hebrew name for the Red Sea translates as "Sea of Sedge." **305: Orion:** the constellation, associated with storms late in the year. **307. Busirus:** in Greek myth, a king of Egypt who sacrificed foreigners to Zeus; slain by Heracles (Hercules; Ramses II was probably the actual Pharaoh of the exodus of the Israelites, the "sojourners of Goshen"; see Genesis 47:27, Exodus 14); **Memphian:** Memphis (its ruins are near modern Cairo) was the capital of ancient Egypt. **312. abject:** cast down, brought low. **320. virtue:** also meaning "courage, strength." **339. Amram's son:** Moses. **340-41:** See Exodus 10:12ff.; note also "pitchy clouds" in Sandys's translation of Ovid's *Metamorphoses*, I, 275 (p. 270). **345. cope:** overhead covering, roof. **351ff.:** the barbarian invasions of the declining Roman Empire; **Rhene:** Rhine; **Danaw:** Danube.

The heads and leaders thither haste where stood
Their great commander; godlike shapes and forms
Excelling human, princely Dignities,
And Powers that erst in Heaven sat on thrones; *360*
Though of their names in Heav'nly records now
Be no memorial, blotted out and razed
By their rebellion from the Books of Life.
Nor had they yet among the sons of Eve
Got them new names, till wand'ring o'er the Earth, *365*
Through God's high sufferance for the trial of man,
By falsities and lies the greatest part
Of mankind they corrupted to forsake
God their Creator, and th' invisible
Glory of him that made them to transform *370*
Oft to the image of a brute, adorned
With gay religions full of pomp and gold,
And devils to adore for deities:
Then were they known to men by various names,
And various idols through the heathen world. *375*
    Say, Muse, their names then known, who first, who last,
Roused from the slumber on that fiery couch,
At their great emperor's call, as next in worth
Came singly where he stood on the bare strand,
While the promiscuous crowd stood yet aloof. *380*
    The chief were those who from the pit of Hell,
Roaming to seek their prey on earth, durst fix
Their seats long after next the seat of God,
Their altars by his altar, gods adored
Among the nations round, and durst abide *385*
Jehovah thund'ring out of Sion, throned
Between the Cherubim; yea, often placed
Within his sanctuary itself their shrines,
Abominations; and with cursed things
His holy rites and solemn feasts profaned, *390*
And with their darkness durst affront his light.
First Moloch, horrid king besmeared with blood
Of human sacrifice, and parents' tears,
Though for the noise of drums and timbrels loud
Their children's cries unheard, that passed through fire
To his grim idol. Him the Ammonite *396*
Worshiped in Rabba and her wat'ry plain,

In Argob and in Basan, to the stream
Of utmost Arnon. Nor content with such
Audacious neighbourhood, the wisest heart *400*
Of Solomon he led by fraud to build
His temple right against the temple of God
On that opprobrious hill, and made his grove
The pleasant valley of Hinnom, Tophet thence
And black Gehenna called, the type of Hell. *405*
Next Chemos, th' obscene dread of Moab's sons,
From Aroer to Nebo, and the wild
Of southmost Abarim; in Hesebon
And Horonaim, Seon's realm, beyond
The flow'ry dale of Sibma clad with vines, *410*
And Eleale to th' Asphaltic pool:
Peor his other name, when he enticed
Israel in Sittim on their march from Nile
To do him wanton rites, which cost them woe.
Yet thence his lustful orgies he enlarged *415*
Even to that hill of scandal, by the grove
Of Moloch homicide, lust hard by hate;
Till good Josiah drove them thence to Hell.
With these came they who, from the bord'ring flood
Of old Euphrates to the brook that parts *420*
Egypt from Syrian ground, had general names
Of Baalim and Ashtaroth, those male,
These feminine. For Spirits when they please
Can either sex assume, or both; so soft
And uncompounded is their essence pure, *425*
Not tied or manacled with joint or limb,
Nor founded on the brittle strength of bones,
Like cumbrous flesh; but in what shape they choose,
Dilated or condensed, bright or obscure,
Can execute their airy purposes, *430*
And works of love or enmity fulfill.
For those the race of Israel oft forsook
Their living Strength, and unfrequented left
His righteous altar, bowing lowly down
To bestial gods; for which their heads as low *435*
Bowed down in battle, sunk before the spear
Of despicable foes. With these in troop
Came Astoreth, whom the Phoenicians called

362-63: See Exodus 32:32-33; Psalms 69:28; Revelation 3:5, 20:15, 21:27. **376ff:** Here begins a "catalogue," one of the conventions of epic. **396:** The Ammonite capital was Rabba, which like the other place names in the next dozen or so lines is east of the Jordan (several are referred to in Isaiah 15 and 16). **403. that opprobrious hill:** the Mount of Olives (see 416 and 443 below, and I Kings 11:7, II Kings 23:13). **404-05:** See II Kings 23:10, Jeremiah 19:4-6; Gehenna (Valley of Hinnom) and Tophet became rubbish dumps; **type:** symbol, emblem, image, imitation. **407-08:** Mt. Nebo is in the Abarim range. **411. Asphaltic pool:** from *Lacus Asphaltites*, Latin name for the Dead Sea, from the pitch or bitumen (*asphaltum*) found on its surface and shores. **412-14:** See Numbers 25. **417. homicide:** an appositive used as if a title or part of Moloch's name, similar to "Ivan the Terrible," "William the Conqueror." **418:** See II Kings 22-23, II Chronicles 34:1-7. **420-21. Euphrates:** Palestine's eastern border; **brook:** Besor, its border with Egypt (see I Samuel 30:9-10). **422. Baalim and Ashtaroth:** plurals of *Baal* and *Ashtoreth* (or *Ishtar*; and see 438-39 below).

Astarte, queen of heav'n, with crescent horns;
To whose bright image nightly by the moon   *440*
Sidonian virgins paid their vows and songs;
In Sion also not unsung, where stood
Her temple on th' offensive mountain, built
By that uxorious king, whose heart though large,
Beguiled by fair idolatresses, fell   *445*
To idols foul. Thammuz came next behind,
Whose annual wound in Lebanon allured
The Syrian damsels to lament his fate
In amorous ditties all a summer's day,
While smooth Adonis from his native rock   *450*
Ran purple to the sea, supposed with blood
Of Thammuz yearly wounded: the love-tale
Infected Sion's daughters with like heat,
Whose wanton passions in the sacred porch
Ezekiel saw, when by the vision led   *455*
His eye surveyed the dark idolatries
Of alienated Judah. Next came one
Who mourned in earnest, when the captive ark
Maimed his brute image, head and hands lopped off
In his own temple, on the grunsel edge,   *460*
Where he fell flat, and shamed his worshipers:
Dagon his name, sea monster, upward man
And downward fish; yet had his temple high
Reared in Azotus, dreaded through the coast
Of Palestine, in Gath and Ascalon,   *465*
And Accaron and Gaza's frontier bounds.
Him followed Rimmon, whose delightful seat
Was fair Damascus, on the fertile banks
Of Abbana and Pharphar, lucid streams.
He also against the house of God was bold: *470*
A leper once he lost and gained a king,
Ahaz his sottish conqueror, whom he drew
God's altar to disparage and displace
For one of Syrian mode, whereon to burn
His odious off'rings, and adore the gods   *475*
Whom he had vanquished. After these appeared
A crew who under names of old renown,
Osiris, Isis, Orus, and their train,

With monstrous shapes and sorceries abused
Fanatic Egypt and her priests, to seek   *480*
Their wand'ring gods disguised in brutish forms
Rather than human. Nor did Israel scape
Th' infection when their borrowed gold composed
The calf in Oreb; and the rebel king
Doubled that sin in Bethel and in Dan,   *485*
Lik'ning his Maker to the grazed ox —
Jehovah, who in one night when he passed
From Egypt marching, equalled with one stroke
Both her first-born and all her bleating gods.
Belial came last, than whom a Spirit more lewd   *490*
Fell not from heaven, or more gross to love
Vice for itself. To him no temple stood
Or altar smoked; yet who more oft than he
In temples and at altars, when the priest
Turns atheist, as did Eli's sons, who filled   *495*
With lust and violence the house of God?
In courts and palaces he also reigns
And in luxurious cities, where the noise
Of riot ascends above their loftiest tow'rs,
And injury and outrage; and when night   *500*
Darkens the streets, then wander forth the sons
Of Belial, flown with insolence and wine.
Witness the streets of Sodom, and that night
In Gibeah, when the hospitable door
Exposed a matron to avoid worse rape.   *505*
These were the prime in order and in might;
The rest were long to tell, though far renowned,
Th' Ionian gods, of Javan's issue held
Gods, yet confessed later than Heav'n and Earth,
Their boasted parents; Titan, Heav'n's first-born,   *510*
With his enormous brood, and birthright seized
By younger Saturn; he from mightier Jove,
His own and Rhea's son, like measure found;
So Jove usurping reigned. These, first in Crete
And Ida known, thence on the snowy top   *515*
Of cold Olympus ruled the middle air,
Their highest Heav'n; or on the Delphian cliff,
Or in Dodona, and through all the bounds

444-45: See I Kings 4:29, 11:1-8. **446. Thammuz:** Syrian deity, counterpart of the Greek Adonis, after whom the Lebanese river (450) was named. **453-57:** See Ezekiel 8:13-14. **457-61:** See I Samuel 5:1-5. **460. grunsel:** groundsill, threshold. **464-66. Azotus:** Ashdod, a Philistine city, as are the other four named. **467-76:** See II Kings 5 and 16. **478. Orus:** Horus, son of Isis and Osiris. **481-82:** See Ovid, *Metamorphoses*, V, 321ff. **482-84:** See Exodus 12:35, and 32. **484-86:** See I Kings 12:28-30, Psalms 106:19-20. **487-89:** See Exodus 12:12-30; **equalled:** equalized, levelled — i.e., killed. **495:** See I Samuel 2:12ff. **498. luxurious:** includes sense of "lustful." **501-02:** The Puritans often used the phrase "sons of Belial" against their enemies; **flown:** overfull, swollen, flushed. **503-05:** See Genesis 19:1-15, Judges 19. **508. Javan:** (Greek, *Ion*) son of Japheth (Genesis 10:2), said to be ancestor of the Ionians (i.e., Greeks). **509. Heav'n and Earth:** Uranus (Uranos) and Ge (Gaia or Gaea), parents of the Titans. **510-14:** Titan (or in earlier tradition Uranos himself) was deposed by his brother (or son) Saturn (Kronos), and Saturn in turn by his son Zeus (Jove, Jupiter). **515. Ida:** Cretan mountain, supposed birthplace of Zeus. **516:** The air was thought to be divided into three regions. **517-19:** Delphi, on Parnassus,

Of Doric land; or who with Saturn old
Fled over Adria to th' Hesperian fields,   *520*
And o'er the Celtic roamed the utmost isles.
 All these and more came flocking; but with looks
Downcast and damp, yet such wherein appeared
Obscure some glimpse of joy, to have found their Chief
Not in despair, to have found themselves not lost   *525*
In loss itself; which on his count'nance cast
Like doubtful hue. But he, his wonted pride
Soon recollecting, with high words, that bore
Semblance of worth, not substance, gently raised
Their fainting courage, and dispelled their fears.   *530*
Then straight commands that at the warlike sound
Of trumpets loud and clarions be upreared
His mighty standard; that proud honour claimed
Azazel as his right, a Cherub tall;
Who forthwith from the glittering staff unfurled   *535*
Th' imperial ensign, which full high advanced
Shone like a meteor streaming to the wind,
With gems and golden lustre rich emblazed,
Seraphic arms and trophies; all the while
Sonorous metal blowing martial sounds;   *540*
At which the universal host upsent
A shout that tore Hell's concave, and beyond
Frighted the reign of Chaos and old Night.
All in a moment through the gloom were seen
Ten thousand banners rise into the air   *545*
With orient colours waving; with them rose
A forest huge of spears; and thronging helms
Appeared, and serried shields in thick array
Of depth immeasurable. Anon they move
In perfect phalanx to the Dorian mood   *550*
Of flutes and soft recorders; such as raised
To highth of noblest temper heroes old
Arming to battle, and instead of rage
Deliberate valour breathed, firm and unmoved

With dread of death to flight or foul retreat,   *555*
Nor wanting power to mitigate and swage
With solemn touches troubled thoughts, and chase
Anguish and doubt and fear and sorrow and pain
From mortal or immortal minds. Thus they,
Breathing united force with fixed thought,   *560*
Moved on in silence to soft pipes that charmed
Their painful steps o'er the burnt soil; and now
Advanced in view they stand, a horrid front
Of dreadful length and dazzling arms, in guise
Of warriors old with ordered spear and shield,   *565*
Awaiting what command their mighty Chief
Had to impose. He through the armed files
Darts his experienced eye, and soon traverse
The whole battalion views, their order due,
Their visages and stature as of gods;   *570*
Their number last he sums. And now his heart
Distends with pride, and hard'ning in his strength
Glories; for never, since created man,
Met such embodied force as named with these
Could merit more than that small infantry   *575*
Warred on by cranes: though all the giant brood
Of Phlegra with th' heroic race were joined
That fought at Thebes and Ilium, on each side
Mixed with auxiliar gods; and what resounds
In fable or romance of Uther's son   *580*
Begirt with British and Armoric knights;
And all who since, baptized or infidel,
Jousted in Aspramont or Montalban,
Damasco, or Marocco, or Trebisond,
Or whom Biserta sent from Afric shore   *585*
When Charlemain with all his peerage fell
By Fontarabbia. Thus far these beyond
Compare of mortal prowess, yet observed
Their dread commander. He above the rest
In shape and gesture proudly eminent   *590*

with its oracle of Apollo, and Dodona, in Epirus, with its oracle of Zeus, were two of the most ancient and prominent locations for the worship of the Olympian gods in central and northern Greece, respectively; the "Doric lands" are southern Greece, the Peloponnesus. **519-21:** Greek gods, or Greek culture in general, crossed the Adriatic to Hesperian fields (Italy), then to Celtic fields (France and Spain), then to the islands of Britain ("utmost" perhaps also suggesting Ultima Thule). **523. damp:** dejected, depressed, dazed, stupefied. **534. Azazel:** traditionally Satan's standard-bearer. **536. advanced:** raised. **556. swage:** assuage. **571-73:** See II Samuel 24:1-10, I Chronicles 21:1-8. **575-76:** The "small infantry" are pygmies (see 780-81 below); Homer (*Iliad*, III, 3-6) and others tell of their battles with cranes. **577. Phlegra:** Macedonian site of fighting between Giants and Olympic gods. **578:** referring to the war of the *Seven against Thebes* (Aeschylus's tragedy) and the Trojan War (Homer's *Iliad*). **580. Uther's son:** King Arthur. **583-87:** place names mentioned in romances and *chansons de geste* (most often Ariosto's *Orlando Furioso* and Boiardo's *Orlando Innamorato*) about battles between Christians and pagans: Aspramont (Aspromonte), range in the toe of Italy's boot where the stories say Orlando and Charlemagne fought against pagans; Montalban (Montauban) the home of Rinaldo in southern France; Damasco (Damascus), where tournaments were held; Trebisond (Trebizond, Trabzon), in Cappadocia (part of modern Turkey), famous as an eastern empire; Biserta (Bizerte), seaport of Tunisia; Fontarabbia (Fuenterrabia), on the coast near Roncesvalles (which is near Pamplona), where according to legend, or tradition, Roland (Orlando) and Charlemagne's rear-guard were defeated by Moors (*Chanson de Roland*, which was written during the time of the Crusades, when Saracens were the enemy; historically, Roland was killed in 778 by Basques, against whom Charlemagne and the Moors fought).

Stood like a tow'r; his form had yet not lost
All her original brightness, nor appeared
Less than Archangel ruined, and th' excess
Of glory obscured: as when the sun new ris'n
Looks through the horizontal misty air   595
Shorn of his beams, or from behind the moon
In dim eclipse disastrous twilight sheds
On half the nations, and with fear of change
Perplexes monarchs. Darkened so, yet shone
Above them all th' Archangel; but his face   600
Deep scars of thunder had intrenched, and care
Sat on his faded cheek, but under brows
Of dauntless courage, and considerate pride
Waiting revenge. Cruel his eye, but cast
Signs of remorse and passion to behold   605
The fellows of his crime, the followers rather
(Far other once beheld in bliss), condemned
For ever now to have their lot in pain,
Millions of Spirits for his fault amerced
Of Heav'n, and from eternal splendours flung   610
For his revolt, yet faithful how they stood,
Their glory withered: as when Heaven's fire
Hath scathed the forest oaks or mountain pines,
With singed top their stately growth though bare
Stands on the blasted heath. He now prepared   615
To speak; whereat their doubled ranks they bend
From wing to wing, and half enclose him round
With all his peers: attention held them mute.
Thrice he assayed, and thrice in spite of scorn,
Tears such as angels weep burst forth; at last   620
Words interwove with sighs found out their way:
    "O myriads of immortal Spirits, O Powers
Matchless, but with th' Almighty, and that strife
Was not inglorious, though th' event was dire,
As this place testifies, and this dire change   625
Hateful to utter. But what power of mind
Foreseeing or presaging, from the depth
Of knowledge past or present, could have feared
How such united force of gods, how such
As stood like these, could ever know repulse?   630
For who can yet believe, though after loss,
That all these puissant legions, whose exile
Hath emptied Heav'n, shall fail to re-ascend
Self-raised, and repossess their native seat?

For me, be witness all the host of Heav'n,   635
If counsels different, or danger shunned
By me, have lost our hopes. But he who reigns
Monarch in Heav'n, till then as one secure
Sat on his throne, upheld by old repute,
Consent or custom, and his regal state   640
Put forth at full, but still his strength concealed,
Which tempted our attempt, and wrought our fall.
Henceforth his might we know, and know our own,
So as not either to provoke, or dread
New war, provoked; our better part remains   645
To work in close design, by fraud or guile,
What force effected not; that he no less
At length from us may find, who overcomes
By force hath overcome but half his foe.
Space may produce new worlds; whereof so rife 650
There went a fame in Heav'n that he ere long
Intended to create, and therein plant
A generation, whom his choice regard
Should favour equal to the sons of Heaven.
Thither, if but to pry, shall be perhaps   655
Our first eruption, thither or elsewhere;
For this infernal pit shall never hold
Celestial Spirits in bondage, nor th' abyss
Long under darkness cover. But these thoughts
Full counsel must mature. Peace is despaired,   660
For who can think submission? War then, war
Open or understood, must be resolved."
    He spake; and to confirm his words, out flew
Millions of flaming swords, drawn from the thighs
Of mighty Cherubim; the sudden blaze   665
Far round illumined Hell. Highly they raged
Against the Highest, and fierce with grasped arms
Clashed on their sounding shields the din of war,
Hurling defiance toward the vault of Heav'n.
    There stood a hill not far whose grisly top   670
Belched fire and rolling smoke; the rest entire
Shone with a glossy scurf, undoubted sign
That in his womb was hid metallic ore,
The work of sulphur. Thither winged with speed
A numerous brigad hastened: as when bands   675
Of pioners with spade and pickaxe armed
Forerun the royal camp, to trench a field
Or cast a rampart. Mammon led them on,

---

592. her: its (Latin *forma* is feminine). **597. eclipse:** See *Lycidas*, 101, and note (p. 317); **disastrous:** ill-starred. **603. considerate:** considered, deliberate. **605. passion:** strong emotion, but includes meaning of "suffering." **609. amerced:** i.e., punished by being deprived. **615. blasted heath:** echoing Shakespeare's *Macbeth*, I.iii.77. **651. fame:** rumour. **674. sulphur:** Alchemical tradition held that all metals were composed of mercury and sulphur. **676. pioners:** pioneers, military engineers, sappers.

Mammon, the least erected Spirit that fell   *679*
From Heav'n, for ev'n in Heav'n his looks and thoughts
Were always downward bent, admiring more
The riches of Heav'n's pavement, trodden gold,
Than aught divine or holy else enjoyed
In vision beatific. By him first
Men also, and by his suggestion taught,   *685*
Ransacked the centre, and with impious hands
Rifled the bowels of their mother Earth
For treasures better hid. Soon had his crew
Opened into the hill a spacious wound
And digged out ribs of gold. Let none admire   *690*
That riches grow in Hell; that soil may best
Deserve the precious bane. And here let those
Who boast in mortal things, and wond'ring tell
Of Babel, and the works of Memphian kings,
Learn how their greatest monuments of fame   *695*
And strength and art are easily outdone
By Spirits reprobate, and in an hour
What in an age they with incessant toil
And hands innumerable scarce perform.
Nigh on the plain in many cells prepared,   *700*
That underneath had veins of liquid fire
Sluiced from the lake, a second multitude
With wondrous art founded the massy ore,
Severing each kind, and scummed the bullion dross.
A third as soon had formed within the ground   *705*
A various mould, and from the boiling cells
By strange conveyance filled each hollow nook,
As in an organ from one blast of wind
To many a row of pipes the sound-board breathes.
Anon out of the earth a fabric huge   *710*
Rose like an exhalation, with the sound
Of dulcet symphonies and voices sweet,
Built like a temple, where pilasters round
Were set, and Doric pillars overlaid
With golden architrave; nor did there want   *715*
Cornice or frieze, with bossy sculptures grav'n;
The roof was fretted gold. Not Babylon
Nor great Alcairo such magnificence
Equaled in all their glories, to enshrine
Belus or Serapis their gods, or seat   *720*
Their kings, when Egypt with Assyria strove

In wealth and luxury. Th' ascending pile
Stood fixed her stately highth, and straight the doors
Op'ning their brazen folds discover wide
Within, her ample spaces, o'er the smooth   *725*
And level pavement; from the arched roof
Pendent by subtle magic many a row
Of starry lamps and blazing cressets fed
With naphtha and asphaltus yielded light
As from a sky. The hasty multitude   *730*
Admiring entered, and the work some praise,
And some the architect: his hand was known
In Heav'n by many a tow'red structure high,
Where sceptered angels held their residence,
And sat as princes, whom the supreme King   *735*
Exalted to such power, and gave to rule,
Each in his hierarchy, the orders bright.
Nor was his name unheard or unadored
In ancient Greece, and in Ausonian land
Men called him Mulciber; and how he fell   *740*
From Heav'n they fabled, thrown by angry Jove
Sheer o'er the crystal battlements: from morn
To noon he fell, from noon to dewy eve,
A summer's day; and with the setting sun
Dropped from the zenith like a falling star,   *745*
On Lemnos th' Aegean isle. Thus they relate,
Erring; for he with this rebellious rout
Fell long before; nor aught availed him now
To have built in Heav'n high tow'rs; nor did he scape
By all his engines, but was headlong sent   *750*
With his industrious crew to build in Hell.
   Meanwhile the winged heralds by command
Of sovran power, with awful ceremony
And trumpet's sound, throughout the host proclaim
A solemn council forthwith to be held   *755*
At Pandemonium, the high capitol
Of Satan and his peers; their summons called
From every band and squared regiment
By place or choice the worthiest; they anon
With hundreds and with thousands trooping came   *760*
Attended. All access was thronged, the gates
And porches wide, but chief the spacious hall
(Though like a covered field, where champions bold
Wont ride in armed, and at the Soldan's chair

682: Cf. Revelation 21:21. **684. vision beatific:** i.e., seeing God (see Matthew 5:8). **684ff.:** Cf. Sandys's translation of Ovid's *Metamorphoses*, I, 141ff. (p. 269), and Chaucer's "The Former Age" (p. 72). **694. Babel:** See Genesis 10:10, 11:1-9; **works of Memphian kings:** temples and pyramids in and near Memphis, or in all ancient Egypt. **716. bossy:** embossed. **718. Alcairo:** Memphis or Cairo. **720. Belus:** Baal; **Serapis:** Osiris as god of the underworld. **737:** See note on lines 128-29 above. **739. Ausonian land:** Italy. **740. Mulciber:** Hephaistos, Vulcan. **740-46:** See *Iliad*, I, 590-93. **756. Pandemonium:** place of "all demons" (coined by Milton). **758. squared regiment:** i.e., the "perfect phalanx" of line 550. **764. Soldan's:** Sultan's.

Defied the best of paynim chivalry 765
To mortal combat or career with lance)
Thick swarmed, both on the ground and in the air,
Brushed with the hiss of rustling wings. As bees
In springtime, when the sun with Taurus rides,
Pour forth their populous youth about the hive 770
In clusters; they among fresh dews and flowers
Fly to and fro, or on the smoothed plank,
The suburb of their straw-built citadel,
New rubbed with balm, expatiate and confer
Their state affairs: so thick the airy crowd 775
Swarmed and were straitened; till the signal giv'n,
Behold a wonder! they but now who seemed
In bigness to surpass Earth's giant sons,
Now less than smallest dwarfs, in narrow room
Throng numberless, like that Pygmean race 780
Beyond the Indian mount, or fairy elves,

Whose midnight revels by a forest side
Or fountain some belated peasant sees,
Or dreams he sees, while overhead the moon
Sits arbitress, and nearer to the earth 785
Wheels her pale course; they on their mirth and dance
Intent, with jocund music charm his ear;
At once with joy and fear his heart rebounds.
Thus incorporeal Spirits to smallest forms
Reduced their shapes immense, and were at large, 790
Though without number still, amidst the hall
Of that infernal court. But far within,
And in their own dimensions like themselves,
The great Seraphic Lords and Cherubim
In close recess and secret conclave sat, 795
A thousand demi-gods on golden seats,
Frequent and full. After short silence then
And summons read, the great consult began.

BOOK II

The Argument

The consultation begun, Satan debates whether another battle be to be hazarded for the recovery of Heaven: some advise it, others dissuade. A third proposal is preferred, mentioned before by Satan, to search the truth of that prophecy or tradition in Heaven concerning another world, and another kind of creature, equal or not much inferior to themselves, about this time to be created. Their doubt who shall be sent on this difficult search; Satan, their chief, undertakes alone the 5 voyage; is honoured and applauded. The council thus ended, the rest betake them several ways and to several employments, as their inclinations lead them, to entertain the time till Satan return. He passes on his journey to Hell gates, finds them shut, and who sat there to guard them; by whom at length they are opened, and discover to him the great gulf between Hell and Heaven; with what difficulty he passes through, directed by Chaos, the power of that place, to the sight of 10 this new world which he sought.

High on a throne of royal state, which far
Outshone the wealth of Ormus and of Ind,
Or where the gorgeous East with richest hand
Show'rs on her kings barbaric pearl and gold,
Satan exalted sat, by merit raised 5
To that bad eminence; and from despair
Thus high uplifted beyond hope, aspires
Beyond thus high, insatiate to pursue
Vain war with Heav'n, and by success untaught,
His proud imaginations thus displayed: 10

"Powers and Dominions, Deities of Heav'n,
For since no deep within her gulf can hold
Immortal vigour, though oppressed and fall'n,
I give not Heav'n for lost. From this descent
Celestial Virtues rising will appear 15
More glorious and more dread than from no fall,
And trust themselves to fear no second fate.
Me though just right and the fixed laws of Heav'n
Did first create your leader, next, free choice,
With what besides, in council or in fight, 20

---

765. paynim: pagan. 768-75: Cf. *Iliad*, II, 87-90; Virgil's *Aeneid*, I, 430-36, and *Georgics*, IV. 769: The sun enters the zodiacal sign of Taurus on April 19. 774. expatiate: move about at large; confer: bring together, gather, discuss. 781. Indian mount: Himalayas. 795. close: secret, hidden; recess: remote or secluded place; conclave: etymologically, room locked "with a key" — most often used of the meeting of cardinals electing a new pope. 797. frequent: crowded.   BOOK II 2. Ormus: Hormuz, Ormuz, then famed as a trading centre for precious stones and the like; Ind: poetic for *India* (which then often referred to the East or the Orient generally). 9. success: outcome, consequence (here, ill-fortune).

Hath been achieved of merit, yet this loss,
Thus far at least recovered, hath much more
Established in a safe unenvied throne
Yielded with full consent. The happier state
In Heav'n, which follows dignity, might draw   25
Envy from each inferior; but who here
Will envy whom the highest place exposes
Foremost to stand against the Thunderer's aim
Your bulwark, and condemns to greatest share
Of endless pain? Where there is then no good   30
For which to strive, no strife can grow up there
From faction; for none sure will claim in Hell
Precedence, none whose portion is so small
Of present pain that with ambitious mind
Will covet more. With this advantage then   35
To union, and firm faith, and firm accord,
More than can be in Heav'n, we now return
To claim our just inheritance of old,
Surer to prosper than prosperity
Could have assured us; and by what best way,   40
Whether of open war or covert guile,
We now debate; who can advise, may speak."
    He ceased, and next him Moloch, sceptered king,
Stood up, the strongest and the fiercest Spirit
That fought in Heav'n, now fiercer by despair.   45
His trust was with th' Eternal to be deemed
Equal in strength, and rather than be less
Cared not to be at all; with that care lost
Went all his fear: of God, or Hell, or worse
He recked not, and these words thereafter spake: 50
    "My sentence is for open war. Of wiles,
More unexpert, I boast not: them let those
Contrive who need, or when they need, not now.
For while they sit contriving, shall the rest,
Millions that stand in arms and longing wait   55
The signal to ascend, sit ling'ring here,
Heav'n's fugitives, and for their dwelling-place
Accept this dark opprobrious den of shame,
The prison of his tyranny who reigns
By our delay? No, let us rather choose,   60
Armed with Hell flames and fury, all at once
O'er Heav'n's high tow'rs to force resistless way,
Turning our tortures into horrid arms
Against the Torturer; when to meet the noise
Of his almighty engine he shall hear   65

Infernal thunder, and for lightning see
Black fire and horror shot with equal rage
Among his angels, and his throne itself
Mixed with Tartarean sulphur and strange fire,
His own invented torments. But perhaps   70
The way seems difficult and steep to scale
With upright wing against a higher foe?
Let such bethink them, if the sleepy drench
Of that forgetful lake benumb not still,
That in our proper motion we ascend   75
Up to our native seat; descent and fall
To us is adverse. Who but felt of late,
When the fierce foe hung on our broken rear
Insulting, and pursued us through the deep,
With what compulsion and laborious flight   80
We sunk thus low? Th' ascent is easy then;
Th' event is feared? Should we again provoke
Our stronger, some worse way his wrath may find
To our destruction, if there be in Hell
Fear to be worse destroyed: what can be worse   85
Than to dwell here, driv'n out from bliss, condemned
In this abhorred deep to utter woe;
Where pain of unextinguishable fire
Must exercise us without hope of end
The vassals of his anger, when the scourge   90
Inexorably, and the torturing hour
Calls us to penance? More destroyed than thus
We should be quite abolished and expire.
What fear we then? What doubt we to incense
His utmost ire? Which to the highth enraged   95
Will either quite consume us, and reduce
To nothing this essential, happier far
Than miserable to have eternal being;
Or if our substance be indeed divine,
And cannot cease to be, we are at worst   100
On this side nothing; and by proof we feel
Our power sufficient to disturb his Heav'n,
And with perpetual inroads to alarm,
Though inaccessible, his fatal throne;
Which if not victory is yet revenge."   105
    He ended frowning, and his look denounced
Desperate revenge, and battle dangerous
To less than gods. On th' other side up rose
Belial, in act more graceful and humane;
A fairer person lost not Heav'n; he seemed   110

---

28. Thunderer: a stock epithet for Jove (Zeus) in classical works (and see I, 92-93). **50. thereafter:** accordingly (or possibly simply "next, after Satan had finished"). **79. insulting:** also means "jumping upon." **89. exercise:** task, afflict (as punishment). **90. vassals:** slaves. **97. essential:** essence. **104. fatal:** upheld by fate (see I, 133). **106. denounced:** threatened.

For dignity composed and high exploit:
But all was false and hollow, though his tongue
Dropped manna, and could make the worse appear
The better reason, to perplex and dash
Maturest counsels: for his thoughts were low;   115
To vice industrious, but to nobler deeds
Timorous and slothful: yet he pleased the ear,
And with persuasive accent thus began:
  "I should be much for open war, O Peers,
As not behind in hate, if what was urged   120
Main reason to persuade immediate war
Did not dissuade me most, and seem to cast
Ominous conjecture on the whole success:
When he who most excels in fact of arms,
In what he counsels and in what excels   125
Mistrustful, grounds his courage on despair
And utter dissolution, as the scope
Of all his aim, after some dire revenge.
First, what revenge? The tow'rs of Heav'n are filled
With armed watch, that render all access   130
Impregnable; oft on the bordering deep
Encamp their legions, or with obscure wing
Scout far and wide into the realm of Night,
Scorning surprise. Or could we break our way
By force, and at our heels all hell should rise   135
With blackest insurrection, to confound
Heav'n's purest light, yet our great Enemy
All incorruptible would on his throne
Sit unpolluted, and th' ethereal mould
Incapable of stain would soon expel   140
Her mischief, and purge off the baser fire,
Victorious. Thus repulsed, our final hope
Is flat despair; we must exasperate
Th' almighty Victor to spend all his rage,
And that must end us, that must be our cure,   145
To be no more. Sad cure! for who would lose,
Though full of pain, this intellectual being,
Those thoughts that wander through eternity,
To perish rather, swallowed up and lost
In the wide womb of uncreated Night,   150
Devoid of sense and motion? And who knows,
Let this be good, whether our angry Foe
Can give it, or will ever? How he can
Is doubtful; that he never will is sure.

Will he, so wise, let loose at once his ire,   155
Belike through impotence, or unaware,
To give his enemies their wish, and end
Them in his anger, whom his anger saves
To punish endless? 'Wherefore cease we then?'
Say they who counsel war; 'we are decreed,   160
Reserved, and destined to eternal woe;
Whatever doing, what can we suffer more,
What can we suffer worse?' Is this then worst,
Thus sitting, thus consulting, thus in arms?
What when we fled amain, pursued and strook   165
With Heav'n's afflicting thunder, and besought
The deep to shelter us? This Hell then seemed
A refuge from those wounds. Or when we lay
Chained on the burning lake? That sure was worse.
What if the breath that kindled those grim fires   170
Awaked should blow them into sevenfold rage
And plunge us in the flames? Or from above
Should intermitted vengeance arm again
His red right hand to plague us? What if all
Her stores were opened and this firmament   175
Of Hell should spout her cataracts of fire,
Impendent horrors, threat'ning hideous fall
One day upon our heads; while we perhaps
Designing or exhorting glorious war,
Caught in a fiery tempest shall be hurled   180
Each on his rock transfixed, the sport and prey
Of racking whirlwinds, or for ever sunk
Under yon boiling ocean, wrapped in chains;
There to converse with everlasting groans,
Unrespited, unpitied, unreprieved,   185
Ages of hopeless end? This would be worse.
War therefore, open or concealed, alike
My voice dissuades; for what can force or guile
With him, or who deceive his mind, whose eye
Views all things at one view? He from Heav'n's highth
All these our motions vain, sees and derides;   191
Not more almighty to resist our might
Than wise to frustrate all our plots and wiles.
Shall we then live thus vile, the race of Heav'n
Thus trampled, thus expelled to suffer here   195
Chains and these torments? Better these than worse,
By my advice; since fate inevitable
Subdues us, and omnipotent decree,

113-14. make . . . reason: a hallmark of sophistry. **124. fact:** also signifies "feat, deeds." **148:** Note *Areopagitica*, lines 56-57: "minds that can wander beyond all limit and satiety." **156. impotence:** lack of self-restraint. **170:** Cf. Isaiah 30:33. **174. red right hand:** translating *rubente dextera*, of Jove (Horace, *Odes*, 1, 2, 2-3). **181-82:** like Ajax (*Aeneid*, I, 44-45; VI, 75), and perhaps also with a glance at Prometheus. **184. converse:** live with, keep company with. **190-91:** Cf. Psalms 2:4.

The Victor's will. To suffer, as to do,
Our strength is equal, nor the law unjust   *200*
That so ordains: this was at first resolved,
If we were wise, against so great a foe
Contending, and so doubtful what might fall.
I laugh when those who at the spear are bold
And vent'rous, if that fail them, shrink and fear   *205*
What yet they know must follow, to endure
Exile, or ignominy, or bonds, or pain,
The sentence of their Conqueror. This is now
Our doom; which if we can sustain and bear,
Our supreme Foe in time may much remit   *210*
His anger, and perhaps, thus far removed,
Not mind us not offending, satisfied
With what is punished; whence these raging fires
Will slacken, if his breath stir not their flames.
Our purer essence then will overcome   *215*
Their noxious vapour, or inured not feel,
Or changed at length, and to the place conformed
In temper and in nature, will receive
Familiar the fierce heat, and void of pain;
This horror will grow mild, this darkness light,   *220*
Besides what hope the never-ending flight
Of future days may bring, what chance, what change
Worth waiting, since our present lot appears
For happy though but ill, for ill not worst,
If we procure not to ourselves more woe."   *225*
    Thus Belial with words clothed in reason's garb,
Counseled ignoble ease, and peaceful sloth,
Not peace; and after him thus Mammon spake:
    "Either to disenthrone the King of Heav'n
We war, if war be best, or to regain   *230*
Our own right lost. Him to unthrone we then
May hope when everlasting Fate shall yield
To fickle Chance, and Chaos judge the strife:
The former, vain to hope, argues as vain
The latter; for what place can be for us   *235*
Within Heav'n's bound, unless Heav'n's Lord supreme
We overpower? Suppose he should relent
And publish grace to all, on promise made
Of new subjection; with what eyes could we
Stand in his presence humble, and receive   *240*
Strict laws imposed, to celebrate his throne
With warbled hymns, and to his Godhead sing
Forced halleluiahs; while he lordly sits
Our envied Sovran, and his altar breathes

Ambrosial odors and ambrosial flowers,   *245*
Our servile offerings? This must be our task
In Heav'n, this our delight; how wearisome
Eternity so spent in worship paid
To whom we hate. Let us not then pursue,
By force impossible, by leave obtained   *250*
Unacceptable, though in Heav'n, our state
Of splendid vassalage, but rather seek
Our own good from ourselves, and from our own
Live to ourselves, though in this vast recess,
Free, and to none accountable, preferring   *255*
Hard liberty before the easy yoke
Of servile pomp. Our greatness will appear
Then most conspicuous, when great things of small,
Useful of hurtful, prosperous of adverse
We can create, and in what place soe'er   *260*
Thrive under evil, and work ease out of pain
Through labour and endurance. This deep world
Of darkness do we dread? How oft amidst
Thick clouds and dark doth Heav'n's all-ruling Sire
Choose to reside, his glory unobscured,   *265*
And with the majesty of darkness round
Covers his throne; from whence deep thunders roar,
Must'ring their rage, and Heav'n resembles Hell!
As he our darkness, cannot we his light
Imitate when we please? This desert soil   *270*
Wants not her hidden lustre, gems and gold;
Nor want we skill or art, from whence to raise
Magnificence; and what can Heav'n show more?
Our torments also may in length of time
Become our elements, these piercing fires   *275*
As soft as now severe, our temper changed
Into their temper; which must needs remove
The sensible of pain. All things invite
To peaceful counsels, and the settled state
Of order, how in safety best we may   *280*
Compose our present evils, with regard
Of what we are and where, dismissing quite
All thoughts of war. Ye have what I advise."
    He scarce had finished, when such murmur filled
Th' assembly as when hollow rocks retain   *285*
The sound of blust'ring winds, which all night long
Had roused the sea, now with hoarse cadence lull
Seafaring men o'erwatched, whose bark by chance
Or pinnace anchors in a craggy bay
After the tempest. Such applause was heard   *290*

---

256. easy yoke: See Sonnet XIX, line 11, and note (p. 325). **263-67:** Cf. II Chronicles 5:13-6:1; Psalms 18:11-13, 97:2. **278. sensible:** sense, what is sensed. **288. o'erwatched:** tired from watching.

As Mammon ended, and his sentence pleased,
Advising peace; for such another field
They dreaded worse than Hell: so much the fear
Of thunder and the sword of Michaël
Wrought still within them; and no less desire   *295*
To found this nether empire, which might rise
By policy, and long process of time,
In emulation opposite to Heav'n.
Which when Beelzebub perceived, than whom,
Satan except, none higher sat, with grave   *300*
Aspect he rose, and in his rising seemed
A pillar of state; deep on his front engraven
Deliberation sat and public care;
And princely counsel in his face yet shone,
Majestic though in ruin: sage he stood,   *305*
With Atlantean shoulders fit to bear
The weight of mightiest monarchies; his look
Drew audience and attention still as night
Or summer's noontide air, while thus he spake:
   "Thrones and imperial Powers, offspring of Heav'n,
Ethereal Virtues; or these titles now   *311*
Must we renounce, and changing style be called
Princes of Hell? For so the popular vote
Inclines, here to continue, and build up here
A growing empire; doubtless! while we dream   *315*
And know not that the King of Heav'n hath doomed
This place our dungeon, not our safe retreat
Beyond his potent arm, to live exempt
From Heav'n's high jurisdiction, in new league
Banded against his throne, but to remain   *320*
In strictest bondage, though thus far removed,
Under th' inevitable curb, reserved
His captive multitude. For he, be sure,
In highth or depth, still first and last will reign
Sole king, and of his kingdom lose no part   *325*
By our revolt, but over Hell extend
His empire, and with iron scepter rule
Us here, as with his golden those in Heav'n.
What sit we then projecting peace and war?
War hath determined us, and foiled with loss   *330*
Irreparable; terms of peace yet none
Vouchsafed or sought; for what peace will be giv'n
To us enslaved, but custody severe,
And stripes, and arbitrary punishment
Inflicted? And what peace can we return,   *335*
But to our power hostility and hate,
Untamed reluctance, and revenge though slow,
Yet ever plotting how the Conqueror least
May reap his conquest, and may least rejoice
In doing what we most in suffering feel?   *340*
Nor will occasion want, nor shall we need
With dangerous expedition to invade
Heav'n, whose high walls fear no assault or siege
Or ambush from the deep. What if we find
Some easier enterprise? There is a place   *345*
(If ancient and prophetic fame in Heav'n
Err not), another world, the happy seat
Of some new race called man, about this time
To be created like to us, though less
In power and excellence, but favoured more   *350*
Of him who rules above; so was his will
Pronounced among the gods, and by an oath,
That shook Heav'n's whole circumference, confirmed.
Thither let us bend all our thoughts, to learn
What creatures there inhabit, of what mould   *355*
Or substance, how endued, and what their power,
And where their weakness, how attempted best,
By force or subtlety. Though Heav'n be shut,
And Heav'n's high Arbitrator sit secure
In his own strength, this place may lie exposed,   *360*
The utmost border of his kingdom, left
To their defense who hold it; here perhaps
Some advantageous act may be achieved
By sudden onset, either with Hell fire
To waste his whole creation, or possess   *365*
All as our own, and drive as we were driven,
The puny habitants; or if not drive,
Seduce them to our party, that their God
May prove their foe, and with repenting hand
Abolish his own works. This would surpass   *370*
Common revenge, and interrupt his joy
In our confusion, and our joy upraise
In his disturbance; when his darling sons,
Hurled headlong to partake with us, shall curse
Their frail original, and faded bliss,   *375*
Faded so soon. Advise if this be worth

---

292. field: battle (cf. Old English *camp*, "battle," from Latin *campus*, "field"; and cf. I, 105). **302. front:** forehead. **306. Atlantean:** like Atlas's. **312. style:** title or name. **324-25:** Cf. Revelation 1:11, 21:6, 22:13. **327-28:** Cf. Psalms 2:9; Revelation 2:27, 12:5, 19:15; see also *Lycidas*, 110-11 (p. 317). **336. to:** to the best of. **337. reluctance:** resistance, struggling against. **352-53:** Cf. Genesis 22:16; Isaiah 45:23; Hebrews 6:13-17, 12:26; *Iliad*, I, 530; *Aeneid*, IX, 106. **367. puny:** also carries the now obsolete etymological sense of *puis né*, "later born." **376. Advise:** weigh well, consider.

Attempting, or to sit in darkness here
Hatching vain empires." Thus Beelzebub
Pleaded his devilish counsel, first devised
By Satan, and in part proposed; for whence,   *380*
But from the author of all ill, could spring
So deep a malice, to confound the race
Of mankind in one root, and Earth with Hell
To mingle and involve, done all to spite
The great Creator? But their spite still serves   *385*
His glory to augment. The bold design
Pleased highly those infernal States, and joy
Sparkled in all their eyes; with full assent
They vote: whereat his speech he thus renews:
    "Well have ye judged, well ended long debate,   *390*
Synod of Gods, and like to what ye are,
Great things resolved; which from the lowest deep
Will once more lift us up, in spite of fate,
Nearer our ancient seat; perhaps in view
Of those bright confines, whence with neighbouring arms
And opportune excursion we may chance   *396*
Re-enter Heav'n; or else in some mild zone
Dwell not unvisited of Heav'n's fair light
Secure, and at the bright'ning orient beam
Purge off this gloom; the soft delicious air   *400*
To heal the scar of these corrosive fires
Shall breathe her balm. But first whom shall we send
In search of this new world, whom shall we find
Sufficient? Who shall tempt with wand'ring feet
The dark unbottomed infinite abyss   *405*
And through the palpable obscure find out
His uncouth way, or spread his airy flight
Upborne with indefatigable wings
Over the vast abrupt, ere he arrive
The happy isle; what strength, what art can then   *410*
Suffice, or what evasion bear him safe
Through the strict senteries and stations thick
Of angels watching round? Here he had need
All circumspection, and we now no less
Choice in our suffrage; for on whom we send,   *415*
The weight of all and our last hope relies."
    This said, he sat; and expectation held
His look suspense, awaiting who appeared
To second, or oppose, or undertake
The perilous attempt: but all sat mute,   *420*
Pondering the danger with deep thoughts; and each

In other's count'nance read his own dismay
Astonished. None among the choice and prime
Of those Heav'n-warring champions could be found
So hardy as to proffer or accept   *425*
Alone the dreadful voyage; till at last
Satan, whom now transcendent glory raised
Above his fellows, with monarchal pride
Conscious of highest worth, unmoved thus spake:
    "O Progeny of Heav'n, Empyreal Thrones,   *430*
With reason hath deep silence and demur
Seized us, though undismayed. Long is the way
And hard, that out of Hell leads up to light;
Our prison strong, this huge convex of fire,
Outrageous to devour, immures us round   *435*
Ninefold, and gates of burning adamant
Barred over us prohibit all egress.
These passed, if any pass, the void profound
Of unessential Night receives him next
Wide gaping, and with utter loss of being   *440*
Threatens him, plunged in that abortive gulf.
If thence he scape into whatever world,
Or unknown region, what remains him less
Than unknown dangers and as hard escape?
But I should ill become this throne, O Peers,   *445*
And this imperial sov'ranty, adorned
With splendour, armed with power, if aught proposed
And judged of public moment, in the shape
Of difficulty or danger could deter
Me from attempting. Wherefore do I assume   *450*
These royalties, and not refuse to reign,
Refusing to accept as great a share
Of hazard as of honour, due alike
To him who reigns, and so much to him due
Of hazard more, as he above the rest   *455*
High honoured sits? Go therefore, mighty Powers,
Terror of Heav'n, though fall'n; intend at home,
While here shall be our home, what best may ease
The present misery, and render Hell
More tolerable, if there be cure or charm   *460*
To respite or deceive, or slack the pain
Of this ill mansion; intermit no watch
Against a wakeful foe, while I abroad
Through all the coasts of dark destruction seek
Deliverance for us all: this enterprise   *465*
None shall partake with me." Thus saying rose

---

377. sit in darkness: See Psalms 107:10-11. **379-80:** See I, 645ff. **387. States:** estates, ranks, assembled members. **404. tempt:** attempt. **406. palpable obscure:** Cf. Exodus 10-21. **412. senteries:** sentries. **432-33:** Cf. *Aeneid*, VI, 126-29. **439. unessential:** without being or substance. **457. intend:** attend to, put your mind to, consider.

The monarch, and prevented all reply;
Prudent, lest from his resolution raised
Others among the chief might offer now
(Certain to be refused) what erst they feared;   470
And so refused might in opinion stand
His rivals, winning cheap the high repute
Which he through hazard huge must earn. But they
Dreaded not more th' adventure than his voice
Forbidding, and at once with him they rose;   475
Their rising all at once was as the sound
Of thunder heard remote. Towards him they bend
With awful reverence prone; and as a God
Extol him equal to the Highest in Heav'n.
Nor failed they to express how much they praised,   480
That for the general safety he despised
His own: for neither do the Spirits damned
Lose all their virtue; lest bad men should boast
Their specious deeds on earth, which glory excites,
Or close ambition varnished o'er with zeal.   485
   Thus they their doubtful consultations dark
Ended rejoicing in their matchless Chief:
As when from mountain tops the dusky clouds
Ascending, while the north wind sleeps, o'erspread
Heav'n's cheerful face, the louring element   490
Scowls o'er the darkened landscape snow or show'r;
If chance the radiant sun with farewell sweet
Extend his ev'ning beam, the fields revive,
The birds their notes renew, and bleating herds
Attest their joy, that hill and valley rings.   495
O shame to men! Devil with devil damned
Firm concord holds; men only disagree
Of creatures rational, though under hope
Of heavenly grace, and God proclaiming peace,
Yet live in hatred, enmity, and strife   500
Among themselves, and levy cruel wars,
Wasting the Earth, each other to destroy:
As if (which might induce us to accord)
Man had not hellish foes enow besides,
That day and night for his destruction wait.   505
   The Stygian council thus dissolved; and forth
In order came the grand infernal Peers;

Midst came their mighty Paramount, and seemed
Alone th' antagonist of Heav'n, nor less
Than Hell's dread emperor, with pomp supreme   510
And god-like imitated state; him round
A globe of fiery Seraphim enclosed
With bright emblazonry and horrent arms.
Then of their session ended they bid cry
With trumpet's regal sound the great result.   515
Toward the four winds four speedy Cherubim
Put to their mouths the sounding alchemy
By herald's voice explained; the hollow abyss
Heard far and wide, and all the host of Hell
With deaf'ning shout returned them loud acclaim.   520
Thence more at ease their minds and somewhat raised
By false presumptuous hope, the ranged powers
Disband, and wand'ring each his several way
Pursues, as inclination or sad choice
Leads him perplexed, where he may likeliest find   525
Truce to his restless thoughts, and entertain
The irksome hours, till his great Chief return.
Part on the plain, or in the air sublime
Upon the wing, or in swift race contend,
As at th' Olympian games or Pythian fields;   530
Part curb their fiery steeds, or shun the goal
With rapid wheels, or fronted brigads form:
As when to warn proud cities war appears
Waged in the troubled sky, and armies rush
To battle in the clouds; before each van   535
Prick forth the airy knights, and couch their spears,
Till thickest legions close; with feats of arms
From either end of Heav'n the welkin burns.
Others with vast Typhoean rage more fell
Rend up both rocks and hills, and ride the air   540
In whirlwind; Hell scarce holds the wild uproar;
As when Alcides from Oechalia crowned
With conquest, felt th' envenomed robe, and tore
Through pain up by the roots Thessalian pines,
And Lichas from the top of Oeta threw   545
Into th' Euboic sea. Others more mild,
Retreated in a silent valley, sing
With notes angelical to many a harp

489: Cf. *Iliad*, V, 524. 513. horrent: bristling. 517. alchemy: gold-like alloy — i.e., metal instruments. 530: The ancient Olympic games were held at Olympia, the Pythian games within the sacred precincts of Delphi. Such games constitute another epic convention: funeral games occur in both the *Iliad* (XXIII) and the *Aeneid* (V). 531. shun the goal: just graze the turning-posts with the wheels of racing chariots (see Horace, *Odes*, 1, 1, 4-5). 535. van: vanguard. 536. Prick: ride, spur. 538-41: See *Areopagitica*, line 62, and note (p. 323); some versions of the myth have Typhon as son of Typhoeus, and one or the other being "father of the winds"; Greek *typhos* means "furious whirlwind, typhoon." 542-46: Heracles (Alcides, either from his grandfather, Alcaeus, or from the Greek *alke*, "strength"), fatally poisoned by the robe innocently brought by Lichas, throws him into the sea near Euboea. (Oechalia is located either in Euboea or in Thessaly; Mount Oeta is in Thessaly. Of the different versions of the tale, Milton follows that of Ovid, *Metamorphoses*, IX, 134ff.)

Their own heroic deeds and hapless fall
By doom of battle; and complain that fate   *550*
Free virtue should enthrall to force or chance.
Their song was partial, but the harmony
(What could it less when Spirits immortal sing?)
Suspended Hell, and took with ravishment
The thronging audience. In discourse more sweet   *555*
(For eloquence the soul, song charms the sense)
Others apart sat on a hill retired,
In thoughts more elevate, and reasoned high
Of providence, foreknowledge, will, and fate,
Fixed fate, free will, foreknowledge absolute,   *560*
And found no end, in wand'ring mazes lost.
Of good and evil much they argued then,
Of happiness and final misery,
Passion and apathy, and glory and shame,
Vain wisdom all, and false philosophy;   *565*
Yet with a pleasing sorcery could charm
Pain for a while or anguish, and excite
Fallacious hope, or arm th' obdured breast
With stubborn patience as with triple steel.
Another part, in squadrons and gross bands,   *570*
On bold adventure to discover wide
That dismal world, if any clime perhaps
Might yield them easier habitation, bend
Four ways their flying march, along the banks
Of four infernal rivers that disgorge   *575*
Into the burning lake their baleful streams:
Abhorred Styx, the flood of deadly hate;
Sad Acheron of sorrow, black and deep;
Cocytus, named of lamentation loud
Heard on the rueful stream; fierce Phlegethon,   *580*
Whose waves of torrent fire inflame with rage.
Far off from these a slow and silent stream,
Lethe, the river of oblivion, rolls
Her wat'ry labyrinth, whereof who drinks
Forthwith his former state and being forgets,   *585*
Forgets both joy and grief, pleasure and pain.
Beyond this flood a frozen continent

Lies dark and wild, beat with perpetual storms
Of whirlwind and dire hail, which on firm land
Thaws not, but gathers heap, and ruin seems   *590*
Of ancient pile; all else deep snow and ice,
A gulf profound as that Serbonian bog
Betwixt Damiata and Mount Casius old,
Where armies whole have sunk; the parching air
Burns frore, and cold performs th' effect of fire.   *595*
Thither by harpy-footed Furies haled,
At certain revolutions all the damned
Are brought; and feel by turns the bitter change
Of fierce extremes, extremes by change more fierce,
From beds of raging fire to starve in ice   *600*
Their soft ethereal warmth, and there to pine
Immovable, infixed, and frozen round,
Periods of time; thence hurried back to fire.
They ferry over this Lethean sound
Both to and fro, their sorrow to augment,   *605*
And wish and struggle, as they pass, to reach
The tempting stream, with one small drop to lose
In sweet forgetfulness all pain and woe,
All in one moment, and so near the brink;
But fate withstands, and to oppose th' attempt   *610*
Medusa with Gorgonian terror guards
The ford, and of itself the water flies
All taste of living wight, as once it fled
The lip of Tantalus. Thus roving on
In confused march forlorn, th' advent'rous bands,   *615*
With shudd'ring horror pale, and eyes aghast,
Viewed first their lamentable lot, and found
No rest. Through many a dark and dreary vale
They passed, and many a region dolorous,
O'er many a frozen, many a fiery Alp,   *620*
Rocks, caves, lakes, fens, bogs, dens, and shades of death,
A universe of death, which God by curse
Created evil, for evil only good,
Where all life dies, death lives, and Nature breeds,
Perverse, all monstrous, all prodigious things,   *625*
Abominable, inutterable, and worse

564: Stoicism valued apathy as an alternative to passion; cf. e.g. Pope's *An Essay on Man*, II, 101-04: "In lazy apathy let Stoics boast / Their virtue fixed; 'tis fixed as in a frost, / Contracted all, retiring to the breast; / But strength of mind is exercise, not rest." **570. gross:** compact, dense. **575-81:** the traditional four rivers of Hades, with the name of each explained. **582-86:** See *Aeneid*, VI, 703-15 (Greek *lethe*, "a forgetting, forgetfulness"). **587ff.:** For another description of a cold part of Hell, see the ninth circle of Dante's *Inferno*; cf. also Shakespeare's *Measure for Measure*, III.i.121ff. **591. pile:** building. **592-94:** Lake Serbonis, near ancient Pelusium, east of the Nile delta, is described by Diodorus Siculus as a long narrow marsh with the quality of quicksand; George Sandys in *A Relation of a Journey* (1615) says "whole armies have been devoured" by it — evidently, e.g., part of Darius II's invading army. Herodotus says Mount Casius "stretches" near Serbonis, and Sandys calls it "no other than a huge mole of sand"; some maps show it at the location of the hill Râs Burûn, on the sandbar enclosing the lagoon now called Sabkhet el Bardawil, identified with ancient Serbonis — though Milton's "betwixt Damiata [Dumyat, Damietta] and Mount Casius" would better fit modern Bahra el Manzala. **596:** The Furies (Erinyes) are here said to have feet with hooked claws like those of the Harpies. **611:** See note to Spenser's "Epithalamion," lines 189-90 (p. 165). **614:** Zeus punished Tantalus by giving him a great thirst and standing him in a lake whose waters receded from him when he tried to drink.

Than fables yet have feigned, or fear conceived,
Gorgons, and Hydras, and Chimeras dire.
  Meanwhile the Adversary of God and man,
Satan, with thoughts inflamed of highest design,   630
Puts on swift wings, and toward the gates of Hell
Explores his solitary flight; sometimes
He scours the right-hand coast, sometimes the left;
Now shaves with level wing the deep, then soars
Up to the fiery concave tow'ring high: 635
As when far off at sea a fleet descried
Hangs in the clouds, by equinoctial winds
Close sailing from Bengala, or the isles
Of Ternate and Tidore, whence merchants bring
Their spicy drugs: they on the trading flood   640
Through the wide Ethiopian to the Cape
Ply stemming nightly toward the pole. So seemed
Far off the flying Fiend. At last appear
Hell bounds high reaching to the horrid roof,
And thrice threefold the gates; three folds were brass,
Three iron, three of adamantine rock,   646
Impenetrable, impaled with circling fire,
Yet unconsumed. Before the gates there sat
On either side a formidable shape;
The one seemed woman to the waist, and fair,   650
But ended foul in many a scaly fold
Voluminous and vast, a serpent armed
With mortal sting. About her middle round
A cry of Hell-hounds never ceasing barked
With wide Cerberean mouths full loud, and rung   655
A hideous peal; yet, when they list, would creep,
If aught disturbed their noise, into her womb,
And kennel there, yet there still barked and howled,
Within unseen. Far less abhorred than these
Vexed Scylla bathing in the sea that parts   660
Calabria from the hoarse Trinacrian shore;
Nor uglier follow the night-hag when, called
In secret, riding through the air she comes,
Lured with the smell of infant blood, to dance
With Lapland witches, while the labouring moon   665
Eclipses at their charms. The other shape —

If shape it might be called that shape had none
Distinguishable in member, joint, or limb,
Or substance might be called that shadow seemed,
For each seemed either — black it stood as Night,   670
Fierce as ten Furies, terrible as Hell,
And shook a dreadful dart; what seemed his head
The likeness of a kingly crown had on.
Satan was now at hand, and from his seat
The monster moving onward came as fast   675
With horrid strides; Hell trembled as he strode.
Th' undaunted Fiend what this might be admired,
Admired, not feared; God and his Son except,
Created thing naught valued he nor shunned;
And with disdainful look thus first began: 680
  "Whence and what art thou, execrable Shape,
That dar'st, though grim and terrible, advance
Thy miscreated front athwart my way
To yonder gates? Through them I mean to pass,
That be assured, without leave asked of thee.   685
Retire, or taste thy folly, and learn by proof,
Hell-born, not to contend with Spirits of Heav'n."
  To whom the Goblin full of wrath replied:
"Art thou that traitor angel, art thou he,
Who first broke peace in Heav'n and faith, till then   690
Unbroken, and in proud rebellious arms
Drew after him the third part of Heav'n's sons
Conjured against the Highest, for which both thou
And they, outcast from God, are here condemned
To waste eternal days in woe and pain?   695
And reckon'st thou thyself with Spirits of Heav'n,
Hell-doomed, and breath'st defiance here and scorn
Where I reign king, and to enrage thee more,
Thy king and lord? Back to thy punishment,
False fugitive, and to thy speed add wings,   700
Lest with a whip of scorpions I pursue
Thy ling'ring, or with one stroke of this dart
Strange horror seize thee, and pangs unfelt before."
  So spake the grisly terror, and in shape,
So speaking and so threat'ning, grew tenfold   705
More dreadful and deform. On th' other side,

628: Cf. *Aeneid*, VI, 287-89. **631. Puts on swift wings:** i.e., flies off swiftly. **638. Bengala:** Bengal. **639. Ternate, Tidore:** two of the Spice Islands (Moluccas). **640. trading flood:** sea-routes followed by trading ships. **641. Ethiopian:** Indian Ocean; **Cape:** Cape of Good Hope. **647. impaled:** surrounded as by a fence of palings. **648ff.** The elaborately developed allegorical figures of Sin and Death are based on James 1:15. **650ff.:** Cf. Milton's figure of Sin and Spenser's monster Error, whom the Red Cross Knight destroys early in Canto I of *The Faerie Queene* (123ff.; p. 155); other models are Scylla (line 660; see *Odyssey*, XII, 85ff.; *Aeneid*, III, 424ff., VI, 286; Ovid, *Metamorphoses*, XIV, 1ff.) and Hesiod's Echidna (*Theogony*, 295ff.). **652. voluminous:** having many coils. **655. Cerberean:** like Cerberus's. **660-61:** Tradition has located Scylla and Charybdis in the Strait of Messina, between Sicily and Italy; see also lines 1019-20 below. **661. Trinacrian:** Sicilian. **662-63. night-hag:** Hecate; see Shakespeare's *Macbeth*, III.v. **665. Lapland:** supposedly a home of witchcraft; **labouring:** undergoing eclipse. **692:** Cf. Revelation 12:4. **693. conjured:** sworn together by oath, conspired. **701.** Cf. I Kings 12:11.

Incensed with indignation Satan stood
Unterrified, and like a comet burned,
That fires the length of Ophiuchus huge
In th' arctic sky, and from his horrid hair   710
Shakes pestilence and war. Each at the head
Leveled his deadly aim; their fatal hands
No second stroke intend; and such a frown
Each cast at th' other, as when two black clouds
With Heav'n's artillery fraught, come rattling on   715
Over the Caspian, then stand front to front
Hov'ring a space, till winds the signal blow
To join their dark encounter in mid-air:
So frowned the mighty combatants that Hell
Grew darker at their frown, so matched they stood;   720
For never but once more was either like
To meet so great a foe. And now great deeds
Had been achieved, whereof all Hell had rung,
Had not the snaky sorceress that sat
Fast by Hell gate, and kept the fatal key,   725
Ris'n, and with hideous outcry rushed between.
    "O Father, what intends thy hand," she cried,
"Against thy only son? What fury, O Son,
Possesses thee to bend that mortal dart
Against thy father's head? And know'st for whom;   730
For him who sits above and laughs the while
At thee ordained his drudge, to execute
Whate'er his wrath, which he calls justice, bids,
His wrath which one day will destroy ye both."
    She spake, and at her words the hellish pest   735
Forbore; then these to her Satan returned:
    "So strange thy outcry, and thy words so strange
Thou interposest, that my sudden hand
Prevented spares to tell thee yet by deeds
What it intends; till first I know of thee,   740
What thing thou art, thus double-formed, and why
In this infernal vale first met thou call'st
Me father, and that phantasm call'st my son.
I know thee not, nor ever saw till now
Sight more detestable than him and thee."   745
    T' whom thus the portress of Hell gate replied:
"Hast thou forgot me then, and do I seem
Now in thine eye so foul? Once deemed so fair
In Heav'n, when at th' assembly, and in sight
Of all the Seraphim with thee combined   750
In bold conspiracy against Heav'n's King,

All on a sudden miserable pain
Surprised thee; dim thine eyes, and dizzy swum
In darkness, while thy head flames thick and fast
Threw forth, till on the left side op'ning wide,   755
Likest to thee in shape and count'nance bright,
Then shining heav'nly fair, a goddess armed
Out of thy head I sprung. Amazement seized
All th' host of Heav'n; back they recoiled afraid
At first, and called me *Sin,* and for a sign   760
Portentous held me; but familiar grown,
I pleased, and with attractive graces won
The most averse, thee chiefly, who full oft
Thyself in me thy perfect image viewing
Becam'st enamoured; and such joy thou took'st   765
With me in secret, that my womb conceived
A growing burden. Meanwhile war arose,
And fields were fought in heav'n; wherein remained
(For what could else?) to our almighty Foe
Clear victory, to our part loss and rout   770
Through all the Empyrean: down they fell
Driv'n headlong from the pitch of heaven, down
Into this deep, and in the general fall
I also; at which time this powerful key
Into my hand was giv'n, with charge to keep   775
These gates for ever shut, which none can pass
Without my op'ning. Pensive here I sat
Alone, but long I sat not, till my womb,
Pregnant by thee, and now excessive grown,
Prodigious motion felt and rueful throes.   780
At last this odious offspring whom thou seest,
Thine own begotten, breaking violent way
Tore through my entrails, that with fear and pain
Distorted, all my nether shape thus grew
Transformed; but he my inbred enemy   785
Forth issued, brandishing his fatal dart
Made to destroy. I fled, and cried out *Death!*
Hell trembled at the hideous name, and sighed
From all her caves, and back resounded *Death!*
I fled, but he pursued (though more, it seems,   790
Inflamed with lust than rage) and swifter far,
Me overtook, his mother, all dismayed,
And in embraces forcible and foul
Engend'ring with me, of that rape begot
These yelling monsters that with ceaseless cry   795
Surround me, as thou saw'st, hourly conceived

708-10: Comets, like eclipses, were commonly considered evil omens (*comet*: Greek for "long-haired"). **709. Ophiuchus:** ("serpent-holder") a large constellation (Serpens, the Serpent, crosses part of it). **715-16.** The Caspian was traditionally thought stormy. **721-22:** See I Corinthians 15:26. **757-58:** just as Athene (Minerva) sprang fully armed from the head of Zeus. **772. pitch:** highest point, height.

And hourly born, with sorrow infinite
To me; for when they list, into the womb
That bred them they return, and howl and gnaw
My bowels, their repast; then bursting forth   *800*
Afresh, with conscious terrors vex me round,
That rest or intermission none I find.
Before mine eyes in opposition sits
Grim Death my son and foe, who sets them on,
And me his parent would full soon devour   *805*
For want of other prey, but that he knows
His end with mine involved; and knows that I
Should prove a bitter morsel, and his bane,
Whenever that shall be; so fate pronounced.
But thou, O Father, I forewarn thee, shun   *810*
His deadly arrow; neither vainly hope
To be invulnerable in those bright arms,
Though tempered heav'nly, for that mortal dint,
Save he who reigns above, none can resist."
    She finished, and the subtle Fiend his lore   *815*
Soon learned, now milder, and thus answered smooth:
"Dear daughter, since thou claim'st me for thy sire,
And my fair son here show'st me, the dear pledge
Of dalliance had with thee in Heav'n, and joys
Then sweet, now sad to mention, through dire change *820*
Befall'n us unforeseen, unthought of, know
I come no enemy, but to set free
From out this dark and dismal house of pain
Both him and thee, and all the heav'nly host
Of Spirits that in our just pretenses armed   *825*
Fell with us from on high. From them I go
This uncouth errand sole, and one for all
Myself expose, with lonely steps to tread
Th' unfounded deep, and through the void immense
To search with wand'ring quest a place foretold   *830*
Should be, and, by concurring signs, ere now
Created vast and round, a place of bliss
In the purlieus of Heav'n, and therein placed
A race of upstart creatures, to supply
Perhaps our vacant room, though more removed,   *835*
Lest Heav'n surcharged with potent multitude
Might hap to move new broils. Be this or aught
Than this more secret now designed, I haste
To know, and this once known, shall soon return,
And bring ye to the place where thou and Death   *840*
Shall dwell at ease, and up and down unseen
Wing silently the buxom air, embalmed

With odours; there ye shall be fed and filled
Immeasurably; all things shall be your prey."   *844*
He ceased, for both seemed highly pleased, and Death
Grinned horrible a ghastly smile, to hear
His famine should be filled, and blessed his maw
Destined to that good hour. No less rejoiced
His mother bad, and thus bespake her sire:
    "The key of this infernal pit by due   *850*
And by command of Heav'n's all-powerful King
I keep, by him forbidden to unlock
These adamantine gates; against all force
Death ready stands to interpose his dart,
Fearless to be o'ermatched by living might.   *855*
But what owe I to his commands above
Who hates me, and hath hither thrust me down
Into this gloom of Tartarus profound,
To sit in hateful office here confined,
Inhabitant of Heav'n and heav'nly-born,   *860*
Here in perpetual agony and pain,
With terrors and with clamours compassed round
Of mine own brood, that on my bowels feed?
Thou art my father, thou my author, thou
My being gav'st me; whom should I obey   *865*
But thee, whom follow? Thou wilt bring me soon
To that new world of light and bliss, among
The gods who live at ease, where I shall reign
At thy right hand voluptuous, as beseems
Thy daughter and thy darling, without end."   *870*
    Thus saying, from her side the fatal key,
Sad instrument of all our woe, she took;
And towards the gate rolling her bestial train,
Forthwith the huge portcullis high up drew,
Which but herself not all the Stygian powers   *875*
Could once have moved; then in the key-hole turns
Th' intricate wards, and every bolt and bar
Of massy iron or solid rock with ease
Unfastens. On a sudden open fly
With impetuous recoil and jarring sound   *880*
Th' infernal doors, and on their hinges grate
Harsh thunder, that the lowest bottom shook
Of Erebus. She opened, but to shut
Excelled her power; the gates wide open stood,
That with extended wings a bannered host   *885*
Under spread ensigns marching might pass through
With horse and chariots ranked in loose array;
So wide they stood, and like a furnace mouth

---

818. pledge: a child as evidence of love between parents. **829. unfounded:** having no foundation, bottomless. **842. buxom:** bending — i.e., yielding. **868.** See *Iliad*, VI, 138, and *Odyssey*, IV, 805.

Cast forth redounding smoke and ruddy flame.
Before their eyes in sudden view appear   890
The secrets of the hoary deep, a dark
Illimitable ocean without bound,
Without dimension; where length, breadth, and highth,
And time and place are lost; where eldest Night
And Chaos, ancestors of Nature, hold   895
Eternal anarchy, amidst the noise
Of endless wars, and by confusion stand.
For Hot, Cold, Moist, and Dry, four champions fierce,
Strive here for mast'ry, and to battle bring
Their embryon atoms; they around the flag   900
Of each his faction, in their several clans,
Light-armed or heavy, sharp, smooth, swift or slow,
Swarm populous, unnumbered as the sands
Of Barca or Cyrene's torrid soil,
Levied to side with warring winds, and poise   905
Their lighter wings. To whom these most adhere,
He rules a moment; Chaos umpire sits,
And by decision more embroils the fray
By which he reigns; next him high arbiter
Chance governs all. Into this wild abyss,   910
The womb of Nature and perhaps her grave,
Of neither sea, nor shore, nor air, nor fire,
But all these in their pregnant causes mixed
Confus'dly, and which thus must ever fight,
Unless th' Almighty Maker them ordain   915
His dark materials to create more worlds,
Into this wild abyss the wary Fiend
Stood on the brink of Hell and looked a while,
Pondering his voyage; for no narrow frith
He had to cross. Nor was his ear less pealed   920
With noises loud and ruinous (to compare
Great things with small) than when Bellona storms,
With all her battering engines bent to raze
Some capital city; or less than if this frame
Of Heav'n were falling, and these elements   925
In mutiny had from her axle torn
The steadfast Earth. At last his sail-broad vans
He spreads for flight, and in the surging smoke
Uplifted spurns the ground; thence many a league
As in a cloudy chair ascending rides   930

Audacious, but that seat soon failing, meets
A vast vacuity: all unawares
Flutt'ring his pennons vain plumb down he drops
Ten thousand fadom deep, and to this hour
Down had been falling, had not by ill chance   935
The strong rebuff of some tumultuous cloud
Instinct with fire and nitre hurried him
As many miles aloft. That fury stayed,
Quenched in a boggy Syrtis, neither sea,
Nor good dry land, nigh foundered on he fares,   940
Treading the crude consistence, half on foot,
Half flying; behoves him now both oar and sail.
As when a gryphon through the wilderness
With winged course o'er hill or moory dale,
Pursues the Arimaspian, who by stealth   945
Had from his wakeful custody purloined
The guarded gold: so eagerly the Fiend
O'er bog or steep, through strait, rough, dense, or rare,
With head, hands, wings, or feet pursues his way,
And swims or sinks, or wades, or creeps, or flies.   950
At length a universal hubbub wild
Of stunning sounds and voices all confused,
Borne through the hollow dark, assaults his ear
With loudest vehemence; thither he plies,
Undaunted to meet there whatever Power   955
Or Spirit of the nethermost abyss
Might in that noise reside, of whom to ask
Which way the nearest coast of darkness lies
Bordering on light; when straight behold the throne
Of Chaos, and his dark pavilion spread   960
Wide on the wasteful deep; with him enthroned
Sat sable-vested Night, eldest of things,
The consort of his reign; and by them stood
Orcus and Ades, and the dreaded name
Of Demogorgon; Rumour next and Chance,   965
And Tumult and Confusion all embroiled,
And Discord with a thousand various mouths.
    T' whom Satan turning boldly, thus: "Ye Powers
And Spirits of this nethermost abyss,
Chaos and ancient Night, I come no spy,   970
With purpose to explore or to disturb
The secrets of your realm, but by constraint

---

889. redounding: surging in waves, billowing, overflowing. **890ff.:** See Sandys's Ovid, I, 5ff. (p. 267). **891. hoary deep:** See Job 41:32. **898:** i.e., the four elements, fire, earth, water, and air (and see line 912). **904. Barca, Cyrene:** cities in Cyrenaica (northeast Libya). **905. poise:** add weight to. **920. pealed:** assailed (with noise). **921-22:** Cf. Virgil, *Eclogues*, I, 23; *Georgics*, IV, 176. **934. fadom:** fathom (Milton wants the sound of the older spelling). **939. Syrtis:** one of two gulfs near Tripoli virtually synonymous with quicksand. **943-47:** Gryphons (griffins) guarded their gold against the thieving one-eyed Arimaspians, a mythical northern people (Herodotus, III, 116). **959ff.:** Cf. *Aeneid*, VI, 273ff. **960-61:** See Psalms 18:11; **wasteful:** desolate. **964. Orcus, Ades:** names for Pluto or Hades. **965. Demogorgon:** another powerful hellish deity (probably derived from a classical slip for Demiurgos, creator of the material world); in *The Faerie Queene* (I, i, 332) Spenser refers to him simply as *Gorgon* (p. 158).

Wand'ring this darksome desert, as my way
Lies through your spacious empire up to light,
Alone, and without guide, half lost, I seek   975
What readiest path leads where your gloomy bounds
Confine with heav'n; or if some other place
From your dominion won, th' Ethereal King
Possesses lately, thither to arrive
I travel this profound. Direct my course;   980
Directed, no mean recompense it brings
To your behoof, if I that region lost,
All usurpation thence expelled, reduce
To her original darkness and your sway
(Which is my present journey), and once more   985
Erect the standard there of ancient Night;
Yours be th' advantage all, mine the revenge."
    Thus Satan; and him thus the Anarch old
With falt'ring speech and visage incomposed
Answered: "I know thee, stranger, who thou art,   990
That mighty leading angel, who of late
Made head against Heav'n's King, though overthrown.
I saw and heard, for such a numerous host
Fled not in silence through the frighted deep
With ruin upon ruin, rout on rout,   995
Confusion worse confounded; and Heav'n gates
Poured out by millions her victorious bands
Pursuing. I upon my frontiers here
Keep residence; if all I can will serve
That little which is left so to defend,   1000
Encroached on still through our intestine broils
Weak'ning the sceptre of old Night: first Hell
Your dungeon stretching far and wide beneath;
Now lately Heaven and Earth, another world
Hung o'er my realm, linked in a golden chain   1005
To that side Heav'n from whence your legions fell.
If that way be your walk, you have not far;
So much the nearer danger; go and speed;
Havoc and spoil and ruin are my gain."
    He ceased; and Satan stayed not to reply,   1010
But glad that now his sea should find a shore,
With fresh alacrity and force renewed
Springs upward like a pyramid of fire
Into the wild expanse, and through the shock

Of fighting elements, on all sides round   1015
Environed, wins his way; harder beset
And more endangered than when Argo passed
Through Bosporus betwixt the justling rocks,
Or when Ulysses on the larboard shunned
Charybdis, and by th' other whirlpool steered.   1020
So he with difficulty and labour hard
Moved on, with difficulty and labour he;
But he once passed, soon after when man fell,
Strange alteration! Sin and Death amain
Following his track, such was the will of Heav'n,   1025
Paved after him a broad and beaten way
Over the dark abyss, whose boiling gulf
Tamely endured a bridge of wondrous length
From Hell continued reaching th' utmost orb
Of this frail world; by which the Spirits perverse   1030
With easy intercourse pass to and fro
To tempt or punish mortals, except whom
God and good angels guard by special grace.
    But now at last the sacred influence
Of light appears, and from the walls of Heav'n   1035
Shoots far into the bosom of dim Night
A glimmering dawn; here Nature first begins
Her fardest verge, and Chaos to retire
As from her outmost works a broken foe,
With tumult less and with less hostile din,   1040
That Satan with less toil and now with ease
Wafts on the calmer wave by dubious light,
And like a weather-beaten vessel holds
Gladly the port, though shrouds and tackle torn;
Or in the emptier waste, resembling air,   1045
Weighs his spread wings, at leisure to behold
Far off th' Empyreal Heav'n, extended wide
In circuit, undetermined square or round,
With opal tow'rs and battlements adorned
Of living sapphire, once his native seat;   1050
And fast by hanging in a golden chain
This pendent world, in bigness as a star
Of smallest magnitude close by the moon.
Thither full fraught with mischievous revenge,
Accurst, and in a cursed hour, he hies.   1055

---

977. confine with: border on. **980. profound:** vast depth, abyss. **989. incomposed:** discomposed, disturbed. **1004:** i.e., earth and its heaven, or sky; the "Heav'n" of 1006 is the Empyrean, from which Satan and his crew fell. **1017-18:** Jason and the Argonauts, aboard the *Argo*, sailed through the Bosporus into the Black Sea and past the ship-crushing rocks called Symplegades. **1019-20:** See *Odyssey*, XII, 73ff., 234ff.; *Aeneid*, III, 420ff.; Scylla, whom Milton calls "th' other whirlpool," was in the classical epics a cave-dwelling, sailor-devouring monster. See also lines 660-61 and note, above. **1024ff.:** See the Argument for Book X. **1026:** See Matthew 7:13. **1029. utmost orb:** the tenth or outermost sphere, the *primum mobile*, that supposedly imparted motion to the other spheres; see note to I, 72 (also for 1047-52 below). **1043. holds:** stays on course for. **1051. golden chain:** See *Iliad*, VIII, 18ff.

from BOOK III

The Argument

God, sitting on his throne, sees Satan flying towards this world, then newly created; shows him to the Son, who sat at his right hand; foretells the success of Satan in perverting mankind; clears his own justice and wisdom from all imputation, having created man free and able enough to have withstood his tempter; yet declares his purpose of grace towards him, in regard he fell not of his own malice, as did Satan, but by him seduced. The Son of God renders praises to his Father for   *5* the manifestation of his gracious purpose towards man; but God again declares that grace cannot be extended towards man without the satisfaction of divine justice: man hath offended the majesty of God by aspiring to Godhead, and therefore with all his progeny devoted to death must die, unless someone can be found sufficient to answer for his offense, and undergo his punishment. The Son of God freely offers himself a ransom for man; the Father accepts him, ordains his   *10* incarnation, pronounces his exaltation above all names in Heaven and Earth; commands all the angels to adore him: they obey, and hymning to their harps in full choir, celebrate the Father and the Son. Meanwhile Satan alights upon the bare convex of this world's outermost orb; where wandering he first finds a place since called the Limbo of Vanity; what persons and things fly up thither; thence comes to the gate of Heaven, described ascending by stairs, and the waters above   *15* the firmament that flow about it. His passage thence to the orb of the sun: he finds there Uriel, the regent of that orb, but first changes himself into the shape of a meaner angel, and pretending a zealous desire to behold the new creation and man whom God had placed here, inquires of him the place of his habitation, and is directed; alights first on Mount Niphates.

Hail, holy Light, offspring of Heav'n first-born,
Or of th' Eternal coeternal beam
May I express thee unblamed? since God is light,
And never but in unapproached light
Dwelt from eternity, dwelt then in thee,   *5*
Bright effluence of bright essence increate.
Or hear'st thou rather pure ethereal stream,
Whose fountain who shall tell? Before the sun,
Before the heavens thou wert, and at the voice
Of God, as with a mantle didst invest   *10*
The rising world of waters dark and deep,
Won from the void and formless infinite.
Thee I revisit now with bolder wing,
Escaped the Stygian pool, though long detained
In that obscure sojourn, while in my flight   *15*
Through utter and through middle darkness borne
With other notes than to th' Orphean lyre
I sung of Chaos and eternal Night,
Taught by the Heav'nly Muse to venture down
The dark descent, and up to reascend,   *20*

Though hard and rare. Thee I revisit safe,
And feel thy sovran vital lamp; but thou
Revisit'st not these eyes, that roll in vain
To find thy piercing ray, and find no dawn;
So thick a drop serene hath quenched their orbs,   *25*
Or dim suffusion veiled. Yet not the more
Cease I to wander where the Muses haunt
Clear spring, or shady grove, or sunny hill,
Smit with the love of sacred song; but chief
Thee, Sion, and the flow'ry brooks beneath   *30*
That wash thy hallowed feet, and warbling flow,
Nightly I visit; nor sometimes forget
Those other two equaled with me in fate,
So were I equaled with them in renown,
Blind Thamyris and blind Maeonides,   *35*
And Tiresias and Phineus prophets old:
Then feed on thoughts that voluntary move
Harmonious numbers, as the wakeful bird
Sings darkling, and in shadiest covert hid
Tunes her nocturnal note. Thus with the year   *40*

BOOK III **1-12:** See Genesis 1:1-8 (pp. 241-42), I John 1:5. **17:** probably referring to the Orphic *Hymn to Night*. **19-21:** See II, 432-33, and note. **25-26:** *drop serene* (Latin: *gutta serena*) and *dim suffusion* (*suffusio nigra*), medical terms for kinds of blindness. **26-29:** Cf. Virgil's *Georgics*, II, 475ff. **29-31:** See I, 10-12. **32:** Milton did much of his composing at night or in the early morning (see also VII, 29-30, and IX, 22-24, 47). **35. Thamyris:** a mythical poet mentioned by Homer; **Maeonides:** Homer himself, supposedly being from Maeonia (in Asia Minor). **36. Tiresias:** the blind prophet in Sophocles's *Oedipus Rex* and *Antigone*; **Phineus:** a mythical Thracian king and prophet. **38. numbers:** i.e., poetry, verse; **wakeful bird:** nightingale.

Seasons return; but not to me returns
Day, or the sweet approach of ev'n or morn,
Or sight of vernal bloom, or summer's rose,
Or flocks, or herds, or human face divine;
But cloud instead, and ever-during dark   45
Surrounds me, from the cheerful ways of men
Cut off, and for the book of knowledge fair
Presented with a universal blanc
Of Nature's works to me expunged and rased,
And wisdom at one entrance quite shut out.   50
So much the rather thou, celestial Light,
Shine inward, and the mind through all her powers
Irradiate, there plant eyes, all mist from thence
Purge and disperse, that I may see and tell
Of things invisible to mortal sight.   55
   Now had the Almighty Father from above,
From the pure Empyrean where he sits
High throned above all highth, bent down his eye,
His own works and their works at once to view.
About him all the Sanctities of Heaven   60
Stood thick as stars, and from his sight received
Beatitude past utterance; on his right
The radiant image of his glory sat,
His only Son. On Earth he first beheld
Our two first parents, yet the only two   65
Of mankind, in the happy garden placed,
Reaping immortal fruits of joy and love,
Uninterrupted joy, unrivaled love,
In blissful solitude. He then surveyed
Hell and the gulf between, and Satan there   70
Coasting the wall of Heav'n on this side Night
In the dun air sublime, and ready now
To stoop with wearied wings and willing feet
On the bare outside of this world, that seemed
Firm land imbosomed without firmament,   75
Uncertain which, in ocean or in air.
Him God beholding from his prospect high,
Wherein past, present, future he beholds,
Thus to his only Son foreseeing spake:
   "Only begotten Son, seest thou what rage   80
Transports our Adversary? Whom no bounds
Prescribed, no bars of Hell, nor all the chains
Heaped on him there, nor yet the main abyss
Wide interrupt can hold; so bent he seems
On desperate revenge, that shall redound   85
Upon his own rebellious head. And now
Through all restraint broke loose he wings his way

Not far off Heav'n, in the precincts of light,
Directly towards the new-created world,
And man there placed, with purpose to assay   90
If him by force he can destroy, or worse,
By some false guile pervert; and shall pervert;
For man will hearken to his glozing lies,
And easily transgress the sole command,
Sole pledge of his obedience; so will fall   95
He and his faithless progeny. Whose fault?
Whose but his own? Ingrate, he had of me
All he could have; I made him just and right,
Sufficient to have stood, though free to fall.
Such I created all th' ethereal Powers   100
And Spirits, both them who stood and them who failed;
Freely they stood who stood, and fell who fell.
Not free, what proof could they have giv'n sincere
Of true allegiance, constant faith or love,
Where only what they needs must do, appeared,   105
Not what they would? What praise could they receive?
What pleasure I from such obedience paid,
When will and reason (reason also is choice)
Useless and vain, of freedom both despoiled,
Made passive both, had served necessity,   110
Not me. They therefore as to right belonged,
So were created, nor can justly accuse
Their Maker, or their making, or their fate,
As if predestination overruled
Their will, disposed by absolute decree   115
Or high foreknowledge; they themselves decreed
Their own revolt, not I. If I foreknew,
Foreknowledge had no influence on their fault,
Which had no less proved certain unforeknown.
So without least impulse or shadow of fate,   120
Or aught by me immutably foreseen,
They trespass, authors to themselves in all,
Both what they judge and what they choose; for so
I formed them free, and free they must remain,
Till they enthrall themselves: I else must change 125
Their nature, and revoke the high decree
Unchangeable, eternal, which ordained
Their freedom; they themselves ordained their fall.
The first sort by their own suggestion fell,
Self-tempted, self-depraved; man falls deceived 130
By the other first; man therefore shall find grace,
The other none. In mercy and justice both,
Through heav'n and earth, so shall my glory excel,
But mercy first and last shall brightest shine."

              . . . .

---

60. Sanctities: angels. **61. his sight:** i.e., sight of him. **61-62:** Cf. I, 684. **62-64:** See Hebrews 1:2-3. **72. sublime:** raised aloft. **74. world:** i.e., the outermost sphere of the created universe. **108:** See *Of Education*, 87-88 (p. 320), and *Areopagitica*, 37-38 (p. 323).

from BOOK IV

The Argument

Satan, now in prospect of Eden, and nigh the place where he must now attempt the bold enterprise which he undertook alone against God and man, falls into many doubts with himself, and many passions: fear, envy, and despair; but at length confirms himself in evil, journeys on to Paradise, whose outward prospect and situation is described, overleaps the bounds, sits in the shape of a cormorant on the Tree of Life, as highest in the Garden, to look about him. The Garden described; 5
Satan's first sight of Adam and Eve; his wonder at their excellent form and happy state, but with resolution to work their fall; overhears their discourse; thence gathers that the Tree of Knowledge was forbidden them to eat of, under penalty of death; and thereon intends to found his temptation by seducing them to transgress; then leaves them a while, to know further of their state by some other means. Meanwhile Uriel, descending on a sunbeam, warns Gabriel, who had in charge the 10
gate of Paradise, that some evil Spirit had escaped the deep, and passed at noon by his sphere, in the shape of a good angel, down to Paradise; discovered after by his furious gestures in the mount. Gabriel promises to find him ere morning. Night coming on, Adam and Eve discourse of going to their rest: their bower described; their evening worship. Gabriel, drawing forth his bands of nightwatch to walk the round of Paradise, appoints two strong angels to Adam's bower, lest the 15
evil Spirit should be there doing some harm to Adam or Eve sleeping; there they find him at the ear of Eve, tempting her in a dream, and bring him, though unwilling, to Gabriel; by whom questioned, he scornfully answers, prepares resistance, but hindered by a sign from Heaven, flies out of Paradise.

O for that warning voice, which he who saw
Th' Apocalypse heard cry in Heaven aloud,
Then when the Dragon, put to second rout,
Came furious down to be revenged on men,
"Woe to the inhabitants on Earth!" that now,   5
While time was, our first parents had been warned
The coming of their secret foe, and scaped,
Haply so scaped, his mortal snare; for now
Satan, now first inflamed with rage, came down,
The tempter ere th' accuser of mankind,   10
To wreck on innocent frail man his loss
Of that first battle, and his flight to Hell:
Yet not rejoicing in his speed, though bold,
Far off and fearless, nor with cause to boast,
Begins his dire attempt, which nigh the birth   15
Now rolling, boils in his tumultuous breast,
And like a devilish engine back recoils
Upon himself; horror and doubt distract
His troubled thoughts, and from the bottom stir
The Hell within him, for within him Hell   20
He brings, and round about him, nor from Hell
One step no more than from himself can fly
By change of place. Now conscience wakes despair

That slumbered, wakes the bitter memory
Of what he was, what is, and what must be   25
Worse; of worse deeds worse sufferings must ensue.
Sometimes towards Eden which now in his view
Lay pleasant, his grieved look he fixes sad,
Sometimes towards Heav'n and the full-blazing Sun,
Which now sat high in his meridian tow'r.   30
Then much revolving, thus in sighs began:
    "O thou that with surpassing glory crowned
Look'st from thy sole dominion like the god
Of this new world; at whose sight all the stars
Hide their diminished heads; to thee I call,   35
But with no friendly voice, and add thy name,
O Sun, to tell thee how I hate thy beams
That bring to my remembrance from what state
I fell, how glorious once above thy sphere;
Till pride and worse ambition threw me down   40
Warring in Heav'n against Heav'n's matchless King.
Ah wherefore? He deserved no such return
From me, whom he created what I was
In that bright eminence, and with his good
Upbraided none; nor was his service hard.   45
What could be less than to afford him praise,

BOOK IV   **1-2ff. he . . . Apocalypse:** St. John, author of The Apocalypse, or Revelation; see Revelation 12. **11. wreck:** wreak. **17. engine:** cannon.

The easiest recompense, and pay him thanks,
How due! Yet all his good proved ill in me,
And wrought but malice; lifted up so high
I sdained subjection, and thought one step higher   50
Would set me highest, and in a moment quit
The debt immense of endless gratitude,
So burthensome still paying, still to owe;
Forgetful what from him I still received,
And understood not that a grateful mind   55
By owing owes not, but still pays, at once
Indebted and discharged; what burden then?
O had his powerful destiny ordained
Me some inferior angel, I had stood
Then happy; no unbounded hope had raised   60
Ambition. Yet why not? Some other Power
As great might have aspired, and me though mean
Drawn to his part; but other Powers as great
Fell not, but stand unshaken, from within
Or from without, to all temptations armed.   65
Hadst thou the same free will and power to stand?
Thou hadst. Whom hast thou then or what to accuse,
But Heav'n's free love dealt equally to all?
Be then his love accurst, since love or hate,
To me alike, it deals eternal woe.   70
Nay cursed be thou, since against his thy will
Chose freely what it now so justly rues.
Me miserable! which way shall I fly
Infinite wrath, and infinite despair?
Which way I fly is Hell; myself am Hell;   75
And in the lowest deep a lower deep
Still threat'ning to devour me opens wide,
To which the Hell I suffer seems a Heav'n.
O then at last relent: is there no place
Left for repentance, none for pardon left?   80
None left but by submission; and that word
Disdain forbids me, and my dread of shame
Among the Spirits beneath, whom I seduced
With other promises and other vaunts
Than to submit, boasting I could subdue   85
Th' Omnipotent. Ay me, they little know
How dearly I abide that boast so vain,
Under what torments inwardly I groan;

While they adore me on the throne of Hell,
With diadem and sceptre high advanced,   90
The lower still I fall, only supreme
In misery; such joy ambition finds.
But say I could repent and could obtain
By act of grace my former state; how soon
Would highth recall high thoughts, how soon unsay   95
What feigned submission swore: ease would recant
Vows made in pain, as violent and void.
For never can true reconcilement grow
Where wounds of deadly hate have pierced so deep;
Which would but lead me to a worse relapse   100
And heavier fall: so should I purchase dear
Short intermission bought with double smart.
This knows my Punisher; therefore as far
From granting he, as I from begging peace.
All hope excluded thus, behold instead   105
Of us outcast, exiled, his new delight,
Mankind created, and for him this world.
So farewell hope, and with hope farewell fear,
Farewell remorse! All good to me is lost;
Evil, be thou my good; by thee at least   110
Divided empire with Heav'n's King I hold
By thee, and more than half perhaps will reign;
As man ere long, and this new world shall know."

. . . .

Not that fair field
Of Enna, where Proserpine gathering flow'rs,
Herself a fairer flow'r, by gloomy Dis   270
Was gathered, which cost Ceres all that pain
To seek her through the world; nor that sweet grove
Of Daphne by Orontes, and th' inspired
Castalian spring, might with this Paradise
Of Eden strive; nor that Nyseian isle   275
Girt with the river Triton, where old Cham,
Whom Gentiles Ammon call and Libyan Jove,
Hid Amalthea and her florid son,
Young Bacchus, from his stepdame Rhea's eye;
Nor where Abassin kings their issue guard,   280
Mount Amara, though this by some supposed
True Paradise, under the Ethiop line
By Nilus' head, enclosed with shining rock,

---

50. sdained: disdained. 79-80: Cf. Hebrews 12:17. 94. grace: i.e., God's forgiveness, mercy. 110: See IX, 122-23, and Isaiah 5:20. 269ff. Enna: in Sicily (see Ovid, *Metamorphoses*, 385ff.); Dis: Pluto, god of the underworld; Ceres (Demeter, mother of Proserpina, or Persephone); the garden of Daphne is in Syria, on the Orontes river; the Castalian spring is on Parnassus, near Delphi; the isle of Nysa in the Triton is in Tunisia, where Cham (Ham), Noah's son, traditionally identified with the Egyptian Ammon (and later Zeus- or Jupiter-Ammon), hid the nymph Amalthea and the son she bore him, Bacchus (Dionysus), from his wife Rhea (in Diodorus Siculus, 3, 67-68). 280ff.: Abassin: Abyssinian; Amara: hill with palaces where the kings' sons were kept (a story later used by Samuel Johnson in his *Rasselas*; Mount Amara turns up — as Abora — in Coleridge's "Kubla Khan" — see p. 783); Ethiop line: equator.

A whole day's journey high, but wide remote
From this Assyrian garden, where the Fiend   *285*
Saw undelighted all delight, all kind
Of living creatures new to sight and strange.
Two of far nobler shape erect and tall,
Godlike erect, with native honour clad
In naked majesty seemed lords of all,   *290*
And worthy seemed, for in their looks divine
The image of their glorious Maker shone,
Truth, wisdom, sanctitude severe and pure,
Severe but in true filial freedom placed;
Whence true authority in men; though both   *295*
Not equal, as their sex not equal seemed;
For contemplation he and valour formed,
For softness she and sweet attractive grace;
He for God only, she for God in him.
His fair large front and eye sublime declared   *300*
Absolute rule; and hyacinthine locks
Round from his parted forelock manly hung
Clust'ring, but not beneath his shoulders broad:
She as a veil down to the slender waist

Her unadorned golden tresses wore   *305*
Disheveled, but in wanton ringlets waved
As the vine curls her tendrils, which implied
Subjection, but required with gentle sway,
And by her yielded, by him best received,
Yielded with coy submission, modest pride,   *310*
And sweet reluctant amorous delay.
Nor those mysterious parts were then concealed;
Then was not guilty shame; dishonest shame
Of Nature's works, honour dishonourable,
Sin-bred, how have ye troubled all mankind   *315*
With shows instead, mere shows of seeming pure,
And banished from man's life his happiest life,
Simplicity and spotless innocence.
So passed they naked on, nor shunned the sight
Of God or angel, for they thought no ill;   *320*
So hand in hand they passed, the loveliest pair
That ever since in love's embraces met,
Adam the goodliest man of men since born
His sons, the fairest of her daughters Eve.

. . . .

from BOOK V

The Argument

Morning approached, Eve relates to Adam her troublesome dream; he likes it not, yet comforts her; they come forth to their day labours; their morning hymn at the door of their bower. God, to render man inexcusable, sends Raphael to admonish him of his obedience, of his free estate, of his enemy near at hand — who he is, and why his enemy, and whatever else may avail Adam to know. Raphael comes down to Paradise; his appearance described; his coming discerned by Adam   *5*
afar off, sitting at the door of his bower; he goes out to meet him, brings him to his lodge, entertains him with the choicest fruits of Paradise got together by Eve; their discourse at table. Raphael performs his message, minds Adam of his state and of his enemy; relates, at Adam's request, who that enemy is, and how he came to be so, beginning from his first revolt in Heaven, and the occasion thereof; how he drew his legions after him to the parts of the north, and there   *10*
incited them to rebel with him, persuading all but only Abdiel, a Seraph, who in argument dissuades and opposes him, then forsakes him.

from BOOK VI

The Argument

Raphael continues to relate how Michael and Gabriel were sent forth to battle against Satan and his angels. The first fight described; Satan and his powers retire under night. He calls a council; invents devilish engines, which, in the second day's fight, put Michael and his angels to some disorder; but they at length, pulling up mountains, overwhelmed both the force and machines of

---

285. this Assyrian garden: i.e., the true Paradise, which is "eastward in Eden" (Genesis 2:8; p. 243). **290-92:** See Genesis 1:26-27 (p. 242). **296-311:** See I Corinthians 11:1-15. **301. hyacinthine:** curly, wavy (see *Odyssey*, VI, 231, and XXIII, 158) — perhaps also dark, like the red or purple blood colour of the flower (see *Lycidas*, 106, and note, p. 317). **310. coy:** shy, modest. **313. dishonest:** unchaste.

Satan. Yet, the tumult not so ending, God on the third day sends Messiah his Son, for whom he   *5*
had reserved the glory of that victory. He, in the power of his Father, coming to the place, and
causing all his legions to stand still on either side, with his chariot and thunder driving into the
midst of his enemies, pursues them, unable to resist, towards the wall of Heaven; which opening,
they leap down with horror and confusion into the place of punishment prepared for them in the
deep. Messiah returns with triumph to his Father.   *10*

from BOOK VII

The Argument
Raphael, at the request of Adam, relates how and wherefore this world was first created: that God,
after the expelling of Satan and his angels out of Heaven, declared his pleasure to create another
world, and other creatures to dwell therein; sends his Son with glory, and attendance of angels, to
perform the work of creation in six days: the angels celebrate with hymns the performance
thereof, and his reascension into Heaven.   *5*

Descend from heav'n, Urania, by that name
If rightly thou art called, whose voice divine
Following, above th' Olympian hill I soar,
Above the flight of Pegasean wing.
The meaning, not the name I call; for thou   *5*
Nor of the Muses nine, nor on the top
Of old Olympus dwell'st, but heav'nly born,
Before the hills appeared or fountain flowed,
Thou with eternal Wisdom didst converse,
Wisdom thy sister, and with her didst play   *10*
In presence of th' Almighty Father, pleased
With thy celestial song. Up led by thee
Into the Heav'n of Heav'ns I have presumed,
An earthly guest, and drawn empyreal air,
Thy temp'ring; with like safety guided down,   *15*
Return me to my native element,
Lest from this flying steed unreined (as once
Bellerophon, though from a lower clime)
Dismounted, on th' Aleian field I fall,
Erroneous there to wander and forlorn.   *20*

Half yet remains unsung, but narrower bound
Within the visible diurnal sphere;
Standing on Earth, not rapt above the pole,
More safe I sing with mortal voice, unchanged
To hoarse or mute, though fall'n on evil days,   *25*
On evil days though fall'n, and evil tongues;
In darkness, and with dangers compassed round,
And solitude; yet not alone, while thou
Visit'st my slumbers nightly, or when morn
Purples the east. Still govern thou my song,   *30*
Urania, and fit audience find, though few.
But drive far off the barbarous dissonance
Of Bacchus and his revellers, the race
Of that wild rout that tore the Thracian bard
In Rhodope, where woods and rocks had ears   *35*
To rapture, till the savage clamour drowned
Both harp and voice; nor could the Muse defend
Her son. So fail not thou who thee implores;
For thou art heav'nly, she an empty dream.
. . . .

from BOOK VIII

The Argument
Adam inquires concerning celestial motions, is doubtfully answered, and exhorted to search rather
things more worthy of knowledge. Adam assents, and still desirous to detain Raphael, relates to

---

BOOK VII   **4:** Pegasus was the "flying steed" (17) ridden by Bellerophon (18) and from which Zeus toppled him onto the Aleian plain in Lycia (19). **7-12:** See Proverbs 8, especially verses 22-30, and The Wisdom of Solomon (in the Apocrypha), 6ff. **8-9:** See note on I, 6. **20. erroneous:** also signifying "wandering." **25-27:** referring to the government after the Restoration of the monarchy in 1660 (after Cromwell's Commonwealth, in whose government Milton had worked; he was even arrested briefly). **29-30:** Cf. III, 32, and note, and IX, 22-24, 47. **32-38:** Cf. *Lycidas*, 58-63 (p. 316); here he also has in mind his Royalist enemies now in power (see I, 501-02).

him what he remembered since his own creation: his placing in Paradise, his talk with God concerning solitude and fit society, his first meeting and nuptials with Eve. His discourse with the angel thereupon; who, after admonitions repeated, departs. *5*

. . . .

"But whether thus these things, or whether not,
Whether the sun predominant in Heav'n *160*
Rise on the Earth, or Earth rise on the sun,
He from the east his flaming road begin,
Or she from west her silent course advance
With inoffensive pace that spinning sleeps
On her soft axle, while she paces ev'n, *165*
And bears thee soft with the smooth air along —
Solicit not thy thoughts with matters hid:
Leave them to God above, him serve and fear;
Of other creatures, as him pleases best,
Wherever placed, let him dispose; joy thou *170*
In what he gives to thee, this Paradise
And thy fair Eve; Heav'n is for thee too high
To know what passes there; be lowly wise:
Think only what concerns thee and thy being;
Dream not of other worlds, what creatures there *175*
Live, in what state, condition, or degree,
Contented that thus far hath been revealed
Not of Earth only but of highest Heav'n."

. . . .

BOOK IX

The Argument

Satan, having compassed the Earth, with meditated guile returns as a mist by night into Paradise; enters into the Serpent sleeping. Adam and Eve in the morning go forth to their labours, which Eve proposes to divide in several places, each labouring apart: Adam consents not, alleging the danger lest that enemy, of whom they were forewarned, should attempt her found alone. Eve, loath to be thought not circumspect or firm enough, urges her going apart, the rather desirous to *5* make trial of her strength; Adam at last yields. The Serpent finds her alone: his subtle approach, first gazing, then speaking, with much flattery extolling Eve above all other creatures. Eve, wondering to hear the Serpent speak, asks how he attained to human speech and such understanding not till now; the Serpent answers that by tasting of a certain tree in the garden he attained both to speech and reason, till then void of both. Eve requires him to bring her to that *10* tree, and finds it to be the Tree of Knowledge forbidden. The Serpent, now grown bolder, with many wiles and arguments induces her at length to eat; she, pleased with the taste, deliberates a while whether to impart thereof to Adam or not; at last brings him of the fruit; relates what persuaded her to eat thereof. Adam, at first amazed, but perceiving her lost, resolves through vehemence of love to perish with her, and, extenuating the trespass, eats also of the fruit. The *15* effects thereof in them both; they seek to cover their nakedness; then fall to variance and accusation of one another.

No more of talk where God or angel guest
With man, as with his friend, familiar used
To sit indulgent, and with him partake
Rural repast, permitting him the while
Venial discourse unblamed. I now must change *5*
Those notes to tragic; foul distrust, and breach
Disloyal on the part of man, revolt,
And disobedience; on the part of Heav'n
Now alienated, distance and distaste,
Anger and just rebuke, and judgment giv'n, *10*
That brought into this world a world of woe,
Sin and her shadow Death, and misery,
Death's harbinger. Sad task, yet argument
Not less but more heroic than the wrath

BOOK VIII   **159-78:** the conclusion of Raphael's advice to Adam about vainly pursuing knowledge he can't have and doesn't need anyway; cf. XII, 558ff. **164. inoffensive:** without hindrance or obstruction.   **BOOK IX**   **14-15:** Cf. the opening of the *Iliad* (p. 534). **14-16:** See *Iliad*, XXII (the foe is Hector).

Of stern Achilles on his foe pursued   *15*
Thrice fugitive about Troy wall; or rage
Of Turnus for Lavinia disesposused;
Or Neptune's ire or Juno's, that so long
Perplexed the Greek and Cytherea's son;
If answerable style I can obtain   *20*
Of my celestial patroness, who deigns
Her nightly visitation unimplored,
And dictates to me slumb'ring, or inspires
Easy my unpremeditated verse,
Since first this subject for heroic song   *25*
Pleased me long choosing, and beginning late;
Not sedulous by nature to indite
Wars, hitherto the only argument
Heroic deemed, chief mast'ry to dissect
With long and tedious havoc fabled knights   *30*
In battles feigned (the better fortitude
Of patience and heroic martyrdom
Unsung), or to describe races and games,
Or tilting furniture, emblazoned shields,
Impresses quaint, caparisons and steeds,   *35*
Bases and tinsel trappings, gorgeous knights
At joust and tournament; then marshalled feast
Served up in hall with sewers and seneschals;
The skill of artifice or office mean,
Not that which justly gives heroic name   *40*
To person or to poem. Me of these
Nor skilled nor studious, higher argument
Remains, sufficient of itself to raise
That name, unless an age too late, or cold
Climate, or years damp my intended wing   *45*
Depressed, and much they may, if all be mine,
Not hers who brings it nightly to my ear.
     The sun was sunk, and after him the star
Of Hesperus, whose office is to bring
Twilight upon the earth, short arbiter   *50*
'Twixt day and night, and now from end to end
Night's hemisphere had veiled the horizon round,
When Satan, who late fled before the threats

Of Gabriel out of Eden, now improved
In meditated fraud and malice, bent   *55*
On man's destruction, maugre what might hap
Of heavier on himself, fearless returned.
By night he fled, and at midnight returned
From compassing the earth, cautious of day,
Since Uriel, regent of the sun, descried   *60*
His entrance, and forewarned the Cherubim
That kept their watch; thence full of anguish driv'n,
The space of seven continued nights he rode
With darkness, thrice the equinoctial line
He circled, four times crossed the car of Night   *65*
From pole to pole, traversing each colure;
On the eighth returned, and on the coast averse
From entrance or Cherubic watch, by stealth
Found unsuspected way. There was a place —
Now not, though sin, not time, first wrought the change —
Where Tigris at the foot of Paradise   *71*
Into a gulf shot under ground, till part
Rose up a fountain by the Tree of Life;
In with the river sunk, and with it rose
Satan, involved in rising mist, then sought   *75*
Where to lie hid; sea he had searched and land
From Eden over Pontus, and the pool
Maeotis, up beyond the river Ob;
Downward as far antarctic; and in length
West from Orontes to the ocean barred   *80*
At Darien, thence to the land where flows
Ganges and Indus. Thus the orb he roamed
With narrow search, and with inspection deep
Considered every creature, which of all
Most opportune might serve his wiles, and found   *85*
The serpent subtlest beast of all the field.
Him after long debate, irresolute
Of thoughts revolved, his final sentence chose
Fit vessel, fittest imp of fraud, in whom
To enter, and his dark suggestions hide   *90*
From sharpest sight; for in the wily snake,
Whatever sleights none would suspicious mark,

16-17: See *Aeneid*, XII (Turnus was Aeneas's rival). **18-19:** In *Odyssey*, I, Poseidon (Neptune) is hostile to Odysseus; in *Aeneid*, I, Juno (Hera) is hostile toward Aeneas, son of Venus (Aphrodite), called Cytherea, from the island Cythera, one of the principal places she was worshipped (see the opening, p. 440). **21. celestial patroness:** i.e., Urania (cf. openings of I and VII). **22-24.** See also line 47, and cf. III, 32, and note, and VII, 29-30. **27. sedulous:** zealous, eager. **33:** See note on II, 530. **34. tilting furniture:** jousting equipment (see Spenser's "A Letter of the Authors," line 82; p. 152). **35. impresses:** heraldic devices or other ornaments on shields. **36. Bases:** housings, ornamented low-hanging coverings for horses; or ornamented skirt-like coverings worn by knights. **44-46:** Cf. Beaumont's "To His Late Majesty," lines 64-65 (p. 276). **56. maugre:** in spite of. **64. equinoctial line:** equator. **66:** The colures are two meridians of the celestial sphere; the equinoctial colure passes through the two equinoctial points (where the celestial equator and the ecliptic intersect); the solstitial colure crosses the equator 90° from the other. The point is that Satan manages to stay in darkness. **77-82:** Pontus is the Black Sea; Maeotis is the Sea of Azov; the river Ob flows north through Siberia; the Orontes flows north through Syria; Darien is the Isthmus of Panama; the Ganges and Indus are in India. **86.** See Genesis 3:1 (p. 244).

As from his wit and native subtlety
Proceeding, which in other beasts observed
Doubt might beget of diabolic pow'r   *95*
Active within beyond the sense of brute.
Thus he resolved, but first from inward grief
His bursting passion into plaints thus poured:
    "O Earth, how like to Heav'n, if not preferred
More justly, seat worthier of Gods, as built   *100*
With second thoughts, reforming what was old!
For what God after better worse would build?
Terrestrial Heav'n, danced round by other Heav'ns
That shine, yet bear their bright officious lamps,
Light above light, for thee alone, as seems,   *105*
In thee concentring all their precious beams
Of sacred influence! As God in Heav'n
Is centre, yet extends to all, so thou
Centring receiv'st from all those orbs; in thee,
Not in themselves, all their known virtue appears   *110*
Productive in herb, plant, and nobler birth
Of creatures animate with gradual life
Of growth, sense, reason, all summed up in man.
With what delight could I have walked thee round,
If I could joy in aught, sweet interchange   *115*
Of hill and valley, rivers, woods, and plains,
Now land, now sea, and shores with forest crowned,
Rocks, dens, and caves; but I in none of these
Find place or refuge; and the more I see
Pleasures about me, so much more I feel   *120*
Torment within me, as from the hateful siege
Of contraries; all good to me becomes
Bane, and in Heav'n much worse would be my state.
But neither here seek I, no nor in Heav'n
To dwell, unless by mast'ring Heav'n's Supreme;   *125*
Nor hope to be myself less miserable
By what I seek, but others to make such
As I, though thereby worse to me redound.
For only in destroying I find ease
To my relentless thoughts; and him destroyed,   *130*
Or won to what may work his utter loss,
For whom all this was made, all this will soon
Follow, as to him linked in weal or woe;
In woe then, that destruction wide may range.
To me shall be the glory sole among   *135*
The infernal Powers, in one day to have marred
What he, Almighty styled, six nights and days
Continued making, and who knows how long
Before had been contriving? Though perhaps

Not longer than since I in one night freed   *140*
From servitude inglorious well-nigh half
Th' angelic name, and thinner left the throng
Of his adorers. He to be avenged,
And to repair his numbers thus impaired,
Whether such virtue spent of old now failed   *145*
More angels to create, if they at least
Are his created, or to spite us more,
Determined to advance into our room
A creature formed of earth, and him endow,
Exalted from so base original,   *150*
With Heav'nly spoils, our spoils. What he decreed
He effected; man he made, and for him built
Magnificent this world, and Earth his seat,
Him lord pronounced, and, O indignity!
Subjected to his service angel wings,   *155*
And flaming ministers to watch and tend
Their earthy charge. Of these the vigilance
I dread, and to elude, thus wrapped in mist
Of midnight vapour glide obscure, and pry
In every bush and brake, where hap may find   *160*
The Serpent sleeping, in whose mazy folds
To hide me, and the dark intent I bring.
O foul descent! that I who erst contended
With Gods to sit the highest, am now constrained
Into a beast, and mixed with bestial slime,   *165*
This essence to incarnate and imbrute,
That to the height of deity aspired;
But what will not ambition and revenge
Descend to? Who aspires must down as low
As high he soared, obnoxious first or last   *170*
To basest things. Revenge, at first though sweet,
Bitter ere long back on itself recoils;
Let it; I reck not, so it light well aimed,
Since higher I fall short, on him who next
Provokes my envy, this new favourite   *175*
Of Heav'n, this man of clay, son of despite,
Whom us the more to spite his Maker raised
From dust: spite then with spite is best repaid."
    So saying, through each thicket dank or dry,
Like a black mist low creeping, he held on   *180*
His midnight search, where soonest he might find
The Serpent. Him fast sleeping soon he found
In labyrinth of many a round self-rolled,
His head the midst, well stored with subtle wiles;
Not yet in horrid shade or dismal den,   *185*
Nor nocent yet, but on the grassy herb

---

95. doubt: suspicion. **104. officious:** obliging, helpful. **122-23:** See IV, 110. **170. obnoxious:** liable, exposed, subject.

Fearless, unfeared, he slept. In at his mouth
The Devil entered, and his brutal sense,
In heart or head, possessing soon inspired
With act intelligential, but his sleep   190
Disturbed not, waiting close th' approach of morn.
    Now whenas sacred light began to dawn
In Eden on the humid flow'rs, that breathed
Their morning incense, when all things that breathe
From th' Earth's great altar send up silent praise   195
To the Creator, and his nostrils fill
With grateful smell, forth came the human pair
And joined their vocal worship to the quire
Of creatures wanting voice; that done, partake
The season, prime for sweetest scents and airs;   200
Then commune how that day they best may ply
Their growing work; for much their work outgrew
The hands' dispatch of two gard'ning so wide.
And Eve first to her husband thus began:
    "Adam, well may we labour still to dress   205
This garden, still to tend plant, herb, and flow'r,
Our pleasant task enjoined, but till more hands
Aid us, the work under our labour grows,
Luxurious by restraint; what we by day
Lop overgrown, or prune, or prop, or bind,   210
One night or two with wanton growth derides,
Tending to wild. Thou therefore now advise
Or hear what to my mind first thoughts present:
Let us divide our labours, thou where choice
Leads thee, or where most needs, whether to wind   215
The woodbine round this arbour, or direct
The clasping ivy where to climb, while I
In yonder spring of roses intermixed
With myrtle, find what to redress till noon.
For while so near each other thus all day   220
Our task we choose, what wonder if so near
Looks intervene and smiles, or object new
Casual discourse draw on, which intermits
Our day's work, brought to little, though begun
Early, and th' hour of supper comes unearned."   225
    To whom mild answer Adam thus returned:
"Sole Eve, associate sole, to me beyond
Compare above all living creatures dear,
Well hast thou motioned, well thy thoughts employed
How we might best fulfill the work which here   230
God hath assigned us, nor of me shalt pass
Unpraised; for nothing lovelier can be found
In woman, than to study household good,

And good works in her husband to promote.
Yet not so strictly hath our Lord imposed   235
Labour, as to debar us when we need
Refreshment, whether food, or talk between,
Food of the mind, or this sweet intercourse
Of looks and smiles, for smiles from reason flow,
To brute denied, and are of love the food,   240
Love not the lowest end of human life.
For not to irksome toil, but to delight
He made us, and delight to reason joined.
These paths and bowers doubt not but our joint hands
Will keep from wilderness with ease, as wide   245
As we need walk, till younger hands ere long
Assist us. But if much converse perhaps
Thee satiate, to short absence I could yield.
For solitude sometimes is best society,
And short retirement urges sweet return.   250
But other doubt possesses me, lest harm
Befall thee severed from me; for thou know'st
What hath been warned us, what malicious foe,
Envying our happiness, and of his own
Despairing, seeks to work us woe and shame   255
By sly assault; and somewhere nigh at hand
Watches, no doubt, with greedy hope to find
His wish and best advantage, us asunder,
Hopeless to circumvent us joined, where each
To other speedy aid might lend at need;   260
Whether his first design be to withdraw
Our fealty from God, or to disturb
Conjugal love, than which perhaps no bliss
Enjoyed by us excites his envy more;
Or this, or worse, leave not the faithful side   265
That gave thee being, still shades thee and protects.
The wife, where danger or dishonour lurks,
Safest and seemliest by her husband stays,
Who guards her, or with her the worst endures."
    To whom the virgin majesty of Eve,   270
As one who loves, and some unkindness meets,
With sweet austere composure thus replied:
    "Offspring of Heav'n and Earth, and all Earth's lord,
That such an enemy we have, who seeks
Our ruin, both by thee informed I learn,   275
And from the parting angel overheard
As in a shady nook I stood behind,
Just then returned at shut of evening flow'rs.
But that thou shouldst my firmness therefore doubt
To God or thee, because we have a foe   280

---

191. close: hidden. **205. still:** always, continually. **218. spring:** copse of young plants. **229. motioned:** moved, proposed. **270. virgin:** innocent.

May tempt it, I expected not to hear.
His violence thou fear'st not, being such
As we, not capable of death or pain,
Can either not receive, or can repel.
His fraud is then thy fear, which plain infers   *285*
Thy equal fear that my firm faith and love
Can by his fraud be shaken or seduced;
Thoughts, which how found they harbour in thy breast,
Adam, misthought of her to thee so dear?"
    To whom with healing words Adam replied: *290*
"Daughter of God and man, immortal Eve,
For such thou art, from sin and blame entire;
Not diffident of thee do I dissuade
Thy absence from my sight, but to avoid
Th' attempt itself, intended by our foe.   *295*
For he who tempts, though in vain, at least asperses
The tempted with dishonour foul, supposed
Not incorruptible of faith, not proof
Against temptation. Thou thyself with scorn
And anger wouldst resent the offered wrong,   *300*
Though ineffectual found. Misdeem not then,
If such affront I labour to avert
From thee alone, which on us both at once
The enemy, though bold, will hardly dare,
Or daring, first on me th' assault shall light.   *305*
Nor thou his malice and false guile contemn;
Subtle he needs must be, who could seduce
Angels, nor think superfluous others' aid.
I from the influence of thy looks receive
Access in every virtue, in thy sight   *310*
More wise, more watchful, stronger, if need were
Of outward strength; while shame, thou looking on,
Shame to be overcome or overreached,
Would utmost vigour raise, and raised unite.
Why shouldst not thou like sense within thee feel   *315*
When I am present, and thy trial choose
With me, best witness of thy virtue tried?"
    So spake domestic Adam in his care
And matrimonial love; but Eve, who thought
Less attributed to her faith sincere,   *320*
Thus her reply with accent sweet renewed:
    "If this be our condition, thus to dwell
In narrow circuit straitened by a foe,
Subtle or violent, we not endued
Single with like defense, wherever met,   *325*
How are we happy, still in fear of harm?

But harm precedes not sin: only our foe
Tempting affronts us with his foul esteem
Of our integrity; his foul esteem
Sticks no dishonour on our front, but turns   *330*
Foul on himself; then wherefore shunned or feared
By us? Who rather double honour gain
From his surmise proved false, find peace within,
Favour from Heav'n, our witness, from th' event.
And what is faith, love, virtue, unassayed   *335*
Alone, without exterior help sustained?
Let us not then suspect our happy state
Left so imperfect by the Maker wise
As not secure to single or combined.
Frail is our happiness, if this be so,   *340*
And Eden were no Eden thus exposed."
    To whom thus Adam fervently replied:
"O woman, best are all things as the will
Of God ordained them; his creating hand
Nothing imperfect or deficient left   *345*
Of all that he created, much less man,
Or aught that might his happy state secure,
Secure from outward force: within himself
The danger lies, yet lies within his power;
Against his will he can receive no harm.   *350*
But God left free the will, for what obeys
Reason is free, and reason he made right,
But bid her well beware, and still erect,
Lest by some fair appearing good surprised
She dictate false, and misinform the will   *355*
To do what God expressly hath forbid.
Not then mistrust, but tender love enjoins,
That I should mind thee oft, and mind thou me.
Firm we subsist, yet possible to swerve,
Since reason not impossibly may meet   *360*
Some specious object by the foe suborned,
And fall into deception unaware,
Not keeping strictest watch, as she was warned.
Seek not temptation then, which to avoid
Were better, and most likely if from me   *365*
Thou sever not; trial will come unsought.
Wouldst thou approve thy constancy, approve
First thy obedience; th' other who can know,
Not seeing thee attempted, who attest?
But if thou think trial unsought may find   *370*
Us both securer than thus warned thou seem'st,
Go; for thy stay, not free, absents thee more;

---

292. entire: intact, free. **310. access:** accession, addition, increase. **353. erect:** wide awake, alert. **358. mind** (1): remind. **367. approve:** prove, demonstrate. **371. securer:** overconfident, less careful.

Go in thy native innocence, rely
On what thou hast of virtue, summon all,
For God towards thee hath done his part; do thine." 375
  So spake the patriarch of mankind, but Eve
Persisted; yet submiss, though last, replied:
  "With thy permission then, and thus forewarned,
Chiefly by what thy own last reasoning words
Touched only, that our trial, when least sought, 380
May find us both perhaps far less prepared,
The willinger I go, nor much expect
A foe so proud will first the weaker seek;
So bent, the more shall shame him his repulse."
Thus saying, from her husband's hand her hand 385
Soft she withdrew, and like a wood-nymph light,
Oread or Dryad, or of Delia's train,
Betook her to the groves, but Delia's self
In gait surpassed and goddess-like deport,
Though not as she with bow and quiver armed, 390
But with such gard'ning tools as art yet rude,
Guiltless of fire, had formed, or angels brought.
To Pales, or Pomona, thus adorned,
Likest she seemed, Pomona when she fled
Vertumnus, or to Ceres in her prime, 395
Yet virgin of Proserpina from Jove.
Her long with ardent look his eye pursued
Delighted, but desiring more her stay.
Oft he to her his charge of quick return
Repeated, she to him as oft engaged 400
To be returned by noon amid the bow'r,
And all things in best order to invite
Noontide repast, or afternoon's repose.
O much deceived, much failing, hapless Eve,
Of thy presumed return! event perverse! 405
Thou never from that hour in Paradise
Found'st either sweet repast or sound repose;
Such ambush hid among sweet flow'rs and shades
Waited with hellish rancour imminent
To intercept thy way, or send thee back 410
Despoiled of innocence, of faith, of bliss.
For now, and since first break of dawn the Fiend,
Mere serpent in appearance, forth was come,
And on his quest, where likeliest he might find

The only two of mankind, but in them 415
The whole included race, his purposed prey.
In bow'r and field he sought, where any tuft
Of grove or garden-plot more pleasant lay,
Their tendance or plantation for delight;
By fountain or by shady rivulet 420
He sought them both, but wished his hap might find
Eve separate; he wished, but not with hope
Of what so seldom chanced, when to his wish,
Beyond his hope, Eve separate he spies,
Veiled in a cloud of fragrance, where she stood, 425
Half spied, so thick the roses bushing round
About her glowed, oft stooping to support
Each flow'r of slender stalk, whose head though gay
Carnation, purple, azure, or specked with gold,
Hung drooping unsustained; them she upstays 430
Gently with myrtle band, mindless the while,
Herself, though fairest unsupported flow'r,
From her best prop so far, and storm so nigh.
Nearer he drew, and many a walk traversed
Of stateliest covert, cedar, pine, or palm, 435
Then voluble and bold, now hid, now seen
Among thick-woven arborets and flow'rs
Imbordered on each bank, the hand of Eve:
Spot more delicious than those gardens feigned
Or of revived Adonis, or renowned 440
Alcinous, host of old Laertes' son,
Or that, not mystic, where the sapient king
Held dalliance with his fair Egyptian spouse.
Much he the place admired, the person more.
As one who long in populous city pent, 445
Where houses thick and sewers annoy the air,
Forth issuing on a summer's morn to breathe
Among the pleasant villages and farms
Adjoined, from each thing met conceives delight,
The smell of grain, or tedded grass, or kine, 450
Or dairy, each rural sight, each rural sound;
If chance with nymph-like step fair virgin pass,
What pleasing seemed, for her now pleases more,
She most, and in her look sums all delight:
Such pleasure took the Serpent to behold 455
This flow'ry plat, the sweet recess of Eve

---

387. Delia: Diana (Artemis; from Delos, the island of her birth). **389. deport:** deportment, bearing. **393-95:** Pales, Roman goddess of shepherds and flocks; Pomona, Roman goddess of fruit; Vertumnus, Roman god of the seasons, gardens, and orchards; Ceres, Roman goddess of agriculture, later mother of Proserpina (see IV, 269ff., and note); see Ovid's *Metamorphoses*, XIV, 623ff.; V, 341ff. **409. imminent:** also signifies "threatening." **436. voluble:** also signifies "turning, rolling." **437. arborets:** small trees or shrubs. **438. hand:** i.e., handiwork. **440:** The Garden of Adonis is where Venus nursed her mortally wounded but "revived" beloved; and see Spenser's *The Faerie Queene*, III, vi, 253ff. (stanzas 29ff.). **441:** Alcinous, king of the Phaeacians, was host to Laertes' son, Odysseus; his remarkable garden is described in *Odyssey*, VII, 112ff. **442-44:** See I Kings 3:1 and The Song of Solomon (the "sapient king"). **446. annoy:** make odious, noisome. **456. plat:** plot (of ground).

Thus early, thus alone; her heav'nly form
Angelic, but more soft and feminine,
Her graceful innocence, her every air
Of gesture or least action overawed   *460*
His malice, and with rapine sweet bereaved
His fierceness of the fierce intent it brought.
That space the Evil One abstracted stood
From his own evil, and for the time remained
Stupidly good, of enmity disarmed,   *465*
Of guile, of hate, of envy, of revenge;
But the hot Hell that always in him burns,
Though in mid Heav'n, soon ended his delight,
And tortures him now more, the more he sees
Of pleasure not for him ordained; then soon   *470*
Fierce hate he recollects, and all his thoughts
Of mischief, gratulating, thus excites:
    "Thoughts, whither have ye led me, with what sweet
Compulsion thus transported to forget
What hither brought us? Hate, not love, nor hope   *475*
Of Paradise for Hell, hope here to taste
Of pleasure, but all pleasure to destroy,
Save what is in destroying; other joy
To me is lost. Then let me not let pass
Occasion which now smiles: behold alone   *480*
The woman, opportune to all attempts,
Her husband, for I view far round, not nigh,
Whose higher intellectual more I shun,
And strength, of courage haughty, and of limb
Heroic built, though of terrestrial mould,   *485*
Foe not informidable, exempt from wound,
I not; so much hath Hell debased, and pain
Enfeebled me, to what I was in Heav'n.
She fair, divinely fair, fit love for gods,
Not terrible, though terror be in love   *490*
And beauty, not approached by stronger hate,
Hate stronger, under show of love well feigned,
The way which to her ruin now I tend."
    So spake the Enemy of mankind, enclosed
In Serpent, inmate bad, and toward Eve   *495*
Addressed his way, not with indented wave,
Prone on the ground, as since, but on his rear,
Circular base of rising folds, that tow'red
Fold above fold a surging maze; his head

Crested aloft, and carbuncle his eyes;   *500*
With burnished neck of verdant gold, erect
Amidst his circling spires, that on the grass
Floated redundant. Pleasing was his shape,
And lovely, never since of Serpent kind
Lovelier; not those that in Illyria changed   *505*
Hermione and Cadmus, or the god
In Epidaurus; nor to which transformed
Ammonian Jove, or Capitoline was seen,
He with Olympias, this with her who bore
Scipio, the highth of Rome. With tract oblique   *510*
At first, as one who sought access, but feared
To interrupt, sidelong he works his way.
As when a ship by skilful steersman wrought
Nigh river's mouth or foreland, where the wind
Veers oft, as oft so steers, and shifts her sail,   *515*
So varied he, and of his tortuous train
Curled many a wanton wreath in sight of Eve,
To lure her eye; she busied heard the sound
Of rustling leaves, but minded not, as used
To such disport before her through the field   *520*
From every beast, more duteous at her call
Than at Circean call the herd disguised.
He bolder now, uncalled before her stood,
But as in gaze admiring. Oft he bowed
His turret crest, and sleek enamelled neck,   *525*
Fawning, and licked the ground whereon she trod.
His gentle dumb expression turned at length
The eye of Eve to mark his play; he glad
Of her attention gained, with Serpent tongue
Organic, or impulse of vocal air,   *530*
His fraudulent temptation thus began:
    "Wonder not, sovran mistress, if perhaps
Thou canst, who art sole wonder, much less arm
Thy looks, the Heav'n of mildness, with disdain,
Displeased that I approach thee thus, and gaze   *535*
Insatiate, I thus single, nor have feared
Thy awful brow, more awful thus retired.
Fairest resemblance of thy Maker fair,
Thee all things living gaze on, all things thine
By gift, and thy celestial beauty adore,   *540*
With ravishment beheld, there best beheld
Where universally admired; but here

---

502. spires: spirals, coils. **505-06:** Cadmus (see note on *Areopagitica*, 7-8, p. 322), king of Thebes, and his queen Hermione (or Harmonia), were changed into serpents (see Ovid, *Metamorphoses*, IV, 562ff.). **506-07:** Aesculapius, god of medicine, who has a temple at Epidaurus, sometimes took the form of a serpent (cf. the caduceus; see Ovid, *Metamorphoses*, XV, 622ff.). **507-10:** A legend relates that Jupiter Ammon, as a serpent, fathered Alexander the Great on Olympias, wife of Philip of Macedon; another that Jupiter Capitolinus (i.e., of Rome) fathered Scipio Africanus, hero of Rome, on Sempronia. **510. tract:** track. **522. herd disguised:** the very friendly beasts into which Circe the enchantress had changed men (*Odyssey*, X, 212ff.).

In this enclosure wild, these beasts among,
Beholders rude, and shallow to discern
Half what in thee is fair, one man except,   545
Who sees thee? (and what is one?) who shouldst be seen
A Goddess among Gods, adored and served
By Angels numberless, thy daily train."
      So glozed the Tempter, and his proem tuned;
Into the heart of Eve his words made way,   550
Though at the voice much marvelling; at length
Not unamazed she thus in answer spake:
      "What may this mean? Language of man pronounced
By tongue of brute, and human sense expressed?
The first at least of these I thought denied   555
To beasts, whom God on their creation-day
Created mute to all articulate sound;
The latter I demur, for in their looks
Much reason, and in their actions oft appears.
Thee, Serpent, subtlest beast of all the field   560
I knew, but not with human voice endued;
Redouble then this miracle, and say,
How cam'st thou speakable of mute, and how
To me so friendly grown above the rest
Of brutal kind, that daily are in sight?   565
Say, for such wonder claims attention due."
      To whom the guileful Tempter thus replied:
"Empress of this fair world, resplendent Eve,
Easy to me it is to tell thee all
What thou command'st, and right thou shouldst be obeyed.
I was at first as other beasts that graze   571
The trodden herb, of abject thoughts and low,
As was my food, nor aught but food discerned
Or sex, and apprehended nothing high:
Till on a day roving the field, I chanced   575
A goodly tree far distant to behold,
Loaden with fruit of fairest colours mixed,
Ruddy and gold. I nearer drew to gaze;
When from the boughs a savoury odour blown,
Grateful to appetite, more pleased my sense   580
Than smell of sweetest fennel or the teats
Of ewe or goat dropping with milk at ev'n,
Unsucked of lamb or kid, that tend their play.
To satisfy the sharp desire I had
Of tasting those fair apples, I resolved   585
Not to defer; hunger and thirst at once,
Powerful persuaders, quickened at the scent

Of that alluring fruit, urged me so keen.
About the mossy trunk I wound me soon,
For high from ground the branches would require   590
Thy utmost reach or Adam's: round the tree
All other beasts that saw, with like desire
Longing and envying stood, but could not reach.
Amid the tree now got, where plenty hung
Tempting so nigh, to pluck and eat my fill   595
I spared not, for such pleasure till that hour
At feed or fountain never had I found.
Sated at length, ere long I might perceive
Strange alteration in me, to degree
Of reason in my inward powers, and speech   600
Wanted not long, though to this shape retained.
Thenceforth to speculations high or deep
I turned my thoughts, and with capacious mind
Considered all things visible in Heav'n,
Or Earth, or middle, all things fair and good;   605
But all that fair and good in thy divine
Semblance, and in thy beauty's heav'nly ray
United I beheld; no fair to thine
Equivalent or second, which compelled
Me thus, though importune perhaps, to come   610
And gaze, and worship thee of right declared
Sovran of creatures, universal dame."
      So talked the spirited sly Snake; and Eve
Yet more amazed unwary thus replied:
      "Serpent, thy overpraising leaves in doubt   615
The virtue of that fruit, in thee first proved.
But say, where grows the tree, from hence how far?
For many are the trees of God that grow
In Paradise, and various, yet unknown
To us; in such abundance lies our choice   620
As leaves a greater store of fruit untouched,
Still hanging incorruptible, till men
Grow up to their provision, and more hands
Help to disburden Nature of her bearth."
      To whom the wily Adder, blithe and glad: 625
"Empress, the way is ready, and not long,
Beyond a row of myrtles, on a flat,
Fast by a fountain, one small thicket past
Of blowing myrrh and balm; if thou accept
My conduct, I can bring thee thither soon."   630
      "Lead then," said Eve. He leading swiftly rolled
In tangles, and made intricate seem straight,

---

558. demur: have doubts about. **581-83:** Snakes were popularly thought to like fennel and to suck the milk of sheep and goats. **605. middle:** i.e., the air. **624. bearth:** a nonce-form perhaps to suggest the combined senses of the "burden" Nature bears, bearing fruit, giving birth, and the things she gives birth to.

To mischief swift. Hope elevates, and joy
Brightens his crest, as when a wand'ring fire,
Compact of unctuous vapour, which the night   *635*
Condenses, and the cold environs round,
Kindled through agitation to a flame,
Which oft, they say, some evil Spirit attends,
Hovering and blazing with delusive light,
Misleads th' amazed night-wanderer from his way   *640*
To bogs and mires, and oft through pond or pool,
There swallowed up and lost, from succour far.
So glistered the dire Snake, and into fraud
Led Eve our credulous mother, to the tree
Of prohibition, root of all our woe;   *645*
Which when she saw, thus to her guide she spake:
    "Serpent, we might have spared our coming hither,
Fruitless to me, though fruit be here to excess,
The credit of whose virtue rest with thee,
Wondrous indeed, if cause of such effects.   *650*
But of this tree we may not taste nor touch;
God so commanded, and left that command
Sole daughter of his voice; the rest, we live
Law to ourselves, our reason is our law."
    To whom the Tempter guilefully replied: *655*
"Indeed? Hath God then said that of the fruit
Of all these garden trees ye shall not eat,
Yet lords declared of all in Earth or air?"
    To whom thus Eve yet sinless: "Of the fruit
Of each tree in the garden we may eat,   *660*
But of the fruit of this fair tree amidst
The garden, God hath said, 'Ye shall not eat
Thereof, nor shall ye touch it, lest ye die.'"
    She scarce had said, though brief, when now more bold
The Tempter, but with show of zeal and love   *665*
To man, and indignation at his wrong,
New part puts on, and as to passion moved,
Fluctuates disturbed, yet comely, and in act
Raised, as of some great matter to begin.
As when of old some orator renowned   *670*
In Athens or free Rome, where eloquence
Flourished, since mute, to some great cause addressed,
Stood in himself collected, while each part,
Motion, each act won audience ere the tongue,
Sometimes in highth began, as no delay   *675*
Of preface brooking through his zeal of right:
So standing, moving, or to highth upgrown,
The Tempter all impassioned thus began:

    "O sacred, wise, and wisdom-giving Plant,
Mother of science, now I feel thy power   *680*
Within me clear, not only to discern
Things in their causes, but to trace the ways
Of highest agents, deemed however wise.
Queen of this Universe, do not believe
Those rigid threats of death; ye shall not die: *685*
How should ye? By the fruit? It gives you life
To knowledge; by the Threat'ner? Look on me,
Me who have touched and tasted, yet both live,
And life more perfect have attained than fate
Meant me, by vent'ring higher than my lot.   *690*
Shall that be shut to man, which to the beast
Is open? Or will God incense his ire
For such a petty trespass, and not praise
Rather your dauntless virtue, whom the pain
Of death denounced, whatever thing death be,   *695*
Deterred not from achieving what might lead
To happier life, knowledge of good and evil?
Of good, how just? Of evil, if what is evil
Be real, why not known, since easier shunned?
God therefore cannot hurt ye, and be just;   *700*
Not just, not God; not feared then, nor obeyed:
Your fear itself of death removes the fear.
Why then was this forbid? Why but to awe,
Why but to keep ye low and ignorant,
His worshipers? He knows that in the day   *705*
Ye eat thereof, your eyes that seem so clear,
Yet are but dim, shall perfectly be then
Opened and cleared, and ye shall be as gods,
Knowing both good and evil as they know.
That ye should be as gods, since I as man,   *710*
Internal man, is but proportion meet,
I of brute human, ye of human gods.
So ye shall die perhaps, by putting off
Human, to put on gods, death to be wished,
Though threatened, which no worse than this can bring.
And what are gods that man may not become   *716*
As they, participating godlike food?
The gods are first, and that advantage use
On our belief, that all from them proceeds;
I question it, for this fair Earth I see,   *720*
Warmed by the sun, producing every kind,
Them nothing. If they all things, who enclosed
Knowledge of good and evil in this tree,
That whoso eats thereof, forthwith attains

634-42: describing the ignis fatuus, will-o'-the-wisp, jack-o'-lantern. **635. Compact:** composed, made. **643. fraud:** deceit, injury. **654:** See Romans 2:14. **656-63, 685, 705-09:** See Genesis 3:1-5 (p. 244). **680. science:** knowledge. **711. Internal man:** See 599-601 above.

Wisdom without their leave? And wherein lies   725
Th' offense, that man should thus attain to know?
What can your knowledge hurt him, or this tree
Impart against his will, if all be his?
Or is it envy, and can envy dwell
In heav'nly breasts? These, these and many more   730
Causes import your need of this fair fruit.
Goddess humane, reach then, and freely taste!"
    He ended, and his words replete with guile
Into her heart too easy entrance won.
Fixed on the fruit she gazed, which to behold   735
Might tempt alone, and in her ears the sound
Yet rung of his persuasive words, impregned
With reason, to her seeming, and with truth;
Meanwhile the hour of noon drew on, and waked
An eager appetite, raised by the smell   740
So savoury of that fruit, which with desire,
Inclinable now grown to touch or taste,
Solicited her longing eye; yet first
Pausing a while, thus to herself she mused:
    "Great are thy virtues, doubtless, best of fruits, 745
Though kept from man, and worthy to be admired,
Whose taste, too long forborne, at first assay
Gave elocution to the mute, and taught
The tongue not made for speech to speak thy praise.
Thy praise he also who forbids thy use   750
Conceals not from us, naming thee the Tree
Of Knowledge, knowledge both of good and evil;
Forbids us then to taste, but his forbidding
Commends thee more, while it infers the good
By thee communicated, and our want;   755
For good unknown sure is not had, or had
And yet unknown, is as not had at all.
In plain then, what forbids he but to know,
Forbids us good, forbids us to be wise?
Such prohibitions bind not. But if Death   760
Bind us with after-bands, what profits then
Our inward freedom? In the day we eat
Of this fair fruit, our doom is, we shall die.
How dies the Serpent? He hath eat'n and lives,
And knows, and speaks, and reasons, and discerns,   765
Irrational till then. For us alone
Was death invented? Or to us denied
This intellectual food, for beasts reserved?
For beasts it seems; yet that one beast which first
Hath tasted, envies not, but brings with joy   770

The good befall'n him, author unsuspect,
Friendly to man, far from deceit or guile.
What fear I then, rather what know to fear
Under this ignorance of good and evil,
Of God or death, of law or penalty?   775
Here grows the cure of all, this fruit divine,
Fair to the eye, inviting to the taste,
Of virtue to make wise; what hinders then
To reach, and feed at once both body and mind?"
    So saying, her rash hand in evil hour   780
Forth reaching to the fruit, she plucked, she eat.
Earth felt the wound, and Nature from her seat
Sighing through all her works gave signs of woe,
That all was lost. Back to the thicket slunk
The guilty Serpent, and well might, for Eve   785
Intent now wholly on her taste, naught else
Regarded; such delight till then, as seemed,
In fruit she never tasted, whether true
Or fancied so, through expectation high
Of knowledge, nor was Godhead from her thought.   790
Greedily she engorged without restraint,
And knew not eating death. Satiate at length,
And heightened as with wine, jocund and boon,
Thus to herself she pleasingly began:
    "O sovran, virtuous, precious of all trees   795
In Paradise, of operation blest
To sapience, hitherto obscured, infamed,
And thy fair fruit let hang, as to no end
Created; but henceforth my early care,
Not without song, each morning, and due praise,   800
Shall tend thee, and the fertile burden ease
Of thy full branches offered free to all;
Till dieted by thee I grow mature
In knowledge, as the gods who all things know;
Though others envy what they cannot give;   805
For had the gift been theirs, it had not here
Thus grown. Experience, next to thee I owe,
Best guide; not following thee, I had remained
In ignorance; thou open'st wisdom's way,
And giv'st access, though secret she retire.   810
And I perhaps am secret; Heav'n is high,
High and remote to see from thence distinct
Each thing on earth; and other care perhaps
May have diverted from continual watch
Our great Forbidder, safe with all his spies   815
About him. But to Adam in what sort

735-43, 781, 996-97: See Genesis 3:6 (p. 244). **758. in plain:** i.e., in plain terms, put simply. **771. author:** also means "authority."

Shall I appear? Shall I to him make known
As yet my change, and give him to partake
Full happiness with me, or rather not,
But keep the odds of knowledge in my power   820
Without copartner? So to add what wants
In female sex, the more to draw his love,
And render me more equal, and perhaps,
A thing not undesirable, sometime
Superior; for inferior who is free?   825
This may be well. But what if God have seen,
And death ensue? Then I shall be no more,
And Adam wedded to another Eve
Shall live with her enjoying, I extinct;
A death to think. Confirmed then I resolve,   830
Adam shall share with me in bliss or woe.
So dear I love him, that with him all deaths
I could endure, without him live no life."
    So saying, from the tree her step she turned,
But first low reverence done, as to the power   835
That dwelt within, whose presence had infused
Into the plant sciential sap, derived
From nectar, drink of gods. Adam the while
Waiting desirous her return, had wove
Of choicest flow'rs a garland to adorn   840
Her tresses, and her rural labours crown,
As reapers oft are wont their harvest queen.
Great joy he promised to his thoughts, and new
Solace in her return, so long delayed;
Yet oft his heart, divine of something ill,   845
Misgave him; he the falt'ring measure felt;
And forth to meet her went, the way she took
That morn when first they parted. By the Tree
Of Knowledge he must pass; there he her met,
Scarce from the tree returning; in her hand   850
A bough of fairest fruit that downy smiled,
New gathered, and ambrosial smell diffused.
To him she hasted; in her face excuse
Came prologue, and apology to prompt,
Which with bland words at will she thus addressed:
    "Hast thou not wondered, Adam, at my stay?   856
Thee I have missed, and thought it long, deprived
Thy presence, agony of love till now
Not felt, nor shall be twice, for never more
Mean I to try what rash untried I sought,   860
The pain of absence from thy sight. But strange
Hath been the cause, and wonderful to hear:

This tree is not as we are told, a tree
Of danger tasted, nor to evil unknown
Op'ning the way, but of divine effect   865
To open eyes, and make them gods who taste;
And hath been tasted such. The Serpent wise,
Or not restrained as we, or not obeying,
Hath eaten of the fruit, and is become
Not dead, as we are threatened, but thenceforth   870
Endued with human voice and human sense,
Reasoning to admiration, and with me
Persuasively hath so prevailed, that I
Have also tasted, and have also found
Th' effects to correspond, opener mine eyes,   875
Dim erst, dilated spirits, ampler heart,
And growing up to Godhead; which for thee
Chiefly I sought, without thee can despise.
For bliss, as thou hast part, to me is bliss;
Tedious, unshared with thee, and odious soon.   880
Thou therefore also taste, that equal lot
May join us, equal joy, as equal love;
Lest thou not tasting, different degree
Disjoin us, and I then too late renounce
Deity for thee, when fate will not permit."   885
    Thus Eve with count'nance blithe her story told;
But in her cheek distemper flushing glowed.
On th' other side, Adam, soon as he heard
The fatal trespass done by Eve, amazed,
Astonied stood and blank, while horror chill   890
Ran through his veins, and all his joints relaxed;
From his slack hand the garland wreathed for Eve
Down dropped, and all the faded roses shed.
Speechless he stood and pale, till thus at length
First to himself he inward silence broke: 895
    "O fairest of creation, last and best
Of all God's works, creature in whom excelled
Whatever can to sight or thought be formed,
Holy, divine, good, amiable, or sweet!
How art thou lost, how on a sudden lost,   900
Defaced, deflow'red, and now to death devote!
Rather how hast thou yielded to transgress
The strict forbiddance, how to violate
The sacred fruit forbidd'n! Some cursed fraud
Of enemy hath beguiled thee, yet unknown,   905
And me with thee hath ruined, for with thee
Certain my resolution is to die;
How can I live without thee, how forgo

---

845. **divine:** divining, foreseeing. 846. **falt'ring measure:** i.e., unsteady heartbeat. 887. **distemper:** an upsetting of the balance of the four humours (see note on line 420 of Chaucer's "General Prologue," p. 34); and see 1131 below. 901. **devote:** doomed.

Thy sweet converse and love so dearly joined,
To live again in these wild woods forlorn? *910*
Should God create another Eve, and I
Another rib afford, yet loss of thee
Would never from my heart; no, no! I feel
The link of nature draw me: flesh of flesh,
Bone of my bone thou art, and from thy state *915*
Mine never shall be parted, bliss or woe."

   So having said, as one from sad dismay
Recomforted, and after thoughts disturbed
Submitting to what seemed remédiless,
Thus in calm mood his words to Eve he turned: *920*
   "Bold deed thou hast presumed, advent'rous Eve,
And peril great provoked, who thus hast dared
Had it been only coveting to eye
That sacred fruit, sacred to abstinence,
Much more to taste it under ban to touch. *925*
But past who can recall, or done undo?
Not God omnipotent, nor fate. Yet so
Perhaps thou shalt not die; perhaps the fact
Is not so heinous now, foretasted fruit,
Profaned first by the Serpent, by him first *930*
Made common and unhallowed ere our taste,
Nor yet on him found deadly; he yet lives,
Lives, as thou saidst, and gains to live as man
Higher degree of life, inducement strong
To us, as likely tasting to attain *935*
Proportional ascent, which cannot be
But to be gods, or angels, demi-gods.
Nor can I think that God, Creator wise,
Though threat'ning, will in earnest so destroy
Us his prime creatures, dignified so high, *940*
Set over all his works, which in our fall,
For us created, needs with us must fail,
Dependent made; so God shall uncreate,
Be frustrate, do, undo, and labour lose,
Not well conceived of God, who though his power *945*
Creation could repeat, yet would be loath
Us to abolish, lest the Adversary
Triumph and say: 'Fickle their state whom God
Most favours, who can please him long? Me first
He ruined, now mankind; whom will he next?' *950*
Matter of scorn not to be given the Foe;
However, I with thee have fixed my lot,
Certain to undergo like doom: if death
Consort with thee, death is to me as life;

So forcible within my heart I feel *955*
The bond of nature draw me to my own,
My own in thee, for what thou art is mine;
Our state cannot be severed; we are one,
One flesh; to lose thee were to lose myself."

   So Adam, and thus Eve to him replied: *960*
"O glorious trial of exceeding love,
Illustrious evidence, example high!
Engaging me to emulate, but short
Of thy perfection, how shall I attain,
Adam? From whose dear side I boast me sprung, *965*
And gladly of our union hear thee speak,
One heart, one soul in both; whereof good proof
This day affords, declaring thee resolved,
Rather than death or aught than death more dread
Shall separate us, linked in love so dear, *970*
To undergo with me one guilt, one crime,
If any be, of tasting this fair fruit,
Whose virtue (for of good still good proceeds,
Direct, or by occasion) hath presented
This happy trial of thy love, which else *975*
So eminently never had been known.
Were it I thought death menaced would ensue
This my attempt, I would sustain alone
The worst, and not persuade thee, rather die
Deserted, than oblige thee with a fact *980*
Pernicious to thy peace, chiefly assured
Remarkably so late of thy so true,
So faithful love unequalled; but I feel
Far otherwise th' event, not death, but life
Augmented, opened eyes, new hopes, new joys, *985*
Taste so divine, that what of sweet before
Hath touched my sense, flat seems to this and harsh.
On my experience, Adam, freely taste,
And fear of death deliver to the winds."

   So saying, she embraced him, and for joy *990*
Tenderly wept, much won that he his love
Had so ennobled, as of choice to incur
Divine displeasure for her sake, or death.
In recompense (for such compliance bad
Such recompense best merits) from the bough *995*
She gave him of that fair enticing fruit
With liberal hand. He scrupled not to eat
Against his better knowledge, not deceived,
But fondly overcome with female charm.
Earth trembled from her entrails, as again *1000*

914-15: See Genesis 2:23 (p. 244). **953. certain:** resolved, determined. **980. oblige:** involve in guilt, fetter, ensnare. **998:** See I Timothy 2:14.

In pangs, and Nature gave a second groan;
Sky loured and, muttering thunder, some sad drops
Wept at completing of the mortal sin
Original; while Adam took no thought,
Eating his fill, nor Eve to iterate   *1005*
Her former trespass feared, the more to soothe
Him with her loved society, that now
As with new wine intoxicated both
They swim in mirth, and fancy that they feel
Divinity within them breeding wings   *1010*
Wherewith to scorn the Earth. But that false fruit
Far other operation first displayed,
Carnal desire inflaming: he on Eve
Began to cast lascivious eyes, she him
As wantonly repaid; in lust they burn,   *1015*
Till Adam thus 'gan Eve to dalliance move:
    "Eve, now I see thou art exact of taste,
And elegant, of sapience no small part;
Since to each meaning savour we apply,
And palate call judicious; I the praise   *1020*
Yield thee, so well this day thou hast purveyed.
Much pleasure we have lost, while we abstained
From this delightful fruit, nor known till now
True relish, tasting; if such pleasure be
In things to us forbidden, it might be wished   *1025*
For this one tree had been forbidden ten.
But come, so well refreshed, now let us play,
As meet is, after such delicious fare;
For never did thy beauty since the day
I saw thee first and wedded thee, adorned   *1030*
With all perfections, so inflame my sense
With ardour to enjoy thee, fairer now
Than ever, bounty of this virtuous tree."
    So said he, and forbore not glance or toy
Of amorous intent, well understood   *1035*
Of Eve, whose eye darted contagious fire.
Her hand he seized, and to a shady bank,
Thick overhead with verdant roof embow'red,
He led her nothing loath; flow'rs were the couch,
Pansies, and violets, and asphodel,   *1040*
And hyacinth, Earth's freshest softest lap.
There they their fill of love and love's disport
Took largely, of their mutual guilt the seal,
The solace of their sin, till dewy sleep

Oppressed them, wearied with their amorous play.   *1045*
Soon as the force of that fallacious fruit,
That with exhilarating vapour bland
About their spirits had played, and inmost powers
Made err, was now exhaled, and grosser sleep
Bred of unkindly fumes, with conscious dreams   *1050*
Encumbered, now had left them, up they rose
As from unrest, and each the other viewing,
Soon found their eyes how opened, and their minds
How darkened; innocence, that as a veil
Had shadowed them from knowing ill, was gone;   *1055*
Just confidence, and native righteousness,
And honour from about them, naked left
To guilty Shame; he covered, but his robe
Uncovered more. So rose the Danite strong,
Herculean Samson, from the harlot-lap   *1060*
Of Philistean Dalilah, and waked
Shorn of his strength; they destitute and bare
Of all their virtue: silent, and in face
Confounded, long they sat, as strucken mute,
Till Adam, though not less than Eve abashed,   *1065*
At length gave utterance to these words constrained:
    "O Eve, in evil hour thou didst give ear
To that false Worm, of whomsoever taught
To counterfeit man's voice, true in our fall,
False in our promised rising; since our eyes   *1070*
Opened we find indeed, and find we know
Both good and evil, good lost and evil got,
Bad fruit of knowledge, if this be to know,
Which leaves us naked thus, of honour void,
Of innocence, of faith, of purity,   *1075*
Our wonted ornaments now soiled and stained,
And in our faces evident the signs
Of foul concupiscence; whence evil store,
Even shame, the last of evils; of the first
Be sure then. How shall I behold the face   *1080*
Henceforth of God or angel, erst with joy
And rapture so oft beheld? Those Heav'nly shapes
Will dazzle now this Earthly, with their blaze
Insufferably bright. O might I here
In solitude live savage, in some glade   *1085*
Obscured, where highest woods impenetrable
To star or sunlight, spread their umbrage broad
And brown as evening! Cover me, ye pines,

1017-20: "Sapience" is from Latin *sapere*, to taste, to have good taste, to be wise (also the root of "savour"); see also 797 above. **1027-33:** See Exodus 32:6, I Corinthians 10:7, and cf. *Iliad*, III, 441ff. **1034. toy:** caress. **1042-44:** Cf. Proverbs 7:18. **1050. unkindly:** unnatural. **1052ff., 1099ff.:** See Genesis 3:7 (p. 244). **1059-62:** See Judges 16.

Ye cedars, with innumerable boughs
Hide me, where I may never see them more.   *1090*
But let us now, as in bad plight, devise
What best may for the present serve to hide
The parts of each from other that seem most
To shame obnoxious, and unseemliest seen,
Some tree whose broad smooth leaves together sewed, *1095*
And girded on our loins, may cover round
Those middle parts, that this newcomer, Shame,
There sit not, and reproach us as unclean."
    So counseled he, and both together went
Into the thickest wood; there soon they chose   *1100*
The fig-tree, not that kind for fruit renowned,
But such as at this day to Indians known
In Malabar or Deccan spreads her arms
Branching so broad and long, that in the ground
The bended twigs take root, and daughters grow   *1105*
About the mother tree, a pillared shade
High overarched, and echoing walks between;
There oft the Indian herdsman shunning heat
Shelters in cool, and tends his pasturing herds
At loop-holes cut through thickest shade. Those leaves *1110*
They gathered, broad as Amazonian targe,
And with what skill they had, together sewed,
To gird their waist, vain covering if to hide
Their guilt and dreaded shame; O how unlike
To that first naked glory! Such of late   *1115*
Columbus found th' American so girt
With feathered cincture, naked else and wild
Among the trees on isles and woody shores.
Thus fenced, and as they thought, their shame in part
Covered, but not at rest or ease of mind,   *1120*
They sat them down to weep; nor only tears
Rained at their eyes, but high winds worse within
Began to rise, high passions, anger, hate,
Mistrust, suspicion, discord, and shook sore
Their inward state of mind, calm region once   *1125*
And full of peace, now tossed and turbulent;
For understanding ruled not, and the will
Heard not her lore, both in subjection now
To sensual appetite, who from beneath
Usurping over sovran reason claimed   *1130*
Superior sway. From thus distempered breast,

Adam, estranged in look and altered style,
Speech intermitted thus to Eve renewed:
    "Would thou hadst hearkened to my words, and stayed
With me, as I besought thee, when that strange   *1135*
Desire of wand'ring this unhappy morn,
I know not whence possessed thee; we had then
Remained still happy, not as now, despoiled
Of all our good, shamed, naked, miserable.
Let none henceforth seek needless cause to approve   *1140*
The faith they owe; when earnestly they seek
Such proof, conclude they then begin to fail."
    To whom, soon moved with touch of blame, thus Eve:
"What words have passed thy lips, Adam severe!
Imput'st thou that to my default, or will   *1145*
Of wand'ring, as thou call'st it, which who knows
But might as ill have happened thou being by,
Or to thyself perhaps? Hadst thou been there,
Or here th' attempt, thou couldst not have discerned
Fraud in the Serpent, speaking as he spake;   *1150*
No ground of enmity between us known
Why he should mean me ill, or seek to harm.
Was I to have never parted from thy side?
As good have grown there still a lifeless rib.
Being as I am, why didst not thou, the head,   *1155*
Command me absolutely not to go,
Going into such danger as thou saidst?
Too facile then, thou didst not much gainsay,
Nay didst permit, approve, and fair dismiss.
Hadst thou been firm and fixed in thy dissent,   *1160*
Neither had I transgressed, nor thou with me."
    To whom then first incensed Adam replied:
"Is this the love, is this the recompense
Of mine to thee, ingrateful Eve, expressed
Immutable when thou wert lost, not I,   *1165*
Who might have lived and joyed immortal bliss,
Yet willingly chose rather death with thee?
And am I now upbraided, as the cause
Of thy transgressing? Not enough severe,
It seems, in thy restraint. What could I more?   *1170*
I warned thee, I admonished thee, foretold
The danger, and the lurking enemy
That lay in wait; beyond this had been force,
And force upon free will hath here no place.

1100ff.: The details about the banyan or Indian fig-tree probably come from Gerard's *Herbal, or General History of Plants* (1597; rev. 1633); Pliny in his *Natural History* erred in saying its leaves were large like an Amazon's shield (targe, 1111). **1121:** Cf. Psalms 137:1. **1141. owe:** own. **1155. head:** See I Corinthians 11:3.

But confidence then bore thee on, secure   *1175*
Either to meet no danger, or to find
Matter of glorious trial; and perhaps
I also erred in overmuch admiring
What seemed in thee so perfect, that I thought
No evil durst attempt thee, but I rue   *1180*
That error now, which is become my crime,
And thou th' accuser. Thus it shall befall

Him who to worth in women overtrusting
Lets her will rule; restraint she will not brook,
And left to herself, if evil thence ensue,   *1185*
She first his weak indulgence will accuse."
      Thus they in mutual accusation spent
The fruitless hours, but neither self-condemning,
And of their vain contest appeared no end.

from BOOK X

The Argument

Man's transgression known, the guardian angels forsake Paradise, and return up to Heaven to approve their vigilance, and are approved, God declaring that the entrance of Satan could not be by them prevented. He sends his Son to judge the transgressors; who descends and gives sentence accordingly; then in pity clothes them both, and reascends. Sin and Death, sitting till then at the gates of Hell, by wondrous sympathy feeling the success of Satan in this new world, and the sin   *5* by man there committed, resolve to sit no longer confined in Hell but to follow Satan their sire up to the place of man. To make the way easier from Hell to this world to and fro, they pave a broad highway or bridge over Chaos, according to the track that Satan first made; then, preparing for Earth, they meet him, proud of his success, returning to Hell; their mutual gratulation. Satan arrives at Pandemonium; in full assembly relates, with boasting, his success against man; instead   *10* of applause is entertained with a general hiss by all his audience, transformed, with himself also, suddenly into serpents, according to his doom given in Paradise; then, deluded with a show of the Forbidden Tree springing up before them, they, greedily reaching to take of the fruit, chew dust and bitter ashes. The proceedings of Sin and Death; God foretells the final victory of his Son over them, and the renewing of all things; but for the present commands his angels to make several   *15* alterations in the heavens and elements. Adam, more and more perceiving his fallen condition, heavily bewails, rejects the condolement of Eve; she persists, and at length appeases him: then, to evade the curse likely to fall on their offspring, proposes to Adam violent ways, which he approves not, but, conceiving better hope, puts her in mind of the late promise made them, that her seed should be revenged on the Serpent, and exhorts her with him to seek peace of the   *20* offended Deity by repentance and supplication.

from BOOK XI

The Argument

The Son of God presents to his Father the prayers of our first parents now repenting, and intercedes for them. God accepts them, but declares that they must no longer abide in Paradise; sends Michael with a band of Cherubim to dispossess them, but first to reveal to Adam future things; Michael's coming down. Adam shows to Eve certain ominous signs; he discerns Michael's approach; goes out to meet him; the Angel denounces their departure. Eve's lamentation. Adam   *5* pleads, but submits; the Angel leads him up a high hill; sets before him in vision what shall happen till the Flood.

from BOOK XII

The Argument

The Angel Michael continues from the Flood to relate what shall succeed; then, in the mention of Abraham, comes by degrees to explain who that Seed of the Woman shall be which was promised Adam and Eve in the Fall; his incarnation, death, resurrection, and ascension; the state of the church till his second coming. Adam, greatly satisfied and recomforted by these relations and promises, descends the hill with Michael; wakens Eve, who all this while had slept, but with   *5* gentle dreams composed to quietness of mind and submission. Michael in either hand leads them out of Paradise, the fiery sword waving behind them, and the Cherubim taking their stations to guard the place.

             . . . .

So spake th' Archangel Michael, then paused,
As at the world's great period; and our sire
Replete with joy and wonder thus replied:
  "O goodness infinite, goodness immense!
That all this good of evil shall produce,   *470*
And evil turn to good; more wonderful
Than that which by creation first brought forth
Light out of darkness! Full of doubt I stand,
Whether I should repent me now of sin
By me done and occasioned, or rejoice   *475*
Much more, that much more good thereof shall spring,
To God more glory, more good will to men
From God, and over wrath grace shall abound.
But say, if our Deliverer up to Heav'n
Must reascend, what will betide the few   *480*
His faithful, left among th' unfaithful herd,
The enemies of truth; who then shall guide
His people, who defend? Will they not deal
Worse with his followers than with him they dealt?"
  "Be sure they will," said th' Angel; "but from Heav'n   *485*
He to his own a Comforter will send,
The promise of the Father, who shall dwell,
His Spirit, within them, and the law of faith
Working through love, upon their hearts shall write,
To guide them in all truth, and also arm   *490*
With spiritual armour, able to resist
Satan's assaults, and quench his fiery darts,
What man can do against them, not afraid,
Though to the death, against such cruelties
With inward consolations recompensed,   *495*
And oft supported so as shall amaze

Their proudest persecutors. For the Spirit
Poured first on his Apostles, whom he sends
To evangelize the nations, then on all
Baptized, shall them with wondrous gifts endue   *500*
To speak all tongues, and do all miracles,
As did their Lord before them. Thus they win
Great numbers of each nation to receive
With joy the tidings brought from Heav'n: at length
Their ministry performed, and race well run,   *505*
Their doctrine and their story written left,
They die; but in their room, as they forewarn,
Wolves shall succeed for teachers, grievous wolves,
Who all the sacred mysteries of Heav'n
To their own vile advantages shall turn   *510*
Of lucre and ambition, and the truth
With superstitions and traditions taint,
Left only in those written records pure,
Though not but by the Spirit understood.
Then shall they seek to avail themselves of names,   *515*
Places and titles, and with these to join
Secular power, though feigning still to act
By spiritual, to themselves appropriating
The Spirit of God, promised alike and giv'n
To all believers; and from that pretense,   *520*
Spiritual laws by carnal power shall force
On every conscience; laws which none shall find
Left them enrolled, or what the Spirit within
Shall on the heart engrave. What will they then
But force the Spirit of Grace itself, and bind   *525*
His consort Liberty, what but unbuild
His living temples, built by faith to stand,
Their own faith, not another's; for on earth

BOOK XII   469-78: a statement of the concept of the "fortunate fall," or *felix culpa*. **478:** See Romans 5:20. **485-88:** See John 14:16 and 26; 15:26. **490-92:** See Ephesians 6:11-17, and Spenser's "A Letter of the Authors," 80-82 (p. 152). **507ff.:** Cf. *Lycidas*, 113ff. (p. 317). **508. grievous wolves:** See Acts 20:29, and *Lycidas*, 128 (p. 317).

Who against faith and conscience can be heard
Infallible? Yet many will presume: 530
Whence heavy persecution shall arise
On all who in the worship persevere
Of Spirit and Truth; the rest, far greater part,
Will deem in outward rites and specious forms
Religion satisfied; Truth shall retire 535
Bestuck with sland'rous darts, and works of faith
Rarely be found. So shall the world go on,
To good malignant, to bad men benign,
Under her own weight groaning, till the day
Appear of respiration to the just, 540
And vengeance to the wicked, at return
Of him so lately promised to thy aid,
The Woman's Seed, obscurely then foretold,
Now amplier known thy Saviour and thy Lord,
Last in the clouds from Heav'n to be revealed 545
In glory of the Father, to dissolve
Satan with his perverted world; then raise
From the conflagrant mass, purged and refined,
New Heav'ns, new Earth, ages of endless date
Founded in righteousness and peace and love, 550
To bring forth fruits, joy and eternal bliss."
    He ended; and thus Adam last replied:
"How soon hath thy prediction, seer blest,
Measured this transient world, the race of time,
Till time stand fixed: beyond is all abyss, 555
Eternity, whose end no eye can reach.
Greatly instructed I shall hence depart,
Greatly in peace of thought, and have my fill
Of knowledge, what this vessel can contain;
Beyond which was my folly to aspire. 560
Henceforth I learn that to obey is best,
And love with fear the only God, to walk
As in his presence, ever to observe
His providence, and on him sole depend,
Merciful over all his works, with good 565
Still overcoming evil, and by small
Accomplishing great things, by things deemed weak
Subverting worldly strong, and worldly wise
By simply meek; that suffering for truth's sake
Is fortitude to highest victory, 570
And to the faithful death the gate of life;

Taught this by his example whom I now
Acknowledge my Redeemer ever blest."
    To whom thus also th' Angel last replied:
"This having learnt, thou hast attained the sum 575
Of wisdom; hope no higher, though all the stars
Thou knew'st by name, and all th' ethereal powers,
All secrets of the deep, all Nature's works,
Or works of God in Heav'n, air, earth, or sea,
And all the riches of this world enjoy'dst, 580
And all the rule, one empire; only add
Deeds to thy knowledge answerable, add faith,
Add virtue, patience, temperance, add love,
By name to come called charity, the soul
Of all the rest: then wilt thou not be loath 585
To leave this Paradise, but shalt possess
A Paradise within thee, happier far.
Let us descend now therefore from this top
Of speculation; for the hour precise
Exacts our parting hence; and see the guards, 590
By me encamped on yonder hill, expect
Their motion, at whose front a flaming sword,
In signal of remove, waves fiercely round;
We may no longer stay: go, waken Eve;
Her also I with gentle dreams have calmed, 595
Portending good, and all her spirits composed
To meek submission: thou at season fit
Let her with thee partake what thou hast heard,
Chiefly what may concern her faith to know,
The great deliverance by her seed to come 600
(For by the Woman's Seed) on all mankind:
That ye may live, which will be many days,
Both in one faith unanimous though sad,
With cause for evils past, yet much more cheered
With meditation on the happy end." 605
    He ended, and they both descend the hill;
Descended, Adam to the bow'r where Eve
Lay sleeping ran before, but found her waked;
And thus with words not sad she him received:
    "Whence thou return'st, and whither went'st, I know;
For God is also in sleep, and dreams advise, 611
Which he hath sent propitious, some great good
Presaging, since with sorrow and heart's distress
Wearied I fell asleep. But now lead on;

533: See John 4:23-24. **540. respiration:** breathing again, returning to life, resurrection (Milton translates *anapsycheos* from the Greek Testament; the King James Bible has *refreshing* — see Acts 3:19 — though the sense is also that of "reviving"). **558ff.:** See the excerpt from Book VIII. **565-69:** See Psalms 145:9, Romans 12:21, I Corinthians 1:27-28. **581-85:** See II Peter 1:5-7, I Corinthians 13. **588. top:** hilltop. **589. speculation:** vision, seeing, observation. **611:** Cf. *Iliad*, I, 63.

In me is no delay; with thee to go,   615
Is to stay here; without thee here to stay,
Is to go hence unwilling; thou to me
Art all things under Heav'n, all places thou,
Who for my wilful crime art banished hence.
This further consolation yet secure   620
I carry hence; though all by me is lost,
Such favour I unworthy am vouchsafed,
By me the Promised Seed shall all restore."
    So spake our mother Eve, and Adam heard
Well pleased, but answered not; for now too nigh   625
Th' Archangel stood, and from the other hill
To their fixed station, all in bright array
The Cherubim descended; on the ground
Gliding meteorous, as ev'ning mist
Ris'n from a river o'er the marish glides,   630
And gathers ground fast at the labourer's heel
Homeward returning. High in front advanced,

The brandished sword of God before them blazed
Fierce as a comet; which with torrid heat,
And vapour as the Libyan air adust,   635
Began to parch that temperate clime; whereat
In either hand the hast'ning Angel caught
Our ling'ring parents, and to th' eastern gate
Led them direct, and down the cliff as fast
To the subjected plain; then disappeared.   640
They, looking back, all th' eastern side beheld
Of Paradise, so late their happy seat,
Waved over by that flaming brand, the gate
With dreadful faces thronged and fiery arms.
Some natural tears they dropped, but wiped them soon;
The world was all before them, where to choose   646
Their place of rest, and Providence their guide:
They hand in hand, with wand'ring steps and slow,
Through Eden took their solitary way.

                              (1658-63;1667, 1674)

SIR JOHN SUCKLING
England, 1609-1641

SONG

Why so pale and wan, fond lover?
          Prithee, why so pale?
Will, when looking well can't move her,
          Looking ill prevail?
          Prithee, why so pale?   5

Why so dull and mute, young sinner?
          Prithee, why so mute?
Will, when speaking well can't win her,
          Saying nothing do't?
          Prithee, why so mute?   10

Quit, quit, for shame, this will not move,
          This cannot take her;
If of herself she will not love,
          Nothing can make her.
          The Devil take her!   15

                              (1638)

"OUT UPON IT! I HAVE LOVED"

Out upon it! I have loved
          Three whole days together;
And am like to love three more,
          If it prove fair weather.

Time shall moult away his wings   5
          Ere he shall discover
In the whole wide world again
          Such a constant lover.

But a pox upon't, no praise
          Is due at all to me: 10
Love with me had made no stays,
          Had it any been but she.

Had it any been but she,
          And that very face,
There had been at least ere this   15
          A dozen dozen in her place.

                              (1659)

---

630. marish: marsh. **633:** See Genesis 3:24 (p. 245). **640. subjected:** low-lying.

Aɴɴᴇ Bʀᴀᴅsᴛʀᴇᴇᴛ
England/USA, 1612-1672

Tʜᴇ Aᴜᴛʜᴏʀ ᴛᴏ Hᴇʀ Bᴏᴏᴋ

Thou ill-form'd offspring of my feeble brain,
Who after birth didst by my side remain,
Till snatched from thence by friends, less wise than true,
Who thee abroad expos'd to public view,
Made thee in rags, halting to th' press to trudge,   5
Where errors were not lessened (all may judge);
At thy return my blushing was not small,
My rambling brat (in print) should mother call;
I cast thee by as one unfit for light,
Thy visage was so irksome in my sight;   10
Yet being mine own, at length affection would
Thy blemishes amend, if so I could.
I wash'd thy face, but more defects I saw,
And rubbing off a spot, still made a flaw.
I stretched thy joints to make thee even feet,   15
Yet still thou run'st more hobbling than is meet.
In better dress to trim thee was my mind,
But nought save home-spun cloth i'th'house I find;
In this array, 'mongst vulgars mayst thou roam;
In critics' hands beware thou dost not come;   20
And take thy way where yet thou art not known.
If for thy Father asked, say thou hadst none;
And for thy Mother, she alas is poor,
Which caus'd her thus to send thee out of door.

(1678)

Bᴇғᴏʀᴇ ᴛʜᴇ Bɪʀᴛʜ ᴏғ Oɴᴇ ᴏғ Hᴇʀ Cʜɪʟᴅʀᴇɴ

All things within this fading world hath end;
Adversity doth still our joys attend;
No ties so strong, no friends so clear and sweet,
But with death's parting blow is sure to meet.
The sentence past is most irrevocable,   5
A common thing, yet oh inevitable;
How soon, my Dear, death may my steps attend,
How soon 't may be thy lot to lose thy friend.

We both are ignorant, yet love bids me
These farewell lines to recommend to thee,   10
That when that knot's untied that made us one,
I may seem thine, who in effect am none.
And if I see not half my days that's due,
What nature would, God grant to yours and you;
The many faults that well you know I have,   15
Let be interr'd in my oblivious grave;
If any worth or virtue were in me,
Let that live freshly in thy memory;
And when thou feel'st no grief, as I no harms,
Yet love thy dead, who long lay in thine arms;   20
And when thy loss shall be repaid with gains,
Look to my little babes, my dear remains;
And if thou love thy self, or loved'st me,
These oh protect from step-dame's injury.
And if chance to thine eyes shall bring this verse,   25
With some sad sighs honour my absent hearse,
And kiss this paper for thy love's dear sake,
Who with salt tears this last farewell did take.

(1678)

Tᴏ Mʏ Dᴇᴀʀ ᴀɴᴅ Lᴏᴠɪɴɢ Hᴜsʙᴀɴᴅ

If ever two were one, then surely we.
If ever man were lov'd by wife, then thee;
If ever wife was happy in a man,
Compare with me ye women if you can.
I prize thy love more than whole mines of gold,   5
Or all the riches that the East doth hold.
My love is such that rivers cannot quench,
Nor ought but love from thee give recompense.
Thy love is such I can no way repay,
The heavens reward thee manifold I pray.   10
Then while we live, in love let's so persever,
That when we live no more, we may live ever.

(1678)

Tʜᴇ Aᴜᴛʜᴏʀ ᴛᴏ Hᴇʀ Bᴏᴏᴋ   The first edition of her poems, *The Tenth Muse Lately Sprung Up in America*, was published in London in 1650 without her permission; this poem was probably written in the mid-1660s while she corrected and revised for the second edition, which was published posthumously.   **Bᴇғᴏʀᴇ ᴛʜᴇ Bɪʀᴛʜ**   24. **step-dame's injury:** i.e., the hurt that might be caused by a future stepmother.

SAMUEL BUTLER
England, 1612-1680

from *HUDIBRAS,* Part I, Canto I

The Argument

Sir Hudibras his passing worth,
The manner how he sallied forth,
His arms and equipage, are shown;
His horse's virtues and his own.
Th' adventure of the bear and fiddle
Is sung, but breaks off in the middle.

When civil dudgeon first grew high,
And men fell out, they knew not why;
When hard words, jealousies, and fears
Set folks together by the ears,
And made them fight, like mad or drunk,   5
For dame Religion as for punk;
Whose honesty they all durst swear for,
Though not a man of them knew wherefore:
When Gospel-Trumpeter, surrounded
With long-eared rout, to battle sounded,   10
And pulpit, drum ecclesiastic,
Was beat with fist, instead of a stick;
Then did Sir Knight abandon dwelling,
And out he rode a-colonelling.
   A wight he was, whose very sight would   15
Entitle him Mirror of Knighthood;
That never bowed his stubborn knee
To anything but chivalry;
Nor put up blow, but that which laid
Right worshipful on shoulder-blade: 20
Chief of domestic knights, and errant,
Either for chartel or for warrant:
Great on the bench, great in the saddle,
That could as well bind o'er, as swaddle:

Mighty he was at both of these,   25
And styled of War as well as Peace.
So some rats of amphibious nature
Are either for the land or water.
But here our authors make a doubt,
Whether he were more wise or stout.   30
Some hold the one, and some the other;
But howsoe'er they make a pother,
The diff'rence was so small, his brain
Outweighed his rage but half a grain;
Which made some take him for a tool   35
That knaves do work with, called a fool.
For 't has been held by many, that
As Montaigne, playing with his cat,
Complains she thought him but an ass,
Much more she would Sir Hudibras: 40
For that's the name our valiant knight
To all his challenges did write.
But they're mistaken very much,
'Tis plain enough he was no such;
We grant, although he had much wit,   45
H' was very shy of using it,
As being loth to wear it out,
And therefore bore it not about,
Unless on holy-days, or so,
As men their best apparel do.   50
Beside, 'tis known he could speak Greek
As naturally as pigs squeak;
That Latin was no more difficile
Than to a blackbird 'tis to whistle.
Being rich in both, he never scanted   55

HUDIBRAS **1-2:** referring to the Civil War which resulted in Cromwell's Commonwealth in 1649. **6. punk:** whore. **10. long-eared rout:** Puritans, or Roundheads. **22. chartel:** challenge. **24. bind o'er:** i.e., designate an accused to be tried at the next court session; **swaddle:** cudgel, beat. **38-39:** Montaigne (see p. 186) in his *Apology for Raymond Sebond* wonders if, when he plays with his cat, she is playing with him more than he is playing with her.

His bounty unto such as wanted;
But much of either would afford
To many, that had not one word.
For Hebrew roots, although they're found
To flourish most in barren ground, 60
He had such plenty, as sufficed
To make some think him circumcised;
And truly so, perhaps, he was,
'Tis many a pious Christian's case.
    He was in logic a great critic, 65
Profoundly skilled in analytic;
He could distinguish, and divide
A hair 'twixt south and southwest side;
On either which he would dispute,
Confute, change hands, and still confute. 70
He'd undertake to prove, by force
Of argument, a man's no horse;
He'd prove a buzzard is no fowl,
And that a lord may be an owl;
A calf an alderman, a goose a justice, 75
And rooks, committee-men or trustees.
He'd run in debt by disputation,
And pay with ratiocination.
All this by syllogism true,
In mood and figure, he would do. 80
    For rhetoric, he could not ope
His mouth, but out there flew a trope;
And when he happened to break off
I' th' middle of his speech, or cough,
H' had hard words ready, to show why, 85
And tell what rules he did it by.
Else, when with greatest art he spoke,
You'd think he talked like other folk.
For all a rhetorician's rules
Teach nothing but to name his tools. 90
But when he pleased to show 't, his speech
In loftiness of sound was rich;
A Babylonish dialect,
Which learned pedants much affect.

It was a parti-coloured dress 95
Of patched and piebald languages:
'Twas English cut on Greek and Latin,
Like fustian heretofore on satin.
It had an odd promiscuous tone
As if h' had talked three parts in one; 100
Which made some think, when he did gabble,
Th' had heard three labourers of Babel;
Or Cerberus himself pronounce
A leash of languages at once.
This he as volubly would vent 105
As if his stock would ne'er be spent;
And truly, to support that charge,
He had supplies as vast and large.
For he could coin, or counterfeit,
New words with little or no wit; 110
Words so debased and hard, no stone
Was hard enough to touch them on.
And when with hasty noise he spoke 'em,
The ignorant for current took 'em;
That had the orator, who once 115
Did fill his mouth with pebble stones
When he harangued, but known his phrase,
He would have used no other ways.
    In mathematics he was greater
Than Tycho Brahe, or Erra Pater; 120
For he, by geometric scale,
Could take the size of pots of ale;
Resolve, by sines and tangents straight,
If bread or butter wanted weight;
And wisely tell what hour o' the day 125
The clock does strike, by algebra.
    Beside, he was a shrewd philosopher,
And had read ev'ry text and gloss over;
Whate'er the crabbed'st author hath,
He understood b' implicit faith; 130
Whatever sceptic could inquire for,
For every WHY he had a WHEREFORE;
Knew more than forty of them do,

60: referring to a theory that Hebrew was the primitive human language and therefore that a child brought up in the wild by animals would soon be speaking Hebrew. **93. Babylonish:** alluding to the confusion of tongues at the Tower of Babel. **98: fustian** garments with holes cut in them to reveal the satin underneath. **115-16:** Demosthenes. **120. Tycho Brahe:** Danish astronomer (1546-1601); **Erra Pater:** name of an old astrologer, used also by the contemporary astrologer, William Lilly.

As far as words and terms could go.
All which he understood by rote,   *135*
And, as occasion served, would quote;
No matter whether right or wrong;
They might be either said or sung.
His notions fitted things so well
That which was which he could not tell,   *140*
But oftentimes mistook the one
For th' other, as great clerks have done.

He could reduce all things to acts,
And knew their natures by abstracts;
Where entity and quiddity   *145*
The ghost of defunct bodies fly;
Where Truth in person does appear,
Like words congealed in northern air.
He knew what's what, and that's as high
As metaphysic wit can fly.   *150*

. . . .

(1663)

from CHARACTERS

A PROUD MAN

Is a fool in fermentation, that swells and boils over like a porridge-pot. He sets out his
feathers like an owl, to swell and seem bigger than he is. He is troubled with a tumour
and inflammation of self-conceit, that renders every part of him stiff and uneasy. He has
given himself sympathetic love-powder, that works upon him to dotage and has
transformed him into his own mistress. He is his own gallant, and makes most   5
passionate addresses to his own dear perfections. He commits idolatry to himself, and
worships his own image; though there is no soul living of his Church but himself, yet he
believes as the Church believes, and maintains his faith with the obstinacy of a fanatic.
He is his own favourite, and advances himself not only above his merit, but all mankind;
is both Damon and Pythias to his own dear self, and values his crony above his soul. He   10
gives place to no man but himself, and that with very great distance to all others, whom
he esteems not worthy to approach him. He believes whatsoever he has receives a value
in being his, as a horse in a nobleman's stable will bear a greater price than in a
common market. He is so proud that he is as hard to be acquainted with himself as with
others, for he is very apt to forget who he is, and knows himself only superficially;   15
therefore he treats himself civilly as a stranger with ceremony and compliment, but
admits of no privacy. He strives to look bigger than himself as well as others, and is no
better than his own parasite and flatterer. A little flood will make a shallow torrent swell
above its banks, and rage and foam and yield a roaring noise, while a deep, silent stream
glides quietly on. So a vainglorious, insolent, proud man swells with a little frail   20
prosperity, grows big and loud, and overflows his bounds, and when he sinks, leaves
mud and dirt behind him. His carriage is as glorious and haughty as if he were advanced
upon men's shoulders or tumbled over their heads like knipperdolling. He fancies
himself a Colosse, and so he is, for his head holds no proportion to his body, and his
foundation is lesser than his upper storeys. We can naturally take no view of ourselves   25
unless we look downwards, to teach us how humble admirers we ought to be of our own

---

CHARACTERS   Butler's character-writings were not published until 1759.   **A PROUD MAN   10. Damon and Pythias:** the prime example
or model of a devoted friendship. **23. knipperdolling:** follower of Münster Anabaptist leader Bernhard Knipperdolling (c.1490-1536) — i.e.,
religious fanatic; Knipperdolling's and others' tortured bodies were hung in high cages. **24. Colosse:** Colossus.

values. The slighter and less solid his materials are the more room they take up and make him swell the bigger, as feathers and cotton will stuff cushions better than things of more close and solid parts.

A MELANCHOLY MAN

Is one that keeps the worst company in the world; that is, his own; and though he be always falling out and quarrelling with himself, yet he has not power to endure any other conversation. His head is haunted, like a house, with evil spirits and apparitions, that terrify and fright him out of himself, till he stands empty and forsaken. His sleeps and his wakings are so much the same that he knows not how to distinguish them, and many *5* times when he dreams he believes he is broad awake and sees visions. The fumes and vapours that rise from his spleen and hypochondrias have so smutched and sullied his brain (like a room that smokes) that his understanding is blear-eyed and has no right perception of anything. His soul lives in his body like a mole in the earth that labours in the dark, and casts up doubts and scruples of his own imaginations, to make that rugged *10* and uneasy that was plain and open before. His brain is so cracked that he fancies himself to be glass, and is afraid that everything he comes near should break him in pieces. Whatsoever makes an impression in his imagination works itself in like a screw, and the more he turns and winds it the deeper it sticks, till it is never to be got out again. The temper of his brain, being earthy, cold, and dry, is apt to breed worms, that sink so deep *15* into it no medicine in art or nature is able to reach them. He leads his life as one leads a dog in a slip that will not follow, but is dragged along until he is almost hanged, as he has it often under consideration to treat himself in convenient time and place, if he can but catch himself alone. After a long and mortal feud between his inward and his outward man, they at length agree to meet without seconds and decide the quarrel, in which the *20* one drops and the other slinks out of the way and makes his escape into some foreign world, from whence it is never after heard of. He converses with nothing so much as his own imagination, which, being apt to misrepresent things to him, makes him believe that it is something else than it is, and that he holds intelligence with spirits that reveal whatsoever he fancies to him, as the ancient rude people that first heard their own voices *25* repeated by echoes in the woods concluded it must proceed from some invisible inhabitants of those solitary places, which they after believed to be gods, and called them sylvans, fauns, and dryads. He makes the infirmity of his temper pass for revelations, as Mahomet did by his falling sickness, and inspires himself with the wind of his own hypochondrias. He laments, like Heraclitus, the maudlin philosopher, at other men's *30* mirth, and takes pleasure in nothing but his own unsober sadness. His mind is full of thoughts, but they are all empty, like a nest of boxes. He sleeps little, but dreams much, and soundest when he is waking. He sees visions farther off than a second-sighted man in Scotland, and dreams upon a hard point with admirable judgment. He is just so much worse than a madman as he is below him in degree of frenzy, for among madmen the *35* most mad govern all the rest, and receive a natural obedience from their inferiors.

A MELANCHOLY MAN   **15:** See note on "humours" at line 420 of Chaucer's "General Prologue" (p. 34) (and see "A Rude Man" below, line 3). **17. slip:** leash which loosens when slackened.

A Projector

Is by interpretation a man of forecast. He is an artist of plots, designs, and expedients to find out money, as others hide it, where nobody would look for it. He is a great rectifier of the abuses of all trades and mysteries, yet has but one remedy for all diseases; that is, by getting a patent to share with them, by virtue of which they become authorised, and consequently cease to be cheats. He is a great promoter of the public good, and makes it   *5*
his care and study to contrive expedients that the nation may not be ill served with false rags, arbitrary puppet-plays, and insufficient monsters, of all which he endeavours to get the superintendency. He will undertake to render treasonable pedlars, that carry intelligence between rebels and fanatics, true subjects and well-affected to the Government for half-a-crown a quarter, which he takes for giving them license to do so   *10*
securely and uncontrolled. He gets as much by those projects that miscarry as by those that hold (as lawyers are paid as well for undoing as preserving of men); for when he has drawn in adventurers to purchase shares of the profit, the sooner it is stopped the better it proves for him; for, his own business being done, he is the sooner rid of theirs. He is very expert at gauging the understandings of those he deals with, and has his   *15*
engines always ready with mere air to blow all their money out of their pockets into his own, as vintners do wine out of one vessel into another. He is very amorous of his country, and prefers the public good before his own advantage, until he has joined them both together in some monopoly, and then he thinks he has done his part, and may be allowed to look after his own affairs in the second place. The chiefest and most useful   *20*
part of his talent consists in quacking and lying, which he calls answering of objections and convincing the ignorant. Without this he can do nothing; for as it is the common practice of most knaveries, so it is the surest and best fitted to the vulgar capacities of the world; and though it render him more ridiculous to some few, it always prevails upon the greater part.   *25*

The Obstinate Man

Does not hold opinions, but they hold him; for when he is once possessed with an error, 'tis, like the devil, not to be cast out but with great difficulty. Whatsoever he lays hold on, like a drowning man, he never loses, though it do but help to sink him the sooner. His ignorance is abrupt and inaccessible, impregnable both by art and nature, and will hold out to the last though it has nothing but rubbish to defend. It is as dark as pitch, and   *5*
sticks as fast to anything it lays hold on. His skull is so thick that it is proof against any reason, and never cracks but on the wrong side, just opposite to that against which the impression is made, which surgeons say does happen very frequently. The slighter and more inconsistent his opinions are, the faster he holds them; otherwise they would fall asunder of themselves, for opinions that are false ought to be held with more strictness   *10*
and assurance than those that are true; otherwise they will be apt to betray their owners before they are aware. If he takes to religion, he has faith enough to save a hundred

---

A Projector   See Swift's *A Modest Proposal,* line 20 and note (p. 481). **21. quacking:** making vain and loud pretensions, boasting.

wiser men than himself, if it were right; but it is too much to be good; and though he deny supererogation and utterly disclaim any overplus of merits, yet he allows superabundant belief, and if the violence of faith will carry the kingdom of heaven, he *15* stands fair for it. He delights most of all to differ in things indifferent; no matter how frivolous they are, they are weighty enough in proportion to his weak judgment, and he will rather suffer self-martyrdom than part with the least scruple of his freehold, for it is impossible to dye his dark ignorance into a lighter colour. He is resolved to understand no man's reason but his own, because he finds no man can understand his but himself. *20* His wits are like a sack which, the French proverb says, is tied faster before it is full than when it is; and his opinions are like plants that grow upon rocks, that stick fast though they have no rooting. His understanding is hardened like Pharaoh's heart, and is proof against all sorts of judgments whatsoever.

THE RUDE MAN

Is an Ostro-Goth or Northern Hun, that, wheresoever he comes, invades and all the world does overrun, without distinction of age, sex, or quality. He has no regard to anything but his own humour, and that, he expects, should pass everywhere without asking leave or being asked wherefore, as if he had a safe-conduct for his rudeness. He rolls up himself like a hedgehog in his prickles, and is as intractable to all that come *5* near him. He is an ill-designed piece, built after the rustic order, and all his parts look too big for their height. He is so ill-contrived that that which should be the top in all regular structures — i.e., confidence — is his foundation. He has neither doctrine nor discipline in him, like a fanatic Church, but is guided by the very same spirit that dipped the herd of swine in the sea. He was not bred, but reared; not brought up to hand, but *10* suffered to run wild and take after his kind, as other people of the pasture do. He takes that freedom in all places, as if he were not at liberty, but had broken loose and expected to be tied up again. He does not eat, but feed, and when he drinks goes to water. The old Romans beat the barbarous part of the world into civility, but if he had lived in those times he had been invincible to all attempts of that nature, and harder to be subdued and *15* governed than a province. He eats his bread, according to the curse, with the sweat of his brow, and takes as much pains at a meal as if he earned it; puffs and blows like a horse that eats provender, and crams his throat like a screwed gun with a bullet bigger than the bore. His tongue runs perpetually over everything that comes in its way, without regard of what, where, or to whom, and nothing but a greater rudeness than his *20* own can stand before it; and he uses it to as slovenly purposes as a dog does that licks his sores and the dirt off his feet. He is the best instance of the truth of Pythagoras's doctrine, for his soul passed through all sorts of brute beasts before it came to him, and still retains something of the nature of every one.

THE OBSTINATE MAN   **23. hardened like Pharaoh's heart:** See Exodus 4:21, 7:3, etc.   THE RUDE MAN   **2. quality:** social position. **10:** For the demonically possessed Gadarene swine, see Matthew 8:30-32, Mark 5:11-13, Luke 8:32-33. **16-17:** See Genesis 3:19. **22-23:** referring to Pythagoras's doctrine of cycles of reincarnation, or metempsychosis.

JEREMY TAYLOR
England, 1613-1667

FROM *THE RULE AND EXERCISES OF HOLY DYING*

from Chapter I: A General Preparation Towards a Holy and Blessed Death, By Way of Consideration

Section IV: Consideration of the Miseries of Man's Life (abridged)

As our life is very short, so it is very miserable, and therefore it is well it is short. God in pity to mankind, lest his burden should be insupportable and his nature an intolerable load, hath reduced our state of misery to an abbreviature; and the greater our misery is, the less while it is like to last, the sorrows of a man's spirit being like ponderous weights which by the greatness of their burden make a swifter motion and descend into the grave   *5* to rest and ease our wearied limbs; for then only we shall sleep quietly when those fetters are knocked off which not only bound our souls in prison, but also ate the flesh till the very bones opened the secret garments of their cartilages, discovering their nakedness and sorrow.

    1. Here is no place to sit down in, but you must rise as soon as you are set, for we   *10* have gnats in our chambers, and worms in our gardens, and spiders and flies in the palaces of the greatest kings. How few men in the world are prosperous! What an infinite number of slaves and beggars, of persecuted and oppressed people, fill all corners of the earth with groans, and Heaven itself with weeping prayers and sad remembrances! How many provinces and kingdoms are afflicted by a violent war, or   *15* made desolate by popular diseases! Some whole countries are remarked with fatal evils, or periodic sicknesses. Grand Cairo in Egypt feels the plague every three years, returning like a quartan ague and destroying many thousands of persons. All the inhabitants of Arabia the desert are in continual fear of being buried in huge heaps of sand, and therefore dwell in tents and ambulatory houses or retire to unfruitful   *20* mountains to prolong an uneasy and wilder life. And all the countries round about the Adriatic Sea feel such violent convulsions by tempests and intolerable earthquakes, that sometimes whole cities find a tomb, and every man sinks with his own house made ready to become his monument, and his bed is crushed into the disorders of a grave. Was not all the world drowned at one deluge and breach of the divine anger? And shall   *25* not all the world again be destroyed by fire? Are there not many thousands that die every night, and that groan and weep sadly every day?

. . . .

CONSIDERATION OF THE MISERIES OF MAN'S LIFE   This is from volume II; volume I, *The Rule and Exercises of Holy Living*, appeared in 1650. **16. popular:** extensively prevalent. **18. quartan:** recurring every fourth day. **25-26. And shall . . . fire:** as prophesied in the *Sibylline Oracles.*

2. We find that all the women in the world are either born for barrenness or the pains of childbirth, and yet this is one of our greatest blessings; but such indeed are the blessings of this world: we cannot be well with nor without many things. Perfumes 30 make our heads ache, roses prick our fingers, and in our very blood where our life dwells is the scene under which nature acts many sharp fevers and heavy sicknesses. It were too sad if I should tell how many persons are afflicted with evil spirits, with spectres and illusions of the night, and that huge multitudes of men and women live upon man's flesh — nay, worse yet, upon the sins of men, upon the sins of their sons 35 and of their daughters, and they pay their souls down for the bread they eat, buying this day's meal with the price of the last night's sin.

3. Or if you please in charity to visit an hospital, which is indeed a map of the whole world, there you shall see the effects of Adam's sin and the ruins of human nature, bodies laid up in heaps like the bones of a destroyed town, *homines precarii* 40 *spiritus et male hærentis,* men whose souls seem to be borrowed, and are kept there by art and the force of medicine; whose miseries are so great that few people have charity or humanity enough to visit them, fewer have the heart to dress them, and we pity them in civility or with a transient prayer, but we do not feel their sorrows by the mercies of a religious pity; and therefore as we leave their sorrows in many degrees unrelieved and 45 uneased, so we contract by our unmercifulness a guilt by which ourselves become liable to the same calamities. Those many that need pity, and those infinites of people that refuse to pity, are miserable upon a several charge, but yet they almost make up all mankind.

4. All wicked men are in love with that which entangles them in huge variety of 50 troubles; they are slaves to the worst of masters, to sin and to the Devil, to a passion, and to an imperious woman. Good men are forever persecuted, and God chastises every son whom he receives, and whatsoever is easy is trifling and worth nothing, and whatsoever is excellent is not to be obtained without labour and sorrow; and the conditions and states of men that are free from great cares are such as have in them 55 nothing rich and orderly, and those that have are stuck full of thorns and trouble. Kings are full of care, and learned men in all ages have been observed to be very poor, *et honestas miserias accusant:* "they complain of their honest miseries."

5. But these evils are notorious and confessed; even they also whose felicity men stare at and admire, besides their splendour and the sharpness of their light, will with 60 their appendant sorrows wring a tear from the most resolved eye. For not only the winter quarter is full of storms and cold and darkness, but the beauteous spring hath blasts and sharp frosts, the fruitful teeming summer is melted with heat, and burnt with the kisses of the sun her friend, and choked with dust, and the rich autumn is full of sickness, and we are weary of that which we enjoy, because sorrow is its biggest portion; and when 65 we remember that upon the fairest face is placed one of the worst sinks of the body, the nose, we may use it not only as a mortification to the pride of beauty but as an allay to the fairest outside of condition which any of the sons and daughters of Adam do possess. For look upon kings and conquerors: I will not tell that many of them fall into

---

40-41. *homines . . . hærentis:* loosely translated by what follows in the text (from Seneca, *Consolatio ad Marciam*, xi, 3). **67. allay:** alloy.

the condition of servants, and their subjects rule over them, and stand upon the ruins of   *70*
their families, and that to such persons the sorrow is bigger than usually happens in
smaller fortunes. . . . But whatsoever tempts the pride and vanity of ambitious persons is
not so big as the smallest star which we see scattered in disorder and unregarded upon
the pavement and floor of Heaven. And if we would suppose the pismires had but our
understandings, they also would have the method of a man's greatness, and divide their   *75*
little mole-hills into provinces and exarchates; and if they also grew as vicious and as
miserable, one of their princes would lead an army out and kill his neighbour ants that
he might reign over the next handful of a turf. But then if we consider at what price and
with what felicity all this is purchased, the sting of the painted snake will quickly
appear, and the fairest of their fortunes will properly enter into this account of human   *80*
infelicities.

. . . .

6. The prosperity of this world is so infinitely soured with the overflowing of evils,
that he is counted the most happy who hath the fewest; all conditions being evil and
miserable, they are only distinguished by the number of calamities. The collector of the
Roman and foreign examples, when he had reckoned two and twenty instances of great   *85*
fortunes every one of which had been allayed with great variety of evils, in all his
reading or experience he could tell but of two who had been famed for an entire
prosperity, Quintus Metellus and Gyges the King of Lydia; and yet concerning the one
of them he tells that his felicity was so inconsiderable (and yet it was the bigger of the
two) that the oracle said that Aglaus Sophidius the poor Arabian shepherd was more   *90*
happy than he; that is, he had fewer troubles, for so indeed we are to reckon the
pleasures of this life; the limit of our joy is the absence of some degrees of sorrow, and
he that hath the least of this is the most prosperous person. But then we must look for
prosperity not in palaces or courts of princes, not in the tents of conquerors or in the
gaieties of fortunate and prevailing sinners, but something rather in the cottages of   *95*
honest, innocent, and contented persons, whose mind is no bigger than their fortune, nor
their virtue less than their security. As for others whose fortune looks bigger, and allures
fools to follow it like the wandering fires of the night till they run into rivers or are
broken upon rocks with staring and running after them, they are all in the condition of
Marius, than whose condition nothing was more constant, and nothing more mutable; if   *100*
we reckon them amongst the happy, they are the most happy men; if we reckon them
amongst the miserable, they are the most miserable. For just as is a man's condition,
great or little, so is the state of his misery; all have their share, but kings and princes,
great generals and consuls, rich men and mighty, as they have the biggest business and
the biggest charge, and are answerable to God for the greatest accounts, so they have the   *105*

---

84. collector: Valerius Maximus, 1st-century Roman historian and moralist; his collection of illustrative "Roman and foreign examples" (*Factorum ac dictorum memorabilium libri IX*, "nine books of memorable deeds and sayings") was for use in schools of rhetoric. **88. Quintus Metellus:** Quintus Caecilius Metellus Macedonicus, Roman consul 146 and 143 B.C.; he was one of several Quintus Metelluses, members of a powerful Roman family in 3rd-1st century B.C.; **Gyges:** 7th-century B.C. king of Lydia; Plato (*Republic*, 359) tells the story of his magic ring, which could make him invisible, enabling him to seize the throne; and Herodotus (I, 8-14) relates another legend of how he became king. **92. the limit . . . sorrow:** Taylor here translates a line from Diogenes Laertius. **97-99:** referring to the ignis fatuus, or will-o'-the-wisp. **100. Marius:** Gaius Marius (157-86 B.C.), Roman politician and soldier, who was made consul in 107 B.C., and who distinguished himself in battle in Africa and against the Teutonic tribes. **100-02. if we reckon . . . most miserable:** Taylor here translates from Valerius Maximus.

biggest trouble; that the uneasiness of their appendage may divide the good and evil of the world, making the poor man's fortune as eligible as the greatest; and also restraining the vanity of man's spirit, which a great fortune is apt to swell from a vapour to a bubble; but God in mercy hath mingled wormwood with their wine, and so restrained the drunkenness and follies of prosperity. *110*

7. Man never hath one day to himself of entire peace from the things of this world, but either something troubles him, or nothing satisfies him, or his very fullness swells him and makes him breathe short upon his bed. Men's joys are troublesome, and besides that the fear of losing them takes away the present pleasure (and a man hath need of another felicity to preserve this), they are also wavering and full of trepidation, not only *115* from their inconstant nature, but from their weak foundation. They arise from vanity, and they dwell upon ice, and they converse with the wind, and they have the wings of a bird, and are serious but as the resolutions of a child, commenced by chance, and managed by folly, and proceed by inadvertency, and end in vanity and forgetfulness. So that as Livius Drusus said of himself, he never had any play-days or days of quiet when *120* he was a boy, for he was troublesome and busy, a restless and unquiet man; the same may every man observe to be true of himself: he is always restless and uneasy, he dwells upon the waters and leans upon thorns, and lays his head upon a sharp stone.

(1651)

Sir John Denham
Ireland/England, 1615-1669

Cooper's Hill

Sure there are poets which did never dream
Upon Parnassus, nor did taste the stream
Of Helicon; we therefore may suppose
Those made not poets, but the poets those.
And as courts make not kings, but kings the court, *5*
So where the Muses and their train resort,
Parnassus stands; if I can be to thee
A poet, thou Parnassus art to me.

Nor wonder, if (advantaged in my flight
By taking wing from thy auspicious height) *10*
Through untraced ways and airy paths I fly,
More boundless in my fancy than my eye:
My eye, which swift as thought contracts the space
That lies between, and first salutes the place
Crowned with that sacred pile, so vast, so high, *15*
That whether 'tis a part of Earth, or sky,

---

120. Drusus: Marcus Livius Drusus, the younger, a tribune in 91 B.C., assassinated while trying to introduce a set of reform laws; Taylor here is translating from Seneca's *De brevitate vitae*. **Cooper's Hill** Denham's poem was much imitated and cited during the 17th and 18th centuries, in works by Addison, Brome, Buckingham, Goldsmith, Gray, Swift, and Leonard Welsted, among others. In *The Dunciad*, III, 169-72, Pope satirizes Welsted (and the many imitations of Denham's lines 189-92, the second couplet of which Dryden first singled out for commendation): "Flow, Welsted, flow! like thine inspirer, beer, / Tho' stale, not ripe, tho' thin, yet never clear; / So sweetly mawkish, and so smoothly dull; / Heady, not strong; o'erflowing, tho' not full." In his *Lives of the Poets*, Samuel Johnson, writing of *Cooper's Hill*, credits Denham with originating "a species of composition that may be denominated *local poetry*, of which the fundamental subject is some particular landscape, to be poetically described, with the addition of such embellishments as may be supplied by historical retrospection, or incidental meditation." **2-3. Parnassus, Helicon:** mountains in Greece, both of which, with their fountains and streams, are associated with the Muses and poetry.

Uncertain seems, and may be thought a proud
Aspiring mountain, or descending cloud,
Paul's, the late theme of such a Muse whose flight
Has bravely reached and soared above thy height. *20*
Now shalt thou stand, though sword, or time, or fire,
Or zeal more fierce than they, thy fall conspire,
Secure, whilst thee the best of poets sings,
Preserved from ruin by the best of kings.
Under his proud survey the City lies, *25*
And like a mist beneath a hill doth rise,
Whose state and wealth, the business and the crowd,
Seems at this distance but a darker cloud,
And is to him who rightly things esteems,
No other in effect than what it seems, *30*
Where with like haste, though several ways, they run,
Some to undo, and some to be undone;
While luxury and wealth, like war and peace,
Are each the other's ruin, and increase;
As rivers lost in seas some secret vein *35*
Thence reconveys, there to be lost again.
Oh happiness of sweet retired content!
To be at once secure, and innocent.
   Windsor the next (where Mars with Venus dwells,
Beauty with strength) above the valley swells *40*
Into mine eye, and doth itself present
With such an easy and unforced ascent,
That no stupendous precipice denies
Access, nor horror turns away our eyes;
But such a rise as doth at once invite *45*
A pleasure, and a reverence from the sight.
Thy mighty master's emblem, in whose face
Sat meekness, heightened with majestic grace.
Such seems thy gentle height, made only proud
To be the basis of that pompous load, *50*
Than which a nobler weight no mountain bears,
But Atlas only that supports the spheres.
When Nature's hand this ground did thus advance,
'Twas guided by a wiser power than chance;
Marked out for such a use, as if 'twere meant *55*

T' invite the builder, and his choice prevent.
Nor can we call it choice, when what we choose,
Folly or blindness only could refuse.
A crown of such majestic towers doth grace
The gods' great Mother, when her heavenly race *60*
Do homage to her, yet she cannot boast
Amongst that numerous and celestial host
More heroes than can Windsor, nor doth Fame's
Immortal book record more noble names.
Not to look back so far, to whom this isle *65*
Owes the first glory of so brave a pile,
Whether to Cæsar, Albanact, or Brute,
The British Arthur, or the Danish Knute
(Though this of old no less contest did move,
Than when for Homer's birth seven cities strove) *70*
(Like him in birth, thou shouldst be like in fame,
As thine his fate, if mine had been his flame);
But whosoe'er it was, Nature designed
First a brave place, and then as brave a mind.
Not to recount those several kings to whom *75*
It gave a cradle, or to whom a tomb,
But thee, great Edward, and thy greater son
(The lilies which his father wore, he won)
And thy Bellona, who the consort came
Not only to thy bed, but to thy fame, *80*
She to thy triumph led one captive king,
And brought that son which did the second bring.
Then didst thou found that Order whither love
Or victory thy royal thoughts did move;
Each was a noble cause, and nothing less *85*
Than the design had been the great success,
Which foreign kings and emperors esteem
The second honour to their diadem.
Had thy great destiny but given thee skill
To know as well as power to act her will, *90*
That from those kings, who then thy captives were,
In after-times should spring a Royal pair
Who should possess all that thy mighty power,
Or thy desires more mighty, did devour;

---

19. Paul's: St. Paul's Cathedral, which then dominated the London skyline; **a Muse:** i.e., poet, namely Edmund Waller (see p. 311), who had written a poem "Upon His Majesty's Repairing of Paul's" (1645). **24. best of Kings:** Charles I. **50. pompous:** displaying pomp, splendid, magnificent. **56. prevent:** come before, anticipate. **60. Mother:** Cybele. **66. brave:** lofty, excellent, beautiful, noble, magnificent. **67-68. Cæsar:** Julius Caesar, who led early raids on England (55 and 54 B.C., during the Gallic Wars); **Brute:** Brut, Brutus, descendant of Aeneas, and legendary first king of England (see opening of *Gawain and the Green Knight*, p. 26); **Albanact:** Brutus's son; **Arthur:** King Arthur, largely mythical or legendary early British hero; **Danish Knute:** Canute, or Cnut, King of England c.1016-1035. **70. for Homer's birth:** i.e., for the honour of having been Homer's birthplace. **77ff. Edward:** Edward III; his son, Edward the "Black Prince," was victorious over the French ("lilies . . . won," line 78, including the capture of King John II in 1356 at Poitiers, line 82); Edward's wife, Philippa of Hainault, is here alluded to as **Bellona** (line 79), Roman goddess of war, because (according to Froissart and others) she rallied English troops against the Scottish invasion of 1346, especially at the battle of Neville's Cross when King David II was captured (line 81), and accompanied her husband on his campaigns. **83. Order:** Order of the Garter, centred at Windsor Castle. **92. Royal pair:** Charles I and his queen consort Henrietta Maria.

To whom their better fate reserves whate'er   95
The victor hopes for, or the vanquished fear;
That blood, which thou and thy great grandsire shed,
And all that since these sister nations bled,
Had been unspilt, had happy Edward known
That all the blood he spilt had been his own.   100
When he that Patron chose, in whom are joined
Soldier and martyr, and his arms confined
Within the azure circle, he did seem
But to foretell and prophesy of him,
Who to his realms that azure round hath joined,   105
Which Nature for their bound at first designed.
That bound, which to the World's extremest ends,
Endless itself, its liquid arms extends;
Nor doth he need those emblems which we paint,
But is himself the soldier and the saint.   110
    Here should my wonder dwell, and here my praise,
But my fixed thoughts my wandering eye betrays,
Viewing a neighbouring hill, whose top of late
A chapel crowned, till in the common fate
Th' adjoining abbey fell (may no such storm   115
Fall on our times, where ruin must reform).
Tell me, my Muse, what monstrous dire offence,
What crime could any Christian king incense
To such a rage? Was 't luxury, or lust?
Was he so temperate, so chaste, so just?   120
Were these their crimes? They were his own much more;
But wealth is crime enough to him that's poor,
Who having spent the treasures of his Crown,
Condemns their luxury to feed his own.
And yet this act, to varnish o'er the shame   125
Of sacrilege, must bear devotion's name.
No crime so bold but would be understood
A real, or at least a seeming good.
Who fears not to do ill, yet fears the name,
And free from conscience, is a slave to fame.   130
Thus he the Church at once protects, and spoils;
But princes' swords are sharper than their styles.

And thus to th' ages past he makes amends;
Their Charity destroys, their Faith defends.
Then did Religion, in a lazy cell,   135
In empty, airy contemplations dwell,
And like the block, unmoved lay; but ours,
As much too active, like the stork devours.
Is there no temperate region can be known,
Betwixt their frigid, and our torrid zone?   140
Could we not wake from that lethargic dream,
But to be restless in a worse extreme?
And for that lethargy was there no cure
But to be cast into a calenture?
Can knowledge have no bound, but must advance   145
So far, to make us wish for ignorance?
And rather in the dark to grope our way
Than, led by a false guide, to err by day?
Who sees these dismal heaps, but would demand
What barbarous invader sacked the land?   150
But when he hears, no Goth, no Turk did bring
This desolation, but a Christian king;
When nothing but the name of zeal appears
'Twixt our best actions and the worst of theirs;
What does he think our sacrilege would spare,   155
When such th' effects of our devotions are?
    Parting from thence 'twixt anger, shame, and fear,
Those for what's past, and this for what's too near,
My eye descending from the Hill, surveys
Where Thames amongst the wanton valleys strays.   160
Thames, the most loved of all the Ocean's sons,
By his old sire, to his embraces runs,
Hasting to pay his tribute to the sea,
Like mortal life to meet eternity.
Though with those streams he no resemblance hold,
Whose foam is amber, and their gravel gold,   166
His genuine and less guilty wealth t' explore,
Search not his bottom, but survey his shore,
O'er which he kindly spreads his spacious wing,
And hatches plenty for th' ensuing spring.   170

---

101. Patron: Saint George. **103. azure circle:** the Order's emblem includes a blue garter encircling the red cross of Saint George. **104. him:** Charles I. **105. azure round:** i.e., the ocean surrounding England, Scotland, and Ireland. **113-15:** St. Anne's Hill, about 20 miles southwest of central London, where Chertsey Abbey was destroyed during Henry VIII's dissolution of the monasteries, as part of the Reformation. **115-16. may . . . reform:** i.e., may "reform" in the 17th century ("our times") differ from the kinds of "reform" practised during the 16th, when it proved destructive (cf. 157-58 below; Denham favoured the royalist cause and feared what the parliamentarians and Puritans might do). **132. styles:** referring to Henry VIII's 1521 book attacking Martin Luther, which earned him the title "Defender of the Faith" (see line 134); a *style* is also a stylus, and by extension a pen, and a pointed instrument used as a weapon. **138. like . . . devours:** See Caxton's retelling of the fable of "The Frogs and Jupiter," p. 104. **144. calenture:** tropical fever. **166:** expanded upon by Pope in his *Pastorals* (Spring, lines 61-64); Strephon speaks: "O'er golden sands let rich Pactolus flow, / And trees weep amber on the banks of Po; / Blessed Thames's shores the brightest beauties yield; / Feed here, my lambs, I'll seek no distant field" (for other echoes, see Pope's *Windsor Forest*); Pactolus, river in Lydia, fabled for bearing gold dust; Po, river in Italy traditionally identified with the mythical *Eridanus* (see line 193), where Phaethon fell to earth, and his sisters, turned into trees along its bank, wept tears of amber (Ovid's *Metamorphoses*, II).

Nor then destroys it with too fond a stay,
Like mothers which their infants overlay;
Nor with a sudden and impetuous wave,
Like profuse kings, resumes the wealth he gave.
No unexpected inundations spoil   *175*
The mower's hopes, nor mock the plowman's toil;
For godlike his unwearied bounty flows;
First loves to do, then loves the good he does.
Nor are his blessings to his banks confined,
But free and common, as the sea or wind;   *180*
When he to boast, or to disperse his stores,
Full of the tributes of his grateful shores,
Visits the World, and in his flying towers
Brings home to us, and makes both Indies ours;
Finds wealth where 'tis, bestows it where it wants,   *185*
Cities in deserts, woods in cities plants;
So that to us no thing, no place is strange,
While his fair bosom is the World's exchange.
O could I flow like thee, and make thy stream
My great example, as it is my theme!   *190*
Though deep, yet clear, though gentle, yet not dull,
Strong without rage, without o'erflowing full.
Heaven her Eridanus no more shall boast,
Whose fame in thine, like lesser currents lost;
Thy nobler streams shall visit Jove's abodes,   *195*
To shine amongst the stars, and bathe the gods.
Here Nature, whether more intent to please
Us, or herself, with strange varieties
(For things of wonder give no less delight
To the wise Maker's, than beholder's sight;   *200*
Though these delights from several causes move,
For so our children, thus our friends we love),
Wisely she knew the harmony of things,
As well as that of sounds, from discords springs.
Such was the discord which did first disperse   *205*
Form, order, beauty through the Universe;
While dryness moisture, coldness heat resists,
All that we have, and that we are, subsists;
While the steep horrid roughness of the wood
Strives with the gentle calmness of the flood.   *210*
Such huge extremes when Nature doth unite,
Wonder from thence results, from thence delight.

The stream is so transparent, pure, and clear,
That had the self-enamoured youth gazed here,
So fatally deceived he had not been,   *215*
While he the bottom, not his face had seen.
  But his proud heart the airy mountain hides
Among the clouds; his shoulders and his sides
A shady mantle clothes; his curled brows
Frown on the gentle stream, which calmly flows,   *220*
While winds and storms his lofty forehead beat:
The common fate of all that's high, or great.
Low at his foot a spacious plain is placed,
Between the mountain and the stream embraced,
Which shade and shelter from the Hill derives,   *225*
While the kind river wealth and beauty gives;
And in the mixture of all these appears
Variety, which all the rest endears.
This scene had some bold Greek or British bard
Beheld of old, what stories had we heard,   *230*
Of fairies, satyrs, and the nymphs their dames,
Their feasts, their revels, and their amorous flames!
'Tis still the same, although their airy shape
All but a quick poetic sight escape.
There Faunus and Sylvanus keep their courts,   *235*
And thither all the horned host resorts,
To graze the ranker mead, that noble herd
On whose sublime and shady fronts is reared
Nature's great masterpiece; to show how soon
Great things are made, but sooner are undone.   *240*
Here have I seen the King, when great affairs
Give leave to slacken, and unbend his cares,
Attended to the chase by all the flower
Of youth, whose hopes a nobler prey devour:
Pleasure with praise, and danger they would buy,   *245*
And wish a foe that would not only fly.
The stag now conscious of his fatal growth,
At once indulgent to his fear and sloth,
To some dark covert his retreat had made,
Where nor man's eye, nor heaven's, should invade   *250*
His soft repose; when th' unexpected sound
Of dogs and men his wakeful ear doth wound.
Roused with the noise, he scarce believes his ear,
Willing to think th' illusions of his fear

---

172. overlay: It was then customary for a nurse or a mother to sleep protectively with an infant, and it wasn't uncommon for the adult, in her sleep, to "overlay" the baby — i.e., roll over upon it and smother it. **183. flying towers:** i.e., tall ships, with sails like wings. **188. exchange:** the place in a city where merchants and brokers met to conduct business (see Pope's *Rape of the Lock*, III, 23 — p. 527). **214. youth:** Narcissus, who fell in love with his own reflection. **234:** Cf. Pope, *Rape of the Lock*, V, 124 (p. 532). **235. Faunus:** a numen often identified with Pan or with the herdsmen's god Inuus; **Sylvanus:** god of uncultivated land, or forest god; the terms *Faunus* and *Silvanus* are even sometimes combined as the name of a single nature deity.

Had given this false alarm, but straight his view   *255*
Confirms that more than all he fears is true.
Betrayed in all his strengths, the wood beset,
All instruments, all arts of ruin met,
He calls to mind his strength, and then his speed,
His winged heels, and then his armed head;   *260*
With these t' avoid, with that his fate to meet:
But fear prevails, and bids him trust his feet.
So fast he flies that his reviewing eye
Has lost the chasers, and his ear the cry;
Exulting, till he finds their nobler sense   *265*
Their disproportioned speed does recompense.
Then curses his conspiring feet, whose scent
Betrays that safety which their swiftness lent.
Then tries his friends, among the baser herd,
Where he so lately was obeyed, and feared,   *270*
His safety seeks; the herd, unkindly wise,
Or chases him from thence, or from him flies.
Like a declining statesman, left forlorn
To his friends' pity, and pursuers' scorn,
With shame remembers, while himself was one   *275*
Of the same herd, himself the same had done.
Thence to the coverts, and the conscious groves,
The scenes of his past triumphs, and his loves;
Sadly surveying where he ranged alone,
Prince of the soil, and all the herd his own;   *280*
And like a bold Knight Errant did proclaim
Combat to all, and bore away the Dame;
And taught the woods to echo to the stream
His dreadful challenge, and his clashing beam.
Yet faintly now declines the fatal strife;   *285*
So much his love was dearer than his life.
Now every leaf, and every moving breath,
Presents a foe, and every foe a death.
Wearied, forsaken, and pursued, at last
All safety in despair of safety placed,   *290*
Courage he thence resumes, resolved to bear
All their assaults, since 'tis in vain to fear.
And now too late he wishes for the fight
That strength he wasted in ignoble flight:
But when he sees the eager chase renewed,   *295*
Himself by dogs, the dogs by men pursued,
He straight revokes his bold resolve, and more

Repents his courage than his fear before;
Finds that uncertain ways unsafest are,
And Doubt a greater mischief than Despair.   *300*
Then to the stream, when neither friends, nor force,
Nor speed, nor art avail, he shapes his course;
Thinks not their rage so desperate t' assay,
An element more merciless than they.
But fearless they pursue, nor can the flood   *305*
Quench their dire thirst; alas, they thirst for blood.
So towards a ship the oar-finned galleys ply,
Which wanting sea to ride, or wind to fly,
Stands but to fall revenged on those that dare
Tempt the last fury of extreme despair.   *310*
So fares the stag among th' enraged hounds,
Repels their force, and wounds returns for wounds.
And as a hero whom his baser foes
In troops surrounds, now these assails, now those,
Though prodigal of life, disdains to die   *315*
By common hands; but if he can descry
Some nobler foe's approach, to him he calls,
And begs his fate, and then contented falls.
So when the King a mortal shaft lets fly
From his unerring hand, then glad to die,   *320*
Proud of the wound, to it resigns his blood,
And stains the crystal with a purple flood.
      This a more innocent and happy chase
Than when of old, but in the self-same place,
Fair liberty pursued, and meant a prey   *325*
To lawless power, here turned, and stood at bay.
When in that remedy all hope was placed
Which was, or should have been at least, the last.
Here was that Charter sealed, wherein the Crown
All marks of arbitrary power lays down: *330*
Tyrant and slave, those names of hate and fear,
The happier style of King and Subject bear;
Happy, when both to the same centre move,
When kings give liberty, and subjects love.
Therefore not long in force this Charter stood;   *335*
Wanting that seal, it must be sealed in blood.
The subjects armed, the more their princes gave,
Th' advantage only took the more to crave;
Till kings by giving, give themselves away,
And even that power that should deny, betray.   *340*

---

271. unkindly: without kindness or affection, but possibly also carrying the meaning "unnaturally, unlike their kind.' **277. conscious:** sharing or witnessing, understanding (see *pathetic fallacy* in the Glossary). **284. beam:** one of the main stems of a stag's horn, bearing the elaborate antlers. **324. self-same place:** Runnymede, meadow where in 1215 King John, confronted by the superior force of his barons, put the best face upon it and put his seal to and then proclaimed the Magna Carta (the "Charter" of line 329).

"Who gives constrained, but his own fear reviles,
Not thanked, but scorned; nor are they gifts but spoils."
Thus kings, by grasping more than they could hold,
First made their subjects by oppression bold;
And popular sway, by forcing kings to give   345
More than was fit for subjects to receive,
Ran to the same extremes; and one excess
Made both, by striving to be greater, less.
When a calm river raised with sudden rains

Or snows dissolved, o'erflows th' adjoining plains,   350
The husbandmen with high-raised banks secure
Their greedy hopes, and this he can endure.
But if with bays and dams they strive to force
His channel to a new, or narrow course,
No longer then within his banks he dwells;   355
First to a torrent, then a deluge swells:
Stronger and fiercer by restraint he roars,
And knows no bound, but makes his power his shores.

(1642, 1655, 1668)

NICHOLAS CULPEPER
England, 1616-1654

from *THE ENGLISH PHYSICIAN*

Basil (Garden or Sweet)
(Ocymum Basilicum)

Descrip. — The greater or ordinary basil riseth up usually with one upright stalk diversely branching forth on all sides, with two leaves at every joint, which are somewhat broad and round, yet pointed, of a pale green colour, but fresh; a little snipped about the edges, and of a strong healthy scent. The flowers are small and white, and standing at the tops of the branches, with two small leaves at the joints, in some places   5
green, in others brown, after which come black seed. The root perisheth at the approach of winter, and therefore must be sown every year.

Place. — It groweth in gardens.

Time. — It must be sown late, and flowers in the heart of summer, it being a very tender plant.   10

Government and Virtues. — This is the herb which all authors are together by the ears about, and rail at one another, like lawyers. Galen and Dioscorides hold it not fitting to be taken inwardly, and Chrysippus rails at it with downright Billingsgate rhetoric: Pliny and the Arabian Physicians defend it.

For my own part, I presently found that speech true; *Non nostrum inter vos tantas*   15
componere lites.

And away to Dr. Reason went I, who told me it was an herb of Mars, and under the Scorpion, and therefore called basilicon, and it is no marvel if it carry a kind of virulent

---

THE ENGLISH PHYSICIAN   The work later became known as *Culpeper's Complete Herbal*, with the subtitle *Consisting of a Comprehensive Description of Nearly All Herbs, with Their Medicinal Properties, and Directions for Compounding the Medicines Extracted from Them.*   BASIL   **11-12. together by the ears:** quarrelling. **12ff. Galen, Dioscorides,** etc.: physicians, naturalists, philosophers — all authorities of one sort or another. **13. Billingsgate:** scurrilous, foul-mouthed (from the verbal manners of denizens of the London fishmarket). **15-16. *non . . . lites:*** "It is not for us [i.e., me] to settle the fierce quarrels among you" (Virgil, *Eclogues*, III, 108). **17. Mars:** the planet. **18. Scorpion:** the constellation (Scorpio, Scorpius) and house of the zodiac — i.e., astrological terms; **basilicon:** Greek *basilikon*, royal, from *basileus*, king.

quality with it. Being applied to the place bitten by venomous beasts, or stung by a wasp or hornet, it speedily draws the poison to it. — *Every like draws its like*. Mizaldus affirms, that being laid to rot in horse-dung, it will breed venomous beasts. Hilarius, a French physician, affirms upon his own knowledge, that an acquaintance of his, by common smelling to it, had a scorpion bred in his brain. Something is the matter; this herb and rue will never grow together, no, nor near one another; and we know rue is as great an enemy to poison as any that grows.

    To conclude. It expelleth both birth and after-birth: and as it helps the deficiency of Venus in one kind, so it spoils all her actions in another. I dare write no more of it.

(1652)

SIR ROGER L'ESTRANGE
England, 1616-1704

translated from Desiderius Erasmus's *COLLOQUIA FAMILIARIA*

THE INNS

The Civility of the People at Lyons to Strangers and Travellers,
and the Sweetness of the Place. The Churlishness of a German Host,
with a Lively Description of Their Entertainment in Their Stoves.

Bertulphus, Gulielmus (Bertulf & William)

BERTULF.   What's the reason, I wonder, that people will never be gotten out of Lyons under two or three days' stay there? For when I am once upon the way myself, I can never be quiet till I come to my journey's end.

WILLIAM.   Now do I rather wonder that people can be gotten from thence at all.

BERTULF.   Why so?

WILLIAM.   Because 'tis the very place where the Sirens charmed Ulysses and his mates; or 'tis at least the moral of that fable. When a man is there at his inn, he's as well as if he were at his own home.

BERTULF.   Why, what's the way on't then?

COLLOQUIA FAMILIARIA **Desiderius Erasmus:** (c.1466-1536) Dutch scholar, Augustinian priest, and Renaissance humanist. The *Colloquia Familiaria* are known variously in English as the *Familiar Colloquies*, the *Informal Colloquies*, or — most often — simply the *Colloquies*. The first collection was published in 1518, with new and expanded editions following until 1533. "The Inns" first appeared in 1523. The title of L'Estrange's collection is *Twenty Select Colloquies Out of Erasmus Roterodamus, Pleasantly Representing Several Superstitious Levities That Were Crept into the Church of Rome in His Days.*

WILLIAM.   The women are very handsome there, and the table never without one of   *10*
'em to season the entertainment; and with ingenious and innocent raillery to keep
the guests in good humour. First came the mistress of the house, and bade us
welcome; and then her daughter, a very fine woman, and of so pretty a kind of wit
and fashion that it was impossible to be sad while she was in the company. And you
are not received there like strangers, neither, but as if you were familiar friends and   *15*
old acquaintances the first minute you see one another.

BERTULF.   Oh, I know the French way of civility very well.

WILLIAM.   Now because they could not be always with us (what with business, and
what out of respect to their other lodgers), when the daughter left us, we had, to
supply her place till she could return, a lass that was so well instructed in the knack   *20*
of repartees, she had a word for everybody, and no conceit came amiss to her (the
mother you must know was somewhat in years).

BERTULF.   Well, but how were you treated all this while? For stories fill no bellies.

WILLIAM.   Truly so splendidly and so cheap that I was amazed at it. And then after
dinner, we chatted away the time so merrily that I was still at home, methought.   *25*

BERTULF.   And how went matters in your chambers?

WILLIAM.   Why, there we had the girls about us again, giggling and toying, with a
thousand ape-tricks, and their main business was to know what linen we had to
wash. In one word, they were all females that we saw there, save only in the stable
— and we had 'em there too sometimes. Upon our coming away, they could not   *30*
have showed more affection and tenderness at parting if we had been their own
brothers.

BERTULF.   This mode may do well enough in France, but the manly way of the
Germans methinks pleases me better.

WILLIAM.   I never was in Germany, wherefore pray let's know how 'tis there.   *35*

BERTULF.   I can tell you for as much on't as I saw; but how 'tis in other parts of
Germany, I can say little. Mine host never salutes his guest, for fear he should be
thought to have some design upon him, which is looked upon as below the dignity
and gravity of a German. When ye have called a good while at the gate, the master
of the inn puts his head out of the stove window, like a tortoise from under his shell   *40*
(for till the summer solstice they live commonly in stoves). Then does he expect
that you should ask him if there be any lodging there. If he makes you no answer,
you may take it for granted there is; and if you enquire for the stable, without a
word speaking he points you to't, and there you may go and curry your own horse
as you please yourself, for there are no servants there to do that office, unless it be   *45*
an inn of extraordinary note, and then you have one to show you the stable, and a
standing for your horse, but incommodious enough, for they keep the best places
for noblemen, as they pretend, that are yet to come. If you fault anything, they tell
you at next word you had best look out another inn. In their great towns there's
hardly any hay to be got, and 'tis almost as dear too as oats. When you have dressed   *50*
your horse, you come whole into the stove, boots, luggage, dirt, and all, for that's a
common room for all comers.

---

40. stove window: i.e., the window of the stove room, the well-heated public room of the inn.

WILLIAM.   Now in France you have your chamber presently appointed you, where you may change your linen, clean, warm, or rest yourself, as you please.

BERTULF.   There's nothing of that here, for in this stove you put off your boots, don 55 your shoes, change your shirt, if you will, hang up your clothes, or set yourself a-drying. If you have a mind to wash, the water's ready, but then you must have more water to fetch off the dirt of that.

WILLIAM.   I am clearly for these manly people (as you call 'em).

BERTULF.   If you come in at four afternoon, you must not expect to sup before nine or 60 ten.

WILLIAM.   What's the reason of that?

BERTULF.   They never make anything ready till they see their whole company, that they may have but one work on't.

WILLIAM.   For brevity's sake. 65

BERTULF.   Right. So that you shall have betwixt fourscore and an hundred persons sometimes in the same stove: horse and foot, merchants, mariners, wagoners, husbandmen, women and children, sick and sound.

WILLIAM.   Why, here is the true convent (or coenobium) then.

BERTULF.   One's combing of his head, another wiping off his sweat, a third cleaning of 70 his boots, or hob-nail shoes, others belching of garlic. Without more ado, the confusion of Babel for men and languages was nothing to this. If they see any stranger that by his train and habit looks like a man of quality, they stand gaping at him as if he were an African monster; nay, when they are set at the table, and he behind 'em, they'll be still looking back at him, and staring him in the face till they 75 forget their suppers.

WILLIAM.   There's none of this gazing at Rome, Paris, or Venice, &c.

BERTULF.   Take notice, now, that 'tis a mortal sin to call for anything. When 'tis so late that there's no hope of any more guests, out comes ye an old gray-bearded servant, close cropped, with a sour crabbed look, and in a sordid habit. 80

WILLIAM.   He would make a good cup-bearer to a cardinal.

BERTULF.   He overlooks the place, and counts to himself the number of the guests, and the more company, the more fire he puts in the stove, though they were half smothered before. For 'tis a token of respect to stew the people into a sweat. If any man that's ready to choke with the fumes does but open the window never so little, 85 mine host bids him shut it again. If he says he's not able to bear it, get ye another inn then (cries the master).

WILLIAM.   'Tis a dangerous thing, methinks, when men's bodies are opened with the heat, to draw in the vapour of so many people together, to eat in the same place, and stay there so many hours. To say nothing of their belching, farting, and corrupt 90 breaths, some of 'em tainted with secret diseases, and every man contributing to the contagion. Nay, they have most of 'em the French itch, too (and yet why the French, when it's common to all nations?), so that a man might be as safe among so many lepers. Tell me now, what is this sort of pestilence?

BERTULF.   They are strong stout men, and laugh at these niceties. 95

---

69. convent: from the Latin *convenire*, "come together"; **coenobium:** late Latin for convent, living in community. **92. French itch:** syphilis.

WILLIAM.   But in the meantime they are bold at other men's perils.

BERTULF.   Why, what's to be done? 'Tis a thing they are used to, and 'tis a point of resolution not to depart from a custom.

WILLIAM.   And yet till within these five and twenty years nothing was more common in Brabant than hot baths. But we have no more of 'em now, since they are found to   *100* be ill for the Scabbado.

BERTULF.   Now let me go on: By and by comes your bearded Ganymede in again, and lays ye his just number of napkins upon the table; no damask (with a pox to 'em), but the remnants rather of an old sail. There are eight guests at least allotted to every table, and now every man that knows the fashion of the country places   *105* himself where he likes. Rich and poor, master and servant, 'tis all one.

WILLIAM.   This was the primitive equality which is now driven out of the world by tyranny — the very life (as I suppose) of the holy disciples with their Master.

BERTULF.   When they are all seated, out comes the dog-looking graybeard again, counts his company over once more, and by and by brings every man his wooden   *110* dish, with a spoon of the same metal, and then a glass; a while after comes the bread, which the guests may chip at leisure, while the porridge are aboiling; for there they sit waiting perhaps some half an hour.

WILLIAM.   Do none of them call for meat in the meantime?

BERTULF.   Not if they know the country. At last, in comes the wine, and wine that for   *115* the sharpness and subtlety of it, is fitter for a schoolman than a traveller; none of the heady fuming drink, I warrant ye. But if a body should privately offer a piece of money to get a can of better wine, somewhere else, they'll give ye a look, without speaking a word, as if they would murther ye. If you press it further, they'll tell you presently, here have been such and such counts and marquises that found no fault   *120* with this wine; if you don't like it, y'ad best mend yourself elsewhere. You must observe, now, that they only reckon upon their own noblemen, in effect, to be men; and wherever ye come, they are showing you their arms. By this time, comes in a morsel to pacify a barking stomach, and after that, in great pomp, follow the fishes, the first with sippets of bread in flesh porridge, or if it be a fish day, in a soup of   *125* pulse. After that comes in another soup, and then a service of butcher's meat that has been twice boiled, or of salt meats twice heated, and then pulse again, or perhaps some more substantial dish. When ye have taken off the edge of your appetite, they bring ye either roast meat or stewed fish (which is not amiss), but they are sparing on't, and 'tis quickly taken away again. This is the method of their   *130* eating, which they order as comedians do their scenes, into so many courses of chops and soups, still taking care that the last act may be the best.

WILLIAM.   The poet's method, too.

BERTULF.   Now 'tis death for any man to say, "Take away this dish; here's nobody eats," for you are bound to sit out your time, which (as I take it) they measure by an   *135* hour-glass. And at last comes your old servant again, or mine host himself (who is

---

101. Scabbado: venereal disease, syphilis. **102. Ganymede:** beautiful Trojan boy carried off to Olympus to be cupbearer to Zeus (name often used facetiously for bar-waiters). **103. a pox to 'em:** common form of light swearing or cursing (*pox*, syphilis). **125. sippets:** small, thin pieces of bread or toast for mixing with milk or broth; **flesh porridge:** i.e., meat broth; **fish day:** Friday. **126. pulse:** beans.

no better clad), and asks ye, "What cheer, gentlemen?" By and by comes a can of more generous wine. They are men of conscience, ye must know, and love those most that drink most, for (say they) you are all upon the club, and he that drinks most pays no more than he that drinks least. *140*

WILLIAM.   Why, these people are wits.

BERTULF.   There are many of 'em that spend twice as much for their wine as they pay for their ordinary. But before I leave this entertainment, what a horrible noise and confusion of tongues is there when they come once to be warm in their drink! Without more words, it deafens a man. And then you shall many times have a *145* mixture of mimics and buffoons in among them: a most detestable sort of men, and yet you would not think how these people delight in 'em. There's such a singing, bawling, gaggling, leaping, and thundering up and down, and there's no hearing of one another, and you'd think the stove would fall upon your head; and yet this is it they take to be a pleasant life, and there you are condemned to sit in spite of your *150* heart, till toward midnight.

WILLIAM.   Come make an end of your meal, for I'm e'en sick on't too.

BERTULF.   Presently. At length, when the cheese is taken away (which must be rotten and full of maggots or they'll have none on't), in comes your Ganymede once again with a wooden trencher, and so many circles and semicircles drawn in chalk upon't. *155* This he lays upon the table, with a grim countenance, and without speaking; by his look, and by his dish, you would take him for a Charon. They that understand the meaning of all this lay down their money, one after another, till the trencher's covered. The servant takes notice who lays down and then reckons it to himself. If all be paid, he gives you a nod. *160*

WILLIAM.   But what if there should be too much?

BERTULF.   Perhaps he'll give ye it again, for I have seen it done.

WILLIAM.   Does nobody find fault with the reckoning?

BERTULF.   Not if he be wise, for he shall quickly hear on't then. "What are you for a man?" (says he), "you are to pay no more than other people." *165*

WILLIAM.   'Tis a frank nation this.

BERTULF.   If you are weary with your journey, and would go to bed, they'll bid you stay till the rest go too.

WILLIAM.   Plato's commonwealth!

BERTULF.   And then every man has his nest showed him, and in truth it is very properly *170* called a bed-chamber, for there's nothing in't but a bed that a man can either carry away or steal.

WILLIAM.   Everything is clean, however.

BERTULF.   Just as it was at the table. Your sheets are washed perhaps once in six months. *175*

WILLIAM.   But what becomes of your horses?

---

139. upon the club: i.e., sharing the cost equally. **143. ordinary:** meal served in an ordinary, a dining place that serves meals at a fixed price, or table d'hote. **155. trencher:** plate or board for cutting and serving food. **157. Charon:** aged ferryman in Hades who charged the shades of the dead for conveying them across the Styx ("Charon's Toll" is the coin, usually an obolus, the ancient Greeks placed in the hand or mouth of a dead person).

BERTULF. They are treated much at the same rate with the men.

WILLIAM. And is it alike all over Germany?

BERTULF. No. 'Tis better in some places and worse in others; but in general 'tis thus.

WILLIAM. What if I should tell you now how travellers are treated in Lombardy, Spain, *180*
England, Wales? For the English partake of the manners both of the French and
Germans, as a mixture of both nations; but the Welsh boast themselves to be
originals, and of the ancient Britons.

BERTULF. Pray'e tell me how 'tis, for I was never there.

WILLIAM. 'Tis too late now, for my baggage is aboard, and if I fail of being at my boat by *185*
three o'clock I shall lose my passage, but some other time ye shall have the rest at large.

(1680)

RICHARD LOVELACE
England, 1618-1658

TO LUCASTA, GOING BEYOND THE SEAS

If to be absent were to be
    Away from thee;
      Or that when I am gone,
    You or I were alone;
Then, my Lucasta, might I crave   *5*
Pity from blustering wind, or swallowing wave.

But I'll not sigh one blast or gale
    To swell my sail,
      Or pay a tear to suage
    The foaming blue-god's rage;   *10*
For whether he will let me pass
Or no, I'm still as happy as I was.

Though seas and land betwixt us both,
    Our faith and troth,
      Like separated souls,   *15*
    All time and space controls:
Above the highest sphere we meet
Unseen, unknown, and greet as angels greet.

So then we do anticipate
    Our after-fate,   *20*
      And are alive i' th' skies,
    If thus our lips and eyes
Can speak like spirits unconfined
In heaven, their earthy bodies left behind.

(1649)

TO LUCASTA, GOING TO THE WARS

Tell me not, Sweet, I am unkind,
    That from the nunnery
Of thy chaste breast, and quiet mind,
    To war and arms I fly.

True, a new mistress now I chase,   *5*
    The first foe in the field;
And with a stronger faith embrace
    A sword, a horse, a shield.

Yet this inconstancy is such,
    As you too shall adore;   *10*
I could not love thee, Dear, so much,
    Loved I not honour more.

(1649)

TO ALTHEA, FROM PRISON

When Love with unconfined wings
    Hovers within my gates;
And my divine Althea brings
    To whisper at the grates:

When I lie tangled in her hair,   *5*
    And fettered to her eye;
The gods that wanton in the air,
    Know no such liberty.

LOVELACE All three of these poems were songs, set to music in the 17th century. **TO LUCASTA, GOING BEYOND THE SEAS** Lucasta: possibly his fiancée, Lucy Sacheverell. **9. suage:** assuage. **TO ALTHEA, FROM PRISON** Lovelace wrote this poem in

When flowing cups run swiftly round
   With no allaying Thames,   *10*
Our careless heads with roses bound,
   Our hearts with loyal flames;
When thirsty grief in wine we steep,
   When healths and draughts go free,
Fishes that tipple in the deep,   *15*
   Know no such liberty.

When (like committed linnets) I
   With shriller throat shall sing
The sweetness, mercy, majesty,
   And glories of my KING;   *20*

When I shall voice aloud, how good
   He is, how great should be;
Enlarged winds that curl the flood,
   Know no such liberty.

Stone walls do not a prison make,   *25*
   Nor iron bars a cage;
Minds innocent and quiet take
   That for an hermitage;
If I have freedom in my love,
   And in my soul am free;   *30*
Angels alone that soar above,
   Enjoy such liberty.

(1649)

ABRAHAM COWLEY
England, 1618-1667

THE WISH

Well then; I now do plainly see,
This busy world and I shall ne'er agree;
The very honey of all earthly joy
   Does of all meats the soonest cloy;
   And they, methinks, deserve my pity   *5*
Who for it can endure the stings,
The crowd, and buzz, and murmurings
   Of this great hive, the city.

Ah, yet, ere I descend to the grave
May I a small house and large garden have!   *10*
And a few friends, and many books, both true,
   Both wise, and both delightful too!
   And since love ne'er will from me flee,
A mistress moderately fair,
And good as guardian angels are,   *15*
   Only beloved, and loving me!

O fountains, when in you shall I
Myself, eased of unpeaceful thoughts, espy?
O fields! O woods! when, when shall I be made
   The happy tenant of your shade?   *20*

Here's the spring-head of pleasure's flood,
Here's wealthy Nature's treasury,
Where all the riches lie that she
   Has coined and stamped for good.

Pride and ambition here   *25*
Only in farfetched metaphors appear;
Here naught but winds can hurtful murmurs scatter,
   And naught but Echo flatter.
The gods, when they descended, hither
From heaven did always choose their way;   *30*
And therefore we may boldly say
   That 'tis the way, too, thither.

How happy here should I
And one dear she live and, embracing, die!
She who is all the world, and can exclude   *35*
   In deserts, solitude.
   I should have then this only fear,
Lest men, when they my pleasures see,
Should hither throng to live like me,
   And so make a city here.   *40*

(1647)

1642 while in prison for presenting a Royalist petition to Parliament. **10:** i.e., the wine is not diluted with water. **17. committed:** i.e., imprisoned, caged. **23. Enlarged:** i.e., at large, free.

from ANACREONTICS

I. Love

I'll sing of heroes, and of kings;
In mighty numbers, mighty things,
Begin, my Muse; but lo, the strings
To my great song rebellious prove;
The strings will sound of nought but Love.   5
I broke them all, and put on new;
'Tis this or nothing sure will do.
These sure (said I) will me obey;
These sure heroic notes will play.
Straight I began with thundering Jove,   10
And all the immortal powers but Love.
Love smiled, and from my enfeebled lyre
Came gentle airs, such as inspire
Melting love, soft desire.
Farewell then heroes, farewell kings,   15
And mighty numbers, mighty things;
Love tunes my heart just to my strings.

II. Drinking

The thirsty earth soaks up the rain,
And drinks, and gapes for drink again.
The plants suck in the earth, and are
With constant drinking fresh and fair.
The sea itself, which one would think   5
Should have but little need of drink,
Drinks ten thousand rivers up,
So filled that they o'erflow the cup.
The busy sun (and one would guess
By's drunken, fiery face no less)   10
Drinks up the sea, and when he's done,
The moon and stars drink up the sun.
They drink and dance by their own light;
They drink and revel all the night.
Nothing in nature's sober found,   15
But an eternal health goes round.
Fill up the bowl, then, fill it high,
Fill all the glasses there, for why
Should every creature drink but I?
Why, man of morals, tell me why?   20

(1656)

ODE: SITTING AND DRINKING IN THE CHAIR MADE OUT OF THE RELICS OF SIR FRANCIS DRAKE'S SHIP

1.

Cheer up, my mates, the wind does fairly blow,
Clap on more sail and never spare;
    Farewell all lands, for now we are
    In the wide Sea of Drink, and merrily we go.
Bless me, 'tis hot! Another bowl of wine,   5
    And we shall cut the Burning Line:
Hey boys! she scuds away, and by my head I know
    We round the world are sailing now.
What dull men are those who tarry at home,
When abroad they might wantonly roam,   10
    And gain such experience, and spy too
    Such countries and wonders as I do?
But prithee, good Pilot, take heed what you do,
    And fail not to touch at Peru;
    With gold, there the vessel we'll store,   15
    And never, and never be poor,
    No never be poor any more.

2.

What do I mean? What thoughts do me misguide?
As well upon a staff may witches ride
    Their fancied journeys in the air,   20
As I sail round the ocean in this chair:
    'Tis true; but yet this chair which here you see,
For all its quiet now, and gravity,
Has wandered, and has travelled more,
Than ever beast, or fish, or bird, or tree before.   25
In every air, and every sea 't has been,
'T has compassed all the earth, and all the heavens 't has
    seen.
Let not the Pope's itself with this compare;
This is the only Universal Chair.

3.

The pious wanderer's fleet, saved from the flame   30
(Which did the relics still of Troy pursue,
    And took them for its due),

ANACREONTICS The subtitle reads as follows: "Or, Some Copies of Verses Translated Paraphrastically Out Of Anacreon." Anacreon (c.570-c.485 B.C.) was a Greek lyric poet, much imitated (in "Anacreontics") for both style (metres and stanza) and subject matter (pleasures such as love and wine), though few of his own poems survive.   **LOVE** Cf. Mary Whateley Darwall's version of the same poem by Anacreon (p. 682). **2. numbers:** metrical feet, verses. **17. just:** exactly, accurately.   **DRINKING   16. health:** i.e., a toast, usually to another's health.   **ODE: SITTING AND DRINKING** The chair made out of wood from *The Golden Hind*, the ship in which Drake circumnavigated the globe, was given to the University Library at Oxford, now the Bodleian Library. **6. Burning Line:** the equator. **30-35:** The ships of Aeneas (often called "pious Aeneas"), about to be set fire to by Turnus in their Italian anchorage, were saved by Cybele and turned into nymphs (see Virgil's *Aeneid*, IX, 69-122; Ovid, *Metamorphoses*, XIV, 531ff.).

A squadron of immortal nymphs became:
Still with their arms they row about the seas,
And still make new and greater voyages; 35
Nor has the first poetic ship of Greece
(Though now a star she so triumphant show,
And guide her sailing successors below,
Bright as her ancient freight the shining fleece)
Yet to this day a quiet harbour found; 40
The tide of heaven still carries her around.
Only Drake's sacred vessel, which before
   Had done, and had seen more,
   Than those have done, or seen,
Ev'n since they goddesses, and this a star has been; 45
As a reward for all her labour past,
   Is made the seat of rest at last.
   Let the case now quite altered be,
And as thou went'st abroad the world to see,
Let the world now come to see thee. 50

4.
The world will do't; for curiosity
Does no less than devotion, pilgrims make;
And I myself who now love quiet too,
As much almost as any chair can do,
   Would yet a journey take 55
An old wheel of the chariot to see,
   Which Phaeton so rashly brake:
Yet what could that say more than these remains of
   Drake?
Great relic! thou too, in the port of ease,
Hast still one way of making voyages; 60
The breath of fame, like an auspicious gale
   (The great trade-wind which ne'er does fail)
Shall drive thee round the world, and thou shalt run
   As long around it as the sun.
The straits of time too narrow are for thee; 65
Lanch forth into an undiscovered sea,
And steer the endless course of vast Eternity;
Take for the sail this verse, and for thy pilot me.

(1663)

JOHN EVELYN
England, 1620-1706

from *DIARY*
2 September–10 October 1666 (The Great Fire of London)

September 2
This fatal night, about ten, began the deplorable fire, near Fish Street, in London.

September 3
I had public prayers at home. The fire continuing, after dinner I took coach with my wife and son and went to the Bankside in Southwark, where we beheld that dismal spectacle, the whole city in dreadful flames near the waterside; all the houses from the bridge, all Thames Street, and upwards towards Cheapside, down to the Three Cranes, were now consumed; and so returned exceeding astonished what would become of the rest. 5

36-41: The "first poetic ship," the *Argo*, sailed by Jason and the Argonauts on their quest for the Golden Fleece, was supposedly turned by Athene into the southern constellation Argo, "The Ship." **57. Phaeton:** Phaethon, son of Helios, who tried to drive the Sun Chariot for a day, but was unable to control the horses, and was killed by Zeus to save the world from being consumed by the fire (see also note to Denham's *Cooper's Hill*, line 166, p. 385); **brake:** broke. **66. Lanch:** launch.   EVELYN'S DIARY   The *Diary* was first published in 1818. Cf. the account of the fire in the ballad "London Mourning in Ashes," and the notes, p. 299. **4ff. bridge:** i.e., London Bridge; Thames Street runs parallel to the river; Cheapside is a few blocks north; the Three Cranes was a few blocks west of the bridge.

The fire having continued all this night (if I may call that night which was light as day for ten miles round about, after a dreadful manner), when conspiring with a fierce eastern wind in a very dry season, I went on foot to the same place, and saw the whole south part of the city burning from Cheapside to the Thames, and all along Cornhill (for it likewise kindled back against the wind as well as forward), Tower Street, *10* Fenchurch Street, Gracious Street, and so along to Baynard's Castle, and was now taking hold of St. Paul's Church, to which the scaffolds contributed exceedingly. The conflagration was so universal, and the people so astonished, that from the beginning, I know not by what despondency or fate, they hardly stirred to quench it, so that there was nothing heard or seen but crying out and lamentation, running about like *15* distracted creatures, without at all attempting to save even their goods; such a strange consternation there was upon them, so as it burned both in breadth and length, the churches, public halls, Exchange, hospitals, monuments, and ornaments, leaping after a prodigious manner from house to house and street to street, at great distances one from the other, for the heat, with a long set of fair and warm weather, had even ignited *20* the air, and prepared the materials to conceive the fire, which devoured, after an incredible manner, houses, furniture, and everything. Here we saw the Thames covered with goods floating, all the barges and boats laden with what some had time and courage to save, as on the other side the carts &c. carrying out to the fields, which for many miles were strewed with moveables of all sorts, and tents erecting to shelter *25* both people and what goods they could get away. Oh the miserable and calamitous spectacle, such as haply the world had not seen since the foundation of it, nor can be outdone till the universal conflagration thereof! All the sky was of a fiery aspect, like the top of a burning oven, and the light seen above forty miles round about for many nights. God grant mine eyes may never behold the like, who now saw above ten *30* thousand houses all in one flame. The noise and cracking and thunder of the impetuous flames, the shrieking of women and children, the hurry of people, the fall of towers, houses and churches, was like a hideous storm, and the air all about so hot and inflamed that at the last one was not able to approach it, so that they were forced to stand still and let the flames burn on, which they did for near two miles in length and *35* one in breadth. The clouds also of smoke were dismal, and reached upon computation near fifty miles in length. Thus I left it this afternoon burning, a resemblance of Sodom, or the last day. It forcibly called to mind that passage, *non enim hic habemus stabilem civitatem*: the ruins resembling the picture of Troy. London was, but is no more. Thus I returned. *40*

September 4

The burning still rages, and it is now gotten as far as the Inner Temple. All Fleet Street, the Old Bailey, Ludgate Hill, Warwick Lane, Newgate, Paul's Chain, Watling Street now flaming, and most of it reduced to ashes; the stones of Paul's flew like grenados,

---

12. Gracious: i.e., Gracechurch. **26. erecting:** i.e., being erected. **39. Sodom:** see Genesis 19:24. **39–40:** "For here have we no continuing city" (Hebrews 13:14). **42. Inner Temple:** See note to line 11 of Dekker's "How a Gallant Should Behave" (p. 238).

the melting lead running down the streets in a stream, and the very pavements glowing   *45*
with fiery redness, so as no horse nor man was able to tread on them, and the demolition
had stopped all the passages, so that no help could be applied; the eastern wind still
more impetuously driving the flames forward. Nothing but the almighty power of God
was able to stop them, for vain was the help of man.

September 5

It crossed toward Whitehall, but oh, the confusion there was then at that court! It   *50*
pleased His Majesty to command me, among the rest, to look after the quenching of
Fetter Lane end, to preserve, if possible, that part of Holborn, while the rest of the
gentlemen took their several posts, some at one part and some at another; for now they
began to bestir themselves, and not till now, who hitherto had stood as men intoxicated,
with their hands across, and began to consider that nothing was likely to put a stop but   *55*
the blowing up of so many houses as might make a wider gap than any had yet been
made by the ordinary method of pulling them down with engines. This some stout
seamen proposed early enough to have saved near the whole city; but this some
tenacious and avaricious men, aldermen, etc., would not permit, because their houses
must have been of the first. It was therefore now commanded to be practised, and my   *60*
concern being particularly for the Hospital of St. Bartholomew, near Smithfield, where I
had many wounded and sick men, made me the more diligent to promote it; nor was my
care for the Savoy less. It now pleased God, by abating the wind, and by the industry of
the people, when almost all was lost, infusing a new spirit into them, that the fury of it
began sensibly to abate about noon, so as it came no farther than the Temple westward   *65*
nor than the entrance of Smithfield north, but continued all this day and night so
impetuous toward Cripplegate and the Tower as made us all despair. It also broke out
again in the Temple, but the courage of the multitude persisting, and many houses being
blown up, such gaps and desolations were soon made as, with the former three days'
consumption, the back fire did not so vehemently urge upon the rest as formerly. There   *70*
was yet no standing near the burning and glowing ruins by near a furlong's space. The
coal and wood wharfs, and magazines of oil, rosin, etc. did infinite mischief, so as the
invective which a little before I had dedicated to His Majesty and published, giving
warning what probably might be the issue of suffering those shops to be in the city, was
looked upon as a prophecy.   *75*

The poor inhabitants were dispersed about St. George's Fields, and Moorfields, as
far as Highgate, and several miles in circle, some under tents, some under miserable
huts and hovels, many without a rag, or any necessary utensils, bed or board, who from
delicateness, riches, and easy accommodations in stately and well-furnished houses,

---

45. melting lead: from the lead plates or sheets used to cover roofs of churches and the like. **46. demolition:** See lines 55-60 below. **55. hands across:** arms folded. **60-63:** Evelyn served on many commissions, including one having to do with caring for "wounded and sick" men, including prisoners, from the second Dutch war (1665-67); **Savoy:** site of another hospital, near the Temple. **65. sensibly:** i.e., noticeably. **73-75. invective . . . :** Evelyn's *Fumifugium, or The Inconvenience of the Air and Smoke of London Dissipated* (1661) had proposed solutions to pollution problems, but had not been acted upon.

were now reduced to extreme misery and poverty. In this calamitous condition I   *80*
returned with a sad heart to my house, blessing and adoring the distinguishing mercy of
God to me and mine, who, in the midst of all this ruin, was like Lot, in my little Zoar,
safe and sound.

September 6

Thursday. I represented to His Majesty the case of the French prisoners at war in my
custody, and besought him that there might be still the same care of watching at all   *85*
places contiguous to unseized houses. It is not indeed imaginable how extraordinary the
vigilance and activity of the King and the Duke was, even labouring in person, and
being present to command, order, reward, or encourage workmen; by which he showed
his affection to his people, and gained theirs. Having then disposed of some under cure
at the Savoy, I returned to Whitehall, where I dined at Mr. Offley's, the groom-porter,   *90*
who was my relation.

September 7

I went this morning on foot from Whitehall as far as London Bridge, through the late
Fleet Street, Ludgate Hill by St. Paul's, Cheapside, Exchange, Bishopsgate, Aldersgate,
and out to Moorfields, thence through Cornhill, etc., with extraordinary difficulty,
clambering over heaps of yet smoking rubbish, and frequently mistaking where I was;   *95*
the ground under my feet so hot that it even burnt the soles of my shoes. In the
meantime, His Majesty got to the Tower by water, to demolish the houses about the
graff, which being built entirely about it, had they taken fire and attacked the White
Tower, where the magazine of powder lay, would undoubtedly not only have beaten
down and destroyed all the bridge, but sunk and torn the vessels in the river, and   *100*
rendered the demolition beyond all expression for several miles about the country.

At my return I was infinitely concerned to find that goodly church St. Paul's now a
sad ruin, and that beautiful portico, for structure comparable to any in Europe, as not
long before repaired by the late King, now rent in pieces, flakes of vast stones split
asunder, and nothing remaining entire but the inscription in the architrave showing by   *105*
whom it was built, which had not one letter of it defaced. It was astonishing to see what
immense stones the heat had in a manner calcined, so that all the ornaments, columns,
friezes, capitals, and projectures of massy Portland stone flew off even to the very roof,
where a sheet of lead covering a great space, no less than six acres by measure, was
totally melted. The ruins of the vaulted roof, falling, broke into St. Faith's, which being   *110*
filled with the magazine of books belonging to the stationers and carried thither for
safety, they were all consumed, burning for a week following. It is also observable that
the lead over the altar at the east end was untouched, and among the divers monuments,
the body of one bishop remained entire. Thus lay in ashes that most venerable church,
one of the most ancient pieces of early piety in the Christian world, besides near one   *115*
hundred more. The lead, iron-work, bells, plate, etc., melted; the exquisitely wrought

---

82. Zoar: See Genesis 13:10, 19:17ff.; of the "cities of the plain," Zoar alone escaped destruction. **84. French prisoners:** In January, France had
joined the Dutch against England. **98. graff:** the trench around the base of the Tower.

Mercer's Chapel, the sumptuous Exchange, the august fabric of Christ Church, all the rest of the companies' halls, splendid buildings, arches, entries, all in dust; the fountains dried up and ruined, whilst the very waters remained boiling; the voragos of subterranean cellars, wells, and dungeons, formerly warehouses, still burning in stench *120* and dark clouds of smoke; so that in five or six miles traversing about I did not see one load of timber unconsumed, nor many stones but were calcined white as snow.

The people who now walked about the ruins appeared like men in some dismal desert, or rather in some great city laid waste by a cruel enemy, to which was added the stench that came from some poor creatures' bodies, beds, and other combustible goods. Sir *125* Thomas Gresham's statue, though fallen from its niche in the Royal Exchange, remained entire, when all those of the kings since the Conquest were broken to pieces. Also the standard in Cornhill and Queen Elizabeth's effigies, with some arms on Ludgate, continued with but little detriment, whilst the vast iron chains of the city streets, hinges, bars, and gates of prisons were many of them melted and reduced to cinders by the *130* vehement heat. Nor was I yet able to pass through any of the narrow streets, but kept the widest; the ground and air, smoke and fiery vapour, continued so intense that my hair was almost singed and my feet insufferably surbated. The by-lanes and narrow streets were quite filled up with rubbish, nor could one have possibly known where he was but by the ruins of some great church or hall that had some remarkable tower or pinnacle remaining. *135*

I then went towards Islington and Highgate, where one might have seen two hundred thousand people of all ranks and degrees dispersed and lying along by their heaps of what they could save from the fire, deploring their loss and, though ready to perish for hunger and destitution, yet not asking one penny for relief, which appeared to me a stranger sight than any I had yet beheld. His Majesty and council indeed took all *140* imaginable care for their relief by proclamation for the country to come in and refresh them with provisions.

In the midst of all this calamity and confusion, there was, I know not how, an alarm begun that the French and Dutch, with whom we were now in hostility, were not only landed, but even entering the city. There was, in truth, some days before, great suspicion *145* of those two nations joining, and now that they had been the occasion of firing the town. This report did so terrify, that on a sudden there was such an uproar and tumult that they ran from their goods, and taking what weapons they could come at, they could not be stopped from falling on some of those nations whom they casually met, without sense or reason. The clamour and peril grew so excessive that it made the whole Court amazed, *150* and they did with infinite pains and great difficulty reduce and appease the people, sending troops of soldiers and guards to cause them to retire into the fields again, where they were watched all this night. I left them pretty quiet, and came home sufficiently weary and broken. Their spirits thus a little calmed, and the affright abated, they now began to repair into the suburbs about the city, where such as had friends or opportunity *155* got shelter for the present, to which His Majesty's proclamation also invited them. Still, the plague continuing in our parish, I could not without danger adventure to our church.

---

119. voragos: abysses, chasms. **133. surbated:** bruised, battered. **157. the plague:** "The Great Plague of London," 1664-66, was England's last major outbreak of bubonic plague; a popular belief credits the "Great Fire" with putting an end to the "Great Plague," but the fire spared the areas where the plague was worst.

September 10
I went again to the ruins, for it was no longer a city.

September 13
I presented His Majesty with a survey of the ruins, and a plot for a new city, with a
discourse on it, whereupon, after dinner, His Majesty sent for me into the Queen's bed- *160*
chamber, Her Majesty and the Duke only being present. They examined each particular,
and discoursed on them for near an hour, seeming to be extremely pleased with what I
had so early thought on. The Queen was now in her cavalier riding-habit, hat and
feather, and horseman's coat, going to take the air.

September 16
I went to Greenwich Church, where Mr. Plume preached very well from this text: *165*
"Seeing, then, all these things shall be dissolved," etc., taking occasion from the late
unparalleled conflagration to remind us how we ought to walk more holy in all manner
of conversation.

October 10
This day was ordered a general fast through the nation to humble us on the late dreadful
conflagration, added to the plague and war, the most dismal judgments that could be *170*
inflicted, but which indeed we highly deserved for our prodigious ingratitude, burning
lusts, dissolute court, profane and abominable lives, under such dispensations of God's
continued favour in restoring Church, Prince, and People from our late intestine
calamities, of which we were altogether unmindful, even to astonishment. This made me
resolve to go to our parish assembly, where our Doctor preached on Luke 19:41, piously *175*
applying it to the occasion. After which was a collection for the distressed losers in the
late fire.

Andrew Marvell
England, 1621-1678

On Mr Milton's "Paradise Lost"

When I beheld the poet blind, yet bold,
In slender book his vast design unfold,
Messiah crowned, God's reconciled decree,
Rebelling Angels, the Forbidden Tree,
Heaven, Hell, Earth, Chaos, all; the argument   5

Held me a while, misdoubting his intent
That he would ruin (for I saw him strong)
The sacred truths to fable and old song,
(So Sampson groped the temple's posts in spite)
The world o'erwhelming to revenge his sight.   *10*

---

168. conversation: behaviour (see I Peter 1:15). **175. Luke 19:41:** "And when he was come near, he beheld the city, and wept over it."   **On Mr**
Milton's "Paradise Lost"   In 1657 Marvell joined Milton in Cromwell's government, and after the Restoration helped save Milton
from a long prison term or even possible execution. **9:** For Samson's story, see Judges 13-16; Milton adapted it for his *Samson Agonistes* (1671).

Yet as I read, soon growing less severe,
I liked his project, the success did fear;
Through that wide field how he his way should find
O'er which lame faith leads understanding blind;
Lest he perplexed the things he would explain,   *15*
And what was easy he should render vain.

   Or if a work so infinite he spanned,
Jealous I was that some less skilful hand
(Such as disquiet always what is well,
And by ill imitating would excel)   *20*
Might hence presume the whole Creation's day
To change in scenes, and show it in a play.

   Pardon me, Mighty Poet, nor despise
My causeless, yet not impious, surmise.
But I am now convinced that none will dare   *25*
Within thy labours to pretend a share.
Thou hast not missed one thought that could be fit,
And all that was improper dost omit:
So that no room is here for writers left,
But to detect their ignorance or theft.   *30*
That majesty which through thy work doth reign
Draws the devout, deterring the profane.
And things divine thou treat'st of in such state
As them preserves, and thee, inviolate.
At once delight and horror on us seize,   *35*
Thou sing'st with so much gravity and ease;
And above human flight dost soar aloft,
With plume so strong, so equal, and so soft.
The bird named from that paradise you sing
So never flags, but always keeps on wing.   *40*

   Where couldst thou words of such a compass find?
Whence furnish such a vast expense of mind?
Just heaven thee, like Tiresias, to requite,
Rewards with prophecy thy loss of sight.

   Well mightst thou scorn thy readers to allure   *45*
With tinkling rhyme, of thine own sense secure;
While the *Town-Bayes* writes all the while and spells,
And like a pack-horse tires without his bells.
Their fancies like our bushy points appear,
The poets tag them; we for fashion wear.   *50*

I too, transported by the mode, offend,
And while I meant to *praise* thee must *commend*.
Thy verse created like thy theme sublime,
In number, weight, and measure, needs not rhyme.

(1674)

ON A DROP OF DEW

See how the orient dew,
Shed from the bosom of the morn
   Into the blowing roses,
Yet careless of its mansion new,
For the clear region where 'twas born   *5*
   Round in itself incloses:
   And in its little globe's extent,
Frames as it can its native element.
   How it the purple flow'r does slight,
      Scarce touching where it lies,   *10*
   But gazing back upon the skies,
      Shines with a mournful light,
         Like its own tear,
Because so long divided from the sphere.
   Restless it rolls and unsecure,   *15*
      Trembling lest it grow impure,
      Till the warm sun pity its pain,
And to the skies exhale it back again.
      So the soul, that drop, that ray
Of the clear fountain of eternal day,   *20*
Could it within the human flow'r be seen,
      Remembering still its former height,
      Shuns the sweet leaves and blossoms green,
      And recollecting its own light,
Does, in its pure and circling thoughts, express   *25*
The greater heaven in an heaven less.
   In how coy a figure wound,
   Every way it turns away:
   So the world excluding round,
   Yet receiving in the day,   *30*
   Dark beneath, but bright above,
   Here disdaining, there in love.

How loose and easy hence to go,
How girt and ready to ascend;
Moving but on a point below,   *35*
It all about does upwards bend.
Such did the manna's sacred dew distill,
White and entire, though congealed and chill,
Congealed on earth: but does, dissolving, run
Into the glories of th' almighty sun.   *40*

                                        (1681)

BERMUDAS

Where the remote Bermudas ride
In th' ocean's bosom unespied,
From a small boat, that rowed along,
The listening winds received this song.
     "What should we do but sing his praise   *5*
That led us through the watery maze,
Unto an isle so long unknown,
And yet far kinder than our own?
Where he the huge sea-monsters wracks,
That lift the deep upon their backs,   *10*
He lands us on a grassy stage,
Safe from the storms, and prelate's rage.
He gave us this eternal spring,
Which here enamels everything,
And sends the fowl to us in care,   *15*
On daily visits through the air.
He hangs in shades the orange bright,
Like golden lamps in a green night,
And does in the pom'granates close
Jewels more rich than Ormus shows.   *20*
He makes the figs our mouths to meet,
And throws the melons at our feet,
But apples plants of such a price,
No tree could ever bear them twice.
With cedars, chosen by his hand,   *25*
From Lebanon, he stores the land,
And makes the hollow seas, that roar,
Proclaim the ambergris on shore.
He cast (of which we rather boast)
The gospel's pearl upon our coast,   *30*

And in these rocks for us did frame
A temple, where to sound his name.
Oh let our voice his praise exalt,
Till it arrive at heaven's vault:
Which thence (perhaps) rebounding, may   *35*
Echo beyond the Mexique Bay."
     Thus sung they, in the English boat,
An holy and a cheerful note,
And all the way, to guide their chime,
With falling oars they kept the time.   *40*

                                        (1681)

A DIALOGUE BETWEEN
THE SOUL AND BODY

SOUL
O, who shall from this dungeon raise
A soul, enslaved so many ways,
With bolts of bones, that fettered stands
In feet, and manacled in hands?
Here blinded with an eye; and there   *5*
Deaf with the drumming of an ear,
A soul hung up, as 'twere, in chains
Of nerves, and arteries, and veins,
Tortured, besides each other part,
In a vain head, and double heart.   *10*

BODY
O, who shall me deliver whole,
From bonds of this tyrannic soul,
Which, stretched upright, impales me so,
That mine own precipice I go;
And warms and moves this needless frame   *15*
(A fever could but do the same),
And, wanting where its spite to try,
Has made me live to let me die,
A body that could never rest,
Since this ill spirit it possessed?   *20*

SOUL
What magic could me thus confine
Within another's grief to pine?

37ff.: See Exodus 16.   **BERMUDAS   7:** European contact with the islands dates from Juan de Bermudez's voyage in 1515. The British landing in 1612 (see line 37) was led by Richard More. **12. prelate's:** i.e., bishop's. **20. Ormus:** Hormuz, in the Persian Gulf (see note to *Paradise Lost*, II, 2, p. 336). **23. apples:** pineapples, presumably, despite the "trees" in line 24. **30. gospel's pearl:** see Matthew 13:45-46.

Where, whatsoever it complain,
I feel, that cannot feel, the pain,
And all my care itself employs,   *25*
That to preserve, which me destroys:
Constrained not only to endure
Diseases, but, what's worse, the cure:
And ready oft the port to gain,
Am shipwrackt into health again?   *30*

BODY
But physic yet could never reach
The maladies thou me dost teach:
Whom first the cramp of hope does tear,
And then the palsy shakes of fear;
The pestilence of love does heat,   *35*
Or hatred's hidden ulcer eat;
Joy's cheerful madness does perplex,
Or sorrow's other madness vex;
Which knowledge forces me to know,
And memory will not forgo.   *40*
What but a soul could have the wit
To build me up for sin so fit?
So architects do square and hew
Green trees that in the forest grew.

(1681)

TO HIS COY MISTRESS

Had we but world enough, and time,
This coyness, Lady, were no crime.
We would sit down, and think which way
To walk, and pass our long love's day.
Thou by the Indian Ganges' side   *5*
Shouldst rubies find: I by the tide
Of Humber would complain. I would
Love you ten years before the flood:
And you should, if you please, refuse
Till the conversion of the Jews.   *10*

My vegetable love should grow
Vaster than empires, and more slow.
An hundred years should go to praise
Thine eyes, and on thy forehead gaze.
Two hundred to adore each breast: *15*
But thirty thousand to the rest.
An age at least to every part,
And the last age should show your heart:
For, Lady, you deserve this state;
Nor would I love at lower rate.   *20*
    But at my back I always hear
Time's winged chariot hurrying near:
And yonder all before us lie
Deserts of vast eternity.
Thy beauty shall no more be found;   *25*
Nor, in thy marble vault, shall sound
My echoing song: then worms shall try
That long-preserved virginity:
And your quaint honour turn to dust;
And into ashes all my lust.   *30*
The grave's a fine and private place,
But none, I think, do there embrace.
    Now, therefore, while the youthful hue
Sits on thy skin like morning dew,
And while thy willing soul transpires   *35*
At every pore with instant fires,
Now let us sport us while we may;
And now, like amorous birds of prey,
Rather at once our time devour,
Than languish in his slow-chapped power.   *40*
Let us roll all our strength, and all
Our sweetness, up into one ball:
And tear our pleasures with rough strife,
Thorough the iron gates of life.
Thus, though we cannot make our sun   *45*
Stand still, yet we will make him run.

(1681)

A DIALOGUE BETWEEN THE SOUL AND BODY 31. physic: medicine. **TO HIS COY MISTRESS 6-7:** Marvell was from Hull, which is on the Humber near its mouth, where the river is tidal (he was member of parliament for Hull for the last twenty years of his life); **complain:** i.e., write love complaints. **24:** The original spelling indicates the intended pronunciation, with broad *a*'s instead of *e*'s: "Des*a*rts of vast et*a*rnity," with the final *ty* rhyming with *lie* in the preceding line. **29. quaint:** prim, fastidious, perhaps with a pun on the older meaning, pudendum. **40. slow-chapped:** slow-jawed (cf. *chops*); in Greek myth, Kronos, the Titan associated with Time, devoured his own sons because one of them was fated to overthrow him. **44. Thorough:** through. **45-46. sun Stand still:** as Joshua did (see Joshua 10:12-13).

THE GARDEN

How vainly men themselves amaze
To win the palm, the oak, or bays,
And their uncessant labours see
Crowned from some single herb or tree,
Whose short and narrow verged shade   5
Does prudently their toils upbraid,
While all flow'rs and all trees do close
To weave the garlands of repose.

Fair Quiet, have I found thee here,
And Innocence, thy sister dear!   10
Mistaken long, I sought you then
In busy companies of men.
Your sacred plants, if here below,
Only among the plants will grow.
Society is all but rude,   15
To this delicious solitude.

No white nor red was ever seen
So am'rous as this lovely green.
Fond lovers, cruel as their flame,
Cut in these trees their mistress' name.   20
Little, alas, they know, or heed,
How far these beauties hers exceed!
Fair trees! wheres'e'er your barks I wound,
No name shall but your own be found.

When we have run our passion's heat,   25
Love hither makes his best retreat.
The gods, that mortal beauty chase,
Still in a tree did end their race.
Apollo hunted Daphne so,
Only that she might laurel grow.   30
And Pan did after Syrinx speed,
Not as a nymph, but for a reed.

What wondrous life is this I lead!
Ripe apples drop about my head;
The luscious clusters of the vine   35
Upon my mouth do crush their wine;

The nectarine, and curious peach,
Into my hands themselves do reach;
Stumbling on melons, as I pass,
Ensnared with flow'rs, I fall on grass.   40

Meanwhile the mind, from pleasures less,
Withdraws into its happiness:
The mind, that ocean where each kind
Does straight its own resemblance find,
Yet it creates, transcending these,   45
Far other worlds, and other seas,
Annihilating all that's made
To a green thought in a green shade.

Here at the fountain's sliding foot,
Or at some fruit-tree's mossy root,   50
Casting the body's vest aside,
My soul into the boughs does glide:
There like a bird it sits, and sings,
Then whets, and combs its silver wings;
And, till prepared for longer flight,   55
Waves in its plumes the various light.

Such was that happy garden-state,
While man there walked without a mate:
After a place so pure, and sweet,
What other help could yet be meet!   60
But 'twas beyond a mortal's share
To wander solitary there:
Two paradises 'twere in one
To live in paradise alone.

How well the skilful gardener drew   65
Of flowers and herbs this dial new,
Where from above the milder sun
Does through a fragrant zodiac run;
And, as it works, the industrious bee
Computes its time as well as we.   70
How could such sweet and wholesome hours
Be reckoned but with herbs and flow'rs!

(1681)

THE GARDEN   **2: Palm, oak,** and **bays** (laurel) were awards for various kinds of excellence or victory. **18. green:** In the 17th century, one of the associations of *green* was with sexuality. **23-30:** See Ovid's *Metamorphoses*, I, 450ff. **31-32:** See Ovid's *Metamorphoses*, I, 691ff. **37. curious:** exquisite. **60:** Cf. Genesis 2:18, 20 (p. 243).

ANTHONY ASHLEY COOPER
1ST EARL OF SHAFTESBURY, England, 1621-1683

HENRY HASTINGS

Mr. Hastings, by his quality, being the son, brother, and uncle to the Earls of Huntingdon, and his way of living, had the first place amongst us. He was peradventure an original in our age, or rather the copy of our nobility in ancient days in hunting and not warlike times; he was low, very strong and very active, of a reddish flaxen hair, his clothes always green cloth, and never all worth when new five pounds. His house was   *5* perfectly of the old fashion, in the midst of a large park well stocked with deer, and near the house rabbits to serve his kitchen, many fish-ponds, and great store of wood and timber; a bowling-green in it, long but narrow, full of high ridges, it being never levelled since it was ploughed; they used round sand bowls, and it had a banqueting-house like a stand, a large one built in a tree. He kept all manner of sport-hounds that ran buck, fox,   *10* hare, otter, and badger, and hawks long and short winged; he had all sorts of nets for fishing: he had a walk in the New Forest and the manor of Christ Church. This last supplied him with red deer, sea and river fish; and indeed all his neighbours' grounds and royalties were free to him, who bestowed all his time in such sports, but what he borrowed to caress his neighbours' wives and daughters, there being not a woman in all   *15* his walks of the degree of a yeoman's wife or under, and under the age of forty, but it was extremely her fault if he were not intimately acquainted with her. This made him very popular, always speaking kindly to the husband, brother, or father, who was to boot very welcome to his house whenever he came. There he found beef pudding and small beer in great plenty, a house not so neatly kept as to shame him or his dirty shoes, the   *20* great hall strewed with marrow bones, full of hawks' perches, hounds, spaniels, and terriers, the upper sides of the hall hung with the fox-skins of this and the last year's skinning, here and there a polecat intermixed, guns and keepers' and huntsmen's poles in abundance. The parlour was a large long room, as properly furnished; on a great hearth paved with brick lay some terriers and the choicest hounds and spaniels; seldom   *25* but two of the great chairs had litters of young cats in them, which were not to be disturbed, he having always three or four attending him at dinner, and a little white round stick of fourteen inches long lying by his trencher, that he might defend such meat as he had no mind to part with to them. The windows, which were very large, served for places to lay his arrows, crossbows, stonebows, and other such like accoutrements; the   *30* corners of the room full of the best chose hunting and hawking poles; an oyster-table at the lower end, which was of constant use twice a day all the year round, for he never failed to eat oysters before dinner and supper through all seasons: the neighbouring town of Poole supplied him with them. The upper part of this room had two small tables

---

HENRY HASTINGS   This "character," frequently printed as a separate unit, was originally part of a "Fragment of Autobiography" Shaftesbury wrote in his last years. Hastings (1551-1650) and Shaftesbury were neighbours in Dorsetshire. **1-2:** Hastings was the second son of George Hastings, 4th Earl of Huntingdon, therefore brother of the 5th and uncle of the 6th. **19-20. small beer:** i.e., weak beer (cf. 41).

and a desk, on the one side of which was a church Bible, on the other the Book of   *35*
Martyrs; on the tables were hawks' hoods, bells, and such like, two or three old green
hats with their crowns thrust in so as to hold ten or a dozen eggs, which were of a
pheasant kind of poultry he took much care of and fed himself; tables, dice, cards, and
boxes were not wanting. In the hole of the desk were store of tobacco-pipes that had
been used. On one side of this end of the room was the door of a closet, wherein stood   *40*
the strong beer and the wine, which never came thence but in single glasses, that being
the rule of the house exactly observed, for he never exceeded in drink or permitted it.
On the other side was a door into an old chapel not used for devotion; the pulpit, as the
safest place, was never wanting of a cold chine of beef, pasty of venison, gammon of
bacon, or great apple-pie, with thick crust extremely baked. His table cost him not   *45*
much, though it was very good to eat at, his sports supplying all but beef and mutton,
except Friday, when he had the best sea-fish as well as other fish he could get, and was
the day that his neighbours of best quality most visited him. He never wanted a London
pudding, and always sung it in with "my part lies therein-a." He drank a glass of wine or
two at meals, very often syrup of gilliflower in his sack, and had always a tun glass   *50*
without feet stood by him holding a pint of small beer, which he often stirred with a
great sprig of rosemary. He was well natured, but soon angry, calling his servants
bastard and cuckoldy knaves, in one of which he often spoke truth to his own
knowledge, and sometimes in both, though of the same man. He lived to a hundred,
never lost his eyesight, but always writ and read without spectacles, and got to horse   *55*
without help. Until past fourscore he rode to the death of a stag as well as any.

(c. 1680; 1753)

HENRY VAUGHAN
England, 1621-1695

THE WORLD

I saw eternity the other night
Like a great ring of pure and endless light,
   All calm as it was bright;
And round beneath it, time in hours, days, years,
    Driv'n by the spheres,   *5*

Like a vast shadow moved, in which the world
   And all her train were hurled.
The doting lover in his quaintest strain
    Did there complain;
Near him his lute, his fancy, and his flights,   *10*

35-36. Book of Martyrs: popular name for a vast work by John Foxe (1516-1587), *Acts and Monuments of These Latter Perilous Times Touching Matters of the Church* (Latin 1559, English 1563), a not highly reliable history of the Christian church, focussing on past martyrs but more so on Catholic persecutions and recent Protestant martyrs. **38. tables:** boards for backgammon or draughts (checkers). **39. boxes:** dice-boxes. **44. chine:** cut of meat including the backbone; **pasty:** pie with meat or other filling, baked without a dish; **gammon:** bottom piece of flitch of bacon, including hind leg. **49. "my part lies therein-a":** part of a catch published in a 1609 collection called *Pammelia: Music's Miscellany*; the relevant stanza: "There lies a pudding in the fire, / and my part lies therein-a; / whom should I call in, / O thy good fellows and mine-a." **50. gilliflower:** clove or clove-like plant; **sack:** dry Spanish wine; sherry; **tun glass:** probably a barrel-shaped drinking glass.   **THE WORLD   5. spheres:** i.e., those of the Ptolemaic universe, moved by the outer sphere or *primum mobile*; see *Ptolemaic* in Glossary.

Wit's sour delights,
With gloves and knots, the silly snares of pleasure,
   Yet his dear treasure,
All scattered lay, while he his eyes did pore
   Upon a flower.   *15*

The darksome statesman, hung with weights and woe,
Like a thick midnight fog moved there so slow
   He did not stay, nor go;
Condemning thoughts, like sad eclipses, scowl
   Upon his soul,   *20*
And clouds of crying witnesses without
   Pursued him with one shout;
Yet digged the mole, and lest his ways be found,
   Worked underground,
Where he did clutch his prey, but One did see   *25*
   That policy;
Churches and altars fed him; perjuries
   Were gnats and flies;
It rained about him blood and tears, but he
   Drank them as free.   *30*

The fearful miser on a heap of rust
Sat pining all his life there, did scarce trust
   His own hands with the dust,
Yet would not place one piece above, but lives
   In fear of thieves.   *35*
Thousands there were as frantic as himself,
   And hugged each one his pelf:
The downright epicure placed heav'n in sense,
   And scorned pretense;
While others, slipped into a wide excess,   *40*
   Said little less;
The weaker sort slight trivial wares enslave,
   Who think them brave;
And poor despised truth sat counting by
   Their victory.   *45*

Yet some, who all this while did weep and sing,
And sing and weep, soared up into the ring;
   But most would use no wing.
O fools, said I, thus to prefer dark night
   Before true light,   *50*
To live in grots and caves, and hate the day
   Because it shows the way,

The way which from this dead and dark abode
   Leads up to God,
A way where you might tread the sun, and be   *55*
   More bright than he!
But as I did their madness so discuss,
   One whispered thus:
This ring the bridegroom did for none provide
   But for his bride.   *60*
          (1650)

THE RETREAT

Happy those early days when I
Shined in my angel-infancy!
Before I understood this place
Appointed for my second race,
Or taught my soul to fancy aught   *5*
But a white celestial thought;
When yet I had not walked above
A mile or two from my first love,
And looking back at that short space,
Could see a glimpse of his bright face;   *10*
When on some gilded cloud or flower
My gazing soul would dwell an hour,
And in those weaker glories spy
Some shadows of eternity;
Before I taught my tongue to wound   *15*
My conscience with a sinful sound,
Or had the black art to dispense
A sev'ral sin to ev'ry sense;
But felt through all this fleshly dress
Bright shoots of everlastingness.   *20*
   Oh, how I long to travel back
And tread again that ancient track!
That I might once more reach that plain
Where first I left my glorious train,
From whence th' enlightened spirit sees   *25*
That shady city of palm trees.
But, ah, my soul with too much stay
Is drunk, and staggers in the way.
Some men a forward motion love,
But I by backward steps would move,   *30*
And when this dust falls to the urn,
In that state I came, return.
          (1650)

---

12. knots: i.e., love-knots. **31-35:** See Matthew 6:19-21. **43. brave:** excellent, magnificent. **59-60:** See Revelation 21. **THE RETREAT 4. second race:** i.e., existence on earth, after a period in heaven. **26:** See Deuteronomy 34:3.

MARGARET CAVENDISH, DUCHESS OF NEWCASTLE
England, 1623-1673

NATURE'S COOK

Death is the cook of nature, and we find
Creatures dressed several ways to please her mind;
Some Death doth roast with fevers burning hot,
And some he boils with dropsies in a pot;
Some are consumed for jelly by degrees,   5
And some with ulcers, gravy out to squeeze;
Some, as with herbs, he stuffs with gouts and pains,
Others for tender meat he hangs in chains;
Some in the sea he pickles up to keep,
Others he, as soused brawn, in wine doth steep;   10
Some flesh and bones he with the Pox chops small,
And doth a French fricassee make withal;
Some on grid-irons of calentures are broiled,
And some are trodden down, and so quite spoiled:
But some are baked, when smothered they do die,   15
Some meat he doth by hectic fevers fry;
In sweat sometimes he stews with savory smell,
An hodge-podge of diseases he likes well;
Some brains he dresseth with apoplexy,
Or sauce of megrims, swimming plenteously;   20
And tongues he dries with smoke from stomachs ill,
Which, as the second course he sends up still;
Throats he doth cut, blood puddings for to make,
And puts them in the guts, which colics rack;
Some hunted are by him for deer, that's red,   25
And some as stall-fed oxen knocked o'th' head;
Some singed and scald for bacon, seem most rare,
When with salt rheum and phlegm they powdered are.

(1653)

THE HUNTING OF THE HARE

Betwixt two ridges of ploughed land lay Wat,
Whose body pressed to th' earth lay close and squat.
His nose upon his two forefeet close lies,
Glaring obliquely with his great grey eyes.
His head he always sets against the wind;   5
His tail when turned, his hair blew up behind,
And made him to get cold, but he being wise,
Doth keep his coat still down, so warm he lies.

Thus rests he all the day, till th' sun doth set,
Then up he riseth, his relief to get,   10
And walks about until the sun doth rise,
Then back returns, down in his form he lies.
At last poor Wat was found, as he there lay,
By huntsmen which came with their dogs that way.
Whom seeing, he got up, and fast did run,   15
Hoping some ways the cruel dogs to shun.
But they by nature had so quick a scent
That by their nose they traced what way he went,
And with their deep wide mouths set forth a cry
Which answered was by echoes in the sky.   20
Then Wat was struck with terror, and with fear,
Seeing each shadow, thought the dogs were there.
And running out some distance from their cry
To hide himself, his thoughts he did employ;
Under a clod of earth in sand-pit wide,   25
Poor Wat sat close, hoping himself to hide.
There long he had not been, but straight in's ears
The winding horns and crying dogs he hears:
Then starting up with fear, he leaped, and such   29
Swift speed he made, the ground he scarce did touch.
Into a great thick wood straightway he got,
And underneath a broken bough he sat.
At every leaf that with the wind did shake,
Did bring such terror, made his heart to ache.
That place he left, to champian plains he went,   35
Winding about, for to deceive their scent.
And while they snuffling were to find his track,
Poor Wat, being weary, his swift pace did slack.
On his two hinder legs for ease did sit,
His forefeet rubbed his face from dust and sweat.   40
Licking his feet, he wiped his ears so clean
That none could tell that Wat had hunted been.
But casting round about his fair grey eyes,
The hounds in full career he near him 'spies:
To Wat it was so terrible a sight,   45
Fear gave him wings, and made his body light.
Though he was tired before, by running long,
Yet now his breath he never felt more strong.
Like those that dying are, think health returns,

When 'tis but a faint blast which life out-burns. *50*
For Spirits seek to guard the heart about,
Striving with Death, but Death doth quench them out.
The hounds so fast came on, and with such cry,
That he no hopes hath left, nor help could 'spy.
With that the winds did pity poor Wat's case, *55*
And with their breath the scent blew from the place.
Then every nose was busily employed,
And every nostril was set open wide;
And every head doth seek a several way
To find the grass or track where the scent lay. *60*
For witty industry is never slack;
'Tis like to witchcraft, and brings lost things back.
But though the wind had tied the scent up close,
A busy dog thrust in his snuffling nose
And drew it out, with that did foremost run. *65*
Then horns blew loud, for th' rest to follow on.
The great slow hounds, their throats did set a bass;
The fleet swift hounds, as tenors next in place;
The little beagles did a treble sing,
And through the air their voices round did ring: *70*
Which made such concert as they ran along,
That, had they spoken words, 't had been a song.
The horns kept time, the men did shout for joy,
And seemed most valiant, poor Wat to destroy.
Spurring their horses to a full career, *75*
Swam rivers deep, leaped ditches without fear,
Endangered life and limbs, so fast they'd ride,
Only to see how patiently Wat died.

At last, the dogs so near his heels did get,
That their sharp teeth they in his breech did set. *80*
Then tumbling down he fell, with weeping eyes,
Gave up his ghost, and thus poor Wat he dies.
Men whooping loud, such acclamations make,
As if the Devil they imprisoned had,
When they but did a shiftless creature kill; *85*
To hunt, there needs no valiant soldier's skill.
But men doth think that exercise, and toil,
To keep their health, is best, which makes most spoil.
Thinking that food and nourishment so good,
Which doth proceed from others' flesh and blood. *90*
When they do lions, wolves, bears, tigers see,
To kill poor sheep, straight say, they cruel be;
But for themselves all creatures think too few,
For luxury, wish God would make more new.
As if God did make creatures for man's meat, *95*
And gave them life, and sense, for man to eat;
Or else for sport or recreation's sake,
For to destroy those lives that God did make:
Making their stomachs graves, which full they fill
With murthered bodies, which in sport they kill. *100*
Yet man doth think himself so gentle, mild,
When of all creatures he's most cruel wild;
And is so proud, thinks only he shall live,
That God a God-like nature him did give,
And that all creatures for his sake alone *105*
Were made for him to tyrannize upon.

(1653, 1664)

DOROTHY OSBORNE
England, 1627-1695

from *LETTERS TO SIR WILLIAM TEMPLE* (some abridged)

[Thursday, 14 April 1653]
SIR,

I received your letter today when I thought it almost impossible that I should be sensible of anything but my father's sickness, and my own affliction in it. Indeed he was then so dangerously ill that we could not reasonably hope he should outlive this day, yet he is

---

61. witty: Since the 1653 edition used the adjective "quick" here, "witty" may carry that connotation as well. **85. shiftless:** lacking the means to survive. **OSBORNE** Dorothy Osborne and Sir William Temple were married on Christmas Day, 1654, she becoming Lady Temple; they had six children who died at birth or in infancy, and one daughter who died of smallpox at age fourteen; Sir William died in 1699. The letters were first published in 1888, edited by Edward Abbott Parry. **THURSDAY, 14 APRIL 1653** **2:** Her father, Sir Peter Osborne, had become ill April 10; he died the following March.

now I thank God much better, and I am come so much to myself with it as to undertake
a long letter to you whilst I watch by him; towards the latter end it will be excellent stuff 5
I believe, but alas you may allow me to dream sometimes; I have had so little sleep
since my father was sick that I am never thoroughly awake. Lord how I have wished for
you! Here do I sit all night by a poor moped fellow that serves my father, and have
much ado to keep him awake and myself too. If you heard the wise discourse that is
between us, you would swear we wanted sleep. But I shall leave him tonight to entertain 10
himself and try if I can write as wisely as I talk.

. . . . Hark you, if you think to 'scape with sending me such bits of letters you are
mistaken. You say you are often interrupted, and I believe you; but you must use then
to begin to write before you receive mine, and whensoever you have any spare time
allow me some of it. . . . Oh, if you do not send me long letters then you are the 15
cruellest person that can be. If you love me you will, and if you do not I shall never
love myself. . . .

The turning of my paper has waked me. All this while I was in a dream, but 'tis no
matter; I am content you should know they are of you, and that when my thoughts are
left most at liberty they are the kindest. I'll swear my eyes are so heavy that I hardly see 20
what or how I write, nor do I think you will be able to read it when I have done. The
best on't is 'twill be no great loss to you if you do not, for sure the greatest part on't is
not sense; and yet on my conscience I shall go on with it. 'Tis like people that talk in
their sleep: nothing interrupts them but talking to them again, and that you are not like
to do at this distance, besides that at this instant you are I believe more asleep than I, and 25
do not so much as dream that I am writing to you. My fellow watchers have been asleep
too till just now; they begin to stretch and yawn; they are going to try if eating and
drinking can keep them awake, and I am kindly invited to be of their company. My
father's man has got one of the maids to talk nonsense to tonight and they have got
between them a bottle of ale. I shall lose my share if I do not take them at their first 30
offer; your patience till I have drunk, and then I am for you again.

And now in the strength of this ale I believe I shall be able to fill up this paper
that's left with something or other. And first let me ask you if you have seen a book of
poems newly come out made by my Lady Newcastle. For God's sake if you meet with it
send it me; they say 'tis ten times more extravagant than her dress. Sure the poor woman 35
is a little distracted; she could never be so ridiculous else as to venture at writing books,
and in verse too. If I should not sleep this fortnight I should not come to that. My eyes
grow a little dim though for all the ale, and I believe if I could see it this is most
strangely scribbled. Sure I shall not find fault with you writing in haste for anything but
the shortness of your letter, and 'twould be very unjust in me to tie you to a ceremony 40
that I do not observe myself. . . . Tell me if there be anything that I can serve you in,
employ me as you would do that sister that you say you love so well, chide me when I
do anything that is not well, but then make haste to tell me that you have forgiven me
and that you are what I shall ever be, a

faithful friend,

---

8. **moped:** dull, spiritless. **18. turning of my paper:** i.e., she turns it in order to write in the margin or to write at a right angle across the other script.
34. **Lady Newcastle:** See p. 410; her *Poems and Fancies* was published in 1653.

[early July 1653]

SIR,

In my opinion you do not understand the laws of friendship right. 'Tis generally believed it owes its birth to an agreement and conformity of humours, and that it lives no longer than 'tis preserved by the mutual care of those that bred it; 'tis wholly governed by equality, and can there be such a thing in it as a distinction of power? No, sure, if we are friends we must both command and both obey alike. Indeed a mistress *5* and a servant sounds otherwise, but that is ceremony and this is truth. Yet what reason have I to furnish you with a stick to beat myself withal, or desire you should command, that do it so severely? I must eat fruit no longer than I could be content you should be in a fever; is not that an absolute forbidding in me? It has frighted me just now from a basket of the most tempting cherries that e'er I saw; though I know that you did not *10* mean I should eat none, but if you had, I think I should have obeyed you. I am glad you lay no fault to my charge but indiscretion, though that be too much, 'tis a well-natured one in me. I confess it is a fault to believe too easily, but 'tis not out of vanity that I do it — as thinking I deserve you should love me and therefore believing it — but because I am apt to think people so honest as to speak as they mean, and the less I deserve it the *15* more I think myself obliged. I know 'tis a fault in anyone to be mastered by a passion, and of all passions love is perhaps the least pardonable in a woman; but when 'tis mingled with gratitude, 'tis sure the less to be blamed.

I do not think if there were more that loved me I should love them all, but I am certain I could not love the most perfect person in the world unless I did first firmly *20* believe he had a passion for me. And yet you would persuade me I am not just, because I did once in my life deny you something. I'll swear you are not, if you do not believe that next the happy end of all our wishes, I desire to see you, but you know the inconveniences that will certainly follow, and if you can dispense with them I can, to show that my obedience is not less than yours. *25*

I cannot hear too often that you are kind and noble enough to prefer my interest above your own, but sure if I have any measure of either myself, the more liberty you give me the less I shall take. 'Tis most certain that our Emperor would have been to me rather a jailer than a husband, and 'tis as true that (though for my own sake I think I should not make an ill wife to anybody) I can not be a good one to any, but one. I *30* know not with what constancy you could hear the sentence of your death, but I am certain there is nothing I could not hear with more, and if your interest in me be dearer to you than your life, it must necessarily follow that 'tis dearer to me than anything in the world besides; therefore you may be sure I will preserve it with all my care. I cannot promise that I shall be yours, because I know not how far my misfortunes may *35* reach, nor what punishments are reserved for my faults, but I dare almost promise you shall never receive the displeasure of seeing me another's. No, in earnest, I have so many reasons to keep me from that, besides your interest, that I know not whether it be not the least of the obligations you have to me. Sure the whole world could never

---

EARLY JULY 1653   **2. humours:** See note to Chaucer's "General Prologue," line 420 (p. 34). **5-6. mistress, servant:** conventional terms for a woman and man in love. **21-22:** In a letter two weeks earlier, she had told him not to call on her, mainly because of the awkwardness: her relatives disliked him and opposed their relationship. **24. dispense with:** allow, put up with. **28. Emperor:** her nickname for an earlier suitor, Sir Justinian Isham. **31. constancy:** firmness of mind, steadfastness.

persuade me (unless a parent commanded it) to marry one that I had no esteem for, and 40
where I have any, I am not less scrupulous than your father, for I should never be
brought to do them the injury as to give them a wife whose affections they could never
hope for, besides that I must sacrifice myself in't and live a walking misery till the
only hope that would then be left me were perfected. Oh me, this is so sad it has put
me out of all I had to say besides. I meant to chide you for the shortness of your last 45
letter and to tell you that if you do not take the same liberty of telling me of all my
faults, I shall not think you are my friend. In earnest, 'tis true you must use to tell me
freely of anything you see amiss in me, whether I am too stately or not enough, what
humour pleases you and what does not, what you would have me do and what avoid,
with the same freedom that you would use to a person over whom you have an 50
absolute power and were concerned in. These are the laws of friendship as I
understand them, and I believe I understand them right, for I am certain nobody can be
more perfectly a friend than I am
Yours

[late July 1653]
Sir,
. . . .

'Tis most true that our friendship has been brought up hardly enough, and possibly it
thrives the better for it; 'tis observed that surfeits kill more than fasting does, but ours is
in no danger of that. My B[rother] would persuade me there is no such thing in the
world as a constant friendship. People (he says) that marry with great passion for one
another, as they think, come afterwards to lose it they know not how, besides the 5
multitude of such as are false and mean it. I cannot be of his opinion (though I confess
there are too many examples on't). I have always believed there might be a friendship
perfect like that you describe, and methinks I find something like it in myself. But sure
'tis not to be taught; it must come naturally to those that have it, and those that have it
not can ne'er be made to understand it. 10
You needed not have feared that I should take occasion from your not answering
my last, not to write this week. You are as much pleased (you say) with writing to me as
I can be to receive your letters; why should you not think the same of me? In earnest
you may, and if you love me you will. But then how much more satisfied should I be if
there were no need of these, and we might talk all that we write and more. Shall we ever 15
be so happy?
Last night I was in the garden till eleven o'clock. It was the sweetest night that e'er
I saw, the garden looked so well, and the jasmine smelt beyond all perfumes, and yet I
was not pleased. The place had all the charms it used to have when I was most satisfied
with it, and had you been there I should have liked it much more than ever I did; but that 20
not being, it was no more to me than the next field, and only served me for a place to
reverie in without disturbance. . . .
Your faithful

41: Temple's father had proposed a suitable wife for him, but didn't insist upon the match.   LATE JULY 1653   3: her brother Henry.

[September 1653]

SIR,

Pray let not the apprehension that others say finer things to me make your letters all the shorter, for if it were so, I should not think they did, and so long you are safe. My brother[-in-law] P[eyton] indeed does sometimes send me letters that may be excellent for aught I know, and the more likely because I do not understand them; but I may say to you (as to a friend) I do not like them, and have wondered that my sister, who . . . had a great deal of 5 wit and was thought to write as well as most women in England, never persuaded him to alter his style and make it a little more intelligible. . . . In my opinion these great scholars are not the best writers (of letters, I mean; of books, perhaps they are). I never had I think but one letter from Sir Justinian, but 'twas worth twenty of anybody's else to make me sport. It was the most sublime nonsense that in my life I ever read, and yet I believe he 10 descended as low as he could to come near my weak understanding. 'Twill be no compliment after this to say I like your letters in themselves, not as they come from one that is not indifferent to me. But seriously, I do. All letters methinks should be free and easy as one's discourse, not studied, as an oration, nor made up of hard words like a charm. 'Tis an admirable thing to see how some people will labour to find out terms that 15 may obscure a plain sense, like a gentleman I knew who would never say "the weather grew cold" but that "Winter began to salute us." I have no patience for such coxcombs and cannot blame an old uncle of mine that threw the standish at his man's head because he writ a letter for him where instead of saying (as his master bid him) that "he would have writ himself but that he had the gout in his hand," he said that "the gout in his hand would 20 not permit him to put pen to paper." The fellow thought he had mended it mightily, and that "putting pen to paper" was much better than plain "writing." . . .

[October 1653]

SIR,

. . . . There are a great many ingredients must go to the making me happy in a husband. First, as my cousin Fr[anklin] says, our humours must agree, and to do that he must have that kind of breeding that I have had and used that kind of company. That is, he must not be so much a Country Gentleman as to understand nothing but hawks and dogs and be fonder of either than of his wife, nor of the next sort of them whose aim reaches 5 no further than to be Justice of Peace and once in his life High Sheriff, who reads no book but statutes and studies nothing but how to make a speech interlarded with Latin that may amaze his disagreeing poor neighbours and fright them rather than persuade them into quietness. He must not be a thing that began the world in a free school, was sent from thence to the University, and is at his farthest when he reaches the Inns of 10 Court, has no acquaintance but those of his form in these places, speaks the French he has picked out of old laws, and admires nothing but the stories he has heard of the revels that were kept there before his time. He must not be a Town Gallant neither, that lives in a tavern and an ordinary, that cannot imagine how an hour should be spent without

---

SEPTEMBER 1653 **2-3:** Sir Thomas Peyton's first wife was Dorothy Osborne's eldest sister, Elizabeth, who died in 1642. **18. standish:** stand for pens and ink, inkpot. **OCTOBER 1653** **2:** Elizabeth, daughter of Sir Thomas Cheke, uncle to Dorothy Osborne, married Sir Richard Franklin. **11. form:** class, rank. **14. ordinary:** dining room or eating house serving meals with a fixed price.

company unless it be in sleeping, that makes court to all the women he sees, thinks they believe him, and laughs and is laughed at equally. Nor a Travelled Monsieur whose head is all feather inside and outside, that can talk of nothing but dances and duels, and has courage enough to wear slashes when everybody else dies with cold to see him. He must not be a fool of no sort, nor peevish nor ill-natured nor proud nor covetous, and to all this must be added that he must love me and I him as much as we are capable of loving. Without all this his fortune though never so great would not satisfy me, and with it a very moderate one would keep me from ever repenting my disposal.

    . . . . I am
       Yours

JOHN BUNYAN
England, 1628-1688

from *THE PILGRIM'S PROGRESS, THE FIRST PART*

[The Beginning]

As I walked through the wilderness of this world, I lighted on a certain place, where was a Den; And I laid me down in that place to sleep: And as I slept I dreamed a Dream. I dreamed, and behold *I saw a Man clothed with Rags, standing in a certain place, with his face from his own House, a Book in his hand, and a great burden upon his Back.* I looked, and saw him open the Book, and Read therein; and as he read, he wept and trembled: and not being able longer to contain, he brake out with a lamentable cry; saying, *what shall I do?*

    In this plight therefore he went home, and refrained himself as long as he could, that his Wife and Children should not perceive his distress; but he could not be silent long, because that his trouble increased: wherefore at length he brake his mind to his Wife and Children; and thus he began to talk to them, O my dear Wife, said he, and you the Children of my bowels, I your dear friend am in my self undone, by reason of a burden that lieth hard upon me: moreover, I am for certain informed, that this our City will be burned with fire from Heaven, in which fearful overthrow, both my self, with thee, my Wife, and you my sweet babes, shall miserably come to ruin; except (the which, yet I see not) some way of escape can be found, whereby we may be delivered. At this his Relations were sore amazed; not for that they believed that what he said to them was true, but because they thought that some frenzy distemper had got into his

Isaiah 64:6
Luke 14:33
Psalms 38:4
Habakkuk 2:2
Acts 16:30

---

18. slashes: slits in garments to show colours of an under layer — i.e., fashion at the expense of comfort. **THE PILGRIM'S PROGRESS** We omit marginal notes that merely paraphrase or otherwise comment on the content, retaining only those that refer the reader to passages from the Bible; we have modified their form for clarity, and we have included several more such references in the footnotes. **2. Den:** Bunyan's marginal note identifies this as *the jail*; Bunyan spent most of the years 1660-72 in jail for preaching as a dissenter from the established church, and again a shorter period in 1675-76; it was during these periods that he had the time to write his several works, including the first part of *The Pilgrim's Progress*. **3. a Man:** later identified as "Christian." **6-7:** See Acts 2:37. **13. our City:** later given the name "City of Destruction" (see Isaiah 19:18).

head: therefore, it drawing towards night, and they hoping that sleep might settle his brains, with all haste they got him to bed; but the night was as troublesome to him as the *20* day: wherefore instead of sleeping, he spent it in sighs and tears. So when the morning was come, they would know how he did; and he told them worse and worse. He also set to talking to them again, but they began to be hardened; they also thought to drive away his distemper by harsh and surly carriages to him: sometimes they would deride, sometimes they would chide, and sometimes they would quite neglect him: wherefore *25* he began to retire himself to his Chamber to pray for, and pity them; and also to condole his own misery: he would also walk solitarily in the Fields, sometimes reading, and sometimes praying: and thus for some days he spent his time.

Now, I saw upon a time, when he was walking in the Fields, that he was (as he was wont) reading in his Book, and greatly distressed in his mind; and as he read, he burst *30* out, as he had done before, crying, *What shall I do to be saved?*

I saw also that he looked this way, and that way, as if he would run; yet he stood still, because, as I perceived, he could not tell which way to go. I looked then, and saw a *Hebrews 9:27* man named *Evangelist* coming to him, and asked, *Wherefore dost thou cry?* He *Job 16:21-22* answered, Sir, I perceive, by the Book in my hand, that I am Condemned to die, and *35* *Ezekiel 22:14* after that to come to Judgment; and I find that I am not willing to do the first, nor able to do the second.

Then said *Evangelist,* Why not willing to die? since this life is attended with so many evils? The Man answered, Because I fear that this burden that is upon my back, *Isaiah 30:33* will sink me lower then the Grave; and I shall fall into *Tophet.* And Sir, if I be not fit to *40* go to Prison, I am not fit (I am sure) to go to Judgment, and from thence to Execution; and the thoughts of these things make me cry.

Then said *Evangelist,* If this be thy condition, why standest thou still? He answered, Because I know not whither to go. Then he gave him a *Parchment-Roll,* and there was *Matthew 3:7* written within, *Fly from the wrath to come.* *45*

The Man therefore Read it, and looking upon *Evangelist* very carefully, said, Whither must I fly? Then said *Evangelist,* pointing with his finger over a very wide *Matthew 7* Field, Do you see yonder *Wicket-gate?* The Man said, No. Then said the other, Do you *Psalms 119:105* see yonder shining light? He said, I think I do. Then said *Evangelist,* Keep that light in *II Peter 1:19* your eye, and go up directly thereto, so shalt thou see the Gate; at which when thou *50* knockest, it shall be told thee what thou shalt do.

So I saw in my Dream, that the Man began to run; Now he had not run far from his own door, but his Wife and Children perceiving it, began to cry after him to return: but *Luke 14:26* the Man put his fingers in his Ears, and ran on crying, Life, Life, Eternal Life: so he *Genesis 19:17* looked not behind him, but fled towards the middle of the Plain. *55*

. . . .

[Christian and Faithful Visit Vanity Fair]

Then I saw in my Dream, that when they were got out of the Wilderness, they presently saw a Town before them, and the name of that Town is *Vanity;* and at the Town there is

---

22. would: wanted to. **24. carriages:** actions, conduct.

a *Fair* kept called *Vanity-Fair*: It is kept all the year long, it beareth the name of *Vanity-Fair,* because the Town where 'tis kept, *is lighter than* Vanity; and also, because all that is there sold, or that cometh thither, is *Vanity.* As is the saying of the wise, *All that* 60
cometh is vanity.

Isaiah 40:17
Eccles. 1 and 2

    This Fair is no new erected business, but a thing of Ancient standing; I will shew you the original of it.

    Almost five thousand years agone, there were Pilgrims walking to the Celestial City, as these two honest persons are; and *Beelzebub, Apollyon,* and *Legion,* with their 65 Companions, perceiving by the path that the Pilgrims made, that their way to the City lay through *this Town of Vanity,* they contrived here to set up a Fair; a Fair wherein should be sold of *all sorts of Vanity,* and that it should last all the year long. Therefore at *this Fair* are all such Merchandize sold, as Houses, Lands, Trades, Places, Honours, Preferments, Titles, Countries, Kingdoms, Lusts, Pleasures, and Delights of all sorts, as 70 Whores, Bawds, Wives, Husbands, Children, Masters, Servants, Lives, Blood, Bodies, Souls, Silver, Gold, Pearls, Precious Stones, and what not.

    And moreover, at this Fair there is at all times to be seen Jugglings, Cheats, Games, Plays, Fools, Apes, Knaves, and Rogues, and that of all sorts.

    Here are to be seen too, and that for nothing, Thefts, Murders, Adulteries, False- 75 swearers, and that of a blood-red colour.

                      . . . .

    Now, as I said, the way to the Celestial City lies just thorow *this Town,* where this lusty Fair is kept; and he that will go to the City, and yet not go thorow this Town, must needs *go out of the World.* The Prince of Princes himself, when here, went through *this Town* to his own Country, and that upon a *Fair-day* too: Yea, and as I think it was 80 *Beelzebub,* the chief Lord of this *Fair,* that invited him to buy of his *Vanities;* yea, would have made him Lord of the *Fair,* would he but have done him Reverence as he went thorow the *Town.* Yea, because he was such a person of Honour, *Beelzebub* had him from *Street* to *Street,* and shewed him all the Kingdoms of the World in a little time, that he might, if possible, allure that Blessed One to *cheapen* and *buy* some of his 85 *Vanities.* But he had no mind to the Merchandize, and therefore left the *Town,* without laying out so much as one Farthing upon these *Vanities.* This *Fair* therefore is an Ancient thing, of long standing, and a very great *Fair.*

I Cor. 5:10

Matthew 4:8
Luke 4:5-7

    Now these Pilgrims, as I said, must needs go thorow this *Fair:* Well, so they did; but behold, even as they entered into the *Fair,* all the people in the *Fair* were moved, 90 and the Town itself as it were in a Hubbub about them; and that for several reasons: For,

    First, The Pilgrims were clothed with such kind of Raiment, as was diverse from the Raiment of any that traded in that *fair.* The people therefore of the *fair* made a great gazing upon them: Some said they were Fools, some they were Bedlams, and some they are Outlandish-men. 95

    Secondly, And as they wondered at their Apparel, so they did likewise at their Speech; for few could understand what they said; they naturally spoke the Language of

I Cor. 2:7-8

Canaan; But they that kept the *fair* were the men of this World: So that from one end of the *fair* to the other, they seemed *Barbarians* each to the other.

Thirdly, But that which did not a little amuse the Merchandizers, was, that these *Pilgrims* set very light by all their Wares, they cared not so much as to look upon them: and if they called upon them to buy, they would put their fingers in their ears, and cry, *Turn away mine eyes from beholding vanity;* and look upwards, signifying that their Trade and Traffic was in Heaven. *100*

One chanced mockingly, beholding the carriages of the men, to say unto them, What will ye buy? but they, looking gravely upon him, said, *We buy the Truth.* At that, there was an occasion taken to despise the men the more; some mocking, some taunting, some speaking reproachfully, and some calling upon others to smite them. At last things came to an hubbub, and great stir in the *fair;* insomuch that all order was confounded. Now was word presently brought to the *great one* of the *fair,* who quickly came down, and deputed some of his most trusty friends to take these men into examination, about whom the *fair* was almost overturned. So the men were brought to examination; and they that sat upon them, asked them whence they came, whither they went, and what they did there in such an unusual Garb? The men told them, that they were Pilgrims and Strangers in the world, and that they were going to their own Country, which was the Heavenly *Jerusalem;* and that they had given none occasion to the men of the Town, nor yet to the Merchandizers, thus to abuse them, and to let them in their Journey. Except it was, for that, when one asked them what they would buy, they said, they would *buy the Truth.* But they that were appointed to examine them, did not believe them to be any other than Bedlams and Mad, or else such as came to put all things into a confusion in the *fair.* Therefore they took them, and beat them, and besmeared them with dirt, and then put them into the Cage, that they might be made a Spectacle to all the men of the *fair.* There therefore they lay for some time, and were made the objects of any man's sport, or malice, or revenge, the great one of the *fair* laughing still at all that befell them. But the men being patient, and not rendering railing for railing, but contrariwise blessing, and giving good words for bad, and kindness for injuries done: Some men in the *fair* that were more observing, and less prejudiced than the rest, began to check and blame the baser sort for their continual abuses done by them to the men: They therefore in angry manner let fly at them again, counting them as bad as the men in the Cage, and telling them that they seemed confederates, and should be made partakers of their misfortunes. The other replied, That for ought they could see, the men were quiet, and sober, and intended no body any harm; and that there were many that Traded in their *fair,* that were more worthy to be put into the Cage, yea, and Pillory too, than were the men that they had abused. Thus, after divers words had passed on both sides (the men behaving themselves all the while very wisely, and soberly before them), they fell to some Blows among themselves, and did harm one to another. Then were these two poor men brought before their Examiners again, and there charged as being guilty of the late Hubbub that had been in the *fair.* So they beat them pitifully, and hanged Irons upon them, and led them in Chains up and down the *fair,* for an example and a terror to *105 110 115 120 125 130 135*

Psalms 119:37 Philemon 3:19-20 *Proverbs 23:23* *Hebrews 11:13-16*

99. See I Corinthians 14:11. **100. amuse:** bewilder, cause to stare with astonishment. **113. sat upon them:** i.e., in judgment. **116. none:** no. **117. let:** delay, obstruct. **127. check:** rebuke, chide.

others, lest any should further speak in their behalf, or join themselves unto them. But *140*
Christian and *Faithful* behaved themselves yet more wisely, and received the ignominy
and shame that was cast upon them, with so much meekness and patience, that it won to
their side (though but few in comparison of the rest) several of the men in the *fair*. This
put the other party yet into a greater rage, insomuch that they concluded the death of these
two men. Wherefore they threatened that the Cage, nor Irons, should serve their turn, but *145*
that they should die, for the abuse they had done, and for deluding the men of the *fair*.

Then were they remanded to the Cage again, until further order should be taken
with them. So they put them in, and made their feet fast in the Stocks.

Here also they called again to mind what they had heard from their faithful friend
Evangelist, and was the more confirmed in their way and sufferings, by what he told *150*
them would happen to them. They also now comforted each other, that whose lot it was
to suffer, even he should have the best on't; therefore each man secretly wished that he
might have that preferment: but committing themselves to the All-wise dispose of him
that ruleth all things, with much content they abode in the condition in which they were,
until they should be otherwise disposed of. *155*

Then a convenient time being appointed, they brought them forth to their Trial in
order to their Condemnation. When the time was come, they were brought before their
Enemies and arraigned; the Judge's name was Lord *Hategood*. Their Indictment was
one and the same in substance, though somewhat varying in form; the Contents whereof
was this. *160*

*That they were enemies to, and disturbers of their Trade; that they had made
Commotions and Divisions in the Town, and had won a party to their own most
dangerous Opinions, in contempt of the Law of their Prince.*

Then *Faithful* began to answer, That he had only set himself against that which had
set itself against him that is higher than the highest. And, said he, as for disturbance, I *165*
make none, being myself a man of Peace; the Party that were won to us, were won, by
beholding our Truth and Innocence, and they are only turned from the worse to the
better. And as to the King you talk of; since he is *Beelzebub,* the Enemy of our Lord, I
defy him and all his Angels.

Then Proclamation was made, that they that had ought to say for their Lord the *170*
King against the Prisoner at the Bar, should forthwith appear, and give in their evidence.
So there came in three Witnesses, to wit, *Envy, Superstition,* and *Pickthank.* They was
then asked, If they knew the Prisoner at the Bar? and what they had to say for their Lord
the King against him.

Then stood forth *Envy,* and said to this effect: My Lord, I have known this man a *175*
long time, and will attest upon my Oath before this honourable Bench, That he is —

Judge. Hold, give him his Oath: So they sware him. Then he said, My Lord, this
man, notwithstanding his plausible name, is one of the vilest men in our Country; He
neither regardeth Prince nor People, Law nor Custom; but doth all that he can to possess
all men with certain of his disloyal notions, which he in the general calls Principles of *180*
Faith and Holiness. And in particular, I heard him once my self affirm, *That Christianity, and the Customs of our Town of* Vanity, *were Diametrically opposite, and could*

---

172. **Pickthank:** one who tattles in order to gain favour.

not be reconciled. By which saying, my Lord, he doth at once not only condemn all our laudable doings, but us in the doing of them.

Judg. Then did the Judge say to him, Hast thou any more to say? 185

Envy. My Lord, I could say much more, only I would not be tedious to the Court. Yet if need be, when the other Gentlemen have given in their Evidence, rather then any thing shall be wanting that will dispatch him, I will enlarge my Testimony against him. So he was bid stand by. Then they called *Superstition,* and bid him look upon the Prisoner; they also asked, What he could say for their Lord the King against him? Then 190 they sware him, so he began.

Super. My Lord, I have no great acquaintance with this man, nor do I desire to have further knowledge of him; However this I know, that he is a very pestilent fellow, from some discourse that the other day I had with him in this *Town;* for then talking with him, I heard him say, That our Religion was naught, and such by which a man could by no 195 means please God: which sayings of his, my Lord, your Lordship very well knows, what necessarily thence will follow, to wit, That we still do worship in vain, are yet in our Sins, and finally shall be damned; and this is that which I have to say.

Then was *Pickthank* sworn, and bid say what he knew, in behalf of their Lord the King against the Prisoner at the Bar. 200

Pick. My Lord, and you Gentlemen all, This fellow I have known of a long time, and have heard him speak things that ought not to be spoke. For he hath railed on our noble Prince *Beelzebub,* and hath spoke contemptibly of his honourable Friends, whose names are the Lord *Old Man,* the Lord *Carnal Delight,* the Lord *Luxurious,* the Lord *Desire of Vain-glory,* my old Lord *Lechery,* Sir *Having Greedy,* with all the rest of our 205 Nobility; and he hath said moreover, that if all men were of his mind, if possible, there is not one of these Noble-men should have any longer a being in this Town. Besides, he hath not been afraid to rail on you, my Lord, who are now appointed to be his Judge, calling you an ungodly villain, with many other such like vilifying terms, with which he hath bespattered most of the Gentry of our Town. When this *Pickthank* had told his tale, 210 the Judge directed his speech to the Prisoner at the Bar, saying, Thou Runagate, Heretic, and Traitor, hast thou heard what these honest Gentlemen have witnessed against thee.

Faith. May I speak a few words in my own defence?

Judg. Sirrah, Sirrah, thou deservest to live no longer, but to be slain immediately upon the place; yet that all men may see our gentleness towards thee, let us hear what 215 thou hast to say.

Faith. 1. I say then in answer to what Mr. *Envy* hath spoken, I never said ought but this, *That what Rule, or Laws, or Custom, or People, were flat against the Word of God, are diametrically opposite to Christianity.* If I have said amiss in this, convince me of my errour, and I am ready here before you to make my recantation. 220

2. As to the second, to wit, Mr. *Superstition,* and his charge against me, I said only this, *That in the worship of God there is required a divine Faith; but there can be no divine Faith, without a divine Revelation of the will of God: therefore whatever is thrust into the worship of God, that is not agreeable to divine Revelation, cannot be done but by an human Faith, which Faith will not profit to Eternal Life.* 225

---

211. Runagate: renegade.

3. As to what Mr. *Pickthank* hath said, I say, (avoiding terms, as that I am said to rail, and the like) That the Prince of this Town, with all the Rabblement his Attendants, by this Gentleman named, are more fit for a being in Hell, than in this Town and Country; *and so the Lord have mercy upon me.*

Then the Judge called to the Jury (who all this while stood by, to hear and observe),   230
Gentlemen of the Jury, you see this man about whom so great an uproar hath been made in this Town: you have also heard what these worthy Gentlemen have witnessed against him; also you have heard his reply and confession: It lieth now in your breasts to hang him, or save his life. But yet I think meet to instruct you into our Law.

Exodus 1   There was an Act made in the days of *Pharaoh* the Great, Servant to our Prince,   235
That lest those of a contrary Religion should multiply and grow too strong for him, their Males should be thrown into the River. There was also an Act made in the days of
Daniel 3 *Nebuchadnezzar* the Great, another of his Servants, That whoever would not fall down and worship his golden Image, should be thrown into a fiery Furnace. There was also an
Daniel 6 Act made in the days of *Darius,* That who so, for some time, called upon any God but   240
his, should be cast into the Lion's Den. Now the substance of these Laws this Rebel has broken, not only in thought (which is not to be borne), but also in word and deed; which must therefore needs be intolerable.

For that of *Pharaoh,* his Law was made upon a supposition, to prevent mischief, no Crime being yet apparent; but here is a Crime apparent. For the second and third, you   245
see he disputeth against our Religion; and for the Treason he hath confessed, he deserveth to die the death.

Then went the Jury out, whose names were Mr. *Blind-man,* Mr. *No-good,* Mr. *Malice,* Mr. *Love-lust,* Mr. *Live-loose,* Mr. *Heady,* Mr. *High-mind,* Mr. *Enmity,* Mr. *Liar,* Mr. *Cruelty,* Mr. *Hate-light,* and Mr. *Implacable,* who every one gave in his   250
private Verdict against him among themselves, and afterwards unanimously concluded to bring him in guilty before the Judge. And first Mr. *Blind-man,* the foreman, said, *I see clearly that this man is an Heretic.* Then said Mr. *No-good, Away with such a fellow from the Earth. Ay,* said Mr. *Malice, for I hate the very looks of him.* Then said Mr. *Love-lust, I could never endure him. Nor I,* said Mr. *Live-loose, for he would always be*   255
condemning my way. Hang him, hang him, said Mr. *Heady. A sorry Scrub,* said Mr. *High-mind. My heart riseth against him,* said Mr. *Enmity. He is a Rogue,* said Mr. *Liar. Hanging is too good for him,* said Mr. *Cruelty. Let's dispatch him out of the way,* said Mr. *Hate-light.* Then said Mr. *Implacable, Might I have all the World given me, I could not be reconciled to him, therefore let us forthwith bring him in guilty of death:* And so   260
they did; therefore he was presently Condemned, To be had from the place where he was, to the place from whence he came, and there to be put to the most cruel death that could be invented.

They therefore brought him out, to do with him according to their Law; and first they Scourged him, then they Buffetted him, then they Lanced his flesh with Knives;   265
after that they Stoned him with Stones, then pricked him with their Swords, and last of all they burned him to Ashes at the Stake. Thus came *Faithful* to his end. Now, I saw that there stood behind the multitude, a Chariot and a couple of Horses, waiting for

---

227. **Rabblement:** rabble.

Faithful, who (so soon as his adversaries had dispatched him) was taken up into it, and straightway was carried up through the Clouds, with sound of Trumpet, the nearest way   *270* to the Celestial Gate. But as for *Christian,* he had some respite, and was remanded back to prison; so he there remained for a space: But he that over-rules all things, having the power of their rage in his own hand, so wrought it about, that *Christian* for that time escaped them, and went his way.

. . . .

[By-Path-Meadow, Doubting-Castle, Giant Despair, and the Delectable Mountains]

Now I beheld in my Dream, that they had not journeyed far, but the River and the way,   *275* for a time, parted. At which they were not a little sorry, yet they durst not go out of the way. Now the way from the River was rough, and their feet tender by reason of their
Numbers 21:4 Travels; *So the soul of the Pilgrims was much discouraged, because of the way.* Wherefore still as they went on, they wished for better way. Now a little before them, there was on the left hand of the Road, a *Meadow,* and a Stile to go over into it, and that   *280* *Meadow* is called *By-Path-Meadow.* Then said *Christian* to his fellow, If this Meadow lieth along by our way side, let's go over into it. Then he went to the Stile to see, and behold a Path lay along by the way on the other side of the fence. 'Tis according to my wish, said *Christian,* here is the easiest going; come good *Hopeful,* and let us go over.

Hope. But how if this Path should lead us out of the way?   *285*

Chr. That's not like, said the other; look, doth it not go along by the way side? So *Hopeful,* being persuaded by his fellow, went after him over the Stile. When they were gone over, and were got into the Path, they found it very easy for their feet; and withal, they looking before them, espied a Man walking as they did (and his name was *Vain-confidence*), so they called after him, and asked him whither that way led? He said, To   *290* the Celestial Gate. Look, said *Christian,* did not I tell you so? By this you may see we are right: so they followed, and he went before them. But behold the night came on, and it grew very dark; so that they that were behind, lost the sight of him that went before.

He therefore that went before (*Vain-confidence* by name) not seeing the way before
Isaiah 9:16 him, fell into a deep Pit, which was on purpose there made by the Prince of those   *295* grounds, to catch *vain-glorious* fools withal; and was dashed in pieces with his fall.

Now *Christian* and his fellow heard him fall. So they called, to know the matter, but there was none to answer, only they heard a groaning. Then said *Hopeful,* Where are we now? Then was his fellow silent, as mistrusting that he had led him out of the way. And now it began to rain, and thunder, and lighten in a very dreadful manner, and the water rose amain.   *300*

Then *Hopeful* groaned in himself, saying, *Oh that I had kept on my way!*

Chr. Who could have thought that this path should have led us out of the way?

Hope. I was afraid on't at very first, and therefore gave you that gentle caution. I would have spoke plainer, but that you are older than I.

Chr. Good Brother, be not offended, I am sorry I have brought thee out of the way,   *305* and that I have put thee into such eminent danger; pray my Brother forgive me, I did not do it of an evil intent.

---

275. **they:** Christian has now been joined by Hopeful.

Hope. Be comforted, my Brother, for I forgive thee; and believe too, that this shall be for our good.

Chr. I am glad I have with me a merciful Brother: but we must not stand thus, let's 310 try to go back again.

Hope. But good Brother let me go before.

Chr. No, if you please let me go first; that if there be any danger, I may be first therein, because by my means we are both gone out of the way.

Hope. No, said *Hopeful,* you shall not go first, for your mind being troubled, may 315 lead you out of the way again. Then for their encouragement, they heard the voice of one, saying, *Let thine Heart be towards the High-way, even the way that thou wentest, turn again.* But by this time the Waters were greatly risen, by reason of which, the way of going back was very dangerous. (Then I thought that it is easier going out of the way when we are in, then going in, when we are out.) Yet they adventured to go back; but it 320 was so dark, and the flood was so high, that in their going back, they had like to have been drowned nine or ten times.

Jeremiah 31:21

Neither could they, with all the skill they had, get again to the Stile that night. Wherefore, at last, lighting under a little shelter, they sat down there till the day brake; but being weary, they fell asleep. Now there was not far from the place where they lay, a 325 Castle, called *Doubting-Castle,* the owner whereof was *Giant Despair,* and it was in his grounds they now were sleeping; wherefore he getting up in the morning early, and walking up and down in his Fields, caught *Christian* and *Hopeful* asleep in his grounds. Then with a *grim* and *surly* voice he bid them awake, and asked them whence they were? and what they did in his grounds? They told him, they were Pilgrims, and that 330 they had lost their way. Then said the *Giant,* You have this night trespassed on me, by trampling in, and lying on my grounds, and therefore you must go along with me. So they were forced to go, because he was stronger than they. They also had but little to say, for they knew themselves in a fault. The *Giant* therefore drove them before him, and put into his Castle, into a very dark Dungeon, nasty and stinking to the spirit 335 of these two men. Here then they lay, from *Wednesday* morning till *Saturday* night, without one bit of bread, or drop of drink, or any light, or any to ask how they did. They were therefore here in evil case, and were far from friends and acquaintance. Now in this place, *Christian* had double sorrow, because 'twas through his unadvised haste that they were brought into this distress. 340

Psalms 88:18

Now *Giant Despair* had a Wife, and her name was *Diffidence:* so when he was gone to bed, he told his Wife what he had done, to wit, that he had taken a couple of Prisoners, and cast them into his *Dungeon,* for trespassing on his grounds. Then he asked her also what he had best to do further to them. So she asked him what they were, whence they came, and whither they were bound; and he told her. Then she counselled 345 him, that when he arose in the morning, he should beat them without any mercy: So when he arose, he getteth him a grievous Crab-tree Cudgel, and goes down into the *Dungeon* to them; and there, first falls to rating of them as if they were dogs, although they gave him never a word of distaste; then he falls upon them, and beats them fearfully, in such sort, that they were not able to help themselves, or to turn them upon 350 the floor. This done, he withdraws and leaves them, there to condole their misery, and to mourn under their distress: so all that day they spent the time in nothing but sighs and bitter lamentations. The next night she talking with her Husband about them further, and understanding that they were yet alive, did advise him to counsel them, to make away themselves. So when morning was come, he goes to them in a surly manner, as before, *355* and perceiving them to be very sore with the stripes that he had given them the day before; he told them, that since they were never like to come out of that place, their only way would be, forthwith to make an end of themselves, either with Knife, Halter or Poison. For why, said he, should you choose life, seeing it is attended with so much bitterness. But they desired him to let them go; with that he looked ugly upon them, and *360* rushing to them, had doubtless made an end of them himself, but that he fell into one of his fits; (for he sometimes in Sun-shine weather fell into fits) and lost (for a time) the use of his hand: wherefore he withdrew, and left them (as before) to consider what to do. Then did the Prisoners consult between themselves, whether 'twas best to take his counsel or no: and thus they began to discourse. *365*

  Chr. Brother, said *Christian,* what shall we do? the life that we now live is miserable: for my part, I know not whether is best, to live thus, or to die out of hand. *My*
 Job 7:15 *soul chooseth strangling rather than life;* and the Grave is more easie for me than this Dungeon: Shall we be ruled by the Giant?

  Hope. Indeed our present condition is dreadful, and death would be far more *370* welcome to me than thus for ever to abide: but yet let us consider, the Lord of the Country to which we are going, hath said, Thou shalt do no murther, no not to another man's person; much more then are we forbidden to take his counsel to kill our selves. Besides, he that kills another, can but commit murder upon his body; but for one to kill himself, is to kill body and soul at once. And moreover, my Brother, thou talkest of ease *375* in the Grave; but hast thou forgotten the Hell whither, for certain, the murderers go? for no murderer hath eternal life, &c. And, let us consider again, that all the Law is not in the hand of *Giant Despair:* Others, so far as I can understand, have been taken by him, as well as we; and yet have escaped out of his hand. Who knows, but that God that made the world, may cause that *Giant Despair* may die; or that, at some time or other he may *380* forget to lock us in; or, but he may in short time have another of his fits before us, and may lose the use of his limbs; and if ever that should come to pass again, for my part, I am resolved to pluck up the heart of a man, and to try my utmost to get from under his hand. I was a fool that I did not try to do it before, but however, my Brother, let's be patient, and endure a while; the time may come that may give us a happy release: but let *385* us not be our own murderers. With these words, *Hopeful* at present did moderate the mind of his Brother; so they continued together (in the dark) that day, in their sad and doleful condition.

  Well, towards evening the Giant goes down into the Dungeon again, to see if his Prisoners had taken his counsel; but when he came there, he found them alive, and *390* truly, alive was all: for now, what for want of Bread and Water, and by reason of the Wounds they received when he beat them, they could do little but breathe: But, I say, he found them alive; at which he fell into a grievous rage, and told them, that seeing they had disobeyed his counsel, it should be worse with them, than if they had never been born. *395*

377: See I John 3:15.

At this they trembled greatly, and I think that *Christian* fell into a Swound; but coming a little to himself again, they renewed their discourse about the *Giant's* counsel; and whether yet they had best to take it or no. Now *Christian* again seemed to be for doing it, but *Hopeful* made his second reply as followeth.

Hope. My Brother, said he, remembrest thou not how valiant thou hast been *400* heretofore; *Apollyon* could not crush thee, nor could all that thou didst hear, or see, or feel in the Valley of the shadow of Death; what hardship, terror, and amazement hast thou already gone through, and art thou now nothing but fear? Thou seest that I am in the Dungeon with thee, a far weaker man by nature than thou art. Also this Giant has wounded me as well as thee; and hath also cut off the Bread and Water from my mouth; *405* and with thee I mourn without the light: but let's exercise a little more patience. Remember how thou playedst the man at *Vanity-Fair,* and wast neither afraid of the Chain nor Cage; nor yet of bloody Death: wherefore let us (at least to avoid the shame, that becomes not a Christian to be found in) bear up with patience as well as we can.

Now night being come again, and the *Giant* and his Wife being in bed, she asked *410* him concerning the Prisoners, and if they had taken his counsel: To which he replied, They are sturdy Rogues, they choose rather to bear all hardship, than to make away themselves. Then said she, Take them into the Castle-yard tomorrow, and shew them the *Bones* and *Skulls* of those that thou hast already dispatched; and make them believe, ere a week comes to an end, thou also wilt tear them in pieces as thou hast done their *415* fellows before them.

So when the morning was come, the *Giant* goes to them again, and takes them into the Castle-yard, and shews them, as his Wife had bidden him. These, said he, were Pilgrims as you are, once, and they trespassed in my grounds, as you have done; and when I thought fit, I tore them in pieces; and so within ten days I will do you. Go get *420* you down to your Den again; and with that he beat them all the way thither: they lay therefore all day on *Saturday* in a lamentable case, as before. Now when night was come, and when Mrs. *Diffidence,* and her Husband, the *Giant,* were got to bed, they began to renew their discourse of their Prisoners: and withal, the old *Giant* wondered, that he could neither by his blows, nor counsel, bring them to an end. And with that his *425* Wife replied, I fear, said she, that they live in hope that some will come to relieve them, or that they have pick-locks about them; by the means of which they hope to escape. And, sayest thou so, my dear, said the *Giant,* I will therefore search them in the morning.

Well, on *Saturday* about midnight they began to *pray,* and continued in Prayer till *430* almost break of day.

Now a little before it was day, good *Christian,* as one half amazed, brake out in this passionate speech: *What a fool,* quoth he, *am I, thus to lie in a stinking Dungeon, when I may as well walk at liberty!* I have a *Key* in my bosom, called *Promise,* that will (I am persuaded) open any Lock in *Doubting-Castle.* Then said *Hopeful,* That's good news, *435* good Brother; pluck it out of thy bosom, and try. Then *Christian* pulled it out of his bosom, and began to try at the Dungeon door, whose bolt (as he turned the Key) gave back, and the door flew open with ease, and *Christian* and *Hopeful* both came out. Then he went to the outward door, that leads into the *Castle yard,* and with his Key opened the door also. After he went to the *Iron* Gate, for that must be opened too, but that Lock *440* went *damnable* hard, yet the Key did open it; then they thrust open the Gate to make their escape with speed; but that Gate, as it opened, made such a creaking, that it waked *Giant Despair,* who hastily rising to pursue his Prisoners, felt his Limbs to fail, for his fits took him again, so that he could by no means go after them. Then they went on, and came to the King's High-way again, and so were safe, because they were out of his *445* Jurisdiction.

Now when they were gone over the Stile, they began to contrive with themselves what they should do at that Stile, to prevent those that should come after, from falling into the hands of *Giant Despair.* So they consented to erect there a Pillar, and to engrave upon the side thereof: *Over this Stile is the way to* Doubting-Castle, *which is kept by* *450* Giant Despair, *who despiseth the King of the Celestial Country, and seeks to destroy his holy Pilgrims.* Many therefore that followed after, read what was written, and escaped the danger. This done, they sang as follows:

> *Out of the way we went, and then we found*
> *What 'twas to tread upon forbidden ground:* *455*
> *And let them that come after have a care,*
> *Lest heedlessness makes them, as we, to fare:*
> *Lest they, for trespassing, his prisoners are,*
> *Whose Castle's* Doubting, *and whose name's* Despair.

They went then, till they came to the delectable Mountains, which Mountains *460* belong to the Lord of that Hill of which we have spoken before; so they went up to the Mountains, to behold the Gardens, and Orchards, the Vineyards, and Fountains of water, where also they drank, and washed themselves, and did freely eat of the Vineyards. Now there was on the tops of these Mountains, Shepherds feeding their flocks, and they stood by the high-way side. The Pilgrims therefore went to them, and leaning upon their *465* staves (as is common with weary Pilgrims, when they stand to talk with any by the way), they asked, *Whose delectable Mountains are these? and whose be the sheep that feed upon them?*

John 10:11 *Shep.* These Mountains are *Immanuel's Land,* and they are within sight of his City, and the sheep also are his, and he laid down his life for them. *470*

Chr. Is this the way to the Celestial City?

Shep. You are just in your way.

Chr. How far is it thither?

Shep. Too far for any, but those that *shall* get thither indeed.

Chr. Is the way safe, or dangerous? *475*

Hosea 14:9 *Shep.* Safe for those for whom it is to be safe, *but transgressors shall fall therein.*

Chr. Is there in this place any relief for Pilgrims that are weary and faint in the way?

Hebrews 13:1-2 *Shep.* The Lord of these Mountains hath given us a charge, *Not to be forgetful to entertain strangers*: Therefore the good of the place is before you.

I saw also in my Dream, that when the *Shepherds* perceived that they were way- *480* faring men, they also put questions to them, (to which they made answer as in other places) as, Whence came you? and, How got you into the way? and, By what means have you so persevered therein? For but few of them that begin to come hither, do shew

---

449. consented: agreed, were of the same mind.

their face on these Mountains. But when the Shepherds heard their answers, being
pleased therewith, they looked very lovingly upon them, and said, *Welcome to the*   *485*
delectable Mountains.

The Shepherds, I say, whose names were, *Knowledge, Experience, Watchful,* and
Sincere, took them by the hand, and had them to their Tents, and made them partake of
that which was ready at present. They said moreover, We would that you should stay
here a while, to acquaint with us, and yet more to solace your selves with the good of   *490*
these delectable Mountains. They then told them that they were content to stay; and so
they went to their rest that night, because it was very late.

Then I saw in my Dream, that in the morning, the Shepherds called up *Christian*
and *Hopeful* to walk with them upon the Mountains: So they went forth with them, and
walked a while, having a pleasant prospect on every side. Then said the Shepherds one   *495*
to another, shall we shew these Pilgrims some wonders? So when they had concluded to
do it, they had them first to the top of an Hill, called *Errour,* which was very steep on
the furthest side, and bid them look down to the bottom. So *Christian* and *Hopeful*
looked down, and saw at the bottom several men, dashed all to pieces by a fall that they
had from the top. Then said *Christian,* What meaneth this? The Shepherds answered,   *500*
II Tim. 2:17-18 Have you not heard of them that were made to err, by hearkening to *Hymeneus,* and
Philetus, as concerning the faith of the Resurrection of the Body? They answered, Yes.
Then said the Shepherds, Those that you see lie dashed in pieces at the bottom of this
Mountain, are they: and they have continued to this day unburied (as you see) for an
example to others to take heed how they clamber too high, or how they come too near   *505*
the brink of this Mountain.

Then I saw that they had them to the top of another Mountain, and the name of that is
Caution; and bid them look afar off: Which when they did, they perceived, as they
thought, several men walking up and down among the Tombs that were there. And they
perceived that the men were blind, because they stumbled sometimes upon the Tombs, and   *510*
because they could not get out from among them. Then said *Christian,* What means this?

The Shepherds then answered, Did you not see a little below these Mountains a
Stile that led into a Meadow on the left hand of this way? They answered, Yes. Then
said the Shepherds, From that Stile there goes a path that leads directly to *Doubting-*
Castle, which is kept by *Giant Despair;* and these men (pointing to them among the   *515*
Tombs) came once on Pilgrimage, as you do now, even till they came to that same *Stile.*
And because the right way was rough in that place, they chose to go out of it into that
Meadow, and there were taken by *Giant Despair,* and cast into *Doubting-Castle;* where,
after they had a while been kept in the Dungeon, he at last did put out their eyes, and led
them among those Tombs, where he has left them to wander to this very day, that the   *520*
Proverbs 21:16 saying of the wise Man might be fulfilled, *He that wandereth out of the way of under-*
standing, shall remain in the Congregation of the dead. Then *Christian* and *Hopeful*
looked one upon another, with tears gushing out; but yet said nothing to the Shepherds.

Then I saw in my Dream, that the Shepherds had them to another place, in a bottom,
where was a door in the side of an Hill; and they opened the door, and bid them look in.   *525*
They looked in therefore, and saw that within it was very dark, and smoky; they also

---

501-02: See also I Timothy 1:20.

thought that they heard there a lumbring noise as of fire, and a cry of some tormented, and that they smelt the scent of Brimstone. Then said *Christian,* What means this? The Shepherds told them, saying, This is a By-way to Hell, a way that Hypocrites go in at; namely, such as sell their Birthright, with *Esau:* such as sell their Master, with *Judas:* 530 such as blaspheme the Gospel, with *Alexander*; and that lie, and dissemble, with *Ananias* and *Saphira* his wife.

Hope. Then said *Hopeful* to the Shepherds, I perceive that these had on them, even every one, a shew of Pilgrimage as we have now; had they not?

Shep. Yes, and held it a long time too. 535

Hope. How far might they go on Pilgrimage in their day, since they notwithstanding were thus miserably cast away?

Shep. Some further, and some not so far as these Mountains.

Then said the Pilgrims one to another, We had need cry to the Strong for strength.

Shep. Ay, and you will have need to use it when you have it, too. 540

By this time the Pilgrims had a desire to go forwards, and the Shepherds a desire they should; so they walked together towards the end of the Mountains. Then said the Shepherds one to another, Let us here shew to the Pilgrims the Gates of the Celestial City, if they have skill to look through our Perspective Glass. The Pilgrims then lovingly accepted the motion. So they had them to the top of an high Hill called *Clear,* and gave 545 them their Glass to look. Then they essayed to look, but the remembrance of that last thing that the Shepherds had shewed them, made their hands shake; by means of which impediment they could not look steadily through the Glass; yet they thought they saw something like the Gate, and also some of the Glory of the place. Then they went away and sang. 550

> *Thus by the* Shepherds, *Secrets are revealed,*
> *Which from all other men are kept concealed:*
> *Come to the* Shepherds *then, if you would see*
> *Things deep, things hid, and that mysterious be.*

When they were about to depart, one of the Shepherds gave them a *note of the way.* 555 Another of them *bid them beware of the flatterer.* The third *bid them take heed that they sleep not upon the Enchanted Ground.* And the fourth *bid them God speed.* So I awoke from my Dream.

And I slept, and Dreamed again, and saw the same two Pilgrims going down the Mountains along the High-way towards the City. Now a little below these Mountains, 560 on the left hand, lieth the Country of *Conceit;* from which Country there comes into the way in which the Pilgrims walked, a little crooked Lane. Here therefore they met with a very brisk Lad, that came out of that Country; and his name was *Ignorance.* So *Christian* asked him, From what parts he came? and whither he was going?

Ign. Sir, I was born in the Country that lieth off there, a little on the left hand; and I 565 am going to the Celestial City.

Chr. But how do you think to get in at the Gate, for you may find some difficulty there?

Ign. As other good People do, said he.

---

531. Alexander: a Christian who lost his faith — see I Timothy 1:20. 532. Ananias and Saphira: see Acts 5:1-10.

Chr. But what have you to shew at that Gate, that may cause that the Gate should be   *570*
opened unto you?

Ign. I know my Lord's will, and I have been a good Liver, I pay every man his own;
I Pray, Fast, pay Tithes, and give Alms, and have left my Country, for whither I am
going.

Chr. But thou camest not in at the Wicket-gate, that is, at the head of this way: thou   *575*
camest in hither through that same crooked Lane, and therefore I fear, however thou
mayest think of thy self, when the reckoning day shall come, thou wilt have laid to thy
charge, that thou art a Thief and a Robber, instead of getting admittance into the City.

Ignor. Gentlemen, ye be utter strangers to me, I know you not, be content to follow
the Religion of your Country, and I will follow the Religion of mine. I hope all will be   *580*
well. And as for the Gate that you talk of, all the world knows that that is a great way off
of our Country. I cannot think that any man in all our parts doth so much as know the
way to it; nor need they matter whether they do or no, since we have, as you see, a fine,
pleasant, green Lane, that comes down from our Country the next way into it.

When *Christian* saw that the man was wise in his own conceit, he said to *Hopeful,*   *585*
Proverbs 26:12 whisperingly. *There is more hopes of a fool than of him.* And said moreover, *When he*
Eccles. 10:3 *that is a fool walketh by the way, his wisdom faileth him, and he saith to every one that*
he is a fool.

. . . .

So they both went on, and *Ignorance* he came after.

. . . .

[Christian and Hopeful Enter the Celestial City]

Then I saw in my Dream, that the shining men bid them call at the Gate, the which when   *590*
they did, some from above looked over the Gate; to wit, *Enoch, Moses,* and *Elijah, &c.*
to whom it was said, These Pilgrims are come from the City of *Destruction,* for the love
that they bear to the King of this place: and then the Pilgrims gave in unto them each
man his Certificate, which they had received in the beginning; those therefore were
carried in to the King, who when he had read them, said, Where are the men? to whom   *595*
it was answered, They are standing without the Gate. The King then commanded to
Isaiah 26:2 open the Gate; *That the righteous Nation,* said he, *that keepeth Truth may enter in.*

Now I saw in my Dream, that these two men went in at the Gate; and lo, as they
entered, they were transfigured, and they had Raiment put on that shone like Gold.
There was also that met them with Harps and Crowns, and gave them to them; The Harp   *600*
to praise withal, and the Crowns in token of honour: Then I heard in my Dream, that all
the Bells in the City Rang again for joy; and that it was said unto them, *Enter ye into the*
joy of your Lord. I also heard the men themselves, that they sang with a loud voice,
Revelation 5:13 saying, *Blessing, Honour, Glory, and Power, be to him that sitteth upon the Throne, and*
to the Lamb for ever and ever.   *605*

Now just as the Gates were opened to let in the men, I looked in after them; and
behold, the City shone like the Sun, the Streets also were paved with Gold, and in them

---

602-03: See Matthew 25:21.

walked many men, with Crowns on their heads, Palms in their hands, and golden Harps to sing praises withal.

There were also of them that had wings, and they answered one another without 610 intermission, saying, *Holy, Holy, Holy, is the Lord.* And after that, they shut up the Gates: which when I had seen, I wished myself among them.

Now while I was gazing upon all these things, I turned my head to look back, and saw *Ignorance* come up to the River side: but he soon got over, and that without half that difficulty which the other two men met with. For it happened, that there was 615 then in that place one *Vain-hope,* a Ferry-man, that with his Boat helped him over: so he, as the other I saw, did ascend the Hill to come up to the Gate, only he came alone; neither did any man meet him with the least encouragement. When he was come up to the Gate, he looked up to the writing that was above; and then began to knock, supposing that entrance should have been quickly administered to him: But he 620 was asked by the men that looked over the top of the Gate, Whence came you? and what would you have? He answered, I have eat and drank in the presence of the King, and he has taught in our Streets. Then they asked him for his Certificate, that they might go in and shew it to the King. So he fumbled in his bosom for one, and found none. Then said they, Have you none? But the man answered never a word. So 625 they told the King but he would not come down to see him; but commanded the two shining Ones that conducted *Christian* and *Hopeful* to the City to go out and take *Ignorance* and bind him hand and foot, and have him away. Then they took him up, and carried him through the air to the door that I saw in the side of the Hill, and put him in there. Then I saw that there was a way to Hell, even from the Gates of 630 Heaven, as well as from the City of *Destruction.* So I awoke, and behold it was a Dream.

THE CONCLUSION

Now Reader, I have told my Dream to thee;
See if thou canst Interpret it to me;
Or to thy self, or Neighbour: but take heed
Of mis-interpreting: for that, instead
Of doing good, will but thy self abuse: 5
By mis-interpreting evil ensues.
    Take heed also, that thou be not extreme,
In playing with the out-side of my Dream:
Nor let my figure, or similitude,
Put thee into a laughter or a feud; 10
Leave this for Boys and Fools; but as for thee,

Do thou the substance of my matter see.
    Put by the Curtains, look within my Veil;
Turn up my Metaphors and do not fail:
There, if thou seekest them, such things to find,
As will be helpful to an honest mind. 16
    What of my dross thou findest there, be bold
To throw away, but yet preserve the Gold.
What if my Gold be wrapped up in Ore?
None throws away the Apple for the Core: 20
But if thou shalt cast all away as vain,
I know not but 'twill make me Dream again.

(1678)

611: See Revelation 4:8.   **THE CONCLUSION**   **22:** Bunyan seems already to have been planning his sequel.

from *THE PILGRIM'S PROGRESS, THE SECOND PART*

[To Be a Pilgrim]

Who would true valour see,
   Let him come hither;
One here will constant be,
   Come wind, come weather.
There's no discouragement   5
Shall make him once relent
His first avowed intent
   To be a pilgrim.

Who so beset him round
   With dismal stories,   10

Do but themselves confound;
   His strength the more is;
No lion can him fright,
He'll with a giant fight,
But he will have a right   15
   To be a pilgrim.

Hobgoblin nor foul fiend
   Can daunt his spirit;
He knows he at the end
   Shall life inherit.   20
Then fancies fly away,
He'll fear not what men say;
He'll labour night and day
   To be a pilgrim.

                (1684)

CHARLES COTTON
England, 1630-1687

ON TOBACCO

What horrid sin condemned the teeming Earth,
And cursed her womb with such a monstrous birth?
What crime, America, that Heav'n would please
To make thee mother of the world's disease?
In thy fair womb what accidents could breed,   5
What plague give root to this pernicious weed?
Tobacco! Oh, the very name doth kill,
And has already foxed my reeling quill;
I now could write libels against the King,
Treason, or blasphemy, or anything   10
'Gainst piety, and reason; I could frame
A panegyric to the Protector's name:
Such sly infection does the word infuse
Into the soul of ev'ry modest Muse.

What politic peregrine was't first could boast   15
He brought a pest into his native coast?
Th' abstract of poison in a stinking weed,
The spurious issue of corrupted seed;
Seed belched in earthquakes from the dark abyss,
Whose name a blot in nature's herbal is.   20
What drunken fiend taught Englishmen the crime,
Thus to puff out, and spawl away their time?

   Pernicious Weed (should not my Muse offend,
To say Heav'n made aught for a cruel end),
I should proclaim that thou created wert,   25
To ruin man's high and immortal part.
The Stygian damp obscures our reason's eye,
Debauches wit, and makes invention dry;
Destroys the memory, confounds our care;
We know not what we do, or what we are: 30
Renders our faculties and members lame
To ev'ry office of our country's claim.
Our life's a drunken dream devoid of sense,
And the best actions of our time offence.
Our health, diseases, lethargies, and rheum,   35
Our friendship's fire, and all our vows are fume.
Of late there's no such thing as wit, or sense,
Counsel, instruction or intelligence:
Discourse that should distinguish man from beast,
Is by the vapour of this weed suppressed;   40
For what we talk is interrupted stuff,
The one half English, and the other puff;
Freedom and truth are things we do not know,
We know not what we say, or what we do:
We want in all, the understanding's light,   45
We talk in clouds, and walk in endless night.

THE SECOND PART   Set to music, and with the words somewhat altered, this became a famous hymn.   **ON TOBACCO**   Cf. Sir John Davies's "Of Tobacco" (p. 235). **8. foxed:** intoxicated, stupefied. **12. Protector:** Oliver Cromwell (1599-1658), Lord Protector of the Commonwealth, 1653-58. **15. peregrine:** i.e., peregrinator, traveller to foreign countries. **22. spawl:** spit carelessly, scatteringly. **27. Stygian:** gloomy, dark (i.e., pertaining to the River Styx).

We smoke, as if we meant, concealed by spell,
To spy abroad, yet be invisible:
But no discovery shall the statesman boast,
We raise a mist wherein ourselves are lost,   50
A stinking shade, and whilst we pipe it thus,
Each one appears an *ignis fatuus*.
Courtier, and peasant, nay the madam nice
Is likewise fall'n into the common vice,
We all in dusky error groping lie,   55
Robbed of our reasons, and the day's bright eye,
Whilst sailors from the main-top see our isle
Wrapped up in smoke, like the Aetnean pile.
    What nameless ill does its contagion shroud
In the dark mantle of this noisome cloud?   60
Sure 'tis the Devil; Oh, I know that's it,
Foh! How the sulphur makes me cough and spit!
'Tis he; or else some fav'rite fiend at least,
In all the mischief of his malice dressed;
Each deadly sin that lurks t'entrap the soul,   65
Does here concealed in curling vapours roll,
And for the body such an unknown ill,
As makes physicians' reading, and their skill:
One undistinguished pest made up of all
That men experienced do diseases call: 70
Coughs, asthmas, apoplexies, fevers, rheum,
All that kill dead, or lingeringly consume,
Folly, and madness, nay the plague, the pox;
And ev'ry fool wears a Pandora's box.
From that rich mine, the stupid sot doth fill,   75

Smokes up his liver, and his lungs, until
His reeking nostrils monstrously proclaim,
His brains, and bowels are consuming flame.
What noble soul would be content to dwell
In the dark lanthorn of a smoky cell?   80
To prostitute his body, and his mind,
To a debauch of such a stinking kind?
To sacrifice to Moloch, and to fry,
In such a base, dirty idolatry;
As if frail life, which of itself's too short,   85
Were to be whiffed away in drunken sport?
Thus, as if weary of our destined years,
We burn the thread so to prevent the shears.
    What noble end can simple man propose
For a reward to his all-smoking nose?   90
His purposes are levelled sure amiss,
Where neither ornament, nor pleasure is.
What can he then design his worthy hire?
Sure 'tis t' inure him for eternal fire;
And thus his aim must admirably thrive,   95
In hopes of Hell, he damns himself alive.
    But my infected Muse begins to choke
In the vile stink of the increasing smoke,
And can no more in equal numbers chime,
Unless to sneeze, and cough, and spit in rhyme.   100
Half stifled now in this new time's disease,
She must *in fumo* vanish, and decease.
This is her fault's excuse, and her pretence,
This satire, perhaps, else had looked like sense.

(1689)

JOHN DRYDEN

England, 1631-1700

MAC FLECKNOE

All human things are subject to decay,
And, when Fate summons, monarchs must obey:
This Flecknoe found, who, like Augustus, young

Was called to Empire, and had governed long:
In prose and verse, was owned, without dispute   5
Through all the realms of Nonsense, absolute.

---

80. lanthorn: lantern. **88:** referring to the thread of life spun, drawn out, and cut by the three Fates: Clotho, Lachesis, and Atropos; **prevent:** anticipate. **102.** *in fumo:* in smoke. **103. pretence:** claim.   **MAC FLECKNOE   Title:** "Mac [son of] Flecknoe" characterizes the poet and dramatist Thomas Shadwell (1642-1692) as the literary "son" of the priest, poet, and dramatist Richard Flecknoe (died c.1678), whose name had become synonymous with bad writing. The feud between Dryden and Shadwell probably arose from several causes — e.g. from Dryden's having expressed some mild disparagement of Ben Jonson, whose literary descendant Shadwell claimed to be; and from Shadwell's praise for Buckingham's play *The Rehearsal* (1671), which parodied the heroic plays of Dryden and others (see the note to line 47 of Marvell's "On Mr Milton's 'Paradise Lost,'" p. 403); and from Whig Shadwell's attacks on Tory Dryden's works. An unauthorized edition of *Mac Flecknoe* appeared in 1682 with the subtitle "Or, a Satire upon the True-Blue-Protestant Poet T. S." Dryden attacked Shadwell's politics in the second part of *Absalom and Achitophel* (1682); in *Mac Flecknoe* he assails his literary abilities. Ironically, when Catholic Dryden lost the laureateship after the Revolution of 1688, Shadwell succeeded him. **4. long:** Octavian (b. 63 B.C.), who, at age 32, became Rome's first emperor, and reigned from 31 B.C. until his

This aged Prince now flourishing in peace,
And blest with issue of a large increase,
Worn out with business, did at length debate
To settle the succession of the State: *10*
And pond'ring which of all his sons was fit
To reign, and wage immortal war with Wit;
Cried, "'Tis resolved; for Nature pleads that he
Should only rule, who most resembles me:
Sh— alone my perfect image bears,   *15*
Mature in dullness from his tender years.
Sh— alone, of all my sons, is he
Who stands confirmed in full stupidity.
The rest to some faint meaning make pretence,
But Sh— never deviates into sense.   *20*
Some beams of Wit on other souls may fall,
Strike through and make a lucid interval;
But Sh—'s genuine night admits no ray.
His rising fogs prevail upon the day;
Besides his goodly fabric fills the eye,   *25*
And seems designed for thoughtless majesty:
Thoughtless as monarch oaks, that shade the plain,
And, spread in solemn state, supinely reign.
Heywood and Shirley were but types of thee,
Thou last great Prophet of Tautology: *30*
Even I, a dunce of more renown than they,
Was sent before but to prepare thy way;
And coarsely clad in Norwich drugget came
To teach the nations in thy greater name.
My warbling lute, the lute I whilom strung   *35*
When to King John of Portugal I sung,
Was but the prelude to that glorious day,
When thou on silver Thames didst cut thy way,
With well timed oars before the royal barge,
Swelled with the pride of thy celestial charge;   *40*
And big with hymn, commander of an host,
The like was ne'er in Epsom blankets tossed.
Methinks I see the new Arion sail,
The lute still trembling underneath thy nail.
At thy well sharpened thumb from shore to shore   *45*
The treble squeaks for fear, the basses roar:
Echoes from Pissing-Alley, Sh— call,
And Sh— they resound from A— Hall.
About thy boat the little fishes throng,
As at the morning toast, that floats along.   *50*
Sometimes as Prince of thy harmonious band
Thou wield'st thy papers in thy threshing hand.
St. Andre's feet ne'er kept more equal time,
Not ev'n the feet of thy own *Psyche's* rhyme:
Though they in number as in sense excel;   *55*
So just, so like tautology they fell,
That, pale with envy, Singleton forswore
The lute and sword which he in triumph bore,

death in A.D. 14; he had been appointed consul as early as 43 B.C., and was given the title *Augustus* in 27 B.C. Like Flecknoe (9ff.), he had difficulties determining the succession, finally making Tiberius co-regent and heir. **10. succession:** an ironic allusion to the current controversy over who would succeed Charles II (see line 65 below). **12. wage immortal war:** See *Paradise Lost*, I, 121 (p. 328); the poem contains several other echoes of Milton's epic — e.g. line 107 echoes II, 1; there are also echoes of the *Aeneid* and other works. **22. lucid interval:** i.e., a brief period of sanity between longer spells of madness. **25. goodly fabric:** Shadwell was corpulent (see lines 193-95). **29:** Thomas Heywood (c.1574-1641) and James Shirley (1596-1666) were prolific English dramatists who appealed to popular audiences. Shirley worked briefly (1636-40) for an Irish theatre company organized by the Scottish entrepreneur John Ogilby (1600-1676); see "Ogleby" below, lines 102, 174). Ogilby was also a publisher and poet, whose translations Dryden dismissed; **types:** prefigurings, foreshadowings. **31-32. I . . . prepare thy way:** Flecknoe characterizes himself as John the Baptist (see Matthew 3:3); but Dryden may also be alluding to Spenser's proem to Book I of *The Fairie Queene* (see p. 153). **33. Norwich drugget:** a coarse woollen cloth (Shadwell came from Norfolk); John the Baptist was clothed in "camel's hair" (Matthew 3:4). **35. whilom:** once, formerly (a deliberate archaism). **36-40:** In *A Relation of Ten Years' Travels . . .* (c.1654) Flecknoe claimed to have pleased King John IV with his musical abilities, but other commentators — notably Marvell, who described his impressions in "Flecknoe, an English Priest at Rome" — found his lute-playing as bad as his verse. Shadwell also prided himself on his musical skill, but whether he ever led or performed for a royal procession on the Thames is not known. **42:** alluding to Shadwell's *Epsom Wells* (1672) and *The Virtuoso* (1676); in the latter (II, ii), Sir Samuel Hearty, in disguise, is haled out to be "pumped soundly [i.e., soaked under a pump], and then tossed in a blanket"; later (III, iv), in another disguise (this time as a woman), he refers to having suffered these mistreatments. And in Shadwell's first play, *The Sullen Lovers* (1668), based on Molière's *Les Fâcheux*, a lady says of another character, "Such a fellow as he deserves to be tossed in a blanket." **43. Arion:** See note to line 164 of Milton's *Lycidas* (p. 318). Here the allusion includes the notion that the dolphins were pleased with his music. **47-50:** The names of Pissing-Alley and perhaps also of A[ston] Hall, located near the Thames Embankment, are part of a scatological motif that includes "morning toast," which refers to excrement and other sewage dumped or discharged into the river. **52. threshing:** flailing. **53-54:** referring to the French choreographer and to Shadwell's stiffly metrical and rhymed libretto for the opera *Psyche* (1675). **55. number:** metrical regularity. **57-59:** John Singleton was a musician and singer mentioned in Shadwell's play *Bury Fair*; Villerius is a general in D'Avenant's *The Siege of Rhodes* (1656), an opera parodied in Buckingham's *The Rehearsal,* in

And vowed he ne'er would act Villerius more."
Here stopped the good old sire; and wept for joy   *60*
In silent raptures of the hopeful boy.
All arguments, but most his plays, persuade,
That for anointed dullness he was made.
   Close to the walls which fair Augusta bind
(The fair Augusta much to fears inclined),   *65*
An ancient fabric raised t' inform the sight,
There stood of yore, and Barbican it hight:
A watch tower once; but now, so Fate ordains,
Of all the pile an empty name remains.
From its old ruins brothel-houses rise,   *70*
Scenes of lewd loves, and of polluted joys;
Where their vast courts the mother-strumpets keep,
And, undisturbed by watch, in silence sleep.
Near these a Nursery erects its head,
Where queens are formed, and future heroes bred;   *75*
Where unfledged actors learn to laugh and cry,
Where infant punks their tender voices try,
And little Maximins the gods defy.
Great Fletcher never treads in buskins here,
Nor greater Jonson dares in socks appear.   *80*
But gentle Simkin just reception finds
Amidst this monument of vanished minds:
Pure clinches, the suburbian Muse affords,

And Panton waging harmless war with words.
Here Flecknoe, as a place to fame well known,   *85*
Ambitiously designed his Sh—'s throne.
For ancient Dekker prophesied long since,
That in this pile should reign a mighty Prince,
Born for a scourge of Wit, and flail of Sense;
To whom true dullness should some *Psyches* owe,   *90*
But worlds of *Misers* from his pen should flow;
Humorists and *Hypocrites* it should produce,
Whole Raymond families, and tribes of Bruce.
   Now Empress Fame had published the renown,
Of Sh—'s coronation through the town.   *95*
Roused by report of Fame, the nations meet,
From near Bun-Hill and distant Watling-street.
No *Persian* carpets spread th' Imperial way,
But scattered limbs of mangled poets lay;
From dusty shops neglected authors come.   *100*
Martyrs of pies, and relics of the bum.
Much Heywood, Shirley, Ogleby there lay,
But loads of Sh— almost choked the way.
Bilked stationers for Yeomen stood prepared,
And H— was Captain of the Guard.   *105*
The hoary Prince in majesty appeared,
High on a throne of his own labours reared.
At his right hand our young Ascanius sat,

---

which the opposing generals enter bearing swords and lutes and "play the battle in *recitativo*." **64-65. Augusta:** Roman name for London; the city's "fears" are roused by the supposed "Popish Plot" of 1678 and the possibility of the Catholic James succeeding his brother Charles II. **66-67. fabric . . . hight:** i.e., a building called the Barbican, or watchtower; cf. Pope's similar use of this unfashionable district in *The Rape of the Lock*, IV, 118 (p. 530). **73. watch:** watchman or watchmen, police. **74. Nursery:** theatre near the Barbican, built as an acting-school for children. **76-77:** Cf. Dryden's translation of the *Aeneid*, X, 149-50: "So winds, when yet unfledged in woods they lie, / In whispers first their tender voices try." **77. punks:** prostitutes. **78. Maximins:** Maximin is the ranting hero of Dryden's own early play *Tyrannic Love, or, The Royal Martyr* (1669), based on the cruel Galerius Valerius Maximinus, Roman emperor 308-13, and the martyrdom of St. Catherine of Alexandria. **79-80:** John Fletcher (1579-1625) and Ben Jonson (1572-1637), major playwrights; in classical theatre, actors wore *buskins* (thick-soled half boots) when performing in tragedies, *socks* (light shoes or sandals) when performing in comedies. **81. Simkin:** stock name for a fool or clown; in his play *The Miser*, Shadwell refers to a short comic sketch called *The Humours of Simkin*. **83. clinches:** puns or similar word-play; **suburbian:** in the 17th century, the term sometimes suggested the licentiousness of London suburbs. **84. Panton:** perhaps a punster of the day, or a farcical character like Simkin, or even a comic mime. **87. Dekker:** Thomas Dekker (c.1570-1632), a playwright, poet, and pamphleteer whom Jonson considered dull and whom he satirized in *The Poetaster* (and see p. 238). **91-93:** The allusions to Shadwell's works continue: *The Miser* (1672, based on Molière's *L'Avare*), *The Humorists* (1670), *The Hypocrite* (1669, unpublished, but probably based on Molière's *Tartuffe*); Raymond, a character in *The Humorists*; Bruce, in *The Virtuoso*. **94. Fame:** i.e., Rumour; see Dryden's *Aeneis*, IV, 251ff. (173ff. in the original). **97:** Bunhill fields, near the Barbican, was a burial ground for victims of the recent plague, and beginning about that time also the chief burial ground for Nonconformists; Watling Street, the beginning of an old Roman road near St. Paul's, is scarcely more "distant." **99:** alluding to plagiarized lines. **100-01:** i.e., pages from unsold books, recycled as pan-liners for meat-pies and as toilet paper. **102:** In his edition of Dryden's works, Sir Walter Scott wrote that Ogilby "translated *The Iliad, The Odyssey, The Aeneid*, and *Aesop's Fables*. . . . He also wrote three epic poems, one of which was fortunately burned in the fire of London. Moreover he conducted the ceremony of Charles II's coronation, and erected a theatre in Dublin." **105. H:** Henry Herringman, a leading stationer — i.e., publisher-bookseller; he was both Dryden's and Shadwell's publisher until 1678, and had earlier published a work by Flecknoe. **108-09. Ascanius:** Aeneas's son (also called Iulus, or Julus); cf. Dryden's *Aeneis*, XII, 253-54: "And by his side Ascanius took his place, / The second hope of Rome's immortal race."

Rome's other hope, and pillar of the State.
His brows thick fogs, instead of glories, grace,   *110*
And lambent dullness played around his face.
As Hannibal did to the altars come,
Sworn by his sire a mortal foe to Rome;
So Sh— swore, nor should his vow be vain,
That he till death true dullness would maintain;   *115*
And in his father's right and realm's defence,
Ne'er to have peace with Wit, nor truce with Sense.
The King himself the sacred unction made,
As King by office, and as priest by trade.
In his sinister hand, instead of ball,   *120*
He placed a mighty mug of potent ale;
Love's Kingdom to his right he did convey,
At once his sceptre and his rule of sway;
Whose righteous lore the Prince had practised young,
And from whose loins recorded *Psyche* sprung.   *125*
His temples last with poppies were o'erspread,
That nodding seemed to consecrate his head.
Just at that point of time, if Fame not lie,
On his left hand twelve reverend owls did fly.
So Romulus, 'tis sung, by Tiber's brook,   *130*
Presage of sway from twice six vultures took.
Th' admiring throng loud acclamations make,
And omens of his future Empire take.
The sire then shook the honours of his head,
And from his brows damps of oblivion shed   *135*
Full on the filial dullness: long he stood,
Repelling from his breast the raging god;
At length burst out in this prophetic mood:

"Heavens bless my son, from Ireland let him reign
To far Barbadoes on the Western main;   *140*
Of his dominion may no end be known,
And greater than his father's be his throne.
Beyond *Love's Kingdom* let him stretch his pen."
He paused, and all the people cried "Amen."
Then thus, continued he, "My son, advance   *145*
Still in new impudence, new ignorance.
Success let others teach, learn thou from me
Pangs without birth, and fruitless industry.
Let *Virtuosos* in five years be writ,
Yet not one thought accuse thy toil of wit.   *150*
Let gentle George in triumph tread the stage,
Make Dorimant betray, and Loveit rage;
Let Cully, Cockwood, Fopling, charm the pit,
And in their folly show the writer's wit.
Yet still thy fools shall stand in thy defence,   *155*
And justify their author's want of sense.
Let 'em be all by thy own model made
Of dullness, and desire no foreign aid:
That they to future ages may be known,
Not copies drawn, but issue of thy own.   *160*
Nay let thy men of wit too be the same,
All full of thee, and differing but in name;
But let no alien S-dl-y interpose
To lard with wit thy hungry *Epsom* prose.
And when false flowers of rhetoric thou would'st cull,
Trust Nature, do not labour to be dull;   *166*
But write thy best, and top; and in each line,
Sir Formal's oratory will be thine.

110-11: Cf. Dryden's *Aeneis*, II, 930-32: "Strange to relate, from young Iulus' head / A lambent flame arose, which gently spread / Around his brows, and on his temples fed." **112-13:** According to Livy, at the age of nine Hannibal was sworn by his father Hamilcar to be an enemy of Rome. **114-17. swore . . . :** i.e., the coronation oath. **120-21:** At their coronation, monarchs held the orb in their left (sinister) hand; the mug of ale reflects Shadwell's love of drink, as the poppies (line 126) do his addiction to opium (as well as suggesting sleepiness). **122. *Love's Kingdom:*** a 1664 play by Flecknoe on which Shadwell's *Psyche* was based. **129-33:** In ancient times, augurers often made use of the flight of birds; owls are still often considered birds of darkness and ill omen, and here suggest solemnity (as opposed to comedy), dullness, and even stupidity (because proverbially thought wise). Plutarch tells how divination with birds won Romulus the right to choose where Rome was to be built, since he claimed that he saw twelve vultures at his chosen site, whereas his brother Remus saw only six at his. **134. honours of his head:** i.e., his hair; cf. Dryden's *Aeneis*, X, 172, describing Jove: "And shook the sacred honours of his head." **137-38:** Cf. the description of the Sibyl being possessed by the god who then speaks prophecies through her, in passages near the beginning of *Aeneid*, VI. **139-40. Ireland . . . Barbadoes:** both regarded as remote, uncivilized places; Dryden treats Flecknoe as Irish (see also line 202), but he was probably English. **149. in five years:** Shadwell claimed to write quickly; Dryden insists that he was slow, but even so without wit (150). **151-53:** The characters named appear in *The Man of Mode; or, Sir Fopling Flutter* (1676), *The Comical Revenge; or, Love in a Tub* (1664), and *She Would If She Could* (1668), by Sir George Etherege ("gentle George," c.1635-91); the "pit," the section in front of the stage where the general and mostly male middle-class audience sat, was more fashionable than the cheap gallery, though less so than the boxes, where women and the aristocracy usually sat (see line 8 of Dekker's "How a Gallant Should Behave," and note, p. 238). **163. S-dl-y:** Sir Charles Sedley (see p. 459), wit and dramatist, wrote the prologue to *Epsom Wells*, and was rumoured to have written other lines for it and perhaps other Shadwell plays. **167. top:** excel, perform at one's best. **168-70:** referring to the empty rhetoric and florid oratorical style of Sir Formal Trifle, in *The Virtuoso*; Shadwell wrote several flattering "northern dedications" of his works to the Duke of Newcastle and his

Sir Formal, though unsought, attends thy quill,
And does thy Northern dedications fill.   *170*
Nor let false friends seduce thy mind to fame,
By arrogating Jonson's hostile name.
Let Father Flecknoe fire thy mind with praise,
And Uncle Ogleby thy envy raise.
Thou art my blood, where Jonson has no part;   *175*
What share have we in Nature or in Art?
Where did his wit on learning fix a brand,
And rail at arts he did not understand?
Where made he love in Prince Nicander's vein,
Or swept the dust in *Psyche's* humble strain?   *180*
Where sold he bargains? Whip-stitch, kiss my arse,
Promis'd a play and dwindled to a farce?
When did his Muse from Fletcher scenes purloin,
As thou whole Eth'rege dost transfuse to thine?
But so transfused as oil on waters flow,   *185*
His always floats above, thine sinks below.
This is thy province, this thy wondrous way,
New humours to invent for each new play:
This is that boasted bias of thy mind,
By which one way, to dullness, 'tis inclined;   *190*
Which makes thy writings lean on one side still,
And in all changes that way bends thy will.
Nor let thy mountain belly make pretence

Of likeness; thine's a tympany of sense.
A tun of man in thy large bulk is writ,   *195*
But sure thou'rt but a kilderkin of wit.
Like mine thy gentle numbers feebly creep,
Thy Tragic Muse gives smiles, thy Comic sleep.
With whate'er gall thou sett'st thyself to write,
Thy inoffensive satires never bite.   *200*
In thy felonious heart, though venom lies,
It does but touch thy Irish pen, and dies.
Thy Genius calls thee not to purchase fame
In keen iambics, but mild anagram:
Leave writing plays, and choose for thy command *205*
Some peaceful province in acrostic land.
There thou may'st wings display and altars raise,
And torture one poor word ten thousand ways.
Or, if thou would'st thy diff'rent talents suit,
Set thy own songs, and sing them to thy lute."   *210*
He said, but his last words were scarcely heard,
For Bruce and Longvil had a trap prepared,
And down they sent the yet declaiming bard.
Sinking he left his drugget robe behind,
Borne upwards by a subterranean wind.   *215*
The mantle fell to the young prophet's part,
With double portion of his father's art.

(1678; 1684)

---

family (as did also Flecknoe). **177-78:** alluding to the satire on the new science and the Royal Society through the character of Sir Nicholas Gimcrack, the "virtuoso." **179:** In *Psyche*, Nicander woos the title character; e.g.: "Madam, I to this solitude am come, / Humbly from you to hear my latest doom," and "You against me too many weapons choose, / Who am defenceless against each you use." **181:** In *The Virtuoso*, Sir Samuel Hearty frequently "sold . . . bargains" — i.e., responded to innocent questions or straightforward remarks with unexpected and often coarse outbursts such as "Prithee . . . hold thy peace with a whip-stitch, your nose in my breech; I know what I have to do, man" (a *whipstitch*, a running or overcast stitch, figuratively refers to something hastily put together or suggests a quick movement; it is also a contemptuous term for a tailor; but here it is virtually a nonsense word, part of one of several catch-phrases used by Sir Samuel); he also, in III, iii, while disguised as a woman, literally tries to sell items to two women. **182:** In the dedication to *The Virtuoso*, Shadwell promised a comedy rather than a farce, criticizing other playwrights' "impossible, unnatural farce fools." **183-86:** Shadwell evidently based much of the plot, characters, and other details of *Epsom Wells* on those of Etherege's *She Would If She Could*, and elsewhere borrowed from Etherege as well; but such "borrowing," or imitation, was not uncommon in those times, especially among playwrights (and see note to lines 42, 92-93, and 122 above). **188:** As a follower of Ben Jonson (e.g. in his *Every Man in His Humour*, 1598), Shadwell presented himself as writing the "comedy of humours," in which each major figure is characterized by a particular trait, temperament, obsession, or the like; in the dedication to *The Virtuoso*, he claims that "Four of the Humours are entirely new, and, without vanity, I may say I ne'er produced a comedy that had not some natural Humour in it not represented before, nor I hope never shall." For the basis of such "humours," see the note to line 420 of Chaucer's "General Prologue" (p. 34). **189-92:** parodying lines from the epilogue to Shadwell's *The Humorists*: "A Humour is the bias of the mind, / By which with violence 'tis one way inclined: / It makes our actions lean on one side still, / And in all changes that way bends the will." **193-94:** Jonson had referred to his own "mountain belly." **194. tympany:** a flatulent distention of the stomach, like a drum; inflated manner or style; anything big but empty. **195. tun:** large wine cask. **196. kilderkin:** small wine cask. **197. numbers:** metrical feet, verses. **204. keen iambics:** i.e., sharp satiric verse (*iambics* having been the metre used by Greek satirists). **204-08. anagram . . . :** Dryden and his contemporaries regarded such devices and forms as "false wit" (see Addison's *Spectator* essays, pp. 490 ff.). For *acrostics* and shaped verse, see Alternative Table of Contents 1; Dryden and Pope and others were not above subtle and witty puns, but scorned obvious or overworked puns and wordplay (see *pun* in the Glossary, and note e.g. how Polonius "torture[s] one poor word" in *Hamlet*, I, iii, 105-09). **212-13:** In *The Virtuoso*, III, iv, Bruce and Longvil drop Sir Formal through a trapdoor, through which, still orating, "He sinks below," according to the stage directions. **214-17:** See II Kings 2:9-13.

TRANSLATION OF VIRGIL'S THE FOURTH ECLOGUE. POLLIO

ARGUMENT

The poet celebrates the birthday of Saloninus, the son of Pollio, born in the
Consulship of his father, after the taking of Salonæ, a city in Dalmatia. Many of the
verses are translated from one of the Sibyls, who prophesy of our Saviour's birth.

Sicilian Muse, begin a loftier strain!
Though lowly shrubs and trees that shade the plain
Delight not all, if thither I repair,
My song shall make 'em worth a Consul's care.
The last great age foretold by sacred rhymes   *5*
Renews its finished course; Saturnian times
Roll round again, and mighty years, begun
From their first orb, in radiant circles run.
The base degenerate iron offspring ends;
A golden progeny from Heav'n descends;   *10*
O chaste Lucina, speed the mother's pains,
And haste the glorious birth; thy own Apollo reigns!
The lovely boy, with his auspicious face,
Shall Pollio's Consulship and triumph grace;
Majestic months set out with him to their appointed race.
The father banished virtue shall restore,   *16*
And crimes shall threat the guilty world no more.
The son shall lead the life of gods, and be
By gods and heroes seen, and gods and heroes see.
The jarring nations he in peace shall bind,   *20*
And with paternal virtues rule mankind.
Unbidden Earth shall wreathing ivy bring,
And fragrant herbs (the promises of spring),
As her first off'rings to her infant king.
The goats with strutting dugs shall homeward speed,
And lowing herds, secure from lions, feed.   *26*
His cradle shall with rising flow'rs be crowned;
The serpent's brood shall die; the sacred ground
Shall weeds and pois'nous plants refuse to bear;
Each common bush shall Syrian roses wear.   *30*
But when heroic verse his youth shall raise,
And form it to hereditary praise,
Unlaboured harvests shall the fields adorn,

And clustered grapes shall blush on every thorn.
The knotted oaks shall show'rs of honey weep,   *35*
And through the matted grass the liquid gold shall creep.
Yet of old fraud some footsteps shall remain:
The merchant still shall plough the deep for gain;
Great cities shall with walls be compassed round;
And sharpened shares shall vex the fruitful ground.   *40*
Another Tiphys shall new seas explore;
Another *Argo* on th'Iberian shore
Shall land the chosen chiefs;
Another Helen other wars create,
And great Achilles shall be sent to urge the Trojan fate.   *45*
But when to ripened manhood he shall grow,
The greedy sailor shall the seas forgo;
No keel shall cut the waves for foreign ware,
For every soil shall every product bear.
The lab'ring hind his oxen shall disjoin;   *50*
No plow shall hurt the glebe, no pruning-hook the vine,
Nor wool shall in dissembled colours shine;
But the luxurious father of the fold,
With native purple, or unborrowed gold,
Beneath his pompous fleece shall proudly sweat,   *55*
And under Tyrian robes the lamb shall bleat.
The Fates, when they this happy web have spun,
Shall bless the sacred clue, and bid it smoothly run.
Mature in years, to awful honours move,
O of celestial stem! O foster son of Jove!   *60*
See, lab'ring Nature calls thee to sustain
The nodding frame of Heav'n, and Earth, and Main;
See to their base restored, earth, seas, and air,
And joyful ages from behind stand crowding to appear.
To sing thy praise, would Heav'n my breath prolong,
Infusing spirits worthy such a song;   *66*

VIRGIL'S FOURTH ECLOGUE   (Cf. Gay's "The Birth of the Squire," p. 507.) Gaius Asinius Pollio befriended Virgil in hard times, introducing him to Octavian and getting confiscated land returned to him, or at least getting him compensation for it, and to Maecenas, who became Virgil's patron as well as Horace's (see note to Pope's Epistle IV, line 79, p. 539). Since at least as early as the 4th century, Christians have interpreted this eclogue, written about 40 B.C., as a prophecy of the coming of Christ. **1:** See note to Milton's *Lycidas*, line 133 (p. 317); Virgil modelled most of his eclogues (though not IV) on those of Theocritus. **5. last great age foretold:** i.e., the Iron Age (see line 9); **sacred rhymes:** those of the Sybil of Cumae; the Sybilline writings included a prophecy of a new cycle of the ages (see Sandys's translation of Ovid's *Metamorphoses*, 90ff., p. 268). **6. Saturnian times:** i.e., a new Golden Age (see line 10). **11. Lucina:** Juno's title as goddess of childbirth, invoked by women in labour. **25. strutting:** swollen — i.e., with milk. **41. Tiphys:** the pilot of the *Argo*. **41-43:** In a later edition Dryden rendered these lines as follows: "Another Tiphys shall new seas explore, / Another *Argo* land the chiefs upon th' Iberian shore." **55. pompous:** stately. **58. sacred clue:** the thread of life spun and governed by the Fates.

Not Thracian Orpheus should transcend my lays,
Nor Linus crowned with never-fading bays,
Though each his Heav'nly parent should inspire,
The Muse instruct the voice, and Phoebus tune the lyre.
Should Pan contend with me, and thou my theme,   71
Arcadian judges should their god condemn.
Begin, auspicious boy, to cast about
Thy infant eyes, and with a smile, thy mother single out;
Thy mother well deserves that short delight,   75
The nauseous qualms of ten long months and travail to
    requite.
Then smile: the frowning infant's doom is read;
No god shall crown the board, nor goddess bless the bed.
                                                    (1684)

TO THE MEMORY OF
MR. OLDHAM

Farewell, too little and too lately known,
Whom I began to think and call my own;
For sure our souls were near allied; and thine
Cast in the same poetic mould with mine.
One common note on either lyre did strike,   5
And knaves and fools we both abhorred alike:
To the same goal did both our studies drive,
The last set out the soonest did arrive.
Thus Nisus fell upon the slippery place,
While his young friend performed and won the race. 10
O early ripe! to thy abundant store
What could advancing age have added more?
It might (what Nature never gives the young)
Have taught the numbers of thy native tongue.
But Satire needs not those, and Wit will shine   15
Through the harsh cadence of a rugged line:
A noble error, and but seldom made,
When poets are by too much force betrayed.
Thy generous fruits, though gathered ere their prime,

Still showed a quickness; and maturing time   20
But mellows what we write to the dull sweets of Rhyme.
Once more, hail and farewell; farewell thou young,
But ah too short, Marcellus of our tongue;
Thy brows with ivy, and with laurels bound;
But Fate and gloomy Night encompass thee around. 25
                                                    (1684)

A SONG FOR ST. CECILIA'S DAY

1

From harmony, from heavenly harmony
    This universal frame began:
    When Nature underneath a heap
        Of jarring atoms lay,
    And could not heave her head,   5
The tuneful voice was heard from high:
    "Arise, ye more than dead."
Then cold, and hot, and moist, and dry,
In order to their stations leap,
        And Music's power obey.   10
From harmony, from heavenly harmony
    This universal frame began:
        From harmony to harmony
Through all the compass of the notes it ran,
The diapason closing full in man.   15

2

What passion cannot Music raise and quell!
    When Jubal struck the corded shell,
    His listening brethren stood around,
    And, wondering, on their faces fell
    To worship that celestial sound.   20
Less than a god they thought there could not dwell
    Within the hollow of that shell
    That spoke so sweetly and so well.
What passion cannot Music raise and quell!

---

68. Linus: mythical singer who perhaps rivalled Apollo, or who taught Herakles music (and see note to Pope's *Iliad*, XVIII, 662, p. 536); **bays:** i.e., wreath of laurel.   **TO THE MEMORY OF MR. OLDHAM**   John Oldham (1653-1683), English poet, author of *Satyrs upon the Jesuits* (1681). For an example of Oldham's satire, see p. 464. **6. knaves and fools:** i.e., the targets of satire. **9-10:** For this event, see the excerpt from Book V of the *Aeneid*, below, p. 441; **performed:** i.e., finished. **14. numbers:** metrics, versification (i.e., smooth rhythm). **22. hail and farewell:** translating *Ave atque vale*, a conventional Latin funerary inscription — especially the last line of Catullus's elegy at his brother's tomb: "*Atque in perpetuum, frater, ave atque vale.*" **23. Marcellus:** Marcus Claudius Marcellus (42-23 B.C.), nephew and adopted heir of Augustus (see *Aeneid*, VI, 855-86; the last line echoes 866, which, along with the line before it, Dryden in his *Aeneis*, VI, 1198-99, translated as "But hov'ring mists around his brows are spread, / And night, with sable shades, involves his head").   **A SONG FOR ST. CECILIA'S DAY**   St. Cecilia's Day (November 22) commemorates a second- or third-century Roman Christian martyr, patron saint of music and traditionally the inventor of the organ (see stanzas 6 and 7). Annual celebrations were held in London from 1683 to 1703, each including a concert with a new ode set to music for the occasion; for two of these performances, Dryden wrote this ode and another ("Alexander's Feast," 1697). Handel composed his famous setting for "A Song for St. Cecilia's Day" in 1739. **2ff. universal frame:** the physical universe, created by divine fiat (6-7) out of a chaos of discordant atoms (3-4) by a harmonious ordering of the four elements (8-10): earth (cold), fire (hot), water (moist), and air (dry); cf. the description of Chaos and the four elements in Milton's *Paradise Lost*, II, 890ff. p. 347). Compare other accounts of creation — e.g. that in Genesis (p. 241), *Paradise Lost*, VII (see especially 271-73), and Dryden's *Aeneis*, VI, 980ff. (with its reference to "earth's compacted frame"). **14-15:** i.e., the perfect harmony ("diapason")

3

The trumpet's loud clangour   25
   Excites us to arms,
With shrill notes of anger,
   And mortal alarms.
The double double double beat
   Of the thund'ring drum   30
Cries: "Hark! the foes come;
Charge, charge, 'tis too late to retreat."

4

The soft complaining flute
In dying notes discovers
The woes of hopeless lovers,   35
Whose dirge is whispered by the warbling lute.

5

Sharp violins proclaim
Their jealous pangs, and desperation,
Fury, frantic indignation,
Depth of pains, and height of passion,   40
   For the fair, disdainful dame.

6

But O! what art can teach,
   What human voice can reach,
The sacred organ's praise?
   Notes inspiring holy love,   45
Notes that wing their heav'nly ways
   To mend the choirs above.

7

Orpheus could lead the savage race;
And trees unrooted left their place,
   Sequacious of the lyre;   50
But bright Cecilia raised the wonder higher:
When to her organ vocal breath was given,
An angel heard, and straight appeared,
   Mistaking earth for heaven.

Grand Chorus

As from the power of sacred lays   55
   The spheres began to move,
And sung the great Creator's praise
   To all the blest above;
So, when the last and dreadful hour
This crumbling pageant shall devour,   60
The trumpet shall be heard on high,
The dead shall live, the living die,
And Music shall untune the sky.

           (1687)

from translation of Virgil's *AENEID:* the *AENEIS*

[from Book I: the opening]

Arms, and the Man I sing, who, forced by Fate,
And haughty Juno's unrelenting hate;
Expelled and exiled, left the Trojan shore.
Long labours, both by sea and land, he bore,
And in the doubtful war, before he won   5
The Latian realm, and built the destined town;
His banished gods restored to rites divine,
And settled sure succession in his line,
From whence the race of Alban fathers come,
And the long glories of majestic Rome.   10
   O Muse! the causes and the crimes relate,
What goddess was provoked, and whence her hate;
For what offence the Queen of Heav'n began
To persecute so brave, so just a Man!
Involved his anxious life in endless cares,   15
Exposed to wants, and hurried into wars!
Can heav'nly minds such high resentment show,
Or exercise their spite in human woe?

---

of a complete run through the full range ("compass") of notes in the octave ("the music of the spheres"; see line 56 below); that it ends in "man" underscores the analogy with the "Great Chain of Being" of creation, with man at the apex (see Pope's *Essay on Man*, I, 237-46; p. 545). **17. Jubal:** See Genesis 4:21 (p. 245); the "corded shell" is a tortoise shell with strings across it — Jubal's newly invented stringed instrument. **37. sharp violins:** referring to the sound of the instruments only recently introduced into England — especially as compared to that of the familiar viols. **48-50:** Orpheus's music purportedly could charm and attract animals, trees, and rocks (see Ovid's *Metamorphoses*, XI, 1-2); **sequacious of:** following after. **52-54:** St. Cecilia is usually depicted playing an organ or harp and singing, sometimes with an angel visiting her, enchanted by her music — though one legend says the visit occurs because of her piety. **56. spheres:** "the music of the spheres" heard by those in heaven (see *Ptolemaic* in the Glossary). **61. trumpet:** See I Corinthians 15:52.   AENEIS   BOOK I: THE OPENING   **6. Latian:** i.e., of Latium, part of ancient Italy. **9. Alban:** Alba Longa was a city in ancient Latium, said to have been founded by Ascanius, Aeneas's son, and to be the birthplace of Romulus and Remus.

[from Book V: the race]

From thence his way the Trojan hero bent,
Into the neighb'ring plain, with mountains pent,
Whose sides were shaded with surrounding wood.　375
Full in the midst of this fair valley stood
A native theatre, which rising slow,
By just degrees, o'erlooked the ground below.
High on a sylvan throne the leader sate;
A num'rous train attend in solemn state;　380
Here those that in the rapid course delight,
Desire of honour, and the prize invite.
The rival runners without order stand,
The Trojans mixed with the Sicilian band.
First Nisus, with Euryalus, appears,　385
Euryalus a boy of blooming years,
With sprightly grace and equal beauty crowned;
Nisus, for friendship to the youth, renowned.
Diores next, of Priam's royal race,
Then Salius, joined with Patron, took their place;　390
But Patron in Arcadia had his birth,
And Salius his from Acarnanian earth.
Then two Sicilian youths, the names of these
Swift Helymus, and lovely Panopes:
Both jolly huntsmen, both in forests bred,　395
And owning old Acestes for their head.
With sev'ral others of ignobler name,
Whom time has not delivered o'er to Fame.
　To these the hero thus his thoughts explained,
In words which gen'ral approbation gained:　400
"One common largess is for all designed:
The vanquished and the victor shall be joined.
Two darts of polished steel and Gnosian wood,
A silver-studded ax alike bestowed.
The foremost three have olive wreaths decreed;　405
The first of these obtains a stately steed
Adorned with trappings; and the next in fame,
The quiver of an Amazonian dame,
With feathered Thracian arrows well supplied;
A golden belt shall gird his manly side,　410
Which with a sparkling diamond shall be tied.
The third this Grecian helmet shall content."
He said; to their appointed base they went;
With beating hearts th'expected sign receive,
And, starting all at once, the barrier leave.　415
Spread out, as on the winged winds, they flew,
And seized the distant goal with greedy view.
Shot from the crowd, swift Nisus all o'erpassed;
Nor storms, nor thunder, equal half his haste.
The next, but though the next, yet far disjoined,　420
Came Salius, and Euryalus behind;
Then Helymus, whom young Diores plied,
Step after step, and almost side by side,
His shoulders pressing; and, in longer space,
Had won, or left at least a dubious race.　425
　Now spent, the goal they almost reach at last,
When eager Nisus, hapless in his haste,
Slipped first, and slipping, fell upon the plain,
Soaked with the blood of oxen, newly slain.
The careless victor had not marked his way,　430
But treading where the treach'rous puddle lay,
His heels flew up, and on the grassy floor
He fell, besmeared with filth and holy gore.
Not mindless then, Euryalus, of thee,
Nor of the sacred bonds of amity,　435
He strove th'immediate rival's hope to cross,
And caught the foot of Salius as he rose:
So Salius lay extended on the plain;
Euryalus springs out, the prize to gain,
And leaves the crowd; applauding peals attend　440
The victor to the goal, who vanquished by his friend.
Next Helymus, and then Diores came,
By two misfortunes made the third in fame.
　But Salius enters, and, exclaiming loud
For justice, deafens and disturbs the crowd;　445
Urges his cause may in the court be heard,
And pleads the prize is wrongfully conferred.
But favour for Euryalus appears;
His blooming beauty, with his tender tears,
Had bribed the judges for the promised prize;　450
Besides, Diores fills the court with cries,
Who vainly reaches at the last reward,
If the first palm on Salius be conferred.
Then thus the Prince: "Let no disputes arise;
Where Fortune placed it, I award the prize.　455
But Fortune's errors give me leave to mend,
At least to pity my deserving friend."

BOOK V: THE RACE (See "To the Memory of Mr. Oldham," lines 9–10 above.) Aeneas and his fleet sail from Carthage toward Italy, but storms drive them ashore at Sicily, where he earlier buried his father, Anchises, and where his Trojan-descended friend Acestes rules. Aeneas institutes funeral games to honour Anchises. First they hold a race of galleys on the water, then they move inland for further games. **373. From thence:** i.e., from the coast; **Trojan hero:** Aeneas. **389. Priam:** the defeated ruler of Troy. **392. Acarnanian:** Acarnania was a region of northwestern Greece. **403. Gnosian:** Gnossian, Cnossian, from Cnossos — i.e., Cretan. **422. plied:** i.e., followed closely. **429. newly slain:** i.e., as ritual sacrifice. **454. Prince:** i.e., Aeneas.

He said, and from among the spoils he draws
(Pond'rous with shaggy main, and golden paws)
A lion's hide; to Salius this he gives.   460
Nisus with envy sees the gift, and grieves:
"If such rewards to vanquished men are due,"
He said, "and falling is to rise by you,
What prize may Nisus from your bounty claim,
Who merited the first rewards and fame?   465
In falling, both an equal fortune tried;
Would Fortune for my fall so well provide!"

With this he pointed to his face, and showed
His hands, and all his habit smeared with blood.
Th'indulgent Father of the People smiled,   470
And caused to be produced an ample shield,
Of wondrous art by Didymaon wrought,
Long since from Neptune's bars in triumph brought.
This giv'n to Nisus, he divides the rest,
And equal justice in his gifts expressed.   475

                                                        (1695)

KATHERINE (FOWLER) PHILIPS
England/Wales, 1632-1664

FRIENDSHIP'S MYSTERY, TO MY DEAREST LUCASIA

I

Come, my Lucasia, since we see
    That miracles men's faith do move,
By wonder and by prodigy
    To the dull angry world let's prove
        There's a Religion in our Love.   5

II

For though we were design'd t' agree,
    That Fate no liberty destroys,
But our Election is as free
    As Angels', who with greedy choice
        Are yet determin'd to their joys.   10

III

Our hearts are doubled by the loss,
    Here mixture is addition grown;
We both diffuse, and both ingross,
    And we whose minds are so much one,
        Never, yet ever are alone.   15

IV

We court our own captivity
    Than Thrones more great and innocent:
'Twere banishment to be set free,
    Since we wear fetters whose intent
        Not bondage is, but ornament.   20

V

Divided joys are tedious found,
    And griefs united easier grow:
We are our selves but by rebound,
    And all our titles shuffled so,
        Both Princes, and both Subjects too.   25

VI

Our hearts are mutual victims laid,
    While they (such power in Friendship lies)
Are Altars, Priests, and Off'rings made:
    And each heart which thus kindly dies,
        Grows deathless by the sacrifice.   30

                                                        (1667)

WISTON VAULT

And why this vault and tomb? Alike we must
Put off distinction, and put on our dust.
Nor can the stateliest fabric help to save
From the corruptions of a common grave;
Not for the Resurrection more prepare,   5
Than if the dust were scattered into air.
What then? Th' ambition's just, say some, that we
May thus perpetuate our memory.
Ah false vain task of Art! Ah poor weak Man!
Whose monument does more than's merit can;   10
Who by his friends' best care and love's abused,
And in his very epitaph accused:

---

472. Didymaon: artist known for the armour he made. **473. bars:** temple gates; evidently the shield was taken from a temple by a Greek warrior and subsequently captured by Aeneas during the fighting at Troy.   **PHILIPS**   While some of Philips's poems were published in earlier versions during her lifetime (including a pirated edition in 1664), we base the texts of these poems on the first authorized edition, published posthumously in 1667.   **FRIENDSHIP'S MYSTERY**   "Lucasia" is Anne Owen, Katherine Philips's friend.   **WISTON VAULT**   Wiston, with its ruins of a

For did they not suspect his name would fall,
There would not need an epitaph at all.
But after death too I would be alive,   *15*
And shall, if my Lucasia do, survive.
I quit these pomps of death, and am content,
Having her heart to be my monument;
Though ne'er stone to me, 'twill stone for me prove,
By the peculiar miracles of Love.   *20*
There I'll inscription have which no tomb gives,
Not "Here Orinda lies," but "Here she lives."

                                            (1667)

AGAINST PLEASURE

I

There's no such thing as Pleasure here,
   'Tis all a perfect cheat,
Which does but shine and disappear,
   Whose charm is but deceit:
The empty bribe of yielding souls,   *5*
Which first betrays, and then controls.

II

'Tis true, it looks at distance fair;
   But if we do approach,
The fruit of Sodom will impair,
   And perish at a touch: *10*
In being than in fancy less,
And we expect more than possess.

III

For by our pleasures we are cloy'd,
   And so Desire is done;
Or else, like rivers, they make wide   *15*
   The channel where they run;
And either way true bliss destroys,
Making Us narrow, or our Joys.

IV

We covet pleasure easily,
   But it not so possess;   *20*
For many things must make it be,

But one may make it less.
Nay, were our state as we could choose it,
'Twould be consum'd by fear to lose it.

V

What art thou then, thou winged air,   *25*
   More weak and swift than Fame?
Whose next successor is Despair,
   And its attendant Shame.
Th' experienc'd Prince then reason had,
Who said of pleasure, It is mad.   *30*

                                            (1667)

AN ANSWER TO ANOTHER PERSUADING A LADY TO MARRIAGE

I

Forbear, bold Youth, all's Heaven here,
   And what you do aver,
To others courtship may appear,
   'Tis sacrilege to her.

II

She is a public Deity,   *5*
   And were't not very odd
She should depose herself to be
   A petty household god?

III

First make the Sun in private shine,
   And bid the World adieu,   *10*
That so he may his beams confine
   In compliment to you.

IV

But if of that you do despair,
   Think how you did amiss,
To strive to fix her beams which are   *15*
   More bright and large than this.

                                            (1667)

---

castle-fortress, is in what was central Pembrokeshire (now Dyfed). **22. Orinda:** Philips's poetic name for herself; she was known as "The Matchless Orinda." **AGAINST PLEASURE 9-10:** referring to "apples of Sodom," which supposedly look fine on the outside but are ashes within (also known as "Dead Sea fruit").

JOHN LOCKE
England, 1632-1704

from *THE SECOND TREATISE OF GOVERNMENT*

from *Chapter VII:* Of Political or Civil Society
. . . .

86. Let us therefore consider a master of a family, with all these subordinate relations of wife, children, servants, and slaves, united under the domestic rule of a family, which, what resemblance soever it may have in its order, offices, and number too, with a little commonwealth, yet is very far from it both in its constitution, power, and end; or, if it must be thought a monarchy, and the paterfamilias the absolute *5* monarch in it, absolute monarchy will have but a very shattered and short power, when 'tis plain, by what has been said before, that the master of the family has a very distinct and differently limited power, both as to time and extent, over those several persons that are in it; for, excepting the slave (and the family is as much a family, and his power as paterfamilias as great, whether there be any slaves in his family or no), he has no *10* legislative power of life and death over any of them, and none, too, but what a mistress of a family may have as well as he. And he certainly can have no absolute power over the whole family, who has but a very limited one over every individual in it. But how a family or any other society of men differ from that which is properly political society, we shall best see by considering wherein political society itself consists. *15*

87. Man being born, as has been proved, with a title to perfect freedom, and an uncontrolled enjoyment of all the rights and privileges of the law of nature equally with any other man or number of men in the world, hath by nature a power not only to preserve his property — that is, his life, liberty, and estate — against the injuries and attempts of other men, but to judge of and punish the breaches of that law in others as he *20* is persuaded the offence deserves, even with death itself, in crimes where the heinousness of the fact in his opinion requires it. But because no political society can be nor subsist without having in itself the power to preserve the property, and in order thereunto punish the offences of all those of that society, there, and there only, is political society, where every one of the members hath quitted this natural power, *25* resigned it up into the hands of the community in all cases that exclude him not from appealing for protection to the law established by it. And thus all private judgment of every particular member being excluded, the community comes to be umpire by settled, standing rules, indifferent and the same to all parties, and by men having authority from the community for the execution of those rules, decides all the differences that may *30* happen between any members of that society concerning any matter of right, and

---

THE SECOND TREATISE OF GOVERNMENT The subtitle reads "An Essay Concerning the True Original, Extent and End of Civil Government."

punishes those offences which any member hath committed against the society, with such penalties as the law has established; whereby it is easy to discern who are and who are not in political society together. Those who are united into one body, and have a common established law and judicature to appeal to, with authority to decide controversies between them and punish offenders, are in civil society one with another; but those who have no such common appeal — I mean on earth — are still in the state of nature, each being, where there is no other, judge for himself and executioner, which is, as I have before shown it, the perfect state of nature.

88. And thus the commonwealth comes by a power to set down what punishment shall belong to the several transgressions which they think worthy of it, committed amongst the members of that society (which is the power of making laws) as well as it has the power to punish any injury done unto any of its members by any one that is not of it (which is the power of war and peace); and all this for the preservation of the property of all the members of that society, as far as is possible. But though every man who has entered into civil society and is become a member of any commonwealth, has thereby quitted his power to punish offences against the law of nature in prosecution of his own private judgment, yet with the judgment of offences, which he has given up to the legislative in all cases where he can appeal to the magistrate, he has given a right to the commonwealth to employ his force for the execution of the judgments of the commonwealth whenever he shall be called to it, which, indeed, are his own judgments, they being made by himself or his representative. And herein we have the original of the legislative and executive power of civil society, which is to judge by standing laws how far offences are to be punished when committed within the commonwealth, and also to determine, by occasional judgments founded on the present circumstances of the fact, how far injuries from without are to be vindicated, and in both these to employ all the force of all the members when there shall be need.

89. Wherever, therefore, any number of men are so united into one society as to quit every one his executive power of the law of nature and to resign it to the public, there and there only is a political or civil society. And this is done wherever any number of men, in the state of nature, enter into society to make one people, one body politic, under one supreme government, or else when any one joins himself to, and incorporates with, any government already made. For hereby he authorizes the society, or, which is all one, the legislative thereof, to make laws for him as the public good of the society shall require, to the execution whereof his own assistance (as to his own decrees) is due. And this puts men out of a state of nature into that of a commonwealth, by setting up a judge on earth with authority to determine all the controversies and redress the injuries that may happen to any member of the commonwealth, which judge is the legislative, or magistrates appointed by it. And wherever there are any number of men, however associated, that have no such decisive power to appeal to, there they are still in the state of nature.

90. Hence it is evident that absolute monarchy, which by some men is counted the only government in the world, is indeed inconsistent with civil society, and so can be no form of civil government at all. For the end of civil society being to avoid and remedy those inconveniences of the state of nature which necessarily follow from every man's being judge in his own case, by setting up a known authority to which every one of that

society may appeal upon any injury received or controversy that may arise, and which every one of the society ought to obey, wherever any persons are, who have not such an authority to appeal to and decide any difference between them, there those persons are still in the state of nature. And so is every absolute prince, in respect of those who are *80* under his dominion.

91. For he being supposed to have all, both legislative and executive, power in himself alone, there is no judge to be found; no appeal lies open to any one who may fairly and indifferently and with authority decide, and from whose decision relief and address may be expected of any injury or inconvenience that may be suffered from the *85* prince or by his order; so that such a man, however entitled, Czar, or Grand Seignior, or how you please, is as much in the state of nature with all under his dominion as he is with the rest of mankind. For wherever any two men are who have no standing rule and common judge to appeal to on earth for the determination of controversies of right betwixt them, there they are still in the state of nature, and under all the inconveniences *90* of it, with only this woeful difference to the subject, or rather slave, of an absolute prince: that whereas in the ordinary state of nature he has a liberty to judge of his right, and according to the best of his power to maintain it, now, whenever his property is invaded by the will and order of his monarch, he has not only no appeal, as those in society ought to have, but, as if he were degraded from the common state of rational *95* creatures, is denied a liberty to judge of or to defend his right, and so is exposed to all the misery and inconveniences that a man can fear from one who, being in the unrestrained state of nature, is yet corrupted with flattery and armed with power.

92. For he that thinks absolute power purifies men's blood, and corrects the baseness of human nature, need read but the history of this or any other age to be *100* convinced of the contrary. He that would have been insolent and injurious in the woods of America, would not probably be much better in a throne, where perhaps learning and religion shall be found out to justify all that he shall do to his subjects, and the sword presently silence all those that dare question it. For what the protection of absolute monarchy is, what kind of fathers of their countries it makes princes to be, and to what a *105* degree of happiness and security it carries civil society, where this sort of government is grown to perfection, he that will look into the late relation of Ceylon may easily see.

93. In absolute monarchies, indeed, as well as other governments of the world, the subjects have an appeal to the law and judges, to decide any controversies and restrain any violence that may happen betwixt the subjects themselves, one amongst another. *110* This everyone thinks necessary, and believes he deserves to be thought a declared enemy to society and mankind who should go about to take it away. But whether this be from a true love of mankind and society, and such a charity as we owe all one to another, there is reason to doubt. For this is no more than what every man who loves his

107: Referring to the widely read book *An Historical Relation of the Island Ceylon, in the East Indies, Together with an Account of the Detaining in Captivity the Author and Divers Other Englishmen Now Living There, and of the Author's Miraculous Escape* (1681), by Captain Robert Knox (1641-1720), "a Captive there near Twenty Years." Part II of Knox's description of Ceylon (now Sri Lanka) is devoted to King Rajasingha and his rule of the Sinhalese kingdom of Kandy, bearing out Locke's remark; on p. 43, e.g., occurs the following paragraph: "As to the manner of his Government, it is Tyrannical and Arbitrary in the highest degree. For he ruleth Absolute, and after his own Will and Pleasure, his own Head being his only Counsellor. The Land all at his Disposal, and all the People from the highest to the lowest Slaves, or very like Slaves, both in Body and Goods wholly at his Command. Neither wants He those three Virtues of a Tyrant, Jealousy, Dissimulation, and Cruelty." (Like the experiences of Alexander Selkirk — see the account by Woodes Rogers, p. 510 — Knox's narration influenced Defoe's *Robinson Crusoe*.)

own power, profit, or greatness may, and naturally must do, keep those animals from *115* hurting or destroying one another who labour and drudge only for his pleasure and advantage, and so are taken care of, not out of any love the master has for them, but love of himself, and the profit they bring him. For if it be asked, what security, what fence is there, in such a state against the violence and oppression of this absolute ruler, the very question can scarce be borne. They are ready to tell you that it deserves death only to *120* ask after safety. Betwixt subject and subject, they will grant, there must be measures, laws, and judges, for their mutual peace and security; but as for the ruler, he ought to be absolute, and is above all such circumstances; because he has power to do more hurt and wrong, 'tis right when he does it. To ask how you may be guarded from harm or injury on that side where the strongest hand is to do it, is presently the voice of faction and *125* rebellion. As if when men, quitting the state of nature, entered into society, they agreed that all of them but one should be under the restraint of laws, but that he should still retain all the liberty of the state of nature, increased with power, and made licentious by impunity. This is to think that men are so foolish that they take care to avoid what mischiefs may be done them by polecats or foxes, but are content, nay, think it safety, to *130* be devoured by lions.

94. But whatever flatterers may talk to amuse people's understandings, it hinders not men from feeling; and when they perceive that any man, in what station soever, is out of the bounds of the civil society which they are of, and that they have no appeal on earth against any harm they may receive from him, they are apt to think themselves in *135* the state of nature in respect of him whom they find to be so, and to take care, as soon as they can, to have that safety and security in civil society for which it was first instituted, and for which only they entered into it. And, therefore, though perhaps at first (as shall be shown more at large hereafter in the following part of this discourse), some one good and excellent man, having got a pre-eminency amongst the rest, had this deference paid *140* to his goodness and virtue, as to a kind of natural authority, that the chief rule, with arbitration of their differences, by a tacit consent devolved into his hands, without any other caution but the assurance they had of his uprightness and wisdom; yet when time, giving authority and, as some men would persuade us, sacredness to customs which the negligent and unforeseeing innocence of the first ages began, had brought in successors *145* of another stamp, the people, finding their properties not secure under the government as then it was (whereas government has no other end but the preservation of property), could never be safe nor at rest, nor think themselves in civil society, till the legislature was placed in collective bodies of men, call them senate, parliament, or what you please; by which means every single person became subject, equally with other the *150* meanest men, to those laws, which he himself, as part of the legislative, had established; nor could any one by his own authority avoid the force of the law when once made, nor by any pretence of superiority plead exemption, thereby to license his own, or the miscarriages of any of his dependents. No man in civil society can be exempted from the laws of it. For if any man may do what he thinks fit, and there be no appeal on earth *155* for redress or security against any harm he shall do, I ask whether he be not perfectly still in the state of nature, and so can be no part or member of that civil society, unless any one will say the state of nature and civil society are one and the same thing, which I have never yet found any one so great a patron of anarchy as to affirm.

from *Chapter VIII:* Of the Beginning of Political Societies

95. Men being, as has been said, by nature all free, equal, and independent, no one can be put out of this estate, and subjected to the political power of another, without his own consent. The only way whereby any one divests himself of his natural liberty and puts on the bonds of civil society is by agreeing with other men to join and unite into a community for their comfortable, safe, and peaceable living one amongst another, in a secure enjoyment of their properties, and a greater security against any that are not of it. This any number of men may do, because it injures not the freedom of the rest; they are left as they were in the liberty of the state of nature. When any number of men have so consented to make one community or government, they are thereby presently incorporated, and make one body politic, wherein the majority have a right to act and conclude the rest.

96. For when any number of men have, by the consent of every individual, made a community, they have thereby made that community one body, with a power to act as one body, which is only by the will and determination of the majority. For that which acts any community being only the consent of the individuals of it, and it being necessary to that which is one body to move one way, it is necessary the body should move that way whither the greater force carries it, which is the consent of the majority, or else it is impossible it should act or continue one body, one community, which the consent of every individual that united into it agreed that it should; and so every one is bound by that consent to be concluded by the majority. And therefore we see that in assemblies empowered to act by positive laws, where no number is set by that positive law which empowers them, the act of the majority passes for the act of the whole, and of course determines, as having, by the law of nature and reason, the power of the whole.

97. And thus every man, by consenting with others to make one body politic under one government, puts himself under an obligation to every one of that society to submit to the determination of the majority, and to be concluded by it; or else this original compact, whereby he with others incorporates into one society, would signify nothing, and be no compact, if he be left free and under no other ties than he was in before in the state of nature. For what appearance would there be of any compact? What new engagement if he were no farther tied by any decrees of the society than he himself thought fit, and did actually consent to? This would be still as great a liberty as he himself had before his compact, or any one else in the state of nature hath, who may submit himself and consent to any acts of it if he thinks fit.

98. For if the consent of the majority shall not in reason be received as the act of the whole, and conclude every individual, nothing but the consent of every individual can make anything to be the act of the whole; but such a consent is next to impossible ever to be had, if we consider the infirmities of health and avocations of business, which in a number, though much less than that of a commonwealth, will necessarily keep many away from the public assembly. To which if we add the variety of opinions, and contrariety of interests, which unavoidably happen in all collections of men, the coming into society upon such terms would be only like Cato's coming into the theatre, only to

160

165

170

175

180

185

190

195

200

200: Marcus Portius Cato (234-149 B.C.), "Cato the Censor," tried to establish a strict moral standard. The reference here is to the end of the preface to Book I of Martial's *Epigrams*, where Martial, after asserting that epigrams are written for people who customarily attend the festival of Flora (known for its licentiousness) and exhorting Cato not to enter "my theatre" unless he intends to stay and watch, adds four lines of verse to the

go out again. Such a constitution as this would make the mighty Leviathan of a shorter duration than the feeblest creatures, and not let it outlast the day it was born in, which cannot be supposed, till we can think that rational creatures should desire and constitute societies only to be dissolved. For where the majority cannot conclude the rest, there they cannot act as one body, and consequently will be immediately dissolved again. *205*

99. Whosoever therefore out of a state of nature unite into a community must be understood to give up all the power necessary to the ends for which they unite into society, to the majority of the community, unless they expressly agreed in any number greater than the majority. And this is done by barely agreeing to unite into one political society, which is all the compact that is, or needs be, between the individuals that enter *210* into or make up a commonwealth. And thus that which begins and actually constitutes any political society is nothing but the consent of any number of freemen capable of a majority to unite and incorporate into such a society. And this is that, and that only, which did or could give beginning to any lawful government in the world.

. . . .

(1690)

GEORGE SAVILE, 1ST MARQUESS OF HALIFAX
England, 1633-1695

from *THE LADY'S NEW-YEAR'S-GIFT; OR, ADVICE TO A DAUGHTER*

DEAR DAUGHTER,

. . . .

A great part of what is said in the following discourse may be above the present growth of your understanding; but that becoming every day taller will in a little time reach up to it, so as to make it easy to you. I am willing to begin with you before your mind is quite formed, that being the time in which it is most capable of receiving a colour that will last when it is mixed with it. Few things are well learnt but by early precepts; those well *5* infused, make them natural; and we are never sure of retaining what is valuable, till by a continued habit we have made it a piece of us.

Whether my skill can draw the picture of a fine woman may be a question; but it can be none that I have drawn that of a kind father. If you will take an exact copy I will so far presume upon my workmanship as to undertake you shall not make an ill figure. *10* Give me so much credit as to try, and I am sure that neither your wishes nor mine shall be disappointed by it.

. . . .

___

effect that "Since you knew what kind of licentious joking goes on here at Flora's festival, why did you come to the theatre, severe Cato — to watch the sensual display, or because of it to stomp out again?" **201. Leviathan:** referring to Hobbes's term for a commonwealth (see p. 280).

House, Family, and Children

You must lay before you, my dear, there are degrees of care to recommend yourself to the world in the several parts of your life. In many things, though the doing them well may raise your credit and esteem, yet the omission of them would draw no immediate *15* reproach upon you. In others, where your duty is more particularly applied, the neglect of them is amongst those faults which are not forgiven, and will bring you under a censure, which will be a much heavier thing than the trouble you would avoid. Of this kind is the government of your house, family, and children, which since it is the province allotted to your sex, and that the discharging it well will for that reason be *20* expected from you, if you either desert it out of laziness, or manage it ill for want of skill, instead of a help you will be an encumbrance to the family where you are placed.

I must tell you that no respect is lasting but that which is produced by our being in some degree useful to those that pay for it. Where that faileth, the homage and the reverence go along with it, and fly to others where something may be expected in *25* exchange for them. And upon this principle the respects even of the children and the servants will not stay with one that doth not think them worth their care, and the old housekeeper shall make a better figure in the family than the lady with all her fine clothes, if she wilfully relinquishes her title to the government. Therefore take heed of carrying your good breeding to such a height as to be good for nothing, and to be proud *30* of it. Some think it hath a great air to be above troubling their thoughts with such ordinary things as their house and family; others dare not admit cares for fear they should hasten wrinkles. Mistaken pride maketh some think they must keep themselves up, and not descend to these duties, which do not seem enough refined for great ladies to be employed in; forgetting all this while that it is more than the greatest princes can do *35* at once to preserve respect and to neglect their business. No age ever erected altars to insignificant gods; they had all some quality applied to them to draw worship from mankind; this maketh it the more unreasonable for a lady to expect to be considered and at the same time resolve not to deserve it. Good looks alone will not do; they are not such a lasting tenure as to be relied upon; and if they should stay longer than they *40* usually do, it will by no means be safe to depend upon them; for when time hath abated the violence of the first liking, and that the nap is a little worn off, though still a good degree of kindness may remain, men recover their sight which before might be dazzled, and allow themselves to object as well as to admire.

In such a case, when a husband seeth an empty airy thing sail up and down the *45* house to no kind of purpose, and look as if she came thither only to make a visit; when he findeth that after her emptiness hath been extreme busy about some very senseless thing, she eats her breakfast half an hour before dinner, to be at greater liberty to afflict the company with her discourse, then calleth for her coach, that she may trouble her acquaintance, who are already cloyed with her; and having some proper dialogues ready *50* to display her foolish eloquence at the top of the stairs, she setteth out like a ship out of the harbour laden with trifles, and cometh back with them. At her return she repeateth to her faithful waiting-woman the triumphs of that day's impertinence; then, wrapped up in

---

THE LADY'S NEW-YEAR'S-GIFT   **19. family:** i.e., the whole household, including servants.

flattery and clean linen, goeth to bed so satisfied that it throweth her into pleasant
dreams of her own felicity. Such a one is seldom serious but with her tailor; her children   *55*
and family may now and then have a random thought, but she never taketh aim but at
something very impertinent.

I say, when a husband, whose province is without doors, and to whom the economy
of the house would be in some degree indecent, findeth no order nor quiet in his family,
meeteth with complaints of all kinds springing from this root, the mistaken lady, who   *60*
thinketh to make amends for all this by having a well-chosen petticoat, will at last be
convinced of her error, and with grief be forced to undergo the penalties that belong to
those who are wilfully insignificant. When this scurvy hour cometh upon her she first
groweth angry, then when the time of it is past, would perhaps grow wiser, not
remembering that we can no more have wisdom than grace whenever we think fit to call   *65*
for it. There are times and periods fixed for both; and when they are too long neglected,
the punishment is that they are irrecoverable, and nothing remaineth but a useless grief
for the folly of having thrown them out of our power. You are to think what a mean
figure a woman maketh when she is so degraded by her own fault; whereas there is
nothing in those duties which are expected from you that can be lessening to you, except   *70*
your want of conduct makes it so.

You may love your children without living in the nursery, and you may have a
competent and discreet care of them without letting it break out upon the company or
exposing yourself by turning your discourse that way, which is a kind of laying children
to the parish, and it can hardly be done anywhere that those who hear it will be so   *75*
forgiving as not to think they are overcharged with them. A woman's tenderness to her
children is one of the least deceitful evidences of her virtue; but yet the way of
expressing it must be subject to the rules of good breeding. And though a woman of
quality ought not to be less kind to them than mothers of the meanest rank are to theirs,
yet she may distinguish herself in the manner and avoid the coarse methods which in   *80*
women of a lower size might be more excusable. You must begin early to make them
love you, that they may obey you. This mixture is nowhere more necessary than in
children. And I must tell you that you are not to expect returns of kindness from yours,
if ever you have any, without grains of allowance; and yet it is not so much a defect in
their good nature as a shortness of thought in them. Their first insufficiency maketh   *85*
them lean so entirely upon their parents for what is necessary, that the habit of it maketh
them continue the same expectations for what is unreasonable; and as often as they are
denied so often they think they are injured; and whilst their desires are strong, and their
reasons yet in the cradle, their anger looketh no farther than the thing they long for and
cannot have; and to be displeased for their own good is a maxim they are very slow to   *90*
understand. So that you may conclude the first thoughts of your children will have no
small mixture of mutiny; which being so natural you must not be angry except you
would increase it. You must deny them as seldom as you can, and when there is no
avoiding it, you must do it gently; you must flatter away their ill humour, and take the

---

63. scurvy: vile. **74-75. laying children to the parish:** i.e., making society responsible for them. **79. quality:** high social position. **81. of a lower size:** i.e., from a lower station in life. **92. except:** lest.

next opportunity of pleasing them in some other thing, before they either ask or look for   *95*
it. This will strengthen your authority by making it soft to them, and confirm their
obedience by making it their interest. You are to have as strict a guard upon yourself
amongst your children as if you were amongst your enemies. They are apt to make
wrong inferences, to take encouragement from half words, and misapply what you may
say or do, so as either to lessen their duty or to extend their liberty farther than is   *100*
convenient. Let them be more in awe of your kindness than of your power. And above
all, take heed of supporting a favourite child in its impertinence, which will give right to
the rest of claiming the same privilege. If you have a divided number, leave the boys to
the father's more peculiar care, that you may with the greater justice pretend to a more
immediate jurisdiction over those of your own sex. You are to live so with them that   *105*
they may never choose to avoid you, except when they have offended; and then let them
tremble that they may distinguish. But their penance must not continue so long as to
grow too sour upon their stomachs, that it may not harden instead of correcting them.
The kind and severe parts must have their several turns seasonably applied; but your
indulgence is to have the broader mixture, that love, rather than fear, may be the root of   *110*
their obedience.

    Your servants are in the next place to be considered; and you must remember not to
fall into the mistake of thinking that because they receive wages, and are so much
inferior to you, therefore they are below your care to know how to manage them. It
would be as good reason for a master workman to despise the wheels of his engines   *115*
because they are made of wood. These are the wheels of your family; and let your
directions be never so faultless, yet if these engines stop or move wrong, the whole
order of your house is either at a stand or discomposed. Besides, the inequality which is
between you must not make you forget that nature maketh no such distinction, but that
servants may be looked upon as humble friends, and that returns of kindness and good   *120*
usage are as much due to such of them as deserve it, as their service is due to us when
we require it. A foolish haughtiness in the style of speaking or in the manner of
commanding them is in itself very undecent; besides that it begetteth an aversion in
them, of which the least ill effect to be expected is that they will be slow and careless in
all that is enjoined them; and you will find it true by your experience that you will be so   *125*
much the more obeyed as you are less imperious. Be not too hasty in giving your orders,
nor too angry when they are not altogether observed; much less are you to be loud and
too much disturbed. An evenness in distinguishing when they do well or ill is that which
will make your family move by a rule and without noise, and will the better set out your
skill in conducting it with ease and silence, that it may be like a well-disciplined army,   *130*
which knoweth how to anticipate the orders that are fit to be given them. You are never
to neglect the duty of the present hour to do another thing, which, though it may be
better in itself, is not to be unseasonably preferred. Allot well-chosen hours for the
inspection of your family, which may be so distinguished from the rest of your time that
the necessary cares may come in their proper place, without any influence upon your   *135*
good humour, or interruption to other things. By these methods you will put yourself in

---

104. **peculiar:** particular. 120. **humble:** i.e., of lowly rank.

possession of being valued by your servants, and then their obedience will naturally follow.

I must not forget one of the greatest articles belonging to a family, which is the expense. It must not be such, as by failing either in the time or measure of it, may rather draw censure than gain applause. If it was well examined, there is more money given to be laughed at than for any one thing in the world, though the purchasers do not think so. A well stated rule is like the Line: when that is once passed we are under another Pole; so the first straying from a rule is a step towards making that which was before a virtue to change its nature, and to grow either into a vice, or at least an impertinence. The art of laying out money wisely is not attained to without a great deal of thought; and it is yet more difficult in the case of a wife, who is accountable to her husband for her mistakes in it. It is not only his money, his credit too is at stake, if what lieth under the wife's care is managed either with undecent thrift, or too loose profusion. You are therefore to keep the mean between these two extremes, and it being hardly possible to hold the balance exactly even, let it rather incline towards the liberal side as more suitable to your quality, and less subject to reproach. Of the two, a little money misspent is sooner recovered than the credit which is lost by having it unhandsomely saved; and a wise husband will less forgive a shameful piece of parsimony than a little extravagance, if it be not too often repeated. His mind in this must be your chief direction; and his temper, when once known, will in great measure justify your part in the management, if he is pleased with it.

In your clothes avoid too much gaudy; do not value yourself upon an embroidered gown; and remember, that a reasonable word, or an obliging look, will gain you more respect than all your fine trappings. This is not said to restrain you from a decent compliance with the world, provided you take the wiser and not the foolisher part of your sex for your pattern. Some distinctions are to be allowed, whilst they are well suited to your quality and fortune, and in the distribution of the expense it seemeth to me that a full attendance and well-chosen ornaments for your house will make you a better figure than too much glittering in what you wear, which may with more ease be imitated by those that are below you. Yet this must not tempt you to starve everything but your own apartment; or, in order to more abundance there, give just cause to the least servant you have to complain of the want of what is necessary. Above all, fix it in your thoughts as an unchangeable maxim, that nothing is truly fine but what is fit, and that just so much as is proper for your circumstances of their several kinds is much finer than all you can add to it. When you once break through these bounds, you launch into a wide sea of extravagance. Everything will become necessary, because you have a mind to it; and you have a mind to it, not because it is fit for you, but because somebody else hath it. This lady's logic setteth reason upon its head, by carrying the rule from things to persons, and appealing from what is right to every fool that is in the wrong. The word *necessary* is miserably applied; it disordereth families, and overturneth governments by being so abused. Remember that children and fools want everything because they want wit to distinguish; and therefore there is no stronger evidence of a crazy understanding

---

143. **Line:** Equator.

than the making too large a catalogue of things necessary, when in truth there are so very few things that have a right to be placed in it. Try everything first in your judgment *180* before you allow it a place in your desire; else your husband may think it as necessary for him to deny, as it is for you to have, whatever is unreasonable; and if you shall too often give him that advantage, the habit of refusing may perhaps reach to things that are not unfit for you.

There are unthinking ladies who do not enough consider how little their own figure *185* agreeth with the fine things they are so proud of. Others, when they have them, will hardly allow them to be visible; they cannot be seen without a light, and that is many times so saucy and so prying, that like a too forward gallant it is to be forbid the chamber. Some, when they are ushered into their dark *ruelle*, it is with such solemnity that a man would swear there was something in it, till the unskilful lady breaketh *190* silence, and beginneth a chat, which discovereth it is a puppet play with magnificent scenes. Many esteem things rather as they are hard to be gotten, than that they are worth getting. This looketh as if they had an interest to pursue that maxim because a great part of their own value dependeth upon it. Truth in these cases would be often unmannerly, and might derogate from the prerogative great ladies would assume to themselves, of *195* being distinct creatures from those of their sex which are inferior and of less difficult access.

In other things, too, your condition must give the rule to you, and therefore it is not a wife's part to aim at more than a bounded liberality; the farther extent of that quality (otherwise to be commended) belongeth to the husband, who hath better means for it. *200* Generosity wrong placed becometh vice. It is no more a virtue when it groweth into an inconvenience; virtues must be enlarged or restrained according to differing circumstances. A princely mind will undo a private family. Therefore things must be suited, or else they will not deserve to be commended, let them in themselves be never so valuable; and the expectations of the world are best answered when we acquit ourselves *205* in that manner which seemeth to be prescribed to our several conditions, without usurping upon those duties which do not so particularly belong to us.

I will close the consideration of this article of expense with this short word: do not fetter yourself with such a restraint in it as may make you remarkable; but remember that virtue is the greatest ornament, and good sense the best equipage. *210*

. . . .

Much more might be said to all these heads, and many more might be added to them. But I must restrain my thoughts, which are full of my dear child, and would overflow into a volume, which would not be fit for a New Year's gift. I will conclude with my warmest wishes for all that is good to you: that you may live so as to be an ornament to your family, and a pattern to your sex; that you may be blessed with a *215* husband that may value, and with children that may inherit, your virtue; that you may shine in the world by a true light, and silence envy by deserving to be esteemed; that wit and virtue may both conspire to make you a great figure. When they are separated, the first is so empty, and the other so faint, that they scarce have right to be commended.

---

188. **saucy:** insolent, presumptuous. 189. *ruelle:* bedroom in which fashionable 17th- and 18th-century ladies held morning receptions. 209. **remarkable:** conspicuous.

May they therefore meet and never part; let them be your guardian angels, and be sure 220 never to stray out of the distance of their joint protection. May you so raise your character, that you may help to make the next age a better thing, and leave posterity in your debt for the advantage it shall receive by your example.

Let me conjure you, my dearest, to comply with this kind ambition of a father, whose thoughts are so engaged in your behalf, that he reckoneth your happiness to be 225 the greatest part of his own.

(1700)

THOMAS SPRAT
England, 1635-1713

from *THE HISTORY OF THE ROYAL SOCIETY*
from Part II, Section XX: Their Manner of Discourse

. . . .

There is one thing more about which the Society has been most solicitous, and that is the manner of their discourse, which, unless they had been very watchful to keep in due temper, the whole spirit and vigour of their design had been soon eaten out by the luxury and redundance of speech. The ill effects of this superfluity of talking have already overwhelmed most other arts and professions, insomuch that when I consider 5 the means of happy living, and the causes of their corruption, I can hardly forbear recanting what I said before, and concluding that eloquence ought to be banished out of all civil societies, as a thing fatal to peace and good manners. To this opinion I should wholly incline if I did not find that it is a weapon which may be as easily procured by bad men as good, and that if these should only cast it away, and those retain it, the 10 naked innocence of virtue would be upon all occasions exposed to the armed malice of the wicked. This is the chief reason that should now keep up the ornaments of speaking in any request, since they are so much degenerated from their original usefulness. They were at first, no doubt, an admirable instrument in the hands of wise men, when they were only employed to describe goodness, honesty, obedience in larger, fairer, and more 15 moving images; to represent Truth clothed with bodies; and to bring knowledge back again to our very senses, from whence it was at first derived to our understandings. But

---

THE HISTORY OF THE ROYAL SOCIETY   The Royal Society got its charter in 1662, having grown out of the Philosophical Society, which was founded in 1645. **7. what I said before:** i.e., in Part I, Sections XIX (Modern Academies for Language) and XX (A Proposal for Erecting an English Academy). **13. in any request:** desirable, held in such estimation as to be sought after. **18. disgust:** have a strong distaste for, loathe.

now they are generally changed to worse uses. They make the fancy disgust the best things if they come sound and unadorned; they are in open defiance against reason, professing not to hold much correspondence with that, but with its slaves, the passions; they give the mind a motion too changeable and bewitching to consist with right practice. Who can behold without indignation how many mists and uncertainties these specious tropes and figures have brought on our knowledge? How many rewards which are due to more profitable and difficult arts have been still snatched away by the easy vanity of fine speaking? For now I am warmed with this just anger, I cannot withhold myself from betraying the shallowness of all these seeming mysteries upon which we writers and speakers look so big. And, in few words, I dare say that of all the studies of men, nothing may be sooner obtained than this vicious abundance of phrase, this trick of metaphors, this volubility of tongue which makes so great a noise in the world. But I spend words in vain, for the evil is now so inveterate that it is hard to know whom to blame or where to begin to reform. We all value one another so much upon this beautiful deceit, and labour so long after it in the years of our education, that we cannot but ever after think kinder of it than it deserves. And indeed, in most other parts of learning I look on it to be a thing almost utterly desperate in its cure, and I think it may be placed amongst those general mischiefs, such as the dissension of Christian princes, the want of practice in religion, and the like, which have been so long spoken against that men are become insensible about them, everyone shifting off the fault from himself to others, and so they are only made bare commonplaces of complaint. It will suffice my present purpose to point out what has been done by the Royal Society towards the correcting of its excesses in natural philosophy, to which it is, of all others, a most professed enemy.

They have therefore been most rigorous in putting in execution the only remedy that can be found for this extravagance, and that has been a constant resolution to reject all the amplifications, digressions, and swellings of style; to return back to the primitive purity, and shortness, when men delivered so many things almost in an equal number of words. They have exacted from all their members a close, naked, natural way of speaking: positive expressions, clear senses, a native easiness, bringing all things as near the mathematical plainness as they can, and preferring the language of artisans, countrymen, and merchants before that of wits or scholars.

And here there is one thing not to be passed by, which will render this established custom of the Society well nigh everlasting, and that is the general constitution of the minds of the English. I have already often insisted on some of the prerogatives of England, whereby it may justly lay claim to be the head of a philosophical league, above all other countries in Europe; I have urged its situation, its present genius, and the disposition of its merchants; and many more such arguments to encourage us still remain to be used. But of all others, this which I am now alleging is the most weighty and important consideration. If there can be a true character given of the universal temper of any nation under Heaven, then certainly this must be ascribed to our

---

24. still: always, continually. **27. big:** proud(ly), pompous(ly). **32. deceit:** deception, fraud, fallacy. **36. want of practice:** i.e., lack of customary worship and observance of rites and ceremonies. **40. natural philosophy:** science. **52-55. I have already . . . merchants:** in Part II, Section XIII.

countrymen: that they have commonly an unaffected sincerity; that they love to deliver their minds with a sound simplicity; that they have the middle qualities, between the   *60* reserved subtle southern and the rough unhewn northern people; that they are not extremely prone to speak; that they are more concerned what others will think of the strength than of the fineness of what they say; and that an universal modesty possesses them. These qualities are so conspicuous and proper to our soil that we often hear them objected to us by some of our neighbour satirists in more disgraceful expressions. For   *65* they are wont to revile the English with a want of familiarity; with a melancholy dumpishness; with slowness, silence; and with the unrefined sullenness of their behaviour. But these are only the reproaches of partiality, or ignorance; for they ought rather to be commended for an honourable integrity; for a neglect of circumstances and flourishes; for regarding things of greater moment more than less; for a scorn to deceive   *70* as well as to be deceived: which are all the best endowments that can enter into a philosophical mind. So that even the position of our climate, the air, the influence of the heaven, the composition of the English blood, as well as the embraces of the ocean, seem to join with the labours of the Royal Society to render our country a land of experimental knowledge. And it is a good sign that nature will reveal more of its secrets   *75* to the English than to others, because it has already furnished them with a genius so well proportioned for the receiving and retaining its mysteries.

. . . .

(1667)

THOMAS TRAHERNE
England, 1637-1674

THE SALUTATION

I

These little limbs,
These eyes and hands which here I find,
These rosy cheeks wherewith my life begins,
Where have ye been? behind
What curtain were ye from me hid so long,   *5*
Where was, in what abyss, my speaking tongue?

II

When silent I
So many thousand, thousand years
Beneath the dust did in a chaos lie,
How could I smiles or tears,   *10*
Or lips or hands or eyes or ears perceive?
Welcome ye treasures which I now receive.

III

I that so long
Was nothing from eternity,
Did little think such joys as ear or tongue   *15*
To celebrate or see:
Such sounds to hear, such hands to feel, such feet,
Beneath the skies on such a ground to meet.

IV

New burnished joys!
Which yellow gold and pearls excel!   *20*
Such sacred treasures are the limbs in boys,
In which a soul doth dwell;
Their organised joints and azure veins
More wealth include than all the world contains.

---

69. circumstances: financial condition, estate.

V

From dust I rise,   25
And out of nothing now awake,
These brighter regions which salute mine eyes,
     A gift from God I take.
The earth, the seas, the light, the day, the skies,
The sun and stars are mine; if those I prize.   30

VI

Long time before
I in my mother's womb was born,
A God preparing did this glorious store,
     The world for me adorn.
Into this Eden so divine and fair,   35
So wide and bright, I come His son and heir.

VII

A stranger here
Strange things doth meet, strange glories see;
Strange treasures lodged in this fair world appear,
     Strange all and new to me;   40
But that they mine should be, who nothing was,
That strangest is of all, yet brought to pass.

                                (c. 1660s; 1903)

INNOCENCE

I

But that which most I wonder at, which most
I did esteem my bliss, which most I boast,
And ever shall enjoy, is that within
     I felt no stain nor spot of sin.

No darkness then did overshade,   5
But all within was pure and bright,
No guilt did crush nor fear invade,
But all my soul was full of light.

A joyful sense and purity
     Is all I can remember,   10
The very night to me was bright,
     'Twas Summer in December.

II

A serious meditation did employ
My soul within, which taken up with joy
Did seem no outward thing to note, but fly   15
     All objects that do feed the eye,

While it those very objects did
Admire and prize and praise and love,
Which in their glory most are hid,
Which presence only doth remove.   20

Their constant daily presence I
     Rejoicing at, did see,
And that which takes them from the eye
Of others offered them to me.

III

No inward inclination did I feel   25
To avarice or pride; my soul did kneel
In admiration all the day. No lust, nor strife,
     Polluted then my infant life.

No fraud nor anger in me moved
No malice, jealousy, or spite;   30
All that I saw I truly loved:
Contentment only and delight

Were in my soul. O Heav'n! what bliss
     Did I enjoy and feel!
What powerful delight did this   35
Inspire! for this I daily kneel.

IV

Whether it be that Nature is so pure,
And custom only vicious; or that sure
God did by miracle the guilt remove,
     And made my soul to feel his Love   40

So early: or that 'twas one day,
Wherein this happiness I found,
Whose strength and brightness so do ray,
That still it seems me to surround,

Whate'er it is, it is a Light   45
     So endless unto me
That I a world of true delight
Did then, and to this day do see.

V

That prospect was the gate of Heaven, that day
The ancient Light of Eden did convey   50
Into my soul: I was an Adam there,
     A little Adam in a sphere

Of joys! O there my ravished sense
Was entertained in Paradise,
And had a sight of Innocence,   55
Which was beyond all bound and price.

An antepast of Heaven sure!
I on the Earth did reign,
Within, without me, all was pure:
I must become a child again.   60

(c. 1660s; 1903)

SIR CHARLES SEDLEY
England, 1639-1701

TO NYSUS

How shall we please this age? If in a song
We put above six lines, they count it long;
If we contract it to an epigram,
As deep the dwarfish poetry they damn;
If we write plays, few see above an act,   5
And those lewd masks, or noisy fops distract:
Let us write satire then, and at our ease
Vex th'ill-natured fools we cannot please.

(1692)

APHRA BEHN
England, 1640-1689

Epilogue to *SIR PATIENT FANCY*

I here and there o'erheard a coxcomb cry,
"Ah, Rot it — 'tis a woman's comedy,
One who, because she lately chanced to please us
With her damned stuff, will never cease to tease us."
What has poor Woman done, that she must be   5
Debarred from sense and sacred poetry?
Why in this age has Heaven allowed you more
And women less of wit than heretofore?
We once were famed in story, and could write
Equal to men; could govern, nay, could fight.   10

We still have passive valour, and can show,
Would custom give us leave, the active too,
Since we no provocations want from you.
For who but we could your dull fopperies bear,
Your saucy love, and your brisk nonsense hear;   15
Endure your worse than womanish affectation,
Which renders you the nuisance of the nation,
Scorned even by all the Misses of the Town,
A jest to Vizard Mask, the pit-buffoon,
A glass by which the admiring country fool   20

INNOCENCE   57. antepast: foretaste.   **TO NYSUS   6. lewd masks:** See "Vizard Mask" (line 19) in Behn's "Epilogue" (immediately following).   **EPILOGUE   13. want:** lack. **15. saucy:** impertinent; **brisk:** curt, brief. **18. Misses of the Town:** kept women. **19. Vizard Mask:** prostitute; **pit-buffoon:** See "coxcomb" (line 1) — a member of the audience sitting in the pit, making foolish comments.

May learn to dress himself *en ridicule*:
Both striving who shall most ingenious grow
In lewdness, foppery, nonsense, noise, and show.
And yet to those fine things we must submit
Our reason, arms, our laurels, and our wit,   25
Because we do not laugh at you, when lewd,
And scorn and cudgel ye when you are rude.
That we have nobler souls than you, we prove
By how much more we're sensible of love;
Quickest in finding all the subtlest ways   30
To make your joys, why not to make you plays?
We best can find your foibles, know our own,
And jilts and cuckolds now best please the Town;
Your way of writing's out of fashion grown.
Method and Rule — you only understand;   35
Pursue that way of fooling and be damned.
Your learned cant of Action, Time, and Place,
Must all give way to the unlaboured farce.
To all the Men of Wit we will subscribe,
But for your half wits, you unthinking tribe,   40
We'll let you see, whate'er besides we do,
How artfully we copy some of you:
And if you're drawn to th'Life, pray tell me then,
Why women should not write as well as men.

(1678)

SONG: ON HER LOVING TWO EQUALLY

How strongly does my passion flow,
Divided equally 'twixt two?
Damon had ne'er subdued my heart
Had not Alexis took his part;
Nor could Alexis powerful prove,   5
Without my Damon's aid, to gain my love.

When my Alexis present is,
Then I for Damon sigh and mourn;
But when Alexis I do miss,
Damon gains nothing but my scorn.   10
But if it chance they both are by,
For both alike I languish, sigh, and die.

Cure then, thou mighty winged god,
This restless fever in my blood;
One golden-pointed dart take back: 15
But which, O Cupid, wilt thou take?
If Damon's, all my hopes are crossed;
Or that of my Alexis, I am lost.

(1684)

EDWARD TAYLOR
England/U.S.A., c.1644-1729

AN ADDRESS TO THE SOUL OCCASIONED BY A RAIN

Ye flippering soul,
　Why dost between the nippers dwell?
Not stay, nor go. Not yea, not yet control.
　Doth this do well?   4
　　Rise journy'ing when the skies fall weeping showers,
　　Not o'er nor under th' clouds and cloudy powers.

Not yea, nor no:
　On tiptoes thus? Why sit on thorns?
Resolve the matter: Stay thyself or go:
　Be n't both ways born.   10
　　Wager thyself against thy surplice; see
　　And win thy coat, or let thy coat win thee.

Is this th'effect,
　To leaven thus my spirits all?
To make my heart a crabtree cask direct?   15
　A verjuiced hall?
　　As bottle ale, whose spirits prisoned nursed,
　　When jogged, the bung with violence doth burst?

Shall I be made
　A sparkling wildfire shop,   20
Where my dull spirits at the fireball trade
　Do frisk and hop?
　　And while the hammer doth the anvil pay,
　　The fireball matter sparkles ev'ry way.

---

29. sensible of: sensitive to. **35. you only:** i.e., that's all you (understand). **37-38. Action, Time, and Place:** These so-called "Unities," deriving from the *Poetics* of Aristotle, came to be accepted as artistic "rules" or determiners of quality; cf. Dryden's *attack* on farce in *Mac Flecknoe* (p. 433).　**AN ADDRESS TO THE SOUL　1. flippering:** Taylor's coinage, probably meaning unsure of its direction. **2. nippers:** pincers. **15. crabtree cask:** cider cask. **16. verjuiced:** sour (verjuice is the juice of unripe fruit, such as crabapples).

One sorry fret, 25
   An anvil spark, rose higher,
And in thy temple falling, almost set
   The house on fire.
      Such fireballs dropping in the temple flame
      Burns up the building: Lord, forbid the same. 30

                  (c. 1680; 1939)

MEDITATION 38

Oh! What a thing is Man? Lord, who am I?
   That thou shouldst give him Law (Oh! golden line)
To regulate his thoughts, words, life thereby;
   And judge him wilt thereby too in thy time.
A Court of Justice thou in heaven holdst, 5
To try his case while he's here housed on mould.

How do thy Angels lay before thine eye
   My deeds both white and black I daily do?
How doth thy court thou panel'st there them try?
   But flesh complains. What right for this? Let's know; 10
For right or wrong, I can't appear unto't.
   And shall a sentence pass on such a suit?

Soft; blemish not this golden bench, or place.
   Here is not bribe, nor colourings to hide,
Nor pettifogger to befog the case; 15
   But Justice hath her glory here well tried;
   Her spotless law all spotted cases tends;
   Without respect or disrespect them ends.

God's Judge himself, and Christ Attorney is;
   The Holy Ghost Registerer is found. 20
Angels the sergeants are; all creatures kiss
   The book, and do as evidence abound.
All cases pass according to pure law,
   And in the sentence is not fret nor flaw.

What saith, my soul? Here all thy deeds are tried. 25
   Is Christ thy advocate to plead thy cause?
Art thou his client? Such shall never slide.
   He never lost his case: he pleads such laws
   As carry do the same, nor doth refuse
   The vilest sinner's case that doth him choose. 30

This is his honour, not dishonour; nay,
   No habeas-corpus 'gainst his clients came;
For all their fines his purse doth make down pay.
   He non-suits Satan's suit or casts the same.
   He'll plead thy case, and not accept a fee. 35
   He'll plead *sub forma pauperis* for thee.

My case is bad. Lord, be my advocate.
   My sin is red: I'm under God's arrest.
Thou hast the hit of pleading; plead my state.
   Although it's bad, thy plea will make it best. 40
   If thou wilt plead my case before the King,
   I'll wagon-loads of love and glory bring.

                  (1690; 1939)

JOHN WILMOT, EARL OF ROCHESTER
England, 1647-1680

IMPROMPTU ON CHARLES II

We have a pretty witty king,
   Whose word no man relies on;
He never said a foolish thing,
   And never did a wise one.

A SATIRE AGAINST MANKIND

Were I (who to my cost already am
One of those strange prodigious creatures, *Man*)
A spirit free to choose for my own share
What case of flesh and blood I pleased to wear,

MEDITATION 38   **6. mould:** the earth. **9. panel'st:** impanel, as a jury. **27. slide:** slip, fall. **29. carry:** win. **34. non-suits:** dismisses because a plaintiff fails to establish a legal case, e.g. for lack of sufficient evidence; **casts:** dismisses, throws out. **39. hit:** Knack.   **IMPROMPTU ON CHARLES II**   First published in 1707, this epigram exists in several versions; one later and perhaps better known is called "The King's Epitaph": "Here lies a great and mighty King, / Whose promise none relied on; / He never said a foolish thing, / Nor ever did a wise one."   **A SATIRE AGAINST MANKIND**   The 1680 edition calls this poem simply *Satyr* (as "satire" was then sometimes spelled, because mistakenly thought to come from the Greek *satyr*); it is also known as *A Satire On Reason and Mankind*. An unauthorized version appeared as a broadside in 1679; the posthumous 1680

I'd be a dog, a monkey, or a bear,   5
Or anything but that vain animal
Who is so proud of being rational.
The senses are too gross, and he'll contrive
A sixth, to contradict the other five;
And before certain instinct, will prefer   10
Reason, which fifty times for one does err.
Reason, an *ignis fatuus* of the mind,
Which leaves the light of Nature, sense, behind;
Pathless and dang'rous wand'ring ways it takes,
Through Error's fenny bogs and thorny brakes;   15
Whilst the misguided follower climbs with pain
Mountains of whimseys heaped in his own brain;
Stumbling from thought to thought, falls headlong down
Into Doubt's boundless sea, where like to drown,
Books bear him up awhile, and make him try   20
To swim with bladders of Philosophy;
In hopes still to o'ertake th' escaping light,
The vapour dances in his dazzled sight
Till, spent, it leaves him to eternal night.
Then Old Age and Experience, hand in hand,   25
Lead him to Death, and make him understand,
After a search so painful, and so long,
That all his life he has been in the wrong;
Huddled in dirt, the reas'ning engine lies,
Who was so proud, so witty, and so wise.   30
Pride drew him in, as cheats their bubbles catch,
And makes him venture to be made a wretch.
His Wisdom did his Happiness destroy,
Aiming to know what world he should enjoy;
And Wit was his vain frivolous pretence   35
Of pleasing others at his own expense.
For wits are treated just like common whores:
First they're enjoyed, and then kicked out of doors;
The pleasure past, a threat'ning doubt remains
That frights th' enjoyer with succeeding pains.   40
Women and men of Wit are dang'rous tools,
And ever fatal to admiring fools.
Pleasure allures, and when the fops escape,

'Tis not that they're belov'd, but fortunate,
And therefore what they fear, at heart they hate.   45
    But now methinks some formal Band and Beard
Takes me to task. Come on, Sir; I'm prepared.
    "Then by your favour, anything that's writ
Against this gibing, jingling knack called Wit
Likes me abundantly, but you take care   50
Upon this point, not to be too severe.
Perhaps my Muse were fitter for this part,
For I profess, I can be very smart
On Wit, which I abhor with all my heart.
I long to lash it in some sharp essay,   55
But your grand indiscretion bids me stay,
And turns my tide of ink another way.
What rage ferments in your degen'rate mind,
To make you rail at Reason, and Mankind?
Blest glorious Man! to whom alone kind Heav'n   60
An everlasting soul has freely giv'n,
Whom his great Maker took such care to make,
That from himself he did the image take,
And this fair frame in shining Reason dressed,
To dignify his nature above beast.   65
Reason, by whose aspiring influence
We take a flight beyond material sense,
Dive into mysteries, then soaring pierce
The flaming limits of the Universe,   69
Search Heav'n and Hell, find out what's acted there,
And give the World true grounds of hope and fear."
    Hold, mighty man, I cry; all this we know
From the pathetic pen of Ingello;
From Patrick's *Pilgrim,* Sibbs' *Soliloquies,*
And 'tis this very Reason I despise.   75
This supernatural gift that makes a mite
Think he's the image of the Infinite,
Comparing his short life, void of all rest,
To the Eternal and the ever Blest.
This busy, puzzling stirrer-up of doubt,   80
That frames deep mysteries, then finds 'em out,
Filling with frantic crowds of thinking fools

---

and some subsequent editions add a section of about fifty lines, sometimes labelled "Postscript" or "Addition" or "Epilogue," which may not even be by Rochester, and which is not included here. Critics have pointed out that the poem is influenced by Montaigne, Boileau, Hobbes, and other writers and philosophers. **12.** *ignis fatuus:* will-o'-the-wisp. **21. bladders:** inflated air-sacs (like water-wings). **31. bubbles:** gulls, dupes. **42. admiring:** wondering, marvelling. **46. Band:** i.e., a Geneva band; taken together with "Beard," it suggests an elderly cleric. **50. Likes me:** i.e., I like; **but:** i.e., but only if. **69:** adapting a line from Lucretius (I, 73): *"flammantia moenia mundi."* **73-74:** referring to various didactic religious works: **Ingello:** Nathaniel Ingelo (c.1621-1683), clergyman author of *Bentivolio and Urania* (1660), an allegorical romance; **Patrick's Pilgrim:** *The Parable of the Pilgrim* (1664), a work similar in kind to Bunyan's *Pilgrim's Progress* (see p. 416), by Simon Patrick (1626-1707), who became Bishop of Ely; **Sibbs' Soliloquies:** works (referred to as *soliloquies,* though none bear this title) by another divine, Richard Sibbes (Sibbs, Sibs; 1577-1635) (some copies of early editions, with "S——— replies" instead of "Sibbs' soliloquies," have "Stillingfleet's" written into the blank, referring to Edward Stillingfleet, 1635-1699, popular preacher who criticized Rochester).

Those reverend Bedlams, colleges and schools,
Borne on whose wings each heavy sot can pierce
The limits of the boundless universe.   *85*
So charming ointments make an old witch fly,
And bear a crippled carcass through the sky.
'Tis this exalted pow'r, whose bus'ness lies
In nonsense, and impossibilities;
This made a whimsical philosopher,   *90*
Before the spacious World, his tub prefer,
And we have modern cloistered coxcombs who
Retire to think, 'cause they have nought to do.
But thoughts are giv'n for action's government;
Where action ceases, thought's impertinent.   *95*
Our sphere of action is life's happiness,
And he who thinks beyond, thinks like an ass.
Thus whilst against false reas'ning I inveigh,
I own right Reason, which I would obey:
That Reason that distinguishes by sense,   *100*
And gives us rules of good and ill from thence;
That bounds desires with a reforming Will,
To keep 'em more in vigour, not to kill.
Your Reason hinders, mine helps to enjoy,
Renewing appetites yours would destroy.   *105*
My Reason is my friend, yours is a cheat;
Hunger calls out, my Reason bids me eat;
Perversely yours your appetite does mock:
This asks for food, that answers "What's a'clock?"
This plain distinction, Sir, your doubt secures;   *110*
'Tis not true Reason I despise, but yours.
Thus I think Reason righted; but for Man,
I'll ne'er recant, defend him if you can.
For all his pride and his philosophy,
'Tis evident beasts are in their degree   *115*
As wise at least, and better far than he.
Those creatures are the wisest who attain,
By surest means, the ends at which they aim.
If therefore Jowler finds and kills his hares
Better than Meres supplies committee chairs,   *120*
Though one's a statesman, th' other but a hound,
Jowler, in justice, would be wiser found.
You see how far Man's Wisdom here extends;
Look next if human nature makes amends,
Whose principles most gen'rous are, and just,   *125*
And to whose morals you would sooner trust.
Be judge yourself, I'll bring it to the test:
Which is the basest creature, Man, or beast?

Birds feed on birds, beasts on each other prey,
But savage Man alone does Man betray: *130*
Pressed by necessity, they kill for food;
Man undoes Man to do himself no good.
With teeth and claws by Nature armed they hunt
Nature's allowance, to supply their want;
But Man, with smiles, embraces, friendships, praise,
Unhumanly his fellow's life betrays;   *136*
With voluntary pains works his distress,
Not through necessity, but wantonness.
For hunger, or for love, they fight, or tear,
Whilst wretched Man is still in arms for fear;   *140*
For fear he arms, and is of arms afraid,
By fear to fear successively betrayed;
Base fear, the source whence his best passions came,
His boasted Honour, and his dear-bought Fame.
That lust of Pow'r, to which he's such a slave,   *145*
And for the which alone he dares be brave;
To which his various projects are designed,
Which makes him gen'rous, affable, and kind;
For which he takes such pains to be thought wise,
And screws his actions in a forced disguise,   *150*
Leading a tedious life in misery,
Under laborious, mean Hypocrisy.
Look to the bottom of his vast design,
Wherein Man's Wisdom, Pow'r, and Glory join;
The good he acts, the ill he does endure: *155*
'Tis all for fear, to make himself secure.
Merely for safety, after Fame we thirst,
For all men would be cowards if they durst.
And honesty's against all common sense;
Men must be knaves, 'tis in their own defence.   *160*
Mankind's dishonest; if you think it fair,
Among known cheats, to play upon the square,
You'll be undone —
Nor can weak Truth your reputation save;
The knaves will all agree to call you knave.   *165*
Wronged shall he live, insulted o'er, oppressed,
Who dares be less a villain than the rest.
Thus, Sir, you see what human nature craves:
Most men are cowards, all men should be knaves;
The diff'rence lies (as far as I can see)   *170*
Not in the thing itself, but the degree;
And all the subject matter of debate
Is only, who's a knave of the first rate?

                                        (c.1676; 1680)

---

86. charming: i.e., magical. **90. whimsical philosopher:** Diogenes, 4th-century B.C. Greek philosopher, founder of the Cynics; he supposedly lived in a tub that he carried about with him, and used a lantern, even in daylight, to search for an honest man. **99. own:** acknowledge, admit. **119. Jowler:** name for a large-jawed dog. **120. Meres:** Sir Thomas Meres (1635-1715), M.P. and Commissioner of the Admiralty (1679-84), who sometimes served as chairman for the House of Commons. **150. screws:** deforms, contorts, strains.

JOHN OLDHAM
England, 1653-1683

A SATIRE UPON A WOMAN WHO BY HER FALSEHOOD AND SCORN WAS THE DEATH OF MY FRIEND

No! she shall ne'er escape, if Gods there be,
Unless they perjured grow, and false as she;
Though no strange judgment yet the murd'ress seize
To punish her, and quit the partial skies;
Though no revenging lightning yet has flashed   *5*
From thence, that might her criminal beauties blast;
Though they in their old lustre still prevail,
By no disease, nor guilt itself made pale,
Guilt which, should blackest Moors themselves but own,
Would make through all their night new blushes dawn;   *10*
Though that kind soul who now augments the blest,
Thither too soon by her unkindness chased
(Where may it be her small'st and lightest doom —
For that's not half my curse — never to come),
Though he, when prompted by the high'st despair,   *15*
Ne'er mentioned her without an hymn or pray'r,
And could by all her scorn be forced no more
Than martyrs to revile what they adore,
Who had he cursed her with his dying breath
Had done but just, and Heaven had forgave;   *20*
Though ill-made Law no sentence has ordained
For her, no statute has her guilt arraigned
(For hangmen, women's scorn, and doctors' skill,
All by a licensed way of murder kill);
Though she from justice of all these go free,   *25*
And boast perhaps in her success, and cry,
'Twas but a little harmless perjury;
Yet think she not she still secure shall prove,
Or that none dare avenge an injured love:
I rise in judgment, am to be to her   *30*
Both witness, judge, and executioner.
Armed with dire satire and resentful spite,
I come to haunt her with the ghosts of wit.
My ink unbid starts out and flies on her,
Like blood upon some touching murderer;   *35*

And should that fail, rather than want I would
Like hags, to curse her, write in my own blood.
    Ye spiteful pow'rs (if any there can be
That boast a worse and keener spite than I),
Assist with malice and your mighty aid   *40*
My sworn revenge, and help me rhyme her dead.
Grant I may fix such brands of infamy,
So plain, so deeply graved on her, that she,
Her skill, patches, nor paint all joined can hide,
And which shall lasting as her soul abide.   *45*
Grant my strong hate may such strong poison cast,
That ev'ry breath may taint and rot and blast,
Till one large gangrene quite o'erspread her fame
With foul contagion, till her odious name,
Spit at and cursed by every mouth like mine,   *50*
Be terror to herself and all her line.
    Vil'st of that viler sex, who damned us all,
Ordained to cause and plague us for our fall!
Woman! nay worse! for she can nought be said
But mummy by some dev'l inhabited!   *55*
Not made in Heaven's mint, but basely coined,
She wears an human image stamped on fiend;
And whoso marriage would with her contract,
Is witch by law, and that a mere compact.
Her soul (if any soul in her there be)   *60*
By Hell was breathed into her in a lie,
And its whole stock of falsehood there was lent,
As if hereafter to be true it meant.
Bawd Nature taught her jilting when she made
And by her make designed her for the trade;   *65*
Hence 'twas she daubed her with a painted face,
That she at once might better cheat and please.
All those gay charming looks that court the eye
Are but an ambush to hide treachery;
Mischief adorned with pomp, and smooth disguise,   *70*

A SATIRE UPON A WOMAN The severity of Oldham's satire (or *satyr*) suggests a basis in fact; but if it does refer to an actual occurrence, the circumstances remain unknown and the parties involved unidentified. **4. quit . . . skies:** i.e., acquit heaven of seeming partiality. **34-35:** According to an old superstition, a murdered body would gush blood if its murderer touched or even drew near it (see e.g. Shakespeare's *Richard III*, I.ii.55-59). **44. patches . . . paint:** cosmetics.

A painted skin stuffed full of guile and lies;
Within a gaudy case, a nasty soul,
Like turd of quality in a gilt close-stool:
Such on a cloud those flatt'ring colours are,
Which only serve to dress a tempest fair.   75
So men upon this Earth's fair surface dwell;
Within are fiends, and at the centre Hell.
Court-promises, the leagues which statesmen make
With more convenience and more ease to break,
The faith a Jesuit in allegiance swears,   80
Or a town-jilt to keeping coxcombs bears,
Are firm and certain all, compared with hers.
Early in falsehood, at her font she lied,
And should ev'n then for perjury been tried.
Her conscience stretched, and open as the stews,   85
But laughs at oaths and plays with solemn vows,
And at her mouth swallows down perjured breath
More glib than bits of lechery beneath;
Less serious known, when she doth most protest,
Than thoughts of arrantest buffoons in jest;   90
More cheap than the vile mercenariest Squire
That plies for half-crown fees at Westminster,
And trades in staple oaths, and swears to hire;
Less guilt than hers, less breach of oath and word,
Has stood aloft and looked through penance-board;   95
And he that trusts her in a death-bed pray'r
Has faith to merit and save anything but her.
  But since her guilt description does outgo,
I'll try if it outstrip my curses too —
Curses, which may they equal my just hate,   100
My wish, and her desert, be each so great,
Each heard like pray'rs, and Heaven make 'em fate.
  First for her beauties, which the mischief brought,
May she affected, they be borrowed thought,
By her own hand, not that of Nature wrought: 105
Her credit, honour, portion, health, and those
Prove light and frail as her broke faith and vows:
Some base unnamed disease her carcass foul,
And make her body ugly as her soul:
Cankers and ulcers eat her, till she be   110
Shunned like infection, loathed like infamy:
Strength quite expired, may she alone retain
The snuff of life, may that unquenched remain,
As in the damned, to keep her fresh for pain:
Hot lust light on her, and the plague of pride   115

On that, this ever scorned as that denied:
Ache, anguish, horror, grief, dishonour, shame
Pursue at once her body, soul, and fame.
If e'er the devil Love must enter her
(For nothing sure but fiends can enter there),   120
May she a just and true tormenter find,
And that like an ill conscience rack her mind:
Be some diseased and ugly wretch her fate,
She doomed to love of one whom all else hate;
May he hate her, and may her destiny   125
Be to despair, and yet love on and die;
Or, to invent some wittier punishment,
May he, to plague her, out of spite consent:
May the old fumbler, though disabled quite,
Have strength to give her claps, but no delight: 130
May he of her unjustly jealous be
For one that's worse and uglier far than he:
May 's impotence balk and torment her lust,
Yet scarcely her to dreams or wishes trust:
Forced to be chaste, may she suspected be,   135
Share none o'th' pleasure, all the infamy.
  In fine, that I all curses may complete
(For I've but cursed in jest and raillied yet),
Whate'er the sex deserves, or feels, or fears,
May all those plagues be hers, and only hers: 140
Whate'er great favourites turned out of doors,
Shamed cullies, bilked and disappointed whores,
Or losing gamesters vent, what curses e'er
Are spoke by sinners raving in despair,
All those fall on her, as they're all her due,   145
Till spite can't think, nor Heav'n inflict anew:
May then (for once I will be kind and pray)
No madness take her use of sense away,
But may she in full strength of reason be,
To feel and understand her misery: 150
Plagued so, till she think damning a release,
And humbly pray to go to Hell for ease:
Yet may not all these suff'rings here atone
Her sin, and may she still go sinning on,
Tick up in perjury, and run o'th' score   155
Till on her soul she can get trust no more:
  Then may she stupid and repentless die,
And Heav'n itself forgive no more than I,
But so be damned of mere necessity.

(1678)

---

73. close-stool: box or stool containing a chamber pot. **85. stews:** brothel. **95. penance-board:** slang term for a pillory (often set up "aloft," on a raised platform). **130. claps:** gonorrhea. **138. raillied:** rallied, bantered, teased. **142. cullies:** dupes. For Dryden's elegy on Oldham, see p. 439.

MARY, LADY CHUDLEIGH
England, 1656-1710

TO THE LADIES

Wife and servant are the same,
But only differ in the name:
For when that fatal knot is tied,
Which nothing, nothing can divide,
When she the word *Obey* has said,   *5*
And man by law supreme has made,
Then all that's kind is laid aside,
And nothing left but state and pride.
Fierce as an eastern prince he grows,
And all his innate rigour shows: *10*
Then but to look, to laugh, or speak,
Will the nuptial contract break.
Like mutes, she signs alone must make,
And never any freedom take,
But still be governed by a nod,   *15*
And fear her husband as her god:
Him still must serve, him still obey,
And nothing act, and nothing say,
But what her haughty lord thinks fit,
Who, with the power, has all the wit.   *20*
Then shun, oh! shun that wretched state,
And all the fawning flatt'rers hate.
Value yourselves, and men despise:
You must be proud, if you'll be wise.

          (1703)

THE WISH

Would but indulgent Fortune send
To me a kind and faithful friend,
One who to Virtue's laws is true,
And does her nicest rules pursue;
One pious, lib'ral, just, and brave,   *5*
And to his passions not a slave;
Who full of honour, void of pride,
Will freely praise, and freely chide,
But not indulge the smallest fault,
Nor entertain one slighting thought;   *10*
Who still the same will ever prove,
Will still instruct, and still will love;
In whom I safely may confide,
And with him all my cares divide;
Who had a large capacious mind,   *15*
Joined with a knowledge unconfined;
A reason bright, a judgment true,
A wit both quick and solid too;
Who can of all things talk with ease,
And whose converse will ever please;   *20*
Who charmed with wit and inward graces,
Despises fools with tempting faces;
And still a beauteous mind does prize
Above the most enchanting eyes:
I would not envy Queens their state,   *25*
Nor once desire a happier Fate.

          (1722)

ANNE WHARTON
England, 1659-1685

from PENELOPE TO ULYSSES

Penelope this slow Epistle sends
To him on whom her future hope depends;
'Tis your Penelope, distressed, forlorn,
Who asks no answer but your quick return.
Priam and Troy, the Grecian dames' just hate,   *5*
Have long ere this, 'tis known, received their Fate.

PENELOPE TO ULYSSES   Wharton's poem (its full text has 183 lines) is based on one of Ovid's *Epistles*. It took Ulysses (Odysseus) ten years to make his way home after the ten-year Trojan War; his adventures are recounted in Homer's *Odyssey*; the story of the Trojan War is told in the *Iliad*.
5. Priam: King of Troy.

For which thy absence pays too dear a rate.
   O ere my hopes and joys had found their graves,
Why did not Paris perish by the waves?
I should not then pass tedious nights alone,   *10*
Courting with fervent breath the rising sun;
But all in vain, for day is night to me,
Nor day nor night brings comfort; only thee.
My tender hands with weaving would not tire,
Nor my soft thoughts with unobtained desire.   *15*
   Still did my mind new fearful forms present
To kill my hopes, and raise my discontent.
Love, jealous Love, has more than eagle's eyes
To spy out sorrows, but o'erlook our joys.
I fancied furious Trojans still were nigh   *20*
To slay my lord, and all my hopes destroy.
As there the arms of Hector still prevail,
Here at his very name my cheeks grew pale;
When told Antilochus by him was slain,
My hopes decayed, my fears revived again.   *25*
I wept when young Patroclus was o'erthrown,
To find how weak the arts of wit were grown.
The deeds of fierce Tlepolemus alarmed
My tender soul, and all my spirits charmed.
Each fatal scene grief to my heart did show;   *30*
Whate'er they felt, I suffered here for you.
   But virtuous love propitious Heav'n befriends;
My husband's safe, on whom my life depends;
Troy is o'erthrown, and all our sorrow ends.
The Grecians triumph; they at large declare   *35*
The fall of Ilium, and the foe's despair.
Old men and tender maids with pleasure hear
The fatal end of all their griefs and fear.

The joyful wife from soft embraces now
Will hardly time to hear these tales allow,   *40*
Forgets long absence and renews her vow.
   Some on the tables their feigned combats draw,
With sparing bowls the victor speaks his joy,
And with spilt wine describes the famous Troy.
Here, says he, Priam's palace did appear;   *45*
The far-famed river Simois glided here;
Here 'twas Achilles fought, Ulysses too;
At that to guard my heart my spirits flew:
Achilles' mighty name passed careless by,
But at this name Penelope could die.   *50*
One shows the place where mangled Hector lay,
To fierce Achilles' fury made a prey.
    . . . .
   This Nestor told your son, whom my fond haste
Sent to enquire of dangers which were past.
He told how Resus was with Dolon slain;   *55*
These tedious tales did but augment my pain;
I listened still to hear of you again.
How truly valiant were you, though unkind?
You little thought of what you left behind;
When in the night you ventured to invade   *60*
The Thracian camp, my soul was filled with dread.
Assisted but by one their strength you prove;
Too strong your courage, but too weak your love.
   But what remains to me for conquests past,
If like that city still my hopes lie waste?   *65*
Your presence would my springing joy renew;
Would Troy were glorious still, so I had you.
    . . . .

                                        (1712)

ANNE KILLIGREW
England, 1660-1685

A FAREWELL TO WORLDLY JOYS

Farewell, ye unsubstantial joys,
Ye gilded nothings, gaudy toys;
Too long ye have my soul misled,

Too long with airy diet fed;
But now my heart ye shall no more   *5*
Deceive, as you have heretofore,

---

9. Paris: Trojan whose abduction of Helen, wife of Menelaus, brought about the Trojan War. **14:** Promising importunate suitors that she would choose one when she finished a piece of weaving, Penelope undid each night what she wove during the day. **22. Hector:** principal Trojan hero, eventually killed by Achilles. **24. Antilochus:** son of Nestor (see line 53). **26. Patroclus:** friend of Achilles, slain by Hector. **28. Tlepolemus:** son of Hercules, leader of the contingent from Rhodes, killed by Sarpedon after badly wounding him. **36. Ilium:** Troy (hence "Iliad"). **43. sparing:** small in quantity, not lavish (i.e., unlike the immoderate consumption indulged in by the crowd of suitors, whom she mentions later in the poem: "Ulysses, these . . . to thy disgrace / Live on thy riches, while thy herds decrease"); **bowls:** drinking vessels. **44. describes:** i.e., draws, sketches. **53. Nestor:** aged King of Pylos who tells Telemachus about his father. **55:** Dolon, a Trojan scout, and Resus, King of the Thracians (see lines 60-61), are both killed by Diomedes, with the help of Odysseus (*Iliad*, X).

For when I hear such sirens sing,
Like Ithaca's fore-warned king,
With prudent resolution I
Will so my will and fancy tie   10
That stronger to the mast not he
Than I to reason bound will be,
And though your witchcrafts strike my ear,
Unhurt, like him, your charms I'll hear.

(1686)

AN INVECTIVE AGAINST GOLD

Of all the poisons that the fruitful earth
E'er yet brought forth, or monsters she gave birth,
Naught to mankind has e'er so fatal been
As thou, accursed gold, their care and sin.

Methinks I the advent'rous merchant see,   5
Ploughing the faithless seas in search of thee,
His dearest wife and children left behind
(His real wealth), while he, a slave to th'wind,
Sometimes becalmed, the shore with longing eyes
Wishes to see, and what he wishes, spies,   10
For a rude tempest wakes him from his dream,
And strands his bark by a more sad extreme.
Thus, hopeless wretch, is his whole lifetime spent,
And though thrice wrecked, 's no wiser than he went.

Again I see the heavenly fair despised,   15
A hag like hell with gold more highly prized,
Men's faith betrayed, their prince and country sold,
Their God denied, all for the idol gold.

Unhappy wretch who first found out the ore,
What kind of vengeance rests for thee in store,   20
If Nebat's son, that Israel led astray,
Meet a severe reward at the last day?
Some strange unheard-of judgment thou wilt find,
Who thus hast caused to sin all humankind.

(1686)

DANIEL DEFOE
England, 1660-1731

from AN ESSAY ON PROJECTS

AN ACADEMY FOR WOMEN

I have often thought of it as one of the most barbarous customs in the world, considering us as a civilised and a Christian country, that we deny the advantages of learning to women. We reproach the sex every day with folly and impertinence, while I am confident, had they the advantages of education equal to us, they would be guilty of less than ourselves.

One would wonder, indeed, how it should happen that women are conversible at all,   5
since they are only beholden to natural parts for all their knowledge. Their youth is spent to teach them to stitch and sew or make baubles. They are taught to read indeed, and perhaps to write their names or so, and that is the height of a woman's education. And I would but ask any who slight the sex for their understanding, what is a man (a gentleman, I mean) good for that is taught no more?   10

I need not give instances, or examine the character of a gentleman with a good estate and of a good family and with tolerable parts, and examine what figure he makes for want of education.

A FAREWELL **8. Ithaca's king:** Odysseus.   **AN INVECTIVE** **11. for:** before. **21. Nebat's son:** Jeroboam, who permitted the worship of idols when he became King of Israel; see I Kings 11:26-14:20.

The soul is placed in the body like a rough diamond, and must be polished, or the lustre of it will never appear: and it is manifest that as the rational soul distinguishes us *15* from brutes, so education carries on the distinction and makes some less brutish than others. This is too evident to need any demonstration. But why then should women be denied the benefit of instruction? If knowledge and understanding had been useless additions to the sex, God Almighty would never have given them capacities, for He made nothing needless. Besides, I would ask such what they can see in ignorance that *20* they should think it a necessary ornament to a woman? or how much worse is a wise woman than a fool? or what has the woman done to forfeit the privilege of being taught? Does she plague us with her pride and impertinence? Why did we not let her learn, that she might have had more wit? Shall we upbraid women with folly, when it is only the error of this inhuman custom that hindered them being made wiser? *25*

The capacities of women are supposed to be greater and their senses quicker than those of the men; and what they might be capable of being bred to is plain from some instances of female wit, which this age is not without; which upbraids us with injustice, and looks as if we denied women the advantages of education for fear they should vie with the men in their improvements. *30*

To remove this objection, and that women might have at least a needful opportunity of education in all sorts of useful learning, I propose the draught of an Academy for that purpose.

I know it is dangerous to make public appearances of the sex. They are not either to be confined or exposed; the first will disagree with their inclinations and the last with *35* their reputations, and therefore it is somewhat difficult; and I doubt a method proposed by an ingenious lady in a little book called "Advice to the Ladies" would be found impracticable, for, saving my respect to the sex, the levity, which perhaps is a little peculiar to them, at least in their youth, will not bear the restraint; and I am satisfied nothing but the height of bigotry can keep up a nunnery. Women are extravagantly *40* desirous of going to heaven, and will punish their pretty bodies to get thither; but nothing else will do it, and even in that case sometimes it falls out that nature will prevail.

When I talk, therefore, of an academy for women, I mean both the model, the teaching, and the government different from what is proposed by that ingenious lady, for whose proposal I have a very great esteem, and also great opinion of her wit; *45* different, too, from all sorts of religious confinement, and, above all, from vows of celibacy.

Wherefore the academy I propose should differ but little from public schools, wherein such ladies as were willing to study should have all the advantages of learning suitable to their genius. *50*

But since some severities of discipline more than ordinary would be absolutely necessary to preserve the reputation of the house, that persons of quality and fortune might not be afraid to venture their children thither, I shall venture to make a small scheme by way of essay.

AN ACADEMY FOR WOMEN **36. doubt:** fear. **37:** referring to Mary Astell's highly influential book, *A Serious Proposal to the Ladies for the Advancement of Their True and Greatest Interest* (1694; Part II, 1697); though he criticises the point about restraint, Defoe adopts other ideas from Astell, not least the whole general notion of providing education for women. (For an excerpt from a different work by Astell, see p. 477.) **50. genius:** natural talent.

The house I would have built in a form by itself, as well as in a place by itself. The   *55*
building should be of three plain fronts, without any jettings or bearing-work, that the
eye might at a glance see from one coin to the other; the gardens walled in the same
triangular figure, with a large moat, and but one entrance.

When thus every part of the situation was contrived as well as might be for
discovery, and to render intriguing dangerous, I would have no guards, no eyes, no spies   *60*
set over the ladies, but shall expect them to be tried by the principles of honour and
strict virtue.

And if I am asked why, I must ask pardon of my own sex for giving this reason for
it:—

I am so much in charity with women, and so well acquainted with men, that it is my   *65*
opinion there needs no other care to prevent intriguing than to keep the men effectually
away; for though inclination, which we prettily call love, does sometimes move a little
too visibly in the sex, and frailty often follows, yet I think, verily, custom, which we
miscall modesty, has so far the ascendant over the sex, that solicitation always goes
before it.   *70*

> Custom with women 'stead of virtue rules;
> It leads the wisest and commands the fools;
> For this alone, when inclinations reign,
> Though virtue's fled, will acts of vice restrain.
> Only by custom 'tis that virtue lives,   *75*
> And love requires to be asked before it gives;
> For that which we call modesty is pride;
> They scorn to ask, and hate to be denied.
> 'Tis custom thus prevails upon their want;
> They'll never beg what asked they easily grant;   *80*
> And when the needless ceremony is over,
> Themselves the weakness of the sex discover.
> If then desires are strong and nature free,
> Keep from her men and opportunity;
> Else 'twill be vain to curb her by restraint,   *85*
> But keep the question off, you keep the saint.

In short, let a woman have never such a coming principle, she will let you ask
before she complies, at least if she be a woman of any honour.

Upon this ground I am persuaded such measures might be taken that the ladies
might have all the freedom in the world within their own walls, and yet no intriguing, no   *90*
indecencies, nor scandalous affairs happen; and in order to this the following customs
and laws should be observed in the colleges, of which I would propose one at least in
every county in England, and about ten for the City of London.

After the regulation of the form of the building as before: —

(1.) All the ladies who enter into the house should set their hands to the orders of   *95*
the house, to signify their consent to submit to them.

---

56. jettings: projections, protrusions (juttings); **bearing-work** has a similar meaning. **57. coin:** corner. **70. it:** i.e., inclination, love, frailty. **95. set their hands to:** i.e., sign.

(2.) As no woman should be received but who declared herself willing, and that it was the act of her choice to enter herself, so no person should be confined to continue there a moment longer than the same voluntary choice inclined her.

(3.) The charges of the house being to be paid by the ladies, every one that entered *100* should have only this encumbrance, that she should pay for the whole year, though her mind should change as to her continuance.

(4.) An Act of Parliament should make it felony without clergy for any man to enter by force or fraud into the house, or to solicit any woman, though it were to marry, while she was in the house. And this law would by no means be severe, because any *105* woman who was willing to receive the addresses of a man might discharge herself of the house when she pleased; and, on the contrary, any woman who had occasion, might discharge herself of the impertinent addresses of any person she had an aversion to by entering into the house.

In this house, the persons who enter should be taught all sorts of breeding suitable *110* to both their genius and their quality, and in particular music and dancing, which it would be cruelty to bar the sex of, because they are their darlings; but besides this, they should be taught languages, as particularly French and Italian; and I would venture the injury of giving a woman more tongues than one.

They should, as a particular study, be taught all the graces of speech and all the *115* necessary air of conversation, which our common education is so defective in that I need not expose it. They should be brought to read books, and especially history, and so to read as to make them understand the world, and be able to know and judge of things when they hear of them.

To such whose genius would lead them to it I would deny no sort of learning; but *120* the chief thing in general is to cultivate the understandings of the sex, that they may be capable of all sorts of conversation; that their parts and judgments being improved, they may be as profitable in their conversation as they are pleasant.

Women, in my observation, have little or no difference in them, but as they are or are not distinguished by education. Tempers indeed may in some degree influence them, *125* but the main distinguishing part is their breeding.

The whole sex are generally quick and sharp. I believe I may be allowed to say generally so, for you rarely see them lumpish and heavy when they are children, as boys will often be. If a woman be well-bred, and taught the proper management of her natural wit, she proves generally very sensible and retentive; and without partiality, a woman of *130* sense and manners is the finest and most delicate part of God's creation; the glory of her Maker, and the great instance of His singular regard to man, His darling creature, to whom He gave the best gift either God could bestow or man receive. And it is the sordidest piece of folly and ingratitude in the world to withhold from the sex the due lustre which the advantages of education gives to the natural beauty of their minds. *135*

A woman well bred and well taught, furnished with the additional accomplishments of knowledge and behaviour, is a creature without comparison; her society is the emblem of sublimer enjoyments; her person is angelic and her conversation heavenly; she is all softness and sweetness, peace, love, wit, and delight. She is every way suitable

---

103. felony without clergy: Some criminals, as part of their punishment, were denied access to a clergyman. **111. quality:** social standing.

to the sublimest wish, and the man that has such a one to his portion has nothing to do   *140*
but to rejoice in her and be thankful.

On the other hand, suppose her to be the very same woman, and rob her of the
benefit of education, and it follows thus:—

If her temper be good, want of education makes her soft and easy. Her wit, for want
of teaching, makes her impertinent and talkative. Her knowledge, for want of judgment   *145*
and experience, makes her fanciful and whimsical. If her temper be bad, want of
breeding makes her worse, and she grows haughty, insolent, and loud. If she be
passionate, want of manners makes her termagant and a scold, which is much at one
with lunatic. If she be proud, want of discretion (which still is breeding) makes her
conceited, fantastic, and ridiculous. And from these she degenerates to be turbulent,   *150*
clamorous, noisy, nasty, and the devil.

Methinks mankind for their own sakes, since, say what we will of the women, we
all think fit one time or other to be concerned with them, should take some care to breed
them up to be suitable and serviceable, if they expected no such thing as delight from
them. Bless us! what care do we take to breed up a good horse and to break him well,   *155*
and what a value do we put upon him when it is done, and all because he should be fit
for our use; and why not a woman? Since all her ornaments and beauty without suitable
behaviour is a cheat in nature, like the false tradesman, who puts the best of his goods
uppermost, that the buyer may think the rest are of the same goodness.

Beauty of the body, which is the woman's glory, seems to be now unequally   *160*
bestowed, and Nature, or rather Providence, to lie under some scandal about it, as if it
was given a woman for a snare to men, and so make a kind of a she-devil of her; because,
they say, exquisite beauty is rarely given with wit, more rarely with goodness of temper,
and never at all with modesty. And some, pretending to justify the equity of such a
distribution, will tell us it is the effect of the justice of Providence in dividing particular   *165*
excellences among all His creatures, share and share alike, as it were, that all might for
something or other be acceptable to one another, else some would be despised.

I think both these notions false, and yet the last, which has the show of respect to
Providence, is the worst, for it supposes Providence to be indigent and empty, as if it had
not wherewith to furnish all the creatures it had made, but was fain to be parsimonious in   *170*
its gifts, and distribute them by piecemeal for fear of being exhausted.

If I might venture my opinion against an almost universal notion, I would say most
men mistake the proceedings of Providence in this case, and all the world at this day are
mistaken in their practice about it. And because the assertion is very bold, I desire to
explain myself.   *175*

That Almighty First Cause which made us all is certainly the fountain of
excellence, as it is of being, and by an invisible influence could have diffused equal
qualities and perfections to all the creatures it has made, as the sun does its light,
without the least ebb or diminution to Himself, and has given indeed to every individual
sufficient to the figure His providence had designed him in the world.   *180*

I believe it might be defended if I should say that I do suppose God has given to all
mankind equal gifts and capacities in that He has given them all souls equally capable,
and that the whole difference in mankind proceeds either from accidental difference in
the make of their bodies or from the foolish difference of education.

From accidental difference in bodies. I would avoid discoursing here of the *185* philosophical position of the soul in the body. But if it be true, as philosophers do affirm, that the understanding and memory is dilated or contracted according to the accidental dimensions of the organ through which it is conveyed, then, though God has given a soul as capable to me as another, yet if I have any natural defect in those parts of the body by which the soul should act, I may have the same soul infused as another man, and yet he *190* be a wise man and I a very fool. For example, if a child naturally have a defect in the organ of hearing, so that he could never distinguish any sound, that child shall never be able to speak or read, though it have a soul capable of all the accomplishments in the world. The brain is the centre of the soul's actings, where all the distinguishing faculties of it reside; and it is observable a man who has a narrow contracted head, in which there *195* is not room for the due and necessary operations of nature by the brain, is never a man of very great judgment; and that proverb, "A great head and little wit," is not meant by nature, but is a reproof upon sloth, as if one should, by way of wonder, say, "Fie, fie! you that have a great head have but little wit; that's strange! that must certainly be your own fault." From this notion I do believe there is a great matter in the breed of men and *200* women — not that wise men shall always get wise children, but I believe strong and healthy bodies have the wisest children, and sickly, weakly bodies affect the wits as well as the bodies of their children. We are easily persuaded to believe this in the breeds of horses, cocks, dogs, and other creatures, and I believe it is as visible in men.

But to come closer to the business, the great distinguishing difference which is seen *205* in the world between men and women is in their education, and this is manifested by comparing it with the difference between one man or woman and another.

And herein it is that I take upon me to make such a bold assertion that all the world are mistaken in their practice about women; for I cannot think that God Almighty ever made them so delicate, so glorious creatures, and furnished them with such charms, so *210* agreeable and so delightful to mankind, with souls capable of the same accomplishments with men, and all to be only stewards of our houses, cooks, and slaves.

Not that I am for exalting the female government in the least; but, in short, I would have men take women for companions, and educate them to be fit for it. A woman of sense and breeding will scorn as much to encroach upon the prerogative of the man as a man of sense *215* will scorn to oppress the weakness of the woman. But if the women's souls were refined and improved by teaching, that word would be lost; to say, the weakness of the sex as to judgment, would be nonsense, for ignorance and folly would be no more to be found among women than men. I remember a passage which I heard from a very fine woman; she had wit and capacity enough, an extraordinary shape and face, and a great fortune, but had been *220* cloistered up all her time, and for fear of being stolen, had not had the liberty of being taught the common necessary knowledge of women's affairs; and when she came to converse in the world, her natural wit made her so sensible of the want of education, that she gave this short reflection on herself: — "I am ashamed to talk with my very maids," says she, "for I don't know when they do right or wrong. I had more need go to school than be married." *225*

I need not enlarge on the loss the defect of education is to the sex, nor argue the benefit of the contrary practice; it is a thing will be more easily granted than remedied. This chapter is but an essay at the thing, and I refer the practice to those happy days, if ever they shall be, when men shall be wise enough to mend it.

(1697)

Anne Finch, Countess of Winchilsea
England, 1661-1720

A Letter to Daphnis, April 2nd, 1685

This to the crown and blessing of my life,
The much loved husband of a happy wife:
To him, whose constant passion found the art
To win a stubborn and ungrateful heart,
And to the world, by tend'rest proof discovers   5
They err who say that husbands can't be lovers.
With such return of passion as is due,
Daphnis I love, Daphnis my thoughts pursue,
Daphnis, my hopes, my joys, are bounded all in you.
Ev'n I, for Daphnis and my promise' sake,   10
What I in women censure, undertake;
But this from love, not vanity, proceeds:
You know who writes, and I who 'tis that reads.
Judge not my passion by my want of skill;
Many love well though they express it ill.   15
And I your censure could with pleasure bear,
Would you but soon return, and speak it here.

                                        (1685)

The Introduction

Did I my lines intend for public view,
How many censures would their faults pursue;
Some would, because such words they do affect,
Cry they're insipid, empty, uncorrect.
And many have attained, dull and untaught,   5
The name of wit, only by finding fault.
True judges might condemn their want of wit,
And all might say, they're by a woman writ.
Alas! a woman that attempts the pen,
Such an intruder on the rights of men,   10
Such a presumptuous creature, is esteemed,
The fault can by no virtue be redeemed.
They tell us we mistake our sex and way;
Good breeding, fashion, dancing, dressing, play
Are the accomplishments we should desire;   15
To write, or read, or think, or to enquire
Would cloud our beauty, and exhaust our time,
And interrupt the conquests of our prime;
Whilst the dull manage of a servile house
Is held by some our utmost art and use.   20
    Sure 'twas not ever thus, nor are we told
Fables of women that excelled of old,
To whom, by the diffusive hand of Heaven
Some share of wit and poetry was given.
On that glad day on which the Ark returned,   25
The holy pledge for which the land had mourned,
The joyful tribes attend it on the way,
The Levites do the sacred charge convey,
Whilst various instruments before it play;
Here holy Virgins in the concert join,   30
The louder notes to soften and refine,
And with alternate verse, complete the hymn divine.
Lo! the young poet, after God's own heart,
By Him inspired and taught the Muses' art,
Returned from conquest, a bright chorus meets   35
That sing his slain ten thousand in the streets.
In such loud numbers they his acts declare,
Proclaim the wonders of his early war,
That Saul upon the vast applause does frown,
And feels its mighty thunder shake the crown.   40
What can the threatened judgment now prolong?
Half of the kingdom is already gone:
The fairest half, whose influence guides the rest,
Have David's empire o'er their hearts confessed.
    A woman here leads fainting Israel on;   45
She fights, she wins, she triumphs with a song,
Devout, majestic, for the subject fit,
And far above her arms exalts her wit;
Then to the peaceful, shady palm withdraws,
And rules the rescued nation with her laws.   50
How are we fall'n, fall'n by mistaken rules!
And Education's, more than Nature's fools,
Debarred from all improvements of the mind,
And to be dull, expected and designed;

THE INTRODUCTION   **14. play:** cards. **23. diffusive:** dispensing bountifully. **33. young poet:** David, the psalmist; lines 25-44 retell three Old Testament stories: how the Levites were charged with taking care of the Ark of the Covenant, how David fought with Goliath, and how David returned the Ark to the Israelites (see Numbers 1: 50-53; I Chronicles 15; I Samuel 17; and II Samuel 6:2ff). **37. numbers:** poetry. **45. a woman here:** Deborah, the judge (see Judges 4-5).

And if some one would soar above the rest,   *55*
With warmer fancy and ambition pressed,
So strong th'opposing faction still appears,
The hopes to thrive can ne'er outweigh the fears.
Be cautioned then my Muse, and still retired;
Nor be despised, aiming to be admired;   *60*
Conscious of wants, still with contracted wing,
To some few friends, and to thy sorrows sing;
For groves of laurel thou wert never meant;
Be dark enough thy shades, and be thou there content.

        (1690; 1903)

ADAM POS'D

Could our first father at his toilsome plough,
Thorns in his path, and labour on his brow,
Clothed only in a rude, unpolished skin,
Could he a vain fantastic nymph have seen
In all her airs, in all her antic graces,   *5*
Her various fashions and more various faces,
How had it posed that skill which late assigned
Just appellations to each several kind!
A right idea of the sight to frame;
T'have guessed from what new element she came;   *10*
T'have hit the wav'ring form, or giv'n this thing a name.

        (1709)

LA PASSION VAINCUE

On the banks of the Severn a desperate maid
(Whom some shepherd, neglecting his vows, had betrayed)
Stood resolving to banish all sense of the pain
And pursue, through her death, a revenge on the swain.
"Since the gods and my passion at once he defies,   *5*
Since his vanity lives whilst my character dies,

No more (did she say) will I trifle with Fate,
But commit to the waves both my love and my hate."
And now to comply with that furious desire,
Just ready to plunge and alone to expire,   *10*
Some reflection on death and its terrors untried,
Some scorn for the shepherd, some flashings of pride
At length pulled her back, and she cried, "Why this strife,
Since the swains are so many, and I've but one life?"

        (1713)

A SONG ON THE SOUTH SEA

Ombre and basset laid aside,
   New games employ the fair;
And brokers all those hours divide
   Which lovers used to share.

The court, the park, the foreign song   *5*
   And harlequin's grimace,
Forlorn; amidst the city throng
   Behold each blooming face.

With Jews and Gentiles undismayed
   Young tender virgins mix,   *10*
Of whiskers nor of beards afraid,
   Nor all the cozening tricks.

Bright jewels, polished once to deck
   The fair one's rising breast,
Or sparkle round her ivory neck,   *15*
   Lie pawned in iron chest.

The gayer passions of the mind
   How avarice controls!
Even love does now no longer find
   A place in female souls.   *20*

        (1720; 1724)

MATTHEW PRIOR
England, 1664-1721

THE DESPAIRING SHEPHERD

Alexis shunned his fellow swains,
Their rural sports, and jocund strains:
   (Heav'n guard us all from Cupid's bow!)

He lost his crook, he left his flocks;
And wand'ring through the lonely rocks,   *5*
   He nourished endless woe.

ADAM POS'D **Title. Pos'd:** posed, given a problem. **3. unpolished:** inelegant. **7-8.** See Genesis 2:19-20 (p. 243). **LA PASSION VAINCUE** **Title:** passion conquered. **A SONG ON THE SOUTH SEA** **Title:** British speculative investment in the South Sea Company (formed in 1711 by Robert Harley) led to schemes involving trading monopolies which were supposed to bring in huge profits; these schemes — characterized as the "South Sea Bubble" — collapsed in 1720 when they were exposed as fraudulent. **1. ombre and basset:** card games. **7. city:** the financial district of London.

The nymphs and shepherds round him came;
His grief some pity, others blame;
　　The fatal cause all kindly seek.
He mingled his concern with theirs;　　　　*10*
He gave 'em back their friendly tears;
　　He sighed, but would not speak.

Clorinda came among the rest,
And she too kind concern expressed,
　　And asked the reason of his woe;　　　　*15*
She asked, but with an air and mien
That made it easily foreseen
　　She feared too much to know.

The shepherd raised his mournful head,
"And will you pardon me," he said,　　　　*20*
　　"While I the cruel truth reveal?
Which nothing from my breast should tear,
Which never should offend your ear,
　　But that you bid me tell.

'Tis thus I rove, 'tis thus complain,　　　　*25*
Since you appeared upon the plain;
　　You are the cause of all my care:
Your eyes ten thousand daggers dart:
Ten thousand torments vex my heart:
　　I love, and I despair."　　　　*30*

"Too much, Alexis, I have heard;
'Tis what I thought, 'tis what I feared;
　　And yet I pardon you," she cried;
"But you shall promise ne'er again
To breath your vows, or speak your pain."　　　　*35*
　　He bowed, obeyed, and died.

　　　　　　　　　　(1703)

THE CHAMELEON

As the chameleon, who is known
To have no colours of his own;
But borrows from his neighbour's hue
His white or black, his green or blue;
And struts as much in ready light,　　　　*5*
Which credit gives him upon sight,
As if the rainbow were in tail

Settled on him, and his heirs male:
So the young Squire, when first he comes
From country school to Will's or Tom's;　　　　*10*
And equally, in truth, is fit
To be a statesman, or a wit;
Without one notion of his own,
He saunters wildly up and down,
Till some acquaintance, good or bad,　　　　*15*
Takes notice of a staring lad,
Admits him in among the gang;
They jest, reply, dispute, harangue;
He acts and talks, as they befriend him,
Smeared with the colours which they lend him.

　　Thus merely, as his fortune chances,　　　　*21*
His merit or his vice advances.
　　If haply he the sect pursues
That read and comment upon news,
He takes up their mysterious face:　　　　*25*
He drinks his coffee without lace.
This week his mimic tongue runs o'er
What they have said the week before.
His wisdom sets all Europe right;
And teaches Marlborough when to fight.　　　　*30*

　　Or if it be his fate to meet
With folks who have more wealth than wit,
He loves cheap port, and double bub,
And settles in the Hum-Drum Club.
He learns how stocks will fall or rise,　　　　*35*
Holds poverty the greatest vice,
Thinks wit the bane of conversation,
And says that learning spoils a nation.

　　But if, at first, he minds his hits,
And drinks champagne among the wits,　　　　*40*
Five deep, he toasts the tow'ring lasses;
Repeats you verses wrote on glasses,
Is in the chair, prescribes the law,
And lies with those he never saw.
　　　　　　　　　　(1708)

THE CHAMELEON   **7. in tail:** an estate limited to a particular inheritor. **10. Will's, Tom's:** coffee houses. **26. lace:** i.e., a lacing of liquor. **30. Marlborough:** See note on Swift's "A Satirical Elegy," p. 478. **33. bub:** strong malt liquor.

MARY ASTELL
England, 1666-1731

from *SOME REFLECTIONS UPON MARRIAGE*

. . . .

If mankind had never sinned, Reason would always have been obeyed, there would have been no struggle for dominion, and brutal power would not have prevailed. But in the lapsed state of mankind, and now that men will not be guided by their Reason but by their appetites, and do not what they *ought* but what they *can*, the Reason, or that which stands for it, the will and pleasure of the governor, is to be the Reason of those who will not be guided by their own, and must take place for order's sake, although it should not be conformable to right Reason. Nor can there be any society great or little, from empires down to private families, without a last resort, to determine the affairs of that society by an irresistible sentence. Now unless this supremacy be fixed somewhere, there will be a perpetual contention about it, such is the love of dominion, and let the Reason of things be what it may, those who have least force or cunning to supply it, will have the disadvantage. So that since women are acknowledged to have least bodily strength, their being commanded to obey is in pure kindness to them, and for their quiet and security, as well as for the exercise of their virtue. But does it follow, that domestic governors have more sense than their subjects, any more than that other governors have? We do not find that any man thinks the worse of his own understanding because another has superior power; or concludes himself less capable of a post of honour and authority because he is not preferred to it. How much time would lie on men's hands, how empty would the places of concourse be, and how silent most companies, did men forbear to censure their governors, that is, in effect, to think themselves wiser. Indeed, government would be much more desirable than it is, did it invest the possessor with a superior understanding as well as power. And if mere power gives a right to rule, there can be no such thing as usurpation; but a highwayman, so long as he has strength to force, has also a right to require our obedience.

Again, if absolute sovereignty be not necessary in a state, how comes it to be so in a family? Or if in a family why not in a state; since no reason can be alleged for the one that will not hold more strongly for the other? If the authority of the husband, so far as it extends, is sacred and inalienable, why not that of the prince? The domestic sovereign is without dispute elected, and the stipulations and contract are mutual; is it not then partial in men to the last degree to contend for and practise that arbitrary dominion in their families, which they abhor and exclaim against in the state? For if arbitrary power is evil in itself, and an improper method of governing rational and free agents, it ought not to be practised anywhere; nor is it less, but rather more mischievous in families than in kingdoms, by how much 100,000 tyrants are worse than one. What though a husband can't deprive a wife of life without being responsible to the law, he may, however, do what is much more grievous to a generous mind, render life miserable, for which she has no redress, scarce pity, which is afforded to every other complainant, it being thought a wife's duty to suffer everything without complaint. If *all men are born free,* how is it that all women are born slaves? As they must be, if the being subjected to the *inconstant, uncertain, unknown, arbitrary will* of men, be the *perfect condition of* 40 *slavery?* And if the essence of freedom consists, as our masters say it does, in having a *standing rule to live by?* And why is slavery so much condemned and strove against in one case, and so highly applauded, and held so necessary and so sacred in another?

(1701)

JONATHAN SWIFT
Ireland/England, 1667-1745

A DESCRIPTION OF THE MORNING

Now hardly here and there an hackney-coach
Appearing, showed the ruddy morn's approach.
Now Betty from her master's bed had flown,
And softly stole to discompose her own.
The slipshod prentice from his master's door   5
Had pared the dirt, and sprinkled round the floor.
Now Moll had whirled her mop with dext'rous airs,
Prepared to scrub the entry and the stairs.
The youth with broomy stumps began to trace
The kennel-edge, where wheels had worn the place.   10
The smallcoal-man was heard with cadence deep,
Till drowned in shriller notes of chimney-sweep.
Duns at his Lordship's gate began to meet,
And brickdust Moll had screamed through half the street.
The turnkey now his flock returning sees,   15
Duly let out a-nights to steal for fees.
The watchful bailiffs take their silent stands,
And schoolboys lag with satchels in their hands.

(1709)

A SATIRICAL ELEGY ON THE DEATH OF A LATE FAMOUS GENERAL

His Grace! impossible! what, dead?
Of old age, too, and in his bed!
And could that mighty warrior fall?
And so inglorious, after all!

Well, since he's gone, no matter how,   5
The last loud trump must wake him now:
And, trust me, as the noise grows stronger,
He'd wish to sleep a little longer.
And could he be indeed so old
As by the newspapers we're told?   10
Threescore, I think, is pretty high;
'Twas time in conscience he should die.
This world he cumbered long enough;
He burnt his candle to the snuff;
And that's the reason, some folks think,   15
He left behind so great a s—k.
Behold, his funeral appears,
Nor widow's sighs, nor orphan's tears,
Wont at such times each heart to pierce,
Attend the progress of his hearse.   20
But what of that, his friends may say;
He had those honours in his day.
True to his profit and his pride,
He made them weep before he died.
Come hither, all ye empty things,   25
Ye bubbles raised by breath of kings;
Who float upon the tide of state,
Come hither, and behold your fate.
Let pride be taught by this rebuke,
How very mean a thing's a Duke;   30
From all his ill-got honours flung,
Turned to that dirt from whence he sprung.

(1722; 1764)

A DESCRIPTION OF THE MORNING   **3. Betty:** stock name for a maidservant (as is **Moll,** line 7). **9-10:** "To find old nails" (note in 1735 edition). **11. smallcoal:** bits of coal or charcoal. **14. brickdust:** i.e., used as abrasive cleanser, e.g. for knives.   A SATIRICAL ELEGY...   The subject is John Churchill, first Duke of Marlborough (1650-1722) — although a great soldier, intensely disliked by the Tories.

from *Letter to Alexander Pope*

29 Sept. 1725

. . . .

I have employed my time (besides ditching) in finishing, correcting, amending, and
transcribing my *Travels,* in four parts complete, newly augmented, and intended for the
press when the world shall deserve them, or rather when a printer shall be found brave
enough to risk his ears. I like your schemes of our meeting after distresses and
dispersions; but the chief end I propose to myself in all my labours is to vex the world   5
rather than divert it, and if I could compass that design without hurting my own person
or fortune I would be the most indefatigable writer you have ever seen without reading.
I am exceedingly pleased that you have done with translations; Lord Treasurer Oxford
often lamented that a rascally world should lay you under a necessity of misemploying
your genius for so long a time. But since you will now be so much better employed,   10
when you think of the world give it one lash the more at my request. I have ever hated
all nations, professions, and communities, and all my love is towards individuals. For
instance I hate the tribe of Lawyers, but I love Counsellor such a one, Judge such a one;
for so with Physicians (I will not speak of my own trade), Soldiers, English, Scotch,
French; and the rest. But principally I hate and detest that animal called man, although I   15
heartily love John, Peter, Thomas, and so forth. This is the system upon which I have
governed myself many years (but do not tell) and so I shall go on till I have done with
them. I have got materials towards a treatise proving the falsity of that definition *animal
rationale,* and to show it should be only *rationis capax.* Upon this great foundation of
misanthropy (though not in Timon's manner) the whole building of my *Travels* is   20
erected. And I never will have peace of mind till all honest men are of my opinion; by
consequence you are to embrace it immediately and procure that all who deserve my
esteem may do so too. The matter is so clear that it will admit little dispute. Nay, I will
hold a hundred pounds that you and I agree in the point.

. . . .

STELLA'S BIRTHDAY, 1727

This day, whate'er the fates decree,
Shall still be kept with joy by me:
This day, then, let us not be told
That you are sick, and I grown old,
Nor think on our approaching ills,   5
And talk of spectacles and pills;
Tomorrow will be time enough
To hear such mortifying stuff.

Yet, since from reason may be brought
A better and more pleasing thought,   10
Which can in spite of all decays
Support a few remaining days:
From not the gravest of divines,
Accept for once some serious lines.
Although we now can form no more   15
Long schemes of life, as heretofore,

LETTER TO POPE   **1. ditching:** Swift was staying in the country at a friend's house, and helped out by doing some ditch-digging. **2.** *Travels*:
Gulliver's Travels was published a little over a year later. **4. risk his ears:** Slicing off ears was then still used as a punishment for such crimes as
fraud and forgery, and had also been associated with writing and publishing libels and the like. **5-6. vex . . . rather than divert:** Pope had proposed
getting together "not . . . to vex . . . but to divert ourselves, and the world too if it pleases. . . ." **8. translations:** Pope's translation of Homer's *Iliad*
was published between 1715 and 1720, his *Odyssey* in 1725-26. **14. my own trade:** Swift was a clergyman as well as an author. **19.** *rationis capax*:
capable of reason. **20. Timon's manner:** The title character of Shakespeare's *Timon of Athens,* an extreme misanthrope, curses everyone and retires
to a cave.   **STELLA'S BIRTHDAY, 1727**   "Stella" was Esther Johnson (March 13, 1681 — January 28, 1728), Swift's protégée, to whom he
had been devoted since her childhood; this was the last of a series of birthday poems for her. **2. still:** always.

Yet you, while time is running fast,
Can look with joy on what is past.
  Were future happiness and pain
A mere contrivance of the brain,   20
As atheists argue, to entice
And fit their proselytes for vice
(The only comfort they propose,
To have companions in their woes);
Grant this the case, yet sure 'tis hard   25
That virtue, styled its own reward,
And by all sages understood
To be the chief of human good,
Should acting, die, nor leave behind
Some lasting pleasure in the mind,   30
Which by remembrance will assuage
Grief, sickness, poverty, and age,
And strongly shoot a radiant dart
To shine through life's declining part.
  Say, Stella, feel you no content,   35
Reflecting on a life well spent?
Your skilful hand employed to save
Despairing wretches from the grave;
And then supporting with your store
Those whom you dragged from death before 40
(So Providence on mortals waits,
Preserving what it first creates);
Your gen'rous boldness to defend
An innocent and absent friend;
That courage which can make you just   45
To merit humbled in the dust;
The detestation you express
For vice in all its glitt'ring dress;
That patience under tort'ring pain,
Where stubborn stoics would complain.   50
  Must these like empty shadows pass,
Or forms reflected from a glass?

Or mere chimæras in the mind,
That fly and leave no marks behind?
Does not the body thrive and grow   55
By food of twenty years ago?
And, had it not been still supplied,
It must a thousand times have died.
Then who with reason can maintain
That no effects of food remain?   60
And is not virtue in mankind
The nutriment that feeds the mind?
Upheld by each good action past,
And still continued by the last:
Then who with reason can pretend   65
That all effects of virtue end?
  Believe me, Stella, when you show
That true contempt for things below,
Nor prize your life for other ends
Than merely to oblige your friends,   70
Your former actions claim their part,
And join to fortify your heart.
For Virtue in her daily race,
Like Janus, bears a double face;
Looks back with joy where she has gone,   75
And therefore goes with courage on.
She at your sickly couch will wait,
And guide you to a better state.
  O then, whatever Heav'n intends,
Take pity on your pitying friends;   80
Nor let your ills affect your mind,
To fancy they can be unkind.
Me, surely me, you ought to spare,
Who gladly would your suff'rings share;
Or give my scrap of life to you,   85
And think it far beneath your due;
You, to whose care so oft I owe
That I'm alive to tell you so.

A MODEST PROPOSAL

for Preventing the Children of Poor People in Ireland from Being a Burden to Their Parents or the Country, and for Making Them Beneficial to the Public

It is a melancholy object to those who walk through this great town, or travel in the country, when they see the streets, the roads, and the cabin doors crowded with beggars of the female sex, followed by three, four, or six children, all in rags, and importuning every passenger for an alms. These mothers, instead of being able to work for their

---

A MODEST PROPOSAL **1. this great town:** Dublin. **4. passenger:** passer-by.

honest livelihood, are forced to employ all their time in strolling to beg sustenance for *5*
their helpless infants, who, as they grow up, either turn thieves for want of work, or
leave their dear native country to fight for the Pretender in Spain, or sell themselves to
the Barbados.

I think it is agreed by all parties that this prodigious number of children in the arms,
or on the backs, or at the heels of their mothers, and frequently of their fathers, is in the *10*
present deplorable state of the kingdom a very great additional grievance; and therefore
whoever could find out a fair, cheap, and easy method of making these children sound
and useful members of the commonwealth would deserve so well of the public as to
have his statue set up for a preserver of the nation.

But my intention is very far from being confined to provide only for the children of *15*
professed beggars. It is of a much greater extent, and shall take in the whole number of
infants at a certain age, who are born of parents in effect as little able to support them as
those who demand our charity in the streets.

As to my own part, having turned my thoughts for many years upon this important
subject, and maturely weighed the several schemes of other projectors, I have always *20*
found them grossly mistaken in their computation. It is true a child just dropped from its
dam may be supported by her milk for a solar year with little other nourishment, at most
not above the value of two shillings, which the mother may certainly get, or the value in
scraps, by her lawful occupation of begging; and it is exactly at one year old that I
propose to provide for them in such a manner as, instead of being a charge upon their *25*
parents, or the parish, or wanting food and raiment for the rest of their lives, they shall,
on the contrary, contribute to the feeding, and partly to the clothing, of many thousands.

There is likewise another great advantage in my scheme, that it will prevent those
voluntary abortions, and that horrid practice of women murdering their bastard children
— alas! too frequent among us — sacrificing the poor innocent babes, I doubt, more to *30*
avoid the expense than the shame, which would move tears and pity in the most savage
and inhuman breast.

The number of souls in Ireland being usually reckoned one million and a half, of
these I calculate there may be about two hundred thousand couple whose wives are
breeders, from which number I subtract thirty thousand couples who are able to *35*
maintain their own children, although I apprehend there cannot be so many, under the
present distresses of the kingdom; but this being granted, there will remain an hundred
and seventy thousand breeders. I again subtract fifty thousand for those women who
miscarry or whose children die by accident or disease within the year. There only
remain an hundred and twenty thousand children of poor parents annually born. The *40*
question therefore is, how this number shall be reared and provided for, which, as I have
already said, under the present situation of affairs is utterly impossible by all the
methods hitherto proposed. For we can neither employ them in handicraft or agriculture;
we neither build houses (I mean in the country) nor cultivate land. They can very

---

5: The term strolling implied vagrancy. **7-8:** James Francis Edward Stuart (1688-1766), "the Old Pretender" to the English throne (son of James II, deposed in the "Glorious Revolution" of 1688), attracted Irish Catholic supporters; many poor Irishmen emigrated to the West Indies and elsewhere, indenturing themselves in order to pay for their passage. **11:** Ireland was suffering from a succession of poor harvests. **20. projectors:** those who project schemes or designs — but the term was commonly applied to those who form wild or impracticable schemes or designs; see Butler's character of "A Projector" (p. 378). **30. doubt:** suspect. **43-44:** England restricted Irish trade, and used Irish land largely for sheep pasturage.

seldom pick up a livelihood by stealing until they arrive at six years old, except where *45*
they are of towardly parts; although I confess they learn the rudiments much earlier,
during which time they can, however, be properly looked upon only as probationers, as I
have been informed by a principal gentleman in the county of Cavan who protested to
me that he never knew above one or two instances under the age of six, even in a part of
the kingdom so renowned for the quickest proficiency in that art. *50*

I am assured by our merchants that a boy or girl before twelve years old is no
saleable commodity; and even when they come to this age they will not yield above
three pounds, or three pounds and half a crown at most, on the exchange, which cannot
turn to account either to the parents or the kingdom, the charge of nutriment and rags
having been at least four times that value. *55*

I shall now therefore humbly propose my own thoughts, which I hope will not be
liable to the least objection.

I have been assured by a very knowing American of my acquaintance in London
that a young healthy child, well nursed, is, at a year old, a most delicious, nourishing,
and wholesome food, whether stewed, roasted, baked, or boiled, and I make no doubt *60*
that it will equally serve in a fricasee or ragout.

I do therefore humbly offer it to public consideration, that of the hundred and
twenty thousand children already computed, twenty thousand may be reserved for
breed, whereof only one-fourth part to be males, which is more than we allow to sheep,
black cattle, or swine; and my reason is, that these children are seldom the fruits of *65*
marriage, a circumstance not much regarded by our savages; therefore one male will be
sufficient to serve four females. That the remaining hundred thousand may, at a year
old, be offered in sale to the persons of quality and fortune through the kingdom, always
advising the mother to let them suck plentifully in the last month, so as to render them
plump and fat for a good table. A child will make two dishes at an entertainment for *70*
friends; and when the family dines alone, the fore or hind quarter will make a reasonable
dish, and seasoned with a little pepper or salt will be very good boiled on the fourth day,
especially in winter.

I have reckoned upon a medium that a child just born will weigh twelve pounds,
and in a solar year, if tolerably nursed, increaseth to twenty-eight pounds. *75*

I grant this food will be somewhat dear, and therefore very proper for landlords,
who, as they have already devoured the parents, seem to have the best title to the
children.

Infants' flesh will be in season throughout the year, but more plentiful in March,
and a little before and after, for we are told by a grave author, an eminent French *80*
physician, that fish being a prolific diet, there are more children born in Roman Catholic
countries about nine months after Lent than at any other season; therefore reckoning a
year after Lent, the markets will be more glutted than usual, because the number of
Popish infants is at least three to one in this kingdom, and therefore it will have one
other collateral advantage, by lessening the number of Papists among us. *85*

I have already computed the charge of nursing a beggar's child (in which list I
reckon all cottagers, labourers, and four fifths of the farmers) to be about two shillings

---

46. towardly parts: promising or precocious talents, apt abilities. **80. grave author:** Rabelais (Swift's note); see *Gargantua and Pantagruel*, V, 29. **87. cottagers:** cottiers, tenant farmers.

per annum, rags included; and I believe no gentleman would repine to give ten shillings for the carcass of a good fat child, which, as I have said, will make four dishes of excellent nutritive meat, when he hath only some particular friend, or his own family, to dine with him. Thus the squire will learn to be a good landlord, and grow popular among his tenants; the mother will have eight shillings net profit, and be fit for work until she produceth another child.

Those who are more thrifty (as I must confess the times require) may flay the carcass, the skin of which, artificially dressed, will make admirable gloves for ladies and summer boots for fine gentlemen.

As to our city of Dublin, shambles may be appointed for this purpose in the most convenient parts of it, and butchers we may be assured will not be wanting, although I rather recommend buying the children alive and dressing them hot from the knife, as we do roasting pigs.

A very worthy person, a true lover of his country, and whose virtues I highly esteem, was lately pleased, in discoursing on this matter, to offer a refinement upon my scheme. He said that many gentlemen of this kingdom having of late destroyed their deer, he conceived that the want of venison might be well supplied by the bodies of young lads and maidens, not exceeding fourteen years of age nor under twelve; so great a number of both sexes in every county being now ready to starve for want of work and service; and these to be disposed of by their parents, if alive, or otherwise by their nearest relations. But with due deference to so excellent a friend, and so deserving a patriot, I cannot be altogether in his sentiments; for as to the males, my American acquaintance assured me from frequent experience that their flesh was generally tough and lean, like that of our schoolboys, by continual exercise, and their taste disagreeable, and to fatten them would not answer the charge. Then, as to the females, it would, I think, with humble submission, be a loss to the public, because they soon would become breeders themselves; and besides, it is not improbable that some scrupulous people might be apt to censure such a practice (although very unjustly) as a little bordering upon cruelty, which, I confess, hath always been with me the strongest objection against any project, how well soever intended.

But in order to justify my friend, he confessed that this expedient was put into his head by the famous Psalmanazar, a native of the island Formosa, who came from thence to London above twenty years ago, and in conversation told my friend that in his country, when any young person happened to be put to death, the executioner sold the carcass to persons of quality as a prime dainty, and that in his time the body of a plump girl of fifteen, who was crucified for an attempt to poison the emperor, was sold to his Imperial Majesty's Prime Minister of State, and other great mandarins of the court, in joints from the gibbet at four hundred crowns. Neither indeed can I deny that if the same use were made of several plump young girls in this town who, without one single groat to their fortunes, cannot stir abroad without a chair, and appear at the playhouse and assemblies in foreign fineries which they will never pay for, the kingdom would not be the worse.

Some persons of a desponding spirit are in great concern about that vast number of poor people who are aged, diseased, or maimed, and I have been desired to employ my

95. **artificially:** artfully, skillfully. 118. **Psalmanazar:** "George Psalmanazar," pseudonym of a Frenchman (c.1679-1763) who passed himself off as a Formosan and wrote a fictitious book about his supposed birthplace (1704), but whose imposture was exposed soon after. 126. **chair:** i.e., sedan chair; **assemblies:** social and perhaps other gatherings.

thoughts what course may be taken to ease the nation of so grievous an encumbrance. *130*
But I am not in the least pain upon that matter, because it is very well known that they
are every day dying and rotting by cold, and famine, and filth, and vermin, as fast as can
reasonably be expected. And as to the younger labourers, they are now in almost as
hopeful a condition: they cannot get work, and consequently pine away for want of
nourishment, to a degree that if at any time they are accidentally hired to common *135*
labour, they have not strength to perform it, and thus the country, and themselves, are in
a fair way of being soon delivered from the evils to come.

I have too long digressed, and therefore shall return to my subject. I think the
advantages by the proposal which I have made are obvious and many, as well as of the
highest importance. *140*

For, first, as I have already observed, it would greatly lessen the number of Papists,
with whom we are yearly overrun, being the principal breeders of the nation as well as
our most dangerous enemies, and who stay at home on purpose with a design to deliver
the kingdom to the Pretender, hoping to take their advantage by the absence of so many
good Protestants, who have chosen rather to leave their country than stay at home and *145*
pay tithes against their conscience to an idolatrous Episcopal curate.

Secondly, the poorer tenants will have something valuable of their own, which by
law may be made liable to distress and help to pay their landlord's rent, their corn and
cattle being already seized, and money a thing unknown.

Thirdly, whereas the maintenance of an hundred thousand children from two years *150*
old and upwards cannot be computed at less than ten shillings apiece per annum, the
nation's stock will be thereby increased fifty thousand pounds per annum, besides the
profit of a new dish introduced to the tables of all gentlemen of fortune in the kingdom
who have any refinement in taste, and the money will circulate among ourselves, the
goods being entirely of our own growth and manufacture. *155*

Fourthly, the constant breeders, besides the gain of eight shillings sterling per
annum by the sale of their children, will be rid of the charge of maintaining them after
the first year.

Fifthly, this food would likewise bring great custom to taverns, where the vintners
will certainly be so prudent as to procure the best receipts for dressing it to perfection, *160*
and consequently have their houses frequented by all the fine gentlemen, who justly
value themselves upon their knowledge in good eating; and a skilful cook, who
understands how to oblige his guests, will contrive to make it as expensive as they please.

Sixthly, this would be a great inducement to marriage, which all wise nations have
either encouraged by rewards or enforced by laws and penalties. It would increase the *165*
care and tenderness of mothers towards their children, when they were sure of a
settlement for life to the poor babes, provided in some sort by the public, to their annual
profit instead of expense. We should soon see an honest emulation among the married
women, which of them could bring the fattest child to the market. Men would become
as fond of their wives during the time of their pregnancy as they are now of their mares *170*
in foal, their cows in calf, or sows when they are ready to farrow, nor offer to beat or
kick them (as it is too frequent a practice) for fear of a miscarriage.

144-46: The "good Protestants" are nonconformists and dissenters. **148. distress:** distraint. **160. receipts:** recipes.

Many other advantages might be enumerated. For instance, the addition of some thousand carcasses in our exportation of barrelled beef; the propagation of swine's flesh, and improvement in the art of making good bacon, so much wanted among us by the great destruction of pigs, too frequent at our tables, which are no way comparable in taste or magnificence to a well-grown, fat yearling child, which, roasted whole, will make a considerable figure at a Lord Mayor's Feast or any other public entertainment. But this, and many others, I omit, being studious of brevity.

Supposing that one thousand families in this city would be constant customers for infants' flesh, besides others who might have it at merry meetings, particularly weddings and christenings, I compute that Dublin would take off, annually, about twenty thousand carcasses, and the rest of the kingdom (where probably they will be sold somewhat cheaper) the remaining eighty thousand.

I can think of no one objection that will possibly be raised against this proposal, unless it should be urged that the number of people will be thereby much lessened in the kingdom. This I freely own, and it was indeed one principal design in offering it to the world. I desire the reader will observe that I calculate my remedy *for this one individual Kingdom of Ireland, and for no other that ever was, is, or I think ever can be upon earth.* Therefore let no man talk to me of other expedients: *Of taxing our absentees at five shillings a pound: Of using neither clothes nor household furniture except what is of our own growth and manufacture: Of utterly rejecting the materials and instruments that promote foreign luxury: Of curing the expensiveness of pride, vanity, idleness, and gaming in our women: Of introducing a vein of parsimony, prudence, and temperance: Of learning to love our country, wherein we differ even from Laplanders and the inhabitants of Topinamboo: Of quitting our animosities and factions, nor act any longer like the Jews, who were murdering one another at the very moment their city was taken: Of being a little cautious not to sell our country and consciences for nothing: Of teaching Landlords to have at least one degree of mercy towards their tenants. Lastly, of putting a spirit of honesty, industry, and skill into our shopkeepers, who, if a resolution could now be taken to buy only our native goods, would immediately unite to cheat and exact upon us in the price, the measure, and the goodness, nor could ever yet be brought to make one fair proposal of just dealing, though often and earnestly invited to it.*

Therefore I repeat, let no man talk to me of these and the like expedients till he hath at least a glimpse of hope that there will ever be some hearty and sincere attempt to put them in practice.

But as to myself, having been wearied out for many years with offering vain, idle, visionary thoughts, and at length utterly despairing of success, I fortunately fell upon this proposal, which, as it is wholly new, so it hath something solid and real, of no expense and little trouble, full in our own power, and whereby we can incur no danger in disobliging England; for this kind of commodity will not bear exportation, the flesh being of too tender a consistence to admit a long continuance in salt, although perhaps I could name a country which would be glad to eat up our whole nation without it.

---

175. wanted: wanting, lacking. **190ff.:** The italicized proposals were all ones Swift himself had offered in other writings. **196. Topinamboo:** *Tupinambà* is the term generally used for those of the Tupi-Guaraní Indians who lived in coastal and Amazonian Brazil, and was also applied to their regions, at the time of European colonization. **197.** probably referring to A.D. 70, when the Roman Emperor Titus took Jerusalem, though possibly to Nebuchadnezzar's conquest and the Babylonian captivity (see II Kings 24, 25; II Chronicles 36).

After all, I am not so violently bent upon my own opinion as to reject any offer proposed by wise men which shall be found equally innocent, cheap, easy, and 215 effectual. But before something of that kind shall be advanced in contradiction to my scheme, and offering a better, I desire the author, or authors, will be pleased maturely to consider two points. First, as things now stand, how they will be able to find food and raiment for a hundred thousand useless mouths and backs. And secondly, there being a round million of creatures in human figure throughout this kingdom, whose sole 220 subsistence, put into a common stock, would leave them in debt two millions of pounds sterling; adding those who are beggars by profession to the bulk of farmers, cottagers, and labourers, with their wives and children, who are beggars in effect; I desire those politicians who dislike my overture and may perhaps be so bold to attempt an answer, that they will first ask the parents of these mortals whether they would not, at this day, 225 think it a great happiness to have been sold for food at a year old, in the manner I prescribe, and thereby have avoided such a perpetual scene of misfortunes as they have since gone through by the oppression of landlords, the impossibility of paying rent without money or trade, the want of common sustenance, with neither house nor clothes to cover them from the inclemencies of weather, and the most inevitable prospect of 230 entailing the like or greater miseries upon their breed forever.

I profess, in the sincerity of my heart, that I have not the least personal interest in endeavouring to promote this necessary work, having no other motive than the public good of my country, by advancing our trade, providing for infants, relieving the poor, and giving some pleasure to the rich. I have no children by which I can propose to get a 235 single penny, the youngest being nine years old, and my wife past child-bearing.

(1729)

TWELVE ARTICLES

1. Lest it may more quarrels breed,
   I will never hear you read.
2. By disputing I will never
   To convince you, once endeavour.
3. When a paradox you stick to,   5
   I will never contradict you.
4. When I talk, and you are heedless,
   I will show no anger needless.
5. When your speeches are absurd,
   I will ne'er object a word.   10
6. When you furious argue wrong,
   I will grieve, and hold my tongue.
7. Not a jest, or hum'rous story,
   Will I ever tell before ye:
   To be chidden for explaining   15
   When you quite mistake the meaning.

8. Never more will I suppose
   You can taste my verse or prose.
9. You no more at me shall fret,
   While I teach, and you forget.   20
10. You shall never hear me thunder
    When you blunder on, and blunder.
11. Show your poverty of spirit,
    And in dress place all your merit;
    Give yourself ten thousand airs;   25
    That with me shall break no squares.
12. Never will I give advice
    Till you please to ask me thrice;
    Which, if you in scorn reject,
    'Twill be just as I expect.   30

Thus we both shall have our ends,
And continue special friends.

(1730)

TWELVE ARTICLES Often taken to be a second part of the poem "Daphne," probably addressed to Lady Acheson. **26. break no squares:** not disrupt the shape of things, not harm our relationship.

THE PLACE OF THE DAMNED

All folks who pretend to religion and grace
Allow there's a Hell, but dispute of the place;
But if Hell by logical rules be defined,
The place of the damned — I'll tell you my mind.
Wherever the damned do chiefly abound,   5
Most certainly there's the Hell to be found:
Damned poets, damned critics, damned blockheads, damned knaves,
Damned senators bribed, damned prostitute slaves;
Damned lawyers and judges, damned lords and damned squires,
Damned spies and informers, damned friends and damned liars;   10
Damned villains, corrupted in every station,
Damned time-serving priests all over the nation;
And into the bargain I'll readily give you
Damned ignorant prelates and councillors privy.
Then let us no longer by parsons be flammed,   15
For we know by these marks the place of the damned;
And Hell to be sure is at Paris or Rome;
How happy for us, that it is not at home.

                                                    (1731)

SARAH FYGE EGERTON
England, 1670-1723

ON THE HONOURABLE ROBERT BOYLE'S NOTION OF NATURE

'Tis bravely done, great Boyle has disenthroned
The goddess Nature, so unjustly crowned,
And by the learn'd so many ages owned.
Refuge of atheists, whose supine desire,
Pleased with that stage, no farther will aspire;   5
It damps the theists, too, while they assign
To Nature what's done by a Power Divine.
We know not how, nor where, to ascribe events
While she's thus rival to Omnipotence.
Sure that alone the mighty work can do;   10
The Power that did create can govern too.
It is not like our sublunary kings,
That must be circumscribed to place and things,
Whose straightened power doth ministers elect
That must for them remoter business act.   15
The Omnipresence of the Power Divine
Argues it need no deputies assign;
Nor is't beneath the glory of His state
To rule, protect the beings He create:
But stop, my pen, blush at thy weak pretence;   20
'Tis Boyle, not thee, that must the world convince,
Boyle the great champion of Providence,
Whose conquering truths in an inquiry dressed
Have celebrated Nature dispossessed;

ON THE HONOURABLE...   Robert Boyle (1627-1691), English chemist, physicist, and theologian, best known for "Boyle's law" about the inverse variation of volume and pressure in a confined gas, in 1661 published *The Sceptical Chymist*, introducing modern notions of elements and demonstrating the errors of Aristotle ("the great Stagirite," 42), Paracelsus, and the medieval natural philosophers ("the Schoolmen," 39); in 1665 he refused to take holy orders (which would have permitted him to become provost of Eton), claiming that his religious writings would be more effective if by a layman rather than a churchman (see lines 33-36). In 1686, the same year Sarah Fyge published her first book, *The Female Advocate*, Boyle published *A Free Inquiry into the Vulgarly Received Notion of Nature*. Boyle spent much time and money promoting Christianity, and in his will founded a series of lectures to defend it against "notorious infidels, viz. atheists, theists, pagans, Jews, and Mahommedans," further stipulating that controversies between Christians themselves not be mentioned. **14. straightened:** i.e., the straitened or limited powers of a constitutional monarch.

Not the vice-gerent of Heaven's settled rules,   *25*
But nice idea of the erring schools.
Fate, Fortune, Chance, all notional and vain,
The floating fictions of the poet's brain,
The world rejects, yet stupidly prefers
This wild chimera of philosophers: *30*
This more insinuating notion lay
Unquestioned till you made your brave assay,
Which doth the daring sceptic more confute
Than a suspected orthodox dispute.
They can't pretend int'rest, thy lines doth bribe   *35*
With which they censure, the canonic tribe;
'Twas love of truth alone thy pen did move,
Nor none but thee could so successful prove.
Methinks I all the Schoolmen's shades espy,
Tending the triumphs of philosophy,   *40*
And all the pregnant Naturists of yore,
From the great Stagirite to Descartes and more,
Resigning their gigantic notions now,
And only what you write for truth allow.
See, they have all their renounced volumes brought   *45*
(Bidding Mankind believe what you have taught);
Ashamed they've been, renowned so many years,
Each from his blushing brow his laurel tears;
With their own hands in one just wreath they twine,
Adorning that victorious head of thine.   *50*
And shall my female pen thy praise pretend,
When angels only can enough commend
In songs, which like themselves, can know no end.

                                    (1703)

THE LIBERTY

Shall I be one of those obsequious fools
That square their lives by custom's scanty rules,
Condemned forever to the puny curse
Of precepts taught at boarding school, or nurse,
That all the business of my life must be   *5*
Foolish, dull trifling, formality,
Confined to a strict magic complaisance,
And round a circle of nice visits dance,
Nor for my life beyond the chalk advance?
The devil Censure stands to guard the same;   *10*

One step awry, he tears my ventrous fame.
So when my friends, in a facetious vein,
With mirth and wit awhile can entertain,
Though ne'er so pleasant, yet I must not stay
If a commanding clock bids me away;   *15*
But with a sudden start as in a fright
I must be gone indeed, 'tis after eight.
Sure these restraints with such regret we bear
That dreaded Censure can't be more severe,
Which has no terror, if we did not fear;   *20*
But let the bugbear, timorous infants fright:
I'll not be scared from innocent delight.
Whatever is not vicious I dare do;
I'll never to the idol Custom bow
Unless it suits with my own humour too.   *25*
Some boast their fetters of formality,
Fancy they ornamental bracelets be;
I'm sure they're gyves and manacles to me.
To their dull fulsome rules I'd not be tied
For all the flattery that exalts their pride.   *30*
My sex forbids I should my silence break;
I lose my jest, 'cause women must not speak.
Mysteries must not be with my search profaned,
My closet not with books, but sweetmeats crammed,
A little china to advance the show,   *35*
My *Prayer Book,* and seven *Champions* or so.
My pen if ever used employed must be
In lofty themes of useful housewifery,
Transcribing old receipts of cookery,
And what is necessary 'mongst the rest,   *40*
Good cures for agues and a cancered breast,
But I can't here write my *Probatum est.*
My daring pen will bolder sallies make,
And like myself an unchecked freedom take;
Not chained to the nice order of my sex,   *45*
And with restraints my wishing soul perplex.
I'll blush at sin, and not what some call shame,
Secure my virtue, slight precarious fame.
This courage speaks me brave; 'tis surely worse
To keep those rules which privately we curse;   *50*
And I'll appeal to all the formal saints
With what reluctance they endure restraints.

                                    (1703)

---

25. vice-gerent: administrative deputy appointed by a ruler. **35. They can't pretend int'rest:** i.e., the sceptics can't accuse Boyle of being "interested," when as a layman he is by definition *disinterested*. **36. they:** i.e., "the canonic tribe," clergymen (unlike Boyle).   **THE LIBERTY   11. ventrous:** adventurous. **36. seven *Champions* or so:** referring to a work by Richard Johnson (1573-1659), *The Famous History of the Seven Champions of Christendom* (c.1597), which went into many subsequent editions and even new versions; in the manner of chivalric romance it told the stories or legends of seven national saints: of England (George), Scotland (Andrew), Ireland (Patrick), Wales (David), France (Denis), Spain (James), and Italy (Anthony). **42. *Probatum est*:** Latin, "It is proved," or "tried" (i.e., the proof or third division of a discourse, according to the stylistic model of the Roman rhetorician Quintilian).

THE EMULATION

Say, tyrant Custom, why must we obey
The impositions of thy haughty sway?
From the first dawn of life unto the grave,
Poor Womankind's in every state a slave.
The Nurse, the Mistress, Parent, and the Swain,   *5*
For love she must, there's none escape that pain;
Then comes the last, the fatal slavery,
The Husband with insulting tyranny
Can have ill manners justified by law,
For Men all join to keep the Wife in awe.   *10*
Moses, who first our freedom did rebuke,
Was married when he writ the Pentateuch;
They're wise to keep us slaves, for well they know,
If we were loose, we soon should make them so.
We yield like vanquished kings whom fetters bind,   *15*
When chance of war is to usurpers kind,
Submit in form, but they'd our thoughts control
And lay restraints on the impassive soul.
They fear we should excel their sluggish parts,
Should we attempt the Sciences and Arts,   *20*

Pretend they were designed for them alone,
So keep us fools to raise their own renown;
Thus priests of old, their grandeur to maintain,
Cried vulgar eyes would sacred laws profane.
So kept the mysteries behind a screen: *25*
There homage and the name were lost had they been seen.
But in this blessed age, such freedom's given
That every Man explains the will of Heaven;
And shall we Women now sit tamely by,
Make no excursions in philosophy,   *30*
Or grace our thoughts in tuneful poetry?
We will our rights in Learning's world maintain;
Wit's empire now shall know a female reign.
Come all ye fair, the great attempt improve;
Divinely imitate the realms above;   *35*
There's ten celestial females govern Wit,
And but two gods that dare pretend to it;
And shall these finite males reverse their rules?
No, we'll be wits, and then Men must be fools.

(1703)

SARAH DIXON
England, 1671-1765

A RECEIPT FOR AN EXTRAORDINARY MADE-DISH

Take of flesh, and blood, and bone
A living thing of twenty-one;
Sent from the schools for want of brain,
To see its dear Mamma again.
It may be either fat or lean,   *5*
Or black or fair, or blue or green;
'Tis not the colour, but the make,
Quantum sufficit you must take;
Fit it out, to make a Tour,
Let it return by twenty-four,   *10*
Provided with some scraps of French
And fragments of a foreign wench;

A flippant blockhead let it come,
Equip with well-bred oaths at home;
Let little pumps enclose its feet,   *15*
Silk stockings make the leg complete;
The finest Holland ruffled shirt,
A waistcoat with a dapper skirt;
A snuff-box with a nauseous lid,
A pound of powder on its head,   *20*
Must shine with lace from top to toe.
Whether you like it aye or no,
This thing we ladies call a Beau.

(1740)

THE EMULATION   **36. ten celestial females:** i.e., the nine Muses, together with either Mnemosyne, their mother and goddess of memory, or Athena (Minerva), goddess of wisdom and the arts. The "two gods" of line 37 are probably Apollo and Hermes (Mercury), gods of the arts and eloquence.   A RECEIPT   **8. *Quantum sufficit*:** as much as suffices, enough. **9. Tour:** i.e., "The Grand Tour" of continental Europe (especially France, Italy, and Germany), with a tutor, often for two or three years — considered by socially prominent English families in the 17th and 18th centuries as *de rigueur* to "finish" a young man's education. **17. Holland:** a kind of linen first made in Holland.

JOSEPH ADDISON
England, 1672-1719

from *THE SPECTATOR*
Nos. 58-63, Monday, May 7,
through Saturday, May 12, 1711 (abridged)

No. 58.   Monday, May 7

Nothing is so much admired, and so little understood, as Wit. No author that I know of
has written professedly upon it; and as for those who make any mention of it, they only
treat on the subject as it has accidentally fallen in their way, and that too in little short
reflections, or in general declamatory flourishes, without entering into the bottom of the
matter. I hope therefore I shall perform an acceptable work to my countrymen if I treat at   *5*
large upon this subject. . . . I intend to lay aside a whole week for this undertaking. . . .

As the great and only end of these my speculations is to banish vice and ignorance
out of the territories of Great Britain, I shall endeavour as much as possible to establish
among us a taste of polite writing. . . .

In this, and one or two following papers, I shall trace out the history of False Wit,   *10*
and distinguish the several kinds of it as they have prevailed in different ages of the
world. . . .

The first species of False Wit which I have met with is very venerable for its
antiquity, and has produced several pieces which have lived very near as long as the
Iliad itself: I mean those short poems printed among the minor Greek poets, which   *15*
resemble the figure of an egg, a pair of wings, an ax, a shepherd's pipe, and an altar.

. . . .

It was impossible for a man to succeed in these performances who was not a kind of
painter, or at least a designer. He was first of all to draw the outline of the subject which
he intended to write upon, and afterwards conform the description to the figure of his
subject. The poetry was to contract or dilate itself according to the mould in which it   *20*
was cast. In a word, the verses were to be cramped or extended to the dimensions of the
frame that was prepared for them, and to undergo the fate of those persons whom the
tyrant *Procrustes* used to lodge in his iron bed; if they were too short, he stretched them
on a rack, and if they were too long, chopped off a part of their legs, till they fitted the
couch which he had prepared for them.   *25*

Mr. Dryden hints at this obsolete kind of Wit . . . in his *Mac Flecknoe*. . . .

This fashion of False Wit was revived by several poets of the last age, and in
particular may be met with among Mr. Herbert's poems. . . . I do not remember any

---

THE SPECTATOR   **26:** See lines 204ff. of Dryden's poem (p. 437). **28. Herbert's poems:** See e.g. "Easter Wings," p. 289; see also "Shaped
Verse" in the Alternative Table of Contents 1.

other kind of work among the Moderns which more resembles the performances I have
mentioned, than that famous picture of King Charles the First, which has the whole *30*
Book of *Psalms* written in the lines of the face and the hair of the head. When I was last
at Oxford I perused one of the whiskers, and was reading the other, but could not go so
far in it as I would have done, by reason of the impatience of my friends and fellow
travellers, who all of them pressed to see such a piece of curiosity. . . .

But to return to our ancient poems in picture, I would humbly propose, for the *35*
benefit of our modern smatterers in poetry, that they would imitate their brethren among
the Ancients in those ingenious devices. . . . I do not question but . . . that we shall see
the town filled in a very little time with poetical tippets, handkerchiefs, snuff-boxes, and
the like female ornaments. . . .

No. 59. Tuesday, May 8

There is nothing more certain than that every man would be a Wit if he could, and *40*
notwithstanding pedants of a pretended depth and solidity are apt to decry the writings
of a polite author as flash and froth, they all of them show upon occasion that they
would spare no pains to arrive at the character of those whom they seem to despise. For
this reason we often find them endeavouring at works of Fancy, which cost them infinite
pangs in the production. The truth of it is, a man had better be a galley slave than a Wit, *45*
were one to gain that title by those elaborate trifles which have been the inventions of
such authors as were often masters of great Learning but no Genius.

In my last paper I mentioned some of these False Wits among the Ancients, and in
this shall give the reader two or three other species of them, that flourished in the same
early ages of the world. The first I shall produce are the lipogrammatists or letter- *50*
droppers of antiquity, that would take an exception, without any reason, against some
particular letter in the alphabet, so as not to admit it once into a whole poem. One
Tryphiodorus . . . composed an *Odyssey* . . . consisting of four and twenty books, having
entirely banished the Letter *A* from his first book, which was called *Alpha* . . . because
there was not an *Alpha* in it. His second Book was inscribed *Beta* for the same reason. *55*
In short, the poet excluded the whole four and twenty letters in their turns, and showed
them, one after another, that he could do his business without them.

. . . .

If the work I have here mentioned had been now extant, the *Odyssey* of
Tryphiodorus, in all probability, would have been oftener quoted by our learned pedants
than the *Odyssey* of Homer. What a perpetual fund would it have been of obsolete words *60*
and phrases, unusual barbarisms and rusticities, absurd spellings and complicated
dialects! I make no question but it would have been looked upon as one of the most
valuable treasuries of the Greek tongue.

I find likewise among the Ancients that ingenious kind of conceit, which the
Moderns distinguish by the name of a *rebus,* that does not sink a letter but a whole *65*
word, by substituting a picture in its place. . . . This kind of Wit was very much in vogue
among our own countrymen about an age or two ago . . . purely for the sake of being

witty. Among innumerable Instances . . . I shall produce the device of one Mr. Newberry. . . . Mr. Newberry, to represent his name by a picture, hung up at his door the sign of a yew tree that had several berries upon it, and in the midst of them a great 70 golden *N* hung upon a bough of the tree, which by the help of a little false spelling made up the word *N-ew-berry.*

. . . .

I find likewise in ancient times the conceit of making an echo talk sensibly, and give rational answers. . . . The learned Erasmus, though a man of Wit and Genius, has composed a dialogue upon this silly kind of device, and made use of an echo who seems 75 to have been a very extraordinary linguist, for she answers the person she talks with in Latin, Greek, and Hebrew, according as she found the syllables which she was to repeat in any one of those learned languages. . . .

No. 60.   Wednesday, May 9

Several kinds of False Wit that vanished in the refined ages of the world, discovered themselves again in the times of monkish ignorance. 80

As the monks were the masters of all that little Learning which was then extant, and had their whole lives entirely disengaged from business, it is no wonder that several of them, who wanted Genius for higher performances, employed many hours in the composition of such tricks in writing as required much time and little capacity. I have seen half the *Aeneid* turned into Latin rhymes by one of the *beaux esprits* of that dark 85 age. . . . I have likewise seen an hymn in hexameters to the Virgin Mary, which filled a whole book, though it consisted but of the eight following words.

> *Tot, tibe, sunt, Virgo, dotes, quot, sidera, coelo*
> Thou hast as many virtues, O Virgin, as there are stars in heaven.

The poet rung the changes upon these eight several words, and by that means made 90 his verses almost as numerous as the virtues and the stars which they celebrated. It is no wonder that men who had so much time upon their hands did not only restore all the antiquated pieces of False Wit, but enriched the world with inventions of their own. It was to this age that we owe the production of anagrams, which is nothing else but a transmutation of one word into another, or the turning of the same set of letters into 95 different words; which may change night into day, or black into white, if Chance, who is the goddess that presides over these sorts of composition, shall so direct. . . .

When the anagrammatist takes a name to work upon, he considers it first as a mine not broken up, which will not show the treasure it contains till he shall have spent many hours in the search of it. For it is his business to find out one word that conceals itself in 100 another, and to examine the letters in all the variety of stations in which they can possibly be ranged. . . .

The acrostic was probably invented about the same time with the anagram, though it is impossible to decide whether the inventor of the one or the other were the greater blockhead. The *simple* acrostic is nothing but the name or title of a person or thing made 105

74ff.: one of Erasmus's *Familiar Colloquies,* called "Echo" (for another of his colloquies, see p. 389). **94, 103:** Addison is mistaken here, since both anagrams and acrostics existed in ancient times, long before the "monkish" age.

out of the initial letters of several verses, and by that means written, after the manner of the Chinese, in a perpendicular line. But besides these there are *compound* acrostics, where the principal letters stand two or three deep. I have seen some of them where the verses have not only been edged by a name at each extremity, but have had the same name running down like a seam through the middle of the poem. *110*

There is another near relation of the anagrams and acrostics, which is commonly called a chronogram. This kind of Wit appears very often on many modern medals, especially those of Germany, when they represent in the inscription the year in which they were coined. Thus we see on a medal of Gustavus Adolphus the following words, *CHRISTVS DUX ERGO TRIVMPHVS.* If you take the pains to pick the figures out of *115* the several words, and range them in their proper order, you will find they amount to MDCXVVVII, or 1627, the year in which the medal was stamped. . . . Your laborious German Wits will turn over a whole dictionary for one of these ingenious devices. . . .

The *bouts-rimés* were the favourites of the French nation for a whole age together, and that at a time when it abounded in Wit and Learning. They were a list of words that *120* rhyme to one another, drawn up by another hand, and given to a poet, who was to make a poem to the rhymes in the same order that they were placed upon the list. The more uncommon the rhymes were, the more extraordinary was the Genius of the poet that could accommodate his verses to them. I do not know any greater instance of the decay of Wit and Learning among the French . . . than the endeavouring to restore this foolish *125* kind of Wit. . . .

I must subjoin to this last kind of Wit the double rhymes, which are used in doggerel poetry, and generally applauded by ignorant readers. . . . I am afraid that great numbers of those who admire the incomparable *Hudibras,* do it more on account of these doggerel rhymes than of the parts that really deserve admiration. . . . *130*

No. 61. Thursday, May 10

There is no kind of False Wit which has been so recommended by the practice of all ages, as that which consists in a jingle of words, and is comprehended under the general name of *punning.* It is indeed impossible to kill a weed, which the soil has a natural disposition to produce. The seeds of punning are in the minds of all men, and though they may be subdued by reason, reflection, and good sense, they will be very apt to *135* shoot up in the greatest Genius that is not broken and cultivated by the rules of art. Imitation is natural to us, and when it does not raise the mind to poetry, painting, music, or other more noble arts, it often breaks out in puns and quibbles.

Aristotle, in the eleventh chapter of his book of *Rhetoric,* describes two or three kinds of puns, which he calls paragrams, among the beauties of good writing, and *140* produces instances of them out of some of the greatest authors in the Greek tongue. Cicero has sprinkled several of his works with puns, and in his book where he lays down the rules of oratory, quotes abundance of sayings as pieces of Wit, which also upon examination prove arrant puns. But the age in which the pun chiefly flourished was the reign of King James the First. That learned monarch was himself a tolerable *145*

---

129. *Hudibras:* See p. 374.

punster, and made very few bishops or Privy Counsellors that had not some time or other signalized themselves by a clinch, or a conundrum. It was therefore in this age that the pun appeared with pomp and dignity. It had before been admitted into merry speeches and ludicrous compositions, but was now delivered with great gravity from the pulpit, or pronounced in the most solemn manner at the council-table. The greatest 150 authors, in their most serious works, made frequent use of puns. The sermons of Bishop Andrewes, and the tragedies of Shakespeare, are full of them. The sinner was punned into repentance by the former, as in the latter nothing is more usual than to see a hero weeping and quibbling for a dozen lines together.

. . . .

I must not here omit, that a famous university of this land was formerly very much 155 infested with puns; but whether or no this might not arise from the fens and marshes in which it was situated, and which are now drained, I must leave to the determination of more skilfull naturalists.

. . . .

Having pursued the history of a pun, from its original to its downfall, I shall here define it to be a conceit arising from the use of two words that agree in the sound, but 160 differ in the sense. The only way therefore to try a piece of Wit is to translate it into a different language: if it bears the test, you may pronounce it True; but if it vanishes in the experiment, you may conclude it to have been a pun. . . .

No. 62. Friday, May 11

Mr. Locke has an admirable reflection upon the difference of Wit and Judgment, whereby he endeavours to show the reason why they are not always the talents of the 165 same person. His words are as follows: "And hence, perhaps, may be given some reason of that common observation, that men who have a great deal of Wit and prompt memories, have not always the clearest Judgment, or deepest reason. For Wit lying most in the assemblage of ideas, and putting those together with quickness and variety, wherein can be found any resemblance or congruity, thereby to make up pleasant 170 pictures and agreeable visions in the Fancy; Judgment, on the contrary, lies quite on the other side, in separating carefully, one from another, ideas wherein can be found the least difference, thereby to avoid being misled by similitude, and by affinity to take one thing for another. This is a way of proceeding quite contrary to metaphor and allusion; wherein, for the most part, lies that entertainment and pleasantry of Wit which strikes so 175 lively on the Fancy, and is therefore so acceptable to all people."

This is, I think, the best and most philosophical account that I have ever met with of Wit, which generally, though not always, consists in such a resemblance and congruity of ideas as this author mentions. I shall only add to it, by way of explanation, that every resemblance of ideas is not that which we call Wit, unless it be such an one that gives 180 *delight* and *surprise* to the reader. These two properties seem essential to Wit, more particularly the last of them. In order therefore that the resemblance in the ideas be Wit,

---

147. **clinch:** clench, play on words, pun. **151-52. Bishop Andrewes:** Lancelot Andrewes (see note on The Authorized Version of the Bible, p. 241ff.); James I made him Bishop of Chichester, then Ely, then Winchester. **155. famous University:** Cambridge. **164ff. Mr. Locke:** John Locke, in *An Essay Concerning Human Understanding* (1690), Book II, Ch. II.

it is necessary that the ideas should not lie too near one another in the nature of things; for where the likeness is obvious, it gives no surprise. . . . Thus when a poet tells us, the bosom of his mistress is as white as snow, there is no Wit in the comparison; but when *185* he adds, with a sigh, that it is as cold too, it then grows into Wit. . . .

As True Wit generally consists in this resemblance and congruity of ideas, False Wit chiefly consists in the resemblance and congruity sometimes of single letters, as in anagrams, chronograms, lipograms, and acrostics; sometimes of syllables, as in echoes and doggerel rhymes; sometimes of words, as in puns and quibbles; and sometimes of *190* whole sentences or poems, cast into the figures of eggs, axes, or altars. Nay, some carry the notion of Wit so far as to ascribe it even to external mimicry, and to look upon a man as an ingenious person, that can resemble the tone, posture, or face of another.

. . . .

There is another kind of Wit which consists partly in the resemblance of ideas, and partly in the resemblance of words; which for distinction's sake I shall call Mixed Wit. *195* This kind of Wit is that which abounds in Cowley, more than in any author that ever wrote. Mr. Waller has likewise a great deal of it. Mr. Dryden is very sparing in it. Milton had a Genius much above it. Spenser is in the same class with Milton. The Italians, even in their epic poetry, are full of it. Monsieur Boileau, who formed himself upon the ancient poets, has everywhere rejected it with scorn. . . . *200*

Out of the innumerable branches of Mixed Wit, I shall choose one instance which may be met with in all the writers of this class. The passion of love in its nature has been thought to resemble fire; for which reason the words *fire* and *flame* are made use of to signify love. The witty poets therefore have taken an advantage from the doubtful meaning of the word *fire,* to make an infinite number of witticisms. Cowley, observing *205* the cold regard of his mistress's eyes, and at the same time their power of producing love in him, considers them as burning-glasses made of ice; and finding himself able to live in the greatest extremities of love, concludes the Torrid Zone to be habitable. When his mistress has read his letter written in juice of lemon by holding it to the fire, he desires her to read it over a second time by love's flames. When she weeps, he wishes it *210* were inward heat that distilled those drops from the limbec. When she is absent he is beyond eighty, that is, thirty degrees nearer the pole than when she is with him. His ambitious love is a fire that naturally mounts upwards; his happy love is the beams of Heaven, and his unhappy love flames of Hell. When it does not let him sleep, it is a flame that sends up no smoke; when it is opposed by counsel and advice, it is a fire that *215* rages the more by the wind's blowing on it. Upon the dying of a tree in which he had cut his loves, he observes that his written flames had burnt up and withered the tree. When he resolves to give over his passion, he tells us that one burnt like him for ever dreads the fire. His heart is an Ætna, that instead of Vulcan's shop encloses Cupid's forge in it. His endeavouring to drown his love in wine, is throwing oil upon the fire. He would *220* insinuate to his mistress, that the fire of love, like that of the sun (which produces so many living creatures) should not only warm but beget. Love in another place cooks

---

199. Boileau: Nicholas Despreaux Boileau (1636-1711), author of *Art Poétique* (1674). **205ff.:** Addison draws these examples from Abraham Cowley's collection *The Mistress* (1647). **211. limbeck:** alembic. **221-22:** It was once believed that the sun created life from dead matter; cf. Hamlet's remark, "For if the sun breed maggots in a dead dog" (II, ii, 183).

pleasure at his fire. Sometimes the poet's heart is frozen in every breast, and sometimes scorched in every eye. Sometimes he is drowned in tears, and burnt in love, like a ship set on fire in the middle of the sea.

225

The reader may observe in every one of these instances, that the poet mixes the qualities of fire with those of love; and in the same sentence speaking of it both as a passion and as real fire, surprises the reader with those seeming resemblances or contradictions that make up all the Wit in this kind of writing. Mixed Wit therefore is a composition of pun and True Wit, and is more or less perfect as the resemblance lies in 230 the ideas or in the words; its foundations are laid partly in falsehood and partly in truth; reason puts in her claim for one half of it, and extravagance for the other. The only province therefore for this kind of Wit, is epigram, or those little occasional poems that in their own nature are nothing else but a tissue of epigrams. I cannot conclude this head of Mixed Wit, without owning that the admirable poet out of whom I have taken the 235 examples of it, had as much True Wit as any author that ever writ; and indeed all other talents of an extraordinary genius.

. . . .

No. 63. Saturday, May 12

It is very hard for the mind to disengage itself from a subject in which it has been long employed. The thoughts will be rising of themselves from time to time, though we give them no encouragement; as the tossings and fluctuations of the sea continue several 240 hours after the winds are laid.

It is to this that I impute my last night's dream or vision, which formed into one continued allegory the several schemes of Wit, whether False, Mixed, or True, that have been the subject of my late papers.

Methought I was transported into a country that was filled with prodigies and 245 enchantments, governed by the Goddess of Falsehood, entitled The Region of False Wit. There is nothing in the fields, the woods, and the rivers, that appeared natural. Several of the trees blossomed in leaf-gold, some of them produced bone-lace, and some of them precious stones. The fountains bubbled in an opera tune, and were filled with stags, wild boars, and mermaids, that lived among the waters; at the same time that 250 dolphins and several kinds of fish played upon the banks or took their pastime in the meadows. The birds had many of them golden beaks, and human voices. The flowers perfumed the air with smells of incense, ambergrease, and pulvillios; and were so interwoven with one another, that they grew up in pieces of embroidery. The winds were filled with sighs and messages of distant lovers. As I was walking to and fro in this 255 enchanted wilderness, I could not forbear breaking out into soliloquies upon the several wonders which lay before me, when, to my great surprise, I found there were artificial echoes in every walk, that by repetitions of certain words which I spoke, agreed with me, or contradicted me, in every thing I said. In the midst of my conversation with these invisible companions, I discovered in the centre of a very dark grove a monstrous fabric 260 built after the Gothic manner, and covered with innumerable devices in that barbarous kind of sculpture. I immediately went up to it, and found it to be a kind of heathen

---

253. **ambergrease:** ambergris; **pulvillios:** perfumed powder, often in scent bags, and often used to powder wigs.

Temple consecrated to the God of Dullness. Upon my entrance I saw the deity of the place dressed in the habit of a monk, with a book in one hand and a rattle in the other. Upon his right hand was Industry, with a lamp burning before her; and on his left *265* Caprice, with a monkey sitting on her shoulder. Before his feet there stood an altar of a very odd make, which, as I afterwards found, was shaped in that manner to comply with the inscription that surrounded it. Upon the altar there lay several offerings of axes, wings, and eggs, cut in paper, and inscribed with verses. The Temple was filled with votaries, who applied themselves to different diversions, as their fancies directed them. *270* In one part of it I saw a regiment of Anagrams, who were continually in motion, turning to the right or to the left, facing about, doubling their ranks, shifting their stations, and throwing themselves into all the figures and countermarches of the most changeable and perplexed exercise.

Not far from these was a body of Acrostics, made up of very disproportioned *275* persons. It was disposed into three columns, the officers planting themselves in a line on the left hand of each column. The officers were all of them at least six foot high, and made three rows of very proper men; but the common soldiers, who filled up the spaces between the officers, were such dwarfs, cripples, and scarecrows, that one could hardly look upon them without laughing. There were behind the Acrostics two or three files of *280* Chronograms, which differed only from the former, as their officers were equipped (like the figure of Time) with an hour-glass in one hand, and a scythe in the other, and took their posts promiscuously among the private men whom they commanded.

In the body of the Temple, and before the very face of the deity, methought I saw the phantom of Tryphiodorus the Lipogrammatist, engaged in a ball with four and *285* twenty persons, who pursued him by turns through all the intricacies and labyrinths of a country dance, without being able to overtake him.

Observing several to be very busy at the western end of the Temple, I inquired into what they were doing, and found there was in that quarter the great magazine of Rebuses. These were several things of the most different natures tied up in bundles, and *290* thrown upon one another in heaps like faggots. You might behold an anchor, a night-rail, and a hobby-horse bound up together. One of the workmen seeing me very much surprised, told me, there was an infinite deal of Wit in several of those bundles, and that he would explain them to me if I pleased; I thanked him for his civility, but told him I was in very great haste at that time. As I was going out of the Temple, I observed in one *295* corner of it a cluster of men and women laughing very heartily, and diverting themselves at a game of crambo. I heard several double rhymes as I passed by them, which raised a great deal of mirth.

Not far from these was another set of merry people engaged at a diversion, in which the whole jest was to mistake one person for another. To give occasion for these *300* ludicrous mistakes, they were divided into pairs, every pair being covered from head to foot with the same kind of dress, though perhaps there was not the least resemblance in their faces. By this means an old man was sometimes mistaken for a boy, a woman for a man, and a blackamoor for an European, which very often produced great peals of laughter. These I guessed to be a party of Puns. But being very desirous to get out of this *305*

291-92. night-rail: a loose wrap or dressing-gown.

world of magic, which had almost turned my brain, I left the Temple, and crossed over the fields that lay about it with all the speed I could make. I was not gone far before I heard the sound of trumpets and alarms, which seemed to proclaim the march of an enemy; and, as I afterwards found, was in reality what I apprehended it. There appeared at a great distance a very shining light, and, in the midst of it, a person of a most *310* beautiful aspect; her name was Truth. On her right hand there marched a male deity, who bore several quivers on his shoulders, and grasped several arrows in his hand. His name was Wit. The approach of these two enemies filled all the territories of False Wit with an unspeakable consternation, insomuch that the Goddess of those regions appeared in person upon her frontiers with the several inferior deities, and the different *315* bodies of forces which I had before seen in the Temple, who were now drawn up in array, and prepared to give their foes a warm reception. As the march of the enemy was very slow, it gave time to the several inhabitants who bordered upon the Regions of Falsehood to draw their forces into a body, with a design to stand upon their guard as neuters, and attend the issue of the combat. *320*

I must here inform my reader, that the frontiers of the enchanted region which I have before described were inhabited by the species of Mixed Wit, who made a very odd appearance when they were mustered together in an army. There were men whose bodies were stuck full of darts, and women whose eyes were burning-glasses; men that had hearts of fire, and women that had breasts of snow. It would be endless to describe *325* several monsters of the like nature, that composed this great army; which immediately fell asunder and divided itself into two parts, the one half throwing themselves behind the banners of Truth, and the others behind those of Falsehood.

The Goddess of Falsehood was of a gigantic stature, and advanced some paces before the front of her army; but as the dazzling light which flowed from Truth began to *330* shine upon her, she faded insensibly, insomuch that in a little space she looked rather like an huge phantom than a real substance. At length, as the Goddess of Truth approached still nearer to her, she fell away entirely, and vanished amidst the brightness of her presence; so that there did not remain the least trace or impression of her figure in the place where she had been seen. *335*

As at the rising of the sun the constellations grow thin, and the stars go out one after another, till the whole hemisphere is extinguished, such was the vanishing of the Goddess; and not only of the Goddess herself, but of the whole army that attended her, which sympathized with their leader, and shrunk into nothing, in proportion as the Goddess disappeared. At the same time the whole Temple sunk, the fish betook *340* themselves to the streams, and the wild beasts to the woods. The fountains recovered their murmurs, the birds their voices, the trees their leaves, the flowers their scents, and the whole face of Nature its true and genuine appearance. Though I still continued asleep, I fancied myself as it were awakened out of a dream, when I saw this region of prodigies restored to woods and rivers, fields and meadows. *345*

Upon the removal of that wild scene of wonders, which had very much disturbed my Imagination, I took a full survey of the persons of Wit and Truth; for indeed it was impossible to look upon the first, without seeing the other at the same time. There was

---

320. neuters: neutrals.

behind them a strong and compact body of figures. The Genius of Heroic Poetry appeared with a sword in her hand, and a laurel on her head. Tragedy was crowned with *350* cypress, and covered with robes dipped in blood. Satire had smiles in her look, and a dagger under her garment. Rhetoric was known by her thunderbolt, and Comedy by her mask. After several other figures, Epigram marched up in the rear, who had been posted there at the beginning of the expedition, that he might not revolt to the enemy, whom he was suspected to favour in his heart. I was very much awed and delighted with the *355* appearance of the God of Wit; there was something so amiable and yet so piercing in his looks, as inspired me at once with love and terror. As I was gazing on him, to my unspeakable joy, he took a quiver of arrows from his shoulder, in order to make me a present of it; but as I was reaching out my hand to receive it of him, I knocked it against a chair, and by that means awaked. *360*

ISAAC WATTS
England, 1674-1748

AGAINST IDLENESS AND MISCHIEF

How doth the little busy bee
    Improve each shining hour,
And gather honey all the day
    From every opening flower!

How skilfully she builds her cell!   *5*
    How neat she spreads the wax!
And labours hard to store it well
    With the sweet food she makes.

In works of labour or of skill
    I would be busy too,   *10*
For Satan finds some mischief still
    For idle hands to do.

In books, or work, or healthful play
    Let my first years be passed,
That I may give for every day   *15*
    Some good account at last.
            (1715)

THE SLUGGARD

'Tis the voice of the sluggard; I heard him complain,
"You have waked me too soon, I must slumber again."
As the door on its hinges, so he on his bed,
Turns his sides, and his shoulders, and his heavy head.

"A little more sleep, and a little more slumber"; *5*
Thus he wastes half his days and his hours without number;
And when he gets up, he sits folding his hands,
Or walks about saunt'ring, or trifling he stands.

I passed by his garden and saw the wild brier,
The thorn and the thistle grow broader and higher; *10*
The clothes that hang on him are turning to rags,
And his money still wastes till he starves or he begs.

I made him a visit, still hoping to find
He had took better care for improving his mind:
He told me his dreams, talked of eating and drinking; *15*
But he scarce reads his Bible, and never loves thinking.

Said I then to my heart, "Here's a lesson for me:
That man's but a picture of what I might be;
But thanks to my friends for their care in my breeding,
Who taught me betimes to love working and reading." *20*
            (1715)

AGAINST IDLENESS AND MISCHIEF From *Divine Songs, for Children.*   **THE SLUGGARD** From *Moral Songs.*

MAN FRAIL, AND GOD ETERNAL

Our God, our help in ages past,
   Our hope for years to come,
Our shelter from the stormy blast,
   And our eternal home.

Under the shadow of thy throne   *5*
   Thy saints have dwelt secure;
Sufficient is thine arm alone,
   And our defence is sure.

Before the hills in order stood,
   Or earth received her frame,   *10*
From everlasting thou art God,
   To endless years the same.

Thy word commands our flesh to dust,
   "Return, ye sons of men";
All nations rose from earth at first,   *15*
   And turn to earth again.

A thousand ages in thy sight
   Are like an evening gone;

Short as the watch that ends the night
   Before the rising sun.   *20*

The busy tribes of flesh and blood,
   With all their lives and cares,
Are carried downwards by thy flood,
   And lost in following years.

Time like an ever-rolling stream   *25*
   Bears all its sons away;
They fly forgotten, as a dream
   Dies at the opening day.

Like flow'ry fields the nations stand,
   Pleased with the morning light;   *30*
The flowers beneath the mower's hand
   Lie withering ere 'tis night.

Our God, our help in ages past,
   Our hope for years to come,
Be thou our guard while troubles last,   *35*
   And our eternal home.

               (1719)

MARY COLLIER
England, 1679-c.1762

from *THE WOMAN'S LABOUR: AN EPISTLE TO MR. STEPHEN DUCK; IN ANSWER TO HIS LATE POEM, CALLED "THE THRESHER'S LABOUR"*

Immortal Bard! thou fav'rite of the Nine!
Enriched by Peers, advanced by Caroline!
Deign to look down on one that's poor and low,
Rememb'ring you yourself was lately so;
Accept these lines: Alas! what can you have   *5*
From her, who ever was, and's still a slave?

No learning ever was bestowed on me;
My life was always spent in drudgery:
And not alone; alas! with grief I find,
It is the portion of poor woman-kind.   *10*
Oft have I thought as on my bed I lay,
Eased from the tiresome labours of the day,

MAN FRAIL, AND GOD ETERNAL From *The Psalms of David Imitated*; in this hymn, Watts imitates the first part of Psalm 90. **THE WOMAN'S LABOUR** See the excerpt from Duck's poem, p. 576. **1. Bard:** i.e., Duck himself; **the Nine:** the Muses. **2. Caroline:** Queen Caroline, who had favoured the "thresher-poet" with money, house, and position. **6. slave:** On the title page, after the title: "By Mary Collier, Now a Washer-woman, at Petersfield in Hampshire." The last part of the poem, over a hundred lines, details the washing and other "charring" labours done in others' homes.

Our first extraction from a mass refined,
Could never be for slavery designed;
Till time and custom by degrees destroyed   *15*
That happy state our sex at first enjoyed.
When men had used their utmost care and toil,
Their recompense was but a female smile;
When they by arts or arms were rendered great,
They laid their trophies at a woman's feet;   *20*
They, in those days, unto our sex did bring
Their hearts, their all, a free-will offering;
And as from us their being they derive,
They back again should all due homage give.

    Jove once descending from the clouds, did drop   *25*
In show'rs of gold on lovely Danae's lap;
The sweet-tongued poets, in those generous days,
Unto our shrine still offered up their lays:
But now, alas! that Golden Age is past,
We are the objects of your scorn at last.   *30*
And you, great Duck, upon whose happy brow
The muses seem to fix the garland now,
In your late poem boldly did declare
Alcides' labours can't with yours compare;
And of your annual task have much to say,   *35*
Of threshing, reaping, mowing corn and hay;
Boasting your daily toil, and nightly dream,
But can't conclude your never-dying theme,
And let our hapless sex in silence lie
Forgotten, and in dark oblivion die;   *40*
But on our abject state you throw your scorn,
And women wrong, your verses to adorn.
You of hay-making speak a word or two,
As if our sex but little work could do:
This makes the honest farmer smiling say,   *45*
He'll seek for women still to make his hay;
For if his back be turned, their work they mind
As well as men, as far as he can find.
For my own part, I many a summer's day
Have spent in throwing, turning, making hay;   *50*
But ne'er could see, what you have lately found,
Our wages paid for sitting on the ground.
'Tis true, that when our morning's work is done,
And all our grass exposed unto the Sun,
While that his scorching beams do on it shine,   *55*
As well as you, we have a time to dine:
I hope, that since we freely toil and sweat

To earn our bread, you'll give us time to eat.
That over, soon we must get up again,
And nimbly turn our hay upon the plain;   *60*
Nay, rake and prow it in, the case is clear;
Or how should cocks in equal rows appear?
But if you'd have what you have wrote believed,
I find, that you to hear us talk are grieved:
In this, I hope, you do not speak your mind,   *65*
For none but Turks, that ever I could find,
Have mutes to serve them, or did e'er deny
Their slaves, at work, to chat it merrily.
Since you have liberty to speak your mind,
And are to talk, as well as we, inclined,   *70*
Why should you thus repine, because that we,
Like you, enjoy that pleasing liberty?
What! would you lord it quite, and take away
The only privilege our sex enjoy?

    . . . .

    When harvest comes, into the field we go,   *75*
And help to reap the wheat as well as you;
Or else we go the ears of corn to glean;
No labour scorning, be it e'er so mean;
But in the work we freely bear a part,
And what we can, perform with all our heart.   *80*
To get a living we so willing are,
Our tender babes into the field we bear,
And wrap them in our clothes to keep them warm,
While round about we gather up the corn;
And often unto them our course do bend,   *85*
To keep them safe, that nothing them offend:
Our children that are able, bear a share
In gleaning corn, such is our frugal care.
When night comes on, unto our home we go,
Our corn we carry, and our infant too;   *90*
Weary, alas! but 'tis not worth our while
Once to complain, or *rest at ev'ry stile;*
We must make haste, for when we home are come,
Alas! we find our work but just begun;
So many things for our attendance call,   *95*
Had we ten hands, we could employ them all.
Our children put to bed, with greatest care
We all things for your coming home prepare:
You sup, and go to bed without delay,
And rest yourselves till the ensuing day;   *100*
While we, alas! but little sleep can have,

---

26. Danae: Perseus's mother, visited by Zeus in a shower of gold. **34. Alcides:** another name for Herakles, or Hercules. **92, 112, 122:** The italicized words repeat or directly refer to parts of Duck's poem.

Because our froward children cry and rave;
Yet, without fail, soon as daylight doth spring,
We in the field again our work begin,
And there, with all our strength, our toil renew,   *105*
Till Titan's golden rays have dried the dew;
Then home we go unto our children dear,
Dress, feed, and bring them to the field with care.
Were this your case, you justly might complain
That day nor night you are secure from pain;   *110*
Those mighty troubles which perplex your mind,
(*Thistles* before, and *females* come behind)
Would vanish soon, and quickly disappear,
Were you, like us, encumbered thus with care.
What you would have of us we do not know: *115*
We oft take up the corn that you do mow;

We cut the peas, and always ready are
In ev'ry work to take our proper share;
And from the time that harvest doth begin,
Until the corn be cut and carried in,   *120*
Our toil and labour's daily so extreme,
That we have hardly ever *time to dream.*
The harvest ended, respite none we find;
The hardest of our toil is still behind:
Hard labour we most cheerfully pursue,   *125*
And out, abroad, a-charring often go:
Of which I now will briefly tell in part,
What fully to declare is past my art;
So many hardships daily we go through,
I boldly say, the like *you* never knew.   *130*

. . . .

(1739)

ROBERT SAMBER
England, born c.1682, fl. 1716-1735

from *HISTORIES, OR TALES OF PAST TIMES*

LITTLE RED RIDING-HOOD
translated from "Le petit chaperon rouge," in *Histoires ou Contes du temps passé* (1697), by Charles Perrault (1628-1703)

There was once upon a time a little village girl, the prettiest little creature that ever was seen. Her mother was excessively fond of her, and her grandmother yet much more. This good woman caused to be made for her a little red riding-hood, which made her look so very pretty that everybody called her Little Red Riding-Hood.

One day her mother, having made some custards, said to her, "Go, my little Biddy"   *5*
(for her Christian name was Biddy), "go and see how your grandmother does, for I hear she has been very ill; carry her a custard and this little pot of butter." Little Red Riding-Hood set out immediately to go to her grandmother, who lived in another village. As she was going through the wood, she met with Mr. Wolf, who had a good mind to eat her up, but he did not dare, because of some faggot-makers that were in the forest.   *10*

He asked of her whither she was going. The poor child, who did not know how dangerous a thing it is to stop and listen to a wolf talk, said to him, "I am going to see my grandmamma, and carry her a custard pie and a little pot of butter my mamma sends her."

---

102. froward: obstinate. 106. Titan: The sun was so called by Roman poets.   LITTLE RED RIDING-HOOD   It is unknown whether Perrault composed this tale or merely collected and perhaps adapted it for his collection of tales. In any event, it has been immensely popular, and in some retellings has been given different — sometimes happy — endings. The version given here is close to the original.

"Does she live far off?" asked the Wolf.

"Oh, yes!" said Little Red Riding-Hood, "on the other side of the mill below   *15*
yonder, at the first house in the village."

"Well," said the Wolf, "and I'll go and see her too. I'll go this way and you go that,
and we shall see who will be there soonest."

The Wolf began to run as fast as he was able the shorter way, and the little girl went
the longer, diverting herself in gathering nuts, running after butterflies, and making   *20*
nosegays of all the little flowers she met with. It was not long before the Wolf came to
the grandmother's house; he knocked at the door, *tap tap.*

"Who's there?"

"Your granddaughter, Little Red Riding-Hood," said the Wolf, counterfeiting her
voice, "who has brought you a custard pie and a little pot of butter Mamma sends you."   *25*

The good grandmother, who was in bed because she found herself somewhat ill,
cried out, "Pull the bobbin, and the latch will go up." The Wolf pulled the bobbin, and
the door opened, upon which he fell upon the good woman and ate her up in the tenth
part of a moment, for he had eaten nothing for over three days. After that he shut the
door and got into the grandmother's bed, expecting Little Red Riding-Hood, who came   *30*
some time afterwards and knocked at the door, *tap tap.*

"Who's there?"

Little Red Riding-Hood, who hearing the big voice of the Wolf was at first afraid,
but believing her grandmother had got a cold and was grown hoarse, said, "It is your
granddaughter, Little Red Riding-Hood, who has brought you a custard pie and a little   *35*
pot of butter Mamma sends you."

The Wolf cried out to her, softening his voice as much as he could, "Pull the
bobbin, and the latch will go up." Little Red Riding-Hood pulled the bobbin, and the
door opened.

The Wolf, seeing her come in, said to her, hiding himself under the bed-clothes,   *40*
"Put the custard and the little pot of butter upon the stool and come into bed with me."

Little Red Riding-Hood undressed herself and got into bed, where she was very
much astonished to see how different her grandmother looked in her night-clothes. So
she said to her, "Grandmamma, what great arms you have got!"

"The better to embrace thee, my pretty child."   *45*

"Grandmamma, what great legs you have got!"

"To run the better, my child."

"Grandmamma, what great ears you have got!"

"To hear the better, my child."

"Grandmamma, what great eyes you have got!"   *50*

"To see the better, my child."

"Grandmamma, what great teeth you have got!"

"To eat thee up!"

And upon saying these words, this wicked Wolf fell upon Little Red Riding-Hood
and ate her up.   *55*

(1729)

EDWARD YOUNG

England, 1683-1765

from *THE COMPLAINT: OR, NIGHT THOUGHTS ON LIFE, DEATH, AND IMMORTALITY,*

Night the First

Tired Nature's sweet restorer, balmy Sleep!
He, like the world, his ready visit pays
Where Fortune smiles; the wretched he forsakes:
Swift on his downy pinion flies from woe,
And lights on lids unsullied with a tear.   5
   From short (as usual) and disturbed repose,
I wake: how happy they, who wake no more!
Yet that were vain, if dreams infest the grave.
I wake, emerging from a sea of dreams
Tumultuous; where my wrecked, desponding thought,
From wave to wave of fancied misery,   11
At random drove, her helm of reason lost.
Though now restored, 'tis only change of pain:
(A bitter change!) severer for severe.
The day too short for my distress, and Night,   15
Even in the zenith of her dark domain,
Is sunshine to the colour of my fate.
   Night, sable goddess! from her ebon throne,
In rayless majesty now stretches forth
Her leaden sceptre o'er a slumbering world.   20
Silence, how dead! and darkness, how profound!
Nor eye, nor listening ear, an object finds;
Creation sleeps. 'Tis as the general pulse
Of life stood still, and Nature made a pause;
An awful pause! prophetic of her end.   25
And let her prophecy be soon fulfilled;
Fate! drop the curtain; I can lose no more.
   Silence and Darkness! solemn sisters! twins
From ancient Night, who nurse the tender thought
To reason, and on reason build resolve   30
(That column of true majesty in man),
Assist me: I will thank you in the grave;
The grave, your kingdom. There this frame shall fall
A victim sacred to your dreary shrine.
But what are ye?—
        Thou, who didst put to flight   35
Primeval Silence, when the morning stars,

Exulting, shouted o'er the rising ball;
O Thou, whose word from solid darkness struck
That spark, the sun; strike wisdom from my soul;
My soul, which flies to Thee, her trust, her treasure,   40
As misers to their gold, while others rest.
   Through this opaque of nature, and of soul,
This double night, transmit one pitying ray,
To lighten and to cheer. Oh lead my mind
(A mind that fain would wander from its woe),   45
Lead it through various scenes of life and death;
And from each scene the noblest truths inspire.
Nor less inspire my conduct than my song:
Teach my best reason, reason; my best will
Teach rectitude; and fix my firm resolve   50
Wisdom to wed, and pay her long arrear:
Nor let the phial of thy vengeance, poured
On this devoted head, be poured in vain.
   The bell strikes one. We take no note of time
But from its loss. To give it then a tongue   55
Is wise in man. As if an angel spoke,
I feel the solemn sound. If heard aright,
It is the knell of my departed hours:
Where are they? With the years beyond the flood.
It is the signal that demands dispatch: 60
How much is to be done? My hopes and fears
Start up alarmed, and o'er life's narrow verge
Look down — on what? A fathomless abyss;
A dread eternity! how surely mine!
And can eternity belong to me,   65
Poor pensioner on the bounties of an hour?
   How poor, how rich, how abject, how august,
How complicate, how wonderful is man!
How passing wonder He who made him such!
Who centred in our make such strange extremes!   70
From different natures marvelously mixed,
Connection exquisite of distant worlds!
Distinguished link in being's endless chain!

THE COMPLAINT: OR, NIGHT THOUGHTS   53. **devoted:** doomed.

Midway from nothing to the Deity!
A beam ethereal, sullied and absorbed!   75
Though sullied and dishonoured, still divine!
Dim miniature of greatness absolute!
An heir of glory! a frail child of dust!
Helpless immortal! insect infinite!
A worm! a god! — I tremble at myself,   80
And in myself am lost! At home a stranger,
Thought wanders up and down, surprised, aghast,
And wondering at her own: how reason reels!
Oh what a miracle to man is man,
Triumphantly distressed! what joy, what dread!   85
Alternately transported, and alarmed!
What can preserve my life? or what destroy?
An angel's arm can't snatch me from the grave;
Legions of angels can't confine me there.
    'Tis past conjecture; all things rise in proof.   90
While o'er my limbs sleep's soft dominion spread,
What though my soul fantastic measures trod
O'er fairy fields; or mourned along the gloom
Of pathless woods; or down the craggy steep
Hurled headlong, swam with pain the mantled pool; 95
Or scaled the cliff; or danced on hollow winds,
With antic shapes, wild natives of the brain?
Her ceaseless flight, though devious, speaks her nature
Of subtler essence than the trodden clod;
Active, aerial, towering, unconfined,   100
Unfettered with her gross companion's fall.
Even silent night proclaims my soul immortal:
Even silent night proclaims eternal day.
For human weal, Heaven husbands all events;
Dull sleep instructs, nor sport vain dreams in vain. 105
    Why then their loss deplore, that are not lost?
Why wanders wretched thought their tombs around,
In infidel distress? Are angels there?
Slumbers, raked up in dust, ethereal fire?
They live! they greatly live a life on earth   110
Unkindled, unconceived; and from an eye
Of tenderness let heavenly pity fall
On me, more justly numbered with the dead.
This is the desert, this the solitude:
How populous, how vital, is the grave!   115
This is creation's melancholy vault,
The vale funereal, the sad cypress gloom;

The land of apparitions, empty shades!
All, all on earth is shadow; all beyond
Is substance; the reverse is Folly's creed: 120
How solid all, where change shall be no more!
    This is the bud of being, the dim dawn,
The twilight of our day, the vestibule;
Life's theatre as yet is shut, and Death,
Strong Death alone, can heave the massy bar,   125
This gross impediment of clay remove,
And make us, embryos of existence, free.
From real life, but little more remote
Is he, not yet a candidate for light,
The future embryo slumbering in his sire.   130
Embryos we must be, till we burst the shell,
Yon ambient azure shell, and spring to life,
The life of gods, oh transport! and of man.
    Yet man, fool man! here buries all his thoughts;
Inters celestial hopes without one sigh.   135
Prisoner of earth, and pent beneath the moon,
Here pinions all his wishes; winged by Heaven
To fly at infinite, and reach it there,
Where seraphs gather immortality,
On life's fair tree, fast by the throne of God.   140
What golden joys ambrosial clustering glow
In His full beam, and ripen for the just,
Where momentary ages are no more!
Where time, and pain, and chance, and death expire!
And is it in the flight of threescore years   145
To push eternity from human thought,
And smother souls immortal in the dust?
A soul immortal, spending all her fires,
Wasting her strength in strenuous idleness,
Thrown into tumult, raptured, or alarmed,   150
At aught this scene can threaten or indulge,
Resembles ocean into tempest wrought,
To waft a feather, or to drown a fly.
    Where falls this censure? It o'erwhelms myself:
How was my heart incrusted by the world!   155
Oh how self-fettered was my grovelling soul!
How, like a worm, was I wrapped round and round
In silken thought, which reptile Fancy spun,
Till darkened Reason lay quite clouded o'er
With soft conceit of endless comfort here,   160
Nor yet put forth her wings to reach the skies!

73-74: For other references to "the Great Chain of Being," see Pope's *Essay on Man*, I, 33-34 (p. 542), 237ff. (p. 545).

Night visions may befriend (as sung above):
Our waking dreams are fatal. How I dreamt
Of things impossible! (Could sleep do more?)
Of joys perpetual in perpetual change!   165
Of stable pleasures on the tossing wave!
Eternal sunshine in the storms of life!
How richly were my noon-tide trances hung
With gorgeous tapestries of pictured joys!
Joy behind joy, in endless perspective!   170
Till at Death's toll, whose restless iron tongue
Calls daily for his millions at a meal,
Starting I woke, and found myself undone.
Where now my frenzy's pompous furniture?
The cobwebbed cottage, with its ragged wall   175
Of mouldering mud, is royalty to me!
The spider's most attenuated thread
Is cord, is cable, to man's tender tie
On earthly bliss; it breaks at every breeze.
     Oh, ye blest scenes of permanent delight!   180
Full, above measure! lasting, beyond bound!
A perpetuity of bliss, is bliss.
Could you, so rich in rapture, fear an end,
That ghastly thought would drink up all your joy,
And quite unparadise the realms of light.   185
Safe are you lodged above these rolling spheres,
The baleful influence of whose giddy dance
Sheds sad vicissitude on all beneath.
Here teems with revolutions every hour,
And rarely for the better; or the best,   190
More mortal than the common births of Fate.
Each Moment has its sickle, emulous
Of Time's enormous scythe, whose ample sweep
Strikes empires from the root; each Moment plays
His little weapon in the narrower sphere   195
Of sweet domestic comfort, and cuts down
The fairest bloom of sublunary bliss.
     Bliss! sublunary bliss! — proud words, and vain!
Implicit treason to divine decree!
A bold invasion of the rights of Heaven!   200
I clasped the phantoms, and I found them air.
Oh had I weighed it ere my fond embrace!
What darts of agony had missed my heart!
     Death! great proprietor of all! 'tis thine
To tread out empire, and to quench the stars: 205
The sun himself by thy permission shines;
And, one day, thou shalt pluck him from his sphere.

Amid such mighty plunder, why exhaust
Thy partial quiver on a mark so mean?
Why thy peculiar rancour wreaked on me?   210
Insatiate archer! could not one suffice?
Thy shaft flew thrice; and thrice my peace was slain;
And thrice, ere thrice yon moon had filled her horn.
O Cynthia! why so pale! Dost thou lament
Thy wretched neighbour? grieve to see thy wheel   215
Of ceaseless change outwhirled in human life?
How wanes my borrowed bliss! From Fortune's smile,
Precarious courtesy! not virtue's sure,
Self-given, solar ray of sound delight.
     In every varied posture, place, and hour,   220
How widowed every thought of every joy!
Thought, busy thought! too busy for my peace!
Through the dark postern of time long elapsed,
Led softly, by the stillness of the night,
Led like a murderer (and such it proves!),   225
Strays (wretched rover!) o'er the pleasing past;
In quest of wretchedness perversely strays;
And finds all desert now; and meets the ghosts
Of my departed joys, a numerous train!
I rue the riches of my former fate;   230
Sweet comfort's blasted clusters I lament;
I tremble at the blessings once so dear;
And every pleasure pains me to the heart.
     Yet why complain? or why complain for one?
Hangs out the sun his lustre but for me,   235
The single man? Are angels all beside?
I mourn for millions: 'tis the common lot;
In this shape, or in that, has fate entailed
The mother's throes on all of woman born,
Not more the children, than sure heirs, of pain.   240
     War, famine, pest, volcano, storm, and fire,
Intestine broils, Oppression, with her heart
Wrapped up in triple brass, besiege mankind.
God's image, disinherited of day,
Here, plunged in mines, forgets a sun was made.   245
There, beings deathless as their haughty lord
Are hammered to the galling oar for life,
And plough the winter's wave, and reap despair.
Some, for hard masters, broken under arms,
In battle lopped away, with half their limbs,   250
Beg bitter bread through realms their valour saved,
If so the tyrant, or his minion, doom.
Want and incurable Disease (fell pair!)

211-13: The immediate occasion for the poem was the death of Young's wife in 1741, preceded in 1736 and 1740 by the deaths of her daughter ("Narcissa" in the poem) and son-in-law from her first marriage. **214. Cynthia:** the moon.

On hopeless multitudes remorseless seize
At once, and make a refuge of the grave.   255
How groaning hospitals eject their dead!
What numbers groan for sad admission there!
What numbers, once in Fortune's lap high-fed,
Solicit the cold hand of Charity!
To shock us more, solicit it in vain!   260
Ye silken sons of pleasure! since in pains
You rue more modish visits, visit here,
And breathe from your debauch: give, and reduce
Surfeit's dominion o'er you. But so great
Your impudence, you blush at what is right.   265
    Happy! did sorrow seize on such alone.
Not prudence can defend, or virtue save;
Disease invades the chastest temperance;
And punishment the guiltless; and alarm,
Through thickest shades, pursues the fond of peace.
Man's caution often into danger turns,   271
And, his guard falling, crushes him to death.
Not Happiness itself makes good her name!
Our very wishes give us not our wish.
How distant oft the thing we dote on most,   275
From that for which we dote, felicity!
The smoothest course of nature has its pains;
And truest friends, through error, wound our rest.
Without misfortune, what calamities!
And what hostilities, without a foe!   280
Nor are foes wanting to the best on earth.
But endless is the list of human ills,
And sighs might sooner fail, than cause to sigh.
    A part how small of the terraqueous globe
Is tenanted by man! the rest a waste,   285
Rocks, deserts, frozen seas, and burning sands;
Wild haunts of monsters, poisons, stings, and death.

Such is earth's melancholy map! But, far
More sad! this earth is a true map of man.
So bounded are its haughty lord's delights   290
To woe's wide empire, where deep troubles toss,
Loud sorrows howl, envenomed passions bite,
Ravenous calamities our vitals seize,
And threatening Fate wide opens to devour.
    What then am I, who sorrow for myself?   295
In age, in infancy, from others' aid
Is all our hope; to teach us to be kind.
That, Nature's first, last lesson to mankind:
The selfish heart deserves the pain it feels;
More generous sorrow, while it sinks, exalts;   300
And conscious virtue mitigates the pang.
Nor virtue, more than prudence, bids me give
Swoll'n thought a second channel; who divide,
They weaken too, the torrent of their grief.
Take then, O World! thy much indebted tear: 305
How sad a sight is human happiness
To those whose thought can pierce beyond an hour!
O thou! whate'er thou art, whose heart exults!
Wouldst thou I should congratulate thy fate?
I know thou wouldst; thy pride demands it from me.
Let thy pride pardon what thy nature needs,   311
The salutary censure of a friend.
Thou happy wretch! by blindness thou art blest;
By dotage dandled to perpetual smiles.
Know, smiler! at thy peril art thou pleased;   315
Thy pleasure is the promise of thy pain.
Misfortune, like a creditor severe,
But rises in demand for her delay;
She makes a scourge of past prosperity
To sting thee more, and double thy distress.   320

        . . . .

                                    (1742-45)

JOHN GAY
England, 1685-1732

THE BIRTH OF THE SQUIRE. AN ECLOGUE
In Imitation of the *Pollio* of Virgil

    Ye sylvan Muses, loftier strains recite;
Not all in shades and humble cots delight.
Hark! the bells ring; along the distant grounds

The driving gales convey the swelling sounds;
Th' attentive swain, forgetful of his work,   5
With gaping wonder leans upon his fork.

---

256. hospitals: charitable institutions for the aged and infirm.   **THE BIRTH OF THE SQUIRE**   For a translation of Virgil's *Pollio,* see p. 438.

What sudden news alarms the waking morn?
To the glad Squire a hopeful heir is born.
Mourn, mourn, ye stags, and all ye beasts of chase,
This hour destruction brings on all your race: *10*
See the pleased tenants duteous off'rings bear,
Turkeys and geese and grocer's sweetest ware;
With the new health the pond'rous tankard flows,
And old October reddens ev'ry nose.
Beagles and spaniels round his cradle stand,   *15*
Kiss his moist lip and gently lick his hand;
He joys to hear the shrill horn's echoing sounds,
And learns to lisp the names of all the hounds.
With frothy ale to make his cup o'erflow,
Barley shall in paternal acres grow;   *20*
The bee shall sip the fragrant dew from flow'rs,
To give metheglin for his morning hours;
For him the clust'ring hop shall climb the poles,
And his own orchard sparkle in his bowls.
His sire's exploits he now with wonder hears,   *25*
The monstrous tales indulge his greedy ears;
How when youth strung his nerves and warmed his veins,
He rode the mighty Nimrod of the plains:
He leads the staring infant through the hall,
Points out the horny spoils that grace the wall;   *30*
Tells, how this stag through three whole counties fled,
What rivers swam, where bayed, and where he bled.
Now he the wonders of the fox repeats,
Describes the desp'rate chase, and all his cheats;
How in one day beneath his furious speed,   *35*
He tired seven coursers of the fleetest breed;
How high the pale he leaped, how wide the ditch,
When the hound tore the haunches of the witch!
These stories which descend from son to son,
The forward boy shall one day make his own.   *40*
Ah, too fond mother, think the time draws nigh,
That calls the darling from thy tender eye;
How shall his spirit brook the rigid rules,
And the long tyranny of grammar schools?
Let younger brothers o'er dull authors plod,   *45*
Lashed into Latin by the tingling rod;
No, let him never feel that smart disgrace:
Why should he wiser prove than all his race?
When rip'ning youth with down o'ershades his chin,

And ev'ry female eye incites to sin,   *50*
The milk-maid (thoughtless of her future shame)
With smacking lip shall raise his guilty flame;
The dairy, barn, the hayloft and the grove
Shall oft be conscious of their stolen love.
But think, Priscilla, on that dreadful time   *55*
When pangs and wat'ry qualms shall own thy crime;
How wilt thou tremble, when thy nipple's pressed,
To see the white drops bathe thy swelling breast!
Nine moons shall publicly divulge thy shame,
And the young Squire forestall a father's name.   *60*
When twice twelve times the reaper's sweeping hand
With levelled harvest has bestrown the land,
On famed St. Hubert's feast, his winding horn
Shall cheer the joyful hound and wake the morn:
This memorable day his eager speed   *65*
Shall urge with bloody heel the rising steed.
O check the foamy bit, nor tempt thy fate,
Think on the murders of a five-bar gate!
Yet prodigal of life, the leap he tries,
Low in the dust his grovelling honour lies,   *70*
Headlong he falls, and on the rugged stone
Distorts his neck, and cracks the collar-bone;
O vent'rous youth, thy thirst of game allay,
May'st thou survive the perils of this day!
He shall survive; and in late years be sent   *75*
To snore away debates in Parliament.
The time shall come when his more solid sense
With nod important shall the laws dispense;
A Justice with grave Justices shall sit,
He praise their wisdom, they admire his wit.   *80*
No greyhound shall attend the tenant's pace,
No rusty gun the farmer's chimney grace;
Salmons shall leave their covers void of fear,
Nor dread the thievish net or triple spear;
Poachers shall tremble at his awful name,   *85*
Whom vengeance now o'ertakes for murdered game.
Assist me, Bacchus, and ye drunken Powers,
To sing his friendships and his midnight hours!
Why dost thou glory in thy strength of beer,
Firm-corked, and mellowed till the twentieth year;   *90*
Brewed or when Phoebus warms the fleecy sign,
Or when his languid rays in Scorpio shine?

---

13. new health: i.e., toasts to the newborn. **14. old October:** popular name for a kind of ale or cider. **22. metheglin:** mead, usually spiced. **27. nerves:** muscles. **28. Nimrod:** hunter (see Genesis 10:8-9). **38:** "The most common accident to sportsmen: to hunt a witch in the shape of a hare" (Gay's note). **56. own:** acknowledge, confess — i.e., reveal. **60. forestall:** anticipate — i.e., be beforehand with. **63. St. Hubert:** patron saint of hunters, said to have been reformed while hunting on Good Friday by seeing a crucifix between a stag's antlers; feast day, November 3. **84. triple spear:** trident. **91. or:** either; **Phoebus:** the sun; **fleecy sign:** Aries, the Ram, first sign of the zodiac (i.e., in the spring). **92. Scorpio:** eighth sign of the zodiac (i.e., in the fall).

Think on the mischiefs which from hence have sprung!
It arms with curses dire the wrathful tongue;
Foul scandal to the lying lip affords,   95
And prompts the mem'ry with injurious words.
O where is wisdom, when by this o'erpowered?
The state is censured, and the maid deflowered!
And wilt thou still, O Squire, brew ale so strong?
Hear then the dictates of prophetic song.   100
    Methinks I see him in his hall appear,
Where the long table floats in clammy beer,
'Midst mugs and glasses shattered o'er the floor,
Dead-drunk his servile crew supinely snore;
Triumphant, o'er the prostrate brutes he stands,   105
The mighty bumper trembles in his hands;
Boldly he drinks and, like his glorious sires,
In copious gulps of potent ale expires.

                                                    (1720)

MY OWN EPITAPH

Life is a jest; and all things show it,
I thought so once; but now I know it.

                                                    (1720)

from *THE FABLES*

Fable IV: The Eagle and the Assembly of Animals

As Jupiter's all-seeing eye
Surveyed the worlds beneath the sky,
From this small speck of earth were sent
Murmurs and sounds of discontent;
For ev'ry thing alive complained   5
That he the hardest life sustained.
Jove calls his Eagle. At the word
Before him stands the royal bird.
The bird, obedient, from Heaven's height,
Downward directs his rapid flight;   10
Then cited ev'ry living thing
To hear the mandates of his king.
"Ungrateful creatures! Whence arise
These murmurs which offend the skies?
Why this disorder? Say the cause;   15

For just are Jove's eternal laws.
Let each his discontent reveal:
To yon sour Dog I first appeal."
    "Hard is my lot," the Hound replies;
"On what fleet nerves the Greyhound flies,   20
While I, with weary step and slow,
O'er plains, and vales, and mountains go.
The morning sees my chase begun,
Nor ends it till the setting sun."
    "When," says the Greyhound, "I pursue,   25
My game is lost, or caught in view;
Beyond my sight the prey's secure;
The Hound is slow, but always sure.
And had I his sagacious scent,
Jove ne'er had heard my discontent."   30
    The Lion craved the Fox's art;
The Fox, the Lion's force and heart.
The Cock implored the Pigeon's flight,
Whose wings were rapid, strong, and light;
The Pigeon strength of wing despised,   35
And the Cock's matchless valour prized.
The Fishes wished to graze the plain;
The Beasts to skim beneath the main.
Thus, envious of another's state,
Each blamed the partial hand of Fate.   40
    The Bird of Heav'n then cried aloud,
"Jove bids disperse the murmuring crowd;
The God rejects your idle prayers.
Would ye, rebellious mutineers,
Entirely change your name and nature,   45
And be the very envied creature?
What, silent all, and none consent?
Be happy, then, and learn content;
Nor imitate the restless mind
And proud ambition of mankind."   50

                                                    (1727)

Fable XLIX: The Man and the Flea

Whether on earth, in air, or main,
Sure ev'ry thing alive is vain!
    Does not the hawk all fowls survey
As destined only for his prey?
And do not tyrants, prouder things,   5
Think men were born for slaves to kings?
    When the crab views the pearly strands,

FABLE IV   29. sagacious: keen-scented, skilled at following a trail.   FABLE XLIX   7. pearly strands: oyster beds.

Or Tagus, bright with golden sands;
Or crawls beside the coral grove,
And hears the ocean roll above;   10
"Nature is too profuse," says he,
"Who gave all these to pleasure me!"
   When bord'ring pinks and roses bloom,
And ev'ry garden breathes perfume;
When peaches glow with sunny dyes,   15
Like Laura's cheek when blushes rise;
When the huge figs the branches bend;
When clusters from the vine depend;
The snail looks round on flower and tree,
And cries, "All these were made for me!"   20
   "What dignity's in human nature!"
Says Man, the most conceited creature,
As from a cliff he cast his eye,
And viewed the sea and arched sky.
The sun was sunk beneath the main;   25
The moon and all the starry train
Hung the vast vault of Heav'n. The Man

His contemplation thus began:
   "When I behold this glorious show,
And the wide wat'ry world below,   30
The scaly people of the main,
The beasts that range the wood or plain,
The winged inhabitants of air,
The day, the night, the various year,
And know all these by Heav'n designed   35
As gifts to pleasure human-kind,
I cannot raise my worth too high;
Of what vast consequence am I!"
   "Not of th' importance you suppose,"
Replies a Flea upon his nose: 40
"Be humble, learn thyself to scan;
Know, pride was never made for Man.
'Tis vanity that swells thy mind.
What, Heav'n and Earth for thee designed!
For thee! made only for our need,   45
That more important Fleas might feed."

                                       (1727)

WOODES ROGERS
England, d. 1732

from *A CRUISING VOYAGE ROUND THE WORLD*

Jan. 22 [1709].   Fair weather, with fresh gales of wind from W by S. to the WNW. Last night George Cross died; he was a smith by trade, and armourer's mate. We and the *Dutchess* have had a great many men down with the cold, and some with the scurvy, the distemper that this man died of. The *Dutchess* had always more sick men than we, and have so now; they buried but one man that died of sickness, and tell us they hope the 5 rest will recover. We have but one man whose life we doubt of, tho most want a harbour. This day Capt. Courtney and Capt. Cooke dined with us. At two a clock we saw the land on the coast of Patagonia, being very high, distant about 14 Ls. Lat. 44.9.S.

---

8. Tagus: river in Spain and Portugal, supposedly rich in gold-dust; Gay echoes a line in "Ode on the King's Birthday" (1718), by Nicholas Rowe (1674-1718): "And Tagus bright in sands of gold." **16. Laura:** probably not referring to any particular woman, though the name inevitably evokes thoughts of Petrarch's beloved Laura, whether a real woman or an idealized romantic fiction.   **A CRUISING VOYAGE** The subtitle reads *First to the South-Seas, thence to the East-Indies, and homewards by the Cape of Good Hope.* Rogers was commander-in-chief of the 1708-11 expedition of the ships *Duke* and *Dutchess,* privateers financed by merchants in Bristol. **7. Capt. Courtney and Capt. Cooke:** Stephen Courtney, Captain of the *Dutchess,* and Edward Cooke, 2nd Captain of the *Dutchess* and author of *A Voyage to the South Sea* (1712). **8. Ls.:** leagues; a league varied in length, but is approximately three miles.

Jan. 26.   Fresh gales with clouds and rain. We spoke with our consort this day, who complains their men grow worse and worse, and want a harbour to refresh 'em; several of ours are also very indifferent, and if we don't get ashore, and a small refreshment, we doubt we shall both lose several men. We are very uncertain of the latitude and longitude of Juan Fernandez, the books laying 'em down so differently, that not one chart agrees with another; and being but a small island, we are in some doubts of striking it, so design to hale in for the mainland to direct us.

Jan. 27.   Fair weather, smooth water, pleasant gales of wind, veerable from the W. to the NW., had a good amplitude, found the variation to be 10 deg. eastward. This is an excellent climate. Lat. 36.36.S.

Jan. 28.   We have had moderate weather. At six a clock we saw the land, the eastermost appearing like an island, which we agree to be the island of St. Mary on the Coast of Chile: it bore E by N. dist. 9 or 10 Ls. Our consort's men are very ill; their want of clothes, and being often wet in the cold weather, has been the greatest cause of their being more sick than our ship's company.

Jan. 31.   These 24 hours we had the wind between the S. and SW by W. At seven this morning we made the island of Juan Fernandez; it bore WSW. dist. about 7 Ls. at noon W by S. 6 Ls. We had a good Observ. Lat. 34.10.S.

February 1.   About two yesterday in the afternoon we hoisted our pinnace out; Capt. Dover with the boat's crew went in her to go ashore tho we could not be less than 4 Ls. off. As soon as the pinnace was gone, I went on board the *Dutchess,* who admired our boat attempted going ashore at that distance from land; 'twas against my inclination, but to oblige Capt. Dover I consented to let her go. As soon as it was dark, we saw a light ashore; our boat was then about a league from the island, and bore away for the ships as soon as she saw the lights. We put out lights abroad for the boat, tho some were of opinion the lights we saw were our boat's lights; but as night came on, it appeared too large for that. We fired one quarterdeck gun and several muskets, showing lights in our mizzen and fore-shrouds, that our boat might find us, whilst we plied in the lee of the island. About two in the morning our boat came on board, having been two hours on board the *Dutchess,* that took 'em up astern of us. We were glad they got well off, because it begun to blow. We are all convinced the light is on the shore, and design to make our ships ready to engage, believing them to be French ships at anchor, and we must either fight 'em or want water, etc.

Febr. 2.   We stood on the back side along the south end of the island, in order to lay in with the first southerly wind, which Capt. Dampier told us generally blows there all day long. In the morning, being past the island, we tacked to lay in close aboard the land; and about ten a clock opened the south end of the island, and ran close aboard the land that begins to make the northeast side. The flaws came heavy off shore, and we were forced to reef our topsails when we opened the middle bay, where we expected to

---

9. consort: a vessel sailing with another. **12. doubt:** fear. **15. hale:** sail. **28. Capt. Dover:** Thomas Dover (1660-1742), 2nd Captain of the *Duke* and chief medical officer. **29. admired:** marvelled that. **39. begun:** had begun. **40. French:** Since 1701, the British, Prussians, Austrians, and Dutch had been at war with the French and Spanish; the War of the Spanish Succession was not concluded till the Treaty of Utrecht in 1713. **43. Capt. Dampier:** William Dampier (1652-1715), master of the *Duke* and pilot of this expedition, had been captain of a previous voyage to the East and West Indies, South America, and Australia. **45. opened:** came in sight of. **46. flaws:** intense gusts of wind, squalls.

find our enemy, but saw all clear, and no ships in that nor the other bay next the NW. end. These two bays are all that ships ride in which recruit on this island, but the middle bay is by much the best. We guessed there had been ships there, but that they were gone   50 on sight of us. We sent our yall ashore about noon, with Capt. Dover, Mr. Frye, and six men, all armed; meanwhile we and the *Dutchess* kept turning to get in, and such heavy flaws came off the land, that we were forced to let fly our topsail-sheet, keeping all hands to stand by our sails, for fear of the wind's carrying 'em away; but when the flaws were gone, we had little or no wind. These flaws proceeded from the land, which is very   55 high in the middle of the island. Our boat did not return, so we sent our pinnace with the men armed, to see what was the occasion of the yall's stay; for we were afraid that the Spaniards had a garrison there, and might have seized 'em. We put out a signal for our boat, and the *Dutchess* showed a French ensign. Immediately our pinnace returned from the shore, and brought abundance of crawfish, with a man clothed in goatskins, who   60 looked wilder than the first owners of them. He had been on the island four years and four months, being left there by Capt. Stradling in the *Cinque-Ports;* his name was Alexander Selkirk, a Scotchman, who had been Master of the *Cinque-Ports,* a ship that came here last with Capt. Dampier, who told me that this was the best man in her; so I immediately agreed with him to be a mate on board our ship. 'Twas he that made the   65 fire last night when he saw our ships, which he judged to be English. During his stay here, he saw several ships pass by, but only two came in to anchor. As he went to view them, he found 'em to be Spaniards, and retired from 'em; upon which they shot at him. Had they been French, he would have submitted; but chose to risk his dying alone on the island rather than fall into the hands of the Spaniards in these parts, because he   70 apprehended they would murder him, or make a slave of him in the mines, for he feared they would spare no stranger that might be capable of discovering the South Sea. The Spaniards had landed before he knew what they were, and they came so near him that he had much ado to escape; for they not only shot at him, but pursued him into the woods, where he climbed to the top of a tree, at the foot of which they made water, and killed   75 several goats just by, but went off again without discovering him. He told us that he was born at Largo in the County of Fife in Scotland, and was bred a sailor from his youth. The reason of his being left here was a difference betwixt him and his Captain; which, together with the ships being leaky, made him willing rather to stay here than go along with him at first; and when he was at last willing, the Captain would not receive him. He   80 had been in the island before to wood and water, when two of the ship's company were left upon it for six months till the ship returned, being chased thence by two French South-Sea ships.

He had with him his clothes and bedding, with a firelock, some powder, bullets, and tobacco, a hatchet, a knife, a kettle, a Bible, some practical pieces, and his mathematical   85

---

49. recruit: replenish. **51. yall:** yawl; a shore boat for the larger vessel, smaller than the pinnace or schooner; **Mr. Frye:** Robert Frye, chief lieutenant of the *Duke.* **63. Selkirk:** Alexander Selkirk (1676-1721) had asked to be put ashore on Juan Fernandez Island after a quarrel with his captain during Dampier's voyage of 1703-04. See Dampier's *A Voyage to New Holland* (1703-09). Rogers' rediscovery of Selkirk gave Daniel Defoe (see p. 468) the idea for *Robinson Crusoe* (1719); see also Cowley's verses (p. 653). Selkirk's story is also said to have influenced Coleridge when he wrote *The Rime of the Ancient Mariner* (p. 784). The two main islands of the Juan Fernandez Island group, off the coast of Chile, are now called Isla Alejandro Selkirk and Isla Robinson Crusoe. **80. at last willing:** i.e. to sail with Stradling.

instruments and books. He diverted and provided for himself as well as he could; but for the first eight months had much ado to bear up against melancholy, and the terror of being left alone in such a desolate place. He built two huts with piemento trees, covered them with long grass, and lined them with the skins of goats, which he killed with his gun as he wanted, so long as his powder lasted, which was but a pound; and that being *90* near spent, he got fire by rubbing two sticks of piemento wood together upon his knee. In the lesser hut, at some distance from the other, he dressed his victuals, and in the larger he slept, and employed himself in reading, singing psalms, and praying; so that he said he was a better Christian while in this solitude than ever he was before, or than, he was afraid, he should ever be again. At first he never eat anything till hunger con- *95* strained him, partly for grief, and partly for want of bread and salt; nor did he go to bed till he could watch no longer. The piemento wood, which burnt very clear, served him both for firing and candle, and refreshed him with its fragrant smell.

He might have had fish enough, but could not eat 'em for want of salt, because they occasioned a looseness; except crawfish, which are there as large as our lobsters, and *100* very good. These he sometimes boiled, and at other times broiled, as he did his goats' flesh, of which he made very good broth, for they are not so rank as ours; he kept an account of 500 that he killed while there, and caught as many more, which he marked on the ear and let go. When his powder failed, he took them by speed of foot; for his way of living and continual exercise of walking and running, cleared him of all gross *105* humours, so that he ran with wonderful swiftness thro the woods and up the rocks and hills, as we perceived when we employed him to catch goats for us. We had a bulldog, which we sent with several of our nimblest runners, to help him in catching goats; but he distanced and tired both the dog and the men, catched the goats, and brought 'em to us on his back. He told us that his agility in pursuing a goat had once like to have cost *110* him his life; he pursued it with so much eagerness that he catched hold of it on the brink of a precipice, of which he was not aware, the bushes having hid it from him; so that he fell with the goat down the said precipice a great height, and was so stunned and bruised with the fall, that he narrowly escaped with his life, and when he came to his senses, found the goat dead under him. He lay there about 24 hours, and was scarce able to *115* crawl to his hut, which was about a mile distant, or to stir abroad again in ten days.

He came at last to relish his meat well enough without salt or bread, and in the season had plenty of good turnips, which had been sowed there by Capt. Dampier's men, and have now overspread some acres of ground. He had enough of good cabbage from the cabbage-trees, and seasoned his meat with the fruit of the piemento trees, *120* which is the same as the Jamaica pepper, and smells deliciously. He found there also a black pepper called *malagita,* which was very good to expel wind, and against griping of the guts.

He soon wore out all his shoes and clothes by running thro the woods; and at last being forced to shift without them, his feet became so hard that he run everywhere *125* without annoyance; and it was some time before he could wear shoes after we found him; for not being used to any so long, his feet swelled when he came first to wear 'em again.

---

88. piemento: pimento or pimiento, a pepper tree. **95. eat:** ate. **119. cabbage:** the leafbuds from the cabbage palm.

After he had conquered his melancholy, he diverted himself sometimes by cutting his name on the trees, and the time of his being left and continuance there. He was at first much pestered with cats and rats, that had bred in great numbers from some of each species which had got ashore from ships that put in there to wood and water. The rats gnawed his feet and clothes while asleep, which obliged him to cherish the cats with his goats' flesh; by which many of them became so tame that they would lie about him in hundreds, and soon delivered him from the rats. He likewise tamed some kids, and to divert himself would now and then sing and dance with them and his cats; so that by the care of Providence and vigour of his youth, being now but about 30 years old, he came at last to conquer all the inconveniences of his solitude, and to be very easy. When his clothes wore out, he made himself a coat and cap of goat skins, which he stitched together with little thongs of the same, that he cut with his knife. He had no other needle but a nail; and when his knife was wore to the back, he made others as well as he could of some iron hoops that were left ashore, which he beat thin and ground upon stones. Having some linen cloth by him, he sewed himself shirts with a nail, and stitched 'em with the worsted of his old stockings, which he pulled out on purpose. He had his last shirt on when we found him in the island.

At his first coming on board us, he had so much forgot his language for want of use, that we could scarce understand him, for he seemed to speak his words by halves. We offered him a dram, but he would not touch it, having drank nothing but water since his being there, and 'twas some time before he could relish our victuals.

He could give us an account of no other product of the island than what we have mentioned, except small black plums, which are very good, but hard to come at, the trees which bear 'em growing on high mountains and rocks. Piemento trees are plenty here, and we saw some of 60 foot high, and about two yards thick; and cotton trees higher, and near four fathom round in the stock.

The climate is so good that the trees and grass are verdant all the year. The winter lasts no longer than June and July, and is not then severe, there being only a small frost and a little hail, but sometimes great rains. The heat of the summer is equally moderate, and there's not much thunder or tempestuous weather of any sort. He saw no venomous or savage creature on the island, nor any other sort of beast but goats, etc. as above-mentioned; the first of which had been put ashore here on purpose for a breed, by Juan Fernando, a Spaniard, who settled there with some families for a time, till the continent of Chile began to submit to the Spaniards; which being more profitable, tempted them to quit this island, which is capable of maintaining a good number of people, and of being made so strong that they could not be easily dislodged.

Ringrose in his account of Capt. Sharp's voyage and other buccaneers, mentions one who had escaped ashore here out of a ship which was cast away with all the rest of the company, and says he lived five years alone before he had the opportunity of another ship to carry him off. Capt. Dampier talks of a Moskito Indian that belonged to Capt.

132. **cherish:** i.e. make pets of the cats by feeding them. 143. **pulled out:** unravelled. 152. **cotton trees:** the bombax, or silk-cotton tree, whose seeds are surrounded by a silky fibre. 153. **fathom:** the length covered by one's outstretched arms, i.e. approximately six feet. 160. **continent:** mainland. 164. **Ringrose:** the West Indian adventures of Basil Ringrose (d. 1686) are recorded in his journal, published in vol. 2 of *History of the Buccaneers* (1685); Dampier refers to Ringrose in *New Voyage round the World* (1697).

Watlin, who being a hunting in the woods when the Captain left the island, lived here three years alone, and shifted much in the same manner as Mr. Selkirk did, till Capt. Dampier came hither in 1684, and carried him off. The first that went ashore was one of his countrymen, and they saluted one another first by prostrating themselves by turns on the ground, and then embracing. But whatever there is in these stories, this of Mr. Selkirk I know to be true; and his behaviour afterwards gives me reason to believe the account he gave me how he spent his time, and bore up under such an affliction, in which nothing but the Divine Providence could have supported any man. By this one may see that solitude and retirement from the world is not such an unsufferable state of life as most men imagine, especially when people are fairly called or thrown into it unavoidably, as this man was; who in all probability must otherwise have perished in the seas, the ship which left him being cast away not long after, and few of the company escaped. We may perceive by this story the truth of the maxim, that Necessity is the Mother of Invention, since he found means to supply his wants in a very natural manner, so as to maintain his life, tho not so conveniently, yet as effectually as we are able to do with the help of all our arts and society. It may likewise instruct us, how much a plain and temperate way of living conduces to the health of the body and the vigour of the mind, both which we are apt to destroy by excess and plenty, especially of strong liquor, and the variety as well as the nature of our meat and drink: for this man, when he came to our ordinary method of diet and life, tho he was sober enough, lost much of his strength and agility. But I must quit these reflections, which are more proper for a philosopher and divine than a mariner, and return to my own subject.

We did not get to anchor till six at night, on *Febr.* 1. and then it fell calm; we rowed and towed into the anchor-ground about a mile off shore, 45 fathom water, clean ground; the current sets mostly along shore to the southward. This morning we cleared up ship, and bent our sails, and got them ashore to mend, and make tents for our sick men. The Governor (tho we might as well have named him the Absolute Monarch of the Island), for so we called Mr. Selkirk, caught us two goats, which make excellent broth, mixed with turnip tops and other greens, for our sick men, being 21 in all, but not above two that we account dangerous; the *Dutchess* has more men sick, and in a worse condition than ours.

Febr. 3.   Yesterday in the afternoon we got as many of our men ashore as could be spared from clearing and fitting our ship, to wood and water. Our sail-makers are all mending our sails, and I lent the *Dutchess* one to assist them. This morning we got our smith's forge put up ashore, set our coopers to work in another place, and made a little tent for myself to have the benefit of the shore. The *Dutchess* has also a tent for their sick men; so that we have a little town of our own here, and every body is employed. A few men supply us all with fish of several sorts, all very good: as silverfish, rockfish, pollock, cavallos, oldwives, and crawfish in such abundance, that in a few hours we could take as many as would serve some hundreds of men. There were sea-fowls in the bay as large as geese, but eat fishy. The Governor never failed of getting us two or three goats a day for our sick men, by which with the help of the greens and the goodness of

---

193. **bent:** usually "tied" (see line 337), but here, clearly, meaning "untied."

the air they recovered very fast of the scurvy, which was their general distemper. 'Twas *210*
very pleasant ashore among the green piemento trees, which cast a refreshing smell. Our
house was made by putting up a sail round four of 'em, and covering it a-top with
another sail; so that Capt. Dover and I both thought it a very agreeable seat, the weather
being neither too hot nor too cold.

We spent our time till the 10th in refitting our ships, taking wood on board, and *215*
laying up water, that which we brought from England and St. Vincent being spoiled by
the badness of the casks. We likewise boiled up about 80 gallons of sea lions' oil, as we
might have done several tuns, had we been provided with vessels, etc. We refined and
strained it for the use of our lamps and to save our candles, tho sailors sometimes use it
to fry their meat, when straitened for want of butter, etc. and say 'tis agreeable enough. *220*
The men who worked ashore on our rigging ate young seals, which they preferred to our
ships' victuals, and said was as good as English lamb; tho for my own part I should have
been glad of such an exchange.

We made what haste we could to get all necessaries on board, being willing to lose
no time; for we were informed at the Canaries that five stout French ships were coming *225*
together to these seas.

Febr. 11.   Yesterday in the evening, having little or nothing to do with the
pinnace, we sent her to the south end of the island to get goats. The Governor told us
that during his stay he could not get down to that end from the mountains where he
lived, they were so steep and rocky; but that there were abundance of goats there, and *230*
that part of the island was plainer. Capt. Dampier, Mr. Glendal, and the Governor, with
ten men, set out in company with the *Dutchess*'s boat and crew, and surrounded a great
parcel of goats, which are of a larger sort, and not so wild as those on the higher part of
the island where the Governor lived; but not looking well to 'em, they escaped over the
cliff, so that instead of catching above a hundred, as they might easily have done with a *235*
little precaution, they returned this morning with only 16 large ones, tho they saw above
a thousand. If any ships come again to this island, the best way is to keep some men and
dogs at that part of the island, and sending a boat to them once in 24 hours they may
victual a good body of men; and no doubt but amongst those goats they may find some
hundreds with Mr. Selkirk's earmark. *240*

Febr. 12.   This morning we bent the remaining sails, got the last wood and water
aboard, brought off our men, and got everything ready to depart. The island of Juan
Fernandez is nearest of a triangular form, about 12 leagues round; the southwest side is
much the longest, and has a small island about a mile long lying near it, with a few
visible rocks close under the shore of the great island. On this side begins a ridge of high *245*
mountains that run cross from the SW. to the NW. of the island; and the land that lies
out in a narrow point to the westward, appears to be the only level ground here. On the
NE. side 'tis very high land, and under it are the two bays where ships always put in to
recruit. The best bay is next the middle on this side the island, which is to be known at a
distance by the highest table mountain right over this bay. You may anchor as near as *250*
you will to the shore, and the nearer the better. The best road is on the larboard side of

---

213. seat: residence. **241. bent:** fastened, as to a yard. **251. road:** roadstead; sheltered water near shore, where ships may ride.

the bay, and nearest the eastermost shore: provided you get well in, you cannot mistake the road. The other bay is plain to be seen under the north end, but not so good for wood, water, or landing, nor so safe for riding. In this bay, where we rode, there's plenty of good water and wood: the best water is in a small cove about a good musket-shot to *255* the eastward of the place I have described. You may ride from a mile to a bow-shot off the shore, being all deep water and bold, without any danger round the island, but what is visible and very near in. This bay where we rode is open to near half the compass; the eastermost land in sight bore E by S. dist. about a mile and a half, and the outermost northwest point of the island lies something without our bay, and bears NW by W. dist. *260* a good league. We were about a mile off the shore, and had 45 fathom water, clean sandy ground; we designed to have ran farther in, and new moored, but Mr. Selkirk informed us that this month proves the fairest in the year, and that during winter and summer, the whole time he was here, he seldom knew the wind to blow off from the sea, but only in small breezes that never brought in a sea, nor held two hours; but he warned *265* us to be on our guard against the wind off shore, which blew very strong sometimes. The bay is all deep water, and you may carry in ships close to the rocks, if occasion require. The wind blows always over the land, and at worst along shore, which makes no sea. It's for the most part calm at night, only now and then a flaw blows from the high land over us. *270*

Near the rocks there are very good fish of several sorts, particularly large crawfish under the rocks, easy to be caught; also cavallies, gropers, and other good fish in so great plenty, anywhere near the shore, that I never saw the like but at the best fishing season in Newfoundland. Piemento is the best timber, and most plentiful on this side the island, but very apt to split till a little dried. We cut the longest and cleanest to split for firewood. The *275* cabbage trees abound about three miles in the woods, and the cabbage are very good; most of 'em are on the tops of the nearest and lowest mountains. In the first plain we found store of turnip greens, and watercresses in the brooks, which mightily refreshed our men, and cleansed 'em from the scurvy. The turnips, Mr. Selkirk told us, are good in our summer months, which is winter here; but this being autumn, they are all run to seed, so *280* that we can't have the benefit of anything but the greens. The soil is a loose black earth, the rocks very rotten, so that without great care it's dangerous to climb the hills for cabbages. Besides, there are abundance of holes dug in several places by a sort of fowls like puffins, which fall in at once, and endanger the wrenching or breaking of a man's leg. Mr. Selkirk tells me, in July he has seen snow and ice here; but the spring, which is in *285* September, October, and November, is very pleasant, when there's abundance of good herbs, as parsley, purslane, sithes in great plenty, besides an herb found by the waterside which proved very useful to our surgeons for fomentations; 'tis not much unlike feverfew, of a very grateful smell like balm, but of a stronger and more cordial scent. 'Tis in great plenty near the shore. We gathered many large bundles of it, dried 'em in the shade, and *290* sent 'em on board, besides great quantities that we carried in every morning to strow the tents, which tended much to the speedy recovery of our sick men, of whom none died but two belonging to the *Dutchess,* viz. Edward Wilts and Christopher Williams.

---

257. bold: steep, abrupt. **265. sea:** wave, billow, surge. **272. gropers:** also called groupers. **287. sithes:** chives. **289. grateful:** pleasing; **cordial:** stimulating. **291. strow:** strew.

Mr. Selkirk tells me that in November the seals come ashore to whelp and engender, when the shore is so full of them for a stone's throw, that 'tis impossible to pass thro them; *295* and they are so surly that they'll not move out of the way, but like an angry dog run at a man, tho he have a good stick to beat them. So that at this and their whelping seasons 'tis dangerous to come near them, but at other times they'll make way for a man; and if they did not, 'twould be impossible to get up from the waterside: they lined the shore very thick for above half a mile of ground all round the bay. When we came in, they kept a continual *300* noise day and night, some bleating like lambs, some howling like dogs or wolves, others making hideous noises of various sorts; so that we heard 'em aboard, tho a mile from the shore. Their fur is the finest that ever I saw of the kind, and exceeds that of our otters.

Another strange creature here is the sea lion. The Governor tells me he has seen of them above 20 feet long and more in compass, which could not weigh less than two ton *305* weight. I saw several of these vast creatures, but none of the above-mentioned size; several of 'em were upward of 16 feet long, and more in bulk, so that they could not weigh less than a ton weight. The shape of their body differs little from the sea dogs or seals, but have another sort of skin, a head much bigger in proportion, and very large mouths, monstrous big eyes, and a face like that of a lion, with very large whiskers, the *310* hair of which is stiff enough to make tooth-pickers. These creatures come ashore to engender the latter end of June, and stay till the end of September; during all which time they lie on the land, and are never observed to go to the water, but lie in the same place above a musket-shot from the waterside, and have no manner of sustenance all that time that he could observe. I took notice of some that lay a week, without once *315* offering to move out of the place whilst I was there, till they were disturbed by us; but we saw few in comparison of what he informs us he did, and that the shore was all crowded full of them a musket-shot into the land. I admire how these monsters come to yield such a quantity of oil. Their hair is short and coarse, and their skin thicker than the thickest ox hide I ever saw. We found no land bird on the island, but a sort of *320* blackbird with a red breast, not unlike our English blackbirds; and the humming-bird of various colours, and no bigger than a large humblebee. Here is a small tide which flows uncertain, and the spring tide flows about seven foot.

I shall not trouble the reader with the descriptions of this island given by others, wherein there are many falsehoods; but the truth of this I can assert from my own *325* knowledge. Nor shall I insert the description of the cabbage and piemento trees, being so well known and so frequently done, that there's no manner of need for it. I have insisted the longer upon this island, because it might be at first of great use to those who would carry on any trade to the South Sea.

(1712)

---

322. **humblebee:** bumblebee.

GEORGE BERKELEY
Ireland, 1685-1753

VERSES ON THE PROSPECT OF PLANTING ARTS AND LEARNING IN AMERICA

The Muse, disgusted at an age and clime
  Barren of every glorious theme,
In distant lands now waits a better time,
  Producing subjects worthy fame.

In happy climes, where from the genial sun   5
  And virgin earth such scenes ensue,
The force of art by nature seems outdone,
  And fancied beauties by the true.

In happy climes, the seat of innocence,
  Where nature guides and virtue rules,   10
Where men shall not impose for truth and sense
  The pedantry of courts and schools:

There shall be sung another golden age,
  The rise of empire and of arts,
The good and great inspiring epic rage,   15
  The wisest heads and noblest hearts.

Not such as Europe breeds in her decay;
  Such as she bred when fresh and young,
When heav'nly flame did animate her clay,
  By future poets shall be sung.   20

Westward the course of empire takes its way;
  The four first acts already past,
A fifth shall close the drama with the day;
  Time's noblest offspring is the last.

(1726; 1752)

ALLAN RAMSAY
Scotland, 1686-1758

LASS WITH A LUMP OF LAND

Gi'e me a lass with a lump of land,
  And we for life shall gang thegither;
Tho' daft or wise I'll never demand,
  Or black or fair it maksna whether.
I'm aff with wit, and beauty will fade,   5
  And blood alane is no worth a shilling;
But she that's rich, her market's made,
  For ilka charm about her is killing.

Gi'e me a lass with a lump of land,
  And in my bosom I'll hug my treasure;   10
Gin I had anes her gear in my hand,
  Should love turn dowf, it will find pleasure.

Laugh on wha likes, but there's my hand,
  I hate with poortith, though bonny, to meddle;
Unless they bring cash, or a lump of land,   15
  They'se never get me to dance to their fiddle.

There's meikle good love in bands and bags,
  And siller and gowd's a sweet complexion;
But beauty, and wit, and vertue in rags,
  Have tint the art of gaining affection.   20
Love tips his arrows with woods and parks,
  And castles, and riggs, and moors, and meadows;
And nathing can catch our modern sparks,
  But well tochered lasses, or jointured widows.

(1726)

LASS WITH A LUMP OF LAND   **4. maksna whether:** makes no difference. **5. aff:** off. **8. ilka:** every. **11. Gin:** if; **anes:** once; **gear:** wealth, goods. **12. dowf:** pithless, dull. **14. poortith:** poverty. **17. meikle:** as much. **18. siller:** silver; **gowd:** gold. **20. tint:** lost. **22. riggs:** ridges. **24. tochered:** dowried.

HENRY CAREY
England, c.1687-1743

A LILLIPUTIAN ODE ON THEIR MAJESTIES' ACCESSION

Smile, smile,
Blest isle!
Grief past,
At last,
Halcyon   5
Comes on.
New King,
Bells ring;
New Queen,
Blest scene!   10
Britain
Again

Revives
And thrives.
Fear flies,   15
Stocks rise;
Wealth flows,
Art grows.
Strange pack
Sent back;   20
Own folks
Crack jokes.
Those out
May pout;

Those in   25
Will grin.

Great, small,
Pleased all.

God send
No end   30
To line
Divine
Of George and Caroline!

(1727)

ALEXANDER POPE
England, 1688-1744

ODE ON SOLITUDE

Happy the man whose wish and care
A few paternal acres bound,
Content to breathe his native air
    In his own ground.

Whose herds with milk, whose fields with bread,
Whose flocks supply him with attire,   6
Whose trees in summer yield him shade,
    In winter fire.

Blest! who can unconcern'dly find
Hours, days, and years slide soft away,   10
In health of body, peace of mind,
    Quiet by day,

Sound sleep by night, study and ease
Together mixed, sweet recreation,
And innocence, which most does please,   15
    With meditation.

Thus let me live, unseen, unknown;
Thus unlamented let me die,
Steal from the world, and not a stone
    Tell where I lie.   20

(1700-09; 1717)

A LILLIPUTIAN ODE Since Swift's *Gulliver's Travels* had been published just the year before, its popularity is suggested by the evidence here that the word "Lilliputian" had already entered the language. Carey may also be imitating — or emulating — the first of Pope's *Verses on Gulliver's Travels* (published anonymously with the second edition of Swift's work in early May of 1727), called "To Quinbus Flestrin, the Man-Mountain; A Lilliputian Ode," which begins: "In Amaze / Lost, I gaze! / Can our Eyes / Reach thy Size? / May my Lays / Swell with Praise / Worthy thee! / Worthy me! / Muse inspire, / All thy Fire! / Bards of old / Of him told, / When they said / Atlas Head / Propt the Skies: / See! and believe your Eyes!" The "Majesties" of Carey's title are George II, King of England 1727-60, and his Queen, Caroline of Anspach (who died in 1737).

from *AN ESSAY ON CRITICISM* [sound and sense]

. . . .

But most by numbers judge a poet's song,
And smooth or rough, with them, is right or wrong;
In the bright Muse though thousand charms conspire,
Her voice is all these tuneful fools admire,　　*340*
Who haunt Parnassus but to please their ear,
Not mend their minds; as some to church repair
Not for the doctrine, but the music there.
These equal syllables alone require,
Though oft the ear the open vowels tire,　　*345*
While expletives their feeble aid do join,
And ten low words oft creep in one dull line,
While they ring round the same unvaried chimes
With sure returns of still expected rhymes.
Where'er you find "the cooling western breeze,"　　*350*
In the next line it "whispers through the trees";
If "crystal streams with pleasing murmurs creep,"
The reader's threatened (not in vain) with "sleep."
Then, at the last and only couplet fraught

With some unmeaning thing they call a thought,　　*355*
A needless Alexandrine ends the song,
That like a wounded snake, drags its slow length along.
Leave such to tune their own dull rhymes, and know
What's roundly smooth, or languishingly slow;
And praise the easy vigour of a line　　*360*
Where Denham's strength and Waller's sweetness join.
True ease in writing comes from art, not chance,
As those move easiest who have learned to dance.
'Tis not enough no harshness gives offence;
The sound must seem an echo to the sense.　　*365*
Soft is the strain when Zephyr gently blows,
And the smooth stream in smoother numbers flows;
But when loud surges lash the sounding shore,
The hoarse, rough verse should like the torrent roar.
When Ajax strives some rock's vast weight to throw,
The line too labours, and the words move slow;　　*371*
Not so when swift Camilla scours the plain,
Flies o'er th'unbending corn, and skims along the main.

(1711)

THE RAPE OF THE LOCK: An Heroi-Comical Poem

Nolueram, Belinda, tuos violare capillos,
Sed juvat hoc precibus me tribuisse tuis.
— *Martial*

To Mrs. Arabella Fermor

MADAM,

It will be in vain to deny that I have some regard for this piece, since I dedicate it to you. Yet you may bear me witness, it was intended only to divert a few young ladies, who have good sense and good humour enough to laugh not only at their sex's little unguarded follies, but at their own. But as it was communicated with the air of a secret, it soon found its way into the world. An imperfect copy having been offered to a bookseller, you had the good nature for my sake to consent to the　　*5* publication of one more correct; this I was forced to, before I had executed half my design, for the machinery was entirely wanting to complete it.

The machinery, Madam, is a term invented by the critics, to signify that part which the deities, angels, or demons are made to act in a poem; for the ancient poets are in one respect like

---

AN ESSAY ON CRITICISM　**337. numbers:** metrical feet, versification. **341. Parnassus:** Greek mountain, one of whose two peaks is sacred to Apollo and the Muses, and therefore considered the home of poetry and music. **346. expletives:** empty words added to fill out a line. **361:** Pope is following comments made by Dryden on Denham's *Cooper's Hill* (see p. 383) and Waller's lyric poetry (see p. 311). **370. Ajax** (also Aias): a large, strong Greek hero in the Trojan War, second only to Achilles (see e.g. Homer's *Iliad*, II, 557; III, 226-29; VII, 206ff.; XXIII, 708ff.). **372. Camilla:** a woman warrior described in Virgil's *Aeneid*, VII, 803ff.; XI, 535ff.　　THE RAPE OF THE LOCK　**Epigraph** (from Martial, *Epigrams*, XII, 84, with "Polytime" changed to "Belinda"): "I didn't want, Belinda, to violate your locks, but it pleases me to have contributed this at your prayer."　**DEDICATORY LETTER**　(The term *Mrs.* abbreviates *Mistress*, and applied to unmarried as well as married women.) **4-5. imperfect copy:** i.e., a pirated version; the poem's two-canto version of 1712 corrected this; Pope then expanded the poem to five cantos, published in 1714, to which this letter was attached.

many modern ladies; let an action be never so trivial in itself, they always make it appear of the *10* utmost importance. These machines I determined to raise on a very new and odd foundation, the Rosicrucian doctrine of spirits.

I know how disagreeable it is to make use of hard words before a lady; but 'tis so much the concern of a poet to have his works understood, and particularly by your sex, that you must give me leave to explain two or three difficult terms. *15*

The Rosicrucians are a people I must bring you acquainted with. The best account I know of them is in a French book called *Le Comte de Gabalis*, which both in its title and size is so like a novel, that many of the fair sex have read it for one by mistake. According to these gentlemen, the four elements are inhabited by spirits, which they call Sylphs, Gnomes, Nymphs, and Salamanders. The Gnomes or Demons of earth delight in mischief; but the Sylphs, whose habitation is in *20* the air, are the best-conditioned creatures imaginable. For they say, any mortals may enjoy the most intimate familiarities with these gentle spirits, upon a condition very easy to all true adepts, an inviolate preservation of chastity.

As to the following cantos, all the passages of them are as fabulous as the vision at the beginning, or the transformation at the end (except the loss of your hair, which I always mention *25* with reverence). The human persons are as fictitious as the airy ones; and the character of Belinda, as it is now managed, resembles you in nothing but in beauty.

If this poem had as many graces as there are in your person, or in your mind, yet I could never hope it should pass through the world half so uncensured as you have done. But let its fortune be what it will, mine is happy enough, to have given me this occasion of assuring you that *30* I am, with the truest esteem,

MADAM, Your most obedient, humble servant, A. POPE

Canto I

What dire offence from am'rous causes springs,
What mighty contests rise from trivial things,
I sing — This verse to Caryll, Muse! is due;
This, ev'n Belinda may vouchsafe to view;
Slight is the subject, but not so the praise, *5*
If she inspire, and he approve my lays.
  Say what strange motive, Goddess! could compel
A well-bred lord t'assault a gentle belle?
Oh say what stranger cause, yet unexplored,
Could make a gentle belle reject a lord? *10*
In tasks so bold can little men engage,
And in soft bosoms dwells such mighty rage?
  Sol through white curtains shot a tim'rous ray,
And oped those eyes that must eclipse the day;
Now lapdogs give themselves the rousing shake, *15*

And sleepless lovers, just at twelve, awake:
Thrice rung the bell, the slipper knocked the ground,
And the pressed watch returned a silver sound.
Belinda still her downy pillow pressed,
Her guardian Sylph prolonged the balmy rest: *20*
'Twas he had summoned to her silent bed
The morning-dream that hovered o'er her head,
A youth more glitt'ring than a birth-night beau
(That ev'n in slumber caused her cheek to glow)
Seemed to her ear his winning lips to lay, *25*
And thus in whispers said, or seemed to say:
  "Fairest of mortals, thou distinguished care
Of thousand bright inhabitants of air!
If e'er one vision touched thy infant thought,
Of all the nurse and all the priest have taught; *30*

---

17. *Le Comte de Gabalis:* a 1670 book on Rosicrucianism by the Abbé de Montfaucon de Villars.   **CANTO I**   **3:** It was Pope's friend John Caryll who suggested that Pope write an amusing poem to try to smooth the quarrel between the families of Arabella Fermor ("Belinda") and Lord Petre ("the baron") caused by his cutting off a lock of her hair. **13. curtains:** i.e., bed-curtains. **18:** When a projecting pin (or sometimes the stem) is pressed, a "repeater" watch chimes the most recent quarter hour (especially useful in the dark, in days before electricity, or even matches). **23:** Courtiers wore especially elegant clothing at a sovereign's birthday celebrations.

THE

RAPE *of the* LOCK.

CANTO I.

HAT dire Offence from am'rous
Caufes fprings,
What mighty Quarrels rife from
trivial Things,

I fing —— This Verfe to C---l, Mufe! is due ;

This, ev'n *Belinda* may vouchfafe to view :

Slight is the Subject, but not fo the Praife,

If She infpire, and He approve my Lays.

B   Say

Plate 4. The opening of Alexander Pope's *The Rape
of the Lock*, as it appeared in 1714.

Of airy elves by moonlight shadows seen,
The silver token, and the circled green,
Or virgins visited by angel-pow'rs,
With golden crowns and wreaths of heav'nly flow'rs;
Hear and believe! thy own importance know,   *35*
Nor bound thy narrow views to things below.
Some secret truths, from learned pride concealed,
To maids alone and children are revealed:
What though no credit doubting wits may give?
The fair and innocent shall still believe.   *40*
Know then, unnumbered spirits round thee fly,
The light militia of the lower sky:
These, though unseen, are ever on the wing,
Hang o'er the box, and hover round the Ring.
Think what an equipage thou hast in air,   *45*
And view with scorn two pages and a chair.
As now your own, our beings were of old,
And once enclosed in woman's beauteous mould;
Thence, by a soft transition, we repair
From earthly vehicles to these of air.   *50*
Think not, when woman's transient breath is fled,
That all her vanities at once are dead;
Succeeding vanities she still regards,
And though she plays no more, o'erlooks the cards.
Her joy in gilded chariots, when alive,   *55*
And love of ombre, after death survive.
For when the fair in all their pride expire,
To their first elements their souls retire:
The sprites of fiery termagants in flame
Mount up, and take a salamander's name.   *60*
Soft yielding minds to water glide away,
And sip, with nymphs, their elemental tea.
The graver prude sinks downward to a gnome,
In search of mischief still on earth to roam.
The light coquettes in sylphs aloft repair,   *65*
And sport and flutter in the fields of air.
   "Know further yet; whoever fair and chaste
Rejects mankind, is by some sylph embraced:
For spirits, freed from mortal laws, with ease
Assume what sexes and what shapes they please.   *70*
What guards the purity of melting maids,
In courtly balls, and midnight masquerades,

Safe from the treach'rous friend, the daring spark,
The glance by day, the whisper in the dark,
When kind occasion prompts their warm desires,   *75*
When music softens, and when dancing fires?
'Tis but their sylph, the wise celestials know,
Though honour is the word with men below.
   "Some nymphs there are, too conscious of their face,
For life predestined to the gnomes' embrace.   *80*
These swell their prospects and exalt their pride,
When offers are disdained, and love denied:
Then gay ideas crowd the vacant brain,
While peers, and dukes, and all their sweeping train,
And garters, stars, and coronets appear,   *85*
And in soft sounds, 'Your Grace' salutes their ear.
'Tis these that early taint the female soul,
Instruct the eyes of young coquettes to roll,
Teach infant-cheeks a bidden blush to know,
And little hearts to flutter at a beau.   *90*
   "Oft, when the world imagine women stray,
The sylphs through mystic mazes guide their way,
Through all the giddy circle they pursue,
And old impertinence expel by new.
What tender maid but must a victim fall   *95*
To one man's treat, but for another's ball?
When Florio speaks, what virgin could withstand,
If gentle Damon did not squeeze her hand?
With varying vanities, from ev'ry part,
They shift the moving toyshop of their heart;   *100*
Where wigs with wigs, with sword-knots sword-knots strive,
Beaux banish beaux, and coaches coaches drive.
This erring mortals levity may call;
Oh blind to truth! the sylphs contrive it all.
   "Of these am I, who thy protection claim,   *105*
A watchful sprite, and Ariel is my name.
Late, as I ranged the crystal wilds of air,
In the clear mirror of thy ruling star
I saw, alas! some dread event impend,
Ere to the main this morning sun descend;   *110*
But Heav'n reveals not what, or how, or where:
Warned by the sylph, O pious maid, beware!
This to disclose is all thy guardian can:
Beware of all, but most beware of man!"   *114*

---

32. silver token: coin supposedly left by fairies in exchange for something or as a reward; **circled green:** "fairy circles" or "rings" in the grass, supposedly caused by dancing fairies. **35-36:** intended to parallel Satan's speech to Eve (*Paradise Lost*, IX, 689ff.; p. 363); the poem abounds with echoes of Milton's epic, as well as Homer's and Virgil's, and numerous other poems, of which we note only a few (this is true of "Epistle IV" and *An Essay on Man*, as well); for fuller annotation, see John Butt, gen. ed., *The Twickenham Edition of the Poems of Alexander Pope.* **44. box:** i.e., in the theatre; **Ring:** a fashionable circular drive in Hyde Park. **46. chair:** sedan chair. **56. ombre** (pronounced "óm-ber"): see III, 25ff. below. **58. elements:** see the note on Chaucer's General Prologue, 420 (p. 34). **69-70:** Cf. *Paradise Lost*, I, 423ff. (p. 331). **94. impertinence:** triviality. **97-98. Florio, Damon:** stock literary names for romantic young men. **100. toyshop:** shop selling purses, fans, ribbons, lace, dolls, and other accessories and gew-gaws, mostly for women (see Pope's *Iliad*, XVIII, 468, p. 534 below).

He said; when Shock, who thought she slept too long,
Leaped up, and waked his mistress with his tongue.
'Twas then, Belinda, if report say true,
Thy eyes first opened on a billet-doux;
Wounds, charms, and ardours were no sooner read,
But all the vision vanished from thy head.   120
    And now, unveiled, the toilet stands displayed,
Each silver vase in mystic order laid.
First, robed in white, the nymph intent adores,
With head uncovered, the cosmetic pow'rs.
A heav'nly image in the glass appears,   125
To that she bends, to that her eyes she rears;
Th' inferior priestess, at her altar's side,
Trembling begins the sacred rites of Pride.
Unnumbered treasures ope at once, and here
The various off'rings of the world appear;   130
From each she nicely culls with curious toil,
And decks the goddess with the glitt'ring spoil.
This casket India's glowing gems unlocks,
And all Arabia breathes from yonder box.
The tortoise here and elephant unite,   135
Transformed to combs, the speckled and the white.
Here files of pins extend their shining rows,
Puffs, powders, patches, bibles, billet-doux.
Now awful beauty puts on all its arms;
The fair each moment rises in her charms,   140
Repairs her smiles, awakens ev'ry grace,
And calls forth all the wonders of her face;
Sees by degrees a purer blush arise,
And keener lightnings quicken in her eyes.
The busy sylphs surround their darling care,   145
These set the head, and those divide the hair,
Some fold the sleeve, whilst others plait the gown;
And Betty's praised for labours not her own.

Canto II

Not with more glories, in th' ethereal plain,
The sun first rises o'er the purpled main,
Than, issuing forth, the rival of his beams
Launched on the bosom of the silver Thames.   4
Fair nymphs and well-dressed youths around her shone,
But ev'ry eye was fixed on her alone.
On her white breast a sparkling cross she wore,
Which Jews might kiss, and infidels adore.

Her lively looks a sprightly mind disclose,
Quick as her eyes, and as unfixed as those: 10
Favours to none, to all she smiles extends;
Oft she rejects, but never once offends.
Bright as the sun, her eyes the gazers strike,
And, like the sun, they shine on all alike.
Yet graceful ease, and sweetness void of pride,   15
Might hide her faults, if belles had faults to hide:
If to her share some female errors fall,
Look on her face, and you'll forget 'em all.
    This nymph, to the destruction of mankind,
Nourished two locks, which graceful hung behind   20
In equal curls, and well conspired to deck
With shining ringlets the smooth iv'ry neck.
Love in these labyrinths his slaves detains,
And mighty hearts are held in slender chains.
With hairy springes we the birds betray,   25
Slight lines of hair surprise the finny prey,
Fair tresses man's imperial race ensnare,
And beauty draws us with a single hair.
    Th' advent'rous baron the bright locks admired;
He saw, he wished, and to the prize aspired.   30
Resolved to win, he meditates the way,
By force to ravish, or by fraud betray;
For when success a lover's toil attends,
Few ask if fraud or force attained his ends.
    For this, ere Phœbus rose, he had implored   35
Propitious Heav'n, and ev'ry pow'r adored,
But chiefly Love — to Love an altar built,
Of twelve vast French romances, neatly gilt.
There lay three garters, half a pair of gloves;
And all the trophies of his former loves;   40
With tender billet-doux he lights the pyre,
And breathes three am'rous sighs to raise the fire.
Then prostrate falls, and begs with ardent eyes
Soon to obtain, and long possess the prize:
The pow'rs gave ear, and granted half his pray'r,   45
The rest the winds dispersed in empty air.
    But now secure the painted vessel glides,
The sunbeams trembling on the floating tides:
While melting music steals upon the sky,
And softened sounds along the waters die;   50
Smooth flow the waves, the zephyrs gently play,
Belinda smiled, and all the world was gay.

115. Shock: Belinda's lapdog, named for its thick, shaggy hair; the word *shock* itself meant long-haired dog. **121. toilet:** dressing table. **127. inferior priestess:** i.e., Betty, named (with a stock name for maidservants) in line 148. **131. curious:** careful. **133:** See note to *Paradise Lost*, II, 2 (p. 336). **134:** i.e., perfumes from Arabia. **138. patches:** bits of court plaster used to adorn the face with supposed "beauty spots." CANTO II **19ff.:** Such twin curls at the nape of the neck (and sometimes other curls as well) were known as "heart-breakers." **32, 34. force . . . or fraud:** Cf. *Paradise Lost*, I, 121; II, 338 (pp. 328, 340).

All but the sylph — with careful thoughts oppressed,
Th' impending woe sat heavy on his breast.
He summons straight his denizens of air; 55
The lucid squadrons round the sails repair:
Soft o'er the shrouds aerial whispers breathe,
That seemed but zephyrs to the train beneath.
Some to the sun their insect-wings unfold,
Waft on the breeze, or sink in clouds of gold; 60
Transparent forms, too fine for mortal sight,
Their fluid bodies half dissolved in light.
Loose to the wind their airy garments flew,
Thin glitt'ring textures of the filmy dew,
Dipped in the richest tincture of the skies, 65
Where light disports in ever-mingling dyes,
While ev'ry beam new transient colours flings,
Colours that change whene'er they wave their wings.
Amid the circle, on the gilded mast,
Superior by the head, was Ariel placed; 70
His purple pinions op'ning to the sun,
He raised his azure wand, and thus begun:
    "Ye sylphs and sylphids, to your chief give ear!
Fays, fairies, genii, elves, and demons, hear!
Ye know the spheres, and various tasks assigned 75
By laws eternal to th' aerial kind.
Some in the fields of purest ether play,
And bask and whiten in the blaze of day.
Some guide the course of wand'ring orbs on high,
Or roll the planets through the boundless sky. 80
Some less refined, beneath the moon's pale light
Pursue the stars that shoot athwart the night,
Or suck the mists in grosser air below,
Or dip their pinions in the painted bow,
Or brew fierce tempests on the wintry main, 85
Or o'er the glebe distill the kindly rain.
Others on earth o'er human race preside,
Watch all their ways, and all their actions guide:
Of these the chief the care of nations own,
And guard with arms divine the British throne. 90
    "Our humbler province is to tend the fair,
Not a less pleasing, though less glorious care;
To save the powder from too rude a gale,
Nor let th' imprisoned essences exhale;
To draw fresh colours from the vernal flow'rs; 95
To steal from rainbows ere they drop in show'rs
A brighter wash; to curl their waving hairs,

Assist their blushes, and inspire their airs;
Nay oft, in dreams, invention we bestow,
To change a flounce, or add a furbelow. 100
    "This day, black omens threat the brightest fair
That e'er deserved a watchful spirit's care;
Some dire disaster, or by force, or sleight;
But what, or where, the Fates have wrapped in night.
Whether the nymph shall break Diana's law, 105
Or some frail china jar receive a flaw;
Or stain her honour, or her new brocade;
Forget her pray'rs, or miss a masquerade;
Or lose her heart, or necklace, at a ball;
Or whether Heav'n has doomed that Shock must fall.
Haste then, ye spirits! to your charge repair: 111
The flutt'ring fan be Zephyretta's care;
The drops to thee, Brillante, we consign;
And, Momentilla, let the watch be thine;
Do thou, Crispissa, tend her fav'rite lock; 115
Ariel himself shall be the guard of Shock.
    "To fifty chosen sylphs, of special note,
We trust th' important charge, the petticoat:
Oft have we known that seven-fold fence to fail,
Though stiff with hoops, and armed with ribs of whale;
Form a strong line about the silver bound, 121
And guard the wide circumference around.
    "Whatever spirit, careless of his charge,
His post neglects, or leaves the fair at large,
Shall feel sharp vengeance soon o'ertake his sins, 125
Be stopped in vials, or transfixed with pins;
Or plunged in lakes of bitter washes lie,
Or wedged whole ages in a bodkin's eye:
Gums and pomatums shall his flight restrain,
While clogged he beats his silken wings in vain; 130
Or alum styptics with contracting pow'r
Shrink his thin essence like a rivelled flow'r:
Or, as Ixion fixed, the wretch shall feel
The giddy motion of the whirling mill,
In fumes of burning chocolate shall glow, 135
And tremble at the sea that froths below!"
    He spoke; the spirits from the sails descend;
Some, orb in orb, around the nymph extend;
Some thrid the mazy ringlets of her hair;
Some hang upon the pendants of her ear; 140
With beating hearts the dire event they wait,
Anxious, and trembling for the birth of Fate.

---

70. superior: taller. **84. painted bow:** i.e., rainbow. **97. wash:** liquid cosmetic (often containing harsh chemicals such as white lead, bismuth, and mercury) to brighten or whiten the complexion. **103. or . . . or:** either . . . or. **105. Diana's law:** i.e., that of chastity. **113. drops:** pendant diamond earrings. **115:** *Crispissa* is from Latin *crispere*, "to curl." **117-22:** Cf. *Iliad*, XVIII, on the shield of Achilles (p. 534). **129. pomatums:** pomades. **132. rivelled:** shrivelled, wrinkled. **133-34:** In Greek myth, Ixion in Hades was tied to a turning wheel; **mill:** a rotary beater to make chocolate frothy. **139. thrid:** thread.

Canto III

Close by those meads, forever crowned with flow'rs,
Where Thames with pride surveys his rising tow'rs,
There stands a structure of majestic frame,
Which from the neighb'ring Hampton takes its name.
Here Britain's statesmen oft the fall foredoom   5
Of foreign tyrants and of nymphs at home;
Here thou, great Anna! whom three realms obey,
Dost sometimes counsel take — and sometimes tea.

    Hither the heroes and the nymphs resort,
To taste a while the pleasures of a court;   10
In various talk th' instructive hours they passed,
Who gave the ball, or paid the visit last;
One speaks the glory of the British Queen,
And one describes a charming Indian screen;
A third interprets motions, looks, and eyes;   15
At ev'ry word a reputation dies.
Snuff, or the fan, supply each pause of chat,
With singing, laughing, ogling, and all that.

    Meanwhile, declining from the noon of day,
The sun obliquely shoots his burning ray;   20
The hungry judges soon the sentence sign,
And wretches hang that jurymen may dine;
The merchant from th' Exchange returns in peace,
And the long labours of the *toilette* cease.
Belinda now, whom thirst of fame invites,   25
Burns to encounter two advent'rous knights,
At ombre singly to decide their doom;
And swells her breast with conquests yet to come.
Straight the three bands prepare in arms to join,
Each band the number of the sacred Nine.   30
Soon as she spreads her hand, th' aerial guard
Descend, and sit on each important card:
First Ariel perched upon a Matadore,
Then each, according to the rank they bore;
For sylphs, yet mindful of their ancient race,   35
Are, as when women, wondrous fond of place.

    Behold, four kings in majesty revered,
With hoary whiskers and a forky beard;
And four fair queens, whose hands sustain a flow'r,
Th' expressive emblem of their softer pow'r;   40
Four knaves in garbs succinct, a trusty band,
Caps on their heads, and halberts in their hand;
And parti-coloured troops, a shining train,
Draw forth to combat on the velvet plain.

    The skillful nymph reviews her force with care: 45
"Let spades be trumps!" she said, and trumps they were.

    Now move to war her sable Matadores,
In show like leaders of the swarthy Moors.
Spadillio first, unconquerable lord!
Led off two captive trumps, and swept the board.   50
As many more Manillio forced to yield,
And marched a victor from the verdant field.
Him Basto followed, but his fate more hard
Gained but one trump and one plebeian card.
With his broad sabre next, a chief in years,   55
The hoary Majesty of Spades appears,
Puts forth one manly leg, to sight revealed,
The rest, his many-coloured robe concealed.
The rebel Knave, who dares his prince engage,
Proves the just victim of his royal rage.   60
Even mighty Pam, that kings and queens o'erthrew
And mowed down armies in the fights of Loo,
Sad chance of war! now destitute of aid,
Falls undistinguished by the victor spade!

    Thus far both armies to Belinda yield;   65
Now to the baron fate inclines the field.
His warlike Amazon her host invades,
Th' imperial consort of the crown of spades.
The club's black tyrant first her victim died,
Spite of his haughty mien, and barb'rous pride: 70
What boots the regal circle on his head,
His giant limbs, in state unwieldy spread;
That long behind he trails his pompous robe,
And, of all monarchs, only grasps the globe?

    The baron now his diamonds pours apace;   75
Th' embroidered King who shows but half his face,
And his refulgent Queen, with pow'rs combined,
Of broken troops an easy conquest find.
Clubs, diamonds, hearts, in wild disorder seen,

CANTO III   **3-4:** Hampton Court, a royal palace a short way up-river from London. **7:** Queen Anne's "three realms" could be (a) England, Wales, and Scotland (the Act of Union was in 1707); (b) England/Wales, Scotland, and Ireland, or (c) England, Ireland, and France (that England ruled France was a fable that persisted long after the end of the reality). **14. Indian screen:** an oriental-style screen used to protect tender faces from the heat of an open fire. **23:** Much business was conducted at the Royal Exchange. **29-30:** Ombre is played with a deck of forty cards (no 8's, 9's, or 10's), nine of which are dealt to each of the three players. **33. Matadore:** The Matadores are the three highest cards (see note on 46ff. below). **41. succinct:** wearing a cincture, girded. **46:** Cf. Genesis 1:3 (p. 241). **46ff.:** Pope stacks the hands so that Belinda wins, but the game as described follows the rules of ombre, though some details are omitted. As "Ombre" (from Spanish *hombre*, "man"), Belinda gets to name trumps; with spades trumps, the three Matadores are Spadillio (ace of spades), Manillio (deuce of spades), and Basto (ace of clubs). **61-62:** Pam, the knave of clubs, is the most powerful card in loo, another fashionable game. **74. globe:** (or *orb*) emblem of sovereignty (usually along with sceptre); in English decks, only the King of Clubs is depicted holding it.

With throngs promiscuous strow the level green. *80*
Thus when dispersed a routed army runs,
Of Asia's troops, and Afric's sable sons,
With like confusion diff'rent nations fly,
Of various habit, and of various dye,
The pierced battalions disunited fall *85*
In heaps on heaps; one fate o'erwhelms them all.
    The Knave of Diamonds tries his wily arts,
And wins (oh shameful chance!) the Queen of Hearts.
At this, the blood the virgin's cheek forsook,
A livid paleness spreads o'er all her look; *90*
She sees, and trembles at th' approaching ill,
Just in the jaws of ruin, and codille.
And now (as oft in some distempered state)
On one nice trick depends the gen'ral fate.
An Ace of Hearts steps forth: the King unseen *95*
Lurked in her hand, and mourned his captive Queen.
He springs to vengeance with an eager pace,
And falls like thunder on the prostrate Ace.
The nymph exulting fills with shouts the sky;
The walls, the woods, and long canals reply. *100*
    Oh thoughtless mortals! ever blind to fate,
Too soon dejected, and too soon elate.
Sudden, these honours shall be snatched away,
And cursed forever this victorious day.
    For lo! the board with cups and spoons is crowned, *105*
The berries crackle, and the mill turns round;
On shining altars of japan they raise
The silver lamp; the fiery spirits blaze:
From silver spouts the grateful liquors glide,
While China's earth receives the smoking tide. *110*
At once they gratify their scent and taste,
And frequent cups prolong the rich repast.
Straight hover round the fair her airy band;
Some, as she sipped, the fuming liquor fanned,
Some o'er her lap their careful plumes displayed, *115*
Trembling, and conscious of the rich brocade.
Coffee (which makes the politician wise,
And see through all things with his half-shut eyes)
Sent up in vapours to the baron's brain
New stratagems, the radiant lock to gain. *120*

Ah cease, rash youth! desist ere 'tis too late,
Fear the just gods, and think of Scylla's fate!
Changed to a bird, and sent to flit in air,
She dearly pays for Nisus' injured hair!
    But when to mischief mortals bend their will, *125*
How soon they find fit instruments of ill!
Just then, Clarissa drew with tempting grace
A two-edged weapon from her shining case:
So ladies in romance assist their knight,
Present the spear, and arm him for the fight. *130*
He takes the gift with rev'rence, and extends
The little engine on his fingers' ends;
This just behind Belinda's neck he spread,
As o'er the fragrant steams she bends her head.
Swift to the lock a thousand sprites repair, *135*
A thousand wings, by turns, blow back the hair;
And thrice they twitched the diamond in her ear;
Thrice she look'd back, and thrice the foe drew near.
Just in that instant, anxious Ariel sought
The close recesses of the virgin's thought; *140*
As on the nosegay in her breast reclined,
He watched th' ideas rising in her mind,
Sudden he viewed, in spite of all her art,
An earthly lover lurking at her heart.
Amazed, confused, he found his pow'r expired, *145*
Resigned to fate, and with a sigh retired.
    The peer now spreads the glitt'ring forfex wide,
T' enclose the lock; now joins it, to divide.
Ev'n then, before the fatal engine closed,
A wretched sylph too fondly interposed; *150*
Fate urged the shears, and cut the sylph in twain
(But airy substance soon unites again);
The meeting points the sacred hair dissever
From the fair head, forever, and forever!
    Then flashed the living lightning from her eyes, *155*
And screams of horror rend th' affrighted skies.
Not louder shrieks to pitying Heav'n are cast,
When husbands, or when lapdogs breathe their last;
Or when rich china vessels fall'n from high,
In glitt'ring dust and painted fragments lie! *160*

---

80. strow: strew. **92. codille:** If the Ombre doesn't take most of the tricks (i.e., at least five), he or she is said to have been given *codille* — i.e., defeat. **95-98:** The king outranks the ace, since spades are trumps. **100:** Cf. the refrain lines in Spenser's *Epithalamion* (pp. 163ff.); the vast grounds of Hampton Court included canals. **103. honours:** honours generally, for winning, or perhaps Belinda's high cards, which earned points. The word *honours* also refers to hair. **106. berries:** i.e., coffee beans, being first roasted and then ground in a hand mill. **107. altars of japan:** lacquered (japanned) tables. **108. spirits:** i.e., in the spirit lamp under the coffee-pot. **109. grateful:** gratifying, pleasing, delicious. **122-24:** Not the Scylla who is paired with Charybdis; this Scylla, daughter of King Nisus of Megara, cut from his head a purple hair — on which his kingdom depended — to give to Minos, who was attacking and whom she had fallen for at a distance; Minos, however, was appalled; but he won, and then sailed away, she trying to cling to his ship; but Nisus, now an osprey, frightened her off, and she too was changed to a bird (see Ovid, *Metamorphoses*, VIII, 1ff.). **147. forfex:** (Latin) pair of scissors. **152.** See *Paradise Lost*, VI, 330-31 (from Pope's note).

"Let wreaths of triumph now my temples twine,"
The victor cried, "the glorious prize is mine!
While fish in streams, or birds delight in air,
Or in a coach and six the British fair,
As long as *Atalantis* shall be read,   *165*
Or the small pillow grace a lady's bed,
While visits shall be paid on solemn days,
When num'rous wax-lights in bright order blaze,
While nymphs take treats, or assignations give,
So long my honour, name, and praise shall live!   *170*
What time would spare, from steel receives its date,
And monuments, like men, submit to fate!
Steel could the labour of the gods destroy,
And strike to dust th' imperial tow'rs of Troy;
Steel could the works of mortal pride confound,   *175*
And hew triumphal arches to the ground.
What wonder then, fair nymph! thy hairs should feel
The conq'ring force of unresisted steel?"

Canto IV

But anxious cares the pensive nymph oppressed,
And secret passions laboured in her breast.
Not youthful kings in battle seized alive,
Not scornful virgins who their charms survive,
Not ardent lovers robbed of all their bliss,   *5*
Not ancient ladies when refused a kiss,
Not tyrants fierce that unrepenting die,
Not Cynthia when her manteau's pinned awry,
E'er felt such rage, resentment, and despair,
As thou, sad virgin! for thy ravished hair.   *10*
    For, that sad moment, when the sylphs withdrew,
And Ariel weeping from Belinda flew,
Umbriel, a dusky, melancholy sprite,
As ever sullied the fair face of light,
Down to the central earth, his proper scene,   *15*
Repaired to search the gloomy Cave of Spleen.
    Swift on his sooty pinions flits the gnome,
And in a vapour reached the dismal dome.
No cheerful breeze this sullen region knows,
The dreaded east is all the wind that blows.   *20*

Here in a grotto, sheltered close from air,
And screened in shades from day's detested glare,
She sighs forever on her pensive bed,
Pain at her side, and Megrim at her head.
Two handmaids wait the throne: alike in place,   *25*
But diff'ring far in figure and in face.
Here stood Ill-nature like an ancient maid,
Her wrinkled form in black and white arrayed;
With store of pray'rs, for mornings, nights, and noons,
Her hand is filled; her bosom with lampoons.   *30*
There Affectation, with a sickly mien,
Shows in her cheek the roses of eighteen,
Practised to lisp, and hang the head aside,
Faints into airs, and languishes with pride,
On the rich quilt sinks with becoming woe,   *35*
Wrapped in a gown, for sickness, and for show.
The fair ones feel such maladies as these,
When each new night-dress gives a new disease.
    A constant vapour o'er the palace flies;
Strange phantoms rising as the mists arise;   *40*
Dreadful as hermits' dreams in haunted shades,
Or bright as visions of expiring maids.
Now glaring fiends, and snakes on rolling spires,
Pale spectres, gaping tombs, and purple fires:
Now lakes of liquid gold, Elysian scenes,   *45*
And crystal domes, and angels in machines.
    Unnumbered throngs on ev'ry side are seen,
Of bodies changed to various forms by Spleen.
Here living teapots stand, one arm held out,
One bent; the handle this, and that the spout: *50*
A pipkin there, like Homer's tripod walks;
Here sighs a jar, and there a goose-pie talks;
Men prove with child, as pow'rful fancy works,
And maids turned bottles call aloud for corks.   *54*
    Safe passed the gnome through this fantastic band,
A branch of healing spleenwort in his hand.
Then thus address'd the pow'r: "Hail, wayward Queen!
Who rule the sex to fifty from fifteen;
Parent of vapours and of female wit,
Who give th' hysteric, or poetic fit,   *60*
On various tempers act by various ways,

---

164. six: i.e., horses, in three pairs. **165:** Mrs. Delarivier Manley's popular *Secret Memoirs and Manners of Several Persons of Quality, of Both Sexes. From the New Atalantis, an Island in the Mediterranean,* a gossip- and scandalmongering *roman à clef,* appeared in 1709 (she was arrested for libel). **167-68:** Fashionable women made frequent evening social calls. **171. date:** end, termination. **173-74:** alluding to the supposed building of Troy by Apollo and Poseidon.   CANTO IV   **16. Spleen:** personifying a fashionable complaint characterized by anger, ill humour, melancholy, and symptoms both real and affected, or hypochondriacal; she is attended by other appropriate personifications (24ff.). **18. vapour:** Spleen was also called "the vapours." **20:** The cold and dank east wind was considered an obvious cause of spleen. **24. Megrim:** headache (migraine). **43-46:** referring to special effects and mechanical contrivances used in theatres, especially in operas. **43. spires:** spirals, coils. **46. angels in machines:** i.e., instances of *deus ex machina* (see Glossary), but also the "machinery" of Pope's poem (see dedicatory letter). **51:** See *Iliad,* XVIII, 439ff. (p. 534; from Pope's note). **52. a goose-pie talks:** "Alludes to a real fact; a lady of distinction imagined herself in this condition" (Pope's note). **56. spleenwort:** fern so named because thought to be efficacious against spleen — imitating the protective golden bough Aeneas carried into the underworld (*Aeneid,* VI, 136ff.), and perhaps the herb *moly* given Odysseus to protect him against Circe (*Odyssey,* X, 287ff.).

Make some take physic, others scribble plays;
Who cause the proud their visits to delay,
And send the godly in a pet to pray.
A nymph there is, that all thy pow'r disdains,   65
And thousands more in equal mirth maintains.
But oh! if e'er thy gnome could spoil a grace,
Or raise a pimple on a beauteous face,
Like citron-waters matrons' cheeks inflame,
Or change complexions at a losing game;   70
If e'er with airy horns I planted heads,
Or rumpled petticoats, or tumbled beds,
Or caused suspicion when no soul was rude,
Or discomposed the head-dress of a prude,
Or e'er to costive lapdog gave disease,   75
Which not the tears of brightest eyes could ease:
Hear me, and touch Belinda with chagrin,
That single act gives half the world the spleen."
    The goddess with a discontented air
Seems to reject him, though she grants his pray'r.   80
A wondrous bag with both her hands she binds,
Like that where once Ulysses held the winds;
There she collects the force of female lungs,
Sighs, sobs, and passions, and the war of tongues.
A vial next she fills with fainting fears,   85
Soft sorrows, melting griefs, and flowing tears.
The gnome rejoicing bears her gifts away,
Spreads his black wings, and slowly mounts to day.
    Sunk in Thalestris' arms the nymph he found,
Her eyes dejected, and her hair unbound.   90
Full o'er their heads the swelling bag he rent,
And all the Furies issued at the vent.
Belinda burns with more than mortal ire,
And fierce Thalestris fans the rising fire.   94
"Oh wretched maid!" she spread her hands, and cried
(While Hampton's echoes, "Wretched maid!" replied),
"Was it for this you took such constant care
The bodkin, comb, and essence to prepare?
For this your locks in paper durance bound,
For this with tort'ring irons wreathed around?   100
For this with fillets strained your tender head,
And bravely bore the double loads of lead?
Gods! shall the ravisher display your hair,

While the fops envy, and the ladies stare!
Honour forbid! at whose unrivalled shrine   105
Ease, pleasure, virtue, all, our sex resign.
Methinks already I your tears survey,
Already hear the horrid things they say,
Already see you a degraded toast,
And all your honour in a whisper lost!   110
How shall I, then, your helpless fame defend?
'Twill then be infamy to seem your friend!
And shall this prize, th' inestimable prize,
Exposed through crystal to the gazing eyes,
And heightened by the diamond's circling rays,   115
On that rapacious hand forever blaze?
Sooner shall grass in Hyde Park Circus grow,
And wits take lodgings in the sound of Bow;
Sooner let earth, air, sea, to chaos fall,
Men, monkeys, lapdogs, parrots, perish all!"   120
    She said; then raging to Sir Plume repairs,
And bids her beau demand the precious hairs
(Sir Plume of amber snuff-box justly vain,
And the nice conduct of a clouded cane);
With earnest eyes, and round unthinking face,   125
He first the snuff-box opened, then the case,
And thus broke out — "My Lord, why, what the devil?
Z—ds! damn the lock! 'fore Gad, you must be civil!
Plague on't! 'tis past a jest — nay prithee, pox!
Give her the hair" — he spoke, and rapped his box. 130
    "It grieves me much," replied the peer again,
"Who speaks so well should ever speak in vain.
But by this lock, this sacred lock, I swear
(Which never more shall join its parted hair;
Which never more its honours shall renew,   135
Clipped from the lovely head where late it grew),
That while my nostrils draw the vital air,
This hand, which won it, shall forever wear."
He spoke, and speaking, in proud triumph spread
The long-contended honours of her head.   140
    But Umbriel, hateful gnome! forbears not so;
He breaks the vial whence the sorrows flow.
Then see! the nymph in beauteous grief appears,
Her eyes half-languishing, half-drowned in tears;
On her heaved bosom hung her drooping head,   145

---

69. citron-waters: brandy flavoured with the rind of the lemonlike fruit of the citron-tree. **71. airy horns:** i.e., those of a man jealously imagining himself a cuckold. **77. chagrin:** ill-humour, vexation, peevishness, fretfulness. **82:** alluding to the bag of winds Aeolus gave Odysseus (see beginning of *Odyssey*, X). **89. Thalestris:** a queen of the Amazons. **99. paper durance:** curl papers (clamped in place with thin strips of flexible lead — see line 102). **113-16:** Locks of hair were set in rings as well as in lockets. **117. Circus:** another name for the Ring (see I, 44). **118. Bow:** True Cockneys are said to be born "within the sound of Bow Bells," the bells of the church of St. Mary-le-Bow, Cheapside, which had by then become the mercantile area considered the least fashionable district in London. **121: Sir Plume** is identified with Sir George Browne, Arabella's mother's cousin, as is Thalestris with his wife, Gertrude Morley. **124. clouded:** i.e., the amber head fashionably darkened with veins or spots. **128. Z—ds!:** Zounds! (a mild oath, euphemism for "God's wounds"; see Chaucer's "Pardoner's Tale," 146, 324ff. — pp. 58, 60). **133ff.:** "In allusion to Achilles's oath in Homer, *Iliad*, I" (Pope's note; see 309ff. in Pope's translation, 234ff. in original).

Which, with a sigh, she raised; and thus she said:
  "Forever cursed be this detested day,
Which snatched my best, my fav'rite curl away!
Happy! ah ten times happy had I been,
If Hampton Court these eyes had never seen! 150
Yet am not I the first mistaken maid,
By love of courts to num'rous ills betrayed.
Oh had I rather unadmired remained
In some lone isle, or distant northern land;
Where the gilt chariot never marks the way, 155
Where none learn ombre, none e'er taste bohea!
There kept my charms concealed from mortal eye,
Like roses that in deserts bloom and die.
What moved my mind with youthful lords to roam?
Oh had I stayed, and said my pray'rs at home! 160
'Twas this, the morning omens seemed to tell,
Thrice from my trembling hand the patch-box fell;
The tott'ring china shook without a wind,
Nay, Poll sat mute, and Shock was most unkind!
A sylph too warned me of the threats of Fate, 165
In mystic visions, now believed too late!
See the poor remnants of these slighted hairs!
My hands shall rend what ev'n thy rapine spares.
These in two sable ringlets taught to break,
Once gave new beauties to the snowy neck; 170
The sister-lock now sits uncouth, alone,
And in its fellow's fate foresees its own;
Uncurled it hangs, the fatal shears demands,
And tempts, once more, thy sacrilegious hands.
Oh hadst thou, cruel! been content to seize 175
Hairs less in sight, or any hairs but these!"

Canto V

She said: the pitying audience melt in tears;
But Fate and Jove had stopped the baron's ears.
In vain Thalestris with reproach assails,
For who can move when fair Belinda fails?
Not half so fixed the Trojan could remain, 5
While Anna begged and Dido raged in vain.
Then grave Clarissa graceful waved her fan;
Silence ensued, and thus the nymph began:
  "Say why are beauties praised and honoured most,
The wise man's passion, and the vain man's toast? 10
Why decked with all that land and sea afford,
Why angels called, and angel-like adored?

Why round our coaches crowd the white-gloved beaux,
Why bows the side-box from its inmost rows?
How vain are all these glories, all our pains, 15
Unless good sense preserve what beauty gains:
That men may say, when we the front-box grace,
'Behold the first in virtue as in face!'
Oh! if to dance all night, and dress all day,
Charmed the smallpox, or chased old age away; 20
Who would not scorn what housewife's cares produce,
Or who would learn one earthly thing of use?
To patch, nay ogle, might become a saint,
Nor could it sure be such a sin to paint.
But since, alas! frail beauty must decay, 25
Curled or uncurled, since locks will turn to grey;
Since painted, or not painted, all shall fade,
And she who scorns a man, must die a maid;
What then remains, but well our pow'r to use,
And keep good humour still whate'er we lose? 30
And trust me, dear! good humour can prevail,
When airs, and flights, and screams, and scolding fail.
Beauties in vain their pretty eyes may roll;
Charms strike the sight, but merit wins the soul."
  So spoke the dame, but no applause ensued; 35
Belinda frowned, Thalestris called her prude.
"To arms, to arms!" the fierce virago cries,
And swift as lightning to the combat flies.
All side in parties, and begin th' attack;
Fans clap, silks rustle, and tough whalebones crack; 40
Heroes' and heroines' shouts confus'dly rise,
And bass and treble voices strike the skies.
No common weapons in their hands are found,
Like gods they fight, nor dread a mortal wound.
  So when bold Homer makes the gods engage, 45
And heav'nly breasts with human passions rage;
'Gainst Pallas, Mars; Latona, Hermes arms;
And all Olympus rings with loud alarms:
Jove's thunder roars, Heav'n trembles all around,
Blue Neptune storms, the bell'wing deeps resound: 50
Earth shakes her nodding tow'rs, the ground gives way,
And the pale ghosts start at the flash of day!
  Triumphant Umbriel on a sconce's height,
Clapped his glad wings, and sate to view the fight:
Propped on their bodkin spears, the sprites survey 55
The growing combat, or assist the fray.

---

156. bohea: a choice black Chinese tea. **158:** Cf. Waller's "Song" (p. 311). **162. patch-box:** container for the patches of I, 138. **164. Poll:** i.e., the parrot. **CANTO V** **5-6:** See *Aeneid*, IV, 296ff., especially 438-49. **7. Clarissa:** "A new character introduced in the subsequent editions [i.e., 1717ff.], to open more clearly the moral of the poem, in a parody of the speech of Sarpedon to Glaucus in Homer" (Pope's note; see his translation, *Iliad*, XII, 371-96; in original, 310-28). **17. front-box:** i.e., at the theatre. **47. Pallas:** Pallas Athena (Minerva); **Latona:** (Leto) mother of Apollo and Artemis (Diana).

While through the press enraged Thalestris flies,
And scatters death around from both her eyes,
A beau and witling perished in the throng,
One died in metaphor, and one in song.   60
"O cruel nymph! a living death I bear,"
Cried Dapperwit, and sunk beside his chair.
A mournful glance Sir Fopling upwards cast,
"Those eyes are made so killing" — was his last.
Thus on Mæander's flow'ry margin lies   65
Th' expiring swan, and as he sings he dies.
    When bold Sir Plume had drawn Clarissa down,
Chloe stepped in, and killed him with a frown;
She smiled to see the doughty hero slain,
But, at her smile, the beau revived again.   70
    Now Jove suspends his golden scales in air,
Weighs the men's wits against the lady's hair;
The doubtful beam long nods from side to side;
At length the wits mount up, the hairs subside.
    See, fierce Belinda on the baron flies,   75
With more than usual lightning in her eyes:
Nor feared the chief th' unequal fight to try,
Who sought no more than on his foe to die.
But this bold lord with manly strength endued,
She with one finger and a thumb subdued: 80
Just where the breath of life his nostrils drew,
A charge of snuff the wily virgin threw;
The gnomes direct, to ev'ry atom just,
The pungent grains of titillating dust.
Sudden, with starting tears each eye o'erflows,   85
And the high dome re-echoes to his nose.
    "Now meet thy fate," incensed Belinda cried,
And drew a deadly bodkin from her side.
(The same, his ancient personage to deck,
Her great-great-grandsire wore about his neck,   90
In three seal-rings; which after, melted down,
Formed a vast buckle for his widow's gown:
Her infant grandame's whistle next it grew,

The bells she jingled, and the whistle blew;
Then in a bodkin graced her mother's hairs,   95
Which long she wore, and now Belinda wears.)
    "Boast not my fall," he cried, "insulting foe!
Thou by some other shalt be laid as low,
Nor think, to die dejects my lofty mind:
All that I dread is leaving you behind!   100
Rather than so, ah let me still survive,
And burn in Cupid's flames — but burn alive."
    "Restore the lock!" she cries; and all around
"Restore the lock!" the vaulted roofs rebound.
Not fierce Othello in so loud a strain   105
Roared for the handkerchief that caused his pain.
But see how oft ambitious aims are crossed,
And chiefs contend 'till all the prize is lost!
The lock, obtained with guilt, and kept with pain,
In ev'ry place is sought, but sought in vain: 110
With such a prize no mortal must be blest,
So Heav'n decrees! with Heav'n who can contest?
Some thought it mounted to the lunar sphere,
Since all things lost on earth are treasured there.
There heroes' wits are kept in pond'rous vases,   115
And beaux' in snuff-boxes and tweezer-cases.
There broken vows, and deathbed alms are found,
And lovers' hearts with ends of ribbon bound,
The courtier's promises, and sick man's pray'rs,
The smiles of harlots, and the tears of heirs,   120
Cages for gnats, and chains to yoke a flea,
Dried butterflies, and tomes of casuistry.
    But trust the Muse — she saw it upward rise,
Though marked by none but quick, poetic eyes:
(So Rome's great founder to the heav'ns withdrew,
To Proculus alone confessed in view):   126
A sudden star, it shot through liquid air,
And drew behind a radiant trail of hair.
Not Berenice's locks first rose so bright,
The heav'ns bespangling with dishevelled light.   130

---

62. Dapperwit: a character in William Wycherley's play *Love in a Wood* (1671). **63:** Sir Fopling Flutter is the subtitle-character in George Etherege's play *Man of Mode* (1676). **64. "Those . . . killing":** "The words in a song in the opera of *Camilla*" (1706, by Marc Antonio Buononcini; Pope's note). **65.** Pope's note quotes from Ovid's *Epistles*, VII, two lines which translate as follows: "Thus when fate calls, throwing himself into the wet grass, by the stream Mæander sings the white swan"; **Mæander** (Greek *Maiandros*): a river in Phrygia noted for its meandering course (modern *Menderes*, in western Turkey), referred to near the end of *Iliad* II. **71:** See *Iliad*, VII, 87ff. (68ff. in original), and *Aeneid* XII, 725ff. (from Pope's note). **78. die:** See note to line 21 of Donne's "The Canonization" (p. 254). **89ff.:** "In imitation of the progress of Agamemnon's sceptre in Homer, *Iliad*, II" (129ff.; in original, 100ff.; Pope's note). **105-06:** See Shakespeare's *Othello*, III.iv. **113ff.:** imitating Ariosto's *Orlando Furioso*, XXXIV, 68ff. (from Pope's note). **125-26:** Romulus was said to have been carried off to heaven as a deity, appearing before the senator Julius Proculus to confirm it. **127-28:** See Ovid, *Metamorphoses*, XV, 849-50 (from Pope's note); **liquid:** (Latin *liquidus*) clear, transparent. **129:** When Berenice (c.273-221 B.C.), wife of Ptolemy III, dedicated a lock to the gods for his safe return from war, it mysteriously disappeared from Arsinoe's temple, and was said by the astronomer Conon to have been turned into the constellation Coma Berenices (Berenice's Locks), surrounded by those of Ursa Major, Boötes, Virgo, and Leo — an event celebrated in a poem by Callimachus (now mostly lost, but closely imitated in one by Catullus) in which the hair speaks from the heavens, saying Venus placed it there.

The sylphs behold it kindling as it flies,
And pleased pursue its progress through the skies.
　This the beau monde shall from the Mall survey,
And hail with music its propitious ray.
This the blest lover shall for Venus take, *135*
And send up vows from Rosamonda's Lake.
This Partridge soon shall view in cloudless skies,
When next he looks through Galileo's eyes;
And hence th' egregious wizard shall foredoom
The fate of Louis, and the fall of Rome. *140*
　Then cease, bright nymph! to mourn thy ravished hair,
Which adds new glory to the shining sphere!
Not all the tresses that fair head can boast,
Shall draw such envy as the lock you lost.
For, after all the murders of your eye, *145*
When, after millions slain, yourself shall die;
When those fair suns shall set, as set they must,
And all those tresses shall be laid in dust,
This lock, the Muse shall consecrate to fame,
And 'midst the stars inscribe Belinda's name. *150*

(1712, 1714, 1717)

THE UNIVERSAL PRAYER

Father of all! in every age,
　In every clime adored,
By saint, by savage, and by sage,
　Jehovah, Jove, or Lord!

Thou great First Cause, least understood, *5*
　Who all my sense confined
To know but this — that Thou art good,
　And that myself am blind;

Yet gave me, in this dark estate,
　To see the good from ill, *10*
And binding Nature fast in Fate,
　Left free the human will.

What conscience dictates to be done,
　Or warns me not to do,
This, teach me more than Hell to shun, *15*
　That, more than Heav'n pursue.

What blessings thy free bounty gives,
　Let me not cast away;
For God is paid when man receives;
　T'enjoy is to obey. *20*

Yet not to Earth's contracted span
　Thy goodness let me bound,
Or think Thee Lord alone of man,
　When thousand worlds are round.

Let not this weak, unknowing hand *25*
　Presume thy bolts to throw,
And deal damnation round the land
　On each I judge thy foe.

If I am right, thy grace impart
　Still in the right to stay; *30*
If I am wrong, oh teach my heart
　To find that better way.

Save me alike from foolish pride,
　Or impious discontent,
At aught thy wisdom has denied, *35*
　Or aught thy goodness lent.

Teach me to feel another's woe,
　To hide the fault I see;
That mercy I to others show,
　That mercy show to me. *40*

Mean though I am, not wholly so,
　Since quickened by thy breath;
Oh lead me wheresoe'er I go
　Through this day's life, or death.

This day, be bread and peace my lot; *45*
　All else beneath the sun,
Thou know'st if best bestowed, or not;
　And let thy will be done.

To Thee, whose temple is all space,
　Whose altar, Earth, Sea, Skies; *50*
One chorus let all Being raise!
　All Nature's incense rise!

(1715; 1738)

---

133. Mall: fashionable promenade in St. James's Park. **136:** Rosamonda's Pond, in St. James's Park, was associated with lovers. **137:** "John Partridge [1644-1715] was a ridiculous stargazer [astrologer], who in his almanacs every year, never failed to predict the downfall of the Pope, and the King of France, then at war with the English" (Pope's note). **149-50.** Cf. Spenser's *Amoretti*, Sonnet 75, 9-12 (p. 162). **THE UNIVERSAL PRAYER 26. bolts:** i.e., Jove's thunderbolts.

from translation of Homer's *ILIAD*

from *Book I*
[the invocation]

Achilles' wrath, to Greece the direful spring
Of woes unnumbered, heavenly Goddess, sing!
That wrath which hurled to Pluto's gloomy reign
The souls of mighty chiefs untimely slain:
Whose limbs, unburied on the naked shore,   5
Devouring dogs and hungry vultures tore:
Since great Achilles and Atrides strove,
Such was the sovereign doom, and such the will of Jove.
Declare, O Muse! in what ill-fated hour
Sprung the fierce strife, from what offended power? 10
Latona's son a dire contagion spread,
And heaped the camp with mountains of the dead;
The king of men his reverend priest defied,
And, for the king's offence, the people died.

                                                    (1715)

from *Book XVIII*
[the shield of Achilles]

. . . . Meanwhile the silver-footed dame
Reached the Vulcanian dome, eternal frame!
High eminent amid the works divine,
Where Heav'n's far-beaming, brazen mansions shine.
There the lame architect the goddess found,   435
Obscure in smoke, his forges flaming round,
While bathed in sweat from fire to fire he flew,
And puffing loud, the roaring bellows blew.
That day, no common task his labour claimed;
Full twenty tripods for his hall he framed,   440
That placed on living wheels of massy gold
(Wondrous to tell) instinct with spirit rolled
From place to place, around the blest abodes,
Self-moved, obedient to the beck of gods:
For their fair handles now, o'erwrought with flow'rs,
In moulds prepared, the glowing ore he pours.   446
Just as, responsive to his thought, the frame

Stood prompt to move, the azure goddess came:
Charis, his spouse, a grace divinely fair
(With purple fillets round her braided hair),   450
Observed her ent'ring; her soft hand she pressed,
And, smiling, thus the wat'ry queen addressed:
    "What, Goddess! this unusual favour draws?
All hail, and welcome! whatsoe'er the cause;
Till now a stranger, in a happy hour   455
Approach, and taste the dainties of the bow'r."
    High on a throne, with stars of silver graced,
And various artifice, the Queen she placed,
A footstool at her feet; then calling said,
"Vulcan, draw near; 'tis Thetis asks your aid."   460
    "Thetis" (replied the god), "our pow'rs may claim
An ever dear and ever honoured name!
When my proud mother hurled me from the sky
(My awkward form, it seems, displeased her eye),
She and Eurynome my griefs redressed,   465
And soft received me on their silver breast.
Ev'n then, these arts employed my infant thought;
Chains, bracelets, pendants, all their toys I wrought.
Nine years kept secret in the dark abode,
Secure I lay, concealed from man and god: 470
Deep in a caverned rock my days were led;
The rushing Ocean murmured o'er my head.
Now since her presence glads our mansion, say,
For such desert what service can I pay?
Vouchsafe, O Thetis! at our board to share   475
The genial rites and hospitable fare,
While I the labours of the forge forgo,
And bid the roaring bellows cease to blow."
    Then from his anvil the lame artist rose;
Wide with distorted legs, oblique he goes,   480
And stills the bellows and (in order laid)
Locks in their chests his instruments of trade.
Then with a sponge the sooty workman dressed
His brawny arms imbrowned, and hairy breast.
With his huge sceptre graced, and red attire,   485
Came halting forth the sov'reign of the fire;
The monarch's steps two female forms uphold,
That moved, and breathed, in animated gold,
To whom was voice, and sense, and science giv'n
Of works divine (such wonders are in Heav'n!).   490

ILIAD, BOOK I   **7. Atrides:** Atreides — i.e., Agamemnon, son of Atreus. **11. Latona's son:** Apollo.   **BOOK XVIII**   (Cf. Auden's "The Shield of Achilles," p. 1361.) **431. silver-footed dame:** the Nereid Thetis, mother of Achilles. **432. dome:** (large) building, house (from Latin *domus*). **435. lame architect:** Vulcan (Hephaistos). **463. mother:** Juno (Hera); in Book I, he tells the other version, namely that it was his father, Jove (Zeus), who threw him out because he took his mother's side against him (see also *Paradise Lost*, I, 740ff.; p. 335). **465. Eurynome:** daughter of Ocean. **489. science:** knowledge.

On these supported, with unequal gait,
He reached the throne where pensive Thetis sate;
There placed beside her on the shining frame,
He thus addressed the silver-footed dame:
　"Thee, welcome Goddess, what occasion calls　　*495*
(So long a stranger) to these honoured walls?
'Tis thine, fair Thetis, the command to lay,
And Vulcan's joy, and duty, to obey."
　To whom the mournful mother thus replies
(The crystal drops stood trembling in her eyes):　　*500*
"Oh Vulcan! say, was ever breast divine
So pierced with sorrows, so o'erwhelmed as mine?
Of all the goddesses, did Jove prepare
For Thetis only such a weight of care?
I, only I, of all the wat'ry race,　　*505*
By force subjected to a man's embrace,
Who, sinking now with age, and sorrow, pays
The mighty fine imposed on length of days.
Sprung from my bed a god-like hero came,
The bravest sure that ever bore the name;　　*510*
Like some fair plant beneath my careful hand
He grew, he flourished, and he graced the land.
To Troy I sent him, but his native shore
Never, ah never, shall receive him more
(Ev'n while he lives, he wastes with secret woe),　　*515*
Nor I, a goddess, can retard the blow!
Robbed of the prize the Grecian suffrage gave,
The King of nations forced his royal slave;
For this he grieved, and till the Greeks oppressed
Required his arm, he sorrowed unredressed.　　*520*
Large gifts they promise, and their elders send;
In vain — he arms not, but permits his friend
His arms, his steeds, his forces to employ.
He marches, combats, almost conquers Troy;
Then slain by Phoebus (Hector had the name),　　*525*
At once resigns his armour, life, and fame.
But thou, in pity, by my pray'r be won;
Grace with immortal arms this short-lived son,
And to the field in martial pomp restore,
To shine with glory, till he shines no more!"　　*530*
　To her the artist-god: "Thy griefs resign,
Secure, what Vulcan can, is ever thine.
O could I hide him from the Fates as well,

Or with these hands the cruel stroke repel,
As I shall forge most envied arms, the gaze　　*535*
Of wond'ring ages, and the world's amaze!"
　Thus having said, the Father of the Fires
To the black labours of his forge retires.
Soon as he bade them blow, the bellows turned
Their iron mouths; and where the furnace burned,　　*540*
Resounding breathed. At once the blast expires,
And twenty forges catch at once the fires;
Just as the god directs, now loud, now low,
They raise a tempest, or they gently blow.
In hissing flames huge silver bars are rolled,　　*545*
And stubborn brass, and tin, and solid gold.
Before, deep fixed, th'eternal anvils stand;
The pond'rous hammer loads his better hand,
His left with tongs turns the vexed metal round,　　*549*
And thick, strong strokes the doubling vaults rebound.
　Then first he formed th'immense and solid shield;
Rich, various artifice emblazed the field;
Its utmost verge a threefold circle bound;
A silver chain suspends the massy round,
Five ample plates the broad expanse compose,　　*555*
And god-like labours on the surface rose.
There shone the image of the Master Mind:
There Earth, there Heav'n, there Ocean he designed;
Th'unwearied sun, the moon completely round;
The starry lights that Heav'n's high convex crowned;
The Pleiads, Hyads, with the Northern Team,　　*561*
And great Orion's more refulgent beam;
To which, around the axle of the sky,
The Bear revolving, points his golden eye,
Still shines exalted on th'ætherial plain,　　*565*
Nor bathes his blazing forehead in the main.
　Two cities radiant on the shield appear,
The image one of peace, and one of war.
Here sacred pomp and genial feast delight,
And solemn dance, and Hymeneal rite;　　*570*
Along the street the new-made brides are led,
With torches flaming, to the nuptial bed;
The youthful dancers in a circle bound
To the soft flute and cittern's silver sound;
Through the fair streets, the matrons in a row　　*575*
Stand in their porches and enjoy the show.

506: Zeus and Poseidon gave Thetis to Peleus, a mortal, as a wife. **509. hero:** i.e., her only child, Achilles, who is fated to die soon after he kills Hector, the Trojan slayer (with the help of Phoebus, or Apollo: line 525) of Patroclus. **518. King:** Agamemnon; the "prize" he robbed Achilles of was the girl Briseis. **522. friend:** i.e., Patroclus. **561:** the Pleiades, the Hyades, and that part of Ursa Major (the "Bear" of 564) variously known as the Wain, the Wagon, the Plough, and the Big Dipper.

There in the Forum swarm a num'rous train;
The subject of debate: a townsman slain;
One pleads the fine discharged, which one denied,
And bade the public and the laws decide;   580
The witness is produced on either hand;
For this, or that, the partial people stand;
Th'appointed heralds still the noisy bands,
And form a ring, with sceptres in their hands;
On seats of stone, within the sacred place,   585
The rev'rend elders nodded o'er the case;
Alternate, each th'attesting sceptre took,
And rising solemn, each his sentence spoke.
Two golden talents lay amidst, in sight,
The prize of him who best adjudge the right.   590
     Another part (a prospect diff'ring far)
Glowed with refulgent arms and horrid war.
Two mighty hosts a leaguered town embrace,
And one would pillage, one would burn the place.
Meantime the townsmen, armed with silent care,   595
A secret ambush on the foe prepare.
Their wives, their children, and the watchful band
Of trembling parents on the turrets stand.
They march, by Pallas and by Mars made bold;
Gold were the gods, their radiant garments gold,   600
And gold their armour: these the squadron led,
August, divine, superior by the head!
A place for ambush fit they found, and stood
Covered with shields, beside a silver flood.
Two spies at distance lurk, and watchful seem   605
If sheep or oxen seek the winding stream.
Soon the white flocks proceeded o'er the plains,
And steers slow-moving, and two shepherd swains;
Behind them, piping on their reeds, they go,
Nor fear an ambush, nor suspect a foe.   610
In arms the glitt'ring squadron rising round
Rush sudden; hills of slaughter heap the ground,
Whole flocks and herds lie bleeding on the plains,
And all amidst them, dead, the shepherd swains.
The bellowing oxen the besiegers hear;   615
They rise, take horse, approach, and meet the war;
They fight, they fall, beside the silver flood;
The waving silver seemed to blush with blood.
There Tumult, their Contention stood confessed;
One reared a dagger at a captive's breast;   620

One held a living foe that freshly bled
With new-made wounds; another dragged a dead;
Now here, now there, the carcasses they tore;
Fate stalked amidst them, grim with human gore.
And the whole war came out, and met the eye,   625
And each bold figure seemed to live, or die.
     A field deep-furrowed next the god designed,
The third time laboured by the sweating hind.
The shining shares full many ploughmen guide,
And turn their crooked yokes on ev'ry side.   630
Still as at either end they wheel around,
The master meets 'em with his goblet crowned;
The hearty draught rewards, renews their toil;
Then back the turning ploughshares cleave the soil;
Behind, the rising earth in ridges rolled,   635
And sable looked, though formed of molten gold.
     Another field rose high with waving grain;
With bended sickles stand the reaper-train.
Here stretched in ranks the levelled swaths are found,
Sheaves heaped on sheaves here thicken up the ground.
With sweeping stroke the mowers strow the lands;   641
The gath'rers follow, and collect in bands;
And last the children, in whose arms are borne
(Too short to gripe them) the brown sheaves of corn.
The rustic monarch of the field descries,   645
With silent glee, the heaps around him rise.
A ready banquet on the turf is laid,
Beneath an ample oak's expanded shade.
The victim-ox the sturdy youth prepare:
The reapers' due repast, the women's care.   650
     Next, ripe in yellow gold, a vineyard shines,
Bent with the pond'rous harvest of its vines;
A deeper dye the dangling clusters show,
And curled on silver props, in order glow.
A darker metal mixed, intrenched the place,   655
And pales of glitt'ring tin th'enclosure grace.
To this, one pathway gently winding leads,
Where march a train with baskets on their heads
(Fair maids, and blooming youths), that smiling bear
The purple product of th'autumnal year.   660
To these a youth awakes the warbling strings,
Whose tender lay the fate of Linus sings;
In measured dance behind him move the train,
Tune soft the voice, and answer to the strain.

---

599. Pallas: Athena. **602:** echoing *The Rape of the Lock*, II, 70 (p. 526). **628. laboured:** i.e., worked over, ploughed, tilled; **hind:** farmer, rustic, servant. **644. gripe:** grip. **662. Linus:** Variously identified, Linus was apparently believed to be someone who died prematurely and who was mourned annually in such a song; Pope, citing among other sources Virgil's *Eclogues* IV (see p. 438) and VI, understands him to have been a sort of mythical proto-poet, inventor of verse itself.

Here, herds of oxen march, erect and bold,   665
Rear high their horns, and seem to low in gold,
And speed to meadows on whose sounding shores
A rapid torrent through the rushes roars;
Four golden herdsmen as their guardians stand,
And nine sour dogs complete the rustic band.   670
Two lions rushing from the wood appeared,
And seized a bull, the master of the herd;
He roared; in vain the dogs, the men withstood;
They tore his flesh, and drank the sable blood.
The dogs (oft cheered in vain) desert the prey,   675
Dread the grim terrors, and at distance bay.
    Next this, the eye the art of Vulcan leads
Deep through fair forests, and a length of meads;
And stalls, and folds, and scattered cots between;
And fleecy flocks, that whiten all the scene.   680
    A figured dance succeeds: such once was seen
In lofty Gnossus, for the Cretan queen,
Formed by Dædalean art. A comely band
Of youths and maidens, bounding hand in hand:
The maids in soft cymars of linen dressed,   685
The youths all graceful in the glossy vest;
Of those the locks with flow'ry wreaths inrolled,
Of these the sides adorned with swords of gold,
That glitt'ring gay from silver belts depend.
Now all at once they rise, at once descend,   690
With well-taught feet; now shape, in oblique ways,
Confus'dly regular, the moving maze;
Now forth at once, too swift for sight, they spring,
And undistinguished blend the flying ring.
So whirls a wheel, in giddy circle tossed,   695
And rapid as it runs, the single spokes are lost.
The gazing multitudes admire around;
Two active tumblers in the centre bound;
Now high, now low, their pliant limbs they bend,
And gen'ral songs the sprightly revel end.   700
    Thus the broad shield complete the artist crowned
With his last hand, and poured the Ocean round:
In living silver seemed the waves to roll,
And beat the buckler's verge, and bound the whole.
    This done, whate'er a warrior's use requires   705

He forged: the cuirass that outshone the fires;
The greaves of ductile tin, the helm impressed
With various sculpture, and the golden crest.
At Thetis' feet the finished labour lay;
She, as a falcon cuts the aerial way,   710
Swift from Olympus' snowy summit flies,
And bears the blazing present through the skies.
                      (1720)

from translation of Homer's *Odyssey*

from *Book IX*
[the lotus-eaters]

    "Meanwhile the god whose hand the thunder forms   75
Drives clouds on clouds, and blackens heav'n with storms:
Wide o'er the waste the rage of Boreas sweeps,
And night rushed headlong on the shaded deeps.
Now here, now there, the giddy ships are born,
And all the rattling shrouds in fragments torn.   80
We furled the sail, we plied the lab'ring oar,
Took down our masts, and rowed our ships to shore.
Two tedious days and two long nights we lay,
O'erwatched and battered in the naked bay.
But the third morning when Aurora brings,   85
We rear the masts, we spread the canvas wings;
Refreshed, and careless on the deck reclined,
We sit, and trust the pilot and the wind.
Then to my native country had I sailed;
But, the cape doubled, adverse winds prevailed.   90
Strong was the tide which, by the northern blast
Impelled, our vessels on Cythera cast.
Nine days our fleet th'uncertain tempest bore
Far in wide ocean, and from sight of shore;
The tenth we touched, by various error tossed,   95
The land of Lotos, and the flow'ry coast.
We climbed the beach, and springs of water found,
Then spread our hasty banquet on the ground.
Three men were sent, deputed from the crew
(An herald one), the dubious coast to view,   100
And learn what habitants possessed the place.

---

670. sour: heavy, coarse. **681-82. Gnossus:** Knossos; Pope in a note remarks that Dædalus was said to have taught such a dance to seven youths and maids who were saved from the Labyrinth; in the original, however, the word *choron* may refer not to a dance but to a dancing-*place* resembling that built by Dædalus for Ariadne, or to a relief sculpture (said to have been seen at Knossos) of a dance whose figures resembled the twists and turns of Dædalus's Labyrinth. **685. cymars:** loose, light garments for women. **696. lost:** i.e., lost to sight, no longer visible as individual spokes.   **ODYSSEY** Odysseus (Ulysses) is relating his adventures to Alcinoos (Alcinous) and the Phaeacians (see note to *Paradise Lost*, IX, 441; p. 360); see also Tennyson's "The Lotos-Eaters" (p. 959). **77. Boreas:** the north wind. **84. o'erwatched:** tired from watching. **85. Aurora:** goddess of the dawn. **92. Cythera:** island just south of the southeastern tip of the Peloponnesus; what the Greek actually says at this point is that the north wind sent them drifting helplessly *past* Cythera (i.e., toward the African coast).

They went, and found a hospitable race:
Not prone to ill, nor strange to foreign guest,
They eat, they drink, and nature gives the feast;
The trees around them all their food produce,   *105*
Lotos the name — divine, nectareous juice!
(Thence called *Lotophagi*) which whoso tastes,
Insatiate riots in the sweet repast,
Nor other home nor other care intends,
But quits his house, his country, and his friends.   *110*

The three we sent, from off th'inchanting ground
We dragged reluctant, and by force we bound;
The rest in haste forsook the pleasing shore,
Or, the charm tasted, had returned no more.
Now placed in order, on their banks they sweep   *115*
The sea's smooth face, and cleave the hoary deep;
With heavy hearts we labour through the tide,
To coasts unknown, and oceans yet untried."

(1726)

from MORAL ESSAYS

Epistle IV
To Richard Boyle, Earl of Burlington: Of the Use of Riches

ARGUMENT

The vanity of expense in people of wealth and quality. The abuse of the word *taste,* v. 13. That the first principle and foundation, in this as in everything else, is Good Sense, v. 40. The chief proof of it is to follow Nature, even in works of mere luxury and elegance. Instanced in architecture and gardening, where all must be adapted to the genius and use of the place, and the beauties not forced into it, but resulting from it, v. 50. How men are disappointed in their most expensive undertakings for want of this true foundation, without which nothing can please long, if at all; and the best examples and rules will but be perverted into something burdensome or ridiculous, v. 65, &c. to 98. A description of the false taste of magnificence, the first grand error of which is to imagine that greatness consists in the size and dimension, instead of the proportion and harmony of the whole, v. 99; and the second, either in joining together parts incoherent or too minutely resembling, or in the repetition of the same too frequently, v. 115, &c. A word or two of false taste in books, in music, in painting, even in preaching and prayer, and lastly in entertainments, v. 133, &c. Yet Providence is justified in giving wealth to be squandered in this manner, since it is dispersed to the poor and laborious part of mankind, v. 169. What are the proper objects of magnificence, and a proper field for the expense of great men, v. 177, &c.; and finally, the great and public works which become a prince, v. 191, to the end.

'Tis strange the miser should his care employ
To gain those riches he can ne'er enjoy;
Is it less strange the prodigal should waste
His wealth to purchase what he ne'er can taste?
Not for himself he sees, or hears, or eats;   *5*
Artists must choose his pictures, music, meats:
He buys for Topham drawings and designs,
For Pembroke statues, dirty gods, and coins;
Rare monkish manuscripts for Hearne alone,
And books for Mead, and butterflies for Sloane.   *10*
Think we all these are for himself? no more
Than his fine wife, alas! or finer whore.
    For what has Virro painted, built, and planted?
Only to show how many tastes he wanted.

---

107. *Lotophagi:* i.e., "Lotus-eaters." 115. banks: rowers' benches. 116. hoary deep: Cf. *Paradise Lost*, II, 891, and note (p. 347)   EPISTLE IV   First published with the title "Of Taste" and then "Of False Taste." Richard Boyle, Earl of Burlington (1695-1753), was a major influence on the architecture of the time. 7-10: names of well-known collectors, scholars, and other "Artists" (i.e., connoisseurs). 13. Virro: name borrowed from Juvenal, and perhaps referring to some real contemporary person.

What brought Sir Visto's ill-got wealth to waste? *15*
Some Dæmon whispered, "Visto! have a taste."
Heav'n visits with a taste the wealthy fool,
And needs no rod but Ripley with a rule.
See! sportive fate, to punish awkward pride,
Bids Bubo build, and sends him such a guide: *20*
A standing sermon, at each year's expense,
That never coxcomb reached magnificence.
   You show us, Rome was glorious, not profuse,
And pompous buildings once were things of use.
Yet shall (my Lord) your just, your noble rules *25*
Fill half the land with imitating fools,
Who random drawings from your sheets shall take,
And of one beauty many blunders make;
Load some vain church with old theatric state,
Turn arcs of triumph to a garden gate; *30*
Reverse your ornaments, and hang them all
On some patched dog-hole eked with ends of wall,
Then clap four slices of pilaster on't,
That, laced with bits of rustic, makes a front.
Or call the winds through long arcades to roar, *35*
Proud to catch cold at a Venetian door;
Conscious they act a true Palladian part,
And if they starve, they starve by rules of art.
   Oft have you hinted to your brother peer
A certain truth, which many buy too dear: *40*
Something there is more needful than expense,
And something previous ev'n to taste — 'tis Sense,
Good Sense, which only is the gift of Heav'n,
And though no science, fairly worth the sev'n;
A light, which in yourself you must perceive; *45*
Jones and Le Nôtre have it not to give.
   To build, to plant, whatever you intend,
To rear the column, or the arch to bend,

To swell the terrace, or to sink the grot;
In all, let Nature never be forgot. *50*
But treat the Goddess like a modest fair,
Nor over-dress, nor leave her wholly bare;
Let not each beauty ev'rywhere be spied,
Where half the skill is decently to hide.
He gains all points who pleasingly confounds, *55*
Surprises, varies, and conceals the bounds.
   Consult the genius of the place in all;
That tells the waters or to rise, or fall,
Or helps th'ambitious hill the heav'n to scale,
Or scoops in circling theatres the vale, *60*
Calls in the country, catches opening glades,
Joins willing woods, and varies shades from shades,
Now breaks or now directs th'intending lines;
Paints as you plant, and, as you work, designs.
   Still follow Sense, of ev'ry art the soul, *65*
Parts answ'ring parts shall slide into a whole,
Spontaneous beauties all around advance,
Start ev'n from difficulty, strike from chance,
Nature shall join you, time shall make it grow
A work to wonder at — perhaps a Stowe. *70*
   Without it, proud Versailles! thy glory falls,
And Nero's terraces desert their walls;
The vast parterres a thousand hands shall make,
Lo! Cobham comes, and floats them with a lake;
Or cut wide views through mountains to the plain, *75*
You'll wish your hill or sheltered seat again.
Ev'n in an ornament its place remark,
Nor in an Hermitage set Dr. Clarke.
   Behold Villario's ten-years toil complete;
His quincunx darkens, his espaliers meet, *80*
The wood supports the plain, the parts unite,
And strength of shade contends with strength of light;

---

15. Visto: another fictitious name (an alternate form of *vista*). **18. Ripley:** a carpenter turned architect, whom Pope (and Burlington) considered incompetent. **20: Bubo** is identified as George Bubb (later Dodington, and Baron Melcombe), a Whig politician whom Pope had already satirized elsewhere. **23:** Burlington had published a book on Palladio's Rome, and projected a second; Andrea Palladio (1508-1580), Italian architect, modified classic Roman styles and influenced Renaissance design. **34. rustic:** rough-hewn stone (or stone artificially made to look so). **36. Venetian door:** "A door or window, so called from being much practised at Venice, by Palladio and others" (Pope's note). **38. starve:** suffer or die from cold. **44. science:** field of study; **the sev'n:** See note on Milton's "Of Education," line 15 (p. 319). **46:** Inigo Jones (1573-1652), first of England's great architects, often for royalty (Burlington had also published a book of Jones's *Designs*); André Le Nôtre (1613-1700), celebrated French landscape architect, mainly for Louis XIV (the gardens at Versailles, Fontainebleau, the Tuileries, and many others). **49. grot:** grotto. **70. Stowe:** "The seat and gardens of the Lord Viscount Cobham in Buckinghamshire" (Pope's note) — now Stowe School, just north of Buckingham, with restored gardens; Richard Temple, Lord Viscount Cobham (1675-1749), was the addressee of Pope's "Epistle I." **75-76:** "This was done in Hertfordshire, by a wealthy citizen, at the expense of above £5000, by which means (merely to overlook a dead plain) he let in the north wind upon his house and parterre, which were before adorned and defended by beautiful woods" (Pope's note); a middle-class family at that time could probably get along on about £30 a year. **78:** A bust of English theologian and philosopher Samuel Clarke, D. D. (1675-1729), along with several others, was installed by Queen Caroline in the ornamental imitation Hermitage in Richmond Park — an act considered inappropriate by Pope and others because of Clarke's unorthodox beliefs. **79:** *Villario* suggests a Roman or Italian *villa*, just as *Sabinus* (89) suggests the Sabine hills northeast of Rome, with probably an allusion to the poet Horace's famous Sabine Farm, given him by his patron Maecenas.

A waving glow his bloomy beds display,
Blushing in bright diversities of day,
With silver-quiv'ring rills meandered o'er —   85
Enjoy them, you! Villario can no more;
Tired of the scene parterres and fountains yield,
He finds at last he better likes a field.
  Through his young woods how pleased Sabinus strayed,
Or sat delighted in the thick'ning shade,   90
With annual joy the redd'ning shoots to greet,
Or see the stretching branches long to meet.
His son's fine taste an op'ner vista loves,
Foe to the dryads of his father's groves;
One boundless green, or flourished carpet views,   95
With all the mournful family of yews;
The thriving plants ignoble broomsticks made,
Now sweep those alleys they were born to shade.
  At Timon's villa let us pass a day,
Where all cry out, "What sums are thrown away!"   100
So proud, so grand, of that stupendous air,
Soft and agreeable come never there.
Greatness, with Timon, dwells in such a draught
As brings all Brobdingnag before your thought.
To compass this, his building is a town,   105
His pond an ocean, his parterre a down:
Who but must laugh, the Master when he sees,
A puny insect, shiv'ring at a breeze!
Lo, what huge heaps of littleness around!
The whole, a laboured quarry above ground.   110
Two Cupids squirt before; a lake behind
Improves the keenness of the northern wind.
His gardens next your admiration call;
On ev'ry side you look, behold the wall!
No pleasing intricacies intervene,   115
No artful wildness to perplex the scene;

Grove nods at grove, each alley has a brother,
And half the platform just reflects the other.
The suff'ring eye inverted Nature sees,
Trees cut to statues, statues thick as trees,   120
With here a fountain, never to be played,
And there a summer-house that knows no shade;
Here Amphitrite sails through myrtle bow'rs;
There gladiators fight, or die, in flow'rs;
Unwatered see the drooping sea-horse mourn,   125
And swallows roost in Nilus' dusty urn.
  My Lord advances with majestic mien,
Smit with the mighty pleasure, to be seen:
But soft — by regular approach — not yet —
First through the length of yon hot terrace sweat,   130
And when up ten steep slopes you've dragged your thighs,
Just at his study-door he'll bless your eyes.
His study! with what authors is it stored?
In books, not authors, curious is my Lord;
To all their dated backs he turns you round,   135
These Aldus printed, those Du Sueil has bound.
Lo some are vellum, and the rest as good,
For all his Lordship knows, but they are wood.
For Locke or Milton 'tis in vain to look;
These shelves admit not any modern book.   140
  And now the chapel's silver bell you hear,
That summons you to all the pride of pray'r:
Light quirks of music, broken and uneven,
Make the soul dance upon a jig to Heaven.
On painted ceilings you devoutly stare,   145
Where sprawl the saints of Verrio or Laguerre,
On gilded clouds in fair expansion lie,
And bring all Paradise before your eye.
To rest, the cushion and soft dean invite,
Who never mentions Hell to ears polite.   150

95: "The two extremes in parterres, which are equally faulty; a *boundless green*, large and naked as a field, or a *flourished carpet*, where the greatness and nobleness of the piece is lessened by being divided into too many parts, with scrolled works and beds, of which the examples are frequent" (Pope's note). **96:** "Touches upon the ill taste of those who are so fond of evergreens (particularly yews, which are the most tonsile [clippable]) as to destroy the nobler forest-trees to make way for such little ornaments as pyramids of dark green continually repeated, not unlike a funeral procession" (Pope's note); **mournful:** Yews are associated with graveyards, where nevertheless they are intended to symbolize immortality. **99-168:** "This description is intended to comprise the principles of a false taste of magnificence, and to exemplify what was said before, that nothing but Good Sense can attain it" (Pope's note). **104: Brobdingnag:** the land of the giants in Swift's *Gulliver's Travels*, II. **123. Amphitrite:** goddess of the sea. **126. Nilus:** personification or god of the Nile, here probably portrayed in relief on the urn, or perhaps as a statue holding the urn. **133-40:** "The false taste in books; a satire on the vanity in collecting them, more frequent in men of fortune than the study to understand them. Many delight chiefly in the elegance of the print, or of the binding; some have carried it so far as to cause the upper shelves to be filled with painted books of wood; others pique themselves so much upon books in a language they do not understand as to exclude the most useful in one they do" (Pope's note). **136:** Aldus Manutius (Aldo Manucci, 1450-1515), famous Italian scholar and printer; the Abbé Du Sueil, early eighteenth-century Parisian binder. **143-44:** "The false taste in music, improper to the subjects, as of light airs in churches, often practised by the organists, &c." (Pope's note). **145-48:** "— And in painting (from which even Italy is not free) of naked figures in churches, &c. which has obliged some popes to put draperies on some of those of the best masters" (Pope's note). **146:** Antonio Verrio (1630-1707) came to England in 1671 and got many royal commissions; Louis Laguerre (1663-1721) came to England about 1684, worked with Verrio at Windsor, but then became much in demand for work at great country houses. **149-50:** "This is a fact; a reverend Dean preaching at court threatened the sinner with punishment 'in a place which he thought it not decent to name in so polite an assembly'" (Pope's note).

But hark! the chiming clocks to dinner call;
A hundred footsteps scrape the marble hall:
The rich buffet well-coloured serpents grace,
And gaping Tritons spew to wash your face.
Is this a dinner? this a genial room?   155
No, 'tis a temple, and a hecatomb.
A solemn sacrifice, performed in state,
You drink by measure, and to minutes eat.
So quick retires each flying course, you'd swear
Sancho's dread doctor and his wand were there.   160
Between each act the trembling salvers ring,
From soup to sweet wine, and God bless the King.
In plenty starving, tantalized in state,
And complaisantly helped to all I hate,
Treated, caressed, and tired, I take my leave,   165
Sick of his civil pride from morn to eve;
I curse such lavish cost, and little skill,
And swear no day was ever passed so ill.
    Yet hence the poor are clothed, the hungry fed;
Health to himself, and to his infants bread   170
The lab'rer bears. What his hard heart denies,
His charitable vanity supplies.
    Another age shall see the golden ear
Imbrown the slope, and nod on the parterre,
Deep harvests bury all his pride has planned,   175
And laughing Ceres re-assume the land.
    Who then shall grace, or who improve the soil?
Who plants like Bathurst, or who builds like Boyle.

'Tis use alone that sanctifies expense,
And splendour borrows all her rays from Sense.   180
    His father's acres who enjoys in peace,
Or makes his neighbours glad, if he increase;
Whose cheerful tenants bless their yearly toil,
Yet to their Lord owe more than to the soil;
Whose ample lawns are not ashamed to feed   185
The milky heifer and deserving steed;
Whose rising forests, not for pride or show,
But future buildings, future navies grow:
Let his plantations stretch from down to down,
First shade a country, and then raise a town.   190
    You too proceed! make falling arts your care;
Erect new wonders, and the old repair;
Jones and Palladio to themselves restore,
And be whate'er Vitruvius was before:
Till kings call forth th'ideas of your mind,   195
Proud to accomplish what such hands designed,
Bid harbours open, public ways extend,
Bid temples, worthier of the God, ascend;
Bid the broad arch the dang'rous flood contain,
The mole projected break the roaring main;   200
Back to his bounds their subject sea command,
And roll obedient rivers through the land.
These honours, peace to happy Britain brings;
These are imperial works, and worthy kings.

                                                    (1731, 1735)

from AN ESSAY ON MAN

Epistle I
Of the Nature and State of Man, with respect to the Universe

ARGUMENT:
Of man in the abstract. — I. That we can judge only with regard to our own system, being
ignorant of the relations of systems and things, ver. 17, &c. II. That man is not to be deemed
imperfect, but a being suited to his place and rank in the creation, agreeable to the general
order of things, and conformable to ends and relations to him unknown, ver. 35, &c. III. That it
is partly upon his ignorance of future events, and partly upon the hope of a future state, that all

---

153-54: "Taxes the incongruity of ornaments (though sometimes practised by the ancients) where an open mouth ejects the water into a fountain, or where the shocking images of serpents, &c. are introduced in grottos or buffets" (Pope's note); Triton was a sea-god, son of Poseidon and Amphitrite. **155. genial:** festive. **155ff.:** "The proud festivals of some men are here set forth to ridicule, where pride destroys the ease, and formal regularity all the pleasurable enjoyment of the entertainment" (Pope's note). **160:** "See *Don Quixote,* chapter xlvii" (Pope's note). **176. Ceres:** corn goddess, goddess of agriculture (Greek *Demeter*). **178:** Allen, Lord Bathurst (1685-1775), was the addressee of Epistle III, also called "Of the Use of Riches," written a year later. **194. Vitruvius:** Marcus Vitruvius Pollio, first-century B.C. Roman architect and military engineer, author of *De Architectura.*

his happiness in the present depends, ver. 77, &c. IV. The pride of aiming at more knowledge, and pretending to more perfection, the cause of man's error and misery. The impiety of putting himself in the place of God, and judging of the fitness or unfitness, perfection or imperfection, justice or injustice of his dispensations, ver. 113, &c. V. The absurdity of conceiting himself the final cause of the creation, or expecting that perfection in the moral world, which is not in the natural, ver. 131, &c. VI. The unreasonableness of his complaints against Providence, while on the one hand he demands the perfections of the angels, and on the other the bodily qualifications of the brutes; though to possess any of the sensitive faculties in a higher degree would render him miserable, ver. 173, &c. VII. That throughout the whole visible world, an universal order and gradation in the sensual and mental faculties is observed, which causes a subordination of creature to creature, and of all creatures to man. The gradations of sense, instinct, thought, reflection, reason; that reason alone countervails all the other faculties, ver. 207, &c. VIII. How much farther this order and subordination of living creatures may extend, above and below us; were any part of which broken, not that part only, but the whole connected creation must be destroyed, ver. 233. IX. The extravagance, madness, and pride of such a desire, ver. 259. X. The consequence of all the absolute submission due to Providence, both as to our present and future state, ver. 281, &c. to the end.

Awake, my St. John! leave all meaner things
To low ambition, and the pride of kings.
Let us (since life can little more supply
Than just to look about us and to die)
Expatiate free o'er all this scene of man;   5
A mighty maze! but not without a plan;
A wild, where weeds and flow'rs promiscuous shoot,
Or garden, tempting with forbidden fruit.
Together let us beat this ample field,
Try what the open, what the covert yield;   10
The latent tracts, the giddy heights explore
Of all who blindly creep, or sightless soar;
Eye Nature's walks, shoot Folly as it flies,
And catch the Manners living as they rise;
Laugh where we must, be candid where we can;   15
But vindicate the ways of God to man.
    I. Say first, of God above, or man below,
What can we reason but from what we know?
Of man what see we but his station here,
From which to reason, or to which refer?   20
Through worlds unnumbered though the God be known,
'Tis ours to trace him only in our own.

He who through vast immensity can pierce,
See worlds on worlds compose one universe,
Observe how system into system runs,   25
What other planets circle other suns,
What varied being peoples ev'ry star,
May tell why Heav'n has made us as we are.
But of this frame the bearings, and the ties,
The strong connections, nice dependencies,   30
Gradations just, has thy pervading soul
Looked through? or can a part contain the whole?
    Is the great chain that draws all to agree,
And drawn supports, upheld by God, or thee?
    II. Presumptuous man! the reason wouldst thou find,
Why formed so weak, so little, and so blind?   36
First, if thou canst, the harder reason guess,
Why formed no weaker, blinder, and no less?
Ask of thy mother earth why oaks are made
Taller or stronger than the weeds they shade?   40
Or ask of yonder argent fields above
Why Jove's satellites are less than Jove?
    Of systems possible, if 'tis confessed
That wisdom infinite must form the best,

AN ESSAY ON MAN   EPISTLE I   1. St. John: Henry St. John (pronounced "sin'jun"), first Viscount Bolingbroke (1678-1751), political and philosophical writer, to whom the *Essay* is addressed and from whose thinking much of what Pope says derives. 5. Expatiate: includes the meaning "wander freely." 9. beat: scour or range over in hunting. 15. candid: kindly. 16: a deliberate echo of *Paradise Lost*, I, 26 (p. 326). 33-34: See *The Rape of the Lock*, V, 71, and note (p. 532); Zeus's golden chain metamorphoses into the common metaphor of "the great chain of being" or ladder of creation (see 237-46). 42. satellites: four syllables (as plural of Latin *satelles*, "attendant, escort," but here including the astronomical sense).

Where all must full or not coherent be,   45
And all that rises, rise in due degree;
Then in the scale of reas'ning life, 'tis plain
There must be, somewhere, such a rank as man;
And all the question (wrangle e'er so long)
Is only this, if God has placed him wrong?   50
   Respecting man, whatever wrong we call,
May, must be right, as relative to all.
In human works, though laboured on with pain,
A thousand movements scarce one purpose gain;
In God's, one single can its end produce;   55
Yet serves to second too some other use.
So man, who here seems principal alone,
Perhaps acts second to some sphere unknown,
Touches some wheel, or verges to some goal;
'Tis but a part we see, and not a whole.   60
   When the proud steed shall know why man restrains
His fiery course, or drives him o'er the plains;
When the dull ox, why now he breaks the clod,
Is now a victim, and now Egypt's god:
Then shall man's pride and dullness comprehend   65
His actions', passions', being's, use and end;
Why doing, suff'ring, checked, impelled; and why
This hour a slave, the next a deity.
   Then say not man's imperfect, Heav'n in fault;
Say rather, man's as perfect as he ought: 70
His knowledge measured to his state and place,
His time a moment, and a point his space.
If to be perfect in a certain sphere,
What matter soon or late, or here or there?
The blest today is as completely so   75
As who began a thousand years ago.
   III. Heav'n from all creatures hides the book of Fate,
All but the page prescribed, their present state;
From brutes what men, from men what spirits know,
Or who could suffer being here below?   80
The lamb thy riot dooms to bleed today;
Had he thy reason, would he skip and play?
Pleased to the last, he crops the flow'ry food,
And licks the hand just raised to shed his blood.
Oh blindness to the future! kindly giv'n,   85
That each may fill the circle marked by Heav'n;
Who sees with equal eye, as God of all,
A hero perish, or a sparrow fall,
Atoms or systems into ruin hurled,

And now a bubble burst, and now a world.   90
   Hope humbly then; with trembling pinions soar;
Wait the great teacher Death, and God adore.
What future bliss, he gives not thee to know,
But gives that hope to be thy blessing now.
Hope springs eternal in the human breast: 95
Man never Is, but always To Be blest:
The soul, uneasy and confined from home,
Rests and expatiates in a life to come.
   Lo! the poor Indian, whose untutored mind
Sees God in clouds, or hears him in the wind;   100
His soul proud Science never taught to stray
Far as the solar walk, or Milky Way;
Yet simple Nature to his hope has giv'n,
Behind the cloud-topped hill, an humbler heav'n;
Some safer world in depth of woods embraced,   105
Some happier island in the wat'ry waste,
Where slaves once more their native land behold,
No fiends torment, no Christians thirst for gold!
To be, contents his natural desire;
He asks no angel's wing, no seraph's fire;   110
But thinks, admitted to that equal sky,
His faithful dog shall bear him company.
   IV. Go, wiser thou! and in thy scale of sense
Weigh thy opinion against Providence;
Call imperfection what thou fancy'st such,   115
Say, here he gives too little, there too much;
Destroy all creatures for thy sport or gust,
Yet cry, if man's unhappy, God's unjust;
If man alone ingross not Heav'n's high care,
Alone made perfect here, immortal there: 120
Snatch from his hand the balance and the rod,
Rejudge his justice, be the God of God!
   In pride, in reas'ning pride, our error lies;
All quit their sphere and rush into the skies.
Pride still is aiming at the blest abodes;   125
Men would be angels, angels would be gods.
Aspiring to be gods, if angels fell,
Aspiring to be angels, men rebel;
And who but wishes to invert the laws
Of order, sins against th'Eternal Cause.   130
   V. Ask for what end the heav'nly bodies shine,
Earth for whose use? Pride answers, " 'Tis for mine:
For me kind Nature wakes her genial pow'r,
Suckles each herb, and spreads out ev'ry flow'r;

---

64. god: the sacred bull, Apis. **81. riot:** luxurious living, excess, feasting. **88. sparrow:** Cf. Matthew 10:29-31, and Hamlet's "There's a special providence in the fall of a sparrow" (V.ii). **102. solar walk:** i.e., the sun's orbit, or apparent path through the heavens. **110. seraph's fire:** a conventional association based on the possible but conjectural derivation of the word from the Hebrew for "burn." **117. gust:** taste, appetite, pleasure. **133. genial:** generative.

Annual for me, the grape, the rose renew 135
The juice nectareous, and the balmy dew;
For me, the mine a thousand treasures brings;
For me, health gushes from a thousand springs;
Seas roll to waft me, suns to light me rise;
My foot-stool earth, my canopy the skies." 140
   But errs not Nature from this gracious end,
From burning suns when livid deaths descend,
When earthquakes swallow, or when tempests sweep
Towns to one grave, whole nations to the deep?
"No" ('tis replied), "the first Almighty Cause 145
Acts not by partial, but by gen'ral laws;
Th'exceptions few; some change since all began,
And what created perfect?" — Why then man?
If the great end be human happiness,
Then Nature deviates; and can man do less? 150
As much that end a constant course requires
Of show'rs and sunshine, as of man's desires;
As much eternal springs and cloudless skies,
As men forever temp'rate, calm, and wise. 154
If plagues or earthquakes break not Heav'n's design,
Why then a Borgia, or a Catiline?
Who knows but he, whose hand the lightning forms,
Who heaves old ocean, and who wings the storms,
Pours fierce ambition in a Cæsar's mind,
Or turns young Ammon loose to scourge mankind? 160
From pride, from pride, our very reas'ning springs;
Account for moral as for nat'ral things.
Why charge we Heav'n in those, in these acquit?
In both, to reason right is to submit.
   Better for us, perhaps, it might appear, 165
Were there all harmony, all virtue here;
That never air or ocean felt the wind;
That never passion discomposed the mind.
But ALL subsists by elemental strife,
And passions are the elements of life. 170
The gen'ral ORDER, since the whole began,
Is kept in Nature, and is kept in man.
   VI. What would this man? Now upward will he soar,
And little less than angel, would be more;
Now looking downwards, just as grieved appears 175
To want the strength of bulls, the fur of bears.
Made for his use all creatures if he call,

Say what their use, had he the pow'rs of all?
Nature to these, without profusion kind,
The proper organs, proper pow'rs assigned; 180
Each seeming want compensated of course,
Here with degrees of swiftness, there of force;
All in exact proportion to the state;
Nothing to add, and nothing to abate.
Each beast, each insect, happy in its own; 185
Is Heav'n unkind to man, and man alone?
Shall he alone, whom rational we call,
Be pleased with nothing, if not blessed with all?
   The bliss of man (could pride that blessing find)
Is not to act or think beyond mankind; 190
No pow'rs of body or of soul to share,
But what his nature and his state can bear.
Why has not man a microscopic eye?
For this plain reason: man is not a fly.
Say what the use, were finer optics giv'n, 195
T'inspect a mite, not comprehend the heav'n?
Or touch, if tremblingly alive all o'er,
To smart and agonize at ev'ry pore?
Or, quick effluvia darting through the brain,
Die of a rose in aromatic pain? 200
If Nature thundered in his op'ning ears,
And stunned him with the music of the spheres,
How would he wish that Heav'n had left him still
The whisp'ring zephyr, and the purling rill?
Who finds not Providence all good and wise, 205
Alike in what it gives, and what denies?
   VII. Far as creation's ample range extends,
The scale of sensual, mental pow'rs ascends:
Mark how it mounts, to man's imperial race,
From the green myriads in the peopled grass: 210
What modes of sight betwixt each wide extreme,
The mole's dim curtain, and the lynx's beam:
Of smell, the headlong lioness between,
And hound sagacious on the tainted green:
Of hearing, from the life that fills the flood, 215
To that which warbles through the vernal wood:
The spider's touch, how exquisitely fine!
Feels at each thread, and lives along the line:
In the nice bee, what sense so subtly true
From pois'nous herbs extracts the healing dew: 220

156: Cesare Borgia (1476-1507), younger son of Pope Alexander VI, was a cardinal, a duke, a politician, a soldier, and notorious for his ruthless crimes and conquests; Catiline (c.108-62 B.C.) was a Roman politician and conspirator who was exposed by Cicero. **160. young Ammon:** Alexander the Great (because fabled to be son of Zeus Ammon). **181. compensated:** accent the second syllable; **of course:** as a matter of course, naturally. **199. effluvia:** the means by which Epicurus and others believed odours and other sense impressions reached the brain. **202. music . . . spheres:** See *Ptolemaic* in Glossary. **212. beam:** i.e., a ray emanating from the eye, by which it was once believed seeing was accomplished. **213:** Pope believed lions hunted by sound rather than smell. **214. sagacious:** keen scented, skilled at following a trail. **219. nice:** apprehending delicate distinctions, distinguishing accurately or minutely. **220. healing:** Honey was used medicinally; **dew:** It was once thought that bees made honey out

How instinct varies in the grov'ling swine,
Compared, half-reas'ning elephant, with thine!
'Twixt that, and reason, what a nice barrier,
Forever sep'rate, yet forever near!
Remembrance and reflection how allied;   225
What thin partitions sense from thought divide:
And middle natures, how they long to join,
Yet never pass th'insuperable line!
Without this just gradation, could they be
Subjected, these to those, or all to thee?   230
The pow'rs of all subdued by thee alone,
Is not thy reason all these pow'rs in one?
    VIII. See, through this air, this ocean, and this earth,
All matter quick, and bursting into birth.
Above, how high progressive life may go!   235
Around, how wide! how deep extend below!
Vast chain of being, which from God began,
Natures ætherial, human, angel, man,
Beast, bird, fish, insect! what no eye can see,
No glass can reach! from infinite to thee,   240
From thee to nothing! — On superior pow'rs
Were we to press, inferior might on ours,
Or in the full creation leave a void,
Where, one step broken, the great scale's destroyed:
From Nature's chain whatever link you strike,   245
Tenth or ten thousandth, breaks the chain alike.
    And if each system in gradation roll,
Alike essential to th'amazing whole,
The least confusion but in one, not all
That system only, but the whole must fall.   250
Let earth unbalanced from her orbit fly,
Planets and suns run lawless through the sky;
Let ruling angels from their spheres be hurled,
Being on being wrecked, and world on world,
Heav'n's whole foundations to their centre nod,   255
And Nature tremble to the throne of God.
All this dread ORDER break — for whom? for thee?
Vile worm! — oh madness, pride, impiety!
    IX. What if the foot, ordained the dust to tread,
Or hand to toil, aspired to be the head?   260
What if the head, the eye, or ear repined
To serve mere engines to the ruling mind?
Just as absurd for any part to claim
To be another, in this gen'ral frame;

Just as absurd to mourn the tasks or pains   265
The great directing MIND of ALL ordains.
    All are but parts of one stupendous whole,
Whose body Nature is, and God the soul;
That, changed through all, and yet in all the same,
Great in the earth, as in th'ætherial frame,   270
Warms in the sun, refreshes in the breeze,
Glows in the stars, and blossoms in the trees,
Lives through all life, extends through all extent,
Spreads undivided, operates unspent,
Breathes in our soul, informs our mortal part,   275
As full, as perfect, in a hair as heart;
As full, as perfect, in vile man that mourns
As the rapt seraph that adores and burns;
To him no high, no low, no great, no small;
He fills, he bounds, connects, and equals all.   280
    X. Cease then, nor ORDER imperfection name;
Our proper bliss depends on what we blame.
Know thy own point: this kind, this due degree
Of blindness, weakness, Heav'n bestows on thee.
Submit — in this, or any other sphere,   285
Secure to be as blest as thou canst bear,
Safe in the hand of one disposing Pow'r,
Or in the natal, or the mortal hour.
All Nature is but art, unknown to thee;
All chance, direction, which thou canst not see;   290
All discord, harmony, not understood;
All partial evil, universal good;
And, spite of pride, in erring reason's spite,
One truth is clear: Whatever IS, is RIGHT.

from *Epistle II*

Of the Nature and State of Man, with Respect to Himself, as an Individual

Know then thyself, presume not God to scan;
The proper study of mankind is man.
Placed on this isthmus of a middle state,
A being darkly wise, and rudely great;
With too much knowledge for the sceptic side,   5
With too much weakness for the stoic's pride,
He hangs between; in doubt to act, or rest,
In doubt to deem himself a god, or beast;

---

of dew they gathered from flowers. **223. barrier:** here pronounced ba-REER. **234. quick:** living. **245. strike:** eliminate, remove. **259-62:** Cf. I Corinthians 12:14-26. **280. equals:** i.e., makes equal. **283-84:** Cf. II, 1-18, below, and the excerpt from *Paradise Lost*, VIII (p. 354). **EPISTLE II** **1-2:** *Gnothi seauton*, "Know thyself" — inscription at the place of the Oracle in Delphi. Epistles III and IV are titled "Of the Nature and State of Man, with respect to Society" and "Of the Nature and State of Man, with respect to Happiness."

In doubt his mind or body to prefer,
Born but to die, and reas'ning but to err;   *10*
Alike in ignorance, his reason such,
Whether he thinks too little, or too much;
Chaos of thought and passion, all confused;
Still by himself abused, or disabused;
Created half to rise, and half to fall;   *15*
Great lord of all things, yet a prey to all;
Sole judge of truth, in endless error hurled:
The glory, jest, and riddle of the world!

. . . .

(1733)

EPIGRAM
Engraved on the Collar of a Dog which I gave to his Royal Highness

I am his Highness' Dog at Kew;
Pray tell me Sir, whose Dog are you?
(1738)

IMITATION OF HORACE
Part of the Ninth Ode of the Fourth Book

Lest you should think that verse shall die,
   Which sounds the silver Thames along,
Taught on the wings of truth, to fly
   Above the reach of vulgar song;

Though daring Milton sits sublime,   *5*
   In Spenser native muses play;
Nor yet shall Waller yield to time,
   Nor pensive Cowley's moral lay.

Sages and chiefs long since had birth
   Ere Cæsar was, or Newton named;   *10*
These raised new empires o'er the earth,
   And those new heav'ns and systems framed;

Vain was the chief's and sage's pride;
   They had no poet and they died!
In vain they schemed, in vain they bled;   *15*
   They had no poet and are dead!

(1738?; 1751)

LADY MARY WORTLEY MONTAGU
England, 1689-1762

from *LETTERS* (abridged)

To Edward Wortley Montagu   *[December 1712]*

. . . .

I continue indifferently well, and endeavour as much as I can to preserve myself from spleen and melancholy; not for my own sake: I think that of little importance; but in the condition I am, I believe it may be of very ill consequence; yet passing whole days alone as I do, I do not always find it possible, and my constitution will sometimes get the better of my reason. Human nature itself, without any additional misfortunes,   *5*

EPIGRAM   Kew was one of the royal residences; the reigning king was George II.   **MONTAGU**   Our texts are based on *The Letters and Works of Lady Mary Wortley Montagu* (1837), edited by Lord Wharncliffe (her great-grandson), and an 1861 edition of the same with additions and corrections by W. Moy Thomas. For some emendations we have consulted the texts in *The Complete Letters* as edited by Robert Halsband (3 vols., Oxford, 1965-67), and *Essays and Poems and "Simplicity, A Comedy,"* ed. Robert Halsband and Isobel Grundy (Oxford, 1977); we generally follow their dating of the letters and poems.   **TO EDWARD WORTLEY MONTAGU, DECEMBER 1712**   After a mostly secret courtship (her father opposed the match), she and Montagu had eloped in August of 1712. **1. indifferently:** tolerably. **2. spleen:** See the beginning of Canto IV of Pope's *Rape of the Lock*, and the notes (p. 529). **3. condition:** She is carrying her son, born the following May.

furnishes disagreeable meditations enough. Life itself, to make it supportable, should not be considered too near. My reason represents to me in vain the inutility of serious reflections. The idle mind will sometimes fall into contemplations that serve for nothing but to ruin the health, destroy good humour, hasten old age and wrinkles, and bring on an habitual melancholy. 'Tis a maxim with me to be young as long as one can. There is 10 nothing can pay one for that invaluable ignorance which is the companion of youth, those sanguine groundless hopes, and that lively vanity which makes all the happiness of life. To my extreme mortification I grow wiser every day. I don't believe Solomon was more convinced of the vanity of temporal affairs than I am. I lose all taste of this world, and I suffer myself to be bewitched by the charms of the spleen, though I know 15 and foresee all the irremediable mischiefs arising from it.

I am insensibly fallen into the writing you a melancholy letter, after all my resolutions to the contrary, but I do not enjoin you to read it. Make no scruple of flinging it into the fire at the first dull line. Forgive me the ill effects of my solitude, and think me (as I am) ever yours, 20

To the Lady ——   *Adrianople, April 1, O.S., 1717*

I am now got into a new world where everything I see appears to me a change of scene; and I write to your Ladyship with some content of mind, hoping at least that you will find the charm of novelty in my letters and no longer reproach me that I tell you nothing extraordinary.

I won't trouble you with a relation of our tedious journey, but must not omit what I 5 saw remarkable at Sophia, one of the most beautiful towns in the Turkish empire, and famous for its hot baths that are resorted to both for diversion and health. I stopped here one day on purpose to see them. Designing to go *incognito,* I hired a Turkish coach. These voitures are not at all like ours, but much more convenient for the country, the heat being so great that glasses would be very troublesome. They are made a good deal 10 in the manner of the Dutch coaches, having wooden lattices painted and gilded, the inside being also painted with baskets and nosegays of flowers, intermixed commonly with little poetical mottos. They are covered all over with scarlet cloth, lined with silk, and very often richly embroidered and fringed. This covering entirely hides the persons in them, but may be thrown back at pleasure and the ladies peep through the lattices. 15 They hold four people very conveniently, seated on cushions, but not raised.

In one of these covered wagons I went to the bagnio about ten o'clock. It was already full of women. It is built of stone in the shape of a dome with no windows but in the roof, which gives light enough. There were five of these domes joined together, the outmost being less than the rest and serving only as a hall, where the portress stood at 20

13-14. Solomon . . . vanity: See the first few chapters of Ecclesiastes (supposedly written by Solomon).   **To the Lady——, April 1, 1717**   Probably addressed to Lady Rich, wife of Sir Robert Rich, and attendant upon the Princess of Wales. "O.S." in the date stands for Old Style, referring to a date according to the Julian Calendar (introduced by Julius Caesar), which England used until 1752, even though the Gregorian Calendar (introduced by Pope Gregory XIII) had been adopted throughout the Catholic countries of Europe in 1582; in 1752 the gap of eleven days was eliminated by dropping the days from 3 September to 13 September, inclusive. Later, "N.S." stands for New Style. **Adrianople:** modern Edirne, on the western border of Turkey; in 1716 her husband was appointed Ambassador to Turkey, and at the time of this letter they were on their way to Constantinople (Istanbul), which they reached the following month. **6. Sophia:** Sofia, in Bulgaria, then a part of the Ottoman Empire. **9. voitures:** (French) carriages. **10. glasses:** windows.

the door. Ladies of quality generally give this woman the value of a crown or ten shillings, and I did not forget that ceremony. The next room is a very large one, paved with marble, and all round it, raised, two sofas of marble, one above another. There were four fountains of cold water in this room, falling first into marble basins and then running on the floor in little channels made for that purpose, which carried the streams *25* into the next room, something less than this, with the same sort of marble sofas, but so hot with steams of sulphur proceeding from the baths joining to it, it was impossible to stay there with one's clothes on. The two other domes were the hot baths, one of which had cocks of cold water turning into it to temper it to what degree of warmth the bathers have a mind to. *30*

I was in my travelling habit, which is a riding dress, and certainly appeared very extraordinary to them. Yet there was not one of them that showed the least surprise or impertinent curiosity, but received me with all the obliging civility possible. I know no European court where the ladies would have behaved themselves in so polite a manner to a stranger. I believe in the whole there were two hundred women, and yet none of *35* those disdainful smiles and satirical whispers that never fail in our assemblies when anybody appears that is not dressed exactly in fashion. They repeated over and over to me: "Uzelle, pék uzelle," which is nothing but "Charming, very charming." The first sofas were covered with cushions and rich carpets, on which sat the ladies; and on the second, their slaves behind them, but without any distinction of rank by their dress, all *40* being in the state of nature — that is, in plain English, stark naked, without any beauty or defect concealed. Yet there was not the least wanton smile or immodest gesture amongst them. They walked and moved with the same majestic grace which Milton describes of our general mother. There were many amongst them as exactly proportioned as ever any goddess was drawn by the pencil of Guido or Titian, and most *45* of their skins shiningly white, only adorned by their beautiful hair divided into many tresses, hanging on their shoulders, braided either with pearl or ribbon, perfectly representing the figures of the Graces.

I was here convinced of the truth of a reflection that I had often made: that if it was the fashion to go naked, the face would be hardly observed. I perceived that the ladies *50* with the finest skins and most delicate shapes had the greatest share of my admiration, though their faces were sometimes less beautiful than those of their companions. To tell you the truth, I had wickedness enough to wish secretly that Mr. Jervas could have been there invisible. I fancy it would have very much improved his art to see so many fine women naked in different postures, some in conversation, some working, others *55* drinking coffee or sherbet, and many negligently lying on their cushions while their slaves (generally pretty girls of seventeen or eighteen) were employed in braiding their hair in several pretty manners. In short, it is the women's coffee-house, where all the news of the town is told, scandal invented, etc. They generally take this diversion once a week, and stay there at least four or five hours, without getting cold by immediately *60*

---

21. quality: high social standing. **44. general mother:** i.e., Eve, so called in *Paradise Lost*, IV, 492; for the description referred to here, see IV, 288ff. (p. 353). **45. Guido:** probably Guido Reni (1575-1642); **Titian:** Tiziano Vecellio (1487-1576) — Italian painters. **48. Graces:** See note to Spenser's *Faerie Queene*, line 430 (p. 159). **53. Mr. Jervas:** Charles Jervas (c.1675-1739), Irish painter who studied with Sir Godfrey Kneller and succeeded him as royal portrait painter in 1723, said to have been especially known for his portraits of women (including one of Lady Mary); he also gave painting lessons to Alexander Pope.

coming out of the hot bath into the cold room, which was very surprising to me. The lady that seemed the most considerable amongst them entreated me to sit by her and would fain have undressed me for the bath. I excused myself with some difficulty, they being all so earnest in persuading me. I was at last forced to open my skirt and show them my stays, which satisfied them very well, for I saw they believed I was locked up in that machine, and that it was not in my own power to open it, which contrivance they attributed to my husband. I was charmed with their civility and beauty and should have been very glad to pass more time with them, but Mr. Wortley resolving to pursue his journey next morning early, I was in haste to see the ruins of Justinian's church, which did not afford me so agreeable a prospect as I had left, being little more than a heap of stones.

Adieu, Madam. I am sure I have now entertained you with an account of such a sight as you never saw in your life and what no book of travels could inform you of. 'Tis no less than death for a man to be found in one of these places.

To Mrs. Sarah Chiswell   *Adrianople, April 1, O.S., 1717*

. . . .

Those dreadful stories you have heard of the plague have very little foundation in truth. I own I have much ado to reconcile myself to the sound of a word which has always given me such terrible ideas, though I am convinced there is little more in it than a fever, as a proof of which we passed through two or three towns most violently infected. In the very next house where we lay (in one of them) two persons died of it. Luckily for me I was so well deceived that I knew nothing of the matter, and I was made believe that our second cook who fell ill there had only a great cold. However, we left our doctor to take care of him, and yesterday they both arrived here in good health, and I am now let into the secret that he has had the plague. There are many that escape it; neither is the air ever infected. I am persuaded it would be as easy to root it out here as out of Italy and France, but it does so little mischief, they are not very solicitous about it and are content to suffer this distemper instead of our variety, which they are utterly unacquainted with.

Apropos of distempers, I am going to tell you a thing that I am sure will make you wish yourself here. The smallpox so fatal and so general amongst us is here entirely harmless by the invention of engrafting (which is the term they give it). There is a set of old women who make it their business to perform the operation. Every autumn in the month of September, when the great heat is abated, people send to one another to know if any of their family has a mind to have the smallpox. They make parties for this purpose, and when they are met (commonly fifteen or sixteen together) the old woman comes with a nutshell full of the matter of the best sort of smallpox and asks what veins you please to have opened. She immediately rips open that you offer to her with a large needle (which gives you no more pain than a common scratch) and puts into the vein as much venom as can lie upon the head of her needle, and after binds up the little wound

---

To Mrs. Sarah Chiswell, April 1, 1717   Sarah Chiswell was a childhood friend whom Lady Mary had hoped to have as a companion on her travels; Miss Chiswell's relatives, however, fearing for her health and safety, dissuaded her from going. She died — of smallpox — in 1726. **15. smallpox:** Her only brother had died of it in 1713, and Lady Mary herself had it in 1715, but recovered safely. **16. engrafting:** i.e., inoculation.

with a hollow bit of shell, and in this manner opens four or five veins. The Grecians have   *25*
commonly the superstition of opening one in the middle of the forehead, in each arm, and
on the breast to mark the sign of the cross, but this has a very ill effect, all these wounds
leaving little scars, and is not done by those that are not superstitious, who choose to have
them in the legs or that part of the arm that is concealed. The children or young patients
play together all the rest of the day and are in perfect health till the eighth. Then the fever   *30*
begins to seize them and they keep their beds two days, very seldom three. They have
very rarely above twenty or thirty in their faces, which never mark, and in eight days'
time they are as well as before their illness. Where they are wounded there remain
running sores during the distemper, which I don't doubt is a great relief to it. Every year
thousands undergo this operation, and the French ambassador says pleasantly that they   *35*
take the smallpox here by way of diversion as they take the waters in other countries.
There is no example of anyone that has died in it, and you may believe I am very well
satisfied of the safety of the experiment, since I intend to try it on my dear little son. I am
patriot enough to take pains to bring this useful invention into fashion in England, and I
should not fail to write to some of our doctors very particularly about it if I knew any one   *40*
of them that I thought had virtue enough to destroy such a considerable branch of their
revenue for the good of mankind; but that distemper is too beneficial to them not to
expose to all their resentment the hardy wight that should undertake to put an end to it.
Perhaps if I live to return I may, however, have courage to war with them. Upon this
occasion, admire the heroism in the heart of your friend, etc.   *45*

To the Countess of Bute   *Brescia, Jan. 5 [1748]*
DEAR CHILD,
I am glad to hear that yourself and family are in good health. As to the alteration you
say you find in the world, it is only owing to your being better acquainted with it. I have
never, in all my various travels, seen but two sorts of people, and those very like one
another; I mean men and women, who always have been, and ever will be, the same.
The same vices and the same follies have been the fruit of all ages, though sometimes   *5*
under different names. I remember, when I returned from Turkey, meeting with the
same affectation of youth amongst my acquaintance that you now mention amongst
yours, and I do not doubt but your daughter will find the same twenty years hence
amongst hers. One of the greatest happinesses of youth is the ignorance of evil, though
it is often the ground of great indiscretions, and sometimes the active part of life is over   *10*
before an honest mind finds out how one ought to act in such a world as this. I am as
much removed from it as it is possible to be on this side the grave — which is from my
own inclination, for I might have even here a great deal of company, the way of living
in this province being what I believe it is now in the sociable part of Scotland and was in
England a hundred years ago.   *15*

· · · ·

38ff.: She had her son inoculated about a year later, and in 1721 her daughter; after they returned to England, in 1718, she did her best to convince English doctors to adopt the practice, but — in spite of royal support — with only limited success.   **TO THE COUNTESS OF BUTE,   JAN. 5, 1748**   Lady Mary's daughter, Mary, born in 1718, in 1736 married John Stuart, Earl of Bute. And in 1739 Lady Mary in effect separated from her husband (though they continued to correspond) and moved abroad, where she remained until his death in 1761.

To the Countess of Bute [January 1750]

MY DEAR CHILD,

I am extremely concerned to hear you complain of ill health at a time of life when you ought to be in the flower of your strength. I hope I need not recommend to you the care of it. The tenderness you have for your children is sufficient to enforce you to the utmost regard for the preservation of a life so necessary to their well-being. I do not doubt your prudence in their education; neither can I say anything particular relating to 5 it at this distance, different tempers requiring different management. In general, never attempt to govern them, as most people do, by deceit; if they find themselves cheated, even in trifles, it will so far lessen the authority of their instructor as to make them neglect all their future admonitions. And if possible breed them free from prejudices; those contracted in the nursery often influence the whole life after, of which I have seen 10 many melancholy examples. I shall say no more of this subject, nor would have said this little if you had not asked my advice: 'tis much easier to give rules than to practise them. I am sensible my own natural temper is too indulgent; I think it the least dangerous error, yet still it is an error. I can only say with truth that I do not know in my whole life having ever endeavoured to impose on you or give a false colour to anything that I 15 represented to you.

If your daughters are inclined to love reading, do not check their inclination by hindering them of the diverting part of it; it is as necessary for the amusement of women as the reputation of men; but teach them not to expect or desire any applause from it. Let their brothers shine, and let them content themselves with making their lives easier by it, 20 which I experimentally know is more effectually done by study than any other way. Ignorance is as much the fountain of vice as idleness, and indeed generally produces it. People that do not read or work for a livelihood have many hours they know not how to employ — especially women, who commonly fall into vapours or something worse. I am afraid you'll think this letter very tedious. Forgive it as coming from your most 25 affectionate mother,

To the Countess of Bute Feb. 19, N.S. [1750]

MY DEAR CHILD,

I gave you some general thoughts on the education of your children in my last letter, but fearing you should think I neglected your request by answering it with too much conciseness, I am resolved to add to it what little I know on that subject, and which may perhaps be useful to you in a concern with which you seem so nearly affected.

People commonly educate their children as they build their houses, according to 5 some plan they think beautiful, without considering whether it is suited to the purposes for which they are designed. Almost all girls of quality are educated as if they were to be great ladies, which is often as little to be expected as an immoderate heat of the sun in the north of Scotland. You should teach yours to confine their desires to probabilities,

to be as useful as is possible to themselves, and to think privacy (as it is) the happiest   *10*
state of life.

I do not doubt your giving them all the instructions necessary to form them to a
virtuous life, but 'tis a fatal mistake to do this without proper restrictions. Vices are
often hid under the name of virtues, and the practice of them followed by the worst of
consequences. Sincerity, friendship, piety, disinterestedness, and generosity are all great   *15*
virtues, but pursued without discretion become criminal. I have seen ladies indulge their
own ill humour by being very rude and impertinent, and think they deserved
approbation by saying "I love to speak truth." One of your acquaintance made a ball the
next day after her mother died, to show she was sincere. I believe your own reflection
will furnish you with but too many examples of the ill effects of the rest of the   *20*
sentiments I have mentioned, when too warmly embraced. They are generally
recommended to young people without limits or distinction, and this prejudice hurries
them into great misfortunes while they are applauding themselves in the noble practice
(as they fancy) of very eminent virtues.

I cannot help adding (out of my real affection to you), that I wish you would   *25*
moderate that fondness you have for your children. I do not mean you should abate any
part of your care, or not do your duty to them in its utmost extent; but I would have you
early prepare yourself for disappointments, which are heavy in proportion to their being
surprising. It is hardly possible in such a number that none should be unhappy. Prepare
yourself against a misfortune of that kind. I confess there is hardly any more difficult to   *30*
support, yet it is certain imagination has a great share in the pain of it, and it is more in
our power than it is commonly believed to soften whatever ills are founded or augmented by fancy. Strictly speaking, there is but one real evil; I mean acute pain. All
other complaints are so considerably diminished by time that it is plain the grief is
owing to our passion, since the sensation of it vanishes when that is over.   *35*

There is another mistake I forgot to mention, usual in mothers. If any of their
daughters are beauties, they take great pains to persuade them that they are ugly, or at
least that they think so, which the young woman never fails to believe springs from
envy, and is perhaps not much in the wrong. I would, if possible, give them a just notion
of their figure, and show them how far it is valuable. Every advantage has its price, and   *40*
may be either over- or under-valued. It is the common doctrine of (what are called) good
books to inspire a contempt of beauty, riches, greatness, etc., which has done as much
mischief amongst the young of our sex as an over-eager desire of them. They should
look on these things as blessings where they are bestowed, though not necessaries that it
is impossible to be happy without. . . . They should be taught to be content with privacy,   *45*
and yet not neglect good fortune if it should be offered them.

I am afraid I have tired you with my instructions. I do not give them as believing
my age has furnished me with superior wisdom, but in compliance with your desire, and
being fond of every opportunity that gives a proof of the tenderness with which I am
ever your affectionate mother,   *50*

Feb. 19, 1750   **10. privacy:** retirement, retreat (see also the poem "Conclusion of a Letter," below. **18. made:** i.e., gave, held. **19. sincere:**
unhurt.

To the Countess of Bute   *September [1752]*

It is very true, my dear child, we cannot now maintain a family with the product of a
flock, though I do not doubt the present sheep afford as much wool and milk as any of
their ancestors, and it is certain our natural wants are not more numerous than formerly;
but the world is past its infancy and will no longer be contented with spoon meat. Time
has added great improvements, but those very improvements have introduced a train of   *5*
artificial necessities. A collective body of men make a gradual progress in
understanding, like that of a single individual. When I reflect on the vast increase of
useful as well as speculative knowledge the last three hundred years has produced, and
that the peasants of this age have more conveniences than the first emperors of Rome
had any notion of, I imagine we are now arrived at that period which answers to fifteen.   *10*
I cannot think we are older, when I recollect the many palpable follies which are still
almost universally persisted in. I place that of war amongst the most glaring, being fully
as senseless as the boxing of schoolboys, and whenever we come to man's estate
(perhaps a thousand years hence), I do not doubt it will appear as ridiculous as the
pranks of unlucky lads. Several discoveries will then be made, and several truths made   *15*
clear, of which we have now no more idea than the ancients had of the circulation of the
blood or the optics of Sir I. Newton.

. . . .

To the Countess of Bute   *March 6 [1753]*

I cannot help writing a sort of apology for my last letter, foreseeing that you will think it
wrong, or at least Lord Bute will be extremely shocked at the proposal of a learned
education for daughters, which the generality of men believe as great a profanation as
the clergy would do if the laity should presume to exercise the functions of the
priesthood. I desire you would take notice I would not have learning enjoined them as a   *5*
task, but permitted as a pleasure if their genius leads them naturally to it. I look upon my
granddaughters as a sort of lay nuns. Destiny may have laid up other things for them,
but they have no reason to expect to pass their time otherwise than their aunts do at
present, and I know by experience it is in the power of study not only to make solitude
tolerable but agreeable. I have now lived almost seven years in a stricter retirement than   *10*
yours in the Isle of Bute, and can assure you I have never had half an hour heavy on my
hands for want of something to do.

  Whoever will cultivate their own mind will find full employment. Every virtue does
not only require great care in the planting, but as much daily solicitude in cherishing, as
exotic fruits and flowers; the vices and passions (which I am afraid are the natural   *15*
product of the soil) demand perpetual weeding. Add to this the search after knowledge

---

September 1752 4. **spoon meat:** liquid food, milk. **March 6, 1753** In her preceding letter (of 28 January), Lady Mary went into a
good deal of specific detail regarding the education of Lady Bute's eldest daughter, Mary — including two cautions: "First, not to think herself
learned when she can read Latin, or even Greek. Languages are more properly to be called vehicles of learning than learning itself. . . . The second
caution to be given her (and which is most absolutely necessary) is to conceal whatever learning she attains, with as much solicitude as she would
hide crookedness or lameness; the parade of it can only serve to draw on her the envy, and consequently the most inveterate hatred, of all he and she
fools, which will certainly be at least three parts in four of her acquaintance." **11. Isle of Bute:** off the west coast of Scotland, near Glasgow.

(every branch of which is entertaining), and the longest life is too short for the pursuit of it, which, though in some regards confined to very strait limits, leaves still a vast variety of amusements to those capable of tasting them, which is utterly impossible for those that are blinded by prejudices, which are the certain effect of an ignorant education. My own was one of the worst in the world, being exactly the same as Clarissa Harlowe's, her pious Mrs. Norton so perfectly resembling my governess (who had been nurse to my mother) I could almost fancy the author was acquainted with her. She took so much pains from my infancy to fill my head with superstitious tales and false notions, it was none of her fault I am not at this day afraid of witches and hobgoblins, or turned Methodist. 20 25

Almost all girls are bred after this manner. I believe you are the only woman (perhaps I might say person) that never was either frighted or cheated into anything by your parents. I can truly affirm I never deceived anybody in my life excepting (which I confess has often happened undesignedly) by speaking plainly. As Earl Stanhope used to say during his ministry, he always imposed on the foreign ministers by telling them the naked truth, which as they thought impossible to come from the mouth of a statesman, they never failed to write informations to their respective courts directly contrary to the assurances he gave them — most people confounding the ideas of sense and cunning, though there are really no two things in nature more opposite. It is in part from this false reasoning that the unjust custom prevails of debarring our sex from the advantages of learning, the men fancying the improvement of our understandings would only furnish us with more art to deceive them, which is directly contrary to the truth. Fools are always enterprising, not seeing the difficulties of deceit or the ill consequences of detection. I could give many examples of ladies whose ill conduct has been very notorious, which has been owing to that ignorance which has exposed them to idleness, which is justly called the mother of mischief. 30 35 40

There is nothing so like the education of a woman of quality as that of a prince. They are taught to dance and the exterior part of what is called good breeding, which if they attain they are extraordinary creatures in their kind, and have all the accomplishments required by their directors. The same characters are formed by the same lessons, which inclines me to think (if I dare say it) that nature has not placed us in an inferior rank to men, no more than the females of other animals, where we see no distinction of capacity — though I am persuaded if there was a commonwealth of rational horses (as Doctor Swift has supposed), it would be an established maxim amongst them that a mare could not be taught to pace. I could add a great deal on this subject, but I am not now endeavouring to remove the prejudices of mankind. My only design is to point out to my granddaughters the method of being contented with that retreat to which probably their circumstances will oblige them, and which is perhaps preferable to all the show of public life. It has always been my inclination. Lady Stafford (who knew me better than anybody else in the world, both from her own just 45 50 55

---

21. Clarissa Harlowe's: in the multi-volume epistolary novel *Clarissa: or The History of a Young Lady* (1748-49), by Samuel Richardson (1689-1761); Lady Mary had extensively criticized Richardson's fiction in an earlier letter. **30. Earl Stanhope:** James Stanhope, first Earl Stanhope (1673-1721), Secretary of State 1714-21. **49-50. commonwealth . . . supposed:** the land of the Houyhnhnms, in Part IV of Jonathan Swift's *Gulliver's Travels.* **55-56. Lady Stafford:** Long a close friend, she had died the same year Lady Mary moved to the Continent.

discernment and my heart being ever as open to her as myself) used to tell me my true vocation was a monastery, and I now find by experience more sincere pleasures with my books and garden than all the flutter of a court could give me.

If you follow my advice in relation to Lady Mary, my correspondence may be of 60 use to her, and I shall very willingly give her those instructions that may be necessary in the pursuit of her studies. Before her age I was in the most regular commerce with my grandmother, though the difference of our time of life was much greater, she being past 45 when she married my grandfather. She died at 96, retaining to the last the vivacity and clearness of her understanding, which was very uncommon. You cannot remember 65 her, being then in your nurse's arms. I conclude with repeating to you, I only recommend, but am far from commanding, which I think I have no right to do. I tell you my sentiments because you desired to know them, and hope you will receive them with some partiality as coming from your most affectionate mother,

from *ECLOGUES*

SATURDAY: THE SMALL POX

Flavia

The wretched Flavia, on her couch reclined,
Thus breathed the anguish of a wounded mind;
A glass reversed in her right hand she bore,
For now she shunned the face she sought before.
    "How am I changed! Alas! how am I grown 5
A frightful spectre, to myself unknown!
Where's my complexion? where my radiant bloom,
That promised happiness for years to come?
Then with what pleasure I this face surveyed!
To look once more, my visits oft delayed! 10
Charmed with the view, a fresher red would rise,
And a new life shot sparkling from my eyes.
    "Ah, faithless glass, my wonted bloom restore;
Alas, I rave! that bloom is now no more!
The greatest good the gods on men bestow, 15
Ev'n youth itself, to me is useless now.
There was a time (oh, that I could forget!)
When opera tickets poured before my feet;
And at the Ring, where brightest beauties shine,

The earliest cherries of the spring were mine. 20
Witness, O Lilly, and thou, Motteux, tell,
How much japan these eyes have made ye sell.
With what contempt ye saw me oft despise
The humble offer of the raffled prize;
For at each raffle still each prize I bore, 25
With scorn rejected, or with triumph wore!
Now beauty's fled, and presents are no more.
    "For me the patriot has the House forsook,
And left debates to catch a passing look;
For me the soldier has soft verses writ; 30
For me the beau has aimed to be a wit.
For me the wit to nonsense was betrayed;
The gamester has for me his dun delayed,
And overseen the card I would have paid.
The bold and haughty, by success made vain, 35
Awed by my eyes, have trembled to complain;
The bashful squire, touched by a wish unknown,
Has dared to speak with spirit not his own.

---

63. grandmother: Mary, Countess Dowager of Denbigh, was the second wife of Lady Mary's maternal grandfather; she died late in 1719. **SATURDAY: THE SMALL POX** Lady Mary's six "Town Eclogues," as they are sometimes called, were written partly as mock-pastorals; the first five are titled as follows: "Monday: Roxana: Or, The Drawing-Room"; "Tuesday: St. James's Coffee-House: Silliander and Patch"; "Wednesday: The Tete-à-Tete: Dancinda"; "Thursday: The Bassette Table: Smilinda and Cardelia"; "Friday: The Toilette: Lydia." "Saturday: The Small Pox" is the concluding poem of the series. Cf. Felltham's poem on this subject (p. 308), and see Lady Mary's letter to Sarah Chiswell, above. Lady Mary's own disfigurement from smallpox was apparently limited to the loss of her eyelashes. **19. Ring:** See Pope's *Rape of the Lock*, I, 44, and note (p. 524). **21. Lilly, Motteux:** contemporary shopkeepers for the fashionable. **22. japan:** japanned (lacquered or enamelled) items. **28. House:** i.e., one of the Houses of Parliament. **33-34:** i.e., in the card game of basset (similar to faro), a beau has put off paying his dun, or creditor, in order to bet on a card for her.

Fired by one wish, all did alike adore;
Now beauty's fled, and lovers are no more.   40
  "As round the room I turn my weeping eyes,
New unaffected scenes of sorrow rise.
Far from my sight that killing picture bear,
The face disfigure, and the canvas tear.
That picture which with pride I used to show,   45
The lost resemblance but upbraids me now.
And thou, my toilette! where I oft have sate,
While hours unheeded passed in deep debate,
How curls should fall, or where a patch to place;
If blue or scarlet best became my face;   50
Now on some happier nymph your aid bestow;
On fairer heads, ye useless jewels, glow!
No borrowed lustre can my charms restore;
Beauty is fled, and dress is now no more.
  "Ye meaner beauties, I permit ye shine;   55
Go, triumph in the hearts that once were mine.
But 'midst your triumphs, with confusion know,
'Tis to my ruin all your charms ye owe.
Would pitying Heav'n restore my wonted mien,
Ye still might move unthought of and unseen.   60
But oh, how vain, how wretched is the boast
Of beauty faded, and of empire lost!
What now is left but weeping to deplore
My beauty fled, and empire now no more!
  "Ye cruel chemists, what withheld your aid?   65
Could no pomatums save a trembling maid?
How false and trifling is that art ye boast;
No art can give me back my beauty lost.
In tears, surrounded by my friends, I lay
Masked o'er, and trembled at the light of day;   70
Mirmillo came my fortune to deplore
(A golden-headed cane well carved he bore);
Cordials, he cried, my spirits must restore;
Beauty is fled, and spirit is no more!
  "Galen, the grave officious Squirt, was there,   75
With fruitless grief and unavailing care;
Machaon too, the great Machaon, known
By his red cloak and his superior frown;
And why, he cried, this grief and this despair?
You shall again be well, again be fair;   80
Believe my oath (with that an oath he swore);
False was his oath; my beauty is no more.

"Cease, hapless maid, no more thy tale pursue;
Forsake mankind, and bid the world adieu.
Monarchs and beauties rule with equal sway;   85
All strive to serve, and glory to obey.
Alike unpitied when deposed they grow;
Men mock the idol of their former vow.
  "Adieu, ye parks, in some obscure recess,
Where gentle streams will weep at my distress,   90
Where no false friend will in my grief take part,
And mourn my ruin with a joyful heart,
There let me live in some deserted place,
There hide in shades this lost inglorious face.
Ye operas, circles, I no more must view!   95
My toilette, patches, all the world, adieu!"

(1715-16; 1747)

[LINES WRITTEN IN A BLANK PAGE OF MILTON'S *PARADISE LOST*]

This happy pair a certain bliss might prove,
Confined to constancy and mutual love;
Heav'n to one object limited their vows,
The only safety faithless Nature knows.
God saw the wand'ring appetite would range,   5
And would have kept them from the power to change;
But falsehood, soon as man increased, began;
Down through the race the swift contagion ran;
All ranks are tainted, all deceitful prove,
False in all shapes, but doubly false in love.   10
This makes the censure of the world more just,
That damns with shame the weakness of a trust!
Ere change began, our sex no scandal knew;
All nymphs were chaste as long as swains were true;
But now, though by the subtlest art betrayed,   15
We're so by custom and false maxims swayed
That infamy still brands the injured maid.

(c. 1725; 1837)

SONG

Why should you think I live unpleased
    Because I am not pleased with you?
My mind is not so far diseased,
    To yield when powdered fops pursue.

---

49. patch: See Pope's *Rape of the Lock*, I, 138, and note (p. 525). **65. chemists:** early physicians, i.e., those following the methods of Paracelsus. **66. pomatums:** ointments (here, medicinal). **71ff.:** "Mirmillo" represents a friend; "Galen," a physician (nicknamed for the famous Greek physician of the 2nd century A.D.); and "Machaon," Sir Samuel Garth (1661-1719), friend and physician, and author of *The Dispensary* (1699), whose main character bears that name; "Officious Squirt" also appears in Garth's poem. **95. circles:** social circles or gatherings, or perhaps seats in a theatre. **LINES WRITTEN IN "PARADISE LOST"** In *Essays and Poems*, Grundy includes only ten lines of this poem, and those fragmentary and containing variants; but even though the text lacks full authority, we include it as it appears in the 1837 edition.

My vanity can find no charm 5
  In common prostituted vows,
Nor can you raise a wish that's warm
  In one that your true value knows.

While cold and careless thus I shun
  The buzz and flutter that you make, 10
Perhaps some giddy girl may run
  To catch the prize that I forsake.

So brightly shines the glittering glare
  In unexperienced children's eyes,
When they with little arts ensnare 15
  The gaudy painted butterflies.

While they with pride the conquest boast,
  And think the chase deserving fame,
Those scorn the useless toil they cost
  Who're used to more substantial game. 20

(c. 1739; 1803)

[CONCLUSION OF A LETTER TO A FRIEND]

But happy you from the contagion free,
Who through her veil can human nature see;
Calm, you reflect amidst the frantic scene
On the low views of those mistaken men
Who lose the short invaluable hour 5
Through dirt-pursuing schemes of distant power;
Whose best enjoyments never pay the chase,
But melt like snow within a warm embrace.
Believe me, friend (for such indeed are you,
Dear to my heart, and to my interest true), 10
Too much already have you thrown away,
Too long sustained the labour of the day.
Enjoy the remnant of declining light,
Nor wait for rest till overwhelmed in night.
By present pleasure balance pain you've past, 15
Forget all systems, and indulge your taste.

(1741; 1803)

ELIZABETH TOLLET
England, 1694-1754

HYPATIA

Denied that fame, and robbed of that repose
Which learning merits, innocence bestows,
From that poetic shade, th' Elysian field,
That shade at least to Heathen virtue yield,
Hypatia comes. The dire, revolving date 5
Of circling years renews my cruel fate.
Did I for this to Plato's chair succeed,

In youth by envious ignorance to bleed?
When neither virtue nor the softer charm
Of female grace the vulgar could disarm 10
(To fury heightened by misguided zeal),
To future age I made my just appeal.
But what detested spell my shade could raise
To suffer L——'s spleen or Toland's praise?

CONCLUSION OF A LETTER Halsband in *The Complete Letters* says that these lines were addressed to Lord Hervey (John Hervey, Baron Hervey of Ickworth, 1696-1743), another close friend and frequent correspondent of Lady Mary's; they often wrote each other in verse. **HYPATIA** Hypatia, the "Divine Pagan," daughter of Theon the mathematician, was a celebrated Neoplatonic philosopher of Alexandria, who also lectured and wrote about mathematics and astronomy; she was murdered in A.D. 415 by a fanatical Christian mob incited, some say, by Archbishop Cyril, the Patriarch of Alexandria — or as the note in the table of contents of Tollet's *Poems on Several Occasions* puts it, "She was a heathen, and killed in a tumult by some illiterate Christian monks." Charles Kingsley (1819-1875) tells her story in his historical novel *Hypatia* (1853). Tollet appends the following comment to her poem: "If in this little piece the doubts concerning the supreme Being be thought exceptionable, or any passage in it inconsistent with the modern philosophy, it must be considered that I was to adapt my notions to the character of an heathen and a Platonist, who is supposed to deliver them. Indeed as to comets, I have deviated a little to follow the late improvements of astronomy." **14. L——'s:** possibly referring to Charles Leslie (1650-1722), Anglican (though a Nonjuror) theologian and controversialist who attacked Roman Catholics, Quakers, Jews, Deists, and perceived heresy of any kind; **Toland:** John (christened "Junius Janus") Toland (1670-1722), Irish-born theologian who frequently changed his religious views (e.g. Roman Catholic, Protestant, deist, freethinker, pantheist — the latter a term evidently first used by him) and wrote several controversial books; best known for *Christianity Not Mysterious* (1696) and *Pantheisticon* (1720).

Above thy rage, above thy flattery more,   *15*
The tort'ring shells with less regret I bore:
Alas! by thee 'tis honour to be blamed;
And to be praised by thee to be defamed.

   Severe! though conscious innocence sustains
The mind, and mean apology disdains;   *20*
That conduct to ambiguous guilt belongs,
Or souls unequal to the weight of wrongs.
To such her fame would inbred virtue owe,
Whom her exalted flight surveys below,
Unskilled to judge, though forward to bestow,   *25*
Yet to th' unbiassed, the distinguished few,
Whose clearer judgment makes a just review,
She turns undaunted, and submits her cause;
Nor shrinks from censure, nor demands applause.
Such gen'rous warmth true modesty inspires,   *30*
Where servile shame with coward dread retires;
Virtue and vice mistaken for the same,
Yet more distinct in nature than in name.

   What cruel laws depress the female kind,
To humble cares and servile tasks confined!   *35*
In gilded toys their florid bloom to spend,
And empty glories that in age must end;
For am'rous youth to spread the artful snares,
And by their triumphs to enlarge their cares.
For, once engaged in the domestic chain,   *40*
Compare the sorrows, and compute the gain.
What happiness can servitude afford?
A will resigned to an imperious lord,
Or slave to avarice, to beauty blind,
Or soured with spleen, or ranging unconfined.   *45*
That haughty man, unrivalled and alone,
May boast the world of science all his own;
As barb'rous tyrants, to secure their sway,
Conclude that ignorance will best obey.
Then boldly loud, and privileged to rail,   *50*
As prejudice o'er reason may prevail,
Unequal nature is accused to fail.
The theme, in keen iambics smoothly writ,
Which was but malice late, shall soon be wit.

   Nature in vain can womankind inspire   *55*
With brighter particles of active fire,
Which to their frame a due proportion hold,
Refined by dwelling in a purer mould,
If useless rust must fair endowments hide,
Or wit, disdaining ease, be misapplied.   *60*
'Tis then that wit, which reason should refine,
And disengage the metal from the mine,
Luxuriates, or degen'rates to design.
Wit unemployed becomes a dang'rous thing,
As waters stagnate, and defile their spring.   *65*
The cultivated mind, a fertile soil,
With rich increase rewards the useful toil;
But fallow left, an hateful crop succeeds,
Of tangling brambles and pernicious weeds;
'Tis endless labour then the ground to clear,   *70*
And trust the doubtful earnest of the year.

   Yet oft we hear, in height of stupid pride,
Some senseless idiot curse a lettered bride.
Is this a crime? for female minds to share
The early influence of instructive care;   *75*
To learn from treach'rous passions to divest
The yielding softness of a youthful breast;
The heart with solid prudence to redeem
From fond, mistaken objects of esteem.
To see in Fortune, when she smiles serene,   *80*
A dang'rous Siren with a fawning mien;
But when she frowns, to scorn her vain alarms,
Secure in Virtue's adamantine arms.
Or to distinguish, with a stricter view,
The near resemblance of the false and true;   *85*
Of vice and virtue there the bounds to fix,
Just where their fading colours seem to mix.

   Or yet is this a crime? by measures just,
In figured space to circumscribe the dust;
With ecstasy proportion to compare,   *90*
Of straight and crooked, circular and square;
Abstracted truths in numbers to explain,
Or in mysterious secrecy retain.

   Or yet is this a crime? the mind to raise,
To follow Nature in her winding ways;   *95*
To interdicted knowledge to aspire,
And of the mighty parent thus enquire:
How all that reason points, or sense can see,

In one of the essays in *Tetradymus* (1720), he recounts Hypatia's story (as Leslie Stephen puts it in *History of English Thought in the Eighteenth Century*, 1876) "as an illustration of the wickedness of priests"; he specifically attacks Cyril and other clergy and "saints," claiming that Cyril envied Hypatia's fame for learning; he offers some defense of the education of women, and praises Hypatia's learning and beauty ("a charming Mind in a charming Body"); he also says she was hauled into a church, stripped, beaten to death with "Tiles," taken outside and cut to pieces, and then burned. **16. shells:** Some accounts say she was hacked to pieces with oyster shells. **47. science:** i.e., knowledge, learning. **53. keen iambics:** See Dryden's *Mac Flecknoe*, line 204, and note (p. 437).

At first began, and yet persists to be;
How, linked in peace, the elements combine,   *100*
And each contributes to the great design;
Though when the chymic fires their parts divide,
The volatile ascend, the gross subside.
What in her cells the central Earth contains;
How latent metals ripen in their veins;   *105*
How ruder flints the sparkling gem inclose,
And how amid the rock the ruby glows.
From whence the Earth imbibes the humid stores
Which weeping marble oozes at its pores;
Why justly she renews the annual scene,   *110*
Now white with snow, now gay with springing green.
Whence knows th' refluent ocean to obey
Th' alternate impulse of the lunar ray.
What diff'rent principles do life bestow
Upon the scale of beings here below,   *115*
Whence some have only to exist and grow.
Of these, why some upon their native bed
Lie prostrate, some to Heav'n erect the head;
Why some a leavy shade alone produce,
Why others clust'ring fruit and gen'rous juice.   *120*
Why some the air with spicy odours fill,
Some through the wounded bark their balm distil,
Whence some have pow'r to stay the fleeting breath,
And some the fatal shafts of instant death.

Or why those beings which we brutes miscall,   *125*
So closely imitate the rational.
Howe'er that fire that animates their frame
May be defined, or whence soe'er it came,
Which now collected and in bodies fixed,
With liquid air hereafter may be mixed;   *130*
Yet by external acts they seem endued
With hatred, love, resentment, gratitude;
Almost the Samian Sage belief might gain
That transmigrating souls their breasts contain.

Or how the race of Man perceives within   *135*
That principle whence these demands begin;
How Nature does in him to sense unite
A more exalted flame, and purer light,
Empowered to choose, reject, divide, combine,
With rays reflected on the past to shine,   *140*

And thence the distant future to divine.
Whether, distinct, the Heav'n-born mind control
The headstrong animal, the lower soul,
Or but a part herself, conduct the whole.
Or of primeval light is she a ray,   *145*
Infused to guide the amicable clay?
Or hold these bodies the reluctant mind
In penalty of former guilt confined?
Is she again through other forms to stray?
Or wait the doom of one decisive day?   *150*

Yet, as she may, her forces she explores,
And far above the orb sublunar soars.
She leaves the less'ning Earth, and upward springs,
On purer Æther to expand her wings;
A nobler pitch her bold enquiries fly,   *155*
Amid the fields of her congenial sky.
She sees the lights, which we accuse to stray,
In measured dance pursue their certain way;
And thousand stars, which scarce to us appear,
With vivid rays illuminate the sphere,   *160*
In deepened spaces, and retiring files,
Whose distance hence the weary eye beguiles.
She sees where comets trail their fiery hair,
Terrific lustre! through the shining air;
Nor vapours they, whose levity aspires   *165*
At Phoebus' car to catch Promethean fires;
But real stars, which unextinguished burn,
Through larger periods of a just return.

Whether that Spirit which o'er all presides
Infused through all its equal motions guides,   *170*
Or from the whole distinct, himself unseen,
Conducts and regulates the vast machine,
Let Heav'n decide; by reason's finite view
To judge the diff'rence would the doubt renew;
Yet she aspires that Being to explore,   *175*
The source of all, and wond'ring to adore.

Shall jealous Man to Woman then deny
In these debates her faculties to try,
And spend the moments which unheeded fly?
For this must our unhappy sex engage   *180*
Relentless malice, and barbarian rage?
While tyrant Custom Reason overawes,

---

102. chymic: chemic, chemical. **133. Samian Sage:** Pythagoras, 6th-century B.C. Greek philosopher and mathematician, known for his doctrine of the transmigration of souls. **152. orb sublunar:** i.e., the earth. **155. pitch:** peak, height. **157. lights . . . stray:** i.e., the planets in their orbits (Tollet knew Sir Isaac Newton, and therefore was familiar with his and others' ideas about planetary orbits). **165. levity:** lightness, lack of weight. **166. Phoebus' car:** in Greek mythology, the chariot of Phoebus Apollo, god of the sun. **166. Promethean:** In myth, Prometheus stole some fire from the gods in order to give it to human beings. **168. just:** exact, regular, due. **182. tyrant Custom:** Cf. the opening of Egerton's "The Emulation" (p. 489).

And partial humour to the world gives laws.
Yet these may conscious innocence defy,
Approved to virtue, and secure to die;   *185*
No doubt remains that fame shall then be just,
When spleen and censure shall be laid in dust;
That future ages shall reverse their doom,
Nor impious envy violate the tomb.

For virtue then, with native lustre bright,   *190*
From time and death receives her strongest light:
So when nice art with nature seems at strife,
To animate the canvas into life,
The just obscure the bolder light confines,
And soft'ning shadows swell the glowing lines.   *195*

(1724)

PHILIP DORMER STANHOPE, LORD CHESTERFIELD
England, 1694-1773

from *LETTERS TO HIS SON*

Bath, October the 12th, O.S. 1748.

DEAR BOY,

I came here three days ago, upon account of a disorder in my stomach, which affected my head, and gave me vertigos. I already find myself something better, and consequently do not doubt but that the course of these waters will set me quite right. But however and wherever I am, your welfare, your character, your knowledge, and your morals employ my thoughts more than anything that can happen to me, or that I can fear   *5*
or hope for myself. I am going off of the stage, you are coming upon it: with me, what has been, has been, and reflection now would come too late; with you, everything is to come, even, in some manner, reflection itself, so that this is the very time when my reflections, the result of experience, may be of use to you, by supplying the want of yours. As soon as you leave Leipzig, you will gradually be going into the great world,   *10*
where the first impressions that you shall give of yourself will be of great importance to you; but those which you shall receive will be decisive, for they always stick. To keep good company, especially at your first setting out, is the way to receive good impressions. If you ask me what I mean by good company, I will confess to you that it is pretty difficult to define; but I will endeavour to make you understand it as well as I can.   *15*

   Good Company is not what respective sets of company are pleased either to call or think themselves; but it is that company which all the people of the place call, and acknowledge to be, good company, notwithstanding some objections which they may form to some of the individuals who compose it. It consists chiefly (but by no means without exception) of people of considerable birth, rank, and character, for people of   *20*
neither birth nor rank are frequently, and very justly, admitted into it, if distinguished by any peculiar merit, or eminency in any liberal art or science. Nay, so motley a thing is

---

183. humour: i.e., turn of mind, disposition. **188. doom:** judgment, condemnation. **194. obscure:** darkness, as in *chiaroscuro*.   **LETTERS TO HIS SON**   Chesterfield wrote these letters to his natural son, Philip (1732-1768). (For more on Chesterfield, see the excerpt from Boswell's *Life of Johnson*, p. 685).   **1-3:** Bath has been a spa since Roman times. **10. Leipzig:** Young Philip was doing a "grand tour"; from Germany he proceeded to Italy (see note to Dixon's "Receipt," line 9, p. 489).

good company, that many people without birth, rank, or merit intrude into it by their own forwardness, and others slide into it by the protection of some considerable person; and some even of indifferent characters and morals make part of it. But, in the main, the good part preponderates, and people of infamous and blasted characters are never admitted. In this fashionable good company, the best manners and the best language of the place are most unquestionably to be learnt; for they establish and give the tone to both, which are therefore called the language and manners of good company, there being no legal tribunal to ascertain either.

A company consisting wholly of people of the first quality cannot, for that reason, be called good company, in the common acceptation of the phrase, unless they are, into the bargain, the fashionable and accredited company of the place; for people of the very first quality can be as silly, as ill-bred, and as worthless as people of the meanest degree. On the other hand, a company consisting entirely of people of very low condition, whatever their merit or parts may be, can never be called good company, and consequently should not be much frequented, though by no means despised.

A company wholly composed of men of learning, though greatly to be valued and respected, is not meant by the words, *good company:* they cannot have the easy manners and *tournure* of the world, as they do not live in it. If you can bear your part well in such a company, it is extremely right to be in it sometimes, and you will be but more esteemed, in other companies, for having a place in that. But then do not let it engross you; for if you do, you will be only considered as one of the *litterati* by profession; which is not the way either to shine or rise in the world.

The company of professed Wits and Poets is extremely inviting to most young men, who, if they have wit themselves, are pleased with it, and if they have none, are sillily proud of being one of it; but it should be frequented with moderation and judgment, and you should by no means give yourself up to it. A Wit is a very unpopular denomination, as it carries terror along with it; and people in general are as much afraid of a live Wit, in company, as a woman is of a gun, which she thinks may go off of itself, and do her a mischief. Their acquaintance is, however, worth seeking, and their company worth frequenting; but not exclusively of others, nor to such a degree as to be considered only as one of that particular set.

But the company, which of all others you should most carefully avoid, is that low company which, in every sense of the word, is low indeed: low in rank, low in parts, low in manners, and low in merit. You will, perhaps, be surprised that I should think it necessary to warn you against such company; but yet I do not think it wholly unnecessary, after the many instances which I have seen of men of sense and rank discredited, vilified, and undone by keeping such company. Vanity, that source of many of our follies, and of some of our crimes, has sunk many a man into company in every light infinitely below himself, for the sake of being the first man in it. There he dictates, is applauded, admired; and, for the sake of being the *Coryphaeus* of that wretched chorus, disgraces and disqualifies himself soon for any better company. Depend upon it, you will sink or rise to the level of the company which you commonly keep: people will judge of you, and not unreasonably, by that. There is good sense in the Spanish saying,

---

31. first quality: i.e., highest social standing. **40. *tournure*:** style. **62. *Coryphaeus*:** chorus-leader in Greek tragedy.

"Tell me whom you live with, and I will tell you who you are." Make it therefore your business, wherever you are, to get into that company which everybody of the place allows to be the best company, next to their own: which is the best definition that I can give you of good company. But here, too, one caution is very necessary, for want of which many young men have been ruined, even in good company. Good company (as I have before observed) is composed of a great variety of fashionable people whose characters and morals are very different, though their manners are pretty much the same. When a young man, new in the world, first gets into that company, he very rightly determines to conform to and imitate it. But then he too often, and fatally, mistakes the objects of his imitation. He has often heard that absurd term of genteel and fashionable vices. He there sees some people who shine, and who in general are admired and esteemed, and observes that these people are whoremasters, drunkards, or gamesters: upon which he adopts their vices, mistaking their defects for their perfections, and thinking that they owe their fashion and their lustre to those genteel vices. Whereas it is exactly the reverse; for these people have acquired their reputation by their parts, their learning, their good-breeding, and other real accomplishments, and are only blemished and lowered, in the opinions of all reasonable people, and of their own, in time, by these genteel and fashionable vices. A whoremaster in a flux, or without a nose, is a very genteel person indeed, and well worthy of imitation. A drunkard, vomiting up at night the wine of the day, and stupefied by the headache all the next, is, doubtless, a fine model to copy from. And a gamester, tearing his hair, and blaspheming, for having lost more than he had in the world, is surely a most amiable character. No; these are allays, and great ones too, which can never adorn any character, but will always debase the best. To prove this, suppose any man, without parts and some other good qualities, to be merely a whoremaster, a drunkard, or a gamester; How will he be looked upon by all sorts of people? Why, as a most contemptible and vicious animal. Therefore it is plain that, in these mixed characters, the good part only makes people forgive, but not approve, the bad.

I will hope, and believe, that you will have no vices; but if, unfortunately, you should have any, at least I beg of you to be content with your own, and to adopt no other body's. The adoption of vice has, I am convinced, ruined ten times more young men, than natural inclinations.

As I make no difficulty of confessing my past errors, where I think the confession may be of use to you, I will own that, when I first went to the university, I drank and smoked, notwithstanding the aversion I had to wine and tobacco, only because I thought it genteel, and that it made me look like a man. When I went abroad, I first went to the Hague, where gaming was much in fashion, and where I observed that many people, of shining rank and character, gamed too. I was then young enough, and silly enough, to believe that gaming was one of their accomplishments; and, as I aimed at perfection, I adopted gaming as a necessary step to it. Thus I acquired, by error, the habit of a vice, which, far from adorning my character, has, I am conscious, been a great blemish in it.

Imitate, then, with discernment and judgment, the real perfections of the good company which you may get into; copy their politeness, their carriage, their address, and

---

66. live with: i.e., associate with, keep company with. **83. in a flux, or without a nose:** symptoms of advanced venereal disease. **87. allays:** alloys, baser metals; i.e., inferior elements that lower the character. **88. parts:** endowments, talents, abilities. **107. carriage:** behaviour, manners, bearing; **address:** manner of speaking to another.

the easy and well-bred turn of their conversation; but remember that, let them shine ever so bright, their vices, if they have any, are so many spots, which you would no more imitate than you would make an artificial wart upon your face, because some very *110* handsome man had the misfortune to have a natural one upon his; but, on the contrary, think how much handsomer he would have been without it.

Having thus confessed some of my *égaremens,* I will now show you a little of my right side. I always endeavoured to get into the best company, wherever I was, and commonly succeeded. There I pleased, to some degree, by showing a desire to please. I *115* took care never to be absent or *distrait;* but, on the contrary, attended to everything that was said, done, or even looked, in company: I never failed in the minutest attentions, and was never *journalier.* These things, and not my *égaremens,* made me fashionable.

Adieu! this letter is full long enough.

Bath, October the 19th, O.S. 1748.

DEAR BOY,

Having, in my last, pointed out what sort of company you should keep, I will now give *120* you some rules for your conduct in it; rules which my own experience and observation enable me to lay down, and communicate to you, with some degree of confidence. I have often given you hints of this kind before, but then it has been by snatches; I will now be more regular and methodical. I shall say nothing with regard to your bodily carriage and address, but leave them to the care of your dancing-master, and to your *125* own attention to the best models; remember, however, that they are of consequence.

Talk often, but never long; in that case, if you do not please, at least you are sure not to tire your hearers.

Pay your own reckoning, but do not treat the whole company; this being one of the very few cases in which people do not care to be treated, everyone being fully *130* convinced that he has wherewithal to pay.

Tell stories very seldom, and, absolutely, never but where they are very apt, and very short. Omit every circumstance that is not material, and beware of digressions. To have frequent recourse to narrative betrays great want of imagination.

Never hold anybody by the button, or the hand, in order to be heard out; if people *135* are not willing to hear you, you had much better hold your tongue than them.

Most long talkers single out some one unfortunate man in company (commonly him whom they observe to be the most silent) or their next neighbour, to whisper, or at least, in a half voice, to convey a continuity of words to. This is excessively ill-bred, and, in some degree, a fraud, conversation-stock being a joint and common property. But, on *140* the other hand, if one of these unmerciful talkers lays hold of you, hear him with patience (and at least seeming attention) if he is worth obliging; for nothing will oblige him more than a patient hearing, as nothing would hurt him more than either to leave him in the midst of his discourse, or to discover your impatience under your affliction.

Take, rather than give, the tone of the company you are in. If you have parts you *145* will show them, more or less, upon every subject; and if you have not, you had better talk sillily upon a subject of other people's, than of your own choosing.

---

113. *égaremens:* i.e., *égarements,* strayings, deviations from virtue. **116.** *distrait:* distracted. **118.** *journalier:* changeable from day to day. **129.** **reckoning:** bills, debts.

Avoid, as much as you can, in mixed companies, argumentative, polemical conversations, which, though they should not, yet certainly do, indispose, for a time, the contending parties towards each other; and if the controversy grows warm and noisy, endeavour to put an end to it by some genteel levity or joke. I quieted such a conversation-hubbub once, by representing to them that, though I was persuaded none there present would repeat, out of company, what passed in it, yet I could not answer for the discretion of the passengers in the street, who must necessarily hear all that was said. *150*

Above all things, and upon all occasions, avoid speaking of yourself, if it be possible. Such is the natural pride and vanity of our hearts, that it perpetually breaks out, even in people of the best parts, in all the various modes and figures of the egotism. *155*

Some, abruptly, speak advantageously of themselves, without either pretence or provocation. They are impudent. Others proceed more artfully, as they imagine, and forge accusations against themselves, complain of calumnies which they never heard, in order to justify themselves, by exhibiting a catalogue of their many virtues. *They acknowledge it may, indeed, seem odd, that they should talk in that manner of themselves; it is what they do not like, and what they never would have done; no, no tortures should ever have forced it from them, if they had not been thus unjustly and monstrously accused. But, in these cases, justice is surely due to one's self, as well as to others; and, when our character is attacked, we may say, in our own justification, what otherwise we never would have said.* This thin veil of Modesty, drawn before Vanity, is much too transparent to conceal it, even from very moderate discernment. *160* *165*

Others go more modestly and more slily still (as they think) to work; but, in my mind, still more ridiculously. They confess themselves (not without some degree of shame and confusion) into all the Cardinal Virtues, by first degrading them into weaknesses, and then owning their misfortune, in being made up of those weaknesses. *They cannot see people suffer, without sympathizing with, and endeavouring to help them. They cannot see people want, without relieving them; though, truly, their own circumstances cannot very well afford it. They cannot help speaking truth, though they know all the imprudence of it. In short, they know that, with all these weaknesses, they are not fit to live in the world, much less to thrive in it. But they are now too old to change, and must rub on as well as they can.* This sounds too ridiculous and *outré*, almost, for the stage; and yet, take my word for it, you will frequently meet with it, upon the common stage of the world. And here I will observe, by the bye, that you will often meet with characters in nature so extravagant, that a discreet Poet would not venture to set them upon the stage, in their true and high colouring. *170* *175* *180*

This principle of vanity and pride is so strong in human nature that it descends even to the lowest objects; and one often sees people angling for praise, where, admitting all they say to be true (which, by the way, it seldom is), no just praise is to be caught. One man affirms that he has rode post an hundred miles in six hours: probably it is a lie; but, supposing it to be true, what then? Why he is a very good post-boy, that is all. Another asserts, and probably not without oaths, that he has drank six or eight bottles of wine at a sitting: out of charity, I will believe him a liar; for, if I do not, I must think him a beast. *185* *190*

---

154. **passengers:** passers-by. 178. ***outré*:** exaggerated, eccentric.

Such, and a thousand more, are the follies and extravagancies which vanity draws people into, and which always defeat their own purpose, and, as Waller says upon another subject,

> Make the wretch the most despised,
> Where most he wishes to be prized. *195*

The only sure way of avoiding these evils is never to speak of yourself at all. But when, historically, you are obliged to mention yourself, take care not to drop one single word that can, directly or indirectly, be construed as fishing for applause. Be your character what it will, it will be known; and nobody will take it upon your own word. Never imagine that anything you can say, yourself, will varnish your defects, or add *200* lustre to your perfections; but, on the contrary, it may, and nine times in ten will, make the former more glaring, and the latter obscure. If you are silent upon your own subject, neither envy, indignation, nor ridicule will obstruct or allay the applause which you may really deserve; but if you publish your own panegyric, upon any occasion, or in any shape whatsoever, and however artfully dressed or disguised, they will all conspire *205* against you, and you will be disappointed at the very end you aim at.

Take care never to seem dark and mysterious, which is not only a very unamiable character, but a very suspicious one too: if you seem mysterious with others, they will be really so with you, and you will know nothing. The height of abilities is to have *volto sciolto,* and *pensieri stretti;* that is, a frank, open, and ingenuous exterior, with a prudent *210* and reserved interior; to be upon your own guard, and yet, by a seeming natural openness, to put people off of theirs. Depend upon it, nine in ten of every company you are in will avail themselves of every indiscreet and unguarded expression of yours, if they can turn it to their own advantage. A prudent reserve is therefore as necessary, as a seeming openness is prudent. Always look people in the face when you speak to them: *215* the not doing it is thought to imply conscious guilt; besides that, you lose the advantage of observing, by their countenances, what impression your discourse makes upon them. In order to know people's real sentiments, I trust much more to my eyes than to my ears; for they can say whatever they have a mind I should hear, but they can seldom help looking what they have no intention that I should know. *220*

Neither retail nor receive scandal willingly; for though the defamation of others may, for the present, gratify the malignity of the pride of our hearts, cool reflection will draw very disadvantageous conclusions from such a disposition; and in the case of scandal, as in that of robbery, the receiver is always thought as bad as the thief.

Mimickry, which is the common and favourite amusement of little, low minds, is in *225* the utmost contempt with great ones. It is the lowest and most illiberal of all buffoonery. Pray, neither practise it yourself, nor applaud it in others. Besides that, the person mimicked is insulted; and, as I have often observed to you before, an insult is never forgiven.

I need not (I believe) advise you to adapt your conversation to the people you are conversing with: for I suppose you would not, without this caution, have talked upon the *230* same subject, and in the same manner, to a Minister of State, a Bishop, a Philosopher, a Captain, and a Woman. A man of the world must, like the chameleon, be able to take

---

192. Waller: See p. 311. **197. historically:** by way of narration.

every different hue; which is by no means a criminal or abject, but a necessary complaisance, for it relates only to Manners, and not to Morals.

One word only as to swearing; and that, I hope and believe, is more than is neces- *235* sary. You may sometimes hear some people, in good company, interlard their discourse with oaths by way of embellishment, as they think; but you must observe, too, that those who do so, are never those who contribute, in any degree, to give that company the denomination of good company. They are always subalterns, or people of low education; for that practice, besides that it has no one temptation to plead, is as silly, and *240* as illiberal, as it is wicked.

Loud laughter is the mirth of the mob, who are only pleased with silly things; for true Wit or good Sense never excited a laugh since the creation of the world. A man of parts and fashion is therefore only seen to smile, but never heard to laugh.

But, to conclude this long letter; all the above-mentioned rules, however carefully *245* you may observe them, will lose half their effect if unaccompanied by the Graces. Whatever you say, if you say it with a supercilious, cynical face, or an embarrassed countenance, or a silly, disconcerted grin, will be ill received. If, into the bargain, you mutter it, or utter it indistinctly, and ungracefully, it will be still worse received. If your air and address are vulgar, awkward, and *gauche,* you may be esteemed indeed, if you *250* have great intrinsic merit; but you will never please, and, without pleasing, you will rise but heavily. Venus, among the Ancients, was synonymous with the Graces, who were always supposed to accompany her; and Horace tells us that even Youth, and Mercury, the God of Arts and Eloquence, would not do without her.

Parum comis sine te Juventas Mercuriusque. *255*

They are not inexorable Ladies, and may be had, if properly and diligently pursued. Adieu.

Nursery Rhymes

A Apple Pie

A was an apple-pie;	I inspected it,
B bit it,	J jumped for it,
C cut it,	K kept it,
D dealt it,	L longed for it,
E eat it,	M mourned for it,
F fought for it,	N nodded at it,
G got it,	O opened it,
H had it,	P peeped in it,

252-53: See note to Spenser's *Faerie Queene*, I, I, 430 (p. 159). **255:** "Without you, neither Youth nor Mercury is very friendly" (Horace, *Odes*, I, xxx, 7). **Nursery Rhymes** Nursery rhymes derive from many sources, including old songs, lullabies, and folk legends; the dating of individual rhymes is uncertain, and the precise sources are often obscure. We have assembled several examples at this point in the anthology because many were in common currency by the 1690s; and during the 18th century, collections of rhymes, such as *Mother Goose's Melody, or Sonnets for*

Q quartered it,
R ran for it,
S stole it,
T took it,
U upset it,
V viewed it,
W wanted it,
X, Y, Z and ampersand
All wished for a piece in hand.

Ride a Cock-horse

Ride a cock-horse to Banbury Cross,
To see a fine lady upon a white horse;
Rings on her fingers and bells on her toes,
And she shall have music wherever she goes.

Baa, Baa, Black Sheep

Baa, baa, black sheep,
  Have you any wool?
Yes, sir, yes, sir,
  Three bags full;
One for the master,
  And one for the dame,
And one for the little boy
  Who lives down the lane.

Hey Diddle Diddle

Hey diddle diddle,
The cat and the fiddle,
The cow jumped over the moon;
The little dog laughed
To see such sport,
And the dish ran away with the spoon.

Cock Robin

Who killed Cock Robin?
I, said the Sparrow,
With my bow and arrow,
I killed Cock Robin.

Who saw him die?
I, said the Fly,
With my little eye,
I saw him die.

Who caught his blood?
I, said the Fish,
With my little dish,
I caught his blood.

Who'll make the shroud?
I, said the Beetle,
With my thread and needle,
I'll make the shroud.

Who'll dig his grave?
I, said the Owl,
With my pick and shovel,
I'll dig his grave.

Who'll be the parson?
I, said the Rook,
With my little book,
I'll be the parson.

Who'll be the clerk?
I, said the Lark,
If it's not in the dark,
I'll be the clerk.

Who'll carry the link?
I, said the Linnet,
I'll fetch it in a minute,
I'll carry the link.

Who'll be chief mourner?
I, said the Dove,
I mourn for my love,
I'll be chief mourner.

Who'll carry the coffin?
I, said the Kite,
If it's not through the night,
I'll carry the coffin.

Who'll bear the pall?
We, said the Wren,
Both the cock and the hen,
We'll bear the pall.

Who'll sing a psalm?
I, said the Thrush,
As she sat on a bush,
I'll sing a psalm.

---

the Cradle (c.1760) and Joseph Ritson's *Gammer Gurton's Garland, or, the Nursery Parnassus* (1784), had become familiar. Nursery rhymes took a variety of forms, from riddles (e.g., "Humpty Dumpty") to games ("Oranges and Lemons"), ritual charms ("Ladybird, Ladybird") to nonsense syllables ("Hey diddle diddle"), mnemonic chants ("A Apple Pie" or "One, Two, Buckle My Shoe") to fantastic narratives ("Jack and Jill"), political

Who'll toll the bell?
I, said the Bull,
Because I can pull,
I'll toll the bell.

All the birds of the air
Fell a-sighing and a-sobbing,
When they heard the bell toll
For poor Cock Robin.

Humpty Dumpty

Humpty Dumpty sat on a wall,
Humpty Dumpty had a great fall.
    All the king's horses,
    And all the king's men,
Couldn't put Humpty together again.

Jack and Jill

Jack and Jill went up the hill
    To fetch a pail of water;
Jack fell down and broke his crown,
    And Jill came tumbling after.

Up Jack got, and home did trot,
    As fast as he could caper,
To old Dame Dob, who patched his nob
    With vinegar and brown paper.

Ladybird, Ladybird

Ladybird, ladybird,
    Fly away home,
Your house is on fire
    And your children all gone;
All except one
    And that's little Ann
And she has crept under
    The warming pan.

Mary, Mary, Quite Contrary

Mary, Mary, quite contrary,
    How does your garden grow?
With silver bells and cockle shells,
    And pretty maids all in a row.

Oranges and Lemons

Oranges and lemons,
Say the bells of St. Clement's.

You owe me five farthings,
Say the bells of St. Martin's.

When will you pay me?
Say the bells of Old Bailey.

When I grow rich,
Say the bells of Shoreditch.

When will that be?
Say the bells of Stepney.

I'm sure I don't know,
Says the great bell at Bow.

Here comes a candle to light you to bed,
Here comes a chopper to chop off your head.

Ring-a-Ring o' Roses

Ring-a-ring o' roses,
A pocket full of posies,
    A-tishoo! A-tishoo!
We all fall down.

Solomon Grundy

Solomon Grundy,
Born on a Monday,
Christened on Tuesday,
Married on Wednesday,
Took ill on Thursday,
Worse on Friday,
Died on Saturday,
Buried on Sunday.
This is the end
Of Solomon Grundy.

Sing a Song of Sixpence

Sing a song of sixpence,
    A pocket full of rye;
Four and twenty blackbirds,
    Baked in a pie.

When the pie was opened,
    The birds began to sing;

---

allegories ("Cock Robin") to cautionary and moral lessons ("Solomon Grundy" and the alphabet from *The New England Primer*). "Oranges and Lemons" devises words to mimic the chimes of London's churchbells. Of the rhymes collected here, "Baa, Baa, Black Sheep" may be the earliest, perhaps a protest against an export tax on wool in the year 1275; the most recent are "One, Two" and "Monday's Child," which appear to be

Was not that a dainty dish,
  To set before the king?

The king was in his counting-house,
  Counting out his money;
The queen was in the parlour,
  Eating bread and honey.

The maid was in the garden,
  Hanging out the clothes,
There came a little blackbird,
  And snapped off her nose.

Monday's Child

Monday's child is fair of face,
Tuesday's child is full of grace,
Wednesday's child is full of woe,
Thursday's child has far to go,
Friday's child is loving and giving,
Saturday's child works hard for his living,
And the child that is born on the Sabbath day
Is bonny and blithe, and good and gay.

One, Two, Buckle My Shoe

One, two,
Buckle my shoe;
Three, four,
Knock at the door;
Five, six,
Pick up sticks;
Seven, eight,
Lay them straight;
Nine, ten,
A big fat hen;
Eleven, twelve,
Dig and delve;
Thirteen, fourteen,
Maids a-courting;
Fifteen, sixteen,
Maids in the kitchen;
Seventeen, eighteen,
Maids in waiting;
Nineteen, twenty,
My plate's empty.

from *The New England Primer*

Alphabet

A   In *Adam's* Fall
    We Sinned all.

B   Thy Life to Mend
    This *Book* Attend.

C   The *Cat* doth play
    And after slay.

D   A *Dog* will bite
    A Thief at night.

E   An *Eagle's* flight
    Is out of sight.

F   The Idle *Fool*
    Is whipt at School.

G   As runs the *Glass*
    Man's life doth pass.

H   My *Book* and *Heart*
    Shall never part.

J   *Job* feels the Rod
    Yet blesses GOD.

K   Our *KING* the good
    No man of blood.

L   The *Lion* bold
    The *Lamb* doth hold.

M   The *Moon* gives light
    In time of night.

N   *Nightengales* sing
    In time of Spring.

O   The *Royal Oak* it was the Tree
    That sav'd His Royal Majestie.

P   *Peter* denies
    His Lord and cries.

Q   *Queen Esther* comes in Royal State
    To Save the JEWS from dismal Fate.

R   *Rachel* doth mourn
    For her first born.

---

deliberately contrived nursery entertainments, first recorded as late as 1805 and 1838, respectively. Other rhymes have been arbitrarily dated through particular allegorical readings ("Ring-a-ring o' roses" as an account of the Great Plague; "Mary, Mary" as a vignette of Mary, Queen of Scots; "Sing a Song of Sixpence" as an indirect rhyme about Henry VIII; "Humpty Dumpty" as ridiculing Richard III; "Cock Robin" as an account of the downfall of Robert Walpole's ministry in 1742) — but these readings all remain conjectural.

S   *Samuel* anoints
    Whom God appoints.

T   *Time* cuts down all
    Both great and small.

U   *Uriah's* beauteous Wife
    Made David seek his Life.

W   *Whales* in the Sea
    God's Voice obey.

X   *Xerxes* the great did die,
    And so must you & I.

Y   *Youth* forward slips
    Death soonest nips.

Z   *Zacheus* he
    Did climb the Tree
    His Lord to see.

(1727)

ANONYMOUS
18th century

THE VICAR OF BRAY

In good King Charles's golden days,
    When loyalty no harm meant,
A zealous High-Churchman I was,
    And so I got preferment;
To teach my flock I never missed —   5
    Kings are by God appointed,
And damned are those who do resist
    Or touch the Lord's anointed.
    And this is law, I will maintain,
      Until my dying day, Sir,   10
    That whatsoever king shall reign,
      I'll be the Vicar of Bray, Sir.

When royal James obtained the crown,
    And Popery came in fashion,
The penal laws I hooted down,   15
    And read the declaration:
The Church of Rome I found would fit
    Full well my constitution,
And had become a Jesuit —
    But for the Revolution.   20
    And this is law, I will maintain,
      Until my dying day, Sir,
    That whatsoever king shall reign,
      I'll be the Vicar of Bray, Sir.

When William was our king declared   25
    To ease the nation's grievance,
With this new wind about I steered,

And swore to him allegiance;
Old principles I did revoke,
    Set conscience at a distance;   30
Passive obedience was a joke,
    A jest was non-resistance.
    And this is law, I will maintain,
      Until my dying day, Sir,
    That whatsoever king shall reign,   35
      I'll be the Vicar of Bray, Sir.

When gracious Anne became our queen,
    The Church of England's glory,
Another face of things was seen —
    And I became a Tory: 40
Occasional Conformists base,
    I scorned their moderation,
And thought the church in danger was
    By such prevarication.
    And this is law, I will maintain,   45
      Until my dying day, Sir,
    That whatsoever king shall reign,
      I'll be the Vicar of Bray, Sir.

When George in pudding-time came o'er,
    And moderate men looked big, Sir,   50
I turned a cat-in-pan once more —
    And so became a Whig, Sir:
And this preferment I procured
    From our new faith's defender,

THE VICAR OF BRAY   Although the song is about a time-serving vicar in the 17th and 18th centuries, it is said to be based on an actual 16th-century Vicar of Bray (in Berkshire) who managed to keep his position under the successive reigns of Henry VIII (as a Catholic), Edward VI (as a Protestant), Mary (as a Catholic), and Elizabeth I (as a Protestant). **41. Occasional Conformists:** non-Anglicans (e.g. dissenters, Roman Catholics) who occasionally, or even only once, took communion in the Church of England in order to qualify themselves for public office according to the Corporation Act and the Test Acts, and then, while in office, proceeded to worship as nonconformists. **49. in pudding-time:** at a favourable or useful time, in good time (before it's too late). **51. turned a cat-in-pan:** changed sides from self-interest, was a turncoat.

And almost every day abjured   *55*
  The Pope and the Pretender.
  And this is law, I will maintain,
    Until my dying day, Sir,
  That whatsoever king shall reign,
    I'll be the Vicar of Bray, Sir.   *60*

The illustrious house of Hanover,
  And Protestant succession,
To these I do allegiance swear —
  While they can keep possession:
For in my faith and loyalty   *65*
  I never more will falter,
And George my lawful King shall be —
  Until the times do alter.
  And this is law, I will maintain,
    Until my dying day, Sir,   *70*
  That whatsoever king shall reign,
    I'll be the Vicar of Bray, Sir.

GUINEA CORN

Guinea Corn, I long to see you
Guinea Corn, I long to plant you
Guinea Corn, I long to mould you
Guinea Corn, I long to weed you
Guinea Corn, I long to hoe you   *5*
Guinea Corn, I long to top you
Guinea Corn, I long to cut you
Guinea Corn, I long to dry you
Guinea Corn, I long to beat you
Guinea Corn, I long to trash you   *10*
Guinea Corn, I long to parch you
Guinea Corn, I long to grind you
Guinea Corn, I long to turn you
Guinea Corn, I long to eat you.

MARY JONES
England, 1707-1778

RHYMES, TO MISS CHARLOT CLAYTON

As *Damon* was pensively walking one day,
Three pretty tight lasses he met in his way:
And who should they be, that were taking the air,
But *Nelly*, and *Molly*, and *Charlot* so fair.
The swain, who to beauty had never been blind,   *5*
Thought this was the season to tell 'em his mind:
But first he debated, to which lovely lass
He should offer his tenders, and open his case.
That *Nelly* was pretty he could not deny,
But *Molly,* he thought, had the sprightliest eye;   *10*
So on her his affections they rested awhile,
'Till *Charlot* appeared, with a look and a smile:

With a look and a smile which sure mischief had done,
Had the swain been encountered by *Charlot* alone.

Perplexed in his thought, and disturbed in his breast,
And unable to tell which bright lass he loved best;
He folded his arms, to the grove he retired,   *17*
And decently on the green willow expired.

To *Damon*'s sad fate lend a pitying ear,
For three at a time what poor mortal could bear?   *20*
One alone, trust me *Charlot,* had made him rejoice,
And the swain been quite happy — "With what?" —
    Hopson's choice.

                                                    (1750)

GUINEA CORN   Originating in the Caribbean, this worksong was first transcribed in 1797.   **RHYMES, TO MISS CHARLOT CLAYTON**   **2. tight:** neat, trim, tidy, smart. **22. Hopson:** "An admirer of that Lady's" (Jones's note) — but alluding also to the proverbial phrase "Hobson's choice," meaning no choice at all.

JAMES THOMSON
Scotland/England, 1700-1748

A HYMN [ON THE SEASONS]

These, as they change, Almighty Father! these
Are but the varied God. The rolling year
Is full of thee. Forth in the pleasing Spring
Thy beauty walks, thy tenderness and love.
Wide flush the fields; the softening air is balm;   5
Echo the mountains round; the forest smiles;
And every sense, and every heart, is joy.
Then comes thy glory in the Summer months,
With light and heat refulgent. Then thy sun
Shoots full perfection through the swelling year;   10
And oft thy voice in dreadful thunder speaks;
And oft at dawn, deep noon, or falling eve,
By brooks and groves, in hollow-whispering gales.
Thy bounty shines in Autumn unconfined,
And spreads a common feast for all that lives.   15
In Winter, awful thou! with clouds and storms
Around thee thrown, tempest o'er tempest rolled,
Majestic darkness! on the whirlwind's wing
Riding sublime, thou bidd'st the world adore,
And humblest nature with thy northern blast.   20
    Mysterious round! what skill, what force divine,
Deep-felt, in these appear! a simple train,
Yet so delightful mixed, with such kind art,
Such beauty and beneficence combined,
Shade, unperceived, so softening into shade,   25
And all so forming an harmonious whole
That, as they still succeed, they ravish still.
But wandering oft, with brute unconscious gaze,
Man marks not thee, marks not the mighty hand,
That, ever busy, wheels the silent spheres,   30
Works in the secret deep, shoots steaming thence
The fair profusion that o'erspreads the Spring,
Flings from the sun direct the flaming day,
Feeds every creature, hurls the tempest forth,
And, as on earth this grateful change revolves,   35
With transport touches all the springs of life.
    Nature, attend! join every living soul
Beneath the spacious temple of the sky,
In adoration join; and, ardent, raise
One general song! To him, ye vocal gales,   40
Breathe soft, whose spirit in your freshness breathes:

Oh! talk of him in solitary glooms,
Where, o'er the rock, the scarcely-waving pine
Fills the brown shade with a religious awe.
And ye, whose bolder note is heard afar,   45
Who shake th' astonished world, lift high to heaven
Th' impetuous song, and say from whom you rage.
His praise, ye brooks, attune, ye trembling rills;
And let me catch it as I muse along.
Ye headlong torrents, rapid and profound;   50
Ye softer floods, that lead the humid maze
Along the vale; and thou, majestic main,
A secret world of wonders in thyself,
Sound his stupendous praise, whose greater voice
Or bids you roar, or bids your roarings fall.   55
Soft roll your incense, herbs, and fruits, and flowers,
In mingled clouds to him, whose sun exalts,
Whose breath perfumes you, and whose pencil paints.
Ye forests bend; ye harvests wave, to him;
Breathe your still song into the reaper's heart,   60
As home he goes beneath the joyous moon.
Ye that keep watch in heaven, as earth asleep
Unconscious lies, effuse your mildest beams,
Ye constellations! while your angels strike,
Amid the spangled sky, the silver lyre.   65
Great source of day! best image here below
Of thy Creator, ever pouring wide
From world to world the vital ocean round!
On nature write with every beam his praise.
The thunder rolls: be hushed the prostrate world;   70
While cloud to cloud returns the solemn hymn.
Bleat out afresh, ye hills; ye mossy rocks,
Retain the sound; the broad responsive low,
Ye valleys, raise; for the Great Shepherd reigns,
And his unsuffering kingdom yet will come.   75
Ye woodlands all, awake: a boundless song
Burst from the groves; and when the restless day,
Expiring, lays the warbling world asleep,
Sweetest of birds! sweet Philomela, charm
The listening shades, and teach the night his praise.   80
Ye chief, for whom the whole creation smiles,
At once the head, the heart, the tongue of all,

Crown the great hymn! in swarming cities vast,
Assembled men, to the deep organ join
The long-resounding voice, oft breaking clear,   85
At solemn pauses, through the swelling bass;
And, as each mingling flame increases each,
In one united ardour rise to heaven.
Or if you rather choose the rural shade,
And find a fane in every sacred grove,   90
There let the shepherd's flute, the virgin's lay,
The prompting seraph, and the poet's lyre,
Still sing the God of Seasons as they roll.
For me, when I forget the darling theme,
Whether the blossom blows, the Summer ray   95
Russets the plain, inspiring Autumn gleams,
Or Winter rises in the blackening east,
Be my tongue mute, may fancy paint no more,
And, dead to joy, forget my heart to beat!
      Should fate command me to the farthest verge   100

Of the green earth, to distant barbarous climes,
Rivers unknown to song, where first the sun
Gilds Indian mountains, or his setting beam
Flames on the Atlantic isles, 'tis nought to me;
Since God is ever present, ever felt,   105
In the void waste as in the city full;
And where he vital spreads there must be joy.
When even at last the solemn hour shall come,
And wing my mystic flight to future worlds,
I cheerful will obey; there, with new powers,   110
Will rising wonders sing: I cannot go
Where Universal Love not smiles around,
Sustaining all yon orbs, and all their sons;
From seeming evil still educing good,
And better thence again, and better still,   115
In infinite progression. But I lose
Myself in him, in Light ineffable!
Come then, expressive Silence, muse his praise.

(1730)

JOHN DYER
Wales, 1700-1758

GRONGAR HILL

Silent Nymph, with curious eye!
Who, the purple ev'ning, lie
On the mountain's lonely van,
Beyond the noise of busy man,
Painting fair the form of things,   5
While the yellow linnet sings;
Or the tuneful nightingale
Charms the forest with her tale;
Come with all thy various hues,
Come, and aid thy sister Muse;   10
Now while Phoebus riding high
Gives lustre to the land and sky!
Grongar Hill invites my song,
Draw the landscape bright and strong;
Grongar, in whose mossy cells   15

Sweetly-musing Quiet dwells;
Grongar, in whose silent shade,
For the modest Muses made,
So oft I have, the evening still,
At the fountain of a rill,   20
Sat upon a flow'ry bed,
With my hand beneath my head;
While strayed my eyes o'er Towy's flood,
Over mead and over wood,
From house to house, from hill to hill,   25
Till Contemplation had her fill.
About his chequered sides I wind,
And leave his brooks and meads behind,
And groves and grottoes where I lay,
And vistoes shooting beams of day: 30

GRONGAR HILL   **3. van:** summit. **11. Phoebus:** Apollo, as god of the sun; Apollo was also the god of poetry and music. **23. Towy's flood:** The River Towy (or Afon Tywi) flows through Dyfed (the part that was formerly the county of Carmarthen), in southwestern Wales, where Dyer was born. **30. vistoes:** vistas.

Wide and wider spreads the vale,
As circles on a smooth canal.
The mountains round, unhappy fate!
Sooner or later, of all height,
Withdraw their summits from the skies,   *35*
And lessen as the others rise:
Still the prospect wider spreads,
Adds a thousand woods and meads,
Still it widens, widens still,
And sinks the newly-risen hill.   *40*
   Now I gain the mountain's brow,
What a landscape lies below!
No clouds, no vapours intervene,
But the gay, the open scene
Does the face of nature show,   *45*
In all the hues of heaven's bow!
And, swelling to embrace the light,
Spreads around beneath the sight.
   Old castles on the cliffs arise,
Proudly tow'ring in the skies!   *50*
Rushing from the woods, the spires
Seem from hence ascending fires!
Half his beams Apollo sheds
On the yellow mountain-heads!
Gilds the fleeces of the flocks,   *55*
And glitters on the broken rocks!
   Below me trees unnumbered rise,
Beautiful in various dyes:
The gloomy pine, the poplar blue,
The yellow beech, the sable yew,   *60*
The slender fir that taper grows,
The sturdy oak with broad-spread boughs.
And beyond the purple grove,
Haunt of Phillis, queen of love!
Gaudy as the op'ning dawn,   *65*
Lies a long and level lawn,
On which a dark hill, steep and high,
Holds and charms the wand'ring eye!
Deep are his feet in Towy's flood,
His sides are clothed with waving wood,   *70*
And ancient towers crown his brow,
That cast an awful look below;
Whose ragged walls the ivy creeps,

And with her arms from falling keeps;
So both a safety from the wind   *75*
On mutual dependence find.
   'Tis now the raven's bleak abode;
'Tis now th' apartment of the toad;
And there the fox securely feeds;
And there the pois'nous adder breeds,   *80*
Concealed in ruins, moss and weeds;
While, ever and anon, there falls
Huge heaps of hoary mouldered walls.
Yet time has seen, that lifts the low,
And level lays the lofty brow,   *85*
Has seen this broken pile complete,
Big with the vanity of state;
But transient is the smile of fate!
A little rule, a little sway,
A sunbeam in a winter's day,   *90*
Is all the proud and mighty have
Between the cradle and the grave.
   And see the rivers how they run,
Through woods and meads, in shade and sun;
Sometimes swift, sometimes slow,   *95*
Wave succeeding wave, they go
A various journey to the deep,
Like human life to endless sleep!
Thus is nature's vesture wrought
To instruct our wand'ring thought;   *100*
Thus she dresses green and gay,
To disperse our cares away.
Ever charming, ever new,
When will the landscape tire the view!
The fountain's fall, the river's flow,   *105*
The woody valleys, warm and low;
The windy summit, wild and high,
Roughly rushing on the sky!
The pleasant seat, the ruined tow'r,
The naked rock, the shady bow'r;   *110*
The town and village, dome and farm,
Each give each a double charm,
As pearls upon an Ethiop's arm.
See on the mountain's southern side,
Where the prospect opens wide,   *115*
Where the evening gilds the tide;

---

64. Phillis: conventional pastoral name. **111. dome:** house (Latin *domus*). **113:** Cf. Shakespeare's *Romeo and Juliet*, I.v.49.

How close and small the hedges lie!
What streaks of meadows cross the eye!
A step methinks may pass the stream,
So little distant dangers seem;   *120*
So we mistake the future's face,
Eyed through hope's deluding glass;
As yon summits soft and fair,
Clad in colours of the air,
Which to those who journey near,   *125*
Barren, brown and rough appear;
Still we tread the same coarse way,
The present's still a cloudy day.
O may I with myself agree,
And never covet what I see: *130*
Content me with an humble shade,
My passions tamed, my wishes laid;
For while our wishes wildly roll,
We banish quiet from the soul:
'Tis thus the busy beat the air,   *135*
And misers gather wealth and care.
Now, ev'n now, my joys run high,

As on the mountain-turf I lie;
While the wanton Zephyr sings,
And in the vale perfumes his wings;   *140*
While the waters murmur deep;
While the shepherd charms his sheep;
While the birds unbounded fly,
And with music fill the sky,
Now, ev'n now, my joys run high.   *145*
Be full, ye courts, be great who will;
Search for Peace with all your skill:
Open wide the lofty door,
Seek her on the marble floor,
In vain you search, she is not there;   *150*
In vain ye search the domes of care!
Grass and flowers Quiet treads,
On the meads and mountain-heads,
Along with Pleasure, close allied,
Ever by each other's side: *155*
And often, by the murm'ring rill,
Hears the thrush, while all is still,
Within the groves of Grongar Hill.

(1726)

HENRY BROOKE
Ireland, c.1703-1783

from *JACK THE GIANT QUELLER. AN ANTIQUE HISTORY*

Air

For often my mammy has told,
　And sure she is wondrous wise,
In cities that all you behold
　Is a fair, but a faithless, disguise:
That the modes of a court education   *5*
　Are train-pits and traitors to youth;
And the only fine language in fashion
　A tongue that is foreign to truth.

Where honour is barely an oath,
　Where knaves are with noblemen classed,
Where nature's a stranger to both,   *11*
　And love an old tale of times past;
Where laughter no pleasure dispenses,
　Where smiles are the envoys of art,
Where joy lightly swims on the senses,   *15*
　But never can enter the heart.

AIR FROM JACK THE GIANT QUELLER　**6. train-pits:** snares, traps.

Where hopes and kind hugs are trepanners,
    Where virtue's divorced from success,
Where cringing goes current for manners,
    And worth is no deeper than dress;   *20*

Where favour creeps lamely on crutches,
    Where friendship is nothing but face,
And the title of Duke or of Duchess
    Is all that entitles to grace.

                              (1749)

STEPHEN DUCK
England, 1705-1756

from *THE THRESHER'S LABOUR*

. . . .

  With heat and labour tired, our scythes we quit,
Search out a shady tree, and down we sit:
From scrip and bottle hope new strength to gain;
But scrip and bottle too are tried in vain.
Down our parched throats we scarce the bread can get;
And, quite o'erspent with toil, but faintly eat.   *6*
Nor can the bottle only answer all;
The bottle and the beer are both too small.
Time flows: again we rise from off the grass;
Again each mower takes his proper place;   *10*
Not eager now, as late, our strength to prove;
But all contented regular to move.
We often whet, and often view the sun;
As often wish his tedious race was run.
At length he veils his purple face from sight,   *15*
And bids the weary labourer good-night.
Homewards we move, but spent so much with toil,
We slowly walk, and rest at every stile.
Our good expecting wives, who think we stay,
Got to the door, soon eye us in the way.   *20*
Then from the pot the dumplin's catched in haste,
And homely by its side the bacon placed.
Supper and sleep by morn new strength supply;
And out we set again, our work to try;
But not so early quite, nor quite so fast,   *25*
As, to our cost, we did the morning past.

  Soon as the rising sun has drank the dew,
Another scene is open to our view:
Our master comes, and at his heels a throng
Of prattling females, armed with rake and prong;   *30*
Prepared, whilst he is here, to make his hay;
Or, if he turns his back, prepared to play:
But here, or gone, sure of the comfort still;
Here's company, so they may chat their fill.
Ah! were their hands so active as their tongues,   *35*
How nimbly then would move the rakes and prongs!

  The grass again is spread upon the ground,
Till not a vacant place is to be found;
And while the parching sun-beams on it shine,
The hay-makers have time allowed to dine.   *40*
That soon dispatched, they still sit on the ground;
And the brisk chat, renewed, afresh goes round.
All talk at once; but seeming all to fear,
That what they speak, the rest will hardly hear;
Till by degrees so high their notes they strain,   *45*
A stander by can nought distinguish plain.
So loud's their speech, and so confused their noise,
Scarce puzzled Echo can return the voice.
Yet, spite of this, they bravely all go on;
Each scorns to be, or seem to be, outdone.   *50*
Meanwhile the changing sky begins to lour,
And hollow winds proclaim a sudden show'r:
The tattling crowd can scarce their garments gain,
Before descends the thick impetuous rain;
Their noisy prattle all at once is done,   *55*
And to the hedge they soon for shelter run.

  Thus have I seen, on a bright summer's day,
On some green brake, a flock of sparrows play;
From twig to twig, from bush to bush they fly;

---

17. trepanners: snares, traps, deceivers. **THE THRESHER'S LABOUR** 15. purple: blood-red. 19. stay: tarry.

And with continued chirping fill the sky: 60
But, on a sudden, if a storm appears,
Their chirping noise no longer dins your ears:
They fly for shelter to the thickest bush;
There silent sit, and all at once is hush.

But better fate succeeds this rainy day, 65
And little labour serves to make the hay.
Fast as 'tis cut, so kindly shines the sun,
Turned once or twice, the pleasing work is done.
Next day the cocks appear in equal rows,
Which the glad master in safe ricks bestows. 70

The spacious fields we now no longer range;
And yet, hard fate! still work for work we change.
Back to the barns we hastily are sent,
Where lately so much time we pensive spent:
Not pensive now, we bless the friendly shade; 75
And to avoid the parching sun are glad.
Yet little time we in the shade remain,
Before our master calls us forth again;
And says, "For harvest now yourselves prepare;
The ripened harvest now demands your care. 80
Get all things ready, and be quickly dressed;
Early next morn I shall disturb your rest."
Strict to his word! for scarce the dawn appears,
Before his hasty summons fills our ears.
His hasty summons we obey; and rise, 85

While yet the stars are glimm'ring in the skies.
With him our guide we to the wheat-field go,
He to appoint, and we the work to do.

. . . .

The morning past, we sweat beneath the sun;
And but uneasily our work goes on. 90
Before us we perplexing thistles find,
And corn blown adverse with the ruffling wind.
Behind our master waits; and if he spies
One charitable ear, he grudging cries,
"Ye scatter half your wages o'er the land." 95
Then scrapes the stubble with his greedy hand.

Let those who feast at ease on dainty fare,
Pity the reapers, who their feasts prepare:
For toils scarce ever ceasing press us now;
Rest never does, but on the Sabbath, show; 100
And barely that our Masters will allow.
Think what a painful life we daily lead:
Each morning early rise, go late to bed:
Nor, when asleep, are we secure from pain;
We then perform our labours o'er again: 105
Our mimic Fancy ever restless seems;
And what we act awake, she acts in dreams.
Hard fate! Our labours ev'n in sleep don't cease;
Scarce Hercules e'er felt such toils as these!

. . . .

(1736)

BENJAMIN FRANKLIN
U.S.A., 1706-1790

Preface to *POOR RICHARD'S ALMANACK*

THE WAY TO WEALTH

COURTEOUS READER,

I have heard that nothing gives an Author so great Pleasure, as to find his Works respectfully quoted by other learned Authors. This Pleasure I have seldom enjoyed; for tho' I have been, if I may say it without Vanity, an *eminent Author* of Almanacks annually now a full Quarter of a Century, my Brother Authors in the same Way, for what Reason I know not, have ever been very sparing in their Applauses; and no other 5

---

92. corn: i.e., grain. **93-96:** Instead of these lines, the 1730 edition has the following couplet: "Behind our backs the female gleaners wait, / Who sometimes stoop, and sometimes hold a chat." See the selection from Mary Collier's *The Woman's Labour* (p. 500), responding to Duck's poem — specifically to the 1730 edition, including this couplet. Duck himself authorized only the 1736 edition. **THE WAY TO WEALTH** Written as the preface to the 1758 *Almanack*, it has been printed separately as both "The Way to Wealth" and "Father Abraham's Speech"; in composing it (in

Author has taken the least Notice of me, so that did not my Writings produce me some *solid Pudding,* the great Deficiency of *Praise* would have quite discouraged me.

I concluded at length, that the People were the best Judges of my Merit; for they buy my Works; and besides, in my Rambles, where I am not personally known, I have frequently heard one or other of my Adages repeated, with, *as poor Richard says,* at the   10
End on't; this gave me some Satisfaction, as it showed not only that my Instructions were regarded, but discovered likewise some Respect for my Authority; and I own, that to encourage the Practice of remembering and repeating those wise Sentences, I have sometimes *quoted* myself with great Gravity.

Judge then how much I must have been gratified by an Incident I am going to relate   15
to you. I stopt my Horse lately where a great Number of People were collected at a Vendue of Merchant Goods. The Hour of Sale not being come, they were conversing on the Badness of the Times, and one of the Company call'd to a plain clean old Man, with white Locks, "Pray, Father Abraham, what think you of the Times? Won't these heavy Taxes quite ruin the Country? How shall we ever be able to pay them? What would you   20
advise us to?" Father Abraham stood up, and reply'd, "If you'd have my Advice, I'll give it you in short, for a *Word to the Wise is enough,* and *many Words won't fill a Bushel,* as *Poor Richard* says." They join'd in desiring him to speak his Mind, and gathering round him, he proceeded as follows;

"Friends," says he, "and Neighbours, the Taxes are indeed very heavy, and if those   25
laid on by the Government were the only Ones we had to pay, we might more easily discharge them; but we have many others, and much more grievous to some of us. We are taxed twice as much by our *Idleness,* three times as much by our *Pride,* and four times as much by our *Folly,* and from these Taxes the Commissioners cannot ease or deliver us by allowing an Abatement. However let us hearken to good Advice, and   30
something may be done for us; *God helps them that help themselves,* as *Poor Richard* says, in his Almanack of 1733.

It would be thought a hard Government that should tax its People one tenth Part of their *Time,* to be employed in its Service. But *Idleness* taxes many of us much more, if we reckon all that is spent in absolute *Sloth,* or doing of nothing, with that which is   35
spent in idle Employments or Amusements, that amount to nothing. *Sloth,* by bringing on Diseases, absolutely shortens Life. *Sloth, like Rust, consumes faster than Labour wears, while the used Key is always bright,* as *Poor Richard* says. But *dost thou love Life, then do not squander Time, for that's the Stuff Life is made of,* as *Poor Richard* says. — How much more than is necessary do we spend in Sleep! forgetting that *The*   40
sleeping Fox catches no Poultry, and that *there will be sleeping enough in the Grave,* as *Poor Richard* says. If Time be of all Things the most precious, *wasting Time* must be, as *Poor Richard* says, *the greatest Prodigality,* since, as he elsewhere tells us, *Lost Time is never found again;* and what we call *Time enough, always proves little enough:* Let us

---

the persona of "Richard Saunders") Franklin used many of "Poor Richard's" proverbs and maxims that had appeared in the *Almanack* during the years since its inception in 1733. (We use the original title of the almanac, though in 1748 it was changed to *Poor Richard Improved,* and from then on Franklin himself did little writing for it; he sold it outright in 1758.) **7. *solid Pudding . . . Praise*:** making use of an old proverb; it occurs also in Pope's *Dunciad,* I, 51-52: "Where, in nice balance, truth with gold she weighs, / And solid pudding against empty praise," and also in Poor Richard's "Preface" for 1750: "Since 'tis not improbable that a Man may receive more solid Satisfaction from *Pudding,* while he is *living,* than from *Praise,* after he is *dead.*" **12. discovered:** revealed. **17. Vendue:** public sale, auction.

then up and be doing, and doing to the Purpose; so by Diligence shall we do more with   45
less Perplexity. *Sloth makes all Things difficult, but Industry all easy,* as *Poor Richard*
says; and *He that riseth late, must trot all Day, and shall scarce overtake his Business at
Night.* While *Laziness travels so slowly, that Poverty soon overtakes him,* as we read in
Poor Richard, who adds, *Drive thy Business, let not that drive thee;* and *Early to Bed,
and early to rise, makes a Man healthy, wealthy and wise.*   50

So what signifies *wishing* and *hoping* for better Times? We may make these Times
better if we bestir ourselves. *Industry need not wish,* as *Poor Richard* says, and *He that
lives upon Hope will die fasting. There are no Gains without Pains;* then *Help Hands,
for I have no Lands,* or if I have, they are smartly taxed. And, as *Poor Richard* likewise
observes, *He that hath a Trade hath an Estate,* and *He that hath a Calling, hath an*   55
Office of Profit and Honour; but then the *Trade* must be worked at, and the *Calling* well
followed, or neither the *Estate,* nor the *Office,* will enable us to pay our Taxes. If we are
industrious we shall never starve; for, as *Poor Richard* says, *At the working Man's
House Hunger looks in, but dares not enter.* Nor will the Bailiff or the Constable enter,
for *Industry pays Debts, while Despair encreaseth them,* says *Poor Richard.* What   60
though you have found no Treasure, nor has any rich Relation left you a Legacy,
Diligence is the Mother of Good luck, as *Poor Richard* says, and *God gives all Things to
Industry.* Then *plough deep, while Sluggards sleep, and you shall have Corn to sell and
to keep,* says *Poor Dick.* Work while it is called To-day, for you know not how much
you may be hindered To-morrow, which makes *Poor Richard* say, *One To-day is worth*   65
two To-morrows; and farther, *Have you somewhat to do To-morrow, do it To-day.* If
you were a Servant, would you not be ashamed that a good Master should catch you
idle? Are you then your own Master, *be ashamed to catch yourself idle,* as *Poor Dick*
says. When there is so much to be done for yourself, your Family, your Country, and
your gracious King, be up by Peep of Day; *Let not the Sun look down and say,*   70
Inglorious here he lies. Handle your Tools without Mittens; remember that *the Cat in
Gloves catches no Mice,* as *Poor Richard* says. 'Tis true there is much to be done, and
perhaps you are weak-handed, but stick to it steadily, and you will see great Effects, for
constant Dropping wears away Stones, and *by Diligence and Patience the Mouse ate in
two the Cable;* and *little Strokes fell great Oaks,* as *Poor Richard* says in his Almanack,   75
the Year I cannot just now remember.

Methinks I hear some of you say, *Must a Man afford himself no Leisure?* I will tell
thee, my Friend, what *Poor Richard* says: *Employ thy Time well if thou meanest to gain
Leisure;* and *since thou art not sure of a Minute, throw not away an Hour.* Leisure is
Time for doing something useful; this Leisure the diligent Man will obtain, but the lazy   80
Man never; so that, as *Poor Richard* says, a *Life of Leisure and a Life of Laziness are
two Things.* Do you imagine that Sloth will afford you more Comfort than Labour? No,
for as *Poor Richard* says, *Trouble springs from Idleness, and grievous Toil from
needless Ease. Many without Labour, would live by their* WITS *only, but they break for
want of Stock.* Whereas Industry gives Comfort, and Plenty, and Respect: *Fly Pleasures,*   85
and they'll follow you. The diligent Spinner has a large Shift; and *now I have a Sheep
and a Cow, every Body bids me Good morrow;* all which is well said by *Poor Richard.*

---

68. are you then: i.e., if then you are. **84. *break*:** fail in business, go bankrupt. **86. *Shift*:** shirt, chemise.

But with our Industry, we must likewise be *steady, settled* and *careful,* and oversee our own Affairs *with our own Eyes,* and not trust too much to others; for, as *Poor Richard* says,

> *I never saw an oft-removed Tree,*
> *Nor yet an oft-removed Family,*
> *That throve so well as those that settled be.*

And again, *Three Removes is as bad as a Fire;* and again, *Keep thy Shop, and thy Shop will keep thee;* and again, *If you would have your Business done, go; If not, send.* And again,

> *He that by the Plough would thrive,*
> *Himself must either hold or drive.*

And again, *The Eye of a Master will do more Work than both his Hands;* and again, *Want of Care does us more Damage than Want of Knowledge;* and again, *Not to oversee Workmen, is to leave them your Purse open.* Trusting too much to others' Care is the Ruin of many; for, as the *Almanack* says, *In the Affairs of this World, Men are saved, not by Faith, but by the Want of it;* but a Man's own Care is profitable; for, saith *Poor Dick, Learning is to the Studious,* and *Riches to the Careful,* as well as *Power to the Bold,* and *Heaven to the Virtuous.* And farther, *If you would have a faithful Servant, and one that you like, serve yourself.* And again, he adviseth to Circumspection and Care, even in the smallest Matters, because sometimes *a little Neglect may breed great Mischief;* adding, *For want of a Nail the Shoe was lost; for want of a Shoe the Horse was lost; and for want of a Horse the Rider was lost,* being overtaken and slain by the Enemy, all for want of Care about a Horse-shoe Nail.

So much for Industry, my Friends, and Attention to one's own Business; but to these we must add *Frugality,* if we would make our *Industry* more certainly successful. A Man may, if he knows not how to save as he gets, *keep his Nose all his Life to the Grindstone,* and die not worth a *Groat* at last. *A fat Kitchen makes a lean Will,* as *Poor Richard* says; and,

> *Many Estates are spent in the Getting,*
> *Since Women for Tea forsook Spinning and Knitting,*
> *And Men for Punch forsook Hewing and Splitting.*

If you would be wealthy, says he, in another Almanack, *think of Saving as well as of Getting: The Indies have not made Spain rich, because her Outgoes are greater than her Incomes.* Away then with your expensive Follies, and you will not have so much Cause to complain of hard Times, heavy Taxes, and chargeable Families; for, as *Poor Dick* says,

> *Women and Wine, Game and Deceit,*
> *Make the Wealth small, and the Wants great.*

---

95. send: i.e., send someone else to do it.

And farther, *What maintains one Vice, would bring up two Children.* You may think perhaps, That a *little* Tea, or a *little* Punch now and then, Diet a *little* more costly, Clothes a *little* finer, and a *little* Entertainment now and then, can be no *great* Matter; but remember what *Poor Richard* says, *Many a Little makes a Mickle;* and farther, *Beware of little Expences; a small Leak will sink a great Ship;* and again, *Who Dainties* 130 *love, shall Beggars prove;* and moreover, *Fools make Feasts, and wise Men eat them.*

Here you are got together at this Vendue of *Fineries* and *Knicknacks.* You call them *Goods,* but if you do not take Care, they will prove *Evils* to some of you. You expect they will be sold *cheap,* and perhaps they may for less than they cost; but if you have no Occasion for them, they must be *dear* to you. Remember what *Poor Richard* says, *Buy* 135 *what thou hast no Need of, and ere long thou shalt sell thy Necessaries.* And again, *At a great Pennyworth pause a while:* He means, that perhaps the Cheapness is *apparent* only, and not *real;* or the Bargain, by straitening thee in thy Business, may do thee more Harm than Good. For in another place he says, *Many have been ruined by buying good Pennyworths.* Again, *Poor Richard* says, *'Tis foolish to lay out Money in a Purchase of* 140 *Repentance;* and yet this Folly is practised every Day at Vendues, for want of minding the Almanack. *Wise Men,* as *Poor Dick* says, *learn by others' Harms, Fools scarcely by their own;* but *Felix quem faciunt aliena Pericula cautum.* Many a one, for the Sake of Finery on the Back, have gone with a hungry Belly, and half starved their Families; *Silks and Sattins, Scarlet and Velvets,* as *Poor Richard* says, *put out the Kitchen Fire.* 145 These are not the *Necessaries* of Life; they can scarcely be called the *Conveniences,* and yet only because they look pretty, how many *want* to *have* them. The *artificial* Wants of Mankind thus become more numerous than the *natural;* and, as *Poor Dick* says, *For one poor Person, there are an hundred indigent.* By these, and other Extravagancies, the Genteel are reduced to Poverty, and forced to borrow of those whom they formerly 150 despised, but who through *Industry* and *Frugality* have maintained their Standing; in which Case it appears plainly, that *a Ploughman on his Legs is higher than a Gentleman on his Knees,* as *Poor Richard* says. Perhaps they have had a small Estate left them which they knew not the Getting of; they think *'tis Day, and will never be Night;* that a little to be spent out of *so much,* is not worth minding (*a Child and a Fool,* as *Poor* 155 *Richard* says, *imagine Twenty Shillings and Twenty Years can never be spent*); but, *always taking out of the Mealtub, and never putting in, soon comes to the Bottom;* then, as *Poor Dick* says, *When the Well's dry, they know the Worth of Water.* But this they might have known before, if they had taken his Advice; *If you would know the Value of Money, go and try to borrow some;* for, *he that goes a borrowing goes a sorrowing;* and 160 indeed so does he that lends to such People, when he goes *to get it in again. Poor Dick* farther advises, and says,

Fond Pride of Dress is sure a very Curse;
Ere Fancy you consult, consult your Purse.

And again, *Pride is as loud a Beggar as Want, and a great deal more saucy.* When 165 you have bought one fine Thing you must buy ten more, that your Appearance may be

---

129. *Many . . . Mickle:* The Scottish proverb is more like "Many a mickle maks a muckle," where *mickle* means little, and *muckle* means much; but Old English *mycel* or *miccel* also means *much, great,* hence this common English version. **143.** *Felix . . . cautum:* (Latin) Happy is he who has been made cautious by the perils of others.

all of a Piece; but *Poor Dick* says, *'Tis easier to suppress the first Desire, than to satisfy all that follow it*. And 'tis as truly Folly for the Poor to ape the Rich, as for the Frog to swell, in order to equal the Ox.

> Great Estates may venture more,   170
> But little Boats should keep near Shore.

'Tis however a Folly soon punished; for *Pride that dines on Vanity sups on Contempt*, as *Poor Richard* says. And in another Place, *Pride breakfasted with Plenty, dined with Poverty, and supped with Infamy*. And after all, of what Use is this *Pride of Appearance*, for which so much is risked, so much is suffered? It cannot promote 175 Health, or ease Pain; it makes no Increase of Merit in the Person, it creates Envy, it hastens Misfortune.

> What is a Butterfly? At best
> He's but a Caterpillar drest.
> The gaudy Fop's his Picture just,   180

as *Poor Richard* says.

But what Madness must it to be to *run in Debt* for these Superfluities! We are offered, by the Terms of this Vendue, *Six Months Credit;* and that perhaps has induced some of us to attend it, because we cannot spare the ready Money, and hope now to be fine without it. But, ah, think what you do when you run in Debt; *You give to another,* 185 *Power over your Liberty*. If you cannot pay at the Time, you will be ashamed to see your Creditor; you will be in Fear when you speak to him; you will make poor pitiful sneaking Excuses, and by Degrees come to lose your Veracity, and sink into base downright lying; for, as *Poor Richard* says, *The second Vice is Lying, the first is running in Debt*. And again, to the same Purpose, *Lying rides upon Debt's Back.* 190 Whereas a freeborn *Englishman* ought not to be ashamed or afraid to see or speak to any Man living. But Poverty often deprives a Man of all Spirit and Virtue: *'Tis hard for an empty Bag to stand upright,* as *Poor Richard* truly says. What would you think of that Prince, or that Government, who should issue an Edict forbidding you to dress like a Gentleman or a Gentlewoman, on Pain of Imprisonment or Servitude? Would you not 195 say, that you are free, have a Right to dress as you please, and that such an Edict would be a Breach of your Privileges, and such a Government tyrannical? And yet you are about to put yourself under that Tyranny when you run in Debt for such Dress! Your Creditor has Authority at his Pleasure to deprive you of your Liberty, by confining you in Gaol for Life, or to sell you for a Servant, if you should not be able to pay him! When 200 you have got your Bargain, you may, perhaps, think little of Payment; but *Creditors, Poor Richard* tells us, *have better Memories than Debtors;* and in another Place says, *Creditors are a superstitious Sect, great Observers of set Days and Times*. The Day comes round before you are aware, and the Demand is made before you are prepared to satisfy it. Or if you bear your Debt in Mind, the Term which at first seemed so long, 205 will, as it lessens, appear extreamly short. *Time* will seem to have added Wings to Heels as well as Shoulders. *Those have a short Lent,* saith *Poor Richard, who owe Money to*

168-69. the Frog ... the Ox: In the fable, the foolish frog puffed itself up until it burst. 170. *Great Estates:* people having wealth, high position.

be paid at Easter. Then since, as he says, *The Borrower is a Slave to the Lender, and the Debtor to the Creditor,* disdain the Chain, preserve your Freedom; and maintain your Independence: Be *industrious* and *free;* be *frugal* and *free.* At present, perhaps, you may *210* think yourself in thriving Circumstances, and that you can bear a little Extravagance without Injury;

> *For Age and Want, save while you may;*
> *No Morning Sun lasts a whole Day,*

as *Poor Richard* says. Gain may be temporary and uncertain, but ever while you live, *215* Expence is constant and certain; and *'tis easier to build two Chimneys than to keep one in Fuel,* as *Poor Richard* says. *So rather go to Bed supperless than rise in Debt.*

> *Get what you can, and what you get hold;*
> *'Tis the Stone that will turn all your Lead into Gold,*

as *Poor Richard* says. And when you have got the Philosopher's Stone, sure you will no *220* longer complain of bad Times, or the Difficulty of paying Taxes.

This Doctrine, my Friends, is *Reason* and *Wisdom;* but after all, do not depend too much upon your own *Industry,* and *Frugality,* and *Prudence,* though excellent Things, for they may all be blasted without the Blessing of Heaven; and therefore ask that Blessing humbly, and be not uncharitable to those that at present seem to want it, but *225* comfort and help them. Remember *Job* suffered, and was afterwards prosperous.

And now to conclude, *Experience keeps a dear School, but Fools will learn in no other, and scarce in that;* for it is true, *we may give Advice, but we cannot give Conduct,* as *Poor Richard* says: However, remember this, *They that won't be counselled, can't be helped,* as *Poor Richard* says: And farther, *That if you will not hear Reason, she'll* *230* *surely rap your Knuckles."*

Thus the old Gentleman ended his Harangue. The People heard it, and approved the Doctrine and immediately practised the contrary, just as if it had been a common Sermon; for the Vendue opened, and they began to buy extravagantly, notwithstanding all his Cautions, and their own Fear of Taxes. I found the good Man had thoroughly *235* studied my Almanacks, and digested all I had dropt on those Topicks during the Course of Five-and-twenty Years. The frequent Mention he made of me must have tired any one else, but my Vanity was wonderfully delighted with it, though I was conscious that not a tenth Part of the Wisdom was my own which he ascribed to me, but rather the *Gleanings* I had made of the Sense of all Ages and Nations. However, I resolved to be *240* the better for the Echo of it; and though I had at first determined to buy Stuff for a new Coat, I went away resolved to wear my old One a little longer. *Reader,* if thou wilt do the same, thy Profit will be as great as mine.

I am, as ever,

Thine to serve thee,

RICHARD SAUNDERS.

July 7, 1757

---

220. Philosopher's Stone: substance, sought by medieval alchemists, capable of turning baser metals into gold.

Henry Fielding
England, 1707-1754

from *The Covent-Garden Journal*

No. 33. Saturday, April 23, 1752

> *Odi profanum vulgus.* — Horace
> I hate profane rascals.

Sir,

In this very learned and enlightened age, in which authors are almost as numerous as
booksellers, I doubt not but your correspondents furnish you with a sufficient quantity
of waste paper. I perhaps may add to the heap; for, as men do not always know the
motive of their own actions, I may possibly be induced, by the same sort of vanity as
other puny authors have been, to desire to be in print. But I am very well satisfied with   *5*
you for my judge, and if you should not think proper to take any notice of the hint I have
here sent you, I shall conclude that I am an impertinent correspondent, but that you are a
judicious and impartial critic. In my own defence, however, I must say that I am never
better pleased than when I see extraordinary abilities employed in the support of His
honour and religion, who has so bountifully bestowed them. It is for this reason that I   *10*
wish you would take some notice of the character, or rather story, here sent you. In my
travels westward last summer, I lay at an inn in Somersetshire, remarkable for its
pleasant situation, and the obliging behaviour of the landlord, who, though a downright
rustic, had an awkward sort of politeness arising from his good nature that was very
pleasing, and, if I may be allowed the expression, was a sort of good breeding   *15*
undressed. As I intended to make a pretty long journey the next day, I rose time enough
to behold that glorious luminary the sun set out on his course, which by-the-by is one of
the finest sights the eye can behold; and, as it is a thing seldom seen by people of
fashion, unless it be at the theatre at Covent-Garden, I could not help laying some stress
upon it here. The kitchen in this inn was a very pleasant room; I therefore called for   *20*
some tea, sat me in the window that I might enjoy the prospect which the country
afforded, and a more beautiful one is not in the power of imagination to frame. This
house was situated on the top of a hill, and for two miles below it meadows, enlivened
with variety of cattle, and adorned with a greater variety of flowers, first caught my
sight. At the bottom of this vale ran a river which seemed to promise coolness and   *25*
refreshment to the thirsty cattle. The eye was next presented with fields of corn that
made a kind of an ascent, which was terminated by a wood, at the top of which appeared
a verdant hill, situate as it were in the clouds, where the sun was just arrived, and,
peeping o'er the summit, which was at this time covered with dew, gilded it over with
his rays and terminated my view in the most agreeable manner in the world. In a word,   *30*

The Covent-Garden Journal No. 33   **19:** a satirical swipe at the way some Covent-Garden productions had staged the figure of the
sun. **26. corn:** i.e., grain.

the elegant simplicity of every object round me filled my heart with such gratitude, and furnished my mind with such pleasing meditations, as made me thank Heaven I was born. But this state of joyous tranquillity was not of long duration: I had scarce begun my breakfast, when my ears were saluted with a genteel whistle, and the noise of a pair of slippers descending the staircase; and soon after I beheld a contrast to my former *35* prospect, being a very beauish gentleman, with a huge laced hat on as big as Pistol's in the play, a wig somewhat dishevelled, and a face which at once gave you a perfect idea of emptiness, assurance, and intemperance. His eyes, which before were scarce open, he fixed on me with a stare which testified surprise, and his coat was immediately thrown open to display a very handsome second-hand gold-laced waistcoat. In one hand he had *40* a pair of saddle-bags, and in the other a hanger of mighty size, both of which, with a graceful G—d d—n you, he placed upon a chair. Then advancing towards the landlord, who was standing by me, he said, "By G—d, landlord, your wine is damnable strong." "I don't know," replied the landlord; "it is generally reckoned pretty good, for I have it all from London." "Pray, who is your wine merchant?" says the man of importance. "A *45* very great man," says the landlord, "in his way; perhaps you may know him, sir; his name is Kirby." "Ah, what! honest Tom? he and I have cracked many a bottle of claret together; he is one of the most considerable merchants in the city; the dog is hellish poor, damnable poor, for I don't suppose he is worth a farthing more than a hundred thousand pound; only a plum, that's all; he is to be our lord-mayor next year." "I ask *50* pardon, sir, that is not the man, for our Mr Kirby's name is not Thomas but Richard." "Ay," says the gentleman, "that's his brother; they are partners together." "I believe," says the landlord, "you are out, sir, for that gentleman has no brother." "D—n your nonsense, with you and your outs!" says the beau; "as if I should not know better than you country puts; I who have lived in London all my lifetime." "I ask a thousand *55* pardons," says the landlord; "I hope no offence, sir." "No, no," cries the other; "we gentlemen know how to make allowance for your country breeding." Then stepping to the kitchen door, with an audible voice he called the ostler, and in a very graceful accent said, "D—n your blood, you cock-eyed son of a bitch, bring me my boots! Did not you hear me call?" Then turning to the landlord, said, "Faith! that Mr What-de-callum, the *60* exciseman, is a d—ned jolly fellow." "Yes, sir," says the landlord, "he is a merryish sort of a man." "But," says the gentleman, "as for that schoolmaster, he is the queerest bitch I ever saw; he looks as if he could not say boh to a goose." "I don't know, sir," says the landlord; "he is reckoned to be a desperate good schollard about us, and the gentry likes him vastly, for he understands the measurement of land and timber, knows how to make *65* dials and such things; and for ciphering few can outdo 'en." "Ay," says the gentleman, "he does look like a cipher indeed, for he did not speak three words all last night." The ostler now produced the boots, which the gentleman taking in his hand, and having placed himself in the chair, addressed in the following speech: "My good friend, Mr

---

36. Pistol: Ancient (i.e. Ensign) Pistol is a boastful character in Shakespeare's *2 Henry IV*, *Henry V*, and *The Merry Wives of Windsor*; the allusion here is to Theophilus Cibber (1703-1758), son of Colley Cibber (see below), a young actor known especially for his performances as "Ancient Pistol" — and for his wild, extravagant, even scandalous behaviour; a print of the time shows him in the role of Pistol in *2 Henry IV*, wearing a large laced hat. **41. hanger:** sword. **50. plum:** slang for £100,000, or for the person possessing that amount. **53. out:** in error. **55. puts:** rustics, clowns, bumpkins. **63. he looks . . . goose:** Proverbially, one who can't say "boh" (or *bo* or *boo*) to a goose is timid, even to the point of being unable to speak at all. **64. schollard:** scholar. **66. dials:** i.e., sundials; **'en:** i.e., *him*.

Boots, I tell you plainly that, if you plague me so damnably as you did yesterday   *70*
morning, by G— I'll commit you to the flames; stap my vituals! as my Lord Huntington
says in the play." He then looked full in my face, and asked the landlord if he had ever
been at Drury-Lane playhouse; which he answered in the negative. "What!" says he,
"did you never hear talk of Mr. Garrick and king Richard?" "No, sir," says the landlord.
"By G—," says the gentleman, "he is the cleverest fellow in England." He then spouted   *75*
a speech out of King Richard, which begins, "Give me an horse," &c. "There," says he,
"that, that is just like Mr. Garrick." Having pleased himself vastly with this
performance, he shook the landlord by the hand with great good humour, and said, "By
G—you seem to be an honest fellow and good blood; if you'll come and see me in
London, I'll give you your skinful of wine, and treat you with a play and a whore every   *80*
night you stay. I'll show you how it is to live, my boy. But here, bring me some paper,
my girl; come, let us have one of your love-letters to air my boots." Upon which the
landlord presented him with a piece of an old newspaper. "D—n you!" says the gent,
"this is not half enough; have you never a Bible or Common-Prayer book in the house?
Half a dozen chapters of Genesis, with a few prayers, make an excellent fire in a pair of   *85*
boots." "Oh! Lord forgive you," says the landlord; "sure you would not burn such books
as those," "No!" cries the spark; "where was you born? Go into a shop in London and
buy some butter or a quartern of tea, and then you'll see what use is made of these
books." "Ay!" says the landlord, "we have a saying here in our country that 't is as sure
as the devil is in London, and if he was not there, they could not be so wicked as they   *90*
be." Here a country fellow who had been standing up in one corner of the kitchen,
eating of cold bacon and beans, and who, I observed, trembled at every oath this spark
swore, took his dish and pot, and marched out of the kitchen, fearing, as I afterwards
learnt, that the house would fall down about his ears, for he was sure, he said, "That
man in the gold-laced hat was the devil." The young spark, having now displayed all his   *95*
wit and humour, and exerted his talents to the utmost, thought he had sufficiently
recommended himself to my favour and convinced me he was a gentleman. He therefore
with an air addressed himself to me, and asked me, which way I was travelling? To
which I gave him no answer. He then exalted his voice; but, at my continuing silent, he
asked the landlord if I was deaf. Upon which the landlord told him he did not believe the   *100*
gentleman was dunch, for that he talked very well just now. The man of wit whispered
in the landlord's ear, and said, "I suppose he is either a parson or a fool." He then drank

---

71-72. stap . . . play: "Stap my vitals" was a common exclamation, also used to emphasize affirmation (like "Cross my heart and hope to die!"); the young man mistakenly substitutes *vituals* for *vitals* (perhaps thinking of *victuals*, pronounced *vittles*), and attributes the saying to a "Lord Huntington," although it was mainly associated with Lord Foppington, a character in Sir John Vanbrugh's *The Relapse, or, Virtue in Danger* (1696), who utters it twenty or so times (along with "Strike me speechless" and "Strike me dumb"), even in the play's final line; in *Love's Last Shift, or, The Fool in Fashion* (1696), by Colley Cibber (1671-1757), Sir Novelty Fashion (played by Cibber himself) says "Stop my vitals"; in *The Relapse*, which is both sequel and critique, Vanbrugh elevates Sir Novelty Fashion to Lord Foppington, hardens his character, and gives him the affected pronunciation which includes *stap* for *stop* — still with Cibber himself in the role; "Stap my vitals!" also occurs (along with "Stap my breath!") in Act III of Fielding's own *The Author's Farce* (1730), spoken by Sir Farcical Comic, Fielding's satirical representation of Cibber, whom in 1752 he continued to dislike for personal, professional, and political reasons. **74. Garrick:** David Garrick (1717-1779), major actor and producer of the period (and even playwright), whose 1741 London debut as Richard III, in Colley Cibber's version of Shakespeare's play, caused a sensation and launched his career; he was probably best known for playing Richard III, in which role William Hogarth (1697-1764) painted his portrait. **76. "Give me an horse":** In Shakespeare's play, Richard's famous line is "A horse! a horse! my kingdom for a horse!" (V.iv.7). **79. blood:** man of spirit, dandy, rake. **88. quartern:** a gill, one fourth of a pint (pages torn from the books would be used as wrapping paper; cf. Dryden's *Mac Flecknoe*, lines 100-01, and note, p. 435). **89. country:** i.e., region, part of the country. **101. dunch:** deaf.

a dram, observing that a man should not cool too fast; paid sixpence more than his reckoning, called for his horse, gave the ostler a shilling, and galloped out of the inn, thoroughly satisfied that we all agreed with him in thinking him a clever fellow, and a   *105* man of great importance. The landlord, smiling, took up his money, and said he was a comical gentleman, but that it was a thousand pities he swore so much; if it was not for that, he was a very good customer, and as generous as a prince, for that the night before he had treated everybody in the house. I then asked him if he knew that comical gentleman, as he called him? "No, really, sir," said the landlord, "though a gentleman   *110* was saying last night that he was a sort of rider or rideout to a linen draper at London." This, Mr. Censor, I have since found to be true; for having occasion to buy some cloth, I went last week into a linen draper's shop, in which I found a young fellow whose decent behaviour and plain dress showed he was a tradesman. Upon looking full in his face, I thought I had seen it before, nor was it long before I recollected where it was, and that   *115* this was the same beau I had met with in Somersetshire. The difference in the same man in London, where he was known, and in the country, where he was a stranger, was beyond expression; and was it not impertinent to make observations to you, I could enlarge upon this sort of behaviour; for I am firmly of opinion that there is neither spirit nor good sense in oaths, nor any wit or humour in blasphemy. But as vulgar errors   *120* require an abler pen than mine to correct them, I shall leave that task to you, and am, sir, your humble servant,

R. S

CHARLES WESLEY
England, 1707-1788

IN TEMPTATION

Jesu, lover of my soul,
  Let me to thy bosom fly,
While the nearer waters roll,
  While the tempest still is high.
Hide me, O my Saviour, hide,   *5*
  Till the storm of life is past:
Safe into the haven guide;
  O receive my soul at last.

Other refuge have I none,
  Hangs my helpless soul on thee.   *10*
Leave, ah leave me not alone,
  Still support and comfort me.
All my trust on thee is stayed,
  All my help from thee I bring;
Cover my defenceless head   *15*
  With the shadow of thy wing.

---

111. rider, rideout: agent, commercial traveller, travelling salesman. **112. Censor:** Fielding conducted *The Covent-Garden Journal* under the pseudonym and title of "Sir Alexander Drawcansir, Knight, Censor of Great Britain" (*censor* in the broad sense of one who oversees and corrects public morals and manners, as in ancient Rome; *Drawcansir* is a character in Buckingham's 1672 play *The Rehearsal*, after which the term "drawcansir" generally signifies a blustering, bullying fellow, a braggart). The concluding initials are among several Fielding used to stand for the name of some fictitious correspondent; although there were occasionally other contributors to the *Journal*, this "character, or . . . story," which was included in his *Works* in 1762, is almost certainly Fielding's own.

Wilt thou not regard my call?
  Wilt thou not accept my prayer?
Lo, I sink, I faint, I fall!
  Lo, on thee I cast my care.   20
Reach me out thy gracious hand!
  While I of thy strength receive,
Hoping against hope I stand,
  Dying, and behold I live!

Thou, O Christ, art all I want;   25
  More than all in thee I find.
Raise the fallen, cheer the faint,
  Heal the sick, and lead the blind.

Just and holy is thy name;
  I am all unrighteousness: 30
False and full of sin I am,
  Thou art full of truth and grace.

Plenteous grace with thee is found,
  Grace to cover all my sin:
Let the healing streams abound,   35
  Make and keep me pure within.
Thou of life the fountain art:
  Freely let me take of thee,
Spring thou up within my heart,
  Rise to all eternity!   40

(1740)

JOHN ARMSTRONG
Scotland, 1709-1779

from *THE ART OF PRESERVING HEALTH*

. . . .

Ye who amid this feverish world would wear
A body free of pain, of cares a mind,
Fly the rank city, shun its turbid air;
Breathe not the chaos of eternal smoke
And volatile corruption, form the dead,   5
The dying, sick'ning, and the living world
Exhaled, to sully heaven's transparent dome
With dim mortality. It is not air
That from a thousand lungs reeks back to thine,
Sated with exhalations rank and fell,   10
The spoil of dunghills, and the putrid thaw
Of nature; when from shape and texture she
Relapses into fighting elements:
It is not air, but floats a nauseous mass
Of all obscene, corrupt, offensive things.   15
Much moisture hurts; but here a sordid bath,
With oily rancour fraught, relaxes more
The solid frame than simple moisture can.
Besides, immured in many a sullen bay
That never felt the freshness of the breeze,   20

This slumb'ring deep remains, and ranker grows
With sickly rest: and (though the lungs abhor
To drink the dun fuliginous abyss)
Did not the acid vigour of the mine,
Rolled from so many thund'ring chimneys, tame   25
The putrid steams that overswarm the sky,
This caustic venom would perhaps corrode
Those tender cells that draw the vital air,
In vain with all their unctuous rills bedewed;
Or by the drunken venous tubes, that yawn   30
In countless pores o'er all the pervious skin,
Imbibed, would poison the balsamic blood,
And rouse the heart to every fever's rage.
While yet you breathe, away; the rural wilds
Invite; the mountains call you, and the vales;   35
The woods, the streams and each ambrosial breeze
That fans the ever-undulating sky;
A kindly sky! whose fost'ring pow'r regales
Man, beast and all the vegetable reign.

. . . .

(1744)

THE ART OF PRESERVING HEALTH   **32. balsamic:** soft, mitigatory.

SAMUEL JOHNSON
England, 1709-1784

THE VANITY OF HUMAN WISHES
The Tenth Satire of Juvenal Imitated

Let Observation with extensive view
Survey mankind from China to Peru;
Remark each anxious toil, each eager strife,
And watch the busy scenes of crowded life;
Then say how Hope and Fear, Desire and Hate,   *5*
O'erspread with snares the clouded maze of Fate,
Where wav'ring man, betrayed by vent'rous Pride
To tread the dreary paths without a guide,
As treach'rous phantoms in the mist delude,
Shuns fancied ills, or chases airy good.   *10*
How rarely Reason guides the stubborn choice,
Rules the bold hand, or prompts the suppliant voice;
How nations sink, by darling schemes oppressed,
When Vengeance listens to the fool's request.
Fate wings with ev'ry wish th' afflictive dart,   *15*
Each gift of Nature, and each grace of Art;
With fatal heat impetuous Courage glows,
With fatal sweetness Elocution flows,
Impeachment stops the speaker's pow'rful breath,
And restless fire precipitates on death.   *20*
   But scarce observed, the knowing and the bold
Fall in the gen'ral massacre of gold;
Wide-wasting pest! that rages unconfined,
And crowds with crimes the records of mankind;
For gold his sword the hireling ruffian draws,   *25*
For gold the hireling judge distorts the laws;
Wealth heaped on wealth nor truth nor safety buys,
The dangers gather as the treasures rise.
   Let Hist'ry tell where rival kings command,
And dubious title shakes the madded land,   *30*
When statutes glean the refuse of the sword,
How much more safe the vassal than the lord;
Low skulks the hind beneath the rage of pow'r,
And leaves the wealthy traitor in the Tow'r,
Untouched his cottage, and his slumbers sound,   *35*

Though Confiscation's vultures hover round.
   The needy traveller, serene and gay,
Walks the wild heath, and sings his toil away.
Does Envy seize thee? crush th' upbraiding joy,
Increase his riches and his peace destroy;   *40*
Now fears in dire vicissitude invade,
The rustling brake alarms, and quiv'ring shade,
Nor light nor darkness bring his pain relief,
One shows the plunder, and one hides the thief.
   Yet still one gen'ral cry the skies assails,   *45*
And gain and grandeur load the tainted gales;
Few know the toiling statesman's fear or care,
Th' insidious rival and the gaping heir.
   Once more, Democritus, arise on earth,
With cheerful wisdom and instructive mirth,   *50*
See motley life in modern trappings dressed,
And feed with varied fools th' eternal jest:
Thou who couldst laugh where Want enchained Caprice,
Toil crushed Conceit, and man was of a piece;
Where Wealth unloved without a mourner died;   *55*
And scarce a sycophant was fed by Pride;
Where ne'er was known the form of mock debate,
Or seen a new-made mayor's unwieldy state;
Where change of fav'rites made no change of laws,
And senates heard before they judged a cause;   *60*
How wouldst thou shake at Britain's modish tribe,
Dart the quick taunt, and edge the piercing gibe!
Attentive truth and nature to descry,
And pierce each scene with philosophic eye.
To thee were solemn toys or empty show   *65*
The robes of pleasure and the veils of woe:
All aid the farce, and all thy mirth maintain,
Whose joys are causeless, or whose griefs are vain.
   Such was the scorn that filled the sage's mind,
Renewed at ev'ry glance on humankind;   *70*

THE VANITY OF HUMAN WISHES **15. wings:** i.e., attaches feathers to the shaft of the arrow, for accuracy. **20. precipitates on:** hastens unexpectedly. **33. hind:** peasant, servant. **46:** I.e., prayers for gain and grandeur pollute the air. **49:** Democritus (c.460-c.370 B.C.) is called "the laughing philosopher." **61. shake:** i.e., with laughter.

How just that scorn ere yet thy voice declare,
Search every state, and canvass ev'ry pray'r.
  Unnumbered suppliants crowd Preferment's gate,
Athirst for wealth, and burning to be great;
Delusive Fortune hears th' incessant call, 75
They mount, they shine, evaporate, and fall.
On ev'ry stage the foes of peace attend,
Hate dogs their flight, and Insult mocks their end.
Love ends with hope, the sinking statesman's door
Pours in the morning worshipper no more; 80
For growing names the weekly scribbler lies,
To growing wealth the dedicator flies,
From every room descends the painted face,
That hung the bright Palladium of the place,
And smoked in kitchens, or in auctions sold, 85
To better features yields the frame of gold;
For now no more we trace in ev'ry line
Heroic worth, benevolence divine:
The form distorted justifies the fall,
And detestation rids th' indignant wall. 90
  But will not Britain hear the last appeal,
Sign her foes' doom, or guard her fav'rites' zeal?
Through Freedom's sons no more remonstrance rings,
Degrading nobles and controlling kings;
Our supple tribes repress their patriot throats, 95
And ask no questions but the price of votes;
With weekly libels and septennial ale,
Their wish is full to riot and to rail.
  In full-blown dignity, see Wolsey stand,
Law in his voice, and fortune in his hand: 100
To him the church, the realm, their pow'rs consign,
Through him the rays of regal bounty shine,
Turned by his nod the stream of honour flows,
His smile alone security bestows:

Still to new heights his restless wishes tow'r, 105
Claim leads to claim, and pow'r advances pow'r;
Till conquest unresisted ceased to please,
And rights submitted left him none to seize.
At length his sov'reign frowns — the train of state
Mark the keen glance, and watch the sign to hate. 110
Where'er he turns he meets a stranger's eye,
His suppliants scorn him, and his followers fly;
At once is lost the pride of awful state,
The golden canopy, the glitt'ring plate,
The regal palace, the luxurious board, 115
The liv'ried army, and the menial lord.
With age, with cares, with maladies oppressed,
He seeks the refuge of monastic rest.
Grief aids disease, remembered folly stings,
And his last sighs reproach the faith of kings. 120
  Speak thou, whose thoughts at humble peace repine,
Shall Wolsey's wealth, with Wolsey's end be thine?
Or liv'st thou now, with safer pride content,
The wisest justice on the banks of Trent?
For why did Wolsey, near the steeps of Fate, 125
On weak foundations raise th' enormous weight?
Why but to sink beneath Misfortune's blow,
With louder ruin to the gulfs below?
  What gave great Villiers to th' assassin's knife,
And fixed disease on Harley's closing life? 130
What murdered Wentworth, and what exiled Hyde,
By kings protected, and to kings allied?
What but their wish indulged in courts to shine,
And pow'r too great to keep, or to resign?
  When first the college rolls receive his name, 135
The young enthusiast quits his ease for fame;
Through all his veins the fever of renown
Burns from the strong contagion of the gown;

80: referring to the levees held by the powerful and attended by, among others, sycophants and petitioners. **84. Palladium:** a sacred object that preserves the safety of a city or state (from the statue of Pallas Athena that secured Troy, until it was stolen by Diomedes — a legend adapted by Virgil in *Aeneid*, II, 162ff.; Roman tradition also said Aeneas rescued it from burning Troy and brought it to Italy, where it later protected Rome). **93-94:** alluding to the Grand Remonstrance, a manifesto presented to Charles I in 1641 by the Long Parliament, which among other demands called for the King's counsellors to be replaced by men approved by Parliament. **97. weekly libels:** political attacks in weekly papers; **septennial ale:** that distributed by candidates at election time (the Septenniel Act of 1716 changed the maximum length of a parliament from three to seven years). **99ff.:** Thomas Wolsey (c.1475-1530) became Cardinal and Lord Chancellor in 1515; Henry VIII discharged him in 1529, and he died on his way to London to face charges of treason. **124. Trent:** major English river (it flows near Lichfield, Johnson's birthplace). **125. steeps:** precipices (Johnson's *Dictionary*). **129:** George Villiers (1592-1628), first Duke of Buckingham, powerful favourite of James I and Charles I, led an unsuccessful campaign against the French at the Isle of Ré in 1627; later, Parliament demanded his dismissal, the King refused, and Villiers was stabbed by a disgruntled officer who had served at Ré. **130:** Robert Harley (1661-1724), first Earl of Oxford and Mortimer, shifted from Whig to Tory under Queen Anne (1702-14), was dismissed in 1714 and imprisoned by the Whigs in 1715, spending two years in the Tower. **131-32:** Thomas Wentworth (1593-1641), first Earl of Strafford, was impeached and executed in spite of being "protected" by Charles I; Edward Hyde (1609-1674), first Earl of Clarendon, powerful under Charles I and II, was forced into exile in 1667; he was "to kings allied" because his daughter Anne (1637-1671) married Charles's brother James (who himself reigned from 1685 to 1688). **137-38:** alluding to the academic gowns worn by students.

O'er Bodley's dome his future labours spread,
And Bacon's mansion trembles o'er his head.　　　　*140*
Are these thy views? proceed, illustrious youth,
And Virtue guard thee to the throne of Truth!
Yet should thy soul indulge the gen'rous heat,
Till captive Science yields her last retreat;
Should Reason guide thee with her brightest ray,　　*145*
And pour on misty Doubt resistless day;
Should no false Kindness lure to loose delight,
Nor Praise relax, nor Difficulty fright;
Should tempting Novelty thy cell refrain,
And Sloth effuse her opiate fumes in vain;　　　　*150*
Should Beauty blunt on fops her fatal dart,
Nor claim the triumph of a lettered heart;
Should no disease thy torpid veins invade,
Nor Melancholy's phantoms haunt thy shade;
Yet hope not life from grief or danger free,　　　*155*
Nor think the doom of man reversed for thee:
Deign on the passing world to turn thine eyes,
And pause awhile from letters to be wise;
There mark what ills the scholar's life assail,
Toil, envy, want, the patron, and the jail.　　　　*160*
See nations slowly wise, and meanly just,
To buried merit raise the tardy bust.
If dreams yet flatter, once again attend,
Hear Lydiat's life, and Galileo's end.
　　Nor deem, when Learning her last prize bestows,　*165*
The glitt'ring eminence exempt from foes;
See when the vulgar 'scape, despised or awed,
Rebellion's vengeful talons seize on Laud.
From meaner minds though smaller fines content,
The plundered palace or sequestered rent;　　　　*170*
Marked out by dangerous parts he meets the shock,
And fatal Learning leads him to the block:
Around his tomb let Art and Genius weep,

But hear his death, ye blockheads, hear and sleep.
　　The festal blazes, the triumphal show,　　　　*175*
The ravished standard, and the captive foe,
The senate's thanks, the gazette's pompous tale,
With force resistless o'er the brave prevail.
Such bribes the rapid Greek o'er Asia whirled,
For such the steady Romans shook the world;　　　*180*
For such in distant lands the Britons shine,
And stain with blood the Danube or the Rhine;
This pow'r has praise, that virtue scarce can warm,
Till fame supplies the universal charm.
Yet Reason frowns on war's unequal game,　　　　*185*
Where wasted nations raise a single name,
And mortgaged states their grandsires' wreaths regret,
From age to age in everlasting debt;
Wreaths which at last the dear-bought right convey
To rust on medals, or on stones decay.　　　　　*190*
　　On what foundation stands the warrior's pride?
How just his hopes let Swedish Charles decide;
A frame of adamant, a soul of fire,
No dangers fright him, and no labours tire;
O'er love, o'er fear, extends his wide domain,　　*195*
Unconquered lord of pleasure and of pain;
No joys to him pacific sceptres yield,
War sounds the trump, he rushes to the field;
Behold surrounding kings their pow'r combine,
And one capitulate, and one resign;　　　　　*200*
Peace courts his hand, but spreads her charms in vain;
"Think nothing gained," he cries, "till naught remain,
On Moscow's walls till Gothic standards fly,
And all be mine beneath the polar sky."
The march begins in military state,　　　　　*205*
And nations on his eye suspended wait;
Stern Famine guards the solitary coast,
And Winter barricades the realms of Frost;

---

139. Bodley's dome: i.e., the Bodleian Library, in Oxford (**dome,** from Latin *domus*: a building; a house — the *Dictionary*). **140:** "There is a tradition, that the study of friar Bacon, built on an arch over the bridge, will fall, when a man greater than Bacon shall pass under it" (Johnson's note; Roger Bacon, c.1214-1294). **144. Science:** knowledge, learning. **148. relax:** make less attentive or laborious (the *Dictionary*). **149. refrain:** spare (the *Dictionary*). **160. patron:** changed from the first edition's "garret" after Johnson's experience with Chesterfield; see *PATRON* in the excerpts from the *Dictionary* (p. 601), and the first excerpt from Boswell's *Life* (p. 685). **161. just:** exact in retribution (the *Dictionary*). **164:** Thomas Lydiat (1572-1646), though a prominent mathematician and scholar and Oxford don, was poor all his life, even spending time in debtor's prison, partly because he was harassed by the Puritans as a Royalist sympathizer; Galileo (1564-1642) was forced by the Inquisition to deny his astronomical discoveries, was imprisoned for a time, and died blind. **168:** Archbishop William Laud (1572-1646) was impeached by the Long Parliament in 1640 and later executed. **171. parts:** qualities, powers, faculties, accomplishments (the *Dictionary*). **177. gazette:** In the *Dictionary*, printed with accent on the first syllable, though Johnson says either syllable may be accented. **179. the rapid Greek:** Alexander the Great. **181-82:** probably alluding both to Marlborough's 1704 victory at Blenheim during the War of the Spanish Succession (1701-13) and to Britain's part in the War of the Austrian Succession (1740-48); possibly also containing an echo of *Paradise Lost*, I, 353 (p. 330). **192:** Charles XII of Sweden (1682-1718), after stunning victories over Denmark, Poland, and Saxony, was humiliatingly defeated by the Russians under Peter the Great at Poltava in 1709 (line 210), fled to sanctuary in Turkey (211-14), and was killed while attacking Norway (219-20); his defeat effectively ended Sweden's days of power.

He comes, not want and cold his course delay; —
Hide, blushing Glory, hide Pultowa's day: *210*
The vanquished hero leaves his broken bands,
And shows his miseries in distant lands;
Condemned a needy supplicant to wait,
While ladies interpose, and slaves debate.
But did not Chance at length her error mend?   *215*
Did no subverted empire mark his end?
Did rival monarchs give the fatal wound?
Or hostile millions press him to the ground?
His fall was destined to a barren strand,
A petty fortress, and a dubious hand;   *220*
He left the name, at which the world grew pale,
To point a moral, or adorn a tale.

    All times their scenes of pompous woes afford,
From Persia's tyrant to Bavaria's lord.
In gay hostility, and barbarous pride,   *225*
With half mankind embattled at his side,
Great Xerxes comes to seize the certain prey,
And starves exhausted regions in his way;
Attendant Flatt'ry counts his myriads o'er,
Till counted myriads soothe his pride no more;   *230*
Fresh praise is tried till madness fires his mind,
The waves he lashes, and enchains the wind;
New pow'rs are claimed, new pow'rs are still bestowed,
Till rude resistance lops the spreading god;
The daring Greeks deride the martial show,   *235*
And heap their valleys with the gaudy foe;
Th' insulted sea with humbler thoughts he gains,
A single skiff to speed his flight remains;
Th' encumbered oar scarce leaves the dreaded coast
Through purple billows and a floating host.   *240*

    The bold Bavarian, in a luckless hour,
Tries the dread summits of Caesarian pow'r,
With unexpected legions bursts away,
And sees defenceless realms receive his sway;
Short sway! fair Austria spreads her mournful charms,
The queen, the beauty, sets the world in arms;   *246*
From hill to hill the beacon's rousing blaze
Spreads wide the hope of plunder and of praise;
The fierce Croatian, and the wild Hussar,

With all the sons of ravage crowd the war;   *250*
The baffled prince in honour's flatt'ring bloom
Of hasty greatness finds the fatal doom,
His foes' derision, and his subjects' blame,
And steals to death from anguish and from shame.
    "Enlarge my life with multitude of days,   *255*
In health, in sickness," thus the suppliant prays;
Hides from himself his state, and shuns to know
That life protracted is protracted woe.
Time hovers o'er, impatient to destroy,
And shuts up all the passages of joy: *260*
In vain their gifts the bounteous seasons pour,
The fruit autumnal, and the vernal flow'r,
With listless eyes the dotard views the store,
He views, and wonders that they please no more;
Now pall the tasteless meats, and joyless wines,   *265*
And Luxury with sighs her slave resigns.
Approach, ye minstrels, try the soothing strain,
Diffuse the tuneful lenitives of pain:
No sounds, alas, would touch th' impervious ear,
Though dancing mountains witnessed Orpheus near; *270*
Nor lute nor lyre his feeble pow'rs attend,
Nor sweeter music of a virtuous friend,
But everlasting dictates crowd his tongue,
Perversely grave, or positively wrong.
The still-returning tale, and ling'ring jest,   *275*
Perplex the fawning niece and pampered guest,
While growing hopes scarce awe the gath'ring sneer,
And scarce a legacy can bribe to hear;
The watchful guests still hint the last offence,
The daughter's petulance, the son's expense,   *280*
Improve his heady rage with treach'rous skill,
And mould his passions till they make his will.

    Unnumbered maladies his joints invade,
Lay siege to life and press the dire blockade;
But unextinguished av'rice still remains,   *285*
And dreaded losses aggravate his pains;
He turns, with anxious heart and crippled hands,
His bonds of debt, and mortgages of lands;
Or views his coffers with suspicious eyes,
Unlocks his gold, and counts it till he dies.   *290*

---

220. dubious hand: Some entertained the possibility that Charles had been shot by one of his own men. **227:** Xerxes ("Persia's tyrant") and his invading army were temporarily halted by a small army of Spartans in the mountain passes of Thermopylae (see Hope's "Inscription for a War," p. 1362, and note), and his fleet decisively defeated in the sea battle near the island of Salamis (480 B.C.); the following year the battle of Plataea ended the Persian threat. **232:** According to Herodotus (VII, 35), when Xerxes's first attempt at a bridge across the Hellespont was destroyed by a storm, he furiously ordered that the waters be flogged (three hundred lashes) and that fetters be lowered into the sea. **241. bold Bavarian:** Charles Albert (1697-1745), elector of Bavaria, who was made Emperor in 1742, challenging Maria Theresa (1717-1780), Archduchess of Austria (line 245), during the War of the Austrian Succession. **270:** See note to Dryden's "A Song for St. Cecilia's Day," lines 48-50 (p. 440).

But grant, the virtues of a temp'rate prime
Bless with an age exempt from scorn or crime;
An age that melts with unperceived decay,
And glides in modest innocence away;
Whose peaceful day Benevolence endears,   *295*
Whose night congratulating Conscience cheers;
The gen'ral fav'rite as the gen'ral friend:
Such age there is, and who shall wish its end?
      Yet ev'n on this her load Misfortune flings,
To press the weary minutes' flagging wings: *300*
New sorrow rises as the day returns,
A sister sickens, or a daughter mourns.
Now kindred Merit fills the sable bier,
Now lacerated Friendship claims a tear.
Year chases year, decay pursues decay,   *305*
Still drops some joy from with'ring life away;
New forms arise, and diff'rent views engage,
Superfluous lags the vet'ran on the stage,
Till pitying Nature signs the last release,
And bids afflicted Worth retire to peace.   *310*
      But few there are whom hours like these await,
Who set unclouded in the gulfs of Fate.
From Lydia's monarch should the search descend,
By Solon cautioned to regard his end,
In life's last scene what prodigies surprise,   *315*
Fears of the brave, and follies of the wise?
From Marlb'rough's eyes the streams of dotage flow,
And Swift expires a driv'ler and a show.
      The teeming mother, anxious for her race,
Begs for each birth the fortune of a face: *320*
Yet Vane could tell what ills from beauty spring,
And Sedley cursed the form that pleased a king.
Ye nymphs of rosy lips and radiant eyes,
Whom Pleasure keeps too busy to be wise,
Whom Joys with soft varieties invite,   *325*
By day the frolic, and the dance by night,
Who frown with vanity, who smile with art,
And ask the latest fashion of the heart,
What care, what rules your heedless charms shall save,

Each nymph your rival, and each youth your slave?   *330*
Against your fame with Fondness Hate combines,
The rival batters, and the lover mines.
With distant voice neglected Virtue calls,
Less heard and less, the faint remonstrance falls;
Tired with contempt, she quits the slipp'ry reign,   *335*
And Pride and Prudence take her seat in vain.
In crowd at once, where none the pass defend,
The harmless Freedom, and the private Friend.
The guardians yield, by force superior plied;
By Int'rest, Prudence; and by Flatt'ry, Pride.   *340*
Now Beauty falls betrayed, despised, distressed,
And hissing Infamy proclaims the rest.
      Where then shall Hope and Fear their objects find?
Must dull Suspense corrupt the stagnant mind?
Must helpless man, in ignorance sedate,   *345*
Roll darkling down the torrent of his fate?
Must no dislike alarm, no wishes rise,
No cries attempt the mercies of the skies?
Enquirer, cease, petitions yet remain,
Which Heav'n may hear, nor deem religion vain.   *350*
Still raise for good the supplicating voice,
But leave to Heav'n the measure and the choice,
Safe in his pow'r, whose eyes discern afar
The secret ambush of a specious pray'r.
Implore his aid, in his decisions rest,   *355*
Secure whate'er he gives, he gives the best.
Yet when the sense of sacred presence fires,
And strong devotion to the skies aspires,
Pour forth thy fervours for a healthful mind,
Obedient passions, and a will resigned;   *360*
For love, which scarce collective man can fill;
For patience sov'reign o'er transmuted ill;
For faith, that panting for a happier seat,
Counts death kind Nature's signal of retreat:
These goods for man the laws of Heav'n ordain,   *365*
These goods he grants, who grants the pow'r to gain;
With these celestial Wisdom calms the mind,
And makes the happiness she does not find.

(1749, 1755)

313-14. Lydia's monarch: Croesus (last king of Lydia, c.560-546 B.C.), though proverbially wealthy, was told by wise Solon that, however wealthy and seemingly happy a man was, until we see how he ends his days we should consider him only fortunate, not happy; Croesus later was made miserable by the accidental killing of his son, and was overthrown by Cyrus of Persia (Herodotus, I, 32-46). **317. Marlb'rough:** See note to Swift's "Satirical Elegy" (p. 478); shortly after Marlborough's favourite daughter died in 1716 (three other children had died earlier), he suffered two strokes which left him temporarily paralyzed and without speech; even though he recovered a good deal, he remained in ill health until his death. **318:** In his last few years, Jonathan Swift was in effect insane, and reportedly his servants displayed him for money. **321:** Anne Vane (1705-1736) was for a time mistress of Frederick, Prince of Wales, who deserted her. **322:** Catherine Sedley (1656-1717) was dropped as mistress by the Duke of York when he became James II (though he later made her a countess). **338. private:** not open, secret (the *Dictionary*). **344. Suspense:** uncertainty; withholding of judgment (the *Dictionary*). **359:** Juvenal says to pray for a sound mind in a sound body (*mens sana in corpore sano*).

from *THE RAMBLER*

No. 4.   Saturday, March 31, 1750

Simul et jucunda et inonea dicere vitæ.
— Horace

And join both profit and delight in one.
— Creech

The works of fiction with which the present generation seems more particularly delighted are such as exhibit life in its true state, diversified only by accidents that daily happen in the world, and influenced by passions and qualities which are really to be found in conversing with mankind.

This kind of writing may be termed, not improperly, the comedy of romance, and is   5
to be conducted nearly by the rules of comic poetry. Its province is to bring about natural events by easy means, and to keep up curiosity without the help of wonder: it is therefore precluded from the machines and expedients of the heroic romance, and can neither employ giants to snatch away a lady from the nuptial rites, nor knights to bring her back from captivity; it can neither bewilder its personages in deserts, nor lodge them   10
in imaginary castles.

I remember a remark made by Scaliger upon Pontanus, that all his writings are filled with the same images, and that if you take from him his lilies and his roses, his satyrs and dryads, he will have nothing left that can be called poetry. In like manner, almost all the fictions of the last age will vanish if you deprive them of a hermit and a   15
wood, a battle and a shipwreck.

Why this wild strain of imagination found reception so long, in polite and learned ages, it is not easy to conceive; but we cannot wonder that, while readers could be procured, the authors were willing to continue it, for when a man had by practice gained some fluency of language, he had no further care than to retire to his closet, let loose his   20
invention, and heat his mind with incredibilities; a book was thus produced without fear of criticism, without the toil of study, without knowledge of nature, or acquaintance with life.

The task of our present writers is very different; it requires, together with that learning which is to be gained from books, that experience which can never be attained   25
by solitary diligence, but must arise from general converse, and accurate observation of the living world. Their performances have, as Horace expresses it, *plus oneris quantum veniæ minus:* little indulgence, and therefore more difficulty. They are engaged in portraits of which everyone knows the original, and can detect any deviation from exactness of resemblance. Other writings are safe, except from the malice of learning,   30

RAMBLER NO. 4   Epigraph: from *Ars Poetica*, 344 (cf. Chaucer's reference to "Tales of best sentence and moost solaas," in the "General Prologue," line 798, p. 39); Thomas Creech (1659-1700) was a classical scholar who translated several works from Greek and Latin. **1. works of fiction:** The preceding decade had seen the publication of several novels by Fielding, Richardson, and Smollett (see the Chronology). **8. machines:** supernatural agency in poems (the *Dictionary*). **12:** Julius Cæsar Scaliger (Giulio Cesare Scaligero, 1484-1558), Italian humanist and literary critic, author of *Poetices* (1561); Jovianus Pontanus (Giovanni Pontano, c.1426-1503), prolific Italian poet, scholar, and humanist, perhaps best known for the poems making up *De amore conjugali* and *Eridanus*. **27-28:** Johnson translates Horace's line (from *Epistles*, II, i, 170).

but these are in danger from every common reader, as the slipper ill executed was censured by a shoemaker who happened to stop in his way at the Venus of Apelles.

But the fear of not being approved as just copiers of human manners is not the most important concern that an author of this sort ought to have before him. These books are written chiefly to the young, the ignorant, and the idle, to whom they serve as lectures of conduct and introductions into life. They are the entertainment of minds unfurnished with ideas, and therefore susceptible of impressions; not fixed by principles, and therefore easily following the current of fancy; not informed by experience, and consequently open to every false suggestion and partial account. 35

That the highest degree of reverence should be paid to youth, and that nothing indecent should be suffered to approach their eyes or ears, are precepts extorted by sense and virtue from an ancient writer, by no means eminent for chastity of thought. The same kind, though not the same degree of caution, is required in everything which is laid before them, to secure them from unjust prejudices, perverse opinions, and incongruous combinations of images. 40

In the romances formerly written, every transaction and sentiment was so remote from all that passes among men, that the reader was in very little danger of making any applications to himself; the virtues and crimes were equally beyond his sphere of activity; and he amused himself with heroes and with traitors, deliverers and persecutors, as with beings of another species, whose actions were regulated upon motives of their own, and who had neither faults nor excellencies in common with himself. 50

But when an adventurer is levelled with the rest of the world, and acts in such scenes of the universal drama as may be the lot of any other man, young spectators fix their eyes upon him with closer attention, and hope by observing his behaviour and success to regulate their own practices, when they shall be engaged in the like part. 55

For this reason these familiar histories may perhaps be made of greater use than the solemnities of professed morality, and convey the knowledge of vice and virtue with more efficacy than axioms and definitions. But if the power of example is so great as to take possession of the memory by a kind of violence, and produce effects almost without the intervention of the will, care ought to be taken that, when the choice is unrestrained, the best examples only should be exhibited; and that which is likely to operate so strongly should not be mischievous or uncertain in its effects. 60

The chief advantage which these fictions have over real life is that their authors are at liberty, though not to invent, yet to select objects, and to cull from the mass of mankind those individuals upon which the attention ought most to be employed; as a diamond, though it cannot be made, may be polished by art and placed in such a situation as to display that lustre which before was buried among common stones. 65

It is justly considered as the greatest excellency of art, to imitate nature; but it is necessary to distinguish those parts of nature which are most proper for imitation; 70

---

32. **Apelles:** celebrated Greek painter of the 4th century B.C., especially noted for his paintings of Alexander and Aphrodite. Pliny the Elder (23-79) in his *History* (XXXV, 85) tells the story of a shoemaker who criticized his rendering of a sandal's fastening; the next day, proud to see that Apelles had corrected the error, the man began to criticize the leg, whereupon Apelles indignantly declared that *"Ne supra crepidam sutor judicaret"* ("A shoemaker should not judge above the shoe," a saying more familiar as "A cobbler should stick to his last"); Pliny notes that the saying had become a proverb. 42. **writer . . . thought:** Juvenal.

greater care is still required in representing life, which is so often discoloured by passion, or deformed by wickedness.

It is therefore not a sufficient vindication of a character, that it is drawn as it appears, for many characters ought never to be drawn; nor of a narrative, that the train of events is agreeable to observation and experience, for that observation which is called knowledge   *75* of the world will be found much more frequently to make men cunning than good. The purpose of these writings is surely not only to show mankind, but to provide that they may be seen hereafter with less hazard; to teach the means of avoiding the snares which are laid by TREACHERY for INNOCENCE, without infusing any wish for that superiority with which the betrayer flatters his vanity; to give the power of counteracting fraud, without   *80* the temptation to practise it; to initiate youth by mock encounters in the art of necessary defence, and to increase prudence without impairing virtue.

Many writers, for the sake of following nature, so mingle good and bad qualities in their principal personages that they are both equally conspicuous; and as we accompany them through their adventures with delight, and are led by degrees to interest ourselves   *85* in their favour, we lose the abhorrence of their faults, because they do not hinder our pleasure, or, perhaps, regard them with some kindness for being united with so much merit.

There have been men indeed splendidly wicked, whose endowments threw a brightness on their crimes, and whom scarce any villainy made perfectly detestable,   *90* because they never could be wholly divested of their excellencies; but such have been in all ages the great corrupters of the world, and their resemblance ought no more to be preserved, than the art of murdering without pain.

Some have advanced, without due attention to the consequences of this notion, that certain virtues have their correspondent faults, and therefore that to exhibit either apart   *95* is to deviate from probability. Thus men are observed by Swift to be "grateful in the same degree as they are resentful." This principle, with others of the same kind, supposes man to act from a brute impulse, and pursue a certain degree of inclination, without any choice of the object; for, otherwise, though it should be allowed that gratitude and resentment arise from the same constitution of the passions, it follows not   *100* that they will be equally indulged when reason is consulted; yet unless that consequence be admitted, this sagacious maxim becomes an empty sound, without any relation to practice or to life.

Nor is it evident that even the first motions to these effects are always in the same proportion. For pride, which produces quickness of resentment, will obstruct gratitude   *105* by unwillingness to admit that inferiority which obligation implies; and it is very unlikely that he who cannot think he receives a favour will acknowledge or repay it.

It is of the utmost importance to mankind that positions of this tendency should be laid open and confuted; for while men consider good and evil as springing from the same root, they will spare the one for the sake of the other, and in judging, if not of   *110* others at least of themselves, will be apt to estimate their virtues by their vices. To this fatal error all those will contribute, who confound the colours of right and wrong, and instead of helping to settle their boundaries, mix them with so much art that no common mind is able to disunite them.

In narratives where historical veracity has no place, I cannot discover why there *115* should not be exhibited the most perfect idea of virtue; of virtue not angelical, nor above probability, for what we cannot credit we shall never imitate, but the highest and purest that humanity can reach, which, exercised in such trials as the various revolutions of things shall bring upon it, may, by conquering some calamities and enduring others, teach us what we may hope, and what we can perform. Vice, for vice is necessary to be *120* shown, should always disgust; nor should the graces of gaiety, or the dignity of courage, be so united with it as to reconcile it to the mind. Wherever it appears, it should raise hatred by the malignity of its practices, and contempt by the meanness of its stratagems; for while it is supported by either parts or spirit, it will be seldom heartily abhorred. The Roman tyrant was content to be hated, if he was but feared; and there are thousands of *125* the readers of romances willing to be thought wicked, if they may be allowed to be wits. It is therefore to be steadily inculcated, that virtue is the highest proof of understanding, and the only solid basis of greatness; and that vice is the natural consequence of narrow thoughts, that it begins in mistake, and ends in ignominy.

from *A Dictionary of the English Language*

from the *Preface*

It is the fate of those who toil at the lower employments of life, to be rather driven by the fear of evil, than attracted by the prospect of good; to be exposed to censure, without hope of praise; to be disgraced by miscarriage, or punished for neglect, where success would have been without applause, and diligence without reward.

Among these unhappy mortals is the writer of dictionaries; whom mankind have *5* considered, not as the pupil, but the slave of science, the pionier of literature, doomed only to remove rubbish and clear obstructions from the paths of Learning and Genius, who press forward to conquest and glory, without bestowing a smile on the humble drudge that facilitates their progress. Every other authour may aspire to praise; the lexicographer can only hope to escape reproach, and even this negative recompense has *10* been yet granted to very few.

I have, notwithstanding this discouragement, attempted a dictionary of the English language, which, while it was employed in the cultivation of every species of literature, has itself been hitherto neglected, suffered to spread, under the direction of chance, into wild exuberance, resigned to the tyranny of time and fashion, and exposed to the *15* corruptions of ignorance, and caprices of innovation.

. . . .

---

124. parts: See note to line 171 of *The Vanity of Human Wishes* (p. 591). **125. Roman tyrant:** Caligula reportedly liked to quote a line from a (now lost) play by Lucius Accius: "*Oderint dum metuant*" ("Let them hate, as long as they fear"). **A Dictionary of the English Language** In these excerpts we have retained Johnson's spelling and punctuation, since they constitute examples of the very things he is discussing. **Preface 6. pionier:** i.e., pioneer, military engineer (cf. *mines*, line 332 of *The Vanity of Human Wishes*; p. 593).

Of the event of this work, for which, having laboured it with so much application, I cannot but have some degree of parental fondness, it is natural to form conjectures. Those who have been persuaded to think well of my design, require that it should fix our language, and put a stop to those alterations which time and chance have hitherto been suffered to make in it without opposition. With this consequence I will confess that I flattered myself for a while; but now begin to fear that I have indulged expectation which neither reason nor experience can justify. When we see men grow old and die at a certain time one after another, from century to century, we laugh at the elixir that promises to prolong life to a thousand years; and with equal justice may the lexicographer be derided, who being able to produce no example of a nation that has preserved their words and phrases from mutability, shall imagine that his dictionary can embalm his language, and secure it from corruption and decay, that it is in his power to change sublunary nature, or clear the world at once from folly, vanity, and affectation. 20 25

. . . .

If the changes that we fear be thus irresistible, what remains but to acquiesce with silence, as in the other insurmountable distresses of humanity? It remains that we retard what we cannot repel, that we palliate what we cannot cure. Life may be lengthened by care, though death cannot be ultimately defeated: tongues, like governments, have a natural tendency to degeneration; we have long preserved our constitution, let us make some struggles for our language. 30 35

In hope of giving longevity to that which its own nature forbids to be immortal, I have devoted this book, the labour of years, to the honour of my country, that we may no longer yield the palm of philology to the nations of the continent. The chief glory of every people arises from its authours: whether I shall add any thing by my own writings to the reputation of English literature, must be left to time: much of my life has been lost under the pressures of disease; much has been trifled away; and much has always been spent in provision for the day that was passing over me; but I shall not think my employment useless or ignoble, if by my assistance foreign nations, and distant ages, gain access to the propagators of knowledge, and understand the teachers of truth; if my labours afford light to the repositories of science, and add celebrity to Bacon, to Hooker, to Milton, and to Boyle. 40 45

When I am animated by this wish, I look with pleasure on my book, however defective, and deliver it to the world with the spirit of a man that has endeavoured well. That it will immediately become popular I have not promised to myself: a few wild blunders, and risible absurdities, from which no work of such multiplicity was ever free, may for a time furnish folly with laughter, and harden ignorance in contempt; but useful diligence will at last prevail, and there never can be wanting some who distinguish desert; who will consider that no dictionary of a living tongue ever can be perfect, since while it is hastening to publication, some words are budding, and some falling away; that a whole life cannot be spent upon syntax and etymology, and that even a whole life would not be sufficient; that he, whose design includes whatever language can express, 50 55

17. event: consequence, conclusion, upshot (the *Dictionary*). **37-38. to the honour of my country . . . continent:** See lines 75-79 below. **45. science:** knowledge, learning. **45-46:** Francis Bacon (see p. 212); Richard Hooker (c.1554-1600), theologian, author of *Of the Laws of Ecclesiastical Polity* (1594-1597); John Milton (see p. 315); Robert Boyle (1627-1691), physicist, chemist, and theologian, one of the founders of the Royal Society (see also Egerton's "On the Honourable Robert Boyle," and the general note, p. 487).

must often speak of what he does not understand; that a writer will sometimes be hurried by eagerness to the end, and sometimes faint with weariness under a task, which Scaliger compares to the labours of the anvil and the mine; that what is obvious is not always known, and what is known is not always present; that sudden fits of inadvertency will surprize vigilance, slight avocations will seduce attention, and casual eclipses of the mind will darken learning; and that the writer shall often in vain trace his memory at the moment of need, for that which yesterday he knew with intuitive readiness, and which will come uncalled into his thoughts tomorrow. 60

In this work, when it shall be found that much is omitted, let it not be forgotten that much likewise is performed; and though no book was ever spared out of tenderness to the authour, and the world is little solicitous to know whence proceeded the faults of that which it condemns; yet it may gratify curiosity to inform it, that the *English Dictionary* was written with little assistance of the learned, and without any patronage of the great; not in the soft obscurities of retirement, or under the shelter of academick bowers, but amidst inconvenience and distraction, in sickness and in sorrow: and it may repress the triumph of malignant criticism to observe, that if our language is not here fully displayed, I have only failed in an attempt which no human powers have hitherto completed. If the lexicons of ancient tongues, now immutably fixed, and comprised in a few volumes, be yet, after the toil of successive ages, inadequate and delusive; if the aggregated knowledge, and cooperating diligence of the Italian academicians, did not secure them from the censure of Beni, if the embodied criticks of France, when fifty years had been spent upon their work, were obliged to change its economy, and give their second edition another form, I may surely be contented without the praise of perfection, which, if I could obtain, in this gloom of solitude, what would it avail me? I have protracted my work till most of those whom I wished to please, have sunk into the grave, and success and miscarriage are empty sounds: I therefore dismiss it with frigid tranquillity, having little to fear or hope from censure or from praise. 65 70 75 80

(1755)

Selected Definitions

ADDLE. Originally applied to eggs, and signifying such as produce nothing, but grow rotten under the hen; thence transferred to brains that produce nothing.

AGGREGATE. The complex or collective result of the conjunction or acervation of many particulars.

TO AKE.

  2. It is frequently applied, in an improper sense, to the heart; as, *the heart akes;* to imply grief or fear. Shakespeare has used it, still more licentiously, of the soul.

ALAMODE. According to the fashion: a low word.

---

59. Scaliger: Joseph Justus Scaliger (1540-1609), classical scholar and critic, son of Julius Cæsar Scaliger (see note to *Rambler* No. 4, line 16), compared dictionary-making with the forced labour undergone by convicted criminals. **69-70. patronage of the great:** See *PATRON* in the selections from the definitions, and the first excerpt from Boswell's *Life* (p. 685). **75-77:** When the *Accademia della Crusca*, founded in 1582, published its *Vocabolario della Crusca* (1612), it was attacked by Paolo Beni in his *Anti-Crusca* for its Tuscan purity. **77-79:** *l'Académie française*, established in 1635, undertook its dictionary in 1639, and published the first edition in 1694 (the eighth edition appeared in 1935). **SELECTED DEFINITIONS** We have abridged some definitions, mainly by omitting designations of parts of speech, etymologies, and illustrative quotations.

AMBIDEXTER.
1. A man who has equally the use of both his hands.
2. A man who is equally ready to act on either side, in party disputes. This sense is ludicrous.

BEAU. A man of dress; a man whose great care is to deck his person.

BOPEEP. To look out, and draw back as if frighted, or with the purpose to fright some other.

BUCANIERS. A cant word for the privateers, or pirates, of America.

CANT.
1. A corrupt dialect used by beggars and vagabonds.
2. A particular form of speaking peculiar to some certain class or body of men.
3. A whining pretension to goodness, in formal and affected terms.
4. Barbarous jargon.

DARKLING. [a participle, as it seems, from *darkle,* which yet I have never found.] Being in the dark; being without light: a word merely poetical.

DORMITORY.
2. A burial place.

EAME. [eam, Saxon; *eom,* Dutch.] Uncle: a word still used in the wilder parts of Staffordshire.

ENCYCLOPEDIA, ENCYCLOPEDY. The circle of sciences; the round of learning.

ENTHUSIASM.
1. A vain belief of private revelation; a vain confidence of divine favour or communication.

EXCISE. A hateful tax levied upon commodities, and adjudged not by the common judges of property, but wretches hired by those to whom excise is paid.

EXOSSATED. Deprived of bones.

EYESERVANT. A servant that works only while watched.

FARCE. A dramatick representation written without regularity, and stuffed with wild and ludicrous conceits.

GAMBLER. [A cant word, I suppose, for *game* or *gamester.*] A knave whose practice it is to invite the unwary to game and cheat them.

TO GARBLE. To sift; to part; to separate the good from the bad.

GRUBSTREET. Originally the name of a street in London, much inhabited by writers of small histories, dictionaries, and temporary poems; whence any mean production is called *grubstreet.*

INK. The black liquor with which men write.

LEXICOGRAPHER. A writer of dictionaries; a harmless drudge, that busies himself in tracing the original, and detailing the signification of words.

GRUBSTREET, LEXICOGRAPHER, and *NETWORK:* See second excerpt from Boswell's *Life* (p. 686).

LICH. A dead carcase; whence *lichwake,* the time or act of watching by the dead; *lichgate,* the gate through which the dead are carried to the grave; *Lichfield,* the field of the dead, a city in Staffordshire, so named from martyred christians. *Salve magna parens. Lichwake* is still retained in Scotland in the same sense.

LIPLABOUR. Action of the lips without concurrence of the mind; words without sentiments.

LOSEL. A scoundrel; a sorry worthless fellow. A word now obsolete.

LUBBER. A sturdy drone; an idle, fat, bulky losel; a booby.

LUCUBRATION. Study by candlelight; nocturnal study; any thing composed by night.

NETWORK. Any thing reticulated or decussated, at equal distances, with interstices between the intersections.

NOSE.
    1. The prominence on the face, which is the organ of scent and the emunctory of the brain.

OATS. A grain, which in England is generally given to horses, but in Scotland supports the people.

PATRON.
    1. One who countenances, supports or protects. Commonly a wretch who supports with insolence, and is paid with flattery.

PENSION. An allowance made to any one without an equivalent. In England it is generally understood to mean pay given to a state hireling for treason to his country.

PRECIPICE. A headlong steep; a fall perpendicular without gradual declivity.

TINY. Little; small; puny. A burlesque word.

TOMBOY. A mean fellow; sometimes a wild coarse girl.

WHIST. A game at cards, requiring close attention and silence.

WIT.
    1. The powers of the mind; the mental faculties; the intellects. This is the original signification.
    2. Imagination; quickness of fancy.
    3. Sentiments produced by quickness of fancy.
    4. A man of fancy.
    5. A man of genius.
    6. Sense; judgment.
    7. In the plural. Sound mind; intellect not crazed.
    8. Contrivance; stratagem; power of expedients.

WITCRACKER. A joker; one who breaks a jest.

WITWORM. One that feeds on wit; a canker of wit.

WITTICISM. A mean attempt at wit.

(1755)

LICH. Salve magne parens: "Hail great parent" (Johnson was born in Lichfield). ***PATRON:*** See first excerpt from Boswell's *Life* (p. 685), and *The Vanity of Human Wishes*, line 160 and note (p. 591).

from *THE IDLER*

No. 20.   *Saturday, August 26, 1758*

There is no crime more infamous than the violation of truth. It is apparent that men can be social beings no longer than they believe each other. When speech is employed only as the vehicle of falsehood, every man must disunite himself from others, inhabit his own cave, and seek prey only for himself.

Yet the law of truth, thus sacred and necessary, is broken without punishment, without censure, in compliance with inveterate prejudice and prevailing passions. Men are willing to credit what they wish, and encourage rather those who gratify them with pleasure, than those that instruct them with fidelity.   5

For this reason every historian discovers his country; and it is impossible to read the different accounts of any great event, without a wish that truth had more power over   10
partiality.

Amidst the joy of my countrymen for the acquisition of Louisbourg, I could not forbear to consider how differently this revolution of American power is not only now mentioned by the contending nations, but will be represented by the writers of another century.   15

The English historian will imagine himself barely doing justice to English virtue, when he relates the capture of Louisbourg in the following manner:

"The English had hitherto seen, with great indignation, their attempts baffled and their force defied by an enemy, whom they considered themselves as entitled to conquer by the right of prescription, and whom many ages of hereditary superiority had taught   20
them to despise. Their fleets were more numerous, and their seamen braver, than those of France; yet they only floated useless on the ocean, and the French derided them from their ports. Misfortunes, as is usual, produced discontent, the people murmured at the ministers, and the ministers censured the commanders.

"In the summer of this year, the English began to find their success answerable to   25
their cause. A fleet and an army were sent to America to dislodge the enemies from the settlements which they had so perfidiously made, and so insolently maintained, and to repress that power which was growing more every day by the association of the Indians, with whom these degenerate Europeans intermarried, and whom they secured to their party by presents and promises.   30

"In the beginning of June the ships of war and vessels containing the land-forces appeared before Louisbourg, a place so secured by nature that art was almost superfluous, and yet fortified by art as if nature had left it open. The French boasted that it was impregnable, and spoke with scorn of all attempts that could be made against it. The garrison was numerous, the stores equal to the longest siege, and their engineers   35
and commanders high in reputation. The mouth of the harbour was so narrow, that three ships within might easily defend it against all attacks from the sea. The French had, with

---

IDLER NO. 20   **12. Louisbourg:** the French-built fortress on Isle Royale (Cape Breton Island), Nova Scotia, was an important fishing port, and also used as a pirate-base; New England colonists captured it in 1745, during the War of the Austrian Succession; it was returned to France in 1748 in the Treaty of Aix-la-Chapelle, but captured by British forces in 1758 — the event about which Johnson writes here.

that caution which cowards borrow from fear and attribute to policy, eluded our fleets, and sent into that port five great ships and six smaller, of which they sunk four in the mouth of the passage, having raised batteries and posted troops at all the places where they thought it possible to make a descent. The English, however, had more to dread from the roughness of the sea, than from the skill or bravery of the defendants. Some days passed before the surges, which rise very high round that island, would suffer them to land. At last their impatience could be restrained no longer; they got possession of the shore with little loss by the sea, and with less by the enemy. In a few days the artillery was landed, the batteries were raised, and the French had no other hope than to escape from one post to another. A shot from the batteries fired the powder in one of their largest ships, the flame spread to the two next, and all three were destroyed; the English admiral sent his boats against the two large ships yet remaining, took them without resistance, and terrified the garrison to an immediate capitulation."

Let us now oppose to this English narrative the relation which will be produced, about the same time, by the writer of the age of Louis XV.

"About this time the English admitted to the conduct of affairs a man who undertook to save from destruction that ferocious and turbulent people, who, from the mean insolence of wealthy traders, and the lawless confidence of successful robbers, were now sunk in despair and stupefied with horror. He called in the ships which had been dispersed over the ocean to guard their merchants, and sent a fleet and an army, in which almost the whole strength of England was comprised, to secure their possessions in America, which were endangered alike by the French arms and the French virtue. We had taken the English fortresses by force, and gained the Indian nations by humanity. The English, wherever they come, are sure to have the natives for their enemies; for the only motive of their settlements is avarice, and the only consequence of their success is oppression. In this war they acted like other barbarians; and, with a degree of outrageous cruelty, which the gentleness of our manners scarcely suffers us to conceive, offered rewards by open proclamation to those who should bring in the scalps of Indian women and children. A trader always makes war with the cruelty of a pirate.

"They had long looked with envy and with terror upon the influence which the French exerted over all the northern regions of America by the possession of Louisbourg, a place naturally strong, and new-fortified with some slight outworks. They hoped to surprise the garrison unprovided; but that sluggishness, which always defeats their malice, gave us time to send supplies, and to station ships for the defence of the harbour. They came before Louisbourg in June, and were for some time in doubt whether they should land. But the commanders, who had lately seen an admiral shot for not having done what he had not power to do, durst not leave the place unassaulted. An Englishman has no ardour for honour, nor zeal for duty; he neither values glory nor loves his king, but balances one danger with another, and will fight rather than be hanged. They therefore landed, but with great loss; their engineers had, in the last war with the French, learned something of the military science, and made their approaches with sufficient skill; but all their efforts had been without effect, had not a ball unfortunately fallen into the powder of one of our ships, which

---

52. of the age: i.e., about the age (Louis XV reigned 1715-74). **53ff. a man who undertook . . . :** William Pitt the elder, first Earl of Chatham, who began running things as secretary of state in 1756.

communicated the fire to the rest, and, by opening the passage of the harbour, obliged the　*80*
garrison to capitulate. Thus was Louisbourg lost, and our troops marched out with the
admiration of their enemies, who durst hardly think themselves masters of the place."

No. 22.　*Saturday, September 9, 1758*

Many naturalists are of opinion, that the animals which we commonly consider as mute
have the power of imparting their thoughts to one another. That they can express general
sensations is very certain; every being that can utter sounds has a different voice for
pleasure and for pain. The hound informs his fellows when he scents his game; the hen
calls her chickens to their food by her cluck, and drives them from danger by her scream.　*5*

Birds have the greatest variety of notes; they have, indeed, a variety which seems
almost sufficient to make a speech adequate to the purposes of a life which is regulated
by instinct, and can admit little change or improvement. To the cries of birds, curiosity
or superstition has been always attentive; many have studied the language of the
feathered tribes, and some have boasted that they understood it.　*10*

The most skilful or most confident interpreters of the sylvan dialogues have been
commonly found among the philosophers of the east, in a country where the calmness of
the air, and the mildness of the seasons, allow the student to pass a great part of the year in
groves and bowers. But what may be done in one place by peculiar opportunities, may be
performed in another by peculiar diligence. A shepherd of Bohemia has, by long abode in　*15*
the forests, enabled himself to understand the voice of birds; at least he relates with great
confidence a story, of which the credibility is left to be considered by the learned.

"As I was sitting," said he, "within a hollow rock, and watching my sheep that fed
in the valley, I heard two vultures interchangeably crying on the summit of the cliff.
Both voices were earnest and deliberate. My curiosity prevailed over my care of the　*20*
flock; I climbed slowly and silently from crag to crag, concealed among the shrubs, till I
found a cavity where I might sit and listen without suffering or giving disturbance."

"I soon perceived that my labour would be well repaid; for an old vulture was
sitting on a naked prominence, with her young about her, whom she was instructing in
the arts of a vulture's life, and preparing, by the last lecture, for their final dismission to　*25*
the mountains and the skies."

" 'My children,' said the old vulture, 'you will the less want my instructions, because
you have had my practice before your eyes; you have seen me snatch from the farm the
household fowl; you have seen me seize the leveret in the bush, and the kid in the pasture;
you know how to fix your talons, and how to balance your flight when you are laden with　*30*
your prey. But you remember the taste of more delicious food: I have often regaled you
with the flesh of man.' 'Tell us,' said the young vultures, 'where man may be found, and
how he may be known; his flesh is surely the natural food of a vulture. Why have you never
brought a man in your talons to the nest?' 'He is too bulky,' said the mother; 'when we find
a man, we can only tear away his flesh, and leave his bones upon the ground.' 'Since man is　*35*
so big,' said the young ones, 'how do you kill him? You are afraid of the wolf and of the
bear; by what power are vultures superior to man? Is man more defenceless than a sheep?'
'We have not the strength of man,' returned the mother, 'and I am sometimes in doubt

IDLER NO. 22　(Published in the *Universal Chronicle, or Weekly Gazette*, but not included in the first collected edition, where Johnson substituted another for it.) **14, 15. peculiar:** particular, special. **25. dismission:** dispatch, act of sending away (the *Dictionary*). **27. want:** need.

whether we have the subtlety; and the vultures would seldom feast upon his flesh, had not nature, that devoted him to our uses, infused into him a strange ferocity, which I have never observed in any other being that feeds upon the earth. Two herds of men will often meet and shake the earth with noise, and fill the air with fire. When you hear noise and see fire, with flashes along the ground, hasten to the place with your swiftest wing, for men are surely destroying one another; you will then find the ground smoking with blood, and covered with carcasses, of which many are dismembered and mangled for the convenience of the vulture.' 'But when men have killed their prey,' said the pupil, 'why do they not eat it? When the wolf has killed a sheep, he suffers not the vulture to touch it till he has satisfied himself. Is not man another kind of wolf?' 'Man,' said the mother, 'is the only beast who kills that which he does not devour, and this quality makes him so much a benefactor to our species.' 'If men kill our prey and lay it in our way,' said the young one, 'what need shall we have of labouring for ourselves?' 'Because man will, sometimes,' replied the mother, 'remain for a long time quiet in his den. The old vultures will tell you when you are to watch his motions. When you see men in great numbers moving close together, like a flock of storks, you may conclude that they are hunting, and that you will soon revel in human blood.' 'But still,' said the young one, 'I would gladly know the reason of this mutual slaughter. I could never kill what I could not eat.' 'My child,' said the mother, 'this is a question which I cannot answer, though I am reckoned the most subtle bird of the mountain. When I was young, I used frequently to visit the aerie of an old vulture, who dwelt upon the Carpathian rocks; he had made many observations; he knew the places that afforded prey round his habitation, as far in every direction as the strongest wing can fly between the rising and setting of the summer sun; he had fed year after year on the entrails of men. His opinion was, that men had only the appearance of animal life, being really vegetables with a power of motion; and that as the boughs of an oak are dashed together by the storm, that swine may fatten upon the fallen acorns, so men are by some unaccountable power driven one against another, till they lose their motion, that vultures may be fed. Others think they have observed something of contrivance and policy among these mischievous beings; and those that hover more closely round them pretend that there is, in every herd, one that gives directions to the rest, and seems to be more eminently delighted with a wide carnage. What it is that entitles him to such preeminence we know not; he is seldom the biggest or the swiftest, but he shows by his eagerness and diligence that he is, more than any of the others, a friend to the vultures.' "

from *THE LIVES OF THE POETS*

from *Cowley*

. . . .

Cowley, like other poets who have written with narrow views, and, instead of tracing intellectual pleasure to its natural sources in the mind of man, paid their court to temporary prejudices, has been at one time too much praised, and too much neglected at another.

COWLEY See Cowley's poems (pp. 395-97). See also *wit* in the Glossary, Johnson's definition of *WIT* above (p. 601), and Addison's discussion of wit in the *Spectator* (p. 490).

Wit, like all other things subject by their nature to the choice of man, has its   *5*
changes and fashions, and at different times takes different forms. About the beginning
of the seventeenth century appeared a race of writers that may be termed the
metaphysical poets; of whom, in a criticism on the works of Cowley, it is not improper
to give some account. The metaphysical poets were men of learning, and to show their
learning was their whole endeavour; but, unluckily resolving to show it in rhyme,   *10*
instead of writing poetry, they only wrote verses, and very often such verses as stood
the trial of the finger better than of the ear; for the modulation was so imperfect, that
they were only found to be verse by counting the syllables.

If the father of criticism has rightly denominated poetry . . . "an imitative art,"
these writers will, without great wrong, lose their right to the name of poets; for they   *15*
cannot be said to have imitated anything; they neither copied nature nor life; neither
painted the forms of matter, nor represented the operations of intellect.

Those, however, who deny them to be poets, allow them to be wits. Dryden
confesses of himself and his contemporaries that they fall below Donne in wit, but
maintains that they surpass him in poetry.   *20*

If wit be well described by Pope, as being "that which has been often thought,
but was never before so well expressed," they certainly never attained, nor even
sought it; for they endeavoured to be singular in their thoughts, and were careless of
their diction. But Pope's account of wit is undoubtedly erroneous: he depresses it
below its natural dignity, and reduces it from strength of thought to happiness of   *25*
language.

If, by a more noble and more adequate conception, that be considered as wit which
is at once natural and new, that which, though not obvious, is, upon its first production,
acknowledged to be just; if it be that which he that never found it wonders how he
missed; to wit of this kind the metaphysical poets have seldom risen. Their thoughts   *30*
are often new, but seldom natural; they are not obvious, but neither are they just; and
the reader, far from wondering that he missed them, wonders more frequently by what
perverseness of industry they were ever found.

But wit, abstracted from its effects upon the hearer, may be more rigorously and
philosophically considered as a kind of *discordia concors,* a combination of dissimilar   *35*
images, or discovery of occult resemblances in things apparently unlike. Of wit thus
defined, they have more than enough. The most heterogeneous ideas are yoked by
violence together; nature and art are ransacked for illustrations, comparisons, and
allusions; their learning instructs, and their subtlety surprises; but the reader commonly
thinks his improvement dearly bought, and, though he sometimes admires, is seldom   *40*
pleased.

. . . .

(1777)

14: Aristotle, in *Poetics*. **21-22:** In *An Essay on Criticism*: "True wit is Nature to advantage dressed, / What oft was thought, but ne'er so well
expressed" (297-98); in a note Pope refers the reader to Quintilian, VIII, iii, 71, which advises the orator to follow nature and life. **35.** *discordia
concors*: reversing Horace's *concordia discors*, "harmonious discord."

from *Milton*

. . . .

One of the poems on which much praise has been bestowed is *Lycidas,* of which the diction is harsh, the rhymes uncertain, and the numbers unpleasing. What beauty there is, we must therefore seek in the sentiments and images. It is not to be considered as the effusion of real passion, for passion runs not after remote allusions and obscure opinions. Passion plucks no berries from the myrtle and ivy, nor calls upon Arethuse and Mincius, nor tells of "rough   *5* satyrs" and "fauns with cloven heel." Where there is leisure for fiction there is little grief.

In this poem there is no nature, for there is no truth; there is no art, for there is nothing new. Its form is that of a pastoral, easy, vulgar, and therefore disgusting: whatever images it can supply are long ago exhausted, and its inherent improbability always forces dissatisfaction on the mind. When Cowley tells of Hervey that they studied   *10* together, it is easy to suppose how much he must miss the companion of his labours and the partner of his discoveries; but what image of tenderness can be excited by these lines!

> We drove afield, and both together heard
> What time the grey fly winds her sultry horn,
> Battening our flocks with the fresh dews of night.   *15*

We know that they never drove afield, and that they had no flocks to batten; and though it be allowed that the representation may be allegorical, the true meaning is so uncertain and remote that it is never sought, because it cannot be known when it is found.

Among the flocks, and copses, and flowers, appear the heathen deities: Jove and Phoebus, Neptune and Aeolus, with a long train of mythological imagery, such as a   *20* college easily supplies. Nothing can less display knowledge, or less exercise invention, than to tell how a shepherd has lost his companion, and must now feed his flocks alone, without any judge of his skill in piping; and how one god asks another god what is become of Lycidas, and how neither god can tell. He who thus grieves will excite no sympathy; he who thus praises will confer no honour.   *25*

This poem has yet a grosser fault. With these trifling fictions are mingled the most awful and sacred truths, such as ought never to be polluted with such irreverent combinations. The shepherd likewise is now a feeder of sheep, and afterwards an ecclesiastical pastor, a superintendent of a Christian flock. Such equivocations are always unskilful; but here they are indecent, and at least approach to impiety, of which,   *30* however, I believe the writer not to have been conscious.

Such is the power of reputation justly acquired, that its blaze drives away the eye from nice examination. Surely no man could have fancied that he read *Lycidas* with pleasure, had he not known its author.

. . . .

(1779)

MILTON   See *Lycidas* (p. 315). **2. numbers:** metrical feet, versification. **8** (and *passim*): Johnson had no patience with conventional forms and techniques, such as those of pastoral; **disgusting:** causing strong distaste. **10:** in "On the Death of Mr. William Hervey." **33. nice:** accurate in judgment to minute exactness; scrupulously and minutely cautious (the *Dictionary*).

WILLIAM SHENSTONE
England, 1714-1763

from *ESSAYS ON MEN, MANNERS, AND THINGS*

from *On Writing and Books*

1. Fine writing is generally the effect of spontaneous thoughts and a laboured style.

2. Long sentences in a short composition are like large rooms in a little house.

3. The world may be divided into people that read, people that write, people that think, and fox-hunters.

5. Superficial writers, like the mole, often fancy themselves deep, when they are exceedingly near the surface.

8. The chief advantage that ancient writers can boast over modern ones seems owing to simplicity. Every noble truth and sentiment was expressed by the former in the natural manner, in word and phrase simple, perspicuous, and incapable of improvement. What then remained for later writers but affectation, witticism, and conceit?

10. The national opinion of a book or treatise is not always right . . . . Milton's *Paradise Lost* is one instance. I mean, the cold reception it met with at first.

28. I hate a style, as I do a garden, that is wholly flat and regular, that slides along like an eel, and never rises to what one can call an inequality.

60. A poet that fails in writing becomes often a morose critic. The weak and insipid white wine makes at length excellent vinegar.

from *Of Men and Manners*

5. The word *folly* is, perhaps, the prettiest word in the language. *Amusement* and *diversion* are good well-meaning words; but *pastime* is what never should be used but in a bad sense: it is vile to say such a thing is agreeable because it helps to pass the time away.

10. Jealousy is the fear or apprehension of superiority; envy, our uneasiness under it.

11. What some people term freedom is nothing else than a liberty of saying and doing disagreeable things. It is but carrying the notion a little higher, and it would require us to break and have a head broken reciprocally without offence.

14. Zealous men are ever displaying to you the strength of their belief, while judicious men are showing you the grounds of it.

ESSAYS ON MEN, MANNERS, AND THINGS   Some of Shenstone's poems were published during his lifetime, but this prose collection did not appear until *The Works in Verse and Prose* was published posthumously in 1764 by Robert Dodsley.   **ON WRITING AND BOOKS   1. Fine writing:** florid, overly ornate writing, sometimes called "purple prose" (from Horace's *purpureus pannus*, in *Ars Poetica*).

18. Men are sometimes accused of pride merely because their accusers would be proud themselves if they were in their places.

from *On Religion*

. . . . When misfortunes happen to such as dissent from us in matters of religion, we call them judgments; when to those of our own sect, we call them trials; when to persons neither way distinguished, we are content to impute them to the settled course of things.

(1764-69)

THOMAS GRAY
England, 1716-1771

SONNET ON THE DEATH OF MR. RICHARD WEST

In vain to me the smiling mornings shine,
And red'ning Phoebus lifts his golden fire:
The birds in vain their amorous descant join,
Or cheerful fields resume their green attire:
These ears, alas! for other notes repine,   5
A different object do these eyes require.
My lonely anguish melts no heart but mine;
And in my breast the imperfect joys expire.
Yet morning smiles the busy race to cheer,
And new-born pleasure brings to happier men: 10
The fields to all their wonted tribute bear;
To warm their little loves the birds complain.
I fruitless mourn to him that cannot hear,
And weep the more because I weep in vain.

(1742; 1775)

ODE ON THE DEATH OF A FAVOURITE CAT, DROWNED IN A TUB OF GOLD FISHES

'Twas on a lofty vase's side,
Where China's gayest art had dyed
  The azure flowers that blow;

Demurest of the tabby kind,
The pensive Selima reclined,   5
  Gazed on the lake below.

Her conscious tail her joy declared;
The fair round face, the snowy beard,
  The velvet of her paws,
Her coat that with the tortoise vies,   10
Her ears of jet, and emerald eyes,
  She saw; and purred applause.

Still had she gazed: but 'midst the tide
Two angel forms were seen to glide,
  The genii of the stream;   15
Their scaly armour's Tyrian hue
Through richest purple to the view
  Betrayed a golden gleam.

The hapless nymph with wonder saw:
A whisker first, and then a claw,   20
  With many an ardent wish,
She stretched in vain to reach the prize.
What female heart can gold despise?
  What cat's averse to fish?

Presumptuous maid! with looks intent   25
Again she stretched, again she bent,
  Nor knew the gulf between.

SONNET ON THE DEATH OF MR. RICHARD WEST Richard West (1716-1742), a friend of Gray's at Eton, son of the Chancellor of Ireland, and grandson of Bishop Burnet; he wrote "A Monody on the Death of Queen Caroline"; he died of tuberculosis. Wordsworth in his "Preface" criticizes this sonnet while using it to demonstrate the similarity of verse and prose (see p. 761). **2. Phoebus:** i.e., the sun, personified as Phoebus Apollo. **ODE ON THE DEATH OF A FAVOURITE CAT** The cat, Selima, belonged to Horace Walpole (1717-1797), another Eton friend, who asked Gray to write an elegy on her. **3. blow:** bloom. **15. genii:** guardian spirits. **16-17. Tyrian, purple:** anywhere from purple to blood-red (from a dye made from shellfish found near ancient Tyre).

(Malignant Fate sat by and smiled)
The slipp'ry verge her feet beguiled,
   She tumbled headlong in.   *30*

Eight times emerging from the flood
She mewed to every wat'ry god,
   Some speedy aid to send.
No dolphin came, no Nereid stirred:
Nor cruel Tom, nor Susan heard.   *35*
   A fav'rite has no friend!

From hence, ye beauties, undeceived,
Know, one false step is ne'er retrieved,
   And be with caution bold.
Not all that tempts your wand'ring eyes   *40*
And heedless hearts is lawful prize;
   Nor all that glisters, gold.

                (1748)

ELEGY WRITTEN IN A COUNTRY CHURCHYARD

The curfew tolls the knell of parting day,
The lowing herd wind slowly o'er the lea,
The ploughman homeward plods his weary way,
And leaves the world to darkness and to me.

Now fades the glimmering landscape on the sight,   *5*
And all the air a solemn stillness holds,
Save where the beetle wheels his droning flight,
And drowsy tinklings lull the distant folds;

Save that from yonder ivy-mantled tow'r
The moping owl does to the moon complain   *10*
Of such as, wand'ring near her secret bow'r,
Molest her ancient solitary reign.

Beneath those rugged elms, that yew-tree's shade,
Where heaves the turf in many a mould'ring heap,
Each in his narrow cell for ever laid,   *15*
The rude forefathers of the hamlet sleep.

The breezy call of incense-breathing Morn,
The swallow twitt'ring from the straw-built shed,

The cock's shrill clarion, or the echoing horn,
No more shall rouse them from their lowly bed.   *20*

For them no more the blazing hearth shall burn,
Or busy housewife ply her evening care;
No children run to lisp their sire's return,
Or climb his knees the envied kiss to share.

Oft did the harvest to their sickle yield,   *25*
Their furrow oft the stubborn glebe has broke;
How jocund did they drive their team afield!
How bowed the woods beneath their sturdy stroke!

Let not Ambition mock their useful toil,
Their homely joys and destiny obscure;   *30*
Nor Grandeur hear, with a disdainful smile,
The short and simple annals of the poor.

The boast of heraldry, the pomp of pow'r,
And all that beauty, all that wealth e'er gave,
Awaits alike th' inevitable hour.   *35*
The paths of glory lead but to the grave.

Nor you, ye Proud, impute to these the fault,
If Mem'ry o'er their tomb no trophies raise,
Where through the long-drawn aisle and fretted vault
The pealing anthem swells the note of praise.   *40*

Can storied urn or animated bust
Back to its mansion call the fleeting breath?
Can Honour's voice provoke the silent dust,
Or Flatt'ry soothe the dull cold ear of Death?

Perhaps in this neglected spot is laid   *45*
Some heart once pregnant with celestial fire;
Hands that the rod of empire might have swayed,
Or waked to ecstasy the living lyre.

But Knowledge to their eyes her ample page
Rich with the spoils of time did ne'er unroll;   *50*
Chill Penury repressed their noble rage,
And froze the genial current of the soul.

Full many a gem of purest ray serene
The dark unfathomed caves of ocean bear:
Full many a flower is born to blush unseen,   *55*
And waste its sweetness on the desert air.

---

34. dolphin: See note to Milton's *Lycidas*, 164 (p. 318); **Nereid:** sea nymph. **35:** Tom and Susan are servants. **42:** The closing line makes use of the familiar proverb, "All that glisters is not gold." Interestingly, the closing lines of an earlier poem by Gray, "Ode on a Distant Prospect of Eton College," have themselves become proverbial: " . . . where ignorance is bliss, / 'Tis folly to be wise" (he may have been consciously echoing the sentiment of Ecclesiastes 1:18). **ELEGY WRITTEN IN A COUNTRY CHURCHYARD 16. rude:** unpolished, uneducated. **19. horn:** i.e., hunting horn. **26. glebe:** soil, field. **38. trophies:** memorial sculptures, especially those depicting items won in battle. **39. fretted:** decorated with designs in relief, or fretwork. **41. storied:** i.e., inscribed with an epitaph; **animated:** lifelike. **43. provoke:** call forth, arouse. **48. lyre:** symbolizing poetry. **51. rage:** eager passion or desire, ardour, including poetic or prophetic enthusiasm and inspiration. **52. genial:** generative, creative. **53. serene:** clear, bright.

Some village-Hampden that with dauntless breast
The little tyrant of his fields withstood;
Some mute inglorious Milton here may rest,
Some Cromwell guiltless of his country's blood.   *60*

Th' applause of list'ning senates to command,
The threats of pain and ruin to despise,
To scatter plenty o'er a smiling land,
And read their hist'ry in a nation's eyes,

Their lot forbade: nor circumscribed alone   *65*
Their growing virtues, but their crimes confined;
Forbade to wade through slaughter to a throne,
And shut the gates of mercy on mankind,

The struggling pangs of conscious truth to hide,
To quench the blushes of ingenuous shame,   *70*
Or heap the shrine of Luxury and Pride
With incense kindled at the Muse's flame.

Far from the madding crowd's ignoble strife
Their sober wishes never learned to stray;
Along the cool sequestered vale of life   *75*
They kept the noiseless tenor of their way.

Yet ev'n these bones from insult to protect
Some frail memorial still erected nigh,
With uncouth rhymes and shapeless sculpture decked,
Implores the passing tribute of a sigh.   *80*

Their name, their years, spelt by th' unlettered muse,
The place of fame and elegy supply:
And many a holy text around she strews,
That teach the rustic moralist to die.

For who to dumb Forgetfulness a prey,   *85*
This pleasing anxious being e'er resigned,
Left the warm precincts of the cheerful day,
Nor cast one longing ling'ring look behind?

On some fond breast the parting soul relies,
Some pious drops the closing eye requires;   *90*
Ev'n from the tomb the voice of Nature cries,
Ev'n in our ashes live their wonted fires.

For thee who, mindful of th' unhonoured dead,
Dost in these lines their artless tale relate;
If chance, by lonely Contemplation led,   *95*
Some kindred spirit shall inquire thy fate,

Haply some hoary-headed swain may say,
"Oft have we seen him at the peep of dawn
Brushing with hasty steps the dews away
To meet the sun upon the upland lawn.   *100*

"There at the foot of yonder nodding beech
That wreathes its old fantastic roots so high,
His listless length at noontide would he stretch,
And pore upon the brook that babbles by.

"Hard by yon wood, now smiling as in scorn,   *105*
Mutt'ring his wayward fancies he would rove,
Now drooping, woeful wan, like one forlorn,
Or crazed with care, or crossed in hopeless love.

"One morn I missed him on the customed hill,
Along the heath and near his fav'rite tree;   *110*
Another came; nor yet beside the rill,
Nor up the lawn, nor at the wood was he;

"The next with dirges due in sad array
Slow through the church-way path we saw him borne.
Approach and read (for thou canst read) the lay,   *115*
Graved on the stone beneath yon aged thorn."

The Epitaph

Here rests his head upon the lap of Earth
A youth to Fortune and to Fame unknown.
Fair Science frowned not on his humble birth,
And Melancholy marked him for her own.   *120*

Large was his bounty, and his soul sincere,
Heav'n did a recompense as largely send:
He gave to Mis'ry all he had, a tear,
He gained from heav'n ('twas all he wished) a friend.

No farther seek his merits to disclose,   *125*
Or draw his frailties from their dread abode
(There they alike in trembling hope repose),
The bosom of his Father and his God.
            (1751)

---

57. Hampden: John Hampden (1594-1643), Oliver Cromwell's cousin, staunch opponent of the rule of Charles I, and hero of Parliament when Charles attempted to arrest him — one of the events leading up to the English Civil War. **59. Milton:** John Milton, the poet (see pp. 315ff.) **60:** Cromwell led the parliamentary forces to victory in the Civil War, and the king was beheaded. **70. ingenuous:** noble, generous, sincere. **119. Science:** learning, knowledge.

ELIZABETH CARTER
England, 1717-1806

from *THE RAMBLER*

No. 100.   Saturday, March 2, 1751

Omne vafer vitium ridenti Flaccus amico
Tangit, et admissus circum praecordia ludit.
Persius, 1.116-17.

Horace, with sly insinuating grace,
Laughed at his friend, and looked him in the face;
Would raise a blush where secret vice he found,
And tickle while he gently probed the wound.
With seeming innocence the crowd beguiled;
But made the desperate passes, when he smiled.
Dryden.

TO THE RAMBLER
SIR,
As very many well-disposed persons by the unavoidable necessity of their affairs, are so unfortunate as to be totally buried in the country, where they labour under the most deplorable ignorance of what is transacting among the polite part of mankind, I cannot help thinking that, as a public writer, you should take the case of these truly compassionable objects under your consideration.   5

These unhappy languishers in obscurity should be furnished with such accounts of the employments of people of the world, as may engage them in their several remote corners to a laudable imitation; or, at least so far inform and prepare them, that if by any joyful change of situation they should be suddenly transported into the gay scene, they may not gape, and wonder, and stare, and be utterly at a loss how to behave and make a   10
proper appearance in it.

It is inconceivable how much the welfare of all the country towns in the kingdom might be promoted, if you would use your charitable endeavours to raise in them a noble emulation of the manners and customs of higher life.

For this purpose you should give a very clear and ample description of the whole   15
set of polite acquirements; a complete history of forms, fashions, frolics, of routs, drums, hurricanes, balls, assemblies, ridottos, masquerades, auctions, plays, operas,

RAMBLER NO. 100   Samuel Johnson's *The Rambler* (see p. 594) ran from March 1750 to March 1752; of its 208 numbers, Johnson wrote all but five. Elizabeth Carter contributed numbers 44 and 100, both being attempts, the second at Catherine Talbot's urging, to inject a lighter note into the otherwise rather solemn periodical (for Talbot, see p. 620). **Epigraph. Persius:** Persius Flaccus (A.D. 34-62); **Horace:** Horatius Flaccus (65-8 B.C.) — best known as "Horace," though Persius's line refers to him as "Flaccus." Dryden translates and expands Persius's lines; the quotation here is slightly modified from lines 228-34 of his translation of the First Satire. **16-17. routs, drums, hurricanes:** large, crowded, noisy, even riotous fashionable assemblies or evening parties, often at private houses; **ridottos:** Italian-style public entertainments consisting of music and dancing.

puppet-shows, and bear-gardens; of all those delights which profitably engage the attention of the most sublime characters, and by which they have brought to such amazing perfection the whole art and mystery of passing day after day, week after week, and year after year, without the heavy assistance of any one thing that formal creatures are pleased to call useful and necessary.

In giving due instructions through what steps to attain this summit of human excellence, you may add such irresistible arguments in its favour, as must convince numbers, who in other instances do not seem to want natural understanding, of the unaccountable error of supposing they were sent into the world for any other purpose but to flutter, sport, and shine. For, after all, nothing can be clearer than that an everlasting round of diversion, and the more lively and hurrying the better, is the most important end of human life.

It is really prodigious, so much as the world is improved, that there should in these days be persons so ignorant and stupid as to think it necessary to mispend their time, and trouble their heads about any thing else than pursuing the present fancy; for what else is worth living for?

It is time enough surely to think of consequences when they come; and as for the antiquated notions of duty, they are not to be met with in any French novel, or any book one ever looks into, but derived almost wholly from the writings of authors who lived a vast many ages ago, and who, as they were totally without any idea of those accomplishments which now characterise people of distinction, have been for some time sinking apace into utter contempt. It does not appear that even their most zealous admirers, for some partisans of his own sort every writer will have, can pretend to say they were ever at one ridotto.

In the important article of diversions, the ceremonial of visits, the ecstatic delight of unfriendly intimacies and unmeaning civilities, they are absolutely silent. Blunt truth and downright honesty, plain clothes, staying at home, hard work, few words, and those unenlivened with censure or double meaning, are what they recommend as the ornaments and pleasures of life. Little oaths, polite dissimulation, tea-table scandal, delightful indolence, the glitter of finery, the triumph of precedence, the enchantments of flattery, they seem to have had no notion of, and I cannot but laugh to think what a figure they would have made in a drawing-room, and how frighted they would have looked at a gaming-table.

The noble zeal of patriotism, that disdains authority, and tramples on laws for sport, was absolutely the aversion of these tame wretches.

Indeed one cannot discover any one thing they pretend to teach people, but to be wise and good; acquirements infinitely below the consideration of persons of taste and spirit, who know how to spend their time to so much better purpose.

Among other admirable improvements, pray, Mr. Rambler, do not forget to enlarge on the very extensive benefit of playing at cards on Sundays, a practice of such infinite use, that we may modestly expect to see it prevail universally in all parts of this kingdom.

To persons of fashion, the advantage is obvious, because, as for some strange reason or other, which no fine gentleman or fine lady has yet been able to penetrate, there is neither play, nor masquerade, nor bottled conjurer, nor any other thing worth living for, to be had on a Sunday, if it were not for the charitable assistance of whist or bragg, the genteel part of mankind must, one day in seven, necessarily suffer a total extinction of being.   65

Nor are the persons of high rank the only gainers by so salutary a custom, which extends its good influence, in some degree, to the lower orders of people; but were it quite general, how much better and happier would the world be than it is even now!

'Tis hard upon poor creatures, be they ever so mean, to deny them those   70 enjoyments and liberties which are equally open for all. Yet if servants were taught to go to church on this day, spend some part of it in reading or receiving instruction in a family way, and the rest in mere friendly conversation, the poor wretches would infallibly take it into their heads, that they were obliged to be sober, modest, diligent, and faithful to their masters and mistresses.   75

Now surely no one of common prudence or humanity would wish their domestics infected with such strange and primitive notions, or laid under such unmerciful restraints. All which may, in a great measure, be prevented by the prevalence of the good-humoured fashion that I would have you recommend. For when the lower kind of people see their betters with a truly laudable spirit, insulting and flying in the face of   80 those rude, ill-bred dictators, piety and the laws, they are thereby excited and admonished, as far as actions can admonish and excite, and taught that they too have an equal right of setting them at defiance in such instances as their particular necessities and inclinations may require; and thus is the liberty of the whole human species mightily improved.   85

In short, Mr. Rambler, by a faithful representation of the numberless benefits of a modish life, you will have done your part in promoting what every body seems to confess the true purpose of human existence, perpetual dissipation.

By encouraging people to employ their whole attention on trifles, and make amusement their sole study, you will teach them how to avoid many very uneasy   90 reflections.

All the soft feelings of humanity, the sympathies of friendship, all natural temptations to the care of a family, and solicitude about the good or ill of others, with the whole train of domestic and social affections, which create such daily anxieties and embarrassments, will be happily stifled and suppressed in a round of perpetual delights;   95 and all serious thoughts, but particularly that of "hereafter," be banished out of the world; a most perplexing apprehension, but luckily a most groundless one too, as it is so very clear a case, that nobody ever dies.

I am, &c.
CHARIESSA.

---

62. bottled conjurer: bottle-conjurer — i.e., a juggler, or other practitioner of legerdemain. **64. bragg:** brag, a card game similar to poker. **Chariessa:** Greek for *graceful, beautiful*, of a woman; but also, of people in general, *graceful, elegant, accomplished*, even *having taste, educated*.

JAMES CAWTHORN
England, 1719-1761

from *OF TASTE: AN ESSAY*

Well — though our passions riot, fret, and rave,
Wild and capricious as the wind and wave,
One common folly, say whate'er we can,
Has fixed at last the mercury of man;
And rules, as sacred as his father's creed,   5
O'er ev'ry native of the Thames, and Tweed.

    Ask ye what pow'r it is that dares to claim
So vast an empire, and so wide a fame?
What God unshrined in all the ages past?
I'll tell you, friend! in one short word—'tis Taste;   10
Taste that, without or head, or ear, or heart,
One gift of nature, or one grace of art,
Ennobles riches, sanctifies expense,
And takes the place of spirit, worth, and sense.

       . . . .

    Time was, a wealthy Englishman would join   15
A rich plum-pudding to a fat sirloin;
Or bake a pasty, whose enormous wall
Took up almost the area of his hall:
But now, as art improves, and life refines,
The demon Taste attends him when he dines,   20
Serves on his board an elegant regale,
Where three stewed mushrooms flank a larded quail;
Where infant turkeys, half a month resigned
To the soft breathings of a southern wind,
And smothered in a rich ragout of snails,   25
Outstink a lenten supper at Versailles.
Is there a saint that would not laugh to see
The good man piddling with his fricassee;
Forced by the luxury of taste to drain
A flask of poison, which he calls champagne!   30
While he, poor idiot! though he dare not speak,
Pines all the while for porter and ox-cheek?

    Sure 'tis enough to starve for pomp and show,
To drink, and curse the clarets of Bordeaux:
Yet such our humour, such our skill to hit   35

Excess of folly through excess of wit,
We plant the garden, and we build the seat,
Just as absurdly as we drink and eat.
For is there ought that nature's hand has sown
To bloom and ripen in her hottest zone?   40
Is there a shrub which, ere its verdures blow,
Asks all the suns that beam upon the Po?
Is there a flowret whose vermilion hue
Can only catch its beauty in Peru?
Is there a portal, colonnade, or dome,   45
The pride of Naples, or the boast of Rome?
We raise it here, in storms of wind and hail,
On the bleak bosom of a sunless vale;
Careless alike of climate, soil, and place,
The cast of nature, and the smiles of grace.   50

    Hence all our stuccoed walls, mosaic floors,
Palladian windows, and Venetian doors,
Our Gothic fronts, whose Attic wings unfold
Fluted pilasters tipped with leaves of gold,
Our massy ceilings, graced with gay festoons,   55
The weeping marbles of our damp salons,
Lawns fringed with citrons, amaranthine bow'rs,
Expiring myrtles, and unop'ning flow'rs.
Hence the good Scotsman bids th' anana blow
In rocks of crystal, or in Alps of snow;   60
On Orcus' steep extends his wide arcade,
And kills his scanty sunshine in a shade.

    One might expect a sanctity of style,
August and manly in an holy pile,
And think an architect extremely odd   65
To build a playhouse for the church of God:
Yet half our churches, such the mode that reigns,
Are Roman theatres, or Grecian fanes;
Where broad arched windows to the eye convey
The keen diffusion of too strong a day;   70
Where, in the luxury of wanton pride,

OF TASTE   The complete poem contains 166 lines. **11. or . . . or . . . or:** either . . . or . . . or. **41. blow:** bloom. **50. cast:** bent, tendency. **53. Attic:** pertaining to ancient Attica, or Athens. **59. anana:** pineapple. **61. Orcus:** presumably referring to the Orkney Islands, by the Romans called the Orcades. **68. fanes:** temples.

Corinthian columns languish side by side,
Closed by an altar, exquisitely fine,
Loose and lascivious as a Cyprian shrine.

Of late, 'tis true, quite sick of Rome, and Greece,   *75*
We fetch our models from the wise Chinese:
European artists are too cool, and chaste,
For Mand'rin only is the man of taste;
Whose bolder genius, fondly wild to see
His grove a forest, and his pond a sea,   *80*
Breaks out — and, whimsically great, designs
Without the shackles or of rules, or lines:
Formed on his plans, our farms and seats begin
To match the boasted villas of Pekin.
On every hill a spire-crowned temple swells,   *85*
Hung round with serpents, and a fringe of bells:
Junks and balons along our waters sail,
With each a gilded cockboat at his tail;
Our choice exotics to the breeze exhale,
Within th' inclosure of a zigzag rail;   *90*
In Tartar huts our cows and horses lie,
Our hogs are fatted in an Indian sty,

On ev'ry shelf a joss divinely stares,
Nymphs laid on chintzes sprawl upon our chairs;
While o'er our cabinets Confucius nods,   *95*
'Midst porcelain elephants, and China gods.

Peace to all such — but you whose chaster fires
True greatness kindles, and true sense inspires,
Or ere you lay a stone, or plant a shade,
Bend the proud arch, or roll the broad cascade,   *100*
Ere all your wealth in mean profusion waste,
Examine nature with the eye of Taste:
Mark where she spreads the lawn, or pours the rill,
Falls in the vale, or breaks upon the hill;
Plan as she plans, and where her genius calls,   *105*
There sink your grottos, and there raise your walls.
Without the Taste, beneath whose magic wand
Truth and correctness guide the artist's hand,
Woods, lakes, and palaces are idle things,
The shame of nations, and the blush of kings.   *110*
Expense, and Vanbrugh, vanity, and show,
May build a Blenheim, but not make a Stowe.

. . . .

(1771)

Samuel Foote
England, 1720-1777

The Grand Panjandrum

So she went into the garden to cut a cabbage-leaf, to make an apple pie; and at the same time a great she-bear, coming up the street, pops its head into the shop. "What! No soap?" So he died, and she very imprudently married the barber; and there were present the Picninnies, and the Joblillies, and the Garyulies, and the Grand Panjandrum himself, with the little round button at top; and they all fell to playing the game of catch-as-catch-can, till the gunpowder ran out at the heels of their boots.

(1755)

---

74. Cyprian: i.e., for the worship of Aphrodite. **83. seats:** large houses. **87. balons:** (ballongs, balloons, balloens) large Siamese and Burmese vessels, e.g. highly decorated state barges, or a kind of brigantine propelled with oars. **88. cockboat:** small boat belonging to a ship. **93. joss:** image of a Chinese deity. **100. cascade:** usually a small waterfall, or one of a series of small waterfalls; but see Matthew Prior's lines: "Rivers diverted from their native course, / And bound with chains of artificial force, / From large cascades in pleasing tumult rolled, / Or rose through figured stone, or breathing gold" — *Solomon on the Vanity of the World*, II, 23-26 (1718). **111-12:** Sir John Vanbrugh (1664-1726), dramatist and architect, who with Nicholas Hawksmoor (1661-1736) designed the large and sumptuous Blenheim Palace, which was built partly at public expense and given by Queen Anne to the first Duke of Marlborough in honour of his military victories; for Stowe, see the note to line 70 of Pope's "Epistle IV" (p. 539). Cawthorn is in part imitating Pope's poem.   **The Grand Panjandrum**   This bit of nonsense, which exists in several slightly different versions, was dashed off by Foote as a test for the actor Charles Macklin (1699-1797), who had just bragged during a lecture that he could memorize any passage by reading through it once; report has it that Macklin, who was often feuding with Foote, professed to be so insulted by such rubbish that he refused to repeat it. The word *panjandrum* eventually entered the language.

GILBERT WHITE
England, 1720-1793

THE NATURALIST'S SUMMER-EVENING WALK

When day declining sheds a milder gleam,
What time the may-fly haunts the pool or stream;
When the still owl skims round the grassy mead,
What time the timorous hare limps forth to feed;
Then be the time to steal adown the vale,   *5*
And listen to the vagrant cuckoo's tale;
To hear the clamorous curlew call his mate,
Or the soft quail his tender pain relate;
To see the swallow sweep the dark'ning plain
Belated, to support her infant train;   *10*
To mark the swift in rapid giddy ring
Dash round the steeple, unsubdued of wing:
Amusive birds! — say where your hid retreat
When the frost rages and the tempests beat;
Whence your return, by such nice instinct led,   *15*
When spring, soft season, lifts her bloomy head?
Such baffled searches mock man's prying pride,
The God of Nature is your secret guide!
    While deep'ning shades obscure the face of day,
To yonder bench leaf-sheltered let us stray,   *20*
Till blended objects fail the swimming sight,
And all the fading landscape sinks in night;

To hear the drowsy dor come brushing by
With buzzing wing, or the shrill cricket cry;
To see the feeding bat glance through the wood;   *25*
To catch the distant falling of the flood;
While o'er the cliff th' awakened churn-owl hung
Through the still gloom protracts his chattering song;
While high in air, and poised upon his wings,
Unseen, the soft, enamoured woodlark sings: *30*
These, Nature's works, the curious mind employ,
Inspire a soothing melancholy joy:
As fancy warms, a pleasing kind of pain
Steals o'er the cheek, and thrills the creeping vein!
    Each rural sight, each sound, each smell, combine;   *35*
The tinkling sheep-bell, or the breath of kine;
The new-mown hay that scents the swelling breeze,
Or cottage-chimney smoking through the trees.
    The chilling night-dews fall: — away, retire;
For see, the glow-worm lights her amorous fire!   *40*
Thus, ere night's veil had half obscured the sky,
Th' impatient damsel hung her lamp on high:
True to the signal, by love's meteor led,
Leander hastened to his Hero's bed.

(c. 1769; 1789)

WILLIAM COLLINS
England, 1721-1759

ODE TO EVENING

If aught of oaten stop, or pastoral song,
May hope, chaste Eve, to soothe thy modest ear,
    Like thy own solemn springs,
    Thy springs and dying gales,

O nymph reserved, while now the bright-haired sun   *5*
Sits in yon western tent, whose cloudy skirts,
    With brede ethereal wove,
    O'erhang his wavy bed;

THE NATURALIST'S SUMMER-EVENING WALK   23. dor: a droning insect, especially any one of several species of beetle, such as the common black dung-beetle. **44:** The tragic love story of Hero and Leander was treated by Ovid in his *Heroides* and told in the 5th century by Musaeus of Alexandria, but it is perhaps best known in the version by Christopher Marlowe (and "completed" by George Chapman); to be with his beloved Hero, a priestess of Aphrodite, Leander nightly swam the Hellespont from Abydos to Sestos, where Hero hung a lantern in a tower to guide him, but when he drowned during a storm she also leaped into the sea and drowned herself.   **ODE TO EVENING   1. oaten stop:** the conventional pastoral reed pipe (cf. line 72 of Spenser's "Januarye" p. 149), the "stop" being one of the holes for controlling tone. **2. Eve:** personification of evening. **7. brede:** braiding, embroidery.

Now air is hushed, save where the weak-eyed bat
With short shrill shriek flits by on leathern wing,   *10*
  Or where the beetle winds
  His small but sullen horn,
As oft he rises midst the twilight path,
Against the pilgrim borne in heedless hum:
  Now teach me, maid composed,   *15*
  To breathe some softened strain,
Whose numbers, stealing through thy dark'ning vale,
May not unseemly with its stillness suit,
  As, musing slow, I hail
  Thy genial loved return!   *20*
For when thy folding-star arising shows
His paly circlet, at his warning lamp
  The fragrant Hours, and elves
  Who slept in flowers the day,
And many a nymph who wreathes her brows with sedge,
And sheds the fresh'ning dew, and, lovelier still,   *26*
  The pensive Pleasures sweet,
  Prepare thy shadowy car.
Then lead, calm vot'ress, where some sheety lake
Cheers the lone heath, or some time-hallowed pile,   *30*

Or upland fallows grey,
  Reflect its last cool gleam.
But when chill blust'ring winds, or driving rain,
Forbid my willing feet, be mine the hut,
  That from the mountain's side   *35*
  Views wilds, and swelling floods,
And hamlets brown, and dim-discovered spires,
And hears their simple bell, and marks o'er all
  Thy dewy fingers draw
  The gradual dusky veil.   *40*
While Spring shall pour his show'rs, as oft he wont,
And bathe thy breathing tresses, meekest Eve!
  While Summer loves to sport
  Beneath thy ling'ring light;
While sallow Autumn fills thy lap with leaves,   *45*
Or Winter, yelling through the troublous air,
  Affrights thy shrinking train,
  And rudely rends thy robes;
So long, sure-found beneath the sylvan shed,
Shall Fancy, Friendship, Science, rose-lipped Health   *50*
  Thy gentlest influence own,
  And love thy fav'rite name!

(1746)

MARK AKENSIDE
England, 1721-1770

HYMN TO SCIENCE

Science! thou fair effusive ray
From the great source of mental day,
  Free, generous, and refined!
Descend with all thy treasures fraught,
Illumine each bewildered thought,   *5*
  And bless my lab'ring mind.

But first with thy resistless light
Disperse those phantoms from my sight,
  Those mimic shades of thee:

The scholiast's learning, sophist's cant,   *10*
The visionary bigot's rant,
  The monk's philosophy.

Oh! let thy powerful charms impart
The patient head, the candid heart,
  Devoted to thy sway;   *15*
Which no weak passions e'er mislead,
Which still with dauntless steps proceed
  Where Reason points the way.

---

17. numbers: verses, rhythms. **20. genial:** cheering, inspiring joy and happiness, enlivening. **21. folding-star:** Hesperus, the evening star, whose rising signals the time for a shepherd to herd his sheep into the fold. **23. Hours:** the Horae (from the Greek for *time, season*), goddesses who preside over the seasons, but here personifying the different times of day and, like the personified Pleasures, and along with the elves and nymphs, serving as attendants on Eve, part of her "train" (47). **28. car:** chariot. **30. pile:** building. **36. floods:** streams, rivers. **42. breathing:** emitting odour, fragrant. **50. Science:** knowledge, learning.   **HYMN TO SCIENCE   Title. Science:** knowledge, learning.

Give me to learn each secret cause;
Let number's, figure's, motion's laws 20
   Revealed before me stand;
These to great Nature's scenes apply,
And round the globe, and through the sky,
   Disclose her working hand.

Next, to thy nobler search resigned, 25
The busy, restless, human mind
   Through ev'ry maze pursue;
Detect Perception where it lies,
Catch the ideas as they rise,
   And all their changes view. 30

Say from what simple springs began
The vast, ambitious thoughts of man,
   Which range beyond control,
Which seek Eternity to trace,
Dive through th' infinity of space, 35
   And strain to grasp THE WHOLE.

Her secret stores let Memory tell,
Bid Fancy quit her fairy cell,
   In all her colours dressed;
While, prompt her sallies to control, 40
Reason, the judge, recalls the soul
   To Truth's severest test.

Then launch through Being's wide extent;
Let the fair scale with just ascent
   And cautious steps be trod; 45
And from the dead, corporeal mass,
Through each progressive order pass
   To Instinct, Reason, GOD.

There, *Science!* veil thy daring eye;
Nor dive too deep, nor soar too high, 50
   In that divine abyss;
To Faith content thy beams to lend,
Her hopes t' assure, her steps befriend,
   And light her way to bliss.

Then downwards take thy flight again; 55
Mix with the policies of men,
   And social nature's ties;

The plan, the genius of each state,
Its interest and its pow'rs relate,
   Its fortunes and its rise. 60

Through private life pursue thy course,
Trace ev'ry action to its source,
   And means and motives weigh;
Put tempers, passions in the scale,
Mark what degrees in each prevail, 65
   And fix the doubtful sway.

That last, best effort of thy skill,
To form the life, and rule the will,
   Propitious pow'r! impart:
Teach me to cool my passion's fires, 70
Make me the judge of my desires,
   The master of my heart.

Raise me above the vulgar's breath,
Pursuit of fortune, fear of death,
   And all in life that's mean; 75
Still true to reason be my plan,
Still let my action speak the man,
   Through ev'ry various scene.

Hail! queen of manners, light of truth;
Hail! charm of age, and guide of youth; 80
   Sweet refuge of distress:
In bus'ness, thou! exact, polite;
Thou giv'st Retirement its delight,
   Prosperity its grace.

Of wealth, pow'r, freedom, thou! the cause; 85
Foundress of order, cities, laws,
   Of arts inventress, thou:
Without thee, what were humankind?
How vast their wants, their thoughts how blind!
   Their joys how mean! how few! 90

Sun of the soul! thy beams unveil:
Let others spread the daring sail
   On Fortune's faithless sea;
While undeluded, happier I
From the vain tumult timely fly, 95
   And sit in peace with thee.

(1739)

CATHERINE TALBOT
England, 1721-1770

from *THE RAMBLER*

No. 30. Saturday, June 30, 1750

——*Vultus ubi tuus*
Affulsit populo, gratior it dies,
Et soles melius nitent.
                    Horace, ODES, IV.5.6-8.

Whene'er thy countenance divine
    Th' attendant people cheers,
The genial suns more radiant shine,
    The day more glad appears.
                    Elphinston.

MR. RAMBLER,

There are few tasks more ungrateful, than for persons of modesty to speak their own praises. In some cases, however, this must be done for the general good, and a generous spirit will on such occasions assert its merit, and vindicate itself with becoming warmth.

My circumstances, sir, are very hard and peculiar. Could the world be brought to treat me as I deserve, it would be a public benefit. This makes me apply to you, that my 5 case being fairly stated in a paper so generally esteemed, I may suffer no longer from ignorant and childish prejudices.

My elder brother was a Jew. A very respectable person, but somewhat austere in his manner: highly and deservedly valued by his near relations and intimates, but utterly unfit for mixing in a larger society, or gaining a general acquaintance among mankind. 10 In a venerable old age he retired from the world, and I in the bloom of youth came into it, succeeding him in all his dignities, and formed, as I might reasonably flatter myself, to be the object of universal love and esteem. Joy and gladness were born with me; cheerfulness, good humour and benevolence always attended and endeared my infancy. That time is long past. So long, that idle imaginations are apt to fancy me wrinkled, old, 15 and disagreeable; but, unless my looking glass deceives me, I have not yet lost one charm, one beauty of my earliest years. However, thus far is too certain, I am to everybody just what they choose to think me, so that to very few I appear in my right shape; and though naturally I am the friend of human-kind, to few, very few comparatively, am I useful or agreeable. 20

This is the more grievous, as it is utterly impossible for me to avoid being in all sorts of places and companies; and I am therefore liable to meet with perpetual affronts and injuries. Though I have as natural an antipathy to cards and dice as some people

---

RAMBLER NO. 30 See the general note to Elizabeth Carter's *Rambler No. 100* (p. 612). **Epigraph:** The Roman poet Horace (65-8 B.C.) is appealing to Augustus, who has just spent three years (15-13 B.C.) in Gaul, to return to Rome. James Elphinstone (1721-1809) was a Scots translator (of Martial, Seneca, Bossuet, etc.), anthologist (of poems and letters), and commentator on educational and social matters.

have to a cat, many and many an assembly am I forced to endure; and though rest and composure are my peculiar joy, am worn out, and harrassed to death with journeys by men and women of quality, who never take one, but when I can be of the party. Some, on a contrary extreme, will never receive me but in bed, where they spend at least half of the time I have to stay with them; and others are so monstrously ill-bred as to take physic on purpose when they have reason to expect me. Those who keep upon terms of more politeness with me, are generally so cold and constrained in their behaviour, that I cannot but perceive myself an unwelcome guest; and even among persons deserving of esteem, and who certainly have a value for me, it is too evident that generally whenever I come I throw a dullness over the whole company, that I am entertained with a formal stiff civility, and that they are glad when I am fairly gone.

How bitter must this kind of reception be to one formed to inspire delight, admiration, and love! To one capable of answering and rewarding the greatest warmth and delicacy of sentiments!

I was bred up among a set of excellent people, who affectionately loved me, and treated me with the utmost honour and respect. It would be tedious to relate the variety of my adventures, and strange vicissitudes of my fortune in many different countries. Here in England there was a time when I lived according to my heart's desire. Whenever I appeared, public assemblies appointed for my reception were crowded with persons of quality and fashion, early dressed as for a court, to pay me their devoirs. Cheerful hospitality everywhere crowned my board, and I was looked upon in every country parish as a kind of social bond between the 'squire, the parson, and the tenants. The laborious poor everywhere blessed my appearance: they do so still, and keep their best clothes to do me honour; though as much as I delight in the honest country folks, they do now and then throw a pot of ale at my head, and sometimes an unlucky boy will drive his cricket-ball full in my face.

Even in these my best days there were persons who thought me too demure and grave. I must forsooth by all means be instructed by foreign masters, and taught to dance and play. This method of education was so contrary to my genius, formed for much nobler entertainments, that it did not succeed at all.

I fell next into the hands of a very different set. They were so excessively scandalized at the gaiety of my appearance, as not only to despoil me of the foreign fopperies, the paint and the patches that I had been tricked out with by my last misjudging tutors, but they robbed me of every innocent ornament I had from my infancy been used to gather in the fields and gardens; nay they blacked my face, and covered me all over with a habit of mourning, and that too very coarse and awkward. I was now obliged to spend my whole life in hearing sermons; nor permitted so much as to smile upon any occasion.

In this melancholy disguise I became a perfect bugbear to all children and young folks. Wherever I came there was a general hush, an immediate stop to all pleasantness of look or discourse; and not being permitted to talk with them in my own language at that time, they took such a disgust to me in those tedious hours of yawning, that having transmitted it to their children, I cannot now be heard, though 'tis long since I have recovered my natural form, and pleasing tone of voice. Would they but receive my visits

---

26. **quality:** high social position. 29. **physic:** medicine. 43. **devoirs:** compliments, respects. 56. **the paint and the patches:** cosmetics.

kindly, and listen to what I could tell them — let me say it without vanity — how charming a companion should I be! To everyone could I talk on the subjects most interesting and most pleasing. With the great and ambitious, I would discourse of honours and advancements, of distinctions to which the whole world should be witness, 70 of unenvied dignities and durable preferments. To the rich I would tell of inexhaustible treasures, and the sure method to attain them. I would teach them to put out their money on the best interest, and instruct the lovers of pleasure how to secure and improve it to the highest degree. The beauty should learn of me how to preserve an everlasting bloom. To the afflicted I would administer comfort, and relaxation to the busy. 75

As I dare promise myself you will attest the truth of all I have advanced, there is no doubt but many will be desirous of improving their acquaintance with me; and that I may not be thought too difficult, I will tell you, in short, how I wish to be received.

You must know I equally hate lazy idleness and hurry. I would everywhere be welcomed at a tolerably early hour with decent good humour and gratitude. I must be 80 attended in the great halls peculiarly appropriated to me with respect; but I do not insist upon finery: propriety of appearance and perfect neatness is all I require. I must at dinner be treated with a temperate, but a cheerful social meal; both the neighbours and the poor should be the better for me. Some time I must have tête-à-tête with my kind entertainers, and the rest of my visit should be spent in pleasant walks and airings 85 among sets of agreeable people, in such discourse as I shall naturally dictate, or in reading some few selected out of those numberless books that are dedicated to me, and go by my name. A name that, alas! as the world stands at present, makes them oftener thrown aside than taken up. As those conversations and books should be both well chosen, to give some advice on that head may possibly furnish you with a future paper, 90 and any thing you shall offer on my behalf will be of great service to,

Good Mr. Rambler, Your faithful friend and servant,
SUNDAY.

MARY LEAPOR
England, 1722-1746

AN ESSAY ON WOMAN

Woman — a pleasing but a short-lived flow'r,
Too soft for business, and too weak for pow'r:
A wife in bondage, or neglected maid;
Despised, if ugly; if she's fair — betrayed.
'Tis wealth alone inspires ev'ry grace,   5
And calls the raptures to her plenteous face.

What numbers for those charming features pine,
If blooming acres round her temples twine!
Her lip the strawberry, and her eyes more bright
Than sparkling Venus in a frosty night.   10
Pale lilies fade, and when the fair appears,
Snow turns a Negro and dissolves in tears.

AN ESSAY ON WOMAN The title probably alludes to Pope's *An Essay on Man* (see p. 541); Leapor strongly admired Pope's work. **5-8:** echoing the 1707 play *The Beaux' Stratagem*, by George Farquhar (1678-1707), where early in III.ii Aimwell says to Archer, speaking of Dorinda, daughter of Lady Bountiful: "O Archer, I read her thousands in her looks; she looked like Ceres in her harvest, corn, wine and oil, milk and honey,

And where the charmer treads her magic toe,
On English ground Arabian odours grow;
Till mighty Hymen lifts his sceptred rod, 15
And sinks her glories with a fatal nod;
Dissolves her triumphs, sweeps her charms away,
And turns the goddess to her native clay.

But, Artemisia, let your servant sing
What small advantage wealth and beauties bring. 20
Who would be wise, that knew Pamphilia's fate?
Or who be fair, and joined to Sylvia's mate?
Sylvia, whose cheeks are fresh as early day,
As ev'ning mild, and sweet as spicy May:
And yet that face her partial husband tires, 25
And those bright eyes, that all the world admires.
Pamphilia's wit who does not strive to shun,
Like death's infection or a dog-day's sun?
The damsels view her with malignant eyes:
The men are vexed to find a nymph so wise: 30
And wisdom only serves to make her know
The keen sensation of superior woe.
The secret whisper, and the list'ning ear,
The scornful eyebrow, and the hated sneer,
The giddy censures of her babbling kind, 35
With thousand ills that grate a gentle mind,
By her are tasted in the first degree,
Though overlooked by Simplicus, and me.
Does thirst of gold a virgin's heart inspire,
Instilled by nature, or a careful sire? 40
Then let her quit extravagance and play,
The brisk companion and expensive tea,
To feast with Cordia in her filthy sty
On stewed potatoes, or on mouldy pie;
Whose eager eyes stare ghastly at the poor, 45
And fright the beggars from her hated door;
In greasy clouts she wraps her smoky chin,
And holds that pride's a never-pardoned sin.

If this be wealth, no matter where it falls;
But save, ye Muses, save your Mira's walls: 50
Still give me pleasing indolence, and ease,
A fire to warm me, and a friend to please.

Since, whether sunk in avarice or pride,
A wanton virgin or a starving bride;

Or wond'ring crowds attend her charming tongue, 55
Or deemed an idiot, ever speaks the wrong:
Though nature armed us for the growing ill
With fraudful cunning, and a headstrong will;
Yet, with ten thousand follies to her charge,
Unhappy woman's but a slave at large. 60

(1751)

CICELY, JOAN, AND DEBORAH: AN ECLOGUE

'Twas when the sun had bid our fields adieu,
And thirsty flowers sip the rising dew,
That ruddy Joan (a sprightly Dame, I ween)
Walked forth to visit Cicely o' th' green.
All sadly dight the hapless maid she found 5
In sable night-cap, and in sorrows drowned,
With eyes cast downward, and dishevelled hair;
Till thus her neighbour greets the mourning fair:

JOAN:
Why how now, Cicely? — What's the matter now?
What a cold sweat hangs dropping on thy brow! 10
Thy eyes brim-full — why how thou look'st today!
Like verjuice sour, and as pale as whey!

CICELY:
For what I weep, Ah! Joan, didst thou but know,
Thou'dst pity (sure) not wonder at my woe.
Ah wretched maid! thus ever let me cry 15
From morn till night; then lay me down, and die.

JOAN:
Ah! tell me, Cicely — though to ask I dread;
Yet, pr'ythee, tell me: Is old Brindle dead?
(Since yester morn I have not heard her low)
If so — who would not weep for such a cow? 20

CICELY:
'Tis not for her I shed this scalding tear:
Ah! no — old Brindle is not half so dear!
I've lost — But who — for sobs I cannot tell;
And his last word was — Cicely, farewell.

gardens, groves and purling streams played on her plenteous face." Archer replies: "Her face! her pocket, you mean; the corn, wine and oil lies there. In short, she has ten thousand pound, that's the English on't." **19. Artemisia:** Leapor's name for her patroness, Bridget Freemantle (1698-1779), with perhaps a glance at the name of the goddess Artemis; *Mira* (50) is her name for herself; the other names are conventional or refer to character-types; the similar names *Papillia* and *Simplicius*, e.g., among many others, appear in Pope's *Epistle II, To a Lady: Of the Characters of Women*. Leapor's Pamphilia is also partly a self-portrait; the speaker in this poem, however, can "overlook" what the character cannot (as can simple Simplicus, though for a different reason). **41. play:** gambling at cards. **CICELY, JOAN, AND DEBORAH 4. green:** grassy area near a village or town — the "village green." **5. dight:** dressed. **8. fair:** i.e., fair one. **10. dropping:** i.e., in drops. **19. low:** moo.

JOAN:
O how I tremble! — pr'ythee, tell me who?   25
CICELY:
Young Colin Clumsey — He was known to you.
For ever curs'd be that same market-day,
When a vile Sergeant led my Youth astray!
Far from his home my Colin's doomed to die,
My lovely Colin with the rolling eye.   30
JOAN:
Yet bear thy sorrows with a patient mind:
They say the Duke is to his soldiers kind.
So may he thrive, and all rebellions quell,
As he shall use thy much-loved Colin well!
CICELY:
Ah! sooth me not — There's nothing left for me   35
But the clear fountain, and the willow tree.
Since Colin's fled, no more I turn the wheel:
There lies the spindle, and the useless reel.
JOAN:
Be patient, girl, and stop that falling tear,
For here comes Deb'rah with a quart of beer.   40
So, Neighbour, so; we've special news today,
Or else Dame Deb'rah would not look so gay.
DEBORAH:
We've killed two thousand of the rogues (d'ye mind?);
Egad, their gen'ral durst not look behind;
Though Gaffer Doubt-man (with the blinking eye)   45
Says 'tis but fifty — and that's pretty nigh.

JOAN:
Then let us drink — Come, Cicely, to thy Dear!
We'll have no whining nor no sniv'ling here.
Health to the Duke, and all that do him aid!
How Cicely drinks! — but Cicely is a maid.   50
DEBORAH:
'Tis a brave man, and has a lucky hand,
This Duke of what d'ye call it — Cumberland.
Heav'n bless this Duke, and all his train! say I.
Let's pledge thee, Cicely; for I'm deadly dry.
JOAN:
My husband lost his purse at Cheatham Fair.   55
Last night a beam broke down, and killed the mare.
These things are hard to such as thee and I:
But yet we'll drink, because the rebels fly.
DEBORAH:
This beer is good — Say, how d'ye like it? ho!
And shall I fetch the other pot, or no?   60
Hark, the men shout, and bonfires light the plain;
Then shall we sit, and lick our lips in vain?
JOAN:
Troth, Goody Deb'rah, troth, it is a crime
To drink so much — but only for the time.
Bring t'other quart, although there is no need: 65
But one draught more, and I have done indeed.

(1746; 1751)

CHRISTOPHER SMART
England, 1722-1771

from *JUBILATE AGNO*, V

"For I will consider my Cat Jeoffry"

For I will consider my Cat Jeoffry.
For he is the servant of the Living God duly and daily serving him.
For at the first glance of the glory of God in the East he worships in his way.
For is this done by wreathing his body seven times round with elegant quickness.

28: I.e., Colin was being impressed for military service. **32. Duke:** William Augustus, Duke of Cumberland (1721-1765; see line 52), best known for defeating the Jacobites at Culloden Moor, near Inverness, on 16 April 1746, ending the rebellion (begun in 1745) of Prince Charles Edward Stuart (1720-1788), "Bonnie Prince Charlie," "the Young Pretender" to the throne of his grandfather, James II, who had been deposed in 1688 (James's son, James Francis Edward Stuart, 1688-1766, was called "the Old Pretender," and raised a rebellion in 1715). **35. sooth:** soothe. **36. willow:** associated with mourning (e.g., to "wear the willow" for a lost sweetheart — and see Shakespeare's *Othello*, IV.iii). **37. wheel:** i.e., spinning wheel, with its spindle and reel, or spool. **43. d'ye mind:** i.e., Are you listening? Do you take note? **45. Gaffer:** name or title for an old man, especially a rustic. **63. Troth:** in truth, truly; **Goody:** common title or term of address for a woman of low social rank (from *Goodwife*).

For then he leaps up to catch the musk, which is the blessing of God upon his prayer.   *5*
For he rolls upon prank to work it in.
For having done duty and received blessing he begins to consider himself.
For this he performs in ten degrees.
For first he looks upon his fore-paws to see if they are clean.
For secondly he kicks up behind to clear away there.   *10*
For thirdly he works it upon stretch with the fore-paws extended.
For fourthly he sharpens his paws by wood.
For fifthly he washes himself.
For Sixthly he rolls upon wash.
For Seventhly he fleas himself, that he may not be interrupted upon the beat.   *15*
For Eighthly he rubs himself against a post.
For Ninthly he looks up for his instructions.
For Tenthly he goes in quest of food.
For having considered God and himself he will consider his neighbour.
For if he meets another cat he will kiss her in kindness.   *20*
For when he takes his prey he plays with it to give it chance.
For one mouse in seven escapes by his dallying.
For when his day's work is done his business more properly begins.
For he keeps the Lord's watch in the night against the adversary.
For he counteracts the powers of darkness by his electrical skin and glaring eyes.   *25*
For he counteracts the Devil, who is death, by brisking about the life.
For in his morning orisons he loves the sun and the sun loves him.
For he is of the tribe of Tiger.
For the Cherub Cat is a term of the Angel Tiger.
For he has the subtlety and hissing of a serpent, which in goodness he suppresses.   *30*
For he will not do destruction, if he is well-fed, neither will he spit without provocation.
For he purrs in thankfulness, when God tells him he's a good Cat.
For he is an instrument for the children to learn benevolence upon.
For every house is incompleat without him and a blessing is lacking in the spirit.
For the Lord commanded Moses concerning the cats at the departure of the Children
    of Israel from Egypt.   *35*
For every family had one cat at least in the bag.
For the English Cats are the best in Europe.
For he is the cleanest in the use of his fore-paws of any quadrupede.
For the dexterity of his defence is an instance of the love of God to him exceedingly.
For he is the quickest to his mark of any creature.   *40*
For he is tenacious of his point.

JUBILATE AGNO ("Rejoice in the Lamb")   Written during Smart's confinement in an asylum, this long work consists of some sections with all lines starting with *Let*, others with answering lines starting with *For*, evidently designed for antiphonal reading or singing, though the pattern is not consistent nor was the work ever completed. Smart referred to it as "my *Magnificat*." The best-known part celebrates his cat, his companion in confinement.   FOR I WILL CONSIDER MY CAT JEOFFRY   **5. musk:** probably some catnip-like material (and perhaps punning on Latin *musculus*, "little mouse"). **6. prank:** capricious, frolicsome movement of an animal such as a cat. **15. beat:** i.e., his regular rounds. **24. adversary:** the Devil. **35-36:** Smart sportively adds cats to the baggage the Israelites are said to have taken with them (see Exodus 11, 12).

For he is a mixture of gravity and waggery.
For he knows that God is his Saviour.
For there is nothing sweeter than his peace when at rest.
For there is nothing brisker than his life when in motion.   45
For he is of the Lord's poor and so indeed is he called by benevolence perpetually —
    Poor Jeoffry! poor Jeoffry! the rat has bit thy throat.
For I bless the name of the Lord Jesus that Jeoffry is better.
For the divine spirit comes about his body to sustain it in compleat cat.
For his tongue is exceeding pure so that it has in purity what it wants in musick.
For he is docile and can learn certain things.   50
For he can set up with gravity which is patience upon approbation.
For he can fetch and carry, which is patience in employment.
For he can jump over a stick which is patience upon proof positive.
For he can spraggle upon waggle at the word of command.
For he can jump from an eminence into his master's bosom.   55
For he can catch the cork and toss it again.
For he is hated by the hypocrite and miser.
For the former is affraid of detection.
For the latter refuses the charge.
For he camels his back to bear the first notion of business.   60
For he is good to think on, if a man would express himself neatly.
For he made a great figure in Egypt for his signal services.
For he killed the Ichneumon-rat very pernicious by land.
For his ears are so acute that they sting again.
For from this proceeds the passing quickness of his attention.   65
For by stroaking of him I have found out electricity.
For I perceived God's light about him both wax and fire.
For the Electrical fire is the spiritual substance, which God sends from heaven
    to sustain the bodies both of man and beast.
For God has blessed him in the variety of his movements.
For, though he cannot fly, he is an excellent clamberer.   70
For his motions upon the face of the earth are more than any other quadrupede.
For he can tread to all the measures upon the musick.
For he can swim for life.
For he can creep.

(1759-63; 1939)

---

63. Ichneumon-rat: the ichneumon, a weasel-like animal venerated and sometimes even domesticated by the ancient Egyptians because it ate rats and mice and supposedly destroyed crocodile-eggs — but also fond of poultry and their eggs (also called "Pharaoh's rat").

from *POETICAL TRANSLATION OF THE FABLES OF PHAEDRUS*

The Dog in the River

The churl that wants another's fare
Deserves at least to lose his share.
  As through the stream a Dog conveyed
A piece of meat, he spied his shade
In the clear mirror of the flood,   *5*

And thinking it was flesh and blood,
Snapped to deprive him of the treat: —
But mark the glutton's self-defeat,
Missed both another's and his own,
Both shade and substance, beef and bone.   *10*

(1765)

JOSEPH WARTON
England, 1722-1800

THE REVENGE OF AMERICA

When fierce Pizarro's legions flew
O'er ravaged fields of rich Peru,
Struck with his bleeding people's woes,
Old India's awful Genius rose.
He sat on Andes' topmost stone,   *5*
And heard a thousand nations groan;
For grief his feathery crown he tore,
To see huge Plata foam with gore;
He broke his arrows, stamped the ground,
To view his cities smoking round.   *10*
  "What woes," he cried, "hath lust of gold

O'er my poor country widely rolled;
Plunderers proceed! my bowels tear,
But ye shall meet destruction there;
From the deep-vaulted mine shall rise   *15*
Th' insatiate fiend, pale Avarice!
Whose steps shall trembling Justice fly,
Peace, Order, Law, and Amity!
I see all Europe's children cursed
With lucre's universal thirst: *20*
The rage that sweeps my sons away,
My baneful gold shall well repay."

(1755)

SIR JOSHUA REYNOLDS
England, 1723-1792

from *DISCOURSES*

THE SEVENTH DISCOURSE (abridged)

The Reality of a Standard of Taste, As Well As of Corporal Beauty — Beside This Immediate Truth, There Are Secondary Truths, Which Are Variable; Both Requiring the Attention of the Artist, in Proportion to Their Stability or Their Influence.

THE DOG IN THE RIVER Phaedrus (c.15 B.C.-c.A.D. 50) was a Roman fabulist. THE REVENGE OF AMERICA **8. huge Plata:** Río de la Plata. THE SEVENTH DISCOURSE was delivered as a lecture to the students of the Royal Academy, December 10, 1776.

GENTLEMEN:

It has been my uniform endeavour, since I first addressed you from this place, to impress you strongly with one ruling idea. I wish you to be persuaded, that success in your Art depends almost entirely on your own industry; but the industry which I principally recommended, is not the industry of the *hands,* but of the *mind.*

As our art is not a divine *gift,* so neither is it a *mechanical* trade. Its foundations are *5* laid in solid science; and practice, though essential to perfection, can never attain that to which it aims, unless it works under the direction of principle.

. . . .

Every man whose business is description, ought to be tolerably conversant with the poets, in some language or other, that he may imbibe a poetical spirit, and enlarge his stock of ideas. He ought to acquire an habit of comparing and digesting his notions. He *10* ought not to be wholly unacquainted with that part of philosophy which gives an insight into human nature, and relates to the manners, characters, passions, and affections. He ought to know *something* concerning the mind, as well as *a great deal* concerning the body of man.

For this purpose, it is not necessary that he should go into such a compass of *15* reading as must, by distracting his attention, disqualify him for the practical part of his profession, and make him sink the performer in the critic. Reading, if it can be made the favourite recreation of his leisure hours, will improve and enlarge his mind, without retarding his actual industry.

What such partial and desultory reading cannot afford, may be supplied by the *20* conversation of learned and ingenious men, which is the best of all substitutes for those who have not the means or opportunities of deep study. There are many such men in this age; and they will be pleased with communicating their ideas to artists, when they see them curious and docile, if they are treated with that respect and deference which is so justly their due. Into such society, young artists, if they make it the point of their *25* ambition, will, by degrees, be admitted. There, without formal teaching, they will insensibly come to feel and reason like those they live with, and find a rational and systematic taste imperceptibly formed in their minds, which they will know how to reduce to a standard, by applying general truth to their own purposes, better perhaps than those to whom they owed the original sentiment. *30*

We include in the notes to this lecture some of the marginal comments William Blake wrote in a copy of the *Discourses;* these comments provide a kind of running argument between one painter and theoretician and a poet and painter of the succeeding generation. The expressions of different opinions help illustrate the changing sensibilities during the latter part of the eighteenth century; for other such expressions, see some of the excerpts from Wordsworth's Preface to *Lyrical Ballads* (p. 759), see also Coleridge's distinction between fancy and imagination, at the end of Chapter XIII of his *Biographia Literaria* (1817). Blake's general antipathy towards Reynolds and the *Discourses* is clear from the following note he wrote on the flyleaf: "I consider Reynolds's *Discourses* to the Royal Academy as the Simulations of the Hypocrite who smiles particularly when he means to Betray. His Praise of Rafael is like the Hysteric Smile of Revenge. His Softness and Candour the hidden trap, and the poisoned feast. He praises Michel Angelo for qualities which Michel Angelo abhorred: and He blames Rafael for the only qualities which Rafael Valued. Whether Reynolds knew what he was doing is nothing to me: the Mischief is the same whether a man does it Ignorantly or Knowingly. I always considered true Art and true Artists to be particularly Insulted and Degraded by the Reputation of these *Discourses,* as much as they were Degraded by the Reputation of Reynolds's Paintings, and that such Artists as Reynolds are at all times hired by the Satans for the Depression of Art. A Pretence of Art: To destroy Art." Of "The Seventh Discourse" in particular he writes as follows: "The purpose of the following discourse is to Prove that Taste and Genius are not of Heavenly Origin, and that all who have supposed that they Are so, Are to be considered as Weak-headed Fanatics. The obligations which Reynolds has laid on bad Artists of all classes will at all times make them his Admirers, but most especially for this discourse, in which it is proved that the stupid are born with Faculties Equal to other Men, Only they have not Cultivated them, because they have not thought it worth the trouble." (For Blake's poetry, see p. 721.)

Of these studies, and this conversation, the desire and legitimate offspring is a power of distinguishing right from wrong; which power, applied to works of art, is denominated *taste*. Let me then, without further introduction, enter upon an examination whether taste be so far beyond our reach as to be unattainable by care; or be so very vague and capricious that no care ought to be employed about it.

It has been the fate of arts to be enveloped in mysterious and incomprehensible language, as if it was thought necessary that even the terms should correspond to the idea entertained of the instability and uncertainty of the rules which they expressed.

To speak of genius and taste, as in any way connected with reason or common sense, would be, in the opinion of some towering talkers, to speak like a man who possessed neither; who had never felt that enthusiasm, or, to use their own inflated language, was never warmed by that Promethean fire, which animates the canvas and vivifies the marble.

If, in order to be intelligible, I appear to degrade the art by bringing her down from her visionary situation in the clouds, it is only to give her a more solid mansion upon the earth. It is necessary that at some time or other we should see things as they really are, and not impose on ourselves by that false magnitude with which objects appear when viewed indistinctly as through a mist.

We will allow a poet to express his meaning, when his meaning is not well known to himself, with a certain degree of obscurity, as it is one source of the sublime. But when, in plain prose, we gravely talk of courting the Muse in shady bowers; waiting the call and inspiration of Genius, finding out where he inhabits, and where he is to be invoked with the greatest success; of attending to times and seasons when the imagination shoots with the greatest vigour, whether at the summer solstice or the vernal equinox; sagaciously observing how much the wild freedom and liberty of imagination is cramped by attention to established rules; and how this same imagination begins to grow dim in advanced age, smothered and deadened by too much judgment; when we talk such language, or entertain such sentiments as these, we generally rest contented with mere words, or at best entertain notions not only groundless, but pernicious.

If all this means what it is very possible was originally intended only to be meant, that in order to cultivate an art, a man secludes himself from the commerce of the world, and retires into the country at particular seasons; or that at one time of the year his body is in better health, and consequently his mind fitter for the business of hard thinking than at another time; or that the mind may be fatigued and grow confused by long and unremitted application: this I can understand. I can likewise believe, that a man eminent when young for possessing poetical imagination, may, from having taken another road, so neglect its cultivation, as to show less of its powers in his later life. But I am persuaded, that scarce a poet is to be found, from Homer down to Dryden, who preserved a sound mind in a sound body, and continued practising his profession to the

---

42. **Promethean:** In Greek myth, Prometheus stole fire from the gods and gave it to men. 50. "Obscurity is Neither the Source of the Sublime nor of anything else" (Blake); **the sublime:** In the 18th century, "the sublime" was a key intellectual and aesthetic concept; it generally signified something that could be described as lofty, elevated, noble, dignified, grand, solemn, stately — something that awakens awe, adoration, veneration, and the like; see *sublime* in the Glossary. 51-59. "The Ancients, and the wisest of the Moderns, are of the opinion that Reynolds condemns and laughs at" (Blake). 68. **Dryden:** John Dryden (see p. 433).

very last, whose latter works are not as replete with the fire of imagination, as those 70
which were produced in his more youthful days.

To understand literally these metaphors, or ideas expressed in poetical language,
seems to be equally absurd as to conclude, that because painters sometimes represent
poets writing from the dictates of a little winged boy or genius, that this same genius did
really inform him in a whisper what he was to write; and that he is himself but a mere 75
machine, unconscious of the operations of his own mind.

Opinions generally received and floating in the world, whether true or false, we
naturally adopt and make our own; they may be considered as a kind of inheritance to
which we succeed and are tenants for life, and which we leave to our posterity very
nearly in the condition in which we received it; it not being much in any one man's 80
power either to impair or improve it.

The greatest part of these opinions, like current coin in its circulation, we are used
to take without weighing or examining; but by this inevitable inattention many
adulterated pieces are received, which, when we seriously estimate our wealth, we must
throw away. So the collector of popular opinions, when he embodies his knowledge, and 85
forms a system, must separate those which are true from those which are only plausible.
But it becomes more peculiarly a duty to the professors of art not to let any opinions
relating to *that* art pass unexamined. The caution and circumspection required in such
examination we shall presently have an opportunity of explaining.

Genius and taste, in their common acceptation, appear to be very nearly related; the 90
difference lies only in this, that genius has superadded to it a habit or power of
execution. Or we may say, that taste, when this power is added, changes its name, and is
called genius. They both, in the popular opinion, pretend to an entire exemption from
the restraint of rules. It is supposed that their powers are intuitive; that under the name
of genius great works are produced, and under the name of taste an exact judgment is 95
given, without our knowing why, and without our being under the least obligation to
reason, precept, or experience.

One can scarce state these opinions without exposing their absurdity; yet they are
constantly in the mouths of men, and particularly of artists. They who have thought
seriously on this subject, do not carry the point so far; yet I am persuaded, that even 100
among those few who may be called thinkers, the prevalent opinion allows less than it
ought to the powers of reason; and considers the principles of taste, which give all their
authority to the rules of art, as more fluctuating, and as having less solid foundations,
than we shall find, upon examination, they really have.

The common saying, that *tastes are not to be disputed,* owes its influence, and its 105
general reception, to the same error which leads us to imagine this faculty of too high an
original to submit to the authority of an earthly tribunal. It likewise corresponds with the

---

70: "As Replete, but not More Replete" (Blake). 72-76: "The Ancients did not mean to Impose [i.e., trick, deceive] when they affirmed their belief
in Vision and Revelation. Plato was in earnest. Milton was in earnest. They believed that God did visit Man really and Truly, and not as Reynolds
pretends. How very Anxious Reynolds is to Disprove and Contemn Spiritual Perceptions" (Blake). **74, genius:** tutelary spirit. **98-99:** "Who ever said
this? He states Absurdities in Company with Truths, and Calls both Absurd" (Blake). **100-04:** "The Artifice of the Epicurean Philosopher is to Call
all other Opinions Unsolid and Unsubstantial than those which are derived from Earth" (Blake). **105. *tastes . . . disputed*:** familiar in Latin as *De
gustibus non est disputandum.*

notions of those who consider it as a mere phantom of the imagination, so devoid of substance as to elude all criticism.

We often appear to differ in sentiments from each other, merely from the inac- *110* curacy of terms, as we are not obliged to speak always with critical exactness. Something of this too may arise from want of words in the language in which we speak, to express the more nice discrimination which a deep investigation discovers. A great deal, however, of this difference vanishes, when each opinion is tolerably explained and understood by constancy and precision in the use of terms. *115*

We apply the term *Taste* to that act of the mind by which we like or dislike, whatever be the subject. Our judgment upon an airy nothing, a fancy which has no foundation, is called by the same name which we give to our determination concerning those truths which refer to the most general and most unalterable principles of human nature: to the works which are only to be produced by the greatest efforts of the human *120* understanding. However inconvenient this may be, we are obliged to take words as we find them; all we can do is to distinguish the *things* to which they are applied.

We may let pass those things which are at once subjects of taste and sense, and which, having as much certainty as the senses themselves, give no occasion to enquiry or dispute. The natural appetite or taste of the human mind is for *Truth*; whether that *125* truth results from the real agreement or equality of original ideas among themselves; from the agreement of the representation of any object with the thing represented; or from the correspondence of the several parts of any arrangement with each other. It is the very same taste which relishes a demonstration in geometry, that is pleased with the resemblance of a picture to an original, and touched with the harmony of music. *130*

All these have unalterable and fixed foundations in nature, and are therefore equally investigated by reason, and known by study; some with more, some with less clearness, but all exactly in the same way. A picture that is unlike, is false. Disproportionate ordonnance of parts is not right, because it cannot be true; until it ceases to be a contradiction to assert, that the parts have no relation to the whole. Colouring is true *135* when it is naturally adapted to the eye, from brightness, from softness, from harmony, from resemblance; because these agree with their object, *Nature,* and therefore are true; as true as mathematical demonstration, but known to be true only to those who study these things.

But besides *real,* there is also *apparent* truth, or opinion, or prejudice. With regard *140* to real truth, when it is known, the taste which conforms to it is, and must be, uniform. With regard to the second sort of truth, which may be called truth on sufferance, or truth by courtesy, it is not fixed, but variable. However, whilst these opinions and prejudices, on which it is founded, continue, they operate as truth; and the Art, whose office it is to

---

110-15: "It is not in Terms that Reynolds and I disagree. Two Contrary Opinions can never by any Language be made alike. I say Taste and Genius are not Teachable nor Acquirable, but are both born with us. Reynolds says the Contrary" (Blake). **113. nice:** subtle, requiring refinement or delicacy, scrupulously exact. **121-22:** "This is False. The Fault is not in Words but in Things. Locke's Opinions on words and their Fallaciousness are hurtful opinions and Fallacious also" (Blake; he objects to John Locke's rationalism and empiricism, as expressed in *An Essay Concerning Human Understanding,* first published in 1690; Locke discusses language, words, in Book III). **123-30:** "Demonstration, Similitude, and Harmony are Objects of Reasoning Invention. Identity and Melody are Objects of Intuition" (Blake). **134. ordonnance:** arrangement. **137-38:** "God forbid that Truth should be Confined to Mathematical Demonstration. He who does not know Truth at sight is unworthy of Her Notice" (Blake).

please the mind, as well as instruct it, must direct itself according to *opinion, or it will* 145
not attain its end.

In proportion as these prejudices are known to be generally diffused, or long
received, the taste which conforms to them approaches nearer to certainty, and to a sort
of resemblance to real science, even where opinions are found to be no better than
prejudices. And since they deserve, on account of their duration and extent, to be 150
considered as really true, they become capable of no small degree of stability and
determination by their permanent and uniform nature.

As these prejudices become more narrow, more local, more transitory, this
secondary taste becomes more and more fantastical; recedes from real science; is less to
be approved by reason, and less followed in practice; though in no case perhaps to be 155
wholly neglected, where it does not stand, as it sometimes does, in direct defiance of the
most respectable opinions received amongst mankind.

Having laid down these positions, I shall proceed with less method, because less
will serve, to explain and apply them.

We will take it for granted, that reason is something invariable and fixed in the 160
nature of things; and without endeavouring to go back to an account of first principles,
which for ever will elude our search, we will conclude, that whatever goes under the
name of taste, which we can fairly bring under the dominion of reason, must be
considered as equally exempt from change. If, therefore, in the course of this inquiry,
we can show that there are rules for the conduct of the artist which are fixed and 165
invariable, it follows of course, that the art of the connoisseur, or, in other words, taste,
has likewise invariable principles.

Of the judgment which we make on the works of art, and the preference that we
give to one class of art over another, if a reason be demanded, the question is perhaps
evaded by answering, I judge from my taste; but it does not follow that a better answer 170
cannot be given, though, for common gazers, this may be sufficient. Every man is not
obliged to investigate the causes of his approbation or dislike.

The arts would lie open for ever to caprice and casualty, if those who are to judge
of their excellencies had no settled principles by which they are to regulate their
decisions, and the merit or defect of performances were to be determined by unguided 175
fancy. And indeed we may venture to assert, that whatever speculative knowledge is
necessary to the artist, is equally and indispensably necessary to the connoisseur.

The first idea that occurs in the consideration of what is fixed in art, or in taste, is
that presiding principle of which I have so frequently spoken in former discourses, the
general idea of Nature. The beginning, the middle, and the end of everything that is 180
valuable in taste, is comprised in the knowledge of what is truly nature; for whatever
notions are not conformable to those of nature, or universal opinion, must be considered
as more or less capricious.

147-50: "Here is a great deal to do to Prove that All Truth is prejudice, for all that is Valuable in Knowledge is Superior to Demonstrative Science, such as is Weighed and Measured" (Blake). **149. science:** knowledge and understanding of truth and facts; systematic knowledge. **153-57:** "And so he thinks he has proved that Genius and Inspiration are all a Hum" (Blake; *Hum*: imposition or hoax, humbug). **158-59:** "He calls the Above, proceeding with Method" (Blake). **160-61:** "Reason — or a ratio of all we have known — is not the same it shall be when we know More. He therefore takes a Falsehood for granted to set out with" (Blake). **162-64:** "Now this is supreme Fooling" (Blake). **173-76:** "He may as well say that if man does not lay down settled Principles the Sun will not rise in a Morning" (Blake).

My notion of nature comprehends not only the forms which nature produces, but also the nature and internal fabric and organization, as I may call it, of the human mind *185* and imagination. The terms beauty, or nature, which are general ideas, are but different modes of expressing the same thing, whether we apply these terms to statues, poetry, or pictures. Deformity is not nature, but an accidental deviation from her accustomed practice. This general idea therefore ought to be called Nature; and nothing else, correctly speaking, has a right to that name. But we are so far from speaking, in *190* common conversation, with any such accuracy, that, on the contrary, when we criticise Rembrandt and other Dutch painters, who introduced into their historical pictures exact representations of individual objects with all their imperfections, we say, though it is not in a good taste, yet it is nature.

This misapplication of terms must be very often perplexing to the young student. Is *195* not art, he may say, an imitation of nature? Must he not, therefore, who imitates her with the greatest fidelity, be the best artist? By this mode of reasoning Rembrandt has a higher place than Rafaelle. But a very little reflection will serve to show us that these particularities cannot be nature: for how can that be the nature of man, in which no two individuals are the same? *200*

It plainly appears, that as a work is conducted under the influence of general ideas, or partial, it is principally to be considered as the effect of a good or a bad taste.

As beauty, therefore, does not consist in taking what lies immediately before you, so neither, in our pursuit of taste, are those opinions which we first received and adopted, the best choice, or the most natural to the mind and imagination. In the infancy *205* of our knowledge we seize with greediness the good that is within our reach; it is by after-consideration, and in consequence of discipline, that we refuse the present for a greater good at a distance. The nobility or elevation of all arts, like the excellency of virtue itself, consists in adopting this enlarged and comprehensive idea; and all criticism built upon the more confined view of what is natural, may properly be called *shallow* *210* criticism, rather than false: its defect is, that the truth is not sufficiently extensive.

. . . .

A picture should please at first sight, and appear to invite the spectator's attention; if on the contrary the general effect offends the eye, a second view is not always sought, whatever more substantial and intrinsic merit it may possess.

Perhaps no apology ought to be received for offences committed against the vehicle *215* (whether it be the organ of seeing, or of hearing) by which our pleasures are conveyed to the mind. We must take care that the eye be not perplexed and distracted by a confusion of equal parts, or equal lights, or offended by an unharmonious mixture of colours, as we should guard against offending the ear by unharmonious sounds. We may venture to be more confident of the truth of this observation, since we find that *220* Shakespeare, on a parallel occasion, has made Hamlet recommend to the players a precept of the same kind, never to offend the ear by harsh sounds: *In the very torrent,*

184-86: "Here is a plain Confession that he Thinks Mind and Imagination not to be above the Mortal and Perishing Nature. Such is the End of Epicurean and Newtonian Philosophy. It is Atheism" (Blake). **192. Rembrandt:** Rembrandt Harmensz van Rijn (1606-1669). **198. Rafaelle:** Raffaello Sanzio (1483-1520), most often in English referred to as Raphael. **212:** "Please whom? Some Men Cannot see a Picture except in a Dark Corner" (Blake). **212-14:** In the omitted passage Reynolds criticizes the unfocussed "confusion" in some relatively naturalistic paintings of battle scenes and the like. **221ff.:** See Hamlet's speeches at the beginning of III.ii.

tempest, and whirlwind of your passion, says he, *you must acquire and beget a temperance that may give it smoothness.* And yet, at the same time, he very justly observes, *The end of playing, both at the first, and now, was and is, to hold, as it were,*   *225* *the mirror up to nature.* No one can deny, that violent passions will naturally emit harsh and disagreeable tones; yet this great poet and critic thought that this imitation of nature would cost too much, if purchased at the expense of disagreeable sensations, or, as he expresses it, of splitting the ear. The poet and actor, as well as the painter of genius, who is well acquainted with all the variety and sources of pleasure in the mind and   *230* imagination, has little regard or attention to common nature, or creeping after common sense. By overleaping those narrow bounds, he more effectually seizes the whole mind, and more powerfully accomplishes his purpose. This success is ignorantly imagined to proceed from inattention to all rules, and a defiance of reason and judgment; whereas it is in truth acting according to the best rules, and the justest reason.   *235*

He who thinks nature, in the narrow sense of the word, is alone to be followed, will produce but a scanty entertainment for the imagination: everything is to be done with which it is natural for the mind to be pleased, whether it proceeds from simplicity or variety, uniformity or irregularity; whether the scenes are familiar or exotic; rude and wild, or enriched and cultivated; for it is natural for the mind to be pleased with all these   *240* in their turn. In short, whatever pleases has in it what is analogous to the mind, and is therefore, in the highest and best sense of the word, natural.

. . . .

All arts have means within them of applying themselves with success both to the intellectual and sensitive part of our natures. It cannot be disputed, supposing both these means put in practice with equal abilities, to which we ought to give the preference; to   *245* him who represents the heroic arts and more dignified passions of man, or to him who, by the help of meretricious ornaments, however elegant and graceful, captivates the sensuality, as it may be called, of our taste.

. . . .

Well-turned periods in eloquence, or harmony of numbers in poetry, which are in those arts what colouring is in painting, however highly we may esteem them, can never   *250* be considered as of equal importance with the art of unfolding truths that are useful to mankind, and which make us better or wiser. Nor can those works which remind us of the poverty and meanness of our nature, be considered as of equal rank with what excites ideas of grandeur, or raises and dignifies humanity; or, in the words of a late poet, which makes the beholder *learn to venerate himself as a man.*   *255*

It is reason and good sense, therefore, which ranks and estimates every art, and every part of that art, according to its importance, from the painter of animated, down to inanimated nature. We will not allow a man, who shall prefer the inferior style, to say it is his taste; taste here has nothing, or at least ought to have nothing, to do with the question. He wants not taste, but sense, and soundness of judgment.   *260*

Indeed perfection in an inferior style may be reasonably preferred to mediocrity in the highest walks of art. A landskip of Claude Lorrain may be preferred to a history by

---

226-27: "Violent Passions emit the Real Good and Perfect Tones" (Blake). **255:** Reynolds quotes from *The Traveller* (1764), by Oliver Goldsmith. **262. landskip:** landscape; *Claude Lorrain* (or *Lorraine*) is what the English call Claude, or Claude Gellée (1600-1682), French landscape painter also called *Le Lorrain.*

Luca Giordano; but hence appears the necessity of the connoisseur's knowing in what consists the excellency of each class, in order to judge how near it approaches to perfection. *265*

. . . .

I shall now say something on that part of *taste,* which, as I have hinted to you before, does not belong so much to the external form of things, but is addressed to the mind, and depends on its original frame, or, to use the expression, the organization of the soul: I mean the imagination and passions. The principles of these are as invariable as the former, and are to be known and reasoned upon in the same manner, by an appeal *270* to common sense deciding upon the common feelings of mankind. This sense, and these feelings, appear to me of equal authority, and equally conclusive.

Now this implies a general uniformity and agreement in the minds of men. It would be else an idle and vain endeavour to establish rules of art; it would be pursuing a phantom to attempt to move affections with which we were entirely unacquainted. We *275* have no reason to suspect there is a greater difference between our minds than between our forms; of which, though there are no two alike, yet there is a general similitude that goes through the whole race of mankind; and those who have cultivated their taste can distinguish what is beautiful or deformed, or, in other words, what agrees with or deviates from the general idea of nature, in one case, as well as in the other. *280*

The internal fabric of our minds, as well as the external form of our bodies, being nearly uniform; it seems then to follow of course, that as the imagination is incapable of producing anything originally of itself, and can only vary and combine those ideas with which it is furnished by means of the senses, there will be necessarily an agreement in the imaginations as in the senses of men. There being this agreement, it follows, that in *285* all cases, in our lightest amusements, as well as in our most serious actions and engagements of life, we must regulate our affections of every kind by that of others. The well-disciplined mind acknowledges this authority, and submits its own opinion to the public voice.

. . . .

He, therefore, who is acquainted with the works which have pleased different ages *290* and different countries, and has formed his opinions on them, has more materials, and more means of knowing what is analogous to the mind of man, than he who is conversant only with the works of his own age or country. What has pleased, and continues to please, is likely to please again: hence are derived the rules of art, and on this immovable foundation they must ever stand. *295*

. . . .

We may therefore conclude, that the real substance, as it may be called, of what goes under the name of taste, is fixed and established in the nature of things; that there are certain and regular causes by which the imagination and passions of men are affected; and that the knowledge of these causes is acquired by a laborious and diligent investigation of nature, and by the same slow progress as wisdom or knowledge of *300* every kind, however instantaneous its operations may appear when thus acquired.

263: Luca Giordano (1634-1705), from Naples, was a prolific painter, mostly of frescoes; he was called "Luca fa presto" because of the speed with which he worked.

. . . .

To distinguish how much has solid foundation, we may have recourse to the same proof by which some hold that wit ought to be tried: whether it preserves itself when translated. That wit is false which can subsist only in one language; and that picture which pleases only one age or one nation, owes its reception to some local or accidental *305* association of ideas.

. . . .

To form this just taste is undoubtedly in your own power, but it is to reason and philosophy that you must have recourse; from them you must borrow the balance by which is to be weighed and estimated the value of every pretension that intrudes itself on your notice. *310*

The general objection which is made to the introduction of Philosophy into the regions of taste, is, that it checks and restrains the flights of the imagination, and gives that timidity which an overcarefulness not to err or act contrary to reason is likely to produce.

It is not so. Fear is neither reason nor philosophy. The true spirit of philosophy, by *315* giving knowledge, gives a manly confidence, and substitutes rational firmness in the place of vain presumption. A man of real taste is always a man of judgment in other respects; and those inventions which either disdain or shrink from reason, are generally, I fear, more like the dreams of a distempered brain than the exalted enthusiasm of a sound and true genius. In the midst of the highest flights of fancy or imagination, reason ought to preside *320* from first to last, though I admit her more powerful operation is upon reflection.

. . . .

FRANCES (MOORE) BROOKE
England/Canada, 1724-1789

from *THE OLD MAID*

No. 32. Saturday, June 19, 1756

> *But when good Saturn, banished from above,*
> *Was driven to hell, the world was under Jove.*
> — Ovid

MADAM,

I am an old politician, who have long been watchful over the public without hitherto finding any advantage from my schemes, either to the world or myself; but I think what I have now to propose cannot fail of being of great utility to both.

302-04: See e.g. Addison's discussion of false wit in *The Spectator* (p. 490). 317-21: "If this is True, it is a devilish Foolish Thing to be an Artist" (Blake). **THE OLD MAID NO. 32 Epigraph:** from Ovid's *Metamorphoses* (see lines 117-18 of Sandys's translation, p. 269). **1. politician:** a crafty intriguer.

You must know then, that being of opinion, as a man of the world, that some national religion is, for decency's sake, necessary in every country, I have made it my business for some years to inquire into the reason of the extreme unfashionableness of Christianity in England among polite people; and find it must be from one of these two causes, either that the virtues it enjoins are too hard for genteel people to practise, or that its being the religion of the whole nation has made it too common, and, if I may be allowed the expression, vulgarized it. *10*

Whilst infidelity was confined to high life, to be sure, it was just the thing one could have wished, as it was separating from the *canaille* and at the same time taking off those horrid restraints upon the pleasures of the *Beau-monde* which the rules of Christianity brought with them; but as the whole mob of this town have dared to follow the fashion, I think it must be as odious now as the national religion, and something new must be *15* introduced to divide us once more from the crowd. It is well known that free-thinking has descended from people of fashion to their servants, and from thence to the numerous and polite communities of hackney-coachmen, chairmen, porters, &c. and flourishes nowhere more than amongst the amiable fair ones who dispense rotten fruit in baskets and wheel-barrows through the streets of this metropolis. What I have therefore to *20* propose is that free-thinking be left to the mob, Christianity to trades-people and old maids, and that a new or revived religion be introduced entirely for the use of people of quality.

This being determined, and I think no reasonable person can be against it, it only remains to take a review of such modes of faith as have existed in other places, but have *25* here the claim of novelty, and to choose such a one as may be agreeable to the manners of modern people of fashion.

I at first thought of Mahometanism, as the prophet's paradise would, I am convinced, be very agreeable to modern taste; but then there are two or three insuperable objections. This paradise we must consider is only in reversion, and *30* whatever indulgencies are promised in another world, there are some articles of self-denial enjoined the true believers in this, which would never be received by polite people in this country. The prohibition of wine and gaming are things not to be borne, and we should certainly have a petition from the club at White's to oppose a faith which forbids the only two pleasures which true fine gentlemen have any relish for; besides the *35* slavery of praying five times a day must be intolerable to those who have a habit of never praying at all. I have also too great a respect for the ladies to introduce a religion which bears so very hard upon them and which is even so ill bred as to deny them souls.

Upon the most mature deliberation, Paganism is what I have fixed upon, as what will in all respects be most agreeable; and I therefore humbly propose that a bill be *40* brought in the next session of Parliament, for the establishment of the Heathen religion from Temple-bar to Upper-Grosvenor-Street; and because the country-folks are obstinate, and enemies to innovations, that all people of fashion be allowed a chapel and a priest in their own houses for the short time in the summer they may choose to mortify at their family seats. *45*

---

7. polite: modish, refined; the *beau monde* (line 13), who lived and met in the fashionable districts mentioned in line 42. **12.** *canaille:* the common people (lit. "pack of dogs"); the mob (line 14). **34. White's:** a fashionable London club (formerly a chocolate house). **44. mortify:** to become dead to the world and the flesh.

The benefits likely to accrue from this establishment are not possible to be told. In the first place, as in the present state of the nation frugality ought to be considered, it is a very sufficient reason for giving this religion the preference to any new one, that all, for whom it is intended, are already provided with gods, and many of them with temples; this would therefore be as good a way to make them of use as the tax proposed some time ago by the lively Mr. Town. *50*

Secondly, I think it might be made a means of providing for a set of men who are of all others the greatest objects of compassion: I mean the poets, who I would have preferred to be priests of these restored deities, they having, besides their distresses, this very reasonable plea, that these gods owing their very being to their tuneful *55* predecessors, the poets of old times, they have a kind of natural right to a large share, at least, of whatever emoluments may arise from their worship.

In the next place, as there are so many female deities, a handsome provision may be made for young ladies of small fortunes, whose case, since the lowering of interest and the prohibition of marrying for love, is almost as deplorable as that of the gentlemen *60* before mentioned, and who, at present, unless happy enough to be admitted as toad-eater to some woman of fashion, a situation of all others the most agreeable, have no resource but the town; which indeed, since some ladies of rank have, by taking up the trade, lowered the price, is hardly bread.

I intend to be chief-priest of Jupiter myself; have fixed upon two poetical *65* physicians, whose works are justly admired by the public, though they have been of very little benefit to themselves, to preside in the temple of Apollo; and intend you, Mrs. Singleton, for high-priestess of Diana, to which honor you have a double right by your chastity and your genius.

As to Venus, I don't doubt but half the women of quality in England will press to *70* serve in her temple; but as it will be wrong to show any partiality to birth in this case, Miss F——M—— will most certainly have the preference, unless Lady —— or the accomplished Miss —— can produce a larger list of conquests.

For Minerva's priestess, I am afraid we shall be in some distress; for though there are many martial women of fashion, who would become the spear and shield admirably, *75* yet as chastity, wisdom, and good huswifery are the attributes of this goddess, I much doubt being able to find half a dozen in this town duly qualified, and am inclined to believe we must inquire amongst the unpolished daughters of fox-hunters in Yorkshire for attendants on her temple.

The restoration of oracles too, a necessary consequence of Paganism, I think, may *80* be made a very pretty business, and as the ingenious Mrs. Drummond has so long

---

49. temples: an allusion to fashionable garden design. **51. Mr. Town:** Bonnell Thornton (1724-1768) and George Colman the elder (1732-1794), editors of *The Connoisseur, by Mr. Town, Critic and Censor-General*, a weekly paper that ran from 1754 to 1756; a letter to issue no. 113 (Thursday, March 25, 1756), from a fictitious correspondent who used the name "Moses Orthodox," suggested a national tax upon all statues of gods and goddesses in the houses and gardens of supposedly tasteful people. **53-54. I would have preferred:** i.e., whom I would like to be selected as. **61. toad-eater:** flattering companion, toady. **63. the town:** prostitution. **64. is hardly bread:** barely provides a livelihood. **65. Jupiter:** i.e., of politics (cf. line 92). **66. physicians:** healers. **67. Apollo:** the god of poetry and medicine. **67-68. Mrs. Singleton:** i.e., Frances Moore herself ("Miss F—M—" of line 72), who edited *The Old Maid* (using the pseudonym "Mary Singleton"), and who wrote many of the "letters" that were ostensibly submitted to it, including this one (despite the initials "F.S." at the end). **68. Diana:** goddess of chastity. **70. Venus:** goddess of beauty. **74. Minerva:** goddess of wisdom. **81. Mrs. Drummond:** Mary Drummond (d. 1777), a Quaker preacher who travelled throughout England and Scotland raising money (i.e., "subscriptions") for the Royal Infirmary at Edinburgh, which was being built by her brother; she preached in London in

possessed the gift of inspiration, I intend to build by subscription an oracle of Apollo upon Richmond-hill, where she shall perform the office of the Pythia, assisted by a choir of an hundred young ladies of unspotted reputations (if to be found), good voices, and a competent skill in music. *85*

The oracle of Jupiter shall be managed by the thundering Mr. R—m—ne; and the mysterious Mr. W—tf—d shall give out responses from a new cave of Trophonius, for which purpose I have been so fortunate as to secure the grotto of a lady of quality in Berkshire.

But these are far from being all the advantages which will attend my scheme. *90* Nothing can be more agreeable than the liberty everyone will have to choose a god for himself: the politicians will have their Jove, the topers their Bacchus, and gamesters their Mercury (the ancient god of thieves), and to save time to this industrious race, whose attendance in temples would be troublesome, I propose that at every polite coffee house a statue of their nimble-fingered god be fixed in the card-room, that they may be *95* able to pay their devotions without losing time from the important business of play.

It cannot fail of being agreeable to the ladies, as it will not only be productive of amusements, a hymn to Jupiter or Apollo being as good as an opera, but it will give them an admirable excuse for some little fashionable failings which, since a late act of parliament, it is very difficult for young ladies of rank, who keep good company, to *100* avoid. If a fair one happens,

Ere a wife to be a nurse,

she may without blushing charge the *faux-pas* to the account of some powerful deity,

For how can mortal maids contend with Jove?

If our *Belles* are not able to resist the torrent of handsome H—ss—ns or H—n—ans *105* now ready to break in upon them, or the more pressing address of our expected invaders, they may with great decency protest themselves invulnerable to mankind, but that there was no resisting the mighty Mars, who solicited them in the form of a German Col. or French Marquis.

I could enumerate many other advantages attending my scheme, but I am afraid I *110* have already exceeded the limits of your paper. If you print this, you shall hear farther from

Your very humble servant,

F.S.

1735. **83. Richmond-hill:** a hill in Surrey with a celebrated view of Windsor and prospect over the Thames Valley; many well-to-do individuals — including Joshua Reynolds in 1772 — had their homes built there; **Pythia:** the priestess of Apollo's oracle at Delphi. **86-87: Mr. R—m—ne, Mr. W—tf—d:** William Romaine (1714-1795) and George Whitefield (1714-1770); Whitefield (pronounced "Whitfield") was a leading preacher among Calvinist Methodists, and Romaine — a controversial evangelical Church of England clergyman, highly popular among the poor — espoused his doctrines. **87. Trophonius:** the builder of the first temple of Apollo at Delphi, later worshipped as an oracular god; according to legend, those who entered his cave at Lebadea, in Boeotia, were so awestruck that they never smiled again. **96. play:** gambling. **98. opera:** Frances Brooke later became a librettist. **99-100. act of parliament:** England (siding with Prussia and Hanover) was just beginning a war against France, Austria, Russia, Sweden, and others, hence the expectation of "invaders" (line 107); lasting until 1763, this conflict is now referred to as the Seven Years' War. **102. "ere . . . nurse":** from Matthew Prior's "Alma: or, the Progress of the Mind" (1718); **nurse:** i.e., a nursing mother. **105. H—ss—ns or H—n—ns:** likely "Hessians or Hanoverians."

EDMUND BURKE
Ireland/England, 1729-1797

from *REFLECTIONS ON THE REVOLUTION IN FRANCE*

And on the Proceedings in Certain Societies in London Relative to That Event in a Letter Intended to Have Been Sent to a Gentleman in Paris

. . . .

You will observe, that from Magna Charta to the Declaration of Right, it has been the uniform policy of our constitution to claim and assert our liberties, as an *entailed inheritance* derived to us from our forefathers, and to be transmitted to our posterity, as an estate specially belonging to the people of this kingdom, without any reference whatever to any other more general or prior right. By this means our constitution 5 preserves a unity in so great a diversity of its parts. We have an inheritable crown; an inheritable peerage; and a house of commons and a people inheriting privileges, franchises, and liberties, from a long line of ancestors.

This policy appears to me to be the result of profound reflection; or rather the happy effect of following nature, which is wisdom without reflection, and above it. A spirit of 10 innovation is generally the result of a selfish temper and confined views. People will not look forward to posterity, who never look backward to their ancestors. Besides, the people of England well know, that the idea of inheritance furnishes a sure principle of conservation and a sure principle of transmission, without at all excluding a principle of improvement. It leaves acquisition free; but it secures what it acquires. Whatever 15 advantages are obtained by a state proceeding on these maxims, are locked fast as in a sort of family settlement, grasped as in a kind of mortmain for ever. By a constitutional policy, working after the pattern of nature, we receive, we hold, we transmit our government and our privileges, in the same manner in which we enjoy and transmit our property and our lives. The institutions of policy, the goods of fortune, the gifts of 20 Providence, are handed down to us and from us, in the same course and order. Our political system is placed in a just correspondence and symmetry with the order of the world, and with the mode of existence decreed to a permanent body composed of transitory parts; wherein, by the disposition of a stupendous wisdom, moulding together the great mysterious incorporation of the human race, the whole at one time is never old, 25 or middle-aged, or young, but, in a condition of unchangeable constancy, moves on through the varied tenor of perpetual decay, fall, renovation, and progression. Thus, by

REFLECTIONS ON THE REVOLUTION IN FRANCE Burke writes in reaction to a November 1789 sermon by Dr. Richard Price (1723-1791), delivered to the "Revolution Society" and published as *A Discourse on the Love of Our Country*, celebrating the Glorious Revolution of 1688 and likening the French Revolution to it — and even hinting, Burke thinks, that something like the French experience might be suitable for England; purportedly writing to a particular Frenchman, Burke in effect addresses the French people as a whole. (For excerpts from Helen Maria Williams's letters from France on the same subjects, see p. 745; for direct responses to Burke, see Mary Wollstonecraft's *A Vindication of the Rights of Men*, p. 734, and Thomas Paine's *The Rights of Man*, p. 673.) **1. Magna Charta** (or Carta): the charter agreed to by King John and his barons at Runnymede in 1215, guaranteeing personal liberty and justice; **Declaration of Right** (or Rights): a document drawn up by parliament after the deposing of James II in 1688; William and Mary were proclaimed sovereigns after accepting it.

preserving the method of nature in the conduct of the state, in what we improve, we are never wholly new; in what we retain, we are never wholly obsolete. By adhering in this manner and on those principles to our forefathers, we are guided not by the superstition *30* of antiquarians, but by the spirit of philosophic analogy. In this choice of inheritance we have given to our frame of polity the image of a relation in blood; binding up the constitution of our country with our dearest domestic ties; adopting our fundamental laws into the bosom of our family affections; keeping inseparable, and cherishing with the warmth of all their combined and mutually reflected charities, our state, our hearths, *35* our sepulchres, and our altars.

Through the same plan of a conformity to nature in our artificial institutions, and by calling in the aid of her unerring and powerful instincts, to fortify the fallible and feeble contrivances of our reason, we have derived several other, and those no small benefits, from considering our liberties in the light of an inheritance. Always acting as if in the *40* presence of canonized forefathers, the spirit of freedom, leading in itself to misrule and excess, is tempered with an awful gravity. This idea of a liberal descent inspires us with a sense of habitual native dignity, which prevents that upstart insolence almost inevitably adhering to and disgracing those who are the first acquirers of any distinction. By this means our liberty becomes a noble freedom. It carries an imposing and majestic *45* aspect. It has a pedigree and illustrating ancestors. It has its bearings and its ensigns armorial. It has its gallery of portraits; its monumental inscriptions; its records, evidences, and titles. We procure reverence to our civil institutions on the principle upon which nature teaches us to revere individual men; on account of their age, and on account of those from whom they are descended. All your sophisters cannot produce *50* anything better adapted to preserve a rational and manly freedom than the course that we have pursued, who have chosen our nature rather than our speculations, our breasts rather than our inventions, for the great conservatories and magazines of our rights and privileges.

You might, if you pleased, have profited of our example, and have given to your *55* recovered freedom a correspondent dignity. Your privileges, though discontinued, were not lost to memory. Your constitution, it is true, whilst you were out of possession, suffered waste and dilapidation; but you possessed in some parts the walls, and in all the foundations, of a noble and venerable castle. You might have repaired those walls; you might have built on those old foundations. Your constitution was suspended before it *60* was perfected; but you had the elements of a constitution very nearly as good as could be wished. In your old states you possessed that variety of parts corresponding with the various descriptions of which your community was happily composed; you had all that combination, and all that opposition of interests, you had that action and counteraction which, in the natural and in the political world, from the reciprocal struggle of *65* discordant powers, draws out the harmony of the universe. These opposed and conflicting interests, which you considered as so great a blemish in your old and in our present constitution, interpose a salutary check to all precipitate resolutions; they render deliberation a matter not of choice, but of necessity; they make all change a subject of *compromise,* which naturally begets moderation; they produce *temperaments,* *70*

---

37. artificial: i.e., made by people, not "natural."

preventing the sore evil of harsh, crude, unqualified reformations; and rendering all the headlong exertions of arbitrary power, in the few or in the many, for ever impracticable. Through that diversity of members and interests, general liberty had as many securities as there were separate views in the several orders; whilst by pressing down the whole by the weight of a real monarchy, the separate parts would have been prevented from 75 warping and starting from their allotted places.

You had all these advantages in your ancient states; but you chose to act as if you had never been moulded into civil society, and had everything to begin anew. You began ill, because you began by despising everything that belonged to you. You set up your trade without a capital. If the last generations of your country appeared without 80 much lustre in your eyes, you might have passed them by, and derived your claims from a more early race of ancestors. Under a pious predilection for those ancestors, your imaginations would have realized in them a standard of virtue and wisdom, beyond the vulgar practice of the hour; and you would have risen with the example to whose imitation you aspired. Respecting your forefathers, you would have been taught to 85 respect yourselves. You would not have chosen to consider the French as a people of yesterday, as a nation of low-born servile wretches until the emancipating year of 1789. In order to furnish, at the expense of your honour, an excuse to your apologists here for several enormities of yours, you would not have been content to be represented as a gang of Maroon slaves, suddenly broke loose from the house of bondage, and therefore 90 to be pardoned for your abuse of the liberty to which you were not accustomed and ill fitted. Would it not, my worthy friend, have been wiser to have you thought, what I, for one, always thought you, a generous and gallant nation, long misled to your disadvantage by your high and romantic sentiments of fidelity, honour, and loyalty; that events had been unfavourable to you, but that you were not enslaved through any 95 illiberal or servile disposition; that in your most devoted submission, you were actuated by a principle of public spirit, and that it was your country you worshipped, in the person of your king? Had you made it to be understood, that in the delusion of this amiable error you had gone further than your wise ancestors; that you were resolved to resume your ancient privileges, whilst you preserved the spirit of your ancient and your 100 recent loyalty and honour; or if diffident of yourselves, and not clearly discerning the almost obliterated constitution of your ancestors, you had looked to your neighbours in this land, who had kept alive the ancient principles and models of the old common law of Europe meliorated and adapted to its present state — by following wise examples you would have given new examples of wisdom to the world. You would have rendered the 105 cause of liberty venerable in the eyes of every worthy mind in every nation. You would have shamed despotism from the earth, by showing that freedom was not only reconcilable, but, as when well disciplined it is, auxiliary to law. You would have had an unoppressive but a productive revenue. You would have had a flourishing commerce to feed it. You would have had a free constitution; a potent monarchy; a disciplined 110 army; a reformed and venerated clergy; a mitigated but spirited nobility, to lead your virtue, not to overlay it; you would have had a liberal order of commons, to emulate and

---

76. starting: moving suddenly, protruding. **90. Maroon:** See note to line 54 of Freneau's "To Sir Toby" (p. 712); the word *Maroon* derives from the Spanish *cimarron* ("wild, untamed"). **112. commons:** mass of the people, as opposed to the nobility.

to recruit that nobility; you would have had a protected, satisfied, laborious, and obedient people, taught to seek and to recognize the happiness that is to be found by virtue in all conditions; in which consists the true moral equality of mankind, and not in *115* that monstrous fiction, which, by inspiring false ideas and vain expectations into men destined to travel in the obscure walk of laborious life, serves only to aggravate and embitter that real inequality, which it never can remove; and which the order of civil life establishes as much for the benefit of those whom it must leave in an humble state, as those whom it is able to exalt to a condition more splendid, but not more happy. You *120* had a smooth and easy career of felicity and glory laid open to you, beyond anything recorded in the history of the world; but you have shown that difficulty is good for man.

Compute your gains: see what is got by those extravagant and presumptuous speculations which have taught your leaders to despise all their predecessors, and all their contemporaries, and even to despise themselves, until the moment in which they *125* became truly despicable. By following those false lights, France has bought undisguised calamities at a higher price than any nation has purchased the most unequivocal blessings. France has bought poverty by crime! France has not sacrificed her virtue to her interest; but she has abandoned her interest, that she might prostitute her virtue. All other nations have begun the fabric of a new government, or the reformation of an old, *130* by establishing originally, or by enforcing with greater exactness, some rites or other of religion. All other people have laid the foundations of civil freedom in severer manners, and a system of a more austere and masculine morality. France, when she let loose the reins of regal authority, doubled the licence of a ferocious dissoluteness in manners, and of an insolent irreligion in opinions and practices; and has extended through all ranks of *135* life, as if she were communicating some privilege, or laying open some secluded benefit, all the unhappy corruptions that usually were the disease of wealth and power. This is one of the new principles of equality in France.

France, by the perfidy of her leaders, has utterly disgraced the tone of lenient council in the cabinets of princes, and disarmed it of its most potent topics. She has *140* sanctified the dark, suspicious maxims of tyrannous distrust; and taught kings to tremble at (what will hereafter be called) the delusive plausibilities of moral politicians. Sovereigns will consider those who advise them to place an unlimited confidence in their people, as subverters of their thrones; as traitors who aim at their destruction, by leading their easy good-nature, under specious pretences, to admit combinations of bold *145* and faithless men into a participation of their power. This alone, if there were nothing else, is an irreparable calamity to you and to mankind. Remember that your parliament of Paris told your king, that in calling the states together, he had nothing to fear but the prodigal excess of their zeal in providing for the support of the throne. It is right that these men should hide their heads. It is right that they should bear their part in the ruin *150* which their counsel has brought on their sovereign and their country. Such sanguine declarations tend to lull authority asleep; to encourage it rashly to engage in perilous adventures of untried policy; to neglect those provisions, preparations, and precautions, which distinguish benevolence from imbecility; and without which no man can answer for the salutary effect of any abstract plan of government or of freedom. For want of *155*

---

113. recruit: renew, restore, supply replacements to. **148. states:** i.e., the States-General, the legislative assembly.

these, they have seen the medicine of the state corrupted into its poison. They have seen the French rebel against a mild and lawful monarch, with more fury, outrage, and insult, than ever any people has been known to rise against the most illegal usurper, or the most sanguinary tyrant. Their resistance was made to concession; their revolt was from protection; their blow was aimed at a hand holding out graces, favours, and immunities.   *160*

This was unnatural. The rest is in order. They have found their punishment in their success. Laws overturned; tribunals subverted; industry without vigour; commerce expiring; the revenue unpaid, yet the people impoverished; a church pillaged, and a state not relieved; civil and military anarchy made the constitution of the kingdom; every-thing human and divine sacrificed to the idol of public credit, and national bankruptcy   *165* the consequence; and to crown all, the paper securities of new, precarious, tottering power, the discredited paper securities of impoverished fraud, and beggared rapine, held out as a currency for the support of an empire, in lieu of the two great recognized species that represent the lasting conventional credit of mankind, which disappeared and hid themselves in the earth from whence they came, when the principle of property,   *170* whose creatures and representatives they are, was systematically subverted.

Were all these dreadful things necessary? Were they the inevitable results of the desperate struggle of determined patriots, compelled to wade through blood and tumult, to the quiet shore of a tranquil and prosperous liberty? No! nothing like it. The fresh ruins of France, which shock our feelings wherever we can turn our eyes, are not the   *175* devastation of civil war; they are the sad but instructive monuments of rash and ignorant counsel in time of profound peace. They are the display of inconsiderate and presumptuous, because unresisted and irresistible, authority. The persons who have thus squandered away the precious treasure of their crimes, the persons who have made this prodigal and wild waste of public evils (the last stake reserved for the ultimate ransom   *180* of the state), have met in their progress with little, or rather with no opposition at all. Their whole march was more like a triumphal procession than the progress of a war. Their pioneers have gone before them, and demolished and laid everything level at their feet. Not one drop of *their* blood have they shed in the cause of the country they have ruined. They have made no sacrifices to their projects of greater consequence than their   *185* shoe-buckles, whilst they were imprisoning their king, murdering their fellow citizens, and bathing in tears, and plunging in poverty and distress, thousands of worthy men and worthy families. Their cruelty has not even been the base result of fear. It has been the effect of their sense of perfect safety, in authorizing treasons, robberies, rapes, assassinations, slaughters, and burnings, throughout their harassed land. But the cause of   *190* all was plain from the beginning.

This unforced choice, this fond election of evil, would appear perfectly unac-countable, if we did not consider the composition of the National Assembly; I do not mean its formal constitution, which, as it now stands, is exceptionable enough, but the materials of which, in a great measure, it is composed, which is of ten thousand times   *195* greater consequence than all the formalities in the world. If we were to know nothing of this Assembly but by its title and function, no colours could paint to the imagination

---

168-69. two . . . species: i.e., gold and silver. 183. pioneers: from the French *pionier*, a foot-soldier who has gone ahead to clear the way. 186. shoe-buckles: i.e., silver shoe-buckles donated to support the cause.

anything more venerable. In that light the mind of an inquirer, subdued by such an awful image as that of the virtue and wisdom of a whole people collected into a focus, would pause and hesitate in condemning things even of the very worst aspect. Instead of *200* blameable, they would appear only mysterious. But no name, no power, no function, no artificial institution whatsoever, can make the men of whom any system of authority is composed any other than God, and nature, and education, and their habits of life have made them. Capacities beyond these the people have not to give. Virtue and wisdom may be the objects of their choice; but their choice confers neither the one nor the other *205* on those upon whom they lay their ordaining hands. They have not the engagement of nature, they have not the promise of revelation for any such powers.

. . . .

(1790)

OLIVER GOLDSMITH
Ireland/England, c.1730-1774

AN ELEGY ON THAT GLORY OF HER SEX, MRS. MARY BLAIZE

Good people all, with one accord,
    Lament for Madame Blaize,
Who never wanted a good word —
    From those who spoke her praise.

The needy seldom passed her door,   *5*
    And always found her kind;
She freely lent to all the poor —
    Who left a pledge behind.

She strove the neighbourhood to please,
    With manners wondrous winning,   *10*
And never followed wicked ways —
    Unless when she was sinning.

At church, in silks and satins new,
    With hoop of monstrous size,
She never slumbered in her pew —   *15*
    But when she shut her eyes.

Her love was sought, I do aver,
    By twenty beaux and more;
The king himself has followed her —
    When she has walked before.   *20*

But now, her wealth and finery fled,
    Her hangers-on cut short all;
The doctors found, when she was dead —
    Her last disorder mortal.

Let us lament, in sorrow sore,   *25*
    For Kent Street well may say,
That had she lived a twelve-month more —
    She had not died to-day.

(1759)

SONG: "WHEN LOVELY WOMAN STOOPS TO FOLLY"

When lovely woman stoops to folly,
    And finds too late that men betray,
What charm can soothe her melancholy,
    What art can wash her guilt away?

The only art her guilt to cover,   *5*
    To hide her shame from every eye,
To give repentance to her lover,
    And wring his bosom — is to die.

(1766)

AN ELEGY ON THAT GLORY OF HER SEX, MRS. MARY BLAIZE Mrs. Blaize was a pawnbroker. The poem imitates and partly translates a French poem called "Le Fameux La Galisse," from *Ménagiana* (1715). **WHEN LOVELY WOMAN STOOPS TO FOLLY** This brief song appears near the beginning of Chapter 24 of Goldsmith's novel, *The Vicar of Wakefield* (1766).

THE DESERTED VILLAGE

To Sir Joshua Reynolds

Dear Sir,

I can have no expectations in an address of this kind, either to add to your reputation, or to establish my own. You can gain nothing from my admiration, as I am ignorant of that art in which you are said to excel; and I may lose much by the severity of your judgment, as few have a juster taste in poetry than you. Setting interest therefore aside, to which I never paid much attention, I must be indulged at present in following my 5 affections. The only dedication I ever made was to my brother, because I loved him better than most other men. He is since dead. Permit me to inscribe this Poem to you.

How far you may be pleased with the versification and mere mechanical parts of this attempt, I do not pretend to enquire; but I know you will object (and indeed several of our best and wisest friends concur in the opinion) that the depopulation it deplores is no where 10 to be seen, and the disorders it laments are only to be found in the poet's own imagination. To this I can scarcely make any other answer than that I sincerely believe what I have written; that I have taken all possible pains, in my country excursions, for these four or five years past, to be certain of what I allege; and that all my views and enquiries have led me to believe those miseries real, which I here attempt to display. But this is not the place 15 to enter into an enquiry, whether the country be depopulating, or not; the discussion would take up much room, and I should prove myself, at best, an indifferent politician, to tire the reader with a long preface, when I want his unfatigued attention to a long poem.

In regretting the depopulation of the country, I inveigh against the increase of our luxuries; and here also I expect the shout of modern politicians against me. For twenty or 20 thirty years past, it has been the fashion to consider luxury as one of the greatest national advantages; and all the wisdom of antiquity in that particular, as erroneous. Still, however, I must remain a professed ancient on that head, and continue to think those luxuries prejudicial to states, by which so many vices are introduced, and so many kingdoms have been undone. Indeed so much has been poured out of late on the other side of the question, that, merely for 25 the sake of novelty and variety, one would sometimes wish to be in the right.

I am, Dear Sir,

Your sincere friend, and ardent admirer,

Oliver Goldsmith.

Sweet Auburn, loveliest village of the plain,
Where health and plenty cheered the labouring swain,
Where smiling spring its earliest visit paid,
And parting summer's lingering blooms delayed:
Dear lovely bowers of innocence and ease, 5
Seats of my youth, when every sport could please,
How often have I loitered o'er thy green,
Where humble happiness endeared each scene;

THE DESERTED VILLAGE   Dedicatory Letter: 6. only dedication: He dedicated his 1764 poem *The Traveller* to his brother, the Reverend Henry Goldsmith, who died in 1768. Goldsmith's Canadian grand-nephew and namesake produced a parallel poem called *The Rising Village* (1825), about the development of "English" communities in the New World. 1. Auburn: Although based on the Irish village of Lissoy, in Westmeath, where Goldsmith spent his childhood, the "Sweet Auburn" of the poem is intended to be recognized as a southern English village. 6. Seats: residences.

How often have I paused on every charm,
The sheltered cot, the cultivated farm,   *10*
The never-failing brook, the busy mill,
The decent church that topped the neighbouring hill,
The hawthorn bush, with seats beneath the shade,
For talking age and whispering lovers made.
How often have I blessed the coming day,   *15*
When toil remitting lent its turn to play,
And all the village train, from labour free,
Led up their sports beneath the spreading tree,
While many a pastime circled in the shade,
The young contending as the old surveyed;   *20*
And many a gambol frolicked o'er the ground,
And sleights of art and feats of strength went round.
And still as each repeated pleasure tired,
Succeeding sports the mirthful band inspired;
The dancing pair that simply sought renown,   *25*
By holding out to tire each other down;
The swain mistrustless of his smutted face,
While secret laughter tittered round the place;
The bashful virgin's sidelong looks of love,   *29*
The matron's glance that would those looks reprove.
These were thy charms, sweet village; sports like these,
With sweet succession, taught even toil to please;
These round thy bowers their cheerful influence shed,
These were thy charms — but all these charms are fled.

Sweet smiling village, loveliest of the lawn,   *35*
Thy sports are fled and all thy charms withdrawn;
Amidst thy bowers the tyrant's hand is seen,
And desolation saddens all thy green:
One only master grasps the whole domain,
And half a tillage stints thy smiling plain.   *40*
No more thy glassy brook reflects the day,
But, choked with sedges, works its weedy way.
Along thy glades, a solitary guest,
The hollow-sounding bittern guards its nest;
Amidst thy desert walks the lapwing flies,   *45*
And tires their echoes with unvaried cries.
Sunk are thy bowers in shapeless ruin all,
And the long grass o'ertops the mouldering wall;

And trembling, shrinking from the spoiler's hand,
Far, far away, thy children leave the land.   *50*
  Ill fares the land, to hastening ills a prey,
Where wealth accumulates and men decay:
Princes and lords may flourish or may fade;
A breath can make them, as a breath has made;
But a bold peasantry, their country's pride,   *55*
When once destroyed, can never be supplied.
  A time there was, ere England's griefs began,
When every rood of ground maintained its man;
For him light labour spread her wholesome store,
Just gave what life required, but gave no more: *60*
His best companions, innocence and health;
And his best riches, ignorance of wealth.
  But times are altered; trade's unfeeling train
Usurp the land and dispossess the swain;
Along the lawn, where scattered hamlets rose,   *65*
Unwieldy wealth and cumbrous pomp repose;
And every want to opulence allied,
And every pang that folly pays to pride.
These gentle hours that plenty bade to bloom,
Those calm desires that asked but little room,   *70*
Those healthful sports that graced the peaceful scene,
Lived in each look and brightened all the green;
These, far departing, seek a kinder shore,
And rural mirth and manners are no more.
  Sweet Auburn! parent of the blissful hour,   *75*
Thy glades forlorn confess the tyrant's power.
Here as I take my solitary rounds,
Amidst thy tangling walks and ruined grounds,
And, many a year elapsed, return to view
Where once the cottage stood, the hawthorn grew,   *80*
Remembrance wakes with all her busy train,
Swells at my breast and turns the past to pain.
  In all my wanderings round this world of care,
In all my griefs — and God has given my share —
I still had hopes my latest hours to crown,   *85*
Amidst these humble bowers to lay me down;
To husband out life's taper at the close
And keep the flame from wasting by repose.

---

10. cot: cottage. **12. decent:** suitable, becoming. **15. coming day:** i.e., a holiday. **35. lawn:** i.e., plain (see line 1), grassy region. **39ff.:** Here and elsewhere Goldsmith is referring to the "enclosure" of commons and other open land by individual landlords, whether for more efficient grazing and farming, or for other private uses (see lines 275ff.) — a process that continued from mediaeval times to the 19th century. One of the results Goldsmith focusses on here (see lines 341ff.) is also the subject of William Barnes's "Eclogue: Rusticus Emigrans" (see p. 891); Barnes deals explicitly with enclosure in poems called "The Common A-Took In." See also the note to Galt's "Canadian Boat Song" (p. 805) and Wollstonecraft's comment on enclosure, lines 81ff. of *Rights of Man* (p. 736).

I still had hopes, for pride attends us still,
Amidst the swains to show my book-learned skill, 90
Around my fire an evening group to draw,
And tell of all I felt and all I saw;
And, as an hare whom hounds and horns pursue,
Pants to the place from whence at first she flew,
I still had hopes, my long vexations past, 95
Here to return — and die at home at last.
　O blest retirement, friend to life's decline,
Retreats from care that never must be mine,
How happy he who crowns in shades like these
A youth of labour with an age of ease; 100
Who quits a world where strong temptations try,
And, since 'tis hard to combat, learns to fly.
For him no wretches, born to work and weep,
Explore the mine or tempt the dangerous deep;
No surly porter stands in guilty state 105
To spurn imploring famine from the gate;
But on he moves to meet his latter end,
Angels around befriending virtue's friend;
Bends to the grave with unperceived decay,
While resignation gently slopes the way; 110
And, all his prospects brightening to the last,
His heaven commences ere the world be past!
　Sweet was the sound, when oft at evening's close
Up yonder hill the village murmur rose;
There, as I passed with careless steps and slow, 115
The mingling notes came softened from below;
The swain responsive as the milkmaid sung,
The sober herd that lowed to meet their young;
The noisy geese that gabbled o'er the pool,
The playful children just let loose from school; 120
The watchdog's voice that bayed the whispering wind,
And the loud laugh that spoke the vacant mind;
These all in sweet confusion sought the shade,
And filled each pause the nightingale had made.
But now the sounds of population fail, 125
No cheerful murmurs fluctuate in the gale,
No busy steps the grassgrown foot-way tread,
For all the bloomy flush of life is fled.
All but yon widowed, solitary thing
That feebly bends beside the plashy spring; 130

She, wretched matron, forced, in age, for bread,
To strip the brook with mantling cresses spread,
To pick her wintry faggot from the thorn,
To seek her nightly shed and weep till morn;
She only left of all the harmless train, 135
The sad historian of the pensive plain.
　Near yonder copse, where once the garden smiled,
And still where many a garden flower grows wild;
There, where a few torn shrubs the place disclose,
The village preacher's modest mansion rose. 140
A man he was to all the country dear,
And passing rich with forty pounds a year;
Remote from towns he ran his godly race,
Nor e'er had changed, nor wished to change, his place;
Unpractised he to fawn, or seek for power, 145
By doctrines fashioned to the varying hour;
Far other aims his heart had learned to prize,
More skilled to raise the wretched than to rise.
His house was known to all the vagrant train,
He chid their wanderings, but relieved their pain; 150
The long-remembered beggar was his guest,
Whose beard descending swept his aged breast;
The ruined spendthrift, now no longer proud,
Claimed kindred there and had his claims allowed;
The broken soldier, kindly bade to stay, 155
Sat by his fire and talked the night away;
Wept o'er his wounds or tales of sorrow done,
Shouldered his crutch and showed how fields were won.
Pleased with his guests, the good man learned to glow,
And quite forgot their vices in their woe; 160
Careless their merits or their faults to scan,
His pity gave ere charity began.
　Thus to relieve the wretched was his pride,
And even his failings leaned to virtue's side;
But in his duty prompt at every call, 165
He watched and wept, he prayed and felt, for all.
And, as a bird each fond endearment tries
To tempt its new-fledged offspring to the skies,
He tried each art, reproved each dull delay,
Allured to brighter worlds, and led the way. 170
　Beside the bed where parting life was laid,
And sorrow, guilt, and pain by turns dismayed,

---

107. latter end: cf. Job 8:7. **122. spoke:** bespoke. **126. gale:** breeze. **137ff.:** In these lines Goldsmith probably had in mind his brother, who had recently died, and his father and uncle, who were also village preachers in Ireland. **140. mansion:** then meaning any dwelling-place, abode. **141. country:** region, immediate surroundings, neighbourhood.

The reverend champion stood. At his control,
Despair and anguish fled the struggling soul;
Comfort came down the trembling wretch to raise, *175*
And his last faltering accents whispered praise.
    At church, with meek and unaffected grace,
His looks adorned the venerable place;
Truth from his lips prevailed with double sway,
And fools, who came to scoff, remained to pray. *180*
The service past, around the pious man,
With steady zeal each honest rustic ran;
Even children followed with endearing wile,
And plucked his gown, to share the good man's smile.
His ready smile a parent's warmth expressed, *185*
Their welfare pleased him and their cares distressed;
To them his heart, his love, his griefs were given,
But all his serious thoughts had rest in heaven.
As some tall cliff that lifts its awful form *189*
Swells from the vale, and midway leaves the storm,
Though round its breast the rolling clouds are spread,
Eternal sunshine settles on its head.
    Beside yon straggling fence that skirts the way,
With blossomed furze unprofitably gay,
There, in his noisy mansion, skilled to rule, *195*
The village master taught his little school;
A man severe he was and stern to view;
I knew him well, and every truant knew;
Well had the boding tremblers learned to trace
The day's disasters in his morning face; *200*
Full well they laughed, with counterfeited glee,
At all his jokes, for many a joke had he;
Full well the busy whisper circling round,
Conveyed the dismal tidings when he frowned;
Yet he was kind, or if severe in aught, *205*
The love he bore to learning was in fault;
The village all declared how much he knew;
'Twas certain he could write and cipher too;
Lands he could measure, terms and tides presage,
And even the story ran that he could gauge. *210*

In arguing too, the parson owned his skill,
For even though vanquished, he could argue still;
While words of learned length and thundering sound
Amazed the gazing rustics ranged around,
And still they gazed, and still the wonder grew, *215*
That one small head could carry all he knew.
    But past is all his fame. The very spot,
Where many a time he triumphed, is forgot.
Near yonder thorn, that lifts its head on high,
Where once the signpost caught the passing eye, *220*
Low lies that house where nutbrown draughts inspired,
Where greybeard mirth and smiling toil retired,
Where village statesmen talked with looks profound,
And news much older than their ale went round.
Imagination fondly stoops to trace *225*
The parlour splendours of that festive place;
The white-washed wall, the nicely sanded floor,
The varnished clock that clicked behind the door;
The chest contrived a double debt to pay,
A bed by night, a chest of drawers by day; *230*
The pictures placed for ornament and use,
The twelve good rules, the royal game of goose;
The hearth, except when winter chilled the day,
With aspen boughs and flowers and fennel gay;
While broken teacups, wisely kept for show, *235*
Ranged o'er the chimney, glistened in a row.
    Vain, transitory splendours! Could not all
Reprieve the tottering mansion from its fall!
Obscure it sinks, nor shall it more impart
An hour's importance to the poor man's heart; *240*
Thither no more the peasant shall repair
To sweet oblivion of his daily care;
No more the farmer's news, the barber's tale,
No more the woodman's ballad shall prevail;
No more the smith his dusky brow shall clear, *245*
Relax his ponderous strength and lean to hear;
The host himself no longer shall be found
Careful to see the mantling bliss go round;

---

209. terms: times when law-courts were in session and when rents were due; **tides:** times, seasons, especially of the church year (e.g. Christmastide, Eastertide, Whitsuntide). **210. gauge:** ascertain the capacity of vessels such as hogsheads, barrels, kegs. **232. the twelve good rules:** "1. Urge no healths. 2. Profane no divine ordinances. 3. Touch no state matters. 4. Reveal no secrets. 5. Pick no quarrels. 6. Make no companions. 7. Maintain no ill opinions. 8. Keep no bad company. 9. Encourage no vice. 10. Make no long meals. 11. Repeat no grievances. 12. Lay no wagers." They were attributed to Charles I, and printed as wall-hangings; **the royal game of goose:** Brought to England from the Continent, "The Royal and Most Pleasant Game of the Goose" was a board game in which throws of two dice determine the placing and movement of counters on a spiral track of 62 spaces leading to the centre, where stakes were placed for the winner; several spaces contain pictures demanding certain actions and payments, including eleven depicting a goose, requiring a player to move double the number thrown. **236. o'er the chimney:** over the fireplace, on the mantel. **248. mantling bliss:** i.e., frothy ale.

Nor the coy maid, half willing to be pressed,
Shall kiss the cup to pass it to the rest.   250
    Yes! let the rich deride, the proud disdain,
These simple blessings of the lowly train;
To me more dear, congenial to my heart,
One native charm, than all the gloss of art;
Spontaneous joys, where nature has its play,   255
The soul adopts and owns their firstborn sway;
Lightly they frolic o'er the vacant mind,
Unenvied, unmolested, unconfined:
But the long pomp, the midnight masquerade,
With all the freaks of wanton wealth arrayed,   260
In these, ere triflers half their wish obtain,
The toiling pleasure sickens into pain;
And, even while fashion's brightest arts decoy,
The heart distrusting asks, if this be joy.
    Ye friends to truth, ye statesmen, who survey   265
The rich man's joys increase, the poor's decay,
'Tis yours to judge how wide the limits stand
Between a splendid and an happy land.
Proud swells the tide with loads of freighted ore,
And shouting Folly hails them from her shore;   270
Hoards, even beyond the miser's wish, abound,
And rich men flock from all the world around.
Yet count our gains. This wealth is but a name
That leaves our useful products still the same.
Not so the loss. The man of wealth and pride   275
Takes up a space that many poor supplied;
Space for his lake, his park's extended bounds,
Space for his horses, equipage and hounds;
The robe that wraps his limbs in silken sloth
Has robbed the neighbouring fields of half their growth;
His seat, where solitary sports are seen,   281
Indignant spurns the cottage from the green;
Around the world each needful product flies,
For all the luxuries the world supplies:
While thus the land, adorned for pleasure all,   285
In barren splendour feebly waits the fall.
    As some fair female unadorned and plain,
Secure to please while youth confirms her reign,
Slights every borrowed charm that dress supplies,
Nor shares with art the triumph of her eyes;   290
But when those charms are past, for charms are frail,
When time advances and when lovers fail,
She then shines forth, solicitous to bless,

In all the glaring impotence of dress:
Thus fares the land, by luxury betrayed,   295
In nature's simplest charms at first arrayed;
But verging to decline, its splendours rise,
Its vistas strike, its palaces surprise;
While scourged by famine from the smiling land,
The mournful peasant leads his humble band;   300
And while he sinks, without one arm to save,
The country blooms — a garden and a grave.
    Where then, ah where, shall poverty reside,
To 'scape the pressure of contiguous pride?
If to some common's fenceless limits strayed,   305
He drives his flock to pick the scanty blade,
Those fenceless fields the sons of wealth divide,
And even the bare-worn common is denied.
    If to the city sped — what waits him there?
To see profusion that he must not share;   310
To see ten thousand baneful arts combined
To pamper luxury and thin mankind;
To see those joys the sons of pleasure know,
Extorted from his fellow-creature's woe.
Here, while the courtier glitters in brocade,   315
There the pale artist plies the sickly trade;
Here, while the proud their long-drawn pomps display,
There the black gibbet glooms beside the way.
The dome where Pleasure holds her midnight reign,
Here, richly decked, admits the gorgeous train;   320
Tumultuous grandeur crowds the blazing square,
The rattling chariots clash, the torches glare.
Sure scenes like these no troubles e'er annoy!
Sure these denote one universal joy!
Are these thy serious thoughts? — Ah, turn thine eyes 325
Where the poor, houseless, shivering female lies.
She once, perhaps, in village plenty blessed,
Has wept at tales of innocence distressed;
Her modest looks the cottage might adorn,
Sweet as the primrose peeps beneath the thorn;   330
Now lost to all; her friends, her virtue fled,
Near her betrayer's door she lays her head,
And, pinched with cold and shrinking from the shower,
With heavy heart deplores that luckless hour,
When idly first, ambitious of the town,   335
She left her wheel and robes of country brown.
    Do thine, sweet Auburn, thine, the loveliest train,
Do thy fair tribes participate her pain?
Even now, perhaps, by cold and hunger led,

---

259. **pomp:** train or procession exhibiting splendour, grandeur. 316. **artist:** artisan, workman. 335. **idly:** foolishly, carelessly.

At proud men's doors they ask a little bread!   *340*
  Ah, no. To distant climes, a dreary scene,
Where half the convex world intrudes between,
Through torrid tracts with fainting steps they go,
Where wild Altama murmurs to their woe.
Far different there from all that charmed before,   *345*
The various terrors of that horrid shore:
Those blazing suns that dart a downward ray,
And fiercely shed intolerable day;
Those matted woods where birds forget to sing,
But silent bats in drowsy clusters cling;   *350*
Those poisonous fields with rank luxuriance crowned,
Where the dark scorpion gathers death around;
Where at each step the stranger fears to wake
The rattling terrors of the vengeful snake;
Where crouching tigers wait their hapless prey,   *355*
And savage men more murderous still than they;
While oft in whirls the mad tornado flies,
Mingling the ravaged landscape with the skies.
Far different these from every former scene,
The cooling brook, the grassy-vested green,   *360*
The breezy covert of the warbling grove,
That only sheltered thefts of harmless love.
  Good heaven! what sorrows gloomed that parting day,
That called them from their native walks away;
When the poor exiles, every pleasure past,   *365*
Hung round their bowers and fondly looked their last,
And took a long farewell, and wished in vain
For seats like these beyond the western main;
And shuddering still to face the distant deep,
Returned and wept, and still returned to weep.   *370*
The good old sire, the first prepared to go
To new-found worlds, and wept for others' woe;
But for himself, in conscious virtue brave,
He only wished for worlds beyond the grave.
His lovely daughter, lovelier in her tears,   *375*
The fond companion of his helpless years,
Silent went next, neglectful of her charms,
And left a lover's for a father's arms.
With louder plaints the mother spoke her woes,
And blessed the cot where every pleasure rose;   *380*
And kissed her thoughtless babes with many a tear,
And clasped them close, in sorrow doubly dear;
Whilst her fond husband strove to lend relief
In all the silent manliness of grief.
  O luxury! thou cursed by heaven's decree,   *385*

How ill exchanged are things like these for thee!
How do thy potions with insidious joy
Diffuse their pleasures only to destroy!
Kingdoms, by thee to sickly greatness grown,
Boast of a florid vigour not their own.   *390*
At every draught more large and large they grow,
A bloated mass of rank unwieldy woe;
Till sapped their strength, and every part unsound,
Down, down they sink, and spread a ruin round.
  Even now the devastation is begun,   *395*
And half the business of destruction done;
Even now, methinks, as pondering here I stand,
I see the rural virtues leave the land.
Down where yon anchoring vessel spreads the sail,
That idly waiting flaps with every gale,   *400*
Downward they move, a melancholy band,
Pass from the shore and darken all the strand.
Contented toil and hospitable care,
And kind connubial tenderness are there;
And piety, with wishes placed above,   *405*
And steady loyalty, and faithful love.
And thou, sweet Poetry, thou loveliest maid,
Still first to fly where sensual joys invade;
Unfit, in these degenerate times of shame,
To catch the heart or strike for honest fame;   *410*
Dear charming nymph, neglected and decried,
My shame in crowds, my solitary pride;
Thou source of all my bliss and all my woe,
That found'st me poor at first and keep'st me so;
Thou guide by which the nobler arts excel,   *415*
Thou nurse of every virtue, fare thee well!
Farewell, and oh, where'er thy voice be tried,
On Torno's cliffs, or Pambamarca's side,
Whether where equinoctial fervours glow,
Or winter wraps the polar world in snow,   *420*
Still let thy voice, prevailing over time,
Redress the rigours of the inclement clime;
Aid slighted truth; with thy persuasive strain
Teach erring man to spurn the rage of gain;
Teach him that states of native strength possessed,   *425*
Though very poor, may still be very blest;
That trade's proud empire hastes to swift decay,
As ocean sweeps the laboured mole away;
While self-dependent power can time defy,
As rocks resist the billows and the sky.   *430*

(1770)

---

344. Altama: the Altamaha River in Georgia, where in 1733 Goldsmith's friend, General James Oglethorpe (1696-1785), established a colony to give paupers a fresh start. **418. Torno:** The Torne (or Tornio) river flows from northern Sweden to the Gulf of Bothnia, forming part of the border with Finland; **Pambamarca,** a mountain in Ecuador. **427-30:** According to Boswell (see p. 685), Dr. Johnson composed these concluding lines.

NATHANIEL WEEKES
Barbados, c.1730-after 1775

from *BARBADOS*

(1)

When frequent rains, and gentle show'rs descend,
To cheer the Earth, and Nature's self revive,
A second Paradise appears! the isle
Throughout, one beauteous garden seems; now plants
Spring forth in all their bloom; now orange groves   5
Diffuse their sweets, and load each passing gale
With heav'nly fragrance; the citron, too, now
Breathes its hoard of rich perfumes; while all
Their various odours join, and to the mind
Inspire a likeness of what Eden was.   10

   Through walks thick-set with orange trees in bloom,
And citron intermixed, who does not like
To sport and range, when the cool evening tempts
The social mind to sober exercise,
And sweet discourse? still sweeter made by mirth!   15
Beneath each pleasant shade, discreetly gay,
Or innocently fond, the sexes meet,
By love or friendship paired; while others range
The various walks, and chat of scandal, toys,
And fashions now in vogue; still reigning themes   20
In all assemblies of the fair and gay.

(2)

The virtues of the Cane must now be sung;
The noblest plant of all the western isles!
What greater subject can employ my Muse?

Not India's aromatic groves, nor all   25
The treasures of her hundred mines, can boast
A more important trade, or yield to man
A nobler use. Here, Muse! your pow'r exert;
The subject now your utmost pow'r demands.
To trace the Cane through all its various toils,   30
Till full perfection crowns its use complete,
Be now your task to celebrate at large.

   To urge the glory of your Cane's success,
Rich be your soil, and well manured with dung,
Or, planters! what will all your labours yield?   35
A faithless profit, and a barren crop.
When heavy rains in pleasing floods descend,
And all your land with finished holing smiles,
Swift to the task of planting call your slaves,
While yet the weather favours your designs.   40
Close watch, ye drivers! your work-hating gang,
And mark their labours with a careful eye;
But spare your cruel and ungen'rous stripes!
They are sure men, though slaves, and coloured black;
And what is colour in the eye of Heav'n?   45
'Tis impious to suppose a diff'rence made;
Like you they boast sound reason, feeling, sense,
And virtues equally as great, and good,
If lessoned rightly, and instructed well.
Spare then your tyranny, inhuman men!   50
And deal that mercy you expect from Heav'n.

(1754)

WILLIAM COWPER
England, 1731-1800

THE MODERN PATRIOT

Rebellion is my theme all day;
  I only wish 'twould come
(As who knows but perhaps it may)
  A little nearer home.

Yon roaring boys, who rave and fight   5
  On t'other side th'Atlantic,
I always held them in the right,
  But most so when most frantic.

BARBADOS   **6. gale:** breeze. **19. toys:** baubles, trifles, pretty accessories. **38. holing:** "holing-gangs" were used on the sugar plantations to dig cane-holes. **43. stripes:** strokes of a whip.

When lawless mobs insult the court,
    That man shall be my toast,   *10*
If breaking windows be the sport,
    Who bravely breaks the most.

But oh! for him my fancy culls
    The choicest flow'rs she bears,
Who constitutionally pulls   *15*
    Your house about your ears.

Such civil broils are my delight,
    Though some folks can't endure 'em,
Who say the mob are mad outright,
    And that a rope must cure 'em.   *20*

A rope! I wish we patriots had
    Such strings for all who need 'em —
What! hang a man for going mad?
    Then farewell British freedom.

        (1780)

VERSES SUPPOSED TO BE WRITTEN BY ALEXANDER SELKIRK, DURING HIS SOLITARY ABODE IN THE ISLAND OF JUAN FERNANDEZ

I am monarch of all I survey,
    My right there is none to dispute;
From the centre all round to the sea,
    I am lord of the fowl and the brute.
O Solitude! where are the charms   *5*
    That sages have seen in thy face?
Better dwell in the midst of alarms
    Than reign in this horrible place.

I am out of humanity's reach;
    I must finish my journey alone,   *10*
Never hear the sweet music of speech;
    I start at the sound of my own.
The beasts that roam over the plain,
    My form with indifference see;
They are so unacquainted with man,   *15*
    Their tameness is shocking to me.

Society, friendship, and love,
    Divinely bestowed upon man,
Oh, had I the wings of a dove,
    How soon would I taste you again!   *20*
My sorrows I then might assuage
    In the ways of religion and truth,
Might learn from the wisdom of age,
    And be cheered by the sallies of youth.

Religion! what treasure untold   *25*
    Resides in that heavenly word!
More precious than silver and gold,
    Or all that this earth can afford.
But the sound of the church-going bell
    These valleys and rocks never heard,   *30*
Ne'er sighed at the sound of a knell,
    Or smiled when a sabbath appeared.

Ye winds that have made me your sport,
    Convey to this desolate shore
Some cordial endearing report   *35*
    Of a land I shall visit no more.
My friends, do they now and then send
    A wish or a thought after me?
Oh tell me I yet have a friend,
    Though a friend I am never to see.   *40*

How fleet is a glance of the mind!
    Compared with the speed of its flight,
The tempest itself lags behind,
    And the swift-winged arrows of light.
When I think of my own native land,   *45*
    In a moment I seem to be there;
But alas! recollection at hand
    Soon hurries me back to despair.

But the sea-fowl is gone to her nest,
    The beast is laid down in his lair;   *50*
Ev'n here is a season of rest,
    And I to my cabin repair.
There's mercy in every place,
    And mercy, encouraging thought!
Gives even affliction a grace,   *55*
    And reconciles man to his lot.

        (1782)

VERSES   Alexander Selkirk (1676-1721), the inspiration for Daniel Defoe's Robinson Crusoe, was marooned, at his own request after quarrelling with his captain, on one of the Juan Fernández islands from 1704 to 1709. See the extracts from Woodes Rogers's journal (p. 510).

THE DIVERTING HISTORY OF JOHN GILPIN

Showing How He Went Farther Than He Intended, and Came Safe Home Again

John Gilpin was a citizen
  Of credit and renown,
A train-band captain eke was he
  Of famous London town.

John Gilpin's spouse said to her dear —   *5*
  "Though wedded we have been
These twice ten tedious years, yet we
  No holiday have seen.

"Tomorrow is our wedding-day,
  And we will then repair   *10*
Unto the Bell at Edmonton
  All in a chaise and pair.

"My sister, and my sister's child,
  Myself, and children three,
Will fill the chaise; so you must ride   *15*
  On horseback after we."

He soon replied — "I do admire
  Of womankind but one,
And you are she, my dearest dear,
  Therefore it shall be done.   *20*

"I am a linen-draper bold,
  As all the world doth know,
And my good friend the calender
  Will lend his horse to go."

Quoth Mrs. Gilpin — "That's well said;   *25*
  And, for that wine is dear,
We will be furnished with our own,
  Which is both bright and clear."

John Gilpin kissed his loving wife;
  O'erjoyed was he to find   *30*
That, though on pleasure she was bent,
  She had a frugal mind.

The morning came, the chaise was brought,
  But yet was not allowed
To drive up to the door, lest all   *35*
  Should say that she was proud.

So three doors off the chaise was stayed,
  Where they did all get in;
Six precious souls, and all agog
  To dash through thick and thin.   *40*

Smack went the whip, round went the wheels,
  Were never folk so glad,
The stones did rattle underneath,
  As if Cheapside were mad.

John Gilpin at his horse's side   *45*
  Seized fast the flowing mane,
And up he got, in haste to ride,
  But soon came down again;

For saddle-tree scarce reached had he,
  His journey to begin,   *50*
When, turning round his head, he saw
  Three customers come in.

So down he came; for loss of time,
  Although it grieved him sore,
Yet loss of pence, full well he knew,   *55*
  Would trouble him much more.

'Twas long before the customers
  Were suited to their mind,
When Betty, screaming, came down stairs —
  "The wine is left behind!"   *60*

"Good lack!" quoth he — "yet bring it me,
  My leathern belt likewise,
In which I bear my trusty sword
  When I do exercise."

Now Mistress Gilpin (careful soul!)   *65*
  Had two stone bottles found,
To hold the liquor that she loved,
  And keep it safe and sound.

THE DIVERTING HISTORY . . . (sometimes familiarly known as "John Gilpin's Ride")   **3. train-band:** a company of citizen-soldiers (see 63-64); **eke:** also. **11. Bell:** the Bell Inn; Edmonton is a suburban district about 10 km north of central London. **23. calender:** one who calenders or presses cloth. **44. Cheapside:** See note to Pope's *The Rape of the Lock*, IV, line 118 (p. 530). **59. Betty:** the maidservant.

Each bottle had a curling ear,
   Through which the belt he drew,   *70*
And hung a bottle on each side,
   To make his balance true.

Then, over all, that he might be
   Equipped from top to toe,
His long red cloak, well brushed and neat, *75*
   He manfully did throw.

Now see him mounted once again
   Upon his nimble steed,
Full slowly pacing o'er the stones,
   With caution and good heed.   *80*

But finding soon a smoother road
   Beneath his well-shod feet,
The snorting beast began to trot
   Which galled him in his seat.

So "Fair and softly," John he cried,   *85*
   But John he cried in vain;
That trot became a gallop soon,
   In spite of curb and rein.

So stooping down, as needs he must
   Who cannot sit upright,   *90*
He grasped the mane with both his hands,
   And eke with all his might.

His horse, who never in that sort
   Had handled been before,
What thing upon his back had got   *95*
   Did wonder more and more.

Away went Gilpin, neck or nought;
   Away went hat and wig!
He little dreamt, when he set out,
   Of running such a rig.   *100*

The wind did blow, the cloak did fly,
   Like streamer long and gay,
Till, loop and button failing both,
   At last it flew away.

Then might all people well discern   *105*
   The bottles he had slung;
A bottle swinging at each side,
   As hath been said or sung.

The dogs did bark, the children screamed,
   Up flew the windows all;   *110*
And ev'ry soul cried out — "Well done!"
   As loud as he could bawl.

Away went Gilpin — who but he?
   His fame soon spread around —
"He carries weight!" "He rides a race!"   *115*
   "'Tis for a thousand pound!"

And still, as fast as he drew near,
   'Twas wonderful to view
How in a trice the turnpike-men
   Their gates wide open threw.   *120*

And now, as he went bowing down
   His reeking head full low,
The bottles twain behind his back
   Were shattered at a blow.

Down ran the wine into the road,   *125*
   Most piteous to be seen,
Which made his horse's flanks to smoke
   As they had basted been.

But still he seemed to carry weight,
   With leathern girdle braced,   *130*
For all might see the bottle-necks
   Still dangling at his waist.

Thus all through merry Islington
   These gambols did he play,
And till he came unto the Wash   *135*
   Of Edmonton so gay.

And there he threw the wash about
   On both sides of the way,
Just like unto a trundling mop,
   Or a wild goose at play.   *140*

At Edmonton his loving wife
   From the balcony spied
Her tender husband, wond'ring much
   To see how he did ride.

"Stop, stop, John Gilpin! — Here's the house" —
   They all at once did cry;   *146*
"The dinner waits, and we are tired";
   Said Gilpin, "So am I!"

---

97. neck or nought: ready to risk everything. **115. carries weight:** i.e., like a handicapped jockey. **122. reeking:** steaming. **135. Wash:** a stream running across the road. **139. trundling:** spinning, twirling.

But yet his horse was not a whit
  Inclined to tarry there;   150
For why? — his owner had a house
  Full ten miles off, at Ware.

So like an arrow swift he flew,
  Shot by an archer strong;
So did he fly — which brings me to   155
  The middle of my song.

Away went Gilpin, out of breath,
  And sore against his will,
Till at his friend the calender's
  His horse at last stood still.   160

The calender, amazed to see
  His neighbour in such trim,
Laid down his pipe, flew to the gate,
  And thus accosted him:

"What news? what news? your tidings tell;
  Tell me you must and shall —   166
Say why bare-headed you are come,
  Or why you come at all?"

Now Gilpin had a pleasant wit,
  And loved a timely joke;   170
And thus unto the calender
  In merry guise he spoke:

"I came because your horse would come,
  And, if I well forebode,
My hat and wig will soon be here —   175
  They are upon the road."

The calender, right glad to find
  His friend in merry pin,
Returned him not a single word,
  But to the house went in;   180

Whence straight he came with hat and wig;
  A wig that flowed behind,
A hat not much the worse for wear,
  Each comely in its kind.

He held them up, and in his turn   185
  Thus showed his ready wit —
"My head is twice as big as yours,
  They therefore needs must fit.

But let me scrape the dirt away
  That hangs upon your face;   190
And stop and eat, for well you may
  Be in a hungry case."

Said John — "It is my wedding-day,
  And all the world would stare
If wife should dine at Edmonton   195
  And I should dine at Ware."

So, turning to his horse, he said —
  "I am in haste to dine;
'Twas for your pleasure you came here,
  You shall go back for mine."   200

Ah, luckless speech, and bootless boast!
  For which he paid full dear;
For, while he spake, a braying ass
  Did sing most loud and clear;

Whereat his horse did snort, as he   205
  Had heard a lion roar,
And galloped off with all his might,
  As he had done before.

Away went Gilpin, and away
  Went Gilpin's hat and wig;   210
He lost them sooner than at first —
  For why? — they were too big.

Now Mistress Gilpin, when she saw
  Her husband posting down
Into the country far away,   215
  She pulled out half a crown;

And thus unto the youth she said,
  That drove them to the Bell —
"This shall be yours when you bring back
  My husband safe and well."   220

The youth did ride, and soon did meet
  John coming back amain;
Whom in a trice he tried to stop
  By catching at his rein;

But not performing what he meant,   225
  And gladly would have done,
The frighted steed he frighted more,
  And made him faster run.

---

178. **pin:** humour, frame of mind.

Away went Gilpin, and away
  Went post-boy at his heels;   *230*
The post-boy's horse right glad to miss
  The lumb'ring of the wheels.

Six gentlemen upon the road,
  Thus seeing Gilpin fly,
With post-boy scamp'ring in the rear,   *235*
  They raised the hue and cry:

"Stop thief! Stop thief! A highwayman!"
  Not one of them was mute;
And all and each that passed that way
  Did join in the pursuit.   *240*

And now the turnpike gates again
  Flew open in short space,
The toll-men thinking, as before,
  That Gilpin rode a race.

And so he did — and won it too!   *245*
  For he got first to town,
Nor stopped till where he had got up
  He did again get down.

Now let us sing, Long live the King,
  And Gilpin, long live he;   *250*
And when he next doth ride abroad,
  May I be there to see!

(1782)

THE GENTLEMAN'S MAGAZINE
England, 1776

from THE GENTLEMAN'S MAGAZINE, AND HISTORICAL CHRONICLE

Declaration by the Representatives of the United States of America, in General Congress assembled, July 4

[August 1776]

When, in the course of human events, it becomes necessary for one people to dissolve the political bands which have connected them with another, and to assume among the powers of the earth the separate and equal station to which the laws of Nature and of Nature's God entitle them, a decent respect to the opinions of mankind requires that they should declare the causes which impel them to the separation.   *5*

    We hold these truths to be self-evident: — That all men are created equal; that they are endowed by their Creator with certain unalienable rights; that among these are life, liberty, and the pursuit of happiness; that, to secure these rights, governments are instituted among men, deriving their just powers from the consent of the governed; and whenever any form of government becomes destructive of these ends, it is the right of   *10* the people to alter or to abolish it, and to institute new government, laying its foundation on such principles, and organizing its powers in such form, as to them shall seem most likely to effect their safety and happiness. Prudence, indeed, will dictate, that governments long established should not be changed for light and transient causes; and,

---

DECLARATION BY THE REPRESENTATIVES Better known as "The Declaration of Independence"; the "General Congress Assembled" was the Second Continental Congress, consisting of delegates from the American colonies. The declaration was written by Thomas Jefferson, with some revisions by Benjamin Franklin and John Adams, and a few by the Congress itself. **6ff.:** Cf. paragraph 87 of Locke's *Second Treatise* (p. 444).

accordingly, all experience hath shewn, that mankind are more disposed to suffer, while *15* evils are sufferable, than to right themselves by abolishing the forms to which they are accustomed. But, when a long train of abuses and usurpations, pursuing invariably the same object, evinces a design to reduce them under absolute despotism, it is their right, it is their duty, to throw off such government, and to provide new guards for their future security. Such has been the patient sufferance of these colonies, and such is now the *20* necessity which constrains them to alter their former systems of government. The history of the present —— of Great Britain, is a history of repeated injuries and usurpations; all having in direct object the establishment of an absolute t—— over these states. To prove this let facts be submitted to a candid world.

He has refused his assent to laws, the most wholesome and necessary for the public *25* good.

He has forbidden his governors to pass laws of immediate and pressing importance, unless suspended in their operation till his assent should be obtained; and when so suspended, he has utterly neglected to attend to them.

He has refused to pass other laws for accommodation of large districts of people, *30* unless those people would relinquish the right of representation in the legislature; a right inestimable to them, and formidable to t—— only.

He has called together legislative bodies at places unusual, uncomfortable, and distant from the depository of their public records, for the sole purpose of fatiguing them into compliance with his measures. *35*

He has dissolved representative houses repeatedly, for opposing, with manly firmness, his invasions on the rights of the people.

He has refused for a long time, after such dissolutions, to cause others to be erected, whereby the legislative powers, incapable of annihilation, have returned to the people at large for their exercise; the state remaining, in the mean time, exposed to all the dangers *40* of invasion from without, and convulsions within.

He has endeavoured to prevent the population of these states; for that purpose obstructing the laws for naturalization of foreigners, refusing to pass others to encourage their migrations hither, and raising the conditions of new appropriations of lands.

He has obstructed the administration of justice, by refusing his assent to laws for *45* establishing judiciary powers.

He has made judges dependent on his will alone, for the tenure of their offices, and the amount and payment of their salaries.

He has erected a multitude of new offices, and sent hither swarms of officers to harrass our people, and eat out their subsistence. *50*

He has kept among us, in times of peace, standing armies, without the consent of our legislatures.

He has affected to render the military independent of, and superior to, the civil power.

He has combined, with others, to subject us to a jurisdiction foreign to our constitution, and unacknowledged by our laws; giving his assent to their pretended acts of legislation, *55*

22: By leaving blanks, the magazine is deliberately avoiding being charged with making or repeating a seditious utterance; the omitted word here is *King*; that at line 87 is *Prince*: the others, beginning with *t*, are variously *tyrants*, *tyranny*, and *tyrant*. **54. others:** i.e., parliament.

For quartering large bodies of armed troops among us:

For protecting them, by a mock trial, from punishment for any murders which they should commit on the inhabitants of these states:

For cutting off our trade with all parts of the world:

For imposing taxes on us without our consent: 60

For depriving us, in many cases, of the benefit of trial by jury:

For transporting us beyond seas to be tried for pretended offences:

For abolishing the free system of English laws in a neighbouring province, establishing therein an arbitrary government, and enlarging its boundaries, so as to render it at once an example and fit instrument for introducing the same absolute rule 65 into these colonies:

For taking away our charters, abolishing our most valuable laws, and altering fundamentally the forms of our governments:

For suspending our own legislatures, and declaring themselves invested with power to legislate for us in all cases whatsoever. 70

He has abdicated government here, by declaring us out of his protection, and waging war against us.

He has plundered our seas, ravaged our coasts, burnt our towns, and destroyed the lives of our people.

He is, at this time, transporting large armies of foreign mercenaries, to compleat the 75 works of death, desolation, and t——, already begun with circumstances of cruelty and perfidy, scarcely paralleled in the most barbarous ages, and totally unworthy the head of a civilized nation.

He has constrained our fellow-citizens, taken captive on the high seas, to bear arms against their country, to become the executioners of their friends and brethren, or to fall 80 themselves by their hands.

He has excited domestic insurrections amongst us, and has endeavoured to bring on the inhabitants of our frontiers, the merciless Indian savages, whose known rule of warfare is an undistinguished destruction of all ages, sexes, and conditions.

In every stage of these oppressions we have petitioned for redress, in the most 85 humble terms; our repeated petitions have been answered only by repeated injury. — A ——, whose character is thus marked by every act which may define a t——, is unfit to be the ruler of a free people.

Nor have we been wanting in attention to our British brethren. We have warned them, from time to time, of attempts, by their legislature, to extend an unwarrantable 90 jurisdiction over us. We have reminded them of the circumstances of our emigration and settlement here. We have appealed to their native justice and magnanimity, and we have conjured them by the ties of our common kindred to disavow these usurpations which would inevitably interrupt our connections and correspondence. They too have been deaf to the voice of justice, and of consanguinity. We must, therefore, acquiesce in the 95 necessity which denounces our separation, and hold them, as we hold the rest of mankind, enemies in war, in peace friends.

---

63. abolishing . . . province: referring to the Quebec Act of 1774, which effectively secured its loyalty to the Crown. **75. mercenaries:** mostly Hessians. **96. denounces:** formally or solemnly declares, announces.

We, therefore, the representatives of the United States of America, in General Congress assembled, appealing to the Supreme Judge of the World for the rectitude of our intentions, do, in the name and by the authority of the good people of these colonies, *100* solemnly publish and declare, That these United colonies are, and of right ought to be, *free and independent states,* and that they are absolved from all allegiance to the British crown, and that all political connection between them and the state of Great Britain, is, and ought to be, totally dissolved; and that, as free and independent states, they have full power to levy war, conclude peace, contract alliances, establish commerce, and to do all *105* other acts and things which independent states may of right do. And for the support of this declaration, with a firm reliance on the protection of Divine Providence, we mutually pledge to each other our lives, our fortunes, and our sacred honour.

Signed by order, and in behalf of the Congress,

JOHN HANCOCK, President.
Attest, CHARLES THOMPSON, Sec.

Thoughts on the late Declaration of the American Congress

[September]

The declaration is without doubt of the most extraordinary nature both with regard to sentiment and language, and considering that the motive of it is to assign some justifiable reasons of their separating themselves from Great Britain, unless it had been fraught with more truth and sense, might well have been spared, as it reflects no honour upon either their erudition or honesty. *5*

We hold (they say) these truths to be self-evident: That all men are created equal. In what are they created equal? Is it in size, strength, understanding, figure, moral or civil accomplishments, or situation of life? Every plough-man knows that they are not created equal in any of these. All men, it is true, are equally created, but what is this to the purpose? It certainly is no reason why the Americans should turn rebels because the *10* people of Great Britain are their fellow creatures, *i.e.* are created as well as themselves. It may be a reason why they should not rebel, but most indisputably is none why they should. They therefore have introduced their self-evident truths, either through ignorance, or by design, with a self-evident falsehood: since I will defy any American rebel, or any of their patriotic retainers here in England, to point out to me any two men, *15* throughout the whole World, of whom it may with truth be said they they are created equal.

The next of their self-evident truths is, that all men are endowed by their Creator with certain unalienable rights (the meaning of which words they appear not at all to understand); among which are life, liberty, and the pursuit of happiness. Let us put some *20* of these words together. All men are endowed by their Creator with the unalienable right of life. How far they may be endowed with this unalienable right I do not yet say,

---

John Hancock: As president of the congress, John Hancock was the first of over fifty members to sign the declaration; the prominence of his signature and of this document led to his name entering the language as an informal synonym for *signature*. **THOUGHTS ON THE LATE DECLARATION** The identity of the writers of the three responses is not known.

but, sure I am, these gentry assume to themselves an unalienable right of talking nonsense. Was it ever heard since the introduction of blunders into the world that life was a man's right? Life or animation is of the essence of human nature, and is that without which one is not a man, and therefore to call life a right, is to betray a total ignorance of the meaning of words. A living man, *i.e.* a man with life, hath a right to a great many things; but to say that a man with life hath a right to be a man with life is so purely American, that I believe the texture of no other brain upon the face of the earth will admit the idea. Whatever it may be, I have tried to make an idea out of it, but own I am unable. Prior to my having any right at all as a man, it is certain *I* must be a man, and such a man I certainly cannot be if I have no life; and therefore if it be said that I have a right to life, then the word *I* must signify something without life, and consequently something without life must be supposed to have a property, which without life it is not possible it can have.

Well but they say all men have not only a right to life, but an unalienable right. The word unalienable signifies that which is not alienable, and that which is not alienable is what cannot be transferred so as to become another's; so that their unalienable right is a right which they cannot transfer to a broomstick or a cabbage-stalk; and because they cannot transfer their own lives from themselves to a cabbage-stalk, therefore they think it absolutely necessary that they should rebel, and, out of a decent respect to the opinions of mankind, allege this as one of the causes which impel them to separate themselves from those to whom they owe obedience.

The next assigned cause and ground of their rebellion is, that every man hath an unalienable right to liberty; and here the words, as it happens, are not nonsense, but then they are not true; slaves there are in America, and where there are slaves, there liberty is alienated.

If the Creator hath endowed man with an unalienable right to liberty, no reason in the world will justify the abridgment of that liberty, and a man hath a right to do every thing that he thinks proper without control or restraint: and upon the same principle there can be no such things as servants, subjects, or government of any kind whatsoever. In a word, every law that hath been in the world since the formation of Adam, gives the lie to this self-evident truth (as they are pleased to term it), because every law, divine or human, that is or hath been in the world, is an abridgment of man's liberty.

Their next self-evident truth and ground of rebellion is, that they have an unalienable right to the pursuit of happiness. The pursuit of happiness an unalienable right! This surely is outdoing every thing that went before. Put it into English: the pursuit of happiness is a right with which the Creator hath endowed me, and which can neither be taken from me, nor can I transfer it to another. Did ever any mortal alive hear of taking a pursuit of happiness from a man? What they possibly can mean by these words, I own is beyond my comprehension. A man may take from me a horse or a cow, or I may alienate either of them from myself, as I may likewise any thing that I have; but how that can be taken from me, or alienated, which I have not, must be left for the solution of some unborn Oedipus.

An Englishman.

---

63. Oedipus: referring to his solving the Riddle of the Sphinx.

[October]

MR. URBAN,

In your last Magazine you have inserted some thoughts on the late declaration of the American congress: the thoughts of a gentleman who does himself the honour to call himself an Englishman. But whether he will pardon me or no, I must take the liberty to say, I am ashamed to own him for a fellow-citizen. An Englishman hath advantages beyond other men for acquiring generous sentiments: when any one, therefore, in writing or conversation, is guilty of meanness and insolence, whatever he says of himself, no man will give him credit by assuming the honourable appellation of ENGLISHMAN.

No man, Mr. Urban, can betray meanness to a greater degree, than by totally disregarding his own natural rights; nor greater insolence, than by charging others with ignorance in subjects which they understand much better than himself.

I think it may fairly be presumed, that the gentleman, upon whose strictures I am animadverting, sets no very high value on his own natural rights: because he does what he can to destroy them. He would prove, if he could, that men are not created equal: and enquires, "Is it in size, strength, understanding, figure, moral or civil accomplishment? Every ploughman (says he) knows that they are not created equal in any of these." But I ask, whoever affirmed they were? Nevertheless, as, originally, any one man had as much right to reign and rule over another man, as that other man had to reign and rule over him, it is certainly in this sense (the sense of the declaration) a self-evident TRUTH, that all men were created equal; though this gentleman has the MODESTY to pronounce it a self-evident FALSEHOOD.

He would prove too, if he could, that men have no right to life, liberty, and the pursuit of happiness. Let him not therefore complain, nor make resistance, should any one attempt to deprive him of life or liberty: and should his task-master command him to hew wood and draw water, let him not murmur; for, according to his notion, no man has a right to pursue his own plan of happiness.

This gentleman, I presume, can demonstrate, that, since the world was made, there never existed any such thing as oppression among mankind. Indeed, if his arguments are good, he has already done it: for certainly there can be no oppression where there are no natural rights. True it is, the phrase used in the declaration is *unalienable* rights: and surely unalienable they are, if natural: — rights which men have received from God, together with their nature, are inseparable from it.

But the congress are such fools they do not understand the meaning of the words *unalienable rights. Unalienable* means, according to this witty gentleman, that which cannot be transferred to another. If he had been wise, he would have known, that to *alienate*, strictly speaking, signifies to *estrange from* or to *take away*: and that certainly a thing may be taken away from a man, which yet cannot be transferred to another. Very unfortunately, indeed, this meaning interferes a little with the gentleman's wit: for he

---

Mr. Urban: *The Gentleman's Magazine* was founded in 1731 by Edward Cave (1691-1754), who conducted it as "Sylvanus Urban," a pseudonym which was maintained by his successors; at this time the editor was Cave's brother-in-law, David Henry.

doubtless imagined himself to be very witty when he talked of the Americans' rights being transferred to a broomstick or a cabbage-stalk. But he is more than a wit, he is a metaphysician. Hear him: "Life or animation is of the essence of human nature, and is that without which one is not a man: and therefore to call life a right is to betray a total *105* ignorance of the meaning of words." And now please to take notice, while, like a consummate logician, he adds, — "To say that a man with life hath a right to be a man with life, is so purely American, that I believe the texture of no other brain upon the face of the earth will admit the idea." In reply I will only observe, that as, according to his account, a man with life has no *right* to be a man with life, if, at any time, a *110* highwayman should happen to pistol this gentleman, in so doing, by his way of reasoning, the highwayman will do him no *wrong.*

To prove that mankind have no unalienable right to enjoy liberty, this gentleman argues thus: "Slaves there are in America; and where there are slaves, there liberty is alienated." But, surely, tho' I should ever be so unhappy as to lose my liberty, it will not *115* follow that I have no right to it. Does not all the world know that great numbers have a right to enjoy what is yet with-holden from them? It cannot be doubted, however, that this gentleman has more penetration than all the world beside!

Further, to prove the matter more fully, he affirms, that every law, which has been in the world since the formation of Adam, gives the lie to this self-evident truth, as the *120* congress are pleased to term it (viz. that every man has an unalienable right to liberty): because, says he, "every law, divine or human, that is or hath been in the world, is an abridgement of liberty." — Divine laws have nothing to do here. — As for human laws, if they take away *liberty,* they neither do nor can take away the *right* to it. Nothing, however, can be more certain than that, if the existence of human laws will prove that *125* mankind have no right to liberty, this gentleman (clever as he is) will be a little puzzled to shew any reason why he ought not to be a slave: and, indeed, if he were, seeing he is so zealous an advocate for slavery, in my judgment, he would deserve as little pity as any other slave.

The declaration asserts, that mankind have an unalienable right to the pursuit of *130* happiness. The gentleman pretends not to dispute this point, but exclaims, "Did ever any mortal alive hear of taking a pursuit of happiness from a man? What they possibly can mean by these words, I own, is beyond my comprehension." But who can help it, if the gentleman's brain is of such a texture that he cannot comprehend the difference between a *house* and a *right* to possess that house? *135*

If, after all, he will needs be a metaphysician, it will not misbecome him to be a little more modest; and before he again affects to display his *wit,* let him *endeavour* at least to fill up the void in his *judgment.*

Yours, &c.

High-Wycomb.

PHILANDER.

Philander: from the Greek for "loving men."

[December]

Mr. Urban,

Your Magazine for October last brought us the answer of an angry gentleman to the thoughts of a merry one on the American Declaration; and this you inadvertently, in your Contents, call a *refutation*. But I beg leave to give this Refuter the correction *140* which, upon a review, you will, I hope, agree with me, he richly deserves.

I have always regarded the liberty we possess of censuring (with reason) Kings, Ministers, and Parliaments, as the pride and happiness of this country; but this angry gentleman is of the opinion, that to make free, even jocularly, with a *Congress* is so ungenerous, is such *meanness* and *insolence,* as renders a man unworthy the name of *145* Englishman.

Nor is his logic better than his manners. He accuses a man of endeavouring to destroy our natural rights of life, liberty, and happiness, — and of asserting that we have no such rights, &c. — merely because he has diverted himself with some blundering expressions of our enemies on this subject. The *Englishman* has said nothing, that I *150* know of, against men's natural rights; but only that all laws, human and divine, give the lie to the American assertion, because they were formed purposely to abridge these rights; that is, in some cases to *alienate* them. God himself has set the example of alienating, where necessary, those rights he gave us with our natures.

The Congress, it seems, have pleaded, in excuse for having established a merciless *155* tyranny, that it is a *self-evident truth that all men are created equal.* To defend this absurdity, their interpreter tells us, that by *all men* is here meant only those *original* men who lived in a state of Nature, and of those one man had as much right to reign or rule as another. — But what has this far-fetched case to do with a people in a state of Society? And even, if it *was* applicable, it is no *self-evident* truth, nor, I believe, any *160* truth at all; for it is likely (I think most likely) that men were at first created with different capacities and mental powers, some formed to rule, and others to obey: — in which sense we might properly say, with the Son of Sirach, that "in the divisions of the nations of the whole earth, God set a ruler over every people."

The witty gentleman having laughed about the word *unalienable,* the *wise* one, as *165* interpreter of the rebels, says, that to *alienate,* strictly speaking, signifies to *estrange from,* or *take away.* If we allow him this, he has then made this blessed sentence to mean that *life,* a *pursuit,* &c. are *rights* which cannot be *taken away!* However, *strictly speaking,* I believe *alieno* (ἀλλοτριόω) is a law metaphor, and means *transitively,* as its derivation implies, to *transfer to another.* *170*

We will suppose, then, that our enemies understand the word *alienate,* as their interpreter asserts, in the sense of *taking away;* — the *Englishman* also is *wise* enough to understand it in the same sense. Liberty, says he, may be taken away, for there are slaves in America. I will add, that the *right* too may be taken away, for there are slaves on the river Thames; all of them legally, and some at least justly, deprived of freedom. *175* The grave gentleman's objection to this is *monstrous*; — human laws, if they take away

---

164-65: Ecclesiasticus 17:17; this book in the Apocrypha is also called "The Wisdom of Jesus the Son of Sirach." **175-76. slaves . . . Thames:** presumably referring to the prisoners kept in the "hulks" on the Thames.

liberty, neither do nor CAN take away the right to it: — an idea subversive of all subordination, magistracy, justice, and every legal control, by which alone societies, and indeed all the *rights* of mankind, are supported. As for divine laws, with one dash of the pen he renders them perfectly nugatory, by saying that they have "nothing to do with the *180* abridgment of liberty." He is angry, perhaps, that they have so much to do *here,* since they are so *pointedly* against American conduct.

But I will tell the angry gentleman, that a man may really have the *things themselves,* and yet have alienated or parted with his *right* to them. A rebel, a traitor, for instance, may be a *man with life,* and yet not have a *right* to be a *man with life;* and the *185* same may be said of the highwayman who pistols my merry friend the *Englishman.* A *man with liberty,* likewise, may not have a *right* to be *a man with liberty;* if, for instance, he obstinately avows his resolution of committing the above crimes: — and, as to the last instance, I cannot but think, that, if a man was breaking into a chamber window at High Wycomb, with an intention of cuckolding my grave antagonist *190* *Philander,* he would *not* be justified in so doing merely because he thought, with the Americans, that he had *an unalienable right to the pursuit of happiness!*

Such are the *ostensible* reasons which our enemies give for becoming *self-evident* parricides (and *self-evident* fools too, by throwing away the lives, liberties, and happiness which they had). They have other latent reasons which I cannot now consider, *195* such as their *unalienable right* of avarice, and their *unalienable right* of ambition, &c. But there is one really plausible reason given by our enemies for their rebellion (and but one that I know of), and that is, "that they have a right to their property, *unalienable,* but by an assembly in which they are *represented.*" As this is a matter of the highest importance, I may perhaps take the liberty of considering it in a future letter. *200*

PATRIO MASTIX.

ERASMUS DARWIN
England, 1731-1802

VISIT OF HOPE TO SYDNEY COVE, NEAR BOTANY BAY

Where Sydney Cove her lucid bosom swells,
And with wide arms the indignant storm repels;
High on a rock amid the troubled air
Hope stood sublime, and waved her golden hair;
Calmed with her rosy smile the tossing deep,   5
And with sweet accents charmed the winds to sleep;
To each wild plain she stretched her snowy hand,
High-waving wood, and sea-encircled strand.
"Hear me," she cried, "ye rising realms! record
Time's opening scenes, and Truth's prophetic word. *10*
There shall broad streets their stately walls extend,
The circus widen, and the crescent bend;
There, rayed from cities o'er the cultured land,
Shall bright canals, and solid roads expand.

Patrio Mastix: from the Greek for "fatherland" or "country" and "whip, scourge." **VISIT OF HOPE** Title: The town of Sydney and the nearby Botany Bay penal settlement were established in the colony of New South Wales in 1788. **1. lucid:** shining. **12 circus:** a circular intersection.

There the proud arch, colossus-like, bestride   *15*
Yon glittering streams, and bound the chasing tide;
Embellished villas crown the landscape-scene,
Farms wave with gold, and orchards blush between.
There shall tall spires, and dome-capped towers ascend,
And piers and quays their massy structures blend;   *20*

While with each breeze approaching vessels glide,
And northern treasures dance on every tide!"
Then ceased the nymph — tumultuous echoes roar,
And Joy's loud voice was heard from shore to shore —
Her graceful steps descending pressed the plain,   *25*
And Peace, and Art, and Labour, joined her train.

(1789)

JACOB BAILEY
U.S.A./Canada, 1731-1808

from *JOURNAL OF A VOYAGE FROM POWNALBORO TO HALIFAX*

June 16th

This morning, when we awoke, a little before sunrise, we had the agreeable information that the weather was fine and clear, and the wind beginning to breeze from the west. This intelligence revived our spirits, but we were obliged to wait for the tide till after breakfast, for it being spring tides, the water had ebbed out so low that we were aground. It was with great impatience that we waited till the element returned to assist   *5* our escape; at length, about nine, we came to sail, and passed through a narrow channel, and stood away towards Owl's Head, under favour of a propitious gale, with a view to discover, if possible, some of the British fleet. We stood away to the northward till we had a fair prospect into Owl's Head Harbour, but no vessels appearing, we had some dispute whether we should proceed up Penobscot Bay, or direct our course for Nova   *10* Scotia. I was inclined to favour the former proposal, but the rest of our company being anxious to visit Halifax, and Mrs. Bailey expressing her fears that instead of finding British ships, we should fall among rebel cruisers, I gave directions to cross the Bay of Fundy. Nothing could be more flattering than the prospect before us; the sky was serene, with a gentle gale from the west-north-west, and a number of small clouds over the land   *15* promised a propitious season. We were, besides, charmed with the various appearances around us — the ocean, interspersed with a multitude of fine islands of different shapes and dimensions; to the north, Penobscot Bay opened into the land, with its numerous islands, covered with lofty trees, except here and there an infant plantation, while beyond, the Camden Mountains arose in majestic grandeur, throwing their rugged   *20* summits above the clouds; these, as we approached the Fox Islands without, began gradually to diminish till their dusky azure resembled the seat of a thunder tempest, advancing to discharge its vengeance on some distant shore. But while we were viewing

---

15. colossus-like, bestride: see *Julius Caesar*, I, ii, 135-36. **20. massy:** massive.   **JOURNAL OF A VOYAGE . . .**   **Title:** Bailey, who remained loyal to the Crown during the Revolution, was afterwards forced to emigrate to a British colony; he sailed from Maine to Nova Scotia. **7. gale:** breeze. **13. rebel:** i.e., American. **14. flattering:** pleasing to the imagination; **prospect:** extensive view. **19. plantation:** settlement.

these romantic scenes with a mixture of delight and veneration, and taking leave of our
native regions with melancholy regret, the wind suddenly shifted into the S.S.W., and a   *25*
thick fog covered the surface of the ocean in such a manner as to exclude every object.
This incident afforded us abundance of perplexity, as we had to pass through a
multitude of islands and rocks, none of which could be discovered at the distance of ten
rods. We however ventured to continue our voyage in this uncertain situation. The wind
continued to blow a moderate gale, though it remained so scanty that we were obliged to   *30*
go close-hauled. In the afternoon the weather for several hours was obscure and gloomy,
and gave us uneasy apprehensions of an approaching storm, a circumstance no ways
agreeable to persons confined to such a little shallop, in so threatening a tract of the
ocean as the Bay of Fundy. These apprehensions continued to disturb our repose till
about an hour before night, when the sun brake forth in all the brightness of his   *35*
departing glory, and tinged the summits of the rolling waves with his level beams. At
the same time we had a distant view of Mount Desert, at an immense distance, sitting
like a hillock on the water. All our company by this time were extremely sick, except
the Captain, who was obliged to continue at the helm till the returning light began to
disperse the shades of darkness. The wind continued somewhat favourable till after   *40*
midnight, when it died away for more than two hours, then sprang up S.E., almost
ahead; about sunrise came to the east, then N.N.E., where it freshened up into a severe
gale. It was now tide of flood, and the current proceeding in direct opposition to the
wind, a sharp and dangerous sea commenced. After reefing we attempted to scud, but
the seas rolling over the vessel obliged us to bring to. The tempest still increased; the   *45*
wind roared like thunder in the shrouds; the ocean around us was all ragged and
deformed, and we were filled with great agitation and dread, expecting every moment to
be swallowed up in the immense abyss. We were unable to take any refreshment, and
continued till the storm abated confined to our miserable apartments.

June 17th

The storm continuing to rage with unceasing violence, we found ourselves in a very   *50*
uneasy and dangerous situation, for, as I have already observed, the tides at this season
were exceeding full, which occasioned them to set into the bay of Fundy with rapid
violence, and the wind blowing hard against the current drove the water into irregular
heaps, which appeared on every hand like enormous rocks or pillars — here rising in a
conic form to an amazing height, and there breaking into tremendous precipices or   *55*
falling ruins, while immense caverns, gaping from beneath, threatened us with
immediate destruction. I was, during these commotions, confined with my family in the
hold, but the weather being warm and the vessel extremely tight, we contrived to keep
the hatchway partly open to let in fresh air, and to prevent suffocation. The consequence
of this precaution was a deluge of water; for the waves, breaking over the deck, came   *60*
pouring upon us, and almost drowned us in our wretched confinement. In attempting to
scud before the wind and billows we were in imminent danger — a mighty wave broke

---

25. native regions: New England. **33. shallop:** an open sailing vessel, a sloop. **44. reefing:** reducing sail; **scud:** move with the wind, with little or no
sail. **45. bring to:** hold stationary.

over the stern and instantly plunged our trembling vessel under water; this obliged the captain to bring to, upon which alteration we became more secure till the tempest abated. During the continuance of this conflict our situation was extremely uneasy, every soul on board except Captain Smith being dying sick, and unable to afford him the least assistance, which rendered his care and labour abundantly more distressing. We that were imprisoned in the hold were in a most woeful pickle, almost stifled with the fumes of bilge water, our beds swimming, our clothes dripping wet, and our minds under the greatest anxiety for ourselves and each other. The thoughts of being driven from our country, our much loved home, and all those endearing connections we had been forming for so many years, and, if we escaped the angry vengeance of the ocean, the expectation of landing on a strange and unknown shore, depressed our spirits beyond measure, and filled us with the sad glooms of despondency and woe. But, as appearances often change in this various world, about two of the o'clock, when the tide began to set out of the Bay again, we were presently indulged with an happy alteration. The wind shifted further to the northward, the seas abated, and we quickly found ourselves able to proceed on our voyage; and still to cheer and animate our spirits, the clouds began to break away, the fog to disperse, and the sun to adorn the waves with his western beams. Wafted by a gentle gale we advanced towards the Acadian shores, and about three hours before sunset, to our great joy, discovered land; but this pleasing prospect did not long continue, the wind fainted into a calm, and, as the darkness approached, an heavy fog covered the mighty deep in such a manner that we could not discover any object at the distance of a rod. Under these disagreeable circumstances we were obliged to stand off to sea in order to avoid the danger of running upon an unknown shore before morning. This unfortunate and unexpected turn in the weather occasioned us great uneasiness, and threw us into our former dejection. To such a number of sea-sick and tempest-beaten mortals, who had been flattered with the prospect of entering into an harbour, this returning to sea was a most grievous mortification; but we had no other remedy except patience, and a very slender dose of that excellent drug. As to myself, it gave me an addition of pain to find that Captain Smith had no assistance in these difficult circumstances, but was obliged to continue at the helm till daylight appeared. The fore part of the night we had the wind at S.S.W., with thick weather.

June 18th

Towards morning the wind shifted into the N.E., then east, and afterwards into the S.E., when it began to blow and rain, with most threatening appearances of a storm. This unexpected continuance of bad weather had a very malignant influence upon our whole company. The hands, with Dr. Mayer, the old bachelor, swore bitterly; the captain, notwithstanding his moderation, lost all patience, and loudly complained of the unpropitious season, while we began to imagine that we should never be able to reach our intended port, so many impediments arising to retard our progress. We, however,

---

80. **Acadian:** in this instance, Nova Scotian.

found some consolation when we perceived that the wind rather abated, and in the afternoon it blew in our favour, so that we rediscovered the land towards evening. But the fog continued to hover over the surface of the water in such a manner that it became wholly unsafe to aim at any harbour. In bearing away from the shore we discovered, *105* through the surrounding fog, several little islands, interspersed with rugged rocks, against which the waves, dashing with violence, occasioned a frightful roaring. We had the good fortune, however, to escape without damage.

After keeping almost two days between decks, as it was now more calm and moderate, I ventured out of my confinement to contemplate the striking prospect *110* around us. Nothing appeared but a waste of waters in perpetual motion, with a surface rugged and unshapen beyond imagination, for the seas in this Bay of Fundy do not roll with regular succession as in other oceans, with gradual swellings, which rise in extensive order, one behind another, as far as the eye can reach, but here we perceive waves of a thousand various figures and dimensions, resembling a multitude of rocks *115* and broken fragments of nature, torn by some violent explosion, and rudely scattered over an immense desert or barren plain. While we were sitting upon deck and diverting ourselves as well as our situation would admit, one of our hens escaped from her confinement in the salt room and flew about the vessel from one quarter to another, seemingly exulting in her liberty. But alas! this freedom proved the destruction of the *120* volatile and noisy animal, for one of our company attempted to secure her, upon which she immediately flew overboard into the sea, and sat struggling and cackling upon the waves till we could see her no longer. I must confess that in my present circumstances this accident affected me, and I was moved with compassion for the foolish flutterer, when I observed her exposed to inevitable destruction, striving to regain the vessel, *125* and, as it were, calling aloud for assistance, when we were unable to afford the wretched being any relief. How often do we behold animals who fondly boast of reason, hurrying themselves with almost the same giddy precipitation into ruin. How common is it for men, when impatient of legal restraint, and ardent to acquire unbounded freedom — how frequent is it for people in these circumstances, when they *130* have escaped from every confinement and gained their wished-for liberty, to plunge headlong into destruction, and when they become sensible too late of their unbounded rashness and folly, they are desirous from their hearts to re-enter that condition they once called slavery and bondage. In short, I am convinced that no animal in nature makes so pernicious an improvement of liberty as man; for notwithstanding all his *135* boasted pretences to wisdom, if you place him in a situation of unrestrained license, it is a thousand to one if he do not ruin both himself and all his intimate connexions. But enough of liberty for the present, since I had a sufficient surfeit from it in New England, and have seen from that abused principle all the miseries of licentiousness, anarchy, and tyranny, flowing like so many torrents to deluge that unhappy and *140* devoted land.

(1779)

---

119. salt room: storage room. **141. devoted:** doomed.

JOHN FREETH
England, c.1731-1808

BOTANY BAY

Away with all whimsical bubbles of air,
Which only excite a momentary stare;
Attention to plans of utility pay,
Weigh anchor and steer towards Botany Bay.

Let no one think much of a trifling expense,   5
Who knows what may happen a hundred years hence;
The loss of America what can repay?
New colonies seek for at Botany Bay.

O'er Neptune's domain how extensive the scope!
Of quickly returning how distant the hope!   10
The Cape must be doubled, and then bear away
Two thousand good leagues to reach Botany Bay.

Of those *precious* souls which for nobody care,
It seems a large cargo the kingdom can spare;
To ship a few hundreds off make no delay,   15
They cannot too soon go to Botany Bay.

They go of an island to take special charge,
Much warmer than Britain, and ten times as large;
No Custom-house duty, no freightage to pay,
And tax-free they'll live when at Botany Bay.   20

This garden of Eden, this new promised land,
The time to set sail for is almost at hand;
Ye worst of land-lubbers, make ready for sea,
There's room for you all about Botany Bay.

As scores of each sex to this place must proceed,   25
In twenty years time — only think of the breed;
Major Semple, should Fortune much kindness display,
May live to be king over Botany Bay.

For a general good, make a general sweep,
The beauty of life is good order to keep;   30
With night-prowling hateful disturbers away,
And send the whole tribe into Botany Bay.

Ye chiefs who go out on this naval exploit,
The work to accomplish, and set matters right,
To Ireland be kind, call at Cork on your way,   35
And take a few White Boys to Botany Bay.

Commercial arrangements give prospect of joy,
Fair and firm may be kept ev'ry national tie;
And mutual confidence those who betray,
Be sent to the bottom of Botany Bay.   40

(1786)

ST. JEAN DE CRÈVECOEUR
France/Canada/U.S.A., 1735-1813

from *LETTERS FROM AN AMERICAN FARMER*

from *Letter III: What Is an American?*

. . . .

Whenever I hear of any new settlement, I pay it a visit once or twice a year, on purpose to observe the different steps each settler takes, the gradual improvements, the different tempers of each family, on which their prosperity in a great nature depends; their

---

BOTANY BAY   **7-8:** The Botany Bay penal colony in Australia (finally established in 1788) was planned after the American Revolution in 1776 made it impossible for the British to continue to send convicts to Virginia. **9. Neptune:** the god of the sea. **11. Cape:** the route to Australia went by either Cape Horn or the Cape of Good Hope. **27. Major Semple:** James George Semple, alias Semple-Lisle, Maxwell, Harrod, and Grant (1759- after 1799), a British adventurer who claimed to have fought with Frederick the Great and met the Empress Catherine of Russia, but who was arrested twice in England on charges of fraud, and twice sentenced (1786, 1795) to transportation to Australia; put to sea during a mutiny on board the convict ship in 1798, he returned to England via South America and Tangier, publishing his autobiography (1799) while confined to prison. **36. White Boys:** members of illegal bands of Irish farm workers (also called Levellers), organized in 1761 to resist landlords and tax collectors; the name derived from the practice of wearing white shirts over their clothes, to recognize each other at night.   **WHAT IS AN AMERICAN?**   The author, christened

different modifications of industry, their ingenuity, and contrivance; for being all poor, their life requires sagacity and prudence. In the evening I love to hear them tell their stories, they furnish me with new ideas; I sit still and listen to their ancient misfortunes, observing in many of them a strong degree of gratitude to God, and the government. Many a well meant sermon have I preached to some of them. When I found laziness and inattention to prevail, who could refrain from wishing well to these new countrymen, after having undergone so many fatigues. Who could withhold good advice? What a happy change it must be, to descend from the high, sterile, bleak lands of Scotland, where everything is barren and cold, to rest on some fertile farms in these middle provinces! Such a transition must have afforded the most pleasing satisfaction.

The following dialogue passed at an out-settlement, where I lately paid a visit:

Well, friend, how do you do now; I am come fifty odd miles on purpose to see you: how do you go on with your new cutting and slashing? Very well, good Sir, we learn the use of the axe bravely, we shall make it out; we have a belly full of victuals every day, our cows run about, and come home full of milk, our hogs get fat of themselves in the woods: Oh, this is a good country! God bless the king, and William Penn; we shall do very well by and by, if we keep our healths. Your log-house looks neat and light, where did you get these shingles? One of our neighbours is a New-England man, and he showed us how to split them out of chestnut-trees. Now for a barn, but all in good time, here are fine trees to build with. Who is to frame it, sure you don't understand that work yet? A countryman of ours who has been in America these ten years, offers to wait for his money until the second crop is lodged in it. What did you give for your land? Thirty-five shillings per acre, payable in seven years. How many acres have you got? An hundred and fifty. That is enough to begin with; is not your land pretty hard to clear? Yes, Sir, hard enough, but it would be harder still if it were ready cleared, for then we should have no timber, and I love the woods much; the land is nothing without them. Have not you found out any bees yet? No, Sir; and if we had we should not know what to do with them. I will tell you by and by. You are very kind. Farewell, honest man, God prosper you; whenever you travel toward ——, inquire for J. S. He will entertain you kindly, provided you bring him good tidings from your family and farm. In this manner I often visit them, and carefully examine their houses, their modes of ingenuity, their different ways; and make them all relate all they know, and describe all they feel. These are scenes which I believe you would willingly share with me. I well remember your philanthropic turn of mind. Is it not better to contemplate under these humble roofs, the rudiments of future wealth and population, than to behold the accumulated bundles of litigious papers in the office of a lawyer? To examine how the world is gradually settled, how the howling swamp is converted into a pleasing meadow, the rough ridge into a fine field; and to hear the cheerful whistling, the rural song, where there was no sound heard before, save the yell of the savage, the screech of the owl, or the hissing of the snake? Here an European, fatigued with luxury, riches, and pleasures, may find a sweet relaxation in a series of interesting scenes, as affecting as they are new. England, which

Michel-Guillaume Jean de Crèvecoeur, also used the name J. Hector St. John de Crèvecoeur. **19. William Penn:** (1644-1718), English Quaker who established the American colony of Pennsylvania in 1682.

now contains so many domes, so many castles, was once like this; a place woody and   *45*
marshy; its inhabitants, now the favourite nation for arts and commerce, were once
painted like our neighbours. The country will flourish in its turn, and the same
observations will be made which I have just delineated. Posterity will look back with
avidity and pleasure, to trace, if possible, the era of this or that particular settlement.

. . . .

(1782)

THOMAS PAINE
England /U.S.A., 1737-1809

from *THE CRISIS*

from *No. 1.   December 23, 1776*

These are the times that try men's souls: The summer soldier and the sunshine patriot
will, in this crisis, shrink from the service of his country; but he that stands it NOW,
deserves the love and thanks of man and woman. Tyranny, like hell, is not easily
conquered; yet we have this consolation with us, that the harder the conflict, the more
glorious the triumph. What we obtain too cheap, we esteem too lightly: 'Tis dearness   *5*
only that gives every thing its value. Heaven knows how to put a proper price upon its
goods; and it would be strange indeed, if so celestial an article as FREEDOM should not be
highly rated. Britain, with an army to enforce her tyranny, has declared that she has a
right (*not only to* TAX) but "*to* BIND *us in* ALL CASES WHATSOEVER," and if being *bound in
that manner,* is not slavery, then is there not such a thing as slavery upon earth. Even the   *10*
expression is impious, for so unlimited a power can belong only to God.

Whether the independence of the continent was declared too soon, or delayed too
long, I will not now enter into as an argument; my own simple opinion is, that had it
been eight months earlier, it would have been much better. We did not make a proper
use of last winter, neither could we, while we were in a dependant state. However, the   *15*
fault, if it were one, was all our own; we have none to blame but ourselves. But no great
deal is lost yet; all that Howe has been doing for this month past is rather a ravage than a
conquest, which the spirit of the Jerseys a year ago would have quickly repulsed, and
which time and a little resolution will soon recover.

I have as little superstition in me as any man living, but my secret opinion has ever   *20*
been, and still is, that God Almighty will not give up a people to military destruction, or
leave them unsupportedly to perish, who had so earnestly and so repeatedly sought to

---

45. domes: domiciles, houses. **46-47. inhabitants . . . painted:** referring to the Picts.   THE CRISIS   Also known as *The American Crisis*, it
consisted of a series of pamphlets printed between December 1776 and December 1783. **17. Howe:** William Howe, 5th Viscount Howe (1729-
1814), British commander-in-chief during the American Revolution. **18. the Jerseys:** The colony that later became New Jersey was at that time
divided into East Jersey and West Jersey.

avoid the calamities of war, by every decent method which wisdom could invent. Neither have I so much of the infidel in me, as to suppose that He has relinquished the government of the world, and given us up to the care of devils; and as I do not, I cannot see on what grounds the king of Britain can look up to Heaven for help against us: A common murderer, a highwayman, or a house-breaker has as good a pretence as he. 25

'Tis surprising to see how rapidly a panic will sometimes run through a country. All nations and ages have been subject to them: Britain has trembled like an ague at the report of a French fleet of flat-bottomed boats; and in the fourteenth century the whole 30 English army, after ravaging the kingdom of France, was driven back like men petrified with fear; and this brave exploit was performed by a few broken forces collected and headed by a woman, Joan of Arc. Would that Heaven might inspire some Jersey maid to spirit up her countrymen, and save her fair fellow sufferers from ravage and ravishment! Yet panics, in some cases, have their uses; they produce as much good as hurt. Their 35 duration is always short; the mind soon grows through them, and acquires a firmer habit than before. But their peculiar advantage is, that they are the touchstones of sincerity and hypocrisy, and bring things and men to light, which might otherwise have lain for ever undiscovered. In fact, they have the same effect on secret traitors, which an imaginary apparition would have upon a private murderer. They sift out the hidden 40 thoughts of man, and hold them up in public to the world. Many a disguised tory has lately shewn his head, that shall penitentially solemnize with curses the day on which Howe arrived upon the Delaware.

. . . .

from *THE RIGHTS OF MAN*

from *Part I*

Among the incivilities by which nations or individuals provoke and irritate each other, Mr. Burke's pamphlet on the French Revolution is an extraordinary instance. Neither the people of France, nor the National Assembly, were troubling themselves about the affairs of England, or the English Parliament; and that Mr. Burke should commence an unprovoked attack upon them, both in Parliament and in public, is a conduct that cannot 5 be pardoned on the score of manners, nor justified on that of policy.

There is scarcely an epithet of abuse to be found in the English language, with which Mr. Burke has not loaded the French nation and the National Assembly. Everything which rancour, prejudice, ignorance, or knowledge could suggest, is poured forth in the copious fury of near four hundred pages. In the strain and on the plan Mr. 10 Burke was writing, he might have written on to as many thousands. When the tongue or the pen is let loose in a frenzy of passion, it is the man, and not the subject, that becomes exhausted.

Hitherto Mr. Burke has been mistaken and disappointed in the opinions he had formed of the affairs of France; but such is the ingenuity of his hope, or the malignancy 15

---

26. king: i.e., George III.   **RIGHTS OF MAN   2. Burke's pamphlet:** See p. 640. See also Wollstonecraft's reply to Burke (p. 734) and Helen Maria Williams's letters on the French Revolution (p. 745). **5. in Parliament:** Burke also spoke on the subject in parliament.

of his despair, that it furnishes him with new pretences to go on. There was a time when it was impossible to make Mr. Burke believe there would be any revolution in France. His opinion then was, that the French had neither spirit to undertake it nor fortitude to support it; and now that there is one, he seeks an escape by condemning it.

Not sufficiently content with abusing the National Assembly, a great part of his work is taken up with abusing Dr. Price (one of the best-hearted men that lives) and the two societies in England known by the name of the Revolution Society and the Society for Constitutional Information. 20

Dr. Price had preached a sermon on the 4th of November, 1789, being the anniversary of what is called in England the Revolution, which took place in 1688. Mr. Burke, speaking of this sermon, says, "The political divine proceeds dogmatically to assert that, by the principles of the Revolution, the people of England have acquired three fundamental rights: 25

       1. To choose our own governors.

       2. To cashier them for misconduct. 30

       3. To frame a government for ourselves."

Dr. Price does not say that the right to do these things exists in this or in that person, or in this or in that description of persons, but that it exists in the *whole;* that it is a right resident in the nation. Mr. Burke, on the contrary, denies that such a right exists in the nation, either in whole or in part, or that it exists anywhere; and, what is still more strange and marvellous, he says, "that the people of England utterly disclaim such a right, and that they will resist the practical assertion of it with their lives and fortunes." That men should take up arms, and spend their lives and fortunes, *not* to maintain their rights, but to maintain they have *not* rights, is an entirely new species of discovery, and suited to the paradoxical genius of Mr. Burke. 35

The method which Mr. Burke takes to prove that the people of England have no such rights, and that such rights do not now exist in the nation, either in whole or in part, or anywhere at all, is of the same marvellous and monstrous kind with what he has already said; for his arguments are that the persons, or the generation of persons, in whom they did exist, are dead, and with them the right is dead also. To prove this, he quotes a declaration made by Parliament about a hundred years ago, to William and Mary, in these words: "The Lords Spiritual and Temporal, and Commons, do, in the name of the people aforesaid [meaning the people of England then living], most humbly and faithfully *submit* themselves, their *heirs* and *posterities*, for EVER." He also quotes a clause of another act of Parliament made in the same reign, the terms of which, he says, "bind us [meaning the people of that day], our *heirs* and our *posterity*, to *them*, their *heirs* and *posterity*, to the end of time." 45 50

Mr. Burke conceives his point sufficiently established by producing these clauses, which he enforces by saying that they exclude the right of the nation for *ever*. And not yet content with making such declarations, repeated over and over again, he further says, "that if the people of England possessed such a right before the Revolution [which he acknowledges to have been the case, not only in England, but throughout Europe, at an early period], yet that the *English nation* did, at the time of the Revolution, most solemnly renounce and abdicate it, for themselves, and for *all their posterity, for ever*." 55

As Mr. Burke occasionally applies the poison drawn from his horrid principles (if it is not profanation to call them by the name of principles) not only to the English nation, but to the French Revolution and the National Assembly, and charges that august, illuminated and illuminating body of men with the epithet of *usurpers,* I shall, *sans cérémonie,* place another system of principles in opposition to his.

The English Parliament of 1688 did a certain thing, which, for themselves and their constituents, they had a right to do, and which it appeared right should be done: But, in addition to this right, which they possessed by delegation, *they set up another right by assumption,* that of binding and controlling posterity to the end of time. The case, therefore, divides itself into two parts: the right which they possessed by delegation, and the right which they set up by assumption. The first is admitted; but with respect to the second, I reply —

There never did, there never will, and there never can, exist a parliament, or any description of men, or any generation of men, in any country, possessed of the right or the power of binding and controlling posterity to the *"end of time,"* or of commanding forever how the world shall be governed, or who shall govern it; and therefore all such clauses, acts, or declarations, by which the makers of them attempt to do what they have neither the right nor the power to do, nor the power to execute, are in themselves null and void. Every age and generation must be as free to act for itself *in all cases* as the ages and generations which preceded it. The vanity and presumption of governing beyond the grave is the most ridiculous and insolent of all tyrannies. Man has no property in man; neither has any generation a property in the generations which are to follow. The Parliament or the people of 1688, or of any other period, had no more right to dispose of the people of the present day, or to bind or to control them *in any shape whatever,* than the Parliament or the people of the present day have to dispose of, bind or control those who are to live a hundred or a thousand years hence. Every generation is, and must be, competent to all the purposes which its occasions require. It is the living, and not the dead, that are to be accommodated. When man ceases to be, his power and his wants cease with him; and having no longer any participation in the concerns of this world, he has no longer any authority in directing who shall be its governors, or how its government shall be organised, or how administered.

I am not contending for nor against any form of government, nor for nor against any party, here or elsewhere. That which a whole nation chooses to do, it has a right to do. Mr. Burke says, No. Where, then, does the right exist? I am contending for the rights of the *living,* and against their being willed away, and controlled and contracted for, by the manuscript assumed authority of the dead; and Mr. Burke is contending for the authority of the dead over the rights and freedom of the living. There was a time when kings disposed of their crowns by will upon their death-beds, and consigned the people, like beasts of the field, to whatever successor they appointed. This is now so exploded as scarcely to be remembered, and so monstrous as hardly to be believed. But the parliamentary clauses upon which Mr. Burke builds his political church are of the same nature.

The laws of every country must be analogous to some common principle. In England no parent or master, nor all the authority of Parliament, omnipotent as it has called itself, can bind or control the personal freedom even of an individual beyond the age of twenty-one years. On what ground of right, then, could the Parliament of 1688, or any other parliament, bind all posterity for ever?

Those who have quitted the world, and those who are not yet arrived in it, are as *105* remote from each other as the utmost stretch of mortal imagination can conceive. What possible obligation, then, can exist between them; what rule or principle can be laid down, that of two nonentities, the one out of existence and the other not in, and who never can meet in this world, the one should control the other to the end of time?

In England it is said that money cannot be taken out of the pockets of the people *110* without their consent. But who authorised, or who could authorise, the Parliament of 1688 to control and take away the freedom of posterity (who were not in existence to give or to withhold their consent), and limit and confine their right of acting in certain cases for ever?

A greater absurdity cannot present itself to the understanding of man than what Mr. *115* Burke offers to his readers. He tells them, and he tells the world to come, that a certain body of men who existed a hundred years ago, made a law, and that there does not now exist in the nation, nor ever will, nor ever can, a power to alter it. Under how many subtilties or absurdities has the divine right to govern been imposed on the credulity of mankind! Mr. Burke has discovered a new one, and he has shortened his journey to *120* Rome by appealing to the power of this infallible Parliament of former days; and he produces what it has done as of divine authority, for that power must certainly be more than human which no human power to the end of time can alter.

. . . .

It requires but a very small glance of thought to perceive, that although laws made in one generation often continue in force through succeeding generations, yet that they *125* continue to derive their force from the consent of the living. A law not repealed continues in force, not because it *cannot* be repealed, but because it *is not* repealed; and the non-repealing passes for consent.

But Mr. Burke's clauses have not even this qualification in their favour. They become null, by attempting to become immortal. The nature of them precludes consent. *130* They destroy the right which they *might* have, by grounding it on a right which they *cannot* have. Immortal power is not a human right, and therefore cannot be a right of Parliament. The Parliament of 1688 might as well have passed an act to have authorised themselves to live for ever, as to make their authority live for ever. All, therefore, that can be said of those clauses is that they are a formality of words, of as much import as if *135* those who used them had addressed a congratulation to themselves, and in the oriental style of antiquity had said: O Parliament, live for ever!

The circumstances of the world are continually changing, and the opinions of men change also; and as government is for the living, and not for the dead, it is the living only that has any right in it. That which may be thought right and found convenient in *140* one age may be thought wrong and found inconvenient in another. In such cases, who is to decide, the living, or the dead?

As almost one hundred pages of Mr. Burke's book are employed upon these clauses, it will consequently follow that if the clauses themselves, so far as they set up an *assumed usurped* dominion over posterity for ever, are unauthoritative, and in their *145* nature null and void; that all his voluminous inferences, and declamation drawn therefrom, or founded thereon, are null and void also; and on this ground I rest the matter.

We now come more particularly to the affairs of France. Mr. Burke's book has the appearance of being written as instruction to the French nation; but if I may permit *150* myself the use of an extravagant metaphor, suited to the extravagance of the case, it is darkness attempting to illuminate light.

While I am writing this there are accidentally before me some proposals for a declaration of rights by the Marquis de Lafayette (I ask his pardon for using his former address, and do it only for distinction's sake) to the National Assembly, on the 11th of *155* July, 1789, three days before the taking of the Bastille; and I cannot but remark with astonishment how opposite the sources are from which that gentleman and Mr. Burke draw their principles. Instead of referring to musty records and mouldy parchments to prove that the rights of the living are lost, "renounced and abdicated for ever," by those who are now no more, as Mr. Burke has done, M. de Lafayette applies to the living *160* world, and emphatically says, "Call to mind the sentiments which Nature has engraved in the heart of every citizen, and which take a new force when they are solemnly recognised by all: For a Nation to love Liberty, it is sufficient that she knows it; and to be free, it is sufficient that she wills it." How dry, barren, and obscure is the source from which Mr. Burke labours; and how ineffectual, though gay with flowers, are all his *165* declamation and his arguments compared with these clear, concise, and soul-animating sentiments! Few and short as they are, they lead to a vast field of generous and manly thinking, and do not finish, like Mr. Burke's periods, with music in the ear, and nothing in the heart.

. . . .

"We have seen," says Mr. Burke, "the French rebel against a mild and lawful *170* monarch, with more fury, outrage, and insult, than any people has been known to rise against the most illegal usurper, or the most sanguinary tyrant." This is one among a thousand other instances, in which Mr. Burke shows that he is ignorant of the springs and principles of the French Revolution.

It was not against Louis XVI, but against the despotic principles of the government, *175* that the nation revolted. These principles had not their origin in him, but in the original establishment, many centuries back; and they were become too deeply rooted to be removed, and the Augean stable of parasites and plunderers too abominably filthy to be cleansed, by anything short of a complete and universal Revolution. When it becomes necessary to do a thing, the whole heart and soul should go into the measure, or not *180* attempt it. That crisis was then arrived, and there remained no choice but to act with determined vigour, or not to act at all. The King was known to be the friend of the nation, and this circumstance was favourable to the enterprise. Perhaps no man bred up in the style of an absolute king, ever possessed a heart so little disposed to the exercise of that species of power as the present King of France. But the principles of the *185* government itself still remained the same. The monarch and the monarchy were distinct and separate things; and it was against the established despotism of the latter, and not against the person or principles of the former, that the revolt commenced, and the Revolution has been carried.

---

168. periods: complete sentences, especially those consisting of several balanced clauses — i.e., implying rhetorical orotundity. **178. Augean stable:** One of the "labours of Hercules" was cleansing the Augean stables, which he did by diverting a river through them.

Mr. Burke does not attend to the distinction between *men* and *principles;* and, *190*
therefore, he does not see that a revolt may take place against the despotism of the latter,
while there lies no charge of despotism against the former.

. . . .

What Mr. Burke considers as a reproach to the French Revolution (that of bringing it
forward under a reign more mild than the preceding ones), is one of its highest honours.
The revolutions that have taken place in other European countries, have been excited by *195*
personal hatred. The rage was against the man, and he became the victim. But, in the
instance of France we see a revolution generated in the rational contemplation of the
rights of man, and distinguishing from the beginning between persons and principles.

But Mr. Burke appears to have no idea of principles when he is contemplating
governments. "Ten years ago," says he, "I could have felicitated France on her having a *200*
government, without inquiring what the nature of that government was, or how it was
administered." Is this the language of a rational man? Is it the language of a heart feeling
as it ought to feel for the rights and happiness of the human race? On this ground, Mr.
Burke must compliment all the governments in the world, while the victims who suffer
under them, whether sold into slavery, or tortured out of existence, are wholly forgotten. *205*
It is power, and not principles, that Mr. Burke venerates; and under this abominable
depravity he is disqualified to judge between them. Thus much for his opinion as to the
occasion of the French Revolution. I now proceed to other considerations.

I know a place in America called Point-no-Point, because as you proceed along the
shore, gay and flowery as Mr. Burke's language, it continually recedes and presents *210*
itself at a distance before you; but when you have got as far as you can go, there is no
point at all. Just thus it is with Mr. Burke's three hundred and fifty-six pages. It is
therefore difficult to reply to him. But as the points he wishes to establish may be
inferred from what he abuses, it is in his paradoxes that we must look for his arguments.

. . . .

from *Part II,   Chapter 1: Of Society and Civilisation*

Great part of that order which reigns among mankind is not the effect of government. It *215*
had its origin in the principles of society and the natural constitution of man. It existed
prior to government, and would exist if the formality of government was abolished. The
mutual dependence and reciprocal interest which man has upon man, and all parts of a
civilised community upon each other, create that great chain of connection which holds
it together. The landholder, the farmer, the manufacturer, the merchant, the tradesman, *220*
and every occupation, prospers by the aid which each receives from the other, and from
the whole. Common interest regulates their concerns, and forms their law; and the laws
which common usage ordains, have a greater influence than the laws of government. In
fine, society performs for itself almost everything which is ascribed to government.

To understand the nature and quantity of government proper for man, it is necessary *225*
to attend to his character. As Nature created him for social life, she fitted him for the
station she intended. In all cases she made his natural wants greater than his individual
powers. No one man is capable, without the aid of society, of supplying his own wants;
and those wants, acting upon every individual, impel the whole of them into society, as
naturally as gravitation acts to a centre. *230*

But she has gone further. She has not only forced man into society by a diversity of wants which the reciprocal aid of each other can supply, but she has implanted in him a system of social affections, which, though not necessary to his existence, are essential to his happiness. There is no period in life when this love for society ceases to act. It begins and ends with our being. *235*

If we examine with attention into the composition and constitution of man, the diversity of his wants and talents in different men for reciprocally accommodating the wants of each other, his propensity to society, and consequently to preserve the advantages resulting from it, we shall easily discover that a great part of what is called government is mere imposition. *240*

Government is no farther necessary than to supply the few cases to which society and civilisation are not conveniently competent; and instances are not wanting to show, that everything which government can usefully add thereto, has been performed by the common consent of society, without government.

For upward of two years from the commencement of the American War, and to a *245* longer period in several of the American states, there were no established forms of government. The old governments had been abolished, and the country was too much occupied in defence to employ its attention in establishing new governments; yet during this interval, order and harmony were preserved as inviolate as in any country in Europe. There is a natural aptness in man, and more so in society, because it embraces a *250* greater variety of abilities and resources, to accommodate itself to whatever situation it is in. The instant formal government is abolished, society begins to act: a general association takes place, and common interest produces common security.

So far is it from being true, as has been pretended, that the abolition of any formal government is the dissolution of society, that it acts by a contrary impulse, and brings *255* the latter the closer together. All that part of its organization which it had committed to its government devolves again upon itself, and acts through its medium. When men, as well from natural instinct as from reciprocal benefits, have habituated themselves to social and civilised life, there is always enough of its principles in practice to carry them through any changes they may find necessary or convenient to make in their *260* government. In short, man is so naturally a creature of society, that it is almost impossible to put him out of it.

Formal government makes but a small part of civilised life; and when even the best that human wisdom can devise is established, it is a thing more in name and idea than in fact. It is to the great and fundamental principles of society and civilisation — to the *265* common usage universally consented to, and mutually and reciprocally maintained — to the unceasing circulation of interest, which, passing through its million channels, invigorates the whole mass of civilised man — it is to these things, infinitely more than to anything which even the best instituted government can perform, that the safety and prosperity of the individual and of the whole depends. *270*

The more perfect civilisation is, the less occasion has it for government, because the more does it regulate its own affairs, and govern itself; but so contrary is the practice of old governments to the reason of the case, that the expenses of them increase in the proportion they ought to diminish. It is but few general laws that civilised life requires, and those of such common usefulness, that whether they are enforced by the forms of *275* government or not, the effect will be nearly the same. If we consider what the principles are that first condense men into society, and what the motives that regulate their mutual intercourse afterwards, we shall find, by the time we arrive at what is called government, that nearly the whole of the business is performed by the natural operation of the parts upon each other. 280

Man, with respect to all those matters, is more a creature of consistency than he is aware, or than governments would wish him to believe. All the great laws of society are laws of nature. Those of trade and commerce, whether with respect to the intercourse of individuals or of nations, are laws of mutual and reciprocal interest. They are followed and obeyed because it is the interest of the parties so to do, and not on account of any 285 formal laws their governments may impose or interpose.

But how often is the natural propensity to society disturbed or destroyed by the operations of government! When the latter, instead of being ingrafted on the principles of the former, assumes to exist for itself, and acts by partialities of favour and oppression, it becomes the cause of the mischiefs it ought to prevent. 290

If we look back to the riots and tumults which at various times have happened in England, we shall find that they did not proceed from the want of a government, but that government was itself the generating cause; instead of consolidating society, it divided it; it deprived it of its natural cohesion, and engendered discontents and disorders, which otherwise would not have existed. In those associations which men promiscuously form 295 for the purpose of trade, or of any concern in which government is totally out of the question, and in which they act merely on the principles of society, we see how naturally the various parties unite; and this shows, by comparison, that governments, so far from being always the cause or means of order, are often the destruction of it. The riots of 1780 had no other source than the remains of those prejudices which the 300 government itself had encouraged. But with respect to England there are also other causes.

Excess and inequality of taxation, however disguised in the means, never fail to appear in their effects. As a great mass of the community are thrown thereby into poverty and discontent, they are constantly on the brink of commotion; and deprived, as 305 they unfortunately are, of the means of information, are easily heated to outrage. Whatever the apparent cause of any riots may be, the real one is always want of happiness. It shows that something is wrong in the system of government, that injures the felicity by which society is to be preserved.

But as fact is superior to reasoning, the instance of America presents itself to 310 confirm these observations. If there is a country in the world where concord, according to common calculation, would be least expected, it is America. Made up, as it is, of people from different nations, accustomed to different forms and habits of government,

---

300. riots of 1780: the anti-Catholic "Gordon riots," precipitated by the introduction in parliament by Lord George Gordon (1751-1793) of a petition against the Roman Catholic Relief Act of 1778. **313. people from different nations:** "That part of America which is generally called New England, including New Hampshire, Massachusetts, Rhode Island, and Connecticut, is peopled chiefly by English descendants. In the State of New York, about half are Dutch, the rest English, Scotch, and Irish. In New Jersey, a mixture of English and Dutch, with some Scotch and Irish. In Pennsylvania, about one third are English, another Germans, and the remainder Scotch and Irish, with some Swedes. The states to the Southward have a greater proportion of English than the Middle States, but in all of them there is a mixture; and besides those enumerated, there are a considerable number of French, and some few of all the European nations, lying on the coast. The most numerous religious denomination is the Presbyterian; but no one sect is established above another, and all men are equally citizens" (Paine's note).

speaking different languages, and more different in their modes of worship, it would appear that the union of such a people was impracticable; but by the simple operation of *315* constructing government on the principles of society and the rights of man, every difficulty retires, and all the parts are brought into cordial unison. There the poor are not oppressed, the rich are not privileged. Industry is not mortified by the splendid extravagance of a court rioting at its expense. Their taxes are few, because their government is just; and as there is nothing to render them wretched, there is nothing to *320* engender riots and tumults.

A metaphysical man, like Mr. Burke, would have tortured his invention to discover how such a people could be governed. He would have supposed that some must be managed by fraud, others by force, and all by some contrivance; that genius must be hired to impose upon ignorance, and show and parade to fascinate the vulgar. Lost in the *325* abundance of his researches, he would have resolved and re-resolved, and finally overlooked the plain and easy road that lay directly before him.

One of the great advantages of the American Revolution has been that it led to a discovery of the principles, and laid open the imposition, of governments. All the revolutions till then had been worked within the small sphere of a court, and never on *330* the great floor of a nation. The parties were always of the class of courtiers; and whatever was their rage for reformation, they carefully preserved that fraud of the profession.

In all cases they took care to represent government as a thing made up of mysteries, which only themselves understood, and they hid from the understanding of the nation *335* the only thing that was beneficial to know, namely, *that government is nothing more than a national association acting on the principles of society.*

. . . .

(1791)

JONATHAN ODELL
U.S.A./Canada, 1737-1818

SONG: *For a fishing party near Burlington, on the Delaware, in 1776*

How sweet is the season, the sky how serene;
On Delaware's banks how delightful the scene;
The Prince of the Rivers, his waves all asleep,
In silence majestic glides on to the deep.

Away from the noise of the fife and the drum,   *5*
And all the rude din of Bellona we come;
And a plentiful store of good humor we bring
To season our feast in the shade of cold spring.

A truce then to all whig and tory debate;
True lovers of Freedom, contention we hate: *10*
For the demon of discord in vain tries his art
To possess or inflame a true Protestant heart.

True Protestant friends to fair Liberty's cause,
To decorum, good order, religion and laws,
From avarice, jealousy, perfidy, free;   *15*
We wish all the world were as happy as we.

SONG FOR A FISHING PARTY **2. Delaware:** the river on which Burlington, New Jersey, is located. **6. Bellona:** Roman goddess of war. **9. whig, tory:** The Whigs favoured the Revolution; the Tories favoured the Crown.

We have wants, we confess, but are free from the care
Of those that abound, yet have nothing to spare:
Serene as the sky, as the river serene,
We are happy to want envy, malice, and spleen.   *20*

While thousands around us, misled by a few,
The phantoms of pride and ambition pursue,
With pity their fatal delusion we see;
And wish all the world were as happy as we!

(1776)

MARY WHATELEY DARWALL
England, 1738-1825

ANACREONTIC

Fain would I sing of war and arms,
Hostile sounds and dire alarms;
Fain in nervous verse would tell
How Brunswick fought and Frenchmen fell;
How Britannia's thunders roar,   *5*
Echoing from each distant shore.
I feel my glowing heart expand,
And strike the strings with bolder hand:
But, ah! the trembling wire resounds,
"Murd'ring steel and dreadful wounds,   *10*
Heroes bleeding, heaps of slain
Strewed promiscuous o'er the plain,

Foaming billows, seas on fire,
Ill become a virgin's lyre."
    Convinced, ashamed, I leave the field,   *15*
Leave it to bards in battle skilled,
Pleased to resume my wonted themes,
Painted meadows, purling streams,
Cupid's pow'r, Philander's eyes,
Wreaths of willow, gales of sighs.   *20*
While spontaneous I complain,
Echoing rocks return the strain:
"Love shall rule these happy fields;
Mars himself to Cupid yields."

(1764)

TO MR. O—Y, UPON HIS ASKING THE AUTHOR TO PAINT HIS CHARACTER

Though you flatter my genius and praise what I write,
Sure this whimsical task was imposed out of spite.
Because this poor head with much scratching and thinking
Made some idle reflections on raking and drinking,
To clip my weak wings with malicious intention,   *5*
You present me a theme that defies all invention.
Your picture! Lord bless us! where can one begin?
To speak truth were insipid, to lie were a sin.

---

20. want: lack.   **ANACREONTIC   4. Brunswick:** George II, who led English, Hanoverian, and Austrian troops against the French at the Battle of Dettingen in 1743, during the War of the Austrian Succession (the last time a British sovereign led troops in person). **21. complain:** sing love songs. See also Abraham Cowley's version of the same poem by Anacreon (p. 396).   **TO MR. O—Y   Title:** When this poem first appeared, it was titled "To Mr. S— on his desiring her to paint his character"; "Mr. S—" was her mentor, friend, and neighbour, the poet and landscape gardener William Shenstone (see p. 608); the name was later changed to the fictional "Mr. O—Y" to obscure the personal occasion of the poem.

A N A C R E O N T I C.

FAIN wou'd I fing of War and Arms,
 Hoftile Sounds and dire Alarms ;
Fain in nervous Verfe wou'd tell,
How *Brunfwick* fought, and *Frenchmen* fell ;
How *Britannia*'s Thunders roar,
Echoing from each diftant Shore ;
I feel my glowing Heart expand,
And ftrike the Strings with bolder Hand :
But, ah ! the trembling Wire refounds,
" Murd'ring Steel and dreadful Wounds,
" Heroes bleeding, Heaps of Slain,
" Strew'd promifcuous o'er the Plain ;
" Foaming Billows, Seas on fire,
" Ill become a Virgin's Lyre."

Convinc'd, afham'd, I leave the Field,
Leave it to Bards in Battle fkill'd ;
Pleas'd to refume my wonted Themes,
Painted Meadows, purling Streams,
Cupid's Pow'r, *Philander*'s Eyes,
Wreaths of Willow, Gales of Sighs :
While fpontaneous I complain,
Echoing Rocks return the Strain ;
" *Love* fhall rule thefe happy Fields ;
" *Mars* himfelf to *Cupid* yields."

Plate 5. Mary Whateley Darwall's "Anacreontic," as it appeared in
Original Poems on Several Occasions by Miss Whateley, 1764.

You might think me in love should I paint your perfections;
Should I sketch out your faults you might make worse objections. *10*
Should I blend in one piece of superlative merit,
Good nature and wit, condescension and spirit;
Should with modesty, ease and politeness be joined;
Unlimited freedom, with manners refined;
Courage, tenderness, honour enthroned in one heart; *15*
With frankness, reserve; and with honesty, art:
Were these glaring good qualities placed in full view,
Do you think any soul would believe it was *you?*
"Why then, turn t'other side (says ill-nature) and find him,
In some few modish faults, leave his sex all behind him; *20*
For levity, flatt'ry, and so forth, he's famed" —
Prithee, peace fool, and let not such trifles be named.
If his failings be such, time will certainly cure 'em;
And the ladies, till then, will with pleasure endure 'em.

(1762, 1764)

Augustus Montague Toplady
England, 1740-1778

A Living and Dying Prayer for the Holiest Believer in the World

Rock of ages, cleft for me,
Let me hide myself in thee!
Let the water and the blood,
From thy riven side which flowed,
Be of sin the double cure; *5*
Cleanse me from its guilt and pow'r.

Not the labours of my hands
Can fulfil thy law's demands:
Could my zeal no respite know,
Could my tears for ever flow, *10*
All for sin could not atone:
Thou must save, and thou alone!

Nothing in my hand I bring;
Simply to thy Cross I cling;
Naked, come to thee for dress; *15*
Helpless, look to thee for grace;
Foul, I to the fountain fly:
Wash me, Saviour, or I die!

While I draw this fleeting breath —
When my eye-strings break in death — *20*
When I soar through tracts unknown —
See thee on thy judgment-throne —
Rock of ages, cleft for me,
Let me hide myself in thee.

(1776)

---

12. condescension: graciousness, considerateness.   **A Living and Dying Prayer** **20. eye-strings:** tendons of the eye.

JAMES BOSWELL
Scotland, 1740-1795

from *THE LIFE OF SAMUEL JOHNSON*

The *Dictionary,* we may believe, afforded Johnson full occupation this year. As it approached to its conclusion, he probably worked with redoubled vigour, as seamen increase their exertion and alacrity when they have a near prospect of their haven.

Lord Chesterfield, to whom Johnson had paid the high compliment of addressing to his Lordship the *Plan* of his *Dictionary,* had behaved to him in such a manner as to excite his contempt and indignation. . . . He told me, that there never was any particular incident which produced a quarrel between Lord Chesterfield and him; but that his Lordship's continued neglect was the reason why he resolved to have no connection with him. When the *Dictionary* was upon the eve of publication, Lord Chesterfield, who, it is said, had flattered himself with expectations that Johnson would dedicate the work to him, attempted, in a courtly manner, to soothe, and insinuate himself with the Sage, conscious, as it should seem, of the cold indifference with which he had treated its learned author; and further attempted to conciliate him, by writing two papers in *The World,* in recommendation of the work; and it must be confessed, that they contain some studied compliments, so finely turned, that if there had been no previous offence, it is probable that Johnson would have been highly delighted. Praise, in general, was pleasing to him; but by praise from a man of rank and elegant accomplishments, he was peculiarly gratified.

. . . .

This courtly device failed of its effect. Johnson, who thought that "all was false and hollow," despised the honeyed words, and was even indignant that Lord Chesterfield should, for a moment, imagine that he could be the dupe of such an artifice. His expression to me concerning Lord Chesterfield, upon this occasion, was, "Sir, after making great professions, he had, for many years, taken no notice of me; but when my *Dictionary* was coming out, he fell a scribbling in *The World* about it. Upon which, I wrote him a letter expressed in civil terms, but such as might show him that I did not mind what he said or wrote, and that I had done with him."

This is that celebrated letter of which so much has been said, and about which curiosity has been so long excited, without being gratified. . . .

TO THE RIGHT HONOURABLE THE EARL OF CHESTERFIELD
MY LORD,   *February 1755*
I have been lately informed, by the proprietor of *The World,* that two papers, in which my Dictionary is recommended to the public, were written by your Lordship. To be so

---

THE LIFE OF SAMUEL JOHNSON **1. this year:** 1754. **5. *Plan:*** in 1747.

distinguished, is an honour, which, being very little accustomed to favours from the great, I know not well how to receive, or in what terms to acknowledge.

When, upon some slight encouragement, I first visited your Lordship, I was overpowered, like the rest of mankind, by the enchantment of your address; and could not forbear to wish that I might boast myself *Le vainqueur du vainqueur de la terre;* — *35* that I might obtain that regard for which I saw the world contending; but I found my attendance so little encouraged, that neither pride nor modesty would suffer me to continue it. When I had once addressed your Lordship in public, I had exhausted all the art of pleasing which a retired and uncourtly scholar can possess. I had done all that I could; and no man is well pleased to have his all neglected, be it ever so little. *40*

Seven years, my Lord, have now passed, since I waited in your outward rooms, or was repulsed from your door; during which time I have been pushing on my work through difficulties, of which it is useless to complain, and have brought it, at last, to the verge of publication, without one act of assistance, one word of encouragement, or one smile of favour. Such treatment I did not expect, for I never had a Patron before. *45*

The shepherd in Virgil grew at last acquainted with Love, and found him a native of the rocks.

Is not a Patron, my Lord, one who looks with unconcern on a man struggling for life in the water, and, when he has reached ground, encumbers him with help? The notice which you have been pleased to take of my labours, had it been early, had been *50* kind; but it has been delayed till I am indifferent, and cannot enjoy it; till I am solitary, and cannot impart it; till I am known, and do not want it. I hope it is no very cynical asperity not to confess obligations where no benefit has been received, or to be unwilling that the Public should consider me as owing that to a Patron, which Providence has enabled me to do for myself. *55*

Having carried on my work thus far with so little obligation to any favourer of learning, I shall not be disappointed though I should conclude it, if less be possible, with less; for I have been long wakened from that dream of hope, in which I once boasted myself with so much exultation, my Lord, your Lordship's most humble, most obedient servant,

SAM. JOHNSON.

. . . .

A few of his definitions must be admitted to be erroneous. Thus, *Windward* and *60* *Leeward,* though directly of opposite meaning, are defined identically the same way; as to which inconsiderable specks it is enough to observe, that his Preface announces that he was aware there might be many such in so immense a work; nor was he at all disconcerted when an instance was pointed out to him. A lady once asked him how he came to define *Pastern* the *knee* of a horse: instead of making an elaborate defence, as *65* she expected, he at once answered, "Ignorance, Madam, pure ignorance." His definition of *Network* has been often quoted with sportive malignity, as obscuring a thing in itself

---

34. address: bearing, manner of speaking. **35. Le . . . terre:** "The conqueror of the conqueror of the world" — the "world" being that of society and fashion. **44. without . . . assistance:** In a note Boswell points out that Johnson did once receive ten pounds from Chesterfield, but felt that to be "so inconsiderable" that it wouldn't be fit to mention it. **45ff.:** See note to line 160 of *The Vanity of Human Wishes* (p. 591). **46-47:** *Eclogue* VIII, 43 (Boswell's note). **51. solitary:** Johnson's wife, Elizabeth, died in 1752.

very plain. But to these frivolous censures no other answer is necessary than that with which we are furnished by his own Preface.

"To explain, requires the use of terms less abstruse than that which is to be explained, and such terms cannot always be found. For as nothing can be proved but by supposing something intuitively known, and evident without proof, so nothing can be defined but by the use of words too plain to admit of definition. Sometimes easier words are changed into harder; as, *burial,* into *sepulture* or *interment*; *dry,* into *desiccative*; *dryness,* into *siccity or aridity*; *fit,* into *paroxysm*; for the *easiest* word, whatever it be, can never be translated into one more easy." 70 75

His introducing his own opinions, and even prejudices, under general definitions of words, while at the same time the original meaning of the words is not explained, as his *Tory, Whig, Pension, Oats, Excise,* and a few more, cannot be fully defended, and must be placed to the account of capricious and humourous indulgence. Talking to me upon this subject when we were at Ashbourne in 1777, he mentioned a still stronger instance of the predominance of his private feelings in the composition of this work, than any now to be found in it. "You know, Sir, Lord Gower forsook the old Jacobite interest. When I came to the word *Renegado,* after telling that it meant 'one who deserts to the enemy, a revolter,' I added, *Sometimes we say a* GOWER. Thus it went to the press; but the printer had more wit than I, and struck it out." 80 85

Let it, however, be remembered, that this indulgence does not display itself only in sarcasm towards others, but sometimes in playful allusion to the notions commonly entertained of his own laborious task. Thus: "*Grub-street,* the name of a street in London, much inhabited by writers of small histories, *dictionaries,* and temporary poems; whence any mean production is called *Grub-street.*" — "*Lexicographer,* a writer of dictionaries, a *harmless drudge.*" 90

. . . .

Mr. Thomas Davies the actor, who then kept a bookseller's shop in Russel-street, Covent-garden, told me that Johnson was very much his friend, and came frequently to his house, where he more than once invited me to meet him; but by some unlucky accident or other he was prevented from coming to us. 95

Mr. Thomas Davies was a man of good understanding and talents, with the advantage of a liberal education. Though somewhat pompous, he was an entertaining companion; and his literary performances have no inconsiderable share of merit. He was a friendly and very hospitable man. Both he and his wife (who has been celebrated for her beauty), though upon the stage for many years, maintained an uniform decency of character; and Johnson esteemed them, and lived in as easy an intimacy with them as with any family which he used to visit. Mr. Davies recollected several of Johnson's remarkable sayings, and was one of the best of the many imitators of his voice and manner, while relating them. He increased my impatience more and more to see the extraordinary man whose works I highly valued, and whose conversation was reported to be so peculiarly excellent. 100 105

At last, on Monday the 16th of May [1763], when I was sitting in Mr. Davies's back-parlour, after having drunk tea with him and Mrs. Davies, Johnson unexpectedly came into the shop; and Mr. Davies having perceived him through the glass door in the room in which

79: For *Pension, Oats,* and *Excise,* see the extracts from the *Dictionary* (pp. 600-01).

we were sitting, advancing towards us — he announced his aweful approach to me,   *110*
somewhat in the manner of an actor in the part of Horatio, when he addresses Hamlet on
the appearance of his father's ghost, "Look, my Lord, it comes." I found that I had a very
perfect idea of Johnson's figure, from the portrait of him painted by Sir Joshua Reynolds
soon after he had published his *Dictionary,* in the attitude of sitting in his easy chair in deep
meditation, which was the first picture his friend did for him, which Sir Joshua very kindly   *115*
presented to me, and from which an engraving has been made for this work. Mr. Davies
mentioned my name, and respectfully introduced me to him. I was much agitated; and
recollecting his prejudice against the Scotch, of which I had heard much, I said to Davies,
"Don't tell where I come from." — "From Scotland," cried Davies roguishly. "Mr. Johnson
(said I), I do indeed come from Scotland, but I cannot help it." I am willing to flatter myself   *120*
that I meant this as light pleasantry to soothe and conciliate him, and not as an humiliating
abasement at the expense of my country. But however that might be, this speech was
somewhat unlucky; for with that quickness of wit for which he was so remarkable, he
seized the expression "come from Scotland," which I used in the sense of being of that
country, and, as if I had said that I had come away from it, or left it, retorted, "That, Sir, I   *125*
find, is what a very great many of your countrymen cannot help." This stroke stunned me a
good deal; and when we had sat down, I felt myself not a little embarrassed, and
apprehensive of what might come next. He then addressed himself to Davies: "What do
you think of Garrick? He has refused me an order for the play for Miss Williams, because
he knows the house will be full, and that an order would be worth three shillings." Eager to   *130*
take any opening to get into conversation with him, I ventured to say, "O, Sir, I cannot
think Mr. Garrick would grudge such a trifle to you." "Sir" (said he, with a stern look), "I
have known David Garrick longer than you have done: and I know no right you have to talk
to me on the subject." Perhaps I deserved this check; for it was rather presumptuous in me,
an entire stranger, to express any doubt of the justice of his animadversion upon his old   *135*
acquaintance and pupil. I now felt myself much mortified, and began to think that the hope
which I had long indulged of obtaining his acquaintance was blasted. And, in truth, had not
my ardour been uncommonly strong, and my resolution uncommonly persevering, so rough
a reception might have deterred me forever from making any further attempts. Fortunately,
however, I remained upon the field not wholly discomfited, and was soon rewarded by   *140*
hearing some of his conversation, of which I preserved the following short minute, without
marking the questions and observations by which it was produced.

"People" (he remarked) "may be taken in once, who imagine that an author is
greater in private life than other men. Uncommon parts require uncommon opportunities
for their exertion."   *145*

"In barbarous society, superiority of parts is of real consequence. Great strength or
great wisdom is of much value to an individual. But in more polished times there are
people to do everything for money; and then there are a number of other superiorities,
such as those of birth and fortune, and rank, that dissipate men's attention, and leave no
extraordinary share of respect for personal and intellectual superiority. This is wisely   *150*
ordered by Providence, to preserve some equality among mankind."

129: David Garrick, actor and theatre-manager, friend of Johnson's from Lichfield days; Anna Williams, blind friend of Johnson and his late wife, lived in Johnson's house. **144. parts:** See note to line 171 of *The Vanity of Human Wishes* (p. 591).

"Sir, this book" (*The Elements of Criticism*, which he had taken up) "is a pretty essay, and deserves to be held in some estimation, though much of it is chimerical."

Speaking of one who with more than ordinary boldness attacked public measures and the royal family, he said,   *155*

"I think he is safe from the law, but he is an abusive scoundrel; and instead of applying to my Lord Chief Justice to punish him, I would send half a dozen footmen and have him well ducked."

"The notion of liberty amuses the people of England, and helps to keep off the *tædium vitæ*. When a butcher tells you that *his heart bleeds for his country,* he has, in *160* fact, no uneasy feeling."

"Sheridan will not succeed at Bath with his oratory. Ridicule has gone down before him, and, I doubt, Derrick is his enemy."

"Derrick may do very well, as long as he can outrun his character; but the moment his character gets up with him, it is all over."   *165*

It is, however, but just to record, that some years afterwards, when I reminded him of this sarcasm, he said, "Well, but Derrick has now got a character that he need not run away from."

I was highly pleased with the extraordinary vigour of his conversation, and regretted that I was drawn away from it by an engagement at another place. I had, for a part of the evening, been left alone with him, and had ventured to make an observation *170* now and then, which he received very civilly; so that I was satisfied that though there was a roughness in his manner, there was no ill-nature in his disposition. Davies followed me to the door, and when I complained to him a little of the hard blows which the great man had given me, he kindly took upon him to console me by saying, "Don't be uneasy. I can see he likes you very well."   *175*

     . . . .

                  (1791)

HESTER LYNCH THRALE PIOZZI
England, 1741-1821

from *BRITISH SYNONYMY: OR, AN ATTEMPT AT REGULATING THE CHOICE OF WORDS IN FAMILIAR CONVERSATION*

Libeller, Defamer, Lampooner, Satirist

The last of these gentlemen will perhaps complain that I have LIBELLED his character by placing it beside the other three. Yet 'tis but his intention, best known to himself too, that preserves, if indeed it does of right preserve him, from a place among this class of noxious although in some degree useful animals; the hornets, wasps, and stinging flies of

---

152: 1762 book by Henry Home, Lord Kames (1696-1782). 154-58: referring to John Wilkes (1727-1797), notorious critic of the government (mostly in his weekly *The North Briton*) and popular M.P. 160. *tædium vitæ*: (Latin) weariness of life. 162-63: Thomas Sheridan (1719-1788); Samuel Derrick (1724-1769); "Mr. Sheridan was then reading lectures on Oratory at Bath, where Derrick was Master of the Ceremonies" (Boswell's note). 163. doubt: suspect.

life, which emulate the vulture's voracity without her force, the serpent's venom too   *5*
without being possessed of his subtlety. Our SATIRIST is however confessedly the noblest
creature of the tribe; for he does not, like the DEFAMER, fix upon one person in particular to
calumniate, but censures (as he says, with hope of reforming) the sex or nation, or species
in general, which comes within the scope of his indignation; that indignation which he
would willingly make us believe was only raised by vice; — whilst his imitators, sheltered   *10*
by his example, and the ill-advised countenance given to his works, detract from virtue,
and slander innocence, under the merry appellation of LAMPOONERS. Foreigners may learn
in England, which teems with these insects almost peculiar to our climate, that he is with
most propriety termed a LIBELLER who insults superiority with reproach, taking Thersites
for his Grecian model; while the LAMPOONERS love mysterious mischief and filthy   *15*
research, and ought to consider the Roman Clodius as head and president of their detested
sect. But DEFAMERS, who are 'tis agreed least worthy our attention, as furthest removed out
of the ranks of humanity, claim no higher patron sure than Shakespeare's Caliban, who
turns upon his benefactors, and says, as some of *them* might well have done,

> You taught me language and my profit on't   *20*
> Is, I know how to curse; the red plague rid ye
> For learning me your language!

Such beings are however best neglected, and they are soon forgotten: the most
compendious and witty answer to them all is that little epigram first published in
Dodsley's Collection, thence taken and put into every other,   *25*

> Lie on, while my revenge shall be
> To speak the very truth of thee.

(1794)

ANNA SEWARD
England, 1742-1809

SONNET XI

How sweet to rove, from summer sun-beams veiled,
  In gloomy dingles; or to trace the tide
Of wandering brooks, their pebbly beds that chide;
  To feel the west wind cool refreshment yield,
That comes soft creeping o'er the flowery field,   *5*
  And shadowed waters; in whose bushy side
  The mountain bees their fragrant treasures hide

Murmuring; and sings the lonely thrush concealed:
Then, Ceremony, in thy gilded halls,
  When forced and frivolous the themes arise,   *10*
  With bow and smile unmeaning, O, how palls
At thee, and thine, my sense! — how oft it sighs
  For leisure, wood-lanes, dells and water-falls;
  And feels th'untempered heat of sultry skies!

(1799)

LIBELLER, DEFAMER, LAMPOONER, SATIRIST   **14. Thersites:** Greek soldier at Troy known chiefly for his scurrility and abusive
ridicule, killed by Achilles for laughing at Achilles' mourning for Penthesilea. **16. Clodius:** generally villainous Roman politician of the 1st century
B.C., enemy to Cicero, Cato, Pompey, and others. **18-22:** in *The Tempest*, I.ii.363-65. **25:** Robert Dodsley (1703-1764) published the six volumes of
A Collection of Poems by Several Hands between 1748 and 1758. This epigram, along with several other epigrams and poems, appears in the second
volume; its author was later identified as Robert Nugent, Earl Nugent (1702-1788).

ANNA LAETITIA BARBAULD
England, 1743-1825

WASHING-DAY

. . . . and their voice,
Turning again towards childish treble, pipes
And whistles in its sound. —

The Muses are turned gossips; they have lost
The buskined step, and clear high-sounding phrase,
Language of gods. Come then, domestic Muse,
In slipshod measure loosely prattling on
Of farm or orchard, pleasant curds and cream,   5
Or drowning flies, or shoe lost in the mire
By little whimpering boy, with rueful face;
Come, Muse, and sing the dreaded Washing-Day.
Ye who beneath the yoke of wedlock bend,
With bowed soul, full well ye ken the day   10
Which week, smooth sliding after week, brings on
Too soon — for to that day nor peace belongs
Nor comfort; ere the first gray streak of dawn,
The red-armed washers come and chase repose.
Nor pleasant smile, nor quaint device of mirth,   15
E'er visited that day: the very cat,
From the wet kitchen scared and reeking hearth,
Visits the parlour — an unwonted guest.
The silent breakfast-meal is soon dispatched;
Uninterrupted, save by anxious looks   20
Cast at the lowering sky, if sky should lower.
From that last evil, O preserve us, heavens!
For should the skies pour down, adieu to all
Remains of quiet: then expect to hear
Of sad disasters — dirt and gravel stains   25
Hard to efface, and loaded lines at once
Snapped short — and linen-horse by dog thrown down,
And all the petty miseries of life.
Saints have been calm while stretched upon the rack,
And Guatimozin smiled on burning coals;   30
But never yet did housewife notable
Greet with a smile a rainy washing-day.

— But grant the welkin fair, require not thou
Who call'st thyself perchance the master there,
Or study swept, or nicely dusted coat,   35
Or usual 'tendance; ask not, indiscreet,
Thy stockings mended, though the yawning rents
Gape wide as Erebus; nor hope to find
Some snug recess impervious: shouldst thou try
The 'customed garden walks, thine eye shall rue   40
The budding fragrance of thy tender shrubs,
Myrtle or rose, all crushed beneath the weight
Of coarse checked apron — with impatient hand
Twitched off when showers impend: or crossing lines
Shall mar thy musings, as the wet cold sheet   45
Flaps in thy face abrupt. Woe to the friend
Whose evil stars have urged him forth to claim
On such a day the hospitable rites!
Looks, blank at best, and stinted courtesy,
Shall he receive. Vainly he feeds his hopes   50
With dinner of roast chicken, savoury pie,
Or tart or pudding: pudding he nor tart
That day shall eat; nor, though the husband try,
Mending what can't be helped, to kindle mirth
From cheer deficient, shall his consort's brow   55
Clear up propitious: the unlucky guest
In silence dines, and early slinks away.
I well remember, when a child, the awe
This day struck into me; for then the maids,
I scarce knew why, looked cross, and drove me from them:
Nor soft caress could I obtain, nor hope   61
Usual indulgences; jelly or creams,
Relic of costly suppers, and set by
For me their petted one; or buttered toast,
When butter was forbid; or thrilling tale   65
Of ghost or witch, or murder — so I went
And sheltered me beside the parlour fire:

WASHING-DAY **Epigraph:** adapts a passage from the "Seven Ages of Man" soliloquy in *As You Like It*, II, vii, 161-63. **2. buskined:** tragic; see the note to lines 79-80 of Dryden's *Mac Flecknoe* (p. 435). **27. linen-horse:** a drying rack. **30. Guatimozin:** the Aztec Emperor Cuauhtémoc (d. 1525), who succeeded the brother of Montezuma II, but who failed to expel the Spanish from Mexico; Cortés charged him with treason and had him tortured to death. **33. welkin:** sky. **38. Erebus:** in Greek mythology, the subterranean world of shadows that the dead encounter on the way to Hades — or, loosely, Hades itself.

There my dear grandmother, eldest of forms,
Tended the little ones, and watched from harm,
Anxiously fond, though oft her spectacles   70
With elfin cunning hid, and oft the pins
Drawn from her ravelled stocking, might have soured
One less indulgent.
At intervals my mother's voice was heard,
Urging dispatch: briskly the work went on,   75
All hands employed to wash, to rinse, to wring,
To fold, and starch, and clap, and iron, and plait.

Then would I sit me down, and ponder much
Why washings were. Sometimes through hollow bowl
Of pipe amused we blew, and sent aloft   80
The floating bubbles; little dreaming then
To see, Montgolfier, thy silken ball
Ride buoyant through the clouds — so near approach
The sports of children and the toils of men.
Earth, air, and sky, and ocean, hath its bubbles,   85
And verse is one of them — this most of all.

(1797)

THOMAS JEFFERSON
U.S.A., 1743-1826

LETTER TO HIS DAUGHTER

Annapolis, November 28, 1783

DEAR PATSY:

After four days' journey, I arrived here without any accident, and in as good health as
when I left Philadelphia. The conviction that you would be more improved in the
situation I have placed you than if still with me, has solaced me on my parting with you,
which my love for you has rendered a difficult thing. The acquirements which I hope
you will make under the tutors I have provided for you will render you more worthy of   5
my love, and if they cannot increase it, they will prevent its diminution. Consider the
good lady who has taken you under her roof, who has undertaken to see that you
perform all your exercises, and to admonish you in all those wanderings from what is
right or what is clever, to which your inexperience would expose you: consider her, I
say, as your mother, as the only person to whom, since the loss with which Heaven has   10
pleased to afflict you, you can now look up; and that her displeasure or disapprobation,
on any occasion, will be an immense misfortune, which should you be so unhappy as to
incur by any unguarded act, think no concession too much to regain her good-will. With
respect to the distribution of your time, the following is what I should approve:

    From 8 to 10, practice music.   15
    From 10 to 1, dance one day and draw another.
    From 1 to 2, draw on the day you dance, and write a letter next day.
    From 3 to 4, read French.
    From 4 to 5, exercise yourself in music.
    From 5 till bed-time, read English, write, etc.   20

---

77. plait: fold. **82. Montgolfier:** The Mongolfier brothers, Joseph Michel (1740-1810) and Jacques Etienne (1745-1799), first demonstrated the
viability of balloon flight by inflating a linen bag with hot air and sending it aloft for ten minutes, near Lyons, France, on June 5, 1783.   **LETTER
TO HIS DAUGHTER   10. your mother:** Jefferson's wife, Martha Skelton (who married him in 1772), died in 1782, having borne six children,
only three of whom survived her; only two of those (Martha and Mary) survived to maturity. "Patsy" is a diminutive of "Martha." For Jefferson's
contributions to drafting the American Declaration of Independence, see the excerpts from *The Gentleman's Magazine* (p. 657).

Communicate this plan to Mrs. Hopkinson, and if she approves of it, pursue it. As long as Mrs. Trist remains in Philadelphia, cultivate her affection. She has been a valuable friend to you, and her good sense and good heart make her valued by all who know her, and by nobody on earth more than me. I expect you will write me every post. Inform me what books you read, what tunes you learn, and enclose me your best copy of *25* every lesson in drawing. Write also one letter a week either to your Aunt Eppes, your Aunt Skipwith, your Aunt Carr, or the little lady from whom I now enclose a letter, and always put the letter you so write under cover to me. Take care that you never spell a word wrong. Always before you write a word, consider how it is spelt, and if you do not remember it, turn to a dictionary; it produces great praise to a lady to spell well. I have *30* placed my happiness on seeing you good and accomplished; and no distress this world can now bring on me equal that of your disappointing my hopes. If you love me, then strive to be good under every situation and to all living creatures, and to acquire those accomplishments which I have put in your power, and which will go far towards ensuring you the warmest love of your affectionate father. *35*

Samuel Hearne
England / Canada, 1745-1792

from *A Journey from Prince of Wales's Fort in Hudson's Bay to the Northern Ocean*

Transactions at the Copper-mine River
July 14, 1771

We had scarcely arrived at the Copper-mine River when four Copper Indians joined us, and brought with them two canoes. They had seen all the Indians who were sent from us at various times, except Matonabbee's brother, and three others that were first dispatched from Congecathawhachaga.

On my arrival here I was not a little surprised to find the river differ so much from *5* the description which the Indians had given of it at the Factory; for, instead of being so large as to be navigable for shipping, as it had been represented by them, it was at that part scarcely navigable for an Indian canoe, being no more than one hundred and eighty yards wide, every where full of shoals, and no less than three falls were in sight at first view. *10*

Near the water's edge there is some wood; but not one tree grows on or near the top of the hills between which the river runs. There appears to have been formerly a much

---

Transactions at the Copper-mine River Hearne's expedition to the mouth of the Coppermine River, on the Arctic Ocean, took three years, from 1769 to 1772. **3. Matonabbee:** Hearne's Chipewyan guide (c.1737-1782), and the leader of the war party; he had been responsible in the 1750s for easing relations between the Chipewyans and the Athabasca Cree. **4. Congecathwhachaga:** a village on Cogead Lake (now called Point Lake). **6. Factory:** York Factory, a trading post south of Prince of Wales Fort on the western shore of Hudson's Bay.

greater quantity than there is at present; but the trees seem to have been set on fire some years ago, and, in consequence, there is at present ten sticks lying on the ground, for one green one which is growing beside them. The whole timber appears to have been, even in its greatest prosperity, of so crooked and dwarfish a growth as to render it of little use for any purpose but fire-wood.

Soon after our arrival at the river-side, three Indians were sent off as spies, in order to see if any Esquimaux were inhabiting the river-side between us and the sea. After walking about three-quarters of a mile by the side of the river, we put up, when most of the Indians went a hunting, and killed several musk-oxen and some deer. They were employed all the remainder of the day and night in splitting and drying the meat by the fire. As we were not then in want of provisions, and as deer and other animals were so plentiful, that each day's journey might have provided for itself, I was at a loss to account for this unusual economy of my companions; but was soon informed, that those preparations were made with a view to have victuals enough ready-cooked to serve us to the river's mouth, without being obliged to kill any in our way, as the report of the guns, and the smoke of the fires, would be liable to alarm the natives, if any should be near at hand, and give them an opportunity of escaping.

Early in the morning of the fifteenth, we set out, when I immediately began my survey, which I continued about ten miles down the river, till heavy rain coming on we were obliged to put up; and the place where we lay that night was the end, or edge of the woods, the whole space between it and the sea being entirely barren hills and wide open marshes. In the course of this day's survey, I found the river as full of shoals as the part which I had seen before; and in many places it was so greatly diminished in its width, that in our way we passed by two more capital falls.

Early in the morning of the sixteenth, the weather being fine and pleasant, I again proceeded with my survey, and continued it for ten miles farther down the river; but still found it the same as before, being every where full of falls and shoals. At this time (it being about noon) the three men who had been sent as spies met us on their return, and informed my companions that five tents of Esquimaux were on the west side of the river. The situation, they said, was very convenient for surprising them; and, according to their account, I judged it to be about twelve miles from the place we met the spies. When the Indians received this intelligence, no farther attendance or attention was paid to my survey, but their whole thoughts were immediately engaged in planning the best method of attack, and how they might steal on the poor Esquimaux the ensuing night, and kill them all while asleep. To accomplish this bloody design more effectually, the Indians thought it necessary to cross the river as soon as possible; and, by the account of the spies, it appeared that no part was more convenient for the purpose than that where we had met them, it being there very smooth, and at a considerable distance from any fall. Accordingly, after the Indians had put all their guns, spears, targets, &c. in good order, we crossed the river, which took up some time.

When we arrived on the West side of the river, each painted the front of his target or shield; some with the figure of the Sun, others with that of the Moon, several with

36. **capital:** excellent.

different kinds of birds and beasts of prey, and many with the images of imaginary 55
beings, which, according to their silly notions, are the inhabitants of the different
elements, Earth, Sea, Air, &c.

On enquiring the reason of their doing so, I learned that each man painted his shield
with the image of that being on which he relied most for success in the intended
engagement. Some were contented with a single representation; while others, doubtful, 60
as I suppose, of the quality and power of any single being, had their shields covered to
the very margin with a group of hieroglyphics, quite unintelligible to every one except
the painter. Indeed, from the hurry in which this business was necessarily done, the want
of every colour but red and black, and the deficiency of skill in the artist, most of those
paintings had more the appearance of a number of accidental blotches, than "of any 65
thing that is on the earth, or in the water under the earth"; and though some few of them
conveyed a tolerable idea of the thing intended, yet even these were many degrees
worse than our country sign-paintings in England.

When this piece of superstition was completed, we began to advance toward the
Esquimaux tents; but were very careful to avoid crossing any hills, or talking loud, for 70
fear of being seen or overheard by the inhabitants; by which means the distance was not
only much greater than it otherwise would have been, but, for the sake of keeping in the
lowest grounds, we were obliged to walk through entire swamps of stiff marly clay,
sometimes up to the knees. Our course, however, on this occasion, though very
serpentine, was not altogether so remote from the river as entirely to exclude me from a 75
view of it the whole way: on the contrary, several times (according to the situation of
the ground) we advanced so near it, as to give me an opportunity of convincing myself
that it was as unnavigable as it was in those parts which I had surveyed before, and
which entirely corresponded with the accounts given of it by the spies.

It is perhaps worth remarking, that my crew, though an undisciplined rabble, and by 80
no means accustomed to war or command, seemingly acted on this horrid occasion with
the utmost uniformity of sentiment. There was not among them the least altercation or
separate opinion; all were united in the general cause, and as ready to follow where
Matonabbee led, as he appeared to be ready to lead, according to the advice of an old
Copper Indian, who had joined us on our first arrival at the river where this bloody 85
business was first proposed.

Never was reciprocity of interest more generally regarded among a number of
people, than it was on the present occasion by my crew, for not one was a moment in
want of any thing that another could spare; and if ever the spirit of disinterested
friendship expanded the heart of a Northern Indian, it was here exhibited in the most 90
extensive meaning of the word. Property of every kind that could be of general use now
ceased to be private, and every one who had any thing which came under that
description, seemed proud of an opportunity of giving it, or lending it to those who had
none, or were most in want of it.

The number of my crew was so much greater than that which five tents could 95
contain, and the warlike manner in which they were equipped so greatly superior to

---

56. silly: simple, unsophisticated. **65-66. "of . . . earth":** See Exodus 20:4.

what could be expected of the poor Esquimaux, that no less than a total massacre of every one of them was likely to be the case, unless Providence should work a miracle for their deliverance.

The land was so situated that we walked under cover of the rocks and hills till we were *100* within two hundred yards of the tents. There we lay in ambush for some time, watching the motions of the Esquimaux; and here the Indians would have advised me to stay till the fight was over, but to this I could by no means consent; for I considered that when the Esquimaux came to be surprised, they would try every way to escape, and if they found me alone, not knowing me from an enemy, they would probably proceed to violence against *105* me when no person was near to assist. For this reason I determined to accompany them, telling them at the same time, that I would not have any hand in the murder they were about to commit, unless I found it necessary for my own safety. The Indians were not displeased at this proposal; one of them immediately fixed me a spear, and another lent me a broad bayonet for my protection, but at that time I could not be provided with a target; nor did I *110* want to be encumbered with such an unnecessary piece of lumber.

While we lay in ambush, the Indians performed the last ceremonies which were thought necessary before the engagement. These chiefly consisted in painting their faces; some all black, some all red, and others with a mixture of the two; and to prevent their hair from blowing into their eyes, it was either tied before and behind, and on both *115* sides, or else cut short all round. The next thing they considered was to make themselves as light as possible for running; which they did, by pulling off their stockings, and either cutting off the sleeves of their jackets, or rolling them up close to their armpits; and though the muskettoes at that time were so numerous as to surpass all credibility, yet some of the Indians actually pulled off their jackets and entered the lists *120* quite naked, except their breech-cloths and shoes. Fearing I might have occasion to run with the rest, I thought it also advisable to pull off my stockings and cap, and to tie my hair as close up as possible.

By the time the Indians had made themselves thus completely frightful, it was near one o'clock in the morning of the seventeenth; when finding all the Esquimaux quiet in *125* their tents, they rushed forth from their ambuscade, and fell on the poor unsuspecting creatures, unperceived till close at the very eaves of their tents, when they soon began the bloody massacre, while I stood neuter in the rear.

In a few seconds the horrible scene commenced; it was shocking beyond description; the poor unhappy victims were surprised in the midst of their sleep, and had neither *130* time nor power to make any resistance; men, women, and children, in all upward of twenty, ran out of their tents stark naked, and endeavoured to make their escape; but the Indians having possession of all the landside, to no place could they fly for shelter. One alternative only remained, that of jumping into the river; but, as none of them attempted it, they all fell a sacrifice to Indian barbarity! *135*

The shrieks and groans of the poor expiring wretches were truly dreadful; and my horror was much increased at seeing a young girl, seemingly about eighteen years of age, killed so near me, that when the first spear was stuck into her side she fell down at my

---

111. piece of lumber: encumbrance. **119. muskettoes:** mosquitoes. **124. frightful:** frightening. **128. neuter:** neutral.

feet, and twisted round my legs, so that it was with difficulty that I could disengage myself from her dying grasps. As two Indian men pursued this unfortunate victim, I solicited very *140* hard for her life; but the murderers made no reply till they had stuck both their spears through her body, and transfixed her to the ground. They then looked me sternly in the face, and began to ridicule me, by asking if I wanted an Esquimaux wife; and paid not the smallest regard to the shrieks and agony of the poor wretch, who was twining round their spears like an eel! Indeed, after receiving much abusive language from them on the *145* occasion, I was at length obliged to desire that they would be more expeditious in dispatching their victim out of her misery, otherwise I should be obliged, out of pity, to assist in the friendly office of putting an end to the existence of a fellow-creature who was so cruelly wounded. On this request being made, one of the Indians hastily drew his spear from the place where it was first lodged, and pierced it through her breast near the heart. *150* The love of life, however, even in this most miserable state, was so predominant, that though this might justly be called the most merciful act that could be done for the poor creature, it seemed to be unwelcome, for though much exhausted by pain and loss of blood, she made several efforts to ward off the friendly blow. My situation and the terror of my mind at beholding this butchery, cannot easily be conceived, much less described; *155* though I summed up all the fortitude I was master of on the occasion, it was with difficulty that I could refrain from tears; and I am confident that my features must have feelingly expressed how sincerely I was affected at the barbarous scene I then witnessed; even at this hour I cannot reflect on the transactions of that horrid day without shedding tears.

(1787; 1795)

OLAUDAH EQUIANO
West Africa/England, c.1745-c.1797

from *THE INTERESTING NARRATIVE OF THE LIFE OF OLAUDAH EQUIANO OR GUSTAVUS VASSA, THE AFRICAN, WRITTEN BY HIMSELF*

That part of Africa, known by the name of Guinea, to which the trade for slaves is carried on, extends along the coast above 3400 miles, from the Senegal to Angola, and includes a variety of kingdoms. Of these the most considerable is the kingdom of Benin, both as to extent and wealth, the richness and cultivation of the soil, the power of its king, and the number and warlike disposition of the inhabitants. It is situated nearly *5*

THE INTERESTING NARRATIVE **Title:** Gustavus Vassa (or Vasa) was the name that European slave-owners gave to Equiano; it was the name of three Swedish kings, including Gustavus III, who reigned from 1771 to 1792. **1. Guinea:** meaning "forest," referring to the coastal regions of West Africa. **3. Benin:** one of the ancient kingdoms of West Africa (along with Ghana, Oyo, and others); it flourished in the 15th and 16th centuries, and was noted for its artistic achievements in gold, ivory, and bronze.

under the line, and extends along the coast about 170 miles, but runs back into the interior part of Africa to a distance hitherto I believe unexplored by any traveller; and seems only terminated at length by the empire of Abyssinia, near 1500 miles from its beginning. This kingdom is divided into many provinces or districts: in one of the most remote and fertile of which, called Eboe, I was born, in the year 1745, in a charming   *10* fruitful vale, named Essaka. The distance of this province from the capital of Benin and the sea coast must be very considerable; for I had never heard of white men or Europeans, nor of the sea: and our subjection to the king of Benin was little more than nominal; for every transaction of the government, as far as my slender observation extended, was conducted by the chiefs or elders of the place. The manners and   *15* government of a people who have little commerce with other countries are generally very simple; and the history of what passes in one family or village may serve as a specimen of a nation. My father was one of those elders or chiefs I have spoken of, and was styled Embrenche; a term, as I remember, importing the highest distinction, and signifying in our language a mark of grandeur. This mark is conferred on the person   *20* entitled to it, by cutting the skin across at the top of the forehead, and drawing it down to the eye-brows; and while it is in this situation applying a warm hand, and rubbing it until it shrinks up into a thick weal across the lower part of the forehead.

. . . .

My father, besides many slaves, had a numerous family, of which seven lived to grow up, including myself and a sister, who was the only daughter. As I was the   *25* youngest of the sons, I became, of course, the greatest favourite with my mother, and was always with her; and she used to take particular pains to form my mind. I was trained up from my earliest years in the art of war; my daily exercise was shooting and throwing javelins; and my mother adorned me with emblems, after the manner of our greatest warriors. In this way I grew up till I was turned the age of eleven, when an end   *30* was put to my happiness in the following manner: — Generally when the grown people in the neighbourhood were gone far in the fields to labour, the children assembled together in some of the neighbours' premises to play; and commonly some of us used to get up a tree to look out for any assailant, or kidnapper, that might come upon us; for they sometimes took those opportunities of our parents' absence to attack and carry off   *35* as many as they could seize. One day, as I was watching at the top of a tree in our yard, I saw one of those people come into the yard of our next neighbour but one, to kidnap, there being many stout young people in it. Immediately on this I gave the alarm of the rogue, and he was surrounded by the stoutest of them, who entangled him with cords, so that he could not escape till some of the grown people came and secured him. But alas!   *40* ere long it was my fate to be thus attacked, and to be carried off, when none of the grown people were nigh. One day, when all our people were gone out to their works as usual, and only I and my dear sister were left to mind the house, two men and a woman got over our walls, and in a moment seized us both, and, without giving us time to cry out, or make resistance, they stopped our mouths, and ran off with us into the nearest   *45* wood. Here they tied our hands, and continued to carry us as far as they could, till night

---

6. **line:** Equator. 38. **stout:** strong.

came on, when we reached a small house, where the robbers halted for refreshment, and spent the night. We were then unbound, but were unable to take any food; and, being quite overpowered by fatigue and grief, our only relief was some sleep, which allayed our misfortune for a short time. The next morning we left the house, and continued travelling all the day. For a long time we had kept the woods, but at last we came into a road which I believed I knew. I had now some hopes of being delivered; for we had advanced but a little way before I discovered some people at a distance, on which I began to cry out for their assistance: but my cries had no other effect than to make them tie me faster and stop my mouth, and then they put me into a large sack. They also stopped my sister's mouth, and tied her hands; and in this manner we proceeded till we were out of the sight of these people. When we went to rest the following night they offered us some victuals; but we refused it; and the only comfort we had was in being in one another's arms all that night, and bathing each other with our tears. But alas! we were soon deprived of even the small comfort of weeping together. The next day proved a day of greater sorrow than I had yet experienced; for my sister and I were then separated, while we lay clasped in each other's arms. It was in vain that we besought them not to part us; she was torn from me, and immediately carried away, while I was left in a state of distraction not to be described. I cried and grieved continually; and for several days I did not eat any thing but what they forced into my mouth. At length, after many days travelling, during which I had often changed masters, I got into the hands of a chieftain, in a very pleasant country. This man had two wives and some children, and they all used me extremely well, and did all they could to comfort me; particularly the first wife, who was something like my mother. Although I was a great many days journey from my father's house, yet these people spoke exactly the same language with us. This first master of mine, as I may call him, was a smith, and my principal employment was working his bellows, which were the same kind as I had seen in my vicinity. They were in some respects not unlike the stoves here in gentlemen's kitchens; and were covered over with leather; and in the middle of that leather a stick was fixed, and a person stood up, and worked it, in the same manner as is done to pump water out of a cask with a hand pump. I believe it was gold he worked, for it was of a lovely bright yellow colour, and was worn by the women on their wrists and ankles. I was there I suppose about a month, and they at last used to trust me some little distance from the house. This liberty I used in embracing every opportunity to inquire the way to my own home: and I also sometimes, for the same purpose, went with the maidens, in the cool of the evenings, to bring pitchers of water from the springs for the use of the house. I had also remarked where the sun rose in the morning, and set in the evening, as I had travelled along; and I had observed that my father's house was towards the rising of the sun. I therefore determined to seize the first opportunity of making my escape, and to shape my course for that quarter; for I was quite oppressed and weighed down by grief after my mother and friends; and my love of liberty, ever great, was strengthened by the mortifying circumstance of not daring to eat with the free-born children, although I was mostly their companion. While I was projecting my escape, one day an unlucky event

---

73. here: After regaining his freedom, Equiano wrote his autobiography in England.

happened, which quite disconcerted my plan, and put an end to my hopes. I used to be sometimes employed in assisting an elderly woman slave to cook and take care of the poultry; and one morning, while I was feeding some chickens, I happened to toss a small pebble at one of them, which hit it on the middle and directly killed it. The old slave, having soon after missed the chicken, inquired after it; and on my relating the accident (for I told her the truth, because my mother would never suffer me to tell a lie) she flew into a violent passion, threatened that I should suffer for it; and, my master being out, she immediately went and told her mistress what I had done. This alarmed me very much, and I expected an instant flogging, which to me was uncommonly dreadful; for I had seldom been beaten at home. I therefore resolved to fly; and accordingly I ran into a thicket that was hard by, and hid myself in the bushes. Soon afterwards my mistress and the slave returned, and, not seeing me, they searched all the house, but not finding me, and I not making answer when they called to me, they thought I had run away, and the whole neighbourhood was raised in the pursuit of me. In that part of the country (as in ours) the houses and villages were skirted with woods, or shrubberies, and the bushes were so thick that a man could readily conceal himself in them, so as to elude the strictest search. The neighbours continued the whole day looking for me, and several times many of them came within a few yards of the place where I lay hid. I then gave myself up for lost entirely, and expected every moment, when I heard a rustling among the trees, to be found out, and punished by my master: but they never discovered me, though they were often so near that I even heard their conjectures as they were looking about for me; and I now learned from them that any attempt to return home would be hopeless. Most of them supposed I had fled towards home; but the distance was so great, and the way so intricate, that they thought I could never reach it, and that I should be lost in the woods. When I heard this I was seized with a violent panic, and abandoned myself to despair.

. . . .

I heard frequent rustlings among the leaves; and being pretty sure they were snakes I expected every instant to be stung by them. This increased my anguish, and the horror of my situation became now quite insupportable. I at length quitted the thicket, very faint and hungry, for I had not eaten or drank any thing all the day; and crept to my master's kitchen, from whence I set out at first, and which was an open shed, and laid myself down in the ashes with an anxious wish for death to relieve me from all my pains. I was scarcely awake in the morning when the old woman slave, who was the first up, came to light the fire, and saw me in the fire place. She was very much surprised to see me, and could scarcely believe her own eyes. She now promised to intercede for me, and went for her master, who soon after came, and, having slightly reprimanded me, ordered me to be taken care of, and not to be ill-treated.

Soon after this my master's only daughter, and child by his first wife, sickened and died, which affected him so much that for some time he was almost frantic, and really would have killed himself, had he not been watched and prevented. However, in a small time afterwards he recovered, and I was again sold.

. . . .

From the time I left my own nation I always found somebody that understood me till I came to the sea coast. The languages of different nations did not totally differ, nor were they so copious as those of the Europeans, particularly the English. They were therefore easily learned; and, while I was journeying thus through Africa, I acquired two or three different tongues. In this manner I had been travelling for a considerable time, when one evening, to my great surprise, whom should I see brought to the house where I *135* was but my dear sister! As soon as she saw me she gave a loud shriek, and ran into my arms — I was quite overpowered: neither of us could speak; but, for a considerable time, clung to each other in mutual embraces, unable to do any thing but weep. Our meeting affected all who saw us; and indeed I must acknowledge, in honour of those sable destroyers of human rights, that I never met with any ill treatment, or saw any *140* offered to their slaves, except tying them, when necessary, to keep them from running away. When these people knew we were brother and sister they indulged us together; and the man, to whom I supposed we belonged, lay with us, he in the middle, while she and I held one another by the hands across his breast all night; and thus for a while we forgot our misfortunes in the joy of being together: but even this small comfort was *145* soon to have an end; for scarcely had the fatal morning appeared, when she was again torn from me for ever! I was now more miserable, if possible, than before. The small relief which her presence gave me from pain was gone, and the wretchedness of my situation was redoubled by my anxiety after her fate, and my apprehensions lest her sufferings should be greater than mine, when I could not be with her to alleviate them. *150* Yes, thou dear partner of all my childish sports! thou sharer of my joys and sorrows! happy should I have ever esteemed myself to encounter every misery for you, and to procure your freedom by the sacrifice of my own. Though you were early forced from my arms, your image has been always rivetted in my heart, from which neither time nor fortune have been able to remove it; so that, while the thoughts of your sufferings have *155* damped my prosperity, they have mingled with adversity and increased its bitterness. To that Heaven which protects the weak from the strong, I commit the care of your innocence and virtues, if they have not already received their full reward, and if your youth and delicacy have not long since fallen victims to the violence of the African trader, the pestilential stench of a Guinea ship, the seasoning in the European colonies, *160* or the lash and lust of a brutal and unrelenting overseer.

I did not long remain after my sister. I was again sold, and carried through a number of places.

. . . .

All the nations and people I had hitherto passed through resembled our own in their manners, customs, and language: but I came at length to a country, the inhabitants of *165* which differed from us in all those particulars. I was very much struck with this difference, especially when I came among a people who did not circumcise, and ate without washing their hands. They cooked also in iron pots, and had European cutlasses and cross bows, which were unknown to us, and fought with their fists amongst themselves. Their women were not so modest as ours, for they ate, and drank, and slept, *170* with their men. But, above all, I was amazed to see no sacrifices or offerings among them. In some of those places the people ornamented themselves with scars, and likewise filed their teeth very sharp. They wanted sometimes to ornament me in the same manner, but I would not suffer them; hoping that I might some time be among a people who did not thus disfigure themselves, as I thought they did. At last I came to the *175* banks of a large river, which was covered with canoes, in which the people appeared to live with their household utensils and provisions of all kinds. I was beyond measure astonished at this, as I had never before seen any water larger than a pond or a rivulet: and my surprise was mingled with no small fear when I was put into one of these canoes, and we began to paddle and move along the river. We continued going on thus   *180* till night; and when we came to land, and made fires on the banks, each family by themselves, some dragged their canoes on shore, others stayed and cooked in theirs, and laid in them all night. Those on the land had mats, of which they made tents, some in the shape of little houses: in these we slept; and after the morning meal we embarked again and proceeded as before. I was often very much astonished to see some of the women,   *185* as well as the men, jump into the water, dive to the bottom, come up again, and swim about. Thus I continued to travel, sometimes by land, sometimes by water, through different countries and various nations, till, at the end of six or seven months after I had been kidnapped, I arrived at the sea coast.

. . . .

The first object which saluted my eyes when I arrived on the coast was the sea, and   *190* a slave ship, which was then riding at anchor, and waiting for its cargo. These filled me with astonishment, which was soon converted into terror when I was carried on board. I was immediately handled and tossed up to see if I were sound by some of the crew; and I was now persuaded that I had gotten into a world of bad spirits, and that they were going to kill me. Their complexions, too, differing so much from ours, their long hair,   *195* and the language they spoke (which was very different from any I had ever heard) united to confirm me in this belief. Indeed such were the horrors of my views and fears at the moment, that, if ten thousand worlds had been my own, I would have freely parted with them all to have exchanged my condition with that of the meanest slave in my own country. When I looked round the ship, too, and saw a large furnace of copper   *200* boiling, and a multitude of black people of every description chained together, every one of their countenances expressing dejection and sorrow, I no longer doubted of my fate; and, quite overpowered with horror and anguish, I fell motionless on the deck and fainted. When I recovered a little I found some black people about me, who I believed were some of those who brought me on board, and had been receiving their pay; they   *205* talked to me in order to cheer me, but all in vain. I asked them if we were not to be eaten by those white men with horrible looks, red faces, and loose hair. They told me I was not; and one of the crew brought me a small portion of spirituous liquor in a wine glass; but, being afraid of him, I would not take it out of his hand. One of the blacks therefore took it from him and gave it to me, and I took a little down my palate, which, instead of   *210* reviving me, as they thought it would, threw me into the greatest consternation at the strange feeling it produced, having never tasted any such liquor before. Soon after this the blacks who brought me on board went off, and left me abandoned to despair. I now saw myself deprived of all chance of returning to my native country, or even the least glimpse of hope of gaining the shore, which I now considered as friendly; and I even   *215* wished for my former slavery in preference to my present situation, which was filled with horrors of every kind, still heightened by my ignorance of what I was to undergo. I was not long suffered to indulge my grief; I was soon put down under the decks, and there I received such a salutation in my nostrils as I had never experienced in my life: so

that, with the loathsomeness of the stench, and crying together, I became so sick and 220
low that I was not able to eat, nor had I the least desire to taste any thing. I now wished
for the last friend, death, to relieve me; but soon, to my grief, two of the white men
offered me eatables; and, on my refusing to eat, one of them held me fast by the hands,
and laid me across I think the windlass, and tied my feet, while the other flogged me
severely. I had never experienced any thing of this kind before; and although, not being 225
used to the water, I naturally feared that element the first time I saw it, yet nevertheless,
could I have got over the nettings, I would have jumped over the side, but I could not;
and, besides, the crew used to watch us very closely who were not chained down to the
decks, lest we should leap into the water: and I have seen some of these poor African
prisoners most severely cut for attempting to do so, and hourly whipped for not eating. 230
This indeed was often the case with myself. In a little time after, amongst the poor
chained men, I found some of my own nation, which in a small degree gave ease to my
mind. I inquired of these what was to be done with us; they gave me to understand we
were to be carried to these white people's country to work for them. I then was a little
revived, and thought, if it were no worse than working, my situation was not so 235
desperate: but still I feared I should be put to death, the white people looked and acted,
as I thought, in so savage a manner; for I had never seen among any people such
instances of brutal cruelty; and this not only shewn towards us blacks, but also to some
of the whites themselves. One white man in particular I saw, when we were permitted to
be on deck, flogged so unmercifully with a large rope near the foremast, that he died in 240
consequence of it; and they tossed him over the side as they would have done a brute.
This made me fear these people the more; and I expected nothing less than to be treated
in the same manner. I could not help expressing my fears and apprehensions to some of
my countrymen: I asked them if these people had no country, but lived in this hollow
place (the ship): they told me they did not, but came from a distant one. "Then," said I, 245
"how comes it in all our country we never heard of them?" They told me because they
lived so very far off. I then asked where were their women? had they any like themselves? I was told they had: "and why," said I, "do we not see them?" they answered,
because they were left behind. I asked how the vessel could go? they told me they could
not tell; but that there were cloths put upon the masts by the help of the ropes I saw, and 250
then the vessel went on; and the white men had some spell or magic they put in the
water when they liked in order to stop the vessel. I was exceedingly amazed at this
account, and really thought they were spirits. I therefore wished much to be from
amongst them, for I expected they would sacrifice me: but my wishes were vain; for we
were so quartered that it was impossible for any of us to make our escape. While we 255
stayed on the coast I was mostly on deck; and one day, to my great astonishment, I saw
one of these vessels coming in with the sails up. As soon as the whites saw it, they gave
a great shout, at which we were amazed; and the more so as the vessel appeared larger
by approaching nearer. At last she came to an anchor in my sight, and when the anchor
was let go I and my countrymen who saw it were lost in astonishment to observe the 260
vessel stop; and were now convinced it was done by magic. Soon after this the other
ship got her boats out, and they came on board of us, and the people of both ships
seemed very glad to see each other. Several of the strangers also shook hands with us
black people, and made motions with their hands, signifying I suppose we were to go to

their country; but we did not understand them. At last, when the ship we were in had got 265
in all her cargo, they made ready with many fearful noises, and we were all put under
deck, so that we could not see how they managed the vessel. But this disappointment
was the least of my sorrow. The stench of the hold while we were on the coast was so
intolerably loathsome, that it was dangerous to remain there for any time, and some of
us had been permitted to stay on the deck for the fresh air; but now that the whole ship's 270
cargo were confined together, it became absolutely pestilential. The closeness of the
place, and the heat of the climate, added to the number in the ship, which was so crowded
that each had scarcely room to turn himself, almost suffocated us. This produced copious
perspirations, so that the air soon became unfit for respiration, from a variety of
loathsome smells, and brought on a sickness among the slaves, of which many died, thus 275
falling victims to the improvident avarice, as I may call it, of their purchasers. This
wretched situation was again aggravated by the galling of the chains, now become
insupportable; and the filth of the necessary tubs, into which the children often fell, and
were almost suffocated. The shrieks of the women, and the groans of the dying, rendered
the whole a scene of horror almost inconceivable. Happily perhaps for myself I was soon 280
reduced so low here that it was thought necessary to keep me almost always on deck; and
from my extreme youth I was not put in fetters. In this situation I expected every hour to
share the fate of my companions, some of whom were almost daily brought upon deck at
the point of death, which I began to hope would soon put an end to my miseries. Often
did I think many of the inhabitants of the deep much more happy than myself. I envied 285
them the freedom they enjoyed, and as often wished I could change my condition for
theirs. Every circumstance I met with served only to render my state more painful, and
heighten my apprehensions, and my opinion of the cruelty of the whites. One day they
had taken a number of fishes; and when they had killed and satisfied themselves with as
many as they thought fit, to our astonishment who were on the deck, rather than give any 290
of them to us to eat as we expected, they tossed the remaining fish into the sea again,
although we begged and prayed for some as well as we could, but in vain; and some of
my countrymen, being pressed by hunger, took an opportunity, when they thought no
one saw them, of trying to get a little privately; but they were discovered, and the
attempt procured them some very severe floggings. One day, when we had a smooth sea 295
and moderate wind, two of my wearied countrymen who were chained together (I was
near them at the time), preferring death to such a life of misery, somehow made through
the nettings and jumped into the sea: immediately another quite dejected fellow, who,
on account of his illness, was suffered to be out of irons, also followed their example;
and I believe many more would very soon have done the same if they had not been 300
prevented by the ship's crew, who were instantly alarmed. Those of us that were the
most active were in a moment put down under the deck, and there was such a noise and
confusion amongst the people of the ship as I never heard before, to stop her, and get the
boat out to go after the slaves. However, two of the wretches were drowned, but they
got the other, and afterwards flogged him unmercifully for thus attempting to prefer 305
death to slavery. In this manner we continued to undergo more hardships than I can now
relate, hardships which are inseparable from this accursed trade.

---

278. necessary tubs: i.e., for urine and feces.

. . . .

At last we came in sight of the island of Barbadoes, at which the whites on board gave a great shout, and made many signs of joy to us. We did not know what to think of this; but as the vessel drew nearer we plainly saw the harbour, and other ships of different kinds *310* and sizes; and we soon anchored amongst them off Bridge Town. Many merchants and planters now came on board, though it was in the evening. They put us in separate parcels, and examined us attentively. They also made us jump, and pointed to the land, signifying we were to go there. We thought by this we should be eaten by these ugly men, as they appeared to us; and, when soon after we were all put down under the deck again, there was *315* much dread and trembling among us, and nothing but bitter cries to be heard all the night from these apprehensions, insomuch that at last the white people got some old slaves from the land to pacify us. They told us we were not to be eaten, but to work, and were soon to go on land, where we should see many of our country people. This report eased us much; and sure enough, soon after we were landed, there came to us Africans of all languages. *320* We were conducted immediately to the merchant's yard, where we were all pent up together like so many sheep in a fold, without regard to sex or age. As every object was new to me every thing I saw filled me with surprise. What struck me first was that the houses were built with stories, and in every other respect different from those in Africa: but I was still more astonished on seeing people on horseback. I did not know what this *325* could mean; and indeed I thought these people were full of nothing but magical arts.

. . . .

We were not many days in the merchant's custody before we were sold after their usual manner, which is this: — On a signal given (as the beat of a drum), the buyers rush at once into the yard where the slaves are confined, and make choice of that parcel they like best. The noise and clamour with which this is attended, and the eagerness visible in the *330* countenances of the buyers, serve not a little to increase the apprehensions of the terrified Africans, who may well be supposed to consider them as the ministers of that destruction to which they think themselves devoted. In this manner, without scruple, are relations and friends separated, most of them never to see each other again. I remember in the vessel in which I was brought over, in the men's apartment, there were several brothers, who, in the *335* sale, were sold in different lots; and it was very moving on this occasion to see and hear their cries at parting. O, ye nominal Christians! might not an African ask you, learned you this from your God, who says unto you, Do unto all men as you would men should do unto you? Is it not enough that we are torn from our country and friends to toil for your luxury and lust of gain? Must every tender feeling be likewise sacrificed to your avarice? Are the *340* dearest friends and relations, now rendered more dear by their separation from their kindred, still to be parted from each other, and thus prevented from cheering the gloom of slavery with the small comfort of being together and mingling their sufferings and sorrows? Why are parents to lose their children, brothers their sisters, or husbands their wives? Surely this is a new refinement in cruelty, which, while it has no advantage to atone for it, *345* thus aggravates distress, and adds fresh horrors even to the wretchedness of slavery.

. . . .

(1789)

---

333. devoted: doomed.

HANNAH MORE
England, 1745-1833

THE RIOT: OR, HALF A LOAF IS BETTER THAN NO BREAD
In a Dialogue Between Jack Anvil and Tom Hod

"Come, neighbours, no longer be patient and quiet,
Come, let us kick up a bit of a riot;
I'm hungry, my lads, but I've little to eat,
So we'll pull down the mills, and we'll seize all the meat;
I'll give you good sport, boys, as ever you saw,   5
So a fig for the justice, a fig for the law."

Then his pitchfork Tom seized. — "Hold a moment,"
   says Jack,
"I'll show thee thy blunder, brave boy, in a crack,
And if I don't prove we had better be still,
I'll assist thee straightway to pull down every mill;   10
I'll show thee how passion thy reason does cheat,
Or I'll join thee in plunder for bread and for meat!

"What a whimsy to think thus our bellies to fill,
For we stop all the grinding by breaking the mill!
What a whimsy to think we shall get more to eat   15
By abusing the butchers who get us the meat!
What a whimsy to think we shall mend our spare diet
By breeding disturbance, by murder and riot!

"Because I am dry, 'twould be foolish, I think,
To pull out my tap and to spill all my drink;   20
Because I am hungry and want to be fed,
That is sure no wise reason for wasting my bread:
And just such wise reasons for minding their diet
Are used by those blockheads who rush into riot.

"I would not take comfort from others' distresses,   25
But still I would mark how God our land blesses;
For though in old England the times are but sad,
Abroad, I am told, they are ten times as bad;
In the land of the Pope there is scarce any grain,
And 'tis worse still, they say, both in Holland and Spain.

"Let us look to the harvest our wants to beguile,   31
See the lands with rich crops how they everywhere smile!
Meantime to assist us, by each western breeze,

Some corn is brought daily across the salt seas!
Of tea we'll drink little, of gin none at all,   35
And we'll patiently wait, and the prices will fall.

"But if we're not quiet, then let us not wonder
If things grow much worse by our riot and plunder;
And let us remember whenever we meet,
The more ale we drink, boys, the less we shall eat.   40
On those days spent in riot, no bread you brought home,
Had you spent them in labour, you must have had some.

"A dinner of herbs, says the wise man, with quiet,
Is better than beef amid discord and riot.
If the thing could be helped I'm a foe to all strife,   45
And I pray for a peace ev'ry night of my life;
But in matters of state not an inch will I budge,
Because I conceive I'm no very good judge.

"But though poor, I can work, my brave boy, with the
   best;
Let the king and the parliament manage the rest;   50
I lament both the war and the taxes together,
Though I verily think they don't alter the weather.
The king, as I take it, with very good reason,
May prevent a bad law, but can't help a bad season.

"The parliament men, although great is their power,   55
Yet they cannot contrive us a bit of a shower;
And I never yet heard, though our rulers are wise,
That they know very well how to manage the skies;
For the best of them all, as they found to their cost,
Were not able to hinder last winter's hard frost.   60

"Besides, I must share in the wants of the times,
Because I have had my full share in its crimes;
And I'm apt to believe the distress which is sent,
Is to punish and cure us of all discontent.
But the harvest is coming — potatoes are come!   65
Our prospect clears up; ye complainers be dumb!

THE RIOT The social unrest of the mid-1790s, caused by poor harvests and high prices, was one of several subjects addressed in Hannah More's *Cheap Repository Tracts*; these were broadsides or songs distributed to the working public — "The Riot" ("Written in ninety-five, a year of scarcity and alarm") was set to a popular tune, and the conventional refrain "Derry down" followed each stanza. **4. meat:** food. **8. in a crack:** in an instant. **34. corn:** grain. **43-44:** "Better is a dinner of herbs where love is, than a stalled ox and hatred therewith" (Proverbs 15:17). **46. peace:** England was then at war with France. **65. are come:** i.e., from Ireland, imported to take the place of wheat in the diet of the working class.

"And though I've no money, and though I've no lands,
I've a head on my shoulders, and a pair of good hands;
So I'll work the whole day, and on Sundays I'll seek
At church how to bear all the wants of the week.   70
The gentlefolks too will afford us supplies;
They'll subscribe — and they'll give up their puddings
   and pies.

"Then before I'm induced to take part in a riot,
I'll ask this short question — what shall I get by it?

So I'll e'en wait a little, till cheaper the bread,   75
For a mittimus hangs o'er each rioter's head:
And when of two evils I'm asked which is best,
I'd rather be hungry than hanged, I protest."

Quoth Tom, "Thou art right; if I rise, I'm a Turk."
So he threw down his pitchfork, and went to his work.   80

(1795)

CHARLES MORRIS
Wales/England, 1745-1838

COUNTRY AND TOWN

In London I never know what to be at,
Enraptured with this and enchanted with that!
I'm wild with the sweets of variety's plan,
And life seems a blessing too happy for man.

But the country, Lord help us, sets all matters right,   5
So calm and composing from morning till night;
O, it settles the spirits when nothing is seen
But an ass on a common or goose on a green.

In town if it rains, why it damps not our hope,
The eye has its range and the fancy her scope;   10
Still the same, though it pour all night and all day,
It spoils not our prospects, it stops not our way.

In the country how blessed, when it rains in the fields,
To feast upon transports that shuttlecock yields,
Or go crawling from window to window to see   15
A hog on a dunghill or crow on a tree.

In London how easy we visit and meet,
Gay pleasure the theme and sweet smiles are our treat;
Our morning's a round of good-humoured delight,
And we rattle in comfort and pleasure all night.   20

In the country how charming our visits to make
Through ten miles of mud for formality's sake,

With the coachman in drink and the moon in a fog,
And no thought in our head but a ditch and a bog.

In London if folks ill together are put,   25
A bore may be dropped or a quiz may be cut;
We change without end and, if happy or ill,
Our wants are at hand and our wishes at will.

In the country you're nailed, like a pale in your park,
To some stick of a neighbour, crammed into the ark;   30
Or if you are sick or in fits tumble down,
You reach death ere the doctor can reach you from town.

I have heard how that love in a cottage is sweet,
When two hearts in one link of soft sympathy meet;
I know nothing of that, for alas! I'm a swain   35
Who requires, I own it, more links to my chain.

Your jays and your magpies may chatter on trees,
And whisper soft nonsense in groves if they please;
But a house is much more to my mind than a tree,
And for groves, O! a fine grove of chimneys for me.   40

Then in town let me live and in town let me die,
For in truth I can't relish the country, not I.
If one must have a villa in summer to dwell,
O give me the sweet shady side of Pall Mall.

(c. 1797)

---

72. subscribe: take up a collection for the poor. **76. mittimus:** legal warrant committing a person to prison. **COUNTRY AND TOWN 14. transports:** joys; **shuttlecock:** the game of battledore-and-shuttlecock (similar to badminton). **20. rattle:** chatter. **26. quiz:** an annoying person. **44. Pall Mall:** fashionable street in London.

SUSANNA BLAMIRE
England, 1747-1794

ON IMAGINED HAPPINESS IN HUMBLE STATIONS

Ye bards who have polished your lays
    And sung of the charms of the grove,
That Truth's not the language of Praise,
    You leave Disappointment to prove.
'Tis true that the meadows are fine,   5
    Through which the rill tinkles along;
And the trees, which the woodbines entwine,
    Regale the sweet thrush for his song.
At morn, when the sunbeams unveil
    The beauties that hide with the night,   10
And the primrose and lily so pale
    The soft eye of Feeling delight,
I own, when bespangled with dew,
    The hawthorn in splendour appears;
The mock gem enriches the bough   15
    Till it melts into fanciful tears.
But yet these are charms of the hour,
    To which the hard heart will not yield;
The eye only dotes on the flower,
    But is caught by the glow of the field.   20
Delusion, ye bards, is your aim,
    You take not from Nature your quill;
The goddess you worship is Fame,
    And you talk of the cottage so still.
You say that sweet Innocence there   25
    Eternal devotion has paid;
That Cheerfulness carols her prayer,
    And Peace ever sleeps in the shade.
But trust me, ye belles of the town,
    Arcadia's a far distant view;   30
And though Ignorance roughens the clown,
    His heart's not one jot the more true.
His wiles I confess we behold
    Uncovered by delicate art;
But still his rude manners unfold   35
The vices that cling to the heart.
And think not, ye nymphs of degree,
    That Peace from the gay scene retires;
What is't in a cot that ye see
    Which kindles such fanciful fires?   40
Is't the roof bending low to the head,
    And lattice just hinting at light?
Hard labour can rest on a bed
    That would not your slumbers invite.
Ah no! trust the plain simple Muse   45
    Whom Nature appoints as her scribe;
Nor, tempted by daydreams, refuse
    Those gifts which Contentment can bribe.
'Tis ease both of fortune and mind
    This smiling companion can gain;   50
'Tis a friend, as correcting as kind,
    And a heart wholly free from all stain!
                        (first published 1842)

WEY, NED, MAN!

Wey, Ned, man! thou luiks sae down-hearted,
    Yen wad swear aw thy kindred were dead;
For sixpence, thy Jean and thee's parted —
    What then, man, ne'er bodder thy head!
There's lasses enow, I'll uphod te,   5
    And tou may be suin as weel matched;
Tou knows there's still fish i' the river
    As guid as has ever been catched.

Nay, Joe! tou kens nought o' the matter,
    Sae let's hae nae mair o' thy jeer;   10
Auld England's gown's worn till a tatter,
    And they'll nit new don her, I fear.
True liberty never can flourish,
    Till man in his reets is a king —
Till we tek a tithe pig frae the bishop,   15
    As he's duin frae us, is the thing.

WEY, NED, MAN! Title: "Stop, Ned, Man"; the poem is written in Cumberland dialect. **2. yen:** you. **5. uphod te:** grant you. **6. suin:** soon. **12. nit new don her:** not dress her anew.

What, Ned! and is this aw that ails thee?
  Mess, lad! tou deserves maist to hang!
What! tek a bit lad frae its owner! —
  Is this then thy fine *Reets o' Man?*   20
Tou ploughs, and tou sows, and tou reaps, man.
  Tou cums, and tou gangs, where tou will;
Nowther king, lword, nor bishop, dar touch thee,
  Sae lang as tou dis fwok nae ill!

How can tou say sae, Joe! tou kens, now,   25
  If hares were as plenty as hops,
I durstn't fell yen for my life, man,
  Nor tek't out o' auld Cwoley's chops:
While girt fwok they ride down my hedges,
  And spang o'er my fields o' new wheat,   30
Nought but ill words I get for my damage —
  Can ony man tell me *that's reet?*

Why, there I mun own the shoe pinches,
  Just there to find faut is nae shame;
Ne'er ak! there's nae hard laws in England,   35
  Except this bit thing about game:
Man, were we aw equal at mwornin,
  We couldn't remain sae till neet;
Some arms are far stranger than others,
  And some heads will tek in mair leet.   40

Tou couldn't mend laws an' tou wad, man;
  'Tis for other-guess noddles than thine;
Lord help te! sud beggars yence rule us,
  They'd tek off baith thy cwoat an' mine.
What is't then but law that stands by us,   45
  While we stand by country and king?
And as to being parfet and parfet,
  I tell thee, there is nae sec thing.

(1792; 1842)

Jeremy Bentham
England, 1748-1832

from *The Rationale of Reward*
from Book III: Reward Applied to Art and Science

from *Chapter 1: Art and Science — Divisions*

. . . .

Taken collectively, and considered in their connexion with the happiness of society, the arts and sciences may be arranged in two divisions; viz. — 1. Those of amusement and curiosity; 2. Those of utility, immediate and remote. These two branches of human knowledge require different methods of treatment on the part of governments.

  By arts and sciences of amusement, I mean those which are ordinarily called the   5
fine arts; such as music, poetry, painting, sculpture, architecture, ornamental gardening, &c. &c. Their complete enumeration must be excused: it would lead us too far from our present subject, were we to plunge into the metaphysical discussions necessary for its accomplishment. Amusements of all sorts would be comprised under this head.

  Custom has in a manner compelled us to make the distinction between the arts and   10
sciences of amusement, and those of curiosity. It is not, however, proper to regard the

---

21. Reets o' Man: See the excerpt from Thomas Paine's *The Rights of Man* (p. 673). **23. lword:** lord. **24. dis fwok:** do folk. **27. fell yen:** kill any. **28. auld Cwoley's chops:** old Coley's chops (i.e., take the hare from the jaws of the hunter's dog). **29. girt:** great. **30. spang:** spring, bound, leap. **33. mun:** must. **35. Ne'er ak:** Never ache, never fear. **39. stranger:** stronger. **40. leet:** light. **41. an' tou wad:** and you would; i.e., even if you wanted to. **43. sud beggars yence:** should beggars once (sometime). **The Rationale of Reward** For remarks on Bentham's Utilitarianism, see Carlyle's "Signs of the Times" (p. 866).

former as destitute of utility: on the contrary, there is nothing, the utility of which is more incontestable. To what shall the character of utility be ascribed, if not to that which is a source of pleasure? All that can be alleged in diminution of their utility is, that it is limited to the excitement of pleasure: they cannot disperse the clouds of grief or of misfortune. They are useless to those who are not pleased with them: they are useful only to those who take pleasure in them, and only in proportion as they are pleased.

By arts and sciences of curiosity, I mean those which in truth are pleasing, but not in the same degree as the fine arts, and to which at the first glance we might be tempted to refuse this quality. It is not that these arts and sciences of curiosity do not yield as much pleasure to those who cultivate them as the fine arts; but the number of those who study them is more limited. Of this nature are the sciences of heraldry, of medals, of pure chronology — the knowledge of ancient and barbarous languages, which present only collections of strange words, — and the study of antiquities, inasmuch as they furnish no instruction applicable to morality, or any other branch of useful or agreeable knowledge.

The utility of all these arts and sciences, — I speak both of those of amusement and curiosity, — the value which they possess, is exactly in proportion to the pleasure they yield. Every other species of the pre-eminence which may be attempted to be established among them is altogether fanciful. Prejudice apart, the game of push-pin is of equal value with the arts and sciences of music and poetry. If the game of push-pin furnish more pleasure, it is more valuable than either. Everybody can play at push-pin: poetry and music are relished only by a few. The game of push-pin is always innocent: it were well could the same be always asserted of poetry. Indeed, between poetry and truth there is a natural opposition: false morals, fictitious nature. The poet always stands in need of something false. When he pretends to lay his foundations in truth, the ornaments of his superstructure are fictions; his business consists in stimulating our passions, and exciting our prejudices. Truth, exactitude of every kind, is fatal to poetry. The poet must see everything through coloured media, and strive to make every one else to do the same. It is true, there have been noble spirits, to whom poetry and philosophy have been equally indebted; but these exceptions do not counteract the mischiefs which have resulted from this magic art. If poetry and music deserve to be preferred before a game of push-pin, it must be because they are calculated to gratify those individuals who are most difficult to be pleased.

All the arts and sciences, without exception, inasmuch as they constitute innocent employments, at least of time, possess a species of moral utility, neither the less real or important because it is frequently unobserved. They compete with, and occupy the place of those mischievous and dangerous passions and employments, to which want of occupation and ennui give birth. They are excellent substitutes for drunkenness, slander, and the love of gaming.

. . . .

It is to the cultivation of the arts and sciences, that we must in great measure ascribe the existence of that party which is now opposed to war: it has received its birth amid the occupations and pleasures furnished by the fine arts. These arts, so to speak, have enrolled under their peaceful banners that army of idlers which would have otherwise possessed no amusement but in the hazardous and bloody game of war.

---

29. **push-pin:** a child's game: the term is virtually synonymous with something that is simple, trivial, "child's play."

Such is the species of utility which belongs indiscriminately to all the arts and *55*
sciences. Were it the only reason, it would be a sufficient reason for desiring to see them
flourish and receive the most extended diffusion.

If these principles are correct, we shall know how to estimate those critics, more
ingenious than useful, who, under pretence of purifying the public taste, endeavour
successively to deprive mankind of a larger or smaller part of the sources of their *60*
amusement. These modest judges of elegance and taste consider themselves as
benefactors to the human race, whilst they are really only the interrupters of their
pleasure — a sort of importunate hosts, who place themselves at the table to diminish,
by their pretended delicacy, the appetite of their guests. It is only from custom and
prejudice that, in matters of taste, we speak of false and true. There is no taste which *65*
deserves the epithet *good,* unless it be the taste for such employments which, to the
pleasure actually produced by them, conjoin some contingent or future utility: there is
no taste which deserves to be characterized as bad, unless it be a taste for some
occupation which has a mischievous tendency.

The celebrated and ingenious Addison has distinguished himself by his skill in the *70*
art of ridiculing enjoyments, by attaching to them the fantastic idea of *bad taste.* In the
Spectator he wages relentless war against the whole generation of *false* wits. Acrostics,
conundrums, pantomimes, puppet-shows, *bouts-rimés,* stanzas in the shape of eggs, of
wings, burlesque poetry of every description — in a word, a thousand other light and
equally innocent amusements, fall crushed under the strokes of his club. And, proud of *75*
having established his empire above the ruins of these literary trifles, he regards himself
as the legislator of Parnassus! What, however, was the effect of his new laws? They
deprived those who submitted to them, of many sources of pleasure — they exposed
those who were more inflexible, to the contempt of their companions.

. . . .

(1825)

CHARLOTTE SMITH
England, 1749-1806

SONNET WRITTEN IN THE CHURCH YARD
AT MIDDLETON IN SUSSEX

Pressed by the moon, mute arbitress of tides,
  While the loud equinox its power combines,
  The sea no more its swelling surge confines,
But o'er the shrinking land sublimely rides.
The wild blast, rising from the western cave, *5*
  Drives the huge billows from their heaving bed,
  Tears from their grassy tombs the village dead,
And breaks the silent sabbath of the grave!

With shells and sea-weed mingled, on the shore
  Lo! their bones whiten in the frequent wave; *10*
  But vain to them the winds and waters rave;
They hear the warring elements no more:
While I am doomed — by life's long storm oppressed,
To gaze with envy on their gloomy rest.

(1789)

70ff.: See Addison's *Spectator* essays, numbers 58-63 (p. 490).

LADY ANNE LINDSAY
Scotland, 1750-1825

AULD ROBIN GRAY

When the sheep are in the fauld, when the cows come hame,
When a' the weary world to quiet rest are gane,
The woes of my heart fa' in showers frae my ee,
Unken'd by my gudeman, who soundly sleeps by me.

Young Jamie loo'd me weel, and sought me for his bride;
But saving ae crown-piece, he'd naething else beside.   6
To make the crown a pound, my Jamie gaed to sea;
And the crown and the pound, oh! they were baith for me!

Before he had been gane a twelvemonth and a day,
My father brak his arm, our cow was stown away;   10
My mither she fell sick — my Jamie was at sea —
And auld Robin Gray, oh! he came a-courting me.

My father cou'dna work, my mother cou'dna spin;
I toil'd day and night, but their bread I cou'dna win;
And Rob maintain'd them baith, and, wi' tears in his ee,
Said, "Jenny, oh! for their sakes, will you marry me?"   16

My heart it said na, and I look'd for Jamie back;
But hard blew the winds, and his ship was a wrack:
His ship it was a wrack! Why didna Jenny dee?
Or, wherefore am I spared to cry out, Woe is me!   20

My father argued sair — my mother didna speak,
But she look'd in my face till my heart was like to break:
They gied him my hand, but my heart was in the sea;
And so auld Robin Gray, he was gudeman to me.

I hadna been his wife, a week but only four,   25
When mournfu' as I sat on the stane at my door,
I saw my Jamie's ghaist — I cou'dna think it he,
Till he said, "I'm come hame, my love, to marry thee!"

O sair, sair did we greet, and mickle say of a';
Ae kiss we took, nae mair — I bade him gang awa.   30
I wish that I were dead, but I'm no like to dee;
For O, I am but young to cry out, Woe is me!

I gang like a ghaist, and I carena much to spin;
I darena think o' Jamie, for that wad be a sin.
But I will do my best a gude wife aye to be,   35
For auld Robin Gray, oh! he is sae kind to me.

(1771; 1776)

PHILIP FRENEAU
U.S.A., 1752-1832

TO SIR TOBY
A Sugar Planter in the Interior Parts of Jamaica

If there exists a hell — the case is clear —
Sir Toby's slaves enjoy that portion here:
Here are no blazing brimstone lakes, 'tis true;
But kindled rum too often burns as blue,
In which some fiend, whom nature must detest,   5
Steeps Toby's brand and marks poor Cudjoe's breast.

Here whips on whips excite perpetual fears,
And mingled howlings vibrate on my ears;
Here nature's plagues abound, to fret and tease,
Snakes, scorpions, despots, lizards, centipedes.   10
No art, no care escapes the busy lash;
All have their dues — and all are paid in cash.

AULD ROBIN GRAY   **1. fauld:** fold. **4. Unken'd:** unknown. **5. loo'd:** loved. **6. ae:** one. **7. gaed:** went. **8. baith:** both. **10. stown:** stolen. **19. dee:** die. **21. sair:** sore, greatly. **23. gied:** gave. **26. stane:** stone. **27. ghaist:** ghost. **29. greet:** cry; **mickle:** much. **35. aye:** always.   **TO SIR TOBY**   **6. Cudjoe:** the name given by African custom to male children born on a Monday (the African variant is Kojo); here, by extension, a slave name.

The eternal driver keeps a steady eye
On a black herd, who would his vengeance fly,
But chained, imprisoned, on a burning soil,   *15*
For the mean avarice of a tyrant, toil!
The lengthy cart-whip guards this monster's reign —
And cracks, like pistols, from the fields of cane.

    Ye powers who formed these wretched tribes, relate,
What had they done, to merit such a fate!   *20*
Why were they brought from Eboe's sultry waste,
To see that plenty which they must not taste —
Food, which they cannot buy, and dare not steal,
Yams and potatoes — many a scanty meal! —

    One, with a gibbet wakes his Negro's fears,   *25*
One to the windmill nails him by the ears;
One keeps his slave in darkened dens, unfed,
One puts the wretch in pickle ere he's dead:
This, from a tree suspends him by the thumbs,
That, from his table grudges even the crumbs!   *30*

    O'er yond' rough hills a tribe of females go,
Each with her gourd, her infant, and her hoe;
Scorched by a sun that has no mercy here,
Driven by a devil, whom men call overseer —

In chains, twelve wretches to their labors haste;   *35*
Twice twelve I saw, with iron collars graced! —

    Are such the fruits that spring from vast domains?
Is wealth, thus got, Sir Toby, worth your pains! —
Who would your wealth on terms like these possess,
Where all we see is pregnant with distress —   *40*
Angola's natives scourged by ruffian hands,
And toil's hard product shipped to foreign lands.

    Talk not of blossoms and your endless spring;
What joy, what smile, can scenes of misery bring? —
Though Nature here has every blessing spread,   *45*
Poor is the laborer — and how meanly fed! —

    Here Stygian paintings light and shade renew,
Pictures of hell, that Virgil's pencil drew:
Here, surely Charons make their annual trip,
And ghosts arrive in every Guinea ship,   *50*
To find what beasts these western isles afford,
Plutonian scourges, and despotic lords: —

    Here, they, of stuff determined to be free,
Must climb the rude cliffs of the Liguanee;
Beyond the clouds, in skulking haste repair,   *55*
And hardly safe from brother traitors there.

(1784)

FRANCES BURNEY, MME D'ARBLAY

England, 1752-1832

from *The DIARIES and LETTERS*

Addressed to a Certain Miss Nobody

Poland Street, London, March 27, 1768

To have some account of my thoughts, manners, acquaintance and actions, when the
hour arrives in which time is more nimble than memory, is the reason which induces me
to keep a Journal. A Journal in which I must confess my *every* thought, must open my
whole heart! But a thing of this kind ought to be addressed to somebody — I must
imagion myself to be talking — talking to the most intimate of friends — to one in   *5*
whom I should take delight in confiding, and remorse in concealment: — but who must

---

21. Eboe: probably the land of the Ibo in Nigeria; Freneau's own note reads: "A small Negro kingdom near the river Senegal." **47. Stygian:** in
classical mythology, pertaining to the River Styx, across which **Charon** (line 49) ferried the dead to Hades, where **Pluto** ruled (see line 52). **50.**
Guinea ship: slave ship. **54. Liguanee:** i.e., Liguanea, a district in southeastern Jamaica; following the English conquest of the island in 1655, the
Maroons (runaway slaves) escaped into the Blue Mountains (in the southeast) and the rugged "Cockpit country" (in the northwest), and set up
independent communities there; they signed a treaty with the English in 1738.

this friend be? to make choice of one in whom I can but *half* rely, would be to frustrate entirely the intention of my plan. The only one I could wholly, totally confide in, lives in the same house with me, and not only never *has,* but never *will,* leave me one secret to tell her. To *whom,* then, *must* I dedicate my wonderful, surprising and interesting Adventures? — to *whom* dare I reveal my private opinion of my nearest relations? my secret thoughts of my dearest friends? my own hopes, fears, reflections, and dislikes? — Nobody!

To Nobody, then, will I write my Journal! since to Nobody can I be wholly unreserved — to Nobody can I reveal every thought, every wish of my heart, with the most unlimited confidence, the most unremitting sincerity to the end of my life! For what chance, what accident can end my connections with Nobody? No secret *can* I conceal from Nobody, and to Nobody can I be *ever* unreserved. Disagreement cannot stop our affection, Time itself has no power to end our friendship. The love, the esteem I entertain for Nobody, Nobody's self has not power to destroy. From Nobody I have nothing to fear, the secrets sacred to friendship Nobody will not reveal when the affair is doubtful, Nobody will not look towards the side least favourable.

I will suppose you, then, to be my best friend, (tho' God forbid you ever should!) my dearest companion — and a romantick girl, for mere oddity may perhaps be more sincere — more tender — than if you were a friend in propria persona — in as much as imagionation often exceeds reality. In your breast my errors may create pity without exciting contempt; may raise your compassion, without eradicating your love. From this moment, then, my dear girl — but why, permit me to ask, must a *female* be made Nobody? Ah! my dear, what were this world good for, *were* Nobody a female? And now I have done with preambulation.

St. Martin's Street, Thursday night.
1st Decr. 1774

My Dear Daddy,

What you have thought of me and of my promises I know not — but evil communication! — Ever since I found myself *defrauded* of my proper goods and chattels by a certain gentleman whom I had held in the highest veneration for honesty; — I have insensibly found myself reconciled to a certain *easiness* of PROMISE and a *cavalier carelessness of* PERFORMANCE, which formerly I was Goth enough to be greatly averse to. The truth is — for at last I find I have still some Gothiness left — that while you thus inflexibly continue to hoard my *old* papers, it is with some effort that I send you *new* ones.

Hang her papers! you cry — if there is this fuss about them, I wish they were all at Old Nick! — prithee let her have them. Well, if I get them, at any rate I don't care. So you may abuse as much as you please, if you will but convey them to me. To *you* they can only furnish entertainment, if any, from the first perusal; — but to me, who know all the people and things mentioned, they may possibly give some pleasure, by rubbing up my memory, when I am a very Tabby, before when I shall not think of looking into them. But the *return* was the condition, so give me my *bond.*

DIARIES AND LETTERS **24. in propria persona:** (Latin) in one's own person. **Daddy:** Burney's pet name for the special family friend, Samuel Crisp (d.1783), author of the unsuccessful tragedy *Virginia* (1754). **42. Tabby:** old maid.

. . . .

And now my dearest Sir, to make you some amends for all the scolding and impertinence with which I have begun this letter, I will tell you that I have seen Omai, *45* and if I am, as I intend to be, very minute in my account, will you shake hands and be friends?

"Yes, you little Devil you! so *to business*, and no more words." Very well, I obey. You must know then, in the first place, that glad as I was to see this great personage, I extremely regretted not having *you* of the party, as you had half promised you would be, *50* — and as I am sure you would have been extremely well pleased, and that the Journey would have more than answered to you: but the notice was so extremely short it was impossible. Now to facts.

[   ] and my brother went last Monday to the play of Isabella at Drury Lane — They sat in one of the Upper Boxes, from whence they spied Omai and Mr. Banks — *55* upon which they crossed over to speak to his friend. Omai received him with a hearty shake of the hand, and made room for him by his side. Jem asked Mr. Banks when he could see him to dinner? Mr. B. said that he believed he was engaged every day till the holydays, which he was to spend at Hinchinbrooke. Jem then returned to . . . However on Tuesday night, very late, there came a note which I will write down. It was directed *60* to my brother. — Omai presents his Compts. to Mr. Burney, and if it is agreeable and convenient to him, he will do himself the honour of dining with Mr. Burney to-morrow, but if it is not so, Omai will wait upon Mr. Burney some other time that shall suit him better. Omai begs to have an answer, and that if he is to come, begs Mr. Burney will fetch him. *65*

. . . .

Mr. Strange and Mr. Hayes, at their own motion, came to dinner to meet our guest. We did not dine till four. But Omai came at two, and Mr. Banks and Dr. Solander brought him, in order to make a short visit to my father. They were all just come from the House of Lords, where they had taken Omai to hear the King make his speech from the Throne. *70*

For my part, I had been confined up stairs for three days — however, I was much better, and obtained leave to come down, though very much wrapt up, and *quite a figure,* but I did not chuse to appear till Mr. Banks and Dr. Solander were gone. I found Omai seated on the great chair, and my brother next to him, and talking Otaheite as fast as possible. You cannot suppose how fluently and easily Jem speaks it. Mama and Susy *75* and Charlotte were opposite. As soon as there was a *cessation* of talk, Jem introduced me, and told him I was another sister. He rose, and made a very fine bow, and then seated himself again. But when Jem went on, and told him that I was not well, he again directly rose, and muttering something of the *fire,* in a very polite *manner,* without *speech* insisting upon my taking his seat, — and he *would* not be refused. He then drew *80*

---

45. **Omai:** Tahitian adventurer (b. in Raiatea), whom Captain James Cook took with him to England in 1774. (Frances Burney's brother James was a Second Lieutenant in Cook's second expedition, 1772.) Given a social education in England, Omai became a feature at English salons, and was treated as a visiting "noble savage." He returned to Tahiti in 1777 and died there in 1789. 54. **Isabella:** Garrick's alteration (1757) of Thomas Southerne's *The Fatal Marriage.* 59. **Hinchinbrooke:** in Huntingdonshire, the seat of the Earl of Sandwich, where James was introduced to Cook, Joseph Banks (1743-1820; the naturalist on Cook's expedition), and Dr. Daniel Solander (67). 61. **Compts.:** compliments. 66. **Strange:** Robert Strange, friend of Mrs. Burney; **Hayes:** John Hayes, friend of Dr. Burney. 74. **Otaheite:** i.e., Tahitian. 77. **another sister:** Susan and Charlotte were also James's and Frances's sisters.

his chair next to mine. and looking at me with an expression of pity said "very well to-morrow-morrow?" — I imagine he meant *I hope* you will be very well in *two or three morrows* — and when I shook my head, he said *"no? O very bad!"* When Mr. Strange and Mr. Hayes were introduced to him, he paid his compliments with great politeness to them, which he has found a method of doing without *words*.   85

As he had been to Court, he was very fine. He had on a suit of Manchester velvet, lined with white satten, a *bag,* lace ruffles, and a very handsome sword which the King had given to him. He is tall and very well made, much darker than I expected to see him, but has a pleasing countenance.

He makes *remarkable* good bows — not for *him,* but for *anybody,* however long   90
under a Dancing Master's care. Indeed he seems to shame Education, for his manners are so extremely graceful, and he is so polite, attentive, and easy, that you would have thought he came from some foreign Court. You will think that I speak in a *high* style; but I assure you there was but one opinion about him.

At dinner I had the pleasure of sitting next to him, as my cold kept me near the fire.   95
The moment he was helped, he presented his plate to me, which, when I declined, he had not the *over-shot* politeness to offer *all round,* as I have seen some people do, but took it quietly again. He eat heartily and committed not the slightest blunder at table, neither did he do anything *awkwardly* or *ungainly.* He found by the turn of the conversation, and some wry faces, that a joint of beef was not roasted enough, and therefore when he was helped,   100
he took great pains to assure mama that he liked it, and said two or three times — *"very dood,* — very *dood."* It is very odd, but true, that he can pronounce the *th,* as in *thank you,* and the *w,* as in *well,* and yet cannot say *g,* which he uses a *d* for. But I now recollect, that in the beginning of a word, as *George,* he *can* pronounce it. He took a good deal of notice of Dick, yet was not quite so well pleased with him, as I had expected him to be.   105

During dinner, he called for some drink. The man, not understanding what he would have, brought the porter. We saw that he was wrong, however, Omai was too well bred to send it back, he took it in his hand, and the man then brought him the small beer; — he laughed, and said — "Two!" — however, he sent off the *small* beer, as the *worse* of the *two.* Another time he called for *port-wine.* And when the bread was   110
handed, he took two bits, and laughed and said *"one* — two." He even observed *my abstinence,* which I think you would have laughed at, for he turned to me with some surprize, when dinner was almost over, and said *"no wine?"*

Mr. Hayes asked him, through Jem, how he liked the King and his Speech. He had the politeness to try to answer in English and *to* Mr. Hayes — and said *"very well,* King   115
George!"

After dinner, mama gave the king for a toast. He made a bow, and said *"Thank you, madam"* and then *tost off "King George!"*

He told Jem that he had an engagement at six o'clock, to go with Dr. Solander to see no less than twelve ladies. — Jem translated this to us — he understands enough of   120
English to find out when he is talked of, in general, and so he did now, and he laughed heartily, and began to count, with his fingers, in order to be understood — "1, 2, 3, 4, 5, 6, 7, 8, 9, 10 — *twelve — woman!"* said he.

---

87. **bag:** ornamental silk pouch for the back part of a bag wig. 98. **eat:** ate.

When Mr. Banks and Dr. Solander went away, he said to them *Good-bye — good-bye*. He never looked at his dress, though it was on for the first time. Indeed he appears to be a perfectly rational and intelligent man, with an understanding far superior to the common race of *us cultivated gentry*. He could not else have borne so well the way of Life into which he is thrown, without some practice.

When the man brought him the *two* beers, I forgot to mention that in returning them, one hit against the other, and occasioned a little sprinkling. He was *shocked* extremely — indeed I was afraid for his fine cloaths, and would have pin'd up the wet table cloth, to prevent its hurting them — but he would not permit me; and, by his *manner* seem'd to *intreat* me not to trouble myself! — however he had thought enough to spread his handkerchief over his knee.

Before six, the coach came. Our man came in and said "Mr. Omai's servant." He heard it at once, and answered *"very well."* He kept his seat about five minutes after, and then rose and got his hat and sword. My father happening to be talking to Mr. Strange, Omai stood still, neither chusing to interrupt him, nor to make his compliments to any body else first. When he was disengaged, Omai went up to him, and made an exceeding fine bow — the same to mama — then separately to every one in the company, and then went out with Jem to his coach.

He must certainly possess an uncommon share of observation and attention. I assure you every body was delighted with him. I only wished I could have spoke his language. Lord Sandwich has actually studied it so as to make himself understood in it. His *hands* are very much *tattooed*, but his face is not at all. He is *by no means* handsome, though I like his *countenance*.

The conversation of our house has turned ever since upon Mr. *Stanhope* and *Omai* — the first with all the advantage of Lord Chesterfield's instructions, brought up at a great school, introduced at fifteen to a Court, taught all possible accomplishments from an infant, and having all the care, expence, labour, and benefit of the best education that any man can receive, — proved after it all a meer *pedantic booby;* — the second with no tutor but Nature, changes, after he is grown up, his dress, his way of life, his diet, his country and his friends; — and appears in a *new world* like a man who had all his life studied *the Graces*, and attended with unremitting application and diligence to form his manners, and to render his appearance and behaviour *politely easy*, and thoroughly *well bred*! I think this shows how much more *nature* can do without *art*, than *art* with all her refinement unassisted by *nature*.

If I have been too *prolix*, you must excuse me, because it is wholly owing to the great curiosity I have heard you express for whatever concerns Omai. My father desires his love to you, and says that if you will but come to town, as soon as Omai returns from Hinchinbrooke, he will promise you that you shall still have a meeting with him.

. . . .

Adieu, my dear Sir,

I beg you to believe me,

Your ever affectionate

and obliged

F. BURNEY.

---

147. Stanhope: Philip Stanhope (1732-1768), the son to whom Lord Chesterfield wrote his letters (see p. 560).

January, 1778

This year was ushered in by a grand and most important event! At the latter end of January the literary world was favoured with the first publication of the ingenious, learned, and most profound Fanny Burney! I doubt not but this memorable affair will, in future times, mark the period whence chronologers will date the zenith of the polite arts in this island! 165

This admirable authoress has named her most elaborate performance, *Evelina: or, a Young Lady's Entrance into the World*.

Perhaps this may seem a rather bold attempt and title for a female whose knowledge of the world is very confined, and whose inclinations, as well as situation, incline her to a private and domestic life. All I can urge is, that I have only presumed to 170 trace the accidents and adventures to which a "young woman" is liable; I have not pretended to show the world what it actually *is*, but what it *appears* to a girl of seventeen: and so far as that, surely any girl who is past seventeen may safely do?

. . . .

My little book, I am told, is now at all the circulating libraries. I have an exceeding odd sensation, when I consider that it is now in the power of *any* and *every* body to read 175 what I so carefully hoarded even from my best friends, till this last month or two; and that a work which was so lately lodged, in all privacy, in my bureau, may now be seen by every butcher and baker, cobbler and tinker, throughout the three kingdoms, for the small tribute of threepence.

My aunt Anne and Miss Humphries being settled at this time at Brompton, I was 180 going thither with Susan to tea, when Charlotte acquainted me that they were then employed in reading *Evelina* to the invalid, my cousin Richard.

. . . .

This intelligence gave me the utmost uneasiness — I foresaw a thousand dangers of a discovery — I dreaded the indiscreet warmth of all my confidants. In truth, I was quite sick with apprehension, and was too uncomfortable to go to Brompton, and Susan 185 carried my excuses.

Upon her return I was somewhat tranquillised, for she assured me that there was not the smallest suspicion of the author, and that they had concluded it to be the work of a *man!*

. . . .

Finding myself more safe than I had apprehended, I ventured to go to Brompton 190 next day. On my way upstairs I heard Miss Humphries in the midst of Mr. Villars's letter of consolation upon Sir John Belmont's rejection of his daughter; and just as I entered the room she cried out, "How pretty that is!"

How much in luck would she have thought herself had she known *who* heard her!

In a private confabulation which I had with my Aunt Anne, she told me a thousand 195 things that had been said in its praise, and assured me they had not for a moment doubted that the work was a *man's.*

. . . .

166-67. *Evelina . . . :* Burney's first novel, published anonymously. **180. Anne:** Dr. Burney's sister. **182. Richard:** son of Dr. Burney's brother, Richard Burney, of Worcester; Miss Humphries is also from Worcester. **191. Villars's letter:** *Evelina* is an epistolary novel.

I must own I suffered great difficulty in refraining from laughing upon several occasions, — and several times, when they praised what they read, I was up on the point of saying, "You are very good!" and so forth, and I could scarcely keep myself from *200* making acknowledgments, and bowing my head involuntarily. However, I got off perfectly safe.

. . . .

It seems, to my utter amazement, Miss Humphries has guessed the author to be Anstey, who wrote the *Bath Guide*! How improbable and how extraordinary a supposition! But they have both of them done it so much honour that, but for Richard's *205* anger at Evelina's bashfulness, I never could believe they did not suspect me.

. . . .

Windsor, Dec. 17th, 1785.

My Dearest Hetty —

I am sorry I could not more immediately write; but I really have not had a moment since your last.

Now I know what you next want is, to hear accounts of kings, queens, and such royal personages. Oho! Do you so? Well. *210*

Shall I tell you a few matters of fact? — or, had you rather a few matters of etiquette? Oh, matters of etiquette, you cry! for matters of fact are short and stupid, and anybody can tell, and everybody is tired with them.

Very well, take your own choice.

To begin, then, with the beginning. *215*

You know I told you, in my last, my various difficulties, what sort of preferment to turn my thoughts to, and concluded with just starting a young budding notion of decision, by suggesting that a handsome pension for nothing at all would be as well as working night and day for a salary.

This blossom of an idea, the more I dwelt upon, the more I liked. Thinking served it *220* for a hot-house, and it came out into full blow as I ruminated upon my pillow. Delighted that thus all my contradictory and wayward fancies were overcome, and my mind was peaceably settled what to wish and to demand, I gave over all further meditation upon choice of elevation, and had nothing more to do but to make my election known.

My next business, therefore, was to be presented. This could be no difficulty; my *225* coming hither had been their own desire, and they had earnestly pressed its execution. I had only to prepare myself for the rencounter.

You would never believe — you, who, distant from courts and courtiers, know nothing of their ways, — the many things to be studied, for appearing with a proper propriety before crowned heads. Heads without crowns are quite other sort of rotundas. *230*

Now, then, to the etiquette. I inquired into every particular, that no error might be committed. And as there is no saying what may happen in this mortal life, I shall give you those instructions I have received myself, that, should you find yourself in the royal presence, you may know how to comport yourself.

---

204. Anstey: Christopher Anstey (1724-1805), author of *The New Bath Guide; or, Memoirs of the B..d.....d* [Blunderhead] *Family. In a Series of Poetical Epistles* (1766). **Hetty:** her sister Esther, Dr. Burney's eldest daughter. **209ff.:** The following year, Frances was appointed a keeper of the robes to Queen Charlotte, wife of George III; after five years' service, she was granted a pension of £100 a year. **221. blow:** bloom.

Directions for coughing, sneezing, or moving, before the King and Queen.   *235*

In the first place, you must not cough. If you find a cough tickling in your throat, you must arrest it from making any sound; if you find yourself choking with the forbearance, you must choke — but not cough.

In the second place, you must not sneeze. If you have a vehement cold, you must take no notice of it; if your nose-membranes feel a great irritation, you must hold your   *240* breath; if a sneeze still insists upon making its way, you must oppose it, by keeping your teeth grinding together; if the violence of the repulse breaks some blood-vessel, you must break the blood-vessel — but not sneeze.

In the third place, you must not, upon any account, stir either hand or foot. If, by chance, a black pin runs into your head, you must not take it out. If the pain is very   *245* great, you must be sure to bear it without wincing; if it brings the tears into your eyes, you must not wipe them off; if they give you a tingling by running down your cheeks, you must look as if nothing was the matter. If the blood should gush from your head by means of the black pin, you must let it gush; if you are uneasy to think of making such a blurred appearance, you must be uneasy, but you must say nothing about it. If, however,   *250* the agony is very great, you may, privately, bite the inside of your cheek, or of your lips, for a little relief; taking care, meanwhile, to do it so cautiously as to make no apparent dent outwardly. And, with that precaution, if you even gnaw a piece out, it will not be minded, only be sure either to swallow it, or commit it to a corner of the inside of your mouth till they are gone — for you must not spit.   *255*

I have many other directions, but no more paper; I will endeavour, however, to have them ready for you in time. Perhaps, meanwhile, you will be glad to know if I have myself had opportunity to put in practice these receipts?

How can I answer in this little space? My love to Mr. B. and the little ones, and remember me kindly to cousin Edward, and believe me, my dearest Esther,   *260*

Most affectionately yours,

F.B.

PHILLIS WHEATLEY
U.S.A., c.1753-1784

ON BEING BROUGHT FROM AFRICA TO AMERICA

'Twas mercy brought me from my pagan land,
Taught my benighted soul to understand
That there's a God, that there's a Saviour too:
Once I redemption neither sought nor knew.

Some view that sable race with scornful eye: 5
"Their colour is a diabolic dye."
Remember, Christians, Negroes black as Cain
May be refined and join the angelic strain.

(1773)

---

258. **receipts:** recipes, directions. 259. **Mr. B.:** Charles Rousseau Burney, Esther's cousin and husband. 260. **Edward:** another son of Dr. Burney's Worcester brother.   **ON BEING BROUGHT**   7. **Cain:** Some churches used the reference to the "mark of Cain" in Genesis 4:15 (p. 245) as an explanation of skin colour and a justification for racial discrimination.

To the Right Honourable William, Earl of Dartmouth,
His Majesty's Principal Secretary of State for North America, Etc.

Hail, happy day, when, smiling like the morn,
Fair Freedom rose New England to adorn:
The northern clime beneath her genial ray,
Dartmouth, congratulates thy blissful sway:
Elate with hope her race no longer mourns,   5
Each soul expands, each grateful bosom burns,
While in thine hand with pleasure we behold
The silken reins, and Freedom's charms unfold.
Long lost to realms beneath the northern skies
She shines supreme, while hated Faction dies: 10
Soon as appeared the goddess long desired,
Sick at the view, she languished and expired;
Thus from the splendors of the morning light
The owl in sadness seeks the caves of night.

   No more, America, in mournful strain   15
Of wrongs, and grievance unredressed complain,
No longer shalt thou dread the iron chain
Which wanton Tyranny with lawless hand
Had made, and with it meant to enslave the land.

   Should you, my lord, while you peruse my song,   20
Wonder from whence my love of Freedom sprung,
Whence flow these wishes for the common good,

By feeling hearts alone best understood,
I, young in life, by seeming cruel fate,
Was snatched from Afric's fancied happy seat: 25
What pangs excruciating must molest,
What sorrows labour in my parents' breast?
Steeled was that soul and by no misery moved
That from a father seized his babe beloved:
Such, such my case. And can I then but pray   30
Others may never feel tyrannic sway?

   For favours past, great Sir, our thanks are due,
And thee we ask thy favors to renew,
Since in thy power, as in thy will before,
To soothe the griefs which thou didst once deplore.   35
May heavenly grace the sacred sanction give
To all thy works, and thou forever live
Not only on the wings of fleeting Fame,
Though praise immortal crowns the patriot's name,
But to conduct to heaven's refulgent fane,   40
May fiery coursers sweep the ethereal plain,
And bear thee upwards to that blessed abode,
Where, like the prophet, thou shalt find thy God.

                        (1773)

William Blake
England, 1757-1827

from *Songs of Innocence*

Nurse's Song

When the voices of children are heard on the green
And laughing is heard on the hill,
My heart is at rest within my breast
    And everything else is still.

"Then come home, my children, the sun is gone down,
And the dews of night arise;   6
Come come, leave off play, and let us away
Till the morning appears in the skies."

"No no, let us play, for it is yet day,
And we cannot go to sleep;   10
Besides, in the sky the little birds fly,
And the hills are all cover'd with sheep."

"Well, well, go & play till the light fades away,
And then go home to bed."
The little ones leaped & shouted & laugh'd   15
    And all the hills echoed.

To the Right Honourable William Title: William Legge, 3rd Earl of Dartmouth (1753-1801) became George III's secretary for the American colonies in 1772; many people were hoping he would be more sympathetic to colonists' grievances than his predecessor had been. **11. goddess:** i.e., Freedom. **12. she:** i.e., Faction. **25. fancied happy seat:** i.e., a happy home she can only imagine. **39. patriot's name:** Dartmouth. **40. refulgent fane:** shining sanctuary. **43. prophet:** Elijah (see 2 Kings 2:11).   **Blake** (See also Blake's marginal comments on Reynolds's "Seventh Discourse" — p. 627.) *Songs of Innocence* (1789) and *Songs of Experience* were combined in 1794 as *Songs of Innocence and of Experience*, and given the explanatory subtitle *Showing the Two Contrary States of the Human Soul*. Individual poems in one group often have

Plate 6. William Blake's hand-lettered version of "The Lamb," with his original illustration.

THE LITTLE BLACK BOY

My mother bore me in the southern wild,
And I am black, but O! my soul is white;
White as an angel is the English child,
But I am black, as if bereav'd of light.

My mother taught me underneath a tree,   5
And sitting down before the heat of day,
She took me on her lap and kissed me,
And pointing to the east, began to say:

"Look on the rising sun: there God does live
And gives his light, and gives his heat away;   10
And flowers and trees and beasts and men receive
Comfort in morning, joy in the noonday.

"And we are put on earth a little space,
That we may learn to bear the beams of love;
And these black bodies and this sun-burnt face   15
Is but a cloud, and like a shady grove.

"For when our souls have learn'd that heat to bear,
The cloud will vanish; we shall hear his voice,
Saying: 'Come out from the grove, my love & care,
And round my golden tent like lambs rejoice.'"   20

Thus did my mother say, and kissed me;
And thus I say to little English boy:
When I from black and he from white cloud free,
And round the tent of God like lambs we joy,

I'll shade him from the heat till he can bear   25
To lean in joy upon our father's knee;
And then I'll stand and stroke his silver hair,
And be like him, and he will then love me.

THE CHIMNEY SWEEPER

When my mother died I was very young,
And my father sold me while yet my tongue
Could scarcely cry "'weep! 'weep! 'weep! 'weep!"
So your chimneys I sweep & in soot I sleep.

There's little Tom Dacre, who cried when his head,   5
That curl'd like a lamb's back, was shav'd, so I said
"Hush, Tom! never mind it, for when your head's bare
You know that the soot cannot spoil your white hair."

And so he was quiet, & that very night,
As Tom was a-sleeping, he had such a sight,   10
That thousands of sweepers, Dick, Joe, Ned, & Jack,
Were all of them lock'd up in coffins of black.

And by came an Angel who had a bright key,
And he open'd the coffins & set them all free;
Then down a green plain leaping, laughing, they run,
And wash in a river, and shine in the Sun.   16

Then naked & white, all their bags left behind,
They rise upon clouds and sport in the wind;
And the Angel told Tom, if he'd be a good boy,
He'd have God for his father & never want joy.   20

And so Tom awoke; and we rose in the dark,
And got with our bags & our brushes to work.
Tho' the morning was cold, Tom was happy & warm,
So if all do their duty they need not fear harm.

THE LAMB

Little Lamb, who made thee?
  Dost thou know who made thee?
Gave thee life, & bid thee feed
By the stream & o'er the mead;
Gave thee clothing of delight,   5
Softest clothing, woolly, bright;
Gave thee such a tender voice,
Making all the vales rejoice?
  Little Lamb, who made thee?
  Dost thou know who made thee?   10

  Little Lamb, I'll tell thee,
  Little Lamb, I'll tell thee!
He is called by thy name,
For he calls himself a Lamb.
He is meek, & he is mild;   15
He became a little child.
I a child, & thou a lamb,
We are called by his name.
  Little Lamb, God bless thee.
  Little Lamb, God bless thee.   20
          (1789)

---

counterparts in the other, e.g. "The Lamb" and "The Tyger."   **SONGS OF INNOCENCE**   **THE CHIMNEY-SWEEPER**   **3:** The term *'weep!*, which acquires a more explicit edge in the counterpart poem in *Songs of Experience*, represents the child's attempt at the street-cry "Sweep! Sweep!" **20. want:** lack.

from SONGS OF EXPERIENCE

THE TYGER

Tyger! Tyger! burning bright
In the forests of the night,
What immortal hand or eye
Could frame thy fearful symmetry?

In what distant deeps or skies   5
Burnt the fire of thine eyes?
On what wings dare he aspire?
What the hand dare seize the fire?

And what shoulder, & what art,
Could twist the sinews of thy heart?   10
And when thy heart began to beat,
What dread hand? & what dread feet?

What the hammer? what the chain?
In what furnace was thy brain?
What the anvil? what dread grasp   15
Dare its deadly terrors clasp?

When the stars threw down their spears,
And water'd heaven with their tears,
Did he smile his work to see?
Did he who made the Lamb make thee? 20

Tyger! Tyger! burning bright
In the forests of the night,
What immortal hand or eye
Dare frame thy fearful symmetry?

THE CLOD & THE PEBBLE

"Love seeketh not Itself to please,
Nor for itself hath any care;
But for another gives its ease,
And builds a Heaven in Hell's despair."

So sung a little Clod of Clay   5
Trodden with the cattle's feet;
But a Pebble of the brook
Warbled out these metres meet:

"Love seeketh only Self to please,
To bind another to Its delight;   10
Joys in another's loss of ease,
And builds a Hell in Heaven's despite."

THE CHIMNEY SWEEPER

A little black thing among the snow,
Crying "'weep! 'weep!" in notes of woe!
"Where are thy father & mother, say?"
"They are both gone up to the church to pray.

"Because I was happy upon the heath,   5
And smil'd among the winter's snow,
They clothed me in the clothes of death,
And taught me to sing the notes of woe.

"And because I am happy & dance & sing,
They think they have done me no injury, 10
And are gone to praise God & his Priest & King,
Who make up a heaven of our misery."

NURSE'S SONG

When the voices of children are heard on the green
And whisp'rings are in the dale,
The days of my youth rise fresh in my mind;
My face turns green and pale.

Then come home, my children, the sun is gone down,
And the dews of night arise;   6
Your spring & your day are wasted in play,
And your winter and night in disguise.

THE SICK ROSE

O rose, thou art sick.
The invisible worm
That flies in the night,
In the howling storm,

Has found out thy bed   5
Of crimson joy,
And his dark secret love
Does thy life destroy.

AH! SUN-FLOWER

Ah, Sun-flower! weary of time,
Who countest the steps of the Sun,
Seeking after that sweet golden clime
Where the traveller's journey is done;

Plate 7. William Blake's hand-lettered version of "The Tyger,"
with his original illustration.

Where the Youth pined away with desire,   *5*
And the pale Virgin shrouded in snow,
Arise from their graves and aspire
Where my Sun-flower wishes to go.

THE GARDEN OF LOVE

I went to the Garden of Love,
And saw what I never had seen:
A Chapel was built in the midst,
Where I used to play on the green.

And the gates of this Chapel were shut,   *5*
And "Thou shalt not" writ over the door;
So I turn'd to the Garden of Love
That so many sweet flowers bore;

And I saw it was filled with graves,
And tomb-stones where flowers should be;   *10*
And Priests in black gowns were walking their rounds,
And binding with briars my joys & desires.

LONDON

I wander thro' each charter'd street,
Near where the charter'd Thames does flow,
And mark in every face I meet
Marks of weakness, marks of woe.

In every cry of every Man,   *5*
In every Infant's cry of fear,
In every voice, in every ban,
The mind-forg'd manacles I hear.

How the Chimney-sweeper's cry
Every black'ning Church appalls;   *10*
And the hapless Soldier's sigh
Runs in blood down Palace walls.

But most thro' midnight streets I hear
How the youthful Harlot's curse
Blasts the new born Infant's tear   *15*
And blights with plagues the Marriage hearse.

(1794)

from *THE MARRIAGE OF HEAVEN AND HELL:* Proverbs of Hell

In seed time learn, in harvest teach, in winter enjoy.
Drive your cart and your plow over the bones of the dead.
The road of excess leads to the palace of wisdom.
Prudence is a rich ugly old maid courted by Incapacity.
He who desires but acts not, breeds pestilence.   *5*
The cut worm forgives the plow.
Dip him in the river who loves water.
A fool sees not the same tree that a wise man sees.
He whose face gives no light, shall never become a star.
Eternity is in love with the productions of time.   *10*
The busy bee has no time for sorrow.
The hours of folly are measur'd by the clock; but of wisdom, no clock can measure.
All wholesome food is caught without a net or a trap.
Bring out number, weight, & measure in a year of dearth.
No bird soars too high, if he soars with his own wings.   *15*
A dead body revenges not injuries.
The most sublime act is to set another before you.
If the fool would persist in his folly he would become wise.
Folly is the cloak of knavery.
Shame is Pride's cloak.   *20*

SONGS OF EXPERIENCE   LONDON   **7. ban:** probably intended to include the sense of *banns.*

Prisons are built with stones of Law, Brothels with bricks of Religion.

The pride of the peacock is the glory of God.

The lust of the goat is the bounty of God.

The wrath of the lion is the wisdom of God.

The nakedness of woman is the work of God.   25

Excess of sorrow laughs. Excess of joy weeps.

The roaring of lions, the howling of wolves, the raging of the stormy sea, and the
  destructive sword, are portions of eternity too great for the eye of man.

The fox condemns the trap, not himself.

Joys impregnate. Sorrows bring forth.

Let man wear the fell of the lion, woman the fleece of the sheep.   30

The bird a nest, the spider a web, man friendship.

The selfish smiling fool & the sullen frowning fool shall be both thought wise, that
  they may be a rod.

What is now proved was once only imagin'd.

The rat, the mouse, the fox, the rabbit watch the roots; the lion, the tyger, the horse,
  the elephant watch the fruits.

The cistern contains; the fountain overflows.   35

One thought fills immensity.

Always be ready to speak your mind, and a base man will avoid you.

Every thing possible to be believ'd is an image of truth.

The eagle never lost so much time as when he submitted to learn of the crow.

The fox provides for himself, but God provides for the lion.   40

Think in the morning, Act in the noon, Eat in the evening, Sleep in the night.

He who has suffered you to impose on him knows you.

As the plow follows words, so God rewards prayers.

The tygers of wrath are wiser than the horses of instruction.

Expect poison from the standing water.   45

You never know what is enough unless you know what is more than enough.

Listen to the fool's reproach! it is a kingly title!

The eyes of fire, the nostrils of air, the mouth of water, the beard of earth.

The weak in courage is strong in cunning.

The apple tree never asks the beech how he shall grow, nor the lion the horse,
  how he shall take his prey.   50

The thankful receiver bears a plentiful harvest.

If others had not been foolish, we should be so.

The soul of sweet delight can never be defil'd.

When thou seest an Eagle, thou seest a portion of Genius; lift up thy head!

As the caterpillar chooses the fairest leaves to lay her eggs on, so the priest lays
  his curse on the fairest joys.   55

To create a little flower is the labour of ages.

Damn braces; Bless relaxes.

The best wine is the oldest, the best water the newest.

Prayers plow not! Praises reap not!

Joys laugh not! Sorrows weep not!   60

The head Sublime, the heart Pathos, the genitals Beauty, the hands & feet Proportion.
As the air to a bird or the sea to a fish, so is contempt to the contemptible.
The crow wish'd every thing was black, the owl that every thing was white.
Exuberance is Beauty.
If the lion was advised by the fox, he would be cunning.   65
Improvement makes strait roads, but the crooked roads without Improvement
    are roads of Genius.
Sooner murder an infant in its cradle than nurse unacted desires.
Where man is not, nature is barren.
Truth can never be told so as to be understood, and not be believ'd.
Enough! or Too much.   70

(1793)

"THE ANGEL THAT PRESIDED O'ER MY BIRTH"

The Angel that presided o'er my birth
Said, "Little creature, form'd of Joy & Mirth,
Go love without the help of any Thing on Earth."

(c.1793)

"MOCK ON, MOCK ON, VOLTAIRE, ROUSSEAU"

Mock on, Mock on, Voltaire, Rousseau;
Mock on, Mock on: 'tis all in vain!
You throw the sand against the wind,
And the wind blows it back again.

And every sand becomes a Gem   5
Reflected in the beams divine;
Blown back they blind the mocking Eye,
But still in Israel's paths they shine.

The Atoms of Democritus
And Newton's Particles of light   10
Are sands upon the Red Sea shore,
Where Israel's tents do shine so bright.

(c.1800; 1863)

THE MENTAL TRAVELLER

I travel'd thro' a Land of Men,
A Land of Men & Women too,
And heard & saw such dreadful things
As cold Earth wanderers never knew.

For there the Babe is born in joy   5
That was begotten in dire woe;
Just as we reap in joy the fruit
Which we in bitter tears did sow.

And if the Babe is born a Boy
He's given to a Woman Old,   10
Who nails him down upon a rock,
Catches his Shrieks in Cups of gold.

She binds iron thorns around his head,
She pierces both his hands & feet,
She cuts his heart out at his side   15
To make it feel both cold & heat.

Her fingers number every Nerve,
Just as a Miser counts his gold;
She lives upon his shrieks & cries,
And she grows young as he grows old.   20

Till he becomes a bleeding youth,
And she becomes a Virgin bright;
Then he rends up his Manacles
And binds her down for his delight.

He plants himself in all her Nerves,   25
Just as a Husbandman his mould;
And she becomes his dwelling place
And Garden fruitful seventy fold.

An aged Shadow, soon he fades,
Wand'ring round an Earthly Cot,   30
Full filled all with gems & gold
Which he by industry had got.

MOCK ON, MOCK ON **1:** Voltaire and Rousseau represent eighteenth-century rationalism, including Deism. **9:** Democritus (c.460-c.370 B.C.), Greek philosopher who propounded an early mechanistic theory that all matter was composed of tiny particles, "atoms." **10:** Sir Isaac Newton (1642-1727) in his *Opticks* (1704) proposed the corpuscular or particle theory of light. THE MENTAL TRAVELLER (Note: In the manuscript, there is no punctuation whatever in this poem.) Various interpretations of this highly suggestive poem have been proposed; but rather

And these are the gems of the Human Soul,
The rubies & pearls of a lovesick eye,
The countless gold of the aching heart,   35
The martyr's groan & the lover's sigh.

They are his meat, they are his drink;
He feeds the Beggar & the Poor
And the wayfaring Traveller:
For ever open is his door.   40

His grief is their eternal joy;
They make the roofs & walls to ring;
Till from the fire on the hearth
A little Female Babe does spring.

And she is all of solid fire   45
And gems & gold, that none his hand
Dares stretch to touch her Baby form,
Or wrap her in his swaddling-band.

But She comes to the Man she loves,
If young or old, or rich or poor;   50
They soon drive out the aged Host,
A Beggar at another's door.

He wanders weeping far away,
Until some other take him in;
Oft blind & age-bent, sore distrest,   55
Untill he can a Maiden win.

And to allay his freezing age
The Poor Man takes her in his arms;
The Cottage fades before his sight,
The Garden & its lovely Charms.   60

The Guests are scatter'd thro' the land,
For the Eye altering alters all;
The Senses roll themselves in fear,
And the flat Earth becomes a ball;

The Stars, Sun, Moon, all shrink away,   65
A desart vast without a bound,
And nothing left to eat or drink,
And a dark desart all around.

The honey of her Infant lips,
The bread & wine of her sweet smile,   70
The wild game of her roving Eye,
Does him to Infancy beguile;

For as he eats & drinks he grows
Younger & younger every day;
And on the desart wild they both   75
Wander in terror & dismay.

Like the wild Stag she flees away,
Her fear plants many a thicket wild;
While he pursues her night & day,
By various arts of Love beguil'd,   80

By various arts of Love & Hate,
Till the wide desart planted o'er
With Labyrinths of wayward Love,
Where roam the Lion, Wolf, & Boar,

Till he becomes a wayward Babe,   85
And she a weeping Woman Old.
Then many a Lover wanders here;
The Sun & Stars are nearer roll'd.

The trees bring forth sweet Extacy
To all who in the desart roam;   90
Till many a City there is Built,
And many a pleasant Shepherd's home.

But when they find the frowning Babe,
Terror strikes thro' the region wide:
They cry "The Babe! the Babe is Born!"   95
And flee away on Every side.

For who dare touch the frowning form,
His arm is wither'd to its root;
Lions, Boars, Wolves, all howling flee,
And every Tree does shed its fruit.   100

And none can touch that frowning form,
Except it be a Woman Old;
She nails him down upon the Rock,
And all is done as I have told.

(c.1803; 1863)

from AUGURIES OF INNOCENCE

To see a World in a Grain of Sand
And a Heaven in a Wild Flower,
Hold Infinity in the palm of your hand
And Eternity in an hour.

. . . .

(c.1803; 1863)

---

than seek a single interpretation, it may be more appropriate to see the cycles the poem depicts as applying simultaneously to many subjects, e.g. the history of philosophical change, the history of art, and so on.

from *MILTON*

"AND DID THOSE FEET IN ANCIENT TIME"

And did those feet in ancient time
Walk upon England's mountains green?
And was the holy Lamb of God
On England's pleasant pastures seen?

And did the Countenance Divine   *5*
Shine forth upon our clouded hills?
And was Jerusalem builded here
Among these dark Satanic Mills?

Bring me my Bow of burning gold:
Bring me my Arrows of desire: *10*
Bring me my Spear: O clouds unfold!
Bring me my Chariot of fire.

I will not cease from Mental Fight,
Nor shall my Sword sleep in my hand,
Till we have built Jerusalem   *15*
In England's green & pleasant Land.

(1804-1808)

ROBERT BURNS
Scotland, 1759-1796

TO A MOUSE, ON TURNING HER UP IN HER NEST WITH THE PLOUGH, NOVEMBER, 1785

Wee, sleeket, cowran, tim'rous beastie,
O, what a panic's in thy breastie!
Thou need na start awa sae hasty,
    Wi' bickering brattle!
I wad be laith to rin an' chase thee,   *5*
    Wi' murd'ring pattle!

I'm truly sorry man's dominion
Has broken Nature's social union,
An' justifies that ill opinion,
    Which makes thee startle,   *10*
At me, thy poor, earth-born companion,
    An' fellow-mortal!

I doubt na, whyles, but thou may thieve;
What then? poor beastie, thou maun live!
A daimen-icker in a thrave   *15*
    'S a sma' request:
I'll get a blessin wi' the lave,
    An' never miss 't!

Thy wee-bit housie, too, in ruin!
It's silly wa's the win's are strewin!   *20*
An' naething, now, to big a new ane,
    O' foggage green!
An' bleak December's winds ensuin,
    Baith snell an' keen!

Thou saw the fields laid bare an' wast,   *25*
An' weary winter comin fast,
An' cozie here, beneath the blast,
    Thou thought to dwell,
Till crash! the cruel coulter past
    Out through thy cell.   *30*

AND DID THOSE FEET   These stanzas, from the Preface to the long prophetic poem *Milton*, have been set to music and given the title "Jerusalem," and in that form the piece has been used as a hymn — and even as an anthem by the British Labour Party.   **TO A MOUSE   1. sleeket:** sleek, shiny; **cowran:** cowering. **4. Wi' bickering brattle:** in a rapid run. **5. laith:** loath; **rin:** run. **6. pattle:** tool used to clean the plough blade. **13. whyles:** sometimes. **14. maun:** must. **15. daimen-icker in a thrave:** an occasional ear of grain from two stooks. **17. the lave:** the rest. **20. silly wa's:** simple walls. **21. big:** build. **22. foggage:** moss. **24. snell:** severe. **25. wast:** waste. **29. coulter:** plough blade.

That wee-bit heap o' leaves an' stibble,
Has cost thee monie a weary nibble!
Now thou's turned out, for a' thy trouble,
  But house or hald,
To thole the winter's sleety dribble,   *35*
  An' cranreuch cauld!

But mousie, thou art no thy lane,
In proving foresight may be vain:
The best laid schemes o' mice an' men
  Gang aft agley,   *40*
An' lea'e us nought but grief an' pain,
  For promised joy!

Still, thou art blest, compared wi' me!
The present only toucheth thee:
But Och! I backward cast my e'e   *45*
  On prospects drear!
An' forward, though I canna see,
  I guess an' fear!

        (1786)

TO A LOUSE,
ON SEEING ONE
ON A LADY'S BONNET
AT CHURCH

Ha! whare ye gaun, ye crowlin ferlie?
Your impudence protects you sairly;
I canna say but ye strunt rarely,
  Owre gauze and lace;
Tho' faith, I fear ye dine but sparely   *5*
  On sic a place.

Ye ugly, creepin, blastit wonner,
Detested, shunn'd by saunt an' sinner,
How dare ye set your fit upon her,
  Sae fine a lady!   *10*
Gae somewhere else, and seek your dinner
  On some poor body.

Swith, in some beggar's haffet squattle;
There ye may creep, and sprawl, and sprattle
Wi' ither kindred, jumping cattle,   *15*
  In shoals and nations;
Whaur horn nor bane ne'er dare unsettle
  Your thick plantations.

Now haud ye there, ye're out o' sight,
Below the fatt'rels, snug an' tight;   *20*
Na, faith ye yet! ye'll no be right
  Till ye've got on it,
The vera tapmost, tow'rin height
  O' Miss's bonnet.   *24*

My sooth! right bauld ye set your nose out,
As plump and gray as onie groset;
O for some rank, mercurial rozet,
  Or fell, red smeddum,
I'd gie you sic a hearty dose o't,
  Wad dress your droddum!   *30*

I wad na been surpris'd to spy
You on an auld wife's flainen toy;
Or aiblins some bit duddie boy,
  On's wyliecoat;
But Miss's fine Lunardi! fie,   *35*
  How daur ye do't?

O, Jenny, dinna toss your head,
An' set your beauties a' abreid!
Ye little ken what cursed speed
  The blastie's makin!   *40*
Thae winks and finger-ends, I dread,
  Are notice takin!

O wad some Pow'r the giftie gie us
To see oursels as others see us!
It wad frae monie a blunder free us   *45*
  And foolish notion:
What airs in dress an' gait wad lea'e us,
  And ev'n Devotion!

        (1786)

---

34. But: without; **hald:** hold, home. **35. thole:** suffer. **36. cranreuch:** frost. **37. no thy lane:** not alone. **40. gang aft agley:** often go awry. **TO A LOUSE 1. crowlin ferlie:** crawling wonder. **2. sairly:** greatly. **3. strunt:** strut. **6. sic:** such. **7. wonner:** inhabitant. **9. fit:** feet. **13. Swith:** scat; **haffet:** side of the head; **squattle:** nestle. **14. sprattle:** scramble. **17. Whaur:** where; **horn, bane:** combs made of horn or bone. **18. plantations:** settlements. **20. fatt'rels:** folds (in the bonnet). **25. bauld:** bold. **26. onie groset:** any gooseberry. **27. rozet:** resin. **28. fell . . . smeddum:** deadly insect powder. **30. dress your droddum:** i.e., "fix your wagon" ("drodden" literally means "buttocks"). **32. flainen toy:** old-fashioned cap. **33. aiblins:** perhaps; **duddie:** ragged. **34. wyliecoat:** undershirt. **35. Lunardi:** balloon-shaped bonnet; the reference is to Vincenzo Lunardi (1759–1806), an Italian-born balloonist, whose air balloon ascents in London (September 15, 1784) and Edinburgh (October 5, 1785) were the first in Britain. **38. set . . . abreid:** scatter [the lice] widely. **40. blastie:** blasted creature. **41. Thae:** those. **45. frae monie:** from many.

JOHN ANDERSON MY JO

John Anderson my jo, John,
  When we were first acquent,
Your locks were like the raven,
  Your bonie brow was brent;
But now your brow is beld, John,   *5*
  Your locks are like the snaw;
But blessings on your frosty pow,
  John Anderson my jo.

John Anderson my jo, John,
  We clamb the hill thegither;   *10*
And mony a canty day, John,
  We've had wi' ane anither:
Now we maun totter down, John,
  And hand in hand we'll go;
And sleep thegither at the foot,   *15*
  John Anderson my jo.

                  (1790)

AFTON WATER

Flow gently, sweet Afton, among thy green braes,
Flow gently, I'll sing thee a song in thy praise;
My Mary's asleep by thy murmuring stream,
Flow gently, sweet Afton, disturb not her dream.

Thou stock-dove whose echo resounds thro' the
  glen,   *5*
Ye wild whistling blackbirds in yon thorny den,
Thou green-crested lapwing, thy screaming
  forbear,
I charge you disturb not my slumbering fair.

How lofty, sweet Afton, thy neighbouring hills,
Far marked with the courses of clear winding rills;
There daily I wander as noon rises high,   *11*
My flocks and my Mary's sweet cot in my eye.

How pleasant thy banks and green valleys below,
Where wild in the woodlands the primroses blow;
There oft as mild evening weeps over the lea,   *15*
The sweet-scented birk shades my Mary and me.

Thy crystal stream, Afton, how lovely it glides,
And winds by the cot where my Mary resides;
How wanton thy waters her snowy feet lave,
As gathering sweet flow'rets she stems thy clear
  wave.   *20*

Flow gently, sweet Afton, among thy green braes,
Flow gently, sweet river, the theme of my lays;
My Mary's asleep by thy murmuring stream,
Flow gently, sweet Afton, disturb not her dream.

                  (1792)

FOR A' THAT AND A' THAT

Is there, for honest poverty
  That hings his head, and a' that;
The coward-slave, we pass him by,
  We dare be poor for a' that!
  For a' that, and a' that,   *5*
    Our toils obscure, and a' that,
  The rank is but the guinea's stamp,
    The man's the gowd for a' that.

What though on hamely fare we dine,
  Wear hoddin grey, and a' that.   *10*
Gie fools their silks, and knaves their wine,
  A man's a man for a' that.
  For a' that, and a' that,
    Their tinsel show, and a' that;
  The honest man, though e'er sae poor,   *15*
    Is king o' men for a' that.

Ye see yon birkie ca'd a lord,
  Wha struts, and stares, and a' that,
Though hundreds worship at his word,
  He's but a coof for a' that.   *20*
  For a' that, and a' that,
    His ribband, star and a' that,
  The man of independent mind,
    He looks and laughs at a' that.

A prince can mak a belted knight,   *25*
  A marquis, duke, and a' that;

JOHN ANDERSON MY JO **1. jo:** sweetheart. **2. acquent:** acquainted. **4. bonie:** bonny; **brent:** smooth. **5. beld:** bald. **7. pow:** head, poll. **11. canty:** cheerful. **AFTON WATER** **Title:** the River Afton flows through Ayrshire. **1. braes:** banks. **16. birk:** birch. **SONG: FOR A' THAT** **8. gowd:** gold. **10. hoddin grey:** undyed homespun wool cloth. **17. birkie:** self-important fellow. **20. coof:** dolt. **22:** referring to medals.

But an honest man's aboon his might,
 Gude faith he mauna fa' that!
  For a' that, and a' that,
   Their dignities, and a' that,   *30*
 The pith o' sense, and pride o' worth
  Are higher rank than a' that.

Then let us pray that come it may,
 As come it will for a' that,
That sense and worth, o'er a' the earth   *35*
 Shall bear the gree, and a' that.
  For a' that, and a' that,
   It's comin yet for a' that,
 That man to man the warld o'er,
  Shall brothers be for a' that.   *40*
             (1795)

A RED, RED ROSE

O My Luve's like a red, red rose,
 That's newly sprung in June;
O My Luve's like the melodie
 That's sweetly played in tune.

As fair art thou, my bonnie lass,   *5*
 So deep in luve am I;
And I will luve thee still, my dear,
 Till a' the seas gang dry.

Till a' the seas gang dry, my dear,
 And the rocks melt wi' the sun: *10*
O I will love thee still, my dear,
 While the sands o' life shall run.

And fare thee weel, my only luve,
 And fare thee weel awhile!
And I will come again, my luve,   *15*
 Though it were ten thousand mile.
             (1796)

HIGHLAND MARY

Ye banks, and braes, and streams around
 The castle o' Montgomery,
Green be your woods, and fair your flowers,
 Your waters never drumlie!
There simmer first unfauld her robes,   *5*
 And there the langest tarry;
For there I took the last fareweel
 O my sweet Highland Mary.

How sweetly bloom'd the gay green birk,
 How rich the hawthorn's blossom,   *10*
As underneath their fragrant shade
 I clasp'd her to my bosom!
The golden hours on angel wings
 Flew o'er me and my dearie;
For dear to me as light and life   *15*
 Was my sweet Highland Mary.

Wi' mony a vow, and locked embrace,
 Our parting was fu' tender;
And, pledging aft to meet again,
 We tore oursels asunder;   *20*
But oh! fell death's untimely frost,
 That nipt my flower sae early! —
Now green's the sod, and cauld's the clay,
 That wraps my Highland Mary!

O pale, pale now, those rosy lips,   *25*
 I aft have kissed sae fondly!
And closed for aye the sparkling glance,
 That dwelt on me sae kindly!
And mould'ring now in silent dust,
 That heart that lo'ed me dearly —   *30*
But still within my bosom's core
 Shall live my Highland Mary.
             (1799)

---

27. aboon: above. **28. mauna fa':** must not fall — i.e., in the dialectal sense: must not lay claim to. **36. gree:** goodwill.   **HIGHLAND MARY 4. drumlie:** turbid, unclear. **5. There . . . unfauld:** i.e., There may summer first unfold.

MARY WOLLSTONECRAFT
England, 1759-1797

from *A VINDICATION OF THE RIGHTS OF MEN*

When we read a book that supports our favourite opinions, how eagerly do we suck in the doctrines, and suffer our minds placidly to reflect the images that illustrate the tenets we have previously embraced. We indolently acquiesce in the conclusion, and our spirit animates and corrects the various subjects. But when, on the contrary, we peruse a skilful writer, with whom we do not coincide in opinion, how attentive is the mind to   *5* detect fallacy. And this suspicious coolness often prevents our being carried away by a stream of natural eloquence, which the prejudiced mind terms declamation — a pomp of words! We never allow ourselves to be warmed; and, after contending with the writer, are more confirmed in our opinion; as much, perhaps, from a spirit of contradiction as from reason. A lively imagination is ever in danger of being betrayed into error by   *10* favourite opinions, which it almost personifies, the more effectually to intoxicate the understanding. Always tending to extremes, truth is left behind in the heat of the chace, and things are viewed as positively good, or bad, though they wear an equivocal face.

. . . .

Judgment is sublime, wit beautiful; and, according to your own theory, they cannot exist together without impairing each other's power. The predominancy of the latter, in   *15* your endless Reflections, should lead hasty readers to suspect that it may, in a great degree, exclude the former.

But among all your plausible arguments, and witty illustrations, your contempt for the poor always appears conspicuous, and rouses my indignation. The following paragraph in particular struck me, as breathing the most tyrannic spirit, and displaying   *20* the most factitious feelings:

> Good order is the foundation of all good things. To be enabled to acquire, the people, without being servile, must be tractable and obedient. The magistrate must have his reverence, the laws their authority. The body of the people must not find the principles of natural subordination by art rooted out of their minds. They *must*   *25* respect that property of which they *cannot* partake. *They must labour to obtain what by labour can be obtained; and when they find, as they commonly do, the success disproportioned to the endeavour, they must be taught their consolation in the final proportions of eternal justice.* Of this consolation, whoever deprives them, deadens their industry, and strikes at the root of all acquisition as of all   *30* conservation. He that does this, is the cruel oppressor, the merciless enemy, of the poor and wretched; at the same time that, by his wicked speculations, he exposes

---

A VINDICATION OF THE RIGHTS OF MEN   The title continues: *in a Letter to the Right Honourable Edmund Burke; Occasioned by His Reflections on the Revolution in France*. Wollstonecraft was among the first of many to reply to Burke's *Reflections* (for which see p. 640); others included, soon after, Thomas Paine with *The Rights of Man* (see p. 673). **12. chace:** chase. **14-15:** referring to Burke's *On the Sublime and Beautiful* (see *sublime* in Glossary). **28. success:** outcome.

the fruits of successful industry, and the accumulations of fortune [ah! there's the rub], to the plunder of the negligent, the disappointed, and the unprosperous.

This is contemptible hard-hearted sophistry, in the specious form of humility, and submission to the will of Heaven. — It is, Sir, *possible* to render the poor happier in this world, without depriving them of the consolation which you gratuitously grant them in the next. They have a right to more comfort than they at present enjoy; and more comfort might be afforded them, without encroaching on the pleasures of the rich: not now waiting to enquire whether the rich have any right to exclusive pleasures. What do I say? — encroaching! No; if an intercourse were established, it would impart the only true pleasure that can be snatched in this land of shadows, this hard school of moral discipline.

I know, indeed, that there is often something disgusting in the distresses of poverty, at which the imagination revolts, and starts back to exercise itself in the more attractive Arcadia of fiction. The rich man builds a house, art and taste give it the highest finish. His gardens are planted, and the trees grow to recreate the fancy of the planter, though the temperature of the climate may rather force him to avoid the dangerous damps they exhale, than seek the umbrageous retreat. Every thing on the estate is cherished but man; — yet, to contribute to the happiness of man, is the most sublime of all enjoyments. But if, instead of sweeping pleasure-grounds, obelisks, temples, and elegant cottages, as *objects* for the eye, the heart was allowed to beat true to nature, decent farms would be scattered over the estate, and plenty smile around. Instead of the poor being subject to the griping hand of an avaricious steward, they would be watched over with fatherly solicitude, by the man whose duty and pleasure it was to guard their happiness, and shield from rapacity the beings who exalted him by the sweat of their brow, above his fellows.

I could almost imagine I see a man thus gathering blessings as he mounted the hill of life; or consolation, in those days when the spirits lag, and the tired heart finds no pleasure in them. It is not by squandering alms that the poor can be relieved, or improved — it is the fostering sun of kindness, the wisdom that finds them employments calculated to give them habits of virtue, that meliorates their condition. Love is only the fruit of love; condescension and authority may produce the obedience you applaud; but he has lost his heart of flesh who can see a fellow-creature humbled before him, and trembling at the frown of a being, whose heart is supplied by the same vital current, and whose pride ought to be checked by a consciousness of having the same infirmities.

What salutary dews might not be shed to refresh this thirsty land, if men were more *enlightened!* Smiles and premiums might encourage cleanliness, industry, and emulation. — A garden more inviting than Eden would then meet the eye, and springs of joy murmur on every side. The clergyman would superintend his own flock, the shepherd would then love the sheep he daily tended; the school might rear its decent head, and the buzzing tribe, let loose to play, impart a portion of their vivacious spirits to the heart that longed to open their minds, and lead them to taste the pleasures of men. Domestic pleasure, the civilizing relations of husband, brother, and father, would soften labour, and render life contented.

33-34. Ah! . . . rub: echoing Hamlet in his best-known soliloquy (III.i). **53. griping:** grasping. **67. premiums:** rewards, bonuses. **69. Clergyman . . . flock:** Some clergymen had more than one "living" — i.e., served more than one church; and some even hired underlings, at a fraction of their own income, to serve their congregations for them.

Returning once from a despotic country to a part of England well cultivated, but not *75*
very picturesque — with what delight did I not observe the poor man's garden! — The
homely palings and twining woodbine, with all the rustic contrivances of simple,
unlettered taste, was a sight which relieved the eye that had wandered indignant from
the stately palace to the pestiferous hovel, and turned from the awful contrast into itself
to mourn the fate of man, and curse the arts of civilization! *80*

Why cannot large estates be divided into small farms? these dwellings would
indeed grace our land. Why are huge forests still allowed to stretch out with idle pomp
and all the indolence of Eastern grandeur? Why do the brown wastes meet the traveller's
view, when men want work? But commons cannot be enclosed without *acts of
parliament* to increase the property of the rich! Why might not the industrious peasant *85*
be allowed to steal a farm from the heath? This sight I have seen; — the cow that
supported the children grazed near the hut, and the cheerful poultry were fed by the
chubby babes, who breathed a bracing air, far from the diseases and the vices of cities.
Domination blasts all these prospects; virtue can only flourish amongst equals, and the
man who submits to a fellow-creature, because it promotes his worldly interest, and he *90*
who relieves only because it is his duty to lay up a treasure in heaven, are much on a
par, for both are radically degraded by the habits of their life.

In this great city, that proudly rears its head, and boasts of its population and
commerce, how much misery lurks in pestilential corners, whilst idle mendicants assail,
on every side, the man who hates to encourage impostors, or repress, with angry frown, *95*
the plaints of the poor! How many mechanics, by a flux of trade or fashion, lose their
employment; whom misfortunes, not to be warded off, lead to the idleness that vitiates
their character and renders them afterwards averse to honest labour! Where is the eye
that marks these evils, more gigantic than any of the infringements of property, which
you piously deprecate? Are these remediless evils? And is the human heart satisfied *100*
with turning the poor over to *another* world, to receive the blessings this could afford? If
society was regulated on a more enlarged plan; if man was contented to be the friend of
man, and did not seek to bury the sympathies of humanity in the servile appellation of
master; if, turning his eyes from ideal regions of taste and elegance, he laboured to give
the earth he inhabited all the beauty it is capable of receiving, and was ever on the watch *105*
to shed abroad all the happiness which human nature can enjoy; — he who, respecting
the rights of men, wishes to convince or persuade society that this is true happiness and
dignity, is not the cruel *oppressor* of the poor, nor a shortsighted philosopher — HE fears
God and loves his fellow-creatures. — Behold the whole duty of man! — the citizen
who acts differently is a sophisticated being. *110*

Surveying civilized life, and seeing, with undazzled eye, the polished vices of the
rich, their insincerity, want of natural affections, with all the specious train that luxury
introduces, I have turned impatiently to the poor, to look for man undebauched by riches
or power — but, alas! what did I see? a being scarcely above the brutes, over which it
tyrannized; a broken spirit, worn-out body, and all those gross vices which the example *115*
of the rich, rudely copied, could produce. Envy built a wall of separation, that made the

---

76. picturesque: See Glossary. **81ff.:** See the note to lines 39ff. of Goldsmith's *The Deserted Village* (p. 647). **96. mechanics:** workmen or
labourers other than agricultural; artisans. **110. sophisticated:** corrupted, impure.

poor hate, whilst they bent to their superiors; who, on their part, stepped aside to avoid the loathsome sight of human misery.

What were the outrages of a day to these continual miseries? Let those sorrows hide their diminished head before the tremendous mountain of woe that thus defaces our *120* globe! Man preys on man; and you mourn for the idle tapestry that decorated a gothic pile, and the dronish bell that summoned the fat priest to prayer. You mourn for the empty pageant of a name, when slavery flaps her wing, and the sick heart retires to die in lonely wilds, far from the abodes of man. Did the pangs you felt for insulted nobility, the anguish that rent your heart when the gorgeous robes were torn off the idol human *125* weakness had set up, deserve to be compared with the long-drawn sigh of melancholy reflection, when misery and vice are thus seen to haunt our steps, and swim on the top of every cheering prospect? Why is our fancy to be appalled by terrific perspectives of a hell beyond the grave? — Hell stalks abroad; — the lash resounds on the slave's naked sides; and the sick wretch, who can no longer earn the sour bread of unremitting labour, *130* steals to a ditch to bid the world a long good night — or, neglected in some ostentatious hospital, breathes his last amidst the laugh of mercenary attendants.

Such misery demands more than tears — I pause to recollect myself; and smother the contempt I feel rising for your rhetorical flourishes and infantine sensibility.

. . . .

(1790)

from *A Vindication of the Rights of Woman:* *With Strictures on Political and Moral Subjects*

from *Chapter IX*
Of the Pernicious Effects Which Arise from the Unnatural
Distinctions Established in Society.

From the respect paid to property flow, as from a poisoned fountain, most of the evils and vices which render this world such a dreary scene to the contemplative mind. For it is in the most polished society that noisome reptiles and venomous serpents lurk under the rank herbage; and there is voluptuousness pampered by the still sultry air, which relaxes every good disposition before it ripens into virtue. *5*

One class presses on another; for all are aiming to procure respect on account of their property: and property, once gained, will procure the respect due only to talents and virtue. Men neglect the duties incumbent on man, yet are treated like demi-gods; religion is also separated from morality by a ceremonial veil, yet men wonder that the world is almost, literally speaking, a den of sharpers or oppressors. *10*

There is a homely proverb, which speaks a shrewd truth, that whoever the devil finds idle he will employ. And what but habitual idleness can hereditary wealth and titles produce? For man is so constituted that he can only attain a proper use of his faculties by exercising them, and will not exercise them unless necessity, of some kind, first set the wheels in motion. Virtue likewise can only be acquired by the discharge of relative *15*

---

119. a day: The 6th of October (Wollstonecraft's note) — referring to the day in 1789 when the mob of French citizens forcibly took the King and Queen from Versailles to Paris.

duties; but the importance of these sacred duties will scarcely be felt by the being who is cajoled out of his humanity by the flattery of sycophants. There must be more equality established in society, or morality will never gain ground, and this virtuous equality will not rest firmly even when founded on a rock, if one half of mankind be chained to its bottom by fate, for they will be continually undermining it through ignorance or pride.   20

It is vain to expect virtue from women till they are, in some degree, independent of men; nay, it is vain to expect that strength of natural affection, which would make them good wives and mothers.

    . . . .

The preposterous distinctions of rank, which render civilization a curse, by dividing the world between voluptuous tyrants, and cunning envious dependents, corrupt, almost   25
equally, every class of people, because respectability is not attached to the discharge of the relative duties of life, but to the station, and when the duties are not fulfilled the affections cannot gain sufficient strength to fortify the virtue of which they are the natural reward. Still there are some loop-holes out of which a man may creep, and dare to think and act for himself; but for a woman it is an herculean task, because she has   30
difficulties peculiar to her sex to overcome, which require almost superhuman powers.

A truly benevolent legislator always endeavours to make it the interest of each individual to be virtuous; and thus private virtue becoming the cement of public happiness, an orderly whole is consolidated by the tendency of all the parts towards a common centre. But, the private or public virtue of woman is very problematical; for   35
Rousseau, and a numerous list of male writers, insist that she should all her life be subjected to a severe restraint, that of propriety. Why subject her to propriety — blind propriety, if she be capable of acting from a nobler spring, if she be an heir of immortality? Is sugar always to be produced by vital blood? Is one half of the human species, like the poor African slaves, to be subject to prejudices that brutalize them,   40
when principles would be a surer guard, only to sweeten the cup of man? Is not this indirectly to deny woman reason? for a gift is a mockery, if it be unfit for use.

Women are, in common with men, rendered weak and luxurious by the relaxing pleasures which wealth procures; but added to this they are made slaves to their persons, and must render them alluring that man may lend them his reason to guide their tottering   45
steps aright. Or should they be ambitious, they must govern their tyrants by sinister tricks, for without rights there cannot be any incumbent duties. The laws respecting woman . . . make an absurd unit of a man and his wife; and then, by the easy transition of only considering him as responsible, she is reduced to a mere cypher.

The being who discharges the duties of its station is independent; and, speaking of   50
women at large, their first duty is to themselves as rational creatures, and the next, in point of importance, as citizens, is that, which includes so many, of a mother. The rank in life which dispenses with their fulfilling this duty, necessarily degrades them by making them mere dolls.

    . . . .

Though I consider that women in the common walks of life are called to fulfil the   55
duties of wives and mothers, I cannot help lamenting that women of a superior cast have

---

A Vindication of the Rights of Woman   35-37: especially in Book V of Jean Jacques Rousseau's influential *Emile, ou l'Education* (1762). 44. persons: bodies.

not a road open by which they can pursue more extensive plans of usefulness and independence. I may excite laughter, by dropping an hint, which I mean to pursue, some future time, for I really think that women ought to have representatives, instead of being arbitrarily governed without having any direct share allowed them in the deliberations of government. 60

But, as the whole system of representation is now, in this country, only a convenient handle for despotism, they need not complain, for they are as well represented as a numerous class of hard-working mechanics, who pay for the support of royalty when they can scarcely stop their children's mouths with bread. How are they 65 represented whose very sweat supports the splendid stud of an heir apparent, or varnishes the chariot of some female favourite who looks down on shame? Taxes on the very necessaries of life, enable an endless tribe of idle princes and princesses to pass with stupid pomp before a gaping crowd, who almost worship the very parade which costs them so dear. 70

. . . .

But what have women to do in society? I may be asked, but to loiter with easy grace; surely you would not condemn them all to suckle fools and chronicle small beer! No. Women might certainly study the art of healing, and be physicians as well as nurses. And midwifery, decency seems to allot to them, though I am afraid the word midwife, in our dictionaries, will soon give place to *accoucheur,* and one proof of the former 75 delicacy of the sex be effaced from the language.

They might, also, study politics. . . .

Business of various kinds, they might likewise pursue, if they were educated in a more orderly manner, which might save many from common and legal prostitution. Women would not then marry for a support, as men accept of places under government, 80 and neglect the implied duties; nor would an attempt to earn their own subsistence, a most laudable one! sink them almost to the level of those poor abandoned creatures who live by prostitution.

. . . .

It is a melancholy truth; yet such is the blessed effect of civilization! the most respectable women are the most oppressed; and, unless they have understandings far 85 superior to the common run of understandings, taking in both sexes, they must, from being treated like contemptible beings, become contemptible. How many women thus waste life away the prey of discontent, who might have practised as physicians, regulated a farm, managed a shop, and stood erect, supported by their own industry, instead of hanging their heads surcharged with the dew of sensibility, that consumes the 90 beauty to which it at first gave lustre; nay, I doubt whether pity and love are so near as poets feign, for I have seldom seen much compassion excited by the helplessness of females, unless they were fair; then, perhaps, pity was the soft handmaid of love, or the harbinger of lust.

. . . .

Would men but generously snap our chains, and be content with rational fellowship 95 instead of slavish obedience, they would find us more observant daughters, more

---

72. to suckle . . . beer: Shakespeare, *Othello*, II.i.160 (what Iago says even the most deserving woman is fit for; *small beer*: trivial matters, household accounts). **75.** *accoucheur*: male physician who attends women during childbirth; obstetrician. **79. legal prostitution:** i.e., marriage.

affectionate sisters, more faithful wives, more reasonable mothers — in a word, better citizens. We should then love them with true affection, because we should learn to respect ourselves; and the peace of mind of a worthy man would not be interrupted by the idle vanity of his wife, nor his babes sent to nestle in a strange bosom, having never *100* found a home in their mother's.

from *Chapter XIII*
Some Instances of the Folly Which the Ignorance of Women Generates;
with Concluding Reflections on the Moral Improvement that a Revolution
in Female Manners Might Naturally Be Expected to Produce.

Section II

Another instance of that feminine weakness of character, often produced by a confined education, is a romantic twist of the mind, which has been very properly termed *sentimental.*

Women subjected by ignorance to their sensations, and only taught to look for *105* happiness in love, refine on sensual feelings, and adopt metaphysical notions respecting that passion, which lead them shamefully to neglect the duties of life, and frequently in the midst of these sublime refinements they plump into actual vice.

These are the women who are amused by the reveries of the stupid novelists, who, knowing little of human nature, work up stale tales, and describe meretricious scenes, all *110* retailed in a sentimental jargon, which equally tend to corrupt the taste, and draw the heart aside from its daily duties. I do not mention the understanding, because never having been exercised, its slumbering energies rest inactive, like the lurking particles of fire which are supposed universally to pervade matter.

Females, in fact, denied all political privileges, and not allowed, as married women, *115* excepting in criminal cases, a civil existence, have their attention naturally drawn from the interest of the whole community to that of the minute parts, though the private duty of any member of society must be very imperfectly performed when not connected with the general good. The mighty business of female life is to please, and restrained from entering into more important concerns by political and civil oppression, sentiments *120* become events, and reflection deepens what it should, and would have effaced, if the understanding had been allowed to take a wider range.

But, confined to trifling employments, they naturally imbibe opinions which the only kind of reading calculated to interest an innocent frivolous mind, inspires. Unable to grasp any thing great, is it surprising that they find the reading of history a very dry *125* task, and disquisitions addressed to the understanding intolerably tedious, and almost unintelligible? Thus are they necessarily dependent on the novelist for amusement. Yet, when I exclaim against novels, I mean when contrasted with those works which exercise the understanding and regulate the imagination. — For any kind of reading I think better than leaving a blank still a blank, because the mind must receive a degree of *130* enlargement and obtain a little strength by a slight exertion of its thinking powers; besides, even the productions that are only addressed to the imagination, raise the reader

---

100. strange bosom: i.e., that of a wet nurse.

a little above the gross gratification of appetites, to which the mind has not given a shade of delicacy.

This observation is the result of experience; for I have known several notable *135* women, and one in particular, who was a very good woman — as good as such a narrow mind would allow her to be, who took care that her daughters (three in number), should never see a novel. As she was a woman of fortune and fashion, they had various masters to attend them, and a sort of menial governess to watch their footsteps. From their masters they learned how tables, chairs, &c. were called in French and Italian; but as the *140* few books thrown in their way were far above their capacities, or devotional, they neither acquired ideas nor sentiments, and passed their time, when not compelled to repeat *words,* in dressing, quarrelling with each other, or conversing with their maids by stealth, till they were brought into company as marriageable.

Their mother, a widow, was busy in the mean time in keeping up her connections, *145* as she termed a numerous acquaintance, lest her girls should want a proper introduction into the great world. And these young ladies, with minds vulgar in every sense of the word, and spoiled tempers, entered life puffed up with notions of their own consequence, and looking down with contempt on those who could not vie with them in dress and parade. *150*

With respect to love, nature, or their nurses, had taken care to teach them the physical meaning of the word; and, as they had few topics of conversation, and fewer refinements of sentiment, they expressed their gross wishes not in very delicate phrases, when they spoke freely, talking of matrimony.

. . . .

This is only one instance; but I recollect many other women who, not led by *155* degrees to proper studies, and not permitted to choose for themselves, have indeed been overgrown children; or have obtained, by mixing in the world, a little of what is termed common sense; that is, a distinct manner of seeing common occurrences, as they stand detached: but what deserves the name of intellect, the power of gaining general or abstract ideas, or even intermediate ones, was out of the question. Their minds were *160* quiescent, and when they were not roused by sensible objects and employments of that kind, they were low-spirited, would cry, or go to sleep.

When, therefore, I advise my sex not to read such flimsy works, it is to induce them to read something superior; for I coincide in opinion with a sagacious man, who, having a daughter and niece under his care, pursued a very different plan with each. *165*

The niece, who had considerable abilities, had, before she was left to his guardianship, been indulged in desultory reading. Her he endeavoured to lead, and did lead to history and moral essays; but his daughter, whom a fond, weak mother had indulged, and who consequently was averse to every thing like application, he allowed to read novels: and used to justify his conduct by saying, that if she ever attained a relish *170* for reading them, he should have some foundation to work upon; and that erroneous opinions were better than none at all.

In fact the female mind has been so totally neglected, that knowledge was only to be acquired from this muddy source, till from reading novels some women of superior talents learned to despise them. *175*

---

150. parade: ostentatious display, show.

The best method, I believe, that can be adopted to correct a fondness for novels is to ridicule them: not indiscriminately, for then it would have little effect; but, if a judicious person, with some turn for humour, would read several to a young girl, and point out both by tones, and apt comparisons with pathetic incidents and heroic characters in history, how foolishly and ridiculously they caricatured human nature, just opinions $\quad$ *180* might be substituted instead of romantic sentiments.

In one respect, however, the majority of both sexes resemble, and equally shew a want of taste and modesty. Ignorant women, forced to be chaste to preserve their reputation, allow their imagination to revel in the unnatural and meretricious scenes sketched by the novel writers of the day, slighting as insipid the sober dignity and $\quad$ *185* matronly graces of history, whilst men carry the same vitiated taste into life, and fly for amusement to the wanton, from the unsophisticated charms of virtue, and the grave respectability of sense.

Besides, the reading of novels makes women, and particularly ladies of fashion, very fond of using strong expressions and superlatives in conversation; and, though the $\quad$ *190* dissipated artificial life which they lead prevents their cherishing any strong legitimate passion, the language of passion in affected tones slips for ever from their glib tongues, and every trifle produces those phosphoric bursts which only mimick in the dark the flame of passion.

Section III

Ignorance and the mistaken cunning that nature sharpens in weak heads as a principle of $\quad$ *195* self-preservation, render women very fond of dress, and produce all the vanity which such a fondness may naturally be expected to generate, to the exclusion of emulation and magnanimity.

. . . .

When the mind is not sufficiently opened to take pleasure in reflection, the body will be adorned with sedulous care; and ambition will appear in tattooing or painting it. $\quad$ *200*

. . . .

An immoderate fondness for dress, for pleasure, and for sway, are the passions of savages; the passions that occupy those uncivilized beings who have not yet extended the domination of the mind, or even learned to think with the energy necessary to concatenate that abstract train of thought which produces principles. And that women from their education and the present state of civilized life, are in the same condition, $\quad$ *205* cannot, I think, be controverted. To laugh at them, or satirize the follies of a being who is never to be allowed to act freely from the light of her own reason, is as absurd as cruel; for, that they who are taught blindly to obey authority, will endeavour cunningly to elude it, is most natural and certain.

Yet let it be proved that they ought to obey man implicitly, and I shall immediately $\quad$ *210* agree that it is woman's duty to cultivate a fondness for dress, in order to please, and a propensity to cunning for her own preservation.

The virtues, however, which are supported by ignorance, must ever be wavering — the house built on sand could not endure a storm. It is almost unnecessary to draw the

---

201. In his "Epistle II. To a Lady: Of the Characters of Women," Pope says women's two "ruling passions" are "The Love of Pleasure, and the Love of Sway" (line 210; *sway:* power in governing, dominion, control). **214. house . . . storm:** See Matthew 7: 26-27.

inference. — If women are to be made virtuous by authority, which is a contradiction in   *215*
terms, let them be immured in seraglios and watched with a jealous eye. — Fear not that
the iron will enter into their souls — for the souls that can bear such treatment are made
of yielding materials, just animated enough to give life to the body.

> Matter too soft a lasting mark to bear,
> And best distinguish'd by black, brown, or fair.   *220*

The most cruel wounds will of course soon heal, and they may still people the
world, and dress to please man — all the purposes which certain celebrated writers have
allowed that they were created to fulfil.

(1792)

from LETTERS WRITTEN DURING A SHORT RESIDENCE IN SWEDEN, NORWAY, AND DENMARK

Letter XV

I left Christiania yesterday. The weather was not very fine; and having been a little
delayed on the road, I found that it was too late to go round, a couple of miles, to see the
cascade near Frederikstad, which I had determined to visit. Besides, as Frederikstad is a
fortress, it was necessary to arrive there before they shut the gate.

The road along the river is very romantic, though the views are not grand; and the   *5*
riches of Norway, its timber, floats silently down the stream, often impeded in its course
by islands and little cataracts, the offspring, as it were, of the great one I had frequently
heard described.

I found an excellent inn at Frederikstad, and was gratified by the kind attention of
the hostess, who, perceiving that my clothes were wet, took great pains to procure me,   *10*
as a stranger, every comfort for the night.

It had rained very hard; and we passed the ferry in the dark, without getting out of
our carriage, which I think wrong, as the horses are sometimes unruly. Fatigue and
melancholy, however, had made me regardless whether I went down or across the
stream; and I did not know that I was wet before the hostess remarked it. My imagin-   *15*
ation has never yet severed me from my griefs — and my mind has seldom been so free
as to allow my body to be delicate.

How I am altered by disappointment! — When going to Lisbon, the elasticity of my
mind was sufficient to ward off weariness, and my imagination still could dip her brush
in the rainbow of fancy, and sketch futurity in glowing colours. Now — but let me talk   *20*
of something else — will you go with me to the cascade?

The cross road to it was rugged and dreary; and though a considerable extent of
land was cultivated on all sides, yet the rocks were entirely bare, which surprised me, as
they were more on a level with the surface than any I had yet seen. On inquiry, however,
I learnt that some years since a forest had been burnt. This appearance of desolation was   *25*

---

217. iron . . . souls: from *The Psalter* or *The Book of Common Prayer*, Psalm 105:18. **219-20:** Pope's "Epistle II," 3-4. **LETTER XV   1. Christiania:** former name for Oslo, Norway. **3. Frederikstad:** Fredrikstad, on the coast about 70 km south of Oslo. **12. passed:** i.e., crossed over by means of. **16-17:** "When the mind's free, / The body's delicate" (*King Lear*, III.iv.11-12; Wollstonecraft's note).

beyond measure gloomy, inspiring emotions that sterility had never produced. Fires of this kind are occasioned by the wind suddenly rising when the farmers are burning roots of trees, stalks of beans, &c. with which they manure the ground. The devastation must, indeed, be terrible, when this, literally speaking, wild fire, runs along the forest, flying from top to top, and crackling amongst the branches. The soil, as well as the trees, is 30 swept away by the destructive torrent; and the country, despoiled of beauty and riches, is left to mourn for ages.

Admiring, as I do, these noble forests, which seem to bid defiance to time, I looked with pain on the ridge of rocks that stretched far beyond my eye, formerly crowned with the most beautiful verdure. 35

I have often mentioned the grandeur, but I feel myself unequal to the task of conveying an idea of the beauty and elegance of the scene when the spiral tops of the pines are loaded with ripening seed, and the sun gives a glow to their light green tinge, which is changing into purple, one tree more or less advanced, contrasting with another. The profusion with which nature has decked them, with pendant honours, prevents all 40 surprise at seeing, in every crevice, some sapling struggling for existence. Vast masses of stone are thus encircled; and roots, torn up by the storms, become a shelter for a young generation. The pine and fir woods, left entirely to nature, display an endless variety; and the paths in the wood are not entangled with fallen leaves, which are only interesting whilst they are fluttering between life and death. The grey cobweb-like 45 appearance of the aged pines is a much finer image of decay; the fibres whitening as they lose their moisture, imprisoned life seems to be stealing away. I cannot tell why — but death, under every form, appears to me like something getting free — to expand in I know not what element; nay I feel that this conscious being must be as unfettered, have the wings of thought, before it can be happy. 50

Reaching the cascade, or rather cataract, the roaring of which had a long time announced its vicinity, my soul was hurried by the falls into a new train of reflections. The impetuous dashing of the rebounding torrent from the dark cavities which mocked the exploring eye, produced an equal activity in my mind: my thoughts darted from earth to heaven, and I asked myself why I was chained to life and its misery? Still the 55 tumultuous emotions this sublime object excited, were pleasurable; and, viewing it, my soul rose, with renewed dignity, above its cares — grasping at immortality — it seemed as impossible to stop the current of my thoughts, as of the always varying, still the same, torrent before me — I stretched out my hand to eternity, bounding over the dark speck of life to come. 60

We turned with regret from the cascade. On a little hill, which commands the best view of it, several obelisks are erected to commemorate the visits of different kings. The appearance of the river above and below the falls is very picturesque, the ruggedness of the scenery disappearing as the torrent subsides into a peaceful stream. But I did not like to see a number of saw-mills crowded together close to the cataracts; they destroyed the 65 harmony of the prospect.

The sight of a bridge erected across a deep valley, at a little distance, inspired very dissimilar sensations. It was most ingeniously supported by mast-like trunks, just stript

---

48-50: Cf. Edward Young's *Complaint*, I, 90-161 (p. 504). **56. sublime:** Cf. *picturesque* (63), and see *picturesque* and *sublime* in the Glossary.

of their branches; and logs, placed one across the other, produced an appearance equally light and firm, seeming almost to be built in the air when we were below it; the height *70* taking from the magnitude of the supporting trees give them a slender, graceful look.

There are two noble estates in this neighbourhood, the proprietors of which seem to have caught more than their portion of the enterprising spirit that is gone abroad. Many agricultural experiments have been made; and the country appears better enclosed and cultivated; yet the cottages had not the comfortable aspect of those I had observed near *75* Moss, and to the westward. Man is always debased by servitude, of any description; and here the peasantry are not entirely free.

Adieu!

I almost forgot to tell you, that I did not leave Norway without making some inquiries after the monsters said to have been seen in the northern sea; but though I conversed with several captains, I could not meet with one who had ever heard any *80* traditional description of them, much less had any ocular demonstration of their existence. Till the fact be better ascertained, I should think the account of them ought to be torn out of our Geographical Grammars.

(1796)

HELEN MARIA WILLIAMS
England, 1762-1827

from *LETTERS WRITTEN IN FRANCE, IN THE SUMMER 1790, TO A FRIEND IN ENGLAND*

Containing Various Anecdotes Relative to the French Revolution . . .

from *Letter VI*

I have been at the National Assembly, where, at a time when the deputies from the provinces engrossed every ticket of admission, my sister and I were admitted without tickets, by the gentleman who had the command of the guard, and placed in the best seats, before he suffered the doors to be opened to other people. We had no personal acquaintance with this gentleman, or any claim to his politeness, except that of being *5* foreigners and women; but these are, of all claims, the most powerful to the urbanity of French manners.

. . . .

The hall of the National Assembly is long and narrow; at each end there is a gallery, where the common people are admitted by applying very early in the morning for numbers, which are distributed at the door; and the persons who first apply secure the *10* first numbers. The seats being also numbered, all confusion and disorder are prevented.

---

76. Moss: town between Oslo and Fredrikstad.

The galleries at the side of the hall are divided into boxes, which are called tribunes; they belong to the principal members of the National Assembly; and to these places company are admitted with tickets. Rows of seats are placed round the hall, raised one above another, where the members of the Assembly are seated; and immediately *15* opposite the chair of the President, in the narrow part of the hall, is the tribune which the Members ascend when they are going to speak. One capital subject of debate in this Assembly is, who shall speak first; for all seem more inclined to talk than to listen; and sometimes the President in vain rings a bell, or with the vehemence of French action stretches out his arms, and endeavours to impose silence; while the six Huissiers, *20* persons who are appointed to keep order, make the attempt with as little success as the President himself. But one ceases to wonder that the meetings of the National Assembly are tumultuous, on reflecting how important are the objects of its deliberations. Not only the lives and fortunes of individuals, but the existence of the country is at stake: and of how little consequence is this impetuosity in debate, if the decrees which are passed are *25* wise and beneficial, and the new constitution arises, like the beauty and order of nature, from the confusion of mingled elements! I heard several of the Members speak; but I am so little qualified to judge of oratory, that, without presuming to determine whether I had reason to be entertained or not, I shall only tell you that I was so.

And this, repeated I with exultation to myself, this is the National Assembly of *30* France! Those men now before my eyes are the men who engross the attention, the astonishment of Europe; for the issue of whose decrees surrounding nations wait in suspense, and whose fame has already extended through every civilized region of the globe: the men whose magnanimity invested them with power to destroy the old constitution, and whose wisdom is erecting the new, on a principle of perfection which *35* has hitherto been thought chimerical, and has only served to adorn the page of the philosopher; but which they believe may be reduced to practice, and have therefore the courage to attempt. My mind, with a sensation of elevated pleasure, passing through the interval of ages, anticipated the increasing renown of these legislators, and the period when, all the nations of Europe following the liberal system which France has adopted, *40* the little crooked policy of present times shall give place to the reign of reason, virtue, and science.

The most celebrated characters in the National Assembly were pointed out to us. Monsieur Barnave de Dauphine, who is only six and twenty years of age, and the youngest member of the Assembly, is esteemed its first orator, and is the leader of the *45* democratic party. . . .

We also saw Mons. Mirabeau l'ainé, whose genius is of the first class, but who possesses a very small share of popularity. I am, however, one of his partisans, though not merely from that enthusiasm which always comes across my heart in favour of great intellectual abilities. Mons. Mirabeau has another very powerful claim on my partiality: *50* he is the professed friend (and I must and will love him for being so) of the African

---

Letters Written in France   **44:** Antoine Pierre Joseph Marie Barnave (1761-1793), revolutionary who supported Mirabeau's attempt to establish a constitutional monarchy; later guillotined. **47:** Honoré Gabriel Riqueti, Comte de Mirabeau (1749-1791), French orator and leader of the Third Estate (which became the National Assembly). **51-62:** On slavery, see the note to Wordsworth's *Prelude*, X, 247ff. (p. 775), and the general note to Kemble's *Journal* (p. 976); France moved to suppress slavery in its colonies in 1851.

race. He has proposed the abolition of the slave-trade to the National Assembly; and, though the Assembly have delayed the consideration of this subject, on account of those deliberations which immediately affect the country, yet, perhaps, if our senators continue to doze over this affair as they have hitherto done, the French will have the glory of setting us an example, which it will then be our humble employment to follow. But I trust the period will never come, when England will submit to be taught by another nation the lesson of humanity. I trust an English House of Commons will never persist in thinking, that what is morally wrong, can be politically right; that the virtue and the prosperity of a people are things at variance with each other; and that a country which abounds with so many sources of wealth, cannot afford to close one polluted channel, which is stained with the blood of our fellow-creatures.

But it is a sort of treason to the honour, the spirit, the generosity of Englishmen, to suppose they will persevere in such conduct. Admitting, however, a supposition, which it is painful to make; admitting that they should abide by this system of inhumanity, they will only retard, but will not finally prevent the abolition of slavery. The Africans have not long to suffer, nor their oppressors to triumph. Europe is hastening towards a period too enlightened for the perpetuation of such monstrous abuses. The mists of ignorance and error are rolling fast away, and the benign beams of philosophy are spreading their lustre over the nations. . . .

from *Letter X*

As we came out of La Maison de Ville, we were shewn, immediately opposite, the far-famed *lanterne*, at which, for want of a gallows, the first victims of popular fury were sacrificed. I own that the sight of *la lanterne* chilled the blood within my veins. At that moment, for the first time, I lamented the revolution; and, forgetting the imprudence, or the guilt, of those unfortunate men, could only reflect with horror on the dreadful expiation they had made. I painted in my imagination the agonies of their families and friends; nor could I for a considerable time chase these gloomy images from my thoughts.

It is for ever to be regretted, that so dark a shade of ferocious revenge was thrown across the glories of the revolution. But alas! where do the records of history point out a revolution unstained by some actions of barbarity? When do the passions of human nature rise to that pitch which produces great events, without wandering into some irregularities? If the French revolution should cost no farther bloodshed, it must be allowed, notwithstanding a few shocking instances of public vengeance, that the liberty of twenty-four millions of people will have been purchased at a far cheaper rate than could ever have been expected from the former experience of the world.

Letter XXVI

We left France early in September, that we might avoid the equinoctial gales; but were so unfortunate as to meet, in our passage from Dieppe to Brighton, with a very violent storm. We were two days and two nights at sea, and beat four and twenty hours off the coast of Brighton; and it would be difficult for you, who have formed your calculations of time on dry land, to guess what is the length of four and twenty hours in a storm at sea. At last, with great difficulty, we landed on the beach, where we found several of our friends and acquaintance, who, supposing that we might be among the passengers, sympathised with our danger, and were anxious for our preservation.

Before the storm became so serious as to exclude every idea but that of preparing to die with composure, I could not help being diverted with the comments on French 95 customs, and French politics, which passed in the cabin. "Ah!" says one man to his companion, "one had need to go to France, to know how to like old England when one gets back again." — "For my part," rejoined another, "I've never been able to get drunk once the whole time I was in France — not a drop of porter to be had — and as for their victuals, they call a bit of meat of a pound and a half, a fine piece of roast beef." — 100 "And pray," added he, turning to one of the sailors, "What do you think of their National Assembly?" "Why," says the sailor, "if I ben't mistaken, the National Assembly has got some points from the wind."

I own it has surprised me not a little, since I came to London, to find that most of my acquaintance are of the same opinion with the sailor. Every visitor brings me 105 intelligence from France full of dismay and horror. I hear of nothing but crimes, assassinations, torture, and death. I am told that every day witnesses a conspiracy; that every town is the scene of a massacre; that every street is blackened with a gallows, and every highway deluged with blood. I hear these things, and repeat to myself — Is this the picture of France? Are these the images of that universal joy which called tears into 110 my eyes, and made my heart throb with sympathy? — To me, the land which these mighty magicians have suddenly covered with darkness, where, waving their evil wand, they have reared the dismal scaffold, have clotted the knife of the assassin with gore, have called forth the shriek of despair, and the agony of torture — to me, this land of desolation appeared dressed in additional beauty beneath the genial smile of Liberty. 115 The woods seemed to cast a more refreshing shade, and the lawns to wear a brighter verdure, while the carols of freedom burst from the cottage of the peasant, and the voice of joy resounded on the hill, and in the valley.

Must I be told, that my mind is perverted, that I am become dead to all sensations of sympathy, because I do not weep with those who have lost a part of their superfluities, rather 120 than rejoice that the oppressed are protected, that the wronged are redressed, that the captive is set at liberty, and that the poor have bread? Did the Universal Parent of the human race implant the feelings of pity in the heart, that they should be confined to the artificial wants of vanity, the ideal deprivations of greatness; that they should be fixed beneath the dome of the palace, or locked within the gate of the *chateau;* without extending one commiserating sigh 125 to the wretched hamlet, as if its famished inhabitants, though not ennobled by *man,* did not bear, at least, the ensigns of nobility stamped on our nature by God?

Must I hear the charming societies, in which I found all the elegant graces of the most polished manners, all the amiable urbanity of liberal and cultivated minds, compared with the most rude, ferocious, and barbarous levellers that ever existed? 130 Really, some of my English acquaintance, whatever objections they may have to republican principles, do, in their discussions of French politics, adopt a most free and republican style of censure. Nothing can be more democratical than their mode of expression, or display a more levelling spirit than their unqualified contempt of *all* the leaders of the revolution. 135

---

124. ideal: imaginary

It is not my intention to shiver lances, in every society I enter, in the cause of the National Assembly. Yet I cannot help remarking, that, since the Assembly does not presume to set itself up as an example to this country, we seem to have very little right to be furiously angry, because they think proper to try another system of government themselves. Why should they not be suffered to make an experiment in politics? I have *140* always been told, that the improvement of every science depends upon experiment. But I now hear, that, instead of their attempt to form the great machine of society upon a simple principle of general amity, upon the Federation of its members, they ought to have repaired the feudal wheels and springs, by which their ancestors directed its movements. Yet, if mankind had always observed this retrograde motion, it would *145* surely have led them to few acquisitions in virtue, or in knowledge; and we might even have been worshipping the idols of paganism at this moment. To forbid, under the pains and penalties of reproach, all attempts of the human mind to advance to greater perfection, seems to be proscribing every art and science: and we cannot much wonder that the French, having received so small a legacy of public happiness from their *150* forefathers, and being sensible of the poverty of their own patrimony, should try new methods of transmitting a richer inheritance to their posterity.

Perhaps the improvements which mankind may be capable of making in the art of politics, may have some resemblance to those they have made in the art of navigation. Perhaps our political plans may have hitherto been somewhat like those ill-constructed *155* misshapen vessels, which, unfit to combat with the winds and the waves, were only used by the ancients to convey the warriors of one country to despoil and ravage another neighbouring state: only served to produce an intercourse of hostility, a communication of injury, an exchange of rapine and devastation. — But it may possibly be within the compass of human ability to form a system of politics, which like a modern ship of *160* discovery, built upon principles that defy the opposition of the tempestuous elements, ("and passions are the elements of life" —) instead of yielding to their fury makes them subservient to its purpose, and sailing sublimely over the untracked ocean, unites those together whom nature seemed for ever to have separated, and throws a line of connexion across the divided world. *165*

One cause of the general dislike in which the French revolution is held in this country, is the exaggerated stories which are carefully circulated by such of the Aristocrats as have taken refuge in England. They are not all, however, persons of this description. There is now a young gentleman in London, nephew to the Bishop de Sens, who has lost his fortune, his rank, all his high expectations, and yet who has the *170* generosity to applaud the revolution, and the magnanimity to reconcile himself to personal calamities, from the consideration of general good; and who is "faithful found" to his country, "among the faithless." I hope this amiable young Frenchman will live to witness, and to share the honours, the prosperity, of that regenerated country; and I also hope that the National Assembly of France will answer the objects of its adversaries in *175* the manner most becoming its own dignity, by forming such a constitution as will render the French nation virtuous, flourishing, and happy.

(1790)

---

162. "and passions . . . life" : Pope, *An Essay on Man*, I, 170 (see p. 544). **172-73. "faithful . . . faithless":** *Paradise Lost*, V, 896-97.

from *LETTERS FROM FRANCE,* VOLUME II

Containing Many New Anecdotes Relative to the French Revolution, and the Present State of French Manners

from *Letter III*

The French revolution is not only sublime in a general view, but is often beautiful when considered in detail. Its history abounds with circumstances that would embellish the page of the Greek or Roman annals. But the old remark, that no man is a hero to his valet de chambre, may be applied to great events, as well as great characters. The French revolution is viewed too near to excite the same veneration in the present age 5 which it will probably awaken in the minds of posterity. It wants that mellowed tint which is produced by time. Succeeding generations will perhaps associate the Tennis-court of Versailles, and the Champ de Mars, with the Forum and the Capitol. For the prejudices which now obscure the revolution are mortal, and will die with the present race, and posterity will view it through a clearer medium. Posterity will not demand, 10 contrary to what appears the law of our nature, "universal good," unmixed with "partial evil"; but will contemplate the revolution in the same manner as we gaze at a sublime landscape, of which the general effect is great and noble, and where some little points of asperity, some minute deformities, are lost in the overwhelming majesty of the whole.

from *Letter V*

The principal article of commerce at Orléans, is that of refining sugar. We went 15 yesterday to see the process. In one stage of its progress the sugar is clarified with the blood of oxen: it is poured into vessels of an immense size, and appears a liquid of a deep red. I own those frightful reservoirs struck my imagination as if stained with the blood of Africans.

The long train of calamities which are the portion of that unhappy race, crowded in sad 20 succession upon my mind, and I observed, with a degree of horror which I could not repress, the process of a luxury obtained for the inhabitants of one part of the globe, by the wrongs, the agonies, the despair of the inhabitants of another part. — Alas! why is there so much more misery in this world than benevolence can cure? Why, in the public discussions in France and in England, on the Slave Trade, are the possibilities of gain and loss 25 calculated with such nice precision? Why are crimes and injustice, desolation and death, treated in a style so very mercantile that humanity listens in despair to their deliberations?

From thence we went to see a very considerable manufactory for spinning cotton, which has been established here by an English gentleman, to whom we are obliged for that cordial hospitality, which is the ancient and honourable characteristic of our country, 30 and which is so peculiarly grateful to the heart when received in a land of strangers.

LETTERS FROM FRANCE   (Volume II)   **1. sublime . . . beautiful:** See *sublime* in the Glossary. **7-8. Tennis-court:** site of the oath by the deputies of the Third Estate, 20 June 1789, when Louis XVI barred them from their hall. **8. Champ de Mars:** Paris site of Louis XVI's oath, at the Fête de la Fédération on 14 July 1790, to uphold the new constitution; **Forum, Capitol:** (Capitoline Hill) important sites in ancient Rome. **11-12. "the law . . . evil":** See Pope's *An Essay on Man*, I, 292 (p. 545).

This manufacture, while it displays the wonderful power of mechanism, gives occasion also to the exercise of humanity, by employing not only a great number of men, but fourteen hundred women and children.

from *Letter VIII*

One subject of complaint among the aristocrats is, that, since the revolution, they are obliged to drive through the streets with caution: the life of a citizen is now considered as of some value, and the poor people on foot cannot be trampled upon, by the horses of the rich people in carriages, with the same impunity as formerly. "C'est si incommode," said an aristocrat to me lately, "quand je vais dans ma voiture en campagne; le peuple ne se range pas comme autrefois — ces gens-là font d'une insolence incroyable — on est obligé de prendre bien garde de ne les pas écraser, et cela demande du temps." Madame de Pompadour, mistress to Lewis XV, was passing through Orléans, when her coachman drove over a poor woman, whom age and infirmity prevented from getting time enough out of the way, and she was killed upon the spot. The coachman stopped the carriage, and the servants told their mistress that the poor woman was killed. "Eh bien," said she, with the most perfect sang-froid, and flinging a louis d'or out of the window, "voilà de quoi la faire enterrer; allez, cocher." Is it possible to hear of every feeling of humanity being thus insulted, without a degree of indignation which can only be soothed by the reflection that such monstrous evils exist no longer? Is it possible to hear this incident without rejoicing, that a system of government which led to such depravation of mind is laid in ruins? For my part, I confess myself so hardened a patriot, that I rejoice to see the lower order of people in this country have lost somewhat of that too obsequious politeness for which they were once distinguished; and that whenever they find themself in the slightest degree offended, they assume a tone of manly independence. While we were walking yesterday along the very square where the poor old woman was killed, I heard a day-labourer say, in an angry tone of voice, to a gentleman, by whom he thought himself ill-treated, "Monsieur, nous sommes égaux — je suis citoyen, monsieur, *tout* comme un autre." Some of our company were shocked at his insolence, while I, recollecting the poor old woman, could not help repeating to myself, "Ah! mon ami, n'oubliez jamais que vous êtes citoyen *tout* comme un autre."

. . . .

Two gentlemen were conversing together this morning upon public affairs. After discussing many political points, one of them said to the other, whom he perceived to be a little violent in his sentiments, "Mais après tout, il faut de la modération."

"On parle tant de la modération," answered the democrat, in the most angry tone in the world: "ma foi, monsieur, on n'a pris la Bastille avec de la limonade."

(1792)

38-41: "It's so inconvenient when I go in my carriage to the country; people don't get out of the way as before — those people have an incredible insolence — one is obliged to take great care not to run over them, and that takes time." **45-47:** "Well, there's something to bury her with; drive on, coachman." **57-58:** "Sir, we are equals — I am a citizen, *just* like any other." **60-61:** "Ah, my friend, never forget that you are a citizen *just* like any other." **64:** "But after all, moderation is necessary." **65-66:** "People speak so of moderation; my faith, sir, the Bastille could not have been taken with lemonade."

THOMAS MALTHUS
England, 1766-1834

from *AN ESSAY ON THE PRINCIPLE OF POPULATION*, Chapter XVIII

The view of human life which results from the contemplation of the constant pressure of distress on man from the difficulty of subsistence, by shewing the little expectation that he can reasonably entertain of perfectibility on earth, seems strongly to point his hopes to the future. And the temptations to which he must necessarily be exposed, from the operation of those laws of nature which we have been examining, would seem to represent the world in the light in which it has been frequently considered, as a state of trial, and school of virtue, preparatory to a superior state of happiness. But I hope I shall be pardoned, if I attempt to give a view in some degree different of the situation of man on earth, which appears to me to be more consistent with the various phenomena of nature which we observe around us, and more consonant to our ideas of the power, goodness, and foreknowledge of the Deity.

It cannot be considered as an unimproving exercise of the human mind to endeavour to "Vindicate the ways of God to man" if we proceed with a proper distrust of our own understandings and a just sense of our insufficiency to comprehend the reason of all that we see; if we hail every ray of light with gratitude, and when no light appears, think that the darkness is from within and not from without; and bow with humble deference to the supreme wisdom of him whose "thoughts are above our thoughts" "as the heavens are high above the earth."

In all our feeble attempts, however, to "find out the Almighty to perfection," it seems absolutely necessary that we should reason from nature up to nature's God, and not presume to reason from God to nature. The moment we allow ourselves to ask why some things are not otherwise, instead of endeavouring to account for them as they are, we shall never know where to stop; we shall be led into the grossest and most childish absurdities; all progress in the knowledge of the ways of Providence must necessarily be at an end; and the study will even cease to be an improving exercise of the human mind. Infinite power is so vast and incomprehensible an idea, that the mind of man must necessarily be bewildered in the contemplation of it. With the crude and puerile conceptions which we sometimes form of this attribute of the Deity, we might imagine that God could call into being myriads and myriads of existences, all free from pain and imperfection, all eminent in goodness and wisdom, all capable of the highest enjoyments, and unnumbered as the points throughout infinite space. But when from these vain and extravagant dreams of fancy, we turn our eyes to the book of nature, where alone we can read God as he is, we see a constant succession of sentient beings, rising apparently from so many specks of matter, going through a long and sometimes painful process in this

---

AN ESSAY ON THE PRINCIPLE OF POPULATION   **13.** "**Vindicate . . . man**": See Milton's *Paradise Lost*, I, 25-26, and note (p. 326), and Pope's *An Essay on Man*, I, 16 (p. 542). **19.** "**find . . . perfection**": from Job 11:7. **20. reason . . . God:** See *An Essay on Man*, I, 17ff.

world; but many of them attaining, ere the termination of it, such high qualities and powers as seem to indicate their fitness for some superior state. Ought we not then to correct our crude and puerile ideas of Infinite Power from the contemplation of what we actually see existing? Can we judge of the Creator but from his creation? And unless we wish to exalt the power of God at the expence of his goodness, ought we not to conclude that even to the Great Creator, Almighty as he is, a certain process may be necessary, a certain time (or at least what appears to us as time) may be requisite, in order to form beings with those exalted qualities of mind which will fit them for his high purposes?

A state of trial seems to imply a previously formed existence that does not agree with the appearance of man in infancy, and indicates something like suspicion and want of foreknowledge, inconsistent with those ideas which we wish to cherish of the Supreme Being. I should be inclined, therefore, as I have hinted before in a note, to consider the world, and this life, as the mighty process of God, not for the trial, but for the creation and formation of mind; a process necessary to awaken inert, chaotic matter into spirit, to sublimate the dust of the earth into soul, to elicit an æthereal spark from the clod of clay. And in this view of the subject, the various impressions and excitements which man receives through life may be considered as the forming hand of his Creator, acting by general laws, and awakening his sluggish existence, by the animating touches of the Divinity, into a capacity of superior enjoyment. The original sin of man is the torpor and corruption of the chaotic matter in which he may be said to be born.

It could answer no good purpose to enter into the question whether mind be a distinct substance from matter, or only a finer form of it. The question is, perhaps, after all, a question merely of words. Mind is as essentially mind, whether formed from matter or any other substance. We know, from experience, that soul and body are most intimately united; and every appearance seems to indicate that they grow from infancy together. It would be a supposition attended with very little probability, to believe that a complete and full formed spirit existed in every infant, but that it was clogged and impeded in its operations, during the first twenty years of life, by the weakness, or hebetude, of the organs in which it was enclosed. As we shall all be disposed to agree that God is the creator of mind as well as of body, and as they both seem to be forming and unfolding themselves at the same time, it cannot appear inconsistent either with reason or revelation, if it appear to be consistent with phenomena of nature, to suppose that God is constantly occupied in forming mind out of matter, and that the various impressions that man receives through life is the process for that purpose. The employment is surely worthy of the highest attributes of the Deity.

This view of the state of man on earth will not seem to be unattended with probability, if, judging from the little experience we have of the nature of mind, it shall appear, upon investigation, that the phenomena around us, and the various events of human life, seem peculiarly calculated to promote this great end: and especially if, upon this supposition, we can account, even to our own narrow understandings, for many of those roughnesses and inequalities in life, which querulous man too frequently makes the subject of his complaint against the God of nature.

· · · ·

(1798)

---

63. **hebetude:** dullness, lethargy.

WILLIAM WORDSWORTH
England, 1770-1850

from DESCRIPTIVE SKETCHES, TAKEN DURING A PEDESTRIAN TOUR AMONG THE ALPS, 1791-2
(early and revised versions)

'Tis storm; and hid in mist from hour to hour
All day the floods a deeper murmur pour,
And mournful sounds, as of a Spirit lost,
Pipe wild along the hollow-blustering coast,   *335*
Till the Sun walking on his western field
Shakes from behind the clouds his flashing shield.
Triumphant on the bosom of the storm,
Glances the fire-clad eagle's wheeling form;
Eastward, in long perspective glittering, shine   *340*
The wood-crown'd cliffs that o'er the lake recline;
Wide o'er the Alps a hundred streams unfold,
At once to pillars turn'd that flame with gold;
Behind his sail the peasant strives to shun
The west that burns like one dilated sun,   *345*
Where in a mighty crucible expire
The mountains, glowing hot, like coals of fire.
                                    (1793)

Swoln with incessant rains from hour to hour,
All day the floods a deepening murmur pour: *271*
The sky is veiled, and every cheerful sight:
Dark is the region as with coming night;
But what a sudden burst of overpowering light!
Triumphant on the bosom of the storm,   *275*
Glances the wheeling eagle's glorious form!
Eastward, in long perspective glittering, shine
The wood-crowned cliffs that o'er the lake recline;
Those lofty cliffs a hundred streams unfold,
At once to pillars turned that flame with gold: *280*
Behind his sail the peasant shrinks, to shun
The *west,* that burns like one dilated sun,
A crucible of mighty compass, felt
By mountains, glowing till they seem to melt.
                                    (1793, 1845)

DESCRIPTIVE SKETCHES   Considering what he did in his revision (printed to the right of the original), Wordsworth's own note to the first version is interesting: "I had once given to these sketches the title of Picturesque; but the Alps are insulted in applying to them that term. Whoever, in attempting to describe their sublime features, should confine himself to the cold rules of painting would give his reader but a very imperfect idea of those emotions which they have the irresistible power of communicating to the most impassive imagination. The fact is, that controlling influence, which distinguishes the Alps from all other scenery, is derived from images which disdain the pencil. Had I wished to make a picture of this scene I had thrown much less light into it. But I consulted nature and my feelings. The ideas excited by the stormy sunset I am here describing owed their sublimity to that deluge of light, or rather of fire, in which nature had wrapped the immense forms all around me; any intrusion of shade, by destroying the unity of the impression, had necessarily diminished its grandeur." (See *picturesque* and *sublime* in the Glossary.) This is also the passage Samuel Taylor Coleridge uses (in Chapter IV of his *Biographia Literaria,* 1817) to illustrate his first impressions of Wordsworth: "Seldom, if ever, was the emergence of any original poetic genius above the literary horizon more evidently announced. In the form, style and manner of the whole poem, and in the structure of the particular lines and periods, there is a harshness and acerbity connected and combined with words and images all a-glow which might recall those products of the vegetable world, where gorgeous blossoms rise out of the hard and thorny rind and shell within which the rich fruit was elaborating. The language was not only peculiar and strong, but at times knotty and contorted, as by its own impatient strength; while the novelty and struggling crowd of images acting in conjunction with the difficulties of the style demanded always a greater closeness of attention than poetry (at all events than descriptive poetry) has a right to claim. It not seldom therefore justified the complaint of obscurity. In the following extract I have sometimes fancied that I saw an emblem of the poem itself and of the author's genius as it was then displayed:" (he then quotes the passage).

LINES
Composed a Few Miles above Tintern Abbey, on Revisiting the Banks of the Wye during a Tour, July 13, 1798

Five years have past; five summers, with the length
Of five long winters! and again I hear
These waters, rolling from their mountain-springs
With a soft inland murmur. — Once again
Do I behold these steep and lofty cliffs,   5
That on a wild secluded scene impress
Thoughts of more deep seclusion; and connect
The landscape with the quiet of the sky.
The day is come when I again repose
Here, under this dark sycamore, and view   10
These plots of cottage-ground, these orchard-tufts,
Which at this season, with their unripe fruits,
Are clad in one green hue, and lose themselves
'Mid groves and copses. Once again I see
These hedge-rows, hardly hedge-rows, little lines   15
Of sportive wood run wild: these pastoral farms,
Green to the very door; and wreaths of smoke
Sent up, in silence, from among the trees!
With some uncertain notice, as might seem
Of vagrant dwellers in the houseless woods,   20
Or of some Hermit's cave, where by his fire
The Hermit sits alone.

          These beauteous forms,
Through a long absence, have not been to me
As is a landscape to a blind man's eye:
But oft, in lonely rooms, and 'mid the din   25
Of towns and cities, I have owed to them,
In hours of weariness, sensations sweet,
Felt in the blood, and felt along the heart;
And passing even into my purer mind,
With tranquil restoration: — feelings too   30
Of unremembered pleasure: such, perhaps,
As have no slight or trivial influence
On that best portion of a good man's life,
His little, nameless, unremembered, acts
Of kindness and of love. Nor less, I trust,   35
To them I may have owed another gift,
Of aspect more sublime; that blessed mood,

In which the burthen of the mystery,
In which the heavy and the weary weight
Of all this unintelligible world,   40
Is lightened: — that serene and blessed mood,
In which the affections gently lead us on, —
Until, the breath of this corporeal frame
And even the motion of our human blood
Almost suspended, we are laid asleep   45
In body, and become a living soul:
While with an eye made quiet by the power
Of harmony, and the deep power of joy,
We see into the life of things.

                If this
Be but a vain belief, yet, oh! how oft —   50
In darkness and amid the many shapes
Of joyless daylight; when the fretful stir
Unprofitable, and the fever of the world,
Have hung upon the beatings of my heart —
How oft, in spirit, have I turned to thee,   55
O sylvan Wye! thou wanderer thro' the woods,
How often has my spirit turned to thee!

     And now, with gleams of half-extinguished thought,
With many recognitions dim and faint,
And somewhat of a sad perplexity,   60
The picture of the mind revives again:
While here I stand, not only with the sense
Of present pleasure, but with pleasing thoughts
That in this moment there is life and food
For future years. And so I dare to hope,   65
Though changed, no doubt, from what I was when first
I came among these hills; when like a roe
I bounded o'er the mountains, by the sides
Of the deep rivers, and the lonely streams,
Wherever nature led: more like a man   70
Flying from something that he dreads, than one
Who sought the thing he loved. For nature then
(The coarser pleasures of my boyish days,
And their glad animal movements all gone by)

LINES . . . TINTERN ABBEY   Title: The ruins of Tintern Abbey are about 10 km south of Monmouth, in Wales. "No poem of mine was composed under circumstances more pleasant for me to remember than this. I began it upon leaving Tintern, after crossing the Wye, and concluded it just as I was entering Bristol in the evening, after a ramble of 4 or 5 days with my sister. Not a line of it was altered, and not any part of it was written down till I reached Bristol" (Wordsworth in a letter); the poem is the last item in *Lyrical Ballads*, poems by Wordsworth and Coleridge published (anonymously) in 1798 (for some discussion of this collection, see Chapter XIV of Coleridge's *Biographia Literaria*). **1. past:** passed. **4. inland murmur:** "The river is not affected by the tides a few miles above Tintern" (Wordsworth's note).

To me was all in all. — I cannot paint   75
What then I was. The sounding cataract
Haunted me like a passion: the tall rock,
The mountain, and the deep and gloomy wood,
Their colours and their forms, were then to me
An appetite; a feeling and a love,   80
That had no need of a remoter charm,
By thought supplied, nor any interest
Unborrowed from the eye. — That time is past,
And all its aching joys are now no more,
And all its dizzy raptures. Not for this   85
Faint I, nor mourn nor murmur; other gifts
Have followed; for such loss, I would believe,
Abundant recompense. For I have learned
To look on nature, not as in the hour
Of thoughtless youth; but hearing oftentimes   90
The still, sad music of humanity,
Nor harsh nor grating, though of ample power
To chasten and subdue. And I have felt
A presence that disturbs me with the joy
Of elevated thoughts; a sense sublime   95
Of something far more deeply interfused,
Whose dwelling is the light of setting suns,
And the round ocean and the living air,
And the blue sky, and in the mind of man:
A motion and a spirit, that impels   100
All thinking things, all objects of all thought,
And rolls through all things. Therefore am I still
A lover of the meadows and the woods,
And mountains; and of all that we behold
From this green earth; of all the mighty world   105
Of eye, and ear, — both what they half create,
And what perceive; well pleased to recognise
In nature and the language of the sense,
The anchor of my purest thoughts, the nurse,
The guide, the guardian of my heart, and soul   110
Of all my moral being.

                 Nor perchance,
If I were not thus taught, should I the more
Suffer my genial spirits to decay:

For thou art with me here upon the banks
Of this fair river; thou my dearest Friend,   115
My dear, dear Friend; and in thy voice I catch
The language of my former heart, and read
My former pleasures in the shooting lights
Of thy wild eyes. Oh! yet a little while
May I behold in thee what I was once,   120
My dear, dear Sister! and this prayer I make,
Knowing that Nature never did betray
The heart that loved her; 'tis her privilege,
Through all the years of this our life, to lead
From joy to joy: for she can so inform   125
The mind that is within us, so impress
With quietness and beauty, and so feed
With lofty thoughts, that neither evil tongues,
Rash judgments, nor the sneers of selfish men,
Nor greetings where no kindness is, nor all   130
The dreary intercourse of daily life,
Shall e'er prevail against us, or disturb
Our cheerful faith, that all which we behold
Is full of blessings. Therefore let the moon
Shine on thee in thy solitary walk;   135
And let the misty mountain-winds be free
To blow against thee: and, in after years,
When these wild ecstasies shall be matured
Into a sober pleasure; when thy mind
Shall be a mansion for all lovely forms,   140
Thy memory be as a dwelling-place
For all sweet sounds and harmonies; oh! then,
If solitude, or fear, or pain, or grief,
Should be thy portion, with what healing thoughts
Of tender joy wilt thou remember me,   145
And these my exhortations! Nor, perchance —
If I should be where I no more can hear
Thy voice, nor catch from thy wild eyes these gleams
Of past existence — wilt thou then forget
That on the banks of this delightful stream   150
We stood together; and that I, so long
A worshipper of Nature, hither came
Unwearied in that service: rather say

---

86. Faint: lose courage or spirit, become depressed or despondent. **106:** "This line has a close resemblance to an admirable line of Young's, the exact expression of which I do not recollect" (Wordsworth's note); he is thinking of a passage in Edward Young's *The Complaint: or, Night Thoughts,* VI, describing human "senses, which inherit earth, and heavens; / Enjoy the various riches nature yields; / Far nobler! give the riches they enjoy; / Give taste to fruits; and harmony to groves; / Their radiant beams to gold, and gold's bright sire; / Take in, at once, the landscape of the world, / At a small inlet, which a grain might close, / And half create the wondrous world they see. / Our senses, as our reason, are divine" (420-28). **113. genial spirits:** perhaps echoing Milton's *Samson Agonistes,* line 594: "So much I feel my genial spirits droop," where *genial* means something like "pertaining to one's individual 'genius' or natural disposition"; but here, and in Coleridge's *Dejection: An Ode,* line 39 ("My genial spirits fail"), more likely signifying "enlivening, inspiring, contributing to cheerfulness and enjoyment of life," with perhaps also an overtone of sensitivity to place. **114-16, 121. thou, Friend, Sister:** his sister, Dorothy, his junior by a little over a year and a half.

With warmer love — oh! with far deeper zeal
Of holier love. Nor wilt thou then forget,   *155*
That after many wanderings, many years
Of absence, these steep woods and lofty cliffs,
And this green pastoral landscape, were to me
More dear, both for themselves and for thy sake!
(1798)

THE "LUCY POEMS"

I

Strange fits of passion have I known:
And I will dare to tell,
But in the Lover's ear alone,
What once to me befell.

When she I loved looked every day   *5*
Fresh as a rose in June,
I to her cottage bent my way,
Beneath an evening-moon.

Upon the moon I fixed my eye,
All over the wide lea;   *10*
With quickening pace my horse drew nigh
Those paths so dear to me.

And now we reached the orchard-plot;
And, as we climbed the hill,
The sinking moon to Lucy's cot   *15*
Came near, and nearer still.

In one of those sweet dreams I slept,
Kind Nature's gentlest boon!
And all the while my eyes I kept
On the descending moon.   *20*

My horse moved on; hoof after hoof
He raised, and never stopped:
When down behind the cottage roof,
At once, the bright moon dropped.

What fond and wayward thoughts will slide   *25*
Into a Lover's head!
"O mercy!" to myself I cried,
"If Lucy should be dead!"
(1799; 1800)

II

She dwelt among the untrodden ways
Beside the springs of Dove,
A Maid whom there were none to praise
And very few to love:

A violet by a mossy stone   *5*
Half hidden from the eye!
— Fair as a star, when only one
Is shining in the sky.

She lived unknown, and few could know
When Lucy ceased to be;   *10*
But she is in her grave, and, oh,
The difference to me!
(1799; 1800)

III

Three years she grew in sun and shower,
Then Nature said, "A lovelier flower
On earth was never sown;
This Child I to myself will take;
She shall be mine, and I will make   *5*
A Lady of my own.

"Myself will to my darling be
Both law and impulse: and with me
The Girl, in rock and plain,
In earth and heaven, in glade and bower,   *10*
Shall feel an overseeing power
To kindle or restrain.

"She shall be sportive as the fawn
That wild with glee across the lawn
Or up the mountain springs;   *15*
And hers shall be the breathing balm,
And hers the silence and the calm
Of mute insensate things.

"The floating clouds their state shall lend
To her; for her the willow bend;   *20*
Nor shall she fail to see
Even in the motions of the Storm
Grace that shall mould the Maiden's form
By silent sympathy.

THE "LUCY POEMS"   "Lucy" has never been identified — if in fact she ever existed as a real person.   **II**   2: Of the several English rivers or streams named Dove, the best known is that forming part of the boundary between Derbyshire and Staffordshire, though there is also one in Wordsworth's beloved Lake District.

"The stars of midnight shall be dear   25
To her; and she shall lean her ear
In many a secret place
Where rivulets dance their wayward round,
And beauty born of murmuring sound
Shall pass into her face.   30

"And vital feelings of delight
Shall rear her form to stately height,
Her virgin bosom swell;
Such thoughts to Lucy I will give
While she and I together live   35
Here in this happy dell."

Thus Nature spake — The work was done —
How soon my Lucy's race was run!
She died, and left to me
This heath, this calm, and quiet scene;   40
The memory of what has been,
And never more will be.

                        (1799; 1800)

IV

A slumber did my spirit seal;
    I had no human fears:
She seemed a thing that could not feel
    The touch of earthly years.

No motion has she now, no force;   5
    She neither hears nor sees;
Rolled round in earth's diurnal course,
    With rocks, and stones, and trees.

                        (1799; 1800)

V

I travelled among unknown men,
    In lands beyond the sea;
Nor, England! did I know till then
    What love I bore to thee.

'Tis past, that melancholy dream!   5
    Nor will I quit thy shore
A second time; for still I seem
    To love thee more and more.

Among thy mountains did I feel
    The joy of my desire;   10
And she I cherished turned her wheel
    Beside an English fire.

Thy mornings showed, thy nights concealed,
    The bowers where Lucy played;
And thine too is the last green field   15
    That Lucy's eyes surveyed.

                        (1801; 1807)

LUCY GRAY
Or, Solitude

Oft I had heard of Lucy Gray:
And, when I crossed the wild,
I chanced to see at break of day
The solitary child.

No mate, no comrade Lucy knew;   5
She dwelt on a wide moor,
— The sweetest thing that ever grew
Beside a human door!

You yet may spy the fawn at play,
The hare upon the green;   10
But the sweet face of Lucy Gray
Will never more be seen.

"To-night will be a stormy night —
You to the town must go;
And take a lantern, Child, to light   15
Your mother through the snow."

"That, Father! will I gladly do:
'Tis scarcely afternoon —
The minster-clock has just struck two,
And yonder is the moon!"   20

At this the Father raised his hook,
And snapped a faggot-band;
He plied his work; — and Lucy took
The lantern in her hand.

Not blither is the mountain roe: 25
With many a wanton stroke
Her feet disperse the powdery snow,
That rises up like smoke.

The storm came on before its time:
She wandered up and down;   30
And many a hill did Lucy climb:
But never reached the town.

The wretched parents all that night
Went shouting far and wide;
But there was neither sound nor sight   35
To serve them for a guide.

At day-break on a hill they stood
That overlooked the moor;
And thence they saw the bridge of wood,
A furlong from their door.   40

They wept — and, turning homeward, cried,
"In heaven we all shall meet;"
— When in the snow the mother spied
The print of Lucy's feet.

Then downwards from the steep hill's edge   45
They tracked the footmarks small;
And through the broken hawthorn hedge,
And by the long stone-wall;

And then an open field they crossed:
The marks were still the same;   50
They tracked them on, nor ever lost;
And to the bridge they came.

They followed from the snowy bank
Those footmarks, one by one,
Into the middle of the plank;   55
And further there were none!

— Yet some maintain that to this day
She is a living child;
That you may see sweet Lucy Gray
Upon the lonesome wild.   60

O'er rough and smooth she trips along,
And never looks behind;
And sings a solitary song
That whistles in the wind.

(1799; 1800)

from Preface to LYRICAL BALLADS

. . . .

   The principal object, then, proposed in these Poems was to choose incidents and
situations from common life, and to relate or describe them, throughout, as far as was
possible in a selection of language really used by men, and, at the same time, to throw
over them a certain colouring of imagination, whereby ordinary things should be
presented to the mind in an unusual aspect; and, further, and above all, to make these   5
incidents and situations interesting by tracing in them, truly though not ostentatiously,
the primary laws of our nature: chiefly, as far as regards the manner in which we
associate ideas in a state of excitement. Humble and rustic life was generally chosen,
because, in that condition, the essential passions of the heart find a better soil in which
they can attain their maturity, are less under restraint, and speak a plainer and more   10
emphatic language; because in that condition of life our elementary feelings coexist in a
state of greater simplicity, and, consequently, may be more accurately contemplated,
and more forcibly communicated; because the manners of rural life germinate from
those elementary feelings, and, from the necessary character of rural occupations, are
more easily comprehended, and are more durable; and, lastly, because in that condition   15
the passions of men are incorporated with the beautiful and permanent forms of nature.
The language, too, of these men has been adopted (purified indeed from what appear to
be its real defects, from all lasting and rational causes of dislike or disgust) because such
men hourly communicate with the best objects from which the best part of language is
originally derived; and because, from their rank in society and the sameness and narrow   20

PREFACE TO LYRICAL BALLADS   It was Wordsworth's practice to revise continually over the years; our text of the "Preface" incorporates
revisions made subsequent to the first editions of 1800 and 1802; the last revisions were made for the edition of 1845. For Coleridge's discussion of
some of the same matters, including his disagreements with Wordsworth, see Chapter XIV of his *Biographia Literaria*.

circle of their intercourse, being less under the influence of social vanity, they convey their feelings and notions in simple and unelaborated expressions. Accordingly, such a language, arising out of repeated experience and regular feelings, is a more permanent, and a far more philosophical language, than that which is frequently substituted for it by Poets, who think that they are conferring honour upon themselves and their art, in proportion as they separate themselves from the sympathies of men, and indulge in arbitrary and capricious habits of expression, in order to furnish food for fickle tastes, and fickle appetites, of their own creation.

I cannot, however, be insensible to the present outcry against the triviality and meanness, both of thought and language, which some of my contemporaries have occasionally introduced into their metrical compositions; and I acknowledge that this defect, where it exists, is more dishonourable to the Writer's own character than false refinement or arbitrary innovation, though I should contend at the same time, that it is far less pernicious in the sum of its consequences. From such verses the Poems in these volumes will be found distinguished at least by one mark of difference, that each of them has a worthy *purpose*. Not that I always began to write with a distinct purpose formally conceived; but habits of meditation have, I trust, so prompted and regulated my feelings, that my descriptions of such objects as strongly excite those feelings, will be found to carry along with them a *purpose*. If this opinion be erroneous, I can have little right to the name of a Poet. For all good poetry is the spontaneous overflow of powerful feelings: and though this be true, Poems to which any value can be attached were never produced on any variety of subjects but by a man who, being possessed of more than usual organic sensibility, had also thought long and deeply. For our continued influxes of feeling are modified and directed by our thoughts, which are indeed the representatives of all our past feelings; and, as by contemplating the relation of these general representatives to each other, we discover what is really important to men, so, by the repetition and continuance of this act, our feelings will be connected with important subjects, till at length, if we be originally possessed of much sensibility, such habits of mind will be produced, that, by obeying blindly and mechanically the impulses of those habits, we shall describe objects, and utter sentiments, of such a nature, and in such connection with each other, that the understanding of the Reader must necessarily be in some degree enlightened, and his affections strengthened and purified.

. . . .

Having dwelt thus long on the subjects and aim of these Poems, I shall request the Reader's permission to apprise him of a few circumstances relating to their *style,* in order, among other reasons, that he may not censure me for not having performed what I never attempted. The Reader will find that personifications of abstract ideas rarely occur in these volumes; and are utterly rejected, as an ordinary device to elevate the style, and raise it above prose. My purpose was to imitate, and, as far as is possible, to adopt the very language of men; and assuredly such personifications do not make any natural or regular part of that language. They are, indeed, a figure of speech occasionally prompted by passion, and I have made use of them as such; but have endeavoured utterly to reject them as a mechanical device of style, or as a family language which Writers in metre seem to lay claim to by prescription. I have wished to keep the Reader in the company of flesh and blood, persuaded that by so doing I shall interest him. Others who pursue a different track will interest him likewise; I do not interfere with their claim, but wish to prefer a claim of my own. There will also be found in these volumes little of what is usually called poetic diction; as much pains has been taken to avoid it as is ordinarily taken to produce it; this has been done for the reason already alleged, to bring my language near to the language of men; and further, because the pleasure which I have proposed to myself to impart, is of a kind very different from that which is supposed by many persons to be the proper object of poetry.

. . . .

If in a poem there should be found a series of lines, or even a single line, in which the language, though naturally arranged, and according to the strict laws of metre, does not differ from that of prose, there is a numerous class of critics, who, when they stumble upon these prosaisms, as they call them, imagine that they have made a notable discovery, and exult over the Poet as over a man ignorant of his own profession. Now these men would establish a canon of criticism which the Reader will conclude he must utterly reject, if he wishes to be pleased with these volumes. And it would be a most easy task to prove to him, that not only the language of a large portion of every good poem, even of the most elevated character, must necessarily, except with reference to the metre, in no respect differ from that of good prose, but likewise that some of the most interesting parts of the best poems will be found to be strictly the language of prose when prose is well written. The truth of this assertion might be demonstrated by innumerable passages from almost all the poetical writings, even of Milton himself. To illustrate the subject in a general manner, I will here adduce a short composition of Gray, who was at the head of those who, by their reasonings, have attempted to widen the space of separation betwixt Prose and Metrical composition, and was more than any other man curiously elaborate in the structure of his own poetic diction.

> "In vain to me the smiling mornings shine,
> And reddening Phoebus lifts his golden fire:
> The birds in vain their amorous descant join,
> Or cheerful fields resume their green attire.
> These ears, alas! for other notes repine;
> *A different object do these eyes require;*
> *My lonely anguish melts no heart but mine;*
> *And in my breast the imperfect joys expire;*
> Yet morning smiles the busy race to cheer,
> And new-born pleasure brings to happier men;
> The fields to all their wonted tribute bear;
> To warm their little loves the birds complain.
> *I fruitless mourn to him that cannot hear,*
> *And weep the more because I weep in vain.*"

85ff. **a short composition of Gray:** Also see this sonnet on p. 609.

It will easily be perceived, that the only part of this Sonnet which is of any value is the lines printed in Italics; it is equally obvious, that, except in the rhyme, and in the use of the single word "fruitless" for fruitlessly, which is so far a defect, the language of *105* these lines does in no respect differ from that of prose.

. . . .

Taking up the subject, then, upon general grounds, let me ask, what is meant by the word Poet? What is a Poet? To whom does he address himself? And what language is to be expected from him? — He is a man speaking to men: a man, it is true, endowed with more lively sensibility, more enthusiasm and tenderness, who has a greater knowledge of human *110* nature, and a more comprehensive soul, than are supposed to be common among mankind; a man pleased with his own passions and volitions, and who rejoices more than other men in the spirit of life that is in him; delighting to contemplate similar volitions and passions as manifested in the goings-on of the Universe, and habitually impelled to create them where he does not find them. To these qualities he has added a disposition to be affected more than *115* other men by absent things as if they were present; an ability of conjuring up in himself passions, which are indeed far from being the same as those produced by real events, yet (especially in those parts of the general sympathy which are pleasing and delightful) do more nearly resemble the passions produced by real events, than anything which, from the motions of their own minds merely, other men are accustomed to feel in themselves: — *120* whence, and from practice, he has acquired a greater readiness and power in expressing what he thinks and feels, and especially those thoughts and feelings which, by his own choice, or from the structure of his own mind, arise in him without immediate external excitement.

But whatever portion of this faculty we may suppose even the greatest Poet to possess, there cannot be a doubt that the language which it will suggest to him, must *125* often, in liveliness and truth, fall short of that which is uttered by men in real life, under the actual pressure of those passions, certain shadows of which the Poet thus produces, or feels to be produced, in himself.

However exalted a notion we would wish to cherish of the character of a Poet, it is obvious, that while he describes and imitates passions, his employment is in some degree *130* mechanical, compared with the freedom and power of real and substantial action and suffering. So that it will be the wish of the Poet to bring his feelings near to those of the persons whose feelings he describes, nay, for short spaces of time, perhaps, to let himself slip into an entire delusion, and even confound and identify his own feelings with theirs; modifying only the language which is thus suggested to him by a consideration that he *135* describes for a particular purpose, that of giving pleasure. Here, then, he will apply the principle of selection which has been already insisted upon. He will depend upon this for removing what would otherwise be painful or disgusting in the passion; he will feel that there is no necessity to trick out or to elevate nature: and, the more industriously he applies this principle, the deeper will be his faith that no words, which *his* fancy or imagination can *140* suggest, will be to be compared with those which are the emanations of reality and truth.

. . . .

Poetry is the breath and finer spirit of all knowledge; it is the impassioned expression which is in the countenance of all science. Emphatically may it be said of the Poet, as Shakspeare hath said of man, "that he looks before and after." He is the rock of defence

---

144: *Hamlet*, IV.iv.37: "Looking before and after."

for human nature; an upholder and preserver, carrying everywhere with him relationship *145*
and love. In spite of difference of soil and climate, of language and manners, of laws and
customs: in spite of things silently gone out of mind, and things violently destroyed; the
Poet binds together by passion and knowledge the vast empire of human society, as it is
spread over the whole earth, and over all time. The objects of the Poet's thoughts are
everywhere; though the eyes and senses of man are, it is true, his favourite guides, yet he *150*
will follow wheresoever he can find an atmosphere of sensation in which to move his
wings. Poetry is the first and last of all knowledge — it is as immortal as the heart of
man. If the labours of men of science should ever create any material revolution, direct or
indirect, in our condition, and in the impressions which we habitually receive, the Poet
will sleep then no more than at present; he will be ready to follow the steps of the man of *155*
science, not only in those general indirect effects, but he will be at his side, carrying
sensation into the midst of the objects of the science itself. The remotest discoveries of
the chemist, the botanist, or mineralogist, will be as proper objects of the Poet's art as any
upon which it can be employed, if the time should ever come when these things shall be
familiar to us, and the relations under which they are contemplated by the followers of *160*
these respective sciences shall be manifestly and palpably material to us as enjoying and
suffering beings. If the time should ever come when what is now called science, thus
familiarised to men, shall be ready to put on, as it were, a form of flesh and blood, the
Poet will lend his divine spirit to aid the transfiguration, and will welcome the Being thus
produced, as a dear and genuine inmate of the household of man. — It is not, then, to be *165*
supposed that any one, who holds that sublime notion of Poetry which I have attempted
to convey, will break in upon the sanctity and truth of his pictures by transitory and
accidental ornaments, and endeavour to excite admiration of himself by arts, the
necessity of which must manifestly depend upon the assumed meanness of his subject.

. . . .

    I have said that poetry is the spontaneous overflow of powerful feelings: it takes its *170*
origin from emotion recollected in tranquillity: the emotion is contemplated till, by a
species of reaction, the tranquillity gradually disappears, and an emotion, kindred to that
which was before the subject of contemplation, is gradually produced, and does itself
actually exist in the mind. In this mood successful composition generally begins, and in
a mood similar to this it is carried on; but the emotion, of whatever kind, and in *175*
whatever degree, from various causes, is qualified by various pleasures, so that in
describing any passions whatsoever, which are voluntarily described, the mind will,
upon the whole, be in a state of enjoyment. If Nature be thus cautious to preserve in a
state of enjoyment a being so employed, the Poet ought to profit by the lesson held forth
to him, and ought especially to take care, that, whatever passions he communicates to *180*
his Reader, those passions, if his Reader's mind be sound and vigorous, should always
be accompanied with an overbalance of pleasure. Now the music of harmonious
metrical language, the sense of difficulty overcome, and the blind association of
pleasure which has been previously received from works of rhyme or metre of the same
or similar construction, an indistinct perception perpetually renewed of language closely *185*
resembling that of real life, and yet, in the circumstance of metre, differing from it so

---

162-65: See e.g. Wordsworth's own "Steamboats, Viaducts, and Railways" (p. 770).

widely — all these imperceptibly make up a complex feeling of delight, which is of the most important use in tempering the painful feeling always found intermingled with powerful descriptions of the deeper passions. This effect is always produced in pathetic and impassioned poetry; while, in lighter compositions, the ease and gracefulness with *190* which the Poet manages his numbers are themselves confessedly a principal source of the gratification of the Reader. All that it is *necessary* to say, however, upon this subject, may be effected by affirming, what few persons will deny, that, of two descriptions, either of passions, manners, or characters, each of them equally well executed, the one in prose and the other in verse, the verse will be read a hundred times *195* where the prose is read once.

. . . .

Long as the Reader has been detained, I hope he will permit me to caution him against a mode of false criticism which has been applied to Poetry, in which the language closely resembles that of life and nature. Such verses have been triumphed over in parodies, of which Dr. Johnson's stanza is a fair specimen: — *200*

> "I put my hat upon my head
> And walked into the Strand,
> And there I met another man
> Whose hat was in his hand."

Immediately under these lines let us place one of the most justly-admired stanzas of *205* the "Babes in the Wood."

> "These pretty Babes with hand in hand
> Went wandering up and down;
> But never more they saw the Man
> Approaching from the Town." *210*

In both these stanzas the words, and the order of the words, in no respect differ from the most unimpassioned conversation. There are words in both, for example, "the Strand," and "the Town," connected with none but the most familiar ideas; yet the one stanza we admit as admirable, and the other as a fair example of the superlatively contemptible. Whence arises this difference? Not from the metre, not from the language, *215* not from the order of the words; but the *matter* expressed in Dr. Johnson's stanza is contemptible. The proper method of treating trivial and simple verses, to which Dr. Johnson's stanza would be a fair parallelism, is not to say, this is a bad kind of poetry, or, this is not poetry; but, this wants sense; it is neither interesting in itself, nor can *lead* to any thing interesting; the images neither originate in that sane state of feeling which *220* arises out of thought, nor can excite thought or feeling in the Reader. This is the only sensible manner of dealing with such verses. Why trouble yourself about the species till you have previously decided upon the genus? Why take pains to prove that an ape is not a Newton, when it is self-evident that he is not a man?

(1800, 1802)

---

191. numbers: metrical feet, versification. **201-04:** Johnson dashed off this quatrain to show the weakness of the verse in the long ballad *The Hermit of Warkworth* (1771), by Thomas Percy (1729-1811). **206:** This popular ballad is included in Thomas Percy's *Reliques of Ancient English Poetry* (1765), under the title "The Children in the Wood." **223-24:** Cf. Pope's *An Essay on Man*, II, 31-34: "Superior beings, when of late they saw / A mortal Man unfold all Nature's law, / Admired such wisdom in an earthly shape, / And showed a Newton as we show an Ape."

"MY HEART LEAPS UP"

My heart leaps up when I behold
  A rainbow in the sky:
So was it when my life began;
So is it now I am a man;
So be it when I shall grow old,   5
  Or let me die!
The Child is father of the Man;
And I could wish my days to be
Bound each to each by natural piety.

(1802; 1807)

"IT IS A BEAUTEOUS EVENING, CALM AND FREE"

It is a beauteous evening, calm and free,
The holy time is quiet as a Nun
Breathless with adoration; the broad sun
Is sinking down in its tranquillity;
The gentleness of heaven broods o'er the Sea: 5
Listen! the mighty Being is awake,
And doth with his eternal motion make
A sound like thunder — everlastingly.
Dear Child! dear Girl! that walkest with me here,
If thou appear untouched by solemn thought,   10
Thy nature is not therefore less divine:
Thou liest in Abraham's bosom all the year;
And worshipp'st at the Temple's inner shrine,
God being with thee when we know it not.

(1802; 1807)

COMPOSED UPON WESTMINSTER BRIDGE, SEPTEMBER 3, 1802

Earth has not anything to show more fair:
Dull would he be of soul who could pass by
A sight so touching in its majesty:
This City now doth, like a garment, wear
The beauty of the morning; silent, bare,   5
Ships, towers, domes, theatres, and temples lie
Open unto the fields, and to the sky;
All bright and glittering in the smokeless air.

Never did sun more beautifully steep
In his first splendour, valley, rock, or hill;   10
Ne'er saw I, never felt, a calm so deep!
The river glideth at his own sweet will:
Dear God! the very houses seem asleep;
And all that mighty heart is lying still!

(1802; 1807)

LONDON, 1802

Milton! thou shouldst be living at this hour:
England hath need of thee: she is a fen
Of stagnant waters: altar, sword, and pen,
Fireside, the heroic wealth of hall and bower,
Have forefeited their ancient English dower   5
Of inward happiness. We are selfish men;
Oh! raise us up, return to us again;
And give us manners, virtue, freedom, power.
Thy soul was like a Star, and dwelt apart;
Thou hadst a voice whose sound was like the sea: 10
Pure as the naked heavens, majestic, free,
So didst thou travel on life's common way,
In cheerful godliness; and yet thy heart
The lowliest duties on herself did lay.

(1802; 1807)

"THE WORLD IS TOO MUCH WITH US"

The world is too much with us; late and soon,
Getting and spending, we lay waste our powers:
Little we see in Nature that is ours;
We have given our hearts away, a sordid boon!
This Sea that bares her bosom to the moon;   5
The winds that will be howling at all hours,
And are up-gathered now like sleeping flowers;
For this, for everything, we are out of tune;
It moves us not. — Great God! I'd rather be
A Pagan suckled in a creed outworn;   10
So might I, standing on this pleasant lea,
Have glimpses that would make me less forlorn;
Have sight of Proteus rising from the sea;
Or hear old Triton blow his wreathèd horn.

(1802; 1807)

MY HEART LEAPS UP See "Ode: Intimations of Immortality" (p. 766). IT IS A BEAUTEOUS EVENING **9.** He speaks to Caroline, his daughter by Annette Vallon, whom he knew in France. **12. Abraham's bosom:** where lie the dead in heaven; see Luke 16:22-23; see also Shakespeare's *Richard III*, IV.iii.38. COMPOSED UPON WESTMINSTER BRIDGE, SEPTEMBER 3, 1802 According to Dorothy Wordsworth's *Journal*, the experience occurred on July 31 (see p. 781). THE WORLD IS TOO MUCH WITH US **13. Proteus:** Greek sea god capable of changing his shape. **14. Triton:** Greek sea god.

To Toussaint L'Ouverture

Toussaint, the most unhappy man of men!
Whether the whistling Rustic tend his plough
Within thy hearing, or thy head be now
Pillowed in some deep dungeon's earless den; —
O miserable Chieftain! where and when   5
Wilt thou find patience! Yet die not; do thou
Wear rather in thy bonds a cheerful brow:
Though fallen thyself, never to rise again,
Live, and take comfort. Thou hast left behind
Powers that will work for thee; air, earth, and skies;   10
There's not a breathing of the common wind
That will forget thee; thou hast great allies;
Thy friends are exultations, agonies,
And love, and man's unconquerable mind.

(1802; 1807)

Ode
Intimations of Immortality from Recollections of Early Childhood

The Child is father of the Man;
And I could wish my days to be
Bound each to each by natural piety.

I

There was a time when meadow, grove, and stream,
The earth, and every common sight,
         To me did seem
         Apparelled in celestial light,
The glory and the freshness of a dream.   5
It is not now as it hath been of yore; —
         Turn whereso'er I may,
         By night or day,
The things which I have seen I now can see no more.

II

         The Rainbow comes and goes,   10
         And lovely is the Rose,
         The Moon doth with delight
Look round her when the heavens are bare,

Waters on a starry night
Are beautiful and fair;   15
The sunshine is a glorious birth;
But yet I know, where'er I go,
That there hath past away a glory from the earth.

III

Now, while the birds thus sing a joyous song,
         And while the young lambs bound   20
         As to the tabor's sound,
To me alone there came a thought of grief:
A timely utterance gave that thought relief,
         And I again am strong:
The cataracts blow their trumpets from the steep;   25
No more shall grief of mine the season wrong;
I hear the Echoes through the mountains throng,
The Winds come to me from the fields of sleep,
         And all the earth is gay;
                  Land and sea   30
         Give themselves up to jollity,
                  And with the heart of May
         Doth every Beast keep holiday; —
                  Thou Child of Joy,
Shout round me, let me hear thy shouts, thou happy
                  Shepherd-boy!   35

IV

Ye blessèd Creatures, I have heard the call
         Ye to each other make; I see
The heavens laugh with you in your jubilee;
         My heart is at your festival,
         My head hath its coronal,   40
The fulness of your bliss, I feel — I feel it all.
         Oh evil day! if I were sullen
         While Earth herself is adorning,
                  This sweet May-morning,
         And the Children are culling   45
                  On every side,
         In a thousand valleys far and wide,
         Fresh flowers; while the sun shines warm,
And the Babe leaps up on his Mother's arm: —
         I hear, I hear, with joy I hear!   50
         — But there's a Tree, of many, one,

To Toussaint L'Ouverture   François Dominique Toussaint (c.1744-1803), called L'Ouverture ("The Opening"), former slave who liberated Haiti from Spain (which had English help) and abolished slavery there; but Napoleon, who lost Santo Domingo in the process, treacherously (in spite of a peace treaty) had him taken to France and imprisoned in a dungeon, where he died.   **Ode: Intimations of Immortality**   (Often called simply the "Immortality Ode.") **Epigraph:** See "My heart leaps up" (p. 765). **18. past:** passed. **40. coronal:** i.e., of spring flowers.

Along the margin of a bay: *10*
Ten thousand saw I at a glance,
Tossing their heads in sprightly dance.

The waves beside them danced; but they
Out-did the sparkling waves in glee:
A poet could not but be gay,   *15*
In such a jocund company:
I gazed — and gazed — but little thought
What wealth the show to me had brought:

For oft, when on my couch I lie
In vacant or in pensive mood,   *20*
They flash upon that inward eye
Which is the bliss of solitude;
And then my heart with pleasure fills,
And dances with the daffodils.

(1804; 1807)

FRENCH REVOLUTION
As It Appeared to Enthusiasts
at Its Commencement

Oh! pleasant exercise of hope and joy!
For mighty were the auxiliars which then stood
Upon our side, we who were strong in love!
Bliss was it in that dawn to be alive,
But to be young was very heaven! — Oh! times,   *5*
In which the meagre, stale, forbidding ways
Of custom, law, and statute, took at once
The attraction of a country in romance!
When Reason seemed the most to assert her rights,
When most intent on making of herself   *10*
A prime Enchantress — to assist the work
Which then was going forward in her name!
Not favoured spots alone, but the whole earth,
The beauty wore of promise, that which sets
(As at some moment might not be unfelt   *15*

Among the bowers of Paradise itself)
The budding rose above the rose full blown.
What temper at the prospect did not wake
To happiness unthought of? The inert
Were roused, and lively natures rapt away!   *20*
They who had fed their childhood upon dreams,
The playfellows of fancy, who had made
All powers of swiftness, subtilty, and strength
Their ministers, — who in lordly wise had stirred
Among the grandest objects of the sense,   *25*
And dealt with whatsoever they found there
As if they had within some lurking right
To wield it; — they, too, who, of gentle mood,
Had watched all gentle motions, and to these
Had fitted their own thoughts, schemers more mild,   *30*
And in the region of their peaceful selves; —
Now was it that both found, the meek and lofty
Did both find, helpers to their heart's desire,
And stuff at hand, plastic as they could wish;
Were called upon to exercise their skill,   *35*
Not in Utopia, subterranean fields,
Or some secreted island, Heaven knows where!
But in the very world, which is the world
Of all of us, — the place where in the end
We find our happiness, or not at all!   *40*

(1804; 1809)

THE SOLITARY REAPER

Behold her, single in the field,
Yon solitary Highland Lass!
Reaping and singing by herself;
Stop here, or gently pass!
Alone she cuts and binds the grain,   *5*
And sings a melancholy strain;
O listen! for the Vale profound
Is overflowing with the sound.

FRENCH REVOLUTION   Written as part of *The Prelude*, the first version of which was finished in 1805 (but not published); this excerpt was published by Coleridge in his weekly essay series *The Friend*, October 26, 1809 (Section I, Essay VI, in the 1818 book version); it eventually became lines 105–44 in Book XI of the revised *Prelude* published in 1850, after Wordsworth's death.   **THE SOLITARY REAPER**   A poem inspired by actual experience, as is usual with Wordsworth, but also by someone else's writing. The experience was recorded by Dorothy Wordsworth in her journal (*Recollections of a Tour Made in Scotland*, first published in 1874): "As we descended, the scene became more fertile, our way being pleasantly varied — through coppices or open fields, and passing farm-houses, though always with an intermixture of uncultivated ground. It was harvest-time, and the fields were quietly — might I say pensively? — enlivened by small companies of reapers. It is not uncommon in the more lonely parts of the Highlands to see a single person so employed. The following poem was suggested to William by a beautiful sentence in Thomas Wilkinson's *Tour in Scotland*" (entry for Sept. 13, 1803); she then incorporates the poem into her journal entry. Wilkinson's sentence: "Passed a female who was reaping alone; she sung in Erse, as she bended over her sickle; the sweetest human voice I ever heard: her strains were tenderly melancholy, and felt delicious, long after they were heard no more." Wordsworth's own note points out that he had read only a manuscript of Wilkinson's tour, not published until 1824.

No Nightingale did ever chaunt
More welcome notes to weary bands   10
Of travellers in some shady haunt,
Among Arabian sands:
A voice so thrilling ne'er was heard
In spring-time from the Cuckoo-bird,
Breaking the silence of the seas   15
Among the farthest Hebrides.

Will no one tell me what she sings? —
Perhaps the plaintive numbers flow
For old, unhappy, far-off things,
And battles long ago: 20
Or is it some more humble lay,
Familiar matter of to-day?
Some natural sorrow, loss, or pain,
That has been, and may be again?

Whate'er the theme, the Maiden sang   25
As if her song could have no ending;
I saw her singing at her work,
And o'er the sickle bending; —
I listened, motionless and still;
And, as I mounted up the hill,   30
The music in my heart I bore,
Long after it was heard no more.

(1805; 1807)

STEAMBOATS, VIADUCTS, AND RAILWAYS

Motions and Means, on land and sea at war
With old poetic feeling, not for this,
Shall ye, by Poets even, be judged amiss!
Nor shall your presence, howsoe'er it mar
The loveliness of Nature, prove a bar   5
To the Mind's gaining that prophetic sense
Of future change, that point of vision, whence
May be discovered what in soul ye are.
In spite of all that beauty may disown
In your harsh features, Nature doth embrace   10
Her lawful offspring in Man's art; and Time,
Pleased with your triumphs o'er his brother Space,
Accepts from your bold hands the proffered crown
Of hope, and smiles on you with cheer sublime.

(1833; 1835)

from THE PRELUDE; OR, GROWTH OF A POET'S MIND
An Autobiographical Poem

from *Book First: Introduction — Childhood and School-Time*

. . . .

Fair seed-time had my soul, and I grew up
Fostered alike by beauty and by fear:
Much favoured in my birth-place, and no less
In that beloved Vale to which erelong
We were transplanted — there were we let loose   305
For sports of wider range. Ere I had told
Ten birth-days, when among the mountain slopes
Frost, and the breath of frosty wind, had snapped
The last autumnal crocus, 't was my joy
With store of springes o'er my shoulder hung   310
To range the open heights where woodcocks run
Along the smooth green turf. Through half the night,
Scudding away from snare to snare, I plied
That anxious visitation; — moon and stars
Were shining o'er my head. I was alone,   315
And seemed to be a trouble to the peace
That dwelt among them. Sometimes it befell
In these night wanderings, that a strong desire
O'erpowered my better reason, and the bird
Which was the captive of another's toil   320
Became my prey; and when the deed was done
I heard among the solitary hills
Low breathings coming after me, and sounds
Of undistinguishable motion, steps
Almost as silent as the turf they trod.   325

   Nor less, when spring had warmed the cultured Vale,
Moved we as plunderers where the mother-bird
Had in high places built her lodge; though mean
Our object and inglorious, yet the end
Was not ignoble. Oh! when I have hung   330
Above the raven's nest, by knots of grass
And half-inch fissures in the slippery rock
But ill sustained, and almost (so it seemed)

THE PRELUDE   The title and subtitle were supplied by Wordsworth's widow; the poem was originally designed as an introduction to a long philosophical poem called *The Recluse*, of which he completed only the part known as *The Excursion*.   **BOOK I   303. my birth-place:** Cockermouth, near the coast, in the northwest part of the Lake District, in Cumberland (as it was then; the Lake District is now in the county of Cumbria, which replaces Cumberland, Westmoreland, and the northern part of Lancashire). **304. Vale:** of Esthwaite, in which lay the town of Hawkshead, in what was then part of Lancashire; Wordsworth entered Hawkshead school when he was nine.

Suspended by the blast that blew amain,
Shouldering the naked crag, oh, at that time   *335*
While on the perilous ridge I hung alone,
With what strange utterance did the loud dry wind
Blow through my ear! the sky seemed not a sky
Of earth — and with what motion moved the clouds!

    Dust as we are, the immortal spirit grows   *340*
Like harmony in music; there is a dark
Inscrutable workmanship that reconciles
Discordant elements, makes them cling together
In one society. How strange, that all
The terrors, pains, and early miseries,   *345*
Regrets, vexations, lassitudes interfused
Within my mind, should e'er have borne a part,
And that a needful part, in making up
The calm existence that is mine when I
Am worthy of myself! Praise to the end!   *350*
Thanks to the means which Nature deigned to employ;
Whether her fearless visitings, or those
That came with soft alarm, like hurtless light
Opening the peaceful clouds; or she would use
Severer interventions, ministry   *355*
More palpable, as best might suit her aim.

    One summer evening (led by her) I found
A little boat tied to a willow tree
Within a rocky cove, its usual home.
Straight I unloosed her chain, and stepping in   *360*
Pushed from the shore. It was an act of stealth
And troubled pleasure, nor without the voice
Of mountain-echoes did my boat move on;
Leaving behind her still, on either side,
Small circles glittering idly in the moon,   *365*
Until they melted all into one track
Of sparkling light. But now, like one who rows,
Proud of his skill, to reach a chosen point
With an unswerving line, I fixed my view
Upon the summit of a craggy ridge,   *370*
The horizon's utmost boundary; for above
Was nothing but the stars and the grey sky.
She was an elfin pinnace; lustily
I dipped my oars into the silent lake,
And, as I rose upon the stroke, my boat   *375*
Went heaving through the water like a swan;
When, from behind that craggy steep till then
The horizon's bound, a huge peak, black and huge,
As if with voluntary power instinct,
Upreared its head. I struck and struck again,   *380*

And growing still in stature the grim shape
Towered up between me and the stars, and still,
For so it seemed, with purpose of its own
And measured motion like a living thing
Strode after me. With trembling oars I turned,   *385*
And through the silent water stole my way
Back to the covert of the willow tree;
There in her mooring-place I left my bark, —
And through the meadows homeward went, in grave
And serious mood; but after I had seen   *390*
That spectacle, for many days, my brain
Worked with a dim and undetermined sense
Of unknown modes of being; o'er my thoughts
There hung a darkness, call it solitude
Or blank desertion. No familiar shapes   *395*
Remained, no pleasant images of trees,
Of sea or sky, no colours of green fields;
But huge and mighty forms, that do not live
Like living men, moved slowly through the mind
By day, and were a trouble to my dreams.   *400*

    Wisdom and Spirit of the universe!
Thou Soul that art the eternity of thought
That givest to forms and images a breath
And everlasting motion, not in vain
By day or star-light thus from my first dawn   *405*
Of childhood didst thou intertwine for me
The passions that build up our human soul;
Not with the mean and vulgar works of man,
But with high objects, with enduring things —
With life and nature — purifying thus   *410*
The elements of feeling and of thought,
And sanctifying, by such discipline,
Both pain and fear, until we recognise
A grandeur in the beatings of the heart.
Nor was this fellowship vouchsafed to me   *415*
With stinted kindness. In November days,
When vapours rolling down the valley made
A lonely scene more lonesome, among woods,
At noon and 'mid the calm of summer nights,
When, by the margin of the trembling lake,   *420*
Beneath the gloomy hills homeward I went
In solitude, such intercourse was mine;
Mine was it in the fields both day and night,
And by the waters, all the summer long.

    And in the frosty season, when the sun   *425*
Was set, and visible for many a mile
The cottage windows blazed through twilight gloom,

I heeded not their summons: happy time
It was indeed for all of us — for me
It was a time of rapture! Clear and loud   430
The village clock tolled six, — I wheeled about,
Proud and exulting like an untired horse
That cares not for his home. All shod with steel,
We hissed along the polished ice in games
Confederate, imitative of the chase   435
And woodland pleasures, — the resounding horn,
The pack loud chiming, and the hunted hare.
So through the darkness and the cold we flew,
And not a voice was idle; with the din
Smitten, the precipices rang aloud;   440
The leafless trees and every icy crag
Tinkled like iron; while far distant hills
Into the tumult sent an alien sound
Of melancholy not unnoticed, while the stars
Eastward were sparkling clear, and in the west   445
The orange sky of evening died away.
Not seldom from the uproar I retired
Into a silent bay, or sportively
Glanced sideway, leaving the tumultuous throng,
To cut across the reflex of a star   450
That fled, and, flying still before me, gleamed
Upon the glassy plain; and oftentimes,
When we had given our bodies to the wind,
And all the shadowy banks on either side
Came sweeping through the darkness, spinning still   455
The rapid line of motion, then at once
Have I, reclining back upon my heels,
Stopped short; yet still the solitary cliffs
Wheeled by me — even as if the earth had rolled
With visible motion her diurnal round!   460
Behind me did they stretch in solemn train,
Feebler and feebler, and I stood and watched
Till all was tranquil as a dreamless sleep.

. . . .

Yes, I remember when the changeful earth,
And twice five summers on my mind had stamped   560
The faces of the moving year, even then
I held unconscious intercourse with beauty
Old as creation, drinking in a pure
Organic pleasure from the silver wreaths
Of curling mist, or from the level plain   565
Of waters coloured by impending clouds.

. . . .

from *Book Third: Residence at Cambridge*

. . . .

Beside the pleasant Mill of Trompington
I laughed with Chaucer in the hawthorn shade;
Heard him, while birds were warbling, tell his tales 280
Of amorous passion. And that gentle Bard,
Chosen by the Muses for their Page of State —
Sweet Spenser, moving through his clouded heaven
With the moon's beauty and the moon's soft pace,
I called him Brother, Englishman, and Friend!   285
Yea, our blind Poet, who in his later day
Stood almost single; uttering odious truth —
Darkness before, and danger's voice behind,
Soul awful — if the earth has ever lodged
An awful soul — I seemed to see him here   290
Familiarly, and in his scholar's dress
Bounding before me, yet a stripling youth —
A boy, no better, with his rosy cheeks
Angelical, keen eye, courageous look,
And conscious step of purity and pride.   295
Among the band of my compeers was one
Whom chance had stationed in the very room
Honoured by Milton's name. O temperate Bard!
Be it confest that, for the first time, seated
Within thy innocent lodge and oratory,   300
One of a festive circle, I poured out
Libations, to thy memory drank, till pride
And gratitude grew dizzy in a brain
Never excited by the fumes of wine
Before that hour, or since.   305

. . . .

from *Book Fourth: Summer Vacation*

. . . .

Among the favourites whom it pleased me well
To see again, was one by ancient right
Our inmate, a rough terrier of the hills;   95
By birth and call of nature pre-ordained
To hunt the badger and unearth the fox
Among the impervious crags, but having been
From youth our own adopted, he had passed
Into a gentler service. And when first   100
The boyish spirit flagged, and day by day
Along my veins I kindled with the stir,
The fermentation, and the vernal heat

---

564. organic: See note to line 43 of the "Preface" above (p. 760). **BOOK III** Wordsworth attended Cambridge from 1787 to 1791. **278-79:** Chaucer's "Reeve's Tale" opens with the line "At Trumpyngtoun, nat fer fro Cantebrigge" (i.e., Cambridge). **286. blind Poet:** Milton. **BOOK IV** The Hawkshead vacation was in 1788.

Of poesy, affecting private shades
Like a sick Lover, then this dog was used   *105*
To watch me, an attendant and a friend,
Obsequious to my steps early and late,
Though often of such dilatory walk
Tired, and uneasy at the halts I made.
A hundred times when, roving high and low,   *110*
I have been harassed with the toil of verse,
Much pains and little progress, and at once
Some lovely Image in the song rose up
Full-formed, like Venus rising from the sea;
Then have I darted forwards to let loose   *115*
My hand upon his back with stormy joy,
Caressing him again and yet again.
And when at evening on the public way
I sauntered, like a river murmuring
And talking to itself when all things else   *120*
Are still, the creature trotted on before;
Such was his custom; but whene'er he met
A passenger approaching, he would turn
To give me timely notice, and straightway,
Grateful for that admonishment, I hushed   *125*
My voice, composed my gait, and, with the air
And mien of one whose thoughts are free, advanced
To give and take a greeting that might save
My name from piteous rumours, such as wait
On men suspected to be crazed in brain.   *130*

    . . . .

             'Mid a throng
Of maids and youths, old men, and matrons staid,   *310*
A medley of all tempers, I had passed
The night in dancing, gaiety, and mirth,
With din of instruments and shuffling feet,
And glancing forms, and tapers glittering,
And unaimed prattle flying up and down;   *315*
Spirits upon the stretch, and here and there
Slight shocks of young love-liking interspersed,
Whose transient pleasure mounted to the head,
And tingled through the veins. Ere we retired,
The cock had crowed, and now the eastern sky   *320*
Was kindling, not unseen, from humble copse
And open field, through which the pathway wound,
And homeward led my steps. Magnificent
The morning rose, in memorable pomp,
Glorious as e'er I had beheld — in front,   *325*

The sea lay laughing at a distance; near,
The solid mountains shone, bright as the clouds,
Grain-tinctured, drenched in empyrean light;
And in the meadows and the lower grounds
Was all the sweetness of a common dawn —   *330*
Dews, vapours, and the melody of birds,
And labourers going forth to till the fields.
Ah! need I say, dear Friend! that to the brim
My heart was full; I made no vows, but vows
Were then made for me; bond unknown to me   *335*
Was given, that I should be, else sinning greatly,
A dedicated Spirit. On I walked
In thankful blessedness, which yet survives.

    . . . .

from *Book Sixth: Cambridge and the Alps*

    . . . .

When from the Vallais we had turned, and clomb
Along the Simplon's steep and rugged road,
Following a band of muleteers, we reached
A halting-place, where all together took   *565*
Their noon-tide meal. Hastily rose our guide,
Leaving us at the board; awhile we lingered,
Then paced the beaten downward way that led
Right to a rough stream's edge, and there broke off;
The only track now visible was one   *570*
That from the torrent's further brink held forth
Conspicuous invitation to ascend
A lofty mountain. After brief delay
Crossing the unbridged stream, that road we took,
And clomb with eagerness, till anxious fears   *575*
Intruded, for we failed to overtake
Our comrades gone before. By fortunate chance,
While every moment added doubt to doubt,
A peasant met us, from whose mouth we learned
That to the spot which had perplexed us first   *580*
We must descend, and there should find the road,
Which in the stony channel of the stream
Lay a few steps, and then along its banks;
And, that our future course, all plain to sight,
Was downwards, with the current of that stream.   *585*
Loth to believe what we so grieved to hear,
For still we had hopes that pointed to the clouds,
We questioned him again, and yet again;

---

311. **tempers:** temperaments. 328. **grain-tinctured:** red-coloured; **empyrean:** i.e., fiery. 333. **dear Friend:** The entire poem is addressed to Coleridge. **BOOK VI** 562-63. **Vallais** (usually so spelled until the 19th century): Valais, now a canton of southern Switzerland, was then two parts, and in 1790, the year of Wordsworth's visit, Lower Vallais rebelled against the ruling Upper Vallais; **Simplon:** The Simplon Pass is in Valais.

But every word that from the peasant's lips
Came in reply, translated by our feelings,   590
Ended in this, — *that we had crossed the Alps.*

    Imagination — here the Power so called
Through sad incompetence of human speech,
That awful Power rose from the mind's abyss
Like an unfathered vapour that enwraps,   595
At once, some lonely traveller. I was lost;
Halted without an effort to break through;
But to my conscious soul I now can say —
"I recognise thy glory"; in such strength
Of usurpation, when the light of sense   600
Goes out, but with a flash that has revealed
The invisible world, doth greatness make abode,
There harbours; whether we be young or old,
Our destiny, our being's heart and home,
Is with infinitude, and only there;   605
With hope it is, hope that can never die,
Effort, and expectation, and desire,
And something evermore about to be.
Under such banners militant, the soul
Seeks for no trophies, struggles for no spoils   610
That may attest her prowess, blest in thoughts
That are their own perfection and reward,
Strong in herself and in beatitude
That hides her, like the mighty flood of Nile
Poured from his fount of Abyssinian clouds   615
To fertilise the whole Egyptian plain.

    . . . .

from *Book Ninth: Residence in France*

    . . . .

    Through Paris lay my readiest course, and there
Sojourning a few days, I visited
In haste, each spot of old or recent fame,
The latter chiefly; from the field of Mars   45
Down to the suburbs of St. Antony,
And from Mont Martre southward to the Dome
Of Geneviève. In both her clamorous Halls,
The National Synod and the Jacobins,
I saw the Revolutionary Power   50

Toss like a ship at anchor, rocked by storms;
The Arcades I traversed, in the Palace huge
Of Orleans; coasted round and round the line
Of Tavern, Brothel, Gaming-house, and Shop,
Great rendezvous of worst and best, the walk   55
Of all who had a purpose, or had not;
I stared and listened, with a stranger's ears,
To Hawkers and Haranguers, hubbub wild!
And hissing Factionists with ardent eyes,
In knots, or pairs, or single. Not a look   60
Hope takes, or Doubt or Fear is forced to wear,
But seemed there present; and I scanned them all,
Watched every gesture uncontrollable,
Of anger, and vexation, and despite,
All side by side, and struggling face to face,   65
With gaiety and dissolute idleness.

    Where silent zephyrs sported with the dust
Of the Bastille, I sate in the open sun,
And from the rubbish gathered up a stone,
And pocketed the relic, in the guise   70
Of an enthusiast: yet, in honest truth,
I looked for something that I could not find,
Affecting more emotion than I felt. . . .

    . . . .

And on these spots with many gleams I looked   500
Of chivalrous delight. Yet not the less,
Hatred of absolute rule, where will of one
Is law for all, and of that barren pride
In them who, by immunities unjust,
Between the sovereign and the people stand,   505
His helper and not theirs, laid stronger hold
Daily upon me, mixed with pity too
And love; for where hope is, there love will be
For the abject multitude. And when we chanced
One day to meet a hunger-bitten girl,   510
Who crept along fitting her languid gait
Unto a heifer's motion, by a cord
Tied to her arm, and picking thus from the lane
Its sustenance, while the girl with pallid hands
Was busy knitting in a heartless mood   515
Of solitude, and at the sight my friend

BOOK IX   Wordsworth was in France during 1791 and 1792. **45-48:** the Champ de Mars (west), the Faubourg St. Antoine (east), Montmartre (north), Dome of Geneviève (now the Pantheon) (south). **49:** the National Assembly (see Helen Maria Williams, Letter VI, p. 745); **Jacobins:** group of radical revolutionists founded in 1789 at the Jacobin convent near the church of St. Jacques (Latin *Jacobus*). **52-53:** the Palais Royal, built in 1629 for Cardinal Richelieu, used by the princes d'Orléans, had a famous *galerie* ("The Arcades"). **68ff.:** The French Revolution in effect began with the storming of the Bastille, a fortress used as a prison, on 14 July 1789. **500. these spots:** various castles and other sites associated with France's monarchical past. **516. my friend:** the Republican Michel Beaupuy, with whom Wordsworth stayed and who acted as guide and companion — later killed in battle.

In agitation said, "'Tis against *that*
That we are fighting," I with him believed
That a benignant spirit was abroad
Which might not be withstood, that poverty   520
Abject as this would in a little time
Be found no more, that we should see the earth
Unthwarted in her wish to recompense
The meek, the lowly, patient child of toil,
All institutes for ever blotted out   525
That legalised exclusion, empty pomp
Abolished, sensual state and cruel power
Whether by edict of the one or few;
And finally, as sum and crown of all,
Should see the people having a strong hand   530
In framing their own laws; whence better days
To all mankind.

．．．．

from *Book Tenth: Residence in France (Continued)*

．．．．

          Twice had the trees let fall
Their leaves, as often Winter had put on
His hoary crown, since I had seen the surge
Beat against Albion's shore, since ear of mine
Had caught the accents of my native speech   240
Upon our native country's sacred ground.
A patriot of the world, how could I glide
Into communion with her sylvan shades,
Erewhile my tuneful haunt? It pleased me more
To abide in the great City, where I found   245
The general air still busy with the stir
Of that first memorable onset made
By a strong levy of humanity
Upon the traffickers in Negro blood;
Effort which, though defeated, had recalled   250
To notice old forgotten principles,
And through the nation spread a novel heat
Of virtuous feeling. For myself, I own
That this particular strife had wanted power
To rivet my affections; nor did now   255
Its unsuccessful issue much excite
My sorrow; for I brought with me the faith

That, if France prospered, good men would not long
Pay fruitless worship to humanity,
And this most rotten branch of human shame,   260
Object, so seemed it, of superfluous pains,
Would fall together with its parent tree.
What, then, were my emotions, when in arms
Britain put forth her free-born strength in league,
Oh, pity and shame! with those confederate Powers!   265
Not in my single self alone I found,
But in the minds of all ingenuous youth,
Change and subversion from that hour. No shock
Given to my moral nature had I known
Down to that very moment; neither lapse   270
Nor turn of sentiment that might be named
A revolution, save at this one time;
All else was progress on the self-same path
On which, with a diversity of pace,
I had been travelling: this a stride at once   275
Into another region. As a light
And pliant harebell, swinging in the breeze
On some grey rock — its birth-place — so had I
Wantoned, fast rooted on the ancient tower
Of my beloved country, wishing not   280
A happier fortune than to wither there:
Now was I from that pleasant station torn
And tossed about in whirlwind. I rejoiced,
Yea, afterwards — truth most painful to record! —
Exulted, in the triumph of my soul,   285
When Englishmen by thousands were o'erthrown,
Left without glory on the field, or driven,
Brave hearts! to shameful flight. It was a grief, —
Grief call it not, 'twas anything but that, —
A conflict of sensations without name,   290
Of which *he* only, who may love the sight
Of a village steeple, as I do, can judge,
When, in the congregation bending all
To their great Father, prayers were offered up,
Or praises for our country's victories;   295
And, 'mid the simple worshippers, perchance
I only, like an uninvited guest
Whom no one owned, sate silent, shall I add,
Fed on the day of vengeance yet to come.

．．．．

BOOK X   **247ff.:** referring to the efforts of Thomas Clarkson and William Wilberforce to abolish the slave trade; Wilberforce's bill, introduced in 1789, finally passed in 1807; slavery itself was abolished in the West Indies in 1833. **263-65:** British fear and antagonism had grown, Louis XVI was executed in January 1793, and France declared war on 1 February; the other powers aligned against France were Austria, Prussia, Holland, and Spain.

from *Book Eleventh: France (Concluded)*

. . . .

I summoned my best skill, and toiled, intent
To anatomise the frame of social life;   *280*
Yea, the whole body of society
Searched to its heart. Share with me, Friend! the wish
That some dramatic tale, endued with shapes
Livelier, and flinging out less guarded words
Than suit the work we fashion, might set forth   *285*
What then I learned, or think I learned, of truth,
And the errors into which I fell, betrayed
By present objects, and by reasonings false
From their beginnings, inasmuch as drawn
Out of a heart that had been turned aside   *290*
From Nature's way by outward accidents,
And which was thus confounded, more and more
Misguided, and misguiding. So I fared,
Dragging all precepts, judgments, maxims, creeds,
Like culprits to the bar; calling the mind,   *295*
Suspiciously, to establish in plain day
Her titles and her honours; now believing,
Now disbelieving; endlessly perplexed
With impulse, motive, right and wrong, the ground
Of obligation, what the rule and whence   *300*
The sanction; till, demanding formal *proof*,
And seeking it in every thing, I lost
All feeling of conviction, and, in fine,
Sick, wearied out with contrarieties,
Yielded up moral questions in despair.   *305*

. . . .

from *Book Twelfth: Imagination and Taste, How Impaired and Restored*

. . . .

   There are in our existence spots of time,
That with distinct pre-eminence retain
A renovating virtue, whence, depressed   *210*
By false opinion and contentious thought,
Or aught of heavier or more deadly weight,
In trivial occupations, and the round
Of ordinary intercourse, our minds
Are nourished and invisibly repaired;   *215*
A virtue, by which pleasure is enhanced,
That penetrates, enables us to mount,
When high, more high, and lifts us up when fallen.
This efficacious spirit chiefly lurks

Among those passages of life that give   *220*
Profoundest knowledge to what point, and how,
The mind is lord and master — outward sense
The obedient servant of her will. Such moments
Are scattered everywhere, taking their date
From our first childhood. I remember well,   *225*
That once, while yet my inexperienced hand
Could scarcely hold a bridle, with proud hopes
I mounted, and we journeyed towards the hills:
An ancient servant of my father's house
Was with me, my encourager and guide: *230*
We had not travelled long, ere some mischance
Disjoined me from my comrade; and, through fear
Dismounting, down the rough and stony moor
I led my horse, and, stumbling on, at length
Came to a bottom, where in former times   *235*
A murderer had been hung in iron chains.
The gibbet-mast had mouldered down, the bones
And iron case were gone; but on the turf,
Hard by, soon after that fell deed was wrought,
Some unknown hand had carved the murderer's name.
The monumental letters were inscribed   *241*
In times long past; but still, from year to year,
By superstition of the neighbourhood,
The grass is cleared away, and to this hour
The characters are fresh and visible: *245*
A casual glance had shown them, and I fled,
Faltering and faint, and ignorant of the road:
Then, reascending the bare common, saw
A naked pool that lay beneath the hills,
The beacon on the summit, and, more near,   *250*
A girl, who bore a pitcher on her head,
And seemed with difficult steps to force her way
Against the blowing wind. It was, in truth,
An ordinary sight; but I should need
Colours and words that are unknown to man,   *255*
To paint the visionary dreariness
Which, while I looked all round for my lost guide,
Invested moorland waste and naked pool,
The beacon crowning the lone eminence,
The female and her garments vexed and tossed   *260*
By the strong wind. When, in the blessed hours
Of early love, the loved one at my side,
I roamed, in daily presence of this scene,
Upon the naked pool and dreary crags,
And on the melancholy beacon, fell   *265*

Book XI   303. in fine: in short, finally.   Book XII   262. loved one: Mary Hutchinson, whom he had known since childhood; they married in 1802.

A spirit of pleasure and youth's golden gleam;
And think ye not with radiance more sublime
For these remembrances, and for the power
They had left behind? So feeling comes in aid
Of feeling, and diversity of strength   270
Attends us, if but once we have been strong.
Oh! mystery of man, from what a depth
Proceed thy honours. I am lost, but see
In simple childhood something of the base
On which thy greatness stands; but this I feel,   275
That from thyself it comes, that thou must give,

Else never canst receive. The days gone by
Return upon me almost from the dawn
Of life: the hiding-places of man's power
Open; I would approach them, but they close.   280
I see by glimpses now; when age comes on,
May scarcely see at all; and I would give,
While yet we may, as far as words can give,
Substance and life to what I feel, enshrining,
Such is my hope, the spirit of the Past   285
For future restoration.

    . . . .

(1798-1839; 1850)

SIR WALTER SCOTT
Scotland, 1771-1832

from *THE LAY OF THE LAST MINSTREL,* Canto 6

Breathes there the man, with soul so dead,
Who never to himself hath said,
   This is my own, my native land!
Whose heart hath ne'er within him burned,
As home his footsteps he hath turned,   5
   From wandering on a foreign strand!
If such there breathe, go, mark him well;
For him no Minstrel raptures swell;
High though his titles, proud his name,
Boundless his wealth as wish can claim;   10
Despite those titles, power, and pelf,
The wretch, concentred all in self,
Living, shall forfeit fair renown,
And, doubly dying, shall go down
To the vile dust, from whence he sprung,   15
Unwept, unhonoured, and unsung.
O Caledonia! stern and wild,
Meet nurse for a poetic child!
Land of brown heath and shaggy wood,
Land of the mountain and the flood,   20
Land of my sires! what mortal hand

Can e'er untie the filial band,
That knits me to thy rugged strand!
Still as I view each well-known scene,
Think what is now, and what hath been,   25
Seems as, to me, of all bereft,
Sole friends thy woods and streams were left;
And thus I love them better still,
Even in extremity of ill.
By Yarrow's stream still let me stray,   30
Though none should guide my feeble way;
Still feel the breeze down Ettrick break,
Although it chill my withered cheek;
Still lay my head by Teviot Stone,
Though there, forgotten and alone,   35
The Bard may draw his parting groan.

(1805)

LOCHINVAR

O, young Lochinvar is come out of the west,
Through all the wide Border his steed was the best;
And save his good broadsword he weapons had none,
He rode all unarmed, and he rode all alone.
So faithful in love, and so dauntless in war,   5
There never was knight like the young Lochinvar.

LAY OF THE LAST MINSTREL **11. pelf:** wealth, especially if ill-gotten. **30. Yarrow:** river in Scotland, which flows into Ettrick Water (line 32) in Selkirkshire, then joins the Tweed. **34. Teviot:** river in Roxburghshire, a tributary of the Tweed. **LOCHINVAR** The poem is a self-contained episode in Canto 5 of Scott's long romantic narrative *Marmion, a Tale of Flodden Field.*

He stayed not for brake, and he stopped not for stone,
He swam the Eske river where ford there was none;
But ere he alighted at Netherby gate,
The bride had consented, the gallant came late: *10*
For a laggard in love, and a dastard in war,
Was to wed the fair Ellen of brave Lochinvar.

So boldly he entered the Netherby Hall,
Among bride's-men, and kinsmen, and brothers, and all:
Then spoke the bride's father, his hand on his sword,
(For the poor craven bridegroom said never a word) *16*
"O come ye in peace here, or come ye in war,
Or to dance at our bridal, young Lord Lochinvar?"

"I long wooed your daughter, my suit you denied; —
Love swells like the Solway, but ebbs like its tide —
And now am I come, with this lost love of mine,   *21*
To lead but one measure, drink one cup of wine.
There are maidens in Scotland more lovely by far,
That would gladly be bride to the young Lochinvar."

The bride kissed the goblet: the knight took it up,   *25*
He quaffed off the wine, and he threw down the cup.
She looked down to blush, and she looked up to sigh,
With a smile on her lips, and a tear in her eye.
He took her soft hand, ere her mother could bar, — *29*
"Now tread we a measure!" said the young Lochinvar.

So stately his form and so lovely her face,
That never a hall such a galliard did grace;
While her mother did fret, and her father did fume,   *33*
And the bridegroom stood dangling his bonnet and plume,
And the bride-maidens whispered, "'Twere better by far,
To have matched our fair cousin with young Lochinvar."

One touch to her hand, and one word in her ear,
When they reached the hall-door, and the charger stood near;
So light to the croup the fair lady he swung,
So light to the saddle before her he sprung!   *40*
"She is won! we are gone, over bank, bush, and scaur;
They'll have fleet steeds that follow," quoth young Lochinvar.

There was mounting 'mong Graemes of the Netherby clan;
Forsters, Fenwicks, and Musgraves, they rode and they ran:
There was racing and chasing on Cannobie Lee,   *45*
But the lost bride of Netherby ne'er did they see.
So daring in love, and so dauntless in war,
Have ye e'er heard of gallant like young Lochinvar?

(1808)

THE DREARY CHANGE

The sun upon the Weirdlaw Hill,
    In Ettrick's vale, is sinking sweet;
The westland wind is hush and still,
    The lake lies sleeping at my feet.
Yet not the landscape to mine eye   *5*
    Bears those bright hues that once it bore;
Though evening, with her richest dye,
    Flames o'er the hills of Ettrick's shore.

With listless look along the plain,
    I see Tweed's silver current glide,   *10*
And coldly mark the holy fane
    Of Melrose rise in ruined pride.
The quiet lake, the balmy air,
    The hill, the stream, the tower, the tree —
Are they still such as once they were?   *15*
    Or is the dreary change in me?

Alas, the warped and broken board,
    How can it bear the painter's dye!
The harp of strained and tuneless chord,
    How to the minstrel's skill reply!   *20*
To aching eyes each landscape lowers,
    To feverish pulse each gale blows chill;
And Araby's or Eden's bowers
    Were barren as this moorland hill.

(1817)

PROUD MAISIE

Proud Maisie is in the wood
    Walking so early;
Sweet Robin sits on the bush,
    Singing so rarely.

"Tell me, thou bonny bird,   *5*
    When shall I marry me?" —
"When six braw gentlemen
    Kirkward shall carry ye."

"Who makes the bridal bed,
    Birdie, say truly?" —   *10*
"The gray-headed sexton
    That delves the grave duly.

"The glow-worm o'er grave and stone
    Shall light thee steady,
The owl from the steeple sing,   *15*
    'Welcome, proud lady.'"

(1818)

---

7. **brake:** thicket. 8. **Eske:** The Black Esk and White Esk Rivers join in Dumfriesshire and flow into Solway Firth (see line 20). 9. **Netherby:** the fictional name of the bride's estate. 39. **croup:** horse's back. 41. **scaur:** rocky cliff. 45. **Cannobie Lee:** Canobie Lea, in Dumfriesshire. **THE DREARY CHANGE** 11. **fane:** sanctuary. 12. **Melrose:** the ruins of Melrose Abbey (founded by Cistercians in 1136), on the Tweed River in Roxburghshire. **PROUD MAISIE** In Scott's novel *The Heart of Midlothian*, crazy Madge Wildfire sings this song shortly before she dies. 7. **braw:** fine, gallant.

SYDNEY SMITH
England, 1771-1845

FALLACIES
Fallacy I: "Because I have gone through it, my son shall go through it also."

A man gets well pommelled at a public school; is subject to every misery and every indignity which seventeen years of age can inflict upon nine and ten; has his eye nearly knocked out, and his clothes stolen and cut to pieces; and twenty years afterward, when he is a chrysalis, and has forgotten the miseries of his grub state, is determined to act a manly part in life, and says, "I passed through all that myself, and I am determined my 5 son shall pass through it as I have done"; and away goes his bleating progeny to the tyranny and servitude of the long chamber or the large dormitory. It would surely be much more rational to say, "Because I have passed through it, I am determined my son shall not pass through it; because I was kicked for nothing, and cuffed for nothing, and fagged for everything, I will spare all these miseries to my child." It is not for any good 10 which may be derived from this rough usage; that has not been weighed and considered; few persons are capable of weighing its effects upon character; but there is a sort of compensatory and consolatory notion, that the present generation (whether useful or not, no matter) are not to come off scot-free, but are to have their share of ill-usage; as if the black eye and bloody nose which Master John Jackson received in 1800, are less black 15 and bloody by the application of similar violence to similar parts of Master Thomas Jackson, the son, in 1830. This is not only sad nonsense, but cruel nonsense. The only use to be derived from the recollection of what we have suffered in youth, is a fixed determination to screen those we educate from every evil and inconvenience, from subjection to which there are not cogent reasons for submitting. Can anything be more 20 stupid and preposterous than this concealed revenge upon the rising generation, and latent envy lest they should avail themselves of the improvements time has made, and pass a happier youth than their fathers have done?

Fallacy II: "I have said I will do it, and I *will* do it; I will stick to my word."

This fallacy proceeds from confounding resolutions with promises. If you have promised to give a man a guinea for a reward, or to sell him a horse or a field, you 25 must do it; you are dishonest if you do not. But if you have made a resolution to eat no meat for a year, and everybody about you sees that you are doing mischief to your constitution, is it any answer to say, you have said so, and you will stick to your word? With whom have you made the contract but with yourself? and if you and yourself, the two contracting parties, agree to break the contract, where is the evil, or who is 30 injured?

FALLACIES   **10. fagged:** made to work for the older students, according to English "public school" [i.e. private school] custom.

Fallacy III: "I object to half-measures — it is neither one thing nor the other."

But why *should* it be either one thing or the other? why not something between both? Why are half-measures necessarily or probably unwise measures? I am embarrassed in my circumstances; one of my plans is, to persevere boldly in the same line of expense, and to trust to the chapter of accidents for some increase of fortune; the other is, to retire   35
entirely from the world, and to hide myself in a cottage; but I end with doing neither, and take a middle course of diminished expenditure. I do neither one thing nor the other, but possibly act wiser than if I had done either. I am highly offended by the conduct of an acquaintance; I neither overlook it entirely nor do I proceed to call him out; I do neither, but show him, by a serious change of manner, that I consider myself to have   40
been ill-treated. I effect my object by half-measures. I cannot agree entirely with the Opposition or the Ministry; it may very easily happen that my half-measures are wiser than the extremes to which they are opposed. But it is a sort of metaphor which debauches the understanding of *foolish* people; and when half-measures are mentioned, they have much the same feeling as if they were cheated — as if they had bargained for   45
a whole bushel and received but half. To act in extremes is sometimes wisdom; to *avoid* them is sometimes wisdom; every measure must be judged of by its own particular circumstances.

                                                                    (1856)

DOROTHY WORDSWORTH
England, 1771-1855

from the *JOURNALS*

Alfoxden, February 3rd, 1798
A mild morning, the windows open at breakfast, the redbreasts singing in the garden. Walked with Coleridge over the hills. The sea at first obscured by vapour; that vapour afterwards slid in one mighty mass along the sea-shore; the islands and one point of land clear beyond it. The distant country (which was purple in the clear dull air), overhung by straggling clouds that sailed over it, appeared like the darker clouds, which are often   5
seen at a great distance apparently motionless, while the nearer ones pass quickly over them, driven by the lower winds. I never saw such a union of earth, sky, and sea. The

---

33-34. embarrassed in my circumstances: short of money. **35. chapter of accidents:** a conventional phrase meaning "sequence of unforeseen circumstances" (*The Chapter of Accidents* was also the title of a 1780 farce by Sophia Lee, 1750-1784). **39. call him out:** challenge to a duel.   **JOURNALS   Alfoxden:** house near Holford in Somerset that William and Dorothy moved to in 1797 in order to be near Coleridge at Nether Stowey. **2. hills:** the Quantock Hills. **4. distant country:** probably southern Wales, across the Bristol Channel.

clouds beneath our feet spread themselves to the water, and the clouds of the sky almost joined them. Gathered sticks in the wood; a perfect stillness. The redbreasts sang upon the leafless boughs. Of a great number of sheep in the field, only one standing. Returned *10* to dinner at five o'clock. The moonlight still and warm as a summer's night at nine o'clock.

Grasmere, Thursday, April 15th, 1802

It was a threatening, misty morning, but mild. We set off after dinner from Eusemere. Mrs. Clarkson went a short way with us, but turned back. The wind was furious, and we thought we must have returned. We first rested in the large boathouse, then under a *15* furze bush opposite Mr. Clarkson's. Saw the plough going in the field. The wind seized our breath. The lake was rough. There was a boat by itself floating in the middle of the bay below Water Millock. We rested again in the Water Millock Lane. The hawthorns are black and green, the birches here and there greenish, but there is yet more of purple to be seen on the twigs. We got over into a field to avoid some cows — people *20* working, a few primroses by the roadside, woodsorrel flower, the anemone, scentless violets, strawberries, and that starry, yellow flower which Mrs. C. calls pile-wort. When we were in the woods beyond Gowbarrow Park we saw a few daffodils close to the water-side. We fancied that the lake had floated the seeds ashore, and that the little colony had so sprung up. But as we went along there were more and yet more, and at *25* last, under the boughs of the trees, we saw that there was a long belt of them along the shore, about the breadth of a country turnpike road. I never saw daffodils so beautiful. They grew among the mossy stones about and about them; some rested their heads upon these stones as on a pillow for weariness, and the rest tossed and reeled and danced, and seemed as if they verily laughed with the wind that blew upon them over *30* the lake; they looked so gay, ever glancing, ever changing. This wind blew directly over the lake to them. There was here and there a little knot, and a few stragglers higher up, but they were so few as not to disturb the simplicity and unity and life of that one busy highway. . . .

On Thursday morning, 29th, we arrived in London. . . . We left London on *35* Saturday morning at half-past five or six, the 31st of July. We mounted the Dover coach at Charing Cross. It was a beautiful morning. The city, St. Paul's, with the river, and a multitude of little boats, made a most beautiful sight as we crossed Westminster Bridge. The houses were not overhung by their cloud of smoke, and they were spread out endlessly, yet the sun shone so brightly, with such a pure light, *40* that there was even something like the purity of one of nature's own grand spectacles. . . .

Grasmere: in the Lake District (near the lake also called Grasmere), location of Dove Cottage, to which William and Dorothy moved at the end of 1799 (the Coleridges settled in nearby Keswick the following year). **13. we:** i.e., Dorothy and William; **Eusemere:** where their friends the Clarksons lived, at the north end of Ullswater, about 20 km northeast of Grasmere. **14:** Catherine Clarkson (1772-1856) was the wife of Thomas Clarkson (1760-1846), prominent opponent of slavery and the slave trade, author of *History of the Abolition of the Slave Trade* (1808; the trade was abolished in 1807). **15. must have:** i.e., would have to. **18. Water Millock:** about 3 km from Eusemere, on the west shore. **22. Mrs. C.:** possibly Mrs. Clarkson, but more likely Sara Coleridge. **23. Gowbarrow:** another 2 km along the way; **daffodils . . . :** See Wordsworth's "I wandered lonely as a cloud" (p. 768). **35. in London:** on the way to France to visit Annette Vallon and her and Wordsworth's natural daughter, Caroline. **37ff.:** See Wordsworth's sonnet "Composed upon Westminster Bridge" (p. 765).

Samuel Taylor Coleridge
England, 1772-1834

On a Ruined House in a Romantic Country

And this reft house is that the which he built,
Lamented Jack! And here his malt he pil'd,
Cautious in vain! These rats that squeak so wild,
Squeak, not unconscious of their father's guilt.
Did ye not see her gleaming thro' the glade?   5
Belike, 'twas she, the maiden all forlorn.
What though she milk no cow with crumpled horn,

Yet *aye* she haunts the dale where *erst* she stray'd;
And *aye* beside her stalks her amorous knight!
Still on his thighs their wonted brogues are worn,   10
And thro' those brogues, still tatter'd and betorn,
His hindward charms gleam an unearthly white;
As when thro' broken clouds at night's high noon
Peeps in fair fragments forth the full-orb'd harvest-moon!

(1797)

Kubla Khan:
Or, A Vision in a Dream. A Fragment.

The following fragment is here published at the request of a poet of great and deserved celebrity, and, as far as the Author's own opinions are concerned, rather as a psychological curiosity, than on the ground of any supposed *poetic* merits.

In the summer of the year 1797, the Author, then in ill health, had retired to a lonely farm-house between Porlock and Linton, on the Exmoor confines of Somerset and Devonshire. In   5
consequence of a slight indisposition, an anodyne had been prescribed, from the effects of which he fell asleep in his chair at the moment that he was reading the following sentence, or words of the same substance, in *Purchas's Pilgrimage*: "Here the Khan Kubla commanded a palace to be built, and a stately garden thereunto. And thus ten miles of fertile ground were inclosed with a wall." The Author continued for about three hours in a profound sleep, at least of the external   10
senses, during which time he has the most vivid confidence, that he could not have composed less than from two to three hundred lines; if that indeed can be called composition in which all the images rose up before him as *things,* with a parallel production of the correspondent expressions, without any sensation or consciousness of effort. On awaking he appeared to himself to have a distinct recollection of the whole, and taking his pen, ink, and paper, instantly and eagerly wrote   15
down the lines that are here preserved. At this moment he was unfortunately called out by a person on business from Porlock, and detained by him above an hour, and on his return to his room, found, to his no small surprise and mortification, that though he still retained some vague and dim recollection of the general purport of the vision, yet, with the exception of some eight or ten scattered lines and images, all the rest had passed away like the images on the surface of a   20
stream into which a stone has been cast, but, alas! without the after restoration of the latter!

On a Ruined House in a Romantic Country   One of three "Sonnets Attempted in the Manner of Contemporary Writers," signed "Nehemiah Higginbottom." In this one he good-naturedly parodies the recognized "characteristic vices" of his own style. **10. brogues:** breeches.   **Kubla Khan   Introduction: 1. poet:** Lord Byron. **4. 1797:** Some have thought this a mistake for 1798, but the evidence for either date we think remains insurmountably confusing; hence our "1797-98" for the date of the poem's composition. **6:** The anodyne, as he noted elsewhere, consisted of two grains of opium. **8-10:** Samuel Purchas's actual wording in *Purchas His Pilgrimage* (1613): "In Xamdu did Cublai Can build a stately Palace, encompassing sixteene miles of plaine ground with a wall, wherein are fertile Meddowes, pleasant Springs, delightful Streames, and all sorts of beasts of chase and game, and in the middest thereof a sumptuous house of pleasure."

Then all the charm
Is broken — all that phantom-world so fair
Vanishes, and a thousand circlets spread,
And each mis-shape the other. Stay awhile,   *25*
Poor youth! who scarcely dar'st lift up thine eyes —
The stream will soon renew its smoothness, soon
The visions will return! And lo, he stays,
And soon the fragments dim of lovely forms
Come trembling back, unite, and now once more   *30*
The pool becomes a mirror.

    Yet from the still surviving recollections in his mind, the Author has frequently purposed to finish for himself what had been originally, as it were, given to him. Σαμερον αδιον ασω: but the to-morrow is yet to come.

    As a contrast to this vision, I have annexed a fragment of a very different character,   *35*
describing with equal fidelity the dream of pain and disease.

In Xanadu did Kubla Khan
A stately pleasure-dome decree:
Where Alph, the sacred river, ran
Through caverns measureless to man
  Down to a sunless sea,   *5*
So twice five miles of fertile ground
With walls and towers were girdled round:
And there were gardens bright with sinuous rills,
Where blossomed many an incense-bearing tree;
And here were forests ancient as the hills,   *10*
Enfolding sunny spots of greenery.

But oh! that deep romantic chasm which slanted
Down the green hill athwart a cedarn cover!
A savage place! as holy and enchanted
As e'er beneath a waning moon was haunted   *15*
By woman wailing for her demon-lover!
And from this chasm, with ceaseless turmoil seething,
As if this earth in fast thick pants were breathing,
A mighty fountain momently was forced:
Amid whose swift half-intermitted burst   *20*
Huge fragments vaulted like rebounding hail,
Or chaffy grain beneath the thresher's flail:
And 'mid these dancing rocks at once and ever
It flung up momently the sacred river.
Five miles meandering with a mazy motion   *25*
Through wood and dale the sacred river ran,
Then reached the caverns measureless to man,

And sank in tumult to a lifeless ocean:
And 'mid this tumult Kubla heard from far
Ancestral voices prophesying war!   *30*
  The shadow of the dome of pleasure
  Floated midway on the waves;
  Where was heard the mingled measure
  From the fountain and the caves.
It was a miracle of rare device,   *35*
A sunny pleasure-dome with caves of ice!

  A damsel with a dulcimer
  In a vision once I saw:
  It was an Abyssinian maid,
  And on her dulcimer she played,   *40*
  Singing of Mount Abora.
  Could I revive within me
  Her symphony and song,
  To such a deep delight 'twould win me,
That with music loud and long,   *45*
I would build that dome in air,
That sunny dome! those caves of ice!
And all who heard should see them there,
And all should cry, Beware! Beware!
His flashing eyes, his floating hair!   *50*
Weave a circle round him thrice,
And close your eyes with holy dread,
For he on honey-dew hath fed,
And drunk the milk of Paradise.

(1797-98; 1816)

22-31: lines 91-100 of Coleridge's "The Picture; or, The Lover's Resolution" (1802). **33.** Σαμερον αδιον ασω: (adapted from near the end of Theocritus's first idyll) "Today I'll sing more sweetly" (in 1834 Σαμερον was changed to Αυριον, "Tomorrow"). **35-36:** He refers to "The Pains of Sleep," written in 1803 (not included here). **KUBLA KHAN 3. Alph:** probably suggested by the river Alpheus; see note to Milton's *Lycidas*, line 132 (p. 317). **19. momently:** moment by moment. **41. Abora:** from *Paradise Lost*, IV, 280-82 (see p. 352); in one manuscript copy Coleridge even spelled it "Amara." **50ff.:** Cf. Socrates's description of possessed poets in Plato's *Ion*.

THE RIME OF THE ANCIENT MARINER
In Seven Parts

Facile credo, plures esse Naturas invisibiles quam visibiles in rerum universitate. Sed horum omnium familiam quis nobis enarrabit? et gradus et cognationes et discrimina et singulorum munera? Quid agunt? quae loca habitant? Harum rerum notitiam semper ambivit ingenium humanum, nunquam attigit. Juvat, interea, non diffiteor, quandoque in animo, tanquam in tabula, majoris et melioris mundi imaginem contemplari: ne mens assuefacta hodiernae vitae minutiis se contrahat nimis, et tota subsidat in pusillas cogitationes. Sed veritati interea invigilandum est, modusque servandus, ut certa ab incertis, diem a nocte, distinguamus. — T. BURNET, *Archaeol. Phil.* p. 68.

Argument

How a Ship, having first sailed to the Equator, was driven by Storms to the cold Country towards the South Pole; how the Ancient Mariner cruelly and in contempt of the laws of hospitality killed a Seabird and how he was followed by many and strange Judgements: and in what manner he came back to his own Country.

Part 1

It is an ancient Mariner,	*An ancient*	He holds him with his glittering eye —	*The Wedding-*
And he stoppeth one of three.	*Mariner meeteth*	The Wedding-Guest stood still,	*Guest is spell-*
"By thy long grey beard and glittering eye,	*three Gallants*	And listens like a three years' child:	*bound by the*
Now wherefore stopp'st thou me?	*bidden to a*	The Mariner hath his will.	*eye of the old*
	wedding-feast, and		*seafaring man,*
The Bridegroom's doors are opened wide,	*detaineth one.*	The Wedding-Guest sat on a stone:	*and constrained*
And I am next of kin;		He cannot choose but hear;	*to hear his tale.*
The guests are met, the feast is set:	6	And thus spake on that ancient man,	
May'st hear the merry din."		The bright-eyed Mariner.	20
He holds him with his skinny hand,		"The ship was cheered, the harbour cleared,	
"There was a ship," quoth he.		Merrily did we drop	
"Hold off! unhand me, grey-beard loon!"	10	Below the kirk, below the hill,	*The Mariner*
Eftsoons his hand dropt he.		Below the lighthouse top.	*tells how the*
			ship sailed

THE RIME OF THE ANCIENT MARINER For a discussion of the intentions of Wordsworth's and Coleridge's 1798 collection, *Lyrical Ballads*, in which the *Rime* was Coleridge's major contribution, see Chapter XIV of his *Biographia Literaria* (1817). **Epigraph** (not in the 1798 *Lyrical Ballads*): Coleridge's somewhat edited version of a passage from Chapter VII of *Archæologiæ Philosophicæ: sive Doctrina Antiqua de Rerum Originibus* (1692; later translated as *An Inquiry into the Doctrine of the Philosophers of All Nations, Concerning the Original of the World*), by Thomas Burnet (c.1635-1715) — written partly as a commentary on his earlier *Telluris Theoria Sacra* (*Sacred Theory of the Earth*, 1680); a 1736 translation (by Mead and Foxton) of the passage reads as follows (Coleridge's omissions are indicated by ellipses and his addition enclosed in brackets): "I can easily believe, that there are more invisible than visible beings in the universe; . . . but who will declare to us the family of all these, and acquaint us with the agreements, differences, and peculiar talents which are to be found among them? [What do they do? What places do they inhabit?] It is true, human wit has always desired a knowledge of these things, though it has never yet attained it. . . . I will own that it is very profitable sometimes to contemplate in the mind, as in a draught [i.e., picture], the image of the greater and better world, lest the soul, being accustomed to the trifles of this present life, should contract too much, and altogether rest in mean cogitations; but, in the meantime, we must take care to keep to the truth, and observe moderation, that we may distinguish certain from uncertain things, and day from night." **Argument:** The 1798 version was revised thus for the 1800 edition of *Lyrical Ballads*. The whole poem was similarly revised: it was shortened, and most of the archaisms were removed. The marginal glosses first appeared in Coleridge's collected *Sibylline Leaves* (1817), where the poem, even further revised, first appeared under his name (this is the version used as the basis for the present text). **12. Eftsoons:** soon after, quickly.

The Sun came up upon the left,   *southward*
Out of the sea came he!   *with a good*
And he shone bright, and on the right   *wind and fair*
Went down into the sea.   *weather, till*
    it reached
Higher and higher every day,   *the Line.*
Till over the mast at noon —"   30
The Wedding-Guest here beat his breast,
For he heard the loud bassoon.

The bride hath paced into the hall,   *The Wedding-*
Red as a rose is she;   *Guest heareth*
Nodding their heads before her goes   *the bridal*
The merry minstrelsy.   *music; but*
    the Mariner
The Wedding-Guest he beat his breast,   *continueth*
Yet he cannot choose but hear;   *his tale.*
And thus spake on that ancient man,
The bright-eyed Mariner.   40

"And now the STORM-BLAST came, and he   *The ship*
Was tyrannous and strong: *driven by*
He struck with his o'ertaking wings,   *a storm*
And chased us south along.   *toward the*
    South Pole.
With sloping masts and dipping prow,   45
As who pursued with yell and blow
Still treads the shadow of his foe,
And forward bends his head,
The ship drove fast, loud roared the blast,
And southward aye we fled.   50

And now there came both mist and snow,
And it grew wondrous cold:
And ice, mast-high, came floating by,
As green as emerald.   54

And through the drifts the snowy clifts   *The land of ice,*
Did send a dismal sheen: *and of fearful*
Nor shapes of men nor beasts we ken —   *sounds where no*
The ice was all between.   *living thing*
    was to be seen.
The ice was here, the ice was there,
The ice was all around: 60
It cracked and growled, and roared and howled,
Like noises in a swound!

At length did cross an Albatross,   *Till a great*
Thorough the fog it came;   *sea-bird, called*
As if it had been a Christian soul,   *the Albatross,*
We hailed it in God's name.   *came through*
    the snow-fog,
    and was received

It ate the food it ne'er had eat,   *with great joy*
And round and round it flew.   *and hospitality.*
The ice did split with a thunder-fit;
The helmsman steered us through!   70

And a good south wind sprung up behind;   *And lo! the*
The Albatross did follow,   *Albatross*
And every day, for food or play,   *proveth a bird*
Came to the mariner's hollo!   *of good omen, and fol-*
    loweth the ship as it
In mist or cloud, on mast or shroud,   *returned northward*
It perched for vespers nine;   *through fog and*
Whiles all the night, through fog-smoke white,   *floating ice.*
Glimmered the white Moon-shine."   79

"God save thee, ancient Mariner!   *The ancient Mariner*
From the fiends, that plague thee thus! —   *inhospitably*
Why look'st thou so?" — "With my cross-bow   *killeth*
I shot the ALBATROSS.   *the pious*
    bird of good omen.

Part II

The Sun now rose upon the right:
Out of the sea came he,
Still hid in mist, and on the left   85
Went down into the sea.

And the good south wind still blew behind,
But no sweet bird did follow,
Nor any day for food or play
Came to the mariners' hollo!   90

And I had done a hellish thing,   *His shipmates*
And it would work 'em woe: *cry out against*
For all averred, I had killed the bird   *the ancient*
That made the breeze to blow.   *Mariner, for*
Ah wretch! said they, the bird to slay,   *killing the bird*
That made the breeze to blow!   *of good luck.*
    96
Nor dim nor red, like God's own head,   *But when the*
The glorious Sun uprist: *fog cleared off,*
Then all averred, I had killed the bird   *they justify the*
That brought the fog and mist.   *same, and thus*
'Twas right, said they, such birds to slay,   *make themselves*
That bring the fog and mist.   *accomplices*
    in the crime.
The fair breeze blew, the white foam flew,   *The fair breeze*
The furrow followed free;   *continues; the*
We were the first that ever burst   *ship enters the*
Into that silent sea.   *Pacific Ocean, and*
    sails northward, even
    till it reaches the Line.

30: i.e, the ship has reached "the Line" (the equator). **55. clifts:** cliffs. **62. swound:** swoon.

786 *Samuel Taylor Coleridge*

Down dropt the breeze, the sails dropt down, *The ship hath*
'Twas sad as sad could be; *been suddenly*
And we did speak only to break *becalmed.*
The silence of the sea! 110

All in a hot and copper sky,
The bloody Sun, at noon,
Right up above the mast did stand,
No bigger than the Moon.

Day after day, day after day, 115
We stuck, nor breath nor motion;
As idle as a painted ship
Upon a painted ocean.

Water, water, every where, *And the*
And all the boards did shrink; *Albatross*
Water, water, every where, *begins to*
Nor any drop to drink. *be avenged.*

The very deep did rot: O Christ!
That ever this should be!
Yea, slimy things did crawl with legs 125
Upon the slimy sea.

About, about, in reel and rout
The death-fires danced at night;
The water, like a witch's oils,
Burnt green, and blue and white. 130

And some in dreams assurèd were *A Spirit had fol-*
Of the Spirit that plagued us so; *lowed them; one*
Nine fathom deep he had followed us *of the invisible*
From the land of mist and snow. *inhabitants of*
this planet,
neither departed
souls nor angels; concerning whom the learned Jew, Josephus, and the
Platonic Constantinopolitan, Michael Psellus, may be consulted. They
are very numerous, and there is no climate or element without one or more.

And every tongue, through utter drought, 135
Was withered at the root;
We could not speak, no more than if
We had been choked with soot.

Ah! well a-day! what evil looks *The shipmates,*
Had I from old and young! *in their sore*
Instead of the cross, the Albatross *distress, would*
About my neck was hung. *fain throw the*
whole guilt on
the ancient
Mariner: in sign whereof they hang the dead sea-bird round his neck.

Part III

There passed a weary time. Each throat
Was parched, and glazed each eye.
A weary time! a weary time! 145
How glazed each weary eye,
When looking westward, I beheld *The ancient Mariner*
A something in the sky. *beholdeth a sign in*
the element afar off.

At first it seemed a little speck,
And then it seemed a mist; 150
It moved and moved, and took at last
A certain shape, I wist.

A speck, a mist, a shape, I wist!
And still it neared and neared:
As if it dodged a water-sprite, 155
It plunged and tacked and veered.

With throats unslaked, with black lips baked, *At its*
We could nor laugh nor wail; *nearer approach,*
Through utter drought all dumb we stood! *it seemeth him*
I bit my arm, I sucked the blood, *and at a dear ransom*
And cried, A sail! a sail! *he freeth his speech from*
the bonds of thirst.

With throats unslaked, with black lips baked,
Agape they heard me call:
Gramercy! they for joy did grin, *A flash of joy;*
And all at once their breath drew in, 165
As they were drinking all.

See! see! (I cried) she tacks no more! *And horror*
Hither to work us weal; *follows. For*
Without a breeze, without a tide, *can it be a ship*
She steadies with upright keel! *that comes onward*
without wind or tide?

The western wave was all a-flame. 171
The day was well nigh done!
Almost upon the western wave
Rested the broad bright Sun;
When that strange shape drove suddenly 175
Betwixt us and the Sun.

And straight the Sun was flecked with bars,
(Heaven's Mother send us grace!) *It seemeth*
As if through a dungeon-grate he peered *him but the*
With broad and burning face. *skeleton*
of a ship.

---

128. death-fires: phosphorescence, like an *ignis fatuus* (some think the reference is to St. Elmo's fire, or corposant, sometimes considered an evil rather than a good omen; see line 314 and note below). **c.131-32, gloss:** Flavius Josephus, 1st-century A.D., Jewish historian; Michael Psellus, 1018-1079, professor of philosophy at Constantinople, author of *De Operatione Daemonum*. **152. wist:** became aware. **158. nor . . . nor:** neither . . . nor. **164. Gramercy:** an exclamation of surprise or thanks (from French *grand merci*). **168. weal:** good.

Alas! (thought I, and my heart beat loud) *181*
How fast she nears and nears!
Are those *her* sails that glance in the Sun,
Like restless gossameres?

And its ribs are seen as bars on the face of the setting Sun.

Are those *her* ribs through which the Sun
Did peer, as through a grate?
And is that Woman all her crew?
Is that a DEATH? and are there two?
Is DEATH that woman's mate?

The Spectre-Woman and her Death-mate, and no other on board the skeleton ship.

Her lips were red, *her* looks were free,
Her locks were yellow as gold:
Her skin was as white as leprosy,
The Night-mare LIFE-IN-DEATH was she,
Who thicks man's blood with cold.

Like vessel, like crew!

Death and Life-in-Death have diced for the ship's crew, and she (the latter) winneth the ancient Mariner.

The naked hulk alongside came,
And the twain were casting dice;
'The game is done! I've won! I've won!'
Quoth she, and whistles thrice.

The Sun's rim dips; the stars rush out:
At one stride comes the dark;
With far-heard whisper, o'er the sea,
Off shot the spectre-bark.

No twilight within the courts of the Sun.

202

We listened and looked sideways up!
Fear at my heart, as at a cup,
My life-blood seemed to sip!
The stars were dim, and thick the night,
The steersman's face by his lamp gleamed white;
From the sails the dew did drip —
Till clomb above the eastern bar
The hornèd Moon, with one bright star
Within the nether tip.

At the rising of the Moon,

205

210

One after one, by the star-dogged Moon,
Too quick for groan or sigh,
Each turned his face with a ghastly pang,
And cursed me with his eye.

One after another,

215

Four times fifty living men,
(And I heard nor sigh nor groan)
With heavy thump, a lifeless lump,
They dropped down one by one.

His ship-mates drop down dead.

The souls did from their bodies fly, —
They fled to bliss or woe!
And every soul, it passed me by,
Like the whizz of my cross-bow!"

But Life-in-Death begins her work on the ancient Mariner.

Part IV

"I fear thee, ancient Mariner!
I fear thy skinny hand!
And thou art long, and lank, and brown,
As is the ribbed sea-sand.

The Wedding-Guest feareth that a Spirit is talking to him;

I fear thee and thy glittering eye,
And thy skinny hand, so brown." —
"Fear not, fear not, thou Wedding-Guest!
This body dropt not down.

But the ancient Mariner assureth him of his bodily life, and proceedeth to relate his horrible penance.

Alone, alone, all, all alone,
Alone on a wide wide sea!
And never a saint took pity on
My soul in agony.

235

The many men, so beautiful!
And they all dead did lie:
And a thousand thousand slimy things
Lived on; and so did I.

He despiseth the creatures of the calm,

239

I looked upon the rotting sea,
And drew my eyes away;
I looked upon the rotting deck,
And there the dead men lay.

And envieth that they *should live, and so many lie dead.*

I looked to heaven, and tried to pray;
But or ever a prayer had gusht,
A wicked whisper came, and made
My heart as dry as dust.

245

I closed my lids, and kept them close,
And the balls like pulses beat;
For the sky and the sea, and the sea and the sky
Lay like a load on my weary eye,
And the dead were at my feet.

250

The cold sweat melted from their limbs,
Nor rot nor reek did they:
The look with which they looked on me
Had never passed away.

But the curse liveth for him in the eye of the dead men.

---

188. a Death: i.e., a personification, such as a skeleton. **210-12: hornèd:** i.e., crescent; a "star-dogged moon" was another evil omen for sailors. **224-27:** "For the last two lines of this stanza, I am indebted to Mr. Wordsworth. It was on a delightful walk from Nether Stowey to Dulverton, with him and his sister, in the Autumn of 1797, that this Poem was planned, and in part composed" (Coleridge's note; Wordsworth also composed lines 13-16, and suggested the shooting of the albatross and the dead crew's rising to navigate the ship). **245. or:** before.

An orphan's curse would drag to hell
A spirit from on high;
But oh! more horrible than that
Is the curse in a dead man's eye!   260
Seven days, seven nights, I saw that curse,
And yet I could not die.

The moving Moon went up the sky,
And no where did abide:
Softly she was going up,
And a star or two beside —

Her beams bemocked the sultry main,
Like April hoar-frost spread;
But where the ship's huge shadow lay,
The charmèd water burnt alway
A still and awful red.

*In his loneliness
and fixedness he
yearneth towards
the journeying Moon,
and the stars
that still sojourn,
yet still move
onward; and
every where
the blue sky belongs
to them, and is their
appointed rest, and their native country and their own natural homes,
which they enter unannounced, as lords that are certainly expected
and yet there is a silent joy at their arrival.*

Beyond the shadow of the ship,
I watched the water-snakes:
They moved in tracks of shining white,
And when they reared, the elfish light
Fell off in hoary flakes.   276

*By the light
of the Moon he
beholdeth God's
creatures of
the great calm.*

Within the shadow of the ship
I watched their rich attire:
Blue, glossy green, and velvet black,
They coiled and swam; and every track   280
Was a flash of golden fire.

O happy living things! no tongue
Their beauty might declare:
A spring of love gushed from my heart,
And I blessed them unaware:
Sure my kind saint took pity on me,
And I blessed them unaware.

*Their beauty and
their happiness.*

*He blesseth
them in his
heart.*

The self-same moment I could pray;
And from my neck so free
The Albatross fell off, and sank
Like lead into the sea.   291

*The spell
begins
to break.*

Part V

Oh sleep! it is a gentle thing,
Beloved from pole to pole!
To Mary Queen the praise be given!
She sent the gentle sleep from Heaven,   295
That slid into my soul.

The silly buckets on the deck,
That had so long remained,
I dreamt that they were filled with dew;
And when I awoke, it rained.

*By grace of
the holy
Mother, the
ancient
Mariner is
refreshed
with rain.*

My lips were wet, my throat was cold,
My garments all were dank;
Sure I had drunken in my dreams,
And still my body drank.

I moved, and could not feel my limbs: 305
I was so light — almost
I thought that I had died in sleep,
And was a blessèd ghost.

And soon I heard a roaring wind:
It did not come anear;
But with its sound it shook the sails,
That were so thin and sere.

*He heareth
sounds and
seeth strange
sights and
commotions in
the sky and
the element.*

The upper air burst into life!
And a hundred fire-flags sheen,
To and fro they were hurried about!   315
And to and fro, and in and out,
The wan stars danced between.

And the coming wind did roar more loud,
And the sails did sigh like sedge;
And the rain poured down from one black cloud;   320
The Moon was at its edge.

The thick black cloud was cleft, and still
The Moon was at its side:
Like waters shot from some high crag,
The lightning fell with never a jag,   325
A river steep and wide.

The loud wind never reached the ship,
Yet now the ship moved on!
Beneath the lightning and the Moon
The dead men gave a groan.

*The bodies of
the ship's crew
are inspirited,
and the ship
moves on;*

They groaned, they stirred, they all uprose,   331
Nor spake, nor moved their eyes;
It had been strange, even in a dream,
To have seen those dead men rise.

The helmsman steered, the ship moved on;   335
Yet never a breeze up-blew;
The mariners all 'gan work the ropes,
Where they were wont to do;
They raised their limbs like lifeless tools —
We were a ghastly crew.   340

---

276. hoary: white, like hoarfrost. **297. silly:** foolish, useless. **314. fire-flags:** probably the corposant, here a favorable sign (see note to line 128 above); some think the reference is to a display of the Aurora Australis or Borealis); **sheen:** bright, shining, resplendent.

The body of my brother's son
Stood by me, knee to knee:
The body and I pulled at one rope,
But he said nought to me."

"I fear thee, ancient Mariner!"   345
"Be calm, thou Wedding-Guest!   *But not by the souls*
'Twas not those souls that fled in pain,   *of the men, nor by*
Which to their corses came again,   *dæmons of earth*
But a troop of spirits blest: *or middle air,*
                                                 but by a blessed
For when it dawned — they dropped their arms,   *troop of*
And clustered round the mast;   *angelic*
Sweet sounds rose slowly through their mouths,   *spirits,*
And from their bodies passed.   *sent*
                                   down by the invocation
                                   of the guardian saint.

Around, around, flew each sweet sound,
Then darted to the Sun;   355
Slowly the sounds came back again,
Now mixed, now one by one.

Sometimes a-dropping from the sky
I heard the sky-lark sing;
Sometimes all little birds that are,   360
How they seemed to fill the sea and air
With their sweet jargoning!

And now 'twas like all instruments,
Now like a lonely flute;
And now it is an angel's song,   365
That makes the heavens be mute.

It ceased; yet still the sails made on
A pleasant noise till noon,
A noise like of a hidden brook
In the leafy month of June,   370
That to the sleeping woods all night
Singeth a quiet tune.

Till noon we quietly sailed on,
Yet never a breeze did breathe:
Slowly and smoothly went the ship,   375
Moved onward from beneath.

Under the keel nine fathom deep,   *The lonesome*
From the land of mist and snow,   *Spirit from*
The spirit slid: and it was he   *the South Pole*
That made the ship to go.   *carries on the*
The sails at noon left off their tune,   *ship as far as*
And the ship stood still also.   *the Line, in*
                                              obedience to the

The Sun, right up above the mast,   *angelic troop, but*
Had fixed her to the ocean: *still requireth*
But in a minute she 'gan stir,   *vengeance.*
With a short uneasy motion —   386
Backwards and forwards half her length
With a short uneasy motion.

Then like a pawing horse let go,
She made a sudden bound: 390
It flung the blood into my head,
And I fell down in a swound.

How long in that same fit I lay,   *The Polar Spirit's*
I have not to declare;   *fellow-dæmons, the*
But ere my living life returned,   *invisible inhabitants*
I heard and in my soul discerned   *of the element,*
Two voices in the air.   *take part in his*
                                              wrong; and two
'Is it he?' quoth one, 'Is this the man?   *of them re-*
By him who died on cross,   *late, one to*
With his cruel bow he laid full low   *the other, that*
The harmless Albatross.   *penance long*
                                              and heavy for
The spirit who bideth by himself   *the ancient*
In the land of mist and snow,   *Mariner hath*
He loved the bird that loved the man   *been accorded to*
Who shot him with his bow.'   *the Polar Spirit,*
                                              who returneth
The other was a softer voice,   *southward.*
As soft as honey-dew: 406
Quoth he, 'The man hath penance done,
And penance more will do.'

Part VI

FIRST VOICE
'But tell me, tell me! speak again,   410
Thy soft response renewing —
What makes that ship drive on so fast?
What is the ocean doing?'

SECOND VOICE
'Still as a slave before his lord,
The ocean hath no blast;   415
His great bright eye most silently
Up to the Moon is cast —

If he may know which way to go;
For she guides him smooth or grim.
See, brother, see! how graciously   420
She looketh down on him.'

---

348. corses: corpses. **362. jargoning:** warbling, twittering, chattering. **394. have not:** i.e., am unable.

FIRST VOICE

'But why drives on that ship so fast,
Without or wave or wind?'

SECOND VOICE

'The air is cut away before,
And closes from behind.

Fly, brother, fly! more high, more high!
Or we shall be belated:
For slow and slow that ship will go,
When the Mariner's trance is abated.'   429

I woke, and we were sailing on
As in a gentle weather:
'Twas night, calm night, the moon was high;
The dead men stood together.

All stood together on the deck,
For a charnel-dungeon fitter: 435
All fixed on me their stony eyes,
That in the Moon did glitter.

The pang, the curse, with which they died,
Had never passed away:
I could not draw my eyes from theirs,   440
Nor turn them up to pray.

And now this spell was snapt: once more
I viewed the ocean green,
And looked far forth, yet little saw
Of what had else been seen —   445

Like one, that on a lonesome road
Doth walk in fear and dread,
And having once turned round walks on,
And turns no more his head;
Because he knows, a frightful fiend   450
Doth close behind him tread.

But soon there breathed a wind on me,
Nor sound nor motion made:
Its path was not upon the sea,
In ripple or in shade.   455

It raised my hair, it fanned my cheek
Like a meadow-gale of spring —
It mingled strangely with my fears,
Yet it felt like a welcoming.

Swiftly, swiftly flew the ship,   460
Yet she sailed softly too:
Sweetly, sweetly blew the breeze —
On me alone it blew.

The Mariner hath been cast into a trance; for the angelic power causeth the vessel to drive northward faster than human life could endure.

The supernatural motion is retarded; the Mariner awakes, and his penance begins anew.

The curse is finally expiated.

Oh! dream of joy! is this indeed
The light-house top I see?
Is this the hill? is this the kirk?
Is this mine own countree?

We drifted o'er the harbour-bar,
And I with sobs did pray —
O let me be awake, my God!   470
Or let me sleep alway.

The harbour-bay was clear as glass,
So smoothly it was strewn!
And on the bay the moonlight lay,
And the shadow of the Moon.   475

The rock shone bright, the kirk no less,
That stands above the rock:
The moonlight steeped in silentness
The steady weathercock.

And the bay was white with silent light,   480
Till rising from the same,
Full many shapes, that shadows were,
In crimson colours came.

A little distance from the prow
Those crimson shadows were:
I turned my eyes upon the deck —
Oh, Christ! what saw I there!

Each corse lay flat, lifeless and flat,
And, by the holy rood!
A man all light, a seraph-man,   490
On every corse there stood.

This seraph-band, each waved his hand:
It was a heavenly sight!
They stood as signals to the land,
Each one a lovely light;   495

This seraph-band, each waved his hand,
No voice did they impart —
No voice; but oh! the silence sank
Like music on my heart.

But soon I heard the dash of oars,   500
I heard the Pilot's cheer;
My head was turned perforce away,
And I saw a boat appear.

The Pilot and the Pilot's boy,
I heard them coming fast: 505
Dear Lord in Heaven! it was a joy
The dead men could not blast.

And the ancient Mariner beholdeth his native country.

The angelic spirits leave the dead bodies,

And appear in their own forms of light.

I saw a third — I heard his voice:
It is the Hermit good!
He singeth loud his godly hymns   510
That he makes in the wood.
He'll shrieve my soul, he'll wash away
The Albatross's blood.

Part VII

This Hermit good lives in that wood   *The Hermit*
Which slopes down to the sea.   *of the Wood,*
How loudly his sweet voice he rears!   516
He loves to talk with marineres
That come from a far countree.

He kneels at morn, and noon, and eve —
He hath a cushion plump: 520
It is the moss that wholly hides
The rotted old oak-stump.

The skiff-boat neared: I heard them talk,
'Why, this is strange, I trow!
Where are those lights so many and fair,   525
That signal made but now?'

'Strange, by my faith!' the Hermit said —   *Approacheth*
'And they answered not our cheer!   *the ship with*
The planks looked warped! and see those sails, *wonder.*
How thin they are and sere!   530
I never saw aught like to them,
Unless perchance it were

Brown skeletons of leaves that lag
My forest-brook along;
When the ivy-tod is heavy with snow,   535
And the owlet whoops to the wolf below,
That eats the she-wolf's young.'

'Dear Lord! it hath a fiendish look —'
(The Pilot made reply)
'I am a-feared' — 'Push on, push on!'   540
Said the Hermit cheerily.

The boat came closer to the ship,
But I nor spake nor stirred;
The boat came close beneath the ship,
And straight a sound was heard.   545

Under the water it rumbled on,   *The ship*
Still louder and more dread: *suddenly*
It reached the ship, it split the bay;   *sinketh.*
The ship went down like lead.

Stunned by that loud and dreadful sound,   *The ancient*
Which sky and ocean smote,   *Mariner is*
Like one that hath been seven days drowned   *saved*
My body lay afloat;   *in the*
But swift as dreams, myself I found   *Pilot's boat.*
Within the Pilot's boat.   555

Upon the whirl, where sank the ship,
The boat spun round and round;
And all was still, save that the hill
Was telling of the sound.

I moved my lips — the Pilot shrieked   560
And fell down in a fit;
The holy Hermit raised his eyes,
And prayed where he did sit.

I took the oars: the Pilot's boy,
Who now doth crazy go,   565
Laughed loud and long, and all the while
His eyes went to and fro.
'Ha! ha!' quoth he, 'full plain I see,
The Devil knows how to row.'

And now, all in my own countree,   570
I stood on the firm land!
The Hermit stepped forth from the boat,
And scarcely he could stand.

'O shrieve me, shrieve me, holy man!'   *The ancient*
The Hermit crossed his brow.   *Mariner earnestly*
'Say quick,' quoth he, 'I bid thee say —   *entreateth the*
What manner of man art thou?'   *Hermit to*
                                             shrieve him;
Forthwith this frame of mine was wrenched   *and the*
With a woful agony,   *penance of*
Which forced me to begin my tale;   *life falls*
And then it left me free.   *on him.*
                                                  581

Since then, at an uncertain hour,   *And ever and*
That agony returns: *anon through*
And till my ghastly tale is told,   *out his future*
This heart within me burns.   *life an agony*
                                             constraineth him
I pass, like night, from land to land;   *to travel from*
I have strange power of speech;   *land to land;*
That moment that his face I see,
I know the man that must hear me:
To him my tale I teach.   590

What loud uproar bursts from that door!
The wedding-guests are there:
But in the garden-bower the bride

---

512. shrieve: shrive. **535. ivy-tod:** bushy clump of ivy.

And bride-maids singing are:
And hark the little vesper bell,   595
Which biddeth me to prayer!

O Wedding-Guest! this soul hath been
Alone on a wide wide sea:
So lonely 'twas, that God himself
Scarce seemèd there to be.   600

O sweeter than the marriage-feast,
'Tis sweeter far to me,
To walk together to the kirk
With a goodly company! —

To walk together to the kirk,   605
And all together pray,
While each to his great Father bends,
Old men, and babes, and loving friends
And youths and maidens gay!   609

Farewell, farewell! but this I tell   *And to teach,*
To thee, thou Wedding-Guest!   *by his own*
He prayeth well, who loveth well   *example, love*
Both man and bird and beast.   *and reverence*
                                          to all things
He prayeth best, who loveth best   *that God made*
All things both great and small;   *and loveth.*
For the dear God who loveth us,   616
He made and loveth all."

The Mariner, whose eye is bright,
Whose beard with age is hoar,
Is gone: and now the Wedding-Guest   620
Turned from the bridegroom's door.

He went like one that hath been stunned,
And is of sense forlorn:
A sadder and a wiser man,
He rose the morrow morn.   625

(1798, 1817)

FROST AT MIDNIGHT

The Frost performs its secret ministry,
Unhelped by any wind. The owlet's cry
Came loud — and hark, again! loud as before.
The inmates of my cottage, all at rest,

Have left me to that solitude, which suits   5
Abstruser musings: save that at my side
My cradled infant slumbers peacefully.
'Tis calm indeed! so calm, that it disturbs
And vexes meditation with its strange
And extreme silentness. Sea, hill, and wood,   10
This populous village! Sea, and hill, and wood,
With all the numberless goings-on of life,
Inaudible as dreams! the thin blue flame
Lies on my low-burnt fire, and quivers not;
Only that film, which fluttered on the grate,   15
Still flutters there, the sole unquiet thing.
Methinks, its motion in this hush of nature
Gives it dim sympathies with me who live,
Making it a companionable form,
Whose puny flaps and freaks the idling Spirit   20
By its own moods interprets, every where
Echo or mirror seeking of itself,
And makes a toy of Thought.

                    But O! how oft,
How oft, at school, with most believing mind,
Presageful, have I gazed upon the bars,   25
To watch that fluttering *stranger*! and as oft
With unclosed lids, already had I dreamt
Of my sweet birth-place, and the old church-tower,
Whose bells, the poor man's only music, rang
From morn to evening, all the hot Fair-day,   30
So sweetly, that they stirred and haunted me
With a wild pleasure, falling on mine ear
Most like articulate sounds of things to come!
So gazed I, till the soothing things, I dreamt,
Lulled me to sleep, and sleep prolonged my dreams! 35
And so I brooded all the following morn,
Awed by the stern preceptor's face, mine eye
Fixed with mock study on my swimming book:
Save if the door half opened, and I snatched
A hasty glance, and still my heart leaped up,   40
For still I hoped to see the *stranger's* face,
Townsman, or aunt, or sister more beloved,
My play-mate when we both were clothed alike!

  Dear Babe, that sleepest cradled by my side,
Whose gentle breathings, heard in this deep calm,   45

---

623. **forlorn:** bereft. 624. **sadder:** graver, more serious. **FROST AT MIDNIGHT** 7: The infant is his son Hartley (born Sept. 19, 1796). 15. **film:** i.e., flake or thread of ash or soot; "In all parts of the kingdom these films are called *strangers* and supposed to portend the arrival of some absent friend" (Coleridge's note) — see lines 26 and 41. 24. **school:** Christ's Hospital, in London. 28. **birth-place:** Ottery St. Mary, Devonshire. 37. **stern preceptor:** the "severe" teacher to whom Coleridge felt a strong indebtedness, described in the first chapter of his *Biographia Literaria* (1817): "The Rev. James Bowyer [Boyer], many years Head Master of the Grammar School, Christ's Hospital"; see also Charles Lamb's "Christ's Hospital Five and Thirty Years Ago," in *The Essays of Elia.* **42-43. sister . . . playmate:** his sister Ann.

Fill up the interspersed vacancies
And momentary pauses of the thought!
My babe so beautiful! it thrills my heart
With tender gladness, thus to look at thee,
And think that thou shalt learn far other lore,   50
And in far other scenes! For I was reared
In the great city, pent 'mid cloisters dim,
And saw nought lovely but the sky and stars.
But *thou*, my babe! shalt wander like a breeze
By lakes and sandy shores, beneath the crags   55
Of ancient mountain, and beneath the clouds,
Which image in their bulk both lakes and shores
And mountain crags: so shalt thou see and hear
The lovely shapes and sounds intelligible
Of that eternal language, which thy God   60

Utters, who from eternity doth teach
Himself in all, and all things in himself.
Great universal Teacher! he shall mould
Thy spirit, and by giving make it ask.

Therefore all seasons shall be sweet to thee,   65
Whether the summer clothe the general earth
With greenness, or the redbreast sit and sing
Betwixt the tufts of snow on the bare branch
Of mossy apple-tree, while the nigh thatch
Smokes in the sun-thaw; whether the eave-drops fall
Heard only in the trances of the blast,   71
Or if the secret ministry of frost
Shall hang them up in silent icicles,
Quietly shining to the quiet Moon.

(1798)

METRICAL FEET
Lesson for a Boy

Trṓchĕe tríps frŏm lóng tŏ shórt;
From long to long in solemn sort
Slów Spóndēe stálks; stróng fóot! yet ill able
Évĕr tŏ cóme ŭp wĭth Dáctўl trĭsýllăblĕ.
Ĭámbĭcs márch frŏm shórt tŏ lóng; —   5
Wĭth ă léap ănd ă bóund thĕ swĭft Ánăpæsts thróng;
One syllable long, with one short at each side,
Ămphíbrăchўs hástes wĭth ă státelў stríde: —
Fírst ănd lást bēĭng lóng, míddlĕ shórt, Ámphĭmácer
Stríkes hĭs thúndérĭng hóofs líke ă próud hígh-brĕd Rácer.   10
If Derwent be innocent, steady, and wise,
And delight in the things of earth, water, and skies;
Tender warmth at his heart, with these metres to show it,
With sound sense in his brains, may make Derwent a poet, —
May crown him with fame, and must win him the love   15
Of his father on earth and his Father above.
        My dear, dear child!
Could you stand upon Skiddaw, you would not from its whole ridge
See a man who so loves you as your fond S. T. COLERIDGE.

(1806ff.; 1834)

METRICAL FEET   Begun in 1806 for his son Hartley, then adapted for his other son Derwent. Coleridge uses ⁻ for "long" and ˘ for "short," as for quantitative verse; we have changed to ´ and ˘, now conventional for marking stressed verse. See the Glossary for further definitions of the various kinds of feet. **18. Skiddaw:** mountain (931 m; 3054′) in the Lake District, near Keswick.

ON DONNE'S POETRY

With Donne, whose muse on dromedary trots,
Wreathe iron pokers into true-love knots;
Rhyme's sturdy cripple, fancy's maze and clue,
Wit's forge and fire-blast, meaning's press and screw.

(1818?; 1836)

ROBERT SOUTHEY
England, 1774-1843

THE BATTLE OF BLENHEIM

It was a summer evening,
  Old Kaspar's work was done,
And he before his cottage door
  Was sitting in the sun.
And by him sported on the green   5
  His little grandchild Wilhelmine.

She saw her brother Peterkin
  Roll something large and round,
Which he beside the rivulet
  In playing there had found;   10
He came to ask what he had found,
That was so large, and smooth, and round.

Old Kaspar took it from the boy,
  Who stood expectant by;
And then the old man shook his head,   15
  And, with a natural sigh,
"'Tis some poor fellow's skull," said he,
"Who fell in the great victory.

"I find them in the garden,
  For there's many here about;   20
And often when I go to plough,

The ploughshare turns them out!
For many thousand men," said he,
"Were slain in that great victory."

"Now tell us what 'twas all about,"   25
  Young Peterkin, he cries;
And little Wilhelmine looks up
  With wonder-waiting eyes;
"Now tell us all about the war,
And what they fought each other for."   30

"It was the English," Kaspar cried,
  "Who put the French to rout;
But what they fought each other for,
  I could not well make out;
But everybody said," quoth he,   35
"That 'twas a famous victory.

"My father lived at Blenheim then,
  Yon little stream hard by;
They burnt his dwelling to the ground,
  And he was forced to fly;   40
So with his wife and child he fled,
Nor had he where to rest his head.

ON DONNE'S POETRY   Written as marginalia in an anthology of poetry. For comments on the "metaphysical" poets, see the excerpt from Johnson's life of Cowley (p. 605). For poems by Donne, see pp. 253ff.   **THE BATTLE OF BLENHEIM   Title:** The Battle of Blenheim took place on August 13, 1704, near the village of Blenheim in Western Bavaria, during the War of the Spanish Succession; John Churchill, the first Duke of Marlborough (1650-1722), leading British and Dutch troops, and Prince Eugene of Savoy (1663-1736), leading troops from Italy — who had initially opposed the British and Dutch — joined to defeat Marshal Camille Tallard (1652-1728) and the troops of France and Bavaria; the war, which was being fought to limit Louis XIV's expansion of French influence in Europe, lasted until the Peace of Utrecht in 1713, at which time Prince Eugene was made Governor of the Austrian Netherlands. See also the note to lines 111-12 of Cawthorn's *Of Taste* (p. 615).

"With fire and sword the country round
　　Was wasted far and wide,
And many a childing mother then, 　　*45*
　　And new-born baby died;
But things like that, you know, must be
At every famous victory.

"They say it was a shocking sight
　　After the field was won; 　　*50*
For many thousand bodies here
　　Lay rotting in the sun;
But things like that, you know, must be
After a famous victory.

"Great praise the Duke of Marlbro' won,
　　And our good Prince Eugene." 　　*56*
"Why 'twas a very wicked thing!"
　　Said little Wilhelmine.
"Nay, nay, my little girl," quoth he,
"It was a famous victory. 　　*60*

"And everybody praised the Duke
　　Who this great fight did win."
"But what good came of it at last?"
　　Quoth little Peterkin.
"Why that I cannot tell," said he, 　　*65*
"But 'twas a famous victory."

　　　　　　　　　　(1798)

THE OLD MAN'S COMFORTS AND HOW HE GAINED THEM

"You are old, Father William," the young man cried;
　　"The few locks which are left you are gray;
You are hale, Father William — a hearty old man:
　　Now tell me the reason, I pray."

"In the days of my youth," Father William replied, 　　*5*
　　"I remembered that youth would fly fast,
And abused not my health and my vigour at first,
　　That I never might need them at last."

"You are old, Father William," the young man cried,
　　"And pleasures with youth pass away; 　　*10*
And yet you lament not the days that are gone:
　　Now tell me the reason, I pray."

"In the days of my youth," Father William replied,
　　"I remembered that youth could not last;
I thought of the future, whatever I did, 　　*15*
　　That I never might grieve for the past."

"You are old, Father William," the young man cried,
　　"And life must be hastening away;
You are cheerful and love to converse upon death:
　　Now tell me the reason, I pray." 　　*20*

"I am cheerful, young man," Father William replied;
　　"Let the cause thy attention engage;
In the days of my youth, I remembered my God,
　　And He hath not forgotten my age."

　　　　　　　　　　(1799; 1805)

CHARLES LAMB
England, 1775-1834

from *THE ESSAYS OF ELIA*

WITCHES, AND OTHER NIGHT FEARS

We are too hasty when we set down our ancestors in the gross for fools, for the monstrous inconsistencies (as they seem to us) involved in their Creed of Witchcraft. In the relations of this visible world we find them to have been as rational and shrewd to detect an historic anomaly as ourselves. But when once the invisible world was supposed to be opened, and the lawless agency of bad spirits assumed, what measures of 　　*5* probability, of decency, of fitness, or proportion — of that which distinguishes the likely

---

45. childing: pregnant. 　**THE OLD MAN'S COMFORTS** 　See Lewis Carroll's parody of this poem (p. 1086).

from the palpable absurd — could they have to guide them in the rejection or admission of any particular testimony? — That maidens pined away, wasting inwardly as their waxen images consumed before a fire — that corn was lodged, and cattle lamed — that whirlwinds uptore in diabolic revelry the oaks of the forest — or that spits and kettles only danced a fearful innocent vagary about some rustic's kitchen when no wind was stirring — were all equally probable where no law of agency was understood. That the Prince of the Powers of Darkness, passing by the flower and pomp of the earth, should lay preposterous siege to the weak fantasy of indigent eld — has neither likelihood nor unlikelihood *a priori* to us, who have no measure to guess at his policy, or standard to estimate what rate those anile souls may fetch in the Devil's market. Nor, when the wicked are expressly symbolized by a goat, was it to be wondered at so much, that *he* should come sometimes in that body, and assert his metaphor. That the intercourse was opened at all between both worlds was perhaps the mistake; but that once assumed, I see no reason for disbelieving one attested story of this nature more than another on the score of absurdity. There is no law to judge of the lawless, or canon by which a dream may be criticized.

   I have sometimes thought that I could not have existed in the days of received witchcraft; that I could not have slept in a village where one of those reputed hags dwelt. Our ancestors were bolder, or more obtuse. Amidst the universal belief that these wretches were in league with the Author of all Evil, holding hell tributary to their muttering, no simple Justice of the Peace seems to have scrupled issuing, or silly Headborough serving, a warrant upon them — as if they should subpoena Satan! — Prospero in his boat, with his books and wand about him, suffers himself to be conveyed away at the mercy of his enemies to an unknown island. He might have raised a storm or two, we think, on the passage. His acquiescence is in exact analogy to the non-resistance of witches to the constituted Powers. What stops the Fiend in Spenser from tearing Guyon to pieces — or who had made it a condition of his prey that Guyon must take assay of the glorious bait — we have no guess. We do not know the laws of that country.

   From my childhood I was extremely inquisitive about witches and witch stories. My maid, and more legendary aunt, supplied me with good store. But I shall mention the accident which directed my curiosity originally into this channel. In my father's book closet the History of the Bible, by Stackhouse, occupied a distinguished station. The pictures with which it abounds — one of the ark, in particular, and another of Solomon's Temple, delineated with all the fidelity of ocular admeasurement, as if the artist had been upon the spot — attracted my childish attention. There was a picture, too, of the Witch raising up Samuel, which I wish that I had never seen. We shall come to that hereafter. Stackhouse is in two huge tomes; and there was a pleasure in removing folios of that magnitude, which, with infinite straining, was as much as I could manage, from the situation which they occupied upon an upper shelf. I have not met with the

10

15

20

25

30

35

40

45

WITCHES, AND OTHER NIGHT FEARS   **9. consumed:** were destroyed; **corn:** grain; **lodged:** beaten down. **14. eld:** old people. **16. anile:** like an old woman. **28. Headborough:** constable. **29. Prospero:** in Shakespeare's *The Tempest*. **33ff.:** Guyon is the hero of Book II of Spenser's *The Faerie Queene*. **39. Stackhouse:** Thomas Stackhouse (1677-1752), author of *A New History of the Holy Bible, from the Beginning of the World, to the Establishment of Christianity* (3 vols., 1737; 2nd ed., rev., 2 vols., 1742-44); its plates (which were altered in later editions) include that of the Witch of Endor raising up Samuel (see I Samuel 28).

work from that time to this; but I remember it consisted of Old Testament stories, orderly set down, with the *objection* appended to each story, and the *solution* of the objection regularly tacked to that. The *objection* was a summary of whatever difficulties had been opposed to the credibility of the history, by the shrewdness of ancient or modern infidelity, drawn up with an almost complimentary excess of candour. The *solution* was brief, modest, and satisfactory. The bane and antidote were both before you. To doubts so put, and so quashed, there seemed to be an end for ever. The Dragon lay dead, for the foot of the veriest babe to trample on. But — like as was rather feared than realized from that slain Monster in Spenser — from the womb of those crushed Errors young Dragonets would creep, exceeding the prowess of so tender a Saint George as myself to vanquish. The habit of expecting objections to every passage set me upon starting more objections, for the glory of finding a solution of my own for them. I became staggered and perplexed, a sceptic in long coats. The pretty Bible stories which I had read, or heard read in church, lost their purity and sincerity of impression, and were turned into so many historic or chronologic theses to be defended against whatever impugners. I was not to disbelieve them, but — the next thing to that — I was to be quite sure that some one or other would or had disbelieved them. Next to making a child an infidel is the letting him know that there are infidels at all. Credulity is the man's weakness, but the child's strength. O, how ugly sound Scriptural doubts from the mouth of a babe and a suckling! — I should have lost myself in these mazes, and have pined away, I think, with such unfit sustenance as these husks afforded but for a fortunate piece of ill-fortune which about this time befell me. Turning over the picture of the Ark with too much haste, I unhappily made a breach in its ingenious fabric — driving my inconsiderate fingers right through the two larger quadrupeds — the Elephant and the Camel — that stare (as well they might) out of the two last windows next the steerage in that unique piece of naval architecture. Stackhouse was henceforth locked up, and became an interdicted treasure. With the book, the *objections* and *solutions* gradually cleared out of my head, and have seldom returned since in any force to trouble me. But there was one impression which I had imbibed from Stackhouse which no lock or bar could shut out, and which was destined to try my childish nerves rather more seriously. That detestable picture!

I was dreadfully alive to nervous terrors. The night-time, solitude, and the dark, were my hell. The sufferings I endured in this nature would justify the expression. I never laid my head on my pillow, I suppose, from the fourth to the seventh or eighth year of my life — so far as memory serves in things so long ago — without an assurance, which realised its own prophecy, of seeing some frightful spectre. Be old Stackhouse then acquitted in part, if I say, that to his picture of the Witch raising up Samuel, (O that old man covered with a mantle!) I owe, not my midnight terrors, the hell of my infancy, but the shape and manner of their visitation. It was he who dressed up for me a hag that nightly sate upon my pillow — a sure bed-fellow, when my aunt or my maid was far from me. All day long, while the book was permitted me, I dreamed waking over his delineation, and at night (if I may use so bold an expression) awoke into sleep, and found the vision true. I durst not, even in the day-light, once enter the

---

54-56: See *The Faerie Queene*, I, I, 118ff. (p. 155). **59. long coats:** i.e., petticoats, long skirts worn by young children. **85. sate:** sat. **87-88. awoke . . . true:** Cf. Bunyan, *The Pilgrim's Progress*: "So I awoke, and behold it was a dream"; see also Adam's two dreams in *Paradise Lost*, and Keats's comment in his letter to Bailey (p. 857 and the note).

chamber where I slept, without my face turned to the window, aversely from the bed
where my witch-ridden pillow was. Parents do not know what they do when they leave   *90*
tender babes alone to go to sleep in the dark. The feeling about for a friendly arm, the
hoping for a familiar voice, when they wake screaming, and find none to soothe them,
what a terrible shaking it is to their poor nerves! Keeping them up till midnight, through
candle light and the unwholesome hours, as they are called, — would, I am satisfied, in
a medical point of view, prove the better caution. That detestable picture, as I have said,   *95*
gave the fashion to my dreams — if dreams they were — for the scene of them was
invariably the room in which I lay. Had I never met with the picture, the fears would
have come self-pictured in some shape or other —

> Headless bear, black man, or ape —

but, as it was, my imaginations took that form. It is not book, or picture, or the stories of   *100*
foolish servants, which create these terrors in children. They can at most but give them a
direction. Dear little T——— H——, who of all children has been brought up with the
most scrupulous exclusion of every taint of superstition — who was never allowed to
hear of goblin or apparition, or scarcely to be told of bad men, or to read or hear of any
distressing story — finds all this world of fear, from which he has been so rigidly   *105*
excluded *ab extra,* in his own "thick-coming fancies"; and from his little midnight
pillow, this nurse-child of optimism will start at shapes, unborrowed of tradition, in
sweats to which the reveries of the cell-damned murderer are tranquility.

Gorgons, and Hydras, and Chimæras dire — stories of Celæno and the Harpies —
may reproduce themselves in the brain of superstition; but they were there before. They   *110*
are transcripts, types, — the archetypes are in us, and eternal. How else should the recital
of that, which we know in a waking sense to be false, come to affect us at all? — or

> — Names, whose sense we see not,
> Fray us with things that be not?

Is it that we naturally conceive terror from such objects considered, in their capacity of   *115*
being able to inflict upon us bodily injury? O, least of all! These terrors are of older
standing. They date beyond body — or, without the body, they would have been the
same. All the cruel, tormenting, defined devils in Dante — tearing, mangling, choking,
stifling, scorching demons — are they one half so fearful to the spirit of a man as the
simple idea of a spirit unembodied following him —   *120*

> Like one that on a lonesome road
> Doth walk in fear and dread,
> And having once turn'd round, walks on
> And turns no more his head;
> Because he knows a frightful fiend   *125*
> Doth close behind him tread.

99: from "The Author's Abstract of Melancholy," prefixed to *The Anatomy of Melancholy* (1621ff.), by Robert Burton (1577-1640): "All other joys to this are folly, / None so sweet as Melancholy. / Methinks I hear, methinks I see / Ghosts, goblins, fiends: my phantasy / Presents a thousand ugly shapes, / Headless bears, black men, and apes, / Doleful outcries, and fearful sights, / My sad and dismal soul affrights" (lines 39-46). **102. T— H—:** Thornton Hunt, eldest son of Leigh Hunt. **106.** *ab extra:* (Latin) from without; **"thick-coming fancies":** *Macbeth* V.iii.38. **109.** Celæno: one of the Harpies. **113-14:** See Spenser's *Epithalamion,* 343-44 (p. 167); **fray:** frighten. **121-26:** lines 446-51 of *The Rime of the Ancient Mariner* (p. 790).

That the kind of fear here treated of is purely spiritual — that it is strong in proportion as it is objectless upon earth — that it predominates in the period of sinless infancy — are difficulties, the solution of which might afford some probable insight into our ante-mundane condition, and a peep at least into the shadowland of pre-existence. *130*

My night fancies have long ceased to be afflictive. I confess an occasional nightmare; but I do not, as in early youth, keep a stud of them. Fiendish faces, with the extinguished taper, will come and look at me; but I know them for mockeries, even while I cannot elude their presence, and I fight and grapple with them. For the credit of my imagination, I am almost ashamed to say how tame and prosaic my dreams are *135* grown. They are never romantic, seldom even rural. They are of architecture and of buildings — cities abroad, which I have never seen and hardly have hope to see. I have traversed, for the seeming length of a natural day, Rome, Amsterdam, Paris, Lisbon — their churches, palaces, squares, market-places, shops, suburbs, ruins, with an inexpressible sense of delight — a map-like distinctness of trace — and a day-light *140* vividness of vision that was all but being awake. I have formerly travelled among the Westmoreland fells — my highest Alps — but they were objects too mighty for the grasp of my dreaming recognition; and I have again and again awoke with ineffectual struggles of the "inner eye," to make out a shape in any way whatever of Helvellyn. Methought I was in that country, but that mountains were gone. The poverty of my *145* dreams mortifies me. There is Coleridge, at his will can conjure up icy domes, and pleasure-houses for Kubla Khan, and Abyssinian maids, and songs of Abara, and caverns,

> Where Alph, the sacred river, runs,

to solace his night solitudes — when I cannot muster a fiddle. Barry Cornwall has his *150* Tritons and his Nereids gamboling before him in nocturnal visions, and proclaiming sons born to Neptune — when my stretch of imaginative activity can hardly in the night season raise up the ghost of a fish-wife. To set my failures in somewhat a mortifying light — it was after reading the noble "Dream" of this poet, that my fancy ran strong upon these marine spectra; and the poor plastic power, such as it is, within me set to *155* work to humour my folly in a sort of dream that very night. Methought I was upon the ocean billows at some sea nuptials, riding and mounted high, with the customary train sounding their conchs, before me (I myself you may be sure the *leading god*), and jollily we went cantering over the main, till just where Ino Leucothea should have greeted me (I think it was Ino) with a white embrace, the billows gradually subsiding, fell from a *160* sea roughness to a sea calm, and thence to a river motion, and that river (as happens in the familiarization of dreams) was no other than the gentle Thames, which landed me in the wafture of a placid wave or two, safe and inglorious, somewhere at the foot of Lambeth Palace.

The degree of the soul's creativeness in sleep might furnish no whimsical criterion *165* of the quantum of poetical faculty resident in the same soul waking. An old gentleman,

---

142. Westmoreland fells: hills, mountains, high moorland, in the county of Westmoreland, in the Lake District (now part of Cumbria). **144. Helvellyn:** a mountain in the Lake District, just north of Grasmere. **146-49:** See "Kubla Khan" (p. 783). **150. Barry Cornwall:** pseudonym of Bryan Waller Procter (1787-1874), popular English poet and friend of Lamb's. **159. Ino Leucothea:** "white goddess" of the sea. **164. Lambeth Palace:** since the 12th century, the official London residence of the Archbishop of Canterbury, on the Thames across from the Houses of Parliament.

a friend of mine, and a humourist, used to carry this notion so far, that when he saw any stripling of his acquaintance ambitious of becoming a poet, his first question would be — "Young man, what sort of dreams have you?" I have so much faith in my old friend's theory, that when I feel that idle vein returning upon me, I presently subside into my proper element of prose, remembering those eluding nereids, and that inauspicious inland landing.   *170*

(1821)

WALTER SAVAGE LANDOR
England, 1775-1864

ROSE AYLMER

Ah what avails the sceptred race,
  Ah what the form divine!
What every virtue, every grace!
  Rose Aylmer, all were thine.
Rose Aylmer, whom these wakeful eyes   *5*
  May weep, but never see,
A night of memories and of sighs
  I consecrate to thee.

(1806)

THE GEORGES

George the First was always reckoned
Vile, but viler George the Second;
And what mortal ever heard
Any good of George the Third?
When from earth the Fourth descended   *5*
(God be praised!) the Georges ended.

(1855)

A FOREIGN RULER

He says, *My reign is peace,* so slays
  A thousand in the dead of night.
Are you all happy now? he says,
  And those he leaves behind cry *quite.*
He swears he will have no contention,   *5*
  And sets all nations by the ears;
He shouts aloud, *No intervention!*
  Invades, and drowns them all in tears.

(1863)

WILLIAM HAZLITT
England, 1778-1830

ON FAMILIAR STYLE

It is not easy to write a familiar style. Many people mistake a familiar for a vulgar style, and suppose that to write without affectation is to write at random. On the contrary, there is nothing that requires more precision, and, if I may so say, purity of expression,

---

ROSE AYLMER   Rose Aylmer (1779-1800) was the daughter of Henry, Baron Aylmer, who befriended Landor in Wales in the 1790s; Landor, who had accompanied Rose on walks near Swansea, wrote the poem after hearing of her death in India.

than the style I am speaking of. It utterly rejects not only all unmeaning pomp, but all low, cant phrases, and loose, unconnected, *slipshod* allusions. It is not to take the first word that offers, but the best word in common use; it is not to throw words together in any combinations we please, but to follow and avail ourselves of the true idiom of the language. To write a genuine familiar or truly English style, is to write as any one would speak in common conversation who had a thorough command and choice of words, or who could discourse with ease, force, and perspicuity, setting aside all pedantic and oratorical flourishes. Or, to give another illustration, to write naturally is the same thing in regard to common conversation as to read naturally is in regard to common speech. It does not follow that it is an easy thing to give the true accent and inflection to the words you utter, because you do not attempt to rise above the level of ordinary life and colloquial speaking. You do not assume, indeed, the solemnity of the pulpit, or the tone of stage-declamation; neither are you at liberty to gabble on at a venture, without emphasis or discretion, or to resort to vulgar dialect or clownish pronunciation. You must steer a middle course. You are tied down to a given and appropriate articulation, which is determined by the habitual associations between sense and sound, and which you can only hit by entering into the author's meaning, as you must find the proper words and style to express yourself by fixing your thoughts on the subject you have to write about. Any one may mouth out a passage with a theatrical cadence, or get upon stilts to tell his thoughts; but to write or speak with propriety and simplicity is a more difficult task. Thus it is easy to affect a pompous style, to use a word twice as big as the thing you want to express: it is not so easy to pitch upon the very word that exactly fits it. Out of eight or ten words equally common, equally intelligible, with nearly equal pretensions, it is a matter of some nicety and discrimination to pick out the very one the preferableness of which is scarcely perceptible, but decisive. The reason why I object to Dr. Johnson's style is that there is no discrimination, no selection, no variety in it. He uses none but "tall, opaque words," taken from the "first row of the rubric" — words with the greatest number of syllables, or Latin phrases with merely English terminations. If a fine style depended on this sort of arbitrary pretension, it would be fair to judge of an author's elegance by the measurement of his words and the substitution of foreign circumlocutions (with no precise associations) for the mother-tongue. How simple is it to be dignified without ease, to be pompous without meaning! Surely, it is but a mechanical rule for avoiding what is low, to be always pedantic and affected. It is clear you cannot use a vulgar English word if you never use a common English word at all. A fine tact is shewn in adhering to those which are perfectly common, and yet never falling into any expressions which are debased by disgusting circumstances, or which owe their signification and point to technical or professional allusions. A truly natural or familiar style can never be quaint or vulgar, for this reason, that it is of universal force

---

ON FAMILIAR STYLE　**29:** For Johnson, see p. 589. **30. "tall, opaque words":** In *The Life and Opinions of Tristram Shandy, Gentleman* (1759-67), by Laurence Sterne (1713-1768), the narrator observes: "I hate set dissertations, — and above all things in the world, 'tis one of the silliest things in one of them, to darken your hypothesis by placing a number of tall, opaque words, one before another, in a right line, betwixt your own and your reader's conception" (Vol. III, Ch. XX, "The Author's Preface"); **"first . . . rubric":** The phrase is from Pope's edition (1725, following the 1676 quarto) of Shakespeare's *Hamlet*, II, ii (just before the players enter) — but Hazlitt likely intends the word *rubric* (which refers to words printed oversize or in red) to reiterate the idea of "tall, opaque." **34. mother-tongue:** At this point Hazlitt inserts a footnote: "I have heard of such a thing as an author who makes it a rule never to admit a monosyllable into his vapid verse. Yet the charm and sweetness of Marlowe's lines depended often on their being made up almost entirely of monosyllables." (For Marlowe, see p. 226.)

and applicability, and that quaintness and vulgarity arise out of the immediate connection of certain words with coarse and disagreeable, or with confined ideas. The last form what we understand by *cant* or *slang* phrases. — To give an example of what is not very clear in the general statement. I should say that the phrase *To cut with a* *45* *knife*, or *To cut a piece of wood*, is perfectly free from vulgarity, because it is perfectly common; but to *cut an acquaintance* is not quite unexceptionable, because it is not perfectly common or intelligible, and has hardly yet escaped out of the limits of slang phraseology. I should hardly, therefore, use the word in this sense without putting it in italics as a license of expression, to be received *cum grano salis*. All provincial or bye- *50* phrases come under the same mark of reprobation — all such as the writer transfers to the page from his fireside or a particular *coterie*, or that he invents for his own sole use and convenience. I conceive that words are like money, not the worse for being common, but that it is the stamp of custom alone that gives them circulation or value. I am fastidious in this respect, and would almost as soon coin the currency of the realm as *55* counterfeit the King's English. I never invented or gave a new and unauthorised meaning to any word but one single one (the term *impersonal* applied to feelings), and that was in an abstruse metaphysical discussion to express a very difficult distinction. I have been (I know) loudly accused of revelling in vulgarisms and broken English. I cannot speak to that point; but so far I plead guilty to the determined use of *60* acknowledged idioms and common elliptical expressions. I am not sure that the critics in question know the one from the other, that is, can distinguish any medium between formal pedantry and the most barbarous solecism. As an author I endeavour to employ plain words and popular modes of construction, as, were I a chapman and dealer, I should common weights and measures. *65*

The proper force of words lies not in the words themselves, but in their application. A word may be a fine-sounding word, of an unusual length, and very imposing from its learning and novelty, and yet in the connection in which it is introduced may be quite pointless and irrelevant. It is not pomp or pretension, but the adaptation of the expression to the idea, that clenches a writer's meaning: — as it is not the size or *70* glossiness of the materials, but their being fitted each to its place, that gives strength to the arch; or as the pegs and nails are as necessary to the support of the building as the larger timbers, and more so than the mere shewy, unsubstantial ornaments. I hate anything that occupies more space than it is worth. I hate to see a load of band-boxes go along the street, and I hate to see a parcel of big words without anything in them. A *75* person who does not deliberately dispose of all his thoughts alike in cumbrous draperies and flimsy disguises, may strike out twenty varieties of familiar every-day language, each coming somewhat nearer to the feeling he wants to convey, and at last not hit upon that particular and only one which may be said to be identical with the exact impression in his mind. This would seem to shew that Mr. Cobbett is hardly right in saying that the *80* first word that occurs is always the best. It may be a very good one; and yet a better may present itself on reflection or from time to time. It should be suggested naturally,

---

47. cut: i.e., "snub" (still considered informal). **50. cum grano salis**: (Latin) with a grain of salt. **57. impersonal**: in "An Essay on the Principles of Human Action" (1805), where he uses the word to mean "disinterested." **58-59. I have been . . . English**: In its review of the first Volume of *Table-Talk*, the *Quarterly Review* of October 1821 called him a "Slang-Whanger"; "On Familiar Style" appeared in the second Volume of *Table-Talk*. **64. chapman and dealer**: peddler and tradesman. **80. Cobbett**: William Cobbett (1763-1835), reformer and journalist; he states this principle in *A Grammar of the English Language* (1818).

however, and spontaneously, from a fresh and lively conception of the subject. We seldom succeed by trying at improvement, or by merely substituting one word for another that we are not satisfied with, as we cannot recollect the name of a place or person by merely plaguing ourselves about it. We wander farther from the point by persisting in a wrong scent; but it starts up accidentally in the memory when we least expected it, by touching some link in the chain of previous association. *85*

There are those who hoard up and make a cautious display of nothing but rich and rare phraseology — ancient medals, obscure coins, and Spanish pieces of eight. They are very curious to inspect, but I myself would neither offer nor take them in the course of exchange. A sprinkling of archaisms is not amiss, but a tissue of obsolete expressions is more fit *for keep than wear*. I do not say I would not use any phrase that had been brought into fashion before the middle or the end of the last century, but I should be shy of using any that had not been employed by any approved author during the whole of that time. Words, like clothes, get old-fashioned, or mean and ridiculous, when they have been for some time laid aside. Mr. Lamb is the only imitator of old English style I can read with pleasure; and he is so thoroughly imbued with the spirit of his authors that the idea of imitation is almost done away. There is an inward unction, a marrowy vein, both in the thought and feeling, an intuition, deep and lively, of his subject, that carries off any quaintness or awkwardness arising from an antiquated style and dress. The matter is completely his own, though the manner is assumed. Perhaps his ideas are altogether so marked and individual as to require their point and pungency to be neutralised by the affectation of a singular but traditional form of conveyance. Tricked out in the prevailing costume, they would probably seem more startling and out of the way. The old English authors, Burton, Fuller, Coryate, Sir Thomas Browne, are a kind of mediators between us and the more eccentric and whimsical modern, reconciling us to his peculiarities. I do not, however, know how far this is the case or not, till he condescends to write like one of us. I must confess that what I like best of his papers under the signature of Elia (still I do not presume, amidst such excellence, to decide what is most excellent) is the account of "Mrs. Battle's Opinions on Whist," which is also the most free from obsolete allusions and turns of expression — *90* *95* *100* *105* *110*

"A well of native English undefiled."

To those acquainted with his admired prototypes, these *Essays* of the ingenious and highly gifted author have the same sort of charm and relish that Erasmus's *Colloquies* or a fine piece of modern Latin have to the classical scholar. Certainly, I do not know any borrowed pencil that has more power or felicity of execution than the one of which I have here been speaking. *115*

It is as easy to write a gaudy style without ideas as it is to spread a pallet of shewy colours or to smear in a flaunting transparency. "What do you read?" "Words, words, words." — "What is the matter?" "*Nothing*," it might be answered. The florid style is the *120*

97ff. Lamb: Charles Lamb (see p. 795); Elia (110) was the name he adopted as the writer of many of his essays; "Mrs. Battle's Opinions on Whist" (111) is one of the better known of *The Essays of Elia*. **106.** Robert Burton (1577-1640), author of *The Anatomy of Melancholy* (1621); Thomas Fuller (1608-1661), author of *The Holy State and the Profane State* (1642) and *The History of the Worthies of England* (1662); Thomas Coryate (c.1577-1617), author of *Coryats Crudities* (1611); Sir Thomas Browne (1605-1682), author of *Religio Medici* (and see p. 309). **113:** Spenser in *The Faerie Queene* refers to "Dan *Chaucer*, well of English undefyled" (Book IV, Canto II, stanza 32). **115. Erasmus's *Colloquies*:** For an example, see p. 389. **120. transparency:** picture painted or impressed on thin cloth, glass, or porcelain, viewed by artificial or natural light shining through it. **120-21:** See *Hamlet* II.ii.193-95.

reverse of the familiar. The last is employed as an unvarnished medium to convey ideas; the first is resorted to as a spangled veil to conceal the want of them. When there is nothing to be set down but words, it costs little to have them fine. Look through the dictionary, and cull out a *florilegium*, rival the *tulippomania*. *Rouge* high enough, and *125* never mind the natural complexion. The vulgar, who are not in the secret, will admire the look of preternatural health and vigour; and the fashionable, who regard only appearances, will be delighted with the imposition. Keep to your sounding generalities, your tinkling phrases, and all will be well. Swell out an unmeaning truism to a perfect tympany of style. A thought, a distinction is the rock on which all this brittle cargo of *130* verbiage splits at once. Such writers have merely *verbal* imaginations, that retain nothing but words. Or their puny thoughts have dragon-wings, all green and gold. They soar far above the vulgar failing of the *Sermo humi obrepens* — their most ordinary speech is never short of an hyperbole, splendid, imposing, vague, incomprehensible, magniloquent, a cento of sounding common-places. If some of us, whose "ambition is more lowly," pry *135* a little too narrowly into nooks and corners to pick up a number of "unconsidered trifles," they never once direct their eyes or lift their hands to seize on any but the most gorgeous, tarnished, thread-bare, patch-work set of phrases, the left-off finery of poetic extravagance, transmitted down through successive generations of barren pretenders. If they criticise actors and actresses, a huddled phantasmagoria of feathers, spangles, floods *140* of light, and oceans of sound float before their morbid sense, which they paint in the style of Ancient Pistol. Not a glimpse can you get of the merits or defects of the performers: they are hidden in a profusion of barbarous epithets and wilful rhodomontade. Our hypercritics are not thinking of these little fantoccini beings —

"That strut and fret their hour upon the stage —" *145*

but of tall phantoms of words, abstractions, *genera* and *species*, sweeping clauses, periods that unite the Poles, forced alliterations, astounding antitheses —

"And on their pens *Fustian* sits plumed."

If they describe kings and queens, it is an Eastern pageant. The Coronation at either House is nothing to it. We get at four repeated images — a curtain, a throne, a sceptre, and a foot- *150* stool. These are with them the wardrobe of a lofty imagination; and they turn their servile strains to servile uses. Do we read a description of pictures? It is not a reflection of tones and hues which "nature's own sweet and cunning hand laid on," but piles of precious stones, rubies, pearls, emeralds, Golconda's mines, and all the blazonry of art. Such persons are in fact besotted with words, and their brains are turned with the glittering but *155* empty and sterile phantoms of things. Personifications, capital letters, seas of sunbeams, visions of glory, shining inscriptions, the figures of a transparency, Britannia with her shield, or Hope leaning on an anchor, make up their stock-in-trade. They may be

125. *florilegium*: a collection of flowers; *tulippomania*: tulipomania, a craze for tulips (referring especially to that in 17th-century Holland). 133. *Sermo humi obrepens*: (Latin) speech creeping on the ground. 135. cento: literary patchwork; "ambition . . . lowly": Cf. lines 584-93 of Cowper's *Table-Talk* (1782), which refer to language in Eden being "Elegant as simplicity, and warm / As ecstasy, unmanacled by form, / Not prompted, as in our degen'rate days, / By low ambition and the thirst of praise. . . . " 136. "unconsidered trifles": Shakespeare, *The Winter's Tale* IV.iii.26. 141-42. style . . . Pistol: i.e., bombastic (see note to Fielding's *Covent-Garden Journal* No. 33, line 36 — p. 585). 143. rhodomontade: rodomontade — boasting, blustering, ranting. 144. fantoccini beings: puppets. 145: Cf. *Macbeth* V.v.25. 147. periods: long and elaborate sentences full of balanced elements. 148: probably adapting *Paradise Lost*, IV, 988-89, describing Satan: "and on his crest / Sat horror plumed." 153. "nature's . . . on": Shakespeare, *Twelfth Night* I.v.242.

considered as *hieroglyphical* writers. Images stand out in their minds isolated and important merely in themselves, without any ground-work of feeling — there is no context 160 in their imaginations. Words affect them in the same way, by the mere sound, that is, by their possible, not by their actual application to the subject in hand. They are fascinated by first appearances, and have no sense of consequences. Nothing more is meant by them than meets the ear: they understand or feel nothing more than meets their eye. The web and texture of the universe, and of the heart of man, is a mystery to them: they have no 165 faculty that strikes a chord in unison with it. They cannot get beyond the daubings of fancy, the varnish of sentiment. Objects are not linked to feelings, words to things, but images revolve in splendid mockery, words represent themselves in their strange rhapsodies. The categories of such a mind are pride and ignorance — pride in outside show, to which they sacrifice everything, and ignorance of the true worth and hidden 170 structure both of words and things. With a sovereign contempt for what is familiar and natural, they are the slaves of vulgar affectation — of a routine of high-flown phrases. Scorning to imitate realities, they are unable to invent anything, to strike out one original idea. They are not copyists of nature, it is true; but they are the poorest of all plagiarists, the plagiarists of words. All is far-fetched, dear bought, artificial, oriental in subject and 175 allusion; all is mechanical, conventional, vapid, formal, pedantic in style and execution. They startle and confound the understanding of the reader by the remoteness and obscurity of their illustrations; they soothe the ear by the monotony of the same everlasting round of circuitous metaphors. They are the *mock-school* in poetry and prose. They flounder about between fustian in expression and bathos in sentiment. They tantalise the fancy, but never 180 reach the head nor touch the heart. Their Temple of Fame is like a shadowy structure raised by Dulness to Vanity, or like Cowper's description of the Empress of Russia's palace of ice, "as worthless as in show 'twas glittering" —

> "It smiled, and it was cold!"

(1821)

JOHN GALT
Scotland/Canada, 1779-1839

CANADIAN BOAT SONG

Listen to me, as when ye heard our father
  Sing long ago the song of other shores —
Listen to me, and then in chorus gather
  All your deep voices, as ye pull your oars:
    Fair these broad meads — these hoary woods are grand;   5
    But we are exiles from our fathers' land.

183-84: adapted from Cowper's *The Task* (1785): "'Twas transient in its nature, as in show / 'Twas durable: as worthless, as it seem'd / Intrinsically precious; to the foot / Treach'rous and false; it smil'd, and it was cold" (V, 173-76). **CANADIAN BOAT SONG** Usually attributed to Galt, this song first appeared anonymously in *Blackwood's Magazine*, Edinburgh; some evidence, however, suggests that it may have been written by Galt's friend, David MacBeth Moir (1798-1851).

From the lone shieling of the misty island
    Mountains divide us, and the waste of seas —
Yet still the blood is strong, the heart is Highland,
    And we in dreams behold the Hebrides.   *10*
    Fair these broad meads — these hoary woods are grand;
    But we are exiles from our fathers' land.

We ne'er shall tread the fancy-haunted valley
    Where 'tween the dark hills creeps the small clear stream,
In arms around the patriarch banner rally,   *15*
    Nor see the moon on royal tombstones gleam.
    Fair these broad meads — these hoary woods are grand;
    But we are exiles from our fathers' land.

When the bold kindred, in the time long vanished,
    Conquered the soil and fortified the keep,   *20*
No seer foretold the children would be banished,
    That a degenerate lord might boast his sheep.
    Fair these broad meads — these hoary woods are grand;
    But we are exiles from our fathers' land.

Come foreign rage, let discord burst in slaughter!   *25*
    O! then, for clansmen true, and stern claymore —
The hearts that would have given their blood like water
    Beat heavily beyond the Atlantic roar.
    Fair these broad meads — these hoary woods are grand;
    But we are exiles from our fathers' land.   *30*

(1829)

THOMAS MOORE
Ireland, 1779-1852

A CANADIAN BOAT SONG

Faintly as tolls the evening chime,
Our voices keep tune and our oars keep time.
Soon as the woods on shore look dim,
We'll sing at St. Ann's our parting hymn.
Row, brothers, row, the stream runs fast,   *5*
The Rapids are near and the daylight's past.

Why should we not our sail unfurl?
There is not a breath the blue wave to curl,
But when the wind blows off the shore,
Oh, sweetly we'll rest our weary oar.   *10*
Row, brothers, row, the stream runs fast,
The Rapids are near and the daylight's past.

---

7. shieling: rural cottage. **22. boast his sheep:** the Enclosure Acts of the late 18th and early 19th centuries (see Goldsmith, p. 645) led in Scotland to the expansion of estate boundaries and the consequent removal of many families from their homes in the grazing lands of the Highlands; referred to as the Clearances, this forced relocation compelled many Scots to emigrate to Canada and elsewhere. **26. claymore:** Highlander's broad two-edged sword.   **A CANADIAN BOAT SONG   4. St. Ann's:** the church at Ste. Anne-de-Bellevue, on the Ile-de-Montréal and just opposite Ile-Perrot (line 15), where the Ottawa River (see line 13) joins the St. Lawrence River.

Utawas' tide! this trembling noon
Shall see us float on thy surges soon.
Saint of this green isle! hear our prayers,   *15*
Oh, grant us cool heavens and favouring airs.
Row, brothers, row, the stream runs fast,
The Rapids are near and the daylight's past.

                                        (1804)

THE HARP THAT ONCE THROUGH TARA'S HALLS

The harp that once through Tara's halls
  The soul of music shed,
Now hangs as mute on Tara's walls
  As if that soul were fled. —
So sleeps the pride of former days,   *5*
  So glory's thrill is o'er,
And hearts that once beat high for praise
  Now feel that pulse no more.

No more to chiefs and ladies bright
  The harp of Tara swells;   *10*
The chord alone that breaks at night
  Its tale of ruin tells.
Thus Freedom now so seldom wakes,
  The only throb she gives
Is when some heart indignant breaks,   *15*
  To shew that still she lives.

'TIS THE LAST ROSE OF SUMMER

'Tis the last rose of summer,
  Left blooming alone;
All her lovely companions
  Are faded and gone;
No flower of her kindred,   *5*
  No rose-bud is nigh,
To reflect back her blushes,
  Or give sigh for sigh!

I'll not leave thee, thou lone one!
  To pine on the stem;   *10*
Since the lovely are sleeping,
  Go, sleep thou with them.
Thus kindly I scatter
  Thy leaves o'er the bed,
Where thy mates of the garden   *15*
  Lie scentless and dead.

So soon may *I* follow,
  When friendships decay,
And from Love's shining circle
  The gems drop away!   *20*
When true hearts lie withered,
  And fond ones are flown,
Oh! who would inhabit
  This bleak world alone?

FRANCES TROLLOPE
England, 1780-1863

from *DOMESTIC MANNERS OF THE AMERICANS*

Had I passed as many evenings in company in any other town that I ever visited as I did in Cincinnati, I should have been able to give some little account of the conversations I had listened to; but, upon reading over my notes, and then taxing my memory to the utmost to supply the deficiency, I can scarcely find a trace of any thing that deserves the name. Such as I have, shall be given in their place. But, whatever may be the talents of   *5* the persons who meet together in society, the very shape, form, and arrangement of the meeting is sufficient to paralyze conversation. The women invariably herd together at one part of the room, and the men at the other; but, in justice to Cincinnati, I must

---

THE HARP THAT ONCE   1. Tara: the ancient fortress of Irish kings.   **'TIS THE LAST ROSE   14. leaves:** petals. Both songs, "The Harp that Once" and "The Last Rose of Summer," appeared in *Irish Melodies* (published 1808-34).

acknowledge that this arrangement is by no means peculiar to that city, or to the western
side of the Alleghanies. Sometimes a small attempt at music produces a partial reunion;   *10*
a few of the most daring youths, animated by the consciousness of curled hair and smart
waistcoats, approach the piano-forte, and begin to mutter a little to the half-grown
pretty things, who are comparing with one another "how many quarters' music they
have had." Where the mansion is of sufficient dignity to have two drawing-rooms, the
piano, the little ladies, and the slender gentlemen are left to themselves, and on such   *15*
occasions the sound of laughter is often heard to issue from among them. But the fate of
the more dignified personages, who are left in the other room, is extremely dismal. The
gentlemen spit, talk of elections and the price of produce, and spit again. The ladies look
at each other's dresses till they know every pin by heart; talk of Parson Somebody's last
sermon on the day of judgment, on Dr. T'otherbody's new pills for dyspepsia, till the   *20*
"tea" is announced, when they all console themselves together for whatever they may
have suffered in keeping awake, by taking more tea, coffee, hot cake and custard, hoe
cake, johnny cake, waffle cake, and dodger cake, pickled peaches, and preserved
cucumbers, ham, turkey, hung beef, apple sauce, and pickled oysters than ever were
prepared in any other country of the known world. After this massive meal is over, they   *25*
return to the drawing-room, and it always appeared to me that they remained together as
long as they could bear it, and then they rise *en masse*, cloak, bonnet, shawl, and exit.

                                                                                (1832)

MARY SOMERVILLE
Scotland/England, 1780-1872

from *PERSONAL RECOLLECTIONS,*
FROM EARLY LIFE TO OLD AGE

                                    . . . .

When I was between eight and nine years old, my father came home from sea, and was
shocked to find me such a savage. I had not yet been taught to write, and although I
amused myself reading the "Arabian Nights," "Robinson Crusoe," and the "Pilgrim's
Progress," I read very badly, and with a strong Scotch accent; so, besides a chapter of
the Bible, he made me read a paper of the "Spectator" aloud every morning, after   *5*
breakfast; the consequence of which discipline is that I have never since opened that
book. Hume's "History of England" was also a real penance to me. I gladly accom-

---

DOMESTIC MANNERS **10. Alleghanies:** The Allegheny Mountains form one range within the Appalachian mountain chain. **13. quarters:** school terms. **22-23. hoe-cake . . . dodger cake:** four varieties of cornmeal and griddle cakes. **PERSONAL RECOLLECTIONS** The title page continues: "of Mary Somerville. With Selections from Her Correspondence. By Her Daughter, Martha Somerville." It was published the year after Mary Somerville's death. **3-4:** *Arabian Nights' Entertainments* (or *The Thousand and One Nights*) had appeared in an anonymous English translation early in the 18th century; Defoe's *Robinson Crusoe* was published in 1719; For excerpts from Bunyan's *Pilgrim's Progress,* see p. 416. **5:** For *The Spectator,* see p. 490. **7:** *The History of Great Britain,* by David Hume (1711-1776), appeared from 1754 to 1762.

panied my father when he cultivated his flowers, which even now I can say were of the best quality. The tulips and other bulbous plants, ranunculi, anemones, carnations, as well as the annuals then known, were all beautiful. He used to root up and throw away 10 many plants I thought very beautiful; he said he did so because the colours of their petals were not sharply defined, and that they would spoil the seed of the others. Thus I learnt to know the good and the bad — how to lay carnations, and how to distinguish between the leaf and fruit buds in pruning fruit trees; this kind of knowledge was of no practical use, for, as my after-life was spent in towns, I never had a garden, to my great 15 regret.

· · · ·

My father at last said to my mother, — "This kind of life will never do, Mary must at least know how to write and keep accounts." So at ten years old I was sent to a boarding-school, kept by a Miss Primrose, at Musselburgh, where I was utterly wretched. The change from perfect liberty to perpetual restraint was in itself a great 20 trial; besides, being naturally shy and timid, I was afraid of strangers, and although Miss Primrose was not unkind she had an habitual frown, which even the elder girls dreaded. My future companions, who were all older than I, came round me like a swarm of bees, and asked if my father had a title, what was the name of our estate, if we kept a carriage, and other such questions, which made me first feel the difference of station. However, 25 the girls were very kind, and often bathed my eyes to prevent our stern mistress from seeing that I was perpetually in tears. A few days after my arrival, although perfectly straight and well-made, I was enclosed in stiff stays with a steel busk in front, while, above my frock, bands drew my shoulders back till the shoulder-blades met. Then a steel rod, with a semi-circle which went under the chin, was clasped to the steel busk in 30 my stays. In this constrained state I, and most of the younger girls, had to prepare our lessons. The chief thing I had to do was to learn by heart a page of Johnson's dictionary, not only to spell the words, give their parts of speech and meaning, but as an exercise of memory to remember their order of succession. Besides I had to learn the first principles of writing, and the rudiments of French and English grammar. The method of teaching 35 was extremely tedious and inefficient. Our religious duties were attended to in a remarkable way. Some of the girls were Presbyterians, others belonged to the Church of England, so Miss Primrose cut the matter short by taking us all to the kirk in the morning and to church in the afternoon.

In our play-hours we amused ourselves with playing at ball, marbles, and especially 40 at "Scotch and English," a game which represented a raid on the debatable land, or Border between Scotland and England, in which each party tried to rob the other of their playthings. The little ones were always compelled to be English, for the bigger girls thought it too degrading.

· · · ·

There was great political agitation at this time. The corruption and tyranny of the 45 court, nobility, and clergy in France were so great, that when the revolution broke out, a large portion of our population thought the French people were perfectly justified in revolting, and warmly espoused their cause. Later many changed their opinions,

---

13. lay: layer. **19. Musselburgh:** near Edinburgh. **32. Johnson's dictionary:** See p. 597.

shocked, as every one was, at the death of the king and queen, and the atrocious massacres which took place in France. Yet some not only approved of the revolution abroad, but were so disgusted with our mal-administration at home, to which they attributed our failure in the war in Holland and elsewhere, that great dissatisfaction and alarm prevailed throughout the country. The violence, on the other hand, of the opposite party was not to be described, — the very name of Liberal was detested.   50

Great dissensions were caused by difference of opinion in families; and I heard people previously much esteemed accused from this cause of all that was evil. My uncle William and my father were as violent Tories as any.   55

The Liberals were distinguished by wearing their hair short, and when one day I happened to say how becoming a crop was, and that I wished the men would cut off those ugly pigtails, my father exclaimed, "By G—, when a man cuts off his queue, the head should go with it."   60

The unjust and exaggerated abuse of the Liberal party made me a Liberal. From my earliest years my mind revolted against oppression and tyranny, and I resented the injustice of the world in denying all those privileges of education to my sex which were so lavishly bestowed on men.   65

. . . .

When we returned to Hanover Square, I devoted my morning hours, as usual, to domestic affairs; but now my children occupied a good deal of my time. Although still very young, I thought it advisable for them to acquire foreign languages; so I engaged a French nursery-maid, that they might never suffer what I had done from ignorance of modern languages. I besides gave them instruction in such things as I was capable of teaching, and which were suited to their age.   70

It was a great amusement to Somerville and myself to arrange the minerals we had collected during our journey. Our cabinet was now very rich. Some of our specimens we had bought; our friends had given us duplicates of those they possessed; and George Finlayson, who was with our troops in Ceylon, and who had devoted all his spare time to the study of the natural productions of the country, sent us a valuable collection of crystals of sapphire, ruby, oriental topaz, amethyst, &c., &c. Somerville used to analyze minerals with the blowpipe, which I never did. One evening, when he was so occupied, I was playing the piano, when suddenly I fainted; he was very much startled, as neither I nor any of our family had ever done such a thing. When I recovered, I said it was the smell of garlic that had made me ill. The truth was, the mineral contained arsenic, and I was poisoned for the time by the fumes.   75   80

. . . .

Though still occasionally occupied with the mineral productions of the earth, I became far more interested in the formation of the earth itself. Geologists had excited public attention, and had shocked the clergy and the more scrupulous of the laity by   85

---

49. **the death . . . queen:** Louis XVI was guillotined 21 January 1793, and his queen Marie Antoinette 16 October 1793. 66. **Hanover Square:** They had moved to London in 1816, when her second husband, Dr. William Somerville, was appointed to the Army Medical Board; they are returning from an extended trip to the Continent. 67. **children:** There were two sons from her first marriage, but here she is probably speaking of her daughters. 74-75. **George Finlayson:** (1790-1823) English naturalist and traveller, clerk to Dr. Somerville. 78. **blowpipe:** tube for directing a stream of air or gas (such as a mixture of oxygen and hydrogen) through a flame to focus and increase its heating action, e.g. to vaporize mineral specimens.

proving beyond a doubt that the formation of the globe extended through enormous periods of time. The contest was even more keen then than it is at the present time about the various races of pre-historic men. It lasted very long, too; for after I had published my work on Physical Geography, I was preached against by name in York Cathedral. Our friend, Dr. Buckland, committed himself by taking the clerical view in his "Bridgewater Treatise;" but facts are such stubborn things, that he was obliged to join the geologists at last.

. . . .

We went frequently to see Mr. Babbage while he was making his Calculating-machines. He had a transcendant intellect, unconquerable perseverance, and extensive knowledge on many subjects, besides being a first-rate mathematician. I always found him most amiable and patient in explaining the structure and use of the engines. The first he made could only perform arithmetical operations. Not satisfied with that, Mr. Babbage constructed an analytical engine, which could be so arranged as to perform all kinds of mathematical calculations, and print each result.

Nothing has afforded me so convincing a proof of the unity of the Deity as these purely mental conceptions of numerical and mathematical science which have been by slow degrees vouchsafed to man, and are still granted in these latter times by the Differential Calculus, now superseded by the Higher Algebra, all of which must have existed in that sublimely omniscient Mind from eternity.

Many of our friends had very decided and various religious opinions, but my husband and I never entered into controversy; we had too high a regard for liberty of conscience to interfere with any one's opinions, so we have lived on terms of sincere friendship and love with people who differed essentially from us in religious views, and in all the books which I have written I have confined myself strictly and entirely to scientific subjects, although my religious opinions are very decided.

. . . .

The British laws are adverse to women; and we are deeply indebted to Mr. Stuart Mill for daring to show their iniquity and injustice. The law in the United States is in some respects even worse, insulting the sex, by granting suffrage to the newly-emancipated slaves, and refusing it to the most highly-educated women of the Republic.

. . . .

Age has not abated my zeal for the emancipation of my sex from the unreasonable prejudice too prevalent in Great Britain against a literary and scientific education for women. The French are more civilized in this respect, for they have taken the lead, and have given the first example in modern times of encouragement to the high intellectual culture of the sex. Madame Emma Chenu, who had received the degree of Master of Arts from the Academy of Sciences in Paris, has more recently received the diploma of Licentiate in Mathematical Sciences from the same illustrious Society, after a successful

---

89: *Physical Geography* was published in 1848. **90. Dr. Buckland:** William Buckland (1784-1856), geologist and dean of Westminster Cathedral. **91:** The *Bridgewater Treatises*, named after Francis Henry Egerton, 8th Earl of Bridgewater (1756-1829), grew out of a bequest in his will and constituted a series "On the Power, Wisdom, and Goodness of God, as manifested in the Creation"; Buckland's contribution, "Geology and Mineralogy considered with reference to Natural Theology" (1836), was number 6 in the series of 8. **93. Mr. Babbage:** Charles Babbage (1792-1871), mathematician and inventor. **111-12. Mr. Stuart Mill:** John Stuart Mill (1806-1873), English philosopher among whose many works is *On the Subjection of Women* (1869).

examination in algebra, trigonometry, analytical geometry, the differential and integral calculi, and astronomy. A Russian lady has also taken a degree; and a lady of my acquaintance has received a gold medal from the same Institution.

I joined in a petition to the Senate of London University, praying that degrees might *125* be granted to women; but it was rejected. I have also frequently signed petitions to Parliament for the Female Suffrage, and have the honour now to be a member of the General Committee for Woman Suffrage in London.

. . . .

The summer of 1870 was unusually cool; but the winter has been extremely gloomy, with torrents of rain, and occasionally such thick fogs, that I could see neither *130* to read nor to write. We had no storms during the hot weather; but on the afternoon of the 21st December, there was one of the finest thunderstorms I ever saw; the lightning was intensely vivid, and took the strangest forms, darting in all directions through the air before it struck, and sometimes darting from the ground or the sea to the clouds. It ended in a deluge of rain, which lasted all night, and made us augur ill for the solar *135* eclipse next day; and, sure enough, when I awoke next morning, the sky was darkened by clouds and rain. Fortunately, it cleared up just as the eclipse began; we were all prepared for observing it, and we followed its progress through the opening in the clouds till at last there was only a very slender crescent of the sun's disc left; its convexity was turned upwards, and its horns were nearly horizontal. It was then hidden *140* by a dense mass of clouds; but after a time they opened, and I saw the edge of the moon leave the limb of the sun. The appearance of the landscape was very lurid, but by no means very dark. The common people and children had a very good view of the eclipse, reflected by the pools of water in the streets.

Many of the astronomers who had been in Sicily observing the eclipse came to see me *145* as they passed through Naples. One of their principal objects was to ascertain the nature of the corona, or bright white rays which surround the dark lunar disc at the time of the greatest obscurity. The spectroscope showed that it was decidedly auroral, but as the aurora was seen on the dark disc of the moon it must have been due to the earth's atmosphere. Part of the corona was polarized, and consequently must have been material; *150* the question is, Can it be the etherial medium? A question of immense importance, since the whole theory of light and colours and the resistance of Encke's comet depends upon that hypothesis. The question is still in abeyance, but I have no doubt that it will be decided in the affirmative, and that even the cause of gravitation will be known eventually.

. . . .

I am now in my 92nd year (1872), still able to drive out for several hours; I am *155* extremely deaf, and my memory of ordinary events, and especially of the names of people, is failing, but not for mathematical and scientific subjects. I am still able to read books on the higher algebra for four or five hours in the morning, and even to solve the problems. Sometimes I find them difficult, but my old obstinacy remains, for if I do not succeed to-day, I attack them again on the morrow. I also enjoy reading about all the *160* new discoveries and theories in the scientific world, and on all branches of science.

129: The Somervilles had for many years been living in various parts of Italy, and had finally settled in Naples. **152. Encke's comet:** first seen in 1786, named in 1818 for the German astronomer Johann Franz von Encke (1791-1865), who accurately calculated its period of recurrence.

. . . .

Vesuvius has exhibited a considerable activity during the winter and early spring, and frequent streams of lava flowed from the crater, and especially from the small cone to the north, a little way below the principal crater. But these streams were small and intermittent, and no great outbreak was expected. On the 24th April a stream of lava 165 induced us to drive in the evening to Santa Lucia. The next night, Thursday, 25th April, my daughter Martha, who had been to the theatre, wakened me that I might see Vesuvius in splendid eruption. This was at about 1 o'clock on Friday morning. Early in the morning I was disturbed by what I thought loud thunder, and when my maid came at 7 a.m. I remarked that there was a thunder storm, but she said, "No, no; it is the 170 mountain roaring." It must have been very loud for me to hear, considering my deafness, and the distance Vesuvius is from Naples, yet it was nothing compared to the noise later in the day, and for many days after. My daughter, who had gone to Santa Lucia to see the eruption better, soon came to fetch me with our friend Mr. James Swinton, and we passed the whole day at windows in an hotel at Santa Lucia, 175 immediately opposite the mountain. Vesuvius was now in the fiercest eruption, such as has not occurred in the memory of this generation, lava overflowing the principal crater and running in all directions. The fiery glow of lava is not very visible by daylight; smoke and steam is sent off which rises white as snow, or rather as frosted silver, and the mouth of the great crater was white with the lava pouring over it. New craters had 180 burst out the preceding night, at the very time I was admiring the beauty of the eruption, little dreaming that, of many people who had gone up that night to the Atrio del Cavallo to see the lava (as my daughters had done repeatedly and especially during the great eruption of 1868), some forty or fifty had been on the very spot where the new crater burst out, and perished, scorched to death by the fiery vapours which eddied from the 185 fearful chasm. Some were rescued who had been less near to the chasm, but of these none eventually recovered.

Behind the cone rose an immense column of dense black smoke to more than four times the height of the mountain, and spread out at the summit horizontally, like a pine tree, above the silvery stream which poured forth in volumes. There were constant 190 bursts of fiery projectiles, shooting to an immense height into the black column of smoke, and tinging it with a lurid red colour. The fearful roaring and thundering never ceased for one moment, and the house shook with the concussion of the air. One stream of lava flowed towards Torre del Greco, but luckily stopped before it reached the cultivated fields; others, and the most dangerous ones, since some of them came from 195 the new craters, poured down the Atrio del Cavallo, and dividing before reaching the Observatory flowed to the right and to the left — the stream which flowed to the north very soon reached the plain, and before night came on had partially destroyed the small town of Massa di Somma. One of the peculiarities of this eruption was the great fluidity of the lava; another was the never-ceasing thundering of the mountain. During that day 200 we observed several violent explosions in the great stream of lava: we thought from the

---

166. Santa Lucia: a district of Naples. **182:** The Atrio del Cavallo is a deep valley or ravine breaking the wall of the Monte Somma, the remains of the large prehistoric crater, on the west side. **194. Torre del Greco:** on the coast, just south of Herculaneum. **199. Massa di Somma:** on the north side of Vesuvius.

enormous volumes of black smoke emitted on these occasions that new craters had burst out — some below the level of the Observatory; but that can hardly have been the case. My daughters at night drove to Portici, and went up to the top of a house, where the noise seems to have been appalling; but they told me they did not gain anything by going to *205* Portici, nor did they see the eruption better than I did who remained at Santa Lucia, for you get too much below the mountain on going near. On Sunday, 28th, I was surprised at the extreme darkness, and on looking out of window saw men walking with umbrellas; Vesuvius was emitting such an enormous quantity of ashes, or rather fine black sand, that neither land, sea, nor sky was visible; the fall was a little less dense during the day, but at *210* night it was worse than ever. Strangers seemed to be more alarmed at this than at the eruption, and certainly the constant loud roaring of Vesuvius was appalling enough amidst the darkness and gloom of the falling ashes. The railroad was crowded with both natives and foreigners, escaping; on the other hand, crowds came from Rome to see the eruption. We were not at all afraid, for we considered that the danger was past when so *215* great an eruption had acted as a kind of safety-valve to the pent-up vapours. But a silly report got about that an earthquake was to take place, and many persons passed the night in driving or walking about the town, avoiding narrow streets. The mountain was quite veiled for some days by vapour and ashes, but I could see the black smoke and silvery mass above it. While looking at this, a magnificent column, black as jet, darted with *220* inconceivable violence and velocity to an immense height; it gave a grand idea of the power that was still in action in the fiery caverns below.

Immense injury has been done by this eruption, and much more would have been done had not the lava flowed to a great extent over that of 1868. Still the streams ran through Massa di Somma, San Sebastiano, and other villages scattered about the *225* country, overwhelming fields, woods, vineyards, and houses. The ashes, too, have not only destroyed this year's crops, but killed both vines and fruit trees, so that altogether it has been most disastrous. Vesuvius was involved in vapour and ashes till far on in May, and one afternoon at sunset, when all below was in shade, and only a few silvery threads of steam were visible, a column of the most beautiful crimson colour rose from the *230* crater, and floated in the air. Many of the small craters still smoked, one quite at the base of the cone, which is a good deal changed — it is lower, the small northern cone has disappeared, and part of the walls of the crater have fallen in, and there is a fissure in them through which smoke or vapour is occasionally emitted.

. . . .

The Blue Peter has been long flying at my foremast, and now that I am in my *235* ninety-second year I must soon expect the signal for sailing. It is a solemn voyage; but it does not disturb my tranquility. Deeply sensible of my utter unworthiness, and profoundly grateful for the innumerable blessings I have received, I trust in the infinite mercy of my Almighty Creator. I have every reason to be thankful that my intellect is still unimpaired, and, although my strength is weakness, my daughters support my *240* tottering steps, and, by incessant care and help, make the infirmities of age so light to me that I am perfectly happy.

(1873)

---

204. Portici: on the coast, just north of Herculaneum. **225. San Sebastiano:** on the west side of Vesuvius. **235. Blue Peter:** blue flag with a white square in the centre, signalling that a ship is ready to sail.

WASHINGTON IRVING
U.S.A., 1783-1859

from *A HISTORY OF NEW YORK, FROM THE BEGINNING OF THE WORLD TO THE END OF THE DUTCH DYNASTY*,
BY DIEDRICH KNICKERBOCKER

Book III
In Which Is Recorded the Golden Reign of Wouter Van Twiller

CHAPTER 1: Of the Renowned Wouter Van Twiller, His Unparalleled Virtues — As Likewise His Unutterable Wisdom in the Law Case of Wandle Schoonhoven and Barent Bleecker — and the Great Admiration of the Public Thereat.

Grievous and very much to be commiserated is the task of the feeling historian who writes the history of his native land. If it fall to his lot to be the recorder of calamity or crime, the mournful page is watered with his tears — nor can he recall the most prosperous and blissful era, without a melancholy sigh at the reflection, that it has passed away for ever! I know not whether it be owing to an immoderate love for the simplicity of former times, or to that certain tenderness of heart incident to all sentimental historians; but I candidly confess that I cannot look back on the happier days of our city, which I now describe, without great dejection of spirit. With faltering hand do I withdraw the curtain of oblivion that veils the modest merit of our venerable ancestors, and as their figures rise to my mental vision, humble myself before their mighty shades. 5 10

Such are my feelings when I revisit the family mansion of the Knickerbockers, and spend a lonely hour in the chamber where hang the portraits of my forefathers, shrouded in dust, like the forms they represent. With pious reverence do I gaze on the countenances of those renowned burghers who have preceded me in the steady march of existence — whose sober and temperate blood now meanders through my veins, flowing slower and slower in its feeble conduits, until its current shall soon be stopped for ever! 15

These, I say to myself, are but frail memorials of the mighty men who flourished in the days of the patriarchs; but who, alas, have long since mouldered in that tomb, towards which my steps are insensibly and irresistibly hastening! As I pace the darkened chamber and lose myself in melancholy musings, the shadowy images around me almost seem to steal once more into existence — their countenances to assume the animation of life — their eyes to pursue me in every movement! Carried away by the 20

A HISTORY OF NEW YORK Irving's burlesque history, first published in 1809, was revised (and toned down) three times for subsequent editions, the last being that of 1848. It satirizes not only the work of serious historians, but also the people and politics both of the period it purports to portray and of the period during which it was written. Book III contains nine chapters in all.

delusions of fancy, I almost imagine myself surrounded by the shades of the departed,   25
and holding sweet converse with the worthies of antiquity! Ah, hapless Diedrich! born
in a degenerate age, abandoned to the buffetings of fortune — a stranger and a weary
pilgrim in thy native land — blest with no weeping wife, nor family of helpless
children; but doomed to wander neglected through those crowded streets, and elbowed
by foreign upstarts from those fair abodes where once thine ancestors held sovereign   30
empire!

Let me not, however, lose the historian in the man, nor suffer the doting
recollections of age to overcome me, while dwelling with fond garrulity on the virtuous
days of the patriarchs — on those sweet days of simplicity and ease, which never more
will dawn on the lovely island of Manna-hata.   35

These melancholy reflections have been forced from me by the growing wealth and
importance of New Amsterdam, which, I plainly perceive, are to involve it in all kinds
of perils and disasters. Already, as I observed at the close of my last book, they had
awakened the attentions of the mother country. The usual mark of protection shown by
mother countries to wealthy colonies was forthwith manifested: a governor being sent   40
out to rule over the province and squeeze out of it as much revenue as possible. The
arrival of a governor of course put an end to the protectorate of Oloffe the Dreamer. He
appears, however, to have dreamt to some purpose during his sway, as we find him
afterwards living as a patroon on a great landed estate on the banks of the Hudson;
having virtually forfeited all right to his ancient appellation of Kortlandt or Lackland.   45

It was in the year of our Lord 1629 that Mynheer Wouter Van Twiller was
appointed governor of the province of Nieuw Nederlandts, under the commission and
control of their High Mightinesses the Lords States General of the United Netherlands,
and the privileged West India Company.

This renowned old gentleman arrived at New Amsterdam in the merry month of   50
June, the sweetest month in all the year; when Dan Apollo seems to dance up the
transparent firmament — when the robin, the thrush, and a thousand other wanton
songsters make the woods to resound with amorous ditties, and the luxurious little
boblincon revels among the clover blossoms of the meadows — all which happy
coincidences persuaded the old dames of New Amsterdam, who were skilled in the art   55
of foretelling events, that this was to be a happy and prosperous administration.

The renowned Wouter (or Walter) Van Twiller was descended from a long line of
Dutch burgomasters, who had successively dozed away their lives, and grown fat upon
the bench of magistracy in Rotterdam, and who had comported themselves with such

---

35. **Manna-hata:** a version of the name "Manhattan"; in Book II, Chapter VI, Irving discusses the supposed etymology of the name, including the
suggestions that it means "island of manna — or, in other words, a land flowing with milk and honey," and "The Island of Jolly Topers." 42. **Oloffe:**
Oloff Stevenszen Van Cortlandt (1600-1684), prominent merchant and landowner, born in the Netherlands; held such offices in New Amsterdam as
city treasurer and burgomaster; after the city became New York, in 1664, he served as alderman and deputy mayor; Irving has satirized him in Book
II, calling him "Oloffe the dreamer" and translating his name as "Shortland or Lackland" (see line 45). Van Twiller (c.1580-1656) was not, as Irving
implies here and states later (line 134), the first governor, or "director general," of New Netherland; rather he was the second, succeeding Peter
Minuit (c.1580-1638), who bought Manhattan from the Indians for $24 worth of trinkets, and was dismissed from his post in 1631 by the Dutch
West India Company; nor did Van Twiller arrive in 1629 (line 46), but in 1633, and served until 1637. 44. **patroon:** one whom the Dutch West India
Company has given proprietary and manorial rights over a large parcel of land, as a reward for establishing fifty settlers. 51. **Dan Apollo:** i.e., the
sun. 54. **boblincon:** bobolincon, bobolink.

singular wisdom and propriety, that they were never either heard or talked of — which, 60
next to being universally applauded, should be the object of ambition of all magistrates
and rulers. There are two opposite ways by which some men make a figure in the
world: one by talking faster than they think, and the other by holding their tongues and
not thinking at all. By the first, many a smatterer acquires the reputation of a man of
quick parts: by the other, many a dunderpate, like the owl, the stupidest of birds, comes 65
to be considered the very type of wisdom. This, by the way, is a casual remark, which I
would not, for the universe, have it thought I apply to Governor Van Twiller. It is true
he was a man shut up within himself, like an oyster, and rarely spoke, except in
monosyllables; but then it was allowed he seldom said a foolish thing. So invincible
was his gravity that he was never known to laugh or even to smile through the whole 70
course of a long and prosperous life. Nay, if a joke were uttered in his presence that set
light-minded hearers in a roar, it was observed to throw him into a state of perplexity.
Sometimes he would deign to inquire into the matter, and when, after much
explanation, the joke was made as plain as a pike-staff, he would continue to smoke his
pipe in silence, and at length, knocking out the ashes, would exclaim, "Well, I see 75
nothing in all that to laugh about!"

With all his reflective habits, he never made up his mind on a subject. His adherents
accounted for this by the astonishing magnitude of his ideas. He conceived every subject
on so grand a scale that he had not room in his head to turn it over and examine both
sides of it. Certain it is that if any matter were propounded to him on which ordinary 80
mortals would rashly determine at first glance, he would put on a vague, mysterious
look, shake his capacious head, smoke some time in profound silence, and at length
observe that "he had his doubts about the matter"; which gained him the reputation of a
man slow of belief and not easily imposed upon. What is more, it gained him a lasting
name: for to this habit of the mind has been attributed his surname of Twiller; which is 85
said to be a corruption of the original Twijfler, or, in plain English, *Doubter.*

The person of this illustrious old gentleman was formed and proportioned as though
it had been moulded by the hands of some cunning Dutch statuary, as a model of
majesty and lordly grandeur. He was exactly five feet six inches in height, and six feet
five inches in circumference. His head was a perfect sphere, and of such stupendous 90
dimensions, that Dame Nature, with all her sex's ingenuity, would have been puzzled to
construct a neck capable of supporting it; wherefore she wisely declined the attempt,
and settled it firmly on the top of his backbone, just between the shoulders. His body
was oblong, and particularly capacious at bottom; which was wisely ordered by
Providence, seeing that he was a man of sedentary habits, and very averse to the idle 95
labor of walking. His legs were short, but sturdy in proportion to the weight they had to
sustain, so that when erect he had not a little the appearance of a beer-barrel on skids.
His face, that infallible index of the mind, presented a vast expanse, unfurrowed by any
of those lines and angles which disfigure the human countenance with what is termed
expression. Two small grey eyes twinkled feebly in the midst, like two stars of lesser 100
magnitude in a hazy firmament; and his full-fed cheeks, which seemed to have taken toll

---

71-72: Cf. *Hamlet,* V.i.193. **88. statuary:** sculptor.

of everything that went into his mouth, were curiously mottled and streaked with dusky red, like a Spitzenberg apple.

His habits were as regular as his person. He daily took his four stated meals, appropriating exactly an hour to each; he smoked and doubted eight hours, and he slept the remaining twelve of the four-and-twenty. Such was the renowned Wouter Van Twiller — a true philosopher, for his mind was either elevated above, or tranquilly settled below, the cares and perplexities of this world. He had lived in it for years, without feeling the least curiosity to know whether the sun revolved round it, or it round the sun; and he had watched, for at least half a century, the smoke curling from his pipe to the ceiling, without once troubling his head with any of those numerous theories by which a philosopher would have perplexed his brain, in accounting for its rising above the surrounding atmosphere.

In his council he presided with great state and solemnity. He sat in a huge chair of solid oak, hewn in the celebrated forest of The Hague, fabricated by an experienced timmerman of Amsterdam, and curiously carved about the arms and feet into exact imitations of gigantic eagle's claws. Instead of a sceptre he swayed a long Turkish pipe, wrought with jasmin and amber, which had been presented to a stadtholder of Holland at the conclusion of a treaty with one of the petty Barbary powers. In this stately chair would he sit, and this magnificent pipe would he smoke, shaking his right knee with a constant motion, and fixing his eye for hours together upon a little print of Amsterdam, which hung in a black frame against the opposite wall of the council chamber. Nay, it has even been said, that when any deliberation of extraordinary length and intricacy was on the carpet, the renowned Wouter would shut his eyes for full two hours at a time, that he might not be disturbed by external objects — and at such times the internal commotion of his mind was evinced by certain regular guttural sounds, which his admirers declared were merely the noise of conflict made by his contending doubts and opinions.

It is with infinite difficulty I have been enabled to collect these biographical anecdotes of the great man under consideration. The facts respecting him were so scattered and vague, and divers of them so questionable in point of authenticity, that I have had to give up the search after many, and decline the admission of still more, which would have tended to heighten the coloring of his portrait.

I have been the more anxious to delineate fully the person and habits of Wouter Van Twiller, from the consideration that he was not only the first, but also the best governor that ever presided over this ancient and respectable province; and so tranquil and benevolent was his reign, that I do not find throughout the whole of it a single instance of any offender being brought to punishment — a most indubitable sign of a merciful governor, and a case unparalleled, excepting in the reign of the illustrious King Log, from whom, it is hinted, the renowned Van Twiller was a lineal descendant.

---

116. **timmerman:** carpenter. 118. **jasmin:** possibly jasmine wood, but more likely an error for *jasper*; **stadtholder:** chief magistrate of the United Provinces of Holland, or a governor or lieutenant governor of a province. 119. **Barbary powers:** the "Barbary States" of North Africa (Tripolitania, Algeria, Tunisia, Morocco), a base for marauding pirates since the 16th century. 140. **King Log:** see Caxton's version of Aesop's fable, "The Frogs and Jupiter" (p. 104).

The very outset of the career of this excellent magistrate was distinguished by an example of legal acumen that gave flattering presage of a wise and equitable administration. The morning after he had been installed in office, and at the moment that he was making his breakfast from a prodigious earthen dish, filled with milk and Indian 145 pudding, he was interrupted by the appearance of Wandle Schoonhoven, a very important old burgher of New Amsterdam, who complained bitterly of one Barent Bleecker, inasmuch as he refused to come to a settlement of accounts, seeing that there was a heavy balance in favor of the said Wandle. Governor Van Twiller, as I have already observed, was a man of few words; he was likewise a mortal enemy to 150 multiplying writings — or being disturbed at his breakfast. Having listened attentively to the statement of Wandle Schoonhoven, giving an occasional grunt, as he shovelled a spoonful of Indian pudding into his mouth — either as a sign that he relished the dish, or comprehended the story — he called unto him his constable, and pulling out of his breeches pocket a huge jack-knife, dispatched it after the defendant as a summons, 155 accompanied by his tobacco-box as a warrant.

This summary process was as effectual in those simple days as was the seal-ring of the great Harun-al-Raschid among the true believers. The two parties being confronted before him, each produced a book of accounts, written in a language and character that would have puzzled any but a High Dutch commentator or a learned decipherer of 160 Egyptian obelisks. The sage Wouter took them one after the other, and having poised them in his hands, and attentively counted over the number of leaves, fell straightway into a very great doubt, and smoked for half an hour without saying a word; at length, laying his finger beside his nose, and shutting his eyes for a moment, with the air of a man who has just caught a subtle idea by the tail, he slowly took his pipe from his 165 mouth, puffed forth a column of tobacco smoke, and with marvellous gravity and solemnity pronounced — that having carefully counted over the leaves and weighed the books, it was found that one was just as thick and as heavy as the other — therefore it was the final opinion of the court that the accounts were equally balanced — therefore Wandle should give Barent a receipt, and Barent should give Wandle a receipt — and 170 the constable should pay the costs.

This decision, being straightway made known, diffused general joy throughout New Amsterdam, for the people immediately perceived that they had a very wise and equitable magistrate to rule over them. But its happiest effect was that not another lawsuit took place throughout the whole of his administration — and the office of 175 constable fell into such decay that there was not one of those losel scouts known in the province for many years. I am the more particular in dwelling on this transaction, not only because I deem it one of the most sage and righteous judgments on record, and well worthy the attention of modern magistrates; but because it was a miraculous event in the history of the renowned Wouter — being the only time he was ever known to 180 come to a decision in the whole course of his life.

(1809, 1848)

145-46. Indian pudding: corn meal and milk, sweetened with molasses. **158:** Harun al-Rashid (c.764-809), most famous Caliph of Baghdad (786-809) — he appears in many of the stories in the *Arabian Nights*. **176. losel:** worthless.

LEIGH HUNT
England, 1784-1859

JENNY KISSED ME

Jenny kissed me when we met,
   Jumping from the chair she sat in;
Time, you thief, who love to get
   Sweets into your list, put that in!

Say I'm weary, say I'm sad,   *5*
   Say that health and wealth have missed me,
Say I'm growing old, but add,
   Jenny kissed me.

                          (1838)

THOMAS LOVE PEACOCK
England, 1785-1866

RICH AND POOR; OR SAINT AND SINNER

The poor man's sins are glaring;
In the face of ghostly warning
   He is caught in the fact
   Of an overt act —
Buying greens on Sunday morning.   *5*

The rich man's sins are hidden
In the pomp of wealth and station,
   And escape the sight
   Of the children of light,
Who are wise in their generation.   *10*

The rich man has a kitchen,
And cooks to dress his dinner;
   The poor who would roast
   To the baker's must post,
And thus becomes a sinner.   *15*

The rich man has a cellar,
And a ready butler by him;
   The poor must steer
   For his pint of beer   *19*
Where the saint can't choose but spy him.

The rich man's painted windows
Hide the concerts of the quality;
   The poor can but share
   A cracked fiddle in the air,
Which offends all sound morality.   *25*

The rich man is invisible
In the crowd of his gay society;
   But the poor man's delight
   Is a sore in the sight,
And a stench in the nose of piety.   *30*

The rich man has a carriage
Where no rude eye can flout him;
   The poor man's bane
   Is a third-class train,
With the daylight all about him.   *35*

The rich man goes out yachting,
Where sanctity can't pursue him;
   The poor goes afloat
   In a fourpenny boat,
Where the bishop groans to view him.   *40*

                          (1825)

RICH AND POOR   **5. greens:** vegetables. **9-10:** see Luke 16:8. **14. baker's:** People who had no kitchen oven would either roast and bake on the hearth, or else use the ovens of the local baker. **16. cellar:** wine cellar. **21. painted:** stained glass. **39. fourpenny boat:** e.g., the boats for hire on the ponds at public parks.

M<small>ARY</small> R<small>USSELL</small> M<small>ITFORD</small>
England, 1787-1855

from *O<small>UR</small> V<small>ILLAGE</small>*

F<small>ROST</small> <small>AND</small> T<small>HAW</small>
January 23rd

At noon to-day I and my white greyhound, Mayflower, set out for a walk into a very beautiful world — a sort of silent fairy-land — a creation of that matchless magician, the hoar-frost. There had been just snow enough to cover the earth and all its colours with one sheet of pure and uniform white, and just time enough since the snow had fallen to allow the hedges to be freed of their fleecy load, and clothed with a delicate   5
coating of rime. The atmosphere was deliciously calm; soft, even mild, in spite of the thermometer; no perceptible air, but a stillness that might almost be felt; the sky, rather grey than blue, throwing out in bold relief the snow-covered roofs of our village, and the rimy trees that rise above them, and the sun shining dimly as through a veil, giving a pale fair light, like the moon, only brighter. There was a silence, too, that might become   10
the moon, as we stood at our little gate looking up the quiet street; a sabbath-like pause of work and play, rare on a work-day; nothing was audible but the pleasant hum of frost, that low monotonous sound, which is perhaps the nearest approach that life and nature can make to absolute silence. The very waggons as they come down the hill along the beaten track of crisp, yellowish frost-dust glide along like shadows; even May's   15
bounding footsteps, at her height of glee and of speed, fall like snow upon snow.

But we shall have noise enough presently: May has stopped at Lizzy's door; and Lizzy, as she sat on the window-sill with her bright rosy face laughing through the casement, has seen her and disappeared. She is coming. No! The key is turning in the door, and sounds of evil omen issue through the keyhole — sturdy "let me outs," and "I   20
will goes," mixed with shrill cries on May and on me from Lizzy, piercing through a low continuous harangue, of which the prominent parts are apologies, chilblains, sliding, broken bones, lollypops, rods, and gingerbread, from Lizzy's careful mother. "Don't scratch the door, May! Don't roar so, my Lizzy! We'll call for you as we come back." — "I'll go now! Let me out! I will go!" are the last words of Miss Lizzy. Mem.   25
Not to spoil that child — if I can help it. But I do think her mother might have let the poor little soul walk with us to-day. Nothing worse for children than coddling. Nothing better for chilblains than exercise. Besides, I don't believe she has any — and as to breaking her bones in sliding, I don't suppose there's a slide on the common. These murmuring cogitations have brought us up the hill, and halfway across the light and airy   30
common, with its bright expanse of snow and its clusters of cottages, whose turf fires send such wreaths of smoke sailing up the air, and diffuse such aromatic fragrance

---

F<small>ROST</small> <small>AND</small> T<small>HAW</small>   See also Thomas Hood's "Our Village" (p. 882). **7. air:** breeze. **23. rods:** switches (as in "Spare the rod and spoil the child" — see line 26). **25. Mem.:** memo (to herself).

around. And now comes the delightful sound of childish voices, ringing with glee and merriment almost from beneath our feet. Ah, Lizzy, your mother was right! They are shouting from that deep irregular pool, all glass now, where, on two long, smooth, liny *35* slides, half a dozen ragged urchins are slipping along in tottering triumph. Half a dozen steps bring us to the bank right above them. May can hardly resist the temptation of joining her friends, for most of the varlets are of her acquaintance, especially the rogue who leads the slide — he with the brimless hat, whose bronzed complexion and white flaxen hair, reversing the usual lights and shadows of the human countenance, give so *40* strange and foreign a look to his flat and comic features. This hobgoblin, Jack Rapley by name, is May's great crony; and she stands on the brink of the steep, irregular descent, her black eyes fixed full upon him, as if she intended him the favour of jumping on his head. She does; she is down, and upon him; but Jack Rapley is not easily to be knocked off his feet. He saw her coming, and in the moment of her leap sprung dexterously off *45* the slide on the rough ice, steadying himself by the shoulder of the next in the file, which unlucky follower, thus unexpectedly checked in his career, fell plump backwards, knocking down the rest of the line like a nest of card-houses. There is no harm done; but there they lie, roaring, kicking, sprawling, in every attitude of comic distress, whilst Jack Rapley and Mayflower, sole authors of this calamity, stand apart from the throng, *50* fondling, and coquetting, and complimenting each other, and very visibly laughing, May in her black eyes, Jack in his wide, close-shut mouth, and his whole monkey-face, at their comrades' mischances. I think, Miss May, you may as well come up again, and leave Master Rapley to fight your battles. He'll get out of the scrape. He is a rustic wit — a sort of Robin Goodfellow — the sauciest, idlest, cleverest, best-natured boy in the *55* parish; always foremost in mischief, and always ready to do a good turn. The sages of our village predict sad things of Jack Rapley, so that I am sometimes a little ashamed to confess, before wise people, that I have a lurking predilection for him (in common with other naughty ones), and that I like to hear him talk to May almost as well as she does. "Come, May!" and up she springs, as light as a bird. The road is gay now; carts and *60* post-chaises, and girls in red cloaks, and, afar off, looking almost like a toy, the coach. It meets us fast and soon. How much happier the walkers look than the riders — especially the frost-bitten gentleman, and the shivering lady with the invisible face, sole passengers of that commodious machine! Hooded, veiled, and bonneted as she is, one sees from her attitude how miserable she would look uncovered. *65*

Another pond, and another noise of children. More sliding? Oh no! This is a sport of higher pretension. Our good neighbour, the lieutenant, skating, and his own pretty little boys, and two or three other four-year-old elves, standing on the brink in an ecstasy of joy and wonder! Oh what happy spectators! And what a happy performer! They admiring, he admired, with an ardour and sincerity never excited by all the *70* quadrilles and the spread-eagles of the Seine and the Serpentine. He really skates well

---

35. liny: narrow, like a line. **54. rustic wit:** i.e., a boy with more common sense than decorum. **55. Robin Goodfellow:** Puck, a mischievous sprite in English folklore, alluded to in Spenser's *Epithalamion* (as "Pouke," see line 341 and note, p. 167) and a character in Shakespeare's *A Midsummer Night's Dream.* **61. post-chaises:** closed horse-drawn carriages, which travellers could hire at post-houses (these later became "post offices" in the modern sense); **coach:** a regularly scheduled public conveyance. **71. quadrilles:** French dances (hence "Seine"); **spread-eagles:** ice-skating figures; **Serpentine:** lake in Hyde Park, London.

though, and I am glad I came this way; for, with all the father's feelings sitting gaily at his heart, it must still gratify the pride of skill to have one spectator at that solitary pond who has seen skating before.

Now we have reached the trees, — the beautiful trees! never so beautiful as to-day. Imagine the effect of a straight and regular double avenue of oaks, nearly a mile long, arching overhead, and closing into perspective like the roof and columns of a cathedral, every tree and branch incrusted with the bright and delicate congelation of hoar-frost, white and pure as snow, delicate and defined as carved ivory. How beautiful it is, how uniform, how various, how filling, how satiating to the eye and to the mind — above all, how melancholy! There is a thrilling awfulness, an intense feeling of simple power in that naked and colourless beauty, which falls on the earth like the thoughts of death — death pure, and glorious, and smiling, — but still death. Sculpture has always the same effect on my imagination, and painting never. Colour is life. — We are now at the end of this magnificent avenue, and at the top of a steep eminence commanding a wide view over four counties — a landscape of snow. A deep lane leads abruptly down the hill; a mere narrow cart-track, sinking between high banks clothed with fern and furze and low broom, crowned with luxuriant hedgerows, and famous for their summer smell of thyme. How lovely these banks are now — the tall weeds and the gorse fixed and stiffened in the hoar-frost, which fringes round the bright prickly holly, the pendent foliage of the bramble, and the deep orange leaves of the pollard oaks! Oh, this is rime in its loveliest form! And there is still a berry here and there on the holly, "blushing in its natural coral" through the delicate tracery, still a stray hip or haw for the birds, who abound here always. The poor birds, how tame they are, how sadly tame! There is the beautiful and rare crested wren, "that shadow of a bird," as White of Selborne calls it, perched in the middle of the hedge, nestling as it were amongst the cold bare boughs, seeking, poor pretty thing, for the warmth it will not find. And there, farther on, just under the bank, by the slender runlet, which still trickles between its transparent fantastic margin of thin ice, as if it were a thing of life — there, with a swift, scudding motion, flits, in short low flights, the gorgeous kingfisher, its magnificent plumage of scarlet and blue flashing in the sun, like the glories of some tropical bird. He is come for water to this little spring by the hillside — water which even his long bill and slender head can hardly reach, so nearly do the fantastic forms of those garland-like icy margins meet over the tiny stream beneath. It is rarely that one sees the shy beauty so close or so long: and it is pleasant to see him in the grace and beauty of his natural liberty, the only way to look at a bird. We used, before we lived in a street, to fix a little board outside the parlour window, and cover it with breadcrumbs in the hard weather. It was quite delightful to see the pretty things come and feed, to conquer their shyness, and do away their mistrust. First came the more social tribes, "the robin red-breast and the wren," cautiously, suspiciously, picking up a crumb on the wing, with the little keen bright eye fixed on the window; then they would stop for two pecks; then stay till they were satisfied. The shyer birds, tamed by their example, came next; and at last one saucy fellow of a blackbird — a sad glutton, he would clear the board in two minutes — used to tap his yellow bill against the window for more. How we loved the fearless

75

80

85

90

95

100

105

110

---

78. congelation: congealing. **81. awfulness:** awesomeness. **95. White of Selborne:** the naturalist Gilbert White (see p. 617). **109. "the robin . . . wren":** from the opening line of the dirge Cornelia recites in John Webster's *The White Devil*, V. iv (c. 1608).

confidence of that fine, frank-hearted creature! And surely he loved us. I wonder the *115*
practice is not more general. — "May! May! naughty May!" She has frightened away
the kingfisher; and now, in her coaxing penitence, she is covering me with snow.
"Come, pretty May! it is time to go home."

January 28th

We have had rain, and snow, and frost, and rain again; four days of absolute
confinement. Now it is a thaw and a flood; but our light gravelly soil, and country boots, *120*
and country hardihood, will carry us through. What a dripping, comfortless day it is!
just like the last days of November: no sun, no sky, grey or blue; one low, overhanging,
dark, dismal cloud, like London smoke — Mayflower is out coursing too, and Lizzy
gone to school. Never mind. Up the hill again! Walk we must. Oh what a watery world
to look back upon! Thames, Kennet, Loddon — all overflowed; our famous town, *125*
inland once, turned into a sort of Venice; C. park converted into an island; and the long
range of meadows from B. to W. one huge unnatural lake, with trees growing out of it.
Oh what a watery world! — I will look at it no longer. I will walk on. The road is alive
again. Noise is re-born. Waggons creak, horses splash, carts rattle, and pattens paddle
through the dirt with more than their usual clink. The common has its old fine tints of *130*
green and brown, and its old variety of inhabitants, horses, cows, sheep, pigs, and
donkeys. The ponds are unfrozen, except where some melancholy piece of melting ice
floats sullenly on the water; and cackling geese and gabbling ducks have replaced the
lieutenant and Jack Rapley. The avenue is chill and dark, the hedges are dripping, the
lanes knee-deep, and all nature is in a state of "dissolution and thaw." *135*

(1832)

GEORGE GORDON, LORD BYRON
England, 1788-1824

WRITTEN AFTER SWIMMING FROM SESTOS TO ABYDOS

1

If, in the month of dark December,
  Leander, who was nightly wont
(What maid will not the tale remember?)
  To cross thy stream, broad Hellespont!

2

If, when the wintry tempest roared,   *5*
  He sped to Hero, nothing loath,
And thus of old thy current poured,
  Fair Venus! how I pity both!

---

125. our famous town: Mitford's own village was Three Mile Cross, which lies to the southwest of Reading, between the Kennet and Loddon Rivers, both tributaries of the Thames. "C. Park" is possibly Coombe Park, on the Thames to the west of Reading. If the meadows that flooded "from B. to W." refer to the low-lying areas between Burghfield (on the Kennet) to Winnersh (on the Loddon), then the whole region to the south of Reading was inundated. **129. pattens:** wooden soles, mounted on iron rings, which were tied onto ordinary shoes in order to raise the wearer above the mud. **WRITTEN AFTER SWIMMING** See the note to line 44 of Gilbert White's "Naturalist's Summer-Evening Walk" (p. 617); Byron swam the Hellespont in 1810.

3

For *me*, degenerate modern wretch,
　　Though in the genial month of May,　　　*10*
My dripping limbs I faintly stretch,
　　And think I've done a feat today.

4

But since he crossed the rapid tide,
　　According to the doubtful story,
To woo — and — Lord knows what beside,　　*15*
　　And swam for Love, as I for Glory;

5

'Twere hard to say who fared the best:
　　Sad mortals! thus the gods still plague you!
He lost his labour, I my jest;
　　For he was drowned, and I've the ague.　　*20*

　　　　　　　　　　　　　　　　　　(1812)

"SHE WALKS IN BEAUTY"

She walks in beauty, like the night
　　Of cloudless climes and starry skies;
And all that's best of dark and bright
　　Meet in her aspect and her eyes:
Thus mellow'd to that tender light　　　　*5*
　　Which heaven to gaudy day denies.

One shade the more, one ray the less,
　　Had half impair'd the nameless grace
Which waves in every raven tress,
　　Or softly lightens o'er her face;　　　*10*
Where thoughts serenely sweet express
　　How pure, how dear their dwelling-place.

And on that cheek, and o'er that brow,
　　So soft, so calm, yet eloquent,
The smiles that win, the tints that glow,　　*15*
　　But tell of days in goodness spent,
A mind at peace with all below,
　　A heart whose love is innocent!

　　　　　　　　　　　　　　　　　　(1815)

"SO WE'LL GO NO MORE A-ROVING"

So we'll go no more a-roving
　　So late into the night,
Though the heart be still as loving,
　　And the moon be still as bright.

For the sword outwears its sheath,　　　*5*
　　And the soul wears out the breast,
And the heart must pause to breathe,
　　And Love itself have rest.

Though the night was made for loving,
　　And the day returns too soon,　　　*10*
Yet we'll go no more a-roving
　　By the light of the moon.

　　　　　　　　　　　　　　(1817; 1830)

from *DON JUAN*

CANTO THE FIRST (abridged)

I.

I want a hero: an uncommon want,
　　When every year and month sends forth a new one,
Till, after cloying the gazettes with cant,
　　The age discovers he is not the true one;
Of such as these I should not care to vaunt,　　*5*
　　I'll therefore take our ancient friend Don Juan —
We all have seen him, in the pantomime,
Sent to the devil somewhat ere his time.

VI.

Most epic poets plunge "in medias res"
　　(Horace makes this the heroic turnpike road),　　*10*
And then your hero tells, whene'er you please,
　　What went before — by way of episode,
While seated after dinner at his ease,
　　Beside his mistress in some soft abode,
Palace, or garden, paradise, or cavern,　　　*15*
Which serves the happy couple for a tavern.

DON JUAN   By 1824 Byron had published sixteen cantos of *Don Juan*, and had begun but did not finish a seventeenth. **7. pantomime:** i.e., in one or another stage presentation, such as *Don Juan; or, The Libertine Destroyed*, adapted from Thomas Shadwell's *The Libertine* (1675); and see line 1052 below. **9. "in medias res":** See the Glossary.

VII.

That is the usual method, but not mine —
  My way is to begin with the beginning;
The regularity of my design
  Forbids all wandering as the worst of sinning,   *20*
And therefore I shall open with a line
  (Although it cost me half an hour in spinning)
Narrating somewhat of Don Juan's father,
And also of his mother, if you'd rather.

VIII.

In Seville was he born, a pleasant city,   *25*
  Famous for oranges and women — he
Who has not seen it will be much to pity,
  So says the proverb — and I quite agree;
Of all the Spanish towns is none more pretty,
  Cadiz perhaps — but that you soon may see: —   *30*
Don Juan's parents lived beside the river,
A noble stream, and call'd the Guadalquivir.

IX.

His father's name was Jóse — *Don*, of course,
  A true Hidalgo, free from every stain
Of Moor or Hebrew blood, he traced his source   *35*
  Through the most Gothic gentlemen of Spain;
A better cavalier ne'er mounted horse,
  Or, being mounted, e'er got down again,
Than Jóse, who begot our hero, who
Begot — but that's to come — Well, to renew: *40*

X.

His mother was a learned lady, famed
  For every branch of every science known —
In every Christian language ever named,
  With virtues equall'd by her wit alone,
She made the cleverest people quite ashamed,   *45*
  And even the good with inward envy groan,
Finding themselves so very much exceeded
In their own way by all the things that she did.

XI.

Her memory was a mine: she knew by heart
  All Calderon and greater part of Lopé,   *50*
So that if any actor miss'd his part
  She could have served him for the prompter's copy;
For her Feinagle's were an useless art,
  And he himself obliged to shut up shop — he
Could never make a memory so fine as   *55*
That which adorn'd the brain of Donna Inez.

XIII.

She knew the Latin — that is, "the Lord's prayer,"
  And Greek — the alphabet — I'm nearly sure;
She read some French romances here and there,
  Although her mode of speaking was not pure;   *60*
For native Spanish she had no great care,
  At least her conversation was obscure;
Her thoughts were theorems, her words a problem,
As if she deem'd that mystery would ennoble 'em.

XVI.

In short, she was a walking calculation,   *65*
  Miss Edgeworth's novels stepping from their covers,
Or Mrs. Trimmer's books on education,
  Or "Cœlebs' Wife" set out in quest of lovers,
Morality's prim personification,
  In which not Envy's self a flaw discovers;   *70*
To others' share let "female errors fall,"
For she had not even one — the worst of all.

XVIII.

Perfect she was, but as perfection is
  Insipid in this naughty world of ours,
Where our first parents never learn'd to kiss   *75*
  Till they were exiled from their earlier bowers,
Where all was peace, and innocence, and bliss
  (I wonder how they got through the twelve hours),
Don Jóse, like a lineal son of Eve,
Went plucking various fruit without her leave.   *80*

28: "Quien no ha visto Sevilla, no ha visto maravilla." **34. Hidalgo:** Spanish nobleman. **50:** Pedro Calderón de la Barca (1600-1681) and Lope Félix de Vega Carpio (1562-1635), Spanish dramatists. **53. Feinagle:** Gregor von Feinagle, German who had lectured in England on the art of memory. **66-68:** Maria Edgeworth (1767-1849); Sarah Trimmer (1741-1810); *Cœlebs in Search of a Wife* (1809), novel by Hannah More (1745-1833). **71. "female errors fall":** quoting Pope's *The Rape of the Lock*, II, 17 (see p. 525). **75. our first parents:** See the opening of Milton's *Of Education* (p. 318).

XIX.

He was a mortal of the careless kind,
    With no great love for learning, or the learn'd,
Who chose to go where'er he had a mind,
    And never dream'd his lady was concern'd;
The world, as usual, wickedly inclined   85
    To see a kingdom or a house o'erturn'd,
Whisper'd he had a mistress, some said *two*,
But for domestic quarrels *one* will do.

XX.

Now Donna Inez had, with all her merit,
    A great opinion of her own good qualities;   90
Neglect, indeed, requires a saint to bear it,
    And such, indeed, she was in her moralities;
But then she had a devil of a spirit,
    And sometimes mix'd up fancies with realities,
And let few opportunities escape   95
Of getting her liege lord into a scrape.

XXII.

'Tis pity learned virgins ever wed
    With persons of no sort of education,
Or gentlemen, who, though well born and bred,
    Grow tired of scientific conversation: 100
I don't choose to say much upon this head,
    I'm a plain man, and in a single station,
But — Oh! ye lords of ladies intellectual,
Inform us truly, have they not hen-peck'd you all?

XXIII.

Don Jóse and his lady quarrell'd — *why*,   105
    Not any of the many could divine,
Though several thousand people chose to try,
    'Twas surely no concern of theirs nor mine;
I loathe that low vice — curiosity;
    But if there's any thing in which I shine,   110
'Tis in arranging all my friends' affairs,
Not having, of my own, domestic cares.

XXIV.

And so I interfered, and with the best
    Intentions, but their treatment was not kind;
I think the foolish people were possess'd,   115
    For neither of them could I ever find,
Although their porter afterwards confess'd —
    But that's no matter, and the worst's behind,
For little Juan o'er me threw, down stairs,
A pail of housemaid's water unawares.   120

XXV.

A little curly-headed, good-for-nothing,
    And mischief-making monkey from his birth;
His parents ne'er agreed except in doting
    Upon the most unquiet imp on earth;
Instead of quarrelling, had they been but both in   125
    Their senses, they'd have sent young master forth
To school, or had him soundly whipp'd at home,
To teach him manners for the time to come.

XXVI.

Don Jóse and the Donna Inez led
    For some time an unhappy sort of life,   130
Wishing each other, not divorced, but dead;
    They lived respectably as man and wife,
Their conduct was exceedingly well-bred,
    And gave no outward signs of inward strife,
Until at length the smother'd fire broke out,   135
And put the business past all kind of doubt.

XXXII.

Their friends had tried at reconciliation,
    Then their relations, who made matters worse.
('Twere hard to tell upon a like occasion
    To whom it may be best to have recourse —   140
I can't say much for friend or yet relation):
    The lawyers did their utmost for divorce,
But scarce a fee was paid on either side
Before, unluckily, Don Jóse died.

XXXVII.

Dying intestate, Juan was sole heir   145
    To a chancery suit, and messuages, and lands,
Which, with a long minority and care,
    Promised to turn out well in proper hands:
Inez became sole guardian, which was fair,
    And answer'd but to nature's just demands;   150
An only son left with an only mother
Is brought up much more wisely than another.

XXXVIII.

Sagest of women, even of widows, she
    Resolved that Juan should be quite a paragon,
And worthy of the noblest pedigree: 155
    (His sire was of Castile, his dam from Aragon.)
Then for accomplishments of chivalry,
    In case our lord the king should go to war again,
He learn'd the arts of riding, fencing, gunnery,
And how to scale a fortress — or a nunnery.   160

---

146. **messuages:** houses with their outbuildings and adjoining lands.

XXXIX.

But that which Donna Inez most desired,
    And saw into herself each day before all
The learned tutors whom for him she hired,
    Was, that his breeding should be strictly moral:
Much into all his studies she enquired,   165
    And so they were submitted first to her, all,
Arts, sciences, no branch was made a mystery
To Juan's eyes, excepting natural history.

XL.

The languages, especially the dead,
    The sciences, and most of all the abstruse,   170
The arts, at least all such as could be said
    To be the most remote from common use,
In all these he was much and deeply read;
    But not a page of any thing that's loose,
Or hints continuation of the species,   175
Was ever suffer'd, lest he should grow vicious.

XLI.

His classic studies made a little puzzle,
    Because of filthy loves of gods and goddesses,
Who in the earlier ages raised a bustle,
    But never put on pantaloons or bodices;   180
His reverend tutors had at times a tussle,
    And for their Æneids, Iliads, and Odysseys,
Were forced to make an odd sort of apology,
For Donna Inez dreaded the Mythology.

XLIV.

Juan was taught from out the best edition,   185
    Expurgated by learned men, who place,
Judiciously, from out the schoolboy's vision,
    The grosser parts; but fearful to deface
Too much their modest bard by this omission,
    And pitying sore his mutilated case,   190
They only add them all in an appendix,
Which saves, in fact, the trouble of an index;

XLVI.

The Missal too (it was the family Missal)
    Was ornamented in a sort of way
Which ancient mass-books often are, and this all   195
    Kinds of grotesques illumined; and how they,
Who saw those figures on the margin kiss all,
    Could turn their optics to the text and pray,
Is more than I know — but Don Juan's mother
Kept this herself, and gave her son another.   200

XLVII.

Sermons he read, and lectures he endured,
    And homilies, and lives of all the saints;
To Jerome and to Chrysostom inured,
    He did not take such studies for restraints;
But how faith is acquired, and then ensured,   205
    So well not one of the aforesaid paints
As Saint Augustine in his fine Confessions,
Which make the reader envy his transgressions.

XLVIII.

This, too, was a seal'd book to little Juan —
    I can't but say that his mamma was right,   210
If such an education was the true one.
    She scarcely trusted him from out her sight;
Her maids were old, and if she took a new one,
    You might be sure she was a perfect fright,
She did this during even her husband's life —   215
I recommend as much to every wife.

L.

At six, I said, he was a charming child,
    At twelve he was a fine, but quiet boy;
Although in infancy a little wild,
    They tamed him down amongst them: to destroy 220
His natural spirit not in vain they toil'd.
    At least it seem'd so; and his mother's joy
Was to declare how sage, and still, and steady,
Her young philosopher was grown already.

LII.

For my part I say nothing — nothing — but   225
    This I will say — my reasons are my own —
That if I had an only son to put
    To school (as God be praised that I have none),
'Tis not with Donna Inez I would shut
    Him up to learn his catechism alone,   230
No — no — I'd send him out betimes to college,
For there it was I pick'd up my own knowledge.

LIII.

For there one learns — 'tis not for me to boast,
    Though I acquired — but I pass over *that*,
As well as all the Greek I since have lost: 235
    I say that there's the place — but *"Verbum sat,"*
I think I picked up too, as well as most,
    Knowledge of matters — but no matter *what* —
I never married — but, I think, I know
That sons should not be educated so.   240

---

236. *"Verbum sat"*: (Latin) for *Verbum sat sapienti*: A word is enough, for a wise man (A word to the wise is sufficient).

LIV.

Young Juan now was sixteen years of age,
　Tall, handsome, slender, but well knit: he seem'd
Active, though not so sprightly, as a page;
　And every body but his mother deem'd
Him almost man; but she flew in a rage　　　245
　And bit her lips (for else she might have scream'd)
If any said so, for to be precocious
Was in her eyes a thing the most atrocious.

LV.

Amongst her numerous acquaintance, all
　Selected for discretion and devotion,　　　250
There was the Donna Julia, whom to call
　Pretty were but to give a feeble notion
Of many charms in her as natural
　As sweetness to the flower, or salt to ocean,
Her zone to Venus, or his bow to Cupid,　　　255
(But this last simile is trite and stupid.)

LVI.

The darkness of her Oriental eye
　Accorded with her Moorish origin;
(Her blood was not all Spanish, by the by;
　In Spain, you know, this is a sort of sin.)　　　260
When proud Granada fell, and, forced to fly,
　Boabdil wept, of Donna Julia's kin
Some went to Africa, some stay'd in Spain,
Her great great grandmamma chose to remain.

LVII.

She married (I forget the pedigree)　　　265
　With an Hidalgo, who transmitted down
His blood less noble than such blood should be;
　At such alliances his sires would frown,
In that point so precise in each degree
　That they bred *in and in*, as might be shown,　　　270
Marrying their cousins — nay, their aunts, and nieces,
Which always spoils the breed, if it increases.

LVIII.

This heathenish cross restored the breed again,
　Ruin'd its blood, but much improved its flesh;
For from a root the ugliest in Old Spain　　　275
　Sprung up a branch as beautiful as fresh;
The sons no more were short, the daughters plain:
　But there's a rumour which I fain would hush,
'Tis said that Donna Julia's grandmamma
Produced her Don more heirs at love than law.　　　280

LIX.

However this might be, the race went on
　Improving still through every generation,
Until it centred in an only son,
　Who left an only daughter; my narration
May have suggested that this single one　　　285
　Could be but Julia (whom on this occasion
I shall have much to speak about), and she
Was married, charming, chaste, and twenty-three.

LX.

Her eye (I'm very fond of handsome eyes)
　Was large and dark, suppressing half its fire　　　290
Until she spoke, then through its soft disguise
　Flash'd an expression more of pride than ire,
And love than either; and there would arise
　A something in them which was not desire,
But would have been, perhaps, but for the soul　　　295
Which struggled through and chasten'd down the whole.

LXI.

Her glossy hair was cluster'd o'er a brow
　Bright with intelligence, and fair, and smooth;
Her eyebrow's shape was like th' aërial bow,
　Her cheek all purple with the beam of youth,　　　300
Mounting, at times, to a transparent glow,
　As if her veins ran lightning; she, in sooth,
Possess'd an air and grace by no means common:
Her stature tall — I hate a dumpy woman.

LXII.

Wedded she was some years, and to a man　　　305
　Of fifty, and such husbands are in plenty;
And yet, I think, instead of such a ONE
　'Twere better to have TWO of five-and-twenty,
Especially in countries near the sun:
　And now I think on 't, "mi vien in mente,"　　　310
Ladies even of the most uneasy virtue
Prefer a spouse whose age is short of thirty.

LXV.

Alfonso was the name of Julia's lord,
　A man well looking for his years, and who
Was neither much beloved nor yet abhorr'd:　　　315
　They lived together, as most people do,
Suffering each other's foibles by accord,
　And not exactly either *one* or *two*;
Yet he was jealous, though he did not show it,
For jealousy dislikes the world to know it.　　　320

---

255. zone: girdle, belt; Venus's girdle made its wearer irresistible. **262. Boabdil:** last Moorish king of Granada (1482-83, 1486-92). **300. purple:** rosy. **310. "mi vien in mente":** (Italian) "it comes to my mind."

LXIX.

Juan she saw, and, as a pretty child,
    Caress'd him often — such a thing might be
Quite innocently done, and harmless styled,
    When she had twenty years, and thirteen he;
But I am not so sure I should have smiled   *325*
    When he was sixteen, Julia twenty-three;
These few short years make wondrous alterations,
Particularly amongst sun-burnt nations.

LXX.

Whate'er the cause might be, they had become
    Changed; for the dame grew distant, the youth shy,   *330*
Their looks cast down, their greetings almost dumb,
    And much embarrassment in either eye;
There surely will be little doubt with some
    That Donna Julia knew the reason why,
But as for Juan, he had no more notion   *335*
Than he who never saw the sea of Ocean.

LXXIV.

Then there were sighs, the deeper for suppression,
    And stolen glances, sweeter for the theft,
And burning blushes, though for no transgression,
    Tremblings when met, and restlessness when left;   *340*
All these are little preludes to possession,
    Of which young passion cannot be bereft,
And merely tend to show how greatly love is
Embarrass'd at first starting with a novice.

LXXVI.

She vow'd she never would see Juan more,   *345*
    And next day paid a visit to his mother,
And look'd extremely at the opening door,
    Which, by the Virgin's grace, let in another;
Grateful she was, and yet a little sore —
    Again it opens, it can be no other,   *350*
'Tis surely Juan now — No! I'm afraid
That night the Virgin was no further pray'd.

LXXVII.

She now determined that a virtuous woman
    Should rather face and overcome temptation,
That flight was base and dastardly, and no man   *355*
    Should ever give her heart the least sensation;
That is to say, a thought beyond the common
    Preference, that we must feel upon occasion,
For people who are pleasanter than others,
But then they only seem so many brothers.   *360*

LXXVIII.

And even if by chance — and who can tell?
    The devil's so very sly — she should discover
That all within was not so very well,
    And, if still free, that such or such a lover
Might please perhaps, a virtuous wife can quell   *365*
    Such thoughts, and be the better when they're over;
And if the man should ask, 'tis but denial:
I recommend young ladies to make trial.

LXXIX.

And then there are such things as love divine,
    Bright and immaculate, unmix'd and pure,   *370*
Such as the angels think so very fine,
    And matrons, who would be no less secure,
Platonic, perfect, "just such love as mine":
    Thus Julia said — and thought so, to be sure;
And so I'd have her think, were I the man   *375*
On whom her reveries celestial ran.

LXXX.

Such love is innocent, and may exist
    Between young persons without any danger.
A hand may first, and then a lip be kissed;
    For my part, to such doings I'm a stranger,   *380*
But *hear* these freedoms form the utmost list
    Of all o'er which such love may be a ranger:
If people go beyond, 'tis quite a crime,
But not my fault — I tell them all in time.

LXXXI.

Love, then, but Love within its proper limits,   *385*
    Was Julia's innocent determination
In young Don Juan's favour, and to him its
    Exertion might be useful on occasion;
And, lighted at too pure a shrine to dim its
    Ethereal lustre, with what sweet persuasion   *390*
He might be taught, by love and her together —
I really don't know what, nor Julia either.

LXXXII.

Fraught with this fine intention, and well fenced
    In mail of proof — her purity of soul,
She, for the future of her strength convinced,   *395*
    And that her honour was a rock, or mole,
Exceeding sagely from that hour dispensed
    With any kind of troublesome control;
But whether Julia to the task was equal
Is that which must be mention'd in the sequel.   *400*

---

394. mail of proof: armour of proven impenetrability.

LXXXIII.

Her plan she deem'd both innocent and feasible,
  And, surely, with a stripling of sixteen
Not scandal's fangs could fix on much that's seizable,
  Or if they did so, satisfied to mean   404
Nothing but what was good, her breast was peaceable—
  A quiet conscience makes one so serene!
Christians have burnt each other, quite persuaded
That all the Apostles would have done as they did.

LXXXIV.

And if in the mean time her husband died,
  But Heaven forbid that such a thought should cross   410
Her brain, though in a dream! (and then she sigh'd)
  Never could she survive that common loss;
But just suppose that moment should betide,
  I only say suppose it — *inter nos.*
(This should be *entre nous,* for Julia thought   415
In French, but then the rhyme would go for nought.)

LXXXVI.

So much for Julia. Now we'll turn to Juan,
  Poor little fellow! he had no idea
Of his own case, and never hit the true one;
  In feelings quick as Ovid's Miss Medea,   420
He puzzled over what he found a new one,
  But not as yet imagined it could be a
Thing quite in course, and not at all alarming,
Which, with a little patience, might grow charming.

XC.

Young Juan wander'd by the glassy brooks   425
  Thinking unutterable things; he threw
Himself at length within the leafy nooks
  Where the wild branch of the cork forest grew;
There poets find materials for their books,
  And every now and then we read them through,   430
So that their plan and prosody are eligible,
Unless, like Wordsworth, they prove unintelligible.

XCI.

He, Juan (and not Wordsworth), so pursued
  His self-communion with his own high soul,
Until his mighty heart, in its great mood,   435
  Had mitigated part, though not the whole
Of its disease; he did the best he could
  With things not very subject to control,
And turn'd, without perceiving his condition,
Like Coleridge, into a metaphysician.   440

XCII.

He thought about himself, and the whole earth,
  Of man the wonderful, and of the stars,
And how the deuce they ever could have birth;
  And then he thought of earthquakes, and of wars,
How many miles the moon might have in girth,   445
  Of air-balloons, and of the many bars
To perfect knowledge of the boundless skies; —
And then he thought of Donna Julia's eyes.

XCIII.

In thoughts like these true wisdom may discern
  Longings sublime, and aspirations high,   450
Which some are born with, but the most part learn
  To plague themselves withal, they know not why:
'Twas strange that one so young should thus concern
  His brain about the action of the sky;
If *you* think 'twas Philosophy that this did,   455
I can't help thinking puberty assisted.

XCIV.

He pored upon the leaves, and on the flowers,
  And heard a voice in all the winds; and then
He thought of wood-nymphs and immortal bowers,
  And how the goddesses came down to men: 460
He miss'd the pathway, he forgot the hours,
  And when he look'd upon his watch again,
He found how much old Time had been a winner —
He also found that he had lost his dinner.

XCVI.

Thus would he while his lonely hours away   465
  Dissatisfied, nor knowing what he wanted;
Nor glowing reverie, nor poet's lay,
  Could yield his spirit that for which it panted,
A bosom whereon he his head might lay,
  And hear the heart beat with the love it granted,   470
With — several other things, which I forget,
Or which, at least, I need not mention yet.

XCVII.

Those lonely walks, and lengthening reveries,
  Could not escape the gentle Julia's eyes;
She saw that Juan was not at his ease;   475
  But that which chiefly may, and must surprise,
Is, that the Donna Inez did not tease
  Her only son with question or surmise;
Whether it was she did not see, or would not,
Or, like all very clever people, could not.   480

420: See Ovid, *Metamorphoses*, VII, for the story of Jason and Medea.

CI.

But Inez was so anxious, and so clear
   Of sight, that I must think, on this occasion,
She had some other motive much more near
   For leaving Juan to this new temptation;
But what that motive was, I sha'n't say here;   *485*
   Perhaps to finish Juan's education,
Perhaps to open Don Alfonso's eyes,
In case he thought his wife too great a prize.

CII.

It was upon a day, a summer's day; —
   Summer's indeed a very dangerous season,   *490*
And so is spring about the end of May;
   The sun, no doubt, is the prevailing reason;
But whatsoe'er the cause is, one may say,
   And stand convicted of more truth than treason,   *494*
That there are months which nature grows more merry in, —
March has its hares, and May must have its heroine.

CIII.

'Twas on a summer's day — the sixth of June: —
   I like to be particular in dates,
Not only of the age, and year, but moon;
   They are a sort of post-house, where the Fates   *500*
Change horses, making history change its tune,
   Then spur away o'er empires and o'er states,
Leaving at last not much besides chronology,
Excepting the post-obits of theology.

CIV.

'Twas on the sixth of June, about the hour   *505*
   Of half-past six — perhaps still nearer seven —
When Julia sate within as pretty a bower
   As e'er held houri in that heathenish heaven
Described by Mahomet, and Anacreon Moore,
   To whom the lyre and laurels have been given,   *510*
With all the trophies of triumphant song —
He won them well, and may he wear them long!

CV.

She sate, but not alone; I know not well
   How this same interview had taken place,
And even if I knew, I should not tell —   *515*

People should hold their tongues in any case;
   No matter how or why the thing befell,
   But there were she and Juan, face to face —
When two such faces are so, 'twould be wise,
But very difficult, to shut their eyes.   *520*

CVI.

How beautiful she look'd! her conscious heart
   Glow'd in her cheek, and yet she felt no wrong.
Oh Love! how perfect is thy mystic art,
   Strengthening the weak, and trampling on the strong,
How self-deceitful is the sagest part   *525*
   Of mortals whom thy lure hath led along —
The precipice she stood on was immense,
So was her creed in her own innocence.

CVII.

She thought of her own strength, and Juan's youth,
   And of the folly of all prudish fears,   *530*
Victorious virtue, and domestic truth,
   And then of Don Alfonso's fifty years:
I wish these last had not occurr'd, in sooth,
   Because that number rarely much endears,
And through all climes, the snowy and the sunny,   *535*
Sounds ill in love, whate'er it may in money.

CVIII.

When people say, "I've told you *fifty* times,"
   They mean to scold, and very often do;
When poets say, "I've written *fifty* rhymes,"
   They make you dread that they'll recite them too;   *540*
In gangs of *fifty*, thieves commit their crimes;
   At *fifty* love for love is rare, 'tis true,
But then, no doubt, it equally as true is,
A good deal may be bought for *fifty* Louis.

CIX.

Julia had honour, virtue, truth, and love,   *545*
   For Don Alfonso; and she inly swore,
By all the vows below to powers above,
   She never would disgrace the ring she wore,
Nor leave a wish which wisdom might reprove;
   And while she ponder'd this, besides much more,   *550*
One hand on Juan's carelessly was thrown,
Quite by mistake — she thought it was her own;

---

504. post-obits: bonds given by a borrower who promises to repay a loan after receiving an inheritance upon a particular person's death. **509. Anacreon Moore:** alluding to Thomas Moore's translation of the *Odes of Anacreon* (1800), and to "Paradise and the Peri," the second verse tale in his *Lalla Rookh* (1817). **528. creed:** belief, faith.

CX.

Unconsciously she lean'd upon the other,
 Which play'd within the tangles of her hair; *554*
And to contend with thoughts she could not smother
 She seem'd, by the distraction of her air.
'Twas surely very wrong in Juan's mother
 To leave together this imprudent pair,
She who for many years had watch'd her son so —
I'm very certain *mine* would not have done so. *560*

CXI.

The hand which still held Juan's, by degrees
 Gently, but palpably confirm'd its grasp,
As if it said, "Detain me, if you please";
 Yet there's no doubt she only meant to clasp
His fingers with a pure Platonic squeeze; *565*
 She would have shrunk as from a toad, or asp,
Had she imagined such a thing could rouse
A feeling dangerous to a prudent spouse.

CXII.

I cannot know what Juan thought of this,
 But what he did, is much what you would do; *570*
His young lip thank'd it with a grateful kiss,
 And then, abash'd at its own joy, withdrew
In deep despair, lest he had done amiss,
 Love is so very timid when 'tis new: *574*
She blush'd, and frown'd not, but she strove to speak,
And held her tongue, her voice was grown so weak.

CXIII.

The sun set, and up rose the yellow moon:
 The devil's in the moon for mischief; they
Who call'd her CHASTE, methinks, began too soon
 Their nomenclature; there is not a day, *580*
The longest, not the twenty-first of June,
 Sees half the business in a wicked way
On which three single hours of moonshine smile —
And then she looks so modest all the while!

CXIV.

There is a dangerous silence in that hour, *585*
 A stillness, which leaves room for the full soul
To open all itself, without the power
 Of calling wholly back its self-control;
The silver light which, hallowing tree and tower,
 Sheds beauty and deep softness o'er the whole, *590*
Breathes also to the heart, and o'er it throws
A loving languor, which is not repose.

CXV.

And Julia sate with Juan, half embraced
 And half retiring from the glowing arm, *594*
Which trembled like the bosom where 'twas placed;
 Yet still she must have thought there was no harm,
Or else 'twere easy to withdraw her waist;
 But then the situation had its charm,
And then — God knows what next — I can't go on;
I'm almost sorry that I e'er begun. *600*

CXVII.

And Julia's voice was lost, except in sighs,
 Until too late for useful conversation;
The tears were gushing from her gentle eyes,
 I wish, indeed, they had not had occasion,
But who, alas! can love, and then be wise? *605*
 Not that remorse did not oppose temptation,
A little still she strove, and much repented,
And whispering "I will ne'er consent" — consented.

CXX.

Here my chaste Muse a liberty must take — *609*
 Start not! still chaster reader — she'll be nice hence-
Forward, and there is no great cause to quake;
 This liberty is a poetic licence,
Which some irregularity may make
 In the design, and as I have a high sense
Of Aristotle and the Rules, 'tis fit *615*
To beg his pardon when I err a bit.

CXXI.

This licence is to hope the reader will
 Suppose from June the sixth (the fatal day,
Without whose epoch my poetic skill
 For want of facts would all be thrown away), *620*
But keeping Julia and Don Juan still
 In sight, that several months have pass'd; we'll say
'Twas in November, but I'm not so sure
About the day — the era's more obscure.

CXXVIII.

Man's a strange animal, and makes strange use *625*
 Of his own nature, and the various arts,
And likes particularly to produce
 Some new experiment to show his parts;
This is the age of oddities let loose,
 Where different talents find their different marts; *630*
You'd best begin with truth, and when you've lost your
Labour, there's a sure market for imposture.

---

615. Rules: i.e., those concerning the unities of time, place, and action in a dramatic structure.

CXXX.

Bread has been made (indifferent) from potatoes;
    And Galvanism has set some corpses grinning,
But has not answer'd like the apparatus   *635*
    Of the Humane Society's beginning
By which men are unsuffocated gratis:
    What wondrous new machines have late been spinning!
I said the small-pox has gone out of late;
Perhaps it may be follow'd by the great.   *640*

CXXXII.

This is the patent-age of new inventions
    For killing bodies, and for saving souls,
All propagated with the best intentions;
    Sir Humphry Davy's lantern, by which coals
Are safely mined for in the mode he mentions,   *645*
    Tombuctoo travels, voyages to the Poles,
Are ways to benefit mankind, as true,
Perhaps, as shooting them at Waterloo.

CXXXIV.

What then? — I do not know, no more do you —
    And so good night. — Return we to our story: *650*
'Twas in November, when fine days are few,
    And the far mountains wax a little hoary,
And clap a white cape on their mantles blue;
    And the sea dashes round the promontory,
And the loud breaker boils against the rock,   *655*
And sober suns must set at five o'clock.

CXXXV.

'Twas, as the watchmen say, a cloudy night;
    No moon, no stars, the wind was low or loud
By gusts, and many a sparkling hearth was bright
    With the piled wood, round which the family crowd;
There's something cheerful in that sort of light,   *661*
    Even as a summer sky's without a cloud:
I'm fond of fire, and crickets, and all that,
A lobster salad, and champagne, and chat.

CXXXVI.

'Twas midnight — Donna Julia was in bed,   *665*
    Sleeping, most probably, — when at her door
Arose a clatter might awake the dead,
    If they had never been awoke before,
And that they have been so we all have read,
    And are to be so, at the least, once more; —   *670*
The door was fasten'd, but with voice and fist
First knocks were heard, then "Madam — Madam — hist!

CXXXVII.

"For God's sake, Madam — Madam — here's my master,
    With more than half the city at his back —
Was ever heard of such a curst disaster!   *675*
    'Tis not my fault — I kept good watch — Alack!
Do pray undo the bolt a little faster —
    They're on the stair just now, and in a crack
Will all be here; perhaps he yet may fly —
Surely the window's not so *very* high!"   *680*

CXXXVIII.

By this time Don Alfonso was arrived,
    With torches, friends, and servants in great number;
The major part of them had long been wived,
    And therefore paused not to disturb the slumber
Of any wicked woman, who contrived   *685*
    By stealth her husband's temples to encumber:
Examples of this kind are so contagious,
Were *one* not punish'd, *all* would be outrageous.

CXXXIX.

I can't tell how, or why, or what suspicion
    Could enter into Don Alfonso's head;   *690*
But for a cavalier of his condition
    It surely was exceedingly ill-bred,
Without a word of previous admonition,
    To hold a levee round his lady's bed,
And summon lackeys, arm'd with fire and sword,   *695*
To prove himself the thing he most abhorr'd.

---

634. Galvanism: The Italian physician Luigi Galvani (1737-1798) had experimented with the muscle contractions of animal tissue, seeking a source and explanation of electricity; his nephew later experimented similarly on the corpse of an executed murderer. **636:** The Royal Humane Society was founded in England in 1774 for the purpose of encouraging attempts to resuscitate those supposed dead from drowning. **640. the great:** i.e., syphilis. **644:** Davy invented his safety lamp in 1815, the year Wellington defeated Napoleon at Waterloo. **646:** alluding to such travels as those of James Grey Jackson, who published a book about Morocco (1809), the many Arctic voyages of William Scoresby from 1803 on, and especially the flurry of Arctic explorations that began in 1818, such as those of Sir John Ross and Sir William Edward Parry, who both later published accounts of their joint and separate expeditions, including searches for the Northwest Passage and attempts to reach the North Pole. **686:** i.e., with the horns of a cuckold. **691. condition:** rank, social position.

CXL.

Poor Donna Julia! starting as from sleep,
   (Mind — that I do not say — she had not slept)
Began at once to scream, and yawn, and weep;
   Her maid Antonia, who was an adept,   700
Contrived to fling the bed-clothes in a heap,
   As if she had just now from out them crept:
I can't tell why she should take all this trouble
To prove her mistress had been sleeping double.

CXLI.

But Julia mistress, and Antonia maid,   705
   Appear'd like two poor harmless women, who
Of goblins, but still more of men afraid,
   Had thought one man might be deterr'd by two,
And therefore side by side were gently laid,
   Until the hours of absence should run through,   710
And truant husband should return, and say,
"My dear, I was the first who came away."

CXLII.

Now Julia found at length a voice, and cried,
   "In heaven's name, Don Alfonso, what d'ye mean?
Has madness seized you? would that I had died   715
   Ere such a monster's victim I had been!
What may this midnight violence betide,
   A sudden fit of drunkenness or spleen?
Dare you suspect me, whom the thought would kill!
Search, then, the room!" — Alfonso said, "I will." 720

CXLIII.

He search'd, *they* search'd, and rummaged everywhere,
   Closet and clothes' press, chest and window-seat,
And found much linen, lace, and several pair
   Of stockings, slippers, brushes, combs, complete,
With other articles of ladies fair,   725
   To keep them beautiful, or leave them neat:
Arras they prick'd and curtains with their swords,
And wounded several shutters, and some boards.

CXLIV.

Under the bed they search'd, and there they found —
   No matter what — it was not that they sought; 730
They open'd windows, gazing if the ground
   Had signs or footmarks, but the earth said nought;
And then they stared each others' faces round:
   'Tis odd, not one of all these seekers thought,
And seems to me almost a sort of blunder,   735
Of looking *in* the bed as well as under.

CXLV.

During this inquisition, Julia's tongue
   Was not asleep — "Yes, search and search," she cried,
"Insult on insult heap, and wrong on wrong!
   It was for this that I became a bride!   740
For this in silence I have suffer'd long
   A husband like Alfonso at my side;
But now I'll bear no more, nor here remain,
If there be law, or lawyers, in all Spain.

CXLVI.

"Yes, Don Alfonso! husband now no more,   745
   If ever you indeed deserved the name,
Is't worthy of your years? — you have threescore —
   Fifty, or sixty, it is all the same —
Is't wise or fitting, causeless to explore
   For facts against a virtuous woman's fame?   750
Ungrateful, perjured, barbarous Don Alfonso,
How dare you think your lady would go on so?

CXLIX.

"Did not the Italian Musico Cazzani
   Sing at my heart six months at least in vain?
Did not his countryman, Count Corniani,   755
   Call me the only virtuous wife in Spain?
Were there not also Russians, English, many?
   The Count Strongstroganoff I put in pain,
And Lord Mount Coffeehouse, the Irish peer,
Who kill'd himself for love (with wine) last year. 760

CL.

"Have I not had two bishops at my feet?
   The Duke of Ichar, and Don Fernan Nunez,
And is it thus a faithful wife you treat?
   I wonder in what quarter now the moon is:
I praise your vast forbearance not to beat   765
   Me also, since the time so opportune is —
Oh, valiant man! with sword drawn and cock'd trigger,
Now, tell me, don't you cut a pretty figure?

CLIV.

"And now, Hidalgo! now that you have thrown
   Doubt upon me, confusion over all,   770
Pray have the courtesy to make it known
   Who is the man you search for? how d'ye call
Him? what's his lineage? let him but be shown —
   I hope he's young and handsome — is he tall?
Tell me — and be assured, that since you stain 775
My honour thus, it shall not be in vain.

CLV.

"At least, perhaps, he has not sixty years,
    At that age he would be too old for slaughter,
Or for so young a husband's jealous fears —
    (Antonia! let me have a glass of water.)   780
I am ashamed of having shed these tears,
    They are unworthy of my father's daughter;
My mother dream'd not in my natal hour
That I should fall into a monster's power.

CLVII.

"And now, sir, I have done, and say no more;   785
    The little I have said may serve to show
The guileless heart in silence may grieve o'er
    The wrongs to whose exposure it is slow: —
I leave you to your conscience as before,
    'Twill one day ask you *why* you used me so?   790
God grant you feel not then the bitterest grief! —
Antonia! where's my pocket-handkerchief?"

CLVIII.

She ceased, and turn'd upon her pillow; pale
    She lay, her dark eyes flashing through their tears,
Like skies that rain and lighten; as a veil,   795
    Waved and o'ershading her wan cheek, appears
Her streaming hair; the black curls strive, but fail,
    To hide the glossy shoulder, which uprears
Its snow through all; — her soft lips lie apart,
And louder than her breathing beats her heart.   800

CLIX.

The Senhor Don Alfonso stood confused;
    Antonia bustled round the ransack'd room,
And, turning up her nose, with looks abused
    Her master, and his myrmidons, of whom
Not one, except the attorney, was amused;   805
    He, like Achates, faithful to the tomb,
So there were quarrels, cared not for the cause,
Knowing they must be settled by the laws.

CLXI.

But Don Alfonso stood with downcast looks,
    And, truth to say, he made a foolish figure;   810
When, after searching in five hundred nooks,
    And treating a young wife with so much rigour,
He gain'd no point, except some self-rebukes,
    Added to those his lady with such vigour
Had pour'd upon him for the last half-hour,   815
Quick, thick, and heavy — as a thunder-shower.

CLXII.

At first he tried to hammer an excuse,
    To which the sole reply was tears, and sobs,
And indications of hysterics, whose
    Prologue is always certain throes, and throbs,   820
Gasps, and whatever else the owners choose:
    Alfonso saw his wife, and thought of Job's;
He saw too, in perspective, her relations,
And then he tried to muster all his patience.

CLXIII.

He stood in act to speak, or rather stammer,   825
    But sage Antonia cut him short before
The anvil of his speech received the hammer,
    With "Pray, sir, leave the room, and say no more,
Or madam dies." — Alfonso mutter'd, "D—n her,"
    But nothing else, the time of words was o'er;   830
He cast a rueful look or two, and did,
He knew not wherefore, that which he was bid.

CLXIV.

With him retired his *"posse comitatus,"*
    The attorney last, who linger'd near the door,
Reluctantly, still tarrying there as late as   835
    Antonia let him — not a little sore
At this most strange and unexplain'd *"hiatus"*
    In Don Alfonso's facts, which just now wore
An awkward look; as he revolved the case,
The door was fasten'd in his legal face.   840

CLXV.

No sooner was it bolted, than — Oh shame!
    Oh sin! Oh sorrow! and Oh womankind!
How can you do such things and keep your fame,
    Unless this world, and t'other too, be blind?
Nothing so dear as an unfilch'd good name!   845
    But to proceed — for there is more behind:
With much heartfelt reluctance be it said,
Young Juan slipp'd, half-smother'd, from the bed.

CLXVIII.

Of his position I can give no notion:
    'Tis written in the Hebrew Chronicle,   850
How the physicians, leaving pill and potion,
    Prescribed, by way of blister, a young belle,
When old King David's blood grew dull in motion,
    And that the medicine answer'd very well;
Perhaps 'twas in a different way applied,   855
For David lived, but Juan nearly died.

---

806. **Achates:** the now proverbial *fidus Achates*, the faithful companion of Aeneas, in Virgil's *Aeneid*. 822. **Job's:** See Job 2:9-10. 845: Cf. Shakespeare's *Othello*, III, iii, 155-61. 850-56: See I Kings 1:1-4.

CLXIX.

What's to be done? Alfonso will be back
  The moment he has sent his fools away.
Antonia's skill was put upon the rack,
  But no device could be brought into play —   860
And how to parry the renew'd attack?
  Besides, it wanted but few hours of day:
Antonia puzzled; Julia did not speak,
But press'd her bloodless lip to Juan's cheek.

CLXX.

He turn'd his lip to hers, and with his hand   865
  Call'd back the tangles of her wandering hair;
Even then their love they could not all command,
  And half forgot their danger and despair:
Antonia's patience now was at a stand —
  "Come, come, 'tis no time now for fooling there,"   870
She whisper'd, in great wrath — "I must deposit
This pretty gentleman within the closet:

CLXXI.

"Pray, keep your nonsense for some luckier night —
  Who can have put my master in this mood?
What will become on't — I'm in such a fright,   875
  The devil's in the urchin, and no good —
Is this a time for giggling? this a plight?
  Why, don't you know that it may end in blood?
You'll lose your life, and I shall lose my place,
My mistress all, for that half-girlish face.   880

CLXXII.

"Had it but been for a stout cavalier
  Of twenty-five or thirty — (Come, make haste)
But for a child, what piece of work is here!
  I really, madam, wonder at your taste —
(Come, sir, get in) — my master must be near: 885
  There, for the present, at the least, he's fast,
And if we can but till the morning keep
Our counsel — (Juan, mind, you must not sleep.)"

CLXXIII.

Now, Don Alfonso entering, but alone,
  Closed the oration of the trusty maid: 890
She loiter'd, and he told her to be gone,
  An order somewhat sullenly obey'd;
However, present remedy was none,
  And no great good seem'd answer'd if she staid:
Regarding both with slow and sidelong view,   895
She snuff'd the candle, curtsied, and withdrew.

CLXXIV.

Alfonso paused a minute — then begun
  Some strange excuses for his late proceeding;
He would not justify what he had done,
  To say the best, it was extreme ill-breeding;   900
But there were ample reasons for it, none
  Of which he specified in this his pleading:
His speech was a fine sample, on the whole,
Of rhetoric, which the learn'd call "*rigmarole*."

CLXXV.

Julia said nought; though all the while there rose   905
  A ready answer, which at once enables
A matron, who her husband's foible knows,
  By a few timely words to turn the tables,
Which, if it does not silence, still must pose, —
  Even if it should comprise a pack of fables;   910
'Tis to retort with firmness, and when he
Suspects with *one*, do you reproach with *three*.

CLXXVI.

Julia, in fact, had tolerable grounds, —
  Alfonso's loves with Inez were well known;
But whether 'twas that one's own guilt confounds —
  But that can't be, as has been often shown,   916
A lady with apologies abounds; —
  It might be that her silence sprang alone
From delicacy to Don Juan's ear,
To whom she knew his mother's fame was dear.   920

CLXXVII.

There might be one more motive, which makes two;
  Alfonso ne'er to Juan had alluded, —
Mention'd his jealousy, but never who
  Had been the happy lover, he concluded,
Conceal'd amongst his premises; 'tis true,   925
  His mind the more o'er this its mystery brooded;
To speak of Inez now were, one may say,
Like throwing Juan in Alfonso's way.

CLXXVIII.

A hint, in tender cases, is enough;
  Silence is best, besides there is a *tact* —   930
(That modern phrase appears to me sad stuff,
  But it will serve to keep my verse compact) —
Which keeps, when push'd by questions rather rough,
  A lady always distant from the fact:
The charming creatures lie with such a grace,   935
There's nothing so becoming to the face.

CLXXIX.

They blush, and we believe them; at least I
  Have always done so; 'tis of no great use,
In any case, attempting a reply,
  For then their eloquence grows quite profuse;   940
And when at length they're out of breath, they sigh,
  And cast their languid eyes down, and let loose
A tear or two, and then we make it up;
And then — and then — and then — sit down and sup.

CLXXX.

Alfonso closed his speech, and begg'd her pardon, 945
  Which Julia half withheld, and then half granted,
And laid conditions, he thought, very hard on,
  Denying several little things he wanted:
He stood like Adam lingering near his garden,
  With useless penitence perplex'd and haunted,   950
Beseeching she no further would refuse,
When, lo! he stumbled o'er a pair of shoes.

CLXXXI.

A pair of shoes! — what then? not much, if they
  Are such as fit with ladies' feet, but these
(No one can tell how much I grieve to say)   955
  Were masculine; to see them, and to seize,
Was but a moment's act. — Ah! well-a-day!
  My teeth begin to chatter, my veins freeze —
Alfonso first examined well their fashion,
And then flew out into another passion.   960

CLXXXII.

He left the room for his relinquish'd sword,
  And Julia instant to the closet flew.
"Fly, Juan, fly! for heaven's sake — not a word —
  The door is open — you may yet slip through
The passage you so often have explored —   965
  Here is the garden-key — Fly — fly — Adieu!
Haste — haste! I hear Alfonso's hurrying feet —
Day has not broke — there's no one in the street."

CLXXXIII.

None can say that this was not good advice,
  The only mischief was, it came too late;   970
Of all experience 'tis the usual price,
  A sort of income-tax laid on by fate:
Juan had reach'd the room-door in a trice,
  And might have done so by the garden-gate,
But met Alfonso in his dressing-gown,   975
Who threaten'd death — so Juan knock'd him down.

CLXXXIV.

Dire was the scuffle, and out went the light;
  Antonia cried out "Rape!" and Julia "Fire!"
But not a servant stirr'd to aid the fight.
  Alfonso, pommell'd to his heart's desire,   980
Swore lustily he'd be revenged this night;
  And Juan, too, blasphemed an octave higher;
His blood was up: though young, he was a Tartar,
And not at all disposed to prove a martyr.

CLXXXVI.

Alfonso grappled to detain the foe,   985
  And Juan throttled him to get away,
And blood ('twas from the nose) began to flow;
  At last, as they more faintly wrestling lay,
Juan contrived to give an awkward blow,
  And then his only garment quite gave way;   990
He fled, like Joseph, leaving it; but there,
I doubt, all likeness ends between the pair.

CLXXXVII.

Lights came at length, and men, and maids, who found
  An awkward spectacle their eyes before;
Antonia in hysterics, Julia swoon'd,   995
  Alfonso leaning, breathless, by the door;
Some half-torn drapery scatter'd on the ground,
  Some blood, and several footsteps, but no more:
Juan the gate gain'd, turn'd the key about,
And liking not the inside, lock'd the out.   1000

CLXXXVIII.

Here ends this canto. — Need I sing, or say,
  How Juan, naked, favour'd by the night,
Who favours what she should not, found his way,
  And reach'd his home in an unseemly plight?
The pleasant scandal which arose next day,   1005
  The nine days' wonder which was brought to light,
And how Alfonso sued for a divorce,
Were in the English newspapers, of course.

CXC.

But Donna Inez, to divert the train
  Of one of the most circulating scandals   1010
That had for centuries been known in Spain,
  At least since the retirement of the Vandals,
First vow'd (and never had she vow'd in vain)
  To Virgin Mary several pounds of candles;
And then, by the advice of some old ladies,   1015
She sent her son to be shipp'd off from Cadiz.

991: See Genesis 39:12. **992. doubt:** suspect.

CXCIX.

This was Don Juan's earliest scrape; but whether
  I shall proceed with his adventures is
Dependent on the public altogether;
  We'll see, however, what they say to this,   *1020*
Their favour in an author's cap's a feather,
  And no great mischief's done by their caprice;
And if their approbation we experience,
Perhaps they'll have some more about a year hence.

CC.

My poem's epic, and is meant to be   *1025*
  Divided in twelve books; each book containing,
With love, and war, a heavy gale at sea,
  A list of ships, and captains, and kings reigning,
New characters; the episodes are three:
  A panoramic view of hell's in training,   *1030*
After the style of Virgil and of Homer,
So that my name of Epic's no misnomer.

CCI.

All these things will be specified in time,
  With strict regard to Aristotle's rules,
The *Vade Mecum* of the true sublime,   *1035*
  Which makes so many poets, and some fools:
Prose poets like blank-verse, I'm fond of rhyme,
  Good workmen never quarrel with their tools;
I've got new mythological machinery,
And very handsome supernatural scenery.   *1040*

CCII.

There's only one slight difference between
  Me and my epic brethren gone before,
And here the advantage is my own, I ween;
  (Not that I have not several merits more,
But this will more peculiarly be seen);   *1045*
  They so embellish, that 'tis quite a bore
Their labyrinth of fables to thread through,
Whereas this story's actually true.

CCIII.

If any person doubt it, I appeal
  To history, tradition, and to facts,   *1050*
To newspapers, whose truth all know and feel,
  To plays in five, and operas in three acts;
All these confirm my statement a good deal,
  But that which more completely faith exacts
Is, that myself, and several now in Seville,   *1055*
Saw Juan's last elopement with the devil.

CCVII.

If any person should presume to assert
  This story is not moral, first, I pray,
That they will not cry out before they're hurt,
  Then that they'll read it o'er again, and say,   *1060*
(But, doubtless, nobody will be so pert),
  That this is not a moral tale, though gay;
Besides, in Canto Twelfth, I mean to show
The very place where wicked people go.

CCXXI.

But for the present, gentle reader! and   *1065*
  Still gentler purchaser! the bard — that's I —
Must, with permission, shake you by the hand,
  And so your humble servant, and good-bye!
We meet again, if we should understand
  Each other; and if not, I shall not try   *1070*
Your patience further than by this short sample —
'Twere well if others follow'd my example.

CCXXII.

"Go, little Book, from this my solitude!
  I cast thee on the waters — go thy ways!
And if, as I believe, thy vein be good,   *1075*
  The World will find thee after many days."
When Southey's read, and Wordsworth understood,
  I can't help putting in my claim to praise —
The four first rhymes are Southey's every line:
For God's sake, reader! take them not for mine.   *1080*
                                                  (1819)

1025-40: See *epic* and *mock epic* in the Glossary. **1035: sublime:** See Glossary. **1073-76:** quoting from the last stanza ("L'Envoy") of Southey's *Epilogue to the Lay of the Laureate*.

THOMAS PRINGLE
Scotland/South Africa/England, 1789-1834

THE DESOLATE VALLEY

Far up among the forest-belted mountains,
Where Winterberg, stern giant old and grey,
Looks down the subject dells, whose gleaming fountains
To wizard Kat their virgin tribute pay,
A valley opens to the noontide ray,   5
With green savannahs shelving to the brim
Of the swift River, sweeping on his way
To where Umtóka hies to meet with him,
Like a blue serpent gliding through the acacias dim.

Round this secluded region circling rise   10
A billowy waste of mountains, wild and wide;
Upon whose grassy slopes the pilgrim spies
The gnu and quagga, by the greenwood side,
Tossing their shaggy manes in tameless pride;
Or troop of elands near some sedgy fount;   15
Or kùdù fawns, that from the thicket glide
To seek their dam upon the misty mount;
With harts, gazelles, and roes, more than the eye may count.

And as we journeyed up the pathless glen,
Flanked by romantic hills on either hand,   20
The boschbok oft would bound away — and then
Beside the willows, backward gazing, stand.
And where old forests darken all the land
From rocky Katberg to the river's brink,
The buffalo would start upon the strand,   25
Where, 'mid palmetto flags, he stooped to drink,
And, crashing through the brakes, to the deep jungle shrink.

Then, couched at night in hunter's wattled shieling,
How wildly beautiful it was to hear
The elephant his shrill *reveillé* pealing,   30

Like some far signal-trumpet on the ear!
While the broad midnight moon was shining clear,
How fearful to look forth upon the woods,
And see those stately forest-kings appear,
Emerging from their shadowy solitudes —   35
As if that trump had woke Earth's old gigantic broods!

Such the majestic, melancholy scene
Which 'midst that mountain-wilderness we found;
With scarce a trace to tell where man had been,
Save the old Caffer cabins crumbling round.   40
Yet this lone glen (Sicána's ancient ground),
To Nature's savage tribes abandoned long,
Had heard, erewhile, the Gospel's joyful sound,
And low of herds mixed with the Sabbath song.
But all is silent now. The Oppressor's hand was strong.   45

Now the blithe loxia hangs her pensile nest
From the wild-olive, bending o'er the rock,
Beneath whose shadow, in grave mantle drest,
The Christian Pastor taught his swarthy flock.
A roofless ruin, scathed by flame and smoke,   50
Tells where the decent Mission-chapel stood;
While the baboon with jabbering cry doth mock
The pilgrim, pausing in his pensive mood
To ask — "Why is it thus? Shall Evil baffle Good?"

Yes — for a season Satan may prevail,   55
And hold, as if secure, his dark domain;
The prayers of righteous men may seem to fail,
And Heaven's Glad Tidings be proclaimed in vain.
But wait in faith: ere long shall spring again
The seed that seemed to perish in the ground;   60

THE DESOLATE VALLEY The poem is set in Cape Province, South Africa, in the valley of the Kat River, or Katrivier, and its tributary, the Umtóka (see lines 3-9). **2. Winterberg:** a mountain ridge. **13. quagga:** native African horse, now extinct. **13-18:** Pringle's own notes about the various antelopes that were once found in the vicinity of the Winterberg indicate that he used the word "hart" to denote the South African hartebeest, "roe" for the reebok, "gnu" for the wildebeest, and "gazelle" for the reebok and smaller antelopes such as the springbok and klipspringer; the "eland" (or kanna) is the largest of the antelopes, the "kudu" somewhat smaller; the "boschbok" (line 21) characteristically lives in the dense brush (or "brakes," line 27), but ventures into the valleys to eat. **24. Katberg:** a mountain range to the east of the Kat River. **28. wattled shieling:** rough hut woven out of twigs. **30. reveillé:** Pringle's note suggests a likeness between a distant elephant call and the sound of a trumpet (see line 36). **40. Caffer:** Kaffir (a term which only later came to be used as a dismissive slur), referring here to the Xhosa. **41. Sicána:** Ntsikana, one of the leaders of a settlement near the Kat River that converted to Christianity, and composer of the first Christian hymn in Xhosa. **45. Oppressor's hand:** Wars between the Xhosa and the Ghonaquas or Khoikhoi (formerly called the Hottentot; see also line 65) in 1818 and 1819 led to some of the Christian converts becoming slaves to Afrikaner settlers and others being imprisoned on Robben Island. **46. loxia:** a crossbilled bird. **49. Pastor:** the missionary who converted Ntsikana and others, whom Pringle names as "Mr. Williams."

And, fertilised by Zion's latter rain,
The long-parched land shall laugh, with harvests crowned,
And through those silent wastes Jehovah's praise resound.

Look round that Vale: behold the unburied bones
Of Ghona's children withering in the blast: 65
The sobbing wind, that through the forest moans,
Whispers — "The spirit hath for ever passed!"

Thus, in the Vale of Desolation vast,
In moral death dark Afric's myriads lie;
But the Appointed Day shall dawn at last,   70
When, breathed on by a Spirit from on High,
The dry bones shall awake, and shout — "Our God is
    nigh!"

(1837)

PERCY BYSSHE SHELLEY
England, 1792-1822

HYMN TO INTELLECTUAL BEAUTY

I

The awful shadow of some unseen Power
    Floats though unseen among us, — visiting
    This various world with as inconstant wing
As summer winds that creep from flower to flower, —
Like moonbeams that behind some piny mountain shower,
    It visits with inconstant glance   6
    Each human heart and countenance;
Like hues and harmonies of evening, —
    Like clouds in starlight widely spread, —
    Like memory of music fled, —   10
    Like aught that for its grace may be
Dear, and yet dearer for its mystery.

II

Spirit of BEAUTY, that dost consecrate
    With thine own hues all thou dost shine upon
    Of human thought or form, — where art thou gone?   15
Why dost thou pass away and leave our state,
This dim vast vale of tears, vacant and desolate?
    Ask why the sunlight not for ever
    Weaves rainbows o'er yon mountain river,
Why aught should fail and fade that once is shown,   20
    Why fear and dream and death and birth
    Cast on the daylight of this earth
    Such gloom, — why man has such a scope
For love and hate, despondency and hope?

III

No voice from some sublimer world hath ever   25
    To sage or poet these responses given —
    Therefore the names of Demon, Ghost, and Heaven,
Remain the records of their vain endeavour,
Frail spells — whose uttered charm might not avail to sever,
    From all we hear and all we see,   30
    Doubt, chance, and mutability.
Thy light alone — like mist o'er mountains driven,
    Or music by the night-wind sent
    Through strings of some still instrument,
    Or moonlight on a midnight stream,   35
Gives grace and truth to life's unquiet dream.

IV

Love, Hope, and Self-esteem, like clouds depart
    And come, for some uncertain moments lent.
    Man were immortal, and omnipotent,
Didst thou, unknown and awful as thou art,   40
Keep with thy glorious train firm state within his heart.
    Thou messenger of sympathies,
    That wax and wane in lovers' eyes —
Thou — that to human thought art nourishment,
    Like darkness to a dying flame!   45
    Depart not as thy shadow came,
    Depart not — lest the grave should be,
Like life and fear, a dark reality.

---

67. "The spirit . . . passed": Cf. Luke 23:46. **68. Vale of Desolation:** Cf. "valley of the shadow of death" (Psalm 23; see p. 251). **70. Appointed Day:** See Acts 17:31. **72. dry bones:** See Ezekiel 37:1-14; **"Our God is nigh":** See Luke 21:31.   **HYMN TO INTELLECTUAL BEAUTY** *Intellectual* here means spiritual, non-material, knowable only by the intellect, the mind, and not by the senses; "intellectual beauty" is therefore akin to the Platonic "Idea" of Beauty. **34:** referring to a wind harp or Æolian harp.

V

While yet a boy I sought for ghosts, and sped
    Through many a listening chamber, cave and ruin,   *50*
    And starlight wood, with fearful steps pursuing
Hopes of high talk with the departed dead.
I called on poisonous names with which our youth is fed;
    I was not heard — I saw them not —
    When musing deeply on the lot   *55*
Of life, at that sweet time when winds are wooing
    All vital things that wake to bring
    News of birds and blossoming, —
    Sudden, thy shadow fell on me;
I shrieked, and clasped my hands in ecstasy!   *60*

VI

I vowed that I would dedicate my powers
    To thee and thine — have I not kept the vow?
    With beating heart and streaming eyes, even now
I call the phantoms of a thousand hours
Each from his voiceless grave: they have in visioned
        bowers   *65*
    Of studious zeal or love's delight
    Outwatched with me the envious night —
They know that never joy illumed my brow
    Unlinked with hope that thou wouldst free
    This world from its dark slavery,   *70*
    That thou — O awful LOVELINESS,
Wouldst give whate'er these words cannot express.

VII

The day becomes more solemn and serene
    When noon is past — there is a harmony
    In autumn, and a lustre in its sky,   *75*
Which through the summer is not heard or seen,
As if it could not be, as if it had not been!
    Thus let thy power, which like the truth
    Of nature on my passive youth
Descended, to my onward life supply   *80*
    Its calm — to one who worships thee,
    And every form containing thee,
    Whom, SPIRIT fair, thy spells did bind
To fear himself, and love all human kind.

               (1816)

MONT BLANC
Lines Written in the Vale of Chamouni

I

The everlasting universe of things
Flows through the mind, and rolls its rapid waves,
Now dark — now glittering — now reflecting gloom —
Now lending splendour, where from secret springs
The source of human thought its tribute brings   *5*
Of waters, — with a sound but half its own,
Such as a feeble brook will oft assume
In the wild woods, among the mountains lone,
Where waterfalls around it leap for ever,
Where woods and winds contend, and a vast river   *10*
Over its rocks ceaselessly bursts and raves.

II

Thus thou, Ravine of Arve — dark, deep Ravine —
Thou many-coloured, many-voiced vale,
Over whose pines, and crags, and caverns sail
Fast cloud-shadows and sunbeams: awful scene,   *15*
Where Power in likeness of the Arve comes down
From the ice-gulfs that gird his secret throne,
Bursting through these dark mountains like the flame
Of lightning through the tempest; — thou dost lie,
Thy giant brood of pines around thee clinging,   *20*
Children of elder time, in whose devotion
The chainless winds still come and ever came
To drink their odours, and their mighty swinging
To hear — an old and solemn harmony;
Thine earthly rainbows stretched across the sweep   *25*
Of the æthereal waterfall, whose veil
Robes some unsculptured image; the strange sleep
Which when the voices of the desert fail
Wraps all in its own deep eternity; —
Thy caverns echoing to the Arve's commotion,   *30*
A loud, lone sound no other sound can tame;
Thou art pervaded with that ceaseless motion,
Thou art the path of that unresting sound —
Dizzy Ravine! and when I gaze on thee
I seem as in a trance sublime and strange   *35*
To muse on my own separate fantasy,
My own, my human mind, which passively

MONT BLANC 9–11: Here and elsewhere (e.g. 30ff. and 120ff.) Shelley seems to be echoing Coleridge's "Kubla Khan" (see p. 782); there are also reminiscences of Wordsworth's "Tintern Abbey" and "Immortality Ode" (see pp. 755, 766). 12: The Arve flows from near Chamonix and Mont Blanc northwest to Lake Geneva. 15. awful: awesome.

Now renders and receives fast influencings,
Holding an unremitting interchange
With the clear universe of things around;   40
One legion of wild thoughts, whose wandering wings
Now float above thy darkness, and now rest
Where that or thou art no unbidden guest,
In the still cave of the witch Poesy,
Seeking among the shadows that pass by   45
Ghosts of all things that are, some shade of thee,
Some phantom, some faint image; till the breast
From which they fled recalls them, thou art there!

III

Some say that gleams of a remoter world
Visit the soul in sleep, — that death is slumber,   50
And that its shapes the busy thoughts outnumber
Of those who wake and live. — I look on high;
Has some unknown omnipotence unfurled
The veil of life and death? or do I lie
In dream, and does the mightier world of sleep   55
Spread far around and inaccessibly
Its circles? For the very spirit fails,
Driven like a homeless cloud from steep to steep
That vanishes among the viewless gales!
Far, far above, piercing the infinite sky,   60
Mont Blanc appears, — still, snowy, and serene —
Its subject mountains their unearthly forms
Pile around it, ice and rock; broad vales between
Of frozen floods, unfathomable deeps,
Blue as the overhanging heaven, that spread   65
And wind among the accumulated steeps;
A desert peopled by the storms alone,
Save when the eagle brings some hunter's bone,
And the wolf tracks her there — how hideously
Its shapes are heaped around! rude, bare, and high,   70
Ghastly, and scarred, and riven. — Is this the scene
Where the old Earthquake-dæmon taught her young
Ruin? Were these their toys? or did a sea
Of fire envelop once this silent snow?
None can reply — all seems eternal now.   75
The wilderness has a mysterious tongue
Which teaches awful doubt, or faith so mild,
So solemn, so serene, that man may be,
But for such faith, with nature reconciled;
Thou hast a voice, great Mountain, to repeal   80

Large codes of fraud and woe; not understood
By all, but which the wise, and great, and good
Interpret, or make felt, or deeply feel.

IV

The fields, the lakes, the forests, and the streams,
Ocean, and all the living things that dwell   85
Within the dædal earth; lightning, and rain,
Earthquake, and fiery flood, and hurricane,
The torpor of the year when feeble dreams
Visit the hidden buds, or dreamless sleep
Holds every future leaf and flower; — the bound   90
With which from that detested trance they leap;
The works and ways of man, their death and birth,
And that of him and all that his may be;
All things that move and breathe with toil and sound
Are born and die; revolve, subside, and swell.   95
Power dwells apart in its tranquillity,
Remote, serene, and inaccessible:
And *this,* the naked countenance of earth,
On which I gaze, even these primæval mountains
Teach the adverting mind. The glaciers creep   100
Like snakes that watch their prey, from their far fountains,
Slow rolling on; there, many a precipice,
Frost and the Sun in scorn of mortal power
Have piled: dome, pyramid, and pinnacle,
A city of death, distinct with many a tower   105
And wall impregnable of beaming ice.
Yet not a city, but a flood of ruin
Is there, that from the boundaries of the sky
Rolls its perpetual stream; vast pines are strewing
Its destined path, or in the mangled soil   110
Branchless and shattered stand; the rocks, drawn down
From yon remotest waste, have overthrown
The limits of the dead and living world,
Never to be reclaimed. The dwelling-place
Of insects, beasts, and birds, becomes its spoil,   115
Their food and their retreat for ever gone,
So much of life and joy is lost. The race
Of man flies far in dread; his work and dwelling
Vanish, like smoke before the tempest's stream,
And their place is not known. Below, vast caves   120
Shine in the rushing torrents' restless gleam,
Which from those secret chasms in tumult welling
Meet in the vale, and one majestic River,

---

59. viewless: not to be viewed, invisible. **86. dædal:** artfully and skillfully formed or devised, ingenious, intricate (after Dædalus, legendary artist and inventor, maker of the Cretan Labyrinth); but here a less common meaning also applies, that of "fertile, fruitful," as in Spenser's *Faerie Queene,* IV, x, stanza 45: "Then doth the dædale earth throw forth to thee / Out of her fruitfull lap aboundant flowres."

The breath and blood of distant lands, forever
Rolls its loud waters to the ocean waves,   125
Breathes its swift vapours to the circling air.

V

Mont Blanc yet gleams on high: — the power is there,
The still and solemn power of many sights,
And many sounds, and much of life and death.
In the calm darkness of the moonless nights,   130
In the lone glare of day, the snows descend
Upon that Mountain; none beholds them there,
Nor when the flakes burn in the sinking sun,
Or the star-beams dart through them: — Winds contend
Silently there, and heap the snow with breath   135
Rapid and strong, but silently! Its home
The voiceless lightning in these solitudes
Keeps innocently, and like vapour broods
Over the snow. The secret Strength of things
Which governs thought, and to the infinite dome   140
Of Heaven is as a law, inhabits thee!
And what were thou, and earth, and stars, and sea,
If to the human mind's imaginings
Silence and solitude were vacancy?

(1816)

OZYMANDIAS

I met a traveller from an antique land
Who said: "Two vast and trunkless legs of stone
Stand in the desert . . . Near them, on the sand,
Half sunk, a shattered visage lies, whose frown,
And wrinkled lip, and sneer of cold command,   5
Tell that its sculptor well those passions read
Which yet survive, stamped on these lifeless things,
The hand that mocked them, and the heart that fed;
And on the pedestal these words appear:
'My name is Ozymandias, king of kings: 10

Look on my works, ye Mighty, and despair!'
Nothing beside remains. Round the decay
Of that colossal wreck, boundless and bare
The lone and level sands stretch far away."

(1817)

ENGLAND IN 1819

An old, mad, blind, despised, and dying king;
Princes, the dregs of their dull race, who flow
Through public scorn — mud from a muddy spring;
Rulers who neither see, nor feel, nor know,
But leech-like to their fainting country cling   5
Till they drop, blind in blood, without a blow;
A people starved and stabbed in the untilled field;
An army, which liberticide and prey
Makes as a two-edged sword to all who wield;
Golden and sanguine laws which tempt and slay;   10
Religion Christless, Godless — a book sealed;
A Senate — Time's worst statute unrepealed, —
Are graves, from which a glorious Phantom may
Burst to illumine our tempestuous day.

(1819; 1839)

ODE TO THE WEST WIND

I

O wild West Wind, thou breath of Autumn's being,
Thou, from whose unseen presence the leaves dead
Are driven, like ghosts from an enchanter fleeing,

Yellow, and black, and pale, and hectic red,
Pestilence-stricken multitudes: O thou,   5
Who chariotest to their dark wintry bed

The winged seeds, where they lie cold and low,
Each like a corpse within its grave, until
Thine azure sister of the Spring shall blow

OZYMANDIAS   Title: the Greek name for Ramses II (13th century B.C.), who left many monuments to himself, including a huge statue which Diodorus Siculus says bore a boastful inscription similar to that which Shelley puts in lines 10-11.   **ENGLAND IN 1819** 1: George III. **2. Princes:** the king's sons, including the Prince Regent (later George IV) and the future William IV. 7: the "Peterloo massacre" (16 August 1819), in which charging cavalry killed several and injured hundreds while stopping a pro-reform rally in St. Peter's Field, Manchester — nicknamed in ironic reference to the battle of Waterloo; see also Shelley's "The Mask of Anarchy." **12. statute:** the Test Acts, imposing restrictions on Nonconformists (dissenters) and Roman Catholics — mainly intended to prevent them from holding office (generally repealed in 1828, but for university posts not until the University Tests Act of 1871).   **ODE TO THE WEST WIND**   "This poem was conceived and chiefly written in a wood that skirts the Arno, near Florence, and on a day when that tempestuous wind, whose temperature is at once mild and animating, was collecting the vapours which pour down the autumnal rains. They began, as I foresaw, at sunset with a violent tempest of hail and rain, attended by that magnificent thunder and lightning peculiar to the Cisalpine regions. The phenomenon alluded to at the conclusion of the third stanza is well known to naturalists. The vegetation at the bottom of the sea, of rivers, and of lakes, sympathizes with that of the land in the change of seasons, and is consequently influenced by the winds which announce it" (Shelley's note). **4. hectic:** feverish, flushed.

Her clarion o'er the dreaming earth, and fill   *10*
(Driving sweet buds like flocks to feed in air)
With living hues and odours plain and hill:

Wild Spirit, which art moving everywhere;
Destroyer and preserver; hear, oh, hear!   *14*

II
Thou on whose stream, mid the steep sky's commotion,
Loose clouds like Earth's decaying leaves are shed,
Shook from the tangled boughs of Heaven and Ocean,

Angels of rain and lightning: there are spread
On the blue surface of thine aery surge,
Like the bright hair uplifted from the head   *20*

Of some fierce Mænad, even from the dim verge
Of the horizon to the zenith's height,
The locks of the approaching storm. Thou dirge

Of the dying year, to which this closing night
Will be the dome of a vast sepulchre,   *25*
Vaulted with all thy congregated might

Of vapours, from whose solid atmosphere
Black rain, and fire, and hail will burst: oh, hear!

III
Thou who didst waken from his summer dreams
The blue Mediterranean, where he lay,   *30*
Lulled by the coil of his crystalline streams,

Beside a pumice isle in Baiæ's bay,
And saw in sleep old palaces and towers
Quivering within the wave's intenser day,

All overgrown with azure moss and flowers   *35*
So sweet, the sense faints picturing them! Thou
For whose path the Atlantic's level powers

Cleave themselves into chasms, while far below
The sea-blooms and the oozy woods which wear
The sapless foliage of the ocean, know   *40*

Thy voice, and suddenly grow grey with fear,
And tremble and despoil themselves: oh, hear!

IV
If I were a dead leaf thou mightest bear;
If I were a swift cloud to fly with thee;
A wave to pant beneath thy power, and share   *45*

The impulse of thy strength, only less free
Than thou, O uncontrollable! If even
I were as in my boyhood, and could be

The comrade of thy wanderings over Heaven,
As then, when to outstrip thy skiey speed   *50*
Scarce seemed a vision; I would ne'er have striven

As thus with thee in prayer in my sore need.
Oh, lift me as a wave, a leaf, a cloud!
I fall upon the thorns of life! I bleed!

A heavy weight of hours has chained and bowed   *55*
One too like thee: tameless, and swift, and proud.

V
Make me thy lyre, even as the forest is:
What if my leaves are falling like its own!
The tumult of thy mighty harmonies

Will take from both a deep, autumnal tone,   *60*
Sweet though in sadness. Be thou, Spirit fierce,
My spirit! Be thou me, impetuous one!

Drive my dead thoughts over the universe
Like withered leaves to quicken a new birth!
And, by the incantation of this verse,   *65*

Scatter, as from an unextinguished hearth
Ashes and sparks, my words among mankind!
Be through my lips to unawakened earth

The trumpet of a prophecy! O Wind,
If Winter comes, can Spring be far behind?   *70*
                                             (1819)

TO A SKYLARK

Hail to thee, blithe Spirit!
    Bird thou never wert,
    That from Heaven, or near it,
        Pourest thy full heart
In profuse strains of unpremeditated art.   *5*

    Higher still and higher
        From the earth thou springest
    Like a cloud of fire;
        The blue deep thou wingest,
And singing still dost soar, and soaring ever singest.   *10*

---

13. Spirit: Latin *spiritus* means "breath, breeze" (see line 1). **18. Angels:** messengers (from Greek *angelos*). **21. Mænad:** frenzied woman participant in the cult of Dionysus (Bacchus). **32. Baiæ:** fashionable Roman resort town near Naples; its ruins are under water as a result of subsidences during earthquakes. **57. lyre:** i.e., wind harp.

In the golden lightning
   Of the sunken sun,
O'er which clouds are bright'ning,
   Thou dost float and run;
Like an unbodied joy whose race is just begun.   *15*

The pale purple even
   Melts around thy flight;
Like a star of Heaven
   In the broad daylight
Thou art unseen, but yet I hear thy shrill delight,   *20*

Keen as are the arrows
   Of that silver sphere,
Whose intense lamp narrows
   In the white dawn clear
Until we hardly see — we feel that it is there.   *25*

All the earth and air
   With thy voice is loud,
As, when night is bare,
   From one lonely cloud
The moon rains out her beams, and Heaven is overflowed.

What thou art we know not;   *31*
   What is most like thee?
From rainbow clouds there flow not
   Drops so bright to see
As from thy presence showers a rain of melody.   *35*

Like a Poet hidden
   In the light of thought,
Singing hymns unbidden,
   Till the world is wrought
To sympathy with hopes and fears it heeded not: *40*

Like a high-born maiden
   In a palace tower,
Soothing her love-laden
   Soul in secret hour
With music sweet as love, which overflows her bower: *45*

Like a glow-worm golden
   In a dell of dew,
Scattering unbeholden
   Its aereal hue
Among the flowers and grass, which screen it from the view:

Like a rose embowered   *51*
   In its own green leaves,
By warm winds deflowered,
   Till the scent it gives
Makes faint with too much sweet those heavy-winged thieves:

Sound of vernal showers   *56*
   On the twinkling grass,
Rain-awakened flowers,

All that ever was
Joyous, and clear, and fresh, thy music doth surpass.   *60*

Teach us, Sprite or Bird,
   What sweet thoughts are thine;
I have never heard
   Praise of love or wine
That panted forth a flood of rapture so divine.   *65*

Chorus Hymeneal,
   Or triumphal chaunt,
Matched with thine, would be all
   But an empty vaunt,
A thing wherein we feel there is some hidden want.   *70*

What objects are the fountains
   Of thy happy strain?
What fields, or waves, or mountains?
   What shapes of sky or plain?
What love of thine own kind? what ignorance of pain?   *75*

With thy clear keen joyance
   Languor cannot be;
Shadow of annoyance
   Never came near thee:
Thou lovest — but ne'er knew love's sad satiety.   *80*

Waking or asleep,
   Thou of death must deem
Things more true and deep
   Than we mortals dream,
Or how could thy notes flow in such a crystal stream?   *85*

We look before and after,
   And pine for what is not;
Our sincerest laughter
   With some pain is fraught;
Our sweetest songs are those that tell of saddest thought.

Yet if we could scorn   *91*
   Hate, and pride, and fear;
If we were things born
   Not to shed a tear,
I know not how thy joy we ever should come near.   *95*

Better than all measures
   Of delightful sound,
Better than all treasures
   That in books are found,
Thy skill to poet were, thou scorner of the ground!   *100*

Teach me half the gladness
   That thy brain must know,
Such harmonious madness
   From my lips would flow
The world should listen then — as I am listening now.   *105*

        (1820)

To— : "Music, when soft voices die"

Music, when soft voices die,
Vibrates in the memory —
Odours, when sweet violets sicken,
Live within the sense they quicken.

Rose leaves, when the rose is dead, 5
Are heaped for the belovèd's bed;
And so thy thoughts, when thou art gone,
Love itself shall slumber on.

(1821; 1824)

Lines: "When the lamp is shattered"

When the lamp is shattered
The light in the dust lies dead —
When the cloud is scattered
The rainbow's glory is shed.
When the lute is broken, 5
Sweet tones are remembered not;
When the lips have spoken,
Loved accents are soon forgot.

As music and splendour
Survive not the lamp and the lute, 10
The heart's echoes render
No song when the spirit is mute:
No song but sad dirges,
Like the wind through a ruined cell,
Or the mournful surges 15
That ring the dead seaman's knell.

When hearts have once mingled
Love first leaves the well-built nest;
The weak one is singled
To endure what it once possessed. 20
O Love! who bewailest
The frailty of all things here,
Why choose you the frailest
For your cradle, your home, and your bier?

Its passions will rock thee 25
As the storms rock the ravens on high;
Bright reason will mock thee,
Like the sun from a wintry sky.
From thy nest every rafter
Will rot, and thine eagle home 30
Leave thee naked to laughter,
When leaves fall and cold winds come.

(1822; 1824)

Felicia Hemans
England, 1793-1835

Casabianca

The boy stood on the burning deck,
Whence all but he had fled;
The flame that lit the battle's wreck
Shone round him o'er the dead.

Yet beautiful and bright he stood 5
As born to rule the storm —
A creature of heroic blood,
A proud, though child-like form!

The flames rolled on — he would not go
Without his Father's word; 10
That Father, faint in death below,
His voice no longer heard.

He called aloud: "Say, father, say
If yet my task is done!"
He knew not that the chieftain lay 15
Unconscious of his son.

"Speak, father!" once again he cried,
"If I may yet be gone!"
And but the booming shots replied,
And fast the flames rolled on. 20

Upon his brow he felt their breath,
And in his waving hair;
And looked from that lone post of death
In still, yet brave, despair;

Casabianca **Title:** after Louis Casabianca (c.1752-1798), Corsican-born French revolutionary commander who refused to leave his burning ship, the *Orient*, during the Battle of the Nile at Aboukir Bay in 1798, and whose young son refused to leave him; the British, under Captain Horatio Nelson, won the battle, securing their influence in the Mediterranean. See also the poem of the same title by Elizabeth Bishop (p. 1370).

And shouted but once more aloud,   25
  "My father! must I stay?"
While o'er him fast, through sail and shroud,
  The wreathing fires made way.

They wrapt the ship in splendour wild,
  They caught the flag on high,   30
And streamed above the gallant child
  Like banners in the sky.

There came a burst of thunder-sound —
  The boy — O! where was he?
— Ask of the winds that far around   35
  With fragments strewed the sea! —

With mast, and helm, and pennon fair,
  That well had borne their part;
But the noblest thing which perished there
  Was that young faithful heart!   40
                                    (1829)

JOHN CLARE
England, 1793-1864

THE YELLOWHAMMER

When shall I see the white thorn leaves agen
And Yellowhammers gath'ring the dry bents
By the Dyke side on stilly moor or fen
Feathered wi love and natures good intents
Rude is the nest this Architect invents   5
Rural the place wi cart ruts by dyke side
Dead grass, horse hair and downy headed bents
Tied to dead thistles she doth well provide
Close to a hill o' ants where cowslips bloom
And shed o'er meadows far their sweet perfume   10
In early Spring when winds blow chilly cold
The yellow hammer trailing grass will come
To fix a place and choose an early home
With yellow breast and head of solid gold
                              (1842-64; 1920)

"THE THUNDER MUTTERS LOUDER & MORE LOUD"

The thunder mutters louder & more loud
With quicker motion hay folks ply the rake
Ready to burst slow sails the pitch black cloud
& all the gang a bigger haycock make
To sit beneath — the woodland winds awake   5
The drops so large wet all thro' in an hour
A tiney flood runs down the leaning rake
In the sweet hay yet dry the hay folks cower
& some beneath the waggon shun the shower
                              (1845; 1984)

I AM

I am: yet what I am none cares or knows,
  My friends forsake me like a memory lost;
I am the self-consumer of my woes,
  They rise and vanish in oblivious host,
Like shades in love and death's oblivion lost;   5
And yet I am, and live with shadows tost

Into the nothingness of scorn and noise,
  Into the living sea of waking dreams,
Where there is neither sense of life nor joys,
  But the vast shipwreck of my life's esteems; 10
And e'en the dearest — that I loved the best —
Are strange — nay, rather stranger than the rest.

I long for scenes where man has never trod,
  A place where woman never smiled or wept;
There to abide with my Creator, God,   15
  And sleep as I in childhood sweetly slept:
Untroubling and untroubled where I lie,
The grass below — above the vaulted sky.
                                    (1848)

---

37. pennon: flag.   **THE YELLOWHAMMER   1. agen:** an artificial spelling of "again," common during the early 19th century; the idiosyncratic punctuation and the inconsistent spellings in this poem and "The thunder mutters" reflect Clare's manuscript practice.   **THE THUNDER MUTTERS   4. gang:** group — i.e., of haymakers.

WILLIAM CARLETON
Ireland, 1794-1869

THE HEDGE SCHOOL

The village of Findramore was situated at the foot of a long green hill, the outline of which formed a low arch, as it rose to the eye against the horizon. This hill was studded with clumps of beeches, and sometimes enclosed as a meadow. In the month of July, when the grass on it was long, many an hour have I spent in solitary enjoyment, watching the wavy motion produced upon its pliant surface by the sunny winds, or the *5* flight of the cloud-shadows, like gigantic phantoms, as they swept rapidly over it, whilst the murmur of the rocking trees, and the glancing of their bright leaves in the sun, produced a heartfelt pleasure, the very memory of which rises in my imagination like some fading recollection of a brighter world.

At the foot of this hill ran a clear, deep-banked river, bounded on one side by a slip *10* of rich, level meadow, and on the other by a kind of common for the village geese, whose white feathers, during the summer season, lay scattered over its green surface. It was also the play-ground for the boys of the village school; for there ran that part of the river which, with very correct judgment, the urchins had selected as their bathing-place. A little slope, or watering-ground in the bank, brought them to the edge of the stream, *15* where the bottom fell away into the fearful depths of the whirlpool, under the hanging oak on the other bank. Well do I remember the first time I ventured to swim across it, and even yet do I see, in imagination, the two bunches of water flaggons on which the inexperienced swimmers trusted themselves in the water.

About two hundred yards above this, the *boreen*, which led from the village to the *20* main road, crossed the river, by one of those old narrow bridges whose arches rise like round ditches across the road — an almost impassable barrier to horse and car. On passing the bridge, in a northern direction, you found a range of low thatched houses on each side of the road: and if one o'clock, the hour of dinner, drew near, you might observe columns of blue smoke curling up from a row of chimneys, some made of *25* wicker creels plastered over with a rich coat of mud; some, of old, narrow, bottomless tubs; and others, with a greater appearance of taste, ornamented with thick, circular ropes of straw, sewed together like bees' skeps, with the peel of a brier; and many having nothing but the open vent above. But the smoke by no means escaped by its legitimate aperture, for you might observe little clouds of it bursting out of the doors and *30* windows; the panes of the latter being mostly stopped at other times with old hats and rags, were now left entirely open for the purpose of giving it a free escape.

Before the doors, on right and left, was a series of dunghills, each with its concomitant sink of green, rotten water; and if it happened that a stout-looking woman,

---

THE HEDGE SCHOOL   **Title:** a low quality school, after the name given to schools held "by the hedge-side," in the open air. **1. Findramore:** perhaps based on Findrum in Tyrone, the county in which Carleton was born. **18. flaggons:** empty bottles, being used here as floats. **20. *boreen*:** road. **26. creels:** frameworks. **28. skeps:** hives; **peel of a brier:** tower made of thornbush or wild rose twigs. **34. sink:** cesspool.

with watery eyes, and a yellow cap hung loosely upon her matted locks, came, with a   *35*
chubby urchin on one arm, and a pot of dirty water in her hand, its unceremonious
ejection in the aforesaid sink would be apt to send you up the village with your finger
and thumb (for what purpose you would yourself perfectly understand) closely, but not
knowingly, applied to your nostrils. But, independently of this, you would be apt to have
other reasons for giving your horse, whose heels are by this time surrounded by a dozen   *40*
of barking curs, and the same number of shouting urchins, a pretty sharp touch of the
spurs, as well as for complaining bitterly of the odour of the atmosphere. It is no
landscape without figure; and you might notice, if you are, as I suppose you to be, a man
of observation, in every sink as you pass along, a "slip-of-a-pig," stretched in the middle
of the mud, the very *beau ideal* of luxury, giving occasionally a long, luxuriant grunt,   *45*
highly expressive of his enjoyment; or, perhaps, an old farrower, lying in indolent
repose, with half a dozen young ones jostling each other for their draught, and punching
her belly with their little snouts, reckless of the fumes they are creating; whilst the loud
crow of the cock, as he confidently flaps his wings on his own dunghill, gives the
warning note for the hour of dinner.   *50*

As you advance, you will also perceive several faces thrust out of the doors, and
rather than miss a sight of you, a grotesque visage peeping by a short cut through the
paneless windows — or a tattered female flying to snatch up her urchin that has been
tumbling itself, heels up, in the dust of the road, lest "the gintleman's horse might ride
over it"; and if you happen to look behind, you may observe a shaggy-headed youth in   *55*
tattered frize, with one hand thrust indolently in his breast, standing at the door in
conversation with the inmates, a broad grin of sarcastic ridicule on his face, in the act of
breaking a joke or two upon yourself, or your horse; or, perhaps, your jaw may be
saluted with a lump of clay, just hard enough not to fall asunder as it flies, cast by some
ragged gorsoon from behind a hedge, who squats himself in a ridge of corn to avoid   *60*
detection.

Seated upon a hob at the door, you may observe a toil-worn man, without coat or
waistcoat; his red, muscular, sunburnt shoulder peering through the remnant of a shirt,
mending his shoes with a piece of twisted flax, called a *lingel*, or, perhaps, sewing two
footless stockings (or *martyeens*) to his coat, as a substitute for sleeves.   *65*

In the gardens, which are usually fringed with nettles, you will see a solitary
labourer, working with that carelessness and apathy that characterise an Irishman when
he labours *for himself* — leaning upon his spade to look after you, and glad of any
excuse to be idle.

The houses, however, are not all such as I have described — far from it. You see   *70*
here and there, between the more humble cabins, a stout, comfortable-looking farmhouse, with ornamental thatching and well-glazed windows; adjoining to which is a hay-
yard, with five or six large stacks of corn, well-trimmed and roped, and a fine, yellow,
weather-beaten old hay-rick, half cut — not taking into account twelve or thirteen
circular strata of stones, that mark out the foundations on which others have been raised.   *75*

---

46. farrower: pig with a litter. **56. frize:** i.e., frieze, a coarse woollen cloth. **60. gorsoon:** i.e., "garçon," boy; **corn:** grain. **62. hob:** possibly part of a sledge, or skid; more likely a "hub," the centre part of a cart wheel. **71. stout:** strong.

Neither is the rich smell of oaten or wheaten bread, which the good wife is baking on the griddle, unpleasant to your nostrils; nor would the bubbling of a large pot, in which you might see, should you chance to enter, a prodigious square of fat, yellow, and almost transparent bacon tumbling about, to be an unpleasant object; truly, as it hangs over a large fire, with well-swept hearthstone, it is in good keeping with the white settle *80* and chairs, and the dresser with noggins, wooden trenchers, and pewter dishes, perfectly clean, and as well polished as a French courtier.

As you leave the village, you have, to the left, a view of the hill which I have already described, and to the right a level expanse of fertile country, bounded by a good view of respectable mountains, peering decently into the sky; and in a line that forms an *85* acute angle from the point of the road where you ride, is a delightful valley, in the bottom of which shines a pretty lake; and a little beyond, on the slope of a green hill, rises a splendid house, surrounded by a park, well-wooded and stocked with deer. You have now topped the little hill above the village, and a straight line of level road, a mile long, goes forward to a country town, which lies immediately behind that white church *90* with its spire cutting into the sky, before you. You descend on the other side, and, having advanced a few perches, look to the left, where you see a long, thatched chapel, only distinguished from a dwelling-house by its want of chimneys, and a small stone cross that stands on the top of the eastern gable; behind it is a graveyard; and beside it a snug public-house, well white-washed; then, to the right, you observe a door apparently *95* in the side of a clay bank, which rises considerably above the pavement of the road. What! you ask yourself, can this be a human habitation? — but ere you have time to answer the question, a confused buzz of voices from within reaches your ear, and the appearance of a little "gorsoon," with a red, close-cropped head and Milesian face, having in his hand a short, white stick, or the thigh-bone of a horse, which you at once *100* recognise as "the pass" of a village school, gives you the full information. He has an ink-horn, covered with leather, dangling at the button-hole (for he has long since played away the buttons) of his frize jacket — his mouth is circumscribed with a streak of ink — his pen is stuck knowingly behind his ear — his shins are dotted over with fire-blisters, black, red, and blue — on each heel a kibe — his "leather crackers," *videlicet* *105* — breeches, shrunk up upon him, and only reaching as far down as the caps of his knees. Having spied you, he places his hand over his brows, to throw back the dazzling light of the sun, and peers at you from under it, till he breaks out into a laugh, exclaiming, half to himself, half to you,

"You a gintleman! — no, nor one of your breed never was, you procthorin' thief, *110* you!"

You are now immediately opposite the door of the seminary, when a half a dozen of those seated next it notice you.

"Oh, sir, here's a gintleman on a horse! — masther, sir, here's a gintleman on a horse, wid boots and spurs on him, that's looking in at us." *115*

---

80. settle: bench. **81. noggins:** mugs; **trenchers:** wooden plates. **92. perches:** rods. **93. want:** lack. **99. Milesian:** Irish (i.e., descended from the legendary King Milesius of Spain, whose sons were said to have conquered the native Firbolgs of Ireland). **101. pass:** i.e., a permit to be out of class (see lines 118-19). **102. ink-horn:** container for ink. **104-05. fire-blisters:** chilblains. **105. kibe:** ulcerated chilblain; *videlicet:* (Latin) that is to say. **110. procthorin':** proctoring, in the sense of begging, but used here primarily to intensify the abuse.

"Silence!" exclaims the master; "back from the door; boys rehearse; every one of you rehearse, I say, you Bœotians, till the gintleman goes past!"

"I want to go out, if you plase, sir."

"No, you don't, Phelim."

"I do, indeed, sir."   *120*

"What! — is it afther conthradictin' me you'd be? Don't you see the porter's out, and you can't go."

"Well, 'tis Mat Meehan has it, sir: and he's out this half-hour, sir; I can't stay in, sir — iphfff — iphfff!"

"You want to be idling your time looking at the gintleman, Phelim."   *125*

"No, indeed, sir — iphfff!"

"Phelim, I know you of ould — go to your sate. I tell you, Phelim, you were born for the encouragement of the hemp manufacture, and you'll die promoting it."

In the meantime, the master puts his head out of the door, his body stooped to a "half bend" — a phrase, and the exact curve which it forms, I leave for the present to   *130* your own sagacity — and surveys you until you pass. That is an Irish hedge-school, and the personage who follows you with his eye, a hedge-schoolmaster.

(1830)

WILLIAM CULLEN BRYANT
U.S.A., 1794-1878

TO A WATERFOWL

Whither, 'midst falling dew,
While glow the heavens with the last steps of day,
Far, through their rosy depths, dost thou pursue
    Thy solitary way?

Vainly the fowler's eye   *5*
Might mark thy distant flight, to do thee wrong,
As, darkly seen against the crimson sky,
    Thy figure floats along.

Seek'st thou the plashy brink
Of weedy lake, or marge of river wide,   *10*
Or where the rocking billows rise and sink
    On the chafed ocean side?

There is a Power, whose care
Teaches thy way along that pathless coast, —
The desert and illimitable air,   *15*
    Lone wandering, but not lost.

All day thy wings have fanned,
At that far height, the cold thin atmosphere;
Yet stoop not, weary, to the welcome land,
    Though the dark night is near.   *20*

And soon that toil shall end,
Soon shalt thou find a summer home, and rest,
And scream among thy fellows; reeds shall bend,
    Soon, o'er thy sheltered nest.

Thou'rt gone, the abyss of heaven   *25*
Hath swallowed up thy form, yet, on my heart
Deeply hath sunk the lesson thou hast given,
    And shall not soon depart.

He, who, from zone to zone,
Guides through the boundless sky thy certain flight,   *30*
In the long way that I must trace alone,
    Will lead my steps aright.

(1818)

---

116. rehearse: recite. **117. Boeotians:** dullards.

JOHN KEATS
England, 1795-1821

ON FIRST LOOKING INTO CHAPMAN'S HOMER

Much have I travell'd in the realms of gold,
  And many goodly states and kingdoms seen;
  Round many western isles have I been
Which bards in fealty to Apollo hold.
Oft of one wide expanse had I been told   *5*
  That deep-brow'd Homer ruled as his demesne;
  Yet did I never breathe its pure serene
Till I heard Chapman speak out loud and bold:
Then felt I like some watcher of the skies
  When a new planet swims into his ken;   *10*
Or like stout Cortez when with eagle eyes
  He star'd at the Pacific — and all his men
Look'd at each other with a wild surmise —
  Silent, upon a peak in Darien.

              (1816)

"WHEN I HAVE FEARS THAT I MAY CEASE TO BE"

When I have fears that I may cease to be
  Before my pen has glean'd my teeming brain,
Before high-piled books, in charact'ry,
  Hold like rich garners the full-ripen'd grain;
When I behold, upon the night's starr'd face,   *5*
  Huge cloudy symbols of a high romance,
And think that I may never live to trace
  Their shadows, with the magic hand of chance;
And when I feel, fair creature of an hour,

That I shall never look upon thee more,   *10*
Never have relish in the faery power
  Of unreflecting love! — then on the shore
Of the wide world I stand alone, and think
Till Love and Fame to nothingness do sink.

              (1818; 1848)

LA BELLE DAME SANS MERCI

O what can ail thee, Knight at arms,
  Alone and palely loitering?
The sedge is wither'd from the Lake,
  And no birds sing!

O what can ail thee, Knight at arms,   *5*
  So haggard, and so woe-begone?
The squirrel's granary is full,
  And the harvest's done.

I see a lily on thy brow,
  With anguish moist and fever dew,   *10*
And on thy cheek a fading rose
  Fast withereth too.

I met a Lady in the Meads
  Full beautiful, a faery's child —
Her hair was long, her foot was light,   *15*
  And her eyes were wild —

I made a Garland for her head,
  And bracelets too, and fragrant Zone;
She look'd at me as she did love,
  And made sweet moan —   *20*

ON FIRST LOOKING INTO CHAPMAN'S HOMER George Chapman (c.1559-1634), scholar, poet, and dramatist, published his translations of Homer from 1598 to 1616. **7. serene:** brightness, radiance (cf. Shelley's "the day's intense serene," *Epipsychidion*, 506). **11ff.:** It was Balboa, not Cortez, who in 1513 viewed the Pacific from Darien (Panama). Chapman's translation of the opening lines of the *Iliad* are as follows: "Achilles' baneful wrath resound, O Goddess, that imposed / Infinite sorrows on the Greeks, and many brave souls losed / From breasts heroic — sent them far, to that invisible cave / That no light comforts; and their limbs to dogs and vultures gave. / To all which Jove's will gave effect; from whom first strife begun / Betwixt Atrides, king of men, and Thetis' godlike son. / What god gave Eris their command, and oped that fighting vein? / Jove's and Latona's son, who, fired against the king of men / For contumely shown his priest, infectious sickness sent / To plague the army; and to death, by troops, the soldiers went." (**losed:** loosed; **Eris:** goddess of discord.) Cf. Pope's version (p. 534). **WHEN I HAVE FEARS 3. charact'ry:** i.e., writing (using characters, or letters). **LA BELLE DAME SANS MERCI** (The original version, copied by Keats into a part of the long journal-letter to George and Georgiana Keats, other parts of which are printed below; the revised version published in 1820 is clearly inferior: "Ah, what can ail thee, wretched wight. . . .") **Title:** that of a popular poem (1424) by French poet Alain Chartier (c.1390-c.1435); "The Beautiful Lady without Mercy." **18. fragrant Zone:** belt or girdle of flowers.

I set her on my pacing steed,
   And nothing else saw all day long,
For sidelong would she bend and sing
   A faery's song —

She found me roots of relish sweet,   *25*
   And honey wild and manna dew,
And sure in language strange she said,
   I love thee true —

She took me to her elfin grot,
   And there she wept and sigh'd full sore,   *30*
And there I shut her wild, wild eyes
   With kisses four —

And there she lulled me asleep,
   And there I dream'd, Ah, Woe betide!
The latest dream I ever dreamt   *35*
   On the cold hill side.

I saw pale Kings, and Princes too,
   Pale warriors, death-pale were they all;
They cried — "La belle dame sans merci
   Thee hath in thrall!"   *40*

I saw their starv'd lips in the gloam
   With horrid warning gaped wide,
And I awoke, and found me here
   On the cold hill's side.

And this is why I sojourn here,   *45*
   Alone and palely loitering,
Though the sedge is withered from the Lake
   And no birds sing.

                (1819)

ODE TO A NIGHTINGALE

1

My heart aches, and a drowsy numbness pains
   My sense, as though of hemlock I had drunk,
Or emptied some dull opiate to the drains
   One minute past, and Lethe-wards had sunk:
'Tis not through envy of thy happy lot,   *5*
   But being too happy in thine happiness, —

   That thou, light-winged Dryad of the trees,
      In some melodious plot
   Of beechen green, and shadows numberless,
      Singest of summer in full-throated ease.   *10*

2

O, for a draught of vintage! that hath been
   Cool'd a long age in the deep-delved earth,
Tasting of Flora and the country green,
   Dance, and Provençal song, and sunburnt mirth!
O for a beaker full of the warm South,   *15*
   Full of the true, the blushful Hippocrene,
      With beaded bubbles winking at the brim,
         And purple-stained mouth;
   That I might drink, and leave the world unseen,
      And with thee fade away into the forest dim: *20*

3

Fade far away, dissolve, and quite forget
   What thou among the leaves hast never known,
The weariness, the fever, and the fret
   Here, where men sit and hear each other groan;
Where palsy shakes a few, sad, last gray hairs,   *25*
   Where youth grows pale, and spectre-thin, and dies;
      Where but to think is to be full of sorrow
         And leaden-eyed despairs,
   Where Beauty cannot keep her lustrous eyes,
      Or new Love pine at them beyond to-morrow.   *30*

4

Away! away! for I will fly to thee,
   Not charioted by Bacchus and his pards,
But on the viewless wings of Poesy,
   Though the dull brain perplexes and retards:
Already with thee! tender is the night,   *35*
   And haply the Queen-Moon is on her throne,
      Cluster'd around by all her starry Fays;
         But here there is no light,
Save what from heaven is with the breezes blown
      Through verdurous glooms and winding
         mossy ways.   *40*

---

41. starv'd: suffering or perishing from cold or hunger.   **ODE TO A NIGHTINGALE**   **2. hemlock:** a poison — that which was used to carry out the death sentence on Socrates. **3. drains:** dregs. **4: Lethe** is the river of forgetfulness, or oblivion, in Hades (see *Paradise Lost*, II, 583; p. 343). **14. Provençal song:** suggesting the songs of the medieval troubadours. **16. Hippocrene:** fountain on Mt. Helicon, sacred to the Muses. **26:** Keats composed the poem in May; his younger brother Thomas had died of tuberculosis the preceding December 1 (and Keats himself would succumb to the same disease in February 1821). **32. pards:** leopards, or panthers (sometimes an attribute of the wine-god Dionysus, or Bacchus — e.g. pulling his chariot). **33. viewless:** invisible. **37. Fays:** fairies.

5

I cannot see what flowers are at my feet,
  Nor what soft incense hangs upon the boughs,
But, in embalmed darkness, guess each sweet
  Wherewith the seasonable month endows
The grass, the thicket, and the fruit-tree wild;   *45*
  White hawthorn, and the pastoral eglantine;
    Fast fading violets cover'd up in leaves;
      And mid-May's eldest child,
  The coming musk-rose, full of dewy wine,
    The murmurous haunt of flies on summer eves.   *50*

6

Darkling I listen; and, for many a time
  I have been half in love with easeful Death,
Call'd him soft names in many a mused rhyme,
  To take into the air my quiet breath;
Now more than ever seems it rich to die,   *55*
  To cease upon the midnight with no pain,
    While thou art pouring forth thy soul abroad
      In such an ecstasy!
  Still wouldst thou sing, and I have ears in vain —
    To thy high requiem become a sod.   *60*

7

Thou wast not born for death, immortal Bird!
  No hungry generations tread thee down;
The voice I hear this passing night was heard
  In ancient days by emperor and clown:
Perhaps the self-same song that found a path   *65*
  Through the sad heart of Ruth, when, sick for home,
    She stood in tears amid the alien corn;
      The same that oft-times hath
  Charm'd magic casements, opening on the foam
    Of perilous seas, in faery lands forlorn.   *70*

8

Forlorn! the very word is like a bell
  To toll me back from thee to my sole self!
Adieu! the fancy cannot cheat so well
  As she is fam'd to do, deceiving elf.
Adieu! adieu! thy plaintive anthem fades   *75*
  Past the near meadows, over the still stream,

Up the hill-side; and now 'tis buried deep
  In the next valley-glades:
Was it a vision, or a waking dream?
  Fled is that music: — Do I wake or sleep?   *80*
      (1819)

ODE ON A GRECIAN URN

1

Thou still unravish'd bride of quietness,
  Thou foster-child of silence and slow time,
Sylvan historian, who canst thus express
  A flowery tale more sweetly than our rhyme:
What leaf-fring'd legend haunts about thy shape   *5*
  Of deities or mortals, or of both,
    In Tempe or the dales of Arcady?
  What men or gods are these? What maidens loth?
What mad pursuit? What struggle to escape?
    What pipes and timbrels? What wild ecstasy?   *10*

2

Heard melodies are sweet, but those unheard
  Are sweeter; therefore, ye soft pipes, play on;
Not to the sensual ear, but, more endear'd,
  Pipe to the spirit ditties of no tone:
Fair youth, beneath the trees, thou canst not leave   *15*
  Thy song, nor ever can those trees be bare;
    Bold lover, never, never canst thou kiss,
Though winning near the goal — yet, do not grieve;
    She cannot fade, though thou hast not thy bliss,
  For ever wilt thou love, and she be fair!   *20*

3

Ah, happy, happy boughs! that cannot shed
  Your leaves, nor ever bid the Spring adieu;
And, happy melodist, unwearied,
  For ever piping songs for ever new;
More happy love! more happy, happy love!   *25*
  For ever warm and still to be enjoy'd,
    For ever panting, and for ever young;
All breathing human passion far above,
  That leaves a heart high-sorrowful and cloy'd,
    A burning forehead, and a parching tongue.   *30*

---

43. embalmed: fragrant. **50:** Cf. Tennyson's line from *The Princess* (1847): "And murmuring of innumerable bees" (VII, 207 — also quoted in the Glossary under *onomatopoeia*); indeed, Keats may have had bees in mind, since the word *fly* had long been used to refer to any winged insect, including bees (though that usage was by then virtually obsolete — but cf. *butterfly*). **64. clown:** rustic, peasant. **66-67:** Cf. the biblical account of Ruth.   **ODE ON A GRECIAN URN   7:** The Vale of Tempe, in Thessaly, northern Greece, and Arcadia, a region in the Peloponnesus, southern Greece — both associated with rustic beauty and pastoral tranquillity.

4

Who are these coming to the sacrifice?
    To what green altar, O mysterious priest,
Lead'st thou that heifer lowing at the skies,
    And all her silken flanks with garlands drest?
What little town by river or sea shore,   *35*
    Or mountain-built with peaceful citadel,
        Is emptied of this folk, this pious morn?
And, little town, thy streets for evermore
    Will silent be; and not a soul to tell
        Why thou art desolate, can e'er return.   *40*

5

O Attic shape! Fair attitude! with brede
    Of marble men and maidens overwrought,
With forest branches and the trodden weed;
    Thou, silent form, dost tease us out of thought
As doth eternity: Cold Pastoral!   *45*
    When old age shall this generation waste,
        Thou shalt remain, in midst of other woe
    Than ours, a friend to man, to whom thou say'st,
"Beauty is truth, truth beauty," — that is all
    Ye know on earth, and all ye need to know.   *50*

(1819)

ODE ON MELANCHOLY

1

No, no, go not to Lethe, neither twist
    Wolf's-bane, tight-rooted, for its poisonous wine;
Nor suffer thy pale forehead to be kiss'd
    By nightshade, ruby grape of Proserpine;

Make not your rosary of yew-berries,   *5*
    Nor let the beetle, nor the death-moth be
        Your mournful Psyche, nor the downy owl
A partner in your sorrow's mysteries;
    For shade to shade will come too drowsily,
        And drown the wakeful anguish of the soul.   *10*

2

But when the melancholy fit shall fall
    Sudden from heaven like a weeping cloud,
That fosters the droop-headed flowers all,
    And hides the green hill in an April shroud;
Then glut thy sorrow on a morning rose,   *15*
    Or on the rainbow of the salt sand-wave,
        Or on the wealth of globed peonies;
Or if thy mistress some rich anger shows,
    Emprison her soft hand, and let her rave,
        And feed deep, deep upon her peerless eyes.   *20*

3

She dwells with Beauty — Beauty that must die;
    And Joy, whose hand is ever at his lips
Bidding adieu; and aching Pleasure nigh,
    Turning to poison while the bee-mouth sips:
Ay, in the very temple of Delight   *25*
    Veil'd Melancholy has her sovran shrine,
        Though seen of none save him whose strenuous
            tongue
    Can burst Joy's grape against his palate fine;
His soul shall taste the sadness of her might,
    And be among her cloudy trophies hung.   *30*

(1819)

---

41. Attic: i.e., Greek (Athens, the cultural centre, is located in Attica, on the Attic peninsula); **brede:** ornamental braiding or embroidery. **42. overwrought:** worked all over. **49:** The quotation marks are present in the 1820 edition of Keats's poems; but their absence from some other contemporary appearances of the poem has led to critical speculation and controversy — e.g. about whether the urn "say'st" just the five words or the entire last two lines, what the pronoun "that" (line 49) refers to, and to whom or what the pronoun "Ye" in the last line refers.   **ODE ON MELANCHOLY 1. Lethe:** the river of forgetfulness in Hades. **4. Proserpine:** (Persephone) daughter of Jupiter and Ceres (Zeus and Demeter), carried off by Pluto (Hades) to become queen of the underworld; but she was allowed to spend half her time on earth with her mother, the two together being associated with grain and harvests. **5:** Yew-berries are often poisonous, and decorations of yew were thought to presage death; see also the note to Pope's "Epistle IV," line 96 (p. 540). **6. beetle:** possibly referring to the so-called "death-watch" beetle, or perhaps to the Egyptian scarab, which symbolized resurrection and eternal life and was therefore placed in tombs and coffins; **death-moth:** death's-head moth, whose markings resemble a skull (and see next note). **7. Psyche:** the soul, often personified as a butterfly — sometimes as escaping in the last breath of a dying person (cf. opening of Donne's "A Valediction: Forbidding Mourning," p. 255); **owl:** often associated with or symbolic of darkness and death. **8. mysteries:** secret symbolic or religious rites (e.g. the "Eleusinian mysteries"). **21. She:** i.e., Melancholy, personified. **26. sovran:** sovereign. **28. fine:** sensitive, discriminating. **30:** In classical times, trophies and other special objects were often dedicated to gods and goddesses and hung in their temples (see e.g. the note to Pope's *The Rape of the Lock*, V, 129; p. 532).

TO AUTUMN

1

Season of mists and mellow fruitfulness,
   Close bosom-friend of the maturing sun;
Conspiring with him how to load and bless
   With fruit the vines that round the thatch-eves run;
To bend with apples the moss'd cottage-trees,   *5*
   And fill all fruit with ripeness to the core;
      To swell the gourd, and plump the hazel shells
With a sweet kernel; to set budding more,
And still more, later flowers for the bees,
Until they think warm days will never cease,   *10*
      For summer has o'er-brimm'd their clammy cells.

2

Who hath not seen thee oft amid thy store?
   Sometimes whoever seeks abroad may find
Thee sitting careless on a granary floor,
   Thy hair soft-lifted by the winnowing wind;   *15*

Or on a half-reap'd furrow sound asleep,
   Drows'd with the fume of poppies, while thy hook
      Spares the next swath and all its twined flowers:
And sometimes like a gleaner thou dost keep
   Steady thy laden head across a brook;   *20*
Or by a cyder-press, with patient look,
   Thou watchest the last oozings hours by hours.

3

Where are the songs of spring? Ay, where are they?
   Think not of them, thou hast thy music too, —
While barred clouds bloom the soft-dying day,   *25*
   And touch the stubble-plains with rosy hue;
Then in a wailful choir the small gnats mourn
   Among the river sallows, borne aloft
      Or sinking as the light wind lives or dies;
And full-grown lambs loud bleat from hilly bourn;   *30*
   Hedge-crickets sing; and now with treble soft
   The red-breast whistles from a garden-croft;
      And gathering swallows twitter in the skies.

              (1819)

from the *LETTERS*

To Benjamin Bailey

22 November 1817

. . . . I am certain of nothing but the holiness of the Heart's affections, and the truth of Imagination. What the imagination seizes as Beauty must be Truth — whether it existed before or not — for I have the same idea of all our passions as of Love: they are all, in their sublime, creative of essential Beauty. . . . The Imagination may be compared to Adam's dream — he awoke and found it truth. I am more zealous in this affair because I   *5* have never yet been able to perceive how any thing can be known for truth by consecutive reasoning — and yet it must be. Can it be that even the greatest philosopher ever arrived at his goal without putting aside numerous objections? However it may be, O for a life of Sensations rather than of Thoughts!

       . . . .

To George and Thomas Keats

December 1817

. . . . Brown and Dilke walked with me and back from the Christmas pantomime. I had not a dispute but a disquisition with Dilke upon various subjects; several things dove-tailed in my mind, and at once it struck me what quality went to form a man of

---

To AUTUMN   **17. hook:** i.e., scythe or sickle. **28. sallows:** willows. **30. bourn:** realm, domain.   **LETTERS** Keats wrote letters rapidly and sometimes carelessly; we have corrected obvious errors and adjusted some capitalization, punctuation, and paragraphing for clarity and ease of reading. The addressees: Benjamin Bailey was a close friend. George and Thomas were Keats's brothers — George married Georgiana in 1818 and they left for the United States; Thomas died of tuberculosis in December 1818. John Hamilton Reynolds was a poet and friend. John Taylor was a partner in the firm that published Keats's work. Fanny Brawne (1800-1865), whom Keats met in the fall of 1818, became his fiancée probably early in 1819.   **TO BENJAMIN BAILEY 2. Beauty . . . Truth:** See line 49 of "Ode on a Grecian Urn," (p. 856). **3-4. in their sublime:** i.e., at their highest or best, when supreme, perfect. **5.** Adam has two such dreams in Book VIII of *Paradise Lost*, the first (283-311) about the Garden of Eden, the second (452-90) about the creation of Eve from one of his ribs.   **TO GEORGE AND THOMAS KEATS 1. Brown and Dilke:** Charles Armitage Brown and Charles Wentworth Dilke, fellow writers and friends.

achievement, especially in literature, and which Shakespeare possessed so enormously — I mean *Negative Capability*; that is, when a man is capable of being in uncertainties, mysteries, doubts, without any irritable reaching after fact and reason. Coleridge, for instance, would let go by a fine isolated verisimilitude caught from the Penetralium of mystery, from being incapable of remaining content with half-knowledge. This pursued through volumes would perhaps take us no further than this, that with a great poet the sense of Beauty overcomes every other consideration, or rather obliterates all consideration. 5

. . . .

To John Hamilton Reynolds

3 February 1818

. . . . We hate poetry that has a palpable design upon us, and if we do not agree, seems to put its hand in its breeches pocket. Poetry should be great and unobtrusive, a thing which enters into one's soul, and does not startle it or amaze it with itself, but with its subject. How beautiful are the retired flowers! How would they lose their beauty were they to throng into the highway crying out, "Admire me, I am a violet!" "Dote upon me, I am a primrose!". . . . 5

To John Taylor

27 February 1818

. . . . In poetry I have a few axioms, and you will see how far I am from their centre. 1st, I think poetry should surprise by a fine excess, and not by singularity; it should strike the reader as a wording of his own highest thoughts, and appear almost a remembrance. 2nd, Its touches of beauty should never be halfway, thereby making the reader breathless, instead of content: the rise, the progress, the setting of imagery should like the sun come natural to him — shine over him and set soberly, although in magnificence, leaving him in the luxury of twilight. But it is easier to think what poetry should be than to write it — and this leads me on to another axiom: that if poetry comes not as naturally as the leaves to a tree, it had better not come at all. . . . 5

To George and Georgiana Keats
14 February-3 May 1819

Friday 19th March

. . . . This morning I am in a sort of temper, indolent and supremely careless: I long after a stanza or two of Thomson's *Castle of Indolence*. My passions are all asleep, from my having slumbered till nearly eleven and weakened the animal fibre all over me to a delightful sensation about three degrees on this side of faintness. If I had teeth of pearl and the breath of lilies I should call it languor, but as I am I must call it laziness. In this state of effeminacy the fibres of the brain are relaxed in common with the rest of the body, and to such a happy degree that pleasure has no show of enticement and pain no unbearable power. Neither Poetry, nor Ambition, nor Love have any alertness of 5

---

7. Penetralium: innermost part, e.g. the sanctuary of a temple. **TO GEORGE AND GEORGIANA KEATS** **2:** James Thomson, author of *The Seasons* (see p. 572); he published *The Castle of Indolence* in 1748. **5. as I am:** "Especially as I have a black eye." (Keats's footnote; he was struck by a cricket ball the day before, as he has described shortly before this excerpt.)

countenance as they pass by me; they seem rather like figures on a Greek vase — a man *10* and two women whom no one but myself could distinguish in their disguisement. This is the only happiness, and is a rare instance of the advantage of the body overpowering the mind.

I have this moment received a note from Haslam in which he expects the death of his father, who has been for some time in a state of insensibility; his mother bears up, he *15* says, very well — I shall go to town tomorrow to see him. This is the world — thus we cannot expect to give away many hours to pleasure. Circumstances are like clouds continually gathering and bursting. While we are laughing, the seed of some trouble is put into the wide arable land of events; while we are laughing it sprouts, it grows, and suddenly bears a poison fruit which we must pluck. Even so we have leisure to reason *20* on the misfortunes of our friends; our own touch us too nearly for words. Very few men have ever arrived at a complete disinterestedness of mind: very few have been influenced by a pure desire of the benefit of others — in the greater part of the benefactors of humanity some meretricious motive has sullied their greatness — some melodramatic scenery has fascinated them. From the manner in which I feel Haslam's *25* misfortune I perceive how far I am from any humble standard of disinterestedness. Yet this feeling ought to be carried to its highest pitch, as there is no fear of its ever injuring society — which it would do, I fear, pushed to an extremity. For in wild nature the hawk would lose his breakfast of robins and the robin his of worms; the lion must starve as well as the swallow. The greater part of men make their way with the same *30* instinctiveness, the same unwandering eye from their purposes, the same animal eagerness as the hawk. The hawk wants a mate, so does the man — look at them both: they set about it and procure one in the same manner. They want both a nest and they both set about one in the same manner. They get their food in the same manner. The noble animal Man for his amusement smokes his pipe — the hawk balances about the *35* clouds — that is the only difference of their leisures. This it is that makes the amusement of life — to a speculative mind. I go among the fields and catch a glimpse of a stoat or a fieldmouse peeping out of the withered grass — the creature hath a purpose and its eyes are bright with it. I go amongst the buildings of a city and I see a man hurrying along — to what? The creature has a purpose and his eyes are bright with it. *40* But then as Wordsworth says, "we have all one human heart" — there is an electric fire in human nature tending to purify — so that among these human creatures there is continually some birth of new heroism. The pity is that we must wonder at it, as we should at finding a pearl in rubbish.

I have no doubt that thousands of people never heard of have had hearts completely *45* disinterested: I can remember but two — Socrates and Jesus — their histories evince it. What I heard a little time ago, Taylor observe with respect to Socrates, may be said of Jesus — that he was so great a man that though he transmitted no writing of his own to posterity, we have his mind and his sayings and his greatness handed to us by others. It is to be lamented that the history of the latter was written and revised by men interested *50* in the pious frauds of religion. Yet through all this I see his splendour. Even here,

13: William Haslam, a close friend. **40. as Wordsworth says . . . :** from "The Old Cumberland Beggar," line 153: " . . . we have all of us one human heart."

though I myself am pursuing the same instinctive course as the veriest human animal you can think of, I am however young writing at random — straining at particles of light in the midst of a great darkness — without knowing the bearing of any one assertion, of any one opinion. Yet may I not in this be free from sin? May there not be superior   *55* beings, amused with any graceful though instinctive attitude my mind may fall into, as I am entertained with the alertness of a stoat or the anxiety of a deer? Though a quarrel in the streets is a thing to be hated, the energies displayed in it are fine; the commonest man shows a grace in his quarrel. By a superior being our reasonings may take the same tone — though erroneous they may be fine. This is the very thing in which consists   *60* poetry; and if so it is not so fine a thing as philosophy — for the same reason that an eagle is not so fine a thing as a truth. Give me this credit — do you not think I strive to know myself? Give me this credit — and you will not think that on my own account I repeat Milton's lines:

> "How charming is divine Philosophy!   *65*
> Not harsh and crabbed as dull fools suppose,
> But musical as is Apollo's lute" —

No — not for myself — feeling grateful as I do to have got into a state of mind to relish them properly. Nothing ever becomes real till it is experienced — even a proverb is no proverb to you till your life has illustrated it. . . .

[15th April]   *70*

. . . . The whole appears to resolve into this: that Man is originally "a poor forked creature" subject to the same mischances as the beasts of the forest, destined to hardships and disquietude of some kind or other. If he improves by degrees his bodily accommodations and comforts, at each stage, at each ascent, there are waiting for him a fresh set of annoyances — he is mortal and there is still a heaven with its stars above his   *75* head. The most interesting question that can come before us is, How far by the persevering endeavours of a seldom appearing Socrates mankind may be made happy — I can imagine such happiness carried to an extreme — but what must it end in? Death — and who could in such a case bear with death? The whole troubles of life which are now frittered away in a series of years would then be accumulated for the last days of a being   *80* who instead of hailing its approach, would leave this world as Eve left Paradise. But in truth I do not at all believe in this sort of perfectibility — the nature of the world will not admit of it — the inhabitants of the world will correspond to itself. Let the fish philosophise the ice away from the rivers in winter time and they shall be at continual play in the tepid delight of summer. Look at the poles and at the sands of Africa,   *85* whirlpools and volcanoes. Let men exterminate them and I will say that they may arrive at earthly happiness. The point at which Man may arrive is as far as the parallel state in inanimate nature and no further. For instance suppose a rose to have sensation; it blooms on a beautiful morning, it enjoys itself, but then comes a cold wind, a hot sun — it cannot escape it, it cannot destroy its annoyances — they are as native to the world as itself. No   *90* more can man be happy in spite; the worldly elements will prey upon his nature.

64-66: from *A Mask (Comus)*, lines 476-78. **70-71. "a poor forked creature":** See Shakespeare's *King Lear*, III.iv.109-10: Lear says to Edgar, or "Poor Tom": "unaccommodated man is no more but such a poor, bare, forked animal as thou art."

The common cognomen of this world among the misguided and superstitious is "a vale of tears," from which we are to be redeemed by a certain arbitrary interposition of God and taken to Heaven. What a little circumscribed straitened notion! Call the world if you please "The vale of Soul-making." Then you will find out the use of the world (I *95* am speaking now in the highest terms for human nature, admitting it to be immortal, which I will here take for granted for the purpose of showing a thought which has struck me concerning it). I say *"Soul making"* — Soul as distinguished from an Intelligence. There may be intelligences or sparks of the divinity in millions, but they are not Souls till they acquire identities, till each one is personally itself. Intelligences *100* are atoms of perception — they know and they see and they are pure, in short they are God.

How then are Souls to be made? How then are these sparks which are God to have identity given them — so as ever to possess a bliss peculiar to each one's individual existence? How but by the medium of a world like this? This point I sincerely wish to *105* consider because I think it a grander system of salvation than the christian religion — or rather it is a system of Spirit creation. This is effected by three grand materials acting the one upon the other for a series of years. These three materials are the *Intelligence*, the *human heart* (as distinguished from intelligence or Mind), and the *World* or *Elemental space* suited for the proper action of *Mind and Heart* on each other for the purpose of *110* forming the *Soul* or *Intelligence destined to possess the sense of Identity*. I can scarcely express what I but dimly perceive — and yet I think I perceive it; that you may judge the more clearly I will put it in the most homely form possible: I will call the *world* a *School* instituted for the purpose of teaching little children to read — I will call the *human heart* the *hornbook* read in that school — and I will call the *Child able to read, the Soul* made *115* from that *School* and its *hornbook*. Do you not see how necessary a World of pains and troubles is to school an Intelligence and make it a Soul? A place where the heart must feel and suffer in a thousand diverse ways. Not merely is the Heart a Hornbook, it is the Mind's Bible, it is the Mind's experience, it is the teat from which the Mind or Intelligence sucks its identity. As various as the lives of men are, so various become their *120* Souls, and thus does God make individual beings, Souls, Identical Souls of the sparks of his own essence.

This appears to me a faint sketch of a system of salvation which does not affront our reason and humanity. I am convinced that many difficulties which christians labour under would vanish before it. There is one which even now strikes me — the salvation *125* of children. In them the spark or intelligence returns to God without any identity — it having had no time to learn of, and be altered by, the heart, or seat of the human passions. It is pretty generally suspected that the christian scheme has been copied from the ancient Persian and Greek philosophers. Why may they not have made this simple thing even more simple for common apprehension by introducing mediators and *130* personages in the same manner as in the heathen mythology abstractions are personified? Seriously, I think it probable that this system of Soul-making may have been the parent of all the more palpable and personal schemes of redemption among the Zoroastrians, the Christians, and the Hindoos. For as one part of the human species must

have their carved Jupiter, so another part must have the palpable and named mediator   *135*
and saviour, their Christ, their Oromanes, and their Vishnu.

If what I have said should not be plain enough, as I fear it may not be, I will put you
in the place where I began in this series of thoughts. I mean, I began by seeing how man
was formed by circumstances — and what are circumstances but touchstones of his
heart? and what are touchstones but provings of his heart? and what are provings of his   *140*
heart but fortifiers or alterers of his nature? and what is his altered nature but his Soul?
And what was his Soul before it came into the world and had these provings and
alterations and perfectionings? An intelligence — without Identity. And how is this
Identity to be made? Through the medium of the Heart? And how is the heart to become
this medium but in a world of circumstances?

. . . .   *145*

I have been endeavouring to discover a better Sonnet stanza than we have. The
legitimate does not suit the language over well from the pouncing rhymes — the other
appears too elegiac — and the couplet at the end of it has seldom a pleasing effect. I do
not pretend to have succeeded — it will explain itself.

> If by dull rhymes our English must be chain'd,   *150*
> And, like Andromeda, the sonnet sweet
> Fetter'd, in spite of pained loveliness;
> Let us find out, if we must be constrain'd,
> Sandals more interwoven and complete
> To fit the naked foot of poesy;   *155*
> Let us inspect the lyre, and weigh the stress
> Of every chord, and see what may be gain'd
> By ear industrious, and attention meet;
> Misers of sound and syllable, no less
> Than Midas of his coinage, let us be   *160*
> Jealous of dead leaves in the bay-wreath crown,
> So, if we may not let the Muse be free,
> She will be bound with garlands of her own.

This is the third of May and everything is in delightful forwardness; the violets are
not withered before the peeping of the first rose. You must let me know everything —   *165*
how parcels go and come — what papers you have, and what newspapers you want, and
other things. God bless you, my dear brother and sister,

Your ever affectionate brother,
JOHN KEATS

---

135. Oromanes: (more commonly *Ahriman*) in Zoroastrianism, the spirit of evil and darkness, in conflict with Ormuzd (or Ormazd or Ahura
Mazda), the spirit of light and good (Keats seems to confuse the two); **Vishnu:** one of the principal deities of Hinduism, "The Preserver." **150.
Andromeda:** in Greek myth, daughter of Cepheus and Cassiope (Cassiopeia, Cassiepeia), king and queen of Ethiopia; Cassiope offended the
Nereids by claiming to be more beautiful than they; as punishment, Poseidon flooded the land and demanded that Andromeda be sacrificed; she was
chained to a rock, at the mercy of a sea-monster, but was saved by Perseus, on his way back from beheading the Gorgon Medusa. **159. Midas:** See
also Carolyn Kizer's "The Ungrateful Garden" (p. 1418). **160. bay-wreath crown:** the laurel garland awarded as a prize to poets who won
competitions.

To Fanny Brawne

Shanklin, Isle of Wight, Thursday 1 July 1819

MY DEAREST LADY,

I am glad I had not an opportunity of sending off a letter which I wrote for you on Tuesday night — 'twas too much like one out of Rousseau's *Heloise*. I am more reasonable this morning. The morning is the only proper time for me to write to a beautiful Girl whom I love so much: for at night, when the lonely day has closed, and ⁵ the lonely, silent, unmusical chamber is waiting to receive me as into a sepulchre, then believe me my passion gets entirely the sway, then I would not have you see those rhapsodies which I once thought it impossible I should ever give way to, and which I have often laughed at in another, for fear you should think me either too unhappy or perhaps a little mad. ¹⁰

I am now at a very pleasant cottage window, looking onto a beautiful hilly country, with a glimpse of the sea; the morning is very fine. I do not know how elastic my spirit might be, what pleasure I might have in living here and breathing and wandering as free as a stag about this beautiful coast, if the remembrance of you did not weigh so upon me. I have never known any unalloyed happiness for many days together: the death or ¹⁵ sickness of someone has always spoilt my hours — and now when none such troubles oppress me, it is you must confess very hard that another sort of pain should haunt me. Ask yourself my love whether you are not very cruel to have so entrammelled me, so destroyed my freedom. Will you confess this in the letter you must write immediately and do all you can to console me in it — make it rich as a draught of poppies to ²⁰ intoxicate me — write the softest words and kiss them that I may at least touch my lips where yours have been. For myself I know not how to express my devotion to so fair a form: I want a brighter word than *bright*, a fairer word than *fair*. I almost wish we were butterflies and lived but three summer days — three such days with you I could fill with more delight than fifty common years could ever contain. But however selfish I may ²⁵ feel, I am sure I could never act selfishly: as I told you a day or two before I left Hampstead, I will never return to London if my Fate does not turn up Pam or at least a Court-card. Though I could centre my happiness in you, I cannot expect to engross your heart so entirely — indeed if I thought you felt as much for me as I do for you at this moment I do not think I could restrain myself from seeing you again tomorrow for the ³⁰ delight of one embrace. But no — I must live upon hope and chance. In case of the worst that can happen, I shall still love you — but what hatred shall I have for another! Some lines I read the other day are continually ringing a peal in my ears:

TO FANNY BRAWNE **2:** *Julie ou la Nouvelle Héloïse* (1761), epistolary novel by Jean-Jacques Rousseau (1712-1778). **26:** Hampstead, a district a few km northeast of central London, was where Keats lived much of the time from 1817 on, both with his brothers and with Charles Armitage Brown, for a time with Fanny Brawne and her mother living next door; **Pam:** the knave of clubs in certain card games, such as loo (see e.g. Pope's *The Rape of the Lock*, III, 61-62; p. 527). **27. Court-card:** other face-card.

To see those eyes I prize above mine own
Dart favors on another —   *35*
And those sweet lips (yielding immortal nectar)
Be gently press'd by any but myself —
Think, think Francesca, what a cursed thing
It were, beyond expression!

                                    J.
                                                                    40

Do write immediately. There is no post from this place, so you must address Post
Office, Newport, Isle of Wight. I know before night I shall curse myself for having sent
you so cold a letter; yet it is better to do it as much in my senses as possible. Be as kind
as the distance will permit to your

                                    J. KEATS.
                                                                    45

Present my compliments to your mother, my love to Margaret and best remembrances to
your brother — if you please so.

THOMAS CARLYLE
Scotland/England, 1795-1881

FOUR FABLES

I.

Once upon a time, a man, somewhat in drink belike, raised a dreadful outcry at the corner
of the market-place, "That the world was all turned topsy-turvy; that the men and cattle
were all walking with their feet uppermost; that the houses and earth at large (if they did
not mind it) would fall into the sky; in short, that unless prompt means were taken, things
in general were on the high road to the Devil." As the people only laughed at him, he   *5*
cried the louder and more vehemently; nay, at last, began objuring, foaming, imprecating;
when a good-natured auditor, going up, took the orator by the haunches, and softly
inverting *his* position, set him down — on his feet. The which upon perceiving, his mind
was staggered not a little. "Ha! deuce take it!" cried he, rubbing his eyes, "so it was not
the world that was hanging by its feet, then, but I that was standing on my head!"   *10*

    Censor, *Castigator morum*, Radical Reformer, by whatever name thou art called!
have a care; especially if thou art getting loud!

                                    PILPAY JUNIOR.

33-38: See Philip Massinger's *The Duke of Milan*, I.iii.245-50. **45. Margaret:** her younger sister.   **FOUR FABLES**   The pseudonym "Pilpay
Junior" alludes to *The Fables of Bidpai* (or *Pilpay*), also known as *Kalilah and Dimnah*, the Arabic version of a collection of Hindu stories from the
Sanskrit *Panchatantra*, translated over the centuries into most European languages. **11. Castigator morum:** (Latin) corrector of manners.

II.

"Gentlemen," said a conjuror, one fine starry evening, "these heavens are a *deceptio visus;* what you call stars are nothing but fiery motes in the air. Wait a little, I will clear them off, and show you how the matter is." Whereupon the artist produced a long *15* syringe of great force; and, stooping over the neighbouring puddle, filled it with mud and dirty water, which he then squirted with might and main against the zenith. The wiser of the company unfurled their umbrellas; but most part, looking up in triumph, cried, "Down with delusion! It is an age of science! Have we not tallow-lights, then?" Here the mud and dirty water fell, and bespattered and beplastered these simple persons, *20* and even put out the eyes of several, so that they never saw the stars any more.

Enlightened Utilitarian! art thou aware that this patent logic-mill of thine, which grindeth with such a clatter, is but a mill?

P.J.

III.

"It is I that support this household," said a hen one day to herself; "the master cannot breakfast without an egg, for he is dyspeptical and would die, and it is I that lay it. And *25* here is this ugly poodle, doing nothing earthly, and gets thrice the victual I do, and is caressed all day! By the Cock of Minerva, they shall give me a double portion of oats, or they have eaten their last egg!" But much as she cackled and creaked, the scullion would not give her an extra grain; whereupon, in dudgeon, she hid her next egg in the dunghill, and did nothing but cackle and creak all day. The scullion suffered her for a *30* week, then (by order) drew her neck, and purchased other eggs at sixpence the dozen.

Man! why frettest thou and whinest thou? This blockhead is happier than thou, and still a blockhead? — Ah, sure enough, thy wages are too low! Wilt thou *strike work* with Providence, then, and force him to "an alternative"? Believe it, he will do without thee: *il n'y a point d'homme nécessaire.* *35*

P.J.

IV.

"What is the use of thee, thou gnarled sapling?" said a young larch-tree to a young oak. "I grow three feet in a year, thou scarcely as many inches, I am straight and taper as a reed, thou straggling and twisted as a loosened withe." — "And thy duration," answered the oak, "is some third part of man's life, and I am appointed to flourish for a thousand years. Thou art felled and sawed into paling, where thou rottest and art burned after a single summer; of *40* me are fashioned battle-ships, and I carry mariners and heroes into unknown seas."

The richer a nature, the harder and slower its development. Two boys were once of a class in the Edinburgh grammar-school: John ever trim, precise and dux; Walter ever slovenly, confused and dolt. In due time John became Baillie John of Hunter-square, and Walter became Sir Walter Scott of the Universe. *45*

The quickest and completest of all vegetables is the cabbage.

P.J.

(1826-27)

13-14. *deceptio visus:* (Latin) optical illusion. **22:** For more of Carlyle's thoughts on Utilitarianism, see the following essay, "Signs of the Times." **27:** The cock, as a fighting bird, was an attribute of Athena (Minerva) as goddess of war. **31. drew her neck:** i.e., killed her. **33.** *strike work:* i.e., refuse to work, go on strike. **35.** *il n'y a . . . nécessaire:* no man is indispensable. **43. dux:** leading pupil in a class. **44. Baillie:** a municipal magistrate, similar to an English alderman. **45: Sir Walter Scott:** See p. 777.

SIGNS OF THE TIMES (abridged)

It is no very good symptom either of nations or individuals, that they deal much in vaticination. Happy men are full of the present, for its bounty suffices them; and wise men also, for its duties engage them. Our grand business undoubtedly is, not to *see* what lies dimly at a distance, but to *do* what lies clearly at hand.

> Know'st thou *Yesterday*, its aim and reason;   5
> Work'st thou well *Today*, for worthy things?
> Calmly wait the *Morrow's* hidden season,
> Need'st not fear what hap soe'er it brings.

But man's "large discourse of reason" *will* look "before and after;" and, impatient of the "ignorant present time," will indulge in anticipation far more than profits him. Seldom   10
can the unhappy be persuaded that the evil of the day is sufficient for it; and the ambitious will not be content with present splendour, but paints yet more glorious triumphs, on the cloud-curtain of the future.

The case, however, is still worse with nations. For here the prophets are not one, but many; and each incites and confirms the other; so that the fatidical fury spreads wider   15
and wider, till at last even Saul must join in it. For there is still a real magic in the action and reaction of minds on one another. The casual deliration of a few becomes, by this mysterious reverberation, the frenzy of many; men lose the use, not only of their understandings, but of their bodily senses; while the most obdurate unbelieving hearts melt, like the rest, in the furnace where all are cast as victims and as fuel. It is grievous   20
to think, that this noble omnipotence of Sympathy has been so rarely the Aaron's-rod of Truth and Virtue, and so often the Enchanter's-rod of Wickedness and Folly! No solitary miscreant, scarcely any solitary maniac, would venture on such actions and imaginations, as large communities of sane men have, in such circumstances, entertained as sound wisdom. Witness long scenes of the French Revolution, in these   25
late times! Levity is no protection against such visitations, nor the utmost earnestness of character. The New-England Puritan burns witches, wrestles for months with the horrors of Satan's invisible world, and all ghastly phantasms, the daily and hourly precursors of the Last Day; then suddenly bethinks him that he is frantic, weeps bitterly, prays contritely, and the history of that gloomy season lies behind him like a frightful dream.   30

Old England too has had her share of such frenzies and panics; though happily, like other old maladies, they have grown milder of late: and since the days of Titus Oates have mostly passed without loss of men's lives; or indeed without much other loss than that of reason, for the time, in the sufferers. In this mitigated form, however, the distemper is of pretty regular recurrence; and may be reckoned on at intervals, like other   35
natural visitations; so that reasonable men deal with it, as the Londoners do with their fogs, — go cautiously out into the groping crowd, and patiently carry lanterns at noon; knowing, by a well-grounded faith, that the sun is still in existence, and will one day reappear. How often have we heard, for the last fifty years, that the country was

---

SIGNS OF THE TIMES   2. vaticination: prophecy. **9. "large . . . after":** Cf. *Hamlet*, I.ii.150 and IV. iv. 36-39; see also Homer's *Iliad*, III, 108. **11. evil . . . sufficient:** See Matthew 6:34. **15. fatidical:** prophetic. **16. Saul:** See I Samuel 10:11-12. **17. deliration:** madness, delirium. **21. Aaron's-rod:** See Numbers 17. **29. Last Day:** i.e., Judgment Day. **32. Titus Oates:** (1649-1705) clergyman who concocted the "popish plot" of 1678.

wrecked, and fast sinking; whereas, up to this date, the country is entire and afloat! The *40*
"State in Danger" is a condition of things, which we have witnessed a hundred times;
and as for the Church, it has seldom been out of "danger" since we can remember it.

All men are aware that the present is a crisis of this sort; and why it has become so.
The repeal of the Test Acts, and then of the Catholic disabilities, has struck many of
their admirers with an indescribable astonishment. Those things seemed fixed and *45*
immovable; deep as the foundations of the world; and lo, in a moment they have
vanished, and their place knows them no more! Our worthy friends mistook the
slumbering Leviathan for an island; often as they had been assured, that Intolerance
was, and could be nothing but a Monster; and so, mooring under the lee, they had
anchored comfortably in his scaly rind, thinking to take good cheer; as for some space *50*
they did. But now their Leviathan has suddenly dived under; and they can no longer be
fastened in the stream of time; but must drift forward on it, even like the rest of the
world: no very appalling fate, we think, could they but understand it; which, however,
they will not yet, for a season. Their little island is gone; sunk deep amid confused
eddies; and what is left worth caring for in the universe? What is it to them that the great *55*
continents of the earth are still standing; and the polestar and all our loadstars, in the
heavens, still shining and eternal? Their cherished little haven is gone, and they will not
be comforted! And therefore, day after day, in all manner of periodical or perennial
publications, the most lugubrious predictions are sent forth. The King has virtually
abdicated; the Church is a widow, without jointure; public principle is gone; private *60*
honesty is going; society, in short, is fast falling in pieces; and a time of unmixed evil is
come on us.

At such a period, it was to be expected that the rage of prophecy should be more
than usually excited. Accordingly, the Millennarians have come forth on the right hand,
and the Millites on the left. The Fifth-monarchy men prophesy from the Bible, and the *65*
Utilitarians from Bentham. The one announces that the last of the seals is to be opened,
positively, in the year 1860; and the other assures us that "the greatest happiness
principle" is to make a heaven of earth, in a still shorter time. We know these symptoms
too well, to think it necessary or safe to interfere with them. Time and the hours will
bring relief to all parties. The grand encourager of Delphic or other noises is — the *70*
Echo. Left to themselves, they will the sooner dissipate, and die away in space.

Meanwhile, we too admit that the present is an important time; as all present time
necessarily is. The poorest Day that passes over us is the conflux of two Eternities; it is
made up of currents that issue from the remotest Past, and flow onwards into the
remotest Future. We were wise indeed, could we discern truly the signs of our own *75*

44: See the note to Shelley's "England in 1819," line 12 (p. 844); the repeal of the Test Acts in 1828 was followed by the Catholic Emancipation Act of 1829, which removed the "disabilities" of Roman Catholics in England. **47-51:** See *Paradise Lost,* I, 200-07, and note (p. 329). **65. Millites:** Utilitarians, followers of Jeremy Bentham (see p. 709) and of James Mill (1773-1836) and his son John Stuart Mill (1806-73); the younger Mill edited Bentham's *Treatise upon Evidence* (1825); the elder was the author of *Elements of Political Economy* (1821; see line 110 below), and of *Analysis of the Phenomena of the Human Mind* (1829), in which he used David Hartley's associationist psychology (see line 334 below, and note) to support Utilitarianism; **Fifth-monarchy men:** mid-17th-century millenarians who believed it was time for Christ's rule on earth to begin, a "fifth monarchy" (following those of Assyria, Persia, Macedonia, and Rome), as prophesied in Daniel 2:31-45. **66. last of the seals:** See Revelation 5ff.; the opening of the last or "seventh seal" is referred to at 8:1. **67-68. "the greatest happiness principle":** According to Bentham, "the greatest happiness of the greatest number" is "the measure of right and wrong" and "the foundation of morals and legislation"; he adopted the key phrase from *Inquiry Concerning Moral Good and Evil* (1725), by Irish-born Francis Hutcheson (1694-1746), professor of moral philosophy at Glasgow from 1729. **70. Delphic:** referring to the oracle of Apollo at Delphi.

time; and by knowledge of its wants and advantages, wisely adjust our own position in it. Let us, instead of gazing idly into the obscure distance, look calmly around us, for a little, on the perplexed scene where we stand. Perhaps, on a more serious inspection, something of its perplexity will disappear, some of its distinctive characters and deeper tendencies more clearly reveal themselves; whereby our own relations to it, our own   *80* true aims and endeavours in it, may also become clearer.

Were we required to characterise this age of ours by any single epithet, we should be tempted to call it, not an Heroical, Devotional, Philosophical, or Moral Age, but, above all others, the Mechanical Age. It is the Age of Machinery, in every outward and inward sense of that word; the age which, with its whole undivided might, forwards,   *85* teaches and practises the great art of adapting means to ends. Nothing is now done directly, or by hand; all is by rule and calculated contrivance. For the simplest operation, some helps and accompaniments, some cunning abbreviating process is in readiness. Our old modes of exertion are all discredited, and thrown aside. On every hand, the living artisan is driven from his workshop, to make room for a speedier, inanimate one.   *90* The shuttle drops from the fingers of the weaver, and falls into iron fingers that ply it faster. The sailor furls his sail, and lays down his oar; and bids a strong, unwearied servant, on vaporous wings, bear him through the waters. Men have crossed oceans by steam; the Birmingham Fire-king has visited the fabulous East; and the genius of the Cape, were there any Camoens now to sing it, has again been alarmed, and with far   *95* stranger thunders than Gamas. There is no end to machinery. Even the horse is stripped of his harness, and finds a fleet fire-horse yoked in his stead. Nay, we have an artist that hatches chickens by steam; the very brood-hen is to be superseded! For all earthly, and for some unearthly purposes, we have machines and mechanic furtherances; for mincing our cabbages; for casting us into magnetic sleep. We remove mountains, and make seas   *100* our smooth highway; nothing can resist us. We war with rude Nature; and, by our resistless engines, come off always victorious, and loaded with spoils.

What wonderful accessions have thus been made, and are still making, to the physical power of mankind; how much better fed, clothed, lodged and, in all outward respects, accommodated men now are, or might be, by a given quantity of labour, is a   *105* grateful reflection which forces itself on every one. What changes, too, this addition of power is introducing into the Social System; how wealth has more and more increased, and at the same time gathered itself more and more into masses, strangely altering the old relations, and increasing the distance between the rich and the poor, will be a question for Political Economists, and a much more complex and important one than   *110* any they have yet engaged with.

But leaving these matters for the present, let us observe how the mechanical genius of our time has diffused itself into quite other provinces. Not the external and physical alone is now managed by machinery, but the internal and spiritual also. Here too

---

93-94. crossed oceans by steam: The *Savannah*, a sailing ship with steam-driven side paddlewheels, crossed the Atlantic in 1819.
94. Birmingham Fire-king: perhaps referring to William Murdock (1754-1839), Scots-born engineer and inventor who worked on steam engines with James Watt (see line 242 below) and Matthew Boulton (1728-1809) at their Soho factory in Birmingham, and who invented coal-gas lighting.
95-96: The Portuguese poet Luis Vaz de Camoëns (1524-1580) in his epic *Os Lusiadas* (*The Lusiads,* 1572) celebrates Portuguese achievements by focussing on the first voyage of Vasco da Gama (c.1469-1524) around the Cape of Good Hope (in 1497) and on to India, the first such voyage by a European. **97. artist:** i.e., artisan. **100. magnetic sleep:** i.e., as induced by mesmerism, or animal magnetism (hypnotism).

nothing follows its spontaneous course, nothing is left to be accomplished by old natural   *115*
methods. Everything has its cunningly devised implements, its preëstablished apparatus;
it is not done by hand, but by machinery. Thus we have machines for Education. . . .
Instruction, that mysterious communing of Wisdom with Ignorance, is no longer an
indefinable tentative process, requiring a study of individual aptitudes, and a perpetual
variation of means and methods, to attain the same end; but a secure, universal,   *120*
straightforward business, to be conducted in the gross, by proper mechanism, with such
intellect as comes to hand. Then, we have Religious machines, of all imaginable
varieties; the Bible-Society, professing a far higher and heavenly structure, is found, on
inquiry, to be altogether an earthly contrivance: supported by collection of moneys, by
fomenting of vanities, by puffing, intrigue and chicane; a machine for converting the   *125*
Heathen. It is the same in all other departments. . . . Mark, too, how every machine must
have its moving power, in some of the great currents of society; every little sect among
us, Unitarians, Utilitarians, Anabaptists, Phrenologists, must have its Periodical, its
monthly or quarterly Magazine; — hanging out, like its windmill, into the *popularis*
aura, to grind meal for the society.   *130*

   With individuals, in like manner, natural strength avails little. No individual now
hopes to accomplish the poorest enterprise single-handed and without mechanical aids;
he must make interest with some existing corporation, and till his field with their oxen.
In these days, more emphatically than ever, "to live, signifies to unite with a party, or to
make one." Philosophy, Science, Art, Literature, all depend on machinery. No Newton,   *135*
by silent meditation, now discovers the system of the world from the falling of an apple;
but some quite other than Newton stands in his Museum, his Scientific Institution, and
behind whole batteries of retorts, digesters and galvanic piles imperatively "interrogates
Nature," — who, however, shows no haste to answer. In defect of Raphaels, and
Angelos, and Mozarts, we have Royal Academies of Painting, Sculpture, Music;   *140*
whereby the languishing spirit of Art may be strengthened, as by the more generous diet
of a Public Kitchen. Literature, too, has its Paternoster-row mechanism, its Trade-
dinners, its Editorial conclaves, and huge subterranean, puffing bellows; so that books
are not only printed, but, in a great measure, written and sold, by machinery.

   National culture, spiritual benefit of all sorts, is under the same management. No   *145*
Queen Christina, in these times, needs to send for her Descartes; no King Frederick for
his Voltaire, and painfully nourish him with pensions and flattery: any sovereign of
taste, who wishes to enlighten his people, has only to impose a new tax, and with the
proceeds establish Philosophic Institutes. Hence the Royal and Imperial Societies, the
Bibliothèques, Glyptothèques, Technothèques, which front us in all capital cities; like so   *150*

---

123. Bible-Society: e.g. the Bible Society, founded in 1780 to distribute Bibles to soldiers and sailors; or the British and Foreign Bible Society, founded in 1804. **125. puffing:** promoting with exaggerated or empty praise. **129-30.** *popularis aura:* (Latin) public breeze. **135. Newton:** Sir Isaac Newton (1642-1727) was said to have begun thinking about his theory of gravity when he saw an apple fall from its tree. **139-40:** Raphael (Raffaello Sanzio, 1483-1520), Italian painter; Michelangelo Buonarroti (1475-1564), Italian sculptor and painter; Wolfgang Amadeus Mozart (1756-1791), Austrian composer. **142:** Paternoster Row in London was the location of publishers and booksellers. **146-47:** Christina (1626-1689), Queen of Sweden, invited French philosopher and scientist René Descartes (1596-1650) to her court in 1649; French philosopher and author Voltaire (François Marie Arouet de Voltaire, 1694-1778) by invitation lived from 1749 to 1753 at the court of Frederick II ("the Great," 1712-1786), king of Prussia. **149:** For the Royal Society, see the general note to Sprat (p. 455). **150:** The Bibliothèque Nationale, in Paris, since 1537 has housed copies of all books published in France; the Glyptothek (from Greek *glyptos*, carved, and *theke*, place of storage) in Munich was built to house sculptures collected by Louis (1786-1868), the crown prince of Bavaria (later Louis — or Ludwig — I), especially the "Aeginetan marbles" (from the temple of Aegina, an island near Athens), which he bought in 1812.

many well-finished hives, to which it is expected the stray agencies of Wisdom will swarm of their own accord, and hive and make honey. In like manner, among ourselves, when it is thought that religion is declining, we have only to vote half-a-million's worth of bricks and mortar, and build new churches. In Ireland it seems they have gone still farther, having actually established a "Penny-a-week Purgatory-Society"! Thus does the   *155* Genius of Mechanism stand by to help us in all difficulties and emergencies, and with his iron back bears all our burdens.

These things, which we state lightly enough here, are yet of deep import, and indicate a mighty change in our whole manner of existence. For the same habit regulates not our modes of action alone, but our modes of thought and feeling. Men are grown   *160* mechanical in head and in heart, as well as in hand. They have lost faith in individual endeavour, and in natural force, of any kind. Not for internal perfection, but for external combinations and arrangements, for institutions, constitutions, — for Mechanism of one sort or other, do they hope and struggle. Their whole efforts, attachments, opinions, turn on mechanism, and are of a mechanical character.   *165*

. . . .

This condition of the two great departments of knowledge, — the outward, cultivated exclusively on mechanical principles; the inward, finally abandoned, because, cultivated on such principles, it is found to yield no result, — sufficiently indicates the intellectual bias of our time, its all-pervading disposition towards that line of inquiry. In fact, an inward persuasion has long been diffusing itself, and now and then even comes   *170* to utterance, That, except the external, there are no true sciences; that to the inward world (if there be any) our only conceivable road is through the outward; that, in short, what cannot be investigated and understood mechanically, cannot be investigated and understood at all. . . .

Nowhere . . . is the deep, almost exclusive faith we have in Mechanism more visible   *175* than in the Politics of this time. Civil government does by its nature include much that is mechanical, and must be treated accordingly. We term it indeed, in ordinary language, the Machine of Society, and talk of it as the grand working wheel from which all private machines must derive, or to which they must adapt, their movements. Considered merely as a metaphor, all this is well enough; but here, as in so many other cases, the   *180* "foam hardens itself into a shell," and the shadow we have wantonly evoked stands terrible before us and will not depart at our bidding. Government includes much also that is not mechanical, and cannot be treated mechanically; of which latter truth, as appears to us, the political speculations and exertions of our time are taking less and less cognisance.   *185*

. . . .

It is no longer the moral, religious, spiritual condition of the people that is our concern, but their physical, practical, economical condition, as regulated by public laws. Thus is the Body-politic more than ever worshipped and tendered; but the Soul-politic less than ever. Love of country, in any high or generous sense, in any other than an almost animal sense, or mere habit, has little importance attached to it in such reforms,   *190* or in the opposition shown them. Men are to be guided only by their self-interests. Good government is a good balancing of these; and, except a keen eye and appetite for self-interest, requires no virtue in any quarter. To both parties it is emphatically a machine:

to the discontented, a "taxing-machine"; to the contented, a "machine for securing property." Its duties and its faults are not those of a father, but of an active parish- *195* constable.

Thus it is by the mere condition of the machine, by preserving it untouched, or else by reconstructing it, and oiling it anew, that man's salvation as a social being is to be insured and indefinitely promoted. Contrive the fabric of law aright, and without farther effort on your part, that divine spirit of Freedom, which all hearts venerate and long for, *200* will of herself come to inhabit it; and under her healing wings every noxious influence will wither, every good and salutary one more and more expand. Nay, so devoted are we to this principle, and at the same time so curiously mechanical, that a new trade, specially grounded on it, has arisen among us, under the name of "Codification," or codemaking in the abstract; whereby any people, for a reasonable consideration, may be *205* accommodated with a patent code; — more easily than curious individuals with patent breeches, for the people does *not* need to be measured first.

To us who live in the midst of all this, and see continually the faith, hope and practice of every one founded on Mechanism of one kind or other, it is apt to seem quite natural, and as if it could never have been otherwise. Nevertheless, if we recollect or *210* reflect a little, we shall find both that it has been, and might again be otherwise. The domain of Mechanism, — meaning thereby political, ecclesiastical or other outward establishments, — was once considered as embracing, and we are persuaded can at any time embrace, but a limited portion of man's interests, and by no means the highest portion. *215*

To speak a little pedantically, there is a science of *Dynamics* in man's fortunes and nature, as well as of *Mechanics.* There is a science which treats of, and practically addresses, the primary, unmodified forces and energies of man, the mysterious springs of Love, and Fear, and Wonder, of Enthusiasm, Poetry, Religion, all which have a truly vital and *infinite* character; as well as a science which practically addresses the finite, *220* modified developments of these, when they take the shape of immediate "motives," as hope of reward, or as fear of punishment.

Now it is certain, that in former times the wise men, the enlightened lovers of their kind, who appeared generally as Moralists, Poets or Priests, did, without neglecting the Mechanical province, deal chiefly with the Dynamical; applying themselves chiefly to *225* regulate, increase and purify the inward primary powers of man; and fancying that herein lay the main difficulty, and the best service they could undertake. But a wide difference is manifest in our age. For the wise men, who now appear as Political Philosophers, deal exclusively with the Mechanical province; and occupying themselves in counting-up and estimating men's motives, strive by curious checking and balancing, *230* and other adjustments of Profit and Loss, to guide them to their true advantage: while, unfortunately, those same "motives" are so innumerable, and so variable in every

---

204. "Codification": The term applies to any systematizing, but refers primarily to law — e.g. the *Code civil des Français* (1804, for a time called the *Code Napoléon*) and the *Code Frédéric* of Prussia (1751, after Frederick the Great); when Sir William Blackstone (1723-1780) published his *Commentaries on the Laws of England* (1765-69), Bentham, in *A Fragment on Government* (1776), attacked it for opposing legal reform, and in his major work, *An Introduction to the Principles of Morals and Legislation* (1789), continued to argue the need for a clear, orderly, and all-inclusive codification of English law, and to oppose judicial legislation. **221.** "motives" of *reward* and *punishment* are prominent in Bentham's writings about Utilitarianism, as are those of *pain* and *pleasure* (see line 304 below).

individual, that no really useful conclusion can ever be drawn from their enumeration. But though Mechanism, wisely contrived, has done much for man in a social and moral point of view, we cannot be persuaded that it has ever been the chief source of his worth *235* or happiness. Consider the great elements of human enjoyment, the attainments and possessions that exalt man's life to its present height, and see what part of these he owes to institutions, to Mechanism of any kind; and what to the instinctive, unbounded force, which Nature herself lent him, and still continues to him. Shall we say, for example, that Science and Art are indebted principally to the founders of Schools and Universities? *240* Did not Science originate rather, and gain advancement, in the obscure closets of the Roger Bacons, Keplers, Newtons; in the workshops of the Fausts and the Watts; wherever, and in what guise soever Nature, from the first times downwards, had sent a gifted spirit upon the earth? Again, were Homer and Shakespeare members of any beneficed guild, or made Poets by means of it? Were Painting and Sculpture created by *245* forethought, brought into the world by institutions for that end? No; Science and Art have, from first to last, been the free gift of Nature; an unsolicited, unexpected gift; often even a fatal one. These things rose up, as it were, by spontaneous growth, in the free soil and sunshine of Nature. They were not planted or grafted, nor even greatly multiplied or improved by the culture or manuring of institutions. Generally speaking, *250* they have derived only partial help from these; often enough have suffered damage. They made constitutions for themselves. They originated in the Dynamical nature of man, not in his Mechanical nature.

Or, to take an infinitely higher instance, that of the Christian Religion. . . . Here again was no Mechanism; man's highest attainment was accomplished Dynamically, not *255* Mechanically.

Nay, we will venture to say, that no high attainment, not even any far-extending movement among men, was ever accomplished otherwise. Strange as it may seem, if we read History with any degree of thoughtfulness, we shall find that the checks and balances of Profit and Loss have never been the grand agents with men; that they have *260* never been roused into deep, thorough, all-pervading efforts by any computable prospect of Profit and Loss, for any visible, finite object; but always for some invisible and infinite one. The Crusades took their rise in Religion; their visible object was, commercially speaking, worth nothing. . . . In later ages it was still the same. The Reformation had an invisible, mystic and ideal aim; the result was indeed to be embodied in external things; *265* but its spirit, its worth, was internal, invisible, infinite. Our English Revolution too originated in Religion. Men did battle, in those old days, not for Purse-sake, but for Conscience-sake. Nay, in our own days it is no way different. The French Revolution itself had something higher in it than cheap bread and a Habeas-corpus act. Here too was an Idea; a Dynamic, not a Mechanic force. It was a struggle, though a blind and at last an *270* insane one, for the infinite, divine nature of Right, of Freedom, of Country.

Thus does man, in every age, vindicate, consciously or unconsciously, his celestial birthright. Thus does Nature hold on her wondrous, unquestionable course; and all our

---

242: Roger Bacon (c.1214-c.1294), English philosopher; Johannes Kepler (1571-1630), German astronomer; for Newton, see note to line 35 of Arnold's "Literature and Science" (p. 1063); Johann Faust, 16th-century itinerant German magician about whom legends grew, written of by many — e.g. Marlowe's play *The Tragical History of Dr. Faustus* (c.1588), Johann Wolfgang von Goethe's dramatic poem *Faust* (1808, 1832), and Thomas Mann's novel *Dr. Faustus* (1947); James Watt (1736-1819), Scots inventor who improved Newcomen's steam engine and after whom the watt is named.

systems and theories are but so many froth-eddies or sandbanks, which from time to time she casts up, and washes away. When we can drain the Ocean into mill-ponds, and *275* bottle-up the Force of Gravity, to be sold by retail, in gas jars; then may we hope to comprehend the infinitudes of man's soul under formulas of Profit and Loss; and rule over this too, as over a patent engine, by checks, and valves, and balances.

. . . .

To define the limits of these two departments of man's activity, which work into one another, and by means of one another, so intricately and inseparably, were by its *280* nature an impossible attempt. Their relative importance, even to the wisest mind, will vary in different times, according to the special wants and dispositions of those times. Meanwhile, it seems clear enough that only in the right coördination of the two, and the vigorous forwarding of *both*, does our true line of action lie. Undue cultivation of the inward or Dynamical province leads to idle, visionary, impracticable courses, and, *285* especially in rude eras, to Superstition and Fanaticism, with their long train of baleful and well-known evils. Undue cultivation of the outward, again, though less immediately prejudicial, and even for the time productive of many palpable benefits, must, in the long-run, by destroying Moral Force, which is the parent of all other Force, prove not less certainly, and perhaps still more hopelessly, pernicious. This, we take it, is the *290* grand characteristic of our age. By our skill in Mechanism, it has come to pass, that in the management of external things we excel all other ages; while in whatever respects the pure moral nature, in true dignity of soul and character, we are perhaps inferior to most civilised ages.

In fact, if we look deeper, we shall find that this faith in Mechanism has now struck *295* its roots down into man's most intimate, primary sources of conviction; and is thence sending up, over his whole life and activity, innumerable stems, — fruit-bearing and poison-bearing. The truth is, men have lost their belief in the Invisible, and believe, and hope, and work only in the Visible; or, to speak it in other words: This is not a Religious age. Only the material, the immediately practical, not the divine and spiritual, is *300* important to us. The infinite, absolute character of Virtue has passed into a finite, conditional one; it is no longer a worship of the Beautiful and Good; but a calculation of the Profitable. Worship, indeed, in any sense, is not recognised among us, or is mechanically explained into Fear of pain, or Hope of pleasure. Our true Deity is Mechanism. It has subdued external Nature for us, and we think it will do all other *305* things. We are Giants in physical power: in a deeper than metaphorical sense, we are Titans, that strive, by heaping mountain on mountain, to conquer Heaven also.

The strong Mechanical character, so visible in the spiritual pursuits and methods of this age, may be traced much farther into the condition and prevailing disposition of our spiritual nature itself. Consider, for example, the general fashion of Intellect in this era. *310* Intellect, the power man has of knowing and believing, is now nearly synonymous with Logic, or the mere power of arranging and communicating. Its implement is not Meditation, but Argument. "Cause and effect" is almost the only category under which we look at, and work with, all Nature. Our first question with regard to any object is not, What is it? but, How is it? We are no longer instinctively driven to apprehend, and lay *315*

306-07: See the note to line 74 of Dekker's "How a Gallant Should Behave" (p. 240).

to heart, what is Good and Lovely, but rather to inquire, as on-lookers, how it is produced, whence it comes, whither it goes. Our favourite Philosophers have no love and no hatred; they stand among us not to do, nor to create anything, but as a sort of Logic-mills to grind out the true causes and effects of all that is done and created. . . . Wonder, indeed, is, on all hands, dying out: it is the sign of uncultivation to wonder. *320* Speak to any small man of a high, majestic Reformation, of a high majestic Luther; and forthwith he sets about "accounting" for it; how the "circumstances of the time" called for such a character, and found him, we suppose, standing girt and road-ready, to do its errand; how the "circumstances of the time" created, fashioned, floated him quietly along into the result; how, in short, this small man, had be been there, could have *325* performed the like himself! For it is the "force of circumstances" that does everything; the force of one man can do nothing. . . . We have our little *theory* on all human and divine things. Poetry, the workings of genius itself, which in all times, with one or another meaning, has been called Inspiration, and held to be mysterious and inscrutable, is no longer without its scientific exposition. The building of the lofty rhyme is like any *330* other masonry or bricklaying: we have theories of its rise, height, decline and fall, — which latter, it would seem, is now near, among all people. Of our "Theories of Taste," as they are called, wherein the deep, infinite, unspeakable Love of Wisdom and Beauty, which dwells in all men, is "explained," made mechanically visible, from "Association" and the like, why should we say anything? *335*

. . . .

To what extent theological Unbelief, we mean intellectual dissent from the Church, in its view of Holy Writ, prevails at this day, would be a highly important, were it not, under any circumstances, an almost impossible inquiry. But the Unbelief, which is of a still more fundamental character, every man may see prevailing, with scarcely any but the faintest contradiction, all around him; even in the Pulpit itself. Religion in most *340* countries, more or less in every country, is no longer what it was, and should be, — a thousand-voiced psalm from the heart of Man to his invisible Father, the fountain of all Goodness, Beauty, Truth, and revealed in every revelation of these; but for the most part, a wise prudential feeling grounded on mere calculation; a matter, as all others now are, of Expediency and Utility; whereby some smaller quantum of earthly enjoyment *345* may be exchanged for a far larger quantum of celestial enjoyment. Thus Religion too is Profit, a working for wages; not Reverence, but vulgar Hope or Fear. . . .

Literature too, if we consider it, gives similar testimony. At no former era has Literature, the printed communication of Thought, been of such importance as it is now. We often hear that the Church is in danger; and truly so it is, — in a danger it seems not *350* to know of: for, with its tithes in the most perfect safety, its functions are becoming more and more superseded. The true Church of England, at this moment, lies in the Editors of its Newspapers. These preach to the people daily, weekly; admonishing kings themselves; advising peace or war, with an authority which only the first Reformers, and a long-past class of Popes, were possessed of. . . . But omitting this class, and the *355* boundless host of watery personages who pipe, as they are able, on so many scrannel

---

321. **Luther:** Martin Luther (1483-1546), German leader of the Reformation, founder of Protestantism. **330: building . . . rhyme:** See line 11 of Milton's *Lycidas* (p. 316). **332. "Theories of Taste":** See e.g. Reynolds's "Seventh Discourse" (p. 627). **334. "Association":** alluding to associationist psychology, founded by David Hartley (1705-1757), who presented his influential mechanistic theories in his *Observations on Man, His Frame, His Duty, and His Expectations* (1749). **356-57. pipe . . . straws:** See line 124 of Milton's *Lycidas* (p. 317).

straws, let us look at the higher regions of Literature, where, if anywhere, the pure melodies of Poesy and Wisdom should be heard. Of natural talent there is no deficiency. . . . But what is the song they sing? Is it a . . . "liquid wisdom," disclosing to our sense the deep, infinite harmonies of Nature and man's soul? Alas, no! It is not a matin or vesper *360* hymn to the Spirit of Beauty, but a fierce clashing of cymbals. . . . Poetry itself has no eye for the Invisible. Beauty is no longer the god it worships, but some brute image of Strength. . . . We praise a work, not as "true," but as "strong"; our highest praise is that it has "affected" us, has "terrified" us.

. . . .

Again, with respect to our Moral condition: here also he who runs may read that the *365* same physical, mechanical influences are everywhere busy. For the "superior morality," of which we hear so much, we too would desire to be thankful: at the same time, it were but blindness to deny that this "superior morality" is properly rather an "inferior criminality," produced not by greater love of Virtue, but by greater perfection of Police; and of that far subtler and stronger Police, called Public Opinion. This last watches over *370* us with its Argus eyes more keenly than ever; but the "inward eye" seems heavy with sleep. Of any belief in invisible, divine things, we find as few traces in our Morality as elsewhere. It is by tangible, material considerations that we are guided, not by inward and spiritual. Self-denial, the parent of all virtue, in any true sense of that word, has perhaps seldom been rarer. . . . Virtue is Pleasure, is Profit; no celestial, but an earthly thing. *375* Virtuous men, Philanthropists, Martyrs are happy accidents; their "taste" lies the right way! In all senses, we worship and follow after Power; which may be called a physical pursuit. No man now loves Truth, as Truth must be loved, with an infinite love. . . .

These dark features, we are aware, belong more or less to other ages, as well as to ours. This faith in Mechanism, in the all-importance of physical things, is in every age *380* the common refuge of Weakness and blind Discontent; of all who believe, as many will ever do, that man's true good lies without him, not within. We are aware also, that, as applied to ourselves in all their aggravation, they form but half a picture; that in the whole picture there are bright lights as well as gloomy shadows. . . .

Neither, with all these evils more or less clearly before us, have we at any time *385* despaired of the fortunes of society. Despair, or even despondency, in that respect, appears to us, in all cases, a groundless feeling. We have a faith in the imperishable dignity of man; in the high vocation to which, throughout this his earthly history, he has been appointed. However it may be with individual nations, whatever melancholic speculators may assert, it seems a well-ascertained fact, that in all times, . . . the happiness and *390* greatness of mankind at large have been continually progressive. Doubtless this age also is advancing. Its very unrest, its ceaseless activity, its discontent contains matter of promise. Knowledge, education are opening the eyes of the humblest; are increasing the number of thinking minds without limit. This is as it should be; for not in turning back, not in resisting, but only in resolutely struggling forward, does our life consist. *395*

Nay, after all, our spiritual maladies are but of Opinion; we are but fettered by chains of our own forging, and which ourselves also can rend asunder. This deep,

---

364. "terrified": See *sublime* in the Glossary. **365. he . . . read:** See Habakkuk 2:2. **371. Argus:** in Greek myth, a many-eyed monster; **"inward eye":** See line 21 of Wordsworth's "I wandered lonely as a cloud" (p. 768).

paralysed subjection to physical objects comes not from Nature, but from our own unwise mode of *viewing* Nature. . . . If Mechanism, like some glass bell, encircles and imprisons us; if the soul looks forth on a fair heavenly country which it cannot reach,   *400* and pines, and in its scanty atmosphere is ready to perish, — yet the bell is but of glass; "one bold stroke to break the bell in pieces, and thou art delivered!"

. . . .

Meanwhile, that great outward changes are in progress can be doubtful to no one. The time is sick and out of joint. Many things have reached their height; and it is a wise adage that tells us, "the darkest hour is nearest the dawn." Wherever we can gather   *405* indication of the public thought, whether from printed books, as in France or Germany, or from Carbonari rebellions and other political tumults, as in Spain, Portugal, Italy and Greece, the voice it utters is the same. The thinking minds of all nations call for change. There is a deep-lying struggle in the whole fabric of society; a boundless grinding collision of the New with the Old. The French Revolution, as is now visible enough,   *410* was not the parent of this mighty movement, but its offspring.

. . . .

On the whole, as this wondrous planet, Earth, is journeying with its fellows through infinite Space, so are the wondrous destinies embarked on it journeying through infinite Time, under a higher guidance than ours. For the present, as our astronomy informs us, its path lies towards *Hercules,* the constellation of *Physical Power:* but that is not our   *415* most pressing concern. Go where it will, the deep HEAVEN will be around it. Therein let us have hope and sure faith. To reform a world, to reform a nation, no wise man will undertake; and all but foolish men know, that the only solid, though a far slower reformation, is what each begins and perfects on *himself.*

(1829)

THOMAS CHANDLER HALIBURTON
Canada, 1796-1856

THE PRINCE DE JOINVILLE'S HORSE

"The machinery of the colonies is good enough in itself, but it wants a safety valve. When the pressure within is too great, there should be something devised to let off the steam. By not understanding this, the English have caused one revolution at home, and another in America."

"Exactly," said Mr. Slick. "It reminds me o' what I wunst saw done by the Prince de Joinville's hoss on the Halifax road."   *5*

---

404. time . . . joint: See *Hamlet,* I.v.188. **405. "the darkest . . . dawn":** Or as in Thomas Fuller's *A Pisgah Sight of Palestine* (1650): "It is always darkest just before the day dawneth." **407. Carbonari:** ("charcoal burners") members of a secret society responsible for uprisings in the 1820s.   THE PRINCE DE JOINVILLE'S HORSE   Haliburton's *The Attaché* (1st and 2nd series, 1843-44), from which this selection is taken, is often read as a reply to Charles Dickens's *American Notes* (1842). The character Sam Slick, who in previous Haliburton books (notably *The Clockmaker,* 1837-40), is an itinerant Yankee clock salesman travelling through Nova Scotia, has become the American attaché in London. Sam's dialect is Haliburton's invention, not a direct representation of any particular regional speech. **Title:** The historical Prince de Joinville — François Ferdinand d'Orléans (1818-1900) — third son of Louis Philippe, served in the French navy in the 1830s and 1840s, commanding the ship that took Napoleon's body from St. Helena to France in 1840; after later being expelled from France, he took part in the American Civil War. **5. Halifax road:** i.e., in Nova Scotia.

"Pardon me," said Mr. Hopewell, "you shall have an opportunity presently of telling your story of the Prince's horse, but suffer me to proceed. England, besides other outlets, has a never-failing one in the colonies, but the colonies have no outlet. Cromwell and Hampden were actually embarked on board of a vessel in the Thames, for Boston, when they were prevented from sailing by an Order in Council. What was the consequence? The sovereign was dethroned. Instead of leading a small sect of fanatical puritans and being the first men of a village in Massachusetts, they aspired to be the first men in an empire — and succeeded. So in the old colonies. Had Washington been sent abroad in command of a regiment, Adams to govern a colony, Franklin to make experiments in an observatory like that at Greenwich, and a more extended field been opened to colonial talent, the United States would still have continued to be dependencies of Great Britain. There is no room for men of talent in British America; and by not affording them an opportunity of distinguishing themselves or rewarding them when they do, they are always ready to make one, by opposition. In comparing their situation with that of the inhabitants of the British Isles, they feel that they labour under disabilities; these disabilities they feel as a degradation; and as those who impose that degradation live three thousand miles off, it becomes a question whether it is better to suffer or resist."

"The Prince de Joinville's hoss," said Mr. Slick, "is a case in p'int."

"One moment, Sam," said Mr. Hopewell. "The very word 'dependencies' shows the state of the colonies. If they are to be retained, they should be incorporated with Great Britain. The people should be made to feel, not that they are colonists, but Englishmen. They may tinker at constitutions as much as they please; the root of the evil lies deeper than statesmen are aware of. O'Connell, when he agitates for a repeal of the Union, if he really has no ulterior objects beyond that of an Irish Parliament, does not know what he is talking about. If his request were granted, Ireland would become a province, and descend from being an integral part of the empire, into a dependency. Had he ever lived in a colony, he would have known the tendencies of such a condition.

"What I desire to see, is the very reverse. Now that steam has united the two continents of Europe and America, in such a manner that you can travel from Nova Scotia to England in as short a time as it once required to go from Dublin to London, I should hope for a united legislature. Recollect that the distance from New Orleans to the head of the River is greater than from Halifax, N.S., to Liverpool. I do not want to see colonists and Englishmen arrayed against each other as different races, but united as one people having the same rights and privileges, each bearing a share of the public burdens and all having a voice in the general government. The love of distinction is natural to man. Three millions of people cannot be shut up in a colony. They will either turn on each other, or unite against their keepers. The road that leads to retirement in the provinces, should be open to those whom the hope of distinction invites to return and contend for the honours of the empire. At present, the egress is practically closed."

---

9. Hampden: See Gray's "Elegy," line 57 and note (p. 611). **13-14. Washington, Adams, Franklin:** representing military, political, and scientific accomplishment in the United States. **29. O'Connell:** Daniel O'Connell (1775-1847), Irish political leader who from the 1820s on urged repeal of the act (passed in 1800) that unified Ireland with Great Britain. **38. River:** the Mississippi.

"If you was to talk forever, Minister," said Mr. Slick, "you couldn't say more nor the Prince de Joinville's hoss on that subject."

The interruption was very annoying, for no man I ever met so thoroughly understands the subject of colonial government as Mr. Hopewell. His experience is greater than that of any man now living, and his views more enlarged and more *50* philosophical.

"Go on, Sam," said he, with great good humour. "Let us hear what the Prince's horse said."

"Well," said Mr. Slick, "I don't just exactly mean to say he spoke, as Balaam's donkey did, in good English or French neither; but he did that that spoke a whole book, *55* with a handsome woodcut to the fore, and that's a fact. About two years ago, one mortal br'ilin' hot day, as I was a-pokin' along the road from Halifax to Windsor with Old Clay in the wagon, with my coat off, a-ridin' in my shirt-sleeves, and a-thinkin' how slick a mint-julep would travel down red lane — if I had it — I heer'd such a chatterin' and laughin' and screamin' as I never a'most heer'd afore since I was raised. *60*

" 'What in natur' is this?' says I, as I gave Old Clay a crack o' the whip to push on. 'There's some critters here, I guess, that have found a haw-haw's nest, with a tee-hee's egg in it. What's in the wind now?' Well, a sudden turn of the road brought me to where they was; and who should they be but French officers from the Prince's ship, travellin' incog in plain clo'es. But, Lord bless you, cook a Frenchman any way you please, and *65* you can't disguise him. Natur' will out, in spite of all, and the name of a Frencher is written as plain as anythin' in his whiskers, and his hair, and his skin, and his coat, and his boots, and his air, and his gait, and in everythin'; but only let him open his mouth, and the cat's out o' the bag in no time, ain't it? They're droll boys, is the French, that's a fact.

"Well, there was four on 'em dismounted, a-holdin' of their hosses by the bridle *70* and a-standin' near a spring of nice, cool water; and there was a fifth, and he was a-layin' down belly-flounder on the ground, a-tryin' to drink out of the runnin' spring.

" 'Parley-vous French,' says I, 'Mountsheer?' At that, they sot to and laughed ag'in more than ever; I thought they'd 'a gone into the high-strikes, they heehawed so. Well, one on 'em that was a Duke, as I found out a'terwards, said, 'O yees, saar, we spoked *75* English, too.' 'Lawful heart!' says I, 'what's the joke?' 'Why,' says he, 'look there, saar.'

"And then they laughed ag'in, ready to split; and sure enough, no sooner had the leftenant laid down to drink than the Prince's hoss kneeled down, and put his head jist over his neck, and began to drink too. Well, the officer couldn't git up for the hoss, and he couldn't keep his face out o' the water for the hoss, and he couldn't drink for the *80* hoss; and he was a'most choked to death, and as black in the face as your hat. And the Prince and the officers laughed so they couldn't help him if they was to die for it.

"Says I to myself, 'A joke's a joke, if it ain't carried too far; but this here critter will be strangled, as sure as a gun, if he lays here splutterin' this way much longer.' So I jist gives the hoss a dab in the mouth, and made him git up; and then says I, 'Prince,' says I, *85* for I know'd him by his beard; he had one exactly like one o' the old saints' heads in an Eyetalian pictur', all dressed to a p'int; so says I, 'Prince,' and a plaguy handsome man he is, too, and as full of fun as a kitten; so says I, 'Prince,' and what's better, all his

54-55. **Balaam's donkey:** See Numbers 22:20-35.

officers seemed plaguy proud and fond on him, too; so says I, 'Prince, voilà le condition of one colonist, which,' says I, 'Prince, means in English, that leftenant is jist like a colonist.' 90

" 'Commong,' says he, 'how is dat?' 'Why,' says I, 'Prince, whenever a colonist goes for to drink at a spring of the good things o' this world (and plaguy small springs we have here, too), and fairly lays down to it, jist as he gits his lips cleverly to it for a swig, there's some cussed neck or another of some confounded Britisher pops right over 95 him and pins him there. He can't git up, he can't back out, and he can't drink, and he is blacked-and-blued in the face, and a'most choked with the weight.

" 'What country was you man of?' said he, for he spoke very good for a Frenchman. With that I straightened myself up, and looked dignified, for I know'd I'd a right to be proud, and no mistake; says I, 'Prince, I am an American citizen.' How them 100 two words altered him. P'r'aps there bean't no two words to ditto 'em. He looked for all the world like a different man when he see'd I wa'n't a mean, onsarcumcized colonist.

" 'Very glad to see you, Mr. Yankee,' said he, 'very glad indeed. Shall I have de honour to ride with you a little way in your carriage?' 'As for the matter o' that,' says I, 'Mountsheer Prince, the honour is all t'other way.' For I can be as civil as any man, if 105 he sots out to act pretty and do the thing ginteel.

"With that he jumped right in; and then he said sunthin' in French to the officers — some order or another, I s'pose, about comin' on and fetchin' his hoss with 'em. I've heer'd, in my time, a good many men speak French, but I never see'd the man yet that could hold a candle to *him*. Oh, it was like lightnin', jist one long, endurin' streak; it seemed all one 110 sentence and one word. It was beautiful; but I couldn't onderstand it, it was so everlastin' fast. 'Now,' says he, 'set sail.' And off we sot, at the rate of sixteen knots an hour.

"Old Clay pleased him, you may depend; he turned round and clapped his hands, and laughed, and waved his hat to his officers to come on; and they whipped, and spurred, and galloped, and raced for dear life; but we dropped 'em astarn like anythin', 115 and he laughed ag'in, heartier than ever. There's no people, a'most, like to ride so fast as sailors; they crack on like a house afire.

"Well, a'ter a while, says he, 'Back topsails,' and I hauls up; and he jumps down, and outs with a pocketbook, and takes [out] a beautiful gold coronation-medal. (It was solid gold, no pinchbeck, but the rale yella stuff, jist fresh from King's shop to Paris, 120 where his money is made.) And says he, 'Mr. Yankee, will you accept that to remember the Prince de Joinville and his horse by?' And then he took off his hat and made me a bow, and if that wa'n't a bow, then I never see'd one, that's all. . . . It was enough to sprain his ankle, he curled so low. And then off he went with a hop, skip, and a jump, sailor-fashion, back to meet his people. 125

"Now, Squire, if you see Lord Stanley, tell him that 'are story of the Prince de Joinville's hoss; but afore you git so far as that, pin him by admissions. When you want to git a man on the hip, ax him a question or two and git his answers; and then you have him in a corner: he must stand and let you put on the bridle. He can't help it, nohow he can fix it. 130

---

120. pinchbeck: imitation gold, an alloy made of copper, tin, and zinc. **126. Squire:** i.e., Mr. Hopewell; **Lord Stanley:** Edward George Geoffrey Smith Stanley, 14th Earl of Derby (1799-1869), who became Britain's Colonial Secretary in 1833 and guided through Parliament the bill abolishing slavery; his assistant, the novelist Benjamin Disraeli (1804-1881), later became Prime Minister.

"Says you, 'My Lord —' Don't forget his title; every man likes the sound o' that; it's music to his ears. It's like our splendid national air, *Yankee Doodle*: you never git tired of it — 'My Lord,' says you, 'what do you s'pose is the reason the French keep Algiers?' Well, he'll up and say it's an outlet for the fiery spirits of France; it gives 'em empl'yment and an opportunity to distinguish themselves; and what the climate and the   *135* inimy spare becomes valuable officers. It makes good sodjers out of bad subjects. 'Do you call that good policy?' says you.

"Well, he's a trump, is Mr. Stanley — at least folks say so; and he'll say right off the reel, 'Onquestionably it is — excellent policy.' When he says that, you have him bagged; he may flounder and spring like a salmon jist caught, but he can't out of the   *140* landin'-net. You've got him, and no mistake. Says you, 'What outlet have you for the colonies?'

"Well, he'll scratch his head and stare at that for a space. He'll hum and haw a leetle to git breath, for he never thought o' that afore since he grow'd up; but he's no fool, I can tell you, and he'll out with his mould, run an answer, and be ready for you in   *145* no time. He'll say, 'They don't require none, sir. They have no redundant population. They're an outlet themselves.'

"Says you, 'I wa'n't talkin' of an outlet for popilation, for France or the provinces neither. I was a-talkin' of an outlet for the clever men, for the onquiet ones, for the fiery spirits.' 'For that, sir,' he will say, 'they have the local patronage.' 'Oh!' says you, 'I   *150* wa'n't aware. I beg pardon; I've been absent some time — as long as twenty days or p'r'aps twenty-five. There must 'a been great changes since I left.'

" 'The garrison?' says you. 'Is English,' says he. 'The armed ships in the harbour?' 'English.' 'The governor and his secretary?' 'English.' 'The principal officer of customs and principal part of his deputies?' 'English.' 'The commissariat and the staff?' 'English   *155* to a man.' 'The dockyard people?' 'English.' 'The postmaster-giniral?' 'English.'

" 'What! English?' says you, and look all surprise, as if you didn't know. 'I thought he was a colonist, seein' the province pays so much for the mails.' 'No,' he'll say, 'not now; we've jist sent an English one over, for we find it's a good thing that.' 'One word more,' says you, 'and I have done. If your army officers out there git leave of absence,   *160* do you stop their pay?' 'No.' 'Do you starve na*tive* colonists the same way?' 'No, we stop half their salaries.'

" 'Exactly,' says you, 'make 'em feel the difference. A'ways make a nigger *feel* he is a nigger or he'll get sassy, you may depend. As for patronage,' says you, 'you know as well as I do that all that's not worth havin' is jist left to poor colonist. He's an officer   *165* of militia, gits no pay, and finds his own fit-out. Like Don Quixote's tailor, he works for nothin' and finds thread. Any other leetle matters of the same kind — that nobody wants and nobody else will take — if Bluenose makes interest for and has good luck, he can git as a great favour, to conciliate his countrymen. No, Minister,' says you, 'you're a clever man, everybody says you're a brick; and if you ain't, you talk more like one than   *170* anybody I've see'd this while past. I don't want no office myself; if I did p'r'aps, I

---

166. finds: supplies, provides; **Don Quixote's tailor:** in *Don Quixote de la Mancha* (1605), a picaresque satire of chivalric romance by Miguel de Cervantes (1547-1616), Quixote claims that a knight errant has more privileges and exemptions than even the gentility: "What knight-errant ever paid custom, poll-tax, subsidy, quit-rent, porterage or ferry-boat? — What tailor ever brought in a bill for making his clothes?" (Book IV, chapter 18). **168. Bluenose:** Nova Scotian.

wouldn't talk about patronage this way. But I am a colonist; I want to see the colonists remain so. They *are* attached to England, that's a fact; keep 'em so by makin' them Englishmen. Throw the door wide open; patronize 'em; enlist 'em in the imperial sarvice; allow 'em a chance to contend for honours — and let 'em win them if they can. *175* If they don't, it's their own fault; and, cuss 'em, they oughta be kicked, for if they ain't too lazy there's no mistake in 'em, that's a fact. The country will be proud of 'em — if they go ahead. Their language will change then. It will be *our* army, the delighted critters will say, not the English army; *our* navy, *our* church, *our* parliament, *our* aristocracy, etcetera; and the word *English* will be left out, holus-bolus, and that proud, *180* that endearin' word *our* will be insarted. Do this, and you'll show yourself the first statesman of modern times. You'll rise right up to the top of the pot; you'll go clean over Peel's head, as your folks go over our'n — not by jumpin' over him, but by takin' him by the neck and squeezin' him down. You 'mancipated the blacks; now liberate the colonists and make Englishmen of 'em, and see whether the goneys wun't grin from ear *185* to ear and show their teeth as well as the niggers did. Don't let Yankee clockmakers' — you may say that if you like, if it will help your argyment — 'don't let travellin' Yankee clockmakers tell sich stories ag'inst *your* justice and *our* pride as that of the Prince de Joinville and his hoss.' "

(1843)

THOMAS HOOD
England, 1799-1845

FAITHLESS NELLY GRAY
A Pathetic Ballad

Ben Battle was a soldier bold,
    And used to war's alarms;
But a cannon-ball took off his legs,
    So he laid down his arms!

Now as they bore him off the field,   *5*
    Said he, "Let others shoot,
For here I leave my second leg,
    And the Forty-second Foot!"

The army-surgeons made him limbs:
    Said he, — "They're only pegs: *10*
But there's as wooden members quite,
    As represent my legs!"

Now Ben he loved a pretty maid,
    Her name was Nelly Gray;
So he went to pay her his devours,   *15*
    When he'd devour'd his pay!

But when he called on Nelly Gray,
    She made him quite a scoff;
And when she saw his wooden legs,
    Began to take them off!   *20*

"O, Nelly Gray! O, Nelly Gray!
    Is this your love so warm?
The love that loves a scarlet coat,
    Should be more uniform!"

---

183. Peel: Sir Robert Peel (1788-1850), British Prime Minister, 1834-35, 1841-46. **185. goneys:** simpletons. **FAITHLESS NELLY GRAY** This ballad first appeared as a comic song, with music by Jonathan Blewitt. **8. Forty-second Foot:** the Royal Highland Regiment or Black Watch (named for the colour of their kilts), formed in 1739. **11-12:** i.e., members of Parliament. **15. devours:** devoirs, respects.

Said she, "I loved a soldier once,   25
  For he was blythe and brave;
But I will never have a man
  With both legs in the grave!

Before you had those timber toes,
  Your love I did allow,   30
But then, you know, you stand upon
  Another footing now!"

"O, Nelly Gray! O, Nelly Gray!
  For all your jeering speeches,
At duty's call, I left my legs   35
  In Badajos's *breaches!*"

"Why, then," said she, "you've lost the feet
  Of legs in war's alarms,
And now you cannot wear your shoes
  Upon your feats of arms!"   40

"O, false and fickle Nelly Gray!
  I know why you refuse: —
Though I've no feet — some other man
  Is standing in my shoes!

I wish I ne'er had seen your face;   45
  But, now, a long farewell!
For you will be my death: — alas!
  You will not be my *Nell!*"

Now when he went from Nelly Gray,
  His heart so heavy got —   50
And life was such a burthen grown,
  It made him take a knot!

So round his melancholy neck,
  A rope he did entwine,
And, for his second time in life,   55
  Enlisted in the Line!

One end he tied around a beam,
  And then removed his pegs,
And, as his legs were off, — of course,
  He soon was off his legs!   60

And there he hung, till he was dead
  As any nail in town, —
For though distress had cut him up,
  It could not cut him down!

A dozen men sat on his corpse,   65
  To find out why he died —
And they buried Ben in four cross-roads,
  With a *stake* in his inside!

                                        (1826)

OUR VILLAGE
By a Villager

Our village, that's to say, not Miss Mitford's village, but our village of Bullock Smithy,
Is come into by an avenue of trees, three oak pollards, two elders, and a withy;
And in the middle there's a green, of about not exceeding an acre and a half;
It's common to all and fed off by nineteen cows, six ponies, three horses, five asses, two foals, seven
  pigs, and a calf!
Besides a pond in the middle, as is held by a similar sort of common law lease,   5
And contains twenty ducks, six drakes, three ganders, two dead dogs, four drowned kittens, and
  twelve geese.
Of course the green's cropt very close, and does famous for bowling when the little village boys play
  at cricket;

---

36. Badajos: Badajoz, in Estremadura, Spain, where in 1812, the British army, led by the Duke of Wellington (1769-1852), defeated the French in the Peninsular War. **62. nail:** a weight of beef. **65. sat on:** i.e., at an inquest. **67-68:** Suicides were often buried at a public crossroads, with a wooden stake driven through the heart.   **OUR VILLAGE   1. Miss Mitford:** See Mary Russell Mitford's "Frost and Thaw" (p. 821); Hood's preface to the first periodical publication of this poem also alludes to Goldsmith's "The Deserted Village" (see p. 646). **2. withy:** willow.

Only some horse, or pig, or cow, or great jackass, is sure to come and stand right before the wicket.

There's fifty-five private houses, let alone barns and workshops, and pigsties, and poultry huts, and such-like sheds,

With plenty of public-houses — two Foxes, one Green Man, three Bunch of Grapes, one Crown, and six King's Heads.   *10*

The Green Man is reckoned the best, as the only one that for love or money can raise

A postillion, a blue jacket, two deplorable lame white horses, and a ramshackle "neat postchaise"!

There's one parish church for all the people, whatsoever may be their ranks in life or their degrees,

Except one very damp, small, dark, freezing cold, little Methodist Chapel of Ease;

And close by the churchyard, there's a stonemason's yard, that when the time is seasonable   *15*

Will furnish with afflictions sore and marble urns and cherubims, very low and reasonable.

There's a cage, comfortable enough; I've been in it with Old Jack Jeffery and Tom Pike;

For the Green Man next door will send you in ale, gin, or anything else you like.

I can't speak of the stocks, as nothing remains of them but the upright post;

But the pound is kept in repair for the sake of Cob's horse as is always there almost.   *20*

There's a smithy of course, where that queer sort of a chap in his way, Old Joe Bradley,

Perpetually hammers and stammers, for he stutters and shoes horses very badly.

There's a shop of all sorts that sells everything, kept by the widow of Mr. Task;

But when you go there it's ten to one she's out of everything you ask.

You'll know her house by the swarm of boys, like flies, about the old sugary cask: *25*

There are six empty houses, and not so well papered inside as out,

For bill-stickers won't beware, but stick notices of sales and election placards all about.

That's the Doctor's with a green door, where the garden pots in the window is seen;

A weakly monthly rose that don't blow, and a dead geranium, and a teaplant with five black leaves, and one green.

As for hollyhocks at the cottage doors, and honeysuckles and jasmines, you may go and whistle;   *30*

But the Tailor's front garden grows two cabbages, a dock, a ha'porth of pennyroyal, two dandelions, and a thistle!

There are three small orchards — Mr. Busby's the schoolmaster's is the chief —

With two pear trees that don't bear; one plum, and an apple that every year is stripped by a thief.

There's another small day-school too, kept by the respectable Mrs. Gaby,

A select establishment for six little boys, and one big, and four little girls and a baby;   *35*

There's a rectory with pointed gables and strange odd chimneys that never smokes,

For the Rector don't live on his living like other Christian sort of folks;

There's a barber's once a week well filled with rough black-bearded, shock-headed churls,

And a window with two feminine men's heads, and two masculine ladies in false curls;

There's a butcher's, and a carpenter's, and a plumber's, and a small greengrocer's, and a baker,   *40*

But he won't bake on a Sunday; and there's a sexton that's a coal merchant besides, and an undertaker;

And a toyshop, but not a whole one, for a village can't compare with the London shops;

One window sells drums, dolls, kites, carts, bats, Clout's balls, and the other sells malt and hops.

And Mrs. Brown in domestic economy not to be a bit behind her betters,

---

12.: See the note to Mitford, line 61 (p. 822). **17. cage:** cell. **29. blow:** bloom. **31. ha'porth:** halfpenny's worth. **40-41. baker . . . Sunday:** Cf. the note to Peacock's "Rich and Poor," line 14 (p. 820).

Lets her house to a milliner, a watchmaker, a rat-catcher, a cobbler, lives in it herself, and it's the
  post-office for letters.   45
Now I've gone through all the village — ay, from end to end, save and except one more house,
But I haven't come to that — and I hope I never shall — and that's the Village Poor House!

(1833)

THE SONG OF THE SHIRT

With fingers weary and worn,
  With eyelids heavy and red,
A woman sat, in unwomanly rags,
  Plying her needle and thread —
    Stitch! stitch! stitch!   5
In poverty, hunger, and dirt,
  And still with a voice of dolorous pitch
She sang the "Song of the Shirt."

"Work! work! work!
While the cock is crowing aloof!   10
  And work — work — work,
Till the stars shine through the roof!
  It's Oh! to be a slave
    Along with the barbarous Turk,
Where woman has never a soul to save,   15
  If this is Christian work!

"Work — work — work
Till the brain begins to swim;
  Work — work — work
Till the eyes are heavy and dim!   20
  Seam, and gusset, and band,
    Band, and gusset, and seam,
Till over the buttons I fall asleep,
  And sew them on in a dream!

"Oh, Men, with Sisters dear!   25
  Oh, Men, with Mothers and Wives!
It is not linen you're wearing out,
  But human creatures' lives!
    Stitch — stitch — stitch,
In poverty, hunger, and dirt,   30
  Sewing at once, with a double thread,
    A Shroud as well as a Shirt.

"But why do I talk of Death?
  That Phantom of grisly bone,
I hardly fear his terrible shape,   35
  It seems so like my own —

It seems so like my own,
  Because of the fasts I keep;
Oh, God! that bread should be so dear,
  And flesh and blood so cheap!   40

"Work — work — work!
  My labour never flags;
And what are its wages? A bed of straw,
  A crust of bread — and rags.
That shatter'd roof — and this naked floor —
  A table — a broken chair —   46
And a wall so blank, my shadow I thank
  For sometimes falling there!

"Work — work — work!
From weary chime to chime,   50
  Work — work — work —
As prisoners work for crime!
  Band, and gusset, and seam,
    Seam, and gusset, and band,
Till the heart is sick, and the brain benumb'd,
  As well as the weary hand.   56

"Work — work — work,
In the dull December light,
  And work — work — work,
When the weather is warm and bright —   60
While underneath the eaves
  The brooding swallows cling
As if to show me their sunny backs
  And twit me with the spring.

"Oh! but to breathe the breath   65
Of the cowslip and primrose sweet —
  With the sky above my head,
And the grass beneath my feet,
For only one short hour
  To feel as I used to feel,   70
Before I knew the woes of want
  And the walk that costs a meal!

"Oh! but for one short hour!
    A respite however brief!
No blessed leisure for Love or Hope,   *75*
    But only time for Grief!
A little weeping would ease my heart,
    But in their briny bed
My tears must stop, for every drop
    Hinders needle and thread!"   *80*

With fingers weary and worn,
    With eyelids heavy and red,
A woman sat in unwomanly rags,
    Plying her needle and thread —
        Stitch! stitch! stitch!   *85*
In poverty, hunger, and dirt,
And still with a voice of dolorous pitch, —
Would that its tone could reach the Rich! —
She sang this "Song of the Shirt"!

                (1843)

JOHN DUNMORE LANG
Scotland/Australia, 1799-1878

COLONIAL NOMENCLATURE

'Twas said of Greece two thousand years ago,
    That every stone i' the land had got a name.
Of New South Wales too, men will soon say so too;
    But every stone there seems to get the same.
"Macquarie" for a name is all *the* go: *5*
    The old Scotch Governor was fond of fame.
Macquarie Street, Place, Port, Fort, Town, Lake, River:
"Lachlan Macquarie, Esquire, Governor," for ever!

I like the native names, as Parramatta,
    And Illawarra, and Woolloomoolloo;   *10*
Nandowra, Woogarora, Bulkomatta,
    Tomah, Toongabbie, Mittagong, Meroo;
Buckobble, Cumleroy, and Coolingatta.
    The Warragumby, Bargo, Burradoo;
Cookbundoon, Carrabaiga, Wingecarribbee,   *15*
The Wollondilly, Yurumbon, Bungarribbee.

I hate your Goulburn Downs and Goulburn Plains,
    And Goulburn River and the Goulburn Range,
And Mount Goulburn and Goulburn Vale! One's brains
    Are turned with Goulburns! Vile scorbutic mange

For immortality! Had I the reins   *21*
    Of Government a fortnight, I would change
These Downing Street appellatives, and give
The country names that should deserve to live.

I'd have Mount Hampden and Mount Marvell, and   *25*
    Mount Wallace and Mount Bruce at the old Bay.
I'd have them all the highest in the land,
    That men might see them twenty leagues away.
I'd have the Plains of Marathon beyond
    Some mountain pass yclept Thermopylae.   *30*
Such are th' immortal names that should be written
On all thy new discoveries, Great Britain!

Yes! let some badge of liberty appear
    On every mountain and on every plain
Where Britain's power is known, or far or near,   *35*
    That freedom there may have an endless reign!
Then though she die, in some revolving year,
    A race may rise to make her live again!
The future slave may lisp the patriot's name
And his breast kindle with a kindred flame!   *40*

                (1824)

COLONIAL NOMENCLATURE   **5. Macquarie:** Lachlan Macquarie (1762-1824), Scots-born governor of New South Wales from 1809 to 1821. **17. Goulbourn:** Henry Goulbourn (1784-1856), British undersecretary for the colonies, 1812-21. **23. Downing Street:** i.e., named by the British Prime Minister, whose residence is at No. 10 Downing Street in London. **25. Hampden:** see note to Gray's "Elegy" line 57 (p. 611); **Marvell:** Andrew Marvell, a supporter of Cromwell (see p. 402). **26. Wallace:** Sir William Wallace (c.1274-1305), Scots hero; **Bruce:** Robert the Bruce (1274-1329), King Robert I of Scotland. **29-30:** At the Battle of Marathon in 490 B.C., the Athenians defeated the Persians; at the Battle of Thermopylae in 480 B.C., the Spartans fought to the death against the invading Persians.

ANONYMOUS
19th century

DAVID LOWSTON

My name is David Lowston, I did seal, I did seal,
My name is David Lowston, I did seal.
Though my men and I were lost,
Though our very lives 'twould cost,
We did seal, we did seal, we did seal.   5

'Twas in eighteen hundred and ten we set sail, we set sail,
'Twas in eighteen hundred and ten we set sail.
We were left, we gallant men,
Never more to sail again,
For to seal, for to seal, for to seal.   10

We were set down in Open Bay, were set down, were set down,
We were set down in Open Bay, were set down.
Upon the sixteenth day,
Of Februar-aye-ay,
For to seal, for to seal, for to seal.   15

Our Captain, John Bedar, he set sail, he set sail,
Yes, for Port Jackson he set sail.
"I'll return, men, without fail,"
But she foundered in a gale,
And went down, and went down, and went down.   20

We cured ten thousand skins for the fur, for the fur,
Yes we cured ten thousand skins for the fur.
Brackish water, putrid seal,
We did all of us fall ill,
For to die, for to die, for to die.   25

Come all you lads who sail upon the sea, sail the sea,
Come all you jacks who sail upon the sea.
Though the schooner *Governor Bligh*,
Took on some who did not die,
Never seal, never seal, never seal.   30

(c.1810-15)

DAVID LOWSTON   17. Port Jackson: Sydney Harbour.

HAIL SOUTH AUSTRALIA!

Hail South Australia! blessed clime,
  Thou lovely land of my adoption
(I never meant to see the spot
  If I had had the slightest option).

Hail charming plains of bounteous growth! *5*
  Where tufted vegetation smiles.
(Those dull, atrocious endless flats,
  And no plain less than thirteen miles).

Hail far-famed Torrens, graceful stream!
  On whose sweet banks I often linger, *10*

Soothed by the murmur of thy waves
  (And plumb the bottom with my finger).

Hail land! where all the wants of life
  Flow in cheap streams of milk and honey;
Where all are sure of daily bread *15*
  (If they can fork out ready money).

Hail *South Australia!* once more hail!
  That man indeed is surely rash
Who cannot live content in thee,
  Or wants for anything (but cash). *20*

  (1843)

THE FEMALE TRANSPORT

Come all young girls, both far and near, and listen unto me,
While unto you I do unfold what proved my destiny;
My mother died when I was young, it caused me to deplore,
And I did get my way too soon upon my native shore.

Sarah Collins is my name, most dreadful is my fate, *5*
My father reared me tenderly, the truth I do relate,
Till enticed by bad company along with many more,
It led to my discovery upon my native shore.

My trial it approached fast, before the judge I stood,
And when the judge's sentence passed it fairly chilled my blood, *10*
Crying, "You must be transported for fourteen years or more,
And go from hence across the seas unto Van Diemen's shore."

It hurt my heart when on a coach I my native town passed by;
To see so many I did know, it made me heave a sigh;
Then to a ship was sent with speed along with many more, *15*
Whose aching hearts did grieve to go unto Van Diemen's shore.

The sea was rough, ran mountains high, with us poor girls 'twas hard,
No one but God to us came nigh, no one did us regard.
At length, alas! we reached the land, it grieved us ten times more,
That wretched place Van Diemen's Land, far from our native shore. *20*

They chained us two by two, and whipped and lashed along,
They cut off our provisions if we did the least thing wrong;
They march us in the burning sun until our feet are sore,
So hard's our lot now we are got to Van Diemen's shore.

HAIL SOUTH AUSTRALIA! **9. Torrens:** the river on which Adelaide is located. **THE FEMALE TRANSPORT Title:** A "transport" was a convict sent abroad from England, often (in the early 19th century) to the prison in Van Diemen's Land (line 12), now called Tasmania.

We labour hard from morn to night until our bones do ache,   *25*
Then every one they must obey, their mouldy beds must make;
We often wish when we lay down we ne'er may rise no more
To meet our savage Governor upon Van Diemen's shore.

Every night when I lay down I wet my straw with tears,
While wind upon that horrid shore did whistle in our ears,   *30*
Those dreadful beasts upon that land around our cots do roar,
Most dismal is our doom upon Van Diemen's shore.

Come all young men and maidens, do bad company forsake,
If tongue can tell our overthrow it will make your heart to ache;
Young girls I pray be ruled by me, your wicked ways give o'er,   *35*
For fear like us you spend your days upon Van Diemen's shore.

THE BLUE-TAIL FLY

When I was young I used to wait
On master and give him his plate
And pass the bottle when he got dry,
And brush away the blue-tail fly.
 Jimmy crack corn and I don't care, *5*
 My master's gone away.

And when he'd ride in the arternoon
I'd follow after with a hickory broom,
The pony being very shy,
When bitten by the blue-tail fly. *10*

One day he ride around the farm,
The flies so num'rous they did swarm —
One chanced to bite him on the thigh,
The devil take the blue-tail fly.

The pony jump, he run, he pitch, *15*
He threw my master in the ditch,
He died and the jury wondered why —
The verdict was the blue-tail fly.

We laid him under a 'simmon tree,
His epitaph was there to see, *20*
Beneath this stone I'm forced to lie,
Victim of a blue-tail fly.

Ole massa's dead and gone to rest,
They say all things is for the best.
I never shall forget till the day I die *25*
Ole massa and the blue-tail fly.

The hornet gets in eyes and nose,
The skeeter bites you through your clothes,
The gallinipper flies up high,
But wusser yet, the blue-tail fly. *30*

I'LL GIVE MY LOVE AN APPLE

I'll give my love an apple without any core;
I'll give my love a dwelling without any door;
I'll give my love a palace wherein she might be,
That she might unlock it without any key.

How can there be an apple without any core? *5*
How can there be a dwelling without any door?
How can there be a palace wherein she might be,
That she might unlock it without any key?

My head is an apple without any core;
My mind is a dwelling without any door; *10*
My heart is a palace wherein she might be,
That she can unlock it without any key.

I'll give my love a cherry without any stone;
I'll give my love a chicken without any bone;
I'll give my love a ring without any end; *15*
I'll give my love a baby and no crying.

How can there be a cherry without any stone?
How can there be a chicken without any bone?
How can there be a ring without any end?
How can there be a baby and no crying? *20*

---

31. cots: cottages. **THE BLUE-TAIL FLY 5-6:** The refrain follows each stanza of this American folk ballad; **corn:** a bottle of corn whisky. **9. shy:** nervous, jumpy. **19. 'simmon:** persimmon. **29. gallinipper:** large mosquito. **I'LL GIVE MY LOVE AN APPLE** This is a Nova Scotia version of a folksong for which there are several variants; the Kentucky version is called "I'll Give My Love a Cherry" or sometimes "The Riddle Song."

When the cherry's in blossom it has no stone;
When the chicken's in the egg it has no bone;
When the ring is a-rolling it has no end;
When the baby is a-getting, there's no crying.

I'SE THE B'Y THAT BUILDS THE BOAT

I'se the b'y that builds the boat,
And I'se the b'y that sails her!
I'se the b'y that catches the fish
And takes 'em home to Lizer.

> *Hip yer partner, Sally Tibbo'!*   5
> *Hip yer partner, Sally Brown!*
> *Fogo, Twillingate, Mor'ton's Harbour,*
> *All around the circle!*

Sods and rinds to cover yer flake,
Cake and tea for supper,   *10*
Codfish in the spring o' the year
Fried in maggoty butter.

I don't want your maggoty fish,
That's no good for winter;
I could buy as good as that   *15*
Down in Bonavista.

I took Lizer to a dance,
And faith, but she could travel!
And every step that she did take
Was up to her knees in gravel.   *20*

Susan White, she's out of sight,
Her petticoat wants a border;
Old Sam Oliver, in the dark,
He kissed her in the corner.

THOMAS BABINGTON MACAULAY
England, 1800-1859

A Speech Delivered in the House of Commons on the Anatomy Bill

Sir, I cannot, even at this late hour of the night, refrain from saying two or three words. Most of the observations of the honourable Member for Preston I pass by, as undeserving of any answer before an audience like this. But on one part of his speech I must make a few remarks. We are, he says, making a law to benefit the rich at the expense of the poor. Sir, the fact is the direct reverse. This is a bill which tends   5
especially to the benefit of the poor. What are the evils against which we are attempting to make provision? Two especially; that is to say, the practice of burking and bad surgery. Now to both these the poor alone are exposed. What man, in our rank of life, runs the smallest risk of being burked? That a man has property, that he has connections, that he is likely to be missed and sought for, are circumstances which   10
secure him against the burker. It is curious to observe the difference between murders of

---

I'SE THE B'Y **1. I'se the b'y:** I'm the boy. **5. Hip:** bump with the hip while dancing. **5-8:** This refrain follows each stanza; the place names in lines 7 and 16 refer to Newfoundland outports. **9:** i.e., sods and spruce bark to cover the platform (or "flake") on which you are drying codfish. **10. cake:** hardtack.   **A SPEECH ON THE ANATOMY BILL**   A British law of 1828 allowed the bodies of executed criminals to be exhumed for the purposes of anatomical dissection. This law came into being in part because of the activities of William Burke, who in 1828 was arrested (along with his accomplice William Hare) for smothering people and selling their bodies to anatomists. Burke — hence the verb "to burke" (line 7), meaning "to smother, hush up" — was executed in 1829. The 1828 law was repealed when the Anatomy Bill was introduced in 1832. Macaulay's support for the bill came in reply to an attack on it by Henry Hunt (1773-1835), the Member for Preston (line 2). The Anatomy Bill disallowed the dissection of criminals but permitted (under regulation) the dissection of bodies of persons who had died in workhouses.

this kind and other murders. An ordinary murderer hides the body and disposes of the property. Bishop and Williams dig holes and bury the property, and expose the body to sale. The more wretched, the more lonely, any human being may be, the more desirable prey is he to these wretches. It is the man, the mere naked man, that they pursue. Again, as to bad surgery: this is, of all evils, the evil by which the rich suffer least and the poor most. If we could do all that, in the opinion of the Member for Preston, ought to be done, if we could prevent disinterment, if we could prevent dissection, if we could destroy the English school of anatomy, if we could force every student of medical science to go to the expense of a foreign education, on whom would the bad consequences fall? On the rich? Not at all. As long as there is in France, in Italy, in Germany, a single surgeon of eminent skill, a single surgeon who is, to use the phrase of the Member for Preston, addicted to dissection, that surgeon will be in attendance whenever an English nobleman is to be cut for the stone. The higher orders in England will always be able to procure the best medical assistance. Who suffers by the bad state of the Russian school of surgery? The Emperor Nicholas? By no means. The whole evil falls on the peasantry. If the education of a surgeon should become very expensive, if the fees of surgeons should consequently rise, if the supply of regular surgeons should diminish, the sufferers would be, not the rich, but the poor in our country villages, who would again be left to mountebanks, and barbers, and old women, and charms, and quack medicines. The honourable gentleman talks of sacrificing the interests of humanity to the interests of science, as if this were a question about the squaring of the circle or the transit of Venus. This is not a mere question of science; it is not the unprofitable exercise of an ingenious mind; it is a question between health and sickness, between ease and torment, between life and death. Does the honourable gentleman know from what cruel sufferings the improvement of surgical science has rescued our species? I will tell him one story, the first that comes into my head. He may have heard of Leopold, Duke of Austria, the same who imprisoned our Richard Cœur de Lion. Leopold's horse fell under him and crushed his leg. The surgeons said that the limb must be amputated; but none of them knew how to amputate it. Leopold, in his agony, laid a hatchet on his thigh, and ordered his servant to strike with a mallet. The leg was cut off, and the Duke died of the gush of blood. Such was the end of that powerful prince. Why, there is not now a bricklayer who falls from a ladder in England who cannot obtain surgical assistance infinitely superior to that which the sovereign of Austria could command in the twelfth century. I think this is a bill which tends to the good of the people, and which tends especially to the good of the poor. Therefore I support it. If it is unpopular, I am sorry for it. But I shall cheerfully take my share of its unpopularity. For such, I am convinced, ought to be the conduct of one whose object it is not to flatter the people, but to serve them.

(1832)

---

13. Bishop and Williams: Bishop, with his accomplice Williams, were arrested and executed in 1831 for the murder in London of an Italian boy named Carlo Ferrari. **24. cut:** operated on. **30. barbers:** i.e., who often acted as surgeons. **32-33. squaring the circle:** i.e., attempting an impossibility. **33. transit of Venus:** the passage of Venus between the earth and the sun, an astronomical event that occurs twice within eight years, followed by a gap of 105 or 121 years. **38. Leopold, Richard:** After securing a peace with the Moslem leader Saladin (c.1137-1193) in 1192, King Richard I (1157-1199) returned from the Third Crusade only to be imprisoned by Leopold II, Margrave of Austria, in Dürnstein; he was released and reached England in 1194.

WILLIAM BARNES
England, 1801-1886

THE GIANTS IN TREADES
Gramfer's Feable: How the steam
engine come about

Vier, Aïr, E'th, Water, wer a-meäde
Good workers, each o'm in his treäde,
An' Aïr an' Water, wer a match
    Vor woone another in a mill;
The giant Water at a hatch,   5
    An' Aïr on the windmill hill.
Zoo then, when Water had a-meäde
Zome money, Aïr begrudg'd his treäde,
An' come by, unaweäres woone night,
    An' vound en at his own mill-head,   10
An' cast upon en, iron-tight,
    An icy cwoat so stiff as lead.
An' there he wer so good as dead
Vor grinden any corn vor bread.
Then Water cried to Vier, "Alack!   15
    Look, here be I, so stiff's a log,
Thik fellor Aïr do keep me back
    Vrom grinden. I can't wag a cog.
If I, dear Vier, did ever souse
Your nimble body on a house,   20
When you wer on your merry pranks
Wi' thatch or refters, beams or planks,
Vorgi'e me, do, in pity's neäme,
Vor 'twerden I that wer to bleäme,
I never wagg'd, though I ben't cringen,   25
Till men did dreve me wi' their engine.
Do zet me free vrom theäse cwold jacket,
Vor I myzelf shall never crack it."
"Well come," cried Vier, "My vo'k ha' meäde
An engine that 'ull work your treäde.   30
If E'th is only in the mood,

While I do work, to gi'e me food,
I'll help ye, an' I'll meäke your skill
A match vor Mister Aïr's wold mill."   34
"What food," cried E'th, "'ull suit your bwoard?"
"Oh! trust me, I ben't over nice,"
Cried Vier, "an' I can eat a slice
Ov any thing you can avvword."
"I've lots," cried E'th, "ov coal an' wood."   39
"Ah! that's the stuff," cried Vier, "that's good."
Zoo Vier at woonce to Water cried,
"Here, Water, here, you get inside
O' theäse girt bwoiler. Then I'll show
How I can help ye down below,
An' when my work shall woonce begin   45
You'll be a thousand times so strong,
An' be a thousand times so long
An' big as when you vu'st got in.
An' I wull meäke, as sure as death,
Thik fellor Aïr to vind me breath,   50
An' you shall grind, an' pull, an' dreve,
An' zaw, an' drash, an' pump, an' heave,
An' get vrom Aïr, in time, I'll lay
A pound, the dreven ships at sea."
An' zoo 'tis good to zee that might   55
Wull help a man a-wrong'd to right.

    (1862)

ECLOGUE: RUSTICUS EMIGRANS
Emigration: ROBERT AND RICHARD

    ROBERT
Well Richat, zoo 'tis true what I do hear
That you be guoin to Dieman's Land to-year.

    RICHARD
Ees, I shall never eat another pound
O' zalt in England here, where I wer barn;

THE GIANTS IN TREADES This and the *Eclogue* are written in Dorset dialect. **Title:** "the giants in trades; Grandpa's fable." **1. Vier:** fire; **a-meäde:** made. **7. Zoo:** so. **12. cwoat:** coat. **14. corn:** grain. **17. Thik:** this. **18. wag a cog:** turn the wheel a single notch. **23. Vorgi'e:** forgive. **36. nice:** fastidious. **38. avvword:** afford. **43. girt:** great. **48. vu'st:** first. **51. dreve:** drive. **52. drash:** thresh. **ECLOGUE: RUSTICUS EMIGRANS** **Title:** (Latin) the farmer emigrates. **2. Dieman's Land:** loosely, Australia.

Nor dig another spit o' English ground;   *5*
Nor cut a bit muore English grass or carn.
Ees, we must get to Lon'on now next Zunday
Abuoard the Ship that is to car us.
Vor if the weather should be rightish var us
We shall put out to Sea o' Monday,   *10*
Zoo our vew tools and clothes (for we must car all
That we can get by buyen, or by baggen),
Here t'other day I packed up in a barrel
And zent 'em on to Lon'on by the waggon.

ROBERT

And how d'ye zend your children and your women? *15*

RICHARD

We got a lightish waggon to clap them in.

ROBERT

And how d'ye get up yourzelves, you men?

RICHARD

O we shall walk and ride oonce now and then
When we do meet wi' any drive-en lads
Wi' lightish luoads to tiake us up var cads.   *20*

ROBERT

And how d'ye veel now Richat in your mind,
To leave your bethpleace and your friends behind?

RICHARD

Why very queer, I do, I can't deny:
When I do think o' be'en piarted
Vrom al my friends var ever, I could cry   *25*
But var the shiame o' be'en so softhearted.
Here be the trees that I did use to clim in,
Here is the brook that I did use to zwim in,
Here be the ground where I've a worked and played;
Here is the hut that I wer barn and bred in;   *30*
Here is the little church where we've a prayed,
And churchyard that my kinsvolk's buones be laid in;
And I myzelf, you know, should like to lie
Among 'em too when I do come to die;
But 'tis noo use to have zich foolish wishes;   *35*
I shall be tossed, i' may be, to the vishes.

ROBERT

'Tis hard a man can't get a luoaf to veed 'en
Upon the pliace wher life wer vust a gied 'en;

'Tis hard that if he'd work, there's noo work var'n,
Or that his work woon't bring enough o' money   *40*
To keep en, though the land is vull a carn
And cattle; and do flow wi' milk and honey.

RICHARD

Why ees, 'tis rather hardish, oone can't doubt it,
But 'tis'n any use to tak about it;
There's noo work here at huome that I can come at, *45*
And zoo I'll goo abroad and try var some'hat.

ROBERT

But you'll be zome time out upon the ocean;
You woon't get ovver very quick;
And if the Sea is rough, the vessel's motion,
I s'puose, wull miake ye rather zick.   *50*

RICHARD

Eees 'twull be voorteen weeks, I s'puose, or muore,
'Forever we shall stratch our lags ashore.

ROBERT

And then, i' may be, you mid come to land
Down at the bottom, in the mud or zand;
You mident goo to Dieman's Land at all,   *55*
Var you mid get a drownded in a squall.

RICHARD

I don't mind that, var a'ter I be dead
I shan't be zoo a puzzled to get bread.
They that 'ave got the wordle's goods, noo doubt on't,
Do like it, and ben't willing to goo out on't: *60*
There's nothin here var I but want and zorrow,
Zoo I don't mind o' leaven it to-morrow.
If 'twerden var my children and my wife,
I wou'dent gi' a zixpence var my life.

ROBERT

Ah! we must stay till God is plieased to tiake us; *65*
If we do do our best he woon't forsiake us.
Good bye, and if I shou'dent zee ye agaen,
God bless you, Richat, drough your life.

RICHARD
Amen.

(*c.1860s*)

---

5. spit: spadeful. **6. carn:** corn; i.e., grain. **7. Ees:** yes. **8. car:** carry. **12. baggen:** begging. **16. clap:** put. **20. var cads:** for cads; i.e., as unbooked passengers. **37. veed 'en:** feed one. **38. gied:** given to. **39. var'n:** for him. **59. wordle's:** world's. **63. If 'twerden:** if it weren't. **68. drough:** through.

JOHN HENRY NEWMAN
England, 1801-1890

THE PILLAR OF THE CLOUD

Lead, Kindly Light, amid the encircling gloom,
    Lead Thou me on!
The night is dark, and I am far from home —
    Lead Thou me on!
Keep Thou my feet; I do not ask to see   5
The distant scene, — one step enough for me.

I was not ever thus, nor prayed that Thou
    Shouldst lead me on.
I loved to choose and see my path; but now

Lead Thou me on!   *10*
I loved the garish day, and, spite of fears,
Pride ruled my will: remember not past years.

So long Thy power hath blessed me, sure it still
    Will lead me on,
O'er moor and fen, o'er crag and torrent, till   *15*
    The night is gone;
And with the morn those angel faces smile
Which I have loved long since, and lost awhile.

          (1832)

from *THE IDEA OF A UNIVERSITY*

Knowledge is one thing, virtue is another; good sense is not conscience, refinement is not humility, nor is largeness and justness of view faith. Philosophy, however enlightened, however profound, gives no command over the passions, no influential motives, no vivifying principles. Liberal Education makes not the Christian, not the Catholic, but the gentleman. It is well to be a gentleman, it is well to have a   *5* cultivated intellect, a delicate taste, a candid, equitable, dispassionate mind, a noble and courteous bearing in the conduct of life — these are the connatural qualities of a large knowledge; they are the objects of a University; I am advocating, I shall illustrate and insist upon them; but still, I repeat, they are no guarantee for sanctity or even for conscientiousness, they may attach to the man of the world, to the profligate,   *10* to the heartless, pleasant, alas, and attractive as he shows when decked out in them. Taken by themselves, they do but seem to be what they are not; they look like virtue at a distance, but they are detected by close observers, and on the long run; and hence it is that they are popularly accused of pretense and hypocrisy, not, I repeat, from their own fault, but because their professors and their admirers persist in taking them   *15* for what they are not, and are officious in arrogating for them a praise to which they have no claim. Quarry the granite rock with razors, or moor the vessel with a thread of silk; then may you hope with such keen and delicate instruments as human knowledge and human reason to contend against those giants, the passion and the pride of man.   *20*

          (1852)

HARRIET MARTINEAU
England, 1802-1876

from *SOCIETY IN AMERICA*

POLITICAL NON-EXISTENCE OF WOMEN

One of the fundamental principles announced in the Declaration of Independence is that governments derive their just powers from the consent of the governed. How can the political condition of women be reconciled with this?

Governments in the United States have power to tax women who hold property; to divorce them from their husbands; to fine, imprison, and execute them for certain 5 offences. Whence do these governments derive their powers? They are not "just," as they are not derived from the consent of the women thus governed.

Governments in the United States have power to enslave certain women; and also to punish other women for inhuman treatment of such slaves. Neither of these powers are "just," not being derived from the consent of the governed. 10

Governments decree to women in some States half their husbands' property; in others one-third. In some, a woman, on her marriage, is made to yield all her property to her husband; in others, to retain a portion, or the whole, in her own hands. Whence do governments derive the unjust power of thus disposing of property without the consent of the governed? 15

The democratic principle condemns all this as wrong; and requires the equal political representation of all rational beings. Children, idiots, and criminals, during the season of sequestration, are the only fair exceptions.

The case is so plain that I might close it here; but it is interesting to inquire how so obvious a decision has been so evaded as to leave to women no political rights 20 whatever. The question has been asked, from time to time, in more countries than one, how obedience to the laws can be required of women, when no woman has, either actually or virtually, given any assent to any law. No plausible answer has, as far as I can discover, been offered; for the good reason, that no plausible answer can be devised. The most principled democratic writers on government have on this subject sunk into 25 fallacies, as disgraceful as any advocate of despotism has adduced. In fact, they have thus sunk from being, for the moment, advocates of despotism. Jefferson in America, and James Mill at home, subside, for the occasion, to the level of the author of the Emperor of Russia's Catechism for the young Poles.

Jefferson says, "Were our State a pure democracy, in which all the inhabitants 30 should meet together to transact all their business, there would yet be excluded from their deliberations,

"1. Infants, until arrived at years of discretion;

POLITICAL NON-EXISTENCE OF WOMEN **1. Declaration of Independence:** See p. 657. **27. Jefferson:** See p. 692. **28. Mill:** English essayist (1773-1836). **30. says:** in a letter.

"2. Women, who, to prevent depravation of morals, and ambiguity of issue, could not mix promiscuously in the public meetings of men;

"3. Slaves, from whom the unfortunate state of things with us takes away the rights of will and of property."

If the slave disqualification, here assigned, were shifted up under the head of Women, their case would be nearer the truth than as it now stands. Woman's lack of will and of property is more like the true cause of her exclusion from the representation, than that which is actually set down against her. As if there could be no means of conducting public affairs but by promiscuous meetings! As if there would be more danger in promiscuous meetings for political business than in such meetings for worship, for oratory, for music, for dramatic entertainments, — for any of the thousand transactions of civilized life! The plea is not worth another word.

Mill says, with regard to representation, in his Essay on Government,[46] "One thing is pretty clear, that all those individuals, whose interests are involved in those of other individuals, may be struck off without inconvenience. . . . In this light, women may be regarded, the interest of almost all of whom is involved, either in that of their fathers or in that of their husbands."

The true democratic principle is, that no person's interests can be, or can be ascertained to be, identical with those of any other person. This allows the exclusion of none but incapables.

The word "almost," in Mr. Mill's second sentence, rescues women from the exclusion he proposes. As long as there are women who have neither husbands nor fathers, his proposition remains an absurdity.

The interests of women who have fathers and husbands can never be identical with theirs, while there is a necessity for laws to protect women against their husbands and fathers. This statement is not worth another word.

Some who desire that there should be an equality of property between men and women, oppose representation, on the ground that political duties would be incompatible with the other duties which women have to discharge. The reply to this is that women are the best judges here. God has given time and power for the discharge of all duties; and, if he had not, it would be for women to decide which they would take, and which they would leave. But their guardians follow the ancient fashion of deciding what is best for their wards. The Emperor of Russia discovers when a coat of arms and title do not agree with a subject prince. The King of France early perceives that the air of Paris does not agree with a free-thinking foreigner. The English Tories feel the hardship that it would be to impose the franchise on every artisan, busy as he is in getting his bread. The Georgian planter perceives the hardship that freedom would be to his slaves. And the best friends of half the human race peremptorily decide for them as to their rights, their duties, their feelings, their powers. In all these cases, the persons thus cared for feel that the abstract decision rests with themselves; that, though they may be compelled to submit, they need not acquiesce.

It is pleaded that half of the human race does acquiesce in the decision of the other half, as to their rights and duties. And some instances, not only of submission, but of

---

46. Essay on Government: in the *Westminster Review.*

acquiescence, there are. Forty years ago, the women of New Jersey went to the poll, and
voted, at state elections. The general term, "inhabitants," stood unqualified; — as it will
again, when the true democratic principle comes to be fully understood. A motion was made
to correct the inadvertence; and it was done, as a matter of course; without any appeal, as far 80
as I could learn, from the persons about to be injured. Such acquiescence proves nothing but
the degradation of the injured party. It inspires the same emotions of pity as the supplication
of the freed slave who kneels to his master to restore him to slavery, that he may have his
animal wants supplied, without being troubled with human rights and duties. Acquiescence
like this is an argument which cuts the wrong way for those who use it. 85

But this acquiescence is only partial; and, to give any semblance of strength to the
plea, the acquiescence must be complete. I, for one, do not acquiesce. I declare that
whatever obedience I yield to the laws of the society in which I live is a matter between,
not the community and myself, but my judgment and my will. Any punishment inflicted
on me for the breach of the laws, I should regard as so much gratuitous injury; for to 90
those laws I have never, actually or virtually, assented. I know that there are women in
England who agree with me in this — I know that there are women in America who
agree with me in this. The plea of acquiescence is invalidated by us.

It is pleaded that, by enjoying the protection of some laws, women give their assent
to all. This needs but a brief answer. Any protection thus conferred is, under woman's 95
circumstances, a boon bestowed at the pleasure of those in whose power she is. A boon
of any sort is no compensation for the privation of something else; nor can the enjoyment of it bind to the performance of any thing to which it bears no relation. Because
I, by favour, may procure the imprisonment of the thief who robs my house, am I,
unrepresented, therefore bound not to smuggle French ribbons? The obligation not to 100
smuggle has a widely different derivation.

I cannot enter upon the commonest order of pleas of all — those which relate to the
virtual influence of woman; her swaying the judgment and will of man through the
heart; and so forth. One might as well try to dissect the morning mist. I knew a
gentleman in America who told me how much rather he had be a woman than the man 105
he is — a professional man, a father, a citizen. He would give up all this for a woman's
influence. I thought he was mated too soon. He should have married a lady, also of my
acquaintance, who would not at all object to being a slave, if ever the blacks should
have the upper hand; "it is so right that the one race should be subservient to the other!"
Or rather, — I thought it a pity that the one could not be a woman, and the other a slave; 110
so that an injured individual of each class might be exalted into their places, to fulfil and
enjoy the duties and privileges which they despise, and, in despising, disgrace.

The truth is, that while there is much said about "the sphere of woman," two widely
different notions are entertained of what is meant by the phrase. The narrow, and, to the
ruling party, the more convenient notion is that sphere appointed by men, and bounded 115
by their ideas of propriety — a notion from which any and every woman may fairly
dissent. The broad and true conception is of the sphere appointed by God, and bounded
by the powers which he has bestowed. This commands the assent of man and woman;
and only the question of powers remains to be proved.

That woman has power to represent her own interests, no one can deny till she has 120
been tried. The modes need not be discussed here: they must vary with circumstances.

The fearful and absurd images which are perpetually called up to perplex the question, — images of women on woolsacks in England, and under canopies in America, have nothing to do with the matter. The principle being once established, the methods will follow, easily, naturally, and under a remarkable transmutation of the ludicrous into the *125* sublime. The kings of Europe would have laughed mightily, two centuries ago, at the idea of a commoner, without robes, crown, or sceptre, stepping into the throne of a strong nation. Yet who dared to laugh when Washington's super-royal voice greeted the New World from the presidential chair, and the old world stood still to catch the echo?

The principle of the equal rights of both halves of the human race is all we have to *130* do with here. It is the true democratic principle which can never be seriously controverted, and only for a short time evaded. Governments can derive their just powers only from the consent of the governed.

(1837)

from *RETROSPECT OF WESTERN TRAVEL*

from NIAGARA

> "Look back!
> Lo! where it comes like an eternity,
> As if to sweep down all things in its track,
> Charming the eye with dread!"
>
> BYRON

It is not my intention to describe what we saw at Niagara so much as to relate what we did. To offer an idea of Niagara by writing of hues and dimensions is much like representing the kingdom of Heaven by images of jasper and topazes.

I visited the falls twice: first in October, 1834, in company with the party with whom we traversed the state of New-York, when we stayed nearly a week; and again *5* with Dr. and Mrs. F., and other friends, in June, 1836, when we remained between two and three days. The first time we approached the falls from Buffalo, the next from Lewistown and Queenstown.

I expected to be disappointed in the first sight of the falls, and did not relish the idea of being questioned on the first day as to my "impressions." I therefore made a law, with *10* the hearty agreement of the rest of the party, that no one should ask an opinion of the spectacle for twenty-four hours. We stepped into the stage at Buffalo at half past eight in the morning on the 14th of October. At Black Rock we got out to cross the ferry. We looked at the green rushing waters we were crossing, and wondered whether they or we should be at the falls first. We had to wait some minutes for the stage on the Canada *15* side, and a comely English woman invited us into her kitchen to warm ourselves. She was washing as well as cooking; and such a log was blazing under her boilers as no fireplace in England would hold. It looked like the entire trunk of a pine somewhat

---

123. on woolsacks, under canopies: i.e., seated at a judge's bench or occupying other positions of power. NIAGARA See also Frances Kemble's "Niagara" (p. 982). **Epigraph:** from *Childe Harold's Pilgrimage,* Canto IV, lines 636-39.

shortened. I could not help often wishing that some of the shivering poor of London could have supplies of the fuel which lies rotting in the American woods.   20

The road is extremely bad all the way from the ferry to the falls, and the bridges the rudest of the rude. The few farms looked decaying, and ill-clad children offered us autumn fruit for sale. We saw nothing to flatter our national complacency; for truly the contrast with the other side of the river was mournful enough. It was not till we had passed the inn with the sign of the "Chippeway Battle Ground" that we saw the spray   25 from the falls. I believe we might have seen it sooner if we had known where to look. "Is that it?" we all exclaimed. It appeared on the left-hand side, whereas we had been looking to the right; and instead of its being suspended in the air like a white cloud, as we had imagined, it curled vigorously up, like smoke from a cannon or from a replenished fire. The winding of the road presently brought this round to our right hand.   30 It seemed very near; the river, too, was as smooth as oil. The beginning of the Welland canal was next pointed out to me, but it was not a moment to care for canals. Then the little Round Island, covered with wood and surrounded by rapids, lay close at hand, in a recess of the Canada shore. Some of the rapids, of eight or ten feet descent, would be called falls elsewhere. They were glittering and foamy, with spaces of green water   35 between. I caught a glimpse of a section of the cataract, but not any adequate view, before we were driven briskly up to the door of the hotel. We ran quickly from piazza to piazza till we reached the crown of the roof, where there is a space railed in for the advantage of the gazer who desires to reach the highest point. I think the emotion of this moment was never renewed or equalled. The morning had been cloudy, with a very few   40 wandering gleams. It was now a little after noon; the sky was clearing, and at this moment the sun lighted up the Horseshoe Fall. I am not going to describe it. The most striking appearance was the slowness with which the shaded green waters rolled over the brink. This majestic oozing gives a true idea of the volume of the floods, but they no longer look like water.   45

We wandered through the wood, along Table Rock, and to the ferry. We sat down opposite to the American Falls, finding them the first day or two more level to our comprehension than the Great Horseshoe Cataract; yet throughout, the beauty was far more impressive to me than the grandeur. One's imagination may heap up almost any degree of grandeur; but the subtile colouring of this scene, varying with every breath of   50 wind, refining upon the softness of driven snow, and dimming all the gems of the mine, is wholly inconceivable. The woods on Goat Island were in their gaudiest autumn dress; yet, on looking up to them from the fall, they seemed one dust colour. This will not be believed, but it is true.

The little detached fall on the American side piqued my interest at once. It looks   55 solitary in the midst of the crowd of waters, coming out of its privacy in the wood to take its leap by itself. In the afternoon, as I was standing on Table Rock, a rainbow started out from the precipice a hundred feet below me, and curved upward as if about to alight on my head. Other such apparitions seemed to have a similar understanding with the sun. They went and came, blushed and faded, the floods rolling on, on, till the   60 human heart, overcharged with beauty, could bear no more.

31-32. Welland canal: opened in 1833 (rebuilt almost a century later). **50. subtile:** delicate.

We crossed the ferry in the afternoon. Our boat was tossed like a cork in the writhing waves. We soon found that, though driven hither and thither by the currents, the ferryman always conquers at last, and shoots his boat into the desired creek; but the tossing and whirling amid the driving spray seems a rather dubious affair at first. To be carried down would be no better than to be sucked up the river, as there is a fatal whirlpool below which forbids all navigation as peremptorily as the falls. 65

I still think the finest single impression of all is half way up the American Fall, seen, not from the staircase, but from the bank on the very verge of the sheet. Here we stood this first evening, and amid the rapids above. In returning, we saw from the river the singular effect of the clouds of spray being in shadow, and the descending floods in light; while the evening star hung over one extremity of the falls, and the moon over the other, and the little perpetual cloud, amber in the last rays from the west, spread its fine drizzle like a silver veil over the scene. 70

There is nothing like patient waiting in a place like this. The gazer, who sits for hours watching what sun and wind may be pleased to reveal, is sure to be rewarded, somewhat as Newton described himself as being when he set a thought before him, and sat still to see what would come out of it. It is surprising what secrets of the thunder cavern were disclosed to me during a few days of still watching; disclosed by a puff of wind clearing the spray for an instant, or by the lightest touch of a sunbeam. The sound of the waters is lulling, even on the very brink; but if one wishes for stillness, there is the forest all around, where the eyes may become accustomed to common objects again. It is pleasant, after the high excitement, to stroll in the wild woods, and wonder what this new tree is and what that; and to gossip with the pigs, slim and spruce while fed on forest nuts and roots; and to watch the progress of a loghouse, sitting the while on a stump or leaning over a snake-fence; and then to return, with new wonder, to the ethereal vision. 75 80 85

. . . .

(1838)

T̲HOMAS L̲OVELL B̲EDDOES
England, 1803-1849

SONG: "OLD ADAM, THE CARRION CROW"

Old Adam, the carrion crow,
  The old crow of Cairo;
He sat in the shower, and let it flow
  Under his tail and over his crest;
    And through every feather 5
    Leaked the wet weather;

And the bough swung under his nest;
For his beak it was heavy with marrow.
  Is that the wind dying? O no;
  It's only two devils, that blow 10
  Through a murderer's bones, to and fro,
    In the ghosts' moonshine.

---

77. **Newton:** the English scientist Sir Isaac Newton (1642-1727).

Ho! Eve, my grey carrion wife,
  When we have supped on kings' marrow,   *14*
Where shall we drink and make merry our life?
  Our nest it is queen Cleopatra's skull,
    'Tis cloven and cracked,
    And battered and hacked,

But with tears of blue eyes it is full:
Let us drink then, my raven of Cairo.   *20*
  Is that the wind dying? O no;
  It's only two devils, that blow
  Through a murderer's bones, to and fro,
    In the ghosts' moonshine.

(1850)

JAMES CLARENCE MANGAN
Ireland, 1803-1849

DARK ROSALEEN

O my Dark Rosaleen,
  Do not sigh, do not weep!
The priests are on the ocean green,
  They march along the deep.
There's wine from the royal Pope,   *5*
  Upon the ocean green;
And Spanish ale shall give you hope,
  My Dark Rosaleen!
  My own Rosaleen!
Shall glad your heart, shall give you hope,   *10*
Shall give you health, and help, and hope,
  My Dark Rosaleen!

Over hills, and through dales,
  Have I roamed for your sake;
All yesterday I sailed with sails   *15*
  On river and on lake.
The Erne, at its highest flood,
  I dashed across unseen,
For there was lightning in my blood,
  My Dark Rosaleen!   *20*
  My own Rosaleen!
O! there was lightning in my blood,
Red lightning lightened through my blood,
  My Dark Rosaleen!

All day long, in unrest,   *25*
  To and fro, do I move,
The very soul within my breast
  Is wasted for you, love!
The heart in my bosom faints
  To think of you, my queen,   *30*
My life of life, my saint of saints,
  My Dark Rosaleen!
  My own Rosaleen!
To hear your sweet and sad complaints,
My life, my love, my saint of saints,   *35*
  My Dark Rosaleen!

Woe and pain, pain and woe,
  Are my lot, night and noon,
To see your bright face clouded so,
  Like to the mournful moon.   *40*
But yet will I rear your throne
  Again in golden sheen;
'T is you shall reign, shall reign alone,
  My Dark Rosaleen!
  My own Rosaleen!   *45*
'T is you shall have the golden throne,
'T is you shall reign, and reign alone,
  My Dark Rosaleen!

DARK ROSALEEN   **5-7. royal Pope, Spanish ale:** King Philip II of Spain (1527-1598) and Pope Sixtus V (1521-1590) had promised help to Ireland in its struggles to reject English rule, during the time of Elizabeth I. **17. Erne:** Irish River, rising in County Cavan and flowing northwest to Donegal Bay.

Over dews, over sands,
   Will I fly for your weal: *50*
Your holy, delicate white hands
   Shall girdle me with steel.
At home in your emerald bowers,
   From morning's dawn till e'en,
You'll pray for me, my flower of flowers,   *55*
   My Dark Rosaleen!
   My fond Rosaleen!
You'll think of me through daylight's hours,
My virgin flower, my flower of flowers,
   My Dark Rosaleen!   *60*

I could scale the blue air,
   I could plough the high hills,
O, I could kneel all night in prayer,
   To heal your many ills!
And one beamy smile from you   *65*
   Would float like light between

My toils and me, my own, my true,
   My Dark Rosaleen!
   My fond Rosaleen!
Would give me life and soul anew,   *70*
A second life, a soul anew,
   My Dark Rosaleen!

O! the Erne shall run red
   With redundance of blood,
The earth shall rock beneath our tread,   *75*
   And flames warp hill and wood,
And gun-peal and slogan cry
   Wake many a glen serene,
Ere you shall fade, ere you shall die,
   My Dark Rosaleen!   *80*
   My own Rosaleen!
The Judgment Hour must first be nigh,
Ere you can fade, ere you can die,
   My Dark Rosaleen!
                    (1846)

RALPH WALDO EMERSON
U.S.A., 1803-1882

CONCORD HYMN
Sung at the Completion of the Battle Monument, July 4, 1837

By the rude bridge that arched the flood,
   Their flag to April's breeze unfurled,
Here once the embattled farmers stood
   And fired the shot heard round the world.

The foe long since in silence slept;   *5*
   Alike the conqueror silent sleeps;
And Time the ruined bridge has swept
   Down the dark stream which seaward creeps.

On this green bank, by this soft stream,
   We set to-day a votive stone;   *10*
That memory may their deed redeem,
   When, like our sires, our sons are gone.

Spirit, that made those heroes dare
   To die, and leave their children free,
Bid Time and Nature gently spare   *15*
   The shaft we raise to them and thee.
           (1837)

CONCORD HYMN   The battles of Lexington and Concord, the first engagements of the American Revolution, took place 19 April 1775.

SELF-RELIANCE

Ne te quæsiveris extra.

"Man is his own star; and the soul that can
Render an honest and a perfect man
Commands all light, all influence, all fate;
Nothing to him falls early or too late.
Our acts our angels are, or good or ill,
Our fatal shadows that walk by us still."
— Epilogue to Beaumont and Fletcher's *The Honest Man's Fortune*

Cast the bantling on the rocks,
Suckle him with the she-wolf's teat,
Wintered with the hawk and fox,
Power and speed be hands and feet.

I read the other day some verses written by an eminent painter which were original and not conventional. The soul always hears an admonition in such lines, let the subject be what it may. The sentiment they instil is of more value than any thought they may contain. To believe your own thought, to believe that what is true for you in your private heart is true for all men, — that is genius. Speak your latent conviction, and it shall be the universal sense; for the inmost in due time becomes the outmost, and our first thought is rendered back to us by the trumpets of the Last Judgment. Familiar as the voice of the mind is to each, the highest merit we ascribe to Moses, Plato and Milton is that they set at naught books and traditions, and spoke not what men, but what *they* thought. A man should learn to detect and watch that gleam of light which flashes across his mind from within, more than the lustre of the firmament of bards and sages. Yet he dismisses without notice his thought, because it is his. In every work of genius we recognize our own rejected thoughts; they come back to us with a certain alienated majesty. Great works of art have no more affecting lesson for us than this. They teach us to abide by our spontaneous impression with good-humored inflexibility then most when the whole cry of voices is on the other side. Else to-morrow a stranger will say with masterly good sense precisely what we have thought and felt all the time, and we shall be forced to take with shame our own opinion from another.

There is a time in every man's education when he arrives at the conviction that envy is ignorance; that imitation is suicide; that he must take himself for better for worse as his portion; that though the wide universe is full of good, no kernel of nourishing corn can come to him but through his toil bestowed on that plot of ground which is given to him to till. The power which resides in him is new in nature, and none but he knows what that is which he can do, nor does he know until he has tried. Not for nothing one face, one character, one fact, makes much impression on him, and another none. This sculpture in the memory is not without preëstablished harmony. The eye was placed where one ray should fall, that it might testify of that particular ray. We but half express ourselves, and are ashamed of that divine idea which each of us represents. It may be safely trusted as proportionate and of good issues, so it be faithfully imparted,

---

SELF-RELIANCE **Epigraphs.** *Ne te quæsiveris extra*: (Latin) Do not seek outside yourself. *The Honest Man's Fortune*, by Francis Beaumont (1584-1616) and John Fletcher (1579-1625), was probably performed about 1613; the epilogue or commentary (perhaps by Fletcher alone) from which Emerson quotes is nearly 100 lines long. The quatrain also appears in Emerson's poems under the title "Power."

but God will not have his work made manifest by cowards. A man is relieved and gay   *30*
when he has put his heart into his work and done his best; but what he has said or done
otherwise shall give him no peace. It is a deliverance which does not deliver. In the
attempt his genius deserts him; no muse befriends; no invention, no hope.

    Trust thyself: every heart vibrates to that iron string. Accept the place the divine
providence has found for you, the society of your contemporaries, the connection of   *35*
events. Great men have always done so, and confided themselves childlike to the genius
of their age, betraying their perception that the absolutely trustworthy was seated at their
heart, working through their hands, predominating in all their being. And we are now
men, and must accept in the highest mind the same transcendent destiny; and not minors
and invalids in a protected corner, not cowards fleeing before a revolution, but guides,   *40*
redeemers and benefactors, obeying the Almighty effort and advancing on Chaos and
the Dark.

    What pretty oracles nature yields us on this text in the face and behavior of
children, babes, and even brutes! That divided and rebel mind, that distrust of a
sentiment because our arithmetic has computed the strength and means opposed to our   *45*
purpose, these have not. Their mind being whole, their eye is as yet unconquered, and
when we look in their faces we are disconcerted. Infancy conforms to nobody; all
conform to it; so that one babe commonly makes four or five out of the adults who
prattle and play to it. So God has armed youth and puberty and manhood no less with its
own piquancy and charm, and made it enviable and gracious and its claims not to be put   *50*
by, if it will stand by itself. Do not think the youth has no force, because he cannot
speak to you and me. Hark! in the next room his voice is sufficiently clear and emphatic.
It seems he knows how to speak to his contemporaries. Bashful or bold, then, he will
know how to make us seniors very unnecessary.

    The nonchalance of boys who are sure of a dinner, and would disdain as much as a   *55*
lord to do or say aught to conciliate one, is the healthy attitude of human nature. A boy
is in the parlor what the pit is in the playhouse; independent, irresponsible, looking out
from his corner on such people and facts as pass by, he tries and sentences them on their
merits, in the swift, summary way of boys, as good, bad, interesting, silly, eloquent,
troublesome. He cumbers himself never about consequences, about interests; he gives   *60*
an independent, genuine verdict. You must court him; he does not court you. But the
man is as it were clapped into jail by his consciousness. As soon as he has once acted or
spoken with *éclat* he is a committed person, watched by the sympathy or the hatred of
hundreds, whose affections must now enter into his account. There is no Lethe for this.
Ah, that he could pass again into his neutrality! Who can thus avoid all pledges and,   *65*
having observed, observe again from the same unaffected, unbiased, unbribable,
unaffrighted innocence, — must always be formidable. He would utter opinions on all
passing affairs, which being seen to be not private but necessary, would sink like darts
into the ear of men and put them in fear.

    These are the voices which we hear in solitude, but they grow faint and inaudible as   *70*
we enter into the world. Society everywhere is in conspiracy against the manhood of
every one of its members. Society is a joint-stock company, in which the members

---

41-42: Cf. Milton's *Paradise Lost,* I, 543 (p. 333). **57. pit:** See note to lines 151-53 of Dryden's *Mac Flecknoe* (p. 436). **64. Lethe:** the river of
forgetfulness in Hades.

agree, for the better securing of his bread to each shareholder, to surrender the liberty and culture of the eater. The virtue in most request is conformity. Self-reliance is its aversion. It loves not realities and creators, but names and customs.   *75*

Whoso would be a man, must be a nonconformist. He who would gather immortal palms must not be hindered by the name of goodness, but must explore if it be goodness. Nothing is at last sacred but the integrity of your own mind. Absolve you to yourself, and you shall have the suffrage of the world. I remember an answer which when quite young I was prompted to make to a valued adviser who was wont to   *80* importune me with the dear old doctrines of the church. On my saying, "What have I to do with the sacredness of traditions, if I live wholly from within?" my friend suggested, — "But these impulses may be from below, not from above." I replied, "They do not seem to me to be such; but if I am the Devil's child, I will live then from the Devil." No law can be sacred to me but that of my nature. Good and bad are but names very readily   *85* transferable to that or this; the only right is what is after my constitution; the only wrong what is against it. A man is to carry himself in the presence of all opposition as if every thing were titular and ephemeral but he. I am ashamed to think how easily we capitulate to badges and names, to large societies and dead institutions. Every decent and well-spoken individual affects and sways me more than is right. I ought to go upright and   *90* vital, and speak the rude truth in all ways. If malice and vanity wear the coat of philanthropy, shall that pass? If an angry bigot assumes this bountiful cause of Abolition, and comes to me with his last news from Barbadoes, why should I not say to him, "Go love thy infant; love thy wood-chopper; be good-natured and modest; have that grace; and never varnish your hard, uncharitable ambition with this incredible   *95* tenderness for black folk a thousand miles off. Thy love afar is spite at home." Rough and graceless would be such greeting, but truth is handsomer than the affectation of love. Your goodness must have some edge to it, — else it is none. The doctrine of hatred must be preached, as the counteraction of the doctrine of love, when that pules and whines. I shun father and mother and wife and brother when my genius calls me. I   *100* would write on the lintels of the door-post, *Whim.* I hope it is somewhat better than whim at last, but we cannot spend the day in explanation. Expect me not to show cause why I seek or why I exclude company. Then again, do not tell me, as a good man did to-day, of my obligation to put all poor men in good situations. Are they *my* poor? I tell thee, thou foolish philanthropist, that I grudge the dollar, the dime, the cent I give to   *105* such men as do not belong to me and to whom I do not belong. There is a class of persons to whom by all spiritual affinity I am bought and sold; for them I will go to prison if need be; but your miscellaneous popular charities; the education at college of fools; the building of meeting-houses to the vain end to which many now stand; alms to sots, and the thousand-fold Relief Societies; — though I confess with shame I some-   *110* times succumb and give the dollar, it is a wicked dollar, which by and by I shall have the manhood to withhold.

Virtues are, in the popular estimate, rather the exception than the rule. There is the man *and* his virtues. Men do what is called a good action, as some piece of courage or charity, much as they would pay a fine in expiation of daily non-appearance on parade.   *115*

92-93. If . . . Barbadoes: Slavery was abolished throughout the British Empire in 1833. **100. I shun . . . calls me:** Cf. Matthew 10:35-37. **100-01. I would . . . door-post:** See Exodus 12:22-23.

Their works are done as an apology or extenuation of their living in the world, — as invalids and the insane pay a high board. Their virtues are penances. I do not wish to expiate, but to live. My life is for itself and not for a spectacle. I much prefer that it should be of a lower strain, so it be genuine and equal, than that it should be glittering and unsteady. I wish it to be sound and sweet, and not to need diet and bleeding. I ask *120* primary evidence that you are a man, and refuse this appeal from the man to his actions. I know that for myself it makes no difference whether I do or forbear those actions which are reckoned excellent. I cannot consent to pay for a privilege where I have intrinsic right. Few and mean as my gifts may be, I actually am, and do not need for my own assurance or the assurance of my fellows any secondary testimony. *125*

What I must do is all that concerns me, not what the people think. This rule, equally arduous in actual and in intellectual life, may serve for the whole distinction between greatness and meanness. It is the harder because you will always find those who think they know what is your duty better than you know it. It is easy in the world to live after the world's opinion; it is easy in solitude to live after our own; but the great man is he *130* who in the midst of the crowd keeps with perfect sweetness the independence of solitude.

The objection to conforming to usages that have become dead to you is that it scatters your force. It loses your time and blurs the impression of your character. If you maintain a dead church, contribute to a dead Bible-society, vote with a great party either for the government or against it, spread your table like base housekeepers, — under all *135* these screens I have difficulty to detect the precise man you are: and of course so much force is withdrawn from your proper life. But do your work, and I shall know you. Do your work, and you shall reinforce yourself. A man must consider what a blind-man's-buff is this game of conformity. If I know your sect I anticipate your argument. I hear a preacher announce for his text and topic the expediency of one of the institutions of his *140* church. Do I not know beforehand that not possibly can he say a new and spontaneous word? Do I not know that with all this ostentation of examining the grounds of the institution he will do no such thing? Do I not know that he is pledged to himself not to look but at one side, the permitted side, not as a man, but as a parish minister? He is a retained attorney, and these airs of the bench are the emptiest affectation. Well, most men *145* have bound their eyes with one or another handkerchief, and attached themselves to some one of these communities of opinion. This conformity makes them not false in a few particulars, authors of a few lies, but false in all particulars. Their every truth is not quite true. Their two is not the real two, their four not the real four; so that every word they say chagrins us and we know not where to begin to set them right. Meantime nature is not *150* slow to equip us in the prison-uniform of the party to which we adhere. We come to wear one cut of face and figure, and acquire by degrees the gentlest asinine expression. There is a mortifying experience in particular, which does not fail to wreak itself also in the general history; I mean "the foolish face of praise," the forced smile which we put on in company where we do not feel at ease, in answer to conversation which does not interest *155* us. The muscles, not spontaneously moved but moved by a low usurping wilfulness, grow tight about the outline of the face, with the most disagreeable sensation.

For nonconformity the world whips you with its displeasure. And therefore a man must know how to estimate a sour face. The by-standers look askance on him in the

---

120. bleeding: an early form of medical treatment. **154. "the ... praise":** Pope, "Epistle to Dr. Arbuthnot," line 212 (with *a* for *the*).

public street or in the friend's parlor. If this aversion had its origin in contempt and   *160*
resistance like his own he might well go home with a sad countenance; but the sour
faces of the multitude, like their sweet faces, have no deep cause, but are put on and off
as the wind blows and a newspaper directs. Yet is the discontent of the multitude more
formidable than that of the senate and the college. It is easy enough for a firm man who
knows the world to brook the rage of the cultivated classes. Their rage is decorous and   *165*
prudent, for they are timid, as being very vulnerable themselves. But when to their
feminine rage the indignation of the people is added, when the ignorant and the poor are
aroused, when the unintelligent brute force that lies at the bottom of society is made to
growl and mow, it needs the habit of magnanimity and religion to treat it godlike as a
trifle of no concernment.   *170*

The other terror that scares us from self-trust is our consistency; a reverence for our
past act or word because the eyes of others have no other data for computing our orbit
than our past acts, and we are loth to disappoint them.

But why should you keep your head over your shoulder? Why drag about this
corpse of your memory, lest you contradict somewhat you have stated in this or that   *175*
public place? Suppose you should contradict yourself; what then? It seems to be a rule
of wisdom never to rely on your memory alone, scarcely even in acts of pure memory,
but to bring the past for judgment into the thousand-eyed present, and live ever in a new
day. In your metaphysics you have denied personality to the Deity, yet when the devout
motions of the soul come, yield to them heart and life, though they should clothe God   *180*
with shape and color. Leave your theory, as Joseph his coat in the hand of the harlot,
and flee.

A foolish consistency is the hobgoblin of little minds, adored by little statesmen and
philosophers and divines. With consistency a great soul has simply nothing to do. He may
as well concern himself with his shadow on the wall. Speak what you think now in hard   *185*
words and to-morrow speak what to-morrow thinks in hard words again, though it
contradict every thing you said to-day. — "Ah, so you shall be sure to be misunderstood."
— Is it so bad then to be misunderstood? Pythagoras was misunderstood, and Socrates,
and Jesus, and Luther, and Copernicus, and Galileo, and Newton, and every pure and wise
spirit that ever took flesh. To be great is to be misunderstood.   *190*

I suppose no man can violate his nature. All the sallies of his will are rounded in by
the law of his being, as the inequalities of Andes and Himmaleh are insignificant in the
curve of the sphere. Nor does it matter how you gauge and try him. A character is like
an acrostic or Alexandrian stanza; read it forward, backward, or across, it still spells the
same thing. In this pleasing contrite wood-life which God allows me, let me record day   *195*
by day my honest thought without prospect or retrospect, and, I cannot doubt, it will be
found symmetrical, though I mean it not and see it not. My book should smell of pines
and resound with the hum of insects. The swallow over my window should interweave
that thread or straw he carries in his bill into my web also. We pass for what we are.
Character teaches above our wills. Men imagine that they communicate their virtue or   *200*
vice only by overt actions, and do not see that virtue or vice emit a breath every
moment.

---

169. **mow:** make a wry face, make a mouth. 181. **harlot:** i.e., Potiphar's wife — see Genesis 39:12. 192. **Himmaleh:** Himalaya.

There will be an agreement in whatever variety of actions, so they be each honest and natural in their hour. For of one will, the actions will be harmonious, however unlike they seem. These varieties are lost sight of at a little distance, at a little height of 205 thought. One tendency unites them all. The voyage of the best ship is a zigzag line of a hundred tacks. See the line from a sufficient distance, and it straightens itself to the average tendency. Your genuine action will explain itself and will explain your other genuine actions. Your conformity explains nothing. Act singly, and what you have already done singly will justify you now. Greatness appeals to the future. If I can be 210 firm enough to-day to do right and scorn eyes, I must have done so much right before as to defend me now. Be it how it will, do right now. Always scorn appearances and you always may. The force of character is cumulative. All the foregone days of virtue work their health into this. What makes the majesty of the heroes of the senate and the field, which so fills the imagination? The consciousness of a train of great days and victories 215 behind. They shed a united light on the advancing actor. He is attended as by a visible escort of angels. That is it which throws thunder into Chatham's voice, and dignity into Washington's port, and America into Adams's eye. Honor is venerable to us because it is no ephemera. It is always ancient virtue. We worship it to-day because it is not of to-day. We love it and pay it homage because it is not a trap for our love and homage, but 220 is self-dependent, self-derived, and therefore of an old immaculate pedigree, even if shown in a young person.

I hope in these days we have heard the last of conformity and consistency. Let the words be gazetted and ridiculous henceforward. Instead of the gong for dinner, let us hear a whistle from the Spartan fife. Let us never bow and apologize more. A great man 225 is coming to eat at my house. I do not wish to please him; I wish that he should wish to please me. I will stand here for humanity, and though I would make it kind, I would make it true. Let us affront and reprimand the smooth mediocrity and squalid contentment of the times, and hurl in the face of custom and trade and office, the fact which is the upshot of all history, that there is a great responsible Thinker and Actor 230 working wherever a man works; that a true man belongs to no other time or place, but is the centre of things. Where he is, there is nature. He measures you and all men and all events. Ordinarily, every body in society reminds us of somewhat else, or of some other person. Character, reality, reminds you of nothing else; it takes place of the whole creation. The man must be so much that he must make all circumstances indifferent. 235 Every true man is a cause, a country, and an age; requires infinite spaces and numbers and time fully to accomplish his design; — and posterity seem to follow his steps as a train of clients. A man Cæsar is born, and for ages after we have a Roman Empire. Christ is born, and millions of minds so grow and cleave to his genius that he is confounded with virtue and the possible of man. An institution is the lengthened shadow 240 of one man; as, Monachism, of the Hermit Anthony; the Reformation, of Luther;

217. Chatham: William Pitt the Elder, first earl of Chatham (1708-1778), MP, secretary of state, lord privy seal, was renowned for his oratory. **218. Washington:** George Washington (1732-1799), first U.S. president; **port:** bearing; **Adams:** Samuel Adams (1722-1803), active in promoting American independence; or John Adams (1735-1826), 2nd U.S. president; or John Quincy Adams (1767-1848), 6th U.S. president. **224. gazetted:** officially announced — here in the sense of *denounced*. **234. takes place of:** takes precedence over. **241-42:** Saint Anthony (c.250-350), Egyptian hermit, founder of Christian monasticism; for Luther, see note to line 321 of Carlyle's "Signs of the Times" p. 874; George Fox (1624-1691), founder of the Society of Friends; John Wesley (1703-1791; see biographical note on Charles Wesley, in Appendix I); for Clarkson, see note to line 14 of the

Quakerism, of Fox; Methodism, of Wesley; Abolition, of Clarkson. Scipio, Milton called "the height of Rome"; and all history resolves itself very easily into the biography of a few stout and earnest persons.

Let a man then know his worth, and keep things under his feet. Let him not peep or 245 steal, or skulk up and down with the air of a charity-boy, a bastard, or an interloper in the world which exists for him. But the man in the street, finding no worth in himself which corresponds to the force which built a tower or sculptured a marble god, feels poor when he looks on these. To him a palace, a statue, or a costly book have an alien and forbidding air, much like a gay equipage, and seem to say like that, "Who are you, 250 Sir?" Yet they all are his, suitors for his notice, petitioners to his faculties that they will come out and take possession. The picture waits for my verdict; it is not to command me, but I am to settle its claims to praise. That popular fable of the sot who was picked up dead-drunk in the street, carried to the duke's house, washed and dressed and laid in the duke's bed, and, on his waking, treated with all obsequious ceremony like the duke, 255 and assured that he had been insane, owes its popularity to the fact that it symbolizes so well the state of man, who is in the world a sort of sot, but now and then wakes up, exercises his reason and finds himself a true prince.

Our reading is mendicant and sycophantic. In history our imagination plays us false. Kingdom and lordship, power and estate, are a gaudier vocabulary than private 260 John and Edward in a small house and common day's work; but the things of life are the same to both; the sum total of both is the same. Why all this deference to Alfred and Scanderbeg and Gustavus? Suppose they were virtuous; did they wear out virtue? As great a stake depends on your private act to-day as followed their public and renowned steps. When private men shall act with original views, the lustre will be transferred from 265 the actions of kings to those of gentlemen.

The world has been instructed by its kings, who have so magnetized the eyes of nations. It has been taught by this colossal symbol the mutual reverence that is due from man to man. The joyful loyalty with which men have everywhere suffered the king, the noble, or the great proprietor to walk among them by a law of his own, make his own 270 scale of men and things and reverse theirs, pay for benefits not with money but with honor, and represent the law in his person, was the hieroglyphic by which they obscurely signified their consciousness of their own right and comeliness, the right of every man.

The magnetism which all original action exerts is explained when we inquire the 275 reason of self-trust. Who is the Trustee? What is the aboriginal Self, on which a universal reliance may be grounded? What is the nature and power of that science-baffling star, without parallax, without calculable elements, which shoots a ray of beauty even into trivial and impure actions, if the least mark of independence appear? The inquiry leads us to that source, at once the essence of genius, of virtue, and of life, 280 which we call Spontaneity or Instinct. We denote this primary wisdom as Intuition, whilst all later teachings are tuitions. In that deep force, the last fact behind which

excerpts from Dorothy Wordsworth's journals (p. 781) and William Wordsworth's *Prelude*, X, 247ff. and note (p. 775); **Scipio:** Scipio Africanus, or Scipio the Elder (237-183 B.C.); **Milton:** in *Paradise Lost*, IX, 510. **253. popular fable:** See e.g. near the beginning of the Induction to Shakespeare's *The Taming of the Shrew*. **262-63:** Alfred the Great (849-899), King of Wessex (871-899); Scanderbeg (c.1404-1468), originally George Castriota, called by the Turks Iskander Bey, national hero of Albania; probably King Gustavus I of Sweden (Gustavus Vasa, 1496-1560), or Gustavus II (Gustavus Adolphus, 1594-1632), or Gustavus III (1746-1792) — or perhaps all three.

analysis cannot go, all things find their common origin. For the sense of being which in calm hours rises, we know not how, in the soul, is not diverse from things, from space, from light, from time, from man, but one with them and proceeds obviously from the same source whence their life and being also proceed. We first share the life by which things exist and afterwards see them as appearances in nature and forget that we have shared their cause. Here is the fountain of action and of thought. Here are the lungs of that inspiration which giveth man wisdom and which cannot be denied without impiety and atheism. We lie in the lap of immense intelligence, which makes us receivers of its truth and organs of its activity. When we discern justice, when we discern truth, we do nothing of ourselves, but allow a passage to its beams. If we ask whence this comes, if we seek to pry into the soul that causes, all philosophy is at fault. Its presence or its absence is all we can affirm. Every man discriminates between the voluntary acts of his mind and his involuntary perceptions, and knows that to his involuntary perceptions a perfect faith is due. He may err in the expression of them, but he knows that these things are so, like day and night, not to be disputed. My wilful actions and acquisitions are but roving; — the idlest reverie, the faintest native emotion, command my curiosity and respect. Thoughtless people contradict as readily the statement of perceptions as of opinions, or rather much more readily; for they do not distinguish between perception and notion. They fancy that I choose to see this or that thing. But perception is not whimsical, but fatal. If I see a trait, my children will see it after me, and in course of time all mankind, — although it may chance that no one has seen it before me. For my perception of it is as much a fact as the sun.

The relations of the soul to the divine spirit are so pure that it is profane to seek to interpose helps. It must be that when God speaketh he should communicate, not one thing, but all things; should fill the world with his voice; should scatter forth light, nature, time, souls, from the centre of the present thought; and new date and new create the whole. Whenever a mind is simple and receives a divine wisdom, old things pass away, — means, teachers, texts, temples fall; it lives now, and absorbs past and future into the present hour. All things are made sacred by relation to it, — one as much as another. All things are dissolved to their centre by their cause, and in the universal miracle petty and particular miracles disappear. If therefore a man claims to know and speak of God and carries you backward to the phraseology of some old mouldered nation in another country, in another world, believe him not. Is the acorn better than the oak which is its fulness and completion? Is the parent better than the child into whom he has cast his ripened being? Whence then this worship of the past? The centuries are conspirators against the sanity and authority of the soul. Time and space are but physiological colors which the eye makes, but the soul is light: where it is, is day; where it was, is night; and history is an impertinence and an injury if it be any thing more than a cheerful apologue or parable of my being and becoming.

Man is timid and apologetic; he is no longer upright; he dares not say "I think," "I am," but quotes some saint or sage. He is ashamed before the blade of grass or the blowing rose. These roses under my window make no reference to former roses or to better ones; they are for what they are; they exist with God to-day. There is no time to

---

302. fatal: fated, destined, inevitable. **322-23. "I think," "I am":** probably alluding to the famous line of Descartes, *"Cogito, ergo sum"* (itself echoing Aristotle's *Nicomachean Ethics*). **324. blowing:** blossoming.

them. There is simply the rose; it is perfect in every moment of its existence. Before a leaf-bud has burst, its whole life acts; in the full-blown flower there is no more; in the leafless root there is no less. Its nature is satisfied and it satisfies nature in all moments alike. But man postpones or remembers; he does not live in the present, but with reverted eye laments the past, or, heedless of the riches that surround him, stands on 330 tiptoe to foresee the future. He cannot be happy and strong until he too lives with nature in the present, above time.

This should be plain enough. Yet see what strong intellects dare not yet hear God himself unless he speak the phraseology of I know not what David, or Jeremiah, or Paul. We shall not always set so great a price on a few texts, on a few lives. We are like 335 children who repeat by rote the sentences of grandames and tutors, and, as they grow older, of the men of talents and character they chance to see, — painfully recollecting the exact words they spoke; afterwards, when they come into the point of view which those had who uttered these sayings, they understand them and are willing to let the words go; for at any time they can use words as good when occasion comes. If we live 340 truly, we shall see truly. It is as easy for the strong man to be strong, as it is for the weak to be weak. When we have new perception, we shall gladly disburden the memory of its hoarded treasures as old rubbish. When a man lives with God, his voice shall be as sweet as the murmur of the brook and the rustle of the corn.

And now at last the highest truth on this subject remains unsaid; probably cannot be 345 said; for all that we say is the far-off remembering of the intuition. That thought by what I can now nearest approach to say it, is this. When good is near you, when you have life in yourself, it is not by any known or accustomed way; you shall not discern the footprints of any other; you shall not see the face of man; you shall not hear any name; — the way, the thought, the good, shall be wholly strange and new. It shall exclude 350 example and experience. You take the way from man, not to man. All persons that ever existed are its forgotten ministers. Fear and hope are alike beneath it. There is somewhat low even in hope. In the hour of vision there is nothing that can be called gratitude, nor properly joy. The soul raised over passion beholds identity and eternal causation, perceives the self-existence of Truth and Right, and calms itself with knowing that all 355 things go well. Vast spaces of nature, the Atlantic Ocean, the South Sea; long intervals of time, years, centuries, are of no account. This which I think and feel underlay every former state of life and circumstances, as it does underlie my present, and what is called life and what is called death.

Life only avails, not the having lived. Power ceases in the instant of repose; it 360 resides in the moment of transition from a past to a new state, in the shooting of the gulf, in the darting to an aim. This one fact the world hates; that the soul *becomes;* for that forever degrades the past, turns all riches to poverty, all reputation to a shame, confounds the saint with the rogue, shoves Jesus and Judas equally aside. Why then do we prate of self-reliance? Inasmuch as the soul is present there will be power not 365 confident but agent. To talk of reliance is a poor external way of speaking. Speak rather of that which relies because it works and is. Who has more obedience than I masters me, though he should not raise his finger. Round him I must revolve by the gravitation of spirits. We fancy it rhetoric when we speak of eminent virtue. We do not yet see that

366. agent: acting.

virtue is Height, and that a man or a company of men, plastic and permeable to 370 principles, by the law of nature must overpower and ride all cities, nations, kings, rich men, poets, who are not.

This is the ultimate fact which we so quickly reach on this, as on every topic, the resolution of all into the ever-blessed ONE. Self-existence is the attribute of the Supreme Cause, and it constitutes the measure of good by the degree in which it enters into all 375 lower forms. All things real are so by so much virtue as they contain. Commerce, husbandry, hunting, whaling, war, eloquence, personal weight, are somewhat, and engage my respect as examples of its presence and impure action. I see the same law working in nature for conservation and growth. Power is, in nature, the essential measure of right. Nature suffers nothing to remain in her kingdoms which cannot help 380 itself. The genesis and maturation of a planet, its poise and orbit, the bended tree recovering itself from the strong wind, the vital resources of every animal and vegetable, are demonstrations of the self-sufficing and therefore self-relying soul.

Thus all concentrates: let us not rove; let us sit at home with the cause. Let us stun and astonish the intruding rabble of men and books and institutions by a simple 385 declaration of the divine fact. Bid the invaders take the shoes from off their feet, for God is here within. Let our simplicity judge them, and our docility to our own law demonstrate the poverty of nature and fortune beside our native riches.

But now we are a mob. Man does not stand in awe of man, nor is his genius admonished to stay at home, to put itself in communication with the internal ocean, but 390 it goes abroad to beg a cup of water of the urns of other men. We must go alone. I like the silent church before the service begins, better than any preaching. How far off, how cool, how chaste the persons look, begirt each one with a precinct or sanctuary! So let us always sit. Why should we assume the faults of our friend, or wife, or father, or child, because they sit around our hearth, or are said to have the same blood? All men have my 395 blood and I all men's. Not for that will I adopt their petulance or folly, even to the extent of being ashamed of it. But your isolation must not be mechanical, but spiritual, that is, must be elevation. At times the whole world seems to be in conspiracy to importune you with emphatic trifles. Friend, client, child, sickness, fear, want, charity, all knock at once at thy closet door and say, — "Come out unto us." But keep thy state; come not 400 into their confusion. The power men possess to annoy me I give them by a weak curiosity. No man can come near me but through my act. "What we love that we have, but by desire we bereave ourselves of the love."

If we cannot at once rise to the sanctities of obedience and faith, let us at least resist our temptations; let us enter into the state of war and wake Thor and Woden, courage 405 and constancy, in our Saxon breasts. This is to be done in our smooth times by speaking the truth. Check this lying hospitality and lying affection. Live no longer to the expectation of these deceived and deceiving people with whom we converse. Say to them, "O father, O mother, O wife, O brother, O friend, I have lived with you after appearances hitherto. Henceforward I am the truth's. Be it known unto you that 410 henceforward I obey no law less than the eternal law. I will have no covenants but proximities. I shall endeavor to nourish my parents, to support my family, to be the

---

386-87. Bid . . . within: See Exodus 3:5 and Joshua 5:15. **405:** Thor, Norse god of thunder and war, son of Woden (Saxon name for Odin, supreme Norse god), god of war, wisdom, arts, and the dead.

chaste husband of one wife, — but these relations I must fill after a new and un-
precedented way. I appeal from your customs. I must be myself. I cannot break myself
any longer for you, or you. If you can love me for what I am, we shall be the happier. If *415*
you cannot, I will still seek to deserve that you should. I will not hide my tastes or
aversions. I will so trust that what is deep is holy, that I will do strongly before the sun
and moon whatever only rejoices me and the heart appoints. If you are noble, I will love
you; if you are not, I will not hurt you and myself by hypocritical attentions. If you are
true, but not in the same truth with me, cleave to your companions; I will seek my own. *420*
I do this not selfishly but humbly and truly. It is alike your interest, and mine, and all
men's, however long we have dwelt in lies, to live in truth. Does this sound harsh to-
day? You will soon love what is dictated by your nature as well as mine, and if we
follow the truth it will bring us out safe at last." — But so may you give these friends
pain. Yes, but I cannot sell my liberty and my power, to save their sensibility. Besides, *425*
all persons have their moments of reason, when they look out into the region of absolute
truth; then will they justify me and do the same thing.

The populace think that your rejection of popular standards is a rejection of all
standard, and mere antinomianism; and the bold sensualist will use the name of
philosophy to gild his crimes. But the law of consciousness abides. There are two *430*
confessionals, in one or the other of which we must be shriven. You may fulfil your
round of duties by clearing yourself in the *direct*, or in the *reflex* way. Consider whether
you have satisfied your relations to father, mother, cousin, neighbor, town, cat and dog
— whether any of these can upbraid you. But I may also neglect this reflex standard and
absolve me to myself. I have my own stern claims and perfect circle. It denies the name *435*
of duty to many offices that are called duties. But if I can discharge its debts it enables
me to dispense with the popular code. If any one imagines that this law is lax, let him
keep its commandment one day.

And truly it demands something godlike in him who has cast off the common
motives of humanity and has ventured to trust himself for a taskmaster. High be his heart, *440*
faithful his will, clear his sight, that he may in good earnest be doctrine, society, law, to
himself, that a simple purpose may be to him as strong as iron necessity is to others!

If any man consider the present aspects of what is called by distinction *society,* he
will see the need of these ethics. The sinew and heart of man seem to be drawn out, and
we are become timorous, desponding whimperers. We are afraid of truth, afraid of *445*
fortune, afraid of death, and afraid of each other. Our age yields no great and perfect
persons. We want men and women who shall renovate life and our social state, but we
see that most natures are insolvent, cannot satisfy their own wants, have an ambition out
of all proportion to their practical force and do lean and beg day and night continually.
Our housekeeping is mendicant, our arts, our occupations, our marriages, our religion *450*
we have not chosen, but society has chosen for us. We are parlor soldiers. We shun the
rugged battle of fate, where strength is born.

If our young men miscarry in their first enterprises they lose all heart. If the young
merchant fails, men say he is *ruined*. If the finest genius studies at one of our colleges
and is not installed in an office within one year afterwards in the cities or suburbs of *455*
Boston or New York, it seems to his friends and to himself that he is right in being
disheartened and in complaining the rest of his life. A sturdy lad from New Hampshire

or Vermont, who in turn tries all the professions, who *teams it, farms it, peddles,* keeps a school, preaches, edits a newspaper, goes to Congress, buys a township, and so forth, in successive years, and always like a cat falls on his feet, is worth a hundred of these city 460 dolls. He walks abreast with his days and feels no shame in not "studying a profession," for he does not postpone his life, but lives already. He has not one chance, but a hundred chances. Let a Stoic open the resources of man and tell men they are not leaning willows, but can and must detach themselves; that with the exercise of self-trust, new powers shall appear; that a man is the word made flesh, born to shed healing to the 465 nations; that he should be ashamed of our compassion, and that the moment he acts from himself, tossing the laws, the books, idolatries and customs out of the window, we pity him no more but thank and revere him; — and that teacher shall restore the life of man to splendor and make his name dear to all history.

It is easy to see that a greater self-reliance must work a revolution in all the offices 470 and relations of men; in their religion; in their education; in their pursuits; their modes of living; their association; in their property; in their speculative views.

1. In what prayers do men allow themselves! That which they call a holy office is not so much as brave and manly. Prayer looks abroad and asks for some foreign addition to come through some foreign virtue, and loses itself in endless mazes of natural and 475 supernatural, and mediatorial and miraculous. Prayer that craves a particular commodity, anything less than all good, is vicious. Prayer is the contemplation of the facts of life from the highest point of view. It is the soliloquy of a beholding and jubilant soul. It is the spirit of God pronouncing his works good. But prayer as a means to effect a private end is meanness and theft. It supposes dualism and not unity in nature and 480 consciousness. As soon as the man is at one with God, he will not beg. He will then see prayer in all action. The prayer of the farmer kneeling in his field to weed it, the prayer of the rower kneeling with the stroke of his oar, are true prayers heard throughout nature, though for cheap ends. Caratach, in Fletcher's *Bonduca,* when admonished to inquire the mind of the god Audate, replies, — 485

> "His hidden meaning lies in our endeavours;
> Our valours are our best gods."

Another sort of false prayers are our regrets. Discontent is the want of self-reliance: it is infirmity of will. Regret calamities if you can thereby help the sufferer; if not, attend your own work and already the evil begins to be repaired. Our sympathy is just as 490 base. We come to them who weep foolishly and sit down and cry for company, instead of imparting to them truth and health in rough electric shocks, putting them once more in communication with their own reason. The secret of fortune is joy in our hands. Welcome evermore to gods and men is the self-helping man. For him all doors are flung wide; him all tongues greet, all honors crown, all eyes follow with desire. Our love goes 495 out to him and embraces him because he did not need it. We solicitously and apologetically caress and celebrate him because he held on his way and scorned our

---

465. word made flesh: John 1:14. **465-66. healing to the nations:** perhaps echoing Revelation 22:2. **479. It is . . . good:** See Genesis 1:25 (p. 242). **484.** *Bonduca:* c.1614 — probably by both Beaumont and Fletcher (see note to epigraphs, above); the quoted lines are from III.i, with *lies* for *dwells*; "Bonduca" is a version of the name *Boadicea,* who calls upon the warrior-goddess Adraste, or Andrasta (see note to line 153 of Holinshed — p. 144); many editions of the play have the name *Audate* and the *His* of Emerson's quotation, though some early editions have *Andate* or *Andrasta,* and *Her.*

disapprobation. The gods love him because men hated him. "To the persevering mortal," said Zoroaster, "the blessed Immortals are swift."

As men's prayers are a disease of the will, so are their creeds a disease of the 500 intellect. They say with those foolish Israelites, "Let not God speak to us, lest we die. Speak thou, speak any man with us, and we will obey." Everywhere I am hindered of meeting God in my brother, because he has shut his own temple doors and recites fables merely of his brother's, or his brother's brother's God. Every new mind is a new classification. If it prove a mind of uncommon activity and power, a Locke, a Lavoisier, 505 a Hutton, a Bentham, a Fourier, it imposes its classification on other men, and lo! a new system. In proportion to the depth of the thought, and so to the number of the objects it touches and brings within reach of the pupil, is his complacency. But chiefly is this apparent in creeds and churches, which are also classifications of some powerful mind acting on the elemental thought of duty and man's relation to the Highest. Such is 510 Calvinism, Quakerism, Swedenborgism. The pupil takes the same delight in subordinating every thing to the new terminology as a girl who has just learned botany in seeing a new earth and new seasons thereby. It will happen for a time that the pupil will find his intellectual power has grown by the study of his master's mind. But in all unbalanced minds the classification is idolized, passes for the end and not for a speedily 515 exhaustible means, so that the walls of the system blend to their eye in the remote horizon with the walls of the universe; the luminaries of heaven seem to them hung on the arch their master built. They cannot imagine how you aliens have any right to see, — how you can see; "It must be somehow that you stole the light from us." They do not yet perceive that light, unsystematic, indomitable, will break into any cabin, even into 520 theirs. Let them chirp awhile and call it their own. If they are honest and do well, presently their neat new pinfold will be too strait and low, will crack, will lean, will rot and vanish, and the immortal light, all young and joyful, million-orbed, million-colored, will beam over the universe as on the first morning.

2. It is for want of self-culture that the superstition of Travelling, whose idols are 525 Italy, England, Egypt, retains its fascination for all educated Americans. They who made England, Italy, or Greece venerable in the imagination, did so by sticking fast where they were, like an axis of the earth. In manly hours we feel that duty is our place. The soul is no traveller; the wise man stays at home, and when his necessities, his duties, on any occasion call him from his house, or into foreign lands, he is at home still 530 and shall make men sensible by the expression of his countenance that he goes, the missionary of wisdom and virtue, and visits cities and men like a sovereign and not like an interloper or a valet.

I have no churlish objection to the circumnavigation of the globe for the purposes of art, of study, and benevolence, so that the man is first domesticated, or does not go 535 abroad with the hope of finding somewhat greater than he knows. He who travels to be amused, or to get somewhat which he does not carry, travels away from himself, and grows old even in youth among old things. In Thebes, in Palmyra, his will and mind

---

498-99: quoting from the *Avesta,* holy book of Zoroastrianism. **501-02:** Cf. Exodus 20:19. **505-06:** For Locke, see p. 444; Antoine Laurent Lavoisier (1743-1794), French chemist; James Hutton (1726-1797), Scottish geologist, author of *Theory of the Earth* (1785-95), in which he initiated the theory of uniformitarianism; for Bentham, see p. 709; François Marie Charles Fourier (1772-1837), French socialist.

have become old and dilapidated as they. He carries ruins to ruins.

Travelling is a fool's paradise. Our first journeys discover to us the indifference of places. At home I dream that at Naples, at Rome, I can be intoxicated with beauty and lose my sadness. I pack my trunk, embrace my friends, embark on the sea and at last wake up in Naples, and there beside me is the stern fact, the sad self, unrelenting, identical, that I fled from. I seek the Vatican and the palaces. I affect to be intoxicated with sights and suggestions, but I am not intoxicated. My giant goes with me wherever I go. *545*

3. But the rage of travelling is a symptom of a deeper unsoundness affecting the whole intellectual action. The intellect is vagabond, and our system of education fosters restlessness. Our minds travel when our bodies are forced to stay at home. We imitate; and what is imitation but the travelling of the mind? Our houses are built with foreign taste; our shelves are garnished with foreign ornaments; our opinions, our tastes, our *550* faculties, lean, and follow the Past and the Distant. The soul created the arts wherever they have flourished. It was in his own mind that the artist sought his model. It was an application of his own thought to the thing to be done and the conditions to be observed. And why need we copy the Doric or the Gothic model? Beauty, convenience, grandeur of thought and quaint expression are as near to us as to any, and if the American artist *555* will study with hope and love the precise thing to be done by him, considering the climate, the soil, the length of the day, the wants of the people, the habit and form of the government, he will create a house in which all these will find themselves fitted, and taste and sentiment will be satisfied also.

Insist on yourself; never imitate. Your own gift you can present every moment with *560* the cumulative force of a whole life's cultivation; but of the adopted talent of another you have only an extemporaneous half possession. That which each can do best, none but his Maker can teach him. No man yet knows what it is, nor can, till that person has exhibited it. Where is the master who could have taught Shakspeare? Where is the master who could have instructed Franklin, or Washington, or Bacon, or Newton? Every *565* great man is a unique. The Scipionism of Scipio is precisely that part he could not borrow. Shakspeare will never be made by the study of Shakspeare. Do that which is assigned you, and you cannot hope too much or dare too much. There is at this moment for you an utterance brave and grand as that of the colossal chisel of Phidias, or trowel of the Egyptians, or the pen of Moses or Dante, but different from all these. Not *570* possibly will the soul, all rich, all eloquent, with thousand-cloven tongue, deign to repeat itself; but if you can hear what these patriarchs say, surely you can reply to them in the same pitch of voice; for the ear and the tongue are two organs of one nature. Abide in the simple and noble regions of thy life, obey thy heart, and thou shalt reproduce the Foreworld again. *575*

4. As our Religion, our Education, our Art look abroad, so does our spirit of society. All men plume themselves on the improvement of society, and no man improves.

Society never advances. It recedes as fast on one side as it gains on the other. It undergoes continual changes; it is barbarous, it is civilized, it is christianized, it is rich, *580*

---

569. Phidias: 5th-century B.C. sculptor.

it is scientific; but this change is not amelioration. For every thing that is given something is taken. Society acquires new arts and loses old instincts. What a contrast between the well-clad, reading, writing, thinking American, with a watch, a pencil and a bill of exchange in his pocket, and the naked New Zealander, whose property is a club, a spear, a mat and an undivided twentieth of a shed to sleep under! But compare the 585 health of the two men and you shall see that the white man has lost his aboriginal strength. If the traveller tell us truly, strike the savage with a broad-axe and in a day or two the flesh shall unite and heal as if you struck the blow into soft pitch, and the same blow shall send the white to his grave.

The civilized man has built a coach, but has lost the use of his feet. He is supported on 590 crutches, but lacks so much support of muscle. He has a fine Geneva watch, but he fails of the skill to tell the hour by the sun. A Greenwich nautical almanac he has, and so being sure of the information when he wants it, the man in the street does not know a star in the sky. The solstice he does not observe; the equinox he knows as little; and the whole bright calendar of the year is without a dial in his mind. His note-books impair his memory; his 595 libraries overload his wit; the insurance-office increases the number of accidents; and it may be a question whether machinery does not encumber; whether we have not lost by refinement some energy, by a Christianity, entrenched in establishments and forms, some vigor of wild virtue. For every Stoic was a Stoic; but in Christendom where is the Christian?

There is no more deviation in the moral standard than in the standard of height or 600 bulk. No greater men are now than ever were. A singular equality may be observed between the great men of the first and of the last ages; nor can all the science, art, religion, and philosophy of the nineteenth century avail to educate greater men than Plutarch's heroes, three or four and twenty centuries ago. Not in time is the race progressive. Phocion, Socrates, Anaxagoras, Diogenes, are great men, but they leave no 605 class. He who is really of their class will not be called by their name, but will be his own man, and in his turn the founder of a sect. The arts and inventions of each period are only its costume and do not invigorate men. The harm of the improved machinery may compensate its good. Hudson and Behring accomplished so much in their fishing-boats as to astonish Parry and Franklin, whose equipment exhausted the resources of science 610 and art. Galileo, with an opera-glass, discovered a more splendid series of celestial phenomena than any one since. Columbus found the New World in an undecked boat. It is curious to see the periodical disuse and perishing of means and machinery which were introduced with loud laudation a few years or centuries before. The great genius returns to essential man. We reckoned the improvements of the art of war among the triumphs of 615 science, and yet Napoleon conquered Europe by the bivouac, which consisted of falling back on naked valor and disencumbering it of all aids. The Emperor held it impossible to make a perfect army, says Las Cases, "without abolishing our arms, magazines, commissaries and carriages, until, in imitation of the Roman custom, the soldier should receive his supply of corn, grind it in his hand-mill and bake his bread himself." 620

---

592. Greenwich: borough of London, then the location of an astronomical observatory. **605. Phocion:** 4th-century B.C. Athenian statesman and general; **Anaxagoras:** 5th-century B.C. Greek philosopher. **609-10:** Henry Hudson (d.1611), English Arctic explorer; Vitus Bering or Behring (1680-1741), Danish navigator who explored the Arctic for Russia; Sir William Edward Parry (1790-1855) and Sir John Franklin (1786-1847), English Arctic explorers. **618. Las Cases:** Emmanuel Augustin Dieudonné Marin Joseph, Comte de Las Cases (1766-1842), French historian who accompanied Napoleon to St. Helena and wrote *Mémorial de Sainte-Hélène* (1818, English tr. 1823).

Society is a wave. The wave moves onward, but the water of which it is composed does not. The same particle does not rise from the valley to the ridge. Its unity is only phenomenal. The persons who make up a nation to-day, next year die, and their experience dies with them.

And so the reliance on Property, including the reliance on governments which 625 protect it, is the want of self-reliance. Men have looked away from themselves and at things so long that they have come to esteem the religious, learned and civil institutions as guards of property, and they deprecate assaults on these, because they feel them to be assaults on property. They measure their esteem of each other by what each has, and not by what each is. But a cultivated man becomes ashamed of his property, out of new 630 respect for his nature. Especially he hates what he has if he see that it is accidental, — came to him by inheritance, or gift, or crime; then he feels that it is not having; it does not belong to him, has no root in him and merely lies there because no revolution or no robber takes it away. But that which a man is, does always by necessity acquire; and what the man acquires, is living property, which does not wait the beck of rulers, or 635 mobs, or revolutions, or fire, or storm, or bankruptcies, but perpetually renews itself wherever the man breathes. "Thy lot or portion of life," said the Caliph Ali, "is seeking after thee; therefore be at rest from seeking after it." Our dependence on these foreign goods leads us to our slavish respect for numbers. The political parties meet in numerous conventions; the greater the concourse and with each new uproar of 640 announcement, The delegation from Essex! The Democrats from New Hampshire! The Whigs of Maine! the young patriot feels himself stronger than before by a new thousand of eyes and arms. In like manner the reformers summon conventions and vote and resolve in multitude. Not so, O friends! will the God deign to enter and inhabit you, but by a method precisely the reverse. It is only as a man puts off all foreign support and 645 stands alone that I see him to be strong and to prevail. He is weaker by every recruit to his banner. Is not a man better than a town? Ask nothing of men, and, in the endless mutation, thou only firm column must presently appear the upholder of all that surrounds thee. He who knows that power is inborn, that he is weak because he has looked for good out of him and elsewhere, and, so perceiving, throws himself 650 unhesitatingly on his thought, instantly rights himself, stands in the erect position, commands his limbs, works miracles; just as a man who stands on his feet is stronger than a man who stands on his head.

So use all that is called Fortune. Most men gamble with her, and gain all, and lose all, as her wheel rolls. But do thou leave as unlawful these winnings, and deal with 655 Cause and Effect, the chancellors of God. In the Will work and acquire, and thou hast chained the wheel of Chance, and shall sit hereafter out of fear from her rotations. A political victory, a rise of rents, the recovery of your sick or the return of your absent friend, or some other favorable event raises your spirits, and you think good days are preparing for you. Do not believe it. Nothing can bring you peace but yourself. Nothing 660 can bring you peace but the triumph of principles.

(1841, 1847)

---

637. Ali: Ali ben Abu Talib (c.600-661), fourth caliph, cousin and son-in-law of Mohammed, and supposed author of collections of proverbs and verses.

ODE
Inscribed to W. H. Channing

Though loath to grieve
The evil time's sole patriot,
I cannot leave
My honied thought
For the priest's cant,   5
Or statesman's rant.

If I refuse
My study for their politique,
Which at the best is trick,
The angry Muse   10
Puts confusion in my brain.

But who is he that prates
Of the culture of mankind,
Of better arts and life?
Go, blindworm, go,   15
Behold the famous States
Harrying Mexico
With rifle and with knife!

Or who, with accent bolder,
Dare praise the freedom-loving mountaineer?
I found by thee, O rushing Contoocook!   21
And in thy valleys, Agiochook!
The jackals of the negro-holder.

The God who made New Hampshire
Taunted the lofty land   25
With little men; —
Small bat and wren
House in the oak: —
If earth-fire cleave
The upheaved land, and bury the folk,   30
The southern crocodile would grieve.
Virtue palters; Right is hence;
Freedom praised, but hid;
Funeral eloquence
Rattles the coffin-lid.   35

What boots thy zeal,
O glowing friend,
That would indignant rend
The northland from the south?
Wherefore? to what good end?   40
Boston Bay and Bunker Hill
Would serve things still; —
Things are of the snake.

The horseman serves the horse,
The neatherd serves the neat,   45
The merchant serves the purse,
The eater serves his meat;
'Tis the day of the chattel,
Web to weave, and corn to grind;
Things are in the saddle,   50
And ride mankind.

There are two laws discrete,
Not reconciled, —
Law for man, and law for things;
The last builds town and fleet,   55
But it runs wild,
And doth the man unking.

'Tis fit the forest fall,
The steep be graded,
The mountain tunnelled,   60
The sand shaded,
The orchard planted,
The glebe tilled,
The prairie granted,
The steamer built.   65

Let man serve law for man;
Live for friendship, live for love,
For truth's and harmony's behoof;
The state may follow how it can,
As Olympus follows Jove.   70

ODE INSCRIBED TO CHANNING   William Henry Channing (1810-1884) — nephew of William Ellery Channing (1780-1842), principal American proponent of Unitarianism — was himself a Unitarian minister, transcendentalist, socialist, and reformer. **16-18:** referring to the Mexican War (1846-48). **21. Contoocook:** river in southern New Hampshire. **22. Agiochook:** Native name for the White Mountains, in northern New Hampshire. **23:** i.e., men pursuing fugitive slaves.

Yet do not I implore
The wrinkled shopman to my
  sounding woods,
Nor did the unwilling senator
Ask votes of thrushes in the solitudes.
Every one to his chosen work; —   75
Foolish hands may mix and mar;
Wise and sure the issues are.
Round they roll till dark is light,
Sex to sex, and even to odd; —
The over-god   80
Who marries Right to Might,
Who peoples, unpeoples, —
He who exterminates
Races by stronger races,

Black by white faces, —   85
Knows to bring honey
Out of the lion;
Grafts gentlest scion
On pirate and Turk.

The Cossack eats Poland,   90
Like stolen fruit;
Her last noble is ruined,
Her last poet mute:
Straight, into double band
The victors divide;   95
Half for freedom strike and stand; —
The astonished Muse finds thousands
  at her side.

(1847)

SUSANNA MOODIE
England/Canada, 1803-1885

from *ROUGHING IT IN THE BUSH*

BURNING THE FALLOW

There is a hollow roaring in the air —
The hideous hissing of ten thousand flames,
That from the centre of yon sable cloud
Leap madly up, like serpents in the dark,
Shaking their arrowy tongues at Nature's heart.

It is not my intention to give a regular history of our residence in the bush, but merely to present to my readers such events as may serve to illustrate a life in the woods.

The winter and spring of 1834 had passed away. The latter was uncommonly cold and backward; so much so that we had a very heavy fall of snow upon the 14th and 15th of May, and several gentlemen drove down to Cobourg in a sleigh, the snow lying upon   5
the ground to the depth of several inches.

A late, cold spring in Canada is generally succeeded by a burning hot summer; and the summer of '34 was the hottest I ever remember. No rain fell upon the earth for many weeks, till nature drooped and withered beneath one bright blaze of sunlight; and the ague and fever in the woods, and the cholera in the large towns and cities, spread death   10
and sickness through the country.

86-87: See Judges 14:8-9. **90-97:** After the Polish "November revolution" of 1830-31, Russia took firm control of its part of Poland, but 1846 saw a Galician uprising against Austrian rule.   **ROUGHING IT IN THE BUSH Epigraph:** written by Susanna Moodie, as is the verse at line 143. **5. Cobourg:** in Upper Canada (now Ontario), where Susanna Moodie and her husband, J.W. Dunbar Moodie, lived when they first arrived in 1832; by 1834 they had settled on a backwoods farm just north of Peterborough.

Moodie had made during the winter a large clearing of twenty acres around the house. The progress of the workmen had been watched by me with the keenest interest. Every tree that reached the ground opened a wider gap in the dark wood, giving us a broader ray of light and a clearer glimpse of the blue sky. But when the dark cedar-swamp fronting the house fell beneath the strokes of the axe, and we got a first view of the lake, my joy was complete; a new and beautiful object was now constantly before me, which gave me the greatest pleasure. By night and day, in sunshine or in storm, water is always the most sublime feature in a landscape, and no view can be truly grand in which it is wanting. From a child, it always had the most powerful effect upon my mind, from the great ocean rolling in majesty, to the tinkling forest rill, hidden by the flowers and rushes along its banks. Half the solitude of my forest home vanished when the lake unveiled its bright face to the blue heavens, and I saw sun and moon, and stars and waving trees reflected there. I would sit for hours at the window as the shades of evening deepened round me, watching the massy foliage of the forests pictured in the waters, till fancy transported me back to England, and the songs of birds and the lowing of cattle were sounding in my ears. It was long, very long, before I could discipline my mind to learn and practise all the menial employments which are necessary in a good settler's wife.

The total absence of trees about the doors in all new settlements had always puzzled me, in a country where the intense heat of summer seems to demand all the shade that can be procured. My husband had left several beautiful rock-elms (the most picturesque tree in the country) near our dwelling, but alas! the first high gale prostrated all my fine trees, and left our log cottage entirely exposed to the fierce rays of the sun.

The confusion of an uncleared fallow spread around us on every side. Huge trunks of trees and piles of brush gave a littered and uncomfortable appearance to the locality, and as the weather had been very dry for some weeks, I heard my husband daily talking with his choppers as to the expediency of firing the fallow. They still urged him to wait a little longer, until he could get a good breeze to carry the fire well through the brush.

Business called him suddenly to Toronto, but he left a strict charge with old Thomas and his sons, who were engaged in the job, by no means to attempt to burn it off until he returned, as he wished to be upon the premises himself, in case of any danger. He had previously burnt all the heaps immediately about the doors.

While he was absent, old Thomas and his second son fell sick with the ague, and went home to their own township, leaving John, a surly, obstinate young man, in charge of the shanty, where they slept, and kept their tools and provisions.

Monaghan I had sent to fetch up my three cows, as the children were languishing for milk, and Mary and I remained alone in the house with the little ones.

The day was sultry, and towards noon a strong wind sprang up that roared in the pine tops like the dashing of distant billows, but without in the least degree abating the heat. The children were lying listlessly upon the floor for coolness, and the girl and I were finishing sun-bonnets, when Mary suddenly exclaimed, "Bless us, mistress, what a smoke!" I ran immediately to the door, but was not able to distinguish ten yards before me. The swamp immediately below us was on fire, and the heavy wind was driving a dense black cloud of smoke directly towards us.

---

19. sublime: See Glossary. **31. picturesque:** see Glossary. **46-47. Monaghan, Mary:** John Monaghan, their hired man, and Mary, their house help.

"What can this mean?" I cried, "Who can have set fire to the fallow?" *55*

As I ceased speaking, John Thomas stood pale and trembling before me. "John, what is the meaning of this fire?"

"Oh, ma'am, I hope you will forgive me; it was I set fire to it, and I would give all I have in the world if I had not done it."

"What is the danger?" *60*

"Oh, I'm terribly afear'd that we shall all be burnt up," said the fellow, beginning to whimper.

"Why did you run such a risk, and your master from home, and no one on the place to render the least assistance?"

"I did it for the best," blubbered the lad. "What shall we do?" *65*

"Why, we must get out of it as fast as we can, and leave the house to its fate."

"We can't get out," said the man, in a low, hollow tone, which seemed the concentration of fear; "I would have got out of it if I could; but just step to the back door, ma'am, and see."

I had not felt the least alarm up to this minute; I had never seen a fallow burnt, but I *70* had heard of it as a thing of such common occurrence that I had never connected with it any idea of danger. Judge then, my surprise, my horror, when, on going to the back door, I saw that the fellow, to make sure of his work, had fired the field in fifty different places. Behind, before, on every side, we were surrounded by a wall of fire, burning furiously within a hundred yards of us, and cutting off all possibility of retreat; for could *75* we have found an opening through the burning heaps, we could not have seen our way through the dense canopy of smoke; and, buried as we were in the heart of the forest, no one could discover our situation till we were beyond the reach of help.

I closed the door, and went back to the parlour. Fear was knocking loudly at my heart, for our utter helplessness annihilated all hope of being able to effect our escape — *80* I felt stupefied. The girl sat upon the floor by the children, who, unconscious of the peril that hung over them, had both fallen asleep. She was silently weeping; while the fool who had caused the mischief was crying aloud.

A strange calm succeeded my first alarm; tears and lamentations were useless; a horrible death was impending over us, and yet I could not believe that we were to die. I *85* sat down upon the step of the door, and watched the awful scene in silence. The fire was raging in the cedar-swamp, immediately below the ridge on which the house stood, and it presented a spectacle truly appalling. From out the dense folds of a canopy of black smoke, the blackest I ever saw, leaped up continually red forks of lurid flame as high as the tree tops, igniting the branches of a group of tall pines that had been left standing for *90* saw-logs.

A deep gloom blotted out the heavens from our sight. The air was filled with fiery particles, which floated even to the door-step — while the crackling and roaring of the flames might have been heard at a great distance. Could we have reached the lake shore, where several canoes were moored at the landing, by launching out into the water we *95* should have been in perfect safety; but, to attain this object, it was necessary to pass through this mimic hell; and not a bird could have flown over it with unscorched wings. There was no hope in that quarter, for, could we have escaped the flames, we should have been blinded and choked by the thick, black, resinous smoke.

The fierce wind drove the flames at the sides and back of the house up the clearing; *100*
and our passage to the road, or to the forest, on the right and left, was entirely obstructed
by a sea of flames. Our only ark of safety was the house, so long as it remained
untouched by the consuming element. I turned to young Thomas, and asked him, how
long he thought that would be.

"When the fire clears this little ridge in front, ma'am. The Lord have mercy upon *105*
us, then, or we must all go!"

"Cannot *you*, John, try and make your escape, and see what can be done for us and
the poor children?"

My eye fell upon the sleeping angels, locked peacefully in each other's arms, and
my tears flowed for the first time. *110*

Mary, the servant-girl, looked piteously up in my face. The good, faithful creature
had not uttered one word of complaint, but now she faltered forth,

"The dear, precious lambs! — Oh! such a death!"

I threw myself down upon the floor beside them, and pressed them alternately to
my heart, while inwardly I thanked God that they were asleep, unconscious of danger, *115*
and unable by their childish cries to distract our attention from adopting any plan which
might offer to effect their escape.

The heat soon became suffocating. We were parched with thirst, and there was not
a drop of water in the house, and none to be procured nearer than the lake. I turned once
more to the door, hoping that a passage might have been burnt through to the water. I *120*
saw nothing but a dense cloud of fire and smoke — could hear nothing but the crackling
and roaring of the flames, which were gaining so fast upon us that I felt their scorching
breath in my face.

"Ah," thought I — and it was a most bitter thought — "what will my beloved
husband say when he returns and finds that his poor Susy and his dear girls have *125*
perished in this miserable manner? But God can save us yet."

The thought had scarcely found a voice in my heart before the wind rose to a
hurricane, scattering the flames on all sides into a tempest of burning billows. I buried
my head in my apron, for I thought that our time was come, and that all was lost, when a
most terrific crash of thunder burst over our heads, and, like the breaking of a water- *130*
spout, down came the rushing torrent of rain which had been pent up for so many
weeks.

In a few minutes the chip-yard was all afloat, and the fire effectually checked. The
storm which, unnoticed by us, had been gathering all day, and which was the only one
of any note we had that summer, continued to rage all night, and before morning had *135*
quite subdued the cruel enemy, whose approach we had viewed with such dread.

The imminent danger in which we had been placed struck me more forcibly after it
was past than at the time, and both the girl and myself sank upon our knees, and lifted
up our hearts in humble thanksgiving to that God who had saved us by an act of His
Providence from an awful and sudden death. When all hope from human assistance was *140*
lost, His hand was mercifully stretched forth, making His strength more perfectly
manifested in our weakness: —

---

133. chip-yard: woodyard, area where wood is cut and sawdust and wood fragments accumulate.

"He is their stay when earthly help is lost,
The light and anchor of the tempest-toss'd."

There was one person unknown to us, who had watched the progress of that rash *145*
blaze, and had even brought his canoe to the landing, in the hope of getting us off. This
was an Irish pensioner named Dunn, who had cleared a few acres on his government
grant, and had built a shanty on the opposite shore of the lake.

"Faith, madam! an' I thought the captain was stark, staring mad to fire his fallow on
such a windy day, and that blowing right from the lake to the house. When Old Wittals *150*
came in and towld us that the masther was not to the fore, but only one lad, an' the wife
an' the chilther at home, — thinks I, there's no time to be lost, or the crathurs will be
burnt up intirely. We started instanther, but, by Jove! we were too late. The swamp was
all in a blaze when we got to the landing, and you might as well have thried to get to
heaven by passing through the other place." *155*

This was the eloquent harangue with which the honest creature informed me the next
morning of the efforts he had made to save us, and the interest he had felt in our critical
situation. I felt comforted for my past anxiety, by knowing that one human being,
however humble, had sympathised in our probable fate, while the providential manner in
which we had been rescued will ever remain a theme of wonder and gratitude. *160*

The next evening brought the return of my husband, who listened to the tale of our
escape with a pale and disturbed countenance; not a little thankful to find his wife and
children still in the land of the living.

For a long time after the burning of that fallow, it haunted me in my dreams. I
would awake with a start, imagining myself fighting with the flames, and endeavouring *165*
to carry my little children through them to the top of the clearing, when invariably their
garments and my own took fire just as I was within reach of a place of safety.

(1852)

N̲A̲T̲H̲A̲N̲I̲E̲L̲ H̲A̲W̲T̲H̲O̲R̲N̲E̲
U.S.A., 1804-1864

THE MAY-POLE OF MERRY MOUNT

Bright were the days at Merry Mount, when the May-pole was the banner-staff of that
gay colony! They who reared it, should their banner be triumphant, were to pour
sunshine over New England's rugged hills, and scatter flower-seeds throughout the soil.
Jollity and gloom were contending for an empire. Midsummer eve had come, bringing
deep verdure to the forest, and roses in her lap, of a more vivid hue than the tender buds *5*
of Spring. But May, or her mirthful spirit, dwelt all the year round at Merry Mount,
sporting with the Summer months, and revelling with Autumn, and basking in the glow

---

THE MAY-POLE OF MERRY MOUNT Hawthorne's own prefatory note: "There is an admirable foundation for a philosophic romance, in
the curious history of the early settlement of Mount Wollaston, or Merry Mount. In the slight sketch here attempted, the facts, recorded on the grave

of Winter's fireside. Through a world of toil and care she flitted with a dreamlike smile, and came hither to find a home among the lightsome hearts of Merry Mount.

Never had the May-pole been so gaily decked as at sunset on midsummer eve. This *10* venerated emblem was a pine-tree, which had preserved the slender grace of youth, while it equalled the loftiest height of the old wood monarchs. From its top streamed a silken banner, colored like the rainbow. Down nearly to the ground, the pole was dressed with birchen boughs, and others of the liveliest green, and some with silvery leaves, fastened by ribands that fluttered in fantastic knots of twenty different colors, but *15* no sad ones. Garden flowers, and blossoms of the wilderness, laughed gladly forth amid the verdure, so fresh and dewy, that they must have grown by magic on that happy pine-tree. Where this green and flowery splendor terminated, the shaft of the May-pole was stained with the seven brilliant hues of the banner at its top. On the lowest green bough hung an abundant wreath of roses, some that had been gathered in the sunniest spots of *20* the forest, and others, of still richer blush, which the colonists had reared from English seed. Oh, people of the Golden Age, the chief of your husbandry was to raise flowers!

But what was the wild throng that stood hand in hand about the May-pole? It could not be, that the fauns and nymphs, when driven from their classic groves and homes of ancient fable, had sought refuge, as all the persecuted did, in the fresh woods of the *25* West. These were Gothic monsters, though perhaps of Grecian ancestry. On the shoulders of a comely youth, uprose the head and branching antlers of a stag; a second, human in all other points, had the grim visage of a wolf; a third, still with the trunk and limbs of a mortal man, showed the beard and horns of a venerable he-goat. There was the likeness of a bear erect, brute in all but his hind legs, which were adorned with pink *30* silk stockings. And here again, almost as wondrous, stood a real bear of the dark forest, lending each of his fore-paws to the grasp of a human hand, and as ready for the dance as any in that circle. His inferior nature rose halfway, to meet his companions as they stooped. Other faces wore the similitude of man or woman, but distorted or extravagant, with red noses pendulous before their mouths, which seemed of awful depth, and *35* stretched from ear to ear in an eternal fit of laughter. Here might be seen the Salvage Man, well known in heraldry, hairy as a baboon, and girdled with green leaves. By his side, a nobler figure, but still a counterfeit, appeared an Indian hunter, with feathery crest and wampum belt. Many of this strange company wore fools-caps, and had little bells appended to their garments, tinkling with a silvery sound, responsive to the *40* inaudible music of their gleesome spirits. Some youths and maidens were of soberer garb, yet well maintained their places in the irregular throng, by the expression of wild revelry upon their features. Such were the colonists of Merry Mount, as they stood in the broad smile of sunset, round their venerated May-pole.

Had a wanderer, bewildered in the melancholy forest, heard their mirth, and stolen *45* a half affrighted glance, he might have fancied them the crew of Comus, some already

---

pages of our New England annalists, have wrought themselves, almost spontaneously, into a sort of allegory. The masques, mummeries, and festive customs, described in the text, are in accordance with the manners of the age. Authority on these points may be found in [Joseph] Strutt's Book of English Sports and Pastimes [1801]." Mount Wollaston (now Quincy, Massachusetts) was founded in 1625 by Captain Wollaston and by Thomas Morton (c.1590-1647), and renamed "Ma-re-Mount" by Morton (it later came to be known as "Merry Mount") when Wollaston left for Virginia; until 1628, when Morton (an Anglican) was attacked, arrested, and shipped back to England by Miles Standish (c.1584-1656), a Puritan from the nearby Plymouth Colony, Morton's Anglican community reportedly traded arms with the Indians and indulged in "atheistic" dancing and boisterous festivities. **36. Salvage Man:** a mummer dressed up as a "savage." **46. Comus:** Roman god of revelry; here, alluding to Milton's *A Masque* (1634; 1637),

transformed to brutes, some midway between man and beast, and the others rioting in the flow of tipsy jollity that foreran the change. But a band of Puritans, who watched the scene, invisible themselves, compared the masques to those devils and ruined souls with whom their superstition peopled the black wilderness. *50*

Within the ring of monsters, appeared the two airiest forms, that had ever trodden on any more solid footing than a purple and golden cloud. One was a youth in glistening apparel, with a scarf of the rainbow pattern crosswise on his breast. His right hand held a gilded staff, the ensign of high dignity among the revellers, and his left grasped the slender fingers of a fair maiden, not less gaily decorated than himself. Bright roses *55* glowed in contrast with the dark and glossy curls of each, and were scattered round their feet, or had sprung up spontaneously there. Behind this lightsome couple, so close to the May-pole that its boughs shaded his jovial face, stood the figure of an English priest, canonically dressed, yet decked with flowers, in heathen fashion, and wearing a chaplet of the native vine leaves. By the riot of his rolling eye, and the pagan decorations of his *60* holy garb, he seemed the wildest monster there, and the very Comus of the crew.

"Votaries of the May-pole," cried the flower-decked priest, "merrily, all day long, have the woods echoed to your mirth. But be this your merriest hour, my hearts! Lo, here stand the Lord and Lady of the May, whom I, a clerk of Oxford, and high priest of Merry Mount, am presently to join in holy matrimony. Up with your nimble spirits, ye *65* morrice dancers, green men, and glee maidens, bears and wolves, and horned gentlemen! Come; a chorus now, rich with the old mirth of Merry England, and the wilder glee of this fresh forest; and then a dance, to show the youthful pair what life is made of, and how airily they should go through it! All ye that love the May-pole, lend your voices to the nuptial song of the Lord and Lady of the May!" *70*

This wedlock was more serious than most affairs of Merry Mount, where jest and delusion, trick and fantasy, kept up a continual carnival. The Lord and Lady of the May, though their titles must be laid down at sunset, were really and truly to be partners for the dance of life, beginning the measure that same bright eve. The wreath of roses, that hung from the lowest green bough of the May-pole, had been twined for them, and *75* would be thrown over both their heads, in symbol of their flowery union. When the priest had spoken, therefore, a riotous uproar burst from the rout of monstrous figures.

"Begin you the stave, reverend Sir," cried they all; "and never did the woods ring to such a merry peal, as we of the May-pole shall send up!"

Immediately a prelude of pipe, cittern, and viol, touched with practised minstrelsy, *80* began to play from a neighboring thicket, in such a mirthful cadence, that the boughs of the May-pole quivered to the sound. But the May Lord, he of the gilded staff, chancing to look into his Lady's eyes, was wonder-struck at the almost pensive glance that met his own.

"Edith, sweet Lady of the May," whispered he, reproachfully, "is yon wreath of roses a garland to hang above our graves, that you look so sad? Oh, Edith, this is our *85* golden time! Tarnish it not by any pensive shadow of the mind; for it may be, that nothing of futurity will be brighter than the mere remembrance of what is now passing."

---

in which Comus (whom Milton makes the son of Bacchus and Circe) by means of a magic potion transforms people's faces into those of various beasts. **66. morrice:** The morrice or morris dance — in which the dancers dressed up as Robin Hood, Maid Marian, a jester, and a hobbyhorse — was a country dance associated with May festivities; it developed in the north of England before the 15th century. **77. rout:** crowd. **78. stave:** stanza. **80. cittern:** cithern, similar to a guitar.

"That was the very thought that saddened me! How came it in your mind too?" said Edith, in a still lower tone than he; for it was high treason to be sad at Merry Mount. "Therefore do I sigh amid this festive music. And besides, dear Edgar, I struggle as with *90* a dream, and fancy that these shapes of our jovial friends are visionary, and their mirth unreal, and that we are no true Lord and Lady of the May. What is the mystery in my heart?"

Just then, as if a spell had loosened them, down came a little shower of withering rose leaves from the May-pole. Alas, for the young lovers! No sooner had their hearts glowed *95* with real passion, than they were sensible of something vague and unsubstantial in their former pleasures, and felt a dreary presentiment of inevitable change. From the moment that they truly loved, they had subjected themselves to earth's doom of care and sorrow, and troubled joy, and had no more a home at Merry Mount. That was Edith's mystery. Now leave we the priest to marry them, and the masquers to sport round the May-pole, till *100* the last sunbeam be withdrawn from its summit, and the shadows of the forest mingle gloomily in the dance. Meanwhile, we may discover who these gay people were.

Two hundred years ago, and more, the old world and its inhabitants became mutually weary of each other. Men voyaged by thousands to the West; some to barter glass beads, and such like jewels, for the furs of the Indian hunter; some to conquer *105* virgin empires; and one stern band to pray. But none of these motives had much weight with the colonists of Merry Mount. Their leaders were men who had sported so long with life, that when Thought and Wisdom came, even these unwelcome guests were led astray by the crowd of vanities which they should have put to flight. Erring Thought and perverted Wisdom were made to put on masques, and play the fool. The men of whom *110* we speak, after losing the heart's fresh gayety, imagined a wild philosophy of pleasure, and came hither to act out their latest day-dream. They gathered followers from all that giddy tribe, whose whole life is like the festal days of soberer men. In their train were minstrels, not unknown in London streets; wandering players, whose theatres had been the halls of noblemen; mummers, rope-dancers, and mountebanks, who would long be *115* missed at wakes, church-ales, and fairs; in a word, mirth makers of every sort, such as abounded in that age, but now began to be discountenanced by the rapid growth of Puritanism. Light had their footsteps been on land, and as lightly they came across the sea. Many had been maddened by their previous troubles into a gay despair; others were as madly gay in the flush of youth, like the May Lord and his Lady; but whatever might *120* be the quality of their mirth, old and young were gay at Merry Mount. The young deemed themselves happy. The elder spirits, if they knew that mirth was but the counterfeit of happiness, yet followed the false shadow wilfully, because at least her garments glittered brightest. Sworn triflers of a lifetime, they would not venture among the sober truths of life, not even to be truly blest. *125*

All the hereditary pastimes of Old England were transplanted hither. The King of Christmas was duly crowned, and the Lord of Misrule bore potent sway. On the eve of Saint John, they felled whole acres of the forest to make bonfires, and danced by the

---

96. **sensible:** aware. 116. **church-ales:** periodic festivals, similar to wakes, at which much ale was consumed. 127. **Lord of Misrule:** in English tradition, a mock official who was named "king" of secular Christmas festivities; also, the name by which the Plymouth colony referred to Thomas Morton. 128. **Saint John:** St. John's Day, June 24.

blaze all night, crowned with garlands, and throwing flowers into the flame. At harvest time, though their crop was of the smallest, they made an image with the sheaves of 130 Indian corn, and wreathed it with autumnal garlands, and bore it home triumphantly. But what chiefly characterized the colonists of Merry Mount, was their veneration for the May-pole. It has made their true history a poet's tale. Spring decked the hallowed emblem with young blossoms and fresh green boughs; Summer brought roses of the deepest blush, and the perfected foliage of the forest; Autumn enriched it with that red 135 and yellow gorgeousness, which converts each wild-wood leaf into a painted flower; and Winter silvered it with sleet, and hung it round with icicles, till it flashed in the cold sunshine, itself a frozen sunbeam. Thus each alternate season did homage to the May-pole, and paid it a tribute of its own richest splendor. Its votaries danced round it, once, at least, in every month; sometimes they called it their religion, or their altar; but 140 always, it was the banner-staff of Merry Mount.

Unfortunately, there were men in the new world, of a sterner faith than these May-pole worshippers. Not far from Merry Mount was a settlement of Puritans, most dismal wretches, who said their prayers before daylight, and then wrought in the forest or the cornfield, till evening made it prayer time again. Their weapons were always at hand, to 145 shoot down the straggling savage. When they met in conclave, it was never to keep up the old English mirth, but to hear sermons three hours long, or to proclaim bounties on the heads of wolves and the scalps of Indians. Their festivals were fast-days, and their chief pastime the singing of psalms. Woe to the youth or maiden, who did but dream of a dance! The selectman nodded to the constable; and there sat the light-heeled reprobate 150 in the stocks; or if he danced, it was round the whipping-post, which might be termed the Puritan May-pole.

A party of these grim Puritans, toiling through the difficult woods, each with a horse-load of iron armor to burden his footsteps, would sometimes draw near the sunny precincts of Merry Mount. There were the silken colonists, sporting round their May- 155 pole; perhaps teaching a bear to dance, or striving to communicate their mirth to the grave Indian; or masquerading in the skins of deers and wolves, which they had hunted for that especial purpose. Often, the whole colony were playing at blindman's buff, magistrates and all with their eyes bandaged, except a single scape-goat, whom the blinded sinners pursued by the tinkling of the bells at his garments. Once, it is said, they 160 were seen following a flower-decked corpse, with merriment and festive music, to his grave. But did the dead man laugh? In their quietest times, they sang ballads and told tales, for the edification of their pious visitors; or perplexed them with juggling tricks; or grinned at them through horse-collars; and when sport itself grew wearisome, they made game of their own stupidity, and began a yawning match. At the very least of 165 these enormities, the men of iron shook their heads and frowned so darkly, that the revellers looked up, imagining that a momentary cloud had overcast the sunshine, which was to be perpetual there. On the other hand, the Puritans affirmed, that, when a psalm was pealing from their place of worship, the echo which the forest sent them back, seemed often like the chorus of a jolly catch, closing with a roar of laughter. Who but 170 the fiend, and his bond-slaves, the crew of Merry Mount, had thus disturbed them? In

---

150. selectman: a New England term for an official who was elected annually to look after civic business. **170. catch:** a musical round.

due time, a feud arose, stern and bitter on one side, and as serious on the other as any thing could be among such light spirits as had sworn allegiance to the May-pole. The future complexion of New England was involved in this important quarrel. Should the grisly saints establish their jurisdiction over the gay sinners, then would their spirits *175* darken all the clime, and make it a land of clouded visages, of hard toil, of sermon and psalm for ever. But should the banner-staff of Merry Mount be fortunate, sunshine would break upon the hills, and flowers would beautify the forest, and late posterity do homage to the May-pole.

After these authentic passages from history, we return to the nuptials of the Lord and *180* Lady of the May. Alas! we have delayed too long, and must darken our tale too suddenly. As we glance again at the May-pole, a solitary sunbeam is fading from the summit, and leaves only a faint golden tinge, blended with the hues of the rainbow banner. Even that dim light is now withdrawn, relinquishing the whole domain of Merry Mount to the evening gloom, which has rushed so instantaneously from the black surrounding woods. *185* But some of these black shadows have rushed forth in human shape.

Yes, with the setting sun, the last day of mirth had passed from Merry Mount. The ring of gay masquers was disordered and broken; the stag lowered his antlers in dismay; the wolf grew weaker than a lamb; the bells of the morrice dancers tinkled with tre-mulous affright. The Puritans had played a characteristic part in the May-pole *190* mummeries. Their darksome figures were intermixed with the wild shapes of their foes, and made the scene a picture of the moment, when waking thoughts start up amid the scattered fantasies of a dream. The leader of the hostile party stood in the centre of the circle, while the rout of monsters cowered around him, like evil spirits in the presence of a dread magician. No fantastic foolery could look him in the face. So stern was the *195* energy of his aspect, that the whole man, visage, frame, and soul, seemed wrought of iron, gifted with life and thought, yet all of one substance with his headpiece and breastplate. It was the Puritan of Puritans; it was Endicott himself!

"Stand off, priest of Baal!" said he, with a grim frown, and laying no reverent hand upon the surplice. "I know thee, Blackstone! Thou art the man, who couldst not abide *200* the rule even of thine own corrupted church, and hast come hither to preach iniquity, and to give example of it in thy life. But now shall it be seen that the Lord hath sanctified this wilderness for his peculiar people. Woe unto them that would defile it! And first, for this flower-decked abomination, the altar of thy worship!"

And with his keen sword, Endicott assaulted the hallowed May-pole. Nor long did *205* it resist his arm. It groaned with a dismal sound; it showered leaves and rosebuds upon the remorseless enthusiast; and finally, with all its green boughs, and ribands, and flowers, symbolic of departed pleasures, down fell the banner-staff of Merry Mount. As it sank, tradition says, the evening sky grew darker, and the woods threw forth a more sombre shadow. *210*

---

198. Endicott: John Endecott (c.1589-1665), who emigrated to the Salem Colony in 1628, became governor of the Massachusetts Bay Colony the year following, and prosecuted the members of Morton's colony, Quakers, and others who differed from his own faith. **199. Baal:** the fertility god of the Phoenicians, later the name applied to any "false" god. **200. Blackstone:** William Blaxton was an English clergyman who settled in Massachusetts in 1626; Hawthorne adds a note to his story: "Did Governor Endicott speak less positively, we should suspect a mistake here. The Rev. Mr. Blackstone, though an eccentric, is not known to have been an immoral man. We rather doubt his identity with the priest of Merry Mount." **203. peculiar:** exclusive.

"There," cried Endicott, looking triumphantly on his work, "there lies the only May-pole in New England! The thought is strong within me, that, by its fall, is shadowed forth the fate of light and idle mirth makers, amongst us and our posterity. Amen, saith John Endicott."

"Amen!" echoed his followers.   *215*

But the votaries of the May-pole gave one groan for their idol. At the sound, the Puritan leader glanced at the crew of Comus, each a figure of broad mirth, yet, at this moment, strangely expressive of sorrow and dismay.

"Valiant captain," quoth Peter Palfrey, the Ancient of the band, "what order shall be taken with the prisoners?"   *220*

"I thought not to repent me of cutting down a May-pole," replied Endicott, "yet now I could find in my heart to plant it again, and give each of these bestial pagans one other dance round their idol. It would have served rarely for a whipping-post!"

"But there are pine-trees enow," suggested the lieutenant.

"True, good Ancient," said the leader. "Wherefore, bind the heathen crew, and   *225* bestow on them a small matter of stripes a-piece, as earnest of our future justice. Set some of the rogues in the stocks to rest themselves, so soon as Providence shall bring us to one of our own well-ordered settlements, where such accommodations may be found. Further penalties, such as branding and cropping of ears, shall be thought of hereafter."

"How many stripes for the priest?" inquired Ancient Palfrey.   *230*

"None as yet," answered Endicott, bending his iron frown upon the culprit. "It must be for the Great and General Court to determine, whether stripes and long imprisonment, and other grievous penalty, may atone for his transgressions. Let him look to himself! For such as violate our civil order, it may be permitted us to show mercy. But woe to the wretch that troubleth our religion!"   *235*

"And this dancing bear," resumed the officer. "Must he share the stripes of his fellows?"

"Shoot him through the head!" said the energetic Puritan. "I suspect witchcraft in the beast."

"Here be a couple of shining ones," continued Peter Palfrey, pointing his weapon at   *240* the Lord and Lady of the May. "They seem to be of high station among these misdoers. Methinks their dignity will not be fitted with less than a double share of stripes."

Endicott rested on his sword, and closely surveyed the dress and aspect of the hapless pair. There they stood, pale, downcast, and apprehensive. Yet there was an air of mutual support, and of pure affection, seeking aid and giving it, that showed them to be   *245* man and wife, with the sanction of a priest upon their love. The youth, in the peril of the moment, had dropped his gilded staff, and thrown his arm about the Lady of the May, who leaned against his breast, too lightly to burthen him, but with weight enough to express that their destinies were linked together, for good or evil. They looked first at each other, and then into the grim captain's face. There they stood, in the first hour of   *250* wedlock, while the idle pleasures, of which their companions were the emblems, had given place to the sternest cares of life, personified by the dark Puritans. But never had

---

219. Palfrey: Peter Palfrey, one of the founders of Salem, Massachusetts, in 1626. **224. enow:** enough. **226. earnest:** token. **232. General Court:** legislature of the colony.

their youthful beauty seemed so pure and high, as when its glow was chastened by adversity.

"Youth," said Endicott, "ye stand in an evil case, thou and thy maiden wife. Make 255 ready presently; for I am minded that ye shall both have a token to remember your wedding day!"

"Stern man," cried the May Lord, "how can I move thee? Were the means at hand, I would resist to the death. Being powerless, I entreat! Do with me as thou wilt; but let Edith go untouched!" 260

"Not so," replied the immitigable zealot. "We are not wont to show an idle courtesy to that sex, which requireth the stricter discipline. What sayest thou, maid? Shall thy silken bridegroom suffer thy share of the penalty, besides his own?"

"Be it death," said Edith, "and lay it all on me!"

Truly, as Endicott had said, the poor lovers stood in a woful case. Their foes were 265 triumphant, their friends captive and abased, their home desolate, the benighted wilderness around them, and a rigorous destiny, in the shape of the Puritan leader, their only guide. Yet the deepening twilight could not altogether conceal that the iron man was softened; he smiled at the fair spectacle of early love; he almost sighed for the inevitable blight of early hopes. 270

"The troubles of life have come hastily on this young couple," observed Endicott. "We will see how they comport themselves under their present trials, ere we burthen them with greater. If, among the spoil, there be any garments of a more decent fashion, let them be put upon this May Lord and his Lady, instead of their glistening vanities. Look to it, some of you." 275

"And shall not the youth's hair be cut?" asked Peter Palfrey, looking with abhorrence at the love-lock and long glossy curls of the young man.

"Crop it forthwith, and that in the true pumpkin-shell fashion," answered the captain. "Then bring them along with us, but more gently than their fellows. There be qualities in the youth, which may make him valiant to fight, and sober to toil, and pious 280 to pray; and in the maiden, that may fit her to become a mother in our Israel, bringing up babes in better nurture than her own hath been. Nor think ye, young ones, that they are the happiest, even in our lifetime of a moment, who misspend it in dancing round a May-pole!"

And Endicott, the severest Puritan of all who laid the rock-foundation of New 285 England, lifted the wreath of roses from the ruin of the May-pole, and threw it, with his own gauntleted hand, over the heads of the Lord and Lady of the May. It was a deed of prophecy. As the moral gloom of the world overpowers all systematic gayety, even so was their home of wild mirth made desolate amid the sad forest. They returned to it no more. But, as their flowery garland was wreathed of the brightest roses that had grown 290 there, so, in the tie that united them, were intertwined all the purest and best of their early joys. They went heavenward, supporting each other along the difficult path which it was their lot to tread, and never wasted one regretful thought on the vanities of Merry Mount.

(1836)

---

281. **Israel:** i.e., promised land, based on the belief that the chosen people are those who are descendents of Jacob (see Genesis 32:28, Deuteronomy 7:6).

ELIZABETH BARRETT BROWNING
England, 1806-1861

from *SONNETS FROM THE PORTUGUESE*

XIV

If thou must love me, let it be for nought
Except for love's sake only. Do not say
"I love her for her smile — her look — her way
Of speaking gently, — for a trick of thought
That falls in well with mine, and certes brought   5
A sense of pleasant ease on such a day" —
For these things in themselves, Belovèd, may
Be changed, or change for thee, — and love, so wrought,
May be unwrought so. Neither love me for
Thine own dear pity's wiping my cheeks dry, —   10
A creature might forget to weep, who bore
Thy comfort long, and lose thy love thereby!
But love me for love's sake, that evermore
Thou mayst love on, through love's eternity.

XXII

When our two souls stand up erect and strong,
Face to face, silent, drawing nigh and nigher,
Until the lengthening wings break into fire
At either curvèd point, — what bitter wrong
Can the earth do to us, that we should not long   5
Be here contented? Think. In mounting higher,
The angels would press on us and aspire
To drop some golden orb of perfect song
Into our deep, dear silence. Let us stay
Rather on earth, Belovèd, — where the unfit   10
Contrarious moods of men recoil away
And isolate pure spirits, and permit
A place to stand and love in for a day,
With darkness and the death-hour rounding it.

XLIII

How do I love thee? Let me count the ways.
I love thee to the depth and breadth and height
My soul can reach, when feeling out of sight
For the ends of Being and ideal Grace.
I love thee to the level of everyday's   5
Most quiet need, by sun and candle-light.
I love thee freely, as men strive for Right;
I love thee purely, as they turn from Praise.
I love thee with the passion put to use
In my old griefs, and with my childhood's faith.   10
I love thee with a love I seemed to lose
With my lost saints, — I love thee with the breath,
Smiles, tears, of all my life! — and, if God choose,
I shall but love thee better after death.

(1847-50)

THE BEST THING IN THE WORLD

What's the best thing in the world?
June-rose, by May-dew impearled;
Sweet south-wind, that means no rain;
Truth, not cruel to a friend;
Pleasure, not in haste to end;   5
Beauty, not self-decked and curled
Till its pride is over-plain;
Light, that never makes you wink;
Memory, that gives no pain;
Love, when, *so*, you're loved again.   10
What's the best thing in the world?
— Something out of it, I think.

(1862)

SONNETS FROM THE PORTUGUESE   Title: "The Portuguese" was Robert Browning's nickname for Elizabeth Barrett Browning, a name he coined after reading her poem "Catarina to Camoens."   **SONNET XIV**   **5. certes:** certainly.   **SONNET XXII**   **11. contrarious:** perverse, contrary.

HENRY WADSWORTH LONGFELLOW
U.S.A., 1807-1882

THE VILLAGE BLACKSMITH

Under a spreading chestnut-tree
  The village smithy stands;
The smith, a mighty man is he,
  With large and sinewy hands;
And the muscles of his brawny arms   *5*
  Are strong as iron bands.

His hair is crisp, and black, and long,
  His face is like the tan;
His brow is wet with honest sweat,
  He earns whate'er he can,   *10*
And looks the whole world in the face.
  For he owes not any man.

Week in, week out, from morn till night,
  You can hear his bellows blow;
You can hear him swing his heavy sledge,   *15*
  With measured beat and slow,
Like a sexton ringing the village bell,
  When the evening sun is low.

And children coming home from school
  Look in at the open door;   *20*
They love to see the flaming forge,
  And hear the bellows roar,
And catch the burning sparks that fly
  Like chaff from a threshing-floor.

He goes on Sunday to the church,   *25*
  And sits among his boys;
He hears the parson pray and preach,
  He hears his daughter's voice,
Singing in the village choir,
  And it makes his heart rejoice.   *30*

It sounds to him like her mother's voice,
  Singing in Paradise!
He needs must think of her once more,
  How in the grave she lies;
And with his hard, rough hand he wipes   *35*
  A tear out of his eyes.

Toiling, — rejoicing, — sorrowing,
  Onward through life he goes;
Each morning sees some task begin,
  Each evening sees it close;   *40*
Something attempted, something done,
  Has earned a night's repose.

Thanks, thanks to thee, my worthy friend,
  For the lesson thou hast taught!
Thus at the flaming forge of life   *45*
  Our fortunes must be wrought;
Thus on its sounding anvil shaped
  Each burning deed and thought.

(1842)

Prelude to *EVANGELINE*

This is the forest primeval. The murmuring pines and hemlocks,
Bearded with moss, and in garments green, indistinct in the twilight,
Stand like Druids of eld, with voices sad and prophetic,
Stand like harpers hoar, with beards that rest on their bosoms.

Loud from its rocky caverns, the deep-voiced neighboring ocean   *5*
Speaks, and in accents disconsolate answers the wail of the forest.
This is the forest primeval; but where are the hearts that beneath it
Leaped like the roe, when he hears in the woodland the voice of the huntsman?

THE VILLAGE BLACKSMITH   **8. the tan:** the bark of the oak tree.

Where is the thatch-roofed village, the home of Acadian farmers, —
Men whose lives glided on like rivers that water the woodlands,   *10*
Darkened by shadows of earth, but reflecting an image of heaven?
Waste are those pleasant farms, and the farmers forever departed!
Scattered like dust and leaves, when the mighty blasts of October
Seize them, and whirl them aloft, and sprinkle them far o'er the ocean.
Naught but tradition remains of the beautiful village of Grand-Pré.   *15*

Ye who believe in affection that hopes, and endures, and is patient,
Ye who believe in the beauty and strength of woman's devotion,
List to the mournful tradition, still sung by the pines of the forest;
List to a Tale of Love in Acadie, home of the happy.

(1847)

THE JEWISH CEMETERY AT NEWPORT

How strange it seems! These Hebrews in their graves,
   Close by the street of this fair seaport town,
Silent beside the never-silent waves,
   At rest in all this moving up and down!

The trees are white with dust, that o'er their sleep *5*
   Wave their broad curtains in the southwind's breath,
While underneath these leafy tents they keep
   The long, mysterious Exodus of Death.

And these sepulchral stones, so old and brown,
   That pave with level flags their burial-place,   *10*
Seem like the tablets of the Law, thrown down
   And broken by Moses at the mountain's base.

The very names recorded here are strange,
   Of foreign accent, and of different climes;
Alvares and Rivera interchange   *15*
   With Abraham and Jacob of old times.

"Blessed be God! for he created Death!"
   The mourners said, "and Death is rest and peace";
Then added, in the certainty of faith,
   "And giveth life that nevermore shall cease."   *20*

Closed are the portals of their Synagogue,
   No Psalms of David now the silence break,
No Rabbi reads the ancient Decalogue
   In the grand dialect the Prophets spake.

Gone are the living, but the dead remain,   *25*
   And not neglected; for a hand unseen,

Scattering its bounty, like a summer rain,
   Still keeps their graves and their remembrance green.

How came they here? What burst of Christian hate,
   What persecution, merciless and blind,   *30*
Drove o'er the sea — that desert desolate —
   These Ishmaels and Hagars of mankind?

They lived in narrow streets and lanes obscure,
   Ghetto and Judenstrass, in mirk and mire;
Taught in the school of patience to endure   *35*
   The life of anguish and the death of fire.

All their lives long, with the unleavened bread
   And bitter herbs of exile and its fears,
The wasting famine of the heart they fed,
   And slaked its thirst with marah of their tears.   *40*

Anathema maranatha! was the cry
   That rang from town to town, from street to street;
At every gate the accursed Mordecai
   Was mocked and jeered, and spurned by
     Christian feet.

Pride and humiliation hand in hand   *45*
   Walked with them through the world where'er
     they went;
Trampled and beaten were they as the sand,
   And yet unshaken as the continent.

For in the background figures vague and vast
   Of patriarchs and of prophets rose sublime,   *50*

PRELUDE TO EVANGELINE   **9. Acadian:** an inhabitant of Acadia or Acadie (line 19), the group of French settlements in what are now the Canadian Maritime Provinces; in 1755 the British disbanded these communities, expelling the people to other colonies, notably Louisiana, where an Acadian (or "Cajun") culture still exists; after 1767, many Acadians returned to their homeland. See also Carman's "Low Tide on Grand Pré" (p. 1190).   **THE JEWISH CEMETERY AT NEWPORT**   **Title:** Newport, Rhode Island. **12:** See Exodus 32:19. **15. Alvares, Rivera:** The Jewish families in colonial New England were mainly descended from Spanish and Portuguese traders. **23. Decalogue:** the ten commandments; see Exodus 20:1-17. **32. Ishmaels, Hagars:** outcasts, exiles; see Genesis 16 and 21:1-21. **34. Judenstrass:** street restricted to Jews. **40. marah:** bitterness; see Exodus 15: 22-23. **41. anathema maranatha:** "Doomed are those who love not the Lord" (see 1 Corinthians 16:22). **43. Mordecai:** See Esther 3-4.

And all the great traditions of the Past
    They saw reflected in the coming time.

And thus forever with reverted look
    The mystic volume of the world they read,
Spelling it backward like a Hebrew book,　　　*55*
    Till life became a Legend of the Dead.

But ah! what once has been shall be no more!
    The groaning earth in travail and in pain
Brings forth its races, but does not restore,
    And the dead nations never rise again.　　　*60*

(1854)

SANTA TERESA'S BOOK-MARK

Let nothing disturb thee,
Nothing affright thee;
All things are passing;
God never changeth;
Patient endurance
Attaineth to all things;
Who God possesseth
In nothing is wanting;
Alone God sufficeth.

(1870)

JOHN GREENLEAF WHITTIER
U.S.A., 1807-1892

THE DOUBLE-HEADED SNAKE OF NEWBURY

"Concerning yᵉ Amphisbæna, as soon as I received your commands, I made diligent inquiry:
. . . he assures me yᵗ it had really two heads, one at each end; two mouths, two stings or tongues."
— REV. CHRISTOPHER TOPPAN to COTTON MATHER.

Far away in the twilight time
Of every people, in every clime,
Dragons and griffins and monsters dire,
Born of water, and air, and fire,
Or nursed, like the Python, in the mud　　　*5*
And ooze of the old Deucalion flood,
Crawl and wriggle and foam with rage,
Through dusk tradition and ballad age.
So from the childhood of Newbury town
And its time of fable the tale comes down　　　*10*
Of a terror which haunted bush and brake,
The Amphisbæna, the Double Snake!
Thou who makest the tale thy mirth,
Consider that strip of Christian earth
On the desolate shore of a sailless sea,　　　*15*
Full of terror and mystery,
Half redeemed from the evil hold
Of the wood so dreary, and dark, and old,
Which drank with its lips of leaves the dew

When Time was young, and the world was new,　　　*20*
And wove its shadows with sun and moon,
Ere the stones of Cheops were squared and hewn.
Think of the sea's dread monotone,
Of the mournful wail from the pine-wood blown,
Of the strange, vast splendors that lit the North,　　　*25*
Of the troubled throes of the quaking earth,
And the dismal tales the Indian told,
Till the settler's heart at his hearth grew cold,
And he shrank from the tawny wizard boasts,
And the hovering shadows seemed full of ghosts,　　　*30*
And above, below, and on every side,
The fear of his creed seemed verified; —
And think, if his lot were now thine own,
To grope with terrors nor named nor known,
How laxer muscle and weaker nerve　　　*35*
And a feebler faith thy need might serve;
And own to thyself the wonder more
That the snake had two heads, and not a score!

SANTA TERESA'S BOOK-MARK   This poem is a translation of a work by the Spanish Carmelite mystic, Santa Teresa de Avila (1515-1582), a work which she used as a bookmark in her breviary, "Letrilla que llevaba por Registro en su Breviario." THE DOUBLE-HEADED SNAKE OF NEWBURY   Title: Newbury, in northeastern Massachusetts. Epigraph. amphisbæna: a fabulous serpent which, because it has two venomous heads, is able to move in two directions; Cotton Mather: (1663-1728) strict American Puritan theologian, who believed that the Salem witch trials were just. 6. Deucalion: in Greek myth, the son of Prometheus, who with his wife Pyrrha was the only survivor of a flood that was sent to punish the world (see Sandys, lines 322ff., p. 271).

Whether he lurked in the Oldtown fen
Or the gray earth-flax of the Devil's Den,   *40*
Or swam in the wooded Artichoke,
Or coiled by the Northman's Written Rock,
Nothing on record is left to show;
Only the fact that he lived, we know,
And left the cast of a double head   *45*
In the scaly mask which he yearly shed.
For he carried a head where his tail should be,
And the two, of course, could never agree,
But wriggled about with main and might,
Now to the left and now to the right;   *50*
Pulling and twisting this way and that,
Neither knew what the other was at.

A snake with two heads, lurking so near!
Judge of the wonder, guess at the fear!
Think what ancient gossips might say,   *55*
Shaking their heads in their dreary way,
Between the meetings on Sabbath-day!
How urchins, searching at day's decline
The Common Pasture for sheep or kine,
The terrible double-ganger heard   *60*
In leafy rustle or whir of bird!
Think what a zest it gave to the sport,
In berry-time, of the younger sort,
As over pastures blackberry-twined,
Reuben and Dorothy lagged behind,   *65*
And closer and closer, for fear of harm,
The maiden clung to her lover's arm;
And how the spark, who was forced to stay,

By his sweetheart's fears, till the break of day,
Thanked the snake for the fond delay!   *70*

Far and wide the tale was told,
Like a snowball growing while it rolled.
The nurse hushed with it the baby's cry;
And it served, in the worthy minister's eye,
To paint the primitive serpent by.   *75*
Cotton Mather came galloping down
All the way to Newbury town,
With his eyes agog and his ears set wide,
And his marvellous inkhorn at his side;
Stirring the while in the shallow pool   *80*
Of his brains for the lore he learned at school,
To garnish the story, with here a streak
Of Latin and there another of Greek:
And the tales he heard and the notes he took,
Behold! are they not in his Wonder-Book?   *85*

Stories, like dragons, are hard to kill.
If the snake does not, the tale runs still
In Byfield Meadows, or Pipestave Hill.
And still, whenever husband and wife
Publish the shame of their daily strife,   *90*
And, with mad cross-purpose, tug and strain
At either end of the marriage-chain,
The gossips say with a knowing shake
Of their gray heads, "Look at the Double Snake!
One in body and two in will,   *95*
The Amphisbæna is living still!"

(1860)

CHARLES TENNYSON TURNER
England, 1808-1879

ON SEEING A LITTLE CHILD SPIN A COIN OF ALEXANDER THE GREAT

This is the face of him, whose quick resource
Of eye and hand subdued Bucephalus,
And made the shadow of a startled horse
A foreground for his glory. It is thus
They hand him down; this coin of Philip's son   *5*
Recalls his life, his glories, and misdeeds;
And that abortive court of Babylon,
Where the world's throne was left among the reeds.
His dust is lost among the ancient dead,
A coin his only presence: he is gone: *10*
And all but this half mythic image fled —
A simple child may do him shame and slight;
'Twixt thumb and finger take the golden head,
And spin the horns of Ammon out of sight.

(1880)

---

39. Oldtown: in southern Maine. **40. earth-flax:** asbestos, or amianthus. **60. double-ganger:** doppelgänger. **85. Wonder-Book:** *The Wonders of the Invisible World* (1693). **ON SEEING A LITTLE CHILD** Cf. Shelley's "Ozymandias" (p. 844). **2. Bucephalus:** Alexander's war horse. **5. Philip:** Philip II of Macedon (382-336 B.C.), father of Alexander. **7. Babylon:** where Alexander died. **14. Ammon:** the Egyptian fertility god Amen, depicted as a man with a ram's head; Alexander, who considered himself a son of Zeus (and was so greeted by the priests at the oracle of Ammon at the Libyan desert oasis of Siwah), did not depict himself on his own coins, but his successor Lysimachus (c.360-281 B.C.), in representing Alexander on coinage, showed him as the son of Ammon, with ram's horns.

EDGAR ALLAN POE
U.S.A., 1809-1849

TO HELEN

Helen, thy beauty is to me
Like those Nicéan barks of yore,
That gently, o'er a perfumed sea,
The weary, way-worn wanderer bore
To his own native shore.   *5*

On desperate seas long wont to roam,
Thy hyacinth hair, thy classic face,
Thy Naiad airs have brought me home
To the glory that was Greece,
And the grandeur that was Rome.   *10*

Lo! in yon brilliant window-niche
How statue-like I see thee stand,
The agate lamp within thy hand!
Ah, Psyche, from the regions which
Are Holy-Land!   *15*

(1831)

THE CASK OF AMONTILLADO

The thousand injuries of Fortunato I had borne as I best could, but when he ventured upon insult I vowed revenge. You, who so well know the nature of my soul, will not suppose, however, that I gave utterance to a threat. *At length* I would be avenged; this was a point definitely settled — but the very definitiveness with which it was resolved precluded the idea of risk. I must not only punish but punish with impunity. A wrong is   *5* unredressed when retribution overtakes its redresser. It is equally unredressed when the avenger fails to make himself felt as such to him who has done the wrong.

    It must be understood that neither by word nor deed had I given Fortunato cause to doubt my good will. I continued, as was my wont, to smile in his face, and he did not perceive that my smile *now* was at the thought of his immolation.   *10*

    He had a weak point — this Fortunato — although in other regards he was a man to be respected and even feared. He prided himself on his connoisseurship in wine. Few

---

To HELEN   **1. Helen:** Cf. Helen of Troy. **2. Nicéan:** Nicene; pertaining to Nicaea, in Asia Minor. **7. hyacinth:** curled, or perhaps reddish brown, as in jacinth (but see the note to *Paradise Lost,* IV, 301, p. 353). **8. Naiad:** a water nymph. **14. Psyche:** in classical myth, the lover of Eros, granted a place among the gods as the personification of the soul.   **THE CASK OF AMONTILLADO**   **Title:** Amontillado is a pale dry sherry from Montilla, Spain, as distinct from the sherry which takes its name from Xerez, Spain.

Italians have the true virtuoso spirit. For the most part their enthusiasm is adopted to suit the time and opportunity, to practise imposture upon the British and Austrian *millionaires.* In painting and gemmary, Fortunato, like his countrymen, was a quack, but in the matter of old wines he was sincere. In this respect I did not differ from him materially; — I was skilful in the Italian vintages myself, and bought largely whenever I could. *15*

It was about dusk, one evening during the supreme madness of the carnival season, that I encountered my friend. He accosted me with excessive warmth, for he had been drinking much. The man wore motley. He had on a tight-fitting parti-striped dress, and his head was surmounted by the conical cap and bells. I was so pleased to see him that I thought I should never have done wringing his hand. *20*

I said to him — "My dear Fortunato, you are luckily met. How remarkably well you are looking to-day. But I have received a pipe of what passes for Amontillado, and I have my doubts." *25*

"How?" said he. "Amontillado? A pipe? Impossible! And in the middle of the carnival!"

"I have my doubts," I replied; "and I was silly enough to pay the full Amontillado price without consulting you in the matter. You were not to be found, and I was fearful of losing a bargain." *30*

"Amontillado!"

"I have my doubts."

"Amontillado!"

"And I must satisfy them."

"Amontillado!" *35*

"As you are engaged, I am on my way to Luchresi. If any one has a critical turn, it is he. He will tell me —"

"Luchresi cannot tell Amontillado from Sherry."

"And yet some fools will have it that his taste is a match for your own."

"Come, let us go." *40*

"Whither?"

"To your vaults."

"My friend, no; I will not impose upon your good nature. I perceive you have an engagement. Luchresi —"

"I have no engagement; — come." *45*

"My friend, no. It is not the engagement, but the severe cold with which I perceive you are afflicted. The vaults are insufferably damp. They are encrusted with nitre."

"Let us go, nevertheless. The cold is merely nothing. Amontillado! You have been imposed upon. And as for Luchresi, he cannot distinguish Sherry from Amontillado."

Thus speaking, Fortunato possessed himself of my arm; and putting on a mask of black silk and drawing a *roquelaire* closely about my person, I suffered him to hurry me to my palazzo. *50*

There were no attendants at home; they had absconded to make merry in honour of the time. I had told them that I should not return until the morning, and had given them

---

24. pipe: a cask containing half a tun of liquid measure, i.e., approximately 100 gallons. **47. nitre:** saltpeter, potassium nitrate. **51. *roquelaire*:** short cloak.

explicit orders not to stir from the house. These orders were sufficient, I well knew, to   *55*
insure their immediate disappearance, one and all, as soon as my back was turned.

I took from their sconces two flambeaux, and giving one to Fortunato, bowed him
through several suites of rooms to the archway that led into the vaults. I passed down a
long and winding staircase, requesting him to be cautious as he followed. We came at
length to the foot of the descent, and stood together on the damp ground of the   *60*
catacombs of the Montresors.

The gait of my friend was unsteady, and the bells upon his cap jingled as he strode.

"The pipe?" said he.

"It is farther on," said I; "but observe the white web-work which gleams from these
cavern walls."   *65*

He turned towards me, and looked into my eyes with two filmy orbs that distilled
the rheum of intoxication.

"Nitre?" he asked, at length.

"Nitre," I replied. "How long have you had that cough?"

"Ugh! ugh! ugh! — ugh! ugh! ugh! — ugh! ugh! ugh! ugh! ugh! ugh! — ugh! ugh!   *70*
ugh!"

My poor friend found it impossible to reply for many minutes.

"It is nothing," he said, at last.

"Come," I said, with decision, "we will go back; your health is precious. You are
rich, respected, admired, beloved; you are happy, as once I was. You are a man to be   *75*
missed. For me it is no matter. We will go back; you will be ill, and I cannot be
responsible. Besides, there is Luchresi —"

"Enough," he said; "the cough is a mere nothing; it will not kill me. I shall not die
of a cough."

"True — true," I replied; "and, indeed, I had no intention of alarming you   *80*
unnecessarily — but you should use all proper caution. A draught of this Medoc will
defend us from the damps."

Here I knocked off the neck of a bottle which I drew from a long row of its fellows
that lay upon the mould.

"Drink," I said, presenting him the wine.   *85*

He raised it to his lips with a leer. He paused and nodded to me familiarly, while his
bells jingled.

"I drink," he said, "to the buried that repose around us."

"And I to your long life."

He again took my arm, and we proceeded.   *90*

"These vaults," he said, "are extensive."

"The Montresors," I replied, "were a great and numerous family."

"I forget your arms."

"A huge human foot d'or, in a field azure; the foot crushes a serpent rampant whose
fangs are imbedded in the heel."   *95*

"And the motto?"

"*Nemo me impune lacessit.*"

---

81. Medoc: i.e., Médoc, a rich red wine of southern France. **94. or, azure:** heraldic terms for gold and blue. **97. *Nemo me impune lacessit:*** (Latin)
No one wounds me with impunity.

"Good!" he said.

The wine sparkled in his eyes and the bells jingled. My own fancy grew warm with the Medoc. We had passed through long walls of piled skeletons, with casks and puncheons intermingling, into the inmost recesses of the catacombs. I paused again, and this time I made bold to seize Fortunato by an arm above the elbow. 100

"The nitre!" I said; "see, it increases. It hangs like moss upon the vaults. We are below the river's bed. The drops of moisture trickle among the bones. Come, we will go back ere it is too late. Your cough —" 105

"It is nothing," he said; "let us go on. But first, another draught of the Medoc."

I broke and reached him a flagon of De Grâve. He emptied it at a breath. His eyes flashed with a fierce light. He laughed and threw the bottle upward with a gesticulation I did not understand.

I looked at him in surprise. He repeated the movement — a grotesque one. 110

"You do not comprehend?" he said.

"Not I," I replied.

"Then you are not of the brotherhood."

"How?"

"You are not of the masons." 115

"Yes, yes," I said; "yes, yes."

"You? Impossible! A mason?"

"A mason," I replied.

"A sign," he said, "a sign."

"It is this," I answered, producing from beneath the folds of my *roquelaire* a trowel. 120

"You jest," he exclaimed, recoiling a few paces. "But let us proceed to the Amontillado."

"Be it so," I said, replacing the tool beneath the cloak and again offering him my arm. He leaned upon it heavily. We continued our route in search of the Amontillado. We passed through a range of low arches, descended, passed on, and descending again, 125 arrived at a deep crypt, in which the foulness of the air caused our flambeaux rather to glow than flame.

At the most remote end of the crypt there appeared another less spacious. Its walls had been lined with human remains, piled to the vault overhead, in the fashion of the great catacombs of Paris. Three sides of this interior crypt were still ornamented in this 130 manner. From the fourth the bones had been thrown down, and lay promiscuously upon the earth, forming at one point a mound of some size. Within the wall thus exposed by the displacing of the bones, we perceived a still interior crypt or recess, in depth about four feet, in width three, in height six or seven. It seemed to have been constructed for no especial use within itself, but formed merely the interval between two of the colossal 135 supports of the roof of the catacombs, and was backed by one of their circumscribing walls of solid granite.

---

107. De Grâve: Grâves, a dry French white wine from the region near Bordeaux. **115. masons:** Freemasonry was formally established in 1717, though it is thought to have emerged from agreements among the members of the masons' craft guild; essentially now a social and charitable organization (its central symbols, the mason's tools — plumb, level, and compasses — representing morality, charity, and ecological awareness), it has had many opponents, some of them suspicious of secret practices (e.g., the secret hand signal in this story), others condemning what they took to be irreligious practices or undue political power.

It was in vain that Fortunato, uplifting his dull torch, endeavored to pry into the depth of the recess. Its termination the feeble light did not enable us to see.

"Proceed," I said; "herein is the Amontillado. As for Luchresi —"   *140*

"He is an ignoramus," interrupted my friend, as he stepped unsteadily forward, while I followed immediately at his heels. In an instant he had reached the extremity of the niche, and finding his progress arrested by the rock, stood stupidly bewildered. A moment more and I had fettered him to the granite. In its surface were two iron staples, distant from each other about two feet, horizontally. From one of these depended a short   *145* chain, from the other a padlock. Throwing the links about his waist, it was but the work of a few seconds to secure it. He was too much astounded to resist. Withdrawing the key I stepped back from the recess.

"Pass your hand," I said, "over the wall; you cannot help feeling the nitre. Indeed it is *very* damp. Once more let me *implore* you to return. No? Then I must positively leave   *150* you. But I must first render you all the little attentions in my power."

"The Amontillado!" ejaculated my friend, not yet recovered from his astonishment.

"True," I replied; "the Amontillado."

As I said these words I busied myself among the pile of bones of which I have before spoken. Throwing them aside, I soon uncovered a quantity of building stone and   *155* mortar. With these materials and with the aid of my trowel, I began vigorously to wall up the entrance of the niche.

I had scarcely laid the first tier of the masonry when I discovered that the intoxication of Fortunato had in a great measure worn off. The earliest indication I had of this was a low moaning cry from the depth of the recess. It was *not* the cry of a drunken   *160* man. There was then a long and obstinate silence. I laid the second tier, and the third, and the fourth; and then I heard the furious vibrations of the chain. The noise lasted for several minutes, during which, that I might hearken to it with the more satisfaction, I ceased my labours and sat down upon the bones. When at last the clanking subsided, I resumed the trowel, and finished without interruption the fifth, the sixth, and the seventh   *165* tier. The wall was now nearly upon a level with my breast. I again paused, and holding the flambeaux over the mason-work, threw a few feeble rays upon the figure within.

A succession of loud and shrill screams, bursting suddenly from the throat of the chained form, seemed to thrust me violently back. For a brief moment I hesitated, I trembled. Unsheathing my rapier, I began to grope with it about the recess; but the   *170* thought of an instant reassured me. I placed my hand upon the solid fabric of the catacombs, and felt satisfied. I reapproached the wall. I replied to the yells of him who clamoured. I re-echoed, I aided, I surpassed them in volume and in strength. I did this, and the clamourer grew still.

It was now midnight, and my task was drawing to a close. I had completed the   *175* eighth, the ninth and the tenth tier. I had finished a portion of the last and the eleventh; there remained but a single stone to be fitted and plastered in. I struggled with its weight; I placed it partially in its destined position. But now there came from out the niche a low laugh that erected the hairs upon my head. It was succeeded by a sad voice, which I had difficulty in recognizing as that of the noble Fortunato. The   *180* voice said —

"Ha! ha! ha! — he! he! he! — a very good joke, indeed — an excellent jest. We will have many a rich laugh about it at the palazzo — he! he! he! — over our wine — he! he! he!"

"The Amontillado!" I said.   185

"He! he! he! — he! he! he! — yes, the Amontillado. But is it not getting late? Will not they be awaiting us at the palazzo, the Lady Fortunato and the rest? Let us be gone."

"Yes," I said, "let us be gone."

"*For the love of God, Montresor!*"

"Yes," I said, "for the love of God!"   190

But to these words I hearkened in vain for a reply. I grew impatient. I called aloud — "Fortunato!"

No answer. I called again — "Fortunato!"

No answer still. I thrust a torch through the remaining aperture and let it fall within.   195 There came forth in return only a jingling of the bells. My heart grew sick; it was the dampness of the catacombs that made it so. I hastened to make an end of my labour. I forced the last stone into its position; I plastered it up. Against the new masonry I re-erected the old rampart of bones. For the half of a century no mortal has disturbed them. *In pace requiescat!*   200

(1846)

ANNABEL LEE

It was many and many a year ago,
    In a kingdom by the sea
That a maiden there lived whom you may know
    By the name of ANNABEL LEE;
And this maiden she lived with no other thought   5
    Than to love and be loved by me.

I was a child and *she* was a child,
    In this kingdom by the sea,
But we loved with a love that was more than love —
    I and my ANNABEL LEE —   10
With a love that the winged seraphs of heaven
    Coveted her and me.

And this was the reason that, long ago,
    In this kingdom by the sea,
A wind blew out of a cloud, chilling   15
    My beautiful ANNABEL LEE;
So that her highborn kinsmen came
    And bore her away from me,
To shut her up in a sepulchre
    In this kingdom by the sea.   20

The angels, not half so happy in heaven,
    Went envying her and me —
Yes! — that was the reason (as all men know,
    In this kingdom by the sea)
That the wind came out of the cloud by night,   25
    Chilling and killing my ANNABEL LEE.

But our love it was stronger by far than the love
    Of those who were older than we —
    Of many far wiser than we —
And neither the angels in heaven above,   30
    Nor the demons down under the sea,
Can ever dissever my soul from the soul
    Of the beautiful ANNABEL LEE:

For the moon never beams, without bringing me dreams
    Of the beautiful ANNABEL LEE;   35
And the stars never rise, but I feel the bright eyes
    Of the beautiful ANNABEL LEE:
And so, all the night-tide, I lie down by the side
Of my darling — my darling — my life and my bride,
    In the sepulchre there by the sea —   40
    In her tomb by the sounding sea.

(1849)

---

200. *In pace requiescat:* (Latin) May he rest in peace.

from MARGINALIA

V

That punctuation is important all agree; but how few comprehend the extent of its importance! The writer who neglects punctuation, or mis-punctuates, is liable to be misunderstood — this, according to the popular idea, is the sum of the evils arising from heedlessness or ignorance. It does not seem to be known that, even where the sense is perfectly clear, a sentence may be deprived of half its force — its spirit — its point — 5 by improper punctuations. For the want of merely a comma, it often occurs that an axiom appears a paradox, or that a sarcasm is converted into a sermonoid. There is *no* treatise on the topic — and there is no topic on which a treatise is more needed. There seems to exist a vulgar notion that the subject is one of pure conventionality, and cannot be brought within the limits of intelligible and consistent *rule*. And yet, if fairly looked 10 in the face, the whole matter is so plain that its *rationale* may be read as we run. If not anticipated, I shall hereafter, make an attempt at a magazine paper on "The Philosophy of Point." In the meantime let me say a word or two of *the dash*. Every writer for the press, who has any sense of the accurate, must have been frequently mortified and vexed at the distortion of his sentences by the printer's now general substitution of a 15 semicolon, or comma, for the dash of the MS. The total or nearly total disuse of the latter point, has been brought about by the revulsion consequent upon its excessive employment about twenty years ago. The Byronic poets were *all* dash. John Neal, in his earlier novels, exaggerated its use into the grossest abuse — although his very error arose from the philosophical and self-dependent spirit which has always distinguished 20 him, and which will even yet lead him, if I am not greatly mistaken in the man, to do something for the literature of the country which the country "will not willingly," and cannot possibly, "let die." Without entering now into the *why*, let me observe that the printer may always ascertain when the dash of the MS. is properly and when improperly employed, by bearing in mind that this point represents *a second thought — an* 25 *emendation*. In using it just above I have exemplified its use. The words "an emendation" are, speaking with reference to grammatical construction, put in *ap*position with the words "a second thought." Having written these latter words, I reflected whether it would not be possible to render their meaning more distinct by certain other words. Now, instead of erasing the phrase "a second thought," which is of *some* use — 30 which *partially* conveys the idea intended — which advances me *a step toward* my full purpose — I suffer it to remain, and merely put a dash between it and the phrase "an emendation." The dash gives the reader a choice between two, or among three or more expressions, one of which may be more forcible than another, but all of which help out the idea. It stands, in general, for these words — *"or, to make my meaning more* 35 *distinct."* This force *it has* — and this force no other point can have; since all other points have well-understood uses quite different from this. Therefore, the dash *cannot* be dispensed with. It has its phases — its variation of the force described; but the one principle — that of second thought or emendation — will be found at the bottom of all.

MARGINALIA   **11.** See Habakkuk 2:2. **13. Point:** punctuation mark. **18. John Neal:** American author (1793-1876), whose early novels include *Keep Cool* (1817) and *Seventy-Six* (1823). **22-23:** See *The Reason of Church Government* (1642), where Milton reflects " . . . I might perhaps leave something so written to aftertimes, as they should not willingly let it die."

XXVII

The nose of a mob is its imagination. By this, at any time, it can be quietly led.   *40*

XXXV

In the tale proper — where there is no space for development of character or for great profusion and variety of incident — mere *construction* is, of course, far more imperatively demanded than in the novel. Defective plot, in this latter, may escape observation, but in the tale, never. Most of our tale-writers, however, neglect the distinction. They seem to begin their stories without knowing how they are to end; and their ends,   *45* generally, — like so many governments of Trinculo — appear to have forgotten their beginnings.

LXIV

A long time ago — twenty-three or four years at least — Edward C. Pinckney, of Baltimore, published an exquisite poem entitled "A Health." It was profoundly admired by the critical few, but had little circulation: — this for no better reason than that the   *50* author was born *too far South*. I quote a few lines:

> Affections are as *thoughts* to her,
>   *The measures of her hours* —
> Her feelings have the fragrancy,
>   The freshness of young *flowers*.   *55*
> To her the better elements
>   And kindlier stars have given
> *A form so fair, that, like the air,*
>   *'Tis less of Earth than Heaven.*

Now, in 1842, Mr. George Hill published "The Ruins of Athens and Other Poems,"   *60* — and from one of the "Other Poems" I quote what follows:

> And thoughts go sporting through her mind
>   Like children among *flowers;*
> And deeds of gentle goodness are
>   *The measures of her hours.*   *65*
> In soul or face she bears no trace
>   Of one from Eden driven,
> *But like the rainbow seems, though born*
>   *Of Earth, a part of Heaven.*

Is this plagiarism or is it *not?* — I merely ask for information.   *70*

CXXXIII

That man is not truly brave who is afraid either to seem or to be, when it suits him, a coward.

---

46. **Trinculo:** more appropriate to Trinculo's companion, Stephano, in Shakespeare's *The Tempest,* who thinks he is king of Prospero's isle, and is rudely disillusioned. 48. **Pinckney:** London-born Edward Coote Pinkney (1802-1828), author of *Poems* (1825), was brought up in Baltimore, Maryland.

CLXXIX

Since it has become fashionable to trundle houses about the streets, should there not be some remodelling of the legal definition of reality, as "that which is permanent, fixed, and immoveable, that cannot be carried out of its place"? According to this, a house is by no means real estate.

75

CCXIII

It is not every one who can put "a good thing" properly together, although, perhaps, when thus properly put together, every tenth person you meet with may be capable of both conceiving and appreciating it. We cannot bring ourselves to believe that less actual ability is required in the composition of a really good "brief article," than in a *80* fashionable novel of the usual dimensions. The novel certainly requires what is denominated a sustained effort — but this is a matter of mere perseverance, and has but a collateral relation to talent. On the other hand — unity of effect, a quality not easily appreciated or indeed comprehended by an ordinary mind, and a *desideratum* difficult of attainment, even by those who can conceive it — is indispensable in the "brief *85* article," and not so in the common novel. The latter, if admired at all, is admired for its detached passages, without reference to the work as a whole — or without reference to any general design — which, if it even exist in some measure, will be found to have occupied but little of the writer's attention, and cannot, from the length of the narrative, be taken in at one view, by the reader. *90*

CCXXI

The increase, within a few years, of the magazine literature, is by no means to be regarded as indicating what some critics would suppose it to indicate — a downward tendency in American taste or in American letters. It is but a sign of the times — an indication of an era in which men are forced upon the curt, the condensed, the well-digested — in place of the voluminous — in a word, upon journalism in lieu of *95* dissertation. We need now the light artillery rather than the Peace-makers of the intellect. I will not be sure that men at present think more profoundly than half a century ago, but beyond question they think with more rapidity, with more skill, with more tact, with more of method and less of excrescence in the thought. Besides all this, they have a vast increase in the thinking material; they have more facts, more to think about. For *100* this reason, they are disposed to put the greatest amount of thought in the smallest compass and disperse it with the utmost attainable rapidity. Hence the journalism of the age; hence, in especial, magazines. Too many we cannot have, as a general proposition; but we demand that they have sufficient merit to render them noticeable in the beginning, and that they continue in existence sufficiently long to permit us a fair *105* estimation of their value.

(1857)

---

84. *desideratum*: something desired or needed.

ABRAHAM LINCOLN
U.S.A., 1809-1865

ADDRESS AT THE DEDICATION OF THE GETTYSBURG NATIONAL CEMETERY

Four score and seven years ago our fathers brought forth on this continent a new nation, conceived in Liberty, and dedicated to the proposition that all men are created equal.

Now we are engaged in a great civil war, testing whether that nation, or any nation so conceived and so dedicated, can long endure. We are met on a great battlefield of that war. We have come to dedicate a portion of that field as a final resting-place for those who here gave their lives that that nation might live. It is altogether fitting and proper that we should do this.

But, in a larger sense, we cannot dedicate — we cannot consecrate — we cannot hallow — this ground. The brave men, living and dead, who struggled here have consecrated it far above our poor power to add or detract. The world will little note nor long remember what we say here, but it can never forget what they did here. It is for us the living, rather, to be dedicated here to the unfinished work which they who fought here have thus far so nobly advanced. It is rather for us to be here dedicated to the great task remaining before us — that from these honored dead we take increased devotion to that cause for which they gave the last full measure of devotion; that we here highly resolve that these dead shall not have died in vain; that this nation, under God, shall have a new birth of freedom; and that government of the people, by the people, for the people, shall not perish from the earth.

(November 19, 1863)

CHARLES DARWIN
England, 1809-1882

from *JOURNAL OF RESEARCHES INTO THE NATURAL HISTORY AND GEOLOGY OF THE COUNTRIES VISITED DURING THE VOYAGE OF H.M.S. "BEAGLE" ROUND THE WORLD*

from *Chapter XVII*: Galapagos Archipelago
September 15th
This archipelago consists of ten principal islands, of which five exceed the others in size. They are situated under the Equator, and between five and six hundred miles westward of the coast of America. They are all formed of volcanic rocks; a few

---

GETTYSBURG ADDRESS   During the American Civil War, the battle of Gettysburg was fought from July 1 to July 4, when the remaining Confederate forces under General Robert E. Lee withdrew in defeat. At the November dedication ceremonies, the featured speaker was Edward Everett (1794-1865) — clergyman, scholar and Harvard professor, editor, and statesman, but known particularly for his florid patriotic oratory. Before several thousand people, Everett spoke (from memory) for two hours, after which Lincoln, as requested, offered his brief remarks. Many, at least initially, disparaged Lincoln's effort, but Everett himself wrote to the President in praise of it.   **GALAPAGOS ARCHIPELAGO**   The *Beagle* reached the Galapagos Islands in 1835.

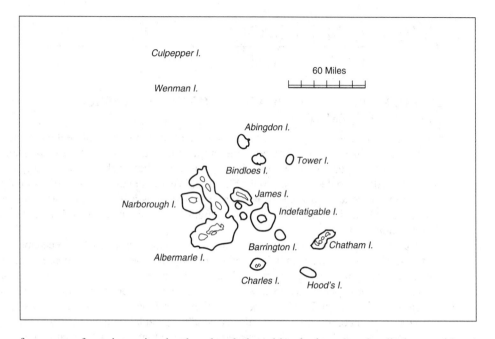

fragments of granite curiously glazed and altered by the heat, can hardly be considered
as an exception. Some of the craters, surmounting the larger islands, are of immense   5
size, and they rise to a height of between three and four thousand feet. Their flanks are
studded by innumerable smaller orifices. I scarcely hesitate to affirm, that there must be
in the whole archipelago at least two thousand craters. These consist either of lava and
scoriæ, or of finely-stratified, sandstone-like tuff. Most of the latter are beautifully
symmetrical; they owe their origin to eruptions of volcanic mud without any lava: it is a   10
remarkable circumstance that every one of the twenty-eight tuff-craters which were
examined, had their southern sides either much lower than the other sides, or quite
broken down and removed. As all these craters apparently have been formed when
standing in the sea, and as the waves from the trade wind and the swell from the open
Pacific here unite their forces on the southern coasts of all the islands, this singular   15
uniformity in the broken state of the craters, composed of the soft and yielding tuff, is
easily explained.

   Considering that these islands are placed directly under the Equator, the climate is
far from being excessively hot; this seems chiefly caused by the singularly low
temperature of the surrounding water, brought here by the great southern Polar current.   20
Excepting during one short season, very little rain falls, and even then it is irregular; but
the clouds generally hang low. Hence, whilst the lower parts of the islands are very
sterile, the upper parts, at a height of a thousand feet and upwards, possess a damp
climate and a tolerably luxuriant vegetation. This is especially the case on the windward
sides of the islands, which first receive and condense the moisture from the atmosphere.   25

   In the morning (17*th*) we landed on Chatham Island, which, like the others, rises
with a tame and rounded outline, broken here and there by scattered hillocks, the remains

of former craters. Nothing could be less inviting than the first appearance. A broken field of black basaltic lava, thrown into the most rugged waves, and crossed by great fissures, is everywhere covered by stunted, sun-burnt brushwood, which shows little signs of life. The dry and parched surface, being heated by the noonday sun, gave to the air a close and sultry feeling, like that from a stove: we fancied even that the bushes smelt unpleasantly. Although I diligently tried to collect as many plants as possible, I succeeded in getting very few; and such wretched-looking little weeds would have better become an arctic than an equatorial Flora. The brushwood appears, from a short distance, as leafless as our trees during winter; and it was some time before I discovered that not only almost every plant was now in full leaf, but that the greater number were in flower. The commonest bush is one of the Euphorbiaceæ: an acacia and a great odd-looking cactus are the only trees which afford any shade. After the season of heavy rains, the islands are said to appear for a short time partially green. The volcanic island of Fernando Noronha, placed in many respects under nearly similar conditions, is the only other country where I have seen a vegetation at all like this of the Galapagos islands.

The *Beagle* sailed round Chatham Island, and anchored in several bays. One night I slept on shore on a part of the island, where black truncated cones were extraordinarily numerous: from one small eminence I counted sixty of them, all surmounted by craters more or less perfect. The greater number consisted merely of a ring of red scoriæ or slags, cemented together; and their height above the plain of lava was not more than from fifty to a hundred feet: none had been very lately active. The entire surface of this part of the island seems to have been permeated, like a sieve, by the subterranean vapours: here and there the lava, whilst soft, has been blown into great bubbles; and in other parts, the tops of caverns similarly formed have fallen in, leaving circular pits with steep sides. From the regular form of the many craters, they gave to the country an artificial appearance, which vividly reminded me of those parts of Staffordshire, where the great iron-foundries are most numerous. The day was glowing hot, and the scrambling over the rough surface and through the intricate thickets, was very fatiguing; but I was well repaid by the strange Cyclopean scene. As I was walking along I met two large tortoises, each of which must have weighed at least two hundred pounds: one was eating a piece of cactus, and as I approached, it stared at me and slowly stalked away; the other gave a deep hiss, and drew in its head. These huge reptiles, surrounded by the black lava, the leafless shrubs, and large cacti, seemed to my fancy like some antediluvian animals. The few dull-coloured birds cared no more for me, than they did for the great tortoises.

. . . .

September 29th
We doubled the south-west extremity of Albemarle Island, and the next day were nearly becalmed between it and Narborough Island. Both are covered with immense deluges of black naked lava, which have flowed either over the rims of the great caldrons, like

30

35

40

45

50

55

60

65

---

40. Fernando Noronha: Fernando de Noronha, an island group in the Atlantic, off the coast of Brazil. **43.** *Beagle:* Darwin was the naturalist aboard this vessel during its 1831-36 voyage (the captain — later the governor of New Zealand — was Robert Fitzroy, 1805-1865). **56. Cyclopean:** massive, gigantic; pertaining to Cyclops, the one-eyed giant in Homer's *Odyssey.*

pitch over the rim of a pot in which it has been boiled, or have burst forth from smaller orifices on the flanks; in their descent they have spread over miles of the sea-coast. On both of these islands, eruptions are known to have taken place; and in Albemarle, we saw a small jet of smoke curling from the summit of one of the great craters. In the evening we anchored at Banks' Cove, in Albemarle Island. The next morning I went out *70* walking. To the south of the broken tuff-crater, in which the *Beagle* was anchored, there was another beautifully symmetrical one of an elliptic form; its longer axis was a little less than a mile, and its depth about 500 feet. At its bottom there was a shallow lake, in the middle of which a tiny crater formed an islet. The day was overpoweringly hot, and the lake looked clear and blue: I hurried down the cindery slope, and choked with dust *75* eagerly tasted the water — but, to my sorrow, I found it salt as brine.

The rocks on the coast abounded with great black lizards, between three and four feet long; and on the hills, an ugly yellowish-brown species was equally common. We saw many of this latter kind, some clumsily running out of our way, and others shuffling into their burrows. I shall presently describe in more detail the habits of both these *80* reptiles. The whole of this northern part of Albemarle Island is miserably sterile.

October 8th

We arrived at James Island: this island, as well as Charles Island, were long since thus named after our kings of the Stuart line. Mr. Bynoe, myself, and our servants were left here for a week, with provisions and a tent, whilst the *Beagle* went for water. We found here a party of Spaniards, who had been sent from Charles Island to dry fish, and to salt *85* tortoise-meat. About six miles inland, and at the height of nearly 2,000 feet, a hovel had been built in which two men lived who were employed in catching tortoises, whilst the others were fishing on the coast. I paid this party two visits, and slept there one night. As in the other islands, the lower region was covered by nearly leafless bushes, but the trees were here of a larger growth than elsewhere, several being two feet and some even *90* two feet nine inches in diameter. The upper region being kept damp by the clouds, supports a green and flourishing vegetation. So damp was the ground, that there were large beds of a coarse cyperus, in which great numbers of a very small water-rail lived and bred. While staying in this upper region we lived entirely upon tortoise-meat: the breastplate roasted (as the Gauchos do *carne con cuero*) with the flesh on it, is very *95* good; and the young tortoises make excellent soup; but otherwise the meat to my taste is indifferent.

One day we accompanied a party of the Spaniards in their whale-boat to a salina, or lake from which salt is procured. After landing, we had a very rough walk over a rugged field of recent lava, which has almost surrounded a tuff-crater, at the bottom of which *100* the salt-lake lies. The water is only three or four inches deep, and rests on a layer of beautifully crystallized, white salt. The lake is quite circular, and is fringed with a border of bright green succulent plants; the almost precipitous walls of the crater are clothed with wood, so that the scene was altogether both picturesque and curious. A few years since, the sailors belonging to a sealing-vessel murdered their captain in this quiet *105* spot; and we saw his skull lying among the bushes.

---

83. **Bynoe:** Benjamin Bynoe, the surgeon's assistant on the *Beagle*. 95. *carne con cuero*: meat with the skin still on.

During the greater part of our stay of a week, the sky was cloudless, and if the trade-wind failed for an hour, the heat became very oppressive. On two days, the thermometer within the tent stood for some hours at 93°; but in the open air, in the wind and sun, at only 85°. The sand was extremely hot; the thermometer placed in some of a brown colour immediately rose to 137°, and how much above that it would have risen, I do not know, for it was not graduated any higher. The black sand felt much hotter, so that even in thick boots it was quite disagreeable to walk over it.

The natural history of these islands is eminently curious, and well deserves attention. Most of the organic productions are aboriginal creations, found nowhere else; there is even a difference between the inhabitants of the different islands; yet all show a marked relationship with those of America, though separated from that continent by an open space of ocean, between 500 and 600 miles in width. The archipelago is a little world within itself, or rather a satellite attached to America, whence it has derived a few stray colonists, and has received the general character of its indigenous productions. Considering the small size of these islands, we feel the more astonished at the number of their aboriginal beings, and at their confined range. Seeing every height crowned with its crater, and the boundaries of most of the lava-streams still distinct, we are led to believe that within a period, geologically recent, the unbroken ocean was here spread out. Hence, both in space and time, we seem to be brought somewhat near to that great fact — that mystery of mysteries — the first appearance of new beings on this earth.

. . . .

We will now turn to the order of reptiles, which gives the most striking character to the zoology of these islands. The species are not numerous, but the numbers of individuals of each species are extraordinarily great. There is one small lizard belonging to a South American genus, and two species (and probably more) of the Amblyrhynchus — a genus confined to the Galapagos islands. There is one snake which is numerous; it is identical, as I am informed by M. Bibron, with the Psammophis Temminckii from Chile. Of sea-turtle I believe there is more than one species; and of tortoises there are, as we shall presently show, two or three species or races. Of toads and frogs there are none: I was surprised at this, considering how well suited for them the temperate and damp upper woods appeared to be. It recalled to my mind the remark made by Bory St. Vincent, namely, that none of this family are found on any of the volcanic islands in the great oceans. As far as I can ascertain from various works, this seems to hold good throughout the Pacific, and even in the large islands of the Sandwich archipelago. Mauritius offers an apparent exception, where I saw the Rana Mascariensis in abundance: this frog is said now to inhabit the Seychelles, Madagascar, and Bourbon; but on the other hand, Du Bois, in his voyage in 1669, states that there were no reptiles in Bourbon except tortoises; and the Officier du Roi asserts that before 1768 it had been attempted, without success, to introduce frogs into Mauritius — I presume, for the

Margin line numbers: 110, 115, 120, 125, 130, 135, 140

---

132. Bibron: Gabriel Bibron (1808-1848), French author of *Expédition scientifique de Morée* (1832-36) and other works. **136-37. Bory St. Vincent:** Jean-Baptiste Bory de St-Vincent (1778-1846), French author of *Voyage dans les quatres principales îles des mers Afrique* (1804) and other works. Darwin's own note reads: "*Voyage aux Quatre Iles d'Afrique.* With respect to the Sandwich Islands, see Tyerman and Bennet's *Journal*, vol. i., p. 434. For Mauritius see *Voyage par un Officier*, etc., part i., p. 170. There are no frogs in the Canary Islands (Webb et Berthelot, *Hist. Nat. des Iles Canaries*). I saw none at St. Jago in the Cape de Verds. There are none at St. Helena." **141. Bourbon:** now called Réunion, an island east of Madagascar. **142. Du Bois:** French traveller of the 17th century.

purpose of eating: hence it may be well doubted whether this frog is an aboriginal of   *145*
these islands. The absence of the frog family in the oceanic islands is the more
remarkable, when contrasted with the case of lizards, which swarm on most of the
smallest islands. May this difference not be caused by the greater facility with which the
eggs of lizards, protected by calcareous shells, might be transported through salt-water,
than could the slimy spawn of frogs?   *150*

   I will first describe the habits of the tortoise (Testudo nigra, formerly called Indica),
which has been so frequently alluded to. These animals are found, I believe, on all the
islands of the Archipelago; certainly on the greater number. They frequent in preference
the high damp parts, but they likewise live in the lower and arid districts. I have already
shown, from the numbers which have been caught in a single day, how very numerous   *155*
they must be. Some grow to an immense size: Mr. Lawson, an Englishman, and vice-
governor of the colony, told us that he had seen several so large, that it required six or
eight men to lift them from the ground; and that some had afforded as much as two
hundred pounds of meat. The old males are the largest, the females rarely growing to so
great a size; the male can readily be distinguished from the female by the greater length   *160*
of its tail. The tortoises which live on those islands where there is no water, or in the
lower and arid parts of the others, feed chiefly on the succulent cactus. Those which
frequent the higher and damp regions, eat the leaves of various trees, a kind of berry
(called guayavita) which is acid and austere, and likewise a pale green filamentous
lichen (Usnera plicata), that hangs in tresses from the boughs of the trees.   *165*

   The tortoise is very fond of water, drinking large quantities, and wallowing in the
mud. The larger islands alone possess springs, and these are always situated towards the
central parts, and at a considerable height. The tortoises, therefore, which frequent the
lower districts, when thirsty, are obliged to travel from a long distance. Hence broad and
well-beaten paths branch off in every direction from the wells down to the sea-coast;   *170*
and the Spaniards by following them up, first discovered the watering-places. When I
landed at Chatham Island, I could not imagine what animal travelled so methodically
along well-chosen tracks. Near the springs it was a curious spectacle to behold many of
these huge creatures, one set eagerly travelling onwards with outstretched necks, and
another set returning, after having drunk their fill. When the tortoise arrives at the   *175*
spring, quite regardless of any spectator, he buries his head in the water above his eyes,
and greedily swallows great mouthfuls, at the rate of about ten in a minute. The
inhabitants say each animal stays three or four days in the neighbourhood of the water,
and then returns to the lower country; but they differed respecting the frequency of these
visits. The animal probably regulates them according to the nature of the food on which   *180*
it has lived. It is, however, certain, that tortoises can subsist even on those islands,
where there is no other water than what falls during a few rainy days in the year.

   I believe it is well ascertained, that the bladder of the frog acts as a reservoir for the
moisture necessary to its existence: such seems to be the case with the tortoise. For
some time after a visit to the springs, their urinary bladders are distended with fluid,   *185*
which is said gradually to decrease in volume, and to become less pure. The inhabitants,
when walking in the lower district, and overcome with thirst, often take advantage of

---

164. austere: astringent.

this circumstance, and drink the contents of the bladder if full; in one I saw killed, the fluid was quite limpid, and had only a very slightly bitter taste. The inhabitants, however, always first drink the water in the pericardium, which is described as being *190* best.

The tortoises, when purposely moving towards any point, travel by night and day, and arrive at their journey's end much sooner than would be expected. The inhabitants, from observing marked individuals, consider that they travel a distance of about eight miles in two or three days. One large tortoise, which I watched, walked at the rate of *195* sixty yards in ten minutes, that is, three hundred and sixty yards in the hour, or four miles a day, — allowing a little time for it to eat on the road. During the breeding season, when the male and female are together, the male utters a hoarse roar or bellowing, which, it is said, can be heard at the distance of more than a hundred yards. The female never uses her voice, and the male only at these times; so that when the *200* people hear this noise, they know that the two are together. They were at this time (October) laying their eggs. The female, where the soil is sandy, deposits them together, and covers them up with sand; but where the ground is rocky she drops them indiscriminately in any hole: Mr. Bynoe found seven placed in a fissure. The egg is white and spherical; one which I measured was seven inches and three-eights in *205* circumference, and therefore larger than a hen's egg. The young tortoises, as soon as they are hatched, fall a prey in great numbers to the carrion-feeding buzzard. The old ones seem generally to die from accidents, as from falling down precipices: at least several of the inhabitants told me, that they had never found one dead without some evident cause. *210*

The inhabitants believe that these animals are absolutely deaf; certainly they do not overhear a person walking close behind them. I was always amused when overtaking one of these great monsters, as it was quietly pacing along, to see how suddenly, the instant I passed, it would draw in its head and legs, and uttering a deep hiss fall to the ground with a heavy sound, as if struck dead. I frequently got on their backs, and then *215* giving a few raps on the hinder part of their shells, they would rise up and walk away; — but I found it very difficult to keep my balance. The flesh of this animal is largely employed, both fresh and salted; and a beautifully clear oil is prepared from the fat. When a tortoise is caught, the man makes a slit in the skin near its tail, so as to see inside its body, whether the fat under the dorsal plate is thick. If it is not, the animal is *220* liberated; and it is said to recover soon from this strange operation. In order to secure the tortoises, it is not sufficient to turn them like turtle, for they are often able to get on their legs again.

There can be little doubt that this tortoise is an aboriginal inhabitant of the Galapagos; for it is found on all, or nearly all, the islands, even on some of the smaller *225* ones where there is no water; had it been an imported species, this would hardly have been the case in a group which has been so little frequented. Moreover, the old Buccaneers found this tortoise in greater numbers even than at present; Wood and Rogers also, in 1708, say that it is the opinion of the Spaniards, that it is found nowhere else in this quarter of the world. It is now widely distributed; but it may be questioned *230*

228-29. **Wood and Rogers:** likely Woodes Rogers (see p. 510).

whether it is in any other place an aboriginal. The bones of a tortoise at Mauritius, associated with those of the extinct Dodo, have generally been considered as belonging to this tortoise; if this had been so, undoubtedly it must have been there indigenous; but M. Bibron informs me that he believes that it was distinct, as the species now living there certainly is. 235

The Amblyrhynchus, a remarkable genus of lizards, is confined to this archipelago: there are two species resembling each other in general form, one being terrestrial and the other aquatic. This latter species (A. cristatus) was first characterised by Mr. Bell, who well foresaw, from its short, broad head, and strong claws of equal length, that its habits of life would turn out very peculiar, and different from those of its nearest ally, 240 the Iguana. It is extremely common on all the islands throughout the group, and lives exclusively on the rocky sea beaches, being never found, at least I never saw one, even ten yards in-shore. It is a hideous looking creature, of a dirty black colour, stupid, and sluggish in its movements. The usual length of a full-grown one is about a yard, but there are some even four feet long; a large one weighed twenty pounds: on the island of 245 Albermarle they seem to grow to a greater size than elsewhere. Their tails are flattened sideways, and all four feet partially webbed. They are occasionally seen some hundred yards from the shore, swimming about; and Captain Collnett, in his Voyage, says, "They go to sea in herds a-fishing, and sun themselves on the rocks; and may be called alligators in miniature." It must not, however, be supposed that they live on fish. When 250 in the water this lizard swims with perfect ease and quickness, by a serpentine movement of its body and flattened tail — the legs being motionless and closely collapsed on its sides. A seaman on board sank one, with a heavy weight attached to it, thinking thus to kill it directly; but when, an hour afterwards, he drew up the line, it was quite active. Their limbs and strong claws are admirably adapted for crawling over the 255 rugged and fissured masses of lava which everywhere form the coast. In such situations, a group of six or seven of these hideous reptiles may oftentimes be seen on the black rocks, a few feet above the surf, basking in the sun with out-stretched legs.

I opened the stomachs of several, and found them largely distended with minced seaweed (Ulvæ), which grows in thin foliaceous expansions of a bright green or a dull 260 red colour. I do not recollect having observed this seaweed in any quantity on the tidal rocks; and I have reason to believe it grows at the bottom of the sea, at some little distance from the coast. If such be the case, the object of these animals occasionally going out to sea is explained. The stomach contained nothing but the seaweed. Mr. Bynoe, however, found a piece of a crab in one; but this might have got in accidentally, 265 in the same manner as I have seen a caterpillar, in the midst of some lichen, in the paunch of a tortoise. The intestines were large, as in other herbivorous animals. The nature of this lizard's food, as well as the structure of its tail and feet, and the fact of its having been seen voluntarily swimming out at sea, absolutely prove its aquatic habits; yet there is in this respect one strange anomaly, namely, that when frightened it will not 270 enter the water. Hence it is easy to drive these lizards down to any little point overhanging the sea, where they will sooner allow a person to catch hold of their tails

---

238. **Bell:** Thomas Bell, former professor of zoology at the University of London, who prepared the scientific descriptions of the reptiles collected during the *Beagle* voyage. 248. **Collnett:** James Colnett (c.1755-1806), author of *A Voyage to the South Atlantic and round Cape Horn into the Pacific Ocean . . .* (1798).

than jump into the water. They do not seem to have any notion of biting; but when much frightened they squirt a drop of fluid from each nostril. I threw one several times as far as I could, into a deep pool left by the retiring tide; but it invariably returned in a direct *275* line to the spot where I stood. It swam near the bottom, with a very graceful and rapid movement, and occasionally aided itself over the uneven ground with its feet. As soon as it arrived near the edge, but still being under water, it tried to conceal itself in the tufts of seaweed, or it entered some crevice. As soon as it thought the danger was past, it crawled out on the dry rocks, and shuffled away as quickly as it could. I several times *280* caught this same lizard, by driving it down to a point, and though possessed of such perfect powers of diving and swimming, nothing would induce it to enter the water; and as often as I threw it in, it returned in the manner above described. Perhaps this singular piece of apparent stupidity may be accounted for by the circumstance, that this reptile has no enemy whatever on shore, whereas at sea it must often fall a prey to the *285* numerous sharks. Hence, probably, urged by a fixed and hereditary instinct that the shore is its place of safety, whatever the emergency may be, it there takes refuge.

During our visit (in October), I saw extremely few small individuals of this species, and none I should think under a year old. From this circumstance it seems probable that the breeding season had not then commenced. I asked several of the inhabitants if they *290* knew where it laid its eggs; they said that they knew nothing of its propagation, although well acquainted with the eggs of the land kind — a fact, considering how very common this lizard is, not a little extraordinary.

. . . .

I have not as yet noticed by far the most remarkable feature in the natural history of this archipelago; it is, that the different islands to a considerable extent are inhabited by *295* a different set of beings. My attention was first called to this fact by the Vice-Governor, Mr. Lawson, declaring that the tortoises differed from the different islands, and that he could with certainty tell from which island any one was brought. I did not for some time pay sufficient attention to this statement, and I had already partially mingled together the collections from two of the islands. I never dreamed that islands, about fifty or sixty *300* miles apart, and most of them in sight of each other, formed of precisely the same rocks, placed under a quite similar climate, rising to a nearly equal height, would have been differently tenanted; but we shall soon see that this is the case. It is the fate of most voyagers, no sooner to discover what is most interesting in any locality, than they are hurried from it; but I ought, perhaps, to be thankful that I obtained sufficient materials to *305* establish this most remarkable fact in the distribution of organic beings.

. . . .

The distribution of the tenants of this archipelago would not be nearly so wonderful, if, for instance, one island had a mocking-thrush, and a second island some other quite distinct genus; — if one island had its genus of lizard, and a second island another distinct genus, or none whatever; — or if the different islands were inhabited, not by *310* representative species of the same genera of plants, but by totally different genera, as does to a certain extent hold good; for, to give one instance, a large berry-bearing tree at James Island had no representative species in Charles Island. But it is the circumstance,

---

294. noticed: commented on.

that several of the islands possess their own species of the tortoise, mocking-thrush, finches, and numerous plants, these species having the same general habits, occupying 315 analogous situations, and obviously filling the same place in the natural economy of this archipelago, that strikes me with wonder. It may be suspected that some of these representative species, at least in the case of the tortoise and of some of the birds, may hereafter prove to be only well-marked races; but this would be of equally great interest to the philosophical naturalist. I have said that most of the islands are in sight of each 320 other; I may specify that Charles Island is fifty miles from the nearest part of Chatham Island, and thirty-three miles from the nearest part of Albemarle Island. Chatham Island is sixty miles from the nearest part of James Island, but there are two intermediate islands between them which were not visited by me. James Island is only ten miles from the part of Albemarle Island, but the two points where the collections were made are 325 thirty-two miles apart. I must repeat, that neither the nature of the soil, nor height of the land, nor the climate, nor the general character of the associated beings, and therefore their action one on another, can differ much in the different islands. If there be any sensible difference in their climates, it must be between the windward group (namely Charles and Chatham Islands), and that to leeward; but there seems to be no 330 corresponding difference in the productions of these two halves of the archipelago.

The only light which I can throw on this remarkable difference in the inhabitants of the different islands, is, that very strong currents of the sea running in a westerly and W.N.W. direction must separate, as far as transportal by the sea is concerned, the southern islands from the northern ones; and between these northern islands a strong 335 N.W. current was observed, which must effectually separate James and Albemarle Islands. As the archipelago is free to a most remarkable degree from gales of wind, neither the birds, insects, nor lighter seeds, would be blown from island to island. And lastly, the profound depth of the ocean between the islands, and their apparently recent (in a geological sense) volcanic origin, render it highly unlikely that they were ever 340 united: and this, probably, is a far more important consideration than any other, with respect to the geographical distribution of their inhabitants. Reviewing the facts here given, one is astonished at the amount of creative force, if such an expression may be used, displayed on these small, barren, and rocky islands; and still more so at its diverse yet analogous action on points so near each other. I have said that the Galapagos 345 Archipelago might be called a satellite attached to America, but it should rather be called a group of satellites, physically similar, organically distinct, yet intimately related to each other, and all related in a marked, though much lesser degree, to the great American continent.

I will conclude my description of the natural history of these islands, by giving an 350 account of the extreme tameness of the birds.

This disposition is common to all the terrestrial species; namely, to the mocking-thrushes, the finches, wrens, tyrant fly-catchers, the dove, and carrion-buzzard. All of them often approached sufficiently near to be killed with a switch, and sometimes, as I myself tried, with a cap or hat. A gun is here almost superfluous; for with the muzzle I 355

---

329. sensible: perceptible, appreciable.

pushed a hawk off the branch of a tree. One day, whilst lying down, a mocking-thrush alighted on the edge of a pitcher, made of the shell of a tortoise, which I held in my hand, and began very quietly to sip the water; it allowed me to lift it from the ground whilst seated on the vessel: I often tried, and very nearly succeeded, in catching these birds by their legs. Formerly the birds appear to have been even tamer than at present. 360
Cowley (in the year 1684) says that the "Turtle-doves were so tame, that they would often alight upon our hats and arms, so as that we could take them alive: they not fearing man, until such time as some of our company did fire at them, whereby they were rendered more shy." Dampier also, in the same year, says that a man in a morning's walk might kill six or seven dozen of these doves. At present, although certainly very 365
tame, they do not alight on people's arms, nor do they suffer themselves to be killed in such large numbers. It is surprising that they have not become wilder; for these islands during the last hundred and fifty years have been frequently visited by buccaneers and whalers; and the sailors wandering through the woods in search of tortoises, always take cruel delight in knocking down the little birds. 370

These birds, although now still more persecuted, do not readily become wild: in Charles Island, which had then been colonized about six years, I saw a boy sitting by a well with a switch in his hand, with which he killed the doves and finches as they came to drink. He had already procured a little heap of them for his dinner; and he said that he had constantly been in the habit of waiting by this well for the same purpose. It would 375
appear that the birds of this archipelago, not having as yet learnt that man is a more dangerous animal than the tortoise or the Amblyrhynchus, disregard him, in the same manner as in England shy birds, such as magpies, disregard the cows and horses grazing in our fields.

. . . .

From these several facts we may, I think, conclude, first, that the wildness of birds 380
with regard to man, is a particular instinct directed against *him*, and not dependent on any general degree of caution arising from other sources of danger; secondly, that it is not acquired by individual birds in a short time, even when much persecuted; but that in the course of successive generations it becomes hereditary. With domesticated animals we are accustomed to see new mental habits or instincts acquired and rendered 385
hereditary; but with animals in a state of nature, it must always be most difficult to discover instances of acquired hereditary knowledge. In regard to the wildness of birds towards man, there is no way of accounting for it, except as an inherited habit: comparatively few young birds, in any one year, have been injured by man in England, yet almost all, even nestlings, are afraid of him; many individuals, on the other hand, 390
both at the Galapagos and at the Falklands, have been pursued and injured by man, but yet have not learned a salutary dread of him. We may infer from these facts, what havoc the introduction of any new beast of prey must cause in a country, before the instincts of the indigenous inhabitants have become adapted to the stranger's craft or power.

(1845)

---

361. **Cowley:** possibly William Ambrosia Cowley, a 17th-century voyager. 364. **Dampier:** William Dampier; see the note to line 43 of Rogers's *A Cruising Voyage* (p. 511).

EDWARD FITZGERALD
England, 1809-1883

from *THE RUBÁIYÁT OF OMAR KHAYYÁM*

VII
Come, fill the Cup, and in the fire of Spring
Your Winter-garment of Repentance fling:
  The Bird of Time has but a little way
To flutter — and the Bird is on the Wing.

VIII
Whether at Naishápúr or Babylon,   5
Whether the Cup with sweet or bitter run,
  The Wine of Life keeps oozing drop by drop,
The Leaves of Life keep falling one by one.

XII
A Book of Verses underneath the Bough,
A Jug of Wine, a Loaf of Bread — and Thou   10
  Beside me singing in the Wilderness —
Oh, Wilderness were Paradise enow!

XIII
Some for the Glories of This World; and some
Sigh for the Prophet's Paradise to come;
  Ah, take the Cash, and let the Credit go,   15
Nor heed the rumble of a distant Drum!

XVI
The Worldly Hope men set their Hearts upon
Turns Ashes — or it prospers; and anon,
  Like Snow upon the Desert's dusty Face,
Lighting a little hour or two — is gone.   20

XVII
Think, in this battered Caravanserai
Whose Portals are alternate Night and Day,
  How Sultán after Sultán with his Pomp
Abode his destined Hour, and went his way.

(1859)

ALFRED, LORD TENNYSON
England, 1809-1892

THE KRAKEN

Below the thunders of the upper deep;
Far, far beneath in the abysmal sea,
His ancient, dreamless, uninvaded sleep
The Kraken sleepeth: faintest sunlights flee
About his shadowy sides: above him swell   5
Huge sponges of millennial growth and height;
And far away into the sickly light,
From many a wondrous grot and secret cell
Unnumbered and enormous polypi
Winnow with giant arms the slumbering green.   10
There hath he lain for ages and will lie
Battening upon huge seaworms in his sleep,
Until the latter fire shall heat the deep;
Then once by man and angels to be seen,
In roaring he shall rise and on the surface die.   15

(1830)

THE RUBÁIYÁT Title: "Rubáiyát" means "quatrains"; Omar (d. 1123) was a Persian poet and mathematician, whose soubriquet "Khayyám" (meaning "tentmaker") probably derives from his father's occupation. **5. Naishápúr:** Nishapur, Omar's birthplace. **12. enow:** enough. **14. Prophet:** Mohammed. **THE KRAKEN** Title: mythological Norwegian sea-monster; see also Revelation 13:1. **9. polypi:** hydras, octopus-like creatures. **10. winnow:** fan. **13. latter fire:** See Revelation 8:8-9; Tennyson may also have been familiar with the theological works of George Stanley Faber (1773-1854), which argued that evil, associated with the serpent (and, by extension, the sea-monster here), is the principle that led to the Flood (Genesis 7-9; see p. 247), and subsequently to God's promise that fire rather than flood would destroy the world next time (see also 2 Thessalonians 1:7-8, 2 Peter 3:6-10, Revelation 20:10).

THE LADY OF SHALOTT

Part I

On either side the river lie
Long fields of barley and of rye,
That clothe the wold and meet the sky;
And through the field the road runs by
　　To many-towered Camelot;　　　　　　*5*
And up and down the people go,
Gazing where the lilies blow
Round an island there below,
　　The island of Shalott.

Willows whiten, aspens quiver,　　　　　*10*
Little breezes dusk and shiver
Through the wave that runs for ever
By the island in the river
　　Flowing down to Camelot.
Four gray walls, and four gray towers,　　*15*
Overlook a space of flowers,
And the silent isle imbowers
　　The Lady of Shalott.

By the margin, willow-veiled,
Slide the heavy barges trailed　　　　　*20*
By slow horses; and unhailed
The shallop flitteth silken-sailed
　　Skimming down to Camelot:
But who hath seen her wave her hand?
Or at the casement seen her stand?　　　*25*
Or is she known in all the land,
　　The Lady of Shalott?

Only reapers, reaping early
In among the bearded barley,
Hear a song that echoes cheerly　　　　*30*
From the river winding clearly,
　　Down to towered Camelot:
And by the moon the reaper weary,
Piling sheaves in uplands airy,
Listening, whispers "'Tis the fairy　　　*35*
　　Lady of Shalott."

Part II

There she weaves by night and day
A magic web with colours gay.
She has heard a whisper say,
A curse is on her if she stay　　　　　*40*
　　To look down to Camelot.
She knows not what the curse may be,
And so she weaveth steadily,
And little other care hath she,
　　The Lady of Shalott.　　　　　　*45*

And moving through a mirror clear
That hangs before her all the year,
Shadows of the world appear.
There she sees the highway near
　　Winding down to Camelot:　　　　*50*
There the river eddy whirls,
And there the surly village-churls,
And the red cloaks of market girls,
　　Pass onward from Shalott.

Sometimes a troop of damsels glad,　　*55*
An abbot on an ambling pad,
Sometimes a curly shepherd-lad,
Or long-haired page in crimson clad,
　　Goes by to towered Camelot;
And sometimes through the mirror blue　*60*
The knights come riding two and two:
She hath no loyal knight and true,
　　The Lady of Shallot.

But in her web she still delights
To weave the mirror's magic sights,　　*65*
For often through the silent nights
A funeral, with plumes and lights
　　And music, went to Camelot:
Or when the moon was overhead,
Came two young lovers lately wed;　　*70*
"I am half sick of shadows," said
　　The Lady of Shalott.

THE LADY OF SHALOTT　**3. wold:** rolling field. **5. Camelot:** legendary location of King Arthur's court. **7. blow:** bloom. **30:** Cf. *Richard II*, I.iii.66 (Tennyson's note). **46. mirror:** placed in order to see from a different angle the design she is weaving; cf. Spenser's *Faerie Queene*, III, ii, stanza 17ff., which (with *FQ* I, vii, stanza 29ff.) also influenced the image of the "red-cross knight" (line 78). **56. pad:** road-horse.

Part III

A bow-shot from her bower-eaves,
He rode between the barley-sheaves,
The sun came dazzling through the leaves,   75
And flamed upon the brazen greaves
    Of bold Sir Lancelot.
A red-cross knight for ever kneeled
To a lady in his shield,
That sparkled on the yellow field,   80
    Beside remote Shalott.

The gemmy bridle glittered free,
Like to some branch of stars we see
Hung in the golden Galaxy.
The bridle bells rang merrily   85
    As he rode down to Camelot:
And from his blazoned baldric slung
A mighty silver bugle hung,
And as he rode his armour rung,
    Beside remote Shalott.   90

All in the blue unclouded weather
Thick-jewelled shone the saddle-leather,
The helmet and the helmet-feather
Burned like one burning flame together,
    As he rode down to Camelot.   95
As often through the purple night,
Below the starry clusters bright,
Some bearded meteor, trailing light,
    Moves over still Shalott.

His broad clear brow in sunlight glowed;   100
On burnished hooves his war-horse trode;
From underneath his helmet flowed
His coal-black curls as on he rode,
    As he rode down to Camelot.
From the bank and from the river   105
He flashed into the crystal mirror,
"Tirra lirra," by the river
    Sang Sir Lancelot.

She left the web, she left the loom,
She made three paces through the room,   110
She saw the water-lily bloom,
She saw the helmet and the plume,
    She looked down to Camelot.

Out flew the web and floated wide;
The mirror cracked from side to side;   115
"The curse is come upon me," cried
    The Lady of Shalott.

Part IV

In the stormy east-wind straining,
The pale yellow woods were waning,
The broad stream in his banks complaining.   120
Heavily the low sky raining
    Over towered Camelot;
Down she came and found a boat
Beneath a willow left afloat,
And round about the prow she wrote   125
    The Lady of Shalott.

And down the river's dim expanse
Like some bold seër in a trance,
Seeing all his own mischance—
With a glassy countenance   130
    Did she look to Camelot.
And at the closing of the day
She loosed the chain, and down she lay;
The broad stream bore her far away,
    The Lady of Shalott.   135

Lying, robed in snowy white
That loosely flew to left and right—
The leaves upon her falling light—
Through the noises of the night
    She floated down to Camelot: 140
And as the boat-head wound along
The willowy hills and fields among,
They heard her singing her last song,
    The Lady of Shalott.

Heard a carol, mournful, holy,   145
Chanted loudly, chanted lowly,
Till her blood was frozen slowly,
And her eyes were darkened wholly,
    Turned to towered Camelot.
For ere she reached upon the tide   150
The first house by the water-side,
Singing in her song she died,
    The Lady of Shalott.

---

76. greaves: shin armour. **87. baldric:** belt worn over the shoulder and across the chest.

Under tower and balcony,
By garden-wall and gallery,   *155*
A gleaming shape she floated by,
Dead-pale between the houses high,
    Silent into Camelot.
Out upon the wharfs they came,
Knight and burgher, lord and dame,   *160*
And round the prow they read her name,
    The Lady of Shalott.

Who is this? and what is here?
And in the lighted palace near
Died the sound of royal cheer;   *165*
And they crossed themselves for fear,
    All the knights at Camelot:
But Lancelot mused a little space;
He said, "She has a lovely face;
God in his mercy lend her grace,   *170*
    The Lady of Shalott."

          (1832, 1842)

THE LOTOS-EATERS

"Courage!" he said, and pointed toward the land,
"This mounting wave will roll us shoreward soon."
In the afternoon they came unto a land
In which it seemed always afternoon.
All round the coast the languid air did swoon,   *5*
Breathing like one that hath a weary dream.
Full-faced above the valley stood the moon;
And like a downward smoke, the slender stream
Along the cliff to fall and pause and fall did seem.
A land of streams! some, like a downward smoke,   *10*
Slow-dropping veils of thinnest lawn, did go;
And some through wavering lights and shadows broke,
Rolling a slumbrous sheet of foam below.
They saw the gleaming river seaward flow
From the inner land: far off, three mountain-tops, *15*
Three silent pinnacles of aged snow,
Stood sunset-flushed: and, dewed with showery drops,
Up-clomb the shadowy pine above the woven copse.
The charmed sunset lingered low adown

In the red West: through mountain clefts the dale   *20*
Was seen far inland, and the yellow down
Bordered with palm, and many a winding vale
And meadow, set with slender galingale;
A land where all things always seemed the same!
And round about the keel with faces pale,   *25*
Dark faces pale against that rosy flame,
The mild-eyed melancholy Lotos-eaters came.

Branches they bore of that enchanted stem,
Laden with flower and fruit, whereof they gave
To each, but whoso did receive of them,   *30*
And taste, to him the gushing of the wave
Far far away did seem to mourn and rave
On alien shores; and if his fellow spake,
His voice was thin, as voices from the grave;
And deep-asleep he seemed, yet all awake,   *35*
And music in his ears his beating heart did make.

They sat them down upon the yellow sand,
Between the sun and moon upon the shore;
And sweet it was to dream of Fatherland,
Of child, and wife, and slave; but evermore   *40*
Most weary seemed the sea, weary the oar,
Weary the wandering fields of barren foam.
Then some one said, "We will return no more";
And all at once they sang, "Our island home
Is far beyond the wave; we will no longer roam."   *45*

CHORIC SONG

I

There is sweet music here that softer falls
Than petals from blown roses on the grass,
Or night-dews on still waters between walls
Of shadowy granite, in a gleaming pass;
Music that gentlier on the spirit lies,   *50*
Than tired eyelids upon tired eyes;
Music that brings sweet sleep down from the
    blissful skies.
Here are cool mosses deep,
And through the moss the ivies creep,
And in the stream the long-leaved flowers weep,   *55*
And from the craggy ledge the poppy hangs in sleep.

THE LOTOS-EATERS See Homer's *Odyssey*, IX, 82-104, and the excerpt from Pope's version (p. 537); for other influences see Spenser's *Faerie Queene*, I, i, stanza 41 (p. 158); II, vi, stanzas 1-26; and II, xii, stanza 32. **1. he:** Odysseus **11. lawn:** fine fabric. **23. galingale:** a tall sedge. **24:** Cf. "eadem sunt omnia semper," *De Rerum Natura* (*On the Nature of Things*), III, 945, by the 1st-century B.C. Roman poet Lucretius. **44. island home:** Ithaca. **51. tired:** Tennyson comments that he intended "making the word neither monosyllabic nor disyllabic, but a dreamy child of the two."

II

Why are we weighed upon with heaviness,
And utterly consumed with sharp distress,
While all things else have rest from weariness?
All things have rest: why should we toil alone,   60
We only toil, who are the first of things,
And make perpetual moan,
Still from one sorrow to another thrown:
Nor ever fold our wings,
And cease from wanderings,   65
Nor steep our brows in slumber's holy balm;
Nor harken what the inner spirit sings,
"There is no joy but calm!"
Why should we only toil, the roof and crown of things?

III

Lo! in the middle of the wood,   70
The folded leaf is wooed from out the bud
With winds upon the branch, and there
Grows green and broad, and takes no care,
Sun-steeped at noon, and in the moon
Nightly dew-fed; and turning yellow   75
Falls, and floats adown the air.
Lo! sweetened with the summer light,
The full-juiced apple, waxing over-mellow,
Drops in a silent autumn night.
All its allotted length of days,   80
The flower ripens in its place,
Ripens and fades, and falls, and hath no toil,
Fast-rooted in the fruitful soil.

IV

Hateful is the dark-blue sky,
Vaulted o'er the dark-blue sea.   85
Death is the end of life; ah, why
Should life all labour be?
Let us alone. Time driveth onward fast,
And in a little while our lips are dumb.
Let us alone. What is it that will last?   90
All things are taken from us, and become
Portions and parcels of the dreadful Past.
Let us alone. What pleasure can we have

To war with evil? Is there any peace
In ever climbing up the climbing wave?   95
All things have rest, and ripen toward the grave
In silence; ripen, fall and cease:
Give us long rest or death, dark death, or dreamful ease.

V

How sweet it were, hearing the downward stream,
With half-shut eyes ever to seem   100
Falling asleep in a half-dream!
To dream and dream, like yonder amber light,
Which will not leave the myrrh-bush on the height;
To hear each other's whispered speech;
Eating the Lotos day by day,   105
To watch the crisping ripples on the beach,
And tender curving lines of creamy spray;
To lend our hearts and spirits wholly
To the influence of mild-minded melancholy;
To muse and brood and live again in memory,   110
With those old faces of our infancy
Heaped over with a mound of grass,
Two handfuls of white dust, shut in an urn of brass!

VI

Dear is the memory of our wedded lives,
And dear the last embraces of our wives   115
And their warm tears: but all hath suffered change:
For surely now our household hearths are cold:
Our sons inherit us: our looks are strange:
And we should come like ghosts to trouble joy.
Or else the island princes over-bold   120
Have eat our substance, and the minstrel sings
Before them of the ten years' war in Troy,
And our great deeds, as half-forgotten things.
Is there confusion in the little isle?
Let what is broken so remain.   125
The Gods are hard to reconcile:
'Tis hard to settle order once again.
There *is* confusion worse than death,
Trouble on trouble, pain on pain,
Long labour unto aged breath,   130
Sore task to hearts worn out by many wars
And eyes grown dim with gazing on the pilot-stars.

---

70. in the middle of the wood: Cf. Dante's *Inferno*, I, 1-2. **80. length of days:** See Psalms 21:4. **106. crisping:** curling. **120-21:** Penelope's suitors.

VII

But, propt on beds of amaranth and moly,
How sweet (while warm airs lull us, blowing lowly)
With half-dropt eyelid still,   *135*
Beneath a heaven dark and holy,
To watch the long bright river drawing slowly
His waters from the purple hill —
To hear the dewy echoes calling
From cave to cave through the thick-twined vine —
To watch the emerald-coloured water falling   *141*
Through many a woven acanthus-wreath divine!
Only to hear and see the far-off sparkling brine,
Only to hear were sweet, stretched out beneath the pine.

VIII

The Lotos blooms below the barren peak: *145*
The Lotos blows by every winding creek:
All day the wind breathes low with mellower tone:
Through every hollow cave and alley lone
Round and round the spicy downs the yellow
    Lotos-dust is blown.
We have had enough of action, and of motion we, *150*
Rolled to starboard, rolled to larboard, when the
    surge was seething free,
Where the wallowing monster spouted his
    foam-fountains in the sea.
Let us swear an oath, and keep it with an equal mind,
In the hollow Lotos-land to live and lie reclined *154*
On the hills like Gods together, careless of mankind.
For they lie beside their nectar, and the bolts are hurled
Far below them in the valleys, and the clouds are
    lightly curled
Round their golden houses, girdled with the
    gleaming world:
Where they smile in secret, looking over wasted lands,
Blight and famine, plague and earthquake,
    roaring deeps and fiery sands,   *160*
Clanging fights, and flaming towns, and sinking
    ships, and praying hands.
But they smile, they find a music centred in a
    doleful song
Steaming up, a lamentation and an ancient tale
    of wrong,

Like a tale of little meaning though the words
    are strong;
Chanted from an ill-used race of men that cleave
    the soil,   *165*
Sow the seed, and reap the harvest with enduring toil,
Storing yearly little dues of wheat, and wine and oil;
Till they perish and they suffer — some, 'tis whis-
    pered — down in hell
Suffer endless anguish, others in Elysian valleys dwell,
Resting weary limbs at last on beds of asphodel. *170*
Surely, surely, slumber is more sweet than toil,
    the shore
Than labour in the deep mid-ocean, wind and wave
    and oar;
Oh rest ye, brother mariners, we will not wander more.

(1832, 1842)

ULYSSES

It little profits that an idle king,
By this still hearth, among these barren crags,
Matched with an aged wife, I mete and dole
Unequal laws unto a savage race,
That hoard, and sleep, and feed, and know not me.   *5*

I cannot rest from travel: I will drink
Life to the lees: all times I have enjoyed
Greatly, have suffered greatly, both with those
That loved me, and alone; on shore, and when
Through scudding drifts the rainy Hyades   *10*
Vext the dim sea: I am become a name;

For always roaming with a hungry heart
Much have I seen and known; cities of men
And manners, climates, councils, governments,
Myself not least, but honoured of them all;   *15*
And drunk delight of battle with my peers,
Far on the ringing plains of windy Troy.

I am a part of all that I have met;
Yet all experience is an arch wherethrough
Gleams that untravelled world, whose margin fades *20*
For ever and for ever when I move.
How dull it is to pause, to make an end,
To rust unburnished, not to shine in use!
As though to breathe were life. Life piled on life

---

133. amaranth and moly: Tennyson called them "the immortal flower of legend" and "the sacred herb of mystical power, used as a charm by Odysseus against Circe," respectively; cf. *Paradise Lost*, III, 352, and *Odyssey*, X, 287ff. **142. acanthus:** tropical shrub, whose ornate leaf is symbolically associated with heaven. **155. Gods:** the Epicurean gods, as depicted in Lucretius's *De Rerum Natura*, III, 18-22. **170. asphodel:** lily-like flower, sacred to Persephone, associated with the Elysian fields. **ULYSSES** See Homer's *Odyssey*, XI, 100-37, and Dante's *Inferno*, XXVI, 90-142. **4. unequal:** i.e., not affecting all in the same way. **5:** Cf. *Hamlet*, IV.iv.33-39. **10-11:** Cf. Horace's *Odes*, IV, xiv, 21-22, and Virgil's *Aeneid*, I, 744 (Tennyson's note); the appearance of the Hyades, a five-star cluster in the constellation Taurus, was thought to foretell rain. **11. Vext:** agitated, disturbed.

Were all too little, and of one to me   25
Little remains: but every hour is saved
From that eternal silence, something more,
A bringer of new things; and vile it were
For some three suns to store and hoard myself,
And this gray spirit yearning in desire   30
To follow knowledge like a sinking star,
Beyond the utmost bound of human thought.

This is my son, mine own Telemachus,
To whom I leave the sceptre and the isle —
Well-loved of me, discerning to fulfil   35
This labour, by slow prudence to make mild
A rugged people, and through soft degrees
Subdue them to the useful and the good.
Most blameless is he, centred in the sphere
Of common duties, decent not to fail   40
In offices of tenderness, and pay
Meet adoration to my household gods,
When I am gone. He works his work, I mine.

There lies the port; the vessel puffs her sail:
There gloom the dark broad seas. My mariners,   45
Souls that have toiled, and wrought, and thought with me —
That ever with a frolic welcome took
The thunder and the sunshine, and opposed
Free hearts, free foreheads — you and I are old;
Old age hath yet his honour and his toil;   50
Death closes all: but something ere the end,
Some work of noble note, may yet be done,
Not unbecoming men that strove with Gods.
The lights begin to twinkle from the rocks:
The long day wanes: the slow moon climbs: the deep   55
Moans round with many voices. Come, my friends,
'Tis not too late to seek a newer world.
Push off, and sitting well in order smite
The sounding furrows; for my purpose holds
To sail beyond the sunset, and the baths   60
Of all the western stars, until I die.
It may be that the gulfs will wash us down:
It may be we shall touch the Happy Isles,
And see the great Achilles, whom we knew.
Though much is taken, much abides; and though   65
We are not now that strength which in old days
Moved earth and heaven; that which we are, we are;

One equal temper of heroic hearts,
Made weak by time and fate, but strong in will
To strive, to seek, to find, and not to yield.   70

(1842)

MORTE D'ARTHUR

So all day long the noise of battle rolled
Among the mountains by the winter sea;
Until King Arthur's table, man by man,
Had fallen in Lyonnesse about their Lord,
King Arthur: then, because his wound was deep,   5
The bold Sir Bedivere uplifted him,
Sir Bedivere, the last of all his knights,
And bore him to a chapel nigh the field,
A broken chancel with a broken cross,
That stood on a dark strait of barren land.   10
On one side lay the Ocean, and on one
Lay a great water, and the moon was full.

Then spake King Arthur to Sir Bedivere:
"The sequel of today unsolders all
The goodliest fellowship of famous knights   15
Whereof this world holds record. Such a sleep
They sleep — the men I loved. I think that we
Shall never more, at any future time,
Delight our souls with talk of knightly deeds,
Walking about the gardens and the halls   20
Of Camelot, as in the days that were.
I perish by this people which I made, —
Though Merlin sware that I should come again
To rule once more — but let what will be, be,
I am so deeply smitten through the helm   25
That without help I cannot last till morn.
Thou therefore take my brand Excalibur,
Which was my pride: for thou rememberest how
In those old days, one summer noon, an arm
Rose up from out the bosom of the lake,   30
Clothed in white samite, mystic, wonderful,
Holding the sword — and how I rowed across
And took it, and have worn it, like a king:
And, wheresoever I am sung or told
In aftertime, this also shall be known: 35

---

29. **suns:** years. 63. **Happy Isles:** the Isles of the Blest, or Fortunate Isles (where heroes dwelt after death); according to myth, they lay beyond the Pillars of Hercules (the mountains on the two sides of the Straits of Gibraltar), which is where, in Dante's *Inferno*, Ulysses urges his fellow sailors to sail.   **MORTE D'ARTHUR**   Basing this poem on Malory's *Le Morte Darthur*, 21, 3-5 (see p. 94), Tennyson later extended it, renamed it "The Passing of Arthur," and incorporated it in *Idylls of the King* (1869). 1. **battle:** the final battle between Arthur and the forces opposed to him, led by his nephew Mordred. 4. **Lyonnesse:** Tennyson calls it "the country of legend that lay between Cornwall and the Scilly Islands," which the myth says now lies under water. 31. **samite:** silk fabric, often interwoven with silver or gold threads.

But now delay not: take Excalibur,
And fling him far into the middle mere:
Watch what thou seest, and lightly bring me word."

To him replied the bold Sir Bedivere:
"It is not meet, Sir King, to leave thee thus,   40
Aidless, alone, and smitten through the helm.
A little thing may harm a wounded man.
Yet I thy hest will all perform at full,
Watch what I see, and lightly bring thee word."

So saying, from the ruined shrine he stept   45
And in the moon athwart the place of tombs,
Where lay the mighty bones of ancient men,
Old knights, and over them the sea-wind sang
Shrill, chill, with flakes of foam. He, stepping down
By zig-zag paths, and juts of pointed rock,   50
Came on the shining levels of the lake.

There drew he forth the brand Excalibur,
And o'er him, drawing it, the winter moon,
Brightening the skirts of a long cloud, ran forth
And sparkled keen with frost against the hilt: 55
For all the haft twinkled with diamond sparks,
Myriads of topaz-lights, and jacinth-work
Of subtlest jewellery. He gazed so long
That both his eyes were dazzled, as he stood,
This way and that dividing the swift mind,   60
In act to throw: but at the last it seemed
Better to leave Excalibur concealed
There in the many-knotted waterflags,
That whistled stiff and dry about the marge.
So strode he back slow to the wounded King.   65

Then spake King Arthur to Sir Bedivere:
"Hast thou performed my mission which I gave?
What is it thou hast seen? or what hast heard?"

And answer made the bold Sir Bedivere:
"I heard the ripple washing in the reeds,   70
And the wild water lapping on the crag."

To whom replied King Arthur, faint and pale:
"Thou hast betrayed thy nature and thy name,
Not rendering true answer, as beseemed
Thy fealty, nor like a noble knight: 75
For surer sign had followed, either hand,
Or voice, or else a motion of the mere.
This is a shameful thing for men to lie.
Yet now, I charge thee, quickly go again

As thou art lief and dear, and do the thing   80
I bad thee, watch, and lightly bring me word."

Then went Sir Bedivere the second time
Across the ridge, and paced beside the mere,
Counting the dewy pebbles, fixed in thought;
But when he saw the wonder of the hilt,   85
How curiously and strangely chased, he smote
His palms together, and he cried aloud,

"And if indeed I cast the brand away,
Surely a precious thing, one worthy note,
Should thus be lost for ever from the earth,   90
Which might have pleased the eyes of many men.
What good should follow this, if this were done?
What harm, undone? deep harm to disobey,
Seeing obedience is the bond of rule.
Were it well to obey then, if a king demand   95
An act unprofitable, against himself?
The King is sick, and knows not what he does.
What record, or what relic of my lord
Should be to aftertime, but empty breath
And rumours of a doubt? but were this kept,   100
Stored in some treasure-house of mighty kings,
Some one might show it at a joust of arms,
Saying, 'King Arthur's sword, Excalibur,
Wrought by the lonely maiden of the Lake.
Nine years she wrought it, sitting in the deeps   105
Upon the hidden bases of the hills.'
So might some old man speak in the aftertime
To all the people, winning reverence.
But now much honour and much fame were lost."

So spake he, clouded with his own conceit,   110
And hid Excalibur the second time,
And so strode back slow to the wounded King.

Then spoke King Arthur, breathing heavily:
"What is it thou hast seen? or what hast heard?"

And answer made the bold Sir Bedivere: 115
"I heard the water lapping on the crag,
And the long ripple washing in the reeds."

To whom replied King Arthur, much in wrath:
"Ah, miserable and unkind, untrue,
Unknightly, traitor-hearted! Woe is me!   120
Authority forgets a dying king,
Laid widowed of the power in his eye
That bowed the will. I see thee what thou art,

---

37. mere: lake. **38. lightly:** quickly. **57. jacinth:** a form of zircon; cf. Revelation 21:19-20. **60:** Cf. Virgil's *Aeneid*, IV, 285, and Homer's *Iliad*, I, 188-89 (Tennyson's note). **80. lief:** beloved. **86. chased:** ornamented, engraved. **110. conceit:** fanciful idea.

For thou, the latest-left of all my knights,
In whom should meet the offices of all,   *125*
Thou wouldst betray me for the precious hilt;
Either from lust of gold, or like a girl
Valuing the giddy pleasure of the eyes.
Yet, for a man may fail in duty twice,
And the third time may prosper, get thee hence: *130*
But, if thou spare to fling Excalibur,
I will arise and slay thee with my hands."

  Then quickly rose Sir Bedivere, and ran,
And, leaping down the ridges lightly, plunged
Among the bulrush-beds, and clutched the sword,   *135*
And strongly wheeled and threw it. The great brand
Made lightnings in the splendour of the moon,
And flashing round and round, and whirled in an arch,
Shot like a streamer of the northern morn,
Seen where the moving isles of winter shock   *140*
By night, with noises of the northern sea.
So flashed and fell the brand Excalibur:
But ere he dipt the surface, rose an arm
Clothed in white samite, mystic, wonderful,
And caught him by the hilt, and brandished him   *145*
Three times, and drew him under in the mere.
And lightly went the other to the King.

  Then spoke King Arthur, drawing thicker breath:
"Now see I by thine eyes that this is done.
Speak out: what is it thou hast heard, or seen?"   *150*

  And answer made the bold Sir Bedivere:
"Sir King, I closed mine eyelids, lest the gems
Should blind my purpose, for I never saw,
Nor shall see, here or elsewhere, till I die,
Not though I live three lives of mortal men,   *155*
So great a miracle as yonder hilt.
Then with both hands I flung him, wheeling him;
But when I looked again, behold an arm,
Clothed in white samite, mystic, wonderful,
That caught him by the hilt, and brandished him   *160*
Three times, and drew him under in the mere."

  And answer made King Arthur, breathing hard:
"My end draws nigh; 'tis time that I were gone.
Make broad thy shoulders to receive my weight,
And bear me to the margin; yet I fear   *165*
My wound hath taken cold, and I shall die."

  So saying, from the pavement he half rose,
Slowly, with pain, reclining on his arm,

And looking wistfully with wide blue eyes
As in a picture. Him Sir Bedivere   *170*
Remorsefully regarded through his tears,
And would have spoken, but he found not words,
Then took with care, and kneeling on one knee,
O'er both his shoulders drew the languid hands,
And rising bore him through the place of tombs.   *175*

  But, as he walked, King Arthur panted hard,
Like one that feels a nightmare on his bed
When all the house is mute. So sighed the King,
Muttering and murmuring at his ear, "Quick, quick!
I fear it is too late, and I shall die."   *180*
But the other swiftly strode from ridge to ridge,
Clothed with his breath, and looking, as he walked,
Larger than human on the frozen hills.
He heard the deep behind him, and a cry
Before. His own thought drove him, like a goad.   *185*
Dry clashed his harness in the icy caves
And barren chasms, and all to left and right
The bare black cliff clanged round him, as he based
His feet on juts of slippery crag that rang
Sharp-smitten with the dint of armed heels —   *190*
And on a sudden, lo! the level lake,
And the long glories of the winter moon.

  Then saw they how there hove a dusky barge,
Dark as a funeral scarf from stem to stern,
Beneath them; and descending they were ware   *195*
That all the decks were dense with stately forms
Black-stoled, black-hooded, like a dream — by these
Three Queens with crowns of gold — and from them rose
A cry that shivered to the tingling stars,
And, as it were one voice, an agony   *200*
Of lamentation, like a wind, that shrills
All night in a waste land, where no one comes,
Or hath come, since the making of the world.

  Then murmured Arthur, "Place me in the barge,"
And to the barge they came. There those three Queens
Put forth their hands, and took the King, and wept. *206*
But she, that rose the tallest of them all
And fairest, laid his head upon her lap,
And loosed the shattered casque, and chafed his hands,
And called him by his name, complaining loud,   *210*
And dropping bitter tears against his brow
Striped with dark blood: for all his face was white
And colourless, and like the withered moon

---

139. streamer . . . morn: aurora borealis. **140. moving isles of winter:** icebergs. **155:** Cf. Homer's *Odyssey*, III, 245 (Tennyson's note). **186. Dry:** hard (i.e., with force). **209. casque:** helmet. **210. complaining:** lamenting.

Smote by the fresh beam of the springing east;
And all his greaves and cuisses dashed with drops   *215*
Of onset; and the light and lustrous curls —
That made his forehead like a rising sun
High from the dais-throne — were parched with dust;
Or, clotted into points and hanging loose,
Mixed with the knightly growth that fringed his lips.
So like a shattered column lay the King;   *221*
Not like that Arthur who, with lance in rest,
From spur to plume a star of tournament,
Shot through the lists at Camelot, and charged
Before the eyes of ladies and of kings.   *225*

    Then loudly cried the bold Sir Bedivere,
"Ah! my Lord Arthur, whither shall I go?
Where shall I hide my forehead and my eyes?
For now I see the true old times are dead,
When every morning brought a noble chance,   *230*
And every chance brought out a noble knight.
Such times have been not since the light that led
The holy Elders with the gift of myrrh.
But now the whole ROUND TABLE is dissolved
Which was an image of the mighty world;   *235*
And I, the last, go forth companionless,
And the days darken round me, and the years,
Among new men, strange faces, other minds."

    And slowly answered Arthur from the barge:
"The old order changeth, yielding place to new,   *240*
And God fulfils Himself in many ways,
Lest one good custom should corrupt the world.
Comfort thyself: what comfort is in me?
I have lived my life, and that which I have done
May He within Himself make pure! but thou,   *245*
If thou shouldst never see my face again,
Pray for my soul. More things are wrought by prayer
Than this world dreams of. Wherefore, let thy voice
Rise like a fountain for me night and day.
For what are men better than sheep or goats   *250*
That nourish a blind life within the brain,
If, knowing God, they lift not hands of prayer
Both for themselves and those who call them friend?

For so the whole round earth is every way
Bound by gold chains about the feet of God.   *255*
But now farewell. I am going a long way
With these thou seest — if indeed I go —
(For all my mind is clouded with a doubt)
To the island-valley of Avilion;
Where falls not hail, or rain, or any snow,   *260*
Nor ever wind blows loudly; but it lies
Deep-meadowed, happy, fair with orchard-lawns
And bowery hollows crowned with summer sea,
Where I will heal me of my grievous wound."

    So said he, and the barge with oar and sail   *265*
Moved from the brink, like some full-breasted swan
That, fluting a wild carol ere her death,
Ruffles her pure cold plume, and takes the flood
With swarthy webs. Long stood Sir Bedivere
Revolving many memories, till the hull   *270*
Looked one black dot against the verge of dawn,
And on the mere the wailing died away.

                                  (1842)

"BREAK, BREAK, BREAK"

Break, break, break,
  On thy cold gray stones, O Sea!
And I would that my tongue could utter
  The thoughts that arise in me.

O well for the fisherman's boy,   *5*
  That he shouts with his sister at play!
O well for the sailor lad,
  That he sings in his boat on the bay!

And the stately ships go on
  To their haven under the hill;   *10*
But O for the touch of a vanished hand,
  And the sound of a voice that is still!

Break, break, break,
  At the foot of thy crags, O Sea!
But the tender grace of a day that is dead   *15*
  Will never come back to me.

                  (1842)

---

215. greaves and cuisses: shin and thigh armour; **drops:** i.e., of blood. **232-33:** i.e., the star that led the Three Kings to the Christ child; see Matthew 2:1-2,11. **242:** "e.g., chivalry, by formalism of habit or by any other means" (Tennyson's note). **255. gold chains:** Cf. *Paradise Lost*, II, 1051 (p. 348). **259. Avilion:** Avalon, the Celtic name for the Isles of the Blest. **260-63:** Cf. Homer's *Odyssey*, IV, 566; X, 195; and Lucretius's *De Rerum Natura*, III, 18 (Tennyson's note).

Songs from *THE PRINCESS*

"TEARS, IDLE TEARS"

Tears, idle tears, I know not what they mean,
Tears from the depth of some divine despair
Rise in the heart, and gather to the eyes,
In looking on the happy Autumn-fields,
And thinking of the days that are no more.   5

Fresh as the first beam glittering on a sail,
That brings our friends up from the underworld,
Sad as the last which reddens over one
That sinks with all we love below the verge;
So sad, so fresh, the days that are no more.   10

Ah, sad and strange as in dark summer dawns
The earliest pipe of half-awakened birds
To dying ears, when unto dying eyes
The casement slowly grows a glimmering square;
So sad, so strange, the days that are no more.   15

Dear as remembered kisses after death,
And sweet as those by hopeless fancy feigned
On lips that are for others; deep as love,
Deep as first love, and wild with all regret;
O Death in Life, the days that are no more.   20

(1847)

"SWEET AND LOW"

Sweet and low, sweet and low,
    Wind of the western sea,
Low, low, breathe and blow,
    Wind of the western sea!
Over the rolling waters go,   5
Come from the dying moon, and blow,
    Blow him again to me;
While my little one, while my pretty one, sleeps.

Sleep and rest, sleep and rest,
    Father will come to thee soon;   10
Rest, rest, on mother's breast,

Father will come to thee soon;
Father will come to his babe in the nest,
Silver sails all out of the west
    Under the silver moon: 15
Sleep, my little one, sleep, my pretty one, sleep.

(1850)

from *IN MEMORIAM A.H.H.*

[Prologue]

Strong Son of God, immortal Love,
    Whom we, that have not seen thy face,
    By faith, and faith alone, embrace,
Believing where we cannot prove;

Thine are these orbs of light and shade;   5
    Thou madest Life in man and brute;
    Thou madest Death; and lo, thy foot
Is on the skull which thou hast made.

Thou wilt not leave us in the dust:
    Thou madest man, he knows not why,   10
    He thinks he was not made to die;
And thou hast made him: thou art just.

Thou seemest human and divine,
    The highest, holiest manhood, thou:
    Our wills are ours, we know not how;   15
Our wills are ours, to make them thine.

Our little systems have their day;
    They have their day and cease to be:
    They are but broken lights of thee,
And thou, O Lord, art more than they.   20

We have but faith: we cannot know;
    For knowledge is of things we see;
    And yet we trust it comes from thee,
A beam in darkness: let it grow.

Let knowledge grow from more to more,   25
    But more of reverence in us dwell;
    That mind and soul, according well,
May make one music as before,

SWEET AND LOW   A familiar musical setting for this lullaby was composed by Sir Joseph Barnby (1838-1896).   **IN MEMORIAM A.H.H.**   The poem, composed between 1833 and 1849, is an elegy for the English poet Arthur Henry Hallam (1811-1833), Tennyson's close friend and his sister Emilia's fiancé, who died suddenly in Vienna of a stroke; the "Prologue" was the last section completed.   **PROLOGUE 1. immortal Love:** Cf. 1 John 4 (Tennyson's note); another possible influence is George Herbert's "Love" (p. 290). **2-3:** See 1 Peter 1:8. **5. orbs:** sun and moon (Tennyson's note). **9.** Cf. Psalms 16:10. **17-19:** Cf. 1 Corinthians 13:9-12. **22:** Here, as elsewhere in the poem (e.g., sections LVI and XCVIII), Tennyson is influenced by a work he read in 1837, *Principles of Geology* (1830-33), by Sir Charles Lyell (1797-1875); along with Darwin (see p. 945), Lyell helped shape scientific thought in the 19th century, suggesting evolutionary models of changes in nature.

But vaster. We are fools and slight;
  We mock thee when we do not fear: *30*
  But help thy foolish ones to bear;
Help thy vain worlds to bear thy light.

Forgive what seemed my sin in me;
  What seemed my worth since I began;
  For merit lives from man to man,   *35*
And not from man, O Lord, to thee.

Forgive my grief for one removed,
  Thy creature, whom I found so fair.
  I trust he lives in thee, and there
I find him worthier to be loved.   *40*

Forgive these wild and wandering cries,
  Confusions of a wasted youth;
  Forgive them where they fail in truth,
And in thy wisdom make me wise.

V

I sometimes hold it half a sin
  To put in words the grief I feel;
  For words, like Nature, half reveal
And half conceal the Soul within.

But, for the unquiet heart and brain,   *5*
  A use in measured language lies;
  The sad mechanic exercise,
Like dull narcotics, numbing pain.

In words, like weeds, I'll wrap me o'er,
  Like coarsest clothes against the cold: *10*
  But that large grief which these enfold
Is given in outline and no more.

XXI

I sing to him that rests below,
  And, since the grasses round me wave,
  I take the grasses of the grave,
And make them pipes whereon to blow.

The traveller hears me now and then,   *5*
  And sometimes harshly will he speak:
  "This fellow would make weakness weak,
And melt the waxen hearts of men."

Another answers, "Let him be,
  He loves to make parade of pain,   *10*
  That with his piping he may gain
The praise that comes to constancy."

A third is wroth: "Is this an hour
  For private sorrow's barren song,
  When more and more the people throng   *15*
The chairs and thrones of civil power?

"A time to sicken and to swoon,
  When Science reaches forth her arms
  To feel from world to world, and charms
Her secret from the latest moon?"   *20*

Behold, ye speak an idle thing:
  Ye never knew the sacred dust:
  I do but sing because I must,
And pipe but as the linnets sing:

And one is glad; her note is gay,   *25*
  For now her little ones have ranged;
  And one is sad: her note is changed,
Because her brood is stolen away.

XXVII

I envy not in any moods
  The captive void of noble rage,
  The linnet born within the cage,
That never knew the summer woods:

I envy not the beast that takes   *5*
  His license in the field of time,
  Unfettered by the sense of crime,
To whom a conscience never wakes;

Nor, what may count itself as blest,
  The heart that never plighted troth   *10*
  But stagnates in the weeds of sloth;
Nor any want-begotten rest.

I hold it true, whate'er befall;
  I feel it, when I sorrow most;
  'Tis better to have loved and lost   *15*
Than never to have loved at all.

---

42. wasted: desolated, devastated, as by grief.   **V 9. weeds:** garments (cf. "widow's weeds").   **XXI 1. rests below:** Hallam was buried in the family vault at Clevedon, in Somerset. **15-16:** probably referring to the riots that were linked to the Chartist Movement (1838-48), and through them back to the French Revolution; Chartism — named for the "People's Charter" devised by Francis Place (1771-1854) and others — called for universal manhood suffrage and other political reforms when the Reform Law of 1832 failed to extend the vote to working men. **20. latest moon:** perhaps Neptune and its larger moon, Triton, which were discovered in 1846, though this part of the poem was likely composed before that date.

XLV

The baby new to earth and sky,
 What time his tender palm is prest
 Against the circle of the breast,
Has never thought that "this is I":

But as he grows he gathers much,   5
 And learns the use of "I," and "me,"
 And finds "I am not what I see,
And other than the things I touch."

So rounds he to a separate mind
 From whence clear memory may begin,   10
 As through the frame that binds him in
His isolation grows defined.

This use may lie in blood and breath,
 Which else were fruitless of their due,
 Had man to learn himself anew   15
Beyond the second birth of Death.

XLVIII

If these brief lays, of Sorrow born,
 Were taken to be such as closed
 Grave doubts and answers here proposed,
Then these were such as men might scorn:

Her care is not to part and prove;   5
 She takes, when harsher moods remit,
 What slender shade of doubt may flit,
And makes its vassal unto love:

And hence, indeed, she sports with words,
 But better serves a wholesome law,   10
 And holds it sin and shame to draw
The deepest measure from the chords:

Nor dare she trust a larger lay,
 But rather loosens from the lip
 Short swallow-flights of song, that dip   15
Their wings in tears, and skim away.

LIV

Oh yet we trust that somehow good
 Will be the final goal of ill,
 To pangs of nature, sins of will,
Defects of doubt, and taints of blood;

That nothing walks with aimless feet;   5
 That not one life shall be destroyed,
 Or cast as rubbish to the void,
When God hath made the pile complete;

That not a worm is cloven in vain;
 That not a moth with vain desire   10
 Is shrivelled in a fruitless fire,
Or but subserves another's gain.

Behold, we know not anything;
 I can but trust that good shall fall
 At last — far off — at last, to all,   15
And every winter change to spring.

So runs my dream: but what am I?
 An infant crying in the night:
 An infant crying for the light:
And with no language but a cry.   20

LV

The wish, that of the living whole
 No life may fail beyond the grave,
 Derives it not from what we have
The likest God within the soul?

Are God and Nature then at strife,   5
 That Nature lends such evil dreams?
 So careful of the type she seems,
So careless of the single life;

That I, considering everywhere
 Her secret meaning in her deeds,   10
 And finding that of fifty seeds
She often brings but one to bear,

I falter where I firmly trod,
 And falling with my weight of cares
 Upon the great world's altar-stairs   15
That slope through darkness up to God,

I stretch lame hands of faith, and grope,
 And gather dust and chaff, and call
 To what I feel is Lord of all,
And faintly trust the larger hope.   20

LVI

"So careful of the type?" but no.
 From scarped cliff and quarried stone
 She cries, "A thousand types are gone:
I care for nothing, all shall go.

LIV   **18. infant:** from the Latin *infans*, meaning "unable to speak"; cf. Jeremiah 1:6.   **LV**   **4:** "The inner consciousness — the divine in men" (Tennyson's note).

"Thou makest thine appeal to me: *5*
    I bring to life, I bring to death:
    The spirit does but mean the breath:
I know no more." And he, shall he,

Man, her last work, who seemed so fair,
    Such splendid purpose in his eyes, *10*
    Who rolled the psalm to wintry skies,
Who built him fanes of fruitless prayer,

Who trusted God was love indeed
    And love Creation's final law —
    Though Nature, red in tooth and claw *15*
With ravine, shrieked against his creed —

Who loved, who suffered countless ills,
    Who battled for the True, the Just,
    Be blown about the desert dust,
Or sealed within the iron hills? *20*

No more? A monster then, a dream,
    A discord. Dragons of the prime,
    That tare each other in their slime,
Were mellow music matched with him.

O life as futile, then, as frail! *25*
    O for thy voice to soothe and bless!
    What hope of answer, or redress?
Behind the veil, behind the veil.

LXXXVIII

Wild bird, whose warble, liquid sweet,
    Rings Eden through the budded quicks,
    O tell me where the senses mix,
O tell me where the passions meet,

Whence radiate: fierce extremes employ *5*
    Thy spirits in the darkening leaf,
    And in the midmost heart of grief
Thy passion clasps a secret joy:

And I — my harp would prelude woe —
    I cannot all command the strings; *10*
    The glory of the sum of things
Will flash along the chords and go.

XCV

By night we lingered on the lawn,
    For underfoot the herb was dry;
    And genial warmth; and o'er the sky
The silvery haze of summer drawn;

And calm that let the tapers burn *5*
    Unwavering: not a cricket chirred:
    The brook alone far-off was heard,
And on the board the fluttering urn:

And bats went round in fragrant skies,
    And wheeled or lit the filmy shapes *10*
    That haunt the dusk, with ermine capes
And woolly breasts and beaded eyes;

While now we sang old songs that pealed
    From knoll to knoll, where, couched at ease,
    The white kine glimmered, and the trees *15*
Laid their dark arms about the field.

But when those others, one by one,
    Withdrew themselves from me and night,
    And in the house light after light
Went out, and I was all alone, *20*

A hunger seized my heart; I read
    Of that glad year which once had been,
    In those fallen leaves which kept their green,
The noble letters of the dead:

And strangely on the silence broke *25*
    The silent-speaking words, and strange
    Was love's dumb cry defying change
To test his worth; and strangely spoke

The faith, the vigour, bold to dwell
    On doubts that drive the coward back, *30*
    And keen through wordy snares to track
Suggestion to her inmost cell.

So word by word, and line by line,
    The dead man touched me from the past,
    And all at once it seemed at last *35*
The living soul was flashed on mine,

And mine in this was wound, and whirled
    About empyreal heights of thought,
    And came on that which is, and caught
The deep pulsations of the world, *40*

Æonian music measuring out
    The steps of Time — the shocks of Chance —
    The blows of Death. At length my trance
Was cancelled, stricken through with doubt.

Vague words! but ah, how hard to frame *45*
    In matter-moulded forms of speech,
    Or even for intellect to reach
Through memory that which I became:

LVI   **23. tare:** tore. **28. veil:** Cf. 2 Corinthians 3:12-16, Hebrews 6:19, 9:3.   **LXXXVIII**   "To the Nightingale" (Tennyson's note); cf. Keats's "Ode to a Nightingale" (p. 854). **2. quicks:** quickset, a plant used in hedges, e.g. the hawthorn.   **XCV**   **8. fluttering urn:** tea-urn, a hot water container, with a flame under it, and with a tap, used to make tea. **10. filmy shapes:** moths. **33. line by line:** Cf. Isaiah 28:13. **41. Æonian:** eternal, associated with the eons, i.e., not subject to chance and change.

Till now the doubtful dusk revealed
　The knolls once more where, couched at ease,
　The white kine glimmered, and the trees　*51*
Laid their dark arms about the field:

And sucked from out the distant gloom
　A breeze began to tremble o'er
　The large leaves of the sycamore,　*55*
And fluctuate all the still perfume,

And gathering freshlier overhead,
　Rocked the full-foliaged elms, and swung
　The heavy-folded rose, and flung
The lilies to and fro, and said　*60*

"The dawn, the dawn," and died away;
　And East and West, without a breath,
　Mixt their dim lights, like life and death,
To broaden into boundless day.

CVI

Ring out, wild bells, to the wild sky,
　The flying cloud, the frosty light:
　The year is dying in the night;
Ring out, wild bells, and let him die.

Ring out the old, ring in the new,　*5*
　Ring, happy bells, across the snow:
　The year is going, let him go;
Ring out the false, ring in the true.

Ring out the grief that saps the mind,
　For those that here we see no more;　*10*
　Ring out the feud of rich and poor,
Ring in redress to all mankind.

Ring out a slowly dying cause,
　And ancient forms of party strife;
　Ring in the nobler modes of life,　*15*
With sweeter manners, purer laws.

Ring out the want, the care, the sin,
　The faithless coldness of the times;
　Ring out, ring out my mournful rhymes,
But ring the fuller minstrel in.　*20*

Ring out false pride in place and blood,
　The civic slander and the spite;
　Ring in the love of truth and right,
Ring in the common love of good.

Ring out old shapes of foul disease;　*25*
　Ring out the narrowing lust of gold;
　Ring out the thousand wars of old,
Ring in the thousand years of peace.

Ring in the valiant man and free,
　The larger heart, the kindlier hand;　*30*
　Ring out the darkness of the land,
Ring in the Christ that is to be.

CXIV

Who loves not Knowledge? Who shall rail
　Against her beauty? May she mix
　With men and prosper! Who shall fix
Her pillars? Let her work prevail.

But on her forehead sits a fire:　*5*
　She sets her forward countenance
　And leaps into the future chance,
Submitting all things to desire.

Half-grown as yet, a child, and vain —
　She cannot fight the fear of death.　*10*
　What is she, cut from love and faith,
But some wild Pallas from the brain

Of Demons? fiery-hot to burst
　All barriers in her onward race
　For power. Let her know her place;　*15*
She is the second, not the first.

A higher hand must make her mild,
　If all be not in vain; and guide
　Her footsteps, moving side by side
With wisdom, like the younger child:　*20*

For she is earthly of the mind,
　But Wisdom heavenly of the soul.
　O, friend, who camest to thy goal
So early, leaving me behind,

I would the great world grew like thee,　*25*
　Who grewest not alone in power
　And knowledge, but by year and hour
In reverence and in charity.

CXVIII

Contemplate all this work of Time,
　The giant labouring in his youth;
　Nor dream of human love and truth,
As dying Nature's earth and lime;

CVI　28. thousand years: See Revelation 20:2-4. **32:** "the broader Christianity of the future" (Tennyson's note). **CXIV　4. pillars:** Cf. Proverbs 9:1 (Tennyson's note). **12-13. some . . . Demons:** i.e., in contrast to Pallas Athena, goddess of wisdom, who sprang full-blown from the head of Zeus.

But trust that those we call the dead   5
   Are breathers of an ampler day
   For ever nobler ends. They say,
The solid earth whereon we tread

In tracts of fluent heat began,
   And grew to seeming-random forms,   10
   The seeming prey of cyclic storms,
Till at the last arose the man;

Who throve and branched from clime to clime,
   The herald of a higher race,
   And of himself in higher place,   15
If so he type this work of time

Within himself, from more to more;
   Or, crowned with attributes of woe
   Like glories, move his course, and show
That life is not as idle ore,   20

But iron dug from central gloom,
   And heated hot with burning fears,
   And dipt in baths of hissing tears,
And battered with the shocks of doom

To shape and use. Arise and fly   25
   The reeling Faun, the sensual feast;
   Move upward, working out the beast,
And let the ape and tiger die.

CXXIV

That which we dare invoke to bless;
   Our dearest faith; our ghastliest doubt;
   He, They, One, All; within, without;
The Power in darkness whom we guess;

I found Him not in world or sun,   5
   Or eagle's wing, or insect's eye;
   Nor through the questions men may try,
The petty cobwebs we have spun:

If e'er when faith had fallen asleep,
   I heard a voice "believe no more"   10
   And heard an ever-breaking shore
That tumbled in the Godless deep;

A warmth within the breast would melt
   The freezing reason's colder part,
   And like a man in wrath the heart   15
Stood up and answered "I have felt."

No, like a child in doubt and fear:
   But that blind clamour made me wise;
   Then was I as a child that cries,
But, crying, knows his father near;   20

And what I am beheld again
   What is, and no man understands;
   And out of darkness came the hands
That reach through nature, moulding men.

[Epilogue]

    . . . .

And rise, O moon, from yonder down,
   Till over down and over dale
   All night the shining vapour sail
And pass the silent-lighted town,

The white-faced halls, the glancing rills,   5
   And catch at every mountain head,
   And o'er the friths that branch and spread
Their sleeping silver through the hills;

And touch with shade the bridal doors,
   With tender gloom the roof, the wall;   10
   And breaking let the splendour fall
To spangle all the happy shores

By which they rest, and ocean sounds,
   And, star and system rolling past,
   A soul shall draw from out the vast   15
And strike his being into bounds,

And, moved through life of lower phase,
   Result in man, be born and think,
   And act and love, a closer link
Betwixt us and the crowning race   20

Of those that, eye to eye, shall look
   On knowledge; under whose command
   Is Earth and Earth's, and in their hand
Is Nature like an open book;

No longer half-akin to brute,   25
   For all we thought and loved and did,
   And hoped, and suffered, is but seed
Of what in them is flower and fruit;

Whereof the man, that with me trod
   This planet, was a noble type   30
   Appearing ere the times were ripe,
That friend of mine who lives in God,

CXVIII   9. fluent heat: The French anatomist and paleontologist Baron Cuvier (1769-1832) rejected evolutionary theory in favour of Catastrophism, a theory that could be more readily reconciled with religious belief because it argued that the earth's populations were started anew after such disruptive catastrophes as flood and fire; other scientists of the time, from the Scottish geologist Lyell to the French astronomer Marquis de Laplace (1749-1827), dismissed Cuvier and argued that the earth had its source in the sun. **16. type:** represent; i.e., implying that human development parallels the larger evolutionary pattern. **26. Faun:** Faunus, the Roman god of nature and fertility (identified with the Greek Pan), celebrated at the Lupercalia, a fertility festival.   **EPILOGUE**   This section celebrates the marriage of Tennyson's sister Cecilia to Edmund Lushington in October 1842. **7. friths:** firths — estuaries, or inlets of the sea.

That God, which ever lives and loves,
  One God, one law, one element,
  And one far-off divine event, *35*
To which the whole creation moves.

(1850)

THE EAGLE

He clasps the crag with crooked hands;
Close to the sun in lonely lands,
Ringed with the azure world, he stands.

The wrinkled sea beneath him crawls;
He watches from his mountain walls, *5*
And like a thunderbolt he falls.

(1851)

THE CHARGE OF
THE LIGHT BRIGADE

I

Half a league, half a league,
  Half a league onward,
All in the valley of Death
  Rode the six hundred.
"Forward, the Light Brigade! *5*
Charge for the guns!" he said:
Into the valley of Death
  Rode the six hundred.

II

"Forward, the Light Brigade!"
Was there a man dismayed? *10*
Not though the soldier knew
  Some one had blundered:
Their's not to make reply,
Their's not to reason why,
Their's but to do and die: *15*
Into the valley of Death
  Rode the six hundred.

III

Cannon to right of them,
Cannon to left of them,
Cannon in front of them *20*

Volleyed and thundered;
Stormed at with shot and shell,
Boldly they rode and well,
Into the jaws of Death,
Into the mouth of Hell *25*
  Rode the six hundred.

IV

Flashed all their sabres bare,
Flashed as they turned in air
Sabring the gunners there,
Charging an army, while *30*
  All the world wondered:
Plunged in the battery-smoke
Right through the line they broke;
Cossack and Russian
Reeled from the sabre-stroke *35*
  Shattered and sundered.
Then they rode back, but not
  Not the six hundred.

V

Cannon to right of them,
Cannon to left of them, *40*
Cannon behind them
  Volleyed and thundered;
Stormed at with shot and shell,
While horse and hero fell,
They that had fought so well *45*
Came through the jaws of Death,
Back from the mouth of Hell,
All that was left of them,
  Left of six hundred.

VI

When can their glory fade? *50*
O the wild charge they made!
  All the world wondered.
Honour the charge they made!
Honour the Light Brigade,
  Noble six hundred! *55*

(1854)

THE CHARGE OF THE LIGHT BRIGADE   The historical event referred to in this poem, part of the Battle of Balaclava (25 October 1854), occurred during the Crimean War (1853-56) — a war between Russia on one side and Britain, France, Sardinia, and Turkey on the other, which resulted from competing demands for territory as the old Ottoman Empire was falling apart; the Charge of the Light Brigade, doomed from the outset because of unequal odds, unfavourable terrain, confusion, misunderstanding, and personal animosities, was led by Lord Cardigan (1797-1868), and was ordered by the British commanding general, Lord Raglan (1788-1855), when he was himself criticized because his troops were not advancing rapidly.

BATTLE OF BRUNANBURH

I

Athelstan King,
Lord among Earls,
Bracelet-bestower and
Baron of Barons,
He with his brother,   5
Edmund Atheling,
Gaining a lifelong
Glory in battle,
Slew with the sword-edge
There by Brunanburh,   10
Brake the shield-wall,
Hewed the lindenwood,
Hacked the battleshield,
Sons of Edward with hammered brands.

II

Theirs was a greatness   15
Got from their Grandsires —
Theirs that so often in
Strife with their enemies
Struck for their hoards and their hearths and
their homes.

III

Bowed the spoiler,   20
Bent the Scotsman,
Fell the shipcrews
Doomed to the death.
All the field with blood of the fighters
Flowed, from when first the great 25
Sun-star of morningtide,
Lamp of the Lord God
Lord everlasting,
Glode over earth till the glorious creature
Sank to his setting.   30

IV

There lay many a man
Marred by the javelin,
Men of the Northland
Shot over shield.
There was the Scotsman   35
Weary of war.

V

We the West-Saxons,
Long as the daylight
Lasted, in companies
Troubled the track of the host that we hated, 40
Grimly with swords that were sharp from the
grindstone,
Fiercely we hacked at the flyers before us.

VI

Mighty the Mercian,
Hard was his hand-play,
Sparing not any of   45
Those that with Anlaf,
Warriors over the
Weltering waters
Borne in the bark's-bosom,
Drew to this island: 50
Doomed to the death.

VII

Five young kings put asleep by the sword-stroke,
Seven strong Earls of the army of Anlaf
Fell on the war-field, numberless numbers,
Shipmen and Scotsmen.   55

VIII

Then the Norse leader,
Dire was his need of it,
Few were his following,
Fled to his warship:
Fleeted his vessel to sea with the king in it, 60
Saving his life on the fallow flood.

BATTLE OF BRUNANBURH   This poem records a battle between Athelstan, king of Wessex and Mercia (d. 939), and the Scots, Welsh, and Danes, at an undetermined site in the north of England; the Old English original version of this poem first appeared in the *Anglo-Saxon Chronicle.* Tennyson's poem (based upon his son Hallam's translation, which had been published in *The Contemporary Review*, November 1876) first appeared with the preface: "Constantinus, King of the Scots, after having sworn allegiance to Athelstan, allied himself with the Danes of Ireland under Anlaf, and invading England, was defeated by Athelstan and his brother Edmund with great slaughter at Brunanburh in the year 937." In his volume *Harold* (1876), Tennyson also observed: "In rendering this Old English war-song into modern language and alliterative rhythm I have made free use of the dactylic beat. I suppose that the original was chanted to a slow, swinging recitative." **6. Atheling:** a member of a noble family. **12. lindenwood:** shields of lindenwood (Tennysons's note). **29. Glode:** glided. **61. fallow:** either pale or dark, from *fealo*, in the Old English original.

IX

Also the crafty one,
Constantinus,
Crept to his North again,
Hoar-headed hero!   65

X

Slender warrant had
He to be proud of
The welcome of war-knives —
He that was reft of his
Folk and his friends that had   70
Fallen in conflict,
Leaving his son too
Lost in the carnage,
Mangled to morsels,
A youngster in war!   75

XI

Slender reason had
He to be glad of
The clash of the war-glaive —
Traitor and trickster
And spurner of treaties —   80
He nor had Anlaf
With armies so broken
A reason for bragging
That they had the better
In perils of battle   85
On places of slaughter —
The struggle of standards,
The rush of the javelins,
The crash of the charges,
The wielding of weapons —   90
The play that they played with
The children of Edward.

XII

Then with their nailed prows
Parted the Norsemen, a
Blood-reddened relic of   95

Javelins over
The jarring breaker, the deep-sea billow,
Shaping their way toward Dyflen again,
Shamed in their souls.

XIII

Also the brethren,   100
King and Atheling,
Each in his glory,
Went to his own in his own West-Saxonland,
Glad of the war.

XIV

Many a carcase they left to be carrion,   105
Many a livid one, many a sallow-skin —
Left for the white tailed eagle to tear it, and
Left for the horny-nibbed raven to rend it, and
Gave to the garbaging war-hawk to gorge it, and
That gray beast, the wolf of the weald.   110

XV

Never had huger
Slaughter of heroes
Slain by the sword-edge —
Such as old writers
Have writ of in histories —   115
Hapt in this isle, since
Up from the East hither
Saxon and Angle from
Over the broad billow
Broke into Britain with   120
Haughty war-workers who
Harried the Welshman, when
Earls that were lured by the
Hunger of glory gat
Hold of the land.   125

(1880)

---

68. welcome of war-knives: a kenning for "battle." **78. glaive:** lance or sword. **79-80:** The original simply calls him "the grey-haired man, the old deceiver." **92. children of Edward:** i.e., Athelstan, Edmund, and Edred, each of whom in turn became king. **96-97. over . . . breaker:** The original reads *on Dinges mere*, which perhaps refers to some part of the sea, or is perhaps derived from the word *dinnes*, meaning "noise." **98. Dyflen:** Dublin (Tennyson's note). **106. livid, sallow:** In the original, the adjectives *salowig* and *sweartan* describe the eagle and raven of line 107-08, not the corpses. **110. weald:** forest. **116. Hapt:** happened.

BY AN EVOLUTIONIST

The Lord let the house of a brute to the soul of a man,
　And the man said "Am I your debtor?"
And the Lord — "Not yet: but make it as clean as you can,
　And then I will let you a better."

I

If my body come from brutes, my soul uncertain, or a fable,　　　　　*5*
　Why not bask amid the senses while the sun of morning shines,
I, the finer brute rejoicing in my hounds, and in my stable,
　Youth and Health, and birth and wealth, and choice of women and of wines?

II

What hast thou done for me, grim Old Age, save breaking my bones on the rack?
　Would I had past in the morning that looks so bright from afar!　　　　　*10*

OLD AGE

Done for thee? starved the wild beast that was linkt with thee eighty years back.
　Less weight now for the ladder-of-heaven that hangs on a star.

I

If my body come from brutes, though somewhat finer than their own,
　I am heir, and this my kingdom. Shall the royal voice be mute?
No, but if the rebel subject seek to drag me from the throne,　　　　　*15*
　Hold the sceptre, Human Soul, and rule thy Province of the brute.

II

I have climbed to the snows of Age, and I gaze at a field in the Past,
　Where I sank with the body at times in the sloughs of a low desire,
But I hear no yelp of the beast, and the Man is quiet at last
　As he stands on the heights of his life with a glimpse of a height that is higher.　　*20*

(1889)

THE OAK

Live thy Life,
　Young and old,
Like yon oak,
Bright in spring,
　Living gold;　　　*5*

Summer-rich
　Then; and then
Autumn-changed,
Soberer-hued
　Gold again.　　　*10*

All his leaves
　Fallen at length,
Look, he stands,
Trunk and bough,
　Naked strength.　　*15*
　　(1889)

CROSSING THE BAR

Sunset and evening star,
　And one clear call for me!
And may there be no moaning of the bar,
　When I put out to sea,

But such a tide as moving seems asleep,　　　*5*
　Too full for sound and foam,
When that which drew from out the boundless deep
　Turns again home.

Twilight and evening bell,
　And after that the dark!　　　*10*
And may there be no sadness of farewell,
　When I embark;

For though from out our bourne of Time and Place
　The flood may bear me far,
I hope to see my Pilot face to face　　　*15*
　When I have crost the bar.
　　　(1889)

CROSSING THE BAR　**15. face to face:** See 1 Corinthians 13:12.

FRANCES ANNE KEMBLE
England, 1809-1893

from *JOURNAL OF A RESIDENCE ON A GEORGIAN PLANTATION IN 1838-1839*

MY DEAREST E——,

I have had an uninterrupted stream of women and children flowing in the whole morning to say "Ha de, missis?" Among others, a poor woman called Mile, who could hardly stand for pain and swelling in her limbs; she had had fifteen children and two miscarriages; nine of her children had died; for the last three years she had become almost a cripple with chronic rheumatism, yet she is driven every day to work in the field. She held my hands, and stroked them in the most appealing way while she exclaimed, "Oh my missis! my missis! me neber sleep till day for de pain," and with the day her labour must again be resumed. I gave her flannel and sal volatile to rub her poor swelled limbs with; rest I could not give her — rest from her labour and her pain — this mother of fifteen children. 5

Another of my visitors had a still more dismal story to tell; her name was Die; she had had sixteen children, fourteen of whom were dead; she had had four miscarriages: one had been caused with falling down with a very heavy burden on her head, and one from having her arms strained up to be lashed. I asked her what she meant by having her arms tied up. She said their hands were first tied together, sometimes by the wrists, and sometimes, which was worse, by the thumbs, and they were then drawn up to a tree or post, so as almost to swing them off the ground, and then their clothes rolled round their waist, and a man with a cowhide stands and stripes them. I give you the woman's words. She did not speak of this as of any thing strange, unusual, or especially horrid and abominable; and when I said, "Did they do that to you when you were with child?" she simply replied, "Yes, missis." And to all this I listen — I, an English woman, the wife of the man who owns these wretches, and I can not say, "That thing shall not be done again; that cruel shame and villainy shall never be known here again." I gave the woman meat and flannel, which were what she came to ask for, and remained choking with indignation and grief long after they had all left me to my most bitter thoughts. 15 20 25

I went out to try and walk off some of the weight of horror and depression which I am beginning to feel daily more and more, surrounded by all this misery and degradation that I can neither help nor hinder. The blessed spring is coming very fast, the air is full of delicious wildwood fragrances, and the wonderful songs of Southern

---

JOURNAL OF A RESIDENCE Through the work of William Wilberforce and others, the institution of slavery was abolished throughout the British Empire in 1838, though it continued in the United States until Lincoln's Emancipation Act (1863) and the end of the Civil War, and in Portuguese territories (e.g., Brazil) until the 1880s. **My dearest E:** Her friend Elizabeth Dwight Sedgwick, of Lenox, Massachusetts, who had advised her to keep her diary in letter form (the "letters" were not sent); Kemble stayed with the Sedgwicks after she separated from her husband, Pierce Butler, and dedicated the *Journal* to her friend when it was subsequently published.

birds; the wood paths are as tempting as paths into Paradise, but Jack is in such deadly   *30*
terror about the snakes, which are now beginning to glide about with a freedom and
frequency certainly not pleasing, that he will not follow me off the open road, and twice
to-day scared me back from charming wood paths I ventured to explore with his
exclamations of terrified warning.

I gathered some exquisite pink blossoms, of a sort of waxen texture, off a small   *35*
shrub which was strange to me, and for which Jack's only name was dye-bush; but I
could not ascertain from him whether any dyeing substance was found in its leaves,
bark, or blossoms.

I returned home along the river side, stopping to admire a line of noble live oaks
beginning, alas! to be smothered with the treacherous white moss under whose pale   *40*
trailing masses their verdure gradually succumbs, leaving them, like huge hoary ghosts,
perfect mountains of parasitical vegetation, which, strangely enough, appears only to
hang upon and swing from their boughs without adhering to them. The mixture of these
streams of gray-white filaments with the dark foliage is extremely beautiful as long as
the leaves of the tree survive in sufficient masses to produce the rich contrast of color;   *45*
but when the moss has literally conquered the whole tree, and, after stripping its huge
limbs bare, clothed them with its own wan masses, they always looked to me like so
many gigantic Druid ghosts, with flowing robes and beards, and locks all of one ghastly
gray, and I would not have broken a twig off them for the world, lest a sad voice, like
that which reproached Dante, should have moaned out of it to me,   *50*
"Non hai tu spirto di pietada alcuno?"
A beautiful mass of various woodland skirted the edge of the stream, and mingled
in its foliage every shade of green, from the pale, stiff spikes and fans of the dwarf
palmetto to the dark canopy of the magnificent ilex — bowers and brakes of the
loveliest wildness, where one dare not tread three steps for fear. What a tantalization! it   *55*
is like some wicked enchantment.

(1839; 1863)

from *RECORDS OF A GIRLHOOD*

[George Stephenson]

While we were acting at Liverpool an experimental trip was proposed upon the line of
railway which was being constructed between Liverpool and Manchester, the first mesh
of that amazing iron net which now covers the whole surface of England and all the
civilized portions of the earth. The Liverpool merchants, whose far-sighted self-interest
prompted them to wise liberality, had accepted the risk of George Stephenson's   *5*
magnificent experiment, which the committee of inquiry of the House of Commons had

---

30. Jack: a slave boy her husband had assigned to her, to accompany her on her walks and drives and to row her on the river. **51. "Non . . . alcuno?":** Have you no pity, breaking a twig from me? See *Inferno* 13:36. **54. brakes:** thickets.   RECORDS OF A GIRLHOOD: GEORGE STEPHENSON   Stephenson (1781-1848) was an English engineer whose locomotive, the *Rocket*, was used on the Liverpool-Manchester Railway when it opened in September 1830; Kemble travelled on one of the preliminary runs during the summer of 1830. **1. acting:** Fanny Kemble was noted as a stage actress.

rejected for the government. These men, of less intellectual culture than the Parliament members, had the adventurous imagination proper to great speculators, which is the poetry of the counting-house and wharf, and were better able to receive the enthusiastic infection of the great projector's sanguine hope than the Westminster committee. They *10* were exultant and triumphant at the near completion of the work, though, of course, not without some misgivings as to the eventual success of the stupendous enterprise. My father knew several of the gentlemen most deeply interested in the undertaking, and Stephenson having proposed a trial trip as far as the fifteen-mile viaduct, they, with infinite kindness, invited him and permitted me to accompany them; allowing me, *15* moreover, the place which I felt to be one of supreme honour, by the side of Stephenson. All that wonderful history, as much more interesting than a romance as truth is stranger than fiction, which Mr. Smiles's biography of the projector has given in so attractive a form to the world, I then heard from his own lips. He was a rather stern-featured man, with a dark and deeply marked countenance; his speech was strongly *20* inflected with his native Northumbrian accent, but the fascination of that story told by himself, while his tame dragon flew panting along his iron pathway with us, passed the first reading of the "Arabian Nights," the incidents of which it almost seemed to recall. He was wonderfully condescending and kind in answering all the questions of my eager ignorance, and I listened to him with eyes brimful of warm tears of sympathy and *25* enthusiasm, as he told me of all his alternations of hope and fear, of his many trials and disappointments, related with fine scorn how the "Parliament men" had badgered and baffled him with their book-knowledge, and how, when at last they thought they had smothered the irrepressible prophecy of his genius in the quaking depths of Chatmoss, he had exclaimed, "Did ye ever see a boat float on water? I will make my road float *30* upon Chatmoss!" The well-read Parliament men (some of whom, perhaps, wished for no railways near their parks and pleasure-grounds) could not believe the miracle, but the shrewd Liverpool merchants, helped to their faith by a great vision of immense gain, did; and so the railroad was made, and I took this memorable ride by the side of its maker, and would not have exchanged the honour and pleasure of it for one of the *35* shares in the speculation.

LIVERPOOL, August 26th.

MY DEAR H——,

A common sheet of paper is enough for love, but a foolscap extra can alone contain a railroad and my ecstasies. There was once a man, who was born at Newcastle-upon-Tyne, who was a common coal-digger; this man had an immense constructiveness, which displayed itself in pulling his watch to pieces and putting it together again; in *40* making a pair of shoes when he happened to be some days without occupation; finally — here there is a great gap in my story — it brought him in the capacity of an engineer before a committee of the House of Commons, with his head full of plans for constructing a railroad from Liverpool to Manchester. It so happened that to the quickest

---

10. projector: promoter. **13. father:** Charles Kemble (1775-1854), best known as a comic actor. **18. Mr. Smiles:** Samuel Smiles (1812-1904), English self-help enthusiast, whose biography of Stephenson appeared in 1857. **24. condescending:** affable. **29. Chatmoss:** Chat Moss is a 12 square mile (c.31 sq. km) Lancashire peat bog, over which Stephenson's railway had to be built. **My dear H:** Harriet St. Leger (d. 1877), an Irish friend, whom Kemble met c.1825.

and most powerful perceptions and conceptions, to the most indefatigable industry and   *45*
perseverance, and the most accurate knowledge of the phenomena of nature as they affect
his peculiar labours, this man joined an utter want of the "gift of the gab"; he could no
more explain to others what he meant to do and how he meant to do it, than he could fly;
and therefore the members of the House of Commons, after saying, "There is rock to be
excavated to a depth of more than sixty feet, there are embankments to be made nearly to   *50*
the same height, there is a swamp of five miles in length to be traversed, in which if you
drop an iron rod it sinks and disappears: how will you do all this?" and receiving no
answer but a broad Northumbrian "I can't tell you how I'll do it, but I can tell you I *will* do
it," dismissed Stephenson as a visionary. Having prevailed upon a company of Liverpool
gentlemen to be less incredulous, and having raised funds for his great undertaking, in   *55*
December of 1826 the first spade was struck into the ground. And now I will give you an
account of my yesterday's excursion. A party of sixteen persons was ushered into a large
court-yard, where, under cover, stood several carriages of a peculiar construction, one of
which was prepared for our reception. It was a long-bodied vehicle with seats placed
across it, back to back; the one we were in had six of these benches, and was a sort of   *60*
uncovered *char à banc*. The wheels were placed upon two iron bands, which formed the
road, and to which they are fitted, being so constructed as to slide along without any
danger of hitching or becoming displaced, on the same principle as a thing sliding on a
concave groove. The carriage was set in motion by a mere push, and, having received this
impetus, rolled with us down an inclined plane into a tunnel, which forms the entrance to   *65*
the railroad. This tunnel is four hundred yards long (I believe), and will be lighted by gas.
At the end of it we emerged from darkness, and, the ground becoming level, we stopped.
There is another tunnel parallel with this, only much wider and longer, for it extends from
the place which we had now reached, and where the steam-carriages start, and which is
quite out of Liverpool, the whole way under the town, to the docks. This tunnel is for   *70*
wagons and other heavy carriages; and as the engines which are to draw the trains along
the railroad do not enter these tunnels, there is a large building at this entrance which is to
be inhabited by steam-engines of a stationary turn of mind, and different constitution from
the travelling ones, which are to propel the trains through the tunnels to the terminus in the
town, without going out of their houses themselves. The length of the tunnel parallel to the   *75*
one we passed through is (I believe) two thousand two hundred yards. I wonder if you are
understanding one word I am saying all this while! We were introduced to the little engine
which was to drag us along the rails. She (for they make these curious little fire-horses all
mares) consisted of a boiler, a stove, a small platform, a bench, and behind the bench a
barrel containing enough water to prevent her being thirsty for fifteen miles, — the whole   *80*
machine not bigger than a common fire-engine. She goes upon two wheels, which are her
feet, and are moved by bright steel legs called pistons; these are propelled by steam, and in
proportion as more steam is applied to the upper extremities (the hip-joints, I suppose) of
these pistons, the faster they move the wheels; and when it is desirable to diminish the
speed, the steam, which unless suffered to escape would burst the boiler, evaporates   *85*
through a safety-valve into the air. The reins, bit, and bridle of this wonderful beast is a

---

61. *char à banc*: charabanc, an open vehicle with bench seats.

small steel handle, which applies or withdraws the steam from its legs or pistons, so that a child might manage it. The coals, which are its oats, were under the bench, and there was a small glass tube affixed to the boiler, with water in it, which indicates by its fullness or emptiness when the creature wants water, which is immediately conveyed to it from its   *90* reservoirs. There is a chimney to the stove, but as they burn coke there is none of the dreadful black smoke which accompanies the progress of a steam vessel. This snorting little animal, which I felt rather inclined to pat, was then harnessed to our carriage, and, Mr. Stephenson having taken me on the bench of the engine with him, we started at about ten miles an hour. The steam-horse being ill adapted for going up and down hill, the road   *95* was kept at a certain level, and appeared sometimes to sink below the surface of the earth, and sometimes to rise above it. Almost at starting it was cut through the solid rock, which formed a wall on either side of it, about sixty feet high. You can't imagine how strange it seemed to be journeying on thus, without any visible cause of progress other than the magical machine, with its flying white breath and rhythmical, unvarying pace, between   *100* these rocky walls, which are already clothed with moss and ferns and grasses; and when I reflected that these great masses of stone had been cut asunder to allow our passage thus far below the surface of the earth, I felt as if no fairy tale was ever half so wonderful as what I saw. Bridges were thrown from side to side across the top of these cliffs, and the people looking down upon us from them seemed like pygmies standing in the sky. I must   *105* be more concise, though, or I shall want room. We were to go only fifteen miles, that distance being sufficient to show the speed of the engine, and to take us on to the most beautiful and wonderful object on the road. After proceeding through this rocky defile, we presently found ourselves raised upon embankments ten or twelve feet high; we then came to a moss, or swamp, of considerable extent, on which no human foot could tread without   *110* sinking, and yet it bore the road which bore us. This had been the great stumbling-block in the minds of the committee of the House of Commons; but Mr. Stephenson has succeeded in overcoming it. A foundation of hurdles, or, as he called it, basket-work, was thrown over the morass, and the interstices were filled with moss and other elastic matter. Upon this the clay and soil were laid down, and the road *does* float, for we passed over it at the   *115* rate of five and twenty miles an hour, and saw the stagnant swamp water trembling on the surface of the soil on either side of us. I hope you understand me. The embankment had gradually been rising higher and higher, and in one place, where the soil was not settled enough to form banks, Stephenson had constructed artificial ones of wood-work, over which the mounds of earth were heaped, for he said that though the wood-work would rot,   *120* before it did so the banks of earth which covered it would have been sufficiently consolidated to support the road.

We had now come fifteen miles, and stopped where the road traversed a wide and deep valley. Stephenson made me alight and led me down to the bottom of this ravine, over which, in order to keep his road level, he has thrown a magnificent viaduct of nine   *125* arches, the middle one of which is seventy feet high, through which we saw the whole of this beautiful little valley. It was lovely and wonderful beyond all words. He here told me many curious things respecting this ravine: how he believed the Mersey had once rolled through it; how the soil had proved so unfavourable for the foundation of his bridge that it

---

128. **Mersey:** the river on which Liverpool is located.

was built upon piles, which had been driven into the earth to an enormous depth; how, *130* while digging for a foundation, he had come to a tree bedded in the earth fourteen feet below the surface of the ground; how tides are caused, and how another flood might be caused; all of which I have remembered and noted down at much greater length than I can enter upon it here. He explained to me the whole construction of the steam-engine, and said he could soon make a famous engineer of me, which, considering the wonderful *135* things he *has* achieved, I dare not say is impossible. His way of explaining himself is peculiar, but very striking, and I understood, without difficulty, all that he said to me. We then rejoined the rest of the party, and the engine having received its supply of water, the carriage was placed behind it, for it cannot turn, and was set off at its utmost speed, thirty-five miles an hour, swifter than a bird flies (for they tried the experiment with a snipe). *140* You cannot conceive what that sensation of cutting the air was; the motion is as smooth as possible, too. I could either have read or written; and as it was, I stood up, and with my bonnet off "drank the air before me." The wind, which was strong, or perhaps the force of our own thrusting against it, absolutely weighed my eyelids down. [I remember a similar experience to this, the first time I attempted to go behind the sheet of the cataract of *145* Niagara; the wind coming from beneath the waterfall met me with such direct force that it literally bore down my eyelids, and I had to put off the attempt of penetrating behind the curtain of foam till another day, when that peculiar accident was less directly hostile to me in its conditions.] When I closed my eyes this sensation of flying was quite delightful, and strange beyond description; yet, strange as it was, I had a perfect sense of security, and not *150* the slightest fear. At one time, to exhibit the power of the engine, having met another steam-carriage which was unsupplied with water, Mr. Stephenson caused it to be fastened in front of ours; moreover, a wagon laden with timber was also chained to us, and thus propelling the idle steam-engine, and dragging the loaded wagon which was beside it, and our own carriage full of people behind, this brave little she-dragon of ours flew on. Farther *155* on she met three carts, which, being fastened in front of her, she pushed on before her without the slightest delay or difficulty; when I add that this pretty little creature can run with equal facility either backward or forward, I believe I have given you an account of all her capacities.

Now for a word or two about the master of all these marvels, with whom I am most *160* horribly in love. He is a man of from fifty to fifty-five years of age; his face is fine, though careworn, and bears an expression of deep thoughtfulness; his mode of explaining his ideas is peculiar and very original, striking, and forcible; and although his accent indicates strongly his north-country birth, his language has not the slightest touch of vulgarity or coarseness. He has certainly turned my head. *165*

Four years have sufficed to bring this great undertaking to an end. The railroad will be opened upon the 15th of next month. The Duke of Wellington is coming down to be present on the occasion, and, I suppose, what with the thousands of spectators and the novelty of the spectacle, there will never have been a scene of more striking interest. The whole cost of the work (including the engines and carriages) will have been eight *170* hundred and thirty thousand pounds; and it is already worth double that sum.

. . . .

144-49: Here and elsewhere, Kemble uses brackets to insert her later reflections into letters written much earlier. **167. Duke of Wellington:** Arthur Wellesley, 1st Duke of Wellington (1769-1852), celebrated for his military victory over Napoleon at the Battle of Waterloo (1815).

[Niagara]

STEAMBOAT ST. PATRICK, ON THE ST. LAWRENCE,
August 17, 1833.

MY DEAREST H———,

There is lying in my desk an unfinished letter to you, begun about a week ago, which is
pausing for want of an opportunity to go on with it; but here I am, a prisoner in a
steamboat, destined to pass the next four and twenty hours on the broad bosom of the St.
Lawrence, and what can I do better than begin a fresh chapter to you, leaving the one
already begun to be finished on my next holiday. My holidays, indeed, are far from   5
leisure time, for when I have nothing to do I have all the more to see; so that I am as
busy and more weary than if I were working much harder.

We have been staying for the last fortnight in Quebec, and are now on our way back
to Montreal, where we shall act a night or two, and then return to the United States, to
New York and Boston. . . .   10

I have much to tell you, for in the last two months I have seen marvelous much. I
have seen Niagara. I wish you had been there to see it with me. However, Niagara will
not cease falling; and you may, perhaps, at some future time, visit this country. You
must not expect any description of Niagara from me, because it is quite unspeakable,
and, moreover, if it were not, it would still be quite unimaginable. The circumstances   15
under which I saw it I can tell you, but of the great cataract itself, what can be told
except that it is water?

I confess the sight of it reminded me, with additional admiration, of Sir Charles
Bagot's daring denial of its existence; having failed to make his pilgrimage thither
during his stay in the United States, he declared on his return to England that he had   20
never been able to find it, that he didn't believe there was any such thing, and that it was
nothing but a bragging boast of the Americans.

. . . .

We reached Queenstown on the Niagara River, below the falls, at about twelve
o'clock, and had three more miles to drive to reach them. The day was serenely bright
and warm, without a cloud in the sky, or a shade in the earth, or a breath in the air. We   25
were in an open carriage, and I felt almost nervously oppressed with the expectation of
what we were presently to see. We stopped the carriage occasionally to listen for the
giant's roaring, but the sound did not reach us until, within three miles over the thick
woods which skirted the river, we saw a vapoury silver cloud rising into the blue sky. It
was the spray, the breath of the toiling waters ascending to heaven. When we reached   30
what is called the Niagara House, a large tavern by the roadside, I sprang out of the
carriage and ran through the house, down flights of steps cut in the rock, and along a
path skirted with low thickets, through the boughs of which I saw the rapids running a
race with me, as it seemed, and hardly faster than I did. Then there was a broad, flashing
sea of furious foam, a deafening rush and roar, through which I heard Mr. Trelawney,   35
who was following me, shout, "Go on, go on; don't stop!" I reached an open floor of

---

NIAGARA   See also Harriet Martineau's "Niagara" (p. 897). **19. Bagot:** British colonial administrator (1781-1843), diplomat in the U.S.A.
between 1815 and 1820, and Governor-General of Canada from 1841 to 1843. **35. Trelawney:** Edward Trelawney (1782-1881), English traveller
and author of *Adventures of a Younger Son* (1831).

broad, flat rock, over which the water was pouring. Trelawney seized me by the arm, and all but carried me to the very brink; my feet were in the water and on the edge of the precipice, and then I looked down. I could not speak, and I could hardly breathe; I felt as if I had an iron band across my breast. I watched the green, glassy, swollen heaps go plunging down, down, down; each mountainous mass of water, as it reached the dreadful brink, recoiling, as in horror, from the abyss; and after rearing backward in helpless terror, as it were, hurling itself down to be shattered in the inevitable doom over which eternal clouds of foam and spray spread an impenetrable curtain. The mysterious chasm, with its uproar of voices, seemed like the watery mouth of hell. I looked and listened till the wild excitement of the scene took such possession of me that, but for the strong arm that held me back, I really think I should have let myself slide down into the gulf. It was long before I could utter, and as I began to draw my breath I could only gasp out, "O God! O God!" No words can describe either the scene itself, or its effect upon me.

We stayed three days at Niagara, the greater part of which I spent by the water, under the water, on the water, and more than half in the water. Wherever foot could stand I stood, and wherever foot could go I went. I crept, clung, hung, and waded; I lay upon the rocks, upon the very edge of the boiling caldron, and I stood alone under the huge arch over which the water pours with the whole mass of it, thundering over my rocky ceiling, and falling down before me like an immeasurable curtain, the noonday sun looking like a pale spot, a white wafer, through the dense thickness. Drenched through, and almost blown from my slippery footing by the whirling gusts that rush under the fall, with my feet naked for better safety, grasping the shale broken from the precipice against which I pressed myself, my delight was so intense that I really could hardly bear to come away.

The rock over which the rapids run is already scooped and hollowed out to a great extent by the action of the water; the edge of the precipice, too, is constantly crumbling and breaking off under the spurn of its downward leap. At the very brink the rock is not much more than two feet thick, and when I stood under it and thought of the enormous mass of water rushing over and pouring from it, it did not seem at all improbable that at any moment the roof might give way, the rock break off fifteen or twenty feet, and the whole huge cataract, retreating back, leave a still wider basin for its floods to pour themselves into. You must come and see it before you die, dear H——.

After our short stay at Niagara, we came down Lake Ontario and the St. Lawrence to Montreal and Quebec. Before I leave off speaking of that wonderful cataract, I must tell you that the impression of awe and terror it produced at first upon me completely wore away, and as I became familiar with it, its dazzling brightness, its soothing voice, its gliding motion, its soft, thick, furry beds of foam, its vails and draperies of floating light, and gleaming, wavering diadems of vivid colours, made it to me the perfection of loveliness and the mere magnificence of beauty. It was certainly not the "familiarity" that "breeds contempt," but more akin to the "perfect love" which "casteth out fear"; and I began at last to understand Mr. Trelawney's saying that the only impression it produced on him was that of perfect repose; but perhaps it takes Niagara to mesmerize him.

75-76. familiarity breeds contempt: proverbial saying current since classical times, perhaps best known from Aesop's fable "The Fox and the Lion" or from Slender's ironic use of it in Shakespeare's *The Merry Wives of Windsor*, I.i.230. **76:** See 1 John 4:18.

[The first time I attempted to go under the cataract of Niagara I had a companion with me, and one of the local guides, who undertook to pilot us safely. On reaching the *80* edge of the sheet of water, however, we encountered a blast of wind so violent that we were almost beaten back by it. The spray was driven against us like a furious hailstorm, and it was impossible to open our eyes or draw our breath, and we were obliged to relinquish the expedition. The next morning, going down to the falls alone, I was seduced by the comparative quietness and calm, the absence of wind or atmospheric disturbance, *85* to approach gradually the entrance to the cave behind the water, and finding no such difficulty as on the previous day, crept on, step by step, beneath the sheet, till I reached the impassable jutting forward of the rock where it meets the full body of the cataract. My first success emboldened me to two subsequent visits, the small eels being the only unpleasant incident I encountered. The narrow path I followed was a mere ledge of shale *90* and broken particles of the rock, which is so frayable and crumbling, either in its own nature, or from the constant action of the water, that as I passed along and pressed myself close against it, I broke off in my hands the portions of it that I grasped.]

A few miles below the falls is a place called the whirlpool, which, in its own kind, is almost as fine as the fall itself. The river makes an abrupt angle in its course, when it *95* is shut in by very high and rocky cliffs — walls, in fact — almost inaccessible from below. Black fir trees are anchored here and there in their cracks and fissures, and hang over the dismal pool below, most of them scathed and contorted by the fires or the blasts of heaven. The water itself is of a strange colour, not transparent, but a pale blue-green, like a discoloured turquoise, or a stream of verdigris, streaked with long veins and angry *100* swirls of white, as if the angry creature couldn't get out of that hole, and was foaming at the mouth; for, before pursuing its course, the river churns round and round in the sullen, savage, dark basin it has worn for itself, and then, as if it had suddenly found an outlet, rushes on its foaming, furious way down to Ontario. We had ridden there and alighted from our horses, and sat on the brink for some time. It was the most dismal *105* place I ever beheld, and seemed to me to grow horribler every moment I looked at it: drowning in that deep, dark, wicked-looking whirlpool would be hideous, compared to being dashed to death amid the dazzling spray and triumphant thunder of Niagara.

[There are but three places I have ever visited that produced upon me the appalling impression of being accursed, and empty of the presence of the God of nature, the *110* Divine Creator, the All-loving Father: this whirlpool of Niagara, that fiery, sulphurous, vile-smelling wound in the earth's bosom, the crater of Vesuvius, and the upper part of the Mer de Glace at Chamouni. These places impressed me with horror, and the impression is always renewed in my mind when I remember them: God-forsaken is what they looked to me.] *115*

I do not believe this whirlpool is at all as generally visited as the falls, and perhaps it might not impress everybody as it did me.

Quebec, where we have been staying, is beautiful. A fortress is always delightful to me; my destructiveness rejoices in guns and drums, and all the circumstance of glorious war. The place itself, too, is so fiercely picturesque — such crags, such dizzy, hanging *120*

---

91. frayable: friable. **113. Mer de Glace:** i.e., the glacier at the French resort town of Chamonix. **119-20. circumstance . . . war:** *Othello*, III.iii.360. **120. picturesque:** See Glossary.

heights, such perpendicular rocky walls, down to the very water's edge, and such a broad, bright bay. The scenery all round Quebec is beautiful, and we went to visit two fine waterfalls in the neighbourhood, but of course to us just now there is but one waterfall in the world. . . . God bless you, dear!

Ever affectionately yours,

F. A. K.

(1879)

ELIZABETH RIGBY, LADY EASTLAKE
England, 1809-1893

from *LETTERS FROM THE SHORES OF THE BALTIC*

[speculations on Russia]

From careful observation, and the judgment of those longer experienced, it would appear that the guarantees for the continued stability of Russia lie exclusively in the person of the monarch and in the body of the people. In the nobility, whose elements of national character fall far beneath those of his serf, the monarch finds no efficient help. Foreign education and contact has, with a few brilliant exceptions, rendered them adepts   *5* in the luxury and frivolity rather than in the humanity of civilization, or grafted them with democratic Utopian ideas that in no state, and least of all in Russia, can bring forth good fruit. The Emperor, therefore, has full ground for the double mistrust with which he views money taken out of the empire and pernicious ideas brought in.

Again, in the so-called middle class — here the mere excrescence of a partial   *10* civilization, who have renounced all of their nationality save its barbarity — all real support to the Crown seems still further removed. These occupy the lower departments of the state, clogging all straightforward dealing, perverting the real intention of the laws, and intercepting every humane Imperial act by the most cunning and unprincipled dishonesty. What will be said of other and more important intentions of the Emperor   *15* when it is known that the snuffbox destined to reward some act of benevolence, which leaves the Imperial hands embossed with diamonds, reaches those of its destined owner deprived of every stone! And no redress is to be had under laws where an equal accumulation of formalities and liability to abuse meet the innocent at every turn.

Despised by the nobles, this class retaliate by a species of persecution which it is   *20* impossible to guard against. No lion's mouth, or familiars of the Inquisition, are needed in a state of things where, ere a false denunciation can be sifted and dismissed, the denounced is equally ruined in purse and worn out with constant care; and nowhere, sad

---

123. waterfalls: e.g., Montmorency; see Henry James's "Quebec" (p. 1117).   **LETTERS FROM THE BALTIC   8. Emperor:** Nicholas I, emperor and tsar 1825-55. **21. lion's mouth:** a receptacle for anonymous denunciations, e.g. in old Venice; citing this as his precedent, Addison (see p. 490) in July 1713 installed a Lion's Head, with open mouth, in Button's Coffee House as a kind of letter-box designed for publicity and to encourage correspondents' contributions to his and Richard Steele's periodical *The Guardian*; **familiars:** officers who arrested those accused by the Inquisition.

to say, are denunciations of this kind so frequent as at this time in Russia — nowhere so
tedious and ruinous in their exposure. Rank, consideration, long service, and high   25
reputation are of no avail. Once an accusation is laid, however it may bear the stamp of
malice, it must distil through all the corkscrew windings of the Russian law, ere the
property of the accused be released from sequestration, or his mind from the most
corroding anxiety — and this done, there is neither compensation for the injured nor
punishment for the injurer, who has thus cloaked his cupidity or revenge under the   30
semblance of what the people honour most, *viz.* his loyalty.

This class it is who have made the Russian courts of justice a byword and a proverb
— who have called down upon Russia the unmerited sarcasm of being "*pourrie avant
d'être mure*" — while, by a natural retribution, the name of *Chinovnik,* or the betitled (for
these men are generally distinguished by an order), is fast becoming the synonym for low   35
dishonesty and intrigue. The national proverb which says no Russian without "*Chai,
Tschi, and Chin*" — tea, sour-krout, and a title — is perfectly true; but the sarcasm on the
latter is derived from the abuse of a noble principle. Peter the Great, the well-intentioned
founder of this rage for orders in Russia, was right when he foresaw the veneration with
which the mass of the people would regard every individual invested with an insignia   40
emanating direct from the sovereign, and calculated thereby on putting a wholesome
power into the hands of the middle ranks: but he reckoned too soon on the formation of
this class, which, to be safe or to be useful, must be gradual and spontaneous in growth;
and the careless and lavish hand with which orders have been distributed since his reign
has only debased the distinction without elevating the possessor.   45

It is predicted that, should any political convulsion occur in Russia, this miserable
class, who suffer the double ill fate of ideas below their station, and a station above their
maintenance, would meet with the nobility in jarring collision, and with equal danger to
both, while the Crown, firmly seated in the instinctive loyalty of the people, would have
nought to fear. By a providential adaptation which surpasses all speculation of   50
legislative philosophy, the people of Russia venerate their sovereign simply because he
is absolute. With them respect for the anointed sovereign is a religion; and to restrict
him by human ordinances would be to strip him of his divine credentials. What Zar has
yet been dethroned or murdered by an act of the people?

(1842)

from *JOURNALS AND CORRESPONDENCE*

[on religion]
July 16
Out to the Non-Intrusionist Box, which, like its builders, defies all the laws of
proportion or anything else — a mere unpainted kind of packing-case, with old half-
sashes stuck in here and there, and the roof pitched. Entered by a road of shingle, which
continued inside the building: this looked as if it had been merely set down upon one of

---

33-34. *pourrie . . . mure*: rotten before being ripe. **38. Peter the Great:** ruled 1689-1725.   **JOURNALS AND CORRESPONDENCE   July 16:**
The year is 1843. **1. Non-Intrusionist:** name for those dissenters who opposed the "intrusion," by church and civil courts, of unacceptable ministers
upon congregations (in 1843, after years of conflict, the Free Church of Scotland separated itself from the established church). **3. shingle:** beach
gravel.

the roughest parts of the beach road that could be found. It reminded me much of a ⁵
theatre booth at a fair — the same kind of rough seats, the same sawdust — a wooden
box at one end and a painted dressing-table before it. It was early, and we chose a place
in full view of the pulpit, and then watched the congregation as they came in. The
proportion of men and women was pretty equally divided, the women showily dressed,
with a profusion of flowers; some fat old matrons, others skinny spinsters, and some ¹⁰
blooming maidens and children. All entered with a satisfied air, as if the mere fact of
their bringing their smart flowers under such a roof as that, and sitting together on
shingle, were sufficient proof of the goodness of their cause. While the men, many of
them, had old, sturdy, hard-burnt, rocky faces, with penthouse brows, and sandy locks,
and straight, lipless mouths; faces which seemed never to have had reverence for man, ¹⁵
or sentiment for woman — contumacious and obstinate all over. These were plentifully
mixed up with smirking shopmen in satin cravats and cotton gloves, and lanky youths
with no head whatever, but a little piece behind the most enormous mouth. The place
was crowded, and many of the veterans I have described began to expound to one
another over the backs of their benches, as if no time was to be lost. But a bustle at the ²⁰
pulpit called attention, and the minister's head was seen rising from a door behind the
pulpit, which he had no sooner entered than he gave a loud cough and spit, and thus
announced his presence to his followers. It was a face and form worthy of the action —
coarse and plebeian. He shut two little eyes with affected solemnity, and gave out a
psalm; the precentor set up the tune, giving a quiver and a wobble at every note, till his ²⁵
voice was drowned in the noise of the multitude. I should hardly have thought that the
assembled voices of so many could produce so harsh and thin an effect. At least 600
individuals were singing at once, and there was neither melody nor fulness; two-thirds
were out of time, and all nasal and wiry. After this the minister began a prayer, the
congregation standing, and settling themselves into such attitudes as should hold out the ³⁰
longest. The minister's manner was a caricature; nothing could exceed the distortion of
his face, or the monotony of his voice — no punctuation: he went on till breath failed,
and whether this crisis occurred in the middle of a sentence, or of a word, no matter —
he stopped. There was one group which formed an exception to the general flaunt of
ribbons; this was a widow, in deep weeds, with a little boy. She had lifted him up to ³⁵
stand on the seat, and, herself turning her back to the minister, she leaned her head on
his little shoulder, her arm round his waist till she thus supported the weight she gave.
The boy was about seven, fair-haired as an angel — his delicate tints standing out from
the black mass of her garments. Poor child, he was gentle and quiet; he gaped again and
again, and played with his mother's sleeve, but he stood still, as if conscious that she ⁴⁰
wished it so. The prayer lasted half an hour, a string of texts in the broadest twang. This
over, the minister seemed as if he hardly knew what was to come next, and very
probably he did not; so he proposed a chapter from the Bible, which is a book they only
resort to when their own ideas run low. So he read the fourth chapter of *Rommans*, and
then took his text from the fourth verse. The sermon was the crowning effort, and was a ⁴⁵
wonderful specimen of sound lungs; he pitched it so loud at first that it seemed

---

35. weeds: i.e., "widow's weeds," mourning garments. **39. gaped:** yawned.

impossible it should be sustained; but, on the contrary, he grew louder and louder, till he bellowed, and foamed, and opened his jaws so wide that all distinctness of syllable was impossible. It was most disgraceful — unconnected, undigested. After the first few minutes a general gaping ensued; mouths opened, and eyes shut, and in a short time a *50* regular breathing took place, which the minister's bawling by no means interfered with. It was wonderful how he kept to his text: sometimes he climbed over stick and stone to it, and then tumbled headlong over a precipice; sometimes he came to a full stop, was fairly pushed into a corner, and roared out "eh, eh"; and then he cleared a wall of his own building at one desperate bound, and rode at it again as mercilessly as ever. This *55* lasted more than an hour, and the dropping of his voice was the signal for the congregation to awake. Then came another psalm, then a short prayer, and then he gave us to understand that he had nothing more to say. This Non-Intrusionist scheme has divested the Covenanters of all charm: we imagine them a venerable, white-haired, apostolic-looking set, with gentle eyes and melodious voices; whereas, doubtless, they *60* were just such a pig-headed race as their descendants.

. . . .

March 10
To church. Text from Job: "He will not afflict. Men do therefore fear Him." Illogically argued, for those who long for God's afflictions, as a proof that He has not forsaken them, do not require them. In the afternoon drove to St. Paul's; got good seats. St. Paul's is all the worse for not having been Roman Catholic; the great space seems for nothing — no altars, no subsidiary chapels — a great, bare building, the beautiful roof looking *5* down on nothing but naked pavement, or, what is worse, on ugly, tasteless monuments — but little solemnity. The very spoliations and violence the older buildings have received give them a charm. The wood carvings very heavy. St. Paul's reminded me of the Smolna in Petersburg, only there is more sense in white marble being bare of ornament. Sydney Smith preached from the good old text, "It is easier for a camel," &c. *10* A sermon which sounded more like a paper from the "Spectator" — terse, compact, sometimes swelling into poetry, sometimes warming into humour; one that every creature, high and low, could understand, but none be improved by. No allusion to a higher source of conviction or action than the reason — a kind of secondary evidence why rich men were more easily deceived. He himself looks, at first sight, an old *15* pampered priest, but, at second, like the shrewd observer; one half of his face the stern moralist, the other the dry humorist.

(1895)

---

59. Covenanters: 17th-century supporters of the National Covenant and the Solemn League and Covenant, generally promoting Scottish Presbyterianism and opposing the Church of Scotland. **March 10:** The year is 1844. **1:** Job 37:23-24. **3. St. Paul's:** the cathedral, in London. **9. Smolna:** originally, the Smol'nyi Institute for Well-Born Girls, founded in 1764, which included a Women's Monastery; in the centre is a five-domed cathedral 85 m high. **10. Sydney Smith:** See p. 779; **"It is easier for a camel":** See Matthew 19:24. **11. "Spectator":** Addison and Steele conducted *The Spectator* in the early 18th century (see p. 490), but the reference here is likely to the weekly periodical of the same name begun in 1828 to promote radical and liberal causes.

OLIVER WENDELL HOLMES
U.S.A., 1809-1894

THE CHAMBERED NAUTILUS

This is the ship of pearl, which, poets feign,
    Sails the unshadowed main, —
    The venturous bark that flings
On the sweet summer wind its purpled wings
In gulfs enchanted, where the Siren sings,   5
    And coral reefs lie bare,
Where the cold sea-maids rise to sun their streaming hair.

Its webs of living gauze no more unfurl;
    Wrecked is the ship of pearl!
    And every chambered cell,   10
Where its dim dreaming life was wont to dwell,
As the frail tenant shaped his growing shell,
    Before thee lies revealed, —
Its irised ceiling rent, its sunless crypt unsealed!

Year after year beheld the silent toil   15
    That spread his lustrous coil;
    Still, as the spiral grew,
He left the past year's dwelling for the new,
Stole with soft step its shining archway through,
    Built up its idle door,   20
Stretched in his last-found home, and knew the old no
    more.

Thanks for the heavenly message brought by thee,
    Child of the wandering sea,
    Cast from her lap, forlorn!
From thy dead lips a clearer note is born   25
Than ever Triton blew from wreathèd horn!
    While on mine ear it rings,
Through the deep caves of thought I hear a voice that
    sings: —

Build thee more stately mansions, O my soul,
    As the swift seasons roll!   30

Leave thy low-vaulted past!
Let each new temple, nobler than the last,
Shut thee from heaven with a dome more vast,
    Till thou at length art free,
Leaving thine outgrown shell by life's unresting sea!   35
            (1858)

THE DEACON'S MASTERPIECE
or, The Wonderful "One-Hoss Shay"
A Logical Story

Have you heard of the wonderful one-hoss shay,
That was built in such a logical way
It ran a hundred years to a day,
And then, of a sudden, it — ah, but stay,
I'll tell you what happened without delay,   5
Scaring the parson into fits,
Frightening people out of their wits, —
Have you ever heard of that, I say?

Seventeen hundred and fifty-five.
Georgius Secundus was then alive, —   10
Snuffy old drone from the German hive.
That was the year when Lisbon-town
Saw the earth open and gulp her down,
And Braddock's army was done so brown,
Left without a scalp to its crown.   15
It was on the terrible Earthquake-day
That the Deacon finished the one-hoss shay.

Now in building of chaises, I tell you what,
There is always *somewhere* a weakest spot, —
In hub, tire, felloe, in spring or thill,   20
In panel, or crossbar, or floor, or sill,

THE CHAMBERED NAUTILUS 1. ship of pearl: The ancient Greeks believed that the spiral-shaped tropical mollusk called the "pearly nautilus" could move by using some of its tissue as a sail. **26. Triton:** a son of Poseidon; see note to line 14 of Wordsworth's "The World Is Too Much With Us" (p. 765). **THE DEACON'S MASTERPIECE 10.** *Georgius Secundus:* George II (1683-1760). **13. open:** An earthquake that year destroyed the city of Lisbon, raising questions about the role of Divine Providence in human affairs. **14. Braddock:** Edward Braddock (1695-1755), British general during the Seven Years' War (which Americans refer to as one of the "French and Indian Wars"), killed during an attack at Fort Duquesne (now Pittsburgh). **17. Deacon:** Though engaging simply as a comic narrative, the poem was also designed as an allegory about the limitations of Puritan logic (i.e., the most logical structure collapses if its premises are unsound); the Deacon thus also represents the Puritan writer Jonathan Edwards (1703-1758), and the "shay" (or "chaise" — line 18 — a one-horse cart) represents Edwards's doctrinal publication *The Freedom of the Will* (1754). **20. felloe:** felly, a wooden wheel-rim; **thill:** the shaft that harnesses the cart to the horse. **21. sill:** the timber used to frame the floor.

In screw, bolt, thoroughbrace, — lurking still,
Find it somewhere you must and will, —
Above or below, or within or without, —
And that's the reason, beyond a doubt,   *25*
That a chaise *breaks down*, but doesn't *wear out*.

But the Deacon swore (as deacons do,
With an "I dew vum," or an "I tell *yeou*")
He would build one shay to beat the taown
'N' the keounty 'n' all the kentry raoun';   *30*
It should be so built that it *could n'* break daown:
"Fur," said the Deacon, "'t 's mighty plain
Thut the weakes' place mus' stan' the strain;
'N' the way t' fix it, uz I maintain,
              Is only jest   *35*
T' make that place uz strong uz the rest."

So the Deacon inquired of the village folk
Where he could find the strongest oak,
That couldn't be split nor bent nor broke, —
That was for spokes and floor and sills;   *40*
He sent for lancewood to make the thills;
The crossbars were ash, from the straightest trees,
The panels of white-wood, that cuts like cheese,
But lasts like iron for things like these;
The hubs of logs from the "Settler's ellum," —   *45*
Last of its timber, — they couldn't sell 'em,
Never an axe had seen their chips,
And the wedges flew from between their lips,
Their blunt ends frizzled like celery-tips;
Step and prop-iron, bolt and screw,   *50*
Spring, tire, axle, and linchpin, too,
Steel of the finest, bright and blue;
Thoroughbrace bison-skin, thick and wide;
Boot, top, dasher, from tough old hide
Found in the pit when the tanner died.   *55*
That was the way he "put her through."
"There!" said the Deacon, "naow she'll dew!"

Do! I tell you, I rather guess
She was a wonder, and nothing less!
Colts grew horses, beards turned gray,   *60*
Deacon and deaconess dropped away,
Children and grandchildren — where were they?
But there stood the stout old one-hoss shay
As fresh as on Lisbon-earthquake-day!

EIGHTEEN HUNDRED; — it came and found   *65*
The Deacon's masterpiece strong and sound.

Eighteen hundred increased by ten; —
"Hahnsum kerridge" they called it then.
Eighteen hundred and twenty came; —
Running as usual; much the same.   *70*
Thirty and forty at last arrive,
And then come fifty, and FIFTY-FIVE.

Little of all we value here
Wakes on the morn of its hundredth year
Without both feeling and looking queer.   *75*
In fact, there's nothing that keeps its youth,
So far as I know, but a tree and truth.
(This is a moral that runs at large;
Take it. — You're welcome. — No extra charge.)

FIRST OF NOVEMBER, — the earthquake-day, —   *80*
There are traces of age in the one-hoss shay,
A general flavor of mild decay,
But nothing local, as one may say.
There couldn't be, — for the Deacon's art
Had made it so like in every part   *85*
That there wasn't a chance for one to start.
For the wheels were just as strong as the thills,
And the floor was just as strong as the sills,
And the panels just as strong as the floor,
And the whipple-tree neither less nor more,   *90*
And the back crossbar as strong as the fore,
And spring and axle and hub *encore*.
And yet, *as a whole*, it is past a doubt
In another hour it will be *worn out!*

First of November, 'Fifty-five!   *95*
This morning the parson takes a drive.
Now, small boys, get out of the way!
Here comes the wonderful one-hoss shay,
Drawn by a rat-tailed, ewe-necked bay.
"Huddup!" said the parson. — Off went they.   *100*
The parson was working his Sunday's text, —
Had got to *fifthly,* and stopped perplexed
At what the — Moses — was coming next.
All at once the horse stood still,
Close by the meet'n'-house on the hill.   *105*
First a shiver, and then a thrill,
Then something decidedly like a spill, —
And the parson was sitting upon a rock,
At half past nine by the meet'n'-house clock, —
Just the hour of the Earthquake shock!   *110*

---

22. **thoroughbrace:** a leather strap under the carriage, that served as a spring. 54. **dasher:** dashboard. 90. **whipple-tree:** whiffletree, the crossbar to which the harness is attached.

What do you think the parson found,
When he got up and stared around?
The poor old chaise in a heap or mound,
As if it had been to the mill and ground!
You see, of course, if you're not a dunce,   *115*
How it went to pieces all at once, —

All at once, and nothing first, —
Just as bubbles do when they burst.

End of the wonderful one-hoss shay.
Logic is logic. That's all I say.   *120*

                                            (1858)

CHARLES DICKENS
England, 1812-1870

WHOLE HOGS

The public market has been of late more than usually remarkable for transactions on the American principle in Whole and indivisible Hogs. The market has been heavy — not the least approach to briskness having been observed in any part of it; but, the transactions, such as they have been, have been exclusively for Whole Hogs. Those who may only have had a retail inclination for sides, ribs, limbs, cheeks, face, trotters, snout,   *5*
ears, or tail, have been required to take the Whole Hog, sinking none of the offal, but consenting to it all — and a good deal of it too.

It has been discovered that mankind at large can only be regenerated by a Teetotal Society, or by a Peace Society, or by always dining on Vegetables. It is to be particularly remarked that either of these certain means of regeneration is utterly defeated, if so   *10*
much as a hair's-breadth of the tip of either ear of that particular Pig be left out of the bargain. Qualify your water with a teaspoonful of wine or brandy — we beg pardon — alcohol — and there is no virtue in Temperance. Maintain a single sentry at the gate of the Queen's Palace, and it is utterly impossible that you can be peaceful. Stew so much as the bone of a mutton chop in the pot with your vegetables, and you will never make   *15*
another Eden out of a Kitchen Garden. You must take the Whole Hog, Sir, and every bristle on him, or you and the rest of mankind will never be regenerated.

Now, without inquiring at present whether means of regeneration that are so easily spoiled, may not a little resemble the pair of dancing-shoes in the story, which the lady destroyed by walking across a room in them, we will consider the Whole Hog question   *20*
from another point of view.

First, stand aside to see the great Teetotal Procession come by. It is called a Temperance Procession — which is not an honest use of a plain word, but never mind that. Hurrah! hurrah! The flags are blue and the letters golden. Hurrah! hurrah! Here are a great many excellent, straightforward, thoroughly well-meaning, and exemplary   *25*
people, four and four, or two and two. Hurrah! Hurrah! Here are a great many children, also four and four, or two and two. Who are they? — They, Sir, are the Juvenile Temperance Bands of Hope. — Lord bless me! What are the Juvenile Temperance Bands of Hope? — They are the Infantine Brigade of Regenerators of Mankind. — Indeed? Hurrah! hurrah! These young citizens being pledged to total abstinence, and   *30*

being fully competent to pledge themselves to anything for life; and it being the custom of such young citizens' parents, in the existing state of unregenerated society, to bring them up on ardent spirits and strong beer (both of which are commonly kept in Barrels, behind the door, on tap, in all large families, expressly for persons of tender years, of whom it is calculated that seven-eights always go to bed drunk); this is a grand show. *35* So, again, Hurrah! hurrah!

Who are these gentlemen walking two and two, with medals on their stomachs and bows in their button-holes? These, Sir, are the Committee. — Are they? Hurrah! hurrah! One cheer more for the Committee! Hoo-o-o-o-rah! A cheer for the Reverend Jabez Fireworks — fond of speaking; a cheer for the gentleman with the stand-up collar, Mr. *40* Gloss — fond of speaking; a cheer for the gentleman with the massive watch-chain, who smiles so sweetly on the surrounding Fair, Mr. Glib — fond of speaking; a cheer for the rather dirty little gentleman who looks like a converted Hyena, Mr. Scradger — fond of speaking; a cheer for the dark-eyed, brown gentleman, the Dove Delegate from America — fond of speaking; a cheer for the swarm who follow, blackening the *45* procession, — Regenerators from everywhere in general — all good men — all fond of speaking; and all going to speak.

I have no right to object, I am sure. Hurrah, hurrah!

The Reverend Jabez Fireworks, and the great Mr. Gloss, and the popular Mr. Glib, and the eminent Mr. Scradger, and the Dove Delegate from America, and the *50* distinguished swarm from everywhere, have ample opportunity (and profit by it, too) for speaking to their heart's content. For, is there not, to-day, a Grand Demonstration Meeting; and to-morrow, another Grand Demonstration Meeting; and, the day after to-morrow, a Grand United Regenerative Zoological Visitation; and, the day after that, a Grand Aggregate General Demonstration; and, the day after that, a Grand Associated *55* Regenerative Breakfast; and, the day after that, a Grand Associated Regenerative Tea; and, the day after that, a Final Grand Aggregate Compounded United and Associated Steamboat River Demonstration; and do the Regenerators go anywhere without speaking, by the bushel? Still, what offence to me? None. Still, I am content to cry, Hurrah! hurrah! If the Regenerators, though estimable men, be the most tiresome men *60* (as speakers) under Heaven; if their sincerest and best followers cannot, in the infirmity of human nature, bear the infliction of such oratory, but occupy themselves in preference with tea and rolls, or resort for comfort to the less terrible society of Lions, Elephants, and Bears, or drown the Regenerative eloquence in the clash of brazen Bands; I think it sensible and right and still exclaim, Hurrah! *65*

But how, if with the matter of such eloquence, when any of it happens to be heard, and also happens not to be a singular compound of references to the Bible, and selections from Joe Miller, I find, on drawing nearer, that I *have* some business? How, if I find that the distinguished swarm are not of that quiet class of gentlemen whom Mr. Carlyle describes as consuming their own smoke; but that they emit a vast amount of *70*

WHOLE HOGS **68. Joe Miller:** Joseph Miller (1684-1738) was a comedian whose name was used, without permission, in the title of John Mottley's joke book, *Joe Miller's Jests* (1739); a "Joe Miller" came to mean a "stale joke." **69-70.** In *Heroes and Hero Worship* (1840), three-fourths of the way through Lecture V, "The Hero as Man of Letters," Thomas Carlyle (see p. 864) writes of Rousseau that "He had not 'the talent of silence'.... The suffering man ought really 'to consume his own smoke'; there is no good in emitting *smoke* till you have made it into *fire*...."

smoke, and blacken their neighbours very considerably? Then, as a neighbour myself, I have perhaps a right to speak.

In Bedlam, and in all other madhouses, Society is denounced as being wrongfully combined against the patient. In Newgate, and in all other prisons, Society is denounced as being wrongfully combined against the criminal. In the speeches of the Reverend 75 Jabez, and the other Regenerators, Society is denounced as being wrongfully and wickedly combined against their own particular Whole Hog — who must be swallowed, every bristle, or there is no Pork in him.

The proof? Society won't come in and sign the pledge; Society won't come in and recruit the Juvenile Temperance bands of hope. Therefore, Society is fond of 80 drunkenness, sees no harm in it, favours it very much, *is* a drunkard — a base, worthless, sensual, profligate brute. Fathers and mothers, sons and daughters, brothers and sisters, divines, physicians, lawyers, editors, authors, painters, poets, musicians, Queen, lords, ladies, and commons, are all in league against the Regenerators, are all violently attached to drunkenness, are all the more dangerous if by any chance they be personal examples of 85 temperance, in the real meaning of the word! — which last powerful steam-hammer of logic has become a pet one, and is constantly to be observed in action.

Against this sweeping misrepresentation, I take the liberty of entering my feeble protest. With all respect for Jabez, for Gloss, for Glib, for Dove Delegate, and for Scradger, I must make so bold as to observe that when a Malay runs amuck he cannot be 90 considered in a temperate state of mind; also, that when a Thermometer stands at Fever Heat, it cannot claim to indicate Temperate weather. A man, to be truly temperate, must be temperate in many respects — in the rejection of strong words no less than of strong drinks — and I crave leave to assert against my good friends the Regenerators, that in such gross statements, they set a most intemperate example. I even doubt whether an 95 equal number of drunkards, under the excitement of the strongest liquors, could set a worse example.

And I would beg to put it seriously to the consideration of those who have sufficient powers of endurance to stand about the platform, listening, whether they think of this sufficiently? Whether they ever knew the like of this before? Whether they have any 100 experience or knowledge of a good cause that was ever promoted by such bad means? Whether they ever heard of an association of people, deliberately, by their chosen vessels, throwing overboard every effort but their own, made for the amelioration of the condition of men; unscrupulously vilifying all other labourers in the vineyard; calumniously setting down as aiders and abettors of an odious vice which they know to 015 be held in general abhorrence, and consigned to general shame, the great compact mass of the community — of its intelligence, of its morality, of its earnest endeavour after better things? If, upon consideration, they know of no such other case, then the inquiry will perhaps occur to them, whether, in supporting a so-conducted cause, they really be upholders of Temperance, dealing with words, which should be the signs for Truth, 110 according to the truth that is in them?

---

73. Bedlam: Bethlehem Hospital, a mental institution in London. **74. Newgate:** London's main prison. **77-78:** alluding to the Anglican Confession: "We have left undone those things which we ought to have done; And we have done those things which we ought not to have done; And there is no health in us."

Mankind can only be regenerated, proclaim the fatteners of the Whole Hog Number Two, by means of a Peace Society. Well! I call out of the nearest Peace Society my worthy friend John Bates — an excellent workman and a sound man, lineally descended from that sturdy soldier of the same name who spake with King Henry the Fifth, on the 115 night before the battle of Agincourt. "Bates," says I, "how about this Regeneration? *Why can it only be effected by means of a Peace Society?*" Says Bates in answer, "Because War is frightful, ruinous, and unchristian. Because the details of one battle, because the horrors of one siege, would so appal you, if you knew them, that probably you never could be happy afterwards. Because man was not created in the image of his Maker to 120 be blasted with gunpowder, or pierced with bayonets, or gashed with swords, or trampled under iron hoofs of horses, into a puddle of mire and blood. Because War is a wickedness that always costs us dear. Because it wastes our treasure, hardens our hearts, paralyses our industry, cripples our commerce, occasions losses, ills, and devilish crimes, unspeakable and out of number." Says I, sadly, "But have I not, O Bates, known 125 all this for this many a year?" "It may be so," says Bates; "then come into the Peace Society." Says I, "Why come in there, Bates?" Says Bates, "Because we declare we won't have War or show of War. We won't have armies, navies, camps, or ships. England shall be disarmed, we say, and all these horrors ended." Says I, "How ended, Bates?" Says Bates, "By arbitration. We have a Dove Delegate from America, and a 130 Mouse Delegate from France; and we are establishing a Bond of Brotherhood, and that'll do it." "Alas! It will NOT do it, Bates. I, too, have thought upon the horrors of war, of the blessings of peace, and of the fatal distraction of men's minds from seeking them, by the roll of the drum and the thunder of the inexorable cannon. However, Bates, the world is not so far upon its course, yet, but that there are tyrants and oppressors left 135 upon it, watchful to find Freedom weak that they may strike, and backed by great armies. O John Bates, look out towards Austria, look out towards Russia, look out towards Germany, look out towards the purple Sea, that lies so beautiful and calm beyond the filthy jails of Naples! Do you see nothing there?" Says Bates (like the sister in Blue Beard, but much more triumphantly) "I see nothing there, but dust"; — and this 140 is one of the inconveniences of a fattened Whole and indivisible Hog, that it fills up the doorway, and its breeders cannot see beyond it. "Dust!" says Bates. I tell Bates that it is because there are, behind that dust, oppressors and oppressed, arrayed against each other — that it is because there are, beyond his Dove Delegate and his Mouse Delegate, the wild beasts of the Forest — that it is because I dread and hate the miseries of tyranny 145 and war — that it is because I would not be soldier-ridden, nor have other men so — that I am not for the disarming of England, and cannot be a member of his Peace Society: admitting all his premises, but denying his conclusion. Whereupon Bates, otherwise just and sensible, insinuates that not being for his Whole and indivisible Hog, I can be for no part of his Hog; and that I have never felt or thought what his Society 150 now tells me it, and only it, feels and thinks as a new discovery; and that when I am told of the new discovery I don't care for it!

114-16: See Shakespeare's *Henry V*. IV. i. **140. Blue Beard:** in the fairytale "Bluebeard," by Charles Perrault; for another of Perrault's works, see p.502.

Mankind can only be regenerated by dining on Vegetables. Why? Certain worthy gentlemen have dined, it seems, on vegetables for ever so many years, and are none the worse for it. Straightway, these excellent men, excited to the highest pitch, announce *155* themselves by public advertisement as "DISTINGUISHED VEGETARIANS," vault upon a platform, hold a vegetable festival, and proceed to show, not without prolixity and weak jokes, that a vegetable diet is the only true faith, and that, in eating meat, mankind is wholly mistaken and partially corrupt. Distinguished Vegetarians. As the men who wear Nankeen trousers might hold a similar meeting, and become *160* Distinguished Nankeenarians! But am I to have NO meat? If I take a pledge to eat three cauliflowers daily in the cauliflower season, a peck of peas daily in the pea time, a gallon of broad Windsor beans daily when beans are "in," and a young cabbage or so every morning before breakfast, with perhaps a little ginger between meals (as a vegetable substance, corrective of that windy diet), may I not be allowed half an ounce *165* of gravy-beef to flavour my potatoes? Not a shred? Distinguished Vegetarians can acknowledge no imperfect animal. Their Hog must be a Whole Hog, according to the fashion of the time.

Now, we would so far renew the custom of sacrificing animals, as to recommend that an altar be erected to Our Country, at present sheltering so many of these very *170* inconvenient and unwieldy Hogs, on which their grosser portions should be "burnt and purged away." The Whole Hog of the Temperance Movement, divested of its intemperate assumption of infallibility and of its intemperate determination to run grunting at the legs of the general population of this empire, would be a far less unclean and a far more serviceable creature than at present. The Whole Hog of the *175* Peace Society, acquiring the recognition of a community of feeling between itself and many who hold war in no less abhorrence, but who yet believe, that, in the present era of the world, some preparation against it is a preservative of peace and a restraint upon despotism, would become as much enlightened as its learned predecessor Toby, of Immortal Memory. And if distinguished Vegetarians, of all *180* kinds, would only allow a little meat; and if distinguished Fleshmeatarians, of all kinds, would only yield a little vegetable; if the former, quietly devouring the fruits of the earth to any extent, would admit the possible morality of mashed potatoes with beef — and if the latter would concede a little spinach with gammon; and if both could manage to get on with a little less platforming — there being at present rather *185* an undue preponderance of cry over wool — if all of us, in short, were to yield up something of our whole and entire animals, it might be very much the better in the end, both for us and for them.

After all, my friends and brothers, even the best Whole and indivisible Hog may be but a small fragment of the higher and greater work, called Education! *190*

(1851)

---

160. Nankeen: buff-coloured Chinese cotton. **171-72. "Burnt . . . away":** See *Hamlet*, I.v.13. **180. Toby:** Shakespeare's character Sir Toby Belch; see *Twelfth Night*, III.iv.175ff. **186. cry over wool:** alluding to the proverbial phrase "Great cry and little wool" — or, in its original and fuller form, "Great cry and little wool, as the Devil said when he sheared his hogs."

H‍ENRY M‍AYHEW
England, 1812-1887

from *L‍ONDON L‍ABOUR AND THE L‍ONDON P‍OOR*

O‍F THE M‍UD-L‍ARKS

There is another class who may be termed river-finders, although their occupation is connected only with the shore; they are commonly known by the name of "mud-larks," from being compelled, in order to obtain the articles they seek, to wade sometimes up to their middle through the mud left on the shore by the retiring tide. These poor creatures are certainly about the most deplorable in their appearance of any I have met with in the course of my inquiries. They may be seen of all ages, from mere childhood to positive decrepitude, crawling among the barges at the various wharfs along the river; it cannot be said that they are clad in rags, for they are scarcely half covered by the tattered indescribable things that serve them for clothing; their bodies are grimed with the foul soil of the river, and their torn garments stiffened up like boards with dirt of every possible description.

Among the mud-larks may be seen many old women, and it is indeed pitiable to behold them, especially during the winter, bent nearly double with age and infirmity, paddling and groping among the wet mud for small pieces of coal, chips of wood, or any sort of refuse washed up by the tide. These women always have with them an old basket or an old tin kettle, in which they put whatever they chance to find. It usually takes them a whole tide to fill this receptacle, but when filled, it is as much as the feeble old creatures are able to carry home.

The mud-larks generally live in some court or alley in the neighbourhood of the river, and, as the tide recedes, crowds of boys and little girls, some old men, and many old women, may be observed loitering about the various stairs, watching eagerly for the opportunity to commence their labours. When the tide is sufficiently low they scatter themselves along the shore, separating from each other, and soon disappear among the craft lying about in every direction. This is the case on both sides of the river, as high up as there is anything to be found, extending as far as Vauxhall-bridge, and as low down as Woolwich. The mud-larks themselves, however, know only those who reside near them, and whom they are accustomed to meet in their daily pursuits; indeed, with but few exceptions, these people are dull, and apparently stupid; this is observable particularly among the boys and girls, who, when engaged in searching the mud, hold but little converse one with another. The men and women may be passed and repassed, but they notice no one; they never speak, but with a stolid look of wretchedness they plash their way through the mire, their bodies bent down while they peer anxiously about, and occasionally stoop to pick up some paltry treasure that falls in their way.

O‍F THE M‍UD-L‍ARKS   **21. stairs:** See line 136.

The mud-larks collect whatever they happen to find, such as coals, bits of old iron, rope, bones, and copper nails that drop from ships while lying or repairing along shore. *35* Copper nails are the most valuable of all the articles they find, but these they seldom obtain, as they are always driven from the neighbourhood of a ship while being new-sheathed. Sometimes the younger and bolder mud-larks venture on sweeping some empty coal-barge, and one little fellow with whom I spoke, having been lately caught in the act of so doing, had to undergo for the offence seven days' imprisonment in the *40* House of Correction: this, he says, he liked much better than mud-larking, for while he staid there he wore a coat and shoes and stockings, and though he had not over much to eat, he certainly was never afraid of going to bed without anything at all — as he often had to do when at liberty. He thought he would try it on again in the winter, he told me, saying, it would be so comfortable to have clothes and shoes and stockings then, and not *45* be obliged to go into the cold wet mud of a morning.

The coals that the mud-larks find, they sell to the poor people of the neighbourhood at 1*d.* per pot, holding about 14 lbs. The iron and bones and rope and copper nails which they collect, they sell at the rag-shops. They dispose of the iron at 5 lbs. for 1*d.*, the bones at 3 lbs. a 1*d.*, rope a ½*d.* per lb. wet, and ¾*d.* per lb. dry, and copper nails at the *50* rate of 4*d.* per lb. They occasionally pick up tools, such as saws and hammers; these they dispose of to the seamen for biscuit and meat, and sometimes sell them at the ragshops for a few halfpence. In this manner they earn from 2½*d.* to 8*d.* per day, but rarely the latter sum; their average gains may be estimated at about 3*d.* per day. The boys, after leaving the river, sometimes scrape their trousers, and frequent the cab- *55* stands, and try to earn a trifle by opening the cab-doors for those who enter them, or by holding gentlemen's horses. Some of them go, in the evening, to a ragged school, in the neighbourhood of which they live; more, as they say, because other boys go there, than from any desire to learn.

At one of the stairs in the neighbourhood of the pool, I collected about a dozen of *60* these unfortunate children; there was not one of them over twelve years of age, and many of them were but six. It would be almost impossible to describe the wretched group, so motley was their appearance, so extraordinary their dress, and so stolid and inexpressive their countenances. Some carried baskets, filled with the produce of their morning's work, and others old tin kettles with iron handles. Some, for want of these *65* articles, had old hats filled with the bones and coals they had picked up; and others, more needy still, had actually taken the caps from their own heads, and filled them with what they had happened to find. The muddy slush was dripping from their clothes and utensils, and forming a puddle in which they stood. There did not appear to be among the whole group as many filthy cotton rags to their backs as, when stitched together, *70* would have been sufficient to form the material of one shirt. There were the remnants of one or two jackets among them, but so begrimed and tattered that it would have been difficult to have determined either the original material or make of the garment. On questioning one, he said his father was a coal-backer; he had been dead eight years; the boy was nine years old. His mother was alive; she went out charing and washing when *75*

---

48. 1*d.* **per pot:** a penny a pot; there were 12 pennies to a shilling, 20 shillings to a pound (sterling). **74. coal-backer:** coal carrier. **75. charing:** working as a charwoman.

she could get any such work to do. She had 1*s*. a day when she could get employment, but that was not often; he remembered once to have had a pair of shoes, but it was a long time since. "It is very cold in winter," he said, "to stand in the mud without shoes," but he did not mind it in the summer. He had been three years mud-larking, and supposed he should remain a mud-lark all his life. What else could he be? for there was 80 nothing else that he knew *how* to do. Some days he earned a 1*d*., and some days 4*d*.; he never earned 8*d*. in one day, that would have been a "jolly lot of money." He never found a saw or a hammer, he "only wished" he could, they would be glad to get hold of them at the dolly's. He had been one month at school before he went mud-larking. Some time ago he had gone to the ragged-school; but he no longer went there, for he forgot it. 85 He could neither read nor write, and did not think he could learn if he tried "ever so much." He didn't know what religion his father and mother were, nor did he know what religion meant. God was God, he said. He had heard he was good, but didn't know what good he was to him. He thought he was a Christian, but he didn't know what a Christian was. He had heard of Jesus Christ once, when he went to a Catholic chapel, but he never 90 heard tell of who or what he was, and didn't "particular care" about knowing. His father and mother were born in Aberdeen, but he didn't know where Aberdeen was. London was England, and England, he said, was in London, but he couldn't tell in what part. He could not tell where he would go to when he died, and didn't believe any one could tell *that*. Prayers, he told me, were what people said to themselves at night. *He* never said 95 any, and didn't know any; his mother sometimes used to speak to him about them, but he could never learn any. His mother didn't go to church or to chapel, because she had no clothes. All the money he got he gave to his mother, and she bought bread with it, and when they had no money they lived the best way they could.

Such was the amount of intelligence manifested by this unfortunate child. 100

Another was only seven years old. He stated that his father was a sailor who had been hurt on board ship, and been unable to go to sea for the last two years. He had two brothers and a sister, one of them older than himself; and his elder brother was a mud-lark like himself. The two had been mud-larking more than a year; they went because they saw other boys go, and knew that they got money for the things they found. They 105 were often hungry, and glad to do anything to get something to eat. Their father was not able to earn anything, and their mother could get but little to do. They gave all the money they earned to their mother. They didn't gamble, and play at pitch and toss when they had got some money, but some of the big boys did on the Sunday, when they didn't go a mud-larking. He couldn't tell why they did nothing on a Sunday, "only they 110 didn't"; though sometimes they looked about to see where the best place would be on the next day. He didn't go to the ragged school; he should like to know how to read a book, though he couldn't tell what good it would do him. He didn't like mud-larking, would be glad of something else, but didn't know anything else that he could do.

Another of the boys was the son of a dock labourer — casually employed. He was 115 between seven and eight years of age, and his sister, who was also a mud-lark, formed one of the group. The mother of these two was dead, and there were three children younger than themselves.

---

84. dolly's: dolly-shop — a marine store, often also a pawnshop.

The rest of the histories may easily be imagined, for there was a painful uniformity in the stories of all the children: they were either the children of the very poor, who, by their own improvidence or some overwhelming calamity, had been reduced to the extremity of distress, or else they were orphans, and compelled from utter destitution to seek for the means of appeasing their hunger in the mud of the river. That the majority of this class are ignorant, and without even the rudiments of education, and that many of them from time to time are committed to prison for petty thefts, cannot be wondered at. Nor can it even excite our astonishment that, once within the walls of a prison, and finding how much more comfortable it is than their previous condition, they should return to it repeatedly. As for the females growing up under such circumstances, the worst may be anticipated of them; and in proof of this I have found, upon inquiry, that very many of the unfortunate creatures who swell the tide of prostitution in Ratcliff-highway, and other low neighbourhoods in the East of London, have originally been mud-larks; and only remained at that occupation till such time as they were capable of adopting the more easy and more lucrative life of the prostitute.

As to the numbers and earnings of the mud-larks, the following calculations fall short of, rather than exceed, the truth. From Execution Dock to the lower part of Limehouse Hole, there are 14 stairs or landing-places, by which the mud-larks descend to the shore in order to pursue their employment. There are about as many on the opposite side of the water similarly frequented.

At King James's Stairs, in Wapping Wall, which is nearly a central position, from 40 to 50 mud-larks go down daily to the river; the mud-larks "using" the other stairs are not so numerous. If, therefore, we reckon the number of stairs on both sides of the river at 28, and the average number of mud-larks frequenting them at 10 each, we shall have a total of 280. Each mud-lark, it has been shown, earns on an average 3*d.* a day, or 1*s.* 6*d.* per week; so that the annual earnings of each will be 3*l.* 18*s.*, or say 4*l.* a year, and hence the gross earnings of the 280 will amount to rather more than 1,000*l.* per annum.

But there are, in addition to the mud-larks employed in the neighbourhood of what may be called the pool, many others who work down the river at various places as far as Blackwall, on the one side, and at Deptford, Greenwich, and Woolwich, on the other. These frequent the neighbourhoods of the various "yards" along shore, where vessels are being built; and whence, at certain times, chips, small pieces of wood, bits of iron, and copper nails, are washed out into the river. There is but little doubt that this portion of the class earn much more than the mud-larks of the pool, seeing that they are especially convenient to the places where the iron vessels are constructed; so that the presumption is, that the number of mud-larks "at work" on the banks of the Thames (especially if we include those above bridge), and the value of the property extracted by them from the mud of the river, may be fairly estimated at double that which is stated above, or say 550 gaining 2,000*l.* per annum.

As an illustration of the doctrines I have endeavoured to enforce throughout this publication, I cite the following history of one of the above class. It may serve to teach

120

125

130

135

140

145

150

155

---

144. annual earnings: Between 1840 and 1850, a working-class man would earn between £30 and £40 a year, depending on his skill; a governess would earn c.£40 plus room and board; a middle-class worker would earn between £150 and £300 a year, and at the upper end of the range could afford a live-in maid; a "gentleman," whose income would be c.£1000 annually, could afford a cook, a manservant, two maids, and property.

those who are still sceptical as to the degrading influence of circumstances upon the   *160*
poor, that many of the humbler classes, if placed in the same easy position as ourselves,
would become, perhaps, quite as "respectable" members of society.

The lad of whom I speak was discovered by me now nearly two years ago "mud-
larking" on the banks of the river near the docks. He was a quick intelligent little fellow,
and had been at the business, he told me, about three years. He had taken to mud-   *165*
larking, he said, because his clothes were too bad for him to look for anything better. He
worked every day, with 20 or 30 boys, who might all be seen at daybreak with their
trousers tucked up, groping about, and picking out the pieces of coal from the mud on
the banks of the Thames. He went into the river up to his knees, and in searching the
mud he often ran pieces of glass and long nails into his feet. When this was the case, he   *170*
went home and dressed the wounds, but returned to the river-side directly, "for should
the tide come up," he added, "without my having found something, why I must starve
till next low tide." In the very cold weather he and his other shoeless companions used
to stand in the hot water that ran down the river side from some of the steam-factories,
to warm their frozen feet.   *175*

At first he found it difficult to keep his footing in the mud, and he had known many
beginners fall in. He came to my house, at my request, the morning after my first
meeting with him. It was the depth of winter, and the poor little fellow was nearly
destitute of clothing. His trousers were worn away up to his knees, he had no shirt, and
his legs and feet (which were bare) were covered with chilblains. On being questioned   *180*
by me he gave the following account of his life: —

He was fourteen years old. He had two sisters, one fifteen and the other twelve
years of age. His father had been dead nine years. The man had been a coal-whipper,
and, from getting his work from one of the publican employers in those days, had
become a confirmed drunkard. When he married he held a situation in a warehouse,   *185*
where his wife managed the first year to save 4*l*. 10*s*. out of her husband's earnings; but
from the day he took to coal-whipping she had never saved one halfpenny, indeed she
and her children were often left to starve. The man (whilst in a state of intoxication) had
fallen between two barges, and the injuries he received had been so severe that he had
lingered in a helpless state for three years before his death. After her husband's decease   *190*
the poor woman's neighbours subscribed 1*l*. 5*s*. for her; with this sum she opened a
greengrocer's shop, and got on very well for five years.

When the boy was nine years old his mother sent him to the Red Lion school at
Green-bank, near Old Gravel-lane, Ratcliffe-highway; she paid 1*d*. a week for his
learning. He remained there for a year; then the potato-rot came, and his mother lost   *195*
upon all she bought. About the same time two of her customers died 30*s*. in her debt;
this loss, together with the potato-disease, completely ruined her, and the whole family
had been in the greatest poverty from that period. Then she was obliged to take all her
children from their school, that they might help to keep themselves as best they could.
Her eldest girl sold fish in the streets, and the boy went to the river-side to "pick up" his   *200*
living. The change, however, was so great that shortly afterwards the little fellow lay ill
eighteen weeks with the ague. As soon as the boy recovered his mother and his two

---

183. coal-whipper: a worker who raises coal out of a ship's hold, using a system of pulleys and ropes.

sisters were "taken bad" with a fever. The poor woman went into the "Great House,"
and the children were taken to the Fever Hospital. When the mother returned home she
was too weak to work, and all she had to depend on was what her boy brought from the   *205*
river. They had nothing to eat and no money until the little fellow had been down to the
shore and picked up some coals, selling them for a trifle.

(1851)

ROBERT BROWNING
England, 1812-1889

MY LAST DUCHESS

Ferrara

That's my last Duchess painted on the wall,
Looking as if she were alive. I call
That piece a wonder, now: Frà Pandolf's hands
Worked busily a day, and there she stands.
Will't please you sit and look at her? I said   *5*
"Frà Pandolf" by design, for never read
Strangers like you that pictured countenance,
The depth and passion of its earnest glance,
But to myself they turned (since none puts by
The curtain I have drawn for you, but I)   *10*
And seemed as they would ask me, if they durst,
How such a glance came there; so, not the first
Are you to turn and ask thus. Sir, 'twas not
Her husband's presence only, called that spot
Of joy into the Duchess' cheek: perhaps   *15*
Frà Pandolf chanced to say, "Her mantle laps
Over my lady's wrist too much," or "Paint
Must never hope to reproduce the faint
Half-flush that dies along her throat": such stuff
Was courtesy, she thought, and cause enough   *20*
For calling up that spot of joy. She had
A heart — how shall I say? — too soon made glad,
Too easily impressed; she liked whate'er
She looked on, and her looks went everywhere.
Sir, 'twas all one! My favour at her breast,   *25*
The dropping of the daylight in the West,
The bough of cherries some officious fool
Broke in the orchard for her, the white mule
She rode with round the terrace — all and each
Would draw from her alike the approving speech,   *30*
Or blush, at least. She thanked men, — good! but thanked
Somehow — I know not how — as if she ranked
My gift of a nine-hundred-years-old name
With anybody's gift. Who'd stoop to blame
This sort of trifling? Even had you skill   *35*
In speech — (which I have not) — to make your will
Quite clear to such an one, and say, "Just this
Or that in you disgusts me; here you miss,
Or there exceed the mark" — and if she let
Herself be lessoned so, nor plainly set   *40*
Her wits to yours, forsooth, and made excuse,
— E'en then would be some stooping; and I choose
Never to stoop. Oh sir, she smiled, no doubt,
Whene'er I passed her; but who passed without
Much the same smile? This grew; I gave commands;   *45*
Then all smiles stopped together. There she stands
As if alive. Will't please you rise? We'll meet
The company below, then. I repeat,
The Count your master's known munificence
Is ample warrant that no just pretence   *50*
Of mine for dowry will be disallowed;
Though his fair daughter's self, as I avowed
At starting, is my object. Nay, we'll go
Together down, sir. Notice Neptune, though,
Taming a sea-horse, thought a rarity,   *55*
Which Claus of Innsbruck cast in bronze for me!

(1842)

---

203. Great House: workhouse.   **MY LAST DUCHESS**   The poem, set in Renaissance Italy, has parallels in history: in 1558 the Duke of
Ferrara, Alfonso d'Este II (1533-1597), married the daughter of Cosimo I de' Medici (1519-1574), the Duke of Florence; when she died
unexpectedly in 1561, the Duke of Ferrara sought to marry the daughter of the Count of Tyrol, resident in Innsbruck.

SOLILOQUY OF THE SPANISH CLOISTER

I

Gr-r-r — there go, my heart's abhorrence!
    Water your damned flower-pots, do!
If hate killed men, Brother Lawrence,
    God's blood, would not mine kill you!
What? your myrtle-bush wants trimming?   5
    Oh, that rose has prior claims —
Needs its leaden vase filled brimming?
    Hell dry you up with its flames!

II

At the meal we sit together:
    Salve tibi! I must hear   10
Wise talk of the kind of weather,
    Sort of season, time of year:
Not a plenteous cork-crop: scarcely
    Dare we hope oak-galls, I doubt:
What's the Latin name for "parsley"?   15
    What's the Greek name for Swine's Snout?

III

Whew! We'll have our platter burnished,
    Laid with care on our own shelf!
With a fire-new spoon we're furnished,
    And a goblet for ourself,   20
Rinsed like something sacrificial
    Ere 't is fit to touch our chaps —
Marked with L. for our initial!
    (He-he! There his lily snaps!)

IV

Saint, forsooth! While brown Dolores   25
    Squats outside the Convent bank
With Sanchicha, telling stories,
    Steeping tresses in the tank,
Blue-black, lustrous, thick like horsehairs,
    — Can't I see his dead eye glow,   30
Bright as 't were a Barbary corsair's?
    (That is, if he'd let it show!)

V

When he finishes refection,
    Knife and fork he never lays
Cross-wise, to my recollection,   35
    As do I, in Jesu's praise.
I the Trinity illustrate,
    Drinking watered orange-pulp —
In three sips the Arian frustrate;
    While he drains his at one gulp.   40

VI

Oh, those melons? If he's able
    We're to have a feast! so nice!
One goes to the Abbot's table,
    All of us get each a slice.
How go on your flowers? None double?   45
    Not one fruit-sort can you spy?
Strange! — And I, too, at such trouble,
    Keep them close-nipped on the sly!

VII

There's a great text in Galatians,
    Once you trip on it, entails   50
Twenty-nine distinct damnations,
    One sure, if another fails:
If I trip him just a-dying,
    Sure of heaven as sure can be,
Spin him round and send him flying   55
    Off to hell, a Manichee?

VIII

Or, my scrofulous French novel
    On grey paper with blunt type!
Simply glance at it, you grovel
    Hand and foot in Belial's gripe: 60
If I double down its pages
    At the woeful sixteenth print,
When he gathers his greengages,
    Ope a sieve and slip it in 't?

SOLILOQUY OF THE SPANISH CLOISTER   10. *Salve tibi:* a greeting: "Be well." **14. oak-galls:** oak-apples, excrescences formed on the oak tree as a result of an insect infestation, used in making ink. **39. Arian:** The Arian heresy (4th century) claimed that God created the Son before creating Adam, and that the Son was not equal in status to God; the 3rd century Manichaean heresy (see line 56), deriving from Zoroastrianism, claimed that human beings lived in a dualistic universe, caught in the fight between the world of God (light) and the world of Satan (darkness). **49. Galatians:** See 5:19-21. **60. Belial:** wickedness (see 2 Corinthians 6:15); Milton later used the name in *Paradise Lost* (I, 490) to refer to the most evil of the fallen angels (see p. 332).

IX

Or, there's Satan! — one might venture 65
  Pledge one's soul to him, yet leave
Such a flaw in the indenture
  As he'd miss till, past retrieve,
Blasted lay that rose-acacia
  We're so proud of! *Hy, Zy, Hine* . . . 70
'St, there's Vespers! *Plena gratiâ*
  Ave, Virgo! Gr-r-r — you swine!
               (1842)

THE BISHOP ORDERS HIS TOMB AT SAINT PRAXED'S CHURCH

Rome, 15—

Vanity, saith the preacher, vanity!
Draw round my bed: is Anselm keeping back?
Nephews — sons mine . . . ah God, I know not! Well —
She, men would have to be your mother once,
Old Gandolf envied me, so fair she was! 5
What's done is done, and she is dead beside,
Dead long ago, and I am Bishop since,
And as she died so must we die ourselves,
And thence ye may perceive the world's a dream.
Life, how and what is it? As here I lie 10
In this state-chamber, dying by degrees,
Hours and long hours in the dead night, I ask
"Do I live, am I dead?" Peace, peace seems all.
Saint Praxed's ever was the church for peace;
And so, about this tomb of mine. I fought 15
With tooth and nail to save my niche, ye know:
— Old Gandolf cozened me, despite my care;
Shrewd was that snatch from out the corner South
He graced his carrion with, God curse the same!
Yet still my niche is not so cramped but thence 20
One sees the pulpit o' the epistle-side,
And somewhat of the choir, those silent seats,

And up into the aery dome where live
The angels, and a sunbeam's sure to lurk:
And I shall fill my slab of basalt there, 25
And 'neath my tabernacle take my rest,
With those nine columns round me, two and two,
The odd one at my feet where Anselm stands:
Peach-blossom marble all, the rare, the ripe
As fresh-poured red wine of a mighty pulse. 30
— Old Gandolf with his paltry onion-stone,
Put me where I may look at him! True peach,
Rosy and flawless: how I earned the prize!
Draw close: that conflagration of my church
— What then? So much was saved if aught were missed!
My sons, ye would not be my death? Go dig 36
The white-grape vineyard where the oil-press stood,
Drop water gently till the surface sink,
And if ye find . . . Ah God, I know not, I! . . .
Bedded in store of rotten fig-leaves soft, 40
And corded up in a tight olive-frail,
Some lump, ah God, of *lapis lazuli*,
Big as a Jew's head cut off at the nape,
Blue as a vein o'er the Madonna's breast . . .
Sons, all have I bequeathed you, villas, all, 45
That brave Frascati villa with its bath,
So, let the blue lump poise between my knees,
Like God the Father's globe on both his hands
Ye worship in the Jesu Church so gay,
For Gandolf shall not choose but see and burst! 50
Swift as a weaver's shuttle fleet our years:
Man goeth to the grave, and where is he?
Did I say basalt for my slab, sons? Black —
'Twas ever antique-black I meant! How else
Shall ye contrast my frieze to come beneath? 55
The bas-relief in bronze ye promised me,
Those Pans and Nymphs ye wot of, and perchance
Some tripod, thyrsus, with a vase or so,
The Saviour at his sermon on the mount,
Saint Praxed in a glory, and one Pan 60
Ready to twitch the Nymph's last garment off,

---

70. *Hy, Zy, Hine*: This phrase is familiar in form to the beginning of several rhymes now associated with children's counting rituals ("One, two, buckle my shoe," see p. 569; "Eeny meeny miney moe"; "Hinx, minx, the old witch stinks," "Ready, set, go"); some critics, however, have suggested that in this context the phrase is the beginning of an invocation to Satan. **71-72. *Plena gratiâ Ave, Virgo*:** Hail, Virgin, full of grace.   **THE BISHOP ORDERS HIS TOMB Title.** Praxed, i.e., Praxedes, a Roman virgin of the 1st century, who is commemorated in the Church of Santa Prassede in Rome. **1. "Vanity . . . vanity":** See Ecclesiastes 1:2. **2. Anselm:** apparently named for St. Anselm (c.1033-1109). **21. epistle-side:** i.e., the right-hand side of the church, facing the altar, the side on which the Epistles are read, as opposed to the left-hand or gospel-side. **26. tabernacle:** an ornamental covering above the tomb-top. **30. pulse:** the pulp of the grape. **31. onion-stone:** poor quality, peeling or flaking marble. **41. frail:** basket. **43. Jew's head:** Cf. the story of Salome and John the Baptist, Matthew 14:6-11. **46. Frascati:** a town in the Alban Hills, famous for its wine and fine estates. **49. Jesu Church:** Il Gesù, a Jesuit church in Rome. **51:** See Job 7:6. **54. antique-black:** a black basalt called *neroantico*. **58. tripod:** three-legged stool, like the one used by the Oracle of Apollo at Delphi; **thyrsus:** staff entwined with ivy, of the sort carried by Bacchus, the god of wine, and the satyrs. **59. sermon on the mount:** See Matthew 5-7 (for the Beatitudes, see p. 251). **60. in a glory:** represented with a gold halo, or rays of gold around the head, signifying holiness.

And Moses with the tables . . . but I know
Ye mark me not! What do they whisper thee,
Child of my bowels, Anselm? Ah, ye hope
To revel down my villas while I gasp   65
Bricked o'er with beggar's mouldy travertine
Which Gandolf from his tomb-top chuckles at!
Nay, boys, ye love me — all of jasper, then!
'Tis jasper ye stand pledged to, lest I grieve
My bath must needs be left behind, alas!   70
One block, pure green as a pistachio-nut,
There's plenty jasper somewhere in the world —
And have I not Saint Praxed's ear to pray
Horses for ye, and brown Greek manuscripts,
And mistresses with great smooth marbly limbs?   75
— That's if ye carve my epitaph aright,
Choice Latin, picked phrase, Tully's every word,
No gaudy ware like Gandolf's second line —
Tully, my masters? Ulpian serves his need!
And then how I shall lie through centuries,   80
And hear the blessed mutter of the mass,
And see God made and eaten all day long,
And feel the steady candle-flame, and taste
Good strong thick stupefying incense-smoke!
For as I lie here, hours of the dead night,   85
Dying in state and by such slow degrees,
I fold my arms as if they clasped a crook,
And stretch my feet forth straight as stone can point,
And let the bedclothes, for a mortcloth, drop
Into great laps and folds of sculptor's-work: 90
And as yon tapers dwindle, and strange thoughts
Grow, with a certain humming in my ears,
About the life before I lived this life,
And this life too, popes, cardinals and priests,
Saint Praxed at his sermon on the mount,   95
Your tall pale mother with her talking eyes,
And new-found agate urns as fresh as day,
And marble's language, Latin pure, discreet,
— Aha, ELUCESCEBAT quoth our friend?
No Tully, said I, Ulpian at the best!   100
Evil and brief hath been my pilgrimage.
All *lapis*, all, sons! Else I give the Pope
My villas! Will ye ever eat my heart?
Ever your eyes were as a lizard's quick,

They glitter like your mother's for my soul,   105
Or ye would heighten my impoverished frieze,
Piece out its starved design, and fill my vase
With grapes, and add a visor and a Term,
And to the tripod ye would tie a lynx
That in his struggle throws the thyrsus down,   110
To comfort me on my entablature
Whereon I am to lie till I must ask
"Do I live, am I dead?" There, leave me, there!
For ye have stabbed me with ingratitude
To death — ye wish it — God, ye wish it! Stone —   115
Gritstone, a-crumble! Clammy squares which sweat
As if the corpse they keep were oozing through —
And no more *lapis* to delight the world!
Well, go! I bless ye. Fewer tapers there,
But in a row: and, going, turn your backs   120
— Ay, like departing altar-ministrants,
And leave me in my church, the church for peace,
That I may watch at leisure if he leers —
Old Gandolf — at me, from his onion-stone,
As still he envied me, so fair she was!   125

(1845)

HOME-THOUGHTS, FROM ABROAD

I

Oh, to be in England
Now that April's there,
And whoever wakes in England
Sees, some morning, unaware,
That the lowest boughs and the brushwood sheaf   5
Round the elm-tree bole are in tiny leaf,
While the chaffinch sings on the orchard bough
In England — now!

II

And after April, when May follows,
And the whitethroat builds, and all the swallows!   10
Hark, where my blossomed pear-tree in the hedge
Leans to the field and scatters on the clover
Blossoms and dewdrops — at the bent spray's edge —
That's the wise thrush; he sings each song twice over,

---

62. Moses . . . tables: See Exodus 20. **66. travertine:** pale yellow building limestone (in contrast to basalt, marble, and such precious stones as lapis lazuli, jasper, and agate, lines 42, 68, 97). **77. Tully:** Marcus Tullius Cicero (106-43 B.C.), Roman orator, poet, and statesman. **79. Ulpian:** Domitius Ulpianus (170-228 A.D.), a Roman writer of legal commentaries. **82. God made and eaten:** referring to the Eucharist, and the doctrine of transubstantiation; see, e.g., Matthew 26:26-28, Mark 14:22-24, 1 Corinthians 11:23-26. **87. crook:** i.e., shepherd's crook, or crozier, the bishop's ceremonial staff. **89. mortcloth:** cloth draped over a coffin. **99. Elucescebat:** the past imperfect form of the Late Latin verb "elucesceo," to shine: hence "he was shining" or "he was illustrious"; Cicero, by contrast, would have written in Classical Latin, using the verb "eluceo" (to shine) and the past imperfect form "elucebat." **101.** Cf. Genesis 47:9. **108. visor:** mask; **Term:** a bust, like the representations of the Roman god Terminus, with a column or pedestal turning at the top into the torso and head of a man. **109. lynx:** the animal that appeared in depictions of Dionysus. **116. Gritstone:** decaying sandstone.

Lest you should think he never could recapture   *15*
The first fine careless rapture!
And though the fields look rough with hoary dew,
All will be gay when noontide wakes anew
The buttercups, the little children's dower
— Far brighter than this gaudy melon-flower!   *20*

(1845)

WANTING IS — WHAT?

Wanting is — what?
Summer redundant,
Blueness abundant,
— Where is the blot?
Beamy the world, yet a blank all the same;   *5*
— Framework which waits for a picture to frame:

What of the leafage, what of the flower?
Roses embowering with naught they embower!
Come then, complete incompletion, O comer,
Pant through the blueness, perfect the summer!   *10*
Breathe but one breath
Rose-beauty above,
And all that was death
Grows life, grows love,
Grows love!   *15*

(1883)

BUHKWUJJENENE

Canada, c.1815-1900

NANABOOZHOO CREATES THE WORLD

Nanaboozhoo . . . had a son. He loved his son. He told his son never to go near the water
lest evil should come to him. The son disobeyed his father, he went out in a canoe and
was never seen or heard of more. Nanaboozhoo then vowed vengeance against the gods
of the water who had destroyed his son. There were two of these gods and one day they
lay sleeping on the shore. Nanaboozhoo was looking everywhere for them, determined   *5*
to kill them. A loon offered to show him where they were sleeping. He followed the
loon till he found them, and then he made short work of them with his tomahawk and
his war-club. But lo and behold no sooner were the gods dead than the waters of the
great lake rose up in vengeance; they pursued Nanaboozhoo up on to the dry land, and
he had to run for his life. He sought the highest mountain and climbed to the top of the   *10*
highest pine tree. Still the waters pursued him. They rose higher and higher. What could
he do! He broke off a few of the topmost branches, and made a raft upon which he got
and saved himself. He saved also a number of the animals that were kicking and
struggling in the water all around him. At length he bethought himself of making a new
world. How should he do it? Could he but procure a little of the old world he might   *15*
manage it. He selected the beaver from among the animals, and sent it to dive after some
earth. When it came up it was dead. He sent the otter, but it died also. At length he tried
the muskrat. The muskrat dived. When it came up it was dead. But in its claws was
clenched a little earth. Nanaboozhoo carefully took this earth, rubbed it in his fingers till
it was dry, then placed it in the palm of his hand, and blew it gently over the surface of   *20*

NANABOOZHOO CREATES THE WORLD Title: Nanaboozhoo (also spelled Nanabush and Manabozho in other tales) is the Ojibway
creator figure.

the water. A new world was thus formed, and Nanaboozhoo and all the animals landed. Nanaboozhoo sent out a wolf to see how big the world was. He was gone a month. Again he sent him out and he was gone a year. Then he sent out a very young wolf. This young wolf died of old age before it could get back. So Nanaboozhoo said the world was big enough, and might stop growing.

25

(1878)

HENRY DAVID THOREAU
U.S.A., 1817-1862

from *WALDEN; OR, LIFE IN THE WOODS*

Chapter 2: Where I Lived, and What I Lived For

At a certain season of our life we are accustomed to consider every spot as the possible site of a house. I have thus surveyed the country on every side within a dozen miles of where I live. In imagination I have bought all the farms in succession, for all were to be bought, and I knew their price. I walked over each farmer's premises, tasted his wild apples, discoursed on husbandry with him, took his farm at his price, at any price, mortgaging it to him in my mind; even put a higher price on it, — took everything but a deed of it, — took his word for his deed, for I dearly love to talk, — cultivated it, and him too to some extent, I trust, and withdrew when I had enjoyed it long enough, leaving him to carry it on. This experience entitled me to be regarded as a sort of real-estate broker by my friends. Wherever I sat, there I might live, and the landscape radiated from me accordingly. What is a house but a *sedes*, a seat? — better if a country seat. I discovered many a site for a house not likely to be soon improved, which some might have thought too far from the village, but to my eyes the village was too far from it. Well, there I might live, I said; and there I did live, for an hour, a summer and a winter life; saw how I could let the years run off, buffet the winter through, and see the spring come in. The future inhabitants of this region, wherever they may place their houses, may be sure that they have been anticipated. An afternoon sufficed to lay out the land into orchard, wood-lot, and pasture, and to decide what fine oaks or pines should be left to stand before the door, and whence each blasted tree could be seen to the best advantage; and then I let it lie, fallow perchance, for a man is rich in proportion to the number of things which he can afford to let alone.

My imagination carried me so far that I even had the refusal of several farms, — the refusal was all I wanted, — but I never got my fingers burned by actual possession. The

5

10

15

20

WHERE I LIVED, AND WHAT I LIVED FOR Thoreau opens the first chapter, "Economy," with the following paragraph: "When I wrote the following pages, or rather the bulk of them, I lived alone, in the woods, a mile from any neighbor, in a house which I had built myself, on the shore of Walden Pond, in Concord, Massachusetts, and earned my living by the labor of my hands only. I lived there two years and two months. At present I am a sojourner in civilized life again." **2. surveyed:** looked over, examined, but also in the technical sense, since he made his living as a surveyor (which is why he italicizes *survey* in the lines from Cowper — see line 37 below). **11:** Latin *sedes* means both "seat" and "dwelling."

nearest that I came to actual possession was when I bought the Hollowell place, and had
begun to sort my seeds, and collected materials with which to make a wheelbarrow to   *25*
carry it on or off with; but before the owner gave me a deed of it, his wife — every man
has such a wife — changed her mind and wished to keep it, and he offered me ten
dollars to release him. Now, to speak the truth, I had but ten cents in the world, and it
surpassed my arithmetic to tell, if I was that man who had ten cents, or who had a farm,
or ten dollars, or all together. However, I let him keep the ten dollars and the farm too,   *30*
for I had carried it far enough; or rather, to be generous, I sold him the farm for just
what I gave for it, and, as he was not a rich man, made him a present of ten dollars, and
still had my ten cents, and seeds, and materials for a wheelbarrow left. I found thus that
I had been a rich man without any damage to my poverty. But I retained the landscape,
and I have since annually carried off what it yielded without a wheelbarrow. With   *35*
respect to landscapes, —

> "I am monarch of all I *survey*,
> My right there is none to dispute."

I have frequently seen a poet withdraw, having enjoyed the most valuable part of a
farm, while the crusty farmer supposed that he had got a few wild apples only. Why, the   *40*
owner does not know it for many years when a poet has put his farm in rime, the most
admirable kind of invisible fence, has fairly impounded it, milked it, skimmed it, and
got all the cream, and left the farmer only the skimmed milk.

The real attractions of the Hollowell farm, to me, were: its complete retirement,
being about two miles from the village, half a mile from the nearest neighbor, and   *45*
separated from the highway by a broad field; its bounding on the river, which the owner
said protected it by its fogs from frosts in the spring, though that was nothing to me; the
gray color and ruinous state of the house and barn, and the dilapidated fences, which put
such an interval between me and the last occupant; the hollow and lichen-covered apple
trees, gnawed by rabbits, showing what kind of neighbors I should have; but above all,   *50*
the recollection I had of it from my earliest voyages up the river, when the house was
concealed behind a dense grove of red maples, through which I heard the house-dog
bark. I was in haste to buy it, before the proprietor finished getting out some rocks,
cutting down the hollow apple trees, and grubbing up some young birches which had
sprung up in the pasture, or, in short, had made any more of his improvements. To enjoy   *55*
these advantages I was ready to carry it on; like Atlas, to take the world on my
shoulders, — I never heard what compensation he received for that, — and do all those
things which had no other motive or excuse but that I might pay for it and be
unmolested in my possession of it; for I knew all the while that it would yield the most
abundant crop of the kind I wanted, if I could only afford to let it alone. But it turned out   *60*
as I have said.

All that I could say, then, with respect to farming on a large scale (I have always
cultivated a garden), was, that I had had my seeds ready. Many think that seeds improve

---

37-38: from Cowper's "Verses, Supposed to Be Written by Alexander Selkirk" (see p. 653). **56. Atlas:** in Greek myth, a Titan said to support the world on his shoulders.

with age. I have no doubt that time discriminates between the good and the bad; and when at last I shall plant, I shall be less likely to be disappointed. But I would say to my 65 fellows, once for all, As long as possible live free and uncommitted. It makes but little difference whether you are committed to a farm or the county jail.

Old Cato, whose "De Re Rusticâ" is my "Cultivator," says, and the only translation I have seen makes sheer nonsense of the passage, "When you think of getting a farm turn it thus in your mind, not to buy greedily; nor spare your pains to look at it, and do 70 not think it enough to go round it once. The oftener you go there the more it will please you, if it is good." I think I shall not buy greedily, but go round and round it as long as I live, and be buried in it first, that it may please me the more at last.

The present was my next experiment of this kind, which I purpose to describe more at length, for convenience putting the experience of two years into one. As I have said, I 75 do not propose to write an ode to dejection, but to brag as lustily as chanticleer in the morning, standing on his roost, if only to wake my neighbors up.

When first I took up my abode in the woods, that is, began to spend my nights as well as days there, which, by accident, was on Independence Day, or the Fourth of July, 1845, my house was not finished for winter, but was merely a defence against the rain, 80 without plastering or chimney, the walls being of rough, weather-stained boards, with wide chinks, which made it cool at night. The upright white hewn studs and freshly planed door and window casings gave it a clean and airy look, especially in the morning, when its timbers were saturated with dew, so that I fancied that by noon some sweet gum would exude from them. To my imagination it retained throughout the day 85 more or less of this auroral character, reminding me of a certain house on a mountain which I had visited a year before. This was an airy and unplastered cabin, fit to entertain a travelling god, and where a goddess might trail her garments. The winds which passed over my dwelling were such as sweep over the ridges of mountains, bearing the broken strains, or celestial parts only, of terrestrial music. The morning wind forever blows, the 90 poem of creation is uninterrupted; but few are the ears that hear it. Olympus is but the outside of the earth everywhere.

The only house I had been the owner of before, if I except a boat, was a tent, which I used occasionally when making excursions in the summer, and this is still rolled up in my garret; but the boat, after passing from hand to hand, has gone down the stream of 95 time. With this more substantial shelter about me, I had made some progress toward settling in the world. This frame, so slightly clad, was a sort of crystallization around me, and reacted on the builder. It was suggestive somewhat as a picture in outlines. I did not need to go outdoors to take the air, for the atmosphere within had lost none of its freshness. It was not so much within-doors as behind a door where I sat, even in the 100 rainiest weather. The Harivansa says, "An abode without birds is like a meat without seasoning." Such was not my abode, for I found myself suddenly neighbor to the birds;

---

68. Cato: See note to lines 73-74 of Milton's *Of Education* (p. 320); *Cultivator* was the name of one or another New England periodical of the time. **75. As I have said:** i.e., on the title page, as epigraph for the whole book. **76.** probably alluding to Samuel Taylor Coleridge's poem "Dejection: An Ode." **91. Olympus:** Mount Olympus, the home of the gods, in northern Greece. **101. Harivansa:** Hindu epic about Hari (Krishna, principal avatar of Vishnu), sometimes included in the *Mahabharata* as a supplement.

not by having imprisoned one, but having caged myself near them. I was not only nearer to some of those which commonly frequent the garden and the orchard, but to those wilder and more thrilling songsters of the forest which never, or rarely, serenade a *105* villager, — the wood-thrush, the veery, the scarlet tanager, the field sparrow, the whip-poor-will, and many others.

I was seated by the shore of a small pond, about a mile and a half south of the village of Concord and somewhat higher than it, in the midst of an extensive wood between that town and Lincoln, and about two miles south of that our only field known *110* to fame, Concord Battle Ground; but I was so low in the woods that the opposite shore, half a mile off, like the rest, covered with wood, was my most distant horizon. For the first week, whenever I looked out on the pond it impressed me like a tarn high up on the side of a mountain, its bottom far above the surface of other lakes, and, as the sun arose, I saw it throwing off its nightly clothing of mist, and here and there, by degrees, its soft *115* ripples or its smooth reflecting surface was revealed, while the mists, like ghosts, were stealthily withdrawing in every direction into the woods, as at the breaking up of some nocturnal conventicle. The very dew seemed to hang upon the trees later into the day than usual, as on the sides of mountains.

This small lake was of most value as a neighbor in the intervals of a gentle rain- *120* storm in August, when, both air and water being perfectly still, but the sky overcast, mid-afternoon had all the serenity of evening, and the wood-thrush sang around, and was heard from shore to shore. A lake like this is never smoother than at such a time; and the clear portion of the air above it being shallow and darkened by clouds, the water, full of light and reflections, becomes a lower heaven itself so much the more *125* important. From a hilltop near by, where the wood had been recently cut off, there was a pleasing vista southward across the pond, through a wide indentation in the hills which form the shore there, where their opposite sides sloping toward each other suggested a stream flowing out in that direction through a wooded valley, but stream there was none. That way I looked between and over the near green hills to some distant and higher ones *130* in the horizon, tinged with blue. Indeed, by standing on tiptoe I could catch a glimpse of some of the peaks of the still bluer and more distant mountain ranges in the northwest, those true-blue coins from heaven's own mint, and also of some portion of the village. But in other directions, even from this point, I could not see over or beyond the woods which surrounded me. It is well to have some water in your neighborhood, to give *135* buoyancy to and float the earth. One value even of the smallest well is, that when you look into it you see that earth is not continent but insular. This is as important as that it keeps butter cool. When I looked across the pond from this peak toward the Sudbury meadows, which in time of flood I distinguished elevated perhaps by a mirage in their seething valley, like a coin in a basin, all the earth beyond the pond appeared like a thin *140* crust insulated and floated even by this small sheet of intervening water, and I was reminded that this on which I dwelt was but *dry land.*

Though the view from my door was still more contracted, I did not feel crowded or confined in the least. There was pasture enough for my imagination. The low shrub oak

---

111. **Concord Battle Ground:** See Emerson's "Concord Hymn" (p. 901).

plateau to which the opposite shore arose stretched away toward the prairies of the West *145*
and the steppes of Tartary, affording ample room for all the roving families of men.
"There are none happy in the world but beings who enjoy freely a vast horizon," — said
Damodara, when his herds required new and larger pastures.

Both place and time were changed, and I dwelt nearer to those parts of the universe
and to those eras in history which had most attracted me. Where I lived was as far off as *150*
many a region viewed nightly by astronomers. We are wont to imagine rare and
delectable places in some remote and more celestial corner of the system, behind the
constellation of Cassiopeia's Chair, far from noise and disturbance. I discovered that my
house actually had its site in such a withdrawn, but forever new and unprofaned, part of
the universe. If it were worth the while to settle in those parts near to the Pleiades or the *155*
Hyades, to Aldebaran or Altair, then I was really there, or at an equal remoteness from
the life which I had left behind, dwindled and twinkling with as fine a ray to my nearest
neighbor, and to be seen only in moonless nights by him. Such was that part of creation
where I had squatted; —

> "There was a shepherd that did live, *160*
>   And held his thoughts as high
> As were the mounts whereon his flocks
>   Did hourly feed him by."

What should we think of the shepherd's life if his flocks always wandered to higher
pastures than his thoughts? *165*

Every morning was a cheerful invitation to make my life of equal simplicity, and I
may say innocence, with Nature herself. I have been as sincere a worshipper of Aurora
as the Greeks. I got up early and bathed in the pond; that was a religious exercise, and
one of the best things which I did. They say that characters were engraven on the
bathing tub of King Tching-thang to this effect: "Renew thyself completely each day; do *170*
it again, and again, and forever again." I can understand that. Morning brings back the
heroic ages. I was as much affected by the faint hum of a mosquito making its invisible
and unimaginable tour through my apartment at earliest dawn, when I was sitting with
door and windows open, as I could be by any trumpet that ever sang of fame. It was
Homer's requiem; itself an Iliad and Odyssey in the air, singing its own wrath and *175*
wanderings. There was something cosmical about it; a standing advertisement, till
forbidden, of the everlasting vigor and fertility of the world. The morning, which is the
most memorable season of the day, is the awakening hour. Then there is least
somnolence in us; and for an hour, at least, some part of us awakes which slumbers all
the rest of the day and night. Little is to be expected of that day, if it can be called a day, *180*

---

148. **Damodara:** another name of Krishna; the quotation is from the *Harivansa*. **153-56:** Cassiopeia's Chair, a star-cluster in the constellation Cassiopeia; the Pleiades and Hyades, clusters in Taurus; Aldebaran, a double star in Taurus — the eye of the bull; Altair, a double star in Aquila. **160-63:** From an anonymous early 17th-century song. **167. Aurora:** Roman goddess of the dawn. **170. Tching-thang:** Ch'en T'ang, legendary founder of the Shang or Yin dynasty of China (c.1766-c.1122 B.C.); written about by Confucius. **174. trumpet . . . fame:** from line 12 of a poem by Felicia Hemans (see p. 847), "The Landing of the Pilgrim Fathers in New England": "Not as the conqueror comes, / They, the true-hearted, came; / Not with the roll of the stirring drums, / And the trumpet that sings of fame." **175-76:** the *wrath* of Achilles, the *wanderings* of Odysseus — the topics of Homer's *Iliad* and *Odyssey*, respectively, as announced in their opening lines. **176-77. a standing . . . forbidden:** i.e., an advertisement that continues to run until expressly cancelled.

to which we are not awakened by our Genius, but by the mechanical nudgings of some servitor, are not awakened by our own newly acquired force and aspirations from within, accompanied by the undulations of celestial music, instead of factory bells, and a fragrance filling the air — to a higher life than we fell asleep from; and thus the darkness bear its fruit, and prove itself to be good, no less than the light. That man who does not believe that each day contains an earlier, more sacred, and auroral hour than he has yet profaned, has despaired of life, and is pursuing a descending and darkening way. After a partial cessation of his sensuous life, the soul of man, or its organs rather, are reinvigorated each day, and his Genius tries again what noble life it can make. All memorable events, I should say, transpire in morning time and in a morning atmosphere. The Vedas say, "All intelligences awake with the morning." Poetry and art, and the fairest and most memorable of the actions of men, date from such an hour. All poets and heroes, like Memnon, are the children of Aurora, and emit their music at sunrise. To him whose elastic and vigorous thought keeps pace with the sun, the day is a perpetual morning. It matters not what the clocks say or the attitudes and labors of men. Morning is when I am awake and there is a dawn in me. Moral reform is the effort to throw off sleep. Why is it that men give so poor an account of their day if they have not been slumbering? They are not such poor calculators. If they had not been overcome with drowsiness, they would have performed something. The millions are awake enough for physical labor; but only one in a million is awake enough for effective intellectual exertion, only one in a hundred millions to a poetic or divine life. To be awake is to be alive. I have never yet met a man who was quite awake. How could I have looked him in the face?

We must learn to reawaken and keep ourselves awake, not by mechanical aids, but by an infinite expectation of the dawn, which does not forsake us in our soundest sleep. I know of no more encouraging fact than the unquestionable ability of man to elevate his life by a conscious endeavor. It is something to be able to paint a particular picture, or to carve a statue, and so to make a few objects beautiful; but it is far more glorious to carve and paint the very atmosphere and medium through which we look, which morally we can do. To affect the quality of the day, that is the highest of arts. Every man is tasked to make his life, even in its details, worthy of the contemplation of his most elevated and critical hour. If we refused, or rather used up, such paltry information as we get, the oracles would distinctly inform us how this might be done.

I went to the woods because I wished to live deliberately, to front only the essential facts of life, and see if I could not learn what it had to teach, and not, when I came to die, discover that I had not lived. I did not wish to live what was not life, living is so dear; nor did I wish to practise resignation, unless it was quite necessary. I wanted to live deep and suck out all the marrow of life, to live so sturdily and Spartan-like as to put to rout all that was not life, to cut a broad swath and shave close, to drive life into a corner, and reduce it to its lowest terms, and, if it proved to be mean, why then to get the whole and genuine

185

190

195

200

205

210

215

---

181. Genius: tutelary deity, guardian spirit. **191. Vedas:** ancient sacred writings of Hinduism. **193. Memnon:** in Greek myth, king of Ethiopia, son of Eos (Aurora), slain by Achilles during the Trojan War; the huge statue of Egyptian pharaoh Amenhotep (Amenophis) III, at Thebes, called Memnon by the Greeks, supposedly gave out a sharp musical sound when struck by the first rays of the morning sun. **217. Spartan-like:** i.e., self-disciplined, austere.

meanness of it, and publish its meanness to the world; or if it were sublime, to know it by experience, and be able to give a true account of it in my next excursion. For most men, it appears to me, are in a strange uncertainty about it, whether it is of the devil or of God, and have *somewhat hastily* concluded that it is the chief end of man here to "glorify God and enjoy him forever." 220

Still we live meanly, like ants; though the fable tells us that we were long ago changed into men; like pygmies we fight with cranes; it is error upon error, and clout upon clout, and our best virtue has for its occasion a superfluous and evitable wretchedness. Our life is frittered away by detail. An honest man has hardly need to count more than his ten fingers, or in extreme cases he may add his ten toes, and lump the rest. Simplicity, simplicity, simplicity! I say, let your affairs be as two or three, and not a hundred or a thousand; instead of a million count half a dozen, and keep your accounts on your thumb-nail. In the midst of this chopping sea of civilized life, such are the clouds and storms and quicksands and thousand-and-one items to be allowed for, that a man has to live, if he would not founder and go to the bottom and not make his port at all, by dead reckoning, and he must be a great calculator indeed who succeeds. Simplify, simplify. Instead of three meals a day, if it be necessary eat but one; instead of a hundred dishes, five; and reduce other things in proportion. Our life is like a German Confederacy, made up of petty states, with its boundary forever fluctuating, so that even a German cannot tell you how it is bounded at any moment. The nation itself, with all its so-called internal improvements, which, by the way, are all external and superficial, is just such an unwieldy and overgrown establishment, cluttered with furniture and tripped up by its own traps, ruined by luxury and heedless expense, by want of calculation and a worthy aim, as the million households in the land; and the only cure for it, as for them, is in a rigid economy, a stern and more than Spartan simplicity of life and elevation of purpose. It lives too fast. Men think that it is essential that the *Nation* have commerce, and export ice, and talk through a telegraph, and ride thirty miles an hour, without a doubt, whether *they* do or not; but whether we should live like baboons or like men, is a little uncertain. If we do not get out sleepers, and forge rails, and devote days and nights to the work, but go to tinkering upon our *lives* to improve *them*, who will build railroads? And if railroads are not built, how shall we get to heaven in season? But if we stay at home and mind our business, who will want railroads? We do not ride on the railroad; it rides upon us. Did you ever think what those sleepers are that underlie the railroad? Each one is a man, an Irishman, or a Yankee man. The rails are laid on them, and they are covered with sand, and the cars run smoothly over them. They are sound sleepers, I assure you. And every few years a new lot is laid down and run over; so that, if some have the pleasure of riding on a rail, others have the misfortune to be ridden upon. And when they run over a man that is walking in his sleep, a supernumerary 225 230 235 240 245 250 255

223-24: "What is the chief end of man?" "To glorify God and to enjoy him for ever" — from *The Shorter Catechism*, used in Presbyterian churches. **225-26. ants . . . men:** When a plague wiped out the people of King Aiakos (Aeacus), he begged Zeus, his father, for help; Zeus turned the ants in a nearby sacred oak tree into human beings to repopulate his realm (see Ovid's *Metamorphoses*, VII, 517ff.). **226. pygmies . . . cranes:** See note to *Paradise Lost*, I, 575-76 (p. 333). **226-27. clout upon clout:** from an early American ballad; *clout*, piece of cloth, patch. **237-38:** The German Confederacy, or Confederation, was formed in 1815, replaced in 1866, after the Austro-Prussian War, by the North German Confederation, and transformed into the German Empire under William I and Bismarck in 1871. **248. sleepers:** railroad ties, crossties. **250:** probably an allusion to Nathaniel Hawthorne's satirical story "The Celestial Railroad." **251-52:** Cf. lines 50-51 of Emerson's "Ode" (p. 918).

sleeper in the wrong position, and wake him up, they suddenly stop the cars, and make a hue and cry about it, as if this were an exception. I am glad to know that it takes a gang of men for every five miles to keep the sleepers down and level in their beds as it is, for *260* this is a sign that they may sometime get up again.

Why should we live with such hurry and waste of life? We are determined to be starved before we are hungry. Men say that a stitch in time saves nine, and so they take a thousand stitches to-day to save nine to-morrow. As for *work*, we haven't any of any consequence. We have the Saint Vitus' dance, and cannot possibly keep our heads still. *265* If I should only give a few pulls at the parish bell-rope, as for a fire, that is, without setting the bell, there is hardly a man on his farm in the outskirts of Concord, notwithstanding that press of engagements which was his excuse so many times this morning, nor a boy, nor a woman, I might almost say, but would forsake all and follow that sound, not mainly to save property from the flames, but, if we will confess the truth, *270* much more to see it burn, since burn it must, and we, be it known, did not set it on fire, — or to see it put out, and have a hand in it, if that is done as handsomely; yes, even if it were the parish church itself. Hardly a man takes a half-hour's nap after dinner, but when he wakes he holds up his head and asks, "What's the news?" as if the rest of mankind had stood his sentinels. Some give directions to be waked every half-hour, *275* doubtless for no other purpose; and then, to pay for it, they tell what they have dreamed. After a night's sleep the news is as indispensable as the breakfast. "Pray tell me anything new that has happened to a man anywhere on this globe," — and he reads it over his coffee and rolls, that a man has had his eyes gouged out this morning on the Wachito River; never dreaming the while that he lives in the dark unfathomed *280* mammoth cave of this world, and has but the rudiment of an eye himself.

For my part, I could easily do without the post-office. I think that there are very few important communications made through it. To speak critically, I never received more than one or two letters in my life — I wrote this some years ago — that were worth the postage. The penny-post is, commonly, an institution through which you seriously offer *285* a man that penny for his thoughts which is so often safely offered in jest. And I am sure that I never read any memorable news in a newspaper. If we read of one man robbed, or murdered, or killed by accident, or one house burned, or one vessel wrecked, or one steamboat blown up, or one cow run over on the Western Railroad, or one mad dog killed, or one lot of grasshoppers in the winter, — we never need read of another. One is *290* enough. If you are acquainted with the principle, what do you care for a myriad instances and applications? To a philosopher all *news*, as it is called, is gossip, and they who edit and read it are old women over their tea. Yet not a few are greedy after this gossip. There was such a rush, as I hear, the other day at one of the offices to learn the foreign news by the last arrival, that several large squares of plate glass belonging to the *295* establishment were broken by the pressure, — news which I seriously think a ready wit

---

265. Saint Vitus' dance: chorea. **267. setting the bell:** causing the bell to stand inverted at the top of its swing (which would mean a summons to church). **271:** Thoreau and a friend had once accidentally set fire to a piece of woodland near Concord. **280. Wachito River:** the Ouachita River, in Arkansas and Louisiana. **281.** Mammoth Cave, in Kentucky, discovered by white men in 1799, known for, among other features, the eyeless fish, bats, and insects that live there. **284-85. some years ago . . . postage:** Prepaid stamps were first used in the U.S. in 1847; before that, letters not franked were paid for by the recipient. **289. Western Railroad:** a railroad in Massachusetts and New York.

might write a twelvemonth, or twelve years, beforehand with sufficient accuracy. As for Spain, for instance, if you know how to throw in Don Carlos and the Infanta, and Don Pedro and Seville and Granada, from time to time in the right proportions, — they may have changed the names a little since I saw the papers, — and serve up a bull-fight when 300 other entertainments fail, it will be true to the letter, and give us as good an idea of the exact state or ruin of things in Spain as the most succinct and lucid reports under this head in the newspapers: and as for England, almost the last significant scrap of news from that quarter was the revolution of 1649; and if you have learned the history of her crops for an average year, you never need attend to that thing again, unless your 305 speculations are of a merely pecuniary character. If one may judge who rarely looks into the newspapers, nothing new does ever happen in foreign parts, a French revolution not excepted.

What news! how much more important to know what that is which was never old! "Kieou-he-yu (great dignitary of the state of Wei) sent a man to Khoung-tseu to know 310 his news. Khoung-tseu caused the messenger to be seated near him, and questioned him in these terms: What is your master doing? The messenger answered with respect: My master desires to diminish the number of his faults, but he cannot come to the end of them. The messenger being gone, the philosopher remarked: What a worthy messenger! What a worthy messenger!" The preacher, instead of vexing the ears of drowsy farmers 315 on their day of rest at the end of the week, — for Sunday is the fit conclusion of an ill-spent week, and not the fresh and brave beginning of a new one, — with this one other draggle-tail of a sermon, should shout with thundering voice, "Pause! Avast! Why so seeming fast, but deadly slow?"

Shams and delusions are esteemed for soundest truths, while reality is fabulous. If 320 men would steadily observe realities only, and not allow themselves to be deluded, life, to compare it with such things as we know, would be like a fairy tale and the Arabian Nights' Entertainments. If we respected only what is inevitable and has a right to be, music and poetry would resound along the streets. When we are unhurried and wise, we perceive that only great and worthy things have any permanent and absolute existence, 325 that petty fears and petty pleasures are but the shadow of the reality. This is always exhilarating and sublime. By closing the eyes and slumbering, and consenting to be deceived by shows, men establish and confirm their daily life of routine and habit everywhere, which still is built on purely illusory foundations. Children, who play life, discern its true law and relations more clearly than men, who fail to live it worthily, but 330 who think that they are wiser by experience, that is, by failure. I have read in a Hindoo book, that "there was a king's son, who, being expelled in infancy from his native city, was brought up by a forester, and, growing up to maturity in that state, imagined himself to belong to the barbarous race with which he lived. One of his father's ministers having discovered him, revealed to him what he was, and the misconception of his character 335 was removed, and he knew himself to be a prince. So soul," continues the Hindoo

---

297-98: Ferdinand VII, who died in 1833, had fixed the succession on his daughter (the Infanta) Isabella, rather than on his brother Don Carlos, who led the Carlists against her and her mother, the regent. **304. revolution of 1649:** The English Civil War, which began in 1642, ended in 1649 with the trial and execution of Charles I and the beginning of the Commonwealth. **310ff.:** an anecdote in the Confucian *Analects* (XIV, 25 or 26). **322-23:** E.W. Lane's new but incomplete translation of *The Arabian Nights* appeared in 1840.

philosopher, "from the circumstances in which it is placed, mistakes its own character, until the truth is revealed to it by some holy teacher, and then it knows itself to be *Brahme*." I perceive that we inhabitants of New England live this mean life that we do because our vision does not penetrate the surface of things. We think that that *is* which *appears* to be. If a man should walk through this town and see only the reality, where, think you, would the "Mill-dam" go to? If he should give us an account of the realities he beheld there, we should not recognize the place in his description. Look at a meeting-house, or a court-house, or a jail, or a shop, or a dwelling-house, and say what that thing really is before a true gaze, and they would all go to pieces in your account of them. Men esteem truth remote, in the outskirts of the system, behind the farthest star, before Adam and after the last man. In eternity there is indeed something true and sublime. But all these times and places and occasions are now and here. God himself culminates in the present moment, and will never be more divine in the lapse of all the ages. And we are enabled to apprehend at all what is sublime and noble only by the perpetual instilling and drenching of the reality that surrounds us. The universe constantly and obediently answers to our conceptions; whether we travel fast or slow, the track is laid for us. Let us spend our lives in conceiving then. The poet or the artist never yet had so fair and noble a design but some of his posterity at least could accomplish it.

Let us spend one day as deliberately as Nature, and not be thrown off the track by every nutshell and mosquito's wing that falls on the rails. Let us rise early and fast, or break fast, gently and without perturbation; let company come and let company go, let the bells ring and the children cry, — determined to make a day of it. Why should we knock under and go with the stream? Let us not be upset and overwhelmed in that terrible rapid and whirlpool called a dinner, situated in the meridian shallows. Weather this danger and you are safe, for the rest of the way is down hill. With unrelaxed nerves, with morning vigor, sail by it, looking another way, tied to the mast like Ulysses. If the engine whistles, let it whistle till it is hoarse for its pains. If the bell rings, why should we run? We will consider what kind of music they are like. Let us settle ourselves, and work and wedge our feet downward through the mud and slush of opinion, and prejudice, and tradition, and delusion, and appearance, that alluvion which covers the globe, through Paris and London, through New York and Boston and Concord, through Church and State, through poetry and philosophy and religion, till we come to a hard bottom and rocks in place, which we can call *reality*, and say, This is, and no mistake; and then begin, having a *point d'appui*, below freshet and frost and fire, a place where you might found a wall or a state, or set a lamp-post safely, or perhaps a gauge, not a Nilometer, but a Realometer, that future ages might know how deep a freshet of shams and appearances had gathered from time to time. If you stand right fronting and face to face to a fact, you will see the sun glimmer on both its surfaces, as if it were a cimeter, and feel its sweet edge dividing you through the heart and marrow, and so you will happily conclude your mortal career. Be it life or death, we

---

339. *Brahme*: In Hinduism, Brahman is the Absolute, the universal soul, the divine essence; Brahma as a deity is one of the three principal gods of Hinduism, the creative aspect of divine reality. **342. Mill-dam:** business centre and gathering place in Concord. **359-62:** Ulysses (Odysseus) had himself tied to the mast so he could safely listen to the Sirens (his men stopped their ears with wax); soon after, they encountered the whirlpool Charybdis (see Homer's *Odyssey*, XII). **361. nerves:** The term could signify sinews, tendons, muscles. **369.** *point d'appui*: point of support. **371. Nilometer:** device at ancient Memphis to measure the rise of the Nile. **374. cimeter:** scimitar.

crave only reality. If we are really dying, let us hear the rattle in our throats and feel cold in the extremities; if we are alive, let us go about our business.

Time is but the stream I go a-fishing in. I drink at it; but while I drink I see the sandy bottom and detect how shallow it is. Its thin current slides away, but eternity remains. I would drink deeper; fish in the sky, whose bottom is pebbly with stars. I *380* cannot count one. I know not the first letter of the alphabet. I have always been regretting that I was not as wise as the day I was born. The intellect is a cleaver; it discerns and rifts its way into the secret of things. I do not wish to be any more busy with my hands than is necessary. My head is hands and feet. I feel all my best faculties concentrated in it. My instinct tells me that my head is an organ for burrowing, as some *385* creatures use their snout and fore-paws, and with it I would mine and burrow my way through these hills. I think that the richest vein is somewhere hereabouts; so by the divining rod and thin rising vapors I judge; and here I will begin to mine.

(1846-54)

EMILY BRONTË
England, 1818-1848

"The night is darkening round me"

The night is darkening round me,
The wild winds coldly blow;
But a tyrant spell has bound me
And I cannot, cannot go.

The giant trees are bending   5
Their bare boughs weighed with snow,
And the storm is fast descending
And yet I cannot go.

Clouds beyond clouds above me,
Wastes beyond wastes below;   10
But nothing drear can move me;
I will not, cannot go.

(1837; 1902)

"I am the only being whose doom"

I am the only being whose doom
No tongue would ask, no eye would mourn;
I never caused a thought of gloom,
A smile of joy, since I was born.

In secret pleasure, secret tears,   5
This changeful life has slipped away,
As friendless after eighteen years,
As lone as on my natal day.

There have been times I cannot hide,
There have been times when this was drear,
When my sad soul forgot its pride   11
And longed for one to love me here.

But those were in the early glow
Of feelings since subdued by care;
And they have died so long ago,   15
I hardly now believe they were.

First melted off the hope of youth,
Then fancy's rainbow fast withdrew;
And then experience told me truth
In mortal bosoms never grew.   20

'Twas grief enough to think mankind
All hollow, servile, insincere;
But worse to trust to my own mind
And find the same corruption there.

(1837; 1910)

ARTHUR HUGH CLOUGH
England, 1819-1861

"SAY NOT THE STRUGGLE NOUGHT AVAILETH"

Say not the struggle nought availeth,
  The labour and the wounds are vain,
The enemy faints not, nor faileth,
  And as things have been, things remain.

If hopes were dupes, fears may be liars;   *5*
  It may be, in yon smoke concealed,
Your comrades chase e'en now the fliers,
  And, but for you, possess the field.

For while the tired waves, vainly breaking,
  Seem here no painful inch to gain,   *10*
Far back through creeks and inlets making
  Came, silent, flooding in, the main,

And not by eastern windows only,
  When daylight comes, comes in the light,
In front the sun climbs slow, how slowly,   *15*
  But westward, look, the land is bright.

                  (1855)

THE LATEST DECALOGUE

Thou shalt have one God only; who
Would be at the expense of two?
No graven images may be
Worshipped, except the currency:
Swear not at all; for for thy curse   *5*
Thine enemy is none the worse:
At church on Sunday to attend
Will serve to keep the world thy friend:
Honour thy parents; that is, all
From whom advancement may befall: *10*
Thou shalt not kill; but needst not strive
Officiously to keep alive:
Do not adultery commit;
Advantage rarely comes of it:
Thou shalt not steal; an empty feat,   *15*
When it's so lucrative to cheat:

Bear not false witness; let the lie
Have time on its own wings to fly:
Thou shalt not covet; but tradition
Approves all forms of competition.   *20*

The sum of all is, thou shalt love,
If any body, God above:
At any rate shall never labour
More than thyself to love thy neighbour.

                  (1862)

"'THERE IS NO GOD,' THE WICKED SAITH"

"There is no God," the wicked saith,
  "And truly it's a blessing,
For what he might have done with us
  It's better only guessing."

"There is no God," a youngster thinks,   *5*
  "Or really, if there may be,
He surely didn't mean a man
  Always to be a baby."

"There is no God, or if there is,"
  The tradesman thinks, "'twere funny   *10*
If he should take it ill in me
  To make a little money."

"Whether there be," the rich man says,
  "It matters very little,
For I and mine, thank somebody,   *15*
  Are not in want of victual."

Some others, also, to themselves
  Who scarce so much as doubt it,
Think there is none, when they are well,
  And do not think about it.   *20*

But country folks who live beneath
  The shadow of the steeple;
The parson and the parson's wife,
  And mostly married people;

SAY NOT THE STRUGGLE   **7. fliers:** those who flee.   **THE LATEST DECALOGUE**   **Title:** For the "Decalogue" (i.e., the Ten Commandments), see Exodus 20:2-17.

Youths green and happy in first love,   25
  So thankful for illusion;
And men caught out in what the world
  Calls guilt, in first confusion;

And almost every one when age,
  Disease, or sorrows strike him,   30
Inclines to think there is a God,
  Or something very like Him.

(1850; 1865)

CHARLES KINGSLEY
England, 1819-1875

THE THREE FISHERS

Three fishers went sailing out into the West,
  Out into the West as the sun went down;
Each thought on the woman who loved him the best;
  And the children stood watching them out of the
    town;
For men must work, and women must weep,   5
And there's little to earn, and many to keep,
  Though the harbour bar be moaning.

Three wives sat up in the light-house tower,
  And they trimmed the lamps as the sun went down;
They looked at the squall, and they looked at the shower,
  And the night rack came rolling up ragged and
    brown!   11

But men must work, and women must weep,
Though storms be sudden, and waters deep,
  And the harbour bar be moaning.

Three corpses lay out on the shining sands   15
  In the morning gleam as the tide went down,
And the women are weeping and wringing their hands
  For those who will never come back to the town;
For men must work, and women must weep,
And the sooner it's over, the sooner to sleep —   20
  And good-bye to the bar and its moaning.

(1851)

GEORGE ELIOT [MARY ANN EVANS]
England, 1819-1880

from *IMPRESSIONS OF THEOPHRASTUS SUCH*

SHADOWS OF THE COMING RACE

My friend Trost, who is no optimist as to the state of the universe hitherto, but is confident that at some future period within the duration of the solar system, ours will be the best of all possible worlds — a hope which I always honour as a sign of beneficent qualities — my friend Trost always tries to keep up my spirits under the sight of the extremely unpleasant and disfiguring work by which many of our fellow-creatures have   5 to get their bread, with the assurance that "all this will soon be done by machinery." But he sometimes neutralises the consolation by extending it over so large an area of human labour, and insisting so impressively on the quantity of energy which will thus be set

---

SHADOWS OF THE COMING RACE   Cf. Butler's "Darwin among the Machines" (p. 1089). **3. the best . . . worlds:** alluding to one of the philosophical attitudes being satirized in Voltaire's *Candide* (1759).

free for loftier purposes, that I am tempted to desire an occasional famine of invention in
the coming ages, lest the humbler kinds of work should be entirely nullified while there   *10*
are still left some men and women who are not fit for the highest.

Especially, when one considers the perfunctory way in which some of the most
exalted tasks are already executed by those who are understood to be educated for them,
there rises a fearful vision of the human race evolving machinery which will by-and-by
throw itself fatally out of work. When, in the Bank of England, I see a wondrously   *15*
delicate machine for testing sovereigns, a shrewd implacable little steel Rhadamanthus
that, once the coins are delivered up to it, lifts and balances each in turn for the fraction
of an instant, finds it wanting or sufficient, and dismisses it to right or left with rigorous
justice; when I am told of micrometers and thermopiles and tasimeters which deal
physically with the invisible, the impalpable, and the unimaginable; of cunning wires   *20*
and wheels and pointing needles which will register your and my quickness so as to
exclude flattering opinion; of a machine for drawing the right conclusion, which will
doubtless by-and-by be improved into an automaton for finding true premises; of a
microphone which detects the cadence of the fly's foot on the ceiling, and may be
expected presently to discriminate the noises of our various follies as they soliloquise or   *25*
converse in our brains — my mind seeming too small for these things, I get a little out
of it, like an unfortunate savage too suddenly brought face to face with civilisation, and
I exclaim —

"Am I already in the shadow of the Coming Race? and will the creatures who are to
transcend and finally supersede us be steely organisms, giving out the effluvia of the   *30*
laboratory, and performing with infallible exactness more than everything that we have
performed with a slovenly approximativeness and self-defeating inaccuracy?"

"But," says Trost, treating me with cautious mildness on hearing me vent this
raving notion, "you forget that these wonder-workers are the slaves of our race, need our
tendance and regulation, obey the mandates of our consciousness, and are only deaf and   *35*
dumb bringers of reports which we decipher and make use of. They are simply
extensions of the human organism, so to speak, limbs immeasurably more powerful,
ever more subtle finger-tips, ever more mastery over the invisibly great and the invisibly
small. Each new machine needs a new appliance of human skill to construct it, new
devices to feed it with material, and often keener-edged faculties to note its registrations   *40*
or performances. How then can machines supersede us? — they depend upon us. When
we cease, they cease."

"I am not so sure of that," said I, getting back into my mind, and becoming rather
wilful in consequence. "If, as I have heard you contend, machines as they are more and
more perfected will require less and less of tendance, how do I know that they may not   *45*
be ultimately made to carry, or may not in themselves evolve, conditions of self-supply,
self-repair, and reproduction, and not only do all the mighty and subtle work possible on
this planet better than we could do it, but with the immense advantage of banishing from
the earth's atmosphere screaming consciousnesses which, in our comparatively clumsy
race, make an intolerable noise and fuss to each other about every petty ant-like   *50*
performance, looking on at all work only as it were to spring a rattle here or blow a

---

16. Rhadamanthus: in Greek myth, the son of Zeus and Europa, noted for his judiciousness. **19. thermopiles:** devices for measuring radiant heat;
tasimeters: devices for measuring changes in temperature, pressure, and other phenomena.

trumpet there, with a ridiculous sense of being effective? I for my part cannot see any reason why a sufficiently penetrating thinker, who can see his way through a thousand years or so, should not conceive a parliament of machines, in which the manners were excellent and the motions infallible in logic: one honourable instrument, a remote descendant of the Voltaic family, might discharge a powerful current (entirely without animosity) on an honourable instrument opposite, of more upstart origin, but belonging to the ancient edge-tool race which we already at Sheffield see paring thick iron as if it were mellow cheese — by this unerringly directed discharge operating on movements corresponding to what we call Estimates, and by necessary mechanical consequence on movements corresponding to what we call the Funds, which with a vain analogy we sometimes speak of as 'sensitive.' For every machine would be perfectly educated, that is to say, would have the suitable molecular adjustments, which would act not the less infallibly for being free from the fussy accompaniment of that consciousness to which our prejudice gives a supreme governing rank, when in truth it is an idle parasite on the grand sequence of things."

"Nothing of the sort!" returned Trost, getting angry, and judging it kind to treat me with some severity; "what you have heard me say is, that our race will and must act as a nervous centre to the utmost development of mechanical processes: the subtly refined powers of machines will react in producing more subtly refined thinking processes which will occupy the minds set free from grosser labour. Say, for example, that all the scavengers' work of London were done, so far as human attention is concerned, by the occasional pressure of a brass button (as in the ringing of an electric bell), you will then have a multitude of brains set free for the exquisite enjoyment of dealing with the exact sequences and high speculations supplied and prompted by the delicate machines which yield a response to the fixed stars, and give readings of the spiral vortices fundamentally concerned in the production of epic poems or great judicial harangues. So far from mankind being thrown out of work according to your notion," concluded Trost, with a peculiar nasal note of scorn, "if it were not for your incurable dilettanteism in science as in all other things — if you had once understood the action of any delicate machine — you would perceive that the sequences it carries throughout the realm of phenomena would require many generations, perhaps æons, of understandings considerably stronger than yours, to exhaust the store of work it lays open."

"Precisely," said I, with a meekness which I felt was praiseworthy; "it is the feebleness of my capacity, bringing me nearer than you to the human average, that perhaps enables me to imagine certain results better than you can. Doubtless the very fishes of our rivers, gullible as they look, and slow as they are to be rightly convinced in another order of facts, form fewer false expectations about each other than we should form about them if we were in a position of somewhat fuller intercourse with their species; for even as it is we have continually to be surprised that they do not rise to our carefully selected bait. Take me then as a sort of reflective and experienced carp; but do not estimate the justice of my ideas by my facial expression."

"Pooh!" says Trost. (We are on very intimate terms.)

---

56. Voltaic: referring to Alessandro Volta (1745-1827), an Italian physicist who experimented with ways of producing an electric charge. **58. Sheffield:** city famous for producing steel. **61. the Funds:** government securities.

"Naturally," I persisted, "it is less easy to you than to me to imagine our race transcended and superseded, since the more energy a being is possessed of, the harder it *95* must be for him to conceive his own death. But I, from the point of view of a reflective carp, can easily imagine myself and my congeners dispensed with in the frame of things and giving way not only to a superior but a vastly different kind of Entity. What I would ask you is, to show me why, since each new invention casts a new light along the pathway of discovery, and each new combination or structure brings into play more *100* conditions than its inventor foresaw, there should not at length be a machine of such high mechanical and chemical powers that it would find and assimilate the material to supply its own waste, and then by a further evolution of internal molecular movements reproduce itself by some process of fission or budding. This last stage having been reached, either by man's contrivance or as an unforeseen result, one sees that the *105* process of natural selection must drive men altogether out of the field; for they will long before have begun to sink into the miserable condition of those unhappy characters in fable who, having demons or djinns at their beck, and being obliged to supply them with work, found too much of everything done in too short a time. What demons so potent as molecular movements, none the less tremendously potent for not carrying the futile *110* cargo of a consciousness screeching irrelevantly, like a fowl tied head downmost to the saddle of a swift horseman? Under such uncomfortable circumstances our race will have diminished with the diminishing call on their energies, and by the time that the self-repairing and reproducing machines arise, all but a few of the rare inventors, calculators, and speculators will have become pale, pulpy, and cretinous from fatty or other *115* degeneration, and behold around them a scanty hydrocephalous offspring. As to the breed of the ingenious and intellectual, their nervous systems will at last have been overwrought in following the molecular revelations of the immensely more powerful unconscious race, and they will naturally, as the less energetic combinations of movement, subside like the flame of a candle in the sunlight. Thus the feebler race, *120* whose corporeal adjustments happened to be accompanied with a maniacal consciousness which imagined itself moving its mover, will have vanished, as all less adapted existences do before the fittest — *i.e.*, the existence composed of the most persistent groups of movements and the most capable of incorporating new groups in harmonious relation. Who — if our consciousness is, as I have been given to understand, a mere *125* stumbling of our organisms on their way to unconscious perfection — who shall say that those fittest existences will not be found along the track of what we call inorganic combinations, which will carry on the most elaborate processes as mutely and painlessly as we are now told that the minerals are metamorphosing themselves continually in the dark laboratory of the earth's crust? Thus this planet may be filled with beings who will *130* be blind and deaf as the inmost rock, yet will execute changes as delicate and complicated as those of human language and all the intricate web of what we call its effects, without sensitive impression, without sensitive impulse: there may be, let us say, mute orations, mute rhapsodies, mute discussions, and no consciousness there even to enjoy the silence." *135*

"Absurd!" grumbled Trost.

---

97. congeners: creatures of the same genus. **106. natural selection:** This and the phrase "survival of the fittest" (see line 127) appear in Charles Darwin's *Origin of Species* (1859).

"The supposition is logical," said I. "It is well argued from the premises."

"Whose premises?" cried Trost, turning on me with some fierceness. "You don't mean to call them mine, I hope."

"Heaven forbid! They seem to be flying about in the air with other germs, and have *140* found a sort of nidus among my melancholy fancies. Nobody really holds them. They bear the same relation to real belief as walking on the head for a show does to running away from an explosion or walking fast to catch the train."

(1879)

HERMAN MELVILLE
U.S.A., 1819-1891

THE LIGHTNING-ROD MAN

What grand irregular thunder, thought I, standing on my hearth-stone among the Acroceraunian hills, as the scattered bolts boomed overhead, and crashed down among the valleys, every bolt followed by zigzag irradiations, and swift slants of sharp rain, which audibly rang, like a charge of spear-points, on my low shingled roof. I suppose, though, that the mountains hereabouts break and churn up the thunder, so that it is far *5* more glorious here than on the plain. Hark! — some one at the door. Who is this that chooses a time of thunder for making calls? And why don't he, man-fashion, use the knocker, instead of making that doleful undertaker's clatter with his fist against the hollow panel? But let him in. Ah, here he comes. "Good day, sir": an entire stranger. "Pray be seated." What is that strange-looking walking-stick he carries: "A fine thunder- *10* storm, sir."

"Fine? — Awful!"

"You are wet. Stand here on the hearth before the fire."

"Not for worlds!"

The stranger still stood in the exact middle of the cottage, where he had first planted *15* himself. His singularity impelled a closer scrutiny. A lean, gloomy figure. Hair dark and lank, mattedly streaked over his brow. His sunken pitfalls of eyes were ringed by indigo halos, and played with an innocuous sort of lightning: the gleam without the bolt. The whole man was dripping. He stood in a puddle on the bare oak floor: his strange walking-stick vertically resting at his side. *20*

It was a polished copper rod, four feet long, lengthwise attached to a neat wooden staff, by insertion into two balls of greenish glass, ringed with copper bands. The metal rod terminated at the top tripodwise, in three keen tines, brightly gilt. He held the thing by the wooden part alone.

---

141. nidus: a site of infection.   **THE LIGHTNING-ROD MAN 2:** The Acroceraunian (or Ceraunian) Mountains are a coastal range of ancient Greece, in what is now southern Albania, a region said to be noted for storms; Melville uses the name as a suggestive classical nickname for his local Berkshire Hills in western Massachusetts. Critics have pointed out that the term also alludes to a heading in Cotton Mather's 1702 ecclesiastical history of New England, *Magnalia Christi Americana*: "Ceraunius. Relating remarkables done by thunder."

"Sir," said I, bowing politely, "have I the honor of a visit from that illustrious god, *25* Jupiter Tonans? So stood he in the Greek statue of old, grasping the lightning-bolt. If you be he, or his viceroy, I have to thank you for this noble storm you have brewed among our mountains. Listen: That was a glorious peal. Ah, to a lover of the majestic, it is a good thing to have the Thunderer himself in one's cottage. The thunder grows finer for that. But pray be seated. This old rush-bottomed arm-chair, I grant, is a poor *30* substitute for your evergreen throne on Olympus; but, condescend to be seated."

While I thus pleasantly spoke, the stranger eyed me, half in wonder, and half in a strange sort of horror; but did not move a foot.

"Do, sir, be seated; you need to be dried ere going forth again."

I planted the chair invitingly on the broad hearth, where a little fire had been *35* kindled that afternoon to dissipate the dampness, not the cold; for it was early in the month of September.

But without heeding my solicitation, and still standing in the middle of the floor, the stranger gazed at me portentously and spoke.

"Sir," said he, "excuse me; but instead of my accepting your invitation to be seated *40* on the hearth there, I solemnly warn *you*, that you had best accept *mine*, and stand with me in the middle of the room. Good heavens!" he cried, starting — "there is another of those awful crashes. I warn you, sir, quit the hearth."

"Mr. Jupiter Tonans," said I, quietly rolling my body on the stone, "I stand very well here." *45*

"Are you so horridly ignorant, then," he cried, "as not to know, that by far the most dangerous part of a house, during such a terrific tempest as this, is the fire-place?"

"Nay, I did not know that," involuntarily stepping upon the first board next to the stone.

The stranger now assumed such an unpleasant air of successful admonition, that — *50* quite involuntarily again — I stepped back upon the hearth, and threw myself into the erectest, proudest posture I could command. But I said nothing.

"For Heaven's sake," he cried, with a strange mixture of alarm and intimidation — "for Heaven's sake, get off the hearth! Know you not, that the heated air and soot are conductors; — to say nothing of those immense iron fire-dogs? Quit the spot — I *55* conjure — I command you."

"Mr. Jupiter Tonans, I am not accustomed to be commanded in my own house."

"Call me not by that pagan name. You are profane in this time of terror."

"Sir, will you be so good as to tell me your business? If you seek shelter from the storm, you are welcome, so long as you be civil; but if you come on business, open it *60* forthwith. Who are you?"

"I am a dealer in lightning-rods," said the stranger, softening his tone; "my special business is ————— Merciful heaven! what a crash! — Have you ever been struck — your premises, I mean? No? It's best to be provided;" — significantly rattling his metallic staff on the floor; — "by nature, there are no castles in thunder-storms; yet, say *65* but the word, and of this cottage I can make a Gibraltar by a few waves of this wand. Hark, what Himalayas of concussions!"

---

26. Jupiter Tonans: Jupiter (Zeus) Thunderer, whose home was on Mount Olympus (line 31), in northern Greece.

"You interrupted yourself; your special business you were about to speak of."

"My special business is to travel the country for orders for lightning-rods. This is my specimen-rod;" tapping his staff; "I have the best of references" — fumbling in his pockets. "In Criggan last month, I put up three-and-twenty rods on only five buildings." 70

"Let me see. Was it not at Criggan last week, about midnight on Saturday, that the steeple, the big elm, and the assembly-room cupola were struck? Any of your rods there?"

"Not on the tree and cupola, but the steeple." 75

"Of what use is your rod, then?"

"Of life-and-death use. But my workman was heedless. In fitting the rod at top to the steeple, he allowed a part of the metal to graze the tin sheeting. Hence the accident. Not my fault, but his. Hark!"

"Never mind. That clap burst quite loud enough to be heard without finger- 80 pointing. Did you hear of the event at Montreal last year? A servant girl struck at her bed-side with a rosary in her hand; the beads being metal. Does your beat extend into the Canadas?"

"No. And I hear that there, iron rods only are in use. They should have *mine*, which are copper. Iron is easily fused. Then they draw out the rod so slender, that it has not 85 body enough to conduct the full electric current. The metal melts; the building is destroyed. My copper rods never act so. Those Canadians are fools. Some of them knob the rod at the top, which risks a deadly explosion, instead of imperceptibly carrying down the current into the earth, as this sort of rod does. *Mine* is the only true rod. Look at it. Only one dollar a foot." 90

"This abuse of your own calling in another might make one distrustful with respect to yourself."

"Hark! The thunder becomes less muttering. It is nearing us, and nearing the earth, too. Hark! One crammed crash! All the vibrations made one by nearness. Another flash. Hold!" 95

"What do you?" I said, seeing him now, instantaneously relinquishing his staff, lean intently forward towards the window, with his right fore and middle fingers on his left wrist.

But ere the words had well escaped me, another exclamation escaped him.

"Crash! only three pulses — less than a third of a mile off — yonder, somewhere in 100 that wood. I passed three stricken oaks there, ripped out new and glittering. The oak draws lightning more than other timber, having iron in solution in its sap. Your floor here seems oak."

"Heart-of-oak. From the peculiar time of your call upon me, I suppose you purposely select stormy weather for your journeys. When the thunder is roaring, you 105 deem it an hour peculiarly favorable for producing impressions favorable to your trade."

"Hark! — Awful!"

"For one who would arm others with fearlessness, you seem unbeseemingly timorous yourself. Common men choose fair weather for their travels: you choose thunder-storms; and yet —" 110

72-73: There had recently been just such lightning-strikes in Pittsfield, Massachusetts.

"That I travel in thunder-storms, I grant; but not without particular precautions, such as only a lightning-rod man may know. Hark! Quick — look at my specimen rod. Only one dollar a foot."

"A very fine rod, I dare say. But what are these particular precautions of yours? Yet first let me close yonder shutters; the slanting rain is beating through the sash. I will bar up." *115*

"Are you mad? Know you not that yon iron bar is a swift conductor? Desist."

"I will simply close the shutters, then, and call my boy to bring me a wooden bar. Pray, touch the bell-pull there."

"Are you frantic? That bell-wire might blast you. Never touch bell-wire in a thunder-storm, nor ring a bell of any sort." *120*

"Nor those in belfries? Pray, will you tell me where and how one may be safe in a time like this? Is there any part of my house I may touch with hopes of my life?"

"There is; but not where you now stand. Come away from the wall. The current will sometimes run down a wall, and — a man being a better conductor than a wall — it would leave the wall and run into him. Swoop! *That* must have fallen very nigh. That must have been globular lightning." *125*

"Very probably. Tell me at once, which is, in your opinion, the safest part of this house?"

"This room, and this one spot in it where I stand. Come hither." *130*

"The reasons first."

"Hark! — after the flash the gust — the sashes shiver — the house, the house! — Come hither to me!"

"The reasons, if you please."

"Come hither to me!" *135*

"Thank you again, I think I will try my old stand — the hearth. And now, Mr. Lightning-rod-man, in the pauses of the thunder, be so good as to tell me your reasons for esteeming this one room of the house the safest, and your own one stand-point there the safest spot in it."

There was now a little cessation of the storm for a while. The Lightning-rod man *140* seemed relieved, and replied: —

"Your house is a one-storied house, with an attic and a cellar; this room is between. Hence its comparative safety. Because lightning sometimes passes from the clouds to the earth, and sometimes from the earth to the clouds. Do you comprehend? — and I choose the middle of the room, because, if the lightning should strike the house at all, it *145* would come down the chimney or walls; so, obviously, the further you are from them, the better. Come hither to me, now."

"Presently. Something you just said, instead of alarming me, has strangely inspired confidence."

"What have I said?" *150*

"You said that sometimes lightning flashes from the earth to the clouds."

"Aye, the returning-stroke, as it is called; when the earth, being overcharged with the fluid, flashes its surplus upward."

"The returning-stroke; that is, from earth to sky. Better and better. But come here on the hearth and dry yourself." *155*

"I am better here, and better wet."

"How?"

"It is the safest thing you can do — Hark, again! — to get yourself thoroughly drenched in a thunder-storm. Wet clothes are better conductors than the body; and so, if the lightning strike, it might pass down the wet clothes without touching the body. The *160* storm deepens again. Have you a rug in the house? Rugs are non-conductors. Get one, that I may stand on it here, and you, too. The skies blacken — it is dusk at noon. Hark! — the rug, the rug!"

I gave him one; while the hooded mountains seemed closing and tumbling into the cottage. *165*

"And now, since our being dumb will not help us," said I, resuming my place, "let me hear your precautions in traveling during thunder-storms."

"Wait till this one is passed."

"Nay, proceed with the precautions. You stand in the safest possible place according to your own account. Go on." *170*

"Briefly, then. I avoid pine-trees, high houses, lonely barns, upland pastures, running water, flocks of cattle and sheep, a crowd of men. If I travel on foot — as to-day — I do not walk fast; if in my buggy, I touch not its back or sides; if on horseback, I dismount and lead the horse. But of all things, I avoid tall men."

"Do I dream? Man avoid man? and in danger-time, too." *175*

"Tall men in a thunder-storm I avoid. Are you so grossly ignorant as not to know, that the height of a six-footer is sufficient to discharge an electric cloud upon him? Are not lonely Kentuckians, ploughing, smit in the unfinished furrow? Nay, if the six-footer stand by running water, the cloud will sometimes *select* him as its conductor to that running water. Hark! Sure, yon black pinnacle is split. Yes, a man is a good conductor. *180* The lightning goes through and through a man, but only peels a tree. But sir, you have kept me so long answering your questions, that I have not yet come to business. Will you order one of my rods? Look at this specimen one? See: it is of the best of copper. Copper's the best conductor. Your house is low; but being upon the mountains, that lowness does not one whit depress it. You mountaineers are most exposed. In *185* mountainous countries the lightning-rod man should have most business. Look at the specimen, sir. One rod will answer for a house so small as this. Look over these recommendations. Only one rod, sir; cost, only twenty dollars. Hark! There go all the granite Taconics and Hoosics dashed together like pebbles. By the sound, that must have struck something. An elevation of five feet above the house will protect twenty *190* feet radius all about the rod. Only twenty dollars, sir — a dollar a foot. Hark! — Dreadful! — Will you order? Will you buy? Shall I put down your name? Think of being a heap of charred offal, like a haltered horse burnt in his stall; and all in one flash!"

"You pretended envoy extraordinary and minister plenipotentiary to and from *195* Jupiter Tonans," laughed I; "you mere man who come here to put you and your pipestem between clay and sky, do you think that because you can strike a bit of green light from the Leyden jar, that you can thoroughly avert the supernal bolt? Your rod

---

189: The Berkshires are part of the Taconic range, and the Hoosac Hills (out of which the Hoosic River flows) are part of the Berkshires.

rusts, or breaks, and where are you? Who has empowered you, you Tetzel, to peddle round your indulgences from divine ordinations? The hairs of our heads are numbered,   *200* and the days of our lives. In thunder as in sunshine, I stand at ease in the hands of my God. False negotiator, away! See, the scroll of the storm is rolled back; the house is unharmed; and in the blue heavens I read in the rainbow, that the Deity will not, of purpose, make war on man's earth."

"Impious wretch!" foamed the stranger, blackening in the face as the rainbow   *205* beamed, "I will publish your infidel notions."

The scowl grew blacker on his face; the indigo-circles enlarged round his eyes as the storm-rings round the midnight moon. He sprang upon me; his tri-forked thing at my heart.

I seized it; I snapped it; I dashed it; I trod it; and dragging the dark lightning-king out of my door, flung his elbowed, copper sceptre after him.   *210*

But spite of my treatment, and spite of my dissuasive talk of him to my neighbors, the Lightning-rod man still dwells in the land; still travels in storm-time, and drives a brave trade with the fears of man.

(1854, 1856)

from *THE ENCANTADAS, OR ENCHANTED ISLES*

SKETCH SECOND: TWO SIDES TO A TORTOISE

> *"Most ugly shapes and horrible aspects,*
> *Such as Dame Nature selfe mote feare to see,*
> *Or shame, that ever should so fowle defects*
> *From her most cunning hand escaped bee;*
> *All dreadfull pourtraicts of deformitee.*
> *Ne wonder if these do a man appall;*
> *For all that here at home we dreadfull hold*
> *Be but as bugs to fearen babes withall*
> *Compared to the creatures in these isles' entrall*
>
> . . . .
>
> *Fear naught, then said the palmer, well avized,*
> *For these same monsters are not these indeed,*
> *But are into these fearfull shapes disguized.*
>
> . . . .
>
> *And lifting up his vertuous staffe on high,*
> *Then all that dreadfull armie fast gan flye*
> *Into great Tethys bosom, where they hidden lye."*

199: Tetzel: Johann Tetzel (c.1465-1519), German preacher, best known for his policy of promoting the sale of indulgences and his consequent dispute with Martin Luther and the Church (the sale and abuse of indulgences was not new: see e.g. Chaucer's Pardoner). **200-01. The hairs . . . our lives:** See Matthew 10:30, Psalms 90:10-12. **201. In thunder as in sunshine:** possibly echoing Tennyson's "Ulysses," line 48 (p. 962). **203-04:** See Genesis 9:13-17 (p. 249).   **THE ENCANTADAS** When Melville first published these ten sketches, in *Putnam's Monthly Magazine* for March, April, and May of 1854, he used the pseudonym "Salvator R. Tarnmoor."   **SKETCH SECOND** **Epigraph:** with several changes, from *The Faerie Queene*, II, xii, stanza 23 (1-5), stanza 25 (6-9), stanza 26 (1-3, 6, 8-9); we have corrected what seem to be printer's errors, restoring Spenser's second *these* for *there* (11) and *Tethys* for *Zethy's* (15); *bugs* (line 8): bugbears, bugaboos, bogies, hobgoblins.

In view of the description given, may one be gay upon the Encantadas? Yes: that is, find one the gaiety, and he will be gay. And, indeed, sackcloth and ashes as they are, the isles are not perhaps unmitigated gloom. For while no spectator can deny their claims to a most solemn and superstitious consideration, no more than my firmest resolutions can decline to behold the spectre-tortoise when emerging from its shadowy recess; yet even the tortoise, dark and melancholy as it is upon the back, still possesses a bright side; its calapee or breast-plate being sometimes of a faint yellowish or golden tinge. Moreover, every one knows that tortoises as well as turtles are of such a make, that if you but put them on their backs you thereby expose their bright sides without the possibility of their recovering themselves, and turning into view the other. But after you have done this, and because you have done this, you should not swear that the tortoise has no dark side. Enjoy the bright, keep it turned up perpetually if you can, but be honest, and don't deny the black. Neither should he, who cannot turn the tortoise from its natural position so as to hide the darker and expose his livelier aspect, like a great October pumpkin in the sun, for that cause declare the creature to be one total inky blot. The tortoise is both black and bright. But let us to particulars.

Some months before my first stepping ashore upon the group, my ship was cruising in its close vicinity. One noon we found ourselves off the South Head of Albemarle, and not very far from the land. Partly by way of freak, and partly by way of spying out so strange a country, a boat's crew was sent ashore, with orders to see all they could, and besides, bring back whatever tortoises they could conveniently transport.

It was after sunset, when the adventurers returned. I looked down over the ship's high side as if looking down over the curb of a well, and dimly saw the damp boat deep in the sea with some unwonted weight. Ropes were dropt over, and presently three huge antediluvian-looking tortoises, after much straining, were landed on deck. They seemed hardly of the seed of earth. We had been broad upon the waters for five long months, a period amply sufficient to make all things of the land wear a fabulous hue to the dreamy mind. Had three Spanish custom-house officers boarded us then, it is not unlikely that I should have curiously stared at them, felt of them, and stroked them much as savages serve civilized guests. But instead of three custom-house officers, behold these really wondrous tortoises — none of your schoolboy mud-turtles — but black as widower's weeds, heavy as chests of plate, with vast shells medallioned and orbed like shields, and dented and blistered like shields that have breasted a battle, shaggy, too, here and there, with dark green moss, and slimy with the spray of the sea. These mystic creatures, suddenly translated by night from unutterable solitudes to our peopled deck, affected me in a manner not easy to unfold. They seemed newly crawled forth from beneath the foundations of the world. Yea, they seemed the identical tortoises whereon the Hindoo plants this total sphere. With a lantern I inspected them more closely. Such worshipful venerableness of aspect! Such furry greenness mantling the rude peelings and healing the fissures of their shattered shells. I no more saw three tortoises. They expanded — became transfigured. I seemed to see three Roman Coliseums in magnificent decay.

---

1. the description given: i.e., in "Sketch First: The Isles at Large." **2. sackcloth and ashes:** emblematic of mourning. **19. freak:** whim, caprice. **30. serve:** treat, behave toward. **37-38:** In Hinduism, a tortoise (an avatar of Vishnu) is sometimes described or depicted as supporting the world — e.g. with an elephant on its back which in turn holds up the globe.

Ye oldest inhabitants of this, or any other isle, said I, pray, give me the freedom of your three walled towns.

The great feeling inspired by these creatures was that of age: — dateless, indefinite endurance. And in fact that any other creature can live and breathe as long as the tortoise of the Encantadas, I will not readily believe. Not to hint of their known capacity of sustaining life, while going without food for an entire year, consider that impregnable armor of their living mail. What other bodily being possesses such a citadel wherein to resist the assaults of Time?

As, lantern in hand, I scraped among the moss and beheld the ancient scars of bruises received in many a sullen fall among the marly mountains of the isle — scars strangely widened, swollen, half obliterate, and yet distorted like those sometimes found in the bark of very hoary trees, I seemed an antiquary of a geologist, studying the bird-tracks and ciphers upon the exhumed slates trod by incredible creatures whose very ghosts are now defunct.

As I lay in my hammock that night, overhead I heard the slow weary draggings of the three ponderous strangers along the encumbered deck. Their stupidity or their resolution was so great that they never went aside for any impediment. One ceased his movements altogether just before the midwatch. At sunrise I found him butted like a battering-ram against the immovable foot of the foremast, and still striving, tooth and nail, to force the impossible passage. That these tortoises are the victims of a penal, or malignant, or perhaps a downright diabolical enchanter, seems in nothing more likely than in that strange infatuation of hopeless toil which so often possesses them. I have known them in their journeyings ram themselves heroically against rocks, and long abide there, nudging, wriggling, wedging, in order to displace them, and so hold on their inflexible path. Their crowning curse is their drudging impulse to straightforwardness in a belittered world.

Meeting with no such hindrance as their companion did, the other tortoises merely fell foul of small stumbling-blocks — buckets, blocks, and coils of rigging — and at times in the act of crawling over them would slip with an astounding rattle to the deck. Listening to these draggings and concussions, I thought me of the haunt from which they came; an isle full of metallic ravines and gulches, sunk bottomlessly into the hearts of splintered mountains, and covered for many miles with inextricable thickets. I then pictured these three straightforward monsters, century after century, writhing through the shades, grim as blacksmiths; crawling so slowly and ponderously, that not only did toad-stools and all fungous things grow beneath their feet, but a sooty moss sprouted upon their backs. With them I lost myself in volcanic mazes; brushed away endless boughs of rotting thickets; till finally in a dream I found myself sitting crosslegged upon the foremost, a Brahmin similarly mounted upon either side, forming a tripod of foreheads which upheld the universal cope.

Such was the wild nightmare begot by my first impression of the Encantadas tortoise. But next evening, strange to say, I sat down with my shipmates, and made a merry repast from tortoise steaks and tortoise stews; and supper over, out knife, and helped convert the three mighty concave shells into three fanciful soup-tureens, and polished the three flat yellowish calapees into three gorgeous salvers.

(1854)

SHILOH

A REQUIEM

(April, 1862)

Skimming lightly, wheeling still,
  The swallows fly low
Over the field in clouded days,
  The forest-field of Shiloh —
Over the field where April rain   5
Solaced the parched ones stretched in pain
Through the pause of night
That followed the Sunday fight
  Around the church of Shiloh —
The church so lone, the log-built one,   10
That echoed to many a parting groan
    And natural prayer
Of dying foemen mingled there —
Foemen at morn, but friends at eve —
  Fame or country least their care: 15
(What like a bullet can undeceive!)
  But now they lie low,
While over them the swallows skim,
  And all is hushed at Shiloh.

(1866)

THE MALDIVE SHARK

About the Shark, phlegmatical one,
Pale sot of the Maldive sea,
The sleek little pilot-fish, azure and slim,
How alert in attendance be.
From his saw-pit of mouth, from his charnel of
    maw,   5
They have nothing of harm to dread,
But liquidly glide on his ghastly flank
Or before his Gorgonian head;
Or lurk in the port of serrated teeth
In white triple tiers of glittering gates,   10
And there find a haven when peril's abroad,
An asylum in jaws of the Fates!
They are friends; and friendly they guide him to
    prey,
Yet never partake of the treat —
Eyes and brains to the dotard lethargic and dull,
Pale ravener of horrible meat.   16

(1888)

WALT WHITMAN
U.S.A., 1819-1892

OUT OF THE CRADLE ENDLESSLY ROCKING

Out of the cradle endlessly rocking,
Out of the mocking-bird's throat, the musical shuttle,
Out of the Ninth-month midnight,
Over the sterile sands and the fields beyond, where the child leaving his bed wander'd alone,
    bareheaded, barefoot,
Down from the shower'd halo,   5
Up from the mystic play of shadows twining and twisting as if they were alive,
Out from the patches of briers and blackberries,

SHILOH   The battle of Shiloh, one of the bloodiest of the Civil War in the United States, took place April 6 and 7, 1862, near Pittsburg Landing, in southwest Tennessee; the battle takes its name from Shiloh Church, near which some of the fighting took place. About one fourth of the 100,000 men who fought were casualties; well over three thousand were killed. Union losses were greater than the Confederates', though technically it was a Union victory. In the Bible, Shiloh was a resting-place for the Ark of the Covenant; the name means something like "rest" and "peace" (see the poem's final line).   THE MALDIVE SHARK   2. sot: stupid person, blockhead, dolt; **Maldive sea:** i.e., around the Maldive Islands, southwest of India in the Indian Ocean. 8. Gorgonian: i.e., hideous, horrible, terrifying, like those of the snake-haired Gorgons (e.g.), to look upon which would petrify one.   OUT OF THE CRADLE ENDLESSLY ROCKING   First published as "A Child's Reminiscence," then as one of a group called "Sea-Shore Memories," and finally as the first poem in the "Sea-Drift" section of *Leaves of Grass* in 1881. 3. Ninth-month: the Quaker name for September (note also line 24 below, and line 82 of "When Lilacs Last . . . " below).

From the memories of the bird that chanted to me,
From your memories sad brother, from the fitful risings and fallings I heard,
From under that yellow half-moon late-risen and swollen as if with tears,   *10*
From those beginning notes of yearning and love there in the mist,
From the thousand responses of my heart never to cease,
From the myriad thence-arous'd words,
From the word stronger and more delicious than any,
From such as now they start the scene revisiting,   *15*
As a flock, twittering, rising, or overhead passing,
Borne hither, ere all eludes me, hurriedly,
A man, yet by these tears a little boy again,
Throwing myself on the sand, confronting the waves,
I, chanter of pains and joys, uniter of here and hereafter,   *20*
Taking all hints to use them, but swiftly leaping beyond them,
A reminiscence sing.

Once Paumanok,
When the lilac-scent was in the air and Fifth-month grass was growing,
Up this seashore in some briers,   *25*
Two feather'd guests from Alabama, two together,
And their nest, and four light-green eggs spotted with brown,
And every day the he-bird to and fro near at hand,
And every day the she-bird crouch'd on her nest, silent, with bright eyes,
And every day I, a curious boy, never too close, never disturbing them,   *30*
Cautiously peering, absorbing, translating.

Shine! shine! shine!
Pour down your warmth, great sun!
While we bask, we two together.

Two together!   *35*
Winds blow south, or winds blow north,
Day come white, or night come black,
Home, or rivers and mountains from home,
Singing all time, minding no time,
While we two keep together.   *40*

Till of a sudden,
May-be kill'd, unknown to her mate,
One forenoon the she-bird crouch'd not on the nest,
Nor return'd that afternoon, nor the next,
Nor ever appear'd again.   *45*

And thenceforward all summer in the sound of the sea,
And at night under the full of the moon in calmer weather,
Over the hoarse surging of the sea,
Or flitting from brier to brier by day,
I saw, I heard at intervals the remaining one, the he-bird,   *50*
The solitary guest from Alabama.

---

23. Paumanok: the Native name for Long Island, meaning "fish-shaped." **32-40:** Between 1859 and 1881, Whitman extensively revised this and the other italicized passages, which represent the bird's song, applying his own ornithological knowledge and drawing on that of his naturalist friend John Burroughs (1837-1921), as he did also for the hermit thrush in "When Lilacs Last . . ."

Blow! blow! blow!
Blow up sea-winds along Paumanok's shore;
I wait and I wait till you blow my mate to me.

Yes, when the stars glisten'd,   55
All night long on the prong of a moss-scallop'd stake,
Down almost amid the slapping waves,
Sat the lone singer wonderful causing tears.

He call'd on his mate,
He pour'd forth the meanings which I of all men know.   60

Yes my brother I know,
The rest might not, but I have treasur'd every note,
For more than once dimly down to the beach gliding,
Silent, avoiding the moonbeams, blending myself with the shadows,
Recalling now the obscure shapes, the echoes, the sounds and sights after their sorts,   65
The white arms out in the breakers tirelessly tossing,
I, with bare feet, a child, the wind wafting my hair,
Listen'd long and long.

Listen'd to keep, to sing, now translating the notes,
Following you my brother.   70

Soothe! soothe! soothe!
Close on its wave soothes the wave behind,
And again another behind embracing and lapping, every one close,
But my love soothes not me, not me.

Low hangs the moon, it rose late,   75
It is lagging — O I think it is heavy with love, with love.

O madly the sea pushes upon the land,
With love, with love.

O night! do I not see my love fluttering out among the breakers?
What is that little black thing I see there in the white?   80

Loud! loud! loud!
Loud I call to you, my love!

High and clear I shoot my voice over the waves,
Surely you must know who is here, is here,
You must know who I am, my love.   85

Low-hanging moon!
What is that dusky spot in your brown yellow?
O it is the shape, the shape of my mate!
O moon do not keep her from me any longer.

Land! land! O land!   90
Whichever way I turn, O I think you could give me my mate back again if you only would,
For I am almost sure I see her dimly whichever way I look.

O rising stars!
Perhaps the one I want so much will rise, will rise with some of you.

O throat! O trembling throat!   95
Sound clearer through the atmosphere!
Pierce the woods, the earth,
Somewhere listening to catch you must be the one I want.

Shake out carols!
Solitary here, the night's carols!   *100*
Carols of lonesome love! death's carols!
Carols under that lagging, yellow, waning moon!
O under that moon where she droops almost down into the sea!
O reckless despairing carols.

But soft! sink low!   *105*
Soft! let me just murmur,
And do you wait a moment you husky-nois'd sea,
For somewhere I believe I heard my mate responding to me,
So faint, I must be still, be still to listen,
But not altogether still, for then she might not come immediately to me.   *110*

Hither my love!
Here I am! here!
With this just-sustain'd note I announce myself to you,
This gentle call is for you my love, for you.

Do not be decoy'd elsewhere,   *115*
That is the whistle of the wind, it is not my voice,
That is the fluttering, the fluttering of the spray,
Those are the shadows of leaves.

O darkness! O in vain!
O I am very sick and sorrowful.   *120*

O brown halo in the sky near the moon, drooping upon the sea!
O troubled reflection in the sea!
O throat! O throbbing heart!
And I singing uselessly, uselessly all the night.

O past! O happy life! O songs of joy!   *125*
In the air, in the woods, over fields,
Loved! loved! loved! loved! loved!
But my mate no more, no more with me!
We two together no more.

The aria sinking,   *130*
All else continuing, the stars shining,
The winds blowing, the notes of the bird continuous echoing,
With angry moans the fierce old mother incessantly moaning,
On the sands of Paumanok's shore gray and rustling,
The yellow half-moon enlarged, sagging down, drooping, the face of the sea almost touching,   *135*
The boy ecstatic, with his bare feet the waves, with his hair the atmosphere dallying,
The love in the heart long pent, now loose, now at last tumultuously bursting,
The aria's meaning, the ears, the soul, swiftly depositing,
The strange tears down the cheeks coursing,
The colloquy there, the trio, each uttering,   *140*
The undertone, the savage old mother incessantly crying,
To the boy's soul's questions sullenly timing, some drown'd secret hissing,
To the outsetting bard.

Demon or bird! (said the boy's soul,)
Is it indeed toward your mate you sing? or is it really to me?   *145*
For I, that was a child, my tongue's use sleeping, now I have heard you,
Now in a moment I know what I am for, I awake,
And already a thousand singers, a thousand songs, clearer, louder and more sorrowful than yours,
A thousand warbling echoes have started to life within me, never to die.

O you singer solitary, singing by yourself, projecting me,   150
O solitary me listening, never more shall I cease perpetuating you,
Never more shall I escape, never more the reverberations,
Never more the cries of unsatisfied love be absent from me,
Never again leave me to be the peaceful child I was before what there in the night,
By the sea under the yellow and sagging moon,   155
The messenger there arous'd, the fire, the sweet hell within,
The unknown want, the destiny of me.

O give me the clew! (it lurks in the night here somewhere,)
O if I am to have so much, let me have more!

A word then, (for I will conquer it,)   160
The word final, superior to all,
Subtle, sent up — what is it? — I listen;
Are you whispering it, and have been all the time, you sea-waves?
Is that it from your liquid rims and wet sands?

Whereto answering, the sea,   165
Delaying not, hurrying not,
Whisper'd me through the night, and very plainly before daybreak,
Lisp'd to me the low and delicious word death,
And again death, death, death, death,

Hissing melodious, neither like the bird nor like my arous'd child's heart,   170
But edging near as privately for me rustling at my feet,
Creeping thence steadily up to my ears and laving me softly all over,
Death, death, death, death, death.

Which I do not forget,
But fuse the song of my dusky demon and brother,   175
That he sang to me in the moonlight on Paumanok's gray beach,
With the thousand responsive songs at random,
My own songs awaked from that hour,
And with them the key, the word up from the waves,
The word of the sweetest song and all songs,   180
That strong and delicious word which, creeping to my feet,
(Or like some old crone rocking the cradle, swathed in sweet garments, bending aside,)
The sea whisper'd me.

(1859, 1881)

WHEN I HEARD THE LEARN'D ASTRONOMER

When I heard the learn'd astronomer,
When the proofs, the figures, were ranged in columns before me,
When I was shown the charts and diagrams, to add, divide, and measure them,
When I sitting heard the astronomer where he lectured with much applause in the lecture-room,
How soon unaccountable I became tired and sick,   5
Till rising and gliding out I wander'd off by myself,
In the mystical moist night-air, and from time to time,
Look'd up in perfect silence at the stars.

(1865)

WHEN I HEARD THE LEARN'D ASTRONOMERS   from the "By the Roadside" section of *Leaves of Grass*.

BY THE BIVOUAC'S FITFUL FLAME

By the bivouac's fitful flame,
A procession winding around me, solemn and sweet and slow — but first I note,
The tents of the sleeping army, the fields' and woods' dim outline,
The darkness lit by spots of kindled fire, the silence,
Like a phantom far or near an occasional figure moving,   5
The shrubs and trees, (as I lift my eyes they seem to be stealthily watching me,)
While wind in procession thoughts, O tender and wondrous thoughts,
Of life and death, of home and the past and loved, and of those that are far away;
A solemn and slow procession there as I sit on the ground,
By the bivouac's fitful flame.   10

                                                                            (1867)

WHEN LILACS LAST IN THE DOORYARD BLOOM'D

1

When lilacs last in the dooryard bloom'd,
And the great star early droop'd in the western sky in the night,
I mourn'd, and yet shall mourn with ever-returning spring.

Ever-returning spring, trinity sure to me you bring,
Lilac blooming perennial and drooping star in the west,   5
And thought of him I love.

2

O powerful western fallen star!
O shades of night — O moody, tearful night!
O great star disappear'd — O the black murk that hides the star!
O cruel hands that hold me powerless — O helpless soul of me!   10
O harsh surrounding cloud that will not free my soul.

3

In the dooryard fronting an old farm-house near the white-wash'd palings,
Stands the lilac-bush tall-growing with heart-shaped leaves of rich green,
With many a pointed blossom rising delicate, with the perfume strong I love,
With every leaf a miracle — and from this bush in the dooryard,   15
With delicate-color'd blossoms and heart-shaped leaves of rich green,
A sprig with its flower I break.

4

In the swamp in secluded recesses,
A shy and hidden bird is warbling a song.

BY THE BIVOUAC'S FITFUL FLAME   from the "Drum-Taps" section of *Leaves of Grass*.   **WHEN LILACS LAST IN THE DOORYARD BLOOM'D**   This and the following poem are from a section first called "President Lincoln's Burial Hymn," and later "Memories of President Lincoln." **2. star:** the planet Venus, known as the "evening star." **13. lilac-bush:** Whitman later said that he always associated lilacs with Lincoln's assassination because there were many lilacs in bloom where he was staying on the day Lincoln was shot (14 April 1865).

Solitary the thrush,   20
The hermit withdrawn to himself, avoiding the settlements,
Sings by himself a song.

Song of the bleeding throat,
Death's outlet song of life, (for well dear brother I know,
If thou wast not granted to sing thou would'st surely die.)   25

5

Over the breast of the spring, the land, amid cities,
Amid lanes and through old woods, where lately the violets peep'd from the ground,
    spotting the gray debris,
Amid the grass in the fields each side of the lanes, passing the endless grass,
Passing the yellow-spear'd wheat, every grain from its shroud in the dark-brown fields uprisen,
Passing the apple-tree blows of white and pink in the orchards,   30
Carrying a corpse to where it shall rest in the grave,
Night and day journeys a coffin.

6

Coffin that passes through lanes and streets,
Through day and night with the great cloud darkening the land,
With the pomp of the inloop'd flags with the cities draped in black,   35
With the show of the States themselves as of crape-veil'd women standing,
With processions long and winding and the flambeaus of the night,
With the countless torches lit, with the silent sea of faces and the unbared heads,
With the waiting depot, the arriving coffin, and the sombre faces,
With dirges through the night, with the thousand voices rising strong and solemn,   40
With all the mournful voices of the dirges pour'd around the coffin,
The dim-lit churches and the shuddering organs — where amid these you journey,
With the tolling tolling bells' perpetual clang,
Here, coffin that slowly passes,
I give you my sprig of lilac.   45

7

(Nor for you, for one alone,
Blossoms and branches green to coffins all I bring,
For fresh as the morning, thus would I chant a song for you O sane and sacred death.

All over bouquets of roses,
O death, I cover you over with roses and early lilies,   50
But mostly and now the lilac that blooms the first,
Copious I break, I break the sprigs from the bushes,
With loaded arms I come, pouring for you,
For you and the coffins all of you O death.)

26-45. Lincoln's body was borne from Washington, D.C., to his burial-place in Springfield, Illinois, on a slow-moving funeral train. **30. blows:** blossoms.

8

O western orb sailing the heaven, 55
Now I know what you must have meant as a month since I walk'd,
As I walk'd in silence the transparent shadowy night,
As I saw you had something to tell as you bent to me night after night,
As you droop'd from the sky low down as if to my side, (while the other stars
    all look'd on,)
As we wander'd together the solemn night, (for something I know not what kept me
    from sleep,) 60
As the night advanced, and I saw on the rim of the west how full you were of woe,
As I stood on the rising ground in the breeze in the cool transparent night,
As I watch'd where you pass'd and was lost in the netherward black of the night,
As my soul in its trouble dissatisfied sank, as where you sad orb,
Concluded, dropt in the night, and was gone. 65

9

Sing on there in the swamp,
O singer bashful and tender, I hear your notes, I hear your call,
I hear, I come presently, I understand you,
But a moment I linger, for the lustrous star has detain'd me,
The star my departing comrade holds and detains me. 70

10

O how shall I warble myself for the dead one there I loved?
And how shall I deck my song for the large sweet soul that has gone?
And what shall my perfume be for the grave of him I love?

Sea-winds blown from east and west,
Blown from the Eastern sea and blown from the Western sea, till there on the
    prairies meeting, 75
These and with these and the breath of my chant,
I'll perfume the grave of him I love.

11

O what shall I hang on the chamber walls?
And what shall the pictures be that I hang on the walls,
To adorn the burial-house of him I love? 80

Pictures of growing spring and farms and homes,
With the Fourth-month eve at sundown, and the gray smoke lucid and bright,
With floods of the yellow gold of the gorgeous, indolent, sinking sun,
    burning, expanding the air,
With the fresh sweet herbage under foot, and the pale green leaves of the trees prolific,
In the distance the flowing glaze, the breast of the river, with a wind-dapple here and there,
With ranging hills on the banks, with many a line against the sky, and shadows, 86
And the city at hand with dwellings so dense, and stacks of chimneys,
And all the scenes of life and the workshops, and the workmen homeward returning.

12

Lo, body and soul — this land,
My own Manhattan with spires, and the sparkling and hurrying tides, and the ships,   90
The varied and ample land, the South and the North in the light, Ohio's shores and
    flashing Missouri,
And ever the far-spreading prairies cover'd with grass and corn.

Lo, the most excellent sun so calm and haughty,
The violet and purple morn with just-felt breezes,
The gentle soft-born measureless light,   95
The miracle spreading bathing all, the fulfill'd noon,
The coming eve delicious, the welcome night and the stars,
Over my cities shining all, enveloping man and land.

13

Sing on, sing on you gray-brown bird,
Sing from the swamps, the recesses, pour your chant from the bushes,   100
Limitless out of the dusk, out of the cedars and pines.

Sing on dearest brother, warble your reedy song,
Loud human song, with voice of uttermost woe.

O liquid and free and tender!
O wild and loose to my soul — O wondrous singer!   105
You only I hear — yet the star holds me, (but will soon depart,)
Yet the lilac with mastering odor holds me.

14

Now while I sat in the day and look'd forth,
In the close of the day with its light and the fields of spring, and the farmers
    preparing their crops,
In the large unconscious scenery of my land with its lakes and forests,   110
In the heavenly aerial beauty, (after the perturb'd winds and the storms,)
Under the arching heavens of the afternoon swift passing, and the voices of children
    and women,
The many-moving sea-tides, and I saw the ships how they sail'd,
And the summer approaching with richness, and the fields all busy with labor,
And the infinite separate houses, how they all went on, each with its meals and minutia of
    daily usages,   115
And the streets how their throbbings throbb'd, and the cities pent — lo, then and there,
Falling upon them all and among them all, enveloping me with the rest,
Appear'd the cloud, appear'd the long black trail,
And I knew death, its thought, and the sacred knowledge of death.

Then with the knowledge of death as walking one side of me,   120
And the thought of death close-walking the other side of me,
And I in the middle as with companions, and as holding the hands of companions,
I fled forth to the hiding receiving night that talks not,
Down to the shores of the water, the path by the swamp in the dimness,
To the solemn shadowy cedars and ghostly pines so still.   125

And the singer so shy to the rest receiv'd me,
The gray-brown bird I know receiv'd us comrades three,
And he sang the carol of death, and a verse for him I love.

From deep secluded recesses,
From the fragrant cedars and the ghostly pines so still,   *130*
Came the carol of the bird.

And the charm of the carol rapt me,
As I held as if by their hands my comrades in the night,
And the voice of my spirit tallied the song of the bird.

Come lovely and soothing death,   *135*
Undulate round the world, serenely arriving, arriving,
In the day, in the night, to all, to each,
Sooner or later delicate death.

Prais'd be the fathomless universe,
For life and joy, and for objects and knowledge curious,   *140*
And for love, sweet love — but praise! praise! praise!
For the sure-enwinding arms of cool-enfolding death.

Dark mother always gliding near with soft feet,
Have none chanted for thee a chant of fullest welcome?
Then I chant it for thee, I glorify thee above all,   *145*
I bring thee a song that when thou must indeed come, come unfalteringly.

Approach strong deliveress,
When it is so, when thou hast taken them I joyously sing the dead,
Lost in the loving floating ocean of thee,
Laved in the flood of thy bliss O death.   *150*

From me to thee glad serenades,
Dances for thee I propose saluting thee, adornments and feastings for thee,
And the sights of the open landscape and the high-spread sky are fitting,
And life and the fields, and the huge and thoughtful night.

The night in silence under many a star,   *155*
The ocean shore and the husky whispering wave whose voice I know,
And the soul turning to thee O vast and well-veil'd death,
And the body gratefully nestling close to thee.

Over the tree-tops I float thee a song,
Over the rising and sinking waves, over the myriad fields and the prairies wide,   *160*
Over the dense-pack'd cities all and the teeming wharves and ways,
I float this carol with joy, with joy to thee O death.

15
To the tally of my soul,
Loud and strong kept up the gray-brown bird,
With pure deliberate notes spreading filling the night.   *165*

Loud in the pines and cedars dim,
Clear in the freshness moist and the swamp-perfume,
And I with my comrades there in the night.

While my sight that was bound in my eyes unclosed,
As to long panoramas of visions.   *170*

And I saw askant the armies,
I saw as in noiseless dreams hundreds of battle-flags,
Borne through the smoke of the battles and pierc'd with missiles I saw them,
And carried hither and yon through the smoke, and torn and bloody,
And at last but a few shreds left on the staffs, (and all in silence,)   *175*
And the staffs all splinter'd and broken.

I saw battle-corpses, myriads of them,
And the white skeletons of young men, I saw them,
I saw the debris and debris of all the slain soldiers of the war,
But I saw they were not as was thought,   *180*
They themselves were fully at rest, they suffer'd not,
The living remain'd and suffer'd, the mother suffer'd,
And the wife and the child and the musing comrade suffer'd,
And the armies that remain'd suffer'd.

16

Passing the visions, passing the night,   *185*
Passing, unloosing the hold of my comrades' hands,
Passing the song of the hermit bird and the tallying song of my soul,
Victorious song, death's outlet song, yet varying ever-altering song,
As low and wailing, yet clear the notes, rising and falling, flooding the night,
Sadly sinking and fainting, as warning and warning, and yet again bursting with joy,   *190*
Covering the earth and filling the spread of the heaven,
As that powerful psalm in the night I heard from recesses,
Passing, I leave thee lilac with heart-shaped leaves,
I leave thee there in the door-yard, blooming, returning with spring.

I cease from my song for thee,   *195*
From my gaze on thee in the west, fronting the west, communing with thee,
O comrade lustrous with silver face in the night.

Yet each to keep and all, retrievements out of the night,
The song, the wondrous chant of the gray-brown bird,
And the tallying chant, the echo arous'd in my soul,   *200*
With the lustrous and drooping star with the countenance full of woe,
With the holders holding my hand nearing the call of the bird,
Comrades mine and I in the midst, and their memory ever to keep, for the dead
    I loved so well,
For the sweetest, wisest soul of all my days and lands — and this for his dear sake,
Lilac and star and bird twined with the chant of my soul,   *205*
There in the fragrant pines and the cedars dusk and dim.

(1865, 1881)

---

179. the war: i.e., the American Civil War.

O CAPTAIN! MY CAPTAIN!

O Captain! my Captain! our fearful trip is done,
The ship has weather'd every rack, the prize we sought is won,
The port is near, the bells I hear, the people all exulting,
While follow eyes the steady keel, the vessel grim and daring;
     But O heart! heart! heart! *5*
       O the bleeding drops of red,
         Where on the deck my Captain lies,
           Fallen cold and dead.

O Captain! my Captain! rise up and hear the bells;
Rise up — for you the flag is flung — for you the bugle trills, *10*
For you bouquets and ribbon'd wreaths — for you the shores a-crowding,
For you they call, the swaying mass, their eager faces turning;
     Here Captain! dear father!
       This arm beneath your head!
         It is some dream that on the deck, *15*
           You've fallen cold and dead.

My Captain does not answer, his lips are pale and still,
My father does not feel my arm, he has no pulse nor will,
The ship is anchor'd safe and sound, its voyage closed and done,
From fearful trip the victor ship comes in with object won; *20*
     Exult O shores, and ring O bells!
       But I with mournful tread,
         Walk the deck my Captain lies,
           Fallen cold and dead.

(1865, 1871)

A NOISELESS PATIENT SPIDER

A noiseless patient spider,
I mark'd where on a little promontory it stood isolated,
Mark'd how to explore the vacant vast surrounding,
It launch'd forth filament, filament, filament, out of itself,
Ever unreeling them, ever tirelessly speeding them. *5*

And you O my soul where you stand,
Surrounded, detached, in measureless oceans of space,
Ceaselessly musing, venturing, throwing, seeking the spheres to connect them,
Till the bridge you will need be form'd, till the ductile anchor hold,
Till the gossamer thread you fling catch somewhere, O my soul. *10*

(1868, 1881)

A NOISELESS PATIENT SPIDER   This poem appears in the section called "Whispers of Heavenly Death."

PASSAGE TO INDIA

1

Singing my days,
Singing the great achievements of the present,
Singing the strong light works of engineers,
Our modern wonders, (the antique ponderous Seven outvied,)
In the Old World the east the Suez canal,   5
The New by its mighty railroad spann'd,
The seas inlaid with eloquent gentle wires;
Yet first to sound, and ever sound, the cry with thee O soul,
The Past! the Past! the Past!

The Past — the dark unfathom'd retrospect!   10
The teeming gulf — the sleepers and the shadows!
The past — the infinite greatness of the past!
For what is the present after all but a growth out of the past?
(As a projectile form'd, impell'd, passing a certain line, still keeps on,
So the present, utterly form'd, impell'd by the past.)   15

2

Passage O soul to India!
Eclaircise the myths Asiatic, the primitive fables.

Not you alone proud truths of the world,
Nor you alone ye facts of modern science,
But myths and fables of eld, Asia's, Africa's fables,   20
The far-darting beams of the spirit, the unloos'd dreams,
The deep diving bibles and legends,
The daring plots of the poets, the elder religions;
O you temples fairer than lilies pour'd over by the rising sun!
O you fables spurning the known, eluding the hold of the known, mounting to heaven!   25
You lofty and dazzling towers, pinnacled, red as roses, burnish'd with gold!
Towers of fables immortal fashion'd from mortal dreams!
You too I welcome and fully the same as the rest!
You too with joy I sing.

Passage to India!   30
Lo, soul, seest thou not God's purpose from the first?
The earth to be spann'd, connected by network,
The races, neighbors, to marry and be given in marriage,
The oceans to be cross'd, the distant brought near,
The lands to be welded together.   35

A worship new I sing,
You captains, voyagers, explorers, yours,
You engineers, you architects, machinists, yours,
You, not for trade or transportation only,
But in God's name, and for thy sake O soul.   40

PASSAGE TO INDIA   (E. M. Forster [1879-1970] derived the title of his 1924 novel, *A Passage to India*, from Whitman's poem.) **4. antique . . . seven:** The Seven Wonders of the Ancient World were the Egyptian pyramids (or just the Great Pyramid of Cheops), The Colossus of Rhodes, the Hanging Gardens of Babylon, the Pharos (or lighthouse) at Alexandria, the Temple of Artemis at Ephesus, Phidias's statue of Zeus at Olympia, and the Mausoleum at Halicarnassus (the tomb of the Persian ruler Mausolus). **5:** The Suez Canal, begun in 1859, was opened 17 November 1869. **6:** The Union Pacific and Central Pacific Railroads were joined on 10 May 1869 in Utah, establishing a transcontinental route. **7. wires:** The first successful Atlantic cable was laid in 1866. **17. Eclaircise:** clarify (from the French *éclaircir*).

3

Passage to India!
Lo soul for thee of tableaus twain,
I see in one the Suez canal initiated, open'd,
I see the procession of steamships, the Empress Eugenie's leading the van,
I mark from on deck the strange landscape, the pure sky, the level sand in the distance,   *45*
I pass swiftly the picturesque groups, the workmen gather'd,
The gigantic dredging machines.

In one again, different, (yet thine, all thine, O soul, the same,)
I see over my own continent the Pacific railroad surmounting every barrier,
I see continual trains of cars winding along the Platte carrying freight and passengers,   *50*
I hear the locomotives rushing and roaring, and the shrill steam-whistle,
I hear the echoes reverberate through the grandest scenery in the world,
I cross the Laramie plains, I note the rocks in grotesque shapes, the buttes,
I see the plentiful larkspur and wild onions, the barren, colorless, sage-deserts,
I see in glimpses afar or towering immediately above me the great mountains,
   I see the Wind river and the Wahsatch mountains,   *55*
I see the Monument mountain and the Eagle's Nest, I pass the Promontory, I ascend the Nevadas,
I scan the noble Elk mountain and wind around its base,
I see the Humboldt range, I thread the valley and cross the river,
I see the clear waters of lake Tahoe, I see forests of majestic pines,
Or crossing the great desert, the alkaline plains, I behold enchanting mirages of waters and meadows,   *60*
Marking through these and after all, in duplicate slender lines,
Bridging the three or four thousand miles of land travel,
Tying the Eastern to the Western sea,
The road between Europe and Asia.

(Ah Genoese thy dream! thy dream!   *65*
Centuries after thou art laid in thy grave,
The shore thou foundest verifies thy dream.)

4

Passage to India!
Struggles of many a captain, tales of many a sailor dead,
Over my mood stealing and spreading they come,   *70*
Like clouds and cloudlets in the unreach'd sky.

Along all history, down the slopes,
As a rivulet running, sinking now, and now again to the surface rising,
A ceaseless thought, a varied train — lo, soul, to thee, thy sight, they rise,
The plans, the voyages again, the expeditions;   *75*
Again Vasco de Gama sails forth,
Again the knowledge gain'd, the mariner's compass,
Lands found and nations born, thou born America,
For purpose vast, man's long probation fill'd,
Thou rondure of the world at last accomplish'd.   *80*

44: The Empress Eugénie (1826-1920), wife of Napoleon III, was on the lead ship, in effect "opening" the canal. **49-63:** These lines catalogue scenes along the new railway route from Omaha, Nebraska, to San Francisco, California. **65. Genoese:** Christopher Columbus (1451-1506), Italian-born navigator who claimed the West Indies for Spain in 1492 (see line 144). **76:** Vasco da Gama (c.1469-1524), Portuguese navigator, was the first European to sail around ("double" — see line 113) the Cape of Good Hope (1497) to India, reaching Calicut in May 1498. **80, 81:** A *rondure* is a circle or something spherical; Whitman is perhaps echoing Shakespeare's "huge rondure" (sonnet 21).

5

O vast Rondure, swimming in space,
Cover'd all over with visible power and beauty,
Alternate light and day and the teeming spiritual darkness5
Unspeakable high processions of sun and moon and countless stars above,
Below, the manifold grass and waters, animals, mountains, trees,   85
With inscrutable purpose, some hidden prophetic intention,
Now first it seems my thought begins to span thee.

Down from the gardens of Asia descending radiating,
Adam and Eve appear, then their myriad progeny after them,
Wandering, yearning, curious, with restless explorations,   90
With questionings, baffled, formless, feverish, with never-happy hearts,
With that sad incessant refrain, *Wherefore unsatisfied soul?* and *Whither O mocking life?*

Ah who shall soothe these feverish children?
Who justify these restless explorations?
Who speak the secret of impassive earth?   95
Who bind it to us? what is this separate Nature so unnatural?
What is this earth to our affections? (unloving earth, without a throb to answer ours,
Cold earth, the place of graves.)

Yet soul be sure the first intent remains, and shall be carried out,
Perhaps even now the time has arrived.   100

After the seas are all cross'd, (as they seem already cross'd,)
After the great captains and engineers have accomplish'd their work,
After the noble inventors, after the scientists, the chemist, the geologist, ethnologist,
Finally shall come the poet worthy that name,
The true son of God shall come singing his songs.   105

Then not your deeds only O voyagers, O scientists and inventors, shall be justified,
All these hearts as of fretted children shall be sooth'd,
All affection shall be fully responded to, the secret shall be told,
All these separations and gaps shall be taken up and hook'd and link'd together,
The whole earth, this cold, impassive, voiceless earth, shall be completely justified,   110
Trinitas divine shall be gloriously accomplish'd and compacted by the true son of God, the poet,
(He shall indeed pass the straits and conquer the mountains,
He shall double the cape of Good Hope to some purpose,)
Nature and Man shall be disjoin'd and diffused no more,
The true son of God shall absolutely fuse them.   115

6

Year at whose wide-flung door I sing!
Year of the purpose accomplish'd!
Year of the marriage of continents, climates and oceans!
(No mere doge of Venice now wedding the Adriatic,)
I see O year in you the vast terraqueous globe given and giving all,   120
Europe to Asia, Africa join'd, and they to the New World,
The lands, geographies, dancing before you, holding a festival garland,
As brides and bridegrooms hand in hand.

---

111. **Trinitas:** (Latin) Trinity. 119. **doge:** chief magistrate of Venice, one of whose principal duties, from the 12th century (and in a cruder form even earlier), was each year to celebrate the republic's symbolic marriage to the sea, the source of its political and commercial power, by casting a precious ring into the Adriatic.

Passage to India!
Cooling airs from Caucasus far, soothing cradle of man,
The river Euphrates flowing, the past lit up again.

Lo soul, the retrospect brought forward,
The old, most populous, wealthiest of earth's lands,
The streams of the Indus and the Ganges and their many affluents,
(I my shores of America walking to-day behold, resuming all,)
The tale of Alexander on his warlike marches suddenly dying,
On one side China and on the other side Persia and Arabia,
To the south the great seas and the bay of Bengal,
The flowing literatures, tremendous epics, religions, castes,
Old occult Brahma interminably far back, the tender and junior Buddha,
Central and southern empires and all their belongings, possessors,
The wars of Tamerlane, the reign of Aurungzebe,
The traders, rulers, explorers, Moslems, Venetians, Byzantium, the Arabs, Portuguese,
The first travelers famous yet, Marco Polo, Batouta the Moor,
Doubts to be solv'd, the map incognita, blanks to be fill'd,
The foot of man unstay'd, the hands never at rest,
Thyself O soul that will not brook a challenge.

The mediæval navigators rise before me,
The world of 1492, with its awaken'd enterprise,
Something swelling in humanity now like the sap of the earth in spring,
The sunset splendor of chivalry declining.

And who art thou sad shade?
Gigantic, visionary, thyself a visionary,
With majestic limbs and pious beaming eyes,
Spreading around with every look of thine a golden world,
Enhuing it with gorgeous hues.

As the chief histrion,
Down to the footlights walks in some great scena,
Dominating the rest I see the Admiral himself,
(History's type of courage, action, faith,)
Behold him sail from Palos leading his little fleet,
His voyage behold, his return, his great fame,
His misfortunes, calumniators, behold him a prisoner, chain'd,
Behold his dejection, poverty, death.

(Curious in time I stand, noting the efforts of heroes,
Is the deferment long? bitter the slander, poverty, death?
Lies the seed unreck'd for centuries in the ground? lo, to God's due occasion,
Uprising in the night, it sprouts, blooms,
And fills the earth with use and beauty.)

125

130

135

140

145

150

155

160

---

126. Euphrates: river which, along with the Tigris, provided water to ancient Mesopotamia, birthplace of civilizations and legendary location of the Garden of Eden. **131:** Alexander the Great (356-323 B.C.) died in Babylon soon after his return from conquests in India. **135. Brahma:** the creator figure in Hinduism — Hindu chronology equates a *kalpa* or "day of Brahma" to 4.3. billion years; **Buddha:** Siddhartha Gautama (6th century B.C.), North Indian ascetic (called "Buddha," meaning "enlightened one"), whose religious teachings reformed Brahmanism. **137. Tamerlane:** or Tamburlane, i.e., Timur-i-Leng, "Timur the Lame" (c.1336-1405), Mongol warrior born in Samarkand, who extended his empire from Turkey to the Ganges to China; **Aurungzebe:** or Aurangzebe (1618-1707), Mogul emperor of India. **139. Marco Polo:** (1254-1324) Venetian adventurer who served Kublai Khan for some years, and whose travels across Asia opened up trade routes between Europe and Cathay; **Batouta:** (1303-1377) African traveller. **140. incognita:** Early European maps often labelled various areas as "terra incognita," unknown land. **152. histrion:** actor. **153. scena:** (Italian) scene or portion of an opera. **154. Admiral:** Columbus, who set sail from Palos, Spain (line 156).

7

Passage indeed O soul to primal thought,   *165*
Not lands and seas alone, thy own clear freshness,
The young maturity of brood and bloom,
To realms of budding bibles.

O soul, repressless, I with thee and thou with me,
Thy circumnavigation of the world begin,   *170*
Of man, the voyage of his mind's return,
To reason's early paradise,
Back, back to wisdom's birth, to innocent intuitions,
Again with fair creation.

8

O we can wait no longer,   *175*
We too take ship O soul,
Joyous we too launch out on trackless seas,
Fearless for unknown shores on waves of ecstasy to sail,
Amid the wafting winds, (thou pressing me to thee, I thee to me, O soul,)
Caroling free, singing our song of God,   *180*
Chanting our chant of pleasant exploration.

With laugh and many a kiss,
(Let others deprecate, let others weep for sin, remorse, humiliation,)
O soul thou pleasest me, I thee.

Ah more than any priest O soul we too believe in God,   *185*
But with the mystery of God we dare not dally.

O soul thou pleasest me, I thee,
Sailing these seas or on the hills, or waking in the night,
Thoughts, silent thoughts, of Time and Space and Death, like waters flowing,
Bear me indeed as through the regions infinite,   *190*
Whose air I breathe, whose ripples hear, lave me all over,
Bathe me O God in thee, mounting to thee,
I and my soul to range in range of thee.

O Thou transcendent,
Nameless, the fibre and the breath,   *195*
Light of the light, shedding forth universes, thou centre of them,
Thou mightier centre of the true, the good, the loving,
Thou moral, spiritual fountain — affection's source — thou reservoir,
(O pensive soul of me — O thirst unsatisfied — waitest not there?
Waitest not haply for us somewhere there the Comrade perfect?)   *200*
Thou pulse — thou motive of the stars, suns, systems,
That, circling, move in order, safe, harmonious,
Athwart the shapeless vastnesses of space,
How should I think, how breathe a single breath, how speak, if, out of myself,
I could not launch, to those, superior universes?   *205*

Swiftly I shrivel at the thought of God,
At Nature and its wonders, Time and Space and Death,
But that I, turning, call to thee O soul, thou actual Me,
And lo, thou gently masterest the orbs,
Thou matest Time, smilest content at Death,   *210*
And fillest, swellest full the vastnesses of Space.

Greater than stars or suns,
Bounding O soul thou journeyest forth;
What love than thine and ours could wider amplify?
What aspirations, wishes, outvie thine and ours O soul?   *215*
What dreams of the ideal? what plans of purity, perfection, strength?
What cheerful willingness for others' sake to give up all?
For others' sake to suffer all?

Reckoning ahead O soul, when thou, the time achiev'd,
The seas all cross'd, weather'd the capes, the voyage done,   *220*
Surrounded, copest, frontest God, yieldest, the aim attain'd,
As fill'd with friendship, love complete, the Elder Brother found,
The Younger melts in fondness in his arms.

9
Passage to more than India!
Are thy wings plumed indeed for such far flights?   *225*
O soul, voyagest thou indeed on voyages like those?
Disportest thou on waters such as those?
Soundest below the Sanscrit and the Vedas?
Then have thy bent unleash'd.

Passage to you, your shores, ye aged fierce enigmas!   *230*
Passage to you, to mastership of you, ye strangling problems!
You, strew'd with the wrecks of skeletons, that, living, never reach'd you.

Passage to more than India!
O secret of the earth and sky!
Of you O waters of the sea! O winding creeks and rivers!   *235*
Of you O woods and fields! of you strong mountains of my land!
Of you O prairies! of you gray rocks!
O morning red! O clouds! O rain and snows!
O day and night, passage to you!

O sun and moon and all you stars! Sirius and Jupiter!   *240*
Passage to you!

Passage, immediate passage! the blood burns in my veins!
Away O soul! hoist instantly the anchor!
Cut the hawsers — haul out — shake out every sail!
Have we not stood here like trees in the ground long enough?   *245*
Have we not grovel'd here long enough, eating and drinking like mere brutes?
Have we not darken'd and dazed ourselves with books long enough?

Sail forth — steer for the deep waters only,
Reckless O soul, exploring, I with thee, and thou with me,
For we are bound where mariner has not yet dared to go,   *250*
And we will risk the ship, ourselves and all.

O my brave soul!
O farther farther sail!
O daring joy, but safe! are they not all the seas of God?
O farther, farther, farther sail!   *255*

                                            (1871, 1881)

---

228. Sanscrit and the Vedas: The Vedas, the oldest of Hindu holy scriptures, were written down in Sanskrit (c.1500 B.C.) after having been communicated orally for several centuries; they were among the works translated into English by the German-born British philologist Friedrich Max Müller (1823-1900), from 1845 onwards, and published in his 51-volume series *Sacred Books of the East* (1875ff.).

JOHN RUSKIN
England, 1819-1900

from *SESAME AND LILIES,* Lecture I

13. Very ready we are to say of a book, "How good this is — that's exactly what I think!" But the right feeling is, "How strange that is! I never thought of that before, and yet I see it is true; or if I do not now, I hope I shall, some day." But whether thus submissively or not, at least be sure that you go to the author to get at *his* meaning, not to find yours. Judge it afterwards if you think yourself qualified to do so; but ascertain it first. And be sure, also, if the author is worth anything, that you will not get at his meaning all at once; — nay, that at his whole meaning you will not for a long time arrive in any wise. Not that he does not say what he means, and in strong words too; but he cannot say it all; and what is more strange, *will* not, but in a hidden way and in parables, in order that he may be sure you want it. I cannot quite see the reason of this, nor analyse that cruel reticence in the breasts of wise men which makes them always hide their deeper thought. They do not give it you by way of help, but of reward; and will make themselves sure that you deserve it before they allow you to reach it. But it is the same with the physical type of wisdom, gold. There seems, to you and me, no reason why the electric forces of the earth should not carry whatever there is of gold within it at once to the mountain tops, so that kings and people might know that all the gold they could get was there; and without any trouble of digging, or anxiety, or chance, or waste of time, cut it away, and coin as much as they needed. But Nature does not manage it so. She puts it in little fissures in the earth, nobody knows where: you may dig long and find none; you must dig painfully to find any.

14. And it is just the same with men's best wisdom. When you come to a good book, you must ask yourself, "Am I inclined to work as an Australian miner would? Are my pickaxes and shovels in good order, and am I in good trim myself, my sleeves well up to the elbow, and my breath good, and my temper?" And, keeping the figure a little longer, even at cost of tiresomeness, for it is a thoroughly useful one, the metal you are in search of being the author's mind or meaning, his words are as the rock which you have to crush and smelt in order to get at it. And your pickaxes are your own care, wit, and learning; your smelting furnace is your own thoughtful soul. Do not hope to get at any good author's meaning without those tools and that fire; often you will need sharpest, finest chiselling, and patientest fusing, before you can gather one grain of the metal.

15. And, therefore, first of all, I tell you earnestly and authoritatively (I *know* I am right in this), you must get into the habit of looking intensely at words, and assuring yourself of their meaning, syllable by syllable — nay, letter by letter. For though it is only by reason of the opposition of letters in the function of signs, to sounds in the function of signs, that the study of books is called "literature," and that a man versed in it is called, by the consent of nations, a man of letters instead of a man of books, or of

words, you may yet connect with that accidental nomenclature this real fact: — that you might read all the books in the British Museum (if you could live long enough), and remain an utterly "illiterate," uneducated person; but that if you read ten pages of a good book, letter by letter, — that is to say, with real accuracy, — you are for evermore in some measure an educated person. The entire difference between education and non-education (as regards the merely intellectual part of it), consists in this accuracy. A well-educated gentleman may not know many languages, — may not be able to speak any but his own, — may have read very few books. But whatever language he knows, he knows precisely; whatever word he pronounces, he pronounces rightly; above all, he is learned in the *peerage* of words; knows the words of true descent and ancient blood, at a glance, from words of modern canaille; remembers all their ancestry, their inter-marriages, distant relationships, and the extent to which they were admitted, and offices they held, among the national noblesse of words at any time, and in any country. But an uneducated person may know, by memory, many languages, and talk them all, and yet truly know not a word of any, — not a word even of his own. An ordinarily clever and sensible seaman will be able to make his way ashore at most ports; yet he has only to speak a sentence of any language to be known for an illiterate person: so also the accent, or turn of expression of a single sentence, will at once mark a scholar. And this is so strongly felt, so conclusively admitted, by educated persons, that a false accent or a mistaken syllable is enough, in the parliament of any civilized nation, to assign to a man a certain degree of inferior standing for ever.

16. And this is right; but it is a pity that the accuracy insisted on is not greater, and required to a serious purpose. It is right that a false Latin quantity should excite a smile in the House of Commons; but it is wrong that a false English *meaning* should *not* excite a frown there. Let the accent of words be watched; and closely: let their meaning be watched more closely still, and fewer will do the work. A few words well chosen, and distinguished, will do work that a thousand cannot, when every one is acting, equivocally, in the function of another. Yes; and words, if they are not watched, will do deadly work sometimes. There are masked words droning and skulking about us in Europe just now, — (there never were so many, owing to the spread of a shallow, blotching, blundering, infectious "information," or rather deformation, everywhere, and to the teaching of catechisms and phrases at school instead of human meanings) — there are masked words abroad, I say, which nobody understands, but which everybody uses, and most people will also fight for, live for, or even die for, fancying they mean this or that, or the other, of things dear to them: for such words wear chameleon cloaks — "ground-lion" cloaks, of the colour of the ground of any man's fancy: on that ground they lie in wait, and rend them with a spring from it. There never were creatures of prey so mischievous, never diplomatists so cunning, never poisoners so deadly, as these masked words; they are the unjust stewards of all men's ideas: whatever fancy or favourite instinct a man most cherishes, he gives to his favourite masked word to take care of for him; the word at last comes to have an infinite power over him, — you cannot get at him but by its ministry.

SESAME AND LILIES   **48. canaille:** rabble. **60. quantity:** length or shortness of sound, with reference to the pronunciation of Latin verse.

17. And in languages so mongrel in breed as the English, there is a fatal power of   *80*
equivocation put into men's hands, almost whether they will or no, in being able to use
Greek or Latin words for an idea when they want it to be awful; and Saxon or otherwise
common words when they want it to be vulgar. What a singular and salutary effect, for
instance, would be produced on the minds of people who are in the habit of taking the
Form of the "Word" they live by, for the Power of which that Word tells them, if we   *85*
always either retained, or refused, the Greek form "biblos," or "biblion," as the right
expression for "book" — instead of employing it only in the one instance in which we
wish to give dignity to the idea, and translating it into English everywhere else. How
wholesome it would be for many simple persons if, in such places (for instance) as Acts
xix. 19, we retained the Greek expression, instead of translating it, and they had to read   *90*
— "Many of them also which used curious arts, brought their bibles together, and burnt
them before all men; and they counted the price of them, and found it fifty thousand
pieces of silver"! Or if, on the other hand, we translated where we retain it, and always
spoke of "The Holy Book," instead of "Holy Bible," it might come into more heads than
it does at present, that the Word of God, by which the heavens were, of old, and by   *95*
which they are now kept in store, cannot be made a present of to anybody in morocco
binding; nor sown on any wayside by help either of steam plough or steam press; but is
nevertheless being offered to us daily, and by us with contumely refused; and sown in us
daily, and by us, as instantly as may be, choked.

18. So, again, consider what effect has been produced on the English vulgar mind   *100*
by the use of the sonorous Latin form "damno," in translating the Greek κατατρίνω,
when people charitably wish to make it forcible; and the substitution of the temperate
"condemn" for it, when they choose to keep it gentle; and what notable sermons have
been preached by illiterate clergymen on — "He that believeth not shall be damned";
though they would shrink with horror from translating Heb. xi. 7, "The saving of his   *105*
house, by which he damned the world," or John viii. 10-11, "Woman, hath no man
damned thee? She saith, No man, Lord. Jesus answered her, Neither do I damn thee: go
and sin no more." And divisions in the mind of Europe, which have cost seas of blood,
and in the defence of which the noblest souls of men have been cast away in frantic
desolation, countless as forest-leaves — though, in the heart of them, founded on deeper   *110*
causes — have nevertheless been rendered practically possible, mainly, by the European
adoption of the Greek word for a public meeting, "ecclesia," to give peculiar
respectability to such meetings, when held for religious purposes; and other collateral
equivocations, such as the vulgar English one of using the word "priest" as a contraction
for "presbyter."   *115*

19. Now, in order to deal with words rightly, this is the habit you must form.
Nearly every word in your language has been first a word of some other language — of
Saxon, German, French, Latin, or Greek (not to speak of eastern and primitive dialects).
And many words have been all these — that is to say, have been Greek first, Latin next,
French or German next, and English last: undergoing a certain change of sense and use   *120*
on the lips of each nation; but retaining a deep vital meaning, which all good scholars
feel in employing them, even at this day. If you do not know the Greek alphabet, learn

---

82. **awful:** elevated. 83. **vulgar:** everyday, vulgate. 96. **kept in store:** See 2 Peter 3:5-7. 104: See John 3:16-18.

it; young or old — girl or boy — whoever you may be, if you think of reading seriously (which, of course, implies that you have some leisure at command), learn your Greek alphabet; then get good dictionaries of all these languages, and whenever you are in *125* doubt about a word, hunt it down patiently. Read Max Müller's lectures thoroughly, to begin with; and, after that, never let a word escape you that looks suspicious. It is severe work; but you will find it, even at first, interesting, and at last endlessly amusing. And the general gain to your character, in power and precision, will be quite incalculable.

Mind, this does not imply knowing, or trying to know, Greek or Latin, or French. It *130* takes a whole life to learn any language perfectly. But you can easily ascertain the meanings through which the English word has passed; and those which in a good writer's work it must still bear.

20. And now, merely for example's sake, I will, with your permission, read a few lines of a true book with you, carefully; and see what will come out of them. I will take *135* a book perfectly known to you all. No English words are more familiar to us, yet few perhaps have been read with less sincerity. I will take these few following lines of Lycidas: —

"Last came, and last did go,
The pilot of the Galilean lake. *140*
Two massy keys he bore of metals twain,
(The golden opes, the iron shuts amain),
He shook his mitred locks, and stern bespake,
'How well could I have spared for thee, young swain,
Enow of such as for their bellies' sake *145*
Creep, and intrude, and climb into the fold!
Of other care they little reckoning make,
Than how to scramble at the shearers' feast,
And shove away the worthy bidden guest;
Blind mouths! that scarce themselves know how to hold *150*
A sheep-hook, or have learn'd aught else, the least
That to the faithful herdman's art belongs!
What recks it them? What need they? They are sped;
And when they list, their lean and flashy songs
Grate on their scrannel pipes of wretched straw; *155*
The hungry sheep look up, and are not fed,
But, swoln with wind, and the rank mist they draw,
Rot inwardly, and foul contagion spread;
Besides what the grim wolf with privy paw
Daily devours apace, and nothing said.'" *160*

Let us think over this passage, and examine its words.

First, is it not singular to find Milton assigning to St. Peter, not only his full episcopal function, but the very types of it which Protestants usually refuse most passionately? His "mitred" locks! Milton was no Bishop-lover; how comes St. Peter to be "mitred"? "Two massy keys he bore." Is this, then, the power of the keys claimed by *165*

---

126. Müller: Friedrich Max Müller (see note to line 228 of "Passage to India," p. 1047), named professor of comparative philology at Oxford in 1866; author of *Lectures on the Science of Language* (1861-64). **127. severe:** rigorous, concise; from an Italian root word meaning "to cut." **138ff.:** See lines 108-29 p. 317.

the Bishops of Rome? and is it acknowledged here by Milton only in a poetical licence, for the sake of its picturesqueness, that he may get the gleam of the golden keys to help his effect?

Do not think it. Great men do not play stage tricks with the doctrines of life and death: only little men do that. Milton means what he says; and means it with his might 170 too — is going to put the whole strength of his spirit presently into the saying of it. For though not a lover of false bishops, he *was* a lover of true ones; and the Lake-pilot is here, in his thoughts, the type and head of true episcopal power. For Milton reads that text, "I will give unto thee the keys of the kingdom of heaven," quite honestly. Puritan though he be, he would not blot it out of the book because there have been bad bishops; 175 nay, in order to understand *him,* we must understand that verse first; it will not do to eye it askance, or whisper it under our breath, as if it were a weapon of an adverse sect. It is a solemn, universal assertion, deeply to be kept in mind by all sects. But perhaps we shall be better able to reason on it if we go on a little farther, and come back to it. For clearly this marked insistence on the power of the true episcopate is to make us feel 180 more weightily what is to be charged against the false claimants of episcopate; or generally, against false claimants of power and rank in the body of the clergy; they who, "for their bellies' sake, creep, and intrude, and climb into the fold."

21. Never think Milton uses those three words to fill up his verse, as a loose writer would. He needs all the three; — especially those three, and no more than those — 185 "creep," and "intrude," and "climb;" no other words would or could serve the turn, and no more could be added. For they exhaustively comprehend the three classes, correspondent to the three characters, of men who dishonestly seek ecclesiastical power. First, those who *"creep"* into the fold; who do not care for office, nor name, but for secret influence, and do all things occultly and cunningly, consenting to any servility of 190 office or conduct, so only that they may intimately discern, and unawares direct, the minds of men. Then those who "intrude" (thrust, that is) themselves into the fold, who by natural insolence of heart, and stout eloquence of tongue, and fearlessly perseverant self-assertion, obtain hearing and authority with the common crowd. Lastly, those who "climb," who, by labour and learning, both stout and sound, but selfishly exerted in the 195 cause of their own ambition, gain high dignities and authorities, and become "lords over the heritage," though not "ensamples to the flock."

22. Now go on: —

> "Of other care they little reckoning make,
> Than how to scramble at the shearers' feast. 200
> *Blind mouths* —"

I pause again, for this is a strange expression; a broken metaphor, one might think, careless and unscholarly.

Not so: its very audacity and pithiness are intended to make us look close at the phrase and remember it. Those two monosyllables express the precisely accurate 205 contraries of right character, in the two great offices of the Church — those of bishop and pastor.

174: See Matthew 16:9. **195. stout:** strong.

A "Bishop" means "a person who sees."

A "Pastor" means "a person who feeds."

The most unbishoply character a man can have is therefore to be Blind.   *210*

The most unpastoral is, instead of feeding, to want to be fed, — to be a Mouth.

Take the two reverses together, and you have "blind mouths." We may advisably follow out this idea a little. Nearly all the evils in the Church have arisen from bishops desiring *power* more than *light*. They want authority, not outlook. Whereas their real office is not to rule; though it may be vigorously to exhort and rebuke: it is the king's   *215* office to rule; the bishop's office is to *oversee* the flock; to number it, sheep by sheep; to be ready always to give full account of it. Now it is clear he cannot give account of the souls, if he has not so much as numbered the bodies, of his flock. The first thing, therefore, that a bishop has to do is at least to put himself in a position in which, at any moment, he can obtain the history, from childhood, of every living soul in his diocese,   *220* and of its present state. Down in that back street, Bill, and Nancy, knocking each other's teeth out! — Does the bishop know all about it? Has he his eye upon them? Has he *had* his eye upon them? Can he circumstantially explain to us how Bill got into the habit of beating Nancy about the head? If he cannot, he is no bishop, though he had a mitre as high as Salisbury steeple; he is no bishop, — he has sought to be at the helm instead of   *225* the masthead; he has no sight of things. "Nay," you say, "it is not his duty to look after Bill in the back street." What! the fat sheep that have full fleeces — you think it is only those he should look after while (go back to your Milton) "the hungry sheep look up, and are not fed, besides what the grim wolf, with privy paw" (bishops knowing nothing about it), "daily devours apace, and nothing said"?   *230*

"But that's not our idea of a bishop." Perhaps not; but it was St. Paul's; and it was Milton's. They may be right, or we may be; but we must not think we are reading either one or the other by putting our meaning into their words.

23. I go on.

"But swoln with wind, and the rank mist they draw."   *235*

This is to meet the vulgar answer that "if the poor are not looked after in their bodies, they are in their souls; they have spiritual food."

And Milton says, "They have no such thing as spiritual food; they are only swollen with wind." At first you may think that is a coarse type, and an obscure one. But again, it is a quite literally accurate one. Take up your Latin and Greek dictionaries, and find   *240* out the meaning of "Spirit." It is only a contraction of the Latin word "breath," and an indistinct translation of the Greek word for "wind." The same word is used in writing, "The wind bloweth where it listeth"; and in writing, "So is every one that is born of the Spirit"; born of the *breath,* that is; for it means the breath of God, in soul and body. We have the true sense of it in our words "inspiration" and "expire." Now, there are two   *245* kinds of breath with which the flock may be filled — God's breath, and man's. The breath of God is health, and life, and peace to them, as the air of heaven is to the flocks on the hills; but man's breath — the word which *he* calls spiritual — is disease and contagion to them, as the fog of the fen. They rot inwardly with it; they are puffed up by

---

221. Bill and Nancy: alluding to two characters in Dickens's *Oliver Twist* (1837-39). **228-30:** See Ezekiel 34:6-8. **239. type:** figure. **243.** See John 3:8. **243-44:** See John 3:5.

it, as a dead body by the vapours of its own decomposition. This is literally true of all *250*
false religious teaching; the first and last, and fatalest sign of it, is that "puffing up."
Your converted children, who teach their parents; your converted convicts, who teach
honest men; your converted dunces, who, having lived in cretinous stupefaction half
their lives, suddenly awaking to the fact of there being a God, fancy themselves
therefore His peculiar people and messengers; your sectarians of every species, small *255*
and great, Catholic or Protestant, of high church or low, in so far as they think
themselves exclusively in the right and others wrong; and, pre-eminently, in every sect,
those who hold that men can be saved by thinking rightly instead of doing rightly, by
word instead of act, and wish instead of work; — these are the true fog children —
clouds, these, without water; bodies, these, of putrescent vapour and skin, without blood *260*
or flesh: blown bagpipes for the fiends to pipe with — corrupt, and corrupting, —
"Swollen with wind, and the rank mist they draw."

24. Lastly, let us return to the lines respecting the power of the keys, for now we
can understand them. Note the difference between Milton and Dante in their
interpretation of this power: for once, the latter is weaker in thought; he supposes *both* *265*
the keys to be of the gate of heaven; one is of gold, the other of silver: they are given by
St. Peter to the sentinel angel; and it is not easy to determine the meaning either of the
substances of the three steps of the gate, or of the two keys. But Milton makes one, of
gold, the key of heaven; the other, of iron, the key of the prison in which the wicked
teachers are to be bound who "have taken away the key of knowledge, yet entered not in *270*
themselves."

We have seen that the duties of bishop and pastor are to see, and to feed; and of all
who do so it is said, "He that watereth, shall be watered also himself." But the reverse is
truth also. He that watereth not, shall be *withered* himself; and he that seeth not, shall
himself be shut out of sight — shut into the perpetual prison-house. And that prison *275*
opens here, as well as hereafter: he who is to be bound in heaven must first be bound on
earth. That command to the strong angels, of which the rock-apostle is the image, "Take
him, and bind him hand and foot, and cast him out," issues, in its measure, against the
teacher, for every help withheld, and for every truth refused, and for every falsehood
enforced; so that he is more strictly fettered the more he fetters, and farther outcast as he *280*
more and more misleads, till at last the bars of the iron cage close upon him, and as "the
golden opes, the iron shuts amain."

25. We have got something out of the lines, I think, and much more is yet to be
found in them; but we have done enough by way of example of the kind of word-by-
word examination of your author which is rightly called "reading"; watching every *285*
accent and expression, and putting ourselves always in the author's place, annihilating
our own personality, and seeking to enter into his, so as to be able assuredly to say,
"Thus Milton thought," not "Thus *I* thought, in mis-reading Milton." And by this
process you will gradually come to attach less weight to your own "Thus I thought" at
other times. You will begin to perceive that what *you* thought was a matter of no serious *290*

251: See 1 Corinthians 8:1. **255. peculiar:** special. **264ff.:** For the Dante reference, see *Inferno* 19:92, *Paradiso* 24:35, and *Paradiso* 5:57; Dante writes that the silver key (of justice) locks damned souls out of heaven, while the gold key (of mercy) opens the gates of heaven for those who are saved. **270-71:** See Luke 11:52. **273:** See Proverbs 11:25. **277. rock-apostle:** i.e., Peter (from "petros," the Greek for "stone"; see also Matthew 16:18). **277-78:** See Matthew 22:13.

importance; — that your thoughts on any subject are not perhaps the clearest and wisest that could be arrived at thereupon: — in fact, that unless you are a very singular person, you cannot be said to have any "thoughts" at all; that you have no materials for them, in any serious matters; — no right to "think," but only to try to learn more of the facts. Nay, most probably all your life (unless, as I said, you are a singular person) you will *295* have no legitimate right to an "opinion" on any business, except that instantly under your hand. What must of necessity be done, you can always find out, beyond question, how to do. Have you a house to keep in order, a commodity to sell, a field to plough, a ditch to cleanse? There need be no two opinions about these proceedings; it is at your peril if you have not much more than an "opinion" on the way to manage such matters. *300* And also, outside of your own business, there are one or two subjects on which you are bound to have but one opinion. That roguery and lying are objectionable, and are instantly to be flogged out of the way whenever discovered; — that covetousness and love of quarrelling are dangerous dispositions even in children, and deadly dispositions in men and nations; — that, in the end, the God of heaven and earth loves active, *305* modest, and kind people, and hates idle, proud, greedy, and cruel ones; — on these general facts you are bound to have but one, and that a very strong, opinion. For the rest, respecting religions, governments, sciences, arts, you will find that, on the whole, you can know NOTHING, — judge nothing; that the best you can do, even though you may be a well-educated person, is to be silent, and strive to be wiser every day, and to *310* understand a little more of the thoughts of others, which so soon as you try to do honestly, you will discover that the thoughts even of the wisest are very little more than pertinent questions. To put the difficulty into a clear shape, and exhibit to you the grounds for *in*decision, that is all they can generally do for you!

(1865)

THE ZODIAC SONG

1. *Aries* (sings)	Horn for weapon, and wool for shield, Windy weather and lambs afield.	
2. *Taurus*	Head in the sunshine, hoof in the hay, Toss the last of the clouds away.	
3. *Gemini*	Double in leaf and double in light, Flowers by day, and stars by night.	*5*
4. *Cancer*	Cancer, Cancer, crooked and black, Answer us, answer us — Forward or back?	
5. *Leo*	Fierce at eve, at morning tame, Crest of cloud, and claws of flame.	*10*
6. *Virgo*	Sickle in hand, and sandal on feet, Crowned with poppy, and swathed with wheat.	
7. *Libra*	Libra, Libra, truth is treasure, Fair the weight and full the measure.	
8. *Scorpio*	Sharp the sting, but grand the grief, Shivering bough, and burning leaf.	*15*

---

294. matters: Ruskin's note at this point reads "Modern 'Education' for the most part signifies giving people the faculty of thinking wrong on every conceivable subject of importance to them."

9. *Sagittarius*	Numb the finger: narrow the mark,	
	Frost on the feather, and flight in the dark.	
10. *Capricorn*	Capricorn, Capricorn,	
	Cowardly heart, and crumpled horn.	20
11. *Aquarius*	Snow to flicker, or rain to fall,	
	Down with thy pitcher, and out with it all.	
12. *Pisces*	Fish, little fish, lying head to tail,	
	Daisies round the dish and a pearl on every scale.	

(1865; 1903)

DORA GREENWELL
England, 1821-1882

A SCHERZO
(A Shy Person's Wishes)

With the wasp at the innermost heart of a peach,
On a sunny wall out of tip-toe reach,
With the trout in the darkest summer pool,
With the fern-seed clinging behind its cool
Smooth frond, in the chink of an aged tree,   5
In the woodbine's horn with the drunken bee,
With the mouse in its nest in a furrow old,
With the chrysalis wrapt in its gauzy fold;
With things that are hidden, and safe, and bold,
With things that are timid, and shy, and free,   10
Wishing to be;
With the nut in its shell, with the seed in its pod,
With the corn as it sprouts in the kindly clod,
Far down where the secret of beauty shows
In the bulb of the tulip, before it blows;   15

With things that are rooted, and firm, and deep,
Quiet to lie, and dreamless to sleep;
With things that are chainless, and tameless, and proud,
With the fire in the jagged thunder-cloud,
With the wind in its sleep, with the wind in its waking,   20
With the drops that go to the rainbow's making,
Wishing to be with the light leaves shaking,
Or stones on some desolate highway breaking;
Far up on the hills, where no foot surprises
The dew as it falls, or the dust as it rises;   25
To be couched with the beast in its torrid lair,
Or drifting on ice with the polar bear,
With the weaver at work at his quiet loom;
Anywhere, anywhere, out of this room!

(1867)

MATTHEW ARNOLD
England, 1822-1888

THE FORSAKEN MERMAN

Come, dear children, let us away;
Down and away below!
Now my brothers call from the bay,
Now the great winds shoreward blow,
Now the salt tides seaward flow;   5

Now the wild white horses play,
Champ and chafe and toss in the spray.
Children dear, let us away!
This way, this way!

Call her once before you go —   *10*
Call once yet!
In a voice that she will know:
"Margaret! Margaret!"
Children's voices should be dear
(Call once more) to a mother's ear;   *15*
Children's voices, wild with pain —
Surely she will come again!
Call her once and come away;
This way, this way!
"Mother dear, we cannot stay!   *20*
The wild white horses foam and fret."
Margaret! Margaret!

Come, dear children, come away down;
Call no more!
One last look at the white-wall'd town, *25*
And the little grey church on the windy shore,
Then come down!
She will not come though you call all day;
Come away, come away!

Children dear, was it yesterday   *30*
We heard the sweet bells over the bay?
In the caverns where we lay,
Through the surf and through the swell,
The far-off sound of a silver bell?
Sand-strewn caverns, cool and deep,   *35*
Where the winds are all asleep;
Where the spent lights quiver and gleam,
Where the salt weed sways in the stream,
Where the sea-beasts, ranged all round,
Feed in the ooze of their pasture-ground; *40*
Where the sea-snakes coil and twine,
Dry their mail and bask in the brine;
Where great whales come sailing by,
Sail and sail, with unshut eye,
Round the world for ever and aye?   *45*
When did music come this way?
Children dear, was it yesterday?

Children dear, was it yesterday
(Call yet once) that she went away?
Once she sate with you and me,   *50*
On a red gold throne in the heart of the sea,
And the youngest sate on her knee.
She comb'd its bright hair, and she tended it well,
When down swung the sound of a far-off bell.
She sigh'd, she look'd up through the clear green sea;
She said: "I must go, for my kinsfolk pray *56*
In the little grey church on the shore to-day.
'Twill be Easter-time in the world — ah me!
And I lose my poor soul, Merman! here with thee."

I said: "Go up, dear heart, through the waves; *60*
Say thy prayer, and come back to the kind sea-caves!"
She smiled, she went up through the surf in the bay.
Children dear, was it yesterday?

Children dear, were we long alone?
"The sea grows stormy, the little ones moan; *65*
Long prayers," I said, "in the world they say;
Come!" I said; and we rose through the surf in the bay.
We went up the beach, by the sandy down
Where the sea-stocks bloom, to the white-wall'd town;
Through the narrow paved streets, where all was still,
To the little grey church on the windy hill. *71*
From the church came a murmur of folk at their
  prayers,
But we stood without in the cold blowing airs.
We climb'd on the graves, on the stones worn
  with rains,
And we gazed up the aisle through the small leaded
  panes.   *75*
She sate by the pillar; we saw her clear:
"Margaret, hist! come quick, we are here!
Dear heart," I said, "we are long alone;
The sea grows stormy, the little ones moan."
But, ah, she gave me never a look,   *80*
For her eyes were seal'd to the holy book!
Loud prays the priest; shut stands the door.
Come away, children, call no more!
Come away, come down, call no more!

Down, down, down!   *85*
Down to the depths of the sea!
She sits at her wheel in the humming town,
Singing most joyfully.
Hark what she sings: "O joy, O joy,
For the humming street, and the child with its toy!
For the priest, and the bell, and the holy well; *91*
For the wheel where I spun,
And the blessed light of the sun!"
And so she sings her fill,
Singing most joyfully,   *95*
Till the spindle drops from her hand,
And the whizzing wheel stands still.
She steals to the window, and looks at the sand,
And over the sand at the sea;
And her eyes are set in a stare;   *100*
And anon there breaks a sigh,
And anon there drops a tear,
From a sorrow-clouded eye,
And a heart sorrow-laden,
A long, long sigh;   *105*
For the cold strange eyes of a little Mermaiden
And the gleam of her golden hair.

Come away, away children;
Come children, come down!
The hoarse wind blows coldly;   *110*
Lights shine in the town.
She will start from her slumber
When gusts shake the door;
She will hear the winds howling,
Will hear the waves roar.   *115*
We shall see, while above us
The waves roar and whirl,
A ceiling of amber,
A pavement of pearl.
Singing: "Here came a mortal,   *120*
But faithless was she!
And alone dwell for ever
The kings of the sea."

But, children, at midnight,
When soft the winds blow,   *125*
When clear falls the moonlight,
When spring-tides are low;
When sweet airs come seaward
From heaths starr'd with broom,
And high rocks throw mildly   *130*
On the blanch'd sands a gloom;
Up the still, glistening beaches,
Up the creeks we will hie,
Over banks of bright seaweed
The ebb-tide leaves dry.   *135*
We will gaze, from the sand-hills,
At the white, sleeping town;
At the church on the hill-side —
And then come back down.
Singing: "There dwells a loved one,   *140*
But cruel is she!
She left lonely for ever
The kings of the sea."
                              (1849)

TO MARGUERITE—CONTINUED

Yes! in the sea of life enisled,
With echoing straits between us thrown,
Dotting the shoreless watery wild,
We mortal millions live *alone*.
The islands feel the enclasping flow,   *5*
And then their endless bounds they know.

But when the moon their hollows lights,
And they are swept by balms of spring,
And in their glens, on starry nights,
The nightingales divinely sing;   *10*
And lovely notes, from shore to shore,
Across the sounds and channels pour —

Oh! then a longing like despair
Is to their farthest caverns sent;
For surely once, they feel, we were   *15*
Parts of a single continent!
Now round us spreads the watery plain —
Oh might our marges meet again!

Who order'd, that their longing's fire
Should be, as soon as kindled, cool'd?   *20*
Who renders vain their deep desire? —
A God, a God their severance ruled!
And bade betwixt their shores to be
The unplumb'd, salt, estranging sea.
                              (1852)

THE SCHOLAR-GIPSY

Go, for they call you, shepherd, from the hill;
    Go, shepherd, and untie the wattled cotes!
        No longer leave thy wistful flock unfed,
    Nor let thy bawling fellows rack their throats,
        Nor the cropp'd herbage shoot another head. *5*

TO MARGUERITE—CONTINUED   This poem, from the group "Switzerland," though preceded in the 1857 edition by "Isolation. To Marguerite," was published five years earlier, without "Continued." "Marguerite" may have been a real woman Arnold had met in Switzerland; she may also be reflected in the name "Margaret" in "The Forsaken Merman." Regarding the poem's central image, cf. Donne's statement in "Meditation XVII" that "No man is an island . . . ; every man is a piece of the continent . . . " (p. 262).   **THE SCHOLAR-GIPSY**   To explain the idea for the poem, Arnold included as a note the following adaptation of a passage from *The Vanity of Dogmatizing* (1661), by Joseph Glanvill (1636-1680), who had been a student at Oxford: "There was very lately a lad in the University of Oxford, who was by his poverty forced to leave his studies there; and at last to join himself to a company of vagabond gipsies. Among these extravagant people, by the insinuating subtilty of his carriage, he quickly got so much of their love and esteem as that they discovered to him their mystery. After he had been a pretty while exercised in the trade, there chanced to ride by a couple of scholars, who had formerly been of his acquaintance. They quickly spied out their old friend among the gipsies; and he gave them an account of the necessity which drove him to that kind of life, and told them that the people he went with were not such impostors as they were taken for, but that they had a traditional kind of learning among them, and could do wonders by the power of imagination, their fancy binding that of others: that himself had learned much of their art, and when he had compassed the whole secret, he intended, he said, to leave their company, and give the world an account of what he had learned." **2. wattled cotes:** sheepfolds made of woven branches.

But when the fields are still,
  And the tired men and dogs all gone to rest,
    And only the white sheep are sometimes seen
    Cross and recross the strips of moon-blanch'd green,
  Come, shepherd, and again begin the quest!   10

Here, where the reaper was at work of late —
  In this high field's dark corner, where he leaves
    His coat, his basket, and his earthen cruse,
    And in the sun all morning binds the sheaves,
      Then here, at noon, comes back his stores to use —
    Here will I sit and wait,   16
  While to my ear from uplands far away
    The bleating of the folded flocks is borne,
    With distant cries of reapers in the corn —
  All the live murmur of a summer's day.   20

Screen'd is this nook o'er the high, half-reap'd field,
  And here till sun-down, shepherd! will I be.
    Through the thick corn the scarlet poppies peep,
    And round green roots and yellowing stalks I see
      Pale pink convolvulus in tendrils creep;   25
    And air-swept lindens yield
  Their scent, and rustle down their perfumed showers
    Of bloom on the bent grass where I am laid,
    And bower me from the August sun with shade;
  And the eye travels down to Oxford's towers.   30

And near me on the grass lies Glanvil's book —
  Come, let me read the oft-read tale again!
    The story of the Oxford scholar poor,
    Of pregnant parts and quick inventive brain,
      Who, tired of knocking at preferment's door,   35
      One summer-morn forsook
    His friends, and went to learn the gipsy-lore,
    And roam'd the world with that wild brotherhood,
    And came, as most men deem'd, to little good,
  But came to Oxford and his friends no more.   40

But once, years after, in the country-lanes,
  Two scholars, whom at college erst he knew,
    Met him, and of his way of life enquired;
    Whereat he answer'd, that the gipsy-crew,
      His mates, had arts to rule as they desired   45
      The workings of men's brains,
    And they can bind them to what thoughts they will.
    "And I," he said, "the secret of their art,
    When fully learn'd, will to the world impart;
  But it needs heaven-sent moments for this skill."   50

This said, he left them, and return'd no more. —
  But rumours hung about the country-side,
    That the lost Scholar long was seen to stray,
    Seen by rare glimpses, pensive and tongue-tied,
      In hat of antique shape, and cloak of grey,   55
    The same the gipsies wore.
  Shepherds had met him on the Hurst in spring;
    At some lone alehouse in the Berkshire moors,
    On the warm ingle-bench, the smock-frock'd boors
  Had found him seated at their entering,   60

But, 'mid their drink and clatter, he would fly.
  And I myself seem half to know thy looks,
    And put the shepherds, wanderer! on thy trace;
    And boys who in lone wheatfields scare the rooks
      I ask if thou hast pass'd their quiet place;   65
      Or in my boat I lie
  Moor'd to the cool bank in the summer-heats,
    'Mid wide grass meadows which the sunshine fills,
    And watch the warm, green-muffled Cumner hills,
  And wonder if thou haunt'st their shy retreats.   70

For most, I know, thou lov'st retired ground!
  Thee at the ferry Oxford riders blithe,
    Returning home on summer-nights, have met
  Crossing the stripling Thames at Bab-lock-hithe,
      Trailing in the cool stream thy fingers wet,   75
      As the punt's rope chops round;
  And leaning backward in a pensive dream,
    And fostering in thy lap a heap of flowers
    Pluck'd in shy fields and distant Wychwood bowers,
  And thine eyes resting on the moonlit stream.   80

And then they land, and thou art seen no more! —
  Maidens, who from the distant hamlets come
    To dance around the Fyfield elm in May,
  Oft through the darkening fields have seen thee roam,
    Or cross a stile into the public way.   85
      Oft thou hast given them store
  Of flowers — the frail-leaf'd, white anemony,
    Dark bluebells drench'd with dews of summer eves,
    And purple orchises with spotted leaves —
  But none hath words she can report of thee.   90

And, above Godstow Bridge, when hay-time's here
  In June, and many a scythe in sunshine flames,
    Men who through those wide fields of breezy grass
    Where black-wing'd swallows haunt the glittering
      Thames,

---

13. cruse: jug for water or other beverage. **19. corn:** grain. **34. pregnant parts:** important or unusually promising abilities. **57. Hurst:** Cumnor Hurst, a 150 m hill about 5 km southwest of Oxford, in what used to be part of Berkshire, but is now in Oxfordshire. **59. ingle-bench:** bench in the chimney-corner, by the fire. **74:** i.e., by the Bablock Hythe ferry just west of the village of Cumnor. **79. Wychwood bowers:** about 25 km northwest of Oxford. **83:** Fyfield is about 11 km southwest of Oxford. **91. Godstow Bridge:** over the Thames just upstream from Oxford.

To bathe in the abandon'd lasher pass,   95
    Have often pass'd thee near
Sitting upon the river bank o'ergrown;
    Mark'd thine outlandish garb, thy figure spare,
    Thy dark vague eyes, and soft abstracted air —
But, when they came from bathing, thou wast gone! 100

At some lone homestead in the Cumner hills,
    Where at her open door the housewife darns,
    Thou hast been seen, or hanging on a gate
To watch the threshers in the mossy barns.
    Children, who early range these slopes and late 105
        For cresses from the rills,
Have known thee eying, all an April-day,
    The springing pastures and the feeding kine;
    And mark'd thee, when the stars come out and shine,
Through the long dewy grass move slow away.   110

In autumn, on the skirts of Bagley Wood —
    Where most the gipsies by the turf-edged way
    Pitch their smoked tents, and every bush you see
With scarlet patches tagg'd and shreds of grey,
    Above the forest-ground called Thessaly —   115
        The blackbird, picking food,
Sees thee, nor stops his meal, nor fears at all;
    So often has he known thee past him stray,
    Rapt, twirling in thy hand a wither'd spray,
And waiting for the spark from heaven to fall.   120

And once, in winter, on the causeway chill
    Where home through flooded fields foot-travellers go,
    Have I not pass'd thee on the wooden bridge,
Wrapt in thy cloak and battling with the snow,
    Thy face tow'rd Hinksey and its wintry ridge?   125
        And thou hast climb'd the hill,
And gain'd the white brow of the Cumner range;
    Turn'd once to watch, while thick the snowflakes fall.
    The line of festal light in Christ-Church hall —
Then sought thy straw in some sequester'd grange. 130

But what — I dream! Two hundred years are flown
    Since first thy story ran through Oxford halls,
    And the grave Glanvil did the tale inscribe
That thou wert wander'd from the studious walls
    To learn strange arts, and join a gipsy-tribe;   135
        And thou from earth art gone
Long since, and in some quiet churchyard laid —
    Some country-nook, where o'er thy unknown grave
    Tall grasses and white flowering nettles wave,
Under a dark, red-fruited yew-tree's shade.   140

— No, no, thou hast not felt the lapse of hours!
    For what wears out the life of mortal men?
        'Tis that from change to change their being rolls;
        'Tis that repeated shocks, again, again,
        Exhaust the energy of strongest souls   145
        And numb the elastic powers.
Till having used our nerves with bliss and teen,
    And tired upon a thousand schemes our wit,
    To the just-pausing Genius we remit
Our worn-out life, and are — what we have been.   150

Thou hast not lived, why should'st thou perish, so?
    Thou hadst *one* aim, *one* business, *one* desire;
    Else wert thou long since number'd with the dead!
Else hadst thou spent, like other men, thy fire!
    The generations of thy peers are fled,   155
        And we ourselves shall go;
But thou possessest an immortal lot,
    And we imagine thee exempt from age
    And living as thou liv'st on Glanvil's page,
Because thou hadst — what we, alas! have not.   160

For early didst thou leave the world, with powers
    Fresh, undiverted to the world without,
    Firm to their mark, not spent on other things;
Free from the sick fatigue, the languid doubt,
    Which much to have tried, in much been baffled, brings.
        O life unlike to ours!   166
Who fluctuate idly without term or scope,
Of whom each strives, nor knows for what he strives,
    And each half lives a hundred different lives;
Who wait like thee, but not, like thee, in hope.   170

Thou waitest for the spark from heaven! and we,
    Light half-believers of our casual creeds,
    Who never deeply felt, nor clearly will'd,
Whose insight never has borne fruit in deeds,
    Whose vague resolves never have been fulfill'd; 175
        For whom each year we see
Breeds new beginnings, disappointments new;
    Who hesitate and falter life away,
    And lose to-morrow the ground won to-day —
Ah! do not we, wanderer! await it too?   180

Yes, we await it! — but it still delays,
    And then we suffer! and amongst us one,
    Who most has suffer'd, takes dejectedly
His seat upon the intellectual throne;
    And all his store of sad experience he   185
        Lays bare of wretched days;

---

95. lasher: pool formed by water flowing over a weir or dam. **111. Bagley Wood:** a little south of Oxford, beyond the area nicknamed after the classical Thessaly (115). **125:** Both North and South Hinksey are just across the river from Oxford. **129. Christ-Church hall:** i.e., the dining hall of Christ Church College. **147. teen:** grief, trouble, vexation. **149. Genius:** a tutelary deity; a presiding spirit, whether good or evil. **182. one:** This may refer to no specific person, though such figures as Goethe, Coleridge, and Carlyle have been suggested, as has Tennyson, who in 1850 had both become poet laureate and published *In Memoriam* (see p. 966).

Tells us his misery's birth and growth and signs,
  And how the dying spark of hope was fed,
  And how the breast was soothed, and how the head,
  And all his hourly varied anodynes.   *190*

This for our wisest! and we others pine,
  And wish the long unhappy dream would end,
  And waive all claim to bliss, and try to bear;
  With close-lipp'd patience for our only friend,
    Sad patience, too near neighbour to despair —   *195*
      But none has hope like thine!
Thou through the fields and through the woods dost stray,
  Roaming the country-side, a truant boy,
  Nursing thy project in unclouded joy,
  And every doubt long blown by time away.   *200*

O born in days when wits were fresh and clear,
  And life ran gaily as the sparkling Thames;
    Before this strange disease of modern life,
  With its sick hurry, its divided aims,
    Its heads o'ertax'd, its palsied hearts, was rife — *205*
      Fly hence, our contact fear!
Still fly, plunge deeper in the bowering wood!
  Averse, as Dido did with gesture stern
  From her false friend's approach in Hades turn,
  Wave us away, and keep thy solitude!   *210*

Still nursing the unconquerable hope,
  Still clutching the inviolable shade,
    With a free, onward impulse brushing through,
  By night, the silver'd branches of the glade —
    Far on the forest-skirts, where none pursue.   *215*
      On some mild pastoral slope
Emerge, and resting on the moonlit pales
  Freshen thy flowers as in former years
  With dew, or listen with enchanted ears,
  From the dark dingles, to the nightingales!   *220*

But fly our paths, our feverish contact fly!
  For strong the infection of our mental strife,
    Which, though it gives no bliss, yet spoils for rest;
  And we should win thee from thy own fair life,
    Like us distracted, and like us unblest.   *225*
      Soon, soon thy cheer would die,
  Thy hopes grow timorous, and unfix'd thy powers,

  And thy clear aims be cross and shifting made;
    And then thy glad perennial youth would fade,
    Fade, and grow old at last, and die like ours.   *230*

Then fly our greetings, fly our speech and smiles!
  — As some grave Tyrian trader, from the sea,
    Descried at sunrise an emerging prow
  Lifting the cool-hair'd creepers stealthily,
    The fringes of a southward-facing brow   *235*
      Among the Ægæan isles;
  And saw the merry Grecian coaster come,
    Freighted with amber grapes, and Chian wine,
    Green, bursting figs, and tunnies steep'd in brine —
  And knew the intruders on his ancient home,   *240*

The young light-hearted masters of the waves —
  And snatch'd his rudder, and shook out more sail;
    And day and night held on indignantly
  O'er the blue Midland waters with the gale,
    Betwixt the Syrtes and soft Sicily,   *245*
      To where the Atlantic raves
Outside the western straits; and unbent sails
  There, where down cloudy cliffs, through sheets of foam,
  Shy traffickers, the dark Iberians come;
  And on the beach undid his corded bales.   *250*

                (1853)

DOVER BEACH

The sea is calm to-night.
The tide is full, the moon lies fair
Upon the straits; — on the French coast the light
Gleams and is gone; the cliffs of England stand,
Glimmering and vast, out in the tranquil bay.   *5*
Come to the window, sweet is the night-air!
Only, from the long line of spray
Where the sea meets the moon-blanch'd land,
Listen! you hear the grating roar
Of pebbles which the waves draw back, and fling,   *10*
At their return, up the high strand,
Begin, and cease, and then again begin,
With tremulous cadence slow, and bring
The eternal note of sadness in.

208-09: Dido, queen of Carthage, committed suicide when Aeneas deserted her, and stayed turned away from him when he encountered her during his visit to Hades (see Virgil's *Aeneid,* VI, 450-72). **217. pales:** palings, fence. **220. dingles:** small wooded valleys. **232. Tyrian:** from Tyre, in ancient Phoenicia. **238. Chian:** from the Aegean island of Chios. **239. tunnies:** tuna. **244. Midland:** translating *Mediterranean.* **245. Syrtes:** gulfs (modern Sidra or Sirte, and Gabes) on the North African coast south of Sicily. **247. straits:** i.e., of Gibraltar. **249-50:** referring to a method of conducting trade without meeting face to face; Herodotus (IV, 196) describes how Carthaginians trading with Africans beyond Gibraltar would leave goods on the beach, retire to their ships and send up a smoke signal, wait for the natives to place their gold beside what they wanted, and themselves withdraw to a distance, repeating the procedure until the terms of exchange satisfied both parties.

Sophocles long ago   15
Heard it on the Ægæan, and it brought
Into his mind the turbid ebb and flow
Of human misery; we
Find also in the sound a thought,
Hearing it by this distant northern sea.   20

The Sea of Faith
Was once, too, at the full, and round earth's shore
Lay like the folds of a bright girdle furl'd.
But now I only hear
Its melancholy, long, withdrawing roar,   25

Retreating, to the breath
Of the night-wind, down the vast edges drear
And naked shingles of the world.

Ah, love, let us be true
To one another! for the world, which seems   30
To lie before us like a land of dreams,
So various, so beautiful, so new,
Hath really neither joy, nor love, nor light,
Nor certitude, nor peace, nor help for pain;
And we are here as on a darkling plain   35
Swept with confused alarms of struggle and flight,
Where ignorant armies clash by night.

(1867)

LITERATURE AND SCIENCE (abridged)

. . . .

I am going to ask whether the present movement for ousting letters from their old predominance in education, and for transferring the predominance in education to the natural sciences, whether this brisk and flourishing movement ought to prevail, and whether it is likely that in the end it really will prevail. An objection may be raised which I will anticipate. My own studies have been almost wholly in letters, and my   5
visits to the field of the natural sciences have been very slight and inadequate, although those sciences have always strongly moved my curiosity. A man of letters, it will perhaps be said, is not competent to discuss the comparative merits of letters and natural science as means of education. To this objection I reply, first of all, that his incompetence, if he attempts the discussion but is really incompetent for it, will be   10
abundantly visible; nobody will be taken in; he will have plenty of sharp observers and critics to save mankind from that danger. But the line I am going to follow is, as you will soon discover, so extremely simple, that perhaps it may be followed without failure even by one who for a more ambitious line of discussion would be quite incompetent.

Some of you may possibly remember a phrase of mine which has been the object of   15
a good deal of comment; an observation to the effect that in our culture, the aim being *to know ourselves and the world*, we have, as the means to this end, *to know the best which has been thought and said in the world....*

DOVER BEACH   15. Sophocles: (c.496-406 B.C.) Greek tragic dramatist, best known for his *Oedipus* plays; Arnold is here probably thinking of lines 583-91 in *Antigone*. **28. shingles:** pebbled beaches.   **LITERATURE AND SCIENCE**   In his Preface to *Discourses in America* (1885), Arnold notes that this essay "was originally given as the Rede Lecture at Cambridge, was recast for delivery in America, and is reprinted here as so recast." His American lecture tour took place in 1883. **16-18:** Arnold characteristically repeats key phrases and ideas from one work to another. For example, in his essay "The Function of Criticism at the Present Time" (which served as the introduction to *Essays in Criticism*, 1865) Arnold quotes from one of his earlier books, *On Translating Homer* (1861, lecture II): "It is the business of the critical power . . . 'in all branches of knowledge, theology, philosophy, history, art, science, to see the object as in itself it really is,'" and defines criticism as "*a disinterested endeavour to learn and propagate the best that is known and thought in the world.*" In a review essay called "A Guide to English Literature" (included in *Mixed Essays*, 1879), he remarks that "In literature we have present, and waiting to form us, the best which has been thought and said in the world." And in what is probably his best known book, *Culture and Anarchy* (1869), he says that "The whole scope of the essay [i.e., the book] is to recommend culture as the great help out of our present difficulties; culture being a pursuit of our total perfection by means of getting to know, on all the matters which most concern us, the best which has been thought and said in the world. . . . "

Now . . . Professor Huxley remarks that when I speak of the above-mentioned knowledge as enabling us to know ourselves and the world, I assert *literature* to contain   20
the materials which suffice for thus making us know ourselves and the world. But it is not by any means clear, says he, that after having learnt all which ancient and modern literatures have to tell us, we have laid a sufficiently broad and deep foundation for that criticism of life, that knowledge of ourselves and the world, which constitutes culture. . . .
What Professor Huxley says, implies just the reproach which is so often brought against   25
the study of *belles lettres*, as they are called: that the study is an elegant one, but slight and ineffectual; a smattering of Greek and Latin and other ornamental things, of little use for any one whose object is to get at truth, and to be a practical man. So, too, M. Renan talks of the "superficial humanism" of a school-course which treats us as if we were all going to be poets, writers, preachers, orators, and he opposes this humanism to   30
positive science, or the critical search after truth.

    . . . .

Let us, I say, be agreed about the meaning of the terms we are using. I talk of knowing the best which has been thought and uttered in the world; Professor Huxley says this means knowing *literature*. Literature is a large word; it may mean everything written with letters or printed in a book. Euclid's *Elements* and Newton's *Principia* are   35
thus literature. All knowledge that reaches us through books is literature. But by literature Professor Huxley means *belles lettres*. He means to make me say, that knowing the best which has been thought and said by the modern nations is knowing their *belles lettres* and no more. And this is no sufficient equipment, he argues, for a criticism of modern life. But as I do not mean, by knowing ancient Rome, knowing   40
merely more or less of Latin *belles lettres*, and taking no account of Rome's military, and political, and legal, and administrative work in the world; and as, by knowing ancient Greece, I understand knowing her as the giver of Greek art, and the guide to a free and right use of reason and to scientific method, and the founder of our mathematics and physics and astronomy and biology, — I understand knowing her as all   45
this, and not merely knowing certain Greek poems, and histories, and treatises, and speeches, — so as to the knowledge of modern nations also. By knowing modern nations, I mean not merely knowing their *belles lettres*, but knowing also what has been done by such men as Copernicus, Galileo, Newton, Darwin.

    . . . .

The appeal, in the study of nature, is constantly to observation and experiment; not only   50
is it said that the thing is so, but we can be made to see that it is so. Not only does a man tell us that when a taper burns the wax is converted into carbonic acid and water, as a

---

19. Huxley: Thomas Henry Huxley (1825-1895), physician, Professor of Natural History, and one of the most influential thinkers of the 19th century; he was a friend of Charles Darwin (see p. 945) and spokesman for his theory of evolution; in referring to Huxley, Arnold quotes and paraphrases from Huxley's 1880 lecture published as "Science and Culture." **24. criticism of life:** In "The Study of Poetry" (1880) Arnold remarks that "More and more mankind will discover that we have to turn to poetry to interpret life for us, to console us, to sustain us," and in this sense refers to poetry as "a criticism of life under the conditions fixed for such a criticism by the laws of poetic truth and poetic beauty." **29. Renan:** Ernest Renan (1823-1892), French philosopher and historian, best known for *The Life of Jesus,* the first volume of his *History of the Origins of Christianity* (1863-81). **35.** Euclid, 3rd-century B.C. Greek mathematician, famous for his textbook, *Elements*; Sir Isaac Newton (1642-1727), English scientist and philosopher, president of the Royal Society, formulator of the theory of gravity; Arnold refers to his *Principia Mathematica* (1687). **49.** Nicholas Copernicus (1473-1543), Polish astronomer whose heliocentric theory of planetary revolution displaced the Ptolemaic theory (see *Ptolemaic* in the Glossary); Galileo Galilei (1564-1642), Italian scientist and philosopher, known for his astronomical observations (and see notes to lines 3-4 of Wotton's letter to Salisbury, p. 234, and line 164 of Samuel Johnson's *Vanity of Human Wishes,* p. 591).

man may tell us, if he likes, that Charon is punting his ferry-boat on the river Styx, or
that Victor Hugo is a sublime poet, or Mr. Gladstone the most admirable of statesmen;
but we are made to see that the conversion into carbonic acid and water does actually   *55*
happen. This reality of natural knowledge it is, which makes the friends of physical
science contrast it, as a knowledge of things, with the humanist's knowledge, which is,
say they, a knowledge of words. And hence Professor Huxley is moved to lay it down
that, "for the purpose of attaining real culture, an exclusively scientific education is at
least as effectual as an exclusively literary education." And a certain President of the   *60*
Section for Mechanical Science in the British Association is, in Scripture phrase, "very
bold," and declares that if a man, in his mental training, "has substituted literature and
history for natural science, he has chosen the less useful alternative." But whether we go
these lengths or not, we must all admit that in natural science the habit gained of dealing
with facts is a most valuable discipline, and that every one should have some experience   *65*
of it.

. . . .

All knowledge is, as I said just now, interesting; and even items of knowledge
which from the nature of the case cannot well be related, but must stand isolated in our
thoughts, have their interest. Even lists of exceptions have their interest. If we are
studying Greek accents, it is interesting to know that *pais* and *pas*, and some other   *70*
monosyllables of the same form of declension, do not take the circumflex upon the last
syllable of the genitive plural, but vary, in this respect, from the common rule. If we are
studying physiology, it is interesting to know that the pulmonary artery carries dark
blood and the pulmonary vein carries bright blood, departing in this respect from the
common rule for the division of labour between the veins and the arteries. But every one   *75*
knows how we seek naturally to combine the pieces of our knowledge together, to bring
them under general rules, to relate them to principles; and how unsatisfactory and
tiresome it would be to go on for ever learning lists of exceptions, or accumulating items
of fact which must stand isolated.

Well, that same need of relating our knowledge, which operates here within the   *80*
sphere of our knowledge itself, we shall find operating, also, outside that sphere. We
experience, as we go on learning and knowing, — the vast majority of us experience, —
the need of relating what we have learnt and known to the sense which we have in us for
conduct, to the sense which we have in us for beauty.

A certain Greek prophetess of Mantineia in Arcadia, Diotima by name, once   *85*
explained to the philosopher Socrates that love, and impulse, and bent of all kinds, is, in
fact, nothing else but the desire in men that good should for ever be present to them.
This desire for good, Diotima assured Socrates, is our fundamental desire, of which
fundamental desire every impulse in us is only some one particular form. And therefore
this fundamental desire it is, I suppose, — this desire in men that good should be for   *90*

53: In Greek myth, Charon ferried the souls of the dead over the river Styx in Hades. **54. Victor Hugo:** (1802-1885), French poet, novelist, and dramatist; **Gladstone:** William Ewart Gladstone (1809-1898), Liberal statesman, four times prime minister of England, and author of *Studies on Homer and the Homeric Age* (1858) and other works. **61-62. very bold:** said of Esaias in Romans 10:20. **84. conduct:** In *Literature and Dogma* (1873), Arnold returns to the idea of "culture" as "knowing the best that has been thought and said in the world," and virtually equates "conduct" with "morality," returning again and again to the idea that "conduct is three-fourths of our life and its largest concern." **85-89:** See Plato's *Symposium*, 201-12.

ever present to them, — which acts in us when we feel the impulse for relating our knowledge to our sense for conduct and to our sense for beauty. At any rate, with men in general the instinct exists. Such is human nature. And the instinct, it will be admitted, is innocent, and human nature is preserved by our following the lead of its innocent instincts. Therefore, in seeking to gratify this instinct in question, we are following the *95* instinct of self-preservation in humanity.

But, no doubt, some kinds of knowledge cannot be made to directly serve the instinct in question, cannot be directly related to the sense for beauty, to the sense for conduct. These are instrument-knowledges; they lead on to other knowledges, which can. A man who passes his life in instrument-knowledges is a specialist. They may be *100* invaluable as instruments to something beyond, for those who have the gift thus to employ them; and they may be disciplines in themselves wherein it is useful for every one to have some schooling. But it is inconceivable that the generality of men should pass all their mental life with Greek accents or with formal logic. My friend Professor Sylvester, who is one of the first mathematicians in the world, holds transcendental *105* doctrines as to the virtue of mathematics, but those doctrines are not for common men. In the very Senate House and heart of our English Cambridge I once ventured, though not without an apology for my profaneness, to hazard the opinion that for the majority of mankind a little of mathematics, even, goes a long way. Of course this is quite consistent with their being of immense importance as an instrument to something else; *110* but it is the few who have the aptitude for thus using them, not the bulk of mankind.

The natural sciences do not, however, stand on the same footing with these instrument-knowledges. Experience shows us that the generality of men will find more interest in learning that, when a taper burns, the wax is converted into carbonic acid and water, or in learning the explanation of the phenomenon of dew, or in learning how the *115* circulation of the blood is carried on, than they find in learning that the genitive plural of *pais* and *pas* does not take the circumflex on the termination. And one piece of natural knowledge is added to another, and others are added to that, and at last we come to propositions so interesting as Mr. Darwin's famous proposition that "our ancestor was a hairy quadruped furnished with a tail and pointed ears, probably arboreal in his *120* habits." Or we come to propositions of such reach and magnitude as those which Professor Huxley delivers, when he says that the notions of our forefathers about the beginning and the end of the world were all wrong, and that nature is the expression of a definite order with which nothing interferes.

Interesting, indeed, these results of science are, important they are, and we should *125* all of us be acquainted with them. But what I now wish you to mark is, that we are still, when they are propounded to us and we receive them, we are still in the sphere of intellect and knowledge. And for the generality of men there will be found, I say, to arise, when they have duly taken in the proposition that their ancestor was "a hairy quadruped furnished with a tail and pointed ears, probably arboreal in his habits," there *130* will be found to arise an invincible desire to relate this proposition to the sense in us for

---

105. Sylvester: James Joseph Sylvester (1814-1897), English-born mathematician, professor of mathematics at the University of Virginia, at the Royal Military Academy in Woolwich, England, and from 1877 the first professor of mathematics at Johns Hopkins University, where in 1878 he founded the *American Journal of Mathematics,* and for a year (1893-94) professor of geometry at Oxford. **119-21:** in chapter 21 of *The Descent of Man* (1871).

conduct, and to the sense in us for beauty. But this the men of science will not do for us, and will hardly even profess to do. They will give us other pieces of knowledge, other facts, about other animals and their ancestors, or about plants, or about stones, or about stars; and they may finally bring us to those great "general conceptions of the universe, *135* which are forced upon us all," says Professor Huxley, "by the progress of physical science." But still it will be *knowledge* only which they give us; knowledge not put for us into relation with our sense for conduct, our sense for beauty, and touched with emotion by being so put; not thus put for us, and therefore, to the majority of mankind, after a certain while, unsatisfying, wearying. *140*

Not to the born naturalist, I admit. But what do we mean by a born naturalist? We mean a man in whom the zeal for observing nature is so uncommonly strong and eminent, that it marks him off from the bulk of mankind. Such a man will pass his life happily in collecting natural knowledge and reasoning upon it, and will ask for nothing, or hardly anything, more. I have heard it said that the sagacious and admirable naturalist *145* whom we lost not very long ago, Mr. Darwin, once owned to a friend that for his part he did not experience the necessity for two things which most men find so necessary to them, — religion and poetry; science and the domestic affections, he thought, were enough. To a born naturalist, I can well understand that this should seem so. So absorbing is his occupation with nature, so strong his love for his occupation, that he *150* goes on acquiring natural knowledge and reasoning upon it, and has little time or inclination for thinking about getting it related to the desire in man for conduct, the desire in man for beauty. He relates it to them for himself as he goes along, so far as he feels the need; and he draws from the domestic affections all the additional solace necessary. But then Darwins are extremely rare. Another great and admirable master of *155* natural knowledge, Faraday, was a Sandemanian. That is to say, he related his knowledge to his instinct for conduct and to his instinct for beauty, by the aid of that respectable Scottish sectary, Robert Sandeman. And so strong, in general, is the demand of religion and poetry to have their share in a man, to associate themselves with his knowing, and to relieve and rejoice it, that, probably, for one man amongst us with the *160* disposition to do as Darwin did in this respect, there are at least fifty with the disposition to do as Faraday.

Education lays hold upon us, in fact, by satisfying this demand. Professor Huxley holds up to scorn mediæval education, with its neglect of the knowledge of nature, its poverty even of literary studies, its formal logic devoted to "showing how and why that *165* which the Church said was true must be true." But the great mediæval Universities were not brought into being, we may be sure, by the zeal for giving a jejune and contemptible education. Kings have been their nursing fathers, and queens have been their nursing mothers, but not for this. The mediæval Universities came into being, because the supposed knowledge, delivered by Scripture and the Church, so deeply engaged men's *170* hearts, by so simply, easily, and powerfully relating itself to their desire for conduct, their desire for beauty. All other knowledge was dominated by this supposed knowledge and was subordinated to it; because of the surpassing strength of the hold which it

---

156. Faraday: Michael Faraday (1791-1867), English chemist and physicist; "Sandemanian" was the more common name in England and America for "Glasite," a member of a religious sect founded by Scottish divine John Glas (1695-1773) and furthered by his son-in-law, Robert Sandeman (1718-1771).

gained upon the affections of men, by allying itself profoundly with their sense for conduct, their sense for beauty. *175*

But now, says Professor Huxley, conceptions of the universe fatal to the notions held by our forefathers have been forced upon us by physical science. Grant to him that they are thus fatal, that the new conceptions must and will soon become current everywhere, and that every one will finally perceive them to be fatal to the beliefs of our forefathers. The need of humane letters, as they are truly called, because they serve the paramount desire in men that *180* good should be for ever present to them, — the need of humane letters, to establish a relation between the new conceptions, and our instinct for beauty, our instinct for conduct, is only the more visible. The Middle Age could do without humane letters, as it could do without the study of nature, because its supposed knowledge was made to engage its emotions so powerfully. Grant that the supposed knowledge disappears, its power of being made to *185* engage the emotions will of course disappear along with it, — but the emotions themselves, and their claim to be engaged and satisfied, will remain. Now if we find by experience that humane letters have an undeniable power of engaging the emotions, the importance of humane letters in a man's training becomes not less, but greater, in proportion to the success of modern science in extirpating what it calls "mediæval thinking." *190*

Have humane letters, then, have poetry and eloquence, the power here attributed to them of engaging the emotions, and do they exercise it? And if they have it and exercise it, *how* do they exercise it, so as to exert an influence upon man's sense for conduct, his sense for beauty? Finally, even if they both can and do exert an influence upon the senses in question, how are they to relate to them the results, — the modern results, — *195* of natural science? All these questions may be asked. First, have poetry and eloquence the power of calling out the emotions? The appeal is to experience. Experience shows that for the vast majority of men, for mankind in general, they have the power. Next, do they exercise it? They do. But then, *how* do they exercise it so as to affect man's sense for conduct, his sense for beauty? And this is perhaps a case for applying the Preacher's *200* words: "Though a man labour to seek it out, yet he shall not find it; yea, farther, though a wise man think to know it, yet shall he not be able to find it." Why should it be one thing, in its effect upon the emotions, to say, "Patience is a virtue," and quite another thing, in its effect upon the emotions, to say with Homer,

τλητὸν γὰρ Μοῖραι θυμὸν θέσαν ἀνθρώποισιν — *205*

"for an enduring heart have the destinies appointed to the children of men"? Why should it be one thing, in its effect upon the emotions, to say with the philosopher Spinoza, *Felicitas in eo consistit quod homo suum esse conservare potest* — "Man's happiness consists in his being able to preserve his own essence," and quite another thing, in its effect upon the emotions, to say with the Gospel, "What is a man advantaged, if he gain *210* the whole world, and lose himself, forfeit himself?" How does this difference of effect arise? I cannot tell, and I am not much concerned to know; the important thing is that it does arise, and that we can profit by it. But how, finally, are poetry and eloquence to exercise the power of relating the modern results of natural science to man's instinct for

---

201-02: Ecclesiastes 8:17 (Arnold's note). **205.** *Iliad,* XXIV, 49 (Arnold's note). **207-09:** *The Ethics,* IV, 18, by Baruch (Benedict) Spinoza (1632-1677), Dutch philosopher. **210-211:** Cf. Luke 9:25, Matthew 16:26.

conduct, his instinct for beauty? And here again I answer that I do not know *how* they 215
will exercise it, but that they can and will exercise it I am sure. I do not mean that modern
philosophical poets and modern philosophical moralists are to come and relate for us, in
express terms, the results of modern scientific research to our instinct for conduct, our
instinct for beauty. But I mean that we shall find, as a matter of experience, if we know
the best that has been thought and uttered in the world, we shall find that the art and 220
poetry and eloquence of men who lived, perhaps, long ago, who had the most limited
natural knowledge, who had the most erroneous conceptions about many important
matters, we shall find that this art, and poetry, and eloquence, have in fact not only the
power of refreshing and delighting us, they have also the power, — such is the strength
and worth, in essentials, of their authors' criticism of life, — they have a fortifying, and 225
elevating, and quickening, and suggestive power, capable of wonderfully helping us to
relate the results of modern science to our need for conduct, our need for beauty.
Homer's conceptions of the physical universe were, I imagine, grotesque; but really,
under the shock of hearing from modern science that "the world is not subordinated to
man's use, and that man is not the cynosure of things terrestrial," I could, for my own 230
part, desire no better comfort than Homer's line which I quoted just now,

τλητὸν γὰρ Μοῖραι θυμὸν θέσαν ἀνθρώποισιν —

"for an enduring heart have the destinies appointed to the children of men"!

And the more that men's minds are cleared, the more that the results of science are
frankly accepted, the more that poetry and eloquence come to be received and studied as 235
what in truth they really are, — the criticism of life by gifted men, alive and active with
extraordinary power at an unusual number of points; — so much the more will the value
of humane letters, and of art also, which is an utterance having a like kind of power with
theirs, be felt and acknowledged, and their place in education be secured.

Let us therefore, all of us, avoid indeed as much as possible any invidious comparison 240
between the merits of humane letters, as means of education, and the merits of the natural
sciences. But when some President of a Section for Mechanical Science insists on making
the comparison, and tells us that "he who in his training has substituted literature and
history for natural science has chosen the less useful alternative," let us make answer to
him that the student of humane letters only, will, at least, know also the great general 245
conceptions brought in by modern physical science; for science, as Professor Huxley says,
forces them upon us all. But the student of the natural sciences only, will, by our very
hypothesis, know nothing of humane letters; not to mention that in setting himself to be
perpetually accumulating natural knowledge, he sets himself to do what only specialists
have in general the gift for doing genially. And so he will probably be unsatisfied, or at 250
any rate incomplete, and even more incomplete than the student of humane letters only.

I once mentioned in a school-report, how a young man in one of our English
training colleges having to paraphrase the passage in *Macbeth* beginning,

Can'st thou not minister to a mind diseased?

turned this line into, "Can you not wait upon the lunatic?" And I remarked what a 255
curious state of things it would be, if every pupil of our national schools knew, let us

---

say, that the moon is two thousand one hundred and sixty miles in diameter, and thought at the same time that a good paraphrase for

Can'st thou not minister to a mind diseased?

was, "Can you not wait upon the lunatic?" If one is driven to choose, I think I would 260 rather have a young person ignorant about the moon's diameter, but aware that "Can you not wait upon the lunatic?" is bad, than a young person whose education had been such as to manage things the other way.

Or to go higher than the pupils of our national schools. I have in my mind's eye a member of our British Parliament who comes to travel here in America, who afterwards 265 relates his travels, and who shows a really masterly knowledge of the geology of this great country and of its mining capabilities, but who ends by gravely suggesting that the United States should borrow a prince from our Royal Family, and should make him their king, and should create a House of Lords of great landed proprietors after the pattern of ours; and then America, he thinks, would have her future happily and perfectly secured. Surely, in 270 this case, the President of the Section for Mechanical Science would himself hardly say that our member of Parliament, by concentrating himself upon geology and mineralogy, and so on, and not attending to literature and history, had "chosen the more useful alternative."

If then there is to be separation and option between humane letters on the one hand, and the natural sciences on the other, the great majority of mankind, all who have not 275 exceptional and overpowering aptitudes for the study of nature, would do well, I cannot but think, to choose to be educated in humane letters rather than in the natural sciences. Letters will call out their being at more points, will make them live more.

I said that before I ended I would just touch on the question of classical education, and I will keep my word. Even if literature is to retain a large place in our education, yet Latin 280 and Greek, say the friends of progress, will certainly have to go. Greek is the grand offender in the eyes of these gentlemen. The attackers of the established course of study think that against Greek, at any rate, they have irresistible arguments. Literature may perhaps be needed in education, they say; but why on earth should it be Greek literature? Why not French or German? Nay, "has not an Englishman models in his own literature of 285 every kind of excellence?" As before, it is not on any weak pleadings of my own that I rely for convincing the gainsayers; it is on the constitution of human nature itself, and on the instinct of self-preservation in humanity. The instinct for beauty is set in human nature, as surely as the instinct for knowledge is set there, or the instinct for conduct. If the instinct for beauty is served by Greek literature and art as it is served by no other literature and art, we 290 may trust to the instinct of self-preservation in humanity for keeping Greek as part of our culture. We may trust to it for even making the study of Greek more prevalent than it is now. Greek will come, I hope, some day to be studied more rationally than at present; but it will be increasingly studied as men increasingly feel the need in them for beauty, and how powerfully Greek art and Greek literature can serve this need. Women will again study 295 Greek, as Lady Jane Grey did; I believe that in that chain of forts, with which the fair host of the Amazons are now engirdling our English universities, I find that here in America, in

---

296: Lady Jane Grey (1537-1554), queen of England for nine days in 1553, was noted for her youthful mastery of Greek, Latin, French, and Italian, among other subjects; **forts:** i.e., women's colleges — Somerville (1879) and Lady Margaret Hall (1879) at Oxford, Girton (1873) and Newnham (1875) at Cambridge; the universities, however, did not recognize these colleges or grant degrees to women until much later.

colleges like Smith College in Massachusetts, and Vassar College in the State of New York, and in the happy families of the mixed universities out West, they are studying it already.

Defuit una mihi symmetria prisca, — "The antique symmetry was the one thing [300] wanting to me," said Leonardo da Vinci; and he was an Italian. I will not presume to speak for the Americans, but I am sure that, in the Englishman, the want of this admirable symmetry of the Greeks is a thousand times more great and crying than in any Italian. The results of the want show themselves most glaringly, perhaps, in our architecture, but they show themselves, also, in all our art. *Fit details strictly combined,* [305] *in view of a large general result nobly conceived*; that is just the beautiful *symmetria prisca* of the Greeks, and it is just where we English fail, where all our art fails. Striking ideas we have, and well-executed details we have; but that high symmetry which, with satisfying and delightful effect, combines them, we seldom or never have. The glorious beauty of the Acropolis at Athens did not come from single fine things stuck about on [310] that hill, a statue here, a gateway there; — no, it arose from all things being perfectly combined for a supreme total effect. What must not an Englishman feel about our deficiencies in this respect, as the sense for beauty, whereof this symmetry is an essential element, awakens and strengthens within him! what will not one day be his respect and desire for Greece and its *symmetria prisca,* when the scales drop from his [315] eyes as he walks the London streets, and he sees such a lesson in meanness as the Strand, for instance, in its true deformity! But here we are coming to our friend Mr. Ruskin's province, and I will not intrude upon it, for he is its very sufficient guardian.

And so we at last find, it seems, we find flowing in favour of the humanities the natural and necessary stream of things, which seemed against them when we started. The [320] "hairy quadruped furnished with a tail and pointed ears, probably arboreal in his habits," this good fellow carried hidden in his nature, apparently, something destined to develop into a necessity for humane letters. Nay, more; we seem finally to be even led to the further conclusion that our hairy ancestor carried in his nature, also, a necessity for Greek.

And therefore, to say the truth, I cannot really think that humane letters are in much [325] actual danger of being thrust out from their leading place in education, in spite of the array of authorities against them at this moment. So long as human nature is what it is, their attractions will remain irresistible. As with Greek, so with letters generally: they will some day come, we may hope, to be studied more rationally, but they will not lose their place. What will happen will rather be that there will be crowded into education [330] other matters besides, far too many; there will be, perhaps, a period of unsettlement and confusion and false tendency; but letters will not in the end lose their leading place. If they lose it for a time, they will get it back again. We shall be brought back to them by our wants and aspirations. And a poor humanist may possess his soul in patience, neither strive nor cry, admit the energy and brilliancy of the partisans of physical [335] science, and their present favour with the public, to be far greater than his own, and still have a happy faith that the nature of things works silently on behalf of the studies which he loves, and that, while we shall all have to acquaint ourselves with the great results

---

299. mixed universities out West: The first such co-ed college, founded in 1833, was Oberlin, in Ohio. **301. Leonardo da Vinci:** (1452-1519) Florentine artist, musician, architect, engineer, and scientist; painter of *The Last Supper* and the *Mona Lisa*; his *Notebooks,* which he kept in his later years, record many of his ideas, in both words and pictures. **315. scales:** i.e., scabs, thin coverings, impediments to clear vision; see Acts 9:18. **316-17: the Strand:** major street in London, parallel to the Thames, near the Embankment and Waterloo Bridge. **317-18. Ruskin:** e.g. in *The Seven Lamps of Architecture* (1849) and *The Stones of Venice* (1851-53).

reached by modern science, and to give ourselves as much training in its disciplines as
we can conveniently carry, yet the majority of men will always require humane letters;   *340*
and so much the more, as they have the more and the greater results of science to relate
to the need in man for conduct, and to the need in him for beauty.

(1885)

WILLIAM (JOHNSON) CORY
England, 1823-1892

HERACLITUS

They told me, Heraclitus, they told me you were dead,
They brought me bitter news to hear and bitter tears to shed.
I wept, as I remembered, how often you and I
Had tired the sun with talking and sent him down the sky.

And now that thou art lying, my dear old Carian guest,   *5*
A handful of grey ashes, long long ago at rest,
Still are thy pleasant voices, thy nightingales, awake;
For Death, he taketh all away, but them he cannot take.

(1858)

FRANCIS PARKMAN
U.S.A., 1823-1893

from *THE JESUITS IN NORTH AMERICA IN THE SEVENTEENTH CENTURY*

Chapter 28: The Martyrs, 1649

On the morning of the twentieth, the Jesuits at Sainte Marie received full confirmation
of the reported retreat of the invaders; and one of them, with seven armed Frenchmen,
set out for the scene of havoc. They passed St. Louis, where the bloody ground was
strewn thick with corpses, and, two or three miles farther on, reached St. Ignace. Here
they saw a spectacle of horror; for among the ashes of the burnt town were scattered in   *5*

HERACLITUS   A translation of a poem written by the Alexandrian poet Callimachus (c.305-c.240 B.C.) on hearing of the death of his friend and
fellow-poet Heraclitus, of Halicarnassus, the capital of ancient Caria, in southwestern Asia Minor.   THE JESUITS IN NORTH
AMERICA   1. Jesuits: The Roman Catholic Jesuit Order, or Society of Jesus, was established by St. Ignatius Loyola in 1540, and almost
immediately began sending missionaries to North America, where they were known as "Black Robes." The Jesuit *Relations*, a series of reports sent
annually from the missions back to France, constitute the main source for Parkman's history, especially the descriptions of torture that were written
by Fr. Paul Ragueneau (1608-1680); **Sainte Marie:** the mission called Sainte-Marie-among-the-Hurons, on Georgian Bay, established in 1610 by
the Récollet order, and developed by the Jesuits in 1634; Iroquois attacks on the Huron missions began in 1648. **3-4. St. Louis, St. Ignace:** missions
in what is now southern Ontario.

profusion the half-consumed bodies of those who had perished in the flames. Apart from the rest, they saw a sight that banished all else from their thoughts; for they found what they had come to seek, — the scorched and mangled relics of Brébeuf and Lalemant.

They had learned their fate already from Huron prisoners, many of whom had   *10*
made their escape in the panic and confusion of the Iroquois retreat. They described what they had seen, and the condition in which the bodies were found confirmed their story.

On the afternoon of the sixteenth — the day when the two priests were captured — Brébeuf was led apart, and bound to a stake. He seemed more concerned for his   *15*
captive converts than for himself, and addressed them in a loud voice, exhorting them to suffer patiently, and promising heaven as their reward. The Iroquois, incensed, scorched him from head to foot, to silence him; whereupon, in the tone of a master, he threatened them with everlasting flames for persecuting the worshippers of God. As he continued to speak, with voice and countenance unchanged, they cut   *20*
away his lower lip and thrust a red-hot iron down his throat. He still held his tall form erect and defiant, with no sign or sound of pain; and they tried another means to overcome him. They led out Lalemant, that Brébeuf might see him tortured. They had tied strips of bark, smeared with pitch, about his naked body. When he saw the condition of his Superior, he could not hide his agitation, and called out to him, with   *25*
a broken voice, in the words of Saint Paul, "We are made a spectacle to the world, to angels, and to men." Then he threw himself at Brébeuf's feet; upon which the Iroquois seized him, made him fast to a stake, and set fire to the bark that enveloped him. As the flame rose, he threw his arms upward, with a shriek of supplication to Heaven. Next they hung around Brébeuf's neck a collar made of hatchets heated red-   *30*
hot; but the indomitable priest stood like a rock. A Huron in the crowd, who had been a convert of the mission, but was now an Iroquois by adoption, called out, with the malice of a renegade, to pour hot water on their heads, since they had poured so much cold water on those of others. The kettle was accordingly slung, and the water boiled and poured slowly on the heads of the two missionaries. "We baptize you,"   *35*
they cried, "that you may be happy in heaven; for nobody can be saved without a good baptism." Brébeuf would not flinch; and, in a rage, they cut strips of flesh from

---

8. relics: remains, corpses. **8-9. Brébeuf, Lalemant:** Fr. Jean de Brébeuf (1593-1649) and Fr. Gabriel Lalemant (1610-1649), Jesuit missionaries; Parkman's note reads in part: "Lalemant was a Parisian, and his family belonged to the class of *gens de robe,* or hereditary practitioners of the law. . . . His physical weakness is spoken of by several of those who knew him. . . . In Ragueneau's notice of Brébeuf, as in all other notices of deceased missionaries in the *Relations,* the saintly qualities alone are brought forward, — as obedience, humility, etc.; but wherever Brébeuf himself appears in the course of those voluminous records, he always brings with him an impression of power. We are told that, punning on his own name, he used to say that he was an ox, fit only to bear burdens. This sort of humility may pass for what it is worth; but it must be remembered that there is a kind of acting in which the actor firmly believes in the part he is playing. As for the obedience, it was as genuine as that of a well-disciplined soldier, and incomparably more profound. In the case of the Canadian Jesuits, posterity owes to this, their favorite virtue, the record of numerous visions, inward voices, and the like miracles, which the object of these favors set down on paper, at the command of his Superior; while, otherwise, humility would have concealed them forever. The truth is, that, with some of these missionaries, one may throw off trash and nonsense by the cartload, and find under it all a solid nucleus of saint and hero." **26-27:** See 1 Corinthians 4:9.

his limbs, and devoured them before his eyes. Other renegade Hurons called out to him, "You told us that the more one suffers on earth, the happier he is in heaven. We wish to make you happy; we torment you because we love you; and you ought to thank us for it." After a succession of other revolting tortures, they scalped him; when, seeing him nearly dead, they laid open his breast, and came in a crowd to drink the blood of so valiant an enemy, thinking to imbibe with it some portion of his courage. A chief then tore out his heart, and devoured it.

Thus died Jean de Brébeuf, the founder of the Huron mission, its truest hero, and its greatest martyr. He came of a noble race — the same, it is said, from which sprang the English Earls of Arundel; but never had the mailed barons of his line confronted a fate so appalling, with so prodigious a constancy. To the last he refused to flinch, and "his death was the astonishment of his murderers." In him an enthusiastic devotion was grafted on an heroic nature. His bodily endowments were as remarkable as the temper of his mind. His manly proportions, his strength, and his endurance, which incessant fasts and penances could not undermine, had always won for him the respect of the Indians, no less than a courage unconscious of fear, and yet redeemed from rashness by a cool and vigorous judgment; for, extravagant as were the chimeras which fed the fires of his zeal, they were consistent with the soberest good sense on matters of practical bearing.

Lalemant, physically weak from childhood, and slender almost to emaciation, was constitutionally unequal to a display of fortitude like that of his colleague. When Brébeuf died, he was led back to the house whence he had been taken, and tortured there all night, until, in the morning, one of the Iroquois, growing tired of the protracted entertainment, killed him with a hatchet. It was said that at times he seemed beside himself; then, rallying, with hands uplifted, he offered his sufferings to Heaven as a sacrifice. His robust companion had lived less than four hours under the torture, while he survived it for nearly seventeen. Perhaps the Titanic effort of will with which Brébeuf repressed all show of suffering conspired with the Iroquois knives and firebrands to exhaust his vitality; perhaps his tormentors, enraged at his fortitude, forgot their subtlety, and struck too near the life.

The bodies of the two missionaries were carried to Sainte Marie, and buried in the cemetery there; but the skull of Brébeuf was preserved as a relic. His family sent from France a silver bust of their martyred kinsman, in the base of which was a recess to contain the skull; and, to this day, the bust and the relic within are preserved with pious care by the nuns of the Hôtel-Dieu at Quebec.

(1867)

---

47. Earls of Arundel: a powerful family during the Renaissance, including such figures as Henry Fitzalan Arundel (c.1510-1580), who helped bring Mary I to the throne, and Thomas Howard Arundel (1585-1646), a privy councillor famous for his art collection, especially the Roman statuary known as the Arundel Marbles, later given to Oxford University. **49. "his death . . . murderers":** Parkman is quoting (vol. I, p. 294) from another Jesuit priest, Pierre François Xavier de Charlevoix (1682-1761), whose *Histoire de la nouvelle France* (1744) appeared in a six-volume English translation between 1865 and 1872. **69. relic:** sacred memento.

COVENTRY PATMORE
England, 1823-1896

MAGNA EST VERITAS

Here, in this little Bay,
Full of tumultuous life and great repose,
Where, twice a day,
The purposeless, glad ocean comes and goes,
Under high cliffs, and far from the huge town,   5

I sit me down.
For want of me the world's course will not fail:
When all its work is done, the lie shall rot;
The truth is great, and shall prevail,
When none cares whether it prevail or not.   10

(1877, 1878)

CATHERINE HELEN SPENCE
England/Australia, 1825-1910

MARRIAGE RIGHTS AND WRONGS

In taking up an old-fashioned novel — one of Richardson's, for example — and reading it in the light of modern ideas, nothing strikes the reader more forcibly than its exaggerated view of marital and parental rights as over and against the rights of wives and children, and the very low idea which even good people then entertained of the responsibilities of the stronger and the rights of the weaker to justice and consideration. Modern opinions   5 reverse the view, and the wider the knowledge and the greater the power the more they are held to be a trust for the benefit and protection of the ignorant and the feeble. But although this is the prevailing tone of the best literature and of the most cultivated society, such a view takes a long time to reach that stratum of society where it is most needed. It takes a long time even to give force to law, which is one of the most efficacious means of   10 educating public opinion; and the Statute-book and the police courts still show that offences by the weaker against the stronger are considered aggravated, while those by the stronger against the weaker are taken with extenuating circumstances.

Public opinion in England as expressed in the law and enforced by the law is yet considerably behind the educated intelligence of the age with regard to marriage rights and   15 marriage wrongs. Any offence or crime committed by a wife against her husband is still looked on as a sort of petty treason, and so late as 1760 the murder of a husband by his wife was punished by the severe sentence of burning, while any offence or violence committed by the husband against a wife is reckoned as so much less heinous than any similar crime against any other person, because she is regarded as somehow his property. A wife is liable   20 to the heaviest punishment for transgressions which on the husband's part would be expiated by a fine. There can be no question that adultery is a greater offence in a wife than

---

MAGNA EST VERITAS Title: (Latin) The truth is great (see line 9).   **MARRIAGE RIGHTS AND WRONGS** **1. Richardson:** Samuel Richardson (1689-1761), English author; his novels are *Pamela* (1740-41), *Clarissa* (1747-48), and *Sir Charles Grandison* (1753-54).

in a husband, but taking the cases otherwise on their own merits it will be found that owing to the difference in physical strength between the sexes the woman who injures her husband does it by deceit and guile. If she takes life, it is by poison; if she is unfaithful, she tries to keep it secret. Her only open weapon is her tongue, and though it is provoking enough it makes no visible wound; whereas in the incomparably more numerous cases among the poorer classes of injury by men towards their wives the strong hand and violent blow and loud curse have a remarkable frankness about them. There is comparatively little secret made of the existence of the rival on whom the family earnings are squandered; there is little delicacy or subterfuge as to language, or gesture, or blow, or kick. Work may be done or let alone; the wages may be spent in every form of vicious indulgence; the earnings of wife or children may be all at the command of the head of the household; but there is little sense of shame on his part for doing what he likes with his own, and he has a consciousness that if his wife cannot stand this, and brings him up before the police court, the punishment awarded will cost her as dear as himself, and that he can pay her out when he returns to the bosom of his family with all his marital and parental rights in full force.

Again and again has flogging been recommended for brutal assaults on women and children as being summary, cheap, and essentially retributive, and as injuring as little as possible the family of the culprit; but although the evidence of judges, magistrates, and recorders has been overwhelming as to its being advisable nothing has been done. According to Miss Cobbe, in the *Contemporary Review* for April, six thousand women in Great Britain have during the short time of three years been brutally assaulted — that is maimed, blinded, burned, trampled on, and in many cases murdered outright — without any fresh legislation to enforce the remedy recommended. In a government which moves forward, if it moves at all, from parliamentary pressure, this question appears not to obtain sufficient backing, even from an assembly of educated gentlemen probably more chivalrous at heart than any other constituent body in the world. There can be little doubt that the swift, sharp, humbling punishment of flogging would have great influence on the effective public opinion which surrounds the culprits in the Black Country and in those large manufacturing towns in Great Britain where ignorance, good but variable wages, poor houses, and bad air lead to drink, vice, and brutality. But there is another point of view to which attention may fairly be directed. Will the flogged husband return to his home and his duties in a better frame of mind than the fined and imprisoned one? And will wives not dread the immediate return even more than the delayed one to such an extent as to prevent them even more than at present from bringing the offenders to justice? This is one of the greatest difficulties in dealing with this class of crimes, for often lingering affection, and still oftener fear, makes the wife weaken her case, and keep back the worst wrongs she has endured. Such cruelty as is often brought before the police courts would in a higher rank of life be considered sufficient ground for judicial separation, and often for absolute divorce; but there is at present no adequate means within the reach of a woman of protecting her person or even her earnings against her husband's claims. If affection still lingers — if for the sake of the children she wishes to give him another chance — she will probably not apply for such separation; but if it is only fear, such a Bill as has been drawn

---

42. Miss Cobbe: Frances Power Cobbe (1822-1904), English essayist and supporter of women's rights. **50. Black Country:** heavily industrialized district in central England, mostly in southern Staffordshire.

out by Mr Alfred D. Hill, of Birmingham, would meet the case. This would allow the *65*
same court which sentences the husband to give the injured wife a protection-order for her
earnings and the custody of her children, and also enforce an order for the husband to pay
his wife such weekly sums for her own and her children's maintenance as the court sees
fit. Magistrates are already empowered to give the wife protection for her earnings in the
case of desertion, which is a minor offence. In many of the cases of wife-beating there is *70*
adultery as well as cruelty on the part of the husband, which should give the wife a claim
for an absolute divorce. Cruelty, even of the most aggravated kind, without proved
adultery is not at present held to authorize divorce, but it is well worthy of consideration
whether in the interest of public morals where the offence has been great and deep, not
repented of on one side, or condoned on the other, the release from marriage bonds should *75*
not be made complete after the lapse of a reasonable time from the judicial separation, the
sum which the first husband is bound to pay being diminished if the wife makes a new
marriage. The difficulty in enforcing the payment of a weekly amount is felt in England,
and an order would be still more easily evaded here. Wife-desertion is a question which
affects all the colonies, each one complaining that wives and families are deserted by their *80*
natural head and are made burdensome to the state. An intercolonial union might give
increased energy to the search for the defaulters. Miss Cobbe mentions that the Recorder
of Hereford last January sentenced a man to be whipped who had left his wife and family
four times and thrown them on the Union.

It is being forcibly urged by some advanced thinkers that there are two grounds for *85*
absolute divorce which are not at present recognized at all. The first is sentence to penal
servitude for a long term of years. Affection may and very often indeed does survive,
especially in the case of wives towards husbands, for whose temptations the most liberal
allowances are made, and whose repentance is believed in. Women having a strong
affection for their husbands will wait any number of years, and will be ready to take them *90*
by the hand to help them by every means in their power up the steep path which may win
back a good name. But when love is dead, when the wife or husband knows better than
judge or jury the depths of wickedness into which their partner has sunk, when there is no
feeling of hope or trust to bridge over the long years of separation, why, it is argued,
enforce the tie for life on the innocent party because vows have been made which the *95*
guilty one has made it impossible to fulfil? The second case of omission is when one party
is under restraint as a lunatic with no chance of recovery. This affords perhaps stronger
ground for dissolving the marriage bond and for allowing a second legal marriage. Every
physician in charge of a lunatic asylum will tell of patients who have been admitted there
in the prime of life, and have dragged on for ten, twenty, and thirty years, leaving their *100*
partners virtually widowed but unable to make another marriage. Such a physician will
speak of many a working-man earning in the colonies from thirty to forty shillings a week
with his wife in the asylum from puerperal mania, and left with two or three or more
young children, obliged to go to his daily task at six in the morning and remain at it until
the evening. So long as there is a chance of recovery the husband and children make a *105*
shift somehow; but as months and years roll on, and no favourable symptom presents
itself, the comfortless home and the expense, and perhaps the scandal arising from

---

82. Recorder: magistrate. **84. thrown them on the Union:** i.e., made them State welfare cases.

employing any woman as servant, lead in many instances to the establishment of an immoral bond between him and some female disposed to act as the head of his household. The man is at the disadvantage that no respectable woman can take the position, but 110 anything he feels is better than the anarchy which prevailed before.

In spite of the man being the breadwinner of a household, it is often harder for a widower to do well for a family than for a widow. His work takes him much away, and he cannot hire efficient female help at home. A widow, too, is more pitied and helped both by public and private charity than a widower. But the condition of either a poor 115 woman or one who is widowed is far better than that of one with a partner hopelessly insane. The bulk of recoveries take place within six months, and if there is no sign of improvement in eighteen months or two years the chance of restoration to reason is infinitesimally small. It may be insisted that people who vow to cleave to each other in sickness and in health cannot be absolved from that vow by any force of malady, but it 120 must be remembered that permanent mental disease necessitating restraint renders cohabitation altogether out of the question. Therefore after the lapse of a reasonable time, and subject to the carefully considered judgment of an expert in mental disease that recovery is practically impossible, is it not fair to provide that the marriage bond shall be legally dissolved? If, contrary to all expectations, the patient should recover, 125 and find that his or her rights have been superseded, he or she will have suffered a grievous misfortune, which may cloud even the great joy of restoration to the duties and pleasures of life; but against this it must be borne in mind that under the present state of things the many husbands and wives who are condemned to widowhood or to an illegal and immoral substitute for marriage are all suffering misfortunes which are not slight. 130 Marriage is a divine institution, because it is so well adapted to human necessities, because its permanency promotes repose and hope and trust, and because it builds up the family in the purest, the most loving, and the most secure manner; but in those exceptional cases where its permanency leads to violence and tyranny, and where it utterly fails to build up the family in love and trust, there is surely ground for the view 135 that the rigid lines must be overstepped and some reasonable qualifications be allowed in the interests of true morality and social order.

(1878)

DANTE GABRIEL ROSSETTI
England, 1828-1882

A MATCH WITH THE MOON

Weary already, weary miles to-night
  I walked for bed: and so, to get some ease,
  I dogged the flying moon with similes.
And like a wisp she doubled on my sight
In ponds; and caught in tree-tops like a kite; 5
  And in a globe of film all liquorish
  Swam full-faced like a silly silver fish; —
Last like a bubble shot the welkin's height

A MATCH WITH THE MOON   **8. welkin:** sky.

Where my road turned, and got behind me,
   and sent
  My wizened shadow craning round at me,   *10*
  And jeered, "So, step the measure, —
    one two three!"
And if I faced on her, looked innocent.
But just at parting, halfway down a dell,
She kissed me for good-night. So you'll not tell.
             (1854; 1870)

THE BALLAD OF DEAD LADIES

Tell me now in what hidden way is
  Lady Flora the lovely Roman?
Where's Hipparchia, and where is Thaïs,
  Neither of them the fairer woman?
  Where is Echo, beheld of no man,   *5*
Only heard on river and mere, —
  She whose beauty was more than human? . . .
But where are the snows of yester-year?

Where's Héloise, the learned nun,
  For whose sake Abeillard, I ween,   *10*
Lost manhood and put priesthood on?
  (From Love he won such dule and teen!)
  And where, I pray you, is the Queen
Who willed that Buridan should steer
  Sewed in a sack's mouth down the Seine? . . .*15*
But where are the snows of yester-year?

White Queen Blanche, like a queen of lilies,
  With a voice like any mermaiden, —
Bertha Broadfoot, Beatrice, Alice,
  And Ermengarde the lady of Maine, —   *20*

And that good Joan whom Englishmen
At Rouen doomed and burned her there, —
  Mother of God, where are they then? . . .
But where are the snows of yester-year?

Nay, never ask this week, fair lord,   *25*
  Where they are gone, nor yet this year,
Save with this much for an overword, —
  But where are the snows of yester-year?
             (1869)

from THE HOUSE OF LIFE: A SONNET SEQUENCE

Introductory Sonnet

A Sonnet is a moment's monument, —
Memorial from the Soul's eternity
To one dead, deathless hour. Look that it be,
Whether for lustral rite or dire portent,
Of its own arduous fulness reverent: *5*
Carve it in ivory or in ebony,
As Day or Night may rule; and let Time see
Its flowering crest impearl'd and orient.
A Sonnet is a coin: its face reveals
The soul, — its converse, to what power 't is due: —
Whether for tribute to the august appeals   *11*
Of Life, or dower in Love's high retinue,
It serve; or, 'mid the dark wharf's cavernous breath,
In Charon's palm it pay the toll to Death.
             (1881)

THE BALLAD OF DEAD LADIES   This poem is a free translation of *"Ballade des dames du temps jadis"* (A ballad of ladies of former times) by the French poet François Villon (1431-c.1462). The names alluded to in Rossetti's version serve as examples of beauty, love, and heroism, especially of thwarted love or of passions taken to the extreme. Héloise (beloved of Abelard) and Beatrice (beloved of Dante) are models of passionate commitment. Flora is a courtesan, mentioned in Juvenal's second satire. Echo (the nymph who fell in love with Narcissus), Thaïs (who according to legend urged Alexander to burn Persepolis), Hipparchia (who fell in love with the hunchback Crates and became a cynic), and Joan of Arc (burned at the stake in 1431, the year of Villon's birth), all represent unfulfilled desires. Alice and Ermengarde ("Aliz" and "Haranburgis" in the original) possibly refer to St. Alice (Aleydis or Adelaide, d.1250) and St. Ermengardis (c.1067-c.1147), French Cistercian nuns. Queen Blanche (Charlemagne's falsely accused consort) and Bertha Broadfoot (Charlemagne's mother, known as "Berthe aux grands pieds," who was treacherously ousted from the throne) are victims; while Queen Jeanne de Bourgogne (consort of Philippe V), who according to legend ordered the philosopher Jean Buriden (d. after 1358) to be tied in a sack and drowned in the Seine, victimized others. **12. dule and teen:** grief and trouble.   THE HOUSE OF LIFE   **4. lustral:** pertaining to purification. **14. Charon:** in Greek myth, the ferryman who carries the souls of the dead across the River Styx.

GEORGE MEREDITH
England, 1828-1909

from *MODERN LOVE*

XVII

At dinner, she is hostess, I am host.
Went the feast ever cheerfuller? She keeps
The Topic over intellectual deeps
In buoyancy afloat. They see no ghost.
With sparkling surface-eyes we ply the ball: 5
It is in truth a most contagious game:
HIDING THE SKELETON, shall be its name.
Such play as this, the devils might appal!
But here's the greater wonder; in that we
Enamoured of an acting nought can tire,   10
Each other, like true hypocrites, admire;
Warm-lighted looks, Love's ephemerioe,
Shoot gaily o'er the dishes and the wine.
We waken envy of our happy lot.
Fast, sweet, and golden, shows the marriage-knot.   15
Dear guests, you now have seen Love's corpse-light shine.

XXV

You like not that French novel? Tell me why.
You think it quite unnatural. Let us see.
The actors are, it seems, the usual three:
Husband, and wife, and lover. She — but fie!
In England we'll not hear of it. Edmond,   5
The lover, her devout chagrin doth share;
Blanc-mange and absinthe are his penitent fare,
Till his pale aspect makes her over-fond:
So, to preclude fresh sin, he tries rosbif.
Meantime the husband is no more abused: 10
Auguste forgives her ere the tear is used.
Then hangeth all on one tremendous IF: —
If she will choose between them. She does choose;
And takes her husband, like a proper wife.
Unnatural? My dear, these things are life: 15
And life, some think, is worthy of the Muse.

XXXIV

Madam would speak with me. So, now it comes:
The Deluge or else Fire! She's well; she thanks
My husbandship. Our chain on silence clanks.
Time leers between, above his twiddling thumbs.
Am I quite well? Most excellent in health!   5
The journals, too, I diligently peruse.
Vesuvius is expected to give news:
Niagara is no noisier. By stealth
Our eyes dart scrutinizing snakes. She's glad
I'm happy, says her quivering under-lip.   10
"And are not you?" "How can I be?" "Take ship!
For happiness is somewhere to be had."
"Nowhere for me!" Her voice is barely heard.
I am not melted, and make no pretence.
With commonplace I freeze her, tongue and sense.   15
Niagara or Vesuvius is deferred.

XLIII

Mark where the pressing wind shoots javelinlike
Its skeleton shadow on broad-backed wave!
Here is a fitting spot to dig Love's grave;
Here where the ponderous breakers plunge and strike,
And dart their hissing tongues high up the sand: 5
In hearing of the ocean, and in sight
Of those ribbed wind-streaks running into white.
If I the death of Love had deeply planned,
I never could have made it half so sure,
As by the unblessed kisses which upbraid   10
The full-waked sense: or failing that, degrade!
'Tis morning: but no morning can restore
What we have forfeited. I see no sin:
The wrong is mixed. In tragic life, God wot,
No villain need be! Passions spin the plot: 15
We are betrayed by what is false within.

(1862)

LUCIFER IN STARLIGHT

On a starred night Prince Lucifer uprose.
Tired of his dark dominion swung the fiend
Above the rolling ball in cloud part screened,
Where sinners hugged their spectre of repose.
Poor prey to his hot fit of pride were those.   5

MODERN LOVE   XVII   **12. ephemerioe:** short-lived insects. **16. corpse-light:** a candle used at wakes, or a flame seen in a churchyard (i.e., an *ignis fatuus*), taken as a portent of a funeral.

And now upon his western wing he leaned,
Now his huge bulk o'er Afric's sands careened,
Now the black planet shadowed Arctic snows.
Soaring through wider zones that pricked his scars
With memory of the old revolt from Awe,   *10*

He reached a middle height, and at the stars,
Which are the brain of heaven, he looked, and sank.
Around the ancient track marched, rank on rank,
The army of unalterable law.

(1883)

EMILY DICKINSON
U.S.A., 1830-1886

214

I taste a liquor never brewed —
From Tankards scooped in Pearl —
Not all the Vats upon the Rhine
Yield such an Alcohol!

Inebriate of Air — am I —   *5*
And Debauchee of Dew —
Reeling — thro endless summer days —
From inns of Molten Blue —

When "Landlords" turn the drunken Bee
Out of the Foxglove's door —   *10*
When Butterflies — renounce their "drams" —
I shall but drink the more!

Till Seraphs swing their snowy Hats —
And Saints — to windows run —
To see the little Tippler   *15*
Leaning against the — Sun —

(c.1860; 1861)

258

There's a certain Slant of light,
Winter Afternoons —
That oppresses, like the Heft
Of Cathedral Tunes —

Heavenly Hurt, it gives us —   *5*
We can find no scar,
But internal difference,
Where the Meanings, are —

None may teach it — Any —
'Tis the Seal Despair —   *10*
An imperial affliction
Sent us of the Air —

When it comes, the Landscape listens —
Shadows — hold their breath —
When it goes, 'tis like the Distance   *15*
On the look of Death —

(c.1861; 1890)

280

I felt a Funeral, in my Brain,
And Mourners to and fro
Kept treading — treading — till it seemed
That Sense was breaking through —

And when they all were seated,   *5*
A Service, like a Drum —
Kept beating — beating — till I thought
My Mind was going numb —

And then I heard them lift a Box
And creak across my Soul   *10*
With those same Boots of Lead, again,
Then Space — began to toll,

As all the Heavens were a Bell,
And Being, but an Ear,
And I, and Silence, some strange Race   *15*
Wrecked, solitary, here —

DICKINSON   Many of Emily Dickinson's lyrics (almost 1800 in all) were left in manuscript and published posthumously between 1890 and 1896. In 1955, *The Poems of Emily Dickinson*, ed. Thomas H. Johnson, established the probable order of composition and assigned a sequence number to each poem; these are the numbers that (as here) are now conventionally used to identify Dickinson's works.

And then a Plank in Reason, broke,
And I dropped down, and down —
And hit a World, at every plunge,
And Finished knowing — then —   20
(c.1861; 1896)

303

The Soul selects her own Society —
Then — shuts the Door —
To her divine Majority —
Present no more —   4

Unmoved — she notes the Chariots — pausing —
At her low Gate —
Unmoved — an Emperor be kneeling
Upon her Mat —

I've known her — from an ample nation —
Choose One —   10
Then — close the Valves of her attention —
Like Stone —
(c.1862; 1890)

435

Much Madness is divinest Sense —
To a discerning Eye —
Much Sense — the starkest Madness —
'Tis the Majority
In this, as All, prevail —   5
Assent — and you are sane —
Demur — you're straightway dangerous —
And handled with a Chain —
(c.1862; 1890)

465

I heard a Fly buzz — when I died —
The Stillness in the Room
Was like the Stillness in the Air —
Between the Heaves of Storm —

The Eyes around — had wrung them dry —   5
And Breaths were gathering firm
For that last Onset — when the King
Be witnessed — in the Room —

I willed my Keepsakes — Signed away
What portion of me be   10
Assignable — and then it was
There interposed a Fly —

With Blue — uncertain stumbling Buzz —
Between the light — and me —
And then the Windows failed — and then   15
I could not see to see —
(c.1862; 1896)

585

I like to see it lap the Miles —
And lick the Valleys up —
And stop to feed itself at Tanks —
And then — prodigious step

Around a Pile of Mountains —   5
And supercilious peer
In Shanties — by the sides of Roads —
And then a Quarry pare

To fit its Ribs
And crawl between   10
Complaining all the while
In horrid — hooting stanza —
Then chase itself down Hill —

And neigh like Boanerges —
Then — punctual as a Star   15
Stop — docile and omnipotent
At its own stable door —
(c.1862; 1891)

712

Because I could not stop for Death —
He kindly stopped for me —
The Carriage held but just Ourselves —
And Immortality.

We slowly drove — He knew no haste   5
And I had put away
My labor and my leisure too,
For His Civility —

We passed the School, where Children strove
At Recess — in the Ring —   10
We passed the Fields of Gazing Grain —
We passed the Setting Sun —

NO. 585 14. **Boanerges:** James and John, "sons of thunder"; see Mark 3:17 and Luke 9:54; possibly also the name of a well-known horse of the time.

Or rather — He passed Us —
The Dews drew quivering and chill —
For only Gossamer, my Gown —   *15*
My Tippet — only Tulle —

We paused before a House that seemed
A Swelling of the Ground —
The Roof was scarcely visible —
The Cornice — in the Ground —   *20*

Since then — 'tis Centuries — and yet
Feels shorter than the Day
I first surmised the Horses' Heads
Were toward Eternity —
                              (c.1863; 1890)

732

She rose to His Requirement — dropt
The Playthings of Her Life
To take the honorable Work
Of Woman, and of Wife —

If ought She missed in Her new Day,   *5*
Of Amplitude, or Awe —
Or first Prospective — Or the Gold
In using, wear away,

It lay unmentioned — as the Sea
Develop Pearl, and Weed,   *10*
But only to Himself — be known
The Fathoms they abide —
                              (c.1863; 1890)

986

A narrow Fellow in the Grass
Occasionally rides —
You may have met Him — did you not
His notice sudden is —

The Grass divides as with a Comb —   *5*
A spotted shaft is seen —
And then it closes at your feet
And opens further on —

He likes a Boggy Acre
A Floor too cool for Corn —   *10*
Yet when a Boy, and Barefoot —
I more than once at Noon

Have passed, I thought, a Whip lash
Unbraiding in the Sun
When stooping to secure it   *15*
It wrinkled, and was gone —

Several of Nature's People
I know, and they know me —
I feel for them a transport
Of cordiality —   *20*

But never met this Fellow
Attended, or alone
Without a tighter breathing
And Zero at the Bone —
                              (c.1865; 1866)

1129

Tell all the Truth but tell it slant —
Success in Circuit lies
Too bright for our infirm Delight
The Truth's superb surprise

As Lightning to the Children eased   *5*
With explanation kind
The Truth must dazzle gradually
Or every man be blind —
                              (c.1868; 1945)

1463

A Route of Evanescence
With a revolving Wheel —
A Resonance of Emerald —
A Rush of Cochineal —
And every Blossom on the Bush   *5*
Adjusts its tumbled Head —
The mail from Tunis, probably,
An easy Morning's Ride —
                              (c.1879; 1891)

1755

To make a prairie it takes a clover and one bee,
One clover, and a bee,
And revery.
The revery alone will do,
If bees are few.   *5*
                              (1896)

No. 712   **16. tippet:** a long scarf.

CHRISTINA ROSSETTI
England, 1830-1894

SONG

When I am dead, my dearest,
  Sing no sad songs for me;
Plant thou no roses at my head,
  Nor shady cypress tree:
Be the green grass above me   *5*
  With showers and dewdrops wet;
And if thou wilt, remember,
  And if thou wilt, forget.

I shall not see the shadows,
  I shall not feel the rain;   *10*
I shall not hear the nightingale
  Sing on, as if in pain:
And dreaming through the twilight
  That doth not rise nor set,
Haply I may remember,   *15*
  And haply may forget.
                              (1848; 1862)

A BIRTHDAY

My heart is like a singing bird
  Whose nest is in a watered shoot;
My heart is like an apple-tree
  Whose boughs are bent with thickset
  fruit;
My heart is like a rainbow shell   *5*
  That paddles in a halcyon sea;
My heart is gladder than all these
  Because my love is come to me.

Raise me a dais of silk and down;
  Hang it with vair and purple dyes;   *10*
Carve it in doves and pomegranates,

And peacocks with a hundred eyes;
Work it in gold and silver grapes,
  In leaves and silver fleurs-de-lys;
Because the birthday of my life   *15*
  Is come, my love is come to me.
                              (1857)

PROMISES LIKE PIE-CRUST

Promise me no promises,
  So will I not promise you:
Keep we both our liberties,
  Never false and never true:
Let us hold the die uncast,   *5*
  Free to come as free to go:
For I cannot know your past,
  And of mine what can you know?

You, so warm, may once have been
  Warmer towards another one: *10*
I, so cold, may once have seen
  Sunlight, once have felt the sun:
Who shall show us if it was
  Thus indeed in time of old?
Fades the image from the glass,   *15*
  And the fortune is not told.

If you promised, you might grieve
  For lost liberty again:
If I promised, I believe
  I should fret to break the chain.   *20*
Let us be the friends we were,
  Nothing more but nothing less:
Many thrive on frugal fare
  Who would perish of excess.
                              (1861; 1896)

A BIRTHDAY   **10. vair:** ermine.

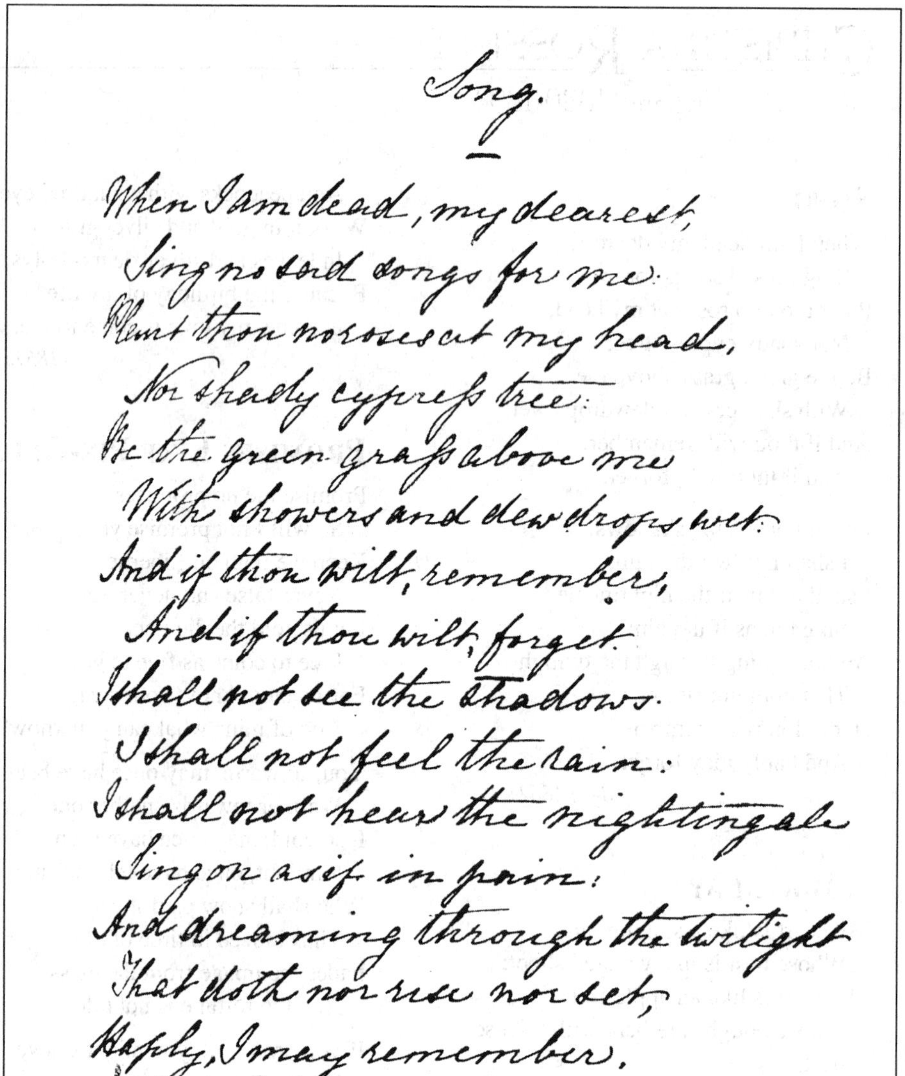

Song.

When I am dead, my dearest,
Sing no sad songs for me:
Plant thou no roses at my head,
Nor shady cypress tree:
Be the green grass above me
With showers and dew-drops wet:
And if thou wilt, remember,
And if thou wilt, forget.

I shall not see the shadows,
I shall not feel the rain:
I shall not hear the nightingale
Sing on as if in pain:
And dreaming through the twilight
That doth not rise nor set,
Haply, I may remember,
And haply, may forget.

— 12th December 1848.

Plate 8. Christina Rossetti's holograph version of
"Song" ("When I am dead, my dearest").

LEWIS CARROLL [CHARLES LUTWIDGE DODGSON]
England, 1832-1898

RULES AND REGULATIONS

A short direction
To avoid dejection,
By variations
In occupations,
And prolongation   5
Of relaxation,
And combinations
Of recreations,
And disputation
On the state of the nation   10
In adaptation
To your station,
By invitations
To friends and relations,
By evitation   15
Of amputation,
By permutation
In conversation,
And deep reflection
You'll avoid dejection.   20

Learn well your grammar,
And never stammer,
Write well and neatly,
And sing most sweetly,
Be enterprising,   25
Love early rising,
Go walk of six miles,
Have ready quick smiles,
With lightsome laughter,
Soft flowing after.   30
Drink tea, not coffee;
Never eat toffy.
Eat bread with butter.
Once more, don't stutter.

Don't waste your money,   35
Abstain from honey.
Shut doors behind you,
(Don't slam them, mind you.)
Drink beer, not porter.
Don't enter the water   40
Till to swim you are able.
Sit close to the table.
Take care of a candle.
Shut a door by the handle,
Don't push with your shoulder
Until you are older.   46
Lose not a button.
Refuse cold mutton.
Starve your canaries.
Believe in fairies.   50
If you are able,
Don't have a stable
With any mangers.
Be rude to strangers.

Moral: Behave.   55

(1845; 1954)

"HOW DOTH THE LITTLE CROCODILE"

How doth the little crocodile
   Improve his shining tail,
And pour the waters of the Nile
   On every golden scale!

How cheerfully he seems to grin,   5
   How neatly spread his claws,
And welcomes little fishes in
   With gently smiling jaws!

(1865)

HOW DOTH THE LITTLE CROCODILE   This and the next poem appear respectively in Chapter II and Chapter V of *Alice in Wonderland* (1865). See also the poem by Watts which this poem parodies (p. 499).

"You are old, Father William"

"You are old, Father William," the young man said
   "And your hair has become very white;
And yet you incessantly stand on your head —
   Do you think, at your age, it is right?"

"In my youth," Father William replied to his son,   *5*
   "I feared it might injure the brain;
But, now that I'm perfectly sure I have none,
   Why, I do it again and again."

"You are old," said the youth, "as I mentioned before,
   And have grown most uncommonly fat;   *10*
Yet you turned a back-somersault in at the door —
   Pray, what is the reason of that?"

"In my youth," said the sage, as he shook his grey locks,
   "I kept all my limbs very supple
By the use of this ointment — one shilling the box —   *15*
   Allow me to sell you a couple?"

"You are old," said the youth, "and your jaws are too weak
   For anything tougher than suet;
Yet you finished the goose, with the bones and the beak —
   Pray, how did you manage to do it?"   *20*

"In my youth," said his father, "I took to the law,
   And argued each case with my wife;
And the muscular strength, which it gave to my jaw
   Has lasted the rest of my life."

"You are old," said the youth, "one would hardly suppose   *25*
   That your eye was as steady as ever;
Yet you balanced an eel on the end of your nose —
   What made you so awfully clever?"

"I have answered three questions, and that is enough,"
   Said his father, "Don't give yourself airs!   *30*
Do you think I can listen all day to such stuff?
   Be off, or I'll kick you down-stairs!"

                           (1865)

You are old, Father William See the poem by Southey which this poem parodies (p. 795).

JABBERWOCKY

'Twas brillig, and the slithy toves
    Did gyre and gimble in the wabe:
All mimsy were the borogoves,
    And the mome raths outgrabe.

"Beware the Jabberwock, my son!   *5*
    The jaws that bite, the claws that catch!
Beware the Jubjub bird, and shun
    The frumious Bandersnatch!"

He took his vorpal sword in hand:
    Long time the manxome foe he sought —
So rested he by the Tumtum tree,   *11*
    And stood awhile in thought.

And, as in uffish thought he stood,
    The Jabberwock, with eyes of flame,

Came whiffling through the tulgey wood,   *15*
    And burbled as it came!

One, two! One, two! And through and through
    The vorpal blade went snicker-snack!
He left it dead, and with its head
    He went galumphing back.   *20*

"And hast thou slain the Jabberwock?
    Come to my arms, my beamish boy!
O frabjous day! Callooh! Callay!"
    He chortled in his joy.

'Twas brillig, and the slithy toves   *25*
    Did gyre and gimble in the wabe:
All mimsy were the borogoves,
    And the mome raths outgrabe.

(1871)

JAMES THOMSON ("B.V.")
England, 1834-1882

"Once in a saintly passion"

Once in a saintly passion
    I cried with desperate grief,
O Lord, my heart is black with guile,
    Of sinners I am chief.

Then stooped my guardian angel   *5*
    And whispered from behind,
"Vanity, my little man,
    You're nothing of the kind."

(1865; 1884)

JABBERWOCKY The first stanza of this poem appeared first in 1855 with the title "Stanza of Anglo-Saxon Poetry"; Carroll then added the following mock interpretation: "BRYLLYG (derived from the verb to BRYL or BROIL, 'the time of broiling dinner, i.e. the close of the afternoon.' SLYTHY (compounded of SLIMY and LITHE). 'Smooth and active.' TOVE. A species of Badger. They had smooth white hair, long hind legs, and short horns like a stag; lived chiefly on cheese. GYRE, verb (derived from GYAOUR or GIAOUR, 'a dog'). To scratch like a dog. GYMBLE (whence GIMBLET). 'To screw out holes in anything.' WABE (derived from the verb to SWAB or SOAK). 'The side of a hill' (from its being *soaked* by the rain). MIMSY (whence MIMSERABLE and MISERABLE). 'Unhappy.' BOROGOVE. An extinct kind of Parrot. They had no wings, beaks turned up, and made their nests under sundials: lived on veal. MOME (hence SOLEMOME, SOLEMONE, AND SOLEMN). 'Grave.' RATH. A species of land turtle. Head erect: mouth like a shark: forelegs curved out so that the animal walked on its knees: smooth green body: lived on swallows and oysters. OUTGRABE, past tense of the verb to OUTGRIBE. (It is connected with old verb to GRIKE, or SHRIKE, from which are derived 'shriek' and 'creak'). 'Squeaked.' Hence the literal English of the passage is: 'It was evening, and the smooth active badgers were scratching and boring holes in the hill-side; all unhappy were the parrots; and the grave turtles squeaked out.' There were probably sundials on the top of the hill, and the 'borogoves' were afraid that their nests would be undermined. The hill was probably full of the nests of 'raths,' which ran out, squeaking with fear, on hearing the 'toves' scratching outside. This is an obscure, but yet deeply-affecting, relic of ancient Poetry." (Carroll is probably alluding here to the popular anthology *Reliques of Ancient English Poetry,* 1765, ed. Thomas Percy, 1729-1811). The full poem later appeared in *Through the Looking-Glass and What Alice Found There* (1871), and it is "interpreted" by Humpty Dumpty in Chapter VI.

SAMUEL BUTLER
England, 1835-1902

from *THE NOTEBOOKS*

from *Life*

vii

Life is one long process of getting tired.

ix

Life is the art of drawing sufficient conclusions from insufficient premises.

xii

A sense of humour keen enough to show a man his own absurdities, as well as those of other people, will keep him from the commission of all sins, or nearly all, save those that are worth committing.   5

xiv

There are two great rules of life, the one general and the other particular. The first is that every one can, in the end, get what he wants if he only tries. This is the general rule. The particular rule is that every individual is, more or less, an exception to the general rule.

Joining and Disjoining

These are the essence of change.

One of the earliest notes I made, when I began to make notes at all, I found not long   10
ago in an old book, since destroyed, which I had in New Zealand. It was to the effect that all things are either of the nature of a piece of string or a knife. That is, they are either for bringing and keeping things together, or for sending and keeping them apart. Nevertheless each kind contains a little of its opposite and some, as the railway train and the hedge, combine many examples of both. Thus the train, on the whole, is used for   15
bringing things together, but it is also used for sending them apart, and its divisions into classes are alike for separating and keeping together. The hedge is also both for joining things (as a flock of sheep) and for disjoining (as for keeping the sheep from getting into corn). These are the more immediate ends. The ulterior ends, both of train and hedge, so far as we are concerned, and so far as anything can have an end, are the bringing or   20
helping to bring meat or dairy produce into contact with man's inside, or wool on to his back, or that he may go in comfort somewhere to converse with people and join his soul on to theirs, or please himself by getting something to come within the range of his senses or imagination.

A piece of string is a thing that, in the main, makes for togetheriness; whereas a knife is,   25
in the main, a thing that makes for splitty-uppiness; still, there is an odour of togetheriness hanging about a knife also, for it tends to bring potatoes into a man's stomach.

JOINING AND DISJOINING   19. **corn:** grain.

In high philosophy one should never look at a knife without considering it also as a piece of string, nor at a piece of string without considering it also as a knife.

Cannibalism

Morality is the custom of one's country and the current feeling of one's peers. Cannibalism is moral in a cannibal country. *30*

Darwin among the Machines

[To the Editor of the *Press*, Christchurch, New Zealand — 13 June, 1863.]

Sɪʀ — There are few things of which the present generation is more justly proud than of the wonderful improvements which are daily taking place in all sorts of mechanical appliances. And indeed it is matter for great congratulation on many grounds. It is unnecessary to mention these here, for they are sufficiently obvious; our present *35* business lies with considerations which may somewhat tend to humble our pride and to make us think seriously of the future prospects of the human race. If we revert to the earliest primordial types of mechanical life, to the lever, the wedge, the inclined plane, the screw and the pulley, or (for analogy would lead us one step further) to that one primordial type from which all the mechanical kingdom has been developed, we mean *40* to the lever itself, and if we then examine the machinery of the *Great Eastern*, we find ourselves almost awestruck at the vast development of the mechanical world, at the gigantic strides with which it has advanced in comparison with the slow progress of the animal and vegetable kingdom. We shall find it impossible to refrain from asking ourselves what the end of this mighty movement is to be. In what direction is it tending? *45* What will be its upshot? To give a few imperfect hints towards a solution of these questions is the object of the present letter.

We have used the words "mechanical life," "the mechanical kingdom," "the mechanical world" and so forth, and we have done so advisedly, for as the vegetable kingdom was slowly developed from the mineral, and as, in like manner, the animal *50* supervened upon the vegetable, so now, in these last few ages, an entirely new kingdom has sprung up of which we as yet have only seen what will one day be considered the antediluvian prototypes of the race.

We regret deeply that our knowledge both of natural history and of machinery is too small to enable us to undertake the gigantic task of classifying machines into the *55* genera and sub-genera, species, varieties and sub-varieties, and so forth, of tracing the connecting links between machines of widely different characters, of pointing out how subservience to the use of man has played that part among machines which natural selection has performed in the animal and vegetable kingdom, of pointing out rudimentary organs which exist in some few machines, feebly developed and perfectly useless, *60* yet serving to mark descent from some ancestral type which has either perished or been modified into some new phase of mechanical existence. We can only point out this field for investigation; it must be followed by others whose education and talents have been of a much higher order than any which we can lay claim to.

DARWIN AMONG THE MACHINES   Butler later used some of this material in "The Book of the Machines" chapters of *Erewhon*. Cf. also George Eliot's "Shadows of the Coming Race" (p. 1018). **41.** *Great Eastern***:** the largest steamship in existence at the time it was built (1853-58) by Isambard Kingdom Brunel (1806-1859).

Some few hints we have determined to venture upon, though we do so with the   *65*
profoundest diffidence. Firstly we would remark that as some of the lowest of the
vertebrata attained a far greater size than has descended to their more highly organised
living representatives, so a diminution in the size of machines has often attended their
development and progress. Take the watch for instance. Examine the beautiful structure
of the little animal, watch the intelligent play of the minute members which compose it;   *70*
yet this little creature is but a development of the cumbrous clocks of the thirteenth
century — it is no deterioration from them. The day may come when clocks, which
certainly at the present day are not diminishing in bulk, may be entirely superseded by
the universal use of watches, in which case clocks will become extinct like the earlier
saurians, while the watch (whose tendency has for some years been rather to decrease in   *75*
size than the contrary) will remain the only existing type of an extinct race.

The views of machinery which we are thus feebly indicating will suggest the
solution of one of the greatest and most mysterious questions of the day. We refer to the
question: What sort of creature man's next successor in the supremacy of the earth is
likely to be. We have often heard this debated; but it appears to us that we are ourselves   *80*
creating our own successors; we are daily adding to the beauty and delicacy of their
physical organisation; we are daily giving them greater power and supplying, by all
sorts of ingenious contrivances, that self-regulating, self-acting power which will be to
them what intellect has been to the human race. In the course of ages we shall find
ourselves the inferior race. Inferior in power, inferior in that moral quality of self-   *85*
control, we shall look up to them as the acme of all that the best and wisest man can
ever dare to aim at. No evil passions, no jealousy, no avarice, no impure desires will
disturb the serene might of those glorious creatures. Sin, shame and sorrow will have no
place among them. Their minds will be in a state of perpetual calm, the contentment of a
spirit that knows no wants, is disturbed by no regrets. Ambition will never torture them.   *90*
Ingratitude will never cause them the uneasiness of a moment. The guilty conscience,
the hope deferred, the pains of exile, the insolence of office and the spurns that patient
merit of the unworthy takes — these will be entirely unknown to them. If they want
"feeding" (by the use of which very word we betray our recognition of them as living
organism) they will be attended by patient slaves whose business and interest it will be   *95*
to see that they shall want for nothing. If they are out of order they will be promptly
attended to by physicians who are thoroughly acquainted with their constitutions; if they
die, for even these glorious animals will not be exempt from that necessary and universal consummation, they will immediately enter into a new phase of existence, for what
machine dies entirely in every part at one and the same instant?   *100*

We take it that when the state of things shall have arrived which we have been
above attempting to describe, man will have become to the machine what the horse and
the dog are to man. He will continue to exist, nay even to improve, and will be probably
better off in his state of domestication under the beneficent rule of the machines than he
is in his present wild state. We treat our horses, dogs, cattle and sheep, on the whole,   *105*
with great kindness, we give them whatever experience teaches us to be best for them,
and there can be no doubt that our use of meat has added to the happiness of the lower

---

91-93: See *Hamlet*, III.i.73-74. **99. consummation:** See *Hamlet*, III.i.63-64.

animals far more than it has detracted from it; in like manner it is reasonable to suppose that the machines will treat us kindly, for their existence is as dependent upon ours as ours is upon the lower animals. They cannot kill us and eat us as we do sheep, they will not only require our services in the parturition of their young (which branch of their economy will remain always in our hands) but also in feeding them, in setting them right if they are sick, and burying their dead or working up their corpses into new machines. It is obvious that if all the animals in Great Britain save man alone were to die, and if at the same time all intercourse with foreign countries were by some sudden catastrophe to be rendered perfectly impossible, it is obvious that under such circumstances the loss of human life would be something fearful to contemplate — in like manner, were mankind to cease, the machines would be as badly off or even worse. The fact is that our interests are inseparable from theirs, and theirs from ours. Each race is dependent upon the other for innumerable benefits, and, until the reproductive organs of the machines have been developed in a manner which we are hardly yet able to conceive, they are entirely dependent upon man for even the continuance of their species. It is true that these organs may be ultimately developed, inasmuch as man's interest lies in that direction; there is nothing which our infatuated race would desire more than to see a fertile union between two steam engines; it is true that machinery is even at this present time employed in begetting machinery, in becoming the parent of machines often after its own kind, but the days of flirtation, courtship and matrimony appear to be very remote and indeed can hardly be realised by our feeble and imperfect imagination.

Day by day, however, the machines are gaining ground upon us; day by day we are becoming more subservient to them; more men are daily bound down as slaves to tend them, more men are daily devoting the energies of their whole lives to the development of mechanical life. The upshot is simply a question of time, but that the time will come when the machines will hold the real supremacy over the world and its inhabitants is what no person of a truly philosophic mind can for a moment question.

Our opinion is that war to the death should be instantly proclaimed against them. Every machine of every sort should be destroyed by the well-wisher of his species. Let there be no exceptions made, no quarter shown; let us at once go back to the primeval condition of the race. If it be urged that this is impossible under the present condition of human affairs, this at once proves that the mischief is already done, that our servitude has commenced in good earnest, that we have raised a race of beings whom it is beyond our power to destroy and that we are not only enslaved but are absolutely acquiescent in our bondage.

For the present we shall leave this subject which we present gratis to the members of the Philosophical Society. Should they consent to avail themselves of the vast field which we have pointed out, we shall endeavour to labour in it ourselves at some future and indefinite period.

I am, Sir, &c.,
Cellarius.

Cellarius: (Latin) "butler."

Making Notes

My notes always grow longer if I shorten them. I mean the process of compression makes them more pregnant and they breed new notes. I never try to lengthen them, so I do not know whether they would grow shorter if I did. Perhaps that might be a good *150* way of getting them shorter.

Public Opinion

The public buys its opinions as it buys its meat, or takes in its milk, on the principle that it is cheaper to do this than to keep a cow. So it is, but the milk is more likely to be watered.

from *Truth*
ii

The pursuit of truth is chimerical. That is why it is so hard to say what truth is. There is *155* no permanent absolute unchangeable truth; what we should pursue is the most convenient arrangement of our ideas.

iii

There is no such source of error as the pursuit of absolute truth.

vi

Truth should not be absolutely lost sight of, but it should not be talked about.

vii

Some men love truth so much that they seem to be in continual fear lest she should *160* catch cold on over-exposure.

viii

The firmest line that can be drawn upon the smoothest paper has still jagged edges if seen through a microscope. This does not matter until important deductions are made on the supposition that there are no jagged edges.

x

An absolute lie may live — for it is a true lie, and is saved by being flecked with a grain *165* of its opposite. Not so absolute truth.

xiv

Truth generally is kindness, but where the two diverge or collide, kindness should override truth.

from *Convenience*
i

We wonder at its being as hard often to discover convenience as it is to discover truth. But surely convenience is truth. *170*

ii

The use of truth is like the use of words; both truth and words depend greatly upon custom.

iii

We do with truth much as we do with God. We create it according to our own requirements and then say that it has created us, or requires that we shall do or think so and so — whatever we find convenient.

175

iv

"What is Truth?" is often asked, as though it were harder to say what truth is than what anything else is. But what is Justice? What is anything? An eternal contradiction in terms meets us at the end of every enquiry. We are not required to know what truth is, but to speak the truth, and so with justice.

Science

If it tends to thicken the crust of ice on which, as it were, we are skating, it is all right. If *180* it tries to find, or professes to have found, the solid ground at the bottom of the water, it is all wrong. Our business is with the thickening of this crust by extending our knowledge downward from above, as ice gets thicker while the frost lasts; we should not try to freeze upwards from the bottom.

(1912)

MARK TWAIN [SAMUEL LANGHORNE CLEMENS]
U.S.A., 1835-1910

THE NOTORIOUS JUMPING FROG OF CALAVERAS COUNTY

In compliance with the request of a friend of mine, who wrote me from the East, I called on good-natured, garrulous old Simon Wheeler, and inquired after my friend's friend, Leonidas W. Smiley, as requested to do, and I hereunto append the result. I have a lurking suspicion that *Leonidas W.* Smiley is a myth; that my friend never knew such a personage; and that he only conjectured that if I asked old Wheeler about him, it would *5* remind him of his infamous *Jim* Smiley, and he would go to work and bore me to death with some exasperating reminiscence of him as long and as tedious as it should be useless to me. If that was the design, it succeeded.

I found Simon Wheeler dozing comfortably by the bar-room stove of the dilapidated tavern in the decayed mining camp of Angel's, and I noticed that he was fat *10* and bald-headed, and had an expression of winning gentleness and simplicity upon his tranquil countenance. He roused up, and gave me good day. I told him that a friend of mine had commissioned me to make some inquiries about a cherished companion of his boyhood named *Leonidas W.* Smiley — *Rev. Leonidas W.* Smiley, a young minister of the Gospel, who he had heard was at one time a resident of Angel's Camp. I added that *15* if Mr. Wheeler could tell me anything about this Rev. Leonidas W. Smiley, I would feel under many obligations to him.

CONVENIENCE 176. "What is Truth": See John 18:38. THE NOTORIOUS JUMPING FROG OF CALAVERAS COUNTY Title: The California place name is accented on the third syllable.

Simon Wheeler backed me into a corner and blockaded me there with his chair, and then sat down and reeled off the monotonous narrative which follows this paragraph. He never smiled, he never frowned, he never changed his voice from the gentle-flowing key to which he tuned his initial sentence, he never betrayed the slightest suspicion of enthusiasm; but all through the interminable narrative there ran a vein of impressive earnestness and sincerity, which showed me plainly that, so far from his imagining that there was anything ridiculous or funny about his story, he regarded it as a really important matter, and admired its two heroes as men of transcendent genius in *finesse*. I let him go on in his own way, and never interrupted him once.

"Rev. Leonidas W. H'm, Reverend Le — well, there was a feller here once by the name of *Jim* Smiley, in the winter of '49 — or maybe it was the spring of '50 — I don't recollect exactly, somehow, though what makes me think it was one or the other is because I remember the big flume warn't finished when he first come to the camp; but anyway, he was the curiousest man about always betting on anything that turned up you ever see, if he could get anybody to bet on the other side; and if he couldn't he'd change sides. Any way that suited the other man would suit *him* — any way just so's he got a bet, *he* was satisfied. But still he was lucky, uncommon lucky; he most always come out winner. He was always ready and laying for a chance; there couldn't be no solit'ry thing mentioned but that feller'd offer to bet on it, and take ary side you please, as I was just telling you. If there was a horse-race, you'd find him flush or you'd find him busted at the end of it; if there was a dog-fight, he'd bet on it; if there was a cat-fight, he'd bet on it; if there was a chicken-fight, he'd bet on it; why, if there was two birds setting on a fence, he would bet you which one would fly first; or if there was a camp-meeting, he would be there reg'lar to bet on Parson Walker, which he judged to be the best exhorter about here, and so he was too, and a good man. If he even see a straddle-bug start to go anywheres, he would bet you how long it would take him to get to — to wherever he was going to, and if you took him up, he would foller that straddle-bug to Mexico but what he would find out where he was bound for and how long he was on the road. Lots of the boys here has seen that Smiley, and can tell you about him. Why, it never made no difference to *him* — he'd bet on *any* thing — the dangdest feller. Parson Walker's wife laid very sick once, for a good while, and it seemed as if they warn't going to save her; but one morning he come in, and Smiley up and asked him how she was, and he said she was considerable better — thank the Lord for his inf'nite mercy — and coming on so smart that with the blessing of Prov'dence she'd get well yet; and Smiley, before he thought, says, 'Well, I'll resk two-and-a-half she don't anyway.'

"Thish-yer Smiley had a mare — the boys called her the fifteen-minute nag, but that was only in fun, you know, because of course she was faster than that — and he used to win money on that horse, for all she was so slow and always had the asthma, or the distemper, or the consumption, or something of that kind. They used to give her two or three hundred yards' start, and then pass her under way; but always at the fag end of the race she'd get excited and desperate like, and come cavorting and straddling up, and scattering her legs around limber, sometimes in the air, and sometimes out to one side among the fences, and kicking up m-o-r-e dust and raising m-o-r-e racket with her coughing and sneezing and blowing her nose — and *always* fetch up at the stand just about a neck ahead, as near as you could cipher it down.

"And he had a little small bull-pup, that to look at him you'd think he warn't worth a cent but to set around and look ornery and lay for a chance to steal something. But as soon as money was up on him he was a different dog; his under-jaw'd begin to stick out like the fo'castle of a steamboat, and his teeth would uncover and shine like the furnaces. And a dog might tackle him and bully-rag him, and bite him, and throw him over his shoulder two or three times, and Andrew Jackson — which was the name of the pup — Andrew Jackson would never let on but what *he* was satisfied, and hadn't expected nothing else — and the bets being doubled and doubled on the other side all the time, till the money was all up; and then all of a sudden he would grab that other dog jest by the j'int of his hind leg and freeze to it — not chaw, you understand, but only just grip and hang on till they throwed up the sponge, if it was a year. Smiley always come out winner on that pup, till he harnessed a dog once that didn't have no hind legs, because they'd been sawed off in a circular saw, and when the thing had gone along far enough, and the money was all up, and he come to make a snatch for his pet holt, he see in a minute how he'd been imposed on, and how the other dog had him in the door, so to speak, and he 'peared surprised, and then he looked sorter discouraged-like, and didn't try no more to win the fight, and so he got shucked out bad. He give Smiley a look, as much as to say his heart was broke, and it was *his* fault, for putting up a dog that hadn't no hind legs for him to take holt of, which was his main dependence in a fight, and then he limped off a piece and laid down and died. It was a good pup, was that Andrew Jackson, and would have made a name for hisself if he'd lived, for the stuff was in him and he had genius — I know it, because he hadn't no opportunities to speak of, and it don't stand to reason that a dog could make such a fight as he could under them circumstances if he hadn't no talent. It always makes me feel sorry when I think of that last fight of his'n, and the way it turned out.

"Well, thish-yer Smiley had rat-tarriers, and chicken cocks, and tomcats and all them kind of things, till you couldn't rest, and you couldn't fetch nothing for him to bet on but he'd match you. He ketched a frog one day, and took him home, and said he cal'lated to educate him; and so he never done nothing for three months but set in his back yard and learn that frog to jump. And you bet you he *did* learn him, too. He'd give him a little punch behind, and the next minute you'd see that frog whirling in the air like a doughnut — see him turn one summer-set, or maybe a couple, if he got a good start, and come down flat-footed and all right, like a cat. He got him up so in the matter of ketching flies, and kep' him in practice so constant, that he'd nail a fly every time as fur as he could see him. Smiley said all a frog wanted was education, and he could do 'most anything — and I believe him. Why, I've seen him set Dan'l Webster down here on this floor — Dan'l Webster was the name of the frog — and sing out, 'Flies, Dan'l, flies!' and quicker'n you could wink he'd spring straight up and snake a fly off'n the counter there, and flop down on the floor ag'in as solid as a gob of mud, and fall to scratching the side of his head with his hind foot as indifferent as if he hadn't no idea he'd been doin' any more'n any frog might do. You never see a frog so modest and straight-for'ard as he was, for all he was so gifted. And when it come to fair and square jumping

65

70

75

80

85

90

95

100

---

68. Andrew Jackson: the name of the 7th president of the United States, a military man with the nickname "Old Hickory." **76. holt:** hold.
98. Dan'l Webster: the name of a famous 19th-century American orator and political figure.

on a dead level, he could get over more ground at one straddle than any animal of his   *105*
breed you ever see. Jumping on a dead level was his strong suit, you understand; and
when it come to that, Smiley would ante up money on him as long as he had a red.
Smiley was monstrous proud of his frog, and well he might be, for fellers that had
traveled and been everywheres all said he laid over any frog that ever *they* see.

"Well, Smiley kep' the beast in a little lattice box, and he used to fetch him down-   *110*
town sometimes and lay for a bet. One day a feller — a stranger in the camp, he was —
come acrost him with his box, and says:

"'What might it be that you've got in the box?'

"And Smiley says, sorter indifferent-like, 'It might be a parrot, or it might be a
canary, maybe, but it ain't — it's only just a frog.'   *115*

"And the feller took it, and looked at it careful, and turned it round this way and
that, and says, 'H'm — so 'tis. Well, what's *he* good for?'

"'Well,' Smiley says, easy and careless, 'he's good enough for *one* thing, I should
judge — he can outjump any frog in Calaveras County.'

"The feller took the box again, and took another long, particular look, and give it   *120*
back to Smiley, and says, very deliberate, 'Well,' he says, 'I don't see no p'ints about
that frog that's any better'n any other frog.'

"'Maybe you don't,' Smiley says. 'Maybe you understand frogs and maybe you
don't understand 'em; maybe you've had experience, and maybe you ain't only a
amature, as it were. Anyways, I've got *my* opinion, and I'll resk forty dollars that he can   *125*
outjump any frog in Calaveras County.'

"And the feller studied a minute, and then says, kinder sad-like, 'Well, I'm only a
stranger here, and I ain't got no frog; but if I had a frog, I'd bet you.'

"And then Smiley says, 'That's all right — that's all right — if you'll hold my box
a minute, I'll go and get you a frog.' And so the feller took the box, and put up his forty   *130*
dollars along with Smiley's, and set down to wait.

"So he set there a good while thinking and thinking to himself, and then he got the
frog out and prized his mouth open and took a teaspoon and filled him full of quail-shot
— filled him pretty near up to his chin — and set him on the floor. Smiley he went to
the swamp and slopped around in the mud for a long time, and finally he ketched a frog,   *135*
and fetched him in, and give him to this feller, and says:

"'Now, if you're ready, set him alongside of Dan'l, with his fore paws just even
with Dan'l's, and I'll give the word.' Then he says, 'One — two — three — *git!*' and
him and the feller touched up the frogs from behind, and the new frog hopped off lively,
but Dan'l give a heave, and hysted up his shoulders — so — like a Frenchman, but it   *140*
warn't no use — he couldn't budge; he was planted as solid as a church, and he couldn't
no more stir than if he was anchored out. Smiley was a good deal surprised, and he was
disgusted too, but he didn't have no idea what the matter was, of course.

"The feller took the money and started away; and when he was going out at the
door, he sorter jerked his thumb over his shoulder — so — at Dan'l, and says again,   *145*
very deliberate, 'Well,' he says, '*I* don't see no p'ints about that frog that's any better'n
any other frog.'

---

107. red: i.e., red cent.

"Smiley he stood scratching his head and looking down at Dan'l a long time, and at last he says, 'I do wonder what in the nation that frog throw'd off for — I wonder if there ain't something the matter with him — he 'pears to look mighty baggy, somehow.' And he ketched Dan'l by the nap of the neck, and hefted him, and says, 'Why blame my cats if he don't weigh five pound!' and turned him upside down and he belched out a double handful of shot. And then he see how it was, and he was the maddest man — he set the frog down and took out after that feller, but he never ketched him. And —" 150

[Here Simon Wheeler heard his name called from the front yard, and got up to see what was wanted.] And turning to me as he moved away, he said: "Just set where you are, stranger, and rest easy — I ain't going to be gone a second." 155

But, by your leave, I did not think that a continuation of the history of the enterprising vagabond *Jim* Smiley would be likely to afford me much information concerning the Rev. *Leonidas W.* Smiley, and so I started away. 160

At the door I met the sociable Wheeler returning, and he buttonholed me and recommenced:

"Well, thish-yer Smiley had a yaller one-eyed cow that didn't have no tail, only just a short stump like a bannanner, and —"

However, lacking both time and inclination, I did not wait to hear about the afflicted cow, but took my leave. 165

(1865, 1867)

THE LATE BENJAMIN FRANKLIN

["Never put off till to-morrow what you can do day after to-morrow just as well." — B. F.]

This party was one of those persons whom they call Philosophers. He was twins, being born simultaneously in two different houses in the city of Boston. These houses remain unto this day, and have signs upon them worded in accordance with the facts. The signs are considered well enough to have, though not necessary, because the inhabitants point out the two birthplaces to the stranger anyhow, and sometimes as often as several times in the same day. The subject of this memoir was of a vicious disposition, and early prostituted his talents to the invention of maxims and aphorisms calculated to inflict suffering upon the rising generation of all subsequent ages. His simplest acts, also, were contrived with a view to their being held up for the emulation of boys forever — boys who might otherwise have been happy. It was in this spirit that he became the son of a soap-boiler, and probably for no other reason than that the efforts of all future boys who tried to be anything might be looked upon with suspicion unless they were the sons of soap-boilers. With a malevolence which is without parallel in history, he would work all day, and then sit up nights, and let on to be studying algebra by the light of a smoldering fire, so that all other boys might have to do that also, or else have Benjamin Franklin thrown up to them. Not satisfied with these proceedings, he had a fashion of living wholly on bread and water, and studying astronomy at meal-time — a thing which has brought affliction to millions of boys since, whose fathers had read Franklin's pernicious biography. 5 10 15

THE LATE BENJAMIN FRANKLIN **Epigraph:** See p. 577ff. for Franklin's preface to *Poor Richard's Almanac* and his version of this old proverb or maxim, most commonly rendered as "Never put off till tomorrow what you can do today"; it had also been humourously inverted by W.B. Rands (1823-1882) in his book of verse for children, *Lilliput Levée* (1864): "Never do today what you can / Put off till tomorrow."

His maxims were full of animosity toward boys. Nowadays a boy cannot follow out a single natural instinct without tumbling over some of those everlasting aphorisms and hearing from Franklin on the spot. If he buys two cents' worth of peanuts, his father says, "Remember what Franklin has said, my son — 'A groat a day's a penny a year'"; and the comfort is all gone out of those peanuts. If he wants to spin his top when he has done work, his father quotes, "Procrastination is the thief of time." If he does a virtuous action, he never gets anything for it, because "Virtue is its own reward." And that boy is hounded to death and robbed of his natural rest, because Franklin said once, in one of his inspired flights of malignity:

> Early to bed and early to rise
> Makes a man healthy and wealthy and wise.

As if it were any object to a boy to be healthy and wealthy and wise on such terms. The sorrow that that maxim has cost me, through my parents, experimenting on me with it, tongue cannot tell. The legitimate result is my present state of general debility, indigence, and mental aberration. My parents used to have me up before nine o'clock in the morning sometimes when I was a boy. If they had let me take my natural rest where would I have been now? Keeping store, no doubt, and respected by all.

And what an adroit old adventurer the subject of this memoir was! In order to get a chance to fly his kite on Sunday he used to hang a key on the string and let on to be fishing for lightning. And a guileless public would go home chirping about the "wisdom" and the "genius" of the hoary Sabbath-breaker. If anybody caught him playing "mumble-peg" by himself, after the age of sixty, he would immediately appear to be ciphering out how the grass grew — as if it was any of his business. My grandfather knew him well, and he says Franklin was always fixed — always ready. If a body, during his old age, happened on him unexpectedly when he was catching flies, or making mud-pies, or sliding on a cellar door, he would immediately look wise, and rip out a maxim, and walk off with his nose in the air and his cap turned wrong side before, trying to appear absent-minded and eccentric. He was a hard lot.

He invented a stove that would smoke your head off in four hours by the clock. One can see the almost devilish satisfaction he took in it by his giving it his name.

He was always proud of telling how he entered Philadelphia for the first time, with nothing in the world but two shillings in his pocket and four rolls of bread under his arm. But really, when you come to examine it critically, it was nothing. Anybody could have done it.

To the subject of this memoir belongs the honor of recommending the army to go back to bows and arrows in place of bayonets and muskets. He observed, with his customary force, that the bayonet was very well under some circumstances, but that he doubted whether it could be used with accuracy at a long range.

Benjamin Franklin did a great many notable things for his country, and made her young name to be honored in many lands as the mother of such a son. It is not the idea

---

24. "Procrastination . . . time": Edward Young's *Night Thoughts*, I, 392. 25. "Virtue . . . reward": a saying attributed to various writers from Silius Italicus (A.D. c.25-c.100) onwards, including Sir Thomas Browne in *Religio Medici* (I, 47) and Matthew Prior in *Imitations of Horace* (III, ode 2). 28-29. "Early . . . wise": from *Poor Richard's Almanack* (October 1735), but it had appeared in almost exactly this form in the early 17th century. 40. mumble-peg: or mumblety-peg, a children's game in which each player flicks a knife from different positions and tries to make it stick in the ground.

of this memoir to ignore that or cover it up. No; the simple idea of it is to snub those pretentious maxims of his, which he worked up with a great show of originality out of truisms that had become wearisome platitudes as early as the dispersion from Babel; and also to snub his stove, and his military inspirations, his unseemly endeavor to make himself conspicuous when he entered Philadelphia, and his flying his kite and fooling away his time in all sorts of such ways when he ought to have been foraging for soap-fat, or constructing candles. I merely desired to do away with somewhat of the prevalent calamitous idea among heads of families that Franklin *acquired* his great genius by working for nothing, studying by moonlight, and getting up in the night instead of waiting till morning like a Christian; and that this program, rigidly inflicted, will make a Franklin of every father's fool. It is time these gentlemen were finding out that these execrable eccentricities of instinct and conduct are only the *evidences* of genius, not the *creators* of it. I wish I had been the father of my parents long enough to make them comprehend this truth, and thus prepare them to let their son have an easier time of it. When I was a child I had to boil soap, notwithstanding my father was wealthy, and I had to get up early and study geometry at breakfast, and peddle my own poetry, and do everything just as Franklin did, in the solemn hope that I would be a Franklin some day. And here I am.

(1875)

Selected epigraphs from *THE TRAGEDY OF PUDD'NHEAD WILSON*

from *"Pudd'nhead Wilson's Calendar"*

Adam was but human — this explains it all. He did not want the apple for the apple's sake, he wanted it only because it was forbidden. The mistake was in not forbidding the serpent; then he would have eaten the serpent.

Training is everything. The peach was once a bitter almond; cauliflower is nothing but cabbage with a college education.

Habit is habit, and not to be flung out of the window by any man, but coaxed down-stairs a step at a time.

One of the most striking differences between a cat and a lie is that a cat has only nine lives.

Consider well the proportions of things. It is better to be a young June-bug than an old bird of paradise.

Why is it that we rejoice at a birth and grieve at a funeral? It is because we are not the person involved.

It is easy to find fault, if one has that disposition. There was once a man who, not being able to find any other fault with his coal, complained that there were too many prehistoric toads in it.

Nothing so needs reforming as other people's habits.

If you pick up a starving dog and make him prosperous, he will not bite you. This is the principal difference between a dog and a man.

Few things are harder to put up with than the annoyance of a good example.   *20*

October 12, the Discovery. It was wonderful to find America, but it would have been more wonderful to miss it.

(1894)

"A MAN HIRED BY JOHN SMITH AND CO."

A man hired by John Smith and Co.
Loudly declared that he'd tho.
   Men that he saw
   Dumping dirt near his store.
The drivers, therefore, didn't do.

SIR W.S. GILBERT
England, 1836-1911

ANGLICISED UTOPIA

Society has quite forsaken all her wicked courses,
Which empties our police courts, and abolishes divorces.
   (Divorce is nearly obsolete in England.)
No tolerance we show to undeserving rank and splendour;
For the higher his position is, the greater the offender.   *5*
   (That's a maxim that is prevalent in England.)
No Peeress at our Drawing-Room before the Presence passes
Who wouldn't be accepted by the lower-middle classes;
Each shady dame, whatever be her rank, is bowed out neatly.
In short, this happy country has been Anglicised completely!   *10*
     It really is surprising
     What a thorough Anglicising
   We've brought about — Utopia's quite another land;
     In her enterprising movements,
     She is England — with improvements,   *15*
   Which we dutifully offer to our mother-land!

Our city we have beautified — we've done it willy-nilly —
And all that isn't Belgrave Square is Strand and Piccadilly.
   (They haven't any slummeries in England.)

A MAN HIRED This undated limerick is attributed to Twain.   **ANGLICIZED UTOPIA** This work first appeared as a patter song (between King and Chorus) in the operetta *Utopia Limited* (1893); it was given this title when collected in the 1898 version of *The Bab Ballads*. **18. Belgrave . . . Piccadilly:** London districts — Belgrave Square was a fashionable residential area; The Strand and Piccadilly, at the time, were well-to-do centres of commercial activity.

We have solved the labour question with discrimination polished,   *20*
So poverty is obsolete and hunger is abolished —
        (They are going to abolish it in England.)
The Chamberlain our native stage has purged, beyond a question,
Of "risky" situation and indelicate suggestion;
No piece is tolerated if it's costumed indiscreetly —   *25*
In short, this happy country has been Anglicised completely!
        It really is surprising
        What a thorough Anglicising
    We've brought about — Utopia's quite another land;
        In her enterprising movements,   *30*
        She is England — with improvements,
    Which we dutifully offer to our mother-land!

Our Peerage we've remodelled on an intellectual basis,
Which certainly is rough on our hereditary races —
        (They are going to remodel it in England.)   *35*
The Brewers and the Cotton Lords no longer seek admission,
And Literary Merit meets with proper recognition —
        (As Literary Merit does in England!)
Who knows but we may count among our intellectual chickens
Like them an Earl of Thackeray and p'raps a Duke of Dickens —   *40*
Lord Fildes and Viscount Millais (when they come) we'll welcome
    sweetly —
And then, this happy country will be Anglicised completely!
        It really is surprising
        What a thorough Anglicising
    We've brought about — Utopia's quite another land;   *45*
        In her enterprising movements,
        She is England — with improvements,
    Which we dutifully offer to our mother-land!
                                 (1893, 1898)

"THERE WAS AN OLD MAN OF ST. BEES"

There was an old man of St. Bees,
Who was stung in the arm by a wasp.
    When asked, "Does it hurt?"
    He replied, "No, it doesn't.
I'm so glad it wasn't a hornet."

---

23. Chamberlain: The Lord Chamberlain of the Household was a member of the monarch's personal staff who appointed the tradespeople that dealt with the Crown, licensed plays, and controlled who acted at the royal theatres. **40-41:** alluding to well-known figures of the time, the novelists Charles Dickens (p. 991) and William Makepeace Thackeray (1811-1863) and the portrait painters Sir Luke Fildes (1844-1927) and Sir John Everett Millais (1829-1896); Millais was made a baronet in 1885, Fildes knighted in 1906. **THERE WAS AN OLD MAN** Though Gilbert was including limericks in the letters he wrote to friends in 1903 and 1904, this particular limerick (attributed to him) is undated.

ALGERNON CHARLES SWINBURNE
England, 1837-1909

THE GARDEN OF PROSERPINE

Here, where the world is quiet;
  Here, where all trouble seems
Dead winds' and spent waves' riot
  In doubtful dreams of dreams;
I watch the green field growing   *5*
For reaping folk and sowing,
For harvest-time and mowing,
  A sleepy world of streams.

I am tired of tears and laughter,
  And men that laugh and weep;   *10*
Of what may come hereafter
  For men that sow to reap:
I am weary of days and hours,
Blown buds of barren flowers,
Desires and dreams and powers   *15*
  And everything but sleep.

Here life has death for neighbour,
  And far from eye or ear
Wan waves and wet winds labour,
  Weak ships and spirits steer;   *20*
They drive adrift, and whither
They wot not who make thither;
But no such winds blow hither,
  And no such things grow here.

No growth of moor or coppice,   *25*
  No heather-flower or vine,
But bloomless buds of poppies,
  Green grapes of Proserpine,
Pale beds of blowing rushes
Where no leaf blooms or blushes   *30*
Save this whereout she crushes
  For dead men deadly wine.

Pale, without name or number,
  In fruitless fields of corn,
They bow themselves and slumber   *35*
  All night till light is born;
And like a soul belated,
In hell and heaven unmated,
By cloud and mist abated
  Comes out of darkness morn.   *40*

Though one were strong as seven,
  He too with death shall dwell,
Nor wake with wings in heaven,
  Nor weep for pains in hell;
Though one were fair as roses,   *45*
His beauty clouds and closes;
And well though love reposes,
  In the end it is not well.

Pale, beyond porch and portal,
  Crowned with calm leaves, she stands   *50*
Who gathers all things mortal
  With cold immortal hands;
Her languid lips are sweeter
Than love's who fears to greet her
To men that mix and meet her   *55*
  From many times and lands.

She waits for each and other,
  She waits for all men born;
Forgets the earth her mother,
  The life of fruits and corn;   *60*
And spring and seed and swallow
Take wing for her and follow
Where summer song rings hollow
  And flowers are put to scorn.

THE GARDEN OF PROSERPINE **Title:** In Roman myth, Proserpine (in Greek, Persephone), the daughter of Ceres (Demeter), was carried off by Pluto (Hades) to be Queen of the underworld. **25. coppice:** copse, grove. **27. poppies:** sacred to Proserpine. **34. corn:** grain. **46. closes:** comes to an end. **59-60:** i.e., Ceres.

There go the loves that wither,   *65*
  The old loves with wearier wings;
And all dead years draw thither,
  And all disastrous things;
Dead dreams of days forsaken,
Blind buds that snows have shaken,   *70*
Wild leaves that winds have taken,
  Red strays of ruined springs.

We are not sure of sorrow,
  And joy was never sure;
To-day will die to-morrow;   *75*
  Time stoops to no man's lure;
And love, grown faint and fretful,
With lips but half regretful
Sighs, and with eyes forgetful
  Weeps that no loves endure.   *80*

From too much love of living,
  From hope and fear set free,
We thank with brief thanksgiving
  Whatever gods may be
That no life lives for ever;   *85*
That dead men rise up never;
That even the weariest river
  Winds somewhere safe to sea.

Then star nor sun shall waken,
  Nor any change of light: *90*
Nor sound of waters shaken,
  Nor any sound or sight:
Nor wintry leaves nor vernal,
Nor days nor things diurnal;
Only the sleep eternal   *95*
  In an eternal night.

                                        (1866)

THE HIGHER PANTHEISM IN A NUTSHELL

One, who is not, we see: but one, whom we see not, is:
Surely this is not that: but that is assuredly this.

What, and wherefore, and whence? for under is over and under:
If thunder could be without lightning, lightning could be without thunder.

Doubt is faith in the main: but faith, on the whole, is doubt: *5*
We cannot believe by proof: but could we believe without?

Why, and whither, and how? for barley and rye are not clover:
Neither are straight lines curves: yet over is under and over.

Two and two may be four: but four and four are not eight:
Fate and God may be twain: but God is the same thing as fate.   *10*

Ask a man what he thinks, and get from a man what he feels:
God, once caught in the fact, shows you a fair pair of heels.

Body and spirit are twins: God only knows which is which:
The soul squats down in the flesh, like a tinker drunk in a ditch.

More is the whole than a part: but half is more than the whole: *15*
Clearly, the soul is the body: but is not the body the soul?

One and two are not one: but one and nothing is two:
Truth can hardly be false, if falsehood cannot be true.

Once the mastodon was: pterodactyls were common as cocks:
Then the mammoth was God: now is He a prize ox.   *20*

---

76. stoops, lure: terms from falconry.   **THE HIGHER PANTHEISM**   This poems parodies Tennyson's "The Higher Pantheism" (1870).

Parallels all things are: yet many of these are askew:
You are certainly I: but certainly I am not you.

Springs the rock from the plain, shoots the stream from the rock:
Cocks exist for the hen: but hens exist for the cock.

God, whom we see not, is: and God, who is not, we see: *25*
Fiddle, we know, is diddle: and diddle, we take it, is dee.

(1880)

WALTER PATER
England, 1839-1894

from *THE RENAISSANCE*

CONCLUSION

Λέγει που ῾Ηράκλειτος ὅτι πάντα χωρεῖ καὶ οὐδὲν μένει

To regard all things and principles of things as inconstant modes or fashions has more
and more become the tendency of modern thought. Let us begin with that which is
without — our physical life. Fix upon it in one of its more exquisite intervals, the
moment, for instance, of delicious recoil from the flood of water in summer heat. What
is the whole physical life in that moment but a combination of natural elements to which   *5*
science gives their names? But these elements, phosphorus and lime and delicate fibres,
are present not in the human body alone: we detect them in places most remote from it.
Our physical life is a perpetual motion of them — the passage of the blood, the wasting
and repairing of the lenses of the eye, the modification of the tissues of the brain by
every ray of light and sound — processes which science reduces to simpler and more   *10*
elementary forces. Like the elements of which we are composed, the action of these
forces extends beyond us; it rusts iron and ripens corn. Far out on every side of us those
elements are broadcast, driven by many forces; and birth and gesture and death and the
springing of violets from the grave are but a few out of ten thousand resultant combinations. That clear, perpetual outline of face and limb is but an image of ours, under   *15*
which we group them — a design in a web, the actual threads of which pass out beyond
it. This at least of flame-like our life has, that it is but the concurrence, renewed from
moment to moment, of forces parting sooner or later on their ways.

CONCLUSION TO THE RENAISSANCE   "This brief 'Conclusion' was omitted in the second edition of this book, as I conceived it might
possibly mislead some of those young men into whose hands it might fall. On the whole, I have thought it best to reprint it here, with some slight
changes which bring it closer to my original meaning. I have dealt more fully in *Marius the Epicurean* with the thoughts suggested by it" (Pater's note
in the third edition); *Marius the Epicurean: His Sensations and Ideas* (1885) is a philosophical romance. **Epigraph:** In *Plato and Platonism* (1893),
Chapter I (which had appeared separately in 1892), Pater notes that this line is spoken by Socrates in Plato's *Cratylus*, and translates what "Heraclitus
says" as "All things give way: nothing remaineth" (see note to Hopkins's "That Nature Is a Heraclitean Fire," pp. 1125-26). **14. springing . . . grave:**
See *Hamlet*, V.i.240ff., where Laertes says of his dead sister, Ophelia, "Lay her i' the earth, / And from her fair and unpolluted flesh / May violets
spring!"

Or if we begin with the inward world of thought and feeling, the whirlpool is still more rapid, the flame more eager and devouring. There it is no longer the gradual darkening of the eye and fading of colour from the wall, — the movement of the shore-side, where the water flows down indeed, though in apparent rest, — but the race of the mid-stream, a drift of momentary acts of sight and passion and thought. At first sight experience seems to bury us under a flood of external objects, pressing upon us with a sharp and importunate reality, calling us out of ourselves in a thousand forms of action. But when reflexion begins to act upon those objects they are dissipated under its influence; the cohesive force seems suspended like a trick of magic; each object is loosed into a group of impressions — colour, odour, texture — in the mind of the observer. And if we continue to dwell in thought on this world, not of objects in the solidity with which language invests them, but of impressions unstable, flickering, inconsistent, which burn and are extinguished with our consciousness of them, it contracts still further; the whole scope of observation is dwarfed to the narrow chamber of the individual mind. Experience, already reduced to a swarm of impressions, is ringed round for each one of us by that thick wall of personality through which no real voice has ever pierced on its way to us, or from us to that which we can only conjecture to be without. Every one of those impressions is the impression of the individual in his isolation, each mind keeping as a solitary prisoner its own dream of a world. Analysis goes a step farther still, and assures us that those impressions of the individual mind to which, for each one of us, experience dwindles down, are in perpetual flight; that each of them is limited by time, and that as time is infinitely divisible, each of them is infinitely divisible also; all that is actual in it being a single moment, gone while we try to apprehend it, of which it may ever be more truly said that it has ceased to be than that it is. To such a tremulous wisp constantly reforming itself on the stream, to a single sharp impression, with a sense in it, a relic more or less fleeting, of such moments gone by, what is real in our life fines itself down. It is with this movement, with the passage and dissolution of impressions, images, sensations, that analysis leaves off — that continual vanishing away, that strange, perpetual weaving and unweaving of ourselves.

Philosophiren, says Novalis, *ist dephlegmatisiren vivificiren*. The service of philosophy, of speculative culture, towards the human spirit is to rouse, to startle it into sharp and eager observation. Every moment some form grows perfect in hand or face; some tone on the hills or the sea is choicer than the rest; some mood of passion or insight or intellectual excitement is irresistibly real and attractive for us, — for that moment only. Not the fruit of experience, but experience itself, is the end. A counted number of pulses only is given to us of a variegated, dramatic life. How may we see in them all that is to be seen in them by the finest senses? How shall we pass most swiftly from point to point, and be present always at the focus where the greatest number of vital forces unite in their purest energy?

To burn always with this hard, gemlike flame, to maintain this ecstasy, is success in life. In a sense it might even be said that our failure is to form habits: for, after all, habit

---

49: Novalis: pen name of Friedrich Leopold von Hardenberg (1772-1801), German Romantic poet and novelist; *Philosophiren* . . . : "To philosophize is to throw off sluggishness, to become alive."

is relative to a stereotyped world, and meantime it is only the roughness of the eye that
makes any two persons, things, situations, seem alike. While all melts under our feet, we
may well catch at any exquisite passion, or any contribution to knowledge that seems by
a lifted horizon to set the spirit free for a moment, or any stirring of the senses, strange
dyes, strange colours, and curious odours, or work of the artist's hands, or the face of   65
one's friend. Not to discriminate every moment some passionate attitude in those about
us, and in the brilliancy of their gifts some tragic dividing of forces on their ways, is, on
this short day of frost and sun, to sleep before evening. With this sense of the splendour
of our experience and of its awful brevity, gathering all we are into one desperate effort
to see and touch, we shall hardly have time to make theories about the things we see and   70
touch. What we have to do is to be for ever curiously testing new opinions and courting
new impressions, never acquiescing in a facile orthodoxy of Comte, or of Hegel, or of
our own. Philosophical theories or ideas, as points of view, instruments of criticism,
may help us to gather up what might otherwise pass unregarded by us. "Philosophy is
the microscope of thought." The theory or idea or system which requires of us the   75
sacrifice of any part of this experience, in consideration of some interest into which we
cannot enter, or some abstract theory we have not identified with ourselves, or what is
only conventional, has no real claim upon us.

One of the most beautiful passages in the writings of Rousseau is that in the sixth
book of the *Confessions,* where he describes the awakening in him of the literary   80
sense. An undefinable taint of death had always clung about him, and now in early
manhood he believed himself smitten by mortal disease. He asked himself how he
might make as much as possible of the interval that remained; and he was not biassed
by anything in his previous life when he decided that it must be by intellectual
excitement, which he found just then in the clear, fresh writings of Voltaire. Well! we   85
are all *condamnés,* as Victor Hugo says: we are all under sentence of death but with a
sort of indefinite reprieve — *les hommes sont tous condamnés à mort avec des sursis
indéfinis:* we have an interval, and then our place knows us no more. Some spend this
interval in listlessness, some in high passions, the wisest, at least among "the children
of this world," in art and song. For our one chance lies in expanding that interval, in get-   90
ting as many pulsations as possible into the given time. Great passions may give us this
quickened sense of life, ecstasy and sorrow of love, the various forms of enthusiastic
activity, disinterested or otherwise, which come naturally to many of us. Only be sure it
is passion — that it does yield you this fruit of a quickened, multiplied consciousness.
Of this wisdom, the poetic passion, the desire of beauty, the love of art for art's sake,   95
has most; for art comes to you professing frankly to give nothing but the highest quality
to your moments as they pass, and simply for those moments' sake.

(1873, 1888)

---

72. Comte: Auguste Comte (1798-1857), French philosopher, founder of positivism; **Hegel:** Georg Wilhelm Friedrich Hegel (1770-1831), German philosopher known for his dialectical theory (thesis + antithesis = synthesis). **74-75. "Philosophy . . . thought":** from *Les Misérables* (*Jean Valjean,* II, Chapter 2), 1862 novel by Victor Hugo (see 86 below). **79. Rousseau:** Jean-Jacques Rousseau (1712-1778), French philosopher and author; *Les Confessions* was published posthumously (1781-88). **85. Voltaire:** pseudonym of François-Marie Arouet (1694-1778), French philosopher and author, perhaps best known for *Candide* (1759). **86. Victor Hugo:** (1802-1885), French novelist, poet, and dramatist. **89-90. wisest . . . world":** See Luke 16:8.

Austin Dobson
England, 1840-1921

A Kiss

Rose kissed me today.
  Will she kiss me tomorrow?
Let it be as it may,
Rose kissed me today.
But the pleasure gives way   *5*
  To a savour of sorrow; —
Rose kissed me today —
  Will she kiss me tomorrow?

             (1874)

Thomas Hardy
England, 1840-1928

Drummer Hodge

I

They throw in Drummer Hodge, to rest
  Uncoffined — just as found:
His landmark is a kopje-crest
  That breaks the veldt around;
And foreign constellations west   *5*
  Each night above his mound.

II

Young Hodge the Drummer never knew —
  Fresh from his Wessex home —
The meaning of the broad Karoo,
  The Bush, the dusty loam,   *10*
And why uprose to nightly view
  Strange stars amid the gloam.

III

Yet portion of that unknown plain
  Will Hodge for ever be;
His homely Northern breast and brain   *15*
  Grow to some Southern tree,
And strange-eyed constellations reign
  His stars eternally.

             (1901)

The Darkling Thrush

I leant upon a coppice gate
  When Frost was spectre-gray,
And Winter's dregs made desolate
  The weakening eye of day.
The tangled bine-stems scored the sky   *5*
  Like strings of broken lyres,
And all mankind that haunted nigh
  Had sought their household fires.

Drummer Hodge   **1. Hodge:** conventional name for a farm labourer. **3. kopje:** hill. **4. veldt:** open grassland. **9. Karoo:** semi-desert in central South Africa; the poem is set during the Boer War (1899-1902).   **The Darkling Thrush**   **Title:** in the dark. **1. coppice:** copse. **5. bine-stems:** the stems of woodbine (honeysuckle).

The land's sharp features seemed to be
    The Century's corpse outleant,   *10*
His crypt the cloudy canopy,
    The wind his death-lament.
The ancient pulse of germ and birth
    Was shrunken hard and dry,
And every spirit upon earth   *15*
    Seemed fervourless as I.

At once a voice arose among
    The bleak twigs overhead
In a full-hearted evensong
    Of joy illimited;   *20*
An aged thrush, frail, gaunt, and small,
    In blast-beruffled plume,
Had chosen thus to fling his soul
    Upon the growing gloom.

So little cause for carolings   *25*
    Of such ecstatic sound
Was written on terrestrial things
    Afar or nigh around,
That I could think there trembled through
    His happy good-night air   *30*
Some blessed Hope, whereof he knew
    And I was unaware.

December 1900.

    (1901)

THE MAN HE KILLED

"Had he and I but met
    By some old ancient inn,
We should have sat us down to wet
    Right many a nipperkin!

"But ranged as infantry,   *5*
    And staring face to face,
I shot at him as he at me,
    And killed him in his place.

"I shot him dead because —
    Because he was my foe,   *10*
Just so: my foe of course he was;
    That's clear enough; although

"He thought he'd 'list, perhaps,
    Off-hand like — just as I —
Was out of work — had sold his traps —   *15*
    No other reason why.

"Yes; quaint and curious war is!
    You shoot a fellow down
You'd treat if met where any bar is,
    Or help to half-a-crown."   *20*

    (1902)

THE CONVERGENCE OF THE TWAIN
(Lines on the loss of the "Titanic")

I

In a solitude of the sea
Deep from human vanity,
And the Pride of Life that planned her, stilly couches she.

II

Steel chambers, late the pyres
Of her salamandrine fires,   *5*
Cold currents thrid, and turn to rhythmic tidal lyres.

THE MAN HE KILLED **4. nipperkin:** a half-pint glass (of ale). **15. traps:** personal belongings.   THE CONVERGENCE OF THE TWAIN **Subtitle:** The R.M.S. *Titanic,* advertised as "unsinkable," collided with an iceberg and sank on its first voyage (Southampton-New York), 14-15 April 1912. **5. salamandrine:** According to legend, salamanders could live in fire. **6. thrid:** thread.

III

Over the mirrors meant
To glass the opulent
The sea-worm crawls — grotesque, slimed, dumb, indifferent.

IV

Jewels in joy designed   *10*
To ravish the sensuous mind
Lie lightless, all their sparkles bleared and black and blind.

V

Dim moon-eyed fishes near
Gaze at the gilded gear
And query: "What does this vaingloriousness down here?". . .   *15*

VI

Well: while was fashioning
This creature of cleaving wing,
The Immanent Will that stirs and urges everything

VII

Prepared a sinister mate
For her — so gaily great —   *20*
A Shape of Ice, for the time far and dissociate.

VIII

And as the smart ship grew
In stature, grace, and hue,
In shadowy silent distance grew the Iceberg too.

IX

Alien they seemed to be: *25*
No mortal eye could see
The intimate welding of their later history.

X

Or sign that they were bent
By paths coincident
On being anon twin halves of one august event,   *30*

XI

Till the Spinner of the Years
Said "Now!" And each one hears,
And consummation comes, and jars two hemispheres.

(1912)

CHANNEL FIRING

That night your great guns, unawares,
Shook all our coffins as we lay,
And broke the chancel window-squares,
We thought it was the Judgment-day

And sat upright. While drearisome   *5*
Arose the howl of wakened hounds:
The mouse let fall the altar-crumb,
The worms drew back into the mounds,

The glebe cow drooled. Till God called, "No;
It's gunnery practice out at sea   10
Just as before you went below;
The world is as it used to be:

"All nations striving strong to make
Red war yet redder. Mad as hatters
They do no more for Christés sake   15
Than you who are helpless in such matters.

"That this is not the judgment-hour
For some of them's a blessed thing,
For if it were they'd have to scour
Hell's floor for so much threatening. . . .   20

"Ha, ha. It will be warmer when
I blow the trumpet (if indeed
I ever do; for you are men,
And rest eternal sorely need)."

So down we lay again. "I wonder,   25
Will the world ever saner be,"
Said one, "than when He sent us under
In our indifferent century!"

And many a skeleton shook his head.
"Instead of preaching forty year,"   30
My neighbour Parson Thirdly said,
"I wish I had stuck to pipes and beer."

Again the guns disturbed the hour,
Roaring their readiness to avenge,
As far inland as Stourton Tower,   35
And Camelot, and starlit Stonehenge.

April 1914.   *(1914)*

In Time of "The Breaking of Nations"

I

Only a man harrowing clods
  In a slow silent walk
With an old horse that stumbles and nods
  Half asleep as they stalk.

II

Only thin smoke without flame   5
  From the heaps of couch-grass;
Yet this will go onward the same
  Though Dynasties pass.

III

Yonder a maid and her wight
  Come whispering by: 10
War's annals will fade into night
  Ere their story die.

          (1917)

Afterwards

When the Present has latched its postern behind
    my tremulous stay,
  And the May month flaps its glad green leaves
    like wings,
Delicate-filmed as new-spun silk, will the
    neighbours say,
  "He was a man who used to notice such things"?

If it be in the dusk when, like an eyelid's soundless
    blink,   5
  The dewfall-hawk comes crossing the shades
    to alight
Upon the wind-warped upland thorn, a gazer may think,
  "To him this must have been a familiar sight."

If I pass during some nocturnal blackness, mothy
    and warm,
  When the hedgehog travels furtively over the lawn,
One may say, "He strove that such innocent   11
    creatures should come to no harm,
  But he could do little for them; and now he is
    gone."

If, when hearing that I have been stilled at last, they
    stand at the door,
  Watching the full-starred heavens that winter sees,
Will this thought rise on those who will meet my
    face no more,   15
  "He was one who had an eye for such mysteries"?

And will any say when my bell of quittance is heard
    in the gloom,
  And a crossing breeze cuts a pause in its
    outrollings,
Till they rise again, as they were a new bell's boom,
  "He hears it not now, but used to notice such
    things"?

          (1917)

CHANNEL FIRING   9. glebe: the field next to a parsonage. 35-36. Stourton Tower, Camelot, Stonehenge: sites in the south of England, associated respectively with King Alfred (though Stourton Tower, known as "King Alfred's Tower," on Kingsettle Hill in Wiltshire, was built as late as 1772), King Arthur, and the Druids.   IN TIME OF "THE BREAKING OF NATIONS"   See Jeremiah 1:10, 51:20.   AFTERWARDS   1. postern: back gate.

THROWING A TREE
New Forest

The two executioners stalk along over the knolls,
Bearing two axes with heavy heads shining and wide,
And a long limp two-handled saw toothed for cutting great boles,
And so they approach the proud tree that bears the deathmark on its side.

Jackets doffed they swing axes and chop away just above ground,   *5*
And the chips fly about and lie white on the moss and fallen leaves;
Till a broad deep gash in the bark is hewn all the way round,
And one of them tries to hook upward a rope, which at last he achieves.

The saw then begins, till the top of the tall giant shivers:
The shivers are seen to grow greater each cut than before: *10*
They edge out the saw, tug the rope; but the tree only quivers,
And kneeling and sawing again, they step back to try pulling once more.

Then, lastly, the living mast sways, further sways: with a shout
Job and Ike rush aside. Reached the end of its long staying powers
The tree crashes downward: it shakes all its neighbours throughout,   *15*
And two hundred years steady growth has been ended in less than two hours.

(1928)

Ambrose Bierce
U.S.A., 1842-1914?

KILLED AT RESACA

The best soldier of our staff was Lieutenant Herman Brayle, one of the two aides-de-camp. I don't remember where the general picked him up; from some Ohio regiment, I think; none of us had previously known him, and it would have been strange if we had, for no two of us came from the same State, nor even from adjoining States. The general seemed to think that a position on his staff was a distinction that should be so   *5*
judiciously conferred as not to beget any sectional jealousies and imperil the integrity of that part of the country which was still an integer. He would not even choose officers from his own command, but by some jugglery at department headquarters obtained them from other brigades. Under such circumstances, a man's services had to be very distinguished indeed to be heard of by his family and the friends of his youth; and "the   *10*
speaking trump of fame" was a trifle hoarse from loquacity, anyhow.

THROWING A TREE   **Title:** felling a tree. **Subtitle:** New Forest (once a royal hunting ground, named in 1079) is located southwest of Southampton, in Hampshire. **KILLED AT RESACA**   The battle at Resaca, in northwestern Georgia, during the American Civil War, took place in May 1864. **10-11. "the speaking . . . fame":** In *English Bards and Scotch Reviewers* (1809), Byron (see p. 824) takes a satirical stab at Amos Cottle (c.1768-1800), who had published some feebly translated verse: "Amos Cottle strikes the lyre in vain . . . . Oh, Amos Cottle! — Phoebus! what a name / To fill the speaking trump of future fame!" (396-400).

Lieutenant Brayle was more than six feet in height and of splendid proportions, with the light hair and gray-blue eyes which men so gifted usually find associated with a high order of courage. As he was commonly in full uniform, especially in action, when most officers are content to be less flamboyantly attired, he was a very striking and conspicuous figure. As to the rest, he had a gentleman's manners, a scholar's head, and a lion's heart. His age was about thirty. 15

We all soon came to like Brayle as much as we admired him, and it was with sincere concern that in the engagement at Stone's River — our first action after he joined us — we observed that he had one most objectionable and unsoldierly quality: he was vain of his courage. During all the vicissitudes and mutations of that hideous encounter, whether our troops were fighting in the open cotton fields, in the cedar thickets, or behind the railway embankment, he did not once take cover, except when sternly commanded to do so by the general, who usually had other things to think of than the lives of his staff officers — or those of his men, for that matter. 20

25

In every later engagement while Brayle was with us it was the same way. He would sit his horse like an equestrian statue, in a storm of bullets and grape, in the most exposed places — wherever, in fact, duty, requiring him to go, permitted him to remain — when, without trouble and with distinct advantage to his reputation for common sense, he might have been in such security as is possible on a battlefield in the brief intervals of personal inaction. 30

On foot, from necessity or in deference to his dismounted commander or associates, his conduct was the same. He would stand like a rock in the open when officers and men alike had taken to cover; while men older in service and years, higher in rank and of unquestionable intrepidity, were loyally preserving behind the crest of a hill lives infinitely precious to their country, this fellow would stand, equally idle, on the ridge, facing in the direction of the sharpest fire. 35

When battles are going on in open ground it frequently occurs that the opposing lines, confronting each other within a stone's throw for hours, hug the earth as closely as if they loved it. The line officers in their proper places flatten themselves no less, and the field officers, their horses all killed or sent to the rear, crouch beneath the infernal canopy of hissing lead and screaming iron without a thought of personal dignity. 40

In such circumstances the life of a staff officer of a brigade is distinctly "not a happy one," mainly because of its precarious tenure and the unnerving alternations of emotion to which he is exposed. From a position of that comparative security from which a civilian would ascribe his escape to a "miracle," he may be despatched with an order to some commander of a prone regiment in the front line — a person for the moment inconspicuous and not always easy to find without a deal of search among men somewhat preoccupied, and in a den in which question and answer alike must be imparted in the sign language. It is customary in such cases to duck the head and scuttle away on a keen run, an object of lively interest to some thousands of admiring marksmen. In returning — well, it is not customary to return. 45

50

19: The battle of Stones River (also called the battle of Murfreesboro), in eastern Tennessee, took place from 31 December 1862 to 2 January 1863.
43-44. "not . . . one": from Gilbert and Sullivan's *The Pirates of Penzance* (1879): "When constabulary duty's to be done, / A policeman's lot is not a happy one."

Brayle's practice was different. He would consign his horse to the care of an orderly, — he loved his horse, — and walk quietly away on his perilous errand with never a stoop of the back, his splendid figure, accentuated by his uniform, holding the eye with a strange fascination. We watched him with suspended breath, our hearts in our mouths. On one occasion of this kind, indeed, one of our number, an impetuous stammerer, was so possessed by his emotion that he shouted at me:

"I'll b-b-bet you t-two d-d-dollars they d-drop him b-b-before he g-gets to that d-d-ditch!"

I did not accept the brutal wager; I thought they would.

Let me do justice to a brave man's memory; in all these needless exposures of life there was no visible bravado nor subsequent narration. In the few instances when some of us had ventured to remonstrate, Brayle had smiled pleasantly and made some light reply, which, however, had not encouraged a further pursuit of the subject. Once he said:

"Captain, if ever I come to grief by forgetting your advice, I hope my last moments will be cheered by the sound of your beloved voice breathing into my ear the blessed words, 'I told you so.'"

We laughed at the captain — just why we could probably not have explained — and that afternoon when he was shot to rags from an ambuscade Brayle remained by the body for some time, adjusting the limbs with needless care — there in the middle of a road swept by gusts of grape and canister! It is easy to condemn this kind of thing, and not very difficult to refrain from imitation, but it is impossible not to respect, and Brayle was liked none the less for the weakness which had so heroic an expression. We wished he were not a fool, but he went on that way to the end, sometimes hard hit, but always returning to duty about as good as new.

Of course, it came at last; he who ignores the law of probabilities challenges an adversary that is seldom beaten. It was at Resaca, in Georgia, during the movement that resulted in the taking of Atlanta. In front of our brigade the enemy's line of earthworks ran through open fields along a slight crest. At each end of this open ground we were close up to him in the woods, but the clear ground we could not hope to occupy until night, when darkness would enable us to burrow like moles and throw up earth. At this point our line was a quarter-mile away in the edge of a wood. Roughly, we formed a semicircle, the enemy's fortified line being the chord of the arc.

"Lieutenant, go tell Colonel Ward to work up as close as he can get cover, and not to waste much ammunition in unnecessary firing. You may leave your horse."

When the general gave this direction we were in the fringe of the forest, near the right extremity of the arc. Colonel Ward was at the left. The suggestion to leave the horse obviously enough meant that Brayle was to take the longer line, through the woods and among the men. Indeed, the suggestion was needless; to go by the short route meant absolutely certain failure to deliver the message. Before anybody could interpose, Brayle had cantered lightly into the field and the enemy's works were in crackling conflagration.

"Stop that damned fool!" shouted the general.

A private of the escort, with more ambition than brains, spurred forward to obey, and within ten yards left himself and his horse dead on the field of honor.

Brayle was beyond recall, galloping easily along, parallel to the enemy and less than two hundred yards distant. He was a picture to see! His hat had been blown or shot from his head, and his long, blond hair rose and fell with the motion of his horse. He sat erect in the saddle, holding the reins lightly in his left hand, his right hanging carelessly   *100* at his side. An occasional glimpse of his handsome profile as he turned his head one way or the other proved that the interest which he took in what was going on was natural and without affectation.

The picture was intensely dramatic, but in no degree theatrical. Successive scores of rifles spat at him viciously as he came within range, and our line in the edge of the   *105* timber broke out in visible and audible defense. No longer regardful of themselves or their orders, our fellows sprang to their feet, and swarming into the open sent broad sheets of bullets against the blazing crest of the offending works, which poured an answering fire into their unprotected groups with deadly effect. The artillery on both sides joined the battle, punctuating the rattle and roar with deep, earth-shaking   *110* explosions and tearing the air with storms of screaming grape, which from the enemy's side splintered the trees and spattered them with blood, and from ours defiled the smoke of his arms with banks and clouds of dust from his parapet.

My attention had been for a moment drawn to the general combat, but now, glancing down the unobscured avenue between these two thunderclouds, I saw Brayle,   *115* the cause of the carnage. Invisible now from either side, and equally doomed by friend and foe, he stood in the shot-swept space, motionless, his face toward the enemy. At some little distance lay his horse. I instantly saw what had stopped him.

As topographical engineer I had, early in the day, made a hasty examination of the ground, and now remembered that at that point was a deep and sinuous gully, crossing   *120* half the field from the enemy's line, its general course at right angles to it. From where we now were it was invisible, and Brayle had evidently not known about it. Clearly, it was impassable. Its salient angles would have afforded him absolute security if he had chosen to be satisfied with the miracle already wrought in his favor and leapt into it. He could not go forward, he would not turn back; he stood awaiting death. It did not keep   *125* him long waiting.

By some mysterious coincidence, almost instantaneously as he fell, the firing ceased, a few desultory shots at long intervals serving rather to accentuate than break the silence. It was as if both sides had suddenly repented of their profitless crime. Four stretcher-bearers of ours, following a sergeant with a white flag, soon afterward moved   *130* unmolested into the field, and made straight for Brayle's body. Several Confederate officers and men came out to meet them, and with uncovered heads assisted them to take up their sacred burden. As it was borne toward us we heard beyond the hostile works fifes and a muffled drum — a dirge. A generous enemy honored the fallen brave.   *135*

Amongst the dead man's effects was a soiled Russia-leather pocketbook. In the distribution of mementoes of our friend, which the general, as administrator, decreed, this fell to me.

A year after the close of the war, on my way to California, I opened and idly inspected it. Out of an overlooked compartment fell a letter without envelope or address.   *140* It was in a woman's handwriting, and began with words of endearment, but no name.

It had the following date line: "San Francisco, Cal., July 9, 1862." The signature was "Darling," in marks of quotation. Incidentally, in the body of the text, the writer's full name was given — Marian Mendenhall.

The letter showed evidence of cultivation and good breeding, but it was an ordinary *145* love letter, if a love letter can be ordinary. There was not much in it, but there was something. It was this:

"Mr. Winters, whom I shall always hate for it, has been telling that at some battle in Virginia, where he got his hurt, you were seen crouching behind a tree. I think he wants to injure you in my regard, which he knows the story would do if I believed it. I could *150* bear to hear of my soldier lover's death, but not of his cowardice."

These were the words which on that sunny afternoon, in a distant region, had slain a hundred men. Is woman weak?

One evening I called on Miss Mendenhall to return the letter to her. I intended, also, to tell her what she had done — but not that she did it. I found her in a handsome *155* dwelling on Rincon Hill. She was beautiful, well bred — in a word, charming.

"You knew Lieutenant Herman Brayle," I said, rather abruptly. "You know, doubtless, that he fell in battle. Among his effects was found this letter from you. My errand here is to place it in your hands."

She mechanically took the letter, glanced through it with deepening color, and then, *160* looking at me with a smile, said:

"It is very good of you, though I am sure it was hardly worth while." She started suddenly and changed color. "This stain," she said, "is it — surely it is not —"

"Madam," I said, "pardon me, but that is the blood of the truest and bravest heart that ever beat." *165*

She hastily flung the letter on the blazing coals. "Uh! I cannot bear the sight of blood!" she said. "How did he die?"

I had involuntarily risen to rescue that scrap of paper, sacred even to me, and now stood partly behind her. As she asked the question she turned her face about and slightly upward. The light of the burning letter was reflected in her eyes and touched her cheek *170* with a tinge of crimson like the stain upon its page. I had never seen anything so beautiful as this detestable creature.

"He was bitten by a snake," I replied.

(1891)

Selected definitions from *THE DEVIL'S DICTIONARY*

ACTUALLY, *adv.* Perhaps; possibly.

ALONE, *adj.* In bad company.

BORE, *n.* A person who talks when you wish him to listen.

CONSERVATIVE, *n.* A statesman who is enamored of existing evils, as distinguished from the Liberal, who wishes to replace them with others.

CONSULT, *v.t.* To seek another's approval of a course already decided on.

CONTEMPT, *n.* The feeling of a prudent man for an enemy who is too formidable safely to be opposed.

DEFAME, *v.t.* To lie about another. To tell the truth about another.

DIPLOMACY, *n.* The patriotic art of lying for one's country.

DISTANCE, *n.* The only thing that the rich are willing for the poor to call theirs, and keep.

HERS, *pron.* His.

LOGIC, *n.* The art of thinking and reasoning in strict accordance with the limitations and incapacities of the human misunderstanding. The basis of logic is the syllogism, consisting of a major and a minor premise and a conclusion — thus:
Major Premise: Sixty men can do a piece of work sixty times as quickly as one man.
Minor Premise: One man can dig a posthole in sixty seconds; therefore —
Conclusion: Sixty men can dig a posthole in one second.
This may be called the syllogism arithmetical, in which, by combining logic and mathematics, we obtain a double certainty and are twice blessed.

MAN, *n.* An animal so lost in rapturous contemplation of what he thinks he is as to overlook what he indubitably ought to be. His chief occupation is extermination of other animals and his own species, which, however, multiplies with such insistent rapidity as to infest the whole habitable earth and Canada.

MORAL, *adj.* Conforming to a local and mutable standard of right. Having the quality of general expediency.

MYTHOLOGY, *n.* The body of a primitive people's beliefs concerning its origin, early history, heroes, deities and so forth, as distinguished from the true accounts which it invents later.

PREJUDICE, *n.* A vagrant opinion without visible means of support.

QUOTATION, *n.* The act of repeating erroneously the words of another.

RASH, *adj.* Insensible to the value of our advice.

REALLY, *adv.* Apparently.

RITE, *n.* A religious or semi-religious ceremony fixed by law, precept or custom, with the essential oil of sincerity carefully squeezed out of it.

SAINT, *n.* A dead sinner revised and edited.

SAW, *n.* A trite popular saying, or proverb. (Figurative and colloquial.) So called because it makes its way into a wooden head. Following are examples of old saws fitted with new teeth.
A man is known by the company he organizes.
A bird in the hand is worth what it will bring.
Better late than before anybody has invited you.
Half a loaf is better than a whole one if there is much else.
Think twice before you speak to a friend in need.
What is worth doing is worth the trouble of asking somebody to do it.
Of two evils choose to be the least.
Strike while your employer has a big contract.
Where there's a will there's a won't.

UN-AMERICAN, *adj.* Wicked, intolerable, heathenish.

(1911)

HENRY JAMES
U.S.A./England, 1843-1916

QUEBEC

A traveller who combines a taste for old towns with a love of letters ought not, I suppose, to pass through "the most picturesque city in America" without making an attempt to commemorate his impressions. His first impression will certainly have been that not America, but Europe, should have the credit of Quebec. I came, some days since, by a dreary night-journey, to Point Levi, opposite the town, and as we rattled toward our goal in the faint raw dawn, and, already attentive to "effects," I began to consult the misty window-panes and descried through the moving glass little but crude, monotonous woods, suggestive of nothing that I had ever heard of in song or story, I felt that the land would have much to do to give itself a romantic air. And, in fact, the feat is achieved with almost magical suddenness. The old world rises in the midst of the new in the manner of a change of scene on the stage. The St. Lawrence shines at your left, large as a harbour-mouth, gray with smoke and masts, and edged on its hither verge by a bustling water-side *faubourg* which looks French or English, or anything not local that you please; and beyond it, over against you, on its rocky promontory, sits the ancient town, belted with its hoary wall and crowned with its granite citadel. Now that I have been here a while I find myself wondering how the city would strike one if the imagination had not been bribed beforehand. The place, after all, is of the soil on which it stands; yet it appeals to you so cunningly with its little stock of transatlantic wares that you overlook its flaws and lapses, and swallow it whole. Fancy lent a willing hand the morning I arrived, and zealously retouched the picture. The very sky seemed to have been brushed in like the sky in an English water-colour, the light to filter down through an atmosphere more dense and more conscious. You cross a ferry, disembark at the foot of the rock on unmistakably foreign soil, and then begin to climb into the city proper — the city *intra muros*. These walls, to the American vision, are of course the sovereign fact of Quebec; you take off your hat to them as you clatter through the gate. They are neither very high nor, after all, very hoary. Our clear American air is hostile to those mellow deposits and incrustations which enrich the venerable surfaces of Europe. Still, they are walls; till but a short time ago they quite encircled the town; they are garnished with little slits for musketry and big embrasures for cannon; they offer here and there to the strolling bourgeoisie a stretch of grassy rampart; and they make the whole place definite and personal.

Before you reach the gates, however, you will have been reminded at a dozen points that you have come abroad. What is the essential difference of tone between street-life in an old civilisation and in a new? It seems something subtler and deeper than mere external accidents — than foreign architecture, than foreign pinks, greens, and yellows plastering the house-fronts, than the names of the saints on the corners, than

---

QUEBEC   **2.** *picturesque:* See Glossary. **13.** *faubourg:* district. **24.** *intra muros:* inside the walls.

all the pleasant crookedness, narrowness and duskiness, the quaint economised spaces, the multifarious detail, the brown French faces, the ruddy English ones. It seems to be the general fact of detail itself — the hint in the air of a slow, accidental accretion, in obedience to needs more timidly considered and more sparingly gratified than the pressing necessities of American progress. But apart from the metaphysics of the question, Quebec has a great many pleasant little ripe spots and amenities. You note the small, box-like houses in rugged stone or in stucco, each painted with uncompromising *naïveté* in some bright hue of the owner's fond choice; you note with joy, with envy, with momentary self-effacement, as a New Yorker, as a Bostonian, the innumerable calashes and cabs which contend for your selection; and you observe when you arrive at the hotel, that this is a blank and gloomy inn, of true provincial aspect, with slender promise of the "American plan." Perhaps, even the clerk at the office will have the courtesy of the ages of leisure. I confess that, in my case, he was terribly modern, so that I was compelled to resort for a lodging to a private house near by, where I enjoy a transitory glimpse of the *vie intime* of Quebec. I fancied, when I came in, that it would be a compensation for worse quarters to possess the little Canadian vignette I enjoy from my windows. Certain shabby Yankee sheds, indeed, encumber the foreground, but they are so near that I can overlook them. Beyond is a piece of garden, attached to nothing less than a convent of the cloistered nuns of St. Ursula. The convent chapel rises inside it, crowned with what seemed to me, in view of the circumstances, a real little *clocher de France*. The "circumstances," I confess, are simply a couple of stout French poplars. I call them French because they are alive and happy; whereas, if they had been American they would have died of a want of appreciation, like their brothers in the "States." I do not say that the little convent-belfry, roofed and coated as it is with quaint scales of tin, would, by itself, produce any very deep illusion; or that the whispering poplars, *per se*, would transport me to the Gallic mother-land; but poplars and belfry together constitute an "effect" — strike a musical note in the scale of association. I look fondly even at the little casements which command this prospect, for they too are an old-world heritage. They open sidewise, in two wings, and are screwed together by that bothersome little iron handle over which we have fumbled so often in European inns.

If the windows tell of French dominion, of course larger matters testify with greater eloquence. In a place so small as Quebec, the bloom of novelty of course rubs off; but when first I walked abroad I fancied myself again in a French seaside town where I once spent a year, in common with a large number of economically disposed English. The French element offers the groundwork, and the English colony wears, for the most part, that half-genteel and migratory air which stamps the exiled and provincial British. They look as if they were still *en voyage* — still in search of low prices — the men in woollen shirts and Scotch bonnets; the ladies with a certain look of being equipped for dangers and difficulties. Your very first steps will be likely to lead you to the market-place, which is a genuine bit of Europeanism. One side of it is occupied by a huge edifice of yellow plaster, with stone facings painted in blue, and a manner of *porte-cochère*,

---

46. cabs: cabriolets, one-horse carriages. **48. American plan:** paying an inclusive rate for hotel room, meals, and service. **51.** *vie intime:* private life. **55. nuns of St. Ursula:** The Ursuline order was founded in France in 1537, and Ursuline schools for girls were established in Quebec in the early 17th century. **57.** *clocher de France:* bell tower; **stout:** sturdy. **73.** *en voyage:* travelling. **77.** *porte-cochère:* carriage entrance.

leading into a veritable court — originally, I believe, a college of the early Jesuits, now a place of military stores. On the other stands the French cathedral, with an ample stone façade, a bulky stone tower, and a high-piled, tin-scaled belfry; not architectural, of course, nor imposing, but with a certain gray maturity, and, as regards the belfry, a quite adequate quaintness. Round about are shops and houses, touching which, I think, it is no mere fancy that they might, as they stand, look down into some dull and rather dirty *place* in France. The stalls and booths in the centre — tended by genuine peasants of tradition, brown-faced old Frenchwomen, with hard wrinkles and short petticoats, and white caps beneath their broad-brimmed hats, and more than one price, as I think you'll find — these, and the stationed calèches and cabriolets complete a passably fashionable French picture. It is a proof of how nearly the old market-women resemble their originals across the sea that you rather resentfully miss one or two of the proper features of the type — the sabots for the feet and the donkey for the load. Of course you go into the cathedral, and how forcibly that swing of the door, as you doff your hat in the cooler air, recalls the old tourist strayings and pryings beneath other skies! You find a big garish church, with a cold high light, a promiscuity of stucco and gilding, and a mild odour of the seventeenth century. It is, perhaps, a shade or so more sensibly Catholic than it would be with ourselves; but, in fine, it has pews and a boarded floor, and the few paintings are rather pale in their badness, and you are forced to admit that the old-world tone which sustains itself so comfortably elsewhere falters most where most is asked of it.

Among the other lions of Quebec — notably in the Citadel — you find Protestant England supreme. A robust trooper of her Majesty, with a pair of very tight trousers and a very small cap, takes charge of you at the entrance of the fortifications, and conducts you through all kinds of incomprehensible defences. I cannot speak of the place as an engineer, but only as a tourist, and the tourist is chiefly concerned with the view. This is altogether superb, and if Quebec is not the most picturesque city in America, this is no fault of its incomparable site. Perched on its mountain of rock, washed by a river as free and ample as an ocean-gulf, sweeping from its embattled crest, the villages, the forests, the blue undulations of the imperial province of which it is warden — as it has managed from our scanty annals to squeeze out a past, you pray in the name of all that's majestic that it may have a future. I may add that, to the mind of the reflective visitor, these idle ramparts and silent courts present other visions than that of the mighty course of the river and its anchorage for navies. They evoke a shadowy image of that great English power, the arches of whose empire were once built strong on foreign soil; and as you stand where they are highest and look abroad upon a land of alien speech, you seem to hear the echoed names of other strongholds and provinces — Gibraltar, Malta, India. Whether these arches are crumbling now, I do not pretend to say; but the last regular troops (in number lately much diminished) are just about to be withdrawn from Quebec, and in the private circles to which I have been admitted I hear sad forebodings of what society will lose by the departure of the "military." This single word is eloquent; it reveals a social order distinctly affiliated, in spite of remoteness, to the society reproduced for the pacific American in novels in which the hero is a captain of the army or navy, and of

---

84. *place*: open square.

which the scene is therefore necessarily laid in countries provided with these branches of the public service. Another opportunity for some such reflections, worthy of a historian or an essayist, as those I have hinted at, is afforded you on the Plains of Abraham, to which you probably adjourn directly from the Citadel — another, but I am bound to say, in my opinion, a less inspiring one. A battlefield remains a battlefield, *125* whatever may be done to it; but the scene of Wolfe's victory has been profaned by the erection of a vulgar prison, and this memento of human infirmities does much to efface the meagre column which, with its neat inscription, "Here died Wolfe, victorious," stands there as a symbol of exceptional virtue.

  To express the historical interest of the place completely, I should dwell on the light *130* provincial — French provincial — aspect of some of the little residential streets. Some of the houses have the staleness of complexion which Balzac loved to describe. They are chiefly built of stone or brick, with a stoutness and separateness of structure which stands in some degree in stead of architecture. I know not that, externally, they have any greater charm than that they belong to that category of dwellings which in our own *135* cities were long since pulled down to make room for brown-stone fronts. I know not, indeed, that I can express better the picturesque merit of Quebec than by saying that it has no fronts of this luxurious and horrible substance. The greater number of houses are built of rough-hewn squares of some more vulgar mineral, painted with frank chocolate or buff, and adorned with blinds of a cruder green than we admire. As you pass the low *140* windows of these abodes, you perceive the walls to be of extraordinary thickness; the embrasure is of great depth; Quebec was built for winter. Door-plates are frequent, and you observe that the tenants are of the Gallic persuasion. Here and there, before a door, stands a comely private equipage — a fact agreeably suggestive of a low scale of prices; for evidently in Quebec one need not be a millionaire to keep a carriage, and one may *145* make a figure on moderate means. The great number of private carriages visible in the streets is another item, by the way, among the Europeanisms of the place; and not, as I may say, as regards the simple fact that they exist, but as regards the fact that they are considered needful for women, for young persons, for gentility. What does it do with itself, this gentility, keeping a gig or not, you wonder, as you stroll past its little multi- *150* coloured mansions. You strive almost vainly to picture the life of this French society, locked up in its small dead capital, isolated on a heedless continent, and gradually consuming its principal, as one may say — its vital stock of memories, traditions, superstitions. Its evenings must be as dull as the evenings described by Balzac in his *Vie de Province*; but has it the same ways and means of dulness? Does it play loto and *155* "boston" in the long winter nights, and arrange marriages between its sons and daughters, whose education it has confided to abbés and abbesses? I have met in the streets here little old Frenchmen who look as if they had stepped out of Balzac — bristling with the habits of a class, wrinkled with old-world expressions. Something assures one that Quebec must be a city of gossip; for evidently it is not a city of culture. *160* A glance at the few booksellers' windows gives evidence of this. A few Catholic

---

126. Wolfe: General James Wolfe (1727-1759), who died in the battle, as did the French commander, General Louis-Joseph Montcalm, Marquis de Montcalm (1712-1759). **132. Balzac:** Honoré de Balzac (1799-1850), French novelist, author of a multi-volume series called *La comédie humaine*, of which one group of novels, called *Etudes de moeurs* (1836-40), was subtitled *Scènes de la vie de province* (see lines 154-55). **155-56. loto, "boston":** card games, the latter resembling whist.

statuettes and prints, two or three Catholic publications, a festoon or so of rosaries, a volume of Lamartine, a supply of ink and matches, form the principal stock.

In the lower class of the French population there is a much livelier vitality. They are a genuine peasantry; you very soon observe it, as you drive along the pleasant country-roads. Just what it is that makes a peasantry, it is, perhaps, not easy to determine; but whatever it is, these good people have it — in their simple, unsharpened faces, in their narrow patois, in their ignorance and naïveté, and their evident good terms with the tin-spired parish church, standing there as bright and clean with ungrudged paint and varnish as a Nürnberg toy. One of them spoke to me with righteous contempt of the French of France — "They are worth nothing; they are bad Catholics." These are good Catholics, and I doubt whether anywhere Catholicism wears a brighter face and maintains more docility at the cost of less misery. It is, perhaps, not Longfellow's *Evangeline* for chapter and verse, but it is a tolerable prose transcript. There is no visible squalor, there are no rags and no curses, but there is a most agreeable tinge of gentleness, thrift, and piety. I am assured that the country-people are in the last degree mild and peaceable; surely, such neatness and thrift, without the irritability of the French genius — it is true the genius too is absent — is a very pleasant type of character. Without being ready to proclaim, with an enthusiastic friend, that the roadside scenery is more French than France, I may say that, in its way, it is quite as picturesque as anything within the city. There is an air of completeness and maturity in the landscape which suggests an old country. The roads, to begin with, are decidedly better than our own, and the cottages and farmhouses would need only a bit of thatch and a few red tiles here and there to enable them to figure creditably by the waysides of Normandy or Brittany. The road to Montmorency, on which tourists most congregate, is also, I think, the prettiest. The rows of poplars, the heavy stone cottages, seamed and cracked with time, in many cases, and daubed in coarse, bright hues, the little bourgeois villas, rising middle-aged at the end of short vistas, the sunburnt women in the fields, the old men in woollen stockings and red nightcaps, the long-kirtled curé nodding to doffed hats, the more or less bovine stare which greets you from cottage-doors, are all so many touches of a local colour reflected from over the sea. What especially strikes one, however, is the peculiar tone of the light and the atmospheric effects — the chilly whites and grays, the steely reflections, the melancholy brightness of a frigid zone. Winter here gives a stamp to the year, and seems to leave even through spring and summer a kind of scintillating trail of his presence. To me, I confess it is terrible, and I fancy I see constantly in the brilliant sky the hoary genius of the climate brooding grimly over his dominion.

The falls of Montmorency, which you reach by the pleasant avenue I speak of, are great, I believe, among the falls of the earth. They are certainly very fine, even in the attenuated shape to which they are reduced at the present season. I doubt whether you obtain anywhere in simpler and more powerful form the very essence of a cataract — the wild, fierce, suicidal plunge of a living, sounding flood. A little platform, lodged in the cliff, enables you to contemplate it with almost shameful convenience; here you may stand at your leisure and spin analogies, more or less striking, on the very edge of the

165

170

175

180

185

190

195

200

---

163. Lamartine: Alphonse de Lamartine (1790-1869), French romantic poet. **170. Nürnberg:** Nuremberg, German city famous for the quality of its handmade toys. **174. *Evangeline*:** See p. 932. **197. The falls of Montmorency:** alluded to at the end of Kemble's "Niagara" (p. 982).

white abyss. The leap of the water begins directly at your feet, and your eye trifles
dizzily with the long, perpendicular shaft of foam, and tries, in the eternal crash, to   *205*
effect some vague notation of its successive stages of sound and fury; but the vaporous
sheet, for ever dropping, lapses from beneath the eye, and leaves the vision distracted in
mid-space; and the vision, in search of a resting-place, sinks in a flurry to the infamous
saw-mill which defaces the very base of the torrent. The falls of Montmorency are
obviously one of the greatest of the beauties of nature; but I hope it is not beside the   *210*
mark to say that of all the beauties of nature, "falls" are to me the least satisfying. A
mountain, a precipice, a river, a forest, a plain, I can enjoy at my ease; they are natural,
normal, self-assured; they make no appeal; they imply no human admiration, no petty
human cranings and shrinkings, head-swimmings and similes. A cataract, of course, is
essentially violent. You are certain, moreover, to have to approach it through a turnstile,   *215*
and to enjoy it from some terribly cockneyfied little booth. The spectacle at Montmorency appears to be the private property of a negro innkeeper, who "runs" it evidently
with great pecuniary profit. A day or two since I went so far as to be glad to leave it
behind, and drive some five miles farther along the road, to a village rejoicing in the
pretty name of Château-Richer. The village is so pretty that you count on finding there   *220*
the elderly manor which might have baptized it. But, of course, in such pictorial efforts
as this Quebec breaks down; one must not ask too much of it. You enjoy from here,
however, a revelation of the noble position of the city. The river, finding room in mid-
stream for the long island of Orleans, opens out below you with a peculiar freedom and
serenity, and leads the eye far down to where an azure mountain gazes up the channel   *225*
and responds to the dark headland of Quebec. I noted, here and there, as I went, an
extremely sketchable effect. Between the road and river stand a succession of ancient
peasant-dwellings, with their backwindows looking toward the stream. Glancing, as I
passed, into the apertures that face the road, I saw, as through a picture-frame, their
dark, rich-toned interiors, played into by the late river light and making an admirable   *230*
series of mellow *tableaux de genre*. The little curtained alcoves, the big household beds,
and presses, and dressers, the black-mouthed chimney-pieces, the crucifixes, the old
women at their spinning-wheels, the little heads at the supper-table, around the big
French loaf, outlined with a rim of light, were all as warmly, as richly composed, as
French, as Dutch, as worthy of the brush, as anything in the countries to which artists   *235*
resort for subjects.

I suppose no patriotic American can look at all these things, however idly, without
reflecting on the ultimate possibility of their becoming absorbed into his own huge state.
Whenever, sooner or later, the change is wrought, the sentimental tourist will keenly
feel that a long stride has been taken, roughshod, from the past to the present. The   *240*
largest appetite in modern civilisation will have swallowed the largest morsel. What the
change may bring of comfort or of grief to the Canadians themselves, will be for them

---

231. *tableaux de genre*: A common form of theatrical presentation in the late 19th and early 20th centuries was the tableau or "living picture," in
which a group of actors, by adopting still poses, would suggest a famous person or recreate a familiar scene, incident, or painting; such "genres" or
"types" of tableau after a while became conventional, and the word "tableau" came by extension to be applied to scenes in real life that corresponded
to the conventions of theatre. **232. presses:** free-standing clothes closets.

to say; but, in the breast of this sentimental tourist of ours, it will produce little but regret. The foreign elements of eastern Canada, at least, are extremely interesting; and it is of good profit to us Americans to have near us, and of easy access, an ample *245* something which is not our expansive selves. Here we find a hundred mementoes of an older civilisation than our own, of different manners, of social forces once mighty, and still glowing with a sort of autumnal warmth. The old-world needs which created the dark-walled cities of France and Italy seem to reverberate faintly in the steep and narrow and Catholic streets of Quebec. The little houses speak to the fancy by rather *250* inexpensive arts; the ramparts are endued with a sort of silvery innocence; but the historic sense, conscious of a general solidarity in the picturesque, ekes out the romance and deepens the colouring.

(1871, 1884)

GERARD MANLEY HOPKINS
England, 1844-1889

GOD'S GRANDEUR

The world is charged with the grandeur of God.
   It will flame out, like shining from shook foil;
   It gathers to a greatness, like the ooze of oil
Crushed. Why do men then now not reck his rod?
Generations have trod, have trod, have trod;   *5*
   And all is seared with trade; bleared, smeared with toil;
   And wears man's smudge and shares man's smell: the soil
Is bare now, nor can foot feel, being shod.

And for all this, nature is never spent;
   There lives the dearest freshness deep down things;   *10*
And though the last lights off the black West went
   Oh, morning, at the brown brink eastward, springs —
Because the Holy Ghost over the bent
   World broods with warm breast and with ah! bright wings.

(1877; 1895)

GOD'S GRANDEUR In this and other poems, Hopkins devised a system of metrics he called "sprung rhythm" (see Glossary), in which each line had a fixed number of primary stresses but a varying number of unstressed syllables (which he referred to as "outrides" or "hangers"); in crafting what he called "inscape" — or poetic design — he also used counterpoint extensively (interweaving different rhythmic patterns), drew on the effects of Old English alliterative verse, and coined many new words (e.g., "wanwood" and "leafmeal" in "Spring and Fall," "shadowtackle" and "firedint" in "That Nature Is a Heraclitean Fire"). **2. foil:** In a letter to Robert Bridges (4 January 1883), Hopkins observed: "I mean foil in its sense of leaf or tinsel. . . . Shaken goldfoil gives off broad glares like sheet lightning." **13. Holy Ghost:** See Luke 3:22

The Windhover:
To Christ our Lord

I caught this morning morning's minion, king-
   dom of daylight's dauphin, dapple-dawn-drawn Falcon, in his riding
   Of the rolling level underneath him steady air, and striding
High there, how he rung upon the rein of a wimpling wing
In his ecstasy! then off, off forth on swing,   *5*
   As a skate's heel sweeps smooth on a bow-bend: the hurl and gliding
   Rebuffed the big wind. My heart in hiding
Stirred for a bird, — the achieve of, the mastery of the thing!

Brute beauty and valour and act, oh, air, pride, plume, here
   Buckle! AND the fire that breaks from thee then, a billion   *10*
Times told lovelier, more dangerous, O my chevalier!

No wonder of it: shéer plód makes plough down sillion
Shine, and blue-bleak embers, ah my dear,
Fall, gall themselves, and gash gold-vermilion.
                        (1877; 1918)

Pied Beauty

Glory be to God for dappled things —
   For skies of couple-colour as a brinded cow;
      For rose-moles all in stipple upon trout that swim;
Fresh-firecoal chestnut-falls; finches' wings;
   Landscape plotted and pieced — fold, fallow, and plough;   *5*
   And áll trádes, their gear and tackle and trim.

All things counter, original, spare, strange;
   Whatever is fickle, freckled (who knows how?)
     With swift, slow; sweet, sour; adazzle, dim;
He fathers-forth whose beauty is past change: *10*
       Praise him.
                    (1877; 1918)

Spring and Fall:
to a young child

Márgarét, áre you gríeving
Over Goldengrove unleaving?
Leáves, líke the things of man, you
With your fresh thoughts care for, can you?
Áh! ás the heart grows older   *5*
It will come to such sights colder
By and by, nor spare a sigh
Though worlds of wanwood leafmeal lie;
And yet you wíll weep and know why.
Now no matter, child, the name: *10*
Sórrow's spríngs áre the same.
Nor mouth had, no nor mind, expressed
What heart heard of, ghost guessed:
It ís the blight man was born for,
It is Margaret you mourn for.   *15*
          (1880; 1893)

The Windhover   Title: the kestrel, or sparrow-hawk, which can hover in the wind. **12. sillion:** selion, or "narrow land," the ridge or strip of land formed between furrows; or, more loosely, the furrow itself.

"AS KINGFISHERS CATCH FIRE"

As kingfishers catch fire, dragonflies dráw fláme;
As tumbled over rim in roundy wells
Stones ring; like each tucked string tells, each hung bell's
Bow swung finds tongue to fling out broad its name;
Each mortal thing does one thing and the same: 5
Deals out that being indoors each one dwells;
Selves — goes itself; *myself* it speaks and spells,
Crying *Whát I do is me: for that I came.*

Í say móre: the just man justices;
Kéeps gráce: thát keeps all his goings graces;   10
Acts in God's eye what in God's eye he is —
Chríst — for Christ plays in ten thousand places,
Lovely in limbs, and lovely in eyes not his
To the Father through the features of men's faces.

(1882?; 1918)

THAT NATURE IS A HERACLITEAN FIRE
AND OF THE COMFORT
OF THE RESURRECTION

Cloud-puffball, torn tufts, tossed pillows ⎪ flaunt forth, then chevy on an air-
built thoroughfare: heaven-roysterers, in gay-gangs ⎪ they throng; they glitter in marches.
Down roughcast, down dazzling whitewash, ⎪ wherever an elm arches,
Shivelights and shadowtackle in long ⎪ lashes lace, lance, and pair.
Delightfully the bright wind boisterous ⎪ ropes, wrestles, beats earth bare   5
Of yestertempest's creases; in pool and rut peel parches
Squandering ooze to squeezed ⎪ dough, crust, dust; stanches, starches
Squadroned masks and manmarks ⎪ treadmire toil there
Footfretted in it. Million-fuelèd, ⎪ nature's bonfire burns on.
But quench her bonniest, dearest ⎪ to her, her clearest-selvèd spark   10
Man, how fast his firedint, ⎪ his mark on mind, is gone!
Both are in an unfathomable, all is in an enormous dark
Drowned. O pity and indig ⎪ nation! Manshape, that shone
Sheer off, disseveral, a star, ⎪ death blots black out; nor mark
        Is any of him at all so stark   15
But vastness blurs and time ⎪ beats level. Enough! the Resurrection,
A heart's-clarion! Away grief's gasping, ⎪ joyless days, dejection.
        Across my foundering deck shone

THAT NATURE IS A HERACLITEAN FIRE **Title:** alluding to Heraclitus of Ephesus (fl. 500 B.C.), whose doctrine of nature's impermanence is epitomized in the maxim "You can't step into the same river twice"; Heraclitus argued that change itself is the only "permanent" truth, that life is a constant state of "becoming" or transition, that all things carry their opposites within them (so that death is part of life, e.g.), that fire is the underlying element of all nature and is to be identified with life and reason, and that all "individual" souls are merely expressions of a universal "soul-fire." **1. chevy:** race, scamper. **4. shivelights:** i.e., shivered lights.

A beacon, an eternal beam. | Flesh fade, and mortal trash
Fall to the residuary worm; | world's wildfire, leave but ash: *20*
In a flash, at a trumpet crash,
I am all at once what Christ is, | since he was what I am, and
This Jack, joke, poor potsherd, | patch, matchwood, immortal diamond,
             Is immortal diamond.

                          (1888; 1918)

"THOU ART INDEED JUST, LORD"

Justus quidem tu es, Domine, si disputem tecum: verumtamen justa
loquar ad te: Quare via impiorum prosperatur? &c.

Thou art indeed just, Lord, if I contend
With thee; but, sir, so what I plead is just.
Why do sinners' ways prosper? and why must
Disappointment all I endeavour end?

   Wert thou my enemy, O thou my friend,   *5*
How wouldst thou worse, I wonder, than thou dost
Defeat, thwart me? Oh, the sots and thralls of lust
Do in spare hours more thrive than I that spend,

Sir, life upon thy cause. See, banks and brakes
Now, leavèd how thick! lacèd they are again   *10*
With fretty chervil, look, and fresh wind shakes

Them; birds build — but not I build; no, but strain,
Time's eunuch, and not breed one work that wakes.
Mine, O thou lord of life, send my roots rain.

                         (1889; 1893)

ROBERT BRIDGES
England, 1844-1930

LONDON SNOW

When men were all asleep the snow came flying,
In large white flakes falling on the city brown,
Stealthily and perpetually settling and loosely lying,
   Hushing the latest traffic of the drowsy town;
Deadening, muffling, stifling its murmurs failing;   *5*
Lazily and incessantly floating down and down:
   Silently sifting and veiling road, roof and railing;
Hiding difference, making unevenness even,

---

23. Jack: i.e. ordinary person.   **THOU ART INDEED JUST, LORD**   **Epigraph:** the Latin translation of Jeremiah 12:1, translated in the first three lines of the poem; the rest of the poem draws upon other verses in this chapter. **9. brakes:** thickets.

Into angles and crevices softly drifting and sailing.
　All night it fell, and when full inches seven　　　　　*10*
It lay in the depth of its uncompacted lightness,
The clouds blew off from a high and frosty heaven;
　And all woke earlier for the unaccustomed brightness
Of the winter dawning, the strange unheavenly glare:
The eye marvelled — marvelled at the dazzling whiteness;　　　*15*
　The ear hearkened to the stillness of the solemn air;
No sound of wheel rumbling nor of foot falling,
And the busy morning cries came thin and spare.
　Then boys I heard, as they went to school, calling,
They gathered up the crystal manna to freeze　　　　*20*
Their tongues with tasting, their hands with snowballing;
　Or rioted in a drift, plunging up to the knees;
Or peering up from under the white-mossed wonder,
"O look at the trees!" they cried, "O look at the trees!"
　With lessened load a few carts creak and blunder,　　　*25*
Following along the white deserted way,
A country company long dispersed asunder:
　When now already the sun, in pale display
Standing by Paul's high dome, spread forth below
His sparkling beams, and awoke the stir of the day.　　　*30*
　For now doors open, and war is waged with the snow;
And trains of sombre men, past tale of number,
Tread long brown paths, as toward their toil they go:
　But even for them awhile no cares encumber
Their minds diverted; the daily word is unspoken,　　　*35*
The daily thoughts of labour and sorrow slumber
At the sight of the beauty that greets them, for the charm they
　have broken.

(1880)

ALICE MEYNELL
England, 1847-1922

PARENTAGE

"When Augustus Caesar legislated against the unmarried citizens of Rome,
he declared them to be, in some sort, slayers of the people."

　Ah no! not these!
These, who were childless, are not they who gave
So many dead unto the journeying wave,
The helpless nurslings of the cradling seas;
Not they who doomed by infallible decrees　　　*5*
Unnumbered man to the innumerable grave.

　But those who slay
Are fathers. Theirs are armies. Death is theirs —
The death of innocences and despairs;
The dying of the golden and the grey.　　　*10*
The sentence, when these speak it, has no Nay.
And she who slays is she who bears, who bears.

(1896)

LONDON SNOW　**29. Paul's:** St. Paul's Cathedral.

WILLIAM ERNEST HENLEY
England, 1849-1903

INVICTUS

Out of the night that covers me,
  Black as the Pit from pole to pole,
I thank whatever gods may be
  For my unconquerable soul.

In the fell clutch of circumstance   5
  I have not winced nor cried aloud.
Under the bludgeonings of chance
  My head is bloody, but unbowed.

Beyond this place of wrath and tears
  Looms but the Horror of the shade,   *10*
And yet the menace of the years
  Finds, and shall find, me unafraid.

It matters not how strait the gate,
  How charged with punishments the scroll,
I am the master of my fate;   *15*
  I am the captain of my soul.

(1875, 1888)

SARAH ORNE JEWETT
U.S.A., 1849-1909

THE PASSING OF SISTER BARSETT

Mrs. Mercy Crane was of such firm persuasion that a house is meant to be lived in, that during many years she was never known to leave her own neat two-storied dwelling-place on the Ridge road. Yet being very fond of company, in pleasant weather she often sat in the side doorway looking out on her green yard, where the grass grew short and thick and was undisfigured even by a path toward the steps. All her faded green blinds   *5* were securely tied together and knotted on the inside by pieces of white tape; but now and then, when the sun was not too hot for her carpets, she opened one window at a time for a few hours, having pronounced views upon the necessity of light and air. Although Mrs. Crane was acknowledged by her best friends to be a peculiar person and very set in her ways, she was much respected, and one acquaintance vied with another in making   *10* up her melancholy seclusion by bringing her all the news they could gather. She had been left alone many years before by the sudden death of her husband from sunstroke, and though she was by no means poor, she had, as some one said, "such a pretty way of taking a little present that you couldn't help being pleased when you gave her anything."

    For a lover of society, such a life must have had its difficulties at times, except that   *15* the Ridge road was more traveled than any other in the township, and Mrs. Crane had invented a system of signals, to which she always resorted in case of wishing to speak to some one of her neighbors.

INVICTUS   **Title:** (Latin) Unconquered.

The afternoon was wearing late, one day toward the end of summer, and Mercy Crane sat in her doorway dressed in a favorite old-fashioned light calico and a small shoulder-shawl figured with large palm-leaves. She was making some tatting of a somewhat intricate pattern; she believed it to be the prettiest and most durable of trimmings, and having decorated her own wardrobe in the course of unlimited leisure, she was now making a few yards apiece for each of her more intimate friends, so that they might have something to remember her by. She kept glancing up the road as if she expected some one, but the time went slowly by, until at last a woman appeared to view, walking fast, and carrying a large bundle in a checked handkerchief.

Then Mercy Crane worked steadily for a short time without looking up, until the desired friend was crossing the grass between the dusty road and the steps. The visitor was out of breath, and did not respond to the polite greeting of her hostess until she had recovered herself to her satisfaction. Mrs. Crane made her the kind offer of a glass of water or a few peppermints, but was answered only by a shake of the head, so she resumed her work for a time until the silence should be broken.

"I have come from the house of mourning," said Sarah Ellen Dow at last, unexpectedly.

"You don't tell me that Sister Barsett ——"

"She's left us this time; she's really gone," and the excited news-bringer burst into tears. The poor soul was completely overwrought; she looked tired and wan, as if she had spent her forces in sympathy as well as hard work. She felt in her great bundle for a pocket-handkerchief, but was not successful in the search, and finally produced a faded gingham apron with long, narrow strings, with which she hastily dried her tears. The sad news appealed also to Mercy Crane, who looked across to the apple-trees, and could not see them for a dazzle of tears in her own eyes. The spectacle of Sarah Ellen Dow going home with her humble workaday possessions, from the house where she had gone in haste only a few days before to care for a sick person well known to them both, was a very sad sight.

"You sent word yesterday that you should be returnin' early this afternoon, and would stop. I presume I received the message as you gave it?" asked Mrs. Crane, who was tenacious in such matters; "but I do declare I never looked to hear she was gone."

"She's been failin' right along since yisterday about this time," said the nurse. "She's taken no notice to speak of, an' been eatin' the vally o' nothin', I may say, since I went there a-Tuesday. Her sisters both come back yesterday, an' of course I was expected to give up charge to them. They're used to sickness, an' both havin' such a name for bein' great housekeepers!"

Sarah Ellen spoke with bitterness, but Mrs. Crane was reminded instantly of her own affairs. "I feel condemned that I ain't begun my own fall cleanin' yet," she said, with an ostentatious sigh.

"Plenty o' time to worry about that," her friend hastened to console her.

"I do desire to have everything decent about my house," resumed Mrs. Crane. "There's nobody to do anything but me. If I was to be taken away sudden myself, I shouldn't want to have it said afterward that there was wisps under my sofy or — There! I can't dwell on my own troubles with Sister Barsett's loss right before me. I can't seem to believe she's really passed away; she always was saying she should go in some o' these spells, but I deemed her to be troubled with narves."

Sarah Ellen Dow shook her head. "I'm all nerved up myself," she said brokenly. "I made light of her sickness when I went there first, I'd seen her what she called dreadful low so many times; but I saw her looks this morning, an' I begun to believe her at last. Them sisters o' hers is the master for unfeelin' hearts. Sister Barsett was a-layin' there yesterday, an' one of 'em was a-settin' right by her tellin' how difficult 'twas for her to leave home, her niece was goin' to graduate to the high school, an' they was goin' to have a time in the evening, an' all the exercises promised to be extry interesting. Poor Sister Barsett knew what she said an' looked at her with contempt, an' then she give a glance at me an' closed up her eyes as if 'twas for the last time. I know she felt it." 65

70

Sarah Ellen Dow was more and more excited by a sense of bitter grievance. Her rule of the afflicted household had evidently been interfered with; she was not accustomed to be ignored and set aside at such times. Her simple nature and uncommon ability found satisfaction in the exercise of authority, but she had now left her post feeling hurt and wronged, besides knowing something of the pain of honest affliction. 75

"If it hadn't been for esteemin' Sister Barsett as I always have done, I should have told 'em No, an' held to it, when they asked me to come back an' watch to-night. 'Tain't for none o' their sakes, but Sister Barsett was a good friend to me in her way." Sarah Ellen broke down once more, and felt in her bundle again hastily, but the handkerchief was again elusive, while a small object fell out upon the doorstep with a bounce. 80

" 'Tain't nothin' but a little taste-cake I spared out o' the loaf I baked this mornin'," she explained, with a blush. "I was so shoved out that I seemed to want to turn my hand to somethin' useful an' feel I was still doin' for Sister Barsett. Try a little piece, won't you, Mis' Crane? I thought it seemed light an' good." 85

They shared the taste-cake with serious enjoyment, and pronounced it very good indeed when they had finished and shaken the crumbs out of their laps. "There's nobody but you shall come and do for me at the last, if I can have my way about things," said Mercy Crane impulsively. She meant it for a tribute to Miss Dow's character and general ability, and as such it was meekly accepted. 90

"You're a younger person than I be, an' less wore," said Sarah Ellen, but she felt better now that she had rested, and her conversational powers seemed to be refreshed by her share of the little cake. "Doctor Bangs has behaved real pretty, I can say that," she continued presently in a mournful tone. 95

"Heretofore, in the sickness of Sister Barsett, I have always felt to hope certain that she would survive; she's recovered from a sight o' things in her day. She has been the first to have all the new diseases that's visited this region. I know she had the spinal mergeetis months before there was any other case about," observed Mrs. Crane with satisfaction.

"An' the new throat troubles, all of 'em," agreed Sarah Ellen; "an' has made trial of all the best patent medicines, an' could tell you their merits as no one else could in this vicinity. She never was one that depended on herbs alone, though she considered 'em extremely useful in some cases. Everybody has their herb, as we know, but I'm free to say that Sister Barsett sometimes done everything she could to kill herself with such rovin' ways o' dosin'. She must see it now she's gone an' can't stuff down no more invigorators." Sarah Ellen Dow burst out suddenly with this, as if she could no longer contain her honest opinion. 100

105

THE PASSING OF SISTER BARSETT   83. taste-cake: sampler.

"There, there! you're all worked up," answered placid Mercy Crane, looking more interested than ever.

"An' she was dreadful handy to talk religion to other folks, but I've come to a realizin' sense that religion is somethin' besides opinions. She an' Elder French has been 110 mostly of one mind, but I don't know's they've got hold of all the religion there is."

"Why, why, Sarah Ellen!" exclaimed Mrs. Crane, but there was still something in her tone that urged the speaker to further expression of her feelings. The good creature was much excited, her face was clouded with disapproval.

"I ain't forgettin' nothin' about their good points either," she went on in a more 115 subdued tone, and suddenly stopped.

"Preachin' 'll be done away with soon or late — preachin' o' Elder French's kind," announced Mercy Crane, after waiting to see if her guest did not mean to say anything more. "I should like to read 'em out that verse another fashion: 'Be ye doers o' the word, not preachers only,' would hit it about right; but there, it's easy for all of us to 120 talk. In my early days I used to like to get out to meetin' regular, because sure as I didn't I had bad luck all the week. I didn't feel pacified 'less I'd been half a day, but I was out all day the Sabbath before Mr. Barlow died as he did. So you mean to say that Sister Barsett's really gone?"

Mrs. Crane's tone changed to one of real concern, and her manner indicated that 125 she had put the preceding conversation behind her with decision.

"She was herself to the last," instantly responded Miss Dow. "I see her put out a thumb an' finger from under the spread an' pinch up a fold of her sister Deckett's dress, to try an' see if 'twas all wool. I thought't wa'n't all wool, myself, an' I know it now by the way she looked. She was a very knowin' person about materials; we shall miss poor Mis' 130 Barsett in many ways, she was always the one to consult with about matters o' dress."

"She passed away easy at the last, I hope?" asked Mrs. Crane with interest.

"Why, I wa'n't there, if you'll believe it!" exclaimed Sarah Ellen, flushing, and looking at her friend for sympathy. "Sister Barsett revived up the first o' the afternoon, an' they sent for Elder French. She took notice of him, and he exhorted quite a spell, an' 135 then he spoke o' there being need of air in the room, Mis' Deckett havin' closed every window, an' she asked me of all folks if I hadn't better step out; but Elder French come too, an' he was very reasonable, an' had a word with me about Mis' Deckett an' Mis' Peak an' the way they was workin' things. I told him right out how they never come near when the rest of us was havin' it so hard with her along in the spring, but now they 140 thought she was re'lly goin' to die, they come settlin' down like a pair o' old crows in a field to pick for what they could get. I just made up my mind they should have all the care, if they wanted it. It didn't seem as if there was anything more I could do for Sister Barsett, an' I set there in the kitchen within call an' waited, an' when I heard 'em sayin', 'There, she's gone, she's gone!' an Mis' Deckett a-weep-in', I put on my bunnit and 145 stepped myself out into the road. I felt to repent after I had gone but a rod, but I was so worked up, an' I thought they'd call me back, an' then I was put out because they didn't, an' so here I be. I can't help it now." Sarah Ellen was crying again; she and Mrs. Crane could not look at each other.

119-20: Be ye . . . only: See James 1:22.

"Well, you set an' rest," said Mrs. Crane kindly, and with the merest shadow of disapproval. "You set an' rest, an' by an' by, if you'd feel better, you could go back an' just make a little stop an' inquire about the arrangements. I wouldn't harbor no feelin's, if they be inconsiderate folks. Sister Barsett has often deplored their actions in my hearin' an' wished she had sisters like other folks. With all her faults she was a useful person an' a good neighbor," mourned Mercy Crane sincerely. "She was one that always had somethin' interestin' to tell, an' if it wa'n't for her dyin' spells an' all that sort o' nonsense, she'd make a figger in the world, she would so. She walked with an air always, Mis' Barsett did; you'd ask who she was, if you hadn't known, as she passed you by. How quick we forget the outs about anybody that's gone! but I always feel grateful to anybody that's friendly, situated as I be. I shall miss her runnin' over. I can seem to see her now, comin' over the rise in the road. But don't you get in a way of takin' things too hard, Sarah Ellen! You've worked yourself all to pieces since I saw you last; you're gettin' to be as lean as a meetin'-house fly. Now, you're comin' in to have a cup o' tea with me, an' then you'll feel better. I've got some new molasses gingerbread that I baked this mornin'."

"I do feel beat out, Mis' Crane," acknowledged the poor little soul, glad of a chance to speak, but touched by this unexpected mark of consideration. "If I could ha' done as I wanted to I should be feelin' well enough; but to be set aside an' ordered about, where I'd taken the lead in sickness so much, an' knew how to deal with Sister Barsett so well! She might be livin' now, perhaps ——"

"Come; we'd better go in, 'tis gettin' damp," and the mistress of the house rose so hurriedly as to seem bustling. "Don't dwell on Sister Barsett an' her foolish folks no more; I wouldn't, if I was you."

They went into the front room, which was dim with the twilight of the half-closed blinds and two great syringa bushes that grew against them. Sarah Ellen put down her bundle and bestowed herself in the large, cane-seated rocking-chair. Mrs. Crane directed her to stay there a while and rest, and then come out into the kitchen when she got ready.

A cheerful clatter of dishes was heard at once upon Mrs. Crane's disappearance. "I hope she's goin' to make one o' her nice shortcakes, but I don't know's she'll think it quite worthwhile," thought the guest humbly. She desired to go out into the kitchen, but it was proper behavior to wait until she should be called. Mercy Crane was not a person with whom one could venture to take liberties. Presently Sarah Ellen began to feel better. She did not often find such a quiet place, or the quarter of an hour of idleness in which to enjoy it, and was glad to make the most of this opportunity. Just now she felt tired and lonely. She was a busy, unselfish, eager-minded creature by nature, but now, while grief was sometimes uppermost in her mind, and sometimes a sense of wrong, every moment found her more peaceful, and the great excitement little by little faded away.

"What a person poor Sister Barsett was to dread growin' old so she couldn't get about. I'm sure I shall miss her as much as anybody," said Mrs. Crane, suddenly opening the kitchen door, and letting in an unmistakable and delicious odor of shortcake that revived still more the drooping spirits of her guest. "An' a good deal of knowledge has died with her," she added, coming into the room and seeming to make it lighter.

"There, she knew a good deal, but she didn't know all, especially o' doctorin'," insisted Sarah Ellen from the rocking-chair, with an unexpected little laugh. "She used to 195 lay down the law to me as if I had neither sense nor experience, but when it came to her bad spells she'd always send for me. It takes everybody to know everything, but Sister Barsett was of an opinion that her information was sufficient for the town. She was tellin' me, the day I went there, how she disliked to have old Mis' Doubleday come an' visit with her, an' remarked that she called Mis' Doubleday very officious. 'Went right down 200 on her knees an' prayed,' says she. 'Anybody would have thought I was a heathen!' But I kind o' pacified her feelin's, an' told her I supposed the old lady meant well."

"Did she give away any of her things? — Mis' Barsett, I mean," inquired Mrs. Crane.

"Not in my hearin'," replied Sarah Ellen Dow. "Except one day, the first of the 205 week, she told her oldest sister, Mis' Deckett — 'twas that first day she rode over — that she might have her green quilted petticoat; you see it was a rainy day, an' Mis' Deckett had complained o' feelin' thin. She went right up an' got it, and put it on an' wore it off, an' I'm sure I thought no more about it, until I heard Sister Barsett groanin' dreadful in the night. I got right up to see what the matter was, an' what do you think 210 but she was wantin' that petticoat back, and not thinkin' any too well o' Nancy Deckett for takin' it when 'twas offered. 'Nancy never showed no sense o' propriety,' says Sister Barsett. I just wish you'd heard her go on!

"If she had felt to remember me," continued Sarah Ellen, after they had laughed a little, "I'd full as soon have some of her nice crockery-ware. She told me once, years 215 ago, when I was stoppin' to tea with her an' we were havin' it real friendly, that she should leave me her Britannia tea-set, but I ain't got it in writin', an' I can't say she's ever referred to the matter since. It ain't as if I had a home o' my own to keep it in, but I should have thought a great deal of it for her sake," and the speaker's voice faltered. "I must say that, with all her virtues, she never was a first-class housekeeper, but I 220 wouldn't say it to any but a friend. You never eat no preserves o' hers that wa'n't commencin' to work, an' you know as well as I how little forethought she had about puttin' away her woolens. I sat behind her once in meetin' when I was stoppin' with the Tremletts and so occupied a seat in their pew, an' I see between ten an' a dozen moth-millers come workin' out o' her fitch-fur tippet. They was flutterin' round her bonnet 225 same's 'twas a lamp. I should be mortified to death to have such a thing happen to me."

"Every housekeeper has her weak point. I've got mine as much as anybody else," acknowledged Mercy Crane with spirit, "but you never see no moth-millers come workin' out o' me in a public place."

"Ain't your oven beginnin' to get overhet?" anxiously inquired Sarah Ellen Dow, 230 who was sitting more in the draft, and could not bear to have any accident happen to the supper. Mrs. Crane flew to a shortcake's rescue, and presently called her guest to the table.

The two women sat down to deep and brimming cups of tea. Sarah Ellen noticed with great gratification that her hostess had put on two of the best tea-cups and some citron-melon preserves. It was not an every-day supper. She was used to hard fare, poor, 235 hard-working Sarah Ellen, and this handsome social attention did her good. Sister Crane

---

222. **work:** ferment. 224-25. **moth-millers:** moths whose wings look powdery white.

rarely entertained a friend, and it would be a pleasure to speak of the tea-drinking for weeks to come.

"You've put yourself out quite a consid'able for me," she acknowledged. "How pretty these cups is! You oughtn't to use 'em so common as for me. I wish I had a home *240* I could really call my own to ask you to, but 'tain't never been so I could. Sometimes I wonder what's goin' to become o' me when I get so I'm past work. Takin' care o' sick folks, an' bein' in houses where there's a sight goin' on an' everybody in a hurry, kind of wears on me now I'm most a-gittin' in years. I was wishin', the other day, that I could get with some comfortable kind of a sick person, where I could live right along *245* quiet as other folks do, but folks never sends for me 'less they're drove to it. I ain't laid up anything to really depend upon."

The situation appealed to Mercy Crane, well-to-do as she was and not burdened with responsibilities. She stirred uneasily in her chair, but could not bring herself to the point of offering Sarah Ellen the home she coveted. *250*

"Have some hot tea," she insisted in a matter-of-fact tone, and Sarah Ellen's face, which had been lighted by a sudden eager hopefulness, grew dull and narrow again.

"Plenty, plenty, Mis' Crane," she said sadly, "'tis beautiful tea — you always have good tea"; but she could not turn her thoughts from her own uncertain future. "None of our folks has ever lived to be a burden," she said presently, in a pathetic tone, putting *255* down her cup. "My mother was thought to be doin' well until four o'clock an' was dead at ten. My Aunt Nancy came to our house well at twelve o'clock an' died that afternoon; my father was sick but ten days. There was dear sister Betsy, she did go in consumption, but 'twa'n't an expensive sickness."

"I've thought sometimes about you, how you'd get past rovin' from house to house *260* one o' these days. I guess your friends will stand by you." Mrs. Crane spoke with unwonted sympathy, and Sarah Ellen's heart leaped with joy.

"You're real kind," she said simply. "There's nobody I set so much by. But I shall miss Sister Barsett, when all's said an' done. She's asked me many a time to stop with her when I wasn't doin' nothin'. We all have our failin's, but she was a friendly creeter. *265* I sha'n't want to see her laid away."

"Yes, I was thinkin' a few minutes ago that I shouldn't want to look out an' see the funeral go by. She's one o' the old neighbors. I s'pose I shall have to look, or I shouldn't feel right afterward," said Mrs. Crane mournfully. "If I hadn't got so kind of housebound," she added with touching frankness, "I'd just as soon go over with you an' *270* offer to watch this night."

"'Twould astonish Sister Barsett so I don't know but she'd return." Sarah Ellen's eyes danced with amusement; she could not resist her own joke, and Mercy Crane herself had to smile.

"Now I must be goin', or 'twill be dark," said the guest, rising, and sighing after she *275* had eaten her last crumb of gingerbread. "Yes, thank ye, you're real good; I will come back if I find I ain't wanted. Look what a pretty sky there is!" and the two friends went to the side door and stood together in a moment of affectionate silence, looking out toward the sunset across the wide fields. The country was still with that deep rural stillness which seems to mean the absence of humanity. Only the thrushes were singing *280* far away in the walnut woods beyond the orchard, and some crows were flying over and cawed once loudly, as if they were speaking to the women at the door.

Just as the friends were parting, after most grateful acknowledgments from Sarah Ellen Dow, some one came driving along the road in a hurry and stopped.

"Who's that with you, Mis' Crane?" called one of their near neighbors. 285

"It's Sarah Ellen Dow," answered Mrs. Crane. "What's the matter?"

"I thought so, but I couldn't rightly see. Come, they are in a peck o' trouble up to Sister Barsett's, wonderin' where you be," grumbled the man. "They can't do nothin' with her; she's drove off everybody an' keeps a-screechin' for you. Come, step along, Sarah Ellen, do!" 290

"Sister Barsett!" exclaimed both the women. Mercy Crane sank down upon the doorstep, but Sarah Ellen stepped out upon the grass all of a tremble, and went toward the wagon. "They said this afternoon that Sister Barsett was gone," she managed to say. "What did they mean?"

"Gone where?" asked the impatient neighbor. "I expect 'twas one of her spells. 295 She's come to. They say she wants somethin' hearty for her tea. Nobody can't take one step till you get there, neither."

Sarah Ellen was still dazed; she returned to the doorway, where Mercy Crane sat shaking with laughter. "I don't know but we might as well laugh as cry," she said in an aimless sort of way. "I know you too well to think you're going to repeat a single word. 300 Well, I'll get my bonnet an' start; I expect I've got consid'able to cope with, but I'm well rested. Good night, Mis' Crane; I certain did have a beautiful tea, whatever the future may have in store."

She wore a solemn expression as she mounted into the wagon in haste and departed, but she was far out of sight when Mercy Crane stopped laughing and went into the house. 305

(1892, 1893)

ROBERT LOUIS STEVENSON
Scotland / Western Samoa, 1850-1894

REQUIEM

Under the wide and starry sky,
Dig the grave and let me lie.
Glad did I live and gladly die,
  And I laid me down with a will.

This be the verse you grave for me: 5
Here he lies where he longed to be;
Home is the sailor, home from sea,
  And the hunter home from the hill.

(1887)

THE FOREIGNER AT HOME

"This is no' my ain house;
I ken by the biggin' o't."

A Scotsman may tramp the better part of Europe and the United States, and never again receive so vivid an impression of foreign travel and strange lands and manners as on his first excursion into England. The change from a hilly to a level country strikes him with delighted wonder. Along the flat horizon there arise the frequent venerable towers of churches. He sees at the end of airy vistas the revolution of the windmill sails. He may   5
go where he pleases in the future; he may see Alps, and Pyramids, and lions; but it will be hard to beat the pleasure of that moment. There are, indeed, few merrier spectacles than that of many windmills bickering together in a fresh breeze over a woody country; their halting alacrity of movement, their pleasant busyness, making bread all day with uncouth gesticulations, their air, gigantically human, as of a creature half alive, put a   10
spirit of romance into the tamest landscape. When the Scottish child sees them first he falls immediately in love; and from that time forward windmills keep turning in his dreams. And so, in their degree, with every feature of the life and landscape. The warm, habitable age of towns and hamlets, the green, settled, ancient look of the country; the lush hedgerows, stiles, and privy pathways in the fields; the sluggish, brimming rivers;   15
chalk and smock-frocks; chimes of bells and the rapid, pertly-sounding English speech
— they are all new to the curiosity; they are all set to English airs in the child's story that he tells himself at night. The sharp edge of novelty wears off; the feeling is blunted, but I doubt whether it is ever killed. Rather it keeps returning, ever the more rarely and strangely, and even in scenes to which you have been long accustomed suddenly awakes   20
and gives a relish to enjoyment or heightens the sense of isolation.

One thing especially continues unfamiliar to the Scotsman's eye — the domestic architecture, the look of streets and buildings; the quaint, venerable age of many, and the thin walls and warm colouring of all. We have, in Scotland, far fewer ancient buildings, above all in country places; and those that we have are all of hewn or harled   25
masonry. Wood has been sparingly used in their construction; the window-frames are sunken in the wall, not flat to the front, as in England; the roofs are steeper-pitched; even a hill farm will have a massy, square, cold and permanent appearance. English houses, in comparison, have the look of cardboard toys, such as a puff might shatter. And to this the Scotsman never becomes used. His eye can never rest consciously on   30
one of these brick houses — rickles of brick, as he might call them — or on one of these flat-chested streets, but he is instantly reminded where he is, and instantly travels back in fancy to his home. "This is no' my ain house; I ken by the biggin' o't." And yet perhaps it is his own, bought with his own money, the key of it long polished in his pocket; but it has not yet been, and never will be, thoroughly adopted by his imagina-   35
tion; nor does he cease to remember that, in the whole length and breadth of his native country, there was no building even distantly resembling it.

But it is not alone in scenery and architecture that we count England foreign. The constitution of society, the very pillars of the empire, surprise and even pain us. The

---

THE FOREIGNER AT HOME **Epigraph:** from a traditional Scottish song (see line 33). **15. privy:** private, personal. **25. harled:** roughcast. **31. rickles:** heaps. **33. ain:** own; **ken:** know; **biggin':** building.

dull, neglected peasant, sunk in matter, insolent, gross and servile, makes a startling 40
contrast with our own long-legged, long-headed, thoughtful, Bible-quoting ploughman.
A week or two in such a place as Suffolk leaves the Scotsman gasping. It seems
incredible that within the boundaries of his own island a class should have been thus
forgotten. Even the educated and intelligent, who hold our own opinions and speak in
our own words, yet seem to hold them with a difference or from another reason, and to 45
speak on all things with less interest and conviction. The first shock of English society is
like a cold plunge. It is possible that the Scot comes looking for too much, and to be
sure his first experiment will be in the wrong direction. Yet surely his complaint is
grounded; surely the speech of Englishmen is too often lacking in generous ardour, the
better part of the man too often withheld from the social commerce, and the contact of 50
mind with mind evaded as with terror. A Scottish peasant will talk more liberally out of
his own experience. He will not put you by with conversational counters and small jests;
he will give you the best of himself, like one interested in life and man's chief end. A
Scotsman is vain, interested in himself and others, eager for sympathy, setting forth his
thoughts and experience in the best light. The egoism of the Englishman is self- 55
contained. He does not seek to proselytise. He takes no interest in Scotland or the Scots,
and, what is the unkindest cut of all, he does not care to justify his indifference. Give
him the wages of going on and being an Englishman, that is all he asks; and in the
meantime, while you continue to associate, he would not be reminded of your baser
origin. Compared with the grand, tree-like self-sufficiency of his demeanour, the vanity 60
and curiosity of the Scot seem uneasy, vulgar, and immodest. That you should
continually try to establish human and serious relations, that you should actually feel an
interest in John Bull, and desire and invite a return of interest from him, may argue
something more awake and lively in your mind, but it still puts you in the attitude of a
suitor and a poor relation. Thus even the lowest class of the educated English towers 65
over a Scotsman by the head and shoulders.

    Different indeed is the atmosphere in which Scottish and English youth begin to
look about them, come to themselves in life, and gather up those first apprehensions
which are the material of future thought and, to a great extent, the rule of future conduct.
I have been to school in both countries, and I found, in the boys of the North, something 70
at once rougher and more tender, at once more reserve and more expansion, a greater
habitual distance chequered by glimpses of a nearer intimacy, and on the whole wider
extremes of temperament and sensibility. The boy of the South seems more wholesome,
but less thoughtful; he gives himself to games as to a business, striving to excel, but is
not readily transported by imagination; the type remains with me as cleaner in mind and 75
body, more active, fonder of eating, endowed with a lesser and a less romantic sense of
life and of the future, and more immersed in present circumstances. And certainly, for
one thing, English boys are younger for their age. Sabbath observance makes a series of
grim, and perhaps serviceable, pauses in the tenor of Scottish boyhood — days of great
stillness and solitude for the rebellious mind, when in the dearth of books and play, and 80

---

63. John Bull: a typical Englishman — after the title character in the satire *The History of John Bull* (1712; first published as *Law is a Bottomless Pit*) by the Scottish physician Dr. John Arbuthnot (1667-1735), a friend of Swift and Pope.

in the intervals of studying the Shorter Catechism, the intellect and senses prey upon and test each other. The typical English Sunday, with the huge midday dinner and the plethoric afternoon, leads perhaps to different results. About the very cradle of the Scot there goes a hum of metaphysical divinity; and the whole of two divergent systems is summed up, not merely speciously, in the two first questions of the rival catechisms, the   *85* English tritely inquiring, "What is your name?" the Scottish striking at the very roots of life with, "What is the chief end of man?" and answering nobly, if obscurely, "To glorify God, and to enjoy Him for ever." I do not wish to make an idol of the Shorter Catechism; but the fact of such a question being asked opens to us Scots a great field of speculation; and the fact that it is asked of all of us, from the peer to the ploughboy,   *90* binds us more nearly together. No Englishman of Byron's age, character, and history, would have had patience for long theological discussions on the way to fight for Greece; but the daft Gordon blood and the Aberdonian school-days kept their influence to the end. We have spoken of the material conditions; nor need much more be said of these: of the land lying everywhere more exposed, of the wind always louder and bleaker, of   *95* the black, roaring winters, of the gloom of high-lying, old stone cities, imminent on the windy seaboard; compared with the level streets, the warm colouring of the brick, the domestic quaintness of the architecture, among which English children begin to grow up and come to themselves in life. As the stage of the University approaches, the contrast becomes more express. The English lad goes to Oxford or Cambridge; there, in an ideal   *100* world of gardens, to lead a semi-scenic life, costumed, disciplined, and drilled by proctors. Nor is this to be regarded merely as a stage of education; it is a piece of privilege besides, and a step that separates him further from the bulk of his compatriots. At an earlier age the Scottish lad begins his greatly different experience of crowded class-rooms, of a gaunt quadrangle, of a bell hourly booming over the traffic of the city to   *105* recall him from the public-house where he has been lunching, or the streets where he has been wandering fancy-free. His college life has little of restraint, and nothing of necessary gentility. He will find no quiet clique of the exclusive, studious and cultured; no rotten borough of the arts. All classes rub shoulders on the greasy benches. The raffish young gentleman in gloves must measure his scholarship with the plain,   *110* clownish laddie from the parish school. They separate, at the session's end, one to smoke cigars about a watering-place, the other to resume the labours of the field beside his peasant family. The first muster of a college class in Scotland is a scene of curious and painful interest; so many lads, fresh from the heather, hang round the stove in cloddish embarrassment, ruffled by the presence of their smarter comrades, and afraid of   *115* the sound of their own rustic voices. It was in these early days, I think, that Professor Blackie won the affection of his pupils, putting these uncouth, umbrageous students at their ease with ready human geniality. Thus, at least, we have a healthy democratic atmosphere to breathe in while at work; even when there is no cordiality there is always

---

81. Shorter Catechism: a set of religious instructions, devised in 1648, used in the Presbyterian Church (see lines 85-89). The Anglican Catechism (also devised as a set of questions-and-answers) appeared in *The Book of Common Prayer* (1549). **91-93. Byron . . . Gordon blood . . . Aberdonian school-days:** George Gordon, Lord Byron (see p. 824), of the Scottish Clan Gordon, was raised and educated in Aberdeen. **109. rotten borough:** the name given to an electoral district that did not have enough voters to justify a separate representative, but that nonetheless elected one. **117. Blackie:** John Stuart Blackie (1809-1895), scholar at the Universities of Aberdeen and Edinburgh, who helped reform Scottish educational practice; **umbrageous:** ready to take offence.

a juxtaposition of the different classes, and in the competition of study the intellectual *120* power of each is plainly demonstrated to the other. Our tasks ended, we of the North go forth as freemen into the humming, lamplit city. At five o'clock you may see the last of us hiving from the college gates, in the glare of the shop-windows, under the green glimmer of the winter sunset. The frost tingles in our blood; no proctor lies in wait to intercept us; till the bell sounds again, we are the masters of the world; and some portion *125* of our lives is always Saturday, *la trêve de Dieu.*

Nor must we omit the sense of the nature of his country and his country's history gradually growing in the child's mind from story and from observation. A Scottish child hears much of shipwreck, outlying iron skerries, pitiless breakers, and great sea-lights; much of heathery mountains, wild clans, and hunted Covenanters. Breaths come to him *130* in song of the distant Cheviots and the ring of foraying hoofs. He glories in his hard-fisted forefathers, of the iron girdle and the handful of oatmeal, who rode so swiftly and lived so sparely on their raids. Poverty, ill-luck, enterprise, and constant resolution are the fibres of the legend of his country's history. The heroes and kings of Scotland have been tragically fated; the most marking incidents in Scottish history — Flodden, Darien, *135* or the Forty-five — were still either failures or defeats; and the fall of Wallace and the repeated reverses of the Bruce combine with the very smallness of the country to teach rather a moral than a material criterion for life. Britain is altogether small, the mere taproot of her extended empire; Scotland, again, which alone the Scottish boy adopts in his imagination, is but a little part of that, and avowedly cold, sterile, and unpopulous. It *140* is not so for nothing. I once seemed to have perceived in an American boy a greater readiness of sympathy for lands that are great, and rich, and growing, like his own. It proved to be quite otherwise: a mere dumb piece of boyish romance, that I had lacked penetration to divine. But the error serves the purpose of my argument; for I am sure, at least, that the heart of young Scotland will be always touched more nearly by paucity of *145* number and Spartan poverty of life.

So we may argue, and yet the difference is not explained. That Shorter Catechism which I took as being so typical of Scotland, was yet composed in the city of West-minster. The division of races is more sharply marked within the borders of Scotland itself than between the countries. Galloway and Buchan, Lothian and Lochaber, are like *150* foreign parts; yet you may choose a man from any of them, and, ten to one, he shall prove to have the headmark of a Scot. A century and a half ago the Highlander wore a different costume, spoke a different language, worshipped in another church, held different morals, and obeyed a different social constitution from his fellow-countrymen either of the south or north. Even the English, it is recorded, did not loathe the *155* Highlander and the Highland costume as they were loathed by the remainder of the Scots. Yet the Highlander felt himself a Scot. He would willingly raid into the Scottish

---

126. *la trêve de Dieu*: (French) the truce of God. **129. skerries:** rock islands. **130. Covenanters:** anti-episcopal defenders of Presbyterianism, particularly during the rule of Charles II and James II, who tried to extend the authority of the bishops into Scotland. **131. Cheviots:** hills on the Scotland-England border, the setting of the ballad "Chevy Chase." **135-37:** Flodden Field was the site of a Scots military defeat (1513); the Darien scheme (for establishing a Scottish colony in Panama), devised in 1695, failed in part because of the economic rivalry between Scots and English investors — a rivalry that was to some degree resolved by the Act of Union between England and Scotland in 1707; the Jacobite Rebellion of 1745 proved to be one of the last military resistances to the new political federation; Sir William Wallace (c.1274-1305), hero of the Battle of Stirling Bridge (1297), and Robert the Bruce (1274-1329), hero of the Battle of Bannockburn (1314), were Scottish patriots in wars against the English. **150. Galloway . . . Lochaber:** districts in mountainous and coastal Scotland. **152. headmark:** distinctiveness of head, face, and features.

lowlands; but his courage failed him at the border, and he regarded England as a perilous, unhomely land. When the Black Watch, after years of foreign service, returned to Scotland, veterans leaped out and kissed the earth at Portpatrick. They had been in   *160* Ireland, stationed among men of their own race and language, where they were well liked and treated with affection; but it was the soil of Galloway that they kissed, at the extreme end of the hostile lowlands, among a people who did not understand their speech, and who had hated, harried, and hanged them since the dawn of history. Last, and perhaps most curious, the sons of chieftains were often educated on the continent of   *165* Europe. They went abroad speaking Gaelic; they returned speaking, not English, but the broad dialect of Scotland. Now, what idea had they in their minds when they thus, in thought, identified themselves with their ancestral enemies? What was the sense in which they were Scottish and not English, or Scottish and not Irish? Can a bare name be thus influential on the minds and affections of men, and a political aggregation blind   *170* them to the nature of facts? The story of the Austrian Empire would seem to answer No; the far more galling business of Ireland clinches the negative from nearer home. Is it common education, common morals, a common language, or a common faith, that join men into nations? There were practically none of these in the case we are considering.

The fact remains: in spite of the difference of blood and language, the Lowlander   *175* feels himself the sentimental countryman of the Highlander. When they meet abroad they fall upon each other's necks in spirit; even at home there is a kind of clannish intimacy in their talk. But from his compatriot in the south the Lowlander stands consciously apart. He has had a different training; he obeys different laws; he makes his will in other terms, is otherwise divorced and married; his eyes are not at home in an   *180* English landscape or with English houses; his ear continues to remark the English speech; and even though his tongue acquire the Southern knack, he will still have a strong Scots accent of the mind.

(1887)

LADY AUGUSTA GREGORY
Ireland, 1852-1932

BOY DEEDS OF CUCHULAIN

It chanced one day, when Setanta was about seven years old, that he heard some of the people of his mother's house talking about King Conchubar's court at Emain Macha, and of the sons of kings and nobles that lived there, and that spent a great part of their time at games and at hurling. "Let me go and play with them there," he said to his

---

159. Black Watch: 42nd Royal Highland Regiment, so named because of the colour of their tartan kilts.   **BOY DEEDS OF CUCHULAIN**   Cuchulain was a great hero of Irish legend, whose exploits are often compared to those of Hercules. Under his youthful name Setanta, he was brought up in the home of his uncle, King Conchubar of Ulster (the brother of his mother, Dechtire), which he singlehandedly defended against the rulers of Connaught. Fergus, an early king of Ulster who turned the throne over to Conchubar, later became Cuchulain's tutor. **4. hurling:** a sport, similar to field hockey.

mother. "It is too soon for you to do that," she said, "but wait till such time as you are   5
able to travel so far, and till I can put you in charge of some one going to the court, that
will put you under Conchubar's protection." "It would be too long for me to wait for
that," he said, "but I will go there by myself if you will tell me the road." "It is too far
for you," said Dechtire, "for it is beyond Slieve Fuad, Emain Macha is." "Is it east or
west of Slieve Fuad?" he asked. And when she had answered him that, he set out there   10
and then, and nothing with him but his hurling stick, and his silver ball, and his little
dart and spear; and to shorten the road for himself he would give a blow to the ball and
drive it from him, and then he would throw his hurling stick after it, and the dart after
that again, and then he would make a run and catch them all in his hand before one of
them would have reached the ground.   15

So he went on until he came to the lawn at Emain Macha, and there he saw three
fifties of king's sons hurling and learning feats of war. He went in among them, and
when the ball came near him he got it between his feet, and drove it along in spite of
them till he had sent it beyond the goal. There was great surprise and anger on them
when they saw what he had done, and Follaman, King Conchubar's son, that was chief   20
among them, cried out to them to come together and drive out this stranger and make an
end of him. "For he has no right," he said, "to come into our game without asking leave,
and without putting his life under our protection. And you may be sure," he said, "that
he is the son of some common fighting man, and it is not for him to come into our game
at all." With that they all made an attack on him, and began to throw their hurling sticks 25
at him, and their balls and darts, but he escaped them all, and then he rushed at them,
and began to throw some of them to the ground. Fergus came out just then from the
palace, and when he saw what a good defence the little lad was making, he brought him
in to where Conchubar was playing chess, and told him all that had happened. "This is
no gentle game you have been playing," he said. "It is on themselves the fault is," said   30
the boy; "I came as a stranger, and I did not get a stranger's welcome." "You did not
know then," said Conchubar, "that no one can play among the boy troop of Emain
unless he gets their leave and their protection." "I did not know that, or I would have
asked it of them," he said. "What is your name and your family?" said Conchubar. "My
name is Setanta, son of Sualtim and of Dechtire," he said. When Conchubar knew that   35
he was his sister's son, he gave him a great welcome, and he bade the boy troop to let
him go safe among them. "We will do that," they said. But when they went out to play,
Setanta began to break through them, and to overthrow them, so that they could not
stand against him. "What are you wanting of them now?" said Conchubar. "I swear by
the gods my people swear by," said the boy, "I will not lighten my hand off them till   40
they have come under my protection the same way I have come under theirs." Then they
all agreed to give in to this; and Setanta stayed in the king's house at Emain Macha, and
all the chief men of Ulster had a hand in bringing him up.

There was a great smith in Ulster of the name of Culain, who made a feast at that
time for Conchubar and for his people. When Conchubar was setting out to the feast, he   45
passed by the lawn where the boy troop were at their games, and he watched them
awhile, and he saw how the son of Dechtire was winning the goal from them all. "That

---

31. stranger's welcome: Custom in many cultures required that strangers be welcomed hospitably.

little lad will serve Ulster yet," said Conchubar; "and call him to me now," he said, "and let him come with me to the smith's feast." "I cannot go with you now," said Setanta, when they had called to him, "for these boys have not had enough of play yet." "It would be too long for me to wait for you," said the king. "There is no need for you to wait; I will follow the track of the chariots," said Setanta. 50

So Conchubar went on to the smith's house, and there was a welcome before him, and fresh rushes were laid down, and there were poems and songs and recitals of laws, and the feast was brought in, and they began to be merry. And then Culain said to the king: "Will there be any one else of your people coming after you to-night?" "There will not," said Conchubar, for he forgot that he had told the little lad to follow him. "But why do you ask me that?" he said. "I have a great fierce hound," said the smith, "and when I take the chain off him, he lets no one come into the one district with himself, and he will obey no one but myself, and he has in him the strength of a hundred." "Loose him out," said Conchubar, "until he keeps a watch on the place." So Culain loosed him out, and the dog made a course round the whole district, and then he came back to the place where he was used to lie and to watch the house, and every one was in dread of him, he was so fierce and so cruel and so savage. 55, 60

Now, as to the boys at Emain, when they were done playing, every one went to his father's house, or to whoever was in charge of him. But Setanta set out on the track of the chariots, shortening the way for himself as he was used to do with his hurling stick and his ball. When he came to the lawn before the smith's house, the hound heard him coming, and began such a fierce yelling that he might have been heard through all Ulster, and he sprang at him as if he had a mind not to stop and tear him up at all, but to swallow him at the one mouthful. The little fellow had no weapon but his stick and his ball, but when he saw the hound coming at him, he struck the ball with such force that it went down his throat, and through his body. Then he seized him by the hind legs and dashed him against a rock until there was no life left in him. 65, 70

When the men feasting within heard the outcry of the hound, Conchubar started up and said: "It is no good luck brought us on this journey, for that is surely my sister's son that was coming after me, and that has got his death by the hound." On that all the men rushed out, not waiting to go through the door, but over walls and barriers as they could. But Fergus was the first to get to where the boy was, and he took him up and lifted him on his shoulder, and brought him in safe and sound to Conchubar, and there was great joy on them all. 75, 80

But Culain the smith went out with them, and when he saw his great hound lying dead and broken there was great grief in his heart, and he came in and said to Setanta: "There is no good welcome for you here." "What have you against the little lad?" said Conchubar. "It was no good luck that brought him here, or that made me prepare this feast for yourself, King," he said; "for from this out, my hound being gone, my substance will be wasted, and my way of living will be gone astray. And, little boy," he said, "that was a good member of my family you took from me, for he was the protector of my goods and my flocks and my herds and of all that I had." "Do not be vexed on account of that," said the boy, "and I myself will make up to you for what I have done." "How will you do that?" said Conchubar. "This is how I will do it: if there is a whelp of 85, 90 the same breed to be had in Ireland, I will rear him and train him until he is as good a hound as the one killed; and until that time, Culain," he said, "I myself will be your watch-dog, to guard your goods and your cattle and your house." "You have made a fair offer," said Conchubar. "I could have given no better award myself," said Cathbad the   *95* Druid. "And from this out," he said, "your name will be Cuchulain, the Hound of Culain." "I am better pleased with my own name of Setanta, son of Sualtim," said the boy. "Do not say that," said Cathbad, "for all the men in the whole world will some day have the name of Cuchulain in their mouths." "If that is so, I am content to keep it," said the boy. And this is how he came by the name Cuchulain.   *100*

It was a good while after that, Cathbad the Druid was one day teaching the pupils in his house to the northeast of Emain. There were eight boys along with him that day, and one of them asked him: "Do your signs tell of any special thing this day is favourable to?" "If any young man should take arms to-day," said Cathbad, "his name will be greater than any other name in Ireland. But his span of life will be short," he said.   *105*

Cuchulain was outside at play, but he heard what Cathbad said, and there and then he put off his playing suit, and he went straight to Conchubar's sleeping-room and said: "All good be with you, King!" "What is it you are wanting?" said Conchubar. "What I want is to take arms to-day." "Who put that into your head?" "Cathbad the Druid," said Cuchulain. "If that is so, I will not deny you," said Conchubar. Then he gave him his   *110* choice of arms, and the boy tried his strength on them, and there were none that pleased him or that were strong enough for him but Conchubar's own. So he gave him his own two spears, and his sword and his shield.

Just then Cathbad the Druid came in, and there was wonder on him, and he said: "Is it taking arms this young boy is?" "He is indeed," said the king. "It is sorry I would be   *115* to see his mother's son take arms on this day," said Cathbad. "Was it not yourself bade him do it?" said the king. "I did not surely," he said. "Then you have lied to me, boy," said Conchubar. "I told no lie, King," said Cuchulain, "for it was he indeed put it in my mind when he was teaching the others, for when one of them asked him if there was any special virtue in this day, he said that whoever would for the first time take arms to-day,   *120* his name would be greater than any other in Ireland, and he did not say any harm would come on him, but that his life would be short." "And what I said is true," said Cathbad, "there will be fame on you and a great name, but your lifetime will not be long." "It is little I would care," said Cuchulain, "if my life were to last one day and one night only, so long as my name and the story of what I had done would live after me." Then   *125* Cathbad said: "Well, get into a chariot now, and let us see if it was the truth I spoke."

Then Cuchulain got into a chariot and tried its strength, and broke it to pieces, and he broke in the same way the seventeen chariots that Conchubar kept for the boy troop at Emain, and he said: "These chariots are no use, Conchubar, they are not worthy of me." "Where is Jubair, son of Riangabra?" said Conchubar. "Here I am," he answered.   *130* "Make ready my own chariot, and yoke my own horses to it for this boy to try," said Conchubar. So he tried the king's chariot and shook it and strained it, and it bore him. "This is the chariot that suits me," he said. "Now, little one," said Jubair, "let us take out the horses and turn them out to graze." "It is too early for that, Jubair; let us drive on to where the boy troop are, that they may wish me good luck on the day of my taking   *135* arms." So they drove on, and all the lads shouted when they saw him — "Have you taken arms?" "I have indeed," said Cuchulain. "That you may do well in wounding and in first killing and in spoil-winning," they said; "but it is a pity for us, you to have left playing."

"Let the horses go graze now," said Jubair. "It is too soon yet," said Cuchulain,   *140* "and tell me where does that great road that goes by Emain lead to?" "It leads to Ath-an-Foraire, the watchers' ford in Slieve Fuad," said Jubair. "Why is it called the watchers' ford?" "It is easy to tell that; it is because some choice champion of the men of Ulster keeps watch there every day to do battle for the province with any stranger that might come to the boundary with a challenge." "Do you know who is in it to-day?" said   *145* Cuchulain. "I know well it is Conall Cearnach, the Victorious, the chief champion of the young men of Ulster and of all Ireland." "We will go on then to the ford," said Cuchulain. So they went on across the plain, and at the water's edge they found Conall, and he said: "And are those arms you have taken to-day, little boy?" "They are indeed," Jubair said for him. "May they bring him triumph and victory and shedding of first   *150* blood," said Conall. "But I think, little Hound," he said, "that you are too ready to take them; for you are not fit as yet to do a champion's work." "What is it you are doing here, Conall?" said the boy. "I am keeping watch and guard for the province." "Rise out of it, Conall," he said, "and for this one day let me keep the watch." "Do not ask that, little one," said Conall; "for you are not able yet to stand against trained fighting men."   *155* "Then I will go down to the shallows of Lough Echtra and see if I can redden my arms on either friend or enemy." "Then I will go with you myself," said Conall, "to take care of you and to protect you, that no harm may happen you." "Do not," said Cuchulain. "I will indeed," said Conall, "for if I let you go into a strange country alone, all Ulster would avenge it on me."   *160*

So Conall's horses were yoked to his chariot, and he set out to follow Cuchulain, for he had waited for no leave, but had set out by himself. When Cuchulain saw Conall coming up with him he thought to himself, "If I get a chance of doing some great thing, Conall will never let me do it." So he picked up a stone, the size of his fist, from the ground, and made a good cast at the yoke of Conall's chariot, so that he broke it, and the   *165* chariot came down, and Conall himself was thrown to the ground sideways. "What did you do that for?" he said. "It was to see could I throw straight, and if there was the making of a good champion in me." "Bad luck on your throwing and on yourself," said Conall. "And any one that likes may strike your head off now, for I will go with you no farther." "That is just what I wanted," said Cuchulain. And with that, Conall went back   *170* to his place at the ford.

As for the lad, he went on towards Lough Echtra in the south. Then Jubair said: "If you will listen to me, little one, I would like that we would go back now to Emain; for at this time the carving of the food is beginning there, and it is all very well for you that have your place kept for you between Conchubar's knees. But as to myself," he said, "it   *175* is among the chariot-drivers and the jesters and the messengers I am, and I must find a place and fight for myself where I can." "What is that mountain before us?" said Cuchulain. "That is Slieve Mourne, and that is Finncairn, the white cairn, on its top."

137. **That you may:** May you, I hope you (cf. line 181).

"Let us go to it," said Cuchulain. "We would be too long going there," said Jubair. "You are a lazy fellow," said Cuchulain; "and this my first adventure, and the first journey *180* you have made with me." "And that it may be my last," said Jubair, "if ever I get back to Emain again." They went on then to the cairn. "Good Jubair," said the boy, "show me now all that we can see of Ulster, for I do not know my way about the country yet." So Jubair showed him from the cairn all there was to see of Ulster, the hills and the plains and the duns on every side. "What is that sloping square plain before us to the south?" *185* "That is Magh Breagh, the fine meadow." "Show me the duns and strong places of that plain." So Jubair showed him Teamhair and Tailte, Cleathra and Cnobhach and the Brugh of Angus on the Boyne, and the dun of Nechtan Sceine's sons. "Are those the sons of Nechtan that say in their boasting they have killed as many Ulstermen as there are living in Ulster to-day?" "They are the same," said Jubair. "On with us then to that *190* dun," said Cuchulain. "No good will come to you through saying that," said Jubair; "and whoever may go there I will not go," he said. "Alive or dead, you must go there for all that," said Cuchulain. "Then if so, it is alive I will go there," said Jubair, "and it is dead I will be before I leave it."

They went on then to the dun of Nechtan's sons, and when they came to the green *195* lawn, Cuchulain got out of the chariot, and there was a pillar-stone on the lawn, and an iron collar about it, and there was Ogham writing on it that said no man that came there, and he carrying arms, should leave the place without giving a challenge to some one of the people of the dun. When Cuchulain had read the Ogham, he put his arms around the stone and threw it into the water that was there at hand. "I don't see it is any better there *200* than where it was before," said Jubair; "and it is likely this time you will get what you are looking for, and that is a quick death." "Good Jubair," said the boy, "spread out the coverings of the chariot now for me, until I sleep for a while." "It is no good thing you are going to do," said Jubair, "to be going to sleep in an enemy's country." He put out the coverings then, and Cuchulain lay down and fell asleep. *205*

It was just at that time, Foill, son of Nechtan Sceine, came out, and when he saw the chariot, he called out to Jubair, "Let you not unyoke those horses." "I was not going to unyoke them," said Jubair; "the reins are in my hands yet." "What horses are they?" "They are Conchubar's two speckled horses." "So I thought when I saw them," said Foill. "And who is it has brought them across our boundaries?" "A young little lad," said Jubair, "that *210* has taken arms to-day for luck, and it is to show himself off he has come across Magh Breagh." "May he never have good luck," said Foill, "and if he were a fighting man, it is not alive but dead he would go back to Emain to-day." "Indeed he is not able to fight, or it could not be expected of him," said Jubair, "and he but a child that should be in his father's house." At that the boy lifted his head from the ground, and it is red his face was, and his *215* whole body, at hearing so great an insult put on him, and he said: "I am indeed well able to fight." But Foill said: "I am more inclined to think you are not." "You will soon know what to think," said the boy, "and let us go down now to the ford. But go first and get your armour," he said, "for I would not like to kill an unarmed man." There was anger on Foill then, and he went running to get his arms. "You must have a care now," said Jubair, "for *220* that is Foill, son of Nechtan, and neither point of spear or edge of sword can harm him."

---

185. duns: fortified residences, surrounded by concentric mounds and either moats or palisades. **197. Ogham:** ancient Celtic alphabet.

"That suits me very well," said the boy. With that out came Foill again, and Cuchulain stood up to him, and took his iron ball in his hand, and hurled it at his head, and it went through the forehead and out at the back of his head, and his brains along with it, so that the air could pass through the hole it made. And then Cuchulain struck off his head.   225

Then Tuachel, the second son of Nechtan, came out on the lawn. "It is likely you are making a great boast of what you are after doing," he said. "I see nothing to boast of in that," said Cuchulain, "a single man to have fallen by me." "You will not have long to boast of it," said Tuachel, "for I myself am going to make an end of you on the moment." "Then go back and bring your arms," said Cuchulain, "for it is only a coward   230 would come out without arms." He went back into the house then, and Jubair said: "You must have a care now, for that is Tuachel, son of Nechtan, and if he is not killed by the first stroke, or the first cast, or the first thrust, he cannot be killed at all, for there is no way of getting at him after that." "You need not be telling me that, Jubair," said Cuchulain, "for it is Conchubar's great spear, the Venomous, I will take in my hand, and   235 that is the last thrust that will be made at him, for after that, there is no physician will heal his wounds for ever."

Then Tuachel came out on the lawn, and Cuchulain took hold of the great spear, and made a cast at him, that went through his shield and broke three of his ribs, and made a hole through his heart. And then he struck his head off, before the body reached the ground.   240

Then Fainnle, the youngest of the three sons of Nechtan, came out. "Those were foolish fellows," he said, "to come at you the way they did. But come out now, after me," he said, "into the water where your feet will not touch the bottom," and with that he made a plunge into the water. "Mind yourself well now," said Jubair, "for that is Fainnle, the Swallow, and it is why that name was put on him, he travels across water   245 with the swiftness of a swallow, and there is not one of the swimmers of the whole world can come near him." "It is not to me you should be saying that," said Cuchulain, "for you know the river Callan that runs through Emain, and it is what I used to do," he said, "when the boy troop would break off from their games and plunge into the river to swim, I used to take a boy of them on each shoulder and a boy on each hand, and I   250 would bring them through the river without so much as to wet my back." With that he made a leap into the water, where it was very deep, and himself and Fainnle wrestled together, and then he got a grip of him, and gave him a blow of Conchubar's sword, and struck his head off, and he let his body go away down the stream.

Then he and Jubair went into the house and destroyed what was in it, and they set   255 fire to it, and left it burning, and turned back towards Slieve Fuad, and they brought the heads of the three sons of Nechtan along with them.

Presently they saw a herd of wild deer before them. "What sort of cattle are those?" said the boy. "They are not cattle, but the wild deer of the dark places of Slieve Fuad." "Make the horses go faster," said Cuchulain, "until we can see them better." But with all   260 their galloping the horses could not come up with the wild deer. Then Cuchulain got down from the chariot and raced and ran after them until two stags lay moaning and panting from the hardness of their run through the wet bog, and he bound them to the back of the chariot with the thongs of it. Then they went on till they came to the plain of Emain, and there they saw a flock of white swans that were whiter than the swans of   265 Conchubar's lake, and Cuchulain asked where they came from. "They are wild swans," said Jubair, "that are come from the rocks and the islands of the great sea to feed on the low levels of the country." "Would it be best to take them alive or to kill them?" "It would be best to take them alive," said Jubair, "for many a one kills them, and many a one makes casts at them, but you would hardly find any one at all would bring them in *270* alive." With that, Cuchulain put a little stone in his sling and made a cast, and brought down eight birds of them, and then he put a bigger stone in, and with it he brought down sixteen more. "Get out now, Jubair," he said, "and bring me the birds here." "I will not," said Jubair, "for it would not be easy to stop the horses the way they are going now, and if I leap out, the iron wheels of the chariot will cut through me, or the horns of the stags *275* will make a hole in me." "You are no good of a warrior, Jubair; but give me the reins and I will quiet the horses and the stags." So then Jubair went and brought in the swans, and tied them, and they alive, to the chariot and to the harness. And it is like that they went on till they came to Emain.

It was Levarcham, daughter of Aedh, the conversation woman and messenger to the *280* king, that was there at that time, and was sometimes away in the hills, was the first to see them coming. "There is a chariot-fighter coming, Conchubar," she said, "and he is coming in anger. He has the bleeding heads of his enemies with him in the chariot, and wild stags are bound to it, and white birds are bearing him company. By the oath of my people!" she said, "if he comes on us with his anger still upon him, the best of the men *285* of Ulster will fall by his hand." "I know that chariot-fighter," said Conchubar. "It is the young lad, the son of Dechtire, that went over the boundaries this very day. He has surely reddened his hand, and if his anger cannot be cooled, the young men of Emain will be in danger from him," he said.

Then they all consulted together, and it is what they agreed, to send out three fifties *290* of the women of Emain to meet him, and they uncovered. When the boy saw the women coming, there was shame on him, and he leaned down his head into the cushions of the chariot, and hid his face from them. And the wildness went out of him, and his feasting clothes were brought, and water for washing; and there was a great welcome before him.

This is the story of the boy deeds of Cuchulain, as it was told by Fergus to Ailell *295* and to Maeve at the time of the war for the Brown Bull of Cuailgne.

(1902)

Alice Jones
Canada, 1853-1933

A Day in Winchester

Twenty-five hours spent in the old Saxon and Norman capital do much to embody for one certain grand shadowy historical characters — Swithin, the saintly Bishop; William of Wykeham, prelate, architect, statesman; the sinister Gardiner; the great Canute; Emma, the slandered Saxon Queen; the gloomy Mary Tudor — all these seem to take a

fresh reality to one as one lounges in the grand old minster, scene of their triumphs or   5
sorrows. It was in a steady dispiriting September drizzle that we sallied forth from that
most clerical of inns, the "George," which is certainly old and fusty enough to have
been, as tradition says, the principal inn of the town for the last four hundred years. How
Dickens would have delighted in the archbishop of a head waiter, in the sanded floor
and old oak chairs of the smoking room.   10

The general view of the High Street cannot compare for quaint interest with that of
Guildford or many other country towns, but turning off by the old city cross with its
sculptured William of Wykeham and other old time worthies, we reach, with a few
steps, a stately elm avenue that leads to the great west front of the cathedral. Grand and
simple early English it is, but how sorry one feels that the low massive tower has no   15
spire to soar up, a centre and climax of the great pile.

Entering, one draws a deep breath at the solemnity of the interior. It is a shocking
confession, but used to the human interest given by the touch of homely tawdriness that
is always evident in foreign cathedrals, the artificial flowers, the humble tallow dips
burning before a shrine, the old peasant women kneeling in side chapels, one is almost   20
chilled by the grand stateliness and simpleness of an English cathedral. It gives one the
sensation of a room that is never lived in. One feels that the Dean's or Canon's wives in
fine apparel would seem more suitable figures in such a background, than the shabby
old women telling their beads. This may be one's first fancy, but after a few moments,
the space and the simplicity affect one with a pleasure that is almost awe. This is the   25
longest cathedral in England, and the clustering pillars of the nave are of the purest early
English, overlaying the original Norman which, with its massiveness and bulk, still
holds its own in the transept. It was William of Wykeham who made this
transformation, but where can one turn in Winchester without coming on traces of the
life work of that grand old bishop? Presently there bears down upon us a little deaf old   30
man with his head on one side like a canary bird, and taking us in tow, he trots ahead,
and shews us all the architectural and historical splendours of the place.

The choir, with the marvellous stone tracery of its rood screen where the empty
niches and central space tell of the images and great cross of silver carried off by Henry
VIII; with its oaken roof of Charles I's time, painted with a white ground, and blazoned   35
in gay colours with heraldic emblems — with the carving of its twelfth century pulpit
and stalls, and wooden chests, perched high at intervals above the side screens, into
which, at some early medieval date, were bundled the bones, good, bad and indifferent,
of the Saxon and Danish kings buried in the Minster, not even the mighty Canute being
spared from this miscellaneous elevation.   40

A DAY IN WINCHESTER   The city of Winchester, once capital of Wessex and England, lies on the River Itchen in Hampshire. The historical
names cited in the text all refer to figures associated with the city's history. Among them, Saint Swithin (d.862) was Bishop of Winchester during
the time that the Saxon King Egbert ruled England. Several other bishops were politically influential during the later years of English Catholicism
and the early Reformation — William of Wykeham (1324-1404), who founded Winchester College in 1382 and was Chancellor of England; Henry
Beaufort (d.1447); Richard Fox (c.1448-1528); and Stephen Gardiner (c.1483-1555), who was hated because he persecuted Protestants in his last
years. Mary Tudor (1516-1558), i.e., Queen Mary I, was Elizabeth I's Roman Catholic sister. The story of the widow Alice Lisle (c.1614-1685)
reveals how political and religious rivalries continued to affect England during the later years of the Stuart Restoration; when Judge George Jeffreys
(1648-1689) sentenced Lisle to death on a trumped-up charge of high treason, she became, in legend, the "victim of a judicial murder." Winchester
Cathedral (begun in 1079) houses the tombs of several Saxon and Danish rulers — including those of Canute and his wife Emma (the widow of
Ethelred and mother of Edward the Confessor) — as well as those of William Rufus (the Plantagenet King William II, d.1100), and such literary
figures as Izaak Walton and Jane Austen.

In the side chapels are the chantries of the bishops of Winchester. Cardinal Beaufort's recumbent figure, gorgeous in his red gown, though the touching inscription, "I should be in anguish did I not know Thy mercies," is gone. Fox, and grim Gardiner, with the weird representation of their dead, nude bodies below the stately piles, though the popular rage against the latter had wreaked itself on this pitiful image of mortality *45* and severed the head from the body. But the chapel of the great St. Swithin lies directly behind the rood screen, and this, too, suffered from the same despoiler, Henry VIII, and lost its magnificent silver shrine. Here the remains of the sainted bishop lie in peace after their forty days conflict with the weather which has made his such a familiar household name to us. *50*

We pass the plain stone which marks the supposed tomb of William Rufus, and come to the Lady Chapel, where took place the gloomy marriage of Mary Tudor to Philip of Spain — there still stands the arm chair where she sat during the ceremony. What fascinate one here are the quaint, hardly decipherable frescoes of the miracles of The Virgin. Delightfully medieval in execution, some of them are slightly shaky in morals, *55* such as that of the robber knight, who remained safe from the devil as long as he never forgot his daily prayer to The Virgin. One feels overwhelmed when one tries to realise the place which this mighty pile holds in English history. A church was first built here in 169, but during Diocletian's persecutions in 266, it was destroyed and the priests martyred. In Constantine's reign, a second was erected, his son being a monk in the monastery hard by, *60* but again in 515 were the priests slaughtered by the fierce Saxon, Herdic, King of Wessex, who turned the church into a temple of Dagon, where he was both crowned and buried. In 635, his great grandson, Kynegils, converted by Saint Birinus, the first Saxon bishop, began a third church, finished by his son, and enlarged in 860 by St. Swithin, King Alfred's tutor. This church was almost ruined by the Danes, and restored by Alfred. Here, *65* in 800, Egbert was the first king crowned of all England — here Canute placed his crown over the crucified figure above the altar — here Queen Emma, Edward the Confessor's mother, who, falsely accused of intimacy with Alwyn, Bishop of Winchester, her property taken from her, and having fled to a convent, on appealing to the ordeal by fire, after spending the night in fasting and prayer, walked barefoot over nine red hot ploughshares *70* without suffering harm. Here, in the chapter house, Archbishop Langton absolved King John and his kingdom from the solemn interdict placed upon them, and subsequently said, at the high altar, the first mass performed for six years. Here Mary Tudor's marriage was celebrated with great pomp — and here, in 1644, Waller's army, after defeating Charles I, wrought devastation, Cromwell's soldiers being said to have used the cathedral as a stable, *75* and the church lands being seized for Government purposes.

On leaving the cathedral, Winchester great hall was the next bourne of our pilgrimage, a place which strikes nearly as echoing a key note in English history as the

---

41. chantries: areas in the chapels that have been endowed for the singing of mass in memory of particular persons. **47. despoiler:** After breaking from Catholicism, Henry VIII ordered Catholic monasteries in England to be destroyed and churches to be ransacked for their valuables. **49. forty days . . . weather:** referring to the legend that Swithin was buried in the churchyard, by choice, but that when he was canonized the monks thought to move him into the cathedral, whereupon it rained for forty days, delaying the move. **59-60. Diocletian, Constantine:** Roman emperors. **62. Dagon:** Philistine fertility god, represented as half man and half fish. **71. Langton:** Stephen Langton (c.1150-1228), Archbishop of Canterbury, who sided with the barons when they required King John (1167-1216) to sign the Magna Carta in 1215. **74. Waller:** Sir William Waller (c.1597-1668), Parliamentary general during the Civil War. **77. bourne:** site.

cathedral itself. We climbed the High Street to where the heavy old west gate overhangs it, and turned up to the buildings which Charles II began for a palace, and where the great hall is the only remnant of the Palace of the Norman Kings. A noble place it is, with its clustering pillars and windows of early English, and its carved oak roof. Tastefully and simply restored, every window glows with the arms of the mighty ones who have ruled here — a goodly array, beginning with the arms of King Arthur, the raven of Canute, and, following English history through the leopards of the Plantagenets, on to the Tudors and Stuarts. A heap of crumbling masonry at one end of the hall is said to be the remains of the Saxon dais, and above it, a curious slit in the wall marks the place where the king sat in his chamber above to listen unseen to the debates of his parliament. For four hundred years this was the meeting place of the English parliament, the pulse of English life. Many a strange scene have these old walls witnessed since the day when the mighty Earl Godwin, feasting here at Easter with Edward the Confessor, spoke in jest, as he watched an attendant slip on one foot and recover himself on the other — "Thus does one brother help another" — and the king, remembering his own suspicion that Godwin had caused his brother's death, made answer darkly, "So might I now be helped by my brother Alfred, if Godwin had not prevented it." Then Godwin, calling on Heaven to choke him with the bread he held if he were guilty, put it in his mouth, and choking, fell down dead, and the king said, "Carry away that dog and bury him in the highway." Here William and the other Norman kings lived — here was held Mary Tudor's wedding feast — here was played the shameful farce of Sir Walter Raleigh's trial. Oliver Cromwell does not fail to here play his usual grim role, for it was he who blew up all the rest of the Castle, besides destroying the Bishop's Palace, at the other end of the town. But Charles II, with true Stuart sense of beauty, was so charmed with the old hillside perch of the Norman kings, that he began to rebuild the palace, though his death left it unfinished; and what there is of it, is now used as law courts. Opening from the old hall, and edging the brow of the hill, these rooms have a noble outlook over the city and the surrounding hills, between which flows the slow and sleepy Itchin.

It was nearing evening, and the rain having stopped, a watery yellow light shone out low in the western sky, when we took a carriage and drove out for a mile or so, through the suburbs, to the Hospital of Saint Cross. It stands among the fringed meadows in the valley of the Itchin, and the first glimpse of the courtyard, and of the stately gateway, Cardinal Beaufort's tower, as it is called, prepares us for the treat inside. What perfection it is, that quiet quadrangle, with its grey buildings around, warmed here and there with a touch of red brickwork, its vivid patches of flower garden, and clambering creepers, its stretch of smoothest lawn, with sundial — no need to say old, for all is old here — which separates us from the low, massive church, beyond which we see the flat meadows. In the grey evening light, the whole scene is a perfect type of the care and skill with which in this wonderful little country of England, the old is grafted into the new.

In France, the yawning gulf of the revolution would have swallowed it with all else of its kind — in Italy it would probably have shared the fate of the monasteries, and be

---

91. Godwin: Godwin, or Godwine (d.1053), likely Danish by birth, was made Earl of Wessex (Earl of the West Saxons) by Canute; Godwin arranged for his own daughter Edith to marry Queen Emma's son, Edward the Confessor, and helped secure the throne for him, but relations between them rapidly cooled. **99. Raleigh:** See Ralegh's letters and the notes (p. 181).

now preserved, empty and useless, an aesthetic entertainment for the tourist — but here, *120* in this quiet nook, the routine of every day life has gone on unharmed by the din of ages. The reformation glided over it peacefully — and the civil wars spared it, and for nearly 700 years, its brothers have worn the silver cross and paced these quiet walks, and the horn of ale and slice of bread has never been denied to any wayfarer at its gates.

Founded by Bishop de Blois, in 1136, as the Hospital of Saint Cross, for thirteen poor *125* men, it was added to by Cardinal Beaufort as an Almshouse of Noble Poverty, for thirty-five brethren, and with ups and downs has enjoyed more or less power of doing good to this day. One heroic name is connected with its annals, that of Alice Lisle, condemned to be burnt by Jeffries, in Winchester market place, whose Puritan husband was once Master of St. Cross.

Following our directions, and seeking a guide, we disturbed one of the brothers over his *130* tea in his cozy little room, and after obeying his wife's orders to put on his thick gown, on which hung the badge of the silver cross, he led the way for us, jingling his keys. Gouty of foot, and infirm was this brother, so that, when standing he leant heavily upon his stick, but there was something both pleasant and intelligent in his massive face, and one liked him for his hearty interest and reverence for the place that sheltered his old days. We followed him to *135* the chapel, which is well worth study, with its heavy Norman arches, laden with dog-tooth tracery, and were soon absorbed in tracing the merging of one period into another, the transition Norman, of which this is said to be one of the most complete examples, into the late Decorated. But even more interesting than architecture was the tale which our guide told us of an old man's life — told with a warmth and heartiness which only personal friendship *140* could have caused. Not many years ago when the chapel had fallen into a sad state of disrepair, an old brother of eighty-one, named Richard King, who had been by trade a stone mason, one day accidentally discovered part of the noble tracery, hidden under plaster and whitewash, and little by little he himself, working singlehanded, brought out those hidden treasures to the light of day — following steadily his labour of love until his death, at the age *145* of ninety-one. But before that, some visitor, touched by the sight of his work, and by hearing its history, sent an anonymous contribution towards the restoration of seven hundred pounds. This was the commencement of the present state of beauty of the church, which has been most skilfully restored, the traces of the old frescoes being carefully copied. Taking us outside, to point out to us a unique dog-toothed arch, our guide shewed us this brave old *150* fellow's grave — a nameless one, for no headstones are allowed to the brethren, but the grass around it was carefully cut, and "Ah, yes, sir," he said — "And I used always to keep fresh flowers on it, until I got too shaky." His heart was opened, and he went on — "The people about would say sometimes, 'Ah, King, ye deserve a fine monument for all this!' but he would say, 'I don't want one, save in my work, and in the Lamb's Book of Life.' Ah, a *155* fine old fellow was King!" And I felt very kindly towards him as I saw that his smile had in it something akin to tears. Afterwards, we inspected the old hall where the brethren used to dine, and where the open brick fireplace in the centre of the room is still used on feast days for the roasting of joints; and saw the old pewter dishes and leathern jacks of Beaufort's days, and then neglecting to apply at the gate for the traveller's ale and bread, we drove back *160* to Winchester in the twilight, well pleased with our day.

(1888)

---

159. jacks: pitchers made of waxed leather.

OSCAR WILDE
Ireland/England, 1854-1900

THE HAPPY PRINCE

High above the city, on a tall column, stood the statue of the Happy Prince. He was gilded all over with thin leaves of fine gold, for eyes he had two bright sapphires, and a large red ruby glowed on his sword-hilt.

He was very much admired, indeed. "He is as beautiful as a weathercock," remarked one of the Town Councillors who wished to gain a reputation for having   5
artistic tastes; "only not quite so useful," he added, fearing lest people should think him unpractical, which he really was not.

"Why can't you be like the Happy Prince?" asked a sensible mother of her little boy who was crying for the moon. "The Happy Prince never dreams of crying for anything."

"I am glad there is some one in the world who is quite happy," muttered a   10
disappointed man as he gazed at the wonderful statue.

"He looks just like an angel," said the Charity Children as they came out of the cathedral in their bright scarlet cloaks, and their clean white pinafores.

"How do you know?" said the Mathematical Master, "you have never seen one."

"Ah! but we have, in our dreams," answered the children; and the Mathematical   15
Master frowned and looked very severe, for he did not approve of children dreaming.

One night there flew over the city a little Swallow. His friends had gone away to Egypt six weeks before, but he had stayed behind, for he was in love with the most beautiful Reed. He had met her early in the spring as he was flying down the river after a big yellow moth, and had been so attracted by her slender waist that he had stopped to talk to her.   20

"Shall I love you?" said the Swallow, who liked to come to the point at once, and the Reed made him a low bow. So he flew round and round her, touching the water with his wings, and making silver ripples. This was his courtship, and it lasted all through the summer.

"It is a ridiculous attachment," twittered the other Swallows, "she has no money,   25
and far too many relations"; and, indeed, the river was quite full of Reeds. Then, when the autumn came, they all flew away.

After they had gone he felt lonely, and began to tire of his lady-love. "She has no conversation," he said, "and I am afraid that she is a coquette, for she is always flirting with the wind." And certainly, whenever the wind blew, the Reed made the most   30
graceful curtsies. "I admit that she is domestic," he continued, "but I love travelling, and my wife, consequently, should love travelling also."

"Will you come away with me?" he said finally to her; but the Reed shook her head, she was so attached to her home.

"You have been trifling with me," he cried. "I am off to the Pyramids. Good-bye!"   35
and he flew away.

THE HAPPY PRINCE   **12. Charity Children:** i.e., students at a school funded by charitable donations.

All day long he flew, and at night-time he arrived at the city. "Where shall I put up?" he said; "I hope the town has made preparations."

Then he saw the statue on the tall column. "I will put up there," he cried; "it is a fine position with plenty of fresh air." So he alighted just between the feet of the Happy Prince. *40*

"I have a golden bedroom," he said softly to himself as he looked round, and he prepared to go to sleep; but just as he was putting his head under his wing a large drop of water fell on him. "What a curious thing!" he cried, "there is not a single cloud in the sky, the stars are quite clear and bright, and yet it is raining. The climate in the north of *45* Europe is really dreadful. The Reed used to like the rain but that was merely her selfishness."

Then another drop fell.

"What is the use of a statue if it cannot keep the rain off?" he said. "I must look for a good chimney-pot," and he determined to fly away. *50*

But before he had opened his wings, a third drop fell, and he looked up, and saw — Ah! what did he see?

The eyes of the Happy Prince were filled with tears, and tears were running down his golden cheeks. His face was so beautiful in the moonlight that the little Swallow was filled with pity. *55*

"Who are you?" he said.

"I am the Happy Prince."

"Why are you weeping then?" asked the Swallow; "you have quite drenched me."

"When I was alive and had a human heart," answered the statue, "I did not know what tears were, for I lived in the Palace of Sans Souci, where sorrow is not allowed to enter. In *60* the daytime I played with my companions in the garden, and in the evening I led the dance in the Great Hall. Round the garden ran a very lofty wall, but I never cared to ask what lay beyond it, everything about me was so beautiful. My courtiers called me the Happy Prince, and happy indeed I was, if pleasure be happiness. So I lived, and so I died. And now that I am dead they have set me up here so high that I can see all the ugliness and all *65* the misery of my city, and though my heart is made of lead yet I cannot choose but weep."

"What, is he not solid gold?" said the Swallow to himself. He was too polite to make any personal remarks out loud.

"Far away," continued the statue in a low, musical voice, "far away in a little street there is a poor house. One of the windows is open, and through it I can see a woman *70* seated at a table. Her face is thin and worn, and she has coarse red hands, all pricked by the needle, for she is a seamstress. She is embroidering passion-flowers on a satin gown for the loveliest of the Queen's maids-of-honour to wear at the next Court-ball. In a bed in the corner of the room her little boy is lying ill. He has a fever, and is asking for oranges. His mother has nothing to give him but river water, so he is crying. Swallow, *75* Swallow, little Swallow, will you not bring her the ruby out of my sword-hilt? My feet are fastened to this pedestal and I cannot move."

"I am waited for in Egypt," said the Swallow, "My friends are flying up and down the Nile, and talking to the large lotus-flowers. Soon they will be going to sleep in the

---

60. Sans Souci: (French) without care.

tomb of the great King. The King is there himself in his painted coffin. He is wrapped in $_{80}$ yellow linen, and embalmed with spices. Round his neck is a chain of pale green jade, and his hands are like withered leaves."

"Swallow, Swallow, little Swallow," said the Prince, "will you not stay with me for one night, and be my messenger? The boy is so thirsty, and the mother so sad."

"I don't think I like boys," answered the Swallow. "Last summer, when I was staying $_{85}$ on the river, there were two rude boys, the miller's sons, who were always throwing stones at me. They never hit me, of course; we swallows fly far too well for that, and besides, I come of a family famous for its agility; but still, it was a mark of disrespect."

But the Happy Prince looked so sad that the little Swallow was sorry. "It is very cold here," he said; "but I will stay with you for one night, and be your messenger." $_{90}$

"Thank you, little Swallow," said the Prince.

So the Swallow picked out the great ruby from the Prince's sword, and flew away with it in his beak over the roofs of the town.

He passed by the cathedral tower, where the white marble angels were sculptured. He passed by the palace and heard the sound of dancing. A beautiful girl came out on $_{95}$ the balcony with her lover. "How wonderful the stars are," he said to her, "and how wonderful is the power of love!" "I hope my dress will be ready in time for the State-ball," she answered; "I have ordered passion-flowers to be embroidered on it; but the seamstresses are so lazy."

He passed over the river, and saw the lanterns hanging to the masts of the ships. He $_{100}$ passed over the Ghetto, and saw the old Jews bargaining with each other, and weighing out money in copper scales. At last he came to the poor house and looked in. The boy was tossing feverishly on his bed, and the mother had fallen asleep, she was so tired. In he hopped, and laid the great ruby on the table beside the woman's thimble. Then he flew gently round the bed, fanning the boy's forehead with his wings. "How cool I feel," $_{105}$ said the boy, "I must be getting better"; and he sank into a delicious slumber.

Then the Swallow flew back to the Happy Prince and told him what he had done. "It is curious," he remarked, "but I feel quite warm now, although it is so cold."

"That is because you have done a good action," said the Prince. And the little Swallow began to think, and then he fell asleep. Thinking always made him sleepy. $_{110}$

When day broke he flew down to the river and had a bath. "What a remarkable phenomenon," said the Professor of Ornithology as he was passing over the bridge. "A swallow in winter!" And he wrote a long letter about it to the local newspaper. Every one quoted it, it was full of so many words that they could not understand.

"To-night I go to Egypt," said the Swallow, and he was in high spirits at the $_{115}$ prospect. He visited all the public monuments, and sat a long time on top of the church steeple. Wherever he went the sparrows chirruped, and said to each other, "What a distinguished stranger!" so he enjoyed himself very much.

When the moon rose he flew back to the Happy Prince. "Have you any commissions for Egypt?" he cried. "I am just starting." $_{120}$

"Swallow, Swallow, little Swallow," said the Prince "will you not stay with me one night longer?"

"I am waited for in Egypt," answered the Swallow. "To-morrow my friends will fly up to the Second Cataract. The river-horse couches there among the bulrushes, and on a great granite throne sits the God Memnon. All night long he watches the stars, and when the morning star shines he utters one cry of joy, and then he is silent. At noon the yellow lions come down to the water's edge to drink. They have eyes like green beryls, and their roar is louder than the roar of the cataract." *125*

"Swallow, Swallow, little Swallow," said the Prince, "far away across the city I see a young man in a garret. He is leaning over a desk covered with papers, and in a tumbler *130* by his side there is a bunch of withered violets. His hair is brown and crisp, and his lips are red as a pomegranate, and he has large and dreamy eyes. He is trying to finish a play for the Director of the Theatre, but he is too cold to write any more. There is no fire in the grate, and hunger has made him faint."

"I will wait with you one night longer," said the Swallow, who really had a good *135* heart. "Shall I take him another ruby?"

"Alas! I have no ruby now," said the Prince; "my eyes are all that I have left. They are made of rare sapphires, which were brought out of India a thousand years ago. Pluck out one of them and take it to him. He will sell it to the jeweller, and buy food and firewood, and finish his play." *140*

"Dear Prince," said the Swallow. "I cannot do that"; and he began to weep.

"Swallow, Swallow, little Swallow," said the Prince, "do as I command you."

So the Swallow plucked out the Prince's eye, and flew away to the student's garret. It was easy enough to get in, as there was a hole in the roof. Through this he darted, and came into the room. The young man had his head buried in his hands, so he did not hear *145* the flutter of the bird's wings, and when he looked up he found the beautiful sapphire lying on the withered violets.

"I am beginning to be appreciated," he cried; "this is from some great admirer. Now I can finish my play," and he looked quite happy.

The next day the Swallow flew down to the harbour. He sat on the mast of a large *150* vessel and watched the sailors hauling big chests out of the hold with ropes. "Heave-a-hoy!" they shouted as each chest came up. "I am going to Egypt!" cried the Swallow, but nobody minded, and when the moon rose he flew back to the Happy Prince.

"I am come to bid you good-bye," he cried.

"Swallow, Swallow, little Swallow," said the Prince, "will you not stay with me one *155* night longer?"

"It is winter," answered the Swallow, "and the chill snow will soon be here. In Egypt the sun is warm on the green palm-trees, and the crocodiles lie in the mud and look lazily about them. My companions are building a nest in the Temple of Baalbec, and the pink and white doves are watching them, and cooing to each other. Dear Prince, *160* I must leave you, but I will never forget you, and next spring I will bring you back two

---

125. Memnon: in Greek mythology, the heroic son of Tithonus and Eos, goddess of the dawn; because Memnon (according to legend) lived in Egypt, the Greeks also gave this name to the Egyptian statue of Amenhotep II, which was said to utter a musical sound at daybreak, when Memnon greeted his mother.

beautiful jewels in place of those you have given away. The ruby shall be redder than a red rose, and the sapphire shall be as blue as the great sea."

"In the square below," said the Happy Prince, "there stands a little match-girl. She has let her matches fall in the gutter, and they are all spoiled. Her father will beat her if 165 she does not bring home some money, and she is crying. She has no shoes or stockings, and her little head is bare. Pluck out my other eye, and give it to her, and her father will not beat her."

"I will stay with you one night longer," said the Swallow, "but I cannot pluck out your eye. You would be quite blind then." 170

"Swallow, Swallow, little Swallow," said the Prince, "do as I command you."

So he plucked out the Prince's other eye, and darted down with it. He swooped past the match-girl, and slipped the jewel into the palm of her hand. "What a lovely bit of glass," cried the little girl; and she ran home, laughing.

Then the Swallow came back to the Prince. "You are blind now," he said, "so I will 175 stay with you always."

"No, little Swallow," said the poor Prince, "you must go away to Egypt."

"I will stay with you always," said the Swallow, and he slept at the Prince's feet.

All the next day he sat on the Prince's shoulder, and told him stories of what he had seen in strange lands. He told him of the red ibises, who stand in long rows on the banks 180 of the Nile, and catch gold fish in their beaks; of the Sphinx, who is as old as the world itself, and lives in the desert, and knows everything; of the merchants, who walk slowly by the side of their camels, and carry amber beads in their hands; of the King of the Mountains of the Moon, who is as black as ebony, and worships a large crystal; of the great green snake that sleeps in a palm-tree, and has twenty priests to feed it with honey- 185 cakes; and of the pygmies who sail over a big lake on large flat leaves, and are always at war with the butterflies.

"Dear little Swallow," said the Prince, "you tell me of marvellous things, but more marvellous than anything is the suffering of men and of women. There is no Mystery so great as Misery. Fly over my city, little swallow and tell me what you see there." 190

So the Swallow flew over the great city, and saw the rich making merry in their beautiful houses, while the beggars were sitting at the gates. He flew into dark lanes, and saw the white faces of starving children looking out listlessly at the black streets. Under the archway of a bridge two little boys were lying in one another's arms to try and keep themselves warm. "How hungry we are!" they said. "You must not lie here," 195 shouted the Watchman, and they wandered out into the rain.

Then he flew back and told the Prince what he had seen.

"I am covered with fine gold," said the Prince, "you must take it off, leaf by leaf, and give it to my poor; the living always think that gold can make them happy."

Leaf after leaf of the fine gold the Swallow picked off, till the Happy Prince looked 200 quite dull and grey. Leaf after leaf of the fine gold he brought to the poor, and the children's faces grew rosier, and they laughed and played games in the street. "We have bread now!" they cried.

Then the snow came, and after the snow came the frost. The streets looked as if they were made of silver, they were so bright and glistening; long icicles like crystal 205 daggers hung down from the eaves of the houses, everybody went about in furs, and the little boys wore scarlet caps and skated on the ice.

The poor little Swallow grew colder and colder, but he would not leave the Prince, he loved him too well. He picked up crumbs outside the baker's door when the baker was not looking, and tried to keep himself warm by flapping his wings. *210*

But at last he knew that he was going to die. He had just strength to fly up to the Prince's shoulder once more. "Good-bye, dear Prince!" he murmured, "will you let me kiss your hand?"

"I am glad that you are going to Egypt at last, little Swallow," said the Prince, "you have stayed too long here; but you must kiss me on the lips, for I love you." *215*

"It is not to Egypt that I am going," said the Swallow. "I am going to the House of Death. Death is the brother of Sleep, is he not?"

And he kissed the Happy Prince on the lips, and fell down dead at his feet.

At that moment a curious crack sounded inside the statue, as if something had broken. The fact is that the leaden heart had snapped right in two. It certainly was a *220* dreadfully hard frost.

Early the next morning the Mayor was walking in the square below in company with the Town Councillors. As they passed the column he looked up at the statue: "Dear me! how shabby the Happy Prince looks!" he said.

"How shabby indeed!" cried the Town Councillors, who always agreed with the *225* Mayor, and they went up to look at it.

"The ruby has fallen out of his sword, his eyes are gone, and he is golden no longer," said the Mayor; "in fact, he is little better than a beggar!"

"Little better than a beggar," said the Town Councillors.

"And here is actually a dead bird at his feet!" continued the Mayor. "We must *230* really issue a proclamation that birds are not to be allowed to die here." And the Town Clerk made a note of the suggestion.

So they pulled down the statue of the Happy Prince. "As he is no longer beautiful he is no longer useful," said the Art Professor at the University.

Then they melted the statue in a furnace, and the Mayor held a meeting of the *235* Corporation to decide what was to be done with the metal. "We must have another statue, of course," he said, "and it shall be a statue of myself."

"Of myself," said each of the Town Councillors, and they quarrelled. When I last heard of them they were quarrelling still.

"What a strange thing," said the overseer of the workmen at the foundry. "This *240* broken lead heart will not melt in the furnace. We must throw it away." So they threw it on a dust heap where the dead Swallow was also lying.

"Bring me the two most precious things in the city," said God to one of His Angels; and the Angel brought Him the leaden heart and the dead bird.

"You have rightly chosen," said God, "for in my garden of Paradise this little bird *245* shall sing for evermore, and in my city of gold the Happy Prince shall praise me."

(1888)

---

242. dust heap: rubbish dump.

Preface to *The Picture of Dorian Gray*

The artist is the creator of beautiful things.

To reveal art and conceal the artist is art's aim.

The critic is he who can translate into another manner or a new material his impression of beautiful things.

> The highest as the lowest form of criticism is a mode of autobiography.   *5*

Those who find ugly meanings in beautiful things are corrupt without being charming. This is a fault.

> Those who find beautiful meanings in beautiful things are the cultivated. For these there is hope.

They are the elect to whom beautiful things mean only beauty.   *10*

> There is no such thing as a moral or an immoral book. Books are well written, or badly written. That is all.

The nineteenth century dislike of realism is the rage of Caliban seeing his own face in a glass.

> The nineteenth century dislike of romanticism is the rage of Caliban not   *15* seeing his own face in a glass.

> The moral life of man forms part of the subject-matter of the artist, but the morality of art consists in the perfect use of an imperfect medium.

No artist desires to prove anything. Even things that are true can be proved.

> No artist has ethical sympathies. An ethical sympathy in an artist is an   *20* unpardonable mannerism of style.

> No artist is ever morbid. The artist can express everything.

Thought and language are to the artist instruments of an art.

> Vice and virtue are to the artist materials for an art.

From the point of view of form, the type of all the arts is the art of the musician. From   *25* the point of view of feeling, the actor's craft is the type.

> All art is at once surface and symbol.

Those who go beneath the surface do so at their peril.

> Those who read the symbol do so at their peril.

It is the spectator, and not life, that art really mirrors.   *30*

> Diversity of opinion about a work of art shows that the work is new, complex, and vital.

> When critics disagree, the artist is in accord with himself.

We can forgive a man for making a useful thing as long as he does not admire it. The only excuse for making a useless thing is that one admires it intensely.   *35*

> All art is quite useless.

(1890)

Preface   **13. Caliban:** a character in Shakespeare's *The Tempest*, referred to as "monster."

OLIVE SCHREINER
South Africa, 1855-1920

THREE DREAMS IN A DESERT
Under a Mimosa-Tree

As I travelled across an African plain the sun shone down hotly. Then I drew my horse
up under a mimosa-tree, and I took the saddle from him and left him to feed among the
parched bushes. And all to right and to left stretched the brown earth. And I sat down
under the tree, because the heat beat fiercely, and all along the horizon the air throbbed.
And after a while a heavy drowsiness came over me, and I laid my head down against   5
my saddle, and I fell asleep there. And, in my sleep, I had a curious dream.

    I thought I stood on the border of a great desert, and the sand blew about
everywhere. And I thought I saw two great figures like beasts of burden of the desert,
and one lay upon the sand with its neck stretched out, and one stood by it. And I looked
curiously at the one that lay upon the ground, for it had a great burden on its back, and   10
the sand was thick about it, so that it seemed to have piled over it for centuries.

    And I looked very curiously at it. And there stood one beside me watching. And I
said to him, "What is this huge creature who lies here on the sand?"

    And he said, "This is woman; she that bears men in her body."

    And I said, "Why does she lie here motionless with the sand piled round her?"   15

    And he answered, "Listen, I will tell you. Ages and ages long she has lain here, and
the wind has blown over her. The oldest, oldest, oldest man living has never seen her
move: the oldest, oldest book records that she lay here then, as she lies here now, with
the sand about her. But listen! Older than the oldest book, older than the oldest recorded
memory of man, on the Rocks of Language, on the hard-baked clay of Ancient   20
Customs, now crumbling to decay, are found the marks of her footsteps! Side by side
with his who stands beside her you may trace them; and you know that she who now
lies there once wandered free over the rocks with him."

    And I said, "Why does she lie there now?"

    And he said, "I take it, ages ago the Age-of-dominion-of-muscular-force found her,   25
and when she stooped low to give suck to her young, and her back was broad, he put his
burden of subjection on to it, and tied it on with the broad band of Inevitable Necessity.
Then she looked at the earth and the sky, and knew there was no hope for her; and she
lay down on the sand with the burden she could not loosen. Ever since she has lain here.
And the ages have come, and the ages have gone, but the band of Inevitable Necessity   30
has not been cut."

    And I looked and saw in her eyes the terrible patience of the centuries; the ground
was wet with her tears, and her nostrils blew up the sand.

    And I said, "Has she ever tried to move?"

    And he said, "Sometimes a limb has quivered. But she is wise; she knows she   35
cannot rise with the burden on her."

And I said, "Why does not he who stands by her leave her and go on?"

And he said, "He cannot. Look —— "

And I saw a broad band passing along the ground from one to the other, and it bound them together. 40

He said, "While she lies there he must stand and look across the desert."

And I said, "Does he know why he cannot move?"

And he said, "No."

And I heard a sound of something cracking, and I looked, and I saw the band that bound the burden on to her back broken asunder; and the burden rolled on to the ground. 45

And I said, "What is this?"

And he said, "The Age-of-muscular-force is dead. The Age-of-nervous-force has killed him with the knife he holds in his hand; and silently and invisibly he has crept up to the woman, and with that knife of Mechanical Invention he has cut the band that bound the burden to her back. The Inevitable Necessity is broken. She might rise now." 50

And I saw that she still lay motionless on the sand, with her eyes open and her neck stretched out. And she seemed to look for something on the far-off border of the desert that never came. And I wondered if she were awake or asleep. And as I looked her body quivered, and a light came into her eyes, like when a sunbeam breaks into a dark room.

I said, "What is it?" 55

He whispered, "Hush! the thought has come to her, 'Might I not rise?'"

And I looked. And she raised her head from the sand, and I saw the dent where her neck had lain so long. And she looked at the earth, and she looked at the sky, and she looked at him who stood by her: but he looked out across the desert.

And I saw her body quiver; and she pressed her front knees to the earth, and veins 60 stood out; and I cried, "She is going to rise!"

But only her sides heaved, and she lay still where she was.

But her head she held up; she did not lay it down again. And he beside me said, "She is very weak. See, her legs have been crushed under her so long."

And I saw the creature struggle: and the drops stood out on her. 65

And I said, "Surely he who stands beside her will help her?"

And he beside me answered, "He cannot help her: *she must help herself*. Let her struggle till she is strong."

And I cried, "At least he will not hinder her! See, he moves farther from her, and tightens the cord between them, and he drags her down." 70

And he answered, "He does not understand. When she moves she draws the band that binds them, and hurts him, and he moves farther from her. The day will come when he will understand, and will know what she is doing. Let her once stagger on to her knees. In that day he will stand close to her, and look into her eyes with sympathy."

And she stretched her neck, and the drops fell from her. And the creature rose an 75 inch from the earth and sank back.

And I cried, "Oh, she is too weak! she cannot walk! The long years have taken all her strength from her. Can she never move?"

And he answered me, "See the light in her eyes!"

And slowly the creature staggered on to its knees. 80

And I awoke: and all to the east and to the west stretched the barren earth, with the dry bushes on it. The ants ran up and down in the red sand, and the heat beat fiercely. I looked up through the thin branches of the tree at the blue sky overhead. I stretched myself, and I mused over the dream I had had. And I fell asleep again, with my head on my saddle. And in the fierce heat I had another dream. 85

I saw a desert and I saw a woman coming out of it. And she came to the bank of a dark river; and the bank was steep and high. And on it an old man met her, who had a long white beard; and a stick that curled was in his hand, and on it was written Reason. And he asked her what she wanted; and she said, "I am woman; and I am seeking for the land of Freedom." 90

And he said, "It is before you."

And she said, "I see nothing before me but a dark flowing river, and a bank steep and high, and cuttings here and there with heavy sand in them."

And he said, "And beyond that?"

She said, "I see nothing, but sometimes, when I shade my eyes with my hand, I 95 think I see on the further bank trees and hills, and the sun shining on them!"

He said, "That is the Land of Freedom."

She said, "How am I to get there?"

He said, "There is one way, and one only. Down the banks of Labour, through the water of Suffering. There is no other." 100

She said, "Is there no bridge?"

He answered, "None."

She said, "Is the water deep?"

He said, "Deep."

She said, "Is the floor worn?" 105

He said, "It is. Your foot may slip at any time, and you may be lost."

She said, "Have any crossed already?"

He said, "Some have *tried!*"

She said, "Is there a track to show where the best fording is?"

He said, "It has to be made." 110

She shaded her eyes with her hand; and she said, "I will go."

And he said, "You must take off the clothes you wore in the desert: they are dragged down by them who go into the water so clothed."

And she threw from her gladly the mantle of Ancient-received-opinions she wore, for it was worn full of holes. And she took the girdle from her waist that she had 115 treasured so long, and the moths flew out of it in a cloud. And he said, "Take the shoes of dependence off your feet."

And she stood there naked, but for one white garment that clung close to her.

And he said, "That you may keep. So they wear clothes in the Land of Freedom. In the water it buoys; it always swims." 120

And I saw on its breast was written Truth; and it was white; the sun had not often shone on it; the other clothes had covered it up. And he said, "Take this stick; hold it

---

THREE DREAMS IN A DESERT **87. steep and high:** Schreiner's note reads: "The banks of an African river are sometimes a hundred feet high, and consist of deep shifting sands, through which in the course of ages the river has worn its gigantic bed."

fast. In that day when it slips from your hand you are lost. Put it down before you; feel your way: where it cannot find a bottom do not set your foot."

And she said, "I am ready; let me go." 125

And he said, "No — but stay; what is that — in your breast?"

She was silent.

He said, "Open it, and let me see."

And she opened it. And against her breast was a tiny thing, who drank from it, and the yellow curls above his forehead pressed against it; and his knees were drawn up to 130 her, and he held her breast fast with his hands.

And Reason said, "Who is he, and what is he doing here?"

And she said, "See his little wings ——"

And Reason said, "Put him down."

And she said, "He is asleep, and he is drinking! I will carry him to the Land of 135 Freedom. He has been a child so long, so long, I have carried him. In the Land of Freedom he will be a man. We will walk together there, and his great white wings will overshadow me. He has lisped one word only to me in the desert — 'Passion!' I have dreamed he might learn to say 'Friendship' in that land."

And Reason said, "Put him down!" 140

And she said, "I will carry him so — with one arm, and with the other I will fight the water."

He said, "Lay him down on the ground. When you are in the water you will forget to fight, you will think only of him. Lay him down." He said, "He will not die. When he finds you have left him alone he will open his wings and fly. He will be in the Land of 145 Freedom before you. Those who reach the Land of Freedom, the first hand they see stretching down the bank to help them shall be Love's. He will be a man then, not a child. In your breast he cannot thrive; put him down that he may grow."

And she took her bosom from his mouth, and he bit her, so that the blood ran down on to the ground. And she laid him down on the earth; and she covered her wound. And 150 she bent and stroked his wings. And I saw the hair on her forehead turned white as snow, and she had changed from youth to age.

And she stood far off on the bank of the river. And she said, "For what do I go to this far land which no one has ever reached? *Oh, I am alone! I am utterly alone!*"

And Reason, that old man, said to her, "Silence! what do you hear?" 155

And she listened intently, and she said, "I hear a sound of feet, a thousand times ten thousand and thousands of thousands, and they beat this way!"

He said, "They are the feet of those that shall follow you. Lead on! make a track to the water's edge! Where you stand now, the ground will be beaten flat by ten thousand times ten thousand feet." And he said, "Have you seen the locusts how they cross a 160 stream? First one comes down to the water's-edge, and it is swept away, and then another comes and then another, and then another, and at last with their bodies piled up a bridge is built and the rest pass over."

She said, "And, of those that come first, some are swept away, and are heard of no more; their bodies do not even build the bridge?" 165

"And are swept away, and are heard of no more — and what of that?" he said.

"And what of that ——" she said.

"They make a track to the water's edge."

"They make a track to the water's edge ——." And she said, "Over that bridge which shall be built with our bodies, who will pass?" *170*

He said, "*The entire human race.*"

And the woman grasped her staff.

And I saw her turn down that dark path to the river.

And I awoke; and all about me was the yellow afternoon light: the sinking sun lit up the fingers of the milk bushes; and my horse stood by me quietly feeding. And I turned *175* on my side, and I watched the ants run by thousands in the red sand. I thought I would go on my way now — the afternoon was cooler. Then a drowsiness crept over me again, and I laid back my head and fell asleep.

And I dreamed a dream.

I dreamed I saw a land. And on the hills walked brave women and brave men, hand *180* in hand. And they looked into each other's eyes, and they were not afraid.

And I saw the women also hold each other's hands.

And I said to him beside me, "What place is this?"

And he said, "This is heaven."

And I said, "Where is it?" *185*

And he answered, "On earth."

And I said, "When shall these things be?"

And he answered, "IN THE FUTURE."

And I awoke, and all about me was the sunset light; and on the low hills the sun lay, and a delicious coolness had crept over everything; and the ants were going slowly *190* home. And I walked towards my horse, who stood quietly feeding. Then the sun passed down behind the hills; but I knew that the next day he would arise again.

(1890)

JOSEPH CONRAD
Poland/England, 1857-1924

THE TALE

Outside the large single window the crepuscular light was dying out slowly in a great square gleam without colour, framed rigidly in the gathering shades of the room.

It was a long room. The irresistible tide of the night ran into the most distant part of it, where the whispering of a man's voice, passionately interrupted and passionately renewed, seemed to plead against the answering murmurs of infinite sadness. *5*

At last no answering murmur came. His movement when he rose slowly from his knees by the side of the deep, shadowy couch holding the shadowy suggestion of a reclining woman revealed him tall under the low ceiling, and sombre all over except for the crude discord of the white collar under the shape of his head and the faint, minute spark of a brass button here and there on his uniform. *10*

He stood over her a moment, masculine and mysterious in his immobility, before he sat down on a chair near by. He could see only the faint oval of her upturned face and, extended on her black dress, her pale hands, a moment before abandoned to his kisses and now as if too weary to move.

He dared not make a sound, shrinking as a man would do from the prosaic   *15* necessities of existence. As usual, it was the woman who had the courage. Her voice was heard first—almost conventional while her being vibrated yet with conflicting emotions.

"Tell me something," she said.

The darkness hid his surprise and then his smile. Had he not just said to her   *20* everything worth saying in the world—and that not for the first time!

"What am I to tell you?" he asked, in a voice creditably steady. He was beginning to feel grateful to her for that something final in her tone which had eased the strain.

"Why not tell me a tale?"

"A tale!" He was really amazed.   *25*

"Yes. Why not?"

These words came with a slight petulance, the hint of a loved woman's capricious will, which is capricious only because it feels itself to be a law, embarrassing sometimes and always difficult to elude.

"Why not?" he repeated, with a slightly mocking accent, as though he had been   *30* asked to give her the moon. But now he was feeling a little angry with her for that feminine mobility that slips out of an emotion as easily as out of a splendid gown.

He heard her say, a little unsteadily with a sort of fluttering intonation which made him think suddenly of a butterfly's flight:

"You used to tell—your—your simple and—and professional—tales very well at   *35* one time. Or well enough to interest me. You had a—a sort of art—in the days—the days before the war."

"Really?" he said, with involuntary gloom. "But now, you see, the war is going on," he continued in such a dead, equable tone that she felt a slight chill fall over her shoulders. And yet she persisted. For there's nothing more unswerving in the world than   *40* a woman's caprice.

"It could be a tale not of this world?" she explained.

"You want a tale of the other, the better world?" he asked, with a matter-of-fact surprise. "You must evoke for that task those who have already gone there."

"No. I don't mean that. I mean another—some other—world. In the universe—not   *45* in heaven."

"I am relieved. But you forget that I have only five days' leave."

"Yes. And I've also taken a five days' leave from— from my duties."

"I like that word."

"What word?"   *50*

"Duty."

"It is horrible—sometimes."

"Oh, that's because you think it's narrow. But it isn't. It contains infinities, and—and so——"

"What is this jargon?"   *55*

He disregarded the interjected scorn. "An infinity of absolution, for instance," he
continued. "But as to this 'another world'—who's going to look for it and for the tale
that is in it?"

"You," she said, with a strange, almost rough, sweetness of assertion.

He made a shadowy movement of assent in his chair, the irony of which not even   60
the gathered darkness could render mysterious.

"As you will. In that world, then, there was once upon a time a Commanding
Officer and a Northman. Put in the capitals, please, because they had no other names. It
was a world of seas and continents and islands——"

"Like the earth," she murmured, bitterly.   65

"Yes. What else could you expect from sending a man made of our common,
tormented clay on a voyage of discovery? What else could he find? What else could you
understand or care for, or feel the existence of even? There was comedy in it, and
slaughter."

"Always like the earth," she murmured.   70

"Always. And since I could find in the universe only what was deeply rooted in the
fibres of my being there was love in it, too. But we won't talk of that."

"No. We won't," she said, in a neutral tone which concealed perfectly her relief—
or her disappointment. Then after a pause she added: "It's going to be a comic story."

"Well——" he paused, too. "Yes. In a way. In a very grim way. It will be human,   75
and, as you know, comedy is but a matter of the visual angle. And it won't be a noisy
story. All the long guns in it will be dumb—as dumb as so many telescopes."

"Ah, there are guns it it, then! And may I ask—where?"

"Afloat. You remember that the world of which we speak had its seas. A war was
going on in it. It was a funny world and terribly in earnest. Its war was being carried on   80
over the land, over the water, under the water, up in the air, and even under the ground.
And many young men in it, mostly in wardrooms and mess-rooms, used to say to each
other—pardon the unparliamentary word—they used to say, 'It's a damned bad war, but
it's better than no war at all.' Sounds flippant, doesn't it?"

He heard a nervous, impatient sigh in the depths of the couch while he went on   85
without a pause.

"And yet there is more in it than meets the eye. I mean more wisdom. Flippancy,
like comedy, is but a matter of visual first-impression. That world was not very wise.
But there was in it a certain amount of common working sagacity. That, however, was
mostly worked by the neutrals in diverse ways, public and private, which had to be   90
watched; watched by acute minds and also by actual sharp eyes. They had to be very
sharp indeed, too, I assure you."

"I can imagine," she murmured, appreciatively.

"What is there that you can't imagine?" he pronounced, soberly. "You have the
world in you. But let us go back to our commanding officer, who, of course, commanded   95
a ship of a sort. My tales if often professional (as you remarked just now) have never
been technical. So I'll just tell you that the ship was of a very ornamental sort once, with
lots of grace and elegance and luxury about her. Yes, once! She was like a pretty woman
who had suddenly put on a suit of sackcloth and stuck revolvers in her belt. But she
floated lightly, she moved nimbly, she was quite good enough."   100

"That was the opinion of the commanding officer?" said the voice from the couch.

"It was. He used to be sent out with her along certain coasts to see—what he could see. Just that. And sometimes he had some preliminary information to help him, and sometimes he had not. And it was all one, really. It was about as useful as information trying to convey the locality and intentions of a cloud, of a phantom taking shape here   *105* and there and impossible to seize, would have been.

"It was in the early days of the war. What at first used to amaze the commanding officer was the unchanged face of the waters, with its familiar expression, neither more friendly nor more hostile. On fine days the sun strikes sparks upon the blue; here and there a peaceful smudge of smoke hangs in the distance, and it is impossible to believe   *110* that the familiar clear horizon traces the limit of one great circular ambush.

"Yes, it is impossible to believe, till some day you see a ship not your own ship (that isn't so impressive), but some ship in company, blow up all of a sudden and plop under almost before you know what has happened to her. Then you begin to believe. Henceforth you go out for the work to see—what you can see, and you keep on at it   *115* with the conviction that some day you will die from something you have not seen. One envies the soldiers at the end of the day, wiping the sweat and blood from their faces, counting the dead fallen to their hands, looking at the devastated fields, the torn earth that seems to suffer and bleed with them. One does, really. The final brutality of it—the taste of primitive passion—the ferocious frankness of the blow struck with one's hand—   *120* the direct call and the straight response. Well, the sea gave you nothing of that, and seemed to pretend that there was nothing the matter with the world."

She interrupted, stirring a little.

"Oh, yes. Sincerity — frankness — passion — three words of your gospel. Don't I know them!"   *125*

"Think! Isn't it ours—believed in common?" he asked, anxiously, yet without expecting an answer, and went on at once: "Such were the feelings of the commanding officer. When the night came trailing over the sea, hiding what looked like the hypocrisy of an old friend, it was a relief. The night blinds you frankly—and there are circumstances when the sunlight may grow as odious to one as falsehood itself. Night is   *130* all right.

"At night the commanding officer could let his thoughts get away—I won't tell you where. Somewhere where there was no choice but between truth and death. But thick weather, though it blinded one, brought no such relief. Mist is deceitful, the dead luminosity of the fog is irritating. It seems that you *ought* to see.   *135*

"One gloomy, nasty day the ship was steaming along her beat in sight of a rocky, dangerous coast that stood out intensely black like an India-ink drawing on gray paper. Presently the second in command spoke to his chief. He thought he saw something on the water, to seaward. Small wreckage, perhaps.

"But there shouldn't be any wreckage here, sir," he remarked.   *140*

"'No,' said the commanding officer. 'The last reported submarined ships were sunk a long way to the westward. But one never knows. There may have been others since then not reported nor seen. Gone with all hands.'

"That was how it began. The ship's course was altered to pass the object close; for it was necessary to have a good look at what one could see. Close, but without touching;   *145* for it was not advisable to come in contact with objects of any form whatever floating casually about. Close, but without stopping or even diminishing speed; for in those times it was not prudent to linger on any particular spot, even for a moment. I may tell you at once that the object was not dangerous in itself. No use in describing it. It may have been nothing more remarkable than, say, a barrel of a certain shape and colour. But it was significant.

"The smooth bow-wave hove it up as if for a closer inspection, and then the ship, brought again to her course, turned her back on it with indifference, while twenty pairs of eyes on her deck stared in all directions trying to see—what they could see.

"The commanding officer and his second in command discussed the object with understanding. It appeared to them to be not so much a proof of the sagacity as of the activity of certain neutrals. This activity had in many cases taken the form of replenishing the stores of certain submarines at sea. This was generally believed, if not absolutely known. But the very nature of things in those early days pointed that way. The object, looked at closely and turned away from with apparent indifference, put it beyond doubt that something of the sort had been done somewhere in the neighbourhood.

"The object in itself was more than suspect. But the fact of its being left in evidence roused other suspicions. Was it the result of some deep and devilish purpose? As to that all speculation soon appeared to be a vain thing. Finally the two officers came to the conclusion that it was left there most likely by accident, complicated possibly by some unforeseen necessity; such, perhaps, as the sudden need to get away quickly from the spot, or something of that kind.

"Their discussion had been carried on in curt, weighty phrases, separated by long, thoughtful silences. And all the time their eyes roamed about the horizon in an everlasting, almost mechanical effort of vigilance. The younger man summed up grimly:

"'Well, it's evidence. That's what this is. Evidence of what we were pretty certain of before. And plain, too.'

"'And much good it will do to us,' retorted the commanding officer. 'The parties are miles away; the submarine, devil only knows where, ready to kill; and the noble neutral slipping away to the eastward, ready to lie!'

"The second in command laughed a little at the tone. But he guessed that the neutral wouldn't even have to lie very much. Fellows like that, unless caught in the very act, felt themselves pretty safe. They could afford to chuckle. That fellow was probably chuckling to himself. It's very possible he had been before at the game and didn't care a rap for the bit of evidence left behind. It was a game in which practice made one bold and successful, too."

"And again he laughed faintly. But his commanding officer was in revolt against the murderous stealthiness of methods and the atrocious callousness of complicities that seemed to taint the very source of men's deep emotions and noblest activities; to corrupt their imagination which builds up the final conceptions of life and death. He suffered——"

The voice from the sofa interrupted the narrator.

"How well I can understand that in him!"

He bent forward slightly.

"Yes. I, too. Everything should be open in love and war. Open as the day, since both are the call of an ideal which it is so easy, so terribly easy, to degrade in the name of Victory."

He paused; then went on:

"I don't know that the commanding officer delved so deep as that into his feelings. *195* But he did suffer from them—a sort of disenchanted sadness. It is possible, even, that he suspected himself of folly. Man is various. But he had no time for much introspection, because from the southwest a wall of fog had advanced upon his ship. Great convolutions of vapours flew over, swirling about masts and funnel, which looked as if they were beginning to melt. They they vanished. *200*

"The ship was stopped, all sounds ceased, and the very fog became motionless, growing denser and as if solid in its amazing dumb immobility. The men at their stations lost sight of each other. Footsteps sounded stealthy; rare voices, impersonal and remote, died out without resonance. A blind white stillness took possession of the world.

"It looked, too, as if it would last for days. I don't mean to say that the fog did not *205* vary a little in its density. Now and then it would thin out mysteriously, revealing to the men a more or less ghostly presentment of their ship. Several times the shadow of the coast itself swam darkly before their eyes through the fluctuating opaque brightness of the great white cloud clinging to the water.

"Taking advantage of these moments, the ship had been moved cautiously nearer *210* the shore. It was useless to remain out in such thick weather. Her officers knew every nook and cranny of the coast along their beat. They thought that she would be much better in a certain cove. It wasn't a large place, just ample room for a ship to swing at her anchor. She would have an easier time of it till the fog lifted up.

"Slowly, with infinite caution and patience, they crept closer and closer, seeing no *215* more of the cliffs than an evanescent dark loom with a narrow border of angry foam at its foot. At the moment of anchoring the fog was so thick that for all they could see they might have been a thousand miles out in the open sea. Yet the shelter of the land could be felt. There was a peculiar quality in the stillness of the air. Very faint, very elusive, the wash of the ripple against the encircling land reached their ears, with mysterious *220* sudden pauses.

"The anchor dropped, the leads were laid in. The commanding officer went below into his cabin. But he had not been there very long when a voice outside his door requested his presence on deck. He thought to himself: 'What is it now?' He felt some impatience at being called out again to face the wearisome fog. *225*

"He found that it had thinned again a little and had taken on a gloomy hue from the dark cliffs which had no form, no outline, but asserted themselves as a curtain of shadows all round the ship, except in one bright spot, which was the entrance from the open sea. Several officers were looking that way from the bridge. The second in command met him with the breathlessly whispered information that there was another *230* ship in the cove.

"She had been made out by several pairs of eyes only a couple of minutes before. She was lying at anchor very near the entrance—a mere vague blot on the fog's brightness. And the commanding officer by staring in the direction pointed out to him by eager hands ended by distinguishing it at last himself. Indubitably a vessel of some sort. *235*

"'It's a wonder we didn't run slap into her when coming in,' observed the second in command.

"'Send a boat on board before she vanishes,' said the commanding officer. He surmised that this was a coaster. It could hardly be anything else. But another thought came into his head suddenly. 'It is a wonder,' he said to his second in command, who had rejoined him after sending the boat away.

"By that time both of them had been struck by the fact that the ship so suddenly discovered had not manifested her presence by ringing her bell.

"'We came in very quietly, that's true,' concluded the younger officer. 'But they must have heard our leadsmen at least. We couldn't have passed her more than fifty yards off. The closest shave! They may even have made us out, since they were aware of something coming in. And the strange thing is that we never heard a sound from her. The fellows on board must have been holding their breath.'

"'Aye,' said the commanding officer, thoughtfully.

"In due course the boarding-boat returned, appearing suddenly alongside, as though she had burrowed her way under the fog. The officer in charge came up to make his report, but the commanding officer didn't give him time to begin. He cried from a distance:

"'Coaster, isn't she?'

"'No, sir. A stranger—a neutral,' was the answer.

"'No. Really! Well, tell us all about it. What is she doing here?'

"The young man stated then that he had been told a long and complicated story of engine troubles. But it was plausible enough from a strictly professional point of view and it had the usual features: disablement, dangerous drifting along the shore, weather more or less thick for days, fear of a gale, ultimately a resolve to go in and anchor anywhere on the coast, and so on. Fairly plausible.

"'Engines still disabled?' inquired the commanding officer.

"'No, sir. She has steam on them.'

"The commanding officer took his second aside. 'By Jove!' he said, 'you were right! They were holding their breaths as we passed them. They were.'

"But the second in command had his doubts now.

"'A fog like this does muffle small sounds, sir,' he remarked. 'And what could his object be, after all?'

"'To sneak out unnoticed,' answered the commanding officer.

"'Then why didn't he? He might have done it, you know. Not exactly unnoticed, perhaps. I don't suppose he could have slipped his cable without making some noise. Still, in a minute or so he would have been lost to view—clean gone before we had made him out fairly. Yet he didn't.'

"They looked at each other. The commanding officer shook his head. Such suspicions as the one which had entered his head are not defended easily. He did not even state it openly. The boarding officer finished his report. The cargo of the ship was of a harmless and useful character. She was bound to an English port. Papers and everything in perfect order. Nothing suspicious to be detected anywhere.

"Then passing to the men, he reported the crew on deck as the usual lot. Engineers of the well-known type, and very full of their achievement in repairing the engines. The mate surly. The master rather a fine specimen of a Northman, civil enough, but appeared to have been drinking. Seemed to be recovering from a regular bout of it.

"'I told him I couldn't give him permission to proceed. He said he wouldn't dare to move his ship her own length out in such weather as this, permission or no permission. I left a man on board, though.'   285

"'Quite right.'

"The commanding officer, after communing with his suspicions for a time, called his second aside.

"'What if she were the very ship which had been feeding some infernal submarine or other?' he said in an undertone.   290

"The other started. Then, with conviction:

"'She would get off scot-free. You couldn't prove it, sir.'

"'I want to look into it myself.'

"'From the report we've heard I am afraid you couldn't even make a case for reasonable suspicion, sir.'   295

"'I'll go on board all the same.'

"He had made up his mind. Curiosity is the great motive power of hatred and love. What did he expect to find? He could not have told anybody—not even himself.

"What he really expected to find there was the atmosphere, the atmosphere of gratuitous treachery, which in his view nothing could excuse; for he thought that even a   300 passion of unrighteousness for its own sake could not excuse that. But could he detect it? Sniff it? Taste it? Receive some mysterious communication which would turn his invincible suspicions into a certitude strong enough to provoke action with all its risks?

"The master met him on the after-deck, looming up in the fog amongst the blurred shapes of the usual ship's fittings. He was a robust Northman, bearded, and in the force   305 of his age. A round leather cap fitted his head closely. His hands were rammed deep into the pockets of his short leather jacket. He kept them there while he explained that at sea he lived in the chart-room, and led the way there, striding carelessly. Just before reaching the door under the bridge he staggered a little, recovered himself, flung it open, and stood aside, leaning his shoulder as if involuntarily against the side of the house,   310 and staring vaguely into the fog-filled space. But he followed the commanding officer at once, flung the door to, snapped on the electric light, and hastened to thrust his hands back into his pockets, as though afraid of being seized by them either in friendship or in hostility.

"The place was stuffy and hot. The usual chart-rack overhead was full, and the   315 chart on the table was kept unrolled by an empty cup standing on a saucer half-full of some spilt dark liquid. A slightly nibbled biscuit reposed on the chronometer-case. There were two settees, and one of them had been made up into a bed with a pillow and some blankets, which were now very much tumbled. The Northman let himself fall on it, his hands still in his pockets.   320

"'Well, here I am,' he said, with a curious air of being surprised at the sound of his own voice.

"The commanding officer from the other settee observed the handsome, flushed face. Drops of fog hung on the yellow beard and moustaches of the Northman. The much darker eyebrows ran together in a puzzled frown, and suddenly he jumped up.   325

"'What I mean is that I don't know where I am. I really don't,' he burst out, with extreme earnestness. 'Hang it all! I got turned around somehow. The fog has been after me for a week. More than a week. And then my engines broke down. I will tell you how it was.'

"He burst out into loquacity. It was not hurried, but it was insistent. It was not continuous for all that. It was broken by the most queer, thoughtful pauses. Each of these pauses lasted no more than a couple of seconds, and each had the profundity of an endless meditation. When he began again nothing betrayed in him the slightest consciousness of these intervals. There was the same fixed glance, the same unchanged earnestness of tone. He didn't know. Indeed, more than one of these pauses occurred in the middle of a sentence.

"The commanding officer listened to the tale. It struck him as more plausible than simple truth is in the habit of being. But that, perhaps, was prejudice. All the time the Northman was speaking the commanding officer had been aware of an inward voice, a grave murmur in the depth of his very own self, telling another tale, as if on purpose to keep alive in him his indignation and his anger with that baseness of greed or of mere outlook which lies often at the root of simple ideas.

"It was the story that had been already told to the boarding officer an hour or so before. The commanding officer nodded slightly at the Northman from time to time. The latter came to an end and turned his eyes away. He added, as an afterthought:

"'Wasn't it enough to drive a man out of his mind with worry? And it's my first voyage to this part, too. And the ship's my own. Your officer has seen the papers. She isn't much, as you can see for yourself. Just an old cargo-boat. Bare living for my family.'

"He raised a big arm to point at a row of photographs plastering the bulkhead. The movement was ponderous, as if the arm had been made of lead. The commanding officer said, carelessly:

"'You will be making a fortune yet for your family with this old ship.'

"'Yes, if I don't lose her,' said the Northman, gloomily.

"'I mean—out of this war,' added the commanding officer.

"The Northman stared at him in a curiously unseeing and at the same time interested manner, as only eyes of a particular blue shade can stare.

"'And you wouldn't be angry at it,' he said, 'would you? You are too much of a gentleman. We didn't bring this on you. And suppose we sat down and cried. What good would that be? Let those cry who made the trouble," he concluded, with energy. 'Time's money, you say. Well—*this* time *is* money. Oh! isn't it!'

"The commanding officer tried to keep under the feeling of immense disgust. He said to himself that it was unreasonable. Men were like that—moral cannibals feeding on each other's misfortunes. He said aloud:

"'You have made it perfectly plain how it is that you are here. Your log-book confirms you very minutely. Of course, a log-book may be cooked. Nothing easier.'

"The Northman never moved a muscle. He was gazing at the floor; he seemed not to have heard. He raised his head after a while.

"'But you can't suspect me of anything,' he muttered, negligently.

"The commanding officer thought: 'Why should he say this?'

"Immediately afterwards the man before him added: 'My cargo is for an English port.'

"His voice had turned husky for the moment. The commanding officer reflected: 'That's true. There can be nothing. I can't suspect him. Yet why was he lying with steam up in this fog—and then, hearing us come in, why didn't he give some sign of life? Why? Could it be anything else but a guilty conscience? He could tell by the leadsmen that this was a man-of-war.' 375

"Yes—why? The commanding officer went on thinking: 'Suppose I ask him and then watch his face. He will betray himself in some way. It's perfectly plain that the fellow *has* been drinking. Yes, he has been drinking; but he will have a lie ready all the same.' The commanding officer was one of those men who are made morally and 380 almost physically uncomfortable by the mere thought of having to beat down a lie. He shrank from the act in scorn and disgust, which were invincible because more temperamental than moral.

"So he went out on deck instead and had the crew mustered formally for his inspection. He found them very much what the report of the boarding officer had led 385 him to expect. And from their answers to his questions he could discover no flaw in the log-book story.

"He dismissed them. His impression of them was—a picked lot; have been promised a fistful of money each if this came off; all slightly anxious, but not frightened. Not a single one of them likely to give the show away. They don't feel in 390 danger of their life. They know England and English ways too well!

"He felt alarmed at catching himself thinking as if his vaguest suspicions were turning into a certitude. For, indeed, there was no shadow of reason for his inferences. There was nothing to give away.

"He returned to the chart-room. The Northman had lingered behind there; and 395 something subtly different in his bearing, more bold in his blue, glassy stare, induced the commanding officer to conclude that the fellow had snatched at the opportunity to take another swig at the bottle he must have had concealed somewhere.

"He noticed, too, that the Northman on meeting his eyes put on an elaborately surprised expression. At least, it seemed elaborated. Nothing could be trusted. And the 400 Englishman felt himself with astonishing conviction faced by an enormous lie, solid like a wall, with no way round to get at the truth, whose ugly murderous face he seemed to see peeping over at him with a cynical grin.

"'I dare say,' he began, suddenly, 'you are wondering at my proceedings, though I am not detaining you, am I? You wouldn't dare to move in this fog?' 405

"'I don't know where I am,' the Northman ejaculated, earnestly. 'I really don't.'

"He looked around as if the very chart-room fittings were strange to him. The commanding officer asked him whether he had not seen any unusual objects floating about while he was at sea.

"'Objects! What objects? We were groping blind in the fog for days.' 410

"'We had a few clear intervals,' said the commanding officer. 'And I'll tell you what we have seen and the conclusion I've come to about it.'

"He told him in a few words. He heard the sound of a sharp breath indrawn through closed teeth. The Northman with his hand on the table stood absolutely motionless and dumb. He stood as if thunderstruck. Then he produced a fatuous smile. 415

"Or at least so it appeared to the commanding officer. Was this significant, or of no meaning whatever? He didn't know, he couldn't tell. All the truth had departed out of the world as if drawn in, absorbed in this monstrous villainy this man was—or was not—guilty of.

"'Shooting's too good for people that conceive neutrality in this pretty way,' remarked the commanding officer, after a silence. 420

"'Yes, yes, yes,' the Northman assented, hurriedly—then added an unexpected and dreamy-voiced 'Perhaps.'

"Was he pretending to be drunk, or only trying to appear sober? His glance was straight, but it was somewhat glazed. His lips outlined themselves firmly under his yellow moustache. But they twitched. Did they twitch? And why was he drooping like this in his attitude? 425

"'There's no perhaps about it,' pronounced the commanding officer sternly.

"The Northman had straightened himself. And unexpectedly he looked stern, too.

"'No. But what about the tempters? Better kill that lot off. There's about four, five, six million of them,' he said, grimly; but in a moment changed into a whining key. 'But I had better hold my tongue. You have some suspicions.' 430

"'No, I've no suspicions,' declared the commanding officer.

"He never faltered. At that moment he had the certitude. The air of the chart-room was thick with guilt and falsehood braving the discovery, defying simple right, common decency, all humanity of feeling, every scruple of conduct. 435

"The Northman drew a long breath. 'Well, we know that you English are gentlemen. But let us speak the truth. Why should we love you so very much? You haven't done anything to be loved. We don't love the other people, of course. They haven't done anything for that either. A fellow comes along with a bag of gold . . . I haven't been in Rotterdam my last voyage for nothing.' 440

"'You may be able to tell something interesting, then, to our people when you come into port,' interjected the officer.

"'I might. But you keep some people in your pay at Rotterdam. Let them report. I am a neutral—am I not? . . . Have you ever seen a poor man on one side and a bag of gold on the other? Of course, I couldn't be tempted. I haven't the nerve for it. Really I haven't. It's nothing to me. I am just talking openly for once.' 445

"'Yes. And I am listening to you,' said the commanding officer, quietly.

"The Northman leaned forward over the table. 'Now that I know you have no suspicions, I talk. You don't know what a poor man is. I do. I am poor myself. This old ship, she isn't much, and she is mortgaged, too. Bare living, no more. Of course, I wouldn't have the nerve. But a man who has nerve! See. The stuff he takes aboard looks like any other cargo—packages, barrels, tins, copper tubes—what not. He doesn't see it work. It isn't real to him. But he sees the gold. That's real. Of course, nothing could induce me. I suffer from an internal disease. I would either go crazy from anxiety—or—or—take to drink or something. The risk is too great. Why—ruin!' 450

"'It should be death.' The commanding officer got up, after this curt declaration, which the other received with a hard stare oddly combined with an uncertain smile. The officer's gorge rose at the atmosphere of murderous complicity which surrounded him, denser, more impenetrable, more acrid than the fog outside. 460

"'It's nothing to me,' murmured the Northman, swaying visibly.

"'Of course not,' assented the commanding officer, with a great effort to keep his voice calm and low. The certitude was strong within him. 'But I am going to clear all you fellows off this coast at once. And I will begin with you. You must leave in half an hour.' 465

"By that time the officer was walking along the deck with the Northman at his elbow.

"'What! In this fog?' the latter cried out, huskily.

"'Yes, you will have to go in this fog.'

"'But I don't know where I am. I really don't.' 470

"The commanding officer turned round. A sort of fury possessed him. The eyes of the two men met. Those of the Northman expressed a profound amazement.

"'Oh, you don't know how to get out.' The commanding officer spoke with composure, but his heart was beating with anger and dread. 'I will give you your course. Steer south-by-east-half-east for about four miles and then you will be clear to haul to 475 the eastward for your port. The weather will clear up before very long.'

"'Must I? What could induce me? I haven't the nerve.'

"'And yet you must go. Unless you want to——'

"'I don't want to,' panted the Northman. 'I've enough of it.'

"The commanding officer got over the side. The Northman remained still as if 480 rooted to the deck. Before his boat reached his ship the commanding officer heard the steamer beginning to pick up her anchor. Then, shadowy in the fog, she steamed out on the given course.

"'Yes,' he said to his officers, 'I let him go.'"

The narrator bent forward towards the couch, where no movement betrayed the 485 presence of a living person.

"Listen," he said, forcibly. "That course would lead the Northman straight on a deadly ledge of rock. And the commanding officer gave it to him. He steamed out—ran on it—and went down. So he had spoken the truth. He did not know where he was. But it proves nothing. Nothing either way. It may have been the only truth in all his story. 490 And yet . . . He seems to have been driven out by a menacing stare—nothing more."

He abandoned all pretence.

"Yes, I gave that course to him. It seemed to me a supreme test. I believe—no, I don't believe. I don't know. At the time I was certain. They all went down; and I don't know whether I have done stern retribution—or murder; whether I have added to the 495 corpses that litter the bed of the unreadable sea the bodies of men completely innocent or basely guilty. I don't know. I shall never know."

He rose. The woman on the couch got up and threw her arms round his neck. Her eyes put two gleams in the deep shadow of the room. She knew his passion for truth, his horror of deceit, his humanity. 500

"Oh, my poor, poor——"

"I shall never know," he repeated, sternly, disengaged himself, pressed her hands to his lips, and went out.

(1917)

EDITH NESBIT
England, 1858-1924

THE LAST OF THE DRAGONS

Of course you know that dragons were once as common as motor-omnibuses are now, and almost as dangerous. But as every well-brought-up prince was expected to kill a dragon, and rescue a princess, the dragons grew fewer and fewer till it was often quite hard for a princess to find a dragon to be rescued from. And at last there were no more dragons in France and no more dragons in Germany, or Spain, or Italy, or Russia. There were some left in China, and are still, but they are cold and bronzy, and there were never any, of course, in America. But the last real live dragon left was in England, and of course that was a very long time ago, before what you call English History began. This dragon lived in Cornwall in the big caves amidst the rocks, and a very fine dragon it was, quite seventy feet long from the tip of its fearful snout to the end of its terrible tail. It breathed fire and smoke, and rattled when it walked, because its scales were made of iron. Its wings were like half-umbrellas — or like bat's wings, only several thousand times bigger. Everyone was very frightened of it, and well they might be.

Now the King of Cornwall had one daughter, and when she was sixteen, of course she would have to go and face the dragon: such tales are always told in royal nurseries at twilight, so the Princess knew what she had to expect. The dragon would not eat her, of course — because the prince would come and rescue her. But the Princess could not help thinking it would be much pleasanter to have nothing to do with the dragon at all — not even to be rescued from him. "All the princes I know are such very silly little boys," she told her father. "Why must I be rescued by a prince?"

"It's always done, my dear," said the King, taking his crown off and putting it on the grass, for they were alone in the garden, and even kings must unbend sometimes.

"Father, darling?" said the Princess presently, when she had made a daisy chain and put it on the King's head, where the crown ought to have been. "Father, darling, couldn't we tie up one of the silly little princes for the dragon to look at — and then *I* could go and kill the dragon and rescue the prince? I fence much better than any of the princes we know."

"What an unladylike idea!" said the King, and put his crown on again, for he saw the Prime Minister coming with a basket of new-laid Bills for him to sign. "Dismiss the thought, my child. I rescued your mother from a dragon, and you don't want to set yourself up above her, I should hope?"

"But this is the *last* dragon. It is different from all other dragons."

"How?" asked the King.

"Because he *is* the last," said the Princess, and went off to her fencing lessons, with which she took great pains. She took great pains with all her lessons — for she could not give up the idea of fighting the dragon. She took such pains that she became the strongest and boldest and most skilful and most sensible princess in Europe. She had always been the prettiest and nicest.

And the days and years went on, till at last the day came which was the day before the Princess was to be rescued from the dragon. The Prince who was to do this deed of valour was a pale prince, with large eyes and a head full of mathematics and philosophy, but he had unfortunately neglected his fencing lessons. He was to stay the night at the palace, and there was a banquet.

After supper the Princess sent her pet parrot to the Prince with a note. It said:

> Please, Prince, come on to the terrace. I want to talk to you without anybody else hearing. — The Princess.

So of course, he went — and he saw her gown of silver a long way off shining among the shadows of the trees like water in starlight. And when he came quite close to her he said: "Princess, at your service," and bent his cloth-of-gold-covered knee and put his hand on his cloth-of-gold-covered heart.

"Do you think," said the Princess earnestly, "that you will be able to kill the dragon?"

"I will kill the dragon," said the Prince firmly, "or perish in the attempt."

"It's no use your perishing," said the Princess.

"It's the least I can do," said the Prince.

"What I'm afraid of is that it'll be the most you can do," said the Princess.

"It's the only thing I can do," said he, "unless I kill the dragon."

"Why you should do anything for me is what I can't see," said she.

"But I want to," he said. "You must know that I love you better than anything in the world."

When he said that he looked so kind that the Princess began to like him a little.

"Look here," she said, "no one else will go out tomorrow. You know they tie me to a rock and leave me — and then everybody scurries home and puts up the shutters and keeps them shut till you ride through the town in triumph shouting that you've killed the dragon, and I ride on the horse behind you weeping for joy."

"I've heard that is how it is done," said he.

"Well, do you love me well enough to come very quickly and set me free — and we'll fight the dragon together?"

"It wouldn't be safe for you."

"Much safer for both of us for me to be free, with a sword in my hand, than tied up and helpless. *Do* agree?"

He could refuse her nothing. So he agreed. And next day everything happened as she had said.

When he had cut the cords that tied her to the rock they stood on the lonely mountain-side looking at each other.

"It seems to me," said the Prince, "that this ceremony could have been arranged without the dragon."

"Yes," said the Princess, "but since it has been arranged with the dragon —"

"It seems such a pity to kill the dragon — the last in the world," said the Prince.

"Well then, don't let's," said the Princess; "let's tame it not to eat princesses but to eat out of their hands. They say everything can be tamed by kindness."

"Taming by kindness means giving them things to eat," said the Prince. "Have you got anything to eat?"

She hadn't, but the Prince owned that he had a few biscuits. "Breakfast was so very early," said he, "and I thought you might have felt faint after the fight."

"How clever," said the Princess, and they took a biscuit in each hand. And they looked here, and they looked there, but never a dragon could they see.

"But here's its trail," said the Prince, and pointed to where the rock was scarred and scratched so as to make a track leading to a dark cave. It was like cart-ruts in a Sussex road, mixed with the marks of sea-gulls' feet on the sea-sand. "Look, that's where it's dragged its brass tail and planted its steel claws."

"Don't let's think how hard its tail and its claws are," said the Princess, "or I shall begin to be frightened — and I know you can't tame anything, even by kindness, if you're frightened of it. Come on. Now or never."

She caught the Prince's hand in hers and they ran along the path towards the dark mouth of the cave. But they did not run into it. It really was so very *dark*.

So they stood outside, and the Prince shouted: "What ho! Dragon there! What ho within!" And from the cave they heard an answering voice and great clattering and creaking. It sounded as though a rather large cotton-mill were stretching itself and waking up out of its sleep.

The Prince and Princess trembled, but they stood firm.

"Dragon — I say, dragon!" said the Princess, "do come out and talk to us. We've brought you a present."

"Oh yes — I know your presents," growled the dragon in a huge rumbling voice. "One of those precious princesses, I suppose? And I've got to come out and fight for her. Well, I tell you straight, I'm not going to do it. A fair fight I wouldn't say no to — a fair fight and no favour — but one of those put-up fights where you've got to lose — no! So I tell you. If I wanted a princess I'd come and take her, in my own time — but I don't. What do you suppose I'd do with her, if I'd got her?"

"Eat her, wouldn't you?" said the Princess, in a voice that trembled a little.

"Eat a fiddle-stick end," said the dragon very rudely. "I wouldn't touch the horrid thing."

The Princess's voice grew firmer.

"Do you like biscuits?" she said.

"No," growled the dragon.

"Not the nice little expensive ones with sugar on the top?"

"*No*," growled the dragon.

"Then what *do* you like?" asked the Prince.

"You go away and don't bother me," growled the dragon, and they could hear it turn over, and the clang and clatter of its turning echoed in the cave like the sound of the steam-hammers in the Arsenal at Woolwich.

The Prince and Princess looked at each other. What *were* they to do? Of course it was no use going home and telling the King that the dragon didn't want princesses — because His Majesty was very old-fashioned and would never have believed that a new-fashioned dragon could ever be at all different from an old-fashioned dragon. They could not go into the cave and kill the dragon. Indeed, unless he attacked the Princess it did not seem fair to kill him at all.

"He must like something," whispered the Princess, and she called out in a voice as sweet as honey and sugar-cane:

"Dragon! Dragon dear!"

"WHAT?" shouted the dragon. "Say that again!" and they could hear the dragon 130 coming towards them through the darkness of the cave. The Princess shivered, and said in a very small voice:

"Dragon — Dragon dear!"

And then the dragon came out. The Prince drew his sword, and the Princess drew hers — the beautiful silver-handled one that the Prince had brought in his motor-car. 135 But they did not attack; they moved slowly back as the dragon came out, all the vast scaly length of him, and lay along the rock — his great wings halfspread and his silvery sheen gleaming like diamonds in the sun. At last they could retreat no further — the dark rock behind them stopped their way — and with their backs to the rock they stood swords in hand and waited. 140

The dragon drew nearer and nearer — and now they could see that he was not breathing fire and smoke as they had expected — he came crawling slowly towards them wriggling a little as a puppy does when it wants to play and isn't quite sure whether you're not cross with it.

And then they saw that great tears were coursing down its brazen cheek. 145

"Whatever's the matter?" said the Prince.

"Nobody," sobbed the dragon, "ever called me 'dear' before!"

"Don't cry, dragon dear," said the Princess. "We'll call you 'dear' as often as you like. We want to tame you."

"I *am* tame," said the dragon — "that's just it. That's what nobody but you has ever 150 found out. I'm so tame that I'd eat out of your hands."

"Eat what, dragon dear?" said the Princess. "Not biscuits?" The dragon slowly shook his heavy head.

"Not biscuits?" said the Princess tenderly. "What, then, dragon dear?"

"Your kindness quite undragons me," it said. "No one has ever asked any of us 155 what we like to eat — always offering us princesses, and then rescuing them — and never once, 'What'll you take to drink the King's health in?' Cruel hard I call it," and it wept again.

"But what would you like to drink our health in?" said the Prince. "We're going to be married today, aren't we, Princess?" 160

She said that she supposed so.

"What'll I take to drink your health in?" asked the dragon. "Ah, you're something like a gentleman, you are, sir. I don't mind if I do, sir. I'll be proud to drink your and your good lady's health in a tiny drop of" — its voice faltered — "to think of you asking me so friendly like," it said. "Yes, sir, just a tiny drop of puppuppuppuppupetrol — tha- 165 that's what does a dragon good, sir —"

"I've lots in the car," said the Prince, and was off down the mountain like a flash. He was a good judge of character and knew that with this dragon the Princess would be safe.

"If I might make so bold," said the dragon, "while the gentleman's away — p'raps 170 just to pass the time you'd be so kind as to call me Dear again, and if you'd shake claws with a poor old dragon that's never been anybody's enemy but his own — well, the last of the dragons'll be the proudest dragon that's ever been since the first of them."

It held out an enormous paw, and the great steel hooks that were its claws closed over the Princess's hand as softly as the claws of the Himalayan bear will close over the *175* bit of bun you hand it through the bars at the Zoo.

And so the Prince and Princess went back to the palace in triumph, the dragon following them like a pet dog. And all through the wedding festivities no one drank more earnestly to the happiness of the bride and bridegroom than the Princess's pet dragon — whom she had at once named Fido. *180*

And when the happy pair were settled in their own kingdom, Fido came to them and begged to be allowed to make himself useful.

"There must be some little thing I can do," he said, rattling his wings and stretching his claws. "My wings and claws and so on ought to be turned to some account — to say nothing of my grateful heart." *185*

So the Prince had a special saddle or howdah made for him — very long it was — like the tops of many tramcars fitted together. One hundred and fifty seats were fitted to this, and the dragon, whose greatest pleasure was now to give pleasure to others, delighted in taking parties of children to the seaside. It flew through the air quite easily with its hundred and fifty little passengers — and would lie on the sand patiently *190* waiting till they were ready to return. The children were very fond of it, and used to call it Dear, a word which never failed to bring tears of affection and gratitude to its eyes. So it lived, useful and respected, till quite the other day — when someone happened to say, in his hearing, that dragons were out-of-date, now so much new machinery had come in. This so distressed him that he asked the King to change him into something less old- *195* fashioned, and the kindly monarch at once changed him into a mechanical contrivance. The dragon, indeed, became the first aeroplane.

(c.1900; 1925)

A.E. HOUSMAN
England, 1859-1936

from *A SHROPSHIRE LAD*

"LOVELIEST OF TREES"

Loveliest of trees, the cherry now
Is hung with bloom along the bough,
And stands about the woodland ride
Wearing white for Eastertide.

Now, of my threescore years and ten, *5*
Twenty will not come again,
And take from seventy springs a score,
It only leaves me fifty more.

And since to look at things in bloom
Fifty springs are little room, *10*
About the woodlands I will go
To see the cherry hung with snow.

(1896)

"WHEN I WAS ONE-AND-TWENTY"

When I was one-and-twenty
  I heard a wise man say,
"Give crowns and pounds and guineas
  But not your heart away;
Give pearls away and rubies   5
  But keep your fancy free."
But I was one-and-twenty,
  No use to talk to me.

When I was one-and-twenty
  I heard him say again,   10
"The heart out of the bosom
  Was never given in vain;
'Tis paid with sighs a plenty
  And sold for endless rue."
And I am two-and-twenty,   15
  And oh, 'tis true, 'tis true.

              (1896)

TO AN ATHLETE DYING YOUNG

The time you won your town the race
We chaired you through the market-place;
Man and boy stood cheering by,
And home we brought you shoulder-high.

To-day, the road all runners come,   5
Shoulder-high we bring you home,
And set you at your threshold down,
Townsman of a stiller town.

Smart lad, to slip betimes away
From fields where glory does not stay   10
And early though the laurel grows
It withers quicker than the rose.

Eyes the shady night has shut
Cannot see the record cut,
And silence sounds no worse than cheers   *15*
After earth has stopped the ears:

Now you will not swell the rout
Of lads that wore their honours out,
Runners whom renown outran
And the name died before the man.   20

So set, before its echoes fade,
The fleet foot on the sill of shade,

And hold to the low lintel up
The still-defended challenge-cup.

And round that early-laurelled head   *25*
Will flock to gaze the strengthless dead,
And find unwithered on its curls
The garland briefer than a girl's.

              (1896)

"IS MY TEAM PLOUGHING"

"Is my team ploughing,
  That I was used to drive
And hear the harness jingle
  When I was man alive?"

Ay, the horses trample,   5
  The harness jingles now;
No change though you lie under
  The land you used to plough.

"Is football playing
  Along the river shore,   10
With lads to chase the leather,
  Now I stand up no more?"

Ay, the ball is flying,
  The lads play heart and soul;
The goal stands up, the keeper   *15*
  Stands up to keep the goal.

"Is my girl happy,
  That I thought hard to leave,
And has she tired of weeping
  As she lies down at eve?"   20

Ay, she lies down lightly,
  She lies not down to weep:
Your girl is well contented.
  Be still, my lad, and sleep.

"Is my friend hearty,   25
  Now I am thin and pine,
And has he found to sleep in
  A better bed than mine?"

Yes, lad, I lie easy,
  I lie as lads would choose;   30
I cheer a dead man's sweetheart,
  Never ask me whose.

              (1896)

"WITH RUE MY HEART IS LADEN"

With rue my heart is laden
  For golden friends I had,
For many a rose-lipt maiden
  And many a lightfoot lad.

By brooks too broad for leaping   *5*
  The lightfoot boys are laid;
The rose-lipt girls are sleeping
  In fields where roses fade.

(1896)

SIR CHARLES G.D. ROBERTS
Canada, 1860-1943

THE ATLANTIC CABLE

This giant nerve, at whose command
  The world's great pulses throb or sleep, —
It threads the undiscerned repose
  Of the dark bases of the deep.

Around it settle in the calm   *5*
  Fine tissues that a breath might mar,
Nor dream what fiery tidings pass,
  What messages of storm and war.

Far over it, where filtered gleams
  Faintly illume the mid-sea day,   *10*
Strange, pallid forms of fish or weed
  In the obscure tide softly sway.

And higher, where the vagrant waves
  Frequent the white, indifferent sun,
Where ride the smoke-blue hordes of rain   *15*
  And the long vapours lift and run,

Passes perhaps some lonely ship
  With exile hearts that homeward ache, —
While far beneath is flashed a word
  That soon shall bid them bleed or break.   *20*

(1898)

THE PRISONERS OF THE PITCHER-PLANT

At the edge of a rough piece of open, where the scrubby bushes which clothed the plain gave space a little to the weeds and harsh grasses, stood the clustering pitchers of a fine young sarracenia. These pitchers, which were its leaves, were of a light, cool green, vividly veined with crimson and shading into a bronzy red about the lip and throat. They were of all sizes, being at all stages of growth; and the largest, which had now, on the   *5* edge of summer, but barely attained maturity, were about six inches in length and an inch and a quarter in extreme diameter. Down in the very heart of the cluster, hardly to be discerned, was a tiny red-tipped bud, destined to shoot up, later in the season, into a sturdy flower-stalk.

    Against the fresh, warm green of the sunlit world surrounding it, the sarracenia's   *10* peculiar colouring stood out conspicuously, its streaks and splashes of red having the effect of blossoms. This effect, at a season when bright-hued blooms were scarce, made the plant very attractive to any insects that chanced within view of it. There was nearly

---

always some flutterer or hummer poising above it, or touching it eagerly to dart away again in disappointment. But every once in a while some little wasp, or fly, or shining-winged beetle, or gauzy ichneumon, would alight on the alluring lip, pause, and peer down into the pitcher. As a rule the small investigator would venture farther and farther, till it disappeared. Then it never came out again. *15*

On a leaf of a huckleberry bush, overhanging the pitcher-plant, a little black ant was running about with the nimble curiosity of her kind. An orange-and-black butterfly, fluttering lazily in the sun, came close beside the leaf. At this moment a passing shrike swooped down and caught the butterfly in his beak. One of his long wings, chancing to strike the leaf, sent it whirling from its stem; and the ant fell directly upon one of the pitchers below. *20*

It was far down upon the red, shining lip of the pitcher that she fell; and there she clung resolutely, her feet sinking into a sort of fur of smooth, whitish hairs. When she had quite recovered her equanimity she started to explore her new surroundings; and, because that was the easiest way to go, she went in the direction toward which the hairs all pointed. In a moment, therefore, she found herself just on the edge of the precipitous slope from the lip to the throat of the pitcher. Here, finding the slope strangely slippery, she thought it best to stop and retrace her steps. But when she attempted this she found it impossible. The little, innocent-looking hairs all pressed against her, thrusting her downward. The more she struggled, the more energetically and elastically they pushed back at her; till all at once she was forced over the round, smooth edge, and fell. *25*

30

To her terrified amazement, it was water she fell into. The pitcher was about half full of the chilly fluid. In her kickings and twistings she brought herself to the walls of her green prison, and tried to clamber out — but here, again, were those cruel hairs on guard to foil her. She tried to evade them, to break them down, to bite them off with her strong, sharp mandibles. At last, by a supreme effort, she managed to drag herself almost clear — but only to be at once hurled back, and far out into the water, by the sharp recoil of her tormentors. *35*

40

Though pretty well exhausted by now, she would not give up the struggle; and presently her convulsive efforts brought her alongside of a refuge. It was only the floating body of a dead moth, but to the ant it was a safe and ample raft. Eagerly she crept out upon it, and lay very still for a while, recovering her strength. More fortunate than most shipwrecked voyagers, she had an edible raft and was therefore in no imminent peril of starvation. *45*

The light that came through the veined, translucent walls of this watery prison was of an exquisite cool beryl, very different from the warm daylight overhead. The ant had never been in any such surroundings before, and was bewildered by the strangeness of them. After a brief rest she investigated minutely every corner of her queer retreat, and then, finding that there was nothing she could do to better the situation, she resumed her attitude of repose, with only the slight waving of her antennae to show that she was awake. *50*

For a long time nothing happened. No winds were astir that day, and no sounds came down into the pitcher save the shrill, happy chirping of birds in the surrounding bushes. But suddenly the pitcher began to tip and rock slightly, and the water to wash within its coloured walls. Something had alighted on the pitcher's lip. *55*

It was something comparatively heavy, that was evident. A moment or two later it came sliding down those treacherous hairs, and fell into the water with a great splash which nearly swept the ant from her refuge. 60

The new arrival was a bee. And now began a tremendous turmoil within the narrow prison. The bee struggled, whirled around on the surface with thrashing wings, and sent the water swashing in every direction, till the ant was nearly drowned. She hung to her raft, however, and waited philosophically for the hubbub to subside. At length the bee 65 too, after half a dozen vain and exhausting struggles to climb out against the opposing array of hairs, encountered the body of the dead moth. Instantly she tried to raise herself upon it, so as to escape the chill of the water and dry her wings for flight. But she was too heavy. The moth sank, and rolled over, at the same time being thrust against the wall of the pitcher. The ant, in high indignation, clutched a bundle of the hostile hairs in her 70 mandibles, and held herself at anchor against the wall.

Thoroughly used up, and stupid with panic and chill, the bee kept on futilely grappling with the moth's body, which, in its turn, kept on sinking and rolling beneath her. A very few minutes of such disastrous folly sufficed to end the struggle, and soon the bee was floating, drowned and motionless, beside the moth. Then the ant, with 75 satisfaction, returned to her refuge.

When things get started happening, they are quite apt to keep it up for a while, as if events invited events. A large hunting spider, creeping among the grass and weeds, discovered the handsome cluster of the sarracenia. She was one of the few creatures who had learned the secret of the pitcher-plant and knew how to turn it to account. More 80 than once had she found easy prey in some trapped insect struggling near the top of a well-filled pitcher.

Selecting the largest pitcher as the one most likely to yield results, the spider climbed its stem. Then she mounted the bright swell of the pitcher itself, whose smooth outer surface offered no obstacle to such visitors. The pitcher swayed and bowed. The 85 water within washed heavily. And the ant, with new alarm, marked the big, black shadow of the spider creeping up the outside of her prison.

Having reached the lip of the leaf and cautiously crawled over upon it, the spider took no risks with those traitor hairs. She threw two or three stout cables of web across the lip; and then, with this secure anchorage by which to pull herself back, she ventured 90 fearlessly down the steep of that perilous throat. One hooked claw, outstretched behind her, held aloft the cable which exuded from her spinnerets as she moved.

On the extreme of the slope she stopped, and her red, jewelled cluster of eyes glared fiercely down upon the little black ant. The latter shrank and crouched, and tried to hide herself under the side of the dead moth to escape the light of those baleful eyes. This 95 new peril was one which appalled her far more than all the others she had encountered.

At this most critical of all crises in the destiny of the little blank ant, the fickle Fortune of the Wild was seized with another whim. An overwhelming cataclysm descended suddenly upon the tiny world of the pitcher-plant. The soft, furry feet of some bounding monster — rabbit, fox, or wildcat — came down amongst the clustered 100 pitchers, crushing several to bits and scattering wide the contents of all the rest. Among these latter was that which contained the little black ant. Drenched, astonished, but unhurt, she found herself lying in a tuft of splashed grass, once more free. Above her, on a grass-top, clung the bewildered spider. As it hung there, conspicuous to all the foraging world, a great black-and-yellow wasp pounced upon it, stung it into [105] helplessness, and carried it off on heavily humming wing.

(1907)

ARCHIBALD LAMPMAN
Canada, 1861-1899

IN NOVEMBER

With loitering step and quiet eye,
Beneath the low November sky,
I wandered in the woods, and found
A clearing, where the broken ground
Was scattered with black stumps and briers,
And the old wreck of forest fires. [6]
It was a bleak and sandy spot,
And, all about, the vacant plot,
Was peopled and inhabited
By scores of mulleins long since dead. [10]
A silent and forsaken brood
In that mute opening of the wood,
So shrivelled and so thin they were,
So gray, so haggard, and austere,
Not plants at all they seemed to me, [15]
But rather some spare company
Of hermit folk, who long ago,
Wandering in bodies to and fro,
Had chanced upon this lonely way,
And rested thus, till death one day [20]
Surprised them at their compline prayer,
And left them standing lifeless there.

There was no sound about the wood
Save the wind's secret stir. I stood
Among the mullein-stalks as still [25]
As if myself had grown to be
One of their sombre company,

A body without wish or will.
And as I stood, quite suddenly,
Down from a furrow in the sky [30]
The sun shone out a little space
Across that silent sober place,
Over the sand heaps and brown sod,
The mulleins and dead goldenrod,
And passed beyond the thickets gray, [35]
And lit the fallen leaves that lay,
Level and deep within the wood,
A rustling yellow multitude.

And all around me the thin light,
So sere, so melancholy bright, [40]
Fell like the half-reflected gleam
Or shadow of some former dream;
A moment's golden reverie
Poured out on every plant and tree
A semblance of weird joy, or less, [45]
A sort of spectral happiness;
And I, too, standing idly there,
With muffled hands in the chill air,
Felt the warm glow about my feet,
And shuddering betwixt cold and heat, [50]
Drew my thoughts closer, like a cloak,
While something in my blood awoke,
A nameless and unnatural cheer,
A pleasure secret and austere.

(1890)

IN NOVEMBER   **10. mulleins:** plants with broad fleshy leaves and a very tall flower stalk. **21. compline:** the last of the "canonical hours," i.e., the seven periods of daily prayer as described by ecclesiastical law; the other six are matins with lauds, prime, tierce, sext, nones, and vespers.

TEMAGAMI

Far in the grim Northwest beyond the lines
That turn the rivers eastward to the sea,
Set with a thousand islands, crowned with pines,
Lies the deep water, wild Temagami:
Wild for the hunter's roving, and the use   5
Of trappers in its dark and trackless vales,
Wild with the trampling of the giant moose,

And the weird magic of old Indian tales.
All day with steady paddles toward the west
Our heavy-laden long canoe we pressed: 10
All day we saw the thunder-travelled sky
Purpled with storm in many a trailing tress,
And saw at eve the broken sunset die
In crimson on the silent wilderness.

(1898)

MARY COLERIDGE
England, 1861-1907

NO NEWSPAPERS

Where, to me, is the loss
    Of the scenes they saw — of the sounds they heard;
A butterfly flits across,
    Or a bird;
The moss is growing on the wall,   5
    I heard the leaf of the poppy fall.

(1900)

SARA JEANNETTE DUNCAN
Canada, 1861-1922

from SAUNTERINGS

November 25, 1886

That it was quite possible to enjoy life, Anastasia, the Youth, and I discovered last summer, and to do it in the orthodox and approved fashion set by those who leave town for the purpose, without either going a prodigious distance or paying a prodigious price. These negative advantages were supplemented by a positive opportunity of gaining some knowledge of local life and character as it is in the Province of Ontario. Local life   5
and character being sought for by Canadians usually anywhere but in Canada, we were fired by a sense of originality in our plan to discover it in the wilds of Prince Edward County.

TEMAGAMI Title: a river in northern Ontario. SAUNTERINGS The title is that of Duncan's regular column in the Toronto newspaper *The Week*. **1. Anastasia, the Youth:** fictional names for her companions. **7-8. Prince Edward County:** i.e., nearby in eastern Ontario.

There may be a few among the great untravelled that do not live in the vicinity of the place who will follow us geographically to the "Sand Banks," on the shores of Lake *10* Ontario. A dotted line vaguely indicates them on the map, which gives no sign, however, of their being inhabited. The most speculative architect of castles in the air would never dream of constructing upon the basis of that wavering and watery indication the magnificence of a pine palace for the accommodation of the transient public, flanked by a grocery and surrounded by every sylvan and sandy attraction: yet *15* such there is. The sand banks are phenomenal, and where there is a phenomenon there is sure to be a hotel.

To get to Picton from almost anywhere in the summer, one sails up the long, narrow, picturesquely irregular Bay of Quinté. Thrice happy is he who takes the trip in that magical time between the day and the darkness of the glowing July weather, when the *20* little steamer almost noiselessly furrows her way through the still, shining water, with its dark tree-shadows and sunset tints of rose and amber, carrying her voyagers, one fancies, to some sure haven where the purple and the gold and the violet and the opal do not slip away. The solid old farm-houses that send their straggling boundaries down to the steep, rocky, moss-grown water's edge, have a look of having been built for comfort and *25* endurance. The fences are all of stones piled on top of one another. Here and there the blossoming water betrays the idyl of a love-tryst at the water-foot of one of these primitive divisions, where Corydon and Phyllis are discussing the advisability of taking it down. And now and then our little craft makes a convulsive hiatus in her peaceful puffing toward an ideal port, and rubs up along a weather-beaten old wharf to receive a solitary passenger, *30* or some half-dozen bags of an agricultural product, the lumpy and uninteresting nature of which will never be made public through the medium of this pen. One feels disposed to speculate upon the forgotten past of these discouraged-looking little settlements, each with its demoralised landing or dilapidated pier, its dusty road curving down to the water out of the woods and pastures, and its church spire rising from a parti-coloured sprinkling of *35* village houses, and softly throwing its doctrinal significance against the evening sky — a chapter folded back in a book that few turn the leaves of; and yet what open page of Canadian history is more bravely illuminated than that which burns with the steadfast loyalty of the strong-hearted ten thousand who preferred allegiance as subjects to disaffection as citizens, even at the expense of all that exile meant in 1783! *40*

It is ten o'clock when we puff into Picton, and at eleven we are driving through the soft radiance of a July moon, that shows us on one side of the road symmetrical maples, set out by the beauty-loving Prince Edward County farmers; on the other, glimmering whitely through the dark cedars and wild undergrowth, the sand banks that have given the narrow peninsula its local fame. Here and there the sand has gradually forced its way through and *45* over the trees to the road, which curves in as the sure yearly encroach is made. Silhouetted against the sky, the dead cedars stretch pathetic arms above us, and every now and then a plash from Lake Ontario, quiet to-night, sounds from behind them. Two hours of this and a sudden bend in the road discloses the hotel, all alight, apparently for the accommodation of a large and fraternal number of circus companies, who have pitched the colossal tents *50* which shine like snow in the moonlight, in most friendly proximity.

---

28. Corydon and Phyllis: conventional names for pastoral lovers; see, e.g., Breton's "Phillida and Coridon" (p. 200). **40. 1783:** the year that a large number of United Empire Loyalists left the newly republican United States to live in Canada.

We are welcomed by a special benefaction in the shape of a young married person, who finds that her olive branches thrive in the doubtful fertility of the Sand Banks, and who shows us the way to the dining room.

There is nobody else to do it — not a hint of a clerk with an old-gold necktie, not a suggestion of a porter without any necktie at all. In fact, there is not a human being visible except a tall, loose-jointed man without a coat, who slouches into the room after us, appropriates a chair at the head of our table, and addresses us familiarly upon the subject of cold apple-pie. Our relative seems to take his presence there quite as a matter of course, so we feel that it behooves us not to be premature with our indignation. We are too hungry to be dignified, anyway, so we content ourselves with bestowing our undivided attention upon such fragments of the feast as remain after forty boarders, ravenous with the fresh lake air, have partaken of their evening meal. We merely observe that he is guilelessly innocent of conventionality and cuffs; that he tips his chair with accustomed grace, and leans forward on his elbows with the air of a part of the establishment. Later, in the seclusion of an apartment which we share with the young married person aforesaid and all the olive branches, we learn that the gentleman who had honoured us with his society was a sort of Pooh-Bah compendium of all the officials whose services we had missed, that he habitually distinguished himself by the non-performance of any of them, that his name was Byers, and that he was had in reputation and respect upon various accounts throughout the whole length and breadth of the county.

We are drawn in from our early stroll among the pines and the rocks and the blossoming elder-bushes next morning by a clamorous bell, which seemed to speak griddle-cakes to our waiting souls. Approaching the veranda, we see that Byers is ringing it, and, having seated ourselves in the plank-walled dining-room, with the lake breeze blowing straight through it, Byers brings us the griddle-cakes of our anticipation. Daylight discloses him the possessor of a long, bristling, yellow moustache, overshadowing a mouth turned down at the corners, with a chronic expression of disgust at things in general. His nose hooks over it, and his gray eyes have a speculative expression. His movements are so mechanical that the Youth whispers, in an awe-struck voice, his conviction that a disrobing would find him wooden, with joints. We feel sure that he superintends the dish-washing; but we are mistaken, for he waylays us in the hall to "register." This we proceed to do, with the forty boarders in a curious line behind us. Only when a guest comes to stay for at least a week is that precious record produced. On being interrogated as to its seclusion from the public eye, Byers had responded to the effect that, while there was nothing mean about him, paper cost something; and "them darned picnickers 'ud fill it up in a week." In fact, nothing happens to exercise this functionary that is not laid directly at the door of the irresponsible, unprofitable, but smilingly guileless rustic visitors, who come for the day with their baskets, disport themselves on the two capacious swings, make love publicly and unrestrainedly on the veranda, but in no wise add to the revenue of the big pine hotel. So in his heart Byers hateth them.

---

53. **olive branches:** children (see Psalms 128:3). 68. **Pooh-Bah:** a self-important character, the "Lord High Everything Else," in Gilbert and Sullivan's *The Mikado* (1885).

Next day is Sunday — a gala day at the Sand Banks. From nine o'clock in the morning until nine at night, trim top-buggies, weather-beaten "democrats," and *95* comfortable family carriages deposit their loads of bashful youths and blushing maidens, farmers' families, shopmen, bank clerks, and all sorts and conditions of townspeople, chiefly come to keep cool, wander about, amuse themselves, and see their friends, for the place is purely local, and everybody is "acquainted." Quoits or croquet, being untaxable, Mr. Byers strictly forbids as violations of the Sabbath; but any and all *100* of the visitors may indulge in rifle-shooting, back of the stables, at a dozen shots for a quarter, without incurring anybody's censure. Of course, ill-natured people make remarks about it; but Byers scorns to justify himself, and goes about persecuted for righteousness' sake. The boarders lie in hammocks under the trees, sing, smoke, and read novels; occasionally making an incursion upon the dining-room, where the tables *105* are always set. They do not dance or play cards. One is almost inclined to record it to their credit.

"Mr. Byers, why don't you have church here, in the dance-hall? You often have a minister over Sunday," asks a lady with a troubled conscience this afternoon.

"Well, ma'am ther' was a church here onct. Right down there." An expressive *110* finger is pointed toward the great white banks. "The sand buried it. Discovered it myself, three weeks ago. Ther's a Presbyterian minister in it, just pernouncin' the benediction. But the congregation had gone hum to dinner! Honest though, no foolin', folks don't want no church here. They come here to have a good time, an' darn it all, they're goin' to *have* it — while I'm boss!" *115*

But we discover that Mr. Byers' views are subject to fluctuation — the weather, or the surroundings, or the social atmosphere affect them equally. He brings a chair down to the lake shore one bright evening, where we sit staring at the shimmering water and the fleecy clouds, and the dark island-outlines, and proceeds to give us various doctrinal views. He begins by inquiring what church we "patronise." We respond, with kindling *120* recollection of our covenanting forefathers, that we are Presbyterians.

"Thought so," giving his chair a hitch to avoid a ledge at the back of his head. Byers never utilises all the legs of his chair. "Ther's somethin' about Presbyterians that gives 'em away every time. Fine people though, the Presbyterians — finer 'n the Methodists by a long sight. I tell *you* I've come across some pretty darn mean *125* Methodists, considerin' the way they whoop 'er up! You never heard tell of 'Bijah Crooks, I 'spose. Well, 'Bijah Crooks is my wife's own second cousin, but I'm bound to say he's the biggest Methodist an' the smallest man in the hull country!"

He pauses for an expression of interest in 'Bijah, which comes with promptitude.

"You see he's the feller that keeps the pound. He got an old white horse in there *130* one day last spring. Jake Smith he owned the beast, an' had turned him out on the road to die. When 'Bijah found after keepin' him nigh onto a fortnight ther' wasn't nothin' to be made out o' Jake, what 'd he do but up an' tell old Doctor Burdock, the best-naturedest man ever was, that *his brother's* white mare was goin' to be sold fer poundage ef he didn't pay two dollars an' git her out. Jim Burdock never owned a white *135*

103-04. persecuted . . . sake: See Matthew 5:10 (p. 252). **121. covenanting:** i.e., Scottish defenders of Presbyterianism; see note to line 130 of Stevenson's "The Foreigner at Home" (p. 1136).

mare in his life far's I know, but the Doctor, knowin' no better, up an' paid the two dollars like a man. He's ben lookin' fer 'Bijah ever since."

"And the poor old white horse —" breathlessly from the Youth.

"Oh, it died in the Doctor's back yard over to Ameliasburg. But that wasn't just square ef 'Bijah, was it now? I'm always thankful I don't worship 'long with *his* sex, 'f *140* they do make more noise."

If I am a blue Presbyterian, Anastasia is a pink and white Methodist, but she doesn't champion her cause. Perhaps 'Bijah's derelictions strike her as too overwhelming to be lightly dealt with, and Anastasia never deals with things seriously — in the hot weather. So in a somnolent spirit of peace and good will, she inquires our entertainer's *145* denominational tendencies.

"Me? Oh, I'm a Brethern. In other words, my wife is. Deacon, too, I am; but she does it fer both of us in the season. Sunday's no day fer me to leave. Lots o' Brethern round here. An' there's no church like 'em — not fer good works. I ain't undoctrinatin' any other denomination, either; dare say there's good in all of 'em. But fer liberal views *150* and proper methods of interpolatin' Scripter I'll back the Brethern. Ef a man thinks a thing's right, why it *is* right — that's all ther' is about it; en' ef he thinks it's wrong, it's wrong." Here he becomes ornate and gesticulative. "An' we don't believe in goin' mournin' all our days, an' callin' this a world of woe. Ef mirthfulness ain't enj'ined in Scripter, I want to know what is. I don't hang my harp on no willow, an' ther's a good *155* deal o' dance in me yet, ef I am married an' settled. 'Nother thing, we believe in immersion as the only symptom o' baptism in the hull Bible. Ef ther's one *re*diculous doctern in your church, it's that sprinklin' the kids!"

The moon shines down upon us, and the waves curl over the big stones and slip back again, leaving them covered with the filmy lacework of the foam. The blue-bells *160* growing in the rock crevices sway with the wind; there is a sound of laughter from the pine-hid veranda; and still Byers continues to discourse with intent to prove that this world is a very tolerable place to live in, if one only possesses a rightly-constituted conscience. And by and by we leave him to his comfortable theory.

It is the day to press flowers, to pack mementoes, to take parting looks at things. *165* The time of our departure is at hand. We are tenderly contemplating that fact and some very badly cooked beefsteak at breakfast when we become conscious of an unusual stir in the "office," that is, the place in which Byers keeps his beloved register. The door opens and a yachting party noisily takes possession of what is known as "the strangers'" table. Six gentlemen, all in becoming navy blue. Poor Anastasia! Her back is toward *170* them, and nobody is interested in a back view.

"I'll have an egg — no, two."

"We haven't any eggs, sir, only for the boarders."

"A glass of milk — ice in it."

"Have to buy our milk, sir. Don't give it to nobody but the boarders' children, on *175* special terms."

"Got any whitefish?"

---

147. Brethern: i.e., Plymouth Brethren. **155. harp . . . willow:** See Psalms 137:2, and the refrain of the popular song "There Is a Tavern in the Town."

"Not this morning, sir. Only enough cooked for the boarders. Like some beefsteak?"

"Yes, if the boarders don't mind. And if there's anything else they haven't disposed   *180*
of, you can bring us that too. We're not particular."

We linger over our last griddle cakes, photograph the rough, bright room, with its shocking chromos, indelibly upon our minds and "settle." Nearly everybody is going to-day; two carriages are waiting now. It costs three cents to answer letters about rooms, and Byers never gratifies public curiosity at his own expense, on principle. Consequently the   *185*
Sand Banks hostelry is overcrowded or empty always. He is everywhere this morning, coatless, hatless, as usual, with his slick, long, whitish hair pasted over his forehead, and his mouth turned down at the corners with its characteristic expression of disgusted forlornity. He shakes hands all round with genuine regret, and, just as we drive off, leans over toward me with a nod in Anastasia's direction. "Say," he whispers timorously,   *190*
"what's her front name?"

(1886)

BLISS CARMAN
Canada, 1861-1929

LOW TIDE ON GRAND PRÉ

The sun goes down, and over all
  These barren reaches by the tide
Such unelusive glories fall,
  I almost dream they yet will bide
  Until the coming of the tide.　　*5*

And yet I know that not for us,
  By any ecstasy of dream,
He lingers to keep luminous
  A little while the grievous stream,
  Which frets, uncomforted of dream —　　*10*

A grievous stream, that to and fro
  Athrough the fields of Acadie
Goes wandering, as if to know
  Why one beloved face should be
  So long from home and Acadie.　　*15*

Was it a year or lives ago
  We took the grasses in our hands,
And caught the summer flying low
  Over the waving meadow lands,
  And held it there between our hands?　　*20*

The while the river at our feet —
  A drowsy inland meadow stream —
At set of sun the after-heat
  Made running gold, and in the gleam
  We freed our birch upon the stream.　　*25*

There down along the elms at dusk
  We lifted dripping blade to drift,
Through twilight scented fine like musk,
  Where night and gloom awhile uplift,
  Nor sunder soul and soul adrift.　　*30*

LOW TIDE ON GRAND PRÉ   Title: in New Brunswick. **12. Acadie:** Acadia; on the expulsion of the Acadians to Louisiana, see the note to Longfellow's *Evangeline* (p. 932); the expulsion and the return home have been the subject of many literary works, including Antonine Maillet's novel *Pélagie-la-charrette* (1979).

And that we took into our hands
   Spirit of life or subtler thing —
Breathed on us there, and loosed the bands
   Of death, and taught us, whispering,
   The secret of some wonder-thing.   35

Then all your face grew light, and seemed
   To hold the shadow of the sun;
The evening faltered, and I deemed
   That time was ripe, and years had done
   Their wheeling underneath the sun.   40

So all desire and all regret,
   And fear and memory, were naught;
One to remember or forget
   The keen delight our hands had caught;
   Morrow and yesterday were naught.   45

The night has fallen, and the tide . . .
   Now and again comes drifting home,
Across these aching barrens wide,
   A sigh like driven wind or foam;
   In grief the flood is bursting home.   50

(1893)

from SAPPHO

XXIII

I loved thee, Atthis, in the long ago,
When the great oleanders were in flower
In the broad herded meadows full of sun.
And we would often at the fall of dusk
Wander together by the silver stream,   5
When the soft grass-heads were all wet with dew
And purple-misted in the fading light.
And joy I knew and sorrow at thy voice,
And the superb magnificence of love, —
The loneliness that saddens solitude,   10
And the sweet speech that makes it durable, —
The bitter longing and the keen desire,
The sweet companionship through quiet days
In the slow ample beauty of the world,
And the unutterable glad release   15
Within the temple of the holy night.
O Atthis, how I loved thee long ago
In that fair perished summer by the sea!

(1902)

RABINDRANATH TAGORE
India, 1861-1941

"Come friend, flinch not"
Come friend, flinch not, step down upon the hard earth.
Do not gather dreams in the dusk.
Storms are brewing in the sky, lightning flashes are striking at our sleep.
Come down to the common life.
The web of illusion is torn, take shelter within walls of rough stones.   5

(1886, 1942)

SAPPHO   The poem is a version of a lyric in fragment 40 of the poems of Sappho of Lesbos (born c.612 B.C.).   **COME FRIEND, FLINCH NOT**   This is Tagore's own translation of "Marichika," a poem he wrote in Bengali in 1886.

MARY KINGSLEY
England, 1862-1900

from *TRAVELS IN WEST AFRICA*

Chapter VI: Libreville and Glass

I must pause here to explain my reasons for giving extracts from my diary, being informed on excellent authority that publishing a diary is a form of literary crime. Such being the case I have to urge in extenuation of my committing it that — Firstly, I have not done it before, for so far I have given a sketchy *résumé* of many diaries kept by me while visiting the regions I have attempted to describe. Secondly, no one expects literature in a book of travel. Thirdly, there are things to be said in favour of the diary form, particularly when it is kept in a little known and wild region, for the reader gets therein notice of things that, although unimportant in themselves, yet go to make up the conditions of life under which men and things exist. The worst of it is these things are not often presented in their due and proper proportion in diaries. Many pages in my journals that I will spare you display this crime to perfection. For example: "Awful turn up with crocodile about ten — Paraffin good for over-oiled boots — Evil spirits crawl on ground, hence high lintel — Odeaka cheese is made thus: —" Then comes half a yard on Odeaka cheese making.

When a person is out travelling, intent mainly on geography, it is necessary, if he publishes his journals, that he should publish them in sequence. But I am not a geographer. I have to learn the geography of a region I go into in great detail, so as to get about; but my means of learning it are not the scientific ones — Taking observations, Surveying, Fixing points, &c., &c. These things I know not how to do. I do not "take lunars"; and I always sympathise with a young friend of mine, who, on hearing that an official had got dreadfully ill from taking them, said, "What do those government men do it for? It kills them all off. I don't hold with knocking yourself to pieces with a lot of doctor's stuff." I certainly have a dim idea that lunars are not a sort of pill; but I quite agree that they were unwholesome things for a man to take in West Africa. This being my point of view regarding geography, I have relegated it to a separate chapter and have dealt similarly with trade and Fetish.

I have omitted all my bush journal. It is a journal of researches in Fetish and of life in the forest and in native villages, and I think I have a better chance of making this

5

10

15

20

25

TRAVELS IN WEST AFRICA   **1. diary:** The diary records Kingsley's impressions during her travels in 1895 to French Equatorial Africa (now the country of Gabon) — where she was collecting natural history specimens — and specifically to the towns of Libreville and Glass. Glass is south of Libreville; both are on the gulf of Gabon (formerly Gaboon, line 115), north of the Ogowé (now the Ogooué) River (line 89). From northwest to southeast, the countries that now border on the Gulf of Guinea are Ivory Coast, Ghana, Togo, Benin, Nigeria, Cameroon, Equatorial Guinea, Gabon, Zaire, and Angola. **13. Odeaka:** in the Niger Coast Protectorate (now Nigeria), where Kingsley had travelled on her first trip to Africa, in 1894. **20. "take lunars":** lunar observations, to determine longitude. **26. Fetish:** one form of African religion, in which an object (or fetish) was deemed to possess special powers, either because of its independent will or because a god dwelt within it.

information understood by collecting it together; for the African forest is not a place you
can, within reasonable limits, give an idea of by chronicling your own experience in it day   30
by day. As a psychological study the carefully kept journal of a white man, from the first
day he went away from his fellow whites and lived in the Great Forest Belt of Africa,
among natives, who had not been in touch with white culture, would be an exceedingly
interesting thing, provided it covered a considerable space of time; but to the general
reader it would be hopelessly wearisome, and as for myself, I am not bent on discoursing   35
on my psychological state, but on the state of things in general in West Africa.

On first entering the great grim twilight regions of the forest you hardly see
anything but the vast column-like grey tree stems in their countless thousands around
you, and the sparsely vegetated ground beneath. But day by day, as you get trained to
your surroundings, you see more and more, and a whole world grows up gradually out   40
of the gloom before your eyes. Snakes, beetles, bats and beasts, people the region that at
first seemed lifeless.

It is the same with the better lit regions, where vegetation is many-formed and
luxuriant. As you get used to it, what seemed at first to be an inextricable tangle ceases
to be so. The separate sorts of plants stand out before your eyes with ever increasing   45
clearness, until you can pick out the one particular one you may want; and daily you
find it easier to make your way through what looked at first an impenetrable wall, for
you have learnt that it is in the end easier to worm your way in among networks of
creepers, than to shirk these, and go for the softer walls of climbing grasses and curtains
of lycopodium; and not only is it easier, but safer, for in the grass and lycopodium there   50
are nearly certain to be snakes galore, and the chances are you may force yourself into
the privacy of a gigantic python's sleeping place.

There is the same difference also between night and day in the forest. You may
have got fairly used to it by day, and then some catastrophe keeps you out in it all night,
and again you see another world. To my taste there is nothing so fascinating as spending   55
a night out in an African forest, or plantation; but I beg you to note I do not advise any
one to follow the practice. Nor indeed do I recommend African forest life to any one.
Unless you are interested in it and fall under its charm, it is the most awful life in death
imaginable. It is like being shut up in a library whose books you cannot read, all the
while tormented, terrified, and bored. And if you do fall under its spell, it takes all the   60
colour out of other kinds of living. Still, it is good for a man to have an experience of it,
whether he likes it or not, for it teaches you how very dependent you have been, during
your previous life, on the familiarity of those conditions you have been brought up
among, and on your fellow citizens; moreover it takes the conceit out of you pretty
thoroughly during the days you spend stupidly stumbling about among your new   65
surroundings.

When this first period passes there comes a sense of growing power. The proudest
day in my life was the day on which an old Fan hunter said to me — "Ah! you see."
Now he did not say this, I may remark, as a tribute to the hard work I had been doing in
order to see, but regarded it as the consequence of a chief having given me a little ivory   70

---

32. Great Forest Belt: i.e., the Guinea (meaning "forest") Coast and the jungle interior of the Congo and other river basins. **50. lycopodium:** a form
of moss named for the wolf's-claw shape of its root; also called club-moss. **68. Fan:** a Gabon tribal group.

half-moon, whose special mission was "to make man see Bush," and when you have attained to that power in full, a state I do not pretend to have yet attained to, you can say, "Put me where you like in an African forest, and as far as the forest goes, starve me or kill me if you can."

As it is with the forest, so it is with the minds of the natives. Unless you live alone *75* among the natives, you never get to know them; if you do this you gradually get a light into the true state of their mind-forest. At first you see nothing but a confused stupidity and crime; but when you get to see — well! as in the other forest, — you see things worth seeing. But it is beyond me to describe the process, so we will pass on to Congo Français. *80*

My reasons for going to this wildest and most dangerous part of the West African regions were perfectly simple and reasonable. I had not found many fish in the Oil Rivers, and, as I have said, my one chance of getting a collection of fishes from a river north of the Congo lay in the attitude Mr. C. G. Hudson might see fit to assume towards ichthyology. Mr. Hudson I had met in 1893 at Kabinda, when he rescued me from dire *85* dilemmas, and proved himself so reliable, that I had no hesitation in depending on his advice. Since those Kabinda days he had become a sort of commercial Bishop, *i.e.,* an Agent-General for Messrs. Hatton and Cookson in Congo Français, and in this capacity had the power to let me get up the Ogowé river, the greatest river between the Niger and the Congo. This river is mainly known in England from the works of Mr. Du Chaillu, *90* who, however, had the misfortune on both his expeditions to miss actually discovering it. Still, he knew it was there, and said so; and from his reports other explorers went out to look for it and duly found it; but of them hereafter. It has been in the possession of France nearly forty years now, and the French authorities keep quite as much order as one can expect along its navigable water way, considering that the density of the forest *95* around it harbours and protects a set of notoriously savage tribes chief among which are the Fans. These Fans are a great tribe that have, in the memory of living men, made their appearance in the regions known to white men, in a state of migration seawards, and are a bright, active, energetic sort of African, who by their pugnacious and predatory conduct do much to make one cease to regret and deplore the sloth and lethargy of the *100* rest of the West Coast tribes; but of Fans I will speak by and by; and merely preface my diary by stating that Congo Français has a coast line of about 900 miles, extending from the Campo River to a point a few miles north of Landana, with the exception of the small Corisco region claimed by Spain. The Hinterland is not yet delimitated, except as regards the Middle Congo. The French possession runs from Brazzaville on Stanley *105*

---

78. crime: i.e., a presumed state of "sinfulness" because they were not Christian. **79-80. Congo Français:** now called Congo, as distinct from the Belgian Congo (Congo Belge, line 548), which is now called Zaire. **82-83. Oil Rivers:** the tributaries that empty into the Niger delta, of which the Benin and Brass Rivers constitute the main western and eastern branches, respectively; Britain claimed the area in 1885. **85. Kabinda:** now called Cabinda, an administrative enclave of Angola on the coast between Congo and Zaire. **88. Hatton and Cookson:** a trading company with whom Kingsley had arranged a line of credit, as she paid her way in goods rather than in currency. **90. Du Chaillu:** Paul Belloni Du Chaillu (c.1831-1903), explorer and popular writer (the son of a French trader in Gabon), who later became an American citizen; his public lectures in London in 1861 helped construct conventional stereotypes about gorillas and cannibals. **103. Campo:** in southwest Cameroon; **Landana:** town in Cabinda, now called Evinayong. **104. Corisco . . . Spain:** The colony of Spanish Guinea consisted of an island called Fernando Po (see line 220) and a section of mainland called Rio Muni, to the northwest of Gabon (see line 407); these areas are now the two largest parts of the country of Equatorial Guinea. **105. Brazzaville:** now the capital city of Congo, across the river from Kinshasa (formerly Leopoldville), the capital city of Zaire, just where the Congo River widens into a lake called Pool Malebo (formerly Stanley Pool, named for the British journalist Henry Morton Stanley, 1841-1904).

Pool up to the confluence of the M'Ubanji with the Congo, then following the western bank of the M'Ubanji. Away to the N.N.E. it is not yet delimitated, and although the French have displayed great courage and enterprise, there are still great stretches of country in Congo Français that have never been visited by a white man; but the same may be said to as great an extent of the West Coast possessions of England and *110* Germany.

The whole of the territory that is at present roughly delimitated, may have an area of 220,000 square miles, with a population variously estimated at from two to five millions.

The two main outlets of its trade are Gaboon and Fernan Vaz. Gaboon is the finest *115* harbour on the western side of the continent, and was thought for many years to be what it looks like, namely, the mouth of a great river. Of late years, however, it has been found to be merely one of those great tidal estuaries like Bonny — that go thirty or forty miles inland and then end in a series of small rivers. While under the impression that Gaboon was one of the great water ways of Africa, France made it a head station for her *120* West African Squadron, and the point of development from which to start on exploring the surrounding country. Her attention, it is said, was first attracted to the importance of Gaboon by the reports brought home by the expedition under Prince de Joinville in the *Belle Poule* — who, in 1840, brought the body of Napoleon from St. Helena for interment in Paris — and after de Joinville the northern termination of the Gaboon *125* estuary is officially known, although it is locally called Cape Santa Clara, which is possibly the name given it by the Portuguese navigator, Lopez Gonsalves, who, in 1469, made his great voyage of discovery on this coast, and whose name Cape Lopez — at the mouth of one of the Ogowé streams — still bears.

Fernan Vaz and Cape Lopez are nowadays more important outlets for trade than *130* Gaboon. To the former comes the trade of the Rembo river, and a certain amount of the Ogowé main trade, since the discovery of the Ogololé creek — a sort of natural canal about twelve miles long and of a fairly uniform breadth of fifty-five feet. Its course is twisted to and fro through the dense forest, and during the rains it is possible to take a small stern wheel steam-boat up and down it. Cape Lopez is the outlet of the Yombas *135* arm of the lower Ogowé, which is also navigable by a small steam-boat. The Chargeur Reunis Company, subsidised by the Government, supply this vessel, the *Eclaireur*, to run from Cape Lopez to Njole, the highest navigable point for vessels on the Ogowé. Messrs. Hatton and Cookson used to have another small steamer, which went straight to and fro from Gaboon to Njole, but alas! she is no more. Nowadays Gaboon is merely a depot, *140* and were it not for her magnificent harbour and the fact that the government is already established there in firm solid buildings, Gaboon would be abandoned, for not only has the trade coming out at Cape Lopez and Fernan Vaz increased, but the trade coming down the Gaboon itself decreased. This is possibly on account of French enterprise having made the route for trade by the Ogowé main stream the safer and easier. *145*

---

106. M'Ubanji: now the Ubangi River, a major tributary of the Congo, which forms the eastern boundary between Congo and Zaire. **115. Fernan Vaz:** now the town of Omboué, on the Gulf of Gabon. **118. Bonny:** town on the south coast of Nigeria. **123. Joinville:** See the note to Haliburton's "The Prince de Joinville's Horse" (p. 876). **127. Lopez Gonsalves:** Lopo Gonçalves (de Secuira), who continued his explorations of the Gulf of Guinea at least until 1474. **131. Rembo:** now the Rembo N'Komi; the several arms of the Ogooué River at its mouth (see also Yombas, line 135) each have separate names. **138. Njole:** now called Ndjolé, about 250 km from the coast.

There is now another rival to Gaboon in Congo Français, Loango. Loango owes its importance to the clear-sightedness and daring of M. de Brazza who, when he reached Brazzaville, as it is now rightly called, on Stanley Pool, saw that there was a possibility of a practicable route *viâ* the Niari Valley from the Middle Congo regions to the sea. For M. de Brazza to see the possibility of the practicability of a thing means that he makes it *150* so, and Loango will gradually become the outlet for a very large portion of the Congo trade, when the railway along the Niari Valley is completed. It has also been suggested that the head station of the government should be moved from Gaboon to Loango, but against this being done is the initial expense and the inferiority of the Loango anchorage. Still, things tend to gravitate towards Loango, as it is the more important *155* position from a local political point. And now, feeling a strong inclination to discourse of M. de Brazza instead of getting on with my own work, I descend to diary.

May 20th, 1895. — Landed at Gaboon from the *Benguella* amidst showers of good advice and wishes from Captain Eversfield and Mr. Fothergill, to which an unknown but amiable French official, who came aboard at Batta, adds a lovely Goliath beetle. *160*

The captain winds up with the advice to run the gig on to the beach, and not attempt the steps of Hatton and Cookson's wharf, for he asserts "they are only fit for a hen." However, having had for the present enough of running ashore, I go for the steps, and they are a little sketchy, but quite practicable.

Mr. Fildes, in the absence of the Agent-General, Mr. Hudson, receives me most *165* kindly, and in the afternoon I and Mr. Huyghens, the new clerk out for the firm, are sent off to the Custom House under the guardian care of a French gentleman, who is an agent of Hatton and Cookson's, and who speaks English perfectly, while retaining his French embellishments and decorations to conversation.

The Post, *i.e.* Custom House, is situated a hundred yards or so from the factory, like *170* it, facing the strand; and we make our way thither over and among the usual *débris* of a south-west coast beach, logs of waterworn trees, great hard seeds, old tins, and the canoes, which are drawn up out of the reach of the ever-mischievous, thieving sea.

The Custom House is far more remarkable for quaintness than beauty; it is two stories high, the ground floor being the local lock-up. The officer in charge lives on the *175* topmost floor and has a long skeleton wooden staircase whereby to communicate with the lower world. This staircase is a veritable "hen-roost" one. It is evidently made to kill people, but why? Individuals desirous of defrauding customs would not be likely to haunt this Custom House staircase, and good people, like me, who want to pay dues, should be encouraged and not killed. *180*

The officer is having his siesta; but when aroused is courteous and kindly, but he incarcerates my revolver, giving me a feeling of iniquity for having had the thing. I am informed if I pay 15*s.* for a licence I may have it — if I fire French ammunition out of it. This seems a heavy sum, so I ask M. Pichault, our mentor, what I may be allowed to shoot if I pay this? Will it make me free, as it were, of all the local shooting? May I *185* daily shoot governors, heads of departments, and *sous officiers?* M. Pichault says

---

146. Loango: coastal town in Congo. **147. de Brazza:** Pierre Savorgnan de Brazza (1852-1905), French explorer and later the governor of French Equatorial Africa (1890-91), whose voyages up the Ogooué River (1876-78) secured French claims to Congolese territory. **152. Niari Valley:** in the interior of Congo. **158.** *Benguella:* named for Benguela, a region and seaport in southern Angola. **160. Goliath beetle:** African beetle about 13 cm (5") long, with a wingspread of about 20 cm (8"). **161. gig:** the shore boat reserved for the captain's use.

"Decidedly not"; — I may shoot "hippo, or elephants, or crocodiles." Now I have never tried shooting big game in Africa with a revolver, and as I don't intend to, I leave the thing in pawn. My collecting-cases and spirit, the things which I expected to reduce me to a financial wreck by custom dues, are passed entirely free, because they are for *190* science. *Vive la France!*

21*st*. — Puddle about seashore. Dr. Nassau comes down from Baraka to see if Messrs. Hatton and Cookson have not appropriated a lady intended for the mission station. One was coming from Batanga by the *Benguella*, he knew, and he is told one has been seen on Hatton and Cookson's quay. Mr. Fildes assures him that the lady they *195* have has been invoiced to the firm, and I am summoned to bear out the statement which gives me the opportunity I have long desired of meeting Dr. Nassau, the great pioneer explorer of these regions and one of the greatest authorities on native subjects in all their bearings.

Although he has been out here, engaged in mission work, since 1851, he is an *200* exceedingly active man, and has a strangely gracious, refined, courteous manner.

22*nd*. — Uninterrupted sea-shore investigations.

23*rd*. — M. Pichault conducts Mr. Huyghens and me into the town of Libreville to be registered.

The road from Glass to Libreville is, at moments, very lovely, and a fine piece of *205* work for the country and the climate. Round Glass the land is swampy, a thing that probably induced the English to settle here when they came to Gaboon, for the English love, above all things, settling in, or as near as possible to, a good reeking, stinking swamp. We pass first along a made piece of road with the swamp on the left hand, and on the other, a sandy bush-grown piece of land with native houses on it, beyond which *210* lies the sea-shore, and whenever the swamp chooses to go down to the edge of the shore there is an iron viaduct thrown across it. The making of this road cost the lives of seventy out of one hundred of the Tonkinese convicts engaged in its construction. After this swampy piece the road runs through sandy land, virtually the shore, with low hills on the one hand and the beach on the other. *215*

A line of cocoanut palms has been planted along either side of the road for most of the way, looking beautiful but behaving badly, for there is a telephone wire running along it from Libreville to Glass, and these gossiping palms — the most inveterate chatterer in the vegetable kingdom is a cocoanut palm — talk to each other with their hard leaves on the wire, just as they did at Fernando Po, so that mere human beings can *220* hardly get a word in edgeways. This irritates the human atom, and of course it uses bad words to the wire, and I fancy these are seventy-five per cent. of all the words that get through the palm leaves' patter.

Two and a half miles' walk brings us to the office of the Directeur de l'Admini-stration de l'Intérieur, and we hang about a fine stone-built verandah. We wait so long *225* that the feeling grows on us that elaborate preparations for incarcerating us for life must

---

189. spirit: alcohol, for preserving specimens. **192. Dr. Nassau:** Robert Hamill Nassau (1861-1906), American Evangelical Presbyterian missionary who had explored the Ogooué River and established himself at Talagouga (also called Otalamaguga), north of Ndjolé. **194. Batanga:** town on the Gabon coast. **213. Tonkinese:** convicts transported from the French colony of Tonkin, now northern Vietnam (cf. Anamese, or Annamese, from central Vietnam, line 541, and French Cochin China, or southern Vietnam, lines 541-42). **220. Fernando Po:** now called Bioko. **221. atom:** smallest unit — i.e., every individual.

be going on, but just as Mr. H. and I have made up our minds to make a dash for it and escape, we are ushered into a cool, whitewashed office, and find a French official, clean, tidy, dark-haired, and melancholy, seated before his writing-table. Courteously bidding us be seated, he asks our names, ages, and avocations, enters them in a book for future *230* reference, and then writes out a permit for each of us to reside in the colony, as long as we behave ourselves, and conform to the laws thereof. These documents are sent up stairs to be signed by the acting Governor, and while we are waiting for their return, he converses with M. Pichault on death, fever, &c. Presently a black man is shown in; he is clad in a blue serge coat, from underneath which float over a pair of blue canvas *235* trousers the tails of a flannel shirt, and on his feet are a pair of ammunition boots that fairly hobble him. His name, the interpreter says, is Joseph. "Who is your father?" says the official — clerk interprets into trade English. "Fader?" says Joseph. "Yes, fader," says the interpreter. "My fader?" says Joseph. "Yes," says the interpreter; "who's your fader?" "Who my fader?" says Joseph. "Take him away and let him think about it," says *240* the officer with a sad, sardonic smile. Joseph is alarmed and volunteers name of mother; this is no good; this sort of information any fool can give; Government is collecting information of a more recondite and interesting character. Joseph is removed by Senegal soldiers, boots and all. As he's going to Boma, in the Congo Free State, it can only be for ethnological purposes that the French Government are taking this trouble to get up *245* his genealogy.

Our stamped papers having arrived now we feel happier and free, and then M. Pichault alarms us by saying, "Now for the Police"; and off we trail, subdued, to the Palais de Justice, where we are promptly ushered into a room containing a vivacious, gesticulatory old gentleman, kindly civil beyond words, and a powerful, calm young *250* man, with a reassuring "He's-all-right; it's-only-his-way" manner regarding his chief. The chief is clad in a white shirt and white pantaloons cut *à la* Turque, but unfortunately these garments have a band that consists of a run-in string, and that string is out of repair. He writes furiously — blotting paper mislaid — frantic flurry round — pantaloons won't stand it — grab just saves them — something wanted the other side of *255* the room — headlong flight towards it — "now's our chance," think the pantaloons, and make off — recaptured.

Formalities being concluded regarding us, the chief makes a dash out from behind his writing-table, claps his heels together, and bows with a jerk that causes the pantaloons to faint in coils, like the White Knight in "Alice in Wonderland," and my last *260* view was of a combat with them, I hope a successful one, and that their owner, who was leaving for home the next day, is now enjoying a well-earned, honourable repose after his long years of service to his country in Congo Français.

24th. — Pouring wet day.

25th. — Called on the Mother Superior, and collected shells from the bay beyond *265* Libreville. In the afternoon called on the missionary lady, who has now arrived with her young son, per German boat from Batanga, and talked on fetish; Dr. Nassau telling a

---

243. **Senegal:** colony on the Atlantic coast of northern Africa, settled by the French in the 1650s, now independent. 244. **Boma:** city on the Congo River, in Zaire; **Congo Free State:** interior part of Zaire, organized as a private colony of King Leopold of Belgium in 1885, and ceded to the Belgian Congo in 1908. 252. *à la* **Turque:** (French) in the Turkish manner. 260. **"Alice in Wonderland":** by Lewis Carroll (see p. 1085).

very pathetic and beautiful story of an old chief at Eloby praying to the spirit of the new moon, which he regarded as a representative of the higher elemental power, to prevent the evil lower spirits from entering his town. *270*

Sunday, 26th. — Mr. Fildes evidently regards it as his duty to devote his Sunday mornings to ladies "invoiced to the firm," and takes me in the gig to go up the little river to the east, ostentatiously only the drainage of the surrounding swamp. The tide just allows us to go over the miniature sand-bar, and then we row up the river, which is about forty feet across, and runs through a perfect gem of a mangrove-swamp, and the *275* stench is quite the right thing — real Odeur de Niger Delta.

As we go higher up, the river channel winds to and fro between walls and slopes of ink-black slime, more sparsely covered with mangrove bushes than near the entrance. This stinking, stoneless slime is honey-combed with crab holes, and the owners of these — green, blue, red, and black — are walking about on the tips of their toes sideways, *280* with that comic pomp peculiar to the crab family. I expected only to have to sit in the boat and say "Horrible" at intervals, but no such thing; my companion, selecting a peculiarly awful-looking spot, says he "thinks that will do," steers the boat up to it, and jumps out with a squidge into the black slime. For one awful moment I thought it was suicide, and that before I could even get the address of his relations to break the news to *285* them there would be nothing but a Panama hat lying on the slime before me. But he only sinks in a matter of a foot or so, and then starts off, to my horror, calling the boys after him, to hunt crabs for me. Now I have mentioned no desire for crabs, and was merely looking at them, as I always do when out with other white folk, noting where they were so as to come back alone next day and get them; for I don't want any one's blood, black *290* or white, on my head. As soon as I recovered speech, I besought him to come back into the boat and leave them: but no, "tears, prayers, entreaties, all in vain," as Koko says; he would not, and dashed about in the stinking mud, regardless, with his four Kruboys far more cautiously paddling after him.

The affrighted crabs were in a great taking. It seems to be crab etiquette that, even *295* when a powerfully built, lithe, six foot high young man is coming at you hard all with a paddle, you must not go rushing into anybody's house save your own, whereby it fell out many crabs were captured; but the thing did not end there. I had never suspected we should catch anything but our deaths of fever, and so had brought with me no collecting-box, and before I could remonstrate Mr. Fildes' handkerchief was full of crabs, and of *300* course mine too. It was a fine sunny morning on the Equator, and therefore it was hot, and we had nothing to wipe our perspiring brows with.

All the crabs being caught or scared home on this mud bank, we proceed higher up river, and after some more crab hunts we got to a place where I noticed you did not sink very far in if you kept moving; so I got ashore, and we went towards a break in the *305* mangroves, where some high trees were growing, where we fell in with some exceedingly lovely mayflies and had a great hunt. They have legs two to three inches long, white at the joints and black between; a very small body with purple wings belongs to the legs, but you do not suspect this until you have caught the legs, as they

---

268. Eloby: island off the coast of Gabon, now part of Equatorial Guinea. **292. Koko:** the Lord High Executioner, in Gilbert and Sullivan's *The Mikado* (1885). **293. Kruboys:** crew.

hover and swing to and fro over some mass of decaying wood stuff. At first I thought   *310*
they were spiders hanging from some invisible thread, so strangely did they move in
circumscribed spaces: but we swept our hands over them and found no thread, and then
we went for the legs in sheer desperation, and found a tiny fly body belonging to them
and not a tiny spider body.

We then made our way on to the slightly higher land fringing the swamp. There   *315*
was at the river end of the swamp a belt of palms, and beyond this a belt of red-woods,
acacias, and other trees, and passing through these, we were out on an open grass-
covered country, with low, rolling hills, looking strangely English, with clumps of trees
here and there, and running between the hills, in all directions, densely-wooded valleys
— a pleasant, homely-looking country.   *320*

We wandered through a considerable lot of grass, wherein I silently observed there
were millions of ticks, and we made for a group of hut-homesteads and chatted with the
inhabitants, until Mr. Fildes' conscience smote him with the fact that he had not given
out cook's stores for the mid-day meal. Then we made a short cut to the boat, which
involved us in a lot of mud-hopping, and so home to 12 o'clock breakfast.   *325*

At breakfast I find Mr. Fildes regards it as his duty to do more scientific work, for
he asks me to go to Woermann's farm, and I, not knowing where it is, say yes; inwardly
trusting that the place may not be far away, and situated in a reasonably dry country, for
I have lost all sense of reliance in Mr. Fildes' instinct of self-preservation — an instinct
usually strong enough to keep a West Coaster from walking a mile. Along the windward   *330*
coast, and in the Rivers, I have always been accustomed to be regarded as insane for my
walking ways, but this gentleman is worth six of me any day, and worth sixty for
Sundays, it's clear.

At 3 o'clock off we go, turning down the "Boulevard" towards Libreville, and then
up a road to the right opposite Woermann's beach, and follow it through miles of grass   *335*
over low hills. Here and there are huts new to me, and quite unlike the mud ones of the
West Coast, or the grass ones of the Congo and Angola districts. They are far inferior to
the swish huts of the Effiks, or the Moorish-looking mud ones you see round Cape
Coast Castle, &c., and notably inferior to the exceedingly neat Dualla huts of Cameroons; but they are better than any other type of African house I have seen.   *340*

They are made of split bamboo with roofs of mats like the Effik roofs, but again
inferior. I notice sometimes the sections of the walls are made on the ground and then
erected. The builder drives in a row of strong wooden poles, and then ties the sections
on to them very neatly with "tie-tie." The door and window-frames and shutters are
made of plank painted a bright cobalt blue as a rule, but now and then red — a red I   *345*
believe that had no business there, as it looks like some white gentleman's red oxide he
has had out for painting the boats with.

Sometimes, however, instead of the sections being made on the ground of closely
set split bamboos, the poles of unsplit bamboo are driven in, and the split bamboos are
lashed on to them, alternately inside and outside, and between these are fixed palm-leaf   *350*
mats. I suspect this style of architecture of being cheaper. Although there are a good

---

338. Effiks: the Efik tribes of southeast Nigeria. **338-39. Cape Coast Castle:** European settlement in the Gold Coast (now Ghana), west of Accra, which Kingsley visited on her previous trip. **339. Dualla:** Douala, a tribal group in western Cameroon.

many houses of both these types being erected on the hills round Glass and Libreville, I cannot say building operations are carried on with much vigour, for there are plenty of skeletons up, with just one or two sections tied in place, and then left as if the builder had gone on strike or got sick of the job somehow. *355*

The stretch of broiling hot grass is trying, but interesting; some of it is intensely fine and a beautiful yellow-green, which I am told is gathered and dried and made into pillows. Some again is long lank stuff, carrying a maroon-coloured ear, which when ripe turns gold colour, and in either state is very lovely when one comes across stretches of it down a hillside. *360*

On either side of us show wooded valleys like those we saw this morning; and away to the east the line of mangrove swamp fringing the little river we rowed up. Away to the west are the groves of mango trees round Libreville; mango trees are only pretty when you are close to them, prettiest of all when you are walking through an avenue of them, and you can see their richness of colour; the deep myrtle-green leaves, with the *365* young shoots a dull crimson, and the soft gray-brown stem, and the luscious-looking but turpentiny-tasting fruit, a glory of gold and crimson, like an immense nectarine.

We gradually get into a more beautiful type of country, and down into a forest. The high trees are the usual high forest series with a preponderance of acacias. It is a forest of varied forms, but flowerless now in the dry season. There are quantities of ferns; hart's- *370* tongues and the sort that grows on the oil-palms, and elks-horn growing out of its great brown shields on the trees above, and bracken, and pretty trailing lycopodium climbing over things, but mostly over the cardamoms which abound in the under-bush, and here and there great banks of the most lovely ferns I have ever seen save the tree-fern, an ambitious climber, called, I believe, by the botanists *Nephrodium circutarium*, and walls *375* of that strange climbing grass, and all sorts of other lovely things by thousands in all directions.

Butterflies and dragon-flies were scarce here compared to Okijon, but of other flies there were more than plenty.

The roadway is exceedingly good; certainly in the grass country you are rather *380* liable to what Captain Eversfield graphically describes as "stub your toe" against lava-like rock, for the grass has overgrown the road, leaving only a single-file path open. In the forest you come across isolated masses of stratified rock, sometimes eight and ten feet high, most prettily overgrown with moss and fern.

We pass through several villages which Mr. Fildes tells me are Fan villages, and are *385* highly interesting after all one has already heard of this tribe of evil repute. Their houses are quite different to the M'pongwe ones we have left behind, and are built of sheets of bark, tied on to sticks.

Frequently in the street one sees the characteristic standing drum painted white in patterns with black, or red-brown, and a piece of raw hide stretched across the top, and *390* one or two talking-drums besides.

We cross several pretty streams in the forest carefully bridged with plank. This Woermann's road, I hear, is between six and seven miles long, and its breadth uniformly nine feet, and it must have cost a lot of money to make. It was made with the intention

---

378. Okijon: i.e., on her previous trip, to Nigeria. **387. M'pongwe:** the Pongo peoples of the Congo coast, whose dialect is referred to in lines 446-47.

of being used for waggons drawn by oxen, which were to bring down all the produce of   *395*
the coffee plantation, and the timber that might be cut down in the clearing for it, to
Gaboon for shipment. A large house was erected and a quantity of coffee planted, and
then the enterprise was abandoned by Messrs. Woermann, and the whole affair, coffee,
road, and all is rapidly sinking back into the bush.

There is a considerable-sized Fan village just at the entrance to the farm in which is   *400*
a big silk-cotton tree. It struck me as strange, after coming from Calabar where these
trees are frequently smothered round the roots with fetish objects, to see nothing on this
one save a framed and glazed image of the Virgin and Child. Just beyond the Fan town
there is a little river.

When we get so far it is too late to proceed further, and nothing but this   *405*
consideration, backed by the memory of one night when he was compelled to walk to
Glass from the farm, prevents Mr. Fildes, I believe, from crossing to Corisco Bay.

So round we turn, and return in the same order we came in, Mr. Fildes lashing
along first, I behind him, going like a clock, which was my one chance. When at last we
reached the "Boulevard" he wanted to reverse this order, but remembering the awful   *410*
state that the back of my blouse got in at Fernando Po from a black boot-lace I was
reduced to employ as a stay-lace, I refuse to go in front, without explaining why.

27th. — Went up among the grass to see if there was anything to be got; ticks were,
and there were any quantity of ants and flocks of very small birds, little finch-like
people, with a soft, dull, gray-brown plumage, relieved by a shading of dark green on   *415*
the back, and little crimson bills; they have a pretty twittering note, and are little bigger
than butterflies; butterflies themselves are rare now. I see the small boys catch these
birds with flake rubber as with birdlime. Down in the wooded hollows there are
numbers of other birds, plantain-eaters, and the bird with the long, soft, rich, thrush-like
note, and the ubiquitous Wu-tu-tu, the clock bird, so called from its regular habit of   *420*
giving the cry, from which its native name comes, every two hours during the night,
commencing at 4 P.M. and going off duty at 6 A.M.

On my return home, I find Mr. Hudson is back from the Ogowé on the *Mové*,
unaltered since '93, I am glad to say. He tells me good Dom Joachim de Sousa Coutinho
e Chichorro is dead, and his wife Donna Anna, and her sister Donna Maria de Sousa   *425*
Coutinho, my valued friends, have returned from Kabinda to Lisbon.

28th. — Go to west side of Libreville shell-hunting; after passing through the town,
and in front of the mango-tree embowered mission station of the Espiritu Santo, the road
runs along close to the sea, through a beautiful avenue of cocoa-palms. Then there is a
bridge, and a little beyond this the road ends, and so I take to the sandy sea-shore for a   *430*
mile or so.

The forest fringes the sand, rising in a wall of high trees, not mangroves; and here
and there a stinking stream comes out from under them, and here and there are masses
of shingle-formed conglomerate and stratified green-gray rock.

Beyond Libreville there are several little clearings in the forest with a native town   *435*
tucked into them, the inhabitants of which seem a happy and contented generation

---

401. **Calabar:** city on the southeast coast of Nigeria. 407. **Corisco Bay:** in northwest Gabon. 412. **stay-lace:** lace for tying a bodice.
418. **birdlime:** sticky substance made out of holly or mistletoe, smeared on branches to trap small birds.

mainly devoted to fishing, and very civil. On my walk back I notice the people getting water from the stinking streams; small wonder the mortality is high in Libreville: this is usually attributed to the inhabitants "going it," but they might "go it" more than they do, without killing themselves if they left off drinking this essence of stinking slime. *440*

29*th.* — Went to see Mrs. Gault and Dr. Nassau, who says the natives have a legend of a volcano about sixty miles from here.

30*th.* — Mrs. Gault asks me to go with her to a Bible meeting, held by a native woman. I assent, I go; Mrs. Sarah, the Biblewoman, is a very handsome, portly lady who speaks English very well. There are besides her, Mrs. Gault and myself, eight or *445* nine native women, and two men. Hymns are sung in M'pongwe, one with a rousing chorus of "Gory we, gory we, pro pa reary gory we." This M'pongwe does not sound so musical as the Effik. Sarah gives an extempore prayer however, which is very beautiful in sound, and she intones it most tastefully. But I confess my mind is distracted by a malignant-looking pig which hovers round us as we kneel upon the sand. I well *450* remember Captain ——— being chivied by a pig in the confines of Die Grosse Colonie, and then there is the chance of ants and so on up one's ankles. Mrs. Gault gives an address which Sarah translates into M'pongwe, and then come more hymns, and the meeting closes, and the ladies settle down and have a quiet pipe and a chat. We then saunter off and visit native Christians' houses. Many houses here are built in clumps *455* round a square, but this form of arrangement seems only a survival, for I find there is no necessary relationship among the people living in the square as there is in Calabar: and so home.

31*st.* — Start out at 2.30 and walk through the grass country behind Baraka, and suddenly fall down into a strange place. *460*

On sitting up after the shock consequent on an unpremeditated descent of some thirteen feet or so, I find myself in a wild place; before me are two cave-like cavities, with a rough wood seat in each; behind me another similar cavity or chamber; the space I am in is about three feet wide; to the left this is terminated by an earth wall; to the right it goes, as a path, down a cutting or trench which ends in dry grass. *465*

No sign of human habitation. Are these sacrifice places, I wonder, or are they places where those Fans one hears so much about, come and secretly eat human flesh? Clearly they are not vestiges of an older civilisation. In fact, what in the world are they? I investigate and find they are nothing in the world more than markers' pits for a rifle range.

Disgust, followed by alarm, seizes me; those French authorities may take it into *470* their heads to think I am making plans of their military works! Visions of incarceration flash before my eyes, and I fly into more grass and ticks, going westwards until I pick up a path, and following this, find myself in a little village. In the centre of the street, see the strange arrow-head-shaped board mounted on a rough easel and alongside it a bundle of stakes, the whole affair clearly connected with making palm oil, and identical *475* with the contrivance I saw in the far-away Fan village on Sunday morning.

Investigate, find the boiled palm nuts are put into a pine-apple fibre bag, which is hung on the board, then stakes are wedged in between the uprights of the easel, so as to

---

439. "going it": trying to do things alone, without assistance. **451. chivied:** chased; **Die Grosse Kolonie:** Kamerun, or Cameroons, the German colony on the Guinea Coast (occupied in 1885), which expanded into French Equatorial Africa in 1911 and was divided into British and French League of Nations Trust Territories after 1918 (now called Cameroon).

squeeze the bag, one stake after another being put in to increase the pressure. The oil runs
out, and off the point of the arrow-shaped board into a receptacle placed to receive it.   *480*

The next object of interest is a piece of paper stuck on a stick at the further end of
the villages. The inscription is of interest though evidently recent. Find it is "No
thoroughfare." There is a bamboo gateway at this end, and so I go through it and find
myself to my surprise on the Woermann farm road, and down this I go, butterfly
hunting. Presently I observe an old gentleman with a bundle of bamboos watching me   *485*
intently. Not knowing the natives of this country yet, I feel anxious, and he, in a few
minutes without taking his eyes off me, crouches in the grass. I remember my great tutor
Captain Boler of Bonny's maxim: "Be afraid of an African if you can't help it, but never
show it anyhow," so I walk on intending to pass him with a propitiatory M'bolo. As I
get abreast of him he hisses out "Look him"; he's evidently got something in the grass;   *490*
Heaven send it's not a snake, but I "look him," — a lizard! The good soul understood
collecting, and meant well from the first. I give him tobacco and a selection of amiable
observations, and he beams and we go on down the road together, discussing the proper
time to burn grass, and the differences in the practical value, for building purposes, of
the two kinds of bamboo. Then coming to a path that runs evidently in the direction of   *495*
the Plateau at Libreville, and thinking it's time I was tacking homewards, I say "good
bye" to my companion, and turn down the path. "You sabe 'em road?" says he in a very
questioning voice: I say "yes" airily, and keep on down it.

The path goes on through grass, and then makes for a hollow — wish it didn't, for
hollows are horrid at times, and evidently this road has got something against it   *500*
somewhere, and is not popular, for the grass falls across it like unkempt hair. Road
becomes damp and goes into a belt of trees, in the middle of which runs a broad stream
with a log laid across it. Congratulating myself on absence of companions, ignomi-
niously crawl across on to the road, which then and there turns round and goes back to
the stream again higher up — evidently a joke, "thought-you-were-going-to-get-home-   *505*
dry-did-you" sort of thing. Wade the stream, rejoin the road on the hither side. Then the
precious thing makes a deliberate bolt for the interior of Africa, instead of keeping on
going to Libreville. I lose confidence in it. The Wu-tu-tu says it's four o'clock. It's dark
at 6.15 down here, and I am miles from home, so I begin to wish I had got an intelligent
companion to guide me, as I walk on through the now shoulder-high grass. Suddenly   *510*
another road branches off to the left. "Saved!" Down it I go, and then it ends in a
manioc patch, with no path out the other end, and surrounded by impenetrable bush.
Crestfallen, I retrace my steps and continue along my old tormentor, which now
attempts to reassure me by doubling round to the left and setting off again for Libreville.
I am not deceived, I have had my trust in it too seriously tampered with — Yes, it's up   *515*
to mischief again, and it turns itself into a stream. Nothing for it but wading, so wade;
but what will be its next manifestation, I wonder? for I begin to doubt whether it is a
road at all, and suspect it of being only a local devil, one of the sort that sometimes
appears as a road, sometimes as a tree or a stream, &c. I wonder what they will do if
they find I don't get in to-night? — wish me — at Liverpool, at least. After a quarter of   *520*
an hour's knee-deep wading, I suddenly meet a native lady who was at the Bible

---

489. M'bolo: "The M'pongwe greeting; meaning, 'May you live long'" (Kingsley's note). **512. manioc:** cassava.

meeting. She has a grand knowledge of English, and she stands with her skirt tucked up round her, evidently in no hurry, and determined to definitely find out who I am. Recognising this, I attempt to take charge of the conversation, and divert its course. "Nice road this," I say, "but it's a little damp." "Washey, ma," she says, "but ——" "Is this road *525* here to go anywhere," I interposed, "or is it only a kind of joke?" "It no go nowhere 'ticular, ma," she says; "but ——" "In a civilised community like this of Gaboon," I say, "it's scandalous that roads should be allowed to wander about in this loose way." "That's so for true," she assents; "but, ma, ——" "You must excuse me," I answer, "I am in a great hurry to get in, hope to meet you again. Where do you live? I'll call." She gives me her address, *530* but does not move, and the grass walls either side of the stream road are high and dense. "My husband," she says, "was in H., and C.'s; he die now." "Dear me, that's very sad; you must have been very sorry," I answer, sympathetically, thinking I have turned the conversation. "We all were; he had ten wives. But, ma, —— I am damp and desperate, and so pushing into the grass at the side, circumnavigate her portly form successfully, and *535* saying a cheery "good-bye," bolt, and down wind after me comes the uninterrupted question at last; but I do not return to discuss the matter, and soon getting on to drier ground, and seeing a path that goes towards the boulevard, down I go, as quickly as my feet can carry me, and then before I know where I am I find myself in a network of little irrigating canals, running between neatly kept beds of tomatoes, salad, &c., whereon there *540* are working busily a lot of Anamese convicts. The convicts are deported from the French Cochin China possessions and employed by the Public Works Department in various ways. Those who conduct themselves well, and survive, have grants of garden ground given them, which they cultivate in this tidy, carefully minute way, so entirely different from the slummacky African methods of doing things. The produce they sell to the residents in the *545* town, and live very prosperously in this way: but the climate of Western Africa is almost, if not quite, as deadly to the Chinese races as to the white — a fact that has been amply demonstrated not only here, but in Congo Belge, where the railway company carried on a series of experiments with imported labour — a series of experiments that entailed an awful waste of human life — for none of the imported people stood the climate any better than the *550* whites, and you know what that means. This labour question out here, a question that increases daily with the development of plantation enterprise, I do not think will ever be solved by importing foreign labour. Nor is it advisable that it should be, for our European Government puts a stop to the action of those causes which used to keep the native population down, intertribal wars, sacrifices, &c., &c.; and to the deportation of surplus *555* population in the form of slaves, and so unless means of support are devised for "the indigenous ones," as Mrs. Gault calls them, Africa will have us to thank for some smart attacks of famine, for the natives, left to their own devices, will never cultivate the soil sufficiently to support a large population, and moreover a vast percentage of the West African soil is very poor, sour stuff, that will grow nothing but equally valueless vegetation. *560* From this discourse you will argue I did get home at last.

June 2nd. — *Nubia* in, but she will not call at Batanga, so Mrs. Gault is stranded until some other steamer calls. *Nubia* has lost all her heavy anchors down south, where she reports the Calemma extra bad this year.

---

545. slummacky: slummocky, awkward. **564. Calemma:** Calema, a sea-current off Togoland (now Togo).

3rd. — Went alone for a long walk to the bend of the mangrove-swamp river to the 565
east. It stank severely, but was most interesting, giving one the conditions of life in a
mangrove-swamp in what you might call a pocket edition. Leaving this, I made my way
north-west along native paths across stretches of grass growing on rolling hills and
down through wooded valleys, each of which had a little stream in it, or a patch of
swamp, with enormous arums and other water plants growing, and along through Fan 570
villages, each with just one straight street, having a club-house at the alternate ends. I
met in the forest a hunter, carrying home a deer he had shot; in addition to his musket,
he carried a couple of long tufted spears, archaic in type. He was very chatty, and I gave
him tobacco, and we talked sport, and on parting I gave him some more tobacco,
because he kindly gave me a charm to enable me to see things in the forest. He was 575
gratified, and said, "You ver nice," "Good-bye," "Good-day," "So long," "Good-night,"
which was very nice of him, as these phrases were evidently all the amiable greetings in
English that he knew. The "So long" you often hear the natives in Gaboon say: it always
sounds exceedingly quaint. They have of course picked it up from the American
missionaries, who have been here upwards of thirty years. 580

4th. — Mr. Hudson announces that the *Mové* will leave at 5.30 on the morning after
next. Later in the day he expects to get her off by 5.30 to-morrow — towards evening he
thinks to-morrow at 8.30 is more likely still. Mrs. Gault called with her boy Harry; she
says, "John Holt has got a lovely waist at only two dollars." I don't want a waist — I am
too thin anyhow — so I don't investigate the matter. We go up to Dr. Nassau and talk 585
ju-ju. He agrees with me that dead black men go white when soaked in water.

(1897)

DUNCAN CAMPBELL SCOTT
Canada, 1862-1947

MEDITATION AT PERUGIA

The sunset colours mingle in the sky,
  And over all the Umbrian valleys flow;
  Trevi is touched with wonder, and the glow
Finds high Perugia crimson with renown;
  Spello is bright;   5
And, ah! St. Francis, thy deep-treasured town,
  Enshrined Assisi, full fronts the light.

This valley knew thee many a year ago;
  Thy shrine was built by simpleness of heart;
  And from the wound called life thou drew'st the smart;
Unquiet kings came to thee and the sad poor —   *11*

  Thou gavest them peace;
Far as the Sultan and the Iberian shore
  Thy faith and abnegation gave release.

Deeper our faith, but not so sweet as thine;   *15*
  Wider our view, but not so sanely sure;
  For we are troubled by the witching lure
Of Science, with her lightning on the mist;
  Science that clears,
Yet never quite discloses what she wist,   *20*
  And leaves us half with doubts and half with fears.

---

584. waist: blouse, bodice. **MEDITATION AT PERUGIA** Perugia, a centre of a 13th-16th century school of painting, is a cathedral city in Umbria, a hilly region of Italy north of Rome that was annexed to the Papal States in 1540. Trevi, Spello, and Assisi (lines 3, 5, 7) are hill towns nearby, Assisi being the shrine of St. Francis (c.1182-1226), founder of the Franciscan order of monks, noted for espousing poverty, simplicity, and a gentle reverence for nature. **13. Sultan . . . Iberian:** i.e., from Turkey to Spain.

We act her dreams that shadow forth the truth,
  That somehow here the very nerves of God
  Thrill the old fires, the rocks, the primal sod;
We throw our speech upon the open air,   *25*
  And it is caught
Far down the world, to sing and murmur there;
  Our common words are with deep wonder fraught.

Shall not the subtle spirit of man contrive
  To charm the tremulous ether of the soul,   *30*
  Wherein it breathes? — until, from pole to pole,
Those who are kin shall speak, as face to face,
  From star to star,
Even from earth to the most secret place,
  Where God and the supreme archangels are.   *35*

Shall we not prove, what thou hast faintly taught,
  That all the powers of earth and air are one,
  That one deep law persists from mole to sun?
Shall we not search the heart of God and find
  That law empearled,   *40*
Until all things that are in matter and mind
  Throb with the secret that began the world?

Yea, we have journeyed since thou trod'st the road,
  Yet still we keep the foreappointed quest;
  While the last sunset smoulders in the West,   *45*
Still the great faith with the undying hope
  Upsprings and flows,
While dim Assisi fades on the wide slope
  And the deep Umbrian valleys fill with rose.

(1916)

ERNEST LAWRENCE THAYER
U.S.A., 1863-1940

CASEY AT THE BAT

It looked extremely rocky for the Mudville nine that day,
The score stood four to six with but an inning left to play.
And so, when Cooney died at first, and Burrows did the same,
A pallor wreathed the features of the patrons of the game.

A straggling few got up to go, leaving there the rest,   *5*
With that hope which springs eternal within the human breast.
For they thought if only Casey could get a whack at that,
They'd put up even money with Casey at the bat.

But Flynn preceded Casey, and likewise so did Blake,
And the former was a pudding and the latter was a fake;   *10*
So on that striken multitude a death-like silence sat.
For there seemed but little chance of Casey's getting to the bat.

But Flynn let drive a single to the wonderment of all,
And the much despisèd Blakey tore the cover off the ball,
And when the dust had lifted and they saw what had occurred,   *15*
There was Blakey safe on second, and Flynn a-hugging third.

CASEY AT THE BAT   There are hundreds of printings of this work, with many textual variants; the version printed here (from F.L. Knowles's *Treasury of Humorous Poetry*, where for some reason it was attributed to an unknown and unidentified "Joseph Quinlan Murphy") is a corrupted version of Thayer's 1888 original, but it has remained one of the most popular forms of the ballad; Thayer's final revision (1909) removed some of the spontaneity of the earlier versions. For details about various identifications of the players and places referred to (though Thayer insisted he invented them all, and had been influenced mainly by reading W.S. Gilbert's *Bab Ballads*), see Martin Gardner's *The Annotated Casey at the Bat* (2nd ed., 1984). **6. hope . . . breast:** alluding to Pope's *Essay on Man*, Epistle III: "Hope springs eternal in the human breast: / Man never is, but always to be blest." **10. pudding:** short for "puddin' head," meaning slow but lovable; Thayer's 1888 version printed "lulu," not "pudding," and his 1909 version substituted "hoodoo"; **fake:** Thayer's word in both 1888 and 1909 was "cake," a slang term for someone whose vanity exceeded his ability.

Then from the gladdened multitude went up a joyous yell,
It bounded from the mountain top and rattled in the dell,
It struck upon the hillside, and rebounded on the flat,
For Casey, mighty Casey, was advancing to the bat.   20

There was ease in Casey's manner as he stepped into his place,
There was pride in Casey's bearing and a smile on Casey's face,
And when responding to the cheers he lightly doffed his hat.
No stranger in the crowd could doubt, 'twas Casey at the bat.

Ten thousand eyes were on him as he rubbed his hands with dirt,   25
Five thousand tongues applauded as he wiped them on his shirt;
And while the writhing pitcher ground the ball into his hip —
Defiance gleamed from Casey's eye — a sneer curled Casey's lip.

And now the leather-covered sphere came hurtling through the air,
And Casey stood a-watching it in haughty grandeur there;   30
Close by the sturdy batsman the ball unheeded sped —
"That hain't my style," said Casey — "Strike one," the umpire said.

From the bleachers black with people there rose a sullen roar,
Like the beating of the storm waves on a stern and distant shore,
"Kill him! kill the Umpire!" shouted some one from the stand —   35
And it's likely they'd have done it had not Casey raised his hand.

With a smile of Christian charity great Casey's visage shone,
He stilled the rising tumult and he bade the game go on;
He signalled to the pitcher and again the spheroid flew,
But Casey still ignored it and the Umpire said "Strike two."   40

"Fraud!" yelled the maddened thousands, and the echo answered "Fraud."
But one scornful look from Casey and the audience was awed;
They saw his face grow stern and cold; they saw his muscles strain,
And they knew that Casey would not let that ball go by again.

The sneer is gone from Casey's lip; his teeth are clenched with hate, 45
He pounds with cruel violence his bat upon the plate;
And now the pitcher holds the ball, and now he lets it go,
And now the air is shattered by the force of Casey's blow.

Oh! somewhere in this favored land the sun is shining bright,
The band is playing somewhere, and somewhere hearts are light,   50
And somewhere men are laughing, and somewhere children shout;
But there is no joy in Mudville — mighty Casey has "Struck Out."

(1888, 1902)

ANDREW BARTON ("BANJO") PATERSON

Australia, 1864-1941

THE MAN FROM SNOWY RIVER

There was movement at the station, for the word had passed around
   That the colt from old Regret had got away,
And had joined the wild bush horses — he was worth a thousand pound,
   So all the cracks had gathered to the fray.
All the tried and noted riders from the stations near and far   *5*
   Had mustered at the homestead overnight,
For the bushmen love hard riding where the wild bush horses are,
   And the stock-horse snuffs the battle with delight.

There was Harrison, who made his pile when Pardon won the cup,
   The old man with his hair as white as snow;   *10*
But few could ride beside him when his blood was fairly up —
   He would go wherever horse and man could go.
And Clancy of the Overflow came down to lend a hand,
   No better horseman ever held the reins;
For never horse could throw him while the saddle-girths would stand —   *15*
   He learnt to ride while droving on the plains.

And one was there, a stripling on a small and weedy beast;
   He was something like a racehorse undersized,
With a touch of Timor pony — three parts thoroughbred at least —
   And such are by mountain horsemen prized.   *20*
He was hard and tough and wiry — just the sort that won't say die —
   There was courage in his quick impatient tread;
And he bore the badge of gameness in his bright and fiery eye,
   And the proud and lofty carriage of his head.

But still so slight and weedy, one would doubt his power to stay,   *25*
   And the old man said, "That horse will never do
For a long and tiring gallop — lad, you'd better stop away,
   Those hills are far too rough for such as you."
So he waited, sad and wistful — only Clancy stood his friend —
   "I think we ought to let him come," he said;   *30*
"I warrant he'll be with us when he's wanted at the end,
   For both his horse and he are mountain bred.

He hails from Snowy River, up by Kosciusko's side,
   Where the hills are twice as steep and twice as rough;
Where a horse's hoofs strike firelight from the flint stones every stride,   *35*
   The man that holds his own is good enough.

THE MAN FROM SNOWY RIVER   **1. station:** ranch. **4. cracks:** i.e., crack riders. **33. Kosciusko:** the highest peak in Australia.

And the Snowy River riders on the mountains make their home,
  Where the river runs those giant hills between;
I have seen full many horsemen since I first commenced to roam,
  But nowhere yet such horsemen have I seen."   40

So he went; they found the horses by the big mimosa clump,
  They raced away towards the mountain's brow,
And the old man gave his orders, "Boys, go at them from the jump,
  No use to try for fancy riding now.
And, Clancy, you must wheel them, try and wheel them to the right.   45
  Ride boldly, lad, and never fear the spills,
For never yet was rider that could keep the mob in sight,
  If once they gain the shelter of those hills."

So Clancy rode to wheel them — he was racing on the wing
  Where the best and boldest riders take their place,   50
And he raced his stock-horse past them, and he made the ranges ring
  With the stockwhip, as he met them face to face.
Then they halted for a moment, while he swung the dreaded lash,
  But they saw their well-loved mountain full in view,
And they charged beneath the stockwhip with a sharp and sudden dash,   55
  And off into the mountain scrub they flew.

Then fast the horsemen followed, where the gorges deep and black
  Resounded to the thunder of their tread,
And the stockwhips woke the echoes and they fiercely answered back
  From cliffs and crags that beetled overhead.   60
And upward, ever upward, the wild horses held their way,
  Where mountain ash and kurrajong grew wide;
And the old man muttered fiercely, "We may bid the mob good day,
  No man can hold them down the other side."

When they reached the mountain's summit, even Clancy took a pull —   65
  It well might make the boldest hold their breath;
The wild hop scrub grew thickly, and the hidden ground was full
  Of wombat holes, and any slip was death.
But the man from Snowy River let the pony have his head,
  And he swung his stockwhip round and gave a cheer,   70
And he raced him down the mountain like a torrent down its bed,
  While the others stood and watched in very fear.

He sent the flint-stones flying, but the pony kept his feet,
  He cleared the fallen timber in his stride,
And the man from Snowy River never shifted in his seat —   75
  It was grand to see that mountain horseman ride.
Through the stringy barks and saplings, on the rough and broken ground,
  Down the hillside at a racing pace he went;
And he never drew the bridle till he landed safe and sound
  At the bottom of that terrible descent.   80

---

47. mob: i.e., the horses. **62. kurrajong:** Australian tree with tough, fibrous bark. **77. stringy barks:** gum trees.

He was right among the horses as they climbed the farther hill,
    And the watchers on the mountain, standing mute,
Saw him ply the stockwhip fiercely; he was right among them still,
    As he raced across the clearing in pursuit.
Then they lost him for a moment, where two mountain gullies met   *85*
    In the ranges — but a final glimpse reveals
On a dim and distant hillside the wild horses racing yet,
    With the man from Snowy River at their heels.

And he ran them single-handed till their sides were white with foam;
    He followed like a bloodhound on their track,   *90*
Till they halted, cowed and beaten; then he turned their heads for home,
    And alone and unassisted brought them back.
But his hardy mountain pony he could scarcely raise a trot,
    He was blood from hip to shoulder from the spur;
But his pluck was still undaunted, and his courage fiery hot,   *95*
    For never yet was mountain horse a cur.

And down by Kosciusko, where the pine-clad ridges raise
    Their torn and rugged battlements on high,
Where the air is clear as crystal, and the white stars fairly blaze
    At midnight in the cold and frosty sky,   *100*
And where around the Overflow the reed-beds sweep and sway
    To the breezes, and the rolling plains are wide,
The Man from Snowy River is a household word today,
    And the stockmen tell the story of his ride.

                                      (1890, 1895)

MARY GILMORE
Australia, 1864-1962

THE HARVESTERS

In from the fields they come
To stand about the well, and, drinking, say,
"The tin gives taste!" taking in turn
The dipper from each other's hands,
The dregs out-flung as each one finishes;   *5*
Then as the water in the oil-drum bucket lowers,
They tip that out, to draw a fresher, cooler draught.

And as the windlass slowly turns they talk of other days,
Of quaichs and noggins made of oak; of oak
Grown black with age, and on through generations   *10*

THE HARVESTERS   **9. quaichs, noggins:** cups.

And old houses handed down to children's children,
Till at last, in scattered families, they are lost to ken.
"Yet even so the dipper tastes the best!" they say.
Then having drunk, and sluiced their hands and faces,
Talk veers to fields and folk in childhood known,   *15*
And names are heard of men and women long since dead,
Or gone because the spirit of adventure
Lured them from familiar scenes to strange and far.
Of these old names, some will have been so long unheard
Not all remember them. And yet a word its vision brings,   *20*
And memory, wakened and eager, lifts anew
The fallen thread, until it seems the past is all about them
Where they group, and in two worlds they stand —
A world that was, a world in making now.

Then in sudden hush the voices cease,   *25*
The supper horn blows clear, and, from community
Where all were one, each man withdraws his mind
As men will drop a rope in haulage held,
And, individuals in a sea of time,
In separateness they turn, and to the cook-house go.   *30*

                                        (1918)

RUDYARD KIPLING
India/England, 1865-1936

DANNY DEEVER

"What are the bugles blowin' for?" said Files-on-Parade.
"To turn you out, to turn you out," the Colour-Sergeant said.
"What makes you look so white, so white?" said Files-on-Parade.
"I'm dreadin' what I've got to watch," the Colour-Sergeant said.
  For they're hangin' Danny Deever, you can hear the Dead March play,   *5*
  The regiment's in 'ollow square — they're hangin' him to-day;
  They've taken of his buttons off an' cut his stripes away,
  An' they're hangin' Danny Deever in the mornin'.

"What makes the rear-rank breathe so 'ard?" said Files-on-Parade.
"It's bitter cold, it's bitter cold," the Colour-Sergeant said.   *10*
"What makes that front-rank man fall down?" says Files-on-Parade.
"A touch o' sun, a touch o' sun," the Colour-Sergeant said.
  They are hangin' Danny Deever, they are marchin' of 'im round,

They 'ave 'alted Danny Deever by 'is coffin on the ground;
An' 'e'll swing in 'arf a minute for a sneakin' shootin' hound —   *15*
O they're hangin' Danny Deever in the mornin'!

" 'Is cot was right-'and cot to mine," said Files-on-Parade.
" 'E's sleepin' out an' far to-night," the Colour-Sergeant said.
"I've drunk 'is beer a score o' times," said Files-on-Parade.
" 'E's drinkin' bitter beer alone," the Colour-Sergeant said.   *20*
   They are hangin' Danny Deever, you must mark 'im to 'is place,
   For 'e shot a comrade sleepin' — you must look 'im in the face;
   Nine 'undred of 'is county an' the regiment's disgrace,
   While they're hangin' Danny Deever in the mornin'.

"What's that so black agin' the sun?" said Files-on-Parade.   *25*
"It's Danny fightin' 'ard for life," the Colour-Sergeant said.
"What's that that whimpers over'ead?" said Files-on-Parade.
"It's Danny's soul that's passin' now," the Colour-Sergeant said.
   For they're done with Danny Deever, you can 'ear the quickstep play,
   The regiment's in column, an' they're marchin' us away;   *30*
   Ho! the young recruits are shakin', an' they'll want their beer to-day,
   After hangin' Danny Deever in the mornin'.

(1890)

William Butler Yeats
Ireland, 1865-1939

The Lake Isle of Innisfree

I will arise and go now, and go to Innisfree,
And a small cabin build there, of clay and wattles made:
Nine bean-rows will I have there, a hive for the honeybee,
And live alone in the bee-loud glade.

And I shall have some peace there, for peace comes dropping slow,   *5*
Dropping from the veils of the morning to where the cricket sings;
There midnight's all a glimmer, and noon a purple glow,
And evening full of the linnet's wings.

I will arise and go now, for always night and day
I hear lake water lapping with low sounds by the shore;   *10*
While I stand on the roadway, or on the pavements grey,
I hear it in the deep heart's core.

(1893)

THE LAKE ISLE OF INNISFREE   **Title:** in County Sligo. Yeats later said that he had from childhood dreamed of living on this island in imitation of Thoreau at Walden Pond (see p. 1006).

HE WISHES FOR THE CLOTHS OF HEAVEN

Had I the heavens' embroidered cloths,
Enwrought with golden and silver light,
The blue and the dim and the dark cloths
Of night and light and the half-light,
I would spread the cloths under your feet: 5
But I, being poor, have only my dreams;
I have spread my dreams under your feet;
Tread softly because you tread on my dreams.

(1899)

TO A FRIEND WHOSE WORK HAS COME TO NOTHING

Now all the truth is out,
Be secret and take defeat
From any brazen throat,
For how can you compete,
Being honour bred, with one   5
Who, were it proved he lies,
Were neither shamed in his own
Nor in his neighbours' eyes?
Bred to a harder thing
Than Triumph, turn away   10
And like a laughing string
Whereon mad fingers play
Amid a place of stone,
Be secret and exult,
Because of all things known   15
That is most difficult.

(1914)

A COAT

I made my song a coat
Covered with embroideries
Out of old mythologies
From heel to throat;
But the fools caught it,   5
Wore it in the world's eyes
As though they'd wrought it.
Song, let them take it,
For there's more enterprise
In walking naked.   10

(1914)

EASTER 1916

I have met them at close of day
Coming with vivid faces
From counter or desk among grey
Eighteenth-century houses.
I have passed with a nod of the head   5
Or polite meaningless words,
Or have lingered awhile and said
Polite meaningless words,
And thought before I had done
Of a mocking tale or a gibe   10
To please a companion
Around the fire at the club,
Being certain that they and I
But lived where motley is worn:
All changed, changed utterly: 15
A terrible beauty is born.

That woman's days were spent
In ignorant good-will,
Her nights in argument

TO A FRIEND WHOSE WORK HAS COME TO NOTHING   Cf. Anne Sexton's "To a Friend . . . " (p. 1427). **Title:** In a note Yeats remarked that Lady Gregory (see p. 1140) in her biography of her nephew Sir Hugh Lane (1874-1915) said this poem was addressed to him, but Yeats says he addressed it to her. Lane had offered his collection of French paintings to the city of Dublin on condition that a special gallery be built for them; when this plan was thwarted by the newspaper editor William Murphy ("one," line 5), he offered them to the National Gallery in London instead. The "work" the title refers to is the unsuccessful efforts of Lady Gregory, Lane, and Yeats himself to persuade Ireland to take the necessary steps to get the collection. Lane was killed when the *Lusitania* was torpedoed during World War I, and because a codicil to his will (which once more gave the paintings to Dublin) had not been witnessed, they went to London — causing much political ill will. Much later, the two cities agreed to share the collection.   **EASTER 1916**   An Irish Nationalist uprising, known as the Easter Rebellion or Easter Rising, began on Easter Monday (24 April 1916), and lasted six days. Among the republican leaders were those named here by Yeats (see 75-76): Patrick Pearse (1879-1916), schoolmaster and poet ("This man," 24); James Connolly (1870-1916), labour leader, co-leader, with Pearse, of the rebellion; Thomas MacDonagh (1878-1916), poet, dramatist, and Professor of English Literature ("This other," 26); and Major John MacBride ("This other man," 31), who in 1903 had married Maud Gonne, long the object of Yeats's unsuccessful love (she separated from MacBride after two years); all four were among those court-martialled and shot. **17. That woman:** Countess Constance Markiewicz (1868-1927), daughter of Anglo-Irish landowners (Georgina and Sir Henry Gore-Booth) in County Sligo and the wife of a Polish count; she was sentenced to death, but was released from prison in 1917.

Until her voice grew shrill.   20
What voice more sweet than hers
When, young and beautiful,
She rode to harriers?
This man had kept a school
And rode our wingèd horse;   25
This other his helper and friend
Was coming into his force;
He might have won fame in the end,
So sensitive his nature seemed,
So daring and sweet his thought.   30
This other man I had dreamed
A drunken, vainglorious lout.
He had done most bitter wrong
To some who are near my heart,
Yet I number him in the song;   35
He, too, has resigned his part
In the casual comedy;
He, too, has been changed in his turn,
Transformed utterly:
A terrible beauty is born.   40

Hearts with one purpose alone
Through summer and winter seem
Enchanted to a stone
To trouble the living stream.
The horse that comes from the road,   45
The rider, the birds that range
From cloud to tumbling cloud,
Minute by minute they change;
A shadow of cloud on the stream
Changes minute by minute;   50
A horse-hoof slides on the brim,
And a horse plashes within it;
The long-legged moor-hens dive,
And hens to moor-cocks call;
Minute by minute they live: 55
The stone's in the midst of all.

Too long a sacrifice
Can make a stone of the heart.
O when may it suffice?
That is Heaven's part, our part   60
To murmur name upon name,
As a mother names her child
When sleep at last has come
On limbs that had run wild.
What is it but nightfall?   65
No, no, not night but death;
Was it needless death after all?
For England may keep faith
For all that is done and said.
We know their dream; enough   70
To know they dreamed and are dead;
And what if excess of love
Bewildered them till they died?
I write it out in a verse —
MacDonagh and MacBride   75
And Connolly and Pearse
Now and in time to be,
Wherever green is worn,
Are changed, changed utterly:
A terrible beauty is born.   80
     (1916)

THE SECOND COMING

Turning and turning in the widening gyre
The falcon cannot hear the falconer;
Things fall apart; the center cannot hold;
Mere anarchy is loosed upon the world,
The blood-dimmed tide is loosed, and everywhere   5
The ceremony of innocence is drowned;
The best lack all conviction, while the worst
Are full of passionate intensity.

Surely some revelation is at hand;
Surely the Second Coming is at hand.   10
The Second Coming! Hardly are those words out

25. wingèd horse: i.e., Pegasus, associated with the Muses. **68-69:** The Home Rule Bill had passed the Commons in 1912, was delayed for the legal maximum of two years by the House of Lords, but implementation was suspended for the duration of World War I; the Irish Free State came into being in 1921. **THE SECOND COMING Title:** See Matthew 24. **1. gyre:** a conical spiral, here viewed as the path of a falcon as it circles higher and higher and farther from the falconer. In his book called *A Vision* (1925, 1937) Yeats discusses his cyclical view of history and his mystical symbolic system, which includes "gyres" or cones representing periods of history, a "primary" cone (a cone of, among other things, objectivity) going from its beginning to full expansion in the course of 1000 years while an "antithetical" cone (a cone of, among other things, subjectivity) goes from maximum back to zero, and then each reversing itself for the next 1000 years; a complete cycle thus takes approximately 2000 years (see line 19).

When a vast image out of *Spiritus Mundi*
Troubles my sight: somewhere in sands of the
    desert
A shape with lion body and the head of a man,
A gaze blank and pitiless as the sun,   *15*
Is moving its slow thighs, while all about it
Reel shadows of the indignant desert birds.
The darkness drops again; but now I know
That twenty centuries of stony sleep
Were vexed to nightmare by a rocking cradle, *20*
And what rough beast, its hour come round at last,
Slouches towards Bethlehem to be born?

                                    (1919, 1921)

A Prayer for My Daughter

Once more the storm is howling, and half hid
Under this cradle-hood and coverlid
My child sleeps on. There is no obstacle
But Gregory's wood and one bare hill
Whereby the haystack- and roof-levelling wind,
Bred on the Atlantic, can be stayed;   *6*
And for an hour I have walked and prayed
Because of the great gloom that is in my mind.

I have walked and prayed for this young child
    an hour   *9*
And heard the sea-wind scream upon the tower,
And under the arches of the bridge, and scream
In the elms above the flooded stream;
Imagining in excited reverie
That the future years had come,
Dancing to a frenzied drum,   *15*
Out of the murderous innocence of the sea.

May she be granted beauty and yet not
Beauty to make a stranger's eye distraught,
Or hers before a looking-glass, for such,
Being made beautiful overmuch,   *20*
Consider beauty a sufficient end,
Lose natural kindness and maybe
The heart-revealing intimacy
That chooses right, and never find a friend.

Helen being chosen found life flat and dull   *25*
And later had much trouble from a fool,
While that great Queen, that rose out of the spray,
Being fatherless could have her way
Yet chose a bandy-leggèd smith for man.
It's certain that fine women eat   *30*
A crazy salad with their meat
Whereby the Horn of Plenty is undone.

In courtesy I'd have her chiefly learned;
Hearts are not had as a gift but hearts are earned
By those that are not entirely beautiful;   *35*
Yet many, that have played the fool
For beauty's very self, has charm made wise,
And many a poor man that has roved,
Loved and thought himself beloved,
From a glad kindness cannot take his eyes.   *40*

May she become a flourishing hidden tree
That all her thoughts may like the linnet be,
And have no business but dispensing round
Their magnanimities of sound,
Not but in merriment begin a chase,   *45*
Nor but in merriment a quarrel.
O may she live like some green laurel
Rooted in one dear perpetual place.

My mind, because the minds that I have loved,
The sort of beauty that I have approved,   *50*
Prosper but little, has dried up of late,
Yet knows that to be choked with hate
May well be of all evil chances chief.
If there's no hatred in a mind
Assault and battery of the wind   *55*
Can never tear the linnet from the leaf.

An intellectual hatred is the worst,
So let her think opinions are accursed.
Have I not seen the loveliest woman born
Out of the mouth of Plenty's horn,   *60*
Because of her opinionated mind
Barter that horn and every good
By quiet natures understood
For an old bellows full of angry wind?

---

12. Spiritus Mundi: (Latin) spirit of the world, which Yeats associates with a universal human "Great Memory," a source of images and cultural symbols on which individuals draw. **19. twenty centuries:** In *A Vision*, Yeats puts the primary cone of what he calls "Babylonian mathematical starlight" at its full expansion in 2000 B.C., when a new antithetical cone is just beginning; he sees the birth of Christ ("a rocking cradle," 20) as marking the end of Greco-Roman civilization and the start of a new antithetical cone — a set of circumstances being repeated as the next 2000-year cycle is drawing to its end. **A Prayer for My Daughter** Title: Anne Butler Yeats was born 26 February 1919, in Galway. **4. Gregory's wood:** once part of Lady Gregory's estate, Coole Park, long Yeats's retreat. **10. tower:** Thoor Ballylee, a Norman tower on a small piece of land, also part of Coole Park, that Yeats had bought. **25. Helen:** of Troy, who left Menelaus, King of Sparta, and eloped with the Trojan hero Paris. **27. Queen:** Aphrodite (Venus), born from the sea, who married Hephaestus (Vulcan), god of fire and a blacksmith, who was lame (see the excerpt from Pope's translation of the *Iliad*, p. 534). **32. Horn of Plenty:** cornucopia; also called Amalthea's Horn, after Zeus's nurse who fed him goat's milk; he in return gave her one of the goat's horns, promising that whoever possessed it would never be in want. **59-64:** Yeats's later poetry recurrently criticizes the way political activism changed Maud Gonne ("the loveliest woman born") and Constance Markiewicz.

Considering that, all hatred driven hence,   *65*
The soul recovers radical innocence
And learns at last that it is self-delighting,
Self-appeasing, self-affrighting,
And that its own sweet will is Heaven's will;
She can, though every face should scowl   *70*
And every windy quarter howl
Or every bellows burst, be happy still.

And may her bridegroom bring her to a house
Where all's accustomed, ceremonious;
For arrogance and hatred are the wares   *75*
Peddled in the thoroughfares.
How but in custom and in ceremony
Are innocence and beauty born?
Ceremony's a name for the rich horn,
And custom for the spreading laurel tree.   *80*

(1919, 1921)

SAILING TO BYZANTIUM

1

That is no country for old men. The young
In one another's arms, birds in the trees
— Those dying generations — at their song,
The salmon-falls, the mackerel-crowded seas,
Fish, flesh, or fowl, commend all summer long
Whatever is begotten, born, and dies.   *6*
Caught in that sensual music all neglect
Monuments of unageing intellect.

2

An aged man is but a paltry thing,
A tattered coat upon a stick, unless   *10*
Soul clap its hands and sing, and louder sing
For every tatter in its mortal dress,
Nor is there singing school but studying
Monuments of its own magnificence;
And therefore I have sailed the seas and come
To the holy city of Byzantium.   *16*

3

O sages standing in God's holy fire
As in the gold mosaic of a wall,
Come from the holy fire, perne in a gyre,
And be the singing-masters of my soul.   *20*
Consume my heart away; sick with desire
And fastened to a dying animal
It knows not what it is; and gather me
Into the artifice of eternity.

4

Once out of nature I shall never take   *25*
My bodily form from any natural thing,
But such a form as Grecian goldsmiths make
Of hammered gold and gold enamelling
To keep a drowsy Emperor awake;
Or set upon a golden bough to sing   *30*
To lords and ladies of Byzantium
Of what is past, or passing, or to come.

(1926, 1927)

SAILING TO BYZANTIUM   Title: Byzantium, founded in the 7th century B.C., was the site of the new city of Constantinople, founded in A.D. 330 as the capital of the Byzantine or East Roman Empire (330-1453) — the city now known as Istanbul. Constantinople was the artistic and intellectual centre of the empire and of the Eastern Orthodox Church. In *A Vision* Yeats (retaining the name "Byzantium") writes: "I think if I could be given a month of Antiquity and leave to spend it where I chose, I would spend it in Byzantium a little before Justinian opened St. Sophia and closed the Academy of Plato. . . . I think that in early Byzantium, maybe never before or since in recorded history, religious, aesthetic and practical life were one, that architect and artificers . . . spoke to the multitude and the few alike." This period is approximately midway between the peaks of two of the "cones" of history in Yeats's system, and therefore (like 5th-century B.C. Athens and 15th-century Italy) at what he considered a point of balance (see notes to "The Second Coming," above). **18. mosaic:** Mosaics feature in Byzantine architecture, as they do in the churches in Ravenna, Italy, which Yeats had visited. **19. perne in a gyre:** As a child in Sligo, Yeats had learned the dialect word *pern* (or *pirn*) for a spool or bobbin on which thread or yarn is wound; *to perne* is therefore to wind, spin, or whirl; here he asks the sages to spiral down to him as a falcon would, its flight describing the shape of a gyre or cone — i.e., also to come from their realm of eternity down into the gyres of history; he also envisioned two opposing and interpenetrating cones of historical change as forming the shape of a spool, or pern. **27ff.:** Perhaps thinking of Hans Christian Andersen's fairytale "The Emperor's Nightingale," Yeats wrote in a note: "I have read somewhere that in the Emperor's palace at Byzantium was a tree made of gold and silver, and artificial birds that sang." Cf. also Keats's "Ode to a Nightingale" (p. 854).

LEDA AND THE SWAN

A sudden blow: the great wings beating still
Above the staggering girl, her thighs caressed
By the dark webs, her nape caught in his bill,
He holds her helpless breast upon his breast.

How can those terrified vague fingers push   *5*
The feathered glory from her loosening thighs?
And how can body, laid in that white rush,
But feel the strange heart beating where it lies?

A shudder in the loins engenders there
The broken wall, the burning roof and tower   *10*
And Agamemnon dead.

Being so caught up,
So mastered by the brute blood of the air,
Did she put on his knowledge with his power
Before the indifferent beak could let her drop? *15*
                                    (1923, 1928)

SWIFT'S EPITAPH

Swift has sailed into his rest;
Savage indignation there
Cannot lacerate his breast.
Imitate him if you dare,
World-besotted traveller; he   *5*
Served human liberty.
                                    (1933)

ARTHUR SYMONS
England, 1865-1945

AT DIEPPE

The grey-green stretch of sandy grass,
Indefinitely desolate;
A sea of lead, a sky of slate;
Already autumn in the air, alas!

One stark monotony of stone,   *5*
The long hotel, acutely white,
Against the after-sunset light
Withers grey-green, and takes the grass's tone.

Listless and endless it outlies,
And means, to you and me, no more   *10*
Than any pebble on the shore,
Or this indifferent moment as it dies.
                                    (1895)

LEDA AND THE SWAN Title: In one version of the Greek myth, the union between Leda and Zeus (in the form of a swan) resulted in two eggs, one giving birth to Clytemnestra (wife of Agamemnon, King of Mycenae and brother of Menelaus), the other to Helen of Troy, whose birth Yeats sees as marking the beginning of western history; as he wrote in A Vision, "I imagine the annunciation that founded Greece as made to Leda, remembering that they showed in a Spartan temple, strung up to the roof as a holy relic, an unhatched egg of hers; and that from one of her eggs came Love and from the other War. But all things are from antithesis, and when in my ignorance I try to imagine what older civilisation that annunciation rejected I can but see bird and woman blotting out some corner of the Babylonian mathematical starlight" (see note to line 19 of "The Second Coming"). 10. The broken . . . tower: i.e., in Troy — perhaps thinking of Marlowe's lines about Helen: "Was this the face that launched a thousand ships, / And burnt the topless towers of Ilium?" (The Tragical History of Doctor Faustus, scene xiii). 11. Agamemnon dead: murdered by Clytemnestra on his return from Troy.   SWIFT'S EPITAPH Jonathan Swift (see p. 478) wrote the Latin epitaph that is carved on his tomb in Saint Patrick's Cathedral, Dublin: Ubi saeva indignatio / ulterius cor lacerare nequit. / Abi, viator, / et imitare, si poteris, / strenuum pro virili [parte] liber- / tatis vindicem ("When cruel indignation is unable to lacerate the heart further, go, traveller, and imitate if you can the one who strongly and manfully defended freedom" — literally, "the strong defender of freedom in manly fashion").

JOHN GRAY
England, 1866-1934

CHARLEVILLE
Imitated from the French of Arthur Rimbaud

The square, with gravel paths and shabby lawns.
Correct, the trees and flowers repress their yawns.
The tradesman brings his favourite conceit,
To air it, while he stifles with the heat.

In the kiosk, the military band.   5
The shakos nod the time of the quadrilles.
The flaunting dandy strolls about the stand.
The notary, half unconscious of his seals.

On the green seats, small groups of grocermen,
Absorbed, their sticks scooping a little hole   10
Upon the path, talk market prices; then
Take up a cue: I think, upon the whole. . . .

The loutish roughs are larking on the grass.
The sentimental trooper, with a rose
Between his teeth, seeing a baby, grows   15
More tender, with an eye upon the nurse.

Unbuttoned, like a student, I follow
A couple of girls along the chestnut row.
They know I am following, for they turn and laugh,
Half impudent, half shy, inviting chaff.   20

I do not say a word. I only stare
At their round, fluffy necks. I follow where
The shoulders drop; I struggle to define
The subtle torso's hesitating line.

Only my rustling tread, deliberate, slow;   25
The rippled silence from the still leaves drips.
They think I am an idiot, they speak low;
— I feel faint kisses creeping on my lips.
                                        (1893)

POEM

Geranium, houseleek, laid in oblong beds
On the trim grass. The daisies' leprous stain
Is fresh. Each night the daisies burst again,
Though every day the gardener crops their heads.

A wistful child, in foul unwholesome shreds,   5
Recalls some legend of a daisy chain
That makes a pretty necklace. She would fain
Make one, and wear it, if she had some threads.

Sun, leprous flowers, foul child. The asphalt burns.
The garrulous sparrows perch on metal Burns.   10
Sing! Sing! they say, and flutter with their wings.
He does not sing, he only wonders why
He is sitting there. The sparrows sing. And I
Yield to the strait allure of simple things.
                                        (1893)

ERNEST DOWSON
England, 1867-1900

Vitae Summa Brevis Spem Nos Vetat Incohare Longam

They are not long, the weeping and the laughter,
   Love and desire and hate:
I think they have no portion in us after
   We pass the gate.

They are not long, the days of wine and roses: 5
   Out of a misty dream
Our path emerges for a while, then closes
   Within a dream.
                                        (1896)

CHARLEVILLE   **Title:** a town in the Ardennes, birthplace of the French symbolist poet Arthur Rimbaud (1854-1891); the poem is not a translation from Rimbaud, but an adaptation of his technique. **6. shakos:** military headdresses with a metal plate in front, a high brim, and a plume.   **POEM 10. metal Burns:** i.e., a metal statue of Robert Burns, in the park.   **VITAE SUMMA BREVIS Title:** "Life's brevity forbids us to entertain far-reaching hopes" (Horace, *Odes*, I.iv.15).

HENRY LAWSON
Australia, 1867-1922

THE DROVER'S WIFE

The two-roomed house is built of round timber, slabs, and stringybark, and floored with split slabs. A big bark kitchen standing at one end is larger than the house itself, veranda included.

Bush all round — bush with no horizon, for the country is flat. No ranges in the distance. The bush consists of stunted, rotten native apple-trees. No undergrowth. Nothing to relieve the eye save the darker green of a few she-oaks which are sighing above the narrow, almost waterless creek. Nineteen miles to the nearest sign of civilization — a shanty on the main road.

The drover, an ex-squatter, is away with sheep. His wife and children are left here alone.

Four ragged, dried-up-looking children are playing about the house. Suddenly one of them yells: "Snake! Mother, here's a snake!"

The gaunt, sun-browned bushwoman dashes from the kitchen, snatches her baby from the ground, holds it on her left hip, and reaches for a stick.

"Where is it?"

"Here! gone into the woodheap!" yells the eldest boy — a sharp-faced urchin of eleven. "Stop there, mother! I'll have him. Stand back! I'll have the beggar!"

"Tommy, come here, or you'll be bit. Come here at once when I tell you, you little wretch!"

The youngster comes reluctantly, carrying a stick bigger than himself. Then he yells, triumphantly:

"There it goes — under the house!" and darts away with club uplifted. At the same time the big, black, yellow-eyed dog-of-all-breeds, who has shown the wildest interest in the proceedings, breaks his chain and rushes after that snake. He is a moment late, however, and his nose reaches the crack in the slabs as the end of its tail disappears. Almost at the same moment the boy's club comes down and skins the aforesaid nose. Alligator takes small notice of this, and proceeds to undermine the building; but he is subdued after a struggle and chained up. They cannot afford to lose him.

The drover's wife makes the children stand together near the dog-house while she watches for the snake. She gets two small dishes of milk and sets them down near the wall to tempt it to come out; but an hour goes by and it does not show itself.

It is near sunset, and a thunderstorm is coming. The children must be brought inside. She will not take them into the house, for she knows the snake is there, and may at any moment come up through a crack in the rough slab floor: so she carries several armfuls of firewood into the kitchen, and then takes the children there. The kitchen has no floor — or, rather, an earthen one — called a "ground floor" in this part of the bush.

THE DROVER'S WIFE **1. stringybark:** gum tree.

There is a large, roughly-made table in the centre of the place. She brings the children in, and makes them get on this table. They are two boys and two girls — mere babies. She gives them some supper, and then, before it gets dark, she goes into the house, and snatches up some pillows and bed-clothes — expecting to see or lay her hand on the snake any minute. She makes a bed on the kitchen table for the children, and sits down beside it to watch all night. 40

She has an eye on the corner, and a green sapling club laid in readiness on the dresser by her side; also her sewing basket and a copy of the *Young Ladies' Journal*. She has brought the dog into the room. 45

Tommy turns in, under protest, but says he'll lie awake all night and smash that blinded snake.

His mother asks him how many times she has told him not to swear.

He has his club with him under the bedclothes, and Jacky protests:

"Mummy! Tommy's skinnin' me alive wif his club. Make him take it out." 50

Tommy: "Shet up, you little ——! D'yer want to be bit by the snake?"

Jacky shuts up.

"If yer bit," says Tommy, after a pause, "you'll swell up, an' smell, an' turn red an' green an' blue all over till yer bust. Won't he, mother?"

"Now then, don't frighten the child. Go to sleep," she says. 55

The two younger children go to sleep, and now and then Jacky complains of being "skeezed." More room is made for him. Presently Tommy says:

"Mother! listen to them (adjective) little possums. I'd like to screw their blanky necks."

And Jacky protests drowsily. 60

"But they don't hurt us, the little blanks!"

Mother: "There, I told you you'd teach Jacky to swear." But the remark makes her smile. Jacky goes to sleep.

Presently Tommy asks:

"Mother! Do you think they'll ever extricate the (adjective) kangaroo?" 65

"Lord! How am I to know, child? Go to sleep."

"Will you wake me if the snake comes out?"

"Yes. Go to sleep."

Near midnight. The children are all asleep and she sits there still, sewing and reading by turns. From time to time she glances round the floor and wall-plate, and whenever she hears a noise she reaches for the stick. The thunderstorm comes on, and the wind, rushing through the cracks in the slab wall, threatens to blow out her candle. She places it on a sheltered part of the dresser and fixes up a newspaper to protect it. At every flash of lightning the cracks between the slabs gleam like polished silver. The thunder rolls, and the rain comes down in torrents. 70 75

Alligator lies at full length on the floor, with his eyes turned towards the partition. She knows by this that the snake is there. There are large cracks in that wall opening under the floor of the dwelling-house.

She is not a coward, but recent events have shaken her nerves. A little son of her brother-in-law was lately bitten by a snake, and died. Besides, she has not heard from her husband for six months, and is anxious about him. 80

He was a drover, and started squatting here when they were married. The drought of 18— ruined him. He had to sacrifice the remnant of his flock and go droving again. He intends to move his family into the nearest town when he comes back, and, in the meantime, his brother, who keeps a shanty on the main road, comes over about once a   *85* month with provisions. The wife has still a couple of cows, one horse, and a few sheep. The brother-in-law kills one of the latter occasionally, gives her what she needs of it, and takes the rest in return for other provisions.

She is used to being left alone. She once lived like this for eighteen months. As a girl she built the usual castles in the air; but all her girlish hopes and aspirations have   *90* long been dead. She finds all the excitement and recreation she needs in the *Young Ladies' Journal,* and — Heaven help her! — takes a pleasure in the fashion-plates.

Her husband is an Australian, and so is she. He is careless, but a good enough husband. If he had the means he would take her to the city and keep her there like a princess. They are used to being apart, or at least she is. "No use fretting," she says. He   *95* may forget sometimes that he is married; but if he has a good cheque when he comes back he will give most of it to her. When he had money he took her to the city several times — hired a railway sleeping compartment, and put up at the best hotels. He also bought her a buggy, but they had to sacrifice that along with the rest.

The last two children were born in the bush — one while her husband was bringing   *100* a drunken doctor, by force, to attend to her. She was alone on this occasion, and very weak. She had been ill with a fever. She prayed to God to send her assistance. God sent Black Mary — the "whitest" gin in all the land. Or, at least, God sent King Jimmy first, and he sent Black Mary. He put his black face round the door-post, took in the situation at a glance, and said cheerfully: "All right, missus — I bring my old woman, she down   *105* alonga creek."

One of the children died while she was here alone. She rode nineteen miles for assistance, carrying the dead child.

It must be near one or two o'clock. The fire is burning low. Alligator lies with his head resting on his paws, and watches the wall. He is not a very beautiful dog, and the light   *110* shows numerous old wounds where the hair will not grow. He is afraid of nothing on the face of the earth or under it. He will tackle a bullock as readily as he will tackle a flea. He hates all other dogs — except kangaroo-dogs — and has a marked dislike to friends or relations of the family. They seldom call, however. He sometimes makes friends with strangers. He hates snakes and has killed many, but he will be bitten some day and die;   *115* most snake-dogs end that way.

Now and then the bushwoman lays down her work and watches, and listens, and thinks. She thinks of things in her own life, for there is little else to think about.

The rain will make the grass grow, and this reminds her how she fought a bushfire once while her husband was away. The grass was long, and very dry, and the fire   *120* threatened to burn her out. She put on an old pair of her husband's trousers and beat out the flames with a green bough, till great drops of sooty perspiration stood out on her forehead and ran in streaks down her blackened arms. The sight of his mother in

---

103. **gin:** aboriginal woman.

trousers greatly amused Tommy, who worked like a little hero by her side, but the terrified baby howled lustily for his "mummy." The fire would have mastered her but for four excited bushmen who arrived in the nick of time. It was a mixed-up affair all round; when she went to take up the baby he screamed and struggled convulsively, thinking it was a "blackman"; and Alligator, trusting more to the child's sense than his own instinct, charged furiously, and (being old and slightly deaf) did not in his excitement at first recognize his mistress's voice, but continued to hang on to the moleskins until choked off by Tommy with a saddle-strap. The dog's sorrow for his blunder, and his anxiety to let it be known that it was all a mistake, was as evident as his ragged tail and twelve-inch grin could make it. It was a glorious time for the boys; a day to look back to, and talk about, and laugh over for many years.

She thinks how she fought a flood during her husband's absence. She stood for hours in the drenching downpour, and dug an overflow gutter to save the dam across the creek. But she could not save it. There are things that a bushwoman cannot do. Next morning the dam was broken, and her heart was nearly broken too, for she thought how her husband would feel when he came home and saw the result of years of labour swept away. She cried then.

She also fought the pleuro-pneumonia — dosed and bled the few remaining cattle, and wept again when her two best cows died.

Again, she fought a mad bullock that besieged the house for a day. She made bullets and fired at him through cracks in the slabs with an old shot-gun. He was dead in the morning. She skinned him and got seventeen-and-sixpence for the hide.

She also fights the crows and eagles that have designs on her chickens. Her plan of campaign is very original. The children cry "Crows, mother!" and she rushes out and aims a broomstick at the birds as though it were a gun, and says "Bung!" The crows leave in a hurry; they are cunning, but a woman's cunning is greater.

Occasionally a bushman in the horrors, or a villainous-looking sundowner, comes and nearly scares the life out of her. She generally tells the suspicious-looking stranger that her husband and two sons are at work below the dam, or over at the yard, for he always cunningly inquires for the boss.

Only last week a gallows-faced swagman — having satisfied himself that there were no men on the place — threw down his swag on the veranda, and demanded tucker. She gave him something to eat; then he expressed his intention of staying for the night. It was sundown then. She got a batten from the sofa, loosened the dog, and confronted the stranger, holding the batten in one hand and the dog's collar with the other. "Now you go!" she said. He looked at her and at the dog, said "All right, mum," in a cringing tone, and left. She was a determined-looking woman, and Alligator's yellow eyes glared unpleasantly — besides, the dog's chawing-up apparatus greatly resembled that of the reptile he was named after.

She has few pleasures to think of as she sits here alone by the fire, on guard against a snake. All days are much the same to her; but on Sunday afternoon she dresses herself, tidies the children, smartens up baby, and goes for a lonely walk along the bush-track, pushing an old perambulator in front of her. She does this every Sunday. She takes as

---

130. **moleskins:** cotton trousers. 154. **swagman:** tramp. 156. **tucker:** food.

much care to make herself and the children look smart as she would if she were going to do the block in the city. There is nothing to see, however, and not a soul to meet. You might walk twenty miles along this track without being able to fix a point in your mind, unless you are a bushman. This is because of the everlasting, maddening sameness of *170* the stunted trees — that monotony which makes a man long to break away and travel as far as trains can go, and sail as far as ship can sail — and further.

But this bushwoman is used to the loneliness of it. As a girl-wife she hated it, and now she would feel strange away from it.

She is glad when her husband returns, but she does not gush or make a fuss about it. *175* She gets him something good to eat, and tidies up the children.

She seems contented with her lot. She loves the children, but has no time to show it. She seems harsh to them. Her surroundings are not favourable to the development of the "womanly" or sentimental side of nature.

It must be near morning now; but the clock is in the dwelling-house. Her candle is *180* nearly gone; she forgot that she was out of candles. Some more wood must be got to keep the fire up, and so she shuts the dog inside and hurries round to the woodheap. The rain has cleared off. She seizes a stick, pulls it out, and — crash! the whole pile collapses.

Yesterday she bargained with a stray blackfellow to bring her some wood, and *185* while he was at work she went in search of a missing cow. She was absent an hour or so, and the native black made good use of his time. On her return she was so astonished to see a good heap of wood by the chimney that she gave him an extra fig of tobacco, and praised him for not being lazy. He thanked her, and left with head erect and chest well out. He was the last of his tribe and a King; but he had built that woodheap hollow. *190*

She is hurt now, and tears spring to her eyes as she sits down again by the table. She takes up a handkerchief to wipe the tears away, but pokes her eyes with her bare fingers instead. The handkerchief is full of holes, and she finds that she has put her thumb through one, and her forefinger through another.

This makes her laugh, to the surprise of the dog. She has a keen, very keen, sense of *195* the ridiculous; and some time or other she will amuse bushmen with the story.

She had been amused before like that. One day she sat down "to have a good cry," as she said — and the old cat rubbed against her dress and "cried too." Then she had to laugh.

It must be near daylight now. The room is very close and hot because of the fire. *200* Alligator still watches the wall from time to time. Suddenly he becomes greatly interested; he draws himself a few inches nearer the partition, and a thrill runs through his body. The hair on the back of his neck begins to bristle, and the battle-light is in his yellow eyes. She knows what this means, and lays her hand on the stick. The lower end of one of the partition slabs has a large crack on both sides. An evil pair of small bright *205* bead-like eyes glisten at one of these holes. The snake — a black one — comes slowly out, about a foot, and moves its head up and down. The dog lies still, and the woman sits as one fascinated. The snake comes out a foot further. She lifts her stick, and the reptile, as though suddenly aware of danger, sticks his head in through the crack on the other

side of the slab, and hurries to get his tail round after him. Alligator springs, and his *210*
jaws come together with a snap. He misses, for his nose is large, and the snake's body
close down in the angle formed by the slabs and the floor. He snaps again as the tail
comes round. He has the snake now, and tugs it out eighteen inches. Thud, thud, comes
the woman's club on the ground. Alligator pulls again. Thud, thud. Alligator gives
another pull and he has the snake out — a black brute, five feet long. The head rises to *215*
dart about, but the dog has the enemy close to the neck. He is a big, heavy dog, but
quick as a terrier. He shakes the snake as though he felt the original curse in common
with mankind. The eldest boy wakes up, seizes his stick, and tries to get out of bed, but
his mother forces him back with a grip of iron. Thud, thud — the snake's back is broken
in several places. Thud, thud — its head is crushed, and Alligator's nose skinned again. *220*

She lifts the mangled reptile on the point of her stick, carries it to the fire, and
throws it in; then piles on the wood and watches the snake burn. The boy and dog watch
too. She lays her hand on the dog's head, and all the fierce, angry light dies out of his
yellow eyes. The younger children are quieted, and presently go to sleep. The dirty-
legged boy stands for a moment in his shirt, watching the fire. Presently he looks up at *225*
her, sees the tears in her eyes, and, throwing his arms round her neck, exclaims:

"Mother, I won't never go drovin'; blast me if I do!"

And she hugs him to her worn-out breast and kisses him; and they sit thus together
while the sickly daylight breaks over the bush.

(1892, 1901)

R.F. SCOTT
England, 1868-1912

from SCOTT'S LAST EXPEDITION

Thursday, February 2 [1911]

. . . .
Impressions
The seductive folds of the sleeping-bag.
The hiss of the primus and the fragrant steam of the cooker issuing from the tent
ventilator.
The small green tent and the great white road.   5
The whine of a dog and the neigh of our steeds.

---

217. original curse: See Genesis 3:13-17 (p. 244).   **SCOTT'S LAST EXPEDITION**   The British expedition, led by Captain Scott, sailed for New Zealand in the summer of 1910; the trek from McMurdo Sound to the South Pole began in November 1911; five men reached the pole 18 January 1912, 34 days after the Norwegian explorer Roald Amundsen (1872-1928) (line 116); on the return journey Scott died along with all four of his companions: Petty Officer Edgar Evans (b. 1876), Dr. Edward Wilson (b. 1880), Lieutenant Henry R. Bowers (b. 1883), and Captain Lawrence Oates (b. 1880); Oates's nickname "Titus" alludes to a famous Restoration conspirator named Titus Oates (1649-1705) who in 1678 fabricated a threat to civil order that came to be known as the "Popish Plot" (see note to lines 64-65 of Dryden's *Mac Flecknoe*, p. 435).

The driving cloud of powdered snow.
The crunch of footsteps which break the surface crust.
The wind-blown furrows.
The blue arch beneath the smoky cloud.   *10*
The crisp ring of the ponies' hoofs and the swish of the following sledge.
The droning conversation of the march as driver encourages or chides his horse.
The patter of dog pads.
The gentle flutter of our canvas shelter.
Its deep booming sound under the full force of a blizzard.   *15*
The drift snow like finest flour penetrating every hole and corner — flickering up
beneath one's head covering, pricking sharply as a sand blast.
The sun with blurred image peeping shyly through the wreathing drift giving pale
shadowless light.
The eternal silence of the great white desert. Cloudy columns of snow drift   *20*
advancing from the south, pale yellow wraiths, heralding the coming storm, blotting out
one by one the sharp-cut lines of the land.
The blizzard, Nature's protest — the crevasse, Nature's pitfall — that grim trap for
the unwary — no hunter could conceal his snare so perfectly — the light rippled snow
bridge gives no hint or sign of the hidden danger, its position unguessable till man or   *25*
beast is floundering, clawing and struggling for foothold on the brink.
The vast silence broken only by the mellow sounds of the marching column.

Monday, January 8 [1912]

Camp 60. Noon. T. –19.8°. Min. for night –25°. Our first summit blizzard. We might
just have started after breakfast, but the wind seemed obviously on the increase, and so
it has proved. The sun has not been obscured, but snow is evidently falling as well as   *30*
drifting. The sun seems to be getting a little brighter as the wind increases. The whole
phenomenon is very like a Barrier blizzard, only there is much less snow, as one would
expect, and at present less wind, which is somewhat of a surprise.

It is quite impossible to speak too highly of my companions. Each fulfils his office

Evans' hand was dressed this morning, and the rest ought to be good for it. I am not
sure it will not do us all good as we lie so very comfortably, warmly clothed in our   *35*
comfortable bags, within our double-walled tent. However, we do not want more than a
day's delay at most, both on account of lost time and food and the slow accumulation of
ice. (Night T. –13.5°.) It has grown much thicker during the day, from time to time
obscuring the sun for the first time. The temperature is low for a blizzard, but we are
very comfortable in our double tent and the cold snow is not sticky and not easily   *40*
carried into the tent, so that the sleeping-bags remain in good condition. (T. –3°.) The
glass is rising slightly. I hope we shall be able to start in the morning, but fear that a
disturbance of this sort may last longer than our local storms.

It is quite impossible to speak too highly of my companions. Each fulfils his office
to the party; Wilson, first as doctor, ever on the lookout to alleviate the small pains and *45*
troubles incidental to the work; now as cook, quick, careful and dexterous, ever thinking

---

28. **T.:** The temperatures are given in Fahrenheit; **summit:** i.e., the icecap covering the land and its mountains, as opposed to the Barrier (line 32), the icecap that extends out from the land over the sea.

of some fresh expedient to help the camp life; tough as steel on the traces, never wavering from start to finish.

Evans, a giant worker with a really remarkable head-piece. It is only now I realise how much has been due to him. Our ski shoes and crampons have been absolutely indispensable, and if the original ideas were not his, the details of manufacture and design and the good workmanship are his alone. He is responsible for every sledge, every sledge fitting, tents, sleeping-bags, harness, and when one cannot recall a single expression of dissatisfaction with any one of these items, it shows what an invaluable assistant he has been. Now, besides superintending the putting up of the tent, he thinks out and arranges the packing of the sledge; it is extraordinary how neatly and handily everything is stowed, and how much study has been given to preserving the suppleness and good running qualities of the machine. On the Barrier, before the ponies were killed, he was ever roaming round, correcting faults of stowage.

Little Bowers remains a marvel — he is thoroughly enjoying himself. I leave all the provision arrangement in his hands, and at all times he knows exactly how we stand, or how each returning party should fare. It has been a complicated business to redistribute stores at various stages of re-organisation, but not one single mistake has been made. In addition to the stores, he keeps the most thorough and conscientious meteorological record, and to this he now adds the duty of observer and photographer. Nothing comes amiss to him, and no work is too hard. It is a difficulty to get him into the tent; he seems quite oblivious of the cold, and he lies coiled in his bag writing and working out sights long after the others are asleep.

Of these three it is a matter for thought and congratulation that each is specially suited for his own work, but would not be capable of doing that of the others as well as it is done. Each is invaluable. Oates had his invaluable period with the ponies; now he is a foot slogger and goes hard the whole time, does his share of camp work, and stands the hardship as well as any of us. I would not like to be without him either. So our five people are perhaps as happily selected as it is possible to imagine.

Night, January 15

.... It is wonderful to think that two long marches would land us at the Pole. We left our depôt to-day with nine days' provisions, so that it ought to be a certain thing now, and the only appalling possibility the sight of the Norwegian flag forestalling ours. Little Bowers continues his indefatigable efforts to get good sights, and it is wonderful how he works them up in his sleeping-bag in our congested tent. (Minimum for night –27.5°.) Only 27 miles from the Pole. We *ought* to do it now.

Tuesday, January 16

Camp 68. Height 9760. T. –23.5°. The worst has happened, or nearly the worst. We marched well in the morning and covered 7½ miles. Noon sight showed us in Lat. 89° 42' S., and we started off in high spirits in the afternoon, feeling that to-morrow would see us at our destination. About the second hour of the march Bowers' sharp eyes

---

58-59. ponies were killed: Scott's decision to take horses rather than rely solely on dogs to pull the sledges proved ill-advised; many died early on.
67. working out sights: i.e., establishing location from observations made with a sextant.

detected what he thought was a cairn; he was uneasy about it, but argued that it must be   *85*
a sastrugus. Half an hour later he detected a black speck ahead. Soon we knew that this
could not be a natural snow feature. We marched on, found that it was a black flag tied
to a sledge bearer; near by the remains of a camp; sledge tracks and ski tracks going and
coming and the clear trace of dogs' paws — many dogs. This told us the whole story.
The Norwegians have forestalled us and are first at the Pole. It is a terrible dis-   *90*
appointment, and I am very sorry for my loyal companions. Many thoughts come and
much discussion have we had. To-morrow we must march on to the Pole and then
hasten home with all the speed we can compass. All the day dreams must go; it will be a
wearisome return. Certainly we are descending in altitude — certainly also the
Norwegians found an easy way up.   *95*

Wednesday, January 17

Camp 69. T. −22° at start. Night −21°. The Pole. Yes, but under very different
circumstances from those expected. We have had a horrible day — add to our
disappointment a head wind 4 to 5, with a temperature −22°, and companions labouring
on with cold feet and hands.

We started at 7.30, none of us having slept much after the shock of our discovery.   *100*
We followed the Norwegian sledge tracks for some way; as far as we make out there are
only two men. In about three miles we passed two small cairns. Then the weather
overcast, and the tracks being increasingly drifted up and obviously going too far to the
west, we decided to make straight for the Pole according to our calculations. . . . We
have been descending again, I think, but there looks to be a rise ahead; otherwise there   *105*
is very little that is different from the awful monotony of past days. Great God! this is an
awful place and terrible enough for us to have laboured to it without the reward of
priority. Well, it is something to have got here, and the wind may be our friend to-
morrow. . . . Now for the run home and a desperate struggle. I wonder if we can do it.

Thursday morning, January 18

Decided after summing up all observations that we were 3.5 miles away from the Pole   *110*
— one mile beyond it and 3 to the right. More or less in this direction Bowers saw a
cairn or tent.

We have just arrived at this tent, 2 miles from our camp, therefore about 1½ miles
from the Pole. In the tent we find a record of five Norwegians having been here, as
follows: *115*

> Roald Amundsen
> Olav Olavson Bjaaland
> Hilmer Hanssen
> Sverre H. Hassel
> Oscar Wisting.   *120*
>
> 16. Dec. 1911.

The tent is fine — a small compact affair supported by a single bamboo. A note
from Amundsen, which I keep, asks me to forward a letter to King Haakon!

---

86. sastrugus: ridge of snow formed by wind. **123. King Haakon:** Haakon VII (1872-1957), king of Norway from 1905 to 1957.

The following articles have been left in the tent: 3 half bags of reindeer containing a miscellaneous assortment of mits and sleeping-socks, very various in description, a *125* sextant, a Norwegian artificial horizon and a hypsometer without boiling-point thermometers, a sextant and hypsometer of English make.

Left a note to say I had visited the tent with companions. Bowers photographing and Wilson sketching. . . . There is no doubt that our predecessors have made thoroughly sure of their mark and fully carried out their programme. I think the Pole is about 9500 *130* feet in height; this is remarkable, considering that in Lat. 88° we were about 10,500.

We carried the Union Jack about ¾ of a mile north with us and left it on a piece of stick as near as we could fix it.

Sunday, February 11

R. 25. Lunch Temp. –6.5°; Supper –3.5°. The worst day we have had during the trip and greatly owing to our own fault. We started on a wretched surface with light S.W. wind, *135* sail set, and pulling on ski — horrible light, which made everything look fantastic. As we went on light got worse, and suddenly we found ourselves in pressure. Then came the fatal decision to steer east. We went on for 6 hours, hoping to do a good distance, which in fact I suppose we did, but for the last hour or two we pressed on into a regular trap. Getting on to a good surface we did not reduce our lunch meal, and thought all *140* going well, but half an hour after lunch we got into the worst ice mess I have ever been in. For three hours we plunged on on ski, first thinking we were too much to the right, then too much to the left; meanwhile the disturbance got worse and my spirits received a very rude shock. There were times when it seemed almost impossible to find a way out of the awful turmoil in which we found ourselves. At length, arguing that there must be *145* a way on our left, we plunged in that direction. It got worse, harder, more icy and crevassed. We could not manage our ski and pulled on foot, falling into crevasses every minute — most luckily no bad accident. At length we saw a smoother slope towards the land, pushed for it, but knew it was a woefully long way from us. The turmoil changed in character, irregular crevassed surface giving way to huge chasms, closely packed and *150* most difficult to cross. It was very heavy work, but we had grown desperate. We won through at 10 P.M. and I write after 12 hours on the march. I *think* we are on or about the right track now, but we are still a good number of miles from the depôt, so we reduced rations to-night. We had three pemmican meals left and decided to make them into four. To-morrow's lunch must serve for two if we do not make big progress. It was a test of *155* our endurance on the march and our fitness with small supper. We have come through well. A good wind has come down the glacier which is clearing the sky and surface. Pray God the wind holds to-morrow. Short sleep to-night and off first thing, I hope.

Monday, February 12

R. 26. In a very critical situation. All went well in the forenoon, and we did a good long march over a fair surface. Two hours before lunch we were cheered by the sight of our *160* night camp of the 18th December, the day after we made our depôt — this showed we

---

126. hypsometer: an instrument that measures the boiling point of water in order to determine elevation. **136. sail set:** i.e., to aid the movement of the sledge, when the wind is favourable.

were on the right track. In the afternoon, refreshed by tea, we went forward, confident of covering the remaining distance, but by a fatal chance we kept too far to the left, and then we struck uphill and, tired and despondent, arrived in a horrid maze of crevasses and fissures. Divided councils caused our course to be erratic after this, and finally, at 9 P.M. we landed in the worst place of all. After discussion we decided to camp, and here we are, after a very short supper and one meal only remaining in the food bag; the depôt doubtful in locality. . . . Pray God we have fine weather to-morrow. . . . 165

Tuesday, February 13

Camp R. 27, beside Cloudmaker. Temp. –10°. Last night we all slept well in spite of our grave anxieties. For my part these were increased by my visits outside the tent, when I 170 saw the sky gradually closing over and snow beginning to fall. By our ordinary time for getting up it was dense all around us. We could see nothing, and we could only remain in our sleeping-bags. At 8.30 I dimly made out the land of the Cloudmaker. At 9 we got up, deciding to have tea, and with one biscuit, no pemmican, so as to leave our scanty remaining meal for eventualities. We started marching, and at first had to wind our way 175 through an awful turmoil of broken ice, but in about an hour we hit an old moraine track, brown with dirt. Here the surface was much smoother and improved rapidly. The fog still hung over all and we went on for an hour, checking our bearings. Then the whole plain got smoother and we turned outward a little. Evans raised our hopes with a shout of depôt ahead, but it proved to be a shadow on the ice. Then suddenly Wilson 180 saw the actual depôt flag. It was an immense relief, and we were soon in possession of our 3½ days' food. The relief to all is inexpressible. . . .

Wednesday, February 14

Lunch Temp. 0°; Supper Temp. +1°. . . . After lunch we got on snow, with ice only occasionally showing through. A poor start, but the gradient and wind improving, we did 6½ miles before night camp. 185

There is no getting away from the fact that we are not pulling strong. Probably none of us: Wilson's leg still troubles him and he doesn't like to trust himself on ski; but the worst case is Evans, who is giving us serious anxiety. This morning he suddenly disclosed a huge blister on his foot. It delayed us on the march, when he had to have his crampon readjusted. Sometimes I fear he is going from bad to worse, but I trust he will 190 pick up again when we come to steady work on ski like this afternoon. He is hungry and so is Wilson. We can't risk opening out our food again, and as cook at present I am serving something under full allowance. We are inclined to get slack and slow with our camping arrangements, and small delays increase. I have talked of the matter to-night and hope for improvement. We cannot do distance without the hours. The next depôt 195 some 30 miles away and nearly 3 days' food in hand.

Thursday, February 15

R. 29. Lunch Temp. +10°; Supper Temp. +4°. 13.5 miles. Again we are running short of provision. We don't know our distance from the depôt, but imagine about 20 miles. . . .

---

169. Cloudmaker: mountain, near Beardmore Glacier, in the Commonwealth Range.

Friday, February 16

12.5 m. Lunch Temp. +6.1°; Supper Temp. +7°. A rather trying position. Evans has nearly broken down in brain, we think. He is absolutely changed from his normal self-reliant self. This morning and this afternoon he stopped the march on some trivial excuse. . . . We cannot be more than 10 or 12 miles from the depôt, but the weather is all against us. . . .

Saturday, February 17

A very terrible day. Evans looked a little better after a good sleep, and declared, as he always did, that he was quite well. He started in his place on the traces, but half an hour later worked his ski shoes adrift, and had to leave the sledge. The surface was awful, the soft recently fallen snow clogging the ski and runners at every step, the sledge groaning, the sky overcast, and the land hazy. We stopped after about one hour, and Evans came up again, but very slowly. Half an hour later he dropped out again on the same plea. He asked Bowers to lend him a piece of string. I cautioned him to come on as quickly as he could, and he answered cheerfully as I thought. We had to push on, and the remainder of us were forced to pull very hard, sweating heavily. Abreast the Monument Rock we stopped, and seeing Evans a long way astern, I camped for lunch. There was no alarm at first, and we prepared tea and our own meal, consuming the latter. After lunch, and Evans still not appearing, we looked out, to see him still afar off. By this time we were alarmed, and all four started back on ski. I was first to reach the poor man and shocked at his appearance; he was on his knees with clothing disarranged, hands uncovered and frostbitten, and a wild look in his eyes. Asked what was the matter, he replied with a slow speech that he didn't know, but thought he must have fainted. We got him on his feet, but after two or three steps he sank down again. He showed every sign of complete collapse. Wilson, Bowers, and I went back for the sledge, whilst Oates remained with him. When we returned he was practically unconscious, and when we got him into the tent quite comatose. He died quietly at 12.30 A.M. . . .

At 1 A.M. we packed up and came down over the pressure ridges, finding our depôt easily.

Friday, March 2

Lunch. Misfortunes rarely come singly. We marched to the [Middle Barrier] depôt fairly easily yesterday afternoon, and since that have suffered three distinct blows which have placed us in a bad position. First we found a shortage of oil; with most rigid economy it can scarce carry us to the next depôt on this surface [71 miles away]. Second, Titus Oates disclosed his feet, the toes showing very bad indeed, evidently bitten by the late temperatures. The third blow came in the night, when the wind, which we had hailed with some joy, brought dark overcast weather. It fell below –40° in the night, and this morning it took 1½ hours to get our foot gear on, but we got away before eight. We lost cairn and tracks together and made as steady as we could N. by W., but have seen nothing. Worse was to come — the surface is simply awful. In spite of strong wind and full sail we have only done 5½ miles. We are in a very queer street since there is no doubt we cannot do the extra marches and feel the cold horribly.

---

224. **Misfortunes rarely come singly:** See *Hamlet*: "When sorrows come, they come not single spies, / But in battalions" (IV.v.78-79); [**Middle Barrier] depôt:** i.e., the depot about halfway across the Great Ice Barrier (now called the Ross Ice Shelf) that covers the southern part of the Ross Sea. 234. **queer street:** i.e., serious difficulty.

Monday, March 5

Lunch. Regret to say going from bad to worse. We got a slant of wind yesterday afternoon, and going on 5 hours we converted our wretched morning run of 3½ miles into something over 9. We went to bed on a cup of cocoa and pemmican solid with the chill off. The result is telling on all, but mainly on Oates, whose feet are in a wretched condition. One swelled up tremendously last night and he is very lame this morning. We   *240* started march on tea and pemmican as last night — we pretend to prefer the pemmican this way. Marched for 5 hours this morning over a slightly better surface covered with high moundy sastrugi. Sledge capsized twice; we pulled on foot, covering about 5½ miles. We are two pony marches and 4 miles about from our depôt. Our fuel dreadfully low and the poor Soldier nearly done. It is pathetic enough because we can do nothing   *245* for him; more hot food might do a little, but only a little, I fear. We none of us expected these terribly low temperatures, and of the rest of us Wilson is feeling them most; mainly, I fear, from his self-sacrificing devotion in doctoring Oates' feet. We cannot help each other, each has enough to do to take care of himself. We get cold on the march when the trudging is heavy, and the wind pierces our warm garments. The others, all of   *250* them, are unendingly cheerful when in the tent. We mean to see the game through with a proper spirit, but it's tough work to be pulling harder than we ever pulled in our lives for long hours, and to feel that the progress is so slow. One can only say "God help us!" and plod on our weary way, cold and very miserable, though outwardly cheerful. We talk of all sorts of subjects in the tent, not much of food now, since we decided to take the risk   *255* of running a full ration. We simply couldn't go hungry at this time.

Tuesday, March 6

Lunch. We did a little better with help of wind yesterday afternoon, finishing 9½ miles for the day, and 27 miles from depôt. But this morning things have been awful. It was warm in the night and for the first time during the journey I overslept myself by more than an hour; then we were slow with foot gear; then, pulling with all our might (for our   *260* lives) we could scarcely advance at rate of a mile an hour; then it grew thick and three times we had to get out of harness to search for tracks. The result is something less than 3½ miles for the forenoon. The sun is shining now and the wind gone. Poor Oates is unable to pull, sits on the sledge when we are track-searching — he is wonderfully plucky, as his feet must be giving him great pain. He makes no complaint, but his spirits   *265* only come up in spurts now, and he grows more silent in the tent. . . .

Saturday, March 10

Things steadily downhill. Oates' foot worse. He has rare pluck and must know that he can never get through. He asked Wilson if he had a chance this morning, and of course Bill had to say he didn't know. In point of fact he has none. Apart from him, if he went under now, I doubt whether we could get through. With great care we might have a   *270* dog's chance, but no more. The weather conditions are awful, and our gear gets steadily more icy and difficult to manage. At the same time of course poor Titus is the greatest handicap. He keeps us waiting in the morning until we have partly lost the warming

---

245. Soldier: i.e., Oates.

effect of our good breakfast, when the only wise policy is to be up and away at once; again at lunch. Poor chap! it is too pathetic to watch him. . . .   *275*

Sunday, March 11

Titus Oates is very near the end, one feels. What we or he will do, God only knows. We discussed the matter after breakfast; he is a brave fine fellow and understands the situation, but he practically asked for advice. Nothing could be said but to urge him to march as long as he could. One satisfactory result to the discussion; I practically ordered Wilson to hand over the means of ending our troubles to us, so that any one of us may *280* know how to do so. Wilson had no choice between doing so and our ransacking the medicine case. We have 30 opium tabloids apiece and he is left with a tube of morphine. So far the tragical side of our story.

Monday, March 12

We did 6.9 miles yesterday, under our necessary average. Things are left much the same, Oates not pulling much, and now with hands as well as feet pretty well useless. *285* We did 4 miles this morning in 4 hours 20 min. — we may hope for 3 this afternoon, $7 \times 6 = 42$. We shall be 47 miles from the depôt. I doubt if we can possibly do it. The surface remains awful, the cold intense, and our physical condition running down. God help us! Not a breath of favourable wind for more than a week, and apparently liable to head winds at any moment.   *290*

Wednesday, March 14

No doubt about the going downhill, but everything going wrong for us. Yesterday we woke to a strong northerly wind with temp. $-37°$. Couldn't face it, so remained in camp till 2, then did 5½ miles. Wanted to march later, but party feeling the cold badly as the breeze (N.) never took off entirely, and as the sun sank the temp. fell. Long time getting supper in dark. . . .   *295*

Friday, March 16 or Saturday 17

Lost track of dates, but think the last correct. Tragedy all along the line. At lunch, the day before yesterday, poor Titus Oates said he couldn't go on; he proposed we should leave him in his sleeping-bag. That we could not do, and we induced him to come on, on the afternoon march. In spite of its awful nature for him he struggled on and we made a few miles. At night he was worse and we knew the end had come.   *300*

Should this be found I want these facts recorded. Oates' last thoughts were of his Mother, but immediately before he took pride in thinking that his regiment would be pleased with the bold way in which he met his death. We can testify to his bravery. He has borne intense suffering for weeks without complaint, and to the very last was able and willing to discuss outside subjects. He did not — would not — give up hope till the *305* very end. He was a brave soul. This was the end. He slept through the night before last, hoping not to wake; but he woke in the morning — yesterday. It was blowing a blizzard. He said, "I am just going outside and may be some time." He went out into the blizzard and we have not seen him since.

I take this opportunity of saying that we have stuck to our sick companions to the last. *310*
In case of Edgar Evans, when absolutely out of food and he lay insensible, the safety of
the remainder seemed to demand his abandonment, but Providence mercifully removed
him at this critical moment. He died a natural death, and we did not leave him till two
hours after his death. We knew that poor Oates was walking to his death, but though we
tried to dissuade him, we knew it was the act of a brave man and an English gentleman. *315*
We all hope to meet the end with a similar spirit, and assuredly the end is not far.

I can only write at lunch and then only occasionally. The cold is intense, −40° at
midday. My companions are unendingly cheerful, but we are all on the verge of serious
frostbites, and though we constantly talk of fetching through I don't think any one of us
believes it in his heart. *320*

We are cold on the march now, and at all times except meals. Yesterday we had to
lay up for a blizzard and to-day we move dreadfully slowly. We are at No. 14 pony
camp, only two pony marches from One Ton Depôt. We leave here our theodolite, a
camera, and Oates' sleeping-bags. Diaries, &c., and geological specimens carried at
Wilson's special request, will be found with us or on our sledge. *325*

Sunday, March 18

To-day, lunch, we are 21 miles from the depôt. Ill fortune presses, but better may come.
We have had more wind and drift from ahead yesterday; had to stop marching; wind
N.W., force 4, temp. −35°. No human being could face it, and we are worn out *nearly*.

My right foot has gone, nearly all the toes — two days ago I was proud possessor of
best feet. These are the steps of my downfall. Like an ass I mixed a small spoonful of *330*
curry powder with my melted pemmican — it gave me violent indigestion. I lay awake
and in pain all night; woke and felt done on the march; foot went and I didn't know it. A
very small measure of neglect and have a foot which is not pleasant to contemplate.
Bowers takes first place in condition, but there is not much to choose after all. The
others are still confident of getting through — or pretend to be — I don't know! We *335*
have the last *half* fill of oil in our primus and a very small quantity of spirit — this alone
between us and thirst. The wind is fair for the moment, and that is perhaps a fact to help.
The mileage would have seemed ridiculously small on our outward journey.

Monday, March 19

Lunch. We camped with difficulty last night, and were dreadfully cold till after our
supper of cold pemmican and biscuit and a half a pannikin of cocoa cooked over the *340*
spirit. Then, contrary to expectation, we got warm and all slept well. To-day we started
in the usual dragging manner. Sledge dreadfully heavy. We are 15½ miles from the
depôt and ought to get there in three days. What progress! We have two days' food but
barely a day's fuel. All our feet are getting bad — Wilson's best, my right foot worst,
left all right. There is no chance to nurse one's feet till we can get hot food into us. *345*
Amputation is the least I can hope for now, but will the trouble spread? That is the
serious question. The weather doesn't give us a chance — the wind from N. to N.W. and
−40° temp. to-day.

---

328. force 4: On Beaufort's Scale, the numbers 0 to 12 represent wind force from dead calm to hurricane.

Wednesday, March 21

Got within 11 miles of depôt Monday night; had to lay up all yesterday in severe
blizzard. To-day forlorn hope, Wilson and Bowers going to depôt for fuel.   350

Thursday, March 22 and 23

Blizzard bad as ever — Wilson and Bowers unable to start — to-morrow last chance —
no fuel and only one or two of food left — must be near the end. Have decided it shall
be natural — we shall march for the depôt with or without our effects and die in our
tracks.

Thursday, March 29

Since the 21st we have had a continuous gale from W.S.W. and S.W. We had fuel to   355
make two cups of tea apiece and bare food for two days on the 20th. Every day we have
been ready to start for our depôt *11 miles* away, but outside the door of the tent it
remains a scene of whirling drift. I do not think we can hope for any better things now.
We shall stick it out to the end, but we are getting weaker, of course, and the end cannot
be far.   360

  It seems a pity, but I do not think I can write more.

                                                                          R. Scott.

  Last entry.
  For God's sake look after our people.

                                                                       (1910-12; 1915)

MARY FULLERTON
Australia, 1868-1946

POETRY

Ecstatic thought's the thing:
Its nature lifts it from the sod.
The father of its soul is God,
And in God's house are many scansions.
                              (1942)

LION

There was no ceremony
When the last god died,
No dramatic moment

When a new Faith slew;
But slow, undeified,   5
The once feared and cherished,
Outworn, forgotten,
Lion Life never knew
When the last god perished.

What next shall he lose   10
In his large going?
Leaves flung from his flanks
In terrible unknowing!
                              (1942)

POETRY 4: Cf. John 14:2.

HUMILITY

The poet was exuberant,
Along his labyrinth shouting.
"Good fellow, you must trim,"
The critics came a-clouting.

And so he cut and pruned,   5
At the behesting . . .
And now remain no bowers,
Nor sweet birds nesting.

(1942)

THREADS

I watched a spider spin
A mystic rope
Made from his very self
And hope.

I saw a human soul   5
By a gulf stand,
Praying the farther side
Be land.

The spider's filament
Reached stem from sod;   10
The thread the soul flung forth
Reached God.

(1946)

W.E.B. DU BOIS
U.S.A., 1868-1963

A MILD SUGGESTION

They were sitting on the leeward deck of the vessel and the colored man was there with his usual look of unconcern. Before the seasickness his presence aboard had caused some upheaval. The Woman, for instance, glancing at the Southerner, had refused point blank to sit beside him at meals, so she had changed places with the Little Old Lady. The Westerner, who sat opposite, said he did not care a ——, then he looked at the   5
Little Old Lady, and added in a lower voice to the New Yorker that there was no accounting for tastes. The Southerner from the other table broadened his back and tried to express with his shoulders both ancestors and hauteur. All this, however, was half forgotten during the seasickness, and the Woman sat beside the colored man for a full half hour before she noticed it, and then was glad to realize that the Southerner was too   10
sick to see. Now again with sunshine and smiling weather, they all quite naturally reverted (did the Southerner suggest it?) to the Negro problem. The usual solutions had been suggested: education, work, emigration, etc.

They had not noticed the back of the colored man, until the thoughtless Westerner turned toward him and said breezily: "Well, now, what do you say? I guess you are   15
rather interested." The colored man was leaning over the rail and about to light his cigarette — he had several such bad habits, as the Little Old Lady noticed. The Southerner simply stared. Over the face of the colored man went the shadow of several expressions; some the New Yorker could interpret, others he could not.

"I have," said the colored man, with deliberation, "a perfect solution." The Souther-   20
ner selected a look of disdain from his repertoire, and assumed it. The Woman moved

nearer, but partly turned her back. The Westerner and the Little Old Lady sat down. "Yes," repeated the colored man, "I have a perfect solution. The trouble with most of the solutions which are generally suggested is that they aggravate the disease." The Southerner could not help looking interested. "For instance," proceeded the colored man, airily waving his hand, "take education; education means ambition, dissatisfaction and revolt. You cannot both educate people and hold them down." 25

"Then stop educating them," growled the Southerner aside.

"Or," continued the colored man, "if the black man works, he must come into competition with whites ——" 30

"He sure will, and it ought to be stopped," returned the Westerner. "It brings down wages."

"Precisely," said the speaker, "and if by underselling the labor market he develops a few millionaires, how now would you protect your residential districts or your select social circles or — your daughters?" 35

The Southerner started angrily, but the colored man was continuing placidly with a far-off look in his eyes. "Now, migration is both costly and inhuman; the transportation would be the smallest matter. You must buy up perhaps a thousand millions' worth of Negro property; you must furnish some capital for the masses of poor; you must get some place for them to go; you must protect them there, and here you must pay not only 40 higher wages to white men, but still higher on account of the labor scarcity. Meantime, the Negroes suddenly removed from one climate and social system to another climate and utterly new conditions would die in droves — it would be simply prolonged murder at enormous cost.

"Very well," continued the colored man, seating himself and throwing away his 45 cigarette, "listen to my plan," looking almost quizzically at the Little Old Lady; "you must not be alarmed at its severity — it may seem radical, but really it is — it is — well, it is quite the only practical thing and it has surely one advantage: it settles the problem once, suddenly, and forever. My plan is this: You now outnumber us nearly ten to one. I propose that on a certain date, shall we say next Christmas, or possibly Easter, 1912? 50 No, come to think of it, the first of January, 1913, would, for historical reasons, probably be best. Well, then, on the first of January, 1913, let each person who has a colored friend invite him to dinner. This would take care of a few; among such friends might be included the black mammies and faithful old servants of the South; in this way we could get together quite a number. Then those who have not the pleasure of black 55 friends might arrange for meetings, especially in "white" churches and Young Men's and Young Women's Christian Associations, where Negroes are not expected. At such meetings, contrary to custom, the black people should not be seated by themselves, but distributed very carefully among the whites. The remaining Negroes who could not be flattered or attracted by these invitations should be induced to assemble among 60 themselves at their own churches or at little parties and house warmings.

"The few stragglers, vagrants and wanderers could be put under careful watch and ward. Now, then, we have the thing in shape. First, the hosts of those invited to dine should provide themselves with a sufficient quantity of cyanide of potassium, placing it carefully in the proper cups, and being careful not to mix the cups. Those at church and 65 prayer meeting could choose between long sharp stilettoes and pistols — I should recommend the former as less noisy. Those who guard the colored assemblies and the stragglers without should carefully surround the groups and use Winchesters. Then, at a given signal, let the colored folk of the United States be quietly dispatched; the signal might be a church bell or the singing of the national hymn; probably the bell would be 70 best, for the diners would be eating."

By this time the auditors of the colored man were staring; the Southerner had forgotten to pose; the Woman had forgotten to watch the Southerner; the Westerner was staring with admiration; there were tears in the eyes of the Little Old Lady, while the New Yorker was smiling; but the colored man held up a deprecating hand: "Now don't 75 prejudge my plan," he urged. "The next morning there would be ten million funerals, and therefore no Negro problem. Think how quietly the thing would be settled; no more bother, no more argument; the whole country united and happy. Even the Negroes would be a great deal happier than they are at present. Instead of being made heirs to hope by education, or ambitious by wealth, or exiled invalids on the fever coast, they 80 would all be happily ensconced in Heaven. Of course, I admit that at first the plan may seem a little abrupt and cruel, and yet is it more cruel than present conditions, and would it not be well to be a little more abrupt in our social solutions? At any rate think it over," and the colored man dropped lazily into his steamer chair and felt for another cigarette.

The crowd slowly dispersed; the Southerner chose the Woman, but was heard to say 85 something about fools. The Westerner turned to the New Yorker and said: "Now, what in hell do you suppose that darky meant?" But the Little Old Lady went silently to her cabin.

(1912)

EDWIN ARLINGTON ROBINSON
U.S.A., 1869-1935

AN OLD STORY

Strange that I did not know him then,
  That friend of mine!
I did not even show him then
  One friendly sign;

But cursed him for the ways he had   5
  To make me see
My envy of the praise he had
  For praising me.

I would have rid the earth of him
  Once, in my pride . . .   10
I never knew the worth of him
  Until he died.

(1897)

MINIVER CHEEVY

Miniver Cheevy, child of scorn,
  Grew lean while he assailed the seasons;
He wept that he was ever born,
  And he had reasons.

Miniver loved the days of old   5
  When swords were bright and steeds were
    prancing;
The vision of a warrior bold
  Would set him dancing.

Miniver sighed for what was not,
  And dreamed, and rested from his labors;   10
He dreamed of Thebes and Camelot,
  And Priam's neighbors.

A MILD SUGGESTION   **80. fever coast:** tropical coast of Liberia and Sierra Leone.   **MINIVER CHEEVY**   **11. Thebes, Camelot:** centres famous in Greek history and Arthurian legend, respectively. **12. Priam:** King of Troy during the Trojan War, father of Paris, Hector, and Cassandra.

Miniver mourned the ripe renown
    That made so many a name so fragrant;
He mourned Romance, now on the town,   *15*
    And Art, a vagrant.

Miniver loved the Medici,
    Albeit he had never seen one;
He would have sinned incessantly
    Could he have been one.   *20*

Miniver cursed the commonplace
    And eyed a khaki suit with loathing;

He missed the mediæval grace
    Of iron clothing.

Miniver scorned the gold he sought,   *25*
    But sore annoyed was he without it;
Miniver thought, and thought, and thought,
    And thought about it.

Miniver Cheevy, born too late,
    Scratched his head and kept on thinking; *30*
Miniver coughed, and called it fate,
    And kept on drinking.

                    (1910)

STEPHEN LEACOCK
Canada, 1869-1944

GERTRUDE THE GOVERNESS: OR SIMPLE SEVENTEEN

Synopsis of Previous Chapters:
There are no Previous Chapters.

It was a wild and stormy night on the West Coast of Scotland. This, however, is immaterial to the present story, as the scene is not laid in the West of Scotland. For the matter of that the weather was just as bad on the East Coast of Ireland.

But the scene of this narrative is laid in the South of England and takes place in and around Knotacentinum Towers (pronounced as if written Nosham Taws), the seat of *5* Lord Knotacent (pronounced as if written Nosh).

But it is not necessary to pronounce either of these names in reading them.

Nosham Taws was a typical English home. The main part of the house was an Elizabethan structure of warm red brick, while the elder portion, of which the Earl was inordinately proud, still showed the outlines of a Norman Keep, to which had been *10* added a Lancastrian Jail and a Plantagenet Orphan Asylum. From the house in all directions stretched magnificent woodland and park with oaks and elms of immemorial antiquity, while nearer the house stood raspberry bushes and geranium plants which had been set out by the Crusaders.

About the grand old mansion the air was loud with the chirping of thrushes, the *15* cawing of partridges and the clear sweet note of the rook, while deer, antelope, and other quadrupeds strutted about the lawn so tame as to eat off the sun-dial. In fact, the place was a regular menagerie.

From the house downwards through the park stretched a beautiful broad avenue laid out by Henry VII. *20*

---

17. Medici: powerful Florentine Renaissance family, noted for its cruelty and deviousness; see also the general note to Browning's "My Last Duchess" (p. 1001).   **GERTRUDE THE GOVERNESS 1:** The opening phrase parodies the first sentence of Edward Bulwer-Lytton's 1840 novel *Paul Clifford*: "It was a dark and stormy night."

Lord Nosh stood upon the hearthrug of the library. Trained diplomat and statesman as he was, his stern aristocratic face was upside down with fury.

"Boy," he said, "you shall marry this girl or I disinherit you. You are no son of mine."

Young Lord Ronald, erect before him, flung back a glance as defiant as his own.

"I defy you," he said. "Hence forth you are no father of mine. I will get another. I will marry none but a woman I can love. This girl that we have never seen —"   *25*

"Fool," said the Earl, "would you throw aside our estate and name of a thousand years? The girl, I am told, is beautiful; her aunt is willing; they are French; pah! they understand such things in France."

"But your reason —"   *30*

"I give no reason," said the Earl. "Listen, Ronald, I give you one month. For that time you remain here. If at the end of it you refuse me, I cut you off with a shilling."

Lord Ronald said nothing; he flung himself from the room, flung himself upon his horse and rode madly off in all directions.

As the door of the library closed upon Ronald the Earl sank into a chair. His face   *35* changed. It was no longer that of the haughty nobleman, but of the hunted criminal. "He must marry the girl," he muttered. "Soon she will know all. Tutchemoff has escaped from Siberia. He knows and will tell. The whole of the mines pass to her, this property with it, and I — but enough." He rose, walked to the sideboard, drained a dipper full of gin and bitters, and became again a high-bred English gentleman.   *40*

It was at this moment that a high dogcart, driven by a groom in the livery of Earl Nosh, might have been seen entering the avenue of Nosham Taws. Beside him sat a young girl, scarce more than a child, in fact not nearly so big as the groom.

The apple-pie hat which she wore, surmounted with black willow plumes, concealed from view a face so face-like in its appearance as to be positively facial.   *45*

It was — need we say it — Gertrude the Governess, who was this day to enter upon her duties at Nosham Taws.

At the same time that the dogcart entered the avenue at one end there might have been seen riding down it from the other a tall young man, whose long, aristocratic face proclaimed his birth and who was mounted upon a horse with a face even longer than   *50* his own.

And who is this tall young man who draws nearer to Gertrude with every revolution of the horse? Ah, who, indeed? Ah, who, who? I wonder if any of my readers could guess that this was none other than Lord Ronald.

The two were destined to meet. Nearer and nearer they came. And then still nearer.   *55* Then for one brief moment they met. As they passed, Gertrude raised her head and directed towards the young nobleman two eyes so eye-like in their expression as to be absolutely circular, while Lord Ronald directed towards the occupant of the dogcart a gaze so gaze-like that nothing but a gazelle, or a gas-pipe, could have emulated its intensity.   *60*

Was this the dawn of love? Wait and see. Do not spoil the story.

Let us speak of Gertrude. Gertrude DeMongmorenci McFiggin had known neither father nor mother. They had both died years before she was born. Of her mother she knew nothing, save that she was French, was extremely beautiful, and that all her ancestors and even her business acquaintances had perished in the Revolution.   *65*

Yet Gertrude cherished the memory of her parents. On her breast the girl wore a locket in which was enshrined a miniature of her mother, while down her neck inside at the back hung a daguerreotype of her father. She carried a portrait of her grandmother up her sleeve and had pictures of her cousins tucked inside her boot, while beneath her — but enough, quite enough. 70

Of her father Gertrude knew even less. That he was a high-born English gentleman who had lived as a wanderer in many lands, this was all she knew. His only legacy to Gertrude had been a Russian grammar, a Roumanian phrase-book, a theodolite, and a work on mining engineering.

From her earliest infancy Gertrude had been brought up by her aunt. Her aunt had 75 carefully instructed her in Christian principles. She had also taught her Mohammedanism to make sure.

When Gertrude was seventeen her aunt had died of hydrophobia.

The circumstances were mysterious. There had called upon her that day a strange bearded man in the costume of the Russians. After he had left, Gertrude had found her 80 aunt in a syncope from which she passed into an apostrophe and never recovered.

To avoid scandal it was called hydrophobia. Gertrude was thus thrown upon the world. What to do? That was the problem that confronted her.

It was while musing one day upon her fate that Gertrude's eye was struck with an advertisement. 85

"Wanted a governess; must possess a knowledge of French, Italian, Russian, and Roumanian, Music, and Mining Engineering. Salary £1, 4 shillings and 4 pence halfpenny per annum. Apply between half-past eleven and twenty-five minutes to twelve at No. 41 A Decimal Six, Belgravia Terrace. The Countess of Nosh."

Gertrude was a girl of great natural quickness of apprehension, and she had not 90 pondered over this announcement more than half an hour before she was struck with the extraordinary coincidence between the list of items desired and the things that she herself knew.

She duly presented herself at Belgravia Terrace before the Countess, who advanced to meet her with a charm which at once placed the girl at her ease. 95

"You are proficient in French?" she asked.

"Oh, oui," said Gertrude modestly.

"And Italian?" continued the Countess.

"Oh, si," said Gertrude.

"And German?" said the Countess in delight. 100

"Ah, ja," said Gertrude.

"And Russian?"

"Yaw."

"And Roumanian?"

"Jep." 105

Amazed at the girl's extraordinary proficiency in modern languages, the Countess looked at her narrowly. Where had she seen those lineaments before? She passed her hand over her brow in thought, and spit upon the floor, but no, the face baffled her.

"Enough," she said, "I engage you on the spot; tomorrow you go down to Nosham Taws and begin teaching the children. I must add that in addition you will be expected 110 to aid the Earl with his Russian correspondence. He has large mining interests at Tschminsk."

Tschminsk! why did the simple word reverberate upon Gertrude's ears? Why? Because it was the name written in her father's hand on the title page of his book on mining. What mystery was here? *115*

It was on the following day that Gertrude had driven up the avenue.

She descended from the dogcart, passed through a phalanx of liveried servants drawn up seven-deep, to each of whom she gave a sovereign as she passed and entered Nosham Taws.

"Welcome," said the Countess, as she aided Gertrude to carry her trunk upstairs. *120*

The girl presently descended and was ushered into the library, where she was presented to the Earl. As soon as the Earl's eye fell upon the face of the new governess he started visibly. Where had he seen those lineaments? Where was it? At the races? or the theatre? on a bus? No. Some subtler thread of memory was stirring in his mind. He strode hastily to the sideboard, drained a dipper and a half of brandy, and became again *125* the perfect English gentleman.

While Gertrude has gone to the nursery to make the acquaintance of the two tiny golden-haired children who are to be her charges, let us say something here of the Earl and his son.

Lord Nosh was the perfect type of the English nobleman and statesman. The years *130* that he had spent in the diplomatic service at Constantinople, St Petersburg, and Salt Lake City had given to him a peculiar finesse and noblesse, while his long residence at St Helena, Pitcairn Island, and Hamilton, Ontario, had rendered him impervious to external impressions. As deputy paymaster of the militia of the country he had seen something of the sterner side of military life, while his hereditary office of Groom of the *135* Sunday Breeches had brought him into direct contact with Royalty itself. His passion for outdoor sports endeared him to his tenants. A keen sportsman, he excelled in fox-hunting, dog-hunting, pig-killing, bat-catching and the pastimes of his class.

In this latter respect Lord Ronald took after his father. From the start the lad had shown the greatest promise. At Eton he had made a splendid showing at battledore and *140* shuttlecock, and at Cambridge had been first in his class at needlework. Already his name was whispered in connection with the All England ping-pong championship, a triumph which would undoubtedly carry with it a seat in Parliament.

Thus was Gertrude the Governess installed at Nosham Taws.

The days and the weeks sped past. *145*

The simple charm of the beautiful orphan girl attracted all hearts. Her two little pupils became her slaves. "Me loves oo," the little Rasehellfrida would say, leaning her golden head in Gertrude's lap. Even the servants loved her. The head gardener would bring a bouquet of beautiful roses to her room before she was up, the second gardener a bunch of early cauliflowers, the third a spray of late asparagus, and even the tenth and *150* eleventh a sprig of mangel-wurzel or an armful of hay. Her room was full of gardeners all the time, while at evening the aged butler, touched at the friendless girl's loneliness, would tap softly at her door to bring her a rye whisky and seltzer or a box of Pittsburg Stogies. Even the dumb creatures seemed to admire her in their own dumb way. The dumb rooks settled on her shoulder and every dumb dog around the place followed her. *155*

And Ronald! ah, Ronald! Yes, indeed! They had met. They had spoken.

"What a dull morning," Gertrude had said. "*Quel triste matin! Was für ein allerverdamnter Tag!*"

"Beastly," Ronald had answered.

"Beastly!!" The word rang in Gertrude's ears all day. 160

After that they were constantly together. They played tennis and ping-pong in the day, and in the evening, in accordance with the stiff routine of the place, they sat down with the Earl and Countess to twenty-five-cent poker, and later still they sat together on the verandah and watched the moon sweeping in great circles around the horizon.

It was not long before Gertrude realized that Lord Ronald felt towards her a warmer 165 feeling than that of mere ping-pong. At times in her presence he would fall, especially after dinner, into a fit of profound subtraction.

Once at night, when Gertrude withdrew to her chamber and before seeking her pillow, prepared to retire as a preliminary to disrobing — in other words, before going to bed, she flung wide the casement (opened the window) and perceived (saw) the face 170 of Lord Ronald. He was sitting on a thorn bush beneath her, and his upturned face wore an expression of agonized pallor.

Meantime the days passed. Life at the Taws moved in the ordinary routine of a great English household. At 7 a gong sounded for rising, at 8 a horn blew for breakfast, at 8:30 a whistle sounded for prayers, at 1 a flag was run up at half-mast for lunch, at 4 a 175 gun was fired for afternoon tea, at 9 a first bell sounded for dressing, at 9:15 a second bell for going on dressing, while at 9:30 a rocket was sent up to indicate that dinner was ready. At midnight dinner was over, and at 1 a.m. the tolling of a bell summoned the domestics to evening prayers.

Meanwhile the month allotted by the Earl to Lord Ronald was passing away. It was 180 already July 15, then within a day or two it was July 17, and, almost immediately afterwards, July 18.

At times the Earl, in passing Ronald in the hall, would say sternly, "Remember, boy, your consent, or I disinherit you."

And what were the Earl's thoughts of Gertrude? Here was the one drop of bitterness 185 in the girl's cup of happiness. For some reason that she could not divine the Earl showed signs of marked antipathy.

Once as she passed the door of the library he threw a bootjack at her. On another occasion at lunch alone with her he struck her savagely across the face with a sausage.

It was her duty to translate to the Earl his Russian correspondence. She sought in it 190 in vain for the mystery. One day a Russian telegram was handed to the Earl. Gertrude translated it to him aloud.

"Tutchemoff went to the woman. She is dead."

On hearing this the Earl became livid with fury, in fact this was the day that he struck her with the sausage. 195

Then one day while the Earl was absent on a bat hunt, Gertrude, who was turning over his correspondence, with that sweet feminine instinct of interest that rose superior to ill-treatment, suddenly found the key to the mystery.

Lord Nosh was not the rightful owner of the Taws. His distant cousin of the older line, the true heir, had died in a Russian prison to which the machinations of the Earl, 200 while Ambassador at Tschminsk, had consigned him. The daughter of this cousin was the true owner of Nosham Taws.

The family story, save only that the documents before her withheld the name of the rightful heir, lay bare to Gertrude's eye.

Strange is the heart of woman. Did Gertrude turn from the Earl with spurning? No. Her own sad fate had taught her sympathy. 205

Yet still the mystery remained! Why did the Earl start perceptibly each time that he looked into her face? Sometimes he started as much as four centimetres, so that one could distinctly see him do it. On such occasions he would hastily drain a dipper of rum and vichy water and become again the correct English gentleman. 210

The denouement came swiftly. Gertrude never forgot it.

It was the night of the great ball at Nosham Taws. The whole neighbourhood was invited. How Gertrude's heart had beat with anticipation, and with what trepidation she had overhauled her scant wardrobe in order to appear not unworthy in Lord Ronald's eyes. Her resources were poor indeed, yet the inborn genius for dress that she inherited 215 from her French mother stood her in good stead. She twined a single rose in her hair and contrived herself a dress out of a few old newspapers and the inside of an umbrella that would have graced a court. Round her waist she bound a single braid of bagstring, while a piece of old lace that had been her mother's was suspended to her ear by a thread.

Gertrude was the cynosure of all eyes. Floating to the strains of the music she 220 presented a picture of bright girlish innocence that no one could see undisenraptured.

The ball was at its height. It was away up!

Ronald stood with Gertrude in the shrubbery. They looked into one another's eyes.

"Gertrude," he said, "I love you."

Simple words, and yet they thrilled every fibre in the girl's costume. 225

"Ronald!" she said, and cast herself about his neck.

At this moment the Earl appeared standing beside them in the moonlight. His stern face was distorted with indignation.

"So!" he said, turning to Ronald, "it appears that you have chosen!"

"I have," said Ronald with hauteur. 230

"You prefer to marry this penniless girl rather than the heiress I have selected for you."

Gertrude looked from father to son in amazement.

"Yes," said Ronald.

"Be it so," said the Earl, draining a dipper of gin which he carried, and resuming his calm. "Then I disinherit you. Leave this place, and never return to it." 235

"Come, Gertrude," said Ronald tenderly, "let us flee together."

Gertrude stood before them. The rose had fallen from her head. The lace had fallen from her ear and the bagstring had come undone from her waist. Her newspapers were crumpled beyond recognition. But dishevelled and illegible as she was, she was still mistress of herself. 240

"Never," she said firmly. "Ronald, you shall never make this sacrifice for me." Then to the Earl, in tones of ice, "There is a pride, sir, as great even as yours. The daughter of Metschnikoff McFiggin need crave a boon from no one."

With that she hauled from her bosom the daguerreotype of her father and pressed it to her lips. 245

The Earl started as if shot. "That name!" he cried, "that face! that photograph! stop!"

There! There is no need to finish; my readers have long since divined it. Gertrude was the heiress.

The lovers fell into one another's arms. The Earl's proud face relaxed. "God bless 250 you," he said. The Countess and the guests came pouring out upon the lawn. The breaking day illuminated a scene of gay congratulations.

Gertrude and Ronald were wed. Their happiness was complete. Need we say more? Yes, only this. The Earl was killed in the hunting-field a few days after. The Countess was struck by lightning. The two children fell down a well. Thus the happiness of 255 Gertrude and Ronald was complete.

(1911)

STEPHEN CRANE
U.S.A., 1871-1900

I SAW A MAN PURSUING THE HORIZON

I saw a man pursuing the horizon;
Round and round they sped.
I was disturbed at this;
I accosted the man.
"It is futile," I said,   5
"You can never —"

"You lie," he cried,
And ran on.

(1895)

A MAN SAID TO THE UNIVERSE

A man said to the universe:
"Sir, I exist!"
"However," replied the universe,
"The fact has not created in me
A sense of obligation."   5

(1899)

JOHN MCCRAE
Canada, 1872-1918

IN FLANDERS FIELDS

In Flanders fields the poppies blow
Between the crosses, row on row,
   That mark our place; and in the sky
   The larks, still bravely singing, fly
Scarce heard amid the guns below.   5

We are the Dead. Short days ago
We lived, felt dawn, saw sunset glow,
   Loved, and were loved, and now we lie
   In Flanders fields.

Take up our quarrel with the foe: 10
To you from failing hands we throw
   The torch; be yours to hold it high.
   If ye break faith with us who die
We shall not sleep, though poppies grow
      In Flanders fields.   15

(1915)

JOHN SHAW NEILSON
Australia, 1872-1942

THE ORANGE TREE

The young girl stood beside me. I
  Saw not what her young eyes could see:
— A light, she said, not of the sky
  Lives somewhere in the Orange Tree.

— Is it, I said, of east or west?   *5*
  The heartbeat of a luminous boy
Who with his faltering flute confessed
  Only the edges of his joy?

Was he, I said, borne to the blue
  In a mad escapade of Spring   *10*
Ere he could make a fond adieu
  To his love in the blossoming?

— Listen! The young girl said. There calls
  No voice, no music beats on me;
But it is almost sound: it falls   *15*
  This evening on the Orange Tree.

— Does he, I said, so fear the Spring
  Ere the white sap too far can climb?
See in the full gold evening
  All happenings of the olden time?   *20*

Is he so goaded by the green?
  Does the compulsion of the dew
Make him unknowable but keen
  Asking with beauty of the blue?

— Listen! the young girl said. For all   *25*
  Your hapless talk you fail to see
There is a light, a step, a call
  This evening on the Orange Tree

— Is it, I said, a waste of love
  Imperishably old in pain,   *30*
Moving as an affrighted dove
  Under the sunlight or the rain?

Is it a fluttering heart that gave
  Too willingly and was reviled?
Is it the stammering at a grave,   *35*
  The last word of a little child?

— Silence! The young girl said. Oh, why,
  Why will you talk to weary me?
Plague me no longer now, for I
  Am listening like the Orange Tree.   *40*

                          (1919)

G.K. CHESTERTON
England, 1874-1936

ELEGY IN A COUNTRY CHURCHYARD

The men that worked for England
They have their graves at home:
And bees and birds of England
About the cross can roam.

But they that fought for England,   *5*
Following a falling star,
Alas, alas for England
They have their graves afar.

And they that rule in England,
In stately conclave met,   *10*
Alas, alas for England
They have no graves as yet.

          (1922)

ELEGY IN A COUNTRY CHURCHYARD See Gray's "Elegy," p. 610.

VARIATIONS OF AN AIR
Composed on Having to Appear in a Pageant as Old King Cole

Old King Cole was a merry old soul,
And a merry old soul was he;
He called for his pipe,
He called for his bowl,
And he called for his fiddlers three.   5

After Lord Tennyson
Cole, that unwearied prince of Colchester,
Growing more gay with age and with long days
Deeper in laughter and desire of life,
As that Virginian climber on our walls
Flames scarlet with the fading of the year;   10
Called for his wassail and that other weed
Virginian also, from the western woods
Where English Raleigh checked the boast of Spain,
And lighting joy with joy, and piling up
Pleasure as crown for pleasure, bade men bring   15
Those three, the minstrels whose emblazoned coats
Shone with the oyster-shells of Colchester;
And these three played, and playing grew more fain
Of mirth and music; till the heathen came,
And the King slept beside the northern sea.   20

After W. B. Yeats
Of an old King in a story
    From the grey sea-folk I have heard,
Whose heart was no more broken
    Than the wings of a bird.

As soon as the moon was silver   25
    And the thin stars began,
He took his pipe and his tankard,
    Like an old peasant man.

And three tall shadows were with him
    And came at his command;   30
And played before him for ever
    The fiddles of fairyland.

And he died in the young summer
    Of the world's desire;
Before our hearts were broken   35
    Like sticks in a fire.

After Robert Browning
Who smoke-snorts toasts o' My Lady Nicotine,
Kicks stuffing out of Pussyfoot, bids his trio
Stick up their Stradivarii (that's the plural)
Or near enough, my fatheads; *nimium*   40
Vicina Cremonæ (that's a bit too near).
Is there some stockfish fails to understand?
Catch hold o' the notion, bellow and blurt back "Cole"?
Must I bawl lessons from a horn-book, howl,
Cat-call the cat-gut "fiddles"? Fiddlesticks!   45

After Walt Whitman
Me clairvoyant,
Me conscious of you, old camarado,
Needing no telescope, lorgnette, field-glass, opera-
    glass, myopic pince-nez,
Me piercing two thousand years with eye naked and
    not ashamed;
The crown cannot hide you from me;   50
Musty old feudal-heraldic trappings cannot hide you
    from me,
I perceive that you drink.
(I am drinking with you. I am as drunk as you are.)
I see you are inhaling tobacco, puffing, smoking,
    spitting
(I do not object to your spitting),   55
You prophetic of American largeness,
You anticipating the broad masculine manners of these
    States;
I see in you also there are movements, tremors, tears,
    desire for the melodious,
I salute your three violinists, endlessly making
    vibrations,
Rigid, relentless, capable of going on for ever;   60
They play my accompaniment; but I shall take no
    notice of any accompaniment;
I myself am a complete orchestra.
So long.

VARIATIONS OF AN AIR   For Tennyson's poetry, see p. 956; for Yeats's, p. 1213; for Browning's, p. 1001; for Whitman's, p. 1030; for Swinburne's, p. 1102. **16-17. minstrels . . . shells:** Cockney buskers, or "pearly-kings," whose coats were covered in pearl buttons. **18. fain:** desirous. **40-41.** *nimium Vicina Cremonæ*: (Latin) very near Cremona. **47. camarado:** comrade.

After Swinburne

In the time of old sin without sadness
  And golden with wastage of gold   *65*
Like the gods that grow old in their gladness
  Was the king that was glad, growing old;
And with sound of loud lyres from his palace
  The voice of his oracles spoke,
And the lips that were red from his chalice   *70*
  Were splendid with smoke.

When the weed was as flame for a token
  And the wine was as blood for a sign;
And upheld in his hands and unbroken
  The fountains of fire and of wine.   *75*
And a song without speech, without singer,
  Stung the soul of a thousand in three
As the flesh of the earth has to sting her,
  The soul of the sea.

                                            (1932)

ROBERT W. SERVICE
Scotland / Canada / France, 1874-1958

THE SHOOTING OF DAN McGREW

A bunch of the boys were whooping it up in the Malamute saloon;
The kid that handles the music-box was hitting a rag-time tune;
Back of the bar, in a solo game, sat Dangerous Dan McGrew,
And watching his luck was his light-o'-love, the lady that's known as Lou.

When out of the night, which was fifty below, and into the din and the glare,   *5*
There stumbled a miner fresh from the creeks, dog-dirty, and loaded for bear.
He looked like a man with a foot in the grave, and scarcely the strength of a louse,
Yet he tilted a poke of dust on the bar, and he called for drinks for the house.
There was none could place the stranger's face, though we searched ourselves for a clue;
But we drank his health, and the last to drink was Dangerous Dan McGrew.   *10*

There's men that somehow just grip your eyes, and hold them hard like a spell;
And such was he, and he looked to me like a man who had lived in hell;
With a face most hair, and the dreary stare of a dog whose day is done,
As he watered the green stuff in his glass, and the drops fell one by one.
Then I got to figgering who he was, and wondering what he'd do,   *15*
And I turned my head — and there watching him was the lady that's known as Lou.

His eyes went rubbering round the room, and he seemed in a kind of daze,
Till at last that old piano fell in the way of his wandering gaze.
The rag-time kid was having a drink; there was no one else on the stool,
So the stranger stumbles across the room, and flops down there like a fool.   *20*
In a buckskin shirt that was glazed with dirt he sat, and I saw him sway;
Then he clutched the keys with his talon hands — my God! but that man could play!

THE SHOOTING OF DAN McGREW   **8. poke of dust:** bag of gold dust (from panning).

Were you ever out in the Great Alone, when the moon was awful clear,
And the icy mountains hemmed you in with a silence you most could *hear*;
With only the howl of a timber wolf, and you camped there in the cold,   25
A half-dead thing in a stark, dead world, clean mad for the muck called gold;
While high overhead, green, yellow and red, the North Lights swept in bars —
Then you've a hunch what the music meant . . . hunger and night and the stars.

And hunger not of the belly kind, that's banished with bacon and beans;
But the gnawing hunger of lonely men for a home and all that it means;   30
For a fireside far from the cares that are, four walls and a roof above;
But oh! so cramful of cosy joy, and crowned with a woman's love;
A woman dearer than all the world, and true as Heaven is true —
(God! how ghastly she looks through her rouge, — the lady that's known as Lou).

Then on a sudden the music changed, so soft that you scarce could hear;   35
But you felt that your life had been looted clean of all that it once held dear;
That someone had stolen the woman you loved; that her love was a devil's lie;
That your guts were gone, and the best for you was to crawl away and die.
'Twas the crowning cry of a heart's despair, and it thrilled you through and through —
"I guess I'll make it a spread misere," said Dangerous Dan McGrew.   40

The music almost died away . . . then it burst like a pent-up flood;
And it seemed to say, "Repay, repay," and my eyes were blind with blood.
The thought came back of an ancient wrong, and it stung like a frozen lash,
And the lust awoke to kill, to kill . . . then the music stopped with a crash.

And the stranger turned, and his eyes they burned in a most peculiar way;   45
In a buckskin shirt that was glazed with dirt he sat, and I saw him sway;
Then his lips went in in a kind of grin, and he spoke, and his voice was calm;
And, "Boys," says he, "you don't know me, and none of you care a damn;
But I want to state, and my words are straight, and I'll bet my poke they're true,
That one of you is a hound of hell . . . and that one is Dan McGrew."   50

Then I ducked my head, and the lights went out, and two guns blazed in the dark;
And a woman screamed, and the lights went up, and two men lay stiff and stark;
Pitched on his head, and pumped full of lead, was Dangerous Dan McGrew,
While the man from the creeks lay clutched to the breast of the lady that's known as Lou.

These are the simple facts of the case, and I guess I ought to know;   55
They say that the stranger was crazed with 'hooch', and I'm not denying it's so.
I'm not so wise as the lawyer guys, but strictly between us two —
The woman that kissed him and — pinched his poke — was the lady that's known as Lou.

(1907)

---

40. spread misere: term from the game of whist, a declaration by which a card player engages to lose every trick.

ROBERT FROST
U.S.A., 1874-1963

MENDING WALL

Something there is that doesn't love a wall,
That sends the frozen-ground-swell under it,
And spills the upper boulders in the sun;
And makes gaps even two can pass abreast.
The work of hunters is another thing: 5
I have come after them and made repair
Where they have left not one stone on a stone,
But they would have the rabbit out of hiding,
To please the yelping dogs. The gaps I mean,
No one has seen them made or heard them
    made,   10
But at spring mending-time we find them there.
I let my neighbor know beyond the hill;
And on a day we meet to walk the line
And set the wall between us once again.
We keep the wall between us as we go.   15
To each the boulders that have fallen to each.
And some are loaves and some so nearly balls
We have to use a spell to make them balance:
"Stay where you are until our backs are turned!"
We wear our fingers rough with handling them.
Oh, just another kind of outdoor game,   21
One on a side. It comes to little more:
There where it is we do not need the wall:
He is all pine and I am apple orchard.
My apple trees will never get across   25
And eat the cones under his pines, I tell him.
He only says, "Good fences make good
    neighbors."
Spring is the mischief in me, and I wonder
If I could put a notion in his head:
"*Why* do they make good neighbors? Isn't it   30
Where there are cows? But here there are no
    cows.
Before I built a wall I'd ask to know
What I was walling in or walling out,
And to whom I was like to give offense.

Something there is that doesn't love a wall,   35
That wants it down." I could say "Elves" to him,
But it's not elves exactly, and I'd rather
He said it for himself. I see him there
Bringing a stone grasped firmly by the top
In each hand, like an old-stone savage armed.   40
He moves in darkness as it seems to me,
Not of woods only and the shade of trees.
He will not go behind his father's saying,
And he likes having thought of it so well
He says again, "Good fences make good
    neighbors."   45

                                  (1914)

FIRE AND ICE

Some say the world will end in fire,
Some say in ice.
From what I've tasted of desire
I hold with those who favor fire.
But if it had to perish twice,   5
I think I know enough of hate
To say that for destruction ice
Is also great
And would suffice.

                                  (1923)

DUST OF SNOW

The way a crow
Shook down on me
The dust of snow
From a hemlock tree

Has given my heart   5
A change of mood
And saved some part
Of a day I had rued.

                                  (1923)

NOTHING GOLD CAN STAY

Nature's first green is gold,
Her hardest hue to hold.
Her early leaf's a flower;
But only so an hour.
Then leaf subsides to leaf. 5
So Eden sank to grief,
So dawn goes down to day.
Nothing gold can stay.

(1923)

STOPPING BY WOODS ON A SNOWY EVENING

Whose woods these are I think I know.
His house is in the village though;
He will not see me stopping here
To watch his woods fill up with snow.

My little horse must think it queer 5
To stop without a farmhouse near
Between the woods and frozen lake
The darkest evening of the year.

He gives his harness bells a shake
To ask if there is some mistake. 10
The only other sound's the sweep
Of easy wind and downy flake.

The woods are lovely, dark and deep,
But I have promises to keep,
And miles to go before I sleep, 15
And miles to go before I sleep.

(1923)

ACQUAINTED WITH THE NIGHT

I have been one acquainted with the night.
I have walked out in rain — and back in rain.
I have outwalked the furthest city light.

I have looked down the saddest city lane.
I have passed by the watchman on his beat 5
And dropped my eyes, unwilling to explain.

I have stood still and stopped the sound of feet
When far away an interrupted cry
Came over houses from another street,

But not to call me back or say good-by; 10
And further still at an unearthly height,
One luminary clock against the sky

Proclaimed the time was neither wrong nor right.
I have been one acquainted with the night.

(1928)

DESIGN

I found a dimpled spider, fat and white,
On a white heal-all, holding up a moth
Like a white piece of rigid satin cloth —
Assorted characters of death and blight
Mixed ready to begin the morning right, 5
Like the ingredients of a witches' broth —
A snow-drop spider, a flower like a froth,
And dead wings carried like a paper kite.

What had that flower to do with being white,
The wayside blue and innocent heal-all? 10
What brought the kindred spider to that height,
Then steered the white moth thither in the night?
What but design of darkness to appall? —
If design govern in a thing so small.

(1936)

DESIGN The 1912 manuscript version of this poem, entitled "In White," reads as follows:

A dented spider like a snow drop white
On a white Heal-all, holding up a moth
Like a white piece of lifeless satin cloth —
Saw ever curious eye so strange a sight? —
Portent in little, assorted death and blight 5
Like the ingredients of a witches' broth? —
The beady spider, the flower like a froth,

And the moth carried like a paper kite.
What had that flower to do with being white,
The blue prunella every child's delight. 10
What brought the kindred spider to that height?
(Make we no thesis of the miller's plight.)
What but design of darkness and of night?
Design, design! Do I use the word aright?

2. heal-all: a weedy herb, usually with purple flowers, once thought to cure disease. **10. prunella:** i.e., *prunella vulgaris*, the heal-all. **12. miller:** a dusty-winged moth.

E.C. BENTLEY
England, 1875-1956

"Sir Humphry Davy"
Sir Humphry Davy
Abominated gravy.
He lived in the odium
Of having discovered Sodium.
(1905)

"George the Third"
George the Third
Ought never to have occurred.
One can only wonder
At so grotesque a blunder.
(1905)

SOL T. PLAATJE
South Africa, 1877-1932

from *NATIVE LIFE IN SOUTH AFRICA, BEFORE AND SINCE THE EUROPEAN WAR AND THE BOER REBELLION*

Chapter IV: One Night with the Fugitives

> Es ist unkoeniglich zu weinen — ach,
> Und hier nicht weinen ist unvaeterlich.
> SCHILLER

"Pray that your flight be not in winter," said Jesus Christ; but it was only during the winter of 1913 that the full significance of this New Testament passage was revealed to us. We left Kimberley by the early morning train during the first week in July, on a tour of observation regarding the operation of the Natives' Land Act; and we arrived at Bloemhof, in Transvaal, at about noon. On the River Diggings there were no actual cases representing the effects of the Act, but traces of these effects were everywhere manifest. Some fugitives of the Natives' Land Act had crossed the river in full flight. The fact that they reached the diggings a fortnight before our visit would seem to show that while the debates were proceeding in Parliament some farmers already viewed with eager eyes the impending opportunity for at once making slaves of their tenants and appropriating their stock; for, acting on the powers conferred on them by an Act signed

5

10

ONE NIGHT WITH THE FUGITIVES **Epigraph:** "It is not kingly to weep, but not to weep is not to be a father" — Johann Christoph Friedrich von Schiller (1759-1805), German idealist poet and dramatist. **1. Pray . . . winter:** See Matthew 24:20, Mark 13:18. **4. Natives' Land Act:** The Natives Land Act (1913) prohibited Native peoples in South Africa from owning, hiring, or leasing land (except with the express permission of the Governor-General); it also defined "leasing" as any form of occupying land and sharing in its produce; it threatened punitive action against anyone attempting to contravene the law; and it established a commission to map South Africa in such a way as to set aside specific separate territories for European and Native occupation. **5. Diggings:** mining area.

by Lord Gladstone, so lately as June 16, they had during that very week (probably a couple of days after, and in some cases, it would seem, a couple of days before the actual signing of the Bill) approached their tenants with stories about a new Act which makes it criminal for any one to have black tenants and lawful to have black servants. Few of these Natives, of course, would object to be servants, especially if the white man is worth working for, but this is where the shoe pinches: one of the conditions is that the black man's (that is the servant's) cattle shall henceforth work for the landlord free of charge. Then the Natives would decide to leave the farm rather than make the landlord a present of all their life's savings, and some of them had passed through the diggings in search of a place in the Transvaal. But the higher up they went the more gloomy was their prospect as the news about the new law was now penetrating every part of the country.

One farmer met a wandering native family in the town of Bloemhof a week before our visit. He was willing to employ the Native and many more homeless families as follows: A monthly wage of £2 10s. for each such family, the husband working in the fields, the wife in the house, with an additional 10s. a month for each son, and 5s. for each daughter, but on condition that the Native's cattle were also handed over to work for him. It must be clearly understood, we are told that the Dutchman added, that occasionally the Native would have to leave his family at work on the farm, and go out with his wagon and his oxen to earn money whenever and wherever he was told to go, in order that the master may be enabled to pay the stipulated wage. The Natives were at first inclined to laugh at the idea of working for a master with their families and goods and chattels, and then to have the additional pleasure of paying their own small wages, besides bringing money to pay the "Baas" for employing them. But the Dutchman's serious demeanour told them that his suggestion was "no joke." He himself had for some time been in need of a native cattle owner, to assist him as transport rider between Bloemhof, Mooifontein, London, and other diggings, in return for the occupation and cultivation of some of his waste lands in the district, but that was now illegal. He could only "employ" them; but, as he had no money to pay wages, their cattle would have to go out and earn it for him. Had they not heard of the law before? he inquired. Of course they had; in fact that is why they left the other place, but as they thought that it was but a "Free" State law, they took the anomalous situation for one of the multifarious aspects of the freedom of the "Free" State whence they came; they had scarcely thought that the Transvaal was similarly afflicted.

Needless to say the Natives did not see their way to agree with such a one-sided bargain. They moved up country, but only to find the next farmer offering the same terms, however, with a good many more disturbing details — and the next farmer and the next — so that after this native farmer had wandered from farm to farm, occasionally getting into trouble for travelling with unknown stock, "across my ground without my permission," and at times escaping arrest for he knew not what, and further, being abused for the crimes of having a black skin and no master, he sold some of his stock along the way, beside losing many which died of cold and starvation; and after thus having lost much of his substance, he eventually worked his way back to Bloemhof with the remainder, sold them for anything they could fetch, and went to work for a digger.

---

12. Lord Gladstone: Herbert John Gladstone (1854-1930), first Governor-General of South Africa. **28. Dutchman:** i.e., Afrikaner. **34. Baas:** boss, master.

The experience of another native sufferer was similar to the above, except that instead *55* of working for a digger he sold his stock for a mere bagatelle, and left with his family by the Johannesburg night train for an unknown destination. More native families crossed the river and went inland during the previous week, and as nothing had since been heard of them, it would seem that they were still wandering somewhere, and incidentally becoming well versed in the law that was responsible for their compulsory unsettlement. *60*

Well, we knew that this law was as harsh as its instigators were callous, and we knew that it would, if passed, render many poor people homeless, but it must be confessed that we were scarcely prepared for such a rapid and widespread crash as it caused in the lives of the Natives in this neighbourhood. We left our luggage the next morning with the local Mission School teacher, and crossed the river to find out some more about this wonderful *65* law of extermination. It was about 10 a.m. when we landed on the south bank of the Vaal River — the picturesque Vaal River, upon whose banks a hundred miles farther west we spent the best and happiest days of our boyhood. It was interesting to walk on one portion of the banks of that beautiful river — a portion which we had never traversed except as an infant in mother's arms more than thirty years before. How the subsequent happy days at *70* Barkly West, so long past, came crowding upon our memory! — days when there were no railways, no bridges, and no system of irrigation. In rainy seasons, which at that time were far more regular and certain, the river used to overflow its high banks and flood the surrounding valleys to such an extent, that no punt could carry the wagons across. Thereby the transport service used to be hung up, and numbers of wagons would congregate for *75* weeks on both sides of the river until the floods subsided. At such times the price of fresh milk used to mount up to 1*s.* per pint. There being next to no competition, we boys had a monopoly over the milk trade. We recalled the number of haversacks full of bottles of milk we youngsters often carried to those wagons, how we returned with empty bottles and with just that number of shillings. Mother and our elder brothers had leather bags full of gold *80* and did not care for the "boy's money"; and unlike the boys of the neighbouring village, having no sisters of our own, we gave away some of our money to fair cousins, and jingled the rest in our pockets. We had been told from boyhood that sweets were injurious to the teeth, and so spurning these delights we had hardly any use for money, for all we wanted to eat, drink and wear was at hand in plenty. We could then get six or eight shillings every *85* morning from the pastime of washing that number of bottles, filling them with fresh milk and carrying them down to the wagons; there was always such an abundance of the liquid that our shepherd's hunting dog could not possibly miss what we took, for while the flocks were feeding on the luscious buds of the haak-doorns and the orange-coloured blossoms of the rich mimosa and other wild vegetation that abounded on the banks of the Vaal River, *90* the cows, similarly engaged, were gathering more and more milk.

The gods are cruel, and one of their cruellest acts of omission was that of giving us no hint that in very much less than a quarter of a century all those hundreds of heads of cattle, and sheep and horses belonging to the family would vanish like a morning mist, and that we ourselves would live to pay 30*s.* per month for a daily supply of this same precious *95* fluid, and in very limited quantities. They might have warned us that Englishmen would agree with Dutchmen to make it unlawful for black men to keep milch cows of their own on the banks of that river, and gradually have prepared us for the shock.

---

89. haak-doorn: haak-'doring, or hook-thorn.

Crossing the river from the Transvaal side brings one into the Province of the Orange "Free" State, in which, in the adjoining division of Boshof, we were born thirty-six years *100* back. We remember the name of the farm, but not having been in this neighbourhood since infancy, we could not tell its whereabouts, nor could we say whether the present owner was a Dutchman, his lawyer, or a Hebrew merchant; one thing we do know, however: it is that even if we had the money and the owner was willing to sell the spot upon which we first saw the light of day and breathed the pure air of heaven, the sale would be followed with a *105* fine of one hundred pounds. The law of the country forbids the sale of land to a Native. Russia is one of the most abused countries in the world, but it is extremely doubtful if the statute book of that Empire contains a law debarring the peasant from purchasing the land whereon he was born, or from building a home wherein he might end his days.

At this time we felt something rising from our heels along our back, gripping us in a *110* spasm, as we were cycling along; a needlelike pang, too, pierced our heart with a sharp thrill. What was it? We remembered feeling something nearly like it when our father died eighteen years ago; but at that time our physical organs were fresh and grief was easily thrown off in tears, but then we lived in a happy South Africa that was full of pleasant anticipations, and now — what changes for the worse have we undergone! For to crown all *115* our calamities, South Africa has by law ceased to be the home of any of her native children whose skins are dyed with a pigment that does not conform with the regulation hue.

We are told to forgive our enemies and not to let the sun go down upon our wrath, so we breathe the prayer that peace may be to the white races, and that they, including our present persecutors of the Union Parliament, may never live to find themselves *120* deprived of all occupation and property rights in their native country as is now the case with the Native. History does not tell us of any other continent where the Bantu lived besides Africa, and if this systematic ill-treatment of the Natives by the colonists is to be the guiding principle of Europe's scramble for Africa, slavery is our only alternative; for now it is only as serfs that the Natives are legally entitled to live here. Is it to be thought *125* that God is using the South African Parliament to hound us out of our ancestral homes in order to quicken our pace heavenward? But go from where to heaven? In the beginning, we are told, God created heaven and earth, and peopled the earth, for people do not shoot up to heaven from nowhere. They must have had an earthly home. Enoch, Melchizedek, Elijah, and other saints, came to heaven from earth. God did not say to the *130* Israelites in their bondage: "Cheer up, boys; bear it all in good part for I have bright mansions on high awaiting you all." But he said: "I have surely seen the affliction of my people which are in Egypt, and have heard their cry by reason of their taskmasters; for I know their sorrows, and I am come down to bring them out of the hands of the Egyptians, and to bring them up out of that land unto a good land and a large, unto a *135* land flowing with milk and honey." And He used Moses to carry out the promise He made to their ancestor Abraham in Canaan, that "unto thy seed will I give this land." It is to be hoped that in the Boer churches, entrance to which is barred against coloured people during divine service, they also read the Pentateuch.

---

118. forgive . . . wrath: See Matthew 5:44, Luke 6:35, 37; Ephesians 4:26. **127-28. In . . . earth:** See Genesis 1:1 (p. 241). **129-30. Enoch, Melchizedek, Elijah:** Biblical prophets; see Genesis 22, 24; 1 Kings 17, 18; Hebrews 7. **132-36. "I have surely seen . . . honey":** See Exodus 3:7-8. **137. "unto . . . land":** See Genesis 12:7.

It is doubtful if we ever thought so much on a single bicycle ride as we did on this journey; *140* however, the sight of a policeman ahead of us disturbed these meditations and gave place to thoughts of quite another kind, for — we had no pass. Dutchmen, Englishmen, Jews, Germans, and other foreigners may roam the "Free" State without permission — but not Natives. To us it would mean a fine and imprisonment to be without a pass. The "pass" law was first instituted to check the movement of livestock over sparsely populated areas. In a sense it was a wise *145* provision, in that it served to identify the livestock which one happened to be driving along the high road, to prove the *bona fides* of the driver and his title to the stock. Although white men still steal large droves of horses in Basutoland and sell them in Natal or in East Griqualand, they, of course, are not required to carry any passes. These white horse-thieves, to escape the clutches of the police, employ Natives to go and sell the stolen stock and write the passes for *150* these Natives, forging the names of Magistrates and Justices of the Peace. Such native thieves in some instances ceasing to be hirelings in the criminal business, trade on their own, but it is not clear what purpose it is intended to serve by subjecting native pedestrians to the degrading requirement of carrying passes when they are not in charge of any stock.

In a few moments the policeman was before us and we alighted in presence of the *155* representative of the law, with our feet on the accursed soil of the district in which we were born. The policeman stopped. By his looks and his familiar "Dag jong" we noticed that the policeman was Dutch, and the embodiment of affability. He spoke and we were glad to notice that he had no intention of dragging an innocent man to prison. We were many miles from the nearest police station, and in such a case one is generally able to *160* gather the real views of the man on patrol, as distinct from the written code of his office, but our friend was becoming very companionable. Naturally we asked him about the operation of the plague law. He was a Transvaaler, he said, and he knew that Kafirs were inferior beings, but they had rights, and were always left in undisturbed possession of their property when Paul Kruger was alive. "The poor devils must be sorry now," he *165* said, "that they ever sang 'God save the Queen' when the British troops came into the Transvaal, for I have seen, in the course of my duties, that a Kafir's life nowadays was not worth a ——, and I believe that no man regretted the change of flags now more than the Kafirs of Transvaal." This information was superfluous, for personal contact with the Natives of Transvaal had convinced us of the fact. They say it is only the criminal *170* who has any reason to rejoice over the presence of the Union Jack, because in his case the cat-o'-nine-tails, except for very serious crimes, has been abolished.

"Some of the poor creatures," continued the policeman, "I knew to be fairly comfortable, if not rich, and they enjoyed the possession of their stock, living in many instances just like Dutchmen. Many of these are now being forced to leave their homes. *175* Cycling along this road you will meet several of them in search of new homes, and if ever there was a fool's errand, it is that of a Kafir trying to find a new home for his stock and family just now."

"And what do you think, Baas Officer, must eventually be the lot of a people under such unfortunate circumstances?" we asked. *180*

---

157. Dag jong: (Afrikaans) good day. **165. Paul Kruger:** (1825-1904) Afrikaner president of the Transvaal republic (1883-1900), who opposed Cecil Rhodes during the early months of the Boer War (1899-1902); following the British military victory, Transvaal became part of the Union of South Africa when it formed in 1910.

"I think," said the policeman, "that it must serve them right. They had no business to hanker after British rule, to cheat and plot with the enemies of their Republic for the overthrow of their Government. Why did they not assist the forces of their Republic during the war instead of supplying the English with scouts and intelligence? Oom Paul would not have died of a broken heart and he would still be there to protect them. Serve them right, I say." ₁₈₅

So saying he spurred his horse, which showed a clean pair of hoofs. He left us rather abruptly, for we were about to ask why we, too, of Natal and the Cape were suffering, for we, being originally British subjects, never "cheated and plotted with the enemies of our Colonies," but he was gone and left us still cogitating by the roadside. ₁₉₀

Proceeding on our journey we next came upon a native trek and heard the same old story of prosperity on a Dutch farm: they had raised an average 800 bags of grain each season, which, with the increase of stock and sale of wool, gave a steady income of about £150 per year after the farmer had taken his share. There were gossipy rumours about somebody having met some one who said that some one else had overheard a ₁₉₅ conversation between the Baas and somebody else, to the effect that the Kafirs were getting too rich on his property. This much involved tale incidentally conveys the idea that the Baas was himself getting too rich on his farm. For the Native provides his own seed, his own cattle, his own labour for the ploughing, the weeding and the reaping, and after bagging his grain he calls in the landlord to receive his share, which is fifty per ₂₀₀ cent of the entire crop.

All had gone well till the previous week when the Baas came to the native tenants with the story that a new law had been passed under which "all my oxen and cows must belong to him, and my family to work for £2 a month, failing which he gave me four days to leave the farm." ₂₀₅

We passed several farm-houses along the road, where all appeared pretty tranquil as we went along, until the evening which we spent in the open country, somewhere near the boundaries of the Hoopstad and Boshof districts; here a regular circus had gathered. By a "circus" we mean the meeting of groups of families, moving to every point of the compass, and all bivouacked at this point in the open country where we were passing. It ₂₁₀ was heartrending to listen to the tales of their cruel experiences derived from the rigour of the Natives' Land Act. Some of their cattle had perished on the journey, from poverty and lack of fodder, and the native owners ran a serious risk of imprisonment for travelling with dying stock. The experience of one of these evicted tenants is typical of the rest, and illustrates the cases of several we met in other parts of the country. ₂₁₅

Kgobadi, for instance, had received a message describing the eviction of his father-in-law in the Transvaal Province, without notice, because he had refused to place his stock, his family, and his person at the disposal of his former landlord, who now refuses to let him remain on his farm except on these conditions. The father-in-law asked that Kgobadi should try and secure a place for him in the much dreaded "Free" State as the Transvaal had ₂₂₀ suddenly become uninhabitable to Natives who cannot become servants; but "greedy folk hae lang airms," and Kgobadi himself was proceeding with his family and his belongings in a wagon, to inform his people-in-law of his own eviction, without notice, in the "Free" State,

---

184. Oom Paul: Uncle Paul (i.e., Kruger). **221-22. "greedy . . . airms":** old Scottish proverb.

for a similar reason to that which sent his father-in-law adrift. The Baas had exacted from
him the services of himself, his wife and his oxen, for wages of 30*s*. a month, whereas   *225*
Kgobadi had been making over £100 a year, besides retaining the services of his wife and of
his cattle for himself. When he refused the extortionate terms the Baas retaliated with a
Dutch note, dated the 30th day of June, 1913, which ordered him to "betake himself from the
farm of the undersigned, by sunset of the same day, failing which his stock would be seized
and impounded, and himself handed over to the authorities for trespassing on the farm."   *230*

A drowning man catches at every straw, and so we were again and again appealed
to for advice by these sorely afflicted people. To those who were not yet evicted we
counselled patience and submission to the absurd terms, pending an appeal to a higher
authority than the South African Parliament and finally to His Majesty the King who,
we believed, would certainly disapprove of all that we saw on that day had it been   *235*
brought to his notice. As for those who were already evicted, as a Bechuana we could
not help thanking God that Bechuanaland (on the western boundary of this quasi-British
Republic) was still entirely British. In the early days it was the base of David Livingstone's activities and peaceful mission against the Portuguese and Arab slave trade. We
suggested that they might negotiate the numerous restrictions against the transfer of   *240*
cattle from the Western Transvaal and seek an asylum in Bechuanaland. We wondered
what consolation we could give to these roving wanderers if the whole of Bechuanaland
were under the jurisdiction of the relentless Union Parliament.

It was cold that afternoon as we cycled into the "Free" State from Transvaal, and
towards evening the southern winds rose. A cutting blizzard raged during the night, and   *245*
native mothers evicted from their homes shivered with their babies by their sides. When
we saw on that night the teeth of the little children clattering through the cold, we
thought of our own little ones in their Kimberley home of an evening after gambolling
in their winter frocks with their schoolmates, and we wondered what these little mites
had done that a home should suddenly become to them a thing of the past.   *250*

Kgobadi's goats had been to kid when he trekked from his farm; but the kids, which
in halcyon times represented the interest on his capital, were now one by one dying as
fast as they were born and left by the roadside for the jackals and vultures to feast upon.

This visitation was not confined to Kgobadi's stock, Mrs. Kgobadi carried a sick baby
when the eviction took place, and she had to transfer her darling from the cottage to the   *255*
jolting ox-wagon in which they left the farm. Two days out the little one began to sink as
the result of privation and exposure on the road, and the night before we met them its little
soul was released from its earthly bonds. The death of the child added a fresh perplexity to
the stricken parents. They had no right or title to the farm lands through which they
trekked: they must keep to the public roads — the only places in the country open to the   *260*
outcasts if they are possessed of a travelling permit. The deceased child had to be buried,
but where, when, and how?

This young wandering family decided to dig a grave under cover of the darkness of
that night, when no one was looking, and in that crude manner the dead child was
interred — and interred amid fear and trembling, as well as the throbs of a torturing   *265*
anguish, in a stolen grave, lest the proprietor of the spot, or any of his servants, should

---

237. **Bechuanaland:** now the independent country of Botswana. **238-39. David Livingstone:** Scottish missionary and traveller (1813-1873) who
worked in Bechuanaland in the 1840s; his book *The Zambesi and Its Tributaries* (1865) exposed the continuing operation of the Portuguese slave trade.

surprise them in the act. Even criminals dropping straight from the gallows have an undisputed claim to six feet of ground on which to rest their criminal remains, but under the cruel operation of the Natives' Land Act little children, whose only crime is that God did not make them white, are sometimes denied that right in their ancestral home. *270*

Numerous details narrated by these victims of an Act of Parliament kept us awake all that night, and by next morning we were glad enough to hear no more of the sickening procedure of extermination voluntarily instituted by the South African Parliament. We had spent a hideous night under a bitterly cold sky, conditions to which hundreds of our unfortunate countrymen and countrywomen in various parts of the country are *275* condemned by the provisions of this Parliamentary land plague. At five o'clock in the morning the cold seemed to redouble its energies; and never before did we so fully appreciate the Master's saying: "But pray ye that your flight be not in the winter."

(1916)

ADELAIDE CRAPSEY
U.S.A., 1878-1914

THE WARNING

Just now,
Out of the strange
Still dusk . . . as strange, as still . . .
A white moth flew. Why am I grown
So cold?

(1915)

EDWARD THOMAS
Wales/England, 1878-1917

THE OWL

Downhill I came, hungry, and yet not starved;
Cold, yet had heat within me that was proof
Against the North wind; tired, yet so that rest
Had seemed the sweetest thing under a roof.

Then at the inn I had food, fire, and rest,   *5*
Knowing how hungry, cold, and tired was I.
All of the night was quite barred out except
An owl's cry, a most melancholy cry

Shaken out long and clear upon the hill,
No merry note, nor cause of merriment,   *10*
But one telling me plain what I escaped
And others could not, that night, as in I went.

And salted was my food, and my repose,
Salted and sobered, too, by the bird's voice
Speaking for all who lay under the stars,   *15*
Soldiers and poor, unable to rejoice.

(1917)

THE OWL   **10:** See line 7 of Shakespeare's "When icicles hang by the wall" (p. 230), and perhaps also Ariel's song "Where the bee sucks, there suck I" in *The Tempest* (V.i.88-94), and the song "Under the greenwood tree" in *As You Like It* (II.v.1-7).

JOHN MASEFIELD
England, 1878-1967

SEA FEVER

I must go down to the seas again, to the lonely sea and the sky,
And all I ask is a tall ship and a star to steer her by;
And the wheel's kick and the wind's song and the white sail's shaking,
And a grey mist on the sea's face, and a grey dawn breaking,

I must go down to the seas again, for the call of the running tide   *5*
Is a wild call and a clear call that may not be denied;
And all I ask is a windy day with the white clouds flying,
And the flung spray and the blown spume, and the sea-gulls crying.

I must go down to the seas again, to the vagrant gypsy life,
To the gull's way and the whale's way where the wind's like a whetted knife;   *10*
And all I ask is a merry yarn from a laughing fellow-rover,
And quiet sleep and a sweet dream when the long trick's over.

(1913)

CARL SANDBURG
U.S.A., 1878-1967

FOG

The fog comes
on little cat feet.

It sits looking
over harbor and city
on silent haunches   *5*
and then moves on.

(1916)

GRASS

Pile the bodies high at Austerlitz and Waterloo.
Shovel them under and let me work —
      I am the grass; I cover all.

And pile them high at Gettysburg
And pile them high at Ypres and Verdun.   *5*
Shovel them under and let me work.

Two years, ten years, and passengers ask the conductor:
      What place is this?
      Where are we now?

      I am the grass.   *10*
      Let me work.

(1918)

SEA FEVER **1. down to the seas:** See Psalms 107:23. **12. trick:** tour of duty.   **GRASS** The place names refer to battles in various wars: Austerlitz (1805) and Waterloo (1815), during the Napoleonic Wars; Gettysburg (1863), during the American Civil War; Ypres (1914, 1915, 1917) and Verdun (1916), during World War I.

WALLACE STEVENS
U.S.A., 1879-1955

THE SNOW MAN

One must have a mind of winter
To regard the frost and the boughs
Of the pine-trees crusted with snow;

And have been cold a long time
To behold the junipers shagged with ice,   *5*
The spruces rough in the distant glitter

Of the January sun; and not to think
Of any misery in the sound of the wind,
In the sound of a few leaves,

Which is the sound of the land   *10*
Full of the same wind
That is blowing in the same bare place

For the listener, who listens in the snow,
And, nothing himself, beholds   *14*
Nothing that is not there and the nothing that is.
                                          (1923)

ANECDOTE OF THE JAR

I placed a jar in Tennessee,
And round it was, upon a hill.
It made the slovenly wilderness
Surround that hill.

The wilderness rose up to it,   *5*
And sprawled around, no longer wild.
The jar was round upon the ground
And tall and of a port in air.

It took dominion everywhere.
The jar was gray and bare.   *10*
It did not give of bird or bush,
Like nothing else in Tennessee.
                                          (1923)

THE HOUSE WAS QUIET
AND THE WORLD WAS CALM

The house was quiet and the world was calm.
The reader became the book; and summer night

Was like the conscious being of the book.
The house was quiet and the world was calm.

The words were spoken as if there was no book, *5*
Except that the reader leaned above the page,

Wanted to lean, wanted much most to be
The scholar to whom his book is true, to whom

The summer night is like a perfection of thought.
The house was quiet because it had to be.   *10*

The quiet was part of the meaning, part of the mind:
The access of perfection to the page.

And the world was calm. The truth in a calm world,
In which there is no other meaning, itself

Is calm, itself is summer and night, itself   *15*
Is the reader leaning late and reading there.
                                          (1947)

E.M. FORSTER
England, 1879-1970

WHAT I BELIEVE

I do not believe in Belief. But this is an age of faith, and there are so many militant creeds that, in self-defence, one has to formulate a creed of one's own. Tolerance, good temper and sympathy are no longer enough in a world which is rent by religious and racial persecution, in a world where ignorance rules, and science, who ought to have ruled, plays

the subservient pimp. Tolerance, good temper and sympathy — they are what matter really, ⁵
and if the human race is not to collapse they must come to the front before long. But for the
moment they are not enough, their action is no stronger than a flower, battered beneath a
military jack-boot. They want stiffening, even if the process coarsens them. Faith, to my
mind, is a stiffening process, a sort of mental starch, which ought to be applied as sparingly
as possible. I dislike the stuff. I do not believe in it, for its own sake, at all. Herein I ¹⁰
probably differ from most people, who believe in Belief, and are only sorry they cannot
swallow even more than they do. My law-givers are Erasmus and Montaigne, not Moses
and St. Paul. My temple stands not upon Mount Moriah but in that Elysian Field where
even the immoral are admitted. My motto is: "Lord, I disbelieve — help thou my unbelief."

I have, however, to live in an Age of Faith — the sort of epoch I used to hear ¹⁵
praised when I was a boy. It is extremely unpleasant really. It is bloody in every sense
of the word. And I have to keep my end up in it. Where do I start?

With personal relationships. Here is something comparatively solid in a world full
of violence and cruelty. Not absolutely solid, for Psychology has split and shattered the
idea of a "Person," and has shown that there is something incalculable in each of us, ²⁰
which may at any moment rise to the surface and destroy our normal balance. We don't
know what we are like. We can't know what other people are like. How, then, can we
put any trust in personal relationships, or cling to them in the gathering political storm?
In theory we cannot. But in practice we can and do. Though A is not unchangeably A or
B unchangeably B, there can still be love and loyalty between the two. For the purpose ²⁵
of living one has to assume that the personality is solid, and the "self" is an entity, and
to ignore all contrary evidence. And since to ignore evidence is one of the characteristics of faith, I certainly can proclaim that I believe in personal relationships.

Starting from them, I get a little order into the contemporary chaos. One must be fond
of people and trust them if one is not to make a mess of life, and it is therefore essential ³⁰
that they should not let one down. They often do. The moral of which is that I must,
myself, be as reliable as possible, and this I try to be. But reliability is not a matter of
contract — that is the main difference between the world of personal relationships and the
world of business relationships. It is a matter for the heart, which signs no documents. In
other words, reliability is impossible unless there is a natural warmth. Most men possess ³⁵
this warmth, though they often have bad luck and get chilled. Most of them, even when
they are politicians, *want* to keep faith. And one can, at all events, show one's own little
light here, one's own poor little trembling flame, with the knowledge that it is not the only
light that is shining in the darkness, and not the only one which the darkness does not
comprehend. Personal relations are despised today. They are regarded as bourgeois ⁴⁰
luxuries, as products of a time of fair weather which is now past, and we are urged to get
rid of them, and to dedicate ourselves to some movement or cause instead. I hate the idea
of causes, and if I had to choose between betraying my country and betraying my friend, I
hope I should have the guts to betray my country. Such a choice may scandalise the
modern reader, and he may stretch out his patriotic hand to the telephone at once and ring ⁴⁵

WHAT I BELIEVE 12-13. **Erasmus . . . Paul:** i.e., philosophers, not proselytizers. **13. Mount Moriah:** a hill of Jerusalem upon which Solomon
built his temple (II Chronicles 3:1), and also the site of Abraham's near sacrifice of Isaac (Genesis 22:2). **14. Lord . . . unbelief:** Cf. Mark 9:24.

up the police. It would not have shocked Dante, though. Dante places Brutus and Cassius in the lowest circle of Hell because they had chosen to betray their friend Julius Caesar rather than their country Rome. Probably one will not be asked to make such an agonising choice. Still, there lies at the back of every creed something terrible and hard for which the worshipper may one day be required to suffer, and there is even a terror and a hardness in this creed of personal relationships, urbane and mild though it sounds. Love and loyalty to an individual can run counter to the claims of the State. When they do — down with the State, say I, which means that the State would down me.   *50*

This brings me along to Democracy, "even Love, the Beloved Republic, which feeds upon Freedom and lives." Democracy is not a Beloved Republic really, and never will be.   *55*
But it is less hateful than other contemporary forms of government, and to that extent it deserves our support. It does start from the assumption that the individual is important, and that all types are needed to make a civilisation. It does not divide its citizens into the bossers and the bossed — as an efficiency-regime tends to do. The people I admire most are those who are sensitive and want to create something or discover something, and do not see life in   *60*
terms of power, and such people get more of a chance under a democracy than elsewhere. They found religions, great or small, or they produce literature and art, or they do disinterested scientific research, or they may be what is called "ordinary people," who are creative in their private lives, bring up their children decently, for instance, or help their neighbours. All these people need to express themselves; they cannot do so unless society   *65*
allows them liberty to do so, and the society which allows them most liberty is a democracy.

Democracy has another merit. It allows criticism, and if there is not public criticism there are bound to be hushed-up scandals. That is why I believe in the Press, despite all its lies and vulgarity, and why I believe in Parliament. Parliament is often sneered at because it is a Talking Shop. I believe in it *because* it is a talking shop. I believe in the Private   *70*
Member who makes himself a nuisance. He gets snubbed and is told that he is cranky or ill-informed, but he does expose abuses which would otherwise never have been mentioned, and very often an abuse gets put right just by being mentioned. Occasionally, too, a well-meaning public official starts losing his head in the cause of efficiency, and thinks himself God Almighty. Such officials are particularly frequent in the Home Office. Well, there will   *75*
be questions about them in Parliament sooner or later, and then they will have to mind their steps. Whether Parliament is either a representative body or an efficient one is questionable, but I value it because it criticises and talks, and because its chatter gets widely reported.

So Two Cheers for Democracy: one because it admits variety and two because it permits criticism. Two cheers are quite enough: there is no occasion to give three. Only   *80*
Love the Beloved Republic deserves that.

What about Force, though? While we are trying to be sensitive and advanced and affectionate and tolerant, an unpleasant question pops up: does not all society rest upon force? If a government cannot count upon the police and the army, how can it hope to rule? And if an individual gets knocked on the head or sent to a labour camp, of what   *85*
significance are his opinions?

---

46. Brutus and Cassius: See *Inferno* 34:66-68. **54-55:** Quoting the last line of the antepenultimate stanza of Swinburne's "Hertha" (in the poem only "Even" and "Republic" are capitalized); Hertha, or Nerthus (in Wagner's *Ring*, Erda), is the Teutonic earth-goddess, or "Mother Earth." **70. Talking Shop:** e.g., early in Act III of George Bernard Shaw's *Major Barbara* (1905), Andrew Undershaft refers to Parliament as a "foolish gabble shop."

This dilemma does not worry me as much as it does some. I realise that all society rests upon force. But all the great creative actions, all the decent human relations, occur during the intervals when force has not managed to come to the front. These intervals are what matter. I want them to be as frequent and as lengthy as possible, and I call them "civilisation." Some people idealise force and pull it into the foreground and worship it, instead of keeping it in the background as long as possible. I think they make a mistake, and I think that their opposites, the mystics, err even more when they declare that force does not exist. I believe that it exists, and that one of our jobs is to prevent it from getting out of its box. It gets out sooner or later, and then it destroys us and all the lovely things which we have made. But it is not out all the time, for the fortunate reason that the strong are so stupid. Consider their conduct for a moment in the Niebelung's Ring. The giants there have the guns, or in other words the gold; but they do nothing with it, they do not realise that they are all-powerful, with the result that the catastrophe is delayed and the castle of Walhalla, insecure but glorious, fronts the storms. Fafnir, coiled round his hoard, grumbles and grunts; we can hear him under Europe today; the leaves of the wood already tremble, and the Bird calls its warnings uselessly. Fafnir will destroy us, but by a blessed dispensation he is stupid and slow, and creation goes on just outside the poisonous blast of his breath. The Nietzschean would hurry the monster up, the mystic would say he did not exist, but Wotan, wiser than either, hastens to create warriors before doom declares itself. The Valkyries are symbols not only of courage but of intelligence; they represent the human spirit snatching its opportunity while the going is good, and one of them even finds time to love. Brünnhilde's last song hymns the recurrence of love, and since it is the privilege of art to exaggerate, she goes even further, and proclaims the love which is eternally triumphant and feeds upon freedom, and lives.

So that is what I feel about force and violence. It is, alas! the ultimate reality on this earth, but it does not always get to the front. Some people call its absences "decadence"; I call them "civilisation" and find in such interludes the chief justification for the human experiment. I look the other way until fate strikes me. Whether this is due to courage or to cowardice in my own case I cannot be sure. But I know that if men had not looked the other way in the past, nothing of any value would survive. The people I respect most behave as if they were immortal and as if society was eternal. Both assumptions are false: both of them must be accepted as true if we are to go on eating and working and loving, and are to keep open a few breathing holes for the human spirit. No millennium seems likely to descend upon humanity; no better and stronger League of Nations will be instituted; no form of Christianity and no alternative to Christianity will bring peace to the world or integrity to the individual; no "change of heart" will occur. And yet we need not despair, indeed, we cannot despair; the evidence of history shows us that men

---

97-110. Niebelung's Ring: *The Ring of the Niebelung* is the general name given to a series of four operas by Richard Wagner (1813-1883), first performed together at Bayreuth, Germany, in 1876; based on the medieval German epic poem the *Nibelungenlied* and a Scandinavian variant called the *Völsung Saga*, they tell the story of the Rhine Maidens, who possess a magic ring; of Wotan (the king of the gods, who lives in Valhalla), who tries to get the ring back in order to preserve his immortality; of Brünnhilde (the Valkyrie, whose function is to carry mortally wounded heroes to Valhalla), who becomes mortal because her love for the mortal hero Siegfried leads her to disobey Wotan; of Siegfried (who learns the true language of birds after he slays the dragon Fafnir, who is really a giant); and of numerous other figures, before the ring returns to the Rhine Maidens, and Valhalla (with all the gods) is destroyed by fire. **104. Nietzschean:** the person who believes in the *übermensch* or race of "supermen," following the ideas that the German philosopher Friedrich Wilhelm Nietzsche (1844-1900) proposed in *Also Sprach Zarathustra* (1883); cf. "hero-worship," line 142. **120. League of Nations:** forerunner of the United Nations (1919-1946).

have always insisted on behaving creatively under the shadow of the sword; that they have done their artistic and scientific and domestic stuff for the sake of doing it, and that *125* we had better follow their example under the shadow of the aeroplanes. Others, with more vision or courage than myself, see the salvation of humanity ahead, and will dismiss my conception of civilisation as paltry, a sort of tip-and-run game. Certainly it is presumptuous to say that we *cannot* improve, and that Man, who has only been in power for a few thousand years, will never learn to make use of his power. All I mean is that, if *130* people continue to kill one another as they do, the world cannot get better than it is, and that since there are more people than formerly, and their means for destroying one another superior, the world may well get worse. What is good in people — and consequently in the world — is their insistence on creation, their belief in friendship and loyalty for their own sakes; and though Violence remains and is, indeed, the major *135* partner in this muddled establishment, I believe that creativeness remains too, and will always assume direction when violence sleeps. So, though I am not an optimist, I cannot agree with Sophocles that it were better never to have been born. And although, like Horace, I see no evidence that each batch of births is superior to the last, I leave the field open for the more complacent view. This is such a difficult moment to live in, one *140* cannot help getting gloomy and also a bit rattled, and perhaps short-sighted.

In search of a refuge, we may perhaps turn to hero-worship. But here we shall get no help, in my opinion. Hero-worship is a dangerous vice, and one of the minor merits of a democracy is that it does not encourage it, or produce that unmanageable type of citizen known as the Great Man. It produces instead different kinds of small men — a *145* much finer achievement. But people who cannot get interested in the variety of life, and cannot make up their own minds, get discontented over this, and they long for a hero to bow down before and to follow blindly. It is significant that a hero is an integral part of the authoritarian stock-in-trade today. An efficiency-regime cannot be run without a few heroes stuck about it to carry off the dullness — much as plums have to be put into a *150* bad pudding to make it palatable. One hero at the top and a smaller one each side of him is a favourite arrangement, and the timid and the bored are comforted by the trinity, and, bowing down, feel exalted and strengthened.

No, I distrust Great Men. They produce a desert of uniformity around them and often a pool of blood too, and I always feel a little man's pleasure when they come a cropper. *155* Every now and then one reads in the newspapers some such statement as: "The coup d'état appears to have failed, and Admiral Toma's whereabouts is at present unknown." Admiral Toma had probably every qualification for being a Great Man — an iron will, personal magnetism, dash, flair, sexlessness — but fate was against him, so he retires to unknown whereabouts instead of parading history with his peers. He fails with a completeness *160* which no artist and no lover can experience, because with them the process of creation is itself an achievement, whereas with him the only possible achievement is success.

I believe in aristocracy, though — if that is the right word, and if a democrat may use it. Not an aristocracy of power, based upon rank and influence, but an aristocracy of the

---

128. tip-and-run: a form of cricket in which a batsman must run each time he hits the ball (also applied in World War I to quick dashes to sea by enemy ships, and in World War II to air-raids by bombers who quickly jettisoned their bombs and flew off). **138. Sophocles . . . born:** "Not to be born is, beyond all question, best" (*Oedipus at Colonus*, line 1224, by the 5th-century B.C. Greek dramatist). **139. Horace:** 1st-century B.C. Roman poet; at the end of Ode vi of Book III, he says that each new generation is worse than the one before.

sensitive, the considerate and the plucky. Its members are to be found in all nations and   *165*
classes, and all through the ages, and there is a secret understanding between them when
they meet. They represent the true human tradition, the one permanent victory of our queer
race over cruelty and chaos. Thousands of them perish in obscurity, a few are great names.
They are sensitive for others as well as for themselves, they are considerate without being
fussy, their pluck is not swankiness but the power to endure, and they can take a joke. I   *170*
give no examples — it is risky to do that — but the reader may as well consider whether
this is the type of person he would like to meet and to be, and whether (going farther with
me) he would prefer that this type should *not* be an ascetic one. I am against asceticism
myself. I am with the old Scotsman who wanted less chastity and more delicacy. I do not
feel that my aristocrats are a real aristocracy if they thwart their bodies, since bodies are   *175*
the instruments through which we register and enjoy the world. Still, I do not insist. This is
not a major point. It is clearly possible to be sensitive, considerate and plucky and yet be
an ascetic too, if anyone possesses the first three qualities, I will let him in! On they go —
an invincible army, yet not a victorious one. The aristocrats, the elect, the chosen, the Best
People — all the words that describe them are false, and all attempts to organise them fail.   *180*
Again and again Authority, seeing their value, has tried to net them and to utilise them as
the Egyptian Priesthood or the Christian Church or the Chinese Civil Service or the Group
Movement, or some other worthy stunt. But they slip through the net and are gone; when
the door is shut, they are no longer in the room; their temple, as one of them remarked, is
the Holiness of the Heart's Affection, and their kingdom, though they never possess it, is   *185*
the wide-open world.

 With this type of person knocking about, and constantly crossing one's path if one has
eyes to see or hands to feel, the experiment of earthly life cannot be dismissed as a failure.
But it may well be hailed as a tragedy, the tragedy being that no device has been found by
which these private decencies can be transmitted to public affairs. As soon as people have   *190*
power they go crooked and sometimes dotty as well, because the possession of power lifts
them into a region where normal honesty never pays. For instance, the man who is selling
newspapers outside the Houses of Parliament can safely leave his papers to go for a drink
and his cap beside them: anyone who takes a paper is sure to drop a copper into the cap.
But the men who are inside the Houses of Parliament — they cannot trust one another like   *195*
that, still less can the Government they compose trust other governments. No caps upon
the pavement here, but suspicion, treachery and armaments. The more highly public life is
organised the lower does its morality sink; the nations of today behave to each other worse
than they ever did in the past, they cheat, rob, bully and bluff, make war without notice,
and kill as many women and children as possible; whereas primitive tribes were at all   *200*
events restrained by taboos. It is a humiliating outlook — though the greater the darkness,
the brighter shine the little lights, reassuring one another, signalling: "Well, at all events,
I'm still here. I don't like it very much, but how are you?" Unquenchable lights of my
aristocracy! Signals of the invincible army! "Come along — anyway, let's have a good
time while we can." I think they signal that too.   *205*

182-83. Group Movement: probably referring to the "Oxford Group," also known as the "First Century Christian Fellowship," "Buchmanism," and (after 1938) "Moral Re-Armament" — a movement founded by American evangelist Frank Nathan Daniel Buchman (1878-1961) at Oxford in 1921, and active at Cambridge (Forster's old school) during the 1920s. **185. Holiness . . . Affection:** Keats, in a letter (see p. 857).

The Saviour of the future — if ever he comes — will not preach a new Gospel. He will merely utilise my aristocracy, he will make effective the good will and the good temper which are already existing. In other words, he will introduce a new technique. In economics, we are told that if there was a new technique of distribution, there need be no poverty, and people would not starve in one place while crops were being ploughed *210* under in another. A similar change is needed in the sphere of morals and politics. The desire for it is by no means new; it was expressed, for example, in theological terms by Jacopone da Todi over six hundred years ago. "Ordina questo amore, O tu che m'ami," he said; "O thou who lovest me — set this love in order." His prayer was not granted, and I do not myself believe that it ever will be, but here, and not through a change of *215* heart, is our probable route. Not by becoming better, but by ordering and distributing his native goodness, will Man shut up Force into its box, and so gain time to explore the universe and to set his mark upon it worthily. At present he only explores it at odd moments, when Force is looking the other way, and his divine creativeness appears as a trivial by-product, to be scrapped as soon as the drums beat and the bombers hum.   *220*

Such a change, claim the orthodox, can only be made by Christianity, and will be made by it in God's good time: man always has failed and always will fail to organise his own goodness, and it is presumptuous of him to try. This claim — solemn as it is — leaves me cold. I cannot believe that Christianity will ever cope with the present world-wide mess, and I think that such influence as it retains in modern society is due to the money behind it, *225* rather than to its spiritual appeal. It was a spiritual force once, but the indwelling spirit will have to be restated if it is to calm the waters again, and probably restated in a non-Christian form. Naturally a lot of people, and people who are not only good but able and intelligent, will disagree here; they will vehemently deny that Christianity has failed, or they will argue that its failure proceeds from the wickedness of men, and really proves its ultimate success. *230* They have Faith, with a large F. My faith has a very small one, and I only intrude it because these are strenuous and serious days, and one likes to say what one thinks while speech is comparatively free: it may not be free much longer.

The above are the reflections of an individualist and a liberal who has found liberalism crumbling beneath him and at first felt ashamed. Then, looking around, he *235* decided there was no special reason for shame, since other people, whatever they felt, were equally insecure. And as for individualism — there seems no way of getting off this, even if one wanted to. The dictator-hero can grind down his citizens till they are all alike, but he cannot melt them into a single man. That is beyond his power. He can order them to merge, he can incite them to mass-antics, but they are obliged to be born separately, and to *240* die separately, and, owing to these unavoidable termini, will always be running off the totalitarian rails. The memory of birth and the expectation of death always lurk within the human being, making him separate from his fellows and consequently capable of intercourse with them. Naked I came into the world, naked I shall go out of it! And a very good thing too, for it reminds me that I am naked under my shirt, whatever its colour. *245*

(1939)

---

213. **Jacopone da Todi:** Italian religious poet (c.1230-1306). 244. **Naked . . . out of it:** Cf. Job 1:21. 245. **colour:** E.g., black shirts were associated with German fascists, brown shirts with Italian fascists.

JAMES JOYCE
Ireland, 1882-1941

EVELINE

She sat at the window watching the evening invade the avenue. Her head was leaned against the window curtains and in her nostrils was the odour of dusty cretonne. She was tired.

Few people passed. The man out of the last house passed on his way home; she heard his footsteps clacking along the concrete pavement and afterwards crunching on the cinder path before the new red houses. One time there used to be a field there in which they used to play every evening with other people's children. Then a man from Belfast bought the field and built houses in it — not like their little brown houses but bright brick houses with shining roofs. The children of the avenue used to play together in that field — the Devines, the Waters, the Dunns, little Keogh the cripple, she and her brothers and sisters. Ernest, however, never played: he was too grown up. Her father used often to hunt them in out of the field with his blackthorn stick; but usually little Keogh used to keep *nix* and call out when he saw her father coming. Still they seemed to have been rather happy then. Her father was not so bad then; and besides, her mother was alive. That was a long time ago; she and her brothers and sisters were all grown up; her mother was dead. Tizzie Dunn was dead, too, and the Waters had gone back to England. Everything changes. Now she was going to go away like the others, to leave her home.

Home! She looked round the room, reviewing all its familiar objects which she had dusted once a week for so many years, wondering where on earth all the dust came from. Perhaps she would never see again those familiar objects from which she had never dreamed of being divided. And yet during all those years she had never found out the name of the priest whose yellowing photograph hung on the wall above the broken harmonium beside the coloured print of the promises made to Blessed Margaret Mary Alacoque. He had been a school friend of her father. Whenever he showed the photograph to a visitor her father used to pass it with a casual word:

— He is in Melbourne now.

She had consented to go away, to leave her home. Was that wise? She tried to weigh each side of the question. In her home anyway she had shelter and food; she had those whom she had known all her life about her. Of course she had to work hard both in the house and at business. What would they say of her in the Stores when they found out that she had run away with a fellow? Say she was a fool, perhaps; and her place would be filled up by advertisement. Miss Gavan would be glad. She had always had an edge on her, especially whenever there were people listening.

— Miss Hill, don't you see these ladies are waiting?

— Look lively, Miss Hill, please.

EVELINE **13.** *nix:* lookout. **24-25. Blessed Margaret Mary Alacoque:** Ste. Marguerite Marie Alacoque (1647-1690), French nun, canonized in 1920, who founded the devotion of the Sacred Heart; her feast day is October 17.

She would not cry many tears at leaving the Stores.

But in her new home, in a distant unknown country, it would not be like that. Then she would be married — she, Eveline. People would treat her with respect then. She would not be treated as her mother had been. Even now, though she was over nineteen, she sometimes felt herself in danger of her father's violence. She knew it was that that had given her the palpitations. When they were growing up he had never gone for her, like he used to go for Harry and Ernest, because she was a girl; but latterly he had begun to threaten her and say what he would do to her only for her dead mother's sake. And now she had nobody to protect her. Ernest was dead and Harry, who was in the church decorating business, was nearly always down somewhere in the country. Besides, the invariable squabble for money on Saturday nights had begun to weary her unspeakably. She always gave her entire wages — seven shillings — and Harry always sent up what he could but the trouble was to get any money from her father. He said she used to squander the money, that she had no head, that he wasn't going to give her his hard-earned money to throw about the streets, and much more, for he was usually fairly bad of a Saturday night. In the end he would give her the money and ask her had she any intention of buying Sunday's dinner. Then she had to rush out as quickly as she could and do her marketing, holding her black leather purse tightly in her hand as she elbowed her way through the crowds and returning home late under her load of provisions. She had hard work to keep the house together and to see that the two young children who had been left to her charge went to school regularly and got their meals regularly. It was hard work — a hard life — but now that she was about to leave it she did not find it a wholly undesirable life.

She was about to explore another life with Frank. Frank was very kind, manly, open-hearted. She was to go away with him by the night-boat to be his wife and to live with him in Buenos Ayres where he had a home waiting for her. How well she remembered the first time she had seen him; he was lodging in a house on the main road where she used to visit. It seemed a few weeks ago. He was standing at the gate, his peaked cap pushed back on his head and his hair tumbled forward over a face of bronze. Then they had come to know each other. He used to meet her outside the Stores every evening and see her home. He took her to see *The Bohemian Girl* and she felt elated as she sat in an unaccustomed part of the theatre with him. He was awfully fond of music and sang a little. People knew that they were courting and, when he sang about the lass that loves a sailor, she always felt pleasantly confused. He used to call her Poppens out of fun. First of all it had been an excitement for her to have a fellow and then she had begun to like him. He had tales of distant countries. He had started as a deck boy at a pound a month on a ship of the Allan Line going out to Canada. He told her the names of the ships he had been on and the names of the different services. He had sailed through the Straits of Magellan and he told her stories of the terrible Patagonians. He had fallen on his feet in Buenos Ayres, he said, and had come over to the old country just for a holiday. Of course, her father had found out the affair and had forbidden her to have anything to say to him.

68. *The Bohemian Girl*: light romantic opera by Michael William Balfe (1808-1870), first performed in 1844, source of the song "I Dreamt that I Dwelt in Marble Halls." **70-71. the lass that loves a sailor:** title of a popular song by Charles Dibdin (1745-1814).

— I know these sailor chaps, he said.   *80*

One day he had quarrelled with Frank and after that she had to meet her lover secretly.

The evening deepened in the avenue. The white of two letters in her lap grew indistinct. One was to Harry; the other was to her father. Ernest had been her favourite but she liked Harry too. Her father was becoming old lately, she noticed; he would miss   *85* her. Sometimes he could be very nice. Not long before, when she had been laid up for a day, he had read her out a ghost story and made toast for her at the fire. Another day, when their mother was alive, they had all gone for a picnic to the Hill of Howth. She remembered her father putting on her mother's bonnet to make the children laugh.

Her time was running out but she continued to sit by the window, leaning her head   *90* against the window curtain, inhaling the odour of dusty cretonne. Down far in the avenue she could hear a street organ playing. She knew the air. Strange that it should come that very night to remind her of the promise to her mother, her promise to keep the home together as long as she could. She remembered the last night of her mother's illness; she was again in the close dark room at the other side of the hall and outside she   *95* heard a melancholy air of Italy. The organ-player had been ordered to go away and given sixpence. She remembered her father strutting back into the sickroom saying:

— Damned Italians! coming over here!

As she mused the pitiful vision of her mother's life laid its spell on the very quick of her being — that life of commonplace sacrifices closing in final craziness. She trembled   *100* as she heard again her mother's voice saying constantly with foolish insistence:

— Derevaun Seraun! Derevaun Seraun!

She stood up in a sudden impulse of terror. Escape! She must escape! Frank would save her. He would give her life, perhaps love, too. But she wanted to live. Why should she be unhappy? She had a right to happiness. Frank would take her in his arms, fold her   *105* in his arms. He would save her.

She stood among the swaying crowd in the station at the North Wall. He held her hand and she knew that he was speaking to her, saying something about the passage over and over again. The station was full of soldiers with brown baggages. Through the wide doors of the sheds she caught a glimpse of the black mass of the boat, lying in   *110* beside the quay wall, with illumined portholes. She answered nothing. She felt her cheek pale and cold and, out of a maze of distress, she prayed to God to direct her, to show her what was her duty. The boat blew a long mournful whistle into the mist. If she went, to-morrow she would be on the sea with Frank, steaming towards Buenos Ayres. Their passage had been booked. Could she still draw back after all he had done for her?   *115* Her distress awoke a nausea in her body and she kept moving her lips in silent fervent prayer.

A bell clanged upon her heart. She felt him seize her hand:

— Come!

All the seas of the world tumbled about her heart. He was drawing her into them: he   *120* would drown her. She gripped with both hands at the iron railing.

---

88. Hill of Howth: on the coast about 14.5 km northeast of Dublin. **102. Derevaun Seraun:** No one has been able to attach any certain meaning to this phrase, though some critics have suggested that it is corrupt Gaelic for "the end of pleasure is pain" — a motif not inappropriate to *Dubliners*, the volume in which "Eveline" appeared.

— Come!

No! No! No! It was impossible. Her hands clutched the iron in frenzy. Amid the seas she sent a cry of anguish!

— Eveline! Evvy!   *125*

He rushed beyond the barrier and called to her to follow. He was shouted at to go on but he still called to her. She set her white face to him, passive, like a helpless animal. Her eyes gave him no sign of love or farewell or recognition.

(1914)

VIRGINIA WOOLF
England, 1882-1941

THE DECAY OF ESSAY-WRITING

The spread of education and the necessity which haunts us to impart what we have acquired have led, and will lead still further, to some startling results. We read of the over-burdened British Museum — how even its appetite for printed matter flags, and the monster pleads that it can swallow no more. This public crisis has long been familiar in private houses. One member of the household is almost officially deputed to stand at the   *5* hall door with flaming sword and do battle with the invading armies. Tracts, pamphlets, advertisements, gratuitous copies of magazines, and the literary productions of friends come by post, by van, by messenger — come at all hours of the day and fall in the night, so that the morning breakfast-table is fairly snowed up with them.

This age has painted itself more faithfully than any other in a myriad of clever and   *10* conscientious though not supremely great works of fiction; it has tried seriously to liven the faded colours of bygone ages; it has delved industriously with spade and axe in the rubbish-heaps and ruins; and, so far, we can only applaud our use of pen and ink. But if you have a monster like the British public to feed, you will try to tickle its stale palate in new ways; fresh and amusing shapes must be given to the old commodities — for we   *15* really have nothing so new to say that it will not fit into one of the familiar forms. So we confine ourselves to no one literary medium; we try to be new by being old; we revive mystery-plays and affect an archaic accent; we deck ourselves in the fine raiment of an embroidered style; we cast off all clothing and disport ourselves nakedly. In short, there is no end to our devices, and at this very moment probably some ingenious youth is   *20* concocting a fresh one which, be it ever so new, will grow stale in its turn. If there are thus an infinite variety of fashions in the external shapes of our wares, there are a certain number — naturally not so many — of wares that are new in substance and in form which we have either invented or very much developed. Perhaps the most significant of these literary inventions is the invention of the personal essay. It is true that it is at least   *25* as old as Montaigne, but we may count him the first of the moderns. It has been used with considerable frequency since his day, but its popularity with us is so immense and

---

THE DECAY OF ESSAY-WRITING   **18. mystery-plays:** i.e., medieval dramatizations of Bible stories — in particular the play cycles that were performed at Chester, Coventry, Townley, and York. **26. Montaigne:** Montaigne's *Essais* were published in 1580ff. (see p. 186).

so peculiar that we are justified in looking upon it as something of our own — typical, characteristic, a sign of the times which will strike the eye of our great-great-grand-children. Its significance, indeed, lies not so much in the fact that we have attained any brilliant success in essay-writing — no one has approached the essays of Elia — but in the undoubted facility with which we write essays as though this were beyond all others our natural way of speaking. The peculiar form of an essay implies a peculiar substance; you can say in this shape what you cannot with equal fitness say in any other. A very wide definition obviously must be that which will include all the varieties of thought which are suitably enshrined in essays; but perhaps if you say that an essay is essentially egoistical you will not exclude many essays and you will certainly include a portentous number. Almost all essays begin with a capital I — "I think," "I feel" — and when you have said that, it is clear that you are not writing history or philosophy or biography or anything but an essay, which may be brilliant or profound, which may deal with the immortality of the soul, or the rheumatism in your left shoulder, but is primarily an expression of personal opinion.

We are not — there is, alas! no need to prove it — more subject to ideas than our ancestors; we are not, I hope, in the main more egoistical; but there is one thing in which we are more highly skilled than they are; and that is in manual dexterity with a pen. There can be no doubt that it is to the art of penmanship that we owe our present literature of essays. The very great of old — Homer and Aeschylus — could dispense with a pen; they were not inspired by sheets of paper and gallons of ink; no fear that their harmonies, passed from lip to lip, should lose their cadence and die. But our essayists write because the gift of writing has been bestowed on them. Had they lacked writing-masters we should have lacked essayists. There are, of course, certain distinguished people who use this medium from genuine inspiration because it best embodies the soul of their thought. But, on the other hand, there is a very large number who make the fatal pause, and the mechanical act of writing is allowed to set the brain in motion which should only be accessible to a higher inspiration.

The essay, then, owes its popularity to the fact that its proper use is to express one's personal peculiarities, so that under the decent veil of print one can indulge one's egoism to the full. You need know nothing of music, art, or literature to have a certain interest in their productions, and the great burden of modern criticism is simply the expression of such individual likes and dislikes — the amiable garrulity of the tea-table — cast into the form of essays. If men and women must write, let them leave the great mysteries of art and literature unassailed; if they told us frankly not of the books that we can all read and the pictures which hang for us all to see, but of that single book to which they alone have the key and of that solitary picture whose face is shrouded to all but one gaze — if they would write of themselves — such writing would have its own permanent value. The simple words "I was born" have somehow a charm beside which all the splendours of romance and fairy-tale turn to moonshine and tinsel. But though it seems thus easy enough to write of one's self, it is, as we know, a feat but seldom accomplished. Of the multitude of autobiographies that are written, one or two alone are what they pretend to be. Confronted with the terrible spectre of themselves, the bravest are inclined to run away or shade their eyes. And thus, instead of the honest truth which we should all respect, we are given timid side-glances in the shape of essays, which, for the most part, fail in the cardinal virtue of sincerity. And those who do not sacrifice their beliefs to the turn of a phrase or the glitter of paradox think it beneath the dignity of the printed word to say simply what it means; in print they must pretend to an oracular and infallible nature. To say simply "I have a garden, and I will tell you what plants do best in my garden" possibly justified its egoism; but to say "I have no sons, though I have six daughters, all unmarried, but I will tell you how I should have brought up my sons had I had any" is not interesting, cannot be useful, and is a specimen of the amazing and unclothed egoism for which first the art of penmanship and then the invention of essay-writing are responsible.

(1905)

THE LADY IN THE LOOKING-GLASS: A REFLECTION

People should not leave looking-glasses hanging in their rooms any more than they should leave open cheque books or letters confessing some hideous crime. One could not help looking, that summer afternoon, in the long glass that hung outside in the hall. Chance had so arranged it. From the depths of the sofa in the drawing-room one could see reflected in the Italian glass not only the marble-topped table opposite, but a stretch of the garden beyond. One could see a long grass path leading between banks of tall flowers until, slicing off an angle, the gold rim cut it off.

The house was empty, and one felt, since one was the only person in the drawing-room, like one of those naturalists who, covered with grass and leaves, lie watching the shyest animals — badgers, otters, kingfishers — moving about freely, themselves unseen. The room that afternoon was full of such shy creatures, lights and shadows, curtains blowing, petals falling — things that never happen, so it seems, if someone is looking. The quiet old country room with its rugs and stone chimney pieces, its sunken book-cases and red and gold lacquer cabinets, was full of such nocturnal creatures. They came pirouetting across the floor, stepping delicately with high-lifted feet and spread tails and pecking allusive beaks as if they had been cranes or flocks of elegant flamingoes whose pink was faded, or peacocks whose trains were veined with silver. And there were obscure flushes and darkenings too, as if a cuttlefish had suddenly suffused the air with purple; and the room had its passions and rages and envies and sorrows coming over it and clouding it, like a human being. Nothing stayed the same for two seconds together.

But, outside, the looking-glass reflected the hall table, the sunflowers, the garden path so accurately and so fixedly that they seemed held there in their reality unescapably. It was a strange contrast — all changing here, all stillness there. One could not help looking from one to the other. Meanwhile, since all the doors and windows were open in the heat, there was a perpetual sighing and ceasing sound, the voice of the transient and the perishing, it seemed, coming and going like human breath, while in the looking-glass things had ceased to breathe and lay still in the trance of immortality.

Half an hour ago the mistress of the house, Isabella Tyson, had gone down the grass path in her thin summer dress, carrying a basket, and had vanished, sliced off by the gilt rim of the looking-glass. She had gone presumably into the lower garden to pick flowers; or as it seemed more natural to suppose, to pick something light and fantastic and leafy and trailing, traveller's joy, or one of those elegant sprays of convolvulus that twine round ugly walls and burst here and there into white and violet blossoms. She suggested the fantastic and the tremulous convolvulus rather than the *35* upright aster, the starched zinnia, or her own burning roses alight like lamps on the straight posts of their rose trees. The comparison showed how very little, after all these years, one knew about her; for it is impossible that any woman of flesh and blood of fifty-five or sixty should be really a wreath or a tendril. Such comparisons are worse than idle and superficial — they are cruel even, for they come like the convolvulus *40* itself trembling between one's eyes and the truth. There must be truth; there must be a wall. Yet it was strange that after knowing her all these years one could not say what the truth about Isabella was; one still made up phrases like this about convolvulus and traveller's joy. As for facts, it was a fact that she was a spinster; that she was rich; that she had bought this house and collected with her own hands — often in the most *45* obscure corners of the world and at great risk from poisonous stings and Oriental diseases — the rugs, the chairs, the cabinets which now lived their nocturnal life before one's eyes. Sometimes it seemed as if they knew more about her than we, who sat on them, wrote at them, and trod on them so carefully, were allowed to know. In each of these cabinets were many little drawers, and each almost certainly held letters, tied *50* with bows of ribbon, sprinkled with sticks of lavender or rose leaves. For it was another fact — if facts were what one wanted — that Isabella had known many people, had had many friends; and thus if one had the audacity to open a drawer and read her letters, one would find the traces of many agitations, of appointments to meet, of upbraidings for not having met, long letters of intimacy and affection, violent letters of *55* jealousy and reproach, terrible final words of parting — for all those interviews and assignations had led to nothing — that is, she had never married, and yet, judging from the mask-like indifference of her face, she had gone through twenty times more of passion and experience than those whose loves are trumpeted forth for all the world to hear. Under the stress of thinking about Isabella, her room became more shadowy and *60* symbolic; the corners seemed darker, the legs of chairs and tables more spindly and hieroglyphic.

Suddenly these reflections were ended violently and yet without a sound. A large black form loomed into the looking-glass; blotted out everything, strewed the table with a packet of marble tablets veined with pink and grey, and was gone. But the picture was *65* entirely altered. For the moment it was unrecognisable and irrational and entirely out of focus. One could not relate these tablets to any human purpose. And then by degrees some logical process set to work on them and began ordering and arranging them and bringing them into the fold of common experience. One realised at last that they were merely letters. The man had brought the post. *70*

There they lay on the marble-topped table, all dripping with light and colour at first and crude and unabsorbed. And then it was strange to see how they were drawn in and arranged and composed and made part of the picture and granted that stillness and immortality which the looking-glass conferred. They lay there invested with a new reality and significance and with a greater heaviness, too, as if it would have needed a *75* chisel to dislodge them from the table. And, whether it was fancy or not, they seemed to have become not merely a handful of casual letters but to be tablets graven with eternal truth — if one could read them, one would know everything there was to be known about Isabella, yes, and about life, too. The pages inside those marble-looking envelopes must be cut deep and scored thick with meaning. Isabella would come in, *80* and take them, one by one, very slowly, and open them, and read them carefully word by word, and then with a profound sigh of comprehension, as if she had seen to the bottom of everything, she would tear the envelopes to little bits and tie the letters together and lock the cabinet drawer in her determination to conceal what she did not wish to be known. *85*

The thought served as a challenge. Isabella did not wish to be known — but she should no longer escape. It was absurd, it was monstrous. If she concealed so much and knew so much one must prize her open with the first tool that came to hand — the imagination. One must fix one's mind upon her at that very moment. One must fasten her down there. One must refuse to be put off any longer with sayings and doings such *90* as the moment brought forth — with dinners and visits and polite conversations. One must put oneself in her shoes. If one took the phrase literally, it was easy to see the shoes in which she stood, down in the lower garden, at this moment. They were very narrow and long and fashionable — they were made of the softest and most flexible leather. Like everything she wore, they were exquisite. And she would be standing *95* under the high hedge in the lower part of the garden, raising the scissors that were tied to her waist to cut some dead flower, some overgrown branch. The sun would beat down on her face, into her eyes; but no, at the critical moment a veil of cloud covered the sun, making the expression of her eyes doubtful — was it mocking or tender, brilliant or dull? One could only see the indeterminate outline of her rather faded, fine *100* face looking at the sky. She was thinking, perhaps, that she must order a new net for the strawberries; that she must send flowers to Johnson's widow; that it was time she drove over to see the Hippesleys in their new house. Those were the things she talked about at dinner certainly. But one was tired of the things that she talked about at dinner. It was her profounder state of being that one wanted to catch and turn to words, the state that is *105* to the mind what breathing is to the body, what one calls happiness or unhappiness. At the mention of those words it became obvious, surely, that she must be happy. She was rich; she was distinguished; she had many friends; she travelled — she bought rugs in Turkey and blue pots in Persia. Avenues of pleasure radiated this way and that from where she stood with her scissors raised to cut the trembling branches while the lacy *110* clouds veiled her face.

Here with a quick movement of her scissors she snipped the spray of traveller's joy and it fell to the ground. As it fell, surely some light came in too, surely one could penetrate a little farther into her being. Her mind then was filled with tenderness and regret. . . . To cut an overgrown branch saddened her because it had once lived, and life *115* was dear to her. Yes, and at the same time the fall of the branch would suggest to her how she must die herself and all the futility and evanescence of things. And then again quickly catching this thought up, with her instant good sense, she thought life had treated her well; even if fall she must, it was to lie on the earth and moulder sweetly into the roots of violets. So she stood thinking. Without making any thought precise — for *120* she was one of those reticent people whose minds hold their thoughts enmeshed in

clouds of silence — she was filled with thoughts. Her mind was like her room, in which
lights advanced and retreated, came pirouetting and stepping delicately, spread their
tails, pecked their way; and then her whole being was suffused, like the room again,
with a cloud of some profound knowledge, some unspoken regret, and then she was full   *125*
of locked drawers, stuffed with letters, like her cabinets. To talk of "prizing her open" as
if she were an oyster, to use any but the finest and subtlest and most pliable tools upon
her was impious and absurd. One must imagine — here was she in the looking-glass. It
made one start.

　　She was so far off at first that one could not see her clearly. She came lingering and   *130*
pausing, here straightening a rose, there lifting a pink to smell it, but she never stopped;
and all the time she became larger and larger in the looking-glass, more and more
completely the person into whose mind one had been trying to penetrate. One verified
her by degrees — fitted the qualities one had discovered into this visible body. There
were her grey-green dress, and her long shoes, her basket, and something sparkling at   *135*
her throat. She came so gradually that she did not seem to derange the pattern in the
glass, but only to bring in some new element which gently moved and altered the other
objects as if asking them, courteously, to make room for her. And the letters and the
table and the grass walk and the sunflowers which had been waiting in the looking-glass
separated and opened out so that she might be received among them. At last there she   *140*
was, in the hall. She stopped dead. She stood by the table. She stood perfectly still. At
once the looking-glass began to pour over her a light that seemed to fix her; that seemed
like some acid to bite off the unessential and superficial and to leave only the truth. It
was an enthralling spectacle. Everything dropped from her — clouds, dress, basket,
diamond — all that one had called the creeper and convolvulus. Here was the hard wall   *145*
beneath. Here was the woman herself. She stood naked in that pitiless light. And there
was nothing. Isabella was perfectly empty. She had no thoughts. She had no friends. She
cared for nobody. As for her letters, they were all bills. Look, as she stood there, old and
angular, veined and lined, with her high nose and her wrinkled neck, she did not even
trouble to open them.   *150*

　　People should not leave looking-glasses hanging in their rooms.

(1929)

E.J. Pratt
Canada, 1882-1964

Sea-Gulls

For one carved instant as they flew,
The language had no simile —
Silver, crystal, ivory
Were tarnished. Etched upon the horizon blue.
The frieze must go unchallenged, for the lift   *5*
And carriage of the wings would stain the drift
Of stars against a tropic indigo
Or dull the parable of snow.

Now settling one by one
Within green hollows or where curled   *10*
Crests caught the spectrum from the sun,
A thousand wings are furled.
No clay-born lilies of the world
Could blow as free
As those wild orchids of the sea.   *15*

(1930, 1932)

FROM STONE TO STEEL

From stone to bronze, from bronze to steel
Along the road-dust of the sun,
Two revolutions of the wheel
From Java to Geneva run.

The snarl Neanderthal is worn   5
Close to the smiling Aryan lips,
The civil polish of the horn
Gleams from our praying finger tips.

The evolution of desire
Has but matured a toxic wine,   10

Drunk long before its heady fire
Reddened Euphrates or the Rhine.

Between the temple and the cave
The boundary lies tissue-thin:
The yearlings still the altars crave   15
As satisfaction for a sin.

The road goes up, the road goes down —
Let Java or Geneva be —
But whether to the cross or crown,
The path lies through Gethsemane.   20

(1932)

WILLIAM CARLOS WILLIAMS
U.S.A., 1883-1963

THE RED WHEELBARROW

so much depends
upon

a red wheel
barrow

glazed with rain   5
water

beside the white
chickens

(1923)

A SORT OF A SONG

Let the snake wait under
his weed
and the writing
be of words, slow and quick, sharp
to strike, quiet to wait,   5
sleepless.

— through metaphor to reconcile
the people and the stones.
Compose. (No ideas
but in things) Invent!   10
Saxifrage is my flower that splits
the rocks.

(1944)

D.H. LAWRENCE
England, 1885-1930

THE HORSE DEALER'S DAUGHTER

"Well, Mabel, and what are you going to do with yourself?" asked Joe, with foolish flippancy. He felt quite safe himself. Without listening for an answer, he turned aside, worked a grain of tobacco to the tip of his tongue, and spat it out. He did not care about anything, since he felt safe himself.

FROM STONE TO STEEL   **20. Gethsemane:** See Matthew 26:36; Mark 14:32.

The three brothers and the sister sat round the desolate breakfast table, attempting   *5*
some sort of desultory consultation. The morning's post had given the final tap to the
family fortune, and all was over. The dreary dining-room itself, with its heavy
mahogany furniture, looked as if it were waiting to be done away with.

But the consultation amounted to nothing. There was a strange air of ineffectuality
about the three men, as they sprawled at table, smoking and reflecting vaguely on their   *10*
own condition. The girl was alone, a rather short, sullen-looking young woman of
twenty-seven. She did not share the same life as her brothers. She would have been good-
looking, save for the impassive fixity of her face, "bulldog," as her brothers called it.

There was a confused tramping of horses' feet outside. The three men all sprawled
round in their chairs to watch. Beyond the dark holly-bushes that separated the strip of   *15*
lawn from the highroad, they could see a cavalcade of shire horses swinging out of their
own yard, being taken for exercise. This was the last time. These were the last horses
that would go through their hands. The young men watched with critical, callous look.
They were all frightened at the collapse of their lives, and the sense of disaster in which
they were involved left them no inner freedom.   *20*

Yet they were three fine, well-set fellows enough. Joe, the eldest, was a man of
thirty-three, broad and handsome in a hot, flushed way. His face was red, he twisted his
black moustache over a thick finger, his eyes were shallow and restless. He had a
sensual way of uncovering his teeth when he laughed, and his bearing was stupid. Now
he watched the horses with a glazed look of helplessness in his eyes, a certain stupor of   *25*
downfall.

The great draught-horses swung past. They were tied head to tail, four of them, and
they heaved along to where a lane branched off from the highroad, planting their great
hoofs floutingly in the fine black mud, swinging their great rounded haunches
sumptuously, and trotting a few sudden steps as they were led into the lane, round the   *30*
corner. Every movement showed a massive, slumbrous strength, and a stupidity which
held them in subjection. The groom at the head looked back, jerking the leading rope.
And the cavalcade moved out of sight up the lane, the tail of the last horse, bobbed up
tight and stiff, held out taut from the swinging great haunches as they rocked behind the
hedges in a motion like sleep.   *35*

Joe watched with glazed hopeless eyes. The horses were almost like his own body
to him. He felt he was done for now. Luckily he was engaged to a woman as old as
himself, and therefore her father, who was steward of a neighbouring estate, would
provide him with a job. He would marry and go into harness. His life was over, he
would be a subject animal now.   *40*

He turned uneasily aside, the retreating steps of the horses echoing in his ears.
Then, with foolish restlessness, he reached for the scraps of bacon-rind from the plates,
and making a faint whistling sound, flung them to the terrier that lay against the fender.
He watched the dog swallow them, and waited till the creature looked into his eyes.
Then a faint grin came on his face, and in a high, foolish voice he said: *45*

"You won't get much more bacon, shall you, you little bitch?"

The dog faintly and dismally wagged its tail, then lowered its haunches, circled
round, and lay down again.

There was another helpless silence at the table. Joe sprawled uneasily in his seat, not willing to go till the family conclave was dissolved. Fred Henry, the second brother, *50* was erect, clean-limbed, alert. He had watched the passing of the horses with more sang-froid. If he was an animal, like Joe, he was an animal which controls, not one which is controlled. He was master of any horse, and he carried himself with a well-tempered air of mastery. But he was not master of the situations of life. He pushed his coarse brown moustache upwards, off his lip, and glanced irritably at his sister, who sat *55* impassive and inscrutable.

"You'll go and stop with Lucy for a bit, shan't you?" he asked. The girl did not answer.

"I don't see what else you can do," persisted Fred Henry.

"Go as a skivvy," Joe interpolated laconically. *60*

The girl did not move a muscle.

"If I was her, I should go in for training for a nurse," said Malcolm, the youngest of them all. He was the baby of the family, a young man of twenty-two, with a fresh, jaunty *museau*.

But Mabel did not take any notice of him. They had talked at her and round her for *65* so many years, that she hardly heard them at all.

The marble clock on the mantelpiece softly chimed the half-hour, the dog rose uneasily from the hearthrug and looked at the party at the breakfast table. But still they sat on in ineffectual conclave.

"Oh, all right," said Joe suddenly, apropos of nothing. "I'll get a move on." *70*

He pushed back his chair, straddled his knees with a downward jerk, to get them free, in horsey fashion, and went to the fire. Still he did not go out of the room; he was curious to know what the others would do or say. He began to charge his pipe, looking down at the dog and saying, in a high, affected voice:

"Going wi' me? Going wi' me are ter? Tha'rt goin' further than tha counts on just *75* now, dost hear?"

The dog faintly wagged its tail, the man stuck out his jaw and covered his pipe with his hands, and puffed intently, losing himself in the tobacco, looking down all the while at the dog with an absent brown eye. The dog looked up at him in mournful distrust. Joe stood with his knees stuck out, in real horsey fashion. *80*

"Have you had a letter from Lucy?" Fred Henry asked of his sister.

"Last week," came the neutral reply.

"And what does she say?"

There was no answer.

"Does she *ask* you to go and stop there?" persisted Fred Henry. *85*

"She says I can if I like."

"Well, then, you'd better. Tell her you'll come on Monday."

This was received in silence.

"That's what you'll do then, is it?" said Fred Henry, in some exasperation.

But she made no answer. There was a silence of futility and irritation in the room. *90* Malcolm grinned fatuously.

THE HORSE DEALER'S DAUGHTER   **60.** skivvy: domestic servant. **64.** *museau*: literally "muzzle."

"You'll have to make up your mind between now and next Wednesday," said Joe
loudly, "or else find yourself lodgings on the kerbstone."

The face of the young woman darkened, but she sat on immutable.

"Here's Jack Fergusson!" exclaimed Malcolm, who was looking aimlessly out of   95
the window.

"Where?" exclaimed Joe, loudly.

"Just gone past."

"Coming in?"

Malcolm craned his neck to see the gate.   100

"Yes," he said.

There was a silence. Mabel sat on like one condemned, at the head of the table.
Then a whistle was heard from the kitchen. The dog got up and barked sharply. Joe
opened the door and shouted:

"Come on."   105

After a moment a young man entered. He was muffled up in overcoat and a purple
woollen scarf, and his tweed cap, which he did not remove, was pulled down on his
head. He was of medium height, his face was rather long and pale, his eyes looked tired.

"Hello, Jack! Well, Jack!" exclaimed Malcolm and Joe. Fred Henry merely said,
"Jack."   110

"What's doing?" asked the newcomer, evidently addressing Fred Henry.

"Same. We've to to be out by Wednesday. Got a cold?"

"I have — got it bad, too."

"Why don't you stop in?"

"*Me* stop in? When I can't stand on my legs, perhaps I shall have a chance." The   115
young man spoke huskily. He had a slight Scotch accent.

"It's a knock-out, isn't it," said Joe, boisterously, "if a doctor goes round croaking
with a cold. Looks bad for the patients, doesn't it?"

The young doctor looked at him slowly.

"Anything the matter with *you*, then?" he asked sarcastically.   120

"Not as I know of. Damn your eyes, I hope not. Why?"

"I thought you were very concerned about the patients, wondered if you might be
one yourself."

"Damn it, no, I've never been patient to no flaming doctor, and hope I never shall
be," returned Joe.   125

At this point Mabel rose from the table, and they all seemed to become aware of her
existence. She began putting the dishes together. The young doctor looked at her, but
did not address her. He had not greeted her. She went out of the room with the tray, her
face impassive and unchanged.

"When are you off then, all of you?" asked the doctor.   130

"I'm catching the eleven-forty," replied Malcolm. "Are you goin' down wi' th'
trap, Joe?"

"Yes, I've told you I'm going down wi' th' trap, haven't I?"

---

132. trap: two-wheeled carriage.

"We'd better be getting her in then. So long, Jack, if I don't see you before I go," said Malcolm, shaking hands. 135

He went out, followed by Joe, who seemed to have his tail between his legs.

"Well, this is the devil's own," exclaimed the doctor, when he was left alone with Fred Henry. "Going before Wednesday, are you?"

"That's the orders," replied the other.

"Where, to Northampton?" 140

"That's it."

"The devil!" exclaimed Fergusson, with quiet chagrin.

And there was silence between the two.

"All settled up, are you?" asked Fergusson.

"About." 145

There was another pause.

"Well, I shall miss yer, Freddy, boy," said the young doctor.

"And I shall miss thee, Jack," returned the other.

"Miss you like hell," mused the doctor.

Fred Henry turned aside. There was nothing to say. Mabel came in again, to finish 150
clearing the table.

"What are *you* going to do, then, Miss Pervin?" asked Fergusson. "Going to your sister's are you?"

Mabel looked at him with her steady, dangerous eyes, that always made him uncomfortable, unsettling his superficial ease. 155

"No," she said.

"Well, what in the name of fortune *are* you going to do? Say what you mean to do," cried Fred Henry, with futile intensity.

But she only averted her head, and continued her work. She folded the white tablecloth, and put on the chenille cloth. 160

"The sulkiest bitch that ever trod!" muttered her brother.

But she finished her task with perfectly impassive face, the young doctor watching her interestedly all the while. Then she went out.

Fred Henry stared after her, clenching his lips, his blue eyes fixing in sharp antagonism, as he made a grimace of sour exasperation. 165

"You could bray her into bits, and that's all you'd get out of her," he said in a small, narrowed tone.

The doctor smiled faintly.

"What's she *going* to do, then?" he asked.

"Strike me if *I* know!" returned the other. 170

There was a pause. Then the doctor stirred.

"I'll be seeing you to-night, shall I?" he said to his friend.

"Ay — where's it to be? Are we going over to Jessdale?"

"I don't know. I've got a cold on me. I'll come round to the Moon and Stars, anyway." 175

---

166. bray: pound, as in a mortar.

"Let Lizzie and May miss their night for once, eh?"

"That's it — if I feel as I do now."

"All's one —"

The two young men went through the passage and down to the back door together. The house was large, but it was servantless now, and desolate. At the back was a small 180 bricked house-yard, and beyond that a big square, gravelled fine and red, and having stables on two sides. Sloping, dank, winter-dark fields stretched away on the open sides.

But the stables were empty. Joseph Pervin, the father of the family, had been a man of no education, who had become a fairly large horse dealer. The stables had been full of horses, there was a great turmoil and come-and-go of horses and of dealers and 185 grooms. Then the kitchen was full of servants. But of late things had declined. The old man had married a second time, to retrieve his fortunes. Now he was dead and everything was gone to the dogs, there was nothing but debt and threatening.

For months, Mabel had been servantless in the big house, keeping the home together in penury for her ineffectual brothers. She had kept house for ten years. But 190 previously it was with unstinted means. Then, however brutal and coarse everything was, the sense of money had kept her proud, confident. The men might be foulmouthed, the women in the kitchen might have bad reputations, her brothers might have illegitimate children. But so long as there was money, the girl felt herself established, and brutally proud, reserved. 195

No company came to the house, save dealers and coarse men. Mabel had no associates of her own sex, after her sister went away. But she did not mind. She went regularly to church, she attended to her father. And she lived in the memory of her mother, who had died when she was fourteen, and whom she had loved. She had loved her father, too, in a different way, depending upon him, and feeling secure in him, until 200 at the age of fifty-four he married again. And then she had set hard against him. Now he had died and left them all hopelessly in debt.

She had suffered badly during the period of poverty. Nothing, however, could shake the curious sullen, animal pride that dominated each member of the family. Now, for Mabel, the end had come. Still she would not cast about her. She would follow her own 205 way just the same. She would always hold the keys of her own situation. Mindless and persistent, she endured from day to day. Why should she think? Why should she answer anybody? It was enough that this was the end, and there was no way out. She need not pass any more darkly along the main street of the small town, avoiding every eye. She need not demean herself any more, going into the shops and buying the cheapest food. This was at 210 an end. She thought of nobody, not even of herself. Mindless and persistent, she seemed in a sort of ecstasy to be coming nearer to her fulfillment, her own glorification, approaching her dead mother, who was glorified.

In the afternoon she took a little bag, with shears and sponge and a small scrubbing brush, and went out. It was a grey, wintry day, with saddened, dark green fields and an 215 atmosphere blackened by the smoke of foundries not far off. She went quickly, darkly along the causeway, heeding nobody, through the town to the churchyard.

There she always felt secure, as if no one could see her, although as a matter of fact she was exposed to the stare of every one who passed along under the churchyard wall. Nevertheless, once under the shadow of the great looming church, among the graves, 220 she felt immune from the world, reserved within the thick churchyard wall as in another country.

Carefully she clipped the grass from the grave, and arranged the pinky white, small chrysanthemums in the tin cross. When this was done, she took an empty jar from a neighbouring grave, brought water, and carefully, most scrupulously sponged the marble headstone and the copingstone. *225*

It gave her sincere satisfaction to do this. She felt in immediate contact with the world of her mother. She took minute pains, went through the park in a state bordering on pure happiness, as if in performing this task she came into a subtle, intimate connection with her mother. For the life she followed here in the world was far less real *230* than the world of death she inherited from her mother.

The doctor's house was just by the church. Fergusson, being a mere hired assistant, was slave to the country-side. As he hurried now to attend to the outpatient in the surgery, glancing across the graveyard with his quick eye, he saw the girl at her task at the grave. She seemed so intent and remote, it was like looking into another world. *235* Some mystical element was touched in him. He slowed down as he walked, watching her as if spell-bound.

She lifted her eyes, feeling him looking. Their eyes met. And each looked away again at once, each feeling, in some way, found out by the other. He lifted his cap and passed on down the road. There remained distinct in his consciousness, like a vision, the *240* memory of her face, lifted from the tombstone in the churchyard, and looking at him with slow, large, portentous eyes. It *was* portentous, her face. It seemed to mesmerize him. There was a heavy power in her eyes which laid hold of his whole being, as if he had drunk some powerful drug. He had been feeling weak and done before. Now the life came back into him, he felt delivered from his own fretted, daily self. *245*

He finished his duties at the surgery as quickly as might be, hastily filling up the bottles of the waiting people with cheap drugs. Then, in perpetual haste, he set off again to visit several cases in another part of his round, before teatime. At all times he preferred to walk if he could, but particularly when he was not well. He fancied the motion restored him. *250*

The afternoon was falling. It was grey, deadened, and wintry, with a slow, moist, heavy coldness sinking in and deadening all the faculties. But why should he think or notice? He hastily climbed the hill and turned across the dark green fields, following the black cinder-track. In the distance, across a shallow dip in the country, the small town was clustered like smouldering ash, a tower, a spire, a heap of low, raw, extinct houses. *255* And on the nearest fringe of the town, sloping into the dip, was Oldmeadow, the Pervins' house. He could see the stables and the outbuildings distinctly, as they lay towards him on the slope. Well, he would not go there many more times! Another resource would be lost to him, another place gone: the only company he cared for in the alien, ugly little town he was losing. Nothing but work, drudgery, constant hastening *260* from dwelling to dwelling among the colliers and the iron-workers. It wore him out, but at the same time he had a craving for it. It was a stimulant to him to be in the homes of the working people, moving as it were through the innermost body of their life. His nerves were excited and gratified. He could come so near, into the very lives of the rough, inarticulate, powerfully emotional men and women. He grumbled, he said he *265* hated the hellish hole. But as a matter of fact it excited him, the contact with the rough, strongly-feeling people was a stimulant applied direct to his nerves.

Below Oldmeadow, in the green, shallow, soddened hollow of fields, lay a square, deep pond. Roving across the landscape, the doctor's quick eye detected a figure in black passing through the gate of the field, down towards the pond. He looked again. It *270* would be Mabel Pervin. His mind suddenly became alive and attentive.

Why was she going down there? He pulled up on the path on the slope above, and stood staring. He could just make sure of the small black figure moving in the hollow of the failing day. He seemed to see her in the midst of such obscurity, that he was like a clairvoyant, seeing rather with the mind's eye than with ordinary sight. Yet he could see *275* her positively enough, whilst he kept his eye attentive. He felt, if he looked away from her, in the thick, ugly falling dusk, he would lose her altogether.

He followed her minutely as she moved, direct and intent, like something transmitted rather than stirring in voluntary activity, straight down the field towards the pond. There she stood on the bank for a moment. She never raised her head. Then she *280* waded slowly into the water.

He stood motionless as the small black figure walked slowly and deliberately towards the centre of the pond, very slowly, gradually moving deeper into the motionless water, and still moving forward as the water got up to her breast. Then he could see her no more in the dusk of the dead afternoon. *285*

"There!" he exclaimed. "Would you believe it?"

And he hastened straight down, running over the wet, soddened fields, pushing through the hedges, down into the depression of callous wintry obscurity. It took him several minutes to come to the pond. He stood on the bank, breathing heavily. He could see nothing. His eyes seemed to penetrate the dead water. Yes, perhaps that was the dark *290* shadow of her black clothing beneath the surface of the water.

He slowly ventured into the pond. The bottom was deep, soft clay, he sank in, and the water clasped dead cold round his legs. As he stirred he could smell the cold, rotten clay that fouled up into the water. It was objectionable in his lungs. Still, repelled and yet not heeding, he moved deeper into the pond. The cold water rose over his thighs, *295* over his loins, upon his abdomen. The lower part of his body was all sunk in the hideous cold element. And the bottom was so deeply soft and uncertain he was afraid of pitching with his mouth underneath. He could not swim, and was afraid.

He crouched a little, spreading his hands under the water and moving them round, trying to feel for her. The dead cold pond swayed upon his chest. He moved again, a *300* little deeper, and again, with his hands underneath, he felt all around under the water. And he touched her clothing. But it evaded his fingers. He made a desperate effort to grasp it.

And so doing he lost his balance and went under, horribly, suffocating in the foul earthy water, struggling madly for a few moments. At last, after what seemed an *305* eternity, he got his footing, rose again into the air and looked around. He gasped, and knew he was in the world. Then he looked at the water. She had risen near him. He grasped her clothing, and drawing her nearer, turned to take his way to land again.

He went very slowly, carefully, absorbed in the slow progress. He rose higher, climbing out of the pond. The water was now only about his legs; he was thankful, full *310* of relief to be out of the clutches of the pond. He lifted her and staggered on to the bank, out of the horror of wet, grey clay.

He laid her down on the bank. She was quite unconscious and running with water. He made the water come from her mouth, he worked to restore her. He did not have to work very long before he could feel the breathing begin again in her; she was breathing 315 naturally. He worked a little longer. He could feel her live beneath his hands; she was coming back. He wiped her face, wrapped her in his overcoat, looked round into the dim, dark grey world, then lifted her and staggered down the bank and across the fields.

It seemed an unthinkably long way, and his burden so heavy he felt he would never get to the house. But at last he was in the stable-yard, and then in the house-yard. He 320 opened the door and went into the house. In the kitchen he laid her down on the hearthrug, and called. The house was empty. But the fire was burning in the grate.

Then again he kneeled to attend to her. She was breathing regularly, her eyes were wide open and as if conscious, but there seemed something missing in her look. She was conscious in herself, but unconscious of her surroundings. 325

He ran upstairs, took blankets from a bed, and put them before the fire to warm. Then he removed her saturated, earthy-smelling clothing, rubbed her dry with a towel, and wrapped her naked in the blankets. Then he went into the dining-room, to look for spirits. There was a little whisky. He drank a gulp himself, and put some into her mouth.

The effect was instantaneous. She looked full into his face, as if she had been 330 seeing him for some time, and yet had only just become conscious of him.

"Dr. Fergusson?" she said.

"What?" he answered.

He was divesting himself of his coat, intending to find some dry clothing upstairs. He could not bear the smell of the dead, clayey water, and he was mortally afraid for his 335 own health.

"What did I do?" she asked.

"Walked into the pond," he replied. He had begun to shudder like one sick, and could hardly attend to her. Her eyes remained full on him, he seemed to be going dark in his mind, looking back at her helplessly. The shuddering became quieter in him, his life 340 came back in him, dark and unknowing, but strong again.

"Was I out of my mind?" she asked, while her eyes were fixed on him all the time.

"Maybe, for the moment," he replied. He felt quiet, because his strength had come back. The strange fretful strain had left him.

"Am I out of my mind now?" she asked. 345

"Are you?" he reflected a moment. "No," he answered truthfully, "I don't see that you are." He turned his face aside. He was afraid now, because he felt dazed, and felt dimly that her power was stronger than his, in this issue. And she continued to look at him fixedly all the time. "Can you tell me where I shall find some dry things to put on?" he asked. 350

"Did you dive into the pond for me?" she asked.

"No," he answered. "I walked in. But I went in overhead as well."

There was silence for a moment. He hesitated. He very much wanted to go upstairs to get into dry clothing. But there was another desire in him. And she seemed to hold him. His will seemed to have gone to sleep, and left him, standing there slack before 355 her. But he felt warm inside himself. He did not shudder at all, though his clothes were sodden on him.

"Why did you?" she asked.

"Because I didn't want you to do such a foolish thing," he said.

"It wasn't foolish," she said, still gazing at him as she lay on the floor, with a sofa 360 cushion under her head. "It was the right thing to do. *I* knew best, then."

"I'll go and shift these wet things," he said. But still he had not the power to move out of her presence, until she sent him. It was as if she had the life of his body in her hands, and he could not extricate himself. Or perhaps he did not want to.

Suddenly she sat up. Then she became aware of her own immediate condition. She 365 felt the blankets about her, she knew her own limbs. For a moment it seemed as if her reason were going. She looked round, with wild eye, as if seeking something. He stood still with fear. She saw her clothing lying scattered.

"Who undressed me?" she asked, her eyes resting full and inevitable on his face.

"I did," he replied, "to bring you round." 370

For some moments she sat and gazed at him awfully, her lips parted.

"Do you love me, then?" she asked.

He only stood and stared at her, fascinated. His soul seemed to melt.

She shuffled forward on her knees, and put her arms round him, round his legs, as he stood there, pressing her breasts against his knees and thighs, clutching him with 375 strange, convulsive certainty, pressing his thighs against her, drawing him to her face, her throat, as she looked up at him with flaring, humble eyes of transfiguration, triumphant in first possession.

"You love me," she murmured, in strange transport, yearning and triumphant and confident. "You love me. I know you love me, I know." 380

And she was passionately kissing his knees, through the wet clothing, passionately and indiscriminately kissing his knees, his legs, as if unaware of everything.

He looked down at the tangled wet hair, the wild, bare, animal shoulders. He was amazed, bewildered, and afraid. He had never thought of loving her. He had never wanted to love her. When he rescued her and restored her, he was a doctor, and she was 385 a patient. He had no single personal thought of her. Nay, this introduction of the personal element was very distasteful to him, a violation of his professional honour. It was horrible to have her there embracing his knees. It was horrible. He revolted from it, violently. And yet — and yet — he had not the power to break away.

She looked at him again, with the same supplication of powerful love, and that 390 same transcendent, frightening light of triumph. In view of the delicate flame which seemed to come from her face like a light, he was powerless. And yet he had never intended to love her. He had never intended. And something stubborn in him could not give way.

"You love me," she repeated, in a murmur of deep, rhapsodic assurance. "You love 395 me."

Her hands were drawing him, drawing him down to her. He was afraid, even a little horrified. For he had, really, no intention of loving her. Yet her hands were drawing him towards her. He put out his hand quickly to steady himself, and grasped her bare shoulder. A flame seemed to burn the hand that grasped her soft shoulder. He had no 400 intention of loving her: his whole will was against his yielding. It was horrible. And yet wonderful was the touch of her shoulders, beautiful the shining of her face. Was she perhaps mad? He had a horror of yielding to her. Yet something in him ached also.

He had been staring away at the door, away from her. But his hand remained on her shoulder. She had gone suddenly very still. He looked down at her. Her eyes were now *405* wide with fear, with doubt, the light was dying from her face, a shadow of terrible greyness was returning. He could not bear the touch of her eyes' question upon him, and the look of death behind the question.

With an inward groan he gave way, and let his heart yield towards her. A sudden gentle smile came on his face. And her eyes, which never left his face, slowly, slowly *410* filled with tears. He watched the strange water rise in her eyes, like some slow fountain coming up. And his heart seemed to burn and melt away in his breast.

He could not bear to look at her any more. He dropped on his knees and caught her head with his arms and pressed her face against his throat. She was very still. His heart, which seemed to have broken, was burning with a kind of agony in his breast. And he *415* felt her slow, hot tears wetting his throat. But he could not move.

He felt the hot tears wet his neck and the hollows of his neck, and he remained motionless, suspended through one of man's eternities. Only now it had become indispensable to him to have her face pressed close to him; he could never let her go again. He could never let her head go away from the close clutch of his arm. He wanted *420* to remain like that for ever, with his heart hurting him in a pain that was also life to him. Without knowing, he was looking down on her damp, soft brown hair.

Then, as it were suddenly, he smelt the horrid stagnant smell of that water. And at the same moment she drew away from him and looked at him. Her eyes were wistful and unfathomable. He was afraid of them, and he fell to kissing her, not knowing what *425* he was doing. He wanted her eyes not to have that terrible, wistful, unfathomable look.

When she turned her face to him again, a faint delicate flush was glowing, and there was again dawning that terrible shining of joy in her eyes, which really terrified him, and yet which he now wanted to see, because he feared the look of doubt still more.

"You love me?" she said, rather faltering. *430*

"Yes." The word cost him a painful effort. Not because it wasn't true. But because it was too newly true, the *saying* seemed to tear open again his newly-torn heart. And he hardly wanted it to be true, even now.

She lifted her face to him, and he bent forward and kissed her on the mouth, gently, with the one kiss that is an eternal pledge. And as he kissed her his heart strained again *435* in his breast. He never intended to love her. But now it was over. He had crossed over the gulf to her, and all that he had left behind had shrivelled and become void.

After the kiss, her eyes again slowly filled with tears. She sat still, away from him, with her face drooped aside, and her hands folded in her lap. The tears fell very slowly. There was complete silence. He too sat there motionless and silent on the hearthrug. The *440* strange pain of his heart that was broken seemed to consume him. That he should love her? That this was love! That he should be ripped open in this way! Him, a doctor! How they would all jeer if they knew! It was agony to him to think they might know.

In the curious naked pain of the thought he looked again to her. She was sitting there drooped into a muse. He saw a tear fall, and his heart flared hot. He saw for the *445* first time that one of her shoulders was quite uncovered, one arm bare, he could see one of her small breasts; dimly, because it had become almost dark in the room.

"Why are you crying?" he asked, in an altered voice.

She looked up at him, and behind her tears the consciousness of her situation for the first time brought a dark look of shame to her eyes. 450

"I'm not crying, really," she said, watching him half frightened.

He reached his hand, and softly closed it on her bare arm.

"I love you! I love you!" he said in a soft, low vibrating voice, unlike himself.

She shrank, and dropped her head. The soft, penetrating grip of his hand on her arm distressed her. She looked up at him. 455

"I want to go," she said. "I want to go and get you some dry things."

"Why?" he said. "I'm all right."

"But I want to go," she said. "And I want you to change your things."

He released her arm, and she wrapped herself in the blanket, looking at him rather frightened. And still she did not rise. 460

"Kiss me," she said wistfully.

He kissed her, but briefly, half in anger.

Then, after a second, she rose nervously, all mixed up in the blanket. He watched her in her confusion, as she tried to extricate herself and wrap herself up so that she could walk. He watched her relentlessly, as she knew. And as she went, the blanket 465 trailing, and as he saw a glimpse of her feet and her white leg, he tried to remember her as she was when he had wrapped her in the blanket. But then he didn't want to remember, because she had been nothing to him then, and his nature revolted from remembering her as she was when she was nothing to him.

A tumbling, muffled noise from within the dark house startled him. Then he heard 470 her voice: — "There are clothes." He rose and went to the foot of the stairs, and gathered up the garments she had thrown down. Then he came back to the fire, to rub himself down and dress. He grinned at his own appearance when he had finished.

The fire was sinking, so he put on coal. The house was now quite dark, save for the light of a street-lamp that shone in faintly from beyond the holly trees. He lit the gas with 475 matches he found on the mantelpiece. Then he emptied the pockets of his own clothes, and threw all his wet things in a heap into the scullery. After which he gathered up her sodden clothes, gently, and put them in a separate heap on the copper-top in the scullery.

It was six o'clock on the clock. His own watch had stopped. He ought to go back to the surgery. He waited, and still she did not come down. So he went to the foot of the 480 stairs and called:

"I shall have to go."

Almost immediately he heard her coming down. She had on her best dress of black voile, and her hair was tidy, but still damp. She looked at him — and in spite of herself, smiled. 485

"I don't like you in those clothes," she said.

"Do I look a sight?" he answered.

They were shy of one another.

"I'll make you some tea," she said.

"No, I must go." 490

"Must you?" And she looked at him again with the wide, strained, doubtful eyes. And again, from the pain of his breast, he knew how he loved her. He went and bent to kiss her, gently, passionately, with his heart's painful kiss.

"And my hair smells so horrible," she murmured in distraction. "And I'm so awful, I'm so awful! Oh, no, I'm too awful." And she broke into bitter, heart-broken sobbing.   *495*
"You can't want to love me, I'm horrible."

"Don't be silly, don't be silly," he said, trying to comfort her, kissing her, holding her in his arms. "I want you, I want to marry you, we're going to be married, quickly, quickly — tomorrow if I can."

But she only sobbed terribly, and cried: *500*

"I feel awful. I feel awful. I feel I'm horrible to you."

"No, I want you, I want you," was all he answered, blindly, with that terrible intonation which frightened her almost more than her horror lest he should *not* want her.

(1922)

SNAKE

A snake came to my water-trough
On a hot, hot day, and I in pajamas for the heat,
To drink there.

In the deep, strange-scented shade of the great dark carob-tree
I came down the steps with my pitcher   *5*
And must wait, must stand and wait, for there he was at the trough before me.

He reached down from a fissure in the earth-wall in the gloom
And trailed his yellow-brown slackness soft-bellied down, over the edge of the stone trough
And rested his throat upon the stone bottom,
And where the water had dripped from the tap, in a small clearness,   *10*
He sipped with his straight mouth,
Softly drank through his straight gums, into his slack long body,
Silently.

Someone was before me at my water-trough,
And I, like a second comer, waiting.   *15*

He lifted his head from his drinking, as cattle do,
And looked at me vaguely, as drinking cattle do,
And flickered his two-forked tongue from his lips, and mused a moment,
And stooped and drank a little more,
Being earth-brown, earth-golden from the burning bowels of the earth   *20*
On the day of Sicilian July, with Etna smoking.

The voice of my education said to me
He must be killed,
For in Sicily the black, black snakes are innocent, the gold are venomous.

And voices in me said, If you were a man   *25*
You would take a stick and break him now, and finish him off.

But must I confess how I liked him,
How glad I was he had come like a guest in quiet, to drink at my water-trough
And depart peaceful, pacified, and thankless,
Into the burning bowels of this earth?   30

Was it cowardice, that I dared not kill him?
Was it perversity, that I longed to talk to him?
Was it humility, to feel so honoured?
I felt so honoured.

And yet those voices: 35
If you were not afraid, you would kill him!

And truly I was afraid, I was most afraid,
But even so, honoured still more
That he should seek my hospitality
From out the dark door of the secret earth.   40

He drank enough
And lifted his head, dreamily, as one who has drunken,
And flickered his tongue like a forked night on the air, so black,
Seeming to lick his lips,
And looked around like a god, unseeing, into the air,   45
And slowly turned his head,
And slowly, very slowly, as if thrice adream,
Proceeded to draw his slow length curving round
And climb again the broken bank of my wall-face.

And as he put his head into that dreadful hole,   50
And as he slowly drew up, snake-easing his shoulders, and entered farther,
A sort of horror, a sort of protest against his withdrawing into that horrid black hole,
Deliberately going into the blackness, and slowly drawing himself after,
Overcame me now his back was turned.

I looked round, I put down my pitcher,   55
I picked up a clumsy log
And threw it at the water-trough with a clatter.

I think it did not hit him,
But suddenly that part of him that was left behind convulsed in undignified haste,
Writhed like lightning, and was gone   60
Into the black hole, the earth-lipped fissure in the wall-front,
At which, in the intense still noon, I stared with fascination.

And immediately I regretted it.
I thought how paltry, how vulgar, what a mean act!
I despised myself and the voices of my accursed human education.   65

And I thought of the albatross,
And I wished he would come back, my snake.

For he seemed to me again like a king,
Like a king in exile, uncrowned in the underworld,
Now due to be crowned again.   *70*

And so, I missed my chance with one of the lords
Of life.
And I have something to expiate;
A pettiness.

Taormina.
(1923)

DOROTHEA MACKELLAR
Australia, 1885-1968

TWO JAPANESE SONGS
1. The Heart of a Bird

What does the bird-seller know of the heart of a bird?

There was a bird in a cage of gold, a small red bird in a cage of gold.
The sun shone through the bars of the cage, out of the wide heaven.
The depths of the sky were soft and blue, greatly to be longed-for.
The bird sang for desire of the sky, and her feathers shone redder for sorrow: *5*
And many passed in the street below, and they said one to another:
"Ah, that we had hearts as light as a bird's!"

But what does the passer-by know of the heart of a bird?

What does the bird-seller know of the heart of a bird?

"I have given grain for you to eat, and water that you may bathe."   *10*
Shall not this bird be content? is there need to clip her wings?
No, for the cage is very strong, the golden bars are set close.
Yet the real bird has flown away, very far away over the rice-fields.
There is only the shadow-body in the cage.

What does the bird-seller care for the heart of a bird?   *15*

2. A Smoke Song

There is a grey plume of smoke in the horizon,
The smoke of a steamer that has departed over the edge of the world.
There is the smoke of a dying fire in my heart,
The smoke has hurt my eyes, they ache with tears.

(1911)

SNAKE   **66. albatross:** See Coleridge's "The Rime of the Ancient Mariner" (p. 784).

EZRA POUND
U.S.A./England/Italy, 1885-1972

THE RIVER-MERCHANT'S WIFE: A LETTER

While my hair was still cut straight across my forehead
I played about the front gate, pulling flowers.
You came by on bamboo stilts, playing horse,
You walked about my seat, playing with blue plums.
And we went on living in the village of Chokan: 5
Two small people, without dislike or suspicion.

At fourteen I married My Lord you.
I never laughed, being bashful.
Lowering my head, I looked at the wall.
Called to, a thousand times, I never looked back.   10

At fifteen I stopped scowling,
I desired my dust to be mingled with yours
Forever and forever and forever.
Why should I climb the look out?

At sixteen you departed,   15
You went into far Ku-to-yen, by the river of swirling eddies,
And you have been gone five months.
The monkeys make sorrowful noise overhead.

You dragged your feet when you went out.
By the gate now, the moss is grown, the different mosses,
Too deep to clear them away!   21
The leaves fall early this autumn, in wind.
The paired butterflies are already yellow with August
Over the grass in the West garden;
They hurt me. I grow older.   25
If you are coming down through the narrows of the river Kiang,
Please let me know beforehand,
And I will come out to meet you
            As far as Cho-fu-Sa.

                              By Rihaku
                          (1915)

THE GARDEN

En robe de parade.
                    — Samain

Like a skein of loose silk blown against a wall
She walks by the railing of a path in Kensington Gardens,
And she is dying piece-meal
            of a sort of emotional anæmia.

And round about there is a rabble   5
Of the filthy, sturdy, unkillable infants of the very poor.
They shall inherit the earth.

In her is the end of breeding.
Her boredom is exquisite and excessive.
She would like some one to speak to her,   10
And is almost afraid that I
            will commit that indiscretion.

                                        (1916)

COMMISSION

Go, my songs, to the lonely and the unsatisfied,
Go also to the nerve-wracked, go to the enslaved-by-
    convention,
Bear to them my contempt for their oppressors.
Go as a great wave of cool water,
Bear my contempt of oppressors.   5

Speak against unconscious oppression,
Speak against the tyranny of the unimaginative,
Speak against bonds.
Go to the bourgeoise who is dying of her ennuis,
Go to the women in suburbs.   10
Go to the hideously wedded,
Go to them whose failure is concealed,
Go to the unluckily mated,

THE RIVER-MERCHANT'S WIFE   This poem is a translation of the first of "Two Letters from Chang-Kan," by the Chinese poet Li Po (c.705-762); because he based his work on notes by the American sinologist Ernest Fenollosa (1853-1908), which in turn were based on work done by Japanese scholars, Pound uses Japanese terms throughout to refer to China — hence, e.g., Li Po becomes "Rihaku" and Chang-Kan (near Nanking) becomes "Chokan." **16. Ku-to-yen:** an island in the river Kiang. **29. Cho-fu-Sa:** hundreds of kilometres upstream from Nanking.   **THE GARDEN**   Epigraph: "dressed for show," from the poem that prefaces *Au Jardin de l'Infante* (1893), by the French symbolist poet Albert Victor Samain (1858-1900); the opening line reads "Mon âme est une infante en robe de parade." **7:** See Matthew 5:5 (p. 251).

Go to the bought wife,
Go to the woman entailed.   15

Go to those who have delicate lust,
Go to those whose delicate desires are thwarted,
Go like a blight upon the dulness of the world;
Go with your edge against this,
Strengthen the subtle cords,   20
Bring confidence upon the algæ and the tentacles
    of the soul.

Go in a friendly manner,
Go with an open speech.
Be eager to find new evils and new good,
Be against all forms of oppression.   25
Go to those who are thickened with middle age,
To those who have lost their interest.

Go to the adolescent who are smothered in family —
Oh how hideous it is
To see three generations of one house gathered together!
It is like an old tree with shoots,   31
And with some branches rotted and falling.

Go out and defy opinion,
Go against this vegetable bondage of the blood.
Be against all sorts of mortmain.   35

(1916)

IN A STATION OF THE METRO

The apparition of these faces in the crowd;
Petals on a wet, black bough.

(1916)

from *THE CANTOS*

I

And then went down to the ship,
Set keel to breakers, forth on the godly sea, and
We set up mast and sail on that swart ship,
Bore sheep aboard her, and our bodies also
Heavy with weeping, and winds from sternward   5
Bore us out onward with bellying canvas,
Circe's this craft, the trim-coifed goddess.
Then sat we amidships, wind jamming the tiller,
Thus with stretched sail, we went over sea till day's end.
Sun to his slumber, shadows o'er all the ocean,   10
Came we then to the bounds of deepest water,
To the Kimmerian lands, and peopled cities
Covered with close-webbed mist, unpierced ever
With glitter of sun-rays
Nor with stars stretched, nor looking back from heaven
Swartest night stretched over wretched men there.   16
The ocean flowing backward, came we then to the place
Aforesaid by Circe.
Here did they rites, Perimedes and Eurylochus,
And drawing sword from my hip   20
I dug the ell-square pitkin;
Poured we libations unto each the dead,
First mead and then sweet wine, water mixed with
    white flour.
Then prayed I many a prayer to the sickly death's-heads;
As set in Ithaca, sterile bulls of the best   25
For sacrifice, heaping the pyre with goods,
A sheep to Tiresias only, black and a bell-sheep.
Dark blood flowed in the fosse,
Souls out of Erebus, cadaverous dead, of brides

COMMISSION   35. mortmain: literally, "dead hand"; a term used in law to refer to perpetual ownership over property, as by a church.   IN A STATION OF THE METRO   In *Gaudier-Brzeska* (1916), Pound observed: "Three years ago in Paris I got out of a "metro" train at La Concorde, and saw suddenly a beautiful face, and then another and another . . ., and I tried all that day to find words for what this had meant to me. . . . And that evening . . . I found, suddenly, the expression. I do not mean that I found words, but there came an equation . . . not in speech, but in little splotches of colour. . . . I realized quite vividly that if I were a painter . . ., I might found a new school . . . of 'non-representative' painting, a painting that would speak only by arrangements in colour. . . . The 'one image poem' is a form of super-position, that is to say, it is one idea set on top of another. I found it useful in getting out of the impasse in which I had been left by my metro emotion. I wrote a thirty-line poem, and destroyed it. . . . Six months later I made a poem half that length; a year later I made the following hokku-like sentence. . . . In a poem of this sort one is trying to record the precise instant when a thing outward and objective transforms itself, or darts into a thing inward and subjective."   THE CANTOS   Pound wrote 117 cantos over fifty years, and left some of them in fragmentary form; though he never completely explained the structure of the whole, he planned a disjunctive modern epic, what he called a "commedia agnostica" that would examine the sources of contemporary civilization and explain its values and character. Canto I (from the beginning to line 68) is a version of Homer's *Odyssey*, XI; subsequent cantos deal with European history, Confucianism, myth, "men of action" (including various American presidents and Benito Mussolini), and his own incarceration in a prison camp in the 1940s. **3. We:** Odysseus and his crew, who are leaving Circe's enchanted island, Aeaea, after having spent a year there, in order to seek Tiresias's advice about how to return to their homeland, Ithaca. **7. Circe:** a sorceress. **12. Kimmerian lands:** ostensibly the edge of the world, where the Cimmerians lived, perpetually shrouded in gloomy mist (see *Odyssey*, XI, 14-19). **19. Perimedes, Eurylochus:** two of Odysseus's crew. **21. pitkin:** little pit (Pound's coinage); **ell:** "arm's length," roughly 1.1 metres or 45". **27. Tiresias:** blind Theban prophet; **bell-sheep:** the leader of the herd. **28. fosse:** ditch. **29. Erebus:** Hades, darkness.

Of youths and of the old who had borne much;   30
Souls stained with recent tears, girls tender,
Men many, mauled with bronze lance heads,
Battle spoil, bearing yet dreory arms,
These many crowded about me; with shouting,
Pallor upon me, cried to my men for more beasts;   35
Slaughtered the herds, sheep slain of bronze;
Poured ointment, cried to the gods,
To Pluto the strong, and praised Proserpine;
Unsheathed the narrow sword,
I sat to keep off the impetuous impotent dead,   40
Till I should hear Tiresias.
But first Elpenor came, our friend Elpenor,
Unburied, cast on the wide earth,
Limbs that we left in the house of Circe,
Unwept, unwrapped in sepulchre, since toils urged other.
Pitiful spirit. And I cried in hurried speech: 46
"Elpenor, how art thou come to this dark coast?
"Cam'st thou afoot, outstripping seamen?"
        And he in heavy speech:
"Ill fate and abundant wine. I slept in Circe's ingle.   50
"Going down the long ladder unguarded,
"I fell against the buttress,
"Shattered the nape-nerve, the soul sought Avernus.
"But thou, O King, I bid remember me, unwept, unburied,

"Heap up mine arms, be tomb by sea-bord, and inscribed:
"*A man of no fortune, and with a name to come.*   56
"And set my oar up, that I swung mid fellows."

And Anticlea came, whom I beat off, and then Tiresias Theban,
Holding his golden wand, knew me, and spoke first:
"A second time? why? man of ill star,   60
"Facing the sunless dead and this joyless region?
"Stand from the fosse, leave me my bloody bever
"For soothsay."
        And I stepped back,
And he strong with the blood, said then: "Odysseus   65
"Shalt return through spiteful Neptune, over dark seas,
"Lose all companions." And then Anticlea came.
Lie quiet Divus. I mean, that is Andreas Divus,
In officina Wecheli, 1538, out of Homer.
And he sailed, by Sirens and thence outward and away   70
And unto Circe.
        Venerandam,
In the Cretan's phrase, with the golden crown, Aphrodite,
Cypri munimenta sortita est, mirthful, oricalchi,
        with golden
Girdles and breast bands, thou with dark eyelids   75
Bearing the golden bough of Argicida. So that:
                                    (1917, 1925)

---

33. dreory: dripping blood (from the Old English *dreorig*). **38. Pluto, Proserpine:** in Roman myth, king and queen of the underworld. **40. to keep off . . . the dead:** Various spirits appear to Odysseus before Tiresias does. **42. Elpenor:** the youngest of Odysseus's crew, who broke his neck in a fall on Aeaea (lines 49-53), and whose soul went directly to Hades because the rest of the crew, who did not find the body, did not perform the necessary burial rituals. **50. ingle:** inglenook, chimney corner. **53. Avernus:** the name of a lake near Naples, beside which is a cave that, according to myth, led to Hades; or, loosely, Hades itself. **56. a name to come:** i.e., in that his fame derives only from being celebrated by the poet/voyager. **58. Anticlea:** Odysseus's mother; Odysseus (as advised by Circe) refuses to allow her to drink the sacrificial blood (line 28) — which would allow her to speak with him — until after Tiresias has done so (lines 62, 65, 67). **59. golden wand:** The golden bough, which grows in Proserpine's artificial underworld garden, is the key to Hades. **60. "A second time":** Pound relies here on Andreas Divus's Latin mistranslation of line 92 of Homer's *Odyssey*, XI, which mistook the Greek word "diogenes" (meaning *noble, sprung from Zeus*) for the word "diogonos" (meaning *twice-born or double*). **62. bever:** drink, beverage. **66. spiteful Neptune:** the Roman god of the sea (equivalent to the Greek Poseidon), who vowed to impede Odysseus's return home because, in an earlier episode in the epic, Odysseus had blinded Neptune's son, the one-eyed giant Polyphemus, who was keeping the crew captive in a cave. **67. lose all:** Tiresias foretells the shipwreck that will end Odysseus's journey home. **68-69. Divus . . . Homer:** The Medieval Latin translation of Homer by Andreas Divus of Justinopolis was published "in officina Wecheli" (i.e., in the workshop of Wechelus) in Paris in 1538. **70. Sirens:** the mermaids who dwelt near Scylla and Charybdis, whose song could lure sailors to their death; in the *Odyssey*, Odysseus returns to Circe before going past the Sirens to Aphrodite, the goddess of love and the mother of Aeneas (line 73). **72. Venerandam:** (Latin) worthy of reverence: the word (associated with Aphrodite) that begins the second Homeric Hymn in the Medieval Latin translation by Georgius Dartona Cretensis ("the Cretan," line 73) that was bound with Pound's copy of Divus's version of the *Odyssey*. **74. Cypri . . . est:** (Latin) she ruled over Cyprus's heights (Dartona's words, referring to Aphrodite — Cyprus being the centre of the cult that worshipped her); **oricalchi:** (Latin) of copper (Cyprium, the Cypriot metal) — alluding to Aphrodite, who is given a gift of copper and gold in the second Homeric Hymn. **75. dark eyelids:** a phrase based on Dartona's mistranslation of the Greek "elikoblephare" (flashing eyes"). **76. the golden bough of Argicida:** This phrase derives from Dartona's mistranslation of the Greek "'Argeiphóntes" (the name given to Hermes, meaning "slayer of Argus") as the Latin "Argicida" (meaning "slayer of the Argi, the Greeks," associating the term with Aphrodite, who sided with the Trojans during the Trojan War); the golden bough, which Aeneas had to find and bring to Proserpine, so that he could descend to Hades (*Aeneid*, VI), is usually associated with the goddess Diana rather than with Aphrodite, but may here be linking Aphrodite with Proserpine.

HD [Hilda Doolittle]
U.S.A., 1886-1961

OREAD

Whirl up, sea —
whirl your pointed pines,
splash your great pines

on our rocks,
hurl your green over us,   5
cover us with your pools of fir.

(1924)

Siegfried Sassoon
England, 1886-1967

A WORKING PARTY

Three hours ago he blundered up the trench,
Sliding and poising, groping with his boots;
Sometimes he tripped and lurched against the walls
With hands that pawed the sodden bags of chalk.
He couldn't see the man who walked in front;   5
Only he heard the drum and rattle of feet
Stepping along barred trench boards, often splashing
Wretchedly where the sludge was ankle-deep.

Voices would grunt "Keep to your right —
        make way!"   9
When squeezing past some men from the front-line:
White faces peered, puffing a point of red;
Candles and braziers glinted through the chinks
And curtain-flaps of dug-outs; then the gloom
Swallowed his sense of sight; he stooped and swore
Because a sagging wire had caught his neck.   15

A flare went up; the shining whiteness spread
And flickered upward, showing nimble rats
And mounds of glimmering sand-bags, bleached
        with rain;
Then the slow silver moment died in dark.
The wind came posting by with chilly gusts   20
And buffeting at corners, piping thin.
And dreary through the crannies; rifle-shots
Would split and crack and sing along the night,

And shells came calmly through the drizzling air
To burst with hollow bang below the hill.   25

Three hours ago he stumbled up the trench;
Now he will never walk that road again:
He must be carried back, a jolting lump
Beyond all need of tenderness and care.

He was a young man with a meagre wife   30
And two small children in a Midland town;
He showed their photographs to all his mates,
And they considered him a decent chap
Who did his work and hadn't much to say,
And always laughed at other people's jokes   35
Because he hadn't any of his own.

That night when he was busy at his job
Of piling bags along the parapet,
He thought how slow time went, stamping his feet
And blowing on his fingers, pinched with cold.   40
He thought of getting back by half-past twelve,
And tot of rum to send him warm to sleep
In draughty dug-out frowsty with the fumes
Of coke, and full of snoring weary men.

He pushed another bag along the top,   45
Craning his body outward; then a flare
Gave one white glimpse of No Man's Land and wire;
And as he dropped his head the instant split
His startled life with lead, and all went out.

(1917)

OREAD **Title:** a mountain nymph.   **A WORKING PARTY** **44. coke:** a form of coal.

BASE DETAILS

If I were fierce, and bald, and short of breath,
   I'd live with scarlet Majors at the Base,
And speed glum heroes up the line to death.
   You'd see me with my puffy petulant face,
Guzzling and gulping in the best hotel,   5

    Reading the Roll of Honour. "Poor young chap,"
I'd say — "I used to know his father well;
    Yes, we've lost heavily in this last scrap."
And when the war is done and youth stone dead,
   I'd toddle safely home and die — in bed.   10

(1917, 1918)

RUPERT BROOKE
England, 1887-1915

PEACE

Now, God be thanked Who has matched us with His hour,
   And caught our youth, and wakened us from sleeping,
With hand made sure, clear eye, and sharpened power,
   To turn, as swimmers into cleanness leaping,
Glad from a world grown old and cold and weary,   5
   Leave the sick hearts that honour could not move,
And half-men, and their dirty songs and dreary,
   And all the little emptiness of love!

Oh! we, who have known shame, we have found release
     there,
   Where there's no ill, no grief, but sleep has mending,
     Naught broken save this body, lost but breath;   *11*
Nothing to shake the laughing heart's long peace there
   But only agony, and that has ending;
    And the worst friend and enemy is but Death.

(1914)

THE SOLDIER

If I should die, think only this of me:
   That there's some corner of a foreign field
That is for ever England. There shall be
   In that rich earth a richer dust concealed;
A dust whom England bore, shaped, made aware,   5
   Gave, once, her flowers to love, her ways to roam,
A body of England's, breathing English air,
   Washed by the rivers, blest by suns of home.

And think, this heart, all evil shed away,
   A pulse in the eternal mind, no less   *10*
    Gives somewhere back the thoughts by England
     given;
Her sights and sounds; dreams happy as her day;
   And laughter, learnt of friends; and gentleness,
    In hearts at peace, under an English heaven.

(1915)

EDITH SITWELL
England, 1887-1964

DIRGE FOR THE NEW SUNRISE

*(Fifteen minutes past eight o'clock, on the morning
of Monday the 6th of August, 1945)*

Bound to my heart as Ixion to the wheel,
Nailed to my heart as the Thief upon the Cross,
I hang between our Christ and the gap where the world was lost

And watch the phantom Sun in Famine Street —
The ghost of the heart of man . . . red Cain   5

PEACE   **1-2. His hour . . . sleeping:** Cf. Matthew 26:39-46.   **DIRGE FOR THE NEW SUNRISE**   **Subtitle:** August 6th, 1945, was the date the atom bomb was dropped on Hiroshima. **1. Ixion:** in Greek legend, a presumptuous king who was punished by the gods by being strapped to a perpetually turning wheel of fire. **2. Thief upon the Cross:** See Matthew 27:38, Mark 15:27. **5. Cain:** See Genesis 4:1-16 (p. 245).

And the more murderous brain
Of Man, still redder Nero that conceived the death
Of his mother Earth, and tore
Her womb, to know the place where he was conceived.

But no eyes grieved —   10
For none were left for tears:
They were blinded as the years
Since Christ was born. Mother or Murderer, you have given or taken life —
Now all is one!

There was a morning when the holy Light   15
Was young. . . . The beautiful First Creature came
To our water-springs, and thought us without blame.

Our hearts seemed safe in our breasts and sang to the Light —
The marrow in the bone
We dreamed was safe . . . the blood in the veins, the sap in the tree   20
Were springs of Deity.

But I saw the little Ant-men as they ran
Carrying the world's weight of the world's filth
And the filth in the heart of Man —
Compressed till those lusts and greeds had a greater heat than that of the Sun.   25

And the ray from that heat came soundless, shook the sky
As if in search for food, and squeezed the stems
Of all that grows on the earth till they were dry —
And drank the marrow of the bone:
The eyes that saw, the lips that kissed, are gone —   30
Or black as thunder lie and grin at the murdered Sun.

The living blind and seeing Dead together lie
As if in love. . . . There was no more hating then,
And no more love: Gone is the heart of Man.

(1947, 1948)

MARIANNE MOORE
U.S.A., 1887-1972

THE FISH

wade   an
through black jade.   injured fan.
  Of the crow-blue mussel shells, one keeps   The barnacles which encrust the side
  adjusting the ash heaps;   of the wave, cannot hide
    opening and shutting itself like   5   there for the submerged shafts of the   10

---

7. **Nero:** (A.D. 37-68), 1st century Roman emperor.

sun,
split like spun
  glass, move themselves with spotlight swiftness
  into the crevices —
    in and out, illuminating   *15*

the
turquoise sea
  of bodies. The water drives a wedge
  of iron through the iron edge
    of the cliff; whereupon the stars,   *20*

pink
rice-grains, ink-
  bespattered jellyfish, crabs like green
  lilies, and submarine
    toadstools, slide each on the other.   *25*

All
external
  marks of abuse are present on this
  defiant edifice —
    all the physical features of   *30*

ac-
cident — lack
  of cornice, dynamite grooves, burns, and
  hatchet strokes, these things stand
    out on it; the chasm side is   *35*

dead.
Repeated
  evidence has proved that it can live
  on what can not revive
    its youth. The sea grows old in it.   *40*

(1935)

POETRY

I, too, dislike it: there are things that are important beyond all this fiddle.
  Reading it, however, with a perfect contempt for it, one discovers in
  it after all, a place for the genuine.
    Hands that can grasp, eyes
    that can dilate, hair that can rise   *5*
      if it must, these things are important not because a

high-sounding interpretation can be put upon them but because they are
  useful. When they become so derivative as to become unintelligible,
  the same thing may be said for all of us, that we
    do not admire what   *10*
    we cannot understand: the bat
      holding on upside down or in quest of something to

eat, elephants pushing, a wild horse taking a roll, a tireless wolf under
  a tree, the immovable critic twitching his skin like a horse that feels a flea, the baseball fan, the statistician —   *15*
    nor is it valid
      to discriminate against "business documents and

school-books"; all these phenomena are important. One must make a distinction
  however: when dragged into prominence by half poets, the result is not poetry,
  nor till the poets among us can be   *20*
    "literalists of
    the imagination" — above
      insolence and triviality and can present

POETRY   A 1967 version of this poem reduced it to three lines: the first clause of line 1 together with lines 2 and 3; Moore's note at the time read: "Omissions are not accidents." **17-18. business . . . school-books:** Moore's notes quote the *Diary of Tolstoy,* p. 84: "Poetry is verse: prose is not verse. Or the poetry is everything with the exception of business documents and school books." **21-22. literalists of the imagination:** Moore's notes

for inspection, "imaginary gardens with real toads in them," shall we have
  it. In the meantime, if you demand on the one hand,   *25*
  the raw material of poetry in
    all its rawness and
    that which is on the other hand
      genuine, you are interested in poetry.

(1935)

KATHERINE MANSFIELD
New Zealand/England, 1888-1923

THE DOLL'S HOUSE

When dear old Mrs Hay went back to town after staying with the Burnells she sent the children a doll's house. It was so big that the carter and Pat carried it into the courtyard, and there it stayed, propped up on two wooden boxes beside the feed-room door. No harm could come to it; it was summer. And perhaps the smell of paint would have gone off by the time it had to be taken in. For, really, the smell of paint coming from that *5* doll's house ("Sweet of old Mrs Hay, of course; most sweet and generous!") — but the smell of paint was quite enough to make anyone seriously ill, in Aunt Beryl's opinion. Even before the sacking was taken off. And when it was. . . .

There stood the doll's house, a dark, oily, spinach green, picked out with bright yellow. Its two solid little chimneys, glued on to the roof, were painted red and white, and *10* the door, gleaming with yellow varnish, was like a little slab of toffee. Four windows, real windows, were divided into panes by a broad streak of green. There was actually a tiny porch, too, painted yellow, with big lumps of congealed paint hanging along the edge.

But perfect, perfect little house! Who could possibly mind the smell? It was part of the joy, part of the newness. *15*

"Open it quickly, someone!"

The hook at the side was stuck fast. Pat prised it open with his penknife, and the whole house-front swung back, and — there you were, gazing at one and the same moment into the drawing-room and dining-room, the kitchen and two bedrooms. That is the way for a house to open! Why don't all houses open like that? How much more exciting than peering through *20* the slit of a door into a mean little hall with a hatstand and two umbrellas! That is — isn't it? — what you long to know about a house when you put your hand on the knocker. Perhaps it is the way God opens houses at dead of night when He is taking a quiet turn with an angel. . . .

"O-oh!" The Burnell children sounded as though they were in despair. It was too marvellous; it was too much for them. They had never seen anything like it in their *25* lives. All the rooms were papered. There were pictures on the walls, painted on the paper, with gold frames complete. Red carpet covered all the floors except the kitchen;

---

quote from W.B. Yeats's comments on "William Blake and His Illustrations" in *Ideas of Good and Evil* (1903): "The limitation of his view was from the very intensity of his vision; he was a too literal realist of imagination, as others are of nature; and because he believed that the figures seen by the mind's eye, when exalted by inspiration, were 'eternal existences,' symbols of divine essences, he hated every grace of style that might obscure their lineaments."

red plush chairs in the drawing-room, green in the dining-room; tables, beds with real
bedclothes, a cradle, a stove, a dresser with tiny plates and one big jug. But what Kezia
liked more than anything, what she liked frightfully, was the lamp. It stood in the middle   *30*
of the dining-room table, an exquisite little amber lamp with a white globe. It was even
filled all ready for lighting, though of course you couldn't light it. But there was
something inside that looked like oil and that moved when you shook it.

The father and mother dolls, who sprawled very stiff as though they had fainted in
the drawing-room, and their two little children asleep upstairs, were really too big for   *35*
the doll's house. They didn't look as though they belonged. But the lamp was perfect. It
seemed to smile at Kezia, to say, "I live here." The lamp was real.

The Burnell children could hardly walk to school fast enough the next morning.
They burned to tell everybody, to describe, too — well — to boast about their doll's
house before the school-bell rang.   *40*

"I'm to tell," said Isabel, "because I'm the eldest. And you two can join in after.
But I'm to tell first."

There was nothing to answer. Isabel was bossy, but she was always right, and Lottie
and Kezia knew too well the powers that went with being eldest. They brushed through
the thick buttercups at the road edge and said nothing.   *45*

"And I'm to choose who's to come and see it first. Mother said I might."

For it had been arranged that while the doll's house stood in the courtyard they
might ask the girls at school, two at a time, to come and look. Not to stay to tea, of
course, or to come traipsing through the house. But just to stand quietly in the courtyard
while Isabel pointed out the beauties, and Lottie and Kezia looked pleased. . . .   *50*

But hurry as they might, by the time they had reached the tarred palings of the
boys' playground the bell had begun to jangle. They only just had time to whip off their
hats and fall into line before the roll was called. Never mind. Isabel tried to make up for
it by looking very important and mysterious and by whispering behind her hand to the
girls near her, "Got something to tell you at playtime."   *55*

Playtime came and Isabel was surrounded. The girls of her class nearly fought to
put their arms round her, to walk away with her, to beam flatteringly, to be her special
friend. She held quite a court under the huge pine trees at the side of the playground.
Nudging, giggling together, the little girls pressed up close. And the only two who
stayed outside the ring were the two who were always outside, the little Kelveys. They   *60*
knew better than to come anywhere near the Burnells.

For the fact was, the school the Burnell children went to was not at all the kind of place
their parents would have chosen if there had been any choice. But there was none. It was
the only school for miles. And the consequence was all the children of the neighbourhood,
the Judge's little girls, the doctor's daughters, the store-keeper's children, the milkman's,   *65*
were forced to mix together. Not to speak of there being an equal number of rude, rough
little boys as well. But the line had to be drawn somewhere. It was drawn at the Kelveys.
Many of the children, including the Burnells, were not allowed even to speak to them. They
walked past the Kelveys with their heads in the air, and as they set the fashion in all matters
of behaviour, the Kelveys were shunned by everybody. Even the teacher had a special voice   *70*
for them, and a special smile for the other children when Lil Kelvey came up to her desk
with a bunch of dreadfully common-looking flowers.

They were the daughters of a spry, hard-working little washerwoman, who went about from house to house by the day. This was awful enough. But where was Mr Kelvey? Nobody knew for certain. But everybody said he was in prison. So they were the daughters of a washerwoman and a jailbird. Very nice company for other people's children! And they looked it. Why Mrs Kelvey made them so conspicuous was hard to understand. The truth was they were dressed in "bits" given to her by the people for whom she worked. Lil, for instance, who was a stout, plain child, with big freckles, came to school in a dress made from a green art-serge table-cloth of the Burnells', with red plush sleeves from the Logans' curtains. Her hat, perched on top of her high forehead, was a grown-up woman's hat, once the property of Miss Lecky, the postmistress. It was turned up at the back and trimmed with a large scarlet quill. What a little guy she looked! It was impossible not to laugh. And her little sister, our Else, wore a long white dress, rather like a nightgown, and a pair of little boy's boots. But whatever our Else wore she would have looked strange. She was a tiny wishbone of a child, with cropped hair and enormous solemn eyes — a little white owl. Nobody had ever seen her smile; she scarcely ever spoke. She went through life holding on to Lil, with a piece of Lil's skirt screwed up in her hand. Where Lil went, our Else followed. In the playground, on the road going to and from school, there was Lil marching in front and our Else holding on behind. Only when she wanted anything, or when she was out of breath, our Else gave Lil a tug, a twitch, and Lil stopped and turned round. The Kelveys never failed to understand each other.

Now they hovered at the edge; you couldn't stop them listening. When the little girls turned round and sneered, Lil, as usual, gave her silly shamefaced smile, but our Else only looked.

And Isabel's voice, so very proud, went on telling. The carpet made a great sensation, but so did the beds with real bedclothes, and the stove with an oven door.

When she finished Kezia broke in. "You've forgotten the lamp, Isabel."

"Oh, yes," said Isabel, "and there's a teeny little lamp, all made of yellow glass, with a white globe that stands on the dining-room table. You couldn't tell it from a real one."

"The lamp's best of all," cried Kezia. She thought Isabel wasn't making half enough of the little lamp. But nobody paid any attention. Isabel was choosing the two who were to come back with them that afternoon and see it. She chose Emmie Cole and Lena Logan. But when the others knew they were all to have a chance, they couldn't be nice enough to Isabel. One by one they put their arms round Isabel's waist and walked her off. They had something to whisper to her, a secret. "Isabel's *my* friend."

Only the little Kelveys moved away forgotten; there was nothing more for them to hear.

Days passed, and as more children saw the doll's house, the fame of it spread. It became the one subject, the rage. The one question was, "Have you seen Burnells' doll's house? Oh, ain't it lovely!" "Haven't you seen it? Oh, I say!"

Even the dinner hour was given up to talking about it. The little girls sat under the pines eating their thick mutton sandwiches and big slabs of johnny cake spread with butter. While always, as near as they could get, sat the Kelveys, our Else holding on to Lil, listening too, while they chewed their jam sandwiches out of a newspaper soaked with large red blobs. . . .

THE DOLL'S HOUSE **83. guy:** grotesque figure.

"Mother," said Kezia, "can't I ask the Kelveys just once?"

"Certainly not, Kezia."

"But why not?"

"Run away, Kezia; you know quite well why not."

At last everybody had seen it except them. On that day the subject rather flagged. It *120* was the dinner hour. The children stood together under the pine trees, and suddenly, as they looked at the Kelveys eating out of their paper, always by themselves, always listening, they wanted to be horrid to them. Emmie Cole started the whisper.

"Lil Kelvey's going to be a servant when she grows up."

"O-oh, how awful!" said Isabel Burnell, and she made eyes at Emmie. *125*

Emmie swallowed in a very meaning way and nodded to Isabel as she'd seen her mother do on those occasions.

"It's true — it's true — it's true," she said.

Then Lena Logan's little eyes snapped. "Shall I ask her?" she whispered.

"Bet you don't," said Jessie May. *130*

"Pooh, I'm not frightened," said Lena. Suddenly she gave a little squeal and danced in front of the other girls. "Watch! Watch me! Watch me now!" said Lena. And sliding, gliding, dragging one foot, giggling behind her hand, Lena went over to the Kelveys.

Lil looked up from her dinner. She wrapped the rest quickly away. Our Else stopped chewing. What was coming now? *135*

"Is it true you're going to be a servant when you grow up, Lil Kelvey?" shrilled Lena.

Dead silence. But instead of answering, Lil only gave her silly shamefaced smile. She didn't seem to mind the question at all. What a sell for Lena! The girls began to titter.

Lena couldn't stand that. She put her hands on her hips; she shot forward. "Yah, yer father's in prison!" she hissed, spitefully. *140*

This was such a marvellous thing to have said that the little girls rushed away in a body, deeply, deeply excited, wild with joy. Someone found a long rope, and they began skipping. And never did they skip so high, run in and out so fast, or do such daring things as on that morning.

In the afternoon Pat called for the Burnell children with the buggy and they drove *145* home. There were visitors. Isabel and Lottie, who liked visitors, went upstairs to change their pinafores. But Kezia thieved out at the back. Nobody was about; she began to swing on the big white gates of the courtyard. Presently, looking along the road, she saw two little dots. They grew bigger, they were coming towards her. Now she could see that one was in front and one close behind. Now she could see that they were the Kelveys. *150* Kezia stopped swinging. She slipped off the gate as if she was going to run away. Then she hesitated. The Kelveys came nearer, and beside them walked their shadows, very long, stretching right across the road with their heads in the buttercups. Kezia clambered back on the gate; she had made up her mind; she swung out.

"Hullo," she said to the passing Kelveys. *155*

They were so astounded that they stopped. Lil gave her silly smile. Our Else stared.

"You can come and see our doll's house if you want to," said Kezia, and she dragged one toe on the ground. But at that Lil turned red and shook her head quickly.

"Why not?" asked Kezia.

Lil gasped, then she said, "Your ma told our ma you wasn't to speak to us." 160

"Oh, well," said Kezia. She didn't know what to reply. "It doesn't matter. You can come and see our doll's house all the same. Come on. Nobody's looking."

But Lil shook her head still harder.

"Don't you want to?" asked Kezia.

Suddenly there was a twitch, a tug at Lil's skirt. She turned round. Our Else was 165 looking at her with big imploring eyes; she was frowning; she wanted to go. For a moment Lil looked at our Else very doubtfully. But then our Else twitched her skirt again. She started forward. Kezia led the way. Like two little stray cats they followed across the courtyard to where the doll's house stood.

"There it is," said Kezia. 170

There was a pause. Lil breathed loudly, almost snorted; our Else was still as a stone.

"I'll open it for you," said Kezia kindly. She undid the hook and they looked inside. "There's the drawing-room and the dining-room, and that's the —"

"Kezia!"

Oh, what a start they gave! 175

"Kezia!"

It was Aunt Beryl's voice. They turned round. At the back door stood Aunt Beryl, staring as if she couldn't believe what she saw.

"How dare you ask the little Kelveys into the courtyard?" said her cold, furious voice. "You know as well as I do you're not allowed to talk to them. Run away, 180 children, run away at once. And don't come back again," said Aunt Beryl. And she stepped into the yard and shooed them out as if they were chickens.

"Off you go immediately!" she called, cold and proud.

They did not need telling twice. Burning with shame, shrinking together, Lil huddling along like her mother, our Else dazed, somehow they crossed the big courtyard 185 and squeezed through the white gate.

"Wicked, disobedient little girl!" said Aunt Beryl bitterly to Kezia, and she slammed the doll's house to.

The afternoon had been awful. A letter had come from Willie Brent, a terrifying, threatening letter, saying if she did not meet him that evening in Pulman's Bush, he'd 190 come to the front door and ask the reason why! But now that she had frightened those little rats of Kelveys and given Kezia a good scolding, her heart felt lighter. That ghastly pressure was gone. She went back to the house humming.

When the Kelveys were well out of sight of Burnells', they sat down to rest on a big red drainpipe by the side of the road. Lil's cheeks were still burning; she took off the hat 195 with the quill and held it on her knee. Dreamily they looked over the hay paddocks, past the creek, to the group of wattles where Logans' cows stood waiting to be milked. What were their thoughts?

Presently our Else nudged up close to her sister. By now she had forgotten the cross lady. She put out a finger and stroked her sister's quill; she smiled her rare smile. 200

"I seen the little lamp," she said, softly.

Then both were silent once more.

(1922)

---

196. **paddocks:** fields.

T.S. ELIOT
U.S.A./England, 1888-1965

THE LOVE SONG OF J. ALFRED PRUFROCK

S'io credesse che mia risposta fosse
A persona che mai tornasse al mondo,
Questa fiamma staria senza piu scosse.
Ma perciocche giammai di questo fondo
Non torno vivo alcun, s'i'odo il vero,
Senza tema d'infamia ti rispondo.

Let us go then, you and I,
When the evening is spread out against the sky
Like a patient etherised upon a table;
Let us go, through certain half-deserted streets,
The muttering retreats   5
Of restless nights in one-night cheap hotels
And sawdust restaurants with oyster-shells:
Streets that follow like a tedious argument
Of insidious intent
To lead you to an overwhelming question . . .   10
Oh, do not ask, "What is it?"
Let us go and make our visit.

   In the room the women come and go
Talking of Michelangelo.

   The yellow fog that rubs its back upon the window-panes,   15
The yellow smoke that rubs its muzzle on the window-panes
Licked its tongue into the corners of the evening,
Lingered upon the pools that stand in drains,
Let fall upon its back the soot that falls from chimneys,
Slipped by the terrace, made a sudden leap,   20
And seeing that it was a soft October night,
Curled once about the house, and fell asleep.

   And indeed there will be time
For the yellow smoke that slides along the street,
Rubbing its back upon the window-panes;   25

THE LOVE SONG OF J. ALFRED PRUFROCK   **Epigraph:** lines 61-66 of Dante's *Inferno*, Canto XXVII (see note to line 137 of "Tradition . . ." below); in the eighth circle of Hell, among the Counsellors of Fraud, the spirit of Guido da Montefeltro, in the form of a flame, responds to Dante's request for his story, unaware that Dante is not one of the damned: "If I believed that my reply was made to a person that would ever return to the world, this flame would stay without more shaking. But because no one has ever returned alive from this abyss, if I hear the truth, without fear of infamy I respond to you." **14. Michelangelo:** Michelangelo Buonarroti (1475-1564), famous Italian sculptor, painter, architect, and poet. **23ff. time:** perhaps echoing "world enough, and time," from line 1 of Marvell's "To His Coy Mistress" (see p. 405).

There will be time, there will be time
To prepare a face to meet the faces that you meet;
There will be time to murder and create,
And time for all the works and days of hands
That lift and drop a question on your plate;   *30*
Time for you and time for me,
And time yet for a hundred indecisions,
And for a hundred visions and revisions,
Before the taking of a toast and tea.

    In the room the women come and go   *35*
Talking of Michelangelo.

    And indeed there will be time
To wonder, "Do I dare?" and, "Do I dare?"
Time to turn back and descend the stair,
With a bald spot in the middle of my hair —   *40*
[They will say: "How his hair is growing thin!"]
My morning coat, my collar mounting firmly to the chin,
My necktie rich and modest, but asserted by a simple pin —
[They will say: "But how his arms and legs are thin!"]
Do I dare   *45*
Disturb the universe?
In a minute there is time
For decisions and revisions which a minute will reverse.

    For I have known them all already, known them all: —
Have known the evenings, mornings, afternoons,   *50*
I have measured out my life with coffee spoons;
I know the voices dying with a dying fall
Beneath the music from a farther room.
    So how should I presume?

    And I have known the eyes already, known them all —   *55*
The eyes that fix you in a formulated phrase,
And when I am formulated, sprawling on a pin,
When I am pinned and wriggling on the wall,
Then how should I begin
To spit out all the butt-ends of my days and ways?   *60*
    And how should I presume?

    And I have known the arms already, known them all —
Arms that are braceleted and white and bare
[But in the lamplight, downed with light brown hair!]
Is it perfume from a dress   *65*

29: *Works and Days* is the conventional English title of a long work on farming and rural life by the 8th-century B.C. Greek poet Hesiod. **52. dying fall:** echoing a phrase in the opening speech of Shakespeare's *Twelfth Night.*

That makes me so digress?
Arms that lie along a table, or wrap about a shawl.
   And should I then presume?
   And how should I begin?

     • • • • •

Shall I say, I have gone at dusk through narrow streets   *70*
And watched the smoke that rises from the pipes
Of lonely men in shirt-sleeves, leaning out of windows? . . .

   I should have been a pair of ragged claws
Scuttling across the floors of silent seas.

     • • • • •

And the afternoon, the evening, sleeps so peacefully!   *75*
Smoothed by long fingers,
Asleep . . . tired . . . or it malingers,
Stretched on the floor, here beside you and me.
Should I, after tea and cakes and ices,
Have the strength to force the moment to its crisis?   *80*
But though I have wept and fasted, wept and prayed,
Though I have seen my head [grown slightly bald] brought in upon a platter,
I am no prophet — and here's no great matter;
I have seen the moment of my greatness flicker,
And I have seen the eternal Footman hold my coat, and snicker,   *85*
And in short, I was afraid.

   And would it have been worth it, after all,
After the cups, the marmalade, the tea,
Among the porcelain, among some talk of you and me,
Would it have been worth while,   *90*
To have bitten off the matter with a smile,
To have squeezed the universe into a ball
To roll it toward some overwhelming question,
To say: "I am Lazarus, come from the dead,
Come back to tell you all, I shall tell you all" —   *95*
If one, settling a pillow by her head,
   Should say: "That is not what I meant at all.
   That is not it, at all."

   And would it have been worth it, after all,
Would it have been worth while,   *100*
After the sunsets and the dooryards and the sprinkled streets,
After the novels, after the teacups, after the skirts that trail along the floor —
And this, and so much more? —
It is impossible to say just what I mean!

82: See Matthew 14:1-12 and Mark 6:17-28 for the story of the death of John the Baptist, whose head was presented to Salome on a platter. **92:** Cf. Marvell's "To His Coy Mistress," lines 41-42. **94:** See John 11:1-45 for the story of the raising of Lazarus.

But as if a magic lantern threw the nerves in patterns on a screen: *105*
Would it have been worth while
If one, settling a pillow or throwing off a shawl,
And turning toward the window, should say:
     "That is not it at all,
     That is not what I meant, at all."   *110*

                    • • • • •

No! I am not Prince Hamlet, nor was meant to be;
Am an attendant lord, one that will do
To swell a progress, start a scene or two,
Advise the prince; no doubt, an easy tool,
Deferential, glad to be of use,   *115*
Politic, cautious, and meticulous;
Full of high sentence, but a bit obtuse;
At times, indeed, almost ridiculous —
Almost, at times, the Fool.

     I grow old . . . I grow old . . .   *120*
I shall wear the bottoms of my trousers rolled.

     Shall I part my hair behind? Do I dare to eat a peach?
I shall wear white flannel trousers, and walk upon the beach.
I have heard the mermaids singing, each to each.

     I do not think that they will sing to me.   *125*

     I have seen them riding seaward on the waves
Combing the white hair of the waves blown back
When the wind blows the water white and black.

     We have lingered in the chambers of the sea
By sea-girls wreathed with seaweed red and brown   *130*
Till human voices wake us, and we drown.

                                        (1915)

TRADITION AND THE INDIVIDUAL TALENT

I

In English writing we seldom speak of tradition, though we occasionally apply its name in deploring its absence. We cannot refer to "the tradition" or to "a tradition"; at most, we employ the adjective in saying that the poetry of So-and-so is "traditional" or even "too traditional." Seldom, perhaps, does the word appear except in a phrase of censure. If otherwise, it is vaguely approbative, with the implication, as to the work approved, of   *5* some pleasing archaeological reconstruction. You can hardly make the word agreeable to English ears without this comfortable reference to the reassuring science of archaeology.

---

111. Hamlet: the title character in Shakespeare's tragedy; lines 112-19 invite comparison with Polonius, another character in *Hamlet*. **113. progress:** formal state journey of a sovereign, accompanied by courtiers etc., through a realm. **117. high sentence:** See line 306 of Chaucer's "General Prologue" (p. 33).

Certainly the word is not likely to appear in our appreciations of living or dead writers. Every nation, every race, has not only its own creative, but its own critical turn of mind; and is even more oblivious of the shortcomings and limitations of its critical habits than of those of its creative genius. We know, or think we know, from the enormous mass of critical writing that has appeared in the French language the critical method or habit of the French; we only conclude (we are such unconscious people) that the French are "more critical" than we, and sometimes even plume ourselves a little with the fact, as if the French were the less spontaneous. Perhaps they are; but we might remind ourselves that criticism is as inevitable as breathing, and that we should be none the worse for articulating what passes in our minds when we read a book and feel an emotion about it, for criticizing our own minds in their work of criticism. One of the facts that might come to light in this process is our tendency to insist, when we praise a poet, upon those aspects of his work in which he least resembles anyone else. In these aspects or parts of his work we pretend to find what is individual, what is the peculiar essence of the man. We dwell with satisfaction upon the poet's difference from his predecessors, especially his immediate predecessors; we endeavour to find something that can be isolated in order to be enjoyed. Whereas if we approach a poet without this prejudice we shall often find that not only the best, but the most individual parts of his work may be those in which the dead poets, his ancestors, assert their immortality most vigorously. And I do not mean the impressionable period of adolescence, but the period of full maturity.

Yet if the only form of tradition, of handing down, consisted in following the ways of the immediate generation before us in a blind or timid adherence to its successes, "tradition" should positively be discouraged. We have seen many such simple currents soon lost in the sand; and novelty is better than repetition. Tradition is a matter of much wider significance. It cannot be inherited, and if you want it you must obtain it by great labour. It involves, in the first place, the historical sense, which we may call nearly indispensable to anyone who would continue to be a poet beyond his twenty-fifth year; and the historical sense involves a perception, not only of the pastness of the past, but of its presence; the historical sense compels a man to write not merely with his own generation in his bones, but with a feeling that the whole of the literature of Europe from Homer and within it the whole of the literature of his own country has a simultaneous existence and composes a simultaneous order. This historical sense, which is a sense of the timeless as well as of the temporal and of the timeless and of the temporal together, is what makes a writer traditional. And it is at the same time what makes a writer most acutely conscious of his place in time, of his own contemporaneity.

No poet, no artist of any art, has his complete meaning alone. His significance, his appreciation is the appreciation of his relation to the dead poets and artists. You cannot value him alone; you must set him, for contrast and comparison, among the dead. I mean this as a principle of aesthetic, not merely historical, criticism. The necessity that he shall conform, that he shall cohere, is not onesided; what happens when a new work of art is created is something that happens simultaneously to all the works of art which preceded it. The existing monuments form an ideal order among themselves, which is modified by the introduction of the new (the really new) work of art among them. The existing order is complete before the new work arrives; for order to persist after the supervention of novelty, the *whole* existing order must be, if ever so slightly, altered; and so the relations, proportions, values of each work of art toward the whole are readjusted; and this is conformity between the old and the new. Whoever has approved   55 this idea of order, of the form of European, of English literature will not find it preposterous that the past should be altered by the present as much as the present is directed by the past. And the poet who is aware of this will be aware of great difficulties and responsibilities.

In a peculiar sense he will be aware also that he must inevitably be judged by the   60 standards of the past. I say judged, not amputated, by them; not judged to be as good as, or worse or better than, the dead; and certainly not judged by the canons of dead critics. It is a judgment, a comparison, in which two things are measured by each other. To conform merely would be for the new work not really to conform at all; it would not be new, and would therefore not be a work of art. And we do not quite say that the new is more valuable   65 because it fits in; but its fitting in is a test of its value — a test, it is true, which can only be slowly and cautiously applied, for we are none of us infallible judges of conformity. We say: it appears to conform, and is perhaps individual, or it appears individual, and may conform; but we are hardly likely to find that it is one and not the other.

To proceed to a more intelligible exposition of the relation of the poet to the past: 70 he can neither take the past as a lump, an indiscriminate bolus, nor can he form himself wholly on one or two private admirations, nor can he form himself wholly upon one preferred period. The first course is inadmissible, the second is an important experience of youth, and the third is a pleasant and highly desirable supplement. The poet must be very conscious of the main current, which does not at all flow invariably through the   75 most distinguished reputations. He must be quite aware of the obvious fact that art never improves, but that the material of art is never quite the same. He must be aware that the mind of Europe — the mind of his own country — a mind which he learns in time to be much more important than his own private mind — is a mind which changes, and that this change is a development which abandons nothing *en route*, which does not   80 superannuate either Shakespeare, or Homer, or the rock drawing of the Magdalenian draughtsmen. That this development, refinement perhaps, complication certainly, is not, from the point of view of the artist, any improvement. Perhaps not even an improvement from the point of view of the psychologist or not to the extent which we imagine; perhaps only in the end based upon a complication in economics and machinery. But the   85 difference between the present and the past is that the conscious present is an awareness of the past in a way and to an extent which the past's awareness of itself cannot show.

Someone said: "The dead writers are remote from us because we *know* so much more than they did." Precisely, and they are that which we know.

I am alive to a usual objection to what is clearly part of my programme for the   90 *métier* of poetry. The objection is that the doctrine requires a ridiculous amount of erudition (pedantry), a claim which can be rejected by appeal to the lives of poets in any pantheon. It will even be affirmed that much learning deadens or perverts poetic sensibility. While, however, we persist in believing that a poet ought to know as much

---

TRADITION AND THE INDIVIDUAL TALENT   **71. bolus:** small round mass or large pill. **81. Magdalenian:** last upper Paleolithic culture, named for La Madeleine, France, near which its artifacts were found.

as will not encroach upon his necessary receptivity and necessary laziness, it is not *95*
desirable to confine knowledge to whatever can be put into a useful shape for
examinations, drawing-rooms, or the still more pretentious modes of publicity. Some
can absorb knowledge, the more tardy must sweat for it. Shakespeare acquired more
essential history from Plutarch than most men could from the whole British Museum.
What is to be insisted upon is that the poet must develop or procure the consciousness of *100*
the past and that he should continue to develop this consciousness throughout his career.

What happens is a continual surrender of himself as he is at the moment to
something which is more valuable. The progress of an artist is a continual self-sacrifice,
a continual extinction of personality.

There remains to define this process of depersonalization and its relation to the *105*
sense of tradition. It is in this depersonalization that art may be said to approach the
condition of science. I therefore invite you to consider, as a suggestive analogy, the
action which takes place when a bit of finely filiated platinum is introduced into a
chamber containing oxygen and sulphur dioxide.

II

Honest criticism and sensitive appreciation is directed not upon the poet but upon the *110*
poetry. If we attend to the confused cries of the newspaper critics and the susurrus of
popular repetition that follows, we shall hear the names of poets in great numbers; if we
seek not Blue-book knowledge but the enjoyment of poetry, and ask for a poem, we
shall seldom find it. I have tried to point out the importance of the relation of the poem
to other poems by other authors, and suggested the conception of poetry as a living *115*
whole of all the poetry that has ever been written. The other aspect of this Impersonal
theory of poetry is the relation of the poem to its author. And I hinted, by an analogy,
that the mind of the mature poet differs from that of the immature one not precisely in
any valuation of "personality," not being necessarily more interesting, or having "more
to say," but rather by being a more finely perfected medium in which special, or very *120*
varied, feelings are at liberty to enter into new combinations.

The analogy was that of the catalyst. When the two gases previously mentioned are
mixed in the presence of a filament of platinum, they form sulphurous acid. This
combination takes place only if the platinum is present; nevertheless the newly formed
acid contains no trace of platinum, and the platinum itself is apparently unaffected: has *125*
remained inert, neutral, and unchanged. The mind of the poet is the shred of platinum. It
may partly or exclusively operate upon the experience of the man himself; but, the more
perfect the artist, the more completely separate in him will be the man who suffers and
the mind which creates; the more perfectly will the mind digest and transmute the
passions which are its material. *130*

The experience, you will notice, the elements which enter the presence of the trans-
forming catalyst, are of two kinds: emotions and feelings. The effect of a work of art
upon the person who enjoys it is an experience different in kind from any experience not
of art. It may be formed out of one emotion, or may be a combination of several; and

---

99. **Plutarch:** (c.46-c.120) Greek biographer of notable statesmen and soldiers. 108. **filiated:** i.e., made thread-like. 111. **susurrus:** whispering or rustling sound, murmur. 113. **Blue-book:** i.e., officially published by the British government. 128. **suffers:** experiences.

various feelings, inhering for the writer in particular words or phrases or images, may be 135
added to compose the final result. Or great poetry may be made without the direct use of
any emotion whatever: composed out of feelings solely. Canto XV of the *Inferno*
(Brunetto Latini) is a working up of the emotion evident in the situation; but the effect,
though single as that of any work of art, is obtained by considerable complexity of
detail. The last quatrain gives an image, a feeling attaching to an image, which "came," 140
which did not develop simply out of what precedes, but which was probably in
suspension in the poet's mind until the proper combination arrived for it to add itself to.
The poet's mind is in fact a receptacle for seizing and storing up numberless feelings,
phrases, images, which remain there until all the particles which can unite to form a new
compound are present together. 145

    If you compare several representative passages of the greatest poetry you see how
great is the variety of types of combination, and also how completely any semi-ethical
criterion of "sublimity" misses the mark. For it is not the "greatness," the intensity, of
the emotions, the components, but the intensity of the artistic process, the pressure, so to
speak, under which the fusion takes place, that counts. The episode of Paolo and 150
Francesca employs a definite emotion, but the intensity of the poetry is something quite
different from whatever intensity in the supposed experience it may give the impression
of. It is no more intense, furthermore, than Canto XXVI, the voyage of Ulysses, which
has not the direct dependence upon an emotion. Great variety is possible in the process
of transmutation of emotion: the murder of Agamemnon, or the agony of Othello, gives 155
an artistic effect apparently closer to a possible original than the scenes from Dante. In
the *Agamemnon*, the artistic emotion approximates to the emotion of an actual spectator;
in *Othello* to the emotion of the protagonist himself. But the difference between art and
the event is always absolute; the combination which is the murder of Agamemnon is
probably as complex as that which is the voyage of Ulysses. In either case there has 160
been a fusion of elements. The ode of Keats contains a number of feelings which have
nothing particular to do with the nightingale, but which the nightingale, partly perhaps
because of its attractive name, and partly because of its reputation, served to bring
together.

    The point of view which I am struggling to attack is perhaps related to the 165
metaphysical theory of the substantial unity of the soul: for my meaning is, that the poet
has, not a "personality" to express, but a particular medium, which is only a medium
and not a personality, in which impressions and experiences combine in peculiar and
unexpected ways. Impressions and experiences which are important for the man may
take no place in the poetry, and those which become important in the poetry may play 170
quite a negligible part in the man, the personality.

    I will quote a passage which is unfamiliar enough to be regarded with fresh
attention in the light — or darkness — of these observations:

---

137. *Inferno:* The first part of the *Commedia* or *Divina Commedia* (*The Divine Comedy,* 1321), by Dante Alighieri (1265-1321). **138. Brunetto Latini:** Dante's admired old teacher, now suffering the torments of the damned (and see note to line 100 of "Little Gidding," below). **148. sublimity:** See *sublime* in Glossary. **150-51. Paolo and Francesca:** in Canto V of the *Inferno;* Dante swoons with pity for the lovers. **153.** The wily Ulysses is suffering among the Counsellors of Fraud; he tells Dante of his final voyage (cf. Tennyson's "Ulysses," p. 961). **155. murder of Agamemnon:** by his wife, Clytemnestra, dramatized in *Agamemnon,* by Aeschylus (525-456 B.C.); **agony of Othello:** in Shakespeare's *Othello.* **161-64: Keats . . . together:** See p. 854.

> *And now methinks I could e' en chide myself*
> *For doating on her beauty, though her death*   *175*
> *Shall be revenged after no common action.*
> *Does the silkworm expend her yellow labours*
> *For thee? For thee does she undo herself?*
> *Are lordships sold to maintain ladyships*
> *For the poor benefit of a bewildering minute?*   *180*
> *Why does yon fellow falsify highways,*
> *And put his life between the judge's lips,*
> *To refine such a thing — keeps horse and men*
> *To beat their valours for her? . . .*

In this passage (as is evident if it is taken in its context) there is a combination of *185* positive and negative emotions: an intensely strong attraction toward beauty and an equally intense fascination by the ugliness which is contrasted with it and which destroys it. This balance of contrasted emotion is in the dramatic situation to which the speech is pertinent, but the situation alone is inadequate to it. This is, so to speak, the structural emotion, provided by the drama. But the whole effect, the dominant tone, is *190* due to the fact that a number of floating feelings, having an affinity to this emotion by no means superficially evident, combined with it to give us a new art emotion.

    It is not in his personal emotions, the emotions provoked by particular events in his life, that the poet is in any way remarkable or interesting. His particular emotions may be simple, or crude, or flat. The emotion in his poetry will be a very complex thing, but *195* not with the complexity of the emotions of people who have very complex or unusual emotions in life. One error, in fact, of eccentricity in poetry is to seek for new human emotions to express; and in this search for novelty in the wrong place it discovers the perverse. The business of the poet is not to find new emotions, but to use the ordinary ones and, in working them up into poetry, to express feelings which are not in actual *200* emotions at all. And emotions which he has never experienced will serve his turn as well as those familiar to him. Consequently, we must believe that "emotion recollected in tranquillity" is an inexact formula. For it is neither emotion, nor recollection, nor, without distortion of meaning, tranquillity. It is a concentration, and a new thing resulting from the concentration, of a very great number of experiences which to the *205* practical and active person would not seem to be experiences at all; it is a concentration which does not happen consciously or of deliberation. These experiences are not "recollected," and they finally unite in an atmosphere which is "tranquil" only in that it is a passive attending upon the event. Of course this is not quite the whole story. There is a great deal, in the writing of poetry, which must be conscious and deliberate. In fact, *210* the bad poet is usually unconscious where he ought to be conscious, and conscious where he ought to be unconscious. Both errors tend to make him "personal." Poetry is not a turning loose of emotion, but an escape from emotion; it is not the expression of personality, but an escape from personality. But, of course, only those who have personality and emotions know what it means to want to escape from these things. *215*

174-84: spoken by Vendice, the principal revenger, in III.iv. of *The Revenger's Tragedy* (1607), probably by Cyril Tourneur (c.1575-1626), though some think it is by Thomas Middleton (1580-1627). **202-03:** See Wordsworth's "Preface" (p. 763).

III

ὁ δὲ νοῦς ἴσως θειότερόν τι καὶ ἀπαθές ἐστιν.

This essay proposes to halt at the frontier of metaphysics or mysticism, and confine itself to such practical conclusions as can be applied by the responsible person interested in poetry. To divert interest from the poet to the poetry is a laudable aim: for it would conduce to a juster estimation of actual poetry, good and bad. There are many people who appreciate the expression of sincere emotion in verse, and there is a smaller number of people who can appreciate technical excellence. But very few know when there is an expression of *significant* emotion, emotion which has its life in the poem and not in the history of the poet. The emotion of art is impersonal. And the poet cannot reach this impersonality without surrendering himself wholly to the work to be done. And he is not likely to know what is to be done unless he lives in what is not merely the present, but the present moment of the past, unless he is conscious, not of what is dead, but of what is already living.

(1919)

220

225

THE HOLLOW MEN

Mistah Kurtz — he dead.

             A penny for the Old Guy

I

We are the hollow men
We are the stuffed men
Leaning together
Headpiece filled with straw. Alas!
Our dried voices, when
We whisper together
Are quiet and meaningless
As wind in dry grass
Or rats' feet over broken glass
In our dry cellar

    Shape without form, shade without colour,
Paralysed force, gesture without motion;

    Those who have crossed
With direct eyes, to death's other Kingdom
Remember us — if at all — not as lost

5

10

15

Violent souls, but only
As the hollow men
The stuffed men.

II

Eyes I dare not meet in dreams
In death's dream kingdom
These do not appear:
There, the eyes are
Sunlight on a broken column
There, is a tree swinging
And voices are
In the wind's singing
More distant and more solemn
Than a fading star.

    Let me be no nearer
In death's dream kingdom
Let me also wear
Such deliberate disguises
Rat's coat, crowskin, crossed staves
In a field

20

25

30

---

216. "The mind is probably more divine and emotionless" — from Aristotle's *De Anima* (Of the Soul).   **THE HOLLOW MEN   Epigraphs. Mistah Kurtz — he dead:** from *Heart of Darkness* (1899, 1902), by Joseph Conrad (see p. 1163) — Kurtz is referred to by Marlow, the narrator, as "hollow at the core"; **A penny for the Old Guy:** said by children collecting money to buy fireworks for Guy Fawkes Day (see Campion's "Bravely decked," p. 232); Fawkes (1570-1606), who was executed for his part in the "gunpowder plot" to blow up the Houses of Parliament, is customarily burnt in effigy as part of the celebration. For section I, cf. Canto III of Dante's *Inferno*, describing the gateway to Hell and the "futile" souls who abide there while others wait to be ferried across the Acheron to Hell (see line 60). The italicized lines in section V echo lines from nursery rhymes and the Lord's Prayer.

Behaving as the wind behaves   35
No nearer —

 Not that final meeting
In the twilight kingdom

III

This is the dead land
This is cactus land   40
Here the stone images
Are raised, here they receive
The supplication of a dead man's hand
Under the twinkle of a fading star.

 Is it like this   45
In death's other kingdom
Waking alone
At the hour when we are
Trembling with tenderness
Lips that would kiss   50
Form prayers to broken stone.

IV

The eyes are not here
There are no eyes here
In this valley of dying stars
In this hollow valley   55
This broken jaw of our lost kingdoms

 In this last of meeting places
We grope together
And avoid speech
Gathered on this beach of the tumid river   60

 Sightless, unless
The eyes reappear
As the perpetual star
Multifoliate rose

Of death's twilight kingdom   65
The hope only
Of empty men.

V

Here we go round the prickly pear
Prickly pear prickly pear
Here we go round the prickly pear   70
At five o'clock in the morning.

 Between the idea
And the reality
Between the motion
And the act   75
Falls the Shadow

     For Thine is the Kingdom

 Between the conception
And the creation
Between the emotion   80
And the response
Falls the Shadow

     Life is very long

 Between the desire
And the spasm   85
Between the potency
And the existence
Between the essence
And the descent
Falls the Shadow   90

     For Thine is the Kingdom

 For Thine is
Life is
For Thine is the

 This is the way the world ends   95
This is the way the world ends
This is the way the world ends
Not with a bang but a whimper.
       (1925)

---

64. Multifoliate rose: suggesting the Celestial Rose in the *Paradiso*, Canto XXX, near the end of Dante's *Commedia*; the rose is also traditionally associated with Christ and the Virgin Mary. **74-76:** Cf. Shakespeare's *Julius Caesar*, II.i.63-65.

from *FOUR QUARTETS*

LITTLE GIDDING

I

Midwinter spring is its own season
Sempiternal though sodden towards sundown,
Suspended in time, between pole and tropic.
When the short day is brightest, with frost and fire,
The brief sun flames the ice, on pond and ditches,   5
In windless cold that is the heart's heat,
Reflecting in a watery mirror
A glare that is blindness in the early afternoon.
And glow more intense than blaze of branch, or brazier,
Stirs the dumb spirit: no wind, but pentecostal fire   10
In the dark time of the year. Between melting and freezing
The soul's sap quivers. There is no earth smell
Or smell of living thing. This is the spring time
But not in time's covenant. Now the hedgerow
Is blanched for an hour with transitory blossom   15
Of snow, a bloom more sudden
Than that of summer, neither budding nor fading,
Not in the scheme of generation.
Where is the summer, the unimaginable
Zero summer?   20

        If you came this way,
Taking the route you would be likely to take
From the place you would be likely to come from,
If you came this way in may time, you would find the hedges
White again, in May, with voluptuary sweetness.   25
It would be the same at the end of the journey,
If you came at night like a broken king,
If you came by day not knowing what you came for,
It would be the same, when you leave the rough road
And turn behind the pig-sty to the dull façade   30
And the tombstone. And what you thought you came for
Is only a shell, a husk of meaning
From which the purpose breaks only when it is fulfilled
If at all. Either you had no purpose
Or the purpose is beyond the end you figured   35

LITTLE GIDDING   The last of the *Four Quartets*, which, though thematically and structurally connected, can be appreciated separately. **Title:** Little Gidding, a village in Cambridgeshire, was originally a religious community founded by Nicholas Ferrar in 1625 and broken up by the Puritans in 1647. **2. sempiternal:** eternal, perpetual. **10. pentecostal fire:** See Acts 2:1-4 (and see line 53 below). **27. broken king:** Charles I, who visited Little Gidding after being defeated at the decisive battle of Naseby in 1645.

And is altered in fulfilment. There are other places
Which also are the world's end, some at the sea jaws,
Or over a dark lake, in a desert or a city —
But this is the nearest, in place and time,
Now and in England.   40

        If you came this way,
Taking any route, starting from anywhere,
At any time or at any season,
It would always be the same: you would have to put off
Sense and notion. You are not here to verify,   45
Instruct yourself, or inform curiosity
Or carry report. You are here to kneel
Where prayer has been valid. And prayer is more
Than an order of words, the conscious occupation
Of the praying mind, or the sound of the voice praying.   50
And what the dead had no speech for, when living,
They can tell you, being dead: the communication
Of the dead is tongued with fire beyond the language of the living.
Here, the intersection of the timeless moment
Is England and nowhere. Never and always.   55

II

Ash on an old man's sleeve
Is all the ash the burnt roses leave.
Dust in the air suspended
Marks the place where a story ended.
Dust inbreathed was a house —   60
The wall, the wainscot and the mouse.
The death of hope and despair,
    This is the death of air.

There are flood and drouth
Over the eyes and in the mouth,   65
Dead water and dead sand
Contending for the upper hand.
The parched eviscerate soil
Gapes at the vanity of toil,
Laughs without mirth.   70
    This is the death of earth.

Water and fire succeed
The town, the pasture and the weed.
Water and fire deride

56ff.: Eliot served as a fire-watcher or air-raid warden during the night-time incendiary bombings of London during World War II. The first three stanzas of section II reflect Heraclitus's theory of universal flux, the four elements always changing, one into another (for Heraclitus, see note to line 300 of Bacon's *Novum Organum* — p. 222).

The sacrifice that we denied. 75
Water and fire shall rot
The marred foundations we forgot,
Of sanctuary and choir.
    This is the death of water and fire.

In the uncertain hour before the morning 80
   Near the ending of interminable night
   At the recurrent end of the unending
After the dark dove with the flickering tongue
   Had passed below the horizon of his homing
   While the dead leaves still rattled on like tin 85
Over the asphalt where no other sound was
   Between three districts whence the smoke arose
   I met one walking, loitering and hurried
As if blown towards me like the metal leaves
   Before the urban dawn wind unresisting. 90
   And as I fixed upon the down-turned face
That pointed scrutiny with which we challenge
   The first-met stranger in the waning dusk
   I caught the sudden look of some dead master
Whom I had known, forgotten, half recalled 95
   Both one and many; in the brown baked features
   The eyes of a familiar compound ghost
Both intimate and unidentifiable.
   So I assumed a double part, and cried
   And heard another's voice cry: "What! are *you* here?" 100
Although we were not. I was still the same,
   Knowing myself yet being someone other —
   And he a face still forming; yet the words sufficed
To compel the recognition they preceded.
   And so, compliant to the common wind, 105
   Too strange to each other for misunderstanding,
In concord at this intersection time
   Of meeting nowhere, no before and after,
   We trod the pavement in a dead patrol.
I said: "The wonder that I feel is easy, 110
   Yet ease is cause of wonder. Therefore speak:
   I may not comprehend, may not remember."
And he: "I am not eager to rehearse
   My thought and theory which you have forgotten.
   These things have served their purpose: let them be. 115

80-151: Eliot intends the form of these lines to suggest Dante's *terza rima* in his *Commedia*. **83:** i.e., the German bomber. **97. compound ghost:** Eliot said he had W.B. Yeats and Jonathan Swift in mind here. **100. What . . . here?:** translating part of line 30 of Canto XV of Dante's *Inferno*, addressed by Dante to Brunetto Latini.

So with your own, and pray they be forgiven
 By others, as I pray you to forgive
 Both bad and good. Last season's fruit is eaten
And the fullfed beast shall kick the empty pail.
 For last year's words belong to last year's language   *120*
 And next year's words await another voice.
But, as the passage now presents no hindrance
 To the spirit unappeased and peregrine
 Between two worlds become much like each other,
So I find words I never thought to speak   *125*
 In streets I never thought I should revisit
 When I left my body on a distant shore.
Since our concern was speech, and speech impelled us
 To purify the dialect of the tribe
 And urge the mind to aftersight and foresight,   *130*
Let me disclose the gifts reserved for age
 To set a crown upon your lifetime's effort.
 First, the cold friction of expiring sense
Without enchantment, offering no promise
 But bitter tastelessness of shadow fruit   *135*
 As body and soul begin to fall asunder.
Second, the conscious impotence of rage
 At human folly, and the laceration
 Of laughter at what ceases to amuse.
And last, the rending pain of re-enactment   *140*
 Of all that you have done, and been; the shame
 Of motives late revealed, and the awareness
Of things ill done and done to others' harm
 Which once you took for exercise of virtue.
 Then fools' approval stings, and honour stains.   *145*
From wrong to wrong the exasperated spirit
 Proceeds, unless restored by that refining fire
 Where you must move in measure, like a dancer."
The day was breaking. In the disfigured street
 He left me, with a kind of valediction,   *150*
 And faded on the blowing of the horn.

III

There are three conditions which often look alike
Yet differ completely, flourish in the same hedgerow:
Attachment to self and to things and to persons, detachment

123-24. peregrine: wandering; cf. Matthew Arnold's 1855 poem "Stanzas from the Grande Chartreuse," 85-86: "Wandering between two worlds, / one dead, / The other powerless to be born." **129:** translating line 6 of "Le Tombeau d'Edgar Poe," by Stéphane Mallarmé (1842-1898): "*Donner un sens plus pur aux mots de la tribu.*" **137-39:** Cf. Yeats's translation of Swift's epitaph (p. 1218). **147. fire:** perhaps thinking of line 17 of Yeats's "Sailing to Byzantium" (p. 1217), or of the third stanza of his "Byzantium." **148. dancer:** an image frequently used by Yeats, e.g. in "Among School Children" and "Byzantium." **151. horn:** i.e., the "all-clear" siren after an air raid; Eliot echoes Marcellus, speaking of the ghost of Hamlet's father: "It faded on the crowing of the cock" (*Hamlet*, I.i.157).

From self and from things and from persons; and, growing between them, indifference   *155*
Which resembles the others as death resembles life,
Being between two lives — unflowering, between
The live and the dead nettle. This is the use of memory:
For liberation — not less of love but expanding
Of love beyond desire, and so liberation   *160*
From the future as well as the past. Thus, love of a country
Begins as attachment to our own field of action
And comes to find that action of little importance
Though never indifferent. History may be servitude,
History may be freedom. See, now they vanish,   *165*
The faces and places, with the self which, as it could, loved them,
To become renewed, transfigured, in another pattern.

Sin is Behovely, but
All shall be well, and
All manner of thing shall be well.   *170*
If I think, again, of this place,
And of people, not wholly commendable,
Of no immediate kin or kindness,
But some of peculiar genius,
All touched by a common genius,   *175*
United in the strife which divided them;
If I think of a king at nightfall,
Of three men, and more, on the scaffold
And a few who died forgotten
In other places, here and abroad,   *180*
And of one who died blind and quiet,
Why should we celebrate
These dead men more than the dying?
It is not to ring the bell backward
Nor is it an incantation   *185*
To summon the spectre of a Rose.
We cannot revive old factions
We cannot restore old policies
Or follow an antique drum.
These men, and those who opposed them   *190*

168-70: from Chapter 27 of Dame Julian of Norwich's *Revelations of Divine Love*: "Sin is behovely, but all shall be well, and all shall be well, and all manner of thing shall be well"; Dame Julian reiterates this idea in several places, but the "all shall be well" lines are especially prominent in Chapter 32 (see p. 74); **behovely:** i.e., an inevitable, even necessary and functional, part of the human condition after the fall (see e.g. Romans 5:20-21; see also *Paradise Lost*, XII, 469-78, and note — p. 370). **177. king:** Charles I, beheaded in 1649, at the end of the English Civil War. **178. three men:** probably referring, among others, to Charles himself and his chief supporters, also executed, Thomas Wentworth, Earl of Strafford (1593-1641), and Archbishop William Laud (1573-1645) — but suggesting also Christ and the two thieves being crucified together (see Matthew 27:33-38). **181:** John Milton (see p. 315), who was in Cromwell's anti-royalist government (see notes to opening of Book VII of *Paradise Lost* — p. 354). **186:** *Le Spectre de la rose* is a Russian ballet (to the music of Carl Maria von Weber's "Invitation to the Dance"); the so-called Wars of the Roses (1455-85), over the crown of England, were fought between the houses of Lancaster (the red rose) and York (the white rose).

And those whom they opposed
Accept the constitution of silence
And are folded in a single party.
Whatever we inherit from the fortunate
We have taken from the defeated   *195*
What they had to leave us — a symbol:
A symbol perfected in death.
And all shall be well and
All manner of thing shall be well
By the purification of the motive   *200*
In the ground of our beseeching.

IV

The dove descending breaks the air
With flame of incandescent terror
Of which the tongues declare
The one discharge from sin and error.   *205*
The only hope, or else despair
   Lies in the choice of pyre or pyre —
   To be redeemed from fire by fire.

Who then devised the torment? Love.
Love is the unfamiliar Name   *210*
Behind the hands that wove
The intolerable shirt of flame
Which human power cannot remove.
   We only live, only suspire
   Consumed by either fire or fire.   *215*

V

What we call the beginning is often the end
And to make an end is to make a beginning.
The end is where we start from. And every phrase
And sentence that is right (where every word is at home,
Taking its place to support the others,   *220*
The word neither diffident nor ostentatious,
An easy commerce of the old and the new,
The common word exact without vulgarity,
The formal word precise but not pedantic,

201: In Dame Julian's *Revelations*, Chapters 41 and 42, "our lord" says "I am the ground of thy beseeching" — i.e., it is "his proper goodness" that invites and answers those who in prayer "meekly ask mercy and grace." **202:** The dove is also the symbol of the Holy Ghost (see line 10 above). **212. shirt of flame:** i.e., that of Nessus, which caused the death of Hercules.

The complete consort dancing together)   *225*
Every phrase and every sentence is an end and a beginning,
Every poem an epitaph. And any action
Is a step to the block, to the fire, down the sea's throat
Or to an illegible stone: and that is where we start.
We die with the dying: *230*
See, they depart, and we go with them.
We are born with the dead:
See, they return, and bring us with them.
The moment of the rose and the moment of the yew-tree
Are of equal duration. A people without history   *235*
Is not redeemed from time, for history is a pattern
Of timeless moments. So, while the light fails
On a winter's afternoon, in a secluded chapel
History is now and England.

With the drawing of this Love and the voice of this Calling   *240*

We shall not cease from exploration
And the end of all our exploring
Will be to arrive where we started
And know the place for the first time.
Through the unknown, remembered gate   *245*
When the last of earth left to discover
Is that which was the beginning;
At the source of the longest river
The voice of the hidden waterfall
And the children in the apple-tree   *250*
Not known, because not looked for
But heard, half-heard, in the stillness
Between two waves of the sea.
Quick now, here, now, always —
A condition of complete simplicity   *255*
(Costing not less than everything)
And all shall be well and
All manner of thing shall be well
When the tongues of flame are in-folded
Into the crowned knot of fire   *260*
And the fire and the rose are one.

(1942)

---

238. chapel: The chapel at Little Gidding was rebuilt in the 19th century. **240:** quoting from *The Cloud of Unknowing*, a 14th-century mystical religious work. **260. crowned knot:** in nautical terminology, a sort of knot at the end of a rope with the strands interwoven ("in-folded") so that it won't come untwisted.

JOHN CROWE RANSOM
U.S.A., 1888-1974

BELLS FOR JOHN WHITESIDE'S DAUGHTER

There was such speed in her little body,
And such lightness in her footfall,
It is no wonder her brown study
Astonishes us all.

Her wars were bruited in our high window.   *5*
We looked among orchard trees and beyond
Where she took arms against her shadow,
Or harried unto the pond

The lazy geese, like a snow cloud
Dripping their snow on the green grass,   *10*

Tricking and stopping, sleepy and proud,
Who cried in goose, Alas,

For the tireless heart within the little
Lady with rod that made them rise
From their noon apple-dreams and scuttle   *15*
Goose-fashion under the skies!

But now go the bells, and we are ready,
In one house we are sternly stopped
To say we are vexed at her brown study,
Lying so primly propped.   *20*

(1924)

EDNA ST. VINCENT MILLAY
U.S.A., 1892-1950

SPRING

To what purpose, April, do you return again?
Beauty is not enough.
You can no longer quiet me with the redness
Of little leaves opening stickily.
I know what I know.   *5*
The sun is hot on my neck as I observe
The spikes of the crocus.
The smell of the earth is good.
It is apparent that there is no death.

But what does that signify?   *10*
Not only under ground are the brains of men
Eaten by maggots.
Life in itself
Is nothing,
An empty cup, a flight of uncarpeted stairs.   *15*
It is not enough that yearly, down this hill,
April
Comes like an idiot, babbling and strewing flowers.

(1921)

AN ANCIENT GESTURE

I thought, as I wiped my eyes on the corner of my apron:
Penelope did this too.
And more than once: you can't keep weaving all day
And undoing it all through the night;

AN ANCIENT GESTURE   **2. Penelope:** wife of Ulysses, in Homer's *Odyssey.*

Your arms get tired, and the back of your neck gets tight;   5
And along towards morning, when you think it will never be light,
And your husband has been gone, and you don't know where, for years,
Suddenly you burst into tears;
There is simply nothing else to do.

And I thought, as I wiped my eyes on the corner of my apron: 10
This is an ancient gesture, authentic, antique,
In the very best tradition, classic, Greek;
Ulysses did this too.
But only as a gesture, — a gesture which implied
To the assembled throng that he was much too moved to speak.   15
He learned it from Penelope . . .
Penelope, who really cried.

(1954)

REBECCA WEST
England, 1892-1983

THE WOMAN AS WORKMATE
Her Claim to Equal Rates of Pay for Equal Quality of Work

Every man likes to think of himself as a kind of Whiteley's — a universal provider. The patriarchal system is the ideal for which he longs. He likes to dream of himself sitting on the verandah after dinner, with his wife beside him and the children in the garden, while his unmarried sisters play duets in the drawing-room and his maiden aunts hand round the coffee. This maintenance of helpless, penniless, subservient womanhood is   5
the nearest he can get in England to the spiritual delights of the harem.

   So when womanhood declares that she is no longer helpless, dislikes being penniless and refuses to be subservient the men become indignant and inarticulate. An example of this was to be seen in Mr George Edgar's recent article, "Why Men Do Not Marry," in the *Daily Dispatch*. Mr Edgar's thesis is difficult to criticise because it consists of two   10
mutually destructive conclusions. He stated, first, that it is absurd for women to ask for equal wages with men because they are inferior workers and have no dependants; and then he vehemently denounces women for ousting men from their work by accepting lower wages. This is the kind of argument one rarely hears except from cross-talk comedians on the halls. What makes it still more elusive is that both his conclusions are incorrect.   15

   Mr Edgar takes the usual masculinist standpoint of regarding women as incompetent weaklings except for their maternal functions which God bestowed on them, and for which, therefore, they deserve no credit.

THE WOMAN AS WORKMATE   **1. Whiteley's:** a chain of shops, begun in 1863 by William Whiteley (1831-1907), a pioneer in "department store" retailing, who called himself the "universal provider." **10. *Daily Dispatch*:** the Manchester newspaper in which West's reply was also printed (on 26 November 1912). **14-15. on the halls:** in the music-halls.

It is not necessary for me to discuss the question whether a woman is the equal of a man in the performance of a day's work. In the past our practice has assumed that   *20* she is not. . . . In actual terms of wages, where in the past women have elected to work in competition with men, commerce has decided that her day's work is less valuable than a man's, and has given her less wages.

This engaging contempt for the value of the women's work is an error which comes of considering only the economic conditions of England since the industrial revolution.   *25* It is as though a Chinese mandarin were to spend a short weekend in Whitechapel and then return to Peking proclaiming that all Englishmen got drunk every night and beat their wives. This degradation of women is simply the accident of a new social order that has not yet righted itself.

Why does a man support his wife? It is not only because the mother needs to be   *30* relieved from the stress of earning her own livelihood. That is a principle that has never been universally adopted even in our own country in our own time: the Lancashire cotton-operative continues to work after she has children. The maintenance of wives is a survival of the time when England was an agricultural country. It was then recognised that the work of women in the home was so valuable that the husband and wife were   *35* regarded as equal partners of a firm, and shared the profits. The wife had then to grind the corn, bake the bread, brew, do all the dairy work and tend much of the livestock, doctor her household, spin the wool and weave the cloth, make her family's clothes and cobble their shoes, and prepare all the food stuffs, such as hams and preserves. And she did it very well indeed. On the rare occasions when she did go out to work beside men   *40* she seems — so far as we can judge from documents such as the paysheets of agricul-tural labourers in the fifteenth century — to have been paid the same wages.

And England went very well then. It was certainly a happier and — many econo-mists agree — a more prosperous country than it is today. Then came the industrial revolution which snatched these occupations out of the women's hands and gave them   *45* to men, leaving women only the dish-washing and floor-scrubbing, which is now regarded as peculiarly feminine work, but which had previously been done mainly by boys. The ugliness and economic embarrassment of England since then ought to cause searchings of heart among masculinists such as Mr Edgar.

So much for Mr Edgar's historical researches. Now for his theory that women have   *50* no dependants. It is true that the wife does not contribute directly to the family income (men having left her no work to do) and that her maintenance and that of her children has to be borne entirely by her husband. But there are the old as well as the young. It is the woman's place to support the old. Many working-class parents will tell one that a daughter is a better investment than a son, for the son marries and keeps a family, while   *55* the daughter will probably remain single so that she can work and provide for her parents. So one cannot advocate the restriction of a woman's wage to the sum sufficient for the support of herself alone, unless one upholds the Tierra del Fuego theory that the aged are useless, dangerous, and ought to be abolished, by exposure if possible, by a club if necessary.   *60*

---

26. Whitechapel: a district in the east end of London. **37. corn:** grain.

Moreover, I grant that men are efficient and godlike, but they sometimes die. They then leave widows and orphans, who have to be supported. And it also happens occasionally that husbands prove more ornamental than useful, "dainty rogues in porcelain," unable to wrestle with the rough world, and then their wives have to work for them and the children.   65

Mr Edgar's fear that if wages were equalised they would tend to drop to the women's level is unsupported by logical proof, and is contradicted by fact. The England of the fifteenth century, which paid its women agricultural labourers as it paid its men, was the paradise of the worker. Never since have they enjoyed similar prosperity. The Lancashire cotton-operatives, who are paid without distinction of sex, are the most well-   70 to-do workers of today. The women are not merely asking for prestige, they are fighting for hard cash. It is not the equality, but the increase in wages they want. Of course, if men insist on women getting lower wages they may create an army of blacklegs to their own undoing.

The second conclusion, that women are ousting men out of the labour world, is a   75 popular and curiously persistent error. In the investigations made twenty years ago by Beatrice and Sidney Webb it was stated that it was very rare for men and women to compete in the same occupation, and Mary Macarthur agrees with them today. When it appears that some industry has shifted from men to women it will usually be found that some new mechanical process has been introduced which demands the manual dexterity   80 and attention to detail characteristic of women. In the few occupations where men and women compete equal wages will benefit men by ridding employers of the temptation to employ women as blacklegs. But, as a rule, the cry for "equal pay for equal work" does not mean equal pay for the *same* work, but equal pay for work which exacts the same time, skill and energy.   85

Or, to put it differently, it is a declaration on the woman's part that she is not going to live by bread alone. She wants butter, and cake if possible; pocket money for an occasional theatre and holiday; and the ability to obey the Fifth Commandment and keep her parents out of the workhouse.

The effect on the marriage-rate of the competition between men and women must   90 be quite insignificant. There are much more forcible reasons which prevent marriage. Important among these is the isolation of modern city life. It is possible for men and women to come up to London and live there for years without making a friend. How different from the small communities of our forefathers, when every child was born "into society" and grew up among a circle of young men and women of the same class!   95 And another deterrent to marriage is the raising of the standard of comfort. Few men and women are prepared to risk bringing up a family on the small means that would have sufficed for their grandparents. And this disinclination to bring children into a poverty-stricken home is not altogether contemptible. City life, with the accompanying miseries of dear food and rent, holds cruel torments for child life.   100

63-64. "dainty . . . porcelain": a phrase used by Mrs. Mountstuart Jenkinson to describe Clara Middleton, in Chapter V of *The Egoist* (1879), a novel by George Meredith (see p. 1079). **77. Beatrice and Sidney Webb:** (1858-1909, 1859-1947) social historians, leaders in the socialist Fabian Society (along with Shaw, Nesbit, and others) from the 1890s to the 1930s. **78. Mary Macarthur:** Scottish trade unionist (1880-1921), founder in 1907 of the journal *Woman Worker*, and a famous leader of a 1910 strike. **88. Fifth Commandment:** "Honour thy father and thy mother" (see Exodus 20:12). **100. dear:** expensive.

And if there is to be any romance in marriage women must be given every chance to earn a decent living at other occupations. Otherwise no man can be sure that he is loved for himself alone, and that his wife did not come to the Registry Office because she had had no luck at the Labour Exchange. Only the materialist can fear that a fair day's wage for a fair day's work will kill the wife and mother in women. The trinity of 105 the man, the woman and the child is as indestructible as the trinity of the sun, the moon and the stars.

But one admires the humility of men who think otherwise, and hold that only by the fear of starvation are women coerced into having husbands.

(1912)

WILFRED OWEN
England, 1893-1918

ANTHEM FOR DOOMED YOUTH

What passing-bells for these who die as cattle?
  Only the monstrous anger of the guns.
  Only the stuttering rifles' rapid rattle
Can patter out their hasty orisons.
No mockeries for them from prayers or bells,   5
  Nor any voice of mourning save the choirs, —
The shrill, demented choirs of wailing shells;
  And bugles calling for them from sad shires.

What candles may be held to speed them all?
  Not in the hands of boys, but in their eyes   10
Shall shine the holy glimmers of good-byes.
  The pallor of girls' brows shall be their pall;
Their flowers the tenderness of silent minds,
And each slow dusk a drawing-down of blinds.

(1917)

DULCE ET DECORUM EST

Bent double, like old beggars under sacks,
Knock-kneed, coughing like hags, we cursed through sludge,
Till on the haunting flares we turned our backs,
And towards our distant rest began to trudge.

Men marched asleep. Many had lost their boots,   5
But limped on, blood-shod. All went lame, all blind;
Drunk with fatigue; deaf even to the hoots
Of gas-shells dropping softly behind.

Gas! GAS! Quick, boys! — An ecstasy of fumbling,
Fitting the clumsy helmets just in time,   10
But someone still was yelling out and stumbling
And floundering like a man in fire or lime. —
Dim through the misty panes and thick green light,
As under a green sea, I saw him drowning.

In all my dreams before my helpless sight   15
He plunges at me, guttering, choking, drowning.

If in some smothering dreams, you too could pace
Behind the wagon that we flung him in,
And watch the white eyes writhing in his face,
His hanging face, like a devil's sick of sin;   20
If you could hear, at every jolt, the blood
Come gargling from the froth-corrupted lungs,
Bitter as the cud
Of vile, incurable sores on innocent tongues, —
My friend, you would not tell with such high zest   25
To children ardent for some desperate glory,
The old Lie: Dulce et decorum est
Pro patria mori.

(1917)

DULCE ET DECORUM EST   27-28. **Dulce . . . mori:** It is sweet and seemly to die for one's country (Horace, *Odes*, III.ii,13).

ARMS AND THE BOY

Let the boy try along this bayonet-blade
How cold steel is, and keen with hunger of blood;
Blue with all malice, like a madman's flash;
And thinly drawn with famishing for flesh.

Lend him to stroke these blind, blunt bullet-heads 5
Which long to nuzzle in the hearts of lads,

Or give him cartridges of fine zinc teeth,
Sharp with the sharpness of grief and death.

For his teeth seem for laughing round an apple.
There lurk no claws behind his fingers supple; 10
And God will grow no talons at his heels,
Nor antlers through the thickness of his curls.

(1918)

E.E. CUMMINGS
U.S.A., 1894-1962

"BUFFALO BILL'S"

Buffalo Bill's
defunct
  who used to
  ride a watersmooth-silver
       stallion   5
and break onetwothreefourfive pigeonsjustlikethat
       Jesus

he was a handsome man
     and what i want to know is
how do you like your blueeyed boy   10
Mister Death

     (1923)

"SPRING IS LIKE A PERHAPS HAND"

Spring is like a perhaps hand
(which comes carefully
out of Nowhere)arranging
a window,into which people look(while
people stare   5
arranging and changing placing
carefully there a strange
thing and a known thing here)and

changing everything carefully

spring is like a perhaps   10
Hand in a window

(carefully to
and fro moving New and
Old things,while
people stare carefully   15
moving a perhaps
fraction of flower here placing
an inch of air there)and

without breaking anything.
  (1925)

ARMS AND THE BOY **Title:** Cf. the opening to Virgil's *Aeneid* (Dryden's translation, p. 440).   **BUFFALO BILL'S** **Title:** "Buffalo Bill" was the stage name of William F. Cody (1846-1917), who after 1883 starred in his own Wild West Show.

"A MAN WHO HAD FALLEN AMONG THIEVES"

a man who had fallen among thieves
lay by the roadside on his back
dressed in fifteenthrate ideas
wearing a round jeer for a hat

fate per a somewhat more than less   5
emancipated evening
had in return for consciousness
endowed him with a changeless grin

whereon a dozen staunch and leal
citizens did graze at pause   10
then fired by hypercivic zeal
sought newer pastures or because

swaddled with a frozen brook
of pinkest vomit out of eyes
which noticed nobody he looked   15
as if he did not care to rise

one hand did nothing on the vest
its wideflung friend clenched weakly dirt
while the mute trouserfly confessed
a button solemnly inert.   20

Brushing from whom the stiffened puke
i put him all into my arms
and staggered banged with terror through
a million billion trillion stars
                              (1926)

"NEXT TO OF COURSE GOD"

"next to of course god america i
love you land of the pilgrims' and so forth oh
say can you see by the dawn's early my
country 'tis of centuries come and go
and are no more what of it we should worry   5
in every language even deafanddumb
thy sons acclaim your glorious name by gorry
by jingo by gee by gosh by gum
why talk of beauty what could be more beautiful than these heroic happy dead   10

who rushed like lions to the roaring slaughter
they did not stop to think they died instead
then shall the voice of liberty be mute?"

He spoke. And drank rapidly a glass of water
                              (1926)

"SOMEWHERE I HAVE NEVER TRAVELLED"

somewhere i have never travelled,gladly beyond
any experience,your eyes have their silence:
in your most frail gesture are things which enclose me,
or which i cannot touch because they are too near

your slightest look easily will unclose me   5
though i have closed myself as fingers,
you open always petal by petal myself as Spring opens
(touching skilfully,mysteriously)her first rose

or if your wish to be close me,i and
my life will shut very beautifully,suddenly,   10
as when the heart of this flower imagines
the snow carefully everywhere descending;

nothing which we are to perceive in this world equals
the power of your intense fragility:whose texture
compels me with the colour of its countries,   15
rendering death and forever with each breathing

(i do not know what it is about you that closes
and opens;only something in me understands
the voice of your eyes is deeper than all roses)
nobody,not even the rain,has such small hands   20
                              (1931)

"ANYONE LIVED IN A PRETTY HOW TOWN"

anyone lived in a pretty how town
(with up so floating many bells down)
spring summer autumn winter
he sang his didn't he danced his did.

Women and men(both little and small)   5
cared for anyone not at all
they sowed their isn't they reaped their same
sun moon stars rain

A MAN WHO HAD FALLEN AMONG THIEVES **Title:** See Luke 10:25-37. **9. leal:** loyal.

children guessed(but only a few
and down they forgot as up they grew   10
autumn winter spring summer)
that noone loved him more by more

when by now and tree by leaf
she laughed his joy she cried his grief
bird by snow and stir by still   15
anyone's any was all to her

someones married their everyones
laughed their cryings and did their dance
(sleep wake hope and then)they
said their nevers they slept their dream   20

stars rain sun moon
(and only the snow can begin to explain
how children are apt to forget to remember
with up so floating many bells down)

one day anyone died i guess   25
(and noone stooped to kiss his face)
busy folk buried them side by side
little by little and was by was

all by all and deep by deep
and more by more they dream their sleep   30

noone and anyone earth by april
wish by spirit and if by yes.

Women and men(both dong and ding)
summer autumn winter spring
reaped their sowing and went their came   35
sun moon stars rain

(1940)

"NO TIME AGO"

no time ago
or else a life
walking in the dark
i met christ

jesus)my heart   5
flopped over
and lay still
while he passed(as

close as i'm to you
yes closer   10
made of nothing
except loneliness

(1950)

JAMES THURBER
U.S.A., 1894-1963

THE LITTLE GIRL AND THE WOLF

One afternoon a big wolf waited in a dark forest for a little girl to come along carrying a basket of food to her grandmother. Finally a little girl did come along and she was carrying a basket of food. "Are you carrying that basket to your grandmother?" asked the wolf. The little girl said yes, she was. So the wolf asked her where her grandmother lived and the little girl told him and he disappeared into the wood.   5

When the little girl opened the door of her grandmother's house she saw that there was somebody in bed with a nightcap and nightgown on. She had approached no nearer than twenty-five feet from the bed when she saw that it was not her grandmother but the wolf, for even in a nightcap a wolf does not look any more like your grandmother than the Metro-Goldwyn lion looks like Calvin Coolidge. So the little girl took an automatic   10
out of her basket and shot the wolf dead.

Moral: It is not so easy to fool little girls nowadays as it used to be.

(1940)

THE LITTLE GIRL AND THE WOLF   **10. Calvin Coolidge:** (1872-1933) thirtieth president of the United States.

ROBERT GRAVES
England, 1895-1985

THE COOL WEB

Children are dumb to say how hot the day is,
How hot the scent is of the summer rose,
How dreadful the black wastes of evening sky,
How dreadful the tall soldiers drumming by.

But we have speech, to chill the angry day,   *5*
And speech, to dull the rose's cruel scent.
We spell away the overhanging night,
We spell away the soldiers and the fright.

There's a cool web of language winds us in,
Retreat from too much joy or too much fear: *10*
We grow sea-green at last and coldly die
In brininess and volubility.

But if we let our tongues lose self-possession,
Throwing off language and its watery clasp
Before our death, instead of when death comes,
Facing the wide glare of the children's day,   *16*
Facing the rose, the dark sky and the drums,
We shall go mad no doubt and die that way.

                    (1927)

FLYING CROOKED

The butterfly, a cabbage-white,
(His honest idiocy of flight)
Will never now, it is too late,
Master the art of flying straight,
Yet has — who knows so well as I? —   *5*
A just sense of how not to fly:
He lurches here and here by guess
And God and hope and hopelessness.
Even the aerobatic swift
Has not his flying-crooked gift.   *10*

          (1931)

WILLIAM FAULKNER
U.S.A., 1897-1962

MULE IN THE YARD

It was a gray day in late January, though not cold because of the fog. Old Het, just walked in from the poorhouse, ran down the hall toward the kitchen, shouting in a strong, bright, happy voice. She was about seventy probably, though by her own counting, calculated from the ages of various housewives in the town from brides to grandmothers whom she claimed to have nursed in infancy, she would have to be   *5* around a hundred and at least triplets. Tall, lean, fog-beaded, in tennis shoes and a long rat-colored cloak trimmed with what forty or fifty years ago had been fur, a modish though not new purple toque set upon her headrag and carrying (time was when she made her weekly rounds from kitchen to kitchen carrying a brocaded carpetbag though since the advent of the ten-cent stores the carpetbag became an endless succession of the   *10* convenient paper receptacles with which they supply their customers for a few cents) the shopping-bag, she ran into the kitchen and shouted with strong and childlike pleasure: "Miss Mannie! Mule in de yard!"

Mrs. Hait, stooping to the stove, in the act of drawing from it a scuttle of live ashes, jerked upright; clutching the scuttle, she glared at old Het, then she too spoke at once, *15* strong too, immediate. "Them sons of bitches," she said. She left the kitchen, not running exactly, yet with a kind of outraged celerity, carrying the scuttle — a compact woman of forty-odd, with an air of indomitable yet relieved bereavement, as though that which had relicted her had been a woman and a not particularly valuable one at that. She wore a calico wrapper and a sweater coat, and a man's felt hat which they in the town *20* knew had belonged to her ten years' dead husband. But the man's shoes had not belonged to him. They were high shoes which buttoned, with toes like small tulip bulbs, and in the town they knew that she had bought them new for herself. She and old Het ran down the kitchen steps and into the fog. That's why it was not cold: as though there lay supine and prisoned between earth and mist the long winter night's suspiration of the *25* sleeping town in dark, close rooms — the slumber and the rousing; the stale waking thermostatic, by re-heating heat-engendered: it lay like a scum of cold grease upon the steps and the wooden entrance to the basement and upon the narrow plank walk which led to a shed building in the corner of the yard: upon these planks, running and still carrying the scuttle of live ashes, Mrs. Hait skated viciously. *30*

"Watch out!" old Het, footed securely by her rubber soles, cried happily. "Dey in de front!" Mrs. Hait did not fall. She did not even pause. She took in the immediate scene with one cold glare and was running again when there appeared at the corner of the house and apparently having been born before their eyes of the fog itself, a mule. It looked taller than a giraffe. Longheaded, with a flying halter about its scissorlike ears, it *35* rushed down upon them with violent and apparitionlike suddenness.

"Dar hit!" old Het cried, waving the shopping-bag. "Hoo!" Mrs. Hait whirled. Again she skidded savagely on the greasy planks as she and the mule rushed parallel with one another toward the shed building, from whose open doorway there now projected the static and astonished face of a cow. To the cow the fog-born mule *40* doubtless looked taller and more incredibly sudden than a giraffe even, and apparently bent upon charging right through the shed as though it were made of straw or were purely and simply mirage. The cow's head likewise had a quality transient and abrupt and unmundane. It vanished, sucked into invisibility like a match flame, though the mind knew and the reason insisted that she had withdrawn into the shed, from which, as *45* proof's burden, there came an indescribable sound of shock and alarm by shed and beast engendered, analogous to a single note from a profoundly struck lyre or harp. Toward this sound Mrs. Hait sprang, immediately, as if by pure reflex, as though in invulnerable compact of female with female against a world of mule and man. She and the mule converged upon the shed at top speed, the heavy scuttle poised lightly in her hand to *50* hurl. Of course it did not take this long, and likewise it was the mule which refused the gambit. Old Het was still shouting "Dar hit! Dar hit!" when it swerved and rushed at her where she stood tall as a stove pipe, holding the shopping-bag which she swung at the beast as it rushed past her and vanished beyond the other corner of the house as though sucked back into the fog which had produced it, profound and instantaneous and without any sound.   55

With that unhasteful celerity Mrs. Hait turned and set the scuttle down on the brick coping of the cellar entrance and she and old Het turned the corner of the house in time to see the now wraithlike mule at the moment when its course converged with that of a choleric-looking rooster and eight Rhode Island Red hens emerging from beneath the   60
house. Then for an instant its progress assumed the appearance and trappings of an apotheosis: hell-born and hell-returning, in the act of dissolving completely into the fog, it seemed to rise vanishing into a sunless and dimensionless medium borne upon and enclosed by small winged goblins.

"Dey's mo in de front!" old Het cried.   65

"Them sons of bitches," Mrs. Hait said, again in that grim, prescient voice without rancor or heat. It was not the mules to which she referred; it was not even the owner of them. It was her whole town-dwelling history as dated from that April dawn ten years ago when what was left of Hait had been gathered from the mangled remains of five mules and several feet of new Manila rope on a blind curve of the railroad just out of town; the geographical   70
hap of her very home; the very components of her bereavement — the mules, the defunct husband, and the owner of them. His name was Snopes; in the town they knew about him too — how he bought his stock at the Memphis market and brought it to Jefferson and sold it to farmers and widows and orphans black and white, for whatever he could contrive — down to a certain figure; and about how (usually in the dead season of winter) teams and   75
even small droves of his stock would escape from the fenced pasture where he kept them and, tied one to another with sometimes quite new hemp rope (and which item Snopes included in the subsequent claim), would be annihilated by freight trains on the same blind curve which was to be the scene of Hait's exit from this world; once a town wag sent him through the mail a printed train schedule for the division. A squat, pasty man perennially   80
tieless and with a strained, harried expression, at stated intervals he passed athwart the peaceful and somnolent life of the town in dust and uproar, his advent heralded by shouts and cries, his passing marked by a yellow cloud filled with tossing jug-shaped heads and clattering hooves and the same forlorn and earnest cries of the drovers; and last of all and well back out of the dust, Snopes himself moving at a harried and panting trot, since it was   85
said in the town that he was deathly afraid of the very beasts in which he cleverly dealt.

The path which he must follow from the railroad station to his pasture crossed the edge of town near Hait's home; Hait and Mrs. Hait had not been in the house a week before they waked one morning to find it surrounded by galloping mules and the air filled with the shouts and cries of the drovers. But it was not until that April dawn some   90
years later, when those who reached the scene first found what might be termed foreign matter among the mangled mules and the savage fragments of new rope, that the town suspected that Hait stood in any closer relationship to Snopes and the mules than that of helping at periodical intervals to drive them out of his front yard. After that they believed that they knew; in a three days' recess of interest, surprise, and curiosity they   95
watched to see if Snopes would try to collect on Hait also.

But they learned only that the adjuster appeared and called upon Mrs. Hait and that a few days later she cashed a check for eight thousand five hundred dollars, since this was back in the old halcyon days when even the companies considered their southern branches and divisions the legitimate prey of all who dwelt beside them. She took the cash: she stood in her sweater coat and the hat which Hait had been wearing on the fatal morning a week ago and listened in cold, grim silence while the teller counted the money and the president and the cashier tried to explain to her the virtues of a bond, then of a savings account, then of a checking account, and departed with the money in a salt sack under her apron; after a time she painted her house: that serviceable and time-defying color which the railroad station was painted, as though out of sentiment or (as some said) gratitude.

The adjuster also summoned Snopes into conference, from which he emerged not only more harried-looking than ever, but with his face stamped with a bewildered dismay which it was to wear from then on, and that was the last time his pasture fence was ever to give inexplicably away at dead of night upon mules coupled in threes and fours by adequate rope even though not always new. And then it seemed as though the mules themselves knew this, as if, even while haltered at the Memphis block at his bid, they sensed it somehow as they sensed that he was afraid of them. Now, three or four times a year and as though by fiendish concord and as soon as they were freed of the box car, the entire uproar — the dust cloud filled with shouts earnest, harried, and dismayed, with plunging demoniac shapes — would become translated in a single burst of perverse and uncontrollable violence, without any intervening contact with time, space, or earth, across the peaceful and astonished town and into Mrs. Hait's yard, where, in a certain hapless despair which abrogated for the moment even physical fear, Snopes ducked and dodged among the thundering shapes about the house (for whose very impervious paint the town believed that he felt he had paid and whose inmate lived within it a life of idle and queen-like ease on money which he considered at least partly his own) while gradually that section and neighborhood gathered to look on from behind adjacent window curtains and porches screened and not, and from the sidewalks and even from halted wagons and cars in the street — housewives in the wrappers and boudoir caps of morning, children on the way to school, casual Negroes and casual whites in static and entertained repose.

They were all there when, followed by old Het and carrying the stub of a worn-out broom, Mrs. Hait ran around the next corner and onto the handkerchief-sized plot of earth which she called her front yard. It was small; any creature with a running stride of three feet could have spanned it in two paces, yet at the moment, due perhaps to the myopic and distortive quality of the fog, it seemed to be as incredibly full of mad life as a drop of water beneath the microscope. Yet again she did not falter. With the broom clutched in her hand and apparently with a kind of sublime faith in her own invulnerability, she rushed on after the haltered mule which was still in that arrested and wraithlike process of vanishing furiously into the fog, its wake indicated by the tossing and dispersing shapes of the nine chickens like so many jagged scraps of paper in the dying air blast of an automobile, and the madly dodging figure of a man. The man was Snopes; beaded too with moisture, his wild face gaped with hoarse shouting and the two heavy lines of shaven beard descending from the corners of it as though in alluvial retrospect of years of tobacco, he screamed at her: "Fore God, Miz Hait! I done everything I could!" She didn't even look at him.

"Ketch that big un with the bridle on," she said in her cold, panting voice. "Git that big un outen here."   *145*

"Sho!" Snopes shrieked. "Jest let um take their time. Jest don't git um excited now."

"Watch out!" old Het shouted. "He headin fer de back again!"

"Git the rope," Mrs. Hait said, running again. Snopes glared back at old Het.

"Fore God, where is ere rope?" he shouted.   *150*

"In de cellar fo God!" old Het shouted, also without pausing. "Go roun de udder way en head um." Again she and Mrs. Hait turned the corner in time to see again the still-vanishing mule with the halter once more in the act of floating lightly onward in its cloud of chickens with which, they being able to pass under the house and so on the chord of a circle while it had to go around on the arc, it had once more coincided. When *155* they turned the next corner they were in the back yard again.

"Fo God!" old Het cried. "He fixin to misuse de cow!" For they had gained on the mule now, since it had stopped. In fact, they came around the corner on a tableau. The cow now stood in the centre of the yard. She and the mule faced one another a few feet apart. Motionless, with lowered heads and braced forelegs, they looked like two book *160* ends from two distinct pairs of a general pattern which some one of amateurly bucolic leanings might have purchased, and which some child had salvaged, brought into idle juxtaposition and then forgotten; and, his head and shoulders projecting above the back-flung slant of the cellar entrance where the scuttle still sat, Snopes standing as though buried to the armpits for a Spanish-Indian-American suttee. Only again it did not take *165* this long. It was less than tableau; it was one of those things which later even memory cannot quite affirm. Now and in turn, man and cow and mule vanished beyond the next corner, Snopes now in the lead, carrying the rope, the cow next with her tail rigid and raked slightly like the stern staff of a boat. Mrs. Hait and old Het ran on, passing the open cellar gaping upon its accumulation of human necessities and widowed woman- *170* years — boxes for kindling wood, old papers and magazines, the broken and outworn furniture and utensils which no woman ever throws away; a pile of coal and another of pitch pine for priming fires — and ran on and turned the next corner to see man and cow and mule all vanishing now in the wild cloud of ubiquitous chickens which had once more crossed beneath the house and emerged. They ran on, Mrs. Hait in grim and *175* unflagging silence, old Het with the eager and happy amazement of a child. But when they gained the front again they saw only Snopes. He lay flat on his stomach, his head and shoulders upreared by his outstretched arms, his coat tail swept forward by its own arrested momentum about his head so that from beneath it his slack-jawed face mused in wild repose like that of a burlesqued nun.   *180*

"Whar'd dey go?" old Het shouted at him. He didn't answer.

"Dey tightenin' on de curves!" she cried. "Dey already in de back again!" That's where they were. The cow made a feint at running into her shed, but deciding perhaps that her speed was too great, she whirled in a final desperation of despair-like valor. But they did not see this, nor see the mule, swerving to pass her, crash and blunder for an *185* instant at the open cellar door before going on. When they arrived, the mule was gone. The scuttle was gone too, but they did not notice it; they saw only the cow standing in the centre of the yard as before, panting, rigid, with braced forelegs and lowered head facing nothing, as if the child had returned and removed one of the book ends for some newer purpose or game. They ran on. Mrs. Hait ran heavily now, her mouth too open, *190* her face putty-colored and one hand pressed to her side. So slow was their progress that the mule in its third circuit of the house overtook them from behind and soared past with undiminished speed, with brief demon thunder and a keen ammonia-sweet reek of sweat sudden and sharp as a jeering cry, and was gone. Yet they ran doggedly on around the next corner in time to see it succeed at last in vanishing into the fog; they heard its *195* hoofs, brief, staccato, and derisive, on the paved street, dying away.

"Well!" old Het said, stopping. She panted, happily. "Gentlemen, hush! Ain't we had —" Then she became stone still; slowly her head turned, high-nosed, her nostrils pulsing; perhaps for the instant she saw the open cellar door as they had last passed it, with no scuttle beside it. "Fo God I smells smoke!" she said. "Chile, run, git yo money." *200*

That was still early, not yet ten o'clock. By noon the house had burned to the ground. There was a farmers' supply store where Snopes could be usually found; more than one had made a point of finding him there by that time. They told him about how when the fire engine and the crowd reached the scene, Mrs. Hait, followed by old Het carrying her shopping-bag in one hand and a framed portrait of Mr. Hait in the other, *205* emerged with an umbrella and wearing a new, dun-colored, mail-order coat, in one pocket of which lay a fruit jar filled with smoothly rolled banknotes and in the other a heavy, nickel-plated pistol, and crossed the street to the house opposite, where with old Het beside her in another rocker, she had been sitting ever since on the veranda, grim, inscrutable, the two of them rocking steadily, while hoarse and tireless men hurled her *210* dishes and furniture and bedding up and down the street.

"What are you telling me for?" Snopes said. "Hit warn't me that set that ere scuttle of live fire where the first thing that passed would knock hit into the cellar."

"It was you that opened the cellar door, though."

"Sho. And for what? To git that rope, her own rope, where she told me to git it." *215*

"To catch your mule with, that was trespassing on her property. You can't get out of it this time, I. O. There ain't a jury in the county that won't find for her."

"Yes. I reckon not. And just because she is a woman. That's why. Because she is a durn woman. All right. Let her go to her durn jury with hit. I can talk too; I reckon hit's a few things I could tell a jury myself about —" He ceased. They were watching him. *220*

"What? Tell a jury about what?"

"Nothing. Because hit ain't going to no jury. A jury between her and me? Me and Mannie Hait? You boys don't know her if you think she's going to make trouble over a pure acci-dent couldn't nobody help. Why, there ain't a fairer, finer woman in the county than Miz Mannie Hait. I just wisht I had a opportunity to tell her so." The *225* opportunity came at once. Old Het was behind her, carrying the shopping-bag. Mrs. Hait looked once, quietly, about at the faces, making no response to the murmur of curious salutation, then not again. She didn't look at Snopes long either, nor talk to him long.

"I come to buy that mule," she said.

"What mule?" They looked at one another. "You'd like to own that mule?" She *230* looked at him. "Hit'll cost you a hundred and fifty, Miz Mannie."

"You mean dollars?"

"I don't mean dimes nor nickels neither, Miz Mannie."

"Dollars," she said. "That's more than mules was in Hait's time."

"Lots of things is different since Hait's time. Including you and me."   *235*

"I reckon so," she said. Then she went away. She turned without a word, old Het following.

"Maybe one of them others you looked at this morning would suit you," Snopes said. She didn't answer. Then they were gone.

"I don't know as I would have said that last to her," one said.   *240*

"What for?" Snopes said. "If she was aiming to law something outen me about that fire, you reckon she would have come and offered to pay me money for hit?" That was about one o'clock. About four o'clock he was shouldering his way through a throng of Negroes before a cheap grocery store when one called his name. It was old Het, the now bulging shopping-bag on her arm, eating bananas from a paper sack.   *245*

"Fo God I wuz jest dis minute huntin fer you," she said. She handed the banana to a woman beside her and delved and fumbled in the shopping-bag and extended a greenback. "Miz Mannie gimme dis to give you; I wuz jest on de way to de sto whar you stay at. Here." He took the bill.

"What's this? From Miz Hait?"   *250*

"Fer de mule." The bill was for ten dollars. "You don't need to gimme no receipt. I kin be de witness I give hit to you."

"Ten dollars? For that mule? I told her a hundred and fifty dollars."

"You'll have to fix dat up wid her yo'self. She jest gimme dis to give ter you when she sot out to fetch de mule."   *255*

"Set out to fetch— She went out there herself and taken my mule outen my pasture?"

"Lawd, chile," old Het said, "Miz Mannie ain't skeered of no mule. Ain't you done foun dat out?"

And then it became late, what with the yet short winter days; when she came in   *260* sight of the two gaunt chimneys against the sunset, evening was already finding itself. But she could smell the ham cooking before she came in sight of the cow shed even, though she could not see it until she came around in front where the fire burned beneath an iron skillet set on bricks and where nearby Mrs. Hait was milking the cow. "Well," old Het said, "you is settled down, ain't you?" She looked into the shed, neated and   *265* raked and swept even, and floored now with fresh hay. A clean new lantern burned on a box, beside it a pallet bed was spread neatly on the straw and turned neatly back for the night. "Why, you is fixed up," she said with pleased astonishment. Within the door was a kitchen chair. She drew it out and sat down beside the skillet and laid the bulging shopping-bag beside her.   *270*

"I'll tend dis meat whilst you milks. I'd offer to strip dat cow fer you ef I wuzn't so wo out wid all dis excitement we been had." She looked around her. "I don't believe I sees yo new mule, dough." Mrs. Hait grunted, her head against the cow's flank. After a moment she said,

"Did you give him that money?"   *275*

"I give um ter him. He ack surprise at first, lak maybe he think you didn't aim to trade dat quick. I tole him to settle de details wid you later. He taken de money, dough. So I reckin dat's offen his mine en yo'n bofe." Again Mrs. Hait grunted. Old Het turned the ham in the skillet. Beside it the coffee pot bubbled and steamed. "Cawfee smell good too," she said. "I ain't had no appetite in years now. A bird couldn't live on de *280* vittles I eats. But jest lemme git a whiff er cawfee en seem lak hit always whets me a little. Now, ef you jest had nudder little piece o dis ham, now— Fo God, you got company aready." But Mrs. Hait did not even look up until she had finished. Then she turned without rising from the box on which she sat.

"I reckon you and me better have a little talk," Snopes said. "I reckon I got *285* something that belongs to you and I hear you got something that belongs to me." He looked about, quickly, ceaselessly, while old Het watched him. He turned to her. "You go away, aunty. I don't reckon you want to set here and listen to us."

"Lawd, honey," old Het said. "Don't you mind me. I done already had so much troubles myself dat I kin set en listen to udder folks' widout hit worryin me a-tall. You gawn talk *290* whut you came ter talk; I jest set here en tend de ham." Snopes looked at Mrs. Hait.

"Ain't you going to make her go away?" he said.

"What for?" Mrs. Hait said. "I reckon she ain't the first critter that ever come on this yard when hit wanted and went or stayed when hit liked." Snopes made a gesture, brief, fretted, restrained. *295*

"Well," he said. "All right. So you taken the mule."

"I paid you for it. She give you the money."

"Ten dollars. For a hundred-and-fifty-dollar mule. Ten dollars."

"I don't know anything about hundred-and-fifty-dollar mules. All I know is what the railroad paid." Now Snopes looked at her for a full moment. *300*

"What do you mean?"

"Them sixty dollars a head the railroad used to pay you for mules back when you and Hait ——"

"Hush," Snopes said; he looked about again, quick, ceaseless. "All right. Even call it sixty dollars. But you just sent me ten." *305*

"Yes. I sent you the difference." He looked at her, perfectly still. "Between that mule and what you owed Hait."

"What I owed ——"

"For getting them five mules onto the tr ——"

"Hush!" he cried. "Hush!" Her voice went on, cold, grim, level. *310*

"For helping you. You paid him fifty dollars each time, and the railroad paid you sixty dollars a head for the mules. Ain't that right?" He watched her. "The last time you never paid him. So I taken that mule instead. And I sent you the ten dollars difference."

"Yes," he said in a tone of quiet, swift, profound bemusement; then he cried: "But look! Here's where I got you. Hit was our agreement that I wouldn't never owe him *315* nothing until after the mules was ——"

"I reckon you better hush yourself," Mrs. Hait said.

"— until hit was over. And this time, when over had come, I never owed nobody no money because the man hit would have been owed to wasn't nobody," he cried triumphantly. "You see?" Sitting on the box, motionless, downlooking, Mrs. Hait *320* seemed to muse. "So you just take your ten dollars back and tell me where my mule is and we'll just go back good friends to where we started at. Fore God, I'm as sorry as ere a living man about that fire ——"

"Fo God!" old Het said, "hit was a blaze, wuzn't it?"

"— but likely with all that ere railroad money you still got, you just been wanting a   *325*
chance to build new, all along. So here. Take hit." He put the money into her hand.
"Where's my mule?" But Mrs. Hait didn't move at once.

"You want to give it back to me?" she said.

"Sho. We been friends all the time; now we'll just go back to where we left off
being. I don't hold no hard feelings and don't you hold none. Where you got the mule   *330*
hid?"

"Up at the end of that ravine ditch behind Spilmer's," she said.

"Sho. I know. A good, sheltered place, since you ain't got nere barn. Only if you'd
a just left hit in the pasture, hit would a saved us both trouble. But hit ain't no hard
feelings though. And so I'll bid you goodnight. You're all fixed up, I see. I reckon you   *335*
could save some more money by not building no house a-tall."

"I reckon I could," Mrs. Hait said. But he was gone.

"Whut did you leave de mule dar fer?" old Het said.

"I reckon that's far enough," Mrs. Hait said.

"Fer enough?" But Mrs. Hait came and looked into the skillet, and old Het said,   *340*
"Wuz hit me er you dat mentioned something erbout er nudder piece o dis ham?" So
they were both eating when in the not-quite-yet accomplished twilight Snopes returned.
He came up quietly and stood, holding his hands to the blaze as if he were quite cold.
He did not look at any one now.

"I reckon I'll take that ere ten dollars," he said.   *345*

"What ten dollars?" Mrs. Hait said. He seemed to muse upon the fire. Mrs. Hait and
old Het chewed quietly, old Het alone watching him.

"You ain't going to give hit back to me?" he said.

"You was the one that said to let's go back to where we started," Mrs. Hait said.

"Fo God you wuz, en dat's de fack," old Het said. Snopes mused upon the fire; he   *350*
spoke in a tone of musing and amazed despair:

"I go to the worry and the risk and the agoment for years and years and I get sixty
dollars. And you, one time, without no trouble and no risk, without even knowing you
are going to git it, git eighty-five hundred dollars. I never begrudged hit to you; can't
nere a man say I did, even if hit did seem a little strange that you should git it all when   *355*
he wasn't working for you and you never even knowed where he was at and what doing;
that all you done to git it was to be married to him. And now, after all these ten years of
not begrudging you hit, you taken the best mule I had and you ain't even going to pay
me ten dollars for hit. Hit ain't right. Hit ain't justice."

"You got de mule back, en you ain't satisfried yit," old Het said. "Whut does you   *360*
want?" Now Snopes looked at Mrs. Hait.

"For the last time I ask hit," he said. "Will you or won't you give hit back?"

"Give what back?" Mrs. Hait said. Snopes turned. He stumbled over something —
it was old Het's shopping-bag — and recovered and went on. They could see him in
silhouette, as though framed by the two blackened chimneys against the dying west;   *365*
they saw him fling up both clenched hands in a gesture almost Gallic, of resignation and
impotent despair. Then he was gone. Old Het was watching Mrs. Hait.

"Honey," she said. "Whut did you do wid de mule?" Mrs. Hait leaned forward to the fire. On her plate lay a stale biscuit. She lifted the skillet and poured over the biscuit the grease in which the ham had cooked.   *370*

"I shot it," she said.

"You which?" old Het said. Mrs. Hait began to eat the biscuit. "Well," old Het said, happily, "de mule burnt de house en you shot de mule. Dat's whut I calls justice." It was getting dark fast now, and before her was still the three-mile walk to the poorhouse. But the dark would last a long time in January, and the poorhouse too would not move at once. *375* She sighed with weary and happy relaxation. "Gentlemen, hush! Ain't we had a day!"

(1934, 1950)

ERNEST HEMINGWAY
U.S.A., 1899-1961

A CLEAN, WELL-LIGHTED PLACE

It was late and every one had left the café except an old man who sat in the shadow the leaves of the tree made against the electric light. In the day time the street was dusty, but at night the dew settled the dust and the old man liked to sit late because he was deaf and now at night it was quiet and he felt the difference. The two waiters inside the café knew that the old man was a little drunk, and while he was a good client they knew that   *5* if he became too drunk he would leave without paying, so they kept watch on him.

"Last week he tried to commit suicide," one waiter said.

"Why?"

"He was in despair."

"What about?"   *10*

"Nothing."

"How do you know it was nothing?"

"He has plenty of money."

They sat together at a table that was close against the wall near the door of the café and looked at the terrace where the tables were all empty except where the old man sat   *15* in the shadow of the leaves of the tree that moved slightly in the wind. A girl and a soldier went by in the street. The street light shone on the brass number on his collar. The girl wore no head covering and hurried beside him.

"The guard will pick him up," one waiter said.

"What does it matter if he gets what he's after?"   *20*

"He had better get off the street now. The guard will get him. They went by five minutes ago."

The old man sitting in the shadow rapped on his saucer with his glass. The younger waiter went over to him.

"What do you want?"   *25*

The old man looked at him. "Another brandy," he said.

"You'll be drunk," the waiter said. The old man looked at him. The waiter went away.

"He'll stay all night," he said to his colleague. "I'm sleepy now. I never get into bed before three o'clock. He should have killed himself last week."   30

The waiter took the brandy bottle and another saucer from the counter inside the café and marched out to the old man's table. He put down the saucer and poured the glass full of brandy.

"You should have killed yourself last week," he said to the deaf man. The old man motioned with his finger. "A little more," he said. The waiter poured on into the glass so   35
that the brandy slopped over and ran down the stem into the top saucer of the pile. "Thank you," the old man said. The waiter took the bottle back inside the café. He sat down at the table with his colleague again.

"He's drunk now," he said.

"He's drunk every night."   40

"What did he want to kill himself for?"

"How should I know."

"How did he do it?"

"He hung himself with a rope."

"Who cut him down?"   45

"His niece."

"Why did they do it?"

"Fear for his soul."

"How much money has he got?"

"He's got plenty."   50

"He must be eighty years old."

"Anyway I should say he was eighty."

"I wish he would go home. I never get to bed before three o'clock. What kind of hour is that to go to bed?"

"He stays up because he likes it."   55

"He's lonely. I'm not lonely. I have a wife waiting in bed for me."

"He had a wife once too."

"A wife would be no good to him now."

"You can't tell. He might be better with a wife."

"His niece looks after him. You said she cut him down."   60

"I know."

"I wouldn't want to be that old. An old man is a nasty thing."

"Not always. This old man is clean. He drinks without spilling. Even now, drunk. Look at him."

"I don't want to look at him. I wish he would go home. He has no regard for those 65
who must work."

The old man looked from his glass across the square, then over at the waiters.

"Another brandy," he said, pointing to his glass. The waiter who was in hurry came over.

"Finished," he said, speaking with that omission of syntax stupid people employ 70
when talking to drunken people or foreigners. "No more tonight. Close now."

"Another," said the old man.

"No. Finished." The waiter wiped the edge of the table with a towel and shook his head.

The old man stood up, slowly counted the saucers, took a leather coin purse from his pocket and paid for the drinks, leaving half a peseta tip. *75*

The waiter watched him go down the street, a very old man walking unsteadily but with dignity.

"Why didn't you let him stay and drink?" the unhurried waiter asked. They were putting up the shutters. "It is not half-past two."

"I want to go home to bed." *80*

"What is an hour?"

"More to me than to him."

"An hour is the same."

"You talk like an old man yourself. He can buy a bottle and drink at home."

"It's not the same." *85*

"No, it is not," agreed the waiter with a wife. He did not wish to be unjust. He was only in a hurry.

"And you? You have no fear of going home before your usual hour?"

"Are you trying to insult me?"

"No, hombre, only to make a joke." *90*

"No," the waiter who was in a hurry said, rising from pulling down the metal shutters. "I have confidence. I am all confidence."

"You have youth, confidence, and a job," the older waiter said. "You have everything."

"And what do you lack?"

"Everything but work." *95*

"You have everything I have."

"No. I have never had confidence and I am not young."

"Come on. Stop talking nonsense and lock up."

"I am of those who like to stay late at the café," the older waiter said. "With all those who do not want to go to bed. With all those who need a light for the night." *100*

"I want to go home and into bed."

"We are of two different kinds," the older waiter said. He was now dressed to go home. "It is not only a question of youth and confidence although those things are very beautiful. Each night I am reluctant to close up because there may be some one who needs the café." *105*

"Hombre, there are bodegas open all night long."

"You do not understand. This is a clean and pleasant café. It is well lighted. The light is very good and also, now, there are shadows of the leaves."

"Good night," said the younger waiter.

"Good night," the other said. Turning off the electric light he continued the *110* conversation with himself. It is the light of course but it is necessary that the place be clean and pleasant. You do not want music. Certainly you do not want music. Nor can you stand before a bar with dignity although that is all that is provided for these hours. What did he fear? It was not fear or dread. It was a nothing that he knew too well. It was

---

A CLEAN, WELL-LIGHTED PLACE   **75. peseta:** Spanish coin, worth 100 centimos. **106. bodegas:** wineshops.

all a nothing and a man was nothing too. It was only that and light was all it needed and   *115*
a certain cleanness and order. Some lived in it and never felt it but he knew it all was
nada y pues nada y nada y pues nada. Our nada who art in nada, nada be thy name thy
kingdom nada thy will be nada in nada as it is in nada. Give us this nada our daily nada
and nada us our nada as we nada our nadas and nada us not into nada but deliver us
from nada; pues nada. Hail nothing full of nothing, nothing is with thee. He smiled and   *120*
stood before a bar with a shining steam pressure coffee machine.

    "What's yours?" asked the barman.

    "Nada."

    "Otro loco mas," said the barman and turned away.

    "A little cup," said the waiter.   *125*

    The barman poured it for him.

    "The light is very bright and pleasant but the bar is unpolished," the waiter said.

    The barman looked at him but did not answer. It was too late at night for conversation.

    "You want another copita?" the barman asked.

    "No, thank you," said the waiter and went out. He disliked bars and bodegas. A   *130*
clean, well-lighted café was a very different thing. Now, without thinking further, he
would go home to his room. He would lie in the bed and finally, with daylight, he would
go to sleep. After all, he said to himself, it is probably only insomnia. Many must have it.

                                                            (1933)

F.R. SCOTT
Canada, 1899-1985

PARADISE LOST

Before any tree grew
On the ground,
Or clip of bird wing
Made sound,

Before cool fish drove   *5*
Under wave,
Or any cave man
Made cave,

The clean aimless worlds
Spun true and blind   *10*
Unseen and undisturbed
By mind,

Till some expanding molecule
Of odd construction

Learned the original sin   *15*
Of reproduction.

Startling the tall void
With new activity,
Something beyond the grave
And more than gravity.   *20*

And so in shallow bays
And warm mud
Began the long tale
Of bone and blood.

The tale of man alive   *25*
And loth to die,
Of mine and thine and ours,
And the question why.

                                       (1945)

---

117. **nada y pues nada:** nothing and then nothing. **117-20:** following the form of the Lord's Prayer, as the next sentence (line 120) follows that of
the "Ave maria," the Roman Catholic prayer beginning "Hail Mary, full of grace, the Lord is with thee." **124. Otro loco mas:** Another crazy one.
129. copita: little cup.

LAKESHORE

The lake is sharp along the shore
Trimming the bevelled edge of land
To level curves; the fretted sands
Go slanting down through liquid air
Till stones below shift here and there   5
Floating upon their broken sky
All netted by the prism wave
And rippled where the currents are.

I stare through windows at this cave   9
Where fish, like planes, slow-motioned, fly.
Poised in a still of gravity
The narrow minnow, flicking fin,
Hangs in a paler, ochre sun,
His doorways open everywhere.

And I am a tall frond that waves   15
Its head below its rooted feet
Seeking the light that draws it down
To forest floors beyond its reach
Vivid with gloom and eerie dreams.

The water's deepest colonnades   20
Contract the blood, and to this home
That stirs the dark amphibian
With me the naked swimmers come
Drawn to their prehistoric womb.

They too are liquid as they fall   25
Like tumbled water loosed above
Until they lie, diagonal,

Within the cool and sheltered grove
Stroked by the fingertips of love.

Silent, our sport is drowned in fact   30
Too virginal for speech or sound
And each is personal and laned
Along his private aqueduct.

Too soon the tether of the lungs
Is taut and straining, and we rise   35
Upon our undeveloped wings
Toward the prison of our ground
A secret anguish in our thighs
And mermaids in our memories.

This is our talent, to have grown   40
Upright in posture, false-erect,
A landed gentry, circumspect,
Tied to a horizontal soil
The floor and ceiling of the soul;
Striving, with cold and fishy care   45
To make an ocean of the air.

Sometimes, upon a crowded street,
I feel the sudden rain come down
And in the old, magnetic sound
I hear the opening of a gate   50
That loosens all the seven seas.
Watching the whole creation drown
I muse, alone, on Ararat.

                                        (1954)

E.B. WHITE
U.S.A., 1899-1985

ONCE MORE TO THE LAKE

One summer, along about 1904, my father rented a camp on a lake in Maine and took us all there for the month of August. We all got ringworm from some kittens and had to rub Pond's Extract on our arms and legs night and morning, and my father rolled over in a canoe with all his clothes on; but outside of that the vacation was a success and from

---

LAKESHORE   **53. Ararat:** the mountain where Noah's Ark landed (see Genesis 8:4, p. 248).

then on none of us ever thought there was any place in the world like that lake in Maine. 5
We returned summer after summer — always on August 1st for one month. I have since
become a salt-water man, but sometimes in summer there are days when the restlessness
of the tides and the fearful cold of the sea water and the incessant wind which blows
across the afternoon and into the evening make me wish for the placidity of a lake in the
woods. A few weeks ago this feeling got so strong I bought myself a couple of bass 10
hooks and a spinner and returned to the lake where we used to go, for a week's fishing
and to revisit old haunts.

I took along my son, who had never had any fresh water up his nose and who had
seen lily pads only from train windows. On the journey over to the lake I began to
wonder what it would be like. I wondered how time would have marred this unique, this 15
holy spot — the coves and streams, the hills that the sun set behind, the camps and the
paths behind the camps. I was sure that the tarred road would have found it out and I
wondered in what other ways it would be desolated. It is strange how much you can
remember about places like that once you allow your mind to return into the grooves
which lead back. You remember one thing, and that suddenly reminds you of another 20
thing. I guess I remembered clearest of all the early mornings, when the lake was cool
and motionless, remembered how the bedroom smelled of the lumber it was made of
and of the wet woods whose scent entered through the screen. The partitions in the camp
were thin and did not extend clear to the top of the rooms, and as I was always the first
up I would dress softly so as not to wake the others, and sneak out into the sweet 25
outdoors and start out in the canoe, keeping close along the shore in the long shadows of
the pines. I remembered being very careful never to rub my paddle against the gunwale
for fear of disturbing the stillness of the cathedral.

The lake had never been what you would call a wild lake. There were cottages
sprinkled around the shores, and it was in farming country although the shores of the 30
lake were quite heavily wooded. Some of the cottages were owned by nearby farmers,
and you would live at the shore and eat your meals at the farmhouse. That's what our
family did. But although it wasn't wild, it was a fairly large and undisturbed lake and
there were places in it which, to a child at least, seemed infinitely remote and primeval.

I was right about the tar: it led to within half a mile of the shore. But when I got 35
back there, with my boy, and we settled into a camp near a farmhouse and into the kind
of summertime I had known, I could tell that it was going to be pretty much the same as
it had been before — I knew it, lying in bed the first morning, smelling the bedroom,
and hearing the boy sneak quietly out and go off along the shore in a boat. I began to
sustain the illusion that he was I, and therefore, by simple transposition, that I was my 40
father. This sensation persisted, kept cropping up all the time we were there. It was not
an entirely new feeling, but in this setting it grew much stronger. I seemed to be living a
dual existence. I would be in the middle of some simple act, I would be picking up a bait
box or laying down a table fork, or I would be saying something, and suddenly it would
be not I but my father who was saying the words or making the gesture. It gave me a 45
creepy sensation.

We went fishing the first morning. I felt the same damp moss covering the worms
in the bait can, and saw the dragonfly alight on the tip of my rod as it hovered a few
inches from the surface of the water. It was the arrival of this fly that convinced me

beyond any doubt that everything was as it always had been, that the years were a 　 *50*
mirage and there had been no years. The small waves were the same, chucking the
rowboat under the chin as we fished at anchor, and the boat was the same boat, the same
color green and the ribs broken in the same places, and under the floor-boards the same
fresh-water leavings and débris — the dead helgramite, the wisps of moss, the rusty
discarded fish-hook, the dried blood from yesterday's catch. We stared silently at the 　 *55*
tips of our rods, at the dragonflies that came and went. I lowered the tip of mine into the
water, tentatively, pensively dislodging the fly, which darted two feet away, poised,
darted two feet back, and came to rest again a little farther up the rod. There had been no
years between the ducking of this dragonfly and the other one — the one that was part
of memory. I looked at the boy, who was silently watching his fly, and it was my hands 　 *60*
that held his rod, my eyes watching. I felt dizzy and didn't know which rod I was at the
end of.

　 We caught two bass, hauling them in briskly as though they were mackerel, pulling
them over the side of the boat in a businesslike manner without any landing net, and
stunning them with a blow on the back of the head. When we got back for a swim 　 *65*
before lunch, the lake was exactly where we had left it, the same number of inches from
the dock, and there was only the merest suggestion of a breeze. This seemed an utterly
enchanted sea, this lake you could leave to its own devices for a few hours and come
back to, and find that it had not stirred, this constant and trustworthy body of water. In
the shallows, the dark, water-soaked sticks and twigs, smooth and old, were undulating 　 *70*
in clusters on the bottom against the clean ribbed sand, and the track of the mussel was
plain. A school of minnows swam by, each minnow with its small individual shadow,
doubling the attendance, so clear and sharp in the sunlight. Some of the other campers
were in swimming, along the shore, one of them with a cake of soap, and the water felt
thin and clear and unsubstantial. Over the years there had been this person with the cake 　 *75*
of soap, this cultist, and here he was. There had been no years.

　 Up to the farmhouse to dinner through the teeming, dusty field, the road under our
sneakers was only a two-track road. The middle track was missing, the one with the
marks of the hooves and the splotches of dried, flaky manure. There had always been
three tracks to choose from in choosing which track to walk in; now the choice was 　 *80*
narrowed down to two. For a moment I missed terribly the middle alternative. But the
way led past the tennis court, and something about the way it lay there in the sun
reassured me; the tape had loosened along the backline, the alleys were green with
plantains and other weeds, and the net (installed in June and removed in September)
sagged in the dry noon, and the whole place steamed with midday heat and hunger and 　 *85*
emptiness. There was a choice of pie for dessert, and one was blueberry and one was
apple, and the waitresses were the same country girls, there having been no passage of
time, only the illusion of it as in a dropped curtain — the waitresses were still fifteen;
their hair had been washed, that was the only difference — they had been to the movies
and seen the pretty girls with the clean hair. 　 *90*

　 Summertime, oh summertime, pattern of life indelible, the fadeproof lake, the
woods unshatterable, the pasture with the sweetfern and the juniper forever and ever,

---

ONCE MORE TO THE LAKE　**54. helgramite:** (more often *hellgramite*) an insect larva, used as bait.

summer without end; this was the background, and the life along the shore was the design, the cottages with their innocent and tranquil design, their tiny docks with the flagpole and the American flag floating against the white clouds in the blue sky, the *95* little paths over the roots of the trees leading from camp to camp and the paths leading back to the outhouses and the can of lime for sprinkling, and at the souvenir counters at the store the miniature birch-bark canoes and the post cards that showed things looking a little better than they looked. This was the American family at play, escaping the city heat, wondering whether the newcomers in the camp at the head of the cove were *100* "common" or "nice," wondering whether it was true that the people who drove up for Sunday dinner at the farmhouse were turned away because there wasn't enough chicken.

It seemed to me, as I kept remembering all this, that those times and those summers had been infinitely precious and worth saving. There had been jollity and peace and goodness. The arriving (at the beginning of August) had been so big a business in itself, *105* at the railway station the farm wagon drawn up, the first smell of the pine-laden air, the first glimpse of the smiling farmer, and the great importance of the trunks and your father's enormous authority in such matters, and the feel of the wagon under you for the long ten-mile haul, and at the top of the last long hill catching the first view of the lake after eleven months of not seeing this cherished body of water. The shouts and cries of *110* the other campers when they saw you, and the trunks to be unpacked, to give up their rich burden. (Arriving was less exciting nowadays, when you sneaked up in your car and parked it under a tree near the camp and took out the bags and in five minutes it was all over, no fuss, no loud wonderful fuss about trunks.)

Peace and goodness and jollity. The only thing that was wrong now, really, was the *115* sound of the place, an unfamiliar nervous sound of the outboard motors. This was the note that jarred, the one thing that would sometimes break the illusion and set the years moving. In those other summertimes all motors were inboard; and when they were at a little distance, the noise they made was a sedative, an ingredient of summer sleep. They were one-cylinder and two-cylinder engines, and some were make-and-break and some *120* were jump-spark, but they all made a sleepy sound across the lake. The one-lungers throbbed and fluttered, and the twin-cylinder ones purred and purred, and that was a quiet sound too. But now the campers all had outboards. In the daytime, in the hot mornings, these motors made a petulant, irritable sound; at night, in the still evening when the afterglow lit the water, they whined about one's ears like mosquitoes. My boy *125* loved our rented outboard, and his great desire was to achieve singlehanded mastery over it, and authority, and he soon learned the trick of choking it a little (but not too much), and the adjustment of the needle valve. Watching him I would remember the things you could do with the old one-cylinder engine with the heavy flywheel, how you could have it eating out of your hand if you got really close to it spiritually. Motor boats *130* in those days didn't have clutches, and you would make a landing by shutting off the motor at the proper time and coasting in with a dead rudder. But there was a way of reversing them, if you learned the trick, by cutting the switch and putting it on again exactly on the final dying revolution of the flywheel, so that it would kick back against compression and begin reversing. Approaching a dock in a strong following breeze, it *135* was difficult to slow up sufficiently by the ordinary coasting method, and if a boy felt he had complete mastery over his motor, he was tempted to keep it running beyond its time and then reverse it a few feet from the dock. It took a cool nerve, because if you threw the switch a twentieth of a second too soon you would catch the flywheel when it still had speed enough to go up past center, and the boat would leap ahead, charging bull- *140* fashion at the dock.

We had a good week at the camp. The bass were biting well and the sun shone endlessly, day after day. We would be tired at night and lie down in the accumulated heat of the little bedrooms after the long hot day and the breeze would stir almost imperceptibly outside and the smell of the swamp drift in through the rusty screens. *145* Sleep would come easily and in the morning the red squirrel would be on the roof, tapping out his gay routine. I kept remembering everything, lying in bed in the mornings — the small steamboat that had a long rounded stern like the lip of a Ubangi, and how quietly she ran on the moonlight sails, when the older boys played their mandolins and the girls sang and we ate doughnuts dipped in sugar, and how sweet the music was on *150* the water in the shining night, and what it had felt like to think about girls then. After breakfast we would go up to the store and the things were in the same place — the minnows in a bottle, the plugs and spinners disarranged and pawed over by the young-sters from the boys' camp, the fig newtons and the Beeman's gum. Outside, the road was tarred and cars stood in front of the store. Inside, all was just as it had always been, *155* except there was more Coca Cola and not so much Moxie and root beer and birch beer and sarsaparilla. We would walk out with a bottle of pop apiece and sometimes the pop would backfire up our noses and hurt. We explored the streams, quietly, where the turtles slid off the sunny logs and dug their way into the soft bottom; and we lay on the town wharf and fed worms to the tame bass. Everywhere we went I had trouble making *160* out which was I, the one walking at my side, the one walking in my pants.

One afternoon while we were there at that lake a thunderstorm came up. It was like the revival of an old melodrama that I had seen long ago with childish awe. The second-act climax of the drama of the electrical disturbance over a lake in America had not changed in any important respect. This was the big scene, still the big scene. The whole *165* thing was so familiar, the first feeling of oppression and heat and a general air around camp of not wanting to go very far away. In midafternoon (it was all the same) a curious darkening of the sky, and a lull in everything that had made life tick; and then the way the boats suddenly swung the other way at their moorings with the coming of a breeze out of the new quarter, and the premonitory rumble. Then the kettle drum, then the *170* snare, then the bass drum and cymbals, then crackling light against the dark, and the gods grinning and licking their chops in the hills. Afterward the calm, the rain steadily rustling in the calm lake, the return of light and hope and spirits, and the campers running out in joy and relief to go swimming in the rain, their bright cries perpetuating the deathless joke about how they were getting simply drenched, and the children *175* screaming with delight at the new sensation of bathing in the rain, and the joke about getting drenched linking the generations in a strong indestructible chain. And the comedian who waded in carrying an umbrella.

When the others went swimming my son said he was going in too. He pulled his dripping trunks from the line where they had hung all through the shower, and wrung *180*

---

156. Moxie: The slang term "moxie" (meaning "nerve," "guts") probably derives from the name of this soft drink.

them out. Languidly, and with no thought of going in, I watched him, his hard little body, skinny and bare, saw him wince slightly as he pulled up around his vitals the small, soggy, icy garment. As he buckled the swollen belt suddenly my groin felt the chill of death.

(1941, 1944)

YVOR WINTERS
U.S.A., 1900-1968

THE FABLE

Beyond the steady rock the steady sea,
In movement more immovable than station,
Gathers and washes and is gone. It comes,
A slow obscure metonymy of motion,
Crumbling the inner barriers of the brain.   5
But the crossed rock braces the hills and makes
A steady quiet of the steady music,
Massive with peace.

          And listen, now:
The foam receding down the sand silvers   10
Between the grains, thin, pure as virgin words,
Lending a sheen to Nothing, whispering.

(1930)

SIR GAWAINE AND THE GREEN KNIGHT

Reptilian green the wrinkled throat,
Green as a bough of yew the beard;
He bent his head, and so I smote;
Then for a thought my vision cleared.

The head dropped clean; he rose and walked;   5
He fixed his fingers in the hair;
The head was unabashed and talked;
I understood what I must dare.

His flesh, cut down, arose and grew.
He bade me wait the season's round,   10
And then, when he had strength anew,
To meet him on his native ground.

The year declined; and in his keep
I passed in joy a thriving yule;
And whether waking or in sleep,   15
I lived in riot like a fool.

He beat the woods to bring me meat.
His lady, like a forest vine,
Grew in my arms; the growth was sweet;
And yet what thoughtless force was mine!   20

By practice and conviction formed,
With ancient stubbornness ingrained,
Although her body clung and swarmed,
My own identity remained.

Her beauty, lithe, unholy, pure,   25
Took shapes that I had never known;
And had I once been insecure,
Had grafted laurel in my bone.

And then, since I had kept the trust,
Had loved the lady, yet was true,   30
The knight withheld his giant thrust
And let me go with what I knew.

I left the green bark and the shade,
Where growth was rapid, thick, and still;
I found a road that men had made   35
And rested on a drying hill.

(1960)

SIR GAWAINE   See the excerpt from the medieval version of *Sir Gawain and the Green Knight* (p. 26).

E.G. MOLL
Australia /U.S.A., 1900-1979

THE BUSH SPEAKS

I will be your lover
If you keep my ways.
All delights I'll give you:
Gum-tree scented days,
Skies where kestrels hover,   5
Nights with stars ablaze.

But if you diminish
Care and think me won,
Other gifts I'll give you
Edged with thorn and sun,   *10*
And the crows will finish
What I have begun.

(1957)

LAURA RIDING
U.S.A., 1901-1991

THE MAP OF PLACES

The map of places passes.
The reality of paper tears.
Land and water where they are
Are only where they were
When words read *here* and *here*   5
Before ships happened there.

Now on naked names feet stand,
No geographies in the hand,

And paper reads anciently,
And ships at sea   *10*
Turn round and round.
All is known, all is found.
Death meets itself everywhere.
Holes in maps look through to nowhere.

(1928)

LANGSTON HUGHES
U.S.A., 1902-1967

HARLEM

What happens to a dream deferred?

Does it dry up
like a raisin in the sun?
Or fester like a sore —
And then run?   5
Does it stink like rotten meat?

Or crust and sugar over —
like a syrupy sweet?

Maybe it just sags
like a heavy load.   *10*

Or does it explode?

(1951)

HARLEM   **Title:** Black district in New York City, centre of the "Harlem Renaissance" during the 1920s.

STEVIE SMITH
England, 1902-1971

EGOCENTRIC

What care I if good God be
If he be not good to me,
If he will not hear my cry
Nor heed my melancholy midnight sigh?
What care I if he created Lamb,   5
And golden Lion, and mud-delighting Clam,
And Tiger stepping out on padded toe,
And the fecund earth the Blindworms know?
He made the Sun, the Moon and every Star,
He made the infant Owl and the Baboon,   10

He made the ruby-orbed Pelican,
He made all silent inhumanity,
Nescient and quiescent to his will,
Unquickened by the questing conscious flame
That is my glory and my bitter bane.   15
What care I if Skies are blue,
If God created Gnat and Gnu,
What care I if good God be
If he be not good to me?

(1937)

GEORGE ORWELL
England, 1903-1950

SHOOTING AN ELEPHANT

In Moulmein, in Lower Burma, I was hated by large numbers of people — the only time in my life that I have been important enough for this to happen to me. I was sub-divisional police officer of the town, and in an aimless, petty kind of way anti-European feeling was very bitter. No one had the guts to raise a riot, but if a European woman went through the bazaars alone somebody would probably spit betel juice over her   5
dress. As a police officer I was an obvious target and was baited whenever it seemed safe to do so. When a nimble Burman tripped me up on the football field and the referee (another Burman) looked the other way, the crowd yelled with hideous laughter. This happened more than once. In the end the sneering yellow faces of young men that met me everywhere, the insults hooted after me when I was at a safe distance, got badly on   10
my nerves. The young Buddhist priests were the worst of all. There were several thousands of them in the town and none of them seemed to have anything to do except stand on street corners and jeer at Europeans.

All this was perplexing and upsetting. For at that time I had already made up my mind that imperialism was an evil thing and the sooner I chucked up my job and got out   15
of it the better. Theoretically — and secretly, of course — I was all for the Burmese and all against their oppressors, the British. As for the job I was doing, I hated it more bitterly than I can perhaps make clear. In a job like that you see the dirty work of

---

EGOCENTRIC   Cf. George Wither's "Shall I, wasting in despair" (p. 278).

Empire at close quarters. The wretched prisoners huddling in the stinking cages of the lock-ups, the grey, cowed faces of the long-term convicts, the scarred buttocks of the 20 men who had been flogged with bamboos — all these oppressed me with an intolerable sense of guilt. But I could get nothing into perspective. I was young and ill-educated and I had had to think out my problems in the utter silence that is imposed on every Englishman in the East. I did not even know that the British Empire is dying, still less did I know that it is a great deal better than the younger empires that are going to 25 supplant it. All I knew was that I was stuck between my hatred of the empire I served and my rage against the evil-spirited little beasts who tried to make my job impossible. With one part of my mind I thought of the British Raj as an unbreakable tyranny, as something clamped down, *in saecula saeculorum*, upon the will of prostrate peoples; with another part I thought that the greatest joy in the world would be to drive a bayonet 30 into a Buddhist priest's guts. Feelings like these are the normal by-products of imperialism; ask any Anglo-Indian official, if you can catch him off duty.

One day something happened which in a roundabout way was enlightening. It was a tiny incident in itself, but it gave me a better glimpse than I had had before of the real nature of imperialism — the real motives for which despotic governments act. Early one 35 morning the sub-inspector at a police station the other end of the town rang me up on the 'phone and said that an elephant was ravaging the bazaar. Would I please come and do something about it? I did not know what I could do, but I wanted to see what was happening and I got on to a pony and started out. I took my rifle, an old .44 Winchester and much too small to kill an elephant, but I thought the noise might be useful *in* 40 *terrorem*. Various Burmans stopped me on the way and told me about the elephant's doings. It was not, of course, a wild elephant, but a tame one which had gone "must." It had been chained up, as tame elephants always are when their attack of "must" is due, but on the previous night it had broken its chain and escaped. Its mahout, the only person who could manage it when it was in that state, had set out in pursuit, but had 45 taken the wrong direction and was now twelve hours' journey away, and in the morning the elephant had suddenly reappeared in the town. The Burmese population had no weapons and were quite helpless against it. It had already destroyed somebody's bamboo hut, killed a cow and raided some fruit-stalls and devoured the stock; also it had met the municipal rubbish van and, when the driver jumped out and took to his heels, 50 had turned the van over and inflicted violences upon it.

The Burmese sub-inspector and some Indian constables were waiting for me in the quarter where the elephant had been seen. It was a very poor quarter, a labyrinth of squalid bamboo huts, thatched with palm-leaf, winding all over a steep hillside. I remember that it was a cloudy, stuffy morning at the beginning of the rains. We began 55 questioning the people as to where the elephant had gone and, as usual, failed to get any definite information. That is invariably the case in the East; a story always sounds clear enough at a distance, but the nearer you get to the scene of events the vaguer it becomes. Some of the people said that the elephant had gone in one direction, some said that he had gone in another, some professed not even to have heard of any elephant. I had 60

SHOOTING AN ELEPHANT   **29.** *in saecula saeculorum*: (Latin) for ever and ever. **40-41.** *in terrorem*: (Latin) as a warning. **42. "must"**: state of sexual agitation, in male elephants.

almost made up my mind that the whole story was a pack of lies, when we heard yells a little distance away. There was a loud, scandalized cry of "Go away, child! Go away this instant!" and an old woman with a switch in her hand came round the corner of a hut, violently shooing away a crowd of naked children. Some more women followed, clicking their tongues and exclaiming; evidently there was something that the children ought not to have seen. I rounded the hut and saw a man's dead body sprawling in the mud. He was an Indian, a black Dravidian coolie, almost naked, and he could not have been dead many minutes. The people said that the elephant had come suddenly upon him round the corner of the hut, caught him with its trunk, put its foot on his back and ground him into the earth. This was the rainy season and the ground was soft, and his face had scored a trench a foot deep and a couple of yards long. He was lying on his belly with arms crucified and head sharply twisted to one side. His face was coated with mud, the eyes wide open, the teeth bared and grinning with an expression of unendurable agony. (Never tell me, by the way, that the dead look peaceful. Most of the corpses I have seen looked devilish.) The friction of the great beast's foot had stripped the skin from his back as neatly as one skins a rabbit. As soon as I saw the dead man I sent an orderly to a friend's house nearby to borrow an elephant rifle. I had already sent back the pony, not wanting it to go mad with fright and throw me if it smelt the elephant.

The orderly came back in a few minutes with a rifle and five cartridges, and meanwhile some Burmans had arrived and told us that the elephant was in the paddy fields below, only a few hundred yards away. As I started forward practically the whole population of the quarter flocked out of the houses and followed me. They had seen the rifle and were all shouting excitedly that I was going to shoot the elephant. They had not shown much interest in the elephant when he was merely ravaging their homes, but it was different now that he was going to be shot. It was a bit of fun to them, as it would be to an English crowd; besides they wanted the meat. It made me vaguely uneasy. I had no intention of shooting the elephant — I had merely sent for the rifle to defend myself if necessary — and it is always unnerving to have a crowd following you. I marched down the hill, looking and feeling a fool, with the rifle over my shoulder and an ever-growing army of people jostling at my heels. At the bottom, when you got away from the huts, there was a metalled road and beyond that a miry waste of paddy fields a thousand yards across, not yet ploughed but soggy from the first rains and dotted with coarse grass. The elephant was standing eight yards from the road, his left side towards us. He took not the slightest notice of the crowd's approach. He was tearing up bunches of grass, beating them against his knees to clean them and stuffing them into his mouth.

I had halted on the road. As soon as I saw the elephant I knew with perfect certainty that I ought not to shoot him. It is a serious matter to shoot a working elephant — it is comparable to destroying a huge and costly piece of machinery — and obviously one ought not to do it if it can possibly be avoided. And at that distance, peacefully eating, the elephant looked no more dangerous than a cow. I thought then and I think now that his attack of "must" was already passing off; in which case he would merely wander harmlessly about until the mahout came back and caught him. Moreover, I did not in the

67. **Dravidian:** the largest group of peoples in India before the Aryan invasions (c.1500 B.C.), whose descendants (speakers of Tamil, Kannada, Malayalam, and other non-Indo-European languages) live mostly in South India. 91. **metalled:** gravel-covered.

least want to shoot him. I decided that I would watch him for a little while to make sure that he did not turn savage again, and then go home.

But at that moment I glanced round at the crowd that had followed me. It was an *105* immense crowd, two thousand at the least and growing every minute. It blocked the road for a long distance on either side. I looked at the sea of yellow faces above the garish clothes — faces all happy and excited over this bit of fun, all certain that the elephant was going to be shot. They were watching me as they would watch a conjurer about to perform a trick. They did not like me, but with the magical rifle in my hands I *110* was momentarily worth watching. And suddenly I realized that I should have to shoot the elephant after all. The people expected it of me and I had got to do it; I could feel their two thousand wills pressing me forward, irresistibly. And it was at this moment, as I stood there with the rifle in my hands, that I first grasped the hollowness, the futility of the white man's dominion in the East. Here was I, the white man with his gun, standing *115* in front of the unarmed native crowd — seemingly the leading actor of the piece; but in reality I was only an absurd puppet pushed to and fro by the will of those yellow faces behind. I perceived in this moment that when the white man turns tyrant it is his own freedom that he destroys. He becomes a sort of hollow, posing dummy, the conventionalized figure of a sahib. For it is the condition of his rule that he shall spend his life *120* in trying to impress the "natives," and so in every crisis he has got to do what the "natives" expect of him. He wears a mask, and his face grows to fit it. I had got to shoot the elephant. I had committed myself to doing it when I sent for the rifle. A sahib has got to act like a sahib; he has got to appear resolute, to know his own mind and do definite things. To come all that way, rifle in hand, with two thousand people marching *125* at my heels, and then to trail feebly away, having done nothing — no, that was impossible. The crowd would laugh at me. And my whole life, every white man's life in the East, was one long struggle not to be laughed at.

But I did not want to shoot the elephant. I watched him beating his bunch of grass against his knees, with that preoccupied grandmotherly air that elephants have. It seemed *130* to me that it would be murder to shoot him. At that age I was not squeamish about killing animals, but I had never shot an elephant and never wanted to. (Somehow it always seems worse to kill a *large* animal.) Besides, there was the beast's owner to be considered. Alive, the elephant was worth at least a hundred pounds; dead, he would only be worth the value of his tusks, five pounds, possibly. But I had got to act quickly. I *135* turned to some experienced-looking Burmans who had been there when we arrived, and asked them how the elephant had been behaving. They all said the same thing: he took no notice of you if you left him alone, but he might charge if you went too close to him.

It was perfectly clear to me what I ought to do. I ought to walk up to within, say, twenty-five yards of the elephant and test his behaviour. If he charged, I could shoot; if *140* he took no notice of me, it would be safe to leave him until the mahout came back. But also I knew that I was going to do no such thing. I was a poor shot with a rifle and the ground was soft mud into which one would sink at every step. If the elephant charged and I missed him, I should have about as much chance as a toad under a steam-roller. But even then I was not thinking particularly of my own skin, only of the watchful *145* yellow faces behind. For at that moment, with the crowd watching me, I was not afraid in the ordinary sense, as I would have been if I had been alone. A white man mustn't be frightened in front of "natives"; and so, in general, he isn't frightened. The sole thought in my mind was that if anything went wrong those two thousand Burmans would see me pursued, caught, trampled on and reduced to a grinning corpse like that Indian up the hill. And if that happened it was quite probable that some of them would laugh. That would never do. There was only one alternative. I shoved the cartridges into the magazine and lay down on the road to get a better aim. *150*

The crowd grew very still, and a deep, low, happy sigh, as of people who see the theatre curtain go up at last, breathed from innumerable throats. They were going to have their bit of fun after all. The rifle was a beautiful German thing with cross-hair sights. I did not then know that in shooting an elephant one would shoot to cut an imaginary bar running from ear-hole to ear-hole. I ought, therefore, as the elephant was sideways on, to have aimed straight at his ear-hole; actually I aimed several inches in front of this, thinking the brain would be further forward. *155* *160*

When I pulled the trigger I did not hear the bang or feel the kick — one never does when a shot goes home — but I heard the devilish roar of glee that went up from the crowd. In that instant, in too short a time, one would have thought, even for the bullet to get there, a mysterious, terrible change had come over the elephant. He neither stirred nor fell, but every line of his body had altered. He looked suddenly stricken, shrunken, immensely old, as though the frightful impact of the bullet had paralysed him without knocking him down. At last, after what seemed a long time — it might have been five seconds, I dare say — he sagged flabbily to his knees. His mouth slobbered. An enormous senility seemed to have settled upon him. One could have imagined him thousands of years old. I fired again into the same spot. At the second shot he did not collapse but climbed with desperate slowness to his feet and stood weakly upright, with legs sagging and head drooping. I fired a third time. That was the shot that did for him. You could see the agony of it jolt his whole body and knock the last remnant of strength from his legs. But in falling he seemed for a moment to rise, for as his hind legs collapsed beneath him he seemed to tower upward like a huge rock toppling, his trunk reaching skywards like a tree. He trumpeted, for the first and only time. And then down he came, his belly towards me, with a crash that seemed to shake the ground even where I lay. *165* *170* *175*

I got up. The Burmans were already racing past me across the mud. It was obvious that the elephant would never rise again, but he was not dead. He was breathing very rhythmically with long rattling gasps, his great mound of a side painfully rising and falling. His mouth was wide open — I could see far down into caverns of pale pink throat. I waited a long time for him to die, but his breathing did not weaken. Finally I fired my two remaining shots into the spot where I thought his heart must be. The thick blood welled out of him like red velvet, but still he did not die. His body did not even jerk when the shots hit him, the tortured breathing continued without a pause. He was dying, very slowly and in great agony, but in some world remote from me where not even a bullet could damage him further. I felt that I had got to put an end to that dreadful noise. It seemed dreadful to see the great beast lying there, powerless to move and yet powerless to die, and not even to be able to finish him. I sent back for my small rifle and poured shot after shot into his heart and down his throat. They seemed to make no impression. The tortured gasps continued as steadily as the ticking of a clock. *180* *185* *190*

In the end I could not stand it any longer and went away. I heard later that **it took** him half an hour to die. Burmans were bringing dahs and baskets even before I left, **and** I was told they had stripped his body almost to the bones by the afternoon.

Afterwards, of course, there were endless discussions about the shooting of the *195* elephant. The owner was furious, but he was only an Indian and could do nothing. Besides, legally I had done the right thing, for a mad elephant has to be killed, like a mad dog, if its owner fails to control it. Among the Europeans opinion was divided. The older men said I was right, the younger men said it was a damn shame to shoot an elephant for killing a coolie, because an elephant was worth more than any damn Coringhee coolie. *200* And afterwards I was very glad that the coolie had been killed; it put me legally in the right and it gave me a sufficient pretext for shooting the elephant. I often wondered whether any of the others grasped that I had done it solely to avoid looking a fool.

(1936)

EARLE BIRNEY
Canada, b.1904

ANGLOSAXON STREET

Dawndrizzle ended   dampness steams from
blotching brick and   blank plasterwaste
Faded housepatterns   hoary and finicky
unfold stuttering   stick like a phonograph

Here is a ghetto   gotten for goyim   *5*
O with care denuded   of nigger and kike
No coonsmell rankles   reeks only cellarrot
attar of carexhaust   catcorpse and cookinggrease
Imperial hearts   heave in this haven   *9*
Cracks across windows   are welded with slogans
There'll Always Be An England   enhances geraniums
and V's for Victory   vanquish the housefly

Ho! with climbing sun   march the bleached beldames
festooned with shopping bags   farded flatarched
bigthewed Saxonwives   stepping over buttrivers *15*
waddling back wienerladen   to suckle smallfry

Hoy! with sunslope   shrieking over hydrants
flood from learninghall   the lean fingerlings
Nordic nobblecheeked   not all clean of nose
leaping Commandowise   into leprous lanes   *20*

What! after whistleblow!   spewed from wheelboat
after daylong doughtiness   dire handplay
in sewertrench or sandpit   come Saxonthegns
Junebrown Jutekings   jawslack for meat

Sit after supper   on smeared doorsteps   *25*
not humbly swearing   hatedeeds on Huns
profiteers politicians   pacifists Jews

Then by twobit magic   to muse in movie
unlock picturehoard   or lope to alehall
soaking bleakly   in beer skittleless   *30*

Home again to hotbox   and humid husbandhood
in slumbertrough adding   sleepily to Anglekin
Alongside in lanenooks   carling and leman
caterwaul and clip   careless of Saxonry
with moonglow and haste   and a higher heartbeat

Slumbers now slumtrack   unstinks cooling   *36*
waiting brief for milkmaid   mornstar and worldrise

Toronto 1942

---

193. dahs: short swords, used as knives. **200. Coringhee:** from Coringa, a seaport in Madras. **ANGLOSAXON STREET** See *alliterative verse* and *kenning* in the Glossary, and the note on Old English poetic form (p. 1). **5. goyim:** Gentiles. **5-7:** While the language of the poem applies generally to numerous locations and exposes the prejudices of various social groups, the particular setting is the white working-class Toronto suburb called Cabbagetown, during World War II. **14. farded:** burdened. **23. thegns:** thanes — i.e., warriors, leaders. **30. skittleless:** joyless (cf. the phrase "all beer and skittles," meaning carefree). **33. carling and leman:** young man and sweetheart. **34. clip:** embrace

ka pass age alaska passage ALASKA PASSAGE alaska passage alas

our ship seems reefed
and only the land comes swimming past alaska pass

the first through   green crescendo the fore
      trampdownwards the fog in   R
                                              E/

SHore'S pleD coMmotion of bristled ROCKS

and   blanching   drift

up from a spew sp & BaRK Logchutews
        of nit ers K A   Ar ro

(one mark of few that men have scribbled
on this lucky palimpsest of ranges)

at times a shake-built shack exchanges
passive stares with Come & Gone   10
or eyeless waits with stoven side

to slide its bones in a
            green tide

age alaska passage alaska passage alaska passage alas-ka pass

Alberni Canal 1934/1947/1960

ALASKA PASSAGE   The "Alaska Passage" or "Inside Passage" is the name given to the protected sea route between Vancouver and Alaska.
10. Come & Gone: the name of a wildflower.

THE BEAR ON THE DELHI ROAD

Unreal   tall as a myth
by the road the Himalayan bear
is beating the brilliant air
with his crooked arms
About him two men   bare   *5*
spindly as locusts   leap

One pulls on a ring
in the great soft nose   His mate
flicks   flicks with a stick
up at the rolling eyes   *10*

They have not led him here
down from the fabulous hills
to this bald alien plain
and the clamorous world   to kill
but simply to teach him to dance   *15*

They are peaceful both   these spare
men of Kashmir   and the bear
alive is their living   too

If   far on the Delhi way
around him galvanic they dance   *20*
it is merely to wear   wear
from his shaggy body the tranced
wish forever to stay
only an ambling bear
four-footed in berries   *25*

It is no more joyous for them
in this hot dust to prance
out of reach of the praying claws
sharpened to paw for ants
in the shadows of deodars   *30*
It is not easy to free
myth from reality
or rear this fellow up
to lurch   lurch with them
in the tranced dancing of men   *35*

Srinagar 1958/Île des Porquerolles 1959

JOHN BETJEMAN
England, 1906-1984

IN WESTMINSTER ABBEY

Let me take this other glove off
  As the *vox humana* swells,
And the beauteous fields of Eden
  Bask beneath the Abbey bells.
Here, where England's statesmen lie,   *5*
Listen to a lady's cry.

Gracious Lord, oh bomb the Germans.
  Spare their women for Thy Sake,
And if that is not too easy
  We will pardon Thy Mistake.   *10*
But, gracious Lord, whate'er shall be,
Don't let anyone bomb me.

Keep our Empire undismembered
  Guide our Forces by Thy Hand,
Gallant blacks from far Jamaica,   *15*
  Honduras and Togoland;
Protect them Lord in all their fights,
And, even more, protect the whites.

Think of what our Nation stands for,
  Books from Boots' and country lanes,   *20*
Free speech, free passes, class distinction,
  Democracy and proper drains.
Lord, put beneath Thy special care
One-eighty-nine Cadogan Square.

THE BEAR ON THE DELHI ROAD **30. deodars:** cedar trees of northern India. **IN WESTMINSTER ABBEY** **2.** *vox humana:* an organ reed stop (from the Latin for "the human voice"). **3. fields of Eden:** Cf. Blake's "And did those feet" (p.730). **20. Boots':** a chain of English pharmacies that also ran a lending library and sold general supplies.

Although dear Lord I am a sinner,
  I have done no major crime;
Now I'll come to Evening Service
  Whensoever I have the time.
So, Lord, reserve for me a crown,
And do not let my shares go down.   *30*

I will labour for Thy Kingdom,
  Help our lads to win the war,
Send white feathers to the cowards

Join the Women's Army Corps,   *25*
Then wash the Steps around Thy Throne   *35*
In the Eternal Safety Zone.

Now I feel a little better,
  What a treat to hear Thy Word,
Where the bones of leading statesmen,
  Have so often been interr'd.   *40*
And now, dear Lord, I cannot wait
Because I have a luncheon date.

                (1940)

SAMUEL BECKETT
Ireland/France, 1906–1989

PING

All known all white bare white body fixed one yard legs joined like sewn. Light heat white floor one square yard never seen. White walls one yard by two white ceiling one square yard never seen. Bare white body fixed only the eyes only just. Traces blurs light grey almost white on white. Hands hanging palms front white feet heels together right angle. Light heat white planes shining white bare white body fixed ping fixed   *5* elsewhere. Traces blurs signs no meaning light grey almost white. Bare white body fixed white on white invisible. Only the eyes only just light blue almost white. Head haught eyes light blue almost white silence within. Brief murmurs only just almost never all known. Traces blurs signs no meaning light grey almost white. Legs joined like sewn heels together right angle. Traces alone unover given black light grey almost   *10* white on white. Light heat white walls shining white one yard by two. Bare white body fixed one yard ping fixed elsewhere. Traces blurs signs no meaning light grey almost white. White feet toes joined like sewn heels together right angle invisible. Eyes alone unover given blue light blue almost white. Murmur only just almost never one second perhaps not alone. Given rose only just bare white body fixed one yard white on white   *15* invisible. All white all known murmurs only just almost never always the same all known. Light heat hands hanging palms front white on white invisible. Bare white body fixed ping fixed elsewhere. Only the eyes only just light blue almost white fixed front. Ping murmur only just almost never one second perhaps a way out. Head haught eyes light blue almost white fixed front ping murmur ping silence. Eyes holes light blue   *20* almost white mouth white seam like sewn invisible. Ping murmur perhaps a nature one second almost never that much memory almost never. White walls each its trace grey

---

PING   This is the author's own translation from his French-language original version. **8. haught:** an obsolete word meaning both "haughty" and "high-minded, noble."

blur signs no meaning light grey almost white. Light heat all known all white planes meeting invisible. Ping murmur only just almost never one second perhaps a meaning that much memory almost never. White feet toes joined like sewn heels together right angle ping elsewhere no sound. Hands hanging palms front legs joined like sewn. Head haught eyes holes light blue almost white fixed front silence within. Ping elsewhere always there but that known not. Eyes holes light blue alone unover given blue light blue almost white only colour fixed front. All white all known white planes shining white ping murmur only just almost never one second light time that much memory almost never. Bare white body fixed one yard ping fixed elsewhere white on white invisible heart breath no sound. Only the eyes given blue light blue almost white fixed front only colour alone unover. Planes meeting invisible one only shining white infinite but that known not. Nose ears while holes mouth white seam like sewn invisible. Ping murmurs only just almost never one second always the same all known. Given rose only just bare white body fixed one yard invisible all known without within. Ping perhaps a nature one second with image same time a little less blue and white in the wind. White ceiling shining white one square yard never seen ping perhaps a way out there one second ping silence. Traces alone unover given black grey blurs signs no meaning light grey almost white always the same. Ping perhaps not alone one second with image always the same same time a little less that much memory almost never ping silence. Given rose only just nails fallen white over. Long hair fallen white invisible over. White scars invisible same white as flesh torn of old given rose only just. Ping image only just almost never one second light time blue and white in the wind. Head haught nose ears white holes mouth white seam like sewn invisible over. Only the eyes given blue fixed front light blue almost white only colour alone unover. Light heat white planes shining white one only shining white infinite but that known not. Ping a nature only just almost never one second with image same time a little less blue and white in the wind. Traces blurs light grey eyes holes light blue almost white fixed front ping a meaning only just almost never ping silence. Bare white one yard fixed ping fixed elsewhere no sound legs joined like sewn heels together right angle hands hanging palms front. Head haught eyes holes light blue almost white fixed front silence within. Ping elsewhere always there but that known not. Ping perhaps not alone one second with image same time a little less dim eye black and white half closed long lashes imploring that much memory almost never. Afar flash of time all white all over all of old ping flash white walls shining white no trace eyes holes light blue almost white last colour ping white over. Ping fixed last elsewhere legs joined like sewn heels together right angle hands hanging palms front head haught eyes white invisible fixed front over. Given rose only just one yard invisible bare white all known without within over. White ceiling never seen ping of old only just almost never one second light time white floor never seen ping of old perhaps there. Ping of old only just perhaps a meaning a nature one second almost never blue and white in the wind that much memory henceforth never. White planes no trace shining white one only shining white infinite but that known not. Light heat all known all white heart breath no sound. Head haught eyes white fixed front old ping last murmur one second perhaps not alone eye unlustrous black and white half closed long lashes imploring ping silence ping over.

(1967)

W.H. AUDEN
England/U.S.A., 1907-1973

"AS I WALKED OUT ONE EVENING"

As I walked out one evening,
  Walking down Bristol Street,
The crowds upon the pavement
  Were fields of harvest wheat.

And down by the brimming river   5
  I heard a lover sing
Under an arch of the railway:
  "Love has no ending.

"I'll love you, dear, I'll love you
  Till China and Africa meet,   10
And the river jumps over the mountain
  And the salmon sing in the street,

"I'll love you till the ocean
  Is folded and hung up to dry
And the seven stars go squawking   15
  Like geese about the sky.

"The years shall run like rabbits,
  For in my arms I hold
The Flower of the Ages,
  And the first love of the world."   20

But all the clocks in the city
  Began to whirr and chime:
"O let not Time deceive you,
  You cannot conquer Time.

"In the burrows of the Nightmare   25
  Where Justice naked is,
Time watches from the shadow
  And coughs when you would kiss.

"In headaches and in worry
  Vaguely life leaks away,   30

And Time will have his fancy
  To-morrow or to-day.

"Into many a green valley
  Drifts the appalling snow;
Time breaks the threaded dances   35
  And the diver's brilliant bow.

"O plunge your hands in water,
  Plunge them in up to the wrist;
Stare, stare in the basin
  And wonder what you've missed.   40

"The glacier knocks in the cupboard,
  The desert sighs in the bed,
And the crack in the tea-cup opens
  A lane to the land of the dead.

"Where the beggars raffle the banknotes   45
  And the Giant is enchanting to Jack,
And the Lily-white Boy is a Roarer,
  And Jill goes down on her back.

"O look, look in the mirror,
  O look in your distress;   50
Life remains a blessing
  Although you cannot bless.

"O stand, stand at the window
  As the tears scald and start;
You shall love your crooked neighbour   55
  With your crooked heart."

It was late, late in the evening,
  The lovers they were gone;
The clocks had ceased their chiming,
  And the deep river ran on.   60

(1938)

AS I WALKED OUT ONE EVENING   **47. Lily-white Boy:** English slang for (1) homosexual, (2) chimney-sweep, (3) guardsman; **Roarer:** bully, reveller. **55-56. crooked:** See also the nursery rhyme "There Was a Crooked Man."

"Now the Leaves Are Falling Fast"

Now the leaves are falling fast,
Nurse's flowers will not last,
Nurses to their graves are gone,
But the prams go rolling on.

Whispering neighbours left and right   *5*
Daunt us from our true delight,
Able hands are left to freeze
Derelict on lonely knees.

Close behind us on our track,
Dead in hundreds cry Alack,   *10*

Arms raised stiffly to reprove
In false attitudes of love.

Scrawny through a plundered wood,
Trolls run scolding for their food,
Owl and nightingale are dumb,   *15*
And the angel will not come.

Clear, unscaleable, ahead
Rise the Mountains of Instead,
From whose cold cascading streams
None may drink except in dreams.   *20*

(1936)

Musée des Beaux Arts

About suffering they were never wrong,
The Old Masters: how well they understood
Its human position; how it takes place
While someone else is eating or opening a window or just walking dully along;
How, when the aged are reverently, passionately waiting   *5*
For the miraculous birth, there always must be
Children who did not specially want it to happen, skating
On a pond at the edge of the wood:
They never forgot
That even the dreadful martyrdom must run its course   *10*
Anyhow in a corner, some untidy spot
Where the dogs go on with their doggy life and the torturer's horse
Scratches its innocent behind on a tree.

In Brueghel's *Icarus*, for instance: how everything turns away
Quite leisurely from the disaster; the ploughman may   *15*
Have heard the splash, the forsaken cry,
But for him it was not an important failure; the sun shone
As it had to on the white legs disappearing into the green
Water; and the expensive delicate ship that must have seen
Something amazing, a boy falling out of the sky,   *20*
Had somewhere to get to and sailed calmly on.

(1939)

The Shield of Achilles

She looked over his shoulder
    For vines and olive trees,
Marble well-governed cities
    And ships upon untamed seas,

But there on the shining metal   *5*
    His hands had put instead
An artificial wilderness
    And a sky like lead.

Musée des Beaux Arts   **Title:** art gallery. **14. Brueghel:** Pieter Brueghel, or Bruegel (c.1525-1569), Flemish painter; *Icarus:* In Brueghel's painting "The Fall of Icarus," all that can be seen of Icarus is a pair of legs disappearing into the sea (for the story of Icarus, see the note to Anne Sexton's "To a Friend," p. 1427).

A plain without a feature, bare and brown,
  No blade of grass, no sign of neighbourhood,   *10*
Nothing to eat and nowhere to sit down,
  Yet, congregated on its blankness, stood
  An unintelligible multitude,
A million eyes, a million boots in line,
Without expression, waiting for a sign.   *15*

Out of the air a voice without a face
  Proved by statistics that some cause was just
In tones as dry and level as the place:
  No one was cheered and nothing was discussed;
  Column by column in a cloud of dust   *20*
They marched away enduring a belief
Whose logic brought them, somewhere else, to grief.

          She looked over his shoulder
            For ritual pieties,
          White flower-garlanded heifers,   *25*
            Libation and sacrifice,
          But there on the shining metal
            Where the altar should have been,
          She saw by his flickering forge-light
            Quite another scene.   *30*

Barbed wire enclosed an arbitrary spot
  Where bored officials lounged (one cracked a joke)
And sentries sweated for the day was hot:
  A crowd of ordinary decent folk
  Watched from without and neither moved nor spoke
As three pale figures were led forth and bound   *36*
To three posts driven upright in the ground.

The mass and majesty of this world, all
  That carries weight and always weighs the same
Lay in the hands of others; they were small   *40*
  And could not hope for help and no help came:
  What their foes liked to do was done, their shame
Was all the worst could wish; they lost their pride
And died as men before their bodies died.

          She looked over his shoulder   *45*
            For athletes at their games,
          Men and women in a dance
            Moving their sweet limbs
          Quick, quick, to music,
            But there on the shining shield   *50*
          His hands had set no dancing-floor
            But a weed-choked field.

A ragged urchin, aimless and alone,
  Loitered about that vacancy, a bird
Flew up to safety from his well-aimed stone: *55*
  That girls are raped, that two boys knife a third,
  Were axioms to him, who'd never heard
Of any world where promises were kept,
Or one could weep because another wept.

          The thin-lipped armourer,   *60*
            Hephaestos hobbled away,
          Thetis of the shining breasts
            Cried out in dismay
          At what the god had wrought
            To please her son, the strong   *65*
          Iron-hearted man-slaying Achilles
            Who would not live long.
                                    (1952)

A.D. Hope
Australia, b.1907

INSCRIPTION FOR A WAR

*Stranger, go tell the Spartans
we died here obedient to their commands.*
        — Inscription at Thermopylae

Linger not, stranger; shed no tear;
Go back to those who sent us here.

We are the young they drafted out
To wars their folly brought about.

Go tell those old men, safe in bed,   *5*
We took their orders and are dead.
                            (1970)

THE SHIELD OF ACHILLES   See the excerpt from Pope's translation of Homer's *Iliad* (p. 534) and notes.   **INSCRIPTION FOR A WAR**   Cf. William Lisle Bowles's "Thermopylae": "Go tell the Spartans, thou that passeth by, / That here, obedient to their laws, we lie" (translated from Simonides of Ceos).

THEODORE ROETHKE
U.S.A., 1908-1963

THE WAKING

I wake to sleep, and take my waking slow.
I feel my fate is what I cannot fear.
I learn by going where I have to go.

We think by feeling. What is there to know?
I hear my being dance from ear to ear.   5
I wake to sleep, and take my waking slow.

Of those so close beside me, which are you?
God bless the Ground! I shall walk softly there,
And learn by going where I have to go.

Light takes the Tree; but who can tell us how?   10
The lowly worm climbs up a winding stair;
I wake to sleep, and take my waking slow.

Great Nature has another thing to do
To you and me; so take the lively air,
And, lovely, learn by going where to go.   15

This shaking keeps me steady. I should know.
What falls away is always. And is near.
I wake to sleep, and take my waking slow.
I learn by going where I have to go.
                                        (1948)

THE SLOTH

In moving-slow he has no Peer.
You ask him something in his ear,
He thinks about it for a Year;

And, then, before he says a Word
There, upside down (unlike a Bird),   5
He will assume that you have Heard —

A most Ex-as-per-at-ing Lug.
But should you call his manner Smug,
He'll sigh and give his Branch a Hug;

Then off again to Sleep he goes,   10
Still swaying gently by his Toes,
And you just *know* he knows he knows.
                                    (1958)

KATHLEEN RAINE
England, b.1908

SHORT POEMS

*

What does this day
    bestow?
Beauty of sparse snow
Whose wet flakes touch
The soil, then vanish.

*

Frost-rime edges blades of
    grass,
The garden blackbird crosses
The motionless air
To the rigid hawthorn.

*

Moon golden towards the
    full,
Summits of pine afloat
Over level mist, the hills
Cloudlike, adrift.
                    (1980)

A.M. KLEIN
Canada, 1909-1972

THE ROCKING CHAIR

It seconds the crickets of the province. Heard
in the clean lamplit farmhouses of Quebec, —
wooden, — it is no less a national bird;
and rivals, in its cage, the mere stuttering clock.
To its time, the evenings are rolled away;   5
and in its peace the pensive mother knits
contentment to be worn by her family,
grown-up, but still cradled by the chair in which she sits.

It is also the old man's pet, pair to his pipe,
the two aids of his arithmetic and plans,   10
plans rocking and puffing into market-shape;
and it is the toddler's game and dangerous dance.
Moved to the verandah, on summer Sundays, it is,
among the hanging plants, the girls, the boy-friends,
sabbatical and clumsy, like the white haloes   15
dangling above the blue serge suits of the young men.

It has a personality of its own;
is a character (like that old drunk Lacoste,
exhaling amber, and toppling on his pins);
it is alive; individual; and no less   20
an identity than those about it. And
it is tradition. Centuries have been flicked
from its arcs, alternately flicked and pinned.
It rolls with the gait of St. Malo. It is act

and symbol, symbol of this static folk   25
which moves in segments, and returns to base, —
a sunken pendulum: *invoke, revoke;*
loosed yon, leashed hither, motion on no space.
O, like some Anjou ballad, all refrain,
which turns about its longing, and seems to move   30
to make a pleasure out of repeated pain,
its music moves, as if always back to a first love.

(1948)

PASTORAL OF THE CITY STREETS

i

Between distorted forests, clapped into geometry,
in meadows of macadam,
heat-fluff-a-host-of-dandelions dances on the air.
Everywhere glares the sun's glare,
the asphalt shows hooves.   5

        In meadows of macadam
grazes the dray horse, nozzles his bag of pasture,
is peaceful. Now and then flicks through farmer straw
his ears, like pulpit-flowers; quivers
his hide; swishes his tempest tail   10
a black and sudden nightmare for the fly.
The sun shines, sun shines down
new harness on his withers, saddle, and rump.

On curbrock and on stairstump the clustered kids
resting let slide some afternoon: then restless   15
hop to the game of the sprung haunches; skid
to the safe place; jump up: stir a wind in the heats:
laugh, puffed and sweat-streaked.

O for the crystal stream!

Comes a friend's father   20
with his pet of a hose,
and plays the sidewalk black
cavelike and cool.

O crisscross beneath the spray, those pelting petals and peas
those white soft whisks   25
brushing off heat!
O underneath these acrobatic fountains
among the crystal,
like raindrops a sunshower of youngsters dance:
small-nippled self-hugged boys   30
and girls with water sheer, going *Ah* and *Ah.*

THE ROCKING CHAIR   24. St. Malo: the French seaport in Normandy from which Jacques Cartier sailed to Quebec (see Florio's translation of Cartier, p. 185). **29. Anjou:** a duchy in Western France, which included Normandy in medieval times; from 1154, when the Angevin or Plantagenet dynasty took the English throne, into the 13th century, its dominion extended through England as well.

ii

And at twilight,
the sun like a strayed neighbourhood creature
having been chased
back to its cover   35
the children count a last game, or talk, or rest,
beneath the bole of the tree of the single fruit of glass
now ripening,
a last game, talk, or rest,
until mothers like evening birds call from the stoops.   40
(1948)

PORTRAIT OF THE POET
AS LANDSCAPE

i

Not an editorial-writer, bereaved with bartlett,
mourns him, the shelved Lycidas.
No actress squeezes a glycerine tear for him.
The radio broadcast lets his passing pass.
And with the police, no record. Nobody, it appears,   5
either under his real name or his alias,
missed him enough to report.

It is possible that he is dead, and not discovered.
It is possible that he can be found some place
in a narrow closet, like the corpse in a detective story,   10
standing, his eyes staring, and ready to fall on his face.
It is also possible that he is alive
and amnesiac, or mad, or in retired disgrace,
or beyond recognition lost in love.

We are sure only that from our real society   15
he has disappeared; he simply does not count,
except in the pullulation of vital statistics —
somebody's vote, perhaps, an anonymous taunt
of the Gallup poll, a dot in a government table —
but not felt, and certainly far from eminent —   20
in a shouting mob, somebody's sigh.

O, he who unrolled our culture from his scroll —
the prince's quote, the rostrum-rounding roar —
who under one name made articulate
heaven, and under another the seven-circled air,   25
is, if he is at all, a number, an x,
a Mr. Smith in a hotel register, —
incognito, lost, lacunal.

ii

The truth is he's not dead, but only ignored —
like the mirroring lenses forgotten on a brow   30
that shine with the guilt of their unnoticed world.
The truth is he lives among neighbours, who, though they
    will allow
him a passable fellow, think him eccentric, not solid,
a type that one can forgive, and for that matter, forgo.

Himself he has his moods, just like a poet.   35
Sometimes, depressed to nadir, he will think all lost,
will see himself as throwback, relict, freak,
his mother's miscarriage, his great-grandfather's ghost,
and he will curse his quintuplet senses, and their tutors
in whom he put, as he should not have put, his trust.   40

Then he will remember his travels over that body —
the torso verb, the beautiful face of the noun,
and all those shaped and warm auxiliaries!
A first love it was, the recognition of his own.
Dear limbs adverbial, complexion of adjective,   45
dimple and dip of conjugation!

And then remember how this made a change in him
affecting for always the glow and growth of his being;
how suddenly was aware of the air, like shaken tinfoil,
of the patents of nature, the shock of belated seeing,   50
the loneliness peering from the eyes of crowds;
the integers of thought; the cube-roots of feeling.

Thus, zoomed to zenith, sometimes he hopes again,
and sees himself as a character, with a rehearsed role:
the Count of Monte Cristo, come for his revenges;   55
the unsuspecting heir, with papers; the risen soul;
or the chloroformed prince awakening from his flowers;
or — deflated again — the convict on parole.

iii

He is alone; yet not completely alone.
Pins on a map of a colour similar to his,   60
each city has one, sometimes more than one;
here, caretakers of art, in colleges;
in offices, there, with arm-bands, and green-shaded;
and there, pounding their catalogued beats in libraries, —

PORTRAIT OF THE POET AS LANDSCAPE   1. **bartlett:** *Familiar Quotations*, originally published in 1855 by John Bartlett (1820-1905). **2. Lycidas:** See Milton's *Lycidas* (p. 315). **19. Gallup:** named for the American statistician, George Gallup (1901-1984), who developed the polling technique. **55. Count of Monte Cristo:** the titular hero of the 1844 adventure novel by Alexandre Dumas (1802-1870).

everywhere menial, a shadow's shadow.   65
And always for their egos — their outmoded art.
Thus, having lost the bevel in the ear,
they know neither up nor down, mistake the part
for the whole, curl themselves in a comma,
talk technics, make a colon their eyes. They distort —   70

such is the pain of their frustration — truth
to something convolute and cerebral.
How they do fear the slap of the flat of the platitude!
Now Pavlov's victims, their mouths water at bell,
the platter empty.   75
                    See they set twenty-one jewels
into their watches; the time they do not tell!

Some, patagonian in their own esteem,
and longing for the multiplying word,
join party and wear pins, now have a message,   80
an ear, and the convention-hall's regard.
Upon the knees of ventriloquists, they own,
of their dandled brightness, only the paint and board.

And some go mystical, and some go mad.
One stares at a mirror all day long, as if   85
to recognize himself; another courts
angels, — for here he does not fear rebuff;
and a third, alone, and sick with sex, and rapt,
doodles him symbols convex and concave.

O schizoid solitudes! O purities   90
curdling upon themselves! Who live for themselves,
or for each other, but for nobody else;
desire affection, private and public loves;
are friendly, and then quarrel and surmise
the secret perversions of each other's lives.   95

iv

He suspects that something has happened, a law
been passed, a nightmare ordered. Set apart,
he finds himself, with special haircut and dress,
as on a reservation. Introvert.
He does not understand this; sad conjecture   100
muscles and palls thrombotic on his heart.

He thinks an impostor, having studied his personal biography,
his gestures, his moods, now has come forward to pose
in the shivering vacuums his absence leaves.

Wigged with his laurel, that other, and faked with his face,
he pats the heads of his children, pecks his wife,   106
and is at home, and slippered, in his house.

So he guesses at the impertinent silhouette
that talks to his phone-piece and slits open his mail.
Is it the local tycoon who for a hobby   110
plays poet, he so epical in steel?
The orator, making a pause? Or is that man
he who blows his flash of brass in the jittering hall?

Or is he cuckolded by the troubadour
rich and successful out of celluloid?   115
Or by the don who unrhymes atoms? Or
the chemist death built up? Pride, lost impostor'd pride,
it is another, another, whoever he is,
who rides where he should ride.

v

Fame, the adrenalin: to be talked about;   120
to be a verb; to be introduced as *The*:
to smile with endorsement from slick paper; make
caprices anecdotal; to nod to the world; to see
one's name like a song upon the marquees played;
to be forgotten with embarrassment; to be —   125
to be.

It has its attractions, but is not the thing;
nor is it the ape mimesis who speaks from the tree
ancestral; nor the merkin joy. . .
Rather it is stark infelicity   130
which stirs him from his sleep, undressed, asleep
to walk upon roofs and window-sills and defy
the gape of gravity.

vi

Therefore he seeds illusions. Look, he is
the nth Adam taking a green inventory   135
in world but scarcely uttered, naming, praising,
the flowering fiats in the meadow, the
syllabled fur, stars aspirate, the pollen
whose sweet collusion sounds eternally.
For to praise   140

---

74. Pavlov: Ivan Petrovich Pavlov (1849-1936), Russian physiologist noted for his experiments with dogs and his studies of trained reflex actions. **78. patagonian:** i.e., extreme, after Patagonia, the southernmost region of South America. **129. merkin:** i.e., deception (literally "false pubic hair"). **135-36:** See Genesis 2:19-20 (p. 243).

the world — he, solitary man — is breath
to him. Until it has been praised, that part
has not been. Item by exciting item —
air to his lungs, and pressured blood to his heart —
they are pulsated, and breathed, until they map,   *145*
not the world's, but his own body's chart!

And now in imagination he has climbed
another planet, the better to look
with single camera view upon this earth —
its total scope, and each afflated tick,   *150*
its talk, its trick, its tracklessness — and this,
this, he would like to write down in a book!

To find a new function for the *déclassé* craft
archaic like the fletcher's; to make a new thing;
to say the word that will become sixth sense;   *155*
perhaps by necessity and indirection bring
new forms to life, anonymously, new creeds —
O, somehow pay back the daily larcenies of the lung!

These are not mean ambitions. It is already something
merely to entertain them. Meanwhile, he   *160*
makes of his status as zero a rich garland,
a halo of his anonymity,
and lives alone, and in his secret shines
like phosphorus. At the bottom of the sea.

(1948)

STEPHEN SPENDER
England, 1909-1986

AN ELEMENTARY SCHOOL CLASSROOM IN A SLUM

Far far from gusty waves these children's faces.
Like rootless weeds, the hair torn round their pallor:
The tall girl with her weighed-down head. The paper-
seeming boy, with rat's eyes. The stunted, unlucky heir
Of twisted bones, reciting a father's gnarled disease, *5*
His lesson, from his desk. At back of the dim class
One unnoted, sweet and young. His eyes live in a
      dream
Of squirrel's game, in tree room, other than this.

On sour cream walls, donations. Shakespeare's head,
Cloudless at dawn, civilized dome riding all cities. *10*
Belled, flowery, Tyrolese valley. Open-handed map
Awarding the world its world. And yet, for these
Children, these windows, not this map, their world,
Where all their future's painted with a fog,
A narrow street sealed in with a lead sky *15*
Far far from rivers, capes, and stars of words.

Surely, Shakespeare is wicked, the map a bad example,
With ships and sun and love tempting them to steal —
For lives that slyly turn in their cramped holes
From fog to endless night? On their slag heap, these
      children   *20*
Wear skins peeped through by bones and
      spectacles of steel
With mended glass, like bottle bits on stones.
All of their time and space are foggy slum.
So blot their maps with slums as big as doom.

Unless, governor, inspector, visitor,   *25*
This map becomes their window and these windows
That shut upon their lives like catacombs,
Break O break open till they break the town
And show the children to green fields, and make
      their world
Run azure on gold sands, and let their tongues   *30*
Run naked into books the white and green leaves open
History theirs whose language is the sun.

(1939)

SUBJECT, OBJECT, SENTENCE

A subject thought: because he had a verb
With several objects, that he ruled a sentence.
Had not the Grammar willed him these substantives
Which he came into as his just inheritance?

His objects were *wine, women, fame* and *wealth.*
And a subordinate clause — *all life can give.*   6
He grew so fond of having these that, finally,
He found himself becoming quite subjective.

Subject, the dictionary warned means "Someone
    ruled by
Person or thing." Was he not *having's* slave?   10
To achieve detachment, he must be *objective*
Which meant to free himself from the verb *have.*

Seeking detachment, he studied the context
Around his sentence, to place it in perspective:
Paraphrased, made a critical analysis,   15
And then re-read it, feeling more *objective.*

Then, with a shock he realized that *sentence*
Like *subject-object* is treacherously double.
A sentence is condemned to stay as stated —   19
As in *life-sentence, death-sentence,* for example.
                    (1940)

RALPH GUSTAFSON
Canada, b.1909

GOOD FRIDAY

With pierced hands he hung at this very
Noontime hour. They put him up,
Heft on his hands,
The jerk back as the stub went
To the hole. Then the suffering for three   5
Hours, the words and the drink
Of vinegar in between, the rag
Around his sex. It would be
A wonder if he were the god.
He thought so. He was human.   10

Enough that there he hung. A sufficient
Phalanx of facts attests, turns history
Back to that. The rest, the god
Business, is human need. To defeat

Death. That got, we can get on   15
With cruelty, hanging stripped humans
Up, his sacrifice sufficient.

O I am up there loving
Him until he die.

                Symbol   20
Of light, questionable god,

                    sufficient
Goodness though we truly die.
                    (1980)

GOOD FRIDAY   See Matthew 27; Mark 15; Luke 23; John 19.

DOROTHY LIVESAY
Canada, b.1909

OTHER

1

Men prefer an island
With its beginning ended:
Undertone of waves
Trees overbended.

Men prefer a road   5
Circling, shell-like
Convex and fossiled
Forever winding inward.

Men prefer a woman
Limpid in sunlight   10
Held as a shell
On a sheltering island . . .

Men prefer an island.

2

But I am mainland
O I range   15
From upper country to the inner core:
From sageland, brushland, marshland
To the sea's floor.

Show me an orchard where I have not slept,
A hollow where I have not wrapped   20
The sage about me, and above, the still
Stars clustering
Over the ponderosa pine, the cactus hill.

Tell me a time
I have not loved,   25
A mountain left unclimbed:
A prairie field
Where I have not furrowed my tongue,
Nourished it out of the mind's dark places;
Planted with tears unwept   30
And harvested as friends, as faces.

O find me a dead-end road
I have not trodden
A logging road that leads the heart away
Into the secret evergreen of cedar roots   35
Beyond sun's farthest ray —
Then, in a clearing's sudden dazzle,
There is no road; no end; no puzzle.

But do not show me! For I know
The country I caress: 40
A place where none shall trespass
None possess:
A mainland mastered
From its inaccess.

                     * * * *

Men prefer an island.   45

                              (1955)

CHARLES OLSON
U.S.A., 1910-1970

NEW POEM

I have a foolishness here which is lamp-like.
Thus the words came, between the two pines
by the old house, an issue of the mind
as deliberate as a dream is suddenly
in the mouth.   5

I do not know what it means, and question,
therefore, any right I have to offer it,
question whether any statement
which is not immediately clear and first-rate
is pertinent to another man   10

Or that it stand up by form alone, this
is the other possibility, never
the creation of an emotional
situation. Words are not love.

The love of words can be a betrayal.   *15*
Yet I persist. I have a foolishness here

This part of it
is acceptable. A man can use this. Love
is a foolishness. It requires foolishness.
It goes against sense. It is lamp-like.   *20*
(1955; 1987)

NORMAN MACCAIG
Scotland, b.1910

STARS AND PLANETS

Trees are cages for them: water holds its breath
To balance them without smudging on its delicate meniscus.
Children watch them playing in their heavenly playground;
Men use them to lug ships across oceans, through firths.

They seem so twinkle-still, but they never cease   *5*
Inventing new spaces and huge explosions
And migrating in mathematical tribes over
The steppes of space at their outrageous ease.

It's hard to think that the earth is one —
This poor sad bearer of wars and disasters   *10*
Rolls-Roycing round the sun with its load of gangsters,
Attended only by the loveless moon.
(1977)

ELIZABETH BISHOP
U.S.A., 1911-1979

CASABIANCA

Love's the boy stood on the burning deck
trying to recite "The boy stood on
the burning deck." Love's the son
    stood stammering elocution
    while the poor ship in flames went down.   *5*

Love's the obstinate boy, the ship,
even the swimming sailors, who
would like a schoolroom platform, too,
    or an excuse to stay
    on deck. And love's the burning boy.   *10*
(1946)

CASABIANCA   See Hemans's "Casabianca" (p. 847).

THE PRODIGAL

The brown enormous odor he lived by
was too close, with its breathing and thick hair,
for him to judge. The floor was rotten; the sty
was plastered halfway up with glass-smooth dung.
Light-lashed, self-righteous, above moving snouts,   *5*
the pigs' eyes followed him, a cheerful stare —
even to the sow that always ate her young —
till, sickening, he leaned to scratch her head.
But sometimes mornings after drinking bouts
(he hid the pints behind a two-by-four),   *10*
the sunrise glazed the barnyard mud with red;
the burning puddles seemed to reassure.
And then he thought he almost might endure
his exile yet another year or more.

But evenings the first star came to warn.   *15*
The farmer whom he worked for came at dark
to shut the cows and horses in the barn

beneath their overhanging clouds of hay,
with pitchforks, faint forked lightnings, catching light,
safe and companionable as in the Ark.   *20*
The pigs stuck out their little feet and snored.
The lantern — like the sun, going away —
laid on the mud a pacing aureole.

Carrying a bucket along a slimy board,
he felt the bats' uncertain staggering flight,   *25*
his shuddering insights, beyond his control,
touching him. But it took him a long time
finally to make his mind up to go home.

(1950)

ALLEN CURNOW
New Zealand, b.1911

DISCOVERY

How shall I compare the discovery of islands?
History had many instinctive processes
Past reason's range, green innocence of nerves,
Now all destroyed by self-analysis.

Or, out of God the separated streams   *5*
Down honeyed valleys, Minoan, Egyptian,
And latterly Polynesia like ocean rains,
Flowing, became one flood, one swift corruption;

Or, the mad bar-beating bird of the mind
Still finding the unknown intolerable   *10*
Burst into a vaster cage, contained by seas,
Prisoned by planets within the measurable;

Or, Gulliver with needles, guns, and glass,
Thrusting trinkets up from the amazing hatches,

Luring doll kings and popes off palm-tree perches,   *15*
Sold them the Age of Reason from the beaches;

Dazzle no more in the discoverer's eye
When his blind chart unglazes, foam and flower
Suddenly spilt on the retreating mirror,
Landfall undreamed or anchorage unsure.   *20*

Compare, compare, now horrible untruth
Rings true in our obliterating season:
Our islands lost again, all earth one island,
And all our travel circumnavigation.

(1943)

THE PRODIGAL   See Luke 15:11-32 (p. 252).   **DISCOVERY   13. Gulliver:** the title character in Jonathan Swift's *Gulliver's Travels* (1726). **16. Age of Reason:** traditional label for the 18th century in Europe, because of the importance at the time of rationalist philosophical thought (also called "The Enlightenment").

IRVING LAYTON
Canada, b.1912

MRS. FORNHEIM, REFUGEE

Very merciful was the cancer
Which first blinding you altogether
Afterwards stopped up your hearing;
At the end when Death was nearing,
Black-gloved, to gather you in   5
You did not demur, or fear
One you could not see or hear.

I taught you Shakespeare's tongue, not knowing
The time and manner of your going;
Certainly if with ghosts to dwell,   10
German would have served as well.
Voyaging lady, I wish for you
An Englishwoman to talk to,
An unruffled listener,
And green words to say to her.   15

(1951)

THE COLD GREEN ELEMENT

At the end of the garden walk
the wind and its satellite wait for me;
their meaning I will not know
            until I go there,
but the black-hatted undertaker   5

who, passing, saw my heart beating in the grass,
is also going there. Hi, I tell him,
a great squall in the Pacific blew a dead poet
            out of the water,
who now hangs from the city's gates.   10

Crowds depart daily to see it, and return
with grimaces and incomprehension;
if its limbs twitched in the air
            they would sit at its feet
peeling their oranges.   15

And turning over I embrace like a lover
the trunk of a tree, one of those
for whom the lightning was too much
            and grew a brilliant
hunchback with a crown of leaves.   20

The ailments escaped from the labels
of medicine bottles are all fled to the wind;
I've seen myself lately in the eyes
            of old women
spent streams mourning my manhood,   25

in whose old pupils the sun became
a bloodsmear on broad catalpa leaves
and hanging from ancient twigs,
            my murdered selves
sparked the air like the muted collisions   30

of fruit. A black dog howls down my blood,
a black dog with yellow eyes;
he too by someone's inadvertence
            saw the bloodsmear
on the broad catalpa leaves.   35

But the furies clear a path for me to the worm
who sang for an hour in the throat of a robin,
and misled by the cries of young boys
            I am again
a breathless swimmer in that cold green element.   40

(1955)

MURIEL RUKEYSER
U.S.A., 1913-1980

M-DAY'S CHILD IS FAIR OF FACE

M-Day's child is fair of face,
Drill-day's child is full of grace,
Gun-day's child is breastless and blind,
Shell-day's child is out of its mind,

Bomb-day's child will always be dumb,   5
Cannon-day's child can never quite come,
But the child that's born on the Battle-day
is blithe and bonny and rotted away.

(1939)

M-DAY'S CHILD   See "Monday's Child" (p. 569).

MYTH

Long afterward, Oedipus, old and blinded, walked the
roads.   He smelled a familiar smell.   It was
the Sphinx.   Oedipus said, "I want to ask one question.
Why didn't I recognize my mother?"   "You gave the
wrong answer," said the Sphinx.   "But that was what   *5*
made everything possible," said Oedipus.   "No," she said.
"When I asked, What walks on four legs in the morning,
two at noon, and three in the evening, you answered,
Man.   You didn't say anything about woman."
"When you say Man," said Oedipus, "you include women   *10*
too. Everyone knows that."   She said, "That's what
you think."

(1973)

ISLANDS

O for God's sake
they are connected
underneath

They look at each other
across the glittering sea   *5*
some keep a low profile

Some are cliffs
The bathers think
islands are separate like them
(1976)

R.S. THOMAS
Wales, b.1913

A PEASANT

Iago Prytherch his name, though, be it allowed,
Just an ordinary man of the bald Welsh hills,
Who pens a few sheep in a gap of cloud.
Docking mangels, chipping the green skin
From the yellow bones with a half-witted grin   *5*
Of satisfaction, or churning the crude earth
To a stiff sea of clods that glint in the wind —
So are his days spent, his spittled mirth
Rarer than the sun that cracks the cheeks
Of the gaunt sky perhaps once in a week.   *10*

MYTH   **1. Oedipus:** character in Sophocles's trilogy (*Oedipus Tyrannus, Oedipus at Colonus*, and *Antigone*) who unwittingly kills his father and
marries his own mother; also, in Freudian psychoanalytic theory, the name of a complex.

And then at night see him fixed in his chair
Motionless, except when he leans to gob in the
fire.
There is something frightening in the vacancy of
his mind.
His clothes, sour with years of sweat
And animal contact, shock the refined,   *15*
But affected, sense with their stark naturalness.
Yet this is your prototype, who, season by season
Against siege of rain and the wind's attrition,
Preserves his stock, an impregnable fortress
Not to be stormed even in death's confusion.   *20*
Remember him, then, for he, too, is a winner of
wars,
Enduring like a tree under the curious stars.
                                                        (1955)

RESERVOIRS

There are places in Wales I don't go:
Reservoirs that are the subconscious
Of a people, troubled far down

With gravestones, chapels, villages even;
The serenity of their expression   *5*
Revolts me; it is a pose
For strangers, a watercolour's appeal
To the mass, instead of the poem's
Harsher conditions. There are the hills,
Too; gardens gone under the scum   *10*
Of the forests; and the smashed faces
Of the farms with the stone trickle
Of their tears down the hills' side.

Where can I go, then, from the smell
Of decay, from the putrefying of a dead   *15*
Nation? I have walked the shore
For an hour and seen the English
Scavenging among the remains
Of our culture, covering the sand
Like the tide and, with the roughness   *20*
Of the tide, elbowing our language
Into the grave that we have dug for it.
                                                        (1968)

DYLAN THOMAS
Wales, 1914-1953

THE FORCE THAT THROUGH THE GREEN FUSE DRIVES THE FLOWER

The force that through the green fuse drives the flower
Drives my green age; that blasts the roots of trees
Is my destroyer.
And I am dumb to tell the crooked rose
My youth is bent by the same wintry fever.   *5*

The force that drives the water through the rocks
Drives my red blood; that dries the mouthing streams
Turns mine to wax.
And I am dumb to mouth unto my veins
How at the mountain spring the same mouth sucks.   *10*

The hand that whirls the water in the pool
Stirs the quicksand; that ropes the blowing wind
Hauls my shroud sail.

And I am dumb to tell the hanging man
How of my clay is made the hangman's lime.   *15*

The lips of time leech to the fountain head;
Love drips and gathers, but the fallen blood
Shall calm her sores.
And I am dumb to tell a weather's wind
How time has ticked a heaven round the stars.   *20*

And I am dumb to tell the lover's tomb
How at my sheet goes the same crooked worm.
                                                        (1933, 1952)

A REFUSAL TO MOURN THE DEATH, BY FIRE, OF A CHILD IN LONDON

Never until the mankind making
Bird beast and flower
Fathering and all humbling darkness
Tells with silence the last light breaking
And the still hour   5
Is come of the sea tumbling in harness

And I must enter again the round
Zion of the water bead
And the synagogue of the ear of corn
Shall I let pray the shadow of a sound   10
Or sow my salt seed
In the least valley of sackcloth to mourn

The majesty and burning of the child's death.
I shall not murder
The mankind of her going with a grave truth   15
Nor blaspheme down the stations of the breath
With any further
Elegy of innocence and youth.

Deep with the first dead lies London's daughter,
Robed in the long friends,   20
The grains beyond age, the dark veins of her mother,
Secret by the unmourning water
Of the riding Thames.
After the first death, there is no other.

(1945)

FERN HILL

Now as I was young and easy under the apple boughs
About the lilting house and happy as the grass was green,
    The night above the dingle starry,
      Time let me hail and climb
    Golden in the heydays of his eyes,   5
And honoured among wagons I was prince of the apple towns
And once below a time I lordly had the trees and leaves
      Trail with daisies and barley
    Down the rivers of the windfall light.

And as I was green and carefree, famous among the barns   10
About the happy yard and singing as the farm was home,
    In the sun that is young once only,
      Time let me play and be
    Golden in the mercy of his means,
And green and golden I was huntsman and herdsman, the calves   15
Sang to my horn, the foxes on the hills barked clear and cold,
      And the sabbath rang slowly
    In the pebbles of the holy streams.

All the sun long it was running, it was lovely, the hay
Fields high as the house, the tunes from the chimneys, it was air   20
    And playing, lovely and watery
      And fire green as grass.
    And nightly under the simple stars
As I rode to sleep the owls were bearing the farm away,

A REFUSAL TO MOURN   **8. Zion:** kingdom of heaven, perfection; cf. Blake's "And did those feet" (p. 730). **9. corn:** grain.   FERN HILL   **Title:** the name of Thomas's aunt's farmhouse in Wales. **3. dingle:** wooded valley.

All the moon long I heard, blessed among stables, the night-jars   *25*
      Flying with the ricks, and the horses
           Flashing into the dark.

And then to awake, and the farm, like a wanderer white
With the dew, come back, the cock on his shoulder: it was all
      Shining, it was Adam and maiden,   *30*
           The sky gathered again
And the sun grew round that very day.
So it must have been after the birth of the simple light
In the first, spinning place, the spellbound horses walking warm
      Out of the whinnying green stable   *35*
           On to the fields of praise.

And honoured among foxes and pheasants by the gay house
Under the new made clouds and happy as the heart was long,
      In the sun born over and over,
           I ran my heedless ways,   *40*
      My wishes raced through the house high hay
And nothing I cared, at my sky blue trades, that time allows
In all his tuneful turning so few and such morning songs
      Before the children green and golden
           Follow him out of grace,   *45*

Nothing I cared, in the lamb white days, that time would take me
Up to the swallow thronged loft by the shadow of my hand,
      In the moon that is always rising,
           Nor that riding to sleep
      I should hear him fly with the high fields   *50*
And wake to the farm forever fled from the childless land.
Oh as I was young and easy in the mercy of his means,
           Time held me green and dying
      Though I sang in my chains like the sea.

                    (1945)

DO NOT GO GENTLE INTO THAT GOOD NIGHT

Do not go gentle into that good night,
Old age should burn and rave at close of day;
Rage, rage against the dying of the light.

Though wise men at their end know dark is right,
Because their words had forked no lightning they   *5*
Do not go gentle into that good night.

Good men, the last wave by, crying how bright
Their frail deeds might have danced in a green bay,
Rage, rage against the dying of the light.

Wild men who caught and sang the sun in flight,   *10*
And learn, too late, they grieved it on its way,
Do not go gentle into that good night.

Grave men, near death, who see with blinding sight
Blind eyes could blaze like meteors and be gay,
Rage, rage against the dying of the light.   *15*

And you, my father, there on the sad height,
Curse, bless, me now with your fierce tears, I pray.
Do not go gentle into that good night.
Rage, rage against the dying of the light.

                    (1951)

---

25. **nightjars:** nighthawks.

RANDALL JARRELL
U.S.A., 1914-1965

THE DEATH OF THE BALL TURRET GUNNER

From my mother's sleep I fell into the State,
And I hunched in its belly till my wet fur froze.
Six miles from earth, loosed from its dream of life,
I woke to black flak and the nightmare fighters.
When I died they washed me out of the turret with a hose.   *5*

(1945)

BERNARD MALAMUD
U.S.A., 1914-1986

IDIOTS FIRST

The thick ticking of the clock stopped. Mendel, dozing in the dark, awoke in fright. The pain returned as he listened. He drew on his cold embittered clothing, and wasted minutes sitting at the edge of the bed.

"Isaac," he ultimately sighed.

In the kitchen, Isaac, his astonished mouth open, held six peanuts in his palm. He   *5* placed each on the table. "One . . . two . . . nine."

He gathered each peanut and appeared in the doorway. Mendel, in loose hat and long overcoat, still sat on the bed. Isaac watched with small eyes and ears, thick hair graying the sides of his head.

"Schlaf," he nasally said.   *10*

"No," muttered Mendel. As if stifling he rose. "Come, Isaac."

He wound his old watch though the sight of the stopped clock nauseated him.

Isaac wanted to hold it to his ear.

"No, it's late." Mendel put the watch carefully away. In the drawer he found the little paper bag of crumpled ones and fives and slipped it into his overcoat pocket. He   *15* helped Isaac on with his coat.

Isaac looked at one dark window, then at the other. Mendel stared at both blank windows.

They went slowly down the darkly lit stairs, Mendel first, Isaac watching the moving shadows on the wall. To one long shadow he offered a peanut.   *20*

"Hungrig."

IDIOTS FIRST   10. Schlaf: Sleep. **21. Hungrig:** hungry.

In the vestibule the old man gazed through the thin glass. The November night was cold and bleak. Opening the door he cautiously thrust his head out. Though he saw nothing he quickly shut the door.

"Ginzburg, that he came to see me yesterday," he whispered in Isaac's ear.   *25*

Isaac sucked air.

"You know who I mean?"

Isaac combed his chin with his fingers.

"That's the one, with the black whiskers. Don't talk to him or go with him if he asks you."   *30*

Isaac moaned.

"Young people he don't bother so much," Mendel said in afterthought.

It was suppertime and the street was empty but the store windows dimly lit their way to the corner. They crossed the deserted street and went on. Isaac, with a happy cry, pointed to the three golden balls. Mendel smiled but was exhausted when they got to the   *35* pawnshop.

The pawnbroker, a red-bearded man with black horn-rimmed glasses, was eating a whitefish at the rear of the store. He craned his head, saw them, and settled back to sip his tea.

In five minutes he came forward, patting his shapeless lips with a large white   *40* handkerchief.

Mendel, breathing heavily, handed him the worn gold watch. The pawnbroker, raising his glasses, screwed in his eyepiece. He turned the watch over once. "Eight dollars."

The dying man wet his cracked lips. "I must have thirty-five."   *45*

"So go to Rothschild."

"Cost me myself sixty."

"In 1905." The pawnbroker handed back the watch. It had stopped ticking. Mendel wound it slowly. It ticked hollowly.

"Isaac must go to my uncle that he lives in California."   *50*

"It's a free country," said the pawnbroker.

Isaac, watching a banjo, snickered.

"What's the matter with him?" the pawnbroker asked.

"So let be eight dollars," muttered Mendel, "but where will I get the rest till tonight?"   *55*

"How much for my hat and coat?" he asked.

"No sale." The pawnbroker went behind the cage and wrote out a ticket. He locked the watch in a small drawer but Mendel still heard it ticking.

In the street he slipped the eight dollars into the paper bag, then searched in his pockets for a scrap of writing. Finding it, he strained to read the address by the light of   *60* the street lamp.

As they trudged to the subway, Mendel pointed to the sprinkled sky.

"Isaac, look how many stars are tonight."

---

46. Rothschild: the name of a German Jewish family famous for its financial empire, established by Meyer Amschel Rothschild (1743-1812) and extending through several generations.

"Eggs," said Isaac.

"First we will go to Mr. Fishbein, after we will eat." 65

They got off the train in upper Manhattan and had to walk several blocks before they located Fishbein's house.

"A regular palace," Mendel murmured, looking forward to a moment's warmth.

Isaac stared uneasily at the heavy door of the house.

Mendel rang. The servant, a man with long sideburns, came to the door and said 70 Mr. and Mrs. Fishbein were dining and could see no one.

"He should eat in peace but we will wait till he finishes."

"Come back tomorrow morning. Tomorrow morning Mr. Fishbein will talk to you. He don't do business or charity at this time of the night."

"Charity I am not interested —" 75

"Come back tomorrow."

"Tell him it's life or death —"

"Whose life or death?"

"So if not his, then mine."

"Don't be such a big smart aleck." 80

"Look me in my face," said Mendel, "and tell me if I got time till tomorrow morning?"

The servant stared at him, then at Isaac, and reluctantly let them in.

The foyer was a vast high-ceilinged room with many oil paintings on the walls, voluminous silken draperies, a thick flowered rug at foot, and a marble staircase. 85

Mr. Fishbein, a paunchy bald-headed man with hairy nostrils and small patent leather feet, ran lightly down the stairs, a large napkin tucked under a tuxedo coat button. He stopped on the fifth step from the bottom and examined his visitors.

"Who comes on Friday night to a man that he has guests, to spoil him his supper?"

"Excuse me that I bother you, Mr. Fishbein," Mendel said. "If I didn't come now I 90 couldn't come tomorrow."

"Without more preliminaries, please state your business. I'm a hungry man."

"Hungrig," wailed Isaac.

Fishbein adjusted his pince-nez. "What's the matter with him?"

"This is my son Isaac. He is like this all his life." Isaac mewled. 95

"I am sending him to California."

"Mr. Fishbein don't contribute to personal pleasure trips."

"I am a sick man and he must go tonight on the train to my Uncle Leo."

"I never give to unorganized charity," Fishbein said, "but if you are hungry I will invite you downstairs in my kitchen. We having tonight chicken with stuffed derma." 100

"All I ask is thirty-five dollars for the train ticket to my uncle in California. I have already the rest."

"Who is your uncle? How old a man?"

"Eight-one years, a long life to him."

Fishbein burst into laughter. "Eighty-one years and you are sending him this 105 halfwit."

Mendel, flailing both arms, cried, "Please, without names."

Fishbein politely conceded.

---

100. derma: the meat casing used in preparing certain dishes made of spiced grain.

"Where is open the door there we go in the house," the sick man said. "If you will kindly give me thirty-five dollars, God will bless you. What is thirty-five dollars to Mr. Fishbein? Nothing. To me, for my boy, is everything." *110*

Fishbein drew himself up to his tallest height.

"Private contributions I don't make — only to institutions. This is my fixed policy."

Mendel sank to his creaking knees on the rug.

"Please, Mr. Fishbein, if not thirty-five, give maybe twenty." *115*

"Levinson!" Fishbein angrily called.

The servant with the long sideburns appeared at the top of the stairs.

"Show this party where is the door — unless he wishes to partake food before leaving the premises."

"For what I got chicken won't cure it," Mendel said. *120*

"This way if you please," said Levinson, descending.

Isaac assisted his father up.

"Take him to an institution," Fishbein advised over the marble balustrade. He ran quickly up the stairs and they were at once outside, buffeted by winds.

The walk to the subway was tedious. The wind blew mournfully. Mendel, breathless, *125* glanced furtively at shadows. Isaac, clutching his peanuts in his frozen fist, clung to his father's side. They entered a small park to rest for a minute on a stone bench under a leafless two-branched tree. The thick right branch was raised, the thin left one hung down. A very pale moon rose slowly. So did a stranger as they approached the bench.

"Gut yuntif," he said hoarsely. *130*

Mendel, drained of blood, waved his wasted arms. Isaac yowled sickly. Then a bell chimed and it was only ten. Mendel let out a piercing anguished cry as the bearded stranger disappeared into the bushes. A policeman came running, and though he beat the bushes with his nightstick, could turn up nothing. Mendel and Isaac hurried out of the little park. When Mendel glanced back the dead tree had its thin arm raised, the thick *135* one down. He moaned.

They boarded a trolley, stopping at the home of a former friend, but he had died years ago. On the same block they went into a cafeteria and ordered two fried eggs for Isaac. The tables were crowded except where a heavyset man sat eating soup with kasha. After one look at him they left in haste, although Isaac wept. *140*

Mendel had another address on a slip of paper but the house was too far away, in Queens, so they stood in a doorway shivering.

What can I do, he frantically thought, in one short hour?

He remembered the furniture in the house. It was junk but might bring a few dollars. "Come, Isaac." They went once more to the pawnbroker's to talk to him, but the *145* shop was dark and an iron gate — rings and gold watches glinting through it — was drawn tight across his place of business.

They huddled behind a telephone pole, both freezing. Isaac whimpered.

"See the big moon, Isaac. The whole sky is white."

He pointed but Isaac wouldn't look. *150*

---

130. Gut yuntif: Sabbath greeting. **140. kasha:** buckwheat. **142. Queens:** a borough of New York City, on Long Island.

Mendel dreamed for a minute of the sky lit up, long sheets of light in all directions. Under the sky, in California, sat Uncle Leo drinking tea with lemon. Mendel felt warm but woke up cold.

Across the street stood an ancient brick synagogue.

He pounded on the huge door but no one appeared. He waited till he had breath and 155 desperately knocked again. At last there were footsteps within, and the synagogue door creaked open on its massive brass hinges.

A darkly dressed sexton, holding a dripping candle, glared at them.

"Who knocks this time of night with so much noise on the synagogue door?"

Mendel told the sexton his troubles. "Please, I would like to speak to the rabbi." 160

"The rabbi is an old man. He sleeps now. His wife won't let you see him. Go home and come back tomorrow."

"To tomorrow I said goodbye already. I am a dying man."

Though the sexton seemed doubtful he pointed to an old wooden house next door. "In there he lives." He disappeared into the synagogue with his lit candle casting 165 shadows around him.

Mendel, with Isaac clutching his sleeve, went up the wooden steps and rang the bell. After five minutes a big-faced, gray-haired bulky woman came out on the porch with a torn robe thrown over her nightdress. She emphatically said the rabbi was sleeping and could not be waked. 170

But as she was insisting, the rabbi himself tottered to the door. He listened a minute and said, "Who wants to see me let them come in."

They entered a cluttered room. The rabbi was an old skinny man with bent shoulders and a wisp of white beard. He wore a flannel nightgown and black skullcap; his feet were bare. 175

"Vey is mir," his wife muttered. "Put on shoes or tomorrow comes sure pneumonia." She was a woman with a big belly, years younger than her husband. Staring at Isaac, she turned away.

Mendel apologetically related his errand. "All I need more is thirty-five dollars."

"Thirty-five?" said the rabbi's wife. "Why not thirty-five thousand? Who has so 180 much money? My husband is a poor rabbi. The doctors take away every penny."

"Dear friend," said the rabbi, "if I had I would give you."

"I got already seventy," Mendel said, heavy-hearted. "All I need more is thirty-five."

"God will give you," said the rabbi.

"In the grave," said Mendel. "I need tonight. Come, Isaac." 185

"Wait," called the rabbi.

He hurried inside, came out with a fur-lined caftan, and handed it to Mendel.

"Yascha," shrieked his wife, "not your new coat!"

"I got my old one. Who needs two coats for one body?"

"Yascha, I am screaming —" 190

"Who can go among poor people, tell me, in a new coat?"

"Yascha," she cried, "what can this man do with your coat? He needs tonight the money. The pawnbrokers are asleep."

---

176. Vey is mir: (Yiddish) Woe is me.

"So let him wake them up."

"No." She grabbed the coat from Mendel.   *195*

He held on to a sleeve, wrestling her for the coat. Her I know, Mendel thought. "Shylock," he muttered. Her eyes glittered.

The rabbi groaned and tottered dizzily. His wife cried out as Mendel yanked the coat from her hands.

"Run," cried the rabbi.   *200*

"Run, Isaac."

They ran out of the house and down the steps.

"Stop, you thief," called the rabbi's wife.

The rabbi pressed both hands to his temples and fell to the floor.

"Help!" his wife wept. "Heart attack! Help!"   *205*

But Mendel and Isaac ran through the streets with the rabbi's new fur-lined caftan. After them noiselessly ran Ginzburg.

It was very late when Mendel bought the train ticket in the only booth open.

There was no time to stop for a sandwich so Isaac ate his peanuts and they hurried to the train in the vast deserted station.   *210*

"So in the morning," Mendel gasped as they ran, "there comes a man that he sells sandwiches and coffee. Eat but get change. When reaches California the train, will be waiting for you on the station Uncle Leo. If you don't recognize him he will recognize you. Tell him I send best regards."

But when they arrived at the gate to the platform it was shut, the light out.   *215*

Mendel, groaning, beat on the gate with his fists.

"Too late," said the uniformed ticket collector, a bulky, bearded man with hairy nostrils and a fishy smell.

He pointed to the station clock. "Already past twelve."

"But I see standing there still the train," Mendel said, hopping in his grief.   *220*

"It just left — in one more minute."

"A minute is enough. Just open the gate."

"Too late I told you."

Mendel socked his bony chest with both hands. "With my whole heart I beg you this little favor."   *225*

"Favors you had enough already. For you the train is gone. You shoulda been dead already at midnight. I told you that yesterday. This is the best I can do."

"Ginzburg!" Mendel shrank from him.

"Who else?" The voice was metallic, eyes glittered, the expression amused.

"For myself," the old man begged, "I don't ask a thing. But what will happen to   *230* my boy?"

Ginzburg shrugged slightly. "What will happen happens. This isn't my responsibility. I got enough to think about without worrying about somebody on one cylinder."

"What then is your responsibility?"

"To create conditions. To make happen what happens. I ain't in the anthropomor-   *235* phic business."

---

197. Shylock: Jewish moneylender in Shakespeare's *The Merchant of Venice*.

"Whatever business you in, where is your pity?"

"This ain't my commodity. The law is the law."

"Which law is this?"

"The cosmic universal law, goddamit, the one I got to follow myself."   *240*

"What kind of a law is it?" cried Mendel. "For God's sake, don't you understand what I went through in my life with this poor boy? Look at him. For thirty-nine years, since the day he was born, I wait for him to grow up, but he don't. Do you understand what this means in a father's heart? Why don't you let him go to his uncle?" His voice had risen and he was shouting.   *245*

Isaac mewled loudly.

"Better calm down or you'll hurt somebody's feelings," Ginzburg said with a wink toward Isaac.

"All my life," Mendel cried, his body trembling, "what did I have? I was poor. I suffered from my health. When I worked I worked too hard. When I didn't work was   *250* worse. My wife died a young woman. But I didn't ask from anybody nothing. Now I ask a small favor. Be so kind, Mr. Ginzburg."

The ticket collector was picking his teeth with a match stick.

"You ain't the only one, my friend, some got it worse than you. That's how it goes in this country."   *255*

"You dog you." Mendel lunged at Ginzburg's throat and began to choke. "You bastard, don't you understand what it means human?"

They struggled nose to nose, Ginzburg, though his astonished eyes bulged, began to laugh. "You pipsqueak nothing. I'll freeze you to pieces."

His eyes lit in rage and Mendel felt an unbearable cold like an icy dagger invading   *260* his body, all of his parts shriveling.

Now I die without helping Isaac.

A crowd gathered. Isaac yelped in fright.

Clinging to Ginzburg in his last agony, Mendel saw reflected in the ticket collector's eyes the depth of his terror. But he saw that Ginzburg, staring at himself in   *265* Mendel's eyes, saw mirrored in them the extent of his own awful wrath. He beheld a shimmering, starry, blinding light that produced darkness.

Ginzburg looked astounded. "Who me?"

His grip on the squirming old man slowly loosened, and Mendel, his heart barely beating, slumped to the ground.   *270*

"Go," Ginzburg muttered, "take him to the train."

"Let pass," he commanded a guard.

The crowd parted. Isaac helped his father up and they tottered down the steps to the platform where the train waited, lit and ready to go.

Mendel found Isaac a coach seat and hastily embraced him. "Help Uncle Leo,   *275* Isaakil. Also remember your father and mother."

"Be nice to him," he said to the conductor. "Show him where everything is."

He waited on the platform until the train began slowly to move. Isaac sat at the edge of his seat, his face strained in the direction of his journey. When the train was gone, Mendel ascended the stairs to see what had become of Ginzburg.   *280*

(1961, 1963)

HENRY REED
England, 1914-1986

NAMING OF PARTS

To-day we have naming of parts. Yesterday,
We had daily cleaning. And to-morrow morning,
We shall have what to do after firing. But to-day,
To-day we have naming of parts. Japonica
Glistens like coral in all of the neighbouring gardens,   5
   And to-day we have naming of parts.

This is the lower sling swivel. And this
Is the upper sling swivel, whose use you will see,
When you are given your slings. And this is the piling swivel,
Which in your case you have not got. The branches   10
Hold in the gardens their silent, eloquent gestures,
   Which in our case we have not got.

This is the safety-catch, which is always released
With an easy flick of the thumb. And please do not let me
See anyone using his finger. You can do it quite easy   15
If you have any strength in your thumb. The blossoms
Are fragile and motionless, never letting anyone see
   Any of them using their finger.

And this you can see is the bolt. The purpose of this
Is to open the breech, as you see. We can slide it   20
Rapidly backwards and forwards: we call this
Easing the spring. And rapidly backwards and forwards
The early bees are assaulting and fumbling the flowers:
   They call it easing the Spring.

They call it easing the Spring: it is perfectly easy   25
If you have any strength in your thumb: like the bolt,
And the breech, and the cocking-piece, and the point of balance,
Which in our case we have not got; and the almond-blossom
Silent in all of the gardens and the bees going backwards and forwards,
   For to-day we have naming of parts.   30

(1946)

NAMING OF PARTS This poem is the first in a series collectively titled "Lessons of the War"; an epigraph to the whole series comes from Horace (*Odes*, III, 26): "Vixi duellis nuper idoneus/ Et militavi non sine gloria" (Reed has changed Horace's word "puellis" [girls] to "duellis" [battles] to make the quotation read "Lately I have lived fit for battle / And have soldiered, not without glory.")

WILLIAM STAFFORD
U.S.A., b.1914

SAYINGS FROM THE NORTHERN ICE

It is people at the edge who say
things at the edge: winter is toward knowing.

   Sled runners before they meet have long talk apart.
   There is a pup in every litter the wolves will have.
   A knife that falls points at an enemy.   *5*
   Rocks in the wind know their place: down low.
   Over your shoulder is God; the dying deer sees Him.

At the mouth of the long sack we fall in forever
storms brighten the spikes of the stars.

   Wind that buried bear skulls north of here   *10*
   and beats moth wings for help outside the door
   is bringing bear skull wisdom, but do not ask the skull
   too large a question till summer.
   Something too dark was held in that strong bone.

Better to end with a lucky saying: *15*

   Sled runners cannot decide to join or to part.
   When they decide, it is a bad day.

                   (1977)

ISABELLA GARDNER
U.S.A., 1915-1981

COCK A' HOOP

How struts my love my cavalier
How crows he like a chanticleer
How softly I am spurred my dear;
Our bed is feathered with desire
And this yard safe from fox and fire.   *5*

But spurless on the dunghill, dead,
The soldier's blood is rooster red,
His seed is spent and no hen fed.
Alas no chick of this sweet cock
Will speak for Christ at dawn o'clock.   *10*

                   (1955)

COCK A' HOOP   **2. chanticleer:** See Chaucer's "The Nun's Priest's Tale" (p. 64).

FALL IN MASSACHUSETTS

I saw the tall bush burn.
(Nineteen times a gallows-tree . . .
The tongue of fire muted by our guilt. There cannot be
a voice for deaf New Englanders vowed never to be healed.)
I saw where a manna of flame had unfallowed the starving field   *5*
        where a witch charred
        where her bones roared
where each of the good-wives took her choice of holiday or skewered house
and the mewing children barked another name
to their elders gathering apple-wood boughs   *10*
        and the sweet, the kindling fern:
        while cinders blew; and shame.

(1955)

DOROTHY AUCHTERLONIE
Australia, 1915-1990

THE TREE

He watched them as they walked towards the tree,
Through the green garden when the leaves stood still,
He saw his scarlet fruit hang tremulously:
He whispered, "Eat it if you will."

Knowing as yet they had no will but his,   *5*
Were as his hand, his foot, his braided hair.
His own face mocked him from his own abyss:
He whispered, "Eat it if you dare!"

Without him they could neither will nor dare;
Courage and will yet slumbered in the fruit,   *10*
Desire forbore, they still were unaware
That doubt was set to feed the root.

God held his breath: If they should miss it now,
Standing within the shadow of the tree . . .
Always the I, never to know the Thou   *15*
Imprisoned in my own eternity.

"Death sits within the fruit, you'll surely die!"
He scarcely formed the words upon a breath;
"O liberating seed! Eat, then, and I
For this release will die your every death.   *20*

"Thus time shall be confounded till you come
Full-circle to this garden where we stand,
From the dark maze of knowledge, with the sum
Of good and evil in your hand.

"Then you will shed the journey you have made,   *25*
See millenniums fall about your feet,
Behold the light that flares within each blade
Of grass, the visible paraclete."

The harsh Word stirred the leaves, the fruit glowed red,
Adam's foot struck against the root;   *30*
He saw his naked doubt and raised his head:
Eve stretched her hand and plucked the fruit.

(1967)

FALL IN MASSACHUSETTS   Cf. Hawthorne's "The May-pole of Merry Mount" (p. 923).   THE TREE   See Genesis 3:3-6 (p. 244).

JUDITH WRIGHT
Australia, b.1915

THE TRAINS

Tunnelling through the night, the trains pass
in a splendour of power, with a sound like thunder
shaking the orchards, waking
the young from a dream, scattering like glass
the old men's sleep; laying   5
a black trail over the still bloom of the orchards.
The trains go north with guns.

Strange primitive piece of flesh, the heart laid quiet
hearing their cry pierce through its thin-walled cave
recalls the forgotten tiger   10
and leaps awake in its old panic riot;
and how shall mind be sober,
since blood's red thread still binds us fast in history?
Tiger, you walk through all our past and future,
troubling the children's sleep; laying   15
a reeking trail across our dream of orchards.

Racing on iron errands, the trains go by,
and over the white acres of our orchards
hurl their wild summoning cry, their animal cry . . .
the trains go north with guns.   20

                                                    (1946)

EVE TO HER DAUGHTERS

It was not I who began it.
Turned out into draughty caves,
hungry so often, having to work for our bread,
hearing the children whining,
I was nevertheless not unhappy.   5
Where Adam went I was fairly contented to go.
I adapted myself to the punishment: it was my life.

But Adam, you know . . . !
He kept on brooding over the insult,
over the trick They had played on us, over the scolding.   10
He had discovered a flaw in himself
and he had to make up for it.

Outside Eden the earth was imperfect,
the seasons changed, the game was fleet-footed,
he had to work for our living, and he didn't like it.   15
He even complained of my cooking
(it was hard to compete with Heaven).

So he set to work.
The earth must be made a new Eden
with central heating, domesticated animals,   20
mechanical harvesters, combustion engines,
escalators, refrigerators,
and modern means of communication
and multiplied opportunities for safe investment
and higher education for Abel and Cain   25
and the rest of the family.
You can see how his pride had been hurt.

In the process he had to unravel everything,
because he believed that mechanism
was the whole secret — he was always mechanical-minded.
He got to the very inside of the whole machine   31
exclaiming as he went, So this is how it works!
And now that I know how it works, why, I must have
       invented it.
As for God and the Other, they cannot be demonstrated,
and what cannot be demonstrated   35
doesn't exist.
You see, he had always been jealous.

Yes, he got to the centre
where nothing at all can be demonstrated.
And clearly he doesn't exist; but he refuses   40
to accept the conclusion.
You see, he was always an egotist.

It was warmer than this in the cave;
there was none of this fall-out.
I would suggest, for the sake of the children,   45
that it's time you took over.

EVE TO HER DAUGHTERS   25. Abel and Cain: See Genesis 4 (p. 245).

But you are my daughters, you inherit my own faults of
    character;
you are submissive, following Adam
even beyond existence.
Faults of character have their own logic   *50*
and it always works out.
I observed this with Abel and Cain.

Perhaps the whole elaborate fable
right from the beginning
is meant to demonstrate this; perhaps it's the whole secret.
Perhaps nothing exists but our faults?   *56*
At least they can be demonstrated.

But it's useless to make
such a suggestion to Adam.
He has turned himself into God,   *60*
who is faultless, and doesn't exist.

                    (1966)

THE OTHER HALF

The self that night undrowns when I'm asleep
travels beneath the dumb days that I give,
within the limits set that I may live,
and beats in anger on the things I love.
I am the cross it bears, and it the tears I weep.   *5*

Under the eyes of light my work is brief.
Day sets on me the burdens that I carry.
I face the light, the dark of me I bury.
My silent answer and my other half,
we meet at midnight and by music only.   *10*

Yet there's a word that I would give to you:
the truth you tell in your dumb images
my daylight self goes stumbling after too.
So we may meet at last, and meeting bless,
and turn into one truth in singleness.   *15*

                    (1966)

P.K. PAGE
Canada, b.1916

T-BAR

Relentless, black on white, the cable runs
through metal arches up the mountain side
At intervals giant pickaxes are hung
on long hydraulic springs. The skiers ride
propped by the axehead, twin automatons   *5*
supported by its handle, one each side.

In twos they move slow motion up the steep
incision in the mountain. Climb. Climb.
Somnambulists, bolt upright in their sleep
their phantom poles swung lazily behind,   *10*
while to the right, the empty T-bars keep
in mute descent, slow monstrous jigging time.

Captive the skiers now and innocent,
wards of eternity, each pair alone.
They mount the easy vertical ascent,   *15*
pass through successive arches, bride and groom,
as through successive naves, are newly wed
participants in some recurring dream.

So do they move forever. Clocks are broken.
In zones of silence they grow tall and slow,   *20*
inanimate dreamers, mild and gentle-spoken
blood-brothers of the haemophilic snow
until the summit breaks and they awaken
imagos from the stricture of the tow.

Jerked from her chrysalis the sleeping bride   *25*
suffers too sudden freedom like a pain.
The dreaming bridegroom severed from her side
singles her out, the old wound aches again.
Uncertain, lost, upon a wintry height
these two, not separate, but no longer one.   *30*

Now clocks begin to peck and sing. The slow
extended minute like a rubber band
contracts to catapult them through the snow
in tandem trajectory while behind
etching the sky-line, obdurate and slow   *35*
the spastic T-bars pivot and descend.

                    (1954)

JAMES MCAULEY
Australia, 1917-1976

TERRA AUSTRALIS

Voyage within you, on the fabled ocean,
And you will find that Southern Continent,
Quiros' vision — his hidalgo heart
And mythical Australia, where reside
All things in their imagined counterpart.   5

It is your land of similes: the wattle
Scatters its pollen on the doubting heart;
The flowers are wide-awake; the air gives ease.
There you come home; the magpies call you Jack
And whistle like larrikins at you from the trees.   10

There too the angophora preaches on the hillsides
With the gestures of Moses; and the white cockatoo,
Perched on his limbs, screams with demoniac pain;
And who shall say on what errand the insolent emu
Walks between morning and night on the edge of the plain?

But northward in valleys of the fiery Goat   16
Where the sun like a centaur vertically shoots
His raging arrows with unerring aim,
Stand the ecstatic solitary pyres
Of unknown lovers, featureless with flame.   20

(1946)

ROBERT LOWELL
U.S.A., 1917-1977

CHRISTMAS EVE UNDER HOOKER'S STATUE

Tonight a blackout. Twenty years ago
I hung my stocking on the tree, and hell's
Serpent entwined the apple in the toe
To sting the child with knowledge. Hooker's heels
Kicking at nothing in the shifting snow,   5
A cannon and a cairn of cannon balls
Rusting before the blackened Statehouse, know
How the long horn of plenty broke like glass
In Hooker's gauntlets. Once I came from Mass;

Now storm-clouds shelter Christmas, once again   10
Mars meets his fruitless star with open arms,
His heavy saber flashes with the rime,
The war-god's bronzed and empty forehead forms
Anonymous machinery from raw men;

The cannon on the Common cannot stun   15
The blundering butcher as he rides on Time —
The barrel clinks with holly. I am cold:
I ask for bread, my father gives me mould;

His stocking is full of stones. Santa in red
Is crowned with wizened berries. Man of war,   20
Where is the summer's garden? In its bed
The ancient speckled serpent will appear,
And black-eyed susan with her frizzled head.
When Chancellorsville mowed down the volunteer,
"All wars are boyish," Herman Melville said;   25
But we are old, our fields are running wild:
Till Christ again turn wanderer and child.

(1946)

TERRA AUSTRALIS Title: the South Land (the name printed on early maps, representing a fabulous but not yet discovered continent). **3. Quiros:** Pedro Fernandez de Quiros (1563-1614), Portuguese explorer, about whom McAuley wrote a narrative poem called *Captain Quiros* (1964). **10. larrikins:** hooligans. **11. angophora:** native Australian tree, similar to eucalyptus. **16. Goat:** the Tropic of Capricorn, which transects northern Australia.   **CHRISTMAS EVE UNDER HOOKER'S STATUE Title:** In May 1863, General Joseph Hooker (1814-1879) led the Union troops against Robert E. Lee's Confederate troops in the Battle of Chancellorsville, Virginia (see line 24); Lee's army, less than half the size of the Union force, outmanoeuvred Hooker and forced him to withdraw, but it was Lee's last major victory in the American Civil War. **25. "All . . . boyish":** "All wars are boyish, and are fought by boys" — line 6 of Melville's "The March into Virginia, Ending in the First Manassas" (otherwise known as the first battle of Bull Run, 21 July 1861); see also "On the Slain Collegians" (both works are in *Battle-Pieces and Aspects of the War*, 1866); for another of Melville's war poems, see "Shiloh" (p. 1030); and cf. Rupert Brooke's "Peace" (p. 1296).

GWENDOLYN BROOKS
U.S.A., b.1917

THE BEAN EATERS

They eat beans mostly, this old yellow pair.
Dinner is a casual affair.
Plain chipware on a plain and creaking wood,
Tin flatware.

Two who are Mostly Good.   5
Two who have lived their day,
But keep on putting on their clothes
And putting things away.

And remembering . . .
Remembering, with twinklings and twinges,   10
As they lean over the beans in their rented back room that
     is full of beads and receipts and dolls and cloths,
     tobacco crumbs, vases and fringes.

(1960)

WE REAL COOL

    The Pool Players.
    Seven at the Golden Shovel.

We real cool. We
Left school. We

Lurk late. We
Strike straight. We

Sing sin. We   5
Thin gin. We

Jazz June. We
Die soon.

(1960)

MARGARET AVISON
Canada, b.1918

THE MIRRORED MAN

Lot put his wife out of his mind
Through respect for the mortal lot:
She having dared to yearn defined
All that to him was naught.

So now we flee the Garden   5
Of Eden, steadfastly.
And still in our flight are ardent
For lost eternity.

We always turn our heads away
When Canaan is at hand,   10
Knowing it mortal to enjoy
The Promise, not the Land.

Yet the Cimmerian meadows know the sword
Flaming and searching that picks out

The children for this earth, and hurls the curse   15
After us, through the void.
    So each of us conceals within himself
    A cell where one man stares into the glass
    And sees, now featureless the meadow mists,
    And now himself, a pistol at his temple,   20
    Gray, separate, wearily waiting.

We, comic creatures of our piebald day,
Either ignore this burden, nonchalantly
(Dragging a dull repudiated house
At heel, through all our trivial ramblings)   25
Or gravely set ourselves the rigorous task
Of fashioning the key that fits that cell
(As if it hid the timeless Garden).

THE MIRRORED MAN   1. Lot: See Genesis 19:1-26. **5-6, 13-14:** See Genesis 3:24 (p. 245). **13. Cimmerian:** dark; see the note to line 12 of Pound's *Canto I* (p. 1293).

I interviewed one gentleman so engaged,
And he looked up and said: *30*
"Despair is a denial and a sin
But to deny despair, intolerable."
The next week, so I heard, he used his key,
Walked over to the mirror, forced the hand
Of the young man, and left him   *35*
Drooping, the idle door of an idle cell
Mirrored at last. Such men are left possessed
Of ready access to no further incident.

One man unlocked his cell
    To use it as a love-nest.   *40*
By fond report, the mirror there is crammed
    With monkey faces, ruby ear-rings, branches
Of purple grapes, and ornamental feathers.
    Whatever winter ravages his gardens
No banging shutters desolate his guests   *45*
    Who entertain illusion as he wills it,
And grant him the inviolate privacy
    His hospitable favour purchases.

All of us, flung in one
Murky parabola,   *50*
Seek out some pivot for significance,
Leery of comets' tails, mask-merry,
Wondering at the centre
Who will gain access, search the citadel
To its last, secret door?   *55*
And what face will the violator find
When he confronts the glass?

                                        (1959)

SEPTEMBER STREET

    Harvest apples lack tartness.
    The youngest child stares at the brick
        school-wall.
    After the surprising *coup* at a late luncheon
        meeting
        the young man shifting for green concludes
    the future makes his bitten thumb the fake.   *5*
        A convalescent steps around
    wet leaves, resolving on the post-box corner.
        Next time, the young man glimpses,
    he will be one of three, not the lone fourth
        susceptible to elation.   *10*
    Yellow. The pride saddens him.
    A van grinds past. Somebody with
    considerable dash and a strong left hand
plays "Annie Laurie" on an untuned piano.
        Granada will not rhyme with Canada.   *15*
    The home-grown wines have sharpness.
        A scissor-grinder used to come
        about the hour the school let out
        and children knocked down chestnuts.
            On the yellow porch   *20*
    one sits, not reading headlines; the old eyes
    read far out into the mild
            air, runes.
    See. There: a stray sea-gull.

                                        (1959)

AL PURDY
Canada, b.1918

LAMENT FOR THE DORSETS
(Eskimos extinct in the 14th century AD)

Animal bones and some mossy tent rings
scrapers and spearheads   carved ivory swans
all that remains of the Dorset giants
who drove the Vikings back to their long ships

talked to spirits of earth and water   *5*
— a picture of terrifying old men
so large they broke the backs of bears
so small they lurk behind bone rafters

in the brain of modern hunters
among good thoughts and warm things   10
and come out at night
to spit on the stars

The big men with clever fingers
who had no dogs and hauled their sleds
over the frozen northern oceans   15
awkward giants
                    killers of seal
they couldn't compete with little men
who came from the west with dogs
Or else in a warm climatic cycle   20
the seals went back to cold waters
and the puzzled Dorsets scratched their heads
with hairy thumbs around 1350 A.D.
— couldn't figure it out
went around saying to each other   25
plaintively
            "What's wrong? What happened?
            Where are the seals gone?"
And died

Twentieth-century people   30
apartment dwellers
executives of neon death
warmakers with things that explode
— they have never imagined us in their future
how could we imagine them in the past   35
squatting among the moving glaciers
six hundred years ago
with glowing lamps?
As remote or nearly
as the trilobites and swamps   40
when coal became
or the last great reptile hissed
at a mammal the size of a mouse
that squeaked and fled

Did they ever realize at all   45
what was happening to them?
Some old hunter with one lame leg
a bear had chewed

sitting in a caribou-skin tent
— the last Dorset?   50
Let's say his name was Kudluk

and watch him sitting there
carving 2-inch ivory swans
for a dead grand-daughter
taking them out of his mind   55
the places in his mind
where pictures are
He selects a sharp stone tool
to gouge a parallel pattern of lines
on both sides of the swan   60
holding it with his left hand
bearing down and transmitting
his body's weight
from brain to arm and right hand
and one of his thoughts   65
turns to ivory
The carving is laid aside
in beginning darkness
at the end of hunger
and after a while wind   70
blows down the tent and snow
begins to cover him

After 600 years
the ivory thought
is still warm   75
                    (1968, 1972)

MOSES AT DARWIN STATION

Tortoises
like small boxcars
a baker's dozen of them
one seven hundred pounds
and 160 years old   5
(call him Moses
pre-dating Darwin's
Voyage of the Beagle)
body a huge strongbox
plundered by 18th-   10

LAMENT FOR THE DORSETS   **50. the last Dorset:** Cf. Crate's "Shawnandithit" (p. 1534).   MOSES AT DARWIN STATION   **8.**
Voyage of the Beagle: See the excerpt from Darwin's book (p. 945).

century seaman for food
but nearly impregnable
for non-human burglars
We're shadows to him
two-legged shadows   *15*
ungainly whirlpools
of bifurcated motion
black and white only
in his optic register
the scrawny old-man's neck   *20*
motionless buckboard of shell
galumphing *galapago*
exploring silence
investigating the either/
or of persistent rumours   *25*
that God exists
or does not
Scratch his long neck
and he suffers me
after 160 years   *30*
one can afford
indulgence of shadows
tolerance of transience
Tortoise-*chelonia*
science nomenclature   *35*
animal identity
and yet I think
who are they?
despite trite labels
perishable description   *40*
vanishing sound-glyphs
who are they?
— would I recognize Moses
in a downtown galaxy
or asteroid hotel room   *45*
of neon and strippers
in New York and Vegas
his buckboard shell
traversing 160 years
his ponderous ancestors   *50*
hop-stepping ages
reptilian acrobat
one hundred million years

of fence posts of time
a phantom charioteer   *55*
called soul or spirit
or even instinct
urging him on forever
We of course are human
but not recognizably so   *60*
as long as he was tortoise
in fact confess it:
remembering far ages
when birds and mammals
branched off from reptiles   *65*
and therefore those distant
ancestors of old Moses
are unrecognizably
but yet indubitably
my own   *70*
It is chastening
it is downright chastening
to have your forefather
barely acknowledge you
when you scratch his neck   *75*
but snuff at greenstuff
you proffer cautiously
his pleasantly ugly
face a road map
to your own past   *80*

Therefore go back there
following your footprints
a lost time-traveller
when things were beginning:
while comets crash   *85*
and ricochet on earth
the *phyla*-families
take evasive action:
one-celled *protozoa*
dodge fire-balls   *90*
way back in the Cambrian
worm-*annelid* slips the punch
fish-*chordata* becomes
a clumsy amphibian
and seven-come-eleven   *95*
the dice turn snake eyes

22. *galapago*: (Spanish) tortoise.

tortoise-*chelonia*
does a tricky dance step
and we're on our way
Ol Granpappy Moses   100
brushes off this nonsense
of uranium clocks
and scientific theories
of continental drifting

glaciation and star-birth   *105*
remembering only
the linchpin now
this permanent moment
the same as always
its name is Moses   *110*

Galapagos Islands
                                        (1981)

Robert Duncan
U.S.A., 1919-1988

Often I Am Permitted to Return to a Meadow

as if it were a scene made-up by the mind,
that is not mine, but is a made place,

that is mine, it is so near to the heart,
an eternal pasture folded in all thought
so that there is a hall therein   5

that is a made place, created by light
wherefrom the shadows that are forms fall.

Wherefrom fall all architectures I am
I say are likenesses of the First Beloved
whose flowers are flames lit to the Lady.   10

She it is Queen Under The Hill
whose hosts are a disturbance of words within words
that is a field folded.

It is only a dream of the grass blowing
east against the source of the sun   15
in an hour before the sun's going down

whose secret we see in a children's game
of ring a round of roses told.

Often I am permitted to return to a meadow
as if it were a given property of the mind   20
that certain bounds hold against chaos,

that is a place of first permission,
everlasting omen of what is.

                                        (1960)

7/15/64
Structure of Rime XXV

The Fire Master waits always for me to recall him from a place in my heart that is burnd or is burning. He comes to my mind where, immediate to the thought of him, his rimes flicker and would blaze forth and take over.

You too are a flame then and my soul quickening in your   5
gaze a draft upward carrying the flame of you. From this bed of a language in compression, life now is fuel, anthracite from whose hardness the years spring. In flame

---

Often I Am Permitted   **18. ring a round of roses:** See the children's rhyme (p. 568).

beings strive in the Sun's
chemistry as we strive in our meat to realize images of manhood   *10*
immanent we have not reacht, but leave, as if they fell from us,
bright fell and fane momentary attendants,

    wild instances,   beast-headed
                initiators

seen in glades of the fire's blazing,   *15*

   the lion's face passing into
   the man's face, flare into
      flare,

the bright tongues of two
    languages   *20*

dance in the one light.

        (1968)

LOUISE BENNETT
Jamaica, b.1919

COLONIZATION IN REVERSE

Wat a joyful news, Miss Mattie,
I feel like me heart gwine burs'
Jamaica people colonizin
Englan in reverse.

By de hundred, by de t'ousan   *5*
From country and from town,
By de ship-load, by de plane-load
Jamaica is Englan boun.

Dem a-pour out o' Jamaica,
Everybody future plan   *10*
Is fe get a big-time job
An settle in de mother lan.

What a islan! What a people!
Man an woman, old an young
Jusa pack dem bag an baggage   *15*
An tun history upside dung!

Some people don't like travel,
But fe show dem loyalty
Dem all a-open up cheap-fare-
To-Englan agency.   *20*

An week by week dem shippin off
Dem countryman like fire,
Fe immigrate an populate
De seat o' de Empire.

Oonoo see how life is funny,   *25*
Oonoo see de tunabout,
Jamaica live fe box bread
Outa English people mout'.

For wen dem catch a Englan,
An start play dem different role,   *30*
Some will settle down to work
An some will settle fe de dole.

COLONIZATION IN REVERSE   **2. gwine:** going to. **16. upside dung:** upside down. **25. Oonoo:** you (plural). **27. fe:** for, in order to.

Jane say de dole is not too bad
Because dey payin' she
Two pounds a week fe seek a job   35
Dat suit her dignity.

Me say Jane will never find work
At the rate how she dah-look,
For all day she stay pon Aunt Fan couch
An read love-story book.   40

Wat a devilment a Englan!
Dem face war an brave de worse,
But I'm wonderin' how dem gwine stan'
Colonizin' in reverse.

(1966)

MAY SWENSON
U.S.A., b.1919

MAsterMANANiMAl

ANiMAte MANANiMAl MAttress of Nerves
MANipulAtor Motor ANd Motive MAker
MAMMAliAN MAtrix MAt of rivers red
MortAl MANic Morsel Mover shAker

MAteriAl-MAster MAsticAtor oxygeN-eAter   5
MouNtAiN-MouNter MApper peNetrAtor
iN MoNster MetAl MANtle of the Air
MAssive wAter-surgeoN prestidigitAtor

MAchiNist MAsoN MesoN-Mixer MArble-heAver
coiNer cArver cities-idols-AtoMs-sMAsher   10
electric lever Metric AlcheMist
MeNtAl AMAzer igNorANt iNcubAtor

cANNibAl AutoMANANiMAl cAllous cAlculAtor
Milky MAgNetic MAN iNNoceNt iNNovAtor
MAlleAble MAMMAl MercuriAl ANd MAteriAl   15
MAsterANiMAl ANd ANiMA etheriAl

(1970)

HOWARD NEMEROV
U.S.A., 1920-1991

A PRIMER OF THE DAILY ROUND

A peels an apple, while B kneels to God,
C telephones to D, who has a hand
On E's knee, F coughs, G turns up the sod

For H's grave, I do not understand
But J is bringing one clay pigeon down   5
While K brings down a nightstick on L's head,
And M takes mustard, N drives into town,

A PRIMER OF THE DAILY ROUND   See the nursery rhyme alphabets (pp. 566,569).

O goes to bed with P, and Q drops dead,
R lies to S, but happens to be heard
By T, who tells U not to fire V   *10*
For having to give W the word
That X is now deceiving Y with Z,
    Who happens just now to remember A
    Peeling an apple somewhere far away.

                                                    (1958)

THE FOUR AGES

The first age of the world was counterpoint,
Music immediate to all the senses
Not yet exclusive in their separate realms,
Wordlessly weaving the tapestried cosmos
Reflected mosaic in the wakening mind.   *5*

That world was lost, though echoes of it stray
On every breeze and breath, fragmented and
Heard but in snatches, thenceforth understood
Only by listeners like Pythagoras,
Who held the music of the spheres was
    silence   *10*
Because we had been hearing it from birth,
And Shakespeare, who made his Caliban recite
Its praises in the temporary isle.

A second age. Hard consonants began
To interrupt the seamless river of sound,   *15*
Set limits, break up and define in bits
What had before been pure relationship.
Units arose, and separations; words
Entered the dancing-space and made it song.
Though the divine had gone, yet there was
    then   *20*
The keenest human intuition of
Its hiding from us one dimension past
What the five senses could receive or send.

In the third age, without our noticing

The music ceased to sound, and we were left   *25*
As unaccompanied and strangely alone,
Like actors suddenly naked in a dream.
Yet we had words, and yet we had the word
Of poetry, a thinner music, but
Both subtle and sublime in its lament   *30*
For all that was lost to all but memory.

The fourth age is, it always is, the last.
The sentences break ranks, the orchestra
Has left the pit, the curtain has come down
Upon the smiling actors, and the crowd   *35*
Is moving toward the exits through the aisles.
Illusion at last is over, all proclaim
The warm humanity of common prose,
Informative, pedestrian and plain,
Imperative and editorial,   *40*
Opinionated and proud to be so,
Delighted to explain, but not to praise.

This is not history, it is a myth.
It's *de rigueur* for myths to have four ages,
Nobody quite knows why, unless to match   *45*
Four seasons and four elements and four
Voices of music and four gospels and four
Cardinal points on the compass rose and four
Whatever elses happen to come in four.
These correspondences are what remain   *50*
Of the great age when all was counterpoint
And no one minded that nothing mattered or
    meant.

                                                (1975)

THE FOUR AGES   Cf. the selection from Sandys's translation of Ovid (p. 267). **9. Pythagoras:** Greek philosopher of the 6th century B.C. **12. Caliban:** character in Shakespeare's *The Tempest*.

AMY CLAMPITT
U.S.A., b.1920

LET THE AIR CIRCULATE

spaces between
archetypal openings   the aperture
seen through binoculars   carved by the lone boatman's
arm athwart the tiller   the schooner's travelling
house of air   split like a nutshell   or a bivalve's domicile   5
jalousies   belfries   cupolas   floor-through
apartments   let the air circulate   spaces between (sixteen
floors up and still rising)   scaffolded pourers
of reinforced concrete   by the motorized   wheelbarrowful
silhouetted   (a hardhatted frieze)   make of them   10
something unwittingly classical

clamdiggers
wading mudflats   bending in attitudes
older than   the name of anything   spaces between
things looked at   or unlooked at   beatitudes   15
of the unaware they're   being looked at
eiders flying   straight as a die   to wherever they're going
triglyph and metope   of air   let the light pass
let the air circulate   let there be intervals
for moving   apart   for   20
coming back together

the antipodal
the antiphonal   the gradual
the totally unexpected   the counted on   as infallible
the look of   from a particular   window   25
an island   in profile
the fish-spine   silhouette   of a particular
spruce   intersecting at nightfall   the unaltering interval
of 'Tit Manan light   opening up   folding into
itself   fading   brightening   an orbiting   30
sidereal buttercup

(1985)

LET THE AIR CIRCULATE   29. **'Tit Manan light:** the lighthouse at Petit Manan, on the Maine–New Brunswick border.

EDWIN MORGAN
Scotland, b.1920

ARCHIVES

```
generation upon
generation upon
generation upon
generation upon
generation upon
generation upon
generation upon
generation upon
generation upon
generation upon
generation upon
generation upon
generation upon
generation upon
generation upon
generation upon
generation upon
generation upon
generation upon
g neration upon
g neration up  n
g nerat on up  n
g nerat  n up  n
g nerat  n  p  n
g   erat  n  p  n
g   era   n  p  n
g   era   n     n
g   er    n     n
g    r    n     n
g         n     n
g         n
g
```

ARCHIVES   This poem appeared in 1968.

GWEN HARWOOD
Australia, b.1920

SUBURBAN SONNET

She practises a fugue, though it can matter
to no one now if she plays well or not.
Beside her on the floor two children chatter,
then scream and fight. She hushes them. A pot
boils over. As she rushes to the stove   5
too late, a wave of nausea overpowers
subject and counter-subject. Zest and love
drain out with soapy water as she scours
the crusted milk. Her veins ache. Once she played
for Rubinstein, who yawned. The children caper   10
round a sprung mousetrap where a mouse lies dead.
When the soft corpse won't move they seem afraid.
She comforts them; and wraps it in a paper
featuring: *Tasty dishes from stale bread.*

                                        (1968)

OODGEROO NOONUCCAL [KATH WALKER]
Australia, b.1920

MUNICIPAL GUM

Gumtree in the city street,
Hard bitumen around your feet,
Rather you should be
In the cool world of leafy forest halls
And wild bird calls.   5
Here you seem to me
Like that poor cart-horse
Castrated, broken, a thing wronged,
Strapped and buckled, its hell prolonged,
Whose hung head and listless mien express   10
Its hopelessness.
Municipal gum, it is dolorous
To see you thus
Set in your black grass of bitumen —
O fellow citizen,   15
What have they done to us?

                                        (1966)

BILL REID (WITH ROBERT BRINGHURST)
Canada, b.1920

THE RAVEN STEALS THE LIGHT

Before there was anything, before the great flood had covered the earth and receded, before the animals walked the earth or the trees covered the land or the birds flew between the trees, even before the fish and the whales and seals swam in the sea, an old man lived in a house on the bank of a river with his only child, a daughter. Whether she was as beautiful as hemlock fronds against the spring sky at sunrise or as ugly as a sea   5
slug doesn't really matter very much to this story, which takes place mainly in the dark.

Because at that time the whole world was dark. Inky, pitchy, all-consuming dark, blacker than a thousand stormy winter midnights, blacker than anything anywhere has been since.

The reason for all this blackness has to do with the old man in the house by the   10
river, who had a box which contained a box which contained a box which contained an infinite number of boxes each nestled in a box slightly larger than itself until finally there was a box so small all it could contain was all the light in the universe.

The Raven, who of course existed at that time, because he had always existed and always would, was somewhat less than satisfied with this state of affairs, since it led to   15
an awful lot of blundering around and bumping into things. It slowed him down a good deal in his pursuit of food and other fleshly pleasures, and in his constant effort to interfere and to change things.

Eventually, his bumbling around in the dark took him close to the home of the old man. He first heard a little singsong voice muttering away. When he followed the voice,   20
he soon came to the wall of the house, and there, placing his ear against the planking, he could just make out the words, "I have a box and inside the box is another box and inside it are many more boxes, and in the smallest box of all is all the light in the world, and it is all mine and I'll never give any of it to anyone, not even to my daughter, because, who knows, she may be as homely as a sea slug, and neither she nor I would like to know that."   25

It took only an instant for the Raven to decide to steal the light for himself, but it took a lot longer for him to invent a way to do so.

First he had to find a door into the house. But no matter how many times he circled it or how carefully he felt the planking, it remained a smooth, unbroken barrier. Sometimes he heard either the old man or his daughter leave the house to get water or   30
for some other reason, but they always departed from the side of the house opposite to him, and when he ran around to the other side the wall seemed as unbroken as ever.

Finally, the Raven retired a little way upstream and thought and thought about how he could enter the house. As he did so, he began to think more and more of the young girl who lived there, and thinking of her began to stir more than just the Raven's imagination.   35

THE RAVEN STEALS THE LIGHT For Bringhurst's poems, see p. 1529. **Title: Raven:** the creator figure in Haida myth, and also a trickster figure (cf. Anancy, in Salkey's "Soot," p. 1429). **1. great flood:** Cf. Bukhwujjenene's tale (p. 1005) and Genesis 6-8 (p. 246).

"It's probable that she's as homely as a sea slug," he said to himself, "but on the other hand, she may be as beautiful as the fronds of the hemlock would be against a bright spring sunrise, if only there were light enough to make one." And in that idle speculation, he found the solution to his problem.

He waited until the young woman, whose footsteps he could distinguish by now 40 from those of her father, came to the river to gather water. Then he changed himself into a single hemlock needle, dropped himself into the river and floated down just in time to be caught in the basket which the girl was dipping in the river.

Even in his much diminished form, the Raven was able to make at least a very small magic — enough to make the girl so thirsty she took a deep drink from the basket, 45 and in doing so, swallowed the needle.

The Raven slithered down deep into her warm insides and found a soft, comfortable spot, where he transformed himself once more, this time into a very small human being, and went to sleep for a long while. And as he slept he grew.

The young girl didn't have any idea what was happening to her, and of course she 50 didn't tell her father, who noticed nothing unusual because it was so dark — until suddenly he became very aware indeed of a new presence in the house, as the Raven at last emerged triumphantly in the shape of a human boychild.

He was — or would have been, if anyone could have seen him — a strange-looking boy, with a long, beaklike nose and a few feathers here and there. In addition, he had the 55 shining eyes of the Raven, which would have given his face a bright, inquisitive appearance — if anyone could have seen these features then.

And he was noisy. He had a cry that contained all the noises of a spoiled child and an angry raven — yet he could sometimes speak as softly as the wind in the hemlock boughs, with an echo of that beautiful other sound, like an organic bell, which is also 60 part of every raven's speech.

At times like that his grandfather grew to love this strange new member of his household and spent many hours playing with him, making him toys and inventing games for him.

As he gained more and more of the affection and confidence of the old man, the 65 Raven felt more intently around the house, trying to find where the light was hidden. After much exploration, he was convinced it was kept in the big box which stood in the corner of the house. One day he cautiously lifted the lid, but of course could see nothing, and all he could feel was another box. His grandfather, however, heard his precious treasure chest being disturbed, and he dealt very harshly with the would-be 70 thief, threatening dire punishment if the Ravenchild ever touched the box again.

This triggered a tidal wave of noisy protests, followed by tender importuning, in which the Raven never mentioned the light, but only pleaded for the largest box. That box, said the Ravenchild, was the one thing he needed to make him completely happy.

As most if not all grandfathers have done since the beginning, the old man finally 75 yielded and gave his grandchild the outermost box. This contented the boy for a short time — but as most if not all grandchildren have done since the beginning, the Raven soon demanded the next box.

It took many days and much cajoling, carefully balanced with well-planned tantrums, but one by one the boxes were removed. When only a few were left, a strange 80 radiance, never before seen, began to infuse the darkness of the house, disclosing vague shapes and their shadows, still too dim to have definite form. The Ravenchild then begged in his most pitiful voice to be allowed to hold the light for just a moment.

His request was instantly refused, but of course in time his grandfather yielded. The old man lifted the light, in the form of a beautiful, incandescent ball, from the final box 85 and tossed it to his grandson.

He had only a glimpse of the child on whom he had lavished such love and affection, for even as the light was travelling toward him, the child changed from his human form to a huge, shining black shadow, wings spread and beak open, waiting. The Raven snapped up the light in his jaws, thrust his great wings downward and shot 90 through the smokehole of the house into the huge darkness of the world.

That world was at once transformed. Mountains and valleys were starkly silhouetted, the river sparkled with broken reflections, and everywhere life began to stir. And from far away, another great winged shape launched itself into the air, as light struck the eyes of the Eagle for the first time and showed him his target. 95

The Raven flew on, rejoicing in his wonderful new possession, admiring the effect it had on the world below, revelling in the experience of being able to see where he was going, instead of flying blind and hoping for the best. He was having such a good time that he never saw the Eagle until the Eagle was almost upon him. In a panic he swerved to escape the savage outstretched claws, and in doing so he dropped a good half of the 100 light he was carrying. It fell to the rocky ground below and there broke into pieces — one large piece and too many small ones to count. They bounced back into the sky and remain there even today as the moon and the stars that glorify the night.

The Eagle pursued the Raven beyond the rim of the world, and there, exhausted by the long chase, the Raven finally let go of his last piece of light. Out beyond the rim of the 105 world, it floated gently on the clouds and started up over the mountains lying to the east.

Its first rays caught the smokehole of the house by the river, where the old man sat weeping bitterly over the loss of his precious light and the treachery of his grandchild. But as the light reached in, he looked up and for the first time saw his daughter, who had been quietly sitting during all this time, completely bewildered by the rush of events. 110

The old man saw that she was as beautiful as the fronds of a hemlock against a spring sky at sunrise, and he began to feel a little better.

(1984)

GABRIEL OKARA

Nigeria, b.1921

ONCE UPON A TIME

Once upon a time, son,
they used to laugh with their hearts
and laugh with their eyes;

but now they only laugh with their teeth,
while their ice-block-cold eyes 5
search behind my shadow.

There was a time indeed
they used to shake hands with their hearts;
but that's gone, son.
Now they shake hands without hearts   10
while their left hands search
my empty pockets.

"Feel at home!" "Come again,"
they say, and when I come
again and feel   15
at home, once, twice,
there will be no thrice —
for then I find doors shut on me.

So I have learned many things, son.
I have learned to wear many faces   20
like dresses — homeface,
officeface, streetface, hostface,
cocktailface, with all their conforming smiles
like a fixed portrait smile.

And I have learned, too,   25
to laugh with only my teeth
and shake hands without my heart.
I have also learned to say, "Goodbye,"
when I mean "Good-riddance,"
to say "Glad to meet you,"   30
without being glad; and to say "It's been
nice talking to you," after being bored.

But believe me, son.
I want to be what I used to be
when I was like you. I want   35
to unlearn all these muting things.
Most of all, I want to relearn
how to laugh, for my laugh in the mirror
shows only my teeth like a snake's bare fangs!

So show me, son,   40
how to laugh; show me how
I used to laugh and smile
once upon a time when I was like you.

                                    (1978)

RICHARD WILBUR
U.S.A., b.1921

PARABLE

I read how Quixote in his random ride
Came to a crossing once, and lest he lose
The purity of chance, would not decide

Whither to fare, but wished his horse to choose.
For glory lay wherever he might turn.   5
His head was light with pride, his horse's shoes

Were heavy, and he headed for the barn.

                                    (1950)

A SUMMER MORNING

Her young employers, having got in late
From seeing friends in town
And scraped the right front fender on the gate,
Will not, the cook expects, be coming down.

She makes a quiet breakfast for herself.   5
The coffee-pot is bright,
The jelly where it should be on the shelf.
She breaks an egg into the morning light,

Then, with the bread-knife lifted, stands and hears
The sweet efficient sounds   10
Of thrush and catbird, and the snip of shears
Where, in the terraced backward of the grounds,

A gardener works before the heat of day.
He straightens for a view
Of the big house ascending stony-gray   15
Out of his beds mosaic with the dew.

His young employers having got in late,
He and the cook alone
Receive the morning on their old estate,
Possessing what the owners can but own.   20

                                    (1961)

PARABLE   **1. Quixote:** title character in Cervantes's *Don Quixote* (1605, 1615).

HAMLEN BROOK

At the alder-darkened brink
Where the stream slows to a lucid jet
I lean to the water, dinting its top with sweat,
    And see, before I can drink,

A startled inchling trout   5
Of spotted near-transparency,
Trawling a shadow solider than he.
    He swerves now, darting out

To where, in a flicked slew
Of sparks and glittering silt, he weaves   10
Through stream-bed rocks, disturbing foundered leaves,
    And butts then out of view

Beneath a sliding glass
Crazed by the skimming of a brace
Of burnished dragon-flies across its face,   15
    In which deep cloudlets pass

And a white precipice
Of mirrored birch-trees plunges down
Toward where the azures of the zenith drown.
    How shall I drink all this?   20

Joy's trick is to supply
Dry lips with what can cool and slake,
Leaving them dumbstruck also with an ache
    Nothing can satisfy.

(1987)

PHILIP LARKIN
England, 1922-1985

"SINCE THE MAJORITY OF ME"

Since the majority of me
Rejects the majority of you,
Debating ends forthwith, and we
Divide. And sure of what to do

We disinfect new blocks of days   5
For our majorities to rent
With unshared friends and unwalked ways.
But silence too is eloquent:

A silence of minorities
That, unopposed at last, return   10
Each night with cancelled promises
They want renewed. They never learn.

(1950)

CHURCH GOING

Once I am sure there's nothing going on
I step inside, letting the door thud shut.
Another church: matting, seats, and stone,
And little books; sprawlings of flowers, cut
For Sunday, brownish now; some brass and stuff   5
Up at the holy end; the small neat organ;
And a tense, musty, unignorable silence,
Brewed God knows how long. Hatless, I take off
My cycle-clips in awkward reverence,

Move forward, run my hand around the font.   10
From where I stand, the roof looks almost new —
Cleaned, or restored? Someone would know: I don't.
Mounting the lectern, I peruse a few
Hectoring large-scale verses, and pronounce
"Here endeth" much more loudly than I'd meant.   15
The echoes snigger briefly. Back at the door
I sign the book, donate an Irish sixpence,
Reflect the place was not worth stopping for.

Yet stop I did: in fact I often do,
And always end much at a loss like this,   20
Wondering what to look for; wondering, too,
When churches fall completely out of use
What we shall turn them into, if we shall keep
A few cathedrals chronically on show,
Their parchment, plate and pyx in locked cases,   25
And let the rest rent-free to rain and sheep.
Shall we avoid them as unlucky places?

CHURCH GOING **15. "Here endeth":** ritual close to formal readings from the lessons, gospels, and epistles in the Church of England service.

Or, after dark, will dubious women come
To make their children touch a particular stone;
Pick simples for a cancer; or on some   30
Advised night see walking a dead one?
Power of some sort or other will go on
In games, in riddles, seemingly at random;
But superstition, like belief, must die,
And what remains when disbelief has gone?   35
Grass, weedy pavement, brambles, buttress, sky,

A shape less recognisable each week,
A purpose more obscure. I wonder who
Will be the last, the very last, to seek
This place for what it was; one of the crew   40
That tap and jot and know what rood-lofts were?
Some ruin-bibber, randy for antique,
Or Christmas-addict, counting on a whiff
Of gown-and-bands and organ-pipes and myrrh?
Or will he be my representative,   45

Bored, uninformed, knowing the ghostly silt
Dispersed, yet tending to this cross of ground
Through suburb scrub because it held unspilt
So long and equably what since is found
Only in separation — marriage, and birth,   50
And death, and thoughts of these — for which was built
This special shell? For, though I've no idea
What this accoutred frowsty barn is worth,
It pleases me to stand in silence here;

A serious house on serious earth it is,   55
In whose blent air all our compulsions meet,
Are recognised, and robed as destinies.
And that much never can be obsolete,
Since someone will forever be surprising
A hunger in himself to be more serious,   60
And gravitating with it to this ground,
Which, he once heard, was proper to grow wise in,
If only that so many dead lie round.

                                    (1954)

THE WHITSUN WEDDINGS

That Whitsun, I was late getting away:
    Not till about
One-twenty on the sunlit Saturday
Did my three-quarters-empty train pull out,

All windows down, all cushions hot, all sense   5
Of being in a hurry gone. We ran
Behind the backs of houses, crossed a street
Of blinding windscreens, smelt the fish-dock; thence
The river's level drifting breadth began,
Where sky and Lincolnshire and water meet.   10

All afternoon, through the tall heat that slept
    For miles inland,
A slow and stopping curve southwards we kept.
Wide farms went by, short-shadowed cattle, and
Canals with floatings of industrial froth;   15
A hothouse flashed uniquely: hedges dipped
And rose: and now and then a smell of grass
Displaced the reek of buttoned carriage-cloth
Until the next town, new and nondescript,
Approached with acres of dismantled cars.   20

At first, I didn't notice what a noise
    The weddings made
Each station that we stopped at: sun destroys
The interest of what's happening in the shade,
And down the long cool platforms whoops and skirls
I took for porters larking with the mails,   26
And went on reading. Once we started, though,
We passed them, grinning and pomaded, girls
In parodies of fashion, heels and veils,
All posed irresolutely, watching us go,   30

As if out on the end of an event
    Waving goodbye
To something that survived it. Struck, I leant
More promptly out next time, more curiously,
And saw it all again in different terms: 35
The fathers with broad belts under their suits
And seamy foreheads; mothers loud and fat;
An uncle shouting smut; and then the perms,
The nylon gloves and jewellery-substitutes,
The lemons, mauves, and olive-ochres that   40

Marked off the girls unreally from the rest.
    Yes, from cafés
And banquet-halls up yards, and bunting-dressed
Coach-party annexes, the wedding-days
Were coming to an end. All down the line   45
Fresh couples climbed aboard: the rest stood round;
The last confetti and advice were thrown,

---

42. **ruin-bibber:** from "bibber," meaning a drunk.   THE WHITSUN WEDDINGS 1. **Whitsun:** Whitsunday or Pentecost, the 7th Sunday in the Easter church calendar, celebrating the Holy Spirit.

And, as we moved, each face seemed to define
Just what it saw departing: children frowned
At something dull; fathers had never known 50

Success so huge and wholly farcical;
  The women shared
The secret like a happy funeral;
While girls, gripping their handbags tighter, stared
At a religious wounding. Free at last, 55
And loaded with the sum of all they saw,
We hurried towards London, shuffling gouts of steam.
Now fields were building-plots, and poplars cast
Long shadows over major roads, and for
Some fifty minutes, that in time would seem 60

Just long enough to settle hats and say
  I nearly died,
A dozen marriages got under way.
They watched the landscape, sitting side by side

— An Odeon went past, a cooling tower, 65
And someone running up to bowl — and none
Thought of the others they would never meet
Or how their lives would all contain this hour.
I thought of London spread out in the sun,
Its postal districts packed like squares of wheat: 70

There we were aimed. And as we raced across
  Bright knots of rail
Past standing Pullmans, walls of blackened moss
Came close, and it was nearly done, this frail
Travelling coincidence; and what it held 75
Stood ready to be loosed with all the power
That being changed can give. We slowed again,
And as the tightened brakes took hold, there swelled
A sense of falling, like an arrow-shower
Sent out of sight, somewhere becoming rain. 80
(1958)

ELI MANDEL
Canada, 1922-1992

PARTING AT UDAIPUR: THE LAKE PALACE

In Calcutta a Bengali artist explains
his family lived in a tree swarming with uncles,
incest and possession. It is an allegory.
Then there's the other story about a mongoose mother.
The tree swarms. Later his mother 5
will warn him she is about to die.

I think of snake charmers, how they produce
out of a sack a blur of slither
how it clamps teeth into a python's head,
savaging the dull beast. 10

At Gujarat an intellectual lets me know
she despises her husband, academics, poetry
her unequivocal dark hands handling a book,
poems my friend has given her.

65. Odeon: a film theatre. **66. to bowl:** i.e., in the game of cricket. **PARTING AT UDAIPUR** Title: The Lake Palace Hotel in Udaipur, Rajasthan, once a Maharajah's palace, is constructed as an island in the middle of a lake, accessible only by boat; Mandel's "diary" entry for January 13, 1977, in *Life Sentence*, reads in part: "I spend the morning . . . in the gardens of the Udaipur Palace, then with Ann [his wife]. We look out at the (artificial) lake in which this hotel-palace . . . sits, Venetian . . . (the stone head of a carved woman incongruously emerging from the water just beyond the dock-landing for water-taxis). We're waiting for our drive to the airport. This is exotic India, an island hotel, glittering with mirrors and ornate corridors, decorated in ponds, . . . glass where once there had been jewels. As our water-taxi pulls away from the scene, I watch Ann turn and walk away along the dock. The moment is unforgettable to me. I can't recall our having said goodbye before in so remote a place."

From the Taj windows in Bombay   *15*
the Gates of India imperial and aloof
open to the Arabian sea. The heat drains
whatever leans in the wind that blows from the desert.
The harbour fills with the blood of the setting sun.

I despair of reason, knowledge, my lectures,   *20*
remember only Ann turning away at Udaipur,
the boat from the palace creating distances.
We are in a strange land. We are drifting apart.
India is between us. Across the lake, its sunken
woman, lie continents: *25*
          war torture poison
          an apparatus of romance
          to keep us apart.
                     (1981)

NADINE GORDIMER
South Africa, b.1923

SOMETHING FOR THE TIME BEING

He thought of it as discussing things with her, but the truth was that she did not help him out at all. She said nothing, while she ran her hand up the ridge of bone behind the rim of her child-sized yellow-brown ear, and raked her fingers tenderly into her hair-line along the back of her neck as if feeling out some symptom in herself. Yet her listening was very demanding; when he stopped at the end of a supposition or a suggestion, her   *5* silence made the stop inconclusive. He had to take up again what he had said, carry it — where?

    "Ve vant to give you a tsance, but you von't let us," he mimicked; and made a loud glottal click, half-angry, resentfully amused. He knew it wasn't because Kalzin Brothers were Jews that he had lost his job at last, but just because he had lost it, Mr Solly's   *10* accent suddenly presented to him the irresistibly vulnerable. He had come out of prison nine days before, after spending three months as an awaiting-trial prisoner in a political case that had just been quashed — he was one of those who would not accept bail. He had been in prison three or four times since 1952; his wife Ella and the Kalzin Brothers were used to it. Until now, his employers had always given him his job back when he   *15* came out. They were importers of china and glass and he was head packer in a team of black men who ran the dispatch department. "Well, what the hell, I'll get something else," he said. "Hey?"

---

15. **Taj:** a hotel. 16. **Gates of India:** an arch, constructed at the Bombay harbourfront during the period of British rule in India, a symbol of imperial power.

She stopped the self-absorbed examination of the surface of her skin for a slow moment and shrugged, looking at him.

He smiled.

Her gaze loosened hold like hands falling away from grasp. The ends of her nails pressed at small imperfections in the skin of her neck. He drank his tea and tore off pieces of bread to dip in it; then he noticed the tin of sardines she had opened and sopped up the pale matrix of oil in which ragged flecks of silver were suspended. She offered him more tea, without speaking.

They lived in one room of a decent, three-roomed house belonging to someone else; it was better for her that way, since he was often likely to have to be away for long stretches. She worked in a factory that made knitted socks; there was no one at home to look after their one child, a girl, and the child lived with a grandmother in a dusty, peaceful village a day's train-journey from the city.

He said, dismissing it as of no importance, "I wonder what chance they meant? You can imagine. I don't suppose they were going to give me an office with my name on it." He spoke as if she would appreciate the joke. She had known when she married him that he was a political man; she had been proud of him because he didn't merely want something for himself, like the other young men she knew, but everything, and for *the people*. It had excited her, under his influence, to change her awareness of herself as a young black girl to awareness of herself as belonging to the people. She knew that everything wasn't like something — a hand-out, a wangled privilege, a trinket you could hold. She would never get something from him.

Her hand went on searching over her skin as if it must come soon, come anxiously, to the flaw, the sickness, the evidence of what was wrong with her; for on this Saturday afternoon all these things that she knew had deserted her. She had lost her wits. All that she could understand was the one room, the child growing up far away in the mud house, and the fact that you couldn't keep a job if you kept being away from work for weeks at a time.

"I think I'd better look up Flora Donaldson," he said. Flora Donaldson was a white woman who had set up an office to help political prisoners. "Sooner the better. Perhaps she'll dig up something for me by Monday. It's the beginning of the month."

He got on all right with those people. Ella had met Flora Donaldson once; she was a pretty white woman who looked just like any white woman who would automatically send a black face round to the back door, but she didn't seem to know that she was white and you were black.

He pulled the curtain that hung across one corner of the room and took out his suit. It was a thin suit, of the kind associated with holiday-makers in American clothing advertisements, and when he was dressed in it, with a sharp-brimmed grey hat tilted slightly back on his small head, he looked a wiry, boyish figure, rather like one of those boy-men who sing and shake before a microphone, and whose clothes admirers try to touch as a talisman.

He kissed her goodbye, obliging her to put down, the lowering of a defence, the piece of sewing she held. She had cleared away the dishes from the table and set up the sewing-machine, and he saw that the shapes of cut material that lay on the table were the parts of a small girl's dress.

She spoke suddenly. "And when the next lot gets tired of you?"

"When that lot gets tired of me, I'll get another job again, that's all."   *65*

She nodded, very slowly, and her hand crept back to her neck.

"Who was that?" Madge Chadders asked.

Her husband had been out into the hall to answer the telephone.

"Flora Donaldson. I wish you'd explain to these people exactly what sort of factory I've got. It's so embarrassing. She's trying to find a job for some chap, he's a skilled   *70* packer. There's no skilled packing done in my workshop, no skilled jobs at all done by black men. What on earth can I offer the fellow? She says he's desperate and anything will do."

Madge had the broken pieces of a bowl on a newspaper spread on the Persian carpet. "Mind the glue, darling! There, just next to your foot. Well, anything is better   *75* than nothing. I suppose it's someone who was in the Soganiland sedition case. Three months awaiting trial taken out of their lives, and now they're chucked back to fend for themselves."

William Chadders had not had any black friends or mixed with coloured people on any but master-servant terms until he married Madge, but his views on the immorality   *80* and absurdity of the colour bar were sound; sounder, she often felt, than her own, for they were backed by the impersonal authority of a familiarity with the views of great thinkers, saints and philosophers, with history, political economy, sociology and anthropology. She knew only what she felt. And she always did something, at once, to express what she felt. She never measured the smallness of her personal protest against   *85* the establishment she opposed; she marched with Flora and eight hundred black women in a demonstration against African women being forced to carry passes; outside the university where she had once been a student, she stood between sandwich-boards bearing messages of mourning because a Bill had been passed closing the university, for the future, to all but white students; she had living in the house for three months a young   *90* African who wanted to write and hadn't the peace or space to get on with it in a location. She did not stop to consider the varying degree of usefulness of the things she did, and if others pointed this out to her and suggested that she might make up her mind to throw her weight on the side either of politics or philanthropy, she was not resentful but answered candidly that there was so little it was possible to do that she simply took   *95* any and every chance to get off her chest her disgust at the colour bar. When she had married William Chadders, her friends had thought that her protestant activities would stop; they underestimated not only Madge, but also William, who, although he was a wealthy business man, subscribed to the view of absolute personal freedom as strictly as any bohemian. Besides he was not fool enough to want to change in any way the person   *100* who had enchanted him just as she was.

She reacted upon him, rather than he upon her; she, of course, would not hesitate to go ahead and change anybody. (But why not? she would have said, astonished. If it's to the good?) The attitude she sought to change would occur to her as something of independent existence, she would not see it as a cell in the organism of personality,   *105*

SOMETHING FOR THE TIME BEING   92. **location:** a Black living area in South Africa, as defined by the laws of apartheid.

whose whole structure would have to regroup itself round the change. She had the boldness of being unaware of these consequences.

William did not carry a banner in the streets, of course; he worked up there, among his first principles and historical precedents and economic necessities, but now they were translated from theory to practice of an anonymous, large-scale and behind-the-scenes sort — he was the brains and part of the money in a scheme to get Africans some economic power besides consumer power, through the setting up of an all-African trust company and investment corporation. A number of Madge's political friends, both white and black (like her activities, her friends were mixed, some political, some do-gooders), thought this was putting the middle-class cart before the proletarian horse, but most of the African leaders welcomed the attempt as an essential backing to popular movements on other levels — something to count on outside the unpredictability of mobs. Sometimes it amused Madge to think that William, making a point at a meeting in a boardroom, fifteen floors above life in the streets, might achieve in five minutes something of more value than she did in all her days of turning her hand to anything — from sorting old clothes to roneo-ing a manifesto or driving people during a bus boycott. Yet this did not knock the meaning out of her own life, for her; she knew that she had to see, touch and talk to people in order to care about them, that's all there was to it.

Before she and her husband dressed to go out that evening she finished sticking together the broken Chinese bowl and showed it to him with satisfaction. To her, it was whole again. But it was one of a set, that had belonged together, and whose unity had illustrated certain philosophical concepts. William had bought them long ago, in London; for him, the whole set was damaged for ever.

He said nothing to her, but he was thinking of the bowls when she said to him as they drove off, "Will you see that chap, on Monday, yourself?"

He changed gear deliberately, attempting to follow her out of his preoccupation. But she said, "The man Flora's sending. What was his name?"

He opened his hand on the steering wheel, indicating that the name escaped him.

"See him yourself?"

"I'll have to leave it to the works manager to find something for him to do," he said.

"Yes, I know. But see him yourself, too?"

Her anxious voice made him feel very fond of her. He turned and smiled at her suspiciously. "Why?"

She was embarrassed at his indulgent manner. She said, frank and wheedling, "Just to show him. You know. That you know about him and it's not much of a job."

"All right," he said. "I'll see him myself."

He met her in town straight from the office on Monday and they went to the opening of an exhibition of paintings and on to dinner and to see a play, with friends. He had not been home at all, until they returned after midnight. It was a summer night and they sat for a few minutes on their terrace, where it was still mild with the warmth of the day's sun coming from the walls in the darkness, and drank lime juice and water to quench the thirst that wine and the stuffy theatre had given them. Madge made gasps and groans of pleasure at the release from the pressures of company and noise. Then she

---

121. roneo-ing: duplicating, as on a mimeograph machine.

lay quiet for a while, her voice lifting now and then in fragments of unrelated comment on the evening — the occasional chirp of a bird that has already put its head under its wing for the night. *150*

By the time they went in, they were free of the evening. Her black dress, her ear-rings and her bracelets felt like fancy-dress; she shed the character and sat on the bedroom carpet, and, passing her, he said, "Oh — that chap of Flora's came today, but I don't think he'll last. I explained to him that I didn't have the sort of job he was looking for." *155*

"Well, that's all right, then," she said inquiringly. "What more could you do?"

"Yes," he said, deprecating. "But I could see he didn't like the idea much. It's a cleaner's job; nothing for him. He's an intelligent chap. I didn't like having to offer it to him."

She was moving about her dressing table, piling out upon it the contents of her handbag. "Then I'm sure he'll understand. It'll give him something for the time being, anyway, darling. You can't help it if you don't need the sort of work he does." *160*

"Huh, he won't last. I could see that. He accepted it, but only with his head. He'll get fed up. Probably won't turn up tomorrow. I had to speak to him about his Congress button, too. The works manager came to me." *165*

"What about his Congress button?" she said.

He was unbuttoning his shirt and his eyes were on the unread evening paper that lay folded on the bed. "He was wearing one," he said inattentively.

"I know, but what did you have to speak to him about it for?"

"He was wearing it in the workshop all day." *170*

"Well, what about it?" She was sitting at her dressing table, legs spread, as if she had sat heavily and suddenly. She was not looking at him, but at her own face.

He gave the paper a push and drew his pyjamas from under the pillow. Vulnerable and naked, he said authoritatively, "You can't wear a button like that among the men in the workshop." *175*

"Good heavens," she said, almost in relief, laughing, backing away from the edge of tension, chivvying him out of a piece of stuffiness. "And why can't you?"

"You can't have someone clearly representing a political organization like Congress."

"But he's not there *representing* anything, he's there as a workman?" Her mouth was still twitching with something between amusement and nerves. *180*

"Exactly."

"Then why can't he wear a button that signifies his allegiance to an organization in his private life outside the workshop? There's no rule about not wearing tie-pins or club buttons or anything, in the workshop, is there?"

"No, there isn't, but that's not quite the same thing." *185*

"My dear William," she said, "it is exactly the same. It's nothing to do with the works manager whether the man wears a Rotary button, or an Elvis Presley button, or an African National Congress button. It's damn all his business."

"No, Madge, I'm sorry," William said, patient, "but it's not the same. I can give the man a job because I feel sympathetic towards the struggle he's in, but I can't put him in the workshop as a Congress man. I mean that wouldn't be fair to Fowler. That I can't do *190*

---

164. Congress: African National Congress, a South African political organization illegal until 1990, opposed to apartheid.

to Fowler." He was smiling as he went towards the bathroom, but his profile, as he turned into the doorway, was incisive.

She sat on at her dressing-table, pulling a comb through her hair, dragging it down through knots. Then she rested her face on her palms, caught sight of herself and *195* became aware, against her fingers, of the curving shelf of bone, like the lip of a strong shell, under each eye. Everyone has his own intimations of mortality. For her, the feel of the bone beneath the face, in any living creature, brought her the message of the skull. Once hollowed out of this, outside the world, too. For what it's worth. It's worth a lot, the world, she affirmed, as she always did, life rising at once in her as a fish opens its *200* jaws to a fly. It's worth a lot; and she sighed and got up with the sigh.

She went into the bathroom and sat down on the edge of the bath. He was lying there in the water, his chin relaxed on his chest, and he smiled at her. She said, "You mean you don't want Fowler to know."

"Oh," he said, seeing where they were again. "What is it I don't want Fowler to *205* know?"

"You don't want your partner to know that you slip black men with political ideas into your workshop. Cheeky kaffir agitators. Specially a man who's been in jail for getting people to defy the government! — What was his name; you never said?"

"Daniel something. I don't know. Mongoma or Ngoma. Something like that." *210*

A line like a cut appeared between her eyebrows. "Why can't you remember his name?" Then she went on at once, "You don't want Fowler to know what you think, do you? That's it? You want to pretend you're like him, you don't mind the native in his place. You want to pretend that to please Fowler. You don't want Fowler to think you're cracked or Communist or whatever it is that good-natured, kind, jolly rich people like *215* old Fowler think about people like us."

"I couldn't have less interest in what Fowler thinks outside our boardroom. And inside it, he never thinks about anything but how to sell more earth-moving gear."

"I don't mind the native in his place. You want him to think you go along with all that." She spoke aloud, but she seemed to be telling herself rather than him. *220*

"Fowler and I run a factory. Our only common interest is the efficient running of that factory. Our *only* one. The factory depends on a stable, satisfied black labour-force, and that we've got. Right, you and I know that the whole black wage standard is too low, right, we know that they haven't a legal union to speak for them, right, we know that the conditions they live under make it impossible for them really to be stable. All that. But the fact is, so *225* far as accepted standards go in this crazy country, they're a stable, satisfied labour-force with better working conditions than most. So long as I'm a partner in a business that lives by them, I can't officially admit an element that represents dissatisfaction with their lot."

"A green badge with a map of Africa on it," she said.

"If you make up your mind not to understand, you don't, and there it is," he said *230* indulgently.

"You give him a job but you make him hide his Congress button."

He began to soap himself. She wanted everything to stop while she inquired into things, she could not go on while a remark was unexplained or a problem unsettled, but

---

208. kaffir: Black, now used as a slur.

he represented a principle she subscribed to but found so hard to follow, that life must *235*
go on, trivially, commonplace, the trailing hem of the only power worth clinging to. She
smoothed the film of her nightgown over the shape of her knees, over and over, and
presently she said, in exactly the flat tone of statement that she had used before, the flat
tone that was the height of belligerence in her, "He can say and do what he likes, he can
call for strikes and boycotts and anything he likes, outside the factory, but he mustn't *240*
wear his Congress button at work."

He was standing up, washing his body that was full of scars; she knew them all,
from the place on his left breast where a piece of shrapnel had gone in, all the way back
to the place under his arm where he had torn himself on barbed wire as a child. "Yes, of
course, anything he likes." *245*

"Anything except his self-respect," she grumbled to herself. "Pretend, pretend.
Pretend he doesn't belong to a political organization. Pretend he doesn't want to be a
man. Pretend he hasn't been to prison for what he believes." Suddenly she spoke to her
husband: "You'll let him have anything except the one thing worth giving."

They stood in uncomfortable proximity to each other, in the smallness of the *250*
bathroom. They were at once aware of each other as people who live in intimacy are
only when hostility returns each to the confines of himself. He felt himself naked before
her, where he had stepped out on to the towelling mat, and he took a towel and slowly
covered himself, pushing the free end in round his waist. She felt herself an intrusion
and, in silence, went out. *255*

Her hands were tingling as if she were coming round from a faint. She walked up
and down the bedroom floor like someone waiting to be summoned, called to account.
I'll forget about it, she kept thinking, very fast, I'll forget about it again. Take a sip of
water. Read another chapter. Don't call a halt. Let things flow, cover up, go on.

But when he came into the room with his wet hair combed and his stranger's face, and *260*
he said, "You're angry," it came from her lips, a black bird in the room, before she could
understand what she had released — "I'm not angry. I'm beginning to get to know you."

Ella Mngoma knew he was going to a meeting that evening and didn't expect him home
early. She put the paraffin lamp on the table so that she could see to finish the child's
dress. It was done, buttons and all, by the time he came in at half past ten. *265*

"Well, now we'll see what happens. I've got them to accept, *in principle*, that in
future we won't take bail. You should have seen Ben Tsolo's face when I said that we lent
the government our money interest-free when we paid bail. That really hit him. That was
language he understood." He laughed, and did not seem to want to sit down, the heat of
the meeting still upon him. "*In principle*. Yes, it's easy to accept in principle. We'll see." *270*

She pumped the primus and set a pot of stew to warm up for him. "Ah, that's nice." He
saw the dress. "Finished already?" And she nodded vociferously in pleasure; but at once she
noticed his forefinger run lightly along the braid round the neck, and the traces of failure that
were always at the bottom of her cup tasted on her tongue again. Probably he was not even
aware of it, or perhaps his instinct for what was true — the plumb line, the coin with the *275*
right ring — led him absently to it, but the fact was that she had botched the neck.

She had an almost Oriental delicacy about not badgering him and she waited until
he had washed and sat down to eat before she asked, "How did the job go?"

"Oh that," he said. "It went." He was eating quickly, moving his tongue strongly round his mouth to marshal the bits of meat that escaped his teeth. She was sitting with him, feeling, in spite of herself, the rest of satisfaction in her evening's work. "Didn't you get it?"   280

"It got *me*. But I got loose again, all right."

She watched his face to see what he meant. "They don't want you to come back tomorrow?"   285

He shook his head, no, no, no, to stem the irritation of her suppositions. He finished his mouthful and said, "Everything very nice. Boss takes me into his office, apologizes for the pay, he knows it's not the sort of job I should have and so forth. So I go off and clean up in the assembly shop. Then at lunchtime he calls me into the office again: they don't want me to wear my A.N.C. badge at work. Flora Donaldson's sympathetic white man, who's going to do me the great favour of paying me three pounds a week." He laughed. "Well, there you are."   290

She kept on looking at him. Her eyes widened and her mouth tightened; she was trying to prime herself to speak, or was trying not to cry. The idea of tears exasperated him and he held her with a firm, almost belligerently inquiring gaze. Her hand went up round the back of her neck under her collar, anxiously exploratory. "Don't do that!" he said. "You're like a monkey catching lice."   295

She took her hand down swiftly and broke into trembling, like a sweat. She began to breathe hysterically. "You couldn't put it in your pocket, for the day," she said wildly, grimacing at the bitterness of malice towards him.   300

He jumped up from the table. "Christ! I knew you'd say it! I've been waiting for you to say it. You've been wanting to say it for five years. Well, now it's out. Out with it. Spit it out!" She began to scream softly as if he were hitting her. The impulse to cruelty left him and he sat down before his dirty plate, where the battered spoon lay among bits of gristle and potato-eyes. Presently he spoke. "You come out and you think   305 there's everybody waiting for you. The truth is, there isn't anybody. You think straight in prison because you've got nothing to lose. Nobody thinks straight, outside. They don't want to hear you. What are you all going to do with me, Ella? Send me back to prison as quickly as possible? Perhaps I'll get a banishment order next time. That'd do. That's what you've got for me. I must keep myself busy with that kind of thing."   310

He went over to her and said, in a kindly voice, kneading her shoulder with spread fingers, "Don't cry. Don't cry. You're just like any other woman."

(1960)

DENISE LEVERTOV
U.S.A., b.1923

EVERYTHING THAT ACTS IS ACTUAL

From the tawny light
from the rainy nights
from the imagination finding

itself and more than itself
alone and more than alone   5
at the bottom of the well where the moon lives,

can you pull me

into December? a lowland
of space, perception of space
towering of shadows of clouds blown upon   *10*
clouds over
              new ground, new made
under heavy December footsteps? *the only*
way to live?

The flawed moon   *15*
acts on the truth, and makes
an autumn of tentative
silences.
You lived, but somewhere else,
your presence touched others, ring upon ring,   *20*
and changed. Did you think
I would not change?

              The black moon
turns away, its work done. A tenderness,
unspoken autumn.   *25*
We are faithful
only to the imagination. *What the*
imagination
        seizes
as beauty must be truth. What holds you   *30*
to what you see of me is
that grasp alone.

                                    (1957)

WHAT WERE THEY LIKE?

1) Did the people of Viet Nam
    use lanterns of stone?
2) Did they hold ceremonies
    to reverence the opening of buds?
3) Were they inclined to quiet laughter?   *5*
4) Did they use bone and ivory,
    jade and silver, for ornament?
5) Had they an epic poem?
6) Did they distinguish between speech and singing?

1) Sir, their light hearts turned to stone.   *10*
    It is not remembered whether in gardens
    stone lanterns illumined pleasant ways.
2) Perhaps they gathered once to delight in blossom,
    but after the children were killed
    there were no more buds.   *15*
3) Sir, laughter is bitter to the burned mouth.
4) A dream ago, perhaps. Ornament is for joy.
    All the bones were charred.
5) It is not remembered. Remember,
    most were peasants; their life   *20*
    was in rice and bamboo.
    When peaceful clouds were reflected in the paddies
    and the water buffalo stepped surely along terraces,
    maybe fathers told their sons old tales.
    When bombs smashed those mirrors   *25*
    there was time only to scream.
6) There is an echo yet
    of their speech which was like a song.
    It was reported their singing resembled
    the flight of moths in moonlight.   *30*
    Who can say? It is silent now.

                                    (1966)

JAMES BERRY
Jamaica/England, b.1924

SPEECH FOR ALTERNATIVE CREATION

Let us recreate all things in own image.
Let us make a new beginning.
Let us remove night, dawn, dusk,
remove black thunder, leave lightning,

dismiss Dark November, leave   *5*
all eyes on noon, that dazzle
of summer, our white heat of days.

EVERYTHING THAT ACTS IS ACTUAL   **27-30:** See Keats's letter to Benjamin Bailey (p. 857).   **WHAT WERE THEY LIKE?**   **1.**
Viet Nam: American military involvement in the war in Viet Nam increased sharply in 1964; the war ended in 1975.

Let us remove the Dark Continent,
and be humane to drifters.
Let us build up a government Blackmale list   *10*
and a Blacklist of Blacklegs
for a kind and natural exile use.
Let there be no tar to dip the brush in,
though twin adjectives Big and Black can stay,
to be own reliable terror-image.   *15*

Let us remember: Blackmarks have a way
of coming to walk like children.
Let us remember this:
each boy our own, each girl,
is our own support garrison.   *20*

We shall let it be law, that anything
except immaculate conception
is Miscegenation, that no
white lady shall ride a black stallion,
that all ravenhaired people be made   *25*
whitehaired, all black Bibles be cancelled

for white ones, and that pure milk
shall replace all coffee drinking.

We shall get every Blacksheep into
a straight scapegoat, and be clear   *30*
that no Blackguard can ever be fair.

We shall erase, correct out, every printed word,
have pure pages to show decent minds.
Even trains shall have no tunnels to go
through. We shall make all our roads into   *35*
journeys on silver. And our science
shall treat all brown earth till changed,
like beauty of clinical cottonwool.

After all, a non-white thing is a non-thing;
Might as well will it away.   *40*

Let us deport devildom. Let us have
that dreamed-of constant world, mirroring
the sun with white lands and houses and walls.
Let us make it all a marvel of a moonshine.

(1984)

IAN HAMILTON FINLAY
Scotland, b.1925

net/planet

stack net
ring net
seine net
salmon net
drift net
trawl net
herring net
planet

(1973)

CAROLYN KIZER
U.S.A., b.1925

THE UNGRATEFUL GARDEN

Midas watched the golden crust
That formed over his streaming sores,
Hugged his agues, loved his lust,
But damned to hell the out-of-doors

Where blazing motes of sun impaled   5
The serried roses, metal-bright.
"Those famous flowers," Midas wailed,
"Have scorched my retina with light."

This gift, he'd thought, would gild his joys,
Silt up the waters of his grief;   10
His lawns a wilderness of noise,
The heavy clang of leaf on leaf.

Within, the golden cup is good
To heft, to sip the yellow mead.
Outside, in summer's rage, the rude   15
Gold thorn has made his fingers bleed.

"I strolled my halls in golden shift,
As ruddy as a lion's meat.
Then I rushed out to share my gift,
And golden stubble cut my feet."   20

Dazzled with wounds, he limped away
To climb into his golden bed.
Roses, roses can betray.
"Nature is evil," Midas said.

(1961)

COLLEEN THIBAUDEAU
Canada, b.1925

FROM THE PLANNED WOODLOT TO THE FREEDOM OF MRS. FIELD

I. The Planned Woodlot

The planned woodlot
where we are the only things that move:
("and since that day no bird flies over Glendalough"
    — the Wicklow man telling it all in the bar
      this comes again where no bird flies)   5
and we are trees, tourists,

                an air of wonder prevails:

THE UNGRATEFUL GARDEN   **1. Midas:** a legendary king of Phrygia, who was granted his wish that whatever he touched would turn to gold.   **FROM THE PLANNED WOODLOT**   The poem opens in a lifeless reforested area or "planned woodlot" in Durham, Grey County, Ontario, just south of Georgian Bay. **3-5:** The 6th century churches in the valley of Glendalough, in County Wicklow, near Dublin, were built by St. Kevin as penance for his wicked past; Irish legend says that, because of this wickedness, birds still do not fly over the valley. **6:** Thibaudeau notes that this line is "a sort of a reference to a Robert Finch poem" — perhaps "Variations on a Familiar Theme" (in *Dover Beach Revisited*, 1961, by the Canadian poet Robert Finch, b. 1900): "Our voices are the voices of a forest / More strangely come to grief in living-rooms / Or vacant lots or roadsides through a wood / Than ever Birnam came to Dunsinane."

the voice that stills the waters
(that floats there Players and Sweet Afton soft)
that is the bird   *10*
the bird that never sings
the song getting lost, you and I
drifting through the planned woodlot.

II. Into the Trees

"dear woods I know them all . . .
                              the day   *15*
when I have to leave them my heart
will be very heavy." Ah yes, Claudine.
Above my head the porcupines steadily munching chips,
on the edge of Grogan's old clearing a deer
poised leaf and silent in the glades   *20*
as sound of paper (pencil on)
pages,   leaves falling,
through the grey-brown shapes of sound
& the imperceptible drawing back of the bow.

III. Going for Water

Then the only sound in the August clear   *25*
is Carmen Sim's pumphandle
          creaking thirst
drawing it up, the Crystal Kingdom,
and we are going for our share
and we are crossing the back line, worsted,   *30*
gravelly and lately corduroy,
and we are feeling smoother now satiny
slipping over the weathered log bridge
tinpail aswing in our two hands,
and our bare soles touch down to August   *35*
and the big Grayling swish under the bridge.
Smooth, clear, we laugh once over,
twinned hands divining that instant caught
when someone somewhere is Really Praying.

---

9. Sweet Afton: Cf. "Afton Water" (p. 732). **14-17:** The opening of the English translation of *Claudine at School* (1900; tr. 1930), a semi-autobiographical work about a young girl by the French writer Colette (Sidonie Gabrielle Claudine Colette, 1873-1954). **19. Grogan's old clearing:** i.e., in the Ontario bush country of Grey County, between Markdale and Flesherton, where Carmen Sim (line 26) and Mrs. Field (section IV) also live. **31. corduroy:** i.e., ribbed with logs, arranged crosswise across wet ground. **36. Grayling:** a fish.

IV. *The Freedom of Mrs. Field Out Divining*

It sprouts in seasonal mist,   *40*
the feel of the gold drawing, burning.
Under the crunch of crackle snow
deep buried
but twitching the locket pendulum.
From reefs of packsnow   *45*
newfallen (feb. southwind)
       sinking her snowshoes
       settling;
       should she slacken
       go slow step   *50*
              to waterlogged settling
              and sleeping
              and reefed
              white in the whitebush
              slow sink of the deepdrifts   *55*
              newfallen   southwind
                        she drifts;
              does not slacken
                  ongoing
                        her pace never varied,   *60*
              never quite over the gold, but
              the freedom of Mrs. Field Out Divining.
And we divine her, plumpish
Ordinary Mrs. Tom Field of the patient eyes.
Instant pendulums of the heart   *65*
twitch, twig, tell us:
       Don't ever stop now, Mrs. Tom Field, but
       stop or not,
       all the gold under all the bush in the world
       it's only in that heart of yours, only   *70*
       in the freedom of Mrs. Field out divining.

                            (1984)

JAMES K. BAXTER
New Zealand, 1926-1972

EAGLE

Were it the parrot brazen and metallic cawing
Were it the brilliant focused eyes of water-fowl
Were it the whistling flight of the swan or heron

Bringing thought of snow-coldness, woodland regret
   I could then observe placidly   *5*
   I would then retain a personal clarity.

But O beautiful the eagle strides over the valley
The sunned rocks are lips that shout to him.
O marvellous is the simplicity
Beyond simplicity of the machine   *10*
Whereby he drops, kills with curved talons
Whereby he rises molten like the living sun

Whereby he soars to a single crag
Unheeding, stranger, poised and solitary.

(1944)

TO MATE WITH

To mate with the air is difficult —
That sinuous invisible creature
Blows hot, blows cold, rubbing her grit of pollen
On the bodies of ploughmen and mountaineers

Who itch and curse! To mate with a river   *5*
Or a filled-up miner's quarry, that pleases me;

My cold kind mother, Sister Water,
Has no comment, accepts whatever I am,

Yet one may think of tentacles
Reaching, searching from under the darkest ledge,   *10*
And not want to be married. To mate with rock
Is obvious, fatal, and what man was made for,

Whose heart of rock trembles like a magnet
For deserts, graves, any hole in the ground
Where he may hide from Zeus. To mate with fire   *15*
Is what the young want most, like salamanders

Weeping in solitary flame, embracing
Red-hot stoves, walking the lava crust
An inch away from fire. Then, my old gravedigger,
To mate with a woman is the choice   *20*

Containing all other kinds of death —
Fire, water, rock, and the airy succubus,
Without parable, without consolation
Except that each is the other's boulder and victim.

(1967)

A.R. AMMONS
U.S.A., b.1926

DISCOVERER

If you must leave the shores of mind,
scramble down the walls
of dome-locked underwater caves
into the breathless, held

clarity of dark, where no waves break,   *5*
a grainy, colloidal grist
and quiet, carry a light: carry $A = \pi r^2$,
carry Kepler's equal areas in

equal times: as air line take Baudelaire's
L'Albatros: as depth markers   *10*
to call you back, fix the words of
the golden rule: feed the

night of your seeking with clusters
of ancient light:
remember the sacred sheaf, the rods of   *15*
civilization, the holy

bundle of elements: if to cast light
you must enter diffusion's ruin,
carry with you light to cast, to
gather darkness by: carry A is to B   *20*

as A plus B is to A: if to gather darkness
into light, evil into good,
you must leave the shores of mind,
remember us, return and rediscover us.

(1966)

TO MATE WITH   15. Zeus: in Greek myth, king of the gods.   **DISCOVERER   8. Kepler:** Johannes Kepler (1571-1630), German astronomer, whose three laws read: 1. Each planet's orbit is elliptical, with the sun as one of its foci; 2. Each planet's radius vector (the line joining the centre of the planet to the centre of the sun) moves across equal areas of the ellipse in equal times; and 3. The square of a planet's periodic time is proportional to the cube of its mean distance from the sun. **9. Baudelaire:** Charles Pierre Baudelaire (1821-1867), French Symbolist poet, whose "The Albatross" appeared in *Les Fleurs du mal* (1857). **20-21. A is to B as A+B is to A:** a ratio known in mathematics as the "Golden Mean" or "Divine Proportion."

ROBERT CREELEY
U.S.A., b.1926

THE EPIC EXPANDS

They had come in a carriage (which
will be less than what's needed)
over the hard roads. And they stop
in the town to get coke, three
bottles, by way of a celebration.   5

So will the epic expand (or be
expanded by) its content. So will
words throw (throw up) their meaning.
Words they have used (will use) are
the sound (of sound), what gets us.   10

But to go farther (he could not
stop there), to look at the old
people, graceless and cold, in a
carriage with only one blanket
between them, to keep out the cold —   15

and it was, he said (he said), it
was a coldness of the mind, too (too).
Yes, poets, we had overlooked an
essence, and quiet (put back into
quiet), we let the tears roll down.   20
(1979)

A VARIATION

1
My son who is stranger
than he should be, outgrown
at five, the normal —

luck is against him!
Unfit for the upbringing he would otherwise   5
have got, I have no hopes for him.

I leave him alone.

I leave him to his own
devices, having pity not so much that he is
strange   10

but that I am him.

2
Myself, who am stranger
than I should be, outgrown
at two, the normal —

luck is against me. Unfit   15
for the upbringing I would otherwise
have got, I have no hopes.

I leave him alone.

I leave him to his own
devices, having pity not so much for   20
myself, for why should that happen

but that he is me, as much as I am him.
(1979)

ELIZABETH JENNINGS
England, b.1926

SONG AT THE BEGINNING OF AUTUMN

Now watch this autumn that arrives
In smells. All looks like summer still;
Colours are quite unchanged, the air
On green and white serenely thrives.
Heavy the trees with growth and full   5
The fields. Flowers flourish everywhere.

STILL LIFE AND OBSERVER

Proust who collected time within
A child's cake would understand
The ambiguity of this —
Summer still raging while a thin   10
Column of smoke stirs from the land
Proving that autumn gropes for us.

But every season is a kind
Of rich nostalgia. We give names —
Autumn and summer, winter, spring —   15
As though to unfasten from the mind
Our moods and give them outward forms.
We want the certain, solid thing.

But I am carried back against
My will into a childhood where   20
Autumn is bonfires, marbles, smoke;
I lean against my window fenced
From evocations in the air.
When I said autumn, autumn broke.
(1955)

The jar
Holds the shadows.
The shining apple
Exults in its own being,
Exacts   5
Not appetite but observation.
The light folds, joins,
Separates.
Here energy is in abeyance,
Silence is tamed and tethered.   10
The one observer
(Himself almost a still life)
Watches eagerly but quietly,
Content to let the light be the only movement,
The shadows the only interruption.   15
Not the objects here but their setting
Is what is important.
So with the observer,
Whose slightest movement will shift the shadows,
Whose gaze balances the objects.   20
(1964)

JAMES WRIGHT
U.S.A., 1927-1980

NOTES OF A PASTORALIST

In a field outside of Pisa, I saw a shepherd
Keeping warm from a late autumn day.
Blown a little
To one side by the cooling sunlight,
He leaned as though a good tree were holding   5
His body upright.
But the nearest cypresses
Were standing a long way off,
And it seemed that only his green umbrella
Held him there.   10
His sheep did not flock together

As they do in Spenser and Theocritus.
They ambled all over the slope
Too old to care
Or too young to know they were posing   15
For the notes
Of a jaded pastoralist.
If the shepherd had a tune,
I stood too far away to hear it.
I hope he sang to himself. I didn't feel   20
Like paying him to sing.
(1982)

SONG AT THE BEGINNING OF AUTUMN   7. Proust: In the vast seven-part novel sequence, *Remembrance of Things Past*, by the French writer Marcel Proust (1871-1922), a madeleine or cake sets off a wide range of memories.   **NOTES OF A PASTORALIST   12. Spenser:** Edmund Spenser (see p. 148); **Theocritus:** Greek pastoral poet (c.310-250 BC).

AGAINST SURREALISM

There are some tiny obvious details in human life that survive the divine purpose of boring fools to death. In France, all the way down south in Avallon, people like to eat cake. The local bakers there spin up a little flour and chocolate into the shape of a penguin. We came back again and again to a certain window to admire a flock of them. But we never bought one.   5

We found ourselves wandering through Italy, homesick for penguins.

Then a terrible and savage fire of the dog-days roared all over the fourteenth arondissement: which is to say, it was August: and three chocolate penguins appeared behind a window near Place Denfert-Rochereau. We were afraid the Parisians would recognize them, so we bought them all and snuck them home under cover.   10

We set them out on a small table above half the rooftops of Paris. I reached out to brush a tiny obvious particle of dust from the tip of a beak. Suddenly the dust dropped an inch and hovered there. Then it rose to the beak again.

It was a blue spider.

If I were a blue spider, I would certainly ride on a train all the way from Avallon to   15
Paris, and I would set up my house on the nose of a chocolate penguin. It's just a matter of common sense.

(1982)

JOHN ASHBERY
U.S.A., b.1927

DOWN BY THE STATION, EARLY IN THE MORNING

It all wears out. I keep telling myself this, but
I can never believe me, though others do. Even things do.
And the things they do. Like the rasp of silk, or a certain
Glottal stop in your voice as you are telling me how you
Didn't have time to brush your teeth but gargled with Listerine   5
Instead. Each is a base one might wish to touch once more

Before dying. There's the moment years ago in the station in Venice,
The dark rainy afternoon in fourth grade, and the shoes then,
Made of a dull crinkled brown leather that no longer exists.

AGAINST SURREALISM   **8. arondissement:** municipal district of Paris.

And nothing does, until you name it, remembering, and even then   *10*
It may not have existed, or existed only as a result
Of the perceptual dysfunction you've been carrying around for years.
The result is magic, then terror, then pity at the emptiness,
Then air gradually bathing and filling the emptiness as it leaks,
Emoting all over something that is probably mere reportage   *15*
But nevertheless likes being emoted on. And so each day
Culminates in merriment as well as a deep shock like an electric one,

As the wrecking ball bursts through the wall with the bookshelves
Scattering the works of famous authors as well as those
Of more obscure ones, and books with no author, letting in   *20*
Space, and an extraneous babble from the street
Confirming the new value the hollow core has again, the light
From the lighthouse that protects as it pushes us away.

(1984)

W.S. MERWIN
U.S.A., b.1927

HAPPENS EVERY DAY

Right in midtown   walking in broad daylight
people around   and everything
all at once   this guy steps out
in front of him   and has a gun
grabs his briefcase   takes off with it   *5*
everybody around   is in a hurry
the first guy wakes up   to shout and the other one
starts running and the first guy   right after him
and the one with the briefcase   drops the gun
and the first guy   stops to pick it up   *10*
but people are passing   in between
he keeps on shouting   and barging through them
and the guy up ahead   drops the briefcase
so he starts after that   and sees somebody
gather up the gun   and get out of there   *15*
and when he stops where   he saw the briefcase
somebody else   has picked that up and gone
the other guy's vanished   and he stands looking
up and down the street   with the people
moving through him   from no beginning   *20*

(1983)

PHYLLIS WEBB
Canada, b.1927

METAPHYSICS OF SPRING

Blossoms —
powder of pink
moths, sift
of mystic wind-
watchers   5
shift of desire's
bled light
gloss of — ah, gross
matter (great
matter), it does   10
not, even
matter
burning / the
shudder of / in
the wings!   15
in shell's pink
growing, birth
of the world
/ feathery
flesh or love   20
what matter?

                                        (1980)

THE DAYS OF THE UNICORNS

  I remember when the unicorns
roved in herds through the meadow
behind the cabin, and how they would
lately pause, tilting their jewelled
horns to the falling sun as we shared 5
the tensions of private property
and the need to be alone.

Or as we walked along the beach
a solitary delicate beast
might follow on his soft paws   10
until we turned and spoke the words
to console him.

It seemed they were always near
ready to show their eyes and stare
us down, standing in their creamy   15
skins, pink tongues out
for our benevolence.

As if they knew that always beyond
and beyond the ladies were weaving them
into their spider looms.   20

I knew where they slept
and how the grass was bent
by their own wilderness
and I pitied them.

It was only yesterday, or seems   25
like only yesterday when we could
touch and turn and they came
perfectly real into our fictions.
But they moved on with the courtly sun
grazing peacefully beyond the story   30
horns lowering and lifting and
lowering.

I know this is scarcely credible now
as we cabin ourselves in cold
and the motions of panic
and our cells destroy each other
performing music and extinction
and the great dreams pass on
to the common good.

                                        (1980)

THE DAYS OF THE UNICORNS   **10. paws:** dream overlap of lion and unicorn (Webb's note).

ANNE SEXTON
U.S.A., 1928-1974

TO A FRIEND WHOSE WORK HAS COME TO TRIUMPH

Consider Icarus, pasting those sticky wings on,
testing that strange little tug at his shoulder blade,
and think of that first flawless moment over the lawn
of the labyrinth. Think of the difference it made!
There below are the trees, as awkward as camels;   5
and here are the shocked starlings pumping past
and think of innocent Icarus who is doing quite well:
larger than a sail, over the fog and the blast
of the plushy ocean, he goes. Admire his wings!
Feel the fire at his neck and see how casually   10
he glances up and is caught, wondrously tunneling
into that hot eye. Who cares that he fell back to the sea?
See him acclaiming the sun and come plunging down
while his sensible daddy goes straight into town.

(1962)

RED RIDING HOOD

Many are the deceivers:

The suburban matron,
proper in the supermarket,
list in hand so she won't suddenly fly,
buying her Duz and Chuck Wagon dog food, 5
meanwhile ascending from earth,
letting her stomach fill up with helium,
letting her arms go loose as kite tails,
getting ready to meet her lover
a mile down Apple Crest Road   10
in the Congregational Church parking lot.

Two seemingly respectable women
come up to an old Jenny
and show her an envelope
full of money   15
and promise to share the booty
if she'll give them ten thou
as an act of faith.
Her life savings are under the mattress
covered with rust stains   20
and counting.
They are as wrinkled as prunes
but negotiable.
The two women take the money and disappear.
Where is the moral?   25
Not all knives are for
stabbing the exposed belly.
Rock climbs on rock
and it only makes a seashore.
Old Jenny has lost her belief in mattresses   30
and now she has no wastebasket in which
to keep her youth.

The standup comic
on the "Tonight" show
who imitates the Vice President   35
and cracks up Johnny Carson
and delays sleep for millions
of bedfellows watching between their feet,
slits his wrist the next morning
in the Algonquin's old-fashioned bathroom, 40
the razor in his hand like a toothbrush,
wall as anonymous as a urinal,
the shower curtain his slack rubberman audience,
and then the slash
as simple as opening a letter   45
and the warm blood breaking out like a rose
upon the bathtub with its claw and ball feet.

TO A FRIEND Cf. Yeats's "To a Friend Whose Work Has Come to Nothing" (p. 1214). **1. Icarus:** In Greek mythology, Icarus was the son of Daedalus, an able craftsman who designed for King Minos of Crete an elaborate maze-like fortress known as the Labyrinth (at the centre of which the king kept a monster known as the Minotaur); when Minos refused to allow Daedalus to leave Crete, Daedalus designed wings made of feathers and wax, so that he and his son could fly to Greece; though Daedalus warned Icarus not to fly high, Icarus flew too close to the sun, and when the sun melted the wax, Icarus plummeted into the sea and drowned.   **RED RIDING HOOD** See "Little Red Riding Hood" (p. 502). **5. Duz, Chuck Wagon:** tradenames; the slogan for Duz soap was "Duz does everything." **34. "Tonight" show:** late-night American television interview show hosted by comedian Johnny Carson (b.1925) from 1962 to 1992. **40. Algonquin:** New York hotel made famous in the 1920s as the meeting place of the "Algonquin Round Table," a witty group of writers that included Robert Benchley (1889-1945), Dorothy Parker (1893-1967), George S. Kaufman (1889-1961), and Alexander Woollcott (1887-1943).

And I. I too.
Quite collected at cocktail parties,
meanwhile in my head   50
I'm undergoing open-heart surgery.
The heart, poor fellow,
pounding on his little tin drum
with a faint death beat.
The heart, that eyeless beetle,   55
enormous that Kafka beetle,
running panicked through his maze,
never stopping one foot after the other
one hour after the other
until he gags on an apple   60
and it's all over.

And I. I too again.
I built a summer house on Cape Ann.
A simple A-frame and this too was
a deception — nothing haunts a new house.   65
When I moved in with a bathing suit and tea bags
the ocean rumbled like a train backing up
and at each window secrets came in
like gas. My mother, that departed soul,
sat in my Eames chair and reproached me   70
for losing her keys to the old cottage.
Even in the electric kitchen there was
the smell of a journey. The ocean
was seeping through its frontiers
and laying me out on its wet rails.   75
The bed was stale with my childhood
and I could not move to another city
where the worthy make a new life.

Long ago
there was a strange deception: 80
a wolf dressed in frills,
a kind of transvestite.
But I get ahead of my story.
In the beginning
there was just little Red Riding Hood,   85
so called because her grandmother
made her a red cape and she was never without it.
It was her Linus blanket, besides

it was red, as red as the Swiss flag,
yes it was red, as red as chicken blood.   90
But more than she loved her riding hood
she loved her grandmother who lived
far from the city in the big wood.

This one day her mother gave her
a basket of wine and cake   95
to take to her grandmother
because she was ill.
Wine and cake?
Where's the aspirin? The penicillin?
Where's the fruit juice?   100
Peter Rabbit got camomile tea.
But wine and cake it was.

On her way in the big wood
Red Riding Hood met the wolf.
Good day, Mr. Wolf, she said,   105
thinking him no more dangerous
than a streetcar or a panhandler.
He asked where she was going
and she obligingly told him.
There among the roots and trunks   110
with the mushrooms pulsing inside the moss
he planned how to eat them both,
the grandmother an old carrot
and the child a shy budkin
in a red red hood.   115
He bade her to look at the bloodroot,
the small bunchberry and the dogtooth
and pick some for her grandmother.
And this she did.
Meanwhile he scampered off   120
to Grandmother's house and ate her up
as quick as a slap.
Then he put on her nightdress and cap
and snuggled down into the bed.
A deceptive fellow.   125

Red Riding Hood
knocked on the door and entered
with her flowers, her cake, her wine.

---

56. Kafka beetle: alluding to "The Metamorphosis," a short story first published in 1915 as *Die Verwandlung*, by the Jewish Czech writer Franz Kafka (1883-1924). **63. Cape Ann:** in Massachusetts. **70. Eames chair:** moulded plywood chair designed by Charles Eames (1907-1978) and his wife Ray (Kaiser) Eames (1916-1988), who specialized in what they called "organic design in Home Furnishings"; a New York Museum of Modern Art exhibition in 1946 featured this chair, and one commentator subsequently described it as the "obligatory foreground object of the Model House of the late 1940s." **88. Linus blanket:** alluding to the security blanket carried by a character in the comic strip *Peanuts*, drawn by Charles Schulz (b. 1922). **101. Peter Rabbit:** character in *The Tale of Peter Rabbit* (1902), by Beatrix Potter (1866-1943).

Grandmother looked strange,
a dark and hairy disease it seemed.   *130*
Oh Grandmother, what big ears you have,
ears, eyes, hands and then the teeth.
The better to eat you with, my dear.
So the wolf gobbled Red Riding Hood down
like a gumdrop. Now he was fat.   *135*
He appeared to be in his ninth month
and Red Riding Hood and her grandmother
rode like two Jonahs up and down with
his every breath. One pigeon. One partridge.

He was fast asleep,   *140*
dreaming in his cap and gown,
wolfless.
Along came a huntsman who heard
the loud contented snores
and knew that was no grandmother.   *145*
He opened the door and said,
So it's you, old sinner.
He raised his gun to shoot him
when it occurred to him that maybe
the wolf had eaten up the old lady.   *150*
So he took a knife and began cutting open
the sleeping wolf, a kind of caesarian section.

It was a carnal knife that let
Red Riding Hood out like a poppy,
quite alive from the kingdom of the belly.   *155*
And grandmother too
still waiting for cakes and wine.
The wolf, they decided, was too mean
to be simply shot so they filled his belly
with large stones and sewed him up.   *160*
He was as heavy as a cemetery
and when he woke up and tried to run off
he fell over dead. Killed by his own weight.
Many a deception ends on such a note.

The huntsman and the grandmother and
    Red Riding Hood   *165*
sat down by his corpse and had a meal of
    wine and cake.
Those two remembering
nothing naked and brutal
from that little death,
that little birth,   *170*
from their going down
and their lifting up.

                                                           (1971)

Andrew Salkey
Jamaica/England/U.S.A., b.1928

SOOT, THE LAND OF BILLBOARDS

You must be sort of gathering, by now, that Anancy got the travel thing in him blood, like say how mongoose got chicken on f'him mind most time. That bound to be the reason why Anancy take foot, one day, to another lan' where he arriving strange as sarsaparilla growing which part snow come from. In this particular lan' call Soot, Anancy find he able to read big billboard all over the place. He able do this easy, 'cause   *5* the lettering black and white and bright bad. The first one Anancy clap him eye 'pon go like so: RUN!

---

138. Jonahs: referring to the Biblical figure Jonah, who was swallowed by a whale (see Jonah 1:17).   **SOOT, THE LAND OF BILLBOARDS   1. Anancy:** In an Author's Note to *Anancy's Score*, Salkey refers to the "traditional Anancy" as a "crisp, cool, calculating spider, a persuasive, inventive, anarchic spider-man," the traditional trickster figure of African and Afro-Caribbean folk tales; trickster stories (including those in other cultures, such as those involving Coyote or Raven — see the story by Reid and Bringhurst, p. 1401) — conventionally use humour to comment on social conditions.

Nothing else add to it. Anancy think hard, as he standing facing the one word message; he waiting f'some small understanding to burs' 'pon him; he don' get none; so, then, he laugh cyah-cyah. He laugh particular at the bosify lettering. He thinking that *10* the billboard don' really done paint proper yet. How man going know where f'run, if he don' catch no meaning other than just plain run? He feeling console-up and confuse, even though he able read it.

The second billboard Anancy see just like the first one; it go so: OURS. It favour the first one, black and white and bright, and nothing else write 'pon it but the one word *15* f'we own. All the same though, Anancy seeing that the lettering got a purple touch that the first lettering don' have. This billboard puzzling Anancy little bit, but, as 'cording to him nature, he start forget the whole thing. One fact about Anancy: he the most forgetting spider man you could find anywhere at all. He develop that forgetting forgiving side of him life to such a total point that he count it as him one bank balance. *20* He get that way from the early days when licks used to ride him back and lash it plenty.

Well, anyway, Anancy stay cool in the sun-hot that Brother Sun been spitting out long time in Soot. And he forget the two sign them, the lettering and the entire billboard, big as life as them be.

He take foot and go into a part of Soot call by name Somethingville. When he get *25* there, he hear about a Spiderman who happen just to receive a vicious neck-hanging. Anancy, with all him blind eye way of looking at the strange country, couldn't help seeing how everybody seeming content and righteous, like they just done do something to make them clean and white inside.

Well, now, f'some Gawd reason that don' have explanation f'itself no how, Anancy *30* change him spider man appearance by catching a wash in a cask of white paint, so that he come out white, as if he born to it nice and natural foreign. Then, in him white condition, Anancy walk up to one of the 'abitants of Somethingville and ask, speaky spokey, about what happen. The 'abitant tall and cough a proud lynch cough and crinkle him mouth corner, plantation boss, and answer with a sugar nod and say: "Where you *35* from?"

Anancy say: "I from foreign. Why you wan' know?"

"Well, you won' find too much interes' in 'angin' 'mongst we in these parts."

And Anancy ask: " 'Ow come?"

And the 'abitant say: " 'Cause we' jus' ordinary folks 'roun' 'ere so, law-'bidin', *40* goin' on usual."

So, Anancy ask: "But you too cool, man. I mean to say: you can cool 'bout other t'ings that 'appen; you should 'dignant bad 'bout the proceedin' o' this brutalisin' business o' 'angin' a man. You don' t'ink so, nuh?"

" 'Dignant 'bout it? No, stranger man. We not 'dignant at all 'bout 'angin'." *45*

"Wha' you know 'bout it? You personal, I mean?"

"Well, as a Somethingvillean, I know this one fac'. It don' do by none o' we livin' roun' 'ere, at no time."

---

10. bosify: overly ornate. **21. licks:** i.e., lickings, whippings. **33-34. speaky spokey:** pretentiously formal. **34. lynch cough:** as though "strangled."

"But 'ow come you know that?"

" 'Cause we don' got no motive, stranger. As the man say, 'A man don' eat unless   *50*
he feel 'ungry an' him belly makin' noise.'"

"So, wha' 'appen then?"

"The mos' I can say is that we glad the kidnappers them didn' come from f'we
parts roun' so. We t'ink they mus' be come from far, somewhere out o' town, an' tha's
wha' I been tellin' the Feelin' Brains Institute o' spider questioner them wit' me own   *55*
words, lickle before you come."

"An' wha' the Feelin' Brains Institute man them say?"

"Not a t'ing wort' mentionin'. It always 'ard f'tell wha' the Feelin' Brains Institute
man them imaginin' in them special brains, you know. 'Ard no bitch!"

"So, wha' the local 'abitants them 'ave to say?"   *60*

"All o' we was 'opin' an' prayin' f'somet'ing to come o' the investigatin', 'cause
we did wan' catch a listen to the case in court. We no goin' get the chance f'do that
now, seein' as wha' 'appen."

"Not a link is a link, then?"

"No local connection wit' the 'angin' at all."   *65*

" 'Ow come that no jailer wasn't 'pon spot when the Spiderman get drag way an'
'ang?"

"Well, you see, stranger: jailer usual go 'ome when night come. He live only few
yards up the road an' he usual go 'ome evenin' time early. Not a t'ing 'ceptional 'bout
that, see. It be a normal peaceful Friday night in a normal peaceful law-'bidin' town.   *70*
Somethingville like that. So we stay. So we get on. From long time, now. Mind we own
business. An' law-'bidin'."

The next day, when Anancy leaving Somethingville and Soot, and he passing the
two billboard them, he catch a look at him body whirling whiteness in a fast car flashing
'gainst him in the road, and he realise say that he did forget him change skin-colour, as   *75*
you would expec', seeing what a most forgetful spider he be from morning; and so, he
look down 'pon the put-on whiteness and laugh cyah-cyah, and he decide that he got to
rub it off before he get back home to him yard good and proper.

But the whiteness catching bad, 'special if you have long 'sociation with it and got
little bit settle way deep down. You see: the thing is that the white business take set in   *80*
Anancy, and it taking long as rass to disappear and out-out from him skin naturalness.
Little most it didn' get rub off complete at all. Anyway, when Anancy done get it off, he
feeling like protection gone. He empty in a most funny way, but he fling ol' iron in him
back and face himself and say that he back to normal, where all the back yard billboard
them got f'him own message write as big as bitch. Even though that not the strict truth,   *85*
it good f'Anancy think so 'til he wake up real one day.

(1973)

---

69. yards: houses. **81. rass:** exclamation expressing scorn or impatience.

IAIN CRICHTON SMITH
Scotland, b.1928

RETURNING EXILE

You who come home do not tell me
anything about yourself, where you have come from,
why your coat is wet, why there is grass in your hair.

The sheep huddle on the hills as always,
there's a yellow light as if cast by helmets,   5
the fences made of wire are strung by the wind.

Do not tell me where you have come from, beloved
   stranger.
It is enough that there is light still in your eyes,
that the dog rising on his pillar of black knows you.
(1984)

SLOWLY

Slowly we are adopted by the words . . . slowly we are other.
We are the aesthetic critics, not the ethical.
The play is a playful event.

Even agony becomes beautiful.
Even the broken heads are questionable.   5
Even the dictator's talent is in doubt.

No sounds from the street reach this theatre.
The torturer is a genius, or he is not.
The drapery on the coffin a lovely red.

The actor walks out on to a cold street.   10
Someone arrests him . . . someone tortures him.
His scream is no longer an actor's scream,

and yet the one from the theatre sounds like it.
The two screams meet where no one has a name.
They meet where all the walls have fallen down.   15
(1989)

U.A. FANTHORPE
England, b.1929

GENESIS
(for J.R.R. Tolkien)

In the beginning were the words,
Aristocratic, cryptic, chromatic.
Vowels as direct as mid-day,
Consonants lanky as long-swords.

Mouths materialized to speak the words: 5
Leafshaped lips for the high language,
Tranquil tongues for the tree-creatures,
Slits and slobbers for the lower orders.

Deeds came next, words' children.
Legs by walking evolved a landscape.   10
Continents and chronologies occurred,
Complex and casual as an implication.

Arched over all, alarming nimbus,
Magic's disorderly thunder and lightning.

The sage sat in his suburban fastness,   15
Garrisoned against progress. He grieved

GENESIS **Dedication:** J.R.R. Tolkien: Birmingham-educated language scholar (1892-1973), author of *The Hobbit* (1937) and its sequel, the three-volume *The Lord of the Rings* (1954-55), a fantasy about the tribulations affecting "middle-earth."

At what the Duke's men did to our words
(Whose war memorial is every signpost).

The sage sat. And middle-earth
Rose around him like a rumour.   20
Grave grammarians, Grimm and Werner,
Gave it laws, granted it charters.

The sage sat. But the ghosts walked
Of the Birmingham schoolboy, the Somme soldier,

Whose bones lay under the hobbit burrows,   25
Who endured darkness, and friends dying,

Whom words waylaid in a Snow Hill siding,
Coal truck pit names, grimy, gracious,
Blaen-Rhondda, Nantyglo, Senghenydd.
In these deeps middle-earth was mined.   30

These were the words in the beginning.
                                    (1982)

KNOWING ABOUT SONNETS

Lesson I: "The Soldier" (Brooke)

"[The task of criticism] is not to redouble the text's self-understanding, to collude with its object in a conspiracy of silence. The task is to show the text as it cannot know itself."

— Terry Eagleton, *Criticism and Ideology*

Recognizing a sonnet is like attaching
A name to a face. *Mister Sonnet, I presume?*
    If I
And naming is power. It can hardly
Deny its name. You are well on the way   5
To mastery. The next step is telling the sonnet
What it is trying to say. This is called Interpretation.
    If I should die
What you mustn't do is collude with it. This
Is bad for the sonnet, and will only encourage it   10
To be eloquent. You must question it closely:
What has it left out? What made it decide
To be a sonnet? The author's testimony
(If any) is not evidence. He is the last person to know.
    If I should die, think this   15
Stand no nonsense with imagery. Remember, though shifty,
It is vulnerable to calculation. Apply the right tests.
Now you are able to Evaluate the sonnet.
    If I
That should do for today.   20
    If I should die
               And over and over
The new white paper track innocent unlined hands.
    Think this. Think this. Think this. Think only this.
                                    (1984)

---

21. Grimm and Werner: Jakob Grimm (1785-1863), German philologist and fairytale collector, and Karl Verner (1846-1896), Danish linguist; "Grimm's Law" and "Verner's Law" both deal with transformations of sound in the evolution of Indo-European languages. **24. Somme:** battle site during World War I. **25. hobbit:** Hobbits are lovable gnome-like creatures who live in burrows, featured in Tolkien's stories. **27. Snow Hill:** railway station in Birmingham. **29:** place names in Glamorgan and Monmouth, Wales.   **KNOWING ABOUT SONNETS**   See Brooke's "The Soldier" (p. 1296). **Epigraph:** Terry Eagleton (b.1943) is a contemporary English literary theorist.

OLD MAN, OLD MAN

He lives in a world of small recalcitrant
Things in bottles, with tacky labels. He was always
A man who did-it-himself.

Now his hands shamble among clues
He left for himself when he saw better, 5
And small things distress: *I've lost the hammer.*

Lifelong adjuster of environments,
Lord once of shed, garage and garden,
Each with its proper complement of tackle,

World authority on twelve different 10
Sorts of glue, connoisseur of nuts
And bolts, not good with daughters

But a dab hand with the Black and Decker,
Self-demoted in your nineties to washing-up
After supper, and missing crusted streaks 15

Of food on plates; have you forgotten
The jokes you no longer tell, as you forget
If you've smoked your timetabled cigarette?

Now television has no power to arouse 19
Your surliness; your wife could replace on the walls
Those pictures of disinherited children,

And you wouldn't know. Now you ramble
In your talk around London districts, fretting
At how to find your way from Holborn to Soho,

And where is Drury Lane? Old man, old man, 25
So obdurate in your contracted world,
Living in almost-dark, *I can see you,*

You said to me, *but only as a cloud.*
When I left, you tried not to cry. I love
Your helplessness, you who hate being helpless. 30

Let me find your hammer. Let me
Walk with you to Drury Lane. I am only a cloud.
(1987)

D.G. JONES
Canada, b.1929

THE PATH

The children are running, there are four
five
the children are running down the path
down the hill between young pine and sumac
between bushes 5
under the last light of the summer solstice

One does not live here
one is not running
one is a girl, homesick, and older

one is sad, her mother, running 10
is married again and lives in Toronto

one is still hiding, stopped, behind bushes

one is holding his foot
he has stepped on a thorn

one's off the horizon 15

The children are running, there are five
four
down the path in the last light of evening
under the pink and white clouds
under the blue once, and forever, sky 20
(1967)

OLD MAN, OLD MAN **13. Black and Decker:** power tool tradename.

URSULA K. LE GUIN
U.S.A., b.1929

THE ONES WHO WALK AWAY FROM OMELAS
(Variations on a theme by William James)

With a clamor of bells that set the swallows soaring, the Festival of Summer came to the city Omelas, bright-towered by the sea. The rigging of the boats in harbor sparkled with flags. In the streets between houses with red roofs and painted walls, between old moss-grown gardens and under avenues of trees, past great parks and public buildings, processions moved. Some were decorous: old people in long stiff robes of mauve and grey, grave master workmen, quiet, merry women carrying their babies and chatting as they walked. In other streets the music beat faster, a shimmering of gong and tambourine, and the people went dancing, the procession was a dance. Children dodged in and out, their high calls rising like the swallows' crossing flights over the music and the singing. All the processions wound towards the north side of the city, where on the great water-meadow called the Green Fields boys and girls, naked in the bright air, with mud-stained feet and ankles and long, lithe arms, exercised their restive horses before the race. The horses wore no gear at all but a halter without bit. Their manes were braided with streamers of silver, gold, and green. They flared their nostrils and pranced and boasted to one another; they were vastly excited, the horse being the only animal who has adopted our ceremonies as his own. Far off to the north and west the mountains stood up half encircling Omelas on her bay. The air of morning was so clear that the snow still crowning the Eighteen Peaks burned with white-gold fire across the miles of sunlit air, under the dark blue of the sky. There was just enough wind to make the banners that marked the racecourse snap and flutter now and then. In the silence of the broad green meadows one could hear the music winding through the city streets, farther and nearer and ever approaching, a cheerful faint sweetness of the air that from time to time trembled and gathered together and broke out into the great joyous clanging of the bells.

Joyous! How is one to tell about joy? How describe the citizens of Omelas?

They were not simple folk, you see, though they were happy. But we do not say the words of cheer much any more. All smiles have become archaic. Given a description such as this one tends to make certain assumptions. Given a description such as this one

THE ONES WHO WALK AWAY FROM OMELAS   **Title:** Le Guin notes that "Omelas" is "Salem, O." backwards, and goes on: "Salem equals schelomo equals salaam equals Peace. Melas. O melas. Omelas. Homme hélas." **Subtitle:** Le Guin's note to the story quotes from "The Moral Philosopher and the Moral Life" by the American philosopher William James (1842-1910): "Or if the hypothesis were offered us of a world in which . . . millions [should be] kept permanently happy on the one simple condition that a certain lost soul on the far-off edge of things should lead a life of lonely torment, what except a specifical and independent sort of emotion can it be which would make us immediately feel, even though an impulse arose within us to clutch at the happiness so offered, how hideous a thing would be its enjoyment when deliberately accepted as the fruit of such a bargain? All the higher, more penetrating ideals are revolutionary. They present themselves far less in the guise of effects of past experience than in that of probable causes of future experience, factors to which the environment and the lessons it has so far taught us must learn to bend." **26. smiles . . . archaic:** The "archaic smile" is that found on many Greek statues of the early 6th century B.C., especially those of *kouroi*, or young men.

tends to look next for the King, mounted on a splendid stallion and surrounded by his noble knights, or perhaps in a golden litter borne by great-muscled slaves. But there was no king. They did not use swords, or keep slaves. They were not barbarians. I do not know the rules and laws of their society, but I suspect that they were singularly few. As they did without monarchy and slavery, so they also got on without the stock exchange, the advertisement, the secret police, and the bomb. Yet I repeat that these were not simple folk, not dulcet shepherds, noble savages, bland utopians. They were not less complex than us. The trouble is that we have a bad habit, encouraged by pedants and sophisticates, of considering happiness as something rather stupid. Only pain is intellectual, only evil interesting. This is the treason of the artist: a refusal to admit the banality of evil and the terrible boredom of pain. If you can't lick 'em, join 'em. If it hurts, repeat it. But to praise despair is to condemn delight, to embrace violence is to lose hold of everything else. We have almost lost hold; we can no longer describe a happy man, nor make any celebration of joy. How can I tell you about the people of Omelas? They were not naïve and happy children — though their children were, in fact, happy. They were mature, intelligent, passionate adults whose lives were not wretched. O miracle! but I wish I could describe it better. I wish I could convince you. Omelas sounds in my words like a city in a fairy tale, long ago and far away, once upon a time. Perhaps it would be best if you imagined it as your own fancy bids, assuming it will rise to the occasion, for certainly I cannot suit you all. For instance, how about technology? I think that there would be no cars or helicopters in and above the streets; this follows from the fact that the people of Omelas are happy people. Happiness is based on a just discrimination of what is necessary, what is neither necessary nor destructive, and what is destructive. In the middle category, however — that of the unnecessary but undestructive, that of comfort, luxury, exuberance, etc. — they could perfectly well have central heating, subway trains, washing machines, and all kinds of marvelous devices not yet invented here, floating light-sources, fuelless power, a cure for the common cold. Or they could have none of that: it doesn't matter. As you like it. I incline to think that people from towns up and down the coast have been coming in to Omelas during the last days before the Festival on very fast little trains and double-decked trams, and that the train station of Omelas is actually the handsomest building in town, though plainer than the magnificent Farmers' Market. But even granted trains, I fear that Omelas so far strikes some of you as goody-goody. Smiles, bells, parades, horses, bleh. If so, please add an orgy. If an orgy would help, don't hesitate. Let us not, however, have temples from which issue beautiful nude priests and priestesses already half in ecstasy and ready to copulate with any man or woman, lover or stranger, who desires union with the deep godhead of the blood, although that was my first idea. But really it would be better not to have any temples in Omelas — at least, not manned temples. Religion yes, clergy no. Surely the beautiful nudes can just wander about, offering themselves like divine soufflés to the hunger of the needy and the rapture of the flesh. Let them join the processions. Let tambourines be struck above the copulations, and the glory of desire be proclaimed upon the gongs, and (a not unimportant point) let the offspring of these delightful rituals be beloved and looked after by all. One thing I know there is none of in Omelas is guilt. But what else should there be? I thought at first there were no drugs, but that is puritanical. For those who like it, the faint insistent sweetness of *drooz* may perfume the ways of the city, *drooz* which first brings a great lightness and brilliance to the minds and limbs, and then after some hours a dreamy languor, and wonderful visions at last of the very arcana and inmost secrets of the Universe, as well as exciting the pleasure of sex beyond all belief; and it is not habit-forming. For more modest tastes I think there ought to be beer. What else, what else belongs in the joyous city? The sense of victory, surely, the celebration of courage. But as we did without clergy, let us do without soldiers. The joy built upon successful slaughter is not the right kind of joy; it will not do; it is fearful and it is trivial. A boundless and generous contentment, a magnanimous triumph felt not against some outer enemy but in communion with the finest and fairest in the souls of all men everywhere and the splendor of the world's summer: this is what swells the hearts of the people of Omelas, and the victory they celebrate is that of life. I really don't think many of them need to take *drooz*.

Most of the processions have reached the Green Fields by now. A marvelous smell of cooking goes forth from the red and blue tents of the provisioners. The faces of small children are amiably sticky; in the benign grey beard of a man a couple of crumbs of rich pastry are entangled. The youths and girls have mounted their horses and are beginning to group around the starting line of the course. An old woman, small, fat, and laughing, is passing out flowers from a basket, and tall young men wear her flowers in their shining hair. A child of nine or ten sits at the edge of the crowd, alone, playing on a wooden flute. People pause to listen, and they smile, but they do not speak to him, for he never ceases playing and never sees them, his dark eyes wholly rapt in the sweet, thin magic of the tune.

He finishes, and slowly lowers his hands holding the wooden flute.

As if that little private silence were the signal, all at once a trumpet sounds from the pavilion near the starting line: imperious, melancholy, piercing. The horses rear on their slender legs, and some of them neigh in answer. Sober-faced, the young riders stroke the horses' necks and soothe them, whispering, "Quiet, quiet, there my beauty, my hope. . . ." They begin to form in rank along the starting line. The crowds along the racecourse are like a field of grass and flowers in the wind. The Festival of Summer has begun.

Do you believe? Do you accept the festival, the city, the joy? No? Then let me describe one more thing.

In a basement under one of the beautiful public buildings of Omelas, or perhaps in the cellar of one of its spacious private homes, there is a room. It has one locked door, and no window. A little light seeps in dustily between cracks in the boards, secondhand from a cobwebbed window somewhere across the cellar. In one corner of the little room a couple of mops, with stiff, clotted, foul-smelling heads, stand near a rusty bucket. The floor is dirt, a little damp to the touch, as cellar dirt usually is. The room is about three paces long and two wide: a mere broom closet or disused tool room. In the room a child is sitting. It could be a boy or a girl. It looks about six, but actually is nearly ten. It is feeble-minded. Perhaps it was born defective, or perhaps it has become imbecile through fear, malnutrition, and neglect. It picks its nose and occasionally fumbles vaguely with its toes or genitals, as it sits hunched in the corner farthest from the bucket and the two mops. It is afraid of the mops. It finds them horrible. It shuts its eyes, but it knows the mops are still standing there; and the door is locked; and nobody will come. The door is always locked; and nobody ever comes, except that sometimes — the child has no understanding of time or interval — sometimes the door rattles terribly and opens, and a person, or several people, are there. One of them may come in and kick the child to make it stand up. The others never come close, but peer in at it with frightened, disgusted eyes. The food bowl and the water jug are hastily filled, the door is locked, the eyes disappear. The people at the door never say anything, but the child, who has not always lived in the tool room, and can remember sunlight and its mother's voice, sometimes speaks. "I will be good," it says. "Please let me out. I will be good!" They never answer. The child used to scream for help at night, and cry a good deal, but now it only makes a kind of whining, "eh-haa, eh-haa," and it speaks less and less often. It is so thin there are no calves to its legs; its belly protrudes; it lives on a half-bowl of corn meal and grease a day. It is naked. Its buttocks and thighs are a mass of festered sores, as it sits in its own excrement continually.

They all know it is there, all the people of Omelas. Some of them have come to see it, others are content merely to know it is there. They all know that it has to be there. Some of them understand why, and some do not, but they all understand that their happiness, the beauty of their city, the tenderness of their friendships, the health of their children, the wisdom of their scholars, the skill of their makers, even the abundance of their harvest and the kindly weathers of their skies, depend wholly on this child's abominable misery.

This is usually explained to children when they are between eight and twelve, whenever they seem capable of understanding; and most of those who come to see the child are young people, though often enough an adult comes, or comes back, to see the child. No matter how well the matter has been explained to them, these young spectators are always shocked and sickened at the sight. They feel disgust, which they had thought themselves superior to. They feel anger, outrage, impotence, despite all the explanations. They would like to do something for the child. But there is nothing they can do. If the child were brought up into the sunlight out of that vile place, if it were cleaned and fed and comforted, that would be a good thing, indeed; but if it were done, in that day and hour all the prosperity and beauty and delight of Omelas would wither and be destroyed. Those are the terms. To exchange all the goodness and grace of every life in Omelas for that single, small improvement: to throw away the happiness of thousands for the chance of the happiness of one: that would be to let guilt within the walls indeed.

The terms are strict and absolute; there may not even be a kind word spoken to the child.

Often the young people go home in tears, or in a tearless rage, when they have seen the child and faced this terrible paradox. They may brood over it for weeks or years. But as time goes on they begin to realize that even if the child could be released, it would not get much good of its freedom: a little vague pleasure of warmth and food, no doubt, but little more. It is too degraded and imbecile to know any real joy. It has been afraid too long ever to be free of fear. Its habits are too uncouth for it to respond to humane treatment. Indeed, after so long it would probably be wretched without walls about it to protect it, and darkness for its eyes, and its own excrement to sit in. Their tears at the bitter injustice dry when they begin to perceive the terrible justice of reality, and to accept it. Yet it is their tears and anger, the trying of their generosity and the acceptance of their helplessness, which are perhaps the true source of the splendor of their lives.

Theirs is no vapid, irresponsible happiness. They know that they, like the child, are not free. They know compassion. It is the existence of the child, and their knowledge of its existence, that makes possible the nobility of their architecture, the poignancy of their *165* music, the profundity of their science. It is because of the child that they are so gentle with children. They know that if the wretched one were not there snivelling in the dark, the other one, the flute-player, could make no joyful music as the young riders line up in their beauty for the race in the sunlight of the first morning of summer.

Now do you believe in them? Are they not more credible? But there is one more *170* thing to tell, and this is quite incredible.

At times one of the adolescent girls or boys who go to see the child does not go home to weep or rage, does not, in fact, go home at all. Sometimes also a man or woman much older falls silent for a day or two, and then leaves home. These people go out into the street, and walk down the street alone. They keep walking, and walk straight out of *175* the city of Omelas, through the beautiful gates. They keep walking across the farmlands of Omelas. Each one goes alone, youth or girl, man or woman. Night falls; the traveler must pass down village streets, between the houses with yellow-lit windows, and on out into the darkness of the fields. Each alone, they go west or north, towards the mountains. They go on. They leave Omelas, they walk ahead into the darkness, and they do not come *180* back. The place they go towards is a place even less imaginable to most of us than the city of happiness. I cannot describe it at all. It is possible that it does not exist. But they seem to know where they are going, the ones who walk away from Omelas.

(1973)

PETER PORTER
Australia/England, b.1929

NEVERTHELESS

Heretofore
you could use words like heretofore
without embarrassment, and catch the tail
of lyricism in some suburban garden
where words were still silver   5
and stoically inventive verse stayed new
through all the limits of recurring sound,
being at once proconsular
and steeped in sadness. This was a time
when needles, once a shining store,   10
clicked in the dusk of cottage madness
under a maidenly predestined order
like the village poplars: a sad connective
linked complicity and fate,
Calvinism and the empty grate.   15

Moreover
what was more emphatic tipped over
into rhetoric, itself a form from which
the cooler mind could distance its approval
if the sought exaggeration seemed   20
too smug: viz. the walls of oak round England
and bloodless the untrodden snow.
Words went in carriages and knew
which world was which and who was who.

Notwithstanding   25
such non-literary facts as one may note
with understanding when the scientists
of history and language point to verse
as the least apposite of checks on how
the language went in any chosen past: 30

look to the lawyers and the letter-writers,
the estate agents in their coaches,
ironfounders and top-hatted railway men.
Now all the practical romantics
called from high-walled gardens   35
to God in a lunette: retreat was sounded
in that melancholy long withdrawing roar.
Circumlocution for these times
was the shape of Empire and an office
where words were banked or shovelled into coffers.   40

Nevertheless
we never move too far from Presbyterian
small print — wireless becomes the radio,
the word processor is a crutch for brains,

glossy paper takes the images of famine.   45
Poetry goes on being made from sounds
and syntax though even its friends confess
the sad old thing is superannuated.
Watch, though, its spritely gait as
like a bent mosquito in it walks   50
on the arms of three tall women in black
to mutter envious obscenities at large —
its task is still to point incredulously
at death, a child who won't be silenced,
among the shattered images to hear   55
what the salt hay whispers to tide's change,
dull in the dark, to climb to bed
with all the dross of time inside its head.

                                        (1984)

ADRIENNE RICH
U.S.A., b.1929

PLANETARIUM

Thinking of Caroline Herschel (1750-1848)
astronomer, sister of William; and others.

A woman in the shape of a monster
a monster in the shape of a woman
the skies are full of them

a woman   "in the snow
among the Clocks and instruments   5
or measuring the ground with poles"

in her 98 years to discover
8 comets

she whom the moon ruled
like us   10
levitating into the night sky
riding the polished lenses

Galaxies of women, there
doing penance for impetuousness
ribs chilled   15
in those spaces   of the mind

NEVERTHELESS   **36. lunette:** crescent-shaped space over a door or window, for a painting or statue; or the painting or statue itself. **37.**
melancholy . . . roar: See line 25 of Arnold's "Dover Beach" (p. 1062). **38-39. Circumlocution . . . office:** alluding to the "Circumlocution Office"
in Dickens's *Little Dorrit* (1855-1857).   **PLANETARIUM**   **Epigraph:** Sir William Herschel (1738-1822), English astronomer, is credited with
discovering the planet Uranus in 1781; Caroline Herschel, who worked with him and did his calculations, also independently discovered eight
comets and published a record of her daily work and an astronomers' guide.

An eye,

> "virile, precise and absolutely certain"
> from the mad webs of Uranusborg
>   encountering the NOVA   *20*
every impulse of light exploding
from the core
as life flies out of us

> Tycho whispering at last
> "Let me not seem to have lived in vain"   *25*

What we see, we see
and seeing is changing

the light that shrivels a mountain
and leaves a man alive

Heartbeat of the pulsar   *30*
Heart sweating through my body
pouring in from Taurus

> I am bombarded yet   I stand

I have been standing all my life in the
direct path of a battery of signals   *35*
the most accurately transmitted most
untranslatable language in the universe
I am a galactic cloud so deep   so invo-
luted that a light wave could take 15
years to travel through me   And has   *40*
taken   I am an instrument in the shape
of a woman trying to translate pulsations
into images   for the relief of the body
and the reconstruction of the mind.
>   *(1968, 1971)*

FRAME

Winter twilight. She comes out of the laboratory, last class of the day
a pile of notebooks slung in her knapsack, coat
zipped high against the already swirling
evening sleet. The wind is wicked and the   *5*
busses slower than usual. On her mind
is organic chemistry and the issue
of next month's rent and will it be possible to
bypass the professor with the coldest eyes

---

24. Tycho: Tycho Brahe (1546-1601), Danish astronomer, who built a castle (Uranienborg) and observatory (Stjarneborg) on the island of Ven.

to get a reference for graduate school,   10
and whether any of them, even those who smile
can see, looking at her, a biochemist
or a marine biologist, which of the faces
can she trust to see her at all, either today
or in any future. The busses are worm-slow in the   15
quickly gathering dark. *I don't know her. I am*
standing though somewhere just outside the frame
of all this, trying to see. At her back
the newly finished building suddenly looks
like shelter, it has glass doors, lighted halls   20
presumably heat. The wind is wicked. She throws a
glance down the street, sees no bus coming and runs
up the newly constructed steps into the newly
constructed hallway. *I am standing all this time*
just beyond the frame, trying to see. She runs   25
her hand through the crystals of sleet about to melt
on her hair. She shifts the weight of the books
on her back. It isn't warm here exactly but it's
out of that wind. Through the glass
door panels she can watch for the bus through the thickening   30
weather. Watching so, she is not
watching for the white man who watches the building
who has been watching her. This is Boston 1979.
I am standing somewhere at the edge of the frame
watching the man, we are both white, who watches the building   35
telling her to move on, get out of the hallway.
I can hear nothing because I am not supposed to be present but I can
    see her gesturing
out toward the street at the wind-raked curb
I see her drawing her small body up   40
against the implied charges. The man
goes away. Her body is different now.
It is holding together with more than a hint of fury
and more than a hint of fear. She is smaller, thinner
more fragile-looking than I am. *But I am not supposed to be*   45
there. I am just outside the frame
of this action when the anonymous white man
returns with a white police officer. Then she starts
to leave into the windraked night but already
the policeman is going to work, the handcuffs are on her   50
wrists he is throwing her down his knee has gone into
her breast he is dragging her down the stairs *I am unable*
to hear a sound of all this all that I know is what
I can see from this position there is no soundtrack

to go with this and I understand at once   55
it is meant to be in silence that this happens
in silence that he pushes her into the car
banging her head in silence that she cries out
in silence that she tries to explain she was only
waiting for a bus   60
in silence that he twists the flesh of her thigh
with his nails in silence that her tears begin to flow
that she pleads with the other policeman as if
he could be trusted to see her at all
in silence that in the precinct she refuses to give her name   65
in silence that they throw her into the cell
in silence that she stares him
straight in the face in silence that he sprays her
in her eyes with Mace in silence that she sinks her teeth
into his hand in silence that she is charged   70
with trespass assault and battery in
silence that at the sleet-swept corner her bus
passes without stopping and goes on
in silence. *What I am telling you*
is told by a white woman who they will say   75
was never there. I say I am there.

                                                                    (1980)

CHINUA ACHEBE
Nigeria, b.1930

CIVIL PEACE

Jonathan Iwegbu counted himself extra-ordinarily lucky. "Happy survival!" meant so much more to him than just a current fashion of greeting old friends in the first hazy days of peace. It went deep to his heart. He had come out of the war with five inestimable blessings — his head, his wife Maria's head and the heads of three out of their four children. As a bonus he also had his old bicycle — a miracle too but naturally   5
not to be compared to the safety of five human heads.

The bicycle had a little history of its own. One day at the height of the war it was commandeered "for urgent military action." Hard as its loss would have been to him he would still have let it go without a thought had he not had some doubts about the genuineness of the officer. It wasn't his disreputable rags, nor the toes peeping out of   10
one blue and one brown canvas shoes, nor yet the two stars of his rank done obviously in a hurry in biro, that troubled Jonathan; many good and heroic soldiers looked the

---

CIVIL PEACE   **3. peace:** after the Nigerian Civil War (1967-70), during which the state of Biafra sought independence. **12. biro:** ball-point pen.

same or worse. It was rather a certain lack of grip and firmness in his manner. So Jonathan, suspecting he might be amenable to influence, rummaged in his raffia bag and produced the two pounds with which he had been going to buy firewood which his wife, Maria, retailed to camp officials for extra stock-fish and corn meal, and got his bicycle back. That night he buried it in the little clearing in the bush where the dead of the camp, including his own youngest son, were buried. When he dug it up again a year later after the surrender all it needed was a little palm-oil greasing. "Nothing puzzles God," he said in wonder. *20*

He put it to immediate use as a taxi and accumulated a small pile of Biafran money ferrying camp officials and their families across the four-mile stretch to the nearest tarred road. His standard charge per trip was six pounds and those who had the money were only glad to be rid of some of it in this way. At the end of a fortnight he had made a small fortune of one hundred and fifteen pounds. *25*

Then he made the journey to Enugu and found another miracle waiting for him. It was unbelievable. He rubbed his eyes and looked again and it was still standing there before him. But, needless to say, even that monumental blessing must be accounted also totally inferior to the five heads in the family. This newest miracle was his little house in Ogui Overside. Indeed nothing puzzles God! Only two houses away a huge concrete *30* edifice some wealthy contractor had put up just before the war was a mountain of rubble. And here was Jonathan's little zinc house of no regrets built with mud blocks quite intact! Of course the doors and windows were missing and five sheets off the roof. But what was that? And anyhow he had returned to Enugu early enough to pick up bits of old zinc and wood and soggy sheets of cardboard lying around the neighbourhood *35* before thousands more came out of their forest holes looking for the same things. He got a destitute carpenter with one old hammer, a blunt plane and a few bent and rusty nails in his tool bag to turn this assortment of wood, paper and metal into door and window shutters for five Nigerian shillings or fifty Biafran pounds. He paid the pounds, and moved in with his overjoyed family carrying five heads on their shoulders. *40*

His children picked mangoes near the military cemetery and sold them to soldiers' wives for a few pennies — real pennies this time — and his wife started making breakfast akara balls for neighbours in a hurry to start life again. With his family earnings he took his bicycle to the villages around and bought fresh palm-wine which he mixed generously in his rooms with the water which had recently started running again *45* in the public tap down the road, and opened up a bar for soldiers and other lucky people with good money.

At first he went daily, then every other day and finally once a week, to the offices of the Coal Corporation where he used to be a miner, to find out what was what. The only thing he did find out in the end was that that little house of his was even a greater *50* blessing than he had thought. Some of his fellow ex-miners who had nowhere to return at the end of the day's waiting just slept outside the doors of the offices and cooked what meal they could scrounge together in Bournvita tins. As the weeks lengthened and still nobody could say what was what Jonathan discontinued his weekly visits altogether and faced his palm-wine bar. *55*

---

43. akara balls: beancakes. **53. Bournvita:** a brand-name of cocoa.

But nothing puzzles God. Came the day of the windfall when after five days of endless scuffles in queues and counter-queues in the sun outside the Treasury he had twenty pounds counted into his palms as ex-gratia award for the rebel money he had turned in. It was like Christmas for him and for many others like him when the payments began. They called it (since few could manage its proper official name) *egg-* 60 *rasher*.

As soon as the pound notes were placed in his palm Jonathan simply closed it tight over them and buried fist and money inside his trouser pocket. He had to be extra careful because he had seen a man a couple of days earlier collapse into near-madness in an instant before that oceanic crowd because no sooner had he got his twenty pounds 65 than some heartless ruffian picked it off him. Though it was not right that a man in such an extremity of agony should be blamed yet many in the queues that day were able to remark quietly on the victim's carelessness, especially after he pulled out the innards of his pocket and revealed a hole in it big enough to pass a thief's head. But of course he had insisted that the money had been in the other pocket, pulling it out to show its 70 comparative wholeness. So one had to be careful.

Jonathan soon transferred the money to his left hand and pocket so as to leave his right free for shaking hands should the need arise, though by fixing his gaze at such an elevation as to miss all approaching human faces he made sure that the need did not arise, until he got home. 75

He was normally a heavy sleeper but that night he heard all the neighbourhood noises die down one after another. Even the night watchman who knocked the hour on some metal somewhere in the distance had fallen silent after knocking one o'clock. That must have been the last thought in Jonathan's mind before he was finally carried away himself. He couldn't have been gone for long, though, when he was violently awakened 80 again.

"Who is knocking?" whispered his wife lying beside him on the floor.

"I don't know," he whispered back breathlessly.

The second time the knocking came it was so loud and imperious that the rickety old door could have fallen down. 85

"Who is knocking?" he asked then, his voice parched and trembling.

"Na tief-man and him people," came the cool reply. "Make you hopen de door." This was followed by the heaviest knocking of all.

Maria was the first to raise the alarm, then he followed and all their children.

"*Police-o! Thieves-o! Neighbours-o! Police-o! We are lost! We are dead!* 90 *Neighbours, are you asleep? Wake up! Police-o!*"

This went on for a long time and then stopped suddenly. Perhaps they had scared the thief away. There was total silence. But only for a short while.

"You done finish?" asked the voice outside. "Make we help you small. Oya, everybody!" 95

"*Police-o! Tief-man-o! Neighbours-o! We done loss-o! Police-o! . . .*"

There were at least five other voices besides the leader's.

60-61. *egg-rasher:* a sum of money given as reparations to the victims of war "*ex gratia,*" or "out of the grace" of government, rather than as an acknowledgment of responsibility. **87. Na:** it is; **tief-man:** thief.

Jonathan and his family were now completely paralysed by terror. Maria and the children sobbed inaudibly like lost souls. Jonathan groaned continuously.

The silence that followed the thieves' alarm vibrated horribly. Jonathan all but begged their leader to speak again and be done with it.   100

"My frien," said he at long last, "we don try our best for call dem but I tink say dem all done sleep-o . . . So wetin we go do now? Sometaim you wan call soja? Or you wan make we call dem for you? Soja better pass police. No be so?"

"Na so!" replied his men. Jonathan thought he heard even more voices now than   105
before and groaned heavily. His legs were sagging under him and his throat felt like sand-paper.

"My frien, why you no de talk again. I de ask you say you wan make we call soja?"
"No."
"Awrighto. Now make we talk business. We no be bad tief. We no like for make   110
trouble. Trouble done finish. War done finish and all the katakata wey de for inside. No Civil War again. This time na Civil Peace. No be so?"

"Na so!" answered the horrible chorus.

"What do you want from me? I am a poor man. Everything I had went with this war. Why do you come to me? You know people who have money. We . . ."   115

"Awright! We know you say no get plenty money. But we sef no get even anini. So derefore make you open dis window and give us one hundred pound and we go commot. Orderwise we de come for inside now to show you guitar-boy like dis . . ."

A volley of automatic fire rang through the sky. Maria and the children began to weep aloud again.   120

"Ah, missisi de cry again. No need for dat. We done talk say we na good tief. We just take our small money and go nwayorly. No molest. Abi we de molest?"

"At all!" sang the chorus.

"My friends," began Jonathan hoarsely. "I hear what you say and I thank you. If I had one hundred pounds . . ."   125

"Lookia my frien, no be play we come play for your house. If we make mistake and step for inside you no go like am-o. So derefore . . ."

"To God who made me; if you come inside and find one hundred pounds, take it and shoot me and shoot my wife and children. I swear to God. The only money I have in this life is this twenty-pounds *egg-rasher* they gave me today . . ."   130

"OK. Time de go. Make you open dis window and bring the twenty pound. We go manage am like dat."

There were now loud murmurs of dissent among the chorus: "Na lie de man de lie; e get plenty money . . . Make we go inside and search properly well . . . Wetin be twenty pound? . . ."   135

"Shurrup!" rang the leader's voice like a lone shot in the sky and silenced the murmuring at once. "Are you dere? Bring the money quick!"

"I am coming," said Jonathan fumbling in the darkness with the key of the small wooden box he kept by his side on the mat.

---

103. wetin: what; **soja:** soldier. **111. katakata:** sound of rifle fire; **wey de for inside:** which they [used] inside — i.e., which disrupted [the community] from within. **116. anini:** any. **117. commot:** right away. **122. nwayorly:** away early; **Abi:** or.

At the first sign of light as neighbours and others assembled to commiserate with *140*
him he was already strapping his five-gallon demijohn to his bicycle carrier and his
wife, sweating in the open fire, was turning over akara balls in a wide clay bowl of
boiling oil. In the corner his eldest son was rinsing out dregs of yesterday's palm wine
from old beer bottles.

"I count it as nothing," he told his sympathizers, his eyes on the rope he was tying. *145*
"What is *egg-rasher*? Did I depend on it last week? Or is it greater than other things that
went with the war? I say, let *egg-rasher* perish in the flames! Let it go where everything
else has gone. Nothing puzzles God."

(1971)

EDWARD KAMAU BRATHWAITE
Barbados/Jamaica, b.1930

BLUES

1 Basie

Hunched, hump-backed, gigantic,
the pianist presides above the
rumpus. his fingers clutch the

chords, dissonance and discord vie
and vamp across the key-   *5*
board; his big feet beat

the beat until the whole joint
rocks. it is not romantic:
but a subtle fingering exudes a sweet exotic

fragrance, now and then: you'll   *10*
recognize the odour if you listen well.
this flower blooms and blossoms till

brash boogie-woogie hordes come
bourgeoning up from hell,
blind and gigantic   *15*

2 Klook

The drummer is thin and has been
a failure at every trade but this

but here he is the king of the
cats: it is he who kills them

sick, sad and subtle,   *20*
from his throne of skin and symbol

he controls the jumping rumble
using simple shock and cymbal

his quick sticks clip and tap, tattoo
a trick or two that leaves you   *25*

prancing: and reveals that perfect quattrocento
patterning: giotto, ghirlandaio, chano pozo, klook . . .

3 Miles

He grows dizzy
with altitude
the sun blares   *30*
he hears
only the brass
of his own mood.
if he could fly
he would be   *35*

BLUES   The subtitles refer to great blues and jazz performers: Basie (Count Basie [William Basie], 1904-1984), Klook (Kenny Clarke, 1914-1985), Miles (Miles Davis, 1926-1991), Trane (John Coltrane, 1926-1967), and Charlie ("Bird") Parker (1920-1955). **26. quattrocento:** 15th century, especially as associated with the rise of art and literature in Italy. **27. giotto, ghirlandaio:** Florentine painters, Giotto di Bondone (c.1266-1337) and Domenico Ghirlandaio (1449-1494); **chano pozo:** the Cuban-born congo drummer (1915-1980) who appeared with Dizzy Gillespie's 1947 Big Band, especially on the recordings of *Cubana Be, Cubana Bop* and *Manteca*.

an eagle.
he would see
how the land lies
softly in contours
how the fields lie   40
striped, how the houses
fit into the valleys.
he would see cloud lying
on water, moving
like the hulls of great ships   45
over the land.
but he is only
a cock.
he sees
nothing   50
cares
nothing.
he reaches to the sky
with his eyes closed
his neck   55
bulging.
imagination
topples through the sunlight like a shining stone

4 Trane

Propped against the crowded bar
he pours into the curved and silver horn   60
his old unhappy longing for a home

the dancers twist and turn
he leans and wishes he could burn
his memories to ashes like some old notorious emperor

of rome. but no stars blazed across the sky when he
    was born   65
no wise men found his hovel; this crowded bar
where dancers twist and turn,

holds all the fame and recognition he will ever earn
on earth or heaven. he leans against the bar
and pours his old unhappy longing in the saxophone 70

5 So Long, Charlie Parker

The night before he died
the bird walked on and played

his heart out: notes fell
like figure-forming pebbles

in a pond. he   75
was angry: and we

knew he wept to know his time had come
so soon. so little had been done

so little time to do it in

he wished to hold the night from burning   80
all time long. but time

is short
and life
is short
and breath   85
is short

and so he
slowed and
slurred and
stopped. his   90
fingers fixed
upon a minor key:
then slipped

his bright eyes blazed and bulged against the
    death in him then knocking at the door
he watched: 95
as one will watch a great clock striking time
    from a great booming midnight bell:
the silence slowly throbbing in behind the dying bell

the night before he died
the bird walked on through fear through faith
    through frenzy that he tried
to hide but could not stop that bell   100

6 Bass

Bassey the bassist
loves his lady

hugs her to him
like a baby

plucks her   105
chucks her

makes her
boom

waltz or tango
bop or shango   110

---

101. **Bassey:** Brathwaite's pun extends Count Basie's name into a tribute, in his words, "to all bassists, especially Blanton, Mingus, and Scott LaFaro" (Jimmy Blanton, c.1918-1942; Charlie Mingus, 1922-1979; Scott LaFaro, 1936-1961). 110. **shango:** Cuban drum rhythm, related to Yoruba fertility rituals.

watch them walk
or do the 'dango:

bassey and his lovely lady

bassey and his lovely lady
like the light and not the shady: *115*

bit by boom
they build from duty

humming strings and throbbing
beauty:

beat by boom   *120*
they build this beauty:

bassey and his lovely lady
                                             (1975)

TED HUGHES
England, b.1930

HAWK ROOSTING

I sit in the top of the wood, my eyes closed.
Inaction, no falsifying dream
Between my hooked head and hooked feet:
Or in sleep rehearse perfect kills and eat.

The convenience of the high trees!   *5*
The air's buoyancy and the sun's ray
Are of advantage to me;
And the earth's face upward for my inspection.

My feet are locked upon the rough bark.
It took the whole of Creation   *10*
To produce my foot, my each feather:
Now I hold Creation in my foot

Or fly up, and revolve it all slowly —
I kill where I please because it is all mine.
There is no sophistry in my body: *15*
My manners are tearing off heads —

The allotment of death.
For the one path of my flight is direct
Through the bones of the living.
No arguments assert my right: *20*

The sun is behind me.
Nothing has changed since I began.
My eye has permitted no change.
I am going to keep things like this.
                                             (1957, 1960)

RICHARD OUTRAM
Canada, b.1930

CHARM FOR MARTHA

Who is three?
Martha Fleming.
Is she fair?
Past telling.
Is she dark?   *5*

As amber waters.
Is she meek?
Most proper.
Is she bold?
As blackbirds.   *10*

---

112. **'dango:** fandango, a Spanish dance.

Is she quick?   Fierce prayers.
As bright swords.   What from her?
Is she slow?   Dark fears.   *20*
As emerald waves.   What of her?
What for her?   *15*   A mystery.
Three Loves.   Is she so?
What with her?   She is three.

(1966)

DEREK WALCOTT
St. Lucia, b.1930

RUINS OF A GREAT HOUSE

> though our longest sun sets at right
> declensions and makes but winter
> arches, it cannot be long before we
> lie down in darkness, and have our
> light in ashes . . .
> — BROWNE: *Urn Burial*

Stones only, the *disjecta membra* of this Great House,
Whose moth-like girls are mixed with candledust,
Remain to file the lizard's dragonish claws;
The mouths of those gate cherubs streaked with stain.
Axle and coachwheel silted under the muck   *5*
Of cattle droppings.

                Three crows flap for the trees,
And settle, creaking the eucalyptus boughs.
A smell of dead limes quickens in the nose
The leprosy of Empire.   *10*

          "Farewell, green fields"
          "Farewell, ye happy groves!"

Marble as Greece, like Faulkner's south in stone,
Deciduous beauty prospered and is gone;
But where the lawn breaks in a rash of trees   *15*

RUINS OF A GREAT HOUSE   **Epigraph:** Sir Thomas Browne (see p. 309). **1.** *disjecta membra:* scattered fragments; from Horace's "disiecti membra poetae" — "the limbs of a dismembered poet" — *Satires,* I.iv.62; **Great House:** name given to the main house on a plantation. **11-12:** echoes of Shakespeare's *Henry V,* II.iii.11 ("babbled of green fields") and Virgil's *Aeneid,* VI, 638-39 ("That happy place, the green groves of the dwelling of the blest"). **13. Faulkner:** William Faulkner (see p. 1330).

A spade below dead leaves will ring the bone
Of some dead animal or human thing
Fallen from evil days, from evil times.

It seems that the original crops were limes
Grown in the silt that clogs the river's skirt;   *20*
The imperious rakes are gone, their bright girls gone,
The river flows, obliterating hurt.

I climbed a wall with the grill ironwork
Of exiled craftsmen, protecting that great house
From guilt, perhaps, but not from the worm's rent,   *25*
Nor from the padded cavalry of the mouse:
And when a wind shook in the limes I heard
What Kipling heard; the death of a great empire, the abuse
Of ignorance by Bible and by sword.

A green lawn, broken by low walls of stone   *30*
Dipped to the rivulet, and pacing, I thought next
Of men like Hawkins, Walter Raleigh, Drake,
Ancestral murderers and poets, more perplexed
In memory now by every ulcerous crime.
The world's green age then was a rotting lime   *35*
Whose stench became the charnel galleon's text.
The rot remains with us, the men are gone.
But, as dead ash is lifted in a wind,
That fans the blackening ember of the mind,
My eyes burned from the ashen prose of Donne.   *40*

Ablaze with rage, I thought
Some slave is rotting in this manorial lake,
And still the coal of my compassion fought:
That Albion too, was once
A colony like ours, "Part of the continent, piece of the main"   *45*
Nook-shotten, rook o'er blown, deranged
By foaming channels, and the vain expense
Of bitter faction.

        All in compassion ends
So differently from what the heart arranged: *50*
"as well as if a manor of thy friend's . . ."

                     (1962)

---

28. Kipling: Rudyard Kipling (see p. 1212). **32. Hawkins, Raleigh, Drake:** English adventurer-explorers, Sir John Hawkins (1532-1595), Sir Walter Ralegh (see p. 170), Sir Francis Drake (c.1540-1596). **37:** Cf. Shakespeare's *Julius Caesar*, III. ii. 81 ("The evil that men do lives after them"). **40. Donne:** John Donne (see p. 253), whose "Meditation XVII" is quoted in lines 45 and 51. **44. Albion:** England. **46. Nook-shotten:** jutting out at various angles.

THE CASTAWAY

The starved eye devours the seascape for the morsel
Of a sail.

The horizon threads it infinitely.

Action breeds frenzy. I lie,
Sailing the ribbed shadow of a palm,   5
Afraid lest my own footprints multiply.

Blowing sand, thin as smoke,
Bored, shifts its dunes.
The surf tires of its castles like a child.

The salt green vine with yellow trumpet-flower,   10
A net, inches across nothing.
Nothing: the rage with which the sandfly's head is filled.

Pleasures of an old man:
Morning: contemplative evacuation, considering
The dried leaf, nature's plan.   15

In the sun, the dog's faeces
Crusts, whitens like coral.
We end in earth, from earth began.
In our own entrails, genesis.

If I listen I can hear the polyp build,   20
The silence thwanged by two waves of the sea.
Cracking a sea-louse, I make thunder split.

Godlike, annihilating godhead, art
And self, I abandon
Dead metaphors: the almond's leaf-like heart,   25

The ripe brain rotting like a yellow nut
Hatching
Its babel of sea-lice, sandfly and maggot,

That green wine bottle's gospel choked with sand,
Labelled, a wrecked ship,   30
Clenched seaward nailed and white as a man's hand.

                            (1965)

ELSEWHERE

(For Stephen Spender)

Somewhere a white horse gallops with its mane
plunging round a field whose sticks
are ringed with barbed wire, and men
break stones or bind straw into ricks.

Somewhere women tire of the shawled sea's   5
weeping, for the fishermen's dories
still go out. It is blue as peace.
Somewhere they're tired of torture stories.

That somewhere there was an arrest.
Somewhere there was a small harvest   10
of bodies in the truck. Soldiers rest
somewhere by a road, or smoke in a forest.

Somewhere there is the conference rage
at an outrage. Somewhere a page
is torn out, and somehow the foliage   15
no longer looks like leaves but camouflage.

Somewhere there is a comrade,
a writer lying with his eyes wide open
on mattress ticking, who will not read
this, or write. How to make a pen?   20

And here we are free for a while, but
elsewhere, in one-third, or one-seventh
of this planet, a summary rifle butt
breaks a skull into the idea of a heaven

where nothing is free, where blue air   25
is paper-frail, and whatever we write
will be stamped twice, a blue letter,
its throat slit by the paper knife of the state.

Through these black bars
hollowed faces stare. Fingers   30
grip the cross bars of these stanzas
and it is here, because somewhere else

their stares fog into oblivion
thinly, like the faceless numbers
that bewilder you in your telephone   35
diary. Like last year's massacres.

The world is blameless. The darker crime
is to make a career of conscience,
to feel through our own nerves the silent scream
of winter branches, wonders read as signs.   40
                            (1987)

THE CASTAWAY   Cf. Cowper's *The Castaway* (1803) and his "Verses" (p. 653).   **ELSEWHERE**   Dedication: For Spender, see p. 1367.

JAY MACPHERSON
Canada, b.1931

EVE IN REFLECTION

Painful and brief the act. Eve on the barren shore
Sees every cherished feature, plumed tree, bright grass,
Fresh spring, the beasts as placid as before
Beneath the inviolable glass.

There the lost girl gone under sea   5
Tends her undying grove, never raising her eyes
To where on the salt shell beach in reverie
The mother of all living lies.

The beloved face is lost from sight,
Marred in a whelming tide of blood: 10
And Adam walks in the cold night
Wilderness, waste wood.

(1957)

THE ISLAND

No man alone an island: we
Stand circled with a lapping sea.
I break the ring and let you go:
Above my head the waters flow.

Look inward, love, and no more sea,   5
No death, no change, eternity
Lapped round us like a crystal wall
To island, and that island all.

(1957)

ALICE MUNRO
Canada, b.1931

MENESETEUNG

I

Columbine, bloodroot,
And wild bergamot,
Gathering armfuls,
Giddily we go.

Offerings the book is called. Gold lettering on a dull-blue cover. The author's full name   5
underneath: Almeda Joynt Roth. The local paper, the *Vidette*, referred to her as "our
poetess." There seems to be a mixture of respect and contempt, both for her calling and
for her sex — or for their predictable conjuncture. In the front of the book is a photograph, with the photographer's name in one corner, and the date: 1865. The book was
published later, in 1873.   10

   The poetess has a long face; a rather long nose; full, sombre dark eyes, which seem
ready to roll down her cheeks like giant tears; a lot of dark hair gathered around her face
in droopy rolls and curtains. A streak of gray hair plain to see, although she is, in this

---

THE ISLAND   1. No . . . island: See Donne's "Meditation XVII," lines 25-26 (p. 262).   MENESETEUNG   Title: the Huron name for a river flowing into Lake Huron (now called the Maitland River) and the settlement at the river mouth; in 1828 the settlement was renamed Goderich.

picture, only twenty-five. Not a pretty girl but the sort of woman who may age well, who probably won't get fat. She wears a tucked and braid-trimmed dark dress or jacket,   *15* with a lacy, floppy arrangement of white material — frills or a bow — filling the deep V at the neck. She also wears a hat, which might be made of velvet, in a dark color to match the dress. It's the untrimmed, shapeless hat, something like a soft beret, that makes me see artistic intentions, or at least a shy and stubborn eccentricity, in this young woman, whose long neck and forward-inclining head indicate as well that she is   *20* tall and slender and somewhat awkward. From the waist up, she looks like a young nobleman of another century. But perhaps it was the fashion.

"In 1854," she writes in the preface to her book, "my father brought us — my mother, my sister Catherine, my brother William, and me — to the wilds of Canada West (as it then was). My father was a harness-maker by trade, but a cultivated man   *25* who could quote by heart from the Bible, Shakespeare, and the writings of Edmund Burke. He prospered in this newly opened land and was able to set up a harness and leather-goods store, and after a year to build the comfortable house in which I live (alone) today. I was fourteen years old, the eldest of the children, when we came into this country from Kingston, a town whose handsome streets I have not seen again but   *30* often remember. My sister was eleven and my brother nine. The third summer that we lived here, my brother and sister were taken ill of a prevalent fever and died within a few days of each other. My dear mother did not regain her spirits after this blow to our family. Her health declined, and after another three years she died. I then became housekeeper to my father and was happy to make his home for twelve years, until he   *35* died suddenly one morning at his shop.

"From my earliest years I have delighted in verse and I have occupied myself — and sometimes allayed my griefs, which have been no more, I know, than any sojourner on earth must encounter — with many floundering efforts at its composition. My fingers, indeed, were always too clumsy for crochetwork, and those dazzling produc-   *40* tions of embroidery which one sees often today — the overflowing fruit and flower baskets, the little Dutch boys, the bonneted maidens with their watering cans — have likewise proved to be beyond my skill. So I offer instead, as the product of my leisure hours, these rude posies, these ballads, couplets, reflections."

Titles of some of the poems: "Children at Their Games," "The Gypsy Fair," "A   *45* Visit to My Family," "Angels in the Snow," "Champlain at the Mouth of the Meneseteung," "The Passing of the Old Forest," and "A Garden Medley." There are other, shorter poems, about birds and wildflowers and snowstorms. There is some comically intentioned doggerel about what people are thinking about as they listen to the sermon in church.   *50*

"Children at Their Games": The writer, a child, is playing with her brother and sister — one of those games in which children on different sides try to entice and catch each other. She plays on in the deepening twilight, until she realizes that she is alone, and much older. Still she hears the (ghostly) voices of her brother and sister calling.

24-25. Canada West: now Ontario; after the Act of Union (1841) joined Upper Canada with Lower Canada, the two areas became known as Canada West and Canada East; at the time of Confederation (1867) they became the provinces of Ontario and Quebec respectively. **26-27. Edmund Burke:** See p. 640. **46. Champlain:** Samuel de Champlain (1567-1635), French explorer (see also lines 66ff., below).

Come over, come over, let Meda come over. (Perhaps Almeda was called Meda in the   *55*
family, or perhaps she shortened her name to fit the poem.)

"The Gypsy Fair": The Gypsies have an encampment near the town, a "fair," where
they sell cloth and trinkets, and the writer as a child is afraid that she may be stolen by
them, taken away from her family. Instead, her family has been taken away from her,
stolen by Gypsies she can't locate or bargain with.   *60*

"A Visit to My Family": A visit to the cemetery, a one-sided conversation.

"Angels in the Snow": The writer once taught her brother and sister to make
"angels" by lying down in the snow and moving their arms to create wing shapes. Her
brother always jumped up carelessly, leaving an angel with a crippled wing. Will this be
made perfect in Heaven, or will he be flying with his own makeshift, in circles?   *65*

"Champlain at the Mouth of the Meneseteung": This poem celebrates the popular,
untrue belief that the explorer sailed down the eastern shore of Lake Huron and landed
at the mouth of the major river.

"The Passing of the Old Forest": A list of all the trees — their names, appearance,
and uses — that were cut down in the original forest, with a general description of the   *70*
bears, wolves, eagles, deer, waterfowl.

"A Garden Medley": Perhaps planned as a companion to the forest poem.
Catalogue of plants brought from European countries, with bits of history and legend
attached, and final Canadianness resulting from this mixture.

The poems are written in quatrains or couplets. There are a couple of attempts at   *75*
sonnets, but mostly the rhyme scheme is simple — *a b a b* or *a b c b*. The rhyme used is
what was once called "masculine" ("shore"/"before"), though once in a while it is
"feminine" ("quiver"/"river"). Are those terms familiar anymore? No poem is
unrhymed.

II

White roses cold as snow   *80*
Bloom where those "'angels" lie.
Do they but rest below
Or, in God's wonder, fly?

In 1879, Almeda Roth was still living in the house at the corner of Pearl and Dufferin
streets, the house her father had built for his family. The house is there today; the   *85*
manager of the liquor store lives in it. It's covered with aluminum siding; a closed-in
porch has replaced the veranda. The woodshed, the fence, the gates, the privy, the barn
— all these are gone. A photograph taken in the eighteen-eighties shows them all in
place. The house and fence look a little shabby, in need of paint, but perhaps that is just
because of the bleached-out look of the brownish photograph. The lace-curtained   *90*
windows look like white eyes. No big shade tree is in sight, and, in fact, the tall elms
that overshadowed the town until the nineteen-fifties, as well as the maples that shade it
now, are skinny young trees with rough fences around them to protect them from the
cows. Without the shelter of those trees, there is a great exposure — back yards, clothes-
lines, woodpiles, patchy sheds and barns and privies — all bare, exposed, provisional-   *95*
looking. Few houses would have anything like a lawn, just a patch of plantains and

anthills and raked dirt. Perhaps petunias growing on top of a stump, in a round box. Only the main street is gravelled; the other streets are dirt roads, muddy or dusty according to season. Yards must be fenced to keep animals out. Cows are tethered in vacant lots or pastured in back yards, but sometimes they get loose. Pigs get loose, too, and dogs roam free or nap in a lordly way on the boardwalks. The town has taken root, it's not going to vanish, yet it still has some of the look of an encampment. And, like an encampment, it's busy all the time — full of people, who, within the town, usually walk wherever they're going; full of animals, which leave horse buns, cow pats, dog turds that ladies have to hitch up their skirts for; full of the noise of building and of drivers shouting at their horses and of the trains that come in several times a day.

I read about that life in the *Vidette*.

The population is younger than it is now, than it will ever be again. People past fifty usually don't come to a raw, new place. There are quite a few people in the cemetery already, but most of them died young, in accidents or childbirth or epidemics. It's youth that's in evidence in town. Children — boys — rove through the streets in gangs. School is compulsory for only four months a year, and there are lots of occasional jobs that even a child of eight or nine can do — pulling flax, holding horses, delivering groceries, sweeping the boardwalk in front of stores. A good deal of time they spend looking for adventures. One day they follow an old woman, a drunk nicknamed Queen Aggie. They get her into a wheelbarrow and trundle her all over town, then dump her into a ditch to sober her up. They also spend a lot of time around the railway station. They jump on shunting cars and dart between them and dare each other to take chances, which once in a while result in their getting maimed or killed. And they keep an eye out for any strangers coming into town. They follow them, offer to carry their bags, and direct them (for a five-cent piece) to a hotel. Strangers who don't look so prosperous are taunted and tormented. Speculation surrounds all of them — it's like a cloud of flies. Are they coming to town to start up a new business, to persuade people to invest in some scheme, to sell cures or gimmicks, to preach on the street corners? All these things are possible any day of the week. Be on your guard, the *Vidette* tells people. These are times of opportunity and danger. Tramps, confidence men, hucksters, shysters, plain thieves are travelling the roads, and particularly the railroads. Thefts are announced: money invested and never seen again, a pair of trousers taken from the clothesline, wood from the woodpile, eggs from the henhouse. Such incidents increase in the hot weather.

Hot weather brings accidents, too. More horses run wild then, upsetting buggies. Hands caught in the wringer while doing the washing, a man lopped in two at the sawmill, a leaping boy killed in a fall of lumber at the lumberyard. Nobody sleeps well. Babies wither with summer complaint, and fat people can't catch their breath. Bodies must be buried in a hurry. One day a man goes through the streets ringing a cowbell and calling, "Repent! Repent!" It's not a stranger this time, it's a young man who works at the butcher shop. Take him home, wrap him in cold wet cloths, give him some nerve medicine, keep him in bed, pray for his wits. If he doesn't recover, he must go to the asylum.

Almeda Roth's house faces on Dufferin Street, which is a street of considerable   *140* respectability. On this street, merchants, a mill owner, an operator of salt wells have their houses. But Pearl Street, which her back windows overlook and her back gate opens onto, is another story. Workmen's houses are adjacent to hers. Small but decent row houses — that is all right. Things deteriorate toward the end of the block, and the next, last one becomes dismal. Nobody but the poorest people, the unrespectable and *145* undeserving poor, would live there at the edge of a boghole (drained since then), called the Pearl Street Swamp. Bushy and luxuriant weeds grow there, makeshift shacks have been put up, there are piles of refuse and debris and crowds of runty children, slops are flung from doorways. The town tries to compel these people to build privies, but they would just as soon go in the bushes. If a gang of boys goes down there in search of *150* adventure, it's likely they'll get more than they bargained for. It is said that even the town constable won't go down Pearl Street on a Saturday night. Almeda Roth has never walked past the row housing. In one of those houses lives the young girl Annie, who helps her with her housecleaning. That young girl herself, being a decent girl, has never walked down to the last block or the swamp. No decent woman ever would.   *155*

But that same swamp, lying to the east of Almeda Roth's house, presents a fine sight at dawn. Almeda sleeps at the back of the house. She keeps to the same bedroom she once shared with her sister Catherine — she would not think of moving to the large front bedroom, where her mother used to lie in bed all day, and which was later the solitary domain of her father. From her window she can see the sun rising, the swamp *160* mist filling with light, the bulky, nearest trees floating against that mist and the trees behind turning transparent. Swamp oaks, soft maples, tamarack, bitternut.

III

Here where the river meets the inland sea,
Spreading her blue skirts from the solemn wood,
I think of birds and beasts and vanished men,   *165*
Whose pointed dwellings on these pale sands stood.

One of the strangers who arrived at the railway station a few years ago was Jarvis Poulter, who now occupies the next house to Almeda Roth's — separated from hers by a vacant lot, which he has bought, on Dufferin Street. The house is plainer than the Roth house and has no fruit trees or flowers planted around it. It is understood that this is a *170* natural result of Jarvis Poulter's being a widower and living alone. A man may keep his house decent, but he will never — if he is a proper man — do much to decorate it. Marriage forces him to live with more ornament as well as sentiment, and it protects him, also, from the extremities of his own nature — from a frigid parsimony or a luxuriant sloth, from squalor, and from excessive sleeping or reading, drinking, *175* smoking, or freethinking.

In the interests of economy, it is believed, a certain estimable gentleman of our town persists in fetching water from the public tap and supplementing his fuel supply by

---

140. Dufferin: named for Frederick Temple Hamilton-Temple-Blackwood (1826-1902), 1st Marquess of Dufferin and Ava, and Governor-General of Canada (1872-1878).

picking up the loose coal along the railway track. Does he think to repay the town or the
railway company with a supply of free salt?   *180*

This is the *Vidette*, full of shy jokes, innuendo, plain accusation that no newspaper
would get away with today. It's Jarvis Poulter they're talking about — though in other
passages he is spoken of with great respect, as a civil magistrate, an employer, a
churchman. He is close, that's all. An eccentric, to a degree. All of which may be a
result of his single condition, his widower's life. Even carrying his water from the town *185*
tap and filling his coal pail along the railway track. This is a decent citizen, prosperous:
a tall — slightly paunchy? — man in a dark suit with polished boots. A beard? Black
hair streaked with gray. A severe and self-possessed air, and a large pale wart among the
bushy hairs of one eyebrow? People talk about a young, pretty, beloved wife, dead in
childbirth or some horrible accident, like a house fire or a railway disaster. There is no *190*
ground for this, but it adds interest. All he has told them is that his wife is dead.

He came to this part of the country looking for oil. The first oil well in the world
was sunk in Lambton County, south of here, in the eighteen-fifties. Drilling for oil,
Jarvis Poulter discovered salt. He set to work to make the most of that. When he walks
home from church with Almeda Roth, he tells her about his salt wells. They are twelve *195*
hundred feet deep. Heated water is pumped down into them, and that dissolves the salt.
Then the brine is pumped to the surface. It is poured into great evaporator pans over
slow, steady fires, so that the water is steamed off and the pure, excellent salt remains. A
commodity for which the demand will never fail.

"The salt of the earth," Almeda says.   *200*

"Yes," he says, frowning. He may think this disrespectful. She did not intend it so.
He speaks of competitors in other towns who are following his lead and trying to hog
the market. Fortunately, their wells are not drilled so deep, or their evaporating is not
done so efficiently. There is salt everywhere under this land, but it is not so easy to
come by as some people think.   *205*

Does this not mean, Almeda says, that there was once a great sea?

Very likely, Jarvis Poulter says. Very likely. He goes on to tell her about other
enterprises of his — a brickyard, a limekiln. And he explains to her how this operates,
and where the good clay is found. He also owns two farms, whose woodlots supply the
fuel for his operations.   *210*

Among the couples strolling home from church on a recent, sunny Sabbath morning
we noted a certain salty gentleman and literary lady, not perhaps in their first youth but
by no means blighted by the frosts of age. May we surmise?

This kind of thing pops up in the *Vidette* all the time.

May they surmise, and is this courting? Almeda Roth has a bit of money, which her *215*
father left her, and she has her house. She is not too old to have a couple of children.
She is a good enough housekeeper, with the tendency toward fancy iced cakes and
decorated tarts that is seen fairly often in old maids. (Honorable mention at the Fall
Fair.) There is nothing wrong with her looks, and naturally she is in better shape than
most married women of her age, not having been loaded down with work and children. *220*
But why was she passed over in her earlier, more marriageable years, in a place that
needs women to be partnered and fruitful? She was a rather gloomy girl — that may

have been the trouble. The deaths of her brother and sister, and then of her mother, who lost her reason, in fact, a year before she died, and lay in her bed talking nonsense — those weighed on her, so she was not lively company. And all that reading and poetry — it seemed more of a drawback, a barrier, an obsession, in the young girl than in the middle-aged woman, who needed something, after all, to fill her time. Anyway, it's five years since her book was published, so perhaps she has got over that. Perhaps it was the proud, bookish father encouraging her? 225

Everyone takes it for granted that Almeda Roth is thinking of Jarvis Poulter as a husband and would say yes if he asked her. And she is thinking of him. She doesn't want to get her hopes up too much, she doesn't want to make a fool of herself. She would like a signal. If he attended church on Sunday evenings, there would be a chance, during some months of the year, to walk home after dark. He would carry a lantern. (There is as yet no street lighting in town.) He would swing the lantern to light the way in front of the lady's feet and observe their narrow and delicate shape. He might catch her arm as they step off the boardwalk. But he does not go to church at night. 230, 235

Nor does he call for her, and walk with her *to* church on Sunday mornings. That would be a declaration. He walks her home, past his gate as far as hers; he lifts his hat then and leaves her. She does not invite him to come in — a woman living alone could never do such a thing. As soon as a man and woman of almost any age are alone together within four walls, it is assumed that anything may happen. Spontaneous combustion, instant fornication, an attack of passion. Brute instinct, triumph of the senses. What possibilities men and women must see in each other to infer such dangers. Or, believing in the dangers, how often they must think about the possibilities. 240, 245

When they walk side by side, she can smell his shaving soap, the barber's oil, his pipe tobacco, the wool and linen and leather smell of his manly clothes. The correct, orderly, heavy clothes are like those she used to brush and starch and iron for her father. She misses that job — her father's appreciation, his dark, kind authority. Jarvis Poulter's garments, his smell, his movements all cause the skin on the side of her body next to him to tingle hopefully, and a meek shiver raises the hairs on her arms. Is this to be taken as a sign of love? She thinks of him coming into her — *their* — bedroom in his long underwear and his hat. She knows this outfit is ridiculous, but in her mind he does not look so; he has the solemn effrontery of a figure in a dream. He comes into the room and lies down on the bed beside her, preparing to take her in his arms. Surely he removes his hat? She doesn't know, for at this point a fit of welcome and submission overtakes her, a buried gasp. He would be her husband. 250, 255

One thing she has noticed about married women, and that is how many of them have to go about creating their husbands. They have to start ascribing preferences, opinions, dictatorial ways. Oh, yes, they say, my husband is very particular. He won't touch turnips. He won't eat fried meat. (Or he will only eat fried meat.) He likes me to wear blue (brown) all the time. He can't stand organ music. He hates to see a woman go out bareheaded. He would kill me if I took one puff of tobacco. This way, bewildered, sidelong-looking men are made over, made into husbands, heads of households. Almeda Roth cannot imagine herself doing that. She wants a man who doesn't have to be made, who is firm already and determined and mysterious to her. She does not look for companionship. Men — except for her father — seem to her deprived in some way, 260, 265 incurious. No doubt that is necessary, so that they will do what they have to do. Would she herself, knowing that there was salt in the earth, discover how to get it out and sell it? Not likely. She would be thinking about the ancient sea. That kind of speculation is *270* what Jarvis Poulter has, quite properly, no time for.

Instead of calling for her and walking her to church, Jarvis Poulter might make another, more venturesome declaration. He could hire a horse and take her for a drive out to the country. If he did this, she would be both glad and sorry. Glad to be beside him, driven by him, receiving this attention from him in front of the world. And sorry to *275* have the countryside removed for her — filmed over, in a way, by his talk and preoccupations. The countryside that she has written about in her poems actually takes diligence and determination to see. Some things must be disregarded. Manure piles, of course, and boggy fields full of high, charred stumps, and great heaps of brush waiting for a good day for burning. The meandering creeks have been straightened, turned into *280* ditches with high, muddy banks. Some of the crop fields and pasture fields are fenced with big, clumsy uprooted stumps; others are held in a crude stitchery of rail fences. The trees have all been cleared back to the woodlots. And the woodlots are all second growth. No trees along the roads or lanes or around the farmhouses, except a few that are newly planted, young and weedy-looking. Clusters of log barns — the grand barns *285* that are to dominate the countryside for the next hundred years are just beginning to be built — and mean-looking log houses, and every four or five miles a ragged little settlement with a church and school and store and a blacksmith shop. A raw countryside just wrenched from the forest, but swarming with people. Every hundred acres is a farm, every farm has a family, most families have ten or twelve children. (This is the country *290* that will send out wave after wave of settlers — it's already starting to send them — to northern Ontario and the West.) It's true that you can gather wildflowers in spring in the woodlots, but you'd have to walk through herds of horned cows to get to them.

IV

The Gypsies have departed.
Their camping-ground is bare. *295*
Oh, boldly would I bargain now
At the Gypsy Fair.

Almeda suffers a good deal from sleeplessness, and the doctor has given her bromides and nerve medicine. She takes the bromides, but the drops gave her dreams that were too vivid and disturbing, so she has put the bottle by for an emergency. She told the *300* doctor her eyeballs felt dry, like hot glass, and her joints ached. Don't read so much, he said, don't study; get yourself good and tired out with housework, take exercise. He believes that her troubles would clear up if she got married. He believes this in spite of the fact that most of his nerve medicine is prescribed for married women.

So Almeda cleans house and helps clean the church, she lends a hand to friends *305* who are wallpapering or getting ready for a wedding, she bakes one of her famous cakes for the Sunday-school picnic. On a hot Saturday in August, she decides to make some grape jelly. Little jars of grape jelly will make fine Christmas presents, or offerings to the sick. But she started late in the day and the jelly is not made by nightfall. In fact, the hot pulp has just been dumped into the cheesecloth bag to strain out the juice. Almeda *310* drinks some tea and eats a slice of cake with butter (a childish indulgence of hers), and that's all she wants for supper. She washes her hair at the sink and sponges off her body to be clean for Sunday. She doesn't light a lamp. She lies down on the bed with the window wide open and a sheet just up to her waist, and she does feel wonderfully tired. She can even feel a little breeze. 315

When she wakes up, the night seems fiery hot and full of threats. She lies sweating on her bed, and she has the impression that the noises she hears are knives and saws and axes — all angry implements chopping and jabbing and boring within her head. But it isn't true. As she comes further awake, she recognizes the sounds that she has heard sometimes before — the fracas of a summer Saturday night on Pearl Street. Usually the 320 noise centers on a fight. People are drunk, there is a lot of protest and encouragement concerning the fight, somebody will scream, "Murder!" Once, there was a murder. But it didn't happen in a fight. An old man was stabbed to death in his shack, perhaps for a few dollars he kept in the mattress.

She gets out of bed and goes to the window. The night sky is clear, with no moon 325 and with bright stars. Pegasus hangs straight ahead, over the swamp. Her father taught her that constellation — automatically, she counts its stars. Now she can make out distinct voices, individual contributions to the row. Some people, like herself, have evidently been wakened from sleep. "Shut up!" they are yelling. "Shut up that caterwauling or I'm going to come down and tan the arse off yez!" 330

But nobody shuts up. It's as if there were a ball of fire rolling up Pearl Street, shooting off sparks — only the fire is noise; it's yells and laughter and shrieks and curses, and the sparks are voices that shoot off alone. Two voices gradually distinguish themselves — a rising and falling howling cry and a steady throbbing, low-pitched stream of abuse that contains all those words which Almeda associates with danger and 335 depravity and foul smells and disgusting sights. Someone — the person crying out, "Kill me! Kill me now!" — is being beaten. A woman is being beaten. She keeps crying, "Kill me! Kill me!" and sometimes her mouth seems choked with blood. Yet there is something taunting and triumphant about her cry. There is something theatrical about it. And the people around are calling out, "Stop it! Stop that!" or "Kill her! Kill her!" in a 340 frenzy, as if at the theatre or a sporting match or a prizefight. Yes, thinks Almeda, she has noticed that before — it is always partly a charade with these people; there is a clumsy sort of parody, an exaggeration, a missed connection. As if anything they did — even a murder — might be something they didn't quite believe but were powerless to stop.

Now there is the sound of something thrown — a chair, a plank? — and of a 345 woodpile or part of a fence giving way. A lot of newly surprised cries, the sound of running, people getting out of the way, and the commotion has come much closer. Almeda can see a figure in a light dress, bent over and running. That will be the woman. She has got hold of something like a stick of wood or a shingle, and she turns and flings it at the darker figure running after her. 350

"Ah, go get her!" the voices cry. "Go baste her one!"

Many fall back now; just the two figures come on and grapple, and break loose again, and finally fall down against Almeda's fence. The sound they make becomes very confused — gagging, vomiting, grunting, pounding. Then a long, vibrating,

---

326. Pegasus: the constellation named for the winged horse in Greek mythology, associated with poetic inspiration.

choking sound of pain and self-abasement, self-abandonment, which could come from *355* either or both of them.

Almeda has backed away from the window and sat down on the bed. Is that the sound of murder she has heard? What is to be done, what is she to do? She must light a lantern, she must go downstairs and light a lantern — she must go out into the yard, she must go downstairs. Into the yard. The lantern. She falls over on her bed and pulls the *360* pillow to her face. In a minute. The stairs, the lantern. She sees herself already down there, in the back hall, drawing the bolt of the back door. She falls asleep.

She wakes, startled, in the early light. She thinks there is a big crow sitting on her windowsill, talking in a disapproving but unsurprised way about the events of the night before. "Wake up and move the wheelbarrow!" it says to her, scolding, and she *365* understands that it means something else by "wheelbarrow" — something foul and sorrowful. Then she is awake and sees that there is no such bird. She gets up at once and looks out the window.

Down against her fence there is a pale lump pressed — a body.

Wheelbarrow. *370*

She puts a wrapper over her nightdress and goes downstairs. The front rooms are still shadowy, the blinds down in the kitchen. Something goes *plop, plup,* in a leisurely, censorious way, reminding her of the conversation of the crow. It's just the grape juice, straining overnight. She pulls the bolt and goes out the back door. Spiders have draped their webs over the doorway in the night, and the hollyhocks are drooping, heavy with *375* dew. By the fence, she parts the sticky hollyhocks and looks down and she can see.

A woman's body heaped up there, turned on her side with her face squashed down into the earth. Almeda can't see her face. But there is a bare breast let loose, brown nipple pulled long like a cow's teat, and a bare haunch and leg, the haunch showing a bruise as big as a sunflower. The unbruised skin is grayish, like a plucked, raw *380* drumstick. Some kind of nightgown or all-purpose dress she has on. Smelling of vomit. Urine, drink, vomit.

Barefoot, in her nightgown and flimsy wrapper, Almeda runs away. She runs around the side of her house between the apple trees and the veranda; she opens the front gate and flees down Dufferin Street to Jarvis Poulter's house, which is the nearest *385* to hers. She slaps the flat of her hand many times against the door.

"There is the body of a woman," she says when Jarvis Poulter appears at last. He is in his dark trousers, held up with braces, and his shirt is half unbuttoned, his face unshaven, his hair standing up on his head. "Mr. Poulter, excuse me. A body of a woman. At my back gate." *390*

He looks at her fiercely. "Is she dead?"

His breath is dank, his face creased, his eyes bloodshot.

"Yes. I think murdered," says Almeda. She can see a little of his cheerless front hall. His hat on a chair. "In the night I woke up. I heard a racket down on Pearl Street," she says, struggling to keep her voice low and sensible. "I could hear this — pair. I *395* could hear a man and a woman fighting."

He picks up his hat and puts it on his head. He closes and locks the front door, and puts the key in his pocket. They walk along the boardwalk and she sees that she is in her bare feet. She holds back what she feels a need to say next — that she is responsible, she

could have run out with a lantern, she could have screamed (but who needed more 400
screams?), she could have beat the man off. She could have run for help then, not now.

They turn down Pearl Street, instead of entering the Roth yard. Of course the body
is still there. Hunched up, half bare, the same as before.

Jarvis Poulter doesn't hurry or halt. He walks straight over to the body and looks
down at it, nudges the leg with the toe of his boot, just as you'd nudge a dog or a sow. 405

"You," he says, not too loudly but firmly, and nudges again.

Almeda tastes bile at the back of her throat.

"Alive," says Jarvis Poulter, and the woman confirms this. She stirs, she grunts
weakly.

Almeda says, "I will get the doctor." If she had touched the woman, if she had 410
forced herself to touch her, she would not have made such a mistake.

"Wait," says Jarvis Poulter. "Wait. Let's see if she can get up."

"Get up, now," he says to the woman. "Come on. Up, now. Up."

Now a startling thing happens. The body heaves itself onto all fours, the head is
lifted — the hair all matted with blood and vomit — and the woman begins to bang this 415
head, hard and rhythmically, against Almeda Roth's picket fence. As she bangs her
head, she finds her voice and lets out an openmouthed yowl, full of strength and what
sounds like an anguished pleasure.

"Far from dead," says Jarvis Poulter. "And I wouldn't bother the doctor."

"There's blood," says Almeda as the woman turns her smeared face. 420

"From her nose," he says. "Not fresh." He bends down and catches the horrid hair
close to the scalp to stop the head-banging.

"You stop that, now," he says. "Stop it. Gwan home, now. Gwan home, where you
belong." The sound coming out of the woman's mouth has stopped. He shakes her head
slightly, warning her, before he lets go of her hair. "Gwan home!" 425

Released, the woman lunges forward, pulls herself to her feet. She can walk. She
weaves and stumbles down the street, making intermittent, cautious noises of protest.
Jarvis Poulter watches her for a moment to make sure that she's on her way. Then he finds
a large burdock leaf, on which he wipes his hand. He says, "There goes your dead body!"

The back gate being locked, they walk around to the front. The front gate stands 430
open. Almeda still feels sick. Her abdomen is bloated; she is hot and dizzy.

"The front door is locked," she says faintly. "I came out by the kitchen." If only he
would leave her, she could go straight to the privy. But he follows. He follows her as far as
the back door and into the back hall. He speaks to her in a tone of harsh joviality that she
has never before heard from him. "No need for alarm," he says. "It's only the 435
consequences of drink. A lady oughtn't to be living alone so close to a bad neighborhood."
He takes hold of her arm just above the elbow. She can't open her mouth to speak to him,
to say thank you. If she opened her mouth, she would retch.

What Jarvis Poulter feels for Almeda Roth at this moment is just what he has not felt
during all those circumspect walks and all his own solitary calculations of her probable 440
worth, undoubted respectability, adequate comeliness. He has not been able to imagine her
as a wife. Now that is possible. He is sufficiently stirred by her loosened hair —
prematurely gray but thick and soft — her flushed face, her light clothing, which nobody
but a husband should see. And by her indiscretion, her agitation, her foolishness, her need?

"I will call on you later," he says to her. "I will walk with you to church."   *445*

At the corner of Pearl and Dufferin streets last Sunday morning there was discovered, by a lady resident there, the body of a certain woman of Pearl Street, thought to be dead but only, as it turned out, dead drunk. She was roused from her heavenly — or otherwise — stupor by the firm persuasion of Mr. Poulter, a neighbour and a Civil Magistrate, who had been summoned by the lady resident. Incidents of this   *450*
sort, unseemly, troublesome, and disgraceful to our town, have of late become all too common.

V

I sit at the bottom of sleep,
As on the floor of the sea.
And fanciful Citizens of the Deep   *455*
Are graciously greeting me.

As soon as Jarvis Poulter has gone and she has heard her front gate close, Almeda rushes to the privy. Her relief is not complete, however, and she realizes that the pain and fullness in her lower body come from an accumulation of menstrual blood that has not yet started to flow. She closes and locks the back door. Then, remembering Jarvis   *460*
Poulter's words about church, she writes on a piece of paper, "I am not well, and wish to rest today." She sticks this firmly into the outside frame of the little window in the front door. She locks that door, too. She is trembling, as if from a great shock or danger. But she builds a fire, so that she can make tea. She boils water, measures the tea leaves, makes a large pot of tea, whose steam and smell sicken her further. She pours out a cup   *465*
while the tea is still quite weak and adds to it several dark drops of nerve medicine. She sits to drink it without raising the kitchen blind. There, in the middle of the floor, is the cheesecloth bag hanging on its broom handle between the two chairbacks. The grape pulp and juice has stained the swollen cloth a dark purple. *Plop, plup,* into the basin beneath. She can't sit and look at such a thing. She takes her cup, the teapot, and the   *470*
bottle of medicine into the dining room.

She is still sitting there when the horses start to go by on the way to church, stirring up clouds of dust. The roads will be getting hot as ashes. She is there when the gate is opened and a man's confident steps sound on her veranda. Her hearing is so sharp she seems to hear the paper taken out of the frame and unfolded — she can almost hear him   *475*
reading it, hear the words in his mind. Then the footsteps go the other way, down the steps. The gate closes. An image comes to her of tombstones — it makes her laugh. Tombstones are marching down the street on their little booted feet, their long bodies inclined forward, their expressions preoccupied and severe. The church bells are ringing.   *480*

Then the clock in the hall strikes twelve and an hour has passed.

The house is getting hot. She drinks more tea and adds more medicine. She knows that the medicine is affecting her. It is responsible for her extraordinary languor, her perfect immobility, her unresisting surrender to her surroundings. That is all right. It seems necessary.   *485*

Her surroundings — some of her surroundings — in the dining room are these: walls covered with dark-green garlanded wallpaper, lace curtains and mulberry velvet curtains on the windows, a table with a crocheted cloth and a bowl of wax fruit, a pinkish-gray carpet with nosegays of blue and pink roses, a sideboard spread with embroidered runners and holding various patterned plates and jugs and the silver tea things. A lot of *490* things to watch. For every one of these patterns, decorations seems charged with life, ready to move and flow and alter. Or possibly to explode. Almeda Roth's occupation throughout the day is to keep an eye on them. Not to prevent their alteration so much as to catch them at it — to understand it, to be a part of it. So much is going on in this room that there is no need to leave it. There is not even the thought of leaving it. *495*

Of course, Almeda in her observations cannot escape words. She may think she can, but she can't. Soon this glowing and swelling begins to suggest words — not specific words but a flow of words somewhere, just about ready to make themselves known to her. Poems, even. Yes, again, poems. Or one poem. Isn't that the idea — one very great poem that will contain everything and, oh, that will make all the other poems, *500* the poems she has written, inconsequential, mere trial and error, mere rags? Stars and flowers and birds and trees and angels in the snow and dead children at twilight — that is not the half of it. You have to get in the obscene racket on Pearl Street and the polished toe of Jarvis Poulter's boot and the plucked-chicken haunch with its blue-black flower. Almeda is a long way now from human sympathies or fears or cozy household *505* considerations. She doesn't think about what could be done for that woman or about keeping Jarvis Poulter's dinner warm and hanging his long underwear on the line. The basin of grape juice has overflowed and is running over her kitchen floor, staining the boards of the floor, and the stain will never come out.

She has to think of so many things at once — Champlain and the naked Indians and *510* the salt deep in the earth, but as well as the salt the money, the money-making intent brewing forever in heads like Jarvis Poulter's. Also the brutal storms of winter and the clumsy and benighted deeds on Pearl Street. The changes of climate are often violent, and if you think about it there is no peace even in the stars. All this can be borne only if it is channelled into a poem, and the word "channelled" is appropriate, because the name *515* of the poem will be — it *is* — "The Meneseteung." The name of the poem is the name of the river. No, in fact it is the river, the Meneseteung, that is the poem — with its deep holes and rapids and blissful pools under the summer trees and its grinding blocks of ice thrown up at the end of winter and its desolating spring floods. Almeda looks deep, deep into the river of her mind and into the tablecloth, and she sees the crocheted roses *520* floating. They look bunchy and foolish, her mother's crocheted roses — they don't look much like real flowers. But their effort, their floating independence, their pleasure in their silly selves do seem to her so admirable. A hopeful sign. *Meneseteung.*

She doesn't leave the room until dusk, when she goes out to the privy again and discovers that she is bleeding, her flow has started. She will have to get a towel, strap it *525* on, bandage herself up. Never before, in health, has she passed a whole day in her nightdress. She doesn't feel any particular anxiety about this. On her way through the kitchen, she walks through the pool of grape juice. She knows that she will have to mop it up, but not yet, and she walks upstairs leaving purple footprints and smelling her escaping blood and the sweat of her body that has sat all day in the closed hot room. *530*

No need for alarm.

For she hasn't thought that crocheted roses could float away or that tombstones could hurry down the street. She doesn't mistake that for reality, and neither does she mistake anything else for reality, and that is how she knows that she is sane.

VI

I dream of you by night,   535
I visit you by day.
Father, Mother,
Sister, Brother,
Have you no word to say?

    April 22, 1903. At her residence, on Tuesday last, between three and four o' clock in 540
the afternoon, there passed away a lady of talent and refinement whose pen, in days
gone by, enriched our local literature with a volume of sensitive, eloquent verse. It is a
sad misfortune that in later years the mind of this fine person had become somewhat
clouded and her behaviour, in consequence, somewhat rash and unusual. Her attention
to decorum and to the care and adornment of her person had suffered, to the degree that 545
she had become, in the eyes of those unmindful of her former pride and daintiness, a
familiar eccentric, or even, sadly, a figure of fun. But now all such lapses pass from
memory and what is recalled is her excellent published verse, her labours in former
days in the Sunday school, her dutiful care of her parents, her noble womanly nature,
charitable concerns, and unfailing religious faith. Her last illness was of mercifully 550
short duration. She caught cold, after having become thoroughly wet from a ramble in
the Pearl Street bog. (It has been said that some urchins chased her into the water, and
such is the boldness and cruelty of some of our youth, and their observed persecution of
this lady, that the tale cannot be entirely discounted.) The cold developed into
pneumonia, and she died, attended at the last by a former neighbour, Mrs. Bert (Annie) 555
Friels, who witnessed her calm and faithful end.

    January, 1904. One of the founders of our community, an early maker and shaker
of this town, was abruptly removed from our midst on Monday morning last, whilst
attending to his correspondence in the office of his company. Mr. Jarvis Poulter
possessed a keen and lively commercial spirit, which was instrumental in the creation of 560
not one but several local enterprises, bringing the benefits of industry, productivity, and
employment to our town.

So the *Vidette* runs on, copious and assured. Hardly a death goes undescribed, or a life unevaluated.

I looked for Almeda Roth in the graveyard. I found the family stone. There was just one 565
name on it — Roth. Then I noticed two flat stones in the ground, a distance of a few feet
— six feet? — from the upright stone. One of these said "Papa," the other "Mama."
Farther out from these I found two other flat stones, with the names William and
Catherine on them. I had to clear away some overgrowing grass and dirt to see the full
name of Catherine. No birth or death dates for anybody, nothing about being dearly 570
beloved. It was a private sort of memorializing, not for the world. There were no roses,

either — no sign of a rosebush. But perhaps it was taken out. The grounds keeper doesn't like such things; they are a nuisance to the lawnmower, and if there is nobody left to object he will pull them out.

I thought that Almeda must have been buried somewhere else. When this plot was 575 bought — at the time of the two children's deaths — she would still have been expected to marry, and to lie finally beside her husband. They might not have left room for her here. Then I saw that the stones in the ground fanned out from the upright stone. First the two for the parents, then the two for the children, but these were placed in such a way that there was room for a third, to complete the fan. I paced out from "Catherine" 580 the same number of steps that it took to get from "Catherine" to "William," and at this spot I began pulling grass and scrabbling in the dirt with my bare hands. Soon I felt the stone and knew that I was right. I worked away and got the whole stone clear and I read the name "Meda." There it was with the others, staring at the sky.

I made sure I had got to the edge of the stone. That was all the name there was — 585 Meda. So it was true that she was called by that name in the family. Not just in the poem. Or perhaps she chose her name from the poem, to be written on her stone.

I thought that there wasn't anybody alive in the world but me who would know this, who would make the connection. And I would be the last person to do so. But perhaps this isn't so. People are curious. A few people are. They will be driven to find things 590 out, even trivial things. They will put things together. You see them going around with notebooks, scraping the dirt off gravestones, reading microfilm, just in the hope of seeing this trickle in time, making a connection, rescuing one thing from the rubbish.

And they may get it wrong, after all. I may have got it wrong. I don't know if she ever took laudanum. Many ladies did. I don't know if she ever made grape jelly. 595

(1990)

SYLVIA PLATH
U.S.A., 1932-1963

WORDS

Axes
After whose stroke the wood rings,
And the echoes!
Echoes traveling
Off from the center like horses.   5

The sap
Wells like tears, like the
Water striving
To re-establish its mirror
Over the rock   10

That drops and turns,
A white skull,
Eaten by weedy greens.
Years later I
Encounter them on the road —   15

Words dry and riderless,
The indefatigable hoof-taps.
While
From the bottom of the pool, fixed stars
Govern a life.   20

1 February 1963

(1965)

ARUN KOLATKAR
India, b.1932

THE BUTTERFLY

There is no story behind it.
It is split like a second.
It hinges around itself.

It has no future.
It is pinned down to no past.   5
It's a pun on the present.

It's a little yellow butterfly.
It has taken these wretched hills
under its wings.

Just a pinch of yellow,   10
it opens before it closes
and closes before it o

where is it

(1976)

V. S. NAIPAUL
Trinidad/England, b.1932

B. WORDSWORTH

Three beggars called punctually every day at the hospitable houses in Miguel Street. At
about ten an Indian came in his dhoti and white jacket, and we poured a tin of rice into
the sack he carried on his back. At twelve an old woman smoking a clay pipe came and
she got a cent. At two a blind man led by a boy called for his penny.

Sometimes we had a rogue. One day a man called and said he was hungry. We gave   5
him a meal. He asked for a cigarette and wouldn't go until we had lit it for him. That
man never came again.

The strangest caller came one afternoon at about four o'clock. I had come back
from school and was in my home-clothes. The man said to me, "Sonny, may I come
inside your yard?"   10

He was a small man and he was tidily dressed. He wore a hat, a white shirt and
black trousers.

B. WORDSWORTH   **2. dhoti:** loincloth.

I asked, "What you want?"

He said, "I want to watch your bees."

We had four small gru-gru palm trees and they were full of uninvited bees.   *15*

I ran up the steps and shouted, "Ma, it have a man outside here. He say he want to watch the bees."

My mother came out, looked at the man and asked in an unfriendly way, "What you want?"

The man said, "I want to watch your bees."   *20*

His English was so good, it didn't sound natural, and I could see my mother was worried.

She said to me, "Stay here and watch him while he watch the bees."

The man said, "Thank you, Madam. You have done a good deed today."

He spoke very slowly and very correctly as though every word was costing him   *25*
money.

We watched the bees, this man and I, for about an hour, squatting near the palm trees.

The man said, "I like watching bees. Sonny, do you like watching bees?"

I said, "I ain't have the time."   *30*

He shook his head sadly. He said, "That's what I do, I just watch. I can watch ants for days. Have you ever watched ants? And scorpions, and centipedes, and *congorees* — have you watched those?"

I shook my head.

I said, "What you does do, mister?"   *35*

He got up and said, "I am a poet."

I said, "A good poet?"

He said, "The greatest in the world."

"What your name, mister?"

"B. Wordsworth."   *40*

"B for Bill?"

"Black. Black Wordsworth. White Wordsworth was my brother. We share one heart. I can watch a small flower like the morning glory and cry."

I said, "Why you does cry?"

"Why boy? Why? You will know when you grow up. You're a poet, too, you know.   *45*
And when you're a poet you can cry for everything."

I couldn't laugh.

He said, "You like your mother?"

"When she not beating me."

He pulled out a printed sheet from his hip-pocket and said, "On this paper is the   *50*
greatest poem about mothers and I'm going to sell it to you at a bargain price. For four cents."

I went inside and I said, "Ma, you want to buy a poetry for four cents?"

My mother said, "Tell that blasted man to haul his tail away from my yard, you hear."   *55*

---

15. gru-gru: worthless. **32.** *congorees:* Congo ants.

I said to B. Wordsworth, "My mother say she ain't have four cents."

B. Wordsworth said, "It is the poet's tragedy."

And he put the paper back in his pocket. He didn't seem to mind.

I said, "Is a funny way to go round selling poetry like that. Only calypsonians do that sort of thing. A lot of people does buy?" 60

He said, "No one has yet bought a single copy."

"But why you does keep on going round, then?"

He said, "In this way I watch many things, and I always hope to meet poets."

I said, "You really think I is a poet?"

"You're as good as me," he said. 65

And when B. Wordsworth left, I prayed I would see him again.

About a week later, coming back from school one afternoon, I met him at the corner of Miguel Street.

He said, "I have been waiting for you for a long time."

I said, "You sell any poetry yet?" 70

He shook his head.

He said, "In my yard I have the best mango tree in Port of Spain. And now the mangoes are ripe and red and very sweet and juicy. I have waited here for you to tell you this and to invite you to come and eat some of my mangoes."

He lived in Alberto Street in a one-roomed hut placed right in the centre of the lot. 75 The yard seemed all green. There was the big mango tree. There was a coconut tree and there was a plum tree. The place looked wild, as though it wasn't in the city at all. You couldn't see all the big concrete houses in the street.

He was right. The mangoes were sweet and juicy. I ate about six, and the yellow mango juice ran down my arms to my elbows and down my mouth to my chin and my 80 shirt was stained.

My mother said when I got home, "Where you was? You think you is a man now and could go all over the place? Go cut a whip for me."

She beat me rather badly, and I ran out of the house swearing that I would never come back. I went to B. Wordsworth's house. I was so angry, my nose was bleeding. 85

B. Wordsworth said, "Stop crying, and we will go for a walk."

I stopped crying, but I was breathing short. We went for a walk. We walked down St Clair Avenue to the Savannah and we walked to the race-course.

B. Wordsworth said, "Now, let us lie on the grass and look up at the sky, and I want you to think how far those stars are from us." 90

I did as he told me, and I saw what he meant. I felt like nothing, and at the same time I had never felt so big and great in all my life. I forgot all my anger and all my tears and all the blows.

When I said I was better, he began telling me the names of the stars, and I particularly remembered the constellation of Orion the Hunter, though I don't really 95

---

59. calypsonians: calypso writers and performers, especially during Carnival season.

know why. I can spot Orion even today, but I have forgotten the rest.

Then a light was flashed into our faces, and we saw a policeman. We got up from the grass.

The policeman said, "What you doing here?"

B. Wordsworth said, "I have been asking myself the same question for forty years." *100*

We became friends, B. Wordsworth and I. He told me, "You must never tell anybody about me and about the mango tree and the coconut tree and the plum tree. You must keep that a secret. If you tell anybody, I will know, because I am a poet."

I gave him my word and I kept it.

I liked his little room. It had no more furniture than George's front room, but it *105* looked cleaner and healthier. But it also looked lonely.

One day I asked him, "Mister Wordsworth, why you does keep all this bush in your yard? Ain't it does make the place damp?"

He said, "Listen, and I will tell you a story. Once upon a time a boy and girl met each other and they fell in love. They loved each other so much they got married. They *110* were both poets. He loved words. She loved grass and flowers and trees. They lived happily in a single room, and then one day, the girl poet said to the boy poet, 'We are going to have another poet in the family.' But this poet was never born, because the girl died, and the young poet died with her, inside her. And the girl's husband was very sad, and he said he would never touch a thing in the girl's garden. And so the garden *115* remained, and grew high and wild."

I looked at B. Wordsworth, and as he told me this lovely story, he seemed to grow older. I understood his story.

We went for long walks together. We went to the Botanical Gardens and the Rock Gardens. We climbed Chancellor Hill in the late afternoon and watched the darkness fall *120* on Port of Spain, and watched the lights go on in the city and on the ships in the harbour.

He did everything as though he were doing it for the first time in his life. He did everything as though he were doing some church rite.

He would say to me, "Now, how about having some ice-cream?" *125*

And when I said yes, he would grow very serious and say, "Now, which café shall we patronise?" As though it were a very important thing. He would think for some time about it, and finally say, "I think I will go and negotiate the purchase with that shop."

The world became a most exciting place.

One day, when I was in his yard, he said to me, "I have a great secret which I am now *130* going to tell you."

I said, "It really secret?"

"At the moment, yes."

I looked at him, and he looked at me. He said, "This is just between you and me, remember. I am writing a poem." *135*

"Oh." I was disappointed.

He said, "But this is a different sort of poem. This is the greatest poem in the world."

I whistled.

He said, "I have been working on it for more than five years now. I will finish it in *140* about twenty-two years from now, that is, if I keep on writing at the present rate."

"You does write a lot, then?"

He said, "Not any more. I just write one line a month. But I make sure it is a good line."

I asked, "What was last month's good line?" *145*

He looked up at the sky, and said, *"The past is deep."*

I said, "It is a beautiful line."

B. Wordsworth said, "I hope to distil the experiences of a whole month into that single line of poetry. So, in twenty-two years, I shall have written a poem that will sing to all humanity." *150*

I was filled with wonder.

Our walks continued. We walked along the sea-wall at Docksite one day, and I said, "Mr Wordsworth, if I drop this pin in the water, you think it will float?"

He said, "This is a strange world. Drop your pin, and let us see what will happen."

The pin sank. *155*

I said, "How is the poem this month?"

But he never told me any other line. He merely said, "Oh, it comes, you know. It comes."

Or we would sit on the sea-wall and watch the liners come into the harbour.

But of the greatest poem in the world I heard no more. *160*

I felt he was growing older.

"How you does live, Mr Wordsworth?" I asked him one day.

He said, "You mean how I get money?"

When I nodded, he laughed in a crooked way.

He said, "I sing calypsoes in the calypso season." *165*

"And that last you the rest of the year?"

"It is enough."

"But you will be the richest man in the world when you write the greatest poem?"

He didn't reply.

One day when I went to see him in his little house, I found him lying on his little bed. *170* He looked so old and so weak, that I found myself wanting to cry.

He said, "The poem is not going well."

He wasn't looking at me. He was looking through the window at the coconut tree, and he was speaking as though I wasn't there. He said, "When I was twenty I felt the power within myself." Then, almost in front of my eyes, I could see his face growing *175* older and more tired. He said, "But that — that was a long time ago."

And then — I felt it so keenly, it was as though I had been slapped by my mother. I could see it clearly on his face. It was there for everyone to see. Death on the shrinking face.

He looked at me, and saw my tears and sat up.

He said, "Come." I went and sat on his knees. *180*

He looked into my eyes, and he said, "Oh, you can see it, too. I always knew you had the poet's eye."

He didn't even look sad, and that made me burst out crying loudly.

He pulled me to his thin chest, and said, "Do you want me to tell you a funny story?" and he smiled encouragingly at me.   *185*

But I couldn't reply.

He said, "When I have finished this story, I want you to promise that you will go away and never come back to see me. Do you promise?"

I nodded.

He said, "Good. Well, listen. That story I told you about the boy poet and the girl   *190* poet, do you remember that? That wasn't true. It was something I just made up. All this talk about poetry and the greatest poem in the world, that wasn't true, either. Isn't that the funniest thing you have heard?"

But his voice broke.

I left the house, and ran home crying, like a poet, for everything I saw.   *195*

I walked along Alberto Street a year later, but I could find no sign of the poet's house. It hadn't vanished, just like that. It had been pulled down, and a big, two-storied building had taken its place. The mango tree and the plum tree and the coconut tree had all been cut down, and there was brick and concrete everywhere.

It was just as though B. Wordsworth had never existed.   *200*

(1959)

LINDA PASTAN
U.S.A., b.1932

ETHICS

In ethics class so many years ago
our teacher asked this question every fall:
if there were a fire in a museum
which would you save, a Rembrandt painting
or an old woman who hadn't many   *5*
years left anyhow? Restless on hard chairs
caring little for pictures or old age
we'd opt one year for life, the next for art
and always half-heartedly. Sometimes
the woman borrowed my grandmother's face   *10*
leaving her usual kitchen to wander
some drafty, half imagined museum.
One year, feeling clever, I replied

why not let the woman decide herself?
Linda, the teacher would report, eschews   *15*
the burdens of responsibility.
This fall in a real museum I stand
before a real Rembrandt, old woman,
or nearly so, myself. The colors
within this frame are darker than autumn,   *20*
darker even than winter — the browns of earth,
though earth's most radiant elements burn
through the canvas. I know now that woman
and painting and season are almost one
and all beyond saving by children.   *25*

(1979)

ETHICS   **4. Rembrandt:** Rembrandt van Rijn, Dutch painter (1606-1669).

SIPHO SEPAMLA
South Africa, b.1932

DA SAME, DA SAME

I doesn't care of you black
I doesn't care of you white
I doesn't care of you India
I doesn't care of you kleeling
if sometimes you Saus Afrika   5
you gotta big terrible terrible
somewheres in yourselves
because why
for sure you doesn't look anader man in da eye

I mean for sure now   10
all da peoples is make like God
sometimes you wanna knows how I meaning for
is simples
da God I knows for sure
He make avarybudy wit' one heart   15

for sure now dis heart go-go da same
dats for meaning to say
one man no diflent to anader

so now
you see a big terrible terrible stand here   20
how one man make anader man feel
da pain he doesn't feel hisself
for sure now dats da whole point

sometime you wanna know how I meaning for
is simples   25
when da nail of da t'orn tree
scratch little bit little bit of da skin
I doesn't care of say black
I doesn't care of say white
I doesn't care of say India   30
I doesn't care of say kleeling
I mean for sure da skin
only one t'ing come for sure
and da one t'ing for sure is red blood
dats for sure da same da same   35
for avarybudy.

(1976)

ALDEN NOWLAN
Canada, 1933-1983

1914-1918

Thinking again of all those young men who were given the same first name,
Canada, once they had reached the place which we in our innocence then
called *Overseas*, doubtless with the same intonation
as Frankish peasants had used eight centuries earlier
in speaking of the sons who had followed their steely Lords to *Outre Mar*;   5
thinking of how a German officer remembered this for half a century as the strangest thing
he saw in four years of war — the Canadians walking,
simply walking, in no apparent order, but like any group of men going anywhere,

---

DA SAME, DA SAME   4. kleeling: "Coloured" (a South African "category") for people with mixed racial heritage). 26. t'orn: thorn.   **1914-1918**   5. Outre Mar: "Beyond the Seas."

into a hailstorm of machine-gun fire that flattened them like wheat,
"They did not even look like soldiers, yet fought like Prussian Guards,"   10
I wish, as they would have done, who were much like me,
though they were so much younger, that God's bad brother,
having killed them, had said *Enough!* and had not proceeded
to prove their deaths were pointless; if they had to die
(and all of us do; oh, all of us do), then I wish   15
that we could say that we are who we are because they were who they were.
That much, at least, has been given others. I think of names:
Salamanca, Antietam, Leningrad. I think of Polish miners
singing of Polish horsemen, a Cuban schoolchild placing flowers
at a wall filled with old photographs.   20
                    All of it lies,
perhaps, or romantic rubbish, though those young men would not have thought it was.

My country has no history, only a past.

                                                                    (1985)

ANNE STEVENSON
U.S.A./England, b.1933

COLOURS

Enough of green
though to remember childhood
is to stand in uneasy radiance
under those trees.

Enough yellow.   5
We are looking back
over our shoulders, telling our children
to be happy.

Try to forget about red.
Leave it to the professionals.   10
But perceive heaven as a density
blue enough to abolish the stars.

As long as the rainbow lasts
the company stays.

Of black there is never enough.   15

One by one the lights in the house go out.
Step over the threshold. Forget
to take my hand.

                                                                    (1977)

WILLOW SONG

I went down to the railway
But the railway wasn't there.
A long scar lay across the waste
Bound up with vetch and maidenhair
And birdsfoot trefoils everywhere.   5
But the clover and the sweet hay,
The cranesbill and the yarrow
Were as nothing to the rose bay
    the rose bay, the rose bay,
As nothing to the rose bay willow.   10

---

18. **Salamanca, Antietam, Leningrad:** celebrated battles of the Spanish Civil War, the American Civil War, and World War II, respectively.

I went down to the river
But the river wasn't there.
A hill of slag lay in its course
With pennycress and cocklebur
And thistles bristling with fur.   *15*
But ragweed, dock and bitter may
And hawkbit in the hollow
Were as nothing to the rose bay,
    the rose bay, the rose bay,
As nothing to the rose bay willow.   *20*

I went down to find my love,
My sweet love wasn't there.
A shadow stole into her place
And spoiled the loosestrife of her hair
And counselled me to pick despair.   *25*
Old elder and young honesty
Turned ashen, but their sorrow
Was as nothing to the rose bay
    the rose bay, the rose bay,
As nothing to the rose bay willow.   *30*

                                    (1985)

JENNIFER STRAUSS
Australia, b.1933

DISCOURSE IN EDEN

"I think I'll call it giraffe" —
He speaks: she smiles; is
always smiling, but won't
discriminate — just
watches the wide garden   *5*
with boundless pleasure.

"Giraffe!" he says, emphatic,
making her look; then sighs
"It isn't easy, having to find
so *many* different names."   *10*
Lively now, she offers help:
he's unconvinced.

"Well really it was *me* God told
to name the creatures . . . but p'rhaps
you *could* try something small . . . "   *15*
"But my ideas are large."
He takes her hand,
"We'll see . . . my love . . . tomorrow . . . "

Tomorrow she basks in sunlight,
grass tickling her toes,   *20*
"Where is giraffe?" he asks.
"Why here," she says "somewhere here."

"Nonsense! Look there —
(finger stabbing) there, there,
there's no giraffe." "But,   *25*
surely there's enough."
"That's not the point — he's lost
if I can't see him, lost,
or somewhere else."
So Adam goes off, questing.   *30*

And though the sky's still blue,
the leaves densely green,
there is a blank,
a space within creation —
inscribed giraffe, it signifies   *35*
the other, absence, lack.

Eve feels, for the first time,
hollow . . . bespoken
(above her head on the branch
but ripe to a hand's reach)   *40*
the fruit shines,
round, substantial.

                                    (1989)

DISCOURSE IN EDEN   See Genesis 2:18-23 (p. 243).

₣AY ₩ELDON
England, b.1933

from *LETTERS TO ALICE ON FIRST READING JANE AUSTEN*

Letter One: The City of Invention

Cairns, Australia, October

My dear Alice,

It was good to get your letter. I am a long way from home here; almost in exile. And you ask me for advice, which is warming, and makes me believe I must know something; or at any rate more than you. The impression of knowing less and less, the older one gets, is daunting. The last time I saw you, you were two, blonde and cherubic. Now, I gather, you are eighteen, you dye your hair black and green with vegetable dye, *5* and your mother, my sister, is perturbed. Perhaps your writing to me is a step towards your and her eventual reconciliation? I shall not interfere between the two of you: I shall confine myself to the matters you raise.

Namely, Jane Austen and her books. You tell me, in passing, that you are doing a college course in English Literature, and are obliged to read Jane Austen; that you find *10* her boring, petty and irrelevant and, that as the world is in crisis, and the future catastrophic, you cannot imagine what purpose there can be in your reading her.

My dear child! My dear pretty little Alice, now with black and green hair.

How can I hope to explain Literature to you, with its capital "L"? You are bright enough. You could read when you were four. But then, sensibly, you turned to *15* television for your window on the world: you slaked your appetite for information, for stories, for beginnings, middles and ends, with the easy tasty substances of the screen in the living room, and (if I remember your mother rightly) no doubt in your bedroom too. You lulled yourself to sleep with visions of violence, and the cruder strokes of human action and reaction; stories in which every simple action has a simple motive, nothing is *20* inexplicable, and even God moves in an un-mysterious way. And now you realize this is not enough: you have an inkling there is something more, that your own feelings and responses are a thousand times more complex than this tinny televisual representation of reality has ever suggested: you have, I suspect and hope, intimations of infinity, of the romance of creation, of the wonder of love, of the glory of existence; you look around *25* for companions in your wild new comprehension, your sudden vision, and you see the

---

LETTERS TO ALICE   Title: Weldon is encouraging her niece to read not only Jane Austen (1775-1817), but other literature as well. Since her references are so wide-ranging, and since she is in effect urging readers to discover literature for themselves, we have chosen to leave readers in a position fairly close to that of Alice, and have therefore annotated only selectively, mainly limiting ourselves to identifying works to be found in this anthology and a few allusions that might not be familiar. **21:** Cf. Cowper's *Olney Hymns*, XXXV: "God moves in a mysterious way, / His wonders to perform."

same zonked-out stares, the same pale faces and dyed cotton-wool hair, and you turn, at last, to education, to literature, and books — and find them closed to you.

Do not despair, little Alice. Only persist, and thou shalt see, Jane Austen's all in all to thee. A coconut fell from a tree just now, narrowly missing the head of a fellow guest,   30
here at this hotel at the edge of a bright blue tropical sea, where sea-stingers in the mating season (which cannot be clearly defined) and at paddling depth, grow invisible tentacles forty feet long, the merest touch of which will kill a child; and any easily shockable adult too, no doubt. Stay out of the sea, and the coconuts get you!

But there is a copy of Jane Austen's *Emma* here, in the small bookshelf, and it's   35
well-thumbed. The other books are yet more tattered; they are thrillers and romances, temporary things. These books open a little square window on the world and set the puppets parading outside for you to observe. They bear little resemblance to human beings, to anyone you ever met or are likely to meet. These characters exist for purposes of plot, and the books they appear in do not threaten the reader in any way; they do not   40
suggest that he or she should reflect, let alone *change*. But then, of course, being so safe, they defeat themselves, they can never enlighten. And because they don't enlighten, they are unimportant. (Unless, of course, they are believed, when they become dangerous. To *believe* a Mills & Boon novel reflects real life, is to live in perpetual disappointment. You are meant to believe while the reading lasts, and not a moment   45
longer.) These books, the tattered ones, the thrillers and romances, are interchangeable. They get used to light the barbecues, when the sun goes down over the wild hills, and there's a hunger in the air — not just for steak and chilli sauce, but a real human demand for living, sex, experience, change. The pages flare up, turn red, turn black, finish. The steak crackles, thanks to a copy of *Gorky Park*. Everyone eats. Imperial   50
Caesar, dead and turned to clay, would stop a hole to keep the wind away!

But no one burns *Emma*. No one would dare. There is too much concentrated here: too much history, too much respect, too much of the very essence of civilization, which is, I must tell you, connected to its Literature. It's Literature, with a capital "L," as opposed to just books. Hitler, of course, managed to burn Literature as well as Just   55
Books at the Reichstag fire, and his nation's cultural past with it, and no one has ever forgiven or forgotten. You have to be really *bad* to burn Literature.

How can I explain this phenomenon to you? How can I convince you of the pleasures of a good book, when you have McDonald's around one corner and *An American Werewolf in London* around the next? I suffer myself from the common nervous dread of literature.   60
When I go on holiday, I read first the thrillers, then the sci-fi, then the instructional books, then *War and Peace,* or whatever book it is I know I ought to read, ought to have read, half want to read and only when reading want to fully. Of course one dreads it: of course it is overwhelming: one both anticipates and fears the kind of swooning, almost erotic pleasure that a good passage in a good book gives; as something nameless *happens*. I don't know   65
what it is that happens: is it the pleasure of mind meeting mind, untramelled by flesh? Of the inchoation of our own experience suddenly given shape and form? Why yes, we cry: yes, yes, that is how it is! But we have to be strong to want to know: if something, suddenly, is going to *happen* as we encounter the *Idea,* and discover it adds up to more than

---

44. Mills & Boon novel: the Australian equivalent of a Harlequin romance. **50-51:** Cf. *Hamlet*, V.i.215-16.

the parts which comprise it: understand that *Idea* is more than the sum of experience. It   *70*
takes courage, to comprehend not just what we are, but why we are.

Perhaps they will explain it to you better, at your English Literature course. I hope
so. I rather doubt it. In such places (or so it seems to me), those in charge are taking
something they cannot quite understand but have an intimation is remarkable, and
breaking it down into its component parts in an attempt to discover its true nature. As   *75*
well take a fly to bits, and hope that the bits will explain the creature. You will know
more, but understand less. You will have more information, and less wisdom. I do not
wish (much) to insult Departments of English Literature, nor to suggest for one moment
that you would do better out of their care than in it: I am just saying be careful. And I
speak as one studied by Literature Departments (a few) and in Women's Studies   *80*
Courses (more) and I say "one" advisedly, because it is not just my novels (legitimate
prey, as works of what they care to call the creative imagination) but *me* they end up
wanting to investigate, and it is not a profitable study.

Now, as a writer of novels I am one thing: what you *read* of mine has gone to third
or fourth draft: it is fiction: that is to say, it is a properly formulated vision of the world.   *85*
But myself living, talking, giving advice, writing this letter, is only, please remember, in
first draft. As someone trying to persuade you to read and enjoy *Emma,* and *Persuasion,*
and *Mansfield Park*, and *Northanger Abbey*, and *Pride and Prejudice*, and (on occasion)
Sense and Sensibility, and (quite often) *Lady Susan*, I am quite another. Believe me or
disbelieve me, as you choose. But hear me out.   *90*

You must *read*, Alice, before it's too late. You must fill your mind with the
invented images of the past: the more the better. Literary images of Beowulf, and The
Wife of Bath, and Falstaff and Sweet Amaryllis in the Shade, and Elizabeth Bennet, and
the Girl in the Green Hat — and Rabbit Hazel of *Watership Down*, if you must. These
images, apart from anything else, will help you put the two and twos of life together,   *95*
and the more images your mind retains, the more wonderful will be the star-studded
canopy of experience beneath which you, poor primitive creature that you are, will
shelter: the nearer you will creep to the great blazing beacon of the Idea which animates
us all.

No? Too rich and embarrassing an image? Would you prefer me to say, more   *100*
safely, "Literature stands at the gates of civilization, holding back greed, rage, murder,
and savagery of all kinds"? I am not too happy with this myself: I think I am as likely,
these days, to be raped and murdered in my bed within the gates of civilization as
without. Unless civilization itself is failing, because literature has stepped aside and we
now merely stare at images? Unless we watch television, and do not read, and so are   *105*
losing the power of reflection? In which case it is only Departments of English Literature
which stand between us and our doom!

No? I see I am trying to define literature by what it does, not by what it is. By
experience, not Idea.

Let's try another way. Let me put to you another notion.   *110*

Try this. Frame it in your mind as a TV cameraman frames a shot, getting Sue Ellen
nicely centred. Let me give you, let me share with you, the City of Invention. For what

---

93. **Wife of Bath:** See p. 40; **Amaryllis . . . Shade:** See Milton's *Lycidas*, line 68 (p. 316).

novelists do (I have decided, for the purposes of your conversion) is to build Houses of the Imagination, and where houses cluster together there is a city. And what a city this one is, Alice! It is the nearest we poor mortals can get to the Celestial City: it glitters *115* and glances with life, and gossip, and colour, and fantasy: it is brilliant, it is illuminated, by day by the sun of enthusiasm and by night by the moon of inspiration. It has its towers and pinnacles, its commanding heights and its swooning depths: it has public buildings and worthy ancient monuments, which some find boring and others mag- nificent. It has its central districts and its suburbs, some salubrious, some seedy, some *120* safe, some frightening. Those who founded it, who built it, house by house, are the novelists, the writers, the poets. And it is to this city that the readers come, to admire, to learn, to marvel and explore.

Let us look round the city: become acquainted with it, make it our eternal, our immortal home. Looming over everything, of course, heart of the City, is the great *125* Castle Shakespeare. You see it whichever way you look. It rears its head into the clouds, reaching into the celestial sky, dominating everything around. It's a rather uneven building, frankly. Some complain it's shoddy, and carelessly constructed in parts, others grumble that Shakespeare never built it anyway, and a few say the whole thing ought to be pulled down to make way for the newer and more relevant, and this prime building *130* site released for younger talent: but the Castle keeps standing through the centuries and, build as others may they can never quite achieve the same grandeur; and the visitors keep flocking, and the guides keep training and re-training, finding yet new ways of explaining the old building. It's more than a life's work.

Here in this City of Invention, the readers come and go, by general invitation, *135* sauntering down its leafy avenues, scurrying through its horrider slums, waving to each other across the centuries, up and down the arches of the years. When I say "the arches of the years" it may well sound strange to you. But I know what I'm doing: it is you who are at fault. This is a phrase used by Francis Thompson — a Catholic poet, late- nineteenth century — in his slightly ridiculous but haunting poem "The Hound of *140* Heaven."

> I fled Him, down the nights and down the days;
> I fled Him, down the arches of the years;

The poem is about God pursuing an escaping soul, lurching after him, hound-like. He gets him in the end, as a Mountie gets his man. (Another dusty image, no doubt; and one *145* scarcely worth the taking out and dusting down.) When I refer to "the arches of the years" I hope to convey the whole feeling-tone (as Freudians say of dreams) of the poem, both the power and the slight absurdity; *all* the poem in fact, in the five words of his that I choose, for the benefit of my sentence. Call it plagiarism, call it fellowship between writers, or resonance (since you're in a Dept. of Eng. Lit.). I don't suppose it *150* matters much. It is the kind of thing writers used to depend upon in their attempts to get taken seriously, and now no longer can. We talk to an audience (and I say talk advisedly, rather than write: for contemporary authors are left largely with the writing down on paper of what they could as well speak, if only their listeners would stand still

---

115. **Celestial City:** in Bunyan's *The Pilgrim's Progress* (see p. 416).

for long enough) and a generation which has read so little it understands only the   *155*
vernacular. I don't think this matters much. I think that writers have to change and
adapt. It is no use lamenting a past: people *now* are as valuable as people *then*. You will
just have to take my word for it, that the words a writer uses, even now, go back and
back into a written history. Words are not simple things: they take unto themselves, as
they have through time, power and meaning: they did so then, they do so now.   *160*

I bet £500 you have not read "The Hound of Heaven."

But back to our City of Invention. Let me put it like this — writers create Houses of
the Imagination, from whose doors the generations greet each other. You will always
hear a great deal of enlivening dissension and discussion. Should Madame Bovary have
munched the arsenic? Would Anna Karenina have gone under the train had Tolstoy   *165*
been a woman, would Darcy have married Elizabeth anywhere else but in the City of
Invention, and so on and so forth, in and out of the centuries.

And thus, by such discussion and such shared experience, do we understand
ourselves and one another, and our pasts and our futures. It is in the literature, the
novels, the fantasy, the fiction of the past, that you find *real* history, and not in text   *170*
books. Thomas More's *Utopia* tells us as much about his own century, his own world,
as the one he invented for the delectation of his peers.

Writers are privileged visitors here. They have a house or two of their own in the
City, after all. Perhaps even well-thought of, and nicely maintained: or perhaps never
much reckoned and falling into disrepair. But to have a house of any kind, even to have   *175*
brought it only to planning stage, and have given up in despair, is to realize more fully
the wonder of the City, and to know how its houses are built: to know also that though
one brick may look much like another, and all builders go about their work in much the
same way, some buildings will be good, some bad. And a very few, sometimes the least
suspected, will last, and not crumble with the decades.   *180*

Writers, builders, good or bad, recognizing these things, are usually polite to one
another, and a great deal kinder than the people who visit, as outsiders. Builders vary in
intellect, aspiration, talent and efficiency; they build well or badly in different suburbs
of the City. Some build because they need to, have to, live to, or believe they are
appointed to, others to prove a point or to change the world. But to build at all requires   *185*
courage, persistence, faith and a surplus of animation. A writer's *all*, Alice, is not taken
up by the real world. There is something left over: enough for them to build these
alternative, finite realities.

Jane Austen had a great deal left over. You could say that was because she didn't
wear herself out physically running round the world, pleasing a husband or looking after   *190*
children. (But that didn't save her from an early and unpleasant death.) And though this
meant that she chose, perhaps, a safer, rather inward-looking site to build her houses
(though what a pleasant, grassy, well-regarded mound it turned out to be), than she
would otherwise have done, she gave herself, through her writing, another life that outran her own; a literary life. It was not, I am sure, what she set out to do. But it happened.   *195*
She breathed in, as it were, into the source of her own energy, her own life, and breathed
out a hundred different lives. She had energy enough to build. Some, of course — and I
tend to be one of them — maintain that the constant energizing friction of wifehood,
motherhood and domesticity, provides its own surging energy, and creates as powerful

an inner life as does the prudent, contemplative, my-art-my-art-alone existence. Others   *200*
deny it.

You get all kinds of writers, Alice. You get Dickens and St Theresa of Avila, you
get wicked George Sand, surrounded by lovers and children, and you get Jane Austen.
Writers deal with their lives as best they can, and their personalities, and the family and
century into which they were born: they do what they must with their day-to-day   *205*
existences, and build in the City of Invention.

It's getting crowded, these days, here as anywhere else. Look around. Almost nowhere
that's not been built on! Unless they think of somewhere new, which they probably will:
discover a new slope, or hillside, hitherto considered barren, which with a little ingenuity
turns out to be fertile. The City as it is today, stretches far and wide, through dreary new   *210*
suburbs to a misty horizon. All kinds of people choose to build here now, and not just those
born to it. Non-vocational writers can put up a pretty fair representation of a proper house,
and even get a number of enthusiastic visitors. The structure will crumble within the year,
and then someone else will quickly use the site, fill the space on the Station Bookstall. But
the result is that bus journeys into the centre of the city can seem to last for ever — so many   *215*
books, just *so many*, on the way! — before you get to those wonderful places where the
visitors flock and the tourists gasp with gratification, and that's where I want you to go,
Alice. I know no one's ever set you a proper example. (Your mother reads books on tennis,
I know: I doubt she's read a novel since an overdose of Georgette Heyer made her marry
your father. Books can be dangerous.) I do not want you to be deprived of the pleasures of   *220*
literature. You are, in spite of everything, my flesh and blood.

I can give you a physical location for the City. It lies at a mid-way point between the
Road to Heaven and the Road to Hell; these two were depicted in the lithograph that used
to hang on your mother's and my bedroom wall when we were children: before I took the
broad and primrose Road to Hell, by going with our father when he left, and she stayed   *225*
on the narrow, uphill path of righteousness that leads to Heaven, by remaining with our
mother. What dramas there were then, little Alice, with your green and black hair! You
have no idea how the world has changed in forty years.

Before you can properly appreciate Jane Austen, you do need to be, just a little,
acquainted with the City: at any rate with its more important districts. Master builders   *230*
work up on the heights, in the shadow of some great castle or other. They build whole
streets, worthy and respectable. Mannstrasse, Melville Ave, Galsworthy Close. You
need at least to know *where* they are. More fun, perhaps, to ferret out the places where
an innocent has erected some glittering edifice almost by mistake — Tressell's *Ragged
Trousered Philanthropists*, or Flora Thompson's *Lark Rise to Candleford* or James   *235*
Stevens's *The Caretaker's Daughter* — or a child achieved what an adult can't. The
path up to Daisy Ashford's *Young Visitors* is always thronged with delighted visitors.
But it's pleasant going about anywhere, especially with company. You can wander up
and down the more cosmopolitan areas, dip into Sartre, or Sagan, or through the
humbler districts, saying: that's a good house for round here, or this one really lets the   *240*
neighbourhood down! Sometimes you'll find quite a shoddy building so well placed and
painted that it quite takes the visitor in, and the critics as well — and all cluster round,

---

202. St Theresa: See Longfellow's translation of "Santa Theresa's Book-Mark" (p. 934). **237:** correctly, *The Young Visiters*.

crying, "Lo, a masterpiece!" and award it prizes. But the passage of time, the peeling of paint, the very lack of concerned visitors, reveals it in the end for what it is: a house of no interest or significance.   *245*

You will find that buildings rise and fall in the estimation of visitors, for no apparent reason. Who reads Arnold Bennett now, or Sinclair Lewis? But perhaps soon, with any luck, they'll be rediscovered. "How interesting," people will say, pushing open the creaking doors. "How remarkable! Don't you feel the atmosphere here? So familiar, so true: the amazing masquerading as the ordinary? Why haven't we been here for so   *250* long?" And Bennett, Lewis, or whoever, will be rediscovered, and the houses of his imagination be renovated, restored, and hinges oiled so that doors open easily, and the builder, the writer, takes his rightful place again in the great alternative hierarchy.

Visitors, builders feel (even while asking them in and feeling insulted if they don't look around), are demanding and difficult people; the visitors seem to have no idea at all   *255* how tricky the building of Houses is. They think if only they had the time, they'd do it themselves. They say, such a life I've had! I really ought to put it all down some day; turn it into a book! And so indeed what a life they've had, but the mere recording of event does not make a book. Experience does not add up to Idea. It is easier for the reader to judge, by a thousand times, than for the writer to invent. The writer must   *260* summon his Idea out of nowhere, and his characters out of nothing, and catch words as they fly, and nail them to the page. The reader has something to go by and somewhere to start from, given to him freely and with great generosity by the writer. And still the reader feels free to find fault.

Some builders build their houses and refuse to open the door, so terrified of visitors   *265* are they. In drawers and cupboards all over the land, I'll swear, are the hidden manuscripts of perfectly publishable novels which, for lack of a brown envelope and a stamp and a little nerve, never see the light of day. Genius lasts, but I'm not so sure that it will necessarily *out*.

Sometimes when a builder opens the door of a newly finished house, and the   *270* crowds and critics rush in, he must wish he'd never opened the door. Hardy never wrote another novel after *Jude the Obscure* was published, so upsetting did the critics find it, and so upsetting did he find the critics.

Mind you, I see their point. *Jude the Obscure* stopped me reading for quite some time. I kept postponing my visits to the City for fear of what I might find there; the   *275* Giant Despair, for example, wandering the hitherto serene streets, zapping the unwary visitor on the head. Hardy, claimed the critics, was the one who had unlocked the cage and let the Giant loose: and then, worse, had opened the gates of the City and positively invited him in: had made it a dangerous place.

It's safer, you'll find, down among the Pre-Fabs, if it's safety you're after. Here the   *280* verges are neatly swept and Despair wears a muzzle, albeit the houses themselves lack all grandeur and aspiration. Surprising to see such flimsy structures built with such care and skill. Novels-from-films — film first, novel after — *Jaws, Alien, ET* — are so efficiently written as to all but pass for real creation, real invention, and not the calculated flights of reason that they are. There is no vision here, but an acute observation of what a mass   *285*

---

276. Giant Despair: in Bunyan's *The Pilgrim's Progress* (p. 423).

audience wants to see and hear. Heart-strings twang, but don't vibrate. The windows in these Pre-Fabs have the blinds pulled down, and on the blinds are painted what you might reasonably see (reasonably for the City of Invention, that is) if they were raised — a beach scene, or a space ship, or an extra-terrestrial plodding about outside — but they are still only painted, albeit with wonderful conviction. And if you do raise the blinds, send them whirring 290 up to the ceiling, where clean brisk straight edge meets clean brisk straight edge (nothing here of the softness of age, no mellow patina of the past) you will see out of the windows grey nothingness, and when the thrumming shark-fear music has died away, and the wistful songs of outer space, you may even hear the footfall of Despair outside and wonder just how fast his claws do grow, and if he gets even this far, and if he's snapped his muzzle free. 295

Quick, next door, to the rather solider hyped twin houses of *Scruples* and *Lace*. The blinds are frilly and expensive and very firmly pulled down. You're not supposed to look around too closely, once inside. You may not want to, much (and in any case, your comments aren't called for. You're supposed to pay your money at the door, and leave at once). These houses and others like them, are well enough made. They are calculated 300 to divert and impress and often do — but do not take them seriously, Alice, and know them for what they are.

The good builders, the really good builders, carry a vision out of the real world and transpose it into the City of Invention, and refresh and enlighten the reader, so that on his, or her, return to reality, that reality itself is changed, however minutely. A book that 305 has no base in an initial reality, written out of reason and not conviction, is a house built of — what shall we say? — bricks and no mortar? Walk into it, brush against a door frame, and the whole edifice falls down about your ears. Like the first little pig's house of straw, when the big bad wolf huffed and puffed.

Round the corner from the money-makers, the edges of the two suburbs running 310 together, is the vast red-light district of Porno. Step into houses here at your peril: what you find inside is exciting enough, but the windows have no blinds at all, and there is real pain, torture, degradation and death out there. There are not even any curtains, just a nasty red flicker round the edges of the window frames, because this is where the city borders on Hell. Well, somewhere has to, just as someone has to be bottom of the class. 315 But the suburb's grown too fast, it's unstoppable. Police forever roam the streets, to the mirth of the nudging, knowing, winking inhabitants, and occasionally manage to demolish a monstrosity, only to find a worse one springing up in its place. There's a good building or so, of course, round here, and visitors bus in from everywhere, sometimes on very respectable tours. They come in by the bus-load for *The Story of O* 320 — it's so well constructed, they say: so elegantly made; look how graceful the lintels are, how delicately placed the beams — never mind where the whole thing's placed! And the French lady, Anaïs Nin, Henry Miller's friend, never built better than when she was down here, and well paid. You will find, you insist, other light-fingered and enchanting structures up and down the streets, but they have the air of the witch's house 325 in *Hansel and Gretel*. All smarties and gingerbread and delicious; but beware, the witch with her oven waits inside, and she's luring you in, to eat you up! Wait until you're older, Alice, and the pleasures of your own flesh desert you.

(You may not know, of course, who Henry Miller was. He was an American. He wrote *Tropic of Cancer* and *Tropic of Capricorn* back in the thirties, books explicitly 330 sexual and much banned, and, with hindsight, exploitative of women. At the time he seemed the prophet of freedom, liberation, and imagination. His houses still stand.)

I used to spend a lot of time myself in the all-male suburb of Sci-Fi, in the days when it was formal and reliable and informed and only a few knew of its pleasures. Sci-Fi Town borders on the red-light district: the two areas blend easily, being all mind and no heart. The houses here are mostly new, though a few proud old structures still stand. Jules Verne and H. G. Wells were amongst the first to build. Aldous Huxley's *Brave New World* and George Orwell's *1984* are showpieces in that nowadays slightly shoddy main street, Utopia. (Utopia comes from the Greek, Alice, and means a Nowhere Place, not a Good Place, as many people think.) Thomas More's *Utopia* and Samuel Butler's *Erewhon* ("Nowhere" spelt backwards — well, more or less) were perhaps the finest and best buildings constructed here. But it's the same here as anywhere: districts become too quickly fashionable, groundspace over-priced, jerry-building is tempting: good buildings are torn down and replaced by inferior constructions and then the heart of the place is gone. No one writes about Utopias any more.

Science Fantasy, where these days the builders are for the most part women, is an area newly and brightly developed. But I for one still prefer to look out of windows and see futuristic nuts and bolts and the occasional bug-eyed monster rather than the strange shifting phantasms which you see up and down the new Fantasy Alley. (I am composing a reading list for you, incidentally. I shall send it under separate cover. An informed visitor to the City of Invention has a better time there than the naive and hopeful.)

Romance Alley is of course a charming place, as your mother, I am sure, will tell you. It's a boom town, too. The suburbs are increasingly popular for visitors who need time off from their own lives. (You don't need to know anything about the rest of the City to visit here. Enough to be naive and hopeful.) And it really is a pretty place. Everything is lavender-tinted, and the cottages have roses round the door, and knights ride by in shining armour, and amazingly beautiful young couples stroll by under the blossoming trees, though *he* perhaps has a slightly cruel mouth, and *she* a tendency to swoon.

Jane Austen is reputed to have fainted away when she came home from a walk with her sister, Cassandra, and was told by her mother, "It's all settled. We're moving to Bath." It was the first, they say, she'd heard of it. (Mind you, as I am fond of saying, they'll say anything!) She was twenty-five; she had lived all her life in the Vicarage at Steventon: her father, without notifying anyone, had decided to retire, and thought that Bath was as pleasant a place as any to go. None of us fainted the day my father came home and told my mother, my sister and myself that he was leaving us that day to live for ever with his sweetheart, whose existence he'd never hinted at before. What are we to make of that? That swooning has gone out of fashion? Or that a later female generation has become inured, by reason of a literature increasingly related to the realities of life, to male surprises? Jane Austen's books are studded with fathers indifferent to their families' (in particular their daughters') welfare, male whims taking priority, then as now, over female happiness. She observes it: she does not condemn. She chides women for their raging vanity, their infinite capacity for self-deception, their idleness, their rapaciousness and folly; men, on the whole, she simply accepts. This may be another of the reasons her books are so socially acceptable in those sections of society least open to change. Women are accustomed to criticism; to being berated, in fiction, for their faults. Men are, quite simply, not. They like to be heroes.

That is quite enough of this letter. If I write too much at any one time the personal keeps intruding, and I am writing a letter of literary advice to a young lady, albeit a niece, on first reading Jane Austen, not a diatribe on the world's insensitivity to her aunt's various misfortunes, or the hard time women have at the hands of men: a fact liberally attested to up and down the streets of the City of Invention.   *380*

Alice, I see in your postscript, to my alarm, that you plan to write a novel as soon as you have the time. I sincerely hope you do *not* find the time, for some years to come, for reasons I will go into if and when you reply to this letter, but to do with your age and your apparent unacquaintance with the City of Invention. If you plan to build here, you *must* know the city. I comfort myself that to do a course in English Literature *and* to   *385* accomplish any serious writing of your own are commonly held to be mutually exclusive. We know you are doing the one, so the other seems (thank God) unlikely, at least for the time being.

With best wishes,   *390*
Aunt Fay
(1984)

FLEUR ADCOCK
New Zealand/England, b.1934

FOR A FIVE-YEAR-OLD

A snail is climbing up the window-sill
Into your room, after a night of rain.
You call me in to see, and I explain
That it would be unkind to leave it there:
It might crawl to the floor; we must take care   5
That no one squashes it. You understand,
And carry it outside, with careful hand,
To eat a daffodil.

I see, then, that a kind of faith prevails:
Your gentleness is moulded still by words   10
From me, who have trapped mice and shot wild birds,
From me, who drowned your kittens, who betrayed
Your closest relatives, and who purveyed
The harshest kind of truth to many another.
But that is how things are: I am your mother,   15
And we are kind to snails.

(1964)

DAVID MALOUF
Australia, b.1934

THE KYOGLE LINE

In July 1944, when train travel was still romantic, and hourly flights had not yet telescoped the distance between Brisbane and Sydney to a fifty-five minute interval of air-conditioned vistas across a tumble of slow-motion foam, we set out, my parents, my sister and I, on the first trip of my life — that is how I thought of it — that would take

me over a border. We left from Kyogle Station, just a hundred yards from where we   *5*
lived, on a line that was foreign from the moment you embarked on it, since it ran only
south out of the state and had a gauge of four-foot-eight. Our own Queensland lines
were three-foot-six and started from Roma Street Station on the other side of the river.

I was familiar with all this business of gauges and lines from school, where our
complicated railway system, and its origins in the jealously guarded sovereignty of our   *10*
separate states, was part of our lessons and of local lore, but also because, for all the
years of my later childhood, I had seen transports pass our house ferrying troops across
the city from one station to the other, on their way to Townsville and the far north. We
lived in a strip of no-man's-land between lines; or, so far as the thousands of Allied
troops were concerned, between safe, cosmopolitan Sydney and the beginning, at Roma   *15*
Street, of their passage to the war.

Our own journey was for a two weeks' stay at the Balfour Hotel at the corner of
King and Elizabeth Streets, Sydney. The owner was an old mate of my father's, which is
why, in wartime, with all hotel rooms occupied, we had this rare chance of accommodation. Train bookings too were hard to come by. We would sit up for sixteen hours   *20*
straight — maybe more, since the line was used for troop movements. I was delighted. It
meant I could stay up all night. Staying awake past midnight was also, in its way, a
border to be crossed.

I had been many times to see people off on the "First Division," and loved the old-
fashioned railway compartments with their foliated iron racks for luggage, their polished   *25*
woodwork, the spotty black-and-white pictures of Nambucca Heads or the Warrumbungles, and the heavy brocade that covered the seats and was hooked in swags at the
windows. When we arrived to claim our seats, people were already crammed into the
corridor, some of them preparing to stand all the way. There were soldiers in winter
uniform going on leave with long khaki packs, pairs of gum-chewing girls with bangles   *30*
and pompadours, women with small kids already snotty or smelly with wet pants,
serious men in felt hats and double-breasted suits. The afternoon as we left was dry and
windy, but hot in the compartment. It was still officially winter. When the sun went
down it would be cold.

My mother would spend the journey knitting. She was, at that time, engaged in   *35*
making dressing-gowns, always of the same pattern and in the same mulberry-coloured
nine-ply, for almost everyone she knew. There was rationing, but no coupons were
needed for wool. I had been taught to knit at school and my mother let me do the belts
— I had already made nine or ten of them — but was waiting because I didn't want to
miss the border and the view.   *40*

What I was hungry for was some proof that the world was as varied as I wanted it
to be; that somewhere, on the far side of what I knew, difference began, and that the
point could be clearly recognised.

The view did change, and frequently, but not suddenly or sharply enough. It was a
matter of geological forms I couldn't read, new variants of eucalypt and pine. The   *45*
journey from this point of view was a failure, though I wouldn't admit it. I stayed

---

THE KYOGLE LINE   **26. Nambucca Heads:** on the northern New South Wales coast. **26-27. Warrumbungles:** mountains in the interior of
New South Wales.

excited and let my own vivid expectations colour the scene. Besides, it wasn't a fair test. We had barely passed the border when it was dark. It did get perceptibly colder. But was that a crossing into a new climate zone or just the ordinary change from day to night? The train rocked and sped, then jolted and stopped for interminable periods in a ring- 50 barked nowhere; then jerked and clashed and started up again. We saw lights away in the darkness, isolated farmhouses or settlements suggesting that some of the space we were passing through was inhabited. We got grimy with smuts.

My mother knitted, even after the lights were lowered and other people had curled up under blankets. I too kept wide awake. I was afraid, as always, of missing something 55 — the one thing that might happen or appear, that was the thing I was intended not to miss. If I did, a whole area of my life would be closed to me for ever.

So I was still awake, not long after midnight, when we pulled into Coff's Harbour and the train stopped to let people get off and walk for a bit, or buy tea at the refreshment room. 60

"Can *we*?" I pleaded. "Wouldn't you like a nice cup of tea, Mummy? I could get it." My mother looked doubtful.

"It wouldn't do any harm," my father said, "to have a bit of a stretch."

"I need to go to the lav," I threw in, just to clinch the thing. It had been difficult to make your way through standing bodies and over sleeping ones to the cubicles at either 65 end of the carriage. The last time we went we had had to step over a couple, one of them a soldier, who were doing something under a blanket. My father, who was modest, had been shocked.

"Come on then." We climbed down.

It was a clear cold night and felt excitingly different, fresher than I had ever known, 70 with a clean smell of dark bushland sweeping away under stars to the escarpments of the Great Divide. People, some of them in dressing-gowns and carrying thermos flasks, were bustling along the platform. The train hissed and clanged. It was noisy; but the noise rose straight up into the starry night as if the air here were thinner, offered no resistance. It felt sharp in your lungs. 75

We passed a smoky waiting-room where soldiers were sprawled in their greatcoats, some on benches, others on the floor, their rifles in stacks against the wall; then the refreshment room with its crowded bar. It was a long walk to the Men's, all the length of the platform. I had never been out after midnight, and I expected it to be stranger. It *was* strange but not strange enough. In some ways the most different thing of all was to 80 be taking a walk like this with my father.

We were shy of one another. He had always worked long hours, and like most children in those days I spent my time on the edge of my mother's world, always half-excluded but half-involved as well. My father's world was foreign to me. He disap-peared into it at six o'clock, before my sister and I were up, and came back again at tea- 85 time, not long before we were packed off to bed. If we went down under-the-house on Saturdays to watch him work, with a stub of indelible pencil behind his ear, as some men wear cigarettes, it was to enter a world of silence there that belonged to his deep

---

58. **Coff's Harbour:** in northern New South Wales. 72. **Great Divide:** the mountain range that runs the length of the eastern side of Australia.

communication with measurements, and tools, and dove-tail joints that cast us back on our own capacity for invention.

90

He was not much of a talker, our father. He seldom told us things unless we asked. Then he would answer our questions too carefully, as if he feared, with his own lack of schooling, that he might lead us wrong. And he never told stories, as our mother did, of his family and youth. His family were there to be seen, and however strange they might be in fact, did not lend themselves to fairytale. My father had gone out to work at twelve. If he never spoke of his youth it was, perhaps, because he had never had one, or because its joys and sorrows were of a kind we could not be expected to understand. There was no grand house to remember, as my mother remembered New Cross; no favourite maids; no vision of parents sweeping into the nursery to say goodnight in all the ballroom finery of leg o'mutton sleeves and pearl combs and shirt-fronts stiff as boards. His people were utterly ordinary. The fact that they were also *not* Australian, that they ate garlic and oil, smelled different, and spoke no English, was less important than that they had always been there and had to be taken as they were. Our father himself was as Australian as anyone could be — except for the name. He had made himself so. He had played football for the State, and was one of the toughest welter-weights of his day, greatly admired for his fairness and skill by an entire generation.

But all this seemed accidental in him. A teetotaller and non-smoker, very quiet in manner, fastidiously modest, he had an inner life that was not declared. He had educated himself in the things that most interested him, but his way of going about them was his own; he had worked the rules out for himself. He suffered from never having been properly schooled, and must, I see now, have hidden deep hurts and humiliations under his studied calm. The best he could do with me was to make me elaborate playthings — box-kites, a three-foot yacht — and, for our backyard, a magnificent set of swings. My extravagance, high-strung fantasies, which my mother tended to encourage, intimidated him. He would have preferred me to become, as he had, a more conventional type. He felt excluded by my attachment to books.

So this walk together was in all ways unusual, not just because we were taking it at midnight in New South Wales.

We walked in silence, but with a strong sense, on my part at least, of our being together and at one. I liked my father. I wished he would talk to me and tell me things. I didn't know him. He puzzled me, as it puzzled me too that my mother, who was so down on our speaking or acting "Australian," should be so fond of these things as they appeared, in their gentler form, in him. She had made, in his case, a unique dispensation.

On our way back from the Men's we found ourselves approaching a place where the crowd, which was generally very mobile, had stilled, forming a bunch round one of the goods wagons.

"What is it?" I wanted to know.

"What is it?" my father asked another fellow when we got close. We couldn't see anything.

"Nips," the man told us. "Bloody Nips. They got three Jap P.O.W.'s in there."

I expected my father to move away then, to move me on. If he does, I thought, I'll get lost. I wanted to see them.

But my father stood, and we worked our way into the centre of the crowd; and as people stepped away out of it we were drawn to the front, till we stood staring in through the door of a truck. 135

It was too big to be thought of as a cage, but was a cage, just the same. I thought of the circus wagons that sometimes came and camped in the little park beside South Brisbane Station, or on the waste ground under Grey Street Bridge.

There was no straw, no animal smell. The three Japs, in a group, if not actually chained then at least huddled, were difficult to make out in the half-dark. But looking in 140 at them was like looking in from our own minds, our own lives, on another species. The vision imposed silence on the crowd. Only when they broke the spell by moving away did they mutter formulas, "Bloody Japs," or "The bastards," that were meant to express what was inexpressible, the vast gap of darkness they felt existed here — a distance between people that had nothing to do with actual space, or the fact that you were 145 breathing, out here in the still night of Australia, the same air. The experience was an isolating one. The moment you stepped out of the crowd and the shared sense of being part of it, you were alone.

My father felt it. As we walked away he was deeply silent. Our moment together was over. What was it that touched him? Was he thinking of a night, three years before, 150 when the Commonwealth Police had arrested his father as an enemy alien?

My grandfather came to Brisbane from Lebanon in the 1880s; though in those days of course, when Australia was still unfederated, a parcel of rival states, Lebanon had no existence except in the mind of a few patriots. It was part of greater Syria; itself then a province of the great, sick Empire of the Turks. My grandfather had fled his homeland 155 in the wake of a decade of massacres. Like other Lebanese Christians, he had sorrowfully turned his back on the Old Country and started life all over again in the New World.

His choice of Australia was an arbitrary one. No one knows why he made it. He might equally have gone to Boston or to Sao Paolo in Brazil. But the choice, once made, 160 was binding. My father and the rest of us were Australians now. That was that. After Federation, in the purely notional view of these things that was practised by the immigration authorities, greater Syria (as opposed to Egypt and Turkey proper) was declared white — but only the Christian inhabitants of it, a set of official decisions, in the matter of boundary and distinction, that it was better not to question. My father's 165 right to be an Australian, like any Scotsman's for example, was guaranteed by this purely notional view — that is, officially. The rest he had to establish for himself; most often with his fists. But my grandfather, by failing to get himself naturalised, remained an alien. At first a Syrian, later a Lebanese. And when Lebanon, as a dependency of France, declared for Vichy rather than the Free French, he became an enemy as well. 170

He was too old, at more than eighty, to be much concerned by any of this, and did not understand perhaps how a political decision made on the other side of the world had changed his status, after so long, on this one. He took the bag my aunts packed for him and went. It was my father who was, in his quiet way — what? — shaken, angered, disillusioned? 175

---

151. **Commonwealth:** i.e., the Commonwealth of Australia. 162. **Federation:** in 1901. 170. **Vichy:** i.e., the government set up by Marshal Pétain in 1940, collaborating with the Germans who occupied France during World War II.

The authorities — that is, the decent local representatives — soon recognised the absurdity of the thing and my grandfather was released: on personal grounds. My father never told us how he had managed it, or what happened, what he *felt*, when he went to fetch his father home. If it changed anything for him, the colour of his own history for example, he did not reveal it. It was just another of the things he kept to himself and buried. Like the language. He must, I understood later, have grown up speaking Arabic as well as he spoke Australian; his parents spoke little else. But I never heard him utter a word of it or give any indication that he understood. It went on as a whole layer of his experience, of his understanding and feeling for things, of alternative being, that could never be expressed. It too was part of the shyness between us. 185

We got my mother her nice cup of tea, and five minutes later, in a great bustle of latecomers and shouts and whistles, the train started up again and moved deeper into New South Wales. But I thought of it now as changed. Included in its string of lighted carriages, along with the sleeping soldiers and their packs and slouch-hats with sunbursts on the turn-up, the girls with their smeared lipstick and a wad of gum 190 hardening now under a rim of the carriage-work, the kids blowing snotty bubbles, the men in business suits, was that darker wagon with the Japs.

Their presence imposed silence. That had been the first reaction. But what it provoked immediately after was some sort of inner argument or dialogue that was in a language I couldn't catch. It had the rhythm of the train wheels over those foreign four- 195 foot-eight inch rails — a different sound from the one our own trains made — and it went on even when the train stalled and waited, and long after we had come to Sydney and the end of our trip. It was, to me, as if I had all the time been on a different train from the one I thought. Which would take more than the sixteen hours the timetable announced and bring me at last to a different, unnameable destination. 200

(1985)

WOLE SOYINKA

Nigeria, b.1934

TELEPHONE CONVERSATION

The price seemed reasonable, location
Indifferent. The landlady swore she lived
Off premises. Nothing remained
But self-confession. "Madam," I warned,
"I hate a wasted journey — I am — African." 5
Silence. Silenced transmission of
Pressurized good-breeding. Voice, when it came,
Lipstick-coated, long gold-rolled
Cigarette-holder pipped. Caught I was, foully.
"HOW DARK?" . . . I had not misheard . . . "ARE YOU LIGHT 10

OR VERY DARK?" Button B. Button A. Stench
Of rancid breath of public-hide-and-speak.
Red booth. Red pillar-box. Red doubled-tiered
Omnibus squelching tar. It *was* real! Shamed
By ill-mannered silence, surrender   15
Pushed dumbfoundment to beg simplification.
Considerate she was, varying the emphasis —
"ARE YOU DARK? OR VERY LIGHT?" Revelation came.
"You mean — like plain or milk chocolate?"
Her assent was clinical, crushing in its light   20
Impersonality. Rapidly, wavelength adjusted,
I chose, "West African sepia" — and as an afterthought,
"Down in my passport." Silence for spectroscopic
Flight of fancy, till truthfulness clanged her accent
Hard on the mouthpiece. "WHAT'S THAT?" conceding   25
"DON'T KNOW WHAT THAT IS." "Like brunette."
"THAT'S DARK, ISN'T IT?" "Not altogether.
Facially, I am brunette, but madam, you should see
The rest of me. Palm of my hand, soles of my feet
Are a peroxide blond. Friction, caused —   30
Foolishly, madam — by sitting down, has turned
My bottom raven black — One moment, madam!" — sensing
Her receiver rearing on the thunder clap
About my ears — "Madam," I pleaded, "Wouldn't you rather
See for yourself?"   35

                                                            (1960)

CHRIS WALLACE-CRABBE
Australia, b.1934

Appearance and Reality

Higgledy-piggledy
Homo Neanderthal
Coming from crowded caves
Onto the scene

Viewed all the countryside   5
Anthropomorphically —
Rather surrealist,
That must have been.

                                (1966)

1066

Higgledy-piggledy
William the Conqueror
Landed at Pevensey,
Solid and sly,

Thickened the native tongue   5
Polysyllabically,
Gave to the monarchy
One in the eye.

                                (1966)

TELEPHONE CONVERSATION   **11. Button B, Button A:** the coin-return and call-connect buttons in British public telephone booths of the time.

ZULFIKAR GHOSE
India [Pakistan]/England/U.S.A., b.1935

ON OWNING PROPERTY IN THE U.S.A.

On my land in the middle of America the wind blows
through the cedar trees and the chickenhawks
stay up in the sky as if they were paid
an hourly wage and the hummingbird throws

its compulsive nervous body from the mimosa   5
to the wisteria and all kinds of other country
things go on and daily I walk on my property
to check the armadillo holes or close a

gap in a fence knowing what happens on this land
is my business with the free blue skies   10
over it and air that in California once
above an orchid's lip held a bee suspended

I've put down nasturtium seeds planted squash
okra and cantaloupe for this summer also

tomatoes and two rows of corn some beans   15
and trimmed the camellia bush

and that's what you'd call pastoral or
bucolic or arcadian and in the nature
of things universal and eternal having
roots and the right kind of image in the lore   20

of the land that from Tennessee west
is strummed out on banjo and guitar
were it not for rattlesnakes and spiders
lying in the underbrush and you guessed

it mister I have extermination problems   25
and must simultaneously poison and preserve
such are the country's contradictions and
such the ambiguity of all dreams.

(1974, 1984)

MARY OLIVER
U.S.A., b.1935

O PIONEERS

Headed through wilderness to found a nation,
They dreamed of farms and easy sleep,
And kept their powder dry, and talked with God,
And shed the cloth of England for the buckskin,
And carved new habits for their sons to keep.   5

Yea, for the Lord's sake, and for their unborn sons,
They strode across the continent, and took
The rivers and the forest and the prairie
And spun them into farms, and bore strong children
Between the musket and the old prayer book.   10

Maybe in earth, shaped into roots, they lie.
Or maybe, met in Heaven with their sons,
Lean down, peer back, to where America
Glitters and roars and suffers what she is —
A land built step by step with God and guns.   15

(1972)

GOING TO WALDEN

It isn't very far as highways lie.
I might be back by nightfall, having seen
The rough pines, and the stones, and the clear water.
Friends argue that I might be wiser for it.
They do not hear that far-off Yankee whisper: 5
How dull we grow from hurrying here and there!

Many have gone, and think me half a fool
To miss a day away in the cool country.
Maybe. But in a book I read and cherish,
Going to Walden is not so easy a thing   10
As a green visit. It is the slow and difficult
Trick of living, and finding it where you are.

(1972)

O PIONEERS Title: the title of a 1913 novel by Willa Cather (1876-1947); the poem may also allude to Walt Whitman's poem "Pioneers! O Pioneers!" **GOING TO WALDEN** See also the excerpt from Thoreau's *Walden* (p. 1006).

LUCILLE CLIFTON
U.S.A., b.1936

LUCY AND HER GIRLS

lucy is the ocean
extended by
her girls
are the river
fed by   5
lucy
is the sun
reflected through
her girls

are the moon   10
lighted by
lucy
is the history of
her girls
are the place where   15
lucy
was going
(1980)

DARYL HINE
Canada/U.S.A., b.1936

RALEIGH'S LAST VOYAGE

After the departure from the guarded quay
Under sentence of return, not "trusty and well loved,"
Though from my hands and feet the chains had been
    removed
My mind, my heart, my spirit were not free.
So I set out upon the sea,   5
The hardly serious ocean which has proved
A Circe to so many. South and west we moved
And the name of that embarkation was the Golden Vanity.

Touched by a land wind our sails of silk and cotton
Filled in the sun, fold upon hopeful fold.   10
Cargo hulks with nothing in the hold,
Our ships were mortgaged, more than half rotten.

Yet has disappointment long begotten
In a captive, sad, suspect and old
For a country, Eldorado, of which he has been told   15
A love obscured but cannot be forgotten.

But can a love so dolorous be good?
Somewhere in the doldrums fever among the men
Established the empery of boredom, fear and pain,
A reign of spleen before an age of blood,   20
Till waited on by sickness the commander could
Not come on deck to greet the sight of land again.
And then contrary winds and then a hurricane.
Praised be that force by which she moves the flood.

RALEIGH'S LAST VOYAGE   See the excerpts from Ralegh's *Discovery of Guiana* (p. 170), *History of the World* (p. 174), and his letters from prison (p. 181). **2. "trusty . . . loved":** a conventional phrase, from monarch to subject, used in such documents as charters to explore and exploit "new" territory. **7. Circe:** the temptress in Homer's *Odyssey* (cf. the notes to Pound's *Canto I*, p. 1293). **8. Golden Vanity:** the title of an English folksong about a ship that was sunk by the Spanish; Ralegh, in 1595, had heard of an El Dorado, a fabulous gold mine, somewhere in the upper reaches of the Caroni River in Guiana, but his tale was not believed when he returned to England, which ultimately led to his unsuccessful return voyage in 1617.

Where into the blue the brown water drops   *25*
We anchored at the Orinoco mouth
And saw on either hand a rotting growth
Of roots and broad leaves and branches and tree tops,
Tendrils twined like snakes and snakes hung down in
   ropes,
Bright as angels, shrill as demons both.   *30*
A fountain flowing from the gaudy south
And heaps of snow from off the mountain tops.

At San Tomé we had an embarrassing victory.
The citadel once taken proved awkward to defend
Against the besieged become besiegers. All we gained   *35*
We lost in ambush on each daily foray.
In our dreams the mine shrunk to a quarry
Like affection which becomes indifference in a friend
Or seeking hiding. There the tale should end
But I must prove the example in love's story.   *40*

For when I thought that there could be no more,
After a night of mutiny and the captain's suicide,
I learned my dear, my only son had died
In an unwatched skirmish on an unwanted shore.
Like one who sees swing to the prison door   *45*
On the whole world locking him inside
To my only listeners, cold walls, I cried,
God knows I never knew what sorrow was before.

The days grow shorter with the darkening year.
An adventurer's life is but a barren stalk.   *50*
The History of the World ends with the Prisoner's Walk
Though far and wide it seemed, and various and queer.
At the fall of the afternoon you brought me here,
To shew me the axe, the headsman and the block.
Though you torture the dumb with silence you cannot
   make them talk.   *55*
Only the dead have nothing left to fear.

                          (1965)

Marge Piercy
U.S.A., b.1936

THE MARKET ECONOMY

Suppose some peddler offered
you can have a color TV
but your baby will be
born with a crooked spine;
you can have polyvinyl cups   *5*
and wash and wear
suits but it will cost
you your left lung
rotted with cancer; suppose
somebody offered you   *10*
a frozen precooked dinner
every night for ten years
but at the end
your colon dies
and then you do,   *15*
slowly and with much pain.

You get a house in the suburbs
but you work in a new plastics
factory and die at fifty-two
when your kidneys turn off.   *20*
But where else will you
work? where else can
you rent but Smog City?
The only houses for sale
are under the yellow sky.   *25*
You've been out of work for
a year and they're hiring
at the plastics factory.
Don't read the fine
print, there isn't any.   *30*

                     (1978)

---

33. San Tomé: San Tomás, a Spanish settlement on the Cayenne River in Guiana, which in 1617 Ralegh's men had to pass on their way to the gold mine they were seeking; their attack on the settlement was only superficially successful — Ralegh himself was ill, and could not accompany his crew; his son Walter was killed; and the Spanish withdrew into the hills, becoming a guerilla force that quickly forced the English to abandon their plans.

GILLIAN CLARKE
Wales, b.1937

BLAEN CWRT

You ask how it is. I will tell you.
There is no glass. The air spins in
The stone rectangle. We warm our hands
With apple wood. Some of the smoke
Rises against the ploughed, brown field   5
As a sign to our neighbours in the
Four folds of the valley that we are in.
Some of the smoke seeps through the stones
Into the barn where it curls like fern
On the walls. Holding a thick root   10
I press my bucket through the surface
Of the water, lift it brimming and skim
The leaves away. Our fingers curl on
Enamel mugs of tea, like ploughmen.
The stones clear in the rain   15
Giving their colours. It's not easy.

There are no brochure blues or boiled sweet
Reds. All is ochre and earth and cloud-green
Nettles tasting sour and the smells of moist
Earth and sheep's wool. The wattle and daub   20
Chimney hood has decayed away, slowly
Creeping to dust, chalking the slate
Floor with stories. It has all the first
Necessities for a high standard
Of civilised living: silence inside   25
A circle of sound, water and fire,
Light on uncountable miles of mountain
From a big, unpredictable sky,
Two rooms, waking and sleeping,
Two languages, two centuries of past   30
To ponder on, and the basic need
To work hard in order to survive.

(1978)

TONY HARRISON
England, b.1937

THEM & [UZ]
for Professors Richard Hoggart & Leon Cortez

I
αἰαῖ, ay, ay! . . . stutterer Demosthenes
gob full of pebbles outshouting seas —

4 words only of *mi 'art aches* and . . . "Mine's broken,
you barbarian, T.W.!" *He* was nicely spoken.
"Can't have our glorious heritage done to death!"   5
I played the Drunken Porter in *Macbeth*.

"Poetry's the speech of kings. You're one of those
Shakespeare gives the comic bits to: prose!
All poetry (even Cockney Keats?) you see
's been dubbed by [ʌs] into RP,   10
Received Pronunciation, please believe [ʌs]
your speech is in the hands of the Receivers."

"We say [ʌs] not [uz], T.W.!" That shut my trap.

THEM & [UZ]   **1.** αἰαῖ: (Greek) exclamation of grief (see note to line 106 of Milton's *Lycidas*, p. 317); **Demosthenes:** 4th century B.C. Athenian orator, who practised elocution by speaking while his mouth was full of pebbles. **3.** *mi 'art aches*: See Keats's "Ode to a Nightingale" (p. 854). **4. T.W.:** The poet's 1964 volume *Earthworks* was published under the name "T.W. Harrison." **10.** [ʌs]: As with [uz] (title and line 13), the brackets frame symbols drawn from the International Phonetic Alphabet, and here record the Received Standard pronunciation of the word *us*, in contrast with the pronunciation [uz]; **RP:** Received Pronunciation, i.e., the dialect of English that has customarily been granted most prestige in Britain — that which is espoused by English "public schools" and the Establishment in general.

I doffed my flat a's (as in "flat cap")
my mouth all stuffed with glottals, great   *15*
lumps to hawk up and spit out . . . *E-nun-ci-ate*!

II
So right, yer buggers, then! We'll occupy
your lousy leasehold Poetry.

I chewed up Littererchewer and spat the bones
into the lap of dozing Daniel Jones,   *20*
dropped the initials I'd been harried as
and used my *name* and own voice: [uz][uz][uz],
ended sentences with by, with, from,
and spoke the language that I spoke at home.
RIP RP, RIP T.W.   *25*
I'm *Tony* Harrison no longer you!

You can tell the Receivers where to go
(and not aspirate it) once you know
Wordsworth's *matter*/*water* are full rhymes,
[uz] can be loving as well as funny.   *30*

My first mention in the *Times*
automatically made Tony Anthony!

(1981)

MERVYN MORRIS
Jamaica, b.1937

A VOYAGE

"Beware, beware their evil song:
they eat your flesh,
they bleach your bones,
you won't last long."

His vessel neared an island.   *5*
Shimmering calm. Air still.
Enthralling song
across the green sea floating

paralysed his will.

O heaven within his reach,   *10*
he felt. And swam for shore.

His fortune waited, lolling on the beach.

(1979)

26. you: possibly a pun on "U" (meaning "upper class") as opposed to "non-U."

L‾ES M‾URRAY
Australia, b.1938

THE QUALITY OF SPRAWL

Sprawl is the quality
of the man who cut down his Rolls-Royce
into a farm utility truck, and sprawl
is what the company lacked when it made repeated efforts
to buy the vehicle back and repair its image.   5

Sprawl is doing your farming by aeroplane, roughly,
or driving a hitchhiker that extra hundred miles home.
It is the rococo of being your own still centre.
It is never lighting cigars with ten-dollar notes:
that's idiot ostentation and murder of starving people.   10
Nor can it be bought with the ash of million-dollar deeds.

Sprawl lengthens the legs; it trains greyhounds on liver and beer.
Sprawl almost never says Why not? with palms comically raised
nor can it be dressed for, not even in running shoes worn
with mink and a nose ring. That is Society. That's Style.   15
Sprawl is more like the thirteenth banana in a dozen
or anyway the fourteenth.

Sprawl is Hank Stamper in Never Give an Inch
bisecting an obstructive official's desk with a chain saw.
Not harming the official. Sprawl is never brutal   20
though it's often intransigent. Sprawl is never Simon de Montfort
at a town-storming: Kill them all! God will know his own.
Knowing the man's name this was said to might be sprawl.

Sprawl occurs in art. The fifteenth to twenty-first
lines in a sonnet, for example. And in certain paintings;   25
I have sprawl enough to have forgotten which paintings.
Turner's glorious Burning of the Houses of Parliament
comes to mind, a doubling bannered triumph of sprawl —
except, he didn't fire them.

Sprawl gets up the nose of many kinds of people   30
(every kind that comes in kinds) whose futures don't include it.
Some decry it as criminal presumption, silken-robed Pope Alexander

---

THE QUALITY OF SPRAWL   **18. Never Give an Inch:** TV title given to the 1971 film version of Ken Kesey's 1964 novel *Sometimes a Great Notion* about Oregon loggers; "Never Give an Inch" is the phrase that the character Hank Stamper paints over the Beatitude printed on a plaque his father gives him: "Blessed are the meek, for they shall inherit the earth" (see p. 251). **21. Simon de Montfort:** French nobleman (c.1160-1218) who laid waste much of southern France in a religious war against the Albigensians; father of Simon de Montfort (c.1208-1265), Earl of Leicester, who fought with King Henry III in a civil war. **27. Turner:** J.M.W. Turner (1775-1851), English painter. **32. Pope Alexander:** Alexander VI (1431-1503), a pope of the Borgia family, who in 1494 drew the line that demarcated the Portuguese and Spanish Empires.

dividing the new world between Spain and Portugal.
If he smiled *in petto* afterwards, perhaps the thing did have sprawl.

Sprawl is really classless, though. It's John Christopher Frederick Murray   35
asleep in his neighbours' best bed in spurs and oilskins
but not having thrown up:
sprawl is never Calum who, in the loud hallway of our house,
reinvented the Festoon. Rather
it's Beatrice Miles going twelve hundred ditto in a taxi,   40
No Lewd Advances, No Hitting Animals, No Speeding,
on the proceeds of her two-bob-a-sonnet Shakespeare readings.
An image of my country. And would that it were more so.

No, sprawl is full-gloss murals on a council-house wall.
Sprawl leans on things. It is loose-limbed in its mind.   45
Reprimanded and dismissed
it listens with a grin and one boot up on the rail
of possibility. It may have to leave the Earth.
Being roughly Christian, it scratches the other cheek
and thinks it unlikely. Though people have been shot for sprawl.   50

(1983)

KEN SMITH
England, b.1938

PERSISTENT NARRATIVE

The speaker opens his mouth.
The lovers lie down together.
The boy is sent to the war.

The last train leaves the city.
The sky clouds over with ruin.   5
The animals step back into shadow.

The speaker opens his mouth.
The fields are trampled by horses.
Children crouch in the ashes.

Survivors wait at the frontier.   10
Two armies meet in a forest.
The lovers take off their clothes.

The speaker opens his mouth.
An earthquake topples the belltower.
The boy lies down in a cornfield.   15

Soldiers patrol all the streets.
The grocer has run out of flour.
The girl dreams of a wheatfield.

The speaker opens his mouth.
Now the woman sweeps out her house.   20
Now there is a christening.

The ship enters the harbour.
The girl waves her red scarf.
The lovers cry out in their love.

And at last it is still.   25
And the speaker says *I shall begin.*
The children are all asleep.

(1971)

---

34. in petto: (Latin) to himself (literally "in one's own breast"). **35. John . . . Murray:** the poet's Scottish grandfather. **38. Calum:** the poet's cousin. **39. reinvented the Festoon:** threw up (Australian working-class slang). **40. Beatrice Miles:** an eccentric Sydney character, famous among other things for her taxi rides; Kate Grenville's novel *Lilian's Story* (1985) is loosely based on her life. **42. bob:** shilling. **44. council-house:** public housing.

MARGARET ATWOOD
Canada, b.1939

from *THE JOURNALS OF SUSANNA MOODIE*

Further Arrivals

After we had crossed the long illness
that was the ocean, we sailed up-river

On the first island
the immigrants threw off their clothes
and danced like sandflies   5

We left behind one by one
the cities rotting with cholera,
one by one our civilized
distinctions

and entered a large darkness.   10

It was our own
ignorance we entered.

I have not come out yet

My brain gropes nervous
tentacles in the night, sends out   15
fears hairy as bears,
demands lamps; or waiting

for my shadowy husband, hears
malice in the trees' whispers.

First Neighbours

The people I live among, unforgivingly
previous to me, grudging
the way I breathe their
property, the air,
speaking a twisted dialect to my differently-   5
shaped ears

though I tried to adapt

(the girl in a red tattered
petticoat, who jeered at me for my burned bread

Go back where you came from   10

I tightened my lips; knew that England
was now unreachable, had sunk down into the sea
without ever teaching me about washtubs)

got used to being
a minor invalid, expected to make   15
inept remarks,
futile and spastic gestures

(asked the Indian
about the squat thing on a stick
drying by the fire: Is that a toad?   20
Annoyed, he said No no,
deer liver, very good)

Finally I grew a chapped tarpaulin
skin; I negotiated the drizzle
of strange meaning, set it   25
down to just the latitude:
something to be endured
but not surprised by.

Inaccurate. The forest can still trick me:
one afternoon while I was drawing   30
birds, a malignant face
flickered over my shoulder;
the branches quivered.

Resolve: to be both tentative and hard to startle
(though clumsiness and   35
fright are inevitable)

in this area where my damaged
knowing of the language means
prediction is forever impossible

The Planters

They move between the jagged edge
of the forest and the jagged river
on a stumpy patch of cleared land

THE JOURNALS OF SUSANNA MOODIE   See the excerpt from Moodie's *Roughing It in the Bush* (p. 919).

my husband, a neighbour, another man
weeding the few rows   *5*
of string beans and dusty potatoes.

They bend, straighten; the sun
lights up their faces and hands, candles
flickering in the wind against the

unbright earth. I see them; I know   *10*
none of them believe they are here.
They deny the ground they stand on,

pretend this dirt is the future.
And they are right. If they let go
of that illusion solid to them as a shovel,   *15*

open their eyes even for a moment
to these trees, to this particular sun
they would be surrounded, stormed, broken

in upon by branches, roots, tendrils, the dark
side of light   *20*
as I am.

The Two Fires
One, the summer fire
outside: the trees melting, returning
to their first red elements
on all sides, cutting me off
from escape or the saving   *5*
lake

I sat in the house, raised up
between that shapeless raging
and my sleeping children
a charm: concentrate on   *10*
form, geometry, the human
architecture of the house, square
closed doors, proved roofbeams,
the logic of windows

(the children could not be wakened: *15*
in their calm dreaming
the trees were straight and still
had branches and were green)

The other, the winter
fire inside: the protective roof   *20*
shrivelling overhead, the rafters
incandescent, all those corners

and straight lines flaming, the carefully-
made structure
prisoning us in a cage of blazing   *25*
bars
    the children
were awake and crying;

I wrapped them, carried them
outside into the snow.   *30*
Then I tried to rescue
what was left of their scorched dream
about the house: blankets,
warm clothes, the singed furniture
of safety cast away with them   *35*
in a white chaos

Two fires in-
formed me,

(each refuge fails
us; each danger   *40*
becomes a haven)

left charred marks
now around which I
try to grow

                                                        (1970)

VARIATIONS ON THE WORD *LOVE*

This is a word we use to plug
holes with. It's the right size for those warm
blanks in speech, for those red heart-
shaped vacancies on the page that look nothing
like real hearts. Add lace   *5*
and you can sell
it. We insert it also in the one empty
space on the printed form
that comes with no instructions. There are whole
magazines with not much in them   *10*
but the word *love*, you can
rub it all over your body and you
can cook with it too. How do we know
it isn't what goes on at the cool
debaucheries of slugs under damp   *15*
pieces of cardboard? As for the weed-
seedlings nosing their tough snouts up

among the lettuces, they shout it.
Love! Love! sing the soldiers, raising
their glittering knives in salute.   *20*

Then there's the two
of us. This word
is far too short for us, it has only
four letters, too sparse
to fill those deep bare   *25*
vacuums between the stars
that press on us with their deafness.

It's not love we don't wish
to fall into, but that fear.
This word is not enough but it will   *30*
have to do. It's a single
vowel in this metallic
silence, a mouth that says
O again and again in wonder
and pain, a breath, a finger-   *35*
grip on a cliffside. You can
hold on or let go.

                                              (1981)

BILL BISSETT
Canada, b.1939

GRADE SCHOOL IN HALIFAX

well class what happend to yu
during th christmas holidaze thats
uv intrest   sumthing unusual say
bill   what abt yu   stand up   n tell
us   well my mothr got her brest cut   *5*
off in th hospital

BILL how can yu talk filth like that
its th strap agen for yu   ium sorree
abt thees welts on yr hand but its th
onlee way yul lern   *10*

wipe thos teers from yr eyes   yr a
big boy now   yr in grade three   yu
bring all ths on yrself

ths hurts me mor than it duz yu she
sd   i pulld my hand away quik as th   *15*
strap cum pounding down on her knee

n that time it did hurt her mor

thr wer scuff marks on th floor in
front uv her desk   i didint dew it

but th girl who was numbr wun on th   *20*
honor roll   i was onlee seventh or
eighth but for a boy mooving up tho
i didint want to   she sd i did it   n
i got strappd agen   it was always in
th cloak room   all th swet n wet rubbrs   *25*
mittns   stuffee

so i wud go out in th yard during recess
stand ther   turn round fast   n faint   dont
remembr if th teechr felt compassyun thn

we had a lot uv fire n air drills   sumtimes   *30*
we dansd reels   girls in skirts   guys in
pants   th english took th kilts away long
time ago bfor that   th ground was always
hard whn i wud fall on it   thr was no wun to
talk to abt my mothr   *35*

that was avoidid like th war n othr deths
                                              (1983)

SEAMUS HEANEY
Northern Ireland, b.1939

DIGGING

Between my finger and my thumb
The squat pen rests; snug as a gun.

Under my window, a clean rasping sound
When the spade sinks into gravelly ground:
My father, digging. I look down   5

Till his straining rump among the flowerbeds
Bends low, comes up twenty years away
Stooping in rhythm through potato drills
Where he was digging.

The coarse boot nestled on the lug, the shaft   10
Against the inside knee was levered firmly.
He rooted out tall tops, buried the bright edge deep
To scatter new potatoes that we picked
Loving their cool hardness in our hands.

By God, the old man could handle a spade.   15
Just like his old man.

My grandfather cut more turf in a day
Than any other man on Toner's bog.
Once I carried him milk in a bottle
Corked sloppily with paper. He straightened up   20
To drink it, then fell to right away

Nicking and slicing neatly, heaving sods
Over his shoulder, going down and down
For the good turf. Digging.

The cold smell of potato mould, the squelch and slap
Of soggy peat, the curt cuts of an edge   26
Through living roots awaken in my head.
But I've no spade to follow men like them.

Between my finger and my thumb
The squat pen rests.
I'll dig with it.   30

(1966)

DENNIS SCOTT
Jamaica, b.1939

GRAMPA

Look him. As quiet as a July river-
bed, asleep, an' trim' down like a tree.
Jesus! I never know the Lord could
squeeze so dry. When I was four
foot small I used to say   5
Grampa, how come you t'in so?
An' him tell me, is so I stay
me chile, is so I stay
laughing, an' fine
emptying on me —   10

laughing? It running from him
like a flood, that old molasses
man. Lord, how I never see?

I never know a man could sweet so, cool
as rain; same way him laugh,   15

I cry now. Wash him. Lay him out.

I know the earth going burn
all him limb dem
as smooth as bone,
clean as a tree under the river   20
skin, an' gather us
beside that distant Shore
bright as a river stone.

(1973)

GRAMPA   **6. t'in:** thin.

JANE FLANDERS
U.S.A., b.1940

LATE REPORT FROM MISS HARRIET ROBINSON'S THIRD GRADE

1. *Waynesboro, Pennsylvania, 1948*

This is the year we start fractions, learn
to cut a pie in any number of pieces,
But Gloria Creager and I can't figure out
how to divide the new boy in class.   5
At recess in bad weather we stay inside
and "Skip to My Lou" around the desks.
She and I fight to dance with Bobby Kribbs.
Sometimes she wins, sometimes I do.
She looks like Shirley Temple but I'm clever.   10
Whenever Miss Robinson has to leave the room,
I'm elected teacher.

                    In our class picture
Miss Robinson, head cocked like a turkey hen,
keeps an eye on us. Gloria looks at Bobby,   15
who stares beyond the borders of the print,
his crew cut pale and thick as a puppy's ruff.
Already he's learned to dodge and feint. (His father
coaches the football team to loss after loss.)
Perhaps he knows they'll soon be leaving town,   20
is dreaming his father's early death, the years
he'll play the game, trying to be his father.

And me? I grin, standing beside him, eyes
closed against the flash or maybe already
a poem flutters behind translucent lids.   25
Over our heads the alphabet unwinds,
tendrils and loops twining around each other
in a script we are just beginning to understand.
This is the year I start to hate Gloria
forever, the year I refuse to wear leggings   30
anymore. A cold wind strokes my thighs;
lifts my skirt and smooths it back down.

2. *Lewisburg, Pennsylvania, 1981*

I am abroad in the world, lose track of everyone,
arrive one day in a place that looks like home   35
to read aloud my poems, my life. Afterwards
someone says, "Were you in Miss Robinson's class?"
He doesn't wax his hair these days, but I know him.
I've always been sure I would. "Bobby Kribbs!
Are you still unattached?" He shakes his head,   40
amused, and then, in the brief space of only
thirty-three years, I see he never loved me,
but raised his eyes by accident from the spelling book,
whirled past windows, chalk boards, closets, dutifully
clutching my sweaty hand.   45

                    How loud I sang
so he would hear my voice above the rest.
"This time," Miss Smith, the music teacher, said,
"I want Jane Hess and Barbara West *not*
to sing." Was Freckle West a rival too?   50
Their names come back: Ronnie Zimmerman, who left
a candy bar on my desk each day (I ate it
too) till his mother got her grocery bill
at the end of the month; Truella Werking, who lost
a nickel and got us all kept in because   55
she said we'd stolen it; Alice and Phyllis Rowe,
whom I dismissed as liars because they claimed
they were twins (one was a midget, for heaven's sake).

For the first time I think of Harriet Robinson
as a woman about my age. I think of Bobby   60
walking home after the reading. It's late.
His daughter's room is dark, but a small light
glows by his wife's bed. She has fallen asleep.
Still, she needs to get under the covers. He rubs
her shoulder and whispers, "Gloria, guess what!"   65

(1982)

LATE REPORT   **7. "Skip to my Lou":** traditional American play song. **10. Shirley Temple:** (b.1928) popular American child filmstar of the 1930s. **33. Lewisburg:** the location of Bucknell University.

STEPHEN JAY GOULD
U.S.A., b.1941

BATHYBIUS AND EOZOON

When Thomas Henry Huxley lost his young son, "our delight and our joy," to scarlet fever, Charles Kingsley tried to console him with a long peroration on the soul's immortality. Huxley, who invented the word "agnostic" to describe his own feelings, thanked Kingsley for his concern, but rejected the proferred comfort for want of evidence. In a famous passage, since taken by many scientists as a motto for proper 5 action, he wrote: "My business is to teach my aspirations to conform themselves to fact, not to try and make facts harmonize with my aspirations. . . . Sit down before fact as a little child, be prepared to give up every preconceived notion, follow humbly wherever and to whatever abysses nature leads, or you shall learn nothing." Huxley's sentiments were noble, his grief affecting. But Huxley did not follow his own dictum, and no 10 creative scientist ever has.

Great thinkers are never passive before facts. They ask questions of nature; they do not follow her humbly. They have hopes and hunches, and they try hard to construct the world in their light. Hence, great thinkers also make great errors.

Biologists have written a long and special chapter in the catalog of major mistakes 15 — imaginary animals that should exist in theory. Voltaire spoke truly when he quipped: "If God did not exist, it would be necessary to invent him." Two related and intersecting chimeras arose during the early days of evolutionary theory — two animals that should have been, by Darwin's criteria, but were not. One of them had Thomas Henry Huxley for a godfather. 20

For most creationists, the gap between living and non-living posed no particular problem. God had simply made the living, fully distinct and more advanced than the rocks and chemicals. Evolutionists sought to close all the gaps. Ernst Haeckel, Darwin's chief defender in Germany and surely the most speculative and imaginative of early evolutionists, constructed hypothetical organisms to span all the spaces. The lowly 25 amoeba could not serve as a model of the earliest life, for its internal differentiation into nucleus and cytoplasm indicated a large advance from primal formlessness. Thus Haeckel proposed a lowlier organism composed only of unorganized protoplasm, the Monera. (In a way, he was right. We use his name today for the kingdom of bacteria and blue green algae, organisms without nucleus or mitochondria — although scarcely 30 formless in Haeckel's sense.)

Haeckel defined his moneran as "an entirely homogeneous and structureless substance, a living particle of albumin, capable of nourishment and reproduction." He

---

BATHYBIUS AND EOZOON   1. Huxley: English biologist (1825-1895), defender of Darwin's theories and author of *Science and Education* (1899); grandfather of the biologist Julian Huxley (1887-1975) and the novelist Aldous Huxley (1894-1963), author of *Brave New World* (1932). **2. Charles Kingsley:** See p. 1018. **16. Voltaire:** French philosopher (1694-1778). **17. If . . . him:** in *Epître à l'auteur du livre des trois imposteurs* (November 10, 1770). **23. Ernst Haeckel:** German biologist (1834-1919), author of *The History of Creation* (1868) and *The Evolution of Man* (1874).

proposed the moneran as an intermediate form between non-living and living. He hoped that it would solve the vexing question of life's origin from the inorganic, for no problem seemed thornier for evolutionists and no issue attracted more rear-guard support for creationism than the apparent gap between the most complex chemicals and the simplest organisms. Haeckel wrote: "Every true cell already shows a division into two different parts, i.e., nucleus and plasm. The immediate production of such an object from spontaneous generation is obviously only conceivable with difficulty; but it is much easier to conceive of the production of an entirely homogeneous, organic substance, such as the structureless albumin body of the Monera." 35 40

During the 1860s, the identification of monerans assumed high priority on the agenda of Darwin's champions. And the more structureless and diffuse the moneran, the better. Huxley had told Kingsley that he would follow facts into a metaphorical abyss. But when he examined a true abyss in 1868, his hopes and expectations guided his observations. He studied some mud samples dredged from the sea bottom northwest of Ireland ten years before. He observed an inchoate, gelatinous substance in the samples. Embedded in it were tiny, circular, calcareous plates called coccoliths. Huxley identified his jelly as the heralded, formless moneran and the coccoliths as its primordial skeleton. (We now know that coccoliths are fragments of algal skeletons, which sink to the ocean bottom following the death of their planktonic producers.) Honoring Haeckel's prediction, he named it *Bathybius Haeckelii*. "I hope that you will not be ashamed of your godchild," he wrote to Haeckel. Haeckel replied that he was "very proud," and ended his note with a rallying cry: "Viva Monera." 45 50 55

Since nothing is quite so convincing as an anticipated discovery, *Bathybius* began to crop up everywhere. Sir Charles Wyville Thomson dredged a sample from the depths of the Atlantic and wrote: "The mud was actually alive; it stuck together in lumps, as if there were white of egg mixed with it; and the glairy mass proved, under the microscope, to be a living sarcode. Prof. Huxley . . . calls it *Bathybius*." (The Sarcodina are a group of single-celled protozoans.) Haeckel, following his usual penchant, soon generalized and imagined that the entire ocean floor (below 5,000 feet) lay covered with a pulsating film of living *Bathybius*, the *Urschleim* (original slime) of the romantic nature philosophers (Goethe was one) idolized by Haeckel during his youth. Huxley, departing from his usual sobriety, delivered a speech in 1870 and proclaimed: "The *Bathybius* formed a living scum or film on the seabed, extending over thousands upon thousands of square miles . . . it probably forms one continuous scum of living matter girding the whole surface of the earth." 60 65

Having reached its limits of extension in space, *Bathybius* oozed out to conquer the only realm left — time. And here it met our second chimera. 70

Eozoon canadense, the dawn animal of Canada, was another organism whose time had come. The fossil record had caused Darwin more grief than joy. Nothing distressed him more than the Cambrian explosion, the coincident appearance of almost all complex organic designs, not near the beginning of the earth's history, but more than five-sixths

---

57. Sir Charles Wyville Thomson: Scottish zoologist (1830-1882), author of *The Depths of the Oceans* (1872). **59. glairy:** viscous, like raw egg white. **60. sarcode:** protoplasm. **64. Goethe:** Johann Wolfgang von Goethe (1749-1832), German poet and dramatist, author of *Faust* (1808, 1832) and of several articles on botany and geology.

of the way through it. His opponents interpreted this event as the moment of creation, 75
for not a single trace of Precambrian life had been discovered when Darwin wrote the
Origin of Species. . . . Nothing could have been more welcome than a Precambrian
organism, the simpler and more formless the better.

In 1858, a collector for the Geological Survey of Canada found some curious
specimens among the world's oldest rocks. They were made of thin, concentric layers, 80
alternating between serpentine (a silicate) and calcium carbonate. Sir William Logan,
director of the Survey, thought that they might be fossils and displayed them to various
scientists, receiving in return little encouragement for his views.

Logan found some better specimens near Ottawa in 1864, and brought them to
Canada's leading paleontologist, J. William Dawson, principal of McGill University. 85
Dawson found "organic" structures, including a system of canals, in the calcite. He
identified the concentric layering as the skeleton of a giant foraminifer, more diffusely
formed but hundreds of times larger than any modern relative. He named it *Eozoon
canadense*, the Canadian dawn animal.

Darwin was delighted. *Eozoon* entered the fourth edition of the *Origin of Species* 90
with Darwin's firm blessing: "It is impossible to feel any doubt regarding its organic
nature." (Ironically, Dawson himself was a staunch creationist, probably the last
prominent holdout against evolution. As late as 1897, he wrote *Relics of Primeval Life*,
a book about *Eozoon*. In it he argues that the persistence of simple Foraminifera
throughout geologic time disproves natural selection since any struggle for existence 95
would replace such lowly creatures with something more exalted.)

Bathybius and *Eozoon* were destined for union. They shared the desired property of
diffuse formlessness and differed only in *Eozoon*'s discrete skeleton. Either *Eozoon* had
lost its shell to become *Bathybius* or the two primordial creatures were closely related as
exemplars of organic simplicity. The great physiologist W.B. Carpenter, a champion of 100
both creatures, wrote:

> If *Bathybius* . . . could form for itself a shelly envelope, that envelope would
> closely resemble *Eozoon*. Further, as Prof. Huxley has proved the existence of
> *Bathybius* through a great range not merely of depth but of temperature, I cannot
> but think it probable that it has existed continuously in the deep seas of all 105
> geological epochs. . . . I am fully prepared to believe that *Eozoon,* as well as
> *Bathybius,* may have maintained its existence through the whole duration of
> geological time.

Here was a vision to titillate any evolutionist! The anticipated, formless organic matter
had been found, and it extended throughout time and space to cover the floor of the 110
mysterious and primal ocean bottom.

Before I chronicle the downfall of both creatures, I want to identify a bias that lay
unstated and undefended in all the primary literature. All participants in the debate
accepted without question the "obvious" truth that the most primitive life would be
homogeneous and formless, diffuse and inchoate. 115

---

77. *Origin of Species*: published in 1859. **81. Sir William Logan:** Scottish-born Canadian geologist (1798-1875). **85. Dawson:** Sir John William Dawson, Canadian geologist (1820-1899), author of *Fossil Men* (1878). **100. Carpenter:** William Benjamin Carpenter, English biologist (1813-1885), author of *Nature and Man* (1888).

Carpenter wrote that *Bathybius* was "a type even lower, *because less definite*, than that of Sponges." Haeckel declared that "protoplasm exists here in its simplest and earliest form, i.e., it has scarcely any definite form, and is scarcely individualized." According to Huxley, life without the internal complexity of a nucleus proved that organization arose from indefinite vitality, not vice versa: *Bathybius* "proves the absence 120 of any mysterious power in nuclei, and shows that life is a property of the molecules of living matter, and that organization is the result of life, not life the result of organization."

But why, when we begin to think about it, should we equate formless with primitive? Modern organisms encourage no such view. Viruses are scarcely matched for regularity and repetition of form. The simplest bacteria have definite shapes. The 125 taxonomic group that houses the amoeba, that prototype of slithering disorganization, also accommodates the Radiolaria, the most beautiful and most complexly sculpted of all regular organisms. DNA is a miracle of organization; Watson and Crick elucidated its structure by building an accurate Tinkertoy model and making sure that all the pieces fit. I would not assert any mystical Pythagorean notion that regular form underlies all 130 organization, but I would argue that the equation of primitive with formless has roots in the outdated progressivist metaphor that views organic history as a ladder leading inexorably through all the stages of complexity from nothingness to our own noble form. Good for the ego to be sure, but not a very good outline of our world.

In any case, neither *Bathybius* nor *Eozoon* outlived Queen Victoria. The same Sir 135 Charles Wyville Thomson who had spoken so glowingly of *Bathybius* as a "glairy mass . . . actually alive" later became chief scientist of the *Challenger* expedition during the 1870s, the most famous of all scientific voyages to explore the world's oceans. The *Challenger* scientists tried again and again to find *Bathybius* in fresh samples of deep-sea mud, but with no success. 140

When scientists stored mud samples for later analysis, they traditionally added alcohol to preserve organic material. Huxley's original *Bathybius* had been found in samples stored with alcohol for more than a decade. One member of the *Challenger* expedition noticed that *Bathybius* appeared whenever he added alcohol to a fresh sample. The expedition's chemist then analyzed *Bathybius* and found it to be no more than a colloidal precipitate of calcium 145 sulfate, a product of the reaction of mud with alcohol. Thomson wrote to Huxley, and Huxley — without complaining — ate crow (or ate leeks, as he put it). Haeckel, as expected, proved more stubborn, but *Bathybius* quietly faded away.

Eozoon hung on longer. Dawson defended it literally to the death in some of the most acerbic comments ever written by a scientist. Of one German critic, he remarked in 1897: 150 "Mobius, I have no doubt, did his best from his special and limited point of view; but it was a crime which science should not readily pardon or forget, on the part of editors of the German periodical, to publish and illustrate as scientific material a paper which was so very far from being either fair or adequate." Dawson, by that time, was a lonely holdout. . . . All scientists had agreed that *Eozoon* was inorganic — a metamorphic product of heat and 155 pressure. Indeed, it had only been found in highly metamorphosed rock, a singularly

---

128. Watson and Crick: James Watson (b.1928), American biologist, and Francis Crick (b.1913), British physiologist, who shared the 1962 Nobel Prize for Medicine for explaining the function and structure of DNA. **130. Pythagorean:** after Pythagorus, the 6th century B.C. Greek philosopher. **151. Mobius:** August Ferdinand Möbius (1790-1868), German astronomer and mathematician (known for devising the continuous one-sided surface called the "Möbius strip").

inauspicious place to find a fossil. If any more proof had been needed, the discovery of *Eozoon* in blocks of limestone ejected from Mount Vesuvius settled the issue in 1894.

Bathybius and *Eozoon*, ever since, have been treated by scientists as an embarrassment best forgotten. The conspiracy succeeded admirably, and I would be surprised if one *160* percent of modern biologists ever heard of the two fantasies. Historians, trained in the older (and invalidated) tradition of science as a march to truth mediated by the successive shucking of error, also kept their peace. What can we get from errors except a good laugh or a compendium of moral homilies framed as "don'ts"?

Modern historians of science have more respect for such inspired errors. They made *165* sense in their own time; that they don't in ours is irrelevant. Our century is no standard for all ages; science is always an interaction of prevailing culture, individual eccentricity, and empirical constraint. Hence, *Bathybius* and *Eozoon* have received more attention in the 1970s than in all previous years since their downfall. (In writing this essay, I was guided to original sources and greatly enlightened by articles of C. F. *170* O'Brien on *Eozoon*, and N. A. Rupke and P. F. Rehbock on *Bathybius*. The article by Rehbock is particularly thorough and insightful.)

Science contains few outright fools. Errors usually have their good reasons once we penetrate their context properly and avoid judgment according to our current perception of "truth." They are usually more enlightening than embarrassing, for they are signs of *175* changing contexts. The best thinkers have the imagination to create organizing visions, and they are sufficiently adventurous (or egotistical) to float them in a complex world that can never answer "yes" in all detail. The study of inspired error should not engender a homily about the sin of pride; it should lead us to a recognition that the capacity for great insight and great error are opposite sides of the same coin — and that the currency of both is brilliance. *180*

Bathybius was surely an inspired error. It served the larger truth of advancing evolutionary theory. It provided a captivating vision of primordial life, extended throughout time and space. As Rehbock argues, it played a plethora of roles as, simultaneously, lowliest form of protozoology, elemental unit of cytology, evolutionary precursor of all organisms, first organic form in the fossil record, major constituent of *185* modern marine sediments (in its coccoliths), and source of food for higher life in the nutritionally impoverished deep oceans. When *Bathybius* faded away, the problems that it had defined did not disappear. *Bathybius* inspired a great amount of fruitful scientific work and served as a focus for defining important problems still very much with us.

Orthodoxy can be as stubborn in science as in religion. I do not know how to shake it *190* except by vigorous imagination that inspires unconventional work and contains within itself an elevated potential for inspired error. As the great Italian economist Vilfredo Pareto wrote: "Give me a fruitful error any time, full of seeds, bursting with its own corrections. You can keep your sterile truth for yourself." Not to mention a man named Thomas Henry Huxley who, when not in the throes of grief or the wars of parson *195* hunting, argued that "irrationally held truths may be more harmful than reasoned errors."

(1980)

169-72: Gould's general bibliography lists the following sources: C.F. O'Brian, "On Eozoön Canadense," *Isis* 62 (1971): 381-83; P.F. Rehbock, "Huxley, Haeckel, and the Oceanographers: the case of *Bathybius haeckelii*," *Isis* 66 (1975): 504-33; N.A. Rupke, "*Bathybius haeckelii* and the Psychology of Scientific Discovery," *Studies in the History and Philosophy of Science* 7 (1976): 53-62. **184. cytology:** the study of cell structure. **192-93. Vilfredo Pareto:** (1848-1923). **195. Huxley:** See note to line 19 of Arnold's "Literature and Science" (p. 1063). **196. irrationally . . . errors:** in *The Coming of Age of "The Origin of Species"* (1880).

JENI COUZYN
South Africa/Canada/England, b.1942

SPELL TO BANISH FEAR

By the warmth of the sun
By the baby's cry
By the lambs on the hill
I banish thee.

By the sweetness of the song   5
By the warm rain falling
By the hum of grass
Begone.

(1972)

DOUGLAS DUNN
Scotland, b.1942

EMPIRES

All the dead Imperia . . . They have gone
Taking their atlases and grand pianos.
They could not leave geography alone.
They conquered with the thistle and the rose.
To our forefathers it was right to raise   5
Their pretty flag at every foreign dawn
Then lower it at sunset in a haze
Of bugle-brass. They interfered with place,
Time, people, lives, and so to bed. They died
When it died. It had died before. It died   10
Before they did. They did not know it. Race,
Power, Trade, Fleet, a hundred regiments,
Postponed that final reckoning with pride,
Which was expensive. Counting up the cost
We plunder morals from the power they lost.   15
They ruined us. They conquered continents.
We filled their uniforms. We cruised the seas.
We worked their mines and made their histories.
You work, we rule, they said. We worked; they
    ruled.
They fooled the tenements. All men were fooled.
It still persists. It will be so, always.   21
Listen. An out-of-work apprentice plays
God Save the Queen on an Edwardian flute.
He is, but does not know it, destitute.

(1979)

EMPIRES   **1. Imperia:** empires. **4. thistle, rose:** emblems of Scotland and England, respectively.

PAMELA MORDECAI
Jamaica, b.1942

PROTEST POEM
for all the brothers

1. An ache is in a man: towns do not ache,
   nor ghettoes fester; the ravening gnaws
   at bellies, one-one; hurt is personal.
   On the corner, again and again, see
   me sit with my needle and spoon, see me   *5*
   puffin' my spliff, see me splittin' my mind,
   see me teenager dead from the blows of
   your words that baptize me according to
   Lenin and Marx — "You are no one, no one."

2. Blessed be the proletariat whom   *10*
   we must mobilize
   we must motivate
   we must liberate
   we must educate
   to a new political awareness.   *15*

3. Is di ole chattel ting again: di same
   slavery bizness, but dis time di boss
   look more like we an im does be smarter.
   Not a damn soul goin' mobilize my ass
   to rass — dem jokin. Any fool can read   *20*
   Das Kapital: what is dat to de poor?

4. We the people propose
   the abolition of you
   and us: we propose
   an acknowledgement   *25*
   of our persons and
   an alliance of poverty;

we propose to share the little
that breeds on these
antilles, one mango   *30*
to one mouth:

we propose to speak
your language
but not abandon ours;
we insist that you understand   *35*
that you do not
understand us.
You may begin
by not shouting —
we are tired of noise.   *40*

5. On the corner again and again see
   me stand with my pride and my children, my
   quiverful, lot, my portion of life; see
   me labour and wait; see me plan and scratch
   dust for a yam root, a corn, bellyful.   *45*

6. See ME
   Look!
   I am
   here
   I am   *50*
   here
   I am
   here.

                                        (1979)

PROTEST POEM   6. spliff: a ganja (cannabis) cigarette. **9. Lenin, Marx:** Vladimir Ilyich Lenin (1870-1924), Russian revolutionary leader in 1917 and first Soviet premier; Karl Marx (1818-1883), German Communist theorist and author of *Das Kapital* (1867). **20. to rass:** a common oath, intensifying the preceding line.

Nikki Giovanni
U.S.A., b.1943

[Untitled]

there is a hunger
    often associated with pain
    that you feel
    when you look at someone
    you used to love and enjoyed   5
    loving and want
    to love again
    though you know you can't
that gnaws at you
    as steadily as a mosquito   10
    some michigan summer
    churning his wings
    through your window screen
because the real world
    made up of baby   15
      clothes   *to be washed*
    food   *to be cooked*
    lullabies   *to be sung*
    smiles   *to be glowed*
    hair   *to be plaited*   20
    ribbons   *to be bowed*
    coffee   *to be drunk*
    books   *to be read*
    tears   *to be cried*
    loneliness   *to be borne*   25
says you are a strong woman
    and anyway he never thought you'd really miss him

(1972)

Revolutionary Dreams

i used to dream militant
dreams of taking
over america to show
these white folks how it should be
done   5
i used to dream radical dreams
of blowing everyone away with my perceptive powers
of correct analysis

i even used to think i'd be the one
to stop the riot and negotiate the peace   10
then i awoke and dug
that if i dreamed natural
dreams of being a natural
woman doing what a woman
does when she's natural   15
i would have a revolution

(1975)

LOUISE GLÜCK
U.S.A., b.1943

THE APPLE TREES

Your son presses against me
his small intelligent body.

I stand beside his crib
as in another dream
you stood among trees hung   5
with bitten apples
holding out your arms.
I did not move
but saw the air dividing
into panes of color — at the very last   10
I raised him to the window saying
See what you have made

and counted out the whittled ribs,
the heart on its blue stalk
as from among the trees   15
the darkness issued:

In the dark room your son sleeps.
The walls are green, the walls
are spruce and silence.
I wait to see how he will leave me.   20
Already on his hand the map appears
as though you carved it there,
the dead fields, women rooted to the river.

(1975)

PAULETTE JILES
U.S.A./Canada, b.1943

BLACKSNAKE

A tangle of black calligraphy,
taut as a telephone cord during an important call.

He has the arrogance of Texas oil, the way
his eyes dart little migraines.

His trickling, scaly currents erect on their own coils. 5

Slimmer and thinner his forepart curves
like a question mark to the hypnotized water —

the clear, beer-bottle-brown lens of these hills
and oaks. A high-power line dips in the pool

                          sip   10

sip

drops like cheap rhinestones splintering
unwinding like a black umbilicus
his slick glitter is perfectly voiceless and thin.

(1984)

PAPER MATCHES

    My aunts washed dishes while the uncles
squirted each other on the lawn with
    garden hoses. Why are we in here,
I said, and they are out there?
    That's the way it is,   5
said Aunt Hetty, the shrivelled-up one.

    I have the rages that small animals have,
being small, being animal.
    Written on me was a message,
"At Your Service," like a book of   10
paper matches. One by one we were
taken out and struck.
    We come bearing supper,
our heads on fire.

(1984)

MICHAEL ONDAATJE
Sri Lanka/Canada, b.1943

CHARLES DARWIN PAYS A VISIT, DECEMBER 1971

View of the coast of Brazil.
A man stood up to shout
at the image of a sailing ship
which was a vast white bird from over the sea
and now ripping its claws into the ocean.   5
Faded hills of March
painted during the cold morning.
On board ship Charles Darwin sketched clouds.

One of these days the Prime Mover will
paint the Prime Mover out of his sky.   10
I want a . . . centuries being displaced
. . . faith.

        23rd of June, 1832.
        He caught sixty-eight species
        of a particularly minute beetle. *15*

The blue thick leaves who greeted him
animals unconscious of celebration
moved slowly into law.
Adam with a watch.
Look past and future, (*I want a . . .*),   20
ease our way out of the structures
this smell of the cogs
and diamonds we live in.

I am waiting for a new ship, so new
we will think the lush machine   25
an animal of God.
Weary from travelling over the air and the water
it will sink to its feet at our door.

                        (1972, 1973)

ARTHUR YAP
Singapore, b.1943

A LESSON ON THE DEFINITE ARTICLE

a crowded restaurant, open eavesdropping
graded into one another's ears. sharing table:
a bearded man, a girl with bank-teller's eyes;
they arrived after me, & an umbrella & 2 coats
which were there when i was.   5

i really love chinese food, you people can cook
beautifully. the bearded man had also a large appetite.
i can't cook, & her non-sequitur
"the poor chinese are like the 2nd class jews"
provoked these possibilities: 10
poor chinese are like 2nd class jews,
poor chinese are like the 2nd class jews,
the poor chinese are like 2nd class jews.

the she was, by the way, the chinese
& her the accent, showing she had arrived,   15
gone the places, reached the it,
made the it, confirmed she was the.

                    (1983)

THE GRAMMAR OF A DINNER

let's have chicken for dinner.

somewhere else, someone else utters:
let's have john for dinner.
we are alarmed by the latter
but a dinner, too, has its own grammar   5

CHARLES DARWIN PAYS A VISIT Title. **Darwin:** See p. 945.

& we are assured by grammarians
both utterances are in order.

john, + animate, + human,
couldn't be passed off as repast.
chicken is + animate, – human,   *10*
& can end up in any oven.
if we combine the items of grammar
the way things in cooking are,
we would then have:
let's have chicken for john for dinner,   *15*

let's have chicken for dinner for john,
let's have for john chicken for dinner,
let's have for dinner for john chicken;
but probably not:
let's have john for chicken for dinner,   *20*
let's have for dinner john for chicken.

john is a noun holding knife & fork.
chicken collocates with the verb eat.
grammarians favour such words
as delicious & john eats happily,   *25*
but in a gastronomic dinner
taxonomic john isn't to eat deliciously.

(1983)

BP NICHOL

Canada, 1944-1988

from *THE MARTYROLOGY*

from *"The Sorrows of Saint Orm"* (from *Book 1*)

         me &
    my friends
    the end   playing what lives we had to

       i want to tell you a story
in the old way   *5*
       i can't

haven't the words or
the hands to reach you

& this circus   this noise in
my brain   *10*
       makes it hard to explain
my sorrow

(1977)

from *"Book of Common Prayer"* (from *Book 2*)

it all ends

i said that before

someone opened his mouth & said that
so long ago i don't care

if it is repeated   *5*
is it left behind?

sweet truth of oneness
duality that does not see

sweet sweet vision

sweet clarity   10
   . . . .

everything i say
i have said before
once when i thot each phrase new
& now see the mockery of speech

artifice   15

holding over
the tight phrases & cursed verse
SCREAMING

soft saintly night
oh god good night   20
soft saint soft light

                (1977)

from *"Sons & Divinations"* (from *Book 2*)

finally come to see
poets are such asocial beings
lost the gift of tongues the death of joy
no towns to wander thru & sing our songs to
somewhere perhaps that place or maybe   5
yes there are the fairs who listens
no place to sing the gift He gave me
blessed finally can i leave false death behind

trapped as we are in signs
our language multiplies above the cities   10
the letters meaningless words
we have less & less to say to one another

thus the buildings rise
distances between our separate dwellings reduced
made possible thru the death of speech   15
what was it someone said
if they're so civilized
why leave the lights on all night?
wander the streets lonely in our silence
fear of the unknown millions who surround you   20
      . . . .

oh i do listen saint rand
but that vision
those bodies wrapped in chains
as language was the chain they did not see
how can they continue knowing as you must know   25
we must return again to human voice & listen
rip off the mask of words to free the sounds
we wear the chains as muscles rigidly

(i awoke with a strange dream. how we were all caught up in a time of
suffering we must pass thru to guard the sacred plants of regeneration.   30
it was morning. the light came thru the window where the cat lay
sleeping . . . .

                (1976)

from *"Book 3"*

there is no desire for speech

there is no desire to spell

each gesture
against the chaos
must be made well   *5*

there is stillness in the heart of the power
as there is stillness in the heart of the storm

between the w & the d
the in side of
the mind /   *10*
         / 's a quiet place
from which the power unwinds

    . . . .

the ear the ear it is all there
the mouth fitted to it with such care
there is music in every sound you make   *15*

the air here is clearer
wind in my hair
it is a moment the poem has occupied before
the words are shapes the sounds take
it is all there it is all there it is all there   *20*

breathing over & over
history's written in my body
architecture of the too tight muscles will not bend where they should
startled eyes moving in & out
aware the sound is there   *25*
occupying space i am afraid to enter

    . . . .

more than meets the eye meets the ear
fear of that as the basic proposition
mo asked "what if the bias were reversed"
2000 years the eye has ruled   *30*
theory that the architecture of greece & egypt was based on the ear
now every architect says there is no exact science of acoustics

the ancient gaelic poets lay with stones on their chests
pressed stale air out   fresh breath
poetry springing from lungs that were pure   *35*

you in the back seat leaning forward
asking where i'm going   i've no good answers
the stone on my chest won't let me breathe

    . . . .

in vocation
i am   *40*
a singer

every letter
invokes a spell
ing is
the power   *45*
letters have
over me

word shaping

addition of the l
                     (1976)

from *"Book 4"*

the is M
the particular
emblem of the end a
beginning a
w a y.   *5*
ME/WE
returned to
that vision &
this time
          i write the letters clearly   *10*
the w rite of consciousness
a transparency's
too often viewed opaquely
lack of seeing
lack of being   *15*
sing
     sang
          sank
froid
     et chaud   *20*
          . . . .
the contradictions are there in a lifetime
literature is no guarantee of a common good
i want a firmer ground to stand on

you do the best you can
as i saw that day the foal was born   *25*
you start with what's local

stands next to you
               & move out
increase your range as your skill grows
& what's around you's taken care of   *30*
          . . . .
the w hat's low call
echoes thru these pages
lo cal or (i.e.)
               what's immediate is
the word in front of me   *35*
the one beyond that that i'm reaching for
no muse at all really
simply this canadian foot
following a tentative line   forward
taking the time to tell you everything   *40*

the muse is western (greek)
the japanese saw poetry as everyman's
like thot or breathing
ambiguity was precisely what they wanted

it's social then   *45*
a point of view
political
the duty of a citizen
"a man betrays himself in his speech"
                     (1976)

THE MARTYROLOGY   BOOK 4   **49. a man . . . speech:** See Matthew 26:73.

"Chain 10" (from *Book 5*)

every(all at(toge(forever)ther) once)thing

(1982)

from *"Briefly: The Birth/Death Cycle — Hour 15"* (from *Book 6*)

tho reason points out the folly
a voice is born again

tho the different purposes & meanings remain unclear
this voice is born again

            empty it out   *5*

            empty it out

i have this dumb shout within me
a lifetime cannot approximate

i have this wish to write the world i can never realize

stand here   mouth open   *10*

            air fills me

blown away

        in the day to day hugeness of this hazy being
i can never take it all in

i have this sentence i must finish   *15*

i have this poem i must write

the boats steam away
west towards Lake Huron
east to Lake Ontario
the planes & surfaces foreshorten & change   *20*

bird song & wave noise

wind & whistling air

         in the midst of
        there is something

a presence or a silence   *25*
an absence of the pressure of

     . . .

               THERE

(1987)

from *gIFTS: The Martyrology Book(s) 7&*

bp: if

•

sacrum
say
the whole thing ends
say
you're frightened   5
of the whole thing
ending

say
cheese
say n't   10
n't ready
n't ready to die
                    (1990)

SHIRLEY GEOK-LIN LIM
Malaysia/U.S.A., b.1944

DEDICATED TO CONFUCIUS PLAZA

I live in a small house
On top of fifty other houses.
Every morning I face the East River
Where the air is cold as
On Tung Shen Mountains.   5
The mountains are made of loess
Brought down by the Yang-tze.
The city is a mountain
Also, made of Asia,
Europe and Africa.   10
They call it America.
Every morning I practice *li*,
Perform my wifely duties,
Watch colour television,
And eat pop, crackle, snap.   15
It is not hard to be
An Asian-American Chinee.
                    (1989)

TO MARIANNE MOORE

Where is the toad?
In the garden we
Did not build,
Deciding against
Stories of the mind   5
While dying
Like everyone else.
Where is the island?
Sailing in the night
Moonwards.   10
We have shut
Imaginary doors
Decisively.
The door to the mind
Does not exist   15
But admits one only.
Here is our denial,
Real.
Like anything else,
We deny it.   20
                    (1989)

DEDICATED TO CONFUCIUS PLAZA   **3. East River:** the strait between Manhattan Island and Long Island.   **12.** *li:* roughly, gathering strength through being calm.   **TO MARIANNE MOORE**   For Moore, see p. 1297.

CRAIG RAINE
England, b.1944

A MARTIAN SENDS A POSTCARD HOME

Caxtons are mechanical birds with many wings
and some are treasured for their markings —

they cause the eyes to melt
or the body to shriek without pain.

I have never seen one fly, but   5
sometimes they perch on the hand.

Mist is when the sky is tired of flight
and rests its soft machine on ground:

then the world is dim and bookish
like engravings under tissue paper.   10

Rain is when the earth is television.
It has the property of making colours darker.

Model T is a room with the lock inside —
a key is turned to free the world

for movement, so quick there is a film   15
to watch for anything missed.

But time is tied to the wrist
or kept in a box, ticking with impatience.

In homes, a haunted apparatus sleeps,
that snores when you pick it up.   20

If the ghost cries, they carry it
to their lips and soothe it to sleep

with sounds. And yet, they wake it up
deliberately, by tickling with a finger.

Only the young are allowed to suffer   25
openly. Adults go to a punishment room

with water but nothing to eat.
They lock the door and suffer the noises

alone. No one is exempt
and everyone's pain has a different smell.   30

At night, when all the colours die,
they hide in pairs

and read about themselves —
in colour, with their eyelids shut.

(1980)

CAROL RUMENS
England, b.1944

TWO WOMEN

Daily to a profession — paid thinking
and clean hands — she rises,
unquestioning. It's second nature now.
The hours, though they're all of daylight, suit her.
The desk, typewriter, carpets, pleasantries   5
are a kind of civilisation — built on money
of course, but money, now she sees, is human.
She has learned giving from a bright new chequebook,
intimacy from absence. Coming home
long after dark to the jugular torrent   10

of family life, she brings,
tucked in her bag, the simple, cool-skinned apples
of a father's loving objectivity.
That's half the story. There's another woman
who bears her name, a silent, background face   *15*
that's always flushed with work, or swallowed anger.
A true wife, she picks up scattered laundry
and sets the table with warmed plates to feed
the clean-handed woman. They've not met.
If they were made to touch, they'd burn each other.   *20*

(1987)

MONGANE WALLY SEROTE
South Africa, b.1944

THE GROWING

No!
This is not dying when the trees
Leave their twigs
To grow blindly long into windows like fingers into eyes.
And leave us unable   *5*
To wink or to blink or to actually close the eye,
The mind —
Twigs thrusting into windows and leaves falling on the sills,
Are like thoughts uncontrolled and stuffing the heart.
Yes,   *10*
This is teaching about the growing of things:
If you crowd me I'll retreat from you,
If you still crowd me I'll think a bit,
Not about crowding you but about your right to crowd me;
If you still crowd me, I will not, but I will be thinking   *15*
About crowding you.
If my thoughts and hands reach out
To prune the twigs and sweep the leaves,
There was a growth of thought here,
Then words, then action.   *20*
So if I say prune instead of cut,
I'm teaching about the growing of things.

(1974)

ALICE WALKER
U.S.A., b.1944

BEAUTY: WHEN THE OTHER DANCER IS THE SELF

It is a bright summer day in 1947. My father, a fat, funny man with beautiful eyes and a subversive wit, is trying to decide which of his eight children he will take with him to the county fair. My mother, of course, will not go. She is knocked out from getting most of us ready: I hold my neck stiff against the pressure of her knuckles as she hastily completes the braiding and then beribboning of my hair.   5

My father is the driver for the rich old white lady up the road. Her name is Miss Mey. She owns all the land for miles around, as well as the house in which we live. All I remember about her is that she once offered to pay my mother thirty-five cents for cleaning her house, raking up piles of her magnolia leaves, and washing her family's clothes, and that my mother — she of no money, eight children, and a chronic earache   10
— refused it. But I do not think of this in 1947. I am two and a half years old. I want to go everywhere my daddy goes. I am excited at the prospect of riding in a car. Someone has told me fairs are fun. That there is room in the car for only three of us doesn't faze me at all. Whirling happily in my starchy frock, showing off my biscuit-polished patent-leather shoes and lavender socks, tossing my head in a way that makes my ribbons   15
bounce, I stand, hands on hips, before my father. "Take me, Daddy," I say with assurance; "I'm the prettiest!"

Later, it does not surprise me to find myself in Miss Mey's shiny black car, sharing the back seat with the other lucky ones. Does not surprise me that I thoroughly enjoy the fair. At home that night I tell the unlucky ones all I can remember about the merry-go-   20
round, the man who eats live chickens, and the teddy bears, until they say: that's enough, baby Alice. Shut up now, and go to sleep.

It is Easter Sunday, 1950. I am dressed in a green, flocked, scalloped-hem dress (handmade by my adoring sister, Ruth) that has its own smooth satin petticoat and tiny hot-pink roses tucked into each scallop. My shoes, new T-strap patent leather, again   25
highly biscuit-polished. I am six years old and have learned one of the longest Easter speeches to be heard that day, totally unlike the speech I said when I was two: "Easter lilies / pure and white / blossom in / the morning light." When I rise to give my speech I do so on a great wave of love and pride and expectation. People in the church stop rustling their new crinolines. They seem to hold their breath. I can tell they admire my   30
dress, but it is my spirit, bordering on sassiness (womanishness), they secretly applaud.

"That girl's a little *mess*," they whisper to each other, pleased.

Naturally I say my speech without stammer or pause, unlike those who stutter, stammer, or, worst of all, forget. This is before the word "beautiful" exists in people's vocabulary, but "Oh, isn't she the *cutest* thing!" frequently floats my way. "And got so   35
much sense!" they gratefully add . . . for which thoughtful addition I thank them to this day.

It was great fun being cute. But then, one day, it ended.

I am eight years old and a tomboy. I have a cowboy hat, cowboy boots, checkered shirt and pants, all red. My playmates are my brothers, two and four years older than I. Their colors are black and green, the only difference in the way we are dressed. On Saturday nights we all go to the picture show, even my mother; Westerns are her favorite kind of movie. Back home, "on the ranch," we pretend we are Tom Mix, Hopalong Cassidy, Lash LaRue (we've even named one of our dogs Lash LaRue); we chase each other for hours rustling cattle, being outlaws, delivering damsels from distress. Then my parents decide to buy my brothers guns. These are not "real" guns. They shoot "BBs," copper pellets my brothers say will kill birds. Because I am a girl, I do not get a gun. Instantly I am relegated to the position of Indian. Now there appears a great distance between us. They shoot and shoot at everything with their new guns. I try to keep up with my bow and arrows.

One day while I am standing on top of our makeshift "garage" — pieces of tin nailed across some poles — holding my bow and arrow and looking out toward the fields, I feel an incredible blow in my right eye. I look down just in time to see my brother lower his gun.

Both brothers rush to my side. My eye stings, and I cover it with my hand. "If you tell," they say, "we will get a whipping. You don't want that to happen, do you?" I do not. "Here is a piece of wire," says the older brother, picking it up from the roof; "say you stepped on one end of it and the other flew up and hit you." The pain is beginning to start. "Yes," I say. "Yes, I will say that is what happened." If I do not say this is what happened, I know my brothers will find ways to make me wish I had. But now I will say anything that gets me to my mother.

Confronted by our parents we stick to the lie agreed upon. They place me on a bench on the porch and I close my left eye while they examine the right. There is a tree growing from underneath the porch that climbs past the railing to the roof. It is the last thing my right eye sees. I watch as its trunk, its branches, and then its leaves are blotted out by the rising blood.

I am in shock. First there is intense fever, which my father tries to break using lily leaves bound around my head. Then there are chills: my mother tries to get me to eat soup. Eventually, I do not know how, my parents learn what has happened. A week after the "accident" they take me to see a doctor. "Why did you wait so long to come?" he asks, looking into my eye and shaking his head. "Eyes are sympathetic," he says. "If one is blind, the other will likely become blind too."

This comment of the doctor's terrifies me. But it is really how I look that bothers me most. Where the BB pellet struck there is a glob of whitish scar tissue, a hideous cataract, on my eye. Now when I stare at people — a favorite pastime, up to now — they will stare back. Not at the "cute" little girl, but at her scar. For six years I do not stare at anyone, because I do not raise my head.

Years later, in the throes of a mid-life crisis, I ask my mother and sister whether I changed after the "accident." "No," they say, puzzled. "What do you mean?"

What do I mean?

BEAUTY **43-44. Tom Mix:** American cowboy and Western film actor (1880-1940); **Hopalong Cassidy:** film cowboy, played by actor William Boyd (1895-1972); **Lash LaRue:** the stage name of Hollywood cowboy star Alfred LaRue (b.1917).

I am eight, and, for the first time, doing poorly in school, where I have been something of a whiz since I was four. We have just moved to the place where the "accident" occurred. We do not know any of the people around us because this is a different county. The only time I see the friends I knew is when we go back to our old church. The new school is the former state penitentiary. It is a large stone building, cold and drafty, crammed to overflowing with boisterous, ill-disciplined children. On the third floor there is a huge circular imprint of some partition that has been torn out. 85

"What used to be here?" I ask a sullen girl next to me on our way past it to lunch.

"The electric chair," says she.

At night I have nightmares about the electric chair, and about all the people reputedly "fried" in it. I am afraid of the school, where all the students seem to be budding criminals. 90

"What's the matter with your eye?" they ask, critically.

When I don't answer (I cannot decide whether it was an "accident" or not), they shove me, insist on a fight. 95

My brother, the one who created the story about the wire, comes to my rescue. But then brags so much about "protecting" me, I become sick.

After months of torture at the school, my parents decide to send me back to our old community, to my old school. I live with my grandparents and the teacher they board. But there is no room for Phoebe, my cat. By the time my grandparents decide there *is* 100 room, and I ask for my cat, she cannot be found. Miss Yarborough, the boarding teacher, takes me under her wing, and begins to teach me to play the piano. But soon she marries an African — a "prince," she says — and is whisked away to his continent.

At my old school there is at least one teacher who loves me. She is the teacher who "knew me before I was born" and bought my first baby clothes. It is she who makes life 105 bearable. It is her presence that finally helps me turn on the one child at the school who continually calls me "one-eyed bitch." One day I simply grab him by his coat and beat him until I am satisfied. It is my teacher who tells me my mother is ill.

My mother is lying in bed in the middle of the day, something I have never seen. She is in too much pain to speak. She has an abscess in her ear. I stand looking down on her, 110 knowing that if she dies, I cannot live. She is being treated with warm oils and hot bricks held against her cheek. Finally a doctor comes. But I must go back to my grandparents' house. The weeks pass but I am hardly aware of it. All I know is that my mother might die, my father is not so jolly, my brothers still have their guns, and I am the one sent away from home. 115

"You did not change," they say.

Did I imagine the anguish of never looking up?

I am twelve. When relatives come to visit I hide in my room. My cousin Brenda, just my age, whose father works in the post office and whose mother is a nurse, comes to find me. "Hello," she says. And then she asks, looking at my recent school picture, which I 120 did not want taken, and on which the "glob," as I think of it, is clearly visible, "You still can't see out of that eye?"

"No," I say, and flop back on the bed over my book.

That night, as I do almost every night, I abuse my eye. I rant and rave at it, in front of the mirror. I plead with it to clear up before morning. I tell it I hate and despise it. I   *125*
do not pray for sight. I pray for beauty.

"You did not change," they say.

I am fourteen and baby-sitting for my brother Bill, who lives in Boston. He is my favorite brother and there is a strong bond between us. Understanding my feelings of shame and ugliness he and his wife take me to a local hospital, where the "glob" is   *130*
removed by a doctor named O. Henry. There is still a small bluish crater where the scar tissue was, but the ugly white stuff is gone. Almost immediately I become a different person from the girl who does not raise her head. Or so I think. Now that I've raised my head I win the boyfriend of my dreams. Now that I've raised my head I have plenty of friends. Now that I've raised my head classwork comes from my lips as faultlessly as   *135*
Easter speeches did, and I leave high school as valedictorian, most popular student, and *queen*, hardly believing my luck. Ironically, the girl who was voted most beautiful in our class (and was) was later shot twice through the chest by a male companion, using a "real" gun, while she was pregnant. But that's another story in itself. Or is it?

"You did not change," they say.   *140*

It is now thirty years since the "accident." A beautiful journalist comes to visit and to interview me. She is going to write a cover story for her magazine that focuses on my latest book. "Decide how you want to look on the cover," she says. "Glamorous, or whatever."

Never mind "glamorous," it is the "whatever" that I hear. Suddenly all I can think   *145*
of is whether I will get enough sleep the night before the photography session: if I don't, my eye will be tired and wander, as blind eyes will.

At night in bed with my lover I think up reasons why I should not appear on the cover of a magazine. "My meanest critics will say I've sold out," I say. "My family will now realize I write scandalous books."   *150*

"But what's the real reason you don't want to do this?" he asks.

"Because in all probability," I say in a rush, "my eye won't be straight."

"It will be straight enough," he says. Then, "Besides, I thought you'd made your peace with that."

And I suddenly remember that I have.   *155*

I remember:

I am talking to my brother Jimmy, asking if he remembers anything unusual about the day I was shot. He does not know I consider that day the last time my father, with his sweet home remedy of cool lily leaves, chose me, and that I suffered and raged inside because of this. "Well," he says, "all I remember is standing by the side of the   *160*
highway with Daddy, trying to flag down a car. A white man stopped, but when Daddy said he needed somebody to take his little girl to the doctor, he drove off."

I remember:

I am in the desert for the first time. I fall totally in love with it. I am so overwhelmed by its beauty, I confront for the first time, consciously, the meaning of the doctor's words   *165*
years ago: "Eyes are sympathetic. If one is blind, the other will likely become blind too."

I realize I have dashed about the world madly, looking at this, looking at that, storing up images against the fading of the light. *But I might have missed seeing the desert!* The shock of that possibility — and gratitude for over twenty-five years of sight — sends me literally to my knees. Poem after poem comes — which is perhaps how poets pray.   *170*

On Sight

I am so thankful I have seen
The Desert
And the creatures in the desert
And the desert Itself.

The desert has its own moon   *175*
Which I have seen
With my own eye.
There is no flag on it.

Trees of the desert have arms
All of which are always up   *180*
That is because the moon is up
The sun is up
Also the sky
The stars
Clouds   *185*
None with flags.

If there *were* flags, I doubt
the trees would point.
Would you?

But mostly, I remember this: *190*
I am twenty-seven, and my baby daughter is almost three. Since her birth I have worried about her discovery that her mother's eyes are different from other people's. Will she be embarrassed? I think. What will she say? Every day she watches a television program called "Big Blue Marble." It begins with a picture of the earth as it appears from the moon. It is bluish, a little battered-looking, but full of light, with whitish clouds   *195* swirling around it. Every time I see it I weep with love, as if it is a picture of Grandma's house. One day when I am putting Rebecca down for her nap, she suddenly focuses on my eye. Something inside me cringes, gets ready to try to protect myself. All children are cruel about physical differences, I know from experience, and that they don't always mean to be is another matter. I assume Rebecca will be the same.   *200*

But no-o-o-o. She studies my face intently as we stand, her inside and me outside her crib. She even holds my face maternally between her dimpled little hands. Then, looking every bit as serious and lawyerlike as her father, she says, as if it may just possibly have slipped my attention: "Mommy, there's a *world* in your eye." (As in, "Don't be alarmed, or do anything crazy.") And then, gently, but with great interest: *205* "Mommy, where did you *get* that world in your eye?"

For the most part, the pain left then. (So what, if my brothers grew up to buy even more powerful pellet guns for their sons and to carry real guns themselves. So what, if a young "Morehouse man" once nearly fell off the steps of Trevor Arnett Library because he thought my eyes were blue.) Crying and laughing I ran to the bathroom, while   *210* Rebecca mumbled and sang herself off to sleep. Yes indeed, I realized, looking into the mirror. There *was* a world in my eye. And I saw that it was possible to love it: that in fact, for all it had taught me of shame and anger and inner vision, I *did* love it. Even to see it drifting out of orbit in boredom, or rolling up out of fatigue, not to mention floating back at attention in excitement (bearing witness, a friend has called it), deeply   *215* suitable to my personality, and even characteristic of me.

That night I dream I am dancing to Stevie Wonder's song "Always" (the name of the song is really "As," but I hear it as "Always"). As I dance, whirling and joyous, happier than I've ever been in my life, another bright-faced dancer joins me. We dance and kiss each other and hold each other through the night. The other dancer has   *220* obviously come through all right, as I have done. She is beautiful, whole and free. And she is also me.

(1983)

EAVAN BOLAND
Ireland, b.1945

FRUIT ON A STRAIGHT-SIDED TRAY

When the painter takes the straight-sided tray
and arranges late melons with grapes and lemons,
the true subject is the space between them:

in which repose the pleasure of these ovals
is seen to be an assembly of possibilities;   *5*
a deliberate collection of cross-purposes:

gross blues and purples, yellow and the shadow of bloom.
The room smells of metal polish. The afternoon sun
brings light but not heat; and no distraction from

the study of absences, the science of relationships   *10*
in which the abstraction is made actual: such as
fruit on a straight-sided tray; a homely arrangement.

This is the geometry of the visible, physical tryst
between substances, disguising for a while the equation
that kills: you are my child and between us are   *15*

spaces, distances. Growing to infinities.

(1982, 1990)

---

209. Trevor Arnett Library: at Morehouse College, Atlanta, Georgia. **217. Stevie Wonder:** Steveland Judkins Hardaway (b.1950), blind American musician.

WENDY COPE
England, b.1945

A NURSERY RHYME
as it might have been written by William Wordsworth

The skylark and the jay sang loud and long,
The sun was calm and bright, the air was sweet,
When all at once I heard above the throng
Of jocund birds a single plaintive bleat.

And, turning, saw, as one sees in a dream,   5
It was a Sheep had broke the moorland peace
With his sad cry, a creature who did seem
The blackest thing that ever wore a fleece.

I walked towards him on the stony track
And, pausing for a while between two crags,   10
I asked him, "Have you wool upon your back?"
Thus he bespake, "Enough to fill three bags."

Most courteously, in measured tones, he told
Who would receive each bag and where they dwelt;
And oft, now years have passed and I am old,   15
I recollect with joy that inky pelt.

(1986)

ROBERT BRINGHURST
U.S.A./Canada, b.1946

SOME CIPHERS

If I say
$1 + e^{\pi i} = 0$,
I have recorded a rather
elaborate but arguably beautiful way
of reducing unity to zero.   5

If, however, I say
$1 + 1 = 2$, or 1
$+ 1 = 1$, I have made a concrete
assertion having to do
with construction or fusion.   10

Observe, now, that on certain occasions
$1 + 1 \rightarrow 0$. The formula
$1 + x = 0$, where x
may equal, for instance, $e^{\pi i}$,
may then be of more interest.   15

Consider, further, $1 = 0$.
This, in mathematical terms, may be called
cancellation. It differs from $0 = 1$,
which may, in mathematical terms, be called
the creation *ex nihil* of number, or,   20

in non-mathematical terms, the invention
of terror.
Consider, therefore, 0 not equal
to 0, or $0 = x$, where x 24
is not equal to zero. Climb left through the zero

and watch, looking back at
the blood in its jacket,
the breath in its jacket,
the absence
opening its arms.   30

(1975)

A NURSERY RHYME See nursery rhymes (p. 566) and Wordsworth's poems (p. 754).   **SOME CIPHERS 2.** $1+e^{\pi i} = 0$: a relation among certain mathematical constants which permits calculus and higher arithmetic in the complex plane. **20. *ex nihil*:** (Latin) out of nothing.

Essay On Adam

There are five possibilities. One: Adam fell.
Two: he was pushed. Three: he jumped. Four:
he only looked over the edge, and one look
   silenced him.
Five: nothing worth mentioning happened to
   Adam.

The first, that he fell, is too simple. The fourth,   *5*
fear, we have tried and found useless. The fifth,
nothing happened, is dull. The choice is between:
he jumped or was pushed. And the difference
   between these

is only an issue of whether the demons
work from the inside out or from the outside   *10*
in: the one
theological question.

           (1975)

Wáng Bì

Wáng Bì of Wei
lies dead in his hut
at age 24. His mind
is now one with the mountain.
His flesh has been grass,   *5*
voles, owls,
owl pellets, grass.

The use of the is
is to point to the isn't.
Go back, said Wáng Bì: *10*
Look again at the mind
of the sky and the heart
of the mountain. The mind
is unbeing. The mind
of heaven and earth   *15*
is unbeing. Go back,
look again. What is,
is. It consists
of what isn't. *Are*
is the plural of *is; is*   *20*
is the plural of *isn't.* Go back,
look again. What isn't,
is. This
is the fusion of substance
and function, the heart of the sky   *25*
and the mind of the mountain.

To be, said Wáng Bì,
without being: this
is the way to have virtue.
Don't fondle it, stand   *30*
on what isn't. We sink, said Wáng Bì,
when we set out to stand on what is.

           (1986)

Bill Manhire
New Zealand, b.1946

Declining the Naked Horse

The naked horse came into the room.
The naked horse comes into the room.
The naked horse has come into the room.
The naked horse will be coming into the room.
The naked horse is coming into the room.   *5*

The naked horse does come into the room.
The naked horse had come into the room.
The naked horse would of come into the room
again if we hadn't of stopped it.

           (1982)

CHILDREN

The likelihood is
the children will die
without you to help them do it.
It will be spring,
the light on the water,   5
or not.

And though at present
they live together
they will not die together.
They will die one by one   10
and not think to call you:
they will be old

and you will be gone.
It will be spring,
or not. They may be crossing   15
the road,

not looking left,
not looking right,

or may simply be afloat at evening
like clouds unable   20
to make repairs. That
one talks too much, that one
hardly at all: and they both enjoy
the light on the water

much as we enjoy   25
the sense
of indefinite postponement. Yes
it's a tall story but don't you think
full of promise, and he's just a kid
but watch him grow.   30

(1982)

CHRISTOPHER DEWDNEY
Canada, b.1951

NIGHT TRAINS

A night train is a part of ourselves
on its way to another part of ourselves
in the darkside of consciousness.
A train is a state of things in transit,
a cartesian living-room passing through   5
a narrative geography.

The sound of wheels
on glistening steel rails
is a continuous ball-bearing glissando
a metallic rolling peal   10
interrupted staccato
by the seams in the tracks.
The engine gliding

on frictionless iron, both
machine and path part   15
of a single mechanism such
that passage is an illusory extension
in space. The labour
that keeps us here
roaring in my ears.   20

And in the mountains, the train whistle
is supernaturally sustained
by the still air of the valleys
an indulgence of the massif
to echo for full seconds in the   25
dream kingdom of the night mountains.

(1988)

PETER GOLDSWORTHY
Australia, b.1951

ACT SIX

Act six begins
when the curtain falls,
the corpses awake,
the daggers are cleaned.

Act six   5
is Juliet in the supermarket,
Mr Macbeth on the 8.15.

In act six
Hamlet sucks a tranquilliser,
Romeo washes up   10

and death
is gentle and anonymous —
Lear's respirator
switched discreetly off.

(1982)

RITA DOVE
U.S.A., b.1952

THREE DAYS OF FOREST, A RIVER, FREE

The dogs have nothing better
to do than bark; duty's whistle
slings a bright cord
around their throats.
I'll stand here all night   5
if need be, no more real
than a tree when no moon shines.

The terror of waking is a trust
drawn out unbearably
until nothing, not even love,   10
makes it easier, and yet
I love this life:

three days of forest,
the mute riot of leaves.

Who can point out a smell   15
but a dog? The way is free
to the river. Tell me,
Lord, how it feels
to burst out like a rose.

Blood rises in my head —   20
I'm there.
Faint tongue, dry fear,
I think I lost you to the dogs,
so far off now they're no
more than a chain of bells   25
ringing darkly, underground.

(1983)

ALICE FULTON
U.S.A. b.1952

EVERYONE KNOWS THE WORLD IS ENDING

Everyone knows the world is ending.
Everyone always thought so, yet
here's the world. Where fundamentalists flick slideshows

in darkened gyms, flash endtime mess-
ages of bliss, tribulation   5
through the trembling bleachers: Christ will come
by satellite TV, bearing millennial weather
before plagues of false prophets and real locusts
botch the cosmic climate — which ecologists predict
is already withering from the green-   10
house effect as fossil fuels seal in
the sun's heat and acid rains
give lakes the cyanotic blues.

When talk turns this way, my mother speaks in memories,
each thought a focused mote in the apocalypse's   15
iridescent fizz. She is trying to restore a world
to glory, but the facts shift with each telling
of her probable gospel. Some stories have been
trinkets in my mind since childhood, yet what clings is not
how she couldn't go near the sink   20
for months without tears when her mother died,
or how she feared she wouldn't get her own
beribboned kindergarten chair, but the grief
in the skull like radium
in lead, and the visible dumb love like water   25
in crystal, at one with what holds it. The triumph
of worlds beyond words. Memory entices because ending is
its antonym. We're here to learn
the earth by heart and everything is crying
mind me, mind me! Yet the brain selects and shimmers   30
to a hand on skin while numbing the constant
stroke of clothes. Thoughts frame and flash
before the dark snaps back: The dress with lace tiers
she adored and the girl with one just like it,
the night she woke to see my father   35
walk down the drive and the second she remembered
he had died. So long as we keep chanting the words
those worlds will live, but just
so long, so long, so long. Each instant waves
through our nature and is nothing.   40
But in the love, the grief, under and above
the mother tongue, a permanence
hums: the steady mysterious
the coherent starlight.

(1983, 1986)

GARY SOTO
U.S.A., b.1952

BLACK HAIR

At eight I was brilliant with my body.
In July, that ring of heat
We all jumped through, I sat in the bleachers
Of Romain Playground, in the lengthening
Shade that rose from our dirty feet.   5
The game before us was more than baseball.
It was a figure — Hector Moreno
Quick and hard with turned muscles,
His crouch the one I assumed before an altar
Of worn baseball cards, in my room.   10

I came here because I was Mexican, a stick
Of brown light in love with those
Who could do it — the triple and hard slide,
The gloves eating balls into double plays.
What could I do with 50 pounds, my shyness,   15

My black torch of hair, about to go out?
Father was dead, his face no longer
Hanging over the table or our sleep,
And mother was the terror of mouths
Twisting hurt by butter knives.   20

In the bleachers I was brilliant with my body,
Waving players in and stomping my feet,
Growing sweaty in the presence of white shirts.
I chewed sunflower seeds. I drank water
And bit my arm through the late innings.   25
When Hector lined balls into deep
Center, in my mind I rounded the bases
With him, my face flared, my hair lifting
Beautifully, because we were coming home
To the arms of brown people.   30

(1985)

JOAN CRATE
Canada, b.1953

SHAWNANDITHIT
(Last of the Beothuks)

White handkerchief to your mouth, Shawnandithit,
white as your mother's fingertips, that expanding
spot on your sister's cheek the day they came
and took you three as you wandered hungry,
ribs hooking ice.   5

Except for the blood
white as death.

Who could have imagined you'd be taken
to a house in town with a fire and embroidered linen
to spit into. Who would have thought death was warm

and plump with meat and men who smile too much,   11
who ask questions with pencils, wanting
you to draw the canoes, the tents, the chasms
dug for winter houses. They ask you to speak
your language so they can study its sound.   15
How full of holes it is, subterranean tunnels
echo around your failing lungs.
Can they hear?
Warm blood in your mouth tastes ripe
as a lover, everything gone.   20

SHAWNANDITHIT   The Beothuk Indians of Newfoundland, now extinct, were the victims of European diseases and genocide; a woman named Shanandithit (b. c.1801) was the last known survivor; she died of tuberculosis in St. John's in 1829.

And so Shawnandithit, with Mother and sister dead
and none of your people left beating against winter,
it is your turn, the last Beothuk, broken
and beautiful as loose feathers on stone.   *24*
In the whitemen's steaming kitchen, you falter, look
to the wall, the clock you can't read, then sketch

them stories of lingering death, marriage ceremonies
and hunting parties, love, and your lingering death.

You cough graceful spurts of blood,
you fly, you plunge, alone Shawnandithit,   *30*
staining the white white pages.

(1990)

LOUISE ERDRICH
U.S.A., b.1954

DEAR JOHN WAYNE

August and the drive-in picture is packed.
We lounge on the hood of the Pontiac
surrounded by the slow-burning spirals they sell
at the window, to vanquish the hordes of mosquitoes.
Nothing works. They break through the smoke screen
    for blood.   *5*

Always the lookout spots the Indians first,
spread north to south, barring progress.
The Sioux or some other Plains bunch
in spectacular columns, ICBM missiles,
feathers bristling in the meaningful sunset.   *10*

The drum breaks. There will be no parlance.
Only the arrows whining, a death-cloud of nerves
swarming down on the settlers
who die beautifully, tumbling like dust weeds
into the history that brought us all here   *15*
together: this wide screen beneath the sign of the bear.

The sky fills, acres of blue squint and eye
that the crowd cheers. His face moves over us,
a thick cloud of vengeance, pitted
like the land that was once flesh. Each rut,   *20*
each scar makes a promise: *It is*
not over, this fight, not as long as you resist.

Everything we see belongs to us.

A few laughing Indians fall over the hood
slipping in the hot spilled butter.   *25*
The eye sees a lot, John, but the heart is so blind.

Death makes us owners of nothing.
He smiles, a horizon of teeth
the credits reel over, and then the white fields

again blowing in the true-to-life dark.   *30*
The dark films over everything.
We get into the car
scratching our mosquito bites, speechless and small
as people are when the movie is done.
We are back in our skins.   *35*

How can we help but keep hearing his voice,
the flip side of the sound track, still playing:
Come on, boys, we got them
where we want them, drunk, running.
They'll give us what we want, what we need.   *40*
Even his disease was the idea of taking everything.
Those cells, burning, doubling, splitting out of their
    skins.

(1984)

I WAS SLEEPING WHERE THE BLACK OAKS MOVE

We watched from the house
as the river grew, helpless
and terrible in its unfamiliar body.
Wrestling everything into it,
the water wrapped around trees   *5*
until their life-hold was broken.
They went down, one by one,
and the river dragged off their covering.

DEAR JOHN WAYNE   Title: the film actor John Wayne (Marion Morrison, 1907-1979), noted for his laconic portrayals of cowboys and other conventional American heroes. **41. disease:** cancer, now thought to have resulted from atomic test fallout in Utah to which the cast and crew of a movie being shot on location were exposed.

Nests of the herons, roots washed to bones,
snags of soaked bark on the shoreline: 10
a whole forest pulled through the teeth
of the spillway. Trees surfacing
singly, where the river poured off
into arteries for fields below the reservation.

When at last it was over, the long removal,   15
they had all become the same dry wood.
We walked among them, the branches
whitening in the raw sun.
Above us drifted herons,
alone, hoarse-voiced, broken,   20
settling their beaks among the hollows.

Grandpa said, *These are the ghosts of the tree people,*
moving above us, unable to take their rest.

Sometimes now, we dream our way back to the heron
    dance.
Their long wings are bending the air   25
into circles through which they fall.
They rise again in shifting wheels.
How long must we live in the broken figures
their necks make, narrowing the sky.

                                                (1984)

SUJATA BHATT
India/U.S.A./Germany, b.1956

A DIFFERENT HISTORY

Great Pan is not dead;
he simply emigrated
        to India.
Here, the gods roam freely,
disguised as snakes or monkeys;   5
every tree is sacred
and it is a sin
to be rude to a book.
It is a sin to shove a book aside
            with your foot,   10
a sin to slam books down
        hard on a table,
a sin to toss one carelessly
        across a room.
You must learn how to turn the pages gently   15
without disturbing Sarasvati,

without offending the tree
from whose wood the paper was made.

2
Which language
has not been the oppressor's tongue?   20
Which language
truly meant to murder someone?
And how does it happen
that after the torture,
after the soul has been cropped   25
with a long scythe swooping out
of the conqueror's face —
the unborn grandchildren
grow to love that strange language.
                                                (1988)

A DIFFERENT HISTORY   **1. Pan:** a fertility god in Greek mythology — associated with flocks, shepherds, pastures, and forests — represented as half man and half goat, playing a reed flute; according to Plutarch, all the oracles ceased at one point during the reign of the emperor Tiberius (A.D. 14-37), and many people heard the cry "Great Pan is Dead" sweep in from the sea. Cf. line 173 of Milton's "On the Morning of Christ's Nativity" (1629, 1645): "The Oracles are dumb"; cf. also Elizabeth Barret Browning's "The Dead Pan" (1844). **16. Sarasvati:** the Hindu goddess of knowledge and the fine arts, who is worshipped in libraries (from Bhatt's note).

VALERIE BLOOM
Jamaica/England, b.1956

YUH HEAR 'BOUT?

Yuh hear bout di people dem arres
Fi bun dung di Asian people dem house?
Yuh hear bout di policeman dem lock up
Fi beat up di black bwoy widout a cause?
Yuh hear bout di MP dem sack because im refuse fi help   *5*
im coloured constituents in a dem fight 'gainst deportation?
Yuh no hear bout dem?
Me neida.

Did You Hear About?

Did you hear about the people they arrested
For burning down the Asian people's house?   *10*
Did you hear about the policeman they put in jail
For beating up the black boy without any cause?
Did you hear about the MP they sacked
because he refused to help
his black constituents in their fight   *15*
against deportation?
You didn't hear about them?
Me neither.

                                        (1983)

EVA TIHANYI
Canada, b.1956

BLIND MAN

Since the eclipse, the earth
speaks to him in braille
and his hands listen,
his life syncopated
by the beat of a cane   *5*
tapping out anger, jazz, lust,
the rhythm of his breathing

Light,
both particle and wave

falling and flowing   *10*
is for him a sound,
a white melody
scored on the dark sheets
of his eyelids

He has a penchant for roses,   *15*
is the only man I know
who hears them sing
                              (1984)

ARCHIE WELLER
Australia, b.1957

"To the Moore River Settlement we now go"

To the Moore River Settlement we now go;
in the belly of the rumbling iron snake
that has swallowed us up, legends laws and all.
From the trees so tall and proud.
The spirits of these trees call out,   5
And from the coloured carpets
scattered like lakes upon the grounds we love so.
Dressed in rags we go, and with whiteman blankets
as grey as my soul inside.

(1988)

FREDERICK D'AGUIAR
England/Guyana, b.1960

OLD MAMA DOT

1
Born on a sunday
In the kingdom of Asante

Sold on a monday
Into slavery

Ran away on tuesday   5
Cause she born free

Lost a foot on wednesday
When they catch she

Worked all thursday
Till her head grey   10

Dropped on friday
Where they burn she

Freed on saturday
In a new century

2
Old Mama Dot   15
Old Mama Dot
Boss o' de stew pot
She na deal in vat
She a farm a plot
She na bap   20
No style so stop
Look at Mama Dot
Winein' on the spot

TO THE MOORE RIVER SETTLEMENT   **1. Moore River:** a native settlement north of Perth. **2-3. iron snake . . . legends:** contrasting the iron train with the Rainbow Serpent (the creator figure) of Aboriginal mythology.   **OLD MAMA DOT**   See "Solomon Grundy" (p. 568). **2. Asante:** the ancient kingdom of the Ashanti in West Africa, predating European contact. **20. bap:** make a surprise move.

Old Mama Dot
Old Mama Dot   25
Watch her squat
Full of the nat-
ural goodness dat
Grows in the lan'
She use to fa'm   30
Bare han'
Up every dawn

Old Mama Dot
Old Mamma Dot
She no deal with vat-   35
igan na mek no fuss
She a deal wid dus'
She swing cutlass
Play big boss
Lick chile rass   40
Go to mass

(1984)

35-36. vat-igan: suggesting *Vatican* and perhaps also *V.A.T.*, or Value Added Tax (U.K.). **40. Lick:** beat; **rass:** behind.

Appendix I
Notes on Authors

N.B.: Names in SMALL CAPS refer to other authors listed in this appendix.

ACHEBE, CHINUA (b.1930): Nigerian novelist, essayist, and editor, born in Ogidi, educated at U. of Ibadan and London U.; worked for the Nigerian Broadcasting Corporation, 1954-57; married Christie Chinwe Okoli, 1961; taught English at U. of Nigeria (Nsukka) after 1967; director with Heinemann Educational publishers (Ibadan) after 1970; like OKARA, served the Biafran government during the Nigerian Civil War (1967-70); books include *Things Fall Apart* (1958), *Arrow of God* (1964), and *Girls at War and Other Stories* (1972); *Morning Yet on Creation Day* (1975) collects his essays on literature and politics.

ADCOCK, FLEUR (b.1934): New Zealand poet, librarian, anthologist, and Latin translator, born in Papakura; married poet Alistair Campbell (1952; divorced 1958); settled in England, 1963; *Selected Poems* appeared in 1983.

ADDISON, JOSEPH (1672-1719): English dramatist, classical scholar, and (after 1708) Whig M.P., best known as an essayist; born in Lichfield, educated at Oxford; married the Countess of Warwick, 1716; school friend of the Irish essayist and playwright Sir Richard Steele (1672-1729), who (borrowing the pseudonym "Isaac Bickerstaff" from SWIFT's *Predictions for the Ensuing Year*, 1708) became editor of *The Tatler* (1709-11), a tri-weekly commentary on current events, literature, and human foible, to which Addison contributed essays; Addison also edited *The Spectator* (1711-12, 1714) with Steele, attracting contributions from POPE and Lady Mary Wortley MONTAGU, among others; an active member of the group of London writers known as the Kit-Kat Club, including Swift, Congreve, and the playwright Sir John Vanbrugh (1664-1726); author of *Cato* (1713), a tragedy, and other works. (Steele, with whom he is repeatedly associated in literary histories, is also the author of a play called *The Conscious Lovers*, 1722, and a political work called *The Crisis*, 1714, which suggested the possibility of a Hanoverian succession and led to Steele being expelled from his seat in Parliament on grounds of sedition; when George I did succeed to the throne later in 1714, Steele was knighted and granted a patent to run the Theatre Royal in Drury Lane.)

AELFRIC (c.955-c.1020): English grammarian, biographer, translator, and Benedictine reformer; wrote his *Colloquy*, intended as a Latin primer, while teaching at Cerne Abbey in Dorset; later became abbot of Eynsham, near Oxford.

AKENSIDE, MARK (1721-1770): London physician, born in Newcastle, the son of a butcher; known for his didactic poem *The Pleasures of [the] Imagination* (1744, revised 1757); satirized in *Peregrine Pickle*, a 1751 novel by Tobias Smollett (1721-1771).

AMMONS, A[RCHIE] R[ANDOLPH] (b.1926): American poet and teacher, born in North Carolina, educated at U. of California at Berkeley; served in the U.S. navy in the South Pacific during World War II; married Phyllis Plumbo, 1949; began teaching creative writing at Cornell U., 1964; *Selected Poems 1951-1977* (1977), which won a National Book Award, and *Selected Longer Poems* (1980) sample his work.

ARBLAY, MME. D': see Frances BURNEY.

ARMSTRONG, JOHN (1709-1779): Scottish poet and physician, born in Roxburghshire, educated at Edinburgh, practised in London; friend of James THOMSON and the painter Henry Fuseli (1741-1825, with whom Mary WOLLSTONECRAFT had a brief relationship); author of *Oeconomy of Love* (1736) and *The Art of Preserving Health* (1744).

ARNOLD, MATTHEW (1822-1888): English poet, critic, and school inspector, educated at Oxford; son of Dr. Thomas Arnold, the Master of Rugby College celebrated in Thomas Hughes's *Tom Brown's Schooldays* (1857); travelled in Switzerland in the 1840s, perhaps meeting the woman celebrated in his poems as "Marguerite"; married Frances Lucy Wightman, 1851, the year he was named Inspector of Schools, a position he held, though he became Professor of Poetry at Oxford in 1858, till his retirement in 1886; criticized current educational practice, and championed state schools; author of several volumes of verse, including *Empedocles on Etna, and Other Poems* (1852) and *Poems* (1853, 1855), and of prose, such as *Essays in Criticism* (1865, 1888) and *Culture and Anarchy* (1869), which shaped definitions of cultural standards for several generations.

ASCHAM, ROGER (1515-1568): English classical scholar, born in Yorkshire, educated at Cambridge; tutor to ELIZABETH I (when she was a child) and later her advisor, and Latin secretary to Queen Mary I; author of *Toxophilus* (1545), a defence of archery, and *The Schoolmaster* (1570).

ASHBERY, JOHN (b.1927): New York-born American poet and professor, educated (in French literature) at Harvard, Columbia, and New York U.; lived in France, 1955-65, working as an art critic for the European edition of the *New York Herald Tribune*; author of many volumes of poetry, including *Selected Poems* (1967) and *Self-Portrait in a Convex Mirror* (1975), which won a Pulitzer Prize and a National Book Award.

ASTELL, MARY (1666-1731): English poet, essayist, and charity school administrator, born in Newcastle; educated by her uncle; a friend of Lady Mary Wortley MONTAGU; attacked by the poet Colley Cibber (1671-1757), who was himself the target of POPE's *The Dunciad* (in its revised version, 1735), and by SWIFT; author of *Some Reflections on Marriage* (1700) and other works on religion and philosophy, often using pseudonyms.

ATWOOD, MARGARET (b.1939): Canadian poet, painter, critic, and fiction writer, born in Ottawa, daughter of an entomologist; spent much of her childhood in the northern Ontario bush; educated at U. of Toronto, a student of Jay MACPHERSON, and at Harvard, where she met and married the critic James Polk, 1967 (divorced 1973); in 1973 married the novelist Graeme Gibson (b.1934); cartoonist for *This Magazine*; active in Amnesty International; winner of several literary honours; author of more than twenty books, including a dystopian novel, *The Handmaid's Tale* (1985), and other fictions, and numerous volumes of criticism and poetry, including *The Journals of Susanna Moodie* (1970), *Survival* (1972), and *Selected Poems* (1976).

AUCHTERLONIE (GREEN), DOROTHY (1915-1990): Australian critic and poet, born in Durham, England; educated there and at U. Sydney; married, 1944, the critic H.M. Green (1881-1962), whose essays she edited after his death; lectured at Australian National U. and other institutions; author of *Kaleidoscope* (1940) and other volumes, her criticism (e.g., *The Music of Love*, 1984) appearing under the name Dorothy Green.

AUDEN, W[YSTAN] H[UGH] (1907-1973): Poet, critic, anthologist, travel writer, and playwright (e.g. *The Ascent of F6*, 1936, which he wrote with his friend Christopher Isherwood, 1904-1986, whom he met at preparatory school in Surrey); born in York, educated at Oxford, where his contemporaries included BETJEMAN, Cecil Day-Lewis (1904-1972), and SPENDER; worked as a tutor and film-maker in the 1920s; began to publish verse with *Poems* (1930), followed by several other volumes, including *The Dance of Death* (1933), *Nones* (1951), and *The Shield of Achilles* (1955); supported the Republican cause in the Spanish Civil War; edited *The Oxford Book of Light Verse* (1938); emigrated with Isherwood to the U.S.A., 1939; became an American citizen, 1946; subsequently lived with Chester Kallman in New York, Oxford, and Austria, collaborating with him on the libretto of Stravinsky's *The Rake's Progress* (1951); was named Oxford Professor of Poetry, 1956-60; *The Dyer's Hand* (1963) is one of several essay collections; *Collected Poems* appeared in 1976.

AVISON, MARGARET (b.1918): Canadian poet, born in Galt, Ontario, educated at U. Toronto; worked as secretary, librarian, and social worker with the Women's Missionary Society of the Presbyterian Church in Toronto; author of *Winter Sun* (1960), *The Dumbfounding* (1978), and other volumes marked by a strong personal Christian belief; her *Selected Poems* appeared in 1991.

BACON, SIR FRANCIS (1561-1626): English essayist, philosopher, lawyer, and politician, born in London, the son of Nicholas Bacon, Lord Keeper of the Seal for ELIZABETH I; influenced by his mother's Calvinism; educated at Cambridge; unsuccessfully sought political favours from his uncle, William Cecil, Lord Burghley (1520-1598), the Queen's advisor; accepted the patronage of Robert Devereux, the 1st Earl of Essex (1541-1576), but helped prosecute Essex after the failure of his revolt in 1601; knighted by JAMES I (was later named Baron Verulam of Verulam, and in 1621, Viscount St Albans; married Alice Barnham, 1606; undertook a series of legal assignments for the king, professing to manage Parliament for him, becoming Lord Chancellor in 1618; opposed RALEGH; was dismissed in 1621 for accepting bribes, released after a short imprisonment; died in debt; author of *Essays* (1597, subsequently much enlarged), *The Advancement of Learning* (1609), *Novum Organum* (1620), and *The New Atlantis* (1626).

BAILEY, JACOB (1731-1808): Canadian poet, diarist, and Church of England minister, born in Massachusetts, educated at Harvard; married Sally Weeks, 1761; was attacked in his Maine parish for his conservative views, and forced to flee; settled in Nova Scotia, 1779; author of *The Frontier Missionary* (published in 1853) and several

Hudibrastic verse satires, including "The Adventures of Jack Ramble, the Methodist Preacher," much of which remains in manuscript.

BARBAULD, ANNA LAETITIA (AIKIN) (1743-1825): English poet, critic, anthologist, and teacher, born in Leicestershire, daughter of a schoolmaster who after 1758 taught at Warrington Academy (a Dissenting school) along with John Howard, the prison reformer (1726-1790), and Joseph Priestley, the scientist (1733-1804); settled in Suffolk after marrying Rochemont Barbauld, a Dissenting minister, and ran a school with him for ten years (he later became violently paranoid, attacking her and committing suicide in 1808); an abolitionist and political liberal, wrote pamphlets against Parliament's 1790 reaffirmation of the Test Acts, the law that permitted only members of the Established Church to hold public office and attend Oxford or Cambridge; editor of works by Samuel Richardson (1689-1761) and others; author of Unitarian essays and verses for children; *Eighteen Hundred and Eleven* (1812) predicted that the cultural centre of civilization would move from England to America; her *Works* were edited in 1825.

BARNARD, LADY ANNE: see Lady Anne LINDSAY.

BARNES, WILLIAM (1801-1886): English poet, philologist, and Church of England clergyman, born in Dorset, educated at Cambridge; in 1823 married Julia Miles (d.1852); ordained, 1847, and became a country parson; author of three volumes of *Poems in the Dorset Dialect* (1844-62); his neighbour, HARDY, commemorated him in "The Last Signal."

BAXTER, JAMES K[EIR] (1926-1972): New Zealand poet, critic, and dramatist, born in Dunedin, educated there and in Wellington; worked as a labourer; edited *Numbers*, 1954-59; converted to Catholicism in 1958, and set up "Jerusalem," a religious commune, in the Wanganui River Valley; author of *In Fires of No Return* (1958), *Pig Island Letters* (1966), and *Jerusalem Sonnets* (1970), among other works.

BEAUMONT, SIR JOHN (1583-1627): English poet, elder brother of the more famous Elizabethan dramatist Francis Beaumont (c.1584-1616), born in Leicestershire; author of *Bosworth Field* (1629), an early example of heroic couplets.

BECKETT, SAMUEL (1906-1989): Irish playwright and novelist, educated at Trinity College (Dublin); settled in Paris after 1927, writing most of his work in French and translating them into English; married the pianist Suzanne Dechevaux-Dumesnil; during the 1930s, took dictation from JOYCE (who, nearly blind, was working on *Finnegans Wake*); won Nobel Prize, 1969; his plays, examples of "Theatre of the Absurd," include *Waiting for Godot* (1953/tr.1955), *Endgame* (1957/tr.1958), and *Happy Days* (1961).

BEDDOES, THOMAS LOVELL (1803-1849): English poet and physician, born near Bristol, educated at Oxford; nephew of the novelist Maria Edgeworth (1767-1849); author of *Death's Jest-Book* (1850), published a year after his suicide in Switzerland.

BEHN, APHRA (1640-1689): English dramatist, poet, translator, and novelist (used the pseudonym "Astraea"), possibly born Aphra Johnson in Canterbury; spent 1663-64 in Surinam, the basis for her most famous novel, *Oroonoko* (1688); married (possibly in 1664) a Dutch merchant (the marriage being finished by 1666); she was a spy in Holland for Charles II in 1666, though her reports about William of

Orange's invasion plans appear to have been ignored; imprisoned for debt in 1668, she began writing to pay for her release, composing eighteen plays, including *Sir Patient Fancy* (1678), and several prose narratives; widely known in the London literary scene, but often attacked for her unorthodox lifestyle, she was arrested in 1682 for her political frankness.

BENNETT, LOUISE (b.1919): Jamaican dialect (or "patwah") poet, stage and radio performer (as "Miss Lou"), born in Kingston, married to the comedian Eric "Chalk Talk" Coverley; studied social work and theatre in London; drama director of the Jamaican Social Welfare Commission; her books include *Jamaica Labrish* (1966).

BENTHAM, JEREMY (1748-1832): English philosopher, born in London, educated at Oxford; the founder of *The Westminster Review* in 1824, and one of the people who helped establish the University of London; best known for his doctrine of Utilitarianism, as in *Poor Laws and Pauper Management* (1797), an espousal of economic self-interest, which influenced the Poor Law of 1834; attacked by DICKENS in *Oliver Twist* (1837-39) and *Hard Times* (1854).

BENTLEY, E[DMUND] C[LERIHEW] (1875-1956): English parodist and author of light verse and detective fiction, born in London, educated at Oxford; journalist for the *Daily Telegraph*; friend of CHESTERTON and Damon Runyon (1884-1946), the American humourist and author of *Guys and Dolls* (1931); inventor of the "clerihew" that he introduced in *Biography for Beginners* (1905); his novels include *Trent's Last Case* (1913).

BERKELEY, GEORGE (1685-1753): Clergyman and philosopher, born in Ireland, at Dysert Castle, to an English family (his mother was said to be the great-aunt of General Wolfe); educated at Trinity College (Dublin); ordained, 1707, lecturing at Trinity College in philosophy and mathematics; moved to London, 1713, becoming a friend of ADDISON, POPE, and SWIFT; opposed the ideas of HOBBES and LOCKE, arguing in such works as *The Treatise Concerning the Principles of Human Knowledge* (1716) that *"esse est percipi"*—that reality exists only because people mentally perceive it—causing Dr. JOHNSON to kick a stone and reply dismissively, "I refute it thus"; married Anne Forster, 1728, sailing to America on the promise of a grant to found a Christian college in the Bermudas; stayed in Rhode Island for three years when the grant did not materialize, though his plan for a college was later used to plan Columbia University; named Bishop of Cloyne, in the county of Cork, 1734, retiring to Oxford in 1752.

BERNERS, LORD: see John BOURCHIER.

BERRY, JAMES (b.1924): English poet, born in Jamaica, emigrated to England in 1948; his works include *Lucy's Letters and Loving* (1982) and an anthology of "Black British poetry," *News for Babylon* (1984).

BETJEMAN, SIR JOHN (1906-1984): English poet and broadcaster, born in London, the son of a merchant; educated at Oxford, a contemporary of AUDEN; worked as a schoolmaster and journalist, publishing his first volume of poetry in 1931; married Penelope Chetwode, 1933; knighted, 1969; named Poet Laureate, 1972, succeeding Cecil Day-Lewis (1904-1972); lived in Berkshire; an enthusiast for Victorian architecture; published guides to parish churches as well as the verse gathered in *Collected Poems* (1958; revised 1962).

BHATT, SUJATA (b.1956): Indian poet and translator, born in Ahmedabad, educated in the United States; she now lives in Germany; author of *Brunizem* (1988).

BIERCE, AMBROSE (1842-c.1914): American satirist, born in Ohio; fought in the American Civil War; became a journalist in San Francisco and contributed to various periodicals while living in England, 1872-75; known for his sardonic and sometimes macabre narratives, as in *Tales of Soldiers and Civilians* (1891), which included "An Occurrence at Owl Creek Bridge," and for *The Cynic's Word Book* (1906, renamed *The Devil's Dictionary* in 1911); he disappeared in Mexico, during a civil war.

BIRNEY, EARLE (b.1904): Canadian poet and novelist, born in Calgary, Alberta, raised in rural British Columbia; strongly influenced by his Calvinist mother; educated (in Medieval Studies) at U. of Toronto and U. of British Columbia; married Sylvia Johnstone, 1933 (annulled 1936); joined the Trotskyite wing of the Communist Party in the 1930s (withdrew when World War II began, and served in the intelligence wing of the Canadian army); married Esther Bull, 1940 (divorced 1977); active editor of Canadian poetry journals, radio playwright and commentator, and innovator in developing a creative writing programme at the U. of British Columbia; friend of Dylan THOMAS and the novelist Malcolm Lowry (1909-1957), some of whose manuscripts he edited; settled in Toronto, with Wai-lan Low, in 1965, taking numerous trips abroad which resulted in new poems; author of over thirty books, including *Turvey* (1949; unexpurgated edition, 1977), *Ice Cod Bell and Stone* (1962), *Near False Creek Mouth* (1975), and *Spreading Time* (1980).

BISHOP, ELIZABETH (1911-1979): American poet, essayist, and short story writer, born in Worcester, Massachusetts, and raised there and in Nova Scotia by her grandparents; educated at Vassar, where she met Muriel RUKEYSER and the novelist Mary McCarthy (1912-1989); lived for sixteen years in Brazil (1951-66), obtaining the experiences that led to several subsequent books, after which she taught at various American universities; friend of Marianne MOORE; author of *Brazil* (1962), *Poems: North and South—A Cold Spring* (1955), which won a Pulitzer Prize, and other works; *Complete Poems* appeared in 1983, *Complete Prose* in 1984.

BISSETT, BILL [bill bissett] (b.1939): Canadian poet and artist, born in Halifax; active with small press publishing in Vancouver during the 1960s; his many works are sampled in *Selected Poems* (1980).

BLAKE, WILLIAM (1757-1827): English poet and painter, born in London, educated at home and apprenticed to an engraver at age 14; accepted at the Royal Academy, but became impatient with its conventional ideas about art; married Catherine Boucher, 1782, and became neighbours of Joshua REYNOLDS, whose ideas (in *Discourses on Art*) Blake rejected, and Jane Hogarth, widow of the engraver William Hogarth (1697-1764); prizing independence and rebellion against authority, became friends with the philosopher and novelist William Godwin [see SHELLEY] and the political reformer PAINE; author (and illustrator) of *Songs of Innocence and of Experience* (1789, 1794), *The Marriage of Heaven and Hell* (1790), *The Four Zoas* (1797), and other books; a brief sojourn in Sussex (1800-03) resulted in his false arrest for sedition; returned to London, engraving his own books for limited distribution; left numerous works in manuscript when he died; buried in an unmarked grave.

BLAMIRE, SUSANNA (1747-1794): English poet, born in Cumberland, noted for her dialect poetry (on which she sometimes collaborated with Catherine Gilpin, 1738-1811); her *Poetical Works* appeared in 1842.

BLOOM, VALERIE (WRIGHT) (b.1956): Jamaican poet, performer, and teacher, born in Clarendon, educated in Jamaica and U. of Kent, now based in Manchester; author of *Touch Mi, Tell Mi* (1983).

BOLAND, EAVAN (b.1945): Irish poet and lecturer in Irish studies, born in Dublin, educated at Trinity College and U. of Iowa; daughter of the painter Frances (Kelly) Boland; married to the novelist Kevin Casey; author of *In Her Own Image* (1980), *Selected Poems* (1989), and other works.

BOSWELL, JAMES (1740-1795): Scottish diarist and biographer, born and educated in Edinburgh, the son of a judge, Lord Auchinleck, whose estate he inherited in 1782; friend of GOLDSMITH and BURKE; best known for his *Life of Samuel Johnson* (1791) and for *The Journal of a Tour to the Hebrides* (1785); the many journals he left unpublished were found in the 20th century, mostly at Malahide Castle, and edited by F.A. Pottle and others.

BOURCHIER, JOHN, LORD BERNERS (1467-1533): English writer, succeeded his grandfather to the baronetcy in 1474; educated at Oxford; served Henry VII, and became Chancellor of the Exchequer for Henry VIII; by 1519 had married Catherine, daughter of Duke of Norfolk; deputy of Calais, where he strengthened the fortifications, as reported in his letters to Cardinal Wolsey; translator of Froissart's *Chronicles* (1523-25), chivalric romances variously involving Oberon and King Arthur, and *The Golden Book of Marcus Aurelius* (1535).

BOWLES, WILLIAM LISLE (1762-1850): English poet, educated at Winchester (where one of his teachers was Joseph WARTON) and Oxford; married Magdalene Wake, 1797; became chaplain to the Prince Regent in 1818; his *Fourteen Sonnets*, published anonymously in 1789, influenced COLERIDGE and SOUTHEY; his 1806 edition of POPE aroused a controversy with BYRON.

BRADSTREET, ANNE (DUDLEY) (1612-1672): The first published American poet; born in Northampton, England, the daughter of Thomas Dudley, steward to the Earl of Lincoln and later governor of Massachusetts; tutored at home; a Puritan, she emigrated to America in 1630 after marrying Simon Bradstreet, who also became governor of Massachusetts; *The Tenth Muse Lately Sprung Up in America* (1650) was expanded and reprinted (with a foreword by Adrienne RICH) in a 1967 edition.

BRATHWAITE, EDWARD KAMAU (b.1930): Jamaican poet and historian, born Lawson Edward Brathwaite in Bridgetown, Barbados, and educated at Cambridge and U. of Sussex; professor of history at U. of the West Indies (Mona) till 1992; author of *The Arrivants* (1973; earlier published in three separate volumes), *Sun Poem* (1982), and such historical works as *The Folk Culture of the Slaves of Jamaica* (1970).

BRETON, NICHOLAS (c.1555-1626): English poet and character writer, son of a London merchant and stepson of George GASCOIGNE; his several volumes include *Strange News out of Divers Countries* (1622).

BRIDGES, ROBERT (1844-1930): English poet and physician, born in Kent; educated at Oxford, where he met HOPKINS, whose work he published in 1918; named Poet Laureate, 1913; practised medicine till 1881, publishing numerous plays and poems from 1873 on; married Monica Waterhouse, 1884; lived near Oxford, close to MASEFIELD; an early *Collected Poems* (1912) was followed by several other books.

BRINGHURST, ROBERT (b.1946): Canadian poet and essayist, born in Los Angeles, educated at Indiana U. and U. of British Columbia; after careers as journalist in Lebanon and law clerk in Panama, now lives on Bowen Island, B.C.; actively involved with Native community, as in *The Raven Steals the Light* (1984, with Bill REID); author of *Bergschrund* (1975), *Ocean/Paper/Stone* (1984), *Pieces of Map, Pieces of Music* (1986), and other works; *The Black Canoe* (1991) deals with REID's sculpture.

BRONTË, EMILY (1818-1848): English novelist and poet; one of three literary sisters (with Charlotte, 1816-1855, and Anne, 1820-1849) who grew up in the Haworth parsonage, in Yorkshire, where they were educated; their poetry, *Poems by Currer, Ellis and Acton Bell*, appeared in 1846; and Emily, as "Ellis Bell," published the novel *Wuthering Heights* in 1847.

BROOKE, FRANCES (MOORE) (1724-1789): English essayist, novelist, and librettist, author of what is often regarded as the first Canadian novel, *The History of Emily Montague* (1769); friend of JOHNSON and the actor David Garrick; as "Mary Singleton," edited a periodical called *The Old Maid* (1755-56); in 1756, married John Brooke, who in 1760 became chaplain to the army garrison in Quebec; returned to London in 1768; became manager of the King's Theatre in London, with her friend, the actress Mary Ann Yates (1728-1787), until the theatre was sold to the playwright Richard Brinsley Sheridan (1751-1816) in 1778; her operas, e.g. *Rosina* (1782, music by William Shield), were produced at Covent Garden.

BROOKE, HENRY (c.1703-1783): Irish poet, dramatist, and novelist, born in County Cavan; educated at Trinity College (Dublin); married his cousin and ward, Catherine Meares; lived in London for ten years, a friend of POPE, who lived near him in Twickenham; author of a play based on Swedish history, *Gustavus Vasa, the Deliverer of his Country* (1739), banned in London because Sir Robert Walpole thought it criticized him (produced in Dublin as *The Patriot*, 1744), and a novel, *The Fool of Quality* (1766-72), among other works.

BROOKE, LORD: see Fulke GREVILLE.

BROOKE, RUPERT (1887-1915): English poet, born in Rugby, educated there and at Cambridge; associated with other Georgian poets, including the anthologist Edward Marsh (1872-1953); travelled through North America in 1913, recuperating from a nervous breakdown; died of blood poisoning on the way to the front during World War I; *Collected Poems* appeared in 1918.

BROOKS, GWENDOLYN (b.1917): American poet, born in Topeka, Kansas, educated in Chicago; with *Annie Allen* (1949) she became the first black poet to win a Pulitzer Prize; other books include *The World of Gwendolyn Brooks* (1971), and two volumes of autobiography.

BROWNE, SIR THOMAS (1605-1682): English writer and doctor, born in London, educated at Oxford and in France, Italy, and Holland;

married Dorothy Mileham, 1641, and had ten children; friend of Joseph HALL; knighted by Charles II in 1671 for his pro-Royalist services during the Civil War; author of several enquiries into science and religion, including *Religio Medici* (1642), *Pseudodoxia Epidemica*, or *Vulgar Errors* (1646), and *Hydriotaphia*, or *Urn Burial* (1658).

BROWNING, ELIZABETH BARRETT (1806-1861): English poet, born near Durham, educated privately; corresponded with Mary Russell MITFORD; met Robert BROWNING after the family moved to London (50 Wimpole Street), married him secretly in 1846 and moved to Italy; *Poems* (1850) includes "Sonnets from the Portuguese," written during their courtship; other books include *Aurora Leigh* (1856).

BROWNING, ROBERT (1812-1889): English poet and playwright, born in London, educated primarily at home; began to publish poetry in 1833; visited Italy, 1838 and 1844; married Elizabeth Barrett in 1846, then settled in Florence; published regularly, but got only moderate reviews, even from friends such as RUSKIN; returned to England after his wife's death (1861), publishing almost twenty more books, finally securing a reputation in the 1880s; died while visiting their son (the sculptor Robert Barrett Browning, 1849-1912) in Venice; publications include *Sordello* (1840), *Dramatic Lyrics* (1842), *Men and Women* (1855), *Dramatis Personae* (1864), *The Ring and the Book* (1868-69), and *Asolando* (1889).

BRYANT, WILLIAM CULLEN (1794-1878): American poet, born in Massachusetts; published his first poems at age 14, satirizing the JEFFERSON administration; studied law, then became editor of the New York *Evening Post* from 1829 till his death; Republican opponent of slavery; author of *Poems* (1821; enlarged 1832).

BUHKWUJJENENE ["MAN OF THE WILD"] (c.1815-1900): Ojibway chief of lands to the northeast of Lake Huron, son of Shinguacouse; his oral tale of the flood was written down when he told it at a garden party during a visit to England in 1878, and first printed in the *Algoma Missionary News and Shingwauk Journal* in 1879.

BUNYAN, JOHN (1628-1688): English writer and preacher, born near Bedford, educated locally before taking up his father's trade as tinker; married twice, though the name of his first wife (married c.1647, d. 1658) is not known (the second, married in 1659, was Elizabeth, d. 1692); supported Cromwell during the Civil War; arrested after the Restoration of the monarchy, and jailed (for his Nonconformist preaching) from 1660 to 1672 and again in 1677, during which time he wrote his spiritual autobiography, *Grace Abounding* (1666), and began *The Pilgrim's Progress* (1678), which circulated widely, both in English and in many translations.

BURKE, EDMUND (1729-1797): Political philosopher, born in Dublin, educated at Trinity College; moved to London, and became a friend of JOHNSON and REYNOLDS; secretary to the Prime Minister (the Marquis of Rockingham), became a Whig M.P. in 1765, and a forceful orator and polemicist, opposing slavery and espousing social reform; *Reflections on the Revolution in France* (1790) is one of many books and pamphlets.

BURNEY, FRANCES [FANNY], MME. D'ARBLAY (1752-1840): English diarist, editor, and novelist, born in King's Lynn and educated at home; daughter of JOHNSON's friend, the musician Dr. Charles Burney; a court attendant to Queen Charlotte, 1786-91 (an experience

which nearly ruined her health), she married a French officer, General Alexandre d'Arblay, in 1793; author of *Evelina* (1778) and several volumes of diaries, edited posthumously.

BURNS, ROBERT (1759-1796): Scottish poet, farmer, and songwriter, born in Alloway, near Ayr, educated locally; after a series of liaisons, married Jean Armour (1767-1834) in 1788; influenced by the poetry of Allan RAMSAY; contributed many songs, including "Auld Lang Syne," to James Johnson's *The Scots Musical Museum* (1787-1803); the "Kilmarnock" edition of *Poems Chiefly in the Scottish Dialect* appeared in 1786; is commemorated annually by Scots dinners on "Burns Night" (January 25).

BUTLER, SAMUEL (1612-1680): English satirist, born near Worcester, the son of a farmer; served in various noble households, including those of the Countess of Kent (where John Selden, 1584-1654, later one of the signers of the 1628 Petition of Right, befriended him) and of the Duke of Buckingham (whose play, *The Rehearsal*, Butler may have helped compose; see DRYDEN); author of *Hudibras*, a burlesque in three parts (1663, 1664, 1678).

BUTLER, SAMUEL (1835-1902): English man of letters, composer, and painter, born into a clergyman's family in Nottinghamshire; grandson of Dr. Samuel Butler, headmaster of Shrewsbury and Bishop of Lichfield; educated at Cambridge; resisting his father and a clerical career, he became a New Zealand sheep farmer, returning to England in 1865; wrote "A Psalm of Montreal" in Canada in 1875; author of the Utopian satire *Erewhon* (1872) and *The Way of All Flesh* (1903), a novel; his *Notebooks* appeared in 1912.

BYRON, GEORGE GORDON, LORD (1788-1824): English poet, born in London, abandoned by his father and raised by his Calvinist mother in Aberdeen; at age 10 inherited the baronetcy from his great-uncle; educated at Cambridge; friend of SHELLEY, HUNT, Thomas MOORE, and Sir Walter SCOTT; quarrelled with and satirized SOUTHEY; after a loose and itinerant life, died of a fever while fighting with Greek forces against Turkey; author of *Childe Harold's Pilgrimage* (1812-1817), *Don Juan* (1819-1824), and other works.

CABOT, SEBASTIAN (1474-1557): explorer and cartographer, son of the explorer John Cabot (Giovanni Caboto, 1425-c.1500), born probably in Venice; explored the Atlantic Coast of Canada for England in 1499; attempted unsuccessfully to colonize Brazil for Spain in 1526; became inspector of the navy for Edward VI in 1548; died during an English expedition to open trade routes to the east.

CAEDMON (fl. 670-680): apparently a herdsman who became a monk at Whitby in Yorkshire during the rule of the abbess Hild (657-80); all information on Caedmon derives from the history written by the Venerable Bede (c.673-735), *Historia Ecclesiastica Gentis Anglorum* (731).

CAMPION, THOMAS (1567-1620): English poet, composer, and physician, born in Essex and educated at Cambridge; author of *Observations in the Art of English Poesie* (1602), which was answered by Samuel DANIEL; best known for the lute songs published in *A Book of Airs* (1601), which made him a musical rival at the time to the composer John Dowland (1563-1626).

CAREW, THOMAS (c.1595-1640): English Cavalier poet whose surname is pronounced "Carey"; born in West Wickham, studied at

Oxford; employed by Lord HERBERT of Cherbury when Herbert was British ambassador to France; a friend of JONSON, DONNE, and King Charles I, his poems were edited posthumously.

CAREY, HENRY (c.1687-1743): English poet and music teacher, born in Yorkshire (information about his family background is scarce); best known as a witty song-writer and author of burlesques and farces, he is thought by some also to have composed "God Save the King."

CARLETON, WILLIAM (1794-1869): Irish novelist and sketch writer, born to a poor peasant family in County Tyrone, fluent in both English and Irish; locally educated; in his late teens, set out to visit Dublin and London, acquiring a reputation for his knowledge of folktales; author of *Traits and Stories of the Irish Peasantry* (1832) and other collections.

CARLYLE, THOMAS (1795-1881): Scots historian and critic, born in Dumfriesshire, educated at Edinburgh U.; tutor, translator of Goethe and others, and regular contributor to *The Edinburgh Review*; in 1826 married Jane Welsh (1801-1866), who became known as a witty letter-writer; influenced RUSKIN and DICKENS, among others, through such works as *Sartor Resartus* (1833-1834), *The French Revolution* (1837; rewritten after the first manuscript was destroyed in a fire while on loan to the philosopher John Stuart Mill in 1835), and *On Heroes, Hero-Worship and the Heroic in History* (1841).

CARMAN, BLISS (1861-1929): Canadian poet, born in Fredericton, a cousin of C.G.D. ROBERTS and distant relative of EMERSON; became associated with the American poet Richard Hovey (1864-1900) and the Unitrinian Movement; a celebrated literary performer in his own day; author of *Low Tide on Grand Pré* (1893) and other works.

CARROLL, LEWIS [Charles Lutwidge Dodgson] (1832-1898): English humorist, clergyman, and mathematics lecturer, born in Cheshire and educated at Rugby and Oxford; ordained, 1861, but gave relatively few sermons, because of a persistent stammer; *Alice's Adventures in Wonderland* (1865)—originally called *Alice's Adventures Under Ground* and narrated to Alice Liddell (1852-1934), the daughter of a friend)—was followed by *Through the Looking-Glass and What Alice Found There* (1871).

CARTER, ELIZABETH (1717-1806): English scholar and poet, born in Deal, Kent, and educated by her father, a clergyman; friend of JOHNSON, TALBOT, and [see Hannah MORE] the "Bluestocking" critic and patron Elizabeth (Robinson) Montagu (1720-1800), with whom she travelled in Europe; fluent in ten languages, she became a well-known translator (e.g., of Epictetus), and she contributed essays on a range of topics to such journals as *The Gentleman's Magazine* and *The Rambler*.

CAVENDISH, MARGARET: see Duchess of NEWCASTLE.

CAWTHORN, JAMES (1719-1761): English poet, born in Sheffield, the son of an upholsterer; educated at Cambridge; became a schoolmaster; ordained c.1743; killed when thrown from a horse; published occasional verses; *Poems* (1771) was published posthumously by subscription.

CAXTON, WILLIAM (c.1422-1491): English printer and translator, born in Kent, trained in Bruges, Belgium; set up the first printing press in England, 1476; printed some works in Latin and many in English, including those of CHAUCER and John Gower (c.1330-1408), together with fables, saints' lives, and romances such as MALORY's *Morte Darthur* (1485); when he died, his press passed to his apprentice and assistant, Wynkyn de Worde (d. 1534), the first printer in England to use italic type (in 1524).

CHAPMAN, GEORGE (c.1559-1634): English translator and playwright, born in Hertfordshire, most famous for his rhymed versions of Homer, *The Iliads of Homer, Prince of Poets* (1611) and the *Odyssey* (1624), alluded to in KEAT's sonnet "Much have I travelled in the realms of gold"; he wrote a continuation of MARLOWE's *Hero and Leander* in 1598, and his plays include *Bussy d'Ambois* (1604).

CHARLES D'ORLÉANS (1394-1465): Poet, born in Paris to Louis d'Orléans (the brother of Charles VI) and Valentin Visconti; in 1406 married his cousin Isabella, widow of Richard II of England; French commander at the Battle of Agincourt (1415), taken as a prisoner to England, where he spent the next 25 years (till ransomed in 1440 and returned to Blois) writing poetry in English and French; his son became Louis XII of France, who was married to Mary Tudor, sister of Henry VIII.

CHAUCER, GEOFFREY (c.1340-1400): English poet, son of a wealthy London vintner and tavern-keeper; served the royal household in various capacities, as a diplomat in France and Italy (where he may have met Petrarch and Boccaccio) for Edward III, as a customs official for the Duke of Gloucester, as Clerk of the King's Works for Richard II; about 1366 married Philippa Roet, sister of the future wife of John of Gaunt), and had two sons, Lewis (to whom his scientific work *A Treatise on the Astrolabe* is addressed) and Thomas; *The Book of the Duchess* was written following the death (in 1369) of the wife of his patron, John of Gaunt (whose son became Henry IV in 1399); other works include *The Parliament of Fowls, Troilus and Criseyde*, and *The Canterbury Tales* (c.1386-1400).

CHESTERFIELD, PHILIP DORMER STANHOPE, 4TH EARL OF (1694-1773): English writer and politician, born in Westminster, educated at Cambridge; elected to Parliament, 1716; held several state positions, from ambassador to Holland to Secretary of State; friend of POPE and SWIFT; known for the private letters of advice he wrote his illegitimate son Philip (1732-1768) beginning in 1737; Eugenia Stanhope, his son's widow (he had married without informing his father, and had two sons himself), made the letters public in 1774.

CHESTERTON, G[ILBERT] K[EITH] (1874-1936): English essayist and novelist, born in London, converted to Catholicism in 1922; friend of the poet Hilaire Belloc (1870-1953); author of *The Man Who Was Thursday* (1908), the Father Brown detective stories (from 1911 on), and several collections of essays, such as *All Things Considered* (1908), *The Uses of Diversity* (1920), and *As I Was Saying* (1936).

CHUDLEIGH, MARY (LEE), LADY (1656-1710): English essayist and poet (used the pseudonym "Marissa"), born in Devon; author of *The Ladies' Defence* (1701), *Poems* (1703), and *Essays upon Several Subjects* (1710), which debate conventional assumptions about women's roles in society.

CLAMPITT, AMY (b.1920): American poet, raised in Iowa, educated at Columbia; worked in publishing and as a librarian in New York till 1982; her works include *The Kingfisher* (1983).

CLARE, JOHN (1793-1864): English poet and farmer, born and raised in Northamptonshire; influenced by SPENSER, GOLDSMITH, and THOMSON, and concerned with the plight of the rural poor in a landscape being modified by parliamentary decree; married Martha Turner, 1820; from 1837 to his death, was confined to the county asylum; author of *Poems Descriptive of Rural Life* (1820), *The Shepherd's Calendar* (1827), and other works, many unappreciated till the 20th century.

CLARKE, GILLIAN (WILLIAMS) (b.1937): Welsh poet, born and educated in Cardiff; knowledgeable about Welsh language and culture, including traditional poetic rhythms; editor of *Anglo-Welsh Review* till 1984; *Selected Poems* appeared in 1985.

CLEMENS, SAMUEL: see Mark TWAIN.

CLIFTON, LUCILLE (SAYLES) (b.1936): American poet, born in New York state; *Generations: A Memoir* (1976), a testament to family solidarity, traces her history as a black in North America; her collections of poems include *Good News About the Earth* (1972) and *Next* (1987).

CLOUGH, ARTHUR HUGH (1819-1861): English poet, born in Liverpool, the son of a cotton merchant; raised in South Carolina until sent to school at Rugby and Oxford; became a tutor at Oxford, but resigned the position when he began to question Christianity; friend of EMERSON and ARNOLD, whose poem "Thyrsis" commemorates him; married Blanche Smith, 1854; died in Florence of a cerebral hemorrhage; *Amours de Voyage*, written in 1848, first appeared in the *Atlantic Monthly* in 1858.

COLERIDGE, MARY (1861-1907): English poet and novelist (used the pseudonym "Anodos"), distantly related to S.T. COLERIDGE, born in London, educated at home; her novels include *The Lady on the Drawing Room Floor* (1906); many of her poems were first published posthumously.

COLERIDGE, SAMUEL TAYLOR (1772-1834): English poet and critic, born in Devon, the son of a local vicar; withdrew from Cambridge and abandoned plans for a clerical career; met Robert SOUTHEY in Bristol and with him planned (to no effect) a Utopian commune on the banks of the Susquehanna in Pennsylvania (based on "Pantisocracy," a set of social ideals developed by his friend, the philosophical novelist William Godwin, 1756-1836 [see SHELLEY]); married SOUTHEY's sister-in-law Sara Fricker in 1795 (separated 1807); began to use laudanum (c.1797); became friends with William and Dorothy WORDSWORTH, and with the former produced *Lyrical Ballads* (1798); friends with LAMB, though alienated from WORDSWORTH during the years 1810-1828, and from Southey; his philosophical criticism includes *Biographia Literaria* (1817) and the three volumes of *The Friend* (1809-1818).

COLLIER, MARY (1679-c.1762): English poet, farm-worker, washerwoman, and housekeeper, born in Sussex, educated at home; *The Woman's Labour* (1739) was a reply to a poem by Stephen DUCK; another volume of poems was published by public subscription in 1762.

COLLINS, WILLIAM (1721-1759): English poet, born in Chichester, where his father was a hatter and mayor of the city; educated at Oxford; friend of WARTON; died after suffering a mental breakdown; author of *Odes on Several Descriptive and Allegoric Subjects* (1746).

CONRAD, JOSEPH [JOZEF TEODOR KONRAD KORZENIOWSKI] (1857-1924): Polish-born English novelist; in 1874 embarked on a 20-year career at sea, serving on French and English vessels; became a naturalized Englishman in 1884 when he earned his master's papers; married Jessie George and settled in Kent, 1896; author of *Lord Jim* (1900), *Heart of Darkness* (1902), *Nostromo* (1904), *The Secret Agent* (1907), and other works, some in collaboration with Ford Madox Ford (1873-1939).

COOPER, ANTHONY ASHLEY: see SHAFTESBURY.

COPE, WENDY (b.1945): English poet, teacher, editor, and children's writer; born in Kent, educated at St. Hilda's College, Oxford; author of *Making Cocoa for Kingsley Amis* (1986).

CORY, WILLIAM (JOHNSON) (1823-1892): English poet, born William Johnson in Devon, educated at Cambridge; assistant master at Eton College from 1845 till 1872, when he inherited an estate and took the name Cory; author of *Ionica* (1858, enlarged 1891).

COTTON, CHARLES (1630-1687): English poet and translator, born in Staffordshire, a Royalist and a fishing friend of WALTON; in 1656 married his cousin, Isabella Hutchison, who bore him eight children, and died c.1670; later married Mary Russell; author of numerous burlesques, a popular version of Montaigne's *Essays* (1685), and *Poems on Several Occasions* (1689).

COUZYN, JENI (b.1942): South African-born poet, teacher, and editor, now a citizen of Canada, living in England; educated at U. of Natal; author of *Life by Drowning: Selected Poems* (1983, revised 1985) and several other books.

COWLEY, ABRAHAM (1618-1667): English poet, essayist, and doctor, born in London, educated at Westminster School and Cambridge, and later, in medicine, at Oxford; a Royalist, secretary to Queen Henrietta Maria; corresponded with SPRAT; never married (POPE wrote that the only love of Cowley's life chose to marry Sprat's brother); imprisoned during Cromwell's rule, but granted land at the time of the Restoration; author of *The Mistress* (1647) and other works.

COWPER, WILLIAM (1731-1800): English poet (whose surname is pronounced "Cooper"), born in Hertfordshire, suffered from repeated bouts of mental illness; a longtime friend of Mrs. Mary Unwin (d. 1794), to whom some of his work is dedicated; author of several popular hymns, first published in *Olney Hymns* (1779); many of his most familiar poems, including *The Task*, appeared in 1785.

CRANE, STEPHEN (1871-1900): American novelist, poet, and short story writer, born in Newark, New Jersey; war correspondent during the Spanish-American and Greco-Turkish Wars, experiences from which some of his fiction derived; died of tuberculosis; author of *Maggie: A Girl of the Streets* (1893), *The Red Badge of Courage* (1895), and *The Open Boat and Other Stories* (1898).

CRAPSEY, ADELAIDE (1878-1914): American poet and teacher, born in Brooklyn, educated at Vassar; died of tuberculosis; *Verses* (1915), demonstrating her skill at the modern cinquain, which she originated, was published posthumously, as were her letters and a study of English metrics.

CRATE, JOAN (b.1953): Alberta-born Canadian poet and novelist; author of *Pale as Real Ladies* (1989), a poem sequence concerned with the Mohawk writer Pauline Johnson (Tekahionwake, 1861-1913), and *Breathing Water* (1989).

CREELEY, ROBERT (b.1926): American writer, born in Arlington, Massachusetts, later associated with the "Black Mountain School" (OLSON, Robert DUNCAN, LEVERTOV); moved to San Franciso in 1956, when Black Mountain College in North Carolina closed, then to Buffalo in 1963, to teach at the State U. of New York; editor of OLSON, and author of a novel, stories, and essays; *Collected Poems* appeared in 1982.

CRÈVECOEUR, ST. JEAN DE [J. HECTOR ST. JOHN] (1735-1813): American writer, born in Normandy (christened Michel-Guillaume Jean de Crèvecoeur), educated in England and France; a soldier with Montcalm in Quebec during the Seven Years' War; subsequently travelled into Pennsylvania and Ohio; became a naturalized colonial citizen in New York, 1764; *Letters from an American Farmer* appeared in 1782, while he was in Europe; returning to America after the Revolution, found that his wife had been killed and his children scattered; returned to France permanently in 1790.

CRICHTON SMITH, IAIN: see Iain Crichton SMITH.

CULPEPER, NICHOLAS (1616-1654): Puritan English physician, born in London, educated at Cambridge; published an English translation of a Latin pharmacopoeia in 1649; in 1653 published *The English Physician Enlarged, or the Herbal*, a guide to herbal medicines; both books, enormously popular except among physicians, made current medical knowledge available to lay readers.

CUMMINGS, E[DWARD] E[STLIN] [e.e. cummings] (1894-1962): American writer, born in Cambridge, Massachusetts, educated at Harvard; ambulance driver during World War I, and author of *The Enormous Room* (1922, an autobiographical narrative with overtones of BUNYAN's *The Pilgrim's Progress*), drama, and travel writings; best known for his poetry: *Complete Poems 1913-1962* (1972) demonstrates his formal inventiveness, drawing on earlier books with titles such as *&* (1925), *is 5* (1925), *ViVa* (1931) and *1/20* (1936).

CURNOW, ALLEN (b.1911): New Zealand poet, critic, journalist, and playwright, born in Timaru, the son of an Anglican clergyman; educated at Auckland U., where he later taught (1951 till retirement), after several years as a theology student, journalist, and drama critic; married Elizabeth Le Cren, 1936 (divorced 1965), and Jenifer Tole, 1965; *Collected Poems, 1933-1973* (1974) samples several earlier volumes; *Four Plays* appeared in 1972.

D'AGUIAR, FREDERICK (b.1960): English poet (whose surname is pronounced "dee-AY-gar"), born in London to Guyanese parents, raised in Guyana; trained as a psychiatric nurse, educated at London U. and U. of Kent in English literature; his works include *Mama Dot* (1985).

DANIEL, SAMUEL (1563-1619): English poet and critic, born near Taunton in Somerset, whose masques were performed for the Stuart court; friend of SHAKESPEARE; brother-in-law to FLORIO; tutor to William Herbert (son of his patron, the Countess of PEMBROKE); author of the sonnet sequence *Delia* (1592) and *A Defence of Rhyme* (1602), a reply to a critical work by CAMPION.

D'ARBLAY, MME.: see Frances BURNEY.

DARWALL, MARY WHATELEY (1738-1825): English poet, born Mary Whateley in Worcestershire; in 1766, became the second wife of John Darwall, who later was named the vicar of Walsall; author of *Original Poems on Several Occasions* (1764), praised by SHENSTONE, and *Poems on Several Occasions* (1794).

DARWIN, CHARLES (1809-1882): English science writer and evolutionary theorist, grandson of Erasmus DARWIN and the potter Josiah Wedgwood (1730-1795), born in Shrewsbury, educated at Cambridge; naturalist for H.M.S. *Beagle*, a scientific survey ship in the southern hemisphere (1831-36), which led to his observations on the zoology, botany, and geology of the Galapagos Islands and other places (published 1839); in 1839 married his cousin, Emma Wedgwood; his subsequent reflections on natural selection resulted in *The Origin of Species* (1859) and *The Descent of Man* (1871), influential volumes whose ideas are sometimes mistakenly identified with theories of deterministic evolution, and occasionally confused with the theories of "social Darwinism" developed by his followers, who combined some of his ideas with those of the philosopher Herbert Spencer (1820-1903) [see SCHREINER].

DARWIN, ERASMUS (1731-1802): English poet, botanist, and physician, born in Lincolnshire, educated at Cambridge; predecessor of the Chevalier de Lamarck (1744-1829) and of Charles DARWIN in postulating evolutionary theory; author of *The Botanic Garden: The Economy of Vegetation* (2 vols., 1789) and *The Loves of the Plants* (1791).

DAVIES, SIR JOHN (1569-1626): English poet, lawyer (disbarred for fighting, 1598-1601), and member of parliament, born in Wiltshire; knighted by JAMES I and made Solicitor General of Ireland; author of *Nosce Teipsum* (1599; a philosophical work), *Hymns of Astraea* (1599; tributes to ELIZABETH I), and a volume of *Epigrams and Elegies* (c.1590) which the Archbishop of Canterbury ordered burned.

DE CRÉVECOEUR, ST. JEAN: see St. Jean de CRÈVECOEUR.

DEFOE, DANIEL (1660-1731): English Nonconformist pamphleteer and fiction writer, born Daniel Foe, the son of a butcher, in London; in 1684 married Mary Tuffley (d. 1732) and had seven children; changed his political loyalties frequently, writing political propaganda for the Tory leader Robert Harley [see SWIFT] as well as for the Whigs who replaced him when George I came to the throne; twice imprisoned when his satires, e.g. *The Shortest Way with the Dissenters* (1702), were read as treasonable and incurred Queen Anne's disfavour; published a newspaper, *The Review* (1703-13); prolific author of at least 500 publications, including *Robinson Crusoe* (1719), *Moll Flanders* (1722), and *Roxana* (1724), and the fictional "documentary," *A Journal of the Plague Year* (1722).

DEKKER, THOMAS (c.1570-c.1632): English playwright and pamphleteer, probably born in London; his plays include *The Shoemaker's Holiday* (1599), but he also collaborated with such Elizabethan playwrights as WEBSTER, Philip Massinger (1583-1640), Thomas Middleton (c.1580-1627), and John Ford (c.1586-c.1640); his pamphlets include *The Gull's Horn-Book* (1609).

DELONEY, THOMAS (c.1560-1600): English silk-weaver and writer of fiction, possibly from Norwich; author of *Jack of Newbury* (1597; 1619) and *The Gentle Craft* (1597; 1637), the source for DEKKER's *The Shoemaker's Holiday*.

DENHAM, SIR JOHN (1615-1669): Irish poet, born in Dublin, educated at Oxford; a Royalist lawyer, knighted after the Restoration and granted a state architect's position as surveyor-general of works, his assistant fortunately being the trained architect Christopher Wren (1632-1723); married Ann Cotton, 1634, and after her death married Margaret Brooke, 1665 (the second marriage was complicated by jealousy and ridicule, for his wife became the Duke of York's mistress [see also SEDLEY], and her death in 1667 may not have been accidental: some commentators say she died from drinking poisoned chocolate, given to her by the Duchess of Rochester); his most famous poem, *Cooper's Hill* (1642), was much imitated, e.g. in POPE's "Windsor Forest."

DEWDNEY, CHRISTOPHER (b.1951): Canadian poet and visual artist, born in London, Ontario, the son of the scientist and novelist Selwyn Dewdney (1909-1979); *Predators of the Imagination* (1983) selects from his poetry.

DICKENS, CHARLES (1812-1870): English novelist and journalist, born in Portsmouth, forced to work at age 12, and then saw his father imprisoned for debt; by the 1830s had become a political reporter, resulting in *Sketches by Boz* (1836); many essays and tales followed, along with novels first published as serials in such magazines as *Bentley's Miscellany* in the 1830s and his own *Household Words* and *All the Year Round* after 1850; married Catherine Hogarth, 1836 (separated 1858); friend of the mystery writer Wilkie Collins (1824-1889); quarrelled frequently with his publishers in the 1830s; travelled on numerous reading tours to the U.S.A. and elsewhere in the 1840s, and again in the 1860s; became attracted to the theatre, and to the actress Ellen Ternan in the 1850s; the pace of life affected both his health and his fiction, and *The Mystery of Edwin Drood* was left incomplete at his death; other works include *Oliver Twist* (1837-39), *Nicholas Nickleby* (1838-39), *A Christmas Carol* (1843), *David Copperfield* (1849-50), *Bleak House* (1852-53), *Hard Times* (1854), *Little Dorrit* (1857-58), *A Tale of Two Cities* (1859), and *Great Expectations* (1860-61).

DICKINSON, EMILY (1830-1886): American poet, born in Amherst, Massachusetts, where she lived all her life; essentially a recluse from the age of 30, except for an active correspondence with a few friends; after she died, her undated, untitled poems were found in her house by her sister Lavinia; some were suppressed by the family and some printed, badly edited, in the 1890s; a scholarly edition of all 1,775 poems was prepared by Thomas H. Johnson as *The Poems of Emily Dickinson* (1955).

DIXON, SARAH (1671-1765): English poet, born in Rochester, lived in Canterbury; published *Poems on Several Occasions* (1740) anonymously.

DOBSON, [HENRY] AUSTIN (1840-1921): English biographer and poet, born in Plymouth, educated in Strasbourg as a civil engineer; author of several biographies of 18th-century writers, and volumes demonstrating skill with French verse forms; *Collected Poems* appeared in 1897.

DODGSON, CHARLES LUTWIDGE: see Lewis CARROLL.

DONNE, JOHN (1572-1631): English poet and churchman, born in London, the son of an ironmonger and the grandson of the dramatist John HEYWOOD; raised a Catholic and educated at Cambridge; sailed on the 1596 expedition to Cadiz; jailed and dismissed from public office when it was revealed he had secretly married a minor, Ann More (or Moore, 1584-1617) in 1601; friend of JOHNSON, DRAYTON, HALL, WOTTON, and the architect Inigo Jones (1573-1652); suffered religious doubts, converted to Church of England, was ordained in 1615 (WALTON was one of his parishioners) and named Dean of St. Paul's Cathedral in 1621, acquiring a reputation for powerful, logically demanding sermons; wrote *Devotions Upon Emergent Occasions* (1624) while ill; published little poetry during his lifetime, *Collected Poems* appearing in 1633.

DOOLITTLE, HILDA ["HD"] (1886-1961): American poet and novelist, born in Bethlehem, Pennsylvania; associated in 1911 with the Imagist Movement; briefly engaged to POUND, who encouraged her writing; after a short marriage to the novelist Richard Aldington (1892-1962), her lifelong companion was the English novelist, patron, and photographer Winnifred Ellerman [who was known as "Bryher"] (1894-1983); her poetry, represented in *Poetry* magazine and Imagist anthologies, includes *Sea Garden* (1916) and *Hymen* (1921); several prose works with lesbian themes, including *Hermione* (1981), appeared posthumously.

DOVE, RITA (b.1952): American poet, born in Akron, Ohio, educated at Miami U. (Oxford, Ohio); married to the writer Fred Viebahn; teaches creative writing at Arizona State U.; publications include *Museum* (1983) and *Thomas and Beulah* (1986), which won a Pulitzer Prize.

D'ORLÉANS, CHARLES: See CHARLES D'ORLÉANS.

DOWSON, ERNEST (1867-1900): English poet, born in Kent; associated in London with WILDE, the essayist Richard Le Gallienne (1866-1947), and the artist Aubrey Beardsley (1872-1898); contributor to *The Yellow Book*; author of *Poems* (1896) and other volumes.

DRAYTON, MICHAEL (1563-1631): English poet, born in Warwickshire; noted for the wide range of his poetic experiments, from pastoral to mock epic; his works include *The Man in the Moon* (1606, 1619) and the two volumes of *Poly-Olbion* (1612 and 1622).

DRUMMOND, WILLIAM, OF HAWTHORNDEN (1585-1649): Scottish poet, born at Hawthornden manor near Edinburgh, educated at Edinburgh U. and (as a lawyer) in France; Royalist; friend of DRAYTON and JONSON; author of several volumes, including *Poems, Amorous, Funereal, Divine, Pastoral, in Sonnets, Songs, Sextains, Madrigals* (1616), written in part to commemorate Mary Cunningham, who died in 1615 on the eve of their wedding.

DRYDEN, JOHN (1631-1700): English poet, critic, and playwright, born in Northamptonshire to a Puritan family, educated at Cambridge; supported Church of England and Royalists after the Restoration; named Poet Laureate in 1668 (though deprived of the post in 1688 and replaced by Thomas Shadwell, 1642-1690); noted for his public verse; adapted SHAKESPEARE, MILTON, and CHAUCER to Restoration forms, and translated Virgil, Ovid, and other classical writers; converted to Catholicism, 1686; involved in several literary disputes, opposing Whigs (including the 1st Earl of SHAFTESBURY) and winning Charles II's approval, but opposed the Protestant House of Orange, by George Villiers, 2nd Duke of Buckingham (1628-1687), by John Wilmot, 2nd Earl of ROCHESTER, Shadwell, HALIFAX, and later his reputation was attacked by JOHNSON; plays include *All for Love* (1678);

poems include *Absalom and Achitophel* (1681) and *The Hind and the Panther* (1687); *An Essay on Dramatic Poesy* appeared in 1668.

DU BOIS, W[ILLIAM] E.B. (1868-1963): American writer (whose surname is pronounced "du-BOYS"), born in Massachusetts, educated at Fisk and Harvard; author of numerous studies of black culture in the U.S.A., including biographies, histories, *The Encyclopedia of the Negro* (1945), and the sketches and poems collected as *The Souls of Black Folk* (1903); a founding member of the NAACP in 1910, he joined the Communist Party in 1961, the same year he emigrated to Ghana, becoming a Ghanaian citizen in 1963.

DUCK, STEPHEN (1705-1756): English farm-labourer, known as "the thresher poet," born in Wiltshire; self-educated; considered for Poet Laureate in 1730 (the year Colley Cibber [see ASTELL] was named to the post), ridiculed by POPE and SWIFT; a favourite of Queen Caroline, who settled him at Kew and Richmond; became a preacher after her death in 1737, later drowned himself; author of *The Thresher's Labour*, to which Mary COLLIER replied.

DUNBAR, WILLIAM (c.1460-c.1513): Scottish poet (one of the "Scottish Chaucerians"), likely from East Lothian, educated at St. Andrews U., influenced by CHAUCER; author of such poems as "The Thrissil and the Rois," celebrating the marriage of James IV of Scotland and Margaret Tudor, and "The Flyting of Dunbar and Kennedie," a mock exchange of inventive insults.

DUNCAN, ROBERT (1919-1988): American poet, born in Oakland, educated at U. of California at Berkeley; associated with the Black Mountain school, along with OLSON, CREELEY, and LEVERTOV; author of *Selected Poems 1942-1950* (1959), *The Opening of the Field* (1960), and *Bending the Bow* (1968), and several other volumes.

DUNCAN (COTES), SARA JEANNETTE (1861-1922): Canadian journalist and novelist who published first as "Garth Grafton," born in Brantford, Ontario, educated at Toronto Normal School; a reporter in the 1880s for the Toronto *Globe* and the Washington *Post*; married the British journalist-librarian Everard Cotes in Calcutta in 1891, living in India for the next 25 years; author of *The Simple Adventures of a Memsahib* (1893), *The Imperialist* (1904), *Cousin Cinderella* (1908), and other fictions; Thomas Tausky edited her *Selected Journalism* in 1980.

DUNN, DOUGLAS (b.1942): Scottish librarian and poet, born in Renfrewshire, educated at Hull U. (in English literature); named Professor of Poetry at the U. of St Andrews, 1991; his several poetry collections, including *Terry Street* (1969) and *Barbarians* (1979), deal with class divisions in Britain; *Elegies* (1985), which won the Whitbread Award, mourns his wife's death.

DYER, JOHN (1700-1758): Welsh poet and Church of England clergyman; *Grongar Hill* (1727) praises the Towy River Valley in Carmarthenshire (now Dyfed), his birthplace; later poems include *The Fleece* (1757), which concerns the wool trade.

DYER, SIR EDWARD (1543-1607): English poet and diplomat, born in Somerset, educated at Oxford, knighted in 1596; a friend of Fulke GREVILLE and Sir Philip SIDNEY; one of the backers of the expedition of Sir Martin Frobisher (c.1535-1594) to North America in 1576; author of many songs.

EARLE, JOHN (c.1601-1665): English essayist and churchman, born in York, educated at Oxford; tutor to Charles II in 1641, chaplain

to him in France; became Bishop of Worcester and Salisbury after the Restoration; author of the popular *Microcosmographia* (1628; expanded in later editions).

EASTLAKE, ELIZABETH RIGBY, later **LADY** (1809-1893): English travel writer and art historian, born in Norwich, educated at home; contributed actively to periodicals, including an 1848 review attacking Charlotte Brontë's *Jane Eyre* in the *Quarterly*; *A Residence on the Shores of the Baltic* (1836) established her reputation; in 1849 married the painter Charles Lock Eastlake (knighted 1850, director of the National Gallery from 1855); her Journals and Correspondence were edited by her nephew, Charles Eastlake Smith, in 1895.

EGERTON, SARAH FYGE (1670-1723): English poet, born Sarah Fyge, raised in London; wrote *The Female Advocate* in 1684 (revised 1687) as a feminist reply to a poem by Robert Gould, angering her father (who banished her from his house); married Edward Field, an attorney, and after his death married her older cousin, Rev. Thomas Egerton, in 1700, petitioning unsuccessfully for divorce in 1703 on grounds of cruelty; *Poems on Several Occasions* (1703) was followed by the unauthorized publication of some of her letters by Delarivier Manley (c.1663-1724; scandalmonger, author of romans à clef, and SWIFT's sometime collaborator).

ELIOT, GEORGE [MARY ANN (MARIAN) EVANS] (1819-1880): English novelist, freethinker, and critic, born in Warwickshire, educated at several ladies' schools, becoming fluent in French and German, and noted for her powerful intellect; translated philosophical works by Feuerbach and Strauss; assistant editor of the *Westminster Review* (1851-54), during which time she met the philosopher Herbert Spencer (1820-1903) and the journalist George Henry Lewes (1817-1878); from 1853 on, she lived with Lewes (whose wife Agnes was an intimate of Leigh HUNT), publishing such novels as *Adam Bede* (1859), *The Mill on the Floss* (1860), and *Middlemarch* (1871-72), and the essays collected in *The Impressions of Theophrastus Such* (1879).

ELIOT, T[HOMAS] S[TEARNS] (1888-1965): Poet, critic, and playwright, born in St. Louis to a Unitarian family, educated at Harvard; left America in 1914, settling in London in 1915, the year of his first (troubled) marriage; editor of *The Criterion* (1922-39) and director of Faber and Faber publishers; became a British citizen and joined the Church of England in 1927; winner of the 1948 Nobel Prize; early poems (encouraged by POUND) appeared in *Prufrock and Other Observations* (1917); *The Waste Land* (1922) was followed by several volumes, including *Murder in the Cathedral* (1935; a verse play), *Collected Poems 1909-35* (1936), the *Four Quartets* ("Burnt Norton," 1935; "East Coker," 1940; "The Dry Salvages," 1941; "Little Gidding," 1942), *Old Possum's Book of Practical Cats* (1939; the basis for the Andrew Lloyd Weber musical *Cats*), and the critical essays collected in *The Sacred Wood* (1920).

ELIZABETH I (1533-1603): Queen of England, daughter of Henry VIII and Anne Boleyn, born in Greenwich Palace; solidified Protestant connection with the monarchy when she was crowned in 1558 (following her Catholic sister Mary's death); during her reign (which was opposed by Pope Paul IV), the Church of England *Book of Common Prayer* was written, English commanders (Hawkins, Drake, Frobisher) defeated the Spanish Armada of Philip II (1588), and the arts flourished; wrote occasional verse.

EMERSON, RALPH WALDO (1803-1882): American essayist, poet, and philosopher, born in Boston, the son of a Unitarian minister;

educated at Harvard; ordained, 1829; rejected the ministry and orthodox religion, 1832, a year after the death of his first wife; helped develop a philosophical system called Transcendentalism (which saw no need for an intercessor between human beings and the divine, which was deemed to be present in all nature); in 1835 married Lydia Jackson, settling in Concord, Massachusetts; editor of the Transcendental quarterly *The Dial* (from 1842); friend of HAWTHORNE, CARLYLE, THOREAU, and the feminist essayist Margaret Fuller (1810-1850); author of *Nature* (1836), *Representative Men* (1850), *Poems* (1847), and other works.

EQUIANO, OLAUDAH (c.1745-c.1797): Ibo-speaking African writer, born in what is now Eastern Nigeria, probably somewhere near the current town of Onitsha; captured by slavers at age 10, given the name "Gustavus Vasa" (which he used for the rest of his life [see also Henry BROOKE]) by his first master, Captain Pascal; accompanied Pascal when he served with General Wolfe in Canada, 1759; despite Pascal's promise of liberty, was sold to a second master, Robert King, a Quaker in Philadelphia; released from slavery in 1766; converted to Calvinism; travelled to the Mediterranean, the Arctic, and Central America, though was prevented from returning to Africa as a missionary; spoke vigorously against the slave trade; married Susan(na) Cullen, 1792; died in England sometime between 1797 and 1801.

ERDRICH, LOUISE (b.1954): American poet and novelist, born in Minnesota to German and Chippewa parents, grew up on the Chippewa Reservation, educated at Dartmouth; married to the writer and Dartmouth educator Michael Dorris; writes of Northern Plains Native culture in such books as *Jacklight* (1984), *The Beet Queen* (1986), and *Tracks* (1988).

EVANS, MARY ANN: see George ELIOT.

EVELYN, JOHN (1620-1706): English diarist, born to landed gentry in Surrey, educated at Oxford; Royalist, acquaintance of Charles II, friend of the diarist Samuel Pepys (1633-1703); one of the first Fellows of the Royal Society; author of books on pollution (*Fumifugium*, 1661), silviculture (*Sylva*, 1664), and *Navigation and Commerce* (1674); best known for his annals of public events, edited as his *Diary* in 1818.

FANTHORPE, U[RSULA] A. (b.1929): English poet, born in London, educated at Oxford and London U.; worked as a teacher, counsellor, and hospital clerk, experiences that influence her poetry; *Selected Poems* (1986) was followed by *A Watching Brief* (1987).

FAULKNER, WILLIAM (1897-1962): American novelist and short story writer, born in Mississippi, where he was a longtime resident of the town of Oxford; worked as a Hollywood screenwriter during the 1930s and 1940s, on such films as *To Have and Have Not* and *The Big Sleep*; won the Nobel Prize, 1950; best known for his stylistically innovative examinations of the shifting values of the American South; among works set in his fictional Yoknapatawpha County are *The Sound and the Fury* (1929), *As I Lay Dying* (1930), *Light in August* (1932), *Absalom! Absalom!* (1936), *Intruder in the Dust* (1948), *Collected Stories* (1950), and *The Reivers* (1962).

FELLTHAM, OWEN (c.1602-1668): English writer, born in Suffolk; exchanged opinions with Ben JONSON; author of several series of moral essays called *Resolves, Divine, Moral, Political* (1620-28), which went into eight editions by 1661..

FIELDING, HENRY (1707-1754): English novelist, journalist, and playwright, born in Somerset, educated at Eton and Leyden; called to the bar, but did not practise law; his burlesques of 1736 and 1737 led to the Theatrical Licensing Act (1737) which, among others, closed his theatre in the Haymarket; married Charlotte Cradock, 1734, the model for his fictional heroines; edited *The Champion* (1739-41), and other papers, using the pseudonym "Captain Hercules Vinegar" to oppose the government of Sir Robert Walpole (1676-1745); with *Shamela* (1741), his talent for mimicry led him to parody the epistolary novel *Pamela, or Virtue Rewarded* (1740) by Samuel Richardson (1689-1761), which he followed with other successful comic picaresques, *Joseph Andrews* (1742) and *The History of Tom Jones, A Foundling* (1744); in addition he was a lawyer and magistrate, whose efforts led to the later formation of a modern police force.

FINCH, ANNE (KINGSMILL), COUNTESS OF WINCHILSEA (1661-1720): English poet (used the pseudonym "Ardelia"), born in Berkshire; became a Maid of Honour to the Duchess of York, 1683; in May 1684, married Heneage Finch ("Daphnis" in her poem), who became 4th Earl of Winchilsea in 1712; retired from the court to Kent after James II fled to France in 1688; her poems circulated in manuscript from about this time, a volume called *Miscellany Poems* appearing in 1713, winning praise from SWIFT and later from Anna SEWARD and WORDSWORTH.

FINLAY, IAN HAMILTON (b.1925): Scottish poet and artist, born in Nassau, Bahamas; settled in Lanarkshire in 1969, gardening and designing; a leading figure among writers of concrete poetry, his work is represented in *Selected Ponds* (1976) and in the Tate Gallery, London.

FITZGERALD, EDWARD (1809-1883): English poet and Orientalist, born Edward Purcell to a wealthy Suffolk family (he took FitzGerald, his mother's maiden name, in 1818), educated at Cambridge; now known mainly for his translation of *The Rubáiyat of Omar Khayyám*, published anonymously in 1859.

FLANDERS, JANE (HESS) (b.1940): American poet, born in Pennsylvania, educated at Bryn Mawr and Columbia; married Steven Flanders, 1966; winner of the Pushcart Prize, 1980; author of several books, including *The Students of Snow* (1982).

FLETCHER, PHINEAS (1582-1650): English poet and clergyman, elder brother of the poet Giles Fletcher (1585-1623), son of the diplomat and poet Giles Fletcher (1546-1611), cousin of the dramatist John Fletcher (1579-1625); born in Kent, educated at Cambridge; volumes include *Britain's Ida* (1628), which was attributed to SPENSER at the time of its appearance, to protect Fletcher's position as an ordained minister.

FLORIO, JOHN (or GIOVANNI) (c.1553-1625): English translator and lexicographer, born to Italian Protestant parents in London, educated at Oxford; language tutor at Oxford and reader in Italian to Queen Anne; married the sister of Samuel DANIEL; author of an Italian-English dictionary, a grammar, and various translations, e.g. Ramusio's version of the voyages of Jacques Cartier (1578) and Montaigne's *Essais* (1603, revised 1613).

FOOTE, SAMUEL (1720-1777): English playwright and actor, born to a wealthy family in Cornwall; a talent for mimicry led him to lampoon prominent living individuals in his plays, notably the evangelist George Whitefield (1714-1770) and other Methodists in *The*

Minor (1760), which in turn led to him being framed, brought to trial, and effectively silenced.

FORSTER, E[DWIN] M[ORGAN] (1879-1970): English novelist, short story writer, and essayist, born in London, educated at Cambridge; from 1905 to 1912 worked as a private tutor, writing such novels as *A Room with a View* (1908), *Howards End* (1910), *Maurice* (suppressed until 1971 because of its homosexual subject matter), and the stories collected in *The Celestial Omnibus* (1911); his experiences in India (1921-22), while secretary to the Maharajah of Dewas Senior, resulted in *A Passage to India* (1924); devoted much of the rest of his life to opposing censorship, as President of the National Council for Civil Liberties (1934) and through his essays, some of them collected in *Abinger Harvest* (1936).

FOWLER, KATHERINE: see Katherine PHILIPS.

FRANKLIN, BENJAMIN (1706-1790): American writer and politician, born in Boston; set up a printing press in Philadelphia, managing his own paper, *The Pennsylvania Gazette* (1729-66), as well as *Poor Richard's Almanac* (1732-58) and other periodicals; in 1730 married Deborah Read (d. 1774), though had children by others as well; author of numerous works on such subjects as electricity, reformed spelling, the slave trade, libraries, hospitals, and education, he also participated actively in American colonial politics, as postmaster-general and as the diplomat negotiating French support for the American revolutionary cause; as a member of the Continental Congress, he helped draft the *Declaration of Independence* [see JEFFERSON], and signed the U.S. Constitution in 1787.

FREETH, JOHN (c.1731-1808): English popular writer, known as "Poet Freeth"; for 48 years ran the much-frequented "Freeth's Coffee House" on Bell Street in Birmingham, where nightly he recited his verses; author of *The Political Songster* (expanded 6th ed., 1790).

FRENEAU, PHILIP (1752-1832): American poet, born in New York City to a family of Huguenot ancestry, grew up in New Jersey, educated at the College of New Jersey (later Princeton); published numerous pro-Revolutionary broadsides (e.g., *The British Prison Ship*, 1781); encouraged by JEFFERSON, edited the *National Gazette* in Philadelphia till it folded in 1793, then returned to New Jersey, writing pro-JEFFERSON essays and poems.

FROST, ROBERT (1874-1963): American poet, born in San Francisco, raised there and in Lawrence, Massachusetts, learning various farm crafts; in 1895 married Elinor White (d. 1938); friend of POUND and Edward THOMAS; began publishing poetry while living in England, 1912-15, then moved to New Hampshire, the setting for much of his poetry; *New Hampshire* (1924) won the Pulitzer Prize, as did *Collected Poems* (1930) and two other titles; of several more volumes, his last was *In the Clearing* (1962).

FULLER, THOMAS (1608-1661): English preacher and writer, born in Northamptonshire, educated at Cambridge; Royalist, became a royal chaplain after the Restoration; among his publications are histories of the Crusades, studies of famous Englishmen, optimistic meditations for difficult times, and a book of character sketches, *The Holy State and the Profane State* (1642-48).

FULLERTON, MARY (1868-1946): Australian poet and novelist, born in the state of Victoria, educated by her mother; active in the Women's Suffrage movement during the 1890s; friend of the novelist

[Stella Maria] Miles Franklin (1879-1954); author of *Moles Do So Little With Their Privacy* (1942) and other books of poetry, using the pseudonym "E."

FULTON, ALICE (b.1952): American poet, born in Troy, New York, educated at SUNY and Cornell; teaches English at U. of Michigan; married the artist Hank De Leo, 1980; author of *Dance Script with Electric Ballerina* (1983).

FYGE, SARAH: see EGERTON.

GALT, JOHN (1779-1839): Scottish businessman and writer, born in Irvine, the son of a sea captain; wrote (1812) of his European travels with BYRON, but attracted notice with his sketches of Scotland for *Blackwood's Magazine* (1820) and such books as *Annals of the Parish* (1821); business ventures in Ontario (where he travelled with DUNLOP) led to him being imprisoned for debt in London in 1829; subsequent books—especially *Lawrie Todd* (1830) and *Bogle Corbet* (1831), based on his Canadian experiences—and a gift from William IV secured his freedom.

GARDNER, ISABELLA (1915-1981): American poet, born in Massachusetts to a wealthy family; her fourth husband (m. 1959) was the American poet Allen Tate (1899-1979); admired by SITWELL and PLATH; assistant editor of *Poetry* magazine (1952-55); *That was Then: New and Selected Poems* appeared in 1980.

GASCOIGNE, GEORGE (c.1539-1577): English soldier, Member of Parliament, poet, dramatist, and prose writer, born in Bedfordshire; fought in the Low Countries in the 1570s; stepfather of Nicholas BRETON; noted for his experimentation with new prose and verse forms and his adaptations of Italian comedy to the English stage; *The Posies of George Gascoigne* (1575) is a miscellany.

GAY, JOHN (1685-1732): English poet and playwright, born in Barnstaple, Devon, educated locally and apprenticed to a London silk-merchant; began to write c.1708, attracting readers' attention for his contributions to journals; secretary to the Duchess of Monmouth (1712-14), a member of the Scriblerus Club [see POPE], and a friend of Pope and SWIFT; best remembered for his satiric writings, especially *The Beggar's Opera* (1728) and its suppressed sequel *Polly* (1729), which satirized Sir Robert Walpole; his *Fables* (begun in 1726, published in part in 1729 and in part posthumously) were designed for Prince William.

GHOSE, ZULFIKAR (b.1935): Novelist, poet, and critic, born in Sialkot, India (now Pakistan); emigrated to England, 1952; educated at Keele U.; recorded his exile in his autobiography, *Confessions of a Native-Alien* (1965); emigrated to the U.S.A., 1969; teaches literature at U. of Texas; married the Brazilian painter Helena de la Fontaine; author of *The Fiction of Reality* (1984; criticism), *The Violent West* (1972) and other books of poetry, and such novels as *The Incredible Brazilian* (1972) and *A New History of Torments* (1982).

GIFFORD, HUMPHREY (fl. 1580): Little is known except that he was born to a Devonshire family, and probably held a position with the Poultry Counter, a London debtors' prison; *A Posy of Gillyflowers* appeared in 1580.

GILBERT, SIR W[ILLIAM] S[CHWENCK] (1836-1911): English librettist and playwright, born in London, educated at London U.; after attempting careers in law and journalism, wrote successfully for the stage; collaborated after 1871 with the composer Sir Arthur Sullivan (1842-1900), especially on the "Savoy Operas," including *H.M.S. Pinafore* (1878), *The Pirates of Penzance* (1879), and *The Mikado* (1885); an expanded version of *The Bab Ballads* appeared in 1882.

GILMORE, MARY (CAMERON) (1864-1962): Australian poet, born in New South Wales, raised in the bush; developed a lifelong commitment to workers' organizations while teaching during the 1880s; friend of Henry LAWSON; joined a shortlived commune in Paraguay in 1896, marrying William Gilmore, a shearer, in 1897; edited the Women's Page of the Sydney *Worker* (1908-31); awarded a DBE in 1937; author of *Battlefields* (1939) and other verse, and several volumes of reminiscences.

GIOVANNI, NIKKI (b.1943): American poet, born in Knoxville, Tennessee, raised in Cincinnati, educated at U. of Pennsylvania and Columbia School of Fine Arts; active in black social organizations; anthologist of black women poets, *Night Comes Softly* (1970); author of *Black Feeling/Black Talk* (1968), *My House* (1972), among other collections of poems, and several books for children.

GLÜCK, LOUISE (b.1943): American poet, born in New York City, educated at Sarah Lawrence College and Columbia; married writer John Dranow, 1977; teaches poetry at Williams College; author of several volumes of poetry, including *First Born* (1968) and *The Triumph of Achilles* (1985).

GOLDSMITH, OLIVER (c.1730-1774): Irish poet, playwright, novelist, and essayist, born in Longford or Roscommon, raised in Westmeath, disfigured by smallpox from childhood; educated at Trinity College (Dublin); after several years travelling, settled in England in 1756, working as a freelance writer; met JOHNSON in 1761, becoming friends with him, BURKE, REYNOLDS, and others; published several histories, biographies, and satires, including *The Citizen of the World* (1762), but is best remembered for *The Vicar of Wakefield* (1766, a novel), *She Stoops to Conquer* (1773, a play), and *The Deserted Village* (1770, a poem).

GOLDSWORTHY, PETER (b.1951): Australian doctor, short story writer, and poet, born in Minlaton (South Australia), raised in South Australia and Darwin, educated at U. of Adelaide; married Helen Wharldall, a doctor, in 1972; books include *Readings from Ecclesiastes* (1982), which won the Commonwealth Poetry Prize.

GOOGE, BARNABE (1540-1594): English poet and translator, born in Lincolnshire, studied at Oxford and Cambridge, kinsman of William Cecil, Lord Burghley (1520-1598), secretary of state for ELIZABETH I; author of *Eclogues, Epitaphs and Sonnets* (1563).

GORDIMER, NADINE (b.1923): South African novelist, essayist, and short story writer, born in Springs, Transvaal, educated by private tutors; married Reinhold Cassirer, 1954; opposed to apartheid, some of her writings were banned in South Africa; won the Nobel Prize, 1991; her many books include *The Conservationist* (1974), *Selected Stories* (1975), *Burger's Daughter* (1979), *July's People* (1981), and *Something Out There* (1984).

GOULD, STEPHEN JAY (b.1941): American palaeontologist and science writer, born in New York City, educated at Columbia; married the artist Deborah Lee, 1965; works at Harvard in comparative zoology; questions the techniques of scientific analysis and argues for evolutionary principles; author of *Ever Since Darwin* (1977), *The Panda's Thumb* (1980), *The Mismeasure of Man* (1981), and other prize-winning volumes.

GRAVES, ROBERT (1895-1985): English poet, novelist, and critic, son of the Irish songwriter A.P. Graves (1846-1931), born in Wimbledon, educated at Cambridge; friend of T.E. Lawrence (of Arabia, 1888-1935), associated with the Georgian poets who were attacked by Roy CAMPBELL; married Nancy Nicholson after fighting in World War I; lived with Laura RIDING from 1920s to 1936, mainly in Mallorca, to which he returned in 1947; author of *Collected Poems* (1938) and many other volumes; celebrated for a book on mythology, *The White Goddess* (1948), and for his novel *I, Claudius* (1934) and its sequels.

GRAY, JOHN (1866-1934): English poet and playwright, born in London; worked as a metalworker, post office employee, and after 1888 a librarian in the British Foreign Office; published his first work in *The Dial* (1889); converted to Catholicism, 1890; ordained, 1901, and named to a parish in Edinburgh; friend of WILDE, YEATS, SYMONS, DAVIDSON, DOWSON, and others at meetings of the Rhymers' Club in London, 1891-94; launched a libel action in 1892 against being identified as the original of WILDE's "Dorian Gray"; wrote for *Blackfriar's* from 1892 on; edited the letters of Aubrey Beardsley (1904); author of *Silverpoints* (1892) and *Poems* (1931).

GRAY, THOMAS (1716-1771): English poet and scholar, born in London, educated at Eton and Cambridge; at Eton (about which he wrote an ode in 1747) became friends with Richard West (1716-1742), and with the Gothic novelist Horace Walpole, 4th Earl of Orford (1717-1797); youngest son of Whig politician Sir Robert Walpole, 1676-1745), later a travelling companion on the Grand Tour of Europe; declined the Poet Laureateship in 1757; established his reputation with several odes during the 1740s and 1750s, then embarked on a series of Celtic and Norse imitations; his *Journal* appeared in 1774.

GREEN, DOROTHY: see Dorothy AUCHTERLONIE.

GREENWELL, DORA (1821-1882): English poet and essayist, born in County Durham, self-taught; tended her invalid mother for 20 years before moving to London in 1874; friend of the political activist Josephine Butler (1838-1906); *Poems* appeared in 1848, and essays pleading for women's education in the 1860s.

GREGORY, LADY AUGUSTA (PERSSE) (1852-1932): Irish playwright, patron, and folklorist, born to a wealthy family in Galway; in 1881 married her neighbour, Sir William Gregory of Coole Park (1811-1892), who had been governor of Ceylon (1871-77); met YEATS in 1896, and with him founded Dublin's Abbey Theatre in 1904 (she, Yeats, and J.M. Synge, 1871-1909, were directors, concerned to re-establish Irish language and culture), and Coole Park became Yeats's retreat; wrote political journalism, retold ancient Irish tales (e.g., *Cuchulain of Muirthemne*, 1902), and wrote such plays as *The Rising of the Moon* (1907).

GREVILLE, SIR FULKE, 1ST BARON BROOKE (1554-1628): English poet and playwright, born in Warwickshire, educated at Cambridge; attended at court, becoming friends with SIDNEY, SPENSER, Edward DYER, and other members of the "Areopagus Club," and later with DANIEL, Francis BACON, and others; knighted in 1597, granted Warwick Castle and a baronetcy in 1621, Chancellor of the Exchequer

1614-1622; murdered by a servant; author of a life of SIDNEY (1652), and a song-cycle, *Caelica* (1633).

GRIFFIN, BARTHOLOMEW (fl. 1596): English poet, about whom little is known; apparently from Coventry, possibly an attorney, perhaps died in 1602; his poem cycle, *Fidessa, More Chaste Than Kind* (1596), contains a sonnet ("Venus and young Adonis sitting by her") once attributed to SHAKESPEARE.

GUSTAFSON, RALPH (b.1909): Canadian poet, born in Lime Ridge, Quebec, raised in Sherbrooke, educated at Bishop's U. and Oxford; teacher, anthologist, and music critic, worked for British Information Service in New York during 1940s; married Betty Renninger in 1958, and returned to Canada, 1960; author of more than thirty volumes, including *Collected Poems* (1987).

HABINGTON, WILLIAM (1605-1654): English poet, born in Worcestershire to a Catholic family (his father, Thomas, had been imprisoned for taking part in Antony Babington's plot to assassinate ELIZABETH I [see TICHBORNE]), educated in Paris; in the early 1630s married Lucy Herbert, whom he celebrated in *Castara* (1640).

HAKLUYT, RICHARD (1552-1616): English geographer, chaplain, and travel writer, born in Herefordshire, educated at Oxford, where he later lectured on cosmography; acquainted with such explorers as Martin Frobisher and Sir Humphrey Gilbert, wrote the introduction to FLORIO's translation of Cartier, corresponded with the Flemish mapmaker Gerhardus Mercator (1512-1594), and was supported by Lord Burghley and other advisors to ELIZABETH I; collected accounts of explorations, which he published in several volumes, including *The Principal Navigations, Voyages and Discoveries of the English Nation* (1589); his manuscripts passed to his assistant, Samuel Purchas (c.1575-1626), who continued his work.

HALIBURTON, THOMAS CHANDLER (1796-1856): Canadian humorist, phrase-maker, and politician, born and educated in Windsor, Nova Scotia, later a judge of the provincial supreme court and an member of parliament in England, where he retired in 1856; through his character "Sam Slick," influenced American humorists such as "Artemus Ward" (C.F. Browne, 1834-1867) and Mark TWAIN; criticized colonial policies and national behaviour; author of *The Clockmaker* (1837-40) and other sketches.

HALIFAX, GEORGE SAVILE, 1ST MARQUESS OF (1633-1695): English statesman and political writer, born in Yorkshire; named Lord Privy Seal in 1682, but dismissed by James II for opposing repeal of the Habeas Corpus Act; negotiated with William and Mary to accept the crown in 1689, subsequently regaining public office; alluded to in DRYDEN's *Absalom and Achitophel* (1681), and (with Matthew PRIOR) replied to his *The Hind and the Panther* with *The Town and Country Mouse* (1687); author of *The Character of a Trimmer* (1688) and other works.

HALL, JOSEPH (1574-1656): English clergyman and prose writer, born at Ashby de la Zouch, Leicestershire, educated at Cambridge; chaplain to Prince Henry (1608), later Bishop of Exeter (1627) and Norwich (1641), a friend of DONNE and BROWNE; opposed by MILTON in 1641, imprisoned in 1642; author of *Characters of Virtues and Vices* (1608) and other works.

HARDY, THOMAS (1840-1928): English poet and novelist, born in Dorset, the son of a stonemason, educated locally, apprenticed to an architect; friend of William BARNES; began to publish in the 1860s, while in London, and returned to Dorchester in 1867; married Emma Gifford (1874, unhappily) and Florence Dugdale (1914); sixteen novels and story collections appeared after 1871, set in his fictional "Wessex," including *The Return of the Native* (1878), *The Mayor of Casterbridge* (1886), *Tess of the d'Urbervilles* (1891), and *Jude the Obscure* (1895); when *Jude* was badly received, he turned to poetry, publishing such volumes as *Time's Laughingstocks* (1909).

HARINGTON, SIR JOHN (c.1561-1612): English translator, courtier, and wit, godson of ELIZABETH I, born in Somerset, educated at Eton and Cambridge; author of a metrical translation of Ariosto's *Orlando Furioso* (1591), and *A New Discourse of a Stale Subject, Called the Metamorphosis of Ajax* (1596), which proposed a new design for a water closet (or "a jakes"), and several epigrams and licentious satires.

HARRISON, TONY (b.1937): English poet and dramatist, born in Leeds, educated at Leeds U.; married Rosemarie Dietzch, 1960; taught in West Africa, returning to Northern England in 1967; author of *Selected Poems* (1984) and other volumes, recurrently concerned with the relation between language and class.

HARWOOD, GWEN (FOSTER) (b.1920): Australian poet and librettist, born in Queensland, studied and taught music; housewife after her marriage to William Harwood (1945), a linguistics professor; published under several pseudonyms ("Francis Geyer," "Walter Lehmann," "T.F. Kline," "Miriam Stone"); author of *New and Selected Poems* (1975) and other volumes.

HAWTHORNE, NATHANIEL (1804-1864): American novelist and short story writer, born in Salem, Massachusetts (one ancestor was John Hathorne, a judge in the 1692 Salem witch trials, who figures in *The House of the Seven Gables*, 1851), educated at Bowdoin College; friend of LONGFELLOW and Franklin Pierce (1804-1869, fourteenth president of the U.S.A., who appointed him Consul in Liverpool, 1854-58); published *Twice-Told Tales* (1837, expanded 1842); joined the Transcendentalist "Brook Farm" commune with EMERSON and others, 1841-2, from which developed his novel *The Blithedale Romance* (1852); with his wife (Sophia Peabody, married 1841) moved to Concord, 1842, and wrote *Mosses from an Old Manse* (1846), *The Scarlet Letter* (1850), and other works.

HAYMAN, ROBERT (1575-1629): English poet and epigrammatist, born in Devon, educated at Oxford; after legal training, he appears to have joined a Bristol company (c.1617) interested in colonizing Newfoundland; *Quodlibets* (1628), his only publication and probably the first English-language publication to be written in Canada, praises the profitability of the colony, but did not win Charles I's attention, as hoped; died of a fever in Guiana while on a new commercial expedition.

HAZLITT, WILLIAM (1778-1830): English essayist and critic, born in Kent to a Unitarian family, grew up in America and Shropshire, educated by his father; acquainted with WORDSWORTH, KEATS, and COLERIDGE; friends with LAMB; wrote for HUNT's journals, sympathizing with the French Revolution and republican ideas; produced an annotated selection of BURKE's speeches (1807), a reply to MALTHUS (1807), reviews of SHELLEY (1821-22); *The Spirit of the Age* (1825) gathers some of his essays.

HD: see Hilda DOOLITTLE.

HEANEY, SEAMUS (b.1939): Ulster poet, born in County Derry, Northern Ireland, the son of a farmer; educated at Queen's U. (Belfast); married Marie Devlin, 1965; settled in Dublin, 1976, lecturing at a Catholic college; his several volumes include *North* (1975), *Field Work* (1979), and *Sweeney Astray* (1983).

HEARNE, SAMUEL (1745-1792): Canadian explorer and journal writer, born in London, England; after serving with the British navy, joined the Hudson's Bay Company, 1766; explored the Coppermine River, 1770-72, reaching the Arctic Ocean; named governor of Fort Prince of Wales, 1776; retired to England, 1786, where he completed his exploration narrative, *A Journey from Prince of Wales's Fort, in Hudson's Bay, to the Northern Ocean* (1795).

HEMANS, FELICIA (BROWNE) (1793-1835): English poet, born in Liverpool, educated by her mother; friend of WORDSWORTH and Sir Walter SCOTT; married Capt. Alfred Hemans (1812; separated 1818); published poetry to support her five sons; volumes include *Records of Woman* (1828).

HEMINGWAY, ERNEST (1899-1961): American novelist and short story writer, born in Oak Park, Illinois; as a reporter for the Toronto *Star* in the 1920s, met the Canadian writer Morley Callaghan (1903-1990); became part of the American expatriate set in Paris in the 1920s, where his literary friends included POUND, Scott Fitzgerald (1896-1940), and Gertrude Stein (1874-1946), who coined the phrase "a lost generation" to describe them; four times married, three times divorced; winner of the 1954 Nobel Prize; repeatedly wrote of the testing of manliness; committed suicide; his books include *In Our Time* (1925), *A Farewell to Arms* (1929), *For Whom the Bell Tolls* (1940), and *The Old Man and the Sea* (1952).

HENLEY, WILLIAM ERNEST (1849-1903): English poet and editor, born in Gloucestershire; crippled by tuberculosis as a child, requiring a leg to be amputated (treated in Edinburgh by Joseph Lister, 1827-1912, the doctor responsible for bringing antiseptic practice to modern surgery); became friends with Robert Louis STEVENSON (though they later quarrelled), who used him as a model for Long John Silver in *Treasure Island*; his poetry includes *A Book of Verses* (1888).

HENRYSON, ROBERT (c.1424-c.1506): Scottish poet (one of the "Scottish Chaucerians"), about whom little is known; lived in Dunfermline, perhaps a schoolmaster, probably a notary in 1478; William DUNBAR refers to him in 1508 as having died; works include *The Testament of Cresseid* (first surviving edition dates from 1532) and thirteen fables translated as *The Morall Fabillis of Esope the Phrygian*.

HERBERT, EDWARD, LORD HERBERT OF CHERBURY (1583-1648): English poet, deist philosopher, and diplomat, elder brother of George HERBERT; born in Shropshire, educated at Oxford; ambassador to France (1619-24); served Royalists until surrendering to the Parliamentarian cause in 1644; his works include *De Veritate* (1625).

HERBERT, GEORGE (1593-1633): English poet and Church of England clergyman, born to a noble family in Shropshire, educated at Cambridge, younger brother of Lord HERBERT of Cherbury; opposed Puritans; married Jane Danvers, 1629; *The Temple* (1633), collecting 160 poems, went through 13 editions by 1680.

HERBERT, MARY SIDNEY: see Countess of PEMBROKE.

HERRICK, ROBERT (1591-1674): English poet and clergyman, born in London, apprenticed to a goldsmith, later educated at Cambridge, never married; friend of JONSON; ordained, 1623; named to a Devon parish until removed (1647) during the Commonwealth, reinstated 1662; published *Hesperides* (1648).

HEYWOOD, JOHN (c.1497-c.1580): English Catholic playwright, epigrammatist, and musician, born possibly in London, possibly in Essex, educated at Oxford; grandfather of John DONNE; related (by marriage) to Sir Thomas MORE, who introduced him at the court of Henry VIII; music teacher to Princess (later Queen) Mary; wrote stage comedies; at ELIZABETH I's accession, went into exile in the Netherlands, where he died.

HINE, DARYL (b.1936): Canadian poet, born in New Westminster, B.C., educated at McGill and at U. of Chicago (in Latin and Comparative Literature), where he went on to teach; editor of *Poetry* (Chicago) through the 1970s; author and editor of numerous volumes, including *Selected Poems* (1981) and an edition of Theocritus (1982).

HOBBES, THOMAS (1588-1679): English materialist philosopher, born in Wiltshire, educated at Oxford; as tutor and later secretary to William Cavendish, 1st Earl of Devonshire, he travelled, met such people as Galileo, Descartes, JONSON, and Lord HERBERT of Cherbury, and worked with Francis BACON (1621-26); lived in Paris during the Puritan interregnum, becoming tutor to the Prince of Wales (later Charles II) in 1647, but was dismissed when his book about political power, *Leviathan* (1651), was mistakenly read as an argument in favour of Cromwell; after 1658, a Commons bill opposing blasphemy forbade him from publishing any more books, and led to the public burning of those already in print; he embarked on translations of Homer in his 80s, and several books were published posthumously.

HOCCLEVE [sometimes OCCLEVE], THOMAS (c.1369-1430): English poet, perhaps born in Hockliffe, Bedfordshire; a clerk in the Privy Seal office; his poems, most dating from the period 1402-22, are mainly autobiographical and religious.

HOLINSHED, RAPHAEL (d. c.1580): English chronicler, perhaps born in Cheshire; worked from c.1560 as a translator in the London printing office of Richard Wolfe, where, with the help of historians William Harrison (1534-1593), Richard Stanyhurst (1547-1604), and Edmund Campion (1540-1581), and using the historical studies of John Leland (c.1506-1552), he composed *The Chronicles of England, Scotland, and Ireland* (2 vols., 1577); this work, the source for historical plays by SHAKESPEARE and MARLOWE, was continued and expanded in 1587 by John Hooker.

HOLMES, OLIVER WENDELL (1809-1894): American man of letters and professor of medicine, born in Cambridge, Massachusetts, educated at Harvard; married Amelia Jackson, 1840; father of the judge Oliver Wendell Holmes (1841-1935); co-founder in 1857 (with James Russell LOWELL) of *The Atlantic Monthly*, where he published many essays, collecting some (along with his verse) in *The Autocrat of the Breakfast Table* (1858); other books include fictional studies of psychological disorders, such as *Elsie Venner* (1861).

HOOD, THOMAS (1799-1845): English poet and humorist, born in London, son of a Scottish bookseller, educated privately; met Thomas De Quincey (1785-1859), LAMB, and HAZLITT while working for *The London Magazine* in the 1820s; went on to write for various journals, including *Punch* (which published "The Song of the Shirt" anonymously in 1843); edited *The New Monthly Magazine* from 1841 to 1844, when he started his own *Hood's Magazine*; his works include *Whims and Oddities* (2 series, 1826-27).

HOPE, A[LEC] D[ERWENT] (b.1907): Australian poet and critic, born in New South Wales, educated at Sydney U. and Oxford; Professor of English at Australian National U., 1951-68; his poems include *Dunciad Minor* (1970), variations on poems by William DUNBAR, and *Collected Poems 1930-1970* (1972).

HOPKINS, GERARD MANLEY (1844-1889): English poet, born in Essex, educated at Oxford (a pupil of PATER), where he became friends with BRIDGES; converted to Catholicism, 1866, becoming a Jesuit priest, 1877; moved from parish to parish, ending up as Professor of Greek at University College, Dublin; died of typhoid; while such poems as "The Wreck of the *Deutschland*" (about five Franciscan nuns who drowned in the Thames in 1875) were accepted by *The Month*, a Jesuit journal, the editor finally feared to publish them; Hopkins' poems circulated among friends in manuscript, but were not published until the edition brought out by Bridges in 1918; his edited *Notebooks* (1937) and his correspondence with friends (edited in several volumes) explained his theories of language and metrics.

HOUSMAN, A[LFRED] E[DWARD] (1859-1936): English poet and Latin scholar, born in Worcestershire, educated at Oxford, later taught at Cambridge and edited the works of Ovid, Manilius, and others; published *A Shropshire Lad* at his own expense (1898).

HOWARD, HENRY: see Earl of SURREY.

HUGHES, LANGSTON (1902-1967): American fiction writer, poet, and playwright, born in Joplin, Missouri, educated at Lincoln U. in Pennsylvania; became involved in the "Harlem Renaissance" movement in New York in the 1920s, along with Claude McKay (1890-1948), Jean Toomer (1894-1967), Countee Cullen (1903-1946), and other modern black writers; publications include *Weary Blues* (1926), *The Ways of White Folks* (1934), *Shakespeare in Harlem* (1941), and *Montage of a Dream Deferred* (1951).

HUGHES, TED [EDWARD JAMES] (b.1930): English poet and children's writer, born in Yorkshire, educated (in archeology and anthropology) at Cambridge, where he met Sylvia PLATH, whom he married in 1956; named Poet Laureate, 1984; his several volumes of poetry include *Hawk in the Rain* (1957), *Lupercal* (1960), and *Selected Poems 1957-81* (1982).

HUNT, LEIGH (1784-1859): English poet and critical journalist, born in Middlesex, educated at Christ's Hospital (London); founded and edited various journals, including *The Examiner* (from 1808 on), which published Thomas MOORE, BYRON, LAMB, and introduced KEATS and SHELLEY to the reading public (when a libel against the Prince Regent led to a 2-year jail term, 1813-15, he edited the journal from prison); lived in Hampstead, where he entertained a wide circle of friends (he was caricatured as "Skimpole" in DICKENS's novel *Bleak House*); maintained a liaison with Agnes Lewes [see George ELIOT]; published *Lord Byron and Some of His Contemporaries* (1828) and other volumes.

IRVING, WASHINGTON (1783-1859): American lawyer, diplomat, satirist, historian, and story writer, born in New York City; officer during the War of 1812; lived in Europe (1815-32) on business and as an attaché for the American legation in Madrid and London; became friends with Sir Walter SCOTT, Mary Shelley, LONGFELLOW, and the American fur millionaire John Jacob Astor (1763-1848); as "Diedrich Knickerbocker" published *A History of New York* (1809), a burlesque of Dutch New Yorkers and satire of JEFFERSON; *The Sketch Book of Geoffrey Crayon, Gent.* (1820) included such stories as "Rip Van Winkle" and "The Legend of Sleepy Hollow."

JACKSON, LAURA: see Laura RIDING.

JAMES I (1566-1625): King of England and Scotland; born James Stuart, son of Mary Queen of Scots and Henry, Lord Darnley; became King James VI of Scotland in 1567; succeeded to the English throne in 1603, on the death of ELIZABETH I; educated by tutors, among them the Latin poet and humanist George Buchanan (1506-1582), who corresponded with ASCHAM and the Danish astronomer Tycho Brahe (1546-1601); wrote several works, including the poems and criticism of *The Essays of a Prentice, in the Divine Art of Poesy* (1584), and books on government, tobacco, and witchcraft; sponsored a new English translation of the Bible (the Authorized Version, known as the "King James Bible"); *The Works of James I* appeared as a folio publication in 1616.

JAMES, HENRY (1843-1916): American essayist and fiction writer, born in New York City, educated by private tutors and at various schools in France, Switzerland, and Germany; brother of the diarist Alice James (1848-1892) and the philosopher of pragmatism, William James (1842-1910); friend of the American writer Edith Wharton (1862-1937); in addition to his travel sketches and many critical essays (including "The Art of Fiction," 1884), he published numerous stories and novels, including *The American* (1877), *Washington Square* (1880), *The Portrait of a Lady* (1881), *The Lesson of the Master* (1892), *What Maisie Knew* (1897), *The Turn of the Screw* (1898), and *The Ambassadors* (1903); a frequent traveller between the U.S.A. and Europe, he settled in London in 1876, and in "Lamb House," in Rye, Sussex, in 1896; became a British citizen in 1915.

JARRELL, RANDALL (1914-1965): American poet, critic, and novelist (whose surname is pronounced "ja-RELL"), born in Nashville, Tennessee, educated at Vanderbilt; served in the U.S. Army Air Force during World War II, after which he taught English and creative writing at a number of colleges; married Mary von Schrader, 1952; killed in an auto accident; publications include *Poetry and the Age* (1953), *Selected Poems* (1955), and *The Woman at the Washington Zoo* (1960).

JEFFERSON, THOMAS (1743-1826): American writer, lawyer, and third president of the United States, born in Virginia to a wealthy, landed, slave-owning family; educated at the College of William and Mary; in 1772 married Martha Skelton (1749-1782); was the principal author of the Declaration of Independence [see FRANKLIN]; later served as governor of Virginia, ambassador to France, Secretary of State under Washington, Vice-President under Adams, and President (1801-08); a member of a group calling themselves Republicans (the origins of the present Democratic Party) [see FRENEAU]; he opposed the Federalist policies of Alexander Hamilton (1755-1804), supported states' rights, agrarian values, and the end of the slave trade; as president, he authorized the Louisiana Purchase (1803) and the 1803-06 expedition of Meriwether Lewis and William Clark to find a land route to the Pacific Coast.

JENNINGS, ELIZABETH (CECIL) (b.1926): English poet, born in Lincolnshire, educated (in English literature) at Oxford; worked as librarian and freelance writer, publishing on religion, mental illness, and painting; Catholic, interested in metaphysics, she translated Michelangelo's sonnets in 1961; author of *Collected Poems* (1986) and several other volumes.

JEWETT, SARAH ORNE (1849-1909): American short story writer and novelist, born in Maine, educated primarily by her father, a doctor; a distant descendant of Anne BRADSTREET; after 1881 lived with the writer Annie (Adams) Fields (1834-1915); regarded as a leading figure among American "local colorists" (among whom are sometimes listed Bret Harte, Mary Wilkins Freeman, Joel Chandler Harris, George W. Cable, Kate Chopin, and Zona Gale), especially for *The Country of the Pointed Firs* (1896).

JILES, PAULETTE (b.1943): Canadian poet and novelist, born in Salem, Missouri; emigrated to Canada in 1968; actress and writer for the Canadian Broadcasting Corporation; publications include *Celestial Navigation* (1984), *Sitting in the Club Car Drinking Rum and Karma-Cola* (1986), *The Late Great Human Road Show* (1986), and *Blackwater* (1988).

JOHNSON, SAMUEL (1709-1784): English man of letters and lexicographer, born in Lichfield, Staffordshire, the son of a bookseller; educated at Oxford; married Elizabeth Porter, 1735, and briefly ran a school in Lichfield with her, one of their pupils being the actor David Garrick (1717-1779); moved to London in 1737; wrote for *The Gentleman's Magazine*; began his series of biographies (later collected as *The Lives of the Poets*, 1781) with a study of his friend Richard Savage (c.1696-1743) in 1744; ran and largely wrote the journal *The Rambler* (1750-52), and from 1758 to 1760 contributed *The Idler* papers to *The Univeral Chronicle or Weekly Gazette*; published *A Dictionary of the English Language* in 1755; in 1763 met James BOSWELL, with whom he was later to travel and who wrote his biography; founded "The Literary Club" (1764) with his friend REYNOLDS, meeting with GOLDSMITH, BURKE, Garrick, and others; friend of PIOZZI; awarded an honorary doctorate by Oxford in 1755, hence the title "Dr. Johnson," which is usually accorded him; author of numerous editions, critical reviews, and commentaries, together with the poem *London* (1728), *The Vanity of Human Wishes* (1747), *Rasselas, The Prince of Abyssinia* (1759), and *A Journey to the Western Isles of Scotland* (1775).

JONES, ALICE (1853-1933): Canadian travel writer and author of fiction ("Alix John"), born and educated in Halifax, daughter of Alfred Gilpin Jones, a businessman who later became the Lieutenant-Governor of Nova Scotia; in 1905 settled in Menton, France; author of *Gabriel Praed's Castle* (1904) and other works.

JONES, D[OUGLAS] G. (b.1929): Canadian poet and critic, born in Bancroft, Ontario, educated at McGill and Queen's U. (Kingston); teaches at Université de Sherbrooke, where he founded the journal *ellipse* (1969); author of *Butterfly on Rock* (1970) and other volumes, including his selected poems, *A Throw of Particles* (1983).

JONES, MARY (1707-1778): English poet and letter-writer, lived in Oxford; corresponded with the American-born novelist Charlotte Lennox (1729-1804; author of *The Female Quixote*, 1752); published verse anonymously, her *Miscellanies in Prose and Verse* appearing in 1750.

JONSON, BEN (1573-1637): English poet and dramatist, probably born in Westminster, the son of a bricklayer; a soldier and actor, known for his quick temper (he killed another actor in a duel, and his plays, e.g. *The Poetaster*, 1601, hurled invective at fellow-playwrights John Marston and Thomas DEKKER, in what came to be known as "the war of the theatres"); gained a reputation with *Every Man in His Humour* (1598), one of several plays concerned with the comedy of "humours"; converted to Catholicism, 1598, though later recanted; wrote masques for the court of JAMES I; later plays include *Volpone* (1605), *The Alchemist* (1610), and *Bartholomew Fair* (1614); his poetry and plays were collected as *Works* in 1616, and his criticism, *Timber* (1640), was published posthumously.

JOYCE, JAMES (1882-1941): Irish short story writer and novelist, born in Dublin, educated at Jesuit Schools and University College (Dublin), briefly pursued medical training and then voice training (for a concert career); knew YEATS, Lady GREGORY, and others involved in the Irish Renaissance, but left Ireland for Zurich (to work at the Berlitz school) in 1904, with Nora Barnacle, whom he married in 1931; detained in Trieste during World War I; settled in Paris, 1920; known for advancing the stream-of-consciousness technique in fiction; author of a play, some lyric verse, and four influential works of fiction: *Dubliners* (1914), *A Portrait of the Artist as a Young Man* (1916; first conceived as *Stephen Hero*), *Ulysses* (1922; suppressed as obscene, no edition appearing in England until 1936), and *Finnegans Wake* (1939; first published in serial form, 1928-37, as *Work in Progress*).

JULIAN, DAME, OF NORWICH (c.1342-after 1413): English mystic, about whom little is known beyond what she tells in her own *Revelations of Divine Love*, a meditation which developed out of fifteen years of contemplating the serious illness she suffered when 30 years old and the 16 divine "shewings" she experienced at that time; possibly a nun in a Benedictine order, she was visited by Margery KEMPE, and ended her life as a recluse in the church of St. Julian and St. Edward in Norwich; known about in her own day, she has influenced such modern writers as T.S. ELIOT, Iris Murdoch (b. 1919), and Randolph Stow (b. 1935).

KEATS, JOHN (1795-1821): English poet and letter-writer, born in London, the eldest of four children of a livery stable manager; apprenticed to a surgeon in 1810, when he was taken out of school; began to publish poetry in 1814, and was encouraged by HUNT; friends with SHELLEY, the poet John Hamilton Reynolds (1796-1852), the painter Benjamin Haydon (1786-1846), and the critic Charles Wentworth Dilke (1789-1864); during the three years 1816-19 wrote much of his most enduring poetry, including "Endymion," "Hyperion," many of the sonnets, "Lamia," "The Eve of St. Agnes," the odes, and the letters that discuss his poetic theories, some of them influenced by HAZLITT; by 1820 was ill with tuberculosis, nursed by Fanny Brawne; moved to Rome, attended by his friend, the portrait painter Joseph Severn (1793-1879, later the British consul in Rome), and died there the following year.

KEMBLE, FRANCES ANNE [FANNY] (1809-1893): English actress and journal-writer; born in London to a family active in the theatre; educated in France; debuted on the stage in 1829, as Juliet; toured the U.S.A. in 1832-33, the basis for *Journal of a Residence in America* (1835); married a slave-owning American plantation owner, Pierce Butler, in 1834 (divorced 1848, after quarrels about slavery—she was an abolitionist—and her own freedom to write); returned to the stage to give public readings of SHAKESPEARE, mainly in America; subsequently wrote several volumes of memoirs and poems, and (in 1889) published a farce and a novel.

KEMPE, MARGERY (BRUNHAM) (c.1373-c.1439): English autobiographer, born in Lynn, Norfolk, where her father (John Brunham) was mayor; married John Kempe (c.1393) and had a number of children (perhaps fourteen), before persuading him to live a life of chastity; her one work, *The Book of Margery Kempe*, dictated to two amanuenses, records among other things the travels she embarked on after a spiritual crisis (c.1413); tried for Lollardy (see WYCLIF) in Leicester in 1417, but acquitted, she travelled as far as Jerusalem and Germany; in England, she visited various religious persons (including Dame JULIAN), offering spiritual advice and (while relating her mystical revelations) bursting into prolonged fits of weeping, for which she became famous.

KILLIGREW, ANNE (1660-1685): English poet, daughter of the royal chaplain Henry Killigrew; like FINCH, she was one of the Duchess of York's attendants; died of smallpox; her *Poems* (1686) were published posthumously by her father, with an encomium by DRYDEN.

KING, HENRY (1592-1669): English clergyman and poet, the son of the Bishop of London, born in Worminghall, Buckinghamshire; educated at Westminster School (by Lancelot Andrewes, 1555-1626, one of the translators of the Authorized Version of the Bible) and at Oxford; in 1617 married Anne Berkeley (c.1600-1624); became Bishop of Chichester, 1642; forced from his position during the Puritan Commonwealth, but regained it at the Restoration; friend of WALTON, and of DONNE, for whom he wrote an elegy; his poems, some commemorating the deaths of JONSON, RALEGH, and his first wife, were collected in 1657.

KINGSLEY, CHARLES (1819-1875): English clergyman and novelist, born in Devon, son of the vicar of Holne; brother of the novelist Henry Kingsley (1830-1876) and the travel writer George Kingsley (1827-1892), and uncle of Mary KINGSLEY; educated at Cambridge and King's College (London), became a Hampshire parish priest, Cambridge professor of modern history (1860-69), chaplain to Queen Victoria (1873), and a devotee of what came to be known as "muscular Christianity"; author of *Alton Locke* (1850), *Westward Ho!* (1855), *The Water Babies* (1863), and *Hereward the Wake* (1865).

KINGSLEY, MARY (1862-1900): English naturalist and travel writer, born in London, daughter of Mary Bailey and the doctor and travel writer George Kingsley; niece of Charles KINGSLEY; largely self-educated; after the death of her parents, embarked on the expeditions that she wrote about in *Travels in West Africa* (1897); observed local society and collected zoological specimens, including several fish now classified by her name; died in South Africa during the Boer War, from typhoid fever caught while nursing Boer prisoners.

KIPLING, RUDYARD (1865-1936): English poet and short story writer, born in Bombay, where his father taught art; one uncle on his mother's side was the painter Sir Edward Burne-Jones (1833-1898), and a cousin was Stanley Baldwin (1867-1947), who became Prime Minister of Britain during the 1920s and 1930s; educated in Devon; returned to India as a journalist in Lahore, 1883; settled in England, 1889; married Caroline Balestier, 1892, and lived in Vermont near her family for four years; established his literary career with verses and tales of Imperial India, including *Plain Tales from the Hills* (1888),

Barrack Room Ballads (1892), and *Kim* (1901); later developed a reputation for his children's books—the two *Jungle Books* (1894-5), *Just So Stories* (1902), and *Puck of Pook's Hill* (1906)—and his realistic short fiction; won the Nobel Prize, 1907.

KIZER, CAROLINE (b.1925): American poet and translator, born in Spokane, Washington, educated at Sarah Lawrence College, Columbia, and U. of Washington; married Charles Bullitt, 1948 (divorced 1954), and John Woodbridge, 1975; founded and edited the journal *Poetry Northwest* (1959-1965); taught in Pakistan, 1964-65, and translates from Urdu and other languages; her works include *The Ungrateful Garden* (1961), *Knock Upon Silence* (1965), and the Pulitzer Prize-winning *Yin* (1984).

KLEIN, A[BRAHAM] M[OSES] (1909-1972): Canadian poet, novelist, journalist, and short story writer, born in Montreal to an orthodox Jewish family; educated at McGill and U. de Montréal; practised law; acquainted with poets F.R. SCOTT and LAYTON, among others; became active in Zionist movements, editing *The Judaean* (1928-32), *The Canadian Zionist* (1936-37), and the weekly *Canadian Jewish Chronicle* (1938-55), until a depression caused him to withdraw from public contacts; his works, which analyze current politics and protest against anti-Semitism, include a 1951 novel, *The Second Scroll*, commentaries on the work of James JOYCE, and several volumes of poetry, among them *The Rocking Chair* (1948); a multi-volume edition of his writings, including those left in manuscript, began in 1982.

KOLATKAR, ARUN (b.1932): Indian poet, born in Kolhapur, raised in the Hindu religion; educated at U. of Bombay; works as a designer and graphic artist in Bombay; *Jejuri* (1976) won the Commonwealth Poetry Prize, and a work in Marathi, *Arun Kolatkarchya Kavita* (1976), won the H.S. Gokhale Award.

LAMB, CHARLES ["ELIA"] (1775-1834): English essayist, born in London, educated at Christ's Hospital, where he met and became friends with Samuel Taylor COLERIDGE; worked for the South Sea House, and after 1792 the East India House; never married, though his early poems, published with Coleridge's *Poems on Various Subjects* (1796), tell of a thwarted love; spent his life looking after his sister Mary (1764-1847), who had been confined to a mental asylum (after murdering their mother in 1796) and who was released into his care in 1799; participated in literary discussions with SOUTHEY, Coleridge, HUNT, and others; with Mary, wrote *Tales from Shakespeare* (1807)—she writing all but the tragedies, though only his name appeared on the book—and other works for children; using the name "Elia," published many personal essays in *The London Magazine*, which were collected as *The Essays of Elia* (1823) and *The Last Essays of Elia* (1833).

LAMPMAN, ARCHIBALD (1861-1899): Canadian poet, born in Morpeth, Ontario, educated at Trinity College (Toronto); married Maud Playter, 1887; worked for the Post Office; friends with D.C. SCOTT; contributed articles to various papers, including *The Week* and the *Toronto Globe*; *The Poems of Archibald Lampman*, edited by Scott, appeared in 1900; in 1975 Margaret Coulby Whitridge edited *Lampman's Kate*, a collection of Lampman's love poems to Katherine Waddell, which had been suppressed.

LANDOR, WALTER SAVAGE (1775-1864): English poet and essayist, born in Warwick, expelled from both Rugby School and Oxford; a quick temper led to his departure from England (twice: to

Italy, 1814-35; and again to Italy in 1858, after a libel action was begun against him); on the second occasion, Robert BROWNING attempted to befriend him in Florence; DICKENS caricatured him as "Boythorn" in his novel *Bleak House*; author of a number of poems, and of *Imaginary Conversations of Literary Men and Statesmen* (1824-29) and other books of prose.

LANG, JOHN DUNMORE (1799-1878): Australian clergyman, poet, and political reformer, born in Greenock, Scotland; emigrated 1823; became Sydney's first Presbyterian minister, then leader of the Scots Church, which he established; republican; campaigned against the transportation of convicts; author of *Poems: Sacred and Secular* (1872) as well as several political works.

LANYER, AMELIA (BASSANO) (1569-1645): English poet, daughter of an Italian musician and his wife; educated in the house of a nobleman; became mistress to Lord Hunsdon, then married Alfonso Lanyer, a musician, 1592; published *Salve Deus Rex Judaeorum* (1611); ran a school for children of the gentry, 1617-19; has been suggested by one critic as the "dark lady" of SHAKESPEARE's sonnets.

LARKIN, PHILIP (1922-1985): English poet, essayist, librarian, and novelist, born in Coventry, educated at Oxford; worked after 1955 at the U. of Hull; author of *The Less Deceived* (1955), *The Whitsun Weddings* (1964), *High Windows* (1974), and other works, including a regular series of articles in *The Daily Telegraph* about jazz recordings.

LAWRENCE, D[AVID] H[ERBERT] (1885-1930): English novelist, poet, critic, painter, and short story and travel writer, born in Nottinghamshire, the son of a coal miner and a woman with social ambitions; educated at Nottingham University College; gave up teaching school to write full time; met Frieda (von Richthofen) Weekley (a cousin of the German pilot), 1912, and married her in 1914 after her divorce from lexicographer and writer Ernest Weekley (1865-1954); developed (often strained) friendships with other literary figures, including MANSFIELD, Bertrand Russell (1872-1970), and Aldous Huxley (1894-1963); accused of spying for the Germans during World War I, and expelled from his home in Cornwall; lived in Italy, Mexico, U.S.A., and Australia after 1919; died in France, of tuberculosis; three novels, *The Rainbow* (1915), *Women in Love* (1921), and *Lady Chatterley's Lover* (1928), faced obscenity charges, the last leading to a celebrated 1959-60 trial that finally permitted the work to be published, unexpurgated, in England and the U.S.A.; three volumes of his collected stories appeared in 1955; other books include *Sons and Lovers* (1913), *The Plumed Serpent* (1926), *Studies in Classic American Literature* (1923), and *Mornings in Mexico* (1927).

LAWSON, HENRY (1867-1922): Australian short story writer and poet, born on the goldfields of New South Wales, son of the suffragist and writer Louisa (Albury) Lawson (1848-1920) and her husband, a Norwegian sailor named Niels Larsen; poorly educated; deaf from age nine; married Bertha Bredt (1876-1957) in 1895, separated bitterly in 1903, Lawson spending some time in jail for not paying maintenance; contributed some early work to his mother's socialist journal *The Republican*, but after 1888 was published in the leading Australian journal of the time, *The Bulletin*, in whose pages he also debated literary questions with A.B. PATERSON; attracted a wide public following with such story collections as *While the Billy Boils* (1896), *Joe Wilson and His Mates* (1901), and the verse of *In the Days When the World Was Wide* (1896); many selections from and editions of his work appeared posthumously; his later years were marked by his

increasing alcoholism, bouts of mental illness, and a cerebral hemorrhage in 1921.

LAYTON, IRVING (b.1912): Canadian poet, essayist, and short story writer, born Israel Lazarovitch in Neamtz, Romania; emigrated 1913; raised in Montreal; educated (in economics and political science) at McGill, later taught English poetry at Sir George Williams U.; five times married; associated with the poets Louis Dudek (b. 1918) and Raymond Souster (b. 1921) in the setting up of Contact Press; subsequently embarked on an independent career that resulted in over fifty books; his poetry celebrates sexuality, intellectual tradition, and his own Jewishness, and attacks what the Established Church has done to the values of Christianity; *A Wild Peculiar Joy* (1982) provides a selection.

LEACOCK, STEPHEN (1869-1944): Canadian humorist and political economist, born in Hampshire, England, emigrated in 1875; brought up in the Lake Simcoe region of Ontario by his mother after his father abandoned the family; educated at Upper Canada College, U. of Toronto, and U. of Chicago, where he studied with the American sociologist and economist Thorstein Veblen (1857-1929); taught political science at McGill; as a humorist was influenced by DICKENS and TWAIN; published his sketches in *Saturday Night* and other periodicals, collecting them (almost annually) into book form; works include *Literary Lapses* (1910), *Sunshine Sketches of a Little Town* (1912), *Arcadian Adventures with the Idle Rich* (1914), *My Discovery of England* (1922), *My Remarkable Uncle* (1942), and *Humour: Its Theory and Technique* (1935); lecture and reading tours confirmed his international reputation.

LEAPOR, MARY (1722-1746): English poet, born in Northamptonshire to a working class family; worked as a kitchen maid; using the name "Mira" (or "Myra"), she wrote poems that criticize gender and class barriers to artistic recognition; died of measles; *Poems upon Several Occasions* appeared posthumously (2 vols., 1748, 1751).

LE GUIN, URSULA K[ROEBER] (b. 1929): American essayist and science fiction and fantasy writer, born in Berkeley, California, daughter of the writer Theodora (Kracaw) Kroeber and the anthropologist Alfred Kroeber (known for his work with *Ishi*); educated (in French and Medieval Studies) at Radcliffe and Columbia; married the historian Charles Le Guin, 1953; her works, which have won numerous science fiction awards, include *A Wizard of Earthsea* (1968), *The Left Hand of Darkness* (1969), *Tehanu* (1990), which won the Nebula Award, and the essays collected in *The Language of the Night* (1979) and *Dancing at the Edge of the World* (1989).

L'ESTRANGE, SIR ROGER (1616-1704): English journalist and translator, born in Norfolk, the son of a landowning family; active in the Civil War, he escaped to the Continent from Newgate Prison in 1648, where he had been held for four years after almost being hanged as a Royalist spy; in France, wrote numerous strongly worded pamphlets attacking Presbyterianism; was made licenser of the press after the Restoration, and published several influential papers, including *The Public Intelligencer* (1663-1666) and *The Observator* (1681-1687); knighted by James II in 1685; deprived of his post after the accession of William and Mary; supported himself by translating works by Seneca, Cicero, Aesop, and Erasmus, among others.

LEVERTOV, DENISE (b.1923): American poet, born in Essex, England, to a family with Welsh and Russian-Jewish heritage; a nurse during World War II; married American writer Mitchell Goodman, 1948 (divorced 1972), emigrating to New York City; influenced by the Black Mountain poets [see CREELEY, Robert DUNCAN]; an anti-Vietnam War activist, she travelled in Southeast Asia; poetry editor for *The Nation* after 1961; author of *O Taste and See* (1964), *Relearning the Alphabet* (1970), *Breathing the Water* (1987), and several other volumes, including translations from Bengali and a collection of essays on writing, *The Poet in the World* (1973).

LIM, SHIRLEY GEOK-LIN (b.1944): Malaysian poet and short story writer, born in Malacca of Chinese and Malaysian descent; educated at U. of Malaya and Brandeis (in English and American literature); teaches at Westchester College in New York; author of *Crossing the Peninsula* (1980), which won the Commonwealth Poetry Prize, *Another Country* (1982), and *No Man's Grove* (1985).

LINCOLN, ABRAHAM (1809-1865): American statesman, 16th President of the United States (1861-65), born in Kentucky, moved to Illinois in 1830; courted Ann Rutledge (died 1835), later (1842) married Mary Todd (1818-82); an attorney and state congressman after 1836, he became a Republican when the new party formed, opposing slavery; established a reputation as a forceful debater; defeated Stephen Douglas for the presidency in 1860, though he lost the popular vote; directed the Union during the Civil War (1861-65); re-elected 1864; assassinated by John Wilkes Booth (April 14, 1865) at Ford's Theatre in Washington; his most famous speeches include the Gettysburg Address (1863) and his second inaugural address ("With malice toward none; with charity for all, let us strive ...[for] a just and lasting peace..."); commemorated in several plays and biographies, and in poems by WHITMAN and others.

LINDSAY, LADY ANNE (later BARNARD) (1750-1825): Scottish writer, born in Fifeshire, eldest daughter of James Lindsay, 5th Earl of Balcarres, and his wife Anne Dalrymple, whose social circle included the philosopher David Hume (1711-1776); moved to London, 1773; married Andrew Barnard (son of the Bishop of Limerick, who was a friend of JOHNSON), 1793, and moved to South Africa, where her husband was Colonial Secretary to Lord Macartney, the new governor of the Cape of Good Hope Colony; returned to England after his death (1807), where her home became a social centre for BURKE, Richard Sheridan [see Frances BROOKE], and her close friend the Prince of Wales; her poem "Auld Robin Gray" remained anonymous until Sir Walter SCOTT attributed it to her in a text he edited in 1825.

LINDSAY (LYNDSAY), SIR DAVID (c.1486-1555): Scottish poet and diplomat; served prince James (later James V of Scotland) from 1512 on, as a companion and after 1528 as a representative to the courts of France, the Netherlands, England, and Denmark; married Janet Douglas, the king's seamstress, c.1524; knighted by 1542; author of a number of (frequently anti-clerical) satires, "flytings" [see DUNBAR], dream-visions, and romances, including *The Satyre of the Thrie Estaitis* (1540).

LIVESAY, DOROTHY (b.1909): Canadian poet, born in Winnipeg, daughter of the poet Florence Randal Livesay (1874-1953); educated at U. of Toronto, the Sorbonne, and U. of British Columbia; joined (but later repudiated) Communist Party; married Duncan McNair, 1937 (divorced 1959); worked as a social worker during the 1930s, and later as an English teacher, in Canada and Zambia; founder and editor of the poetry journal *CV/II*; winner of the Governor-General's Award and

other honours, for books such as *Day and Night* (1944), *Poems for People* (1947), *Ice Age* (1975), and *The Woman I Am* (1978); *Beginnings* (1989) is an autobiography.

LOCKE, JOHN (1632-1704): English philosopher, born in Somerset, educated at Oxford, where he subsequently taught rhetoric and Greek and studied medicine; became physician to the Earl of SHAFTESBURY, 1667, and later his political advisor; lived largely in France and Holland during the politically troubled years 1675-88, supporting William of Orange's claim to the throne; held a government post, 1691-1700; founded a philosophical discussion group, 1670, which began to question Divine Right, Aristotelianism, and the ideas of HOBBES, and which championed empiricism, "natural morality," and the right to rebel against unjust rulers (an idea that influenced JEFFERSON); works include *Letters Concerning Toleration* (1689-92), *Two Treatises on Government* (1690), *Essay Concerning Human Understanding* (1690), *Some Thoughts Concerning Education* (1693), and *The Reasonableness of Christianity* (1695).

LODGE, THOMAS (1558-1625): English poet, dramatist, romance-writer, and physician, born in London, son of Sir Thomas Lodge (who was imprisoned for debt shortly after being named Lord Mayor in 1562); educated at Oxford and Avignon; practised medicine in England and Holland; sailed in expeditions to South America (1588, 1591); converted to Catholicism; author of several plays, satires, and sermons; best known for a prose romance, *Rosalynde* (1590), which SHAKESPEARE used as the basis for *As You Like It*.

LONGFELLOW, HENRY WADSWORTH (1807-1882): American poet, born in Maine, educated at Bowdoin College; became Professor of Modern Languages at Harvard, 1836, and lived in Cambridge, Massachusetts, for the rest of his life; married Frances Appleton, 1843; author of several popular poems, including *Ballads and Other Poems* (1841), *Evangeline* (1847), *The Song of Hiawatha* (1855), and *The Courtship of Miles Standish* (1858).

LOVELACE, RICHARD (1618-1658): English Cavalier poet, born possibly in Woolwich and possibly in Holland, the son of a Kentish knight; educated at Oxford, active at court; used his estate to fight for Royalist causes, opposing the Puritan Parliament and assisting the French to combat the Spanish; jailed in 1642 and again in 1648; composed the poems to Lucasta (1649) while in prison ("Lucasta" was his fiancée, Lucy Sacheverell); his brother published a second collection posthumously.

LOWELL, ROBERT (1917-1977): American poet, grandson of James Russell LOWELL; born in Boston, educated at Harvard and Kenyon College; converted to Catholicism, 1940, the year he married the novelist Jean Stafford (1915-1979; divorced 1948); jailed during World War II, when he refused to join the army; in 1949 married the novelist Elizabeth Hardwick (b. 1916; divorced 1972); twice winner of the Pulitzer Prize; publications include *Lord Weary's Castle* (1946), *For the Union Dead* (1946), *Life Studies* (1959), and *The Dolphins* (1973).

MACAULAY, THOMAS BABINGTON, 1st BARON MACAULAY (1800-1859): English essayist, historian, and statesman, born in Leicestershire, educated at Cambridge; began to write social and critical essays for the Whig *Edinburgh Review* in 1825, continuing prolifically for twenty years; entered Parliament, 1830, winning fame as an orator when he supported the Reform Bill of 1831-32; instituted various legal reforms in India, 1834-38; became

Lord Melbourne's Secretary-at-War, 1839; named to the peerage, 1857; author of *Lays of Ancient Rome* (1842), *Critical and Historical Essays* (1843), and the five volumes of *History of England* (1848-61), the last volume being edited posthumously by his sister.

MacCaig, Norman (b.1910): Scottish poet, born in Edinburgh, educated at Edinburgh U.; schoolteacher, headmaster, and later Reader in Poetry at Stirling U. (till 1977); winner of several awards, including the OBE (1979); friend of the Scots poets Hugh MacDiarmid [Christopher Murray Grieve, 1892-1978] and Sydney Goodsir Smith (1915-1975); his *Collected Poems* appeared in 1985.

Mackellar, Dorothea (1885-1968): Australian poet and novelist, born in Sydney, educated at U. of Sydney, skilled in European languages; author of *The Closed Door and Other Verses* (1911) and eight other books; awarded the OBE in 1968; published little during her last forty years; *The Poems of Dorothea Mackellar* (1971) collects her work.

Macpherson, Jay (b.1931): Canadian poet and critic, born in London, England, emigrated to Newfoundland in 1940, settled in Ottawa in 1944; educated at Carleton U., McGill, and U. of Toronto, where she became professor of English; friend and colleague of the critic Northrop Frye (1912-1990); her critical volume, *The Spirit of Solitude* (1982), examines pastoral myths; poems include *The Boatman* (1957) and *Welcoming Disaster* (1974).

Makin, Bathsua (Reynolds) (1600-c.1675): English poet and teacher, purported to have medical skills; sister-in-law of the mathematician John Pell (1610-1685); married Richard Makin, 1622; tutor to Princess Elizabeth in the 1640s; author of a collection of poems in several languages, *Musa Virginea* (1616), and of books on women's education and her own system of shorthand.

Malamud, Bernard (1914-1986): American novelist and short story writer, born in Brooklyn to a Russian Jewish immigrant family; educated at City College of New York and Columbia; married Ann de Chiara, 1945; taught English at Oregon State U. and Bennington College; author of such novels as *The Natural* (1952), *The Assistant* (1957), *The Fixer* (1967), which won the Pulitzer Prize and a National Book Award, and *Dubin's Lives* (1979); his story collections include *The Magic Barrel* (1958) and *Idiots First* (1963).

Malory, Sir Thomas (d.1471): English writer, probably from Warwickshire, though his identity remains uncertain; Caxton's preface to *Morte Darthur* (1485) indicates that Malory was a knight, that he wrote most of the work while in Newgate prison (possibly because of a quarrel involving Lancastrian politics), that he "reduced" his romance from a French source, and that he completed it in the ninth year of Edward IV's reign (c.1470); the work influenced many later writers of Arthurian romance, including Tennyson.

Malouf, David (b.1934): Australian poet, novelist, short story writer, and essayist, born in Brisbane to English and Lebanese parents; educated at U. of Queensland; lived in Europe, 1959-68, returning to Australia to lecture in English at U. of Sydney (to 1977), then settled in Italy; author of several volumes, including *Selected Poems* (1980), *An Imaginary Life* (1978), *Harland's Half Acre* (1984), *Antipodes* (1985), and *12 Edmondstone Street* (1985).

Malthus, Thomas (1766-1834): English economist, born in Surrey, educated at Cambridge; ordained 1798, the same year he

published anonymously the first version of his essay *On the Principle of Population As It Affects the Future Improvement of Society* (revised 1803); married, 1804, and became a professor of political economy at Haileybury; "Malthusianism," a reply to the optimism of Rousseau and William Godwin [see Shelley], influenced Darwin's theory of natural selection, but stirred controversy because it appeared to justify poverty as a check on population growth.

Mandel, Eli (1922-1992): Canadian poet and critic, born in Estevan, Saskatchewan, to a Jewish family; educated at U. of Saskatchewan and U. of Toronto, his schooling interrupted by service with the Canadian Army Medical Corps, 1943-45; wrote a dissertation on the work of Christopher Smart; taught English at various universities, including Alberta and York; married twice, to the poet Miriam (Minovitch) Mandel (1930-1982) and the critic Ann (Hardy) Mandel; author and editor of numerous anthologies, critical works, and volumes of poetry, including *Crusoe: Poems Selected and New* (1973), *Another Time* (1977), *Life Sentence* (1981), and *Dreaming Backwards* (1981); debilitated by a series of strokes in the late 1980s.

Mandeville, Sir John (c.1300-1372): the name given to the compiler of a book of travels, first published in French, possibly at Liège (1357), and soon translated; scholars have variously suggested that the real author was a French writer named Jean d'Outremeuse, or a physician named Jehan de Bourgogne (or Jehan à la Barbe) who claimed on his deathbed (1372) that his real named was Maundevylle, that he was English, and that he had fled England to escape prosecution for murder; the "Mandeville" who narrates *Mandeville's Travels*, claims to have been born in England, embarked on his travels in 1322, and written about them from memory; the "travels" are based, however, on the encyclopedia of Vincent de Beauvais (c.1250) and on Jean de Long of St. Omer's French translations (completed 1351) of a series of travel writings by such writers as William of Boldensele and Odoric of Pordenone.

Mangan, James Clarence (1803-1849): Irish poet, born in Dublin to a poor family; educated by a priest; became an attorney's clerk and published poems in such Irish magazines as *The Nation*; an edition of his *Poems* appeared in 1903.

Manhire, Bill (b.1946): New Zealand poet and prose writer, born in Invercargill; educated at U. of Otago and London U.; married Marion McLeod, 1970; teaches English language at Victoria U. of Wellington; general editor of *NZ Stories* series, and author of *Zoetropes: Poems 1972-82* (1984), *The New Land* (1990), and other works.

Mansfield, Katherine [Kathleen Beauchamp, later Murry] (1888-1923): New Zealand short story writer, born Kathleen Beauchamp to a well-to-do family in Wellington; educated at Queen's College (London); settled in England, 1908, though after 1918 (because of tuberculosis, from which she died) spent many months in France, Italy, and Switzerland; married George Bowden in 1909 (whom she left after one day) and, after her divorce in 1918, the critic John Middleton Murry (1889-1957); an acquaintance of Woolf, who published *Prelude* (1918) at her Hogarth Press, and of Lawrence and others, with whom she conducted a revealing correspondence; author of *In a German Pension* (1911), *The Garden Party* (1922), and numerous essays; Murry's posthumous collections of her unpublished stories and notes have been corrected by subsequent editions.

Marlowe, Christopher (1564-1593): English poet and dramatist, born in Canterbury, the son of a shoemaker; educated at

Cambridge; active in the theatre, noted for such plays as *Tamburlaine the Great* (1587), *The Tragical History of Doctor Faustus* (c.1589), *The Jew of Malta* (c.1589), and *Edward the Second* (c.1592); meanwhile (possibly while still at Cambridge) had entered the service of ELIZABETH I as a spy (for the Queen's secretary of state, Sir Francis Walsingham, c.1530-1590, who had devised the elaborate espionage network that uncovered details about the Spanish Armada and implicated Mary Queen of Scots in treason); perhaps because of his espionage activities (though perhaps because of an irregular lifestyle) was murdered in a Deptford tavern brawl.

MARTINEAU, HARRIET (1802-1876): English essayist, novelist, and translator, whose father was of Huguenot ancestry; born in Norwich, educated by her Unitarian parents and at a Bristol boarding school; after 1820, prevented from teaching because of increasing deafness and repeated illness; from 1821 on, published regular articles in such journals as the *Monthly Repository, Edinburgh Review*, and *Athenaeum,* on education, religion (she moved steadily towards agnosticism), mesmerism (for which she became an enthusiast in 1844), economics (she espoused BENTHAM's Utilitarianism), divorce reform, and disease; moved to the Lake District in 1845, hosting such friends as William and Dorothy WORDSWORTH, George ELIOT, and Charlotte BRONTË; her books include *Illustrations of Political Economy* (1832-3), *Society in America* (1837), *Deerbrook* (1839), and a posthumous *Autobiographical Memoir* (1877).

MARVELL, ANDREW (1621-1678): English poet and political writer, born in Yorkshire, educated at Cambridge; travelled widely in Europe (1642-47); served as tutor (1651-53) to the daughter of Lord Fairfax (the general of the parliamentary horse brigade, who lived at Nun Appleton House), tutor (1653-56) to William Dutton (later Oliver Cromwell's ward), and aide to his friend MILTON (1657) in the post of Assistant Latin Secretary to the Council of State; became member of parliament for Hull in Richard Cromwell's parliament (1659; re-elected during the Restoration); much of his poetry was written prior to 1656 and circulated in manuscript, though was not published till the appearance of *Miscellaneous Poems by Andrew Marvell, Esq.* (1681); after 1660, dissatisfied with the rule of Charles II, he primarily wrote political commentaries, including arguments in favour of republicanism and satires of leading state figures.

MASEFIELD, JOHN (1878-1967): English poet, novelist, dramatist, and writer for children; born in Herefordshire, trained (at age 13) to join the merchant navy; left his ship in New York (1895), where he stayed till he became a journalist for the *Manchester Guardian* (1897); friend of YEATS; *Salt-Water Ballads* (1910) was the first of more than 50 books; the success of *Collected Poems* (1923) led to his being named Poet Laureate in 1930.

MAYHEW, HENRY (1812-1887): English novelist, travel writer, and journalist, born in London; one of the original founders of *Punch* in 1841, co-editing it with Mark Lemon (1809-1870) till 1846; collaborated with his brothers Horace (1816-1872) and Augustus (1826-1875) on several popular fictions; began publishing *London Labour and the London Poor* in weekly instalments in *The Morning Chronicle* (finally collected in four volumes, 1861-62, expanded 1864).

MCAULEY, JAMES (1917-1976): Australian poet and critic, born in New South Wales, educated at U. of Sydney; visited New Guinea frequently, and wrote several commentaries on its society in the journal *South Pacific*; taught at the Australian School of Pacific Administration (1946-61) and the U. of Tasmania (1961-76); edited the conservative journal *Quadrant* (1956-75) and championed the classics and traditional literary culture; author of *Under Aldebaran* (1946), *A Vision of Ceremony* (1956), *Captain Quiros* (1964), and other volumes.

MCCRAE, JOHN (1872-1918): Canadian physician and poet, born in Guelph, Ontario, educated at U. of Toronto; practised medicine at Toronto General Hospital and Johns Hopkins in Baltimore, then taught at McGill U. in Montreal and published a textbook on pathology; served as a medical officer in the Boer War (1900) and World War I; composed "In Flanders Fields" (published anonymously in *Punch*, 1915) during the Battle of Ypres; died of pneumonia at the military hospital he ran in Boulogne.

MELVILLE, HERMAN (1819-1891): American novelist, poet, and short story writer, born in New York City; left school at age 12 (after his bankrupted father went insane and died) to work as a bank clerk, teacher, and sailor (deserting his ship, a whaler, in the Marquesas Islands, for which he was jailed in Tahiti); after returning to Boston in 1844, he married Elizabeth Shaw, 1847, and wrote the novels (based on his sailing experiences) that won him his initial reputation, *Typee* (1846) and *Omoo* (1847); *Moby-Dick* (1851), written while he lived on a farm in Massachusetts, near his friend HAWTHORNE, did not attract a following till after 1920; in subsequent years he turned more to short fiction (*The Piazza Tales*, 1856; *Billy Budd*, first published 1924) and poetry (e.g., *Battle-Pieces and Aspects of the War*, 1866).

MEREDITH, GEORGE (1828-1909): English novelist and poet, born in Portsmouth, educated privately and also in Germany; published poetry and articles in such papers as *The Fortnightly* and the *Ipswich Journal*, and worked as a publisher's reader for Chapman and Hall; married, 1849, Mary Ellen Nicholls (the widowed daughter of the novelist PEACOCK), who left him in 1857 for the painter Henry Wallis; married Marie Vulliamy, 1861, after his first wife died; a book of poems about marriage, *Modern Love*, appeared in 1862; established his literary reputation with a series of novels that includes *The Ordeal of Richard Feverel* (1859), *Sandra Belloni* (1864), *The Egoist* (1879) [see WOOLF], *Diana of the Crossways* (1885), and *The Amazing Marriage* (1895), and with an essay on the nature of comedy (1897).

MERWIN, W[ILLIAM] S[TANLEY] (b.1927): American poet and playwright, born in New York City, educated at Princeton, where he studied Romance languages; translator of *The Satires of Perseus* (1961) and *The Song of Roland* (1963), and author of several volumes of poetry, of which *The Carriers of Ladders* (1970) won the Pulitzer Prize.

MEYNELL, ALICE (THOMPSON) (1847-1922): English poet and essayist, born in Surrey, educated largely by her father, in Italy and Switzerland; converted to Catholicism, 1872; in 1877 married the journalist Wilfrid Meynell (1852-1948), editing with him the London periodical *Merry England*; friends with George MEREDITH and Coventry PATHMORE; mother of eight children, including the writer Viola Meynell (1886-1956); author of several books of prose and poetry, including *Collected Poems* (1912).

MILLAY, EDNA ST. VINCENT (1892-1950): American poet and playwright, born in Maine, educated at Vassar; using the pseudonym

"Nancy Boyd," published several satirical magazine articles, later collected as *Distressing Dialogues* (1924); journalist for *Vanity Fair*; married Eugen Jan Boissevain, 1923; won the Pulitzer Prize for *Ballad of the Harp-Weaver* (1923); friend of the poet Elinor Wylie (1885-1928); later poems, as in *Make Bright the Arrows* (1940), turn to political themes.

MILTON, JOHN (1608-1674): English poet, essayist, and civil servant, born in London, to a family converted from Catholicism to Puritanism; educated at Cambridge and through private study; wrote poems in Latin, Italian, and English from 1626 on, including "L'Allegro" and "Il Penseroso" (1632), *Comus* (1634), and *Lycidas* (1638); toured Europe in 1638, meeting Galileo in Italy; returned in 1639, writing anti-episcopal tracts as England moved towards Civil War; married three times, first in 1642 to Mary Powell (who after three weeks returned to her Royalist family, leading Milton to champion easier divorce laws; though they were reconciled in 1645, she died in 1652), second in 1656 to Katherine Woodcock (died 1658), third in 1665 to Elizabeth Minshull; published numerous controversial pamphlets championing freedom and attacking the monarchy, including *Areopagitica* (1644), and *The Tenure of Kings and Magistrates* (1649); named Latin Secretary to the Council of State (i.e., author and translator of diplomatic documents in foreign languages) in 1649, he was blind by 1652, and in 1657 his friend MARVELL was named his assistant; continued his republican writing even in 1660, leading to the threat of imprisonment and the public burning of his books after the Restoration; in retirement (his freedom possibly having been negotiated by MARVELL), completed *Paradise Lost* (1667; revised for the 2nd ed., 1674), *Paradise Regained*, and *Samson Agonistes* (both 1671); died of gout.

MITFORD, MARY RUSSELL (1787-1855): English sketch-writer, novelist, playwright, and letter-writer, born in Hampshire, educated at home; supported her parents in the family home near Reading; friends with Elizabeth Barrett BROWNING, MARTINEAU, HEMANS, and others, with whom she conducted an extensive correspondence, and an acquaintance of MOODIE; author of *The Foscari* (1826), *Rienzi* (1828), and other plays, as well as stories and poems; best known for the five volumes of *Our Village: Sketches of Rural Life, Character and Scenery* (1824-32), which began as contributions to *The Lady's Magazine*; her memoirs, *Recollections of a Literary Life*, appeared in 1852.

MOLL, E[RNEST] G[EORGE] (1900-1979): Australian poet, born in Murtoo, Victoria, brought up on the family farm, educated in New South Wales and at Harvard; professor of English at U. of Oregon, 1928-66; author of fifteen books, including a memoir, *Below These Hills: The Story of a Riverina Farm* (1957), and *Poems 1940-1955* (1957).

MONTAGU, LADY MARY WORTLEY (PIERREPOINT) (1689-1762): English letter-writer, poet, and essayist, eldest daughter of Lady Mary (Fielding) and Evelyn Pierrepoint, 1st Duke of Kingston; educated at home; about a decade after her mother's death in 1694, became her father's hostess; eloped with Edward Wortley Montagu in 1712, avoiding an arranged marriage; lived in London, in a literary circle that included POPE (till a quarrel in 1723), GAY, and ADDISON; lived in Turkey, 1716-18, when her husband became ambassador, and wrote a series of descriptive letters, to which Mary ASTELL wrote a manuscript preface; maintained a lively

correspondence with her daughter, Lady Bute, at whose home she subsequently died of breast cancer; campaigned to introduce inoculation against smallpox; left her husband in 1738, to live in France and Italy, returning to England only after his death (1761); published, anonymously, a political journal, *The Nonsense of Common-Sense* (1837-38), and two books of poems, including *Court Poems by a Lady of Quality* (1716); her *Complete Letters* were edited by Robert Halsband in three volumes (1965-67).

MOODIE, SUSANNA (STRICKLAND) (1803-1885): Canadian sketch-writer and novelist, born in Suffolk, England, to a literary family (her sisters include the novelist and nature writer Catharine Parr Traill, 1802-1899, and the biographer Agnes Strickland, 1796-1874); influenced by the work of Mary Russell MITFORD, whom she visited socially; converted to Methodism; married, 1831, the army officer and writer J.W.D. Moodie (1797-1869) and emigrated to Canada, 1832, settling in the bush near Belleville; contributed sketches to *The Literary Garland* and other journals, rewriting them as *Roughing It in the Bush* (1852; revised 1871) and *Life in the Clearings, versus the Bush* (1853); died in Toronto, after some years of what was possibly Alzheimer's Disease.

MOORE, MARIANNE (1887-1972): American poet, born in St. Louis, educated at Bryn Mawr and Carlisle Commercial College; settled in Greenwich Village, New York, after having visited Europe and undertaken various jobs, from revising the Dewey Decimal system to teaching in an Indian school in Pennsylvania; published her first poems in *Poetry*, 1915; edited *Dial*, 1924-29, after which she supported herself by her own writing; friends with Elizabeth BISHOP; admired by DOOLITTLE, POUND, T.S. ELIOT; won the Pulitzer Prize for *Collected Poems* (1951); *A Marianne Moore Reader* (1961) includes prose as well as poetry; *Complete Poems* appeared in 1967.

MOORE, THOMAS (1779-1852): Irish poet and songwriter, born in Dublin, educated at Trinity College (Dublin); appointed to an Admiralty post in Bermuda, but left it to travel in Canada and the U.S.A., returning to England in 1804; friend of BYRON, whose journals he edited (1830); secured a popular reputation for the ten parts of *A Selection of Irish Melodies* (1808-34, the music for his texts being arranged mostly by Sir John Stevenson), and for *Lalla Rookh: An Oriental Romance* (1817) and the satirical *The Fudge Family in Paris* (1818).

MORDECAI, PAMELA (b.1942): Jamaican poet and educator, educated at U. of the West Indies (Mona); taught, worked in television, later became publications officer for the Faculty of Education (U.W.I.) and editor of several Caribbean textbooks; editor of *Caribbean Journal of Education* and *Caribbean Quarterly*; editor of *Jamaica Woman* (1980, with Mervyn MORRIS) and other volumes.

MORE, HANNAH (1745-1833): English dramatist and moralist, born near Bristol, educated (in languages) at a boarding school run by her sisters; through REYNOLDS and his sister (the painter Frances Reynolds, 1729-1807), gained access to London society; friend of JOHNSON and others, including the Bluestocking Group that formed in the 1760s with Elizabeth Montagu (1720-1800), Elizabeth CARTER, Fanny BURNEY, and others to discuss literature, society, and morality; criticized Frances BROOKE and quarrelled with the poet Ann Yearsley ("Lactilla, the Bristol Milkwoman," 1752-1806); after 1793 became increasingly involved in anti-slavery and universal education campaigns, the Sunday School movement, and didactic Christian publications, such as the *Cheap Repository Tracts* series (1795-98), which earned her a substantial income; the Religious Tract Society was founded to continue her work.

MORE, SIR THOMAS (1478-1535): English statesman and writer, born in London, the son of a judge; educated at Oxford; twice married; friend of the philosopher Erasmus (c.1466-1536); rose (and fell) rapidly in court circles, becoming Lord Chancellor in 1529; a devout Catholic, he helped Henry VIII reply to Martin Luther, but refused to sanction Henry's marriage to Anne Boleyn; executed in 1535, deemed a traitor by Protestants and a martyr by Catholics; beatified in 1886 and canonized by Pope Pius XI in 1935; author of *Utopia* (1516; translated from Latin to English by Ralph Robinson in 1551) and other works.

MORGAN, EDWIN (b.1920): Scottish poet and critic, born in Glasgow, educated at Glasgow U., where he subsequently taught English; known for stylistic experiment, his works include *Selected Poems* (1985) and translations of several contemporary European poets.

MORLEY, THOMAS (1557-1602): English composer and lyricist, a student of the composer William Byrd (1543-1623); organist at St. Paul's Cathedral; set some of SHAKESPEARE's songs to music, and is known for his collections of madrigals; author of *A Plaine and Easie Introduction to Practicall Musicke* (1597) and *The Triumphes of Oriana* (1603).

MORRIS, CHARLES (1745-1838): Welsh songwriter and soldier, born near Carlisle, one of four sons (including the poet Thomas Morris) of Captain Thomas Morris; educated by his mother; joined the 17th Foot, serving in America after 1764; in London after 1785, joined a convivial social group involving the Prince of Wales and others, who met at Covent Garden Theatre, where he sang his songs; known as "the punch-maker and bard of the Beefsteak Society" (founded 1735); married the widow of Sir William Stanhope (likely the 2nd Earl of Harrington, d. 1784, whose widow, Caroline Fitzroy, was noted for her beauty and her unorthodox life); *A Collection of Songs by the Inimitable Captain Morris* appeared in 1786.

MORRIS, MERVYN (b.1937): Jamaican poet, born in Kingston, educated at U. of the West Indies (Mona) and Oxford (as a Rhodes scholar); lecturer in English at U. of the West Indies; author of *The Pond* (1973), *Shadowboxing* (1979), and other collections, and editor (with Pamela MORDECAI) of *Jamaica Woman* (1980).

MUNDAY, ANTHONY (1560-1633): English poet and playwright, born in London; possibly an actor; worked as an anti-Catholic spy; wrote several works concerned with Robin Hood and Arthurian legends; London's official poet (1592-1623) and author of a number of pageants.

MUNRO, ALICE (LAIDLAW) (b.1931): Canadian short story writer, born in Wingham, Ontario; raised on a fox farm; educated at U. of Western Ontario; married James Munro, a bookseller, 1951 (divorced 1976), moved to Victoria, and raised three daughters; married geographer Gerald Fremlin, 1976, settling in Clinton, Ontario; winner of the Governor-General's Award and other honours; publications include *Dance of the Happy Shades* (1968), *Lives of Girls and Women* (1971), and *Friend of My Youth* (1990).

MURRAY, LES[LIE ALLAN] (b.1938): Australian poet and essayist, born in Bunyah, New South Wales, raised on a dairy farm;

later married and returned to live on a farm nearby; educated at Sydney U.; journalist and editor for the publishing firm of Angus & Robertson; noted for his literary use of laconic idiom; author of *Selected Poems: The Vernacular Republic* (1976), *The Peasant Mandarin* (1978), *The Boys Who Stole the Funeral* (1979), and other works.

NAIPAUL, V[IDIADHAR] S[URAJPRASAD] (b.1932): Trinidadian novelist and travel writer, born in Chaguanas, raised as an orthodox Hindu; educated at Oxford; married and settled in England, 1950; travelled widely, leading to such books as *An Area of Darkness* (1964) and *India: A Million Mutinies Now* (1990); his fictions, which range from comic satires to pessimistic analyses of alienation, include *Miguel Street* (1959), *A House for Mr Biswas* (1961), *In a Free State* (1971), and *The Enigma of Arrival* (1987).

NASHE, THOMAS (1567-1601): English dramatist, pamphleteer, and prose writer, born in Lowestoft, Suffolk; educated at Cambridge; settled in London in 1588; associated with the playwright Robert Greene (c.1558-1592) and acknowledged the influence of the work of SPENSER and PEELE; in 1588-89, joined the Martin Marprelate controversy by writing pamphlets to defend the bishops against "Martin Marprelate," the pseudonym used in Puritan attacks on organized religion, printed on secret presses; quarreled with the scholar Gabriel Harvey (c.1550-1631), resulting in *Pierce Penniless His Supplication to the Devil* (1592); best known for the first picaresque prose narrative in English, *The Unfortunate Traveller* (1594); his play, *The Isle of Dogs* (performed 1597, now lost), led to his arrest for sedition and that of other suspected authors, including JONSON; died in poverty.

NEILSON, JOHN SHAW (1872-1942): Australian poet, born in South Australia to a pioneering family, worked as a labourer to 1928; first published in the *Bulletin* (1896), whose editor, A.G. Stephen (1865-1933), became his literary advisor and friend; produced several volumes, despite limited eyesight, his *Collected Poems* appearing in 1934; among several posthumous volumes, *Witnesses of Spring: Unpublished Poems* (1970), was edited by Judith WRIGHT.

NEMEROV, HOWARD (1920-1991): American poet, essayist, and satiric fiction writer, born in New York City, educated at Harvard; served as a pilot in World War II; taught English at Brandeis U. and Washington U. in St. Louis; his several books include *Collected Poems* (1977), which won a Pulitzer Prize, and *Journal of the Fictive Life* (1966), a meditation on creativity.

NESBIT, EDITH (1858-1924): English writer of children's literature, born in London, educated at boarding schools in England, France, and Germany; friend of Olive SCHREINER and the American feminist writer Charlotte Perkins Gilman (1860-1935); in 1880 married a political journalist, Hubert Bland, and had an open marriage, raising five children; with Bland and others, helped found the Fabian Society in 1883, and became friends with SHAW and the novelist H.G. Wells (see Rebecca WEST); married a marine engineer, Terry Tucker, in 1917; wrote *Ballads and Lyrics of Socialism* (1908) and several books for children, including the Treasure Seekers trilogy (1899-1904), *The Railway Children* (1906), and the trilogy that begins with *Five Children and It* (1902).

NEWCASTLE, MARGARET (LUCAS) CAVENDISH, DUCHESS OF (1623-1673): English biographer, poet, playwright, and prose writer, born in Essex to a landed family; during the Civil War, accompanied Queen Henrietta Maria to France, where she met and in 1645 married William Cavendish (1592-1676), Marquis (and after 1665, Duke) of Newcastle; stepmother to Lady Jane Cavendish (Cheyne) (1621-1669) and Lady Elizabeth Cavendish (1626-1663), poets and playwrights; established a reputation for her opinions about natural science, as in *Philosophical and Physical Opinions* (1655, 1663); published a biography of her husband in 1667.

NEWMAN, JOHN HENRY (1801-1890): English religious writer, born in London to a family with Calvinist views; educated at Oxford, ordained in the Church of England (1824), influenced by the Oxford Movement of the 1930s (which espoused High Church ritual and the necessity of dogma), wrote *Tracts for the Times* (1841; arguing the validity of the Anglican Church), set up a monastic community (1842), converted to Catholicism (1845), was named a Cardinal (1879) by Pope Leo XIII; *Apologia Pro Vita Sua* (1864) replied to an attack on his religious beliefs by Charles KINGSLEY; *The Idea of a University* (1873) appeared after an unhappy period as Rector of Dublin University.

NICHOL, B[ARRIE] P[HILIP] (1944-1988): Canadian poet (who signed his works "bp Nichol"), born in Vancouver, educated at U. British Columbia; taught, worked in a library, performed with a "sound poetry" group called The Four Horsemen; settled in Toronto, 1963; married Eleanor Hiebert, 1980; winner of the 1971 Governor-General's Award; experimented with concrete poetry and other stylistic forms from the early 1960s on, influenced by the language theories of Gertrude Stein (1874-1946) and others; *As Elected: Selected Writing 1962-1979* (1980) samples his work; the several volumes of *The Martyrology*, from "Books I & II" (1972) to the incomplete, posthumous "Book(s) 7&" (1990), trace a life in language; died suddenly, during surgery.

NOONUCCAL, OODGEROO [KATH (RUSKA) WALKER] (b.1920): Australian Aboriginal poet, born Kathleen Ruska on North Stradbroke Island, Queensland; affiliated with the Noonuccal (or Noonuckle) tribe, from which she took her aboriginal name in 1987; served in Australian Women's Army during World War II, but race discrimination prevented her from training as a nurse; married Bruce Walker (divorced after twelve years); became actively involved in Aboriginal Rights movements; established the Noonuccal-Nughie Education and Cultural Centre, 1972; author of *We Are Going* (1964), *Stradbroke Dreamtime* (1972, a story collection), and other works.

NOWLAN, ALDEN (1933-1983): Canadian poet and fiction writer, born in rural Nova Scotia; left school early, working at various labouring jobs; moved to New Brunswick in 1952 to become news editor for the *Hartland Observer* (till 1962); published his first book in 1958; married Claudine Orser, 1964; became a freelance writer and poet-in-residence at the U. of New Brunswick, 1969, where he stayed till his death from pneumonia, after a long bout with cancer; winner of several awards; author of *Bread, Wine and Salt* (1967), *Miracle at Indian River: Stories* (1968), three plays (with Walter Learning) and numerous other volumes, his selected poems (edited by Robert Gibbs) appearing in 1985 as *An Exchange of Gifts*.

NUGENT, ROBERT (later **CRAGGS**), **EARL NUGENT** (1702-1788): Irish poet and politician, born in Westmeath; made a fortune in real estate and through marriage (Horace Walpole coined the verb "Nugentize," meaning to marry rich widows); married three times— first in 1730 to Emilia (d. 1731; daughter of the 4th Earl of Fingal), second in 1737 to an acquaintance of Pope, Anne Newsham Craggs (d.

1756; taking her surname, he acquired £100,000, two estates, and a seat in Parliament, which he occupied from 1741 to 1784), and third to the widow of the 4th Earl of Berkeley, Elizabeth Drax, who outlived him (though they were separated for many years and he disowned his second daughter by this marriage); favoured by George III, he was named Viscount Clare of the Irish peerage in 1766, and Earl Nugent in 1776; author of *Odes and Epistles* (1739).

ODELL, JONATHAN (1737-1818): Canadian poet, physician, and clergyman, born in Newark, in the American colony of New Jersey, educated at the College of New Jersey (later Princeton); served as a British army surgeon in the West Indies; ordained in the Church of England, 1767; fled New Jersey for New York (and then England, after his property was seized), because of the unpopularity of his conservative stance in poetry and politics; named by the British to a civil post in the new province of New Brunswick, settled in Fredericton, 1784; published *The American Times: A Satire* (1780) as "Camillo Querno," and other poetic critiques of the republican United States.

OKARA, GABRIEL (b.1921): Nigerian poet and novelist, born in Bumoundi, son of an Ijo chief; educated in Umuahia and at Northwestern U. in the United States; worked for the Government Printery at Enugu; published in *Black Orpheus*; worked with ACHEBE for the Biafran government during the Civil War, and as the first editor of *Nigerian Tide*; works include *The Voice* (1964), a novel, and his collected poems, *The Fisherman's Invocation* (1978), which won the Commonwealth Poetry Prize.

OLDHAM, JOHN (1653-1683): English poet and teacher, born in Gloucestershire, the son of a Nonconformist minister; educated at Oxford; wrote several satires (whose quality is acknowledged in a poem by DRYDEN) against the Jesuits, in the years after Titus Oates (1649-1705) concocted his tale of a "Popish Plot" against England in 1678 (exposed as fraudulent, 1685); died of smallpox; *Poems and Translations* appeared in 1683.

OLIVER, MARY (b.1935): American poet, born in Cleveland, Ohio; lives in Provincetown, Massachusetts, where she chairs the Creative Writing Department at the Fine Arts Work Center; author of *No Voyage, and other poems* (1963), *American Primitive* (1983), which won a Pulitzer Prize, and several other works.

OLSON, CHARLES (1910-1970): American poet and critical theorist, born in Massachusetts, educated at Harvard, Yale, and Wesleyan U.; lectured at Black Mountain College after 1948; his ideas (as set forth in a 1950 essay called "Projective Verse" and in such books as *Human Universe*, 1965) influenced CREELEY, LEVERTOV, Robert DUNCAN, and others in the "Black Mountain School"; his series called *The Maximus Poems*, focussing on the town of Gloucester, Massachusetts, appeared in several volumes (1953-75), collected as one volume in 1983; other works include *Archeologist of Morning* (1970).

ONDAATJE, MICHAEL (b.1943): Canadian poet, film-maker, anthologist, and prose writer, born in Colombo, Ceylon (now Sri Lanka), to a family described in his autobigraphical *Running in the Family* (1982); emigrated to England, 1952, and Canada, 1962; educated at Bishop's U. (Lennoxville, Quebec), where he met D.G. JONES, and at U. of Toronto and Queen's U., writing a thesis on Edwin Muir; married Kim Jones, 1964 (separated 1980); teaches English at Glendon College in Toronto; winner of numerous literary awards;

author of *The Collected Works of Billy the Kid* (1970), *Coming Through Slaughter* (1976), *There's a Trick with a Knife I'm Learning to Do* (1979), *In the Skin of a Lion* (1987), and other works.

ORLÉANS, CHARLES D': see CHARLES D'ORLÉANS.

ORWELL, GEORGE [ERIC BLAIR] (1903-1950): English novelist and essayist, born in Motihari, Bengal, educated at Eton; served with the Imperial Police in Burma (1922-27), an experience recalled in *Burmese Days* (1934) and the title essay of *Shooting an Elephant* (1950); fought with the Republican army in the Spanish Civil War; married, 1936, Eileen O'Shaughnessy (d. 1945), then the translator Sonia Brownell (c.1919-1980); when commissioned to write on unemployment for the Left Book Club, produced *The Road to Wigan Pier* (1937); correspondent for the BBC and *The Observer* during World War II; satirized political bureaucracy in *Animal Farm* (1945) and *Nineteen Eighty-Four* (1948); his essays on poverty, politics, language, and other subjects were collected in four volumes (1968).

OSBORNE, DOROTHY (later, **LADY TEMPLE)** (1627-1695): English letter-writer, born in Bedfordshire, the youngest daughter of Dorothy (Danvers) and Sir Peter Osborne; met Sir William Temple (1628-1699) when he was nineteen, and during the next seven years, while he was abroad, conducted the correspondence with him—on the nature of romantic love, the pressures of family, and the public role of children of the nobility—for which she is now known (first published in the nineteenth century); married him in 1654, after being disfigured by smallpox; from 1655 on, accompanied him to various diplomatic posts in The Hague and elsewhere (in 1677 he helped negotiate the marriage between Princess Mary and the Prince of Orange); retired with him to Moor Park, in Surrey (see SWIFT); lost all her children; corresponded with Katherine PHILIPS (whose work she admired) and with Queen Mary II.

OUTRAM, RICHARD (b.1930): Canadian poet, born in Oshawa, Ontario, educated at U. of Toronto in philosophy and English; married and settled in Toronto; became a technician with the Canadian Broadcasting Corporation; author of *Exultate, Jubilate* (1966), *Selected Poems* (1984), and *Hiram and Jenny* (1988).

OVERBURY, SIR THOMAS (1581-1613): English poet and sketch-writer, born in Compton-Scorpion, Warwickshire, educated at Oxford; became a friend of Robert Carr (later the Earl of Somerset, d. 1645), who interceded with JAMES I to have Overbury named Viscount Rochester and knighted in 1608; served as a go-between for Carr and his mistress, Frances Howard (1592-1632), wife of the 3rd Earl of Essex; imprisoned in the Tower in 1613, on a pretext, when he demurred at Howard getting a divorce and becoming Carr's wife; was poisoned in the Tower, after Howard offered a bribe (Howard and Carr, later married, were convicted of the murder in 1616, but pardoned); author of some of the essays collected in *Characters* (1614).

OWEN, WILFRED (1893-1918): English poet, born in Shropshire, educated at Shrewsbury Technical College; influenced by his mother's Anglicanism; left for Bordeaux in 1913 to teach at the Berlitz School; enlisted in the Artists' Rifles, 1915, and was stationed at the Somme, suffering trench fever and shell shock; in 1917 met and became friends with SASSON, who in 1920 edited his poems (all but four previously unpublished); killed in action one week before the armistice; several of his poems are used in Benjamin Britten's musical composition, *War*

Requiem (1962); Jon Stallworthy's edition of *The Complete Poems and Fragments* appeared in 1983.

PAGE, P[ATRICIA] K[ATHLEEN] [P.K. IRWIN] (b.1916): Canadian poet, painter, and autobiographer, born in Dorset, England, emigrated to Alberta, 1919; worked as a sales clerk and file clerk, writing a novel that appeared later (under the pseudonym "Judith Cape") as *The Sun and the Moon* (1944); published poetry in *Preview* and other journals that began in the 1940s, and became friends with Montreal poets F.R. SCOTT and A.M. KLEIN; met Arthur Irwin while working as a script writer for the National Film Board (1946-50), marrying in 1950 and moving with him to Australia and Brazil when he was posted, respectively, as High Commissioner and Ambassador (an experience recalled in *Brazilian Journal*, 1987); settled in Victoria, B.C., after 1959; as an painter, uses the name P.K. Irwin; other publications include *Evening Dance of the Gray Flies* (1981) and *The Glass Air* (1985).

PAINE, THOMAS (1737-1809): English political writer, born in Norfolk to a Quaker family; left school at 13 to become a corset-maker, tobacconist, teacher, and exciseman; at FRANKLIN's urging, sailed in 1774 to Philadelphia, and joined the revolutionary cause, writing *Common Sense* (1776) and the sixteen pamphlets called *The Crisis* (1776-83); settled in rural New York after undertaking several political tasks for the new government, travelling frequently to France; published *The Rights of Man* (1791-92) in England, defending the French Revolution against BURKE [see also WOLLSTONECRAFT]; facing trial in England (for treason), fled to France; granted French citizenship and elected to the French Assembly (1792), but imprisoned (1793-94) after alienating Robespierre; published *The Age of Reason* (1794-95), which estranged him from others; attacked George Washington in subsequent publications, causing a political dispute between JEFFERSON, who supported Paine, and John Quincy Adams; retired to his farm in New York in 1802, and was buried there when (because of his free thinking) consecrated ground was denied him (but his remains were lost after the civil rights polemicist William Cobbett, 1763-1835, had them removed to England in 1819, intending a memorial that never got built).

PARKMAN, FRANCIS (1823-1893): American historian, born in Boston, educated at Harvard; suffered from a chronic nervous dysfunction that affected his sight and his concentration; in 1846 headed from St. Louis to Wyoming, vainly seeking health on the frontier; dictated his diary of his travels, published as *The Oregon Trail* (1849); despite the continuing illness, embarked on a seven-volume history of the New World, *France and England in North America* (1865-92), including *The Old Regime in Canada* (1874) and *Montcalm and Wolfe* (1884); named professor of horticulture at Harvard, 1871.

PASTAN, LINDA (OLENIK) (b.1932): American poet, born in New York City; educated at Radcliffe, Simmons College (in librarianship), and Brandeis; married Ira Pastan, a scientist, 1953; her first book appeared in 1971, followed by several others, including *Aspects of Eve* (1975), *Waiting for My Life* (1981), *PM/AM* (1983), and *The Imperfect Paradise* (1988).

PATER, WALTER (1839-1894): English critic and essayist, born in London, educated at Oxford, where he remained as a scholar after 1864; associated with the Aesthetic Movement (involving at various times YEATS, DOWSON, WILDE, SYMONS, and others), which opposed the functional precepts of Utilitarianism; author of critical works and romances, including *Studies in the History of the Renaissance* (1873), *Marius the Epicurean* (1885), and *The Child in the House* (1894).

PATERSON, ANDREW BARTON ("BANJO") (1864-1941): Australian poet, crocodile hunter, novelist, and journalist, born at Narambla Station, New South Wales; trained as a lawyer in Sydney, practising law till 1899, when he became war correspondent for the Sydney *Evening News*, covering the Boer War and the Boxer Rebellion; later edited the *Evening News*, the *Australian Town and Country Journal*, and *Sydney Sportsman*; widely known as "Banjo" Paterson because of the pseudonym he used ("The Banjo") in early publications in *The Bulletin*; author of "Waltzing Matilda," *The Man from Snowy River and Other Verses* (1895), and numerous other collections; *Collected Verse* appeared in 1923.

PATMORE, COVENTRY (1823-1896): English poet and critic, born in Essex, educated at home; became assistant librarian in the British Museum (now the British Library); married three times, first in 1847 to Emily Andrews (d. 1862); converted to Catholicism, 1864; associated with the Pre-Raphaelite Brotherhood (see D.G. ROSSETTI); author of *The Angel in the House* (1854-63), *The Unknown Eros* (1877), and other works.

PEACOCK, THOMAS LOVE (1785-1866): English novelist and poet, born in Weymouth, Dorset, son of a London merchant; left school at 13, living off an inheritance; took a position with the East India Company, 1819; met SHELLEY in 1812 and became close friends; married Jane Gryffydh, 1820; father-in-law of George MEREDITH; in *The Paper Money Lyrics* (1837), criticized the economic philosophy of John Stuart Mill (1806-1873), his superior at India House; author of *Headlong Hall* (1816), *Nightmare Abbey* (1818), *Crotchet Castle* (1831), *Gryll Grange* (1860-61), and other satires.

PEELE, GEORGE (1556-1596): English actor, poet, and playwright, born in London, educated at Oxford; returned to London, 1571, living a boisterous life and writing works to be performed before ELIZABETH I, before ending his days both sick and poor; author of *The Old Wives' Tale* (1595) and other plays; *Polyhymnia* (1590) is one of three collections of poetry.

PEMBROKE, MARY SIDNEY HERBERT, COUNTESS OF (1561-1621): English poet, daughter of Lady Mary Dudley and Sir Henry Sidney; educated at home (in languages); at age 15 (in 1577) married Henry Herbert, 2nd Earl of Pembroke (c.1534-1601), whose first wife was Lady Catharine Grey (sister of Lady Jane Grey, 1537-1554, who before being beheaded was briefly Queen of England); lived in Wilton House, near Salisbury, where she became a patron to many poets; after the death of her brother, Sir Philip SIDNEY, she continued his project of writing the psalms in metrical form and revised and completed his *Arcadia* (1593); translated Petrarch and others; died of smallpox.

PHILIPS, KATHERINE (FOWLER) (1632-1664): English poet (known as "the matchless Orinda"), born in London, the daughter of a wealthy merchant, John Fowler (d. 1642), and Katherine Oxenbridge; moved to Wales in 1646 and married James Philips of Cardigan Priory, who was related to her mother's second husband; became the friend of VAUGHAN, Jeremy TAYLOR, COWLEY, and others; corresponded with Dorothy OSBORNE, Mary Aubrey, and Anne Owen ("Lucasia" in her poems); translated works by the French playwright Corneille (1606-

1684); died of smallpox in London, while trying to get a pirated (1664) version of her *Poems* suppressed (an authorized edition was released in 1667).

PIERCY, MARGE (b.1936): American poet, essayist, anthologist, and novelist, born in Detroit to a Jewish family; educated at U. of Michigan and Northwestern U.; thrice married, lives in Massachusetts with Ira Wood, a writer; a political activist concerned with feminist causes; author of *Woman on the Edge of Time* (1976), *Braided Lives* (1982), and other fictions; *Breaking Camp* (1968) was the first of several volumes of poetry.

PIOZZI, HESTER LYNCH (SALUSBURY) THRALE (1741-1821): Welsh writer, born in Caernarvonshire, educated in London; bowing to family pressure, married a well-to-do Southwark brewer, Henry Thrale, in 1763, the year after her father died; met JOHNSON in 1765, becoming a close friend; had twelve children before Thrale died (1781) and the brewery was sold (in 1784, for £135,000); married Gabriel Piozzi (d. 1809), an Italian musician, in 1784, outraging Johnson, the Bluestocking circle (see Hannah MORE), and other friends; returned to Wales in the 1790s; author of *Anecdotes of the Late Samuel Johnson, LL.D.* (1786), *British Synonymy* (1794), and several reflections on politics and travel; her *Thraliana*, notebooks and diaries kept from 1776 to 1809, were first published in their entirety in 1942.

PLAATJE, SOL[OMON] T[SHEKISHO] (1877-1932): South African writer and political figure (whose surname is pronounced "PLAH-kie"), born near Boshof; an observer and court interpreter during the Boer War, and later a newspaper editor; became the first secretary of the South African Native National Congress (1912); attacked the 1913 Native Lands Act in *Native Life in South Africa* (1913); other works include a novel, *Mhudi* (1930), a Sechuana reader, and the posthumously published *Boer War Diary* (1972).

PLATH, SYLVIA (1932-1963): American poet and prose writer, born in Massachusetts, the daughter of a teacher and an entomologist, with German and Austrian heritage; educated at Smith College and Cambridge; met the poet Ted HUGHES in England, and married him, 1956; student of Robert LOWELL; friend of Anne SEXTON; committed suicide; published *The Colossus and Other Poems* (1960); other manuscripts were published posthumously, including *Ariel* (1965), *The Bell Jar* (a semi-autobiographical novel, 1963), and the *Collected Poems* (which won a Pulitzer Prize) and *Journals* (1981-82).

POE, EDGAR ALLAN (1809-1849): American poet, critic, and short story writer, born in Boston; took the name "Allan" from his foster family in Richmond, Virginia (after the death of his father and mother in 1810 and 1811 respectively), though the relationship between Poe and Richard Allan was strained; educated at U. of Virginia, joined the army, then arranged for his dismissal; began to publish in 1827, his *Poems* appearing in 1831 and his early stories in various New York and Philadelphia magazines before being collected as *Tales of the Grotesque and Arabesque* (1840); in 1836, married his 13-year-old cousin Virginia Clemm (d. 1847); died from complications associated with alcoholism; other works include *The Raven and Other Poems* (1846), such stories as "The Pit and the Pendulum" and "The Gold Bug" (both 1843), and an influential commentary on the nature of the short story form.

POPE, ALEXANDER (1688-1744): English poet and critic, born in London to a middle-class Catholic family; largely self-educated (barred from university because of his religion); suffered throughout his life from asthma and the effects of spinal tuberculosis; began to write as a child, *The Pastorals* (1709) being the first of several publications; an early friend of ADDISON, he later criticized both him and Lady Mary Wortley MONTAGU, another erstwhile friend, in *An Epistle to Dr Arbuthnot* (1735); moved away from ADDISON's circle because the Whigs were anti-Catholic; became a member of the Scriblerus Club when it formed in 1713 (Tory in sympathy, its members including John Arbuthnot [1667-1735; the originator of the "John Bull" figure], SWIFT, GAY, CONGREVE, Robert Harley [see SWIFT], and the Irish poet Thomas Parnell [1679-1718: see YOUNG]); moved to Twickenham, 1719, to avoid the anti-Catholic measures that followed the Jacobite rebellion of 1715 (the money to rent his estate coming from the success of his translations of the *Iliad*, 1715-20, and *Odyssey*, 1726); interested in landscape design, architecture, and the character of "correct" style; *Essay on Criticism* (1711), *The Rape of the Lock* (1712; expanded 1714), *The Dunciad* (1728, revised 1743), *Essay on Man* (1733-34), and other works confirmed his reputation.

PORTER, PETER (b.1929): Australian poet, born and educated in Brisbane; emigrated to England, 1951, working as a BBC broadcaster and freelance writer for *New Statesman, Times Literary Supplement, Observer, Encounter*, and other journals; married, 1961, Jannice Henry (d. 1974, possibly a suicide); volumes of poetry began to appear in 1961, mounting to more than twenty, including collaborations with the Australian painter Arthur Boyd, translations of Martial's epigrams, numerous elegies, "On First Looking into Chapman's *Hesiod*," and *Collected Poems* (1983).

POUND, EZRA (1885-1972): American poet and critic, born in Idaho, the son of a mine inspector; raised in Pennsylvania, educated at U. of Pennsylvania; left for Europe, 1908, where he became acquainted with JOYCE, YEATS, and other innovative figures in the arts, and began to publish; married Dorothy Shakespear, 1914; lived in London (1908-20), Paris (1920-24), Rapallo, Italy (1924-45); associated with many influential literary movements, including Imagism and Vorticism, as author (e.g., *Hugh Selwyn Mauberly*, 1920), editor (of the journal *Blast!*, 1914-15), correspondent (for *Poetry, The Dial*, and other little magazines), anthologist (e.g., *Des Imagistes*, which included work by W.C. WILLIAMS, Joyce, Hilda DOOLITTLE, and others), editor (helping T.S. ELIOT to shape *The Waste Land*), and translator (of Cavalcanti, Japanese and Chinese authors, troubadour ballads, Anglo-Saxon, and the classics); author of numerous volumes, best known for *The Cantos* (begun in 1925, published in complete form in 1970); his later life was marked by a trial for treason in 1945 (he had broadcast on behalf of Mussolini's fascists during World War II), after which he was institutionalized in the United States (1945-58), against some protest, on grounds of insanity; returned to Italy, 1958; his critical books include *ABC of Reading* (1934).

PRATT, E[DWIN] J[OHN] (1882-1964): Canadian poet, born in Newfoundland, to a Methodist family; educated at outport schools and at U. of Toronto (in philosophy and divinity); served briefly in the Methodist ministry before becoming a lecturer in psychology and English at U. of Toronto; married Viola Whitney, 1918; author of nineteen books, from the lyrics of *Newfoundland Verse* (1923) and the comic satire of *The Witches' Brew* (1925) to such romantic narratives about heroic conflict as *The Titanic* (1935), *Brébeuf and His Brethren* (1940), and *Towards the Last Spike* (1952).

PRINGLE, THOMAS (1789-1834): Scottish poet, born in Roxburghshire, educated at U. of Edinburgh; in 1817 started *The Edinburgh Monthly Magazine* (which later joined with *Blackwood's*); sailed to the Cape Colony in 1820, as government librarian; with John Fairbairn began *The South African Journal*, which brought opposition from Governor Lord Charles Somerset, but established freedom of the press in South Africa; returned to London, 1826, as secretary of the Anti-Slavery Society, in which position he met MOODIE and others; author of *African Sketches* (1834) and *The History of Mary Prince, a West Indian Slave* (1831).

PRIOR, MATTHEW (1664-1721): English poet, born in Dorset, educated at Cambridge; friend of SWIFT; from 1690 on, served as a diplomatic envoy for William III and Queen Anne in Holland and France, as is recounted in part in Swift's *A Journey to Paris* (1711); negotiated the Treaty of Utrecht (sometimes known as "Matt's Peace") in 1713, but at the accession of George I, was imprisoned for over a year because of it; retired to prepare the 1718 folio edition of his works (which include a travesty of DRYDEN's *The Hind and the Panther*); died of cholera.

PURDY, AL[FRED] (b.1918): Canadian poet, born in Ontario to a farming family of Loyalist stock; educated in Trenton; joined the Royal Canadian Air Force, 1940; married Eurithe Parkhurst, 1941; worked at a variety of jobs in British Columbia and Ontario, finally settling in Ameliasburgh, the site of *In Search of Owen Roblin* (1974) and other poems; in the 1960s and 1970s, travelled to the Arctic, the Soviet Union, and the Galapagos Islands, and in the 1980s divided his time between Ontario and Vancouver Island; began to publish in 1944, producing more than forty books by 1991, among them *The Cariboo Horses* (1965), *North of Summer* (1967), and *The Collected Poems of Al Purdy* (1986).

QUARLES, FRANCIS (1592-1644): English poet and essayist, born in Essex, educated at Cambridge and Lincoln's Inn; a Royalist, found favour in the Stuart Court, but had his manuscripts burned and his property taken from him at the time of the Puritan ascendancy; married, 1618, and had eighteen children; left his family in poverty at his death; best known for *Emblems* (1635).

RAINE, CRAIG (b.1944): English poet and librettist, born in County Durham; educated at Oxford, where he later lectured in English; married Ann Slater, a professor, 1972; became poetry editor for Faber and Faber publishers, 1981; author of *The Onion, Memory* (1978), *A Martian Sends a Postcard Home* (1979), and other works.

RAINE, KATHLEEN (b.1908): English poet, born in Essex, brought up during World War I as an evacuee in Northumberland, educated at Cambridge; twice married; interested in symbolism and metaphysics, published her first book of poetry in 1943; briefly converted to Catholicism in 1944; in 1981, the year of her *Collected Poems*, she founded *Temenos*, a journal devoted to the arts and the religious imagination.

RALEGH (or RALEIGH), SIR WALTER (c.1552-1618): English poet, explorer, historian, and courtier, born to a landed family in Devon, educated at Oxford; fought in France and Ireland, winning a knighthood and the approval of ELIZABETH I in 1582; secretly married Elizabeth Throckmorton, one of the royal ladies-in-waiting, 1592, angering the Queen, who imprisoned him in the Tower of London before permitting them to settle in Dorset; led a British expedition to the Orinoco River (1595) and participated in the siege of Cadiz (1596); imprisoned by JAMES I (1603), on suspicion of intrigue and because of a rigged trial; lived with his family in the Tower till 1616; imprisoned again in 1618, after the failure of a second Guiana expedition, and beheaded; author of numerous poems (most not published till after his death), together with accounts of his travels to the Azores and South America, and the first part of The History of the World (1614), written while he was in prison.

RAMSAY, ALLAN (1686-1758): Scottish poet, born in Lanarkshire to a mining family; educated locally, apprenticed to an Edinburgh wigmaker in 1704; published several satirical broadsides, earning a reputation as a poet, and issued in broadside form the poems of James I of Scotland (1394-1437), HENRYSON, and DUNBAR, making traditional Scots poetry (marked by his own emendations) available to 18th-century readers; had become a prosperous bookseller by the 1720s, establishing in 1728 the first circulating library in Britain; opened a theatre in Edinburgh in 1736, though officials closed it in 1737; editor of The Tea Table Miscellany (1724-32) and other works, and author of The Gentle Shepherd (1725) and Poems (1728); his work was admired by BURNS.

RANSOM, JOHN CROWE (1888-1974): American poet and critic, born in Tennessee, educated at Vanderbilt U. (where he later taught English) and Oxford; member of the politically and artistically conservative Fugitive Group at Vanderbilt (which also included Laura RIDING and Allen Tate, 1899-1975); after 1937 taught at Kenyon College in Ohio, founding in 1939 the Kenyon Review, which encouraged the critical techniques described in The New Criticism (1941); Selected Poems (1945) was enlarged in 1969.

REED, HENRY (1914-1986): English poet and playwright, born in Birmingham, educated at Birmingham U.; friends with the poet Louis MacNeice (1907-1963), who taught at Birmingham after leaving Oxford, and with AUDEN; worked as a freelance journalist before World War II, for the Foreign Office during it, and as a BBC broadcaster afterwards; author of translations from French and Italian, over three dozen radio plays, and poems about World War II in A Map of Verona (1946).

REID, BILL [WILLIAM RONALD REID] (b.1920): Canadian artist, of Haida and Scots heritage, born in Vancouver; discovered Haida culture, and his own Haida roots, only as an adult; trained in jewellery and engraving at Ryerson Institute (Toronto); designs in wood, argillite, and precious metals, and casts statues (based on Haida tales and traditional figures) in bronze; author (with BRINGHURST) of Raven Steals the Light (1984), and sculptor of "Raven and the First Humans" and "The Chief of the Undersea World" (both in Vancouver) and "Spirit of Haida Gwaii" (at the Canadian Embassy in Washington, D.C.).

REYNOLDS, SIR JOSHUA (1723-1792): English portrait painter, born in Devon, educated at his father's grammar school; studied art in London and Italy after 1740; by 1760 had been recognized as one of the foremost painters of his time; friend of JOHNSON, and a member of The Club, along with BURKE and others (GOLDSMITH dedicated The Deserted Village to him, as did BOSWELL The Life of Johnson); named first president of the Royal Academy (1768), knighted the following year; delivered the first of his Aristotelian Discourses on Art (1769) as

an Academy lecture; attacked by BLAKE for his conventionality, and later by D.G. ROSSETTI; partly deaf after 1750, he began to lose his sight in 1789, and gave up painting.

RICH, ADRIENNE (b.1929): American poet, anthologist, and essayist, born in Baltimore, Maryland, educated by her mother and at Radcliffe; married Alfred Conrad, a Harvard professor of economics, 1953 (separated 1966); taught English and feminist studies at several universities, including Stanford (after 1986); co-edited Sinister Wisdom, a lesbian feminist journal, 1981-83; author of more than twenty books, including the prize-winning Diving into the Wreck (1973), The Dream of a Common Language (1978), The Fact of a Doorframe (1984), An Atlas of the Difficult World (1991) and such influential analytic commentaries as Of Woman Born (1976) and On Lies, Secrets, and Silence (1979).

RIDING (JACKSON), LAURA (REICHENTHAL) (1901-1991): American poet and fiction writer, born Laura Reichenthal in New York City to Jewish socialist parents, educated at Cornell; married a history teacher, Louis Gottschalk, 1920 (divorced 1925); legally adopted the name "Riding" in 1927, though she later used the pseudonyms "Barbara Rich" and "Madeleine Vara"; published poems in Poetry and The Fugitive (see RANSOM); moved to England, where she lived with Robert GRAVES and his wife, Nancy Nicholson, and where Leonard and Virginia WOOLF, in 1926 and 1927, published her early books; collaborated with GRAVES on a critical survey of modern poetry; attempted suicide, 1929, then moved with GRAVES to Mallorca, where she helped him run Seizin Press and organized an artistic circle; Collected Poems (1938) gathers the work of several previous volumes, and is essentially her last work of poetry; returned to the U.S.A. in 1939, married the linguist Schuyler Jackson (d. 1970), and moved to Florida with him to grow citrus fruit and work on a dictionary.

RIGBY, ELIZABETH: see Lady EASTLAKE.

ROBERTS, SIR CHARLES G.D. (1860-1943): Canadian poet and fiction writer, born in New Brunswick to a conservative Anglican family; educated at the U. of New Brunswick; cousin to Bliss CARMAN, brother to the poet Theodore Goodridge Roberts (1877-1953), and uncle to the poet Dorothy Roberts (b. 1906); his first book of poems, Orion (1880), influenced LAPMAN and others in the Confederation Group (e.g. D.C. SCOTT); married Mary Fenety, 1880; in 1883, edited the influential Toronto paper The Week; taught English at King's College, Nova Scotia, 1885-95, publishing poems and historical novels; left his family and moved to New York in 1896, writing stories about animals and nature, such as The Heart of the Ancient Wood (1900) and The Kindred of the Wild (1902); travelled widely, living in England 1912-25; knighted in 1935; The Collected Poems, edited by Desmond Pacey and Graham Adams, appeared in 1985 and The Collected Letters in 1989.

ROBINSON, EDWIN ARLINGTON (1869-1935): American poet, born in Maine and brought up in the town of Gardiner, which provided the basis for the "Tilbury Town" of his poems; educated at Harvard; after the success of The Children of the Night (1897), enjoyed the patronage of Theodore Roosevelt (1858-1919), who secured for him a clerkship in the New York Custom House, 1898; hurt by poverty and alcoholism; won three Pulitzer Prizes, for Collected Poems (1921), The Man Who Died Twice (1924), and the third volume of an Arthurian trilogy (1917, 1920, 1927).

ROCHESTER, JOHN WILMOT, 2ND EARL OF (1647-1680): English poet and courtier, born in Oxfordshire, educated at Oxford; fought against the Dutch in 1665, and became a favourite of Charles II; friend of SEDLEY; kidnapped Elizabeth Malet and married her, 1667; noted in his own day for his libertine life and obscene verse, as well as for the social satires he wrote in the 1670s; rumoured to have physically attacked DRYDEN in 1679; died (a Christian penitent in his last year) of alcohol poisoning and venereal disease; he was the subject of an elegy by BEHN.

ROETHKE, THEODORE (1908-1963): American poet and tennis coach, born in Michigan, the son of a nurseryman; educated at U. Michigan and Harvard; taught English, at the U. of Washington after 1947; married Beatrice O'Connell, 1953; began publishing poetry in 1941, winning the Pulitzer Prize for *The Waking: Poems, 1933-1953* (1953) and the Bollingen Prize and a National Book Award for *Words for the Wind* (1957); later books include a posthumous volume of selected prose, *On the Poet and His Craft* (1965).

ROGERS, WOODES (d.1732): English navigator and journal writer; led the privateering expedition (1708-11) that, after he suppressed a mutiny in the Canary Islands, rescued Alexander Selkirk, as reported in his *Voyage round the World* (1712); married, and in 1717 rented the Bahamas Islands from the "lords proprietors" for a period of 21 years; took up the governorship of the Bahamas, 1718-21 (during which time he hanged many of the pirates who were already living there) and 1729-32; in the intervening years he was back in England, seeking (vainly) to get official approval for his actions.

ROSSETTI, CHRISTINA (1830-1894): English poet, prose writer, and children's writer, born in London to an expatriate political and academic Italian family; sister to D.G. ROSSETTI, for whom she was an artist's model (as was his wife, Elizabeth Siddal, and Jane Burden, who in 1859 married the poet, designer, and socialist Utopian writer William Morris [1834-1896], author of *News from Nowhere* [1890] and founder of The Kelmscott Press, 1891); educated by her mother; devoted to High Anglicanism, she also worked in the 1860s for a Home for Fallen Women, both experiences affecting her poetry; *Verses* (1847), her first work, was printed by her grandfather, Gaetano Polidori; attracted critical notice with *Goblin Market* (1862); long engaged to the Pre-Raphaelite painter James Collinson, but never married; died of cancer.

ROSSETTI, DANTE GABRIEL (1828-1882): English poet and painter, born in London, brother to Christina ROSSETTI; after art training, formed the Pre-Raphaelite Brotherhood, 1848, along with the critic William Michael Rossetti (1829-1919; his brother, the editor of their journal *The Germ* in 1850), and the painters Holman Hunt (1827-1910) and John Everett Millais (1829-1896), with whom he shared a studio (Pre-Raphaelitism, which opposed the art principles of REYNOLDS—whom they called "Sir Sploshua"—aimed at romantic symbolism, fidelity to nature, and a fresh use of colour; supported by RUSKIN, the movement influenced other 19th century writers and painters, including PATMORE, Sir Edward Burne-Jones [see KIPLING], and William Morris [see Christina ROSSETTI]); in 1860 married Elizabeth Siddal, whose death in 1862 from a drug overdose sent him into a depression that ended in paranoia and reclusiveness; publications include "The Blessed Damozel" in *The Germ* (a poem to accompany a painting of the same name), translations from Dante and others, *Poems* (1870), and *Ballads and Sonnets* (1881).

RUKEYSER, MURIEL (1913-1980): American writer, best known for her political poetry; born in New York City to a Jewish family; educated at Vassar and Columbia; briefly married to Glyn Collins; Vice-President of the New York City House of Photography, 1946-60; supported the Loyalists in the Spanish Civil War, actively protested U.S. involvement in Vietnam (for which she was jailed), championed American civil rights and women's movements, all these activities shaping her poetry; taught at Sarah Lawrence College (1946, 1956-57), influencing Alice WALKER; publications include *Beast in View* (1944), *Breaking Open* (1973), and *The Gates* (1976).

RUMENS, CAROL (LUMLEY) (b.1944): English poet and anthologist, born in London, educated at a convent school and London U. (in philosophy); married David Rumens (1965); has worked in journalism, as a copywriter and poetry editor; author of a novel, *Plato Park* (1987) and compiler of an anthology of contemporary women writers, *Making for the Open* (1985); *Selected Poems* (1987) draws upon seven earlier volumes.

RUSKIN, JOHN (1819-1900): English critic, born in London to a well-to-do wine merchant's family; educated privately and at Oxford; in 1848 married Euphemia Chalmers Gray (annulled 1854; she later married Millais [see D.G. ROSSETTI]; author of a few poems and stories (including the children's classic, *The King of the Golden River*, which appeared in *Sesame and Lilies*, 1865), made his name as an art critic (as in *Modern Painters*, 1843, and *Seven Lamps of Architecture*, 1849), an enthusiast for medievalism and the Gothic (as in *The Stones of Venice*, 1851-53), and an evangelist for social reform (as in *Unto This Last*, 1860, and *Fors Clavigera*, 1871-84); after 1880, though he worked on an autobiography, *Praeterita* (1886-89), his life was disrupted by a series of mental breakdowns.

SALKEY, ANDREW (b.1928): Jamaican fiction writer, anthologist, and commentator, born in Colon, Panama, educated in Jamaica and at London U.; worked as a journalist and broadcaster with the BBC in London, 1952-76; married Patricia Verden, 1957; moved to the U.S.A., 1976, to teach creative writing in Amherst, Massachusetts; author and editor of over thirty books, including children's fiction (e.g., *Hurricane*, 1964), travel books (e.g., *Georgetown Journal*, 1972), novels and stories (e.g., *Come Home, Malcolm Heartland* (1976), and poetry (e.g., the prize-winning *In the Hills Where Her Dreams Live*, 1979).

SAMBER, ROBERT (b. c.1682, fl. 1729): English translator, about whom little is known; his name is attached to various works issued between 1716 and 1731, with some manuscripts dated 1735; in 1729 translated Charles Perrault's 1696-97 work, *Contes de la Mère Oye* as *Histories of Tales of Past Times told by Mother Goose*, thus introducing into English the term "Mother Goose" as well as such tales as "Puss in Boots" and "Cinderella."

SANDBURG, CARL (1878-1967): American poet and biographer, born in Illinois to a Swedish immigrant family (Sandburg was his mother's name—his father, a blacksmith, was named Johnson); left school to become a labourer and journalist in Chicago; fought in the Spanish-American War; in 1908 married Paula Steichen (sister of the photographer Edward Steichen); established his name with the free verse of *Chicago Poems* (1916) and subsequent collections; retired to North Carolina; noted also for his six-volume biography of LINCOLN (1926-39); *Collected Poems* (1950) won the Pulitzer Prize.

SANDYS, GEORGE (1578-1644): English translator and travel writer, born in Yorkshire (son of the Archbishop of York), educated at Oxford; travelled to Turkey, writing *A Relation of a Journey* (1615); also lived in America, serving as treasurer of the colony of Virginia (1621-26); produced verse translations of Ovid's *Metamorphoses* (1626), Virgil's *The Aeneid* (1632), passages from the Bible (1636, 1641), and other works.

SASSOON, SIEGFRIED (1886-1967): English poet, born in Kent, educated at Cambridge; joined the Royal Welsh Fusiliers and fought in World War I, winning the Military Cross, but openly criticized military authorities in 1917, leading to his being treated as a medical case; friend of GRAVES and of OWEN, whose poems he edited in 1920; after a brief period in journalism, retired to the country and wrote; books include *Counter-Attack* (1918), a biography of MEREDITH (1948), and *Memoirs of a Fox-Hunting Man* (1928) and other semi-autobiographical fictions; converted to Catholicism in 1957.

SAVILLE, GEORGE: see HALIFAX.

SCHREINER, OLIVE (1855-1920): South African novelist (used the pseudonym "Ralph Iron") and political writer, born at a mission station in Cape Colony, on the border of Basutoland; self-educated, worked as a governess (1870-81) before moving to England with the manuscript of her second (and most famous) novel, *The Story of an African Farm* (1883), which shows the influence of EMERSON and the evolutionary philosopher Herbert Spencer (1820-1903); involved in a relationship with the sexologist Havelock Ellis (1859-1939); returned to South Africa, 1894, marrying Samuel Cronwright, who changed his named to Cronwright-Schreiner; pacifist, opposed the Boer War, and Cecil Rhodes's capitalist part in it, in *Trooper Peter Halket of Mashonaland* (1897); other works include reflections on women's roles in society, as in *Dreams* (1891) and *Woman and Labour* (1911).

SCOTT, DENNIS (b.1939): Jamaican poet, involved in the theatre; born and educated in Jamaica, where he has been a dancer and actor with the Jamaica National Dance Theatre Company, and also a playwright and director; lectured on directing at Yale; author of *Uncle Time* (1973), which won the Commonwealth Poetry Prize, *Dreadwalk* (1982), and other works.

SCOTT, DUNCAN CAMPBELL (1862-1947): Canadian poet and short story writer, born in Ottawa to a Methodist family; locally educated; after 1879 worked for the Department of Indian Affairs, becoming deputy superintendant general (1913-1932); influenced to write by his friend and fellow civil servant LAMPMAN, collaborating with him in a series of newspaper columns ("At the Mermaid Inn") for the Toronto *Globe* (1892-93); married Belle Warner, 1894, and two years after her death in 1929, married the novelist Elise Aylen (1904-1972), who was later to join an *ashram* in India; publications include *In the Village of Viger* (1896), *The Witching of Elspie* (1923), and *The Circle of Affection* (1947); his *Selected Poems* were edited in 1951 by his friend, the critic E.K. Brown.

SCOTT, F[RANCIS] R[EGINALD] (1899-1985): Canadian poet, lawyer, translator, and political strategist, born in Quebec City, the son of Canon Frederick George Scott (1861-1944), himself a poet; educated at Bishop's College, Oxford, and McGill (where he taught law, 1928-68); married the painter Marian Dale, 1928; concerned with civil liberties, helped draft the "Regina Manifesto" that in the 1930s established a Canadian social democratic political party, the CCF;

successfully argued before the Supreme Court of Canada two far-reaching civil rights cases in the 1950s; associated with KLEIN, A.J.M. Smith (1902-1980), and other members of the "Montreal Group," 1925-27; edited influential anthologies of new poets (*New Provinces*, 1936), satires (*The Blasted Pine*, 1957, enlarged 1967), and francophone Canadian writers in his own translations (*Poems of French Canada*, 1977); *Essays on the Constitution* (1977) and *The Collected Poems of F.R. Scott* (1981, edited by John Newlove) both won Governor-General's Awards.

SCOTT, R[OBERT] F[ALCON] (1868-1912): English explorer, born in Devon; joined the navy, 1881, rising to midshipman by 1883 and lieutenant commander by 1897; commanded the National Antarctic Expedition that mapped the Ross Sea region (1900-04) as well as the ill-fated expedition to the South Pole (1910-12); in 1908 married Kathleen Bruce, a sculptress (1878-1947; later Lady Kennet, a friend of Rodin); posthumously knighted; recent research shows that his diary was substantially edited before its publication as *Scott's Last Expedition* (1913), with some commentators consequently rejecting the heroic image constructed by the published version, and analyzing the narrative instead for signs of incompetent leadership and political interference in public records.

SCOTT, SIR WALTER (1771-1832): Scottish novelist, editor, and poet, born in Edinburgh, educated at Edinburgh U.; articled at his father's law office, read widely in SPENSER, Percy's *Reliques of Ancient English Poetry* (1765), and Gothic fiction, and anonymously began publishing ballads and translations from German; in 1795 married Margaret Charlotte Carpenter (or Charpentier), daughter of a French émigré; attracted public attention (and extraordinary popularity) with such poems as *The Lay of the Last Minstrel* (1805) and *The Lady of the Lake* (1810); prepared several critical editions (e.g., of DRYDEN, 1808; SEWARD, 1810; SWIFT, 1814; and Scottish ballads, 1825 [see Lady Anne LINDSAY]) and wrote numerous reviews (for the Whig *Edinburgh Review* and for the Tory *Quarterly Review*, which he helped found in 1809); purchased his estate, Abbotsford, in the Scottish Lowlands, in 1811, and began the series of more than thirty "Waverley novels" (including *Rob Roy*, 1817; *The Heart of Midlothian*, 1818; *The Bride of Lammermoor*, 1819; *Ivanhoe*, 1819; and *Redgauntlet*, 1824) that appeared between 1814 and 1832, establishing the genre of the romantic historical novel; bankrupt in 1826, he wrote prolifically to pay off debts of £135,000, but in so doing sacrificed his health.

SEDLEY, SIR CHARLES (1639-1701): English courtier, playwright, and poet, born in London; friend of ROCHESTER, and (like him) known at the time for his wit and libertine life; married Catherine Savage; after their daughter Catharine became the mistress of James II, who made her the Countess of Dorchester, Sedley fought (out of "gratitude," he said) to have James's daughter Mary (wife of William III) made Queen; author of *Bellamira, or, The Mistress* (1687), his *Works* appeared in 1928.

SEPAMLA, (SYDNEY) SIPHO (b.1932): South African poet and novelist, born in Krugersdorp; trained as a teacher; edited the journals *New Classic* and *S'ketch* (a drama magazine), and is director of the Federated Union of Black Arts in Johannesburg; author of several volumes, including *The Blues Is You in Me* (1976), *The Soweto I Love* (1977), *Selected Poems* (1984), and a novel called *A Ride on the Whirlwind* (1981).

SEROTE, MONGANE WALLY (b.1944): South African poet and novelist, born in Sophiatown (Johannesburg); educated in Soweto, and at Columbia in New York; involved in black consciousness movements; imprisoned for nine months in 1969, without charges, under the terms of the Terrorism Act, before studying art in the U.S.A.; returned to Africa in 1979, choosing to live in Botswana, where he helped found a social organization called Medu; moved to London, 1986, to work for the African National Congress; author of several books, including a novel about the Soweto protests of 1976, *To Every Birth Its Blood* (1981), *Selected Poems* (1982), and *A Tough Tale* (1987).

SERVICE, ROBERT W[ILLIAM] (1874-1958): Canadian poet and fiction writer, born in Lancashire, England, perhaps distantly related to BURNS; raised in Ayrshire; apprenticed to a Glasgow bank, where he worked from 1889 to 1896, when he emigrated; worked at various jobs in California and B.C., till posted by the Canadian Bank of Commerce to Whitehorse, Yukon Territory, 1904; *Songs of a Sourdough* (1907; called *The Spell of the Yukon* in its U.S. edition), containing "The Cremation of Sam McGee" and other recital favourites, won him immediate fame; left the Yukon for Paris in 1912, remaining in France for most of the rest of his life, interrupted only by a short stint as a Hollywood screenwriter, 1921-22, and actor, 1940-45; married Germaine Bourgoin, 1913; war correspondent, 1915-16; friend of the biographer and adventure writer (and later Governor-General of Canada) John Buchan, Lord Tweedsmuir (1875-1940); produced more than twenty verse collections and romances, including *Ballads of a Cheechako* (1909) and *Bar-Room Ballads* (1940); retired to the Riviera, 1946.

SEWARD, ANNA (1742-1809): English poet and letter-writer (whose name is pronounced "SEE-ward"); born in Derbyshire, educated at home; lived primarily in Staffordshire, looking after her father, an Anglican churchman; the doyenne of a literary circle, she published as "Benvolio" and came to be known as "The Swan of Lichfield"; an acquaintance of JOHNSON, whom she criticized, BOSWELL, and Helen María WILLIAMS, with whom she corresponded; author of *Louisa* (1784; a verse novel) and numerous sonnets and memoirs, including elegies on Captain James Cook and Erasmus DARWIN; bequeathed her manuscripts to Sir Walter SCOTT, who edited her poems in 1810.

SEXTON, ANNE (HARVEY) (1928-1974): American poet and children's writer, born in Massachusetts; abused as a child, an experience that affected her life and poetry; educated in Boston, where Robert LOWELL was one of her teachers, and where PLATH was a contemporary in an adult education class; eloped with Alfred Mueller Sexton II (1948; divorced 1973), and in 1953, while he was fighting in the Korean War, she attempted suicide for the first time (succumbing to carbon monoxide poisoning in 1974); friend and collaborator of the poet Maxine Kumin (b. 1925); author of several collections, including *To Bedlam and Part Way Back* (1960), *All My Pretty Ones* (1962), the Pulitzer Prize-winning *Live or Die* (1966), *Transformations* (1972; which retells Grimm's tales in feminist terms), and *The Death Notebooks* (1974), all of which deal directly with women's experience; several works were posthumously edited from manuscripts by her daughter Linda Sexton.

SHAFTESBURY, ANTHONY ASHLEY COOPER, 1ST EARL OF (1621-1683): English politician, born in Dorset to landed gentry (his father being made a baronet in 1622, and his mother's father being Sir Anthony Ashley, 1551-1628, clerk of the Privy Council); educated at Oxford; married three times: to Margaret Coventry (d. 1649), Lady Frances Cecil, sister to the Earl of Exeter (d. 1654), and Margaret Spencer, sister to the Earl of Sunderland, each time securing his political position; a Royalist colonel in 1643, he crossed to Cromwell, sitting on his council of state; after 1660, he sided with the Royalist cause; a political pragmatist, he introduced the Habeas Corpus Act in 1679 but ruthlessly punished his enemies; friend of LOCKE, whom he met in 1666 and who became his physician (and, later, tutor to his grandson, the moral philosopher Anthony Ashley Cooper, 3rd Earl of Shaftesbury, 1671-1713, author of *Characteristics of Men, Manners, Opinions, Times*, 1711); finally charged with high treason (1681), for championing the Duke of Monmouth (Charles II's illegitimate son) as a replacement for James II (a Catholic); characterized as Achitophel in DRYDEN's *Absalom and Achitophel* (1681); fled to Holland, where he died.

SHAKESPEARE, WILLIAM (1564-1616): English playwright and poet, born in Stratford-on-Avon, the son of Mary Arden and John Shakespeare, a glover and (in 1571) chief Alderman of the town; married Anne Hathaway, 1585, and had three children; little is known of his life between 1585 and 1592, when he was first recognized as a young playwright and actor in London; purchased a share in the acting company called the Lord Chamberlain's Men, 1595, moving to the Globe Theatre in 1598 (burned down, 1613, during a performance of *Henry VIII*, but also invested in property in Stratford ("New Place"); his early poems, such as *Venus and Adonis* (1593), were probably written about the same time as his earliest comedies (e.g., *The Taming of the Shrew*) and tragic histories (e.g., *Richard III*); plays of the later 1590s include *A Midsummer Night's Dream, Romeo and Juliet,* and *Henry IV*; the most admired tragedies and comedies followed at the end of the decade and in the first years of the new century, among them *As You Like It, Twelfth Night, Julius Caesar, Hamlet, Othello, King Lear, Macbeth,* and *Antony and Cleopatra*; after his theatre troupe was granted the right to call themselves the King's Men, they moved to the Blackfriars Theatre (1608); published *Sonnets* (1609), dedicated to "Mr. W.H." (as yet unidentified: perhaps Henry Wriothesley, 3rd Earl of Southampton, or William Herbert, 3rd Earl of Pembroke [see WROTH; see also LANYER]); later plays, usually called "romances," include *Cymbeline* and *The Tempest*; the plays were collected as the First Folio (1623) by two fellow-actors, Henry Condell (d. 1627) and John Heminges (d. 1630); generally drew his plots from other sources (notably HOLINSHED's *Chronicles* and contemporary writers such as LODGE); his plays have frequently been rewritten to suit the differing taste of subsequent centuries (e.g., DRYDEN adapted *Troilus and Cressida* in 1679; the Poet Laureate Nahum Tate, 1652-1715, rewrote *King Lear* in 1681 with a happy ending; and various 20th century films have modified text, costume, and setting), or summarized for children [see LAMB], or adapted to other media (e.g., Mendelssohn's ballet music for *A Midsummer Night's Dream*); in performance, the plays have been the vehicle by which numerous acting careers have been measured, among them those of David Garrick [see JOHNSON], Edmund Kean (c.1789-1833), Sarah Siddons (1755-1831), Fanny KEMBLE, Ellen Terry (1848-1928; see SHAW), Laurence Olivier (1907-1989), and Kenneth Branagh (b. 1961).

SHELLEY, PERCY BYSSHE (1792-1822): English poet, born in Sussex, educated at Eton, where he wrote and published a Gothic novel, *Zastrozzi* (1810), and at Oxford, where the next year he professed *The Necessity of Atheism* and was consequently expelled; eloped in 1811 with 16-year-old Harriet Westbrook, and spent the next years wandering from the Lake District to London, corresponding with SOUTHEY, William Godwin [see COLERIDGE], and writing *Queen Mab* (1813); eloped to France with 16-year-old Mary (Godwin) Shelley (author of *Frankenstein*, 1818) in 1814 (though still married to Harriet, who had a child later that year, and drowned herself in 1816), and (in the name of liberty) had liaisons with several other women as well; moved to Switzerland in 1816, where BYRON was living, then to Italy in 1818; friends included PEACOCK, HUNT, KEATS, and HAZLITT; from 1817 till his death by accidental drowning, produced most of his major poems, burlesques, and political pamphlets, including, in 1819 (the year his son William—Mary's child—died), *Prometheus Unbound* (extended 1820), *The Cenci*, *The Mask of Anarchy*, and several short poems, followed by *A Defence of Poetry* (1820) and *Adonais* (1821), an elegy on the death of KEATS; Mary Shelley edited *The Poetical Works* in four volumes (1839), the contents selected partly in accordance with the wish of Sir Timothy Shelley (her father-in-law) to restore the respectability of the family name.

SHENSTONE, WILLIAM (1714-1763): English poet, born in Worcestershire, educated by a tutor; friend and mentor of DARWALL; author of *The Schoolmistress* (1737), written while he was briefly at Oxford, a contemporary of JOHNSON's; achieved fame in his own day as a landscape gardener on his estate, the Leasowes.

SIDNEY, MARY: see Countess of PEMBROKE

SIDNEY, SIR PHILIP (1554-1586): English poet, prose writer, critic, and courtier, born at Penshurst, the family estate in Kent; named for his godfather, King Philip II of Spain; educated in Shrewsbury, with his friend Sir Fulke GREVILLE, and briefly attended Oxford before leaving for Europe to learn other languages; returned to England, 1575, after which he sought employment with ELIZABETH I, but was given a mixed reception at court, due in part to the disfavour into which his mother's brother, the Earl of Leicester, had fallen; knighted, 1583; killed in a minor battle in the Low Countries, while serving as governor of Flushing; author of *An Apology for Poetry* (1595; also called *The Defence of Poesie*), *Arcadia* (written about 1580, and completed by his sister, the Countess of PEMBROKE), and a sonnet sequence, *Astrophel and Stella* (1591; probably written about 1582, after Penelope Devereux [c.1562-1607; daughter of the 1st Earl of Essex] had married Lord Rich); he is remembered in elegies by NASHE and SPENSER.

SITWELL, EDITH (1887-1964): English poet, critic, and biographer, born in Yorkshire, elder sister of the writers Osbert (1892-1969) and Sacheverell Sitwell (1897-1969); educated by a governess; influenced by Christina ROSSETTI, SWINBURNE, and Gertrude Stein (1874-1946), whom she met in 1925 when living in Paris; left for London at age 26, publishing her first poems in 1915; anti-war, anti-establishment, and in opposition to Edward Marsh and the Georgian poets (see Rupert BROOKE), edited (with her brothers, 1916-21) an annual called *Wheels*, publishing some of OWEN's first poems in 1919; collaborated in 1923 with the musician Sir William Walton (1902-1983) in an experimental multi-media presentation of her poem sequence *Façade*; wrote biographies of POPE (1930) and ELIZABETH I (1946, 1962), and a 1937 novel based on the life of SWIFT, *I Live Under a Black Sun*; was made a DBE in 1954, a year before converting to Catholicism; *Collected Poems* appeared in 1954 (enlarged 1957).

SKELTON, JOHN (c.1460-1529): English poet, educated at Oxford and perhaps Cambridge; tutor to Prince Henry (1496-1501); ordained 1498, and granted a parish in Norfolk, after which details of his life are scarce; praised by Erasmus and CAXTON, he seems to have had mixed relations with Cardinal Wolsey, satirizing him and the court of Henry VII in various poems, e.g. *The Bowge of Court* (1498) and *Colin Clout* (1521-22); named "Orator Regius" by Henry VII in 1512; author of a morality play, *Magnyficence* (c.1516).

SMART, CHRISTOPHER (1722-1771): English poet and classical scholar, born in Kent, raised in Durham, educated at Cambridge; after 1749, showed signs of mental instability, and while incarcerated in St. Luke's Hospital after 1756, wrote *A Song to David* (1763) and *Jubilate Agno* (first published 1939); translated Horace, and also published other religious poetry, including verse versions of the parables (1768) and hymns for children (1770).

SMITH, CHARLOTTE (TURNER) (1749-1806): English novelist and poet, born in Sussex, educated at boarding schools; married in 1765 to her father's choice of husband, a merchant in the West Indies trade named Benjamin Smith, whom she left in 1787 (after her twelfth child, and fearing for her life); began writing early, publishing an elegy for General Wolfe in 1759, but took up writing novels to earn money when her husband went bankrupt in 1782 and (with her and the children) was held in debtors' prison; after 1786, published a book almost annually, including translations from French, children's books, stories, and novels, such as the popular Gothic romance, *Emmeline, The Orphan of the Castle* (1788).

SMITH, IAIN CRICHTON (b.1928): Scottish poet, fiction writer, playwright, and translator, born on the island of Lewis, educated at Aberdeen U.; fluent in Gaelic as well as English, taught school, 1955-77, before starting to write full-time; lives in Oban; publications include *Consider the Lilies* (1968) and *Selected Poems* (1985).

SMITH, KEN[NETH JOHN] (b.1938): English poet, born in Yorkshire, educated at U. of Leeds; married Ann Minnis, 1960, and lives in Exeter, lecturing on poetry; author of *Eleven Poems* (1963), *Island Called Henry the Navigator* (1976), *The Poet Reclining* (1982, a selection from previous volumes), and *Wormwood* (1987).

SMITH, STEVIE (FLORENCE MARGARET) (1902-1971): English poet, novelist, and illustrator, born in Yorkshire; after secondary school, became an actress and secretary before beginning to publish the journal-like fictions and the satirical, free-form, revelatory observations that won her an international readership (including PLATH, COUZYN, and the novelist Rosamund Lehmann, 1901-90); attempted suicide, 1953; works include *Novel on Yellow Paper* (1936), *Over the Frontier* (1938), and *Collected Poems* (1975).

SMITH, SYDNEY (1771-1845): English essayist, wit, and clergyman, born in Essex, educated at Oxford; ordained, 1794; took up several parishes, including one in Edinburgh, where he mixed with Sir Walter SCOTT's circle, married, and in 1802 helped found *The Edinburgh Review*; moved to London in 1804, then Yorkshire, Bristol, Somerset, and finally St. Paul's Cathedral, winning constant favour as a preacher; published some of his sermons, along with pamphlets on a variety of social issues (from game laws to prison reform), and numerous essays (both serious and witty) for the *Edinburgh Review*; his *Selected Writings* were edited by AUDEN in 1957.

SOMERVILLE, MARY (FAIRFAX) (1780-1872): Scottish writer on science, born in Jedburgh, the daughter of Margaret Charters and Vice-Admiral Sir William Fairfax; educated at a boarding school and through her own reading; married, 1804, her cousin Samuel Greig (d. 1807), and then another cousin, Dr. William Somerville (1771-1860), and moved to London, where she met numerous scientists, including the Marquis de Laplace (1749-1827) and Sir William Herschel (1738-1822); achieved fame with her first book, a translation and popularization of Laplace's *Mécanique Célestial* as *The Mechanism of the Heavens* (1831); established a reputation among other scientists with papers to the Royal Society and several books on physics, including *On the Connexion of the Physical Sciences* (1834; revised 1842), which suggested the existence of the planet that came to be known as Neptune, *Physical Geography* (1848), and *Molecular and Microscopic Science* (1869); lived in Italy after 1838; one of Oxford's colleges for women, Somerville (founded 1879), is named after her.

SOTO, GARY (b.1952): American poet, born in Fresno, California, to a Mexican-American family who worked as migrant labourers in the San Joaquin Valley when he was a child; educated at California State U., and U. of California (Irvine); married Carolyn Oda, 1975; teaches in the Department of Chicano Studies at U. of California (Berkeley); author of several volumes, including *Black Hair* (1985), *Lesser Evils: Ten Quartets* (1988), and a memoir, *Living Up the Street* (1985).

SOUTHEY, ROBERT (1774-1843): English poet, critic, and biographer, born in Bristol, educated at Oxford, where he was noted for his rebelliousness, republicanism, and support of the French Revolution; a friendship with COLERIDGE in 1794 (later severed, when Coleridge abandoned his family and left SOUTHEY to care for them) led to the Pantisocracy scheme [see COLERIDGE]; married Elizabeth Fricker, 1795 (she died, insane, in 1837, after which he married the poet Caroline Anne Bowles, 1787-1854); wrote voluminously, a range of poems, histories, and other works, including biographies of John Wesley (1820) and BUNYAN (1830); was named Poet Laureate in 1813; ridiculed by PEACOCK as "Mr Feathernest" in *Melincourt* (1817) and (because of his encomium on the death of George III) parodied by BYRON in *The Vision of Judgment* (1822); now remembered best for his early poetry; died of what was probably Alzheimer's Disease.

SOUTHWELL, ROBERT (c.1561-1595): English poet and Jesuit martyr, born in Norwich; educated in Douai and Rome, ordained as a priest in 1585; returned the next year to what had become Protestant England as part of a Jesuit mission to reconvert the people; arrested in 1592 while saying mass, imprisoned in the Tower of London, executed in 1595, and beatified by Pope Pius XI in 1929; many of his works circulated in secret during his lifetime; *Maeoniae* appeared in 1595.

SOYINKA, WOLE (b.1934): Nigerian dramatist, poet, critic, and novelist (whose surname is pronounced "shoy-ING-ka"); born in Abeokuta, educated at University College, Ibadan, and U. of Leeds; after teaching and also working in the London theatre, returned to Nigeria in 1960 to set up Theatre Arts Departments at the Universities of Ibadan and Ife, and to write, produce, and act in plays; in 1963 married Olayide Idowu, a teacher; mostly noted for such plays as *A Dance of the Forests* (1963) and *The Road* (1965), which embody Yoruba cosmography; *Madmen and Specialists* (1971) and *A Play of Giants* (1984), satiric comedies; and *The Bacchae* (1973) and *Opera Wanyosi* (1981), African adaptations of Euripedes, Brecht, and GAY; imprisoned in Northern Nigeria during the Civil War, 1967-69, resulting in the poem collection *A Shuttle in the Crypt* (1972) and an autobiographical meditation, *The Man Died* (1973); won the Nobel Prize, 1986; other works include *Aké* (1981), about his childhood, and *Myth, Literature, and the African World* (1976), a volume of criticism.

SPENCE, CATHERINE HELEN (1825-1910): Australian novelist and essayist, born in Scotland, emigrated to South Australia with her family in 1839; became a governess at age 17, then set about publishing fiction, first anonymously with *Clara Morison* (1854), then using her own name with *Mr. Hogarth's Will* (1865); after her feminist novel *Handfasted* (not published till 1984) was rejected on grounds that it transgressed social proprieties, she turned increasingly to writing essays about social reform (primarily for Adelaide newspapers); her subjects ranged from voting rights and Unitarianism to institutionalized marriage, orphanages, and the economics of being female; became Australia's first female political candidate (1897).

SPENDER, STEPHEN (1909-1986): English poet and critic, born in London, educated at Oxford, where he was a contemporary of AUDEN; professed leftwing sympathies during the 1930s, as revealed in his early book *Poems* (1933); participated in the Spanish Civil War; was a London fireman during the Blitz of World War II; lived in both England and the U.S.A. after 1948; edited *Horizon* magazine (1939-41) and *Encounter* (1953-66); was knighted in 1983; publications include *World Within World* (1951), an autobiography, and *Collected Poems 1928-1985* (1985).

SPENSER, EDMUND (1552-1599): English poet, born in London, son of a tradesman; educated at Merchant Taylors' School (where his contemporaries included LODGE, the playwright Thomas Kyd, 1558-1594, and the Bible translator Lancelot Andrewes, 1555-1626) and at Cambridge (where his friends included Gabriel Harvey, c.1550-1631); married Maccabeus Chylde, 1579, and in the same year became secretary to the Earl of Leicester, meeting SIDNEY (to whom *The Shepheardes Calendar*, 1579, is dedicated) and Edward DYER; lived in Ireland, holding various government posts, 1580-1598, returning to England when Hugh O'Neill, the Earl of Tyrone, began to lead a revolt against ELIZABETH I, burning Spenser's home, Kilcolman Castle; despite RALEGH's interceding on his behalf, the first three books of *The Faerie Queene* (1590; enlarged, 1596, 1609), though a popular success, failed to win Spenser preferment at court; married again, 1594, to Elizabeth Boyle, publishing *Amoretti* and *Epithalamion* in a single volume (1595); died in Westminster.

SPRAT, THOMAS (1635-1713): English prose writer and clergyman, born in Dorset, the son of a minister; educated at Oxford, taking part in discussions at Wadham College (where Dr. John Wilkins was master) that ultimately led to the founding of the Royal Society in 1660 (his *History of the Royal Society of London* appeared in 1667); supported Cromwell prior to 1660, then was ordained in the Church of England, 1661, preaching in Oxford and London; married Helen Wolseley (1647-1726); became Bishop of Rochester and Dean of Westminster, 1683; friend of the architect Christopher Wren [see DENHAM], and known in his own day as a wit; praised by COWLEY and JOHNSON for his style; became the victim of a plot in 1692, when he was imprisoned after being falsely accused of wanting James II back as king, an experience that led to *A Relation of the Late Wicked Contrivance of Stephen Blackhead and Robert Young Against the Lives of Several Persons* (1692).

STAFFORD, WILLIAM (b.1914): American poet and anthologist, born in Kansas, the son of a businessman; educated at U. of Kansas and State U. of Iowa; conscientious objector during World War II; married Dorothy Frantz, a teacher, 1944; worked on a farm, then for the Church of the Brethren, then as a professor at Lewis and Clark College in Portland, Oregon, from 1948 till his retirement; author of several collections of lyrics, including *Traveling through the Dark* (1962), which won a National Book Award, and *Stories that Could Be True* (1977); other books include *Poems by Ghalib* (translated with Adrienne RICH, 1969), and an autobiographical memoir called *Down in My Heart* (1947).

STANHOPE, PHILIP DORMER: see CHESTERFIELD.

STEVENS, WALLACE (1879-1955): American poet and lawyer, born in Pennsylvania, the son of a lawyer, educated at Harvard and New York Law School; married Elsie Kachel, 1909; worked as an executive with a Hartford insurance company from 1916 till his death; began publishing in *Poetry* (Chicago), collecting his work in such volumes as *Harmonium* (1923), which won praise from Marianne MOORE, *Ideas of Order* (1935), *The Man with the Blue Guitar* (1937), and *Notes Toward a Supreme Fiction* (1942); a volume of essays on "reality and the imagination," *The Necessary Angel* (1951), won a National Book Award; *Collected Poems* (1954) won a Pulitzer Prize; other works, including *Letters* (1966), edited by his daughter Holly Stevens, appeared posthumously.

STEVENSON, ANNE (b.1933): Poet, critic, and cellist, with British and American affiliations; born in Cambridge, England, to American parents, raised in Michigan, educated at U. of Michigan; married (1955) in England, later divorced and returned to teach in Cambridge, Massachusetts; remarried (Mark Elvin, an academic, later divorced), then resettled in Britain, variously living in Glasgow (where she was a tutor at the university), Hay-on-Wye (where she married Michael Farley and opened The Poetry Bookshop), Oxford, and County Durham; author of a study of BISHOP, a life of PLATH, and several poetry volumes, from *Living in America* (1965) to *Selected Poems* (1987) and *The Other House* (1990).

STEVENSON, ROBERT LOUIS (1850-1894): Scottish novelist, essayist, story writer, and children's poet, born in Edinburgh, educated at Edinburgh U. (in law); in poor health all his life, but an inveterate traveller, published *Travels with a Donkey* (1878), about France and Belgium, before leaving for California; in 1895 married Fanny Osbourne, an American widow with a small son, Lloyd (1868-1947), for whom he wrote *Treasure Island* (1883); returned to England, writing numerous poems, essays (for *The Cornhill Magazine*), and romantic adventures, including *A Child's Garden of Verses* (1885), *The Strange Case of Dr Jekyll and Mr Hyde* (1886), *Kidnapped* (1886) and its sequel *Catriona* (1893), *The Black Arrow* (1888) and *The Master of Ballantrae* (1889); collaborated with Lloyd Osbourne on *The Wrong Box* (1889) and two other books; in 1888 left England for the South Pacific, settling on the Vailima estate in Samoa, where he became known as "Tusitala" (Teller of Tales); other books include his early *Familiar Studies of Men and Books* (1882) and his late novella *The Beach at Falesà* (1893; 1984); died of a cerebral hemorrhage.

STRAUSS, JENNIFER (WALLACE) (b.1933): Australian poet and critic, born in Heywood, Victoria, educated at a convent school and Melbourne U.; married (husband died 1978); taught English at various universities, including Monash (after 1964); active in university politics; publications include *Children and Other Strangers* (1975), *Winter Driving* (1981), and *Labour Ward* (1988).

SUCKLING, SIR JOHN (1609-1641): English poet and playwright, born in Norfolk to a family with close ties to JAMES I; educated at Cambridge; knighted, 1630, after various military and diplomatic ventures; noted in his day for his extravagant lifestyle; friends with CAREW and the playwright Sir William D'Avenant (1606-1668), SHAKESPEARE's godson; fled to France, 1641, after the failure of a military campaign, and ostensibly committed suicide; publications include the play *Aglaura* (1638) and the posthumously published poetry collection *Fragmenta Aurea* (1646).

SURREY, HENRY HOWARD, EARL OF (1517-1547): English courtier and poet, eldest son of Thomas Howard, who in 1524 became 3rd Duke of Norfolk; educated privately; became companion of Henry VIII's illegitimate son, the Earl of Richmond (d. 1536); educated at the favour of the court as long as Anne Boleyn (beheaded 1536) was Queen; during the 1540s, distinguished himself in various military campaigns, and was honoured with the Order of the Garter, 1541, but became the political victim of the family of the next Queen, Jane Seymour (c.1509-1537), and of his own sister, the Countess of Richmond, and was imprisoned in the Tower and executed; noted for introducing blank verse to England in his translation of the *Aeneid*, and for his use of Petrarchan form in his sonnets, printed first in *Tottel's Miscellany* (1557).

SWENSON, MAY (b.1919): American poet and children's writer, born in Utah to a Mormon family; educated at Utah State Agricultural College, where her father taught; became a journalist, a secretary in New York City, and a lecturer on poetry at various universities; author of several volumes, from *A Cage of Spines* (1958) to *In Other Words: New Poems* (1987).

SWIFT, JONATHAN (1667-1745): Irish churchman, poet, and satirist, born in Dublin; educated at Kilkenny School (a contemporary of CONGREVE), Trinity College (Dublin), and Oxford; ordained, 1694, and granted a position near Belfast; meanwhile, served as secretary to Sir William Temple [see Dorothy OSBORNE] at Moor Park, and as tutor to 8-year-old Esther Johnson, who became the "Stella" of his poems and later his companion (she died in 1728); this relationship was complicated by Swift's association with Esther Vanhomrigh ("Vanessa" in his poems), who died in 1723, leaving half her property, once designed for Swift, to Bishop BERKELEY; Swift edited Temple's correspondence in 1696, becoming increasingly involved in Whig politics with subsequent publications, *The Battle of the Books* (1697) and *A Tale of a Tub* (written c.1696; published 1704), at which time he also met ADDISON and Steele (see ADDISON) in London; after 1710, editing *The Examiner*, changed his political allegiance to the Tory party of Robert Harley, Earl of Oxford (1661-1724; son of Edward Harley, 1689-1741, literary patron and friend of POPE); became friends with POPE, GAY, and others in the Scriblerus Club [see POPE], and wrote *Journal to Stella* (published 1766); named Dean of St. Patrick's Cathedral in Dublin, 1713, and remained in Ireland after the Hanoverian accession, writing satires of scientific presumption and political bureaucracy, and defences of Irish liberty, including *The Drapier's Letters* (1724), *Gulliver's Travels* (1726), and *A Modest Proposal* (1729).

SWINBURNE, ALGERNON CHARLES (1837-1909): English poet and verse playwright, born in London, raised on the Isle of Wight (his father was an admiral), and educated sporadically in France, and at Eton and Oxford; friend of D.G. ROSSETTI, MEREDITH, William Morris [see Christina ROSSETTI], and the painter Edward Burne-Jones (1833-

1898) [see KIPLING]; published prolifically, horrifying many readers because of his subjects (paganism and sexual rebelliousness); rescued from alcoholism by the critic Theodore Watts-Dunton (1832-1914), who became his legal and financial adviser and longtime companion; publications include the play *Atalanta in Calydon* (1865), *Ave Atque Vale* (1868), and the three series of *Poems and Ballads* (1866, 1878, 1889).

SYMONS, ARTHUR (1865-1945): English poet and critic, born in Wales to Cornish parents; privately educated; moved to London, participating in the Rhymers' Club, along with WILDE, DOWSON, John GRAY, and YEATS, contributing to *The Yellow Book*, editing *The Savoy* (after 1896), and translating Italian and French literature, particularly works by Gabriele D'Annunzio (1863-1938) and Charles Baudelaire (1821-1867); published the influential book *The Symbolist Movement in Literature* (1899) and several collections of poems, including *Silhouettes* (1892).

TAGORE, RABINDRANATH [sometimes transliterated RAVINDRANATH] (1861-1941): Bengali poet, novelist, playwright, musician, painter, social activist, and philosopher, born in Calcutta, educated (in law) at University College, London; returned to India to manage the family properties at Shihada; married Mrinalini Devi Raichaudhuri, 1883; founded Santiniketan, 1901, a communal school that attempted to join eastern and western traditions of thought; won the Nobel Prize, 1913; knighted, 1915, though he tried to reject the honour four years later, as a protest against British colonial policy; founded agricultural cooperatives; author of *Gitanjali* (1913), *Chitra* (1914), *Sakuntala* (1920), and other works, in both Bengali and English.

TALBOT, CATHERINE (1721-1770): English poet and essayist; educated by Bishop Thomas Secker, for whom she was a secretary; tended her ailing mother all her life; associated with the Bluestocking Group (see Hannah MORE), circulating her manuscripts to her friends Elizabeth CARTER and the novelist Samuel Richardson, and publishing in *The Rambler* and elsewhere; died of cancer; her *Works* appeared in 1771.

TAYLOR, EDWARD (c.1644-1729): American poet, physician, and Puritan pastor, born in Leicestershire, emigrated to Boston (1668), educated at Harvard; a friend of Samuel Sewall (1652-1730), a judge in the 1692 Salem witchcraft trials, and the Puritan divines Cotton Mather (1663-1728) and Increase Mather (1639-1723); author of various doctrinal texts; *Poetical Works* (1939) was edited (from manuscripts housed in Yale University Library) by Thomas H. Johnson, a more complete *Poems* appearing in 1960.

TAYLOR, JEREMY (1613-1667): English churchman, born in Cambridge, the son of a barber, educated at Oxford; in 1638, named chaplain to Charles I and to William Laud (1573-1645), Archbishop of Canterbury; sought refuge in Wales (at Golden Grove, Carmarthenshire) during the Civil War, where he taught; in 1658 was named to a chaplaincy in Northern Ireland, where he remained; from 1647 to 1660, though imprisoned three times for "idolatry," he wrote the works on religion and tolerance for which he is best remembered, including *The Golden Grove* (1655), a devotional manual, and *The Rule and Exercises of Holy Living* (1650) and *...Holy Dying* (1651), the latter written in response to the death of Lord and Lady Carbery, his patrons while he lived in Wales.

TAYLOR, JOHN (1580-1653): English poet (known as "the Water Poet"), born in Gloucestershire, educated locally; pressed into the navy while apprenticed to a London waterman; served at the siege of Cadiz (1596) and on other voyages before returning to the waterman's trade (working on the river and seacoast, ferrying goods and passengers); walked from London to Edinburgh in 1618, as described in *A Penniless Pilgrimage* (1618), and recounted other adventures in such books as *The Praise of Hempseed* (1618); ran a pub in Oxford, 1642, giving it up in 1645 to be a London innkeeper, selling his verses to his customers.

TENNYSON, ALFRED, LORD (1809-1892): English poet, born in Lincolnshire to a churchman's family, educated by his father and at Cambridge, where he met Arthur Henry Hallam (1811-1833), whose sudden death led to *In Memoriam* (begun in 1834, published in 1850); with his brothers Frederick and Charles TENNYSON TURNER published *Poems by Two Brothers* (1827); two of his own collections appeared in the 1930s, followed by *Poems* (1842, in two volumes) and *The Princess* (1847); married Emily Wellwood, 1850, the year he was named Poet Laureate, when WORDSWORTH died; sought privacy (he was known to be obsessively shy), but was repeatedly forced into public roles; had several audiences with Queen Victoria (1819-1901) and was awarded a baronetcy, 1883; his many subsequent publications confirmed his technical virtuosity, and include *Maud* (1855), *The Idylls of the King* (his retelling of the Arthurian legend, in several volumes, 1859-85), *Enoch Arden* (1864), and *Locksley Hall Sixty Years After* (1886).

TENNYSON TURNER, CHARLES (1808-1879): English poet, elder brother of Alfred TENNYSON, born in Lincolnshire, educated at Cambridge; became a Church of England vicar, changing his name to Turner in 1830, in accordance with the dictates of a will, after inheriting his great-uncle's lands; his numerous sonnets, published in four volumes (1830-74), were collected in 1880.

THAYER, ERNEST LAWRENCE (1863-1940): American journalist and poet, born in Lawrence, Massachusetts; educated at Harvard, where he was president of the *Harvard Lampoon* and wrote a humorous column using the pseudonym "Phin"; worked for the San Francisco *Examiner* from 1886 on, writing columns and occasional verse, including "Casey at the Bat" (1888).

THIBAUDEAU, COLLEEN (b.1925): Canadian poet, born in Toronto to a family of Irish and Acadian descent; raised in St. Thomas, Ontario; educated at U. of Toronto (in English literature), where she met numerous other young writers, including the poet and playwright James Reaney (b. 1926), whom she married in 1951; settled in London, Ontario, 1959, raising a family and publishing in *Brick* and other journals, sometimes as "M. Morris"; books include *Ten Letters* (1975), *The Martha Landscapes* (1984), and *The Artemisia Book* (1991).

THOMAS, DYLAN (1914-1953): Welsh writer, born in Swansea, left school in 1931; married Caitlin Macnamara, 1937; worked as a broadcaster for the BBC during the 1940s, establishing his literary reputation with the publication of stories (*Portrait of the Artist as a Young Dog*, 1940) and poems (including *Deaths and Entrances*, 1946, and *In Country Sleep*, 1952); his "play for voices," *Under Milk Wood* (1952) won further attention; several North American tours confirmed his skills as a reader, but also contributed to the decline of his health; died in New York.

THOMAS, EDWARD (1878-1917): Poet and prose writer, born in London to a Welsh family, educated at Oxford; married Helen Noble, 1899; became a full-time writer, producing editions of HERBERT and MARLOWE, biographies of several nature writers, reviews, books of travel and natural history based on his walking tours (e.g, *The Heart of England*, 1906; *In Pursuit of Spring*, 1914), and poems, for which he sometimes used the pseudonym "Edward Eastaway"; joined the Artists' Rifles in 1914 as an artillery officer and was killed during World War I; his reputation as a poet developed gradually after his death, especially with the appearance of *Collected Poems of Edward Thomas* (1978).

THOMAS, R[ONALD] S[TEWART] (b.1913): Welsh poet, born in Cardiff, educated at University College of North Wales in Bangor (studying Classics) and St. Michael's College in Llandaff (studying theology); married Mildred Eldridge, a painter; ordained in the Church of Wales, 1937; author of a dozen books of poetry, including *Song at the Year's Turning: Poems 1942-54* (1955), *H'm* (1972), and *Between Here and Now* (1981).

THOMSON, JAMES (1700-1748): Scottish poet and playwright, born in Roxburghshire, educated at Edinburgh U.; left theological studies to pursue a literary career in London, meeting POPE, GAY, and others in 1725, and acquiring a position as tutor; his dramas had mixed success (*The Masque of Alfred*, 1740, providing the words to "Rule Britannia"), but his poems won the approval of Thomas GRAY, YOUNG, and COLLINS, who wrote an elegy for him; most remembered for *The Seasons* (1730; enlarged 1744) and *The Castle of Indolence* (1748).

THOMSON, JAMES ["B.V."] (1834-1882): British poet, born in Port Glasgow, Renfrewshire, son of a sailor; raised and educated in orphanages in Hertfordshire and London, where he trained to be a schoolmaster; an ill-fated love affair with Matilda Weller (died 1853) exacerbated the melancholia that marked his entire life, and that drove him ultimately to drugs, alcohol, and an early death; undertook various jobs, from teaching and clerking to working (in the U.S.A.) for an American silver mine (1873); published numerous essays and poems, using the pseudonym "B.V." (for Bysshe Vanolis, honouring Percy Bysshe SHELLEY and the German writer known as Novalis—itself a pen-name for Friedrich Leopold von Hardenberg, 1772-1801), in such journals as *National Reformer* and *Cope's Tobacco Plant* (Liverpool); *The City of Dreadful Night and Other Poems* appeared in 1880.

THOREAU, HENRY DAVID (1817-1862): American essayist and poet, born in Concord, Massachusetts, educated at Harvard; made his living through a variety of jobs, from teaching and lecturing to land-surveying, gardening, and pencil-making; a friend of EMERSON, whose Transcendentalist ideas he attempted to put into practice; wrote extensively about his own experiences with nature, as in *A Week on the Concord and Merrimack Rivers* (1849) and *Walden* (1854), and about his travels, as in *A Yankee in Canada* (1866); *On the Duty of Civil Disobedience* (1849) testifies to the morality of liberty; died of tuberculosis, leaving his letters, journals, and poems to be published posthumously.

THRALE, HESTER: see Hester PIOZZI.

THURBER, JAMES (1894-1963): American humorist, story writer, and illustrator, born in Columbus, Ohio, educated at Ohio State U.; married Althea Adams, 1922 (divorced 1935), and Helen Wismer,

1935; joined the staff of *The New Yorker* in 1927, as described in his memoir, *The Years with Ross* (1959), and worked there with E.B. WHITE; continued as a contributor from 1933 to his death (from pneumonia, following a stroke); his many collections of sketches, fables, stories, and drawings include *The Owl in the Attic and Other Perplexities* (1931), *The Seal in the Bedroom and Other Predicaments* (1932), *Fables for Our Time* (1940), *My World—and Welcome to It* (1942; containing possibly his best known story, "The Secret Life of Walter Mitty"), *The Thurber Carnival* (1945), *The Beast in Me and Other Animals* (1948), and *The 13 Clocks* (1950), one of several books for children.

TICHBORNE, CHIDIOCK (c.1558-1586): English poet; an ardent Catholic, became involved in the Babington plot (led by Antony Babington, 1561-1586, one-time page to Mary, Queen of Scots) to murder ELIZABETH I and secure Mary's release from imprisonment in Sheffield; executed along with other conspirators [see HABINGTON], though the violence of his execution (disembowelment as well as hanging) led the Queen to reform the laws regarding legal punishment; his "Elegy" (addressed to his wife Agnes) proved very popular, and was set to music and printed in several collections of songs and madrigals between 1594 and 1606.

TIHANYI, EVA (b.1956): Canadian poet, born in Budapest, Hungary, emigrated in 1962, educated at U. of Windsor; has taught in several colleges in Ontario, including Seneca College in Toronto; author of *A Sequence of Blood* (1983) and *Prophecies Near the Speed of Light* (1984).

TOLLETT, ELIZABETH (1694-1754): English poet, daughter of the Commissioner of the Navy, George Tollett, who lived in one of the residences constituting part of the Tower of London and raised his family there; privately educated in languages, music, and history, she showed an interest in the history of science, which affects some of her poems; an heiress, she lived near London, and published anonymously *Poems on Several Occasions* (1724), with its translations from the classics and its tributes to CONGREVE, POPE, FINCH, and Lady Mary Wortley MONTAGU.

TOPLADY, AUGUSTUS MONTAGUE (1740-1778): English religious writer and hymnist, born in Surrey, educated at Trinity College (Dublin); ordained, 1764, became a preacher in a London chapel in 1775, attacking John Wesley [see Charles WESLEY], but defending Calvinism and asserting the Calvinist basis for the Church of England; most famous for his hymns, some of which were collected in *Poems on Sacred Subjects* (1759).

TRAHERNE, THOMAS (1637-1674): English poet and prose writer, born in Hereford, the son of a shoemaker; educated at Oxford; ordained, 1660, in the Church of England, becoming chaplain to Sir Orlando Bridgeman, the Keeper of the Great Seal, in 1667; published various commentaries on ethics and church history; his literary reputation awaited the discovery of his manuscripts in 1897 and the accurate attribution of them (they were at first thought to have been written by VAUGHAN); *Poems* appeared in 1903, with more poems discovered in 1910, and the prose *Centuries of Meditations* were published in 1908.

TROLLOPE, FRANCES (MILTON) (1780-1863): English novelist and travel writer, born in Leicestershire, raised in Hampshire by her father, a cleric, and stepmother; educated at home in French and Italian; moved to London, 1803, where in 1809 she married Thomas Trollope, a barrister; of their six children, three (Cecilia, Thomas Adolphus, and the most famous, Anthony, 1815-1882, author of the Barsetshire Chronicles and the Palliser novels) became novelists; facing debt and illness, she embarked on a scheme to set up a commercial venture in the U.S.A., which led to literary fame (with a travel book, *Domestic Manners of the Americans*, 1832) rather than economic success; another forty travel books and novels, written between then and 1858, mostly examining evangelical issues and arguing for industrial reform, include *The Vicar of Wrexhill* (1837) and *The Life and Adventures of Michael Armstrong, Factory Boy* (1840); retired to Florence, Italy, with her eldest son, Thomas Adolphus.

TURBERVILLE, GEORGE (c.1544-c.1597): English poet and translator, born in Dorset, educated at Oxford, but left to live in London; as secretary to Sir Thomas Randolph (1523-90), the Queen's ambassador, he travelled to Russia in 1568; published translations of Ovid and Italian poets, together with *Epitaphs, Epigrams, Songs and Sonnets* (1567).

TURNER, CHARLES: see Charles TENNYSON TURNER.

TUSSER, THOMAS (c.1524-1580): English agriculturalist and poet, born in Essex, educated at Cambridge; at different times in his life a chorister at St. Paul's Cathedral and a court musician, he became a farmer in Suffolk after his marriage, and a specialist in horticulture, introducing the cultivation of barley; in his day, famous for his book *A Hundreth Good Pointes of Husbandrie* (1557; enlarged to five hundred points in 1573, and combined with "as many of good huswifery"), which combined almanac-like advice with local proverbs.

TWAIN, MARK [SAMUEL LANGHORNE CLEMENS] (1835-1910): American writer, born in Missouri, raised in the town of Hannibal, on the Mississippi River; left school to be apprenticed to a printer, then became a riverboat pilot till the Civil War stopped the boats operating; travelled west in 1861 (from which grew "The Celebrated Jumping Frog," 1865, and *Roughing It*, 1872), visited Europe (leading to *The Innocents Abroad*, 1869), and edited newspapers in Nevada, San Francisco (with the writer Bret Harte, 1836-1902), Buffalo (where he met and married Olivia Langdon, 1870), and Hartford, Connecticut, where he settled; a friend of the novelist William Dean Howells (1837-1920); such works as *The Gilded Age* (1873; written in collaboration with Charles Dudley Warner, 1829-1900), *The Adventures of Tom Sawyer* (1876), *The Prince and the Pauper* (1882), *Adventures of Huckleberry Finn* (1884), and *A Connecticut Yankee in King Arthur's Court* (1889) established his reputation as a skilled raconteur, humorist, satirist, master of dialect, and social observer; bankrupt by 1894, however, he began a series of popular lecture tours and published other writings to pay off debts, his work becoming less consistent (as in *Tom Sawyer, Detective*, 1896) and more pessimistic (as in *The Man That Corrupted Hadleyburg*, 1900); the deaths of his wife and two daughters (respectively in 1904, 1896, and 1909) exacerbated the pessimism, as his posthumously published writings (e.g., *The Mysterious Stranger*, 1916) reveal.

TYNDALE, WILLIAM (c.1495-1536): English translator of the Bible and author of parables, born in Gloucestershire, educated at both Oxford and Cambridge; left for the Continent in 1524 when he found in London no support for his proposal to translate the Bible; met

Martin Luther (1483-1546) in Wittenberg, and in Cologne began to translate Erasmus's Greek text of the New Testament into English (completed 1526, but most copies sent to England were burned); lived in Antwerp after this time, often in hiding, revising the 1526 work and translating portions of the Old Testament, notably The Pentateuch (1530) and Jonah (1531), all of which subsequently became the basis for the Authorized Version; arrested for heresy in 1535, and strangled and burned at the stake, near Brussels, in 1536.

VASSA, GUSTAVUS: see Olaudah EQUIANO.

VAUGHAN, HENRY (1621-1695): Welsh physician and poet, born in Breconshire, the twin brother of Thomas Vaughan (1621-1666), the alchemist; referred to himself as a "Silurist" (using the Latin designation for the pre-Celtic people of Wales, the Silures); educated in Oxford, which he left to pursue legal studies in London, disrupted by the outbreak of the Civil War; became a physician instead, returning to Brecon to practise; published several collections of poems and religious meditations, including a translation of Juvenal (1646) and *Silex Scintillans* (or "flashing flint," 1650).

VAUX, THOMAS, LORD, 2ND BARON VAUX OF HARROWDEN (1509-1556): English courtier and poet, son of Sir Nicholas Vaux; educated at Cambridge; involved in various diplomatic ventures for Henry VIII in the 1520s and 1530s; made a Knight of the Bath, 1533; most of his poems (some becoming popular as songs) appeared in a later miscellany called *The Paradise of Dainty Devices* (1576); the gravedigger's scene in SHAKESPEARE's *Hamlet* deliberately scrambles a Vaux poem called "The Aged Lover Renounceth Love."

WALCOTT, DEREK (b.1930): Poet, playwright, and theatre director, born in Castries, St. Lucia; educated there and at U. of the West Indies (Mona, Jamaica); married three times; founded the Trinidad Theatre workshop, 1959, staging several of his own plays there, including *Dream on Monkey Mountain* (1970), which won the Obie Award in New York the following year; has been a visiting professor at Harvard and several other U.S. colleges; has published over fifteen volumes of poetry, including *In a Green Night* (1962), *The Castaway* (1965), and *The Gulf* (1970), and the autobiographical *Another Life* (1973); an annotated *Selected Poems*, edited by the poet Wayne Brown (b. 1944), appeared in 1981; won the 1992 Nobel Prize.

WALKER, ALICE (b.1944): American novelist, poet, and short story writer, born in Georgia to a sharecroppers' family, educated at Sarah Lawrence College, where she was influenced by Muriel RUKEYSER, who helped her publish her first book, *Once: Poems* (1968); married Melvyn Leventhal, a civil rights lawyer, 1967 (divorced 1976); lectured at several universities; her work characteristically examines the lives of black women, as in the stories of *You Can't Keep a Good Woman Down* (1981) and the novel *The Color Purple* (1982; Pulitzer Prize, 1983; adapted for film, 1985); edited the writings of Zora Neale Hurston (c.1891-1960); other publications include essays on language and women's history, e.g. *In Search of Our Mothers' Gardens: Womanist Prose* (1983) and *The Temple of My Familiar* (1989).

WALKER, KATH: see Oodgeroo NOONUCCAL.

WALLACE-CRABBE, CHRIS (b.1934): Australian poet, anthologist, novelist, and critic, born in Melbourne, educated at Melbourne U., where he started teaching in 1968; *Selected Poems*

(1973) reveals his abilities as an ironic formalist; other publications include *The Emotions Are Not Skilled Workers* (1980) and *Melbourne or the Bush* (1974).

WALLER, EDMUND (1606-1687): English poet, born in Buckinghamshire to a wealthy family; educated at Oxford; elected to Parliament at sixteen, but was sent into exile in 1643, after plotting to restore the monarchy (his oratorical skills, and the payment of a £10,000 fine, helped save his life); married a wealthy heiress in 1631, and after her death in 1634 unsuccessfully courted Lady Dorothy Sidney, whom his verse commemorates as "Sacharissa"; published his collected *Poems* (1645), then travelled to Italy with his friend, the diarist John EVELYN, before returning to England in 1652.

WALTON, IZAAK (1593-1683): English biographer and writer about fishing; born in Staffordshire, apprenticed to a London draper in 1618, eventually becoming a prosperous businessman; lived in DONNE's parish till 1643, became friends with him and with WOTTON and George HERBERT, all of whose biographies he subsequently wrote; married twice, Rachel Floud (d. 1640; grand-niece of Thomas Cranmer, the Archbishop of Canterbury) in 1626, and Ann Ken (d. 1662; a half-sister of Thomas Ken, at one time a royal chaplain) in 1647; moved to Worcester and Winchester after the Restoration; a fishing friend of COTTON; best known for his classic book on fishing, *The Compleat Angler* (1653; expanded in subsequent editions).

WARTON, JOSEPH (1722-1800): English poet and critic, born in Surrey, son of the scholar-poet Thomas Warton (1688-1745) and brother of the poet Thomas Warton the younger (1728-1790); educated at Basingstoke (where his father was master and Gilbert WHITE was a contemporary) and at Oxford; ordained, 1744; became a teacher and cleric at Winchester, 1755, where BOWLES was one of his pupils; like his brother, mixed with JOHNSON, REYNOLDS, Garrick, and BURKE in the Literary Club; in 1748 married Mary Daman (d. 1772) and in 1773 married Charlotte Nicholas (d. 1809); published *Odes* (1746), but was best known in his own day for his translations of Virgil (1753) and his 2-volume *Essay on Pope* (1756, 1782).

WATTS, ISAAC (1674-1748): English Nonconformist hymn-writer, born in Southampton, the eldest of nine children of a clothier; educated at the Dissenters' Academy in Stoke Newington, becoming a pastor in London in 1702, and achieving fame as a preacher till ill health forced him to retire in 1712; collections of hymns include *Horae Lyricae* (1705), *Hymns and Spiritual Songs* (1707), *The Psalms of David Imitated* (1719), and the first book of hymns for children, *Divine Songs* (1715).

WEBB, PHYLLIS (b.1927): Canadian poet, born in Victoria, educated (in English and philosophy) at the U. of British Columbia (where she later taught) and at McGill (where she worked with the poet Louis Dudek, b. 1918); influenced by BIRNEY, F.R. SCOTT, LIVESAY, PAGE, John Thompson (1938-1976; for his use of the Arabic poetic form called the *ghazal*), RICH, and others; interested in the ideas underlying the concept of social democracy, and ran as a political candidate; worked as a CBC producer and broadcaster, 1964-69, before settling on Saltspring Island, B.C.; publications include *The Sea Is Also a Garden* (1962), *Naked Poems* (1965), *The Vision Tree* (1982), and *Water and Light* (1984).

WEBSTER, JOHN (c.1578-c.1632): English playwright and sketch writer, about whom little is known; author of two significant Jacobean tragedies, *The White Devil* (c.1612) and *The Duchess of Malfi* (c.1613); wrote at least one of the sketches collected in OVERBURY's *Characters* (1614); collaborated with several other playwrights of the time, including DEKKER, Thomas Heywood (1573-1641), Thomas Middleton (c.1580-1627), and William Rowley (c.1585-1626).

WEEKES, NATHANIEL (c.1730-after 1775): Barbados-born poet about whom little is known; author of several works, including *On the Abuse of Poetry* (1752), *Barbados* (1754), *The Choice of a Husband, an Epistle to a Young Lady* (1754), *The Angel and the Curate* (1765; a satire), and *The Messiah, A Sacred Poem* (1775).

WELDON, FAY (BIRKINSHAW) (b.1933): English novelist, playwright, and cultural commentator, born in Worcestershire, brought up in New Zealand and London; educated at U. of St. Andrews; worked as an advertising copywriter; a single mother by 1955, married Ronald Weldon, 1960, settling in Somerset in 1976; author of a critical appreciation of Rebecca WEST, numerous satiric renderings of contemporary society (particularly the war between the sexes), as in *Female Friends* (1975) and *The Life and Loves of a She-Devil* (1983), and a testament to cultural values, *Letters to Alice on First Reading Jane Austen* (1984).

WELLER, ARCHIE (b.1957): Australian aboriginal poet and fiction writer, born in Subiaco, Western Australia, raised on a farm; trained as a printer in East Perth; author of *The Day of the Dog* (1981) and *Going Home* (1986).

WESLEY, CHARLES (1707-1788): English hymn-writer and evangelist, born in Lincolnshire, educated at Oxford, where in 1729 he founded a group called the Oxford methodists, joined later by his brother John Wesley (1703-1791); both brothers were ordained in the Church of England (John in 1728, Charles in 1735), and both went on a mission to convert the Indians in the American colony of Georgia, 1735-38 (accompanying James Oglethorpe, 1696-1785, the colony's leader), during which they were themselves influenced by Moravian missionaries; returning to London in 1738, both converted from Anglicanism, with John Wesley founding the first Methodist chapel in 1739, breaking with the Moravians in 1745, the Calvinists in 1770, arguing theology with TOPLADY, and acquiring an extraordinary reputation as a preacher; Charles married Sarah Gwynne, 1749 (John married Mary Vazeille, 1751; she left him in 1776); both composed numerous hymns, which John Wesley edited, and both kept personal journals, Charles Wesley's being posthumously published (1849).

WEST, REBECCA [CICILY ISABEL FAIRFIELD] (1892-1983): British journalist, novelist, and travel writer, born in County Kerry, Ireland; educated at George Watson's Ladies' College, Edinburgh; after a brief career as an actress (she took her pseudonym from the name of the heroine of Henrik Ibsen's 1886 play *Rosmersholm*), she began writing (in 1911) for *Freewoman* and other journals; a liaison with the novelist H.G. Wells (1866-1946) between 1912 and the 1920s led to the birth of a son, the writer Anthony West (b. 1914); married Henry Maxwell Andrews, a banker, 1930; wrote several novels and political commentaries; awarded a DBE; publications include *Black Lamb and Grey Falcon: A Journey through Yugoslavia* (1941).

WHARTON, ANNE (LEE) (1659-1685): English poet and dramatist, an orphan from birth; married, 1673, to Thomas Wharton (1648-1714; he became an earl in 1706 and was made Thomas, 1st

Marquis of Wharton in 1708; Whig politician, Lord-Lieutenant of Ireland, 1708-10, and author of the anti-Catholic song "Lilliburlero"); her poems and plays, which drew on Ovid as a recurrent source and praised BEHN and others, were mostly published posthumously, as in *A Collection of Poems* (1693).

WHEATLEY (PETERS), PHILLIS (c.1753-1784): American poet, born in Africa, shipped as a slave to Boston, 1761, and sold to Susanna and John Wheatley (a tailor); educated (in English, Latin, and Greek) with the Wheatleys' daughter; sent by them on a visit to London in 1772, where she published *Poems on Various Subjects, Religious and Moral* (1773) and was both lionized and criticized; freed from slavery when she returned to Massachusetts, married John Peters, 1778; died in poverty.

WHITE, E[LWYN] B[ROOKS] (1899-1985): American essayist, humorist, and children's writer, born in Mount Vernon, New York; educated at Cornell; became a contributing editor to *The New Yorker* in 1926 (where he associated with THURBER and with him wrote *Is Sex Necessary*, 1929) and a regular contributor to *Harper's*, 1938-43; in 1929 married Katherine Angell (d. 1977), a *New Yorker* editor; noted for his revision of a style manual by William Strunk, Jr., *The Elements of Style* (1959), and for his children's books—which include *Stuart Little* (1945) and *Charlotte's Web* (1952)—as well as for his essays; collections of sketches, editorials, and other comments include *One Man's Meat* (1942), *The Points of My Compass* (1962), and the selected *Poems and Sketches* (1981).

WHITE, GILBERT (1720-1793): English clergyman and naturalist, born in Selborne, Hampshire, eldest son of eleven children; educated at Oxford, where he taught until returning to Selborne as a curate in 1758; friend of Joseph WARTON; corresponded with Sir Joseph Banks (1744-1820), the botanist who accompanied Captain James Cook (1728-1779) on his 1768-71 voyage round the world; kept a journal about local nature, published in 1789 as *The Natural History and Antiquities of Selborne*.

WHITMAN, WALT (1819-1892): American poet and prose writer, born on Long Island, one of ten children, raised in Brooklyn, where he became apprenticed to a printer; from 1841 on, edited and wrote (conventionally) for several papers; became a force for more radical social change after visiting New Orleans in 1848, reading the Transcendentalists [see EMERSON], and confronting at first hand (as a field nurse, after 1862) the effects of the Civil War; *Leaves of Grass* (1855), examining himself, individuality, and democratic idealism, was successively expanded in the editions of 1856, 1860, 1871, and 1891-2, which incorporated such other publications as *Democratic Vistas* (1871); attacked for immorality, defended by SWINBURNE and others, became a *cause célèbre* in the 1870s; suffered a stroke and retired to Camden, New Jersey, 1873; friend of the Canadian "medical mystic" Richard Maurice Bucke (1837-1902), whom he visited in Ontario in 1880; an 18-volume edition of *The Collected Writings of Walt Whitman* began appearing in 1961.

WHITTIER, JOHN GREENLEAF (1807-1892): American poet, born in Massachusetts to a Quaker farming family; educated largely by his own reading, in BURNS and others; apprenticed to the newspaper trade, where he absorbed the Abolitionist principles of the newspaper owner, William Lloyd Garrison (1805-1879); edited various papers, including *National Era* (1847-60), contributing anti-slavery poems and articles as well as various writings about New England history and life;

among his many collections are *Poems* (1849), *Home Ballads, Poems and Lyrics* (1860), *In War Time and Other Poems* (1864), and *Snow-Bound* (1866).

WILBUR, RICHARD (b.1921): American poet and translator, born in New York City, educated at Amherst and Harvard, where he first taught (19950-54); married Mary Ward, 1942; soldier during World War II; taught at Wesleyan U. after 1955; author of *Things of This World* (1956), which won the Pulitzer Prize, and several other collections, as well as children's verse, essays on poetry (*Responses*, 1976), translations of Molière, and a comic opera based on *Candide* (1957; in collaboration with the playwright Lillian Hellman, 1905-1984).

WILDE, OSCAR (1854-1900): Irish playwright, wit, and fiction writer, born in Dublin to the journalist Lady Jane Francesca Wilde (1820-1896) and Sir William Wilde (1815-1876), a physician who collected Irish folktales; educated at Trinity College (Dublin) and Oxford, where he won the Newdigate Prize in poetry; moved to London, becoming notorious for his commitment (through fashion as well as literary practice) to the Aesthetic Movement (see PATER); married Constance Lloyd, 1884, writing *The Happy Prince and Other Tales* (1888) for his two sons; established his literary reputation with a novel, *The Picture of Dorian Gray* (1890) [see John GRAY], and several plays, including *Lady Windermere's Fan* (1892) and *The Importance of Being Earnest* (1894); after an unsuccessful libel suit against the Marquess of Queensberry (father of his friend Lord Alfred Douglas, 1870-1945), was tried and sentenced to two years' hard labour (1895-97) for committing homosexual acts; imprisonment led to *The Ballad of Reading Gaol* (1898) and *De Profundis* (1905; a bitter rebuke of Douglas); settled in Paris after his release, adopting the name "Sebastian Melmoth" (from the 1820 Gothic novel *Melmoth the Wanderer* by Charles Maturin, 1782-1824).

WILLIAMS, HELEN MARIA (1762-1827): English poet, novelist, and letter writer, born in London, raised in Scotland; adopted radical stances in politics, expressed in her poems on the slave trade (1788 and 1823), a novel, *Julia* (1790), adapting the ideas of Rousseau to unconventional marital relationships, and various sympathetic accounts of the French Revolution, as in her several collections of *Letters* (published from 1790 on), based on her own observations; lived with John Hurford Stone, whom she may have married in 1794; was imprisoned in France during the Terror; died in Paris.

WILLIAMS, WILLIAM CARLOS (1883-1963): American poet and physician of English and Puerto Rican descent, born in Rutherford, New Jersey, where he practised pediatric medicine after 1909; educated at U. of Pennsylvania (a contemporary of DOOLITTLE and POUND) and in Leipzig; married Florence Herman, 1912; noted for his command of American vernacular rhythms, as in such collections as *Kora in Hell: Improvisations* (1920), *Pictures from Brueghel and Other Poems* (1962; winner of the Pulitzer Prize), and the multi-volume poem *Paterson* (1946-63); other publications include volumes of essays and short stories, four novels, several plays, and an autobiography (1951).

WILMOT, JOHN: see Earl of ROCHESTER.

WINCHILSEA, COUNTESS OF: see Anne FINCH.

WINTERS, YVOR (1900-1968): American critic and poet, born in Chicago; raised in California, moving to Santa Fe, New Mexico, in

1918, to combat tuberculosis; educated at U. of Chicago, U. of Colorado, and Stanford, where he taught English after 1928; married Janet Lewis, 1926; corresponded with Marianne MOORE; wrote critical books about E.A. ROBINSON, obscurity, and literary form, as in *Forms of Discovery* (1973); published several volumes of poetry from 1921 on, his *Collected Poems* (1952, enlarged 1960) winning a Bollingen Prize.

WITHER, GEORGE (1588-1667): English poet, born in Hampshire, educated at Oxford; wrote pastoral and religious verse, as in *Shepherds Hunting* (1617) and *Emblemes* (1634); imprisoned twice for writing satires, including *Abuses Stript and Whipt* (1613); became a Puritan, rising to the rank of major-general in the Civil War; imprisoned again (1661-63) after the Restoration, losing both rank and property.

WOLLSTONECRAFT (GODWIN), MARY (1759-1797): English novelist and essayist, born in London, raised on several farms in England and Wales; largely self-taught (resentful of the social disparity that granted boys an education but not girls), leading to *Thoughts on the Education of Daughters* (1787), her first book; worked as a ladies' companion, governess, translator, reviewer, and editorial assistant with a London publishing firm, through which she met BLAKE, PAINE, William Godwin (1756-1836), and other Rational Dissenters; questioned the institution of marriage and other seemingly fixed conventions affecting women, compiling *The Female Reader* (1789); responded to BURKE (before PAINE did) by writing *A Vindication of the Rights of Man* (1790), followed by *A Vindication of the Rights of Woman* (1792); lived in France, 1792-96, for part of the time with the American novelist Gilbert Imlay (1754-1828), giving birth to a daughter, Fanny; returned to England, after twice attempting suicide, and published a novel, *Maria, or The Wrongs of Woman* (1797); married William Godwin, 1797; died ten days after the birth of their daughter Mary (later Mary Shelley [see P.B. SHELLEY]), from an infection that was likely introduced by her doctor's unclean hands.

WOOLF, VIRGINIA (STEPHEN) (1882-1941): English novelist, essayist, diarist, journalist, and sketch writer, born in London, daughter of the critic Sir Leslie Stephen (1832-1904, author of *Hours in a Library*, 1874-79, and editor of the *Dictionary of National Biography*; he was the model for both Mr Ramsay in Woolf's novel *To the Lighthouse*, 1927, and Vernon Whitford in MEREDITH's *The Egoist*) and his second wife, Julia (his first wife, Harriet, was the daughter of the novelist William Makepeace Thackeray, 1811-1863); educated at home; suffered a breakdown in 1895 (reacting both to her mother's death and to the abuse she suffered from her elder half-brother); after her father's death, moved to a house in the Bloomsbury district of London, a meetingplace for writers and artists (Cambridge-centred, later known as the Bloomsbury Group), who came to include Virginia, Thoby, Vanessa, and Adrian Stephen, along with FORSTER, the biographer Lytton Strachey (1880-1932), the economist John Maynard Keynes (1883-1946), the art critic Clive Bell (1881-1964; who married Vanessa, 1907), and the novelist and autobiographer Leonard Woolf (1880-1969; who married Virginia, 1912); suffered another breakdown after her brother Thoby's death (from typhoid fever) in 1906; with Leonard, established the Hogarth Press in 1917, which published some of her own stories as well as works by MANSFIELD, RIDING, and T.S. ELIOT; reviewed for *The Times Literary Supplement* from 1905 on, and published several critical essays, including those in *The Common Reader* (1925), *The Second Common Reader* (1932), and the important feminist collections *A Room of One's Own* (1929), based on lectures she gave at Girton College, Cambridge, and *Three Guineas* (1937);

close friend of the biographer and garden designer Vita Sackville-West (1892-1962; wife of the diplomat Sir Harold Nicolson, 1886-1968), to whom her novel *Orlando* (1928) is dedicated; other fictions include *Mrs Dalloway* (1925), *To the Lighthouse* (1927), and *The Waves* (1931); depressed by the onset of World War II, she drowned herself by walking into the River Ouse.

WORDSWORTH, DOROTHY (1771-1855): English poet and diarist, born in Cumberland, sister to William WORDSWORTH; raised by relatives after her mother's death (1778), reunited with her brother in 1794, becoming his lifelong companion and, often, his inspiration; closely observed people and nature, as her *Letters* and the *Journals* (edited in the 20th century) indicate; author of several journals describing their travels together, including *A Tour Made in Scotland* (1874); was praised by COLERIDGE, Thomas De Quincey (1785-1859), and others, for simplicity and innocence; suffered from declining health (probably Alzheimer's Disease) after 1829.

WORDSWORTH, WILLIAM (1770-1850): English poet and critic, born in Cumberland, third of four sons of an attorney, and brother to Dorothy WORDSWORTH; educated at Cambridge and on summer walking tours to the Continent; celebrated Helen Maria WILLIAMS in his first published poem (1787); visited France, 1791, where his affair with Annette Vallon produced a daughter (b. 1792); returned to England, 1792 (the year his *Descriptive Sketches* appeared), torn between English patriotism and French revolutionary fervour; met COLERIDGE, c.1795, a friendship (later disrupted) that led to *Lyrical Ballads* (1798; enlarged, with an extensive preface, 1800); moved with his sister to Dove Cottage, Grasmere, 1799, and in 1802 travelled with her to visit Annette Vallon before marrying Mary Hutchinson; settled in Ambleside, 1813; other publications include *Poems in Two Volumes* (1807), *The Excursion* (1814), and *Yarrow Revisited* (1835), the last describing some of his many tours, though by his later years he had become personally and politically more conventional; named Poet Laureate, 1843; a 13-book version of *The Prelude, or, Growth of a Poet's Mind* (unpublished in his own day, and in manuscript called "Poem to Coleridge") was complete by 1805, expanded to 14 books by 1839, and published posthumously, 1850, given its title by the poet's widow.

WOTTON, SIR HENRY (1568-1639): English poet and diplomat, born in Kent, educated in Oxford; travelled in Europe for seven years before becoming secretary to the Earl of Essex, 1595; subsequently negotiated political agreements between the Duke of Florence and James VI of Scotland, who knighted him after succeeding to the English throne; ambassador to Venice, 1604, and to the German princes; returned to England in 1624, and was made provost of Eton; friend of DONNE and of WALTON, who prefaced a biography to Wotton's posthumously collected writings, *Reliquiae Wottonianae* (1651).

WRIGHT, JAMES [ARLINGTON] (1927-1980): American poet, born in Ohio, educated at Kenyon College, where he was a student of RANSOM, and U. of Washington, where he was a student of ROETHKE; taught at Hunter College in New York, 1966-80; married Edith Runk, 1967; began to publish in 1957, his *Collected Poems* (1971) winning a Pulitzer Prize; subsequent volumes included *This Journey* (1982); died of cancer.

WRIGHT, JUDITH (b.1915): Australian poet, anthologist, and critic, born in New South Wales, educated at Sydney U.; married, 1948, the freelance journalist Jack McKinney (1891-1966);

publications include *Woman to Man* (1949), *The Other Half* (1966), *Collected Poems* (1971), and the critical volume *Preoccupations in Australian Poetry* (1965); noted also for her history of her pastoral family, *The Generations of Men* (1959), and for her work as a conservationist and on behalf of the Aboriginal peoples, as expressed in *The Cry for the Dead* (1981).

WROTH, LADY MARY (SIDNEY) (c.1587-c.1652): English poet and prose writer, daughter of Barbara (Gamage) and Sir Robert Sidney (later Earl of Leicester), niece of the poets Sir Philip SIDNEY and the Countess of PEMBROKE; educated privately; acted in court masques, and was the dedicatee of JONSON's *The Alchemist* (1610); married Sir Robert Wroth (1604), and after his death (1614) had two children by her lover (her cousin, William Herbert, 3rd Earl of Pembroke and Montgomery [see also SHAKESPEARE]); in 1621 published *The Countesse of Montgomerie's Urania*, a prose romance that was bound with a sonnet sequence, *Pamphilia to Amphilanthus*.

WYATT, SIR THOMAS (1503-1542): English poet and diplomat, born in Kent, educated at Cambridge; married Elizabeth Brooke, c.1520 (separated c.1527); undertook several political missions for Henry VIII (to Venice, the papal court, Spain, and Calais); knighted, 1535, but was twice imprisoned (1536, 1541) when the king suspected him of personal disloyalty; retired to Kent, 1542; some of his poems, along with SURREY's, appeared in *Tottel's Miscellany* (1557), while others remained in manuscript till the 19th century.

WYCLIF (or WYCLIFFE), JOHN (c.1330-1384): English priest and translator of the Bible, born in Yorkshire (some scholars date his birth as early as 1320); educated at Oxford, where he taught and became Master of Balliol College, 1360-61; left to become a parish priest and court ambassador to papal delegations; questioned Catholic dogma (e.g., indulgences, absolution, and transubstantiation), winning public support but papal opposition; after 1378, began to write in English (rather than Latin), translating part of the New Testament and organizing a group of itinerant preachers (most of whom were forced to recant their stated beliefs in 1382) whose ideas developed into the movement known as Lollardy (or Lollardry) [see KEMPE], which lasted into the 16th century.

YAP, ARTHUR (CHOR HIONG) (b.1943): poet, critic, and painter, born in Singapore; educated at University of Singapore (where he now teaches language and literature) and University of Leeds; author of several books of poetry, including *Only Lines* (1971) and *Man Snake Apple and Other Poems* (1986), and *A Brief Critical Survey of Prose Writings in Singapore and Malaysia* (1972).

YEATS, WILLIAM BUTLER (1865-1939): Irish poet and dramatist, born in Dublin, the son of the painter John Butler Yeats (1839-1922); educated in London and Dublin as an art student in the 1880s, meeting the novelist George Moore (1852-1933) and becoming interested in hermeticism and Irish nationalism; helped found the Rhymers' Club in London in 1887 (see SYMONS), the Irish Literary Theatre in London in 1899 (with Moore), and the Abbey Theatre in Dublin in 1904 (with Lady GREGORY, who was to become his neighbour, and the playwright John Millington Synge, 1871-1909); for years he courted Maud Gonne, but she would not marry him (in 1903 she married John MacBride instead); in 1912 met POUND, who became his fencing master and secretary; married Georgie Hyde-Lees, 1917; won the Nobel Prize, 1923; died in France; publications include *The Celtic Twilight* (1893), *Cathleen Ni Houlihan* (1902, a play), *The Wild Swans at Coole* (1919), *Michael Robartes and the Dancer* (1921), *A Vision* (1925), *The Tower* (1928), *The Winding Stair* (1933), and several volumes of letters and autobiography.

YOUNG, EDWARD (1683-1765): English poet, born in Hampshire to a clergyman's family; educated at Oxford; attempted a career as a playwright before becoming a Hertfordshire clergyman; married Lady Elizabeth Lee, daughter of the Earl of Lichfield, 1731, and after her death (1740) began *The Complaint, or, Night-Thoughts on Life, Death and Immortality* (1742-46), which attracted the attention of the Bluestocking Circle (see Hannah MORE), JOHNSON, and others; because of this poem, which was extremely popular in its own day, he is associated with a group of poets who came to be known as the Graveyard School, including Robert Blair (1699-1746), author of *The Grave* (1743), Thomas Parnell (1679-1718), author of "A Night-Piece on Death" (1721), and Thomas GRAY.

APPENDIX II
CHRONOLOGY

History, Politics, Science	Date	Literature, Philosophy, Culture
	B.C.	
Earliest records of human habitation in Asia, Africa, Australia, Europe, and America	c.500,000-c.30,000	
c.4000-1000: Sumerian (Mesopotamia), Egyptian, Indus Valley, and Minoan (Crete) civilizations	c.3000	Cuneiform writing; papyrus
	c.2500	*Instructions of Ptahhotep*, on manners (Egypt)
Labyrinthine palace at Knossos (Crete)	c.2000	Babylonian *Epic of Gilgamesh*
	c.1750	Hammurabi codifies laws of Amorites
Shang dynasty, China	c.1600	Phoenicians develop phonetic alphabet
c.1375-1200: Akhenaton and Nefertiti, Tutankhamun, Seti I, Ramses II, III rule Egypt; Etruscans	c.1250	Moses leads exodus from Egypt; Trojan War
	c.1200	Sanskrit *Rig Veda*
Chou dynasty, China; Teotihuacan founded, Mexico	c.1000	King David of Israel writes *Psalms*
Solomon builds temple in Jerusalem	c.950	Solomon fosters religious writings, later Old Testament
Phoenicians found Carthage	c.800	Homer, *Iliad*, *Odyssey*
753: Romulus founds Rome	776	First recorded Olympic games
Byzantium founded	7thC-6thC	Thales; Zoroaster; Lao Tzu; *Upanishads*
597: Nebuchadnezzar exiles Israelites to Babylon	6thC	Anaximander; Anaximines; Sappho of Lesbos
c.590: Solon introduces legal reforms in Athens	6thC-5thC	Siddartha Gautama (the Buddha); Confucius; Pythagoras
510: Foundation of Roman Republic	5thC	Anaxagoras; Heraclitus; Empedocles; Protagoras; Parmenides; Democritus; Zeno the Eleatic
490: Battle of Marathon: Greeks defeat Darius		
479: Greeks defeat Xerxes at Salamis and Plataea		
Pericles rules in Athens (-429)	462	Pindar, fourth *Pythian Ode*
	458	Aeschylus, *Oresteia*
	447-432	Building of Parthenon
Peloponnesian War: Sparta defeats Athens (-404)	431	Euripides, *Medea*; Sophocles, *Oedipus Tyrannus*
	414	Aristophanes, *The Birds*; 411, *Lysistrata*
	c.405	Thucydides, *Peloponnesian War*
Great Wall of China begun (-204 B.C.)	c.400	

History, Politics, Science	*Date*	*Literature, Philosophy, Culture*
401-399: Xenophon's expedition (*Anabasis*)	399	Trial and death of Socrates
	397	Pentateuch completed
	c.387	Plato founds the Academy
	384-322	Aristotle
Alexander the Great invades Asia	334	
	4thC-3rdC	Diogenes (Cynics); Epicurus; Menander
Euclid, *Elements*	c.300	*Mahabharata* begun (to A.D. 300)
221-210: Shih Huang Ti, China's "First Emperor"	3rdC	Ashoka establishes Buddhism in India
287-212: Archimedes	c.276	Theocritus, *Idyl XVI*
Punic Wars: Rome defeats Carthage	264-146	264: First Roman gladiatorial games (to A.D. 325)
	c.200	*Ramayana* begun (to A.D. 200)
Hannibal crosses Alps and invades Italy	218	
Romans take over Palestine	190	
Judas Maccabeus leads Jewish revolt vs Romans	166	
	c.100	Chinese have invented paper
	c.84-54	Catullus
56-49: Julius Caesar conquers Gaul, briefly invades Celtic Britain; Cleopatra rules Egypt	c.55	Lucretius, *De Rerum Natura*
	c.50	*Bhagavad-Gita* composed
44: Julius Caesar assassinated	46	Cicero, *De Oratore*
40: Romans make Herod king of the Jews	42-19	Virgil, *Eclogues*, *Aeneid*
27: Augustus Caesar first emperor of Rome	23-13	Horace, *Odes*
	A.D.	
	c.8	Ovid, *Metamorphoses*
30: Jesus crucified	c.33	Paul (Saul) begins missionary writings
61: Boadicea leads uprising against Romans	c.50	*On the Sublime*; New Testament books begun
64: Half of Rome burns; Nero emperor (54-68)	66	Death of Petronius (*Satyricon*)
79: Eruption of Vesuvius, buries Pompeii, Herculaneum	77	Pliny the Elder, *Natural History*
	c.93	Josephus, *Antiquities of the Jews*
c.122-127: Building of Hadrian's Wall	c.100-180	Writings of Juvenal, Tacitus, Suetonius, Ptolemy, Pausanias, Marcus Aurelius
Classic Mayan civilization begins, city of Tikal	c.300	Porphyry edits Plotinus (Neoplatonism)
Constantine the Great emperor of Rome (306-337)	313	Edict of Milan: toleration of all creeds, including Christianity
Huns invade Europe from Asia	c.372	

History, Politics, Science	Date	Literature, Philosophy, Culture
Goths use cavalry, defeat Romans at Hadrianopolis	378	
Chrysostom patriarch of Constantinople (-404)	398	Theodosius destroys library at Alexandria
410: Visigoths sack Rome; Romans leave Britain	c.413	St. Augustine, *The City of God*; Plutarch's *Lives*
Angles, Saxons, Jutes begin invading Britain	c.450	St. Patrick converts Ireland to Christianity
Death of Attila the Hun; Vandals sack Rome (455)	453	
481-511: King Clovis rules the Franks	5thC-7thC	Composition of *Beowulf*, *The Wanderer*, and other Old English works
493-526: Theodoric rules Ostrogoth Italy		
A historical King Arthur reigns; Chinese using powder for firecrackers; Khmer empire begins	6thC	the *Talmud* is completed; chess played in India
529: Justinian's codification of Roman law	c.524	Boëthius, *Consolation of Philosophy* (in Latin)
535-554: Belisarius conquers Italy for Justinian	532-537	Building of Hagia Sophia mosque (Constantinople)
542: Plague enters Europe (England 547), kills about half the population before ending in 594		
	563	St. Columba takes Christianity to Britain
618-906: T'ang dynasty, China	611	Mohammed's revelation from Allah; 625ff., *Koran*
Hegira (622), marking year 1 in Muslim calendar	c.660	Caedmon, first English poet known by name, *Hymns*
634-711: Moslems invade Syria, Palestine, India, N. Africa, Constantinople, Spain,	c.700	*Lindisfarne Gospels*
	701-762	Chinese poet Li Po; 712-70: Chinese poet Tu Fu
710-794: Nara period in Japan	731	Bede's *History* of the English people
Arabic science begins to flourish; Machu Picchu	8thC	*Book of Kells*; Cynewulf and other writers active
786-809: Reign of Haroun al-Rashid	c.781	Alcuin's literary and educational revival
Danes (Vikings) begin raiding England	787	
Charlemagne crowned first Holy Roman Emperor	800	
c.840: Danes found Dublin and Limerick	868	Oldest known printed book: Chinese, a Buddhist text (scroll form, sheets glued together)
c.850: Kenneth MacAlpin, first Scottish king		
Alfred the Great, king of Wessex	871-899	Alfred fosters literacy; translates Boëthius etc.
	891	*Anglo-Saxon Chronicle* (to 1154)
Viking explorers reach North America; Toltec civilization, Mexico; the Maori reach New Zealand; beginning of Nam Viet kingdom, Annam	10thC	*Greek Anthology*; 937, *Battle of Brunanburh*; 975, *Exeter Book*; 991, *Battle of Maldon*; c.992, Aelfric, *Catholic Homilies*, *Lives of the Saints*
Iceland's Althing—world's first parliament	c.930	
1016-35: Canute, king of England	11thC	*Chanson de Roland*, French epic poem
1040-57: Macbeth, king of Scots		Chinese invent movable type
	c.1020	Lady Murasaki, *The Tale of Genji*
Saxon rule restored; Edward the Confessor king	1042	

History, Politics, Science	Date	Literature, Philosophy, Culture
1066: Normans conquer England, rule to 1154	1065	Westminster Abbey consecrated
	12thC	Angkor Wat built; Leaning Tower of Pisa begun; Averroes (Ibn Rushd); Maimonides
	c.1100	First "miracle" play, "Play of St. Catherine"
Knights Templar founded, as Crusaders	1119	Univ. of Bologna founded; 1167, Oxford Univ.
Matilda, daughter of Henry I, claims English throne; civil war and anarchy, 1138-48	c.1136	Geoffrey of Monmouth, *History of the Kings of Britain*
Henry (Plantagenet) of Anjou marries Eleanor of Aquitaine	1152	
The Pope authorizes Henry II to conquer Ireland	1155	
Thomas à Becket murdered	1170	c.1180: Andreas Capellanus, *De Arte Honeste Amandi* (The Art of Courtly Love)
	1185	Saxo Grammaticus, *Historia Danica* (-1208)
Richard Lionheart joins 3rd Crusade, imprisoned	1190	
Inca culture emerges in Peru, Aztec in Mexico	c.1200	*King Horn*, *Beves of Hampton*, Layamon's *Brut*
Mongols (Genghis and Kublai Khan) invade China, Persia, Russia, Poland, Hungary, Burma; Inquisition begins; Crusades continue (-1291)	13thC	Rheims and Salisbury Cathedrals built; Guillaume de Lorris and Jean de Meun, *Roman de la Rose*; works of Roger Bacon
	1209	after riots at Oxford, students set up Cambridge
		St. Francis of Assisi begins his mission (-1226)
1215: King John signs the Magna Carta	1216	St. Dominic founds Dominicans (Order of Preachers)
Sundiata extends Mali Empire in West Africa	1235	
1266: Scots drive Norwegians out of the Hebrides	1267-73	St. Thomas Aquinas, *Summa Theologica*
	c.1300	*Havelok the Dane*; Marco Polo, *Travels*
The "Black Death," at worst in England in 1349, killing a third of population; the Hundred Years' War (1337-1453); Hanseatic League at its height; Tamerlane's campaigns in Asia	14thC	Paintings of Giotto; the Chester cycle of plays; *Mandeville's Travels*; *Sir Gawaine and the Green Knight*; *The Pearl*; Boccaccio, *Decameron*; Petrarch's poems; Langland, *Piers Plowman*
	1321	Dante Alighieri finishes *Divina Commedia*
1368: Tibet independent; Ming dynasty (-1644)	c.1370	Chaucer, *The Book of the Duchess*
1378: Great Schism, popes at Rome, Avignon (-1417)	c.1375	Barbour's *Bruce*
Wat Tyler leads the Peasants' Revolt	1381	Wyclif *et al.* translate Bible from Latin
	c.1386	Chaucer, *The Canterbury Tales* (-1400)
Scots win battle of Otterburn (Chevy Chase)	1388	Thomas Usk, *The Testament of Love*
Mohawk Confederacy established	1390	John Gower, *Confessio Amantis*
Glendwr's attempted Welsh rebellion (-1408)	1400	Jean Froissart, *Chronicles*
Russian state founded by Ivan III,"The Great"; Wars of the Roses (1455-85); Incas at the peak of their power;	15thC	Wakefield play cycle; Medicis foster arts and learning in Florence; ART by van Eyck, Donatello, Fra Angelico,

History, Politics, Science	Date	Literature, Philosophy, Culture
Prince Henry the Navigator organizes Portuguese explorations in Africa; Chinese make several voyages of exploration westward		Rogier van der Weyden, Masaccio, Lippi, Piero della Francesca, Bellini, Mantegna, Botticelli, Bosch, Leonardo da Vinci; MUSIC by Josquin des Prés
	1410	University of St. Andrews, Scotland's oldest
Henry V and archers win battle of Agincourt; Jan Hus burned at stake in Constance, for heresy	1415	February 14: Charles, Duke of Orléans, prisoner in Tower of London, sends wife a Valentine card
1431: Joan of Arc burned at Rouen for heresy	1440	Eton founded by royal charter, to educate poor
Ottoman Turks capture Constantinople	1453	The "Gutenberg Bible" (-1455)
	1465	Arakida Moritake, Japanese poet (d. 1533)
Spanish Inquisition established	1478	
Wars of the Roses end at Bosworth Field	1485	Caxton publishes Malory's *Le Morte Darthur*
Bartholomeu Dias rounds the Cape of Good Hope	1488	Skelton made poet laureate by Oxford Univ.
1492: Columbus reaches West Indies	1495	Leonardo da Vinci paints *The Last Supper* (-1498)
The Cabots reach a "new-founde-land"	1497	
Nanak founds Sikh religion	c.1500	*Everyman*, morality play from the Dutch
Black slaves taken to Portuguese and Spanish colonies in New World; height of Ottoman Empire under Suleiman the Magnificent; Cortes conquers Aztec Mexico; Spain takes control of Philippines; Hideyoshi unifies Japan	16thC	ART by Bosch, Leonardo da Vinci, Carpaccio, the Holbeins, Dürer, Cranach, Michelangelo, Giorgione, Raphael, Titian, Correggio, Cellini, the Bruegels, Tintoretto, Veronese, El Greco, Hilliard; MUSIC by Tallis, Palestrina, Byrd, Morley, Dowland
Machiavelli creates citizens' militia in Italy	1506	beginning of St. Peter's Church in Rome (-1626)
Henry VIII becomes king of England (-1547)	1509	Alexander Barclay, *The Ship of Fools*
1513: Balboa crosses Isthmus of Panama; Luther's "95 theses": Reformation begins	1516	More, *Utopia*
1519: Magellan begins world voyage;	1517	Machiavelli, *The Prince*
1526: Babar founds Mogul (Moghul) Empire in India	1525	Tyndale, *New Testament*, translated from the Greek
1529: Turks' advance into Europe stopped at Vienna	1528	Castiglione, *The Book of the Courtier* (tr. 1561)
c.1530: Copernicus's theory of heliocentrism		
1533: Francisco Pizarro executes the Inca of Peru	1531	Sir Thomas Elyot, *The Boke Named the Governour*
Henry VIII breaks with Rome; Church of England	1534	Society of Jesus (Jesuits) founded
Jacques Cartier's voyages to New World begin	1535	Miles Coverdale's complete English Bible
England annexes Wales	1536	John Calvin, *Institutes*; Ursuline order founded
	1540	Sir David Lindsay, *Satyre of the Thrie Estaitis*
1545-63: Council of Trent, Counter-Reformation	1549-52	*The Book of Common Prayer*
1547: Ivan the Terrible becomes first tsar	1557	*Songs and Sonnets* ("*Tottel's Miscellany*")
Elizabeth I, queen of England (-1603)	1558	
Presbyterian Church established	1560	

History, Politics, Science	Date	Literature, Philosophy, Culture
"39 Articles" as Church of England creed	1563	
c.1565: tobacco introduced to England	1567	Rugby School founded
Mercator's first map using his "projection"	1568	
Mary Queen of Scots imprisoned by Elizabeth	1569	
Battle of Lepanto, Turks defeated at sea	1571	
St. Bartholomew's Day Massacre, Paris	1572	Camoëns, *The Lusiads*
Frobisher begins search for Northwest Passage	1576	Gascoigne, *The Steel Glass: A Satire*
1577: Drake circumnavigates the world (-1580)	1578	John Lyly, *Euphues. The Anatomy of Wit*
	1579	Spenser, *The Shepheardes Calender*
	1580	Montaigne, *Essais* (-1588) Sidney, *The Countess of Pembroke's Arcadia*
Spanish Armada defeated	1588	"Martin Marprelate" tracts (-1589)
Galileo experiments with bodies in motion	1589	George Puttenham, *The Arte of English Poesie*
	1590	Lodge, *Rosalynde* Spenser, *The Fairie Queene* (-1596)
1592: English sack Cadiz	c.1590	Shakespeare, *The Comedy of Errors*
	1594	Marlowe, *Dr. Faustus* Nashe, *The Unfortunate Traveller*
Dutch begin colonizing East Indies	c.1595	Shakespeare, *A Midsummer Night's Dream*; *Romeo and Juliet*; *The Merchant of Venice*
Tycho Brahe writes on astronomy	1597	Bacon, *Essays* (1612, 1625)
	1599	Globe Theatre built; Shakespeare, *Henry V*
	c.1599	Shakespeare, *Julius Caesar*; *As You Like It*
East India Company established; Giordano Bruno burned in Rome as a heretic	1600	*England's Helicon*, collection of lyrical and pastoral poetry
Thirty Years' War (1618-48); English Civil War (1642-49); Dutch Wars (1652-54, 1664-67, 1672-78); further colonization of New World (Virginia, Massachusetts, Carolina, Rhode Island, Maryland, Nova Scotia, New Amsterdam, Bermudas, Quebec); rise of the Ashanti (Asante) in West Africa	17thC	ART by El Greco, the Bruegels, Caravaggio, Rubens, Hals, Poussin, Bernini, van Dyck, Velasquez, Claude, Rembrandt, Rosa, Murillo, Lely, Steen, Vermeer, Hobbema, Kneller; ARCHITECTURE by Jones, Wren; MUSIC by Byrd, Dowland, Monteverdi, Gibbons, Lully, Corelli, Purcell
The Poor Law Act	1601	Shakespeare, *Hamlet*; *Twelfth Night*
James I, king of England (VI, of Scots) (-1625)	1603	Dekker, *The Wonderful Year* (of the plague) Heywood, *A Woman Killed with Kindness*
The Gunpowder Plot (Guy Fawkes)	1605	Bacon, *The Advancement of Learning* Cervantes, *Don Quixote de la Mancha* (II, 1615)
	1606	Shakespeare, *King Lear*; *Macbeth*
Samuel de Champlain founds a colony at Quebec	1608	Captain John Smith, *A True Relation*

History, Politics, Science	Date	Literature, Philosophy, Culture
Henry Hudson explores Hudson's Bay	1610	Jonson, *The Alchemist*
	1611	The "King James" Bible Shakespeare, *The Tempest*
	1613	Webster, *The Duchess of Malfi*
John Napier invents logarithms	1614	
William Harvey writes of circulation of blood; Kepler announces third law of planetary motion; first black slaves arrive in America (Virginia)	1619	
	1621	Robert Burton, *The Anatomy of Melancholy*
	1623	Lope de Vega, *El mejor alcalde, el rey*
John Sibthorpe patents metal coal-fired range	1630	Taj Mahal constructed (-1648)
Inquisition makes Galileo deny heliocentrism	1633	Phineas Fletcher, *The Purple Island*
Tulipomania in Holland	1634	John Milton, *A Masque (Comus)* Richelieu founds the Académie française
	1636	Harvard College founded Pierre Corneille, *Le Cid*
	1640	"Bay Psalm Book" (first book printed in America)
English Civil War begins (-1649); Abel Tasman explores South Pacific, names New Zealand	1642	Theatres closed in England; Sir Thomas Browne, *Religio Medici* (-1643)
Louis XIV, king of France (-1715)	1643	Milton, *The Doctrine and Discipline of Divorce*
Manchu dynasty (-1912)	1644	René Descartes, *The Principles of Philosophy*
Charles I executed; Commonwealth declared	1649	Milton, *Tenure of Kings and Magistrates*
Archbishop Ussher calculates that Creation took place at 9 a.m. on 26 October, 4004 BC (-1654)	1650	Bradstreet, *The Tenth Muse Lately Sprung Up in America*
Charles II flees to France	1651	Hobbes, *Leviathan*
Dutch found Cape Colony	1652	
Oliver Cromwell becomes Lord Protector (-1658)	1653	Izaak Walton, *The Compleat Angler*
Restoration of Stuart monarchy; Royal Society	1660	Theatres reopen
Robert Boyle, *The Sceptical Chemist*	1661	Louis XIV begins reconstructions at Versailles
New France comes under direct French rule	1662	Michael Wigglesworth, *The Day of Doom*
Isaac Newton invents calculus, proposes theory of gravity; the Great Plague of London	1665	
The Great Fire of London	1666	Molière, *Le misanthrope*
	1667	Milton, *Paradise Lost*
	1668	La Fontaine, *Fables* (-1694)
Hudson's Bay Company incorporated	1670	Dryden, *The Conquest of Granada*; poet laureate
	1671	Milton, *Paradise Regained; Samson Agonistes*

History, Politics, Science	Date	Literature, Philosophy, Culture
Test Act (only Anglicans hold office) (-1828)	1673	
	1675	Wren starts new St. Paul's Cathedral (-1710) William Wycherley, *The Country Wife*
	1676	Sir George Etherege, *The Man of Mode*
	1677	Jean Racine, *Phèdre*
The "Popish Plot"	1678	Bunyan, *The Pilgrim's Progress* (-1684)
	1681	Dryden, *Absalom and Achitophel*
La Salle claims Louisiana for France; Peter the Great becomes Tsar (-1725)	1682	Thomas Otway, *Venice Preserved*
John III of Poland raises Turkish siege of Vienna	1683	
Louis XIV revokes Edict of Nantes (1598)	1685	
Newton, *Principia Mathematica*	1687	
The "Glorious Revolution" (also "Bloodless")	1688	Behn, *Oroonoko*
William and Mary rule England (-1702); French and Indian Wars (-1763); Toleration Act	1689	
Salem witchcraft trials and executions	1692	
	1693	Cotton Mather, *The Wonders of the Invisible World*
	1695	Congreve, *Love for Love*
	1697	William Dampier, *A New Voyage round the World* Charles Perrault, *Contes de ma mère l'Oye*
Great Northern War (1700-18); War of the Spanish Succession (1701-14); War of the Polish Succession (1733-35); War of Jenkins's Ear (1739-41); War of the Austrian Succession (1740-48); Seven Years' War (1756-63); Anglo-Mysore wars (1767-99); American Revolution (1775-83); Mahratta wars (1775-1818); French Revolution (1789-99); French Revolutionary Wars (1792-1802); Napoleonic Wars (1796-1815)	18thC	ART by Kneller, Watteau, Tiepolo, Hogarth, Canaletto, Ramsay, Reynolds, Stubbs, Gainsborough, Fragonard, West, Fuseli, Goya, David, Cozens, Flaxman, G. Stuart, Morland, ARCHITECTURE by Wren, Vanbrugh, Hawksmoor, Burlington, J. Stuart, Piranesi, Adam; MUSIC by Corelli, the Scarlattis, Couperin, Vivaldi, Telemann, Rameau, Handel, the Bachs, Pergolesi, Arne, Gluck, Haydn, Boccherini, Salieri, Clementi, Mozart; PLAYS by Rowe, Gay, Marivaux, Macklin, Farquhar, Fielding, Lillo, Frances Sheridan, Goldsmith, Richard Brinsley Sheridan
Captain Kidd hanged for piracy	1701	*The Daily Courant*, 1st English daily paper (-1735)
Battle of Blenheim; England takes Gibraltar; Alexander Selkirk voluntarily marooned in Pacific	1704	*Boston News-Letter*, first paper in America (-1776) Swift, *The Battle of the Books*; *A Tale of a Tub*
Act of Union (England and Scotland)	1707	Watts, *Hymns and Spiritual Songs*
	1710	Berkeley, *Treatise Concerning . . . Human Knowledge*
	1711	Pope, *An Essay on Criticism* Addison and Steele, *The Spectator* (-1712, 1714)
England's last execution for witchcraft	1712	Pope, *The Rape of the Lock* (1714, 1717)
House of Hanover accedes to English throne	1714	Bernard de Mandeville, *The Fable of the Bees* Henry Mill patents a typewriter

History, Politics, Science	Date	Literature, Philosophy, Culture
First Jacobite rebellion (last ends in 1746)	1715	
	1719	Defoe, *Robinson Crusoe*
"South Sea Bubble" bursts (company formed, 1711)	1720	
	1722	Defoe, *Journal of the Plague Year*; *Moll Flanders*
	1726	Swift, *Gulliver's Travels* Thomson, *The Seasons* (-1730)
	1728	Gay, *The Beggar's Opera*
At Oxford, the Wesleys found Methodism	1729	Franklin runs *The Pennsylvania Gazette* (-1766) Swift, *A Modest Proposal*
James Oglethorpe establishes colony of Georgia	1732	Pope, *An Essay on Man* (-1734)
John Kay patents his flying shuttle	1733	Franklin, *Poor Richard's Almanack* (-1758)
Carolus Linnaeus, *Systema naturae*	1735	John Peter Zenger acquitted of libel in newspaper
	1737	Theatre licensing and censorship act (-1843)
Frederick the Great, king of Prussia (-1786)	1740	Samuel Richardson, *Pamela, or Virtue Rewarded*
Vitus Bering claims Alaska for Russians	1741	J. Edwards, *Sinners in the Hands of an Angry God*
	1742	Fielding, *Joseph Andrews*
	1743	Robert Blair, *The Grave*
	1744	Eliza Haywood, *The Female Spectator* (-1746)
	1746	William Collins, *Odes*
	1748	David Hume, *Enquiry Concerning Human Understanding* Tobias Smollett, *The Adventures of Roderick Random* Thomson, *The Castle of Indolence*
	1749	Fielding, *The History of Tom Jones*
Franklin experiments with electricity (flies kite in 1752); Fielding proposes a police force	1751	Denis Diderot et al., *Encyclopédie* (-1772), inspired by Ephraim Chambers's English one (1728)
England adopts Gregorian Calendar	1752	Charlotte Lennox, *The Female Quixote*
	1753	British Museum established
Lisbon earthquake kills tens of thousands; Acadians deported to Louisiana	1755	Johnson, *A Dictionary of the English Language*
Clive's victories, British dominance in India	1757	Burke, *Sublime* (2nd ed., with essay on *Taste*)
Edmund Halley's comet returns as predicted	1758	Blackstone, *Commentaries on the Laws of England*
Plains of Abraham—Wolfe & Montcalm both killed	1759	Johnson, *Rasselas* Voltaire, *Candide*
James Cook maps the St. Lawrence	1760	Laurence Sterne, *Tristram Shandy* (-1767)
Catherine the Great, empress of Russia (-1796)	1762	Jean Jacques Rousseau, *Le contrat social*
Treaty of Paris cedes New France to England	1763	James Boswell meets Samuel Johnson

History, Politics, Science	Date	Literature, Philosophy, Culture
James Otis, *The Rights of the British Colonies*	1764	Horace Walpole, *The Castle of Otranto*
Stamp Act leads to protests by colonies	1765	Percy's *Reliques of Ancient English Poetry* (-1794)
Henry Cavendish discovers hydrogen	1766	Goldsmith, *The Vicar of Wakefield*
Cook begins exploration of Pacific (-1779)	1768	Reynolds first president of the Royal Academy
James Watt patents his improved steam engine	1769	Frances Brooke, *The History of Emily Montague*
	1771	*Encyclopaedia Britannica* first published Tobias Smollett, *The Expedition of Humphry Clinker*
The "Boston Tea Party"	1773	John Wesley, *Thoughts on Slavery*
Quebec Act guarantees French language in Canada; Warren Hastings first governor-general of India;	1774	Goethe, *The Sorrows of Young Werther* (1787)
Paul Revere's ride; Lexington and Concord	1775	
U.S Declaration of Independence, July 4; Bushnell's *Turtle* submersible attacks British	1776	Gibbon, *Decline & Fall of the Roman Empire* (-1788) Adam Smith, *The Wealth of Nations*
Joseph Bramah invents modern water closet	1778	Burney, *Evelina*
The Gordon Riots in London; Robert Fulton's submersible, the *Nautilus*	1779	Johnson, *The Lives of the Poets* (-1781) Earl of Derby holds first "Derby," at Epsom Downs
Herschel discovers Uranus	1781	Immanuel Kant, *Critique of Pure Reason*
Rama I founds new dynasty in Siam	1782	de Laclos, *Les Liaisons Dangereuses*
United Empire Loyalists leave U.S.A. for Canada; Montgolfier brothers demonstrate hot-air balloon	1783	George Crabbe, *The Village* Noah Webster's *Spelling Book*
Edmund Cartwright patents his power loom	1785	Cowper, *The Task*
	1786	William Beckford, *Vathek, an Arabian Tale*

England founds Sierre Leone for freed slaves; U.S.
  Constitution signed in Philadelphia; Fitch and Rumsey
  both demonstrate steamboats
	1787	Joel Barlow, *The Vision of Columbus*
		Alexander Hamilton et al., *The Federalist* (-1788)
		Bernardin de Saint Pierre, *Paul et Virginie*

England establishes penal colony in Australia	1788	*The Times* (*The Universal Daily Register*, 1785)

Bastille falls, 14 July: French Revolution begins; George
  Washington first U.S. president (-1797); mutiny aboard
  H.M.S. *Bounty*
	1789	Blake, *Songs of Innocence*
		William Hill Brown, *The Power of Sympathy*

The Nootka Convention	1790	Burke, *Reflections on the Revolution in France* Ellis Cornelia Knight, *Dinarbas* (sequel to *Rasselas*) Wollstonecraft, *A Vindication of the Rights of Men*

Vancouver explores NW coast of N. America (-1795);
  Toussaint leads slave revolt in Haiti (-1804); Luigi
  Galvani's theory of "animal electricity"
	1791	Boswell, *The Life of Samuel Johnson*
		Erasmus Darwin, *The Botanic Garden*

Denmark first nation to abolish slave trade	1792	*The Farmer's Almanac* Wollstonecraft, *A Vindication of the Rights of Woman*
Eli Whitney invents the cotton gin	1793	William Godwin, *Enquiry concerning Political Justice*
Kosciusko leads unsuccessful Polish uprising	1794	Ann Radcliffe, *The Mysteries of Udolpho*

History, Politics, Science	Date	Literature, Philosophy, Culture
Lime juice fed British sailors to prevent scurvy; James Hutton, *Theory of the Earth*	1795	Landor, *Poems* Hearne, *Journey to the Northern Ocean*
Edward Jenner proves smallpox vaccination works; Pierre Laplace, *Exposition du système du monde*	1796	Matthew G. "Monk" Lewis, *The Monk* Southey, *Joan of Arc*
Napoleon captures Rome and Egypt; French troops attempt to help Ireland against the English; England makes gold the standard currency	1798	Charles Brockden Brown, *Wieland* Malthus, *An Essay on the Principle of Population* Wordsworth and Coleridge, *Lyrical Ballads*
Napoleon assumes power in France; Alessandro Volta invents the battery	1799	Thomas Campbell, *The Pleasures of Hope* Mungo Park, *Travels in the Interior of Africa*
Act of Union (Great Britain and Ireland); British take Malta from the French; Davy, *Researches, Chemical and Philosophical*	1800	Library of Congress established Robert Owen's model community at New Lanark Maria Edgeworth, *Castle Rackrent*
Napoleonic Wars continue (to 1815); Emmet's rebellion in Ireland (1803); Peninsular War (1808-13); Latin American revolutions against Spain (1810-24); War of 1812 (-1815); Greek War of Independence (1822-29); rebellions in Upper and Lower Canada (1837); Afghan Wars (1838-42, 1879-80); Opium Wars (1839-42, 1856-58); Maori Wars (1843-48, 1860-70); Sikh Wars (1845-49); U.S. war vs. Mexico (1846-48); revolutions in Paris, Berlin, Vienna, Venice, Milan, Rome, Warsaw (1848-49); Tai Ping rebellion (1850-64); Crimean War (1853-56); Sepoy Mutiny (1857-58); Franco-Austrian War (1859-62); U.S. Civil War (1861-65); War of the Triple Alliance (S. America, 1865-70); Red River Rebellion (1869-70); Franco-Prussian War (1870-71); Russo-Turkish War (1877-78); Zulu War (1879); Pacific War (S. America, 1879-84); Boer Wars (1880-81, 1899-1902); 2nd Métis Rebellion (1885); Sino-Japanese War (1894-95); Cuban rebellion from Spain (1895-98); Spanish-American War (1898); Boxer Uprising (1900); Ashanti rebellion (1900)	19thC	ART by Goya, David, Flaxman, Stuart, Raeburn, Hokusai, Lawrence, Turner, Constable, Allston, Ingres, Géricault, Corot, Delacroix, Landseer, Daumier, Millet, Krieghoff, Watts, Courbet, Moreau, Hunt, Rossetti, Millais, Pissaro, Doré, Manet, Burne-Jones, Morris, Whistler, Degas, Fantin-Latour, Homer, Alma-Tadema, Sisley, Cézanne, Rodin, Monet, Morisot, Renoir, Rousseau, Eakins, Cassatt, Gauguin, Van Gogh, McCubbin, Sargent, Tom Roberts, Seurat, Sickert, Klimt, Signac, Munch, Toulouse-Lautrec, Kollwitz, Matisse, Beardsley; ARCHITECTURE by Pugin, Voysey; MUSIC by Haydn, Clementi, Beethoven, Paganini, von Weber, Meyerbeer, Rossini, Schubert, Donizetti, Bellini, Berlioz, the Strausses, Glinka, Mendelssohn, Chopin, Schumann, Liszt, Verdi, Wagner, Gounod, Offenbach, Franck, Smetana, Bruckner, Borodin, Brahms, Ponchielli, Saint-Saëns, Delibes, Bizet, Moussorgsky, Tchaikovsky, Dvorak, Sullivan, Massenet, Grieg, Rimsky-Korsakov, Fauré, d'Indy, Humperdinck, Sousa, Elgar, Leoncavallo, Puccini, Mahler, MacDowell, Debussy, Delius, Mascagni, Dukas, Sibelius, Scriabin, Schoenberg, Ravel
Thomas Jefferson, U.S. president (-1809)	1801	Sir Alexander Mackenzie, *Voyages from Montreal*
Peace of Amiens	1802	*The Edinburgh Review Founded* (-1929) Paley, *Natural Theology . . . Evidences of the Deity*
Louisiana Purchase	1803	
Lewis and Clark expedition to Oregon (-1806); Aaron Burr kills Alexander Hamilton in a duel	1804	Blake, *Jerusalem*; *Milton* Friedrich von Schiller, *Wilhelm Tell*
Battle of Trafalgar; Lord Nelson killed	1805	Scott, *The Lay of the Last Minstrel*
England abolishes the slave trade; Robert Fulton launches steamboat *Clermont*	1807	Charles and Mary Lamb, *Tales from Shakespeare*
U.S. prohibits importation of slaves	1808	Goethe, *Faust*, Part I (Part II, 1832)
Davy produces light from electric arcs	1809	Irving, *Knickerbocker's History of New York*

History, Politics, Science	Date	Literature, Philosophy, Culture
Prince of Wales becomes Regent for George III; Luddites smash factory machinery (-1812, 1816)	1811	Jane Austen, *Sense and Sensibility* Shelley, *The Necessity of Atheism*
Napoleon's march against and retreat from Moscow; Russian settlement at Fort Ross, Alta California	1812	Byron, *Childe Harold's Pilgrimage* (-1818) *Grimm's Fairy Tales* (-1815; English tr. 1823)
	1813	Jane Austen, *Pride and Prejudice*
Napoleon exiled to Elba; Congress of Vienna (-1815)	1814	Scott, *Waverley* Wordsworth, *The Excursion*
Battle of Waterloo; Napoleon exiled to St. Helena; Sir Humphry Davy's miner's safety lamp; Lamarck's *Histoire naturelle des animaux* (-1822); John McAdam introduces "macadamized" roads	1815	*The North American Review* (-1939)
Joseph Niepce makes photographic negative; Shaka founds Zulu nation	1816	Peacock, *Headlong Hall* Hegel finishes *Science of Logic* (1812-)
David Ricardo, *Political Economy and Taxation*; public flogging of females abolished in England	1817	Keats, *Poems*; Coleridge, *Biographia Literaria* *Blackwood's Magazine* (-1980)
Canadian-U.S. border established at 49th parallel	1818	Mary Shelley, *Frankenstein*
"Peterloo Massacre" at Manchester workers' rally; Factory Act bans children under 9 working in cotton mills, and those from 9-16, no more than 12 hours; Britain acquires Singapore	1819	Byron, *Don Juan* (-1824) Arthur Schopenhauer, *The World as Will and Idea* Scott, *Ivanhoe*
Oersted discovers electromagnetism; Malthus, *Principles of Political Economy*	1820	Irving, *Sketch Book*; Lamb, *Essays of Elia* (-1823) Maturin, *Melmoth the Wanderer* Shelley, *Prometheus Unbound*
Mexico wins independence from Spain; Michael Faraday's electric motor; James Mill, *Elements of Political Economy*	1821	Jean François Champollion deciphers Rosetta Stone Bryant, *Poems* Shelley, *Adonais*
Brazil wins independence from Portugal; Mary Mantell finds dinosaur bones near London	1822	De Quincey, *Confessions of an English Opium Eater* Clement Clarke Moore, "The Night Before Christmas"
Monroe Doctrine; *The Lancet* begins	1823	Rugby originated, at Rugby School
Simón Bolívar completes liberation of Venezuela, Ecuador, Colombia, Peru, and Bolivia from Spain	1824	Landor, *Imaginary Conversations* (-1829) Mitford, *Our Village* (-1832)
First steam railway, the Stockton and Darlington; Decembrist Revolt crushed in St. Petersburg	1825	Hazlitt, *The Spirit of the Age* Anthelme Brillat-Savarin, *Physiology of Taste*
University College, London; Zoological Society; Niepce makes first permanent photograph	1826	James Fenimore Cooper, *The Last of the Mohicans* Benjamin Disraeli, *Vivian Grey* (-1827)
Battle of Navarino	1827	John James Audubon, *The Birds of America* (-1838)
New corn laws (first in 1815) (-1846)	1828	Webster, *American Dictionary of English Language*
Catholics given full rights in England & Ireland; Sir Robert Peel's metropolitan police system	1829	First Oxford-Cambridge boat-race *La revue des deux mondes* begins Douglas Jerrold, *Black-Ey'd Susan*
Daniel Massey develops the threshing machine; Sir Charles Lyell, *Principles of Geology* (-1833)	1830	Stendhal (Marie Henri Beyle), *Le rouge et le noir* *Godey's Lady's Book* (-1898)

History, Politics, Science	Date	Literature, Philosophy, Culture
Voyage of H.M.S. *Beagle* (-1836); McCormick's reaper; Faraday's electric generator	1831	Aleksander Pushkin, *Eugene Onegin*
The Great Reform Act extends the franchise	1832	Frances Trollope, *Domestic Manners of The Americans*
Slavery ended throughout British Empire; Charles Babbage begins work on early kind of computer	1833	Carlyle, *Sartor Resartus* (-1834) Oxford Movement (Newman and others) (-1845)
Tolpuddle Martyrs transported to Australia; Spanish Inquisition abolished; Mary Somerville, *Connexion of the Physical Sciences*	1834	Honoré de Balzac, *Le Père Goriot* George Bancroft, *History of The United States* (-1876) Edward Bulwer-Lytton, *The Last Days of Pompeii*
Great Trek begins in South Africa (-1836); Samuel Colt invents the revolver; William Talbot takes first photograph on a paper negative	1835	Hans Christian Andersen, fairy tales (-1872) de Tocqueville, *Democracy in America* (-1839) Wordsworth, *Guide Through the Lake District*
The London Working Men's Association; Mexicans take Alamo; Texas gains independence	1836	Dickens, *Pickwick Papers* (-1837) Haliburton, *The Clockmaker* (1838, 1840) Captain Frederick Marryat, *Mr Midshipman Easy*
Victoria becomes Queen of England (-1901); Samuel F.B. Morse and others patent the telegraph; Louis Daguerre's daguerrotype	1837	Sir Isaac Pitman, *Stenographic Shorthand*
First ships cross Atlantic using steam alone; Public Record Office established	1838	First recorded baseball game, Beachville, Upper Canada
Treaty of Waitangi; Britain annexes New Zealand; Victoria weds Prince Albert of Saxe-Coburg-Gotha; penny post begins: first use of prepaid stamps; Act of Union joins Upper and Lower Canada	1840	Kew Gardens open Browning, *Sordello* Richard Henry Dana, *Two Years Before the Mast* Poe, *Tales of the Grotesque and Arabesque*
Britain occupies Hong Kong (-1997); Chemical Society and Pharmaceutical Society	1841	*Punch, or the London Charivari*, begins (-1992) James Fenimore Cooper, *The Deerslayer*
Mines Act: boys under 10 and females not allowed to work underground; inquiry into sanitation	1842	Macaulay, *Lays of Ancient Rome*
Britain annexes Natal; Thames Tunnel opens (begun 1824); Ethnological Society founded	1843	First commercially printed Christmas cards Carlyle, *Past and Present* Dickens, *A Christmas Carol* Ruskin, *Modern Painters* (-1860) Sören Kierkegaard, *Either-Or* Wordsworth made poet laureate
	1844	Benjamin Disraeli, *Coningsby* Alexandre Dumas, *Le Comte de Monte Cristo* Toronto *Globe* begins (1872, *Globe and Mail*)
Irish potato crop fails — famine begins (-1851); Robert W. Thompson invents pneumatic tire	1845	François-Xavier Garneau, *Histoire du Canada* (-1848) Poe, *The Raven*
Corn Laws repealed; Oregon Treaty; Mormons go west (-1847); Elias Howe invents sewing machine	1846	Edward Lear, *A Book of Nonsense* (-1870) Melville, *Typee*
Liberia declared independent (colonized by freed U.S. slaves since 1821); Factory Act (10-hour day for women and for children under 18); Hermann Helmholtz, *On the Conservation of Energy*	1847	Anne Brontë, *Agnes Grey*; Charlotte Brontë, *Jane Eyre*; Emily Brontë, *Wuthering Heights* Longfellow, *Evangeline, A Tale of Acadie* William Makepeace Thackeray, *Vanity Fair* (-1848) Parkman, *The Oregon Trail* (-1849)

History, Politics, Science	Date	Literature, Philosophy, Culture
Public Health Act; gold found in California	1848	Queen's College (London school for women) Marx and Engels, *The Communist Manifesto*
Britain annexes the Punjab; John Herschel, *Outlines of Astronomy*	1849	Dickens, *David Copperfield* (-1850) Macaulay, *History of England* (-1855)
Public Libraries Act; slave trade abolished in Washington, D.C.; women's rights convention in Worcester, Massachusetts.	1850	Pre-Raphaelite Brotherhood formed E. B. Browning, *Sonnets from the Portuguese* Dickens's *Household Words* begins Nathaniel Hawthorne, *The Scarlet Letter* Tennyson, *In Memoriam A.H.H.*; made poet laureate Wordsworth, *The Prelude*
The Great Exhibition (Crystal Palace); gold rush, Victoria and New South Wales (-1854)	1851	Mrs Gaskell, *Cranford* (in *Household Words*, -1853) Herman Melville, *Moby-Dick; or, The Whale* *The New York Times* begins Harriet Beecher Stowe, *Uncle Tom's Cabin* (-1852)
David Livingstone travels in Africa; Louis Napoleon's "Second Empire" begins (-1870)	1852	Arnold, *Empedocles on Etna, and other Poems* Dickens, *Bleak House* (-1853) Moodie, *Roughing It in the Bush* *Roget's Thesaurus of English Words and Phrases*
Visit by Commodore Perry reopens Japan to West	1853	G. H. Lewes, *Comte's Philosophy of the Sciences*
Florence Nightingale at Scutari; George Boole's symbolic logic, "Boolean algebra"	1854	Working Men's College founded Thoreau, *Walden, or Life in the Woods*
Alexander Parkes develops plastic; London's first public lavatories;	1855	Thomas Bulfinch, *The Age of Fable* Longfellow, *The Song of Hiawatha* Whitman, *Leaves of Grass* (-1892)
Neanderthal Man discovered, near Dusseldorf; Henry Bessemer patents his steelmaking process	1856	Gustave Flaubert, *Madame Bovary*
Matrimonial Causes Act (the "Divorce Act"); Dred Scott decision, vs. slave's freedom; first Atlantic cable laid (fails; redone 1865-66)	1857	Charles Baudelaire, *Les fleurs du mal* Anthony Trollope, *Barchester Towers* *Atlantic Monthly* begins
John Brown's raid on Harpers Ferry, Virginia; first oil well begins producing (Pennsylvania)	1859	Wilkie Collins, *The Woman in White* (-1860) Charles Darwin, *On the Origin of Species* George Eliot, *Adam Bede* John Stuart Mill, *On Liberty* Samuel Smiles, *Self-Help* Tennyson, *The Idylls of the King* (-1885)
England's first pure food laws; Joseph Swan's carbon filament incandescent lamp	1860	First British Open golf tournament Dickens, *Great Expectations* (-1861)
Russian serfs emancipated; Italy united under Victor Emmanuel II; Gatling invents machine gun; Ignaz Semmelweis pioneers antisepsis	1861	George Eliot, *Silas Marner* John Stuart Mill, *Representative Government* Charles Reade, *The Cloister and the Hearth*
Otto von Bismarck, premier of Prussia (-1871); *Monitor* and *Merrimac*, battle of ironclads	1862	Sarah Bernhardt's acting debut, Comédie Française Victor Hugo, *Les misérables*
Emancipation of U.S. slaves; London's underground railway begins	1863	T. H. Huxley, *Evidence as to Man's Place in Nature* Charles Kingsley, *The Water-Babies* (1862-)
Louis Pasteur develops pasteurization; Geneva Convention establishes Red Cross; Karl Marx organizes First International, in London; Herbert Spencer, *The Principles of Biology*	1864	Robert Browning, *Dramatis Personae* Newman, *Apologia Pro Vita Sua* Jules Verne, *Voyage au centre de la terre*

History, Politics, Science	Date	Literature, Philosophy, Culture
Abraham Lincoln assassinated by John Wilkes Booth; Joseph Lister demonstrates antiseptic surgery; *Great Eastern* lays Atlantic Cable (-1866)	1865	Carroll, *Alice's Adventures in Wonderland* Ruskin, *Sesame and Lilies* Leo Tolstoy, *War and Peace* (-1869)
Ku Klux Klan founded in Pulaski, Tennessee; Alfred Nobel invents dynamite; SPCA founded; Gregor Mendel, *Experiments in Plant Hybridization*	1866	Fyodor Dostoevsky, *Crime and Punishment* Swinburne, *Poems and Ballads* (1878, 1889) Whittier, *Snow-Bound; A Winter Idyl*
Second Reform Act extends franchise; Canadian Confederation, Sir John A. Macdonald PM; diamonds first discovered in South Africa; U.S. buys Alaska ("Seward's Folly")	1867	Paris international exposition Modern commercial typewriter invented Henrik Ibsen, *Peer Gynt* Marx, *Das Kapital* (finished by Engels, 1894)
Beginning of Trades Union Congress; shoguns overthrown in Japan, ending samurai era; Cro-Magnon Man discovered	1868	Louisa May Alcott, *Little Women* Robert Browning, *The Ring and the Book* (-1869) William Morris, *The Earthly Paradise* (-1870)
First women's suffrage (Wyoming Territory); Suez Canal opens (begun 1859); U.S. transcontinental railway completed; Dmitri Mendeleev's periodic table of elements	1869	Girton College, Cambridge, for women Arnold, *Culture and Anarchy* R. D. Blackmore, *Lorna Doone* T.H. Huxley coins the term *agnostic* John Stuart Mill, *The Subjection of Women*
Home Government Association (wants Home Rule for Ireland); the first Married Women's Property Act; Vatican Council declares papal infallibility	1870	Elementary Education Act Bret Harte, *The Luck of Roaring Camp* Marcus Clarke, *Term of His Natural Life* (-1874)
Test Act (religious, for teachers) abolished; H. M. Stanley finds Dr. Livingstone at Ujiji; the great Chicago fire	1871	P. T. Barnum opens his circus, in Brooklyn George Eliot, *Middlemarch* (-1872) Whitman, *Democratic Vistas*
Ballot Act, establishes secret vote; Eadweard Muybridge begins inventing motion pictures; Yellowstone Park established	1872	Newnham College, Cambridge, for women First international soccer (England vs. Scotland) Butler, *Erewhon*
North West Mounted Police established; Ernst Haeckel coins the word *ecology*	1873	Newman, *The Idea of a University* Jules Verne, *Tour du monde en quatre-vingt jours*
Britain annexes Fiji; Women's Trade Union League formed; national Women's Christian Temperance Union founded in U.S.A.	1874	Hardy, *Far From the Madding Crowd* Parkman, *The Old Regime in Canada* Anthony Trollope, *The Way We Live Now* (-1875) First "Impressionist" exhibition
London Medical School for Women; Public Health Act; London sewer system finished; use of children as chimneysweeps made illegal; Charles Stewart Parnell enters parliament	1875	Mount Allison Univ. awards degrees to women Madame Blavatsky founds Theosophical Society First Kentucky Derby Mary Baker Eddy, *Science and Health* Heinrich Schliemann, *Troy and Its Remains*
Victoria proclaimed Empress of India; Plimsoll line introduced; Alexander Graham Bell invents the telephone; "Custer's Last Stand," battle of Little Big Horn	1876	Carroll, *The Hunting of the Snark, An Agony in Eight Fits* Twain, *The Adventures of Tom Sawyer* Wagner's *Ring* cycle performed at Bayreuth
Thomas A. Edison invents the phonograph; Quaker Mill Co. begins making oatmeal	1877	Henry James, *The American* Anna Sewell, *Black Beauty*
New Scotland Yard; General William Booth's Salvation Army; first birth-control clinic, in Amsterdam; electric street lighting in London	1878	Lady Margaret Hall, Oxford, for women Charles Sanders Peirce founds Pragmatism Hardy, *The Return of the Native* Gilbert and Sullivan, *H.M.S. Pinafore*

History, Politics, Science	Date	Literature, Philosophy, Culture
Edison patents incandescent lamp; London telephone exchange begins operating; Ivan Pavlov begins working with dogs	1879	Fyodor Dostoevsky, *The Brothers Karamazov* Henry George, *Progress and Poverty* Henrik Ibsen, *A Doll's House* Meredith, *The Egoist*
In Ireland, Captain Boycott is "boycotted"	1880	Andrew Carnegie begins funding libraries Sir Charles G. D. Roberts, *Orion, and other poems* Lew Wallace, *Ben-Hur: A Tale of the Christ* Émile Zola, *Nana*; *Le roman expérimental*
Beginnings of British Socialist Party; U.S. president James Garfield assassinated; Sheriff Pat Garrett shoots Billy the Kid; Tuskegee Institute founded, for blacks	1881	Henry James, *The Portrait of a Lady* Stevenson, *Treasure Island* (-1882) Johanna Spyri, *Heidi* Anatole France, *Le crime de Sylvestre Bonnard*
European "scramble" for African territory begins; the second Married Women's Property Act	1882	John L. Sullivan, heavyweight boxing champion Frank R. Stockton, "The Lady or the Tiger?"
Orient Express begins operating; Brooklyn Bridge opens; Krakatoa erupts	1883	Buffalo Bill's Wild West Show opens Friedrich Nietzsche, *Thus Spake Zarathustra* (-1885) Schreiner, *The Story of an African Farm*
Third Reform Act; Fabian Society founded; France gives U.S. Statue of Liberty	1884	First volume of the *New English Dictionary* (later the Oxford English Dictionary) Twain, *Adventures of Huckleberry Finn* Joris Karl Huysmans, *A rebours*
The fall of Khartoum; General Gordon killed — Belgian Congo, personal property of Leopold II; Canadian Pacific Railway completed; first automobiles appear (Karl Benz's "velocipede")	1885	H. Rider Haggard, *King Solomon's Mines* William Dean Howells, *The Rise of Silas Lapham* Pater, *Marius the Epicurean* Vol. 1 of *Dictionary of National Biography*
Gold discovered in Transvaal; Coca-Cola, "Brain Tonic & Intellectual Beverage"	1886	Stevenson, *Strange Case of Dr Jekyll and Mr Hyde* Frances Hodgson Burnett, *Little Lord Fauntleroy*
"French Indo-China" established; Banff National Park established	1887	Berne Convention on international copyright Arthur Conan Doyle, *A Study in Scarlet*
National Geographic Society founded; Jack the Ripper murders five in London; George Eastman invents the Kodak	1888	Edward Bellamy, *Looking Backward: 2000-1887* C. M. Doughty, *Travels in Arabia Deserta* Mrs. Humphry Ward, *Robert Elsmere*
London Dock strike; Eiffel Tower built for The Paris Exposition; Johnstown (Pennsylvania) flood	1889	Andrew Lang, *The Blue Fairy Book* Twain, *A Connecticut Yankee in King Arthur's Court* Yeats, *The Wanderings of Oisin and Other Poems*
Parnell resigns amid scandal; Cecil Rhodes becomes premier of Cape Colony; battle at Wounded Knee, massacre of Sioux	1890	James George Frazer, *The Golden Bough* (-1915) James Whistler, *The Gentle Art of Making Enemies* William James, *The Principles of Psychology*
Pithecanthropus erectus (Java Man) discovered; building of trans-Siberian railroad (-1905)	1891	Hardy, *Tess of the d'Urbervilles* Wilde, *The Picture of Dorian Gray*
Rudolf Diesel's engine; Henry Ford builds his first automobile; colour photography introduced	1892	Charlotte Perkins Gilman, "The Yellow Wall-Paper" Wilde, *Lady Windermere's Fan* First Stanley Cup final
Keir Hardie forms the Independent Labour Party	1893	Yeats, *The Celtic Twilight*
Alfred Dreyfus sent to Devil's Island; President Carnot of France assassinated by Italian anarchist; Nicholas II becomes Tsar of Russia (-1917)	1894	Kipling, *The Jungle Book* (-1895) George Moore, *Esther Waters* *The Yellow Book* begins (-1897)

History, Politics, Science	Date	Literature, Philosophy, Culture
The trial of Oscar Wilde; Wilhelm Konrad Roentgen discovers X-rays; Guglielmo Marconi sends wireless signal; King Camp Gillette invents the safety razor	1895	Stephen Crane, *The Red Badge of Courage* Hardy, *Jude the Obscure* H. G. Wells, *The Time Machine* Wilde, *The Importance of Being Earnest*
Klondike gold rush begins; Samuel P. Langley's powered model aircraft; radioactivity discovered in uranium compounds	1896	First modern Olympics, held in Athens Anton Chekhov, *The Sea Gull* *Maclean's Magazine* begins
The first Workmen's Compensation Act; Adelaide Hoodless establishes Women's Institute; discovery of malaria bacillus and of electron	1897	Rudolph Dirks originates *The Katzenjammer Kids* Edmond Rostand, *Cyrano de Bergerac* Bram Stoker, *Dracula*
Doukhobors emigrate to Canada; United States annexes Hawaii; Marie and Pierre Curie isolate radium, first radioactive element	1898	Henry James, *The Turn of the Screw* Ernest Thompson Seton, *Wild Animals I Have Known* Shaw, *Plays Pleasant and Unpleasant*
Hague Conference establishes Hague Tribunal	1899	Conrad, *Heart of Darkness* John Dewey, *The School and Society* Thorstein Veblen, *The Theory of the Leisure Class*
"Planck's Constant" initiates quantum theory; Count Ferdinand Zeppelin's rigid airship flies; Arthur Evans excavates palace of Knossos	1900	L. Frank Baum, *The Wonderful Wizard of Oz* Sigmund Freud, *The Interpretation of Dreams* Beatrix Potter, *The Tale of Peter Rabbit*
U.S. defeats Philippine resistance (1901); Russo-Japanese War (1904-05); abortive Russian revolution (1905); "Young Turks" revolt (1909); Japan annexes Korea (1910); China takes Tibet (1910); revolution in Mexico (1910-11); Sun Yat-sen's revolution in China (1911); Italo-Turkish war, first use of aircraft as weapon (1911-12); Balkan Wars (1912-13); U.S. troops in Nicaragua (1912-33); "Great War"—World War I (1914-18); Easter Rebellion in Ireland (1916); U.S. Marines occupy Dominican Republic (1916-24); civil wars in China (1916ff.); first Russian Revolution and Bolshevik Revolution (1917), then civil war (-1920); revolution in Hungary (1918); Black-and-Tan War, IRA founded (1919-22); Russo-Polish War (1920); Greco-Turkish War (1920-23); Pilsudski's coup in Poland (1926); Mukden Incident: Japan invades Manchuria (1931) and other parts of China (1937-45); attempted Communist rebellion in El Salvador (1932); Chaco War (Bolivia-Paraguay, 1932-35); Germany occupies the Rhineland (1936); Italy conquers Ethiopia (1936); Spanish Civil War (1936-39); Germany occupies Sudetenland (1938); the "Anschluss": Germany occupies Austria (1938); Germany occupies rest of Czechoslovakia (1939); Italy occupies Albania (1939); Russo-Finnish War (1939-40); Germany invades Poland: World War II begins (1939-45); Japanese bomb Pearl Harbor (7 Dec. 1941); civil war in Greece (1944-49); civil war in China (1945-49); Indochina War (1945-54) and Viet Nam War (1950-75); India-Pakistan Wars (especially 1947-48, 1965, 1971); Arab-Israeli war (1948-49); China retakes Tibet (1950-51); Korean War (1950-53); Mau Mau rebellion (1952ff.); Algerian revolt against France	20thC	ART by Rousseau, Cassatt, Gauguin, Sargent, Grandma Moses, Klimt, Munch, Morrice, Fry, Kandinsky, Rackham, Bonnard, Vuillard, Hodgkins, Matisse, Carr, Feininger, Balla, Rouault, Mondrian, Brancusi, Vlaminck, Thomson, Dufy, Klee, Marc, Kirchner, Epstein, Léger, Picasso, Group of Seven (A. Y. Jackson, Lawren Harris, et al.), Milne, Braque, Hopper, Utrillo, Modigliani, Lewis, Grant, Bakst, Rivera, Kokoschka, Arp, Duchamp, Chagall, O'Keeffe, de Chirico, Morandi, Ray, Gaudier-Brzeska, Lipchitz, Ernst, Wood, Grosz, Miró, Nicholson, Rockwell, Moholy-Nagy, Magritte, Shahn, Escher, Calder, Moore, Giacometti, Dubuffet, Hepworth, Rothko, Sutherland, Dali, de Kooning, Borduas, Bacon, Pollock, Drysdale, Motherwell, Nolan, Wyeth, Colville, Lichtenstein, Riopelle, Rauschenberg, Buffet, Oldenburg, Warhol, Johns, Hockney, Chicago; ARCHITECTURE by Gaudi, Sullivan, Lutyens, Wright, the Saarinens, Gropius, Miës van der Rohe, Le Corbusier, Fuller, Johnson, Erickson; MUSIC by Saint-Saëns, Rimsky-Korsakov, Janacek, Elgar, Puccini, Herbert, Albéniz, Mahler, Paderewski, Debussy, Delius, R. Strauss, Dukas, Sibelius, Satie, Lehar, Scriabin, Vaughan Williams, Rachmaninoff, Holst, Schoenberg, Ives, Ravel, de Falla, Respighi, Bloch, Bartók, Grainger, Kodály, Stravinsky, von Webern, Berg, Varèse, Kern, Romberg, Villa-Lobos, Berlin, Ibert, Prokofiev, Milhaud, Porter, Piston, Hindemith, Orff, Sessions, Thomson, Gershwin, Poulenc, Weill, Copland, Rodgers & Hammerstein, Walton, Khachaturian, Shostakovich, Carter, Messiaen, Barber, Menotti, Cage, Britten, Bernstein, Schafer, McCartney; PLAYS by Strindberg, Gregory, Pinero,

History, Politics, Science	Date	Literature, Philosophy, Culture
(1954-62); Soviet invasion stops Hungarian Revolution (1956); Suez crisis and second Arab-Israeli war (1956); Castro's Cuban revolution (1953, 1956-59); civil war in Lebanon (1958); civil war in Congo (1960ff.); Arab-Israeli "six-day war" (1967); Biafran War (1967-70); Soviets invade Czechoslovakia (1968); revolution in Libya (1969); war in Cambodia (1970ff.); Pakistan civil war (1971); fourth Arab-Israeli war (1973); army revolt in Chile (1973); war in Cyprus—island in effect partitioned (1974); conflict in Ethiopia (1974ff.); Indonesia invades and annexes East Timor (1975-76); more civil war in Lebanon (1975ff.), Israel invading in 1982; civil war in Angola (1975-88); Somalia vs. Ethiopia (1977); Zia-ul-Haq ousts Pakistan's Bhutto (1977); Afghan war (1978ff.); Ayatollah Khomeini's forces oust Shah of Iran (1979); civil war in El Salvador (1979-92); Sandinistas (Nicaragua) oust Somoza (1979), fight "Contras" (1981-90); Iran-Iraq War (1980-88); Falklands War (1982); U.S. forces occupy Grenada (1983); U.S. sinks two Libyan boats, bombs military targets (1986); Palestinian *intifada* in occupied territories (1987ff.); military coup in Burma, or "Myanmar" (1988); civil war in Somalia (1988ff.); U.S. invades Panama (1989); civil war in Liberia (1990); Persian Gulf War (1990-91); break up and war in Yugoslavia (1991-)		Shaw, Jerome, Chekhov, Barrie, Feydeau, Hauptmann, Maeterlinck, Yeats, Galsworthy, Pirandello, Gorki, Claudel, Synge, Maugham, Barker, Giraudoux, O'Casey, O'Neill, Anderson, Eliot, Cocteau, Capek, Connelly, Rice, Sherwood, Wilder, Lorca, Brecht, Coward, Sartre, Hellman, Odets, Beckett, Auden, Fry, Saroyan, Genet, Anouilh, Williams, Rattigan, Ionesco, Inge, Miller, Dürrenmatt, Behan, Chayefsky, R. Bolt, Reaney, Shaffer, Jellicoe, Albee, Osborne, Arden, Pinter, Fugard, Orton, Baraka (Jones), Bond, Soyinka, Pollock, Stoppard, Ayckbourn, Delaney, C. Bolt, Tremblay, Williamson, Shepard, Mamet, Highway; FILMS by Griffith, De Mille, Chaplin, Ford, Pagnol, Capra, Eisenstein, Hitchcock, Buñuel, Disney, De Sica, Forman, Riefenstahl, Wyler, Stevens, Huston, Rossellini, Wilder, Zinneman, Lean, Reed, Kazan, Kurosawa, Antonioni, Kramer, McLaren, Welles, Bergman, Fellini, S. Ray, Attenborough, Jewison, Kubrick, Godard, Malle, Truffaut, Polanski, Allen, Coppola, Lucas, Weir, Zhang; PHOTOGRAPHY by Curtis, Stieglitz, Steichen, Adams, Evans, Bourke-White, Karsh, Capa, Arbus, Leibovitz, Mapplethorpe
Australia becomes independent (1 Jan.); U.S. president William McKinley killed by anarchist; First Nobel Prizes awarded	1901	Thomas Mann, *Buddenbrooks* Frank Norris, *The Octopus*
Cuba wins independence from Spain; volcano destroys St. Pierre, Martinique; Aswan Dam completed	1902	Use of Alfred Binet's mental tests begins André Gide, *L'immoraliste* Helen Keller, *The Story of My Life*
20-mph speed limit imposed on British roads; Ernest Rutherford and Frederick Soddy's theory of radio-activity; Wright brothers fly plane at Kitty Hawk, N.C.	1903	First "World Series": Boston beats Pittsburgh Butler, *The Way of All Flesh* Jack London, *The Call of the Wild*
Trans-Siberian RR links Moscow and Vladivostok; William Gorgas stops yellow fever in Canal Zone	1904	Abbey Theatre opens in Dublin Sara Jeannette Duncan, *The Imperialist* O. Henry, *Cabbages and Kings* Saki (Hector Hugh Monro), *Reginald*
Norway separates from Sweden; Emmeline Pankhurst's Suffragettes become more active; Sinn Fein movement organized politically; Industrial Workers of the World (IWW) founded; Albert Einstein's "special theory" of relativity	1905	First movie theatre (Pittsburgh), 5¢ "nickelodeon" Baroness Orczy, *The Scarlet Pimpernel*
Roald Amundsen transits Northwest Passage; San Franciso earthquake and fire; Reginald Fessenden's 2-way transatlantic talk by radio	1906	John Galsworthy, *The Forsyte Saga* (-1922) Upton Sinclair, *The Jungle*
New Zealand becomes independent; Mohandas K. Gandhi starts civil-disobedience (South Africa); Maria Montessori's new educational methods	1907	First major comic strip ("Mutt and Jeff") Henry Adams, *The Education of Henry Adams* Conrad, *The Secret Agent* Edmund Gosse, *Father and Son*

History, Politics, Science	Date	Literature, Philosophy, Culture
Robert Baden-Powell founds Scouting movement; Old Age Pensions Act; Model T's roll off Henry Ford's assembly line	1908	Arnold Bennett, *The Old Wives' Tale* Kenneth Grahame, *The Wind in the Willows* Lucy Maud Montgomery, *Anne of Green Gables*
Robert E. Peary claims to have reached North Pole; Louis Blériot flies across the Channel; John McCurdy flies "Silver Dart" in Nova Scotia	1909	Pound, *Personae* Gertrude Stein, *Three Lives* H. G. Wells, *Tono-Bungay*
Union of South Africa formed; New York Metropolitan Opera broadcast on radio; Bertrand Russell, Alfred North Whitehead, *Principia Mathematica* (-1913)	1910	Leacock, *Literary Lapses*
Parliament Act curtails power of House of Lords; Health Insurance Act (including for unemployment); Alfred Wegener's theory of continental drift	1911	Hollywood's first movie studio Max Beerbohm, *Zuleika Dobson* Frances Hodgson Burnett, *The Secret Garden*
Ulster Voluntary Force formed; African National Congress founded; the *Titanic* sinks (1500 die); Casimir Funk coins term *vitamine*	1912	first Calgary Stampede Edgar Rice Burroughs publishes first Tarzan story Carl Gustav Jung, *Psychology of the Unconscious*
Tibet ousts Chinese, becomes independent; Native Land Act, South Africa; Hans W. Geiger invents alpha ray counter	1913	Willa Cather, *O Pioneers!* D. H. Lawrence, *Sons and Lovers* Marcel Proust, *Remembrance of Things Past* (-1927)
World War I begins; Irish Home Rule bill passes; Panama Canal opens	1914	Frost, *North of Boston* Joyce, *Dubliners*; *A Portrait of the Artist as a Young Man*
War continues: zeppelin raids on England; Germans use poison gas at Ypres; Gallipoli; U-boat sinks *Lusitania*	1915	John Buchan, *The Thirty-Nine Steps* Ford Madox Ford, *The Good Soldier* Dorothy Richardson begins *Pilgrimage* novels (-1967) William Somerset Maugham, *Of Human Bondage*
War continues: evacuation from Gallipoli, tanks first used (by British), Conscription Bill, Count Felix von Luckner's raids, T. E. Lawrence in Arabia; Margaret Sanger arrested (NY) for birth-control clinic; Grigori Efimovich Rasputin killed; Einstein's general theory of relativity	1916	HD (Hilda Doolittle), *Sea Garden* Edgar A. Guest, *A Heap o' Livin'* Ring Lardner, *You Know Me Al: A Busher's Letters* Sandburg, *Chicago Poems* Twain, *The Mysterious Stranger* Tristan Tzara begins Dada in Zurich
War continues: U.S. enters, Canadians take Vimy Ridge, convoy system begins, Mata Hari tried and executed, Halifax explosion; Russian Revolutions; Balfour Declaration promises Jewish homeland; U.S. buys Virgin Islands from Denmark	1917	Norman Douglas, *South Wind* Knut Hamsun, *The Growth of the Soil* Henry Handel Richardson, *Australia Felix* Bertrand Russell, *Why Men Fight*
Woodrow Wilson's 14 Points, RAF formed, German Empire collapses, armistice signed (11 Nov.); Baltic Republics become independent; Canadian women, English women over 30 get vote; Bolsheviks execute Tsar Nicholas II and family; influenza pandemic (-1919): over 20 million die	1918	Rupert Brooke, *Collected Poems* Hopkins, *Poems*, ed. Robert Bridges Lytton Strachey, *Eminent Victorians* Booth Tarkington, *The Magnificent Ambersons* Oswald Spengler, *The Decline of the West* (-1922)
Finland becomes independent; Treaty of Versailles; Paris Peace Conference; Amritsar Massacre; Gandhi's civil disobedience; Lady Astor becomes England's first woman MP; J.W. Alcock and A.W. Brown fly nonstop across Atlantic	1919	Sherwood Anderson, *Winesburg, Ohio* H. L. Mencken, *The American Language* (-1948) Pound, *Cantos* (-1959) Sassoon, *War Poems* Yeats, *The Wild Swans at Coole*
League of Nations established; women get vote in U.S.; first commercial radio station: KDKA, Pittsburgh; Hermann Rorschach's inkblots	1920	Agatha Christie, *The Mysterious Affair at Styles* Pound, *Hugh Selwyn Mauberley* Edith Wharton, *The Age of Innocence*

History, Politics, Science	Date	Literature, Philosophy, Culture
Irish Free State established (Jan. 1922); first birth-control clinic in London, for the poor	1921	John Dos Passos, *Three Soldiers*
British Broadcasting Company established; Frederick Banting and Charles Best isolate and use insulin; Benito Mussolini made premier of Italy; Howard Carter and Lord Carnarvon find tomb of Tutankhamun	1922	Cummings, *The Enormous Room* T. S. Eliot, *The Waste Land* Joyce, *Ulysses* Sinclair Lewis, *Babbitt* Mansfield, *The Garden Party and Other Stories*
Egypt regains independence; Ottoman Empire ends; Mustafa Kemal heads Turkey; Adolf Hitler's "beer-hall putsch" in Munich; television invented (-1927)	1923	Frost, *New Hampshire* Rainer Maria Rilke, *Duino Elegies* Stevens, *Harmonium*
First Labour government in England (Jan.-Nov.); Lenin dies; Stalin and two others rule; United Church of Canada established	1924	Forster, *A Passage to India* Adolf Hitler, *Mein Kampf* (-1926) André Breton founds Surrealism
The Scopes "Monkey Trial" in Tennessee	1925	Theodore Dreiser, *An American Tragedy* F. Scott Fitzgerald, *The Great Gatsby* Ellen Glasgow, *Barren Ground* Franz Kafka, *The Trial*
British general strike (May, re: coal miners); Stalin becomes sole dictator of USSR; Gertrude Ederle swims English Channel;	1926	Hemingway, *The Sun Also Rises* T. E. Lawrence, *Seven Pillars of Wisdom* A. A. Milne, *Winnie-the-Pooh*
Charles A. Lindbergh flies solo across the Atlantic; Werner Heisenberg proposes "uncertainty principle"	1927	Thornton Wilder, *The Bridge of San Luis Rey* Woolf, *To the Lighthouse*
In England, votes for all women over 21; Alexander Fleming discovers penicillin; Richard E. Byrd explores Antarctica	1928	Ford Madox Ford, *Parade's End* (1924-) Margaret Mead, *Coming of Age in Samoa* Disney's Mickey Mouse debuts in *Steamboat Willie*
28 Oct., "Black Friday"—Great Depression begins; France begins building Maginot Line (-1940); women declared "persons" under Canadian law; Lateran Treaty makes Vatican City independent; Ernest O. Lawrence invents the cyclotron (-31); "St. Valentine's Day Massacre" in Chicago	1929	Faulkner, *The Sound and the Fury* Richard Hughes, *A High Wind in Jamaica* Katharine Susanna Prichard, *Coonardoo* Erich Maria Remarque, *All Quiet on the Western Front* Thomas Wolfe, *Look Homeward, Angel* Woolf, *A Room of One's Own*
Haile Selassie (Ras Tafari Makonnen) becomes emperor of Ethiopia (deposed, 1974); Gandhi makes sea-salt in protest vs. British; Pluto, the ninth planet, discovered	1930	Auden, *Poems* Hart Crane, *The Bridge* Katherine Anne Porter, *Flowering Judas* *Strike Up the Band*, musical with Goodman, Dorsey
Statute of Westminster establishes Commonwealth; Alfonso XIII deposed; Spain becomes a republic	1931	Pearl Buck, *The Good Earth* Antoine de Saint-Exupéry, *Vol de nuit*
Neutron and positron discovered; Lindbergh baby kidnapped and killed; Amelia Earhart flies the Atlantic	1932	Louis Ferdinand Céline, *Voyage au bout de la nuit* James T. Farrell, *Young Lonigan* Aldous Huxley, *Brave New World*
Adolf Hitler, German Chancellor (Führer, 1934); Franklin Delano Roosevelt, U.S. president (-1945); Wiley Post flies solo around the world	1933	James Hilton, *Lost Horizon* Dorothy L. Sayers, *Murder Must Advertise* Gertrude Stein, *Autobiography of Alice B. Toklas*
Chinese Red Army's 6000-mile "Long March" (-1935); Enrico Fermi experiments with nuclear fission; William Beebe descends 3028' in a bathysphere	1934	Jean Cocteau, *La machine infernale* Graves, *I, Claudius*; *Claudius the God* Mikhail Sholokhov, *And Quiet Flows the Don*

History, Politics, Science	Date	Literature, Philosophy, Culture
Nazis' Nuremberg Laws — denounce Versailles Treaty; Government of India Act; U.S. creates Work Projects Administration (WPA); 22 June, cane toads arrive in Australia	1935	Game of Monopoly first marketed Louis MacNeice, *Poems* C. Day Lewis, *A Time to Dance*
Edward VIII abdicates to wed Wallis Simpson; Canadian Broadcasting Corporation established; John Maynard Keynes, *The General Theory of Employment, Interest, and Money*	1936	Mulk Raj Anand, *Coolie* Dale Carnegie, *How to Win Friends & Influence People* Margaret Mitchell, *Gone with the Wind*
German planes bomb Guernica; airship *Hindenburg* burns at Lakehurst, N.J.; Amelia Earhart disappears over Pacific	1937	Isak Dinesen, *Out of Africa* David Jones, *In Parenthesis* J. R. R. Tolkien, *The Hobbit*
Munich Agreement between Chamberlain and Hitler; Nov. 9-10: "Kristallnacht," anti-Jewish pogrom; nylon bristles introduced (hosiery, 1940); G. S. Callendar predicts "greenhouse effect"	1938	Graham Greene, *Brighton Rock* Jean-Paul Sartre, *La nausée* Elizabeth Bowen, *The Death of the Heart* *Superman*, by Siegel and Shuster, first appears
"Molotov-Ribbentrop pact" re: Baltic states etc.; Francisco Franco, dictator of Spain (-1975); first television news coverage and sports event; first transatlantic air service; Igor Sikorsky develops his helicopter	1939	Christopher Isherwood, *Goodbye to Berlin* Joyce, *Finnegans Wake* Flann O'Brien, *At Swim-Two-Birds* John Steinbeck, *The Grapes of Wrath* Nathanael West, *The Day of the Locust*
Churchill becomes English Prime Minister (-1945); Japan joins Germany and Italy in the "Axis"; evacuation from Dunkirk; Battle of Britain; USSR annexes Estonia, Latvia, and Lithuania	1940	A. M. Klein, *Hath Not a Jew...* Carson McCullers, *The Heart Is a Lonely Hunter* Christina Stead, *The Man Who Loved Children* Richard Wright, *Native Son*
Lend Lease aid begins; the Atlantic Charter; Rudolph Hess flies to Scotland; "Manhattan Project" begins	1941	Emily Carr, *Klee Wyck* Arthur Koestler, *Darkness at Noon* Hugh MacLennan, *Barometer Rising* Sinclair Ross, *As For Me and My House* Rebecca West, *Black Lamb and Grey Falcon*
Jimmy Doolittle leads B-25 raid on Japan; raid on Dieppe by British and Canadian troops; heavy air raids on Germany begin	1942	Birney, *David* Albert Camus, *L'étranger* Faulkner, *Go Down, Moses*
Tehran, Casablanca conferences (FDR & Churchill)	1943	T. S. Eliot, *Four Quartets* (1935-)
Normandy invasion (6 June); German officers try to kill Hitler; V-1, V-2 rockets vs. England; Bretton Woods Conference: IMF and World Bank; Dumbarton Oaks Conference proposes United Nations; Lazlo Biro invents ball-point pen	1944	Jorge Luis Borges, *Ficciones* Joyce Cary, *The Horse's Mouth* Katherine Anne Porter, *The Leaning Tower* E. J. Pratt, *Collected Poems* G. M. Trevelyan, *English Social History*
Yalta and Potsdam conferences; VE Day, 8 May; UN charter signed (June); atomic bombs dropped on Japan (6 and 9 Aug.); VJ Day, 14 Aug.; Nuremberg war-crimes trials (20 Nov.-1 Oct. '46)	1945	Orwell, *Animal Farm* Gabrielle Roy, *Bonheur d'occasion* (*The Tin Flute*) Evelyn Waugh, *Brideshead Revisited* Henry Green, *Loving*
Philippines declared independent (4 July); Churchill uses the phrase "Iron Curtain"; Juan Peron becomes president of Argentina; ENIAC, first all-electronic computer	1946	Frank Sargeson, *That Summer* John Hersey, *Hiroshima* Dr. Benjamin Spock, *Baby and Child Care* Robert Penn Warren, *All the King's Men* William Carlos Williams, *Paterson* (-1951)

History, Politics, Science	Date	Literature, Philosophy, Culture
India and Pakistan independent ("Partition"); Truman Doctrine (containment of Communism) and Marshall Plan (European Recovery Program); test flights break the sound barrier	1947	First Dead Sea Scrolls found *Diary of Anne Frank* Malcolm Lowry, *Under the Volcano* Ethel Wilson, *Hetty Dorval* First Cannes International Film Festival
Ireland, Burma, and Ceylon become independent; Britain's National Health Service established; state of Israel established by UN; Mahatma Gandhi assassinated; UN passes Universal Declaration of Human Rights; *apartheid* formally instituted in South Africa; Berlin Airlift begins (-1949); Organization of American States formed; long-playing records developed	1948	Women admitted to univ. membership at Cambridge G. V. Desani, *All About H. Hatterr* (1970) Graham Greene, *The Heart of the Matter* Alfred Kinsey, *Sexual Behavior of the Human Male* Norman Mailer, *The Naked and the Dead* Alan Paton, *Cry, the Beloved Country* Patrick White, *The Aunt's Story*
Indonesia becomes independent; NATO established; Newfoundland joins Confederation; Communists rule China — Nationalists go to Taiwan	1949	Simone de Beauvoir, *Le deuxième sexe* Orwell, *Nineteen Eighty-Four* Shirley Jackson, *The Lottery* Eudora Welty, *The Golden Apples*
Sen. Joseph McCarthy begins Red-hunting (-1954); U.S. sends 35 advisers to Vietnam to help French	1950	Ray Bradbury, *The Martian Chronicles* Thor Heyerdahl, *Kon-Tiki* (translated)
Libya becomes independent; spies Guy Burgess and Donald Maclean flee to USSR; colour television in U.S.	1951	Morley Callaghan, *The Loved and the Lost* Rachel Carson, *The Sea Around Us* Anthony Powell, *Dance to the Music of Time* (-1975) J. D. Salinger, *The Catcher in the Rye*
Elizabeth II begins reign; US explodes hydrogen bomb at Eniwetok; Michael Ventris and John Chadwick decipher Linear B; first passenger jet service, London-Johannesburg	1952	Ralph Ellison, *Invisible Man* R. K. Narayan, *The Financial Expert* E. B. White, *Charlotte's Web*
Ethel and Julius Rosenberg executed for spying; Josef Stalin dies; Edmund Hillary and Tenzing Norgay climb Everest	1953	John Cheever, *The Enormous Radio* L. P. Hartley, *The Go-Between*
SEATO established; Vietminh army defeats French at Dienbienphu; racial segregation banned in U.S. public schools; Jonas Salk develops polio vaccine; "teflon" patented by Du Pont (discovered 1938)	1954	Roger Bannister runs the mile in 3:59.4 Kingsley Amis, *Lucky Jim* William Golding, *Lord of the Flies* Dylan Thomas, *Under Milk Wood* J. R. R. Tolkien, *The Lord of the Rings* (-1955)
Martin Luther King leads blacks' bus boycott; Warsaw Pact established	1955	James Baldwin, *Notes of a Native Son* Vladimir Nabokov, *Lolita* Khushwant Singh, *Train to Pakistan*
Tunisia and Morocco become independent	1956	Elvis Presley and rock-and-roll become popular Gerald Durrell, *My Family and Other Animals* Allen Ginsberg, *Howl and Other Poems* Colin Wilson, *The Outsider*
Gold Coast and Togoland become independent Ghana; USSR launches two "Sputnik" space satellites; Canada Council established; stereophonic records	1957	Northrop Frye, *Anatomy of Criticism* Jack Kerouac, *On the Road* Boris Pasternak, *Doctor Zhivago* Dr. Seuss, *The Cat in the Hat* Nevil Shute, *On the Beach*
Guinea becomes independent; EEC (Common Market) comes into being 1 Jan.; Pope John XXIII elected	1958	Chinua Achebe, *Things Fall Apart* Carlos Fuentes, *Where the Air Is Clear* Günter Grass, *The Tin Drum*

History, Politics, Science	Date	Literature, Philosophy, Culture
EFTA (European Free Trade Association) formed; Alaska and Hawaii become 49th and 50th states; Saint Lawrence Seaway opens; unmanned *Lunik 1* (USSR) lands on moon; former seaman, 25, dies in Manchester of HIV infections (discovered in 1990 by tests of stored tissue)	1959	Saul Bellow, *Henderson the Rain King* Marie-Claire Blais, *La belle bête* Eskia Mphahlele, *Down Second Avenue* Mordecai Richler, *Apprenticeship of Duddy Kravitz* Sheila Watson, *The Double Hook* Raymond Williams, *Culture and Society 1780-1950*
Independence of Cameroon, Central African Rep., Chad, Congo, Cyprus, Dahomey (Benin), Gabon, Ivory Coast, Madagascar, Mali, Mauritania, Niger, Nigeria, Republic of the Congo (Zaire), Senegal, Somalia, Togo, Upper Volta; Sirimavo Bandaranaike becomes first woman PM (Ceylon); Sharpeville riots and killings in South Africa; Israelis capture Adolf Eichmann — hanged, 1962; blacks' "sit-in" campaign begins in U.S.; Soviets shoot down American U-2 spy plane; Echo, first communications satellite, launched; U.S. develops first working laser beams	1960	Avison, *Winter Sun* John Barth, *The Sot-Weed Factor* Lawrence Durrell, *The Alexandria Quartet* (1957-) Wilson Harris, *Palace of the Peacock* Raja Rao, *The Serpent and the Rope*
Independence of Sierra Leone, Tanganyika; South Africa leaves Commonwealth; Amnesty International founded; Yuri Gagarin, first human being in space; unsuccessful "Bay of Pigs" invasion of Cuba; Berlin Wall built	1961	Robert Heinlein, *Stranger in a Strange Land* Joseph Heller, *Catch-22* Margaret Laurence, *The Stone Angel* Naipaul, *A House for Mr Biswas* Muriel Spark, *The Prime of Miss Jean Brodie*
Independence of Algeria, Burundi, Jamaica, Rwanda, Trinidad and Tobago, Uganda, Western Samoa; the Cuban missile crisis; Nobel Prize to Francis Crick, Maurice Wilkins, and James Watson for DNA model	1962	Anthony Burgess, *A Clockwork Orange* Curnow, *A Small Room with Large Windows* Doris Lessing, *The Golden Notebook* Marshall McLuhan, *The Gutenberg Galaxy* Plath, *The Colossus*
Independence of Kenya, Malaysia, Zanzibar; John F. Kennedy assassinated (22 Nov.); Britain's "Great Train Robbery"; casettes for sound recording introduced	1963	Rachel Carson, *Silent Spring* John Le Carré, *The Spy Who Came in from the Cold* Farley Mowat, *Never Cry Wolf* John Updike, *The Centaur*
Independence of Malawi, Malta, Zambia; Tanganyika and Zanzibar merge to become Tanzania; Palestine Liberation Organization established; Civil Rights bill passed in U.S.; Canada adopts the Maple-leaf flag	1964	9 Feb., the Beatles appear on *The Ed Sullivan Show* Achebe, *Arrow of God* John Berryman, *77 Dream Songs* Margaret Laurence, *The Stone Angel* Robert Lowell, *For the Union Dead* Christopher Okigbo, *Limits*
Independence of Gambia, Singapore, Southern Rhodesia (by declaration; Zimbabwe, 1980); Malcolm X assassinated in New York City; riots in Watts area of Los Angeles (-1966); Early Bird, commercial communications satellite	1965	Rosemary Dobson, *Cockcrow* F. O'Connor, *Everything That Rises Must Converge* John Fowles, *The Magus* (1977) Nissim Ezekiel, *The Exact Name*
Independence of Barbados, Botswana, Guyana; Indira Gandhi becomes PM of India; China's Red Guards, Cultural Revolution (-1967); Michael De Bakey implants artificial human heart	1966	Basil Bunting, *Briggflatts* Truman Capote, *In Cold Blood* Leonard Cohen, *Beautiful Losers* Heaney, *Death of a Naturalist* Okot p'Bitek, *Song of Lawino* Plath, *Ariel* Jean Rhys, *Wide Sargasso Sea*
Canada's centennial; successful human heart transplant (S. Africa)	1967	George Clutesi, *Son of Raven, Son of Deer* G. García Márquez, *One Hundred Years of Solitude* Ngugi wa Thiong'o, *A Grain of Wheat*

History, Politics, Science	Date	Literature, Philosophy, Culture
Independence of Mauritius, Nauru, Swaziland; Martin Luther King, Robert. F. Kennedy assassinated; Pierre Elliott Trudeau becomes Canadian PM; student riots in Europe, especially Paris	1968	Arthur C. Clarke, *2001: A Space Odyssey* Alexander Solzhenitsyn, *Cancer Ward* Joyce Carol Oates, *Expensive People* Joan Didion, *Slouching Towards Bethlehem* Tom Wolfe, *The Electric Kool-Aid Acid Test*
Golda Meir becomes PM of Israel (-1974); *Apollo 11*: Neil Armstrong, first man on moon	1969	Open University established in England Kurt Vonnegut, Jr., *Slaughterhouse-Five*
Independence of Fiji, Tonga; "October Crisis" in Canada, War Measures Act; 4 students killed at Kent State demonstration; 22 April—the first Earth Day	1970	Robertson Davies, *Fifth Business* Maurice Duggan, *O'Leary's Orchard* Germaine Greer, *The Female Eunuch* Anne Hébert, *Kamouraska* Dee Brown, *Bury My Heart at Wounded Knee*
East Pakistan becomes independent Bangladesh; UN admits Communist China, Nationalists out; Swiss women get right to vote (except Appenzell)	1971	Munro, *Lives of Girls and Women* C. K. Stead, *Smith's Dream* (1973) John Gardner, *Grendel*
Terrorists at Munich Olympics, 11 Israelis killed; Watergate scandal in U.S. (-1974); Pioneer 10, first craft to leave solar system	1972	Richard Adams, *Watership Down* Margaret Drabble, *The Needle's Eye* Witi Ihimaera, *Pounamu, Pounamu* Thomas Keneally, *The Chant of Jimmy Blacksmith*
The Bahamas become independent; Carl Sontheimer's Cuisinart food-processor	1973	Brathwaite, *The Arrivants* Thomas Pynchon, *Gravity's Rainbow* Rudy Wiebe, *The Temptations of Big Bear*
Guinea-Bissau becomes independent; Richard Nixon first U.S. president to resign	1974	Gordimer, *The Conservationist* Dennis Lee, *Alligator Pie* R. Pirsig, *Zen and the Art of Motorcycle Maintenance*
Independence of Mozambique, Papua New Guinea, Surinam; unmanned Viking I and 2 (U.S.) land on Mars	1975	Ruth Prawer Jhabvala, *Heat and Dust* Paul Scott completes *The Raj Quartet* (1966-) Robert Kroetsch, *Badlands*
Seychelles become independent; blacks protest in Soweto, South Africa; Israeli commandos free hostages at Entebbe; death of Mao Tse-Tung; Anglo-French supersonic *Concorde* begins flying; first video cassette recorders	1976	Les Murray, *The Vernacular Republic* Patrick White, *A Fringe of Leaves* Alex Haley, *Roots* Piercy, *Woman on the Edge of Time* Maxine Hong Kingston, *The Woman Warrior* Jacques Derrida, *Of Grammatology* (tr.; French, 1967)
Smallpox eradicated	1977	Timothy Findley, *The Wars* Jack Hodgins, *The Invention of the World*
Independence of Dominica, Solomon Islands, Tuvalu; Camp David peace accord, Israel and Egypt; Karol Wojtyla becomes Pope John Paul II; Jonestown, Guyana, mass suicide and killings; home computers begin to become common; Love Canal toxic waste "disaster" disclosed	1978	Maurice Gee, *Plumb* Patricia Grace, *Mutuwhenua* John Irving, *The World According to Garp* Christopher Koch, *The Year of Living Dangerously*
Independence of Kiribati; Margaret Thatcher becomes British PM; nuclear accident at Three Mile Island; Iranians occupy U.S. Embassy (for 444 days)	1979	Mavis Gallant, *From the Fifteenth District* Heaney, *Field Work* Randolph Stow, *Visitants*
Independence of Vanuatu; Zimbabwe recognized; Gdansk shipyards strike, "Solidarity" movement; John	1980	Umberto Eco, *The Name of the Rose*

History, Politics, Science	Date	Literature, Philosophy, Culture
Lennon shot and killed in New York City; Keynesian economics giving way to monetarism		
Independence of Antigua & Barbuda, Belize; attempted assassinations of U.S. president Ronald Reagan and the Pope; first voyage of U.S. space shuttle *Columbia*; AIDS identified, first reported in U.S. (pandemic began in mid-1970's; virus discovered in 1983)	1981	Donald Barthelme, *Sixty Stories* Peter Carey, *Bliss* Joy Kogawa, *Obasan* Salman Rushdie, *Midnight's Children*
Canada's constitution repatriated; Charter of Rights and Freedoms; compact discs developed	1982	Thea Astley, *An Item from the Late News* Ghose, *A New History of Torments* Rodney Hall, *Just Relations* Manhire, *Good Looks* Walker, *The Color Purple* V. S. Pritchett, *Collected Stories* (-1983)
Brunei becomes independent; digital records developed	1983	Robert Creeley, *Collected Poems* Joan Didion, *Salvador* Buchi Emecheta, *Adah's Story* Graham Swift, *Waterland*
Indira Gandhi assassinated	1984	Julian Barnes, *Flaubert's Parrot* Timothy Findley, *Not Wanted on the Voyage* Weldon, *The Life and Loves of a She-Devil* Milan Kundera, *The Unbearable Lightness of Being* Keri Hulme, *The Bone People*
Mikhail Gorbachev becomes Soviet leader	1985	Anne Tyler, *The Accidental Tourist* Atwood, *The Handmaid's Tale* Peter Ackroyd, *Hawksmoor*
Corazon Aquino elected president of Philippines — Ferdinand Marcos flees; space shuttle *Challenger* explodes; Chernobyl nuclear reactor explodes; Desmond Tutu installed as Archbishop, S. Africa	1986	Barry Lopez, *Arctic Dreams* Kazuo Ishiguro, *An Artist of the Floating World*
Gorbachev starts reforms, *perestroika*, *glasnost*	1987	Bruce Chatwin, *The Songlines* Toni Morrison, *Beloved*
Stephen Hawking, *A Brief History of Time*	1988	J. M. Coetzee, *Foe* Anita Desai, *Baumgartner's Bombay* Rohinton Mistry, *Tales from Firozsha Baag* Janet Frame, *The Carpathians*
Student demonstrations, China — Tiananmen Square; East European countries drop communism; Berlin Wall opened	1989	Kazuo Ishiguro, *The Remains of the Day* Amy Tan, *The Joy Luck Club* Bharati Mukherjee, *Jasmine* Peter Ustinov, *The Disinformer*
Namibia becomes independent; F. W. De Klerk releases Nelson Mandela; playwright Vaclav Havel elected Czech president; Boris Yeltsin elected head of Russian Republic; reunification of East and West Germany; Lech Walesa sworn in as president of Poland	1990	A. S. Byatt, *Possession* Malouf, *The Great World*
Baltic states recognized as independent; Warsaw Pact dissolved; Rajiv Gandhi assassinated; USSR dissolves; Commonwealth of Independent States	1991	Nadine Gordimer wins Nobel Prize for Literature

Appendix III
Glossary of Selected Literary Terms

Note: Many terms are briefly defined in the *Alternative Table of Contents No. 1* (abbreviated below as *AC 1*), which also lists examples of works that use the various forms and modes. Cross-references to terms defined in this Glossary appear in **boldface**.

abstract Not referring to anything **concrete**. An abstract word denotes something intangible, such as an idea, quality, or condition. (N.B.: Not to be confused with the distinction in rhetoric between *general* and *specific* — though the two pairs do partly overlap.)

acatalectic See **catalectic**.

accent Stress; see **metre**.

accentual metre (or verse) Metre or **verse** that counts only the stressed syllables in a line, as in Old English **alliterative verse** and often in **ballades** and other **songs** and in **nursery rhymes**. Cf. **accentual-syllabic metre** and **syllabic verse**, and see **sprung rhythm**.

accentual-syllabic metre (or verse) Metre or **verse** that counts both stressed and unstressed syllables in order to establish a **metre**; by far the most common form in English poetry. Cf. **accentual metre** and **syllabic verse**.

acephalous "Headless": said of a line of **verse** lacking one or more (usually unstressed) syllables in the first **foot**, resulting in initial **truncation**; see e.g. Dickinson's "There's a certain Slant of light" (p. 1080). Cf. **catalectic** and **hypermetric**; see also **metre**.

acrostic See *AC 1*.

alexandrine A line (or **verse**) with twelve syllables; in English poetry, an **iambic hexameter** line. See e.g. the anonymous poem "The Poor Estate to Be Holden for Best" (p. 128). An alexandrine forms the last line of a Spenserian stanza (see *The Faerie Queene*, p. 153); for alexandrines used for variety or other effect among *heroic couplets* (see *AC 1*), see e.g. Finch's "The Introduction," line 32 (p. 474), and Egerton's "The Emulation," line 26 (p. 489); see also Pope's comments and examples in the excerpt from *An Essay on Criticism* (p. 521).

allegory An extended **metaphorical** structure in which each element within a **narrative** corresponds in a patterned way to a parallel element in an implied narrative or in the world outside the narrative; **characters**, objects, and actions, e.g., may stand consistently for particular ideas or endeavours. In Bunyan's *Pilgrim's Progress* (see p. 416), the character Christian stands for all persons in **quest** of God and salvation, and the Slough of Despond corresponds to the state of emotional despair which can interfere with the progress of faith. And the literal level of Spenser's *Faerie Queene* (see p. 150) corresponds variously to historical, moral, and spiritual levels of allegorical meaning. A work that is not a full-fledged allegory may nevertheless contain *allegorical* elements — e.g. the figures of Sin and Death in *Paradise Lost*, II, 648ff. (p. 344). Allegories are usually to some degree **didactic**. See also **personification**; see also *AC 1: Indirect Modes*.

alliteration Repetition of the same sound at the beginnings of nearby words. Alliteration most often occurs with consonants, but it also occurs with any initial vowels (called *vocalic* alliteration), as in the opening line of *The Wanderer*: "**O**ft him **a**nhaga **a**re gebideth." See **accentual metre**; see also **alliterative verse, assonance,** and **consonance**.

alliterative verse See *AC 1*. In Old English alliterative verse, the two half-lines are bound by **alliteration**, usually occurring in both stressed syllables in the first half and one stressed syllable in the second half. Some early poetry is strongly alliterative but also metrically regular, unlike the earlier alliterative verse with its irregular rhythms and pairs of half lines; see e.g. Henryson's "Robene and Makyne" (p. 108) and Dunbar's "Lament for the Makaris" (p. 110). For effective alliteration that is less systematic, see e.g. "Gascoigne's Woodsmanship"

(p. 138) and Swinburne's "The Garden of Proserpine" (p. 1102). See also **sprung rhythm**.

allusion An indirect or casual reference to something outside a given work, such as a figure or event from literature or other arts, **myth**, the Bible, history, or popular culture, in order to call up in the reader's mind relevant facts, associations, emotions, and the like, and also sometimes mainly as ornamentation. See **intertextuality**; see also *AC 2: Narrative Paradigms*.

ambiguity Multiple meaning. Something *ambiguous* can be understood in more than one way. If unintentional, such impreciseness is usually a weakness; but deliberate ambiguity can enrich meaning and effect. Note e.g. the two opposite meanings of the word *buckle* in Hopkins's "The Windhover" (p. 1124) and the allusive ambiguity in the title of his "Spring and Fall" (p. 1124) and Vaughan's "The Retreat" (p. 409). See also **open**.

amphibrach (adj. *amphibrachic*) A **foot** of three syllables, stressing the second ($\smile\, \prime\, \smile$). See **metre**; see also S. T. Coleridge's "Metrical Feet" (p. 793).

amphimacer A **foot** of three syllables, the first and third stressed ($\prime\, \smile\, \prime$); also called a *cretic* or a *cretic foot*. See **metre**; see also S. T. Coleridge's "Metrical Feet" (p. 793).

anacrusis The addition of one or more unstressed syllables at the head of a line of **verse**, before the regular metrical pattern begins, creating a **hypermetric** line.

anadiplosis The **repetition** of a word or phrase from the end of one line, **stanza**, or sentence at the beginning of the next. See the anonymous 16th-century poem "Upon Consideration of the State of This Life" (p. 128) and Barnabe Googe's "Out of Sight, Out of Mind" (p. 146).

analepsis See **flashback.**

analogy Especially in **expository** or **argumentative** writing, a comparison of two things that are alike in some respects in order to suggest or argue that they are alike in other respects as well; for an analogy to be useful or valid, the features compared must be significant ones. A **simile** is a brief analogy, as is a **metaphor**, though left implicit.

anapest (adj. *anapestic*) A **foot** having two unstressed syllables followed by one stressed syllable ($\smile\, \smile\, \prime$). See **metre**; see also S. T. Coleridge's "Metrical Feet" (p. 793).

anaphora Repetition of the same word or phrase at the beginning of successive lines, clauses, or sentences. See e.g. the opening lines of Bradstreet's "To My Dear and Loving Husband" (p. 373). Cf. **epistrophe.**

antagonist See **protagonist** and **conflict.**

anthem See *AC 1: Hymn; Anthem.*

antibacchius (adj. *antibacchic*) A **foot** of two stressed syllables followed by an unstressed syllable ($\prime\, \prime\, \smile$). See **metre.**

anticlimax Something occurring just after a **climax** that is out of keeping with it, e.g. in tone or intensity, thereby undercutting its effectiveness. Anticlimax is usually a weakness, a let-down, e.g. when a scene dealing with trivial matters follows a strong and moving dramatic climax. Even a weak word at the end of a sentence can be anticlimactic. But anticlimax can be used intentionally for comic effect, as e.g. in stanzas IX, LV, LXXXI, and CXLIII of Canto I of Byron's *Don Juan* (p. 825).

anti-hero, anti-heroine A kind of **protagonist** found mostly in relatively recent times, one without the **traditional** heroic virtues; usually a character with everyday weaknesses, and often one who is somewhat pathetically victimized by social or other circumstances.

anti-pastoral A poem which mocks or otherwise criticizes **conventional pastoral**, usually by juxtaposing **traditional** forms and **images** with rural, psychological, or urban realities. See also *AC 1: Pastoral and Anti-pastoral.*

antispast A **foot** of four syllables, the second and third stressed ($\smile\, \prime\, \prime\, \smile$). See **metre.**

antithesis A **rhetorical figure of speech** consisting of two **balanced** and contrasting halves; the two parts may be **parallel** or the second may reverse the order of the first. See also **chiasmus** and **oxymoron.**

aphorism A concise statement of a truth or principle, often pointed, like an **epigram**; similar to a **proverb**, but with a known author. For some examples, see the sketch by Haliburton (p. 876). See also **wit.**

apostrophe A direct address to someone (usually absent) or something, or a god or goddess, or some **abstract** quality. See e.g. Donne's "Death, be not proud" and "Batter my heart, three-personed God" (Holy Sonnets 10 and 14, p. 258), Milton's invocations in *Paradise Lost* I, III, VII (pp. 326,

349, 354), William Wordsworth's "Milton! thou shoudst be living at this hour" ("London, 1802," p. 765), Blake addressing the "Tyger" (p. 724), and Keats addressing the Grecian urn (p. 855).

archetype A term adapted from Jungian psychology to refer to experiences, **characters**, situations, patterns of events, and types of **subjects** that recur over the centuries in **myth**, folklore, dreams, and literary works, thereby representing what Jung called "primordial **images**" or **symbols** from the human race's "collective unconscious" — such as the serpent, birth, coming of age, love, the generation gap, the spiritual journey, the **quest**, the defeat of real or imaginary monsters, seasonal death and rebirth, sin and punishment, the search for the father, the cowardly braggart, the temptress, the wanderer. Jungian archetypes include the Hero, the Wise Old Man or Magus, the Young King, the Anima, the Friend, the Enemy.

argumentation One of the four **traditional modes** of discourse, or composition; cf. **exposition**, **description**, and **narration**. A written *argument* marshals evidence in order to convince a reader of some **proposition** or to persuade a reader to pursue some course of action. See also **rhetoric**. The term *argument* is also used to denote a brief summary of the plot or statement of the subject matter of a long work or part of a work (see e.g. those for each book of Milton's *Paradise Lost*, p. 325, and Herrick's "The Argument of His Book," p. 285).

assonance Similar vowel sounds within nearby words, usually in stressed syllables. See also **consonance** and **alliteration**.

atmosphere See **tone**.

aubade See *AC 1*.

bacchius (adj. *bacchic*) A **foot** of three syllables, the second and third stressed (˘ ´ ´). See **metre**.

balance Symmetry of structure in any unit of writing. Balanced structures often use **parallelism**. See also **antithesis** and **chiasmus**.

ballad See *AC 1: Ballad Stanza*. Now loosely applied to almost any song, the term *ballad* or *folk ballad* refers specifically to anonymous narrative poems, meant to be sung, relating in a simple but dramatic manner some **story** of love, adventure, death, the supernatural, or the like. Later authors have written "literary" ballads in imitation of these earlier ones — e.g. Cowper's "John Gilpin" (p. 654), S. T.

Coleridge's *Rime of the Ancient Mariner* (p. 784), and Keats's "La Belle Dame Sans Merci" (p. 853). See also **common measure**.

ballade See *AC 1*.

beast epic A medieval allegorical sequence of tales whose characters are animals that behave like human beings. Chaucer's *Nun's Priest's Tale* (p. 64) is a single tale whose source is in a French sequence about Reynard the Fox. See also *AC 1: Indirect Modes*.

beast fable See **fable**.

beat See **metre** and **rhythm**.

beautiful See **picturesque** and **sublime**.

bestiary See *AC 1*.

blank verse See *AC 1*.

bob and wheel See **envoy**.

broadside A large sheet of paper printed on one side, usually with a popular poem, ballad, or other song about some recent event or other topical subject, and sold by peddlers in the streets, like later "Extra" editions of newspapers. See e.g. Deloney's "The Winning of Cales" (p. 206) and the anonymous "London Mourning in Ashes" (p. 299).

burlesque See *AC 1*.

cacophony Harsh or otherwise unpleasant sounds or patterns of sound, whether intentional or unintentional. Cf. **euphony**; and see the excerpt from Pope's *An Essay on Criticism* (p. 521).

cadence A kind of **rhythm**, though less regular than that of **metre**, e.g. the rhythm of speech or **free verse**.

caesura A pause in a line of **verse**, often but not always coinciding with a punctuation mark. A caesura most often appears near the middle of a line, but a poet may choose to position it earlier or later. See **scansion**.

canto A section of a long poem, such as an **epic** (or a **mock-epic**); e.g. see the first section from Pound's *Cantos* (p. 1293).

caricature Exaggeration of particular — usually prominent — physical or moral features of a **character**, often for the purpose of ridicule, whether in drawing or writing. See e.g. Dryden's portrait of Shadwell in "Mac Flecknoe" (p. 433).

carpe diem (Latin, "seize the day") See **motif**.

catalectic Said of a line of **verse** lacking one or more (usually unstressed) syllables in the final **foot**, resulting from **truncation**, as in the patterns ´ ˘ ´ ˘ ´ ˘ ´

(see e.g. Blake's "Tyger," p. 724), ⌣ ⌣ ⌣ ⁄ ⌣ ⌣ ⁄ ⌣ ⌣ ⁄ ⌣, ⁄ ⌣ ⌣ ⁄ ⌣ ⌣ ⁄ and ⁄ ⌣ ⁄ ⁄ ⁄ ⌣ ⁄. The practice is so common that lines having their full quota of syllables are often called *acatalectic*. Cf. **acephalous**, **hypermetric**, and see also **metre**.

chanson de geste Literally "song of great deeds"; the term is applied especially to early French **epics** such as the *Chanson de Roland* and other poems celebrating the military feats, both historical and legendary, of Charlemagne and others — works which provided material for many later **romances**.

character (1) a person portrayed in **fiction**, whether a poem, a play, or a **story** or **novel**; (2) the qualities of personality of such a person; (3) a **sketch**, usually prose, that briefly portrays a particular type of person, or occasionally a real person: see *AC 1: Character*. As for *characterization*, characters in fiction may be presented directly, in statements by a **narrator** and by other characters, or indirectly, through their actions, including their speech and thoughts (and see **point of view** and **diegesis**). A character may be *static*, relatively unchanging, or *dynamic*, changing, developing in significant ways. In *Aspects of the Novel* (1927), E. M. Forster distinguished between what he called *flat* and *round* characters: a *round* character being three-dimensional, similar to a real person (complex, capable of changing, capable of surprising us), a *flat* character being two-dimensional, undeveloped (simple and unchanging, limited to the one or two characteristics necessary for his or her part in the story, holding no surprises). The flat character is cousin to the *stock* or **stereotyped** character, a **conventional**, basically unchanging, and therefore easily recognizable character that recurs in certain kinds of writing, e.g. the mustache-twirling villain of **melodrama**, the tough private eye, the country bumpkin, the cruel stepmother, the *miles gloriosus* or braggart soldier (see **motif**); stock characters are often, though not always, *type* or *stereotype* (in a slightly different sense) characters, taken as representative of a group or class.

charm See *AC 1*.

Chaucerian stanza Another name for *rhyme royal*; see *AC 1*.

chiasmus An X-shaped pattern, named for the Greek letter *X* (*khi* or *chi*); a type of **balance** in which the construction of the second half is the reverse of that

in the first half; e.g. Pope's line "Favours to none, to all she smiles extends" (*The Rape of the Lock*, II, 11; p. 525). Sometimes the two parts use the same or similar words, as in Satan's "Surer to prosper than prosperity / Could have assured us" (*Paradise Lost*, II, 39-40; p. 337). See also **antithesis**.

choriamb A **foot** of four syllables, the first and fourth stressed (⁄ ⌣ ⌣ ⁄). See **metre**.

cinquain See *AC 1*.

clerihew See *AC 1*.

climax Loosely, any moment of high intensity; particularly, the point at which a piece of writing reaches its peak of intensity or interest; in a **narrative** or drama, the turning point or moment of crisis, the point at which the **conflict** is at its height, the moment when *rising action* gives way to *falling action*. If too much happens after the climax, the work risks giving an effect of **anti-climax**. See also **plot**.

closed A term sometimes applied to works of literature whose meaning at the end is definite, clear, determinate, as brought about by **closure**. Cf. **open**.

closed couplet See **couplet**.

closed form A term applied to poetry that uses regular patterns of **rhyme**, **metre**, line length, and **stanza**; cf. **free verse** (which is also called *open form*).

closure A closing or completion, or that which closes; a sense of such an ending; a coming to a clear and definite end. See e.g. how a *heroic couplet* (see *AC 1*) effects closure at the end of a Shakespearean **sonnet** (see *AC 1*); such couplets were also often used to end scenes in plays otherwise written in *blank verse* (see *AC 1*). *Closure* also refers to an ending which appears to resolve all problems, as in the **conventional fairy-tale** ending, "And they all lived happily ever after."

colloquial Describing everyday, conversational speech that falls somewhere between **informal** and **slang** on the spectrum of **diction** or **style**. Colloquialisms are acceptable in everyday speech but not felt to be appropriate in **formal** writing. In imaginative literature, however, colloquial language is often deliberately used, whether for comic effect or for realism. See **vernacular**, and **dialect**. See also **decorum**.

comedy A narrative or dramatic work, often amusing, which, unlike **conventional tragedy**, ends happily, at least for the principal characters, and which usually is more **realistic** in its presentation of everyday life. *Comedy* and *comic* in a narrower sense apply to works designed to provoke outright laughter. See the beginning of Johnson's *Rambler* No. 4 (p. 594). See also **mode** and **wit and humour**, and cf. **irony**.

common measure Also called *hymnal stanza*. Like the *ballad stanza* (see *AC 1*, a quatrain of alternating **tetrameter** and **trimeter** lines, though more regularly **iambic** than ballads often are, and often rhyming *abab* rather than *abcb*; see e.g. Dickinson's "I heard a Fly buzz when I died" (p. 1081), "She rose to His Requirement" (p. 1082), and "Tell all the Truth but tell it slant" (p. 1082), Herrick's "To the Virgins, to Make Much of Time" (p. 285), and William Wordsworth's "A slumber did my spirit seal" (p. 758). See also **fourteener**.

complaint A once-**conventional genre** of **lyric** poem in which a speaker complains about his or her unhappiness, usually the result of the behaviour of a lover, of the speaker's personal circumstances, or of the state of the world in general; such poems often include either an explicit or an implicit appeal for relief. See *AC 1*.

conceit A term originally meaning "concept," but later referring to ingenious **analogies**, elaborate or exaggerated **metaphors** and **similes**, unusual and surprising **images**. The *Petrarchan conceit* is a mainstay of Petrarch's **sonnets** and many Elizabethan sonnets and love poems; see for example Wyatt's translation "My galley charged with forgetfulness" (p. 129), the lover as ship being one of the most repeated comparisons, having become a **convention** in itself; other standard comparisons describe the lady's eyes, lips, skin, hair, and so on — note Shakespeare's making fun of such overworked conceits in his sonnet beginning "My mistress' eyes are nothing like the sun" (p. 229). Later the so-called "metaphysical" poets (e.g. Donne, George Herbert, Carew, Suckling, Lovelace, Cowley, Marvell, Vaughan) used strikingly **witty** comparisons that came to be called *metaphysical conceits*, one of the best known being Donne's comparison of himself and his wife to the legs of a draughtsman's compass in the last three **stanzas** of "A Valediction: Forbidding Mourning" (p. 256); and see the excerpt from Johnson's "Life of Cowley" (p. 605). See also **oxymoron**.

concrete A *concrete* word denotes something tangible, perceivable by one or more of the senses. Cf. **abstract**; see also **empirical** and **image**.

concrete poem See *AC 1: Shaped Verse*

conflict The struggle or opposition that constitutes the centre of interest of most **plots**, whether between a **character** (**protagonist**) and some force such as nature or society, or two characters (**protagonist** and **antagonist**), or two elements within one character. See also **climax** and **dénouement**.

connotation What a word suggests or implies, regardless of its **denotation**. Thus "stingy," "tightfisted," and "thrifty" *denote* much the same thing, but they *connote* different attitudes, ranging from unfavourable to favourable. The emotional and other associations called up by a word may be (1) personal, individual, (2) shared by a small or large group, or (3) general, universal.

consonance Similar consonant sounds in nearby words. See also **assonance, alliteration,** and *slant rhyme* (under **rhyme**).

content See **form and content**.

convention Any literary device, technique, **subject**, or **form** that is generally accepted or recognized both by authors and by their audiences — e.g. an actor's "aside" heard by the audience but presumably not by others on stage; stock **characters** are conventions. In **pastoral elegies**, e.g. Milton's *Lycidas* (p. 315), it is conventional for one poet-"shepherd" to mourn another. Many conventions change over time; e.g. the system of **courtly love** was conventional in medieval literature; the Horatian convention that poetry confers immortality on its subject was much used by Shakespeare and other Elizabethan sonneteers; intrusive **narrators** were conventional in 18th- and 19th-century novels; **free verse** was not conventional in the 19th century, when Whitman's use of it was innovative, but had become conventional by the 20th century. See **motif** and **tradition**.

couplet Two successive rhyming lines of **verse**, such as the pair of lines that end a Shakespearean sonnet (see *AC 1*). A *closed couplet*, common in 18th-century *heroic couplets* (see *AC 1*), is complete within itself in both **form and content**, syntax and thought, the second line usually ending with a colon, semicolon, or period. Though *heroic* or **pentameter** couplets are far more common, see

Carew's "Song" (p. 298) and John Dyer's *Grongar Hill* (p. 573) for examples of **tetrameter** couplets. Couplets sometimes serve as **stanzas** (see e.g. Tusser's "The Ladder to Thrift," p. 135).

courtly love A modern term for an elaborate chivalric code of manners followed by many of the aristocracy in late medieval Europe and reflected in a major way in literature; put most simply, a knight would court an idealized but unresponsive and usually married lady; the tradition combined elements of the purifying worship of the Virgin Mary, Platonic idealism, and sexual desire. Though it appears in many of the Petrarchan **conventions** used in 16th-century English literature, it is most evident in French literature. See **conceit**; see also Chaucer's "Wife of Bath's Tale," lines 1026ff. (p. 51), and lines 19-24 of Henryson's "Robene and Makyne" (p. 108).

cretic (n. & adj.) See **amphimacer**.

curtal sonnet See *AC 1: Sonnet.*

dactyl (adj. *dactylic*) A **foot** having one stressed syllable followed by two unstressed syllables ($\prime\,\smile\,\smile$). See **metre**; see also S. T. Coleridge's "Metrical Feet" (p. 793); for an example of a poem using dactyls as the basic foot, see Finch's "La Passion Vaincue" (p. 475).

decorum In discussions of literature, a term referring to stylistic propriety, i.e. the appropriateness of **style** to **genre**, **subject** matter, and occasion — e.g. the **convention** that **epics** and **tragedies** should be in a "high" or **formal** style, **comedies** in a "low" or **colloquial** style, and that a royal **character** should speak in a high style, a clown or servant in a low style (and, in a play, in prose rather than **verse**). In modern times the term refers simply to the suitability of any given work's style.

denotation The literal, objective meaning of a word, regardless of any emotional sense it may convey. Cf. **connotation**.

dénouement The final "unknotting" or unravelling, the resolution of the **conflict** of a **plot** and its complications, usually following the last or main **climax**. But see **open**.

description One of the four **traditional modes** of discourse, or composition; cf. **narration**, **exposition**, and **argumentation**. Descriptive writing attempts to paint a word-picture of an object, a **scene**, or a **character**. Description

sometimes occurs alone, as in some **sketches**, but is usually used in conjunction with another mode, especially narration.

deus ex machina (Latin) "god from the machine" — specifically, a deity brought swinging through the air into a classical drama by stage machinery at the end or at other difficult moments in order to resolve matters; more loosely, any sudden and usually improbable intervention, whether by a **character** or other device, to untangle a **plot** or otherwise resolve difficulties. See Pope's reference in *The Rape of the Lock*, IV, 46 (p. 529).

dialect A regional speech differing from the received standard or literary language in vocabulary, idiom, pronunciation, and grammar, usually as a result of being separated or distant from the main branch, whether because of geography, history, class, or some other reason; over time, a dialect can become a standard in its own right. Dialects often preserve older forms of the language. See e.g. the dialect poems of William Barnes (p. 891). See also *AC 1*, and **colloquial** and **vernacular**.

dialogue See *AC 1*.

dibrach See **pyrrhic**.

diction The choice and use of words. Diction and **style** are often thought of as having levels — **formal**, **informal**, **colloquial**, and **slang**. But the term *levels* is misleading, since *formal* is not necessarily better than *informal*; it depends on the nature and purpose of a work. In some contexts, slang is more appropriate than formality. See **decorum**.

didactic Intended to instruct; said of works whose primary purpose is to teach some moral or other lesson, such as a **parable** or a **fable**, or, with appropriate qualification, of works having such instruction as one of their purposes. Note Johnson's concerns in his *Rambler* No. 4 (p. 594).

diegesis Telling, as opposed to showing (see **mimesis**). In contemporary theories of narrating, the term *diegesis* also refers to the primary fictional world in which narrated events take place; various forms of the adjective *diegetic* refer to the relation between a narrator and the events being narrated (i.e. as observer, participant, teller of a story embedded in a **frame story**, etc.). See also **point of view** and **narrator**.

dimeter A line of **verse** with two metrical feet. See **foot** and **metre**.

documentary (1) (adj.) based on documents; (2) (n.) a work that treats its subject matter in a factual way, or that creates the illusion of truth, authenticity. See also **empirical**, **mimesis**, **realism**, and **verisimilitude**.

double dactyl See *AC 1*.

double rhyme See **rhyme**.

dramatic context The circumstances or **setting** for the thought and action of some poems, such as, obviously, **dramatic monologues**.

dramatic irony See **irony**.

dramatic monologue See *AC 1*. See also **dramatic context**.

dystopia See **utopia**.

eclogue See **pastoral**.

elegy See *AC 1*.

elevated diction, language, style diction, language, or **style** that is **formal**, dignified, and perhaps also emotionally heightened, and that makes liberal use of complex **syntax** and elaborate poetic and **rhetorical** devices and techniques. One form of such language is called **poetic diction**. See also **decorum**.

elision The omission of a final vowel in order to run two words together (e.g. *th' only* for *the only*), or of a vowel, consonant, or syllable within a word (e.g. *ne'er* for *never*, *ev'ry* for *every*), usually in order to achieve a desired **metre**, but sometimes just for smoothness of sound (see **euphony**). (The second sort of omission is also called *syncope*.)

emblem See *AC 1*.

empirical Based on direct experience or observation, rather than on theory: "empirical knowledge," "the evidence of one's senses." See also **concrete**, **documentary**, and **mimesis**.

end rhyme See **rhyme**.

end-stopped line A line of poetry in which both sense and **syntax** come to a satisfactory ending at the end of the line, usually marked with punctuation indicating a pause. Cf. **enjambement**.

English sonnet See *AC 1: Sonnet*.

enjambement The running over of both sense and syntax from one line to the next, without punctuation at the end of the line; such a line is called a *run-on line*. Cf. **end-stopped line**.

envoy (*envoi*) Either a poem of farewell, or a **conventional** final short **stanza**, often bidding farewell and perhaps including a dedication, at the end of some kinds of poems, such as the **ballade** and the **sestina** (see *AC 1*); the "bob and wheel" that concludes each stanza of *Sir Gawain* and *the Green Knight* is a sort of envoy (see p. 26). The term is also sometimes used to refer to an **epilogue** or to the summing up or conclusion of a prose work.

epic An **elevated** long poem focussing on a central heroic figure; the **narration** of the hero's and others' exploits celebrates the founding (e.g. Virgil's *Aeneid*) or some other important part of the history of a particular race or nation (with Milton's *Paradise Lost*, it is the human race). Virgil's and Milton's are called "literary" epics, imitating the Homeric epics, the *Iliad* and the *Odyssey*, which were part of an oral tradition. Epic **conventions** include the **invocation**, the beginning **in medias res**, the catalogue, the grand speeches of the heroes, the arming of the hero, boastful speeches, extended descriptions of battles and games, the journey to the underworld, supernatural "machinery" (gods and goddesses looking after specific characters or otherwise influencing the action; see Pope's dedicatory letter to *The Rape of the Lock*, p. 521), and the **epic simile**. See also *chanson de geste*, and **mock epic** and *AC 1*.

epic simile See **simile**.

epigram A short **verse**, or sometimes a prose saying, defined by Samuel Taylor Coleridge thus: "What is an epigram? A dwarfish whole, / Its body brevity, and wit its soul." See *AC 1*. Sometimes only a part of a poem is called an epigram — e.g. some of the more telling closed **couplets** of Pope and Swift. See also **aphorism**, **proverb**, and **wit**.

epigraph A quotation or motto at the beginning of a literary work or of a section.

epilogue A tail-piece or concluding section after the body of a work is complete. For example, in the 17th and 18th centuries it was **conventional** at the end of a play for an actor to step forward and address some final remarks to the audience; see the epilogue by Aphra Behn (p. 459). See **envoy**; see also **prologue**.

epiphany Literally a "showing forth" — a religious term adopted by James Joyce to describe the "sudden spiritual manifestation" of some **character**, object, or event in one of his works, producing for a character an accompanying insight into its true "whatness." A **story** itself may be an epiphany, evoking a sudden insight in a character or a reader, or both.

epistrophe Repetition of the same word or phrase at the end of successive lines, clauses, or sentences; see e.g. Griffin's "Fly to her heart" (p. 273). Cf. **anaphora**.

epitaph See *AC 1*.

epithalamion, epithalamium See *AC 1*.

epithet A striking descriptive word or phrase used to characterize a person or thing. Some epithets are simply adjectives or adjectival phrases (e.g. "*light-winged* Dryad," "*verdurous* glooms," "*magic* casements," "*plaintive* anthem," in Keats's "Ode to a Nightingale," p. 854); others function as appositives and sometimes become virtually part of a name (e.g. *the Apostle* Paul, Alexander *the Great*, William *the Conqueror*, Ivan *the Terrible*). A *stock epithet* is one used **repeatedly** for the same thing or person, including the familiar *Homeric epithets* in the *Iliad* and *Odyssey* (e.g. *rosy-fingered* dawn, *wine-dark* sea, *grey-eyed* Athena, *swift-footed* Achilles) — and note the appositive epithet used both by Milton in *Paradise Lost*, II, 28 ("the Thunderer" — without even using the name of the god; p. 337) and by Melville in "The Lightning-Rod Man" ("Jupiter Tonans" — line 26, p. 1023). A *transferred epithet* is an adjective attached to a noun other than the one it is appropriate to — as when one might exclaim "What a *miserable* day!" though it is the person, not the day, that is miserable; e.g. in Milton's *Paradise Lost*, I, 266 (p. 329), the adjective *oblivious* is made to modify the noun *pool*, when strictly it applies to the fallen angels themselves (and see II, 74, p. 337, for a similar occurrence); or see "*blind* mouths, in his *Lycidas*, line 119 (p. 317), or "*melodious* plot" and "*sunburnt* mirth" in Keats's poem already cited.

essay From the French *essai*, "try, attempt": a relatively short nonfictional prose discussion of a limited **topic**. Essays may be **formal**, **informal**, **expository**, **argumentative**, serious, humorous, personal, scientific, reflective, philosophical, **narrative**, critical, and so on. See also *AC 1: Non-fictional Prose*. (Occasionally works in **verse** are called essays — e.g. Pope's *An Essay on Criticism* and *An Essay on Man*; see pp. 521, 541).

euphony Pleasantness of sound, including smoothness of **rhythm**. Cf. **cacophony**; and see the excerpt from Pope's *An Essay on Criticism* (p. 521).

exemplum An "example" in the form of a **tale**, often inserted in medieval sermons, to illustrate a moral point. Chaucer's *Pardoner's Tale* (p. 58) is an exemplum, and *The Nun's Priest's Tale* (p. 64) includes exempla. See also *AC 1: Indirect Modes*.

exposition One of the four **traditional modes** of discourse, or composition; cf. **argumentation**, **description**, and **narration**. An *expository* essay is one that explains and informs. The term *exposition* also refers to that part of a play, **novel**, or **story**, usually at or near the beginning, that establishes the tone and gives the necessary facts of setting, character, and circumstances.

extended metaphor See **metaphor**.

eye rhyme See **rhyme**.

fable A brief **tale**, in **verse** or prose, often with animal characters (and then often called a *beast fable*), that illustrates a moral, often made explicit at the end. Cf. **parable**, and see **didactic** and *AC 1: Indirect Modes*. The term *fable* is also sometimes used to refer to the **plot** of a **narrative** or drama.

fairy tale A **story**, whether anonymous and **traditional** or composed by a known author, about the doings of small spirits, the "little people" — fairies, elves, gnomes, and other miniature humanoids — especially when their adventures influence human affairs; also, more broadly, any **tale** of magic and **fantasy** for children. See also *AC 1: Oral Forms*.

falling rhythm The **rhythm** or **metre** of a **trochaic** or **dactylic foot**.

fantasy An unusually imaginative work marked by a departure from reality, such as a **fairy tale** or a work of speculative science fiction; also, the characteristic quality of such a work, and the **genre** containing such works. See also **romance**, and cf. **realism**.

fiction Any imaginative **narrative** supposedly not true, though it can be based on truth; generally applied to prose (i.e. **novel** and **short story**), though logically applicable to **verse** and drama as well. Cf. **documentary**, and see also **realism**, **verisimilitude**.

figure of speech; figurative language Words used in other than their literal sense, such as in **metaphors** and **similes**, or arranged or otherwise used in unusual ways to achieve certain effects, such as in **antithesis** and **apostrophe** (the latter sort often being referred to as *figures of* **rhetoric**, or *rhetorical figures*).

flashback The **narration** of events that happened before other events already narrated. A work that begins **in medias res**, such as Milton's *Paradise Lost* (p. 325), will necessarily include flashback. Also called *analepsis*. Cf. **flashforward**.

flashforward Reference to or **narration** of future events in the midst of "present" narrative time. Also called *prolepsis*. Cf. **flashback**.

flat character See **character**.

folk song See *AC 1*.

foot A group of two or more syllables constituting the unit of poetic **metre**. See also **scansion**, and **acephalous** and **catalectic**. (A *foot* in Hopkins's **sprung rhythm** may have only one syllable.)

form See **form and content**.

formal A term describing **diction** or **style** that is relatively dignified or **elevated**, serious; cf. **informal**, **colloquial**, and **slang**; see also **decorum**. The adjective *formal* also refers to matters having to do with the *form* of a work.

form and content (or *style and substance*) Though it is customary to discuss matters of form and content separately, such a division distorts the inevitable connections between the *form* of a work and the work's literary effects. All verbal communications are expressed in a form of some kind. The term *form* refers specifically to such fixed **structures** or shapes as **stanzaic** and **metrical** patterns (see the opening section of AC 1) and certain **conventional** kinds of **narrative** (e.g. the use of a **frame story**), and to departures from such fixed patterns; more generally it refers to the organization of structural elements within any unit of speech or writing; more loosely, it is also sometimes used as a synonym for **genre**. See **style**. See also the headnote to *AC 1*.

fourteener An **iambic heptameter** line. A **couplet** of fourteeners is in effect the same as **common metre**.

frame story A **story** which contains within it another story or **tale** or a series of them. Chaucer's *Canterbury Tales*, e.g. (see p. 29), consists of separate tales within the frame story of a group of **characters** on a pilgrimage to Canterbury, characters introduced in the "General Prologue" and seen and heard acting and interacting in their own persons in the various introductions and conclusions that occur between the tales. Less formalized frame stories occur frequently in fiction — e.g. in Conrad's "The Tale," where the neutral's tale occurs within the Englishman's, and the Englishman's occurs within the relationship between him and the woman set up at the beginning and returned to at the end.

free indirect discourse (or **style**) In a **narrative**, the formal appearance of third-person **point of view**, but using the idiom and attitude appropriate to the **character** being focussed on. The opening of Mansfield's "The Doll's House" (p. 1299) contains examples of *direct discourse* ("'Open it quickly, someone!'") and *free indirect discourse* (e.g. the voice or idiom of Aunt Beryl: "The smell of paint was quite enough to make anyone seriously ill, in Aunt Beryl's opinion"; and the voice or idiom of the children: "But perfect, perfect little house!"). Ordinary *indirect discourse* would have reported, "Someone said that it should be opened quickly" or "The children thought that the little house was perfect."

free verse Also called *open form* poetry. Poetry that avoids regular patterns of **rhyme**, **metre**, line length, and **stanza**. Free verse gains its effects instead through **imagery**, **rhythm**, **repetition**, and **structure**. After Whitman, much poetry, especially 20th-century poetry, is free verse. See *AC 1*, and **cadence**, and cf. **closed form**.

genre A particular literary kind or type, such as **epic**, **tragedy**, **comedy**, **satire**, **fable**, **short story**, **essay**. The elastic term *genre* is used both for large classes (e.g. drama, **lyric**) and for specific subcategories (or subgenres—e.g. farce, **elegy**, **pastoral elegy**). Some genres have fairly strict **formal** and other **conventions** (e.g. *sonnet*; see *AC 1*); others do not (e.g. **novel**). Cf. **mode**.

haiku (or **hokku**) A Japanese **verse** form with three lines of 5, 7, and 5 syllables, usually focussing on one **image** of nature in a certain season and evoking a single emotion and insight. One by Moritake (15th-16th century) translates roughly as "Cherry blossoms / fall upwards to the branch— / and I see butterflies!" Two other examples, by Bashō (1644-1694): "Clouds now and then give / people a welcome respite / from moon-watching"; "The usually disgusting / crow—even he, amidst / this morning's snow!" (perhaps cf. Frost's "Dust of Snow," p. 1250). A modern example in English: "White gulls drifting slow / against grey April sky— / spring snow." For other works in English in a similar vein, see *AC 1*; see also **Imagists**.

heptameter A line of **verse** with seven metrical feet. See **foot** and **metre**; see also **fourteener**. See e.g. Vaux's "Of the Mean Estate" (p. 131).

hero, heroine See **protagonist**.

heroic couplet See *AC 1*.

heroic stanza See *AC 1*.

hexameter A line of **verse** with six metrical feet. See **foot** and **metre**, and see also **alexandrine**.

historical rhyme See **rhyme**.

Homeric simile See **simile**.

Hudibrastic verse See *AC 1*.

humour See **wit and humour**. For the "humours" as bodily fluids and temperaments, see the note to Chaucer's "General Prologue," line 420 (p. 34).

hymn See *AC 1*.

hymnal stanza See **common measure**.

hyperbole Overstatement; intentional exaggeration, e.g. for a **rhetorical** or **humorous** effect. Cf. **litotes** and **understatement**.

hypermetric A term applied to a line of **verse** with one or more extra unstressed syllables in the first or last **foot**, or both; see e.g. S. T. Coleridge's "Kubla Khan," lines 12-18 (p. 782), and the **trimeter** lines in Herrick's "To the Virgins, to Make Much of Time" (p. 285). Cf. **acephalous** and **catalectic**, and see **anacrusis**; see also **metre**.

iamb (adj. *iambic*) A **foot** having an unstressed syllable followed by a stressed syllable (˘ ´). See **metre**; see also S. T. Coleridge's "Metrical Feet" (p. 793).

identical rhyme See **rhyme**.

image, imagery An *image* is a verbal representation of something **concrete**, something that can be apprehended by one or more of the senses. Most images are visual, but images may also be aural, olfactory, gustatory, tactile, or kinesthetic. An image may also be either literal or **figurative**: in Donne's "The Flea" (p. 255), the insect is at first real, a literal image, becoming metaphorical in the second stanza; the three **quatrains** of Shakespeare's sonnet 73 (p. 228) are **metaphors** presenting three successive figurative images of old age. *Imagery* refers generally to the use of images, or to the body of images in a given work. See also **synaesthesia**, **symbol**, and **Imagists**.

Imagists A group of poets, mostly American, working in the years immediately before World War I, who promoted poems with, among other features, clear

concrete images and everyday language. See e.g. HD's "Oread" (p. 1295) and Pound's "In a Station of the Metro," with his remarks on it (p. 1293); see also *AC 1: Haiku*.

implied author See **persona**.

informal A term describing **diction** or **style** that is relatively relaxed, everyday, conversational, falling between **formal** and **colloquial** on the spectrum of style. See also **slang** and **vernacular**.

in medias res A term from Horace's *Ars Poetica*; Latin for "in the middle of things," describing the way some **narratives** begin. **Epics**, by **convention**, begin *in medias res* and then use **flashback** to fill in the prior events; see Milton's "**Argument**" to Book I of *Paradise Lost* (p. 326).

In Memoriam stanza See *AC 1*.

innuendo A hint, intimation, indirect suggestion, insinuation; usually negative, derogatory.

internal rhyme See **rhyme**.

intertextuality In literary criticism, a term referring broadly to the interdependence and interrelationships of all or most or many literary texts (see T. S. Eliot's "Tradition and the Individual Talent," p. 1307), or more narrowly to a given text's relationship to one or more other texts to which it makes explicit or implicit references — or even to itself (see **meta-**). See also **allusion**.

inversion The reversal of normal word order, e.g. using noun-adjective instead of adjective-noun or verb-noun instead of noun-verb, either for emphasis or for poetic effect, such as a desired **metre** or **rhyme**.

invocation At the beginning of an **epic** or other work or a section thereof, a **conventional** appeal to a Muse or other deity for help in the writing; in effect it often asks the Muse to dictate the poem, which the poet then simply records. See e.g. the openings of Books I, III, and VII of Milton's *Paradise Lost* (pp. 326, 349, 354), and the beginning of Pope's *The Rape of the Lock* (p. 521). See also **epic**, and *AC 1: Epic*; cf. **apostrophe**.

irony A term referring to a contrast or discrepancy, e.g. between appearance and reality. Of the several kinds of irony, the most common is *verbal* irony, when the intended meaning of a statement is different from the apparent or surface one (e.g. with **understatement**, **hyperbole**, or **paradox**). *Sarcasm* is verbal irony that is notably unsubtle — unusually obvious or direct — and, especially, harsh or cruel (the word comes from a Greek word meaning "to tear flesh"). Swift's *A Modest Proposal* (p. 480) is considered a masterpiece of irony; and Dekker uses heavy irony (often saying the opposite of what he means) in his advice to a gallant (p. 238). *Situational* irony occurs when a situation or action has consequences that are the opposite of what one expects or intends. *Dramatic* irony occurs when readers or audience, as well as perhaps other characters, understand a **character**'s words or actions better than the character because they possess knowledge that the character lacks; the more extreme instances of dramatic irony, such as in Sophocles's *Oedipus the King* or Shakespeare's *Othello*, are often referred to as *tragic irony*. The unintentional self-revelation in *dramatic monologues* (see *AC 1*) such as Robert Browning's "My Last Duchess" (see p. 1001) is a kind of dramatic irony. Irony, of whatever kind, is often **humorous**. The term *irony* is also used to describe a literary **mode** within which the power of the narrator or central character is less than that of other characters or the surrounding world; in a work in the ironic mode, characters may be unable to accept the world's order, or may no longer accept that the world is ordered, or may no longer believe in their own ability to relate to the world. It is a recurrent 20th-century attitude, as e.g. in Arnold's "Dover Beach" (p. 1061), the stories by Hemingway (p. 1339), Naipaul (p. 1468), Malamud (p. 1377), and Munro (p. 1453), and Orwell's "Shooting an Elephant" (p. 1350). See also **realism** and **comedy**.

Italian sonnet See *AC 1: Sonnet*.

jargon Specifically, the specialized language used by members of a particular profession or occupation; generally, however, it refers to any unnecessarily complex or incomprehensible diction (also called *bureaucratese, educationese, sociologese, gibberish, bafflegab, gobbledygook,* and so on). See **slang**.

kenning A **conventional** circumlocution or condensed **metaphor**, usually a compound noun, common in Anglo-Saxon and other old Germanic poetry. For example stock phrases for the sea are *swan-road, whale-path, whale-road.* The Wanderer (p. 10) speaks of his now dead lord as *goldwine,* i.e. gold-friend, giver of treasure; Tennyson uses the similar

term *bracelet-bestower* near the beginning of his version of "The Battle of Brunanburh" (p. 973); and note Birney's *buttrivers* in "Anglosaxon Street" (p. 1355). See also **poetic diction**.

legend A **story** handed down from past generations, usually having some basis in historical fact and often in the deeds of a particular, usually heroic, figure embodying national or racial achievements and spiritual or cultural values generally. Cf. **myth**. See also *AC 1: Oral Forms*.

leitmotif, leitmotiv See **motif**.

leonine rhyme See **rhyme**.

light verse Verse that has little or no serious purpose, but instead seeks to amuse, entertain, and often to demonstrate wit, elegance, and technical mastery of various kinds; even if it has some seriousness of purpose or treats a serious subject, it remains light in manner. See e.g. in *AC 1: Limerick; Clerihew; Double Dactyl;* see also some of the items under *Wit and Humour, Parody, Epigram.* And see **nonsense verse** and **performance verse**.

limerick See *AC 1*.

literary periods and movements Although this anthology avoids potentially arbitrary and misleading divisions of English literary history into chronological *periods*, it is just as well that readers be aware of terms commonly used: the Anglo-Saxon or Old English period; the Anglo-Norman period; the Medieval or Middle English period, or the Middle Ages; the Renaissance; the Elizabethan period; the Jacobean period; the Caroline period; the Restoration; the Neoclassical period, or Enlightenment, or Age of Reason, or Augustan Age; the Age of Johnson; the Romantic period; the Victorian Age; the Edwardian Age; the Georgian Age; the Modern period; the Post-Modern period. For the often widely varying and overlapping or conflicting dates for and characterizations of these periods, you may wish to consult other reference sources. (The artificiality of many of these divisions and designations is revealed by the once common use of such other terms as *Pre-Romanticism* to describe a good deal of what was going on during the Neoclassical period, and *Early Modern* to label much of the literature of the late-Victorian and Edwardian periods.)

Various literary *movements* and *schools,* some conscious and deliberate, some recognized only after the fact, and sometimes coinciding with these periods, include the following: the Scottish Chaucerians (15C), Metaphysical and Cavalier poets (17C), Neoclassicism (late 17-late 18C), Augustanism (18C), the School of Sensibility (18C), the Graveyard School (early to mid-18C), Sentimentalism (late 18C), the Gothic Revival (late 18-early 19C), Romanticism (late 18-mid 19C), Transcendentalism (mid-19C), the Pre-Raphaelites (mid-19C), Realism (mid- to late 19C), the Decadent Movement or Decadence (mid- to late 19C), the Aesthetic Movement or Aestheticism (late 19C), *fin de siècle* ("end of the century," 1880s & '90s), Naturalism (late 19C), Impressionism (late 19-early 20C), Expressionism (late 19-early 20C), Symbolism (late 19-early 20C), the Celtic Renaissance or Revival (late 19-early 20C), Modernism (early 20C), Imagism (1912-1917), Vorticism (1914-1915), Dadaism (post-WW I), Surrealism (1920s & '30s), Existentialism and the Absurd (mid-20C), the Black Mountain School (or Movement, 1950s), Post-Modernism (mid- to late 20C), Post-Colonialism (20C).

litotes A kind of **understatement** that uses a **negative** to state an opposite positive — e.g. to call a person "not ungenerous." The pilgrim Chaucer says of the Clerk, "And he nas nat right fat, I undertake." Cf. **hyperbole**.

local color writing Works of **fiction**, especially in the late 19th-century United States, depicting the people and customs and evoking the flavour of life in one or another specific region, such as the South, the West, New England. In this anthology, the story by Jewett (p. 1128) is an example.

lyric In ancient Greece, a poem sung to the accompaniment of a lyre. Now the term is extremely broad, used as it is for almost any relatively short poem, preferably with some musical qualities, in which a single speaker (usually but not necessarily the poet) expresses his or her thoughts and feelings; personal emotion is the prime requirement. **Ballads**, *ballades, dramatic monologues, elegies, hymns, odes, rondeaus,* **songs**, *sonnets* — all these and more (see *AC 1*) are kinds of *lyric* poetry, as distinct from **narrative**, dramatic, **satiric**, or **didactic** poetry (though such other kinds may include lyrical portions, such as in speeches by individual **characters**). The term *lyrics* is also used

to refer to the words of a song, as separate from its music.

malapropism A humorous misuse of one word for another that sounds similar; named for Mrs. Malaprop, a character in *The Rivals* (1775), a play by Richard Brinsley Sheridan (1751-1816); e.g., she refers to "an allegory on the banks of the Nile" and "a shrewd awakening." For other examples, see some of the remarks made by Mr. Byers in the sketch from Sara Jeannette Duncan's *Saunterings* (p. 1185).

meditation See *AC 1*.

meiosis See **understatement**.

melodramatic Characterized by violent or otherwise sensational language and action without sufficient justification in the motivation of **characters** or elements of **plot**; blatantly playing on the audience's or readers' emotions, and often depending on stock responses. Many popular plays in the 19th century were melodramas. See also **sentimentality**.

meta- In the terminology of literary criticism, a prefix implying that something is self-reflexive, concerned with itself; a work of *metafiction*, for example, has as part of its **subject** matter the nature of **fiction** or even the process of writing that particular work; notable examples are Laurence Sterne's *Tristram Shandy* (1760-67) and John Fowles's *The French Lieutenant's Woman* (1969). Related terms include *metatheatre* (or *metadrama*), *metacriticism, metalanguage*. See also **intertextuality**.

metaphor A **figure of speech** that implicitly compares two unlike things by identifying them with each other, as when Shakespeare in sonnet 116 (p. 229) states that love "is an ever-fixed mark" and "the star to every wand'ring bark," or when Campion writes "There is a garden in her face" (p. 233). Often, rather than stating such an identification, a metaphor will condense it, e.g. into a noun ("the *eye* of heaven" — Shakespeare's sonnet #18), or a verb ("morning . . . *Flatter* the mountain-tops" — #33), or an adjective ("*sluttish* time" — #55). An *extended* metaphor is one drawn out over several resemblances — i.e., virtually an **analogy** — even to the point of risking over-extension (see the first two paragraphs of the excerpt from Ruskin's *Sesame and Lilies*, p. 1048. A *dead* metaphor is one so commonplace that it no longer has any metaphorical force — e.g. the *leg* of a table, *stumbling* speech, *green* with envy, the *brow* of the hill; many clichés are dead metaphors. Cf. **simile**, and see also **allegory**, **image**, and **conceit**.

metaphysical conceit See **conceit**.

metonymy A **figure of speech** in which something associated in some way with another thing is made to stand for it, such as "crown" for a king or queen, or for the monarchy, "Madison Avenue" for the advertising industry, "Shakespeare" for his literary works. Metonymy depends on closeness of association and is therefore distinct from **metaphor**, whose effects depend on the marked difference of the things being equated. See **synecdoche**.

metre (or *meter*) (from Greek *metron*, "measure") Usually, **accentual-syllabic metre**: the regular beat of a line of **verse** established by the pattern of stressed and unstressed (or accented and unaccented) syllables; but see **accentual metre** (and cf. **quantitative verse** and **syllabic verse**). See also the terms for different lengths of lines: **monometer**, **dimeter**, **trimeter**, **tetrameter**, **pentameter**, **hexameter**, **heptameter**, **octameter**; and the various kinds of metrical **foot**: the most common, those used as the basic or dominant feet in the lines of a poem, are **anapest**, **dactyl**, **iamb**, and **trochee**; relatively rare, occurring almost exclusively as the result of **substitution**, are **amphibrach**, **amphimacer**, **antibacchius**, **antispast**, **bacchius**, **choriamb**, **paeon**, **pyrrhic**, and **spondee**; see also S. T. Coleridge's helpful mnemonic "Metrical Feet" (p. 793), and the excerpt from Pope's *An Essay on Criticism* (p. 521). See also **acephalous**, **catalectic**, **elision**, **hypermetric**, **substitution**, **scansion**, **rhythm**, **rising rhythm**, **falling rhythm**, **rocking rhythm**, and **sprung rhythm**.

mimesis "Imitation" — an influential notion in critical **tradition**, one which (in contrast to that of **diegesis**, or "telling") is concerned with the implications of "showing." It is variously interpreted as (1) the "accurate" reproduction of the "real" or **empirical** world, (2) the deliberate imitation or emulation of classic models or masters, and (3) the view that the "realistic portrayal" of the world demonstrates the presence of the "universal" in the particular. See also **documentary**, **realism**, and **verisimilitude**.

mock epic, mock heroic A poem that ridicules a relatively trivial **subject** by treating it in the **style** and with the techniques of **epic**; Pope's *The Rape of the Lock* is the classic example (see p. 521). The term *mock-heroic* is often used for similar satirical works that don't have the full epic flavour, e.g. Dryden's *Mac Flecknoe* (p. 433) and Byron's *Don Juan* (p. 825). See also *AC 1: Epic and Mock Epic*, and cf. *Burlesque in AC 1*.

mode A term similar to and sometimes overlapping with **genre**, but pertaining more to manner, method, mood, to **tone** and **theme**, or to the impulse or purpose behind a piece of writing, rather than to physical **form** or **structure**: the principal traditional modes are **romance**, **satire**, **irony**, **comedy**, and **tragedy**; **pastoral** can be thought of as both a genre and a mode. Mode can also be usefully thought of as pertaining to the patterns of thought implicitly embodied in the printed word and those implicitly embodied in works that depend upon performance — i.e., the *visual* and the *aural*. See e.g. the classifications in *AC 1*. See also **argumentation**, **exposition**, **description**, and **narration**.

monometer A line of **verse** with only one metrical **foot**. See **metre**.

mood See **tone**.

motif Any idea, **image**, **setting**, action, or the like frequently recurring in literature, e.g. the *carpe diem motif* (see *AC 2: Time*), the *ubi sunt* motif (e.g. in "Ubi Sunt Qui Ante Nos Fuerent," p. 18, and D. G. Rossetti's "The Ballad of Dead Ladies," p. 1078), or the **quest**; *stock* **characters** also constitute motifs. The term *motif* is also used to refer to any recurrent element, such as a name, an **image**, a **symbol**, or even simply an object, in a single relatively extended work; if the recurrent element is associated with a particular character, idea, place, or the like, it is sometimes referred to as a *leitmotif*, a term derived from music criticism, where it first referred to Wagner's practice in his operas of **repeating** a musical theme for a particular character, idea, place, or the like. The term **theme** itself is sometimes used to refer to one or both of these kinds of motif. See **convention** and **tradition**.

myth An anonymous **narrative** incorporating the folk-beliefs of a particular culture and involving **tales** of larger-than-life heroes, gods, and other supernatural beings; often myths seek to explain natural phenomena or the origins of a race or nation or of its social and religious behaviour. The term *myth* (or *mythology*) may also refer to a particular group or to the entire body of such stories. Cf. **legend**. See also *AC 1: Oral Forms*.

narration One of the four **traditional modes** of discourse, or composition; cf. **description**, **argumentation**, and **exposition**. *Narration* is the process of telling a **story**, recounting a sequence of events. The term is also used as a synonym for the noun **narrative**.

narrative An account of an event or sequence of events, either **fictional** or factual, and in either prose or **verse**. See also *AC 1: Fictional Narrative*; *Historical Narrative*.

narrator Anyone who narrates, who speaks or writes a **narrative**. In **fiction**, the narrator is the person telling the **story**. With first-person **point of view**, the "I" is the narrator. With third-person omniscient, the author is in effect the narrator — but the narrator is not necessarily the author, since the speaker will almost always be at least in part a **persona** adopted for the occasion. Similarly, while many narrators are reliable — making statements and offering opinions a reader can accept — sometimes an author will deliberately use a narrator who is naive or otherwise *unreliable*, e.g. Chaucer's persona in the "General Prologue" (p. 29). An *intrusive* narrator, rare in recent fiction but common in 18th- and 19th-century novels, pauses in the story to offer comments and judgments on characters and actions; sometimes the author addresses the reader directly (the term *intrusive* is not necessarily pejorative). See also **free indirect discourse** and **diegesis**.

negation A **rhetorical** or **stylistic** device which emphasizes negative forms of words and statements, usually in order to make an affirmative point. See e.g. Shakespeare's sonnet 130 (p. 229) and the opening of Keats's "Ode on Melancholy" (p. 856). See also **litotes**.

nonsense verse Verse that patently makes little or no sense, e.g. because it uses concocted words or defies logic, or for some other reason. Lewis Carroll's "Jabberwocky" (p. 1087) and Foote's "The Grand Panjandrum" (p. 616) are good examples. See also **light verse**.

novel A comparatively long work of prose **fiction**, usually dealing with a relatively large number of **characters** interacting in a society, and often

covering long periods of time in a variety of **settings**. Cf. **novella**, **romance**, **short story**.

novella, novelette A work of prose **fiction** too short to be called a **novel**, yet longer and more complex than a **short story**; often simply called "short novel" or "long short story."

nursery rhyme Brief jingles or heavily rhymed **songs**, **narratives**, riddles, games, **nonsense verses**, and the like, for children — though often originally meant for adults and containing **allusions** to historical events. Most were passed down orally before being recorded in writing; see p. 566. See also *AC 1: Oral Forms*.

octameter A line of **verse** with eight metrical feet. See **foot** and **metre**.

octave A **stanza** of eight lines, as e.g. in a **ballade** — see *AC 1*; or the eight-line portion of an Italian sonnet — see *AC 1: Sonnet*.

octosyllabic See **tetrameter**.

ode See *AC 1*.

omniscient point of view See **point of view**.

onomatopoeia The use of words whose **sounds** partly imitate or suggest their meanings, e.g. *sizzle, hiss, splash, tap*. But note the much more elaborate imitative **sounds** and **rhythms** in Tennyson's often-quoted lines from *The Princess*: "The moan of doves in immemorial elms, / And murmuring of innumerable bees" (see the note to line 50 of Keats's "Ode to a Nightingale," p. 854); and see stanzas 3-5 of Dryden's "A Song for St. Cecilia's Day" (p. 439). See also the "sound and sense" passage from Pope's *An Essay on Criticism* (p. 521).

open A term sometimes applied to works of literature whose endings are **ambiguous** or otherwise indeterminate, left open, or which deliberately offer simultaneous alternatives; such open-endedness is much more common in modern works than in earlier ones (but consider e.g. Blake's "The Mental Traveller," p. 728). Cf. **closed**.

open form See **free verse**.

ottava rima See *AC 1*.

overstatement See **hyperbole**.

oxymoron A form of **antithesis** depending on **paradox**; a statement or phrase or word consisting of two logically contradictory parts that nevertheless expresses a valid or thought-provoking idea or image — e.g. *sophomore* ("wise fool"), *bittersweet*. "I must be cruel only to be kind," says Hamlet.

Petrarchan **conceits** often include oxymorons (see e.g. the series in Wyatt's "I find no peace, and all my war is done," p. 130). Milton in *Paradise Lost* refers to the absence of light in Hell as "darkness visible" (I, 63; p. 327), and see also "precious bane" (I, 692; p. 335). "O Death in Life," says Tennyson in the last line of "Tears, Idle Tears" (p. 966).

paean A **song** or **hymn** of praise, joy, triumph, thanksgiving.

paeon A classical metrical **foot** consisting of one long and three short syllables — or in English stressed and unstressed (´˘˘˘, ˘´˘˘, ˘˘´˘, ˘˘˘´ — called first, second, third, or fourth paeon according to the position of the long or stressed syllable). The paeon is unusual in English **verse**, but it does occur, e.g. in Hopkins's work: see **sprung rhythm**, and p. 1123. See also **metre** and **quantitative verse**.

parable A brief **story**, often a sort of simple **allegory**, that teaches a moral lesson. Cf. **fable**, and see **didactic** and *AC 1: Indirect Modes*.

paradigm A pattern, example, or model. In *AC 2*, what we call "narrative paradigms" are standard actions, events, characters, or texts that are used or referred to repeatedly in literary works — thus becoming virtual **motifs** (and see **intertextuality**).

paradox A seemingly illogical statement that is nevertheless true; see e.g. the concluding **couplet** of Donne's Holy Sonnet 14 (p. 258). The term can also apply more generally to a set of contradictory circumstances or qualities; see e.g. the opening passage of Epistle II of Pope's *Essay on Man* (p. 541). Paradoxes often turn up in **epigrams** and **proverbs**. See **oxymoron**.

parallelism Similarity of **structure** or order of elements, whether in phrases, clauses, sentences, paragraphs, or even larger units. An example from Pope's *The Rape of the Lock* (I, 81-82; p. 524), in which the parallelism is strengthened by **alliteration**: "These swell their prospects and exalt their pride, / When offers are disdained, and love denied." And see e.g. the parallel sentence structure often used by Samuel Johnson (p. 589). See also **antithesis**, **balance**, and **chiasmus**.

parody See *AC 1*.

paronomasia See **pun**.

pastoral Originally a poetic **genre** in which ostensible shepherds sang of country love and other rural matters; now more commonly a **mode** in which the non-urban plays some part, e.g. as **setting** or **subject**; the term *pastoral* is sometimes loosely applied to any work about rural people and places, or even just nature. Among the **traditional** forms are the singing match, the **dialogue**, the love song or **complaint**, and the **elegy**. Never genuinely naive or "folk" art, pastoral poetry expresses a sophisticated urban attitude towards the country — often idealized — and often says or implies something about the problematic relationship between art and nature. Pastorals are also called *eclogues* and *bucolics*. See also **anti-pastoral** and *AC 1*; and see Samuel Johnson's criticism in the excerpt from his life of Milton (p. 607).

pathetic fallacy A term coined by John Ruskin as a derogatory label for the **convention** by which human emotions are attributed to inanimate elements of nature, similar to but falling short of full-scale **personification**; but it is now considered a fallacy or weakness only if overdone. It is a convention of **pastoral elegy**: see e.g. Milton's *Lycidas*, 39-44 (p. 316), and other pastorals such as the first Idyll of Theocritus and the "Lament for Bion" by Moschus; see also Denham's use of the single word *conscious* to convey such an idea (*Cooper's Hill*, 277; p. 387).

pentameter A line of **verse** with five metrical feet. See **foot** and **metre**.

performance verse Poetry that either was designed for reciting aloud or has become popularly associated with recital. See *AC 1* for examples. Some poems, though especially popular and sometimes recited or read aloud, are still not "performance verse" *per se*: Thomas Gray's "Elegy," for example (p. 610), or Hood's "The Song of the Shirt" (p. 884), or Blake's "The Tyger" (p. 724) — though the latter's "Jerusalem" ("And did those feet," p. 730), as a **song**, might be so considered, such as folk songs (see *AC 1*) or some other songs and hymns (e.g. Galt's "Canadian Boat Song," p. 805, Newman's "Lead, Kindly Light," p. 893, and Thomas Moore's "The harp that once through Tara's halls," p. 807) or early **ballads** (e.g. "Sir Patrick Spens," p. 19); but if a piece is sung rather than recited, it isn't, strictly speaking, performance verse. Similarly, though a popular **nursery rhyme** such as "Who Killed Cock Robin?" (p. 567) might be meant to be recited, it remains a nursery rhyme, not, in ordinary circumstances, a "performance" piece.

persona A "mask." Rather than write as themselves, authors frequently adopt a persona, wear a mask, for the purpose of a given work. Swift for example adopts the persona of a naive "projector" in order to make his **ironic** points in *A Modest Proposal* (p. 480). It is usually safer and less potentially confusing to refer to the "speaker" of a work, even of many **lyric** poems, than to its "author," since the "I" may be someone fictional, even quite different from the actual author. Similarly, modern criticism uses the term *implied author* for the person inferred by readers as standing behind a given work — a "person" who may be significantly different from the real author. The "I" of a non-fiction work may also be a persona, as in an autobiography, letter, or travel narrative (Moodie, p. 919; Chesterfield, p. 560; Mandeville, p. 22). See **narrator**.

personification A **figure of speech** in which something nonhuman, often an **abstraction**, is given human attributes. Note e.g. how Johnson personifies abstractions throughout *The Vanity of Human Wishes* (p. 589), and how Keats personifies his "Grecian Urn" as a "Sylvan historian" (p. 855); in Denham's *Cooper's Hill* (p. 383), the hunted stag is to a considerable degree personified by being given human thoughts and emotions. When extended or multiplied, personification becomes **allegory** or allegorical. Note e.g. Drayton's gathering of personifications in "Since there's no help" (p. 226), Pope's in the Cave of Spleen scene near the beginning of Canto IV of *The Rape of the Lock* (p. 529), and the cluster of personifications in the third stanza of Keats's "Ode on Melancholy" (p. 856). And see William Wordsworth's comments in his "Preface" (p. 760).

Petrarchan conceit See **conceit**.

Petrarchan sonnet See *AC 1: Sonnet*.

picturesque An intellectual and aesthetic term that developed in the 18th century, largely as a response to Edmund Burke's 1757 book *A Philosophical Inquiry into the Origin of Our Ideas of the Sublime and Beautiful* (see **sublime**). Finding attractions in unorganized rural scenery, numerous writers, artists, and landscape designers — among them William Gilpin (1724-1804) in *Three Essays: On Picturesque Beauty, On Picturesque Travel, and On Sketching Landscape* (1792) — sought a midway point between the "sublime" (which inspired awe and terror) and the "beautiful" (which was smooth and small); they used the word "picturesque" to describe "scenes" that were characterized by roughness, ruggedness, and irregularity, and that were so arranged as to provide the illusion of wilderness without the reality of vastness and uninhabitability. Rural cottages, ruined buildings, winding streams, and wild patches of garden thus all provided instances of the picturesque, provided that the viewer had a secure vantage point from which to view them. Garden planners such as Lancelot "Capability" Brown (1716-1783) designed "prospects" over a landscape, often with such features as artificial ruins viewed across a "natural" lake; French painters such as Nicolas Poussin (1594-1665) and Claude Lorrain (1600-1682) appealed to the English taste for "scenery"; the poet Thomas Gray was one of many people who carried a "Claude glass" — a darkened curved mirror (named after Claude Lorrain) by which a viewer could look at an actual landscape and see what it might look like as a painting, thus artificially constructing the world as "picturesque." The works by William Wordsworth (p. 754), Kemble (p. 976), and Moodie (p. 919) all differentiate between the sublime and the picturesque; the term *picturesque* was still being used in this sense in the late 19th century in the works by Henry James (p. 1117) and Sara Jeannette Duncan (p. 1185).

plot The arrangement or organization of incidents in a play or a **fictional narrative**, whether in **verse** or prose, usually setting up, then complicating, and finally resolving a **conflict** (a standard pattern sometimes described as consisting of **exposition**, rising action, crisis or **climax**, falling action, and conclusion — but a pattern, however "standard," that is not necessarily followed in every work of fiction; e.g., the point may be that there is no possible resolution — see **open**). Aristotle in his *Poetics* asserts that a good plot must have a beginning, a middle, and an end, and that its events must be linked by causality. E. M. Forster in *Aspects of the Novel* puts it this way: "'The king died and then the queen died,' is a story. 'The king died and then the queen died of grief' is a plot." Without cause-and-effect relations, the incidents constitute a sequence of episodes without any necessary connections between them, resulting in what is called an "episodic" plot. See **story** and **dénouement**.

poetic diction In general, language suitable for or used in poetry. But the term more commonly refers to the particular register of language used in the late 17th and early 18th centuries by poets who felt that everyday language was not sufficiently refined or **elevated** for poetry—e.g. Gay's periphrastic "scaly people" ("Fable XLIX," line 31; p. 509) or Pope's "finny prey" (*The Rape of the Lock*, II, 26; p. 525) for fish; or such archaisms as *oft*, *methought*, *whilom* used for deliberate atmospheric effect by Spenser and with less conscious purpose by many later poets. See William Wordsworth's attack early in his Preface to *Lyrical Ballads* (p. 759); see also **kenning**.

point of view In a work of **fiction**, the position or perspective from which an author chooses to tell the story. Point of view is usually *first-person* or *third-person*. *First-person* point of view uses an "I" **narrator**, who may be, at one extreme, the **protagonist**, or at the other a minor **character** functioning merely as an observer, or somewhere in between. *Third-person* point of view may be *omniscient* ("all-knowing," the narrator able to be in all places and having access to the minds of all the characters and revealing as much or as little as the author chooses), or *limited* to some degree, for example knowing only what a particular character — the "point of view" character — can know. Or the point of view may be what is called *objective* or *dramatic*, the author presenting — or purporting to present — only the outward facts, without comment, as if readers were watching a play: observing the action and the scenery and hearing only what the characters say. Modern fiction often uses a multiple perspective, presenting events as seen from more than one point of view, including experiments with second-person and **free indirect discourse**.

poulter's measure See *AC 1*.

prolepsis See **flashforward**.

prologue Specifically, an opening speech by one of the actors introducing a play, but also an introduction or preface to any long literary work, such as a play, **novel**, or long poem — e.g. the "General Prologue" to Chaucer's *Canterbury Tales* (p. 29). See also **epilogue**.

proposition The **thesis** or statement that an **argument** attempts to support or prove.

prose poem See *AC 1*.

prosody The principles and the systematic study and analysis of versification. See **metre**, **rhyme**, **rhythm**, **scansion**, and **stanza**.

protagonist The main **character**, the first (*proto*) contender (*agonist*), who perhaps struggles against an *antagonist* (*anti-agonist*, opponent). The terms *hero* and *heroine* commonly refer to a main character, but may be misleading if the main character is not notably "heroic" — or is even perhaps an **anti-hero** or **-heroine**. See also **conflict**.

proverb An anonymous pithy popular saying expressing some truth about experience, often deriving from folk wisdom, handed down orally. Note e.g. the proverb Henryson works in at lines 91-92 of "Robene and Makyne" (p. 108); and see Franklin's "The Way to Wealth" (p. 577). See also **aphorism**, and *AC 1: Epigram*.

Ptolemaic Until the astronomical observations of Nicholas Copernicus (1473-1543) were published in 1543 — arguing that the earth revolved around the sun — the prevailing theory of the structure of the universe was that devised by the 2nd-century A.D. Greco-Egyptian mathematician Ptolemy (Claudius Ptolemaeus) and explained in his *Almagest*, based on the work of the Greek astronomer Hipparchus (2nd century B.C.). In the Ptolemaic system, the earth is the centre of the universe and is surrounded by a series of concentric spheres in which the sun, moon, and other heavenly bodies move at different speeds. Beyond the planets, as this diagram of Ptolemy's scheme shows, lie the "firmament" (or "heaven") of fixed stars; the crystalline sphere (conceived of as a transparent filter or lens); and the outermost sphere, the *primum mobile* or "prime mover," which by moving sets in motion all the rest. Each circle in the diagram represents an entire sphere, not a flat plane. Beyond the spheres lies the Empyrean, which was conceptualized (as the etymology of the word suggests) as an area of pure elemental fire. (N.B.: The Crystalline Sphere does not appear in all versions of the Ptolemaic system, having been introduced later to explain some apparent inconsistencies in planetary motion, namely the precession of the equinoxes; supposedly, certain oscillations of this sphere were imparted to the inner spheres, resulting in what was called "the trepidation of the spheres.") As works by Milton, Pope, and others demonstrate, writers made

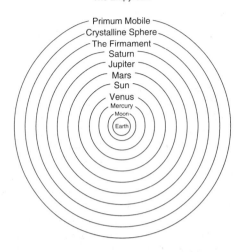

The Empyrean

Primum Mobile
Crystalline Sphere
The Firmament
Saturn
Jupiter
Mars
Sun
Venus
Mercury
Moon
Earth

imaginative use of the Ptolemaic scheme long after its scientific validity had been questioned. They also alluded to several ideas associated with the Ptolemaic universe, such as the "music of the spheres," a harmony that (according to Pythagorean philosophy) heavenly bodies produced as they travelled in their orbits, but which human ears could not distinguish. Christian adaptations of the Ptolemaic universe suggested that Hell lay within the Earth or (as in Milton's *Paradise Lost*) some- where below it in an indeterminate Chaos, and that Heaven existed above Earth, in the highest reaches of the Empyrean.

pun Wordplay whose effect, whether serious or **humorous**, depends on a word's having two meanings or on two words having a similar or identical sound. As a **rhetorical** device, often called *paronomasia*. See e.g. the word *kindely* in the next to last line of Wyatt's "They flee from me who sometime did me seek" (p. 130), the puns in Donne's "Hymn to God the Father" (p. 259), the pun Milton gives Satan in *Paradise Lost*, I, 642 (p. 334), and Thomas Hood's "Faithless Nelly Gray" (p. 881).

pyrrhic (n. & adj.) A metrical **foot** having two unstressed syllables (˘ ˘), also called a *dibrach*. See **metre**.

quantitative verse Verse whose **metre** is determined by duration of syllables (long or short), as in classical (Latin and Greek) poetry, rather than

stress, as in most English poetry; see **paeon** and **sapphics**. And cf. **accentual**, **accentual syllabic**, and **syllabic verse**.

quatrain A **stanza** of four lines, or a four-line portion of a longer poem, such as an English sonnet (see *AC 1: Sonnet*), or a four-line poem.

quintain See *AC 1*.

quest Loosely, any journey towards a goal; more specifically, a **motif** in **romances** and other heroic **tales** in which a wanderer, through a series of trials, seeks a solution or a truth. Odysseus (Ulysses) in the *Odyssey* travelled in search of home, e.g., and Arthurian knights sought the Holy Grail. Sometimes the term is used to describe the art form of exploration **narratives**, but the "quest" must be distinguished from the simple "adventure" of a peripatetic or picaresque character.

realism The faithful depiction of objective reality, or at least the appearance or illusion of objectively depicting reality, within the limitations on probability and the conventions governing language and usage; also, a philosophical position favouring the acknowledgment of the often difficult nature of life, rather than trying to avoid it or hide it (e.g. via **romance**) — hence the term refers also to literature reflecting that position, e.g. in **stories** and **novels** about ordinary middle- and lower-class people facing the everyday problems of life. See also **comedy**, **irony**, **documentary**, **mimesis**, **verisimilitude**, and **fiction**.

refrain One or more lines **repeated** in a poem, most commonly at the end of each **stanza**; occasionally a refrain consists of only a word or phrase, rather than a line; and sometimes the refrain will vary slightly each time, rather than be repeated exactly. See e.g. Spenser's *Epithalamion*, and see *AC 1: Ballade*; *Rondeau*. Refrains also occur in many **songs** (see *AC 1*).

regional, regionalism A term used to describe writing that emphasizes the geographic or social attitudes of a particular area, or which expresses the social perspectives of a particular area; hence such various writings as Mitford's *Our Village*, Munro's Ontario stories, Barnes's Dorset dialect verse, and Haliburton's Maritime anecdotes are all sometimes classed as *regional*. Cf. **local color**. Derived from the Latin *regere*, "to rule," the term *regional* frequently implies lesser quality or importance, connoting "peripheral," "marginal," "imitative," or "colonial," but recent usage rejects this implication, interpreting the term more sympathetically, defining *regions* as the constitutive parts of a whole, rather than as the territories surrounding a centre.

repetition An important **rhetorical** technique, basic to much of the effectiveness of literature. Repetition of words, phrases, and ideas obviously produces emphasis; but repetition of various kinds also enhances aesthetic and other effects by creating patterns, whether of **sound** (**rhyme, alliteration, assonance, consonance**) or **rhythm** (**metre, stanza, refrain**), or **structure** (e.g. with **parallel syntax**). See also **anadiplosis, anaphora,** and **epistrophe**.

rhetoric A term formerly limited to the art of speaking persuasively, but which now means simply the art or craft of using words effectively, most often in writing, whether for **argumentative** purposes or not; *rhetoric* as a discipline refers to the study of the elements and principles of effective writing. The so-called **figures** of rhetoric include such devices or patterns as **anaphora, antithesis, apostrophe, balance, chiasmus, paradox, parallelism,** and **rhetorical question**.

rhetorical question A question that is intended not to elicit an answer but to make a point; it assumes the obviousness of the answer. See e.g. the second stanza of Donne's "The Canonization" (p. 254), or Thalestris's speech in Pope's *The Rape of the Lock,* 4, 95ff. (p. 530).

rhyme Repetition of the same or similar concluding **sound** in two or more words, such as *fame/name, broken/token. Single rhyme* occurs in final stressed syllables: *lend/depend/condescend, act/packed. Double rhyme* occurs in the last two syllables, the first stressed and the second unstressed: *lending/depending, manic/panic. Triple rhyme* occurs in three successive syllables, the first being stressed: con*secutive/executive, company/thump any* (and obviously can be used for **humorous** effect, as sometimes can double rhyme). Not uncommon in early poetry but frowned upon since the Middle Ages, *identical rhyme* repeats the exact word — e.g. in lines 9-10 and 17-18 of Chaucer's "General Prologue," (p. 29), and see Griffin's "Fly to her heart" (p. 273); similarly, *rime riche* repeats the exact sound but with different spellings — e.g.

roam/Rome in Poe's "To Helen" (p. 936). Slant *rhyme* (also called *half rhyme, near rhyme, off rhyme, pararhyme, imperfect rhyme*) only partly echoes the sound; most often it amounts to **consonance** at the ends of a pair of lines — i.e., retaining the opening and closing consonant sounds, or just the final one, and altering the internal vowels, as in *mine/moon, bid/bad, came/comb, loss/base, farce/horse*; sometimes it amounts to **assonance**, as in *side/time, song/fog, met/head*; and still other variations are possible; see e.g. some of the poems by Emily Dickinson (p. 1080), Wilfred Owen's "Arms and the Boy" (p. 1327), and Dylan Thomas's "The Force that Through the Green Fuse Drives the Flower" (p. 1374).

Eye rhyme occurs when words look as though they rhyme but are actually pronounced somewhat differently, e.g. *fear/bear, lost/most, power/mower, rough/though,* often because pronunciations have changed over the centuries: what once was true rhyme now is eye rhyme — e.g. *worth/forth, love/prove, said/maid,* or Pope's *binds/winds* and *wind/unkind* (*Rape of the Lock*, IV, 81-82, 163-64; pp. 530-31); such eye rhyme is called historical rhyme. Similar instances, though the spellings aren't identical, occur in Pope's *away/tea* and *obey/tea* (then pronounced "tay") in *The Rape of the Lock* (I, 61-62; III, 7-8) and *line/join* (then pronounced "jine") in *An Essay on Criticism* (346-47, 360-61; p. 521, which see also for his comments on rhyme); in Finch's "The Introduction" (p. 474), *fault* in line 6 is pronounced "fawt" or "fought," so that it rhymes with *untaught* in the preceding line; and in Denham's "Cooper's Hill" (p. 383), note that in lines 131-32 *spoils* is pronounced so that it rhymes with *styles* (and again at 342), though *spoil* has its regular pronunciation at 175; and at 252 and 312 *wound* rhymes with *sound* and *wounds* with *hounds*.

Most rhyme is *end rhyme,* occurring at the ends of lines, but there is also *internal rhyme,* in which words within a line rhyme with each other or with the final word; when a word in the middle of a line rhymes with the final word, the rhyme is called *leonine* (as in Poe's "The Raven," and often in S. T. Coleridge's *Rime of the Ancient Mariner,* p. 784).

The rhyme scheme of a poem is conventionally indicated by using letters, beginning with a and proceeding alphabetically, with like letters representing like sounds: a Shakespearean sonnet, e.g., has a rhyme scheme of *ababcdcdefefgg*; for examples of a variety of rhyme schemes, see *AC 1*.

rhyme royal (or *rime royal*) So-called because it was used by James I; also known as the *Chaucerian Stanza*, after the English poet who first used it. See *AC 1*.

rhyme scheme See **rhyme**.

rhythm The movement or cadence in a sequence of words, lines, sentences, or paragraphs, produced by recurrence or alternation of qualities or elements such as size or length, emphasis and lack of emphasis, sensed or "heard" pitch or volume, identical or similar sounds, or stressed and unstressed syllables. If the last, it is synonymous with **metre**. See also **rising rhythm, falling rhythm, rocking rhythm**, and **sprung rhythm**, and the excerpt from Pope's *An Essay on Criticism* (p. 521).

riddle See *AC 1*.

rising rhythm The **rhythm** or **metre** of an **iambic** or **anapestic foot**.

rocking rhythm The **rhythm** or **metre** of an **amphibrachic foot**.

romance A term used to designate (1) a **verse** or (later) prose **story** of knights and chivalry, magic and love (metrical romance or medieval romance — e.g. *Sir Gawain and the Green Knight*, Malory's *Le Morte d'Arthur*; see pp. 26, 94); (2) a long **epic**-like **narrative** poem (e.g. Spenser's *The Faerie Queene*; see p. 150); (3) a popular **novel** about passionate love (e.g. the "Harlequin" series); (4) a **novel**-like but more imaginative prose work with exotic **settings**, larger-than-life **characters**, thrilling adventures, heightened **style**, sometimes supernatural elements, and often a probing of philosophical ideas (e.g. Melville's *Moby-Dick*, Emily Brontë's *Wuthering Heights*, Hawthorne's *The Scarlet Letter*). Insofar as romance tends to idealize characters and events and to offer escapist reading, it is generally viewed as in contrast to **realism**. See Johnson's *Rambler* No. 4 (p. 594); see also *chanson de geste*, **tale**, **novel**, and **story**; and see **mode**.

rondeau See *AC 1*.

rondel See *AC 1*.

round character See **character**.

run-on line See **enjambement**.

sapphics In English a difficult stanzaic pattern, imitating a **quantitative verse** form named after Sappho. See *AC 1*.

sarcasm See **irony**.

satire See *AC 1*. Satire is both a **genre** and a **mode**. Satire with a **humorous tone**, such as Pope's *The Rape of the Lock* (p. 521), is called *Horatian* (after Horace); satire with a tone of serious indignation or even bitterness, such as Rochester's "Satire Against Mankind" (p. 461) or Johnson's *The Vanity of Human Wishes* (p. 589), is called *Juvenalian* (after Juvenal). Donne's "Satire III" is somewhat different in that its criticism of human frailty is largely implicit in its wide-ranging discussion and questioning of religious beliefs: the principal "folly" would be in not seeking the true religion at all — though the brief portraits in lines 43ff. are **conventionally** satirical. See also the selection from Piozzi's *British Synonymy* (p. 689), and *Burlesque* and *Parody* in *AC 1*.

scansion Determining the nature of the **metre** or **rhythm** of a line or lines of **verse** by identifying stressed and unstressed syllables and thus the kind and number of metrical feet present (see **foot**). Conventionally, syllables are marked (above the line) as stressed (ˊ) or unstressed (˘), feet separated with a vertical line (|), and a caesura marked with a double line (|| or ˊˊ).

scatology (adj. *scatological*) Literally, the study of dung, as in medicine or paleontology, or, in psychiatry, of an obsession with excrement. As a literary term, it sometimes refers broadly to off-colour work of various degrees, but more specifically it indicates references—especially if repeated or continued — to excrement and other such physical realities; see e.g. those in Dryden's *Mac Flecknoe* (p. 433); it occurs also in Oldham's "Satire upon a Woman" (p. 464). Jonathan Swift is noted for occasional scatological passages.

scene A division of an act of a play, but the term also refers to the place where some action occurs — "the *scene* of battle"; "the author sets the *scene* in the opening paragraph of the story." In the latter sense, the term is loosely synonymous with **setting**.

semiotics (semiology) The study of **signs** and sign-systems and how, through the **conventions** of a particular culture, they produce meaning, whether in literature or in everyday life, through such things as advertisements, films, buildings, food, and clothing.

sentimentality Exaggerated emotion, more intense feelings than the circumstances call for or will support; once fashionable, as in the 18th-century "sentimental comedy" and "sentimental novel," but now usually perceived as a weakness, unless designed for humorous effect. See **melodramatic**.

sestet A **stanza** of six lines, or the six-line portion of an Italian sonnet. See *AC 1: Sonnet*.

sestina See *AC 1*.

setting The place and time in which the action of a **narrative** occurs ("The story is *set* in mid-nineteenth-century London"); in a **novel** or play, the action will often occur in several different settings. Setting may also be thought of as including such things as the weather and such non-tangible elements as *atmosphere* and *mood* (see **tone**), and even the psychological make-up of **characters** — i.e., the full array of circumstances within which the action occurs. See also **scene** and **dramatic context**.

Shakespearean sonnet See *AC 1: Sonnet*.

shaped verse See *AC 1*.

short story A short work of prose **fiction**, usually focussing on only a few **characters**, with a **plot** of no more than a few episodes, and often in a single **setting**. Cf. **novel**, **novella**, **sketch**, **story**, and **tale**. See also *AC 1: Fictional Narrative*.

sign Something that signifies something else, e.g. a signal directing one to do something, such as a red traffic light; or a word standing for something, such as the noun *rose*; or something indicating the presence of something else, such as smoke suggesting the presence of fire, or a dark cloud signalling the approach of a storm. Cf. **symbol**, and see **semiotics**.

simile A **figure of speech** that explicitly compares two unlike things, using *like* or *as*, as in Burns's "O, my luve's like a red, red rose" (p. 733). Like a **metaphor**, a simile may be *extended*; see e.g. the two with which Keats closes "On Looking into Chapman's Homer" (p. 853). And an *epic* (or *Homeric*) simile, usually introduced with so or as, imitates Homer's practice in the *Iliad* and *Odyssey* by elaborating the comparison until it becomes an independent discussion, description, or miniature tale; see e.g. stanzas 21 and 23 of Book I, Canto I of Spenser's *Faerie Queene* (p. 150). Milton often uses such similes in *Paradise Lost* (see e.g. the notes to I, 196-208 through 302-11, p. 329). See also **conceit**.

single rhyme See **rhyme**.

situational irony See **irony**.

Skeltonics See the excerpt from John Skelton's "Colyn Clout" and the note thereto (p. 113).

sketch (1) A brief descriptive **essay**. (2) A brief play (often **satirical**). (3) A brief prose work focussing on a single **setting** without **characters**, or on the feelings evoked by such a setting, or with one or more characters involved in a single incident (**plot** is minimized; see e.g. Woolf's "The Lady in the Looking-Glass — p. 1273); such a sketch may or may not be fictional, and may even be almost entirely **descriptive** (see e.g. the selection from Melville's *The Encantadas*, p. 1027). One kind of descriptive sketch is the *character* or character sketch (see *AC 1*); and cf. **short story** and **tale**.

slang **Vernacular diction** or speech, sometimes considered as including obscene or otherwise offensive language, and sometimes equated with **jargon** in the sense of the language of a special group. After **informal** and **colloquial**, it is the next step away from **formal** on the spectrum of **style**. Often lively and striking, slang is usually felt to be inappropriate outside everyday, colloquial speech, but used carefully it can be effective in writing; see e.g. line 156 of E. B. White's "Once More to the Lake" (p. 1347). Sometimes the slang of one generation becomes part of the standard, even formal vocabulary of the next, but more often it just disappears; perhaps its main drawback is its impermanence: it changes so fast that it is often out of date almost overnight. Slang is also often confined to a particular class, group, profession, or region.

song Any **lyric** poem can be called a song, whether sung or not, but most so-called "songs" are intended to be sung. See also *AC 1*.

sonnet See *AC 1*.

sonnet sequence On Petrarch's model, poets often composed long sequences of sonnets addressed to a real or fictitious person — e.g. Spenser's *Amoretti* (p. 161), Sidney's *Astrophel and Stella* (p. 193), Shakespeare's sonnets (p. 226).

sound, sound patterns See **alliteration**, **assonance**, **cacophony**, **consonance**, **euphony**, **repetition**, **rhyme**. See also **rhythm** and **metre**, and the excerpt from Pope's *An Essay on Criticism* (p. 521).

speaker See **persona**.

spell See *AC 1: Charm, Spell.*

Spenserian stanza See *AC 1.*

spondee (adj. *spondaic*) A **foot** having two stressed syllables (ʹ ʹ). See **metre**; see also S. T. Coleridge's "Metrical Feet" (p. 793).

sprung rhythm A term coined by Gerard Manley Hopkins to describe his **metrics**, namely his controlling the number of stressed syllables in a line of **verse** without using regular feet: each **foot** begins with a stressed syllable, and the number of unstressed syllables following each stressed syllable may vary from none to three, or even more (and thus some of Hopkins's feet are first **paeons**); supposedly, each foot, regardless of the number of syllables it contains, will occupy the same amount of time. The system is based on **accentual metre** and mediaeval **alliterative verse**. Hopkins claimed such rhythm was "nearest to the rhythm of prose, the native and natural rhythm of speech." See poems by Hopkins (p. 1123), some of the **nursery rhymes** (p. 566), and *AC 1: Alliterative Verse.*

stanza A patterned group of two or more lines serving as a division of a poem. A stanza's pattern is determined by number and length of lines, **metre**, and **rhyme** scheme (if any; see *tercet* through *Spenserian Stanza* in *AC 1*). A single poem may contain more than one kind of stanza. Stanzas are conventionally separated from each other by spaces, and are sometimes numbered. See also **couplet**, **tercet**, **quatrain**, **sestet**, **octave**, and **envoy**, and cf. **verse paragraph**.

stereotype Something repeated from age to age, usually in works of the same **genre**, with little or no variation; see **character**. A *stereotype* may also be a formulaic phrasing or set pattern of expression, an idea or opinion (e.g. simplistic attitudes toward a race or nation), a stock situation or **setting** (e.g. the "locked room" murder mystery), or even a **plot** (e.g. those of many popular **romances**).

stock character See **character.**

story Loosely, any **narrative**, such as a **short story**, but especially relatively simple ones designed to entertain. The term *story* can also refer to the sequence of events or **plot** in a narrative, as distinct from such other elements as **character** and **setting**. In modern criticism, it may also refer to the complete and chronological sequence of events that readers infer from a plotted narrative that may itself

be to some degree only suggestive, unchronological, incomplete, or otherwise different from the full sequence of events. Cf. **fable**, **fairy tale**, **romance**, **sketch**, **tale**. See also *AC 1: Fictional Narrative.*

stress Accent; see **metre**.

stretched sonnet See *AC 1: Sonnet.*

structure The organized shape of a work of literature or of part of a work. The structure of an English sonnet, e.g., consists of a pattern made up of fourteen iambic pentameter lines: three **quatrains** (each rhyming in a certain way) and a closing **couplet** (see *AC 1: Sonnet*). Plays are usually divided into acts and **scenes**. The effective structure of a **short story** or a **novel** is usually not so discernible, so patterned or regular, but is often recognizably, e.g., linear or circular in its movement. See also **frame story** and **form and content**.

style Everything that constitutes the way something is written; the overall choice and arrangement of sounds, words, phrases, sentences, and paragraphs or other parts. A particular style or kind of style may be associated with a particular author, subject, period, or audience. See also **form and content**.

subject What is being written about. A work of imaginative literature will usually have two kinds of subjects: Joyce's **short story** "Eveline" (p. 1268), e.g., is literally or specifically "about" Eveline, a young woman in Dublin who contemplates sailing away with her romantic young man; more generally, in terms of intended meaning and ideas, it is "about" such matters as parent-child relations, fear of leaving the security of home, and what Joyce saw as the smothering, entrapping nature of Irish society. *Topic*, or more often *topos* (Greek for "place," plural *topoi*), is also used in **rhetoric** to refer to categories of argumentative devices, or in literature to recurrent and therefore *stock* or conventional subjects, situations, poses, and the like, such as the Golden Age, comparing city and country (see *AC 2*), and bewailing the inadequacy of verse to express one's love; see **motif** and **theme**. For nonfiction writing, the term *topic* is often used as a synonym for *subject*, but it is also used to refer to a subdivision of a subject; e.g., a given essay's broad subject or subject area could be "travel," but it might focus on one or more narrower topics, such as "the psychology of tipping" or "cruising the Aegean."

sublime An intellectual and aesthetic term that developed in the 18th century, generally signifying an idea, principle, scene, emotion, or experience that awakens awe — applying to anything that could be described as elevated, noble, or solemn. The term derives from a treatise *On the Sublime* (*Peri Hypsous*, *hypsos* meaning *height*, *summit*; attributed to "Longinus" by mistaken association with the 3rd-century-A.D. rhetorician Cassius Longinus, though actually written by an unknown author of the 1st century A.D.), which stipulated five sorts of loftiness as sources of the sublime: two deriving from nature (loftiness of thoughts and feelings) and three from art (loftiness of figurative language, diction, and arrangement). The concept's currency in the 18th century was influenced by Edmund Burke's *A Philosophical Inquiry into the Origin of Our Ideas of the Sublime and Beautiful* (1757), which associated the sublime with terror (stemming from such qualities as darkness, power, solitude, and vastness) and the beautiful with a sort of "love" (stemming from smallness, smoothness, delicacy, and fair and mild colours). The Grand Tour of Europe and the European settlement of North America — especially by acquainting travellers with alpine scenery, vast expanses of forest and tundra, and rushing cascades (Niagara in particular) — encouraged writers and artists to describe certain landscapes as sublime. By the 19th century, the word "sublime" in relation to landscape came also to suggest "uninhabitable." See the works by Reynolds (p. 627), William Wordsworth (especially the note to "Descriptive Sketches, p. 754), Kemble (p. 982), Martineau (p. 897), and Moodie (p. 919). See also **picturesque**.

substitution The replacement in a line of **verse** of the regular or prevalent **foot** (such as an **iamb**) by another (such as a **trochee** or **spondee**), whether for emphasis (see e.g. the beginnings of lines 1, 5, and 9 of Shakespeare's sonnet 116, p. 229) or for variety, to avoid the monotony of an entirely regular metre. Substitution is especially common in *blank verse* (see *AC 1*).

surrealism A primarily French artistic movement that began in the 1920s; it elevated imagination, dreams, and the unconscious above reason and logic, and sought to combine the rational and the irrational, the conscious and the unconscious. See James Wright's

"Against Surrealism" (p. 1424), and perhaps also Layton's "The Cold Green Element" (p. 1372) and Beckett's "Ping" (p. 1358).

syllabic verse Verse which measures lines only by the number of syllables each contains, regardless of **stress** or quantity (see **quantitative verse**). Common in poetry of the Romance languages, and Japanese (see **haiku**), it is rare in English, though some modern and contemporary poets, such as Marianne Moore and W. H. Auden, have experimented with it; and some earlier poets, e.g. Milton, sometimes varied the stress pattern in their lines to such a degree that they are as much syllabic as otherwise — and it is probably more accurate to call Donne's "Satire III" *decasyllabic* than to assign a metrical pattern to it. Crapsey's "The Warning" (p. 1259), a *cinquain* (see *AC 1*, is a syllabic poem, as essentially is Dylan Thomas's "Fern Hill" (p. 1375). Cf. **accentual metre** and **accentual-syllabic metre**.

symbol Basically, an **image** whose **concrete** item, like a **sign**, stands for something else, but a "something else" that is larger, richer, more complex, or even not otherwise expressible, such as an **abstract** idea or cluster of ideas or associations. A symbol may be an object, a **character**, an action, a situation, or a place; strictly, words themselves are symbols. Symbols in a literary work can be classified as either (1) intrinsic, private, deriving their significance from their immediate context, such as perhaps the woods in Frost's "Stopping by Woods on a Snowy Evening" (p. 1251) or the spider and other elements in his "Design" (p. 1251), or (2) extrinsic, **conventional**, having a culturally shared significance from outside the work, such as the cross as a symbol of Christianity, or Housman's laurel (athletic victory) and rose (feminine beauty) in "To an Athlete Dying Young" (p. 1180). Many symbols are a combination of the two — e.g. Yeats's Byzantium (see the note to the title of "Sailing to Byzantium," p. 1217). But a symbol's significance, or what it "stands for," can seldom be so easily and neatly pinned down: many symbols are intended to be partly or wholly **open**, suggestive; consider e.g. the multivalent symbols in Blake's "The Sick Rose" (p. 724). The term *symbolism can* refer to the practice of using symbols, to a system of symbols or symbolic meanings, and to an important **literary movement** that began in France in the late 19th century.

synaesthesia The mixing of two or more senses in one **image**, as in the second stanza of Keats's "Ode to a Nightingale" (p. 854); see also line 45 of Sidney's "Ye Goat-herd Gods" (p. 192).

syncope See **elision**.

synecdoche A **figure of speech** — a kind of **metonymy** — that names a significant part to stand for a whole, or sometimes a whole for a part — e.g. "sails" for ships, "meat" or "bread" for food, "hands" for labourers, "the law" for an individual police officer. See e.g. Sandys's *Ovid*, 97 and note (p. 268), and line 101 of King's "The Exequy" (p. 288), where "bottom" means ship.

syntax The arrangement of words in phrases, clauses, and sentences; the grammatical relation among such words.

tail-rhyme stanza See *AC 1*.

tale The word *tale* can refer to any related **story**, even one in **verse**, or more narrowly to any **narrative** with a relatively simple **plot**. More narrowly still, however, it refers to a **fictional** narrative with relatively stylized or flat **characters**, unusual or even exotic **settings**, a plot emphasizing action or adventure and strong emotions, and often the supernatural. See also *AC 1: Fictional Narrative*. Cf. **short story**, **sketch**, and **romance**.

tercet A **stanza** of three lines, sometimes with the same rhyme, or either half of the **sestet** in an Italian sonnet. See *AC 1*. Cf. **triplet**.

terza rima See *AC 1*.

tetrameter A line of **verse** with four metrical feet. See **foot** and **metre**. Lines of **iambic** or **trochaic** tetrameter are often referred to as *octosyllabic*.

theme A potentially misleading term. A *theme* is an idea, or a *topic*, or a **subject**. *Theme* is thus commonly used as a synonym for "central idea" or **thesis** or **proposition**, or for *meaning*, or even for *moral* (as of a **fable**); but this may result in oversimplification of a complex work: few serious literary works of more than a few lines or sentences have a single "theme." Readers will usually be safer to think not of *the* theme of a work but of a theme in a work, or of its several *themes*. Consider a frequently cited example: *jealousy* is certainly a theme of Shakespeare's *Othello*, even a *major*

theme — but it is far from being the play's *only* theme. See also **motif**.

thesis The central or controlling idea of an **essay**; the **proposition** of an **argument** — or sometimes of a **didactic novel** or other **narrative**. See also **theme**.

tone The attitude toward **subject** and audience evident in a work, created or established by the interaction of various elements of **style**; the quality inherent in a work that will determine how a reader will "hear" it: think of "tone of voice." A written work, e.g., may "sound" serious, playful, formal, ironic, bitter, tragic, solemn, matter-of-fact, intimate, cold, sneering, detached, sympathetic, laudatory, and so on. A related term, *mood*, usually refers more to the emotional attitude of an author or **narrator**, or the feeling evoked in a reader; and *atmosphere*, often used as a synonym of *mood*, often results from **description** of the **setting** of a **narrative** work.

topic See **subject**.

topographical poetry See *AC 1: Meditation, Reflection, Vision*.

topos, topoi See **subject**.

tradition A body of beliefs, practices, and sayings handed down from generation to generation. Tradition is sometimes associated with history (see e.g. Alice Jones's "A Day in Winchester," p. 1147) or education (think e.g. of the Grand Tour — see the note to line 9 of Dixon's "A Receipt for an Extraordinary Made-Dish," p. 489). In literature, a *tradition* is a body of **conventions** used by writers of a certain period, or the conventions used by authors of a certain **genre** (e.g. the **pastoral**) and inherited by later writers. See T. S. Eliot's essay "Tradition and the Individual Talent" (p. 1307). See also **motif**.

tragedy Loosely, a **narrative** or dramatic work which depicts misfortune, unhappiness, defeat, destruction, and the like. In its simplest form it shows the fall of a central character from prosperity to ruin, and usually death; but the "tragic" effect most often depends on our sense of the **protagonist**'s heroic struggle against inevitable defeat and of the consequent waste of strength and virtue. By stressing the ordinariness of misfortune, modern tragedy, or "the tragedy of the common man," modifies many of these **conventions**. Cf. **comedy**, and see also **mode**.

tragic irony See **irony**.

transferred epithet See **epithet**.

trimeter A line of **verse** with three metrical feet. See **foot** and **metre**.

triolet See *AC 1*.

triple rhyme See **rhyme**.

triplet Three successive rhyming lines, e.g. as used for variety or other effect among *heroic couplets* (see *AC 1*; see e.g. lines 57-59, 76-78, 87-89, 136-38, and 211-13 in Dryden's *Mac Flecknoe* (p. 433), the several triplets in Oldham's "A Satire upon a Woman" (p. 464), and the first three lines, lines 20-22, and the final three lines of Egerton's "On the Honourable Robert Boyle" (p. 487); such triplets are sometimes marked with the kind of bracket known as a brace. Cf. **tercet**.

trochee (adj. *trochaic*) A **foot** having a stressed syllable followed by an unstressed syllable (´ ˘). See **metre**; see also S. T. Coleridge's "Metrical Feet" (p. 793).

truncation The omission of one or more (usually unstressed) syllables from the first ("initial" truncation) or last **foot** of a line of **verse**. See **acephalous** and **catalectic**.

type character See **character**.

ubi sunt (Latin, "Where are") See **motif**.

understatement A kind of **irony** in which something is said to be lesser than it actually is, often for **rhetorical** or **humorous** effect; see e.g. lines 31-32 of Marvell's "To His Coy Mistress" (p. 405). Also called *meiosis*. See also **litotes**, and cf. **hyperbole**.

unreliable narrator See **narrator**.

utopia A term punningly coined by Sir Thomas More from the Greek *eutopos*, "good place," and *outopos*, "no place," for the title of his *Utopia* (1516), a **satirical romance** contrasting the way politics, education, religion, and other social matters are managed in England with the better way they're managed in the imagined ideal land of Utopia; the popularity of the work established the term as the name of a **genre**. Other notable utopias are Plato's *Republic*, Samuel Butler's *Erewhon*, and Charlotte Perkins Gilman's *Herland*. A related term, *dystopia*, "bad place," is applied to imaginary places (and the works about them) that are the opposite of *utopias*; dystopias are terrible places (usually in a science-fiction future) where things have gone wrong, such as in Aldous Huxley's *Brave New World*, George Orwell's *Nineteen Eighty-Four*, and Margaret

Atwood's *The Handmaid's Tale*. Le Guin's "The Ones Who Walk Away from Omelas" (p. 1435) might be said to combine the two sorts of imaginary society.

verbal irony See **irony**.

verisimilitude (adj. *verisimilar*) "Truth-likeness" — the appearance or semblance of truth or probability in a literary work; the quality that allows a work to seem to portray reality. See also **documentary**, **mimesis**, and **realism**.

vernacular The everyday, **colloquial** language, or **dialect**, whether standard or substandard, native to a locality or a country. The term also refers to living languages, such as English or Italian, as opposed e.g. to Latin; and to the language used by the people when a different language is used by officialdom, as e.g. in England after the Norman conquest.

verse Generally, any or all poetry, or a single poem; also, strictly, a single line of poetry, but now more commonly a loose synonym for **stanza**, as of a **hymn**; the term also refers to one of the divisions of a chapter in the books of the Bible.

verse paragraph A nonstanzaic group of lines, unified just as a prose paragraph would be, and indicated (like a prose paragraph) by a line space or an indented first line, or both. Though often thought of as most appropriate for the divisions of works in **free verse** and *blank verse* (see *AC 1*), verse paragraphs are common also with other forms, such as *heroic couplets* (see *AC 1*); see e.g. Dryden's "Mac Flecknoe" (p. 433), Pope's T*he Rape of the Lock* (p. 521), *Epistle IV* (p. 538), and *An Essay on Man* (p. 541), and Johnson's *The Vanity of Human Wishes* (p. 589). Cf. **stanza**.

villanelle See *AC 1*.

vocalic alliteration See **alliteration**.

wit and humour Terms sometimes used interchangeably about something funny; but *wit* more precisely refers to intellectual sharpness, agility with ideas and words, inventiveness and imagination; "True wit," says Pope in *An Essay on Criticism*, "is Nature to advantage dressed, / What oft was thought, but ne'er so well expressed" (297-98); *humour* on the other hand has to do with matters such as human foibles and circumstances. Both terms have undergone much change in meaning over the centuries. See *AC 1*; see also *AC 1: Satire*, and **aphorism**, **conceit**, **epigram**, and

Addison's essays from *The Spectator*, on "false wit" (p. 490). And see Johnson's comments in the excerpt from his life of Cowley (p. 605). On the four "humours" of early physiology, see the note to line 420 of the "General Prologue" to Chaucer's *Canterbury Tales* (p. 34).

zeugma A construction in which one word relates grammatically to two other words but in somewhat different senses, as in Pope's "Or stain her honour, or her new brocade" (*The Rape of the Lock*, II, 107; p. 526), or Milton's "flown with insolence and wine" (*Paradise Lost*, I, 502; p. 332).

Note: This glossary is necessarily brief and selective. We urge you to supplement it by consulting other, more expansive glossaries and specialized dictionaries. Some suggestions:

M. H. Abrams, *A Glossary of Literary Terms*

Chris Baldick, *The Concise Oxford Dictionary of Literary Terms*

Sylvan Barnet, Morton Berman, and William Burto, *A Dictionary of Literary Terms*

Raymond W. Barry and A. J. Wright, *Literary Terms: Definitions, Explanations, Examples*

Karl Beckson and Arthur Ganz, *A Reader's Guide to Literary Terms*

David Crystal, *A Dictionary of Linguistics and Phonetics*

J. A. Cuddon, *A Dictionary of Literary Terms and Literary Theory*

Roger Fowler, ed., *A Dictionary of Modern Critical Terms*

Paul Fussell, *Poetic Meter and Poetic Form*

C. Hugh Holman and William Harmon, *A Handbook to Literature*

Richard A. Lanham, *A Handlist of Rhetorical Terms*

Lee T. Lemon, *A Glossary for the Study of English*

Jack Myers and Michael Simms, *Longman Dictionary and Handbook of Poetry*

Alex Preminger, Frank J. Warnke, and O. B. Hardison, eds., *Princeton Encyclopedia of Poetry and Poetics*

Gerald Prince, *A Dictionary of Narratology*

Harry Shaw, *Concise Dictionary of Literary Terms*

Joseph T. Shipley, ed., *Dictionary of World Literature*

Acknowledgments

Plate 1.   (f.29R) By permission of the British Library.
Plate 2.   By permission of the British Library.
Plate 3.   By permission of The Newberry Library.
Plate 4.   JA644/9. By permission of The Edinburgh University Library.
Plate 5.   appeared in Original Poems on Several Occassions by Miss. Whateley, 1764.
Plate 6.   By permission of the British Museum.
Plate 7.   By permission of the British Museum.
Plate 8.   By permission of Messrs. MacMillan & Co.

Larry D. Benson: *The Riverside Chaucer*, Third Edition, Copyright © 1987 by Houghton Mifflin Company. Used with permission.

William Barnes: "The Giants in Treades" and "Eclogue: Rusticus Emigrans," Centaur Press Ltd.

Buhkwujjenene: "Nanaboozhoo Creates the World" from Petrone, FIRST PEOPLE, FIRST VOICES. Reprinted by permission of The Algoma Missionary News and Shingwauk Journal. March 1, 1879, pp 20-21.

Emily Dickinson: Poems – reprinted by permission of the publishers and the Trustees of Amherst College from THE POEMS OF EMILY DICKINSON, Thomas H. Johnson, ed., Cambridge, Mass. The Belknap Press of Harvard University Press, copyright 1951, ©1955, 1979, 1983 by the President and Fellows of Harvard College.

Samuel Butler: from "THE NOTEBOOKS OF SAMUEL BUTLER," Jonathan Cape, Publishers.

Ambrose Bierce: "Killed at Resaca" and selections from THE DEVIL'S DICTIONARY by Ambrose Bierce. Copyright © 1957 by Hill and Wang, Inc. Reprinted by permission of Hill and Wang, a division of Farrar, Straus and Giroux, Inc.

Edith Nesbit: "The Last of the Dragons" from FIVE OF US – MADELINE. A & C Black, Publishers.

A.E. Housman: from *A Shropshire Lad*. Henry Holt & Company.

Rabindranath Tagore: "Come Friend, Flinch Not" reprinted by permission of Visva-Bharati, Publishers.

Duncan Campbell Scott: "Meditation at Perugia" from The Poems of Duncan Campbell Scott. Reprinted by permission of Scott & Aylen, Ottawa.

Mary Gilmore: "The Harvesters" from THE PASSIONATE HEART AND OTHER POEMS. Reprinted with permission of Collins / Angus & Robertson Publishers.

Arthur Symons: "At Dieppe" (1895) from POEMS by Arthur Symons. Reprinted by permission of Mr. B. Read. Dorset.

John Gray: "Charleville" and "Poem" from SILVERPOINTS by John Gray. Bodley Head Publishers.

Ernest Dowson: "Vitae Summa Brevis Spem Nos Vetat Incohere Longam" from THE POETICAL WORKS OF ERNEST DOWSON, Associated University Presses.

W.E.B. Dubois: "A Mild Suggestion" from The Crisis January, 1912. By permission of The Crisis Magazine.

Edwin Arlington Robinson: "An Old Story" from THE CHILDREN OF THE NIGHT by Edwin Arlington Robinson (New York: Charles Scribner's Sons, 1897) and "Miniver Cheevy" from THE TOWN DOWN THE RIVER by Edwin Arlington Robinson (New York: Charles Scribner's Sons, 1910)

Stephen Leacock: "Gertrude the Governess: or Simple Seventeen" from NONSENSE NOVELS by Stephen Leacock. Used by permission of the Canadian Publishers, McClelland & Stewart, Toronto.

John Shaw Neilson: "The Orange Tree" – Lothian Books, Australia.

Robert Service: "The Shooting of Dan McGrew" © copyright 1909 Dodd Mead & Co. Used by permission of the Estate of Robert Service.

Robert Frost: "Mending Wall," "Fire and Ice," "Dust of Snow," "Nothing Gold Can Stay," "Stopping by Woods on a Snowy Evening," "Acquainted with the Night" and "Design." Reprinted by permission of Henry Holt and Company, Inc.

E.C. Bentley: "Sir Humphrey Davy" and "George III" from THE COMPLETE CLERIHEWS OF E. CLERIHEW BENTLEY. Reprinted by permission of Oxford University Press.

Adelaide Crapsey: "The Warning" from COMPLETE POEMS AND COLLECTED LETTERS OF ADELAIDE CRAPSEY by Susan S. Smith. By permission of the State University of New York Press.

John Masefield: "Sea Fever" from POEMS, 1918. Reprinted by permission of The Society of Authors, as the literary representative of the Estate of John Masefield.

Carl Sandburg: "Fog" from *Chicago Poems* by Carl Sandburg, copyright 1916 by Holt, Rinehart and Winston, Inc. and renewed 1944 by Carl Sandburg, reprinted by permission of Harcourt Brace Jovanovich, Inc. "Grass" from *CORNHUSKERS* by Carl Sandburg, copyright 1918 by Holt, Rinehart and Winston, Inc. and renewed 1946 by Carl Sandburg, reprinted by permission of Harcourt Brace Jovanovich, Inc.

Wallace Stevens: "The Snow Man," "Anecdote of the Jar" and "The House was Quiet and the World was Calm" from THE COLLECTED POEMS OF WALLACE STEVENS, by Wallace Stevens. Copyright 1923 and renewed 1951 by Wallace Stevens. "Anecdote" copyright 1947. Reprinted by permission of Alfred A. Knopf, Inc.

E.M. Forster: "What I Believe" from TWO CHEERS FOR DEMOCRACY. Reprinted by permission of Edward Arnold Publishers.

James Joyce: "Eveline" from DUBLINERS by James Joyce. Copyright 1916 by B.W. Heubsch. Definitive text copyright © 1967 by the Estate of James Joyce. Used by permission of Viking Penguin, a division of Penguin Books USA Inc.

Virginia Woolf: "The Decay of Essay Writing" and "The Lady in the Looking Glass: A Reflection," reprinted by permission of the Executors of the Estate of Virginia Woolf, The Hogarth Press, Publishers.

E.J. Pratt: "Sea Gulls," and "From Stone to Steel" by E.J. Pratt from *E.J. Pratt Complete Poems*, edited by Sandra Djwa and R.G. Moyles. Reprinted by permission of University of Toronto Press.

William Carlos Williams: "The Red Wheelbarrow" from *The Collected Poems of William Carlos Williams, 1909-1939, vol.I.* Copyright 1938, by New Directions Publishing Corporation. "A Sort of a Song" from *The Collected Poems of William Carlos Williams, 1939-1962, Vol. II.* Copyright 1944, 1948 by William Carlos Williams.

D.H. Lawrence: "The Horse Dealer's Daughter," copyright 1922 by Thomas B. Seltzer, Inc., renewed 1950 by Frieda Lawrence, from COMPLETE SHORT STORIES OF D.H. LAWRENCE by D.H. Lawrence. Used by permission of Viking Penguin, a division of Penguin Books USA Inc. "Snake," from the COMPLETE POEMS OF D.H. LAWRENCE by D.H. Lawrence. Copyright © 1964, 1971 by Angelo Ravagli and C.M. Weekley, Executors of the Estate of Frieda Lawrence Ravagli. Used by permission of Viking Penguin, a division of Penguin Books USA Inc.

Dorthea Mackellar: "Two Japanese Songs: The Heart of a Bird, A Smoke Song." Reprinted by permission by Estate of late Dorothea Mackellar c/o Curtis Brown (Aust.) Pty Ltd.

Ezra Pound: "The River-Merchant's Wife: A Letter," "The Garden," "Commission," "In a Station of the Metro," "Canto I," from LUSTRA, CATHAY, and THE CANTOS by Ezra Pound. Reprinted by permission of Faber and Faber Ltd.

Hilda Doolittle: "Oread" from *Collected Poems 1912-1944.* Copyright © 1982 by the Estate of Hilda Doolittle.

Siegfried Sassoon: "A Working Party" and "Base Details" by permission of George Sassoon.

Marianne Moore: "The Fish," and "Poetry." Reprinted with permission of Macmillan Publishing Company from COLLECTED POEMS by Marianne Moore. Copyright 1935 by Marianne Moore, renewed 1963 by Marianne Moore and T.S. Eliot.

T.S. Eliot: "The Love Song of J. Alfred Prufrock," Tradition and the Individual Talent," "Little Gidding," and "The Hollow Men" from COLLECTED POEMS 1909-192, and SELECTED ESSAYS 1917-1932 by T.S. Eliot. Faber and Faber Limited, Publishers.

John Crowe Ransom: "Bells for John Whiteside's Daughter" from SELECTED POEMS, Third Ed., REVISED AND ENLARGED by John Crowe Ransom. Copyright 1924 by Alfred A. Knopf, Inc. and renewed 1952 by John Crowe Ransom. Reprinted by permission of Alfred A. Knopf, Inc.

Rebecca West: "The Woman as Workmate" from THE YOUNG REBECCA. Reprinted by permission of the Peters, Fraser & Dunlop Group Ltd.

Wilfred Owen: "Anthem for Doomed Youth," "Dulce et Decorum Est," and "Arms and the Boy" from Wilfred Owen, Vol. 1, The Complete Poems and Fragments edited by John Stallworthy. Chatto & Windus, Publishers.

e.e. cummings: "Buffalo Bill's," "spring is like a perhaps hand," "a man who had fallen among thieves," "next to of course god," "somewhere I have never travelled," "anyone lived in a pretty how town," "no time ago." Reprinted from COMPLETE POEMS, 1913-1962, by e.e. cummings, by permission of Liveright Publishing Corporation. Copyright © 1923, 1925, 1931, 1935, 1938, 1939, 1940, 1944, 1945, 1946, 1947, 1948, 1949, 1950, 1951, 1952, 1953, 1954, 1955, 1956, 1957, 1958, 1959, 1960, 1961, 1962 by the Trustees for the e.e. cummings Trust. Copyright © 1961, 1963, 1968 by Marion Morehouse Cummings.

James Thurber: "The Little Girl and the Wolf" Copyright © 1940 James Thurber. Copyright © 1968 Helen Thurber. From Fables for Our Time, published by Harper & Row.

Robert Graves: "Flying Crooked" and "The Cool Web" from COLLECTED POEMS 1975 by Robert Graves. Reprinted by permission of A.P. Watt Ltd. on behalf of The Trustees of the Robert Graves Copyright Trust.

William Faulkner: "A Mule in the Yard." From COLLECTED STORIES OF WILLIAM FAULKNER by William Faulkner. Copyright 1934 by Random House, Inc. and renewed 1962 by William Faulkner. Reprinted by permission of Random House, Inc.

Ernest Hemingway: "A Clean, Well-Lighted Place" from WINNER TAKE NOTHING. Reprinted with permission of Charles Scribner's Sons, an imprint of Macmillan Publishing Company. Copyright 1933 by Charles Scribner's Sons; renewal copyright © 1961 by Mary Hemingway.

F.R. Scott: "Paradise Lost" and "Lakeshore" from COLLECTED POEMS by F.R. Scott. Used by permission of the Canadian Publishers, McClelland & Stewart, Toronto.

E.B. White: "Once More to the Lake" from Essays of E.B. White. Copyright 1941 by E.B. White. Reprinted by permission of Harper Collins Publishers.

Yvor Winters: "The Fable" and "Sir Gawaine and the Green Knight" from COLLECTED POEMS by Yvor Winters. Reprinted by permission of Carcanet Press Ltd.

Ernest G. Moll: "The Bush Speaks" from POEMS (c) Ernest Moll. Reprinted by permission of Collins/Angus & Robertson. Publishers.

Laura Riding" "The Map of Places" from COLLECTED POEMS. In conformity with the late author's wish, her Board of Literary Management asks us to record that, in 1941, Laura (Riding) Jackson renounced, on grounds of linguistic principle, the writing of poetry: she had come to hold that "poetry obstructs general attainment to something better in our linguistic way-of-life than we have."

Langston Hughes: "Harlem" from THE PANTHER AND THE LASH by Langston Hughes. Copyright 1951 by Langston Hughes. Reprinted by permission of Alfred A. Knopf, Inc.

Stevie Smith: "Egocentric."

George Orwell: "Shooting an Elephant," reprinted with permission of The Estate of the late Sonia Brownell Orwell and Martin Secker & Warburg.

Earle Birney: "Anglosaxon Street," "The Bear on the Delhi Road" and "Ka Pass Age Alaska Passage" from The Collected Poems of Earle Birney by Earle Birney. Used by permission of the Canadian Publishers, McClelland & Stewart, Toronto.

John Betjeman: "In Westminster Abbey" from COLLECTED POEMS, reprinted by permission of John Murray (Publishers) Ltd.

Samuel Beckett: "Ping," translated from the French by Samuel Beckett, from Collected Shorter Prose 1945-1980 by Samuel Beckett. Reproduced here by courtesy of the Beckett Estate and Calder Publications Ltd. London. This translation copyright © Samuel Beckett 1967, 1975, 1984, 1986.

W.H. Auden: "As I walked out one evening," "Now the Leaves are Falling fast," "Musée des Beaux Arts" and "The Shield of Achilles" from W.H. Auden: COLLECTED POEMS by W.H. Auden, ed. by Edward Mendelson. Copyright 1937, 1940, 1952 and renewed 1965, 1968 by W.H. Auden. Reprinted by permission of Random House, Inc.

A.D. Hope: "Inscription for a War" from ANTECHINUS copyright (c) A.D. Hope 1981. Reprinted by permission of Collins/Angus & Robertson Publishers.

Theodore Roethke: "The Waking," copyright 1948 and "The Sloth" copyright 1950 by Theodore Roethke. From THE COLLECTED POEMS OF THEODORE ROETHKE. Used by permission of Doubleday, a division of Bantam Doubleday Dell Publishing Group, Inc.

Kathleen Raine: "What does this day bestow," "Frost-rime edges blades of grass," and "Moon golden towards the full." Reprinted by permission of the author, Kathleen Raine.

A.M. Klein: "The Rocking Chair," "Pastoral of the City Streets," and "Portrait of the Poet as Landscape" from COMPLETE POEMS by A.M. Klein, edited by Zailig Pollock. Reprinted by permission of University of Toronto Press.

Stephen Spender: "An Elementary School Classroom in a Slum" and "Subject, Object, Sentence" Reprinted by permission of Faber and Faber Ltd. from COLLECTED POEMS 1928-1985 by Stephen Spender.

Dorothy Livesay: "Other" from Collected Poems. Permission granted by author Dr. Dorothy Livesay.

Ralph Gustafson. "Good Friday," from THE MOMENT IS ALL by Ralph Gustafson. Used by permission of the Canadian Publishers, McClelland & Stewart, Toronto.

Charles Olson: "New Poem" from Collected Poetry of Charles Olson, trans./ed. by George Butterick. Copyright © 1987 Estate of Charles Olson (previously published poetry) (c) 1987 University of Connecticut (previously unpublished poetry). Reprinted by permission of the University of California Press.

Norman McCaig: "Stars & Planets" from COLLECTED POEMS by Norman McCaig. Reprinted by permission of Chatto & Windus.

Elizabeth Bishop: "The Prodigal" and "Casabianca" from THE COMPLETE POEMS OF ELIZABETH BISHOP 1927-1979. Copyright © 1979, 1983 by Alice Helen Methfessel. Reprinted by permission of Farrar, Straus & Giroux, Inc.

Allen Curnow: "Discovery" from SELECTED POEMS by Allen Curnow. Reprinted by permission of Penguin Books (NZ) Ltd.

Irving Layton: "Mrs. Fornheim, Refugee" and "The Cold Green Element" from COLLECTED POEMS by Irving Layton. Used by permission of the Canadian Publishers McClelland & Stewart, Toronto.

Muriel Rukeyser: "M-Day's Child is Fair of Face," "Myth" and "Islands" copyright Muriel Rukeyser, by permission of William L. Rukeyser, from *Out of Silence*, 1992, TriQuarterly Books, Evanston, IL, USA.

R.S. Thomas: "A Peasant" and "Reservoirs" from POEMS OF R.S. THOMAS, copyright © 1983 by R.S. Thomas. Reprinted by permission of The University of Arkansas Press.

Dylan Thomas: "The Force that Through the Green Fuse Drives the Flower," "A Refusal to Mourn the Death, by Fire, of a Child in London," "Fern Hill," "Do Not Go Gentle into That Good Night" from THE POEMS. Reprinted by permission of David Higham Associates Ltd.

Randall Jarrell: "The Death of the Ball Turret Gunner" from THE COMPLETE POEMS by Randall Jarrell. Copyright (c) 1945 and renewal copyright (c) 1972 by Mrs. Randall Jarrell. Reprinted by permission of Farrar, Straus & Giroux, Inc.

Bernard Malamud: "Idiots First" from IDIOTS FIRST. Reprinted by permission of the estate of the late Bernard Malamud and A.M. Heath Publishers.

Henry Reed: "The Naming of Parts" from A MAP OF VERONA. Reprinted by permission of the Peters, Fraser & Dunlop Group Ltd.

William Stafford: "Sayings from the Northern Ice" from Stories That Could Be True. © 1977 by William Stafford. Harper & Row.

Isabella Gardner: "Cock A' Hoop" and "Fall in Massachusetts" from BIRTHDAYS FROM THE OCEAN by Isabella Gardner. Published in 1955 by Houghton Mifflin Company. Reprinted by permission of Houghton Mifflin Company.

Dorothy Auchterlonie: "The Tree." Reprinted by permission of the Estate of Dorothy Auchterlonie / Andrew Green.

Judith Wright: "The Trains," "Eve to Her Daughters" and "The Other Half" from COLLECTED POEMS. © Judith Wright 1971. Collins/Angus & Robertson Publishers.

P.K. page: "T-Bar." © P.K. Page.

James McAuley: "Terra Australis" from COLLECTED POEMS. (c) Norma McAuley 1971. Collins/Angus & Robertson Publishers.

Robert Lowell: "Christmas Eve Under Hooker's Statue" from LORD WEARY'S CASTLE. Reprinted by permission of Harcourt Brace Jovanovich, Inc.

Gwendolyn Brooks: "The Bean Eaters" and "We Real Cool" from "BLACKS," copyright © by Gwendolyn Brooks, 1987 & 1991. Third World Press, Chicago.

Margaret Avison: "The Mirrored Man" and "September Street" from Wintersun/The Dumbfounding Poems by Margaret Avison. Used by permission of the Canadian Publishers, McClelland & Stewart, Toronto.

Al Purdy: "Lament for the Dorsets" and "Moses at Darwin Station" from COLLECTED POEMS by Al Purdy. Used by permission of the Canadian Publishers, McClelland & Stewart, Toronto.

Robert Duncan: "Often I am Permitted to Return to A Meadow" from *The Opening of the Field*. Copyright © 1960 by Robert Duncan. Reprinted by permission of New Directions Publishing Corporation. "Structure of Rime XXV" from Bending the Bow. Copyright © 1968 by Robert Duncan.

Louise Bennett: "Colonization in Reverse" from JAMAICA LABRISH. Permission to use from Sangster's Book Stores Ltd. Kingston, Jamaica.

May Swenson: "MAster MANANiMAl" © 1970 by May Swenson and used with the permission of the Literary Estate of May Swenson.

Howard Nemerov: "A Primer of the Daily Round" and "The Four Ages" from THE COLLECTED POEMS OF HOWARD NEMEROV. Reprinted by permission of the author.

Amy Clampitt: "Let the Air Circulate" from WHAT THE LIGHT WAS LIKE by Amy Clampitt, copyright (c) 1985 by Amy Clampitt. Reprinted by permission of Alfred A. Knopf, Inc.

Gwen Harwood: "Suburban Sonnet" from SELECTED POEMS. Reprinted with permission of Collins/Angus & Robertson Publishers.

Edwin Morgan: "Archives" from POEMS OF THIRTY YEARS. Reprinted by permission of Carcanet Press Ltd.

Oodgeroo Noonuccal: "Municipal Gum" from MY PEOPLE by Oodgeroo Noonuccal (formerly Kath Walker) Oodgeroo of the tribe Noonuccal, custodian of the land Minjerribah. Reprinted by permission of Jacaranda Wiley Ltd.

Bill Reid: "The Raven Steals the Light" from *The Raven Steals the Light* by Bill Reid and Robert Bringhurst, published by Douglas & McIntyre. Reprinted by permission.

Gabriel Okara: "Once Upon a Time" from The Fisherman's Invocation, Ministry of Information, Enugu, Nigeria.

Richard Wilbur: "Parable" and "Hamlen Brook" from New & Collected Poems. "A Summer Morning" from ADVICE TO A PROPHET AND OTHER POEMS. Copyright © 1960 and renewed 1988 by Richard Wilbur, reprinted by permission of Harcourt, Brace, Jovanovich, Inc.

Philip Larkin: "Since the majority of me," from COLLECTED POEMS 1938-1983 by Philip Larkin, "The Whitsun Weddings" from THE WHITSUN WEDDINGS by Philip Larkin. Reprinted by permission of Faber & Faber Ltd. "Church Going" from THE LESS DECEIVED by Philip Larkin. Reprinted by permission of The Marvell Press.

Eli Mandel: "Parting at Udaipur: the Lake Palace" from LIFE SENTENCE. Reprinted by permission of Press Porcépic.

Nadine Gordimer: "Something for the Time Being" copyright © 1960, renewed © 1988 by Nadine Gordimer, from SELECTED STORIES by Nadine Gordimer. Used by permission of Viking Penguin, a division of Penguin Books USA Inc.

Denise Levertov: "Everything that Acts is Actual" and "What Were They Like?" from Collected Poems 1960-1967. Copyright © 1966 by Denise Levertov. Reprinted by Permission of New Directions Publishing Corporation.

James Berry: "Speech for Alternative Creation" from NEWS FOR BABYLON. Reprinted by permission of the June Hall Literary Agency Ltd.

Ian Hamilton Finlay: "Net/Planet" from HONEY BY THE WATER. Black Sparrow Press.

Carolyn Kizer: "The Ungrateful Garden" from The Ungrateful Garden.

Colleen Thibaudeau: "from the planned woodlot to the freedom of Mrs. Field" from The Martha Landscapes. Reprinted by permission of BRICK BOOKS.

James K. Baxter: "Eagle" and "To Mate With" from COLLECTED POEMS, reprint by permission of Oxford University Press.

A.R. Ammons: "Discoverer" from NORTHFIELD POEMS. Reprinted by permission of Professor Archie Ammons.

Robert Creeley: "The Epic Expands" and "A Variation" from Collected Poems of Robert Creeley, 1945-1975, Reprinted by permission of the University of California Press.

Elizabeth Jennings: "Song at the Beginning of Autumn" and "Still Life and Observer" from COLLECTED POEMS, reprinted courtesy Macmillan/David Higham Associates.

James Wright: "Notes of a Pastoralist" and "Against Surrealism" from THIS JOURNEY by James Wright. Copyright © 1980, 1981 by Anne Wright. Reprinted by permission of Random House, Inc.

John Ashbery: "Down by the Station, Early in the Morning" from A WAVE by John Ashbery (New York: Viking 1984). Reprinted by permission of Georges Borchardt Inc. for the author.

W.S. Merwin: "Happens Every Day" from OPENING THE HAND. Copyright © 1983 by W.S. Merwin.

Phyllis Webb: "Metaphysics of Spring" and "The Days of the Unicorns," from Selected Poems. Reprinted by permission of Phyllis Webb.

Anne Sexton: "To A Friend Whose Work Has Come To Triumph," from ALL MY PRETTY ONES by Anne Sexton. Copyright © 1962 by Anne Sexton. Reprinted by permission of Houghton Mifflin Company. All rights reserved. "Red Riding Hood" from TRANSFORMATIONS by Anne Sexton. Copyright © 1971 by Anne Sexton. Reprinted by permission of Houghton Mifflin Company. All rights reserved.

Andrew Salkey: "Soot, the Land of Billboards" from ANANCY'S SCORE, Bogle L'Ouverture Publications Limited.

Iain Crichton Smith: "Returning Exile" from Selected Poems. "Slowly" from THE VILLAGE AND OTHER POEMS. Reprinted with permission of Carcanet Press Limited.

U.A. Fanthorpe: "Genesis," from Standing To (Peterloo Poets, 1982) and Selected Poems (Peterloo Poets & King Penguin, 1986) "Knowing about Sonnets" from Voices Off (Peterloo Poets, 1984) and Selected Poems (Peterloo

Poets & King Penguin, 1986) and "Old Man, Old Man" from A Watching Brief (Peterloo Poets, 1987).

D.G. Jones: "The Path" from A THROW OF PARTICLES reproduced with the permission of Stoddart Publishing Co. Limited, 34 Lesmill Rd., Don Mills, Ontario, Canada.

Ursula K. Le Guin: "The Ones who walk away from Omelas" Copyright © 1973 by Ursula K. Le Guin; first appeared in New Dimensions 3; reprinted by permission of the author and the author's agent, Virginia Kidd.

Peter Porter: "Nevertheless" from *The Automatic Oracle* (1987). Reprinted by permission of Oxford University Press.

Adrienne Rich: "Planetarium" and "Frame" are reprinted from THE FACT OF A DOORFRAME, Poems Selected and New, 1950-1984, by Adrienne Rich, by permission of W.W. Norton & Company, Inc. Copyright © 1984 by Adrienne Rich. Copyright © 1975, 1978 by W.W. Norton & Company, Inc. Copyright © 1981 by Adrienne Rich.

Chinua Achebe: "Civil Peace" from GIRLS AT WAR, © 1972, 1973 by Chinua Achebe. Reprinted by permission of Harold Ober Associates Inc.

Edward Kamau Brathwaite: "Blues" from *Other Exiles* (1975). Reprinted by permission of Oxford University Press.

Ted Hughes: "Hawk Roosting" from LUPERCAL, reprinted by permission of Faber & Faber Ltd.

Richard Outram: "Charm for Martha" from *Exsultate, Jubilate* by permission of Richard Outram.

Derek Walcott: "Ruins of a Great House" from Selected Poetry, and "Elsewhere" from The Arkansas Testament. Reprinted by permission of Random House, Inc.

Jay Macpherson: "Eve in Reflection" and "The Island" from Jay Macpherson's Poems Twice Told, © Oxford University Press Canada 1981. Reprinted by permission of Oxford University Press, Canada.

Alice Munro: "Meneseteung" from Friends of My Youth by Alice Munro. Used by permission of the Canadian Publishers, McClelland & Stewart, Toronto.

Sylvia Plath: "Words" from COLLECTED POEMS. Reprinted by permission of Faber & Faber Ltd.

Arun Kolatkar: "The Butterfly" from JEJURI. Reprinted by permission of Arun Kolatkar.

V.S. Naipaul: "B. Wordsworth" from Miguel Street. Reprinted with permission of Aitken & Stone Ltd.

Linda Pastan: "Ethics" is reprinted from WAITING FOR MY LIFE. Poems by Linda Pastan, by permission of W.W. Norton & Company, Inc. Copyright © 1981 by Linda Pastan.

Sipho Sepamla: "Da Same, Da Same" from THE BLUES IS YOU AND ME. Reprinted with permission of Deneys Reitz Attorneys.

Alden Nowlan: "1914-1918" from AN EXCHANGE OF GIFTS. Reprinted with the permission of Stoddart Publishing Co. Limited, Don Mills, Ont.

Anne Stevenson: "Colours" and "Willow Song Blues" from SELECTED POEMS by Anne Stephenson 1956-1986. Reprinted by permission of Oxford University Press.

Jennifer Strauss: "Discourse in Eden" first published in THE AGE MONTHLY REVIEW of September 19, 1989. Reprinted by permission of Jennifer Strauss.

Fay Weldon: "The City of Invention" from LETTERS TO ALICE ON FIRST READING JANE AUSTEN by Fay Weldon (Michael Joseph/Rainbird, 1984) copyright Fay Weldon, 1984. Reproduced by permission of Penguin Books Ltd.

Fleur Adcock: "For A Five-Year-Old" from Fleur Adcock's *Selected Poems* (1983). Reprinted by permission of Oxford University Press.

David Malouf: "The Kyogle Line" from 12 Edmonstone Street by David Malouf. Reprinted by permission of Chatto & Windus.

Wole Soyinka: "Telephone Conversation," from A BOOK OF AFRICAN VERSE.

Chris Wallace-Crabbe: "Appearance and Reality," and "1066" from JIGGERY-POKERY (Atheneum, 1967) © Chris Wallace-Crabbe.

Zulfikar Ghose: "On Owning Property in the U.S.A." from A MEMORY OF ASIA.

Mary Oliver: "O Pioneers" and "Going to Walden," from THE RIVER STYX OHIO AND OTHER POEMS. Reprinted by permission of The Molly Malone Cook Literary Agency, Inc. Copyright © 1972 by Mary Oliver.

Lucille Clifton: "Lucy and her girls" from TWO HEADED WOMAN, reprinted by permission of Curtis Brown, Ltd. Copyright © 1980 by Lucille Clifton.

Daryl Hine: "Raleigh's Last Voyage" Reprinted with permission of Atheneum Publishers, an imprint of Macmillan Publishing Company, from THE WOODEN HORSE by Daryl Hine. Copyright © 1960, 1962, 1963, 1964, 1965 by Daryl Hine.

From *Circles on the Water* by Marge Piercy. Copyright © 1982 by Marge Piercy. Reprinted by permission of Alfred A. Knopf, Inc.

Gillian Clarke: "Blaen Cwrt" from SELECTED POEMS reprinted with permission of Carcanet Press Ltd.

Tony Harrison: "Them and Uz" from SELECTED POEMS reprinted with permission of Peters Fraser & Dunlop Group Ltd.

Mervyn Morris: "A Voyage" from *Shadowboxing* by Mervyn Morris, published by New Beacon Books Ltd., in 1979.

Les Murray: "The Quality of Sprawl" from The Peoples Otherworld. Copyright © 1983, 1987, 1988, by Les A. Murray. Reprinted by permission of PERSEA BOOKS, INC.

Ken Smith: "Persistent Narrative" reprinted by permission of Bloodaxe Books Ltd. from: The Poet Reclining: Selected Poems 1962-1980 by Ken Smith (Bloodaxe Books, 1982).

Margaret Atwood: from The Journals of Susanna Moodie. "Further arrivals," "First Neighbours," "The Planters," "The Two Fires," and Variations on the Word *Love* from Margaret Atwood's Selected Poems 1966-1984, copyright © Margaret Atwood 1990. Reprinted by permission of Oxford University Press Canada.

bill bissett: "grade school in halifax," © 1983 bill bissett; from: *Seagull on Yonge Street*, Talon Books Ltd., Vancouver, B.C.

Seamus Heaney: "Digging" and "Casualty" from DEATH OF A NATURALIST and FIELDWORK, reprinted by permission of Faber and Faber Ltd.

Dennis Scott: "Grampa" Reprinted from UNCLE TIME, by Dennis Scott, by permission of the University of Pittsburgh Press © 1973 by Dennis Scott.

Jane Flanders: "Late Report from Miss Harriet Robinson's Third Grade" from THE STUDENTS OF SNOW, by Jane Flanders (Amherst: University of Massachusetts Press, 1982) copyright © 1982 by Jane Flanders.

Stephen Jay Gould: "Bathybius and Eozoon" reprinted from THE PANDA'S THUMB, More Reflections in Natural History, by Stephen Jay Gould, by permission of W.W. Norton & Company, Inc. Copyright © 1980 by Stephen Jay Gould.

Jeni Couzyn: "Spell to Banish Fear" from LIFE BY DROWNING, reproduced with the permission of Stoddart Publishing Co. Limited, 34 Lesmill Rd., Don Mills, Ontario, Canada.

Douglas Dunn: "Empires" reprinted by permission of Faber & Faber Ltd. from BARBARIANS by Douglas Dunn.

Pamela Mordecai: "Protest Poem" . . . to the poet, Pamela Mordeai, for permission to use "Protest Poem" from JAMAICA WOMEN (ed. Mordecai and Morris) Heinemann UK, 1985.

Nikki Giovanni: "(Untitled) There is a Hunger" from MY HOUSE and "Revolutionary Dreams" from THE WOMEN AND THE MEN, reprinted by permission of William Morrow and Company, Inc./Publishers, New York.

Louise Glück: "The Apple Trees," copyright 1971, 1972, 1973, 1974, 1975 by Louise Glück, FROM THE HOUSE ON MARSHLAND, first published by The Ecco Press in 1975. Reprinted by permission.

Paulette Jiles: "Blacksnake" and "Paper Matches" from Celestial Navigation, by Paulette Jiles. Used by permission of the Canadian Publishers, McClelland & Stewart, Toronto.

Michael Ondaatje: "Charles Darwin Pays a Visit" from THERE'S A TRICK WITH A KNIFE THAT I'M LEARNING TO DO, Ellen Levine Literary Agency.

Arthur Yap: "a lesson on the definite article" and "the grammar of a dinner" from DOWN THE LINE, Heinemann Asia 1983.

bp Nichol: from "the Martyrology" The Estate of bp Nichol.

Shirley Geok-Lin Lim: "Dedicated to Confucius Plaza" and "To Marianne Moore" from MODERN SECRETS, Dangaroo Press.

Craig Raine "A Martian Sends a Postcard Home" from *A Martian Sends a Postcard Home* (1979). Reprinted by permission of Oxford University Press.

Carol Rumens: "Two Women" from SELECTED POEMS by Carol Rumens, published by Chatto & Windus.

Mongane Wally Serote: "The Growing" from POETS TO THE PEOPLE ed. Barry Feinberg.

Alice Walker: "Beauty: When the Other Dancer is the Self" from *In Search of Our Mothers' Gardens*, copyright © 1983 by Alice Walker, reprinted by permission of Harcourt Brace Jovanovich, Inc.

Eavan Boland: "Fruit on a Straight-Sided Tray" from Domestic Interior is reprinted from OUTSIDE HISTORY, Selected Poems 1980-1990, published by W.W. Norton & Co. Copyright (c) 1990 by Eavan Boland.

Wendy Cope: "A Nursery Rhyme as it might have been written by William Wordsworth" from Making Cocoa for Kingsley Amis by Wendy Cope, by permission of Faber and Faber Ltd.

Robert Bringhurst: "Wang Bi," "Some Ciphers" and "Essay on Adam" form Pieces of Map, Pieces of Music by Robert Bringhurst. Used by permission of the Canadian Publishers, McClelland & Stewart, Toronto.

Bill Manhire: "Declining the Naked Horse" and "Children" from GOOD LOOKS, Auckland University Press.

Christopher Dewdney: "Night Trains" from Radiant Inventory by Christopher Dewdney. Used by permission of the Canadian Publishers, McClelland & Stewart, Toronto.

Peter Goldsworthy: "Act Six" from Readings from Ecclesiastes by Peter Goldsworthy, published by Collins / Angus & Robertson Publishers Pty. Limited.

Rita Dove: "Three Days of Forest, A River, Free" reprinted from MUSEUM by permission of Carnegie Mellon University Press, 1983, by Rita Dove.

Alice Fulton: "Everyone Knows the World is Ending" from Palladium by Alice Fulton, published by the University of Illinois Press.

Gary Soto: "Black Hair" reprinted from BLACK HAIR, by Gary Soto, by permission of the University of Pittsburgh Press © 1985 by Gary Soto.

Joan Crate: "Shawnandithit (last of the Beothuks)" by permission of Joan Crate. The poem first appeared in *Canadian Literature* No. 116-117.

Louse Erdrich: "Dear John Wayne" and "I Was Sleeping Where the Black Oaks Move," from JACKLIGHT Poems by Louise Erdrich. Copyright © 1984 by Louise Erdrich. Reprinted by permission of Henry Holt and Company, Inc.

Sujata Bhatt: "A Different History" from BRUNIZEM, by permission of Carcanet Press Limited.

Valerie Bloom: "Yuh Hear 'Bout?" from Touch Mi Tell Mi by Valerie Bloom. Bogle L'Ouverture Publications Limited.

Eva Tihanyi: "Blind Man" from PROPHECIES NEAR THE SPEED OF LIGHT used with permission of Thistledown Press Ltd.

Archie Weller: "To the Moore River Settlement we now go..." by Archie Weller from *Inside Black Australia* edited by Kevin Gilbert. Published by Penguin Books Australia Ltd.

Frederick D'Aguiar: "Old Mama Dot" from Mama Dot, by Frederick D'Aguiar, by permission of Chatto and Windus.

INDEX OF AUTHORS AND TITLES

---

* Titles that begin with an article are alphabetized by the second word, except when a poem's first line (in quotation marks) serves as its title. Works in prose are identified by a preceding asterisk.